Time-Saver Standards for Interior Design and Space Planning

Other McGraw-Hill Books of Interest

Binder • Corporate Facility Planning
Breyer • Design of Wood Structures
Burden • Entourage
Callender • Time-Saver Standards for Architectural Design Data
Colley • Practical Manual of Site Development
De Chiara • Handbook of Architectural Details for Commercial Buildings
De Chiara • Time-Saver Standards for Residential Development
De Chiara and Callender • Time-Saver Standards for Building Types
De Chiara and Koppelman • Time-Saver Standards for Site Planning
Dines • Landscape Perspective Drawing
Ehrenkrantz • Architectural Systems
Halse and George • Architectural Rendering
Harris • Dictionary of Architecture and Construction
Harris and Dines • Time-Saver Standards for Landscape Architecture
Izenour • Theater Technology
Leach • Photographic Perspective Drawing Techniques
Merritt • Building Design and Systems Handbook
Merritt • Standard Handbook for Civil Engineers
Nolon and Dickinson • Common Walls/Private Homes
Simonds • Landscape Architecture
Spaulding and D'Elia • Advanced Marketing Techniques for Architecture and
  Engineering Firms
Wentling • Housing By Lifestyle

Time-Saver Standards for Interior Design and Space Planning

Joseph De Chiara
Julius Panero
Martin Zelnik

McGraw-Hill, Inc.
New York St. Louis San Francisco Auckland Bogotá
Caracas Hamburg Lisbon London Madrid Mexico
Milan Montreal New Delhi Paris San Juan
São Paulo Singapore Sydney Tokyo Toronto

Time-Saver Standards For Interior Design And Space Planning

International Editions 1992

6 7 8 9 0 KHL FC 9 8 7 6

The sponsoring editor for this book was Joel Stein, the editing supervisor was Stephen M. Smith, the designer was Ron Lane, and the production supervisor was Suzanne W. Babeuf. It was set in Univers Light.

Library of Congress Cataloging-in-Publication Data

De Chiara, Joseph, date
    Time-saver standards for interior design and space planning/ Joseph De Chiara, Julius Panero, Martin Zelnik.
      p.   cm.
    Includes index.
    ISBN 0-07-016299-9
    1. Interior decoration—Standards—Handbook, manuals, etc.
2. Interior architecture—Standards—Handbook, manuals, etc.
I. Panero, Julius. II. Zelnik, Martin, date. III. Title.
NK2110.D35 1991
729—dc20
                                      91-15189

When ordering this title, use ISBN 0-07-112589-2

Printed in Singapore

Contents

Contributors

Marvin Affrime
Andrew Alpern, AIA
Amon & Graecen *Architects*
David Appel, DLF, IALD
Bertram L. Bassuk *Architect*
Anthony Beaumont *Architect*
Jeannie Bochette *Steelcase*
Louis Bowman *Architect*
Scott Bromley *Architect*
Bromley Jacobsen *Architecture and Design*
Jerry Caldari *Architect*
Toni Chi/Albert Chen Associates
Will Ching *Planning and Design*
Barbara Cianci, IALD
Cameron Clark *Architect*
Davis, Brody & Wisniewski *Architects*
Majorie Earthlife
Brad Elias, ASID
David Engel *Landscape Architect*
Engel/GGP *Landscape Architects*
Paul Eshelman, IDEC
Evans, Moore, Peterson & Woodbridge *Architects*
Charles D. Flayhan Associates, Inc.
Frank J. Forster *Architect*
Ulrich Franzen *Architect*
Gensler Associates
Franklin H. Gottschall
Adrienne Grad
Julius Gregory *Architect*
Albert Halse
Hochheiser Elias Design Group, Inc.
Caleb Hornbolstel *Architect*
Lees Horton
ISD Incorporated
Lawrence Israel, FAIA *Architect*
Francis Joannes *Architect*
Ely Jacques Kahn *Architect*
Mary Jean Kamin, ASID
William H. Kapple, AIA
Joseph Kleiman
Dorothy Lee
Sammy Lee *Architect*
Lori Lennon, ASID

Howard Litton, ASID
Steve Louie
Ronald Lubman *Architect*
Harry Lunstead Design, Inc.
Michael Lynn *Architect*
Michael Lynn & Associates
Nathan Jerry Maltz, AIA *Architect*
William M. Manley, FASID
Mays, Simpson & Hunsicker *Architects*
Merrill, Humble, and Taylor *Architects*
Montgomery Winecoff & Associates, Inc.
William Morgan, FAIA
Bernhardt E. Muller *Architect*
Richard J. Neutra *Architect*
Julius Panero *Architect*
Panero Zelnik Associates
Parish Hadley Associates, Inc.
Perkins & Will *Architects*
Dennis Piermont, ASLA
Nicholas Politis *Professor, Fashion Institute of Technology*
John Russel Pope *Architect*
William Pulgram *Architect*
Ramey, Himes & Buchner *Architects*
Antonin Raymond *Architect*
Frank Rispoli
Saarinin, Swanson & Saarinen *Architects*
Jacqueline Siles
The Space Design Group
Richard Stonis
William Tarr
Andrew J. Thomas *Architect*
Thompson, Robinson, Toraby, Inc.
Darius Toraby *Architect*
Michael Trencher *Professor, Pratt Institute*
Verna, Cook, Salomosky *Architects*
Walker & Gillette *Architects*
Walker Group/CNI
Leroy P. Ward *Architect*
Edgar I. Williams *Architect*
Charlie Wing
Martin Zelnik *Architect*
Simon B. Zelnik, FAIA *Architect*

Organizations

A & J Washroom Accessories
Access America
Alvarado Manufacturing Co., Inc.
American Olean Tile Company
American Parquet Association
American Sanitary Partition Corporation
American Specialties, Inc.
American Standard, Inc.
Architectural Paneling, Inc.
Architectural Woodwork Institute
Armor Elevator Company
Ascente
Bauman
Brown Manufacturing Co.
Buckingham-Virginia Slate Co.
Camden Window and Millwork
Clairson International
Closet Maid Systems
Conde Nast Publications, Inc.
Culter Manufacturing Corp.
Curvoflite
Designers Sign Company
Dover Elevator Systems
Eggers Industries
Eljer Plumbingware Division of Wallace-Murray Corporation
Euroflair
Focal Point, Inc.
Formica Corporation
Franciscan Tile Company
General Electric Lighting
General Services Administration
Glencoe Publishing Co.
Habitat
Hafele
Hartco Flooring/Tibbals Flooring Co.
Haws
Herman Miller, Inc.
Hollow Metal Manufacturers Association
Horton Lees Lighting Designs, Inc.
Howe Furniture Company

Hussey Seating Company
Illinois Agricultural Experiment Station
Iittala, Inc.
Indiana Limestone Institute of America
Insulated Steel Door Systems Institute
Intergraph Corporation
Interkal, Inc.
JG Furniture Systems, Inc.
Just Bulbs Ltd.
Kinney Shoe Corporation
Kirsch Division of Cooper Industries, Inc.
Kohler
Lapeyre Stair Co.
Lehigh Furniture Corporation
Library Bureau, Inc.
Maclevy Health and Fitness Products
Manville
Marble Institute of America, Inc.
Marvin Windows
McGraw-Hill, Inc.
McKinney/Parker
Merillat
Midwest Plan Service
Modernfold
National Association of Architectural Metal Manufacturers
National Association of Ornamental Metal Manufacturers
National Cathode Corp.
National Retail Merchants Association
National Terrazzo and Mosaic Association, Inc.
Nesson Lamps, Inc.
New York City Housing Authority
Nichols Publishing
Niland Company
Osram Corporation
PAM International
Parker/Nutone
Philips Lighting Co.
Phillips & Brooks, Inc.
Pittcon Softforms
Pittsburg Corning Corp.

Putnam Rolling Ladder Co., Inc.
Railex Corporation
Roberts Step-Lite Systems
Roppe Rubber Corporation
St. Charles Kitchens
Schlage Lock Company
Schulte
Selby Furniture Hardware Co., Inc.
Simon and Schuster
Sister Kenny Institute
Steel Door Institute
Steelcase
Sweet's Division of McGraw-Hill, Inc.

Tarkett
Tile Council of America, Inc.
Triangle Pacific Corp.
Western Wood Products Association
Whirlpool
White Consolidated Industries, Inc.
Winebarger Church Furniture
Woodwork Institute of California
United States Dept. of Agriculture
United States Dept. of Commerce
United States Dept. of Housing and Urban Development
United States Dept. of the Interior
United States Dept. of Transportation

Foreword

A resource of incredible range and detail, this volume was compiled by three remarkably inspired designers and educators. Because of their great knowledge of interior design and their sensitivity to the subject matter, they have created the most comprehensive source book for the field ever.

The editors spent three years bringing this volume to fruition, culling the best project drawings by outstanding designers to illustrate much of the subject matter and tapping their own anthropometric expertise to address space planning and special function areas. They also address the importance of historic influence on present-day design with an impressive review of period furniture and interior details. All of these things have produced a reference work of such scope and inclusiveness that the reader will be relieved of many hours in the pursuit of details and information, time saved that can be used for more innovation and creativity in developing solutions for client needs.

The authority and abundance of this book are a testimony to the maturation of this profession of ours and to the editors' appreciation and understanding of its importance.

Jack Lowery, FASID, IDEC

My pleasure in being invited to write part of the Foreword swiftly changed to respect and, in turn, awe at the scope and depth of this book.

To say that it is an encyclopedic compilation and mass of information is obvious. But it is especially and uniquely user-friendly. It presents the written and illustrative data without a trace of pedantry; it meets a real need in our interior designer professional resources. The editors' effort, dedication, and patience, sustained during a period of over three years, are truly heroic. An astonishing number of hours of input have produced a reference of incalculable value.

I offer the same cautionary advice mentioned in the Preface: If the book is a wonderfully comprehensive reference and support for interior design standards, historical material, suggested plan and design criteria, and regulatory limitations, it is not—it will never be—a substitute for the inspired, creative design act, for imaginative solutions are always driven by new cultural conditions, programs, and functional requirements.

So to all you designers: Continue to spin your dreams, but do not stray far from this great resource.

Lawrence J. Israel, AIA, FISP

Preface

Time-Saver Standards for Interior Design and Space Planning is a professional handbook dealing with the planning, design, and detailing of interior spaces. Its primary goal is to provide, within a single reference, information that typically is found dispersed throughout a multitude of sources, including manufacturers' catalogs, technical literature, books dealing with historic styles, and documents and drawings from various projects.

This handbook can be used by the small and medium-size interior design or architectural firm to establish an instant reference library of design data and details by providing a broad selection of detail types and techniques. In addition, the large firm will be able to substantially augment and modify an existing library of details.

Perhaps the most unique feature of this handbook is the vast array of construction and woodwork details reproduced directly from actual working drawings contributed by some of the nation's leading interior design and architectural firms. It is this that makes the handbook particularly useful to the interior designer, architect, and student alike.

This book consists of five sections. The first, entitled Planning and Design of Interior Spaces, deals with residential, office, hospitality, and retail spaces in terms of the relevant planning, design, and detailing data specifically associated with each. The second section, entitled Construction Details and Finishes, deals with various basic interior construction components associated with most interior spaces. These components include partitions, wall openings, wall finishes, floors and floor finishes, doors, ceilings, stairs, fireplaces, and lighting. Details relevant to each component have been contributed by practicing interior designers and architects as well as manufacturers.

The third section, entitled Architectural Woodwork, deals with standard joinery and casework details, customized woodwork details, cornices and mouldings, and furniture hardware. The fourth section, entitled Specialties, deals with various specialized areas of equipment, systems, furnishings, and decoration, including signage and graphics, audio-visual systems, window treatments, and accessories. Information for these subject areas is drawn from manufacturers, suppliers, and designers.

The fifth section, entitled General Reference Data, provides the most comprehensive set of time-saving reference materials found in handbooks of this type, including tables, charts, formulas, and planning guidelines. Of particular interest to the architect, interior designer, and facility manager are tables that can be easily used to determine carpet and wall covering yardage. Charts and drawings relative to human factors and planning standards are also provided.

It should be noted that since the details and other information presented in this book have been compiled from so many different sources, it is difficult to ensure that all the data are entirely accurate or appropriate; for example, in some instances planning guidelines may reflect minimum acceptable standards and not necessarily ideal or preferred standards. In other instances the details indicated may have been perfectly adequate in the context of the total building design of which they were a part, but they may well require modification to reflect design conditions and the reader's intended use. It should also be noted that building codes, fire safety regulations, barrier-free standards, and many other laws governing the design and construction of buildings vary from state to state. Accordingly, the reader should consult all applicable local, state, and federal codes for conformance prior to applying any of the information contained in this book. Moreover, the reader is cautioned that the dimensional information provided in connection with furniture, equipment, appliances, accessories, etc., has been obtained from manufacturers and technical literature and thus varies from supplier to supplier and from source to source. Certain items may have been discontinued, others modified, and still others replaced. Although every effort has been made to ensure the reasonableness of the information, the reader is cautioned to consult the manufacturer of the item specified for current dimensional data.

The reader is also advised that most drawings and other illustrative material have been enlarged or reduced for reasons of page layout and page size. The reader is cautioned, therefore, to disregard any scale designations and not to scale the drawings in order to determine any additional dimensional information.

Finally, as mentioned before, the plans and details contained in this book were extracted from complete sets of actual working drawings prepared by many different contributors. They were selected both because they were representative of typical situations faced by the designer of interior spaces and because they were particularly informative. The authors would like to underscore the fact that these plans and details, as well as all the other material presented in this book, are intended to serve only as a helpful point of departure in connection with the design process, and not as a substitute for original thinking and creativity.

Although every effort has been made to present reasonably accurate information, the editors and publisher assume no liability or responsibility for damage to persons or property alleged to have occurred as a direct or indirect consequence of the use and application of any of the contents of this book. The reader is advised to view the subject matter primarily as guidelines for preliminary planning and detailing, and to properly review, modify, and process it to ensure conformance with local codes and practices and appropriateness of applicability.

Joseph De Chiara
Julius Panero
Martin Zelnik

1

Planning and Design of Interior Spaces

Residential Spaces

THE EXTERIOR

THE 17th Century immigrants brought to America the building traditions of their native lands. The Parson Capen house (1683) at Topsfield, Mass., for example, closely resembles English houses of the same period. But the clapboards are typically American. In the panels at right are close-up details of the Early Colonial background.

Moldings and trim

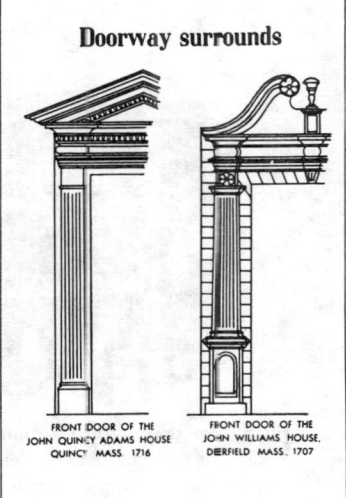

CHIMNEY ARCHITRAVE PANEL MOLDING DOOR AND WINDOW TRIM DADO CHIMNEY ARCHITRAVE FIREPLACE SURROUND MOLDING BASEBOARD

Doorway surrounds

FRONT DOOR OF THE JOHN QUINCY ADAMS HOUSE QUINCY MASS. 1716 FRONT DOOR OF THE JOHN WILLIAMS HOUSE, DEERFIELD MASS. 1707

THE LIVING ROOM

THIS living room is typical of those in the more elaborate Early Colonial homes. The crewel-embroidered curtains are blue-green with touches of red. This is taken up by the upholstery—blue-green damask for the sofas, red tapestry for the chairs. The Oriental rug and the portrait above the fireplace are both in tones of red, brown and yellow, with red dominant.

An alternative color scheme would have blue and yellow upholstery (needlework for the chairs, satin for the sofas). The walls would be pine-paneled, adorned with silver sconces, the curtains a bright cotton print in red, yellow, blue and white.

Living-room fabrics

PETIT-POINT ON SATIN

NEEDLEWORK PANEL

NEEDLEPOINT TAPESTRY

Wing chairs, sofas, armchairs, stools

SLAT-BACK COURTING CHAIR JOINT STOOL ARMCHAIR WITH CANE SEAT AND BACK UPHOLSTERED STOOL SLAT-BACK ROCKING CHAIR WALNUT SOFA WAINSCOT CHAIR C. 1650 TALL-BACK WING CHAIR SETTEE CHAIR WITH WIDE SEAT CABRIOLE-LEG WING CHAIR DOUBLE CHAIR SETTEE HOGARTH TYPE SIDE CHAIR PANELED-OAK SETTEE

Furniture made in America during the Early Colonial period (the seventeenth century and the first quarter of the eighteenth century) was necessarily, and possibly also by choice, of the simplest type. The early colonists, particularly those in New England, had not time or equipment to spare for any but the essentials of life.

Turning on the lathe was the simplest to achieve and thus the most common form of furniture decoration. It was also a process capable of infinite variations of design (some are shown in Fig. 1).

Characteristic types of stretcher

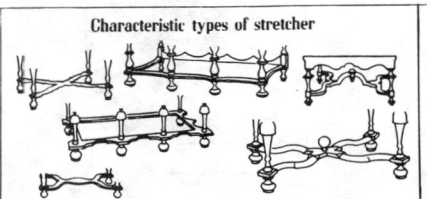

Turnings used for decoration

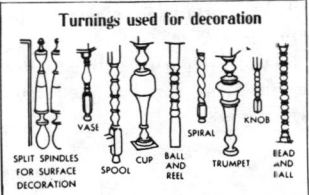

SPLIT SPINDLES FOR SURFACE DECORATION VASE SPOOL CUP BALL AND REEL SPIRAL TRUMPET KNOB BEAD AND BALL

Fig. 1 Motifs characteristic of Early Colonial furniture.

THE DINING ROOM

The color scheme in this dining room is keyed to the low tones of the pine paneling and walnut furniture, the soft gleam of the smooth polished brass chandelier. The bannister back chairs have rush-bottom seats. Brilliant red and white printed cotton is used for the curtains. The hooked rug is in reds and greens.

Alternatively the curtains might be of red and yellow crewel embroidery, the upholstery of red brocade. In the panels at right are furniture and fabrics suited to an Early Colonial dining room.

Dining-room fabrics

NEEDLEPOINT TAPESTRY

CUT VELVET

COTTON PRINT

Dining tables, table chairs

OAK TABLE

TABLE CHAIRS —
THE BACK SWINGS
DOWN OVER THE ARMS

SIDE TABLE
WITH CABRIOLE LEGS

OVAL TABLE, QUEEN ANNE STYLE,
WITH CABRIOLE LEGS

MAPLE BUTTERFLY TABLE,
FROM NEW ENGLAND

PLANK-TOP REFECTORY TABLE

ENGLISH GATE-LEG TABLE C 1670

THE BEDROOM

This little bedroom with its pine paneling and low ceiling is typical of the Early Colonial period. The bed, decorated with hangings of crewel work in an Oriental design, is the most important feature of the room. The chairs are upholstered in yellow damask. The green printed cotton used for the little draped window curtains is echoed by the greens in the hooked rug on the floor.

Alternatively the walls might be painted a dark gray-blue, the curtain material being a red printed cotton on a gray ground. The furniture is of walnut and oak.

Bedroom fabrics

DAMASK

PRINTED CALICO

CREWEL EMBROIDERY BASED ON TREE OF LIFE DESIGN

Beds, daybed, cradle

PRIMITIVE TRUNDLE BED

FOLDING PRESS BED

CANOPY BED

PANELED CRADLE

WALNUT FOUR-POSTER
C. 1710

DAYBED OF "CAIN" STYLE C. 1690

Even the most costly furniture in this Early Colonial period was usually of solid wood unfinished except for stain or waxing. Veneering and shellacking, to gain carefully patterned graining and high finish, were still unexploited. The pine paneling on the walls might be left unfinished, waxed, or painted. Other woods near at hand in the forests and so commonly used were oak, birch, maple, and walnut. Generally, American work is patterned upon English work of 10 or 20 years earlier. In Pennsylvania and Delaware, which were settled by colonists of Swedish and German descent (in addition to the English), much of the simple furniture was painted with its motifs transferred from European peasant art.

In the later years of the Early Colonial period, when New Englanders were already beginning to trade with the Orient, much Chinese porcelain was imported. The Oriental influence was strong in textiles; the Tree of Life pattern was very popular at this period. Native textiles copied the patterns

Armchair, side chairs

"CAIN" CHAIRS, FLEMISH SCROLLS AND FEET, CANE BACKS AND SEATS

BANNISTER BACK, SIMPLE TURNED LEGS

EARLY TYPE CABRIOLE LEGS

CANE SEAT, PLAIN SPLAT

LATE QUEEN ANNE TYPE, FLATTENED BALL AND CLAW FEET

BANNISTER BACK, SPANISH FEET

EARLY QUEEN ANNE TYPE WITH DUTCH SPLAT BACK

UPHOLSTERED CHAIR WITH DUTCH FEET

SHELL CRESTING, SHALLOW SEAT

PIERCED BACK, BALL-AND-CLAW FEET

Sideboards, dressers, chests

OAK SIDEBOARD CABRIOLE LEGS C 1650

LOW CHEST WITH DRAWERS

NEW ENGLAND OAK PRESS CUPBOARD

HEAVY OAK CHEST OF DRAWERS WITH APPLIED MOLDINGS

OAK SIDEBOARD, TWISTED LEGS

WILLIAM AND MARY TYPE GLASS-FRONTED CABINET

PENNSYLVANIA SPICE CUPBOARD C. 1700

WALNUT DRESSER, PANELED DOORS

Dining-room accessories

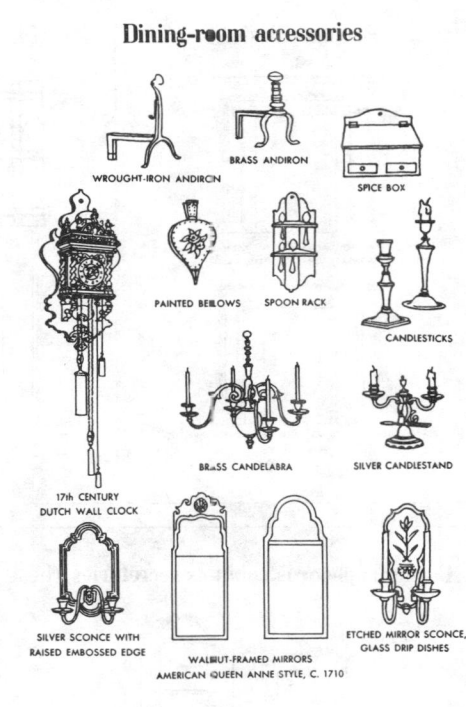

WROUGHT-IRON ANDIRON

BRASS ANDIRON

SPICE BOX

PAINTED BELLOWS

SPOON RACK

CANDLESTICKS

17TH CENTURY DUTCH WALL CLOCK

BRASS CANDELABRA

SILVER CANDLESTAND

SILVER SCONCE WITH RAISED EMBOSSED EDGE

WALNUT-FRAMED MIRRORS AMERICAN QUEEN ANNE STYLE, C. 1710

ETCHED MIRROR SCONCE, GLASS DRIP DISHES

Chests, kas, highboy, chests of drawers

MAPLE CHEST OF DRAWERS

BOX TABLE OF OAK AND MAPLE C 1670

INLAID CHEST OF DRAWERS WITH DROP HANDLES

CHEST ON FRAME, DECORATED WITH SCRATCH CARVING

CONNECTICUT PAINTED CHEST

HIGHBOY WITH TRUMPET-TURNED LEGS

DUTCH KAS WITH BALL FEET

DUTCH KAS FROM NEW YORK PAINTED IN GRAY AND WHITE

Desk, lowboys, night tables, stools

WALNUT CORNER CHAIR

OAK JOINT STOOL

LOWBOY IN BURL WALNUT

NIGHT TABLE

ARMCHAIR QUEEN ANNE STYLE

CANDLESTAND

STOOL WILLIAM AND MARY TYPE

NIGHT TABLE

CARVED OAK WRITING BOX C. 1650

UPHOLSTERED JACOBEAN SIDE CHAIR

LOWBOY WITH SHELL FRONT

SLANT-TOP DESK ON A TURNED FRAME

Bedroom accessories

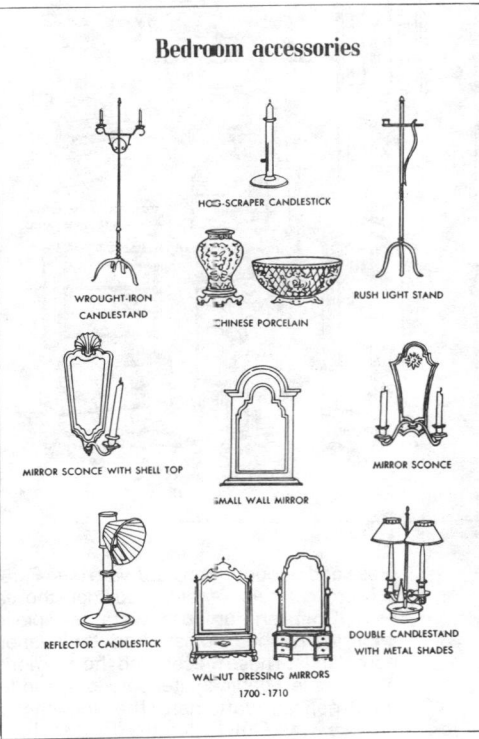

WROUGHT-IRON CANDLESTAND

CHINESE PORCELAIN

HOG-SCRAPER CANDLESTICK

RUSH LIGHT STAND

MIRROR SCONCE WITH SHELL TOP

SMALL WALL MIRROR

MIRROR SCONCE

REFLECTOR CANDLESTICK

WALNUT DRESSING MIRRORS 1700 - 1710

DOUBLE CANDLESTAND WITH METAL SHADES

---

and colors of India, Persia, and China. The originals, or good copies of them, were usually imported from England.

The colors in common use were of a piece with the solid, sturdy furniture. They seldom escaped from the conventional round of blue, red, gold, and natural gray. The only exceptions were imported fabrics and the occa-

sional hard brilliance of the Chinese porcelain found in the great houses of the day. Whatever luxury there was at this time expressed itself in textiles and silver rather than in furniture. Settlers in the South, many of them English aristocrats, maintained a higher standard of comfort than those in the North; they imported most of their furniture and fabrics

from England and continued to do so for a long time.

Early Colonial furniture taken as a whole is sturdy, but not subtle. Furniture patterns in this country changed slowly. Paneling relieved the larger flat areas such as cupboard doors and drawer fronts. The latter were further decorated by quite elaborate fretted

PERIOD FURNITURE

17th Century American: Colonial

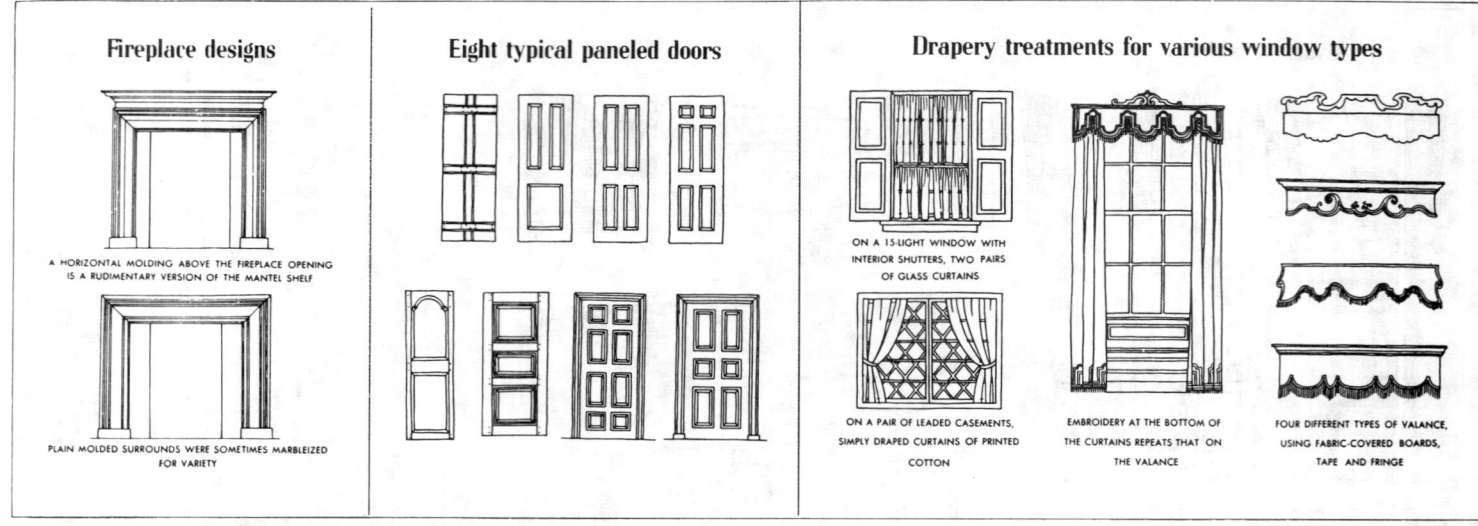

Fireplace designs

A HORIZONTAL MOLDING ABOVE THE FIREPLACE OPENING IS A RUDIMENTARY VERSION OF THE MANTEL SHELF

PLAIN MOLDED SURROUNDS WERE SOMETIMES MARBLEIZED FOR VARIETY

Eight typical paneled doors

Drapery treatments for various window types

ON A 15-LIGHT WINDOW WITH INTERIOR SHUTTERS, TWO PAIRS OF GLASS CURTAINS

ON A PAIR OF LEADED CASEMENTS, SIMPLY DRAPED CURTAINS OF PRINTED COTTON

EMBROIDERY AT THE BOTTOM OF THE CURTAINS REPEATS THAT ON THE VALANCE

FOUR DIFFERENT TYPES OF VALANCE, USING FABRIC-COVERED BOARDS, TAPE AND FRINGE

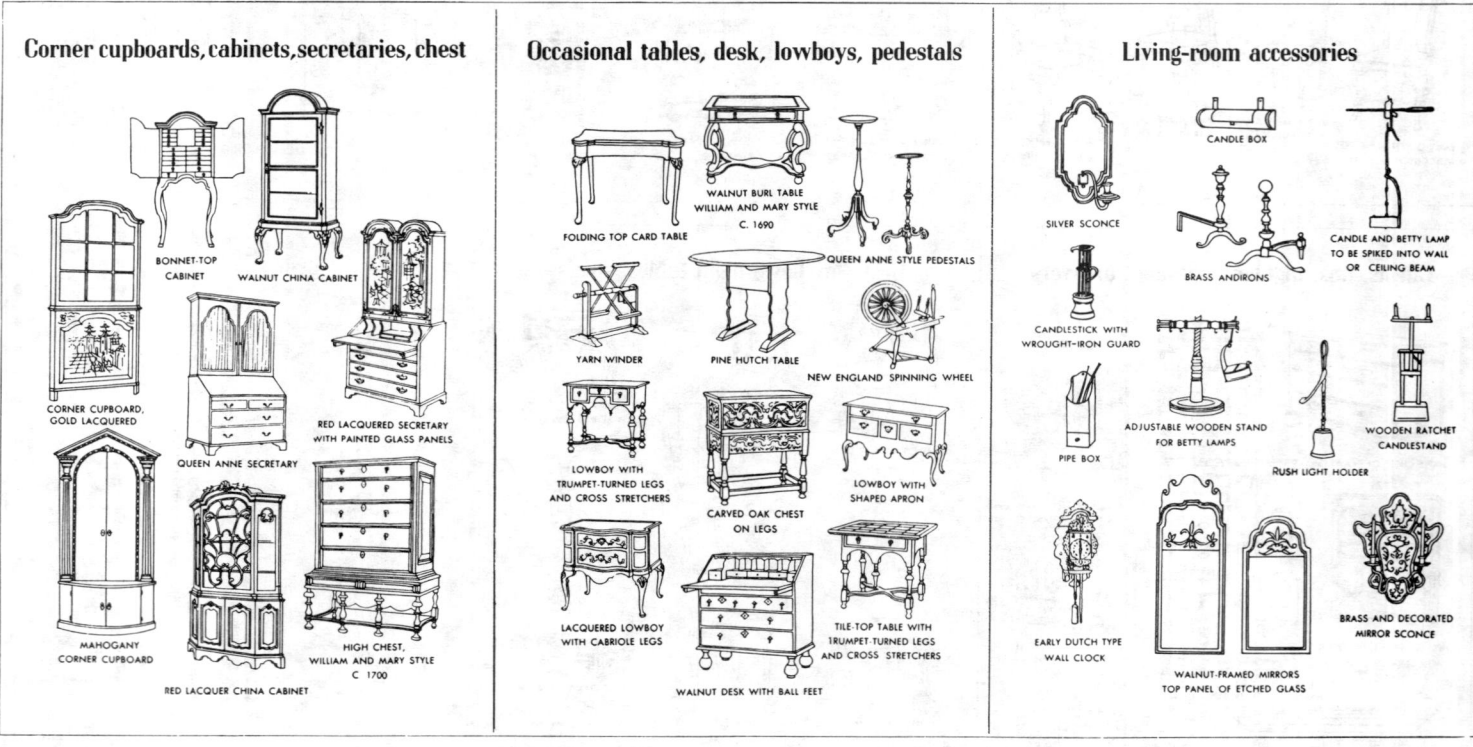

Corner cupboards, cabinets, secretaries, chest

BONNET-TOP CABINET

WALNUT CHINA CABINET

CORNER CUPBOARD, GOLD LACQUERED

QUEEN ANNE SECRETARY

RED LACQUERED SECRETARY WITH PAINTED GLASS PANELS

MAHOGANY CORNER CUPBOARD

RED LACQUER CHINA CABINET

HIGH CHEST, WILLIAM AND MARY STYLE C 1700

Occasional tables, desk, lowboys, pedestals

FOLDING TOP CARD TABLE

WALNUT BURL TABLE WILLIAM AND MARY STYLE C. 1690

QUEEN ANNE STYLE PEDESTALS

YARN WINDER

PINE HUTCH TABLE

NEW ENGLAND SPINNING WHEEL

LOWBOY WITH TRUMPET-TURNED LEGS AND CROSS STRETCHERS

CARVED OAK CHEST ON LEGS

LOWBOY WITH SHAPED APRON

LACQUERED LOWBOY WITH CABRIOLE LEGS

TILE-TOP TABLE WITH TRUMPET-TURNED LEGS AND CROSS STRETCHERS

WALNUT DESK WITH BALL FEET

Living-room accessories

CANDLE BOX

SILVER SCONCE

BRASS ANDIRONS

CANDLE AND BETTY LAMP TO BE SPIKED INTO WALL OR CEILING BEAM

CANDLESTICK WITH WROUGHT-IRON GUARD

ADJUSTABLE WOODEN STAND FOR BETTY LAMPS

PIPE BOX

RUSH LIGHT HOLDER

WOODEN RATCHET CANDLESTAND

EARLY DUTCH TYPE WALL CLOCK

WALNUT-FRAMED MIRRORS TOP PANEL OF ETCHED GLASS

BRASS AND DECORATED MIRROR SCONCE

brass and wrought-iron hardware (see Fig. 1).

More carefully embellished than the earliest American furniture were the pieces imported by the colonists from their various homelands. These pieces, and the memories of others left behind, later served as models for American craftsmen. The dominant influence was Dutch, for the English had a Hollander, William of Orange, as king. He and his queen, Mary, gave their names to a style of which elaborate stretchers (particularly on highboys, lowboys, and occasional tables) and scrolled legs are among the most obvious characteristics.

Also from Dutch, Spanish, and Portuguese sources are derived most of the carved feet

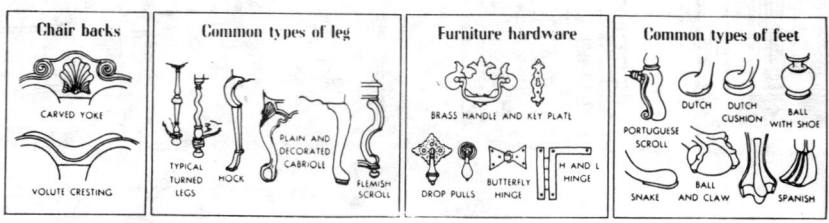

Chair backs

CARVED YOKE

VOLUTE CRESTING

Common types of leg

TYPICAL TURNED LEGS

MOCK

PLAIN AND DECORATED CABRIOLE

FLEMISH SCROLL

Furniture hardware

BRASS HANDLE AND KEY PLATE

DROP PULLS

BUTTERFLY HINGE

H AND L HINGE

Common types of feet

DUTCH

DUTCH CUSHION

BALL WITH SHOE

PORTUGUESE SCROLL

SNAKE

BALL AND CLAW

SPANISH

Fig. 1 *(Continued)*

which distinguish this Early Colonial furniture and often give clues to its date and place of origin.

THE EXTERIOR

The architectural details shown in the five panels at right are characteristic of the background for 18th Century Colonial decoration. As one of the finest houses of the period we have pictured (at right) "Westover" the great mansion erected by William Byrd in Charles City Co., Virginia. Typical of this period are the brick walls and chimneys, the stone or white painted brick trim. In the North wood was in more common use than brick for the exterior, and the interior wooden trim was finely detailed.

Typical Colonial architecture

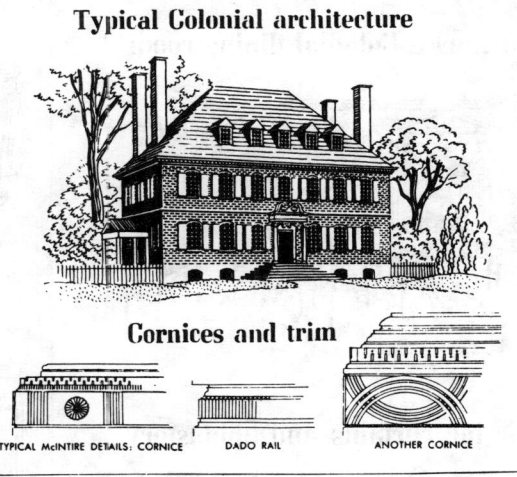

Cornices and trim

TYPICAL McINTIRE DETAILS: CORNICE   DADO RAIL   ANOTHER CORNICE

Interior doorways

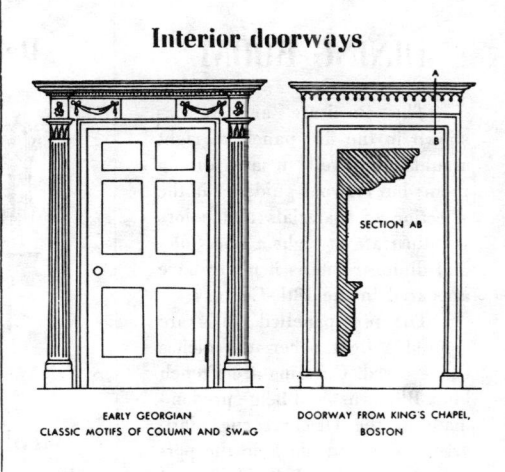

EARLY GEORGIAN
CLASSIC MOTIFS OF COLUMN AND SWAG

DOORWAY FROM KING'S CHAPEL, BOSTON

SECTION AB

THE LIVING ROOM

The furniture, fabrics and accessories shown in these panels are all suitable to the living room, and they are all typical of the 18th Century Colonial style.

The interior pictured at right is a fine Colonial living room carefully restored to its 18th Century state. The walls are Naples yellow, the columns and fireplace white. Red and green are dominant in the Oriental rug, dark greens and browns in the portrait above the fireplace. So the sofa is upholstered in striped satin, the armchair in yellow Venetian brocade, the wing chair in a printed linen. The urns are of Chinese porcelain.

Another color scheme might be: pearly gray walls, oyster white columns and fireplace. Red would be dominant in the Oriental carpet, dark greens and red in the portrait. There would be red damask on the sofa, green rep on the wing chair, and gold damask for the armchair.

Decorating a Colonial living room

Fabrics for curtains and upholstery

EMBROIDERY   SATIN   BLOCK PRINT

Wing chairs, armchairs, sofas

CONNECTICUT WING CHAIR   PHILADELPHIA VERSION OF HEPPLEWHITE   MARTHA WASHINGTON CHAIR

CABRIOLE LEG SOFA 1760-1770   SETTEE CHIPPENDALE INFLUENCE

HEPPLEWHITE STYLE   PHILADELPHIA TYPE DESK CHAIR CABRIOLE LEG   PHILADELPHIA MAKE CHIPPENDALE STYLE

PHILADELPHIA TYPE WING CHAIR CHIPPENDALE INFLUENCE   MAHOGANY CHIPPENDALE SOFA

Whereas furniture of the Early Colonial period was often so primitive as to be referred to as "kitchen Colonial," in this succeeding era dignity and luxury prevail in the centers of taste. The furnishings reflect the fashionable contemporary styles of England and stately country homes, whether on New England farms or Virginian and Carolina plantations, followed these styles. This gave rise to a number of notable architects, craftsmen, and workers in metal and wood.

The eighteenth century Colonial period was the first of the really great eras in American cabinetmaking.

The manufacture of wallpaper in this country was begun by 1763. Before this it was from Europe. The "Pennsylvania fireplace" or "Franklin stove" was invented by Benjamin Franklin in 1742 and immediately became popular up and down the Atlantic seaboard. Philadelphia was a furniture style center, in fact the most active in the creation of taste, with Boston and Charleston following.

A number of artists and craftsmen of this period bear mentioning. Among the architects were Samuel McIntire, Charles Bulfinch, John James, Richard Mundy, Peter Harrison, John Kirk, and Isaac Royall. These men were greatly influenced by the English architects Isaac Ware, James Gibbs, Robert Morris, Abraham Swan, William Halfpenny, Batty Langley, and William Pain, who in turn were in debt to the Italian masters Palladio and Giacomo Leoni. Among the cabinetmakers were Moses Dodge, Stephen Dwight, Henry Hardcastle, Gilbert Ash, Robert Wallace, Charles Shipman, John Brinner, John Tremain, Charles Warham, John Brown, Bemsley Wells, Thomas and Benjamin Laskey, Jonathan Goodhue, and Job Trask. Among the upholsterers were Stephen Callow, Richard Wenman, Joseph Cox, and John Taylor; among the metalworkers were William Coffin, Wilkins, Joseph Liddell, William Bradford, John Bassett, and Peter Harby; and among the painters were John Singleton Copley, Joseph Blackburn, John

DINING ROOM

The furniture and fabrics shown in the five panels at right would look well in any dining room; but for your guidance in the selection of materials and colors we illustrate at right a fine Colonial dining room as it might have appeared in the 18th Century.

The pine-panelled walls are colored a light ocher, the niches Chinese red. Curtains are French blue. Blue, rust and beige predominate in the Oriental rug, dark green, blue and black in the portrait over the fireplace. Table and chairs are of walnut, the sideboard of mahogany.

An alternative color scheme would be light blue-gray walls with cream niches. Curtains would be oyster white silk, the Oriental rug having a greenish tan background.

Decorating a Colonial dining room

Fabric for curtains and upholstery

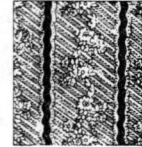 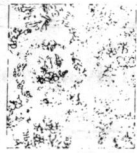 

BROCADE   PRINTED LINEN   STRIPED BROCADE

Dining tables, consoles

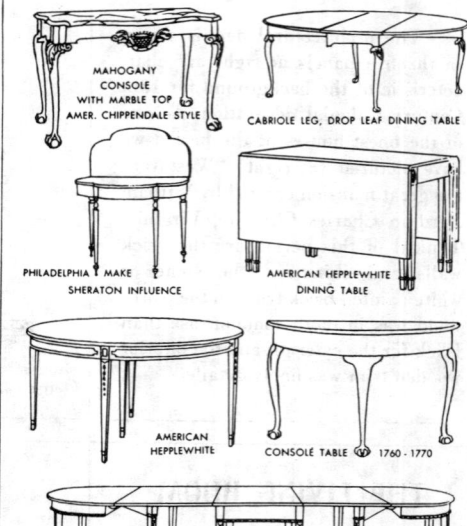

MAHOGANY CONSOLE WITH MARBLE TOP AMER. CHIPPENDALE STYLE

CABRIOLE LEG, DROP LEAF DINING TABLE

PHILADELPHIA MAKE SHERATON INFLUENCE

AMERICAN HEPPLEWHITE DINING TABLE

AMERICAN HEPPLEWHITE

CONSOLE TABLE 1760 - 1770

EXTENSIBLE DINING TABLE 1770

BEDROOM

In the bedroom at right, choice of color and textures was designed to achieve an impression of warmth and intimacy. The paneled walls are in two tones of gray-green, the ceiling ocher. Curtains are antique gray-green satin.

Furniture is walnut, except for the mahogany bed, which has a yellow taffeta spread. Fireside chairs are covered in crimson damask, side chairs in turkey work.

An alternative color scheme would be: warm gray walls with oyster white moldings. The ceiling would be cream, the carpet solid taupe, and the curtains of blue damask. The bed would have a white moire spread and blue valance. The side chairs would be upholstered in yellow damask, the wing chair in turkey work.

Decorating a Colonial bedroom

Fabrics for curtains, upholstery, canopy

  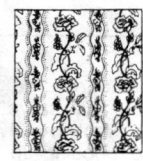

PRINTED LINEN   TOILE DE JOUY   DAMASK

Four-poster beds

MAPLE LOW POSTER BED

FIELD BED AND TESTER

FIELD BED AND TESTER

LATE 18TH CENTURY TYPE

Ramage, James Peale, and Charles Wilson Peale. Important manufacturers were, of wallpaper, Jackson of Battersea (England) and, of window and bottle glass, Baron Stiegel and Caspar Wistar.

Fabrics most commonly used during the Colonial period were damask, camblet, Indian gimp and binding, moreen (woolen drapery cloth), harrateen cloth, block-printed cotton and linen, cashmere, calico, dimity, durance, stout worsted cloth, turkey work (tufted "pilelike"), paduasoy (strong silk), soy, shalloon, watchet, linsey-woolsey, fustian, silk muslin, chintz, Indian calico, tabby, sarcanet, taffeta, horsehair, camak, bancours, and brocade.

Woods most commonly used were oak, ash, elm, red cedar, mahogany, walnut, maple, pine, and cherry.

The Chippendale style merges at one end with Queen Anne, at the other with Hepplewhite, Sheraton, and Duncan Phyfe. The Rococo mounts to its zenith and starts to decline within these years. Walnut has a new rival in mahogany. And American craftsmen produced pieces of a quality which compares favorably with English work.

Armchairs, side chairs

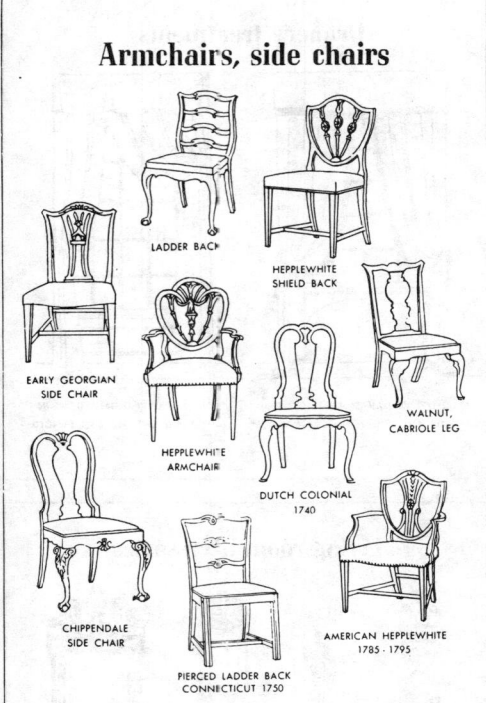

LADDER BACK

HEPPLEWHITE SHIELD BACK

EARLY GEORGIAN SIDE CHAIR

HEPPLEWHITE ARMCHAIR

WALNUT, CABRIOLE LEG

DUTCH COLONIAL 1740

CHIPPENDALE SIDE CHAIR

PIERCED LADDER BACK CONNECTICUT 1750

AMERICAN HEPPLEWHITE 1785 - 1795

Sideboards, lowboys, chests

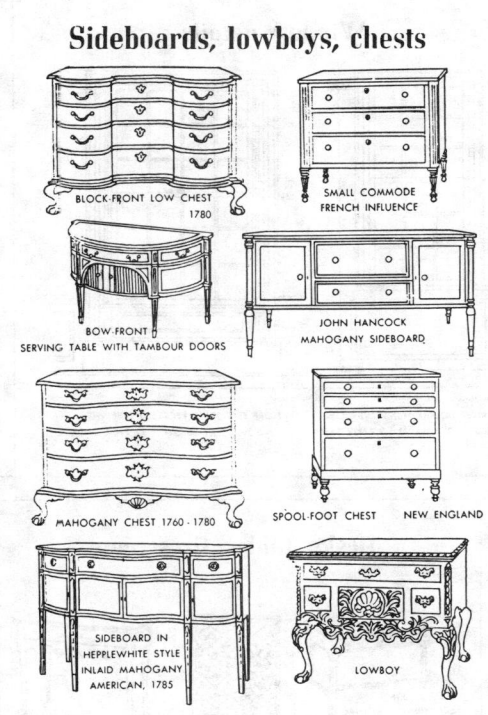

BLOCK-FRONT LOW CHEST 1780

SMALL COMMODE FRENCH INFLUENCE

BOW-FRONT SERVING TABLE WITH TAMBOUR DOORS

JOHN HANCOCK MAHOGANY SIDEBOARD

MAHOGANY CHEST 1760 - 1780

SPOOL-FOOT CHEST   NEW ENGLAND

SIDEBOARD IN HEPPLEWHITE STYLE INLAID MAHOGANY AMERICAN, 1785

LOWBOY

Dining room accessories

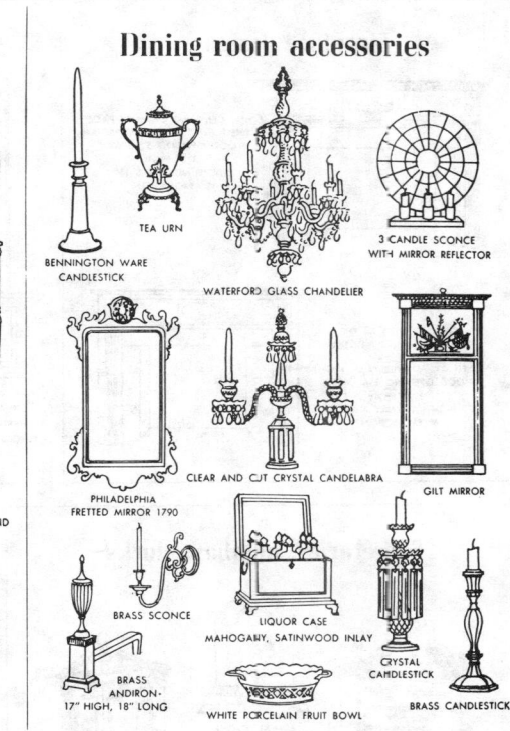

TEA URN

3 CANDLE SCONCE WITH MIRROR REFLECTOR

BENNINGTON WARE CANDLESTICK

WATERFORD GLASS CHANDELIER

PHILADELPHIA FRETTED MIRROR 1790

CLEAR AND CUT CRYSTAL CANDELABRA

GILT MIRROR

BRASS SCONCE

LIQUOR CASE MAHOGANY, SATINWOOD INLAY

CRYSTAL CANDLESTICK

BRASS ANDIRON· 17" HIGH, 18" LONG

WHITE PORCELAIN FRUIT BOWL

BRASS CANDLESTICK

Chests, kas, secretary

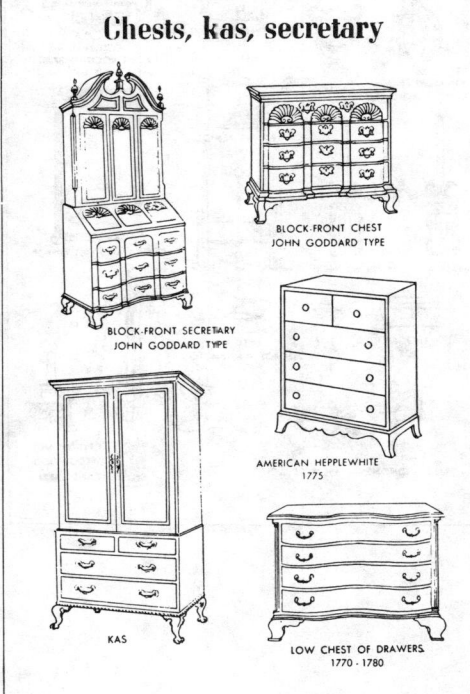

BLOCK-FRONT CHEST JOHN GODDARD TYPE

BLOCK-FRONT SECRETARY JOHN GODDARD TYPE

AMERICAN HEPPLEWHITE 1775

KAS

LOW CHEST OF DRAWERS 1770 - 1780

Wing chairs, armchairs, tables

JEFFERSON'S LEATHER TOP COMBINATION WRITING DESK AND DRAWING TABLE

SIDE TABLE

SEWING STAND HEPPLEWHITE STYLE 1770 - 1780

AMERICAN CHIPPENDALE

QUEEN TYPE COLONIAL WING CHAIR

TABLE BELONGING TO JEFFERSON

CANDLE STAND

DRESSING TABLE

CAPE COD WING CHAIR

CHAIR OWNED BY GEORGE WASHINGTON

Bedroom accessories

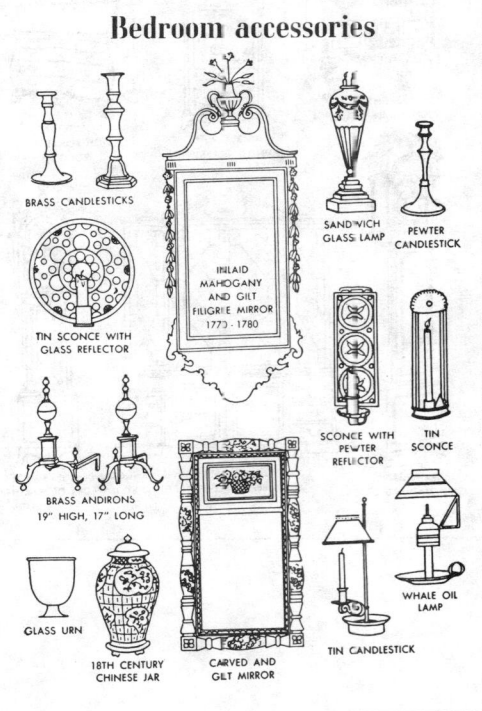

BRASS CANDLESTICKS

SANDWICH GLASS LAMP

PEWTER CANDLESTICK

TIN SCONCE WITH GLASS REFLECTOR

INLAID MAHOGANY AND GILT FILIGREE MIRROR 1770 - 1780

SCONCE WITH PEWTER REFLECTOR

TIN SCONCE

BRASS ANDIRONS 19" HIGH, 17" LONG

GLASS URN

18TH CENTURY CHINESE JAR

CARVED AND GILT MIRROR

WHALE OIL LAMP

TIN CANDLESTICK

Marble was imported until after the Revolution when domestic marbles began to be used. Marble chimney pieces, window sash, lead roofing, and hardware were all imported from London. The size of glass window panes gradually increased as the century progressed.

An order of small pilasters or columns supporting the mantel in a chimney piece was found only in imported work prior to the Revolution. Fireplace openings with neither cornice nor mantel shelf were long common. Ears on the architraves were almost universal, and a pediment (always broken) was very common. After 1760 the scroll pediment, or a similar treatment of the architrave, occurs.

PERIOD FURNITURE
18th Century American: Colonial

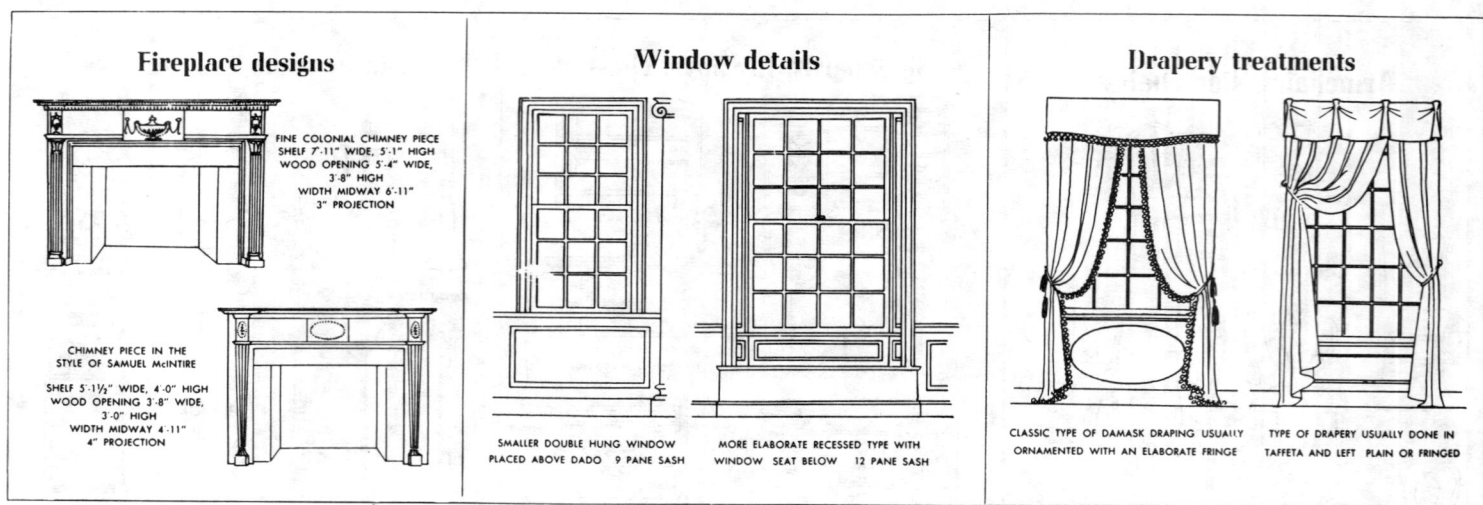

Fireplace designs

FINE COLONIAL CHIMNEY PIECE
SHELF 7'-11" WIDE, 5'-1" HIGH
WOOD OPENING 5'-4" WIDE,
3'-8" HIGH
WIDTH MIDWAY 6'-11"
3" PROJECTION

CHIMNEY PIECE IN THE
STYLE OF SAMUEL McINTIRE

SHELF 5'-1½" WIDE, 4'-0" HIGH
WOOD OPENING 3'-8" WIDE,
3'-0" HIGH
WIDTH MIDWAY 4'-11"
4" PROJECTION

Window details

SMALLER DOUBLE HUNG WINDOW
PLACED ABOVE DADO   9 PANE SASH

MORE ELABORATE RECESSED TYPE WITH
WINDOW SEAT BELOW   12 PANE SASH

Drapery treatments

CLASSIC TYPE OF DAMASK DRAPING USUALLY
ORNAMENTED WITH AN ELABORATE FRINGE

TYPE OF DRAPERY USUALLY DONE IN
TAFFETA AND LEFT PLAIN OR FRINGED

Secretaries, highboy, clocks

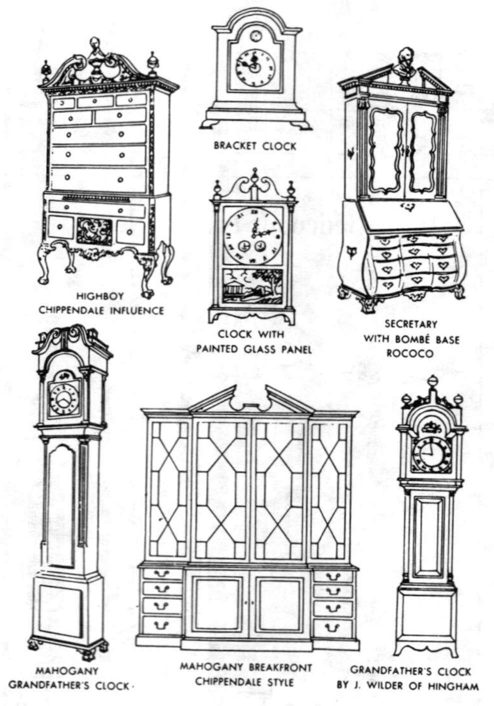

BRACKET CLOCK

HIGHBOY
CHIPPENDALE INFLUENCE

CLOCK WITH
PAINTED GLASS PANEL

SECRETARY
WITH BOMBÉ BASE
ROCOCO

MAHOGANY
GRANDFATHER'S CLOCK

MAHOGANY BREAKFRONT
CHIPPENDALE STYLE

GRANDFATHER'S CLOCK
BY J. WILDER OF HINGHAM

Desks, tables, firescreen

LATE
SOUTHERN COLONIAL
1760

MAHOGANY
SIDE TABLE

WALL TABLE

POLE FIRE SCREEN
1775

LATE
SOUTHERN COLONIAL
CARD TABLE

SLANT TOP DESK
1750

KNEEHOLE MAHOGANY DESK
RHODE ISLAND BLOCKFRONT

TIP TOP TEA TABLE
C. 1775

MAHOGANY CONSOLE TABLE

Living room accessories

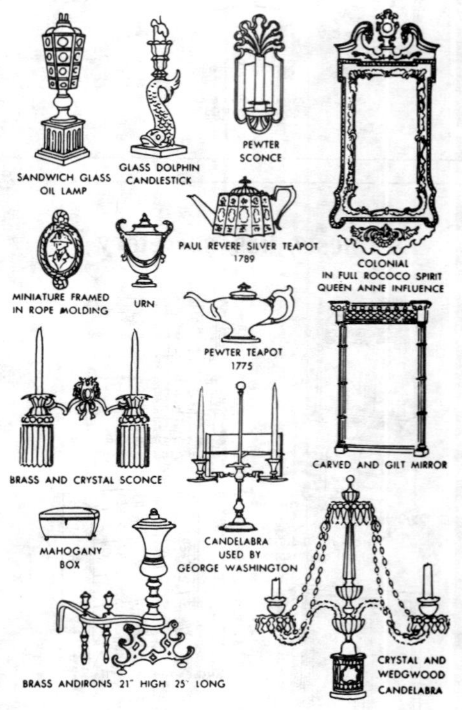

SANDWICH GLASS
OIL LAMP

GLASS DOLPHIN
CANDLESTICK

PEWTER
SCONCE

COLONIAL
IN FULL ROCOCO SPIRIT
QUEEN ANNE INFLUENCE

MINIATURE FRAMED
IN ROPE MOLDING

URN

PAUL REVERE SILVER TEAPOT
1789

PEWTER TEAPOT
1775

BRASS AND CRYSTAL SCONCE

CARVED AND GILT MIRROR

MAHOGANY
BOX

CANDELABRA
USED BY
GEORGE WASHINGTON

BRASS ANDIRONS 21" HIGH 25" LONG

CRYSTAL AND
WEDGWOOD
CANDELABRA

THE EXTERIOR

As a typical mansion of the Federal period we show Mappa Hall in Trenton, N.Y. It was started in the closing years of the 18th Century and completed in 1809. The portico and the simple pediment exemplify the prevailing Classic trend. In the panels to the right are some typical details from the Federal period background

Cornices and trim

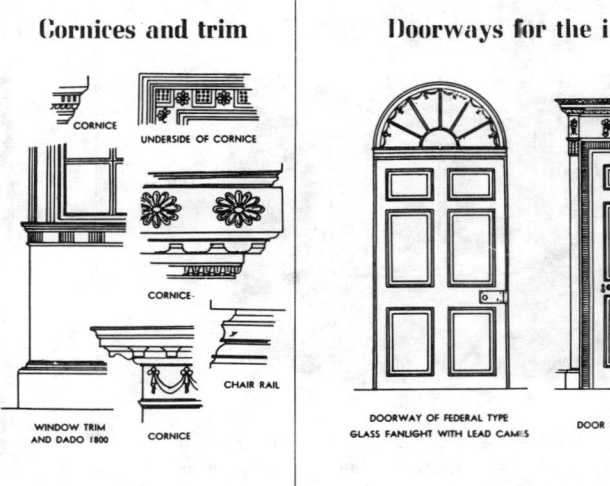

CORNICE

UNDERSIDE OF CORNICE

CORNICE

CHAIR RAIL

WINDOW TRIM AND DADO 1800

CORNICE

Doorways for the interior

DOORWAY OF FEDERAL TYPE
GLASS FANLIGHT WITH LEAD CAMES

DOOR BY SAMUEL McINTIRE

THE LIVING ROOM

THIS is a fine Federal interior in its original condition. The walls and woodwork are painted pistachio green. The curtains are of beige damask, the sofa upholstered in red and gold damask. Gold damask is used for the armchairs, yellow damask for the side chairs. The Oriental rug is wine red in tone, the furniture, mahogany. The clock is of ox-blood marble.

An alternate scheme would have light gray-blue walls and woodwork. The draperies would be yellow damask, the chairs upholstered in green damask. The furniture and fabrics shown in panels at right would also be suitable for the Federal living room

Living room fabrics

SATIN DAMASK

VELOUR

SILK DAMASK

Armchairs, side chair, sofas

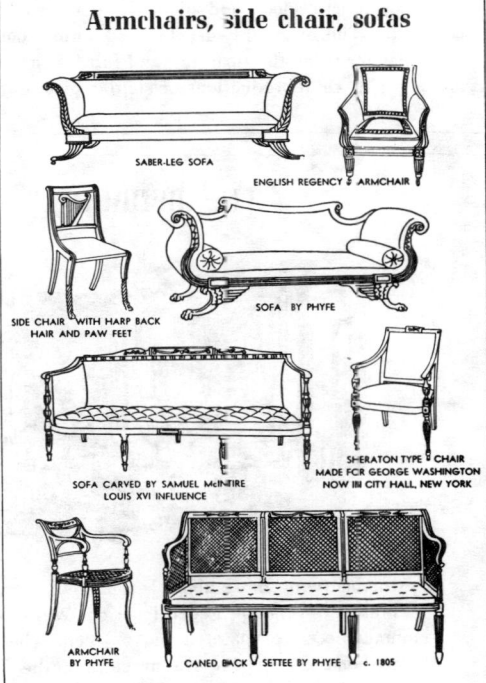

SABER-LEG SOFA

ENGLISH REGENCY ARMCHAIR

SIDE CHAIR WITH HARP BACK HAIR AND PAW FEET

SOFA BY PHYFE

SOFA CARVED BY SAMUEL McINTIRE LOUIS XVI INFLUENCE

SHERATON TYPE CHAIR MADE FOR GEORGE WASHINGTON NOW IN CITY HALL, NEW YORK

ARMCHAIR BY PHYFE

CANED BACK SETTEE BY PHYFE c. 1805

The Federal style is at its most suave and elegant in the furniture of Duncan Phyfe, a Scotch cabinetmaker who arrived in New York about 1795. He did not originate a style; he translated prevailing fashions into fine craftsmanship. Thomas Sheraton, then the current English favorite, and the French Directoire cabinetmakers set the style. All these designers were profoundly influenced by a rediscovery of the classic splendors of Greece and Italy.

Reeding of table, chair, and sofa legs and other framing members gives elegance to Federal furniture. Contrasting color veneer is used to outline the edges of tables and desks and to lend interest to large plain surfaces.

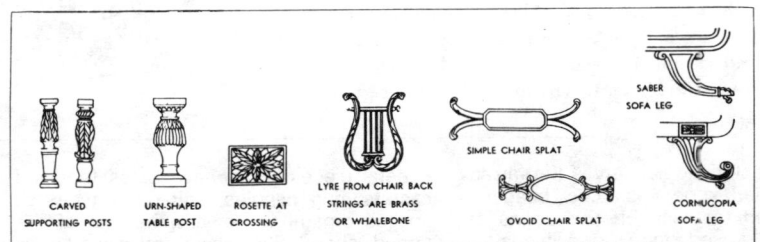

CARVED SUPPORTING POSTS

URN-SHAPED TABLE POST

ROSETTE AT CROSSING

LYRE FROM CHAIR BACK STRINGS ARE BRASS OR WHALEBONE

SIMPLE CHAIR SPLAT

OVOID CHAIR SPLAT

SABER SOFA LEG

CORNUCOPIA SOFA LEG

Fig. 2   Motifs characteristic of Federal furniture.

THE DINING ROOM

I N THE dining room shown above the walls are mist gray, the chimneypiece ochre and white marble. The drapery and upholstery are both cherry silk damask. The Oriental rug is in tones of brown, blue and beige. The furniture is mahogany.

An alternate scheme would include: soft gray-green walls, beige silk damask curtains, red damask upholstery. The sconces, clock and picture frames would be gilt.

This original Federal period dining room will give you ideas for using the furniture and fabrics shown in the panels at right. Or reproductions of similar pieces are appropriate.

Dining room fabrics

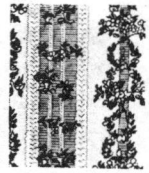

SATIN

PRINTED SILK

BROCATELLE

Dining tables, side tables, console

PEDESTAL DINING TABLE

LYRE END TABLE BY PHYFE

CONSOLE WITH EGYPTIAN CARYATIDS

EXTENSION TYPE TABLE BY PHYFE

SOFA TABLE BY PHYFE

PEDESTAL DINING TABLE

FOUR SOFA TABLES JOINED TO FORM A DINING TABLE

FOLDING TOP OCCASIONAL TALLE

THE BEDROOM

T HIS bedroom shown above is typical of those found in fine houses during the Federal period. Walls, woodwork and chimneypiece are painted moss green. The upholstery is beige damask, except for yellow satin on the desk chair. The rug is in two tones of burgundy with a design of green, pink and white. On the walls are engravings in gilt frames.

An alternate color scheme would have walls and woodwork painted peach color. The rug would then be olive green with a design in yellow and pink. The upholstery would be blue, except for red satin on the seat of the desk chair. Other furniture and fabrics suitable for this room are shown at right

Bedroom fabrics

SILK

SATIN

DAMASK

Four-poster and other types of bed

FOUR-POSTER BED BY PHYFE

BED BY PHYFE, LOUIS XVI AFFINITY

MAHOGANY BED ONE OF A PAIR BY PHYFE

BED BY PHYFE FRENCH INFLUENCE

Another characteristic subtlety is the raised hairline of wood, known as a cock beading, which is used to finish off the edges of drawers. Phyfe used white wood linings for the drawers in his furniture, instead of the pine linings universally employed by other American cabinetmakers of this period.

Brass ornaments (probably for the most part imported) are used extensively on Federal pieces. They have brass feet and casters, ring handles, and other types of applied ornament. Toward the end of the period, about 1825, china and glass knobs began to supplant brass rings as drawer pulls.

The new United States was in its first throes of nationalism; consequently its emblem, the eagle, appears everywhere — on transparencies in windows, painted on fans, inlaid in mirrors, desks, knife boxes, and brass work. The "Spread Eagle" became a favorite tavern sign. All kinds of historic scenes and patriotic emblems appear as decoration on clocks.

And yet, the Classic influence was even stronger than the patriotic. Earthenware and porcelain such as Crown-Derby, Worcester,

Armchairs, side chairs

TYPICAL CHAIRS OF AMERICAN FEDERAL DESIGN 1790-1830

Sideboards, chests of drawers

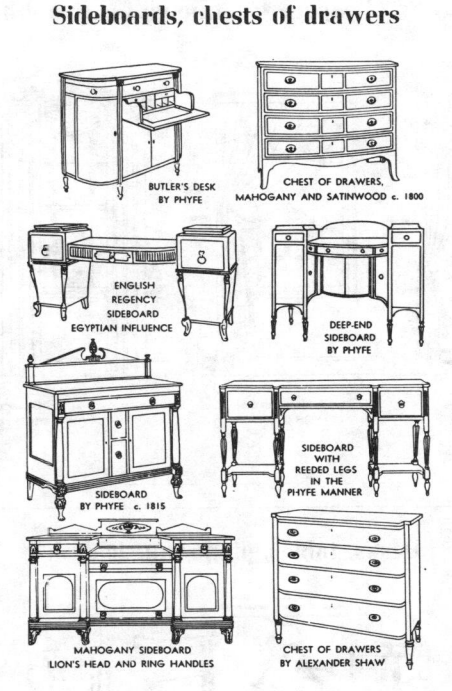

BUTLER'S DESK BY PHYFE

CHEST OF DRAWERS, MAHOGANY AND SATINWOOD c. 1800

ENGLISH REGENCY SIDEBOARD EGYPTIAN INFLUENCE

DEEP-END SIDEBOARD BY PHYFE

SIDEBOARD BY PHYFE c. 1815

SIDEBOARD WITH REEDED LEGS IN THE PHYFE MANNER

MAHOGANY SIDEBOARD LION'S HEAD AND RING HANDLES

CHEST OF DRAWERS BY ALEXANDER SHAW

Dining room accessories

WALL SCONCE FROM MOUNT VERNON

PORCELAIN BASKET BOWL

PINE AND METAL SCONCE c. 1800

CONVEX MIRROR WITH CRYSTAL CANDLE BRACKETS

CRYSTAL TOP CANDLESTICK c. 1830

CHINESE LOWESTOFT JAR 1820

SANDWICH MOLDED GLASS WHALE OIL LAMP

SILVER PLATED SCONCE

PORCELAIN URN

CLOCK, FRENCH EMPIRE STYLE

GILT SCONCE c. 1800

TORCHERE, PAINTED BLACK AND GOLD

SARCOPHAGUS GRATE

MIRROR IN GILT FRAME

Dressing tables, wardrobe, chests

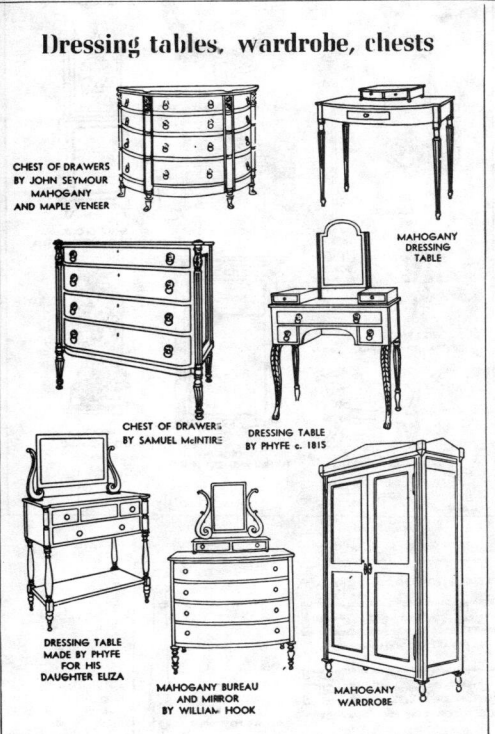

CHEST OF DRAWERS BY JOHN SEYMOUR MAHOGANY AND MAPLE VENEER

MAHOGANY DRESSING TABLE

CHEST OF DRAWERS BY SAMUEL McINTIRE

DRESSING TABLE BY PHYFE c. 1815

DRESSING TABLE MADE BY PHYFE FOR HIS DAUGHTER ELIZA

MAHOGANY BUREAU AND MIRROR BY WILLIAM HOOK

MAHOGANY WARDROBE

Chairs, stools, tables, desks

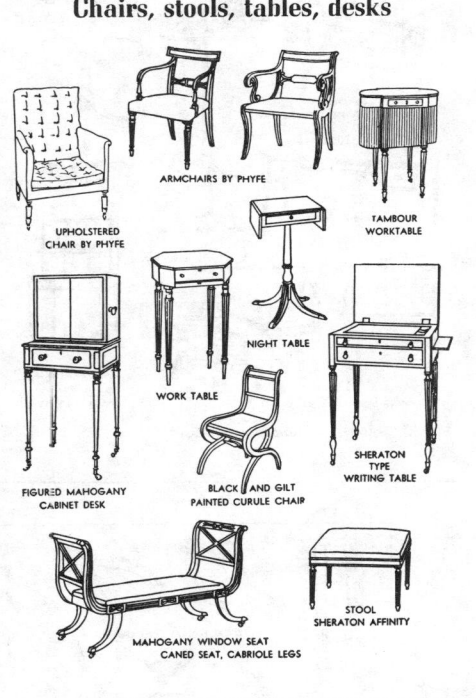

ARMCHAIRS BY PHYFE

UPHOLSTERED CHAIR BY PHYFE

TAMBOUR WORKTABLE

NIGHT TABLE

WORK TABLE

FIGURED MAHOGANY CABINET DESK

BLACK AND GILT PAINTED CURULE CHAIR

SHERATON TYPE WRITING TABLE

MAHOGANY WINDOW SEAT CANED SEAT, CABRIOLE LEGS

STOOL SHERATON AFFINITY

Bedroom accessories

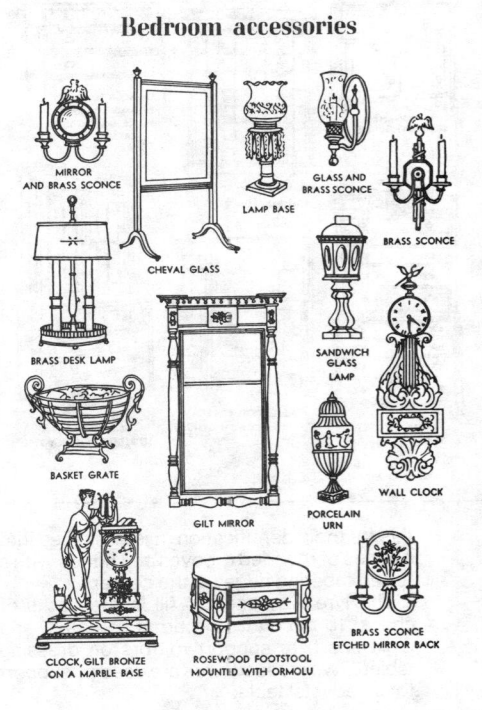

MIRROR AND BRASS SCONCE

GLASS AND BRASS SCONCE

LAMP BASE

CHEVAL GLASS

BRASS SCONCE

BRASS DESK LAMP

SANDWICH GLASS LAMP

BASKET GRATE

GILT MIRROR

PORCELAIN URN

WALL CLOCK

CLOCK, GILT BRONZE ON A MARBLE BASE

ROSEWOOD FOOTSTOOL MOUNTED WITH ORMOLU

BRASS SCONCE ETCHED MIRROR BACK

---

and Wedgwood were molded in Classic forms and painted with delicate sepia figures in Classic robes. Silver and Sheffield plate (the latter replacing pewter) also followed Classic forms. Ireland sent Waterford glass.

Fabrics most used were damask, brocade, satin, taffeta, haircloth, toile de Jouy, printed cotton, and silk.

Woods most used were mahogany, cherry, and maple; and fruit woods in less splendid furniture. Curly maple often replaced the satinwood used in European models. After 1800 rosewood was used for the more costly furniture.

The Federal motifs derive almost exclusively from classical sources. The acanthus leaf, the lyre, the saber leg, the lion's mask and paw, the bowknot, rosettes, thunderbolts, trumpets, and drapery swags are all to be found on the list of standard Federal furniture motifs.

After the War of 1812, when the Federal era rose to its zenith of popularity, the laurel, cornucopia, and eagle motifs became especially popular. (See Fig. 2.)

Phyfe's treatment of the acanthus leaf is so typical that many of his pieces depend upon

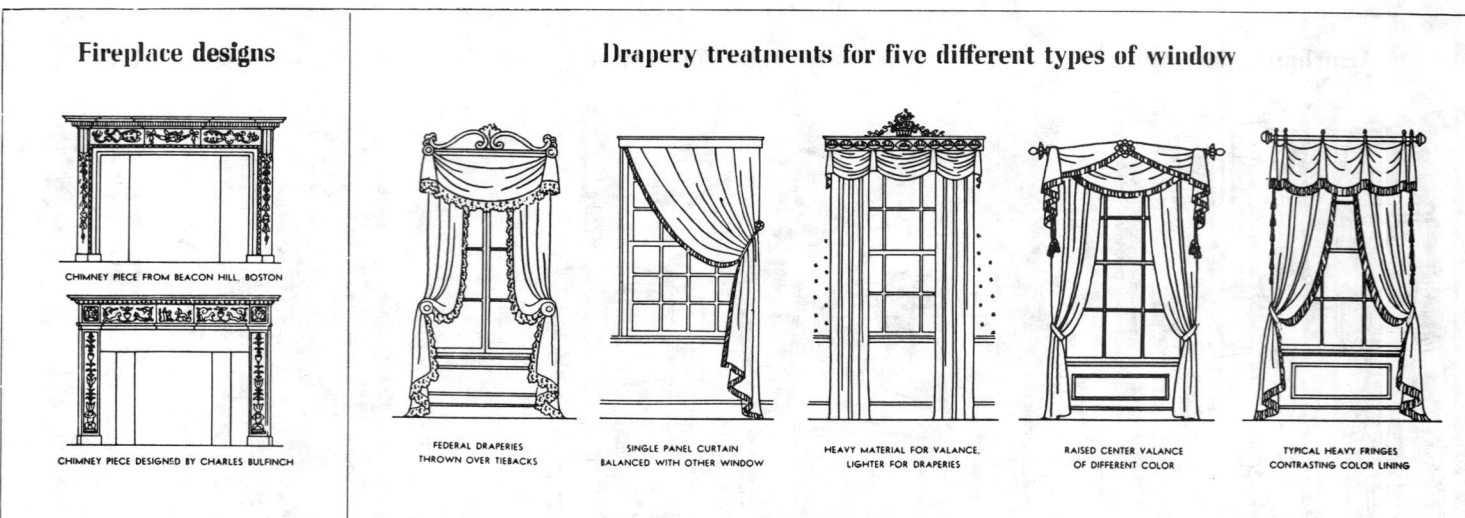

Fireplace designs

CHIMNEY PIECE FROM BEACON HILL, BOSTON

CHIMNEY PIECE DESIGNED BY CHARLES BULFINCH

Drapery treatments for five different types of window

FEDERAL DRAPERIES THROWN OVER TIEBACKS

SINGLE PANEL CURTAIN BALANCED WITH OTHER WINDOW

HEAVY MATERIAL FOR VALANCE, LIGHTER FOR DRAPERIES

RAISED CENTER VALANCE OF DIFFERENT COLOR

TYPICAL HEAVY FRINGES CONTRASTING COLOR LINING

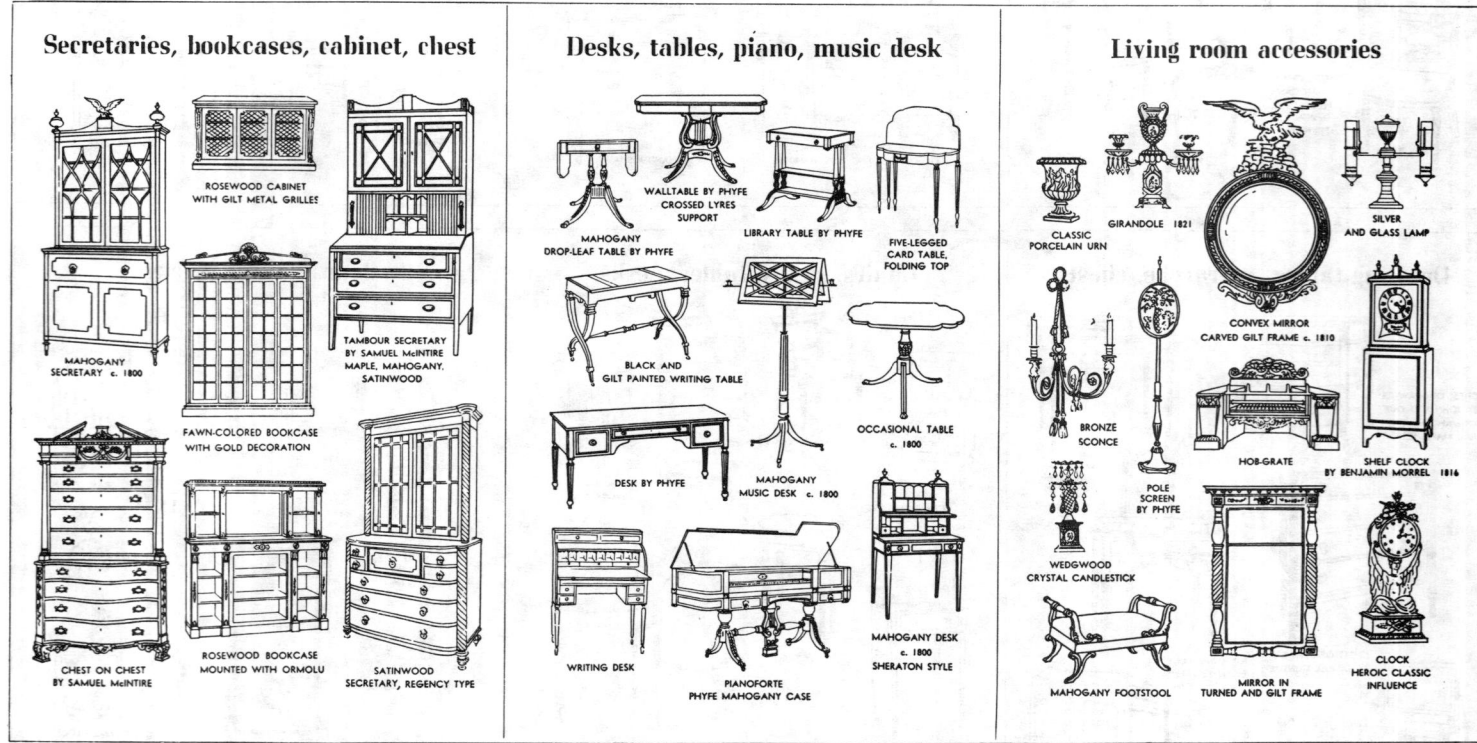

Secretaries, bookcases, cabinet, chest

MAHOGANY SECRETARY c. 1800

ROSEWOOD CABINET WITH GILT METAL GRILLES

TAMBOUR SECRETARY BY SAMUEL McINTIRE MAPLE, MAHOGANY, SATINWOOD

FAWN-COLORED BOOKCASE WITH GOLD DECORATION

CHEST ON CHEST BY SAMUEL McINTIRE

ROSEWOOD BOOKCASE MOUNTED WITH ORMOLU

SATINWOOD SECRETARY, REGENCY TYPE

Desks, tables, piano, music desk

MAHOGANY DROP-LEAF TABLE BY PHYFE

WALLTABLE BY PHYFE CROSSED LYRES SUPPORT

LIBRARY TABLE BY PHYFE

FIVE-LEGGED CARD TABLE, FOLDING TOP

BLACK AND GILT PAINTED WRITING TABLE

DESK BY PHYFE

MAHOGANY MUSIC DESK c. 1800

OCCASIONAL TABLE c. 1800

WRITING DESK

PIANOFORTE PHYFE MAHOGANY CASE

MAHOGANY DESK c. 1800 SHERATON STYLE

Living room accessories

CLASSIC PORCELAIN URN

GIRANDOLE 1821

SILVER AND GLASS LAMP

CONVEX MIRROR CARVED GILT FRAME c. 1810

BRONZE SCONCE

POLE SCREEN BY PHYFE

HOB-GRATE

SHELF CLOCK BY BENJAMIN MORREL 1816

WEDGWOOD CRYSTAL CANDLESTICK

MAHOGANY FOOTSTOOL

MIRROR IN TURNED AND GILT FRAME

CLOCK HEROIC CLASSIC INFLUENCE

this for their identification. It is simplified into a series of rounded grooves and ridges with a raised tapering ridge up the center.

The lyre was used to fill in the backs of chairs, to decorate the arms of sofas, and (split apart) to support mirrors on dressing tables. Two crossed lyres are used as support for a pedestal table.

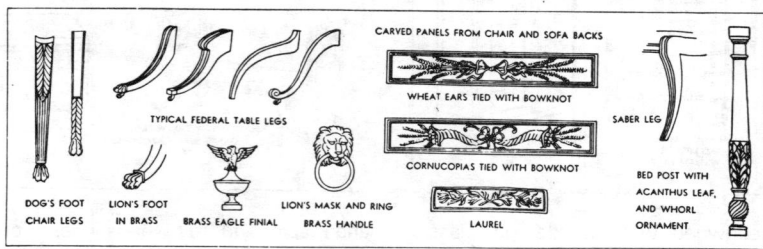

TYPICAL FEDERAL TABLE LEGS

CARVED PANELS FROM CHAIR AND SOFA BACKS

WHEAT EARS TIED WITH BOWKNOT

SABER LEG

DOG'S FOOT CHAIR LEGS

LION'S FOOT IN BRASS

BRASS EAGLE FINIAL

LION'S MASK AND RING BRASS HANDLE

CORNUCOPIAS TIED WITH BOWKNOT

LAUREL

BED POST WITH ACANTHUS LEAF, AND WHORL ORNAMENT

Fig. 2 *(Continued)*

THE EXTERIOR

Tʏᴘɪᴄᴀʟ of the better country houses in the second half of the 18th Century, is this design from Abraham Swan's *British Architect,* one of the many handbooks of builders' designs, which at this period carried news of architectural fashions from England to America. At right are close-up details of the Georgian background

Moldings and trim

CORNICE OF FIREPLACE AT ONE CORNER OF THE MANTELSHELF

DADO RAIL

BASE MOLDING

CORNER OF A DOORHEAD WITH PULVINATED FRIEZE BELOW

MOLDINGS AROUND NICHES

CORNICE WITH ACANTHUS LEAF DECORATION AND MODILLIONS

Interior doorway

CARVED PINE DECORATION COMBINES CLASSIC AND ORIENTAL MOTIFS

THE LIVING ROOM

Tʜᴇ pine-paneled walls in this characteristic Georgian living room are left unstained. The silk curtains are richly embroidered in many colors on a yellow ground which echoes the gilt frames used for pictures and mirrors. The crimson upholstery of the mahogany furniture is given added quality by the olive green carpet.

An alternative color scheme would be to have the walls painted dark gray-green with carving picked out in gold. The wall-to-wall carpet would be taupe, the upholstery of the wing chairs yellow Italian damask. In both color schemes needlepoint and natural leather would be used for upholstering other chairs in the room

Living-room fabrics

CHINTZ

DAMASK

PRINTED SILK

Armchairs, sofas, settees

TRIPLE CHAIR-BACK SETTEE, GOTHIC FRET SPLATS

DOUBLE CHAIR-BACK SETTEE, SWEPT WHORL TOP RAIL

CHIPPENDALE ARMCHAIR WITH CANTED ARMS

GEORGIAN TYPE DOUBLE CHAIR-BACK SETTEE

CHIPPENDALE WING-CHAIR

UPHOLSTERED ARMCHAIR, CABRIOLE LEGS

CHIPPENDALE SOFA WITH CHINESE FRET

MAHOGANY CHIPPENDALE SETTEE

MAHOGANY CHIPPENDALE SOFA

Chippendale was a dominating factor in the history of Georgian furniture design and his name serves as a convenient tag for the period centering in the reign of the second of the three Georges who provide the period title. Yet this English cabinetmaker achieved eminence not so much by his own work as by that of his copyists.

They all used the designs in *The Gentleman and Cabinet-Makers' Director,* published by Chippendale in 1754. To fill this book Chippendale commandeered all the ideas he could lay his hands on and then embroidered them with his own fancy, adapted them to his own forms. He plundered the design manuals of China and the French rococo, of the ancient Gothic masters, and of his immediate predecessors in the English furniture trade.

Georgian profiles

ROCOCO FRENCH

FRENCH BOMBÉ

CANTED CORNER

COMBINATION OF S AND C CURVES

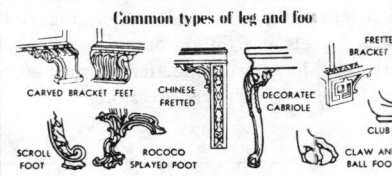

Common types of leg and foot

CARVED BRACKET FEET

CHINESE FRETTED

DECORATED CABRIOLE

FRETTED BRACKET FOOT

CLUB FOOT

SCROLL FOOT

ROCOCO SPLAYED FOOT

CLAW AND BALL FOOT

Fig. 3   Motifs characteristic of Georgian furniture.

From the craftsmen of the early eighteenth century Chippendale borrowed such tested forms as the cabriole leg, the claw-and-ball foot, and the typical acanthus leaf ornament. But to each of them he added a grace and charm of which the earlier furniture makers had never been capable.

Thomas Chippendale was a typical product of that brilliant English society which flourished during the mid–eighteenth century. He

PERIOD FURNITURE
18th Century English: Georgian

THE DINING ROOM

HERE the walls are pine-paneled, the wood being left its natural honey color. The consoles are also of pine. But brilliant against this pale background are the red damask curtains, and the mahogany furniture with its red and yellow striped silk upholstery.

Alternatively, the walls might be painted light blue as a background for yellow brocade curtains. The mahogany table and chairs stand on an Oriental rug which repeats colors found in the needlepoint upholstery. In the panels at right is furniture suitable for a room of this style

Dining-room fabrics

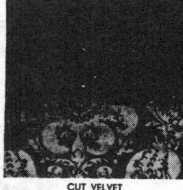
CUT VELVET

CHINTZ

SILK BROCADE

Armchairs, side chairs

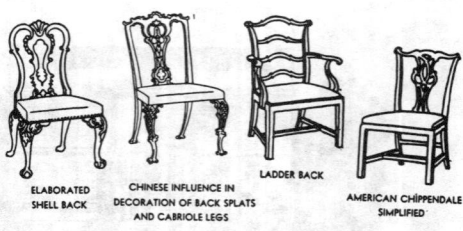
ELABORATED SHELL BACK — CHINESE INFLUENCE IN DECORATION OF BACK SPLATS AND CABRIOLE LEGS — LADDER BACK — AMERICAN CHIPPENDALE SIMPLIFIED

OTHER CHARACTERISTIC EARLY GEORGIAN DESIGNS

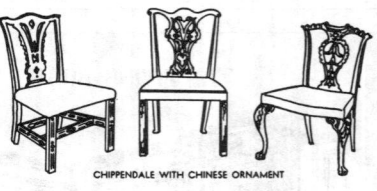
CHIPPENDALE WITH CHINESE ORNAMENT

THE BEDROOM

CHARACTERISTIC of the Georgian period are the richly embroidered Chinese silk draperies and the delicately fretted four-poster bed in this room. The dominant tone is yellow, against which is posed green upholstery, with a gun-metal carpet for base, putty walls for background.

Alternatively the walls could be pale green, the carpet brown, the upholstery blue-green and yellow, the ceiling pale apricot. In the panels at right are other pieces suitable for a room of this type. Modern reproductions of such authentic pieces are available in good furniture stores

Bedroom fabrics

CHINESE SILK BROCADE

PRINTED TAFFETA

PAINTED SATIN

Four-poster and canopy beds

CHIPPENDALE BED WITH PAINTED SILK HANGINGS

CHIPPENDALE FIELD BED WITH CANOPY

COUCH BED DESIGNED FOR AN ALCOVE

CHIPPENDALE IN ROCOCO MANNER

was a contemporary of Josiah Wedgwood, the potter, and of Edmund Burke, the orator. Boswell and Johnson, Benjamin Franklin, Garrick, Gibbon, and Goldsmith, all added their wit and intelligence to the creation of a sturdy culture.

Thomas Chippendale served their changing taste and their fashionable whims. In his later years he was engaged in making furniture of classic, elegant simplicity for the brothers Adam. His earlier work to his own designs, his love of gilt and gaudy color, his fascination with the exotic — all typical of the age in which he lived — suggest that he might have made a brilliant stage designer.

Chippendale is the first personality in the history of furniture style. This was due less to his fine craftsmanship than to his ability as a publicist. He was the first cabinetmaker to publish a book of furniture designs. The influence of his *Director* was particularly strong in Philadelphia, but the American cabinetmakers usually simplified his exuberant ornament to suit their clients' taste and

Dining tables, side tables, console

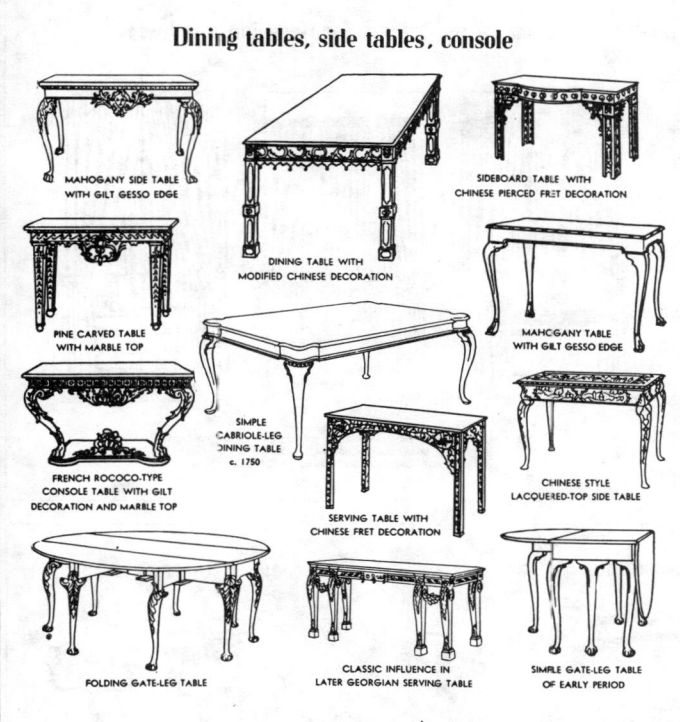

MAHOGANY SIDE TABLE WITH GILT GESSO EDGE

DINING TABLE WITH MODIFIED CHINESE DECORATION

SIDEBOARD TABLE WITH CHINESE PIERCED FRET DECORATION

PINE CARVED TABLE WITH MARBLE TOP

MAHOGANY TABLE WITH GILT GESSO EDGE

FRENCH ROCOCO-TYPE CONSOLE TABLE WITH GILT DECORATION AND MARBLE TOP

SIMPLE CABRIOLE-LEG DINING TABLE c. 1750

SERVING TABLE WITH CHINESE FRET DECORATION

CHINESE STYLE LACQUERED-TOP SIDE TABLE

FOLDING GATE-LEG TABLE

CLASSIC INFLUENCE IN LATER GEORGIAN SERVING TABLE

SIMPLE GATE-LEG TABLE OF EARLY PERIOD

Pedestals, wine coolers

COMMODE WITH FOLDING TOP WHICH OPENS OUT TO FORM A TABLE

MAHOGANY METAL-LINED WINE COOLERS WITH BRASS ORNAMENT

"CHINESE" FRETTED PEDESTALS BY EDWARDS & DARLEY

Dining-room accessories

MAHOGANY TEA CADDY WITH BRASS ORNAMENT

PORCELAIN

BRACKET CLOCK IN MAHOGANY WITH BRASS FITTINGS

PORCELAIN COFFEE POTS FANTASTIC CHINCISERIE

SILVER TEA URN

CANDLESTICKS IN SILVER IN BRASS

PIERCED SILVER FRUIT BASKET

MIRROR-BACK SCONCE 1775

CARVED AND GILT MIRROR

CRYSTAL CHANDELIER

CHANDELIER BY CHIPPENDALE IN THE "GOTHICK" TASTE

Chests of drawers, secretary, desk

MAHOGANY CHEST OF DRAWERS FRENCH ROCOCO INFLUENCE

BOMBÉ WRITING TABLE

MAHOGANY WITH WATER-GILT, HAND-CHASED MOUNTS

MAHOGANY SECRETARY BY CHIPPENDALE

CHIPPENDALE CHEST-ON-CHEST

MAHOGANY CABINET WITH CHINESE DETAIL

CHIPPENDALE KNEE-HOLE CHESTS OF DRAWERS

MAHOGANY CHEST OF DRAWERS 1760

Dressing tables, night stands, stools

SHELL-TYPE CHAIR OF CARVED WOOD

CHIPPENDALE STOOLS

MAHOGANY FIRESCREEN WITH TRIPOD POLE AND PETIT-POINT PANEL

CANDLESTAND BY CHIPPENDALE

RUSTIC WALL TABLE BY THOMAS JOHNSON

RIBBON BACK CHAIR

CHIPPENDALE MAHOGANY STAND

BASIN STAND

CANOPIED HANGING SHELVES

MAHOGANY NIGHT STANDS

FOLDING-TOP DRESSING TABLE BY INCE & MAYHEW

Bedroom accessories

CHINESE PORCELAIN

CRYSTAL SCONCE

IRON GRATE WITH BRASS DECORATIONS

AESOP MIRROR BY CHIPPENDALE

CHINESE CHIPPENDALE MIRRORS, CARVED AND GILT

WALL BRACKET CHINESE CHIPPENDALE

GILT BRONZE CLOCKS CHINESE AND FRENCH ROCOCO IN STYLE

SILVER CANDLESTICK 1773

their workers' skill in carving. For it must be remembered that many of the published designs were too complex for reproduction in the solid, even by the most highly skilled English carvers. Such designs were intended for inspiration only.

The introduction of mahogany about 1725 was a fundamental influence on furniture design. Rosewood was another material in favor. Pine was used for paneling and also for intricate carving as, for example, on mirror frames. In the latter case it was usually gilt. Amboyna was occasionally used, mostly for inlays. But the considerable use of inlay is not found until the late Georgian period.

From China come the rectangular leg and an infinite variety of fretted ornament, as well as the more obviously Oriental pagoda forms. From the France of Louis XV come the elaborate combinations of foliated C and S scrolls so typical of the rococo style of ornament. These came to a lush flowering in furniture hardware and gilt mirror frames. Serpentine fronts and sides broke down

PERIOD FURNITURE
18th Century English : Georgian

Fireplaces and wall paneling

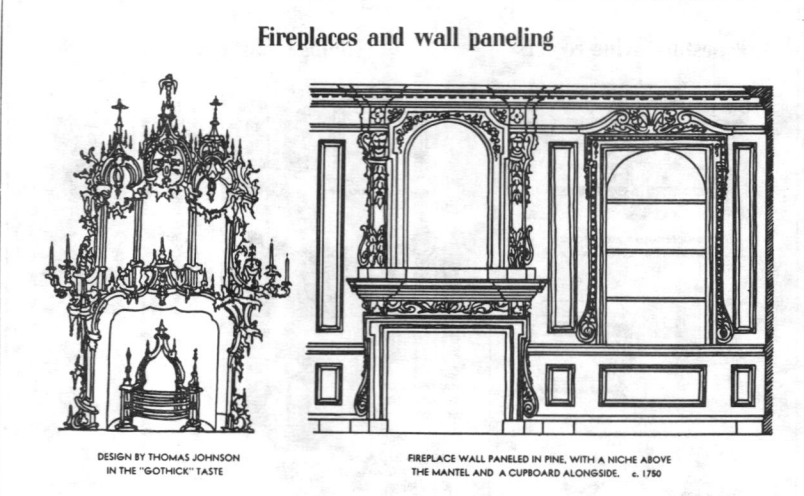

DESIGN BY THOMAS JOHNSON
IN THE "GOTHICK" TASTE

FIREPLACE WALL PANELED IN PINE, WITH A NICHE ABOVE
THE MANTEL AND A CUPBOARD ALONGSIDE. c. 1750

Drapery treatments for Georgian windows

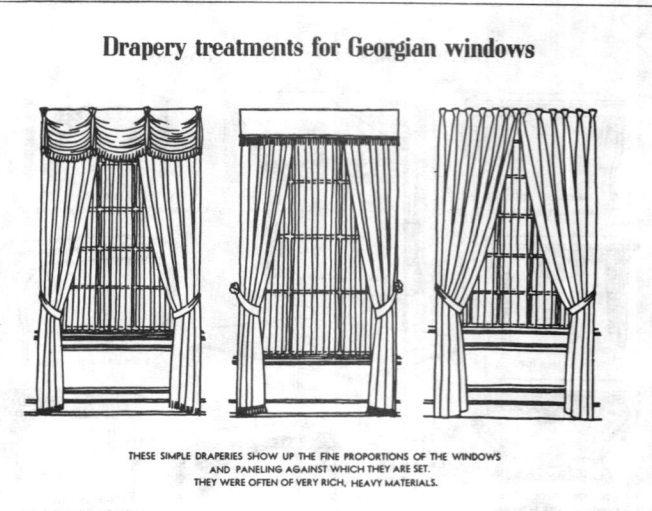

THESE SIMPLE DRAPERIES SHOW UP THE FINE PROPORTIONS OF THE WINDOWS
AND PANELING AGAINST WHICH THEY ARE SET.
THEY WERE OFTEN OF VERY RICH, HEAVY MATERIALS.

Secretaries, desks, bookcases

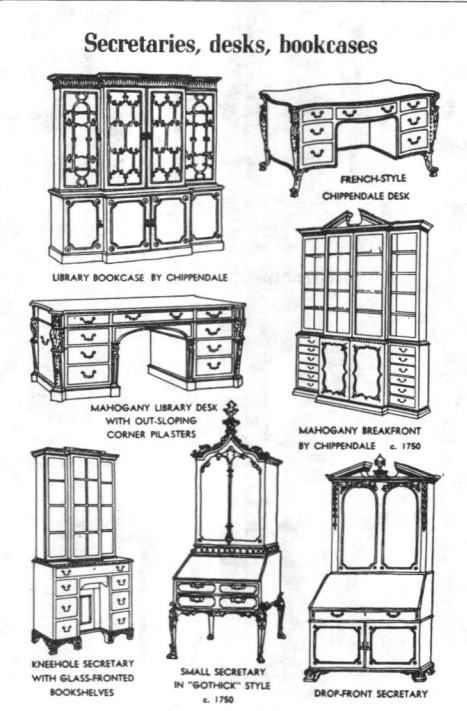

LIBRARY BOOKCASE BY CHIPPENDALE

FRENCH-STYLE
CHIPPENDALE DESK

MAHOGANY LIBRARY DESK
WITH OUT-SLOPING
CORNER PILASTERS

MAHOGANY BREAKFRONT
BY CHIPPENDALE c. 1750

KNEEHOLE SECRETARY
WITH GLASS-FRONTED
BOOKSHELVES

SMALL SECRETARY
IN "GOTHICK" STYLE
c. 1750

DROP-FRONT SECRETARY

Grandfather clocks, shelves, tables

POLE SCREEN
WITH PIERCED
TRIPOD BASE

PAGODA CHINA CABINET
1750

FOLDING-TOP
CARD TABLE
WITH CABRIOLE LEGS

CANOPIED WALL SHELVES
FOR KNICKKNACKS

TILT-TOP TABLE
WITH TRIPOD BASE

MAHOGANY
BY CHIPPENDALE

INLAID WALNUT

LOUIS XV TYPE
WITH BRASS MOUNTS

PIECRUST TRIPOD TABLE
BY CHIPPENDALE

CHIPPENDALE TEA TABLE
WITH GALLERY EDGE

Living-room accessories

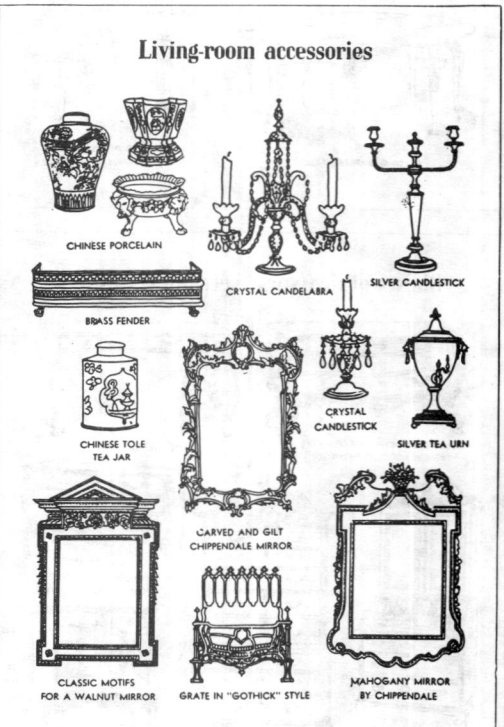

CHINESE PORCELAIN

CRYSTAL CANDELABRA

SILVER CANDLESTICK

BRASS FENDER

CHINESE TOLE
TEA JAR

CRYSTAL
CANDLESTICK

SILVER TEA URN

CARVED AND GILT
CHIPPENDALE MIRROR

CLASSIC MOTIFS
FOR A WALNUT MIRROR

GRATE IN "GOTHICK" STYLE

MAHOGANY MIRROR
BY CHIPPENDALE

even the solid rectangular forms of such traditionally four-square pieces as chests of drawers and tables. (For typical profiles and decorative motifs see Fig. 3.)

Romance was sought in the past as well as the East; the pointed Gothic arch and burgeoning crockets turn up in all kinds of furniture and decoration.

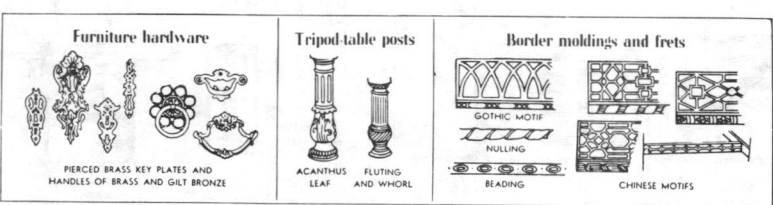

Furniture hardware

PIERCED BRASS KEY PLATES AND
HANDLES OF BRASS AND GILT BRONZE

Tripod-table posts

ACANTHUS
LEAF

FLUTING
AND WHORL

Border moldings and frets

GOTHIC MOTIF

NULLING

BEADING

CHINESE MOTIFS

Fig. 3 *(Continued)*

THE EXTERIOR

THE exterior of a later Georgian house, such as the one shown above, would have been finished in cream-painted stucco with stone trim. The Classic detail was in carved stone or molded stucco. At right are details of the architectural background at this period.

Wall paneling and painted decoration

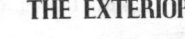

FIREPLACE WALL IN THE LIBRARY OF SYON HOUSE, ISLEWORTH, ENGLAND
DESIGNED BY THE BROTHERS ADAM FOR THE DUKE OF NORTHUMBERLAND

THE LIVING ROOM

GREEN brocade curtains, bound with gold, and green brocade upholstery on the sofa and adjacent chairs stand out brilliantly against the French white of these walls. A damask in tones of coffee and gold is used for the other chairs, a red moire for the other sofa. All these colors are repeated in the rug. The dark brown red of polished mahogany appears in the doors and furniture. Some of the smaller pieces are inlaid with satinwood.

Alternatively the walls might be pale pink with white moldings. Upholstery would be blue green except for the chairs by the fire in lemon yellow brocade and the sofa in gold satin.

Living-room fabrics

SILK AND LINEN DAMASK

BROCADED SATIN

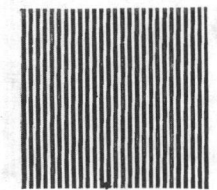

SILK AND VELVET STRIPE

Armchairs, love-seats, sofas

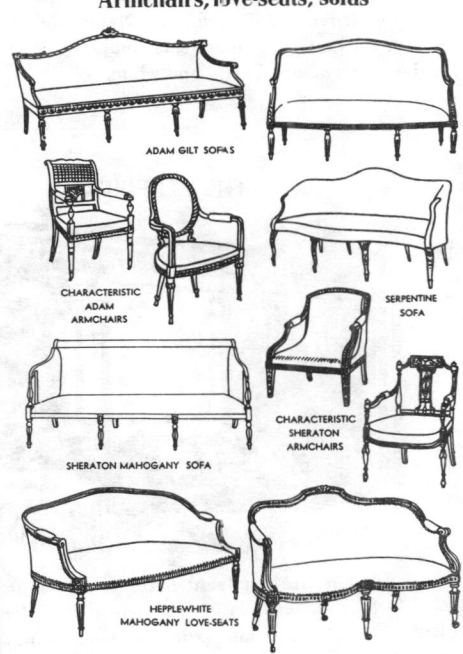

ADAM GILT SOFAS

CHARACTERISTIC ADAM ARMCHAIRS

SERPENTINE SOFA

SHERATON MAHOGANY SOFA

CHARACTERISTIC SHERATON ARMCHAIRS

HEPPLEWHITE MAHOGANY LOVE-SEATS

Chippendale went for inspiration to Chinese and Gothic decoration. The great designers of the later Georgian period — the brothers Adam, George Hepplewhite, and Thomas Sheraton — were entranced by the recently discovered Classic glories of Pompeii and Herculaneum, and by the slim prettiness in vogue at the French court.

The motifs most characteristic of the later Georgian period (see Fig. 4) are all of Classic origin: acanthus leaf and honeysuckle, ram's head, winged griffin and lion, laurel, and garland.

Characteristic of this period is the perfect coordination between architects, painters, and furniture designers. The four Adam brothers — John, Robert, James, and William, who trademarked themselves the Adelphi (Greek for brothers) — were Scots by

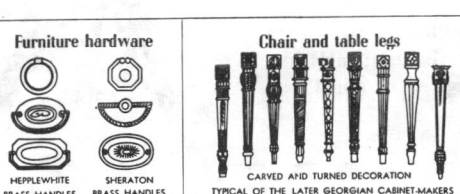

Furniture hardware

HEPPLEWHITE BRASS HANDLES

SHERATON BRASS HANDLES

Chair and table legs

CARVED AND TURNED DECORATION TYPICAL OF THE LATER GEORGIAN CABINET-MAKERS

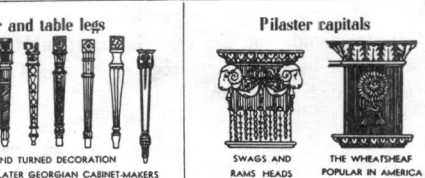

Pilaster capitals

SWAGS AND RAMS HEADS

THE WHEATSHEAF POPULAR IN AMERICA

Fig. 4   Motifs characteristic of the later Georgian period.

birth, architects by profession. They did not consider their job at an end when they had designed the shell of a house. Every detail of furnishing, decoration, and lighting was especially designed by the Adams to give a rounded effect. Nothing was too small or

unimportant to deserve their attention. The best craftsmen would then be employed to carry out their designs. Chippendale and Hepplewhite, perhaps Sheraton also, made furniture for the Adams.

All these designers followed Chippen-

THE DINING ROOM

T HESE pale blue-green walls are relieved by grisaille paint-ings in delicate Classic taste. Gold appears in the leather chair seats, in the mirror above the consoles and in the binding of the white curtains. Green and beige enliven the carpet and painted ceiling design.

Alternatively the wall paintings might be brighter and more varied in color, including Naples yellow, mauve and green. Curtains and chair seats would be cherry, the ceiling painting cinnamon brown and white.

Dining-room fabrics

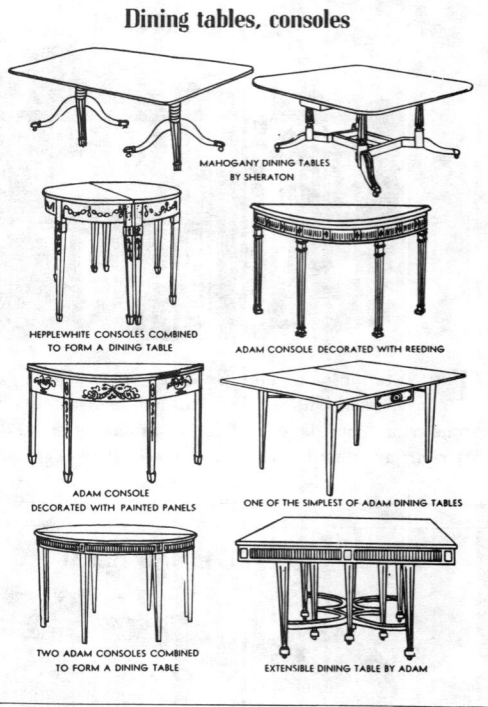

SILK DAMASK

PRINTED COTTON

BROCATELLE

Dining tables, consoles

MAHOGANY DINING TABLES BY SHERATON

HEPPLEWHITE CONSOLES COMBINED TO FORM A DINING TABLE

ADAM CONSOLE DECORATED WITH REEDING

ADAM CONSOLE DECORATED WITH PAINTED PANELS

ONE OF THE SIMPLEST OF ADAM DINING TABLES

TWO ADAM CONSOLES COMBINED TO FORM A DINING TABLE

EXTENSIBLE DINING TABLE BY ADAM

THE BEDROOM

P ALE colors are dominant here. The sofa, painted oyster white, is upholstered in apple green satin. The mahogany bed is covered in white taffeta trimmed with apple green, and the armchair upholstery is cinnamon and gold-striped damask. Curtains are white silk, gold-trimmed.

Alternatively the color scheme might be based on gold and white with blue green silk on the bed and yellow satin upholstery on the armchair for contrast. In the panels to the right are a number of authentic pieces which might be used in a Georgian bedroom such as this.

Bedroom fabrics

SATIN BROCADE

SATIN DAMASK

CHINTZ

Four-poster beds and canopies

CANOPY BY SHERATON

DRAPED FOUR-POSTER BY ADAM

CARVED MAHOGANY BED BY SHERATON

SOFA BED WITH CUPOLA BY SHERATON

CANOPY BY ADAM

dale's lead by publishing design handbooks for the use of other less experienced and less imaginative craftsmen in this country and in the English provinces outside London. Here is seen the changing fashion: lowboys are being supplanted by dressing tables, high-boys by wardrobes. Color and inlay become more popular than carving, with Sheraton as the champion of inlay against painting.

Hepplewhite's work is usually charac-terized by his affection for curves, Sheraton's by a preference for straight lines. This was probably because Hepplewhite was more strongly influenced than Sheraton by con-temporary French work, which was enlivened by a profusion of delicate curves. Of particular interest in Sheraton's work are his designs for ingenious folding and multi-

purpose furniture such as folding beds, com-bined bookcases and washstand, and couches that folded up to become tables. These were designed for use in those bed-rooms which were now doubling as parlors during the day.

This later Georgian period has often been labeled the Age of Satinwood. All the design-ers eagerly exploited the possibilities of ve-

Armchairs, side chairs

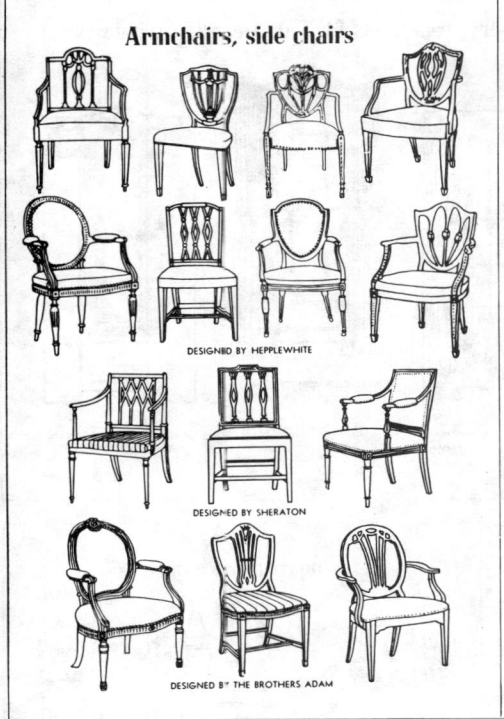

DESIGNED BY HEPPLEWHITE

DESIGNED BY SHERATON

DESIGNED BY THE BROTHERS ADAM

Commodes, sideboards, cupboard

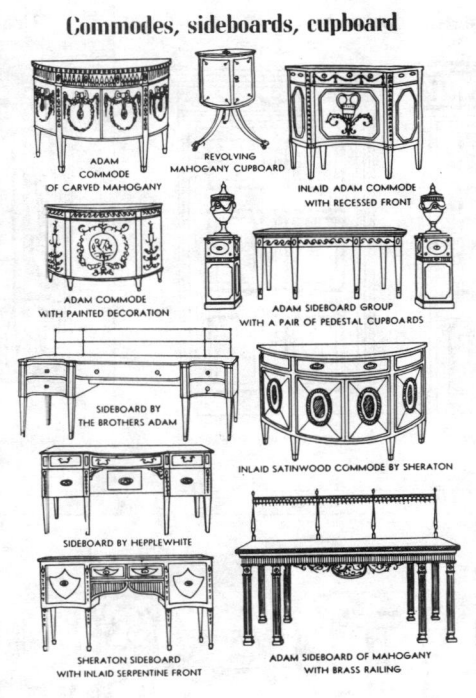

ADAM COMMODE OF CARVED MAHOGANY

REVOLVING MAHOGANY CUPBOARD

INLAID ADAM COMMODE WITH RECESSED FRONT

ADAM COMMODE WITH PAINTED DECORATION

ADAM SIDEBOARD GROUP WITH A PAIR OF PEDESTAL CUPBOARDS

SIDEBOARD BY THE BROTHERS ADAM

INLAID SATINWOOD COMMODE BY SHERATON

SIDEBOARD BY HEPPLEWHITE

SHERATON SIDEBOARD WITH INLAID SERPENTINE FRONT

ADAM SIDEBOARD OF MAHOGANY WITH BRASS RAILING

Dining-room accessories

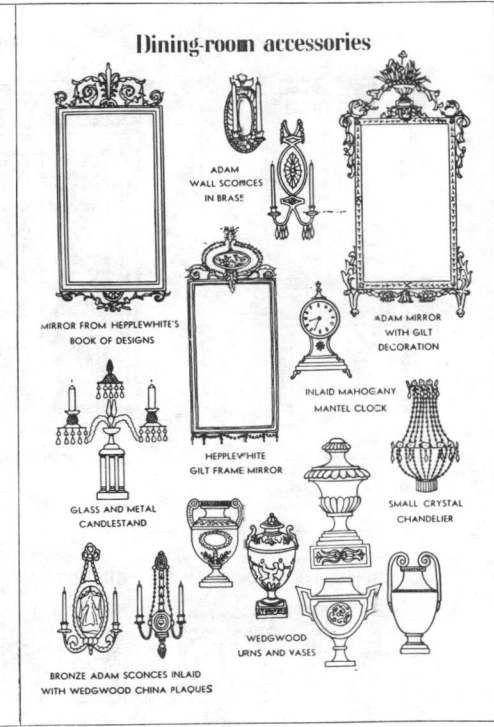

MIRROR FROM HEPPLEWHITE'S BOOK OF DESIGNS

ADAM WALL SCONCES IN BRASS

ADAM MIRROR WITH GILT DECORATION

INLAID MAHOGANY MANTEL CLOCK

HEPPLEWHITE GILT FRAME MIRROR

GLASS AND METAL CANDLESTAND

SMALL CRYSTAL CHANDELIER

WEDGWOOD URNS AND VASES

BRONZE ADAM SCONCES INLAID WITH WEDGWOOD CHINA PLAQUES

Chests of drawers, wardrobes, commodes

HEPPLEWHITE INLAID MAHOGANY CHEST OF DRAWERS

ADAM COMMODE OF INLAID SATINWOOD WITH PANELING IN "ZUCCHI" STYLE

INLAID MAHOGANY SWELL-FRONT CHEST OF DRAWERS BY HEPPLEWHITE

SERPENTINE CHEST OF DRAWERS BY HEPPLEWHITE

WARDROBE OF CARVED PINE PAINTED

SHERATON CABINET OF SATINWOOD WITH TULIPWOOD BASE

INLAID SERPENTINE-FRONT COMMODE BY SHERATON

ADAM WARDROBE WITH DRAWERS BELOW

Dressing tables, secretaries, candlestands

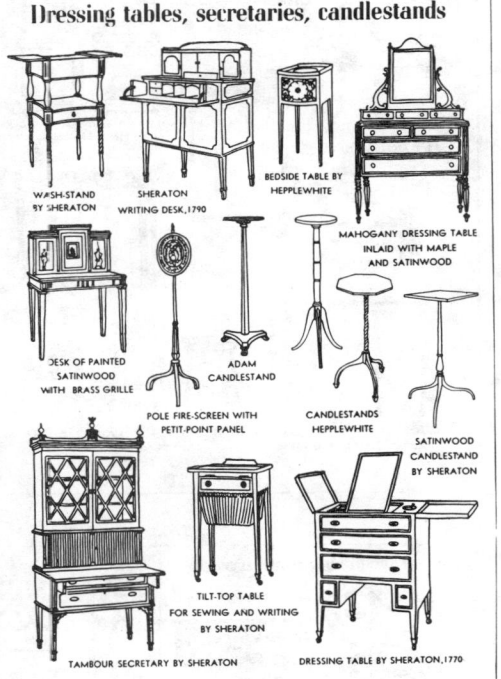

WASH-STAND BY SHERATON

SHERATON WRITING DESK, 1790

BEDSIDE TABLE BY HEPPLEWHITE

MAHOGANY DRESSING TABLE INLAID WITH MAPLE AND SATINWOOD

DESK OF PAINTED SATINWOOD WITH BRASS GRILLE

ADAM CANDLESTAND

POLE FIRE-SCREEN WITH PETIT-POINT PANEL

CANDLESTANDS HEPPLEWHITE

SATINWOOD CANDLESTAND BY SHERATON

TILT-TOP TABLE FOR SEWING AND WRITING BY SHERATON

TAMBOUR SECRETARY BY SHERATON

DRESSING TABLE BY SHERATON, 1770

Bedroom accessories

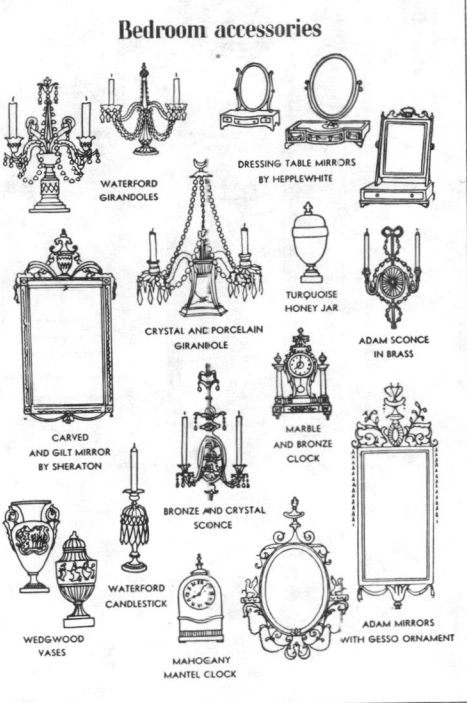

WATERFORD GIRANDOLES

DRESSING TABLE MIRRORS BY HEPPLEWHITE

TURQUOISE HONEY JAR

CRYSTAL AND PORCELAIN GIRANDOLE

ADAM SCONCE IN BRASS

CARVED AND GILT MIRROR BY SHERATON

MARBLE AND BRONZE CLOCK

BRONZE AND CRYSTAL SCONCE

WATERFORD CANDLESTICK

WEDGWOOD VASES

MAHOGANY MANTEL CLOCK

ADAM MIRRORS WITH GESSO ORNAMENT

neering and inlay with woods such as satinwood and amboyna, ebony, sycamore, holly, kingwood, and lime. Ivory and brass inlay were often used to mark key plates.

Some of these motifs (the acanthus leaf, for example) had been in use by English designers for more than half a century. But now, reintroduced from Italy by means of measured drawings, they take on a fresh elegance. Italian painters were brought in — Pergolesi, Zucchi, and Cipriani — to provide the background of decoration. Angelica Kaufmann, a Swiss, filled their wreathed panels with neo-Classic figures.

Yet the solid tradition of English craftsmanship remained intact beneath all these changing fashions. The basic proportions remain almost inviolate. Hepplewhite attempted (in his own words) "to unite elegance with utility, and to blend the useful with the agreeable."

PERIOD FURNITURE

18th Century English: Late Georgian

Fireplace designs

ADAM MANTEL OF STATUARY MARBLE
AND ANTIQUE GREEN
BEVERLY HALL, ENGLAND, 1770

ADAM MANTEL OF WHITE, SIENNA
AND BROCATELLE MARBLE

Interior doorways

DESIGNED BY PERGOLESI

DESIGNED BY THE BROTHERS ADAM

Drapery treatments for Late Georgian windows

OUTSIDE THESE TALL WINDOWS
WERE SLENDER IRON BALCONIES

ELABORATE CORNICE OF METAL
OR OF CARVED, GILT WOOD

LAMBREQUINS, FABRIC-COVERED,
USED TO CUT DOWN DRAFTS

Secretaries, bookcases, desks, cabinets

LIBRARY DESK BY SHERATON
OF INLAID SATINWOOD

HEPPLEWHITE SECRETARY

ADAM WRITING TABLE
WITH ROLL TOP AT BACK

HEPPLEWHITE SECRETARY
INLAID MAHOGANY

MAHOGANY LIBRARY CABINET
BY SHERATON

PAINTED CABINET
BY THE BROTHERS ADAM

SATINWOOD SECRETARY
MIRROR PANELS IN THE BOOKCASE DOORS

Occasional tables, grandfather clocks

SHERATON LEATHER-TOPPED
CARD TABLE

HEPPLEWHITE SIDE TABLE
INLAID WITH TULIP
AND SATIN WOODS

SHERATON WALL TABLE

MAHOGANY GRANDFATHER CLOCKS
BY SHERATON

DROP-LEAF
OCCASIONAL TABLES

ADAM CONSOLE
PAINTED DECORATION, FOLDING TOP

ADAM PROJECTING-FRONT CONSOLE WITH
DELICATE CLASSIC DECORATION

SHERATON OCCASIONAL TABLES IN
MAHOGANY AND SATINWOOD

Living-room accessories

WEDGWOOD
VASES

PAINTED
BRONZE AND CRYSTAL
SCONCES

PLASTER URN DESIGNED BY
THE BROTHERS ADAM

ADAM MIRROR
WITH GILT DECORATION

BILBOA MIRROR

BRASS AND CRYSTAL
SCONCE

ADAM MIRROR CANDLE
SCONCE

PEDESTAL
FOR ANTIQUE STATUES

CLASSIC DETAIL
IN BRONZE
AND MARBLE CLOCK

GILT WALL SCONCE
BY HEPPLEWHITE, 1785

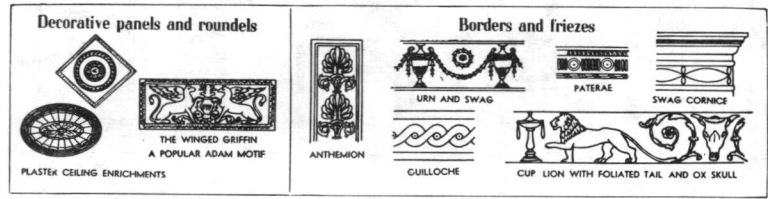

Decorative panels and roundels

PLASTER CEILING ENRICHMENTS

THE WINGED GRIFFIN
A POPULAR ADAM MOTIF

Borders and friezes

ANTHEMION

URN AND SWAG

PATERAE

SWAG CORNICE

GUILLOCHE

CUP LION WITH FOLIATED TAIL AND OX SKULL

Fig. 4 *(Continued)*

THE EXTERIOR

THE typical Directoire château shows French Renaissance tradition crossed with the newer Classic vogue. The center panel of this façade is of stone, the remainder in two shades of painted stucco, perhaps in such gay colors as salmon, tan and blue.

Typical Directoire wall treatments

VERY SIMPLE PANELING ELABORATELY PAINTED
WITH MULTICOLOR DECORATION OF CLASSIC AND EGYPTIAN DERIVATION

PLAIN COLOR DRAPERY PINNED UP WITH METAL ROSETTES
PILASTERS AND CORNICE GILT

THE LIVING ROOM

A CHARACTERISTICALLY pale range of colors keeps this room in period. The walls are a pinkish gray, the doors gray and gold. The curtains are oyster white bound in gray and the rug predominantly white except for green and gold in the center. Green recurs in the upholstery of the armchair, side chairs and sofa, and gold (satin) in the sofa and méridienne by the fireplace.

For added color the fireside pieces might be upholstered in red satin, the other furniture in gold and blue striped satin. In panels at right are other pieces suitable for such a room.

Living-room fabrics

DAMASK

SATIN STRIPED DAMASK

TAPESTRY

Settees, méridienne, sofas

MAHOGANY SOFA
WITH BRASS MOUNTS
LION FEET

MÉRIDIENNE DESIGNED FOR
THE EMPRESS JOSEPHINE

SETTEE OF ITALIAN TYPE
WITH SWAN AND LYRE BACK

DULL BLACK LOVE-SEAT WITH
TAN STRIPING AND MAROON ROSETTES

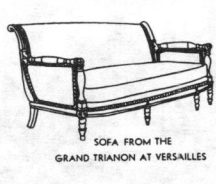

SOFA FROM THE
GRAND TRIANON AT VERSAILLES

ITALIAN-TYPE SETTEE
PAINTED AND PARCEL GILT

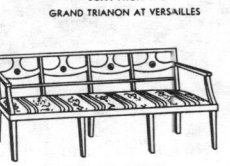

SIMPLE DIRECTOIRE SETTEE
UPHOLSTERED IN STRIPED SATIN

GOLD AND WHITE PAINTED SOFA
WITH GOLD SATIN UPHOLSTERY

The Directoire was France's recovery period after the shock of a six-year revolution. The Directoire, established in 1795, lasted only a brief four years; but this was long enough for the designers to sketch in the outlines of a new style. Those outlines were to be filled in later as Directoire merged into Empire; these are but two stages in a single style.

With the rise of Napoleon to absolute power, the delicate style of the Directoire was taken over and developed "for the good of the State." It was to be made into a French national style thoroughly imbued with the political principles which were to guide the new state.

Imperial Rome was found to provide the dignity and impressiveness required in the

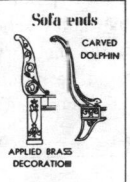

Friezes and borders

GREEK FRET

ROSETTES

SWANS AND BOWL

FLORIATED ROUNDEL

CLASSIC LEAVES
AND FLOWER

Furniture
hardware

BRASS HANDLES

BRASS KEY PLATES

Sofa ends

CARVED
DOLPHIN

APPLIED BRASS
DECORATION

Fig. 5 Motifs characteristic of Directoire and Empire.

prototype, so all the Imperial symbols were converted to use. The symmetrical shapes of heavy proportion were taken over unchanged, copied in wood instead of being reproduced in stone or bronze.

Most pieces displayed large surfaces of highly polished wood, usually mahogany. They were not, as a rule, decorated by molding or paneling, or even by carving. Ornamentation was almost always applied or inlaid. Most typically it took the form of gilded bas reliefs tacked to the smooth wood sur-

PERIOD FURNITURE
Late 18th–Early 19th Century French: Directoire and Empire

THE DINING ROOM

THE rich brown of polished mahogany in this table is surrounded by chairs painted gold and white, upholstered in blue satin. The walls are painted oyster white picked out with yellow moldings. Above the doors are white Classic figure paintings with a blue background which is echoed in the blue taffeta curtains.

Alternatively the walls might be painted green with the cornice picked out in white and gold. The chairs would then be upholstered in red. Other pieces suitable for a room of this type are shown in the panels at right.

Dining-room fabrics

PAINTED SILK

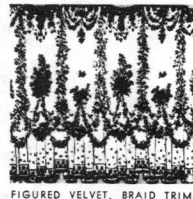
FIGURED VELVET, BRAID TRIM

BROCADE

Side chairs, armchair

ARMCHAIR WITH LEATHER SEAT DESIGN INSPIRED BY ENGLISH PRECEDENT

FROM THE PALACE OF FONTAINEBLEAU

DESIGNED FOR NAPOLEON UPHOLSTERED WITH BEAUVAIS TAPESTRY

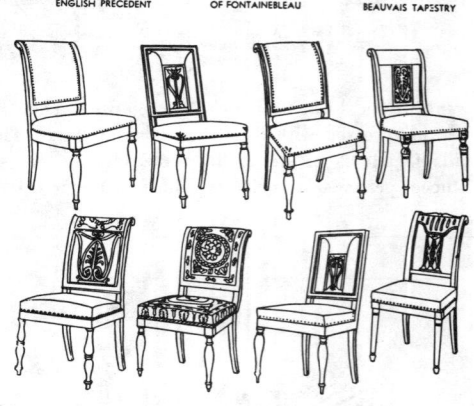
A GROUP OF MAHOGANY CHAIRS DESIGNED BY JACOB BROTHERS MANY WERE PAINTED WHITE. UPHOLSTERY WAS SATIN OR TAPESTRY

THE BEDROOM

PINK WALLS decorated in white and gold provide a good background for this mahogany and rosewood furniture relieved with brass mounts. Fabrics are gayly colored here: blue taffeta for curtains and bed canopy, striped yellow and red satin for the chairs, and yellow satin for the two stools (which have white-painted frames).

An alternative color scheme would have dark beige walls, green taffeta for the curtains and bed canopy. Most of the furniture would be painted white and gold. At right are other pieces and fabrics suitable for this type of room.

Bedroom fabrics

MOIRÉ

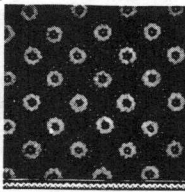
PRINTED SILK

SILK DAMASK

Beds, chaises longues, méridiennes

MAHOGANY BED WITH SWAN AND LYRE DECORATION

MÉRIDIENNE OF MAHOGANY WITH BRONZE MOUNTS

CHAISE LONGUE WITH SWAN'S NECK DECORATION

MAHOGANY CHAISE LONGUE WITH BOLDLY PATTERNED RED UPHOLSTERY

PAINTED WOOD DIVAN

MAHOGANY COUCH UPHOLSTERED IN YELLOW SATIN

MÉRIDIENNE WITH GOLD AND WHITE FRAME, GREEN UPHOLSTERY

MAHOGANY BEDS WITH UPHOLSTERED ENDS

faces. Painted decoration was more commonly used on walls and ceilings than for furniture.

The general color scheme is rich, dark, and somewhat heavy. Rich deep mahogany, French polished and often stained red, was the favorite material. Rosewood and ebony were also in favor. Where other woods were used, their nature was concealed by staining to imitate the more popular species.

Round tables were popular. They usually stood on a pedestal or tripod vase. The top was commonly of porphyry or marble. Beds developed into Classic ceremonial couches with scrolled ends. The popular craze for all things Roman extended to include women's dresses and Lucullan banquets.

In the early (Directoire) part of the period fabrics were quite delicately colored, the decorative motifs still possessed some Gre-

cian delicacy of form, and much of the furniture was painted and gilt. Later, under Napoleon's fist, fabrics were usually in deep primary colors, the motifs of Imperial Roman heaviness, the furniture of dark red polished mahogany.

From each of his campaigns he brought home some new decorative motif which he would turn over to his craftsmen for use in the net batch of furniture made to his order.

PERIOD FURNITURE
Late 18th–Early 19th Century French: Directoire and Empire

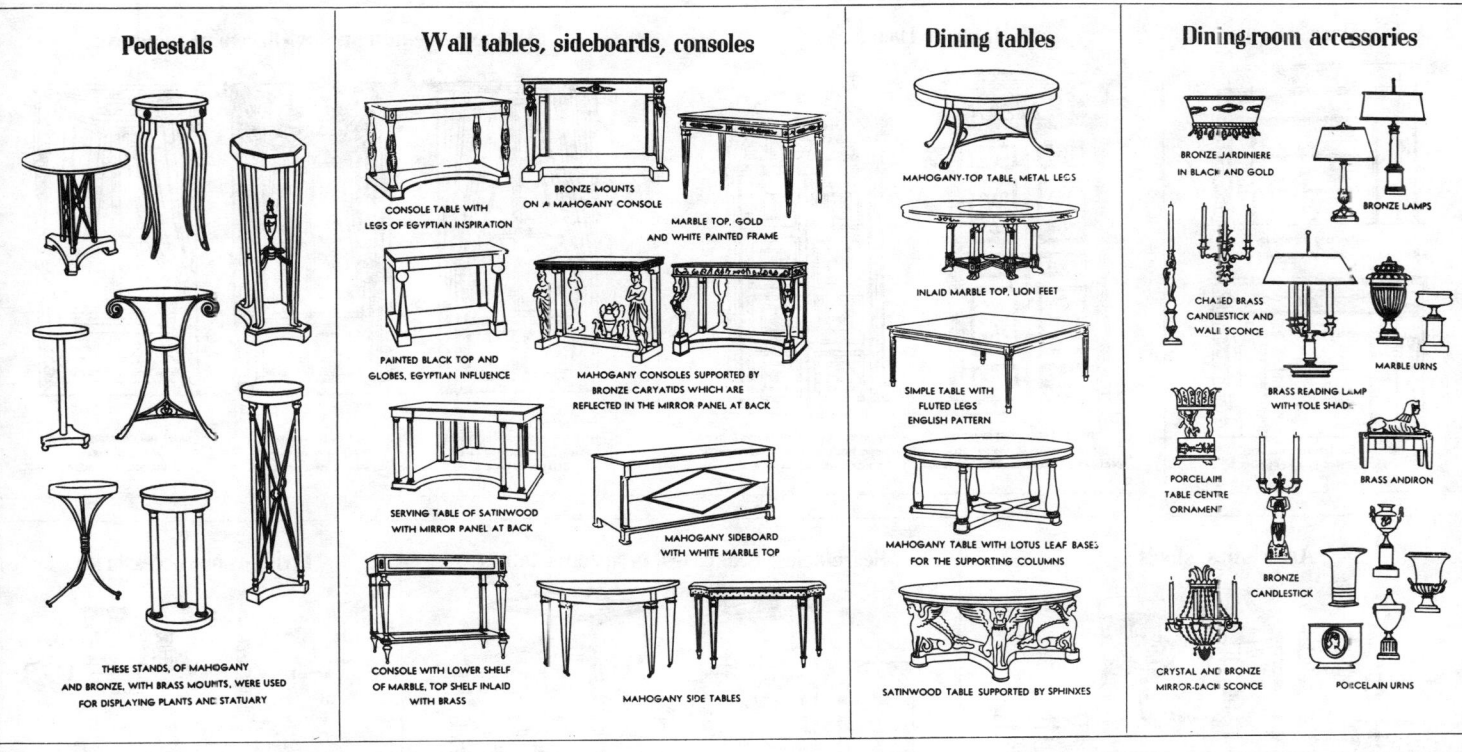

Pedestals

THESE STANDS, OF MAHOGANY
AND BRONZE, WITH BRASS MOUNTS, WERE USED
FOR DISPLAYING PLANTS AND STATUARY

Wall tables, sideboards, consoles

CONSOLE TABLE WITH
LEGS OF EGYPTIAN INSPIRATION

BRONZE MOUNTS
ON A MAHOGANY CONSOLE

MARBLE TOP, GOLD
AND WHITE PAINTED FRAME

PAINTED BLACK TOP AND
GLOBES, EGYPTIAN INFLUENCE

MAHOGANY CONSOLES SUPPORTED BY
BRONZE CARYATIDS WHICH ARE
REFLECTED IN THE MIRROR PANEL AT BACK

SERVING TABLE OF SATINWOOD
WITH MIRROR PANEL AT BACK

MAHOGANY SIDEBOARD
WITH WHITE MARBLE TOP

CONSOLE WITH LOWER SHELF
OF MARBLE, TOP SHELF INLAID
WITH BRASS

MAHOGANY SIDE TABLES

Dining tables

MAHOGANY-TOP TABLE, METAL LEGS

INLAID MARBLE TOP, LION FEET

SIMPLE TABLE WITH
FLUTED LEGS
ENGLISH PATTERN

MAHOGANY TABLE WITH LOTUS LEAF BASES
FOR THE SUPPORTING COLUMNS

SATINWOOD TABLE SUPPORTED BY SPHINXES

Dining-room accessories

BRONZE JARDINIERE
IN BLACK AND GOLD

BRONZE LAMPS

CHASED BRASS
CANDLESTICK AND
WALL SCONCE

MARBLE URNS

BRASS READING LAMP
WITH TOLE SHADE

PORCELAIN
TABLE CENTRE
ORNAMENT

BRASS ANDIRON

BRONZE
CANDLESTICK

CRYSTAL AND BRONZE
MIRROR-BACK SCONCE

PORCELAIN URNS

Cabinets, chests of drawers, secretaries, desk

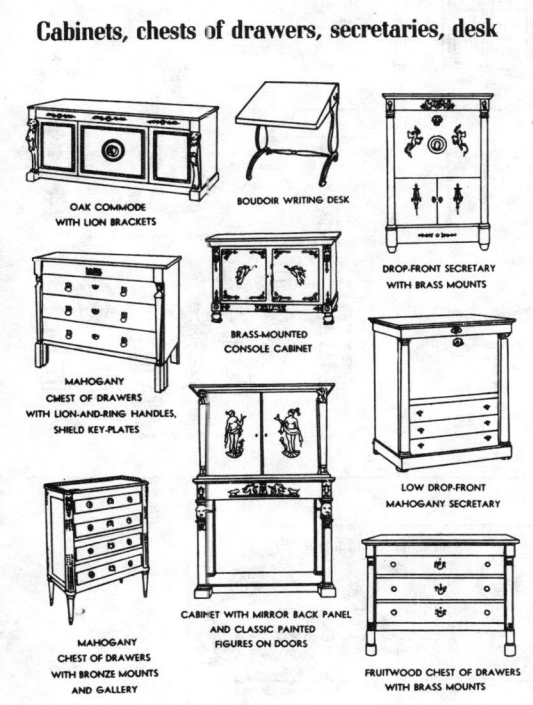

OAK COMMODE
WITH LION BRACKETS

BOUDOIR WRITING DESK

DROP-FRONT SECRETARY
WITH BRASS MOUNTS

BRASS-MOUNTED
CONSOLE CABINET

MAHOGANY
CHEST OF DRAWERS
WITH LION-AND-RING HANDLES,
SHIELD KEY-PLATES

LOW DROP-FRONT
MAHOGANY SECRETARY

MAHOGANY
CHEST OF DRAWERS
WITH BRONZE MOUNTS
AND GALLERY

CABINET WITH MIRROR BACK PANEL
AND CLASSIC PAINTED
FIGURES ON DOORS

FRUITWOOD CHEST OF DRAWERS
WITH BRASS MOUNTS

Dressing tables, stools, night tables, mirrors

DRESSING TABLE MIRROR
WITH SPHINX HEAD SUPPORTS

WALNUT NIGHT TABLE

MAHOGANY NIGHT TABLE
WITH PILLAR SUPPORTS

NIGHT TABLE WITH BRASS
BUSTS, FEET AND KEY PLATE

DRESSING TABLE WITH
BRONZE MOUNTS FOR THE LEGS

CANDLESTAND

BEDSIDE
CHAIR

ADJUSTABLE PIER GLASS
IN MAHOGANY STAND

BLACK PAINTED TABLE
WITH GILT LINING

NIGHT TABLES WITH TAMBOUR DOORS

UPHOLSTERED PAINTED CHAIR

DRESSING STOOLS IN PAINTED MAHOGANY

Bedroom accessories

BRASS READING LAMP
WITH TOLE SHADE

MARBLE-BASE
LAMP

BRONZE HEAD
ON MARBLE STAND

BRASS WALL
SCONCE

BRONZE
CANDLESTICKS

TOLE VASES

GOLD AND MARBLE
MANTEL CLOCK

PORCELAIN URNS

SMALL BRONZE
WALL LAMP
WITH TOLE SHADE

BRONZE SCONCE

FOOTSTOOLS WITH WHITE-PAINTED FRAMES
UPHOLSTERED IN STRIPED SATIN AND TAPESTRY

The Egyptian campaign yielded an impressive collection of sphinxes, pyramids, obelisks, and lotus leaf capitals. From Italy came all the paraphernalia of Imperial Roman decoration, acanthus leaves, laurel wreaths, torches, winged victories, cornucopias, and the rest, including the famous wreath of bees Napoleon is usually accused of having appropriated from the arms of an old Italian family, the Barberini.

The early Empire pieces (Directoire) are simplified versions of the styles current under Louis XVI. These pieces have grace, simplicity, and charm. The hampering restrictions on foreign trade led to the use of native fruitwoods instead of mahogany.

PERIOD FURNITURE

Late 18th–Early 19th Century French: Directoire and Empire

Fireplace designs

MARBLEIZED SURROUND
SLIDING METAL SCREEN IN FIREPLACE OPENING

GILT METAL APPLIED ORNAMENT
RELIEVES THIS SIMPLE DESIGN

Interior Doorways

THE FRIEZE COMBINES CLASSIC
AND EGYPTIAN MOTIFS. PAINTED
DECORATION IN GREEN, GOLD AND BEIGE

PANELED DOOR WITH PAINTING OF
CLASSIC FIGURES ABOVE DECORATION IN
GOLD, WHITE, BLUE AND YELLOW

Drapery treatments for Directoire windows

SIMPLE LIGHT BLUE CURTAINS EDGED
WITH YELLOW BINDING TAPE
YELLOW TIEBACK

GREEN OVERDRAPERY
EDGED WITH GOLD AND
WHITE EMBROIDERY TAPE

WHITE SILK CURTAINS TRIMMED
WITH GOLD BRAID
SIMPLE WOODEN CORNICE BOARD

Armchairs, stools

PAINTED GONDOLA CHAIRS

MAHOGANY DESK CHAIR

CROSS-LEGGED
CURULE STOOLS

WHITE AND GOLD CHAIR
FROM HOTEL DES MONNAIES, PARIS

MAHOGANY ARMCHAIR
PAINTED GREEN AND GOLD

WHITE-PAINTED
MAHOGANY ARMCHAIR
BY JACOB BROTHERS

WHITE-PAINTED FRAME
GREEN UPHOLSTERY

ARMCHAIR, WHITE-PAINTED FRAME
THE GRAND TRIANON, VERSAILLES

BERGÈRE
PAINTED FRAME

FAUTEUIL UPHOLSTERED
IN STRIPED SATIN

Secretaries, bookcases, occasional tables

GLASS-FRONTED CABINET
PAINTED OLIVE GREEN
AND GOLD

MAHOGANY
SECRETARY WITH
PAINTED DECORATION

LIBRARY WRITING TABLE
WITH LEATHER INLAID TOP

MAHOGANY BOOKCASES OF CLASSIC STYLE

MAHOGANY SECRETARY

SIDE TABLES IN MAHOGANY WITH BRONZE MOUNTS
DESIGNED BY RIESENER

MAHOGANY OCCASIONAL TABLES WITH BRASS ORNAMENT

Living-room accessories

BRASS WALL
SCONCE

POLISHED
MARBLE OBELISK

DARK RED
AND GOLD TOLE

WHITE MARBLE
CLOCK

BRASS
CANDLESTICK

SMALL
BRONZE HEAD

TOLE LAMP

BRONZE LAMP

BRONZE CHANDELIER

BRASS
CANDELABRA

PORCELAIN URNS AND VASES

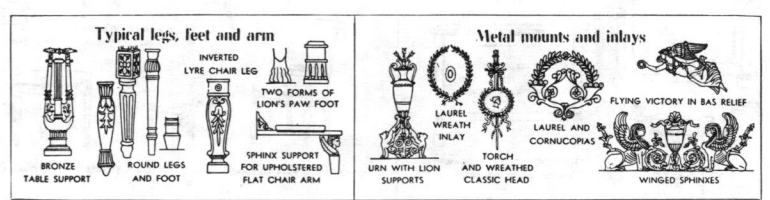

Typical legs, feet and arm

INVERTED
LYRE CHAIR LEG

TWO FORMS OF
LION'S PAW FOOT

BRONZE
TABLE SUPPORT

ROUND LEGS
AND FOOT

SPHINX SUPPORT
FOR UPHOLSTERED
FLAT CHAIR ARM

Metal mounts and inlays

LAUREL
WREATH INLAY

FLYING VICTORY IN BAS RELIEF

LAUREL AND
CORNUCOPIAS

URN WITH LION
SUPPORTS

TORCH
AND WREATHED
CLASSIC HEAD

WINGED SPHINXES

Fig. 5 *(Continued)*

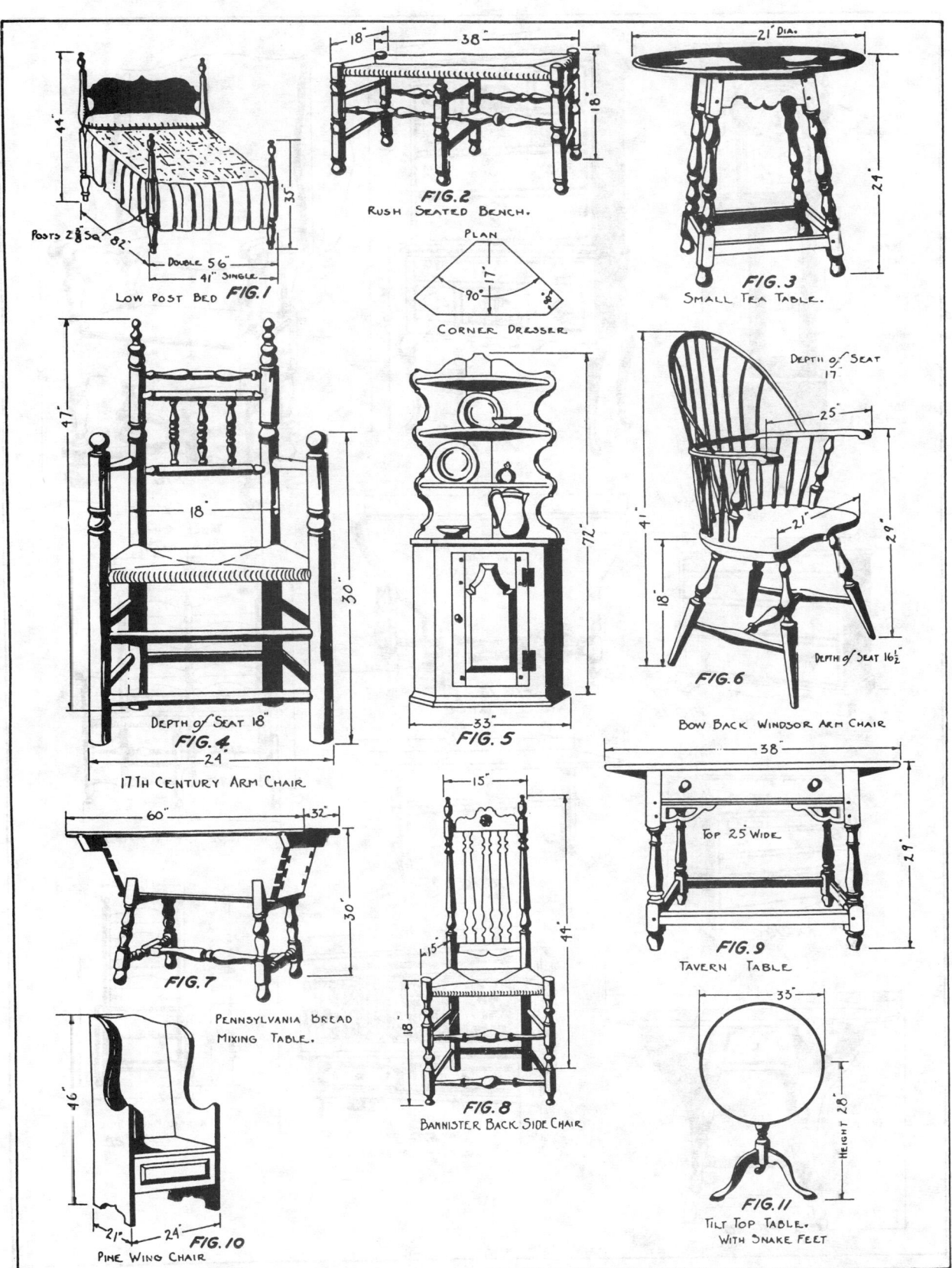

FIG.1
Low Post Bed
44"
Posts 2⅜"Sq. 82"
Double 56"
41" Single
35"

FIG.2
Rush Seated Bench.
18" 38" 18"

FIG.3
Small Tea Table.
21" Dia.
24"

PLAN
Corner Dresser
17"
90"

FIG.4
17th Century Arm Chair
Depth of Seat 18"
47"
18"
30"
24"

FIG.5
33"
72"

FIG.6
Bow Back Windsor Arm Chair
Depth of Seat 17
25"
41"
18"
2'9"
Depth of Seat 16½"

FIG.7
Pennsylvania Bread Mixing Table.
60" 32"
30"

FIG.8
Bannister Back Side Chair
15"
15"
41"
18"

FIG.9
Tavern Table
38"
Top 25 Wide
2'9"

FIG.10
Pine Wing Chair
46"
21" 24"

FIG.11
Tilt Top Table.
With Snake Feet
33"
Height 28"

Colonial style

29

PERIOD FURNITURE
17th and 18th Century American: Colonial

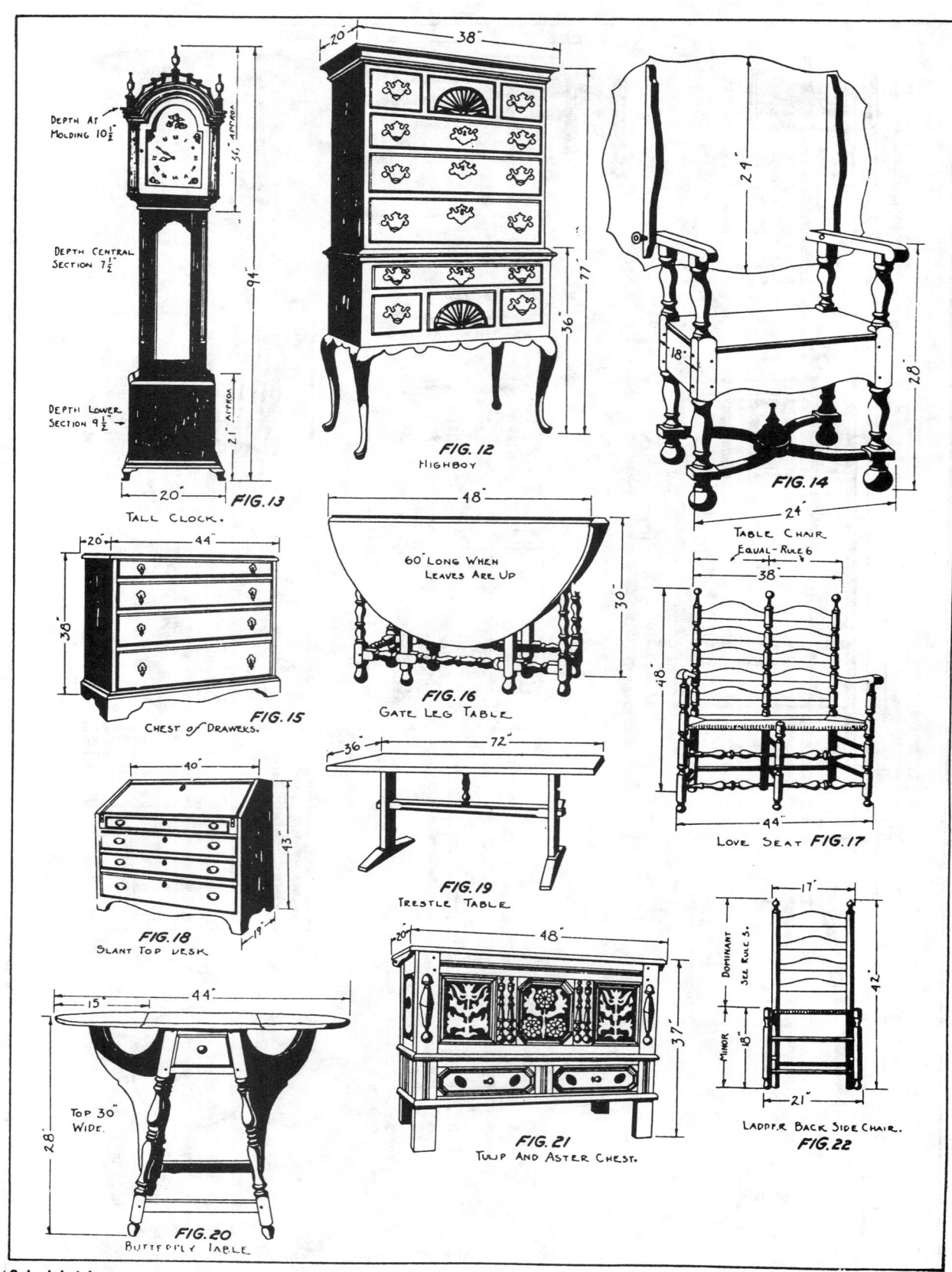

FIG. 13
TALL CLOCK.

FIG. 12
HIGHBOY

FIG. 14
TABLE CHAIR
EQUAL-RULE 6

FIG. 15
CHEST OF DRAWERS.

FIG. 16
GATE LEG TABLE

LOVE SEAT *FIG. 17*

FIG. 18
SLANT TOP DESK

FIG. 19
TRESTLE TABLE

FIG. 20
BUTTERFLY TABLE

FIG. 21
TULIP AND ASTER CHEST.

LADDER BACK SIDE CHAIR.
FIG. 22

Colonial style

FIG.1
Duncan Phyfe Side Chair
Reeded Horseshoe Shaped
Seat.

FIG.2
Side Chair With Lyre Back.

FIG.3
Duncan Phyfe Arm Chair.

FIG.4
Two Back Setter With Lyre Ends. These May Be Made
With Three Backs & Are Sometimes Caned. They
Sometimes Have Animal Feet.

FIG. 5
Console Table. Veneered Apron.

FIG.6
Sewing Table. The Silk Bag
Is Fastened To The Lower Drawer
Which Has No Bottom. The
Semi-Circular Ends Are Boxes &
The Lids Have Invisible Hinges.

*Though Duncan
Phyfe Adapted
Freely From The
Work of Sheraton.
Heppelwhite & Others
He Developed A
Distinct Style.*

FIG.7
Library Table With Lyre Ends.

FIG.8
Small Veneered Sideboard.

FIG.9
Lyre Base Card Table

FIG.10
Dining Table. These May Be Made In Two, Three Or
Five Sections. Wide Boards May Also Be Added
Between Each Section To Lengthen The Tables.

The Principle Pieces of Furniture Made
By Phyfe Were Chairs. Tables. Sofas
& Setters. He Also Made Sideboards.
Bedsteads. Mirrors. Washstands. Writing
Desks. Etc. Some of His Favorite
Motifs Were The Lyre. The Acanthus
Leaf. Turned & Reeded Legs. Turned
Pedestals Supported On Curved Legs.
& Animal Feet of Brass. The Principal
Wood Used Was Mahogany Often
Veneered.

Duncan Phyfe style

PERIOD FURNITURE
16th Century English: Early Jacobean

CHEST
FIG. 1

FIG. 2
CHEST ON FRAME

FIG. 3
CHEST OF DRAWERS

FIG. 4
COURT CUPBOARD

REFECTORY TABLE
FIG. 5

SETTLE   FIG. 6

FIG. 7
CROMWELLAN CHAIR

SMALL TABLE
FIG. 8

FIG. 9   LONG FORM

FIG. 10
STOOL

Early Jacobean period

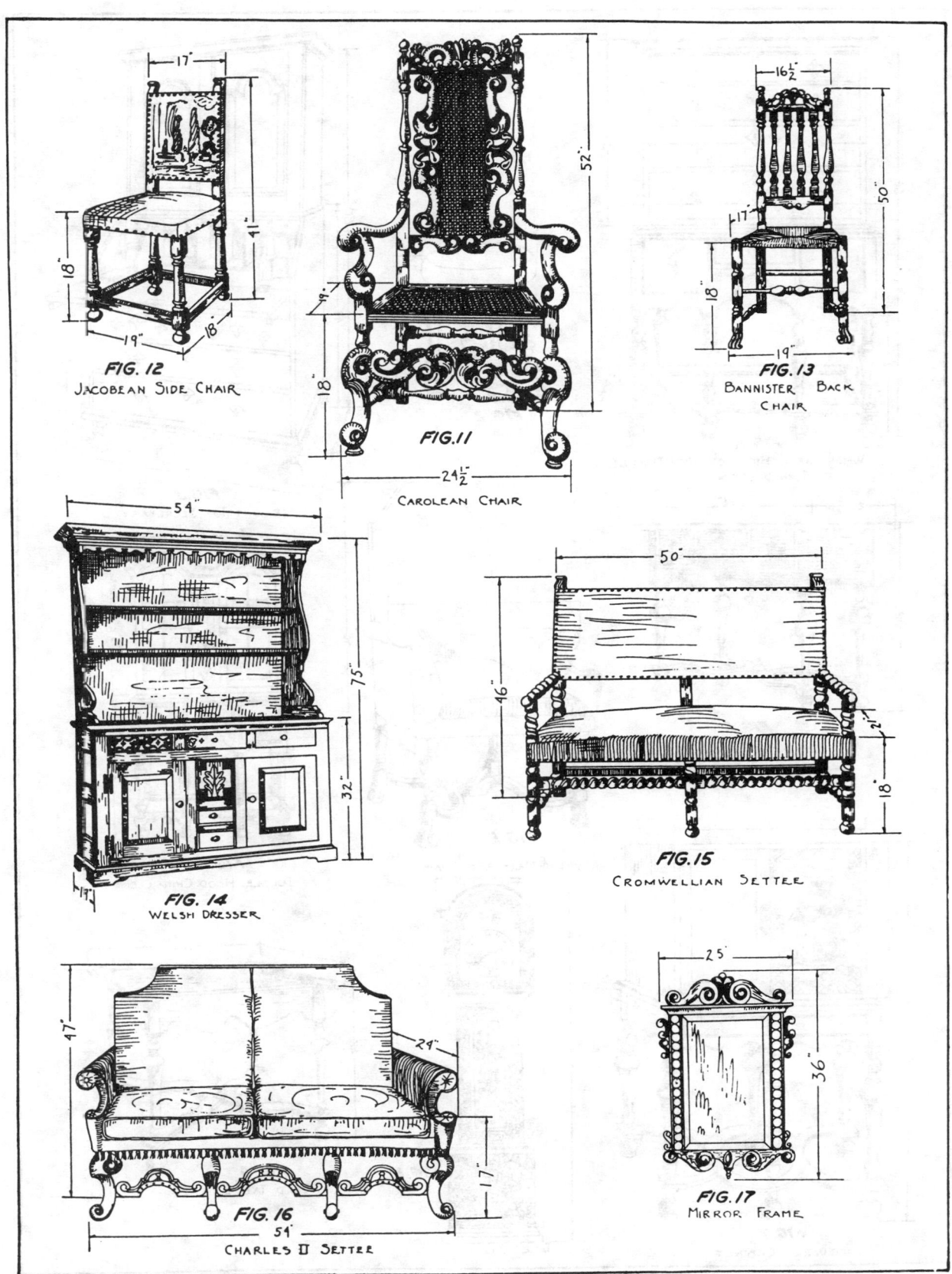

FIG. 12
JACOBEAN SIDE CHAIR

FIG. 11
CAROLEAN CHAIR

FIG. 13
BANNISTER BACK
CHAIR

FIG. 14
WELSH DRESSER

FIG. 15
CROMWELLIAN SETTEE

FIG. 16
CHARLES II SETTEE

FIG. 17
MIRROR FRAME

Jacobean period

PERIOD FURNITURE
17th Century English: William & Mary

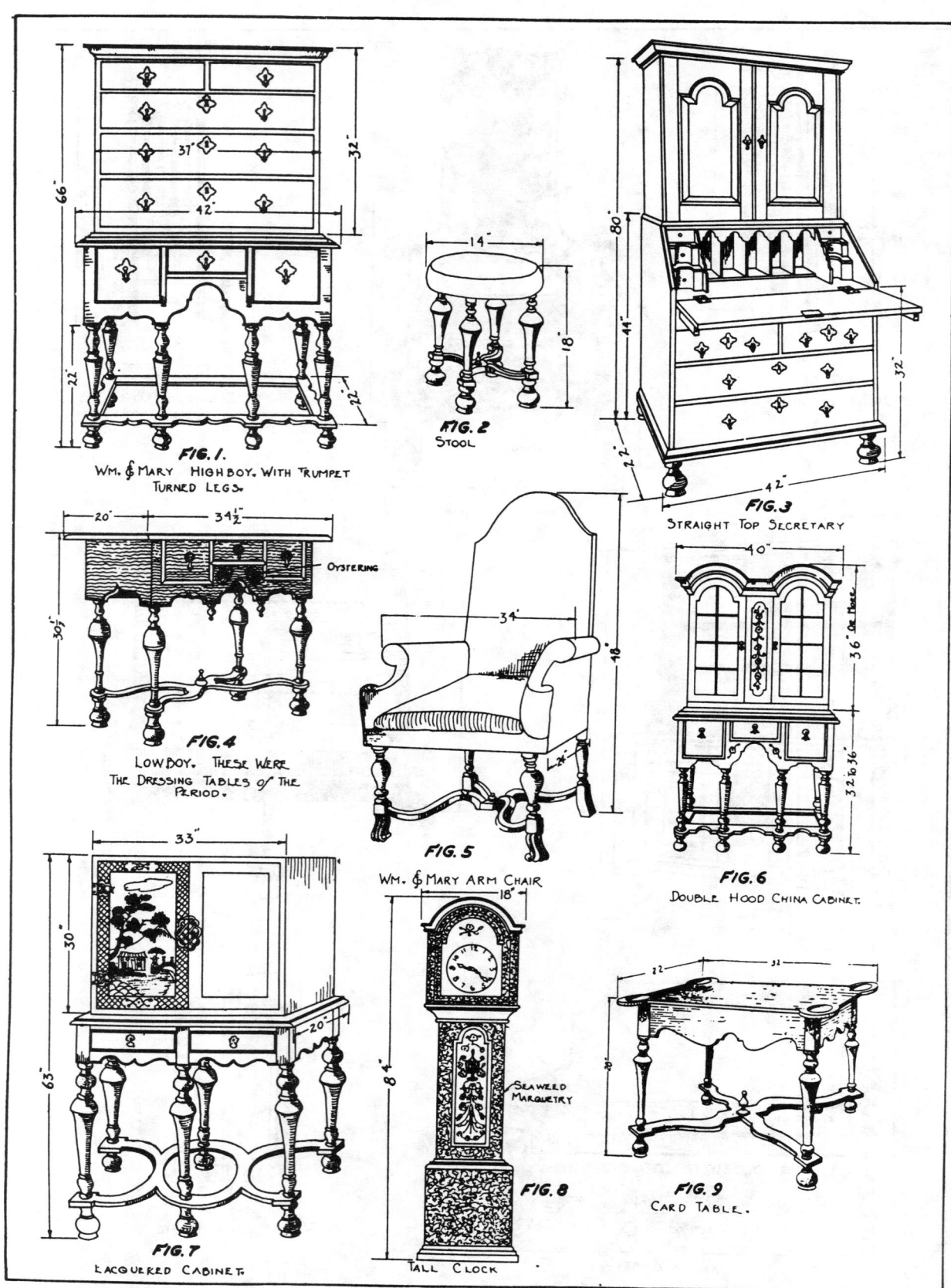

FIG. I.
WM. & MARY HIGHBOY. WITH TRUMPET
TURNED LEGS.

FIG. 2
STOOL

FIG. 3
STRAIGHT TOP SECRETARY

FIG. 4
LOWBOY. THESE WERE
THE DRESSING TABLES of THE
PERIOD.

OYSTERING

FIG. 5
WM. & MARY ARM CHAIR

FIG. 6
DOUBLE HOOD CHINA CABINET.

FIG. 7
LACQUERED CABINET.

FIG. 8
TALL CLOCK

SEAWEED
MARQUETRY

FIG. 9
CARD TABLE.

William and Mary period

FIG. 1
HIGHBOY

FIG. 2
LOWBOY

FIG. 3
SMALL TABLE

FIG 4
SOFA

FIG. 5
HALL TABLE

FIG. 6
SMALL TEA TABLE

Top 40" In Diameter When Open.

FIG. 7
LIGHT DROP-LEAF TABLE

FIG. 8
GATE LEG TABLE

FIG. 9
ARM CHAIR

Seat 18" High
40 To 46" High
Seat 24" Wide
18" Deep

Top 22 By 72

FIG. 10
SIDEBOARD

FIG. 11
WRITING DESK

FIG. 12
Width of Seat 21"
Depth 17"

FIG. 13
STOOL

SIDE CHAIR
THE PROPER WOOD FOR QUEEN ANNE
FURNITURE IS WALNUT. MAHOGANY
WAS SOMETIMES USED.

Queen Anne period

PERIOD FURNITURE

18th Century English: Georgian (Chippendale)

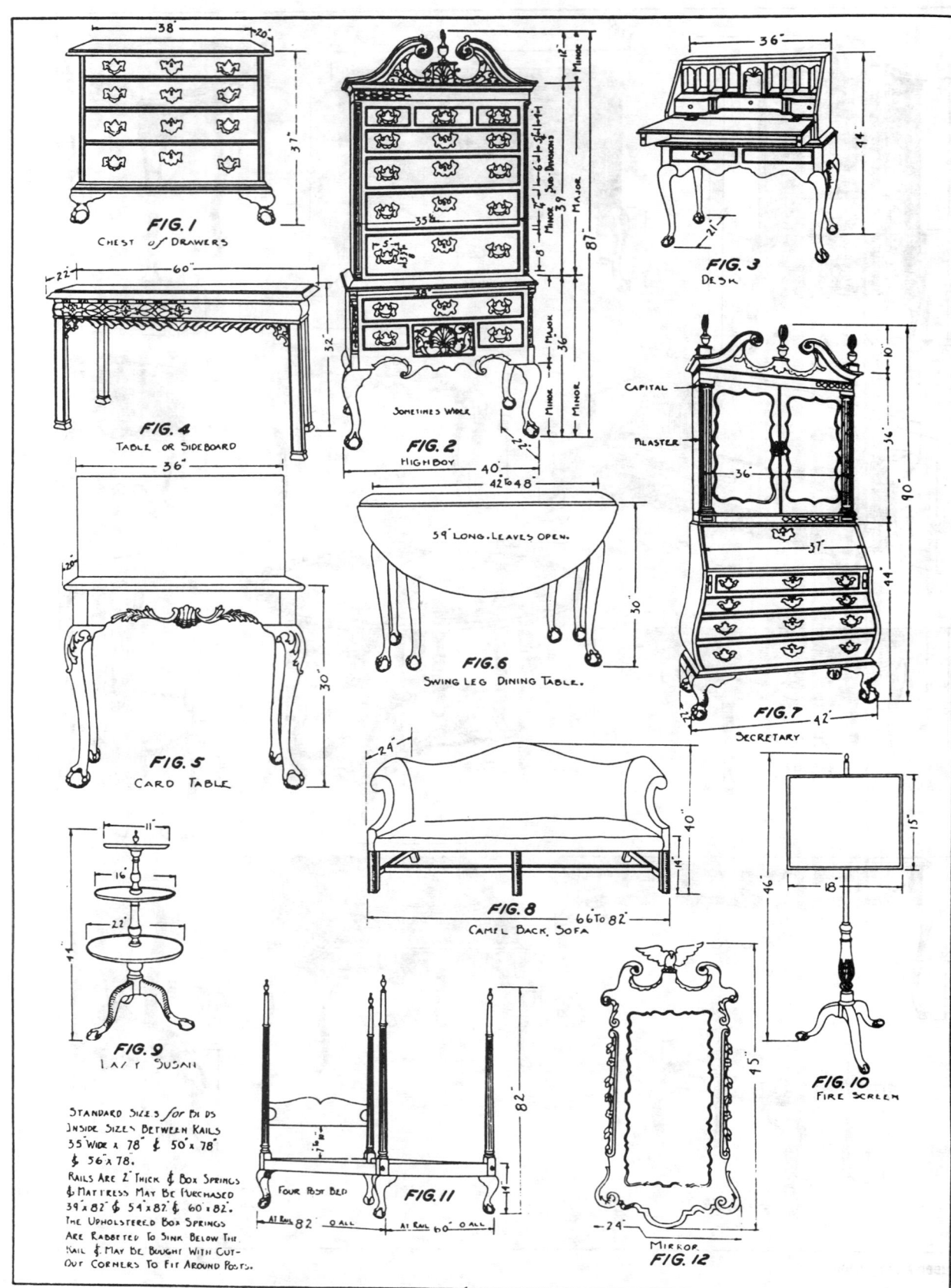

FIG. 1
CHEST OF DRAWERS

FIG. 2
HIGHBOY

FIG. 3
DESK

FIG. 4
TABLE OR SIDEBOARD

FIG. 5
CARD TABLE

FIG. 6
SWING LEG DINING TABLE.

FIG. 7
SECRETARY

FIG. 8
CAMEL BACK SOFA

FIG. 9
LAZY SUSAN

FIG. 10
FIRE SCREEN

FIG. 11
FOUR POST BED

FIG. 12
MIRROR

STANDARD SIZES FOR BEDS
INSIDE SIZES BETWEEN RAILS
35" WIDE x 78" & 50" x 78"
& 56" x 78.
RAILS ARE 2" THICK & BOX SPRINGS
& MATTRESS MAY BE PURCHASED
39"x82" & 54"x82" & 60"x82".
THE UPHOLSTERED BOX SPRINGS
ARE RABBETED TO SINK BELOW THE
RAIL & MAY BE BOUGHT WITH CUT-
OUT CORNERS TO FIT AROUND POSTS.

Chippendale style

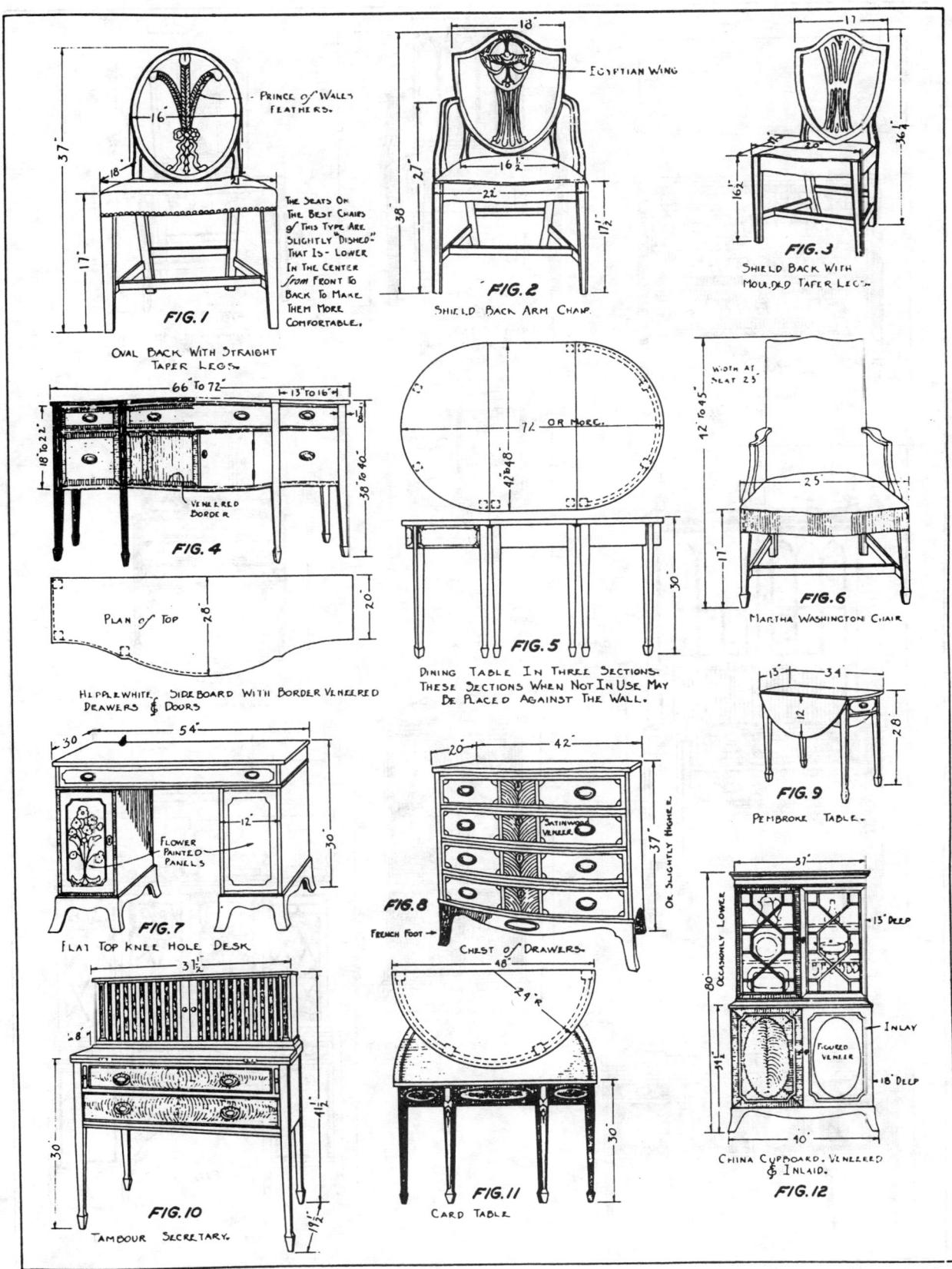

FIG. 1 — OVAL BACK WITH STRAIGHT TAPER LEGS.
PRINCE OF WALES FEATHERS.
THE SEATS ON THE BEST CHAIRS OF THIS TYPE ARE SLIGHTLY "DISHED" THAT IS- LOWER IN THE CENTER *from* FRONT TO BACK TO MAKE THEM MORE COMFORTABLE.

FIG. 2 — SHIELD BACK ARM CHAIR. EGYPTIAN WING

FIG. 3 — SHIELD BACK WITH MOULDED TAPER LEGS.

FIG. 4 — HEPPLEWHITE SIDEBOARD WITH BORDER VENEERED DRAWERS & DOORS. VENEERED BORDER. PLAN OF TOP.

FIG. 5 — DINING TABLE IN THREE SECTIONS. THESE SECTIONS WHEN NOT IN USE MAY BE PLACED AGAINST THE WALL.

FIG. 6 — MARTHA WASHINGTON CHAIR. WIDTH AT SEAT 25"

FIG. 7 — FLAT TOP KNEE HOLE DESK. FLOWER PAINTED PANELS.

FIG. 8 — CHEST OF DRAWERS. SATINWOOD VENEER. FRENCH FOOT. OR SLIGHTLY HIGHER.

FIG. 9 — PEMBROKE TABLE.

FIG. 10 — TAMBOUR SECRETARY.

FIG. 11 — CARD TABLE.

FIG. 12 — CHINA CUPBOARD. VENEERED & INLAID. OCCASIONLY LOWER. INLAY. FIGURED VENEER.

Hepplewhite style

37

PERIOD FURNITURE
18th Century English: Late Georgian (Sheraton)

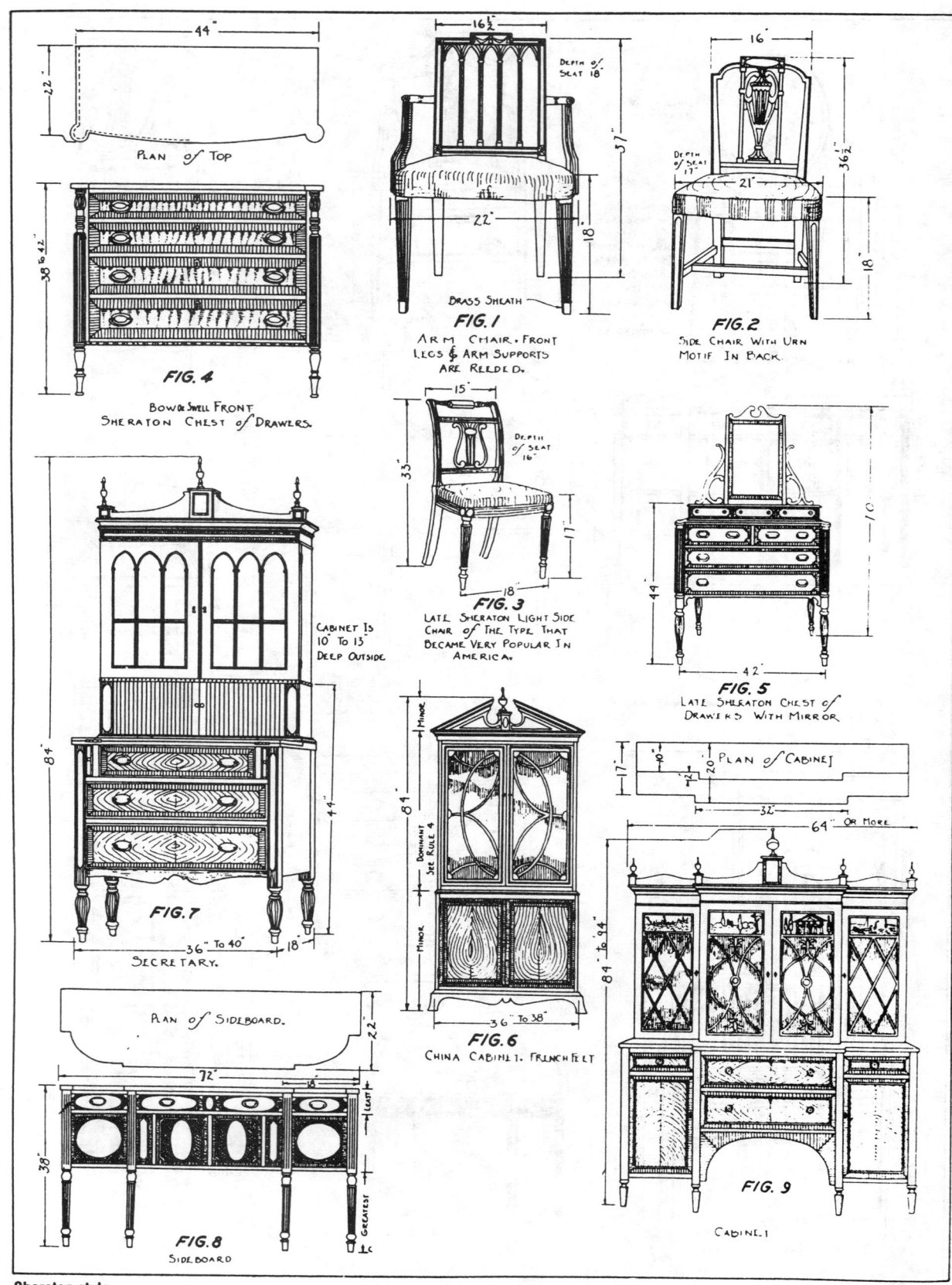

PLAN OF TOP

FIG. 4

BOW & SWELL FRONT
SHERATON CHEST OF DRAWERS.

BRASS SHEATH

FIG. I
ARM CHAIR. FRONT
LEGS & ARM SUPPORTS
ARE REEDED.

FIG. 2
SIDE CHAIR WITH URN
MOTIF IN BACK.

FIG. 3
LATE SHERATON LIGHT SIDE
CHAIR OF THE TYPE THAT
BECAME VERY POPULAR IN
AMERICA.

CABINET IS
10" TO 13"
DEEP OUTSIDE

FIG. 7
SECRETARY.

PLAN OF SIDEBOARD.

FIG. 8
SIDEBOARD

FIG. 6
CHINA CABINET. FRENCH FEET

FIG. 5
LATE SHERATON CHEST OF
DRAWERS WITH MIRROR

PLAN OF CABINET

FIG. 9

CABINET

Sheraton style

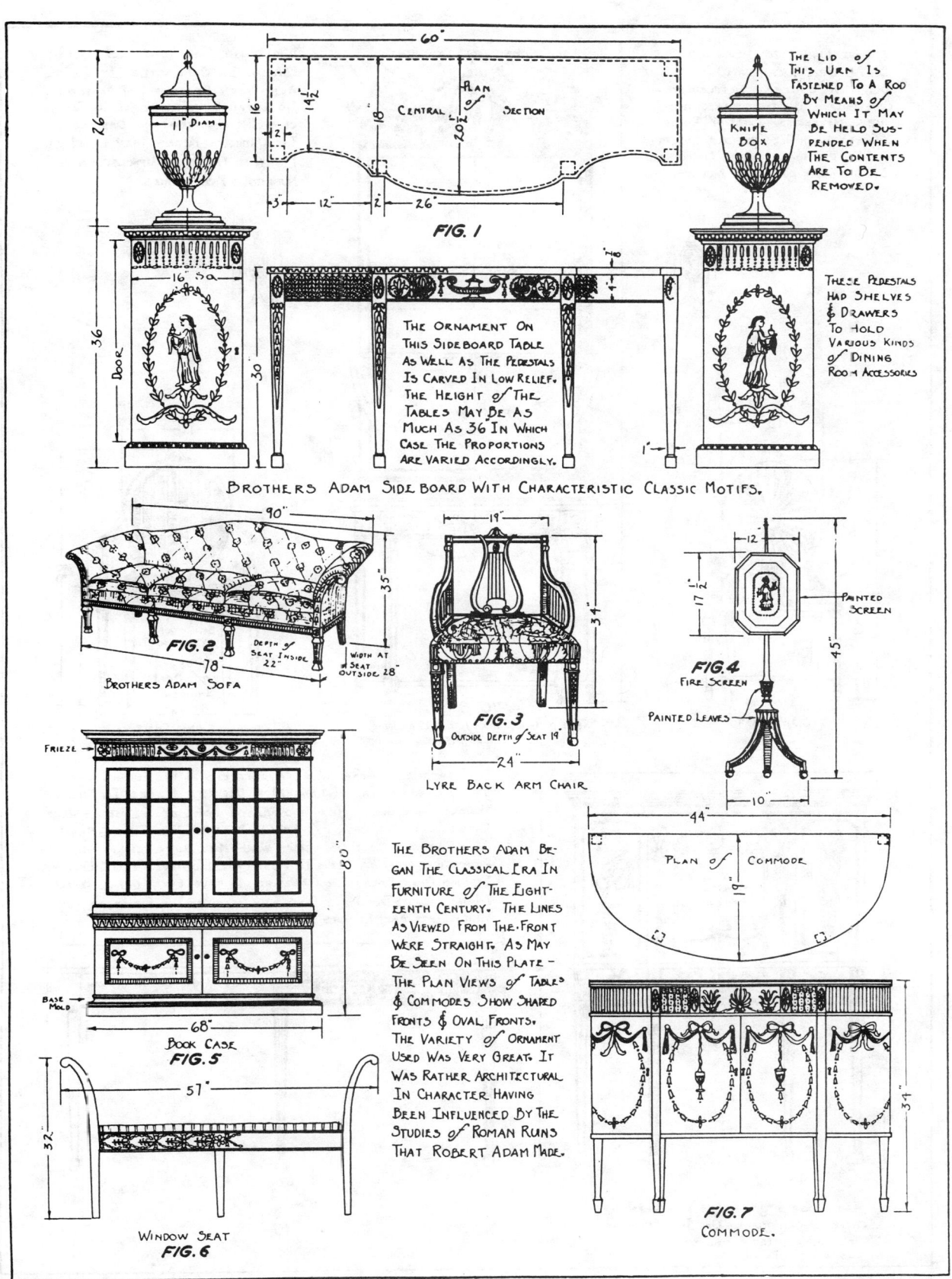

THE LID of THIS URN IS FASTENED TO A ROD BY MEANS of WHICH IT MAY BE HELD SUSPENDED WHEN THE CONTENTS ARE TO BE REMOVED.

60"

PLAN of CENTRAL SECTION

KNIFE BOX

FIG. 1

16" Sq

Door 36

30

THE ORNAMENT ON THIS SIDEBOARD TABLE AS WELL AS THE PEDESTALS IS CARVED IN LOW RELIEF. THE HEIGHT of THE TABLES MAY BE AS MUCH AS 36 IN WHICH CASE THE PROPORTIONS ARE VARIED ACCORDINGLY.

THESE PEDESTALS HAD SHELVES & DRAWERS TO HOLD VARIOUS KINDS of DINING ROOM ACCESSORIES

BROTHERS ADAM SIDEBOARD WITH CHARACTERISTIC CLASSIC MOTIFS.

90"

35"

78"
DEPTH of SEAT INSIDE 22"
WIDTH AT SEAT OUTSIDE 28"

BROTHERS ADAM SOFA
FIG. 2

19"

34"

24"
FIG. 3
Outside Depth of Seat 19"

LYRE BACK ARM CHAIR

12

17 1/2"

45

PAINTED SCREEN

FIG. 4
FIRE SCREEN

PAINTED LEAVES

10"

FRIEZE

80"

BASE MOLD

68"

BOOK CASE
FIG. 5

THE BROTHERS ADAM BEGAN THE CLASSICAL ERA IN FURNITURE of THE EIGHTEENTH CENTURY. THE LINES AS VIEWED FROM THE FRONT WERE STRAIGHT, AS MAY BE SEEN ON THIS PLATE – THE PLAN VIEWS of TABLES & COMMODES SHOW SHAPED FRONTS & OVAL FRONTS. THE VARIETY of ORNAMENT USED WAS VERY GREAT. IT WAS RATHER ARCHITECTURAL IN CHARACTER HAVING BEEN INFLUENCED BY THE STUDIES of ROMAN RUINS THAT ROBERT ADAM MADE.

44"

PLAN of COMMODE

34"

FIG. 7
COMMODE.

57"

32"

WINDOW SEAT
FIG. 6

Brothers Adam

39

PERIOD FURNITURE
18th Century English: Late Georgian (Brothers Adam)

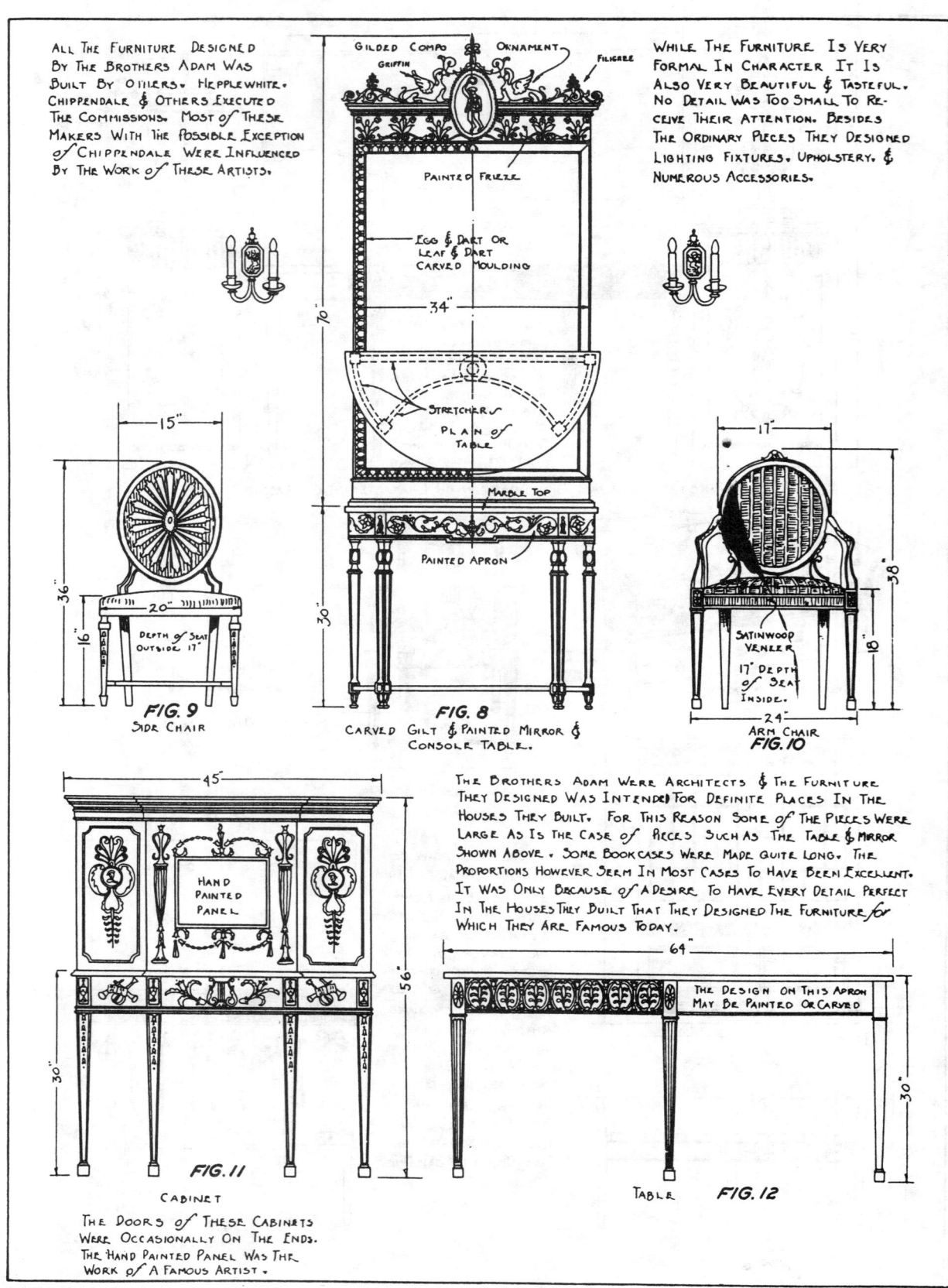

ALL THE FURNITURE DESIGNED BY THE BROTHERS ADAM WAS BUILT BY OTHERS. HEPPLEWHITE, CHIPPENDALE & OTHERS EXECUTED THE COMMISSIONS. MOST OF THESE MAKERS WITH THE POSSIBLE EXCEPTION OF CHIPPENDALE WERE INFLUENCED BY THE WORK OF THESE ARTISTS.

WHILE THE FURNITURE IS VERY FORMAL IN CHARACTER IT IS ALSO VERY BEAUTIFUL & TASTEFUL. NO DETAIL WAS TOO SMALL TO RECEIVE THEIR ATTENTION. BESIDES THE ORDINARY PIECES THEY DESIGNED LIGHTING FIXTURES, UPHOLSTERY, & NUMEROUS ACCESSORIES.

GILDED COMPO ORNAMENT
GRIFFIN
FILIGREE
PAINTED FRIEZE
EGG & DART OR LEAF & DART CARVED MOULDING
34"
STRETCHERS
PLAN OF TABLE
MARBLE TOP
PAINTED APRON
70"
30"

FIG. 9
SIDE CHAIR
15"
36"
16"
20"
DEPTH OF SEAT OUTSIDE 17"

FIG. 8
CARVED GILT & PAINTED MIRROR & CONSOLE TABLE.

FIG. 10
ARM CHAIR
17"
38"
18"
24"
SATINWOOD VENEER
17" DEPTH OF SEAT INSIDE.

THE BROTHERS ADAM WERE ARCHITECTS & THE FURNITURE THEY DESIGNED WAS INTENDED FOR DEFINITE PLACES IN THE HOUSES THEY BUILT. FOR THIS REASON SOME OF THE PIECES WERE LARGE AS IS THE CASE OF PIECES SUCH AS THE TABLE & MIRROR SHOWN ABOVE. SOME BOOKCASES WERE MADE QUITE LONG. THE PROPORTIONS HOWEVER SEEM IN MOST CASES TO HAVE BEEN EXCELLENT. IT WAS ONLY BECAUSE OF A DESIRE TO HAVE EVERY DETAIL PERFECT IN THE HOUSES THEY BUILT THAT THEY DESIGNED THE FURNITURE FOR WHICH THEY ARE FAMOUS TODAY.

45"
HAND PAINTED PANEL
56"
30"

FIG. 11
CABINET
THE DOORS OF THESE CABINETS WERE OCCASIONALLY ON THE ENDS. THE HAND PAINTED PANEL WAS THE WORK OF A FAMOUS ARTIST.

64"
THE DESIGN ON THIS APRON MAY BE PAINTED OR CARVED
30"
TABLE **FIG. 12**

Brothers Adam

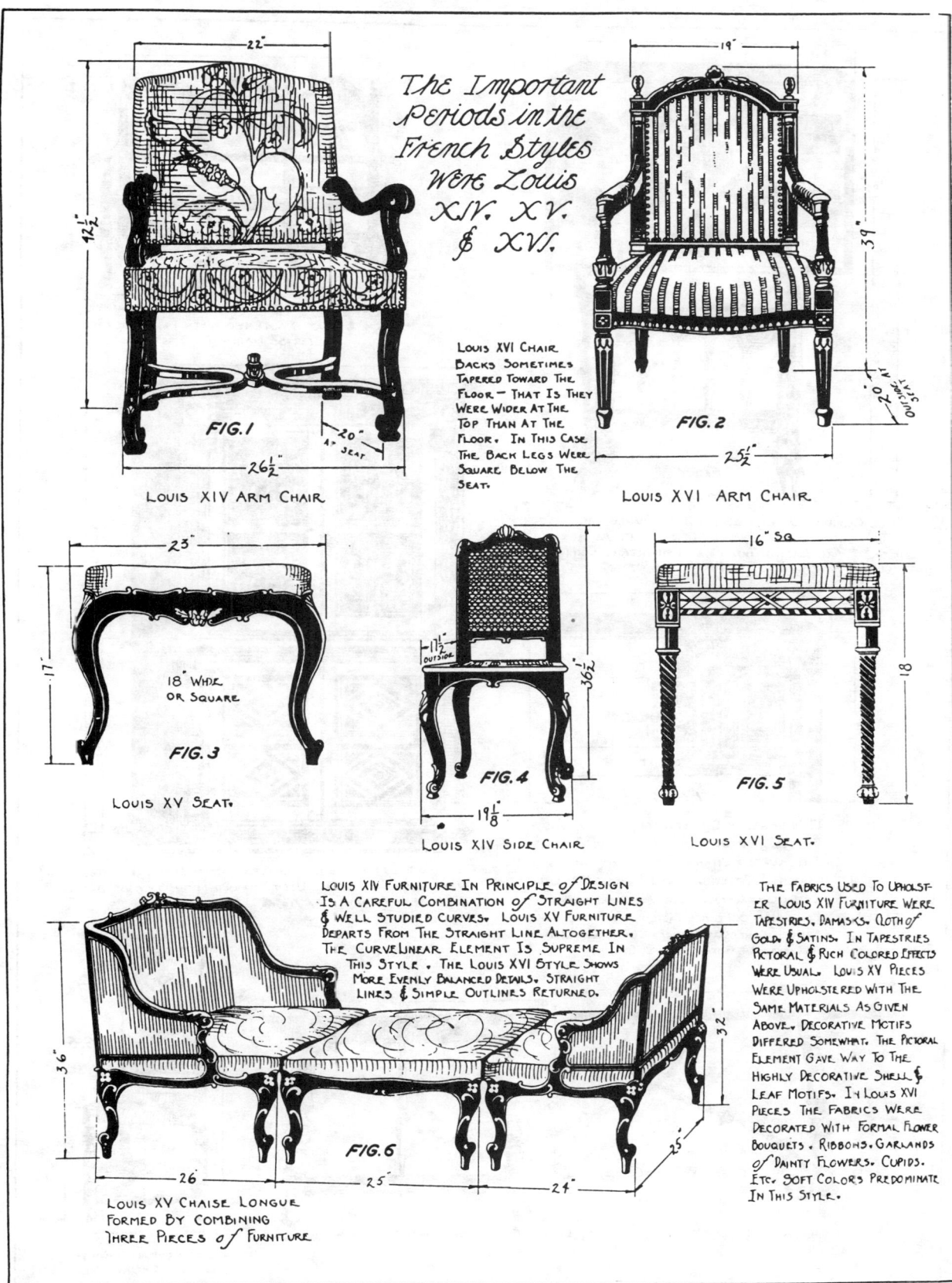

The Important Periods in the French Styles were Louis XIV, XV, & XVI.

LOUIS XVI CHAIR BACKS SOMETIMES TAPERED TOWARD THE FLOOR — THAT IS THEY WERE WIDER AT THE TOP THAN AT THE FLOOR. IN THIS CASE THE BACK LEGS WERE SQUARE BELOW THE SEAT.

FIG. 1
LOUIS XIV ARM CHAIR

FIG. 2
LOUIS XVI ARM CHAIR

FIG. 3
18" WIDE OR SQUARE
LOUIS XV SEAT.

FIG. 4
LOUIS XIV SIDE CHAIR

FIG. 5
16" SQ.
LOUIS XVI SEAT.

LOUIS XIV FURNITURE IN PRINCIPLE OF DESIGN IS A CAREFUL COMBINATION OF STRAIGHT LINES & WELL STUDIED CURVES. LOUIS XV FURNITURE DEPARTS FROM THE STRAIGHT LINE ALTOGETHER. THE CURVELINEAR ELEMENT IS SUPREME IN THIS STYLE. THE LOUIS XVI STYLE SHOWS MORE EVENLY BALANCED DETAILS. STRAIGHT LINES & SIMPLE OUTLINES RETURNED.

THE FABRICS USED TO UPHOLSTER LOUIS XIV FURNITURE WERE TAPESTRIES, DAMASKS, CLOTH OF GOLD & SATINS. IN TAPESTRIES PICTORAL & RICH COLORED EFFECTS WERE USUAL. LOUIS XV PIECES WERE UPHOLSTERED WITH THE SAME MATERIALS AS GIVEN ABOVE. DECORATIVE MOTIFS DIFFERED SOMEWHAT. THE PICTORAL ELEMENT GAVE WAY TO THE HIGHLY DECORATIVE SHELL & LEAF MOTIFS. IN LOUIS XVI PIECES THE FABRICS WERE DECORATED WITH FORMAL FLOWER BOUQUETS, RIBBONS, GARLANDS OF DAINTY FLOWERS, CUPIDS, ETC. SOFT COLORS PREDOMINATE IN THIS STYLE.

FIG. 6
LOUIS XV CHAISE LONGUE FORMED BY COMBINING THREE PIECES OF FURNITURE

French styles

PERIOD FURNITURE
16th and 17th Century Spanish

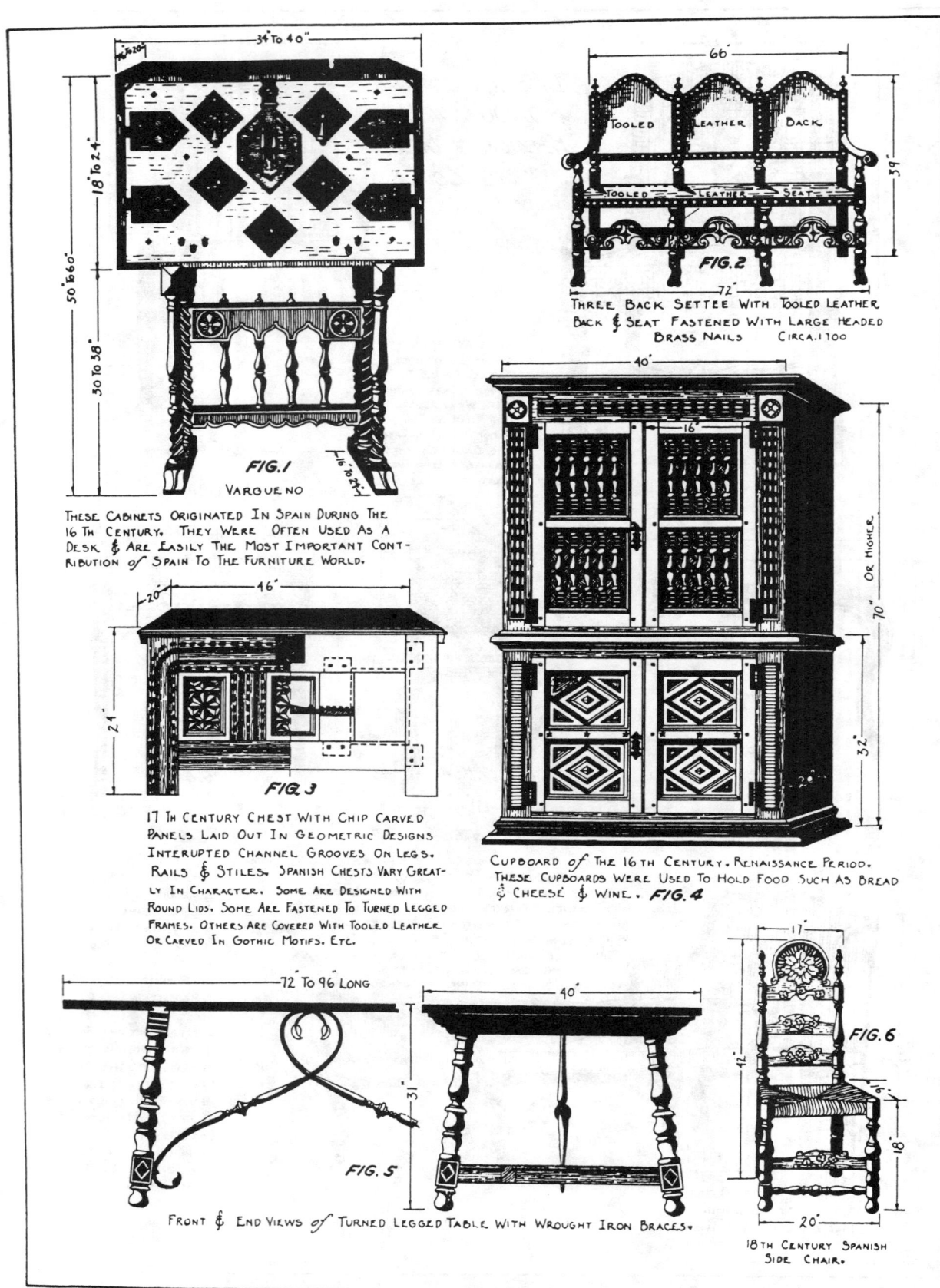

FIG.1
VARGUENO

These Cabinets Originated In Spain During The 16 Th Century. They Were Often Used As A Desk & Are Easily The Most Important Contribution of Spain To The Furniture World.

FIG.2
Three Back Settee With Tooled Leather Back & Seat Fastened With Large Headed Brass Nails   Circa.1700

TOOLED   LEATHER   BACK
TOOLED   LEATHER   SEAT

FIG 3
17 Th Century Chest With Chip Carved Panels Laid Out In Geometric Designs Interupted Channel Grooves On Legs. Rails & Stiles. Spanish Chests Vary Greatly In Character. Some Are Designed With Round Lids. Some Are Fastened To Turned Legged Frames. Others Are Covered With Tooled Leather Or Carved In Gothic Motifs. Etc.

Cupboard of The 16 th Century. Renaissance Period. These Cupboards Were Used To Hold Food Such As Bread & Cheese & Wine. FIG.4

FIG.5
Front & End Views of Turned Legged Table With Wrought Iron Braces.

FIG.6
18th Century Spanish Side Chair.

Spanish styles

TABLE 1 Period Style and Finishes

Period style	Associated styles	Walls and ceilings	Floors	Floor coverings
Early English Tudor Jacobean Charles II	Italian Renaissance Spanish Renaissance William & Mary Larger pieces of Queen Anne	Oak panels Rough plaster with oak trim Parquetry ceilings	Hardwood stained, dark strips and planks on flooring Stone Tiles	Oriental and large-patterned domestic rugs Plain rugs
Anglo-Dutch William & Mary Queen Anne	Chippendale Early Georgian Louis XVI Smaller pieces of Jacobean, such as gate-leg table or Windsor chair	Papered Painted (in light tones) Hung with fabrics Paneled	Hardwood flooring Parquetry	Oriental and large-patterned domestic rugs Plain rugs
Early Georgian Chippendale	Chippendale Early Georgian Louis XVI Smaller pieces of Jacobean, such as gate-leg table or Windsor chair	Painted dado Painted Paneled Papered upper section	Hardwood flooring Parquetry	Plain or small-patterned rugs or carpets Oriental rugs
Late Georgian Adam Hepplewhite Sheraton Empire Federal	Chinese Chippendale Louis XVI Duncan Phyfe Directoire	Plain plaster Painted Papered Large wood panels painted Gesso ceilings	Hardwood flooring Parquetry	Plain or small-patterned rugs or carpets Oriental rugs
Louis XIV, XV, and XVI	All late Georgian styles 1 or 2 pieces of Directoire	Large wood panels painted and decorated Wallpaper in Chinese motifs	Hardwood flooring Parquetry	Plain or small-patterned rugs or carpets Oriental rugs
Spanish Renaissance	Italian Renaissance Early English Louis XIV	Rough plaster painted Ceilings same or beamed	Hardwood flooring Tiles Vinyls in tile pattern	Spanish or Oriental rugs
Early Colonial	All Early English styles William & Mary Queen Anne wing chair	Oak panels Rough plaster with oak Parquetry ceilings	Hardwood flooring or planks Vinyls in jaspe pattern	Braided or hooked rugs
Early American	Late Georgian Chippendale Queen Anne Duncan Phyfe French Provincial	Smooth plaster, light trim Wallpaper, scenic and Chinese designs Paneling Ceiling plaster	Dark hardwood flooring Vinyls in plain or jaspe patterns	Hooked, braided, Oriental, or domestic rugs Carpet, plain, two-toned patterned
Modern	Swedish Modern Chinese Chippendale	Painted solid colors, striped, figured Plain papers Combinations of above	Hardwood flooring Parquetry Vinyls in modern pattern	Carpet Rugs in solid colors, geometric patterns
French Provincial	18th-century American Colonial Federal	Smooth plaster Wallpaper in scenic or geometric designs	Hardwood flooring Parquetry	Aubussons Homespun carpet, small-patterned Oriental rugs
Victorian	Colonial William & Mary Queen Anne	Large-patterned paper	Hardwood flooring	Carpet in large patterns Oriental rugs

FURNITURE DIMENSIONS
Children's Furniture and Tables

CHILDREN'S FURNITURE

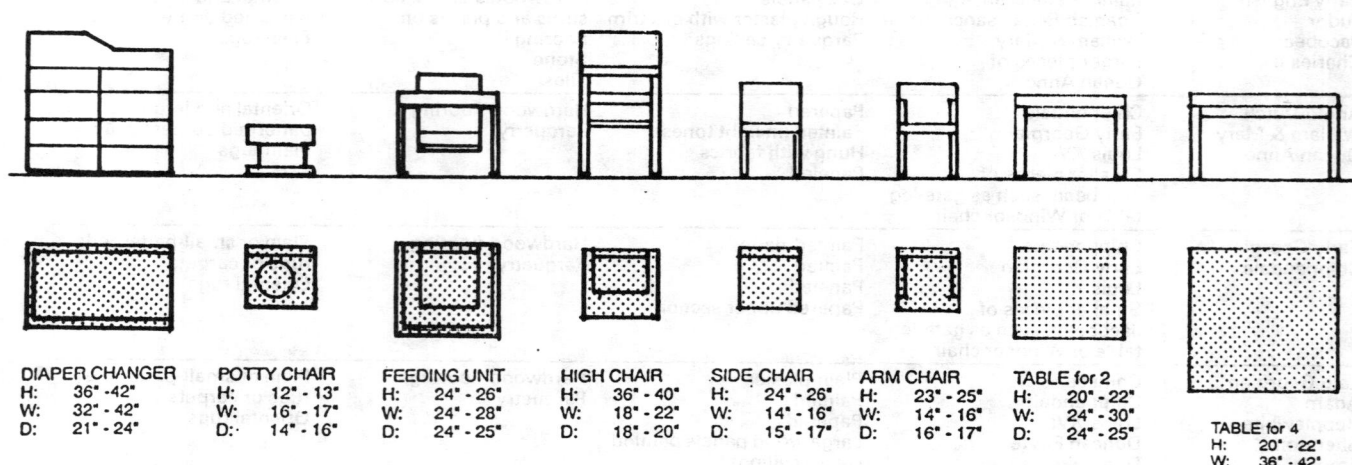

DIAPER CHANGER	POTTY CHAIR	FEEDING UNIT	HIGH CHAIR	SIDE CHAIR	ARM CHAIR	TABLE for 2
H: 36" -42"	H: 12" - 13"	H: 24" - 26"	H: 36" - 40"	H: 24" - 26"	H: 23" - 25"	H: 20" - 22"
W: 32" - 42"	W: 16" - 17"	W: 24" - 28"	W: 18" - 22"	W: 14" - 16"	W: 14" - 16"	W: 24" - 30"
D: 21" - 24"	D: 14" - 16"	D: 24" - 25"	D: 18" - 20"	D: 15" - 17"	D: 16" - 17"	D: 24" - 25"

TABLE for 4
H: 20" - 22"
W: 36" - 42"
D: 36" - 42"

TABLES

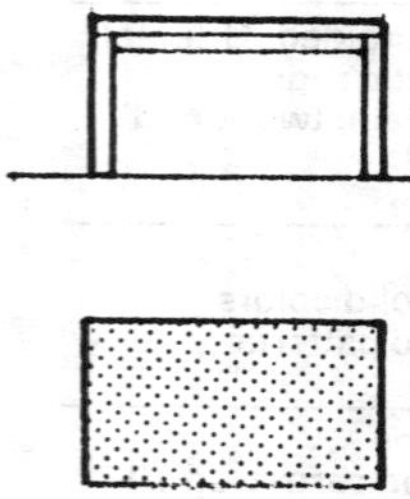

END/SIDE	END/SIDE	END/SIDE	LOW/COFFEE	LOW/COFFEE	LOW/COFFEE
H: 20"	H: 18"	H: 18"	H: 18"	H: 18"	H: 18"
W: 36"	W: 20"	Diam. 18"	W: 36"	W: 36"	Diam. 36"
D: 20"	D: 20"		D: 24"	D: 36"	

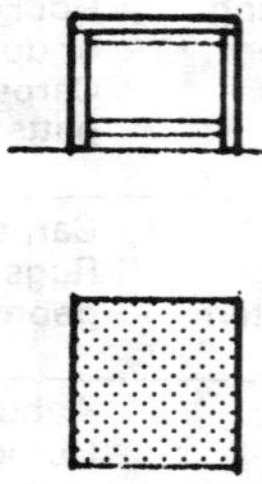

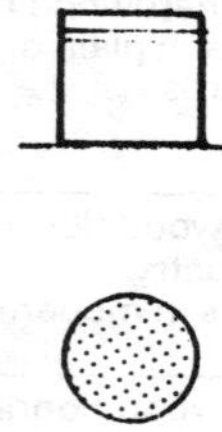

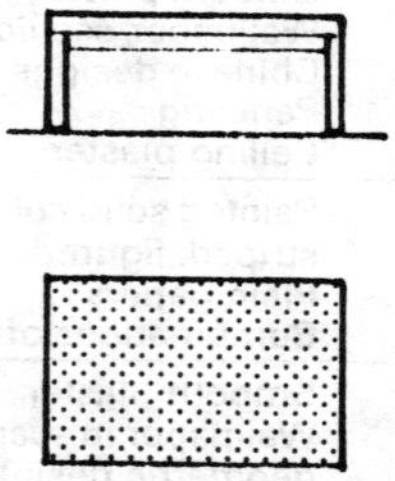

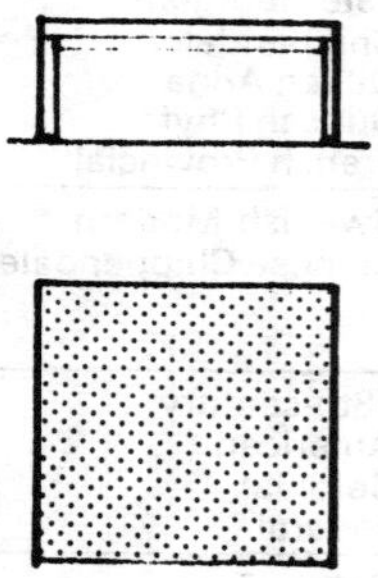

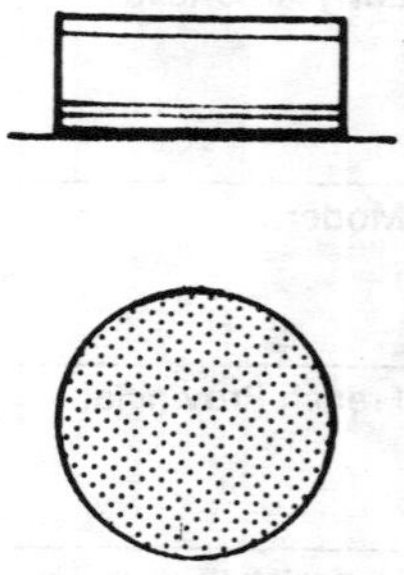

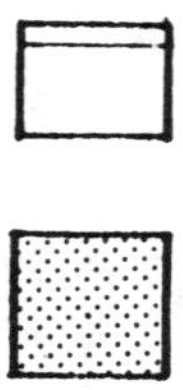

STOOLS	STOOLS	ENTRY/HALLWAY
H: 18"	H: 38"	H: 33"
W: 18"	W: 18"	W: 48"
D: 18"	D: 20"	D: 20"

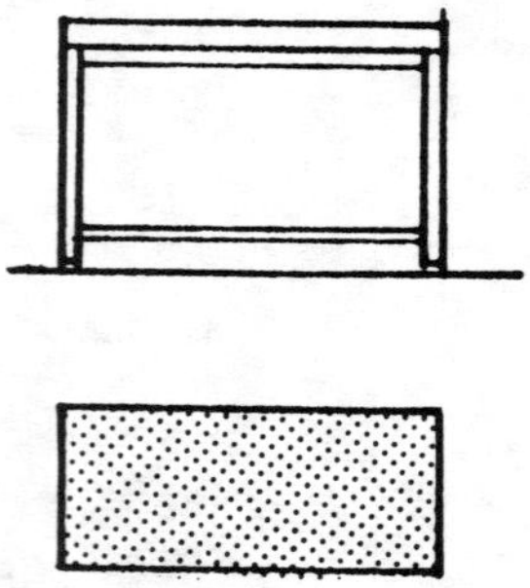

FURNITURE DIMENSIONS

Sofas, Loveseats, Lounge Chairs, and Arm Chairs

SOFAS

30-33"
92-96"
32-36"
92-96"

Sectional sofa

30-33"
72-80"
32-36"

Apartment-size sofa

30-33"
90-108"
32-36"

Full-size sofa

LOVESEATS, LOUNGE CHAIRS, AND ARM CHAIRS

30-33"
60-66"
32-36"

Loveseat

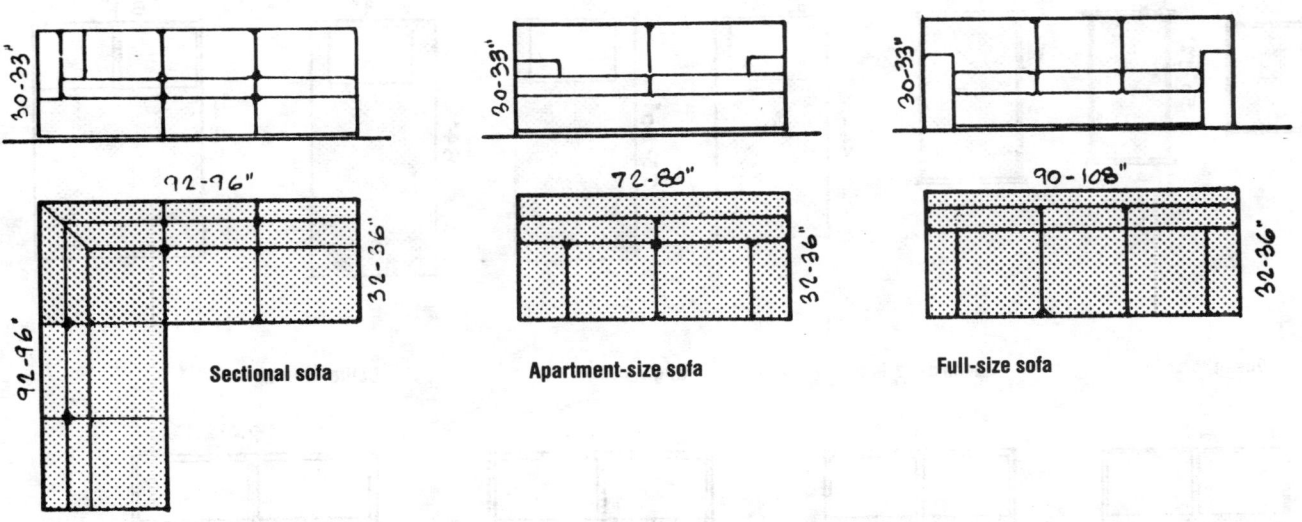

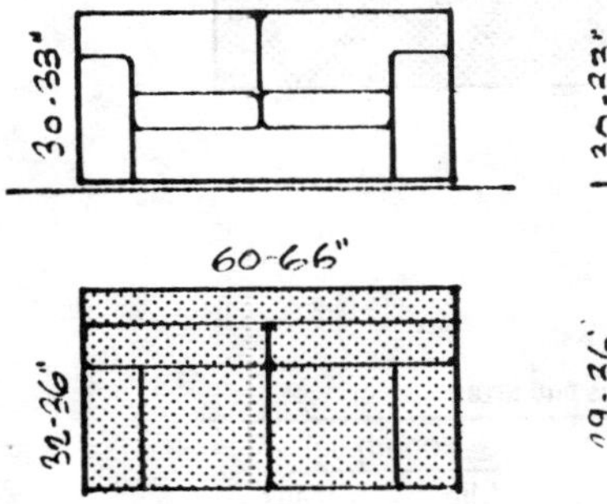

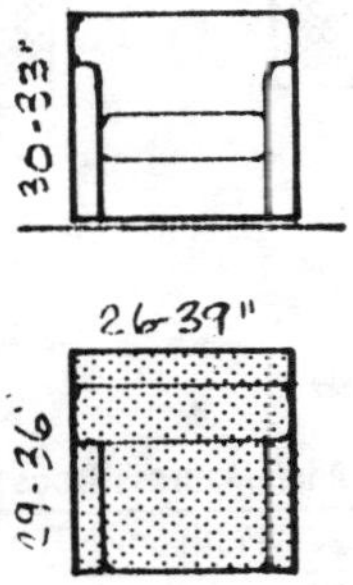

30-33"
26-39"
29-36"

Upholstered chair

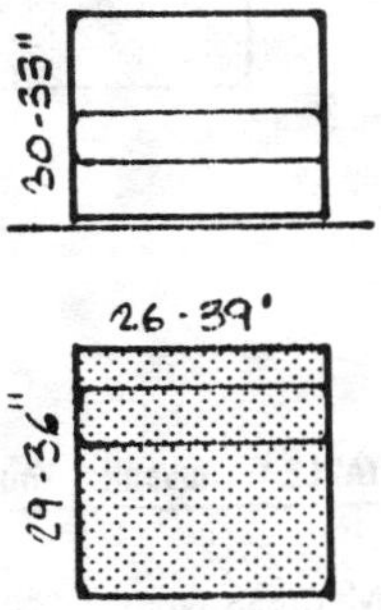

30-33"
26-39"
29-36"

Lounge chair

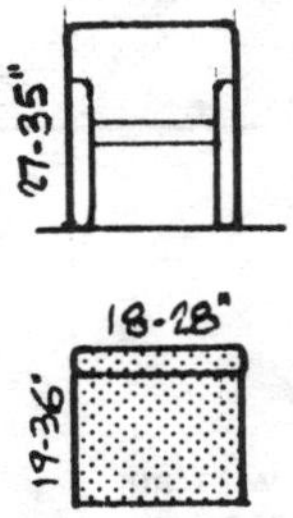

27-35"
18-28"
19-36"

Arm chair

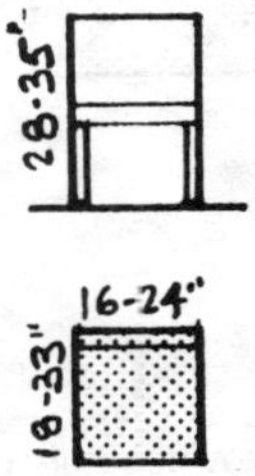

28-35"
16-24"
18-33"

Side chair

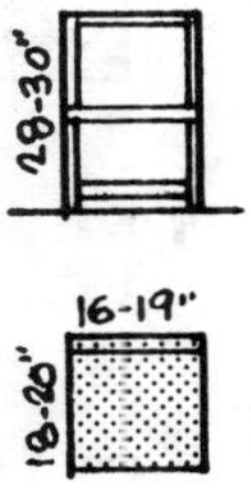

28-30"
16-19"
18-20"

Folding chair

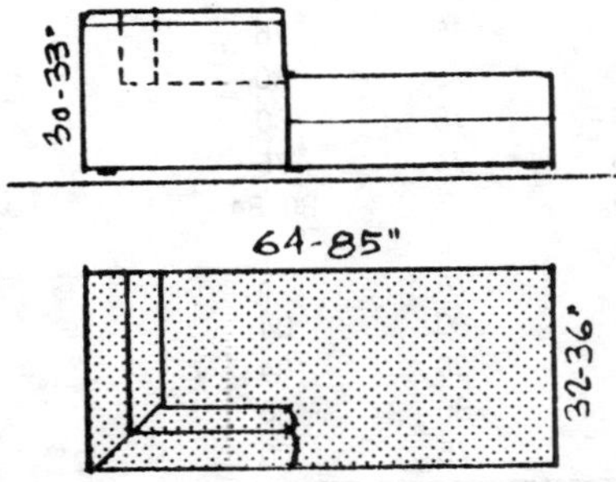

30-33"
64-85"
32-36"

Chaise lounge

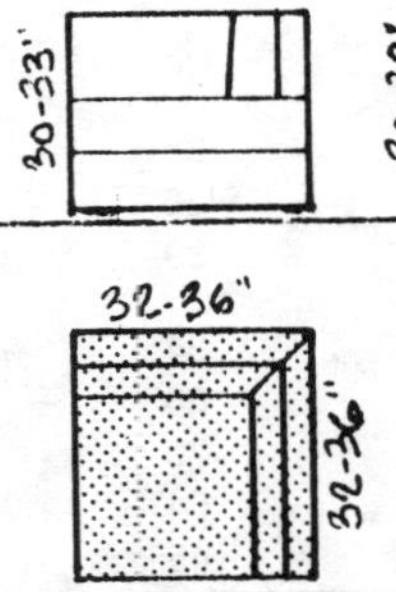

30-33"
32-36"
32-36"

Right corner

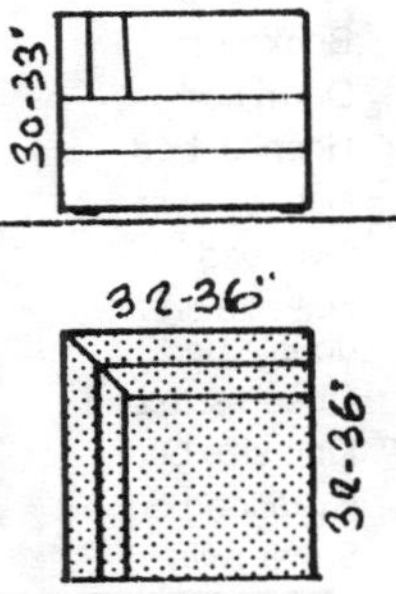

30-33"
32-36"
32-36"

Left corner

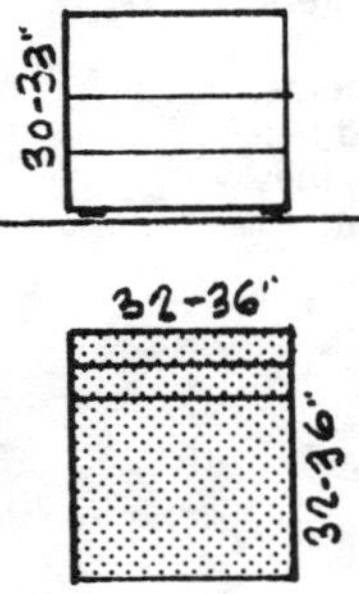

30-33"
32-36"
32-36"

Armless

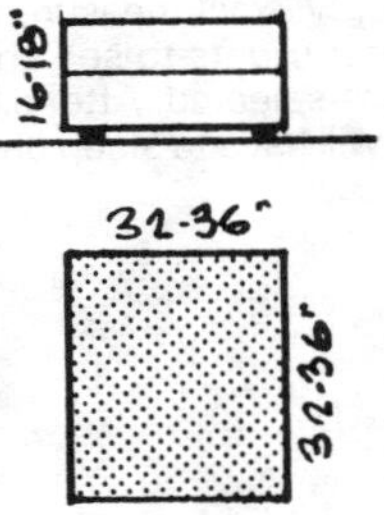

16-18"
32-36"
32-36"

Ottoman

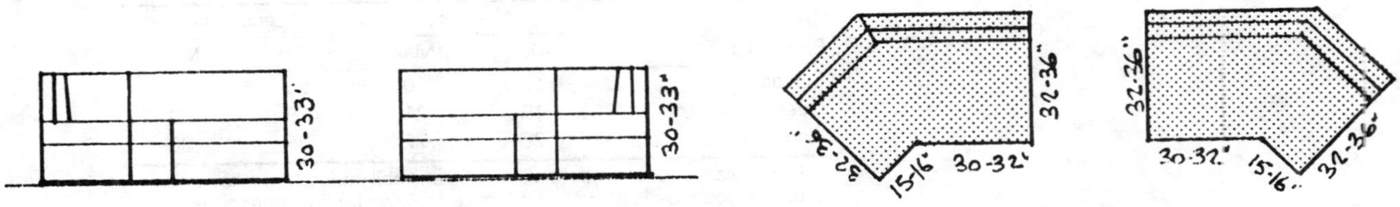

30-33"
30-33"
32-36"
32-36"
15-16"
30-32"
32-36"
30-32"
15-16"
32-36"

Angled sectionals

FURNITURE DIMENSIONS
Bed/Mattress Types and Sizes

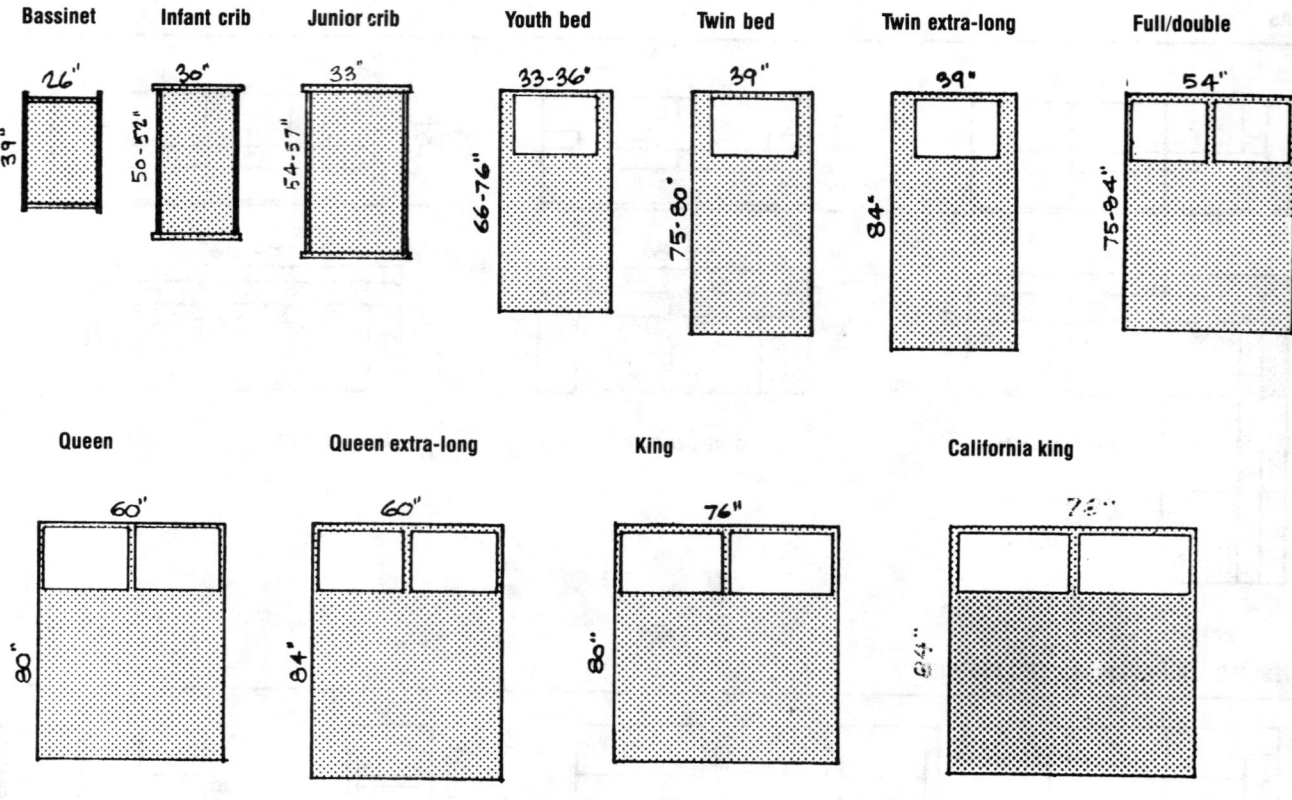

Fig. 1

Figure 1 provides the designer with an array of typical bed and mattress sizes with which rooms can be planned. Tables 1 and 2, however, suggest that within the bedding and mattress industries there exists a wide range of sizes from which to select. Many manufacturers use bed/mattress terminology that reflects different dimensional standards than that of other manufacturers. Ultimately, the designer, in consultation with the client, must verify exact measurements. Be sure to take your clients to see and test the bed or mattress selected. After all, they are the ones who will have to sleep on it.

TABLE 1 Juvenile, Youth, and Adult Mattress Types and Sizes

Mattress type	Width (in)		Length (in)	
	Min	Max	Min	Max
Bassinet	17	23	36	40
Portable crib	22	26	45	52
Junior crib	24	32½	46	58
Youth bed	33	36	66	76
Bunk bed	30	33	75	76
Dorm bed	32	36	75	80
Hospital bed	36	36	75	80
Narrow twin	36	36	74	75
Twin bed	39	39	75	80, 84
Full-size or double bed	54	54	74	75
Queen-size bed	60	60	80	84
King-size bed	76	78	80	84
Extra-long double	54	54	80	80
Super twin	45	45	75	80

TABLE 2 Pillow Types and Sizes

Pillow type	Width (in)		Length (in)	
	Min	Max	Min	Max
Standard	18	20	26	27
Queen	19	21	29	30
King	20	22	35	36

Note: Many manufacturers also make and sell undersized pillows for cribs and youth beds as well as oversized pillows for the larger beds.

FURNITURE DIMENSIONS
Waterbeds, Sofa Beds/Convertible Sofas, and Wall Beds

WATERBEDS

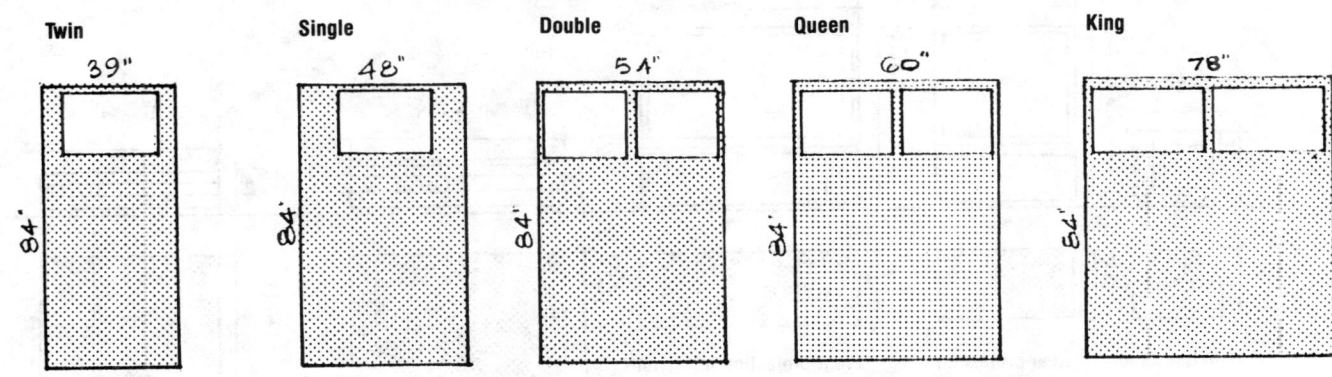

Twin	Single	Double	Queen	King
39"	48"	51"	60"	78"
84'	84'	84'	84'	84'

SOFA BEDS/CONVERTIBLE SOFAS

96-in-diam round

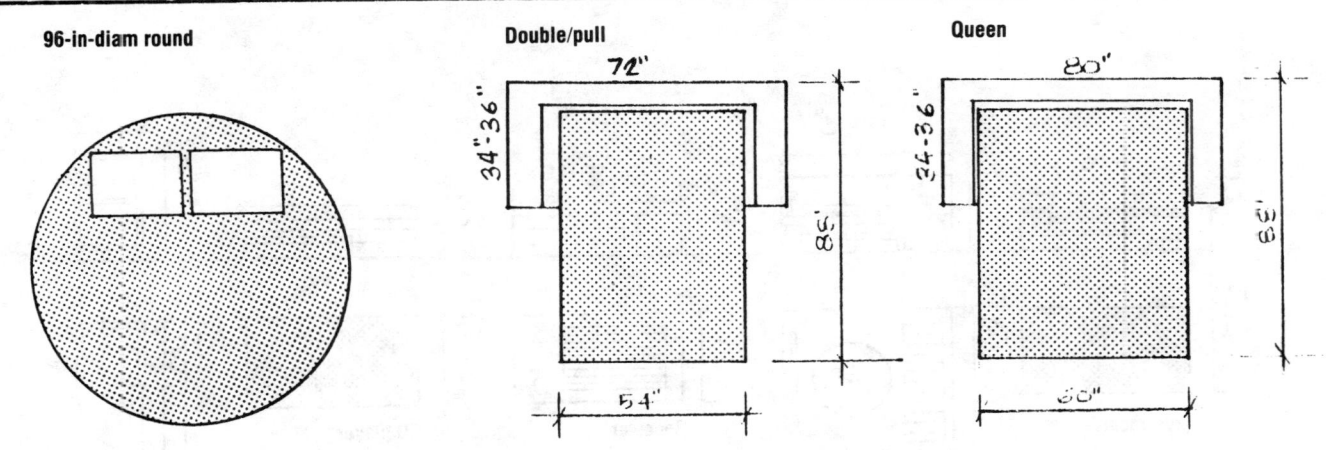

Double/pull
- 72"
- 34"-36"
- 86'
- 54"

Queen
- 80"
- 34"-36"
- 86'
- 80"

WALL AND SIDE BEDS

Side

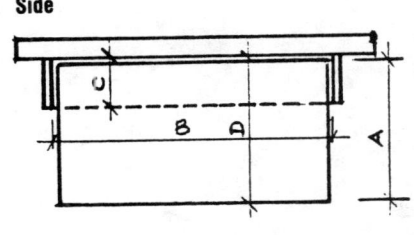

A Width of Bed	B Width of Clear Door Opening	C Depth From Back Of Closet To Back of Doors	D Projection of Bed in Use From Back of Closet
39"	79"	13"	43½"
48"	79"	13"	52½"
54"	79"	13"	57"

HEIGHT: FLOOR TO TOP OF OPENING
44½" for 39" Bed. 53½" for 48" Bed. 59" for 54" Bed.

Wall

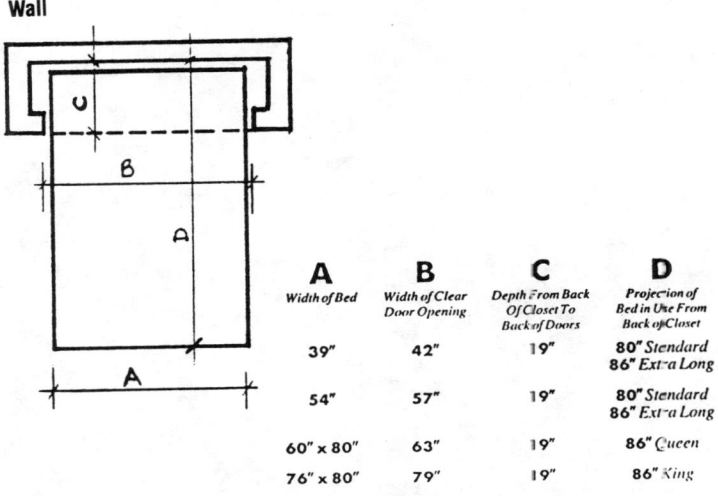

A Width of Bed	B Width of Clear Door Opening	C Depth From Back Of Closet To Back of Doors	D Projection of Bed in Use From Back of Closet
39"	42"	19"	80" Standard 86" Extra Long
54"	57"	19"	80" Standard 86" Extra Long
60" x 80"	63"	19"	86" Queen
76" x 80"	79"	19"	86" King

HEIGHT: FLOOR TO TOP OF OPENING
80" - For 39" and 54" Beds of Standard 75" Length
86" - For Queen, King and Extra Long Beds 80" in Length

FURNITURE DIMENSIONS
Audio-Visual Equipment

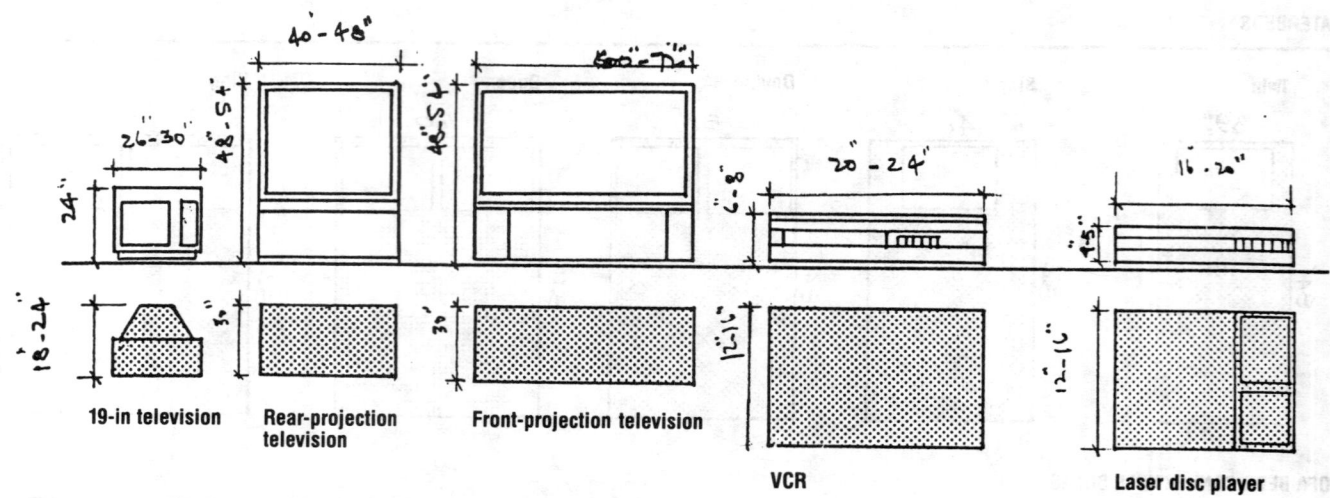

19-in television   Rear-projection television   Front-projection television   VCR   Laser disc player

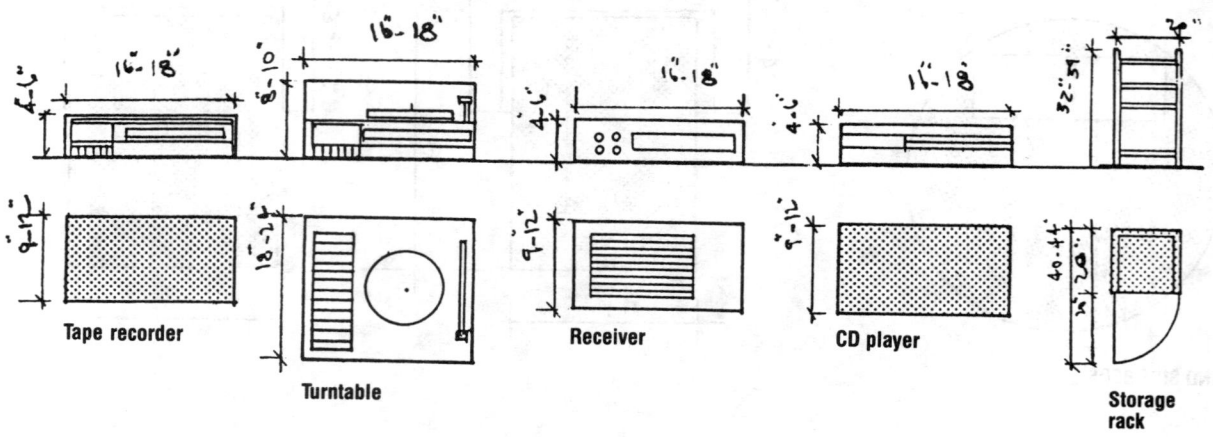

Tape recorder   Turntable   Receiver   CD player   Storage rack

The shape of the viewing area is approximately as shown in Fig. 2. Its size is always based on the size of the image to be viewed. The human eye comprehends detail only within a limited cone angle (about 2½ minutes of arc), and the length of chord subtending this arc, i.e., the image of width, varies with its distance from the observer. Thus an object 20 feet away and 6 feet long appears the same as a similar object 10 feet away and 3 feet long. The size of the viewing area is determined by three dimensions:

■ the minimum distance (1), which is the distance from the nearest part of the image to the eye of the closest viewer

■ the maximum distance (2), which is the distance from the furthermost part of the image to the most distant viewer

■ the maximum viewing angle (3), which is the angle between the projection axis and the line of sight of a person located as far from this axis as can be and still see all image detail in proper brilliance

Practical minimum and maximum distances are both expressed as multiples of the image width (W). They vary both with the medium being used and with the type and quality of material being projected, and may be affected also, in some degree, by personal preferences. They have not yet been precisely determined by scientific methods, and it's doubtful that such data would have much practical value anyway. The generally accepted values, resulting from numerous studies, are these:

Fig. 2

	Film, slides, and projected TV	TV receivers
Minimum distance	2W	4W
Maximum distance	6W to 10W	12W

Size of TV tube	Minimum viewing distance 4W	Maximum viewing distance 12W
17 in	4 ft 11 in	14 ft 9 in
19 in	5 ft 1 in	15 ft 2 in
21 in	6 ft 4 in	19 ft 0 in
23 in	6 ft 6 in	19 ft 4 in
24 in	7 ft 5 in	21 ft 5 in
27 in	9 ft 8 in	24 ft 5 in

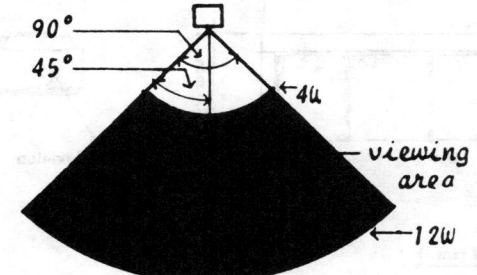

FURNITURE DIMENSIONS

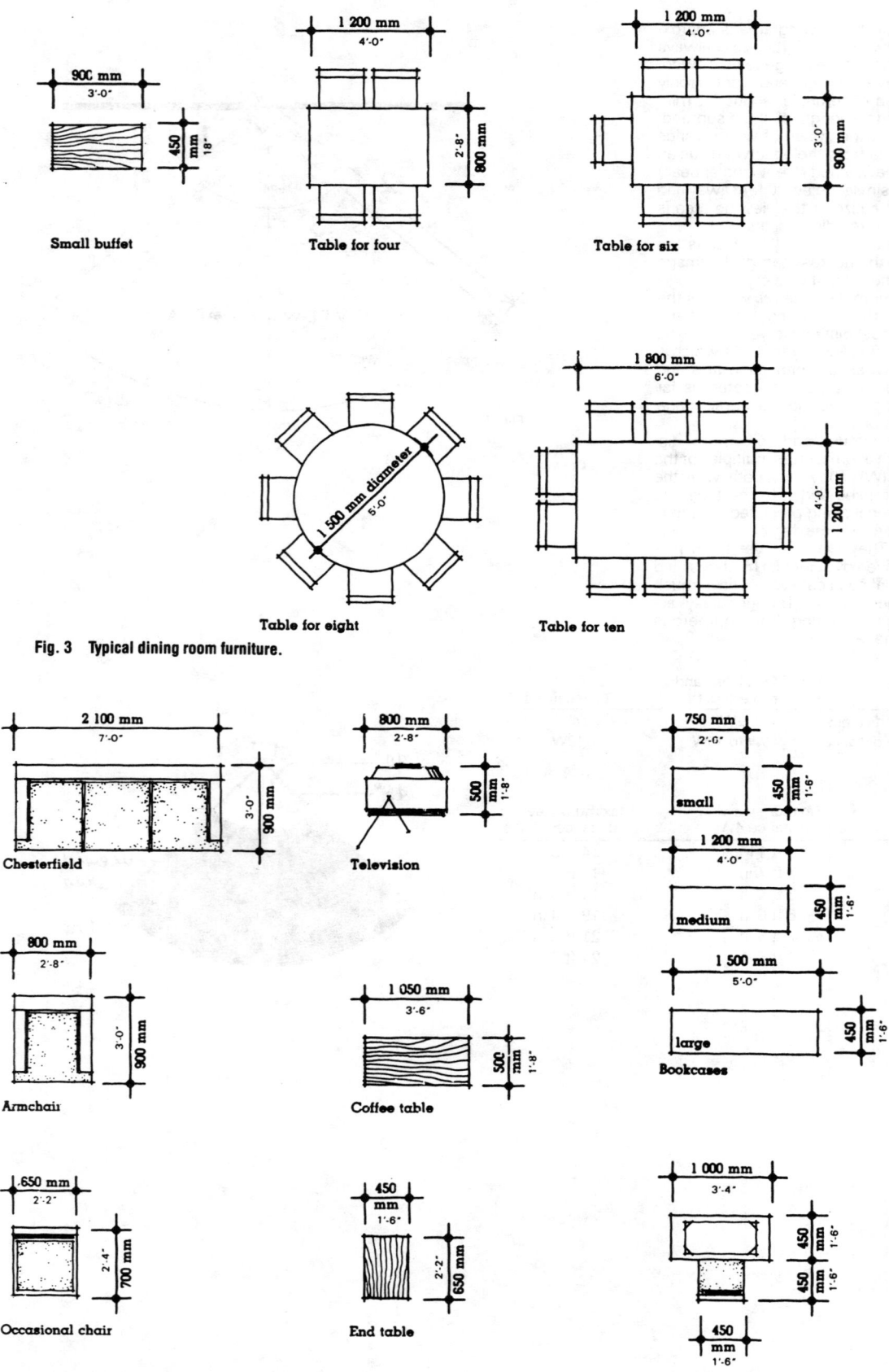

900 mm
3'-0"

450 mm
18"

Small buffet

1 200 mm
4'-0"

800 mm
2'-8"

Table for four

1 200 mm
4'-0"

900 mm
3'-0"

Table for six

1 500 mm diameter
5'-0"

Table for eight

1 800 mm
6'-0"

1 200 mm
4'-0"

Table for ten

Fig. 3   Typical dining room furniture.

2 100 mm
7'-0"

900 mm
3'-0"

Chesterfield

800 mm
2'-8"

500 mm
1'-8"

Television

750 mm
2'-6"

450 mm
1'-6"

small

1 200 mm
4'-0"

450 mm
1'-6"

medium

1 500 mm
5'-0"

450 mm
1'-6"

large

Bookcases

800 mm
2'-8"

900 mm
3'-0"

Armchair

1 050 mm
3'-6"

500 mm
1'-8"

Coffee table

650 mm
2'-2"

700 mm
2'-4"

Occasional chair

450 mm
1'-6"

650 mm
2'-2"

End table

1 000 mm
3'-4"

450 mm
1'-6"

450 mm
1'-6"

450 mm
1'-6"

Desk   Chair

Fig. 4   Typical living room furniture.

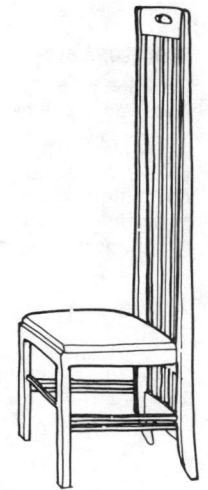

INGRAM HIGH CHAIR
DESIGNER:
Charles R. Macintosh
YEAR: 1900
MANUFACTURER:
Atelier International
DIMENSIONS:
18½"W x 17½"D x 59¼"H

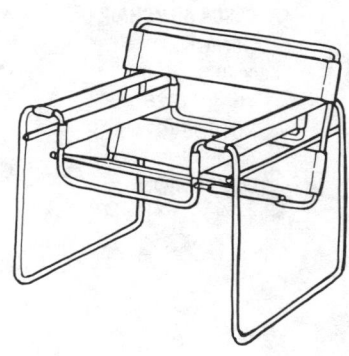

WASSILY CHAIR
DESIGNER:
Marcel Breuer
YEAR: 1925
MANUFACTURER:
Knoll International
DIMENSIONS:
30¾"W x 29"D x 28½"H

KUBUS CHAIR
DESIGNER:
Joseph Hoffman
YEAR: 1910
DIMENSIONS:
36"W x 30½"D x 28½"H

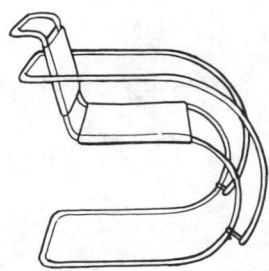

MR. CHAIR
DESIGNER:
Mies Van Der Rohe
YEAR: 1927
MANUFACTURER:
Stendig
DIMENSIONS:
21¾"W x 32¼"D x 32¼"H

HAU KOLLER CHAIR
DESIGNER:
Joseph Hoffman
YEAR: 1911
DIMENSIONS:
35½"W x 32"D x 37"H

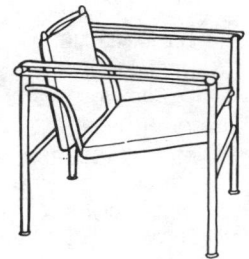

LC1 SLING CHAIR
DESIGNER:
Le Corbusier
YEAR: 1928
MANUFACTURER:
Atelier International
DIMENSIONS:
23⅝"W x 25⅝"D x 25¼"H

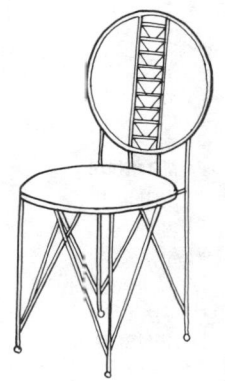

MIDWAY CHAIR
DESIGNER:
Frank Lloyd Wright
YEAR: 1914
MANUFACTURER:
Atelier International
DIMENSIONS:
16"W x 13"D x 35"H

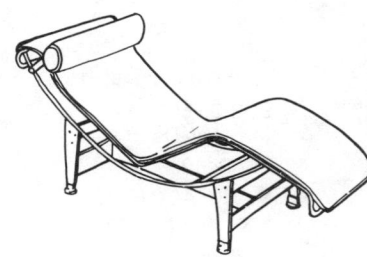

LC9 LOUNGE CHAIR
DESIGNER:
Le Corbusier
YEAR: 1928
MANUFACTURER:
Atelier International
DIMENSIONS:
22"W x 63"D

FURNITURE DIMENSIONS
20th Century Classic Chairs

CESCA ARMCHAIR
DESIGNER:
Marcel Breuer
YEAR: 1928
MANUFACTURER:
Knoll International
DIMENSIONS:
22⅝"W x 21⅝"D x 31¾"H

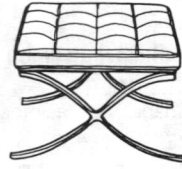

BARCELONA STOOL
DESIGNER:
Mies Van Der Rohe
YEAR: 1929
MANUFACTURER:
Knoll International
DIMENSIONS:
23"W x 22"D x 14½"H

BRNO ARMCHAIR
DESIGNER:
Mies Van Der Rohe
YEAR: 1929
MANUFACTURER:
Stendig
DIMENSIONS:
18"W x 23"D x 31½"H

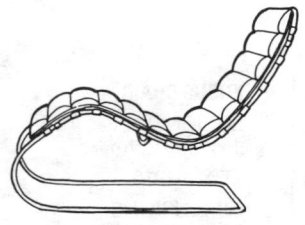

CHAISE LOUNGE
DESIGNER:
Mies Van Der Rohe
YEAR: 1931
MANUFACTURER:
Knoll International
DIMENSIONS:
23⅝"W x 47½"D x 37½"H

LC2 ARMCHAIR
DESIGNER:
Le Corbusier
YEAR: 1929
MANUFACTURER:
Atelier International
DIMENSIONS:
30"W x 27½"D x 26½"H

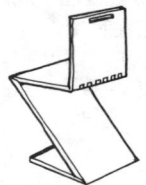

ZIG-ZAG CHAIR
DESIGNER:
Gerrit Rietveld
YEAR: 1934
MANUFACTURER:
Atelier International
DIMENSIONS:
14½"W x 17"D x 29"H

BARCELONA CHAIR
DESIGNER:
Mies Van Der Rohe
YEAR: 1929
MANUFACTURER:
Knoll International
DIMENSIONS:
30"W x 30"D x 30"H

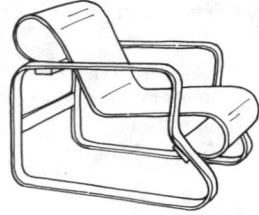

PAIMO CHAIR
DESIGNER:
Alvar Aalto
YEAR: 1935
MANUFACTURER:
Palazetti
DIMENSIONS:
23½"W x 31½"D x 25"H

BARREL CHAIR
DESIGNER:
Frank Lloyd Wright
YEAR: 1937
MANUFACTURER:
Atelier International
DIMENSIONS:
21½"W x 22"D x 32"H

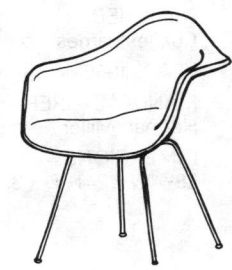

MOLDED FIBERGLAS CHAIR
DESIGNER:
Charles Eames
YEAR: 1949
MANUFACTURER:
Herman Miller
DIMENSIONS:
25"W x 25½"D x 31"H

BUTTERFLY CHAIR
DESIGNER:
Harday, Boner & Kurchan
YEAR: 1938
DIMENSIONS:
28"W x 27½"D x 35½"H

DIAMOND CHAIR
DESIGNER:
Harry Bertoia
YEAR: 1952
MANUFACTURER:
Knoll International
DIMENSIONS:
33¾"W x 28"D x 30½"H

MOLDED PLYWOOD CHAIR
DESIGNER:
Charles Eames
YEAR: 1946
MANUFACTURER:
Herman Miller
DIMENSIONS:
21½"W x 19¼"D x 29⅜"H

LOUNGE CHAIR
DESIGNER:
Charles Eames
YEAR: 1956
MANUFACTURER:
Herman Miller
DIMENSIONS:
32½"W x 32¾"D x 33½"H

WOMB CHAIR
DESIGNER:
Eero Saarinen
YEAR: 1948
MANUFACTURER:
Knoll International
DIMENSIONS:
40"W x 39"D x 35½"H

OTTOMAN
DESIGNER:
Charles Eames
YEAR: 1956
MANUFACTURER:
Herman Miller
DIMENSIONS:
26"W x 21"D x 15"H

FURNITURE DIMENSIONS
20th Century Classic Chairs

ALUMINUM GROUP CHAIR
DESIGNER:
Charles Eames
YEAR: 1958
MANUFACTURER:
Herman Miller
DIMENSIONS:
28½"W x 24¾"D x 33¾"H

LOUNGE CHAIR
DESIGNER:
Richard Schultz
YEAR: 1966
MANUFACTURER:
Knoll International
DIMENSIONS:
26"W x 28¼"D x 26½"H

SHERRIFF CHAIR
DESIGNER:
Sergio Rodriguez
YEAR: 1958
MANUFACTURER:
OCA

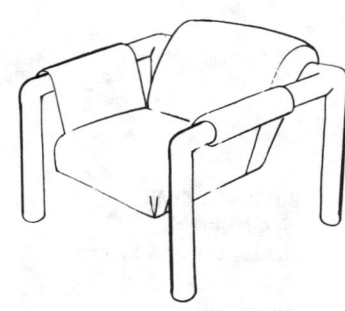

TUBO CHAIR
DESIGNER:
John Mascheroni
YEAR: 1968
MANUFACTURER:
Vecta
DIMENSIONS:
32"W x 32"D x 32"H

HAND CHAIR
DESIGNER:
Pedro Freidberg
YEAR: 1963
MANUFACTURER:
Hand Crafted

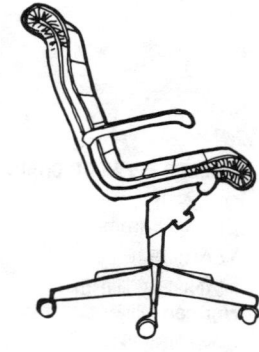

SAPPER COLLECTION
DESIGNER:
Richard Sapper
YEAR: 1977
MANUFACTURER:
Knoll International
DIMENSIONS:
28⅜"W x 27½"D x 38½-41⅜"H

PLATNER CHAIR
DESIGNER:
Warren Platner
YEAR: 1966
MANUFACTURER:
Knoll International
DIMENSIONS:
36½"W x 25½"D x 30½"H

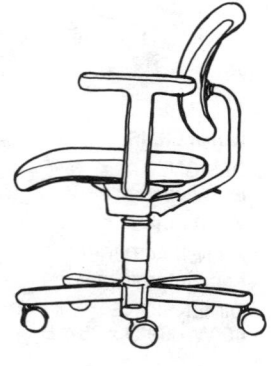

BASIC OPERATIONAL
DESIGNER:
Niels Diffrient
YEAR: 1979
MANUFACTURER:
Knoll International
DIMENSIONS:
25½"W x 21"D x 32½-36½"H

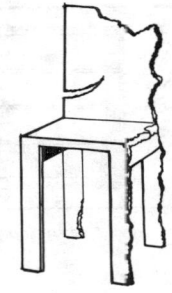

**NOTHING CONTINUES TO
HAPPEN CHAIR**
DESIGNER:
Horward Meisper
YEAR: 1981
MANUFACTURER:
Art et Industre
DIMENSIONS:
17"W x 16"D x 37"H

OTTOMAN
DESIGNER:
Niels Diffrient
YEAR: 1986
MANUFACTURER:
Sunar/Hauserman
DIMENSIONS:
25"W x 24"D x 17⅛"H

LOUNGE CHAIR
DESIGNER:
Michael Graves
YEAR: 1982
MANUFACTURER:
Sunar/Hauserman
DIMENSIONS:
32"W x 29"D x 29"H

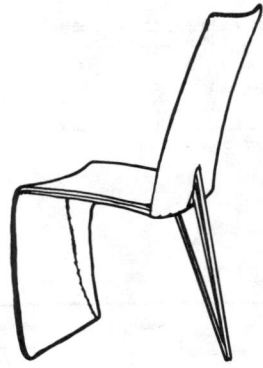

ED ARCHER CHAIR
DESIGNER:
Philippe Starck
YEAR: 1987
MANUFACTURER:
Driade Italy
DIMENSIONS:
18½"W x 21½"D x 38½"H

QUEENE ANNE CHAIR
DESIGNER:
Robert Venturi
YEAR: 1984
MANUFACTURER:
Knoll International
DIMENSIONS:
26½"W x 23½"D x 38½"H

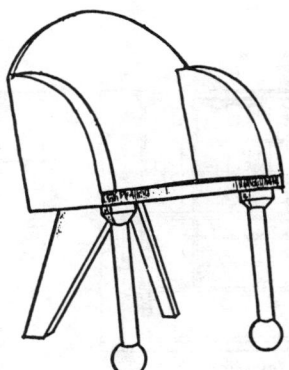

STONE CHAIR
DESIGNER:
James Kutasi
YEAR: 1988
MANUFACTURER:
James Kutasi Australia
DIMENSIONS:
19⅝"W x 19⅝"D x 35½"H

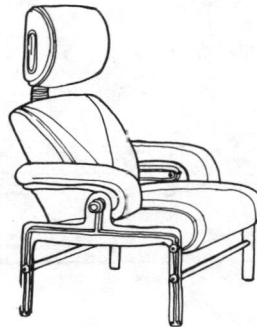

JEFFERSON CHAIR
DESIGNER:
Neils Diffrient
YEAR: 1986
MANUFACTURER:
Sunar/Hauserman
DIMENSIONS:
32⅜"W x 34"D x 43½"H

FURNITURE DIMENSIONS
Traditional Bedroom and Dining Room Furniture

BEDROOM FURNITURE

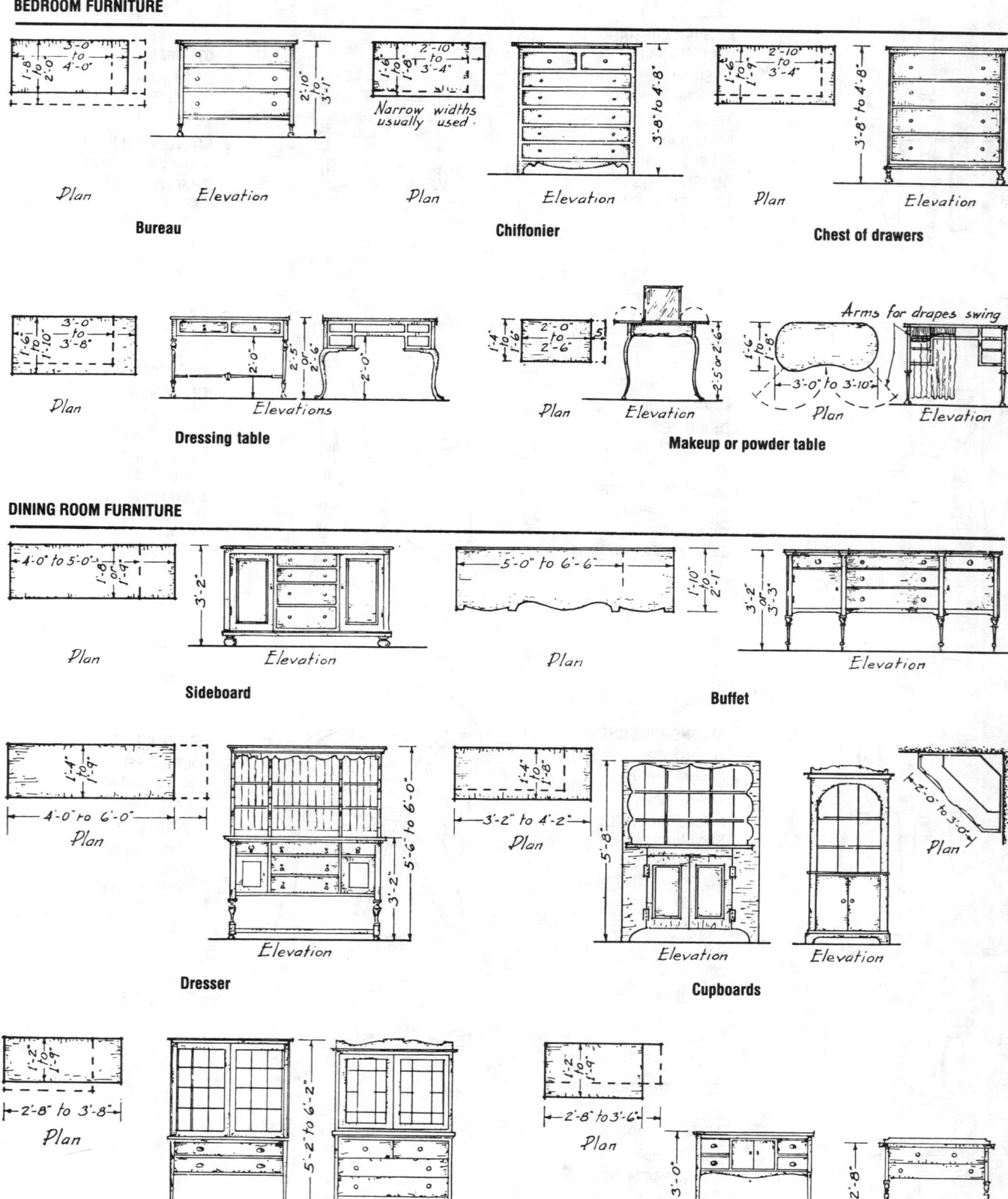

Plan   Elevation
Bureau

Narrow widths usually used.
Plan   Elevation
Chiffonier

Plan   Elevation
Chest of drawers

Plan   Elevations
Dressing table

Plan   Elevation   Arms for drapes swing   Plan   Elevation
Makeup or powder table

DINING ROOM FURNITURE

Plan   Elevation
Sideboard

Plan   Elevation
Buffet

Plan   Elevation
Dresser

Plan   Elevation   Elevation   Plan
Cupboards

Plan   Elevations
China cabinets

Plan   Elevations
Servers

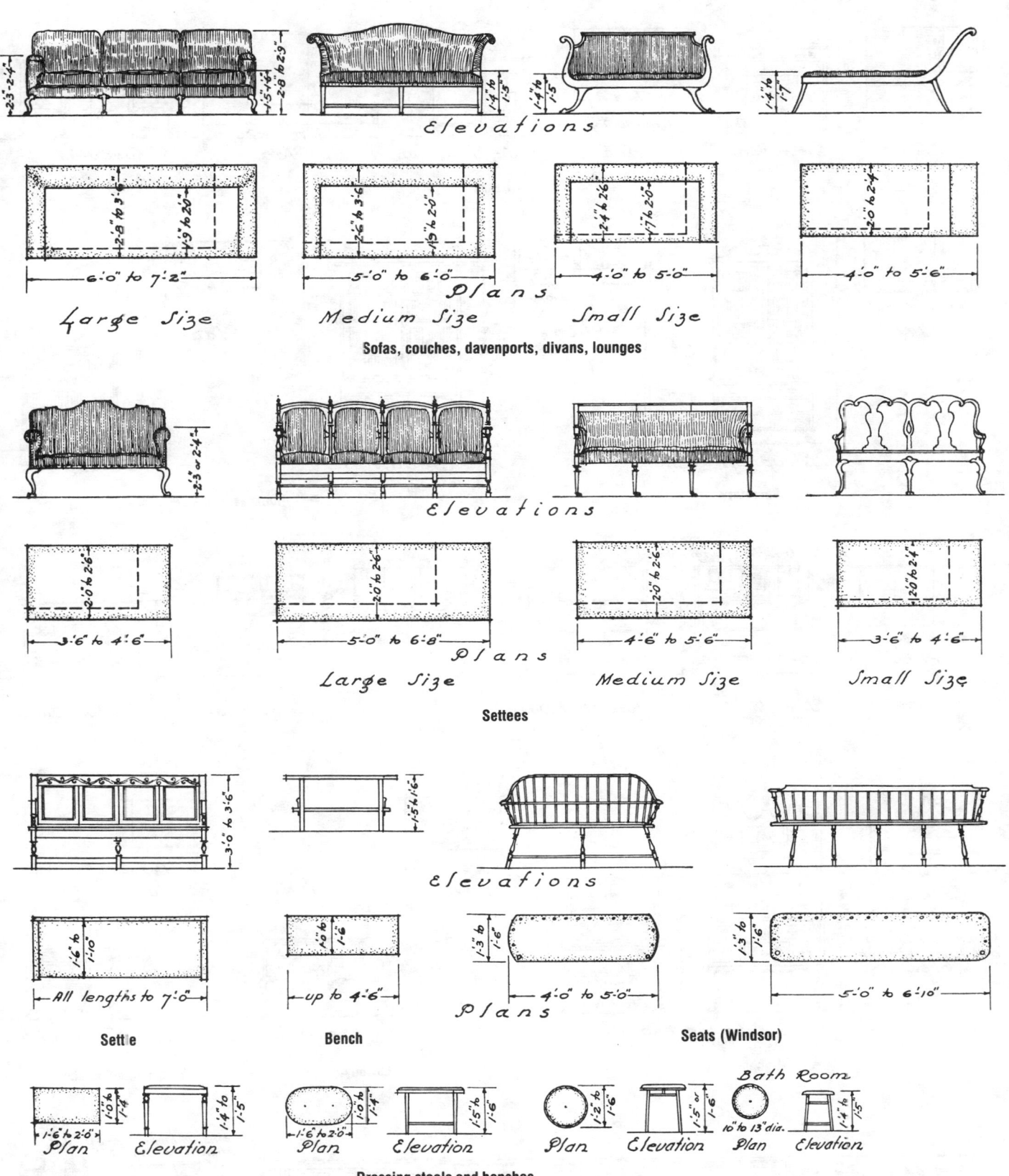

Elevations

Plans

Large Size   Medium Size   Small Size

Sofas, couches, davenports, divans, lounges

Elevations

Plans

Large Size   Medium Size   Small Size

Settees

Elevations

Plans

Settle   **Bench**   **Seats (Windsor)**

Plan   *Elevation*   *Plan*   *Elevation*   *Plan*   *Elevation*   *Plan*   *Elevation*

Bath Room

Dressing stools and benches

FURNITURE DIMENSIONS
Traditional Desks, Bookcases, and Chests

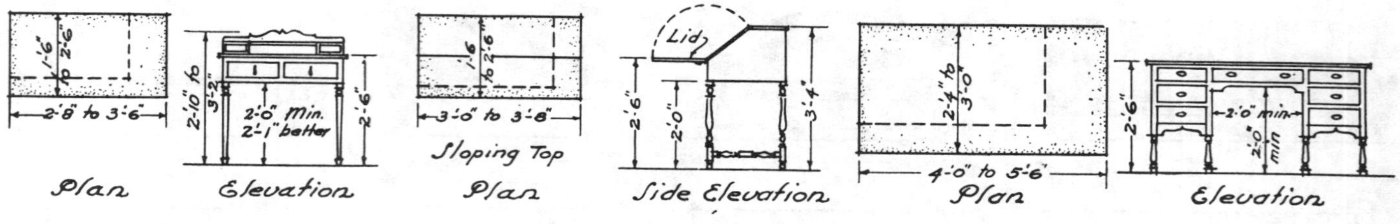

Plan   1'-6" to 2'-6"   2'-6" to 3'-6"

Elevation   2'-10" to 3'-2"   2'-0" Min. 2'-1" better   2'-6"

Plan — Sloping Top   1'-6" to 2'-6"   3'-0" to 3'-6"

Side Elevation   Lid   2'-6" to 2'-0"   3'-4"

Plan   2'-4" to 3'-0"   4'-0" to 5'-6"

Elevation   2'-6"   2'-0" min   2'-0" min

Desks

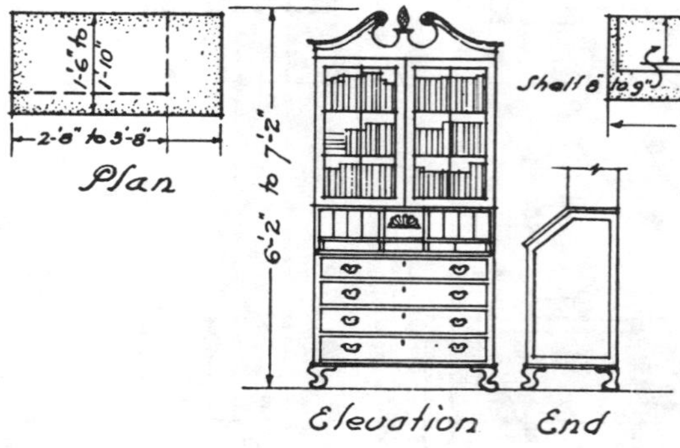

Plan   1'-6" to 1'-10"   2'-8" to 3'-8"

Elevation — **End**   6'-2" to 7'-2"

Secretary

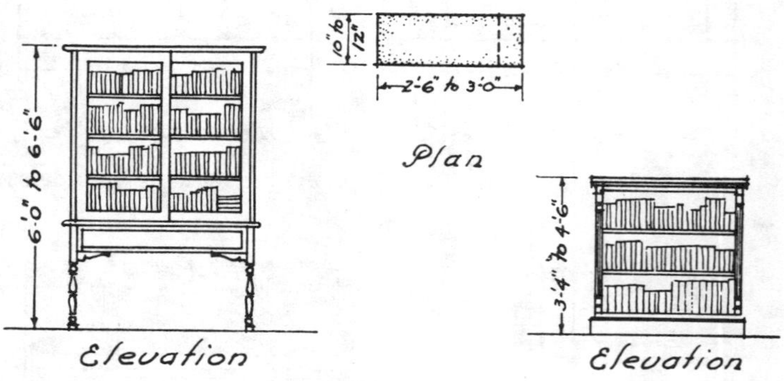

Plan   Shelf 6" to 9"   Variable   6" to 12"   3'-0" to 5'-0"

Elevation   6'-0" to 6'-6"

Plan   10" to 12"   2'-6" to 3'-0"

Elevation   3'-4" to 4'-6"

Bookcases

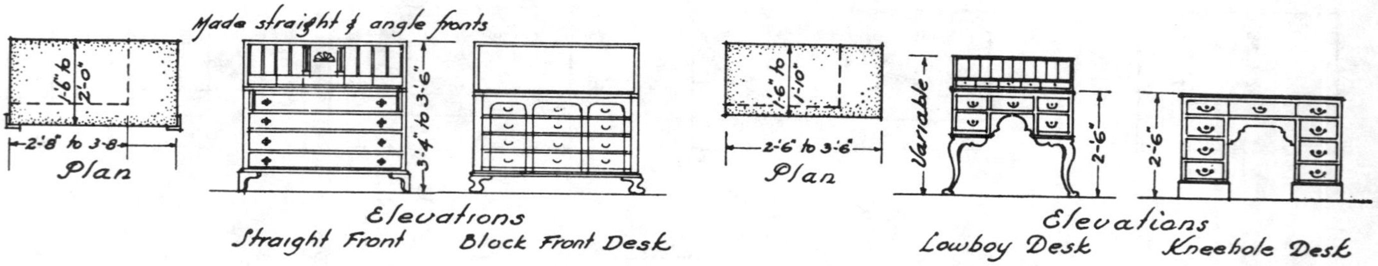

Made straight & angle fronts

Plan   1'-6" to 2'-0"   2'-8" to 3'-8"

Elevations   3'-4" to 3'-6"

Straight Front   **Block Front Desk**

Plan   1'-6" to 2'-0"   2'-6" to 3'-6"

Elevations   Variable   2'-6"   2'-6"

Lowboy Desk   **Kneehole Desk**

Desks

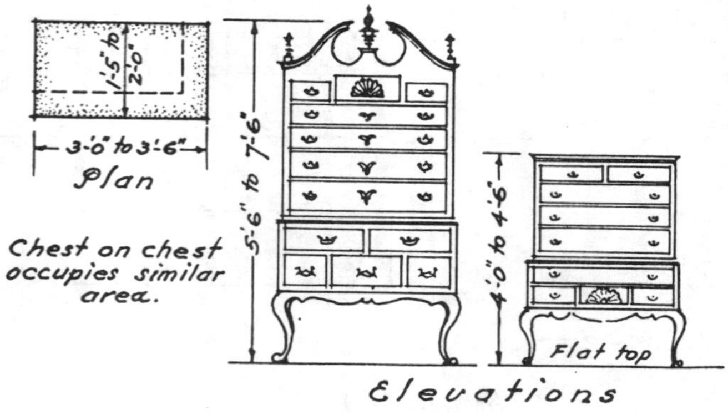

Plan   1'-5" to 2'-0"   3'-0" to 3'-6"

Chest on chest occupies similar area.

Elevations   5'-6" to 7'-6"   4'-0" to 4'-6"

Flat top

Highboys

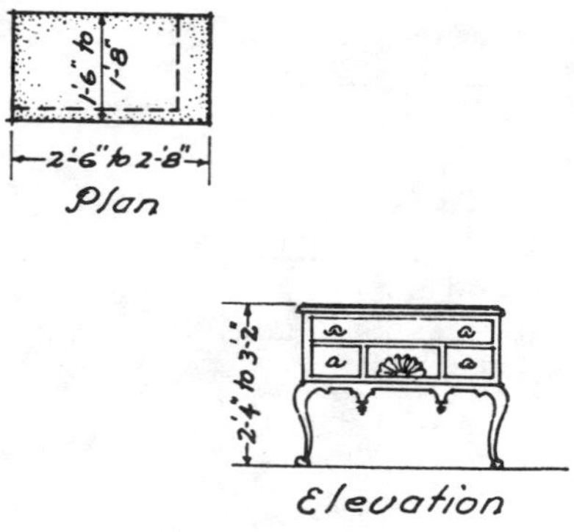

Plan   1'-6" to 1'-8"   2'-6" to 2'-8"

Elevation   2'-4" to 3'-2"

Lowboy

Plan   1'-3" to 1'-6"   2'-0" to 2'-6"

Elevation   2'-0" to 2'-6"

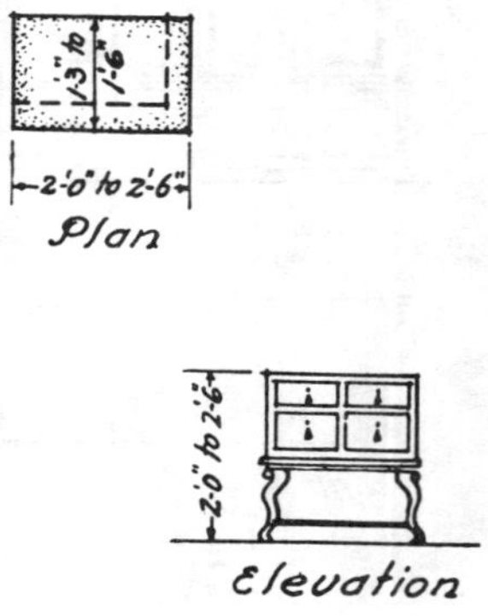

Cabinet or chest

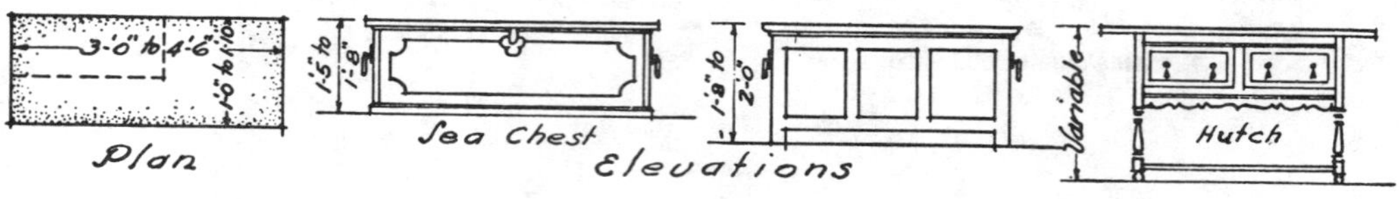

Plan   1'-6" to 2'-0"   3'-0" to 4'-6"

Elevations   1'-5" to 1'-8"   1'-8" to 2'-0"   Variable

Sea Chest   **Hutch**

Chests

Mens' Umbrellas 2'-8"–3'-0"
Womens' " 1'-10"–2'-4"

Plan   1'-5"   2'-1"

| 1 | 2 | 3 |
| 4 | 5 | 6 |

Elevation

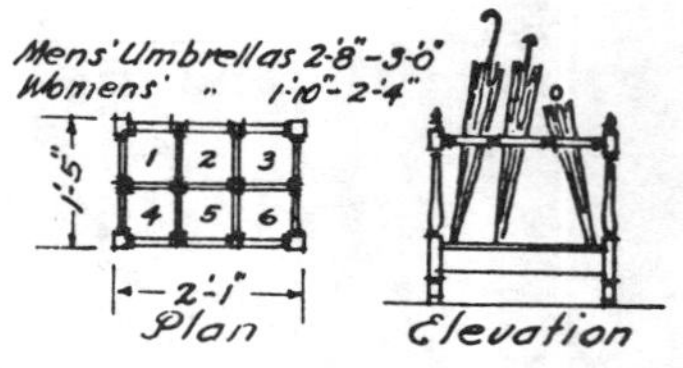

Umbrella stand

UNUPHOLSTERED CHAIRS

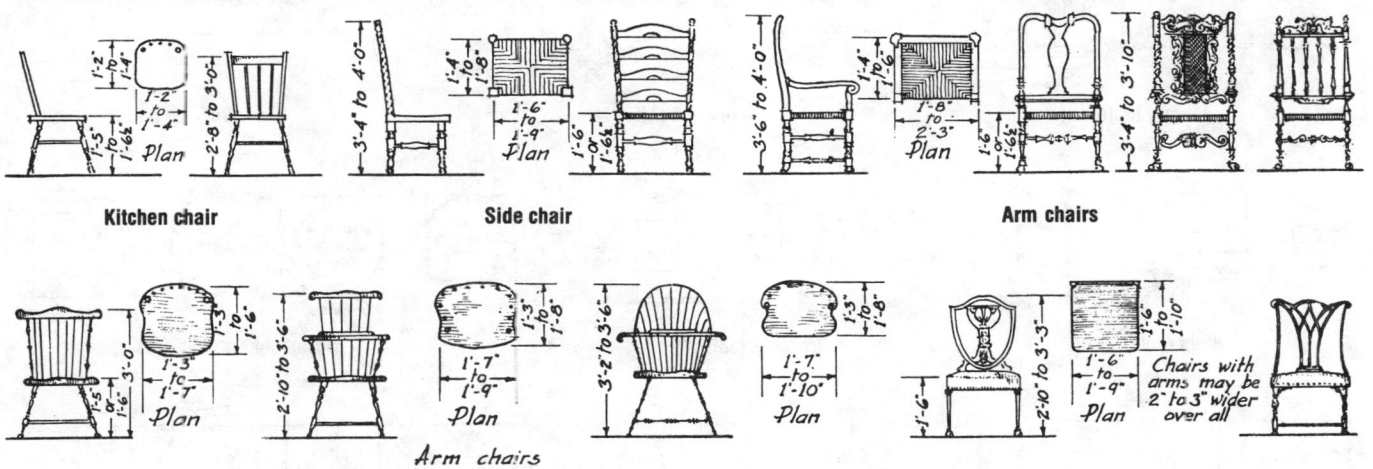

Kitchen chair   **Side chair**   **Arm chairs**

Windsor chairs   **Dining room chairs**

UPHOLSTERED CHAIRS

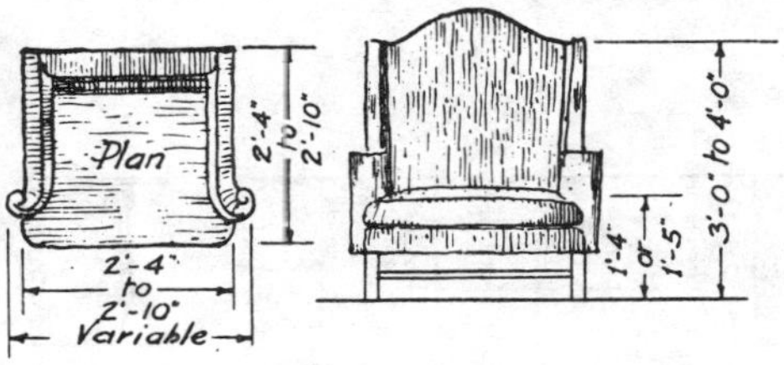

Wing chair 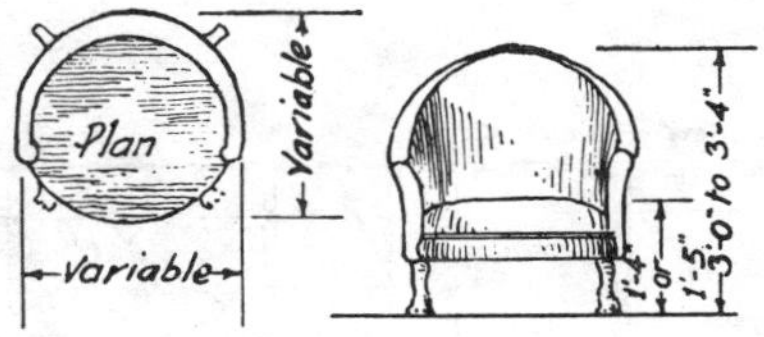   **Barrel chair** 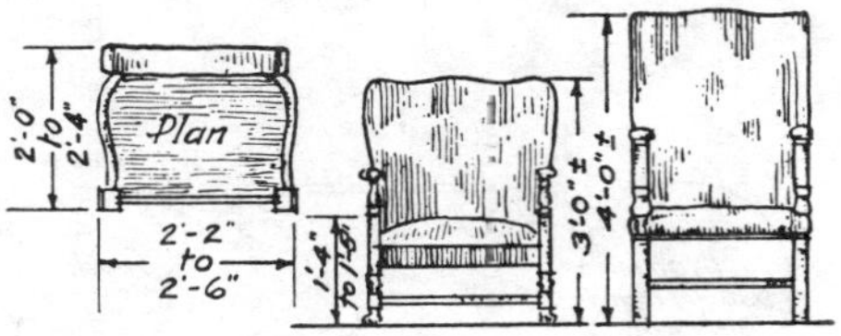   **Arm chairs**

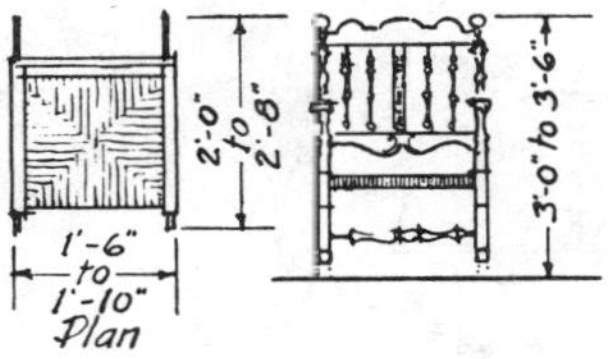

Rocking chair 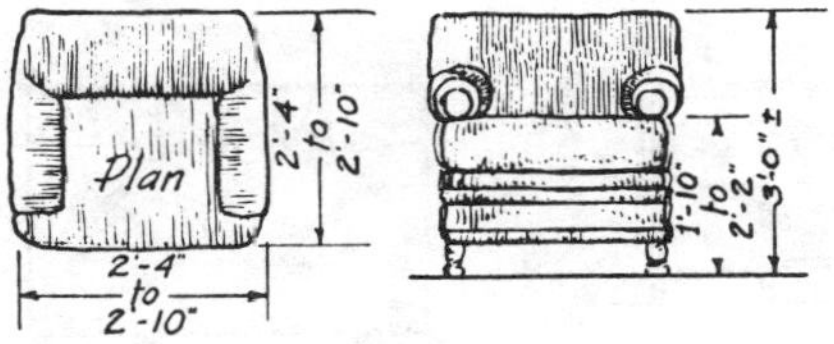   **Club chair** 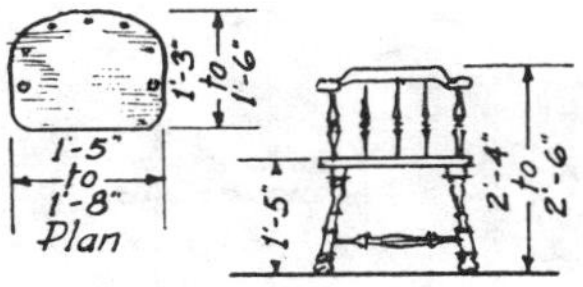   **Tavern chair** 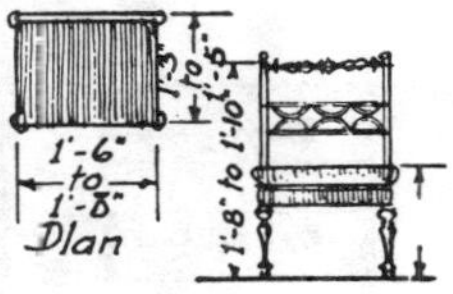   **Side chair**

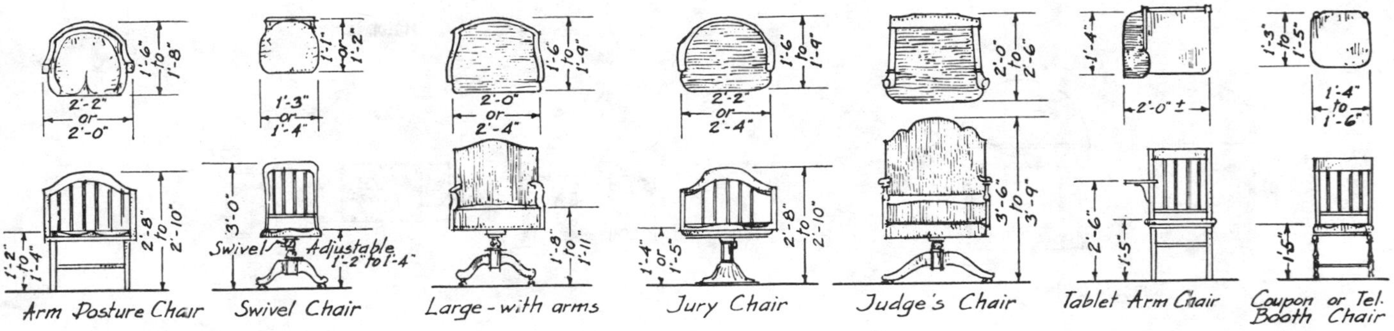

Arm Posture Chair   Swivel Chair   Large - with arms   Jury Chair   Judge's Chair   Tablet Arm Chair   Coupon or Tel. Booth Chair

Office chairs   **Special chairs**

FURNITURE DIMENSIONS

Traditional Tables

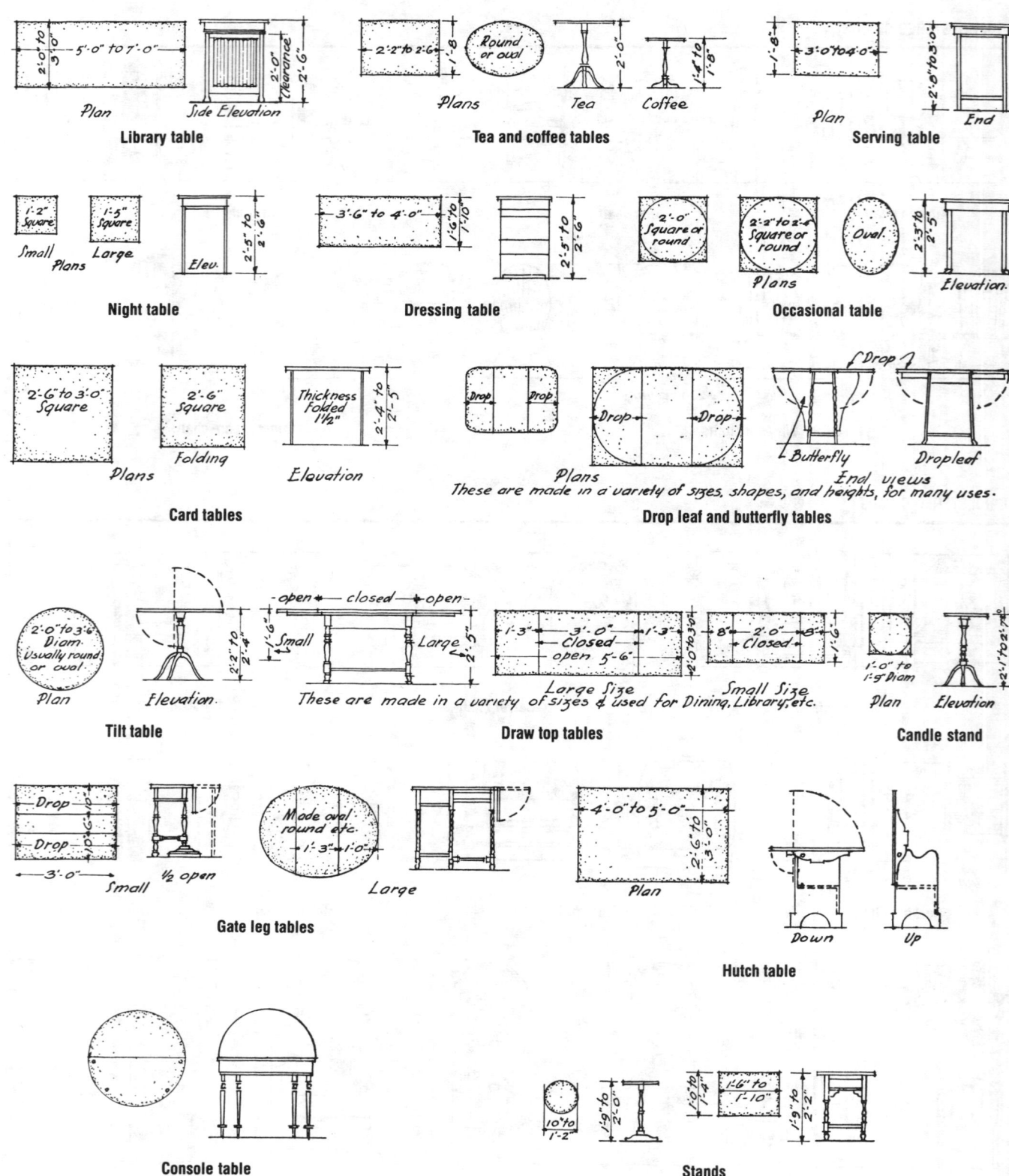

Library table

Tea and coffee tables

Serving table

Night table

Dressing table

Occasional table

Card tables

Drop leaf and butterfly tables

These are made in a variety of sizes, shapes, and heights, for many uses.

Tilt table

Draw top tables

These are made in a variety of sizes & used for Dining, Library, etc.

Candle stand

Gate leg tables

Hutch table

Console table

Stands

The size of living rooms and the furniture arrangements contained within such spaces vary dramatically, depending on the size of the dwelling, the economic status and lifestyle of the user, and the relationship of the room to other areas of the dwelling. With regard to the luxury end of the scale, there are few limitations and no attempt has been made to identify the endless planning options possible. There are, however, minimum requirements and basic planning considerations that are applicable whatever the size of the space.

Minimum Requirements

A living room for a three- or four-bedroom dwelling unit requires more space for its occupants than one for a one- or two-bedroom dwelling unit. Luxury units will necessarily need more space to accommodate more furnishings. In any case, the minimum living room with no dining facilities should be approximately 180 ft² but preferably around 200 ft². Figures 1 and 2 show two living rooms· with typical furniture groupings (no dining facilities).

Figure 3 shows a living room with one end used for dining. This area often is arranged in an "L" shape to achieve greater definition or privacy from the living activities. Dwelling units with three or more bedrooms should have separate dining rooms or clearly defined dining areas.

The minimum width of a living room should be 11–12 ft. This is extremely tight, however, and if at all possible the width should be at least 14 ft.

Planning Considerations

Planning considerations should include adequate floor and wall space for furniture groupings, separation of trafficways from centers of activity, and ease of access to furniture and windows.

Circulation within the living room should be as direct as possible and yet not interfere with furniture placement. Ideally, there should be no through traffic. If such traffic is necessary, it should be at one end, with the remaining portion of the room a "dead-end" space.

During social activities, people tend to gather or congregate in relatively small groups. Desirable conversation distance is also relatively small, approximately 10 ft in diameter.

When the living room is combined with the dining area, the dining area should be offset into an alcove or be clearly identified as an entity in itself.

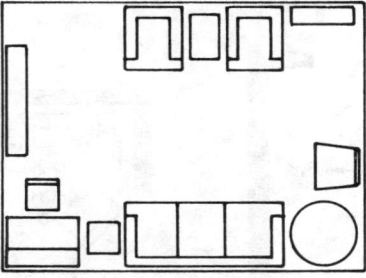

Fig. 1 Typical furniture arrangement for a one- or two-bedroom apartment (12.5 ft x 16 ft, 200 ft²).

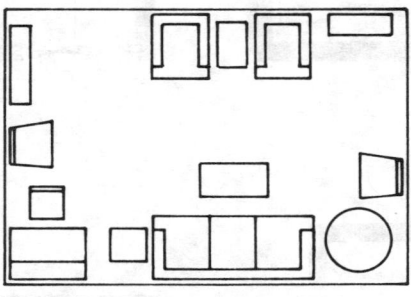

Fig. 2 Typical furniture arrangement for a three-bedroom apartment (12.5 ft x 20 ft, 250 ft²).

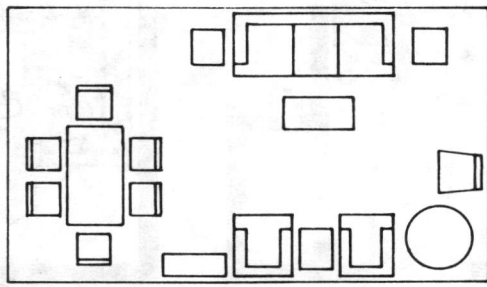

Fig. 3 Another typical furniture arrangement for a three-bedroom apartment (12.5 ft x 22 ft, 275 ft²).

LIVING ROOMS
Circulation

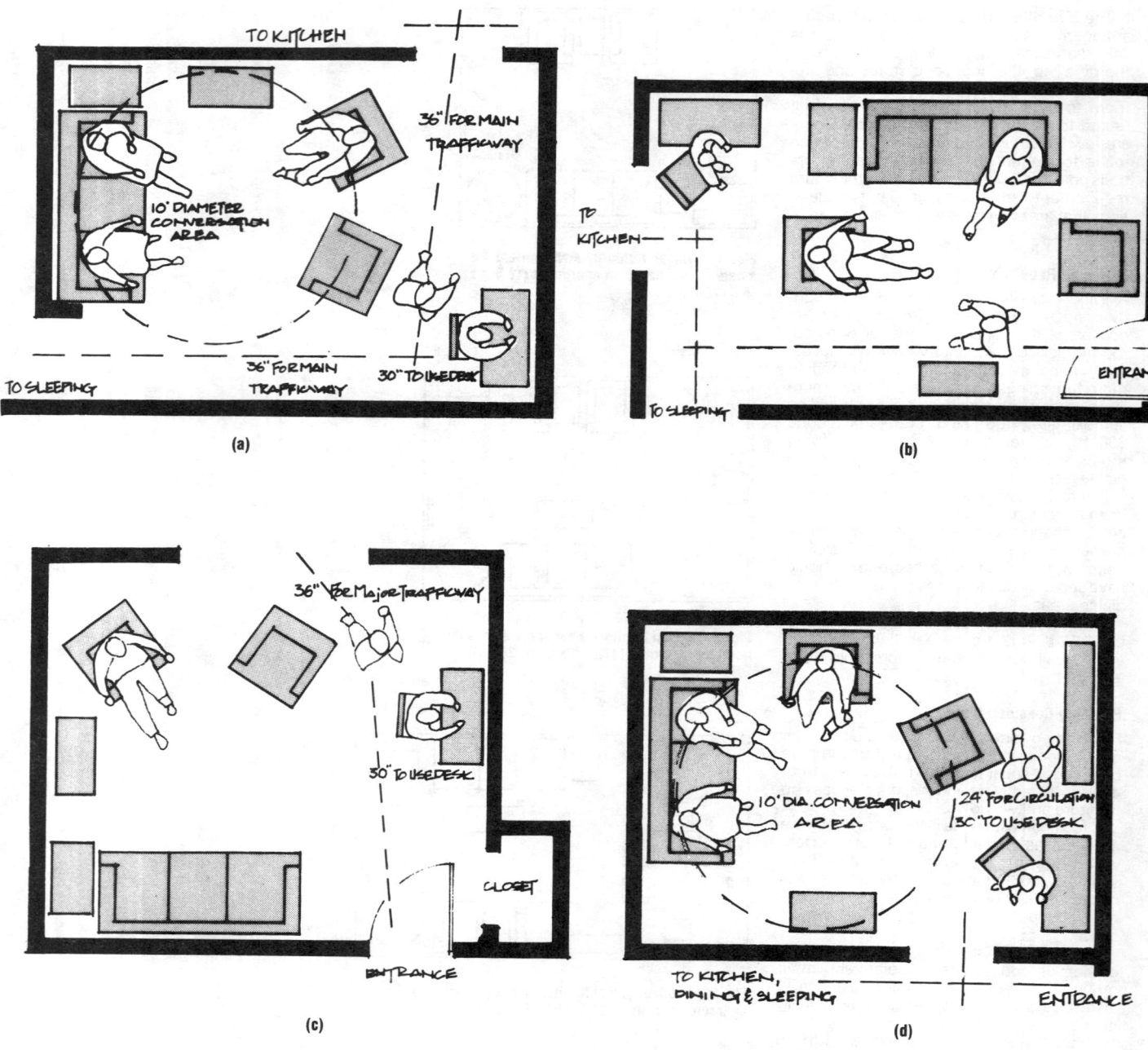

Fig. 4 When through traffic is unavoidable, pathways should skirt conversational or activity centers, as illustrated in *(a)*, *(b)*, and *(c)*. *(d)* illustrates a more ideal layout in which the entire room is bypassed.

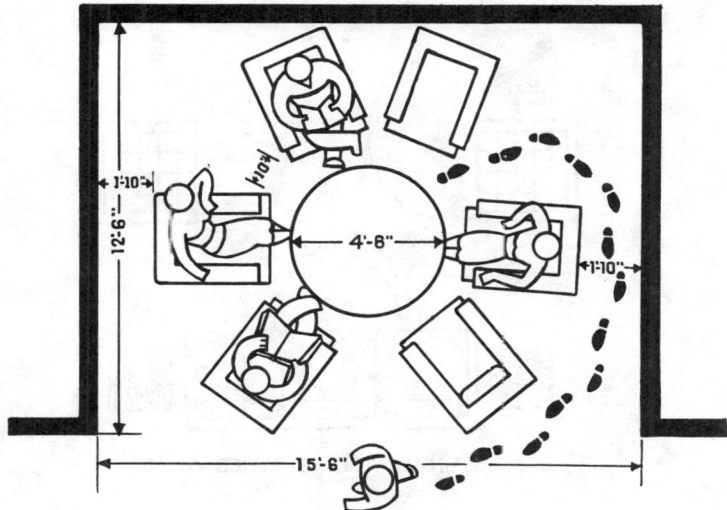

Fig. 5

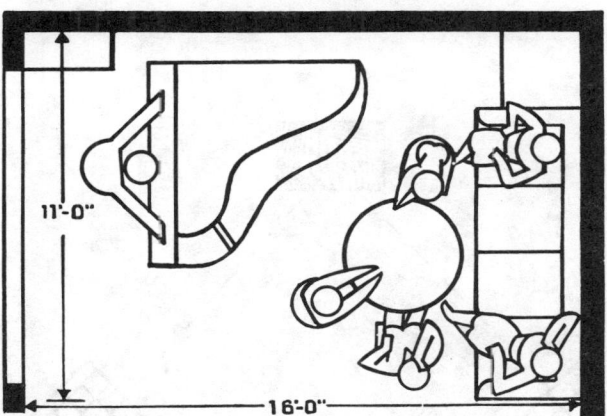

Fig. 6

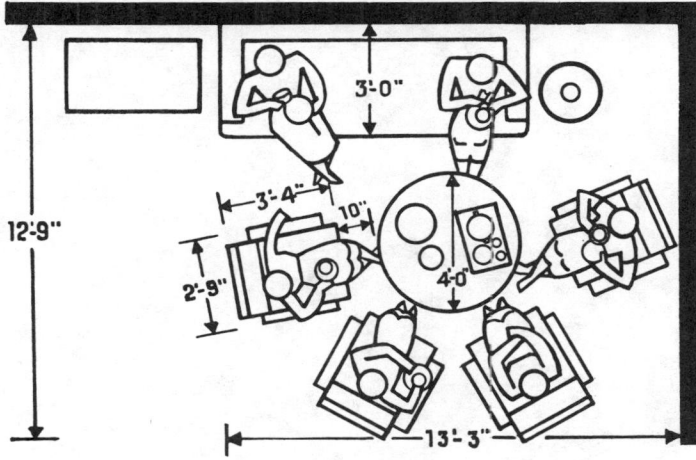

Fig. 7

Figures 5 to 10 show various groupings and related clearances. Figure 5 shows that a space 12'6" x 15'6" should be provided in order to accommodate seating for five around a 56-in-diameter cocktail table. The piano, sofa, and cocktail table arrangement shown in Fig. 6 requires a space at least 11'0" x 16'0". Figure 7 suggests that a space at least 12'9" x 13'3" is required to accommodate a grouping to seat 6 or 7 persons, while Fig. 8 indicates that a corner arrangement for two requires a space at least 6'3" x 6'6".

When planning furniture arrangements, allowances for clearances should take into account the human dimension as well, as illustrated in Figs. 9 and 10.

It should be noted that these diagrams are not intended as models for complete living room layouts. They are intended only as guidelines to illustrate minimum clearances for preliminary planning purposes.

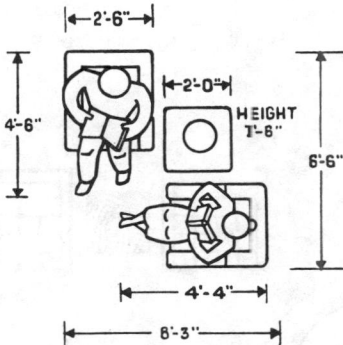

Fig. 8

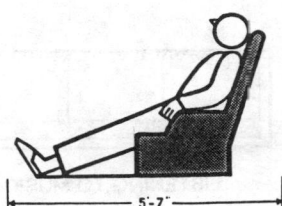

Fig. 9

Fig. 10

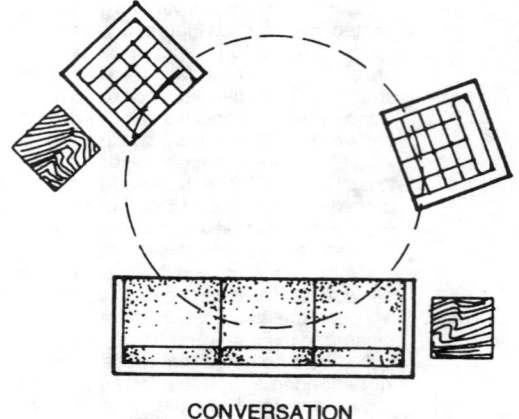

CONVERSATION

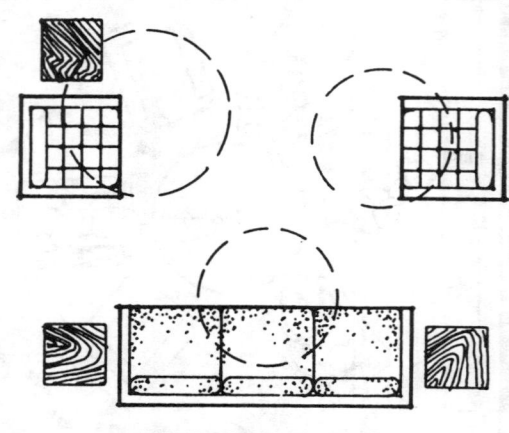

UNRELATED ACTIVITIES

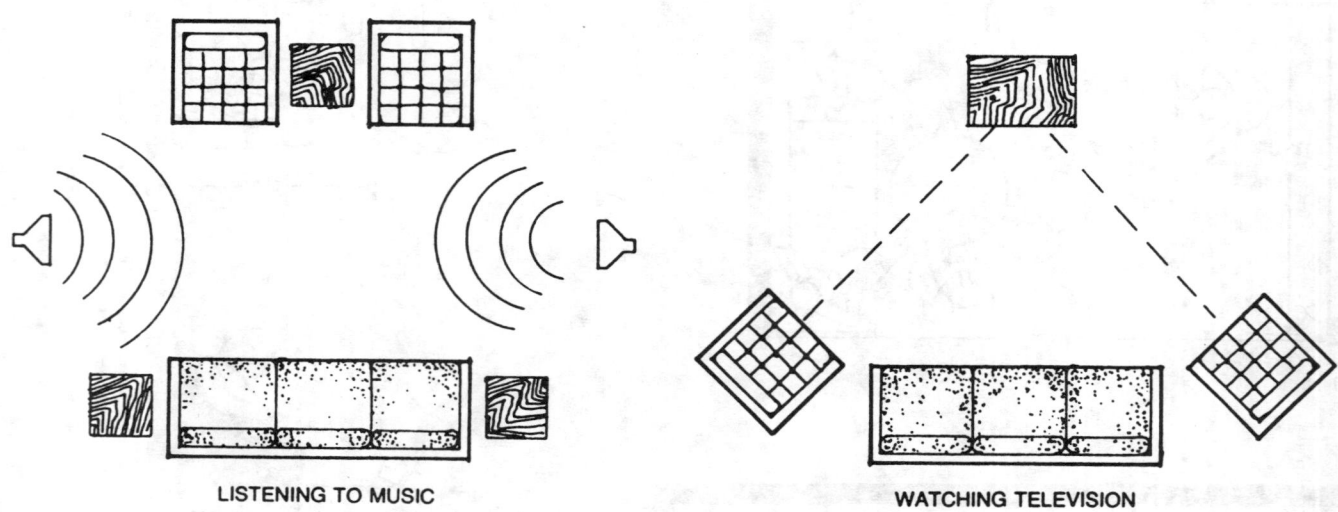

LISTENING TO MUSIC

WATCHING TELEVISION

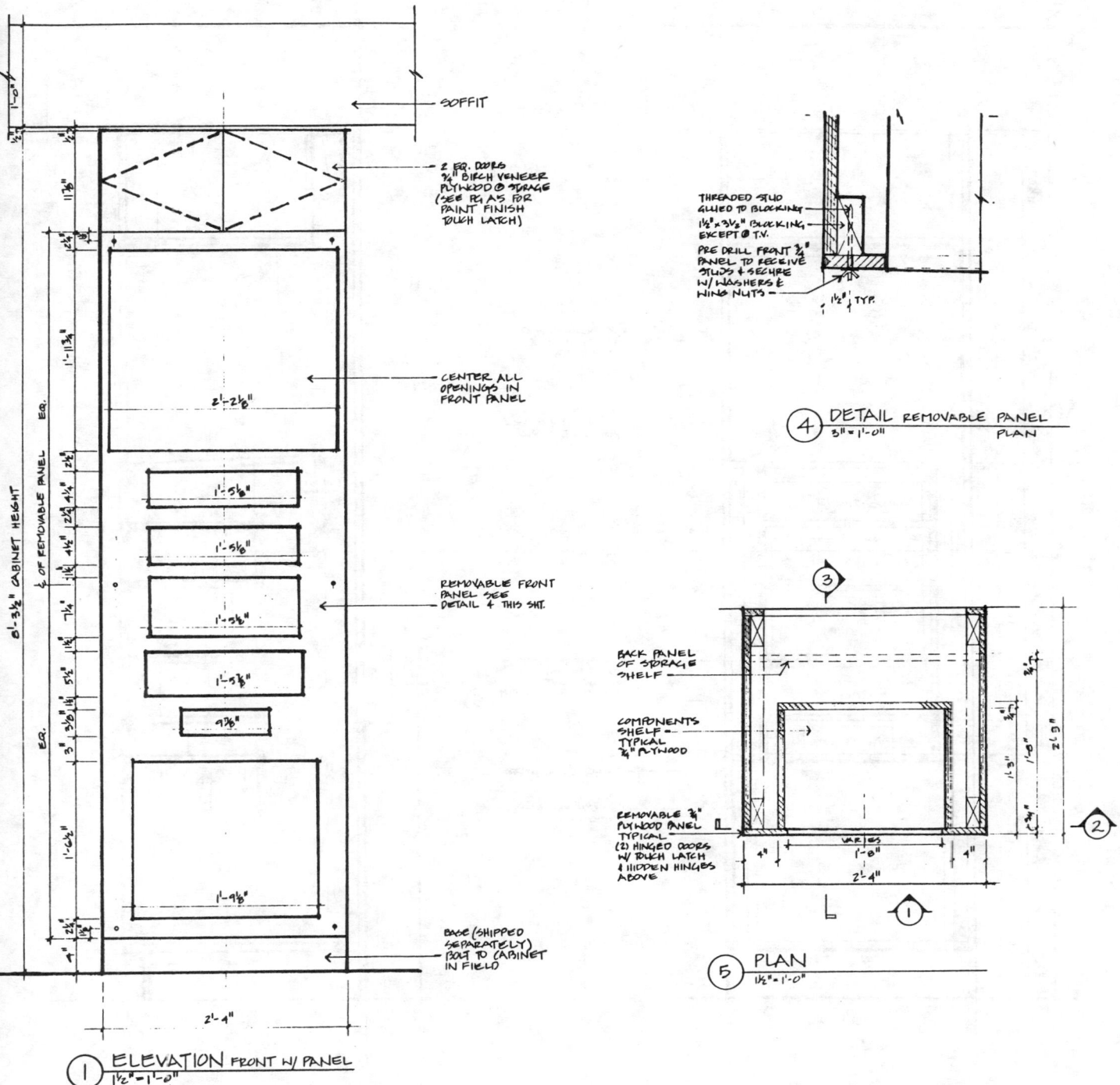

SOFFIT

2 EQ. DOORS ¾" BIRCH VENEER PLYWOOD @ STORAGE (SEE PG. A5 FOR PAINT FINISH TOUCH LATCH)

THREADED STUD GLUED TO BLOCKING

1½" x 3½" BLOCKING EXCEPT @ T.V.

PRE DRILL FRONT ¾" PANEL TO RECEIVE STUDS & SECURE W/ WASHERS & WING NUTS

1½" TYP.

CENTER ALL OPENINGS IN FRONT PANEL

4 DETAIL REMOVABLE PANEL
   3" = 1'-0"   PLAN

REMOVABLE FRONT PANEL SEE DETAIL 4 THIS SHT.

BACK PANEL OF STORAGE SHELF

COMPONENTS SHELF - TYPICAL ¾" PLYWOOD

REMOVABLE ¾" PLYWOOD PANEL TYPICAL (2) HINGED DOORS W/ TOUCH LATCH & HIDDEN HINGES ABOVE

BASE (SHIPPED SEPARATELY) BOLT TO CABINET IN FIELD

VARIES
4"
1'-0"
4"
2'-4"

5 PLAN
   1½" = 1'-0"

1 ELEVATION FRONT W/ PANEL
   1½" = 1'-0"

2'-4"

Fig. 11   Working drawings of a media cabinet, including plans, elevations, and sections of the installation. The design of the cabinet should take into account the actual electronic and other equipment to be housed and the clearances involved for operation. Power outlets should be coordinated and located so as to conceal unsightly wires and cables.

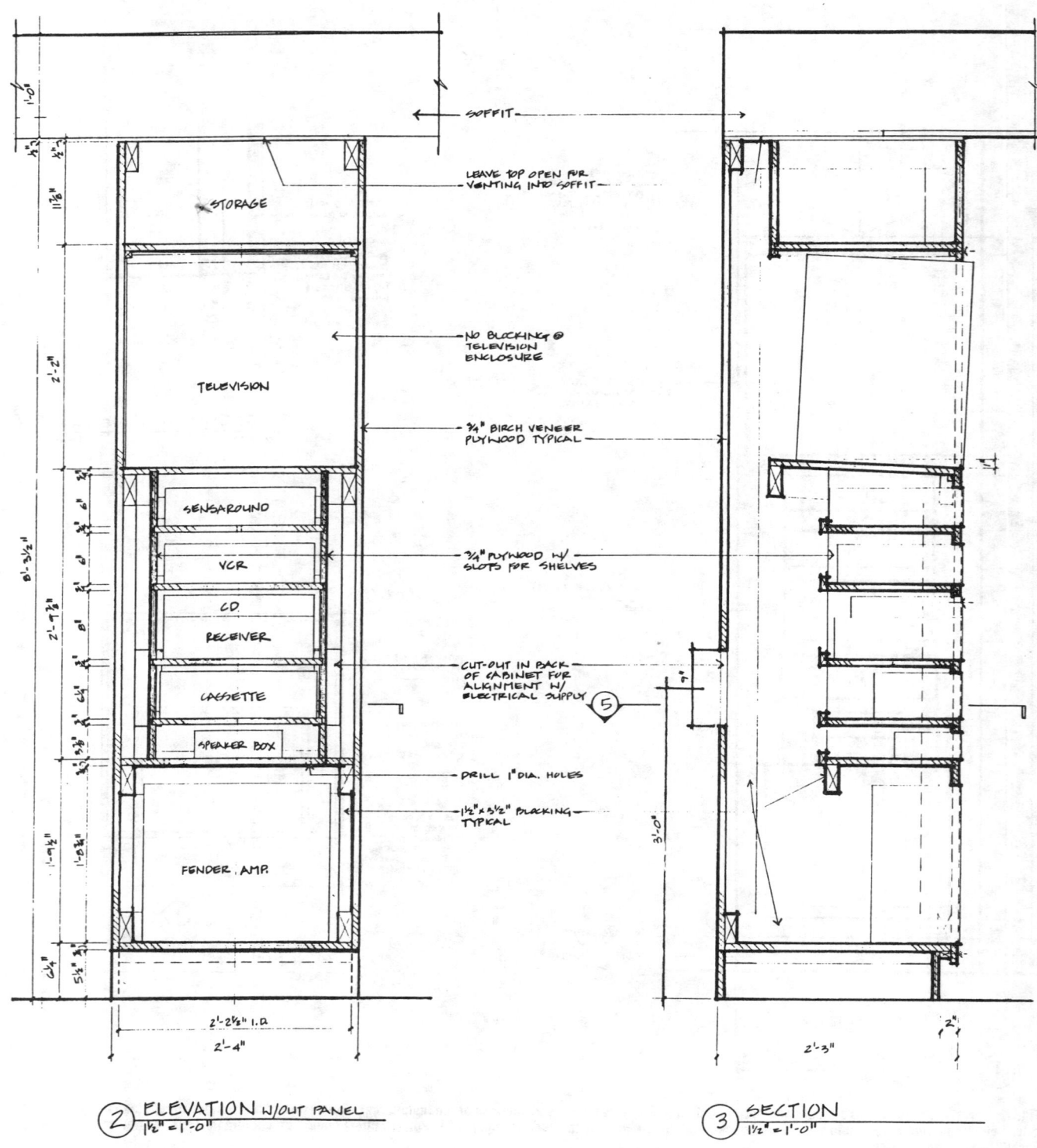

SOFFIT

LEAVE TOP OPEN FOR VENTING INTO SOFFIT

STORAGE

NO BLOCKING @ TELEVISION ENCLOSURE

TELEVISION

3/4" BIRCH VENEER PLYWOOD TYPICAL

SENSAROUND

VCR

3/4" PLYWOOD W/ SLOTS FOR SHELVES

C.D.

RECEIVER

CUT-OUT IN BACK OF CABINET FOR ALIGNMENT W/ ELECTRICAL SUPPLY

CASSETTE

SPEAKER BOX

DRILL 1" DIA. HOLES

1½" x 3½" BLOCKING TYPICAL

FENDER , AMP.

2'-2½" I.D.

2'-4"

② ELEVATION W/OUT PANEL
1½" = 1'-0"

3'-0"

2"

2'-3"

③ SECTION
1½" = 1'-0"

Fig. 11 *(Continued)*

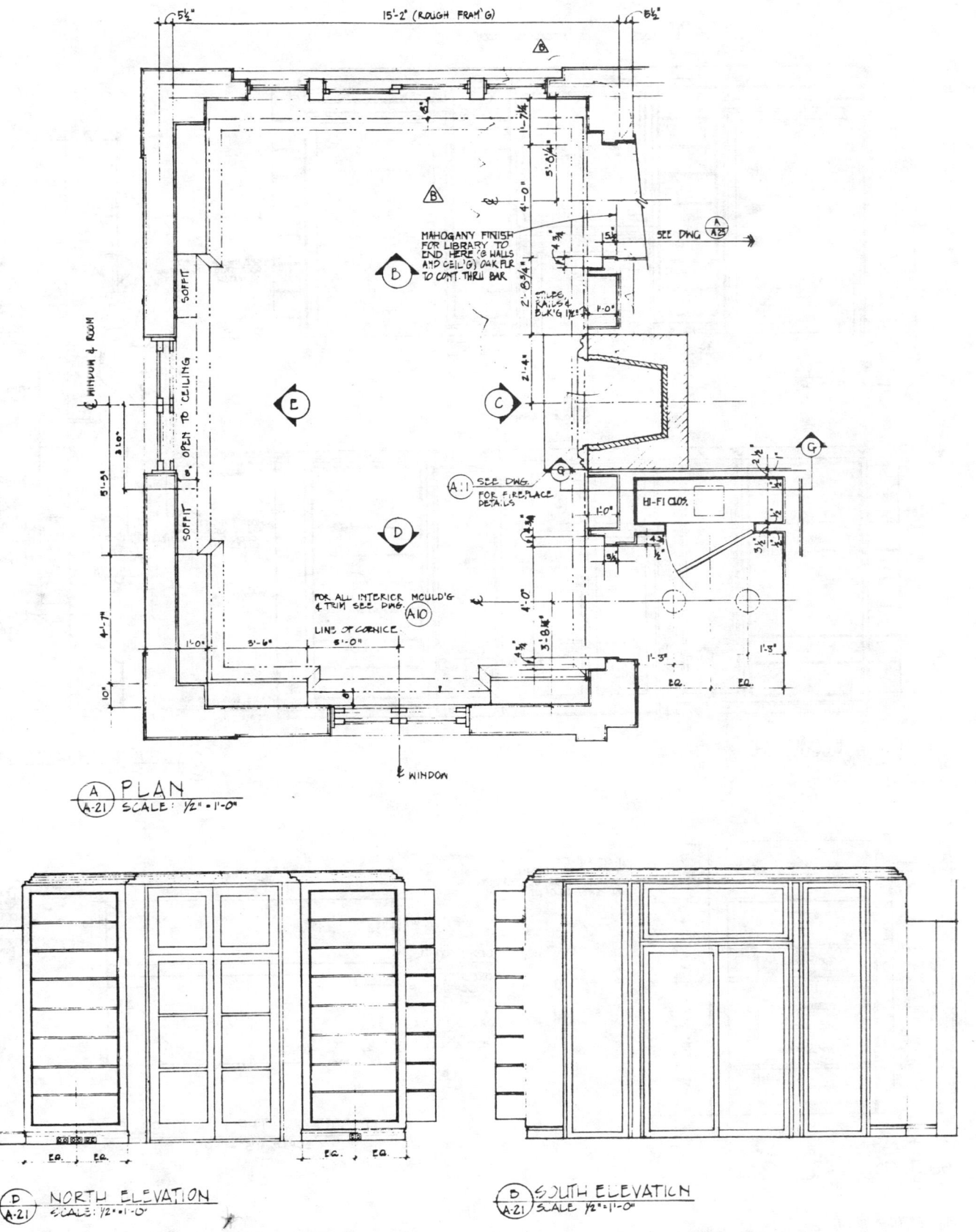

Fig. 12 Working drawings of a library/living room, including a plan of the space, wall elevations, and some of the many details involved.

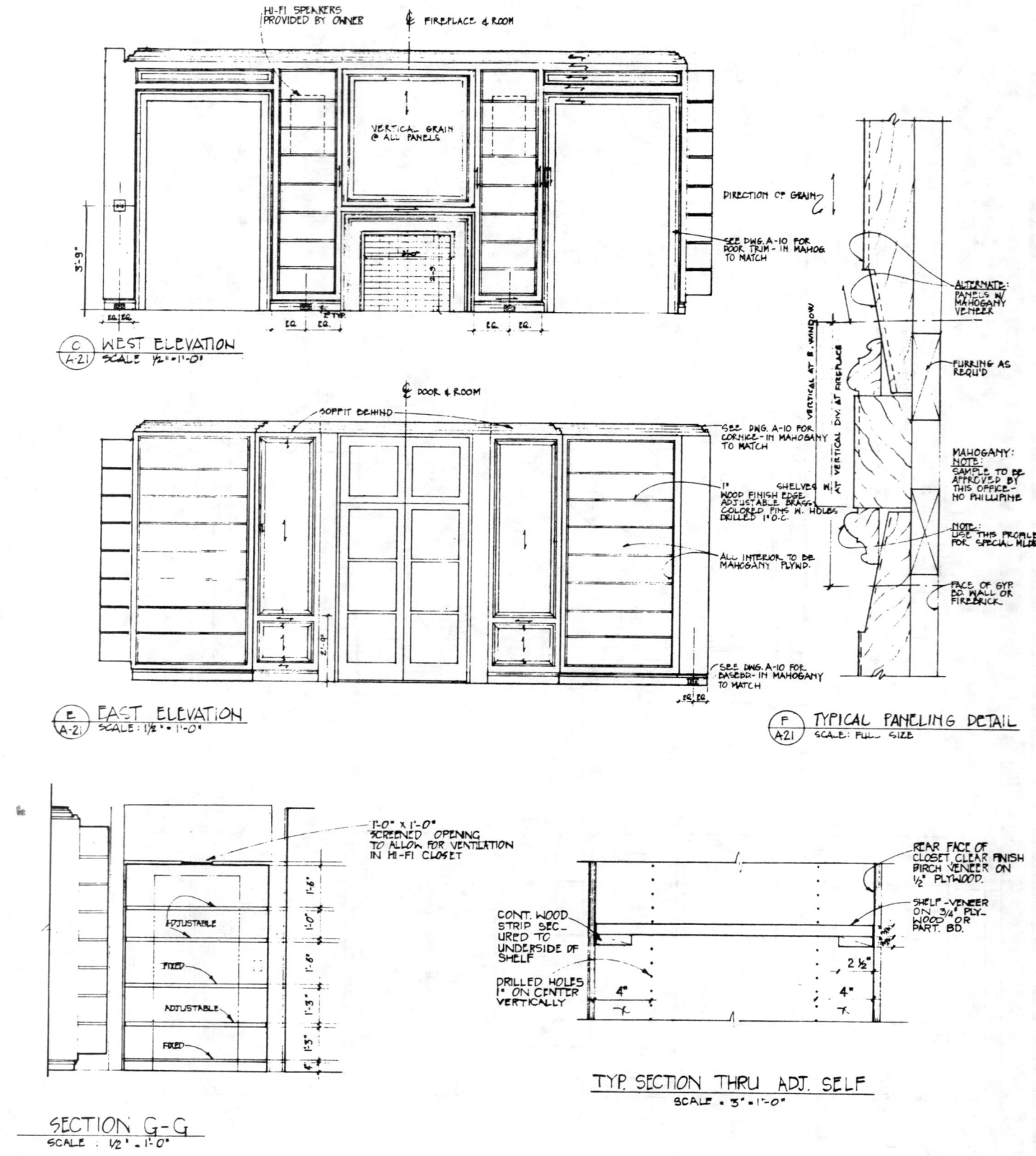

Fig. 12 (Continued)

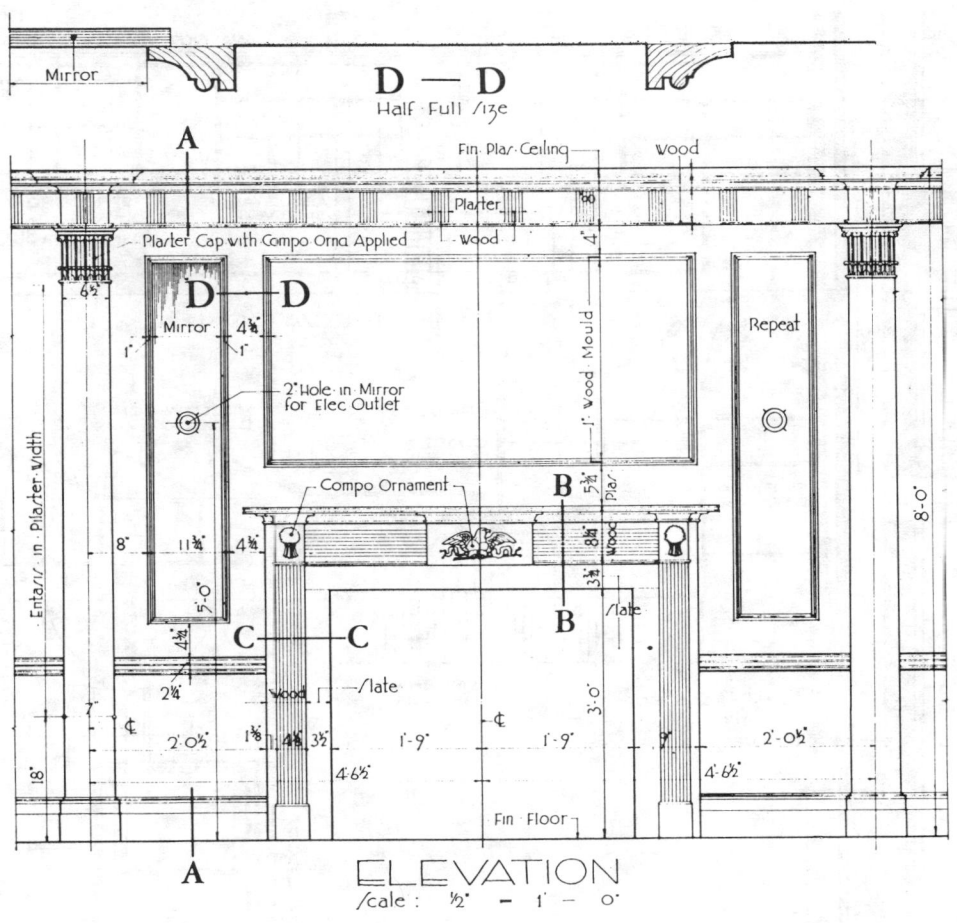

D — D
Half Full Size

ELEVATION
Scale: ½" = 1'-0"

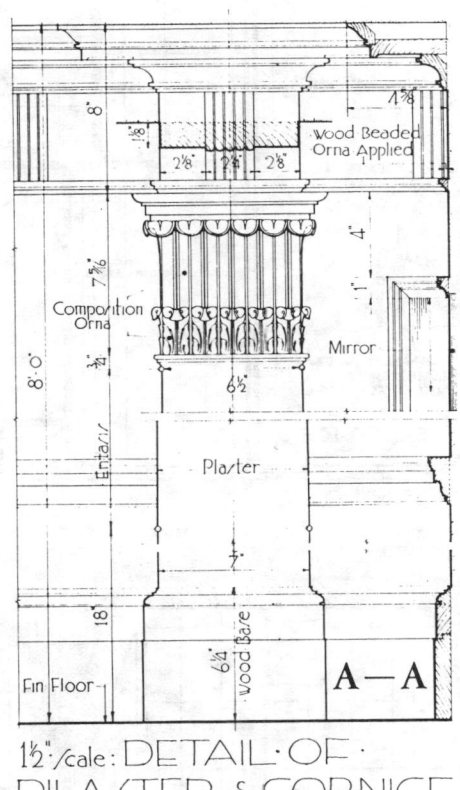

A — A

1½" Scale: DETAIL OF
PILASTER & CORNICE

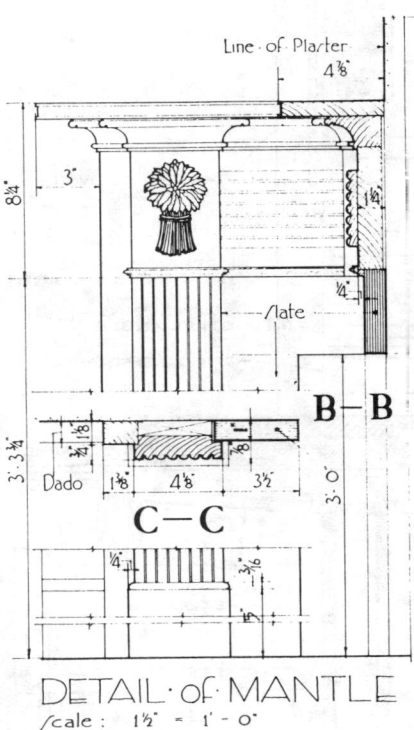

DETAIL of MANTLE
Scale: 1½" = 1'-0"

LIVING ROOMS
Fireplace Wall Sections and Details

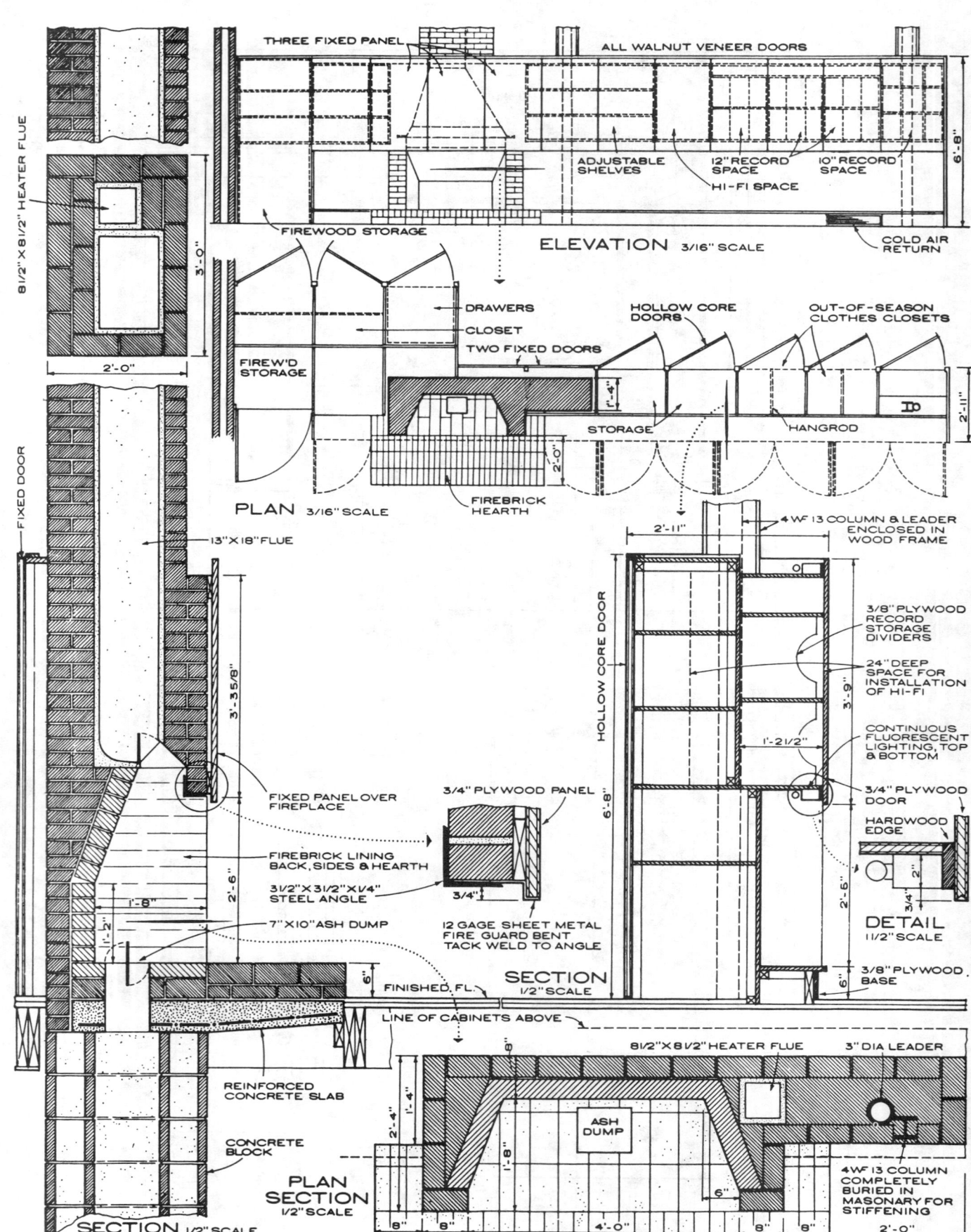

81/2" X 81/2" HEATER FLUE

3'-0"

2'-0"

THREE FIXED PANEL

ALL WALNUT VENEER DOORS

6'-8"

ADJUSTABLE
SHELVES

12" RECORD
SPACE

10" RECORD
SPACE

HI-FI SPACE

FIREWOOD STORAGE

COLD AIR
RETURN

ELEVATION 3/16" SCALE

DRAWERS

CLOSET

TWO FIXED DOORS

HOLLOW CORE
DOORS

OUT-OF-SEASON
CLOTHES CLOSETS

FIREW'D
STORAGE

2'-11"

STORAGE

HANGROD

2'-0"

PLAN 3/16" SCALE

FIREBRICK
HEARTH

FIXED DOOR

13" X 18" FLUE

3'-3 5/8"

FIXED PANEL OVER
FIREPLACE

FIREBRICK LINING
BACK, SIDES & HEARTH

3 1/2" X 3 1/2" X 1/4"
STEEL ANGLE

7" X 10" ASH DUMP

1'-8"

2'-6"

1'-2"

6"

FINISHED FL.

3/4" PLYWOOD PANEL

3/4"

12 GAGE SHEET METAL
FIRE GUARD BENT
TACK WELD TO ANGLE

SECTION
1/2" SCALE

2'-11"

4 WF 13 COLUMN & LEADER
ENCLOSED IN
WOOD FRAME

HOLLOW CORE DOOR

3/8" PLYWOOD
RECORD
STORAGE
DIVIDERS

24" DEEP
SPACE FOR
INSTALLATION
OF HI-FI

3'-9"

6'-8"

1'-2 1/2"

CONTINUOUS
FLUORESCENT
LIGHTING, TOP
& BOTTOM

3/4" PLYWOOD
DOOR

HARDWOOD
EDGE

2"

3/4"

2'-6"

DETAIL
11/2" SCALE

3/8" PLYWOOD
BASE

6"

LINE OF CABINETS ABOVE

REINFORCED
CONCRETE SLAB

CONCRETE
BLOCK

**PLAN
SECTION**
1/2" SCALE

SECTION 1/2" SCALE

8"

81/2" X 81/2" HEATER FLUE

3" DIA LEADER

1'-4"

2'-4"

1'-8"

ASH
DUMP

4 WF 13 COLUMN
COMPLETELY
BURIED IN
MASONARY FOR
STIFFENING

8" 8" 4'-0" 8" 8"

6"

2'-0"

Figure 13 shows a plan and elevations of modifications to an existing fireplace. Based on these drawings and inspection and measurement of existing conditions, the contractor prepares and submits shop drawings for the designer's approval. Since at least two trades are involved, coordination of the trades by the contractor and a thorough review of the shop drawings by both contractor and designer are essential. It is important, also, that modifications conform with all applicable codes. The extent of hearth extension, the materials used, and the distance of combustible materials from the fire box are among the numerous items governed by codes.

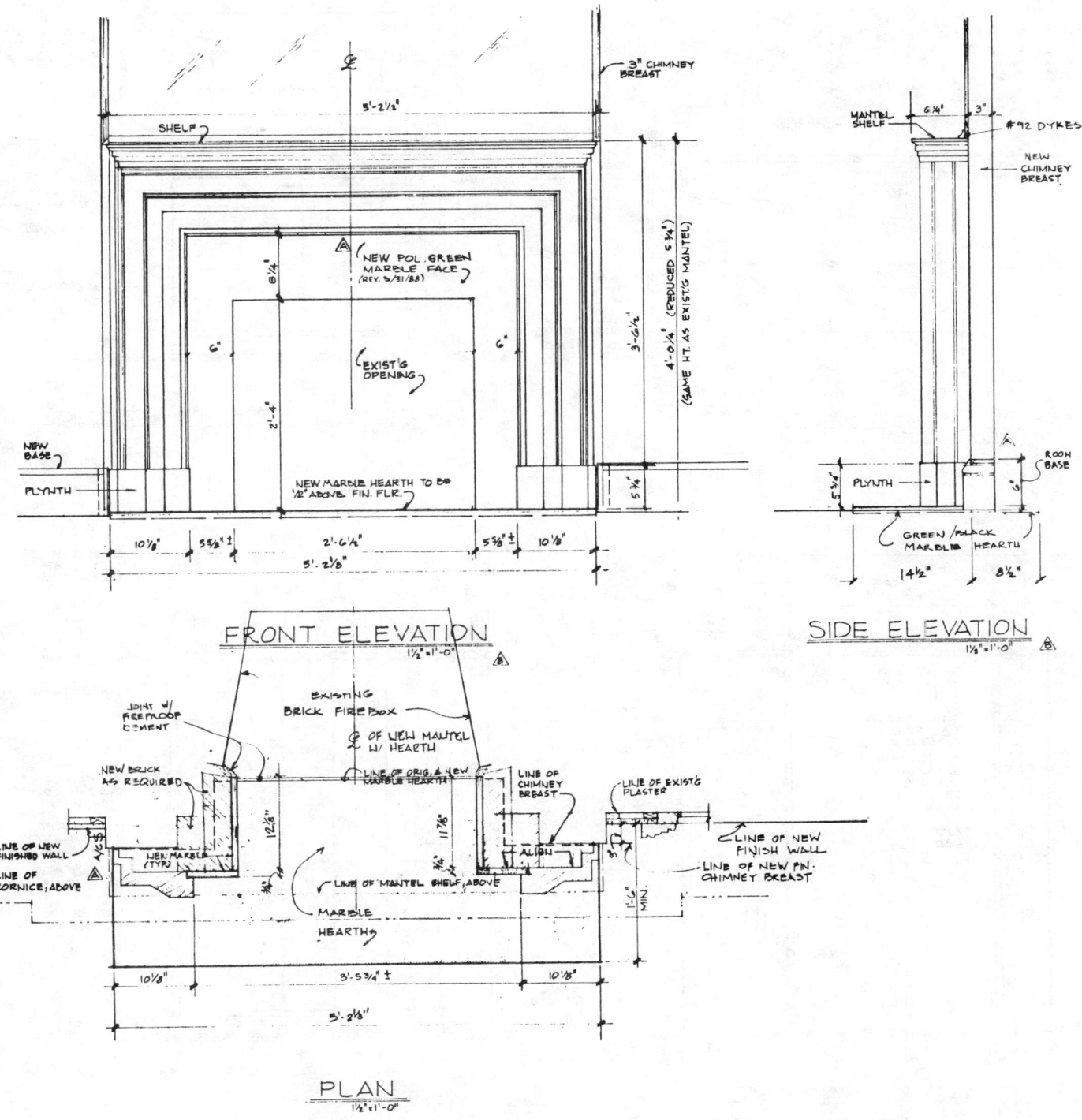

FRONT ELEVATION
1½"=1'-0"

SIDE ELEVATION
1½"=1'-0"

PLAN
1½"=1'-0"

Fig. 13

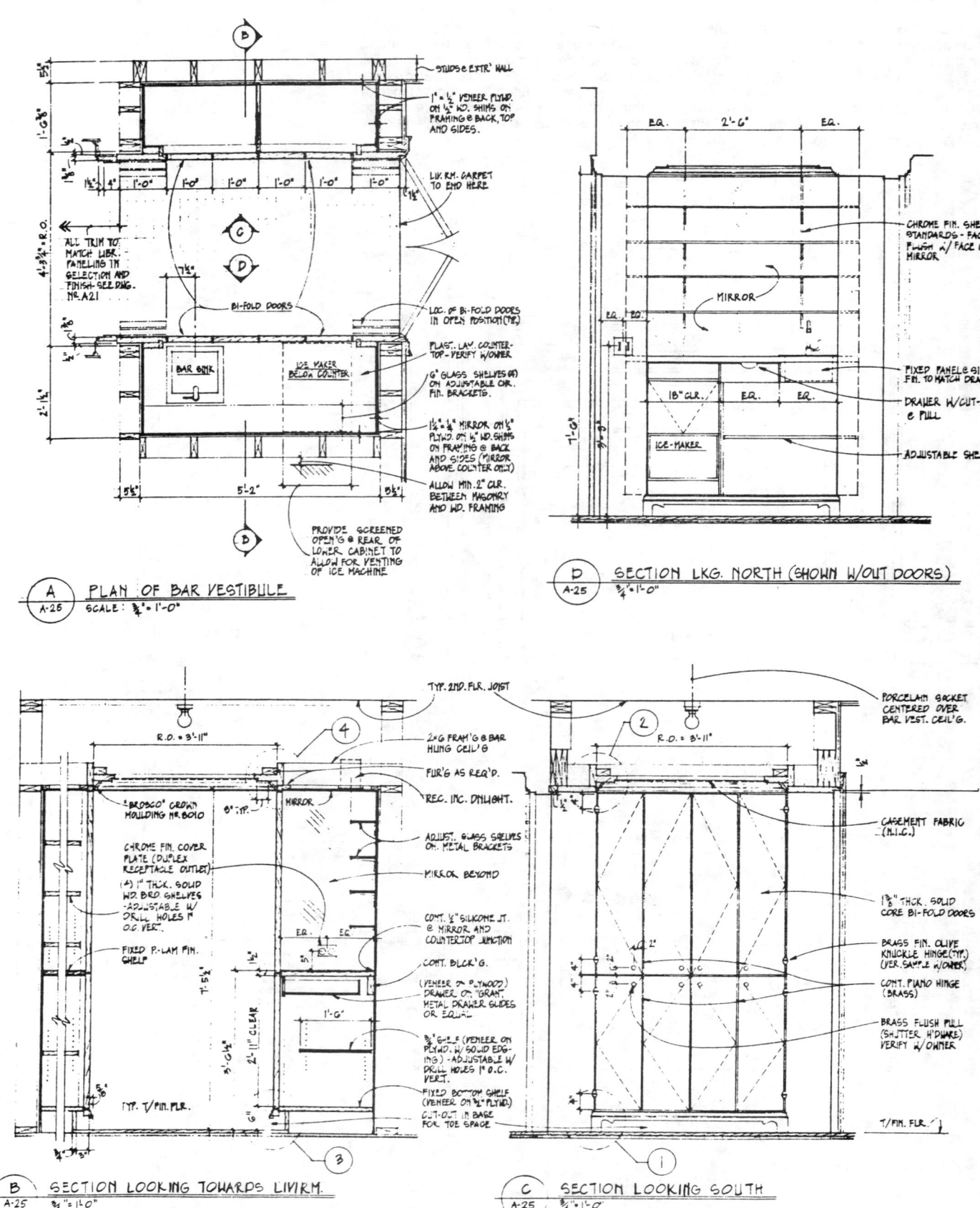

A PLAN OF BAR VESTIBULE
A-25   SCALE: ¾"=1'-0"

D SECTION LKG. NORTH (SHOWN W/OUT DOORS)
A-25   ¾"=1'-0"

B SECTION LOOKING TOWARDS LIV.RM.
A-25   ¾"=1'-0"

C SECTION LOOKING SOUTH
A-25   ¾"=1'-0"

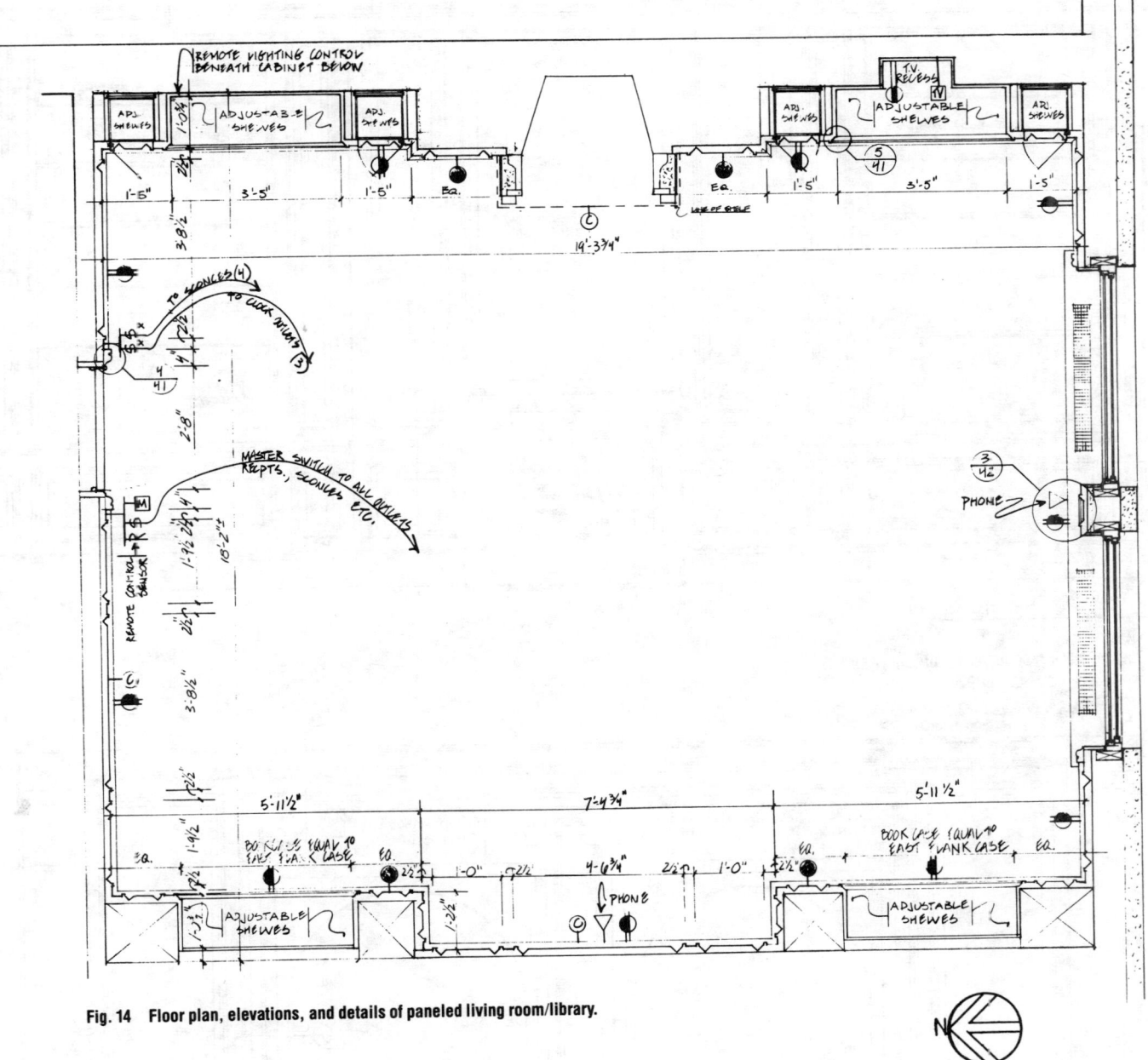

Fig. 14   Floor plan, elevations, and details of paneled living room/library.

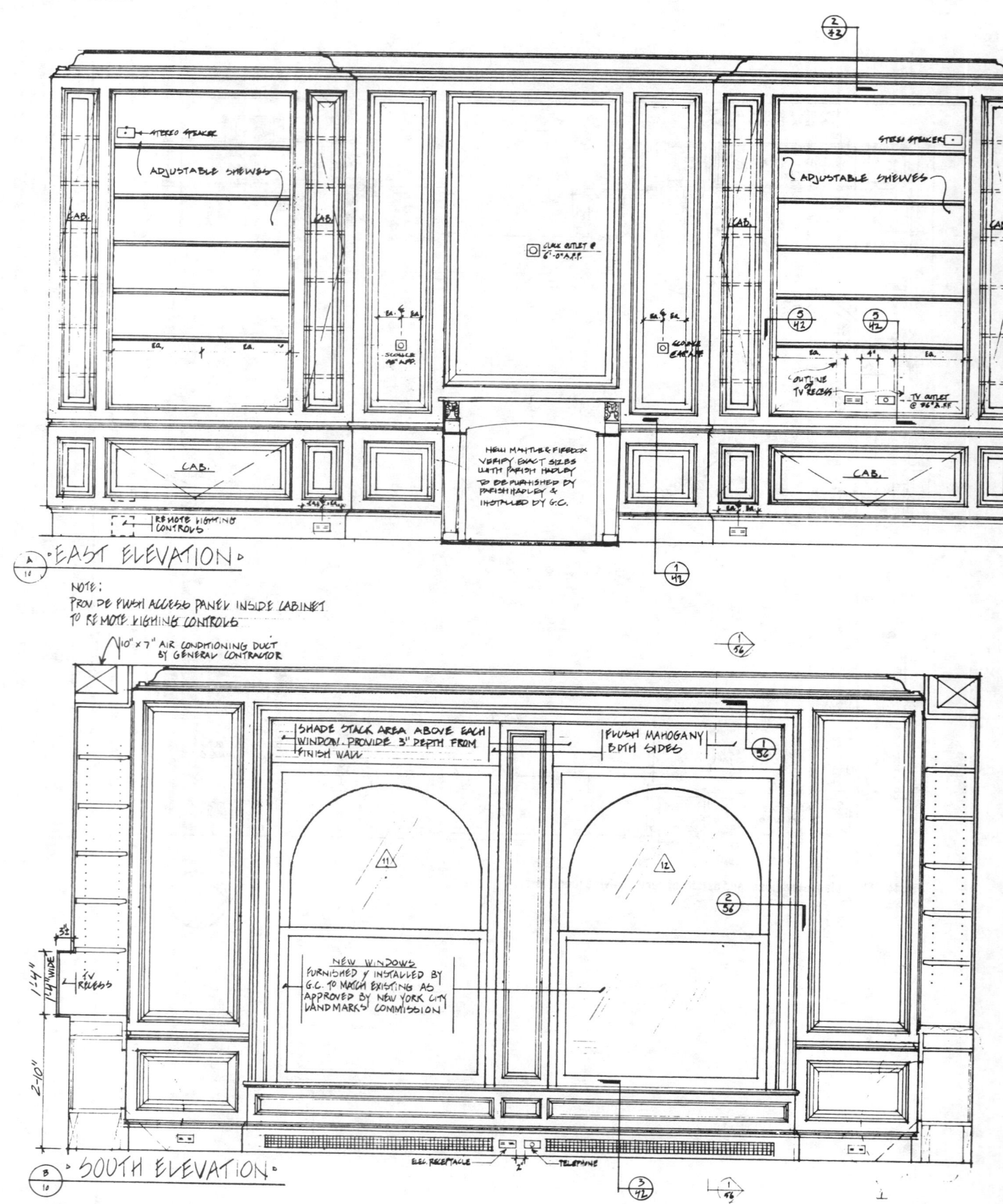

EAST ELEVATION

NOTE:
PROVIDE FLUSH ACCESS PANEL INSIDE CABINET
TO REMOTE LIGHTING CONTROLS

SOUTH ELEVATION

Fig. 14 (Continued)

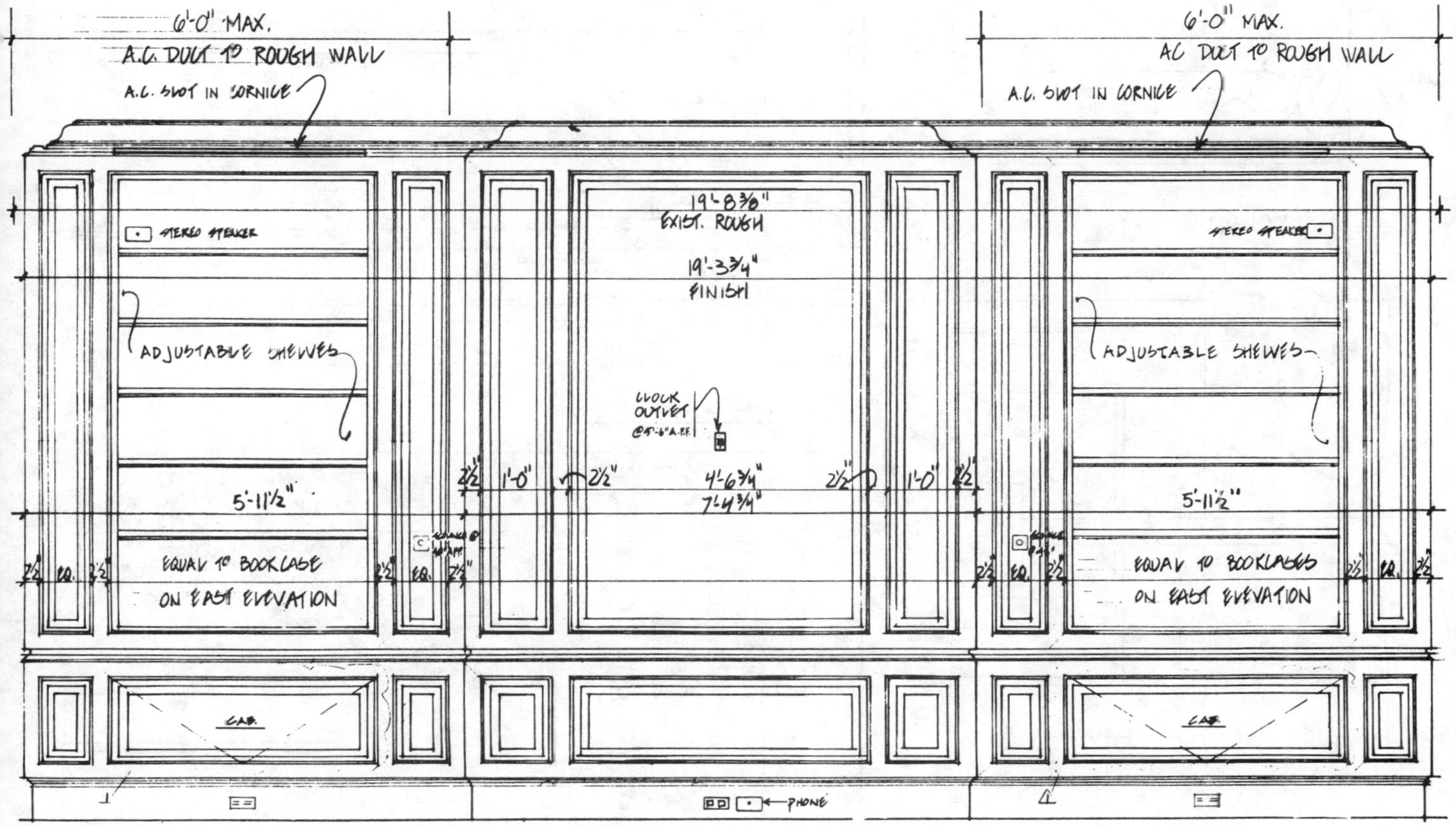

6'-0" MAX.
A.C. DUCT TO ROUGH WALL

A.C. SLOT IN CORNICE

6'-0" MAX.
AC DUCT TO ROUGH WALL

A.C. SLOT IN CORNICE

STEREO SPEAKER

19'-8⅜"
EXIST. ROUGH

19'-3¾"
FINISH

STEREO SPEAKER

ADJUSTABLE SHELVES

CLOCK
OUTLET
@ 5'-6" A.F.F.

ADJUSTABLE SHELVES

5'-11½"

2½" 1'-0" 2½"   4'-6¾"   2½" 1'-0"
                7'-4¾"

5'-11½"

EQUAL TO BOOKCASE
ON EAST ELEVATION

EQUAL TO BOOKCASES
ON EAST ELEVATION

CAB.

CAB.

PHONE

· WEST ELEVATION ·

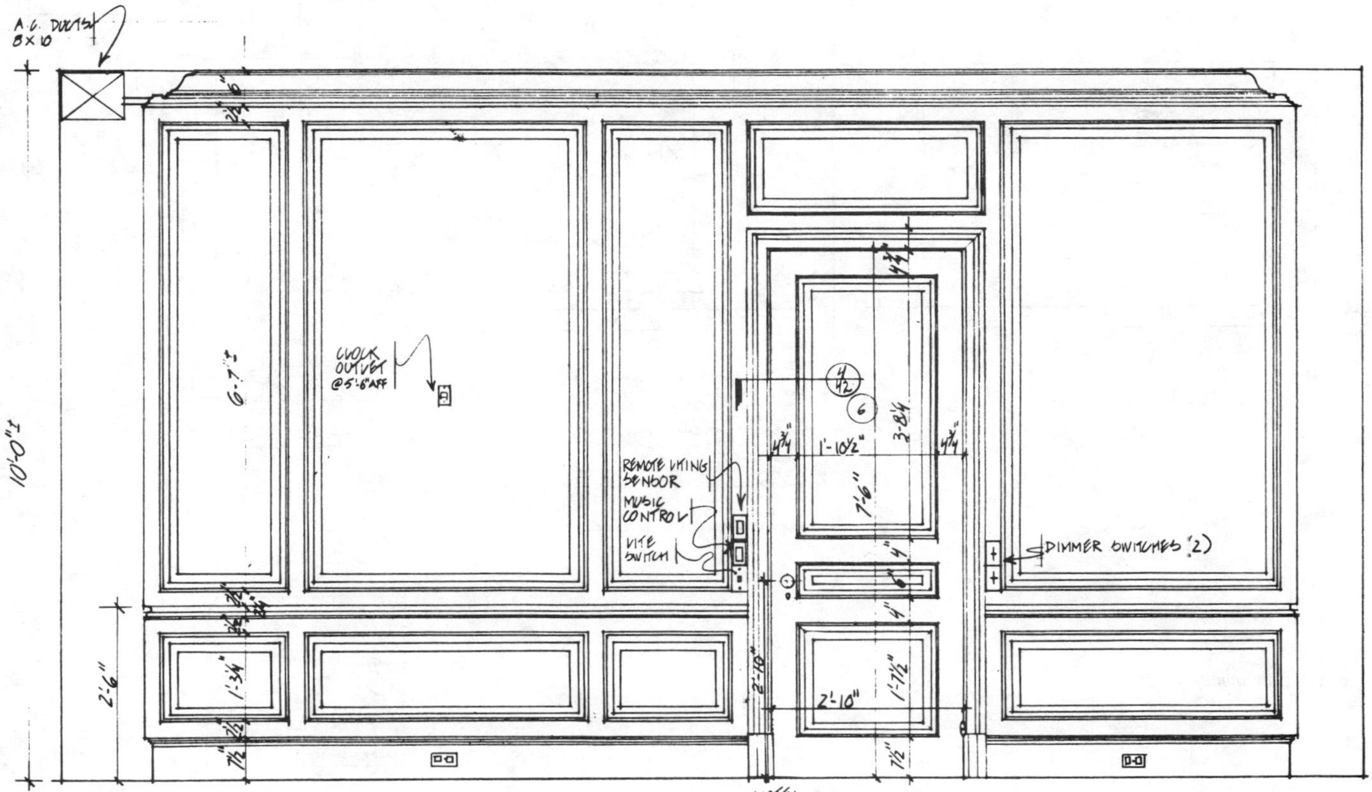

A.C. DUCTS
8×10

CLOCK
OUTLET
@ 5'-6" AFF

6'-7"

10'-0" ±

REMOTE DIMMING
SENSOR
MUSIC
CONTROL
LITE
SWITCH

4"
1'-10½"   3-8¾"   4"
7'-6"

4/2
6

DIMMER SWITCHES (2)

2'-10"

2'-6"

1-3¼"

2'-10"   1'-7½"

7½"

· NORTH ELEVATION ·

D
10

Fig. 14 *(Continued)*

· NOTE:
· DOOR PANEL PROFILES TO
  MATCH WALL PANELS
· DOOR & JAMB TO BE FURNISHED & INSTALLED
  BY GENERAL CONTRACTOR

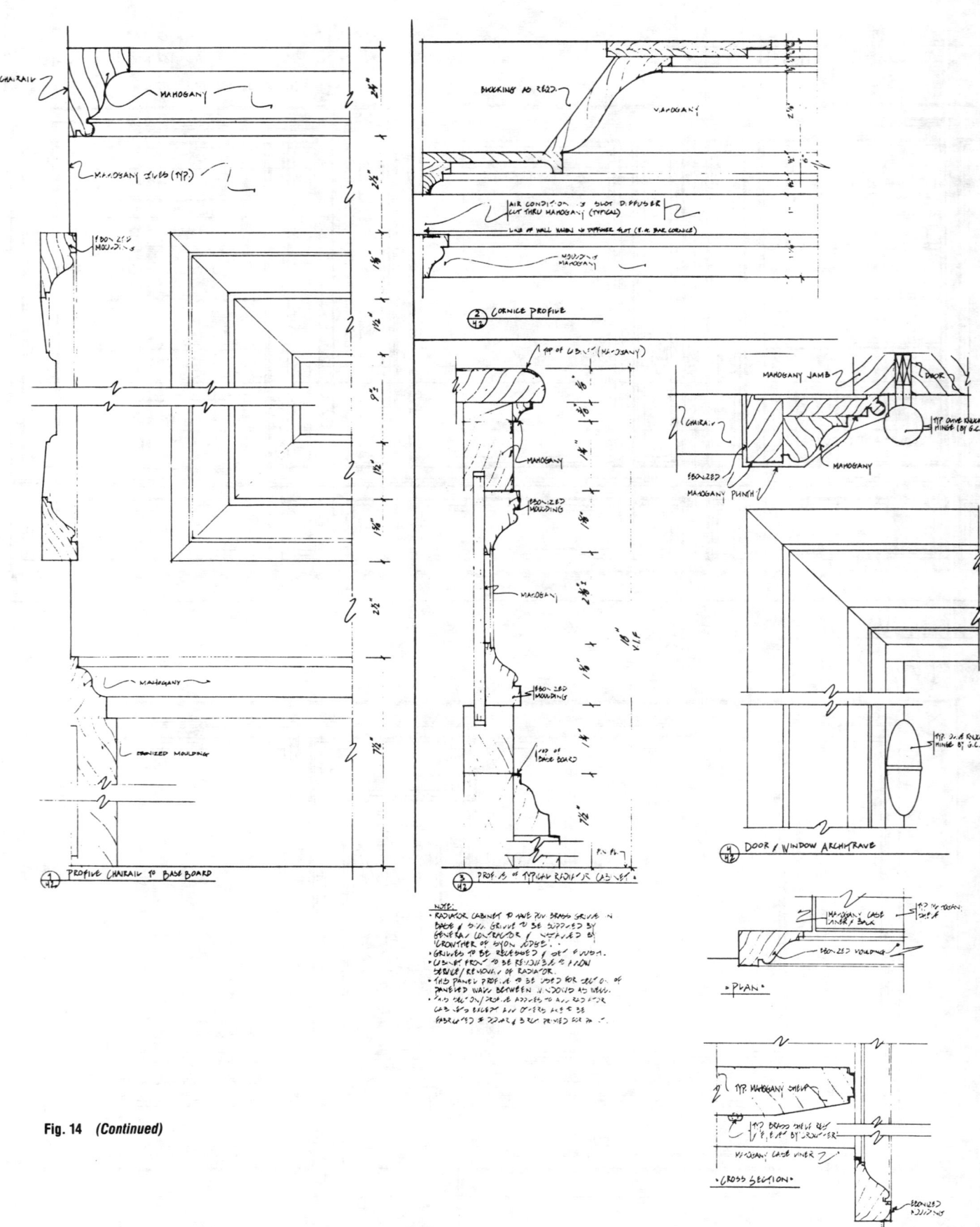

Fig. 14 *(Continued)*

Traditional: roll arms, loose-cushion back, kidney shape, solid base

Traditional: roll arms, fixed-cushion back, tailored skirt

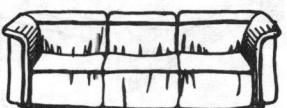

Contemporary: curved arms, fixed-cushion back, solid base

Contemporary: dome arms, solid back, solid base

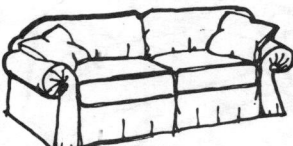

Traditional: roll arms, fixed-cushion back, tailored skirt

Traditional: roll arms, tufted

Traditional: roll arms, one-piece back, skirted base

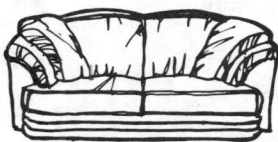

Contemporary: slanted cushion arms, fixed-cushion back, solid base

Traditional: roll arms, one-piece back, solid base

Traditional: roll arms, loose-pillow back, shirred base

Contemporary: curved arms, fixed-cushion back, solid base

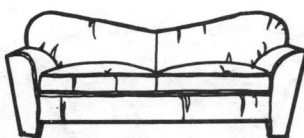

Contemporary: shaped sofa, shaped front view

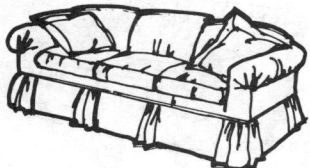

Traditional: roll arms

Traditional: roll arms, loose-pillow back, tailored skirt

Traditional: roll arms

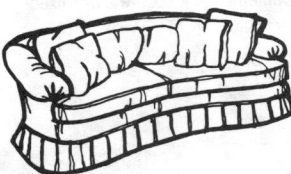

Traditional: roll arms, loose-cushion back, kidney shape, pleated skirt, solid base

Traditional: roll arms

Contemporary: shaped sofa, shaped base

Traditional: roll arms, fixed-cushion back, solid base

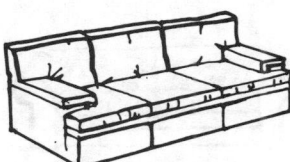

Contemporary: square arms, loose-cushion back, solid base

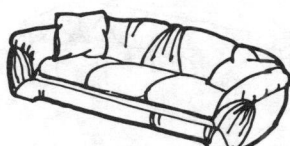

Contemporary: miscellaneous slanted arms

Traditional: roll arms, fixed-cushion back, shirred skirt

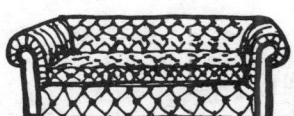

Traditional: roll arms, tufted

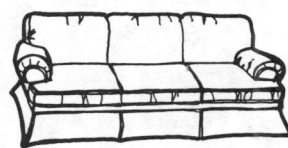

Traditional: roll arms, fixed-cushion back, tailored skirt

LIVING ROOMS
Planning Data: Sofas

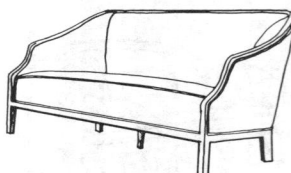

Contemporary: straight arms, one-piece back, open base

Traditional: roll arms, loose-pillow back, full skirt

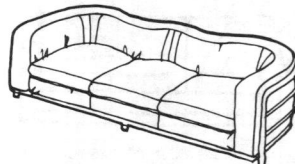

Contemporary: shaped sofa, shaped plan

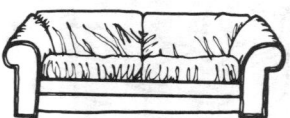

Contemporary: roll arms, fixed-cushion back, solid base

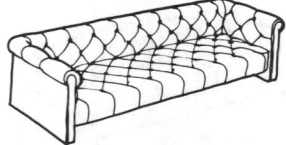

Traditional: roll arms, tufted

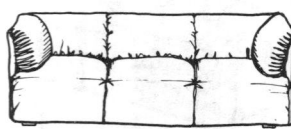

Contemporary: miscellaneous slanted arms

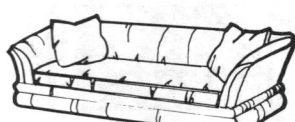

Contemporary: shaped sofa, partitioned back

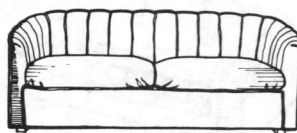

Contemporary: curved arms, fixed-cushion back, solid base

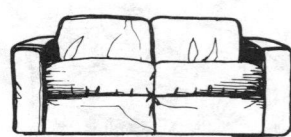

Contemporary: square arms, loose-cushion back, solid base

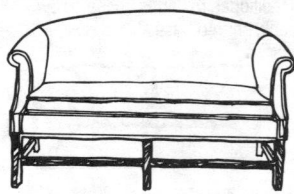

Contemporary: straight arms, one-piece back, open base

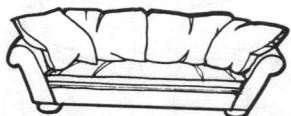

Contemporary: miscellaneous slanted arms

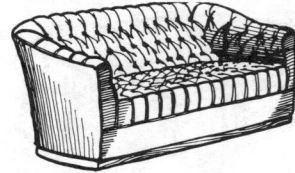

Contemporary: dome arms, one-piece tufted back, solid base

Contemporary: roll arms, loose-cushion back, solid base

Contemporary: square arms, fixed-cushion back, open base

Contemporary: dome arms, loose-cushion back, solid base

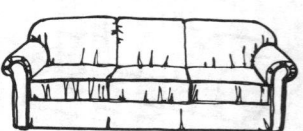

Traditional: roll arms, fixed-cushion back

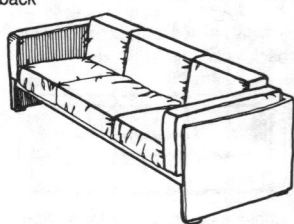

Contemporary: square arms, fixed-cushion back, open base

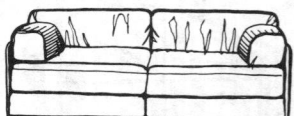

Contemporary: curved arms, fixed-cushion back, solid base

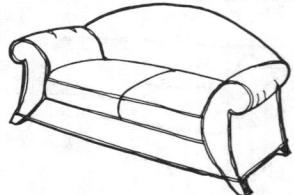

Contemporary: roll arms, fixed-cushion back, solid base

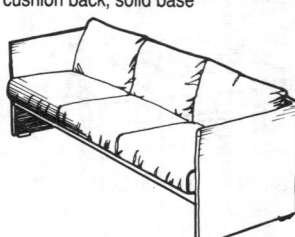

Contemporary: square arms, fixed-cushion back, open base

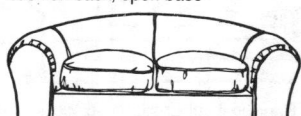

Contemporary: dome arms, solid back, solid base

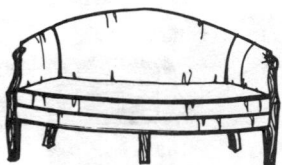

Contemporary: wood frame arms
and legs, one-piece curved back,
open base

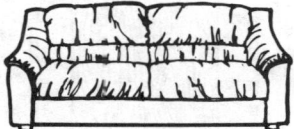

Contemporary: curved arms, fixed-
cushion back, solid base

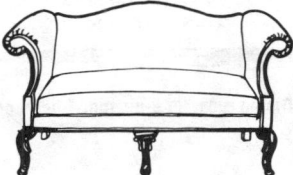

Traditional: roll arms, one-piece
back, open base

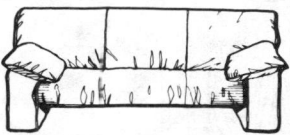

Contemporary: slanted cushion
arms, fixed-cushion back, open base

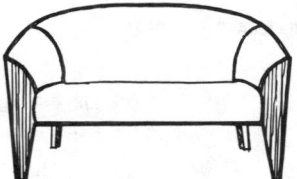

Contemporary: one-piece curved
back and arms, wood legs, open
base

Contemporary: slanted cushion
arms, fixed-cushion back, open base

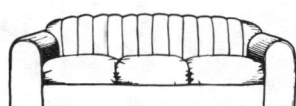

Contemporary: dome arms, solid
back

Contemporary: square arms, fixed-
cushion back, wood trim, open base

Traditional: roll arms, one-piece
back, open base

Contemporary: dome arms, channel
quilted back, seat, and arms, solid
base

Contemporary: curved arms, fixed-
cushion back, solid base

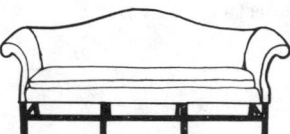

Traditional: roll arms, one-piece
back, open base

Contemporary: curved arms, fixed-
cushion back, solid base

Contemporary: modular

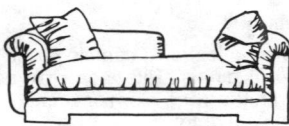

Contemporary: sofa/daybed

Contemporary: slanted cushion
arms, fixed-cushion back, solid base

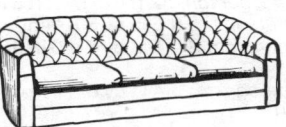

Contemporary: dome arms, one-
piece tufted back and seat, solid
base

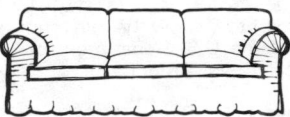

Contemporary: roll arms, fixed-
cushion back, soft skirt

Contemporary: shaped sofa,
partitioned back

Contemporary: curved arms, fixed-
cushion back, solid base

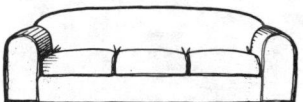

Contemporary: dome arms, solid
back

DINING ROOMS
Furniture Clearances

SPATIAL CHARACTERISTICS AND ARRANGEMENT

Requirement

Each living unit should contain space for the purpose of dining. This area may be combined with the living room or kitchen, or may be a separate room.

Criterion

The amount of space allocated to dining should be based on the number of persons to be served and the proper circulation space. Appropriate space should be provided for the storage of china and large dining articles either in the dining area itself or in the adjacent kitchen.

Space for accommodating the following sizes of tables and chairs in the dining area should be provided, according to the intended occupancy, as shown:

1 or 2 persons: 2 ft 6 in by 2 ft 6 in
4 persons: 2 ft 6 in by 3 ft 2 in
6 persons: 3 ft 4 in by 4 ft 0 in or 4 ft 0 in round
8 persons: 3 ft 4 in by 6 ft 0 in or 4 ft 0 in by 4 ft 0 in
10 persons: 3 ft 4 in by 8 ft 0 in or 4 ft 0 in by 6 ft 0 in
12 persons: 4 ft 0 in by 8 ft 0 in
Dining chairs: 1 ft 6 in by 1 ft 6 in
Buffet or storage unit: 1 ft 6 in by 3 ft 6 in

Figures 1 to 6 show the minimum requirements of the U.S. Department of Housing and Urban Development.

Commentary

Size of the individual eating space on the table should be based upon a frontage of 24 in and an area of approximately 2 ft². In addition, table space should be large enough to accommodate serving dishes.

Desirable room for seating is a clear 42 in all around the dining table. The following minimum clearances from the edge of the table should be provided: 32 in for chairs plus access thereto, 38 in for chairs plus access and passage, 42 in for serving from behind chair, 24 in for passage only, 48 in from table to base cabinet (in kitchen).

In sizing the separate dining room, provision should be made for circulation through the room in addition to space for dining.

The location of the dining area in the kitchen is desirable for small houses and small apartments. This preference appears to stem from two needs: (1) housekeeping advantages; (2) the dining table in the kitchen provides a meeting place for the entire family. Where only one dining location is feasible, locating the dining table in the living room is not recommended.

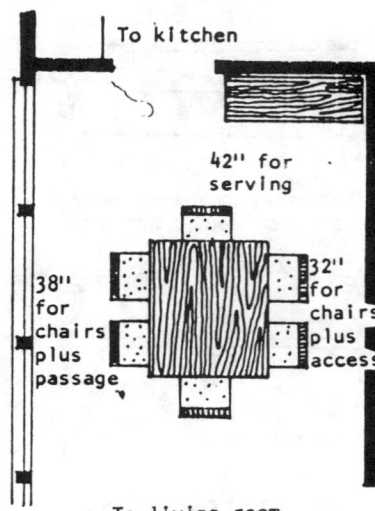

Fig. 1 Dining room for 6-person, 3-bedroom living unit.

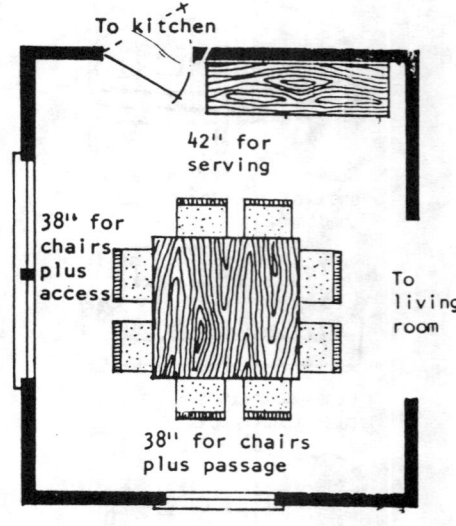

Fig. 2 Dining room for 8-person, 4-bedroom living unit.

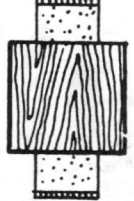

Fig. 3 Table for 2, 2'6" × 2'6".

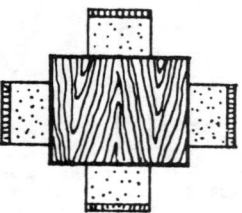

Fig. 4 Table for 4, 2'6" × 3'2".

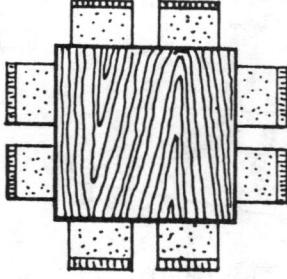

Fig. 5 Table for 8, 4'0" × 4'0".

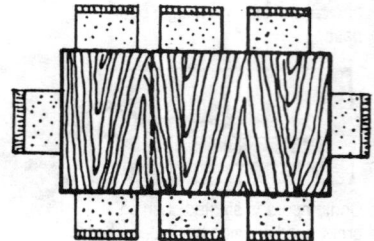

Fig. 6 Table for 8, 3'4" × 6'0".

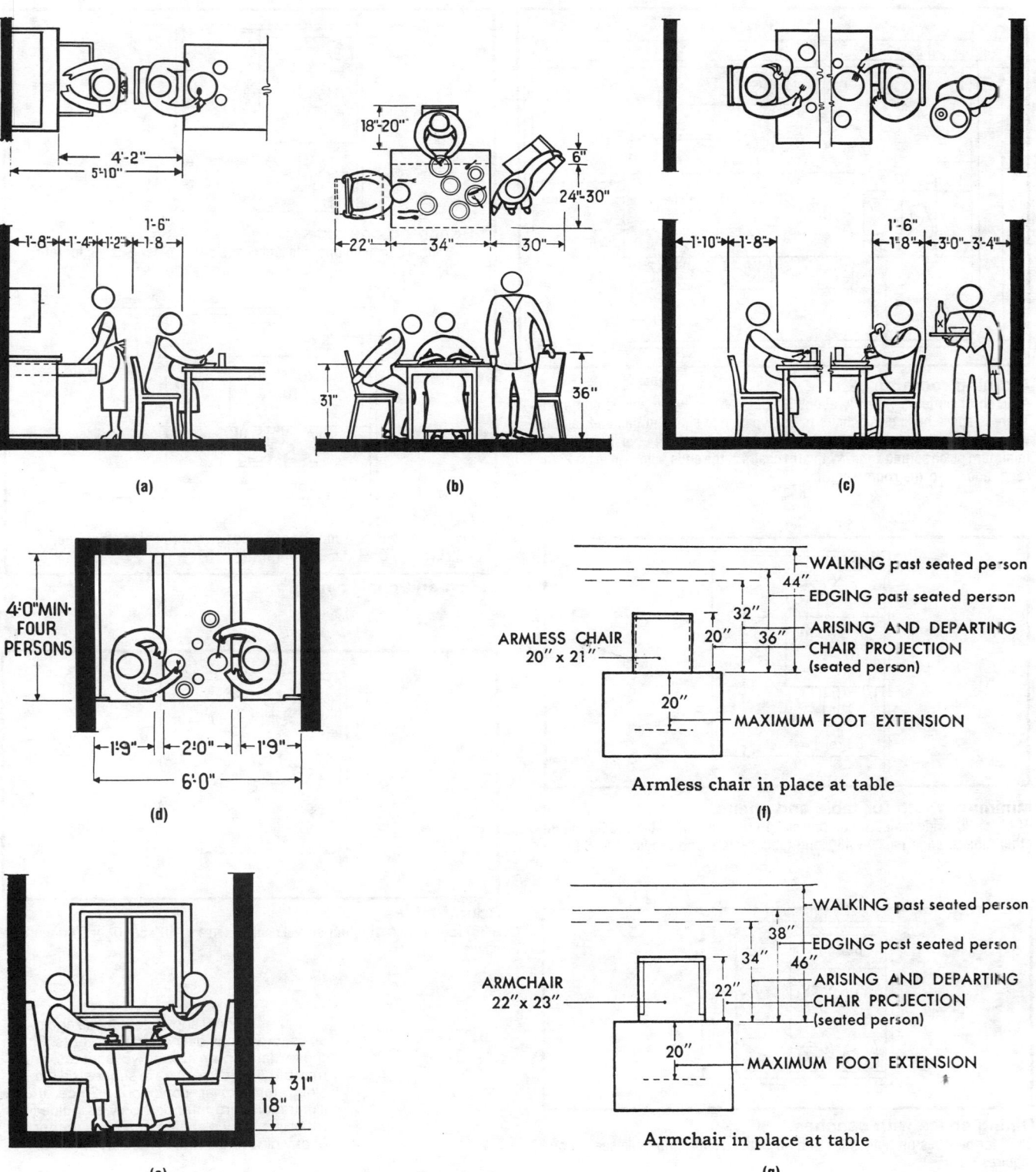

Fig. 7 *(a)* to *(e)* illustrate, in plan and elevation, seating requirements and clearances for various dining table arrangements. *(f)* and *(g)* illustrate clearance guidelines for a typical armless dining chair and a dining chair with arms, respectively. It should be noted that the clearances indicated relate to chairs with depth dimensions of 20″ and 22″; clearances should be adjusted depending on the chair size finally selected.

DINING ROOMS
Furniture Clearances

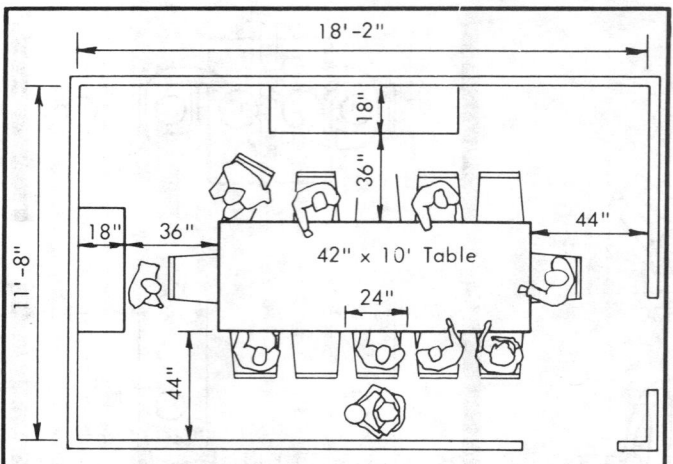

A dining room for 12.
A hutch or buffet is typically about 18″ deep. A 42″ wide table is common. There is space behind the chairs to edge past one side and one end, and to walk past on the other side and end. Table space is 24″ per person, the minimum place setting zone. With arm chairs at the ends, allow an extra 2″ for each; add 4″ to the room length.

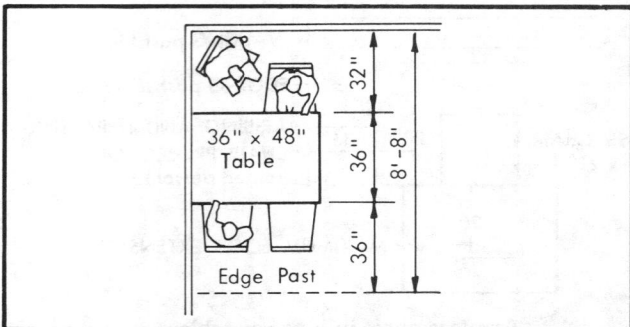

Minimum width for table and chairs.
8′-8″ for 36″ wide table, 32″ on one side to rise from the table and 36″ on the other side to edge past. A 48″ long table seats 4 and requires 34.6 ft².

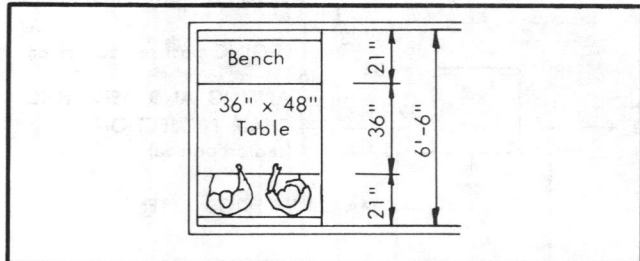

Dining space with benches.
6′-6″ for benches on both sides of a 36″ table. A 48″ long table seats 4 and requires 26 ft².

Fig. 8

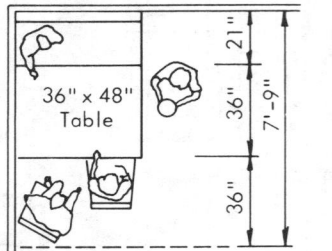

Bench on one side.
7′-9″ for a bench on one side and chairs on the other. Seating for four requires 31 ft².

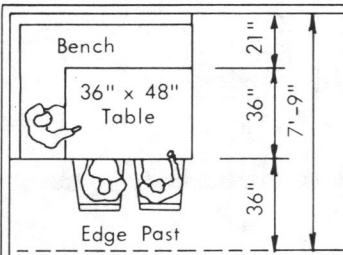

Corner bench.
Benches on one side and one end, and two chairs on the other side, seat five at a 3′x4′ table in 44.5 ft².

Bench and chair dining.

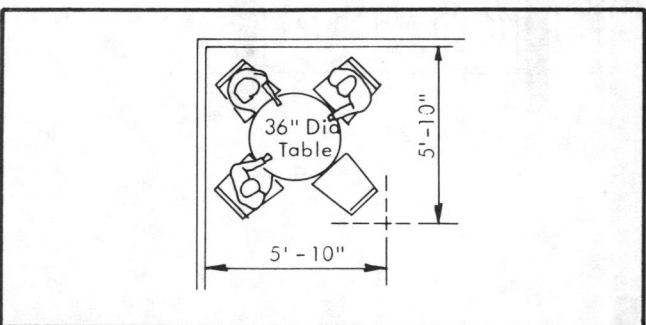

Round tables.
A 36″ round table with four swivel chairs fit in a 5′-10″x5′-10″ or 34 ft² corner space.

Figures 8 and 9 show clearances and room sizes for various dining arrangements. Since these data come from two sources, there may be slight disparities in suggested dimensions for similar conditions. Since these illustrations are intended only as guidelines for preliminary planning purposes, either set of any differing dimensions can be used.

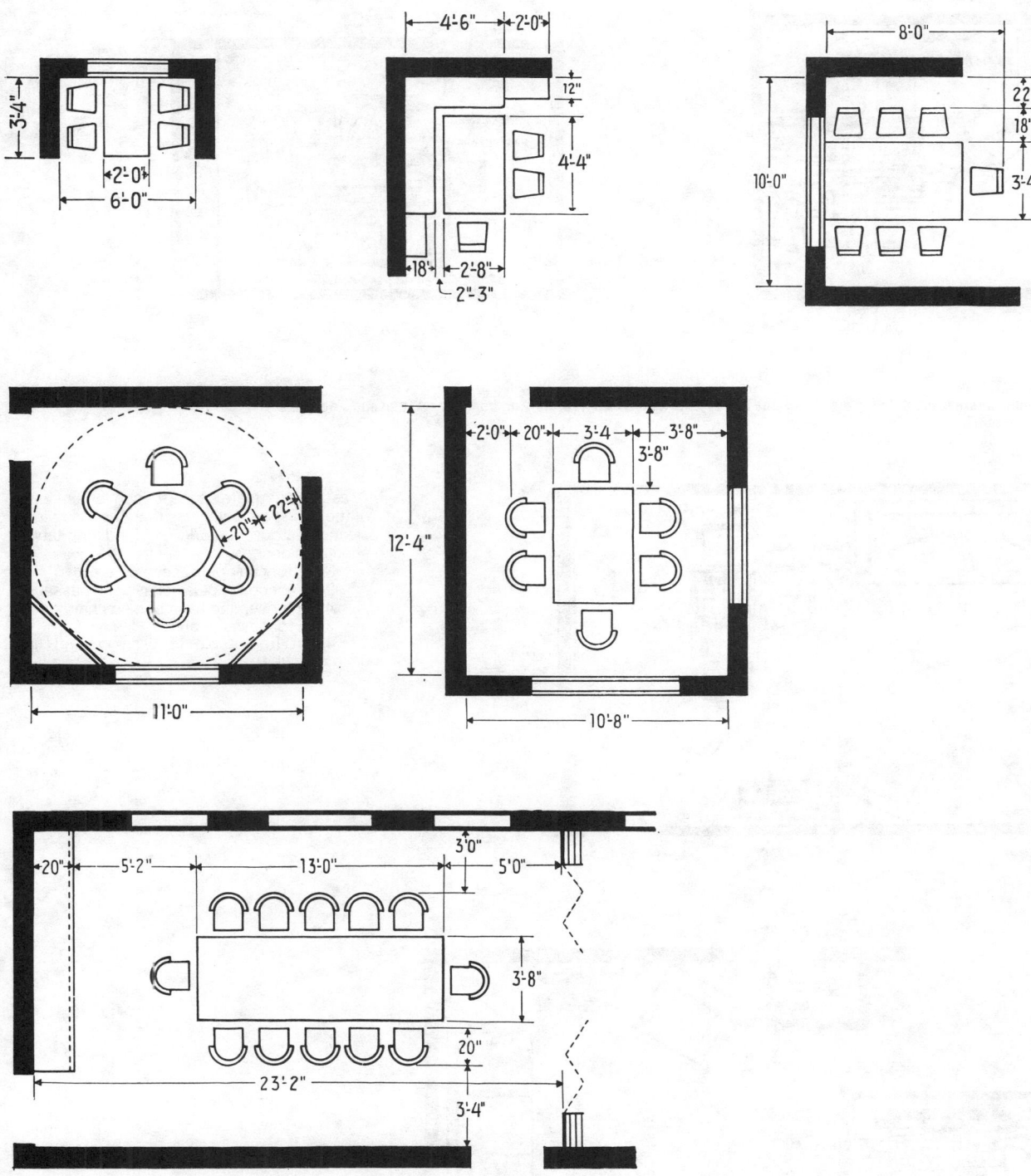

Fig. 9

DINING ROOMS
Furniture Clearances

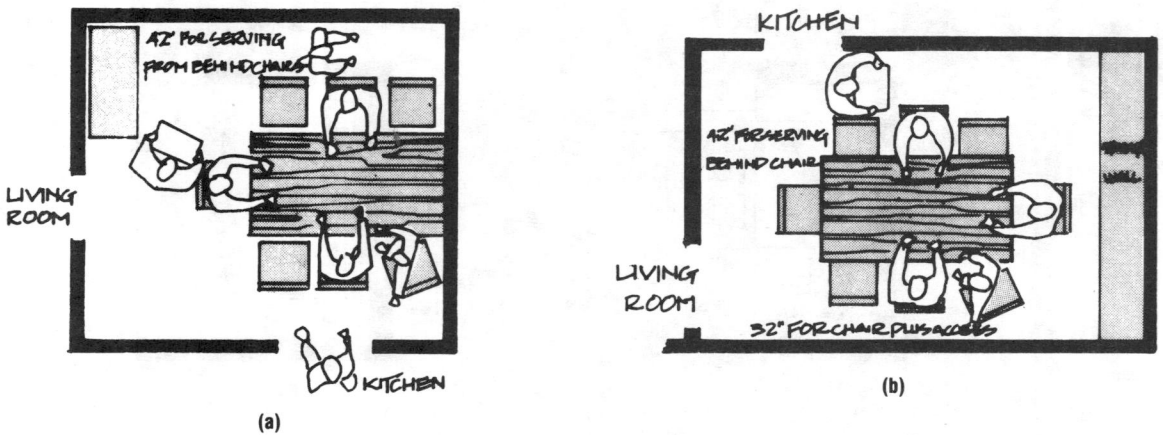

Fig. 10 Minimum clearances for dining areas. *(a)* One end of table against wall. *(b)* Serving from one end and one side of table.

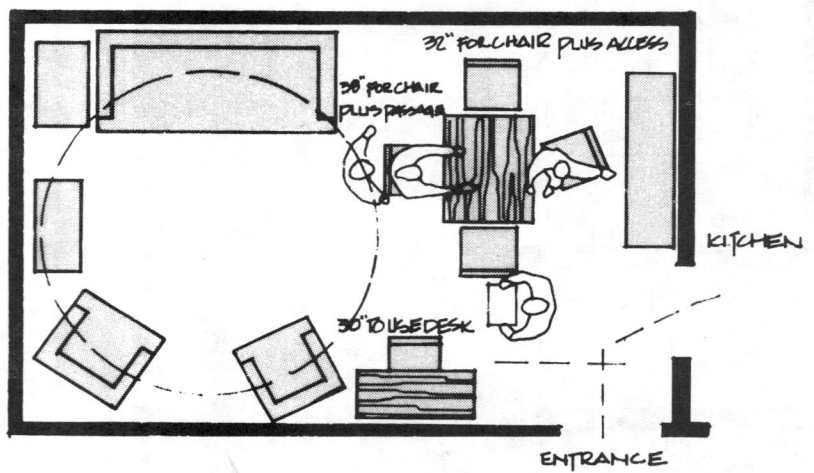

To assure adequate space for convenient use of the dining area, not less than the following clearances from the edge of the dining table should be observed:

    32 in for chair plus access thereto
    38 in for chairs plus access and passage
    42 in for serving from behind chair
    24 in for passage only
    48 in from table to base cabinet (in dining-kitchen)

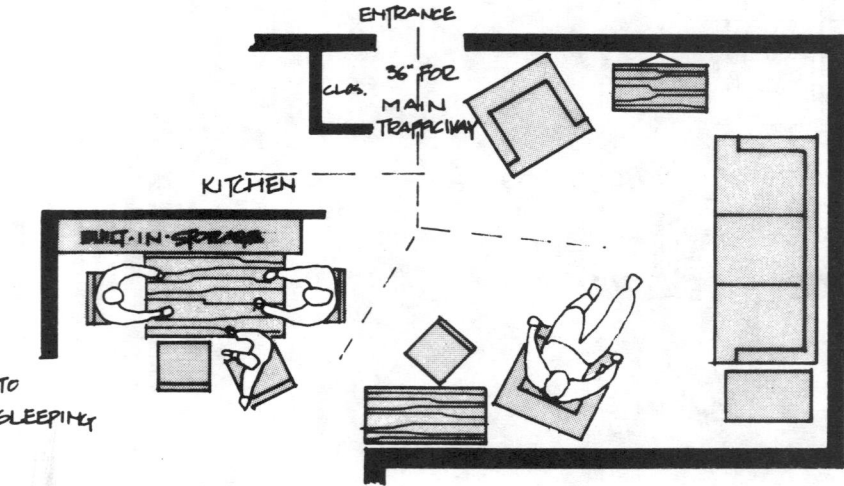

Fig. 11 Minimum clearances and circulation for combined living-dining areas.

ROUND TABLES

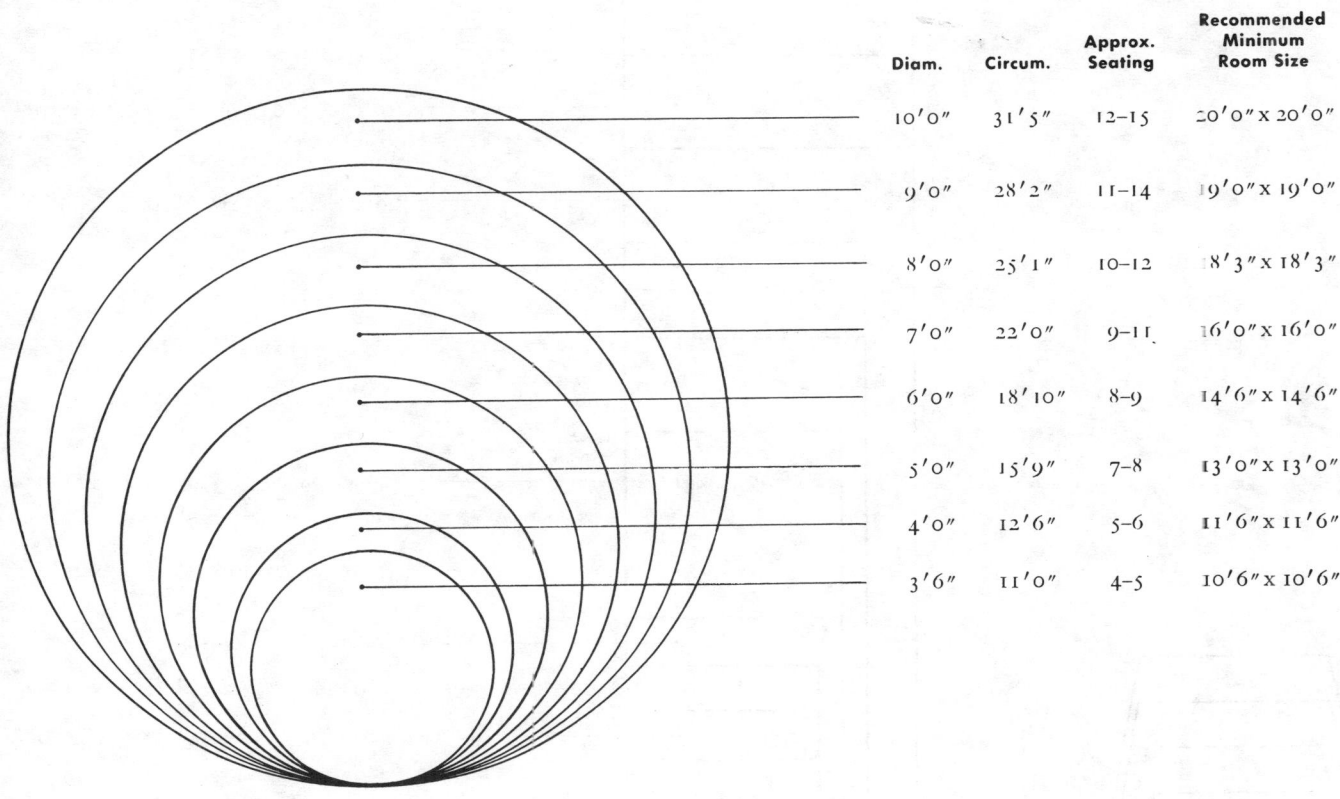

Diam.	Circum.	Approx. Seating	Recommended Minimum Room Size
10'0"	31'5"	12–15	20'0" x 20'0"
9'0"	28'2"	11–14	19'0" x 19'0"
8'0"	25'1"	10–12	18'3" x 18'3"
7'0"	22'0"	9–11	16'0" x 16'0"
6'0"	18'10"	8–9	14'6" x 14'6"
5'0"	15'9"	7–8	13'0" x 13'0"
4'0"	12'6"	5–6	11'6" x 11'6"
3'6"	11'0"	4–5	10'6" x 10'6"

SQUARE TABLES

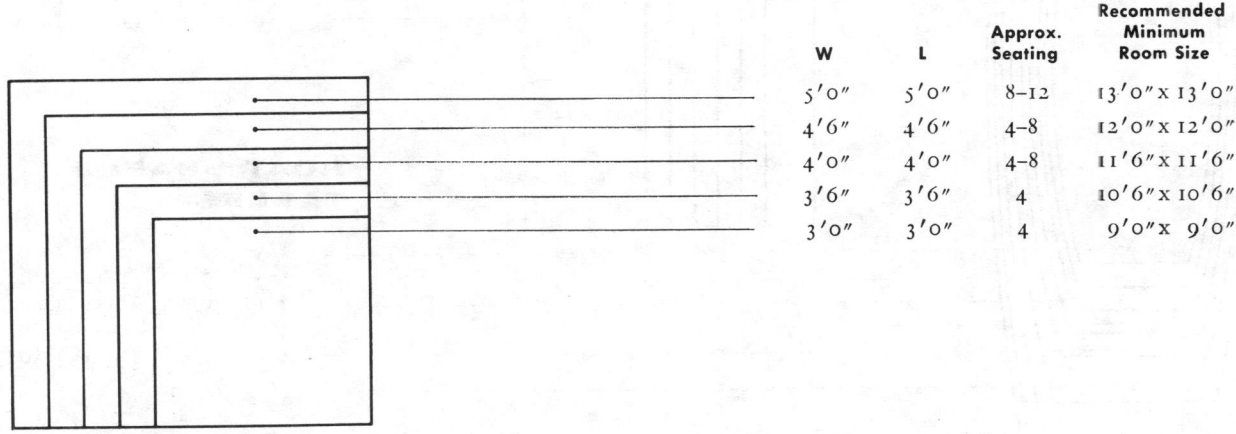

W	L	Approx. Seating	Recommended Minimum Room Size
5'0"	5'0"	8–12	13'0" x 13'0"
4'6"	4'6"	4–8	12'0" x 12'0"
4'0"	4'0"	4–8	11'6" x 11'6"
3'6"	3'6"	4	10'6" x 10'6"
3'0"	3'0"	4	9'0" x 9'0"

Fig. 12 Seating capacities for round, square, rectangular, and boat-shaped tables of various sizes and the recommended minimum room sizes to accommodate each.

DINING ROOMS
Dining Tables and Room Sizes

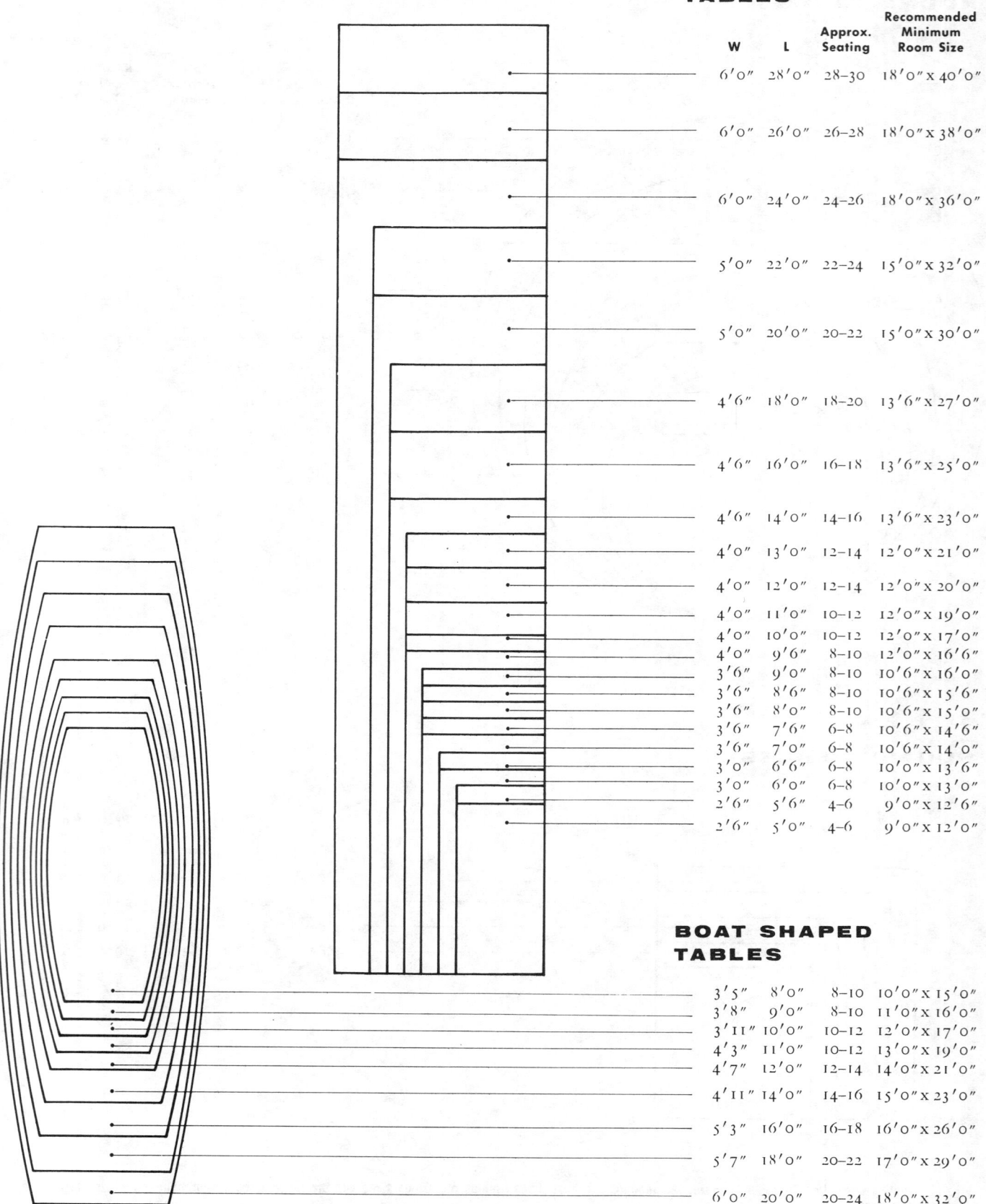

RECTANGULAR TABLES

W	L	Approx. Seating	Recommended Minimum Room Size
6'0"	28'0"	28–30	18'0" x 40'0"
6'0"	26'0"	26–28	18'0" x 38'0"
6'0"	24'0"	24–26	18'0" x 36'0"
5'0"	22'0"	22–24	15'0" x 32'0"
5'0"	20'0"	20–22	15'0" x 30'0"
4'6"	18'0"	18–20	13'6" x 27'0"
4'6"	16'0"	16–18	13'6" x 25'0"
4'6"	14'0"	14–16	13'6" x 23'0"
4'0"	13'0"	12–14	12'0" x 21'0"
4'0"	12'0"	12–14	12'0" x 20'0"
4'0"	11'0"	10–12	12'0" x 19'0"
4'0"	10'0"	10–12	12'0" x 17'0"
4'0"	9'6"	8–10	12'0" x 16'6"
3'6"	9'0"	8–10	10'6" x 16'0"
3'6"	8'6"	8–10	10'6" x 15'6"
3'6"	8'0"	8–10	10'6" x 15'0"
3'6"	7'6"	6–8	10'6" x 14'6"
3'6"	7'0"	6–8	10'6" x 14'0"
3'0"	6'6"	6–8	10'0" x 13'6"
3'0"	6'0"	6–8	10'0" x 13'0"
2'6"	5'6"	4–6	9'0" x 12'6"
2'6"	5'0"	4–6	9'0" x 12'0"

BOAT SHAPED TABLES

W	L	Approx. Seating	Recommended Minimum Room Size
3'5"	8'0"	8–10	10'0" x 15'0"
3'8"	9'0"	8–10	11'0" x 16'0"
3'11"	10'0"	10–12	12'0" x 17'0"
4'3"	11'0"	10–12	13'0" x 19'0"
4'7"	12'0"	12–14	14'0" x 21'0"
4'11"	14'0"	14–16	15'0" x 23'0"
5'3"	16'0"	16–18	16'0" x 26'0"
5'7"	18'0"	20–22	17'0" x 29'0"
6'0"	20'0"	20–24	18'0" x 32'0"

Fig. 12 *(Continued)*

Most of the clearances and bedroom sizes shown here are minimum and intended primarily for preliminary planning purposes. Some building codes permit rooms of even smaller sizes, while rooms in many private homes and luxury apartments are much larger. Moreover, in the final analysis lifestyle, the size and scale of furniture, the activities to be accommodated, and barrier-free design are all factors that should be taken into account during the design process.

Ideally, the recommended minimum bedroom size should be 10'0" x 12"0" exclusive of closets, while the recommended minimum size for a larger bedroom or master bedroom should be 12'0" x 16'0" exclusive of closets.

A larger proportion of the bedroom floor area is occupied by furniture than is the case with any other room; windows and doors account for a large percentage of the wall and partition space. These two factors complicate the planning of bedrooms, especially when the rooms are small.

Because of the room layout, some bedrooms with smaller areas better meet the needs than larger ones. The location of doors, windows, and closets must be properly planned to allow the best placement of the bed and other furniture.

Privacy, both visual and sound, are desirable for the bedroom. Children's bedrooms should be located away from the living room, because conversation in the living room prevents the children from sleeping. Closets should be used between all bedrooms wherever possible.

Each child needs a space that is his or her own to develop a sense of responsibility and a respect for the property rights of others. The ideal plan would provide a bedroom for each child, but since this is not always possible, there should be a bed for each.

The minimum room width shall be determined by the space required for the bed, activity space, and any furniture facing the bed. Widths less than 9'0" will usually require extra area to accommodate comparable furniture.

Aside from sleeping, the bedroom is the center of dressing and undressing activities. An interrelationship exists between dressing, storage of clothes, and the bedroom.

Inevitably, in a small apartment, it is not only economical but necessary to plan the use of the bedroom for more than one activity. It is essential to incorporate in the bedroom other functions such as relaxation, work, or entertainment.

A master bedroom should accommodate at least one double bed 4'6" x 6'6" or two single beds 3'3" x 6'6" each, one crib 2'4" x 1'5" if necessary, one dresser 3'6" x 1'10", one chest of drawers 2'6" x 1'10", one or two chairs 1'6" x 1'6" each, two night tables, and possibly a small desk or table 1'6" x 3'0". Figures 1 to 3 illustrate three configurations and the furniture clearances and room sizes required.

Ample storage is essential. Each bedroom requires at least one clothes closet. For master bedrooms, at least five linear feet of closet length is needed. For secondary bedrooms, at least three linear feet is needed. Clothes closets require a clear depth of two feet.

Each bedroom shall have at least one closet that meets or exceeds the following standards:
1. Depth: 2 feet clear
2. Length (for primary bedroom): 5 linear feet clear
3. Height:
   a. At least 5'4" clear hanging space
   b. Lowest shelf shall not be over 6'2" above the floor of room
4. One shelf and rod with at least 12 inches clear space above shelf
5. At least one-half the closet floor shall be level and not more than 12 inches above floor of adjacent room

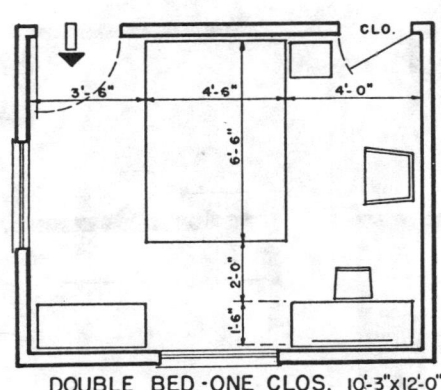

DOUBLE BED - ONE CLOS. 10'-3"x12'-0"

Fig. 1

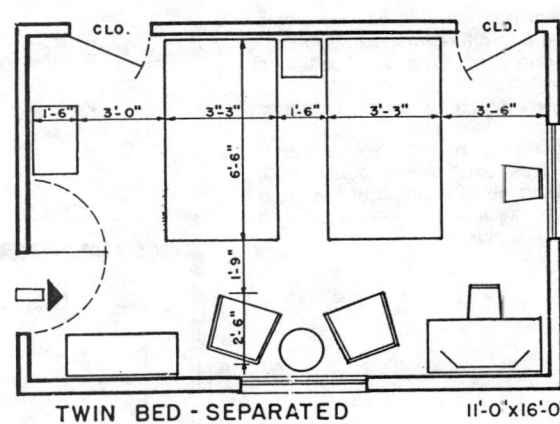

TWIN BED - SEPARATED   11'-0"x16'-0"

Fig. 2

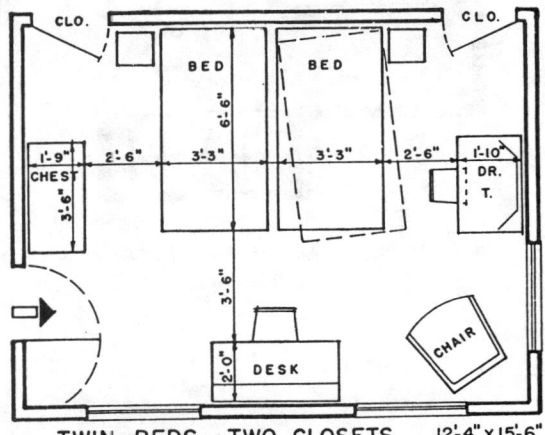

TWIN BEDS - TWO CLOSETS   12'-4"x15'-6"

Fig. 3

BEDROOMS

Furniture Clearances and Arrangements

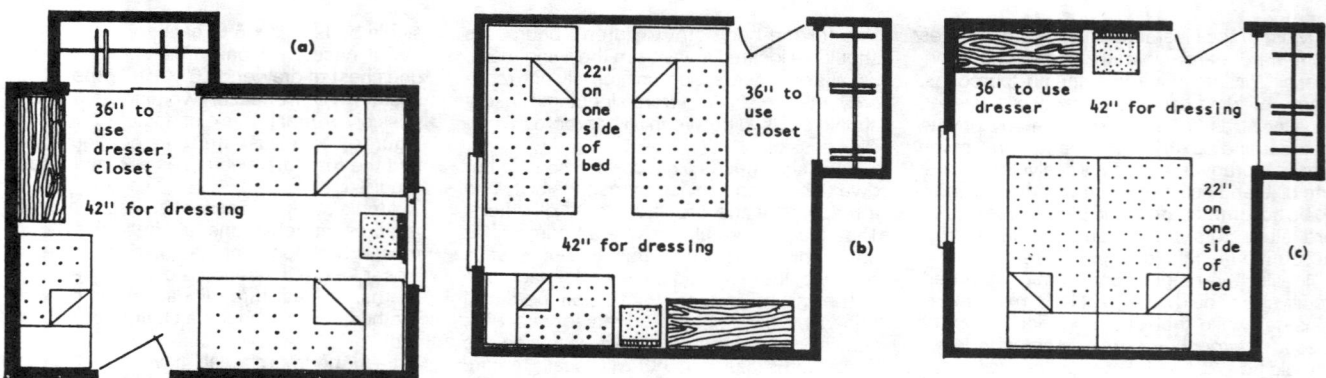

Fig. 4 *(a)*, *(b)* Primary bedroom; *(c)* primary bedroom without crib.

FURNITURE CLEARANCES

To assure adequate space for convenient use of furniture in the bedroom, not less than the following clearances should be observed (Figs. 4 and 5):

42 in at one side or foot of bed for dressing

6 in between side of bed and side of dresser or chest

FURNITURE ARRANGEMENTS

The location of doors and windows should permit alternate furniture arrangements.

36 inches in front of dresser, closet, and chest of drawers

24 in for major circulation path (door to closet, etc.)

22 in on one side of bed for circulation

12 in on least used side of double bed. The least-used side of a single or twin bed can be placed against the wall except in bedrooms for the elderly.

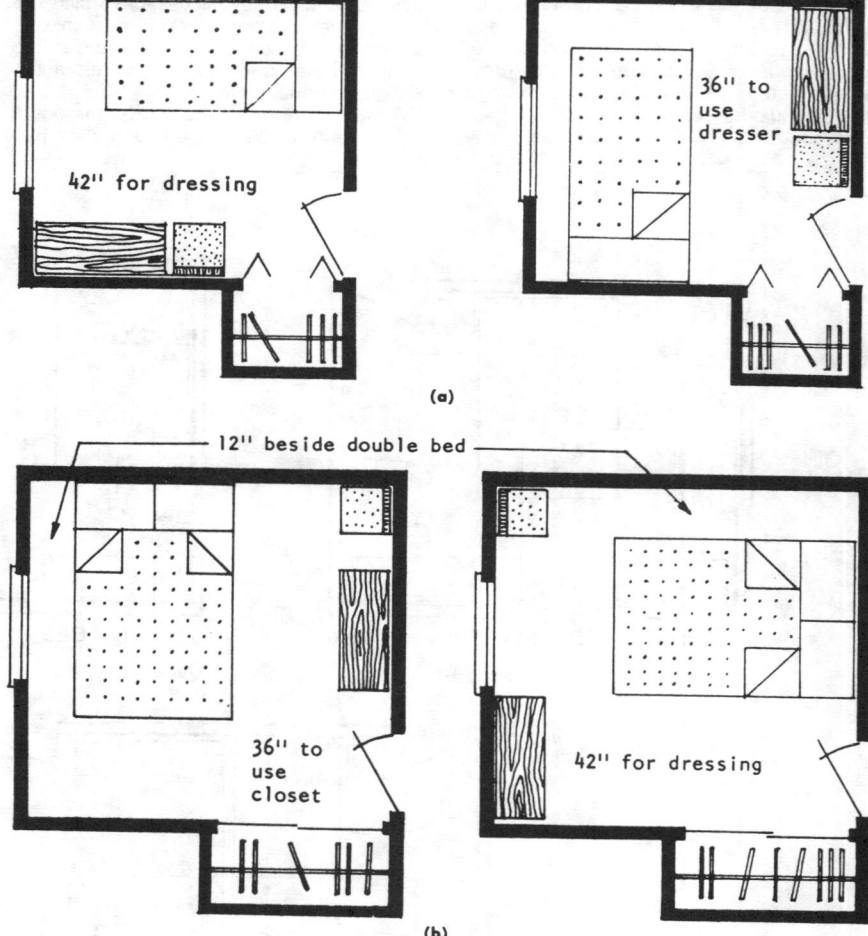

Fig. 5 *(a)* Single-occupancy bedroom; *(b)* double-occupancy bedroom.

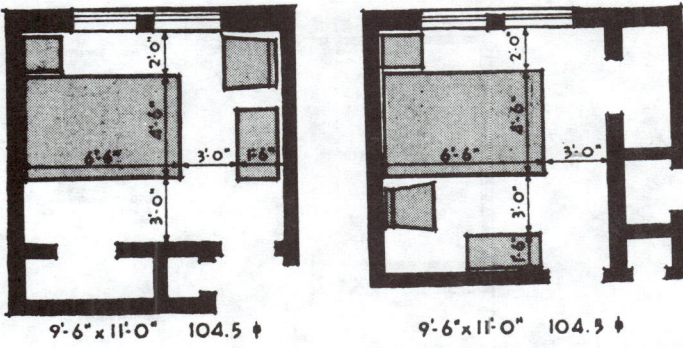

9'-6" x 11'-0" 104.5 ♦   9'-6"x 11'-0" 104.5 ♦

Fig. 6 Although the recommended minimum size for a secondary bedroom is 10'0" x 12'0", these diagrams indicate how a double bed, night table, chair, and dresser can be accommodated in a room only 9'6" x 11'0".

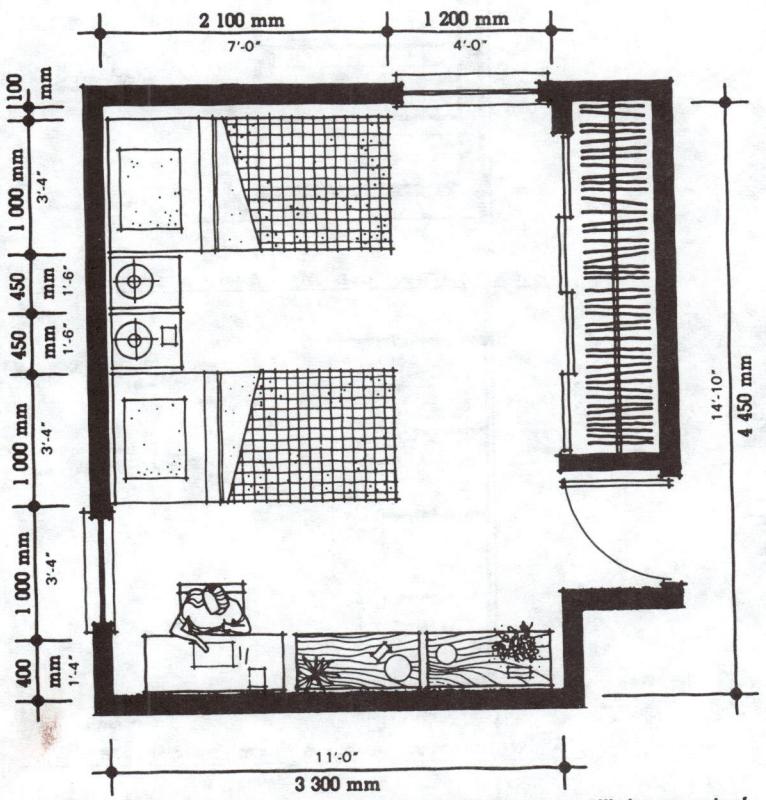

Fig. 7 Double occupancy bedroom. Net area: 14.7 m² (160 ft²). The most likely occupants of this type of bedroom are adults, school-age children of the same sex, children of different sexes who are less than 9 years old, and preschoolers.

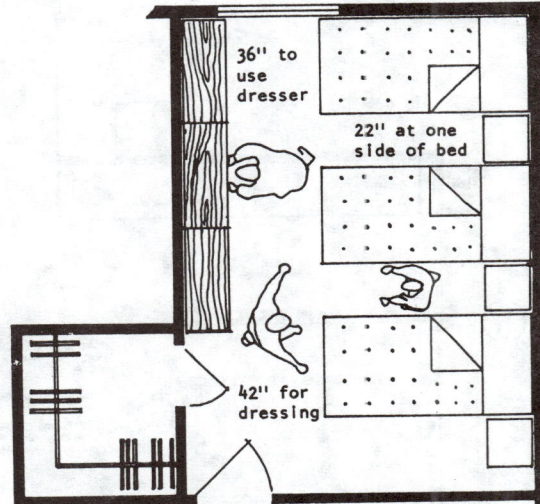

36" to use dresser

22" at one side of bed

42" for dressing

Fig. 8 Occupancy of a bedroom by more than two persons is not recommended. In cases where budgetary and/or space limitations offer no alternative, however, a dormitory arrangement may be necessary. The U.S. Department of Housing and Urban Development recommends the arrangement illustrated in this diagram.

BEDROOMS
Built-In Storage Details

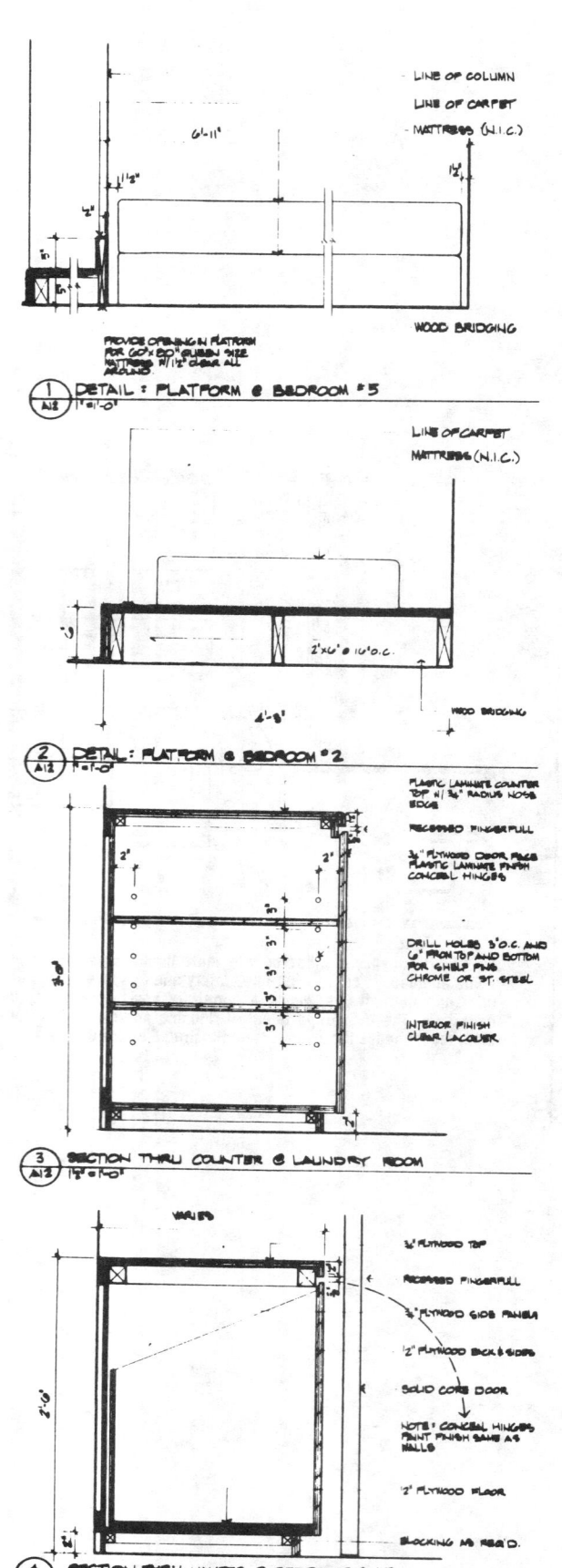

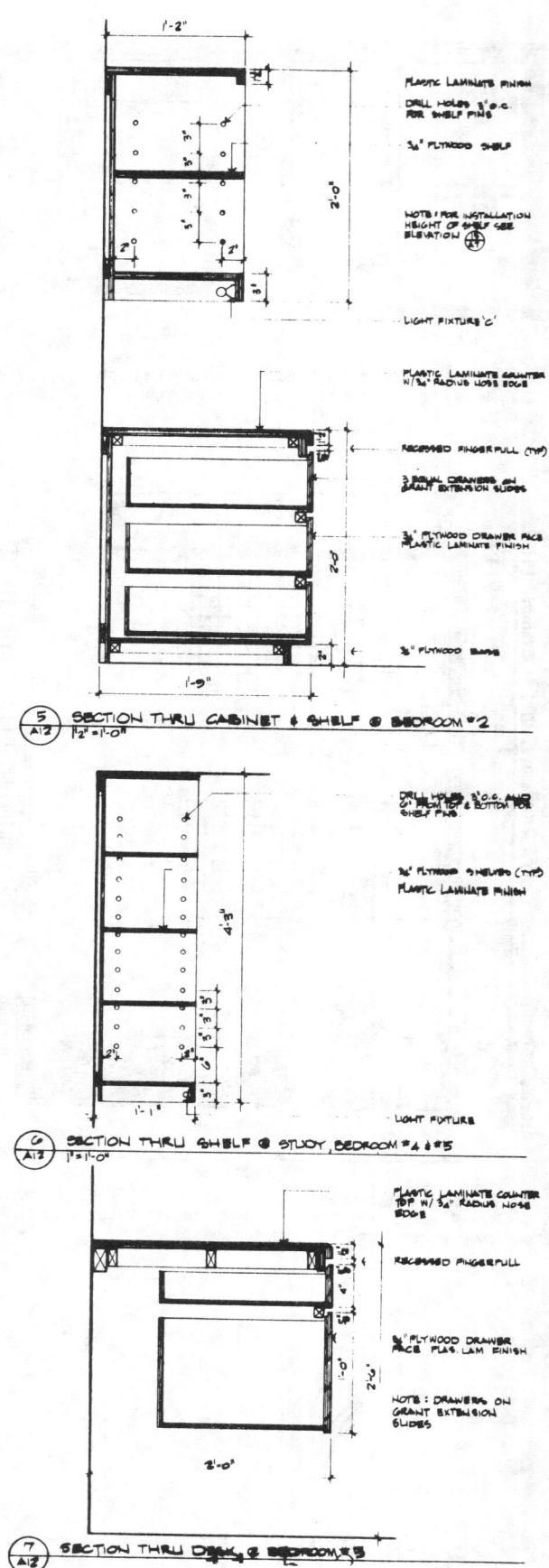

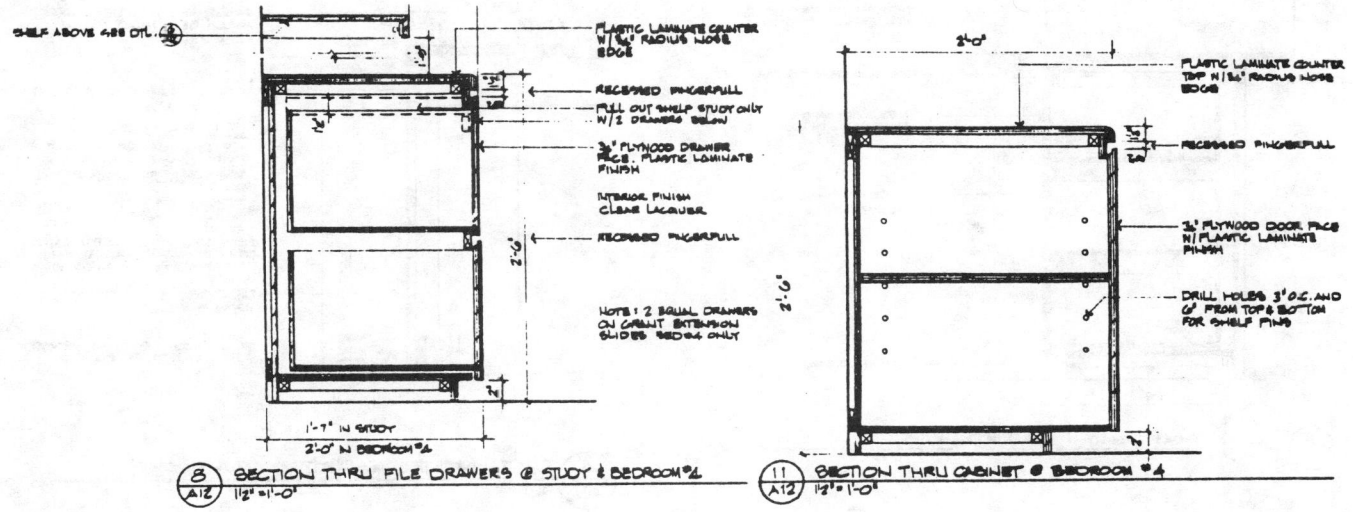

SHELF ABOVE -SEE DTL.

PLASTIC LAMINATE COUNTER W/ ¾" RADIUS NOSE EDGE

RECESSED FINGERPULL

PULL OUT SHELF STUDY ONLY W/2 DRAWERS BELOW

¾" PLYWOOD DRAWER FACE. PLASTIC LAMINATE FINISH

INTERIOR FINISH CLEAR LACQUER

RECESSED FINGERPULL

NOTE: 2 EQUAL DRAWERS ON GRANT EXTENSION SLIDES BEDRM ONLY

1'-7" IN STUDY
2'-0" IN BEDROOM #4

8 / A12 SECTION THRU FILE DRAWERS @ STUDY & BEDROOM #1
1½" = 1'-0"

2'-0"

PLASTIC LAMINATE COUNTER TOP W/ ¾" RADIUS NOSE EDGE

RECESSED FINGERPULL

¾" PLYWOOD DOOR FACE W/ PLASTIC LAMINATE FINISH

DRILL HOLES 3" O.C. AND 6" FROM TOP & BOTTOM FOR SHELF PINS

11 / A12 SECTION THRU CABINET @ BEDROOM #4
1½" = 1'-0"

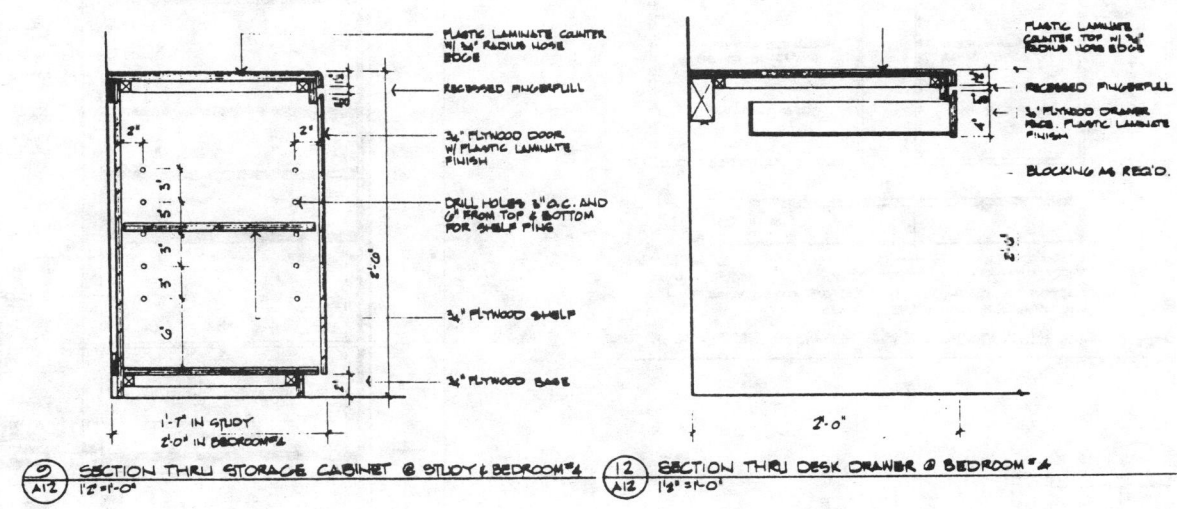

PLASTIC LAMINATE COUNTER W/ ¾" RADIUS NOSE EDGE

RECESSED FINGERPULL

¾" PLYWOOD DOOR W/ PLASTIC LAMINATE FINISH

DRILL HOLES ½" O.C. AND 6" FROM TOP & BOTTOM FOR SHELF PINS

¾" PLYWOOD SHELF

¾" PLYWOOD BASE

1'-7" IN STUDY
2'-0" IN BEDROOM #4

9 / A12 SECTION THRU STORAGE CABINET @ STUDY & BEDROOM #4
1½" = 1'-0"

PLASTIC LAMINATE COUNTER TOP W/ ¾" RADIUS NOSE EDGE

RECESSED FINGERPULL

¾" PLYWOOD DRAWER FACE. PLASTIC LAMINATE FINISH

BLOCKING AS REQ'D.

2'-0"

12 / A12 SECTION THRU DESK DRAWER @ BEDROOM #4
1½" = 1'-0"

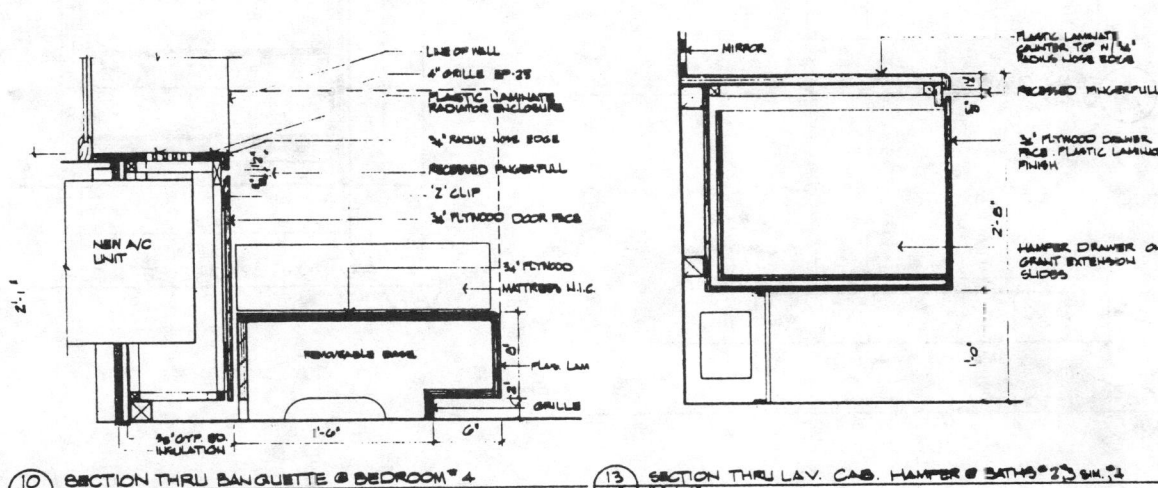

LINE OF WALL

6" GRILLE SP-25

PLASTIC LAMINATE RADIATOR ENCLOSURE

¾" RADIUS NOSE EDGE

RECESSED FINGERPULL

'Z' CLIP

¾" PLYWOOD DOOR FACE

¾" PLYWOOD

MATTRESS N.I.C.

NEW A/C UNIT

REMOVEABLE BASE

PLAS. LAM.

GRILLE

½" GYP. BD. INSULATION

1'-6"   6"

10 / A12 SECTION THRU BANQUETTE @ BEDROOM #4
1½" = 1'-0"

MIRROR

PLASTIC LAMINATE COUNTER TOP W/ ¾" RADIUS NOSE EDGE

RECESSED FINGERPULL

¾" PLYWOOD DRAWER FACE. PLASTIC LAMINATE FINISH

HAMPER DRAWER ON GRANT EXTENSION SLIDES

13 / A12 SECTION THRU LAV. CAB. HAMPER @ BATHS #2 & BM. #4
1½" = 1'-0"

BEDROOMS
Built-In Furniture

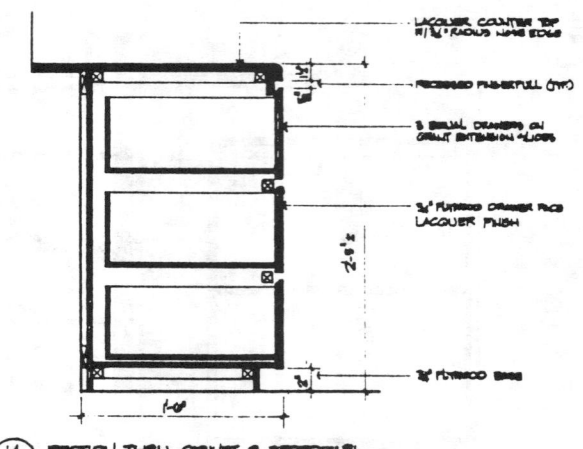

LACQUER COUNTER TOP W/ 1/4" RADIUS NOSE EDGE

RECESSED FINGERPULL (TYP)

3 EQUAL DRAWERS ON GRANT EXTENSION SLIDES

3/4" PLYWOOD DRAWER FACE LACQUER FINISH

3/4" PLYWOOD BASE

2'-0 1/2"

1'-0"

14 — SECTION THRU CABINET @ BEDROOM #1
A12   1 1/2" = 1'-0"

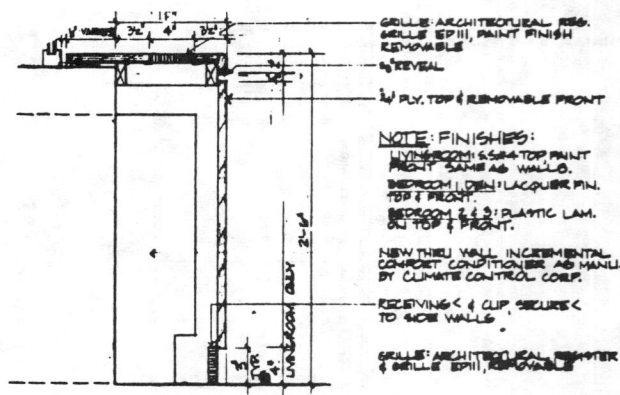

GRILLE: ARCHITECTURAL REG. GRILLE EP III, PAINT FINISH REMOVABLE

1/2" REVEAL

3/4" PLY. TOP & REMOVABLE FRONT

NOTE: FINISHES:
LIVING ROOM: SEMI-GLOSS TOP PAINT FRONT SAME AS WALLS.
BEDROOM 1, DEN: LACQUER FIN. TOP & FRONT.
BEDROOM 2 & 3: PLASTIC LAM. ON TOP & FRONT.

NEW THRU WALL INCREMENTAL COMFORT CONDITIONER AS MANU. BY CLIMATE CONTROL CORP.

RECEIVING < & CLIP SECURE < TO SIDE WALLS.

GRILLE: ARCHITECTURAL REGISTER & GRILLE EP III, REMOVABLE

3 — SECTION THRU RADIATOR COVER, TYP.
A7   1 1/2" = 1'-0"

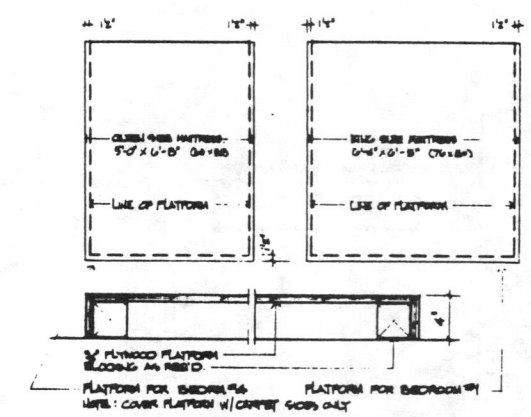

QUEEN SIZE MATTRESS 5'-0" x 6'-8" (60 x 80)

KING SIZE MATTRESS 6'-4" x 6'-8" (76 x 80)

LINE OF PLATFORM   LINE OF PLATFORM

3/4" PLYWOOD PLATFORM BLOCKING AS REQ'D.

PLATFORM FOR BEDROOM #4   PLATFORM FOR BEDROOM #1
NOTE: COVER PLATFORM W/ CARPET SIDES ONLY

15 — PLAN & ELEVATION OF PLATFORMS @ BED #1 & #4
A12   1 1/2" = 1'-0"

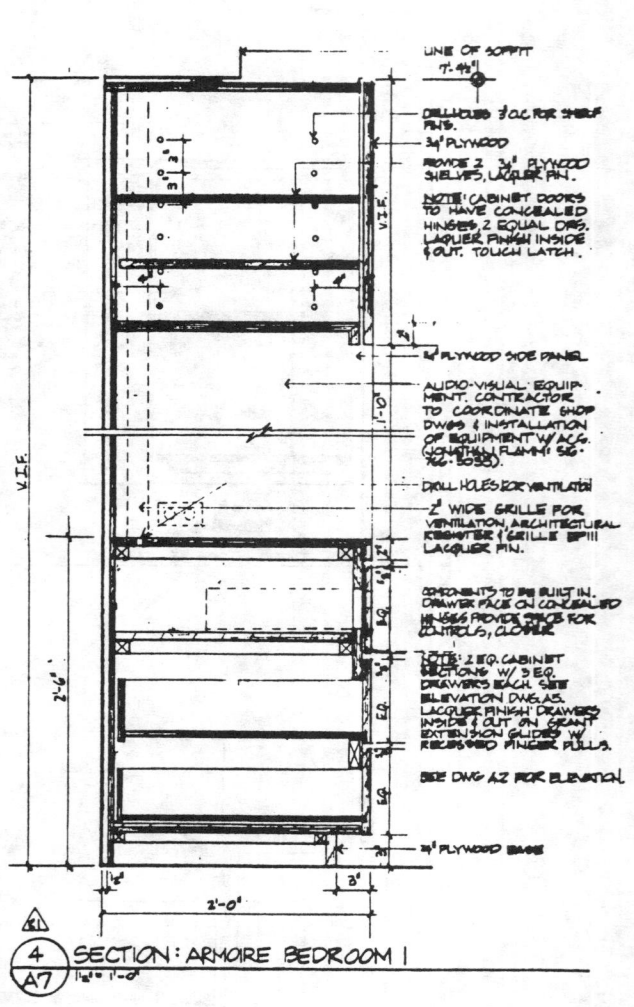

LINE OF SOFFIT 7'-4 1/2"

DRILL HOLES 3/4" O.C. FOR SHELF PINS.

3/4" PLYWOOD

PROVIDE 2 3/4" PLYWOOD SHELVES, LACQUER FIN.

NOTE: CABINET DOORS TO HAVE CONCEALED HINGES, 2 EQUAL DRS. LACQUER FINISH INSIDE & OUT. TOUCH LATCH.

3/4" PLYWOOD SIDE PANEL

AUDIO-VISUAL EQUIPMENT: CONTRACTOR TO COORDINATE SHOP DWGS & INSTALLATION OF EQUIPMENT W/ A.C.G. (JONATHAN FLAMM) SIG. 962-5035).

DRILL HOLES FOR VENTILATION

2" WIDE GRILLE FOR VENTILATION, ARCHITECTURAL REGISTER & GRILLE EP III LACQUER FIN.

COMPONENTS TO BE BUILT IN. DRAWER FACE ON CONCEALED HINGES PROVIDE SPACE FOR CONTROLS, CLOSED.

NOTE: 2 EQ. CABINET SECTIONS W/ 3 EQ. DRAWERS EACH. SEE ELEVATION DWG. AS LACQUER FINISH. DRAWERS INSIDE & OUT ON GRANT EXTENSION SLIDES W/ RECESSED FINGER PULLS.

SEE DWG. A2 FOR ELEVATION

3/4" PLYWOOD BASE

2'-0"

4 — SECTION: ARMOIRE BEDROOM 1
A7   1 1/2" = 1'-0"

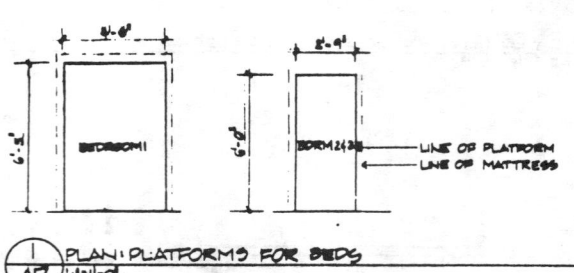

4'-0"   2'-9"

BEDROOM 1   BEDRM 2 & 3

LINE OF PLATFORM
LINE OF MATTRESS

6'-8"   6'-8"

1 — PLAN: PLATFORMS FOR BEDS
A7   1/4" = 1'-0"

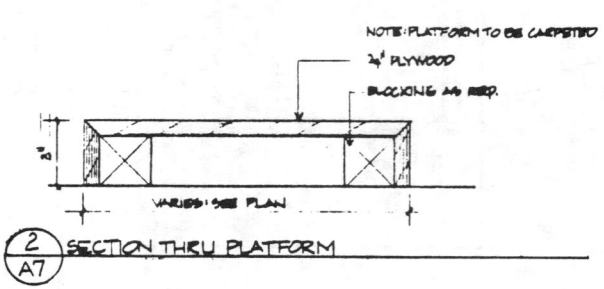

NOTE: PLATFORM TO BE CARPETED

3/4" PLYWOOD

BLOCKING AS REQ.

VARIES: SEE PLAN

2 — SECTION THRU PLATFORM
A7

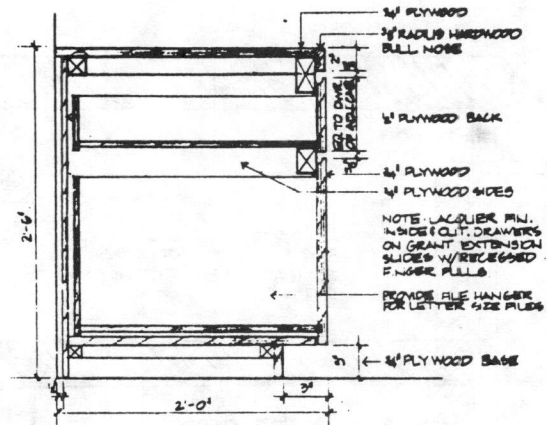

- 3/4" PLYWOOD
- 3/8" RADIUS HARDWOOD BULL NOSE
- 1/4" PLYWOOD BACK
- 3/4" PLYWOOD
- 1/4" PLYWOOD SIDES
- NOTE: LACQUER FIN. INSIDE & OUT. DRAWERS ON GRANT EXTENSION SLIDES W/ RECESSED FINGER PULLS
- PROVIDE FILE HANGER FOR LETTER SIZE FILES
- 3/4" PLYWOOD BASE

⑤ / A6   SECTION THRU FILE CAB @ BEDROOM 1
1 1/2" = 1'-0"

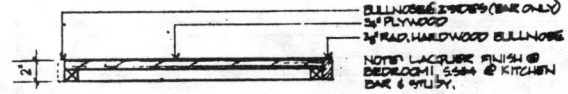

- BULLNOSE 3 SIDES (BAR ONLY)
- 3/4" PLYWOOD
- 3/8" RAD. HARDWOOD BULLNOSE
- NOTE: LACQUER FINISH @ BEDROOM 1, SSB4 @ KITCHEN BAR & STUDY.

⑦ / A7   SECTION THRU DESK TOP - BDRM 1, BAR, STUDY
1 1/2" = 1'-0"

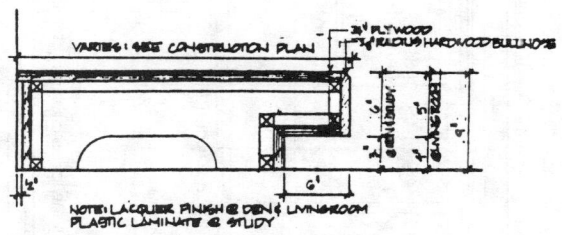

- VARIES: SEE CONSTRUCTION PLAN
- 3/4" PLYWOOD
- 3/8" RADIUS HARDWOOD BULLNOSE
- NOTE: LACQUER FINISH @ DEN & LIVINGROOM PLASTIC LAMINATE @ STUDY

⑧ / A7   SECTION THRU BANQUETTE - TYPICAL
1 1/2" = 1'-0"

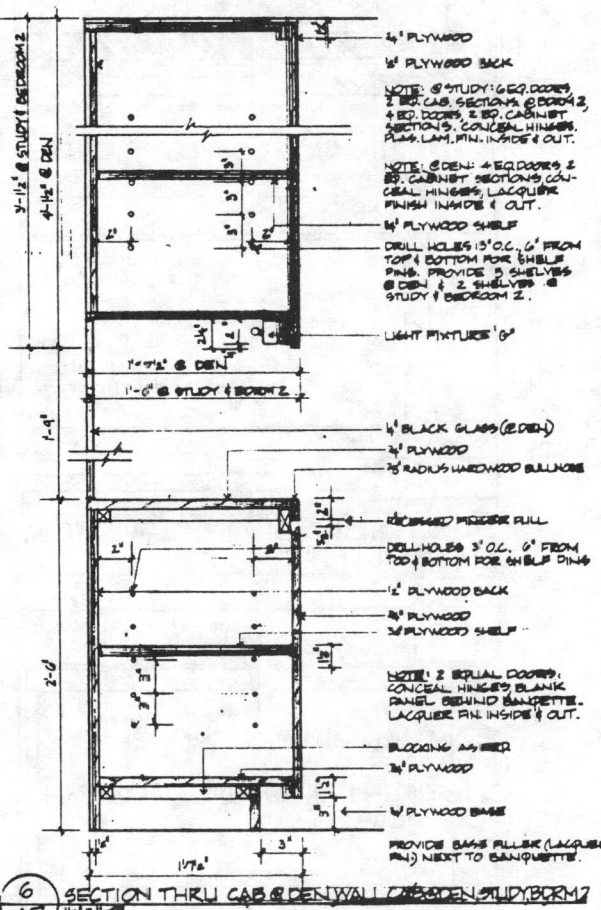

- 3/4" PLYWOOD
- 1/4" PLYWOOD BACK
- NOTE: @ STUDY: 6 EQ. DOORS, 2 EQ. CAB. SECTIONS @ BDRM 2, 4 EQ. DOORS, 2 EQ. CABINET SECTIONS. CONCEAL HINGES. PLAS. LAM. FIN. INSIDE & OUT.
- NOTE: @ DEN: 4 EQ. DOORS 2 EQ. CABINET SECTIONS CONCEAL HINGES, LACQUER FINISH INSIDE & OUT.
- 3/4" PLYWOOD SHELF
- DRILL HOLES 13" O.C., 6" FROM TOP & BOTTOM FOR SHELF PINS. PROVIDE 5 SHELVES @ DEN & 2 SHELVES @ STUDY & BEDROOM 2.
- LIGHT FIXTURE 'G'
- 1/4" BLACK GLASS (@ DEN)
- 3/4" PLYWOOD
- 3/8" RADIUS HARDWOOD BULLNOSE
- RECESSED FINGER PULL
- DRILL HOLES 3" O.C., 6" FROM TOP & BOTTOM FOR SHELF PINS
- 1/2" PLYWOOD BACK
- 3/4" PLYWOOD
- 3/4" PLYWOOD SHELF
- NOTE: 2 EQUAL DOORS, CONCEAL HINGES. BLANK PANEL BEHIND BANQUETTE. LACQUER FIN. INSIDE & OUT.
- BLOCKING AS REQ'D
- 3/4" PLYWOOD
- 3/4" PLYWOOD BASE
- PROVIDE BASE FILLER (LACQUER FIN.) NEXT TO BANQUETTE.

⑥ / A7   SECTION THRU CAB @ DEN WALL @ BDRM @ DEN, STUDY, BDRM 2
1 1/2" = 1'-0"

BEDROOMS

Built-In Wardrobe Details

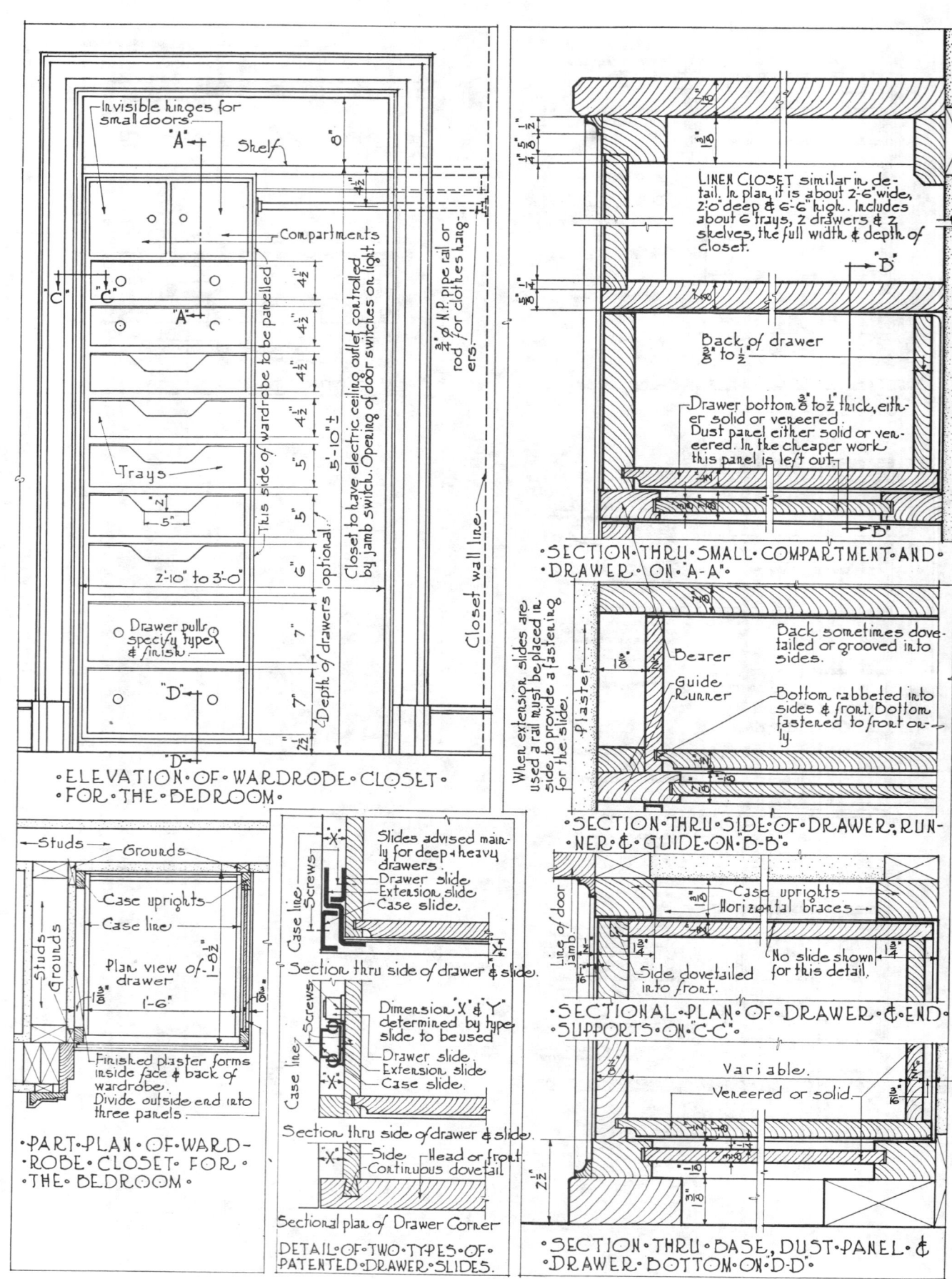

Invisible hinges for small doors.

"A"

Shelf

Compartments

"C" "C"

"A"

Trays

Drawer pulls specify type & finish

"D"

This side of wardrobe to be panelled.

Closet to have electric ceiling outlet controlled by jamb switch. Opening of door switches on light.

$\frac{3}{4}$"⌀ N.P. pipe rail or rod for clothes hangers.

Closet wall line

Depth of drawers optional.

·ELEVATION·OF·WARDROBE·CLOSET· ·FOR·THE·BEDROOM·

LINEN CLOSET similar in detail. In plan, it is about 2'-6" wide, 2'-0" deep & 6'-6" high. Includes about 6 trays, 2 drawers & 2 shelves, the full width & depth of closet.

Back of drawer $\frac{3}{8}$ to $\frac{1}{2}$

Drawer bottom $\frac{3}{8}$ to $\frac{1}{2}$ thick, either solid or veneered. Dust panel either solid or veneered. In the cheaper work this panel is left out.

·SECTION·THRU·SMALL·COMPARTMENT·AND· ·DRAWER·ON·"A-A"·

When extension slides are used a rail must be placed in side, to provide a fastening for the slide.

Plaster

Bearer

Guide Runner

Back sometimes dovetailed or grooved into sides.

Bottom rabbeted into sides & front. Bottom fastened to front only.

·SECTION·THRU·SIDE·OF·DRAWER;·RUN-· ·NER·&·GUIDE·ON·"B-B"·

Studs
Grounds

Case uprights

Case line

Plan view of drawer

Finished plaster forms inside face & back of wardrobe.
Divide outside end into three panels.

·PART·PLAN·OF·WARD-· ·ROBE·CLOSET·FOR· ·THE·BEDROOM·

Slides advised mainly for deep & heavy drawers.
-Drawer slide
-Extension slide
-Case slide.

Case line
Screws

Section thru side of drawer & slide.

Dimension "X" & "Y" determined by type slide to be used.
-Drawer slide
-Extension slide
-Case slide.

Case line
Screws

"X"

Section thru side of drawer & slide.

"X" -Side -Head or front
Continuous dovetail

Sectional plan of Drawer Corner

·DETAIL·OF·TWO·TYPES·OF· ·PATENTED·DRAWER·SLIDES.

Line of door jamb

Case uprights
Horizontal braces

No slide shown for this detail.

Side dovetailed into front.

·SECTIONAL·PLAN·OF·DRAWER·&·END· ·SUPPORTS·ON·"C-C"·

Variable.

Veneered or solid.

·SECTION·THRU·BASE,·DUST·PANEL·&· ·DRAWER·BOTTOM·ON·"D-D"·

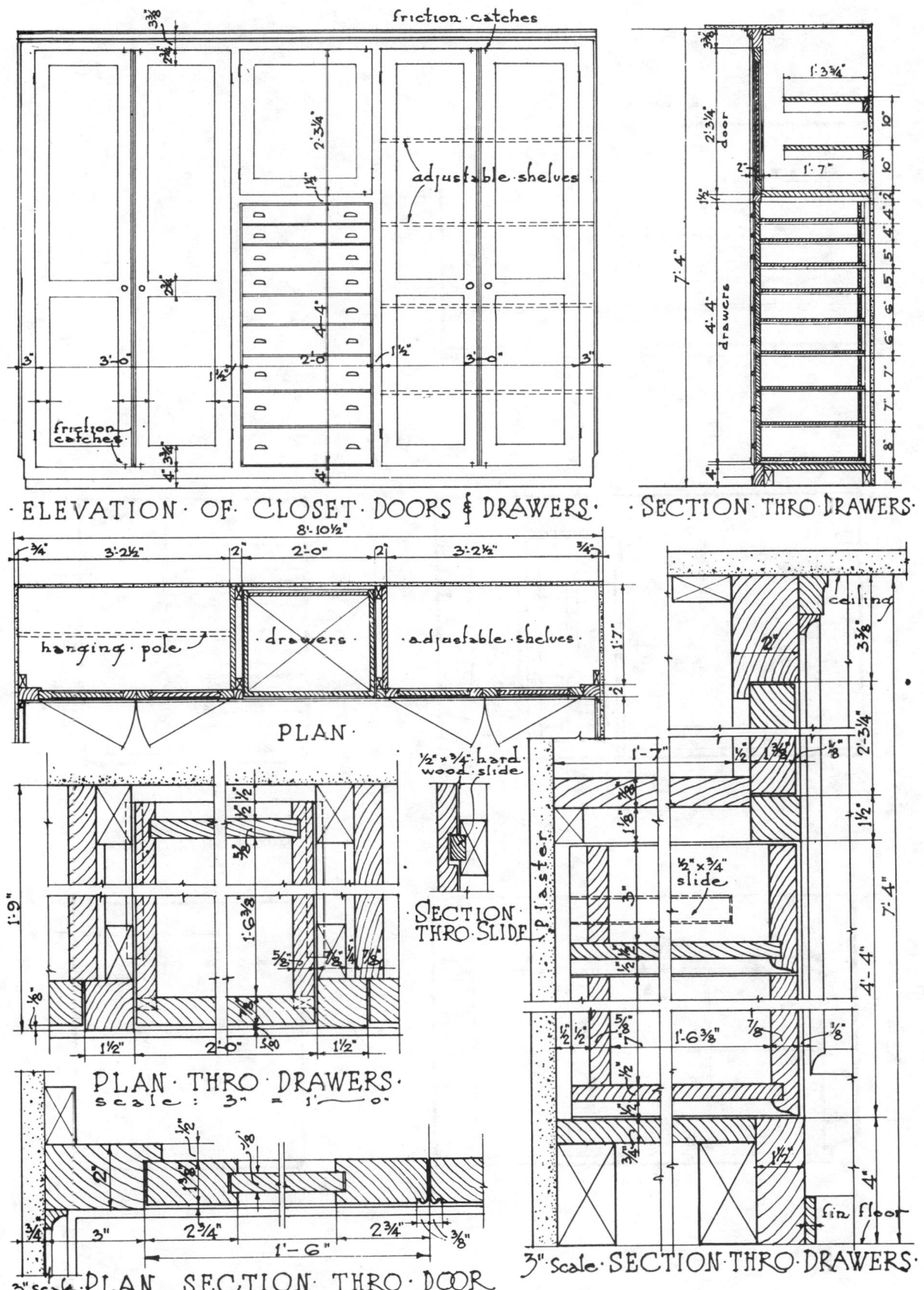

ELEVATION · OF · CLOSET · DOORS § DRAWERS ·

SECTION · THRO · DRAWERS ·

PLAN

PLAN · THRO · DRAWERS ·
scale : 3" = 1' 0"

SECTION THRO · SLIDE ·

3" scale PLAN SECTION THRO · DOOR ·

3" Scale SECTION · THRO · DRAWERS ·

BEDROOMS
Plan and Elevation of Walk-In Closet

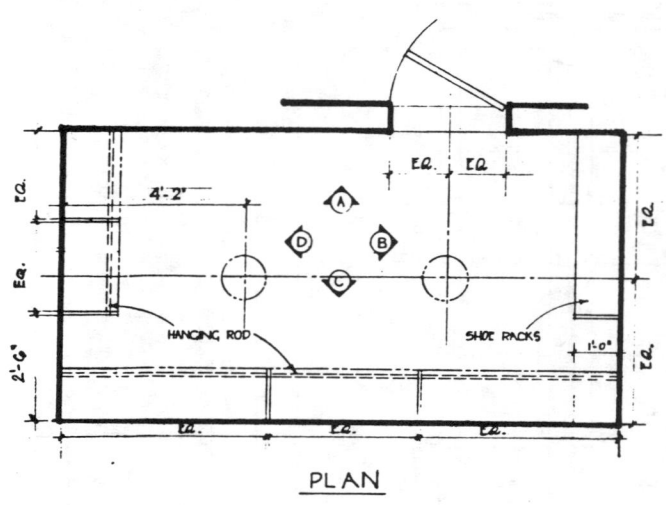

PLAN

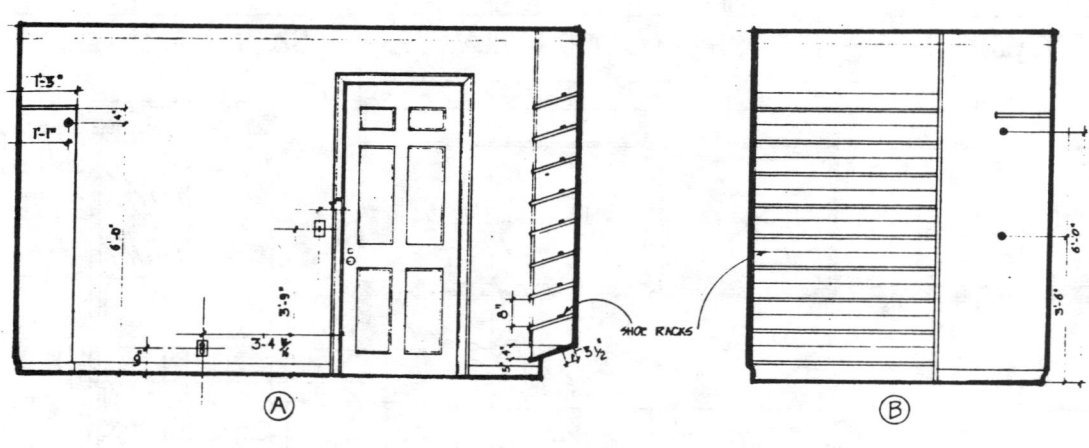

NOTE: ALL HANG'G RODS
TO BE METAL

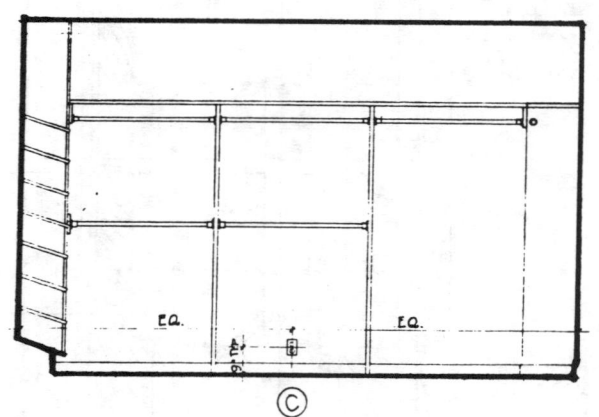

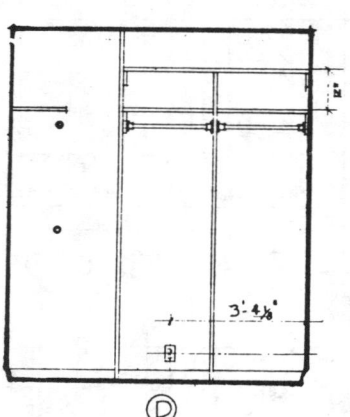

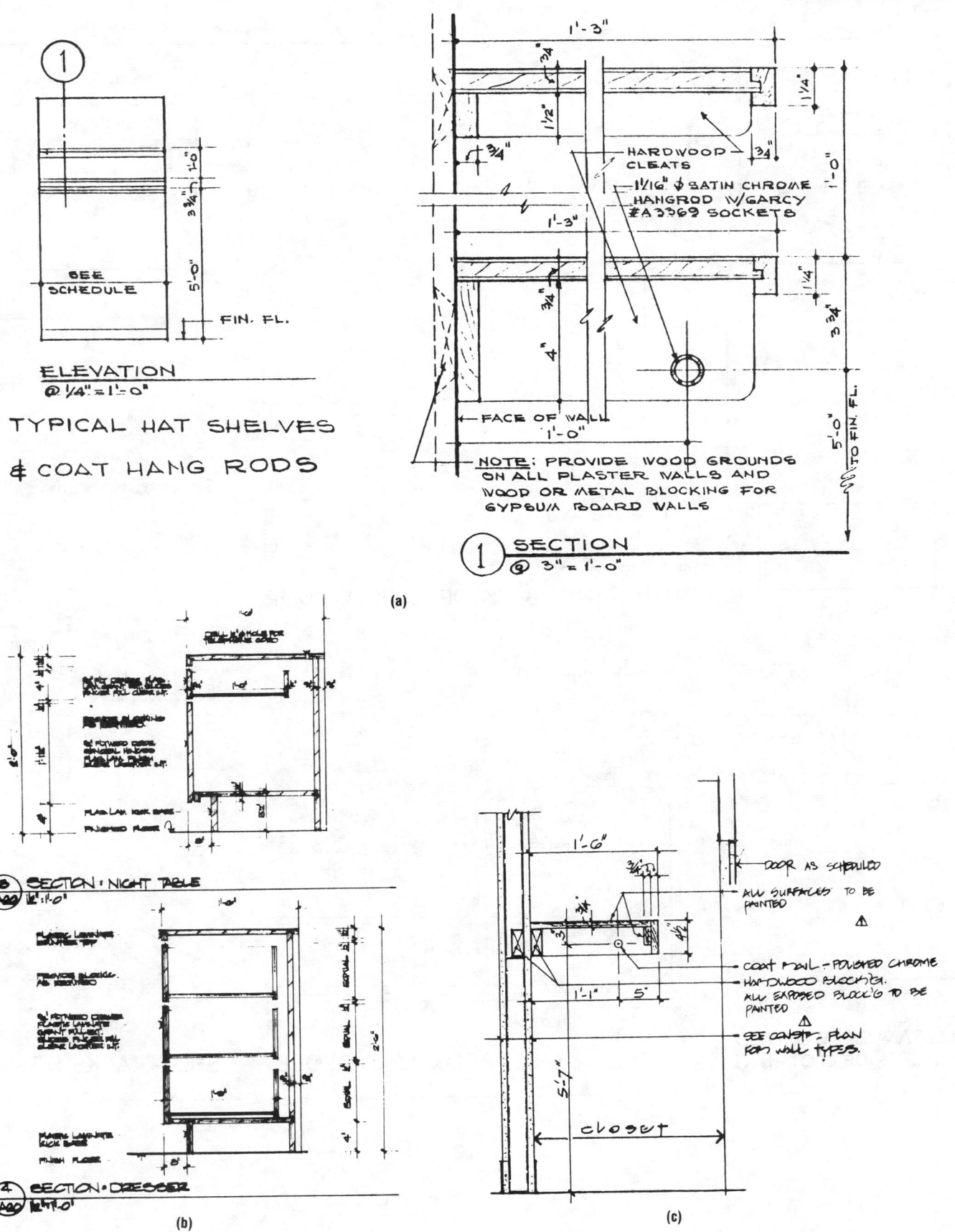

(a)

(b)

(c)

Fig. 9 *(a)* illustrates a typical hat shelf and coat rod, while *(b)* shows relatively typical sections through a night table and a dresser. *(c)* illustrates a typical closet.

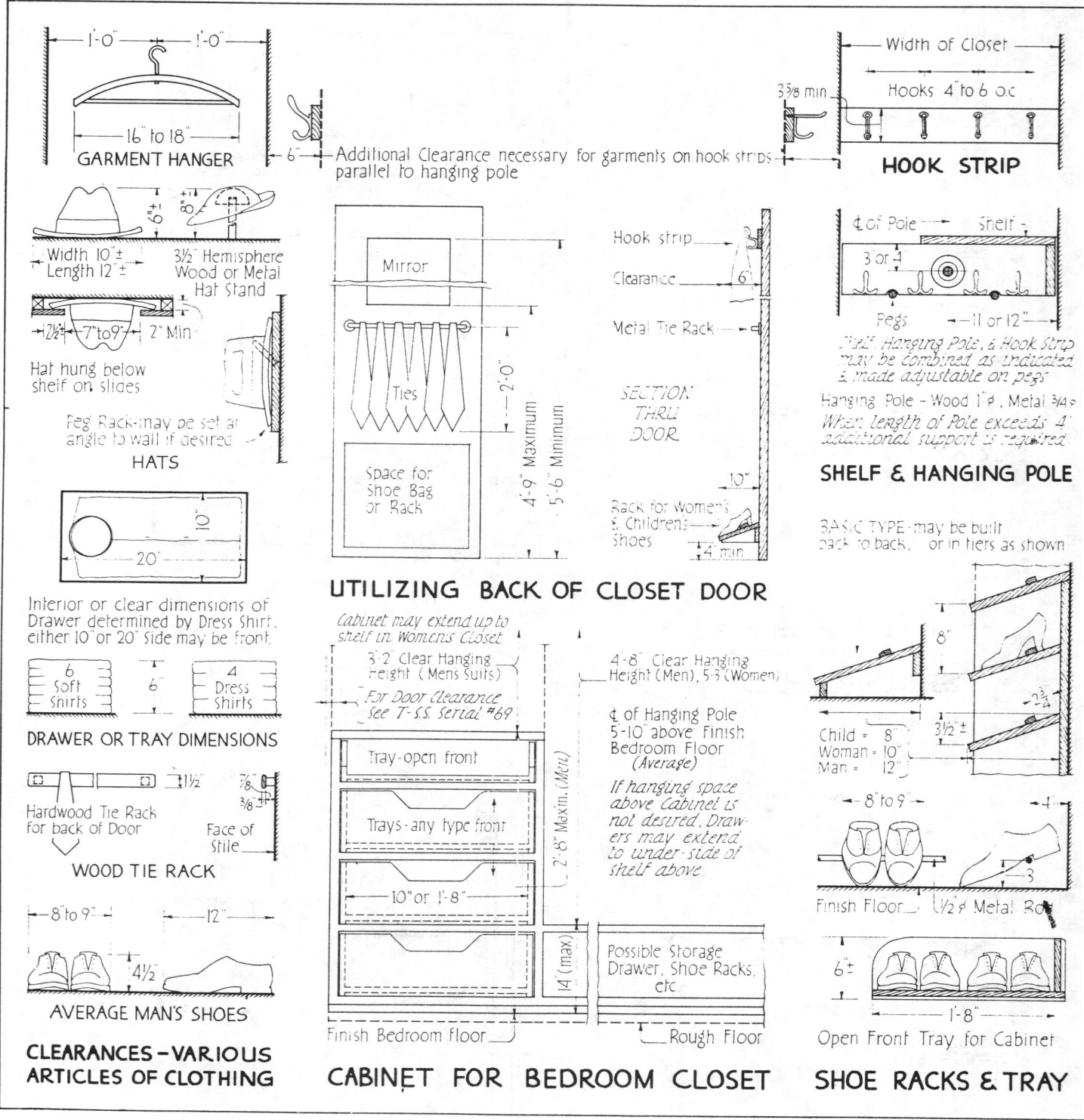

GARMENT HANGER

16" to 18"

1'-0"   1'-0"

Additional Clearance necessary for garments on hook strips parallel to hanging pole

6"

HOOK STRIP

Width of Closet

Hooks 4" to 6" o.c.

3⅝" min

HATS

6"±   8"±

Width 10"±
Length 12"±

3½" Hemisphere
Wood or Metal
Hat Stand

2½"   7"to 9"   2" Min

Hat hung below
shelf on slides

Peg Rack may be set at
angle to wall if desired

Interior or clear dimensions of
Drawer determined by Dress Shirt,
either 10" or 20" Side may be front.

20"   10"

6
Soft
Shirts

6"

4
Dress
Shirts

DRAWER OR TRAY DIMENSIONS

1½"   ⅞"   ⅜"

Hardwood Tie Rack
for back of Door

Face of
Stile

WOOD TIE RACK

8" to 9"   12"

4½"

AVERAGE MAN'S SHOES

CLEARANCES – VARIOUS ARTICLES OF CLOTHING

Mirror

Ties

Space for
Shoe Bag
or Rack

4'-9" Maximum
5'-6" Minimum

2'-0"

UTILIZING BACK OF CLOSET DOOR

Hook strip

Clearance   6"

Metal Tie Rack

SECTION
THRU
DOOR

10"

Rack for Women's
& Children's
Shoes

4" min

Cabinet may extend up to
shelf in Womens Closet

3'-2" Clear Hanging
Height (Mens Suits)

For Door Clearance
see T-S.S. Serial #69

Tray - open front

Trays - any type front

10" or 1'-8"

2'-8" Maximum (Men)

14" (max)

Finish Bedroom floor

4'-8" Clear Hanging
Height (Men), 5'-3" (Women)

¢ of Hanging Pole
5'-10" above Finish
Bedroom Floor
(Average)

If hanging space
above Cabinet is
not desired, Draw-
ers may extend
to under-side of
shelf above

Possible Storage
Drawer, Shoe Racks,
etc

Rough Floor

CABINET FOR BEDROOM CLOSET

¢ of Pole   Shelf

3 or 4

Pegs   11 or 12"

Shelf, Hanging Pole, & Hook Strip
may be combined as indicated
& made adjustable on pegs

Hanging Pole - Wood 1"ø, Metal ¾"ø
When length of Pole exceeds 4'
additional support is required

SHELF & HANGING POLE

BASIC TYPE may be built
back to back, or in tiers as shown

8"

2¾"

Child = 8"
Woman = 10"
Man = 12"

3½"±

8" to 9"

Finish Floor   ½"ø Metal Rod

6"±

1'-8"

Open Front Tray for Cabinet

SHOE RACKS & TRAY

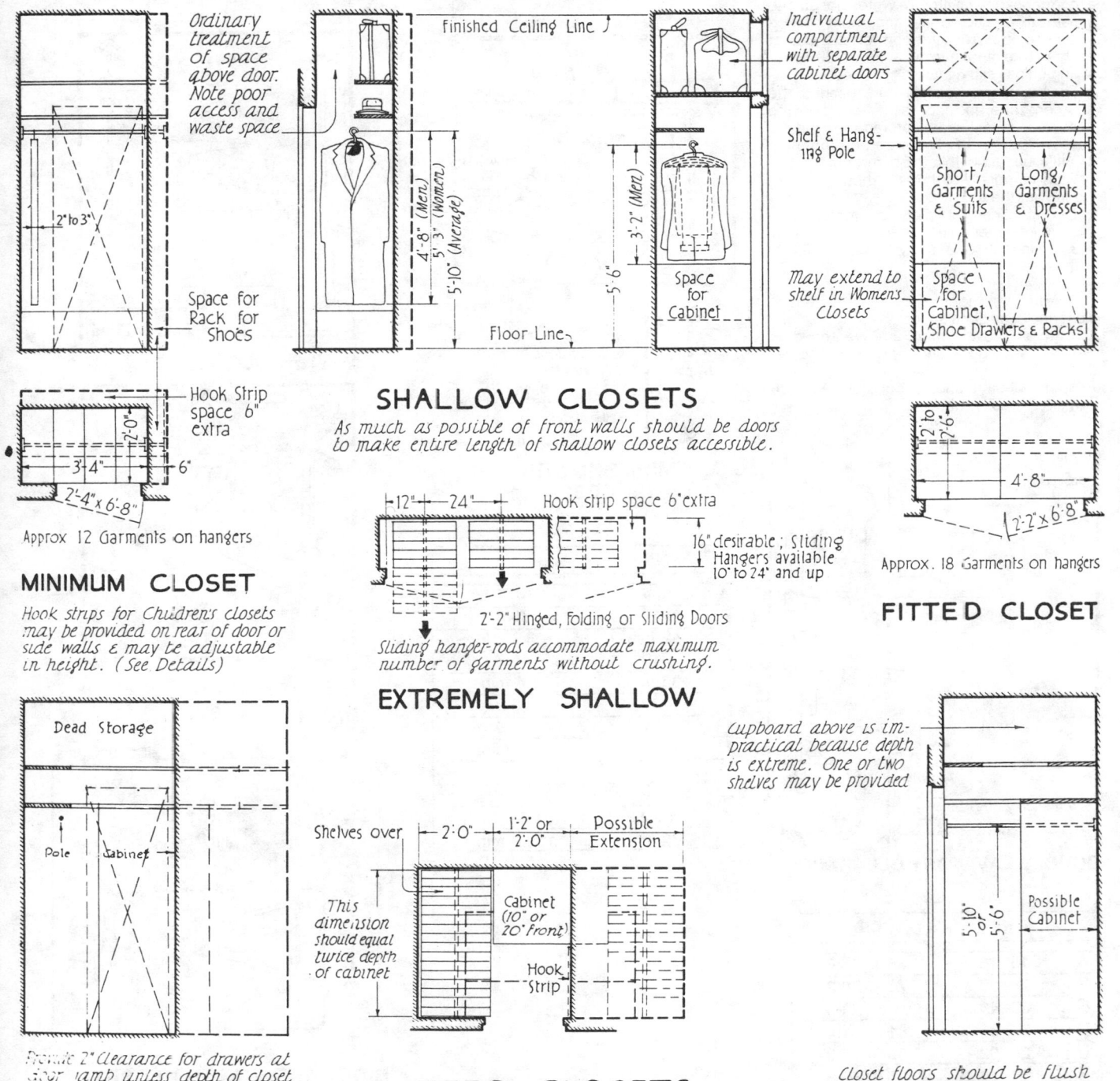

Ordinary treatment of space above door. Note poor access and waste space

2" to 3"

Space for Rack for Shoes

Hook Strip space 6" extra

2'-0"

3' 4"   6"

2'-4" x 6'-8"

Approx 12 Garments on hangers

MINIMUM CLOSET

Hook strips for Children's closets may be provided on rear of door or side walls & may be adjustable in height. (See Details)

Dead Storage

Pole   Cabinet

Provide 2" clearance for drawers at door jamb unless depth of closet permits complete removal

Finished Ceiling Line

4'-8" (Men.)
5'-3" (Women.)
5'-10" (Average)

Floor Line

SHALLOW CLOSETS

As much as possible of front walls should be doors to make entire length of shallow closets accessible.

12" 24"   Hook strip space 6" extra

16" desirable; Sliding Hangers available 10" to 24" and up

2'-2" Hinged, folding or Sliding Doors

Sliding hanger-rods accommodate maximum number of garments without crushing.

EXTREMELY SHALLOW

Shelves over   2'-0"   1'-2" or 2'-0"   Possible Extension

This dimension should equal twice depth of cabinet

Cabinet (10" or 20" front)

Hook Strip

DEEP CLOSETS

Closet lights desirable; controlled preferably by door switch

Individual compartment with separate cabinet doors

Shelf & Hanging Pole

Short Garments & Suits   Long Garments & Dresses

May extend to shelf in Women's Closets

Space for Cabinet, Shoe Drawers & Racks

3'-2" (Men.)

5'-6"

Space for Cabinet

2' to 2'-6"

4'-8"

2'-2" x 6'-8"

Approx. 18 Garments on hangers

FITTED CLOSET

Cupboard above is impractical because depth is extreme. One or two shelves may be provided

5'-10" or 5'-6"

Possible Cabinet

Closet floors should be flush with top of the door saddle.

BATHROOMS
Planning Data and Fixture Arrangements

A bathroom should have enough area to accommodate a lavatory, a water closet, and a bathtub or shower. Arrangement for fixtures should provide for comfortable use of each fixture and permit at least 90° door swing unless sliding doors are used.

The bathroom should be convenient to the bedroom zone, and accessible from the living and work areas. Linen storage should be accessible from the bathroom, but not necessarily located within the bathroom.

Each complete bathroom should be provided with the following:
1. Grab-bar and soap dish at bathtub
2. Toilet paper holder at water closet
3. Soap dish at lavatory (may be integral with lavatory)
4. Towel bar
5. Mirror and medicine cabinet or equivalent enclosed shelf space
6. In all cases where shower head is installed, provide a shower rod or shower door

Each half-bath should be provided with items 2 to 6 listed above.

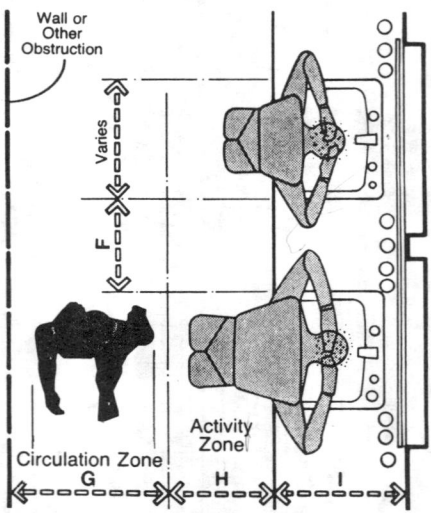

DOUBLE LAVATORY CLEARANCES

	in	cm
A	15–18	38.1–45.7
B	28–30	71.1–76.2
C	37–43	94.0–109.2
D	32–36	81.3–91.4
E	26–32	66.0–81.3
F	14–16	35.6–40.6
G	30	76.2
H	18	45.7
I	21–26	53.3–66.0

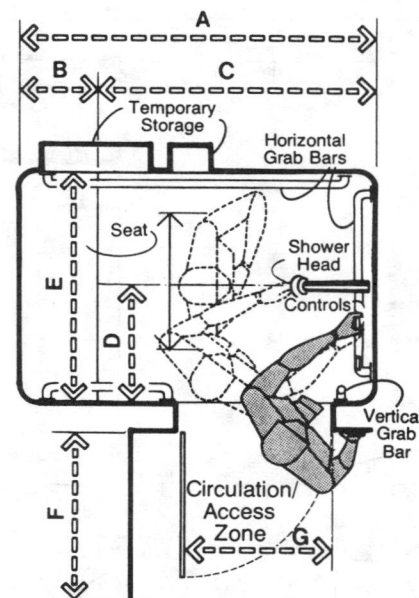

MINIMUM SHOWER CLEARANCES

	in	cm
A	54	137.2
B	12	30.5
C	42 min.	106.7 min.
D	18	45.7
E	36 min.	91.4 min.
F	30	76.2
G	24	61.0
H	12 min.	30.5 min.
I	15	38.1
J	40–48	101.6–121.9
K	40–50	101.6–127.0
L	72 min.	182.9 min.

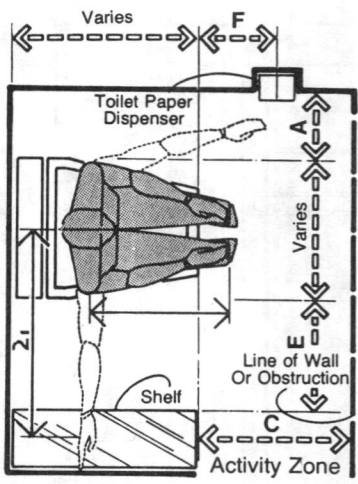

WATER CLOSET

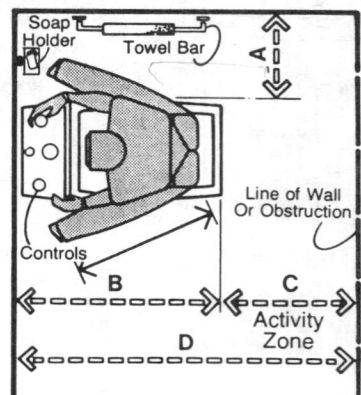

BIDET

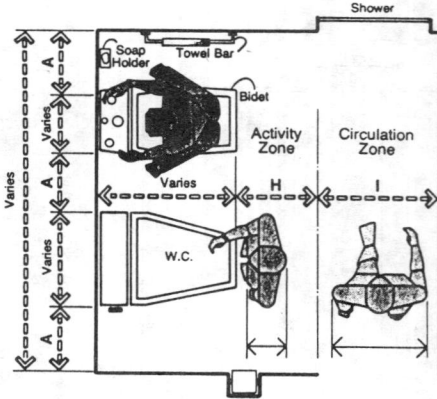

BIDET AND WATER CLOSET

	in	cm
A	12 min.	30.5 min.
B	28 min.	71.1 min.
C	24 min.	61.0 min.
D	52 min.	132.1 min.
E	12–18	30.5–45.7
F	12	30.5
G	40	101.6
H	18	45.7
I	30	76.2

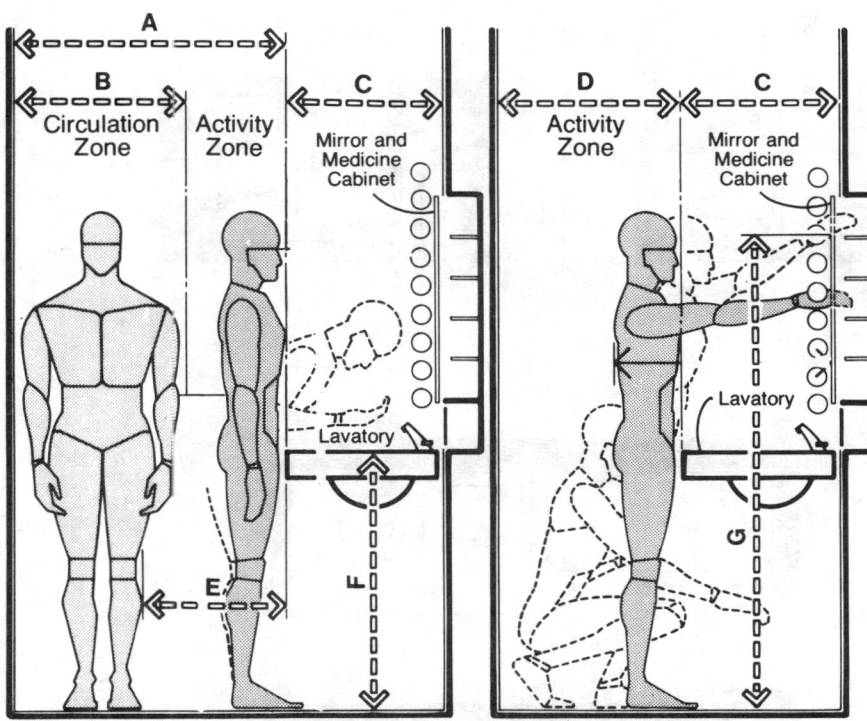

Fig. 1 Lavatory: male anthropometric considerations.

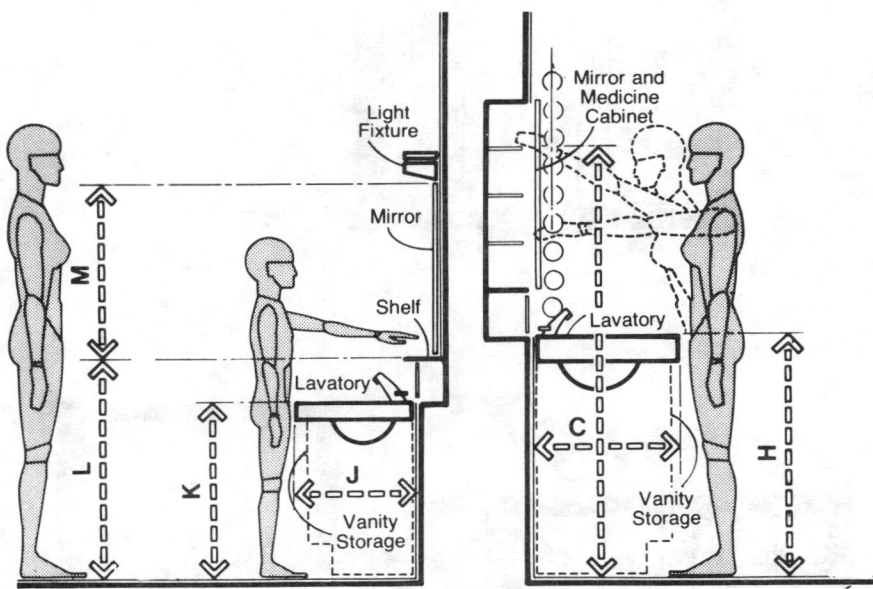

Fig. 2 Lavatory: female and child anthropometric considerations.

Figure 1 deals primarily with some of the more critical male anthropometric considerations. A lavatory height above the floor of 37 to 43 in, or 94 to 109.2 cm, is suggested to accommodate the majority of users. It should be noted, however, that common practice is to locate the lavatory in the neighborhood of 31 in above the floor. In order to establish the location of mirrors above the lavatory, eye height should be taken into consideration.

Figure 2 explores, in much the same manner, the anthropometric considerations related to women and children. Given the great variability in body sizes to be accommodated within a single family, a strong case can be presented for the development of a height adjustment capability for the lavatory. Until that is developed, there is no reason, on custom installations, why the architect or interior designer cannot take anthropometric measurements of the client to ensure proper interface between the user and the lavatory.

	in	cm
A	48	121.9
B	30	76.2
C	19–24	48.3–61.0
D	27 min.	68.6 min.
E	18	45.7
F	37–43	94.0–109.2
G	72 max.	182.9 max.
H	32–36	81.3–91.4
I	69 max.	175.3 max.
J	16–18	40.6–45.7
K	26–32	66.0–81.3
L	32	81.3
M	20–24	50.8–61.0

BATHROOMS
Typical Plans and Fixture Arrangements

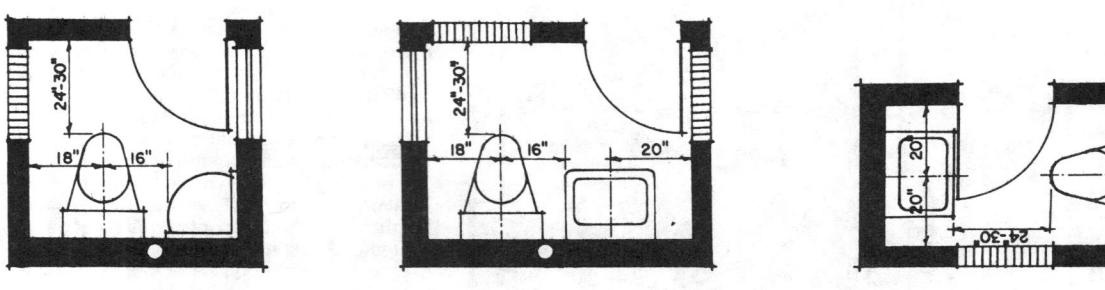

Fig. 3   Two-fixture plans: water closet and washbasin.

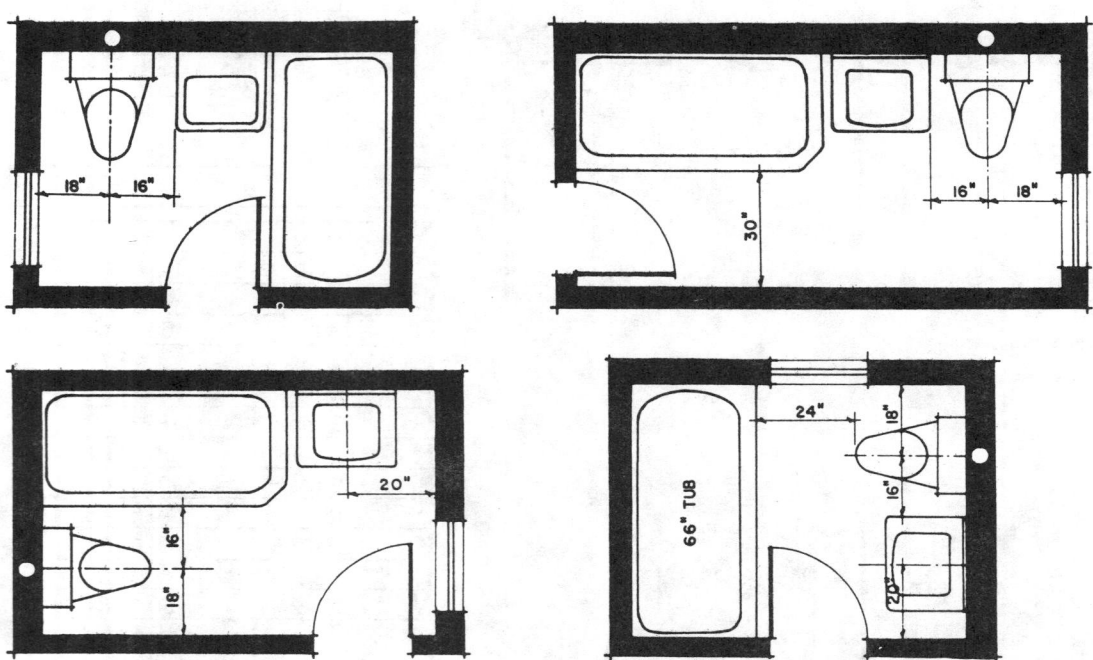

Fig. 4   Three-fixture plans: water closet, washbasin and tub.

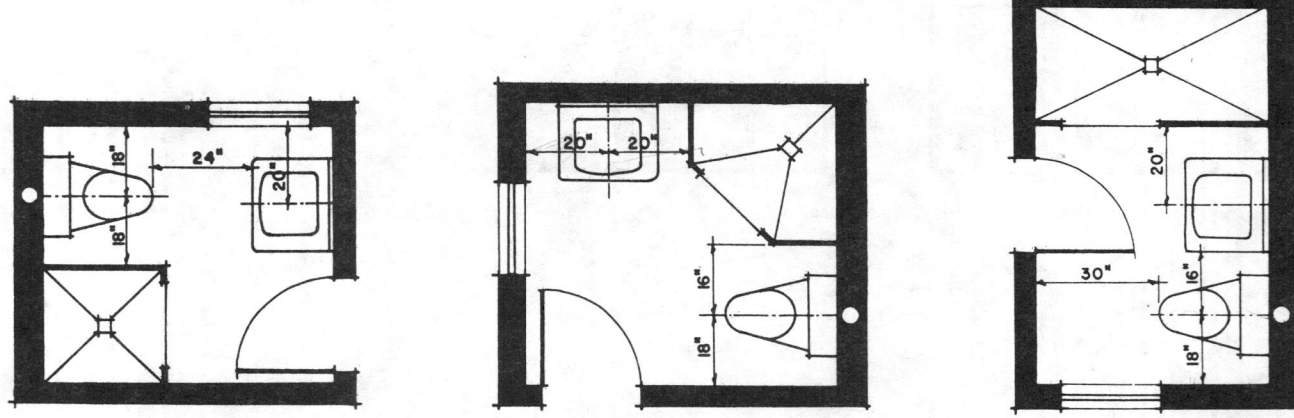

Fig. 5   Two- and three-fixture noncompartmented plans: water closet, washbasin, and shower.

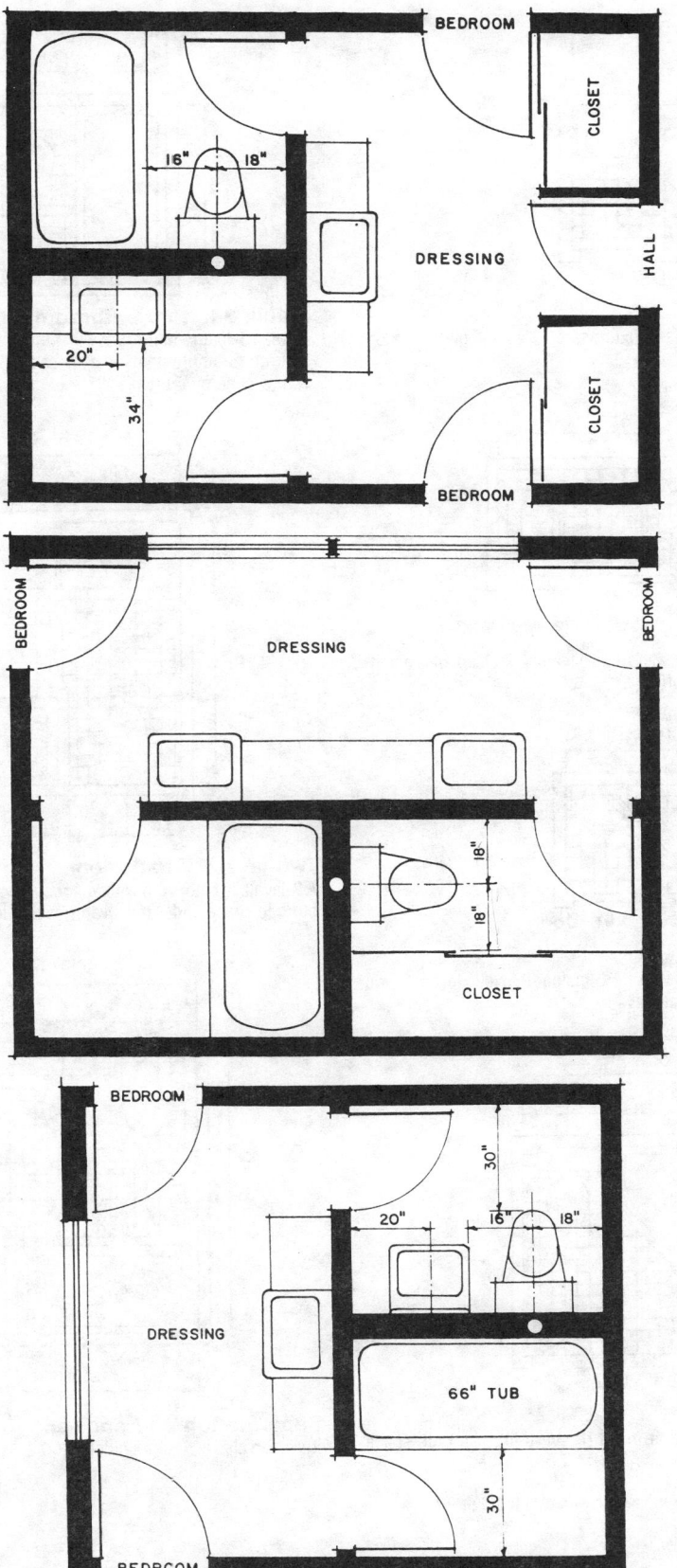

Fig. 6 Four-fixture compartmented plans: water closet, tub, and two washbasins.

BATHROOMS
Typical Plans and Fixture Arrangements

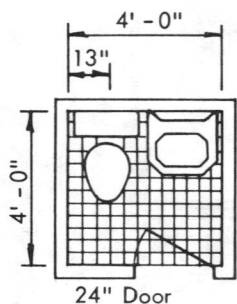

Minimum half-bath.
16 ft² is about minimum for standard fixtures; 4'-6"x4'-6" gives a more spacious feeling.

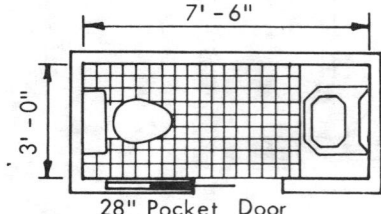

Generous half-bath.
22.5 ft² is a generous half-bath. A wall-hung lavatory instead of a vanity squeezes into 2'-6" width and 16.3 ft².

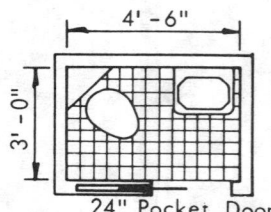

Corner toilet in a half-bath.
A corner toilet and a small lavatory fit 13.5 ft². Consider this idea for installing a half-bath in a closet or under a stairway.

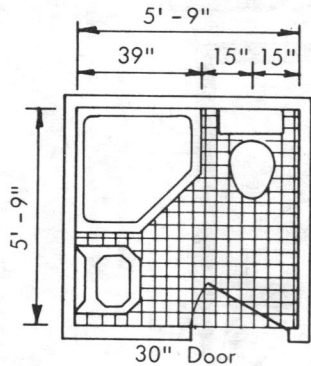

Corner shower.
A corner shower, toilet, and lavatory fit in 33 ft². Very little storage space available.

Fig. 7   A wide array of two-, three-, four-, and five-fixture toilet plans.

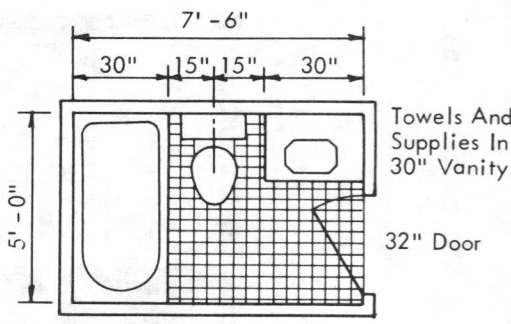

Small, 3-fixture bathroom.
A small 3-fixture bathroom with limited storage in a built-in vanity meets basic bathroom requirements in a space 37.5 ft². The door is 32" wide for a person with a cane or crutches. This bathroom is too small for a wheelchair.

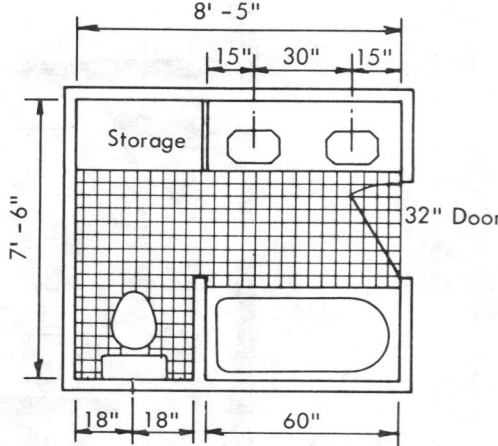

Two-lavatory bathroom.
A 2-lavatory bathroom with adequate room at the toilet and each lavatory. Note storage space under the lavatories and in a floor-to-ceiling unit. Area: 63 ft².

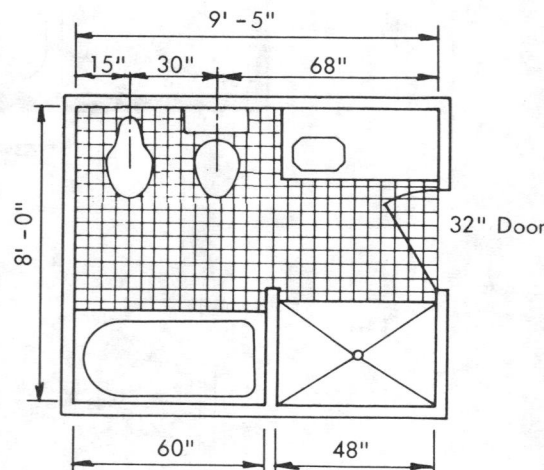

Separate tub and shower.
This plan also includes a bidet. Storage is in the 48" long vanity. Area: 75.3 ft².

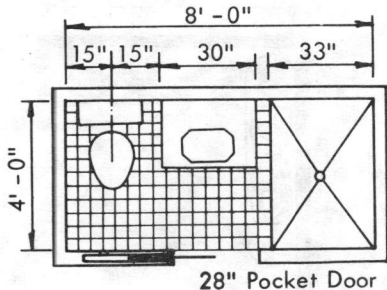

Large shower.
A generous 33"x48" shower is featured in this 32 ft² bathroom. Storage is under the 30" vanity and on shelves over the toilet.

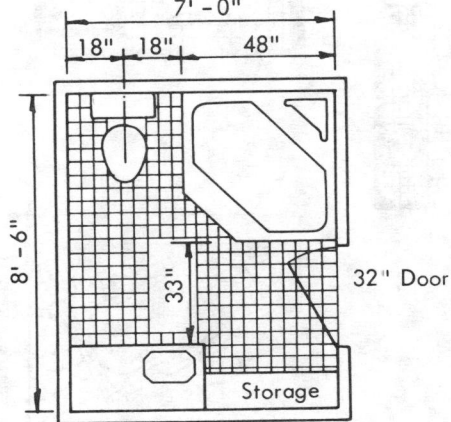

Corner square tub.
Although not usually a space saver, a square tub fits some situations better than a rectangular one. This 3-fixture bathroom has excellent storage but is only 59.5 ft².

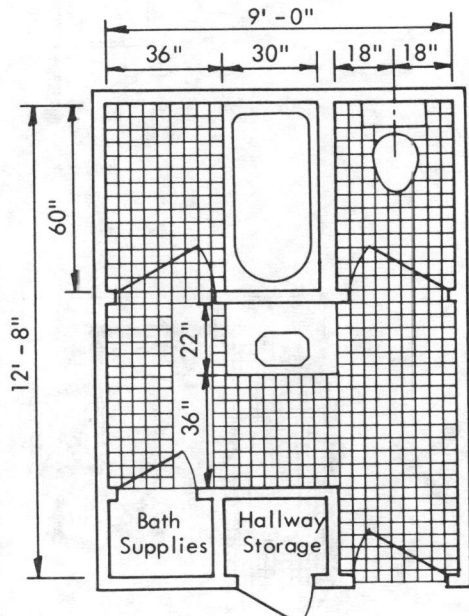

Large 3-fixture bathroom.
With fixtures in separate compartments, this layout can replace a second bath by accommodating more than one person at a time. It is as large as two bathrooms but costs less because of fewer fixtures and less plumbing. Area: 106 ft² plus hallway storage.

Fig. 7 (Continued)

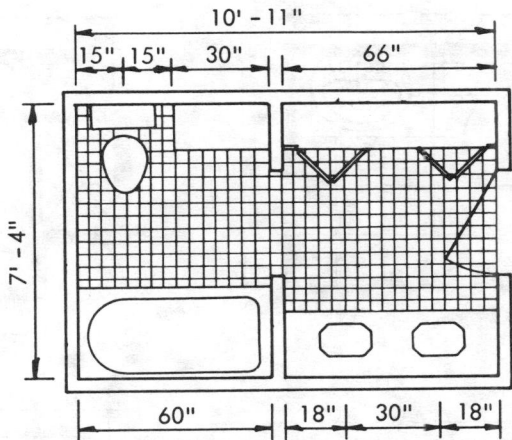

Four-fixtures, two compartments.
Three people can use this bathroom at the same time. Consider a pocket door between the compartments. Even with generous storage space it takes only the same space as many non-compartmented bathrooms, about 80.5 ft².

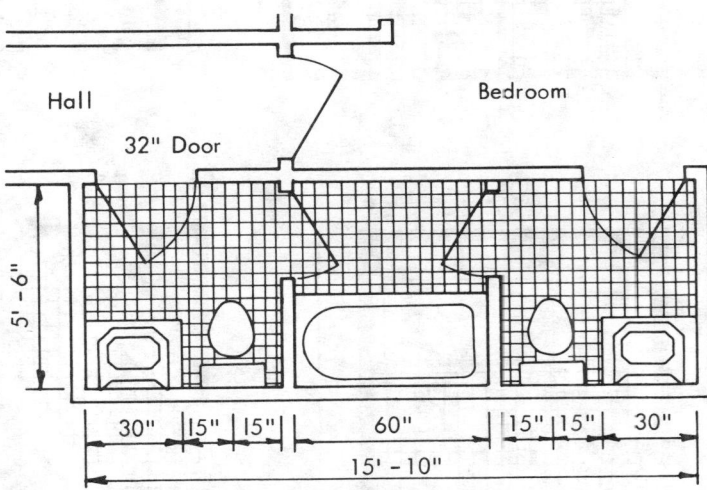

Five fixtures, three compartments.
This bathroom serves as two full bathrooms in 87 ft². Two doors to each compartment are undesirable. Limited storage space available.

BATHROOMS
Custom Designs

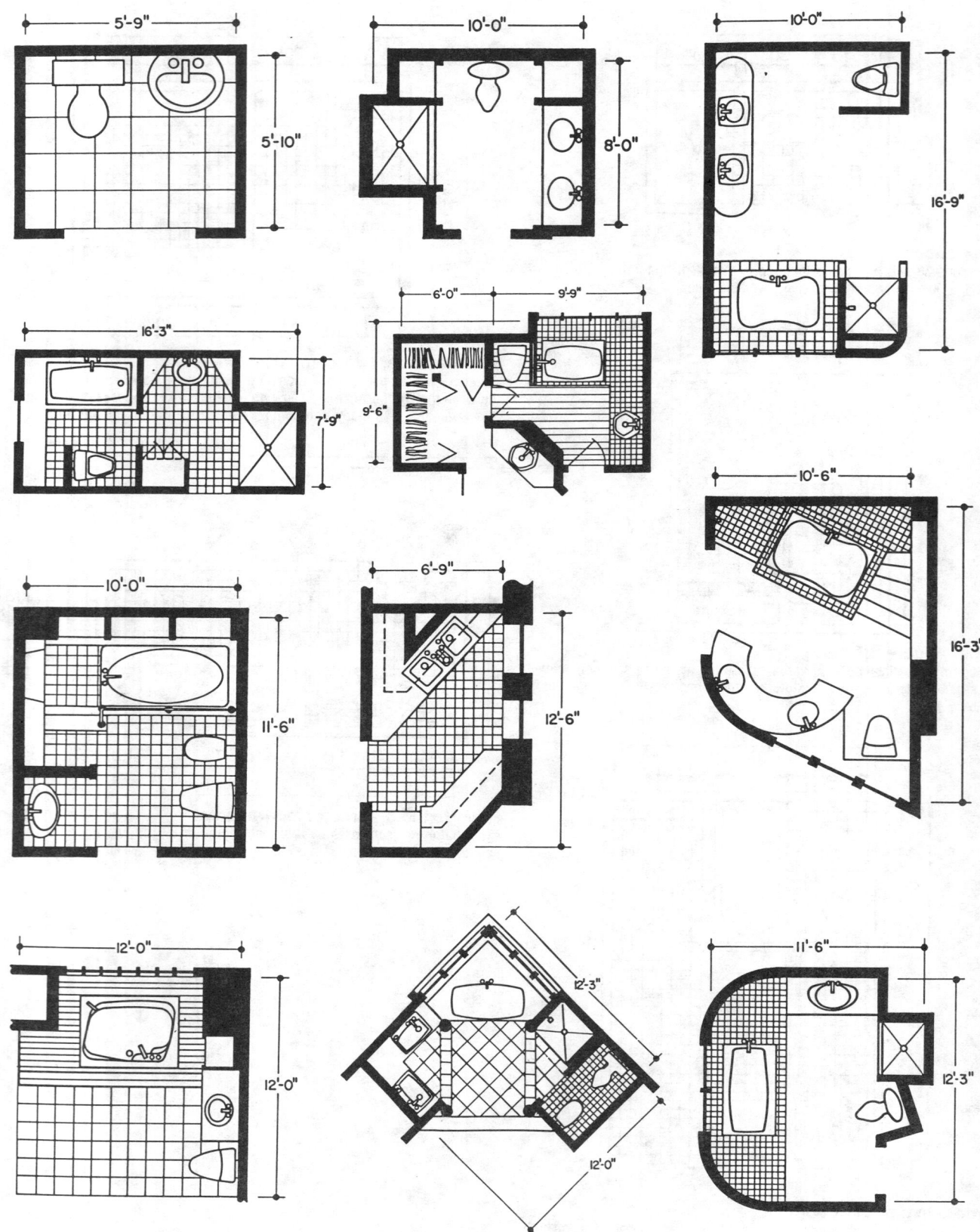

Fig. 8   A variety of design possibilities for the more customized bathroom.

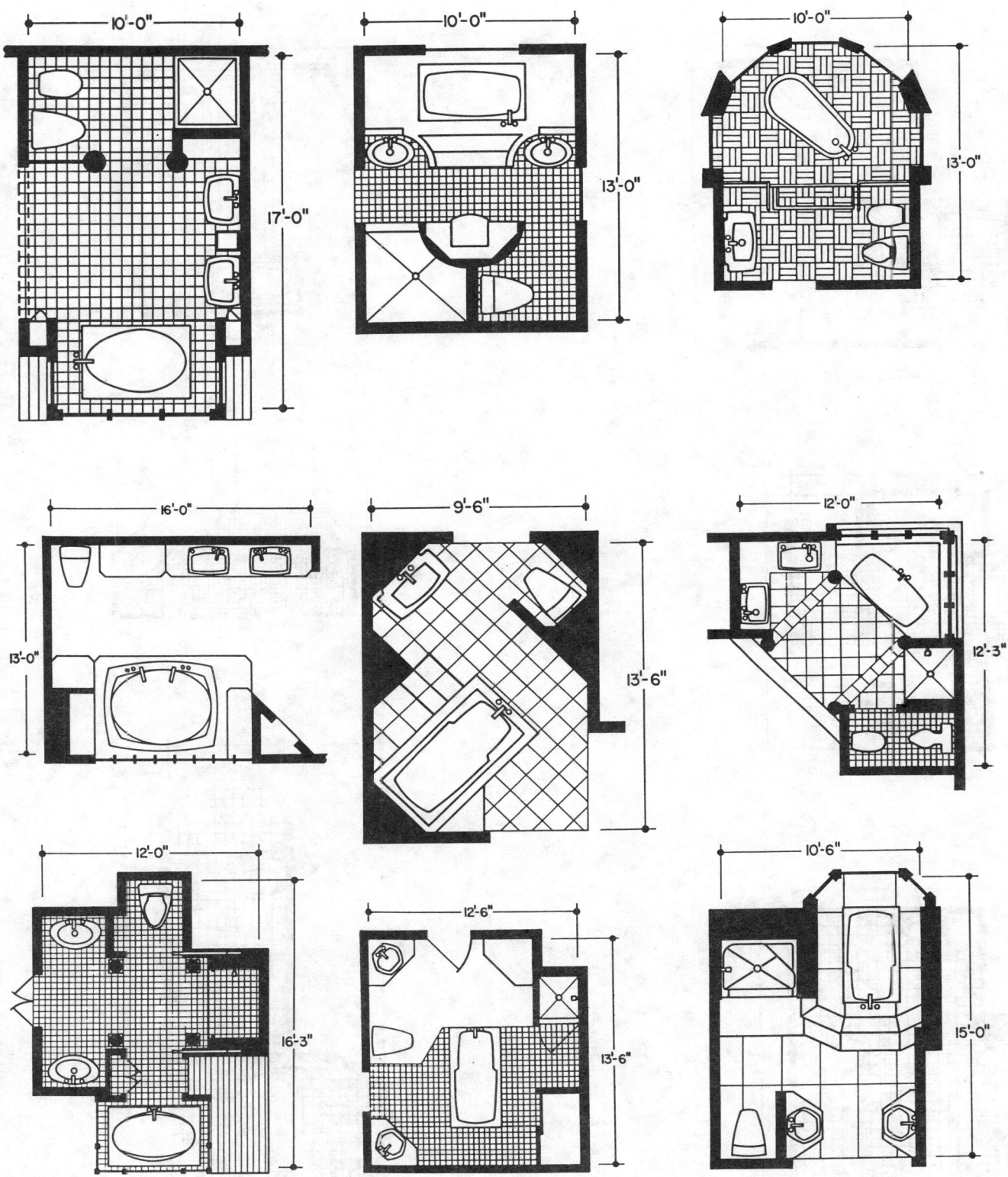

Fig. 8 *(Continued)*

BATHROOMS
Custom Designs

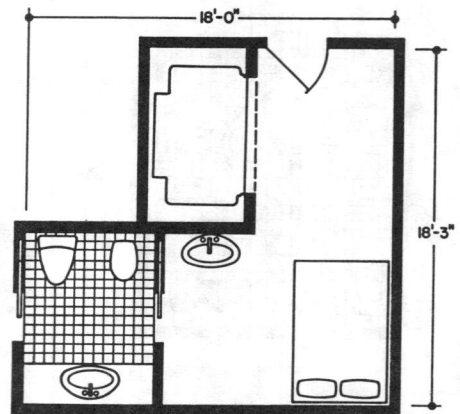

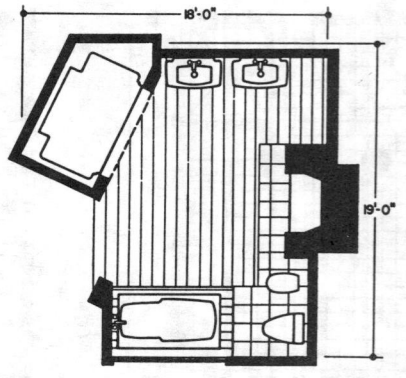

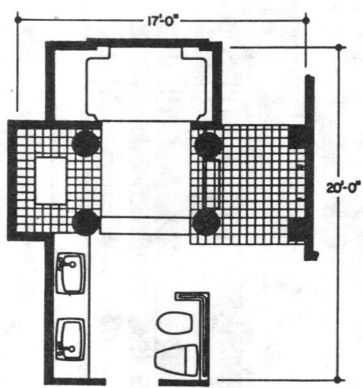

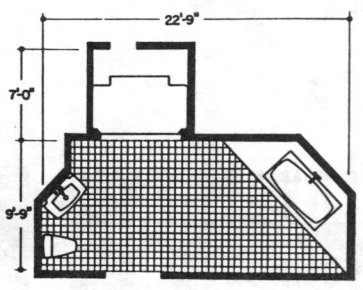

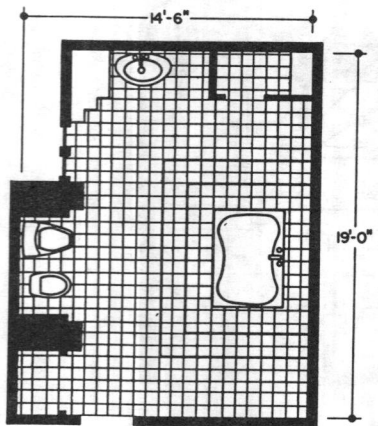

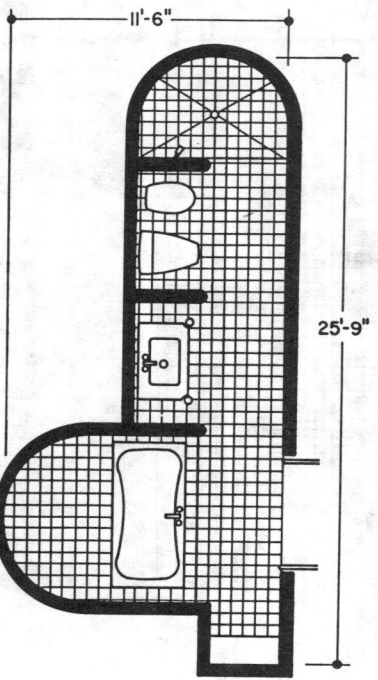

Fig. 8 *(Continued)*

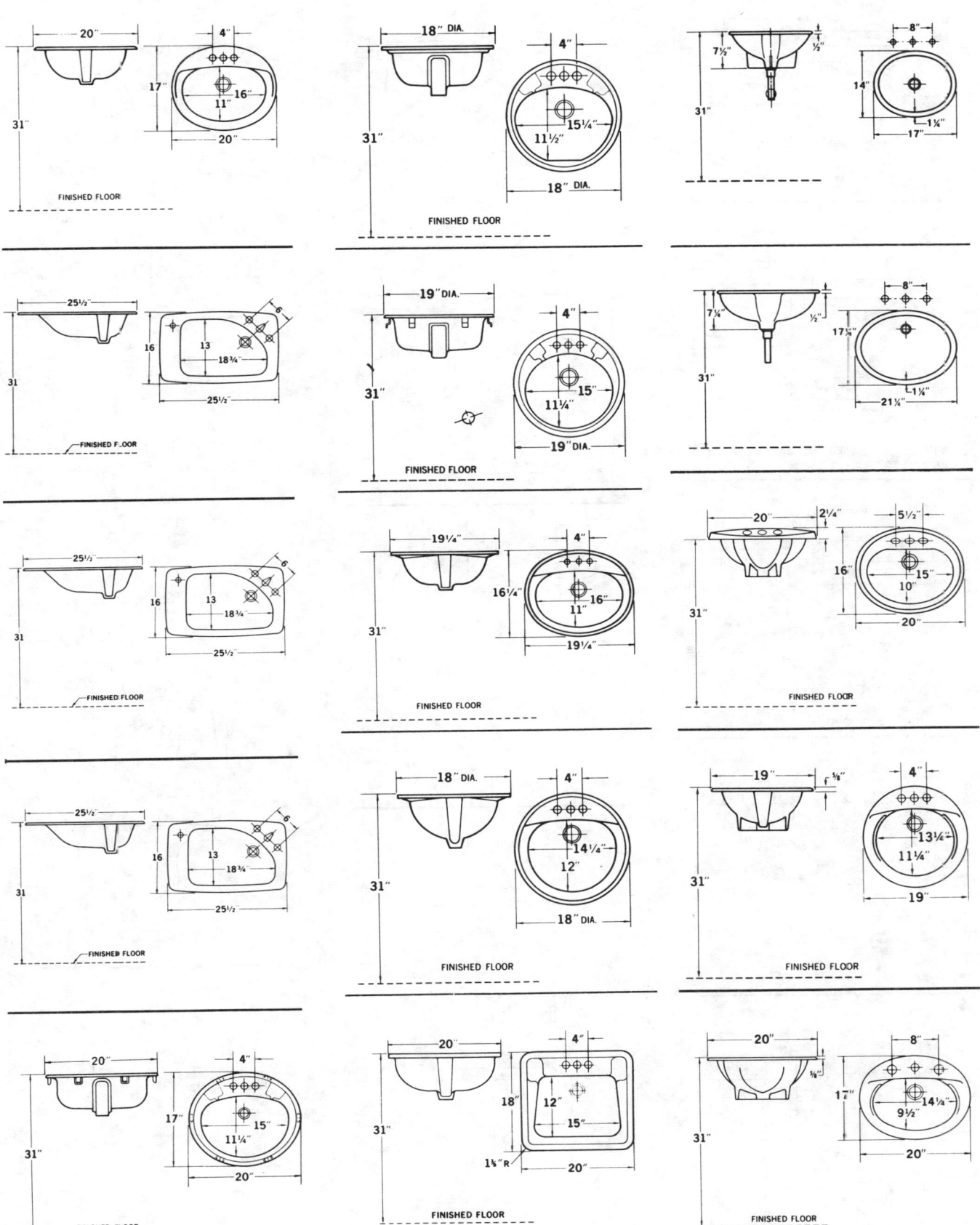

Fig. 9   A selection of countertop lavatories.

BATHROOMS
Lavatory Types and Dimensions

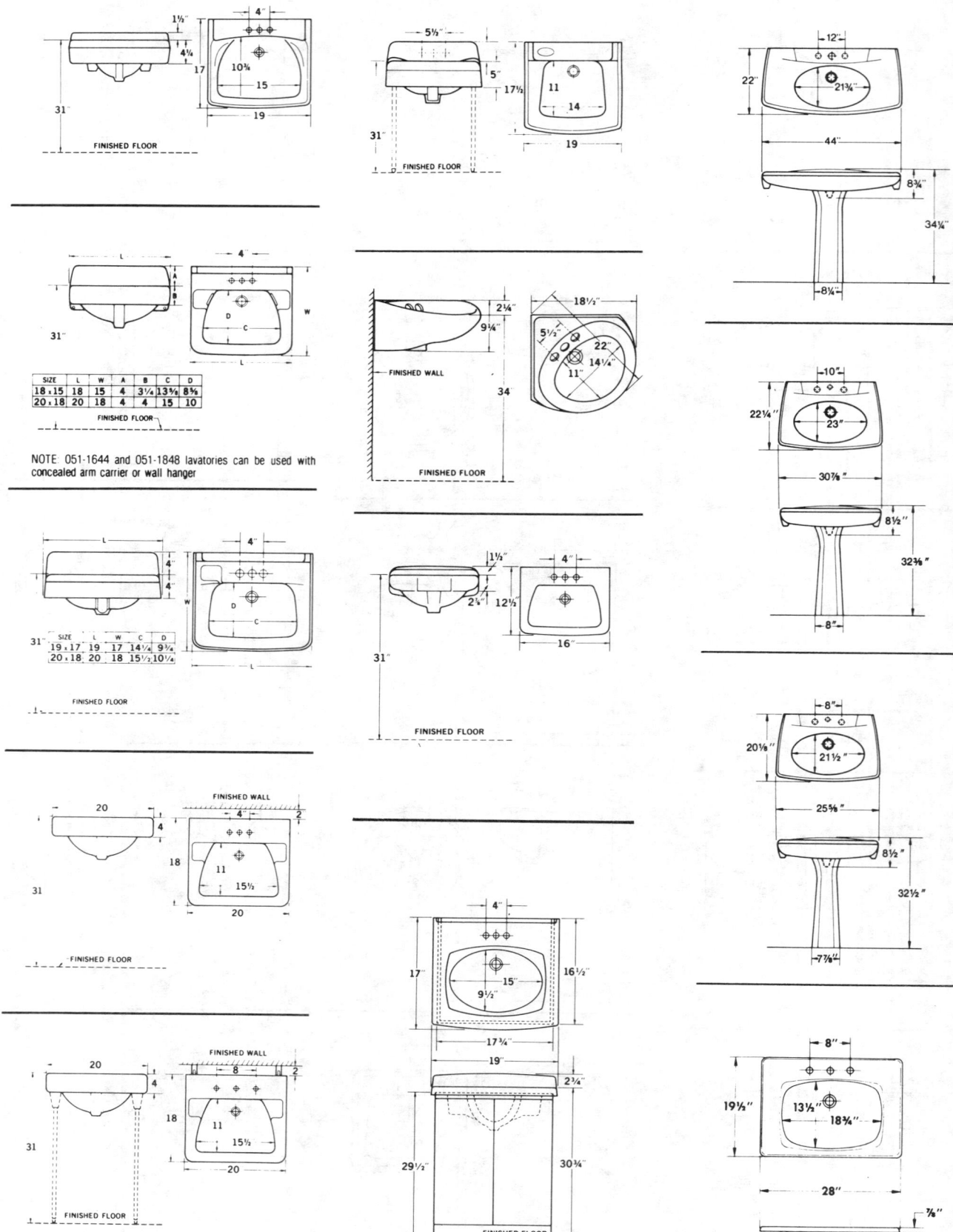

Fig. 10   A selection of wall-hung and pedestal-type lavatories.

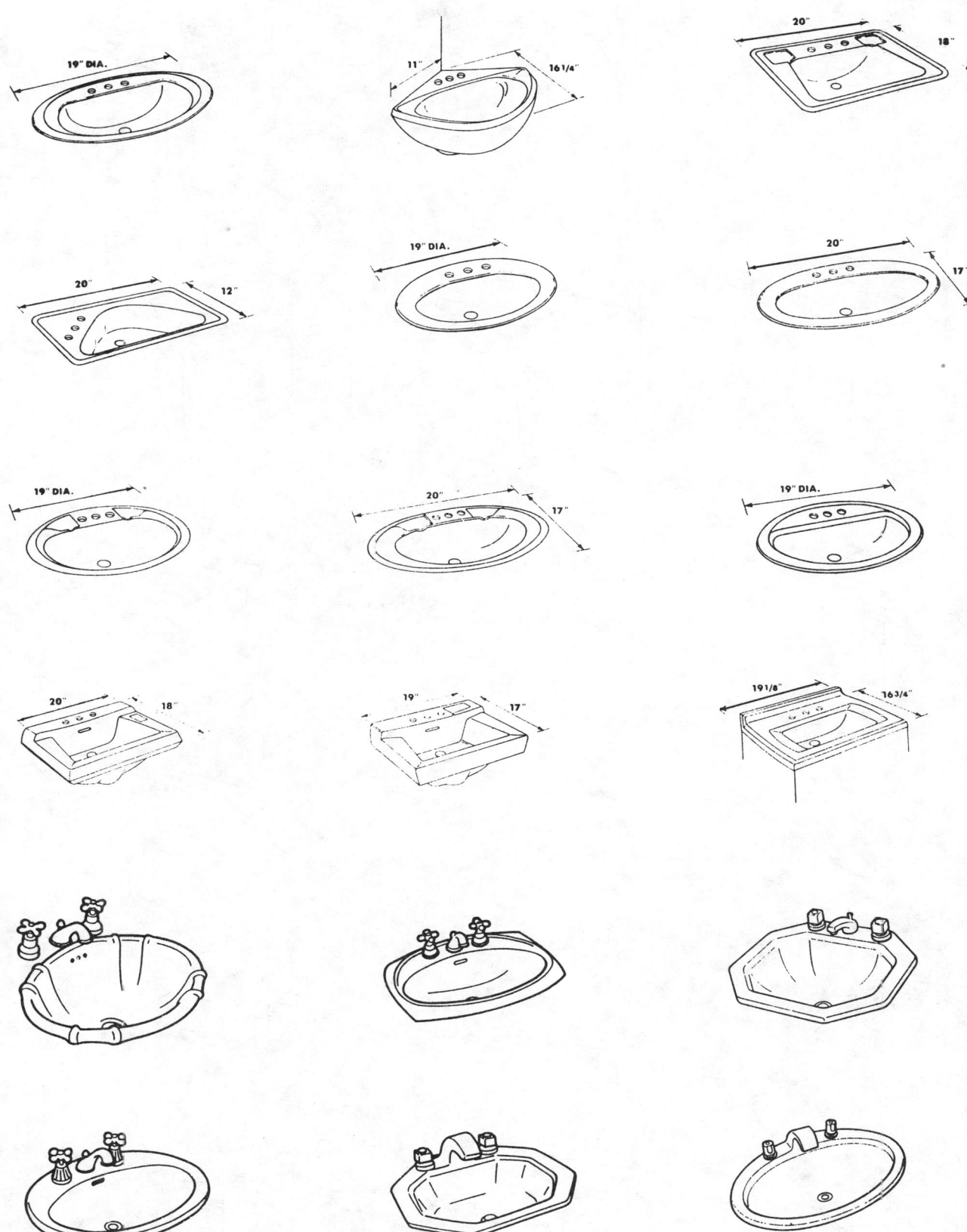

Fig. 11   Another selection of lavatories.

BATHROOMS
Lavatory Types and Dimensions

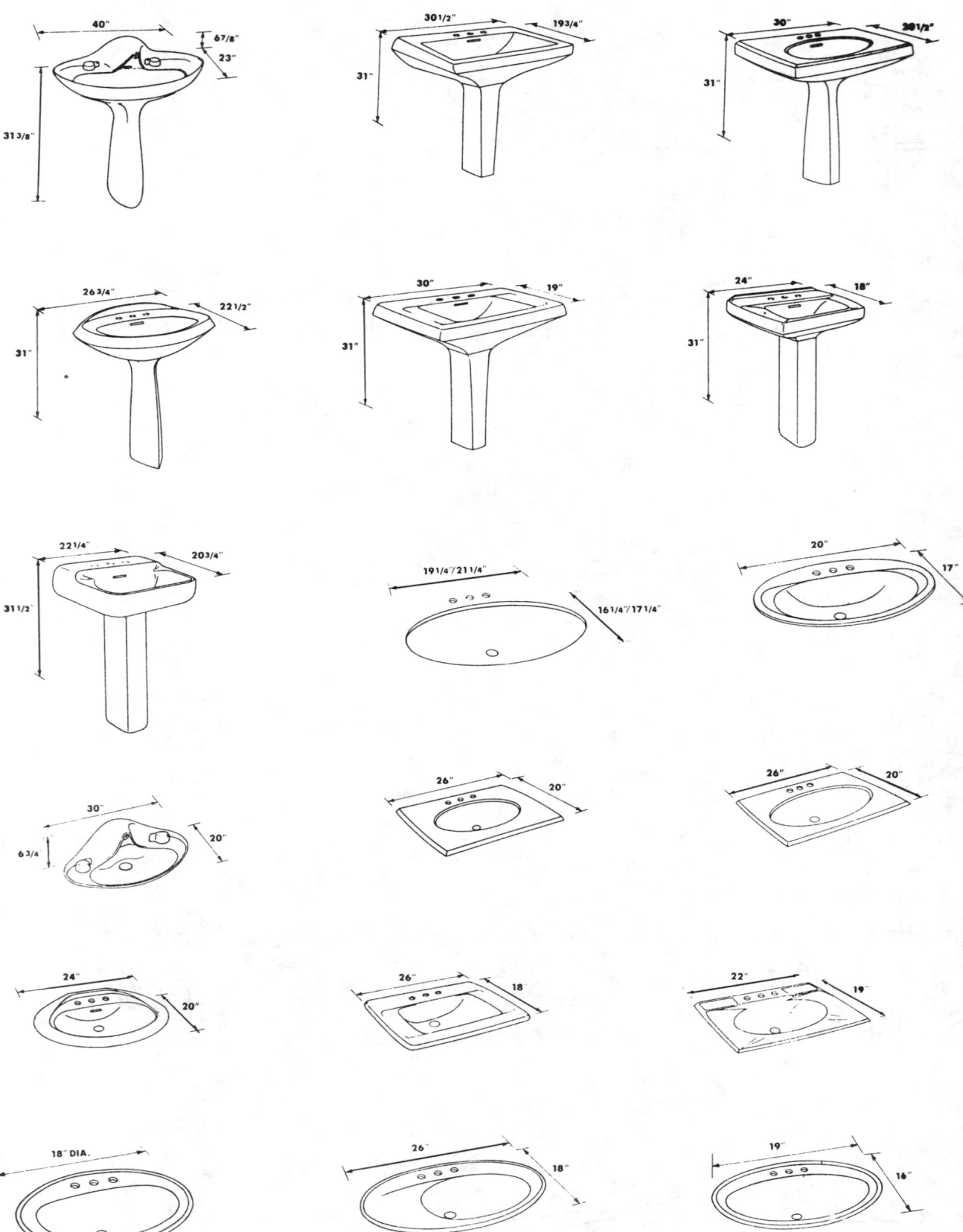

Fig. 11 (Continued)

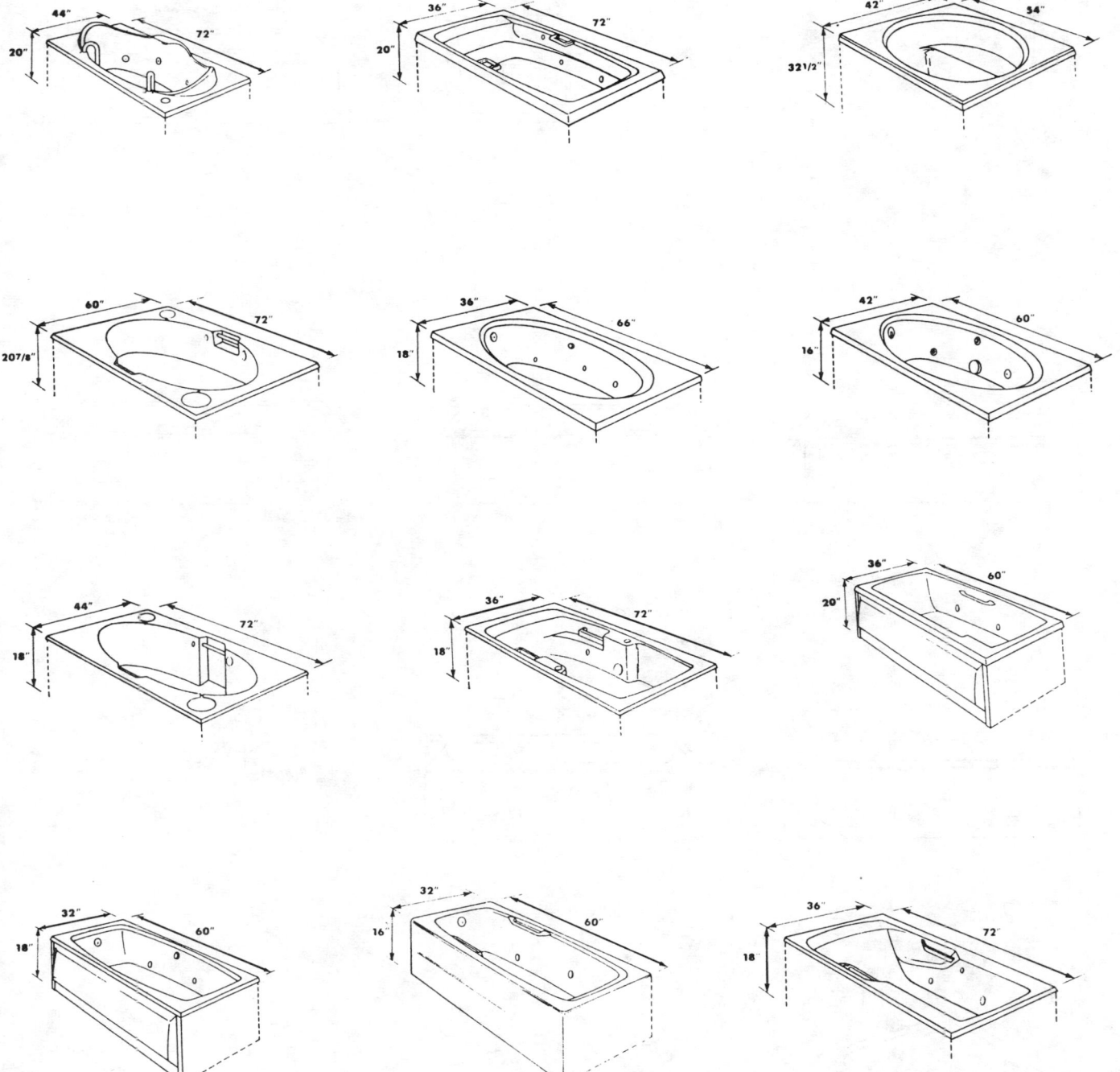

Fig. 12　A selection of whirlpool baths.

BATHROOMS
Bathtub Types and Dimensions

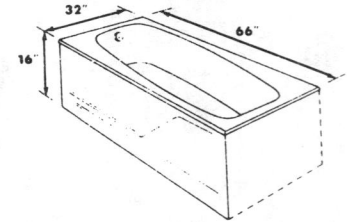

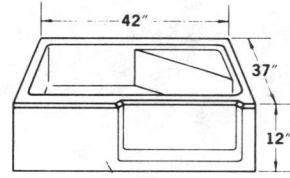

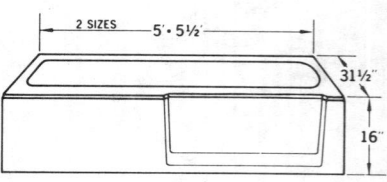

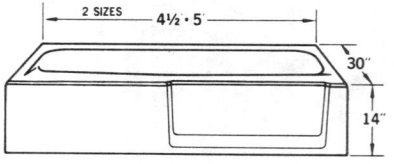

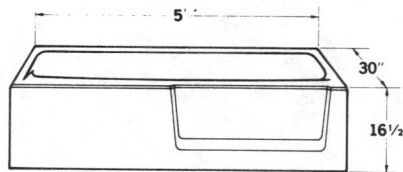

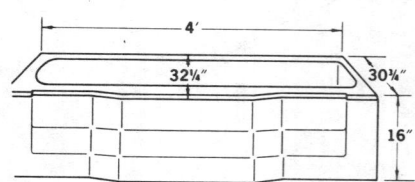

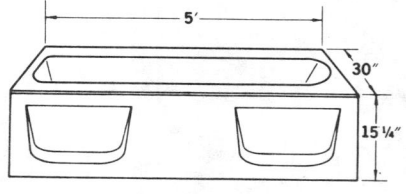

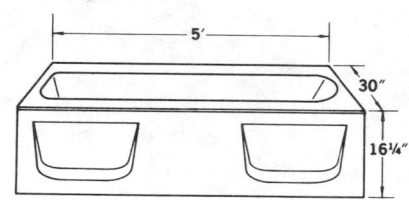

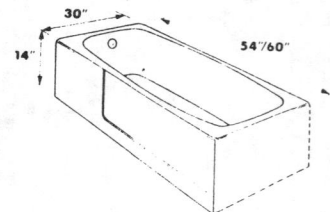

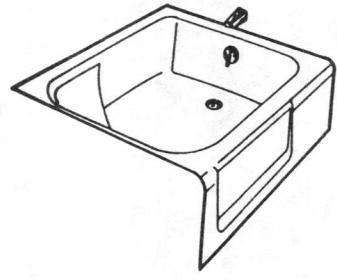

Dimensions: 42" x 37" x 12"

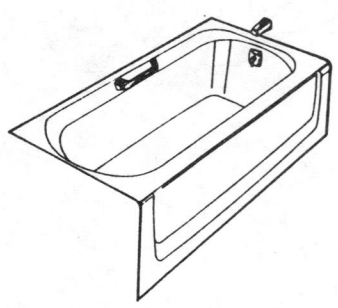

Dimensions: 60" x 31½" x 16"

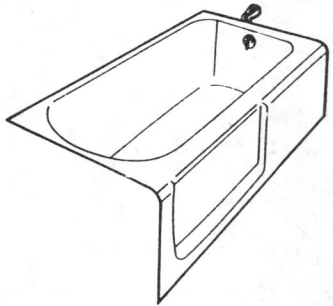

Dimensions: 60" x 31½" x 16"

Fig. 13   A selection of standard baths.

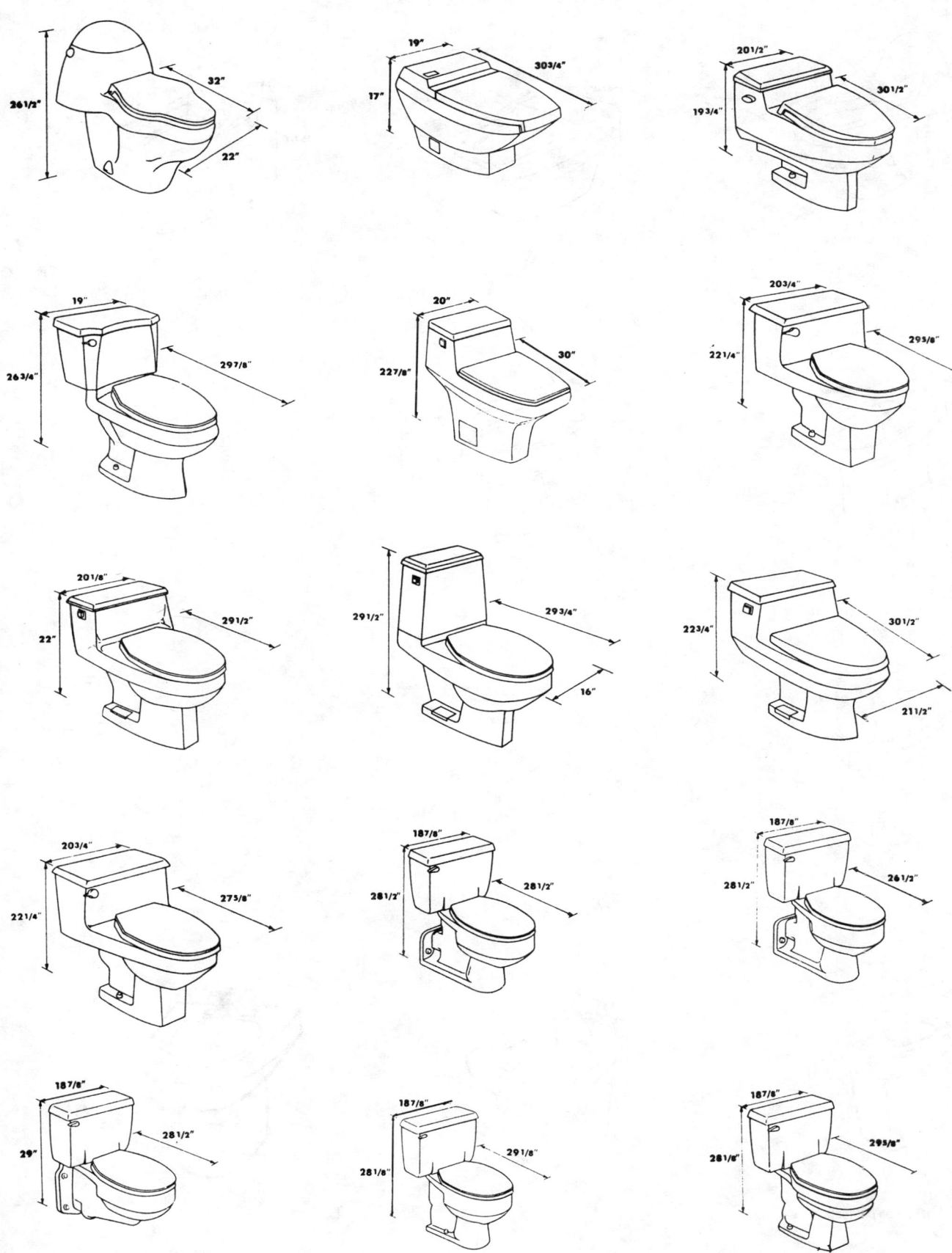

Fig. 14   A selection of waterclosets.

BATHROOMS
Bidet Types and Dimensions

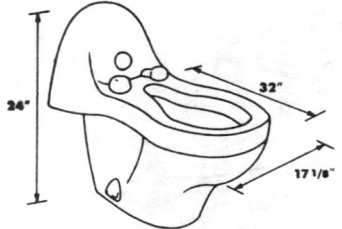

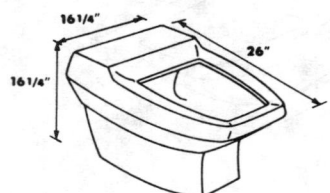

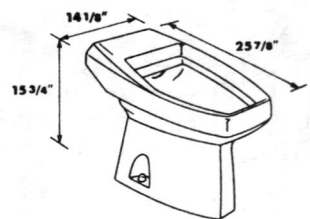

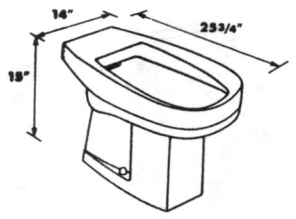

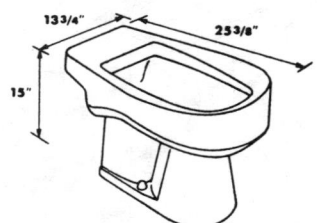

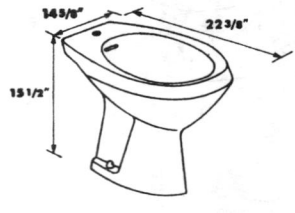

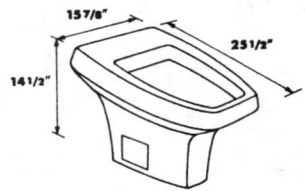

Fig. 15   A selection of bidets.

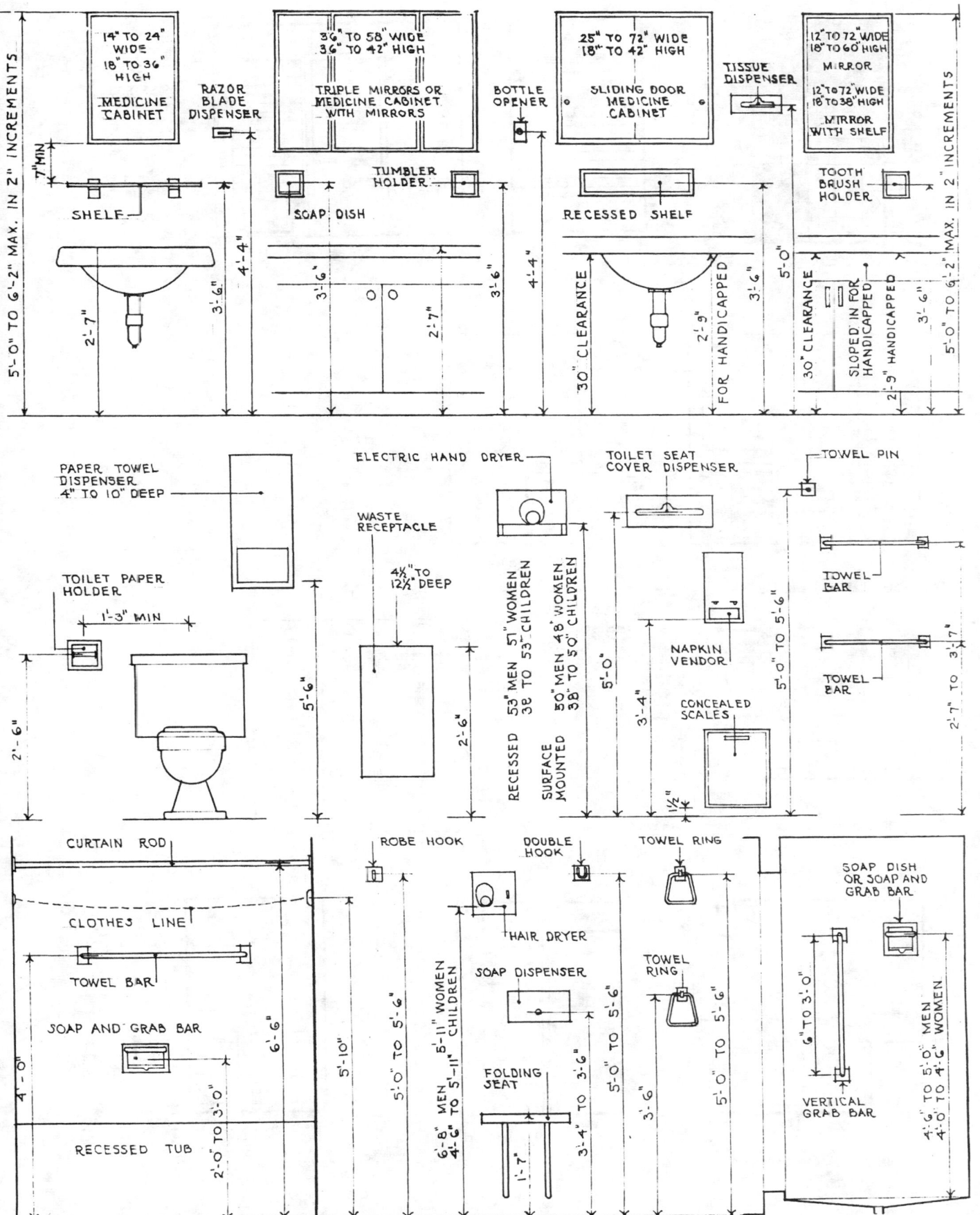

BATHROOMS

Plans, Elevations, and Details

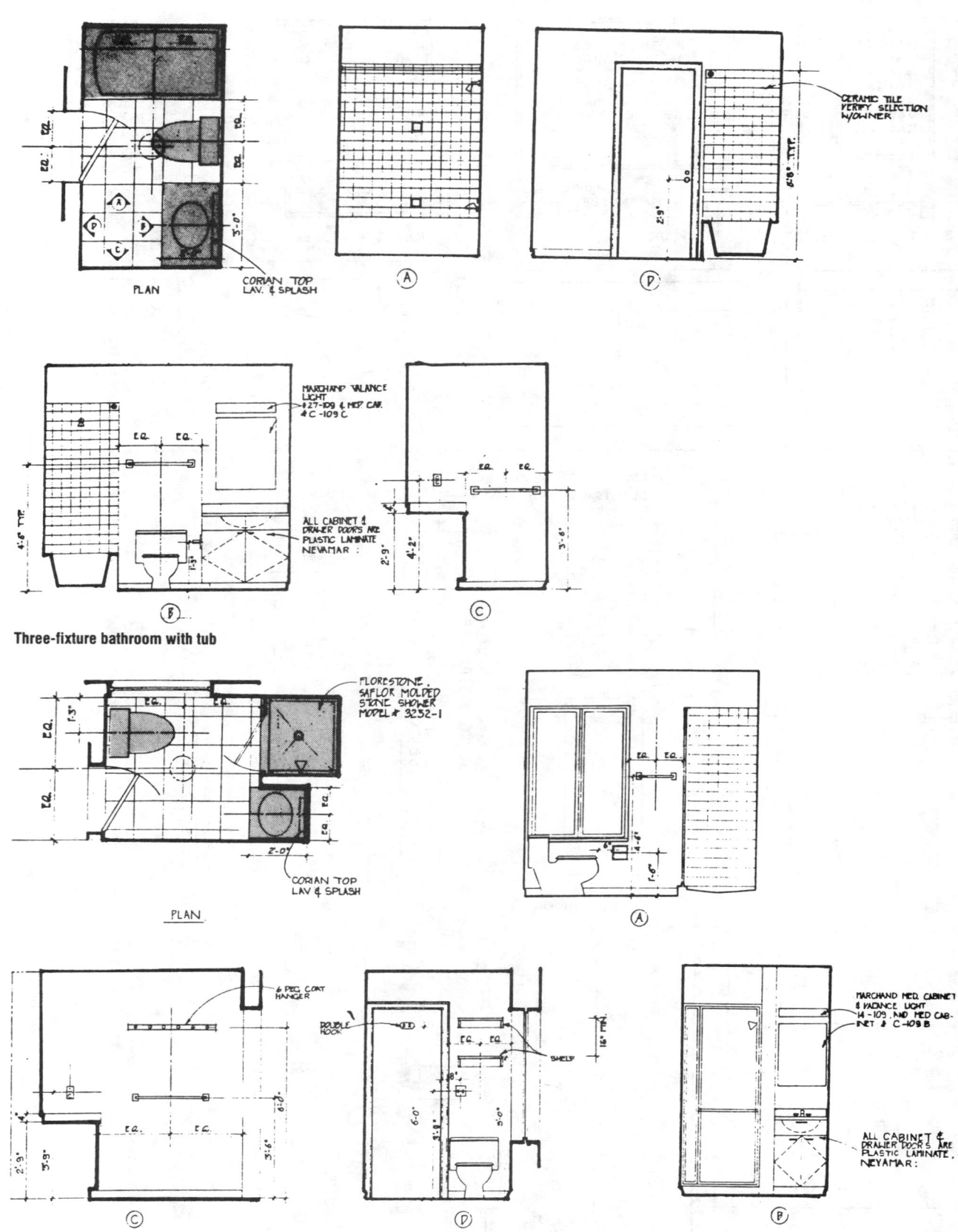

PLAN

CORIAN TOP
LAV. & SPLASH

CERAMIC TILE
VERIFY SELECTION
W/OWNER

Ⓐ

Ⓓ

MARCHAND VALANCE
LIGHT
#27-109 & MED CAB.
C-109 C

ALL CABINET &
DRAWER DOORS ARE
PLASTIC LAMINATE
NEVAMAR

Ⓑ

Ⓒ

Three-fixture bathroom with tub

FLORESTONE
SAFLOR MOLDED
STONE SHOWER
MODEL # 3232-1

CORIAN TOP
LAV & SPLASH

PLAN

Ⓐ

6 PEG COAT
HANGER

DOUBLE
HOOK

SHELF

MARCHAND MED. CABINET
& VALANCE LIGHT
14-109 AND MED CAB-
INET # C-109 B

ALL CABINET &
DRAWER DOORS ARE
PLASTIC LAMINATE
NEVAMAR

Ⓒ

Ⓓ

Ⓑ

Three-fixture bathroom with shower

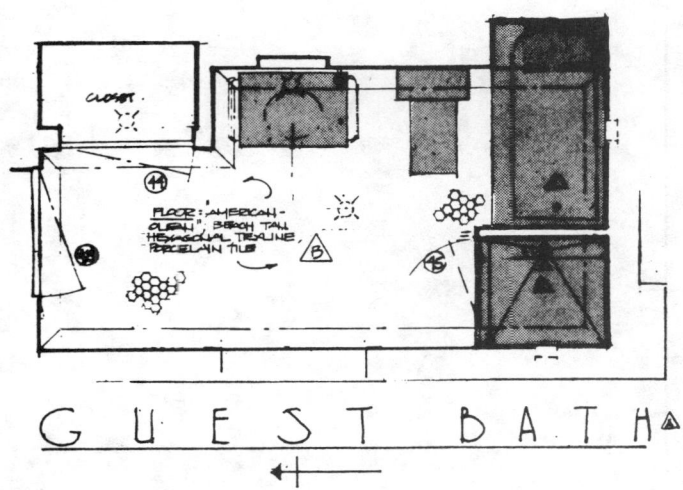

G U E S T   B A T H

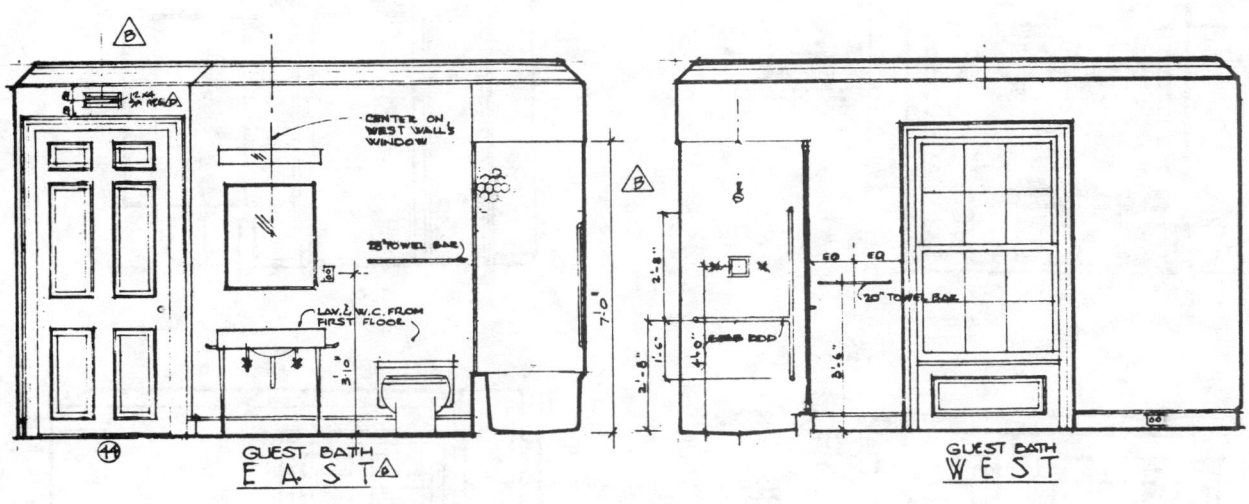

GUEST BATH
E A S T

GUEST BATH
W E S T

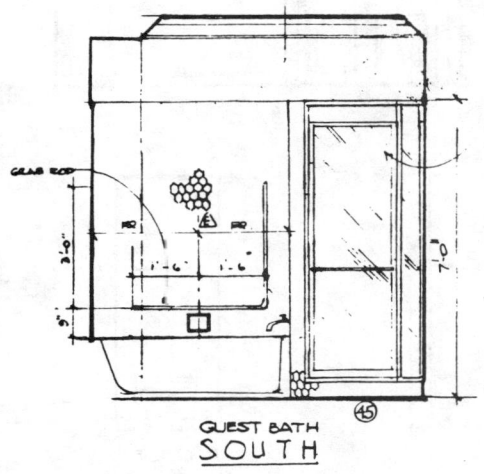

GUEST BATH
S O U T H

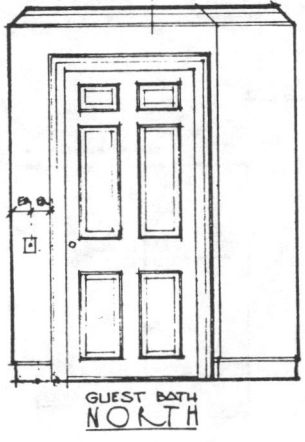

GUEST BATH
N O R T H

Four-fixture bathroom with tub and shower

BATHROOMS

Plans, Elevations, and Details

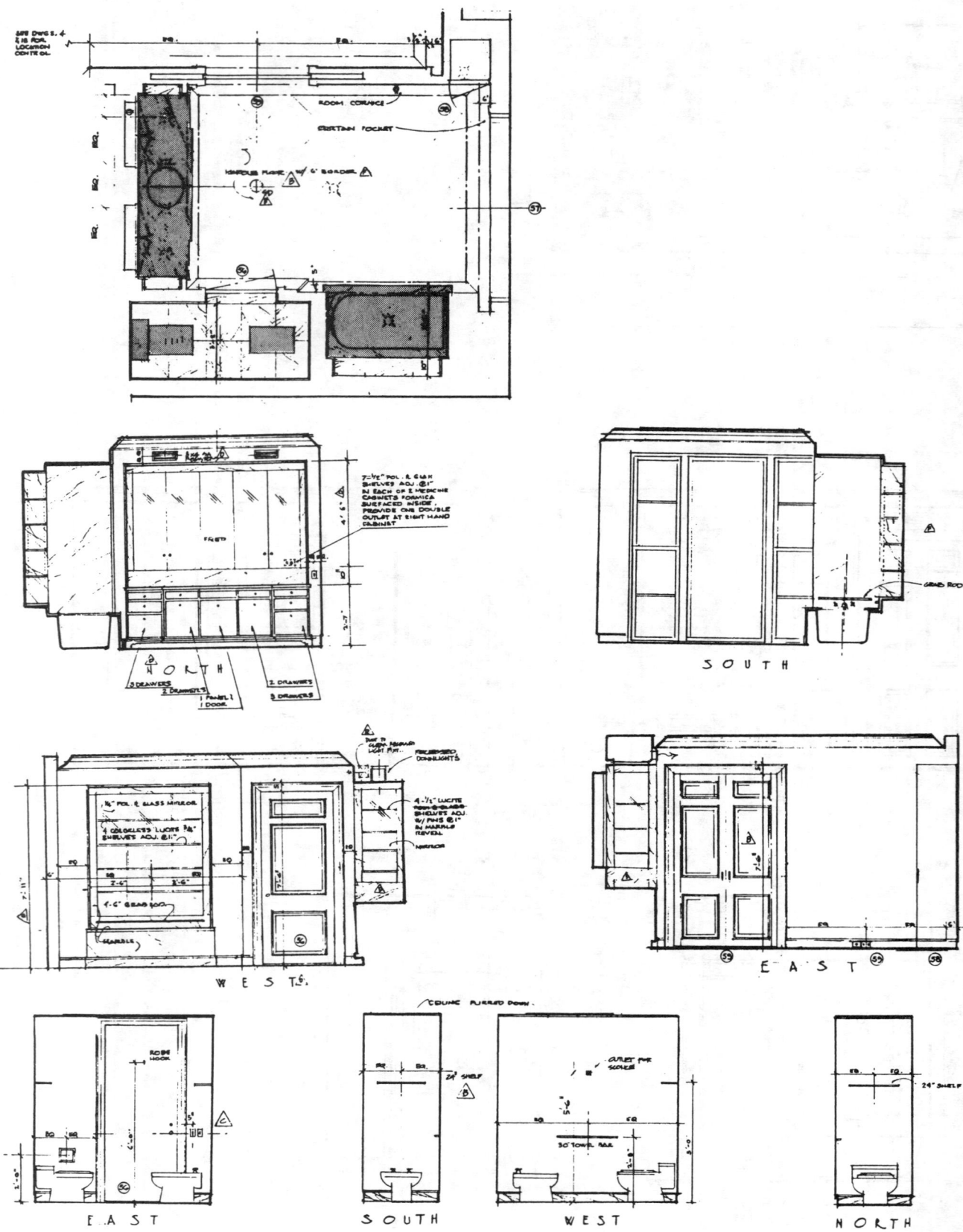

Four-fixture bathroom with bidet and tub

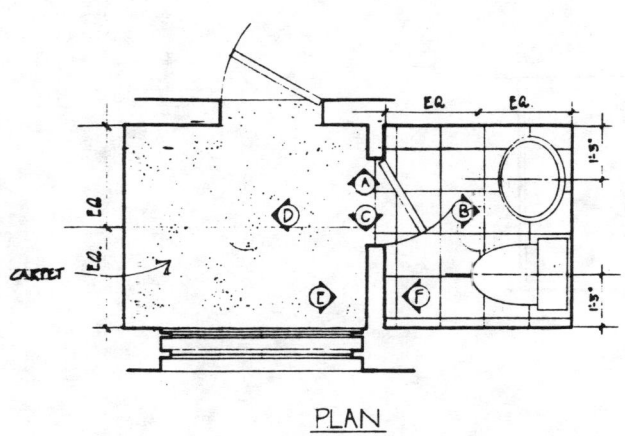

EQ. | EQ.

1'-3"

EQ.

EQ.

EQ.

CARPET

PLAN

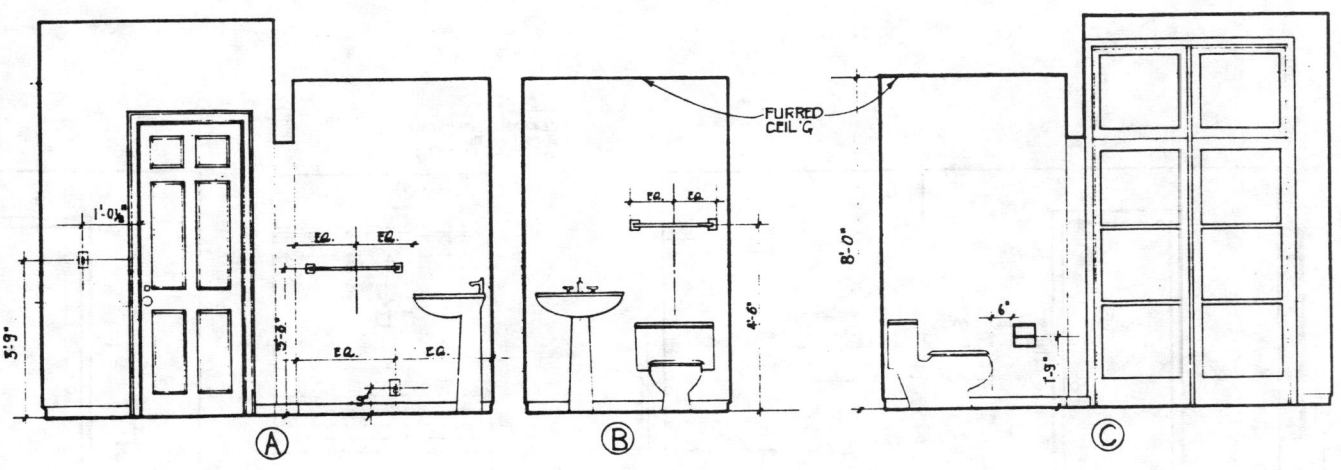

1'-0"

5'-9"

5'-3"

EQ. | EQ.

EQ. | EQ.

Ⓐ

EQ. | EQ.

4'-6"

Ⓑ

FURRED CEIL'G

8'-0"

6"

1'-9"

Ⓒ

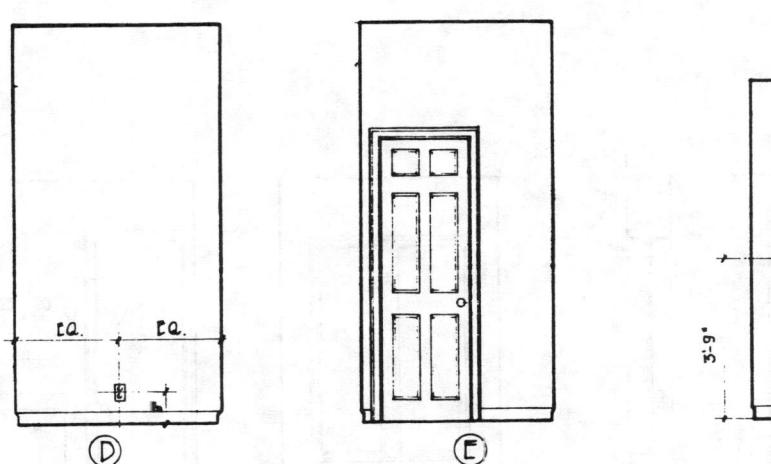

EQ. | EQ.

Ⓓ

Ⓔ

1'-0"

3'-9"

Ⓕ

Powder room

BATHROOMS

Plans, Elevations, and Details

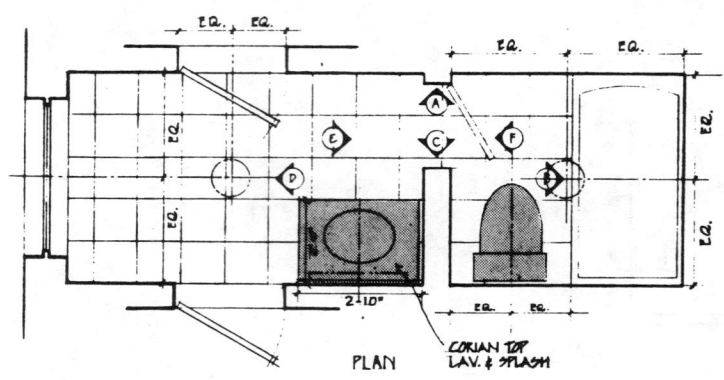

PLAN

CORIAN TOP
LAV. & SPLASH

B A T H R O O M

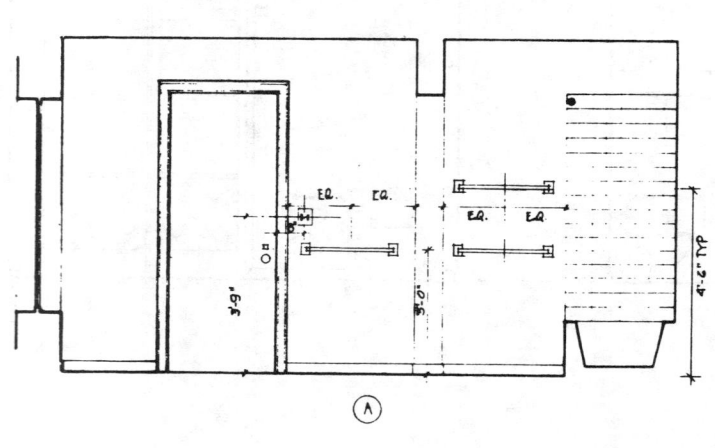

(A)

CERAMIC SOAP DISH
TO MATCH TILE
(CONSULT OWNER)

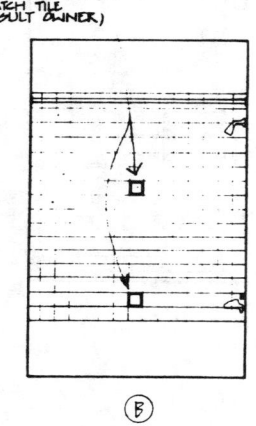

(B)

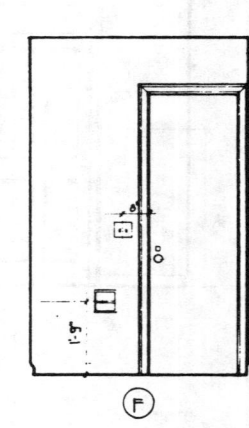

(F)

MARCHAND VALANCE
LIGHT
ZT-109 & MED. CAB.
C-109 C

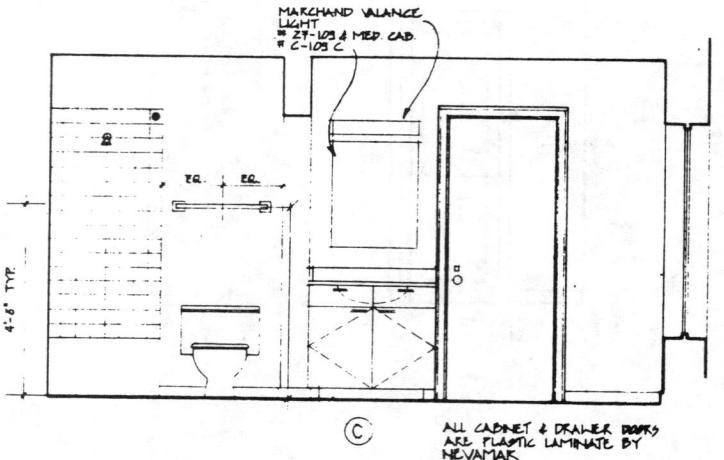

(C)

ALL CABINET & DRAWER DOORS
ARE PLASTIC LAMINATE BY
NEVAMAR

(D)

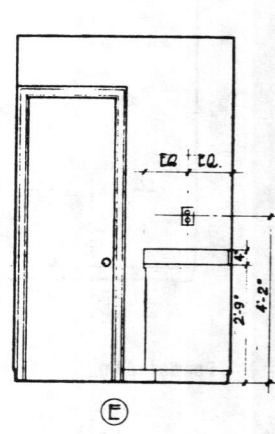

(E)

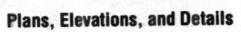

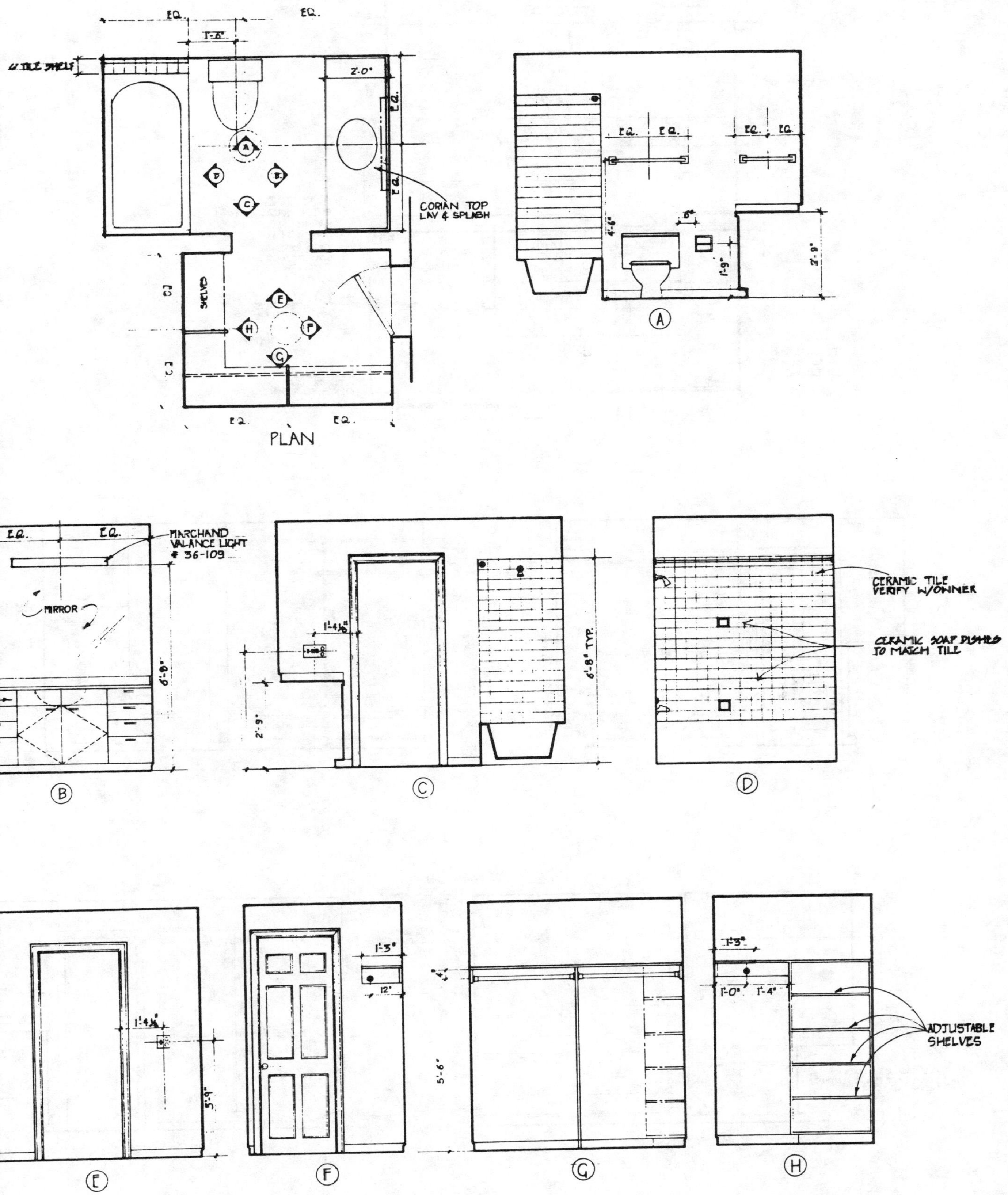
EQ.
EQ.
1'-8"
4" TILE SHELF
2'-0"
CORIAN TOP LAV & SPLASH
SHELVES
PLAN
4'-6"
6"
1'-9"
3'-9"
A
MARCHAND VALANCE LIGHT # 36-109
MIRROR
6'-8"
B
1'-4 1/8"
2'-9"
6'-8" TYP.
C
CERAMIC TILE VERIFY W/OWNER
CERAMIC SOAP DISHES TO MATCH TILE
D
1'-4 1/8"
3'-9"
E
1'-3"
12"
F
5'-6"
G
1'-3"
1'-0"
1'-4"
ADJUSTABLE SHELVES
H

Her bathroom

BATHROOMS
Plans, Elevations, and Details

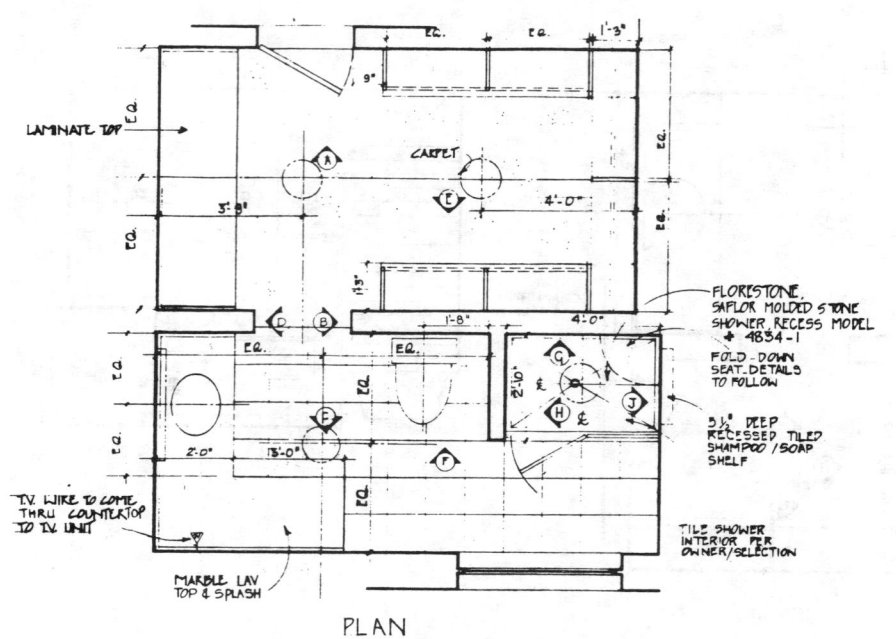

LAMINATE TOP

CARPET

FLORESTONE, SAFLOR MOLDED STONE SHOWER, RECESS MODEL # 4834-1

FOLD-DOWN SEAT. DETAILS TO FOLLOW

5½" DEEP RECESSED TILED SHAMPOO/SOAP SHELF

TILE SHOWER INTERIOR PER OWNER/SELECTION

T.V. WIRE TO COME THRU COUNTERTOP TO T.V. UNIT

MARBLE LAV TOP & SPLASH

PLAN

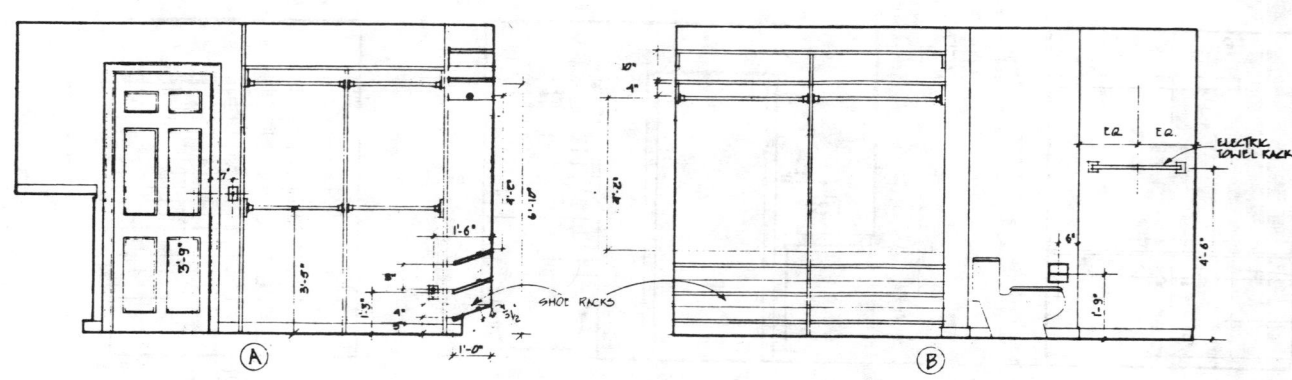

SHOE RACKS

(A)

ELECTRIC TOWEL RACK

(B)

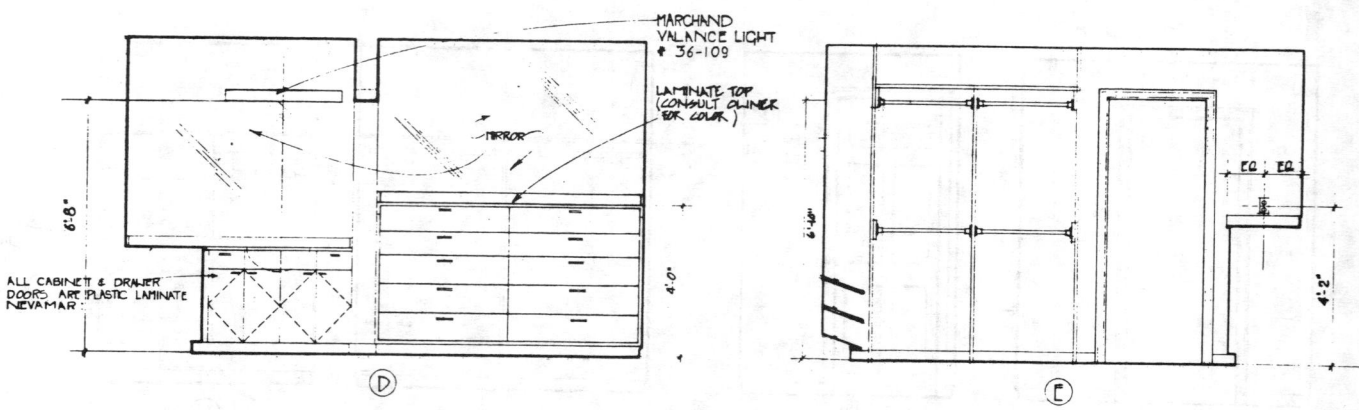

MARCHAND VALANCE LIGHT # 36-109

LAMINATE TOP (CONSULT OWNER FOR COLOR)

MIRROR

ALL CABINET & DRAWER DOORS ARE PLASTIC LAMINATE NEVAMAR

(D)

(E)

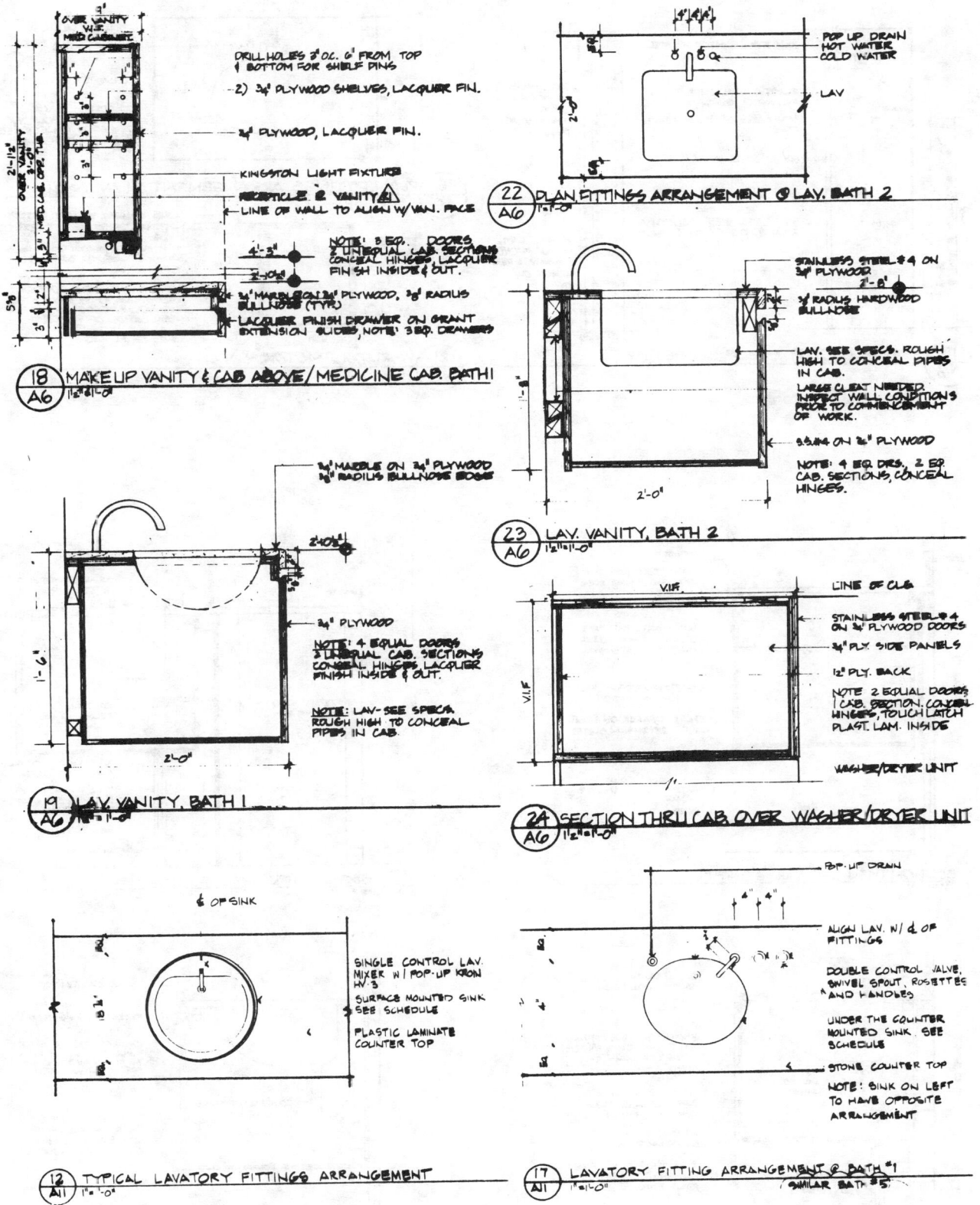

18 / A6 MAKE UP VANITY & CAB ABOVE / MEDICINE CAB. BATH 1 1½"=1'-0"

DRILL HOLES 2" O.C. 6" FROM TOP & BOTTOM FOR SHELF PINS

2) ¾" PLYWOOD SHELVES, LACQUER FIN.

¾" PLYWOOD, LACQUER FIN.

KINGSTON LIGHT FIXTURE

RECEPTICLE @ VANITY

LINE OF WALL TO ALIGN W/ VAN. FACE

NOTE: 3 EQ. DOORS, 3 UNEQUAL CAB. SECTIONS CONCEAL HINGES, LACQUER FINISH INSIDE & OUT.

¾" MARBLE ON ¾" PLYWOOD, ⅜" RADIUS BULLNOSE (TYP.)

LACQUER FINISH DRAWER ON GRANT EXTENSION SLIDES, NOTE: 3 EQ. DRAWERS

22 / A6 PLAN FITTINGS ARRANGEMENT @ LAV. BATH 2 1½"=1'-0"

POP UP DRAIN
HOT WATER
COLD WATER

LAV

19 / A6 LAV. VANITY, BATH 1 1½"=1'-0"

¾" MARBLE ON ¾" PLYWOOD ⅜" RADIUS BULLNOSE EDGE

¾" PLYWOOD

NOTE: 4 EQUAL DOORS 3 UNEQUAL CAB. SECTIONS CONCEAL HINGES, LACQUER FINISH INSIDE & OUT.

NOTE: LAV - SEE SPECS. ROUGH HIGH TO CONCEAL PIPES IN CAB.

23 / A6 LAV. VANITY, BATH 2 1½"=1'-0"

STAINLESS STEEL #4 ON ¾" PLYWOOD

⅜" RADIUS HARDWOOD BULLNOSE

LAV. SEE SPECS. ROUGH HIGH TO CONCEAL PIPES IN CAB.

LARGE CLEAT NEEDED. INSPECT WALL CONDITIONS PRIOR TO COMMENCEMENT OF WORK.

SS #4 ON ¾" PLYWOOD

NOTE: 4 EQ. DRS, 2 EQ. CAB. SECTIONS, CONCEAL HINGES.

24 / A6 SECTION THRU CAB OVER WASHER/DRYER UNIT 1½"=1'-0"

LINE OF CLG

STAINLESS STEEL #4 ON ¾" PLYWOOD DOORS

¾" PLY. SIDE PANELS

½" PLY. BACK

NOTE: 2 EQUAL DOORS, 1 CAB. SECTION, CONCEAL HINGES, TOUCH LATCH PLAST. LAM. INSIDE

WASHER/DRYER UNIT

12 / A11 TYPICAL LAVATORY FITTINGS ARRANGEMENT 1"=1'-0"

¢ OF SINK

SINGLE CONTROL LAV. MIXER W/ POP-UP KROIN HV-3

SURFACE MOUNTED SINK SEE SCHEDULE

PLASTIC LAMINATE COUNTER TOP

17 / A11 LAVATORY FITTING ARRANGEMENT @ BATH #1 1"=1'-0" (SIMILAR BATH #5)

POP-UP DRAIN

ALIGN LAV. W/ ¢ OF FITTINGS

DOUBLE CONTROL VALVE, SWIVEL SPOUT, ROSETTES AND HANDLES

UNDER THE COUNTER MOUNTED SINK. SEE SCHEDULE

STONE COUNTER TOP

NOTE: SINK ON LEFT TO HAVE OPPOSITE ARRANGEMENT

BATHROOMS

Vanities

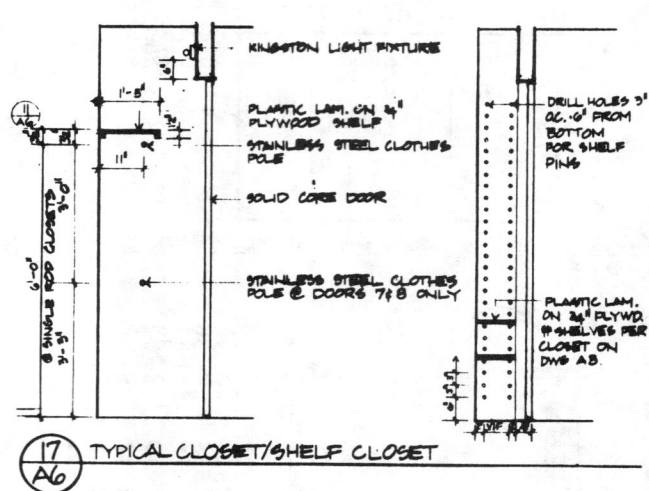

KINGSTON LIGHT FIXTURE

PLASTIC LAM. ON 3/4"
PLYWOOD SHELF

STAINLESS STEEL CLOTHES
POLE

SOLID CORE DOOR

STAINLESS STEEL CLOTHES
POLE @ DOORS 7 & 8 ONLY

DRILL HOLES 3"
OC. 6" FROM
BOTTOM
FOR SHELF
PINS

PLASTIC LAM.
ON 3/4" PLYWD.
SHELVES PER
CLOSET ON
DWG AB.

17 / A6 — TYPICAL CLOSET/SHELF CLOSET

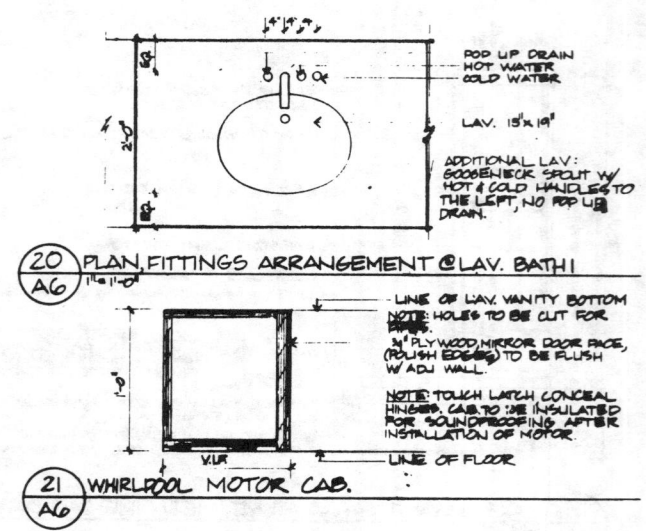

POP UP DRAIN
HOT WATER
COLD WATER

LAV. 15"x 19"

ADDITIONAL LAV:
GOOSENECK SPOUT W/
HOT & COLD HANDLES TO
THE LEFT, NO POP UP
DRAIN.

20 / A6 — PLAN, FITTINGS ARRANGEMENT @ LAV. BATH 1
1½"=1'-0"

LINE OF LAV. VANITY BOTTOM
NOTE: HOLES TO BE CUT FOR
PIPES.

3/4" PLYWOOD, MIRROR DOOR FACE,
(POLISH EDGES) TO BE FLUSH
W/ ADJ WALL.

NOTE: TOUCH LATCH CONCEAL
HINGES. CAB. TO BE INSULATED
FOR SOUNDPROOFING AFTER
INSTALLATION OF MOTOR.

LINE OF FLOOR

21 / A6 — WHIRLPOOL MOTOR CAB.

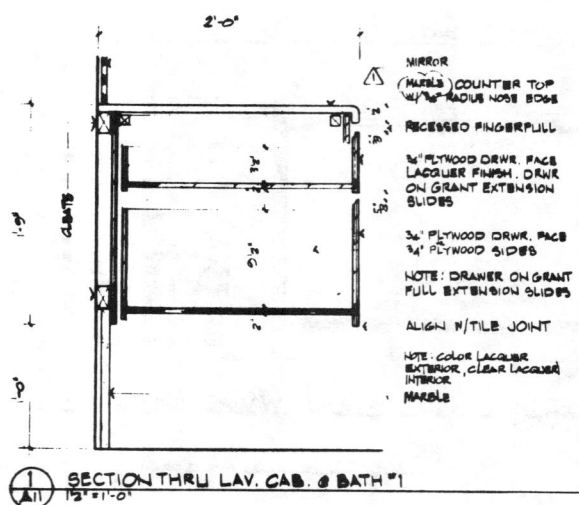

2'-0"

MIRROR

MARBLE COUNTER TOP
W/ 3/8" RADIUS NOSE EDGE

RECESSED FINGERPULL

3/4" PLYWOOD DRWR. FACE
LACQUER FINISH . DRWR
ON GRANT EXTENSION
SLIDES

3/4" PLYWOOD DRWR. FACE
3/4" PLYWOOD SIDES

NOTE: DRAWER ON GRANT
FULL EXTENSION SLIDES

ALIGN W/TILE JOINT

NOTE: COLOR LACQUER
EXTERIOR, CLEAR LACQUER
INTERIOR

MARBLE

1 / A11 — SECTION THRU LAV. CAB. @ BATH #1
1½"=1'-0"

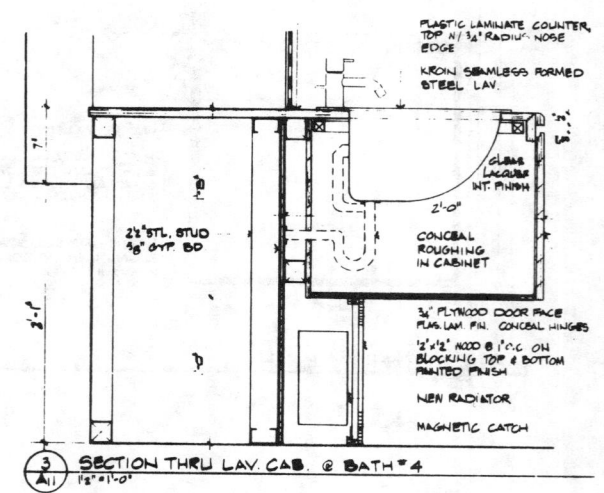

PLASTIC LAMINATE COUNTER
TOP W/ 3/4" RADIUS NOSE
EDGE

KROIN SEAMLESS FORMED
STEEL LAV.

CLEAR
LACQUER
INT. FINISH

CONCEAL
ROUGHING
IN CABINET

2½" STL. STUD
5/8" GYP. BD

3/4" PLYWOOD DOOR FACE
PLAS. LAM. FIN. CONCEAL HINGES

2"x 2" WOOD @ 1" O.C. ON
BLOCKING TOP & BOTTOM
PAINTED FINISH

NEW RADIATOR

MAGNETIC CATCH

3 / A11 — SECTION THRU LAV. CAB. @ BATH #4
1½"=1'-0"

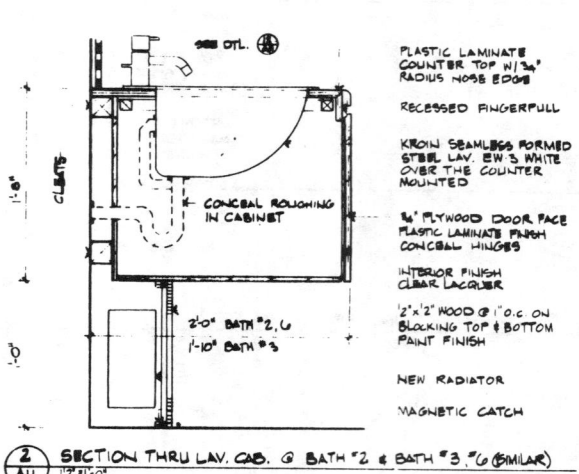

SEE DTL. A

PLASTIC LAMINATE
COUNTER TOP W/ 3/4"
RADIUS NOSE EDGE

RECESSED FINGERPULL

KROIN SEAMLESS FORMED
STEEL LAV. EW-3 WHITE
OVER THE COUNTER
MOUNTED

CONCEAL ROUGHING
IN CABINET

2'-0" BATH #2, 6
1'-10" BATH #3

3/4" PLYWOOD DOOR FACE
PLASTIC LAMINATE FINISH
CONCEAL HINGES

INTERIOR FINISH
CLEAR LACQUER

2"x 2" WOOD @ 1" O.C. ON
BLOCKING TOP & BOTTOM
PAINT FINISH

NEW RADIATOR

MAGNETIC CATCH

2 / A11 — SECTION THRU LAV. CAB. @ BATH #2 & BATH #3, #6 (SIMILAR)
1½"=1'-0"

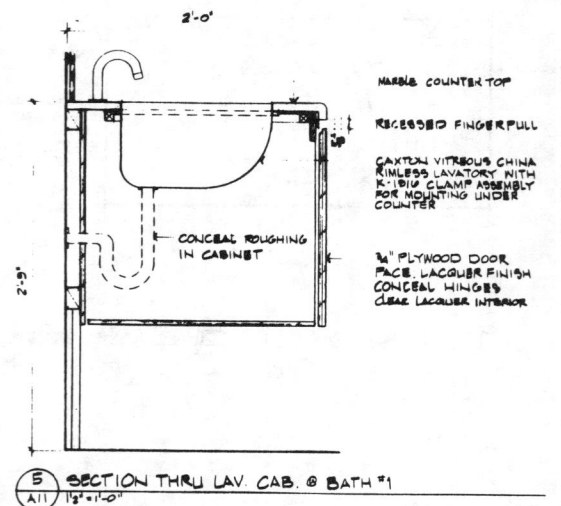

2'-0"

MARBLE COUNTER TOP

RECESSED FINGERPULL

CAXTON VITREOUS CHINA
RIMLESS LAVATORY WITH
K-1016 CLAMP ASSEMBLY
FOR MOUNTING UNDER
COUNTER

CONCEAL ROUGHING
IN CABINET

3/4" PLYWOOD DOOR
FACE LACQUER FINISH
CONCEAL HINGES
CLEAR LACQUER INTERIOR

5 / A11 — SECTION THRU LAV. CAB. @ BATH #1
1½"=1'-0"

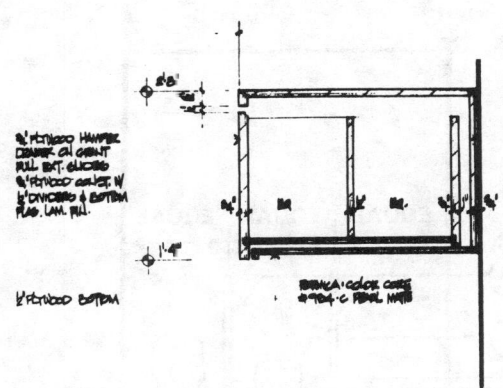

(5) DETAIL: VANITY HAMPER
A17 1/2":1'-0"

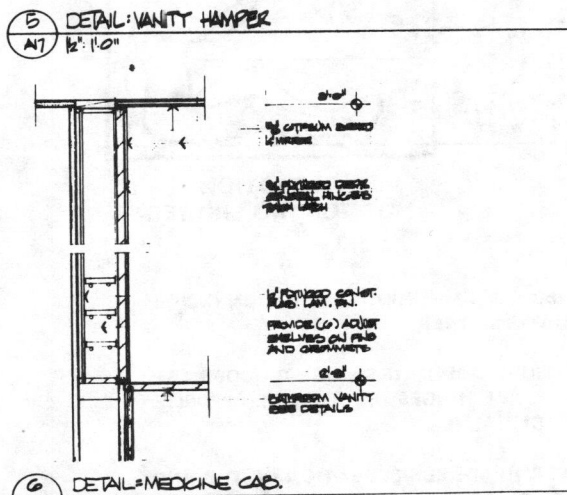

(6) DETAIL: MEDICINE CAB.
A17 1/2":1'-0"

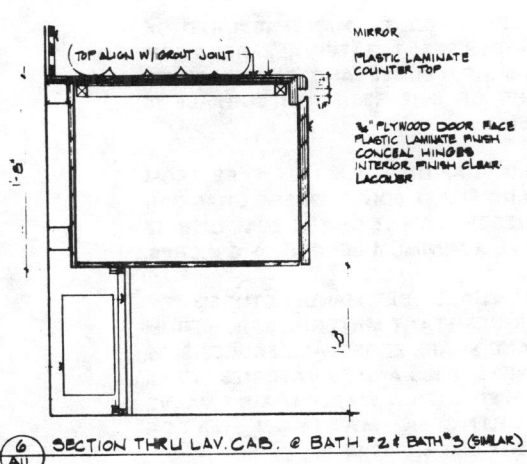

MIRROR

PLASTIC LAMINATE
COUNTER TOP

3/4" PLYWOOD DOOR FACE
PLASTIC LAMINATE FINISH
CONCEAL HINGES
INTERIOR FINISH CLEAR
LACQUER

(6) SECTION THRU LAV. CAB. @ BATH #2 & BATH #3 (SIMILAR)
A11

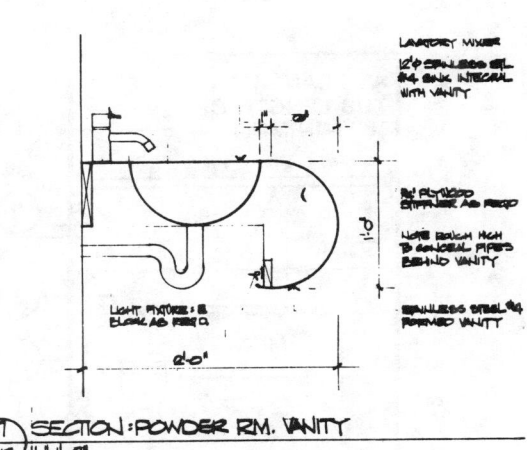

(7) SECTION: POWDER RM. VANITY
A17 1/2":1'-0"

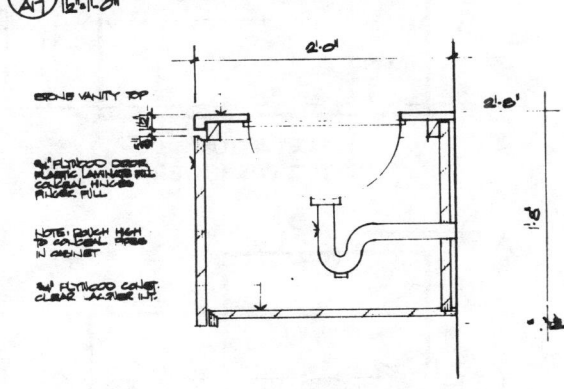

(8) DETAIL: VANITY MASTER BATHROOM
A17 1/2":1'-0"

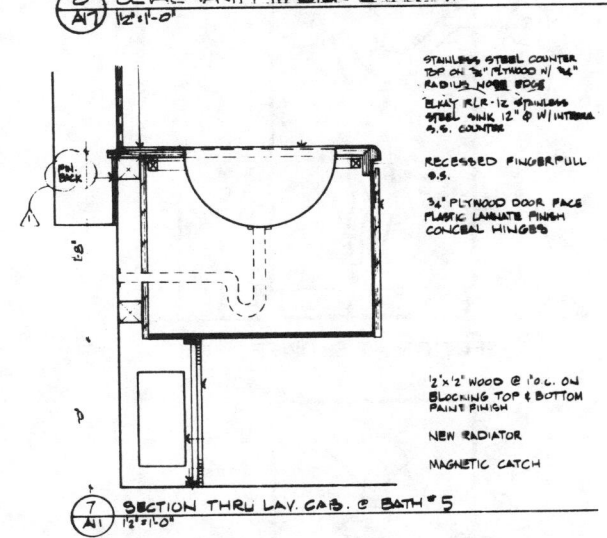

STAINLESS STEEL COUNTER
TOP ON 3/4" PLYWOOD W/ 3/4"
RADIUS NOSE EDGE

ELKAY RLR-12 STAINLESS
STEEL SINK 12" Ø W/ INTEGRAL
S.S. COUNTER

RECESSED FINGERPULL
S.S.

3/4" PLYWOOD DOOR FACE
PLASTIC LAMINATE FINISH
CONCEAL HINGES

1/2" x 2" WOOD @ 1'-0 c. ON
BLOCKING TOP & BOTTOM
PAINT FINISH

NEW RADIATOR

MAGNETIC CATCH

(7) SECTION THRU LAV. CAB. @ BATH #5
A11 1/2":1'-0"

BATHROOMS
Accessory and Control Placement

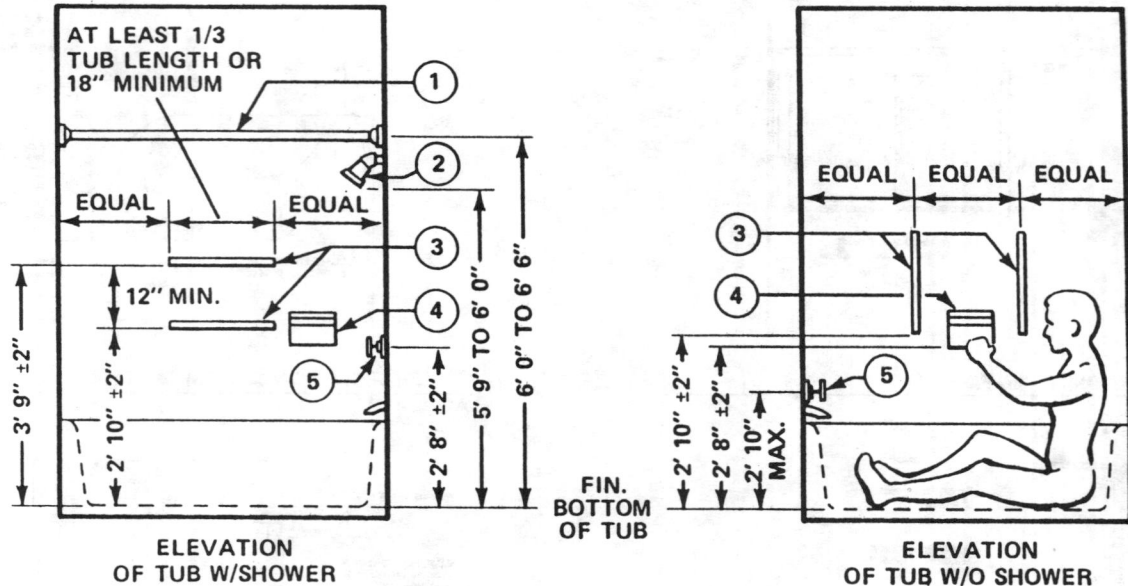

AT LEAST 1/3 TUB LENGTH OR 18" MINIMUM

EQUAL   EQUAL

12" MIN.

3' 9" ±2"

2' 10" ±2"

5' 9" TO 6' 0"

6' 0" TO 6' 6"

2' 8" ±2"

FIN. BOTTOM OF TUB

ELEVATION OF TUB W/SHOWER

EQUAL   EQUAL   EQUAL

2' 10" ±2"

2' 8" ±2"

2' 10" MAX.

ELEVATION OF TUB W/O SHOWER

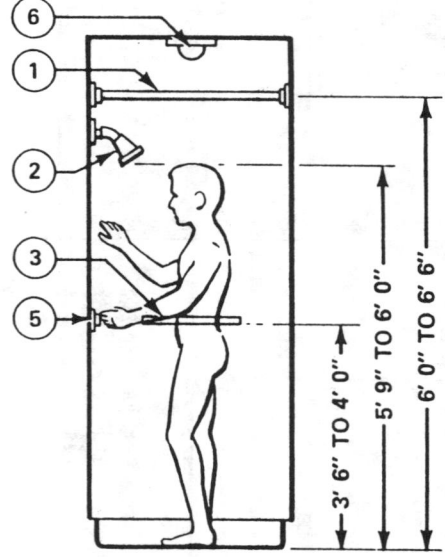

3' 6" TO 4' 0"

5' 9" TO 6' 0"

6' 0" TO 6' 6"

SECTION AT SHOWER

PLAN

1. SHOWER CURTAIN ROD: KEEP WITHIN INSIDE OF TUB OR SHOWER.

1a. ENCLOSURE DOORS: IF SWINGING DOORS ARE USED, PLACE HINGES ON THE SIDE OPPOSITE CONTROL VALVES.

2. SHOWER HEAD: SEE ELEVATION OF TUB AND SHOWER STALL FOR RECOMMENDED HEIGHTS.

3. GRAB BARS SHALL BE MANUFACTURED OF SHATTER-RESISTANT MATERIAL, FREE FROM BURRS, SHARP EDGES AND PINCH POINTS. KNURLING OR SLIP-RESISTANT SURFACE IS DESIRABLE.

4. RECESSED SOAP DISH SHALL BE FREE FROM BURRS AND SHARP EDGES. WHERE GRAB BAR IS AN INTEGRAL PART OF THE SOAP DISH, IT MAY HAVE A MINIMUM LENGTH OF 6 INCHES.

5. FAUCET SHALL BE MANUFACTURED OF SHATTER-RESISTANT MATERIAL, FREE FROM BURRS AND SHARP EDGES. ALL FAUCET SETS IN SHOWERS, TUBS AND LAVATORIES SHALL BE EQUIPPED WITH A WATER-MIXING VALVE DELIVERING A MAXIMUM WATER TEMPERATURE OF 110° ±5°F.

6. SHOWER STALL LIGHT: SHALL BE OF A VAPOR-PROOF FIXTURE WITH THE ELECTRICAL LIGHT SWITCH A MINIMUM OF 72 INCHES AWAY FROM SHOWER STALL.

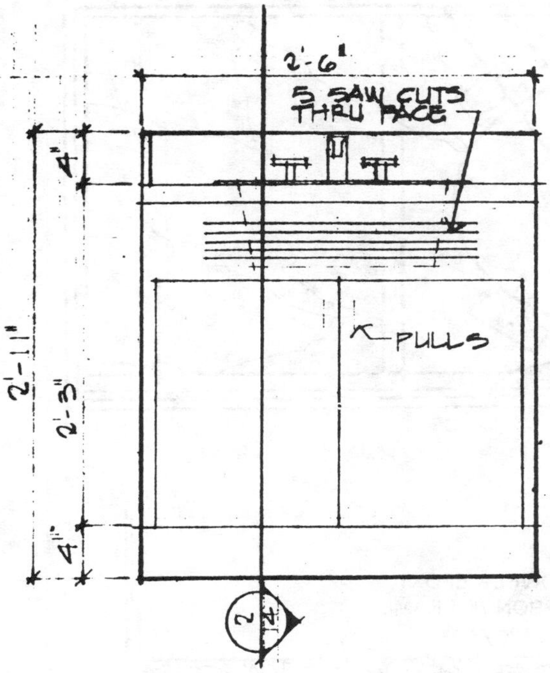

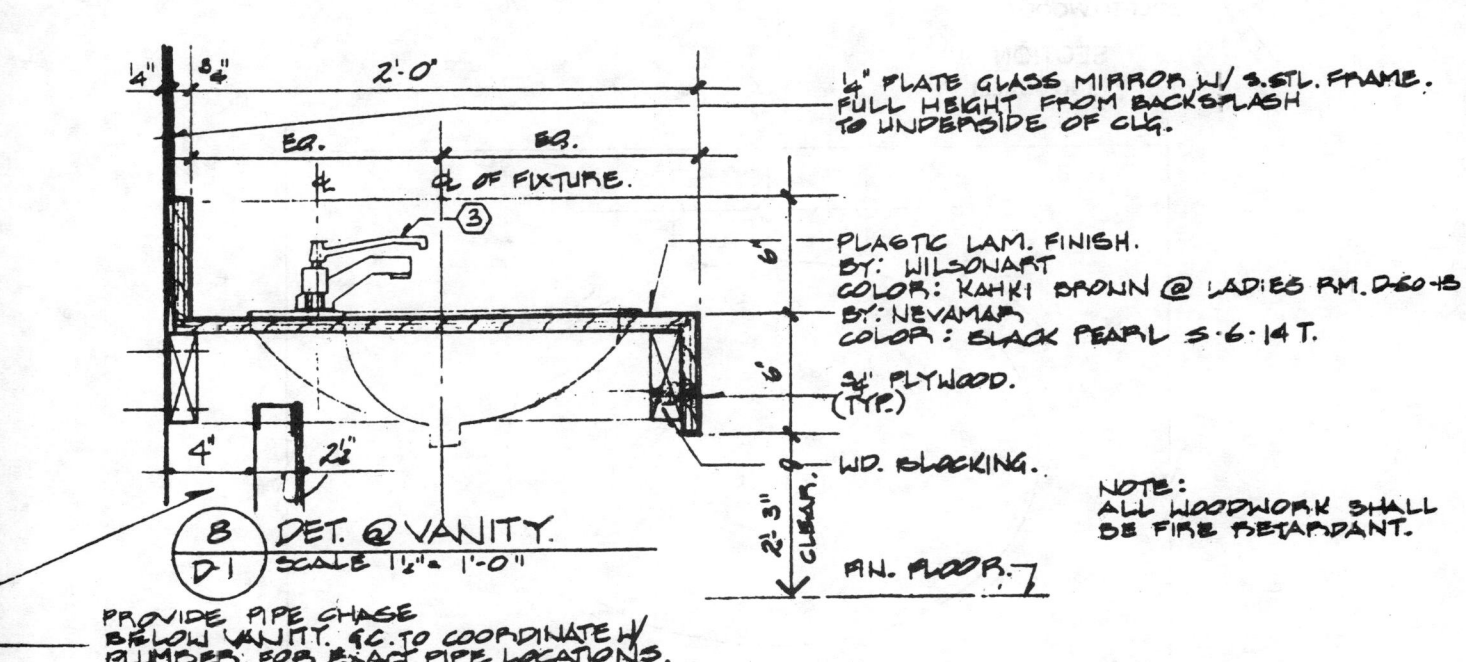

2'-6"

5 SAW CUTS THRU FACE

4"

PULLS

2'-11"

2'-5"

4"

PLASTIC LAM.

SPLASH RETURN @ WALL

3/4" RED OAK PLYWD. W/ RED OAK EDGES

LAV.

3/8" FIR PLYWD

3/4" FIR PLYWD

DETAIL @ 3/4"-0"

4" BASE

1'-9"

1
14
TOILET ROOM CAB. ELEV.

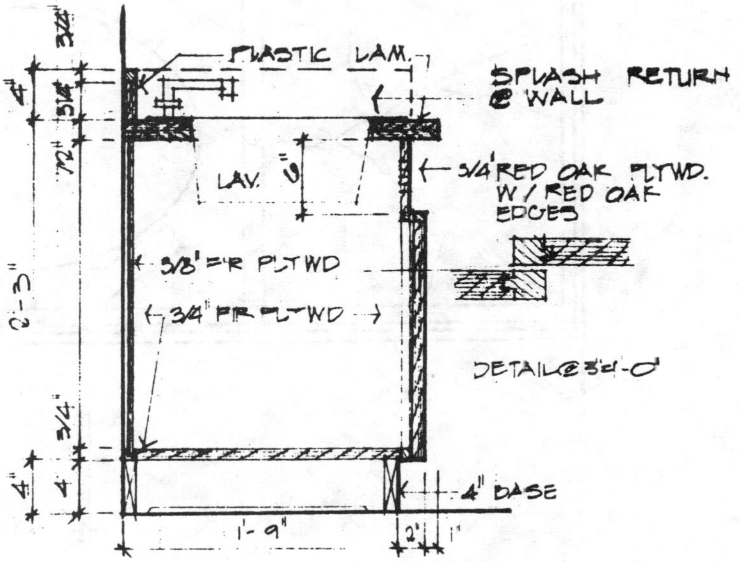

2
14
TOILET ROOM CAB. SECT.

2'-0"

EQ.   EQ.

℄ OF FIXTURE.

3

4" PLATE GLASS MIRROR W/ S.STL. FRAME. FULL HEIGHT FROM BACKSPLASH TO UNDERSIDE OF CLG.

PLASTIC LAM. FINISH.
BY: WILSONART
COLOR: KAHKI BROWN @ LADIES RM. D-60-B
BY: NEVAMAR
COLOR: BLACK PEARL S-6-14 T.

3/4" PLYWOOD.
(TYP.)

WD. BLOCKING.

2'-3" CLEAR.

FIN. FLOOR.

NOTE:
ALL WOODWORK SHALL BE FIRE RETARDANT.

4"   2½"

B
D1
DET. @ VANITY.
SCALE 1½" = 1'-0"

PROVIDE PIPE CHASE BELOW VANITY. GC. TO COORDINATE W/ PLUMBER. FOR EXACT PIPE LOCATIONS.

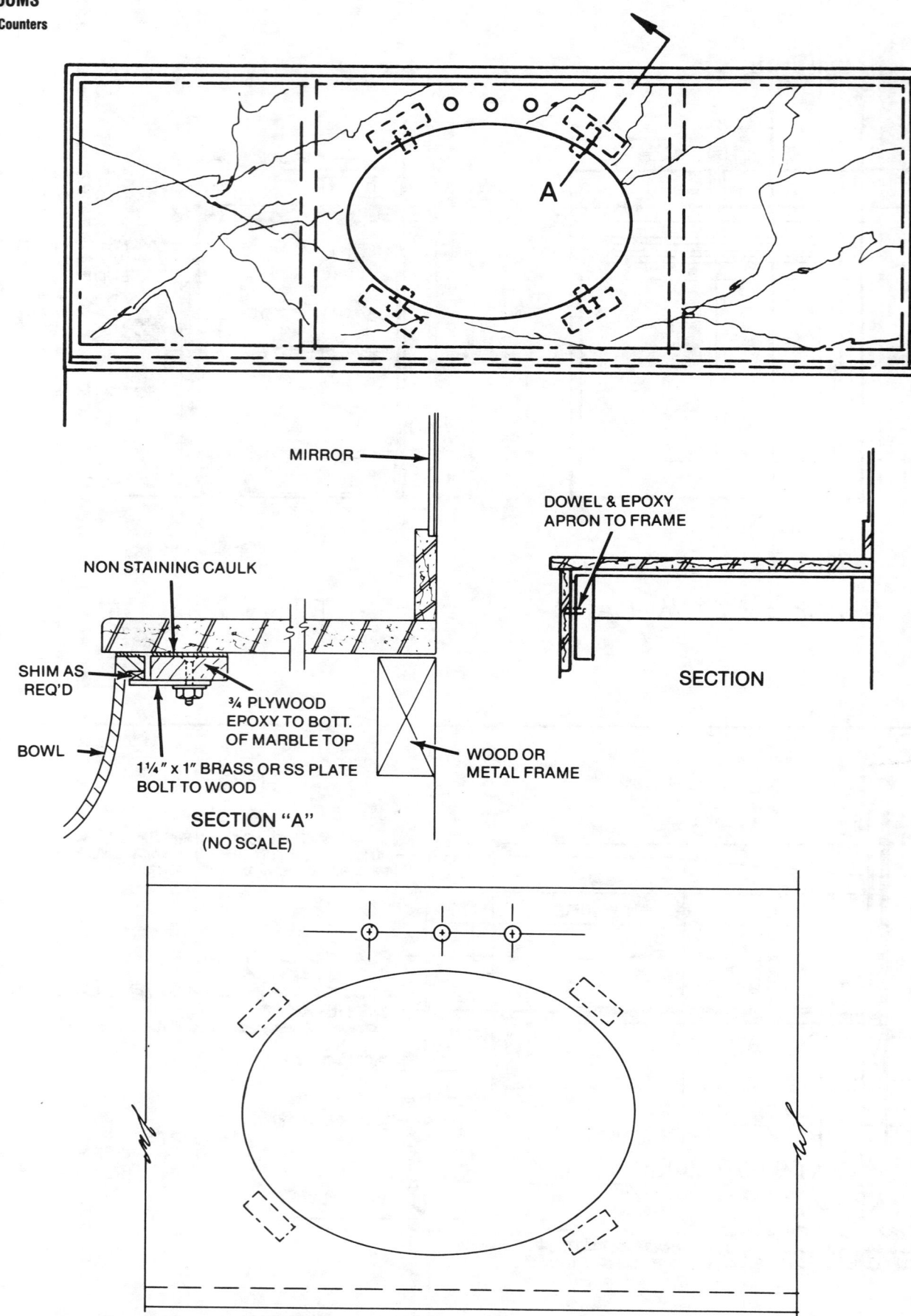

Fig. 16 Typical details of a marble vanity-top installation.

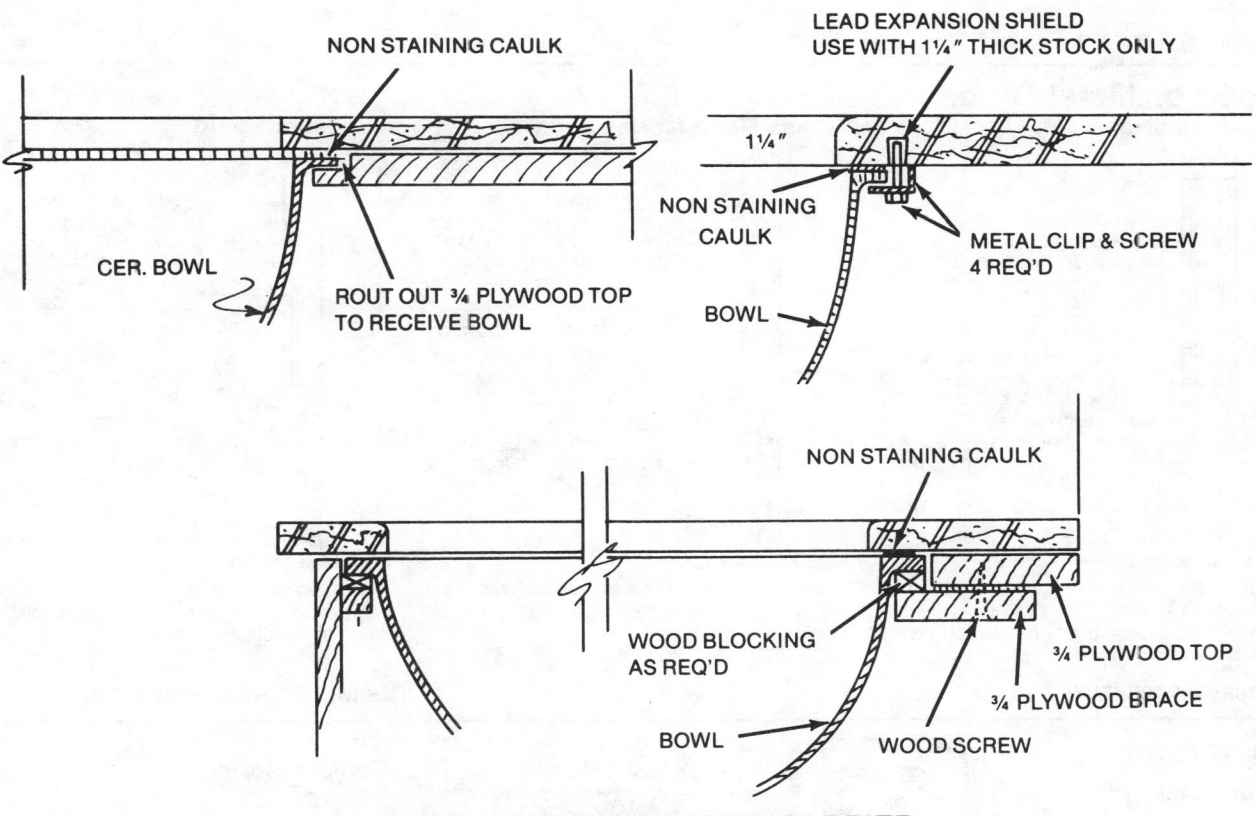

NON STAINING CAULK

LEAD EXPANSION SHIELD
USE WITH 1¼" THICK STOCK ONLY

1¼"

CER. BOWL

ROUT OUT ¾ PLYWOOD TOP
TO RECEIVE BOWL

NON STAINING
CAULK

BOWL

METAL CLIP & SCREW
4 REQ'D

NON STAINING CAULK

WOOD BLOCKING
AS REQ'D

¾ PLYWOOD TOP

¾ PLYWOOD BRACE

BOWL

WOOD SCREW

TYPICAL SECTIONS BOWL CARRIER

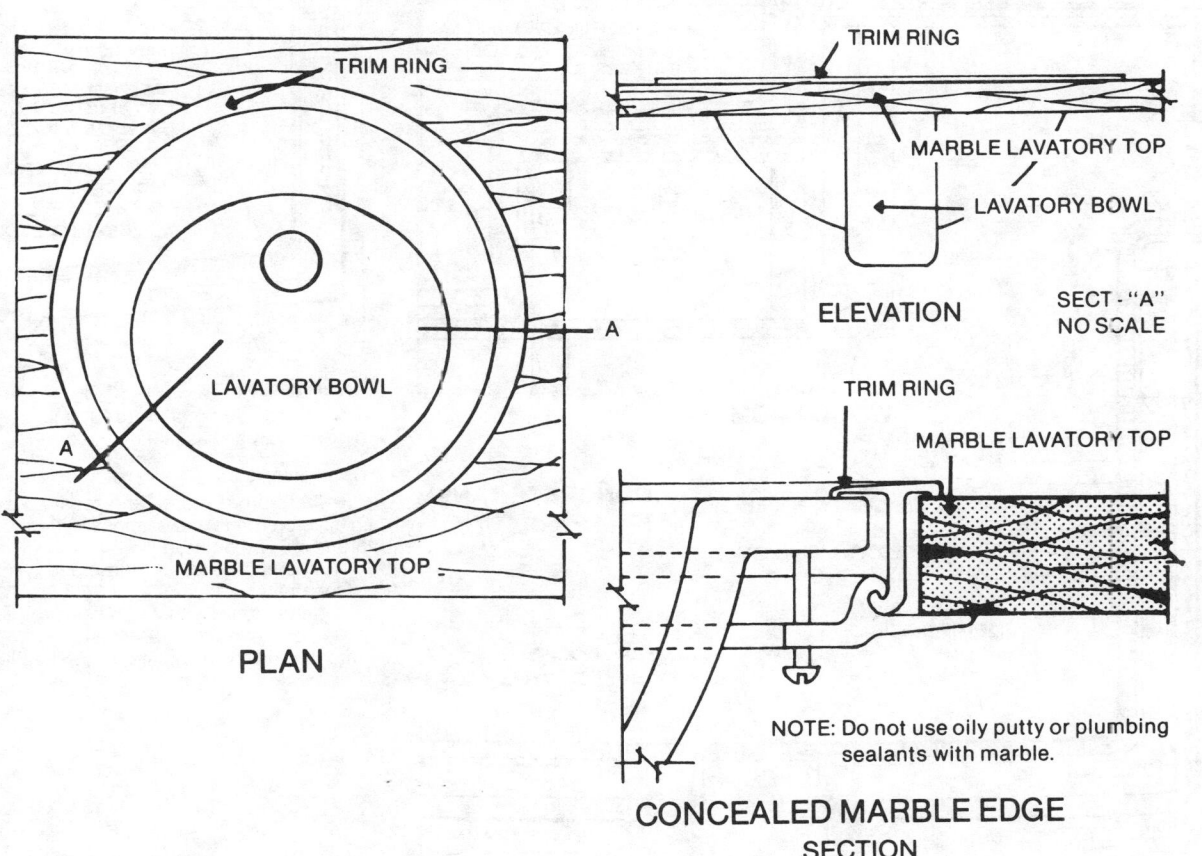

TRIM RING

TRIM RING

MARBLE LAVATORY TOP

LAVATORY BOWL

A

A

LAVATORY BOWL

MARBLE LAVATORY TOP

PLAN

ELEVATION

SECT - "A"
NO SCALE

TRIM RING

MARBLE LAVATORY TOP

NOTE: Do not use oily putty or plumbing
sealants with marble.

CONCEALED MARBLE EDGE
SECTION

Fig. 16 *(Continued)*

BATHTUB WALLS

Wood or Metal Studs
Cement Mortar

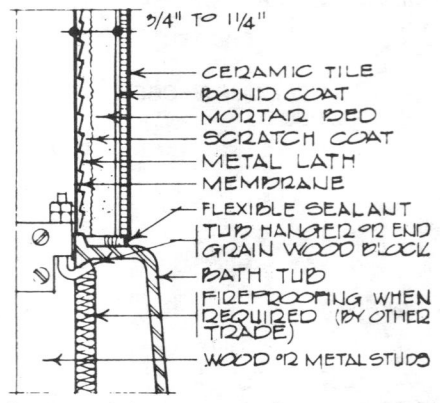

- CERAMIC TILE
- BOND COAT
- MORTAR BED
- SCRATCH COAT
- METAL LATH
- MEMBRANE
- FLEXIBLE SEALANT
- TUB HANGER OR END GRAIN WOOD BLOCK
- BATH TUB
- FIREPROOFING WHEN REQUIRED (BY OTHER TRADE)
- WOOD OR METAL STUDS

3/4" TO 1 1/4"

Recommended uses

■ over dry, well-braced wood studs, furring, or metal studs
■ preferred method of installation over wood studs for bathtubs

Glass Mesh Mortar Units

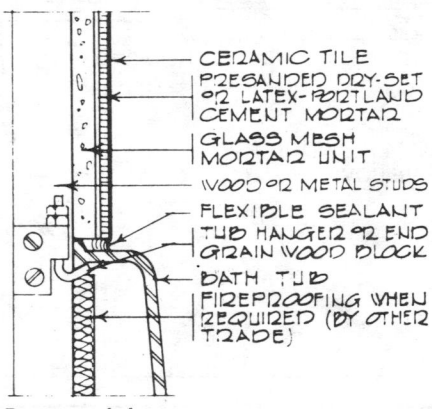

- CERAMIC TILE
- PRESANDED DRY-SET OR LATEX-PORTLAND CEMENT MORTAR
- GLASS MESH MORTAR UNIT
- WOOD OR METAL STUDS
- FLEXIBLE SEALANT
- TUB HANGER OR END GRAIN WOOD BLOCK
- BATH TUB
- FIREPROOFING WHEN REQUIRED (BY OTHER TRADE)

Recommended use

■ in tub enclosures and tub showers over dry, well-braced wood studs, furring, or metal studs

Gypsum Board

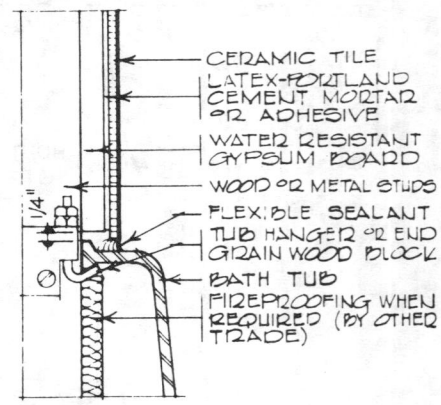

- CERAMIC TILE
- LATEX-PORTLAND CEMENT MORTAR OR ADHESIVE
- WATER RESISTANT GYPSUM BOARD
- WOOD OR METAL STUDS
- FLEXIBLE SEALANT
- TUB HANGER OR END GRAIN WOOD BLOCK
- BATH TUB
- FIREPROOFING WHEN REQUIRED (BY OTHER TRADE)

1/4"

Recommended use

■ in tub enclosures and tub showers over water-resistant gypsum backing board on wood or metal studs

TILE TUBS AND FOUNTAINS

Membrane
Cement Mortar

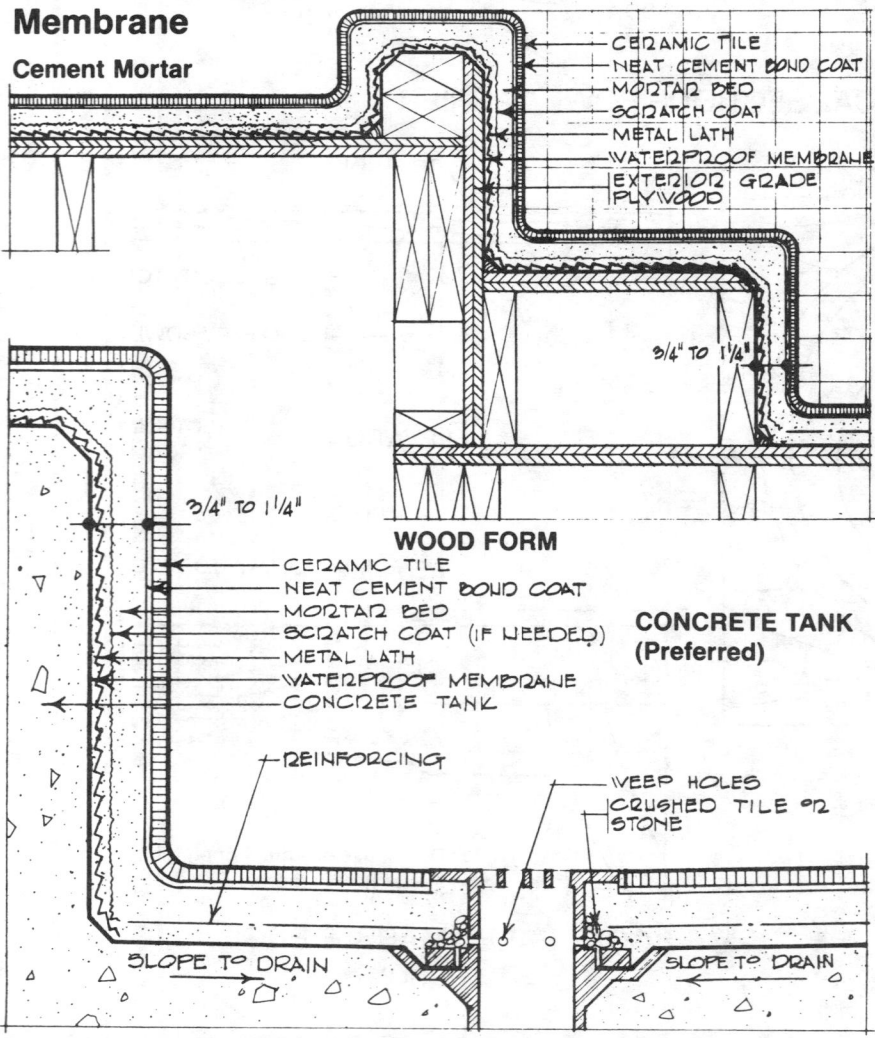

- CERAMIC TILE
- NEAT CEMENT BOND COAT
- MORTAR BED
- SCRATCH COAT
- METAL LATH
- WATERPROOF MEMBRANE
- EXTERIOR GRADE PLYWOOD

3/4" TO 1 1/4"

WOOD FORM

- CERAMIC TILE
- NEAT CEMENT BOND COAT
- MORTAR BED
- SCRATCH COAT (IF NEEDED)
- METAL LATH
- WATERPROOF MEMBRANE
- CONCRETE TANK

3/4" TO 1 1/4"

**CONCRETE TANK
(Preferred)**

- REINFORCING
- WEEP HOLES
- CRUSHED TILE OR STONE

SLOPE TO DRAIN   SLOPE TO DRAIN

SHOWER RECEPTOR RENOVATION

Cement Mortar

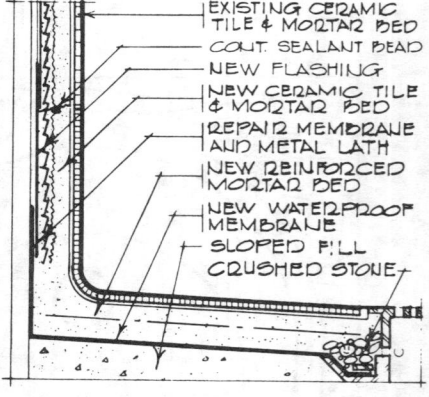

- EXISTING CERAMIC TILE & MORTAR BED
- CONT. SEALANT BEAD
- NEW FLASHING
- NEW CERAMIC TILE & MORTAR BED
- REPAIR MEMBRANE AND METAL LATH
- NEW REINFORCED MORTAR BED
- NEW WATERPROOF MEMBRANE
- SLOPED FILL CRUSHED STONE

Recommended use

■ over wood or concrete subfloors; where old shower pan has failed

Requirements

■ waterproof membrane required except in slab-on-grade installations where membrane may be omitted
■ slope tank so that membrane will slope to the drain
■ flange drain with weep holes required
■ wood framing, if used, should be pressure treated and designed to resist deflection and movement

SHOWER RECEPTORS, WALLS

Wood or Metal Studs

Cement Mortar

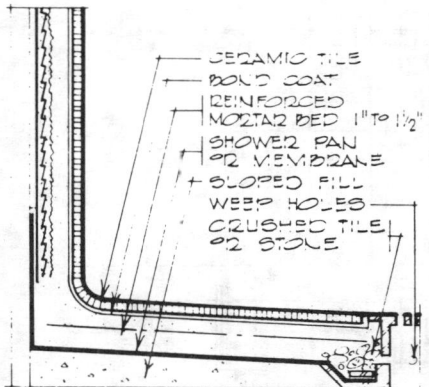

CERAMIC TILE
BOND COAT
REINFORCED
MORTAR BED 1" TO 1½"
SHOWER PAN
OR MEMBRANE
SLOPED FILL
WEEP HOLES
CRUSHED TILE
OR STONE

Recommended use
- over wood or concrete subfloors

Glass Mesh Mortar Units

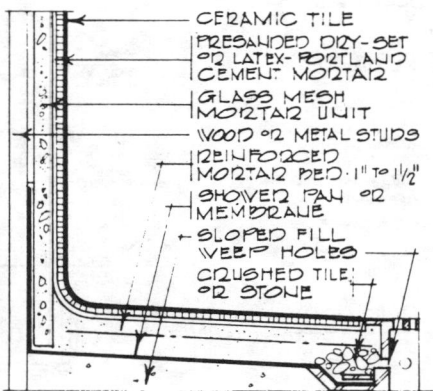

CERAMIC TILE
PRESANDED DRY-SET
OR LATEX- PORTLAND
CEMENT MORTAR
GLASS MESH
MORTAR UNIT
WOOD OR METAL STUDS
REINFORCED
MORTAR BED 1" TO 1½"
SHOWER PAN OR
MEMBRANE
SLOPED FILL
WEEP HOLES
CRUSHED TILE
OR STONE

Recommended use
- in showers over dry, well-braced wood studs, furring, or metal studs

**Gypsum Board
Organic Adhesive**

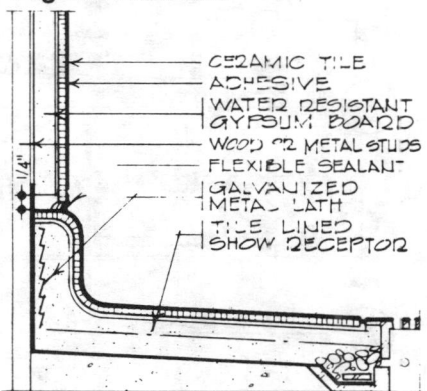

CERAMIC TILE
ADHESIVE
WATER RESISTANT
GYPSUM BOARD
WOOD OR METAL STUDS
FLEXIBLE SEALANT
GALVANIZED
METAL LATH
TILE LINED
SHOWER RECEPTOR

Recommended use
- in showers over water-resistant gypsum backing board on wood or metal studs

COUNTERTOPS

Wood Base

Cement Mortar

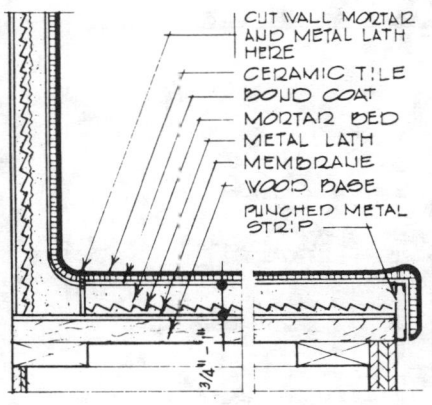

CUT WALL MORTAR
AND METAL LATH
HERE
CERAMIC TILE
BOND COAT
MORTAR BED
METAL LATH
MEMBRANE
WOOD BASE
PUNCHED METAL
STRIP

Recommended uses
- on countertops, drainboards, lavatory tops, etc.
- preferred method where sink or lavatory is to be recessed

Thin-Bed

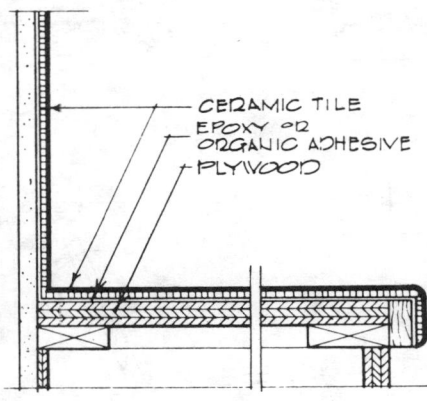

CERAMIC TILE
EPOXY OR
ORGANIC ADHESIVE
PLYWOOD

Recommended use
- on countertops where thin-set method is desired

Glass Mesh Mortar Unit

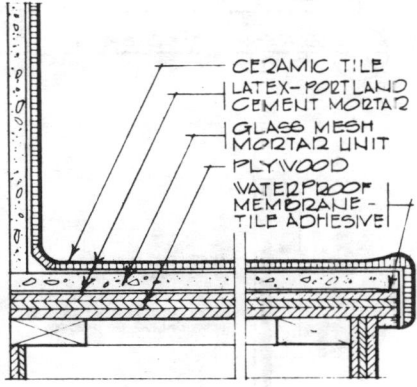

CERAMIC TILE
LATEX-PORTLAND
CEMENT MORTAR
GLASS MESH
MORTAR UNIT
PLYWOOD
WATERPROOF
MEMBRANE -
TILE ADHESIVE

Recommended uses
- preferred thin-set mortar method on countertops, drainboards, lavatory tops, and similar uses
- preferred method where self-rimming sinks and lavatories are desired

Fig. 18 Typical installation details for shower receptors, walls, and countertops.

BATHROOMS
Bathtub and Shower Details

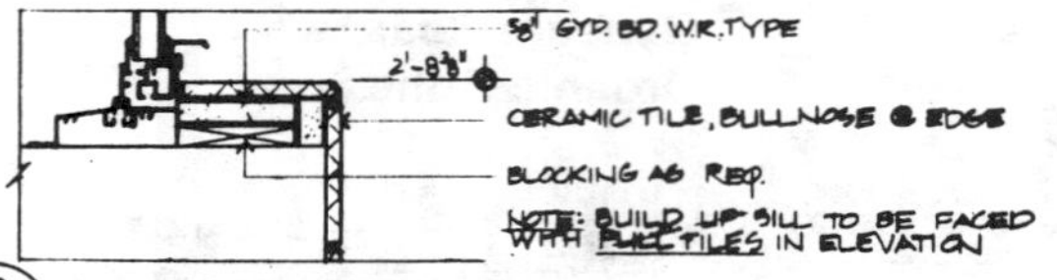

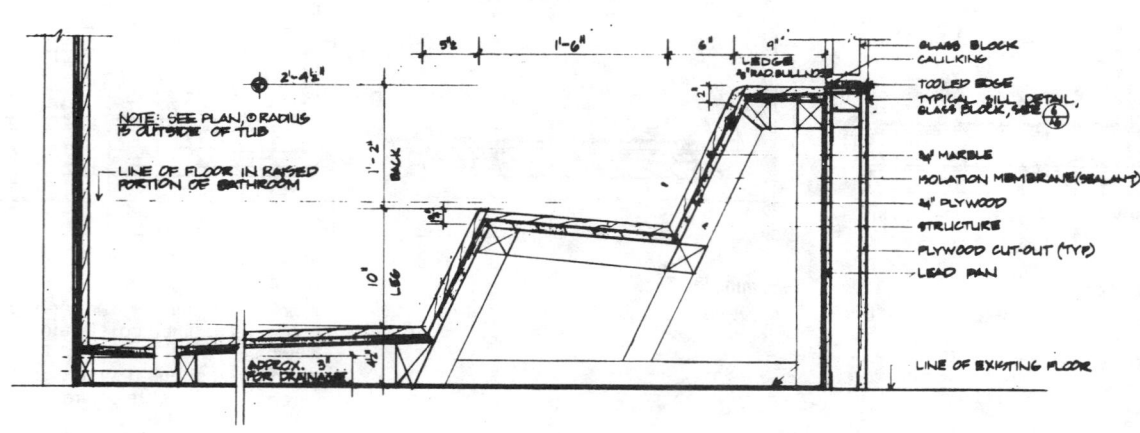

⁵/₈" GYP. BD. W.R. TYPE

2'-8¾"

CERAMIC TILE, BULLNOSE @ EDGE

BLOCKING AS REQ.

NOTE: BUILD UP SILL TO BE FACED WITH FULL TILES IN ELEVATION

⑩ SILL DETAIL @ BATH 2
A6   3"=1'-0"

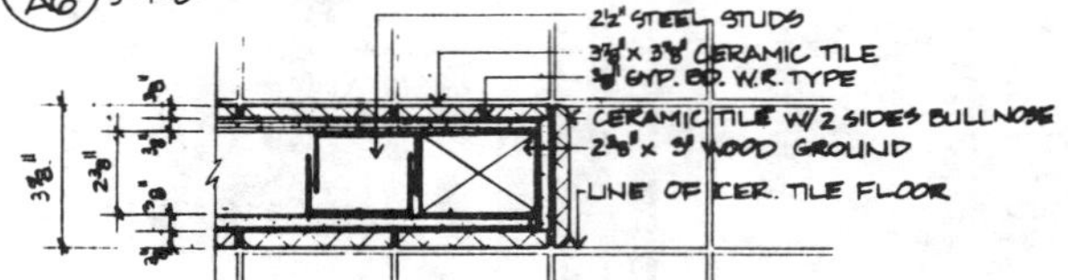

2½" STEEL STUDS
3¾" x 3¾" CERAMIC TILE
⅝" GYP. BD. W.R. TYPE
CERAMIC TILE W/2 SIDES BULLNOSE
2⅜" x 9" WOOD GROUND
LINE OF CER. TILE FLOOR

⑪ WING WALL @ BATH 2 · TYP.
A6   3"=1'-0"

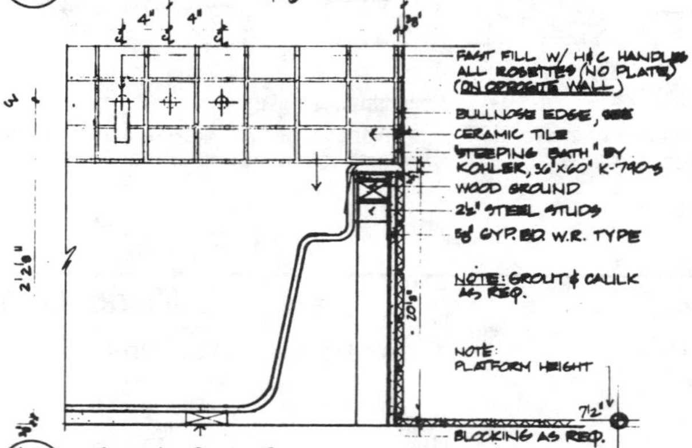

1'-6"

FAST FILL W/ H&C HANDLES
ALL ROSETTES (NO PLATE)
(ON OPPOSITE WALL)

BULLNOSE EDGE, SEE
CERAMIC TILE

STEEPING BATH" BY
KOHLER, 36"x60" K-790-5

WOOD GROUND

2½" STEEL STUDS

⅝" GYP. BD. W.R. TYPE

NOTE: GROUT & CAULK AS REQ.

NOTE: PLATFORM HEIGHT

BLOCKING AS REQ.

⑫ SECTION: BATH @ BATH 2
A6   1½"=1'-0"

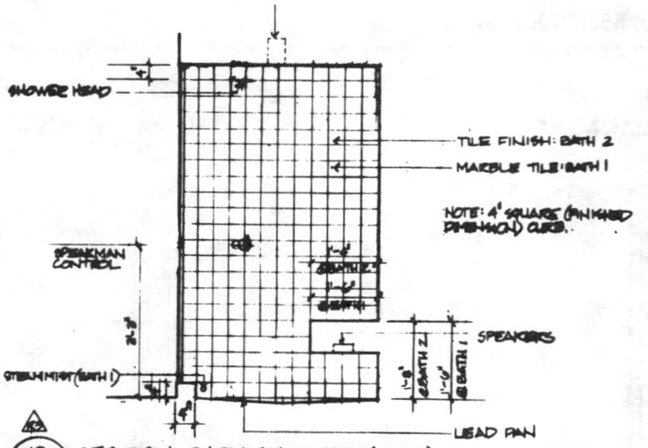

SHOWER HEAD

TILE FINISH: BATH 2

MARBLE TILE: BATH 1

NOTE: 4" SQUARES (FINISHED DIMENSION) CURB

SPEAKMAN CONTROL

SPEAKERS

STEAM MIST (BATH 1)

LEAD PAN

⑬ SECTION THRU SHOWER (TYP.)
A6   ½"=1'-0"

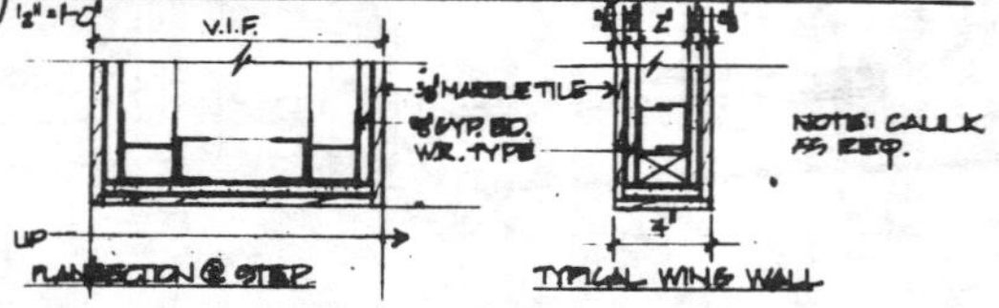

V.I.F.

⅜" MARBLE TILE
⅝" GYP BD. W.R. TYPE

NOTE: CAULK AS REQ.

UP
PLAN SECTION @ STEP   TYPICAL WING WALL

⑭ SECTION THRU MARLE TILE WALL @ BATH 1
A6   ½"=1'-0"

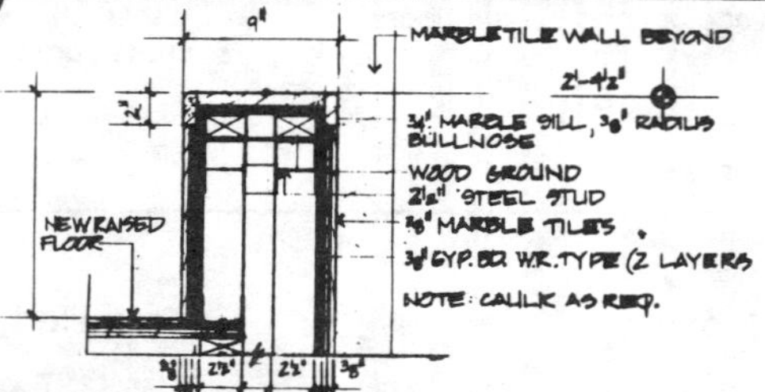

MARBLE TILE WALL BEYOND

2'-4½"

¾" MARBLE SILL, ⅜" RADIUS BULLNOSE
WOOD GROUND
2½" STEEL STUD
⅜" MARBLE TILES
⅝" GYP. BD. W.R. TYPE (2 LAYERS)

NEW RAISED FLOOR

NOTE: CAULK AS REQ.

⑮ SECTION THRU KNEE WALL & SILL @ BATH 1
A6   ½"=1'-0"

NOTE: SEE PLAN, Ø RADIUS IS OUTSIDE OF TUB

LINE OF FLOOR IN RAISED PORTION OF BATHROOM

2'-4½"

5½"   1'-6"   6"   9"

LEDGE
½" RAD BULLNOSE

GLASS BLOCK
CAULKING

TOOLED EDGE

TYPICAL SILL DETAIL,
GLASS BLOCK, SEE

¾" MARBLE

ISOLATION MEMBRANE (SEALANT)

¾" PLYWOOD

STRUCTURE

PLYWOOD CUT-OUT (TYP.)

LEAD PAN

LINE OF EXISTING FLOOR

APPROX. 3" FOR DRAINAGE

⑯ SECTION THRU BATHTUB @ BATH #1 (TYP.)
A6   1½"=1'-0"

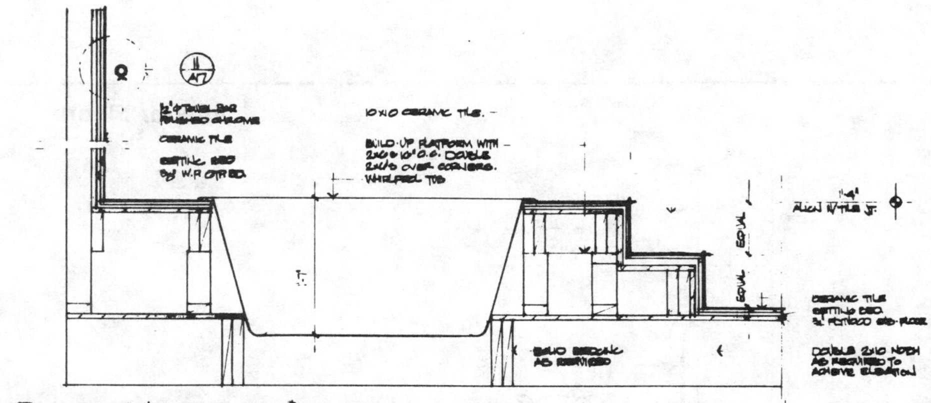

12 / SECTION: WHIRLPOOL BATH #1
A17   1"=1'-0"

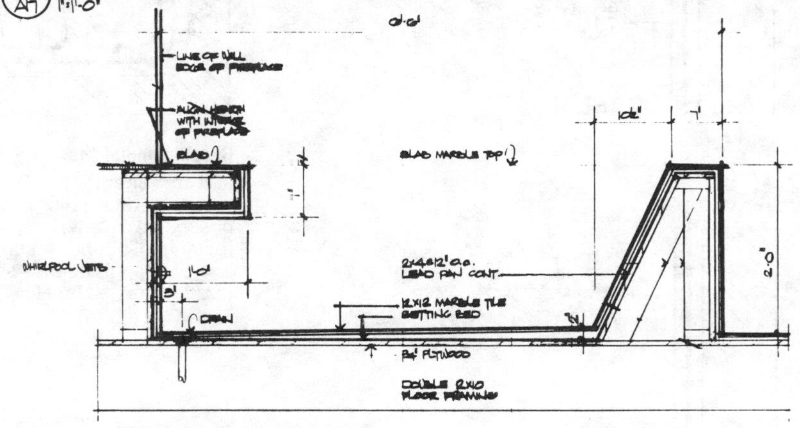

10X10 CERAMIC TILE.

BUILD-UP PLATFORM WITH
2X6 @ 16" O.C. DOUBLE
2X6 OVER CORNERS.
WHIRLPOOL TUB

12'-0" TOWEL BAR
BRUSHED CHROME

CERAMIC TILE

SETTING BED
BY W.R. CERT'D.

ALIGN W/TILE JT.

CERAMIC TILE
SETTING BED
3/4" PLYWOOD SUB-FLOOR

BUILD BEDDING
AS REQUIRED

DOUBLE 2X10 NOTCH
AS REQUIRED TO
ACHIEVE ELEVATION

13 / SECTION: WHIRLPOOL TUB, MASTER BATH
A17   1"=1'-0"

LINE OF WALL
EDGE OF FIREPLACE

ALIGN WIDTH
WITH INSIDE
OF FIREPLACE

SLAB MARBLE TOP

SLAB MARBLE TOP

WHIRLPOOL JETS

2X4 @ 12" O.C.
LEAD PAN CONT.

DRAIN

12X12 MARBLE TILE
SETTING BED

3/4" PLYWOOD

DOUBLE 2X10
FLOOR FRAMING

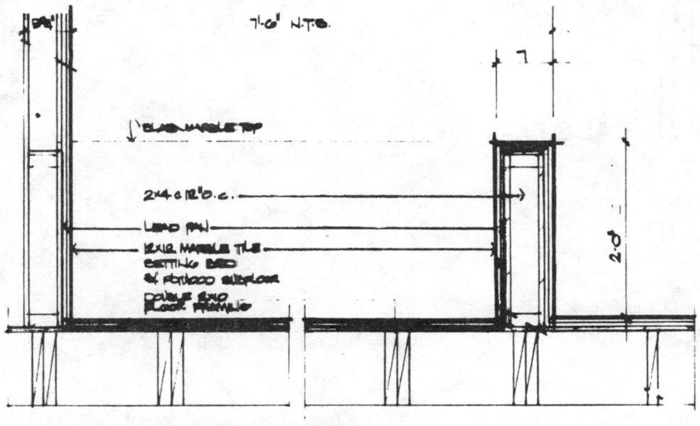

14 / SECTION: WHIRLPOOL TUB, MASTER BATH
A17   1"=1'-0"

SLAB MARBLE TOP

2X4 @ 12" O.C.

LEAD PAN

12X12 MARBLE TILE
SETTING BED
3/4" PLYWOOD SUBFLOOR
DOUBLE 2X10
FLOOR FRAMING

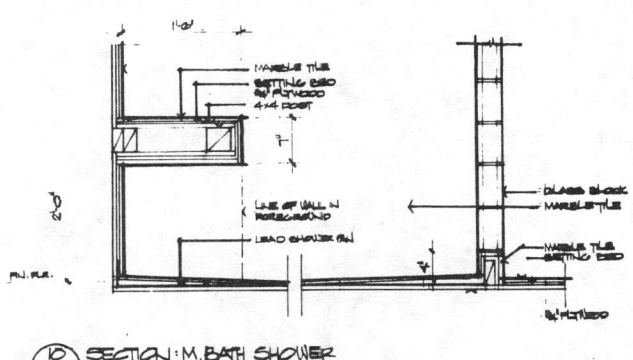

10 / SECTION: M. BATH SHOWER
A17   1"=1'-0"

MARBLE TILE
SETTING BED
3/4" PLYWOOD
4X4 POST

GLASS BLOCK
MARBLE TILE

MARBLE TILE
SETTING BED

LINE OF WALL IN
FOREGROUND

LEAD SHOWER PAN

3/4" PLYWOOD

FIN. FLR.

BATHROOMS
Ceramic Tile Details

TILE OVER TILE

Interior Walls

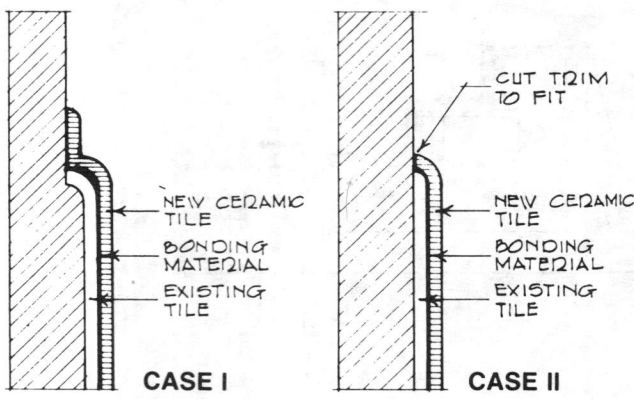

CUT TRIM TO FIT

NEW CERAMIC TILE

BONDING MATERIAL

EXISTING TILE

CASE I

CASE II

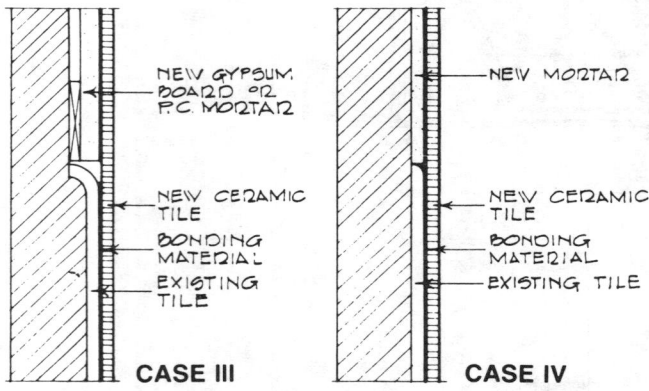

NEW GYPSUM BOARD OR P.C. MORTAR

NEW CERAMIC TILE

BONDING MATERIAL

EXISTING TILE

NEW MORTAR

NEW CERAMIC TILE

BONDING MATERIAL

EXISTING TILE

CASE III

CASE IV

Recommended uses
■ for alteration of ceramic-tiled areas where modernization or a change of design is desired in residences, motels and hotels, restaurants, public rest rooms, etc.
■ also applicable to smooth walls of marble, stone, slate, etc.

Requirements
■ existing installation must be sound, well bonded, and without major structural cracks

Materials, grouting, expansion joints, installation specifications
■ for organic adhesive installation see Method W223
■ for Dry-Set or latex-portland cement mortar installation see Method W202
■ for epoxy adhesive installation refer to manufacturer's literature

Fig. 19 Typical installation details for tile over tile.

Interior Floors

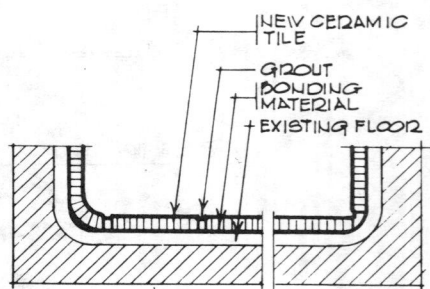

NEW CERAMIC TILE

GROUT

BONDING MATERIAL

EXISTING FLOOR

Recommended uses
■ for alteration of ceramic-tiled areas where modernization or a change of design is desired in residences, motels and hotels, restaurants, public rest rooms, etc.
■ also applicable to smooth floors of terrazzo, stone, slate, etc.

ACCESSIBILITY

It is essential that the design of interior spaces, as well as exterior spaces, be responsive to the needs of those having physical disabilities. There is a proliferation of state and local legislation in this regard, and, more recently, federal legislation (Americans with Disabilities Act of 1990), that provides design guidelines and requirements. The designer should become familiar with those codes and other requirements in her or his area prior to initiation of design and, where possible, go beyond the very minimum standards.

The design of the bathroom is perhaps one of those areas where the interface between the physically disabled and the interior space is the most critical. Accordingly, on this page and the following pages are design guidelines prepared by the Veterans Administration and the U.S. Department of Housing and Urban Development.

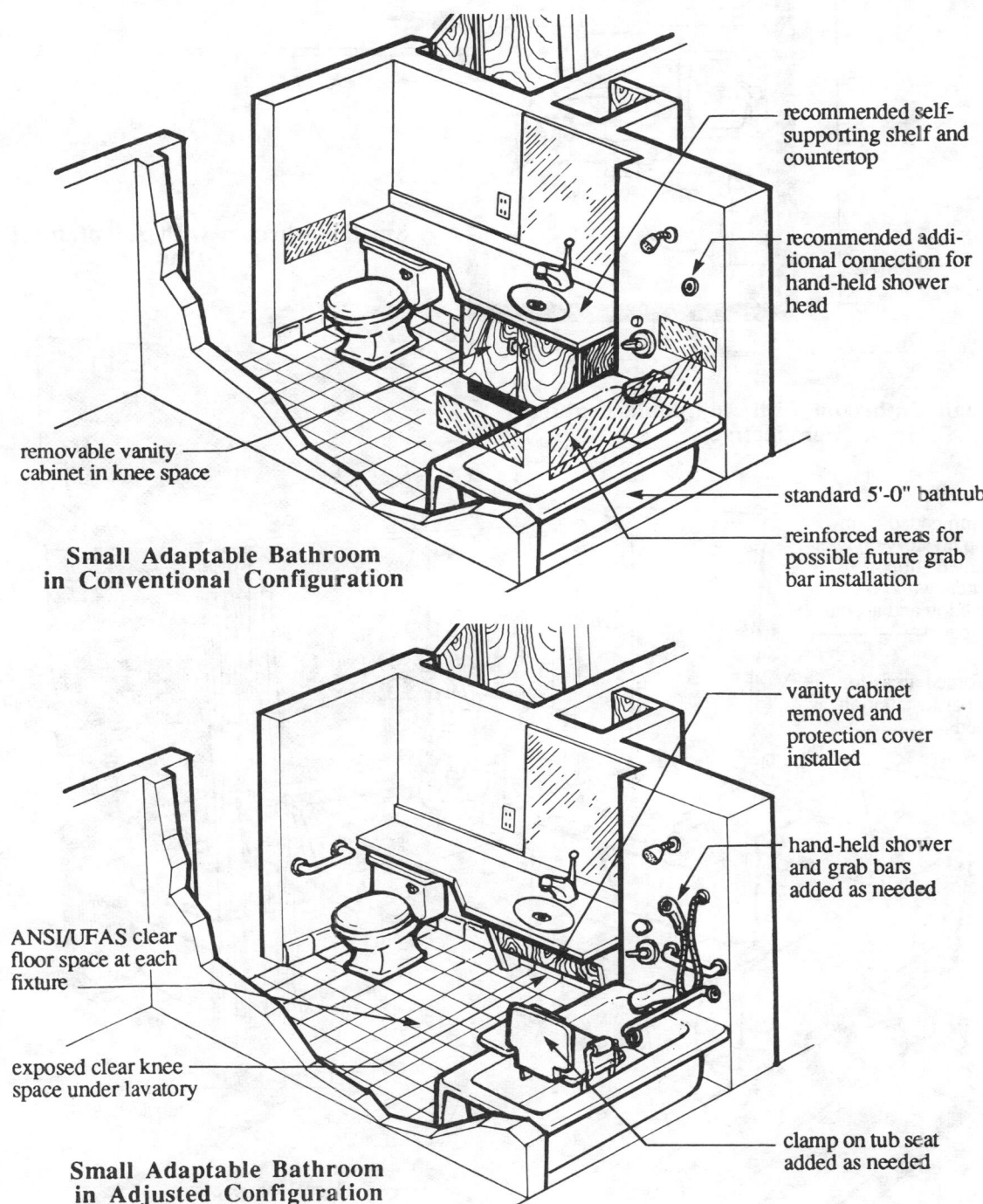

recommended self-supporting shelf and countertop

recommended additional connection for hand-held shower head

removable vanity cabinet in knee space

standard 5'-0" bathtub

reinforced areas for possible future grab bar installation

Small Adaptable Bathroom in Conventional Configuration

vanity cabinet removed and protection cover installed

hand-held shower and grab bars added as needed

ANSI/UFAS clear floor space at each fixture

exposed clear knee space under lavatory

clamp on tub seat added as needed

Small Adaptable Bathroom in Adjusted Configuration

BATHROOMS
Adaptable Bathrooms

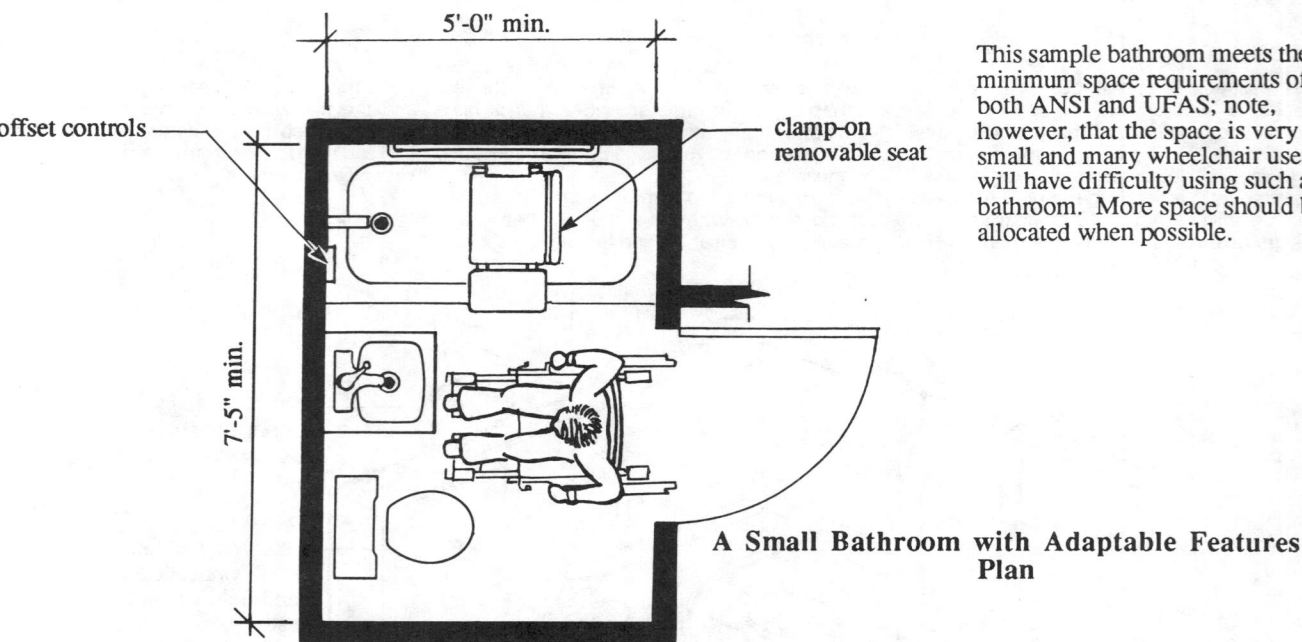

offset controls

5'-0" min.

7'-5" min.

clamp-on removable seat

This sample bathroom meets the minimum space requirements of both ANSI and UFAS; note, however, that the space is very small and many wheelchair users will have difficulty using such a bathroom. More space should be allocated when possible.

A Small Bathroom with Adaptable Features
Plan

A Small Bathroom with Adaptable Features
Perspective

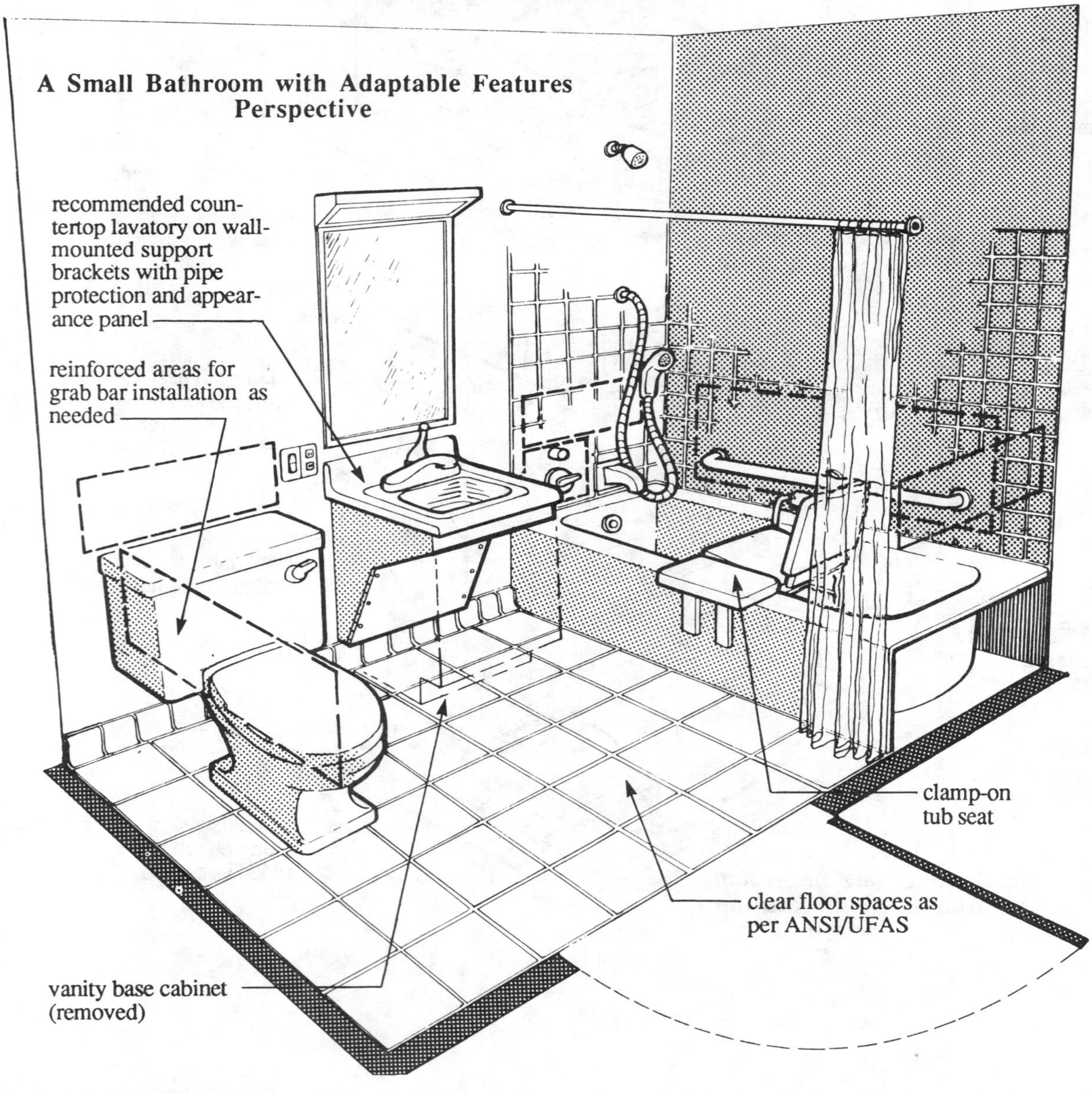

recommended countertop lavatory on wall-mounted support brackets with pipe protection and appearance panel

reinforced areas for grab bar installation as needed

clamp-on tub seat

clear floor spaces as per ANSI/UFAS

vanity base cabinet (removed)

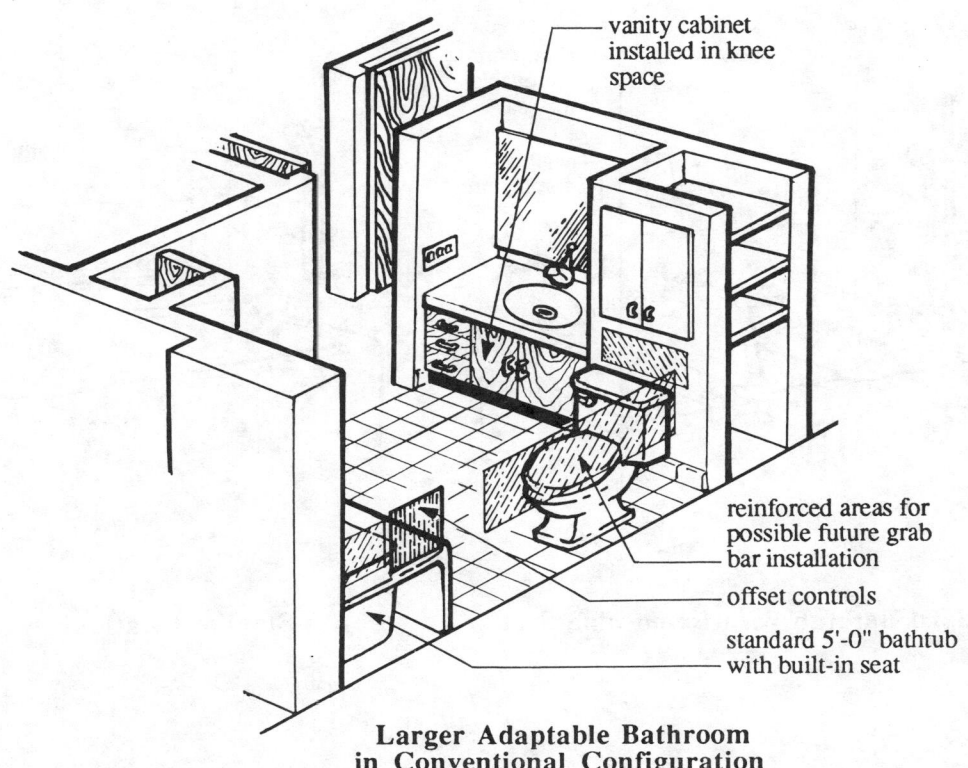

vanity cabinet
installed in knee
space

reinforced areas for
possible future grab
bar installation

offset controls

standard 5'-0" bathtub
with built-in seat

**Larger Adaptable Bathroom
in Conventional Configuration**

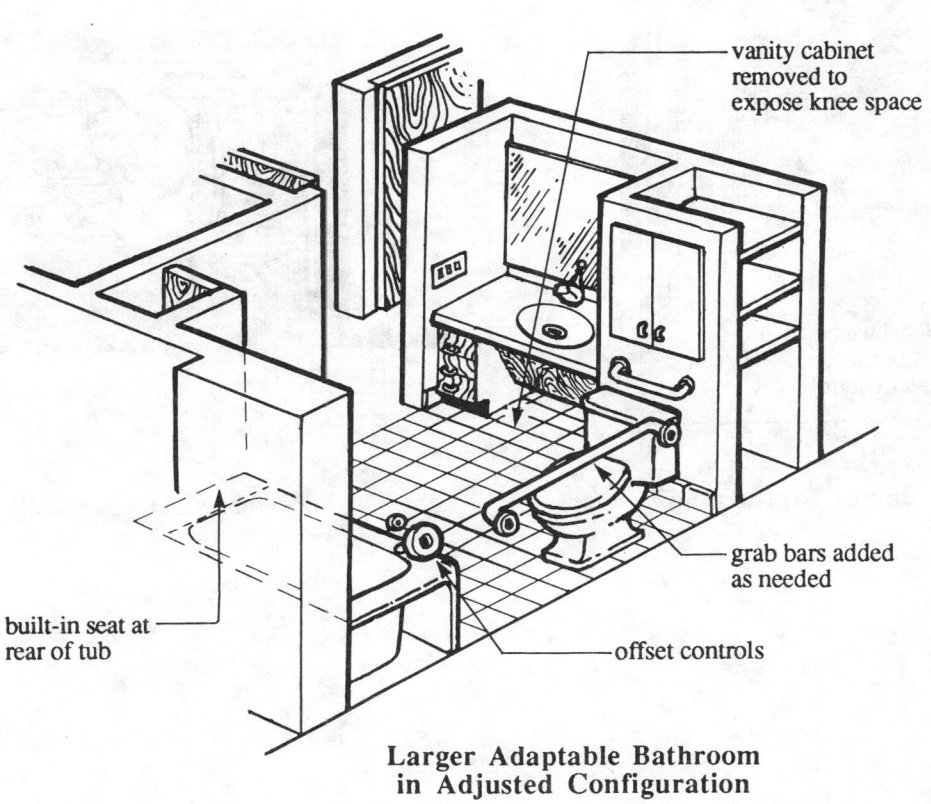

vanity cabinet
removed to
expose knee space

grab bars added
as needed

built-in seat at
rear of tub

offset controls

**Larger Adaptable Bathroom
in Adjusted Configuration**

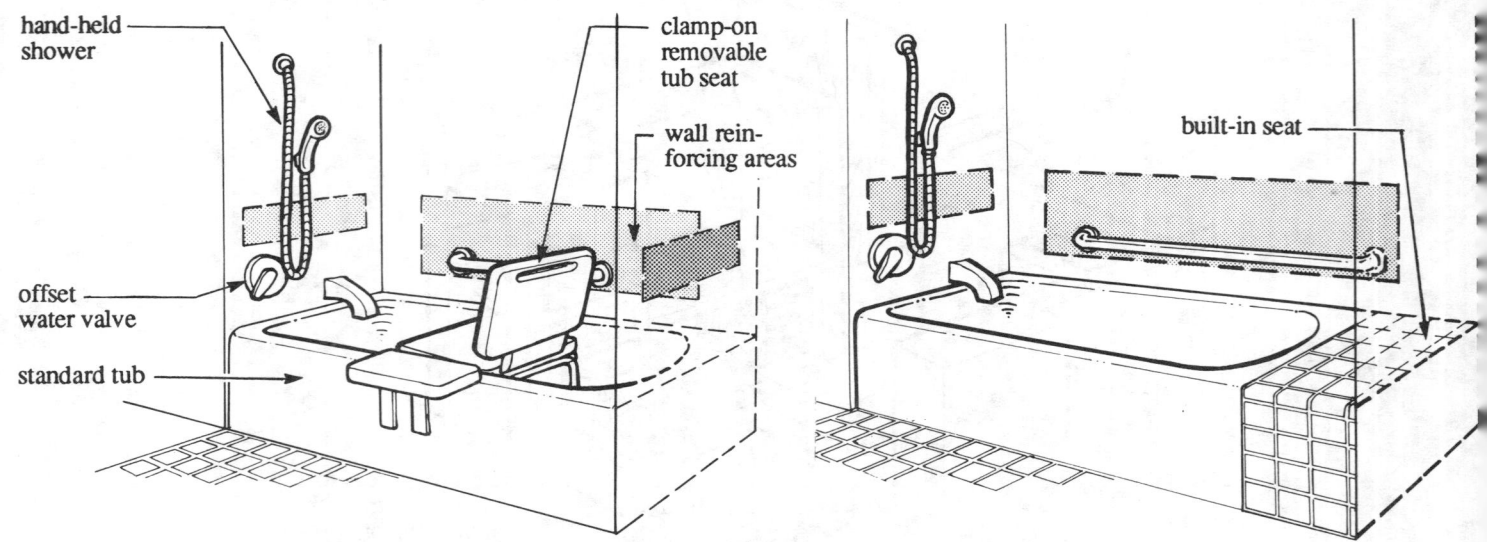

hand-held shower

clamp-on removable tub seat

wall rein-forcing areas

built-in seat

offset water valve

standard tub

Standard Bathtub with Removable Seat

Standard Bathtub with Built-in Seat

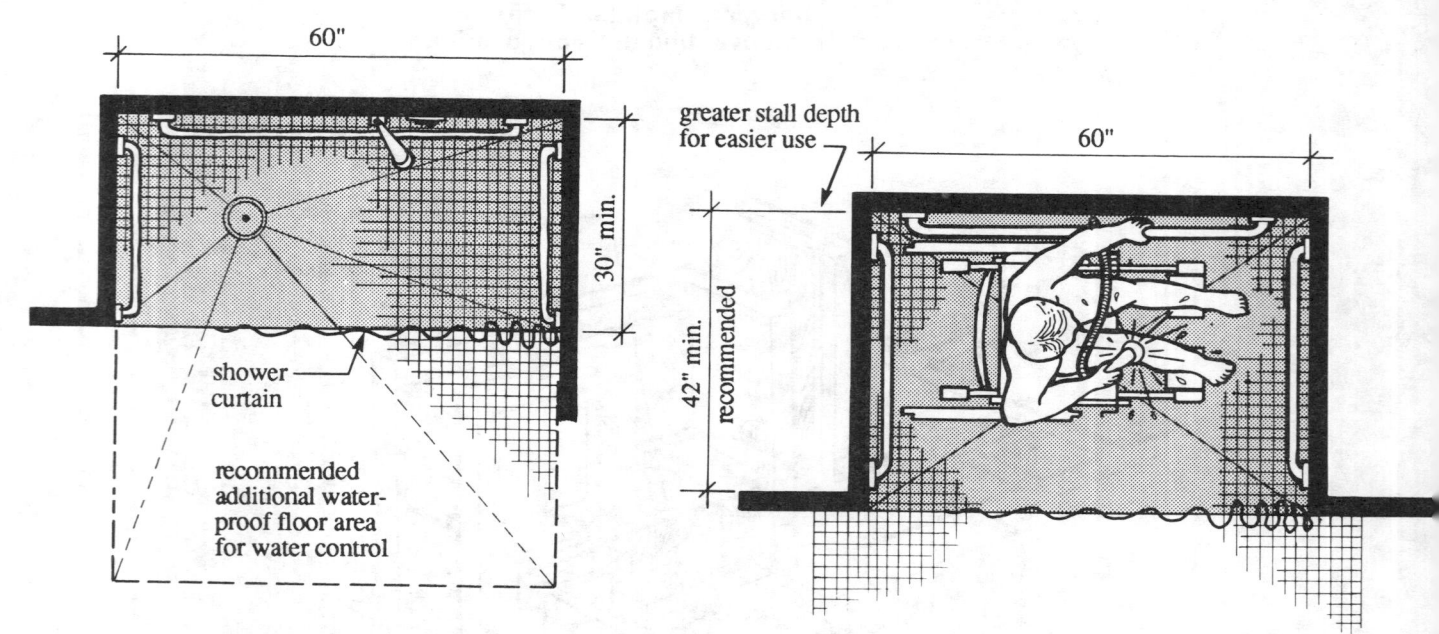

60"

30" min.

shower curtain

recommended additional water-proof floor area for water control

ANSI Minimum Roll-in Shower

greater stall depth for easier use

60"

42" min. recommended

Preferred Deeper Roll-in Shower

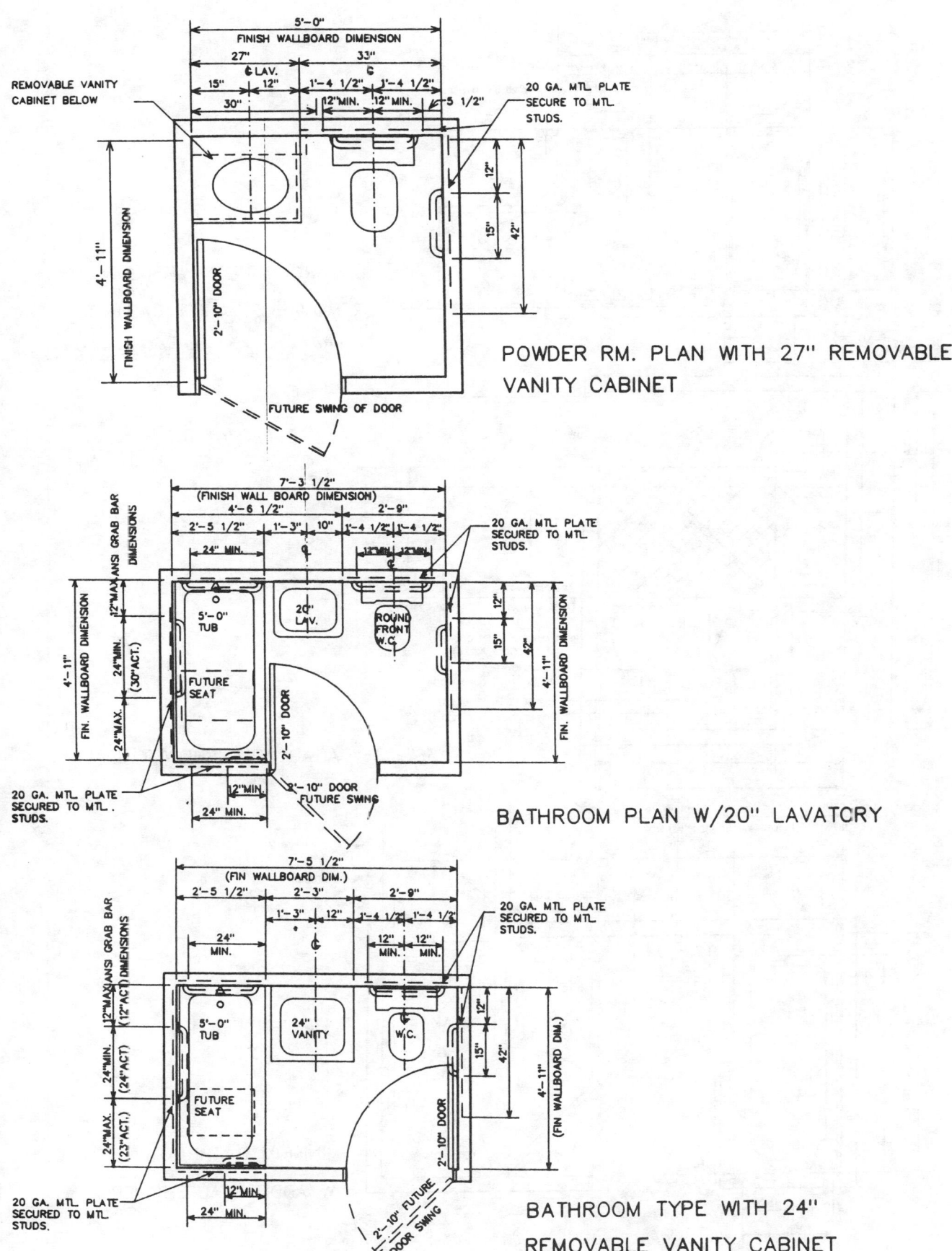

POWDER RM. PLAN WITH 27" REMOVABLE
VANITY CABINET

BATHROOM PLAN W/20" LAVATORY

BATHROOM TYPE WITH 24"
REMOVABLE VANITY CABINET

141

BATHROOMS
Adaptable Bathrooms

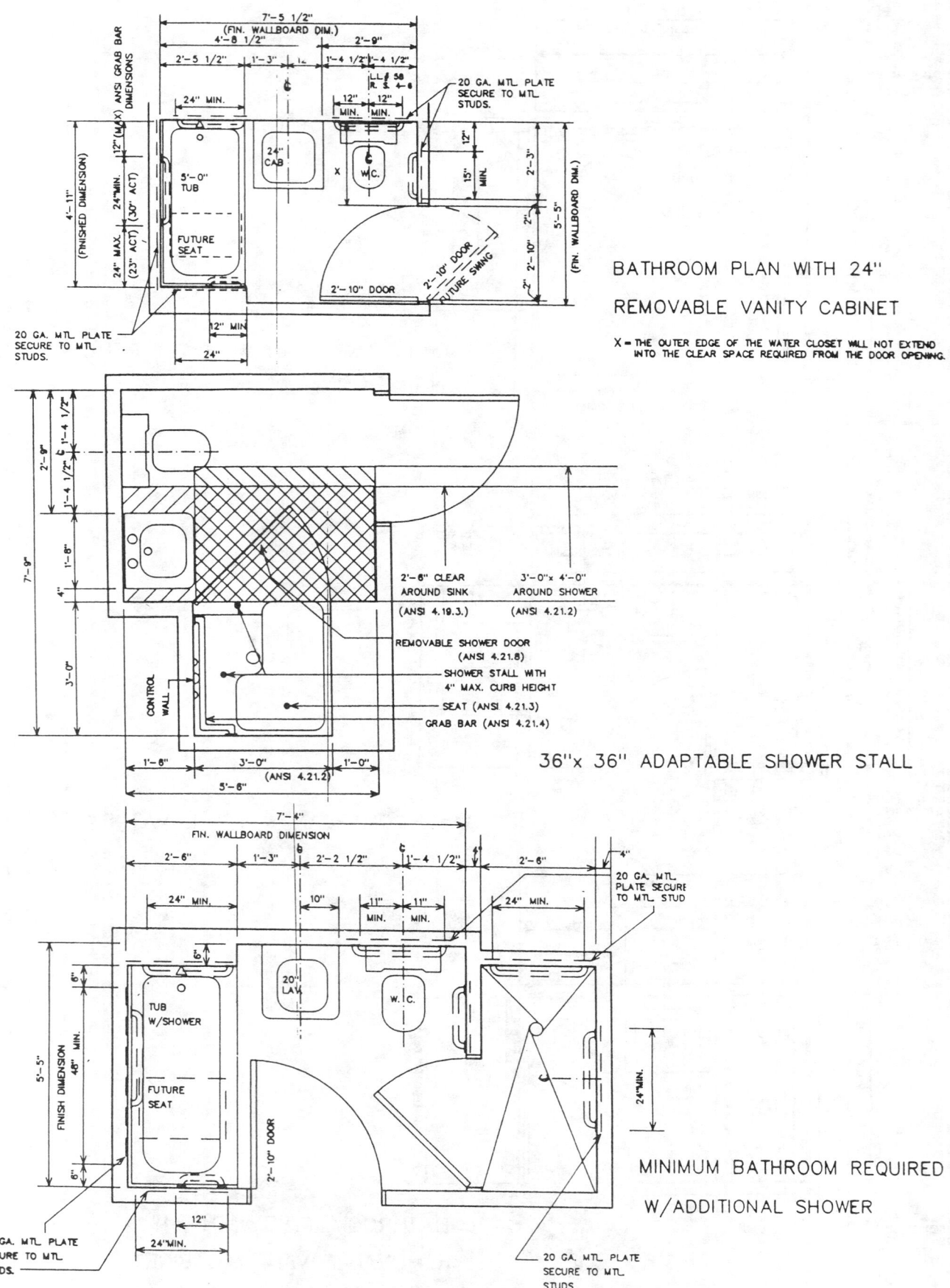

BATHROOM PLAN WITH 24"

REMOVABLE VANITY CABINET

X = THE OUTER EDGE OF THE WATER CLOSET WILL NOT EXTEND INTO THE CLEAR SPACE REQUIRED FROM THE DOOR OPENING.

2'-6" CLEAR AROUND SINK (ANSI 4.19.3.)

3'-0"x 4'-0" AROUND SHOWER (ANSI 4.21.2)

REMOVABLE SHOWER DOOR (ANSI 4.21.8)

SHOWER STALL WITH 4" MAX. CURB HEIGHT

SEAT (ANSI 4.21.3)

GRAB BAR (ANSI 4.21.4)

36"x 36" ADAPTABLE SHOWER STALL

MINIMUM BATHROOM REQUIRED

W/ADDITIONAL SHOWER

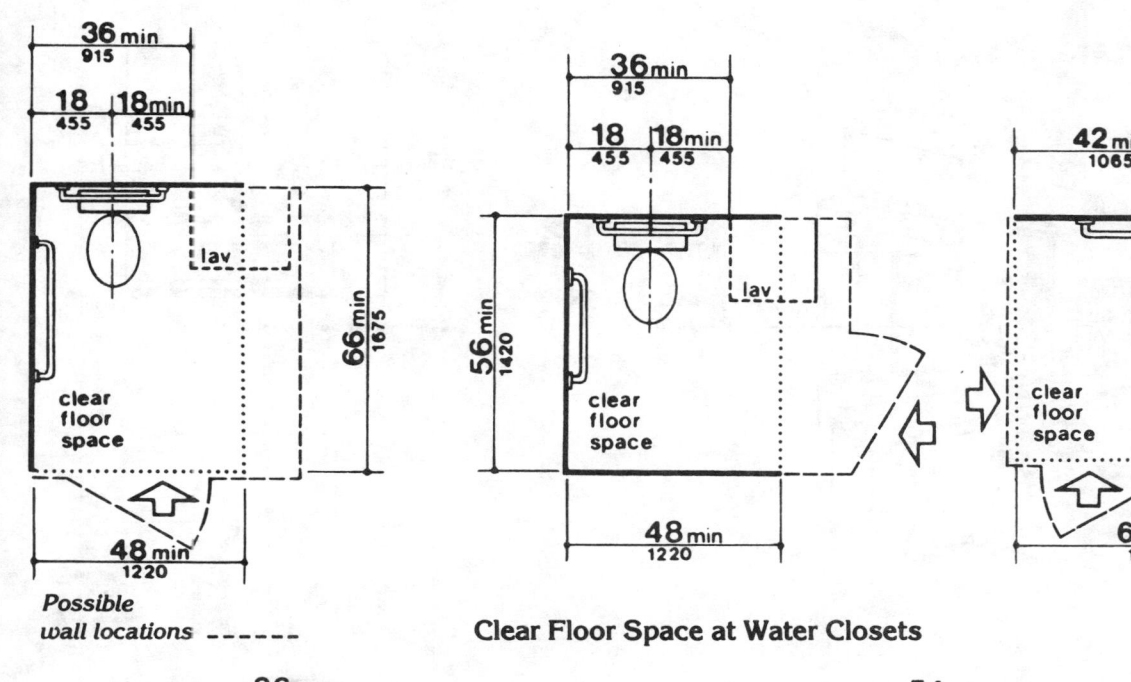

Clear Floor Space at Water Closets

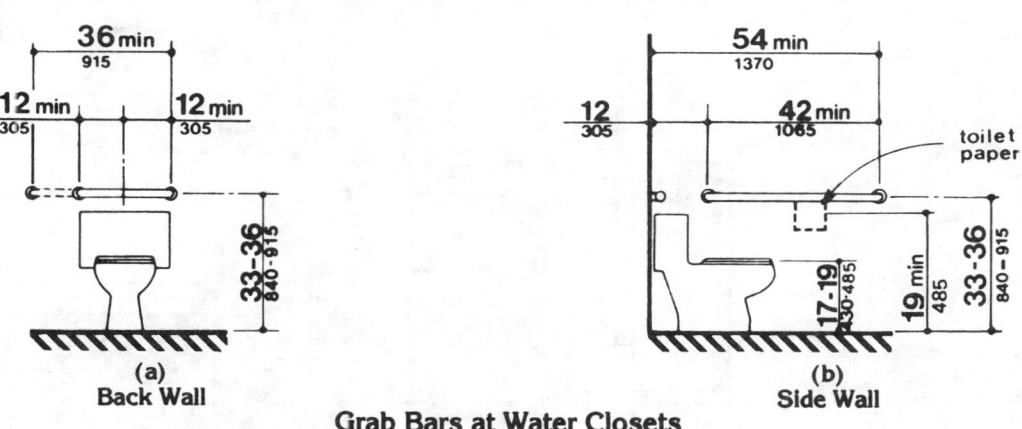

(a)
Back Wall

(b)
Side Wall

Grab Bars at Water Closets

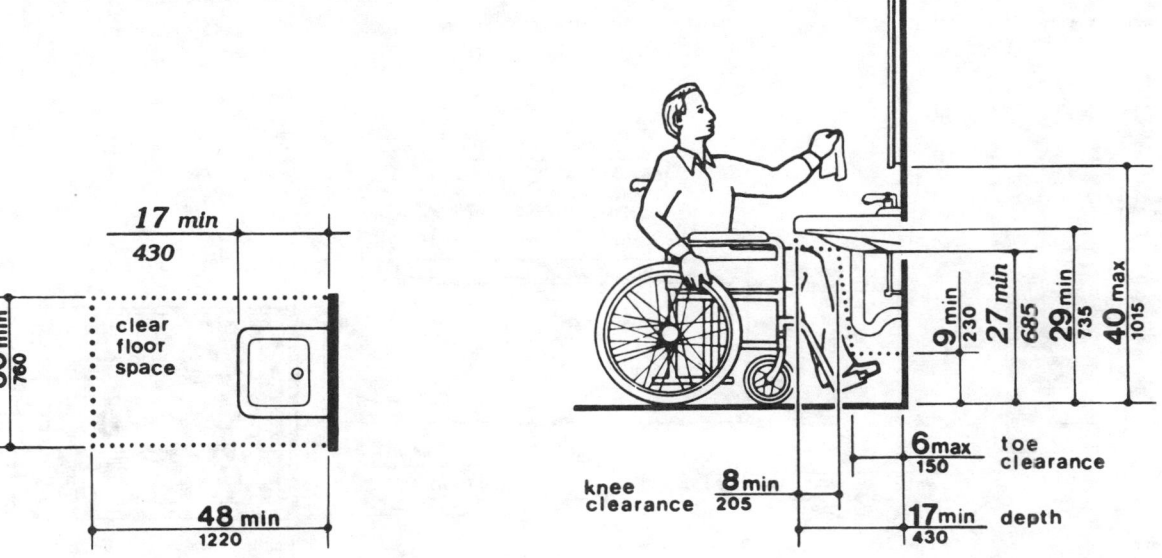

Clear Floor Space at Lavatories

Lavatory Clearances

BATHROOMS
Wheelchair Accessible Clearances

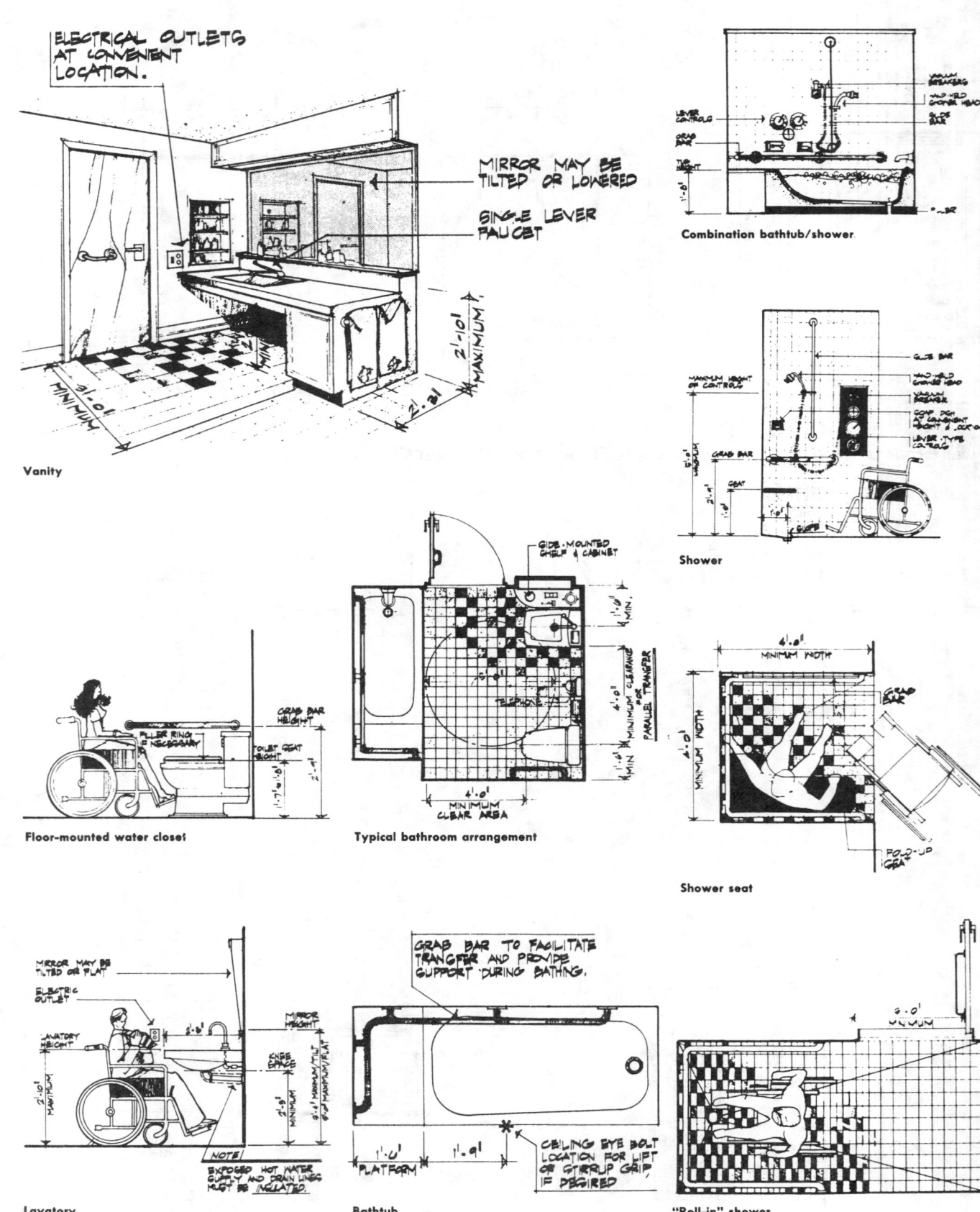

Vanity

Combination bathtub/shower

Shower

Floor-mounted water closet

Typical bathroom arrangement

Shower seat

Lavatory

Bathtub

"Roll-in" shower

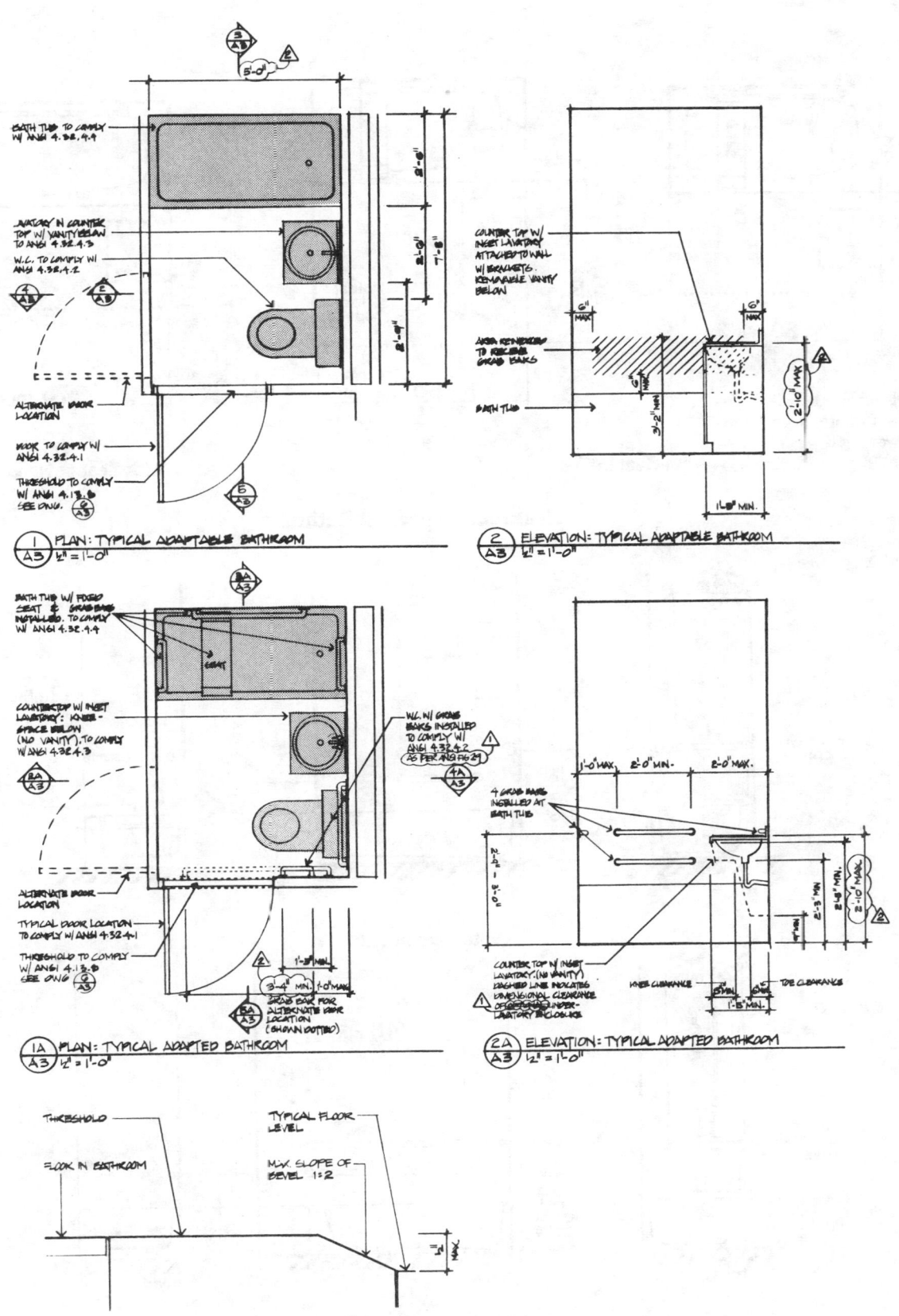

BATH TUB TO COMPLY W/ ANSI 4.32.4.4

LAVATORY IN COUNTER TOP W/ VANITY BELOW TO ANSI 4.32.4.3

W.C. TO COMPLY W/ ANSI 4.32.4.2

ALTERNATE DOOR LOCATION

DOOR TO COMPLY W/ ANSI 4.32.4.1

THRESHOLD TO COMPLY W/ ANSI 4.13.8 SEE DWG.

1/A3 PLAN: TYPICAL ADAPTABLE BATHROOM ¼" = 1'-0"

COUNTER TOP W/ INSET LAVATORY ATTACHED TO WALL W/ BRACKETS. REMOVABLE VANITY BELOW

AREA REINFORCED TO RECEIVE GRAB BARS

BATH TUB

2/A3 ELEVATION: TYPICAL ADAPTABLE BATHROOM ¼" = 1'-0"

BATH TUB W/ FIXED SEAT & GRAB BARS INSTALLED. TO COMPLY W/ ANSI 4.32.4.4

COUNTERTOP W/ INSET LAVATORY: KNEE-SPACE BELOW (NO VANITY). TO COMPLY W/ ANSI 4.32.4.3

W.C. W/ GRAB BARS INSTALLED TO COMPLY W/ ANSI 4.32.4.2 AS PER ANSI FIG.29

ALTERNATE DOOR LOCATION

TYPICAL DOOR LOCATION TO COMPLY W/ ANSI 4.32.4.1

THRESHOLD TO COMPLY W/ ANSI 4.13.8 SEE DWG.

GRAB BAR FOR ALTERNATE DOOR LOCATION (SHOWN DOTTED)

1A/A3 PLAN: TYPICAL ADAPTED BATHROOM ¼" = 1'-0"

4 GRAB BARS INSTALLED AT BATH TUB

COUNTER TOP W/ INSET LAVATORY (NO VANITY) DASHED LINE INDICATES DIMENSIONAL CLEARANCE OF GENERAL UNDER-LAVATORY ENCLOSURE

KNEE CLEARANCE

TOE CLEARANCE

2A/A3 ELEVATION: TYPICAL ADAPTED BATHROOM ¼" = 1'-0"

THRESHOLD

TYPICAL FLOOR LEVEL

FLOOR IN BATHROOM

MAX. SLOPE OF BEVEL 1:2

6/A3 SECTION THRU THRESHOLD: TO COMPLY W/ ANSI 4.13.8 FULL SIZE

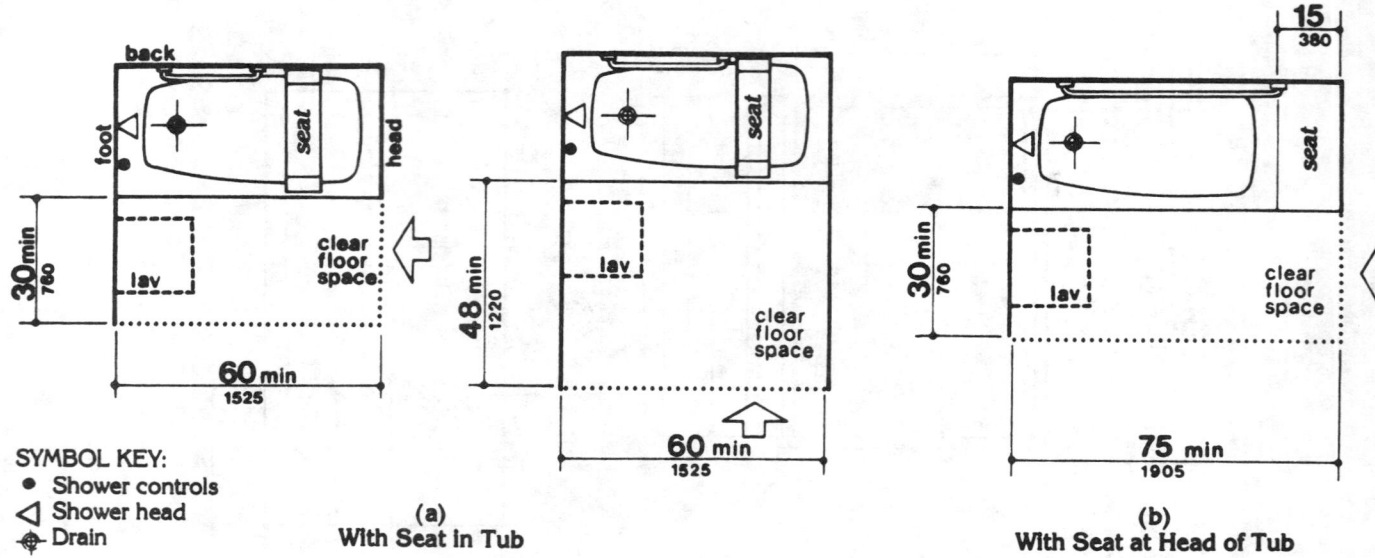

SYMBOL KEY:
- Shower controls
- Shower head
- Drain

(a)
With Seat in Tub

(b)
With Seat at Head of Tub

Clear Floor Space at Bathtubs

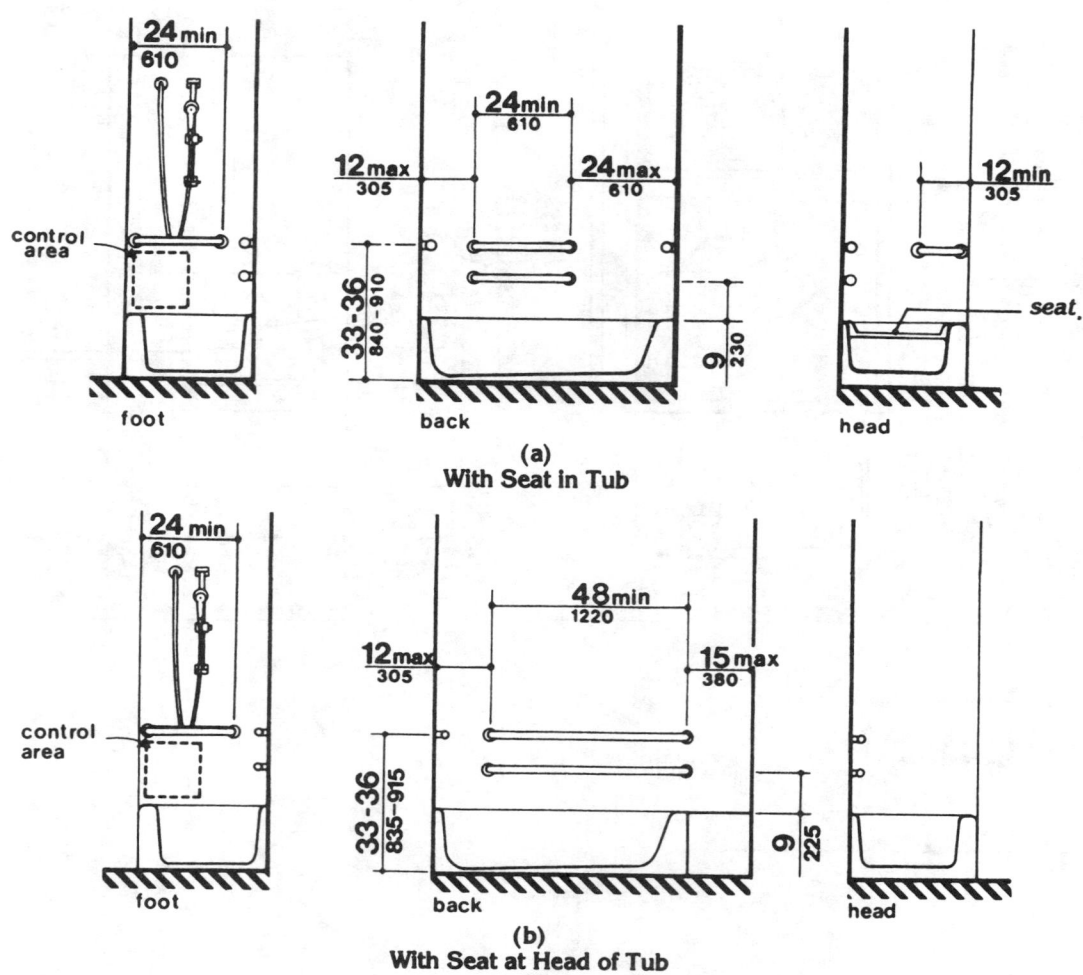

(a)
With Seat in Tub

(b)
With Seat at Head of Tub

Grab Bars at Bathtubs

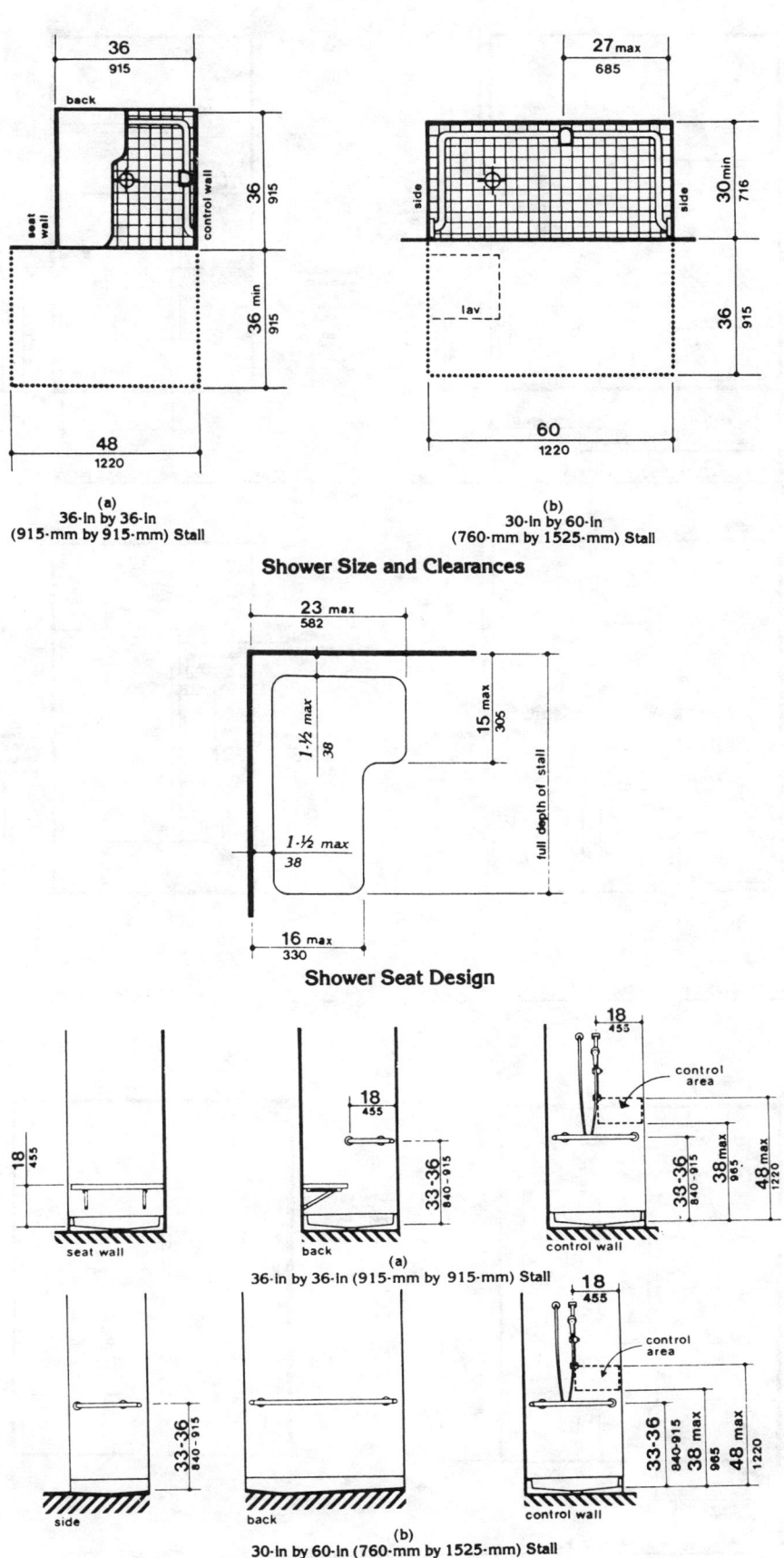

Shower Size and Clearances

(a)
36-In by 36-In
(915-mm by 915-mm) Stall

(b)
30-In by 60-In
(760-mm by 1525-mm) Stall

Shower Seat Design

(a)
36-In by 36-In (915-mm by 915-mm) Stall

(b)
30-In by 60-In (760-mm by 1525-mm) Stall

Grab Bars at Shower Stalls

BATHROOMS
Wheelchair Accessible Design

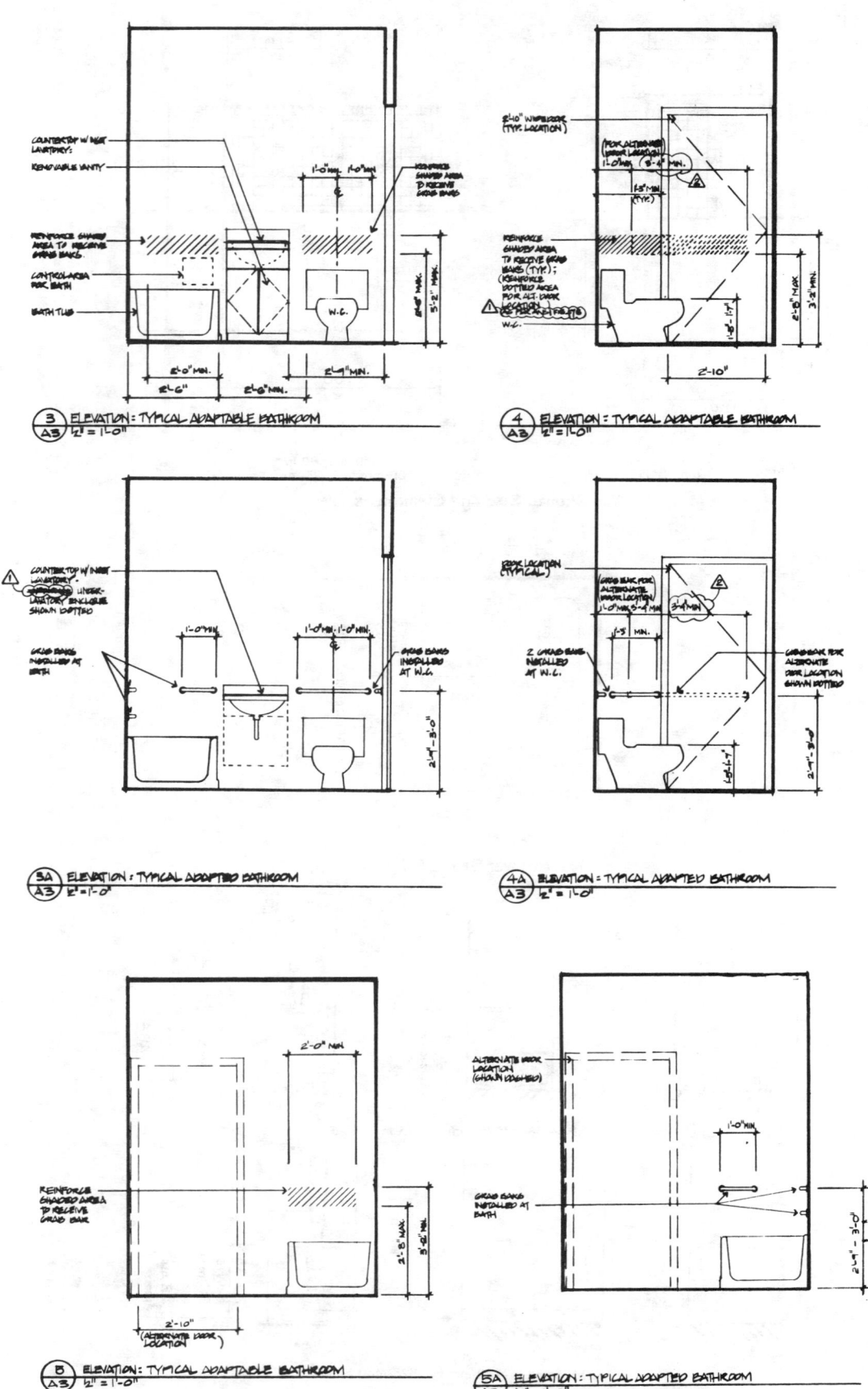

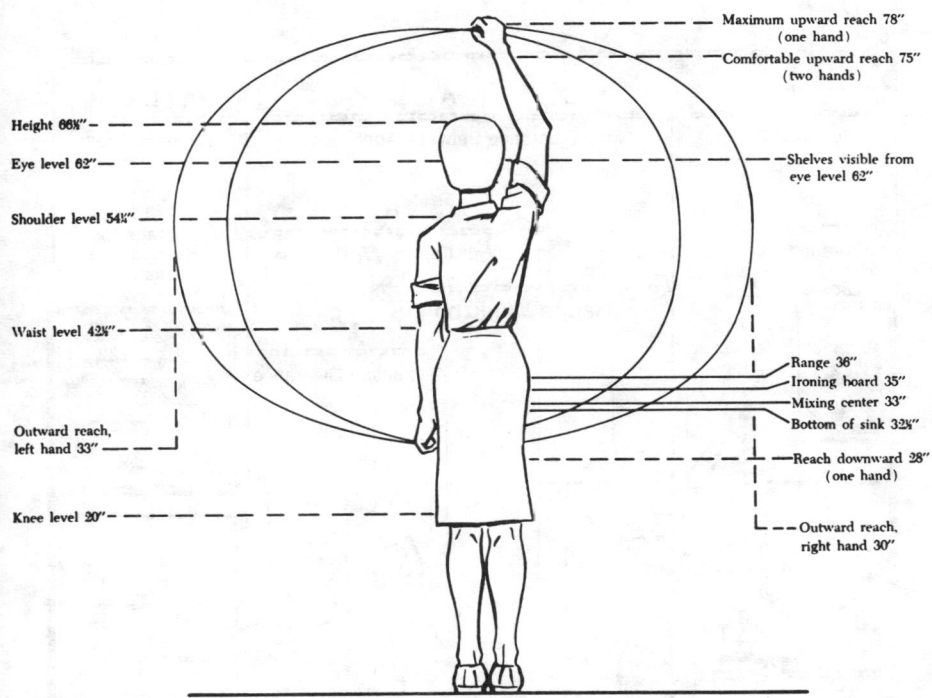

Maximum upward reach 78"
(one hand)

Comfortable upward reach 75"
(two hands)

Height 66¾"

Eye level 62"

Shelves visible from
eye level 62"

Shoulder level 54½"

Waist level 42¾"

Range 36"
Ironing board 35"
Mixing center 33"
Bottom of sink 32½"

Reach downward 28"
(one hand)

Outward reach,
left hand 33"

Knee level 20"

Outward reach,
right hand 30"

Fig. 1

The height of a kitchen workcounter, the proper clearance between cabinets or appliances for circulation, the accessibility to overhead or undercounter storage, and proper visibility are among the primary considerations in the design of cooking spaces. All must be responsive to human dimens on and body size if the quality of interface between the user and the components of the interior space are to be adequate. In establishing clearances between counters, the maximum body breadth and depth of the user of larger body size must be taken into account as well as the projections of the appliances. Refrigerator doors, cabinet drawers, dishwashing machine doors, and cabinet doors all project to some degree in their open position into the space within which the user must circulate and must be accommodated.

Standard kitchen counter heights manufactured are all about 36 in, or 91.4 cm. But such a height does not necessarily accommodate the body dimension of all users for all tasks. Certain cooking activities, for example, may be more efficiently performed from a standing position, but with a counter height less than 36 in. In overhead cabinets the upper shelves are usually inaccessible to the smaller person, while the lower shelves are usually inaccessible to most without bending or kneeling. The logical answer is the development of kitchen cabinet systems capable of total adjustability to accommodate the human dimension of the individual user. Such a system could accommodate not only those of smaller and larger body size, but also elderly and disabled people.

Figure 1 provides some general anthropometric data for establishing basic heights of cabinetry and appliances above the floor. Figures 2 and 3 show in more detail the interface of the human body and the kitchen environment.

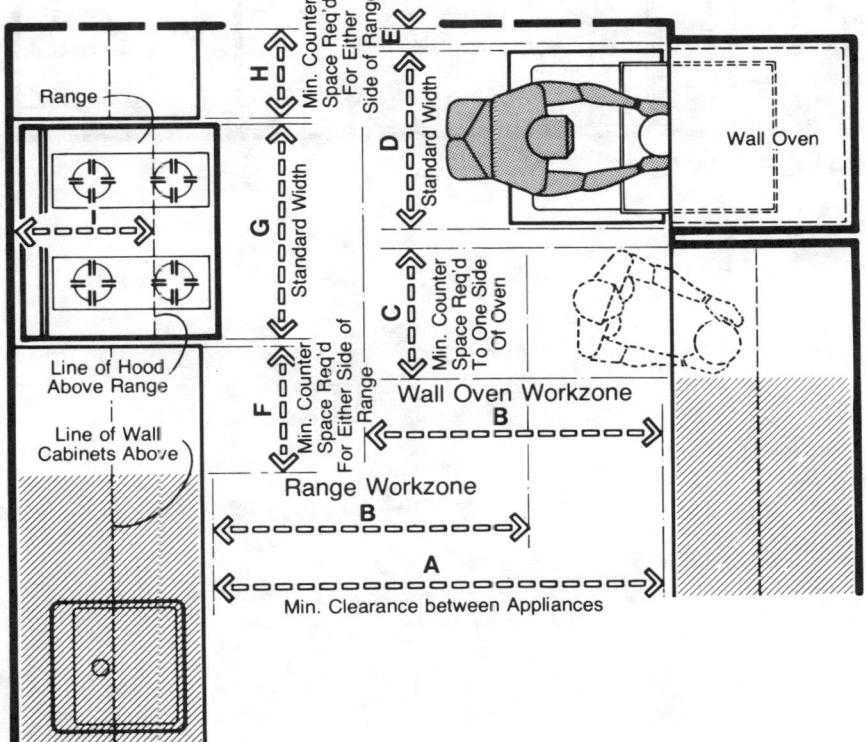

Min. Counter Space Req'd For Either Side of Range

Range

H

Standard Width

E

D

Standard Width

Wall Oven

G

Min. Counter Space Req'd To One Side Of Oven

C

Line of Hood Above Range

F

Min. Counter Space Req'd For Either Side of Range

Wall Oven Workzone

B

Line of Wall Cabinets Above

Range Workzone

B

A

Min. Clearance between Appliances

RANGE CENTER

Fig. 2

	in	cm
A	48 min.	121.9 min.
B	40	101.6
C	15	38.1 min.
D	21–30	53.3–76.2
E	1–3	2.5–7.6
F	15 min.	38.1 min.
G	19.5–46	49.5–116.8
H	12 min.	30.5 min.
I	17.5 max.	44.5 max
J	96–101.5	243.8–257 8
K	24–27.5	61.0–69.9
L	24–26	61.0–66.0
M	30	76.2
N	60 min.	152.4 min.
O	35–36.25	88.9–92.1
P	24 min.	61.0 min
Q	35 max.	88.9 max.

KITCHENS

Anthropometric Data

Figures 2 and 3 illustrate the clearances related to range centers. Figure 2 indicates a minimum clearance between appliances of 48 in, or 121. 9 cm. The anthropometric basis for the clearances are amplified in Fig. 3.

The 40-in, or 101.6-cm, wall oven workzone clearance is adequate to accommodate the projected wall oven door, in addition to the maximum body depth dimension of the user. The standing figure shown in broken line, however, indicates both dimensionally and graphically that the 40-in clearance will not permit comfortable circulation when appliances on both sides are in operation at the same time. The range workzone clearance, also 40 in, is adequate to accommodate the open range door and the body size of the kneeling user.

An extremely important, but frequently overlooked, anthropometric consideration in kitchen design is eye height. In this regard, the distance from the top of the range to the underside of the hood should allow the rear burners to be visible to the user.

	in	cm
A	48 min. (4')	121.9 min.
B	40	101.6
C	15	38.1 min.
D	21–30	53.3–76.2
E	1–3	2.5–7.6
F	15 min.	38.1 min.
G	19.5–46	49.5–116.8
H	12 min.	30.5 min.
I	17.5 max.	44.5 max
J	(8') 96–101.5	243.8–257.8
K	24–27.5	61.0–69.9
L	24–26	61.0–66.0
M	30	76.2
N	60 min.	152.4 min.
O	35–36.25 (3')	88.9–92.1
P	24 min.	61.0 min.
Q	35 max.	88.9 max.

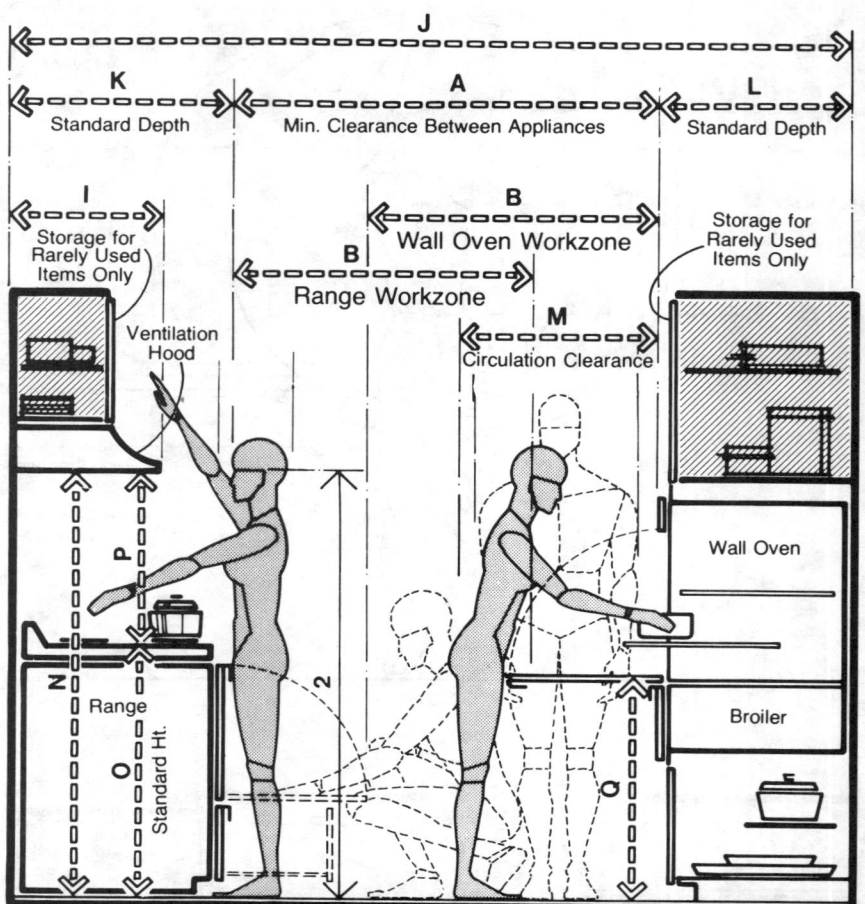

RANGE CENTER

Fig. 3

The U-shaped plan is the most efficient. When not broken, it provides the opportunity and floor space for several simultaneous activities. The corridor or gallery kitchen is typically accessible from both ends, often converting it from a work space to a corridor. It sometimes is closed off on one end, thereby creating a variation of the U-plan, which although small can produce a fairly comfortable kitchen.

The broken U-shaped plan often results from the necessity of locating a door along one or two of the three walls of a typical U-shaped scheme. The resulting through traffic reduces the compactness and efficiency of the plan.

The typical L-shaped kitchen allows for the location of a small breakfast area in the opposite corner.

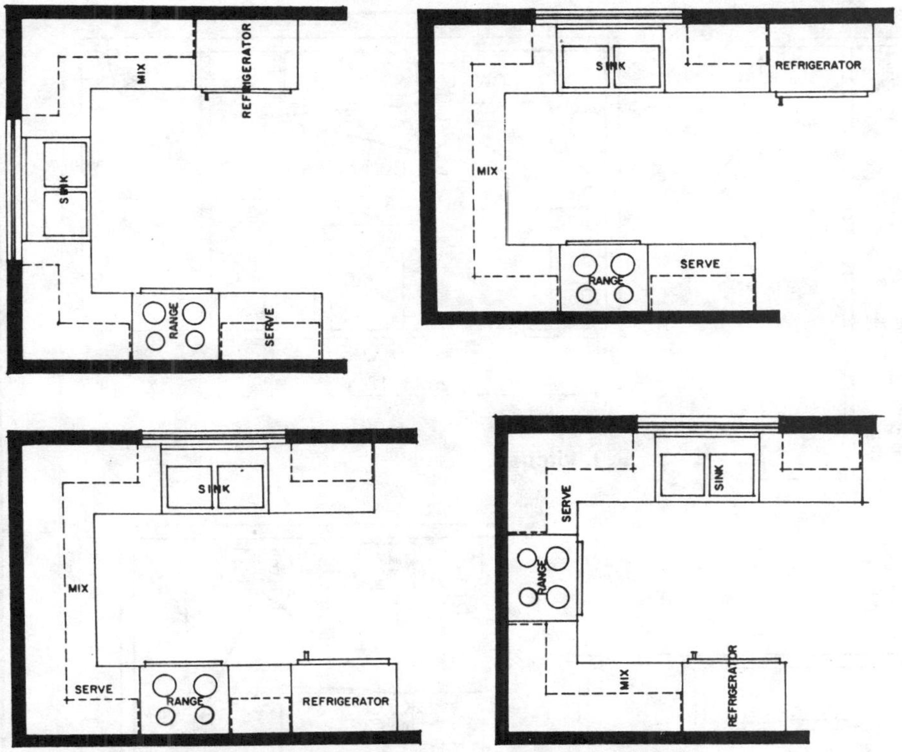

Fig. 4   U-shaped plans. If dishwasher is desired, it should be located at sink center.

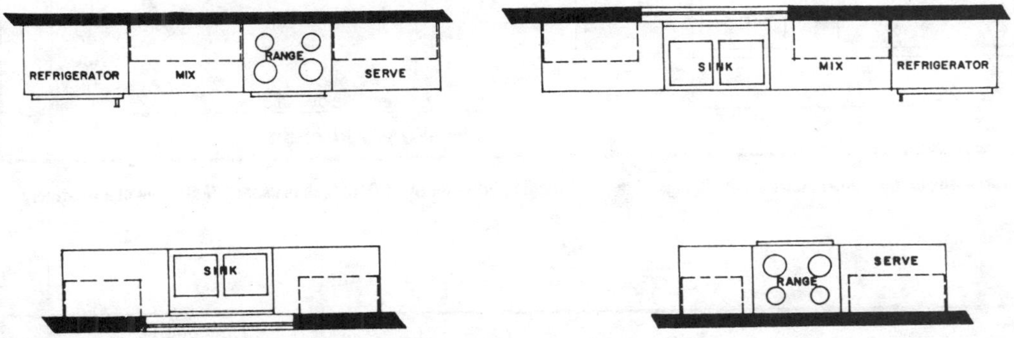

Fig. 5   Corridor plans. If dishwasher is desired, it should be located at sink center.

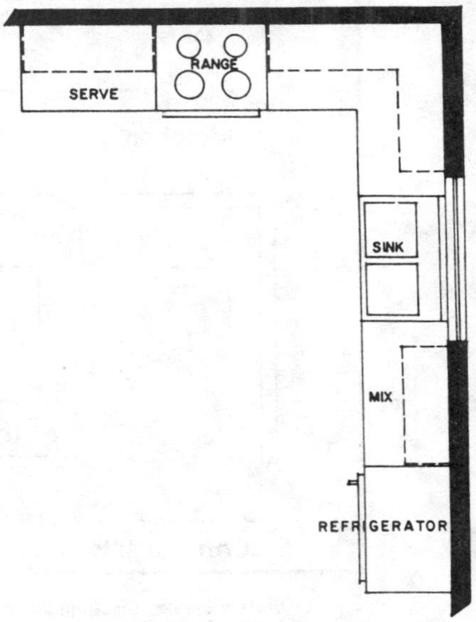

Fig. 7   L-shaped plan. If dishwasher is desired, it should be located at sink center.

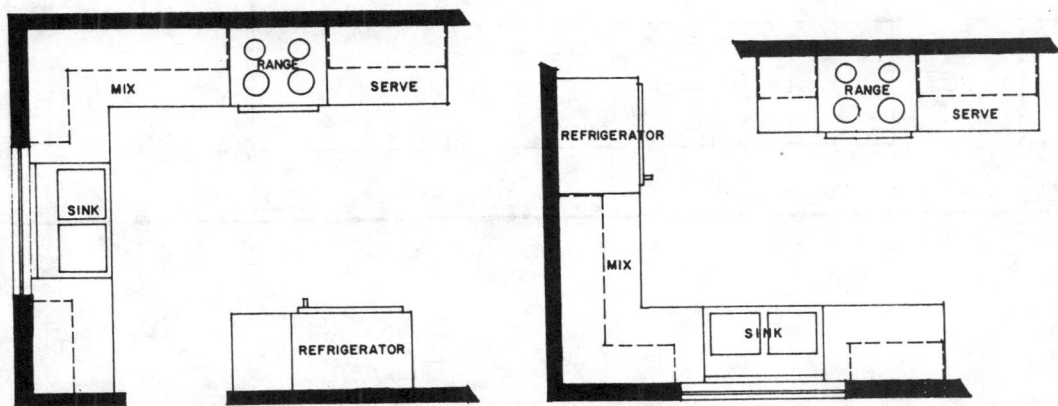

Fig. 6   Broken U-shaped plans. If dishwasher is desired, it should be located at sink center.

KITCHENS

Typical Layouts

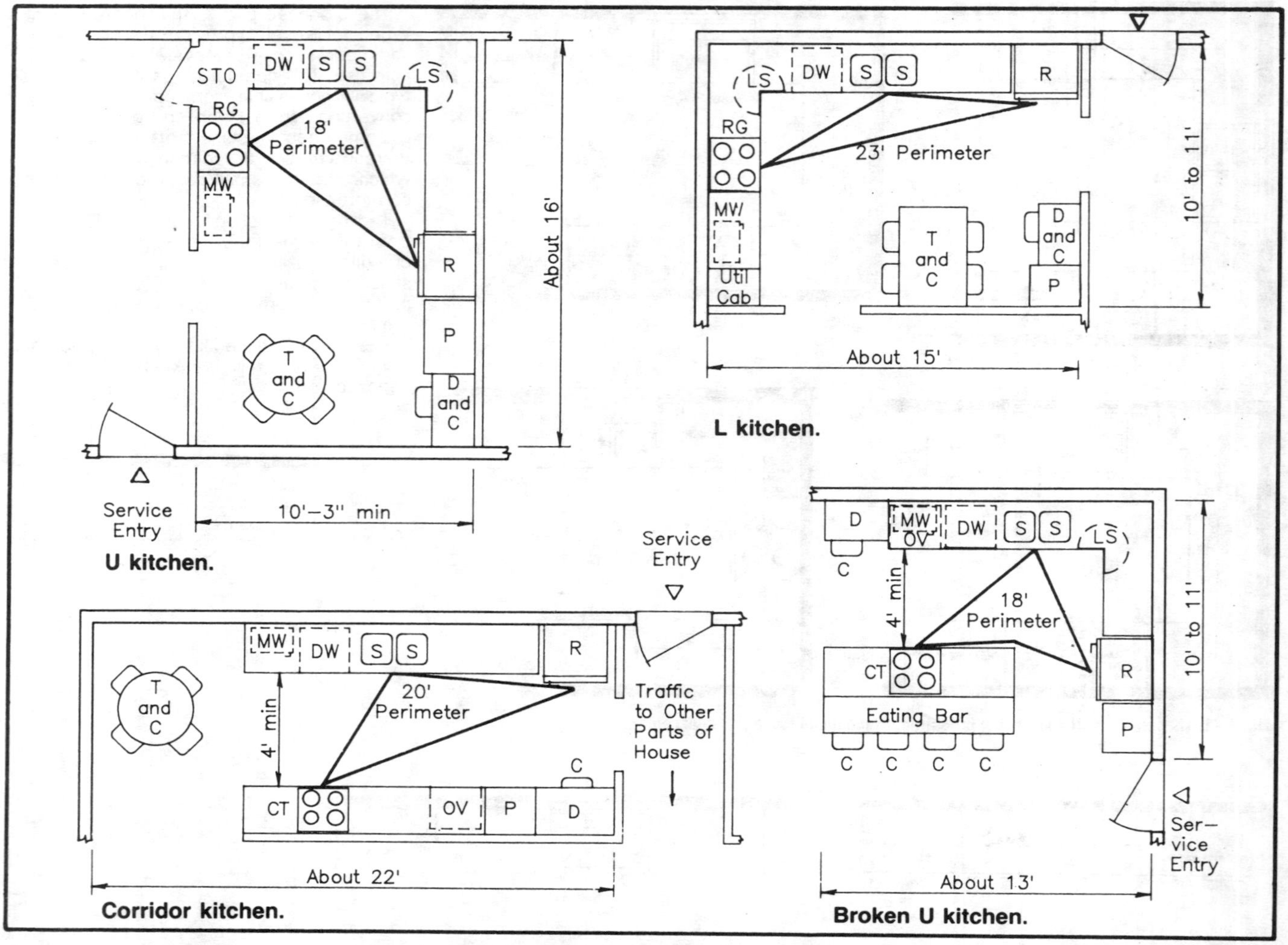

U kitchen.

Service Entry

10'-3" min

About 16'

STO DW S S (LS)
RG
18' Perimeter
MW
R
P
D and C
T and C

L kitchen.

About 15'

10' to 11'

(LS) DW S S R
RG
23' Perimeter
MW/
Util Cab
T and C
D and C
P

Corridor kitchen.

About 22'

Service Entry

Traffic to Other Parts of House

T and C
4' min
MW DW S S R
20' Perimeter
CT OV P D
C

Broken U kitchen.

About 13'

10' to 11'

Service Entry

D
C
MW OV DW S S (LS)
4' min
CT
18' Perimeter
R
P
Eating Bar
C C C C

Fig. 8   These diagrams illustrate further variations of the typical plans shown in Figs. 4 to 7. A triangle perimeter of 23'0" or less is usually indicative of a relatively efficient kitchen layout.

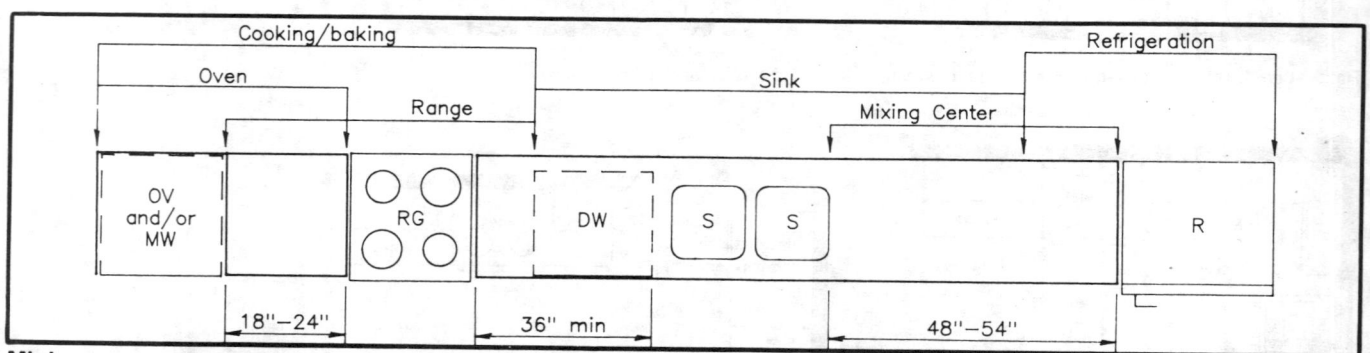

Cooking/baking
Refrigeration
Oven
Sink
Range
Mixing Center

OV and/or MW RG DW S S R

18"-24"   36" min   48"-54"

Minimum counter frontage.
For combined work centers.

Space Criterion

The size of the kitchen should be determined by the number of bedrooms provided in the living unit. Work centers for the following equipment, cabinets, and space for their use should be provided:

1. Range space with base and wall cabinet at one side for serving and storage of utensils and staples.

2. Sink and base cabinet with counter space on each side for cleanup. Wall cabinets for storage of dinnerware.

3. Refrigerator space with counter space at latch side of the refrigerator door.

4. Mixing counter and base cabinet for electrical appliances and utensil storage. Wall cabinet for staple storage.

Recommended minimum edge distance
Equipment should be placed to allow for efficient operating room between it and any adjacent corner cabinet. At least 9 in from the edge of the sink and range and 16 in at the side of the refrigerator is recommended.

Circulation space A minimum of 40 in should be provided between base cabinets or appliances opposite each other. This same minimum clearance applies when a wall,

storage wall, or work table is opposite a base cabinet.

Traffic Traffic in the kitchen should be limited to kitchen work only. Serving circulation to the dining area should be without any cross traffic.

Height of shelving and counter tops

1. Maximum height of wall shelving 74 in. Height of counter tops should be 36 in.

2. Minimum clearance height between sink and wall cabinet 24 in; between base and wall cabinets 15-in clearance.

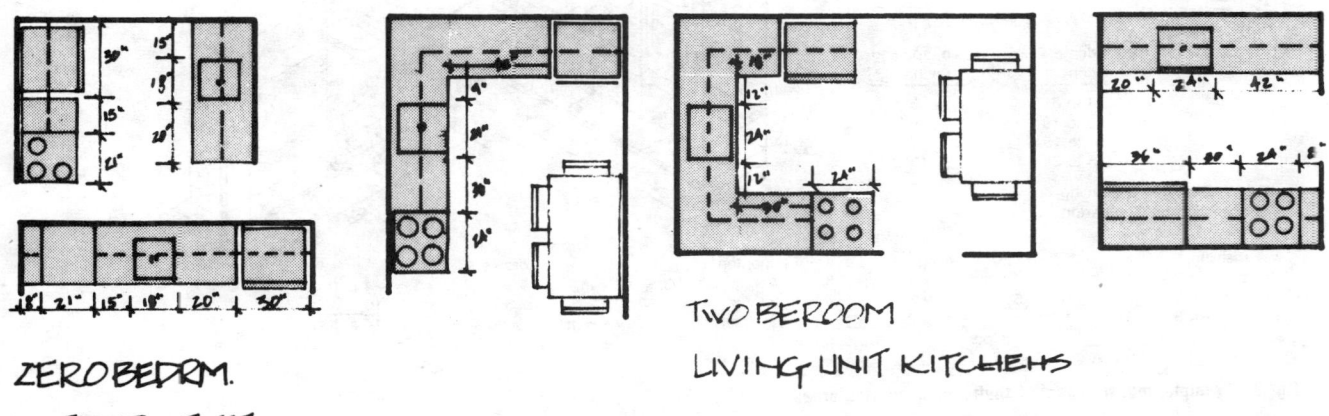

ZERO BEDRM. KITCHENETTE

TWO BEDROOM LIVING UNIT KITCHENS

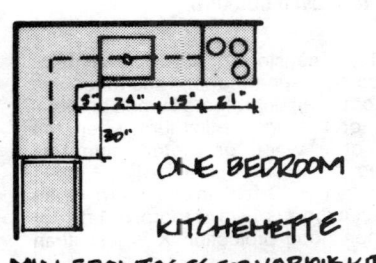

ONE BEDROOM KITCHENETTE

MIN. FRONTAGES for VARIOUS KITCHENS

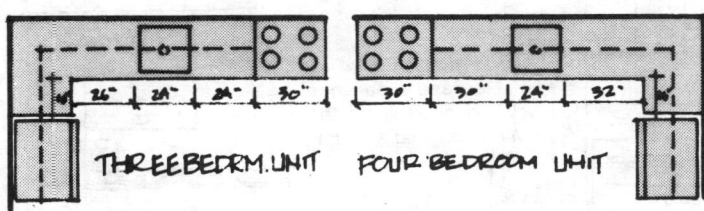

THREE BEDRM. UNIT   FOUR BEDROOM UNIT

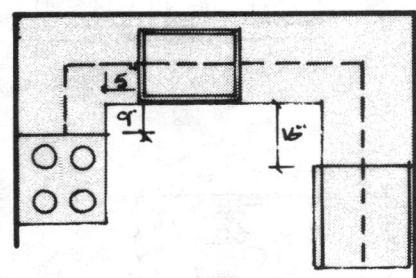

MIN. EDGE DISTANCES

KITCHENS
Storage and Cabinets

KITCHEN STORAGE

Each kitchen or kitchenette should have (1) accessible storage space for food and utensils, (2) sufficient space for the average kitchen accessories, (3) sufficient storage space for those items of household equipment normally used and for which storage is not elsewhere provided.

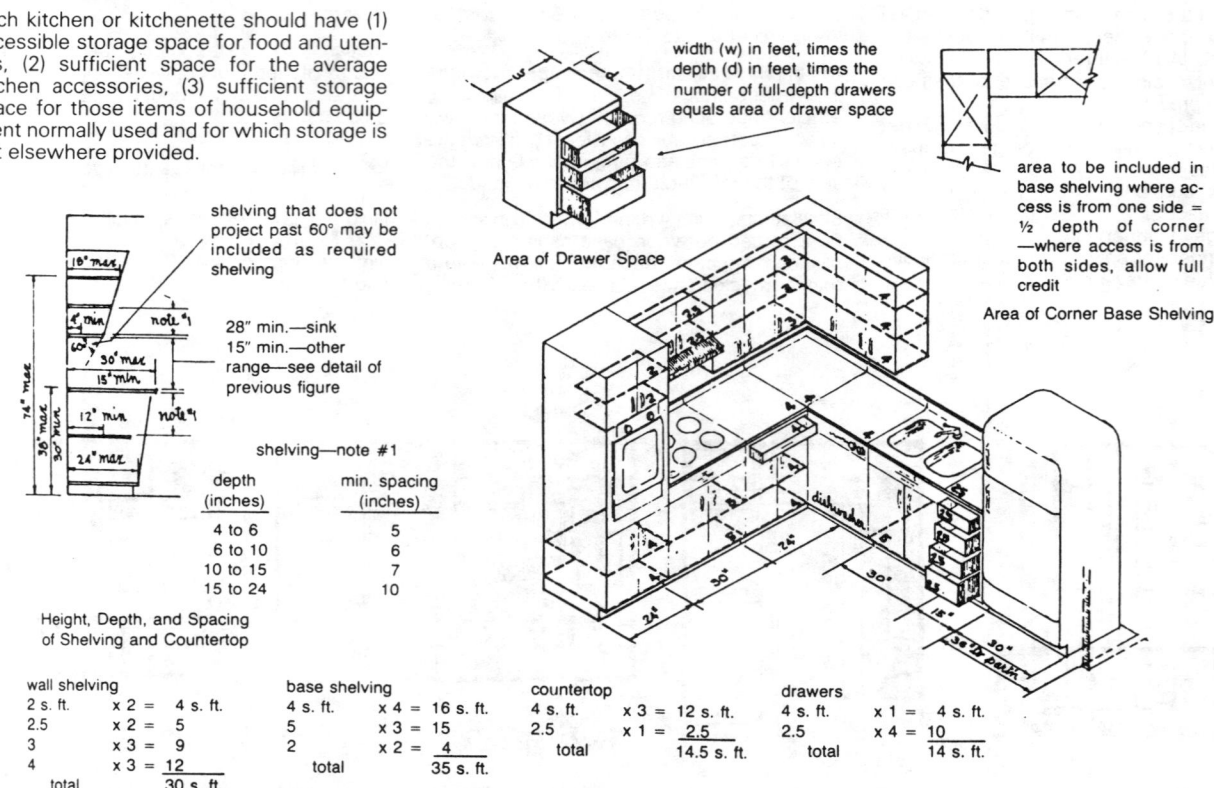

width (w) in feet, times the depth (d) in feet, times the number of full-depth drawers equals area of drawer space

Area of Drawer Space

area to be included in base shelving where access is from one side = ½ depth of corner —where access is from both sides, allow full credit

Area of Corner Base Shelving

shelving that does not project past 60° may be included as required shelving

28" min.—sink
15" min.—other
range—see detail of previous figure

shelving—note #1

depth (inches)	min. spacing (inches)
4 to 6	5
6 to 10	6
10 to 15	7
15 to 24	10

Height, Depth, and Spacing of Shelving and Countertop

wall shelving				base shelving				countertop				drawers			
2 s. ft.	x 2 =	4 s. ft.		4 s. ft.	x 4 =	16 s. ft.		4 s. ft.	x 3 =	12 s. ft.		4 s. ft.	x 1 =	4 s. ft.	
2.5	x 2 =	5		5	x 3 =	15		2.5	x 1 =	2.5		2.5	x 4 =	10	
3	x 3 =	9		2	x 2 =	4		total		14.5 s. ft.		total		14 s. ft.	
4	x 3 =	12		total		35 s. ft.									
total		30 s. ft.													

Fig. 9 Example: measurement of shelf and countertop areas.

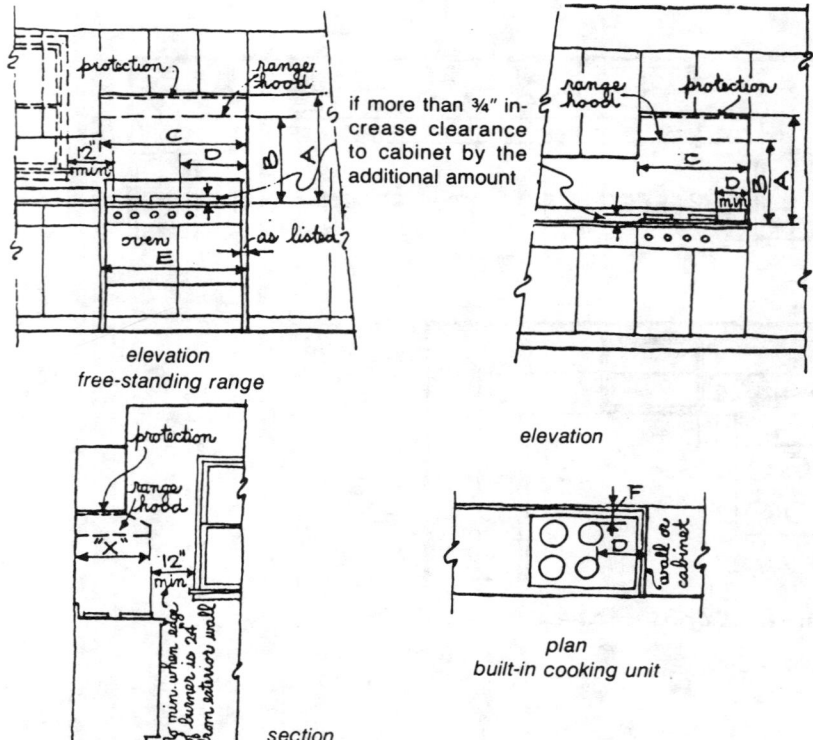

if more than ¾" increase clearance to cabinet by the additional amount

elevation
free-standing range

elevation

plan
built-in cooking unit

section

Fig. 10

CLEARANCES OVER COOKING RANGES

In Fig. 10, dimension A: 2 ft 6 in minimum clearance between the top of the range and the bottom of an unprotected wood or metal cabinet, or 2 ft 0 in minimum when the bottom of a wood or metal cabinet is protected.

Dimension B: 2 ft 0 in minimum when hood projection X is 18 in or more, or 1 ft 10 in min. when hood projection X is less than 18 in.

Dimension C: not less than width of range or cooking unit.

Dimension D: 10 in minimum when vertical side surface extends above countertops.

Dimension E: when range is not provided by builder, 40 in minimum.

Dimension F: Minimum clearance should be not less than 3 in.

Cabinet protection should be at least ¼ in asbestos millboard covered with not less than 28-gauge sheet metal (0.015 stainless steel, 0.024 aluminum, or 0.020 copper).

Clearance for D, E, or F should be not less than listed UL or AGA clearances.

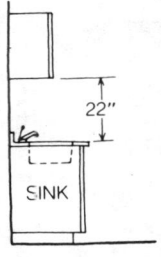

ABOVE SINK

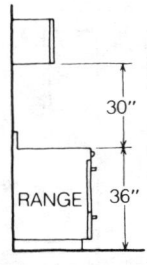

ABOVE RANGE

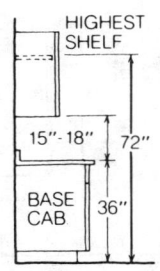

ABOVE BASE CAB

Above a sink, plan for a minimum of 22 in. to the bottom of a wall cabinet. Since the wall behind a sink often holds a window, measurement for a cabinet is academic. But if wall space is minimal, a cabinet over the sink makes good sense.

The use of large pans, pancake flips and similar cooking maneuvers dictate a distance of 30 in. between rangetop and wall cabinet bottom. A fan mounted in the wall is the means here to exhaust cooking fumes to the outside.

A range of 15 in. to 18 in. is the proper span between standard base and wall cabinets. Opt for the 15 in. distance if you are 5 ft. 4 in. or less; a wider span if you're taller. The highest shelf: 6 ft. from the floor, is a reachable distance.

Kitchen activities become tiresome in poor light. A single fixture, centered on the ceiling is insufficient. Your need for light is greatest over the work centers. A good light there reduces the danger of cutting yourself; eases the task of monitoring color changes during a mix, and so on. The best place to install fixtures for this purpose is beneath the wall cabinets (with a shield to prevent glare when you're seated in the kitchen). A workable alternative is found in fixtures installed in an extended soffit. Plan for light above a rangetop and over the sink, as well. Choose incandescent, deluxe warm white or deluxe cool white lamps for the fixtures to avoid poor color rendition.

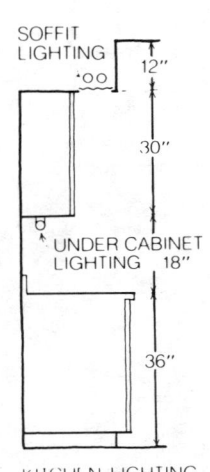

KITCHEN LIGHTING

Utensil and General Storage

Space for utensils includes storage for dishes, pots and pans, utensils, and appliances. With the increased use of such electrical appliances, their storage becomes a significant problem. General storage requires space for linens, towels, and kitchen supplies. Included in this category are brooms, mops, and other cleaning equipment and supplies.

TABLE 1   Minimum Kitchen Storage Required

	40 to 60 ft² Area — Kitchenette	
Item	0-bedroom living unit,* ft²	1-bedroom living unit,* ft²
Total shelving in wall and base cabinets	24	30
Shelving in either wall or base cabinets	10	12
Drawer area	4	5
Countertop area	5	6
	60 ft² Area and Over — Kitchen	
Item	1- and 2-bedroom living units, ft²	3- and 4-bedroom living units, ft²
Total shelving in wall and base cabinets	48	54
Shelving in either wall or base cabinets	18	20
Drawer area	8	10
Countertop area	10	12

*Kitchen unit assemblies serving the kitchen function and occupying less than 40 ft² area in 0-BR living units shall not be less than 5 ft in length and shall provide at least 12 ft² of total shelving in wall and base cabinets. Drawer and countertop space shall also be provided. No room count is allowable for this type facility.

KITCHENS

Cabinet Dimensions

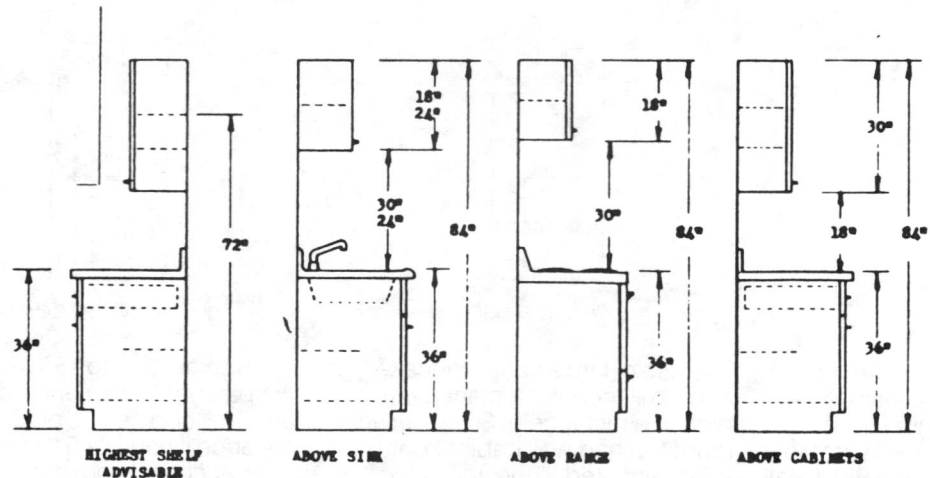

HIGHEST SHELF ADVISABLE   ABOVE SINK   ABOVE RANGE   ABOVE CABINETS

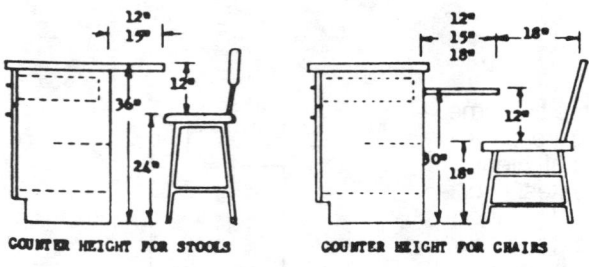

COUNTER HEIGHT FOR STOOLS   COUNTER HEIGHT FOR CHAIRS

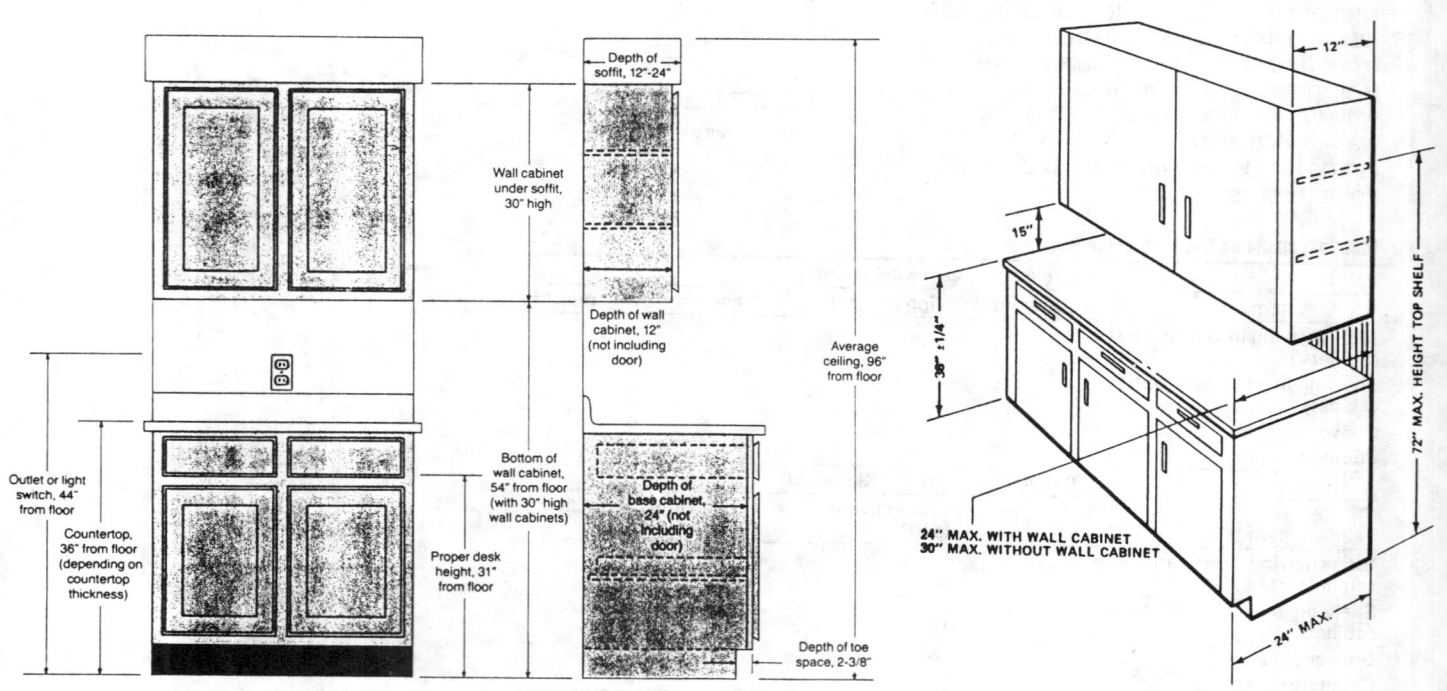

Outlet or light switch, 44" from floor

Countertop, 36" from floor (depending on countertop thickness)

Wall cabinet under soffit, 30" high

Depth of soffit, 12"–24"

Depth of wall cabinet, 12" (not including door)

Bottom of wall cabinet, 54" from floor (with 30" high wall cabinets)

Proper desk height, 31" from floor

Depth of base cabinet, 24" (not including door)

Depth of toe space, 2-3/8"

Average ceiling, 96" from floor

12"

15"

36" ± 1/4"

72" MAX. HEIGHT TOP SHELF

24" MAX. WITH WALL CABINET
30" MAX. WITHOUT WALL CABINET

24" MAX.

Example of the proper dimensional limits and relative placement of kitchen base cabinets and wall cabinets

FRAMED CABINETRY

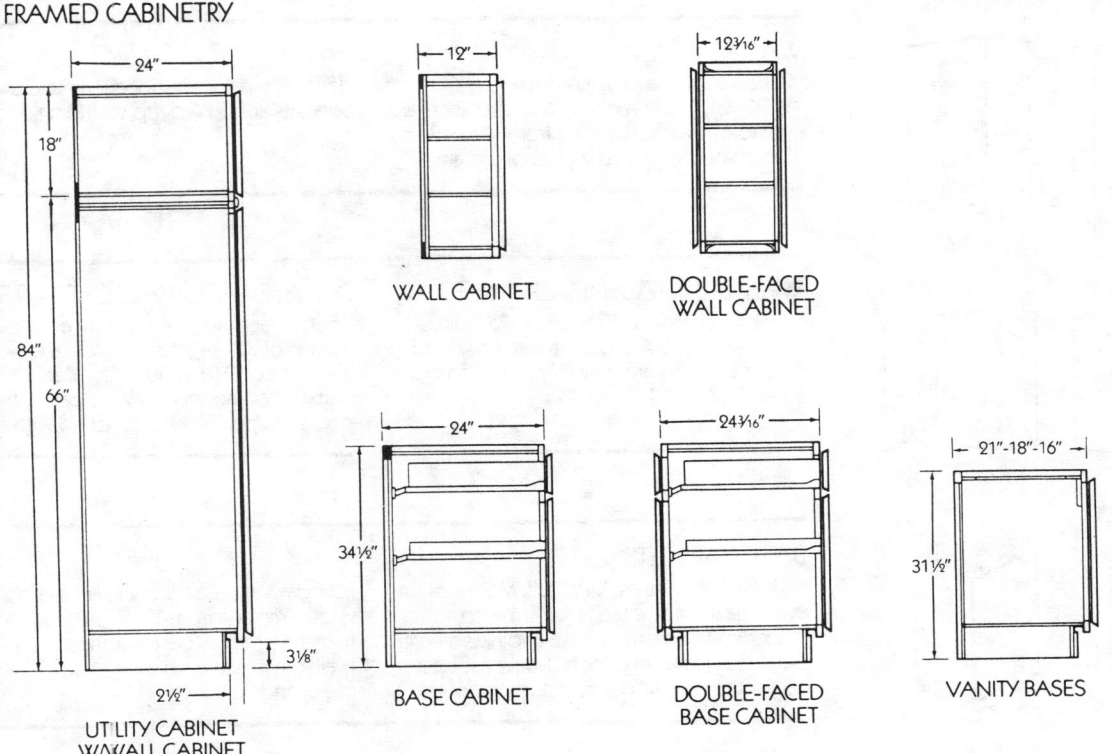

UTILITY CABINET
W/WALL CABINET

WALL CABINET

DOUBLE-FACED
WALL CABINET

BASE CABINET

DOUBLE-FACED
BASE CABINET

VANITY BASES

FRAMELESS CABINETRY

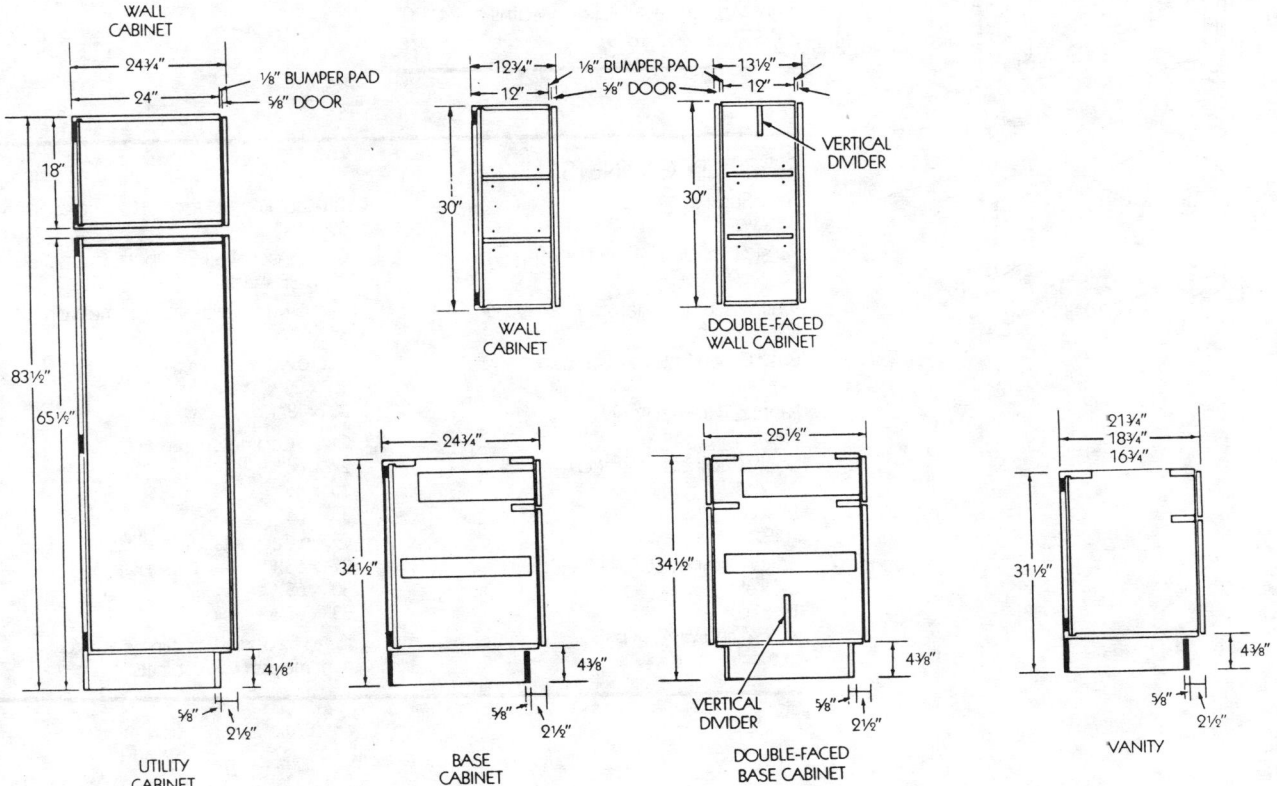

UTILITY
CABINET

WALL
CABINET

DOUBLE-FACED
WALL CABINET

BASE
CABINET

DOUBLE-FACED
BASE CABINET

VANITY

KITCHENS
Cabinet Sizes

FRAMED   FRAMELESS

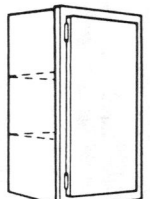 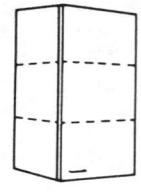

 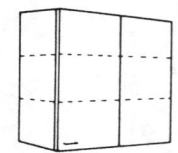

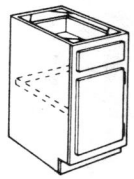 

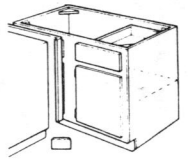 

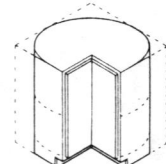 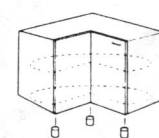

WALL CABINETS

Wall cabinets are available in heights of 42", 30", 24", 18", 15", and 12". Most cabinets are available in widths ranging from 9" to 48", in 3" increments. Framed wall cabinets are 12" deep, not including doors. Frameless wall cabinets are 12¾" deep, including doors.

WALL BLIND CORNER CABINETS

Wall blind corner cabinets are available in heights of 42", 30" and 24". Most wall blind corner cabinets are available in widths of 24", 27", 30", 33", 36", 42", and 48".

DOUBLE-FACE WALL CABINETS

Double-face wall cabinets are available in heights of 30", 24" and 18". Most are available in widths of 18", 24", 30", 36", 42" and 48". Framed cabinets are 13¹⁵/₁₆" deep with doors. Frameless are 13½" deep with doors.

BASE CABINETS

All base cabinets are 34½" tall. Most are available in widths ranging from 9" to 48", in 3" increments. Framed base cabinets are 24" deep, not including doors. Frameless base cabinets are 24¾" deep, including doors.

Four-drawer base cabinets are available in widths ranging from 12" to 24", in 3" increments. Frameless base cabinets are also available in a three-drawer style in widths of 30" and 36".

BASE BLIND CORNER CABINETS

All base blind corner cabinets are 34½" high. Most are available in widths of 24", 30", 36", 39", 42", and 48".

SPECIALTY CABINETS

Lazy Susans:
36"-Wide

Range Hoods: (framed only)
36" & 30"-Wide

Wall What-Not Shelves: (framed only)
30"-High

Base Open Shelves: (framed only)
34½"-High

Pantries: (framed only)
36" x 66"

Utility Cabinets: (framed)
24" x 66"
18" x 66"
In 12" and 24" Depths

Utility Cabinets: (frameless)
24" x 65½"
18" x 65½"
In 12¾" and 24¾" Depths

Tilt-Out Range Hoods: (frameless only)
30" x 24"

Glass Door Wall Cabinets: (frameless only)
30" & 36"-Wide

Microwave Cabinets: (framed only)
30" x 21"

Microwave Shelves:
30" x 22⅝" (framed)
30" x 18" (frameless)

Oven Cabinets: (framed)
27" x 66"
30" x 66"
33" x 66"

Oven Cabinets: (frameless)
27" x 65½"
30" x 65½"
33" x 65½"

Up to six 6" drawers can be added to frameless oven cabinets.

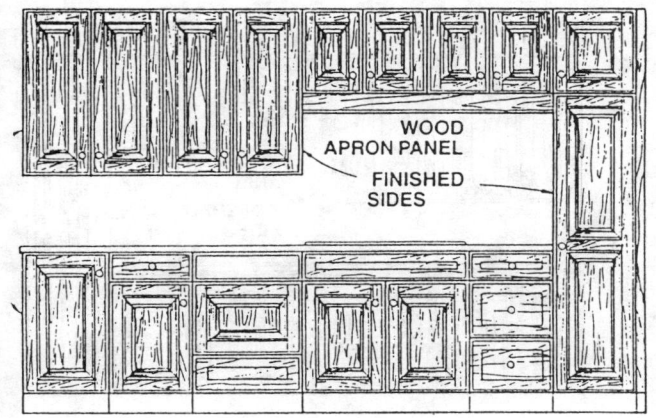

WOOD
APRON PANEL

FINISHED
SIDES

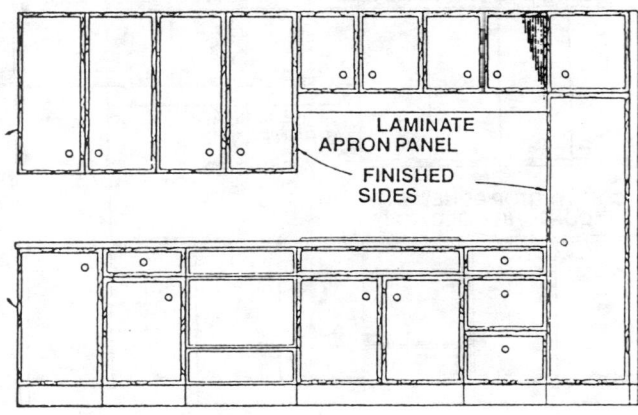

LAMINATE
APRON PANEL

FINISHED
SIDES

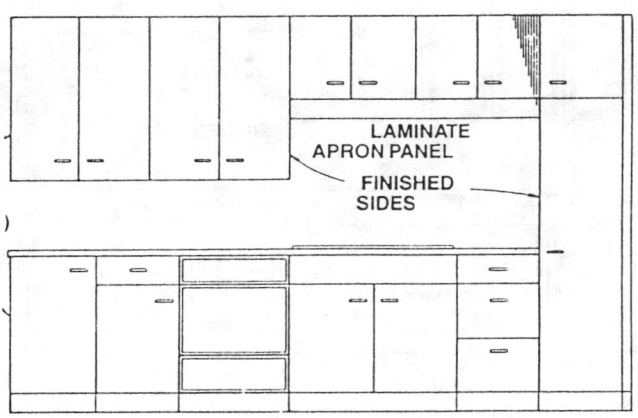

LAMINATE
APRON PANEL

FINISHED
SIDES

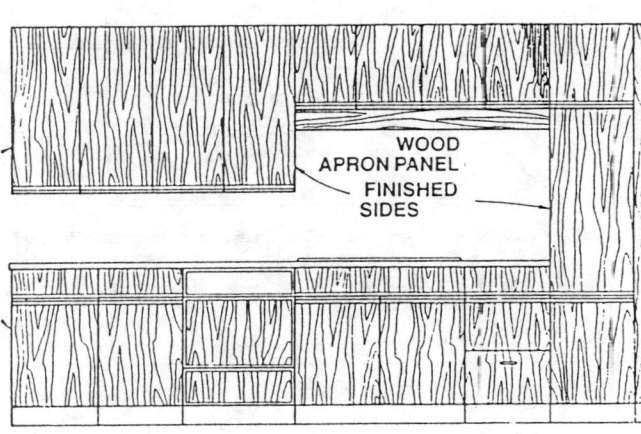

WOOD
APRON PANEL

FINISHED
SIDES

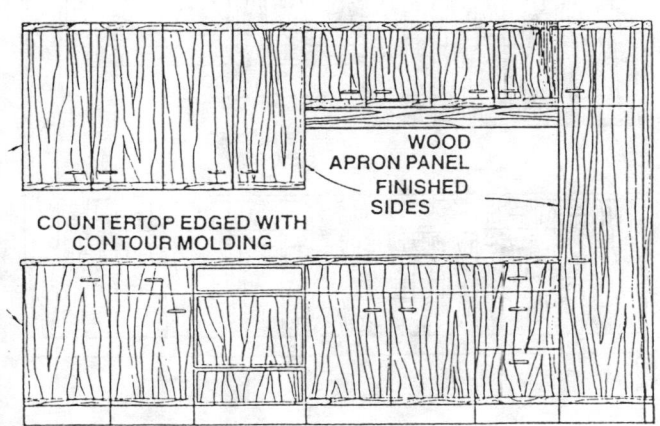

WOOD
APRON PANEL

FINISHED
SIDES

COUNTERTOP EDGED WITH
CONTOUR MOLDING

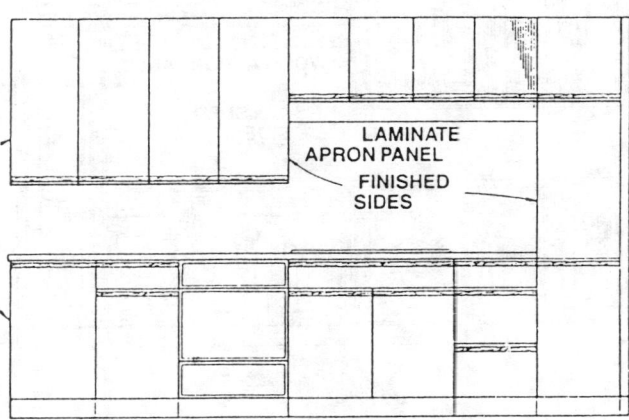

LAMINATE
APRON PANEL

FINISHED
SIDES

KITCHENS
Cabinet Types and Dimensions

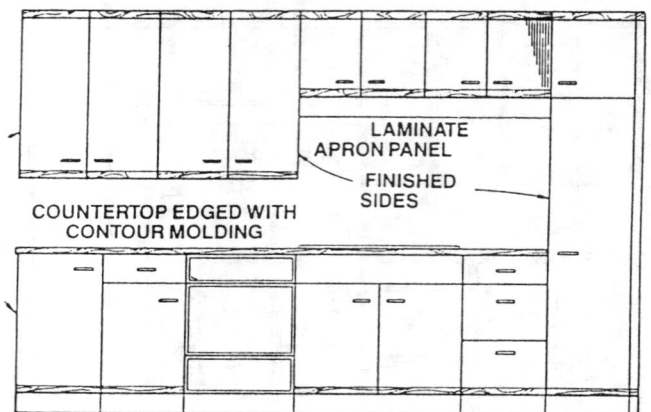

COUNTERTOP EDGED WITH
CONTOUR MOLDING

LAMINATE
APRON PANEL

FINISHED
SIDES

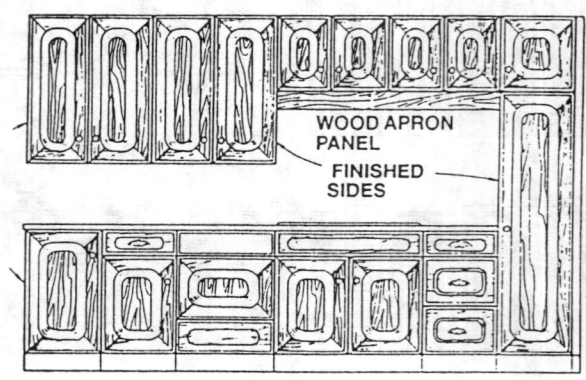

WOOD APRON
PANEL

FINISHED
SIDES

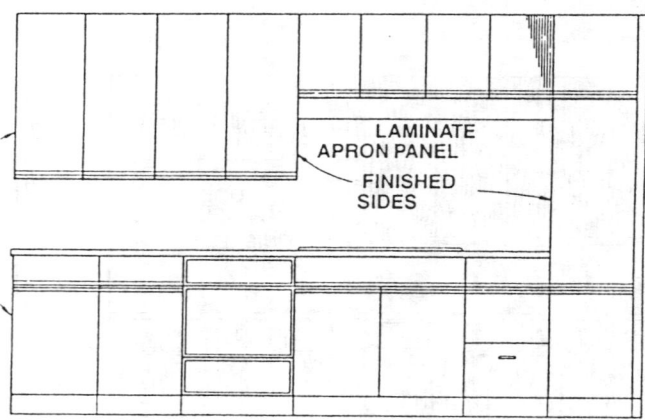

LAMINATE
APRON PANEL

FINISHED
SIDES

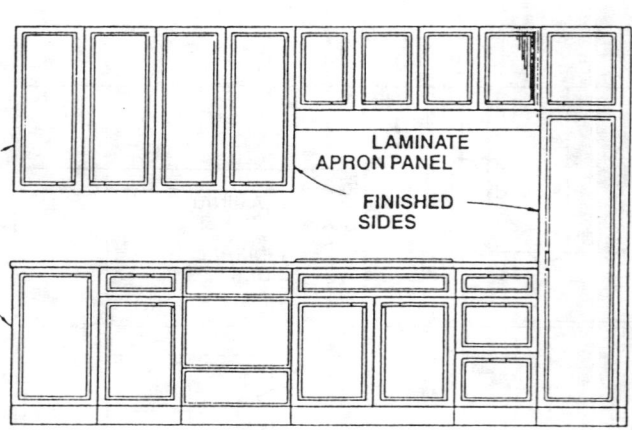

LAMINATE
APRON PANEL

FINISHED
SIDES

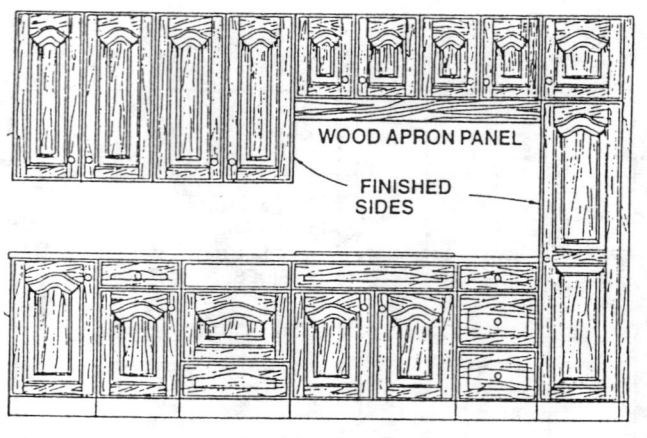

WOOD APRON PANEL

FINISHED
SIDES

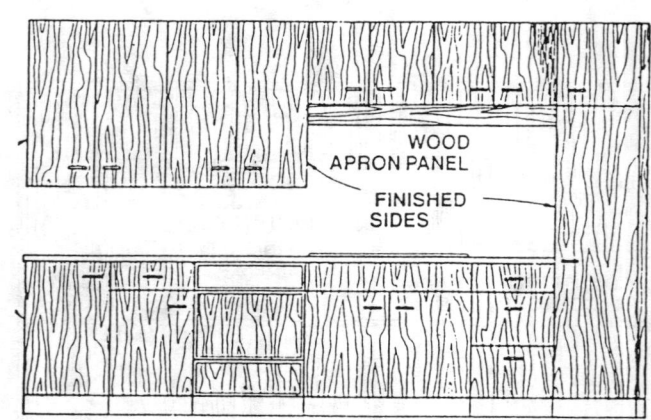

WOOD
APRON PANEL

FINISHED
SIDES

Sink Cabinets & Fronts

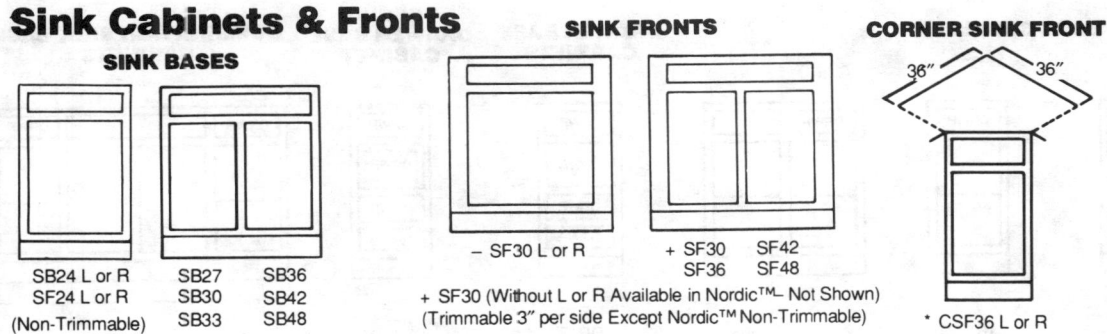

SINK BASES

SB24 L or R
SF24 L or R
(Non-Trimmable)

SB27
SB30
SB33

SB36
SB42
SB48

SINK FRONTS

– SF30 L or R

+ SF30   SF42
  SF36   SF48

+ SF30 (Without L or R Available in Nordic™– Not Shown)
(Trimmable 3″ per side Except Nordic™ Non-Trimmable)

CORNER SINK FRONT

36″   36″

* CSF36 L or R

Oven Cabinets & Drop-In Range Fronts

OVEN CABINETS

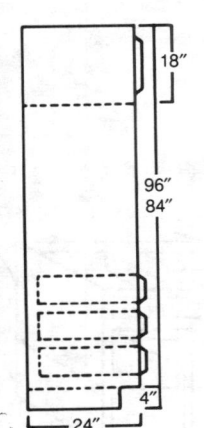

18″

96″
84″

4″

24″

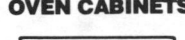
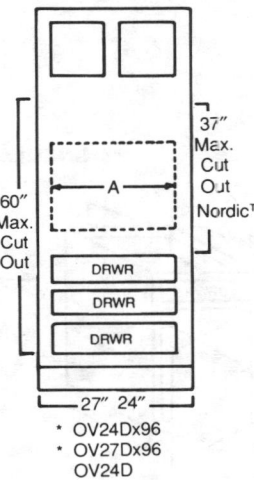

60″
Max.
Cut
Out

37″
Max.
Cut
Out
Nordic™

A

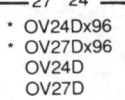

DRWR

DRWR

DRWR

27″ 24″

* OV24Dx96
* OV27Dx96
  OV24D
  OV27D

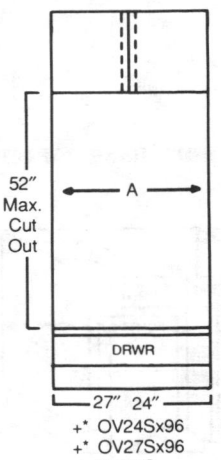

52″
Max.
Cut
Out

A

DRWR

27″ 24″

+* OV24Sx96
+* OV27Sx96
 + OV24S
 + OV27S

DROP-IN RANGE FRONT

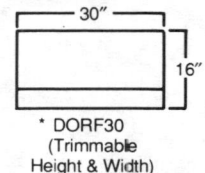

30″

16″

* DORF30
(Trimmable
Height & Width)

UNIVERSAL DROP-IN RANGE FRONTS

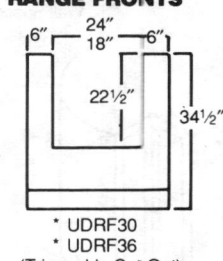

6″ 24″ 6″
18″

22½″

34½″

* UDRF30
* UDRF36
(Trimmable Cut-Out)

Utility Cabinets/Fronts & Pantry Cabinet

UTILITY CABINETS/FRONTS

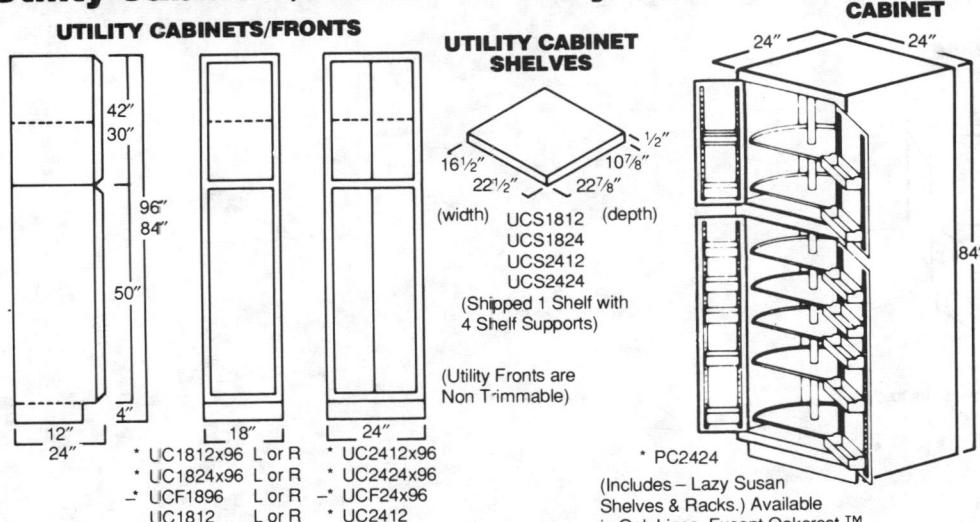

42″
30″

96″
84″

50″

4″

12″
24″

* UC1812x96   L or R
* UC1824x96   L or R
-* UCF1896   L or R
  UC1812   L or R
  UC1824   L or R
-* UCF18   L or R

18″

* UC2412x96
* UC2424x96
-* UCF24x96
* UC2412
* UC2424
-* UCF24

24″

UTILITY CABINET SHELVES

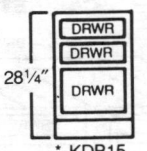

½″
16½″   10⅞″
22½″   22⅞″

(width)   (depth)

UCS1812
UCS1824
UCS2412
UCS2424

(Shipped 1 Shelf with
4 Shelf Supports)

(Utility Fronts are
Non Trimmable)

PANTRY CABINET

24″   24″

84″

* PC2424

(Includes – Lazy Susan
Shelves & Racks.) Available
in Oak Lines, Except Oakcrest,™
Euro,™ X-Line,™ & Spartan™

Desk Cabinets

DESK UNIT

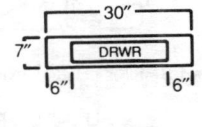

DRWR
DRWR
DRWR

28¼″

* KDB15

KNEEHOLE DRAWER

30″
7″
DRWR
6″   6″

* KD30

(Trimmable 3″ per side)

DESK END PANEL

KITCHENS

Cabinet Types and Dimensions

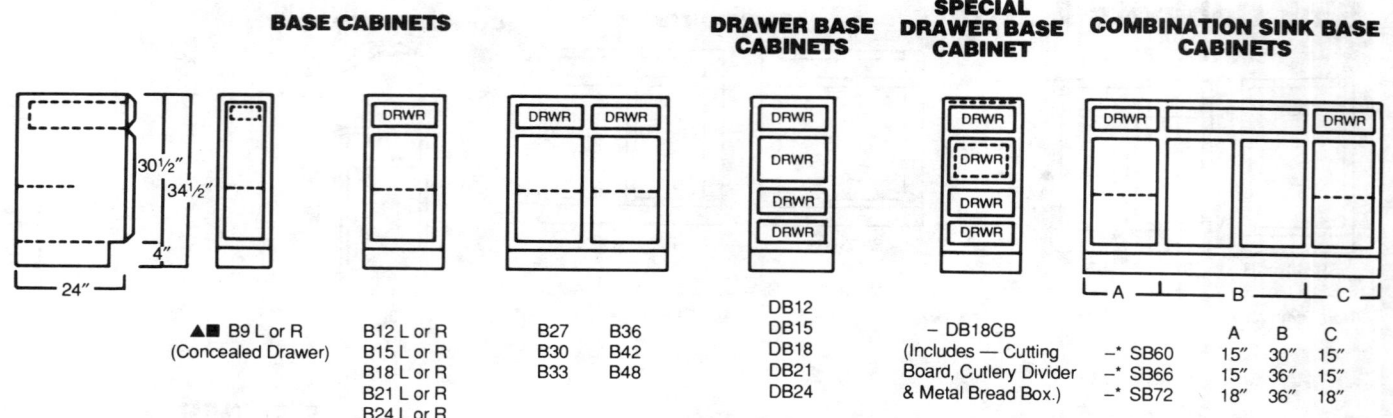

BASE CABINETS

30½"
34½"
4"
24"

▲■ B9 L or R
(Concealed Drawer)

B12 L or R
B15 L or R
B18 L or R
B21 L or R
B24 L or R

B27　B36
B30　B42
B33　B48

DRAWER BASE CABINETS

DRWR

DB12
DB15
DB18
DB21
DB24

SPECIAL DRAWER BASE CABINET

DRWR
DRWR
DRWR
DRWR

– DB18CB
(Includes — Cutting
Board, Cutlery Divider
& Metal Bread Box.)

COMBINATION SINK BASE CABINETS

DRWR　　　　DRWR

A　　B　　C

	A	B	C
–* SB60	15"	30"	15"
–* SB66	15"	36"	15"
–* SB72	18"	36"	18"

▲ No Arched Door.
■ No Center Medallion. (Saxony)

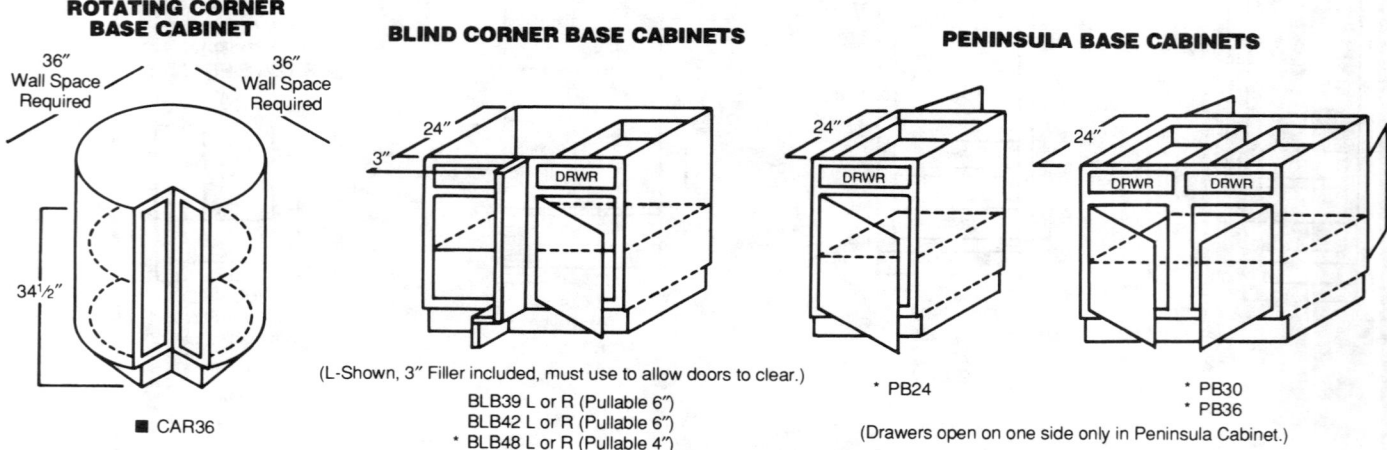

ROTATING CORNER BASE CABINET

36"
Wall Space
Required

36"
Wall Space
Required

34½"

■ CAR36

BLIND CORNER BASE CABINETS

24"
3"
DRWR

(L-Shown, 3" Filler included, must use to allow doors to clear.)
BLB39 L or R (Pullable 6")
BLB42 L or R (Pullable 6")
* BLB48 L or R (Pullable 4")

PENINSULA BASE CABINETS

24"
DRWR

* PB24

24"
DRWR　DRWR

* PB30
* PB36

(Drawers open on one side only in Peninsula Cabinet.)

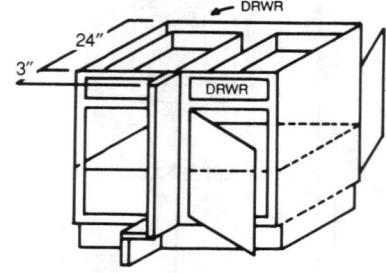

BLIND PENINSULA BASE CABINETS

DRWR
24"
3"
DRWR

(L-Shown, 3" Filler included, must use to allow doors to clear.)

* BLPB42 L or R (Pullable 6")
* BLPB48 L or R (Pullable 6")

WALL CABINETS

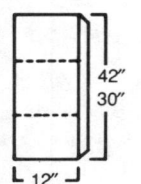 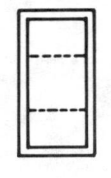 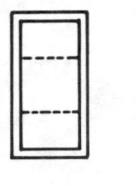 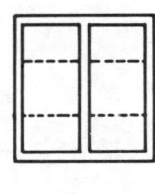 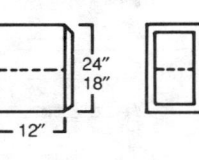 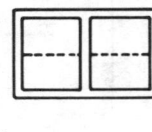 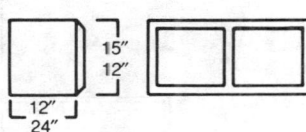

* W1242 L or R	▲■ * W930 L or R	* W2742	W2730	* W1224 L or R	W3024	W2418
* W1542 L or R	W1230 L or R	* W3042	W3030	* W1524 L or R	* W3624	W3018
* W1842 L or R	W1530 L or R	* W3342	W3330	* W1824 L or R	* W4224	W3318
* W2142 L or R	W1830 L or R	* W3642	W3630	* W2124 L or R	* W4824	W3618
* W2442 L or R	W2130 L or R	* W4242	W4230	* W2424 L or R		W4218
	W2430 L or R	* W4842	W4330			

W3015	* W3015x24	■ W3012
W3315	* W3315x24	■ W3612
W3615	* W3615x24	

COMBINATION WALL CABINETS

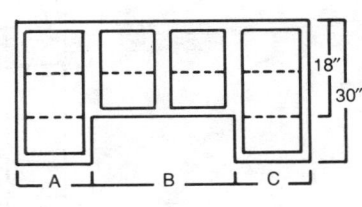

	A	B	C
–* CWC60	15″	30″	15″
–* CWC66	18″	30″	18″
–* CWC72	21″	30″	21″

(Fixed Shelves)

CORNER WALL CABINET

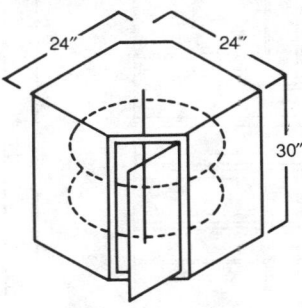

* CW2442 L or R
CW2430 L or R
(Fixed Shelves)

CWS2430 L or R
(2 Adjustable
Rotary Shelves)

BLIND CORNER WALL CABINETS

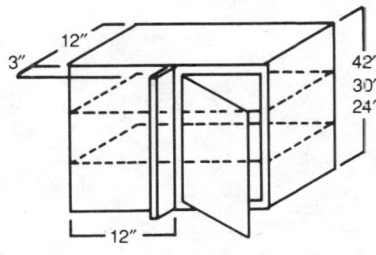

(L-Shown, 3″ Filler included, must use to allow doors to clear.)

* BLW2742 L or R	BLW2730 L or R	* BLW2724 L or R
* BLW3042 L or R	BLW3030 L or R	* BLW3624 L or R
* BLW3642 L or R	BLW3630 L or R	
* BLW4242 (2 Doors) L or R	BLW4230 (2 Doors) L or R	
* BLW4842 (2 Doors) L or R	* BLW4830 (2 Doors) L or R	

PENINSULA WALL CABINETS

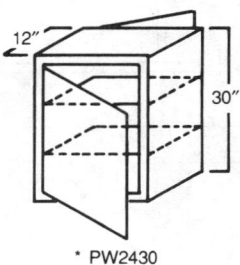 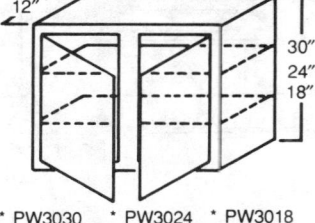

* PW2430

* PW3030	* PW3024	* PW3018
* PW3630	PW3624	* PW3618
		* PW4218

BLIND PENINSULA CORNER WALL CABINET

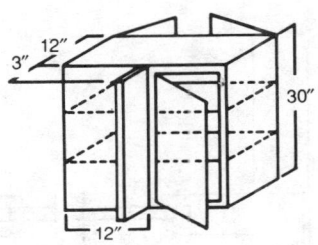

(L-Shown, 3″ Filler included, must use to allow doors to clear.)

* BLPW2730 L or R

MICROWAVE CABINET

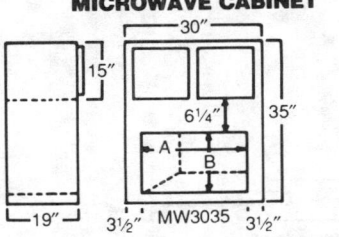

MW3035

A: 22″ Minimum   B: 13¾″ Minimum
   28″ Maximum   19⅛″ Maximum

MICROWAVE CABINET W/SHELF

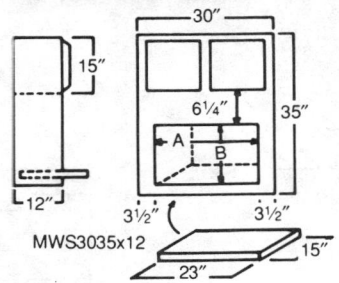

MWS3035x12

KITCHENS
Cabinet Types and Dimensions

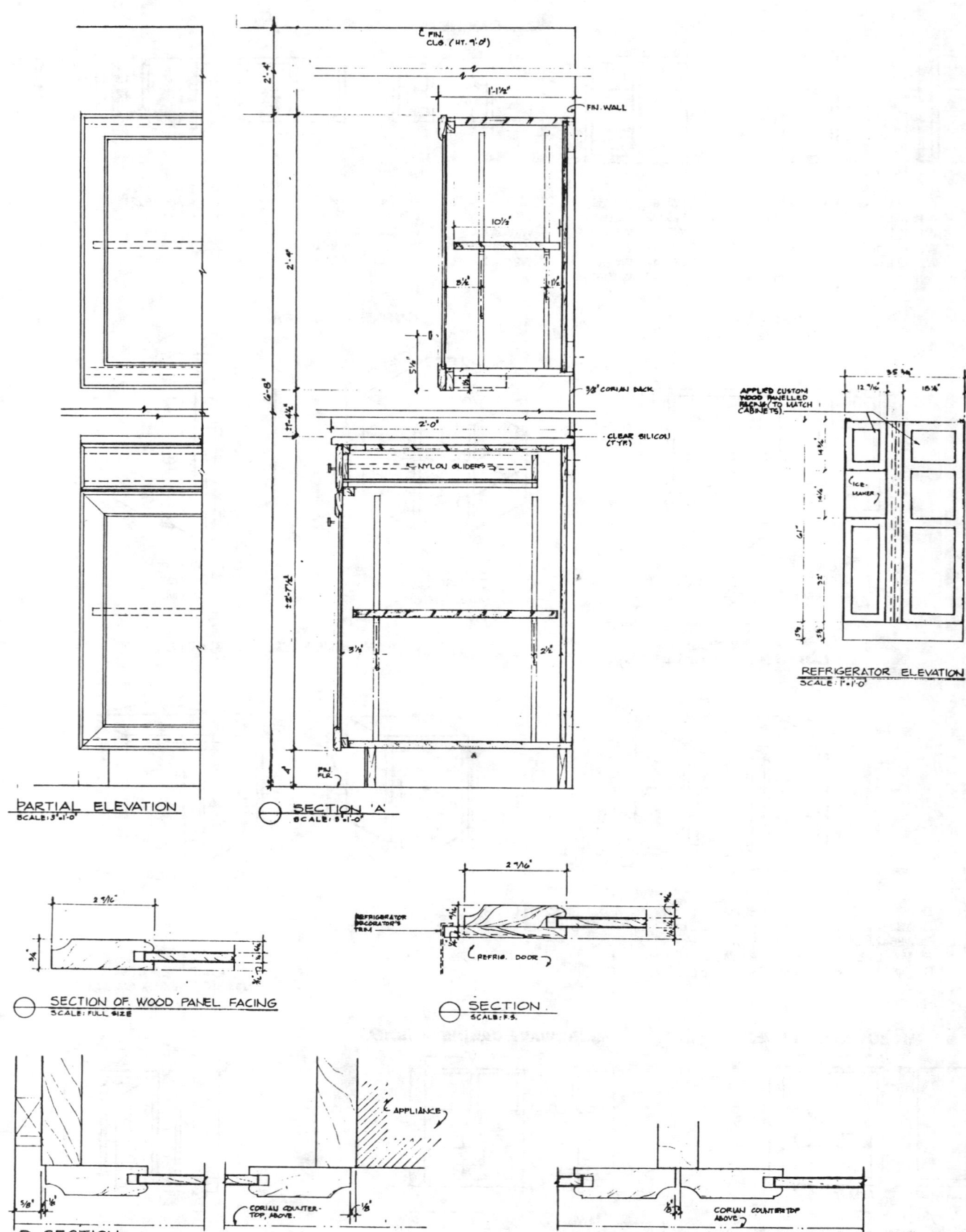

PARTIAL ELEVATION
SCALE: 3"=1'-0"

SECTION 'A'
SCALE: 3"=1'-0"

REFRIGERATOR ELEVATION
SCALE: 1"=1'-0"

SECTION OF WOOD PANEL FACING
SCALE: FULL SIZE

SECTION
SCALE: F.S.

SECTION
SCALE: F.S.

SECTION
SCALE: F.S.

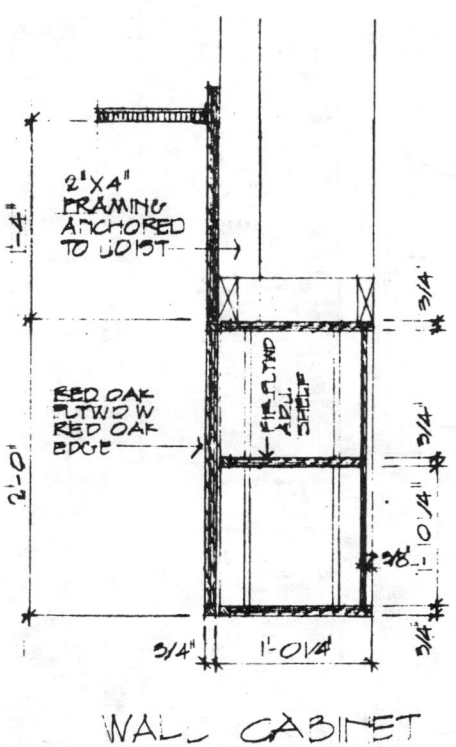

2'X4" FRAMING ANCHORED TO JOIST

3/4"

RED OAK PLYWD W RED OAK EDGE

3/4"

FIR PLYWD ADJ. SHELF

1'-4"

2'-0"

0 1/4"

3/4" 1'-0 1/4" 3/4"

WALL CABINET

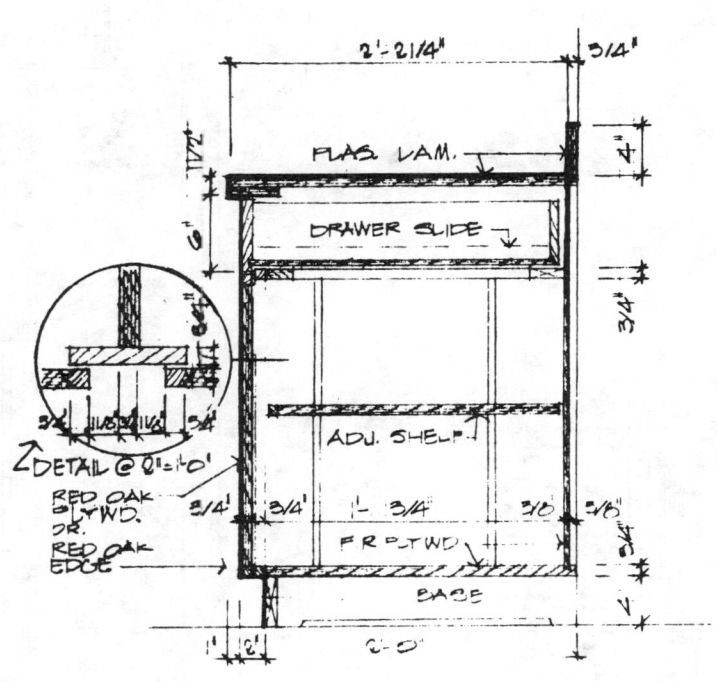

2'-2 1/4" 3/4"

PLAS. LAM.

4"

DRAWER SLIDE

3/4"

1 1/2"

6"

DETAIL @ 0"=1'-0'

3/4" 1/2" 1/2" 3/4"

RED OAK PLYWD. DR.

RED OAK EDGE

ADJ. SHELF

3/4" 3/4" 3/4" 3/4" 3/4"

FIR PLYWD

BASE

1" 2" 2'-0"

BASE CABINET

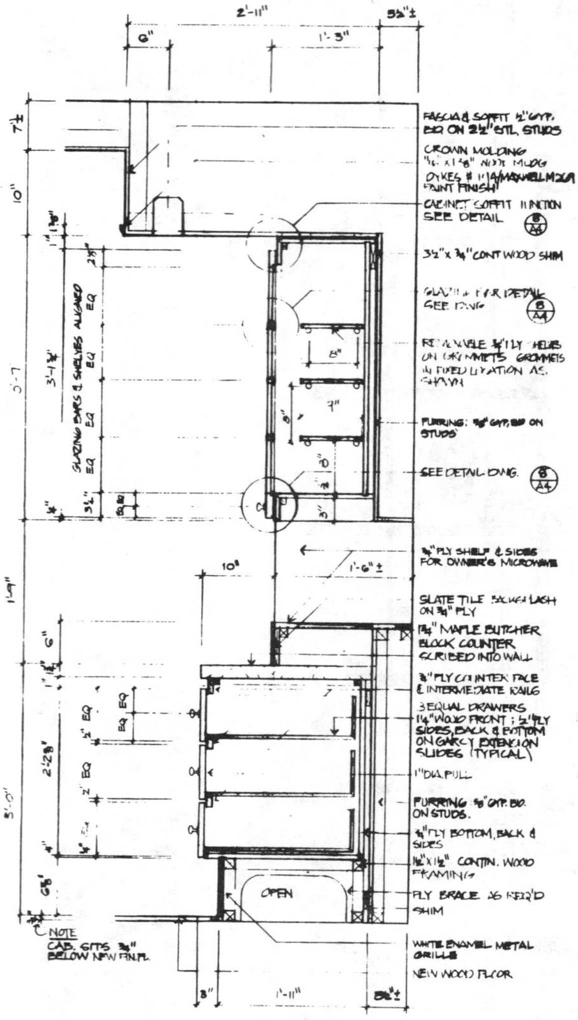

FASCIA & SOFFIT ½" GYP. BD ON 2½" STL. STUDS

CROWN MOLDING "⅝" X 1'-8" ANDR MLDG DYKES # 114/MAXWELLM2G9 PAINT FINISH

CABINET SOFFIT JUNCTION SEE DETAIL ⑤ A4

3½" X ¾" CONT WOOD SHIM

GRAC 112 FOR DETAIL SEE DWG ⑥ A4

REMOVABLE ¾" PLY SHELVES ON DRY MOUNTS GROMMETS IN FIXED LOCATION AS SHOWN

FURRING ⅝" GYP. BD ON STUDS

SEE DETAIL DWG ⑧ A4

¾" PLY SHELF & SIDES FOR OWNER'S MICROWAVE

SLATE TILE BACKSPLASH ON ¾" PLY

1¾" MAPLE BUTCHER BLOCK COUNTER SCRIBED INTO WALL

¾" PLY COUNTER FACE & INTERMEDIATE RAILS

3 EQUAL DRAWERS 1¼" WOOD FRONT; ½" PLY SIDES, BACK & BOTTOM ON GARCY EXTENSION SLIDES (TYPICAL)

1" DIA PULL

FURRING ⅝" GYP. BD. ON STUDS.

¾" PLY BOTTOM, BACK & SIDES

1½"X 1½" CONTIN. WOOD FRAMING

PLY BRACE AS REQ'D SHIM

WHITE ENAMEL METAL GRILLE

NEW WOOD FLOOR

NOTE CAB. SITS ¾" BELOW NEW FIN. FL.

① SECTION: TYPICAL KITCHEN CABINET @ DRAWERS
A4   1" = 1'-0"

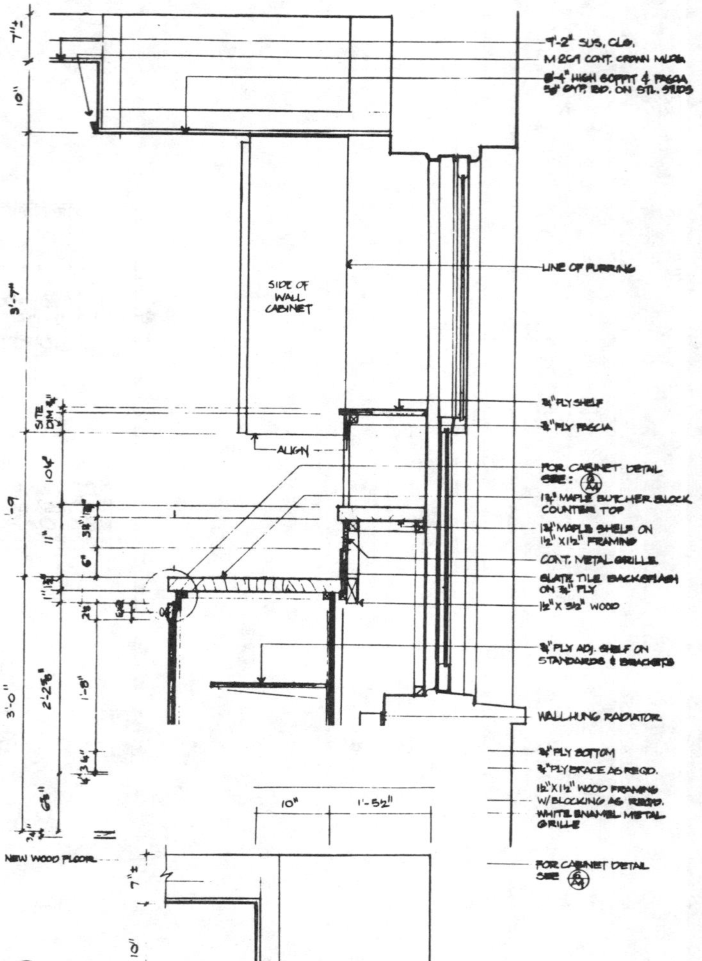

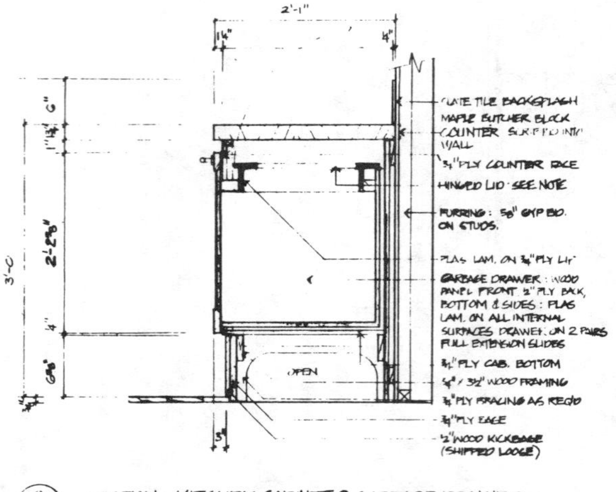

SLATE TILE BACKSPLASH
MAPLE BUTCHER BLOCK COUNTER SCRIBED INTO WALL
¾" PLY COUNTER FACE
HINGED LID - SEE NOTE
FURRING ⅝" GYP BD. ON STUDS.
PLAS LAM. ON ¾" PLY LID
GARBAGE DRAWER : WOOD PANEL FRONT ½" PLY BACK, BOTTOM & SIDES : PLAS LAM. ON ALL INTERNAL SURFACES DRAWER ON 2 PAIRS FULL EXTENSION SLIDES
¾" PLY CAB. BOTTOM
¾" / 3½" WOOD FRAMING
¾" PLY FRAMING AS REQ'D
¾" PLY FACE
½" WOOD KICKBASE (SHIPPED LOOSE)

② SECTION: KITCHEN CABINET @ GARBAGE DRAWER
A4   1" = 1'-0"

*NOTE: PLAS LAM. ON ¾" PLY W/ CUT OUT FOR GARBAGE BAG, ATTACH LID TO DRAWER W/ CONTIN. PIANO HINGE

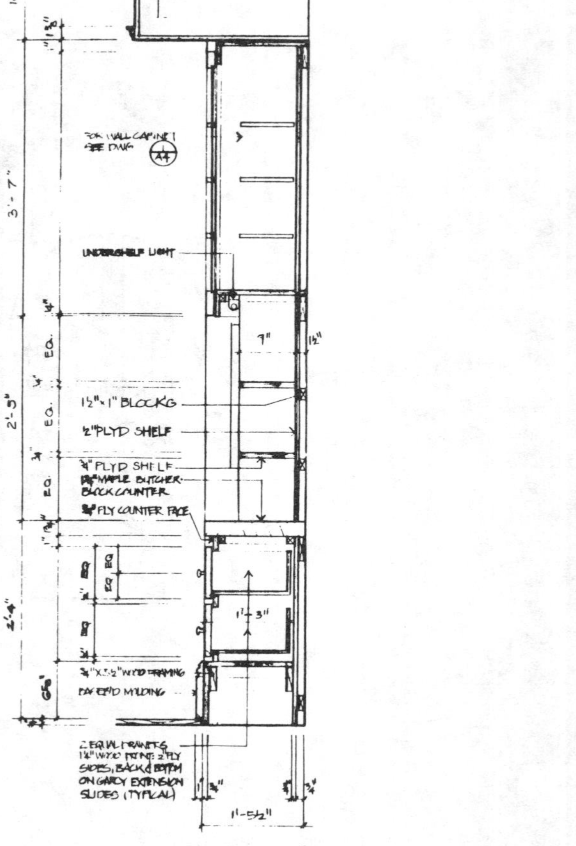

7'-2" SUS. CLG.
M 2G9 CONT. CROWN MLDG
8'-4" HIGH SOFFIT & FASCIA ⅝" GYP. BD. ON STL. STUDS
LINE OF FURRING
SIDE OF WALL CABINET
ALIGN
¾" PLY SHELF
¾" PLY FASCIA
FOR CABINET DETAIL SEE : ② A4
1¾" MAPLE BUTCHER BLOCK COUNTER TOP
1¾" MAPLE SHELF ON 1½"X1½" FRAMING
CONT. METAL GRILLE
SLATE TILE BACKSPLASH ON ¾" PLY
1½" X 5½" WOOD
¾" PLY ADJ. SHELF ON STANDARDS & BRACKETS
WALL HUNG RADIATOR
¾" PLY BOTTOM
¾" PLY BRACE AS REQ'D
1½"X1½" WOOD FRAMING W/BLOCKING AS REQD.
WHITE ENAMEL METAL GRILLE
FOR CABINET DETAIL SEE : ②
NEW WOOD FLOOR

③ SECTION
A4   1" = 1'-0"

FOR WALL CABINET SEE DWG ① A4
UNDERSHELF LIGHT
1½" X 1" BLOCKG
½" PLYD SHELF
½" PLYD SHELF
1¾" MAPLE BUTCHER BLOCK COUNTER
¾" PLY COUNTER FACE
¾"X 3½" WOOD FRAMING
PAINTED MOLDING
2 EQUAL DRAWERS 1¼" WOOD FRONT ½" PLY SIDES, BACK & BOTTOM ON GARCY EXTENSION SLIDES (TYPICAL)

④ SECTION @ NEW WOOD DESK
A4   1" = 1'-0"

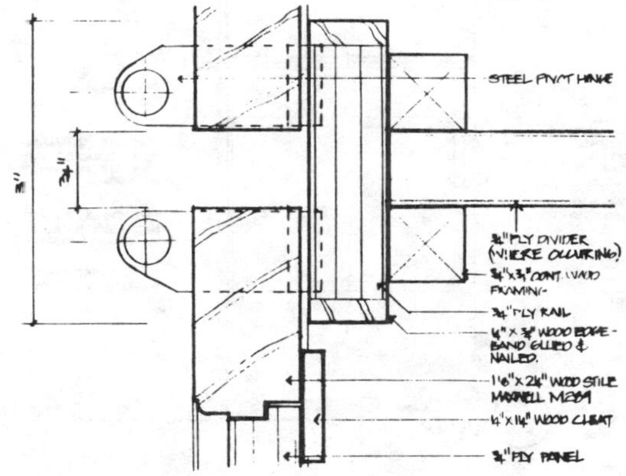
STEEL PIVOT HINGE
3/4" PLY DIVIDER (WHERE OCCURRING)
3/4"x3/4" CONT. WOOD FRAMING
3/4" PLY RAIL
1/4" x 3/4" WOOD EDGE-BAND GLUED & NAILED.
1 1/8" x 2 1/4" WOOD STILE MAXWELL M289
1/4" x 1 1/4" WOOD CLEAT
3/4" PLY PANEL

5/A4 KITCHEN CABINET - PLAN @ JAMB (TYPICAL)
FULL SIZE

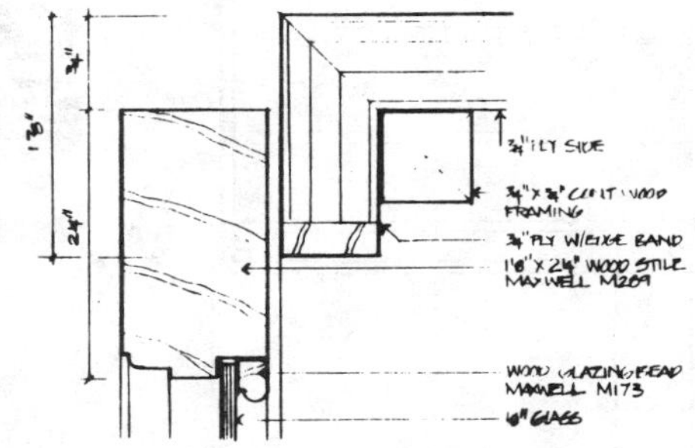
3/4" PLY SIDE
3/4" x 3/4" CONT. WOOD FRAMING
3/4" PLY W/EDGE BAND
1 1/8" x 2 1/4" WOOD STILE MAXWELL M289
WOOD GLAZING BEAD MAXWELL M173
1/8" GLASS

7/A4 KITCHEN CABINET - PLAN @ CORNER JAMB (TYPICAL)
FULL SIZE

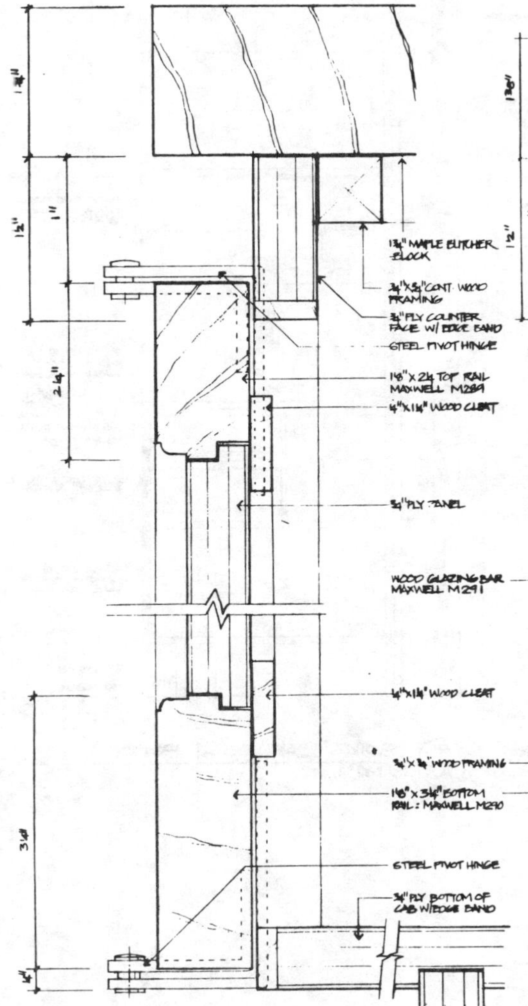
1 3/4" MAPLE BUTCHER BLOCK
3/4"X3/4" CONT. WOOD FRAMING
3/4" PLY COUNTER FACE W/ EDGE BAND
STEEL PIVOT HINGE
1 1/8" X 2 1/4 TOP RAIL MAXWELL M289
1/4"X1 1/4" WOOD CLEAT
3/4" PLY PANEL
WOOD GLAZING BAR MAXWELL M291
1/4"X1 1/4" WOOD CLEAT
3/4"X3/4" WOOD FRAMING
1 1/8" X 3 1/4" BOTTOM RAIL: MAXWELL M290
STEEL PIVOT HINGE
3/4" PLY BOTTOM OF CAB W/EDGE BAND
3/4" PLY BASE

6/A4 KITCHEN BASE CABINET @ DOOR - TYPICAL SECTION
FULL SIZE

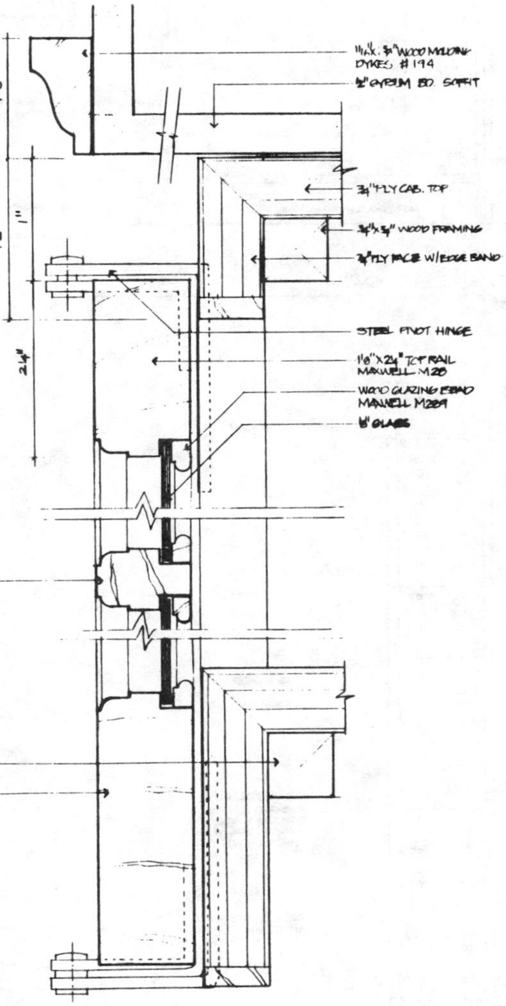
WOOD MOLDING DYKES #194
1/2" GYPSUM BD. SOFFIT
3/4" PLY CAB. TOP
3/4"x3/4" WOOD FRAMING
3/4" PLY FACE W/EDGE BAND
STEEL PIVOT HINGE
1 1/8" X 2 1/4" TOP RAIL MAXWELL M28
WOOD GLAZING BEAD MAXWELL M289
1/8" GLASS

8/A4 WALL CABINET - TYPICAL SECTION
FULL SIZE

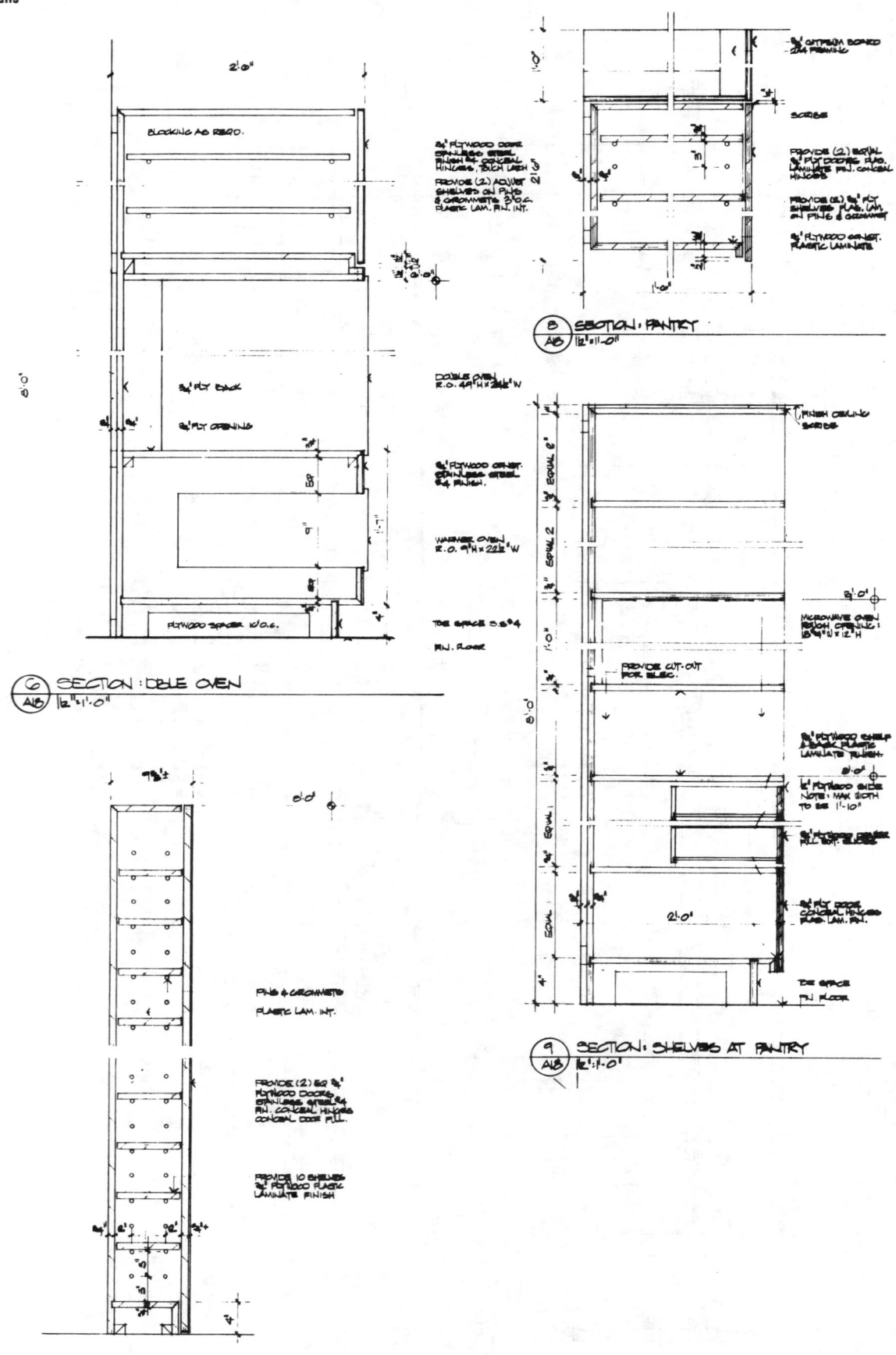

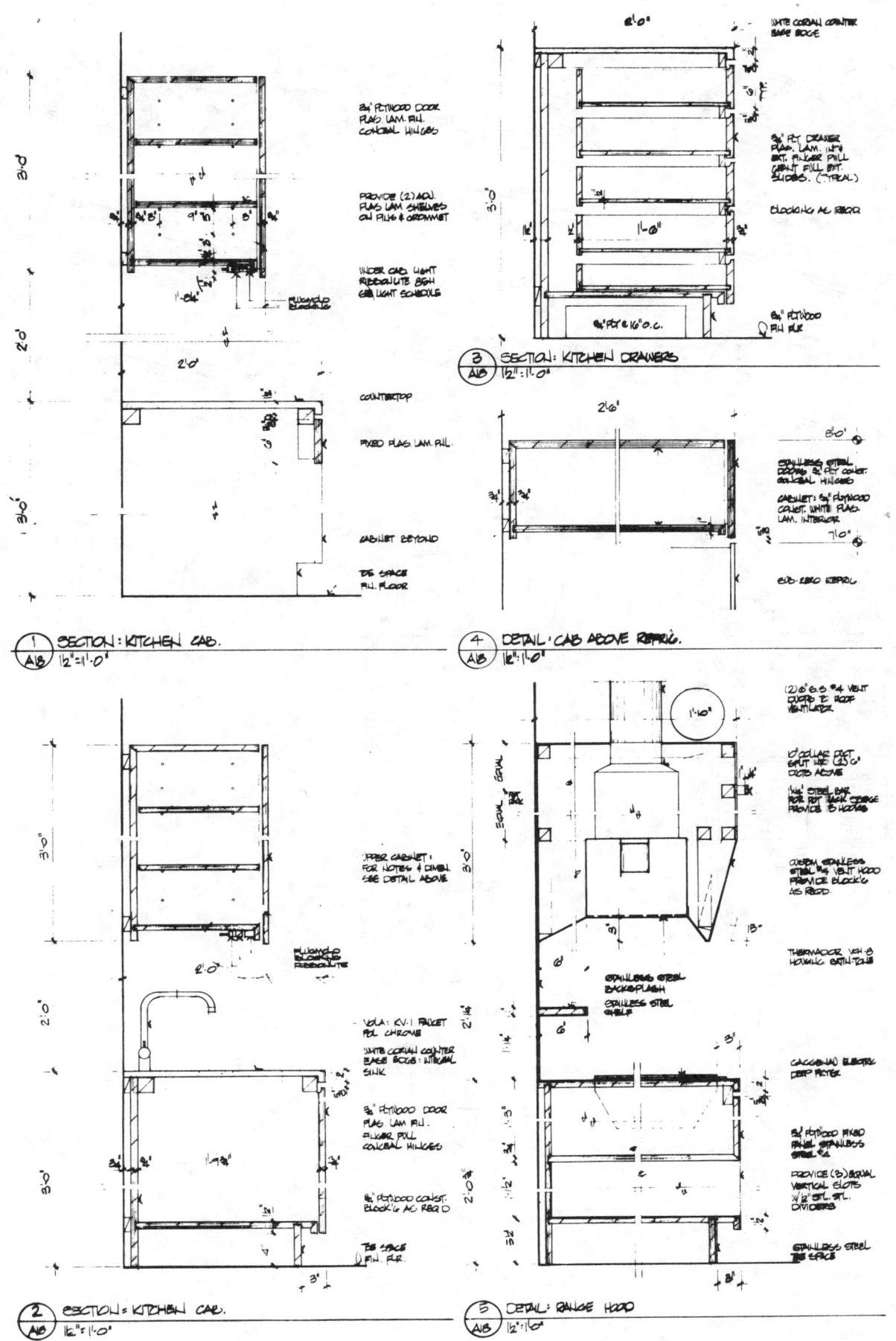

SECTION: KITCHEN CAB.

SECTION: KITCHEN DRAWERS

SECTION: KITCHEN CAB.

DETAIL: CAB ABOVE REFRIG.

DETAIL: RANGE HOOD

KITCHENS

Sink Types and Dimensions

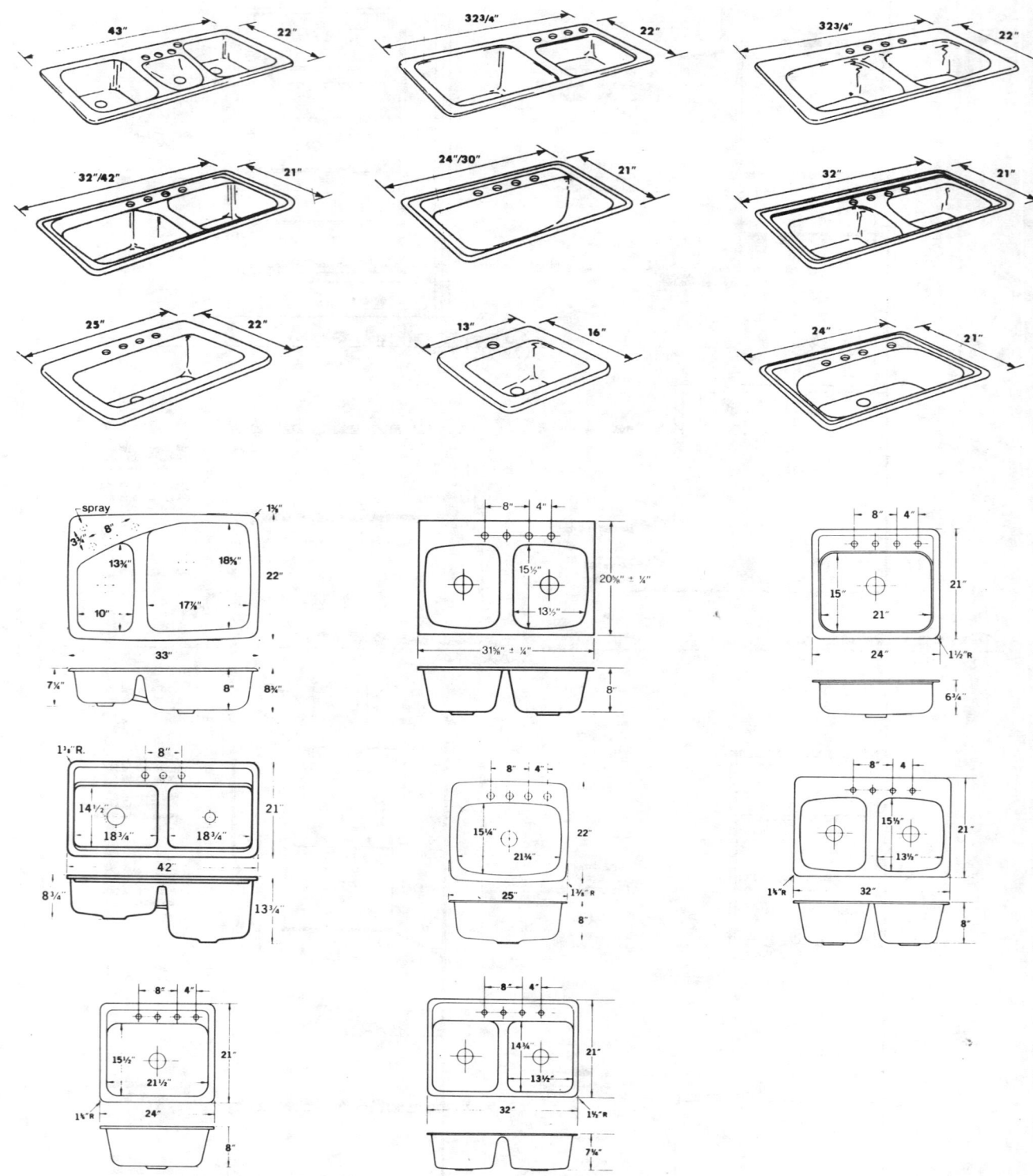

Ranges and Built-In Ovens

Freestanding ranges and built-in ovens come in a variety of sizes and configurations. Some of the larger ranges consist of modular cooktops providing anywhere from two to seven heating elements as well as modular grills, griddles, and even downdraft built-in ventilators. Normally, a minimum clearance of 30" is required above any range or cooktop, but the designer is cautioned to carefully verify local code requirements. Manufacturers' specifications should be carefully reviewed for rough opening requirements and any venting requirements, particularly for self-cleaning ovens.

Dishwashers

Built-in, freestanding, and undersink dishwashers are fairly well standardized in terms of overall dimensions. Access to plumbing and waste lines is the major consideration, as is the method of securing the dishwasher in order to minimize vibration.

Refrigerators

Refrigerator door swings and clearances are of critical importance. While a 90° door swing may provide sufficient room for a person to observe storage within a refrigerator or freezer, a 180° door swing may be required to clean a refrigerator and remove storage bins.

This is particularly true of the side-by-side door configuration. In addition, adequate clearance should be allowed between the sides and top of the refrigerator and any adjoining cabinetwork, especially if a built-in look is desired. The designer should check requirements with the manufacturer.

While these drawings can be used for preliminary planning, final dimensions and clearance must be verified with the manufacturer. Often overlooked are clearances for refrigerator handles or pulls as well as coils mounted at the rear of the refrigerator.

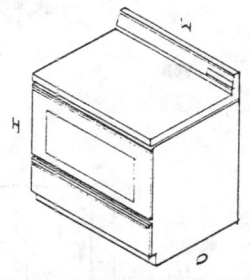

STANDARD FREESTANDING RANGE
W: 18' - 42'
D: 24" - 27 1/2"
H: 35" - 36"

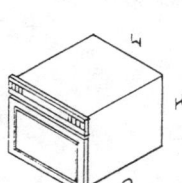

BUILT-IN SINGLE OVEN
W: 20' - 24'
D: 21" - 24"
H: 22" - 28"

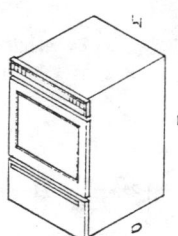

BUILT-IN OVEN/BROILER
W: 18' - 24'
D: 21" - 24"
H: 36" - 41"

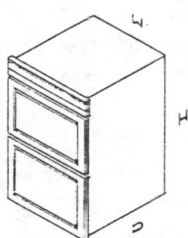

BUILT-IN DOUBLE OVEN
W: 18' - 24'
D: 21" - 24"
H: 38" - 51"

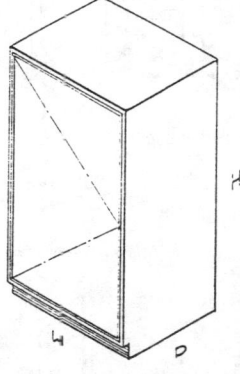

STANDARD REFRIGERATOR
W: 18"   SINGLE DOOR
D: 24"
H: 68 1/2"

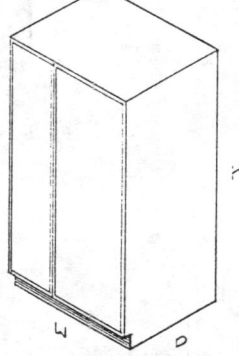

STANDARD REFRIGERATOR
W: 29 1/2' - 39 1/2' (SIDE BY SIDE)
D: 29"   - 33"
H: 64"   - 69 1/2"

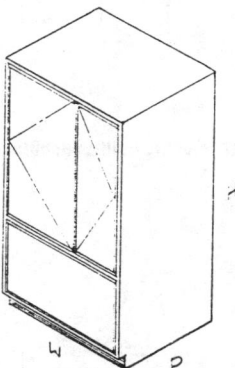

STANDARD REFRIGERATOR
W: 24" - 33 1/2" (BOTTOM FREEZER)
D: 29" - 33"
H: 64" - 69 1/2"

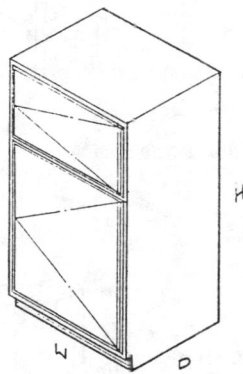

STANDARD REFRIGERATOR
W: 24' - 33' (FREEZER AT TOP)
D: 27 3/4" - 32"
H: 63 1/2" - 68 1/2"

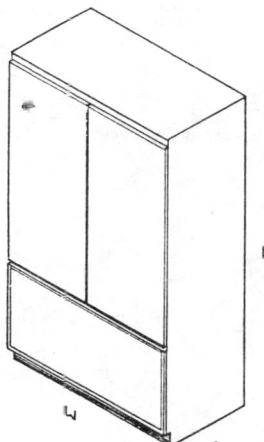

BUILT-IN/RECESSED REFRIGERATOR
W: 30 1/2' - 72'
D: 23 1/2" - 24"
H: 84"

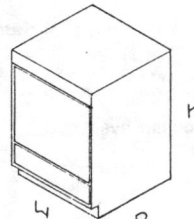

UNDER COUNTER DISHWASHER
W: 23' - 24'
D: 23 1/2" - 26 1/2"
H: 33 1/2" - 34 1/2"

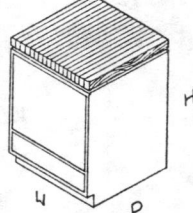

FREE STANDING DISHWASHER
W: 23' - 24'
D: 23 1/2" - 26 1/2"
H: 33 1/2" - 34 1/2"

KITCHENS

Appliances

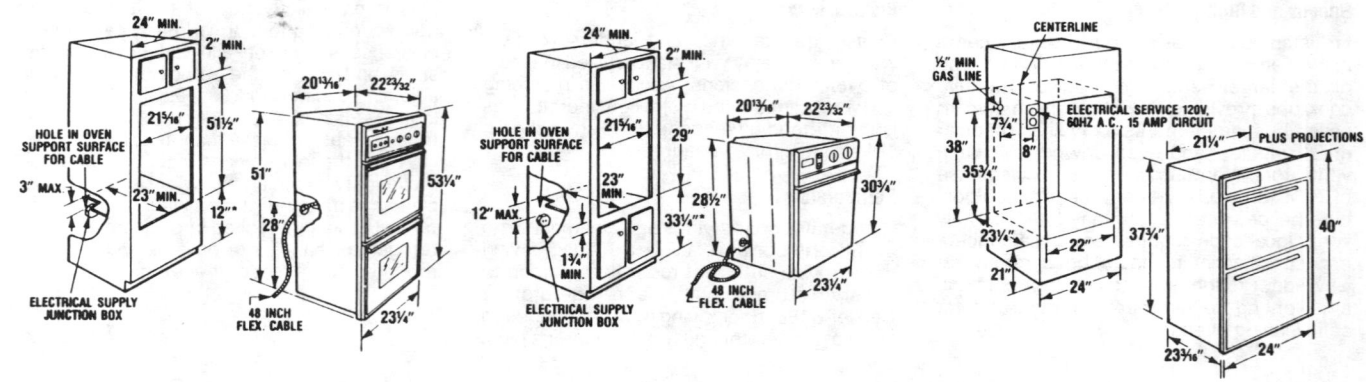

24" electric built-in double oven

24" electric built-in single oven

Gas built-in oven

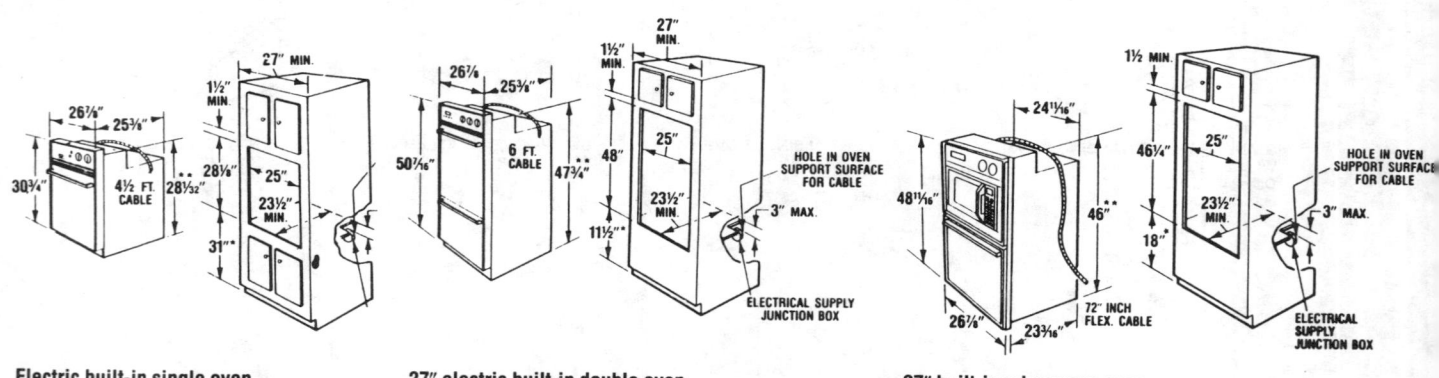

Electric built-in single oven

27" electric built-in double oven

27" built-in microwave oven

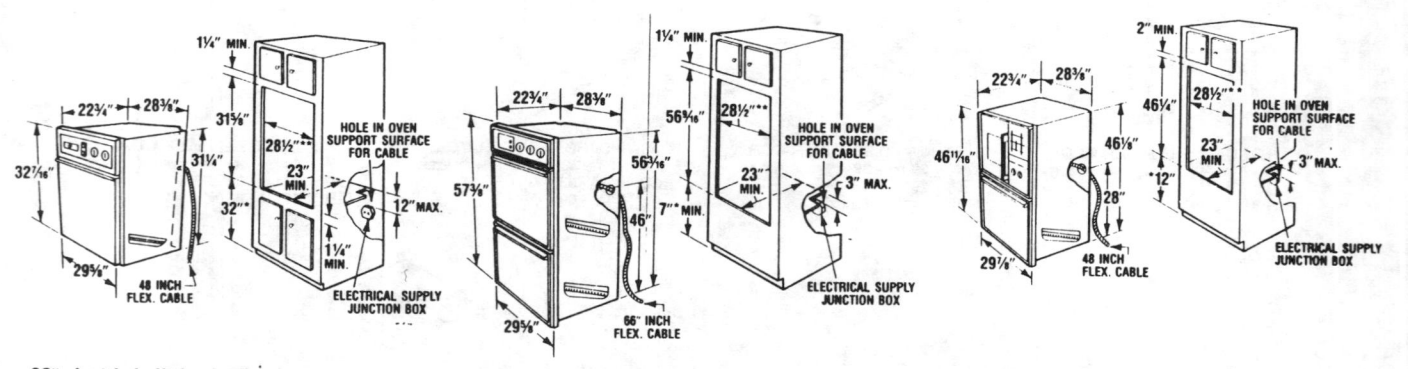

30" electric built-in single oven

30" electric built-in double oven

30" built-in microwave oven

Note: Dimensions shown are for planning purposes only.

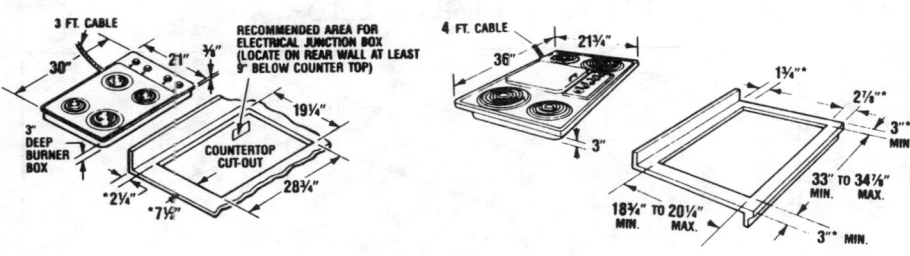

Conventional electric cooktop

36" electric cooktop

Glass cooktop

30" solid elements/glass cooktop

36" solid element/glass cooktop

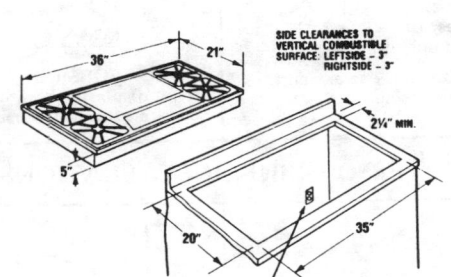

30" gas cooktop

30" gas cooktop

Note: Dimensions shown are for planning purposes only.

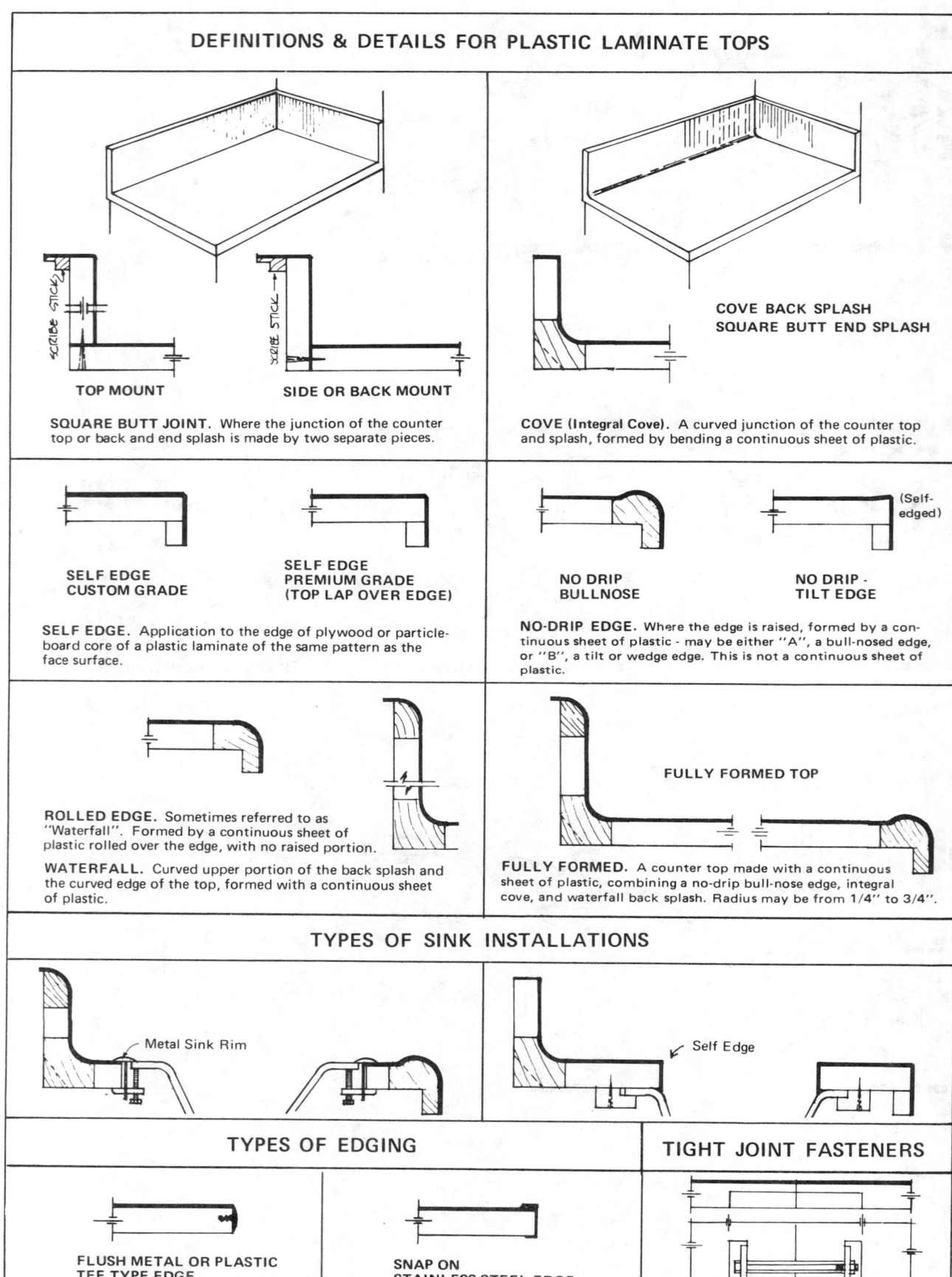

DEFINITIONS & DETAILS FOR PLASTIC LAMINATE TOPS

TOP MOUNT

SIDE OR BACK MOUNT

SQUARE BUTT JOINT. Where the junction of the counter top or back and end splash is made by two separate pieces.

COVE BACK SPLASH SQUARE BUTT END SPLASH

COVE (Integral Cove). A curved junction of the counter top and splash, formed by bending a continuous sheet of plastic.

SELF EDGE CUSTOM GRADE

SELF EDGE PREMIUM GRADE (TOP LAP OVER EDGE)

SELF EDGE. Application to the edge of plywood or particle-board core of a plastic laminate of the same pattern as the face surface.

NO DRIP BULLNOSE

NO DRIP - TILT EDGE

(Self-edged)

NO-DRIP EDGE. Where the edge is raised, formed by a continuous sheet of plastic - may be either "A", a bull-nosed edge, or "B", a tilt or wedge edge. This is not a continuous sheet of plastic.

ROLLED EDGE. Sometimes referred to as "Waterfall". Formed by a continuous sheet of plastic rolled over the edge, with no raised portion.

WATERFALL. Curved upper portion of the back splash and the curved edge of the top, formed with a continuous sheet of plastic.

FULLY FORMED TOP

FULLY FORMED. A counter top made with a continuous sheet of plastic, combining a no-drip bull-nose edge, integral cove, and waterfall back splash. Radius may be from 1/4" to 3/4".

TYPES OF SINK INSTALLATIONS

Metal Sink Rim

Self Edge

TYPES OF EDGING

FLUSH METAL OR PLASTIC TEE TYPE EDGE

SNAP ON STAINLESS STEEL EDGE

TIGHT JOINT FASTENERS

Draw-Bolt

Fig. 11 Definitions and details for plastic laminate tops.

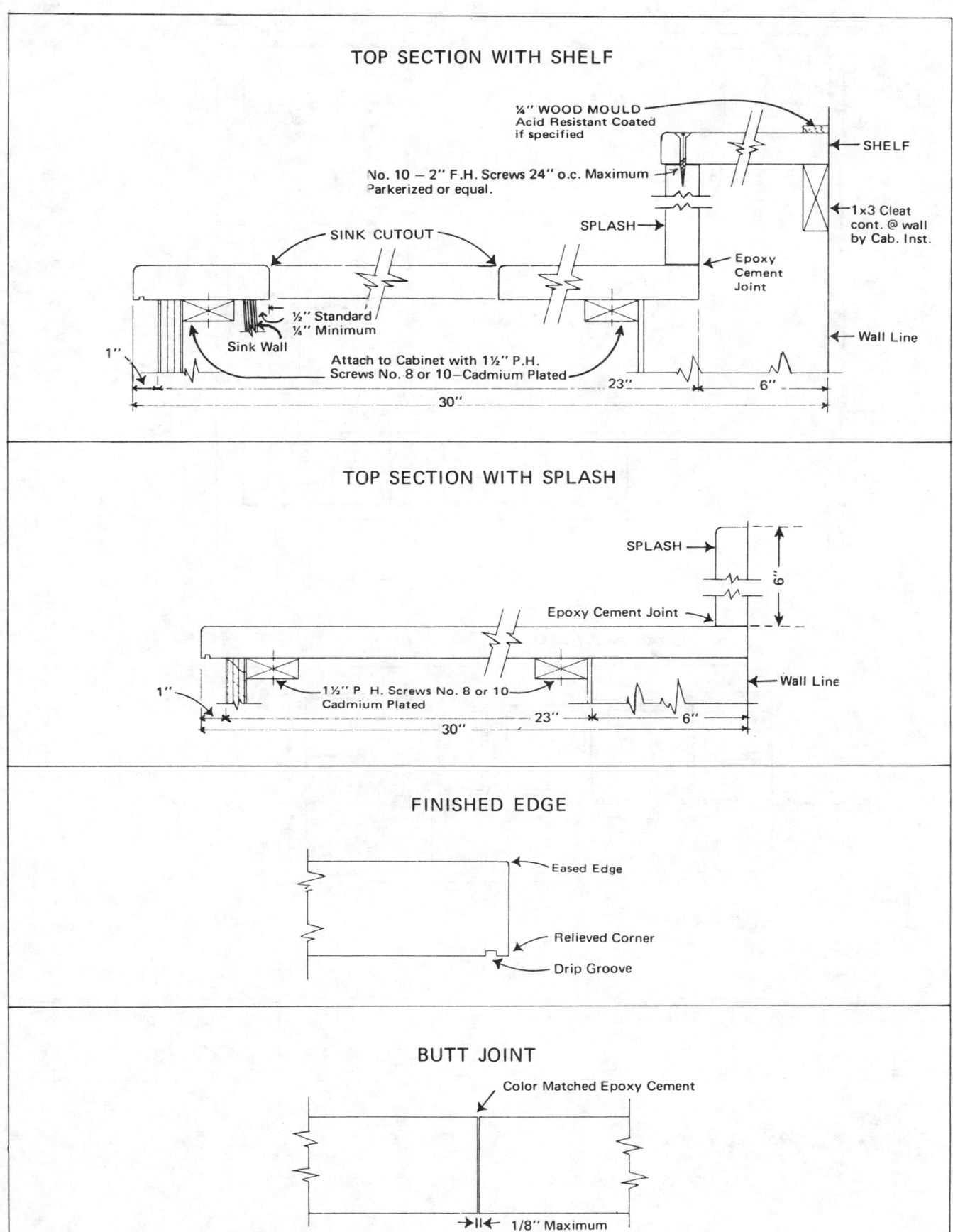

TOP SECTION WITH SHELF

¼" WOOD MOULD
Acid Resistant Coated
if specified

No. 10 – 2" F.H. Screws 24" o.c. Maximum
Parkerized or equal.

SINK CUTOUT

SPLASH

SHELF

1x3 Cleat
cont. @ wall
by Cab. Inst.

Epoxy
Cement
Joint

½" Standard
¼" Minimum

Sink Wall

Wall Line

1"

Attach to Cabinet with 1½" P.H.
Screws No. 8 or 10—Cadmium Plated

23"   6"

30"

TOP SECTION WITH SPLASH

SPLASH

6"

Epoxy Cement Joint

1½" P.H. Screws No. 8 or 10
Cadmium Plated

Wall Line

1"

30"   23"   6"

FINISHED EDGE

Eased Edge

Relieved Corner

Drip Groove

BUTT JOINT

Color Matched Epoxy Cement

1/8" Maximum

Fig. 12 Composition stone top and sink details.

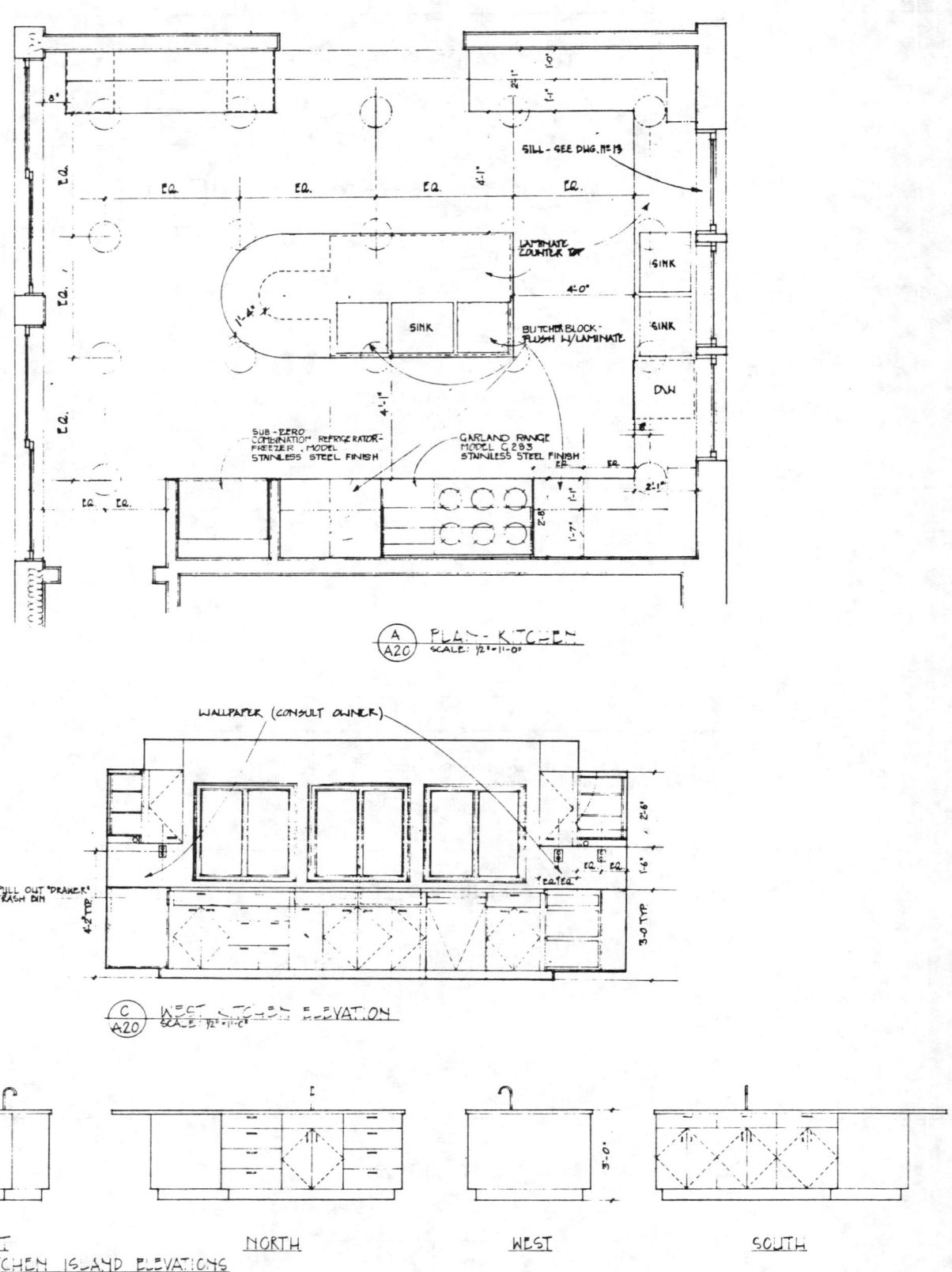

SILL - SEE DWG. Nº 19

LAMINATE COUNTER TOP

SINK

SINK

SINK

BUTCHER BLOCK - FLUSH W/LAMINATE

DW

SUB-ZERO COMBINATION REFRIGERATOR - FREEZER, MODEL STAINLESS STEEL FINISH

GARLAND RANGE MODEL G283 STAINLESS STEEL FINISH

Ⓐ PLAN - KITCHEN
A20 SCALE: ½"=1'-0"

WALLPAPER (CONSULT OWNER)

PULL OUT "DRAWER" TRASH BIN

Ⓒ WEST KITCHEN ELEVATION
A20 SCALE: ½"=1'-0"

EAST   NORTH   WEST   SOUTH

Ⓕ KITCHEN ISLAND ELEVATIONS
A-20 SCALE: ½"=1'-0"

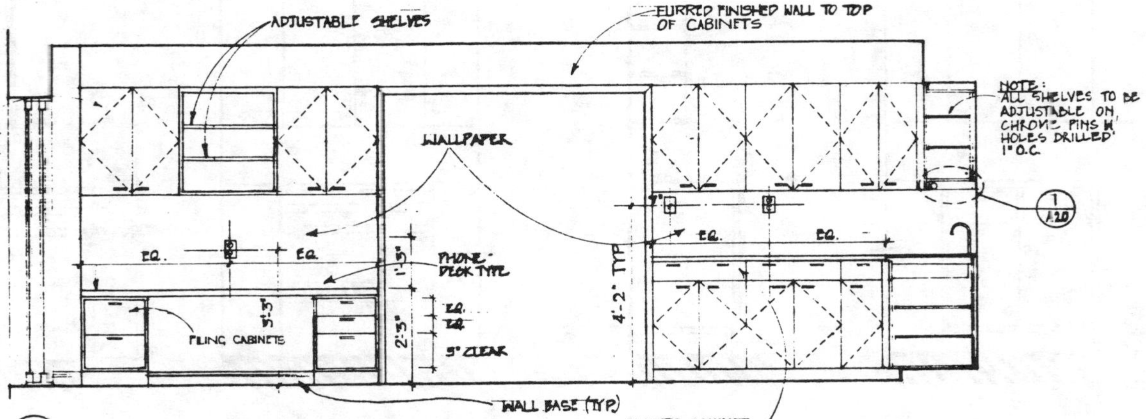

ADJUSTABLE SHELVES

FURRED FINISHED WALL TO TOP OF CABINETS

NOTE:
ALL SHELVES TO BE ADJUSTABLE ON CHROME PINS W/ HOLES DRILLED 1" O.C.

PLASTIC LAMINATE CABINET DOORS, COUNTER TOPS, AND DRAWER FRONTS

WALLPAPER

EQ.   EQ.

PHONE DESK TYPE.

1'-3"

EQ.
TA.

2'-3"

5" CLEAR

FILING CABINETS

4'-2" TYP.

1
A20

WALL BASE (TYP.)

PLASTIC LAMINATE CABINET DOORS, COUNTER TOPS, AND DRAWER DOORS, LAMINATED COLOR & TEXTURE SELECTED BY OWNER (TYP.)

B
A20 SOUTH KITCHEN ELEVATION
SCALE: 1/2" = 1'-0"

BRUSHED STAINLESS STEEL TO MATCH RANGE, RANGE HOOD.

2'-6"

1'-6"

3'-0" TYP.

EQ.   EQ.

RANGE

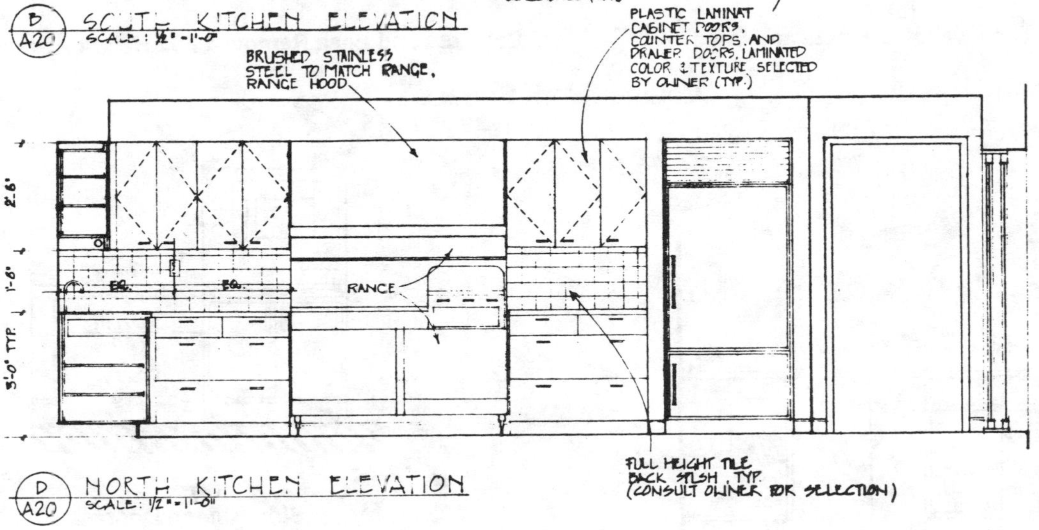

D
A20 NORTH KITCHEN ELEVATION
SCALE: 1/2" = 1'-0"

FULL HEIGHT TILE BACK SPLSH, TYP. (CONSULT OWNER FOR SELECTION)

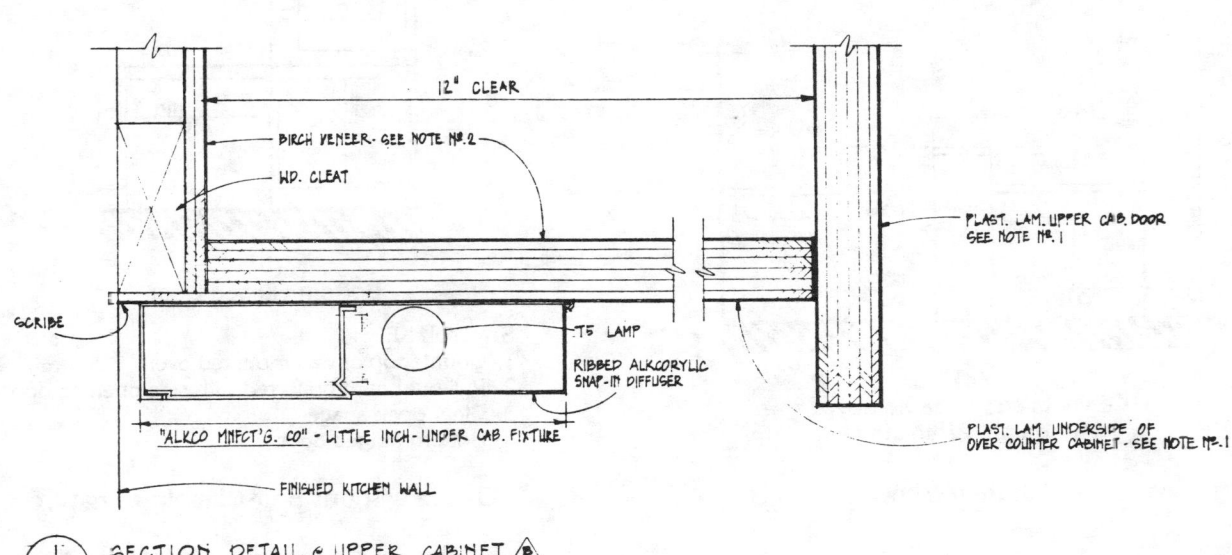

12" CLEAR

BIRCH VENEER- SEE NOTE Nº 2

WD. CLEAT

SCRIBE

T5 LAMP

RIBBED ALKCORYLIC SNAP-IN DIFFUSER

"ALKCO MNFCT'G. CO" - LITTLE INCH - UNDER CAB. FIXTURE

FINISHED KITCHEN WALL

PLAST. LAM. UPPER CAB. DOOR SEE NOTE Nº 1

PLAST. LAM. UNDERSIDE OF OVER COUNTER CABINET - SEE NOTE Nº 1

1
A20 SECTION DETAIL @ UPPER CABINET B
FULL SIZE

KITCHENS
Wheelchair Accessible Design

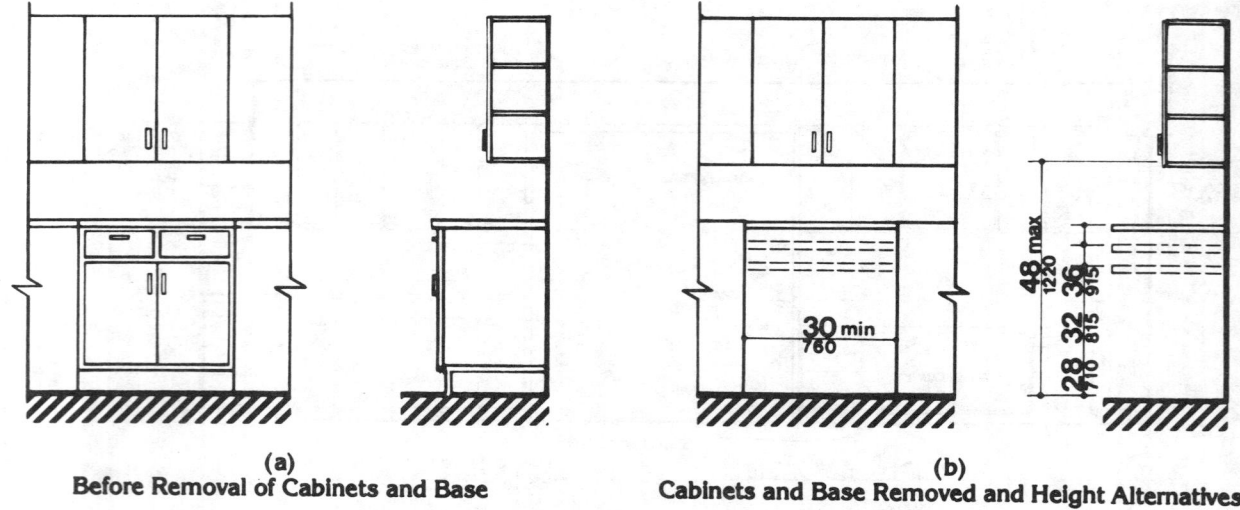

(a)
Before Removal of Cabinets and Base

(b)
Cabinets and Base Removed and Height Alternatives

Counter Work Surface

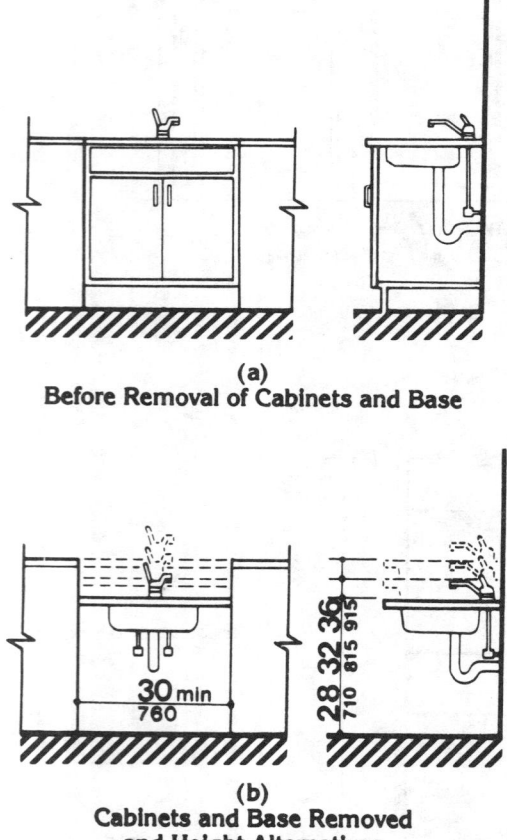

(a)
Before Removal of Cabinets and Base

(b)
Cabinets and Base Removed
and Height Alternatives

Kitchen Sink

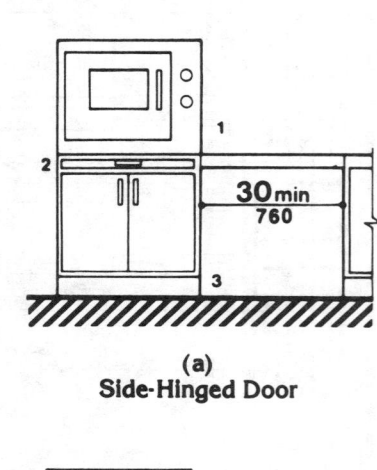

(a)
Side-Hinged Door

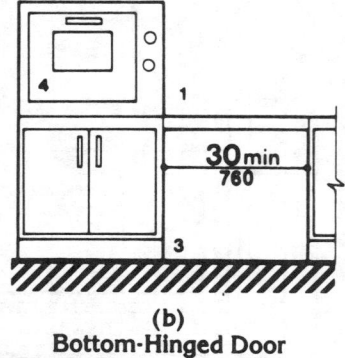

(b)
Bottom-Hinged Door

SYMBOL KEY:
1. Countertop or wall-mounted oven.
2. Pull-out board preferred with side-opening door.
3. Clear open space.
4. Bottom-hinged door.

Ovens without Self-Cleaning Feature

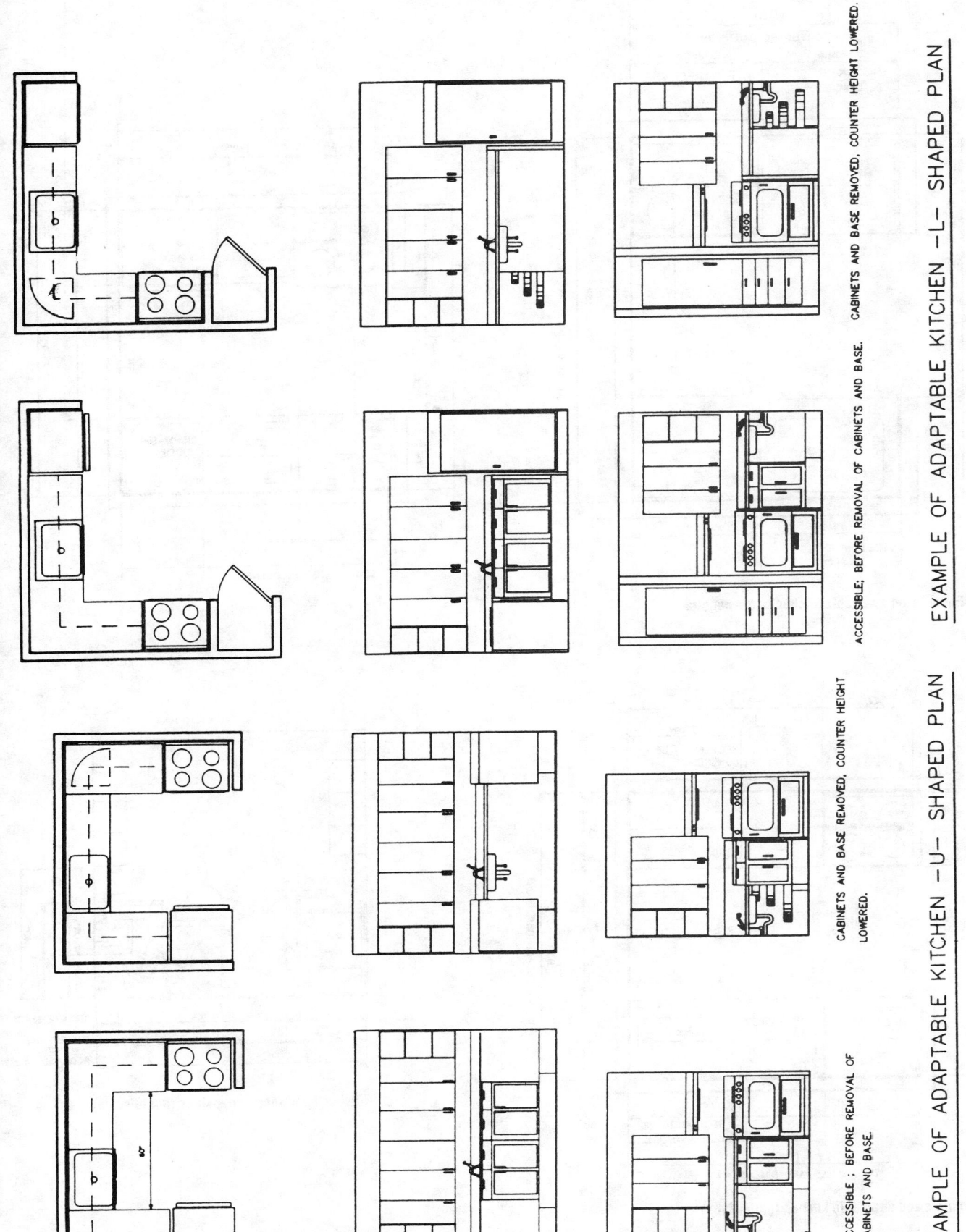

CABINETS AND BASE REMOVED, COUNTER HEIGHT LOWERED.

ACCESSIBLE; BEFORE REMOVAL OF CABINETS AND BASE.

EXAMPLE OF ADAPTABLE KITCHEN –L– SHAPED PLAN

CABINETS AND BASE REMOVED, COUNTER HEIGHT LOWERED.

ACCESSIBLE ; BEFORE REMOVAL OF CABINETS AND BASE.

EXAMPLE OF ADAPTABLE KITCHEN –U– SHAPED PLAN

KITCHENS

Wheelchair Accessible Design

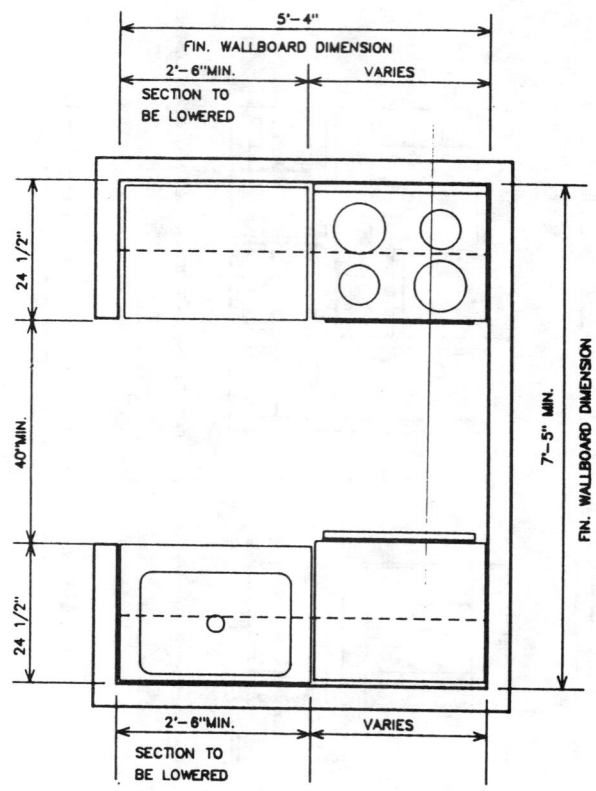

Minimum-sized adaptable kitchen or kitchenette

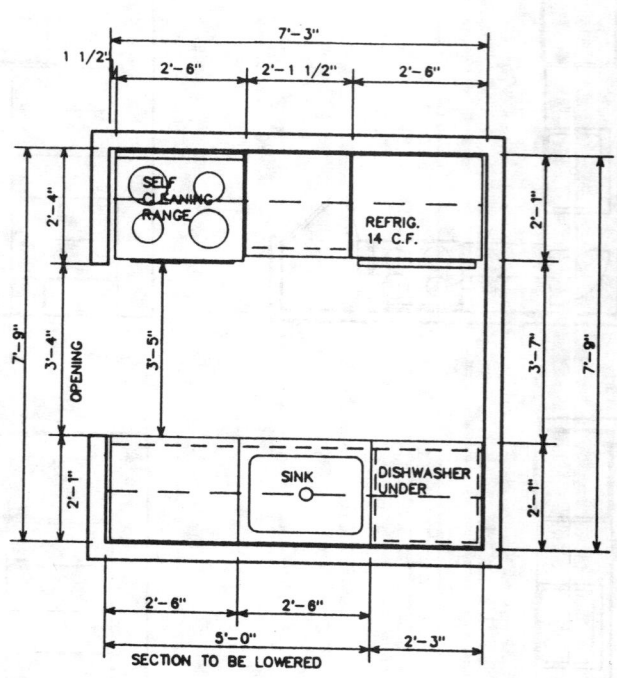

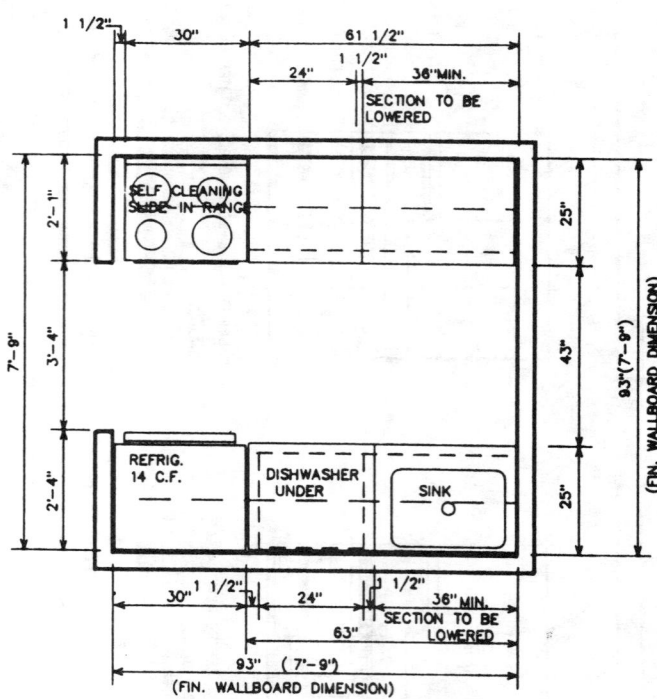

Minimum-sized adaptable kitchen (galley type)

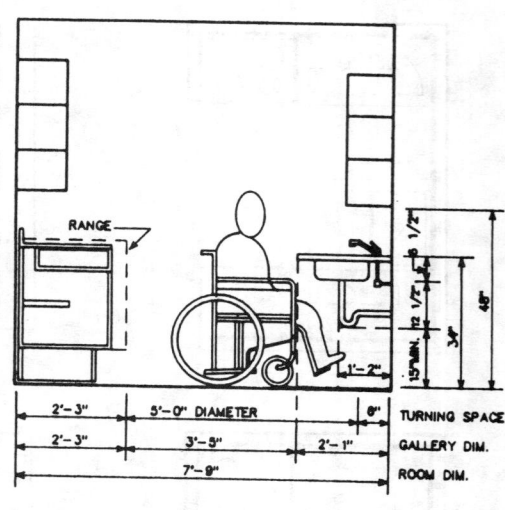

Kitchen clearance dimensions (not to scale)

Requirements

The ANSI and UFAS standards require accessible and adaptable features which make the kitchen usable by most people. The fixed accessible features specified in ANSI 4.32 5 and UFAS 4.34.6 include requirements for doors, clearances, clear floor space, appliances, storage, controls, and knee space. The adaptable features are removable base cabinets at knee spaces and counters that can be adjusted in height or fixed at a lower than standard height.

The adaptable features for kitchens specified in the standards are shown in Figs. 13 and 14. In Fig. 13, the kitchen is shown in a standard configuration with the counter height at 36 inches and the knee spaces covered with base cabinets.

In Fig. 14, the kitchen has been adapted by exposing the knee spaces and lowering the work surface and sink counter segments. No other changes have been made to the kitchen.

Since removable base cabinets and adjustable height counters are not now products that are readily available for purchase, they are usually custom-made items.

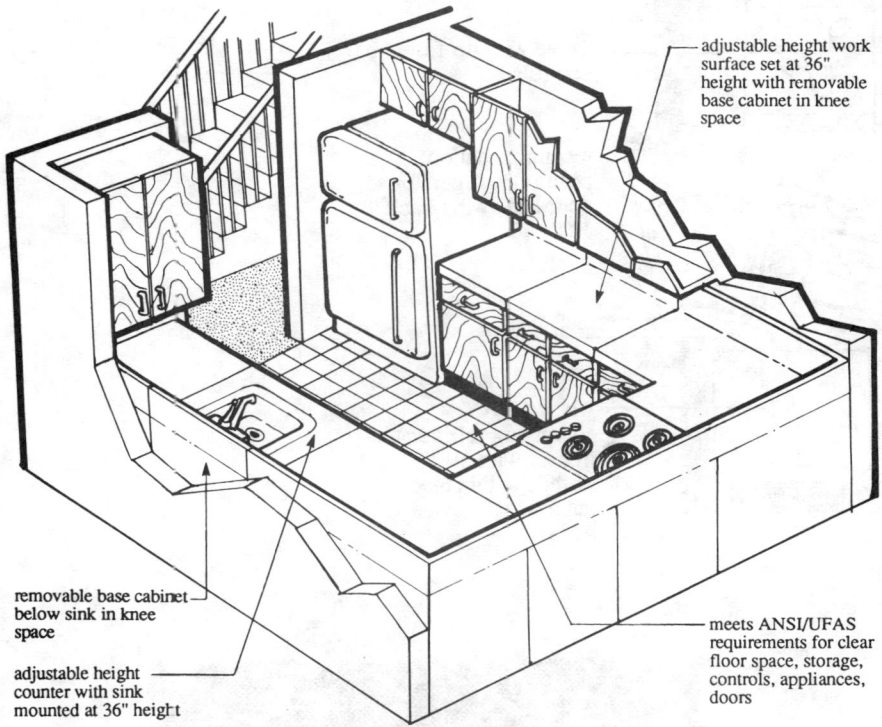

adjustable height work surface set at 36" height with removable base cabinet in knee space

removable base cabinet below sink in knee space

adjustable height counter with sink mounted at 36" height

meets ANSI/UFAS requirements for clear floor space, storage, controls, appliances, doors

Fig. 13   An adaptable kitchen in conventional configuration.

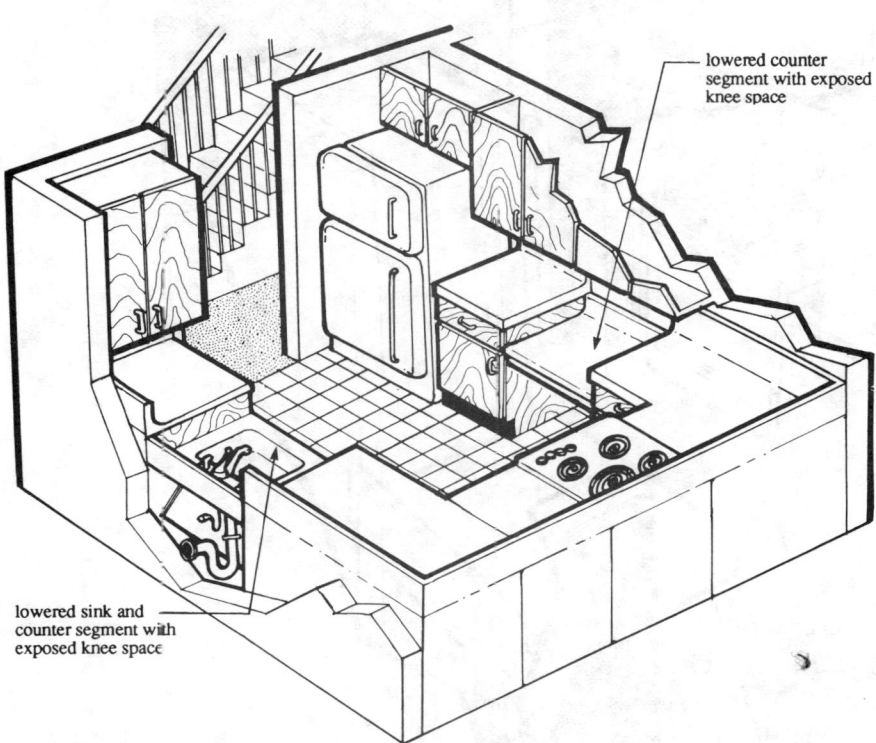

lowered counter segment with exposed knee space

lowered sink and counter segment with exposed knee space

Fig. 14   An adaptable kitchen in the adjusted configuration.

KITCHENS
Wheelchair Accessible Design

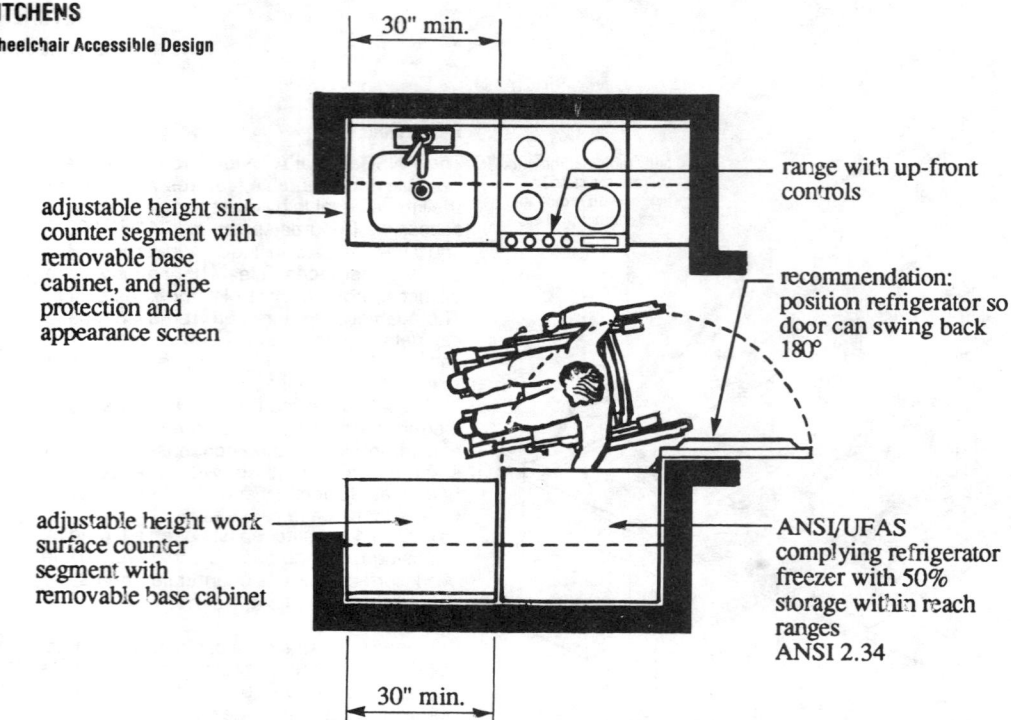

30" min.

adjustable height sink counter segment with removable base cabinet, and pipe protection and appearance screen

range with up-front controls

recommendation: position refrigerator so door can swing back 180°

adjustable height work surface counter segment with removable base cabinet

ANSI/UFAS complying refrigerator freezer with 50% storage within reach ranges ANSI 2.34

30" min.

Fig. 15   A small kitchen with adaptable features: plan.

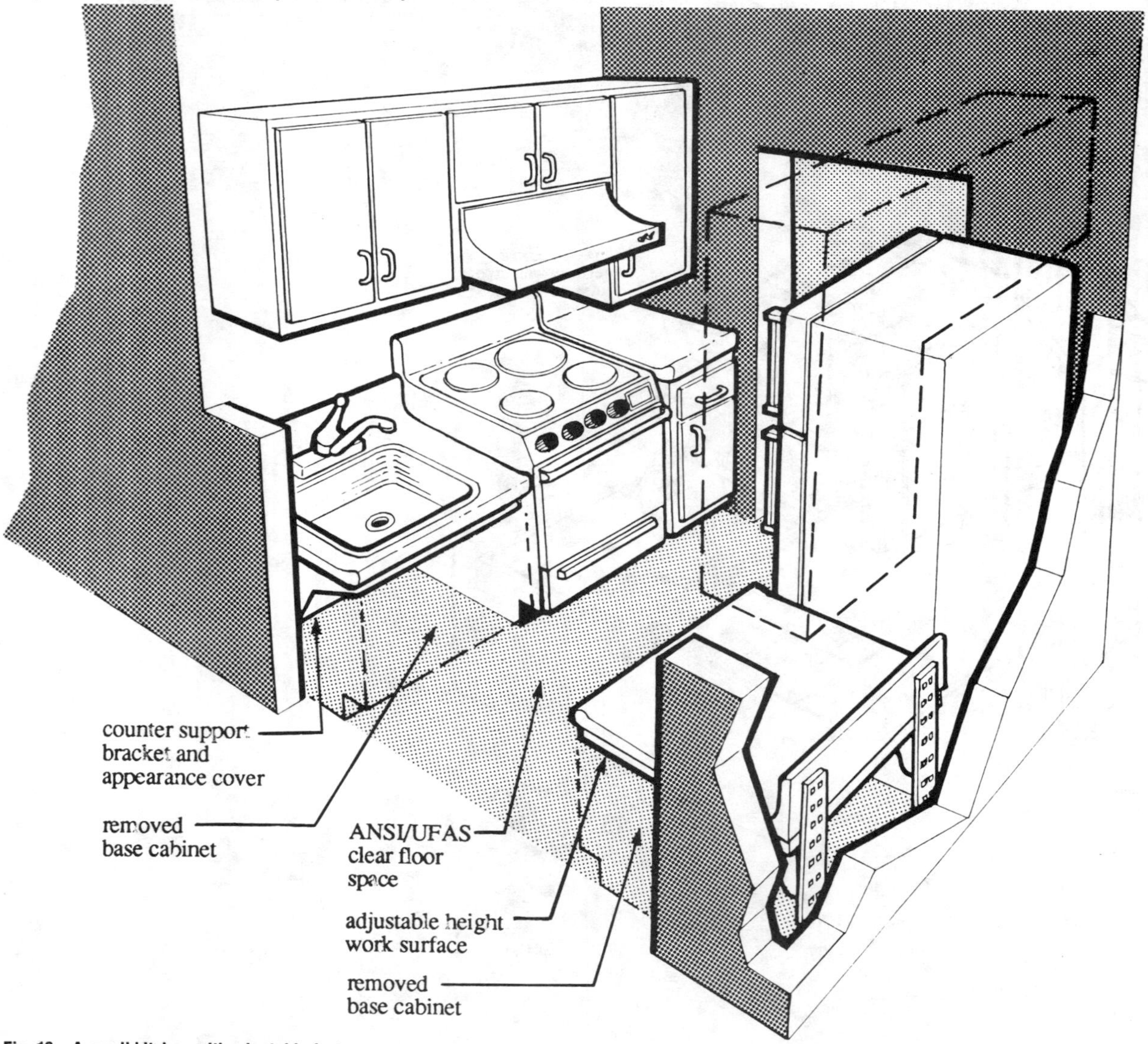

counter support bracket and appearance cover

removed base cabinet

ANSI/UFAS clear floor space

adjustable height work surface

removed base cabinet

Fig. 16   A small kitchen with adaptable features: perspective.

The kitchen shown in Figs. 17 and 18 is an example of a more elaborate kitchen having ANSI/UFAS accessible/adaptable features. This kitchen exceeds the ANSI/UFAS minimum requirements.

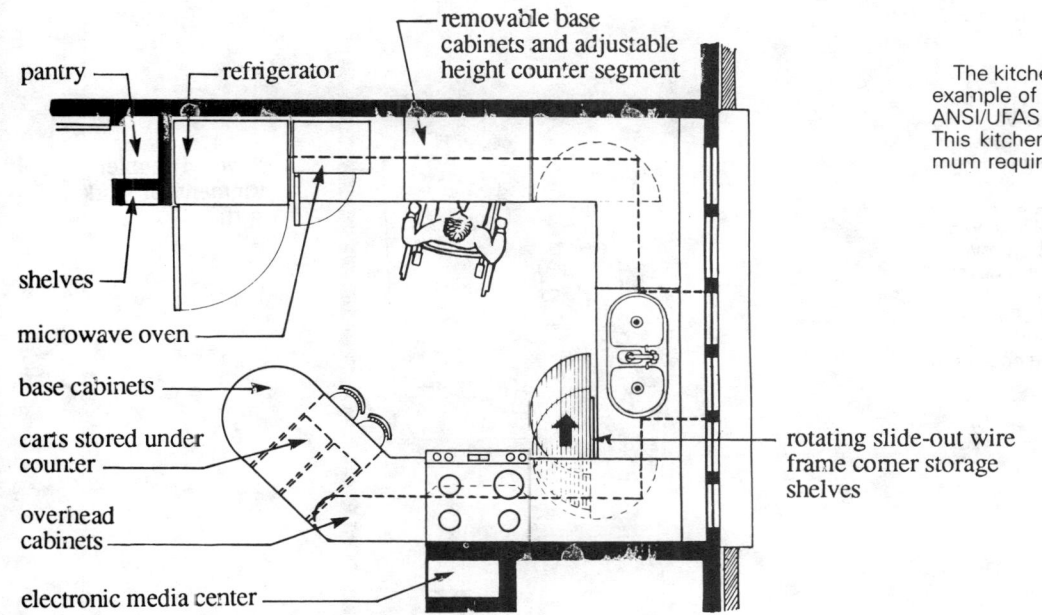

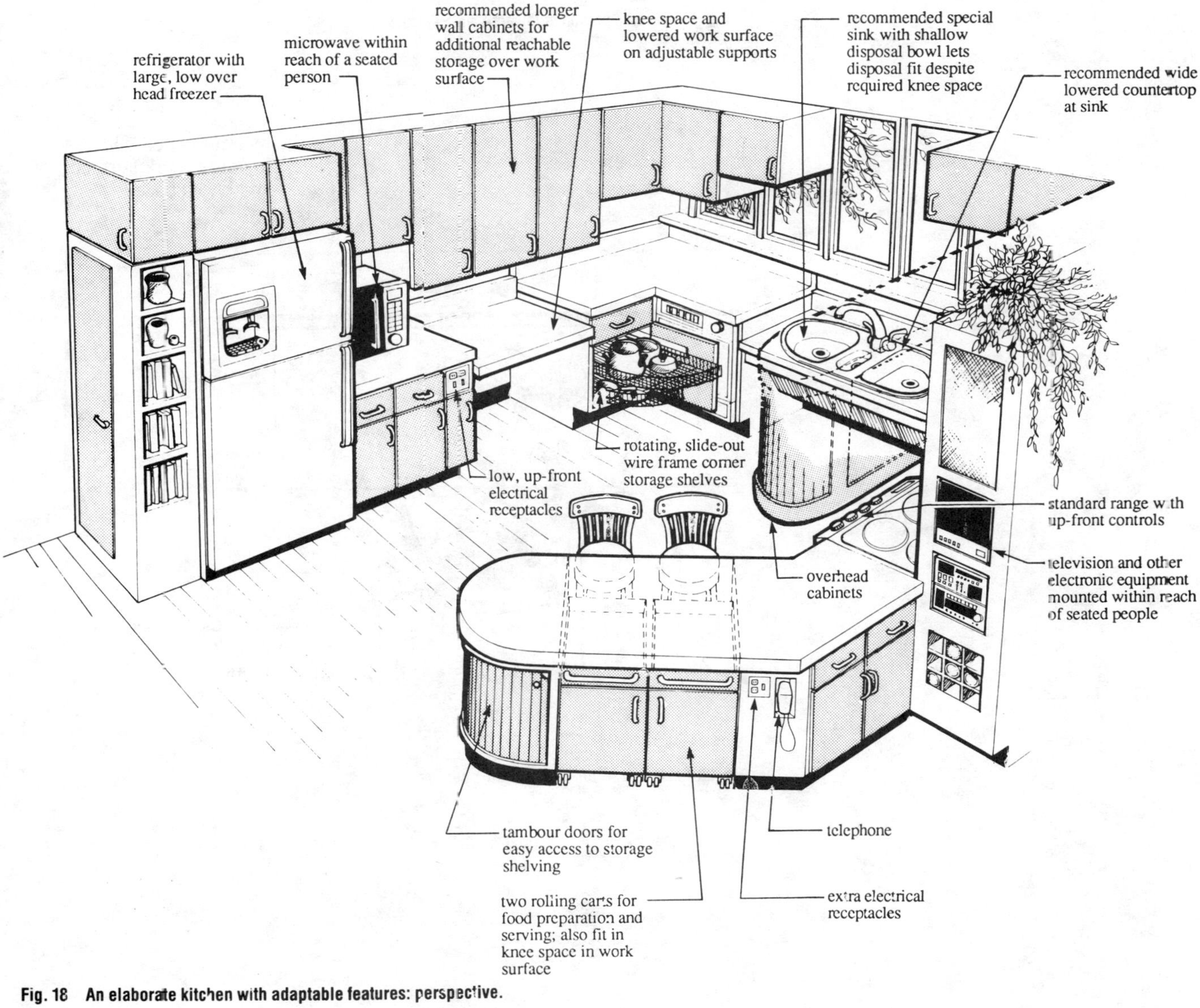

pantry

refrigerator

removable base cabinets and adjustable height counter segment

shelves

microwave oven

base cabinets

carts stored under counter

overhead cabinets

electronic media center

rotating slide-out wire frame corner storage shelves

Fig. 17   An elaborate kitchen with adaptable features: plan.

refrigerator with large, low over head freezer

microwave within reach of a seated person

recommended longer wall cabinets for additional reachable storage over work surface

knee space and lowered work surface on adjustable supports

recommended special sink with shallow disposal bowl lets disposal fit despite required knee space

recommended wide lowered countertop at sink

low, up-front electrical receptacles

rotating, slide-out wire frame corner storage shelves

overhead cabinets

standard range with up-front controls

television and other electronic equipment mounted within reach of seated people

tambour doors for easy access to storage shelving

telephone

two rolling carts for food preparation and serving; also fit in knee space in work surface

extra electrical receptacles

Fig. 18   An elaborate kitchen with adaptable features: perspective.

KITCHENS
Wheelchair Accessible Design

Work Surfaces

People who use wheelchairs and other people who must or wish to sit down while preparing food need at least one work surface lower than the usual 36-in-high counter (Fig. 19).

The standards (ANSI 4.32.5.4 and UFAS 4.34.6.4) require that at least one 30-in-wide, adjustable-height work surface be provided in an adaptable kitchen, although a wider size is preferred. The wider work surface provides space for pots, dishes, and other utensils as well as small appliances, and makes it easier to work on several things at once or to cook using many ingredients.

lowered counter segment for work surface

Fig. 19   Seated person at lowered work surface.

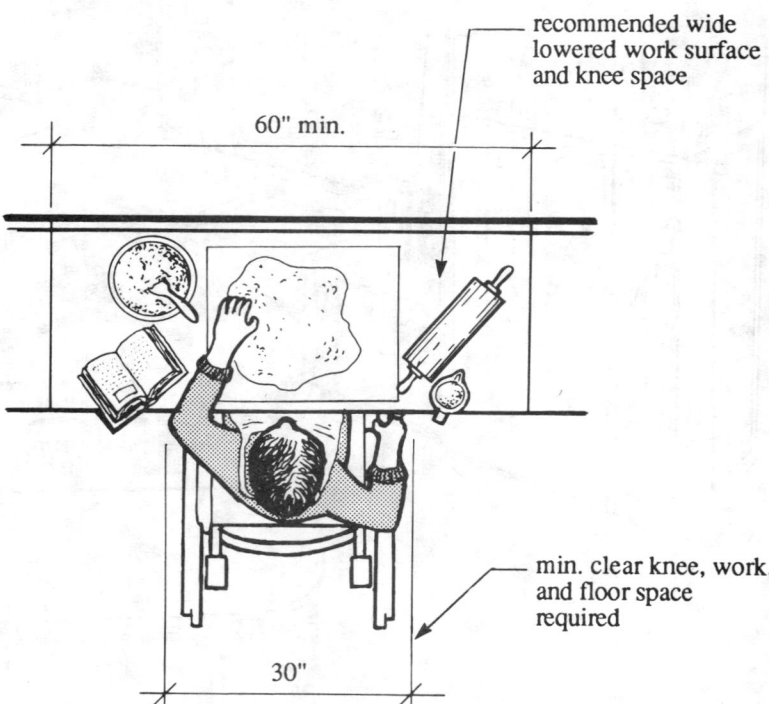

recommended wide lowered work surface and knee space

60" min.

30"

min. clear knee, work, and floor space required

Fig. 20   Use of a wider, lowered work surface.

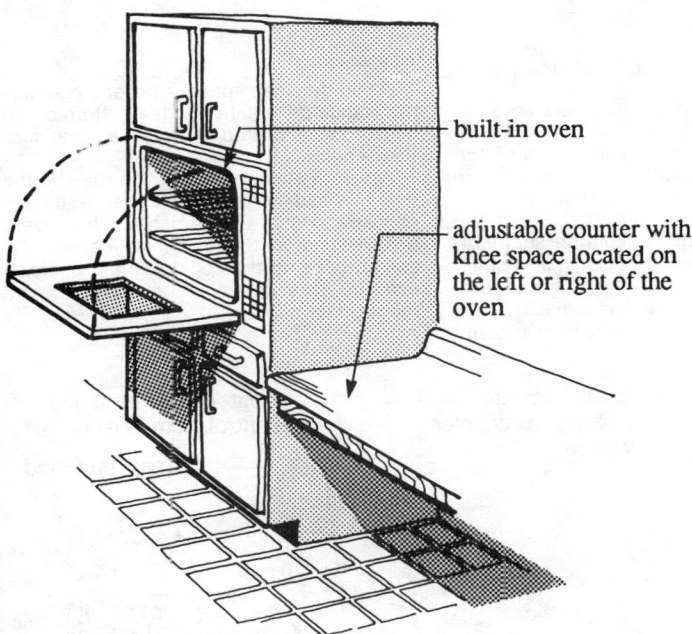

built-in oven

adjustable counter with knee space located on the left or right of the oven

Fig. 21 Work surface at non-self-cleaning oven with drop-front door.

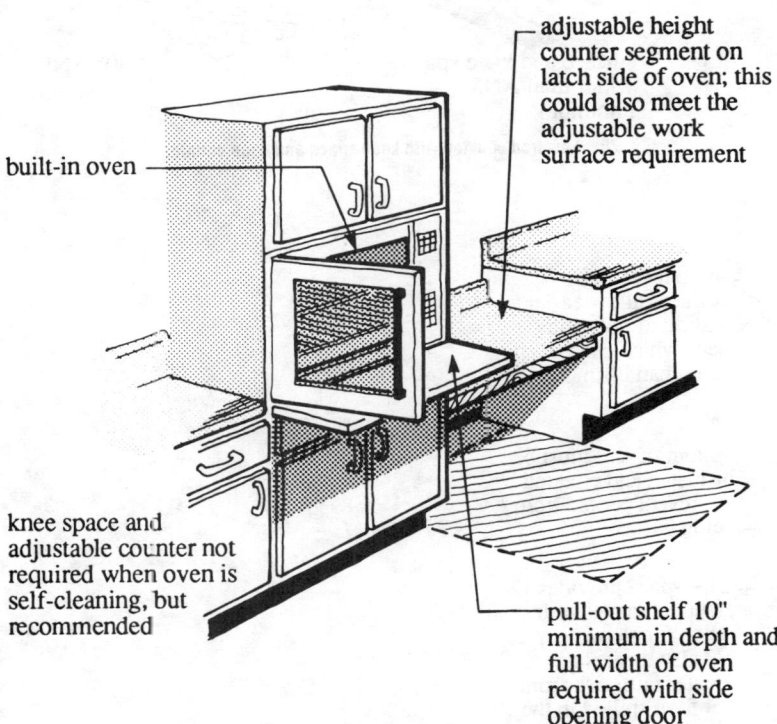

built-in oven

knee space and adjustable counter not required when oven is self-cleaning, but recommended

adjustable height counter segment on latch side of oven; this could also meet the adjustable work surface requirement

pull-out shelf 10" minimum in depth and full width of oven required with side opening door

Fig. 23 Pull-out shelf at non-self-cleaning oven with side-opening door.

Work surfaces at ovens If a wall oven is installed, a lowered work surface with knee space should be installed next to the wall oven. The standards specify that when the wall oven is not self-cleaning, a knee space must be located next to the oven to permit a disabled person in a wheelchair to pull up close enough to clean the oven.

Even if a self-cleaning oven is installed, locating the knee space next to the oven makes it easier and safer for a disabled person to remove hot items from the oven.

When an oven with a side-opening door is used, a pull-out shelf located beneath the oven must be installed. The shelf is used as a transfer surface for dishes as they are placed into or taken out of the oven. When not needed, the shelf is pushed back into the oven cabinet (Fig. 23). When an oven with a drop-front door is used (Fig. 21), the pullout shelf is not needed because the door serves as a transfer shelf.

See ANSI 4.32.5.7 and UFAS 4.34.6.7 for dimensions and details of oven.

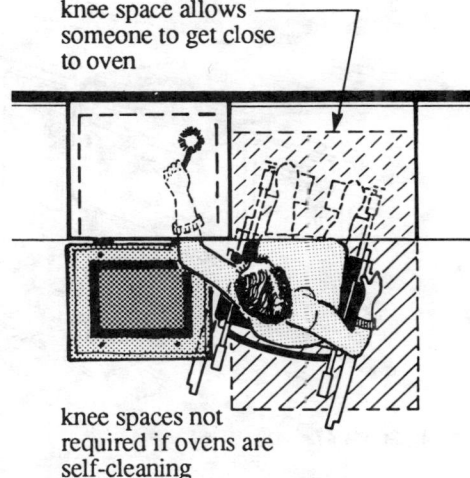

knee space allows someone to get close to oven

knee spaces not required if ovens are self-cleaning

Fig. 22 Use of knee space next to oven.

KITCHENS

Wheelchair Accessible Design

Cooktops in Adjustable Height Counter Segments

ANSI 4.32.5.6 and UFAS 4.34.6.6 permit use of a standard range if the controls comply with ANSI 4.25 or UFAS 4.27. The controls must be placed along the front or the side of the range so that a seated person need not reach across a hot burner to adjust the controls (Fig. 24).

Some wheelchair users cannot use conventional ranges because the surface is too high and there is no knee space for maneuvering. Cooktops in lowered counter segments with knee space below allow some wheelchair users to get close enough to operate the controls and move heavy pots and pans (Fig. 25).

Cooktops with smooth surfaces are preferred by people with limited hand and arm strength because they can slide pots of hot food on and off the cooktop rather than lifting them over raised burners and knobs.

When a cooktop is installed in a lowered counter, the width of the counter segment and knee space should be at least 30 inches and should provide space to the side of the cooktop for utensils and maneuvering. An additional 30 inches to the side is recommended (Fig. 26).

When the knee space is under a cooktop, the standards require that the bottom of the cooktop be insulated to protect against accidental burns.

While this type of installation may be the only way that some people can cook, it does expose a person in a wheelchair to the hazard of spilling hot food in his/her lap. People who pull up beneath the cooktop must exercise extreme care and cool hot foods before moving them.

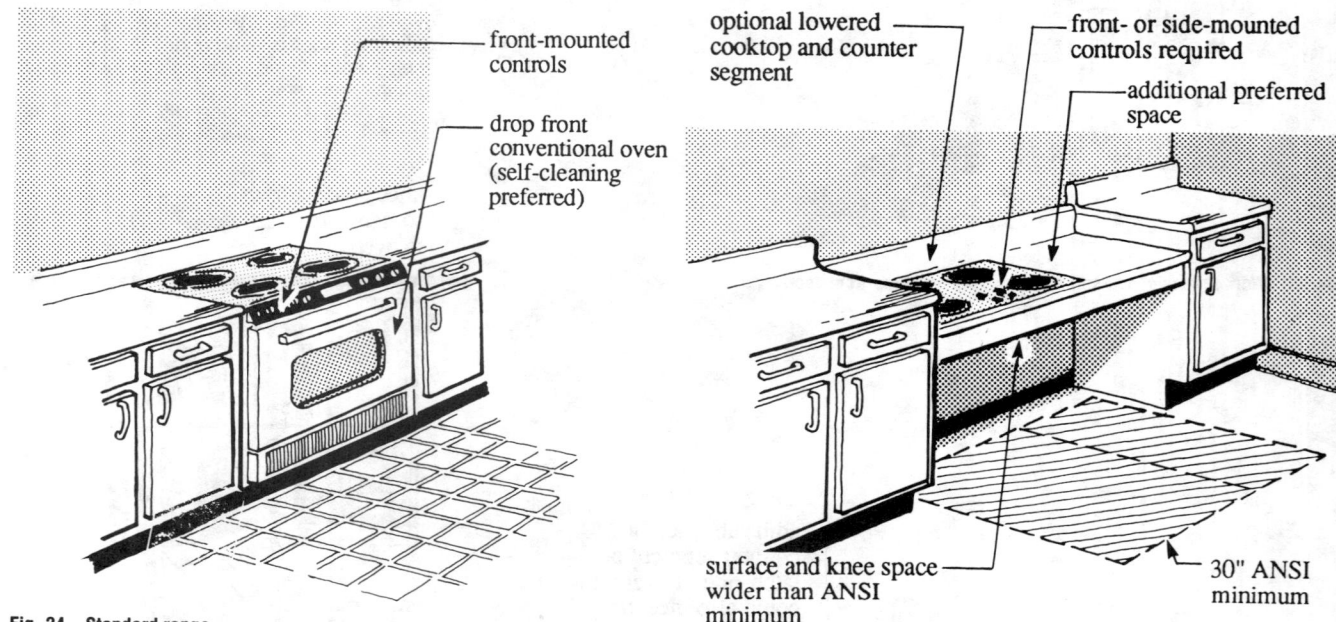

front-mounted controls

drop front conventional oven (self-cleaning preferred)

optional lowered cooktop and counter segment

front- or side-mounted controls required

additional preferred space

surface and knee space wider than ANSI minimum

30" ANSI minimum

Fig. 24   Standard range.

Fig. 26   Lowered cooktop with knee space and wide counter.

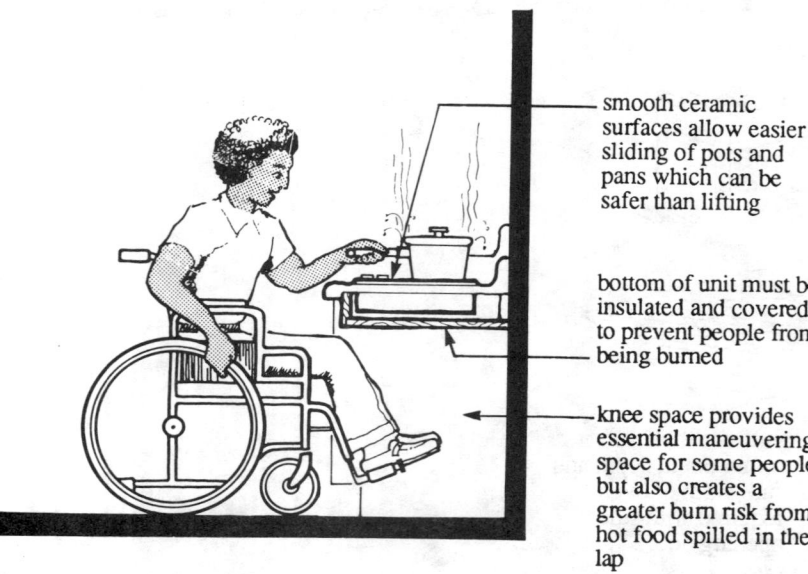

smooth ceramic surfaces allow easier sliding of pots and pans which can be safer than lifting

bottom of unit must be insulated and covered to prevent people from being burned

knee space provides essential maneuvering space for some people, but also creates a greater burn risk from hot food spilled in the lap

Fig. 25   Use of cooktop with knee space.

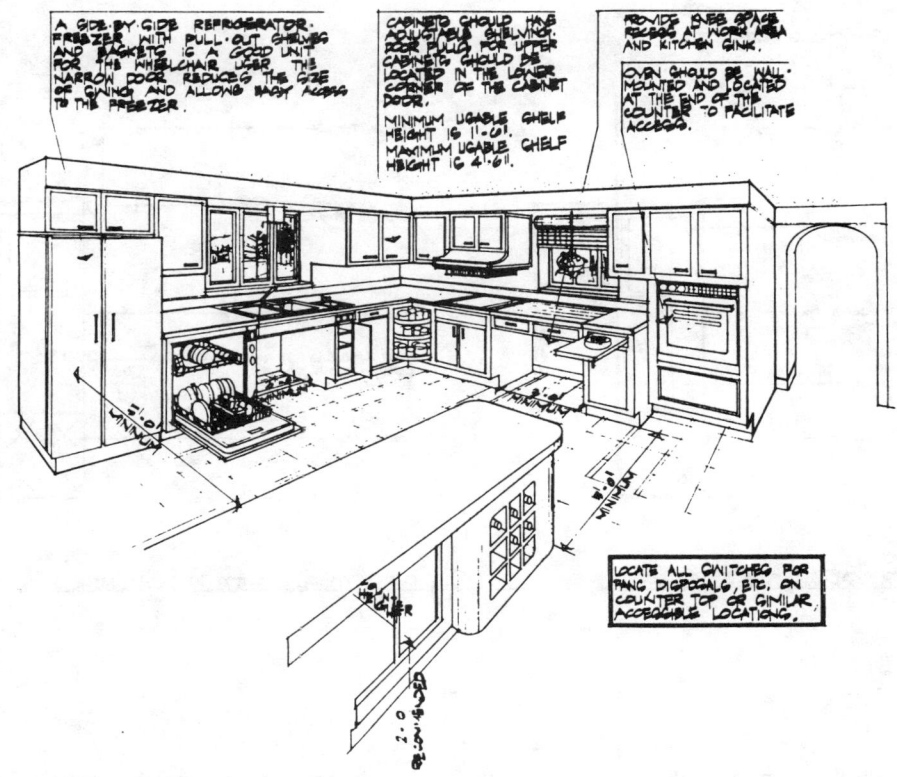

Kitchen arrangements

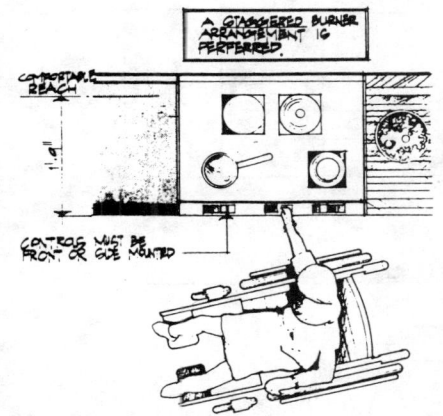

Counter-mounted cook top

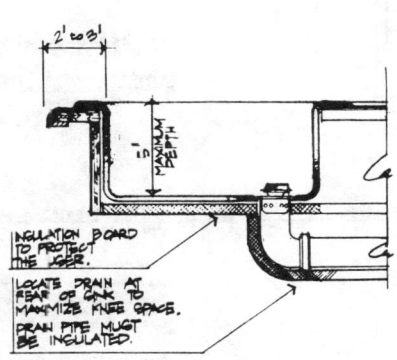

Sink

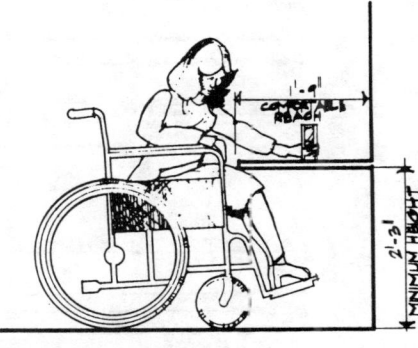

Knee-space clearance

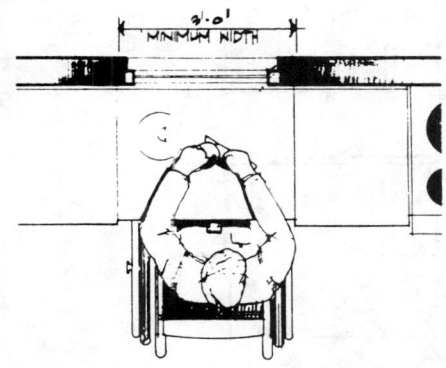

Knee-recess work area

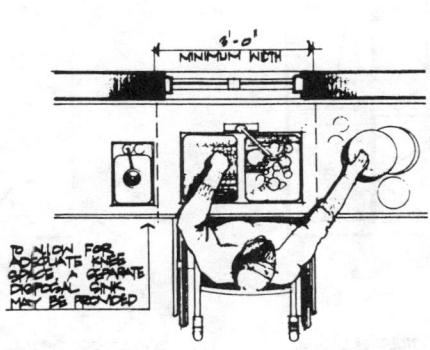

Disposal sink

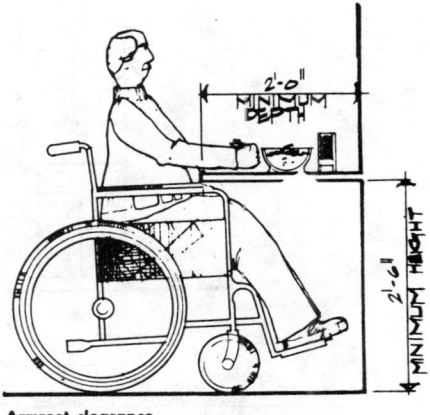

Armrest clearance

KITCHENS
Wheelchair Accessible Design

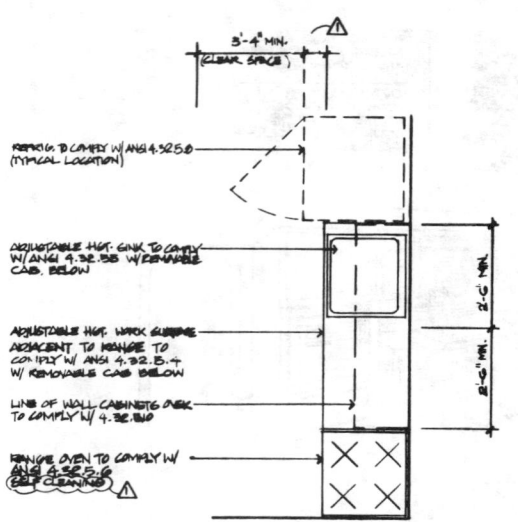

REFRIG. TO COMPLY W/ ANSI 4.32.5.8
(TYPICAL LOCATION)

ADJUSTABLE HGT. SINK TO COMPLY
W/ ANSI 4.32.5.8 W/ REMOVABLE
CAB. BELOW

ADJUSTABLE HGT. WORK SURFACE
ADJACENT TO RANGE TO
COMPLY W/ ANSI 4.32.5.4
W/ REMOVABLE CAB BELOW

LINE OF WALL CABINETS OVER
TO COMPLY W/ 4.32.5.8

RANGE OVEN TO COMPLY W/
ANSI 4.32.5.6
SELF CLEANING

3'-4" MIN.
(CLEAR SPACE)

2'-6" MIN.

① **PLAN: TYPICAL ADAPTABLE KITCHEN: LINEAR**
A4   ½" = 1'-0"

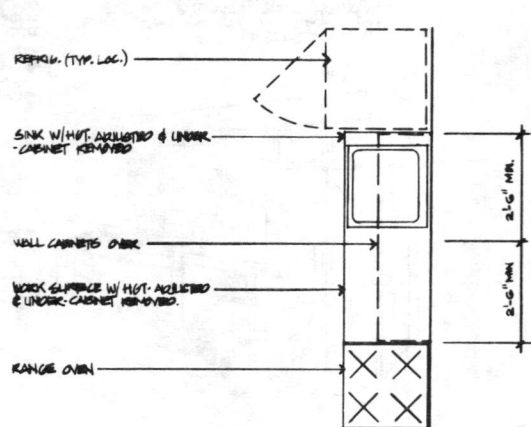

REFRIG. (TYP. LOC.)

SINK W/HGT. ADJUSTED & UNDER
-CABINET REMOVED

WALL CABINETS OVER

WORK SURFACE W/ HGT. ADJUSTED
& UNDER-CABINET REMOVED.

RANGE OVEN

2'-6" MIN.

2'-6" MIN.

①A **PLAN: TYPICAL ADAPTED KITCHEN: LINEAR**
A4   ½" = 1'-0"

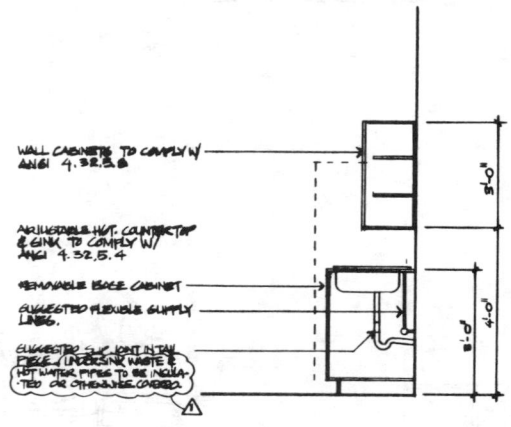

WALL CABINETS TO COMPLY W/
ANSI 4.32.5.8

ADJUSTABLE HGT. COUNTERTOP
& SINK TO COMPLY W/
ANSI 4.32.5.4

REMOVABLE BASE CABINET

SUGGESTED FLEXIBLE SUPPLY
LINES.

SUGGESTED SLIP JOINT IN TAIL
PIECE. UNDERSINK WASTE &
HOT WATER PIPES TO BE INSULA-
TED OR OTHERWISE COVERED.

5'-0"

4'-0"

② **SECTION: TYPICAL ADAPTABLE KITCHEN: LINEAR**
A4   ½" = 1'-0"

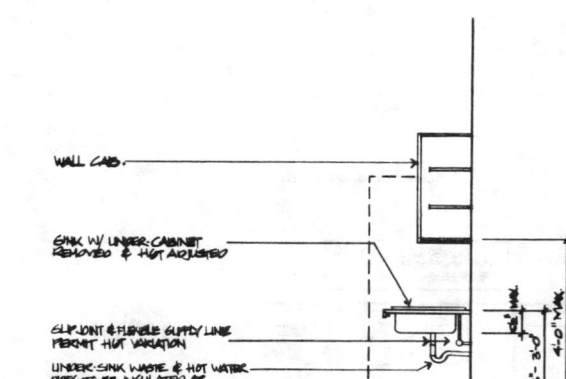

WALL CAB.

SINK W/ UNDER-CABINET
REMOVED & HGT ADJUSTED

SLIP JOINT & FLEXIBLE SUPPLY LINE
PERMIT HGT VARIATION

UNDER-SINK WASTE & HOT WATER
PIPES TO BE INSULATED OR
OTHERWISE COVERED

4'-0" MAX.

2'-6" - 3'-0"

②A **SECTION: TYPICAL ADAPTED KITCHEN: LINEAR**
A4   ½" = 1'-0"

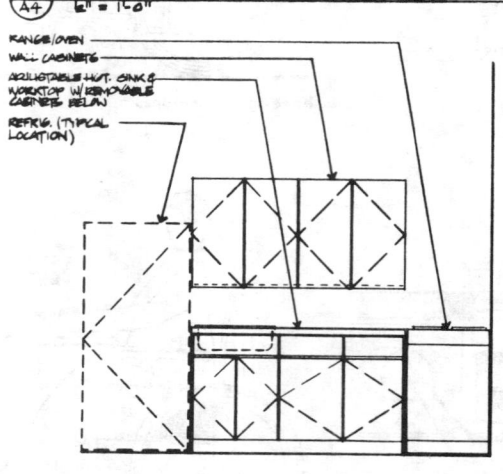

RANGE/OVEN
WALL CABINETS
ADJUSTABLE HGT. SINK &
WORKTOP W/ REMOVABLE
CABINETS BELOW
REFRIG. (TYPICAL
LOCATION)

③ **ELEVATION: TYPICAL ADAPTABLE KITCHEN: LINEAR**
A4   ½" = 1'-0"

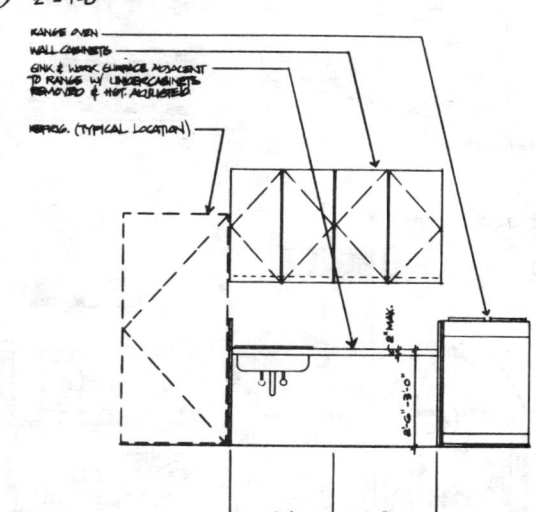

RANGE OVEN
WALL CABINETS
SINK & WORK SURFACE ADJACENT
TO RANGE W/ UNDER-CABINETS
REMOVED & HGT. ADJUSTED
REFRIG. (TYPICAL LOCATION)

2'-8" MAX.

2'-6" - 3'-0"

2'-6" MIN.   2'-6" MIN.

③A **ELEVATION: TYPICAL ADAPTED KITCHEN: LINEAR**
A4   ½" = 1'-0"

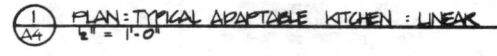

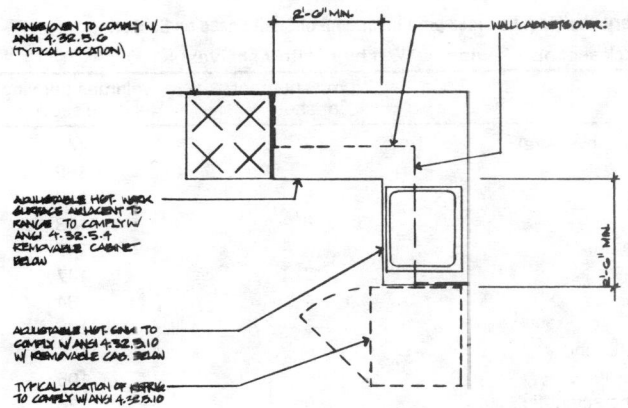

RANGE/OVEN TO COMPLY W/ ANSI 4.32.5.6 (TYPICAL LOCATION)

WALL CABINETS OVER:

2'-0" MIN.

2'-6" MIN.

ADJUSTABLE HGT. WORK SURFACE ADJACENT TO RANGE TO COMPLY W/ ANSI 4.32.5.4 REMOVABLE CABINET BELOW

ADJUSTABLE HGT. SINK TO COMPLY W/ ANSI 4.32.3.10 W/ REMOVABLE CAB. BELOW

TYPICAL LOCATION OF REFRIG. TO COMPLY W/ ANSI 4.32.5.10

④ **PLAN : TYPICAL ADAPTABLE KITCHEN : L-SHAPED**
A4   ½" = 1'-0"

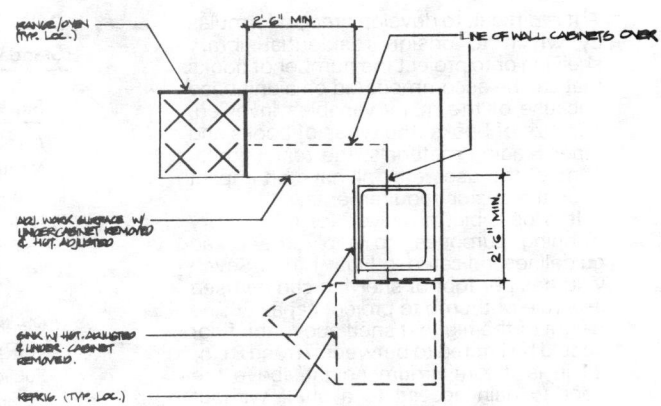

RANGE/OVEN (TYP. LOC.)

2'-6" MIN.

LINE OF WALL CABINETS OVER

ADJ. WORK SURFACE W/ UNDERCABINET REMOVED & HGT. ADJUSTED

2'-6" MIN.

SINK W/ HGT. ADJUSTED & UNDER-CABINET REMOVED.

REFRIG. (TYP. LOC.)

④A **PLAN : TYPICAL ADAPTED KITCHEN : L-SHAPED**
A4   ½" = 1'-0"

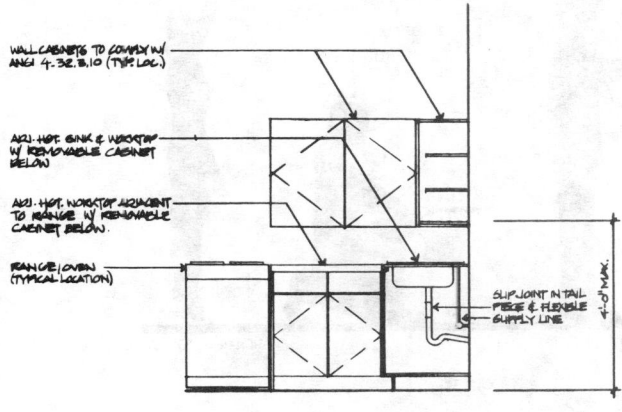

WALL CABINETS TO COMPLY W/ ANSI 4.32.3.10 (TYP. LOC.)

ADJ. HGT. SINK & WORKTOP W/ REMOVABLE CABINET BELOW

ADJ. HGT. WORKTOP ADJACENT TO RANGE W/ REMOVABLE CABINET BELOW

RANGE/OVEN (TYPICAL LOCATION)

4'-8" MAX.

SLIP JOINT IN TAIL PIECE & FLEXIBLE SUPPLY LINE

⑤ **ELEVATION : TYPICAL ADAPTABLE KITCHEN : L-SHAPED**
A4   ½" = 1'-0"

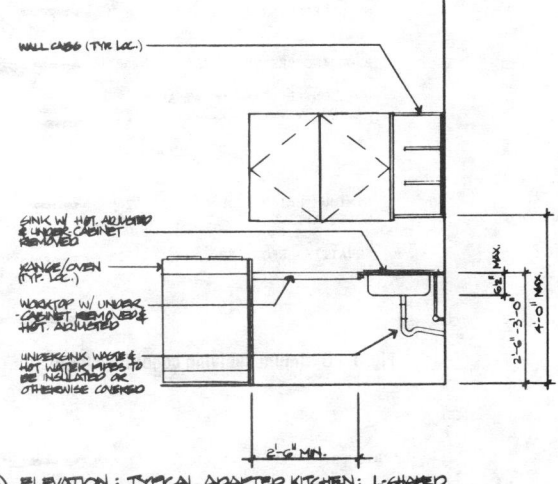

WALL CABS (TYP. LOC.)

SINK W/ HGT. ADJUSTED & UNDER-CABINET REMOVED.

RANGE/OVEN (TYP. LOC.)

WORKTOP W/ UNDER-CABINET REMOVED & HGT. ADJUSTED

UNDERSINK WASTE & HOT WATER PIPES TO BE INSULATED OR OTHERWISE COVERED

3'-2" MAX.

2'-6" / 3'-0"

4'-8" MAX.

2'-6" MIN.

⑤A **ELEVATION : TYPICAL ADAPTED KITCHEN : L-SHAPED**
A4   ½" = 1'-0"

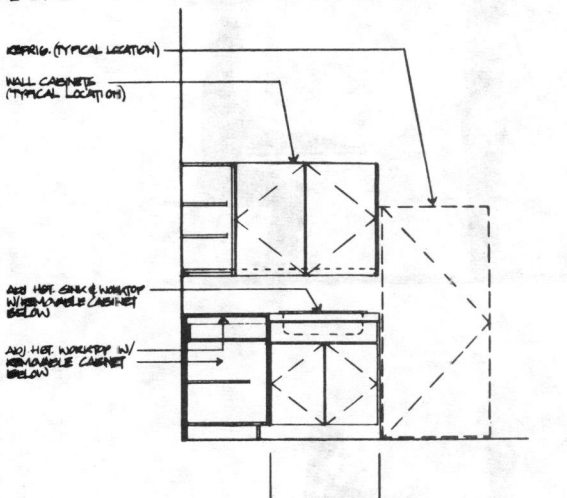

REFRIG. (TYPICAL LOCATION)

WALL CABINETS (TYPICAL LOCATION)

ADJ. HGT. SINK & WORKTOP W/ REMOVABLE CABINET BELOW

ADJ. HGT. WORKTOP W/ REMOVABLE CABINET BELOW

2'-6" MIN.

⑥ **ELEVATION : TYPICAL ADAPTABLE KITCHEN : L-SHAPED**
A4   ½" = 1'-0"

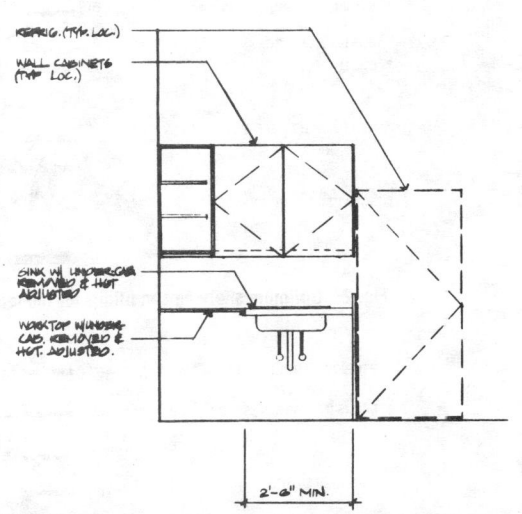

REFRIG. (TYP. LOC.)

WALL CABINETS (TYP. LOC.)

SINK W/ UNDERCAB. REMOVED & HGT. ADJUSTED

WORKTOP W/ UNDER CAB. REMOVED & HGT. ADJUSTED

2'-6" MIN.

⑥A **ELEVATION : TYPICAL ADAPTED KITCHEN : L-SHAPED**
A4   ½" = 1'-0"

It is difficult to develop precise formulas by which to design residential library shelving or to project the number of books that can be accommodated on a unit base because of the many variables involved. The size of books, the types of books and other reading materials, the reach limitations of the user, etc., all have an impact upon the design requirements.

It is possible, however, for preliminary planning purposes, to apply the broad guidelines indicated in Figs. 1 to 3. Seven volumes per foot of shelving can be used as a rule-of-thumb to project capacity. The height of the highest shelf above the floor should be limited to between 78 and 81 in; 24 in is the minimum height above the floor to gain access to a shelf without squatting. Limitations for shelving to serve children will differ and are indicated in Fig. 3.

TABLE 1 Library Shelving: Volumes per Linear Foot of Shelf Based on Subject

(Standard stack section 3 ft wide × 7½ ft high with 7 shelves)

Subject	Volumes per foot of shelf	Volumes per single face section
Art (excluding oversize)	7	147
Nonfiction	8	168
Economics	8	168
Fiction	8	168
General literature	7	147
History	7	147
Law	4	84
Medical	5	105
Periodicals, bound	5	105
Public documents	5	105
Technical and scientific	6	126
Average for overall estimating		125

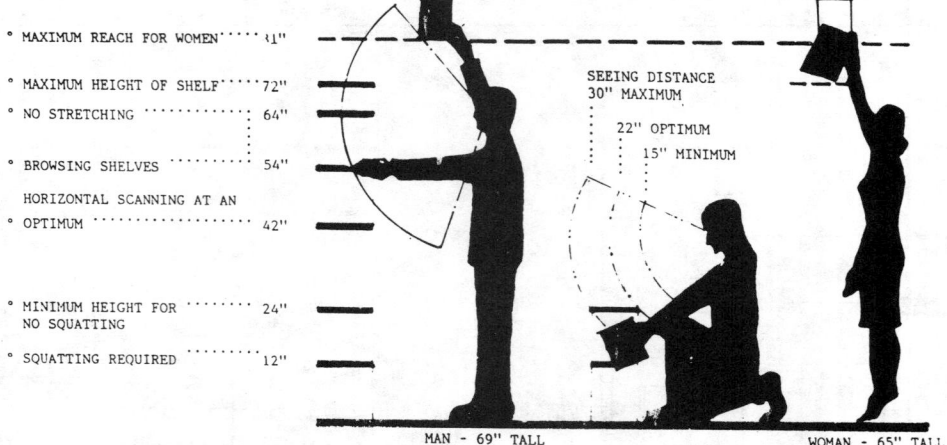

Fig. 1 Optimum shelving conditions for adults.

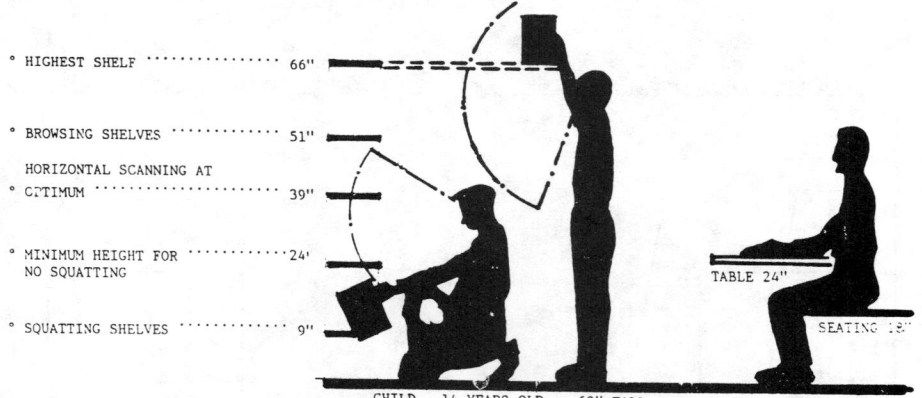

Fig. 2 Optimum shelving conditions for teenagers.

Fig. 3 Optimum shelving conditions for children.

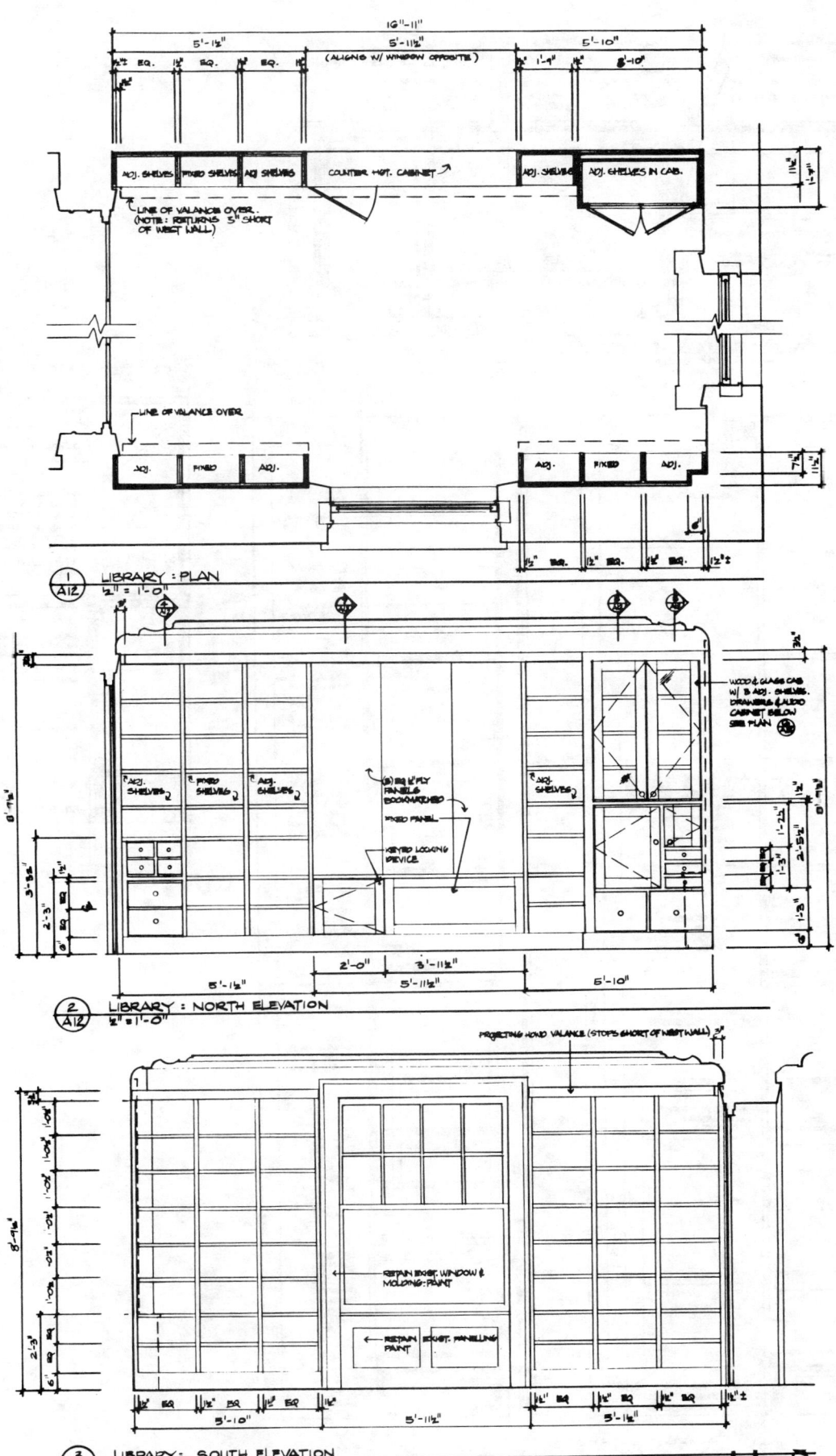

1 LIBRARY: PLAN
A12 ½" = 1'-0"

2 LIBRARY: NORTH ELEVATION
A12 ½" = 1'-0"

3 LIBRARY: SOUTH ELEVATION
A12 ½" = 1'-0"

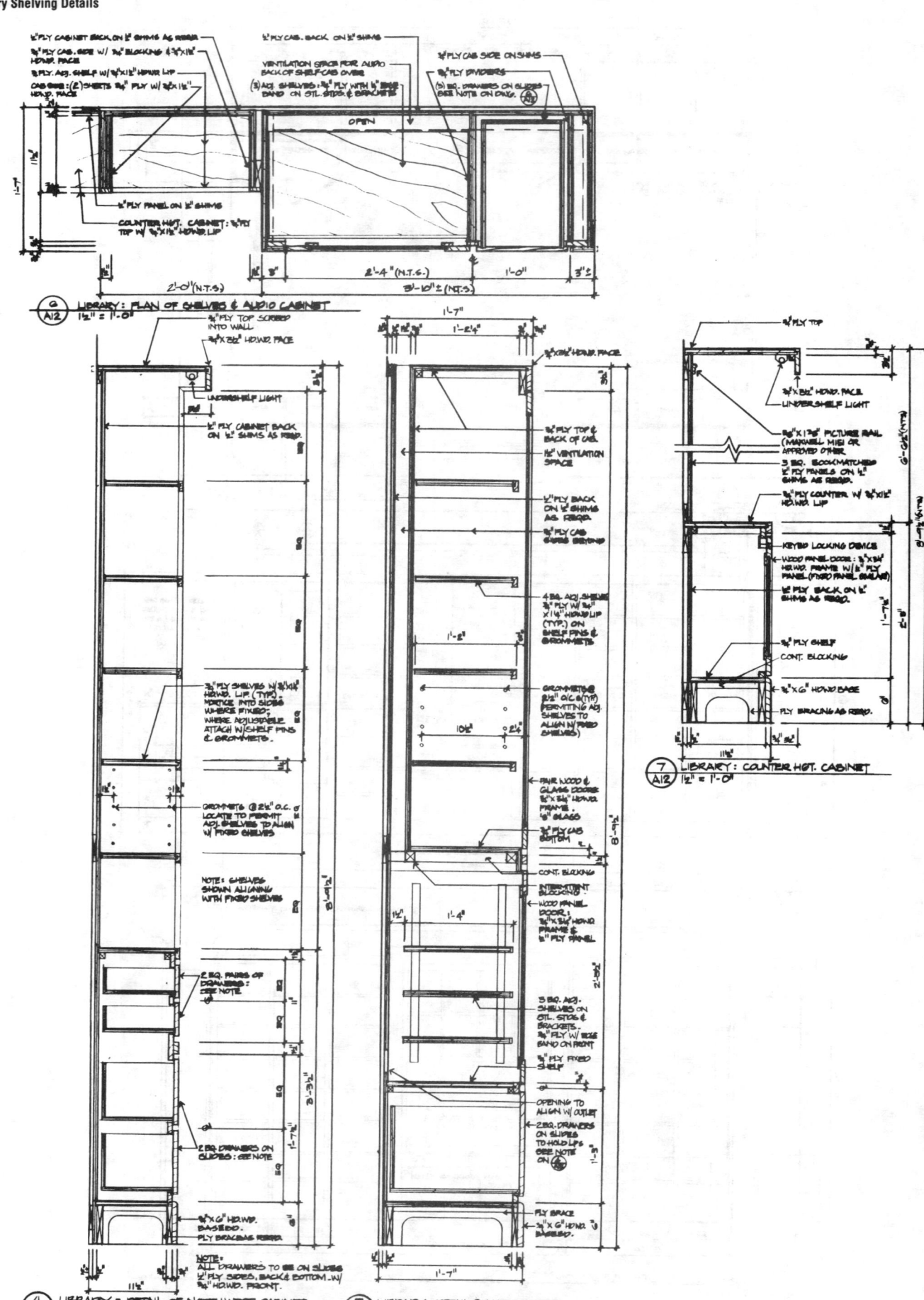

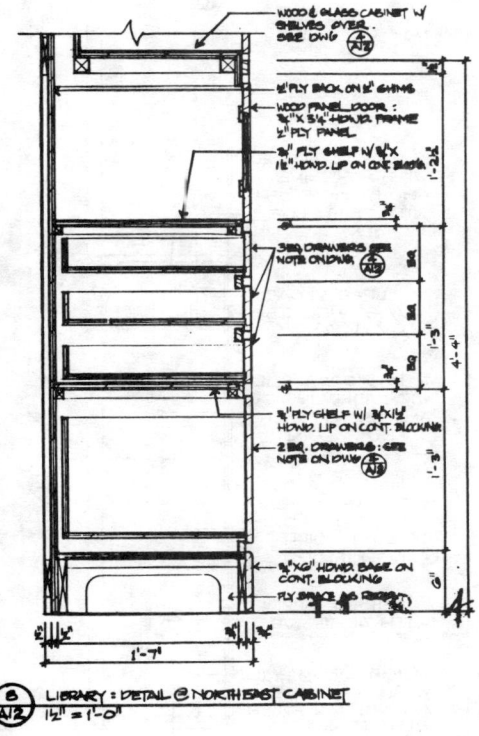

WOOD & GLASS CABINET W/ SHELVES OVER. SEE DWG

½" PLY BACK ON 1" SHIMS

WOOD PANEL DOOR :
¾" X 3½" HARDW. FRAME
½" PLY PANEL

¾" PLY SHELF W/ ¾X X
1½" HARDW. LIP ON CONT. BLOCKING

3 EQ. DRAWERS SEE NOTE ON DWG

¾" PLY SHELF W/ ¾X½ HARDW. LIP ON CONT. BLOCKING

2 EQ. DRAWERS: SEE NOTE ON DWG

¾"X6" HARDW. BASE ON CONT. BLOCKING

PLY SPACE AS REQD

B / A12 LIBRARY : DETAIL @ NORTHEAST CABINET
1½" = 1'-0"

DETAIL OF SHELVING

⅞" Shelving
5'-0"

shelf

Face of Cupboard below

· PLAN ·

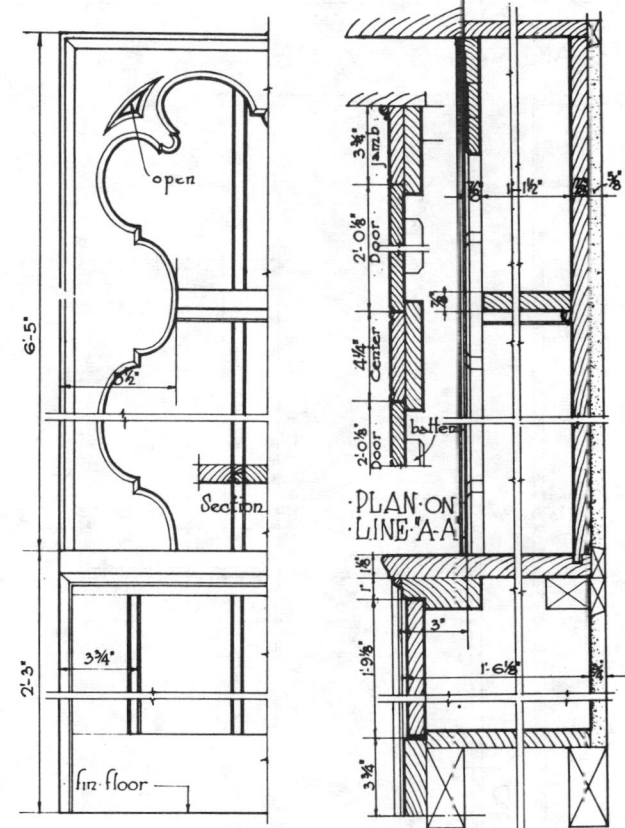

open

Section

6'-5"

2'-3"

3¾"

fin. floor

PLAN ON LINE "A-A"

3¾" jamb

2'-0⅛" Door

4¼" Center

2'-0⅛" Door

batten

1'-9⅝"

3"

1'-6⅛"

3¾"

Note: All woodwork in bookcase and Cupboards is White Oak

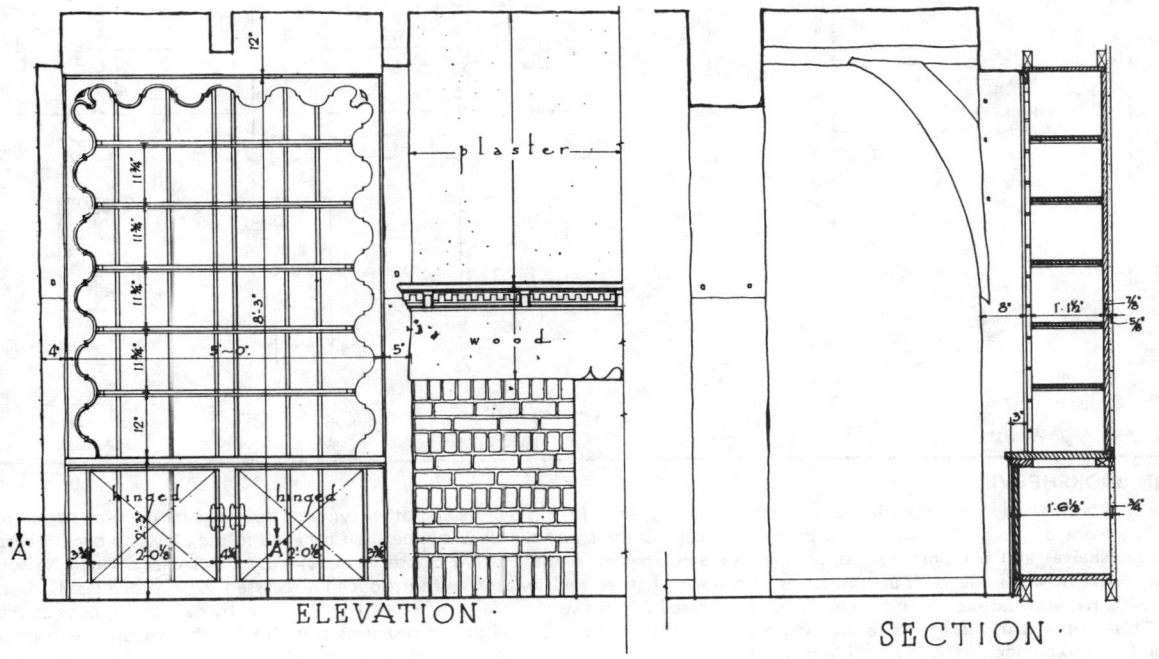

plaster

wood

12'

11⅜"

11⅜"

11⅜"

8'-3"

11⅜"

5'-0"

12'

4

5

hinged   hinged

2'-3"

2'-0⅛"   4¼"   2'-0⅛"

3¾"   · A·

· ELEVATION ·

· SECTION ·

8"   1'-1½"   ⅞"
                ⅝"

1'-6⅛"   ⅞"

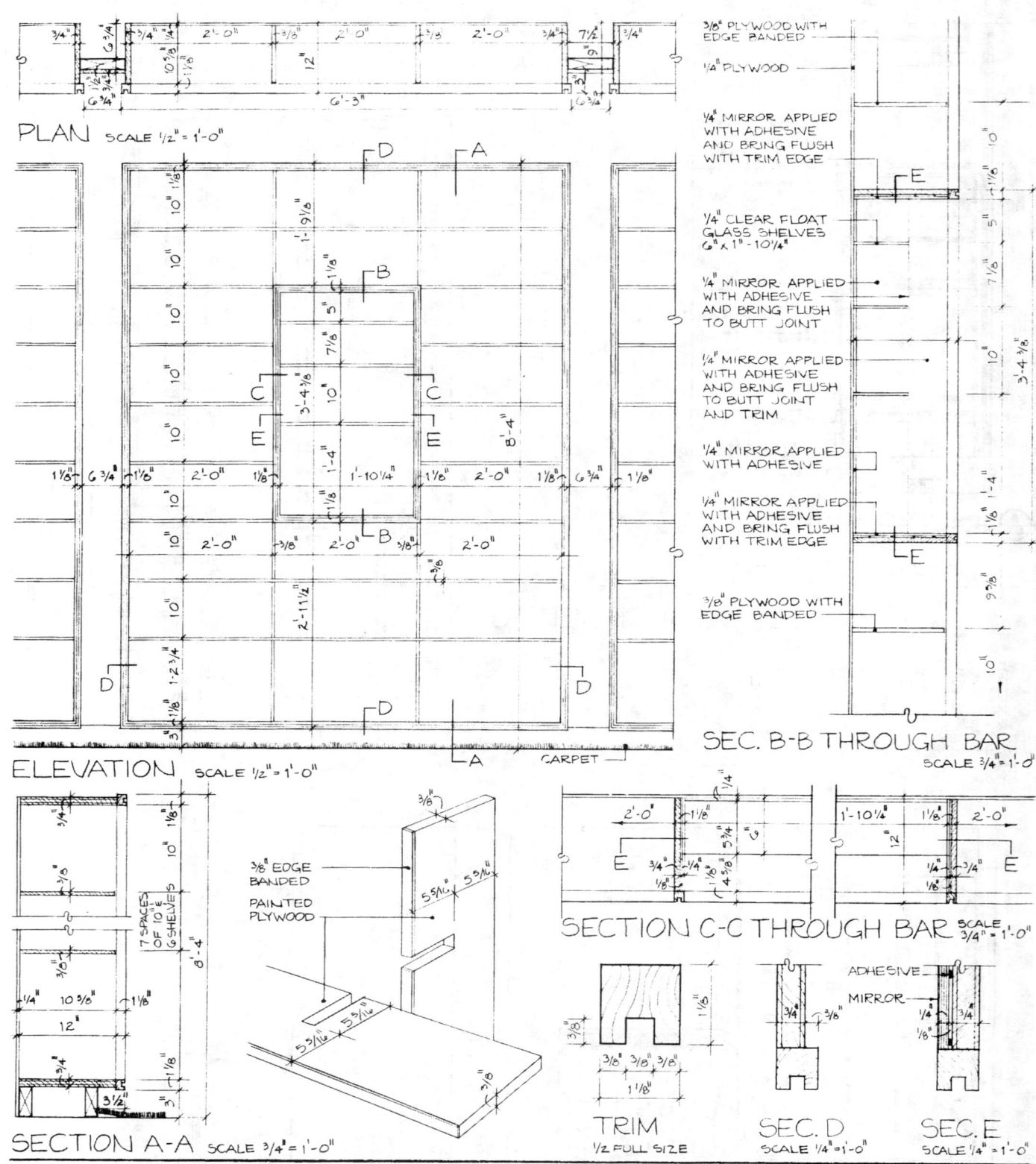

PLAN SCALE 1/2" = 1'-0"

3/8" PLYWOOD WITH EDGE BANDED

1/4" PLYWOOD

1/4" MIRROR APPLIED WITH ADHESIVE AND BRING FLUSH WITH TRIM EDGE

1/4" CLEAR FLOAT GLASS SHELVES 6" X 1" - 10 1/4"

1/4" MIRROR APPLIED WITH ADHESIVE AND BRING FLUSH TO BUTT JOINT

1/4" MIRROR APPLIED WITH ADHESIVE AND BRING FLUSH TO BUTT JOINT AND TRIM

1/4" MIRROR APPLIED WITH ADHESIVE

1/4" MIRROR APPLIED WITH ADHESIVE AND BRING FLUSH WITH TRIM EDGE

3/8" PLYWOOD WITH EDGE BANDED

SEC. B-B THROUGH BAR
SCALE 3/4" = 1'-0"

ELEVATION SCALE 1/2" = 1'-0"

CARPET

SECTION C-C THROUGH BAR SCALE 3/4" = 1'-0"

3/8" EDGE BANDED

PAINTED PLYWOOD

7 SPACES OF 10" 6 SHELVES

SECTION A-A SCALE 3/4" = 1'-0"

TRIM
1/2 FULL SIZE

SEC. D
SCALE 1/4" = 1'-0"

ADHESIVE

MIRROR

SEC. E
SCALE 1/4" = 1'-0"

BUILT-IN BOOKSHELVES

Here is a simple method of building in bookshelves, bar units, etc., for residences and other types of buildings by using an egg-crate system. The front of the shelf is supported by the vertical members and the back of the shelf is nailed to the plywood back. These built-in bookshelves and bar unit were developed for a residence on the Eastern Shore of Maryland. In this design Hugh Newell Jacobsen, FAIA, divided the built-in bookcases into units of three shelf widths and introduced a recessed vertical divider 3" deep by 7 1/2" wide between bookcase units. The major trim piece is solid wood 1 1/8" X 1 1/8" with a 3/8" wide by 3/8" deep groove at the middle. This simple trim piece acts as framing for sides, top, and bottom of the bookshelves and also for the bar unit with glass shelves and mirrored back, sides, top, and bottom.

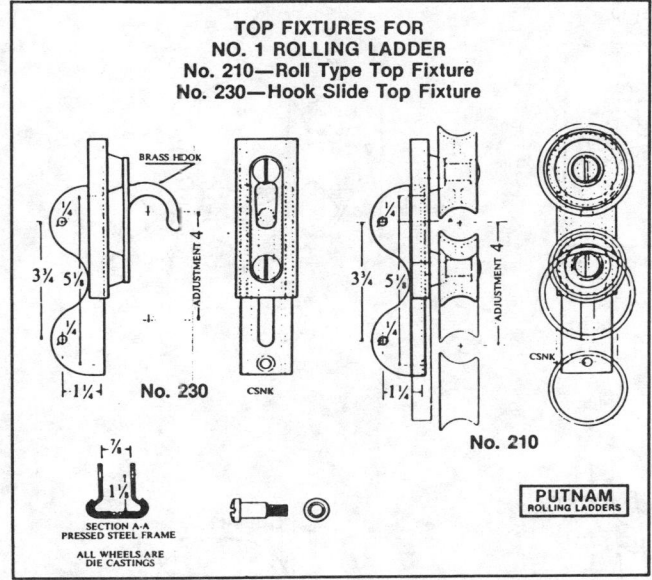

TOP FIXTURES FOR
NO. 1 ROLLING LADDER
No. 210—Roll Type Top Fixture
No. 230—Hook Slide Top Fixture

No. 230

No. 210

SECTION A-A
PRESSED STEEL FRAME
ALL WHEELS ARE
DIE CASTINGS

PUTNAM
ROLLING LADDERS

BOTTOM FIXTURES FOR NO. 1 ROLLING LADDER

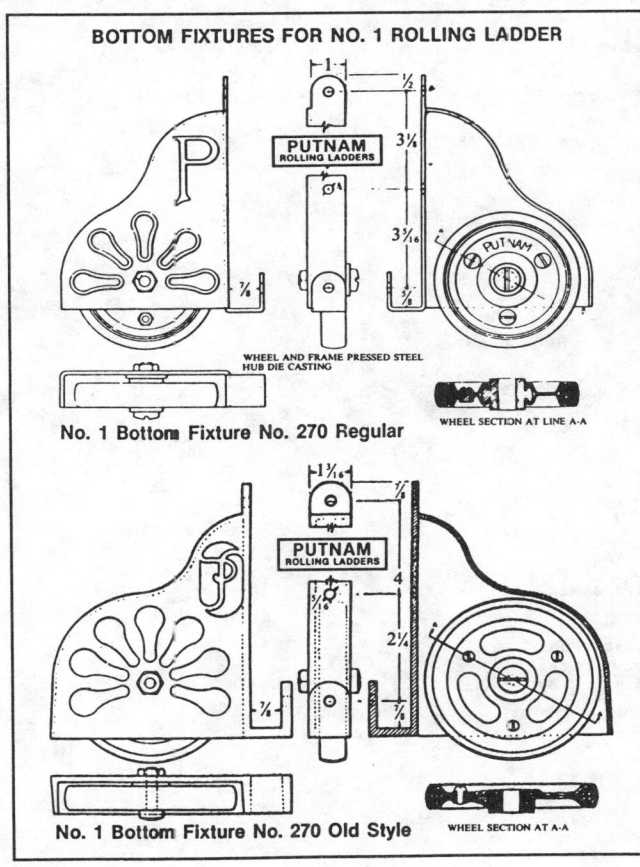

PUTNAM
ROLLING LADDERS

WHEEL AND FRAME PRESSED STEEL
HUB DIE CASTING

No. 1 Bottom Fixture No. 270 Regular

WHEEL SECTION AT LINE A-A

PUTNAM
ROLLING LADDERS

No. 1 Bottom Fixture No. 270 Old Style

WHEEL SECTION AT A-A

BRACKETS FOR TRACK

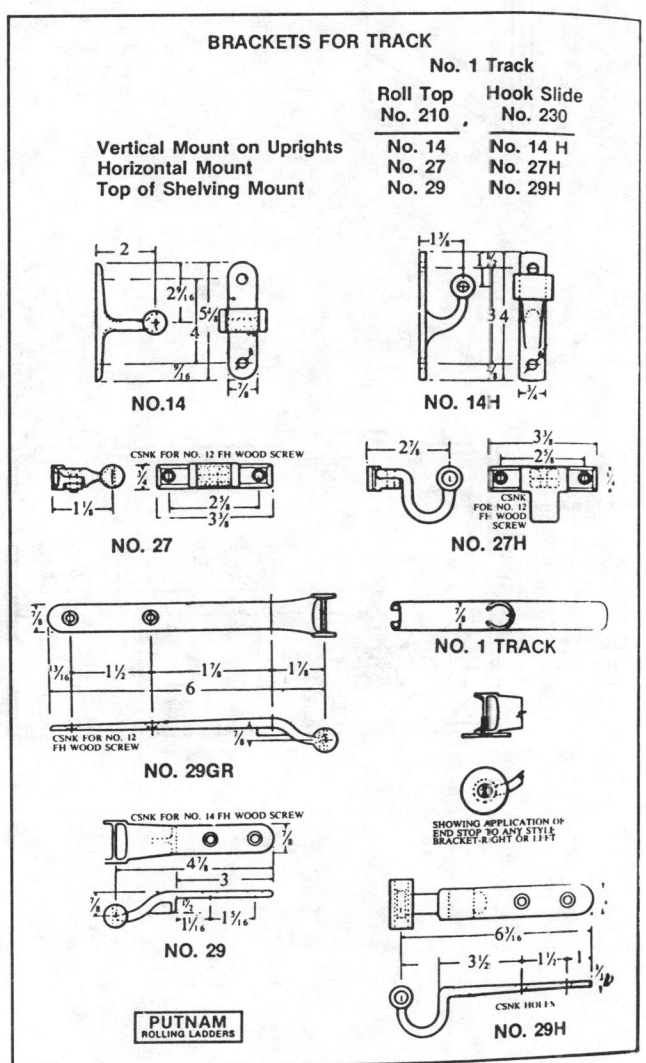

	No. 1 Track	
	Roll Top No. 210	Hook Slide No. 230
Vertical Mount on Uprights	No. 14	No. 14 H
Horizontal Mount	No. 27	No. 27H
Top of Shelving Mount	No. 29	No. 29H

NO.14

NO. 14H

NO. 27

NO. 27H

NO. 1 TRACK

NO. 29GR

SHOWING APPLICATION OF
END STOP TO ANY STYLE
BRACKET-RIGHT OR LEFT

NO. 29

NO. 29H

PUTNAM
ROLLING LADDERS

FAMILY/RECREATION ROOMS
Arrangements and Clearances

Recreational Activities

Indoor recreational activities invariably require definite spaces for equipment and clearances for using it. Not all games occupy floor areas indicated as necessary for those diagramed on this page. But if interiors are planned to accommodate large units of equipment such as that required for table tennis, and provide necessary playing clearances, spaces will be adequate for many other uses as well.

Dimensions of game equipment and floor areas required for its use are both subject to variation. Sizes noted here are comfortable averages, not absolute minima.

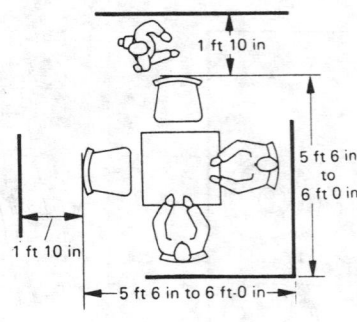

Clearances for playing bridge

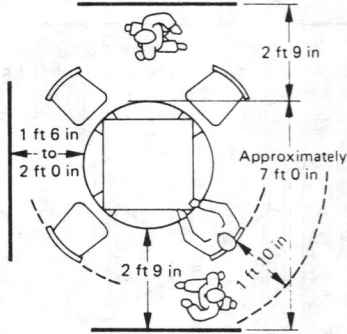

Clearances for playing poker

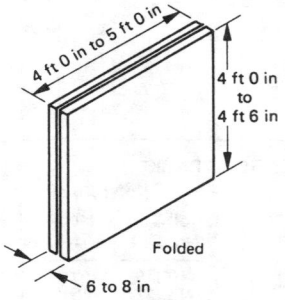

Folded

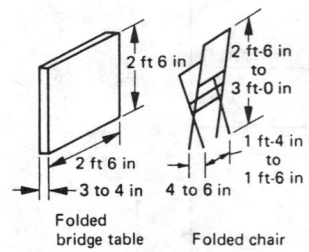

Folded bridge table   Folded chair

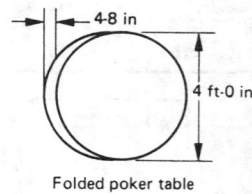

Folded poker table

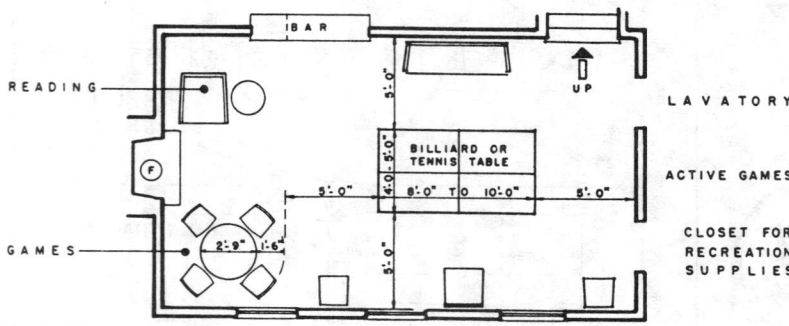

Fig. 1   Play room.

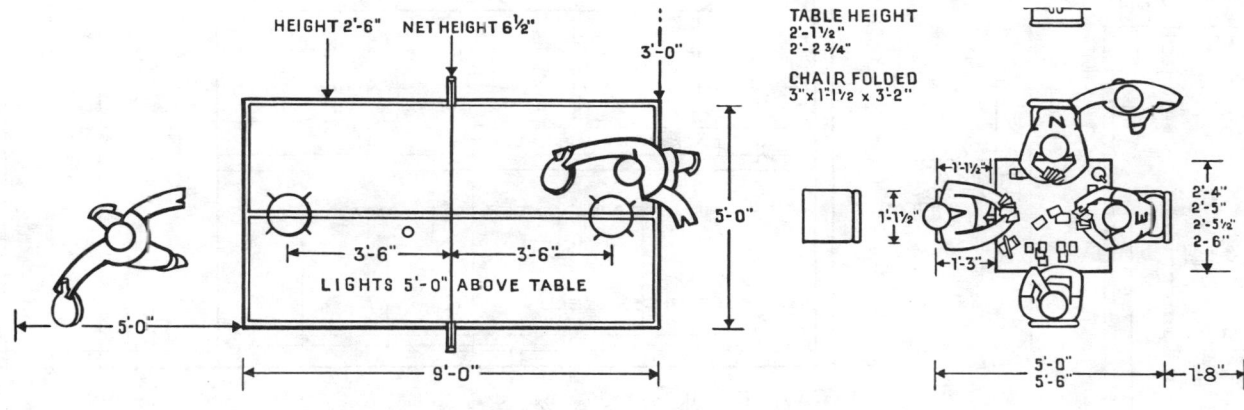

PING PONG

CARD PLAYING

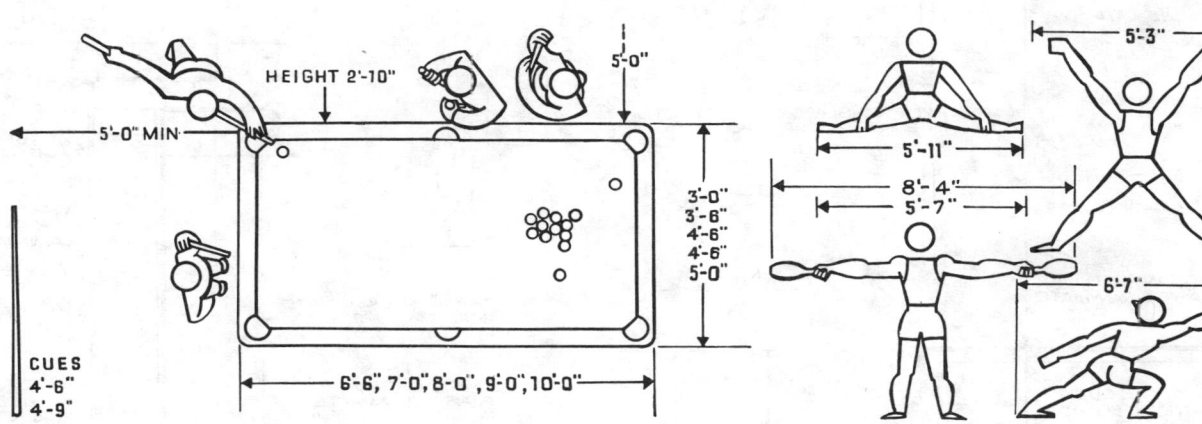

POOL AND BILLIARDS

GYMNASTICS

TABLE 1   Pool and Billiard Table Sizes (in feet)

Size	Where used
3 × 6	Home
3½ × 7	Home
4 × 8	Home
	Commercial standard in South America, Mexico, and Spain
4½ × 9	Popular U.S. commercial standard
5 × 10	U.S. professional standard
6 × 12	Commercial standard in Canada and England

Standard ping pong table sizes are 3 ft × 6 ft; 3 ft 6 in × 7 ft 0 in; 4 ft 0 in × 8 ft 0 in; 4 ft 8 in × 8 ft 6 in; 5 ft 0 in × 9 ft 2 in; 5 ft 6 in × 10 ft 2 in; 6 ft 8 in × 12 ft 8 in.

FAMILY/RECREATION ROOMS
Residential Bar

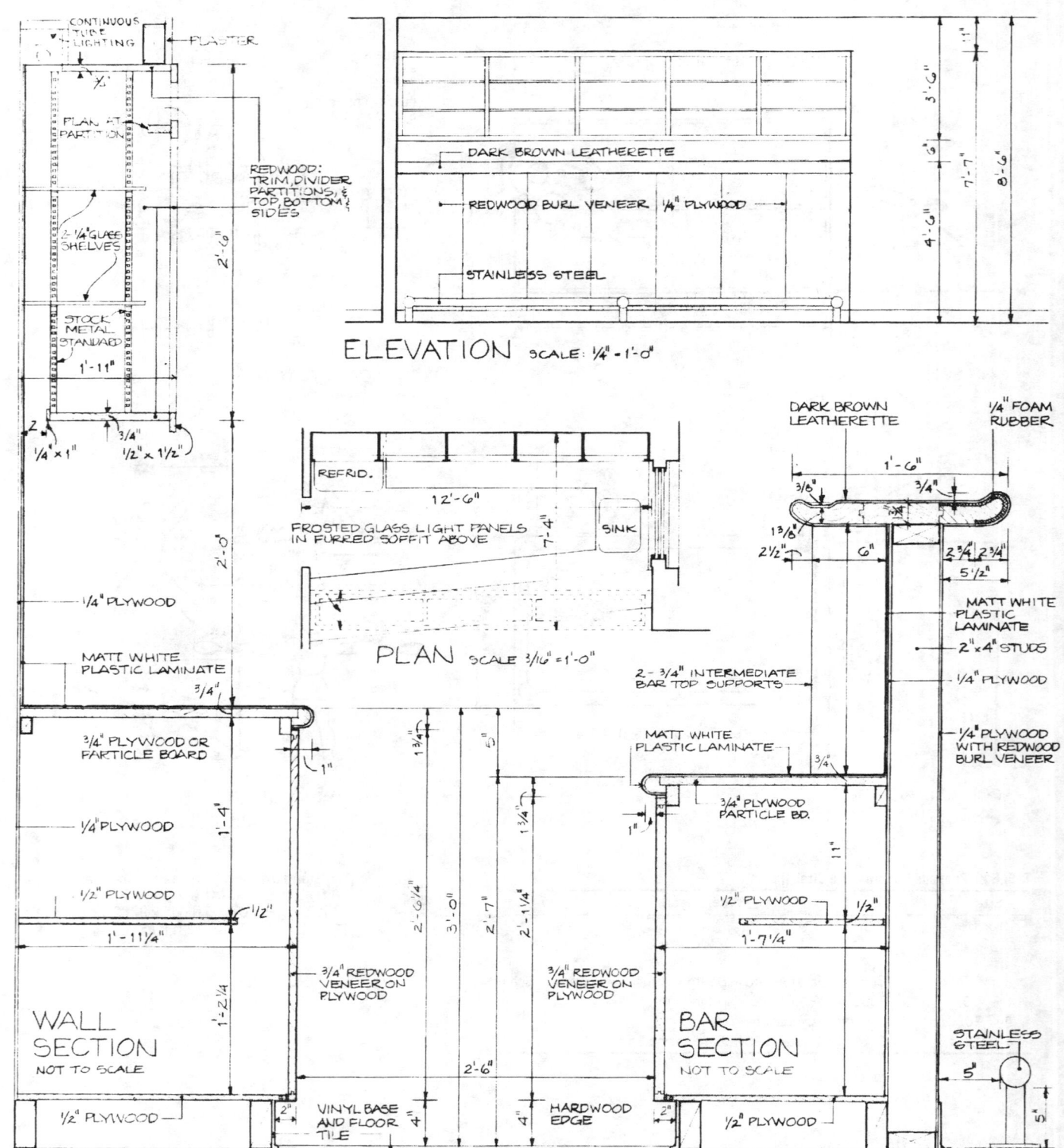

CONTINUOUS TUBE LIGHTING — PILASTER

PLAN AT PARTITION

REDWOOD: TRIM, DIVIDER PARTITIONS, & TOP, BOTTOM, SIDES

2 1/4" GLASS SHELVES

STOCK METAL STANDARD

1'-11"

2'-6"

2" 1/4" x 1" 3/4" 1/2" x 1/2"

ELEVATION SCALE: 1/4" = 1'-0"

DARK BROWN LEATHERETTE

REDWOOD BURL VENEER 1/4" PLYWOOD

STAINLESS STEEL

1" 3'-0" 6" 7'-7" 8'-0" 4'-6"

REFRID.

12'-6"

FROSTED GLASS LIGHT PANELS IN FURRED SOFFIT ABOVE

SINK

7'-4"

PLAN SCALE 3/16" = 1'-0"

DARK BROWN LEATHERETTE

1/4" FOAM RUBBER

3/8" 3/4" 1'-6" 1 3/8" 2 1/2" 6" 5 1/2" 2 3/4" 2 3/4"

MATT WHITE PLASTIC LAMINATE

2" x 4" STUDS

1/4" PLYWOOD

1/4" PLYWOOD WITH REDWOOD BURL VENEER

2 - 3/4" INTERMEDIATE BAR TOP SUPPORTS

MATT WHITE PLASTIC LAMINATE

3/4"

3/4" PLYWOOD PARTICLE BD.

11"

1/2" PLYWOOD 1/2"

1'-7 1/4"

WALL SECTION
NOT TO SCALE

1/4" PLYWOOD

MATT WHITE PLASTIC LAMINATE

3/4"

3/4" PLYWOOD OR PARTICLE BOARD

1'-4"

1/4" PLYWOOD

1/2" PLYWOOD

1/2"

1'-11 1/4"

1'-2 1/4"

2'-0"

3/4" REDWOOD VENEER ON PLYWOOD

1'-9 1/4" 1 3/4" 5" 2'-6 1/4" 3'-0" 2'-7" 2'-1 1/4" 1 3/4" 1"

3/4" REDWOOD VENEER ON PLYWOOD

2'-6"

1/2" PLYWOOD

2" VINYL BASE AND FLOOR TILE

4" HARDWOOD EDGE

BAR SECTION
NOT TO SCALE

2" 1/2" PLYWOOD

STAINLESS STEEL

5"

5"

RESIDENTIAL BAR

This small residential bar with double lighting was designed so that the back bar shelves would display all the types of bar glasses and the liquor bottles as a decorative element. Note how the recessed fluorescent tube fixtures indirectly light up all the glasses and the 2" open slot in the bottom shelf indirectly lights up the liquor bottles on the back bar shelf. The entire front bar has recessed light fixtures in the ceiling above; this allows for two different methods of lighting the bar area. Note also that the bar front is slightly padded with foam rubber and the entire bar top is finished with dark brown leatherette.

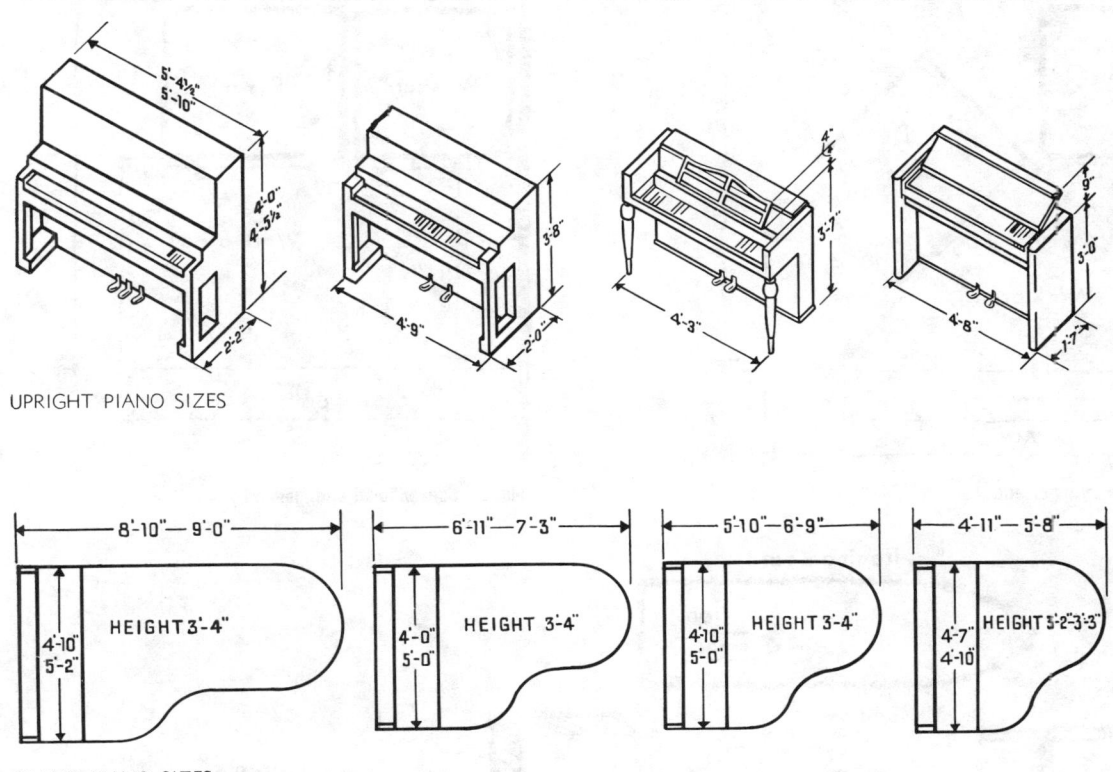

UPRIGHT PIANO SIZES

GRAND PIANO SIZES

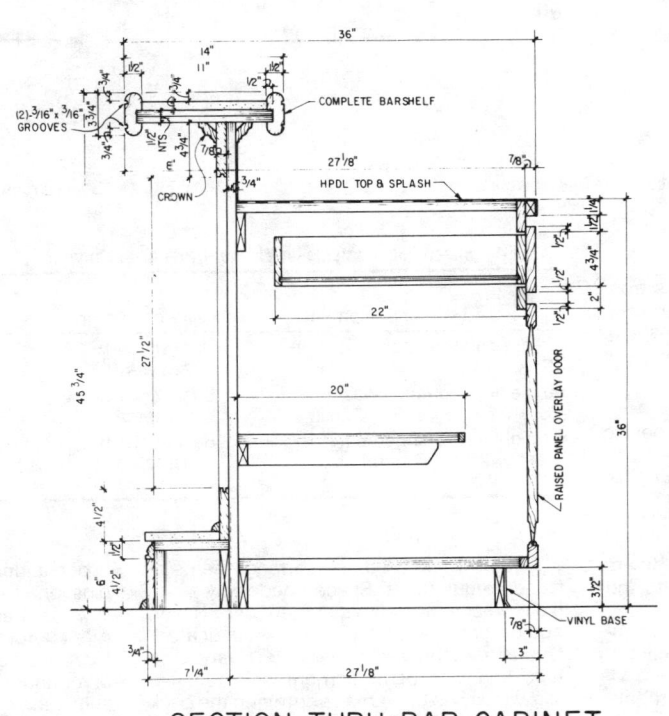

SECTION THRU BAR CABINET

LAUNDRY/SEWING ROOMS
Laundry Room Layouts

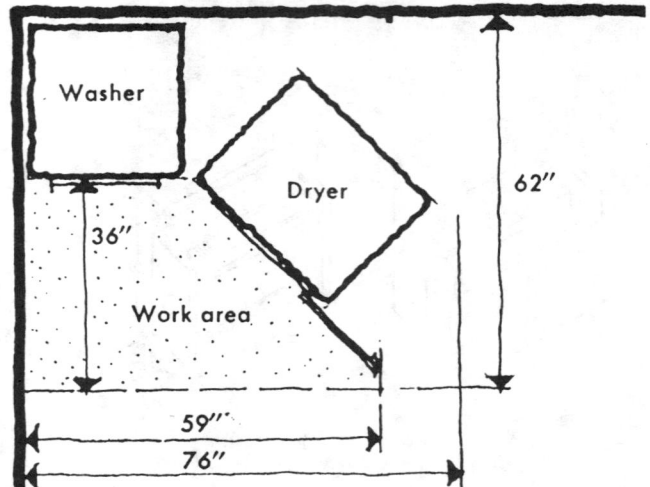

Fig. 1   Angle arrangement.

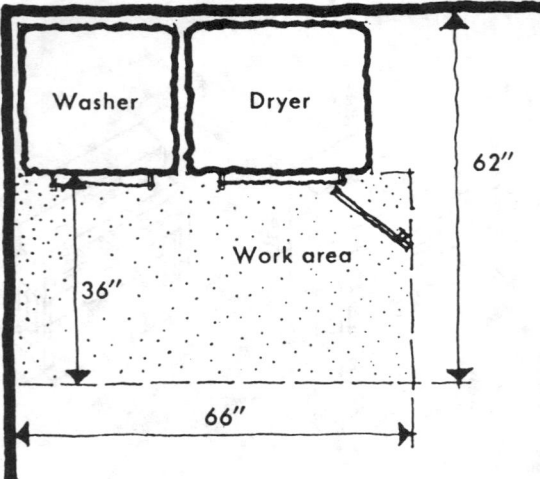

Fig. 2   Conventional arrangement.

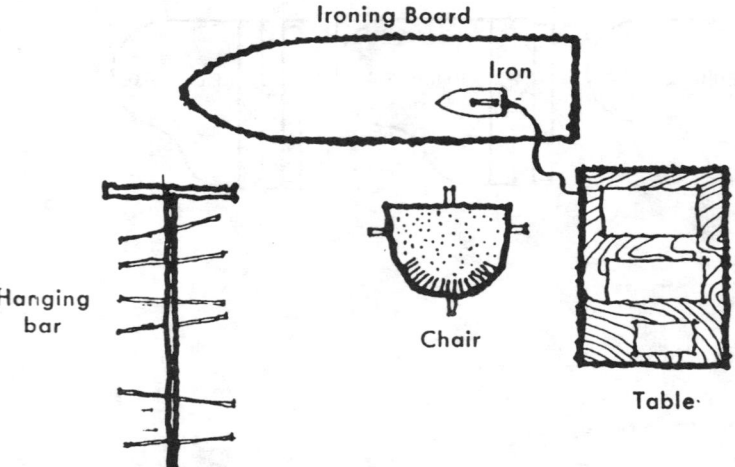

Fig. 3   Arrangement of ironing equipment based on flow of work.

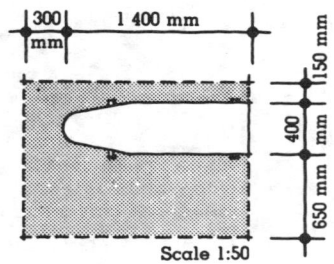

Fig. 4.   Space around ironing board.

HOME LAUNDRY ACTIVITIES

Home laundry includes the processes from sorting through ironing of clothes and household linens, including pretreating, washing, drying, and sprinkling.

General Planning Suggestions

1. It is desirable to plan space for specific laundry processes.
2. Moistureproof surfaces are needed for pretreating and sprinkling of clothes.
3. Drying areas should be accessible for use under all climatic conditions.
4. To control moisture in the room, dryers should be located to permit venting to the outside of the house.
5. Adequate storage for washing equipment and supplies should be located near the place of first use.
6. Facilities for hanging drip-dry garments after washing should be provided.
7. In locating the washing equipment consideration should be given to convenience of inter-related household activities, distances from the source of soiled clothes and the drying areas, and the isolation of clutter.

TABLE 1   Space Requirements for Washer-Dryer Arrangements

Type and size of equipment	Auxiliary equipment	Work area, in	Total floor area, in Width	Total floor area, in Depth
Stacked arrangement: washer, 31 × 26 in; dryer, 31 × 26 in	Basket, 19-in diameter	43 × 37	43	63
Angle arrangement: washer 26 × 26 in; dryer, 31 × 26 in	Basket, 19-in diameter	36 × 59	62	76
Straight-line arrangement: washer, 26 × 26 in; dryer, 31 × 26 in	Basket, 19-in diameter	36 × 66	62	66

Figures 1 and 2 illustrate arrangements of laundry equipment. Space needed by a single worker in front of equipment or between equipment placed opposite is indicated. Overall dimensions of areas will vary with type and size of equipment selected. No allowance has been made between the back of equipment and the wall for electrical, plumbing, and dryer vent connections. The space required will depend on the type of installation used.

Counter space is provided for sorting and folding three washer loads of clothes. The space under the counters has been used for bins, one for soiled clothing and the other for dry, clean articles that require further treatment before use or storage. Additional counter space can be provided by the tops of the dryer and washer, depending upon the type selected.

A tall storage cabinet for laundry supplies would complement each arrangement. In this cabinet, an ironing board, iron, mops, and buckets (needed for cleaning the laundry area) may also be stored.

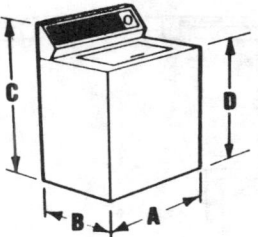

Fig. 5   Automatic washer. A = 24–30 in, B = 26–30 in, C = 42 in, D = 36 in.

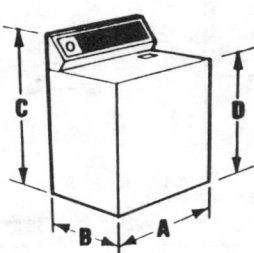

Fig. 6   Automatic dryer. A = 24–28 in, B = 24–26 in, C = 42 in, D = 36 in.

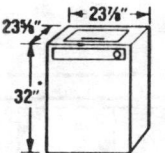

Fig. 7   Compact washer.

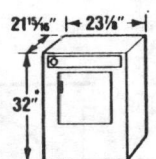

Fig. 8   Compact dryer.

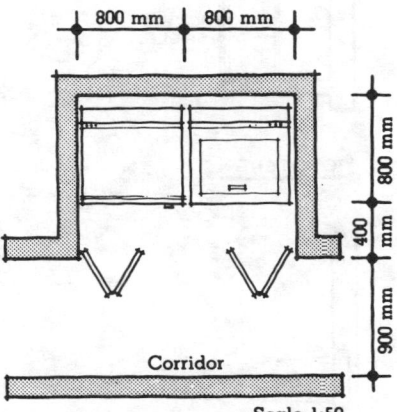

Corridor

Scale 1:50

Fig. 9   When space is limited, it may be possible to locate the laundry space next to a corridor.

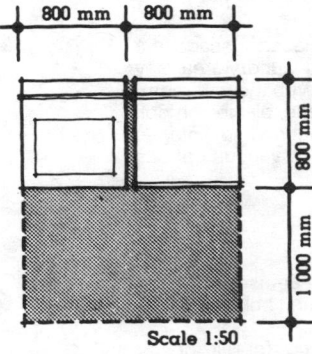

Scale 1:50

Fig. 10   Clearance in front of automatic washer and dryer. If the space in front of the automatic washer and dryer is a corridor, this dimension should be increased to at least 1200 mm (4 ft). This will permit a second person to pass through when someone is doing the laundry. If a washer and dryer are located opposite each other, this dimension should also be 1200 mm (4 ft).

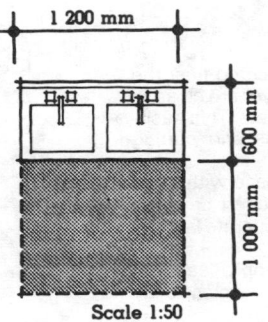

Scale 1:50

Fig. 11   Clearance in front of laundry tub.

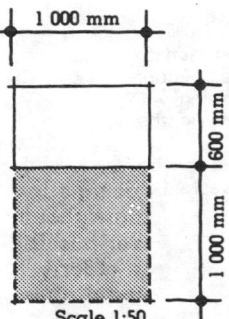

Scale 1:50

Fig. 12   Clearance in front of sorting counter or table.

LAUNDRY/SEWING ROOMS

Laundry Room Layouts

LAUNDRY LOCATION

The ideal location of the laundry space is a matter of preference. The laundry area may be separate or combined with the bathroom, the kitchen, the utility space, or the corridor. The most frequently mentioned advantages and disadvantages of these various options are listed below.

Separate Laundry

Advantages

A separate space can be used for other activities such as sewing and hobbies, if it is large enough.

Clothes may be hung for air drying without interfering with other household activities.

Noise from laundry appliances can be shut off from the rest of the dwelling.

Temporary holding or storage of clothing to be washed or ironed is made easier.

Disadvantages

Providing this extra room increases the cost of the dwelling.

Laundry in Combination with Bathroom

Advantages

When the bathroom is located near the bedrooms, the washer and dryer are close to where most laundry originates. This facilitates gathering soiled articles and putting away clean linen and clothing.

Combining the laundry space with a half bathroom adjacent to the kitchen provides many of the advantages of a separate laundry room.

The tops of the laundry appliances provide useful horizontal space on which to lay clothes.

Floor and wall finishes in bathrooms are usually resistant to high humidities.

Usually, additional plumbing costs are minimal.

The bathroom sink may be used for hand washing.

Mechanical ventilation can be provided economically for both functions.

Disadvantages

A bathroom will usually accommodate only washing and drying facilities. Other laundry related activities such as ironing, will have to be carried out elsewhere in the dwelling.

Occupants may wish to use the bathroom when laundry is being washed or dried.

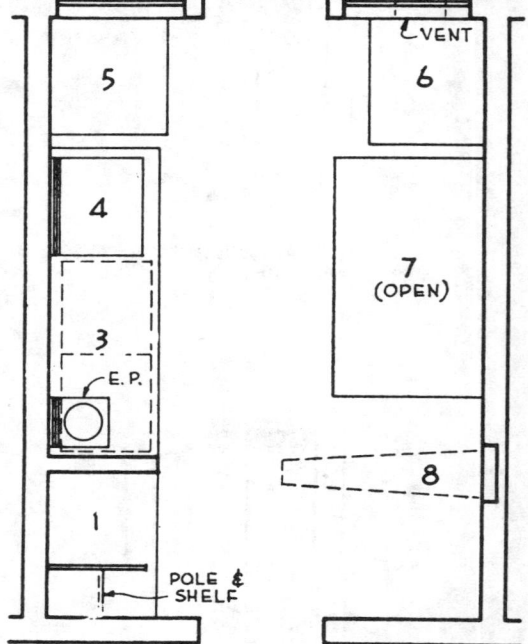

KEY

1. STORAGE CLOSET
2. CLOTHES CHUTE
3. SORTING SHELF
4. LAUNDRY TRAY
5. WASHING MACHINE
6. DRYER
7. IRONER
8. IRONING BOARD

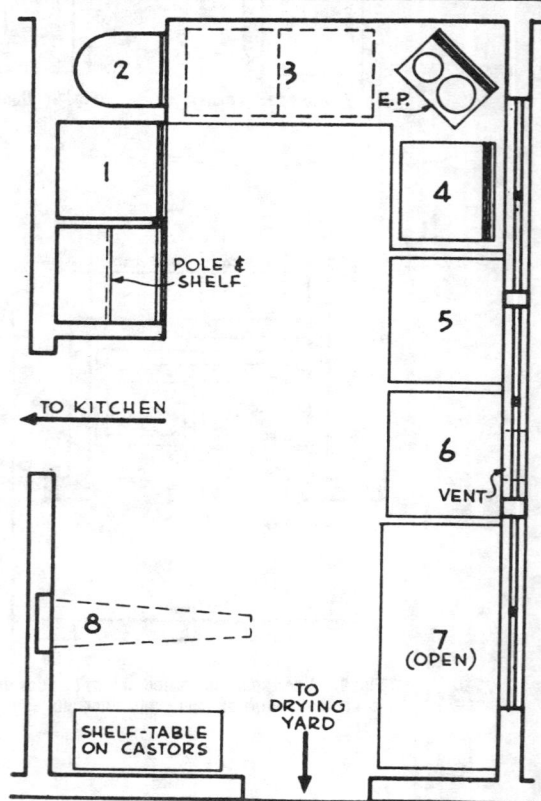

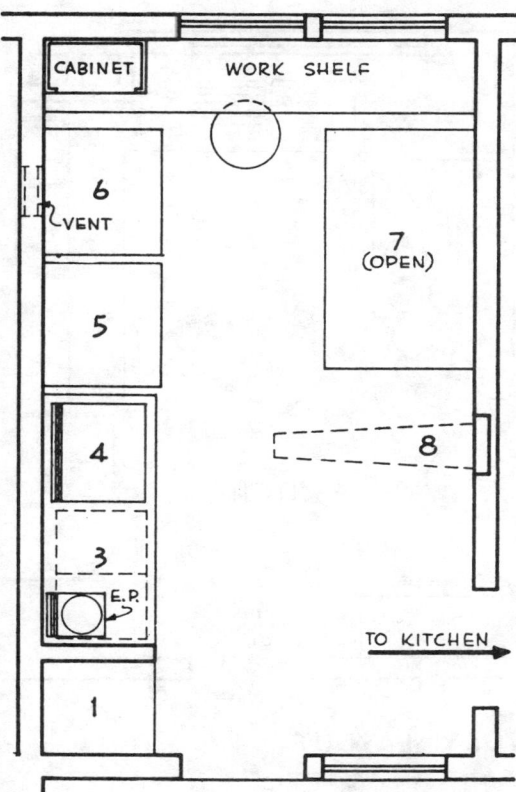

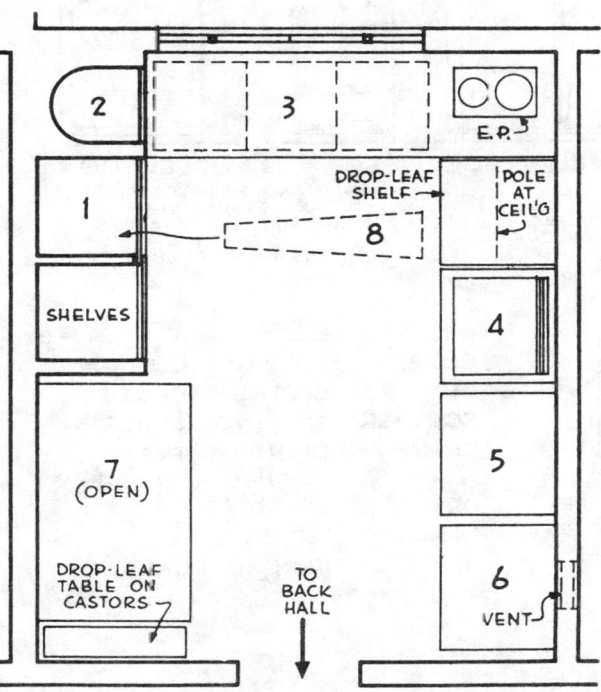

Laundry in Combination with Kitchen
Advantages

Suitable in housing for young families because the person doing the laundry can keep an eye on the washing machine while doing other jobs and supervising the children.

Direct access to the outside for clothes drying is likely to be easier than from laundries located in a basement or on a second storey.

Kitchen sinks are usually sizeable and can be used for laundering.

Additional plumbing costs are usually small.

Disadvantages

Danger of cross-contamination through the handling of dirty washing during food preparation.

Grease and cooking smells can be passed on to clean clothes.

Noise generated by running appliances cannot easily be shut off from the rest of the dwelling.

Laundry in Combination with Utility Space in Basement
Advantages

Generally, as much space as needed can be provided.

Noise generated by running appliances can be easily shut off from the rest of the dwelling.

Disadvantages

Laundry must be carried up and down stairs, although automatic dryers have eased the problem of carrying heavy baskets of damp clothes to outdoor clotheslines.

Laundry in Combination with Corridor
Advantages

The space is used more economically (Fig. 9).

The space above the appliances may be used as a linen closet.

The appliances can be hidden from sight when they are not in use; they can be recessed into the wall and enclosed with doors.

Disadvantages

Noise generated by running appliances cannot be easily shut off from the rest of the dwelling.

An alcove adjacent to a corridor will accommodate only a minimum-sized laundry area. Other laundry related activities, such as ironing, will have to be carried out elsewhere in the dwelling.

LAUNDRY/SEWING ROOMS

Laundry Room Layouts

Planning for Efficiency

The sequence of laundering operations determines the planning of space and facilities and the placing of equipment. Convenience and time-and-step saving are easily achieved by placing the elements in their natural order of use: (1) clothes chute (with or without bins or hampers), (2) sorting table or counter, (3) washing machine, (4) laundry trays, (5) dryer, (6) ironer or mangle, (7) ironing board, (8) rack, "horse," or table for finished laundry. In addition, storage closet or cabinets will be necessary for soaps, powders, bluing, bleaches, starch, basket, clothespins, iron, etc.

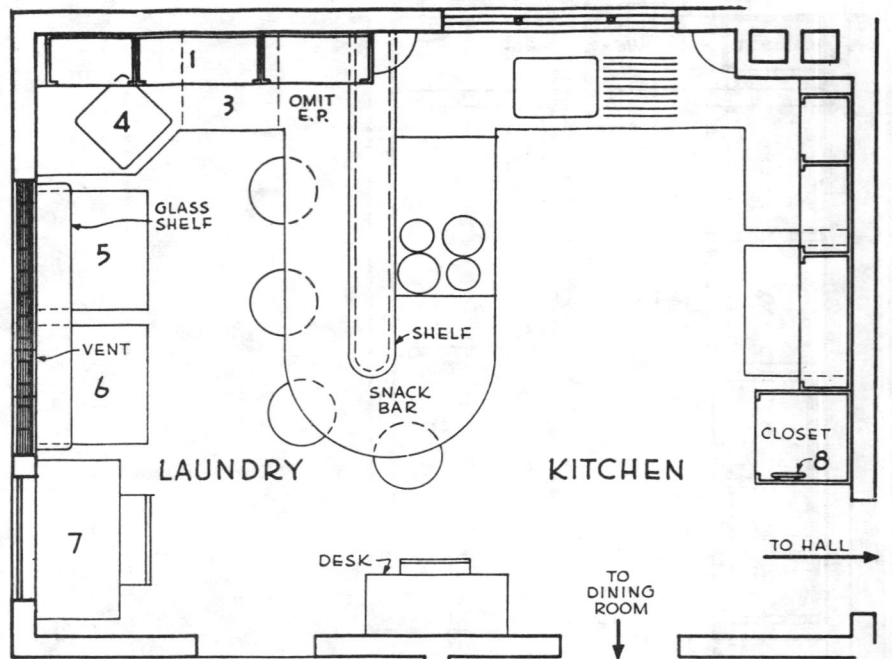

KEY

1. STORAGE CLOSET
2. CLOTHES CHUTE
3. SORTING SHELF
4. LAUNDRY TRAY
5. WASHING MACHINE
6. DRYER
7. IRONER
8. IRONING BOARD

KITCHEN AND LAUNDRY LAYOUT

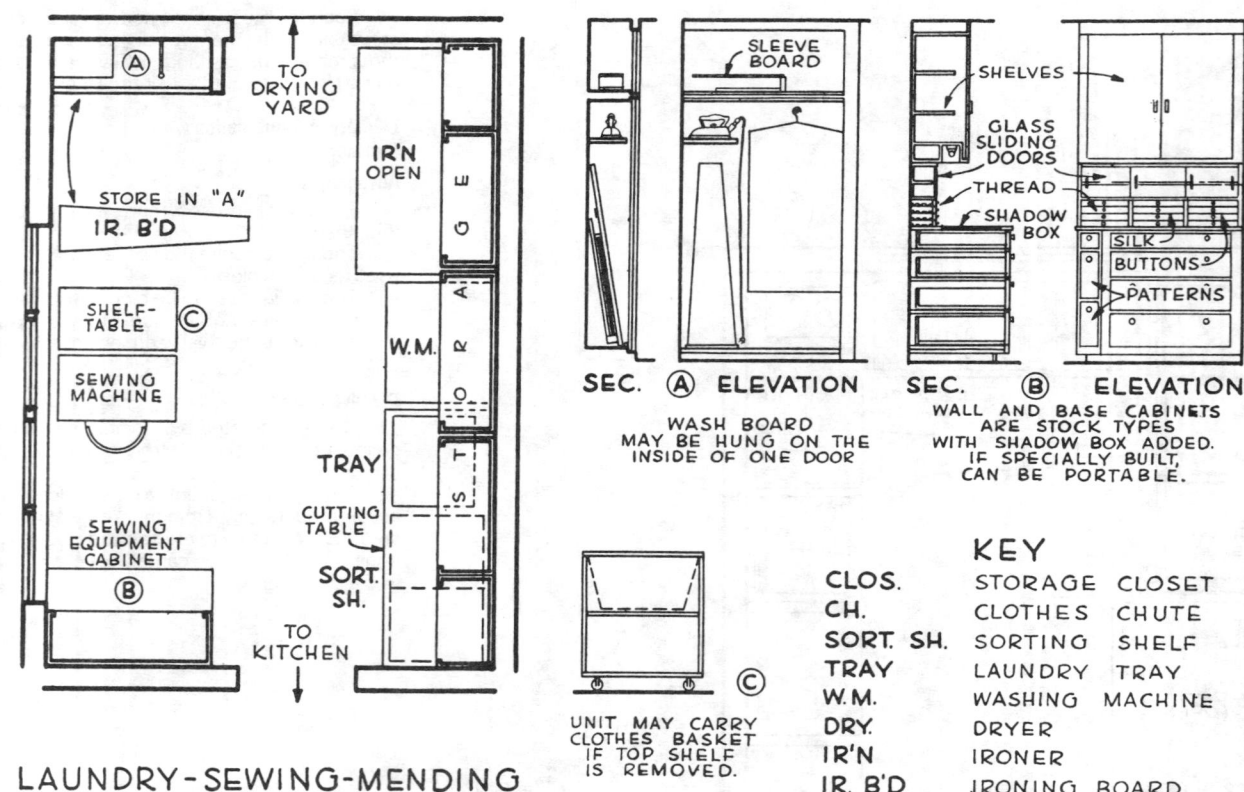

LAUNDRY-SEWING-MENDING

SEC. (A) ELEVATION
WASH BOARD
MAY BE HUNG ON THE
INSIDE OF ONE DOOR

SEC. (B) ELEVATION
WALL AND BASE CABINETS
ARE STOCK TYPES
WITH SHADOW BOX ADDED.
IF SPECIALLY BUILT,
CAN BE PORTABLE.

UNIT MAY CARRY
CLOTHES BASKET
IF TOP SHELF
IS REMOVED.

KEY

CLOS.	STORAGE CLOSET
CH.	CLOTHES CHUTE
SORT. SH.	SORTING SHELF
TRAY	LAUNDRY TRAY
W.M.	WASHING MACHINE
DRY.	DRYER
IR'N	IRONER
IR. B'D	IRONING BOARD

General Planning Suggestions

1. An area especially planned for sewing, convenient to other activity areas, is desirable.

2. Most houses need storage space for sewing materials and equipment. The amount and kind of storage required varies according to the quality and frequency of sewing.

3. A minimum sewing area should include the machine, auxiliary work surfaces, a chair that permits freedom of motion, and storage arrangements. The work surface for layout and cutting may be outside the area for sewing machine operations and serve multiple purposes.

4. Consideration should be given to work surfaces at comfortable heights for the varying activities of sewing.

5. Light should be adequate for the activity.

TABLE 2   Dimensions of Area for Layout and Cutting Garments

Measurement	Dimensions, in	
	Minimum	Adequate
Working surface		
Length	56	72
Width		
Table, free-standing	28	36
Table obstructed on one side	28	32
Height	34–40 (range)	36 (median)
Clearance for worker	18	24

TABLE 3   Dimensions of Fitting Space

Use of Space	Minimum	Adequate
Viewing in mirror:		
Mirror dimensions, in		
Width	16	18
Length	42	60
Top to floor	70	72
Clearance in front of mirror, ft		
Width	3	4
Length	6–8	10
Clearance while fitting self, ft	6 × 4	
Clearance while being fitted, ft	8½ × 4	
Fitting garment on dress form, ft	5 × 4	7 × 6

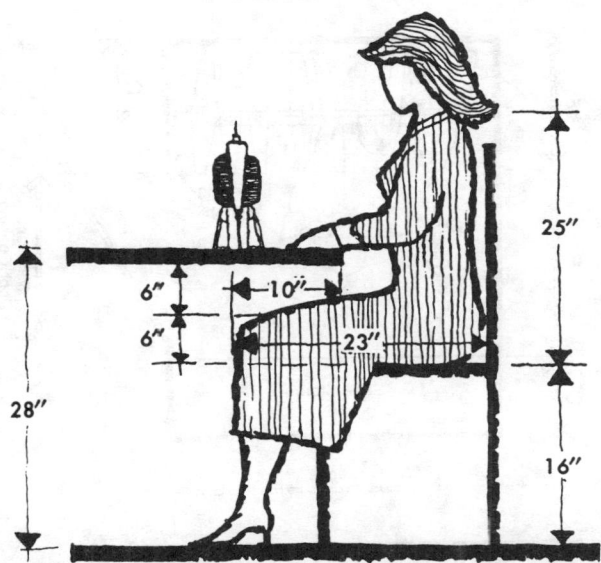

Fig. 13   Mean heights and clearances for sewing machine use.

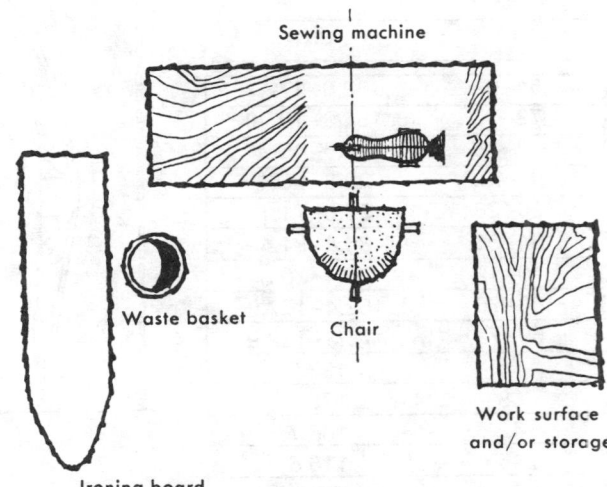

Fig. 14   Arrangement of sewing equipment based on flow of work.

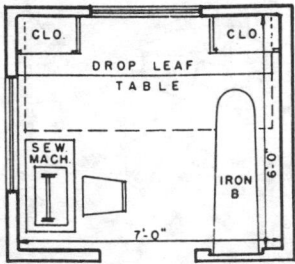

Fig. 15   Sewing room.

Figures 1 and 2 show the vertical clearances related to male and female closet and storage facilities. Wherever possible or practical, the closet shelf should be located within human reach. The height shown for the high shelf has been established based on fifth percentile male and female data in order to place it within reach of individuals of smaller body size. Any shelf located at a greater distance should be used primarily for storage that requires only infrequent access. The location of the shelf just above the rod is essentially a function of rod height. The clearance between the bottom of the shelf and the top of the rod should allow for easy removal of the hanger.

Figure 3 illustrates two various types of walk-in storage facilities. Undoubtably, it can be argued that the 36-in, or 91.4-cm, clearance shown between the hanging garment and the storage shelf or between opposite garments could be reduced about 50 percent. The authors contend, however, that in order to achieve any degree of comfort in the selection and removal of the desired garment, a minimum of 36 in should be maintained. The degree to which this dimension can be reduced is a question of the level of comfort the user is prepared to tolerate in exchange for the floor space saved. The two drawings of the plan view of the human figure illustrate clearances required for donning a coat or putting on a pair of stockings.

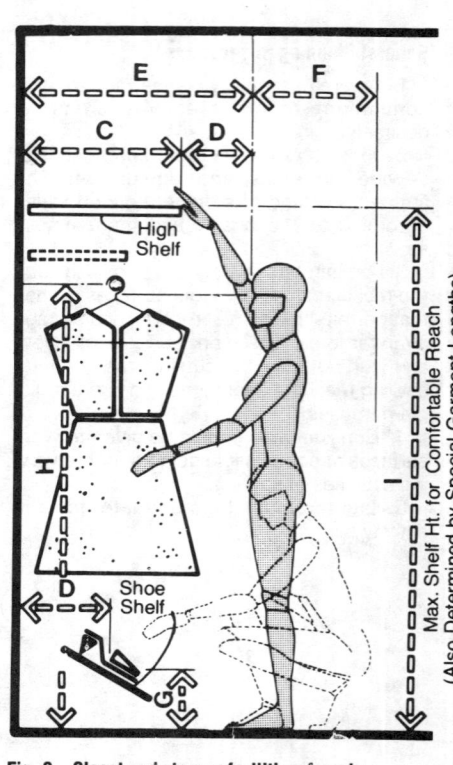

Fig. 1 Closet and storage facilities: male.

Fig. 2 Closet and storage facilities: female.

	in	cm
A	64–68	162.6–172.7
B	72–76	182.9–193.0
C	12–18	30.5–45.7
D	8–10	20.3–25.4
E	20–28	50.8–71.1
F	34–36	86.4–91.4
G	10–12	25.4–30.5
H	60–70	152.4–177.8
I	69–72	175.3–182.9
J	76	193.0
K	68	172.7
L	42	106.7
M	46	116.8
N	30	76.2
O	18	45.7

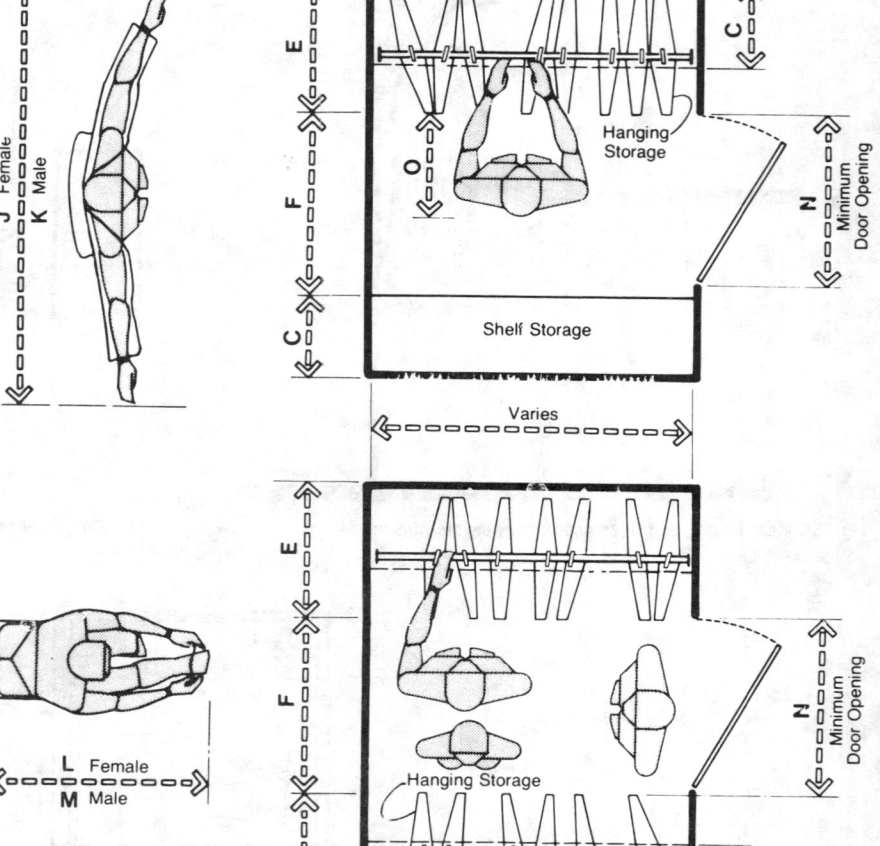

Fig. 3 Walk-in closet and storage facilities.

CLOTHES CLOSETS

The capacity of a clothes closet depends upon the accessible length of rod. Three types of closets are common.

Reach-in closet The minimum front-to-back depth of space for hanging clothes is 24". The accessible rod length is equal to the width of the door opening plus 6" on each side.

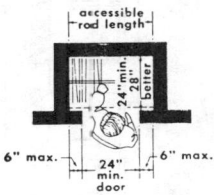

Edge-in closet By providing an edge-in space of at least 18", the accessible rod length can be much longer than the door width. This requires less wall space than a full front opening.

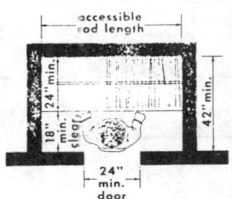

Walk-in closet This type provides rods on one or both sides of an access path at least 20" wide. A wider access space within the closet may be used as a dressing area.

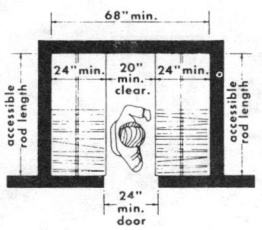

Rod Lengths and Heights

The Minimum Property Standards of HUD (1973) require that each bedroom have a closet, with rod and shelf, with minimum dimensions of

For double-occupancy bedrooms:
24" by 60"
For single-occupancy bedrooms:
24" by 36"
For closet at entrance to house:
24" by 24"

A more desirable front-to-back depth would be 28" for bedroom closets and 30" for entrance closets to accommodate bulky outer garments.

The average rod space per garment is about 2" for women's clothing, 2¼" for men's clothing, and 4" for heavy coats.

Recommended heights of rods are 68" for long robes, 63" for adult clothing, and 32" for children's clothing.

Shelf Space and Lighting

The shelf is normally located 2" above the rod, and another shelf may be located 12" higher. Shelves higher than the rod may also be installed at the end of the closet.

A fluorescent fixture over the door is recommended for lighting a closet. Deluxe cool white tubes match daylight for selecting clothes.

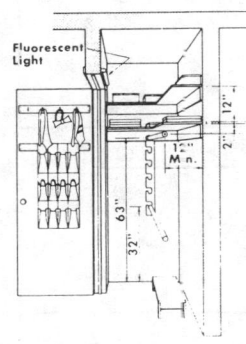

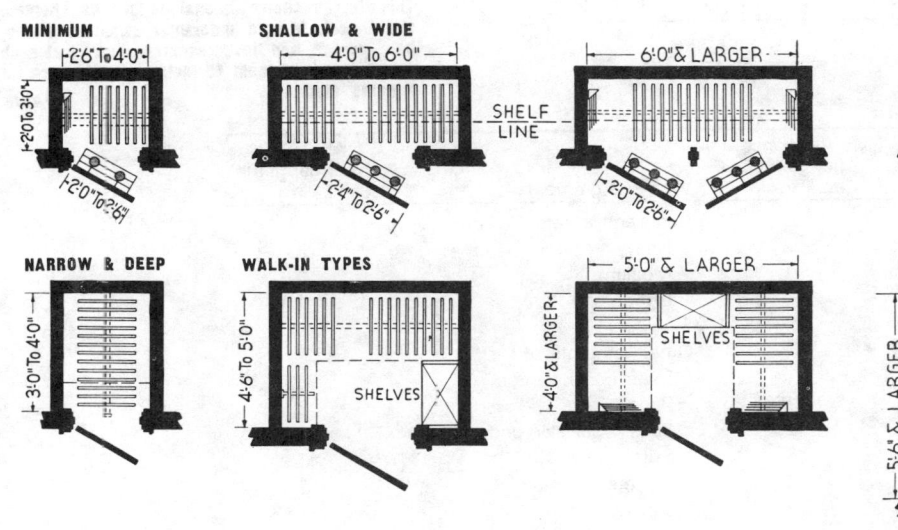

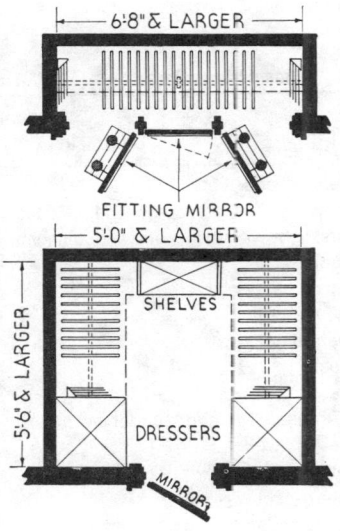

CLOSETS/STORAGE AREAS
Clothes Closet Details

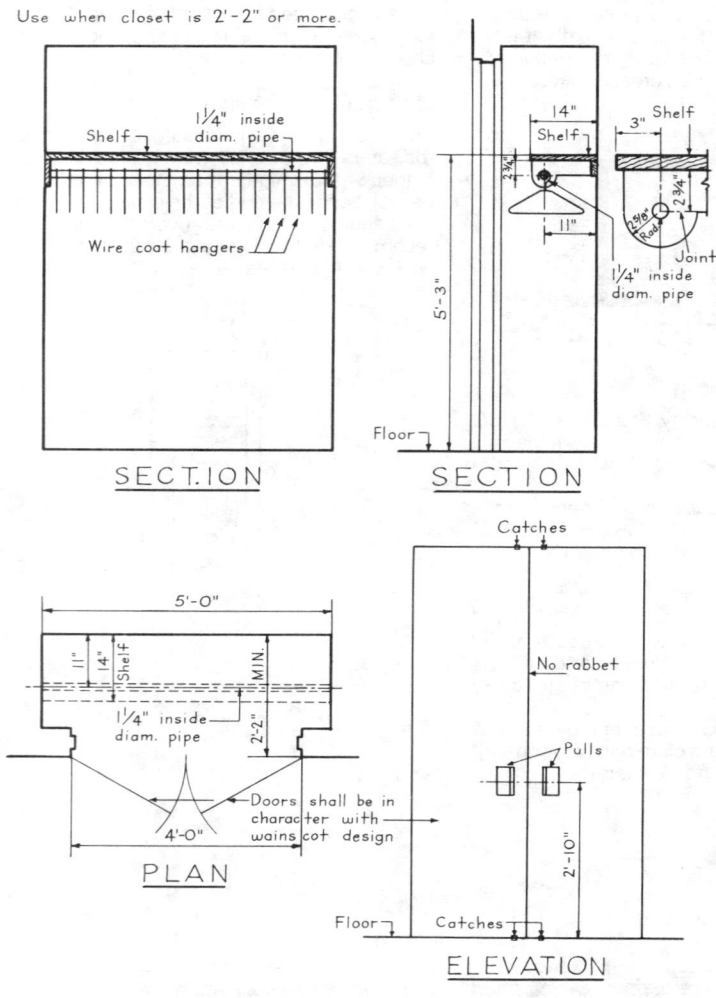

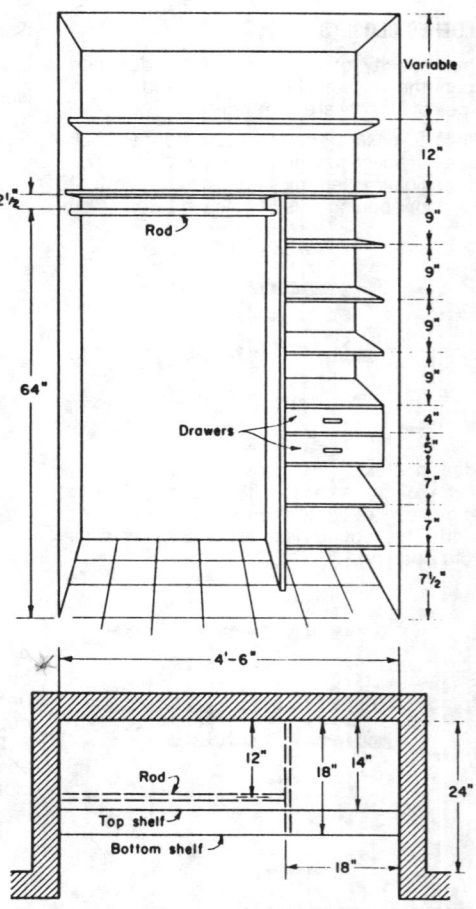

Fig. 4 Bedroom closet designed for one person. This diagram shows dimensions for rods, shelves, and drawers to hold underwear, sweaters, shoes, hats, purses, and ties. Research shows that each person needs at least 48 inches of rod space for hanging clothing.

TABLE 1 Garment Dimensions

Men's garments	Allowance per garment, in	Women's garments	Allowance per garment, in
Heavy jackets and coats	3	Coats and jackets:	
Medium-weight jackets, coats, and raincoats	2	Heavy	3
Sweaters, light-weight jackets, and raincoats	1	Medium	2
Work pants:		Light	1
Folded on hanger	2¼	Sweaters	1¼
Hung full length	1¾	Other garments:	
Other garments:		Dress coats, winter	3½
Top coats	2½	Robes	2
Robes	2	Suits, wool (skirt under jacket)	2½
Suits (trousers full length under jacket)	3	Skirts	1
Trousers	1½	Jackets	2
Jackets	2	Blouses	1
Sweater jacket	1	House dresses	1¾
Shirts (all kinds)	1½	Other dresses:	
		Average	2
		Full-skirted	2½
		Straight-line	1¼

Men's garments	Range of lengths, in	Women's garments	Range of lengths, in
Suit jackets, other jackets, shirts	31–40	Blouses, jackets	25–35
Trousers:		Skirts, medium and short coats	31–43
Folded over hanger	29–37	Dresses, long coats, short robes	48–55
Full length	47–53	Long robes, long evening dresses	61–68
Overcoats, robes	48–54		

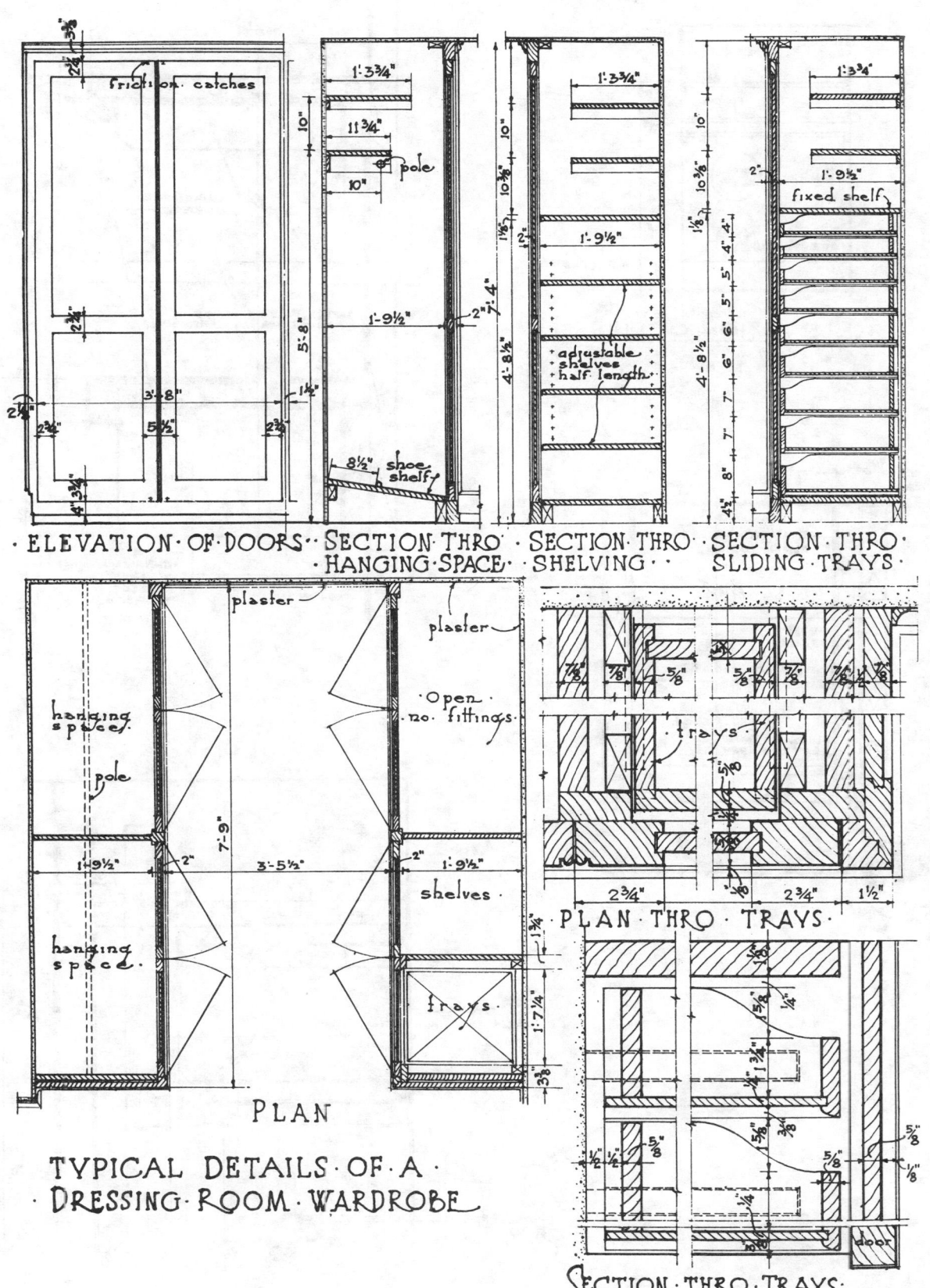

· ELEVATION · OF · DOORS · · SECTION · THRO · HANGING · SPACE · · SECTION · THRO · SHELVING · · · SECTION · THRO · SLIDING · TRAYS ·

PLAN

TYPICAL · DETAILS · OF · A · DRESSING · ROOM · WARDROBE

PLAN · THRO · TRAYS ·

SECTION · THRO · TRAYS ·

CLOSETS/STORAGE AREAS
Clothes Closet Details

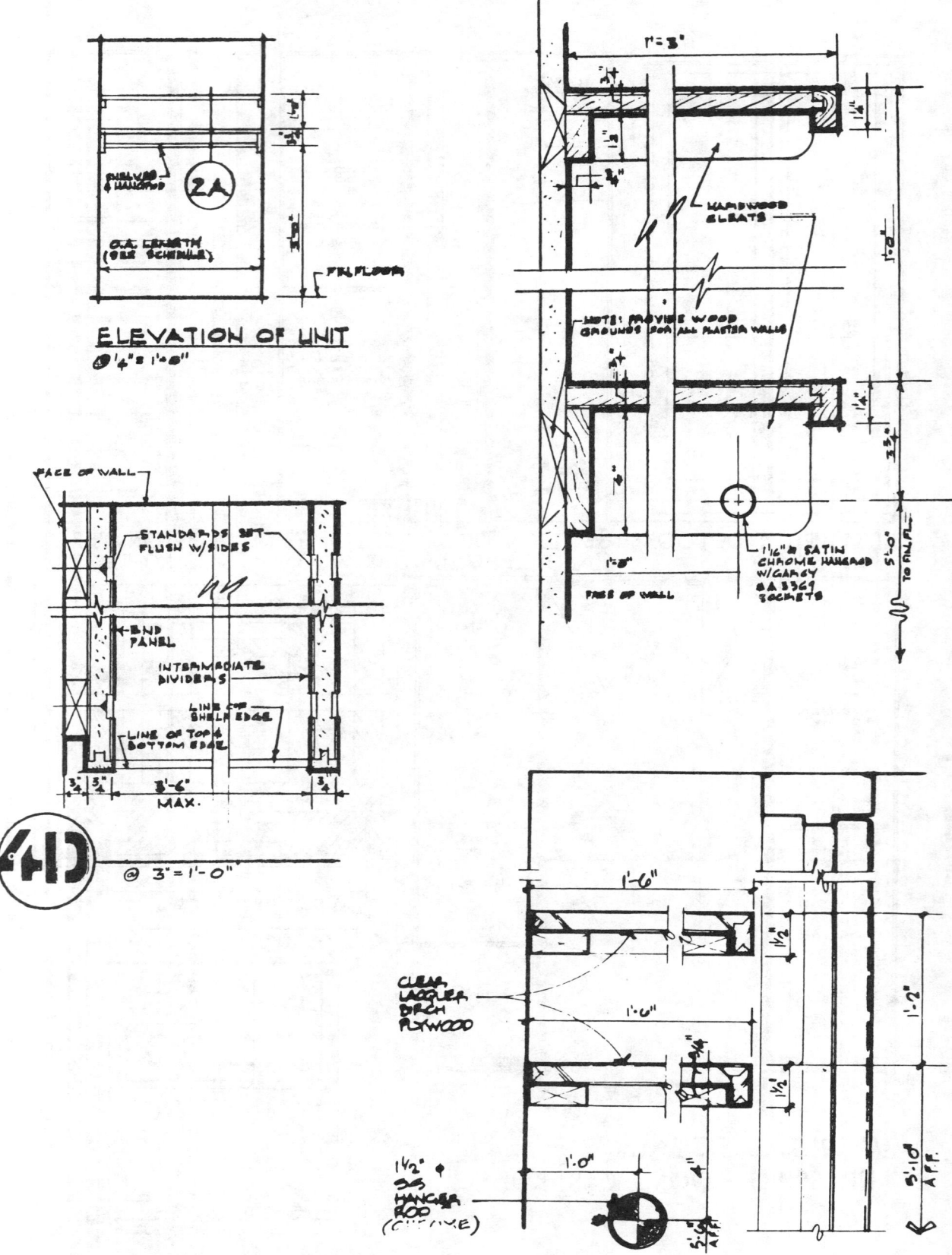

ELEVATION OF UNIT
@ 1/4" = 1'-0"

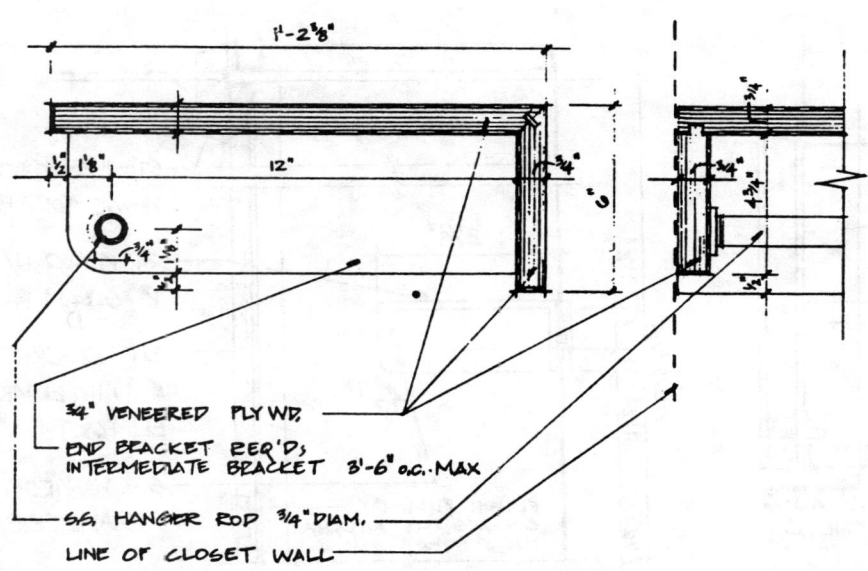

3/4" VENEERED PLY WD.

END BRACKET REQ'D;
INTERMEDIATE BRACKET 3'-6" O.C. MAX

S.S. HANGER ROD 3/4" DIAM.

LINE OF CLOSET WALL

CLOSET SHELF DETAIL

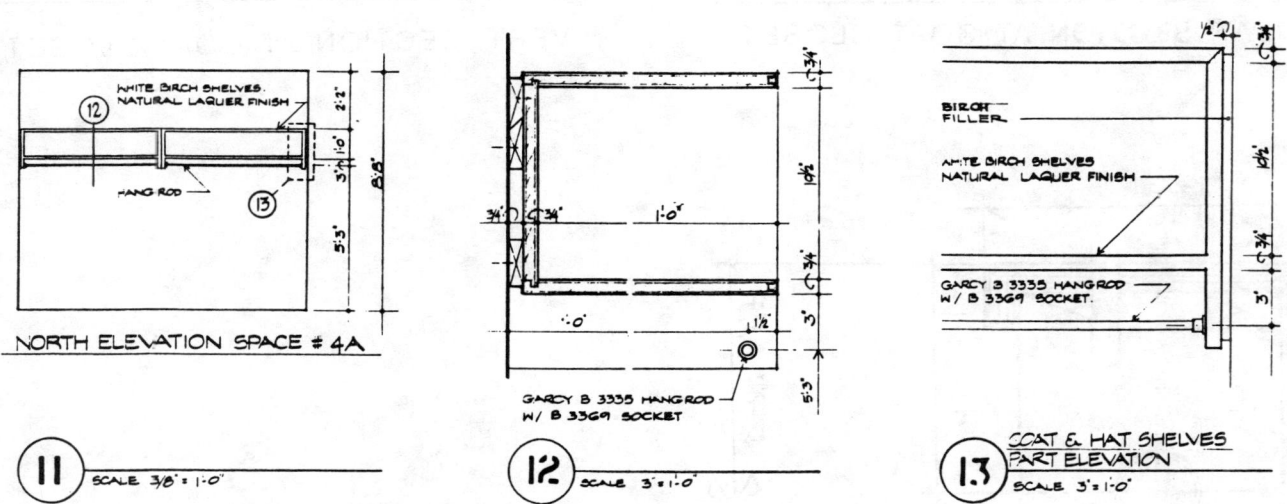

NORTH ELEVATION SPACE # 4A

WHITE BIRCH SHELVES.
NATURAL LAQUER FINISH

HANG ROD

GARCY B 3335 HANGROD
W/ B 3369 SOCKET

BIRCH
FILLER

WHITE BIRCH SHELVES
NATURAL LAQUER FINISH

GARCY B 3335 HANGROD
W/ B 3369 SOCKET.

COAT & HAT SHELVES
PART ELEVATION

(11) SCALE 3/8" = 1'-0"

(12) SCALE 3" = 1'-0"

(13) SCALE 3" = 1'-0"

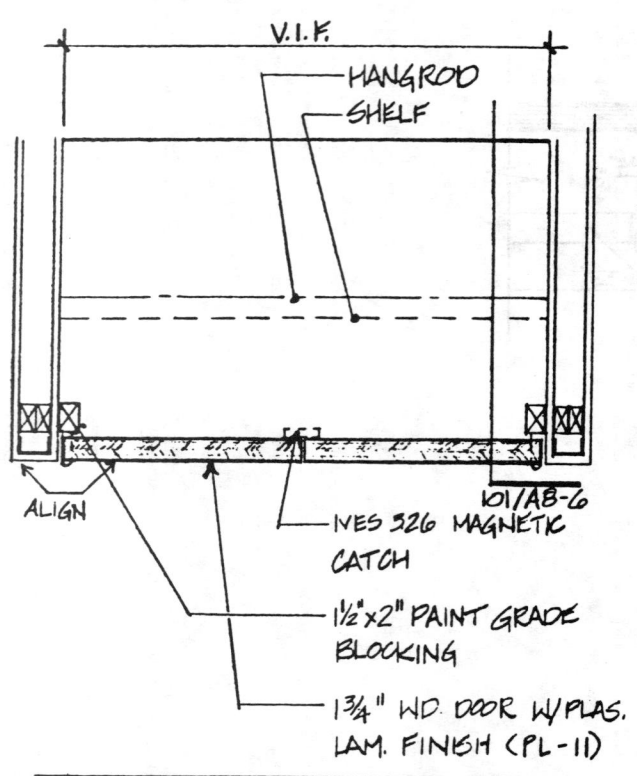

V.I.F.

HANGROD

SHELF

ALIGN

101/AB-6

IVES 326 MAGNETIC CATCH

1½" x 2" PAINT GRADE BLOCKING

1¾" WD. DOOR W/PLAS. LAM. FINISH (PL-11)

PLAN SECTION AT COAT CLOSET

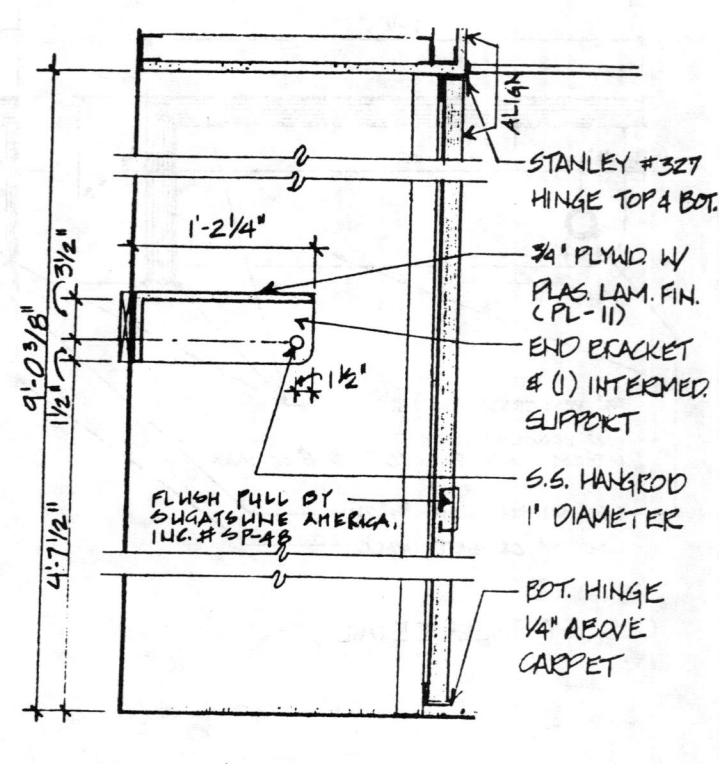

ALIGN

STANLEY #327 HINGE TOP & BOT.

¾" PLYWD W/ PLAS. LAM. FIN. (PL-11)

END BRACKET & (1) INTERMED. SUPPORT

S.S. HANGROD 1" DIAMETER

BOT. HINGE ¼" ABOVE CARPET

1'-2¼"

3½"

9'-0⅜"

½"

1½"

4'-7½"

FLUSH PULL BY SUGATSUHE AMERICA, INC. #SP-48

VERT. SECTION AT COAT CLOSET

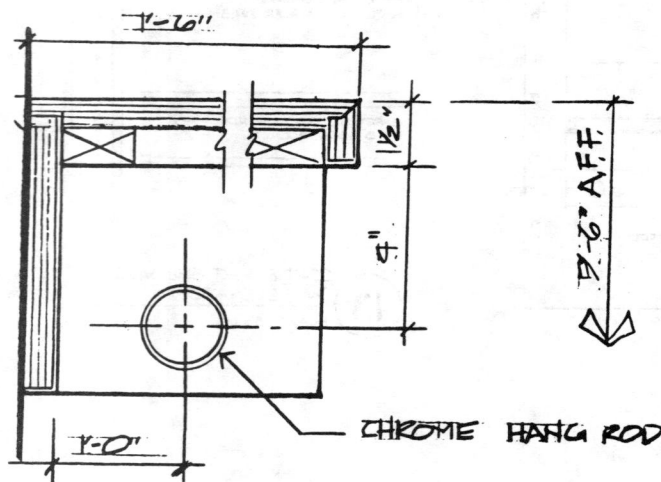

1'-6"

1½"

4"

1'-0"

7'-6" A.F.F.

CHROME HANG ROD

PROVIDE INTERMEDIATE SUPPORT FOR SPANS GREATER THAN 54"

COAT CLOSET SHELF

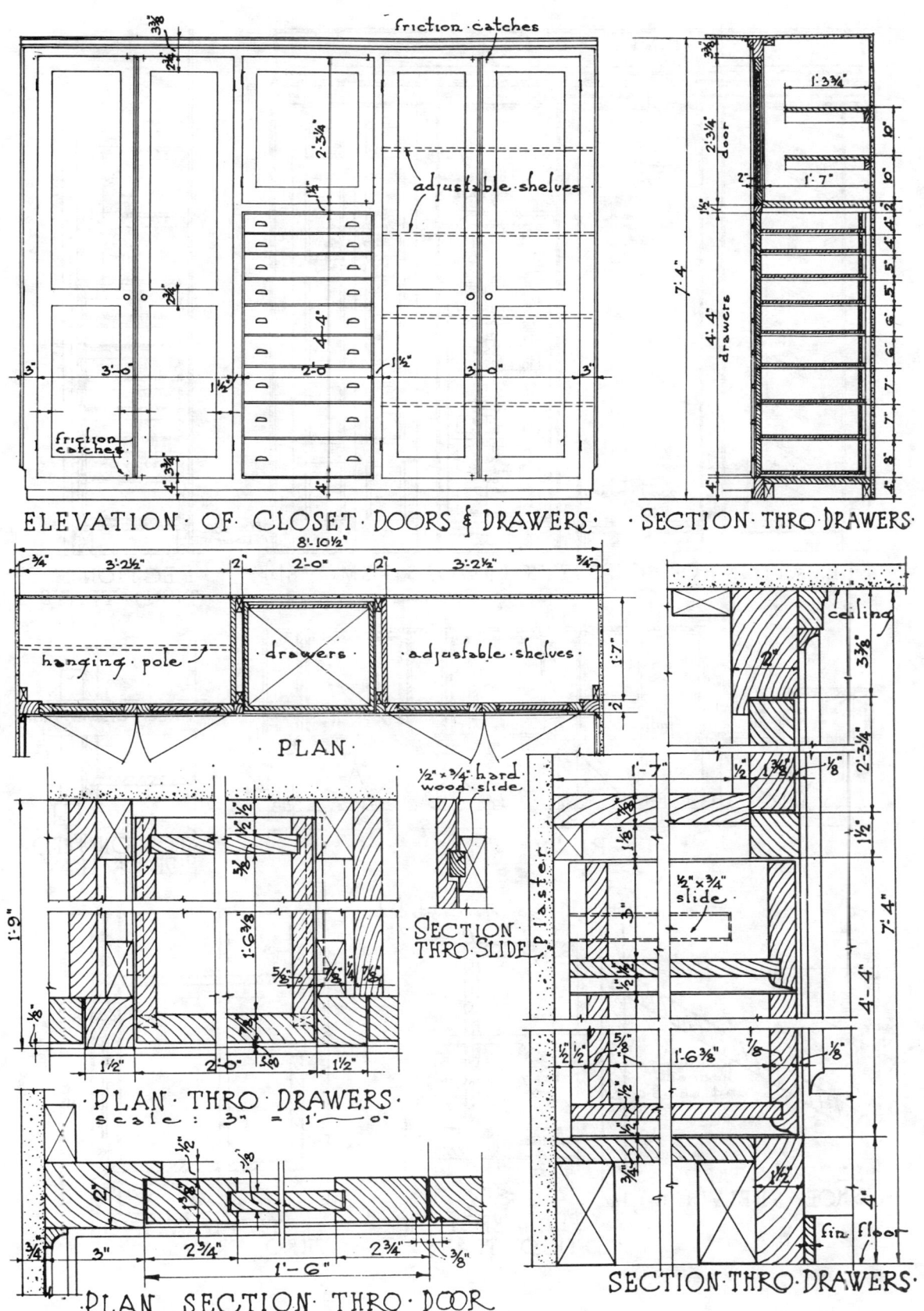

ELEVATION · OF · CLOSET · DOORS & DRAWERS ·

SECTION · THRO · DRAWERS ·

friction catches

adjustable shelves

friction catches

PLAN

hanging pole

drawers

adjustable shelves

ceiling

½" × ¾" hard wood slide

SECTION THRO SLIDE

½" × ¾" slide

Plaster

PLAN · THRO · DRAWERS ·
scale · 3" = 1'—0"

PLAN SECTION · THRO · DOOR

SECTION THRO DRAWERS ·

fin floor

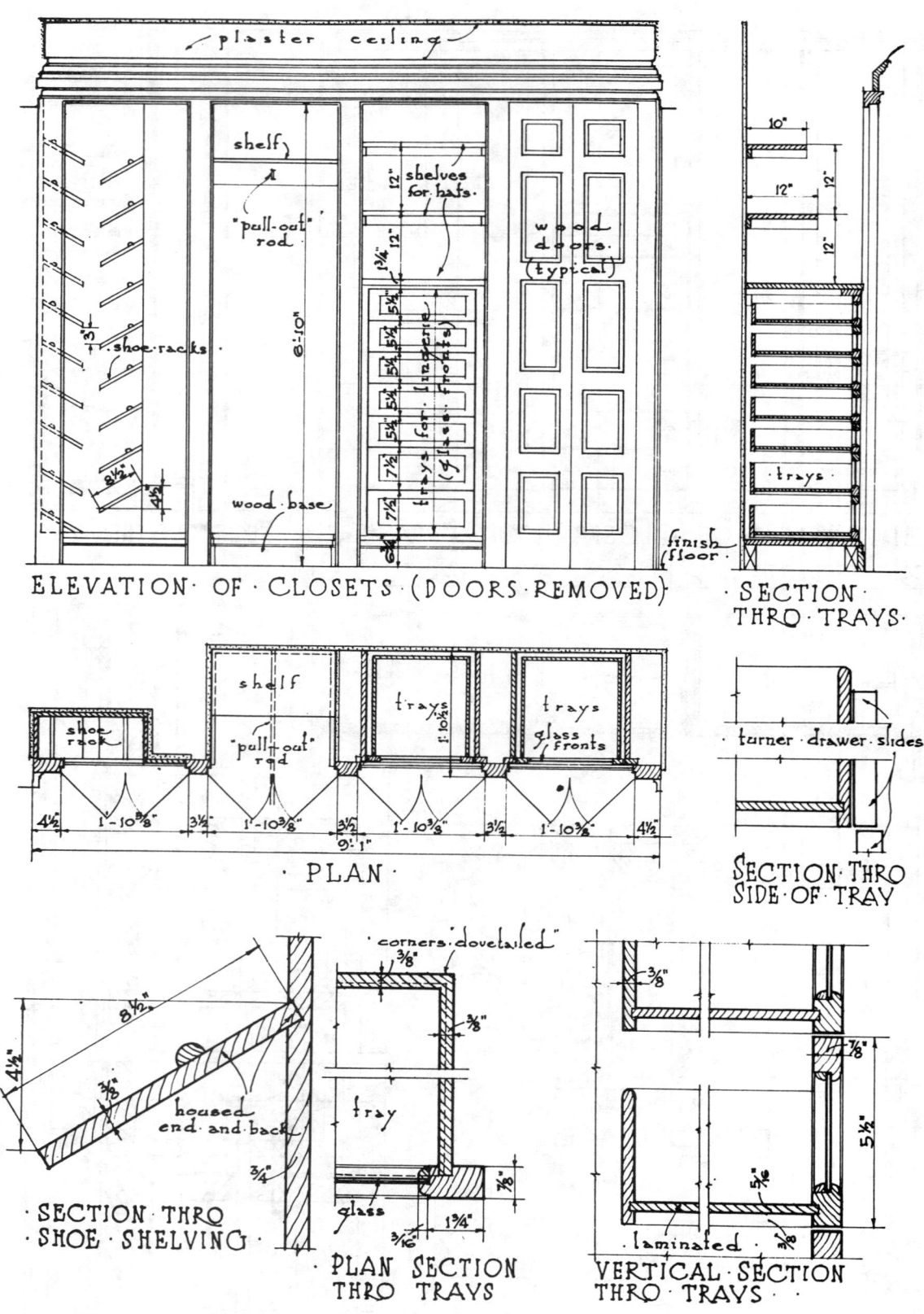

ELEVATION · OF · CLOSETS · (DOORS · REMOVED)

· SECTION ·
THRO · TRAYS ·

· PLAN ·

SECTION · THRO
SIDE · OF · TRAY

· SECTION · THRO
· SHOE · SHELVING ·

· PLAN SECTION
THRO TRAYS

VERTICAL · SECTION
THRO · TRAYS ·

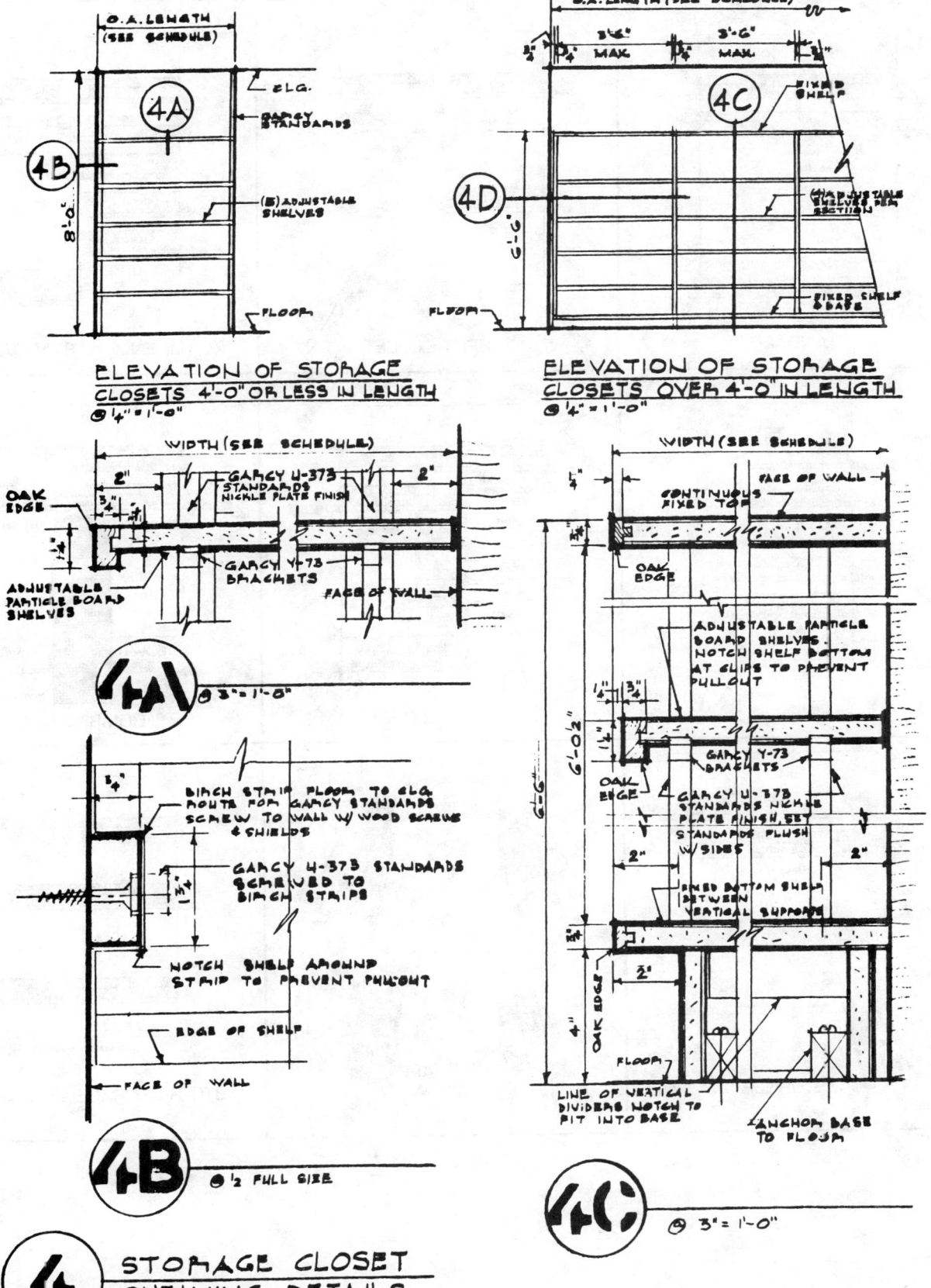

ELEVATION OF STORAGE
CLOSETS 4'-0" OR LESS IN LENGTH
@ 1/4" = 1'-0"

ELEVATION OF STORAGE
CLOSETS OVER 4'-0" IN LENGTH
@ 1/4" = 1'-0"

STORAGE CLOSET
SHELVING DETAILS

CLOSETS/STORAGE AREAS
Wire Basket and Shelving Systems

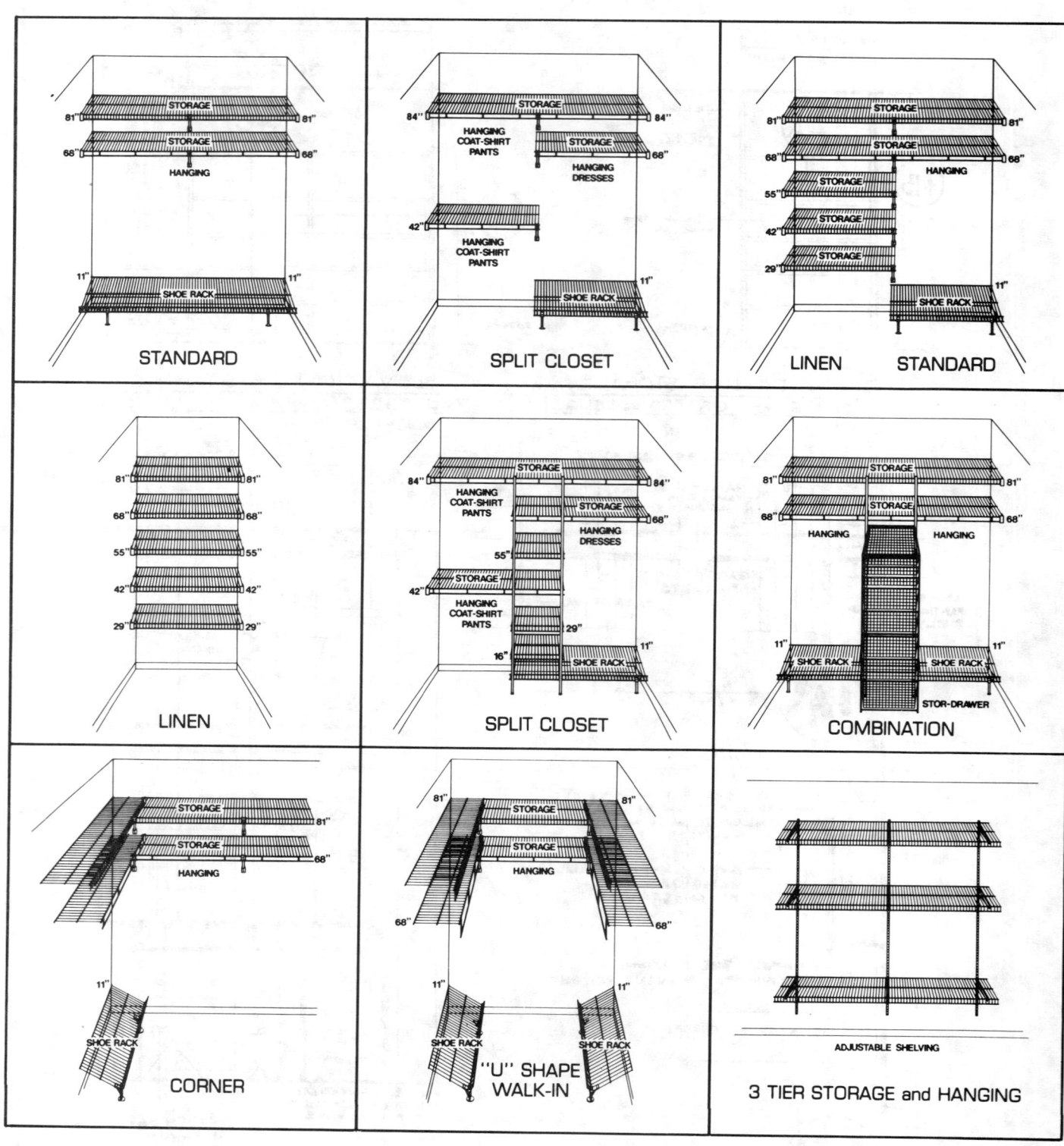

STANDARD

SPLIT CLOSET

LINEN   STANDARD

LINEN

SPLIT CLOSET

COMBINATION

CORNER

"U" SHAPE WALK-IN

3 TIER STORAGE and HANGING

PANTRY

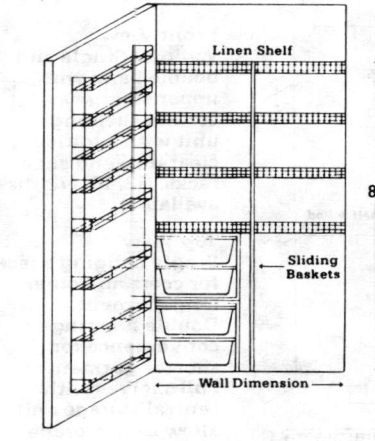

Front View
Multiple-stacked, wrap-around storage shelving. Optional baskets and door racks. (9", 12", 16" and 20" widths available)

Top View
All the shelving you'll ever need for full-size family food storage. Sliding baskets hold fruit, vegetables and other kitchen supplies. Optional door racks maximize storage area by utilizing all available space.

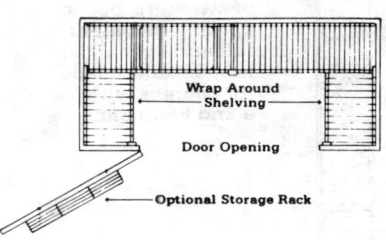

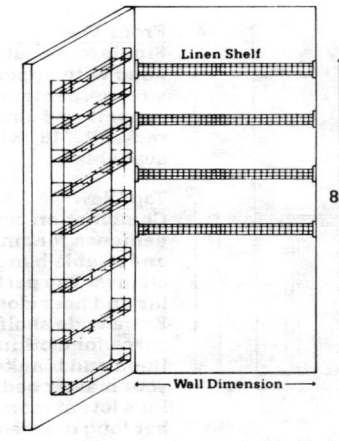

Front View
Multiple-stacked storage shelving. Optional full-height door storage rack. (9", 12", 16" and 20" widths available)

Top View
Standard pantry design provides ample shelving and storage for canned goods and other food items. Center pole gives extra support. Optional door racks provide easy access to your most needed items.

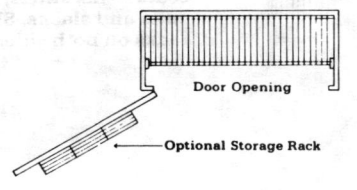

HOUSEKEEPING/UTILITY ROOM

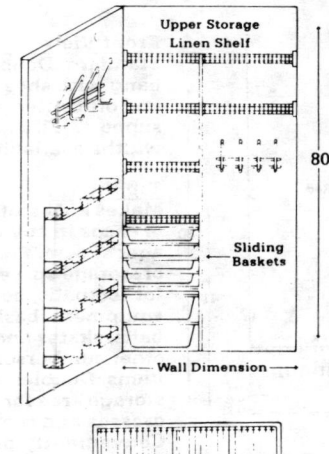

Front View
Double, full-width upper storage shelving with stacked storage shelving. (12", 16" widths available)

Top View
Makes housework easier to handle by storing household cleaning items just where you need them. Plenty of shelving space for cloths, detergents and brushes. Wide storage area holds vacuum cleaner, brooms, mops and small appliances.

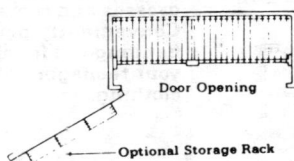

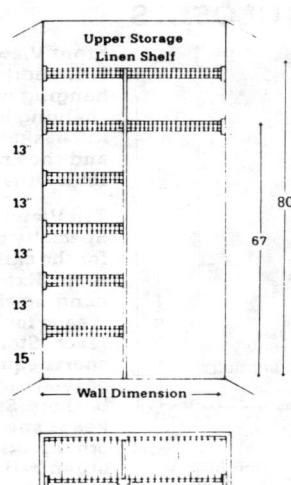

Front View
Double, full-width storage shelving with side-mounted shelving and basket unit and optional door/wall storage rack. (12", 16" widths available)

Top View
Make a clean sweep of cleaning with full-length shelves that hold a variety of utensils. Storage baskets pack brushes, cloths and sundry items. Bottled detergents and cleaning products can be stored neatly and safely in optional door racks.

BEDROOM APPLICATIONS

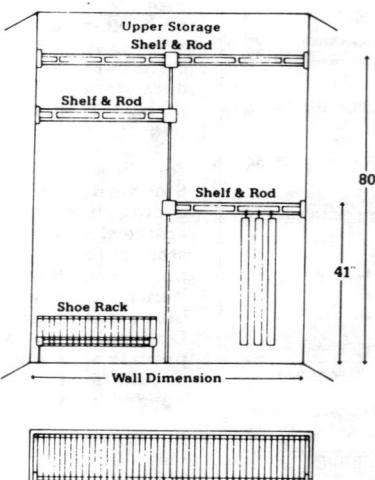

Front View
Single and double hang with upper storage, center pole support and shoe racks. (12", 16" widths available)

Top View
Combination convenience for single and double hanging clothes. The perfect his and hers closet. Extra wide shelf space for clothing, linen and blankets in your master bedroom. Plus lots of room for her long dresses and coats — his shirts, suits and slacks. Shoe racks on both sides.

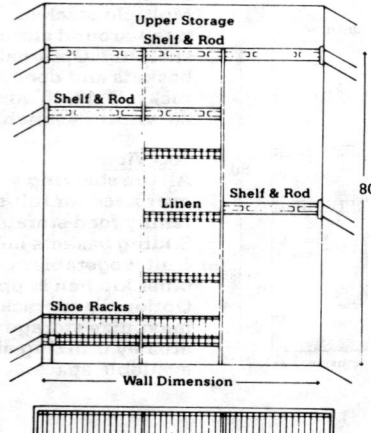

Front View
Walk-In. Single and double hang with upper storage and central shelving unit with additional clearance and shoe racks. (12", 16" widths available)

Top View
Single hanging space for coats and other long garments. Double hanging convenience for shorter garments. Full shelves with central storage unit allow easy storage of sweaters, boots, sports equipment, tall and over-sized items. Tailor-made for couples with a 2nd bedroom.

CHILDREN'S CLOSETS

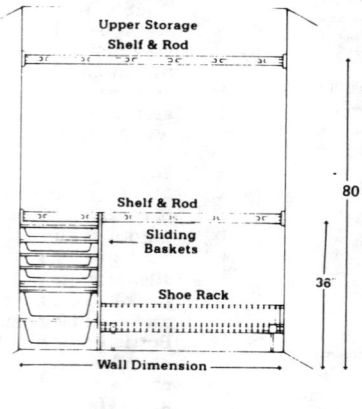

Front View
Full-width, double hanging with lower shelving height. Sliding basket system and shoe racks. (12", 16" widths available)

Top View
Specially designed for the children's room. Extra low-hanging shelf makes it easy for kids to reach. Stores toys and sports equipment in easy-access sliding baskets. Shoe rack keeps sneakers and other footwear neatly organized.

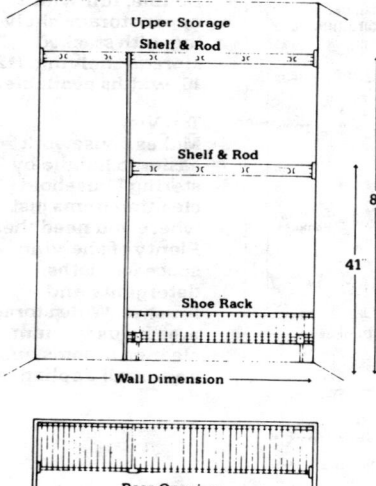

Front View
Standard. Double hang with shoe rack and off-center pole support. (12", 16" widths available)

Top View
Makes kids stuff out of chaos in any teenager's room. Plenty of storage space for footballs, beach equipment, basketballs, skates and other cumbersome items. Doubles as storage area for dresses and coats. Conveniently placed hanging rod for all your teenager's clothing.

LINEN

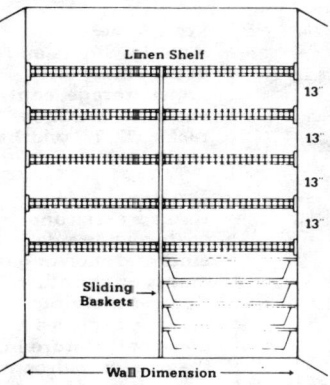

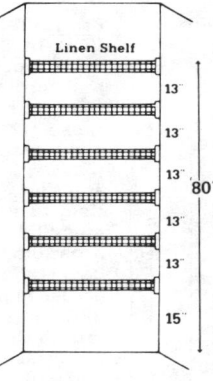

Front View
Multiple-stacked linen shelving with pole support and sliding basket system. (9″, 12″, 16″ and 20″ widths available)

Top View
Four extra-wide shelves for linen and blankets. Storage baskets slide out and hold dish cloths, pillowcases and smaller items. The perfect linen closet.

Front View
Multiple-stacked linen shelving. (9″, 12″, 16″ and 20″ widths available)

Top View
Bathroom linen closet stores towels, sheets and cleaning supplies in one easy-access area.

Door Opening

Door Opening

FOYER/FRONT ENTRY CLOSET

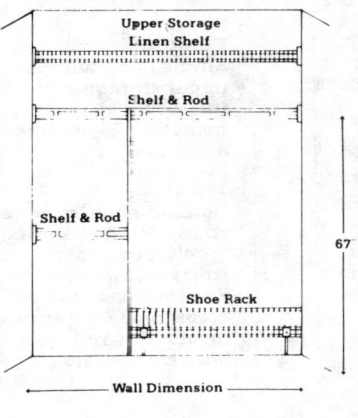

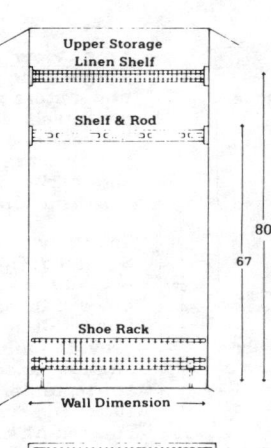

Front View
Single hang with upper storage and off-center storage unit and shoe racks. (12″, 16″ widths available)

Top View
A welcome addition to any home. Full-width, upper storage holds hats, gloves and sweaters. Off-center storage for umbrellas and winter items. Shelves, shoe racks and generous hanging space lets guests know they're welcome.

Front View
Single hang with half-length shoe racks and upper storage. (12″, 16″ widths available)

Top View
Holds coats, hats, shoes and guest clothing with care. Upper storage area for visitor's bags and small cases.

Door Opening

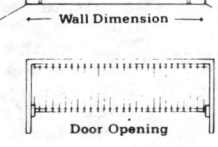

Door Opening

MASTER BEDROOMS

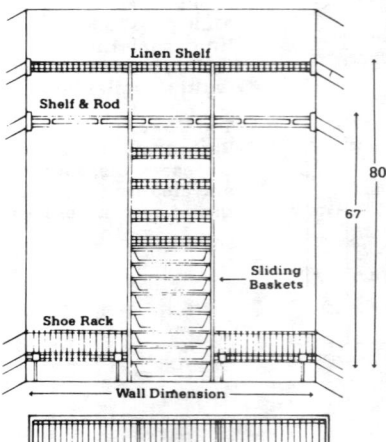

Front View
Walk-In. Single hang with upper storage and central shelving/basket unit and shoe racks. (12", 16" widths available)

Top View
Keeps shoes, shirts and clothing neatly organized. Sliding baskets for easy access to linen, underwear, etc. Full-length clothes storage for dresses, shirts and suits. Ideal for master bedroom.

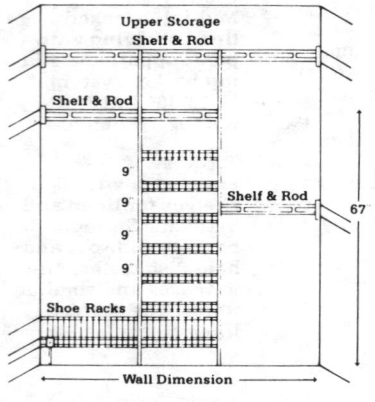

Front View
Walk-In. Single and double hang with upper storage, central shelving and shoe racks. (12", 16" widths available)

Top View
Hang dresses and coats on one side, suits and shorter garments on the other. Central shelving actually replaces a piece of furniture in the master bedroom!

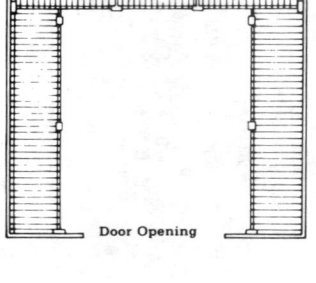

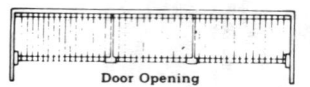

Front View
Single hang with upper storage and central shelving and basket unit, additional clearance and shoe racks. (12", 16" widths available)

Top View
So well designed it actually replaces a piece of furniture! Four sliding baskets provide multiple storage capacity for shirts, underwear, socks and sweaters. Full-length clothes hanging space, full-width shoe racks and lots of shelf space make this system a must for your 2nd bedroom.

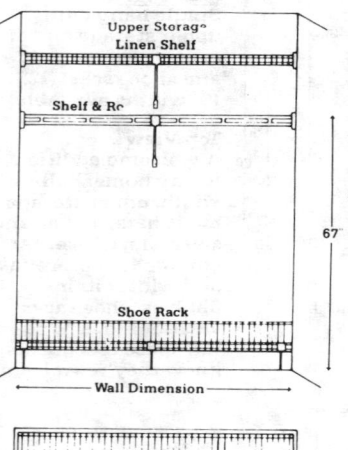

Front View
Single hang with upper storage and full-width shoe racks. (12", 16" widths available)

Top View
Doubles shelf/storage space. Single hanging for clothes, coats, shirts and jackets. Expands easily to accommodate future needs. Two full-length shoe racks.

Office Spaces

INTRODUCTION

The amount of office space built during the past few decades can be measured in the hundreds of billions of square feet. Within these buildings, workers spend nearly half their waking hours and a third of their entire lives.

Over the life span of a typical office building, the same spaces may be occupied by a succession of different tenants, each with their own programmatic requirements. Consequently, interior spaces may be recycled and redesigned many times, simply to accommodate the changing needs of new corporate users. In many instances redesign may be necessitated solely by the effect of technological change on the methodology of transacting business. Moreover, the escalating costs of land acquisition and construction and the increasing scarcity of urban building sites make it essential that the redesign reflects an efficient, cost-effective utilization of space, as well as one that is responsive to the human factors involved. It is necessary, therefore, for the designer to be familiar not only with the general planning criteria associated with office design, but with the architectural detailing of some of the typical interior elements contained within these spaces.

Accordingly, this section includes general planning criteria and examples of actual working drawings of typical interior conditions, prepared by various design professionals. The details alluded to include such items as trading desks, elevated computer floors, library furniture, built-in storage cabinets, work counters, wall paneling, vanities, reception desks, and conference room elements. Also included are illustrations and dimensional data pertaining to typical office furniture, equipment, and electronic media storage.

The so-called general office takes on a variety of forms and configurations. In its simplest variation it may be nothing more complex than several standard desks with returns located within a room or space. In its more sophisticated and ergonomically designed form, the general office may be based on an open planning or office landscaping concept, involving a system of workstations. The workstations include desk surfaces, files, acoustic partitions, and a host of other optional components to suit the nature of the particular work tasks involved. The systems are extremely flexible, allowing the workstations to be configured in a variety of shapes. Provision for power and lighting is quite common.

The design of the general office, like the design of the private office, requires a knowledge of the basic dimensional requirements and clearances of the workstation and, where applicable, of the visitor seating to be accommodated.

In certain instances, where customized and/or built-in storage elements, work coun-

ters, credenzas, etc., are required, a knowledge of architectural woodworking, as may be related to the design of such elements, can be quite helpful.

Accordingly, this part includes basic planning criteria for general office design, in addition to examples of architectural woodwork details in connection with some of the more common customized components of general office spaces.

The basic workstation, as illustrated in plan in Fig. 1, is the fundamental building block in understanding the anthropometric considerations for the planning and design of the general office. The worktask zone must be large enough to accommodate the paperwork, equipment, and other accessories that support the user's function. The work/activity zone dimension, shown in Fig. 1, is established by the space requirements needed for use of the typical return. In no case should this distance be less than the 30 in, or 76.2 cm, needed to provide adequate space for the chair clearance zone. The visitor seating zone, ranging in depth from 30 to 42 in, or

76.2 to 106.7 cm, requires the designer to accommodate both the buttock-knee and buttock-toe length body dimensions of the larger user. If an overhang is provided or the desk's modesty panel is recessed, the visitor seating zone can be reduced due to the additional knee and toe clearances provided. The specific type and size of the seating (i.e., if it swivels or if it has casters) also influence these dimensions.

Figure 2 shows the typical workstation expanded into the basic U-shaped configuration. The work/activity zone dimension range is shown as 46 to 58 in, or 116.8 to 147.3 cm additional space is needed to allow for drawer extension of the lateral file. Not only does it provide more storage, the lateral file unit is generally the same height as that of the worksurface and is often utilized as a supplementary worksurface. The distance between this unit and that of the primary worksurface must be sufficient to allow for movement and rotation of the chair.

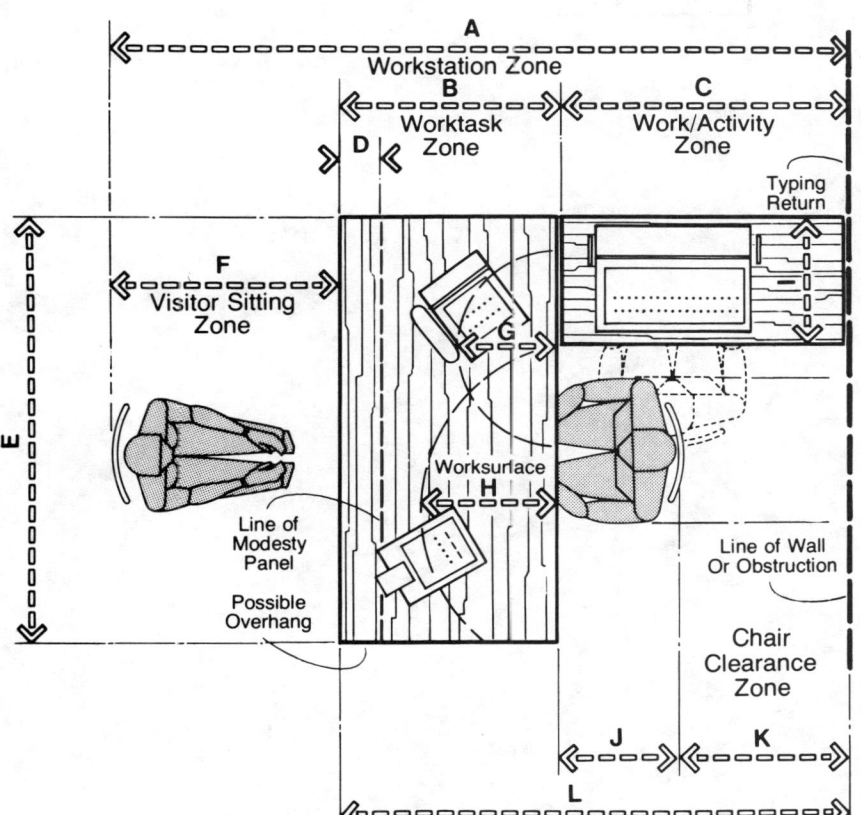

Fig. 1   Basic workstation with visitor seating.

	in	cm
A	90–126	228.6–320.0
B	30–36	76.2–91.4
C	30–48	76.2–121.9
D	6–12	15.2–30.5
E	60–72	152.4–182.9
F	30–42	76.2–106.7
G	14–18	35.6–45.7
H	16–20	40.6–50.8
I	18–22	45.7–55.9
J	18–24	45.7–61.0
K	6–24	15.2–61.0
L	60–84	152.4–213.4
M	24–30	61.0–76.2
N	29–30	73.7–76.2
O	15–18	38.1–45.7

GENERAL OFFICES AND MULTIPLE WORKSTATIONS

Planning Data: Basic Workstations

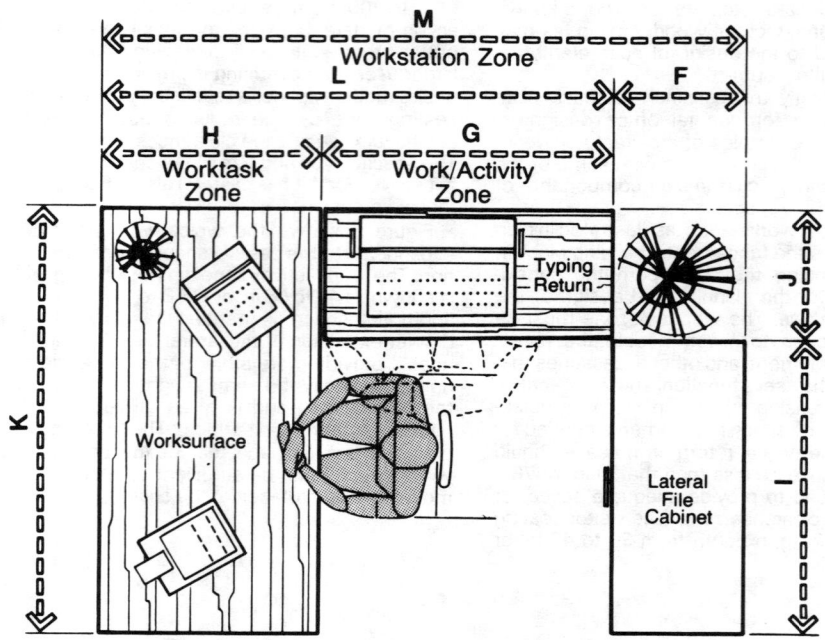

	in	cm
A	26–27	66.0–68.6
B	14–20	35.6–50.8
C	7.5 min.	19.1 min
D	29–30	73.7–76.2
E	7 min.	17.8 min.
F	18–24	45.7–61.0
G	46–58	116.8–147.3
H	30–36	76.2–91.4
I	42–50	106.7–127.0
J	18–22	45.7–55.9
K	60–72	152.4–182.9
L	76–94	193.0–238.8
M	94–118	238.8–299.7

Fig. 2   Basic U-shaped workstation.

Minimum Square Footage Standards for the Open and Screened Workstation

The Nonautomated Task. *Square footage workstation standards for the nonautomated task are developed primarily according to task profile, equipment, conferencing, and privacy requirements.*

Open

No requirement of equipment or task for privacy, concentration

Screened

Privacy required for reading, working, thinking, calculating, meetings, confidential phone calls, elimination of visual and acoustical distractions

---

Task Profile: Processing paper on work surface with quick turnaround.
- Continued flow of material is processed as it arrives at the workspace and is passed on to either another function or to group storage.
- Storage for permanent files and reference materials minimal.
- Reference material accessed infrequently. Telephone tasks may require concentration.

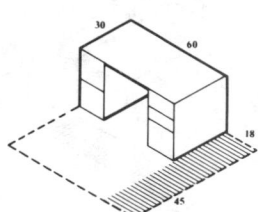
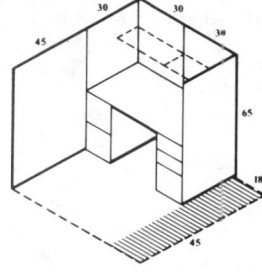

No	Guest chair
30 x 60	Primary work surface
(76 x 152 cm)	
No	Secondary work surface
3–4	File drawers
0–2	Shelves

41 sq. ft.

Task Profile: Typewriter the primary tool for processing paper.
- Continued flow of material is processed as it arrives at the workspace and is passed on to either another function or to group storage.
- Storage for permanent files and reference materials minimal.
- Reference material access may be frequent. Tasks may require concentration.

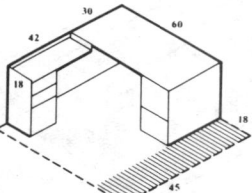
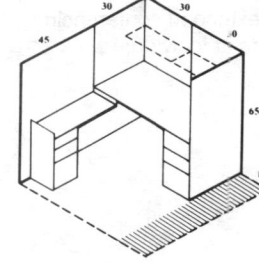

No	Guest chair
30 x 60	Primary work surface
18 x 42	Secondary work surface
(46 x 107 cm)	
3–4	File drawers
0–2	Shelves

41 sq. ft.

Task Profile: Typewriter the primary tool for processing paper.
- Continued flow of material is processed as it arrives at the workspace and is passed on to either another function or to group storage.
- Storage for permanent files and reference materials minimal.
- Reference material access may be frequent. Tasks may require concentration. Limited conferencing required at the workspace.
- Need to see and hear co-workers or subordinates of secondary priority.

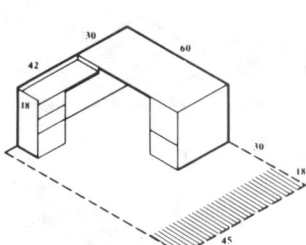
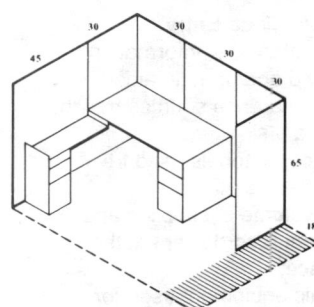

1	Guest chair
30 x 60	Primary work surface
18 x 42	Secondary work surface
3–4	File drawers
0–2	Shelves

56 sq. ft.

GENERAL OFFICES AND MULTIPLE WORKSTATIONS
Planning Data: Basic Workstations

The Nonautomated Task	**Open** No requirement of equipment or task for privacy, concentration	**Screened** Privacy required for reading, working, thinking, calculating, meetings, confidential phone calls, elimination of visual and acoustical distractions

Task Profile: Same as 1 with addition of extended conferencing requirements at individual workstation.

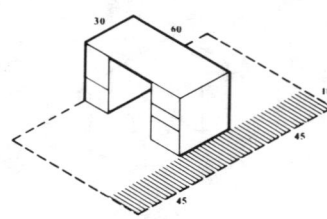

2	Guest chair
30 x 60	Primary work surface
No	Secondary work surface
3–4	File drawers
No	Shelves

65 sq. ft.

Task Profile: Same as 3 with addition of extended conferencing requirements at individual workstation.

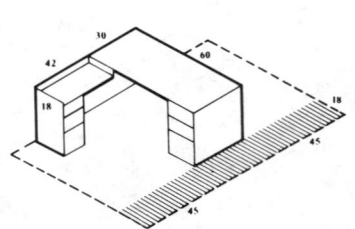
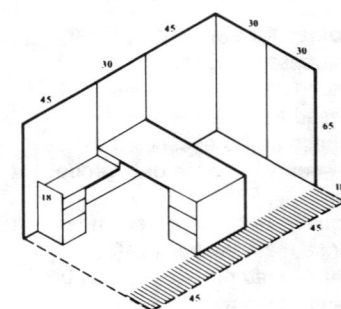

2	Guest chair
30 x 60	Primary work surface
18 x 42	Secondary work surface
3–4	File drawers
No	Shelves

65 sq. ft.

Task Profile: Data Entry.
- Paper, material, or information processed and/or maintained.
- Multiple reference sources may be used on a task.
- Reference materials used frequently.
- Limited volume of supplies and permanent records kept at the workspace.
- Electronic equipment used for keeping records current, information inputting, and maintaining data and records.
- Ability to see and hear co-workers may be desirable.
- Tasks may also require screening for concentration.

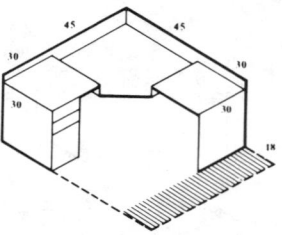
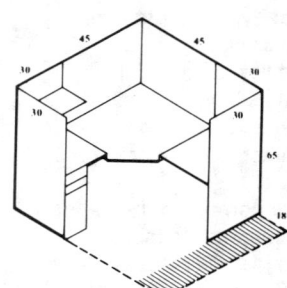

No	Guest chair
45 x 45	Primary work surface
(114 x 114 cm)	
30 x 30	Secondary work surface
(76 x 76 cm)	
1–2	File drawers
0–2	Shelves

48 sq. ft.

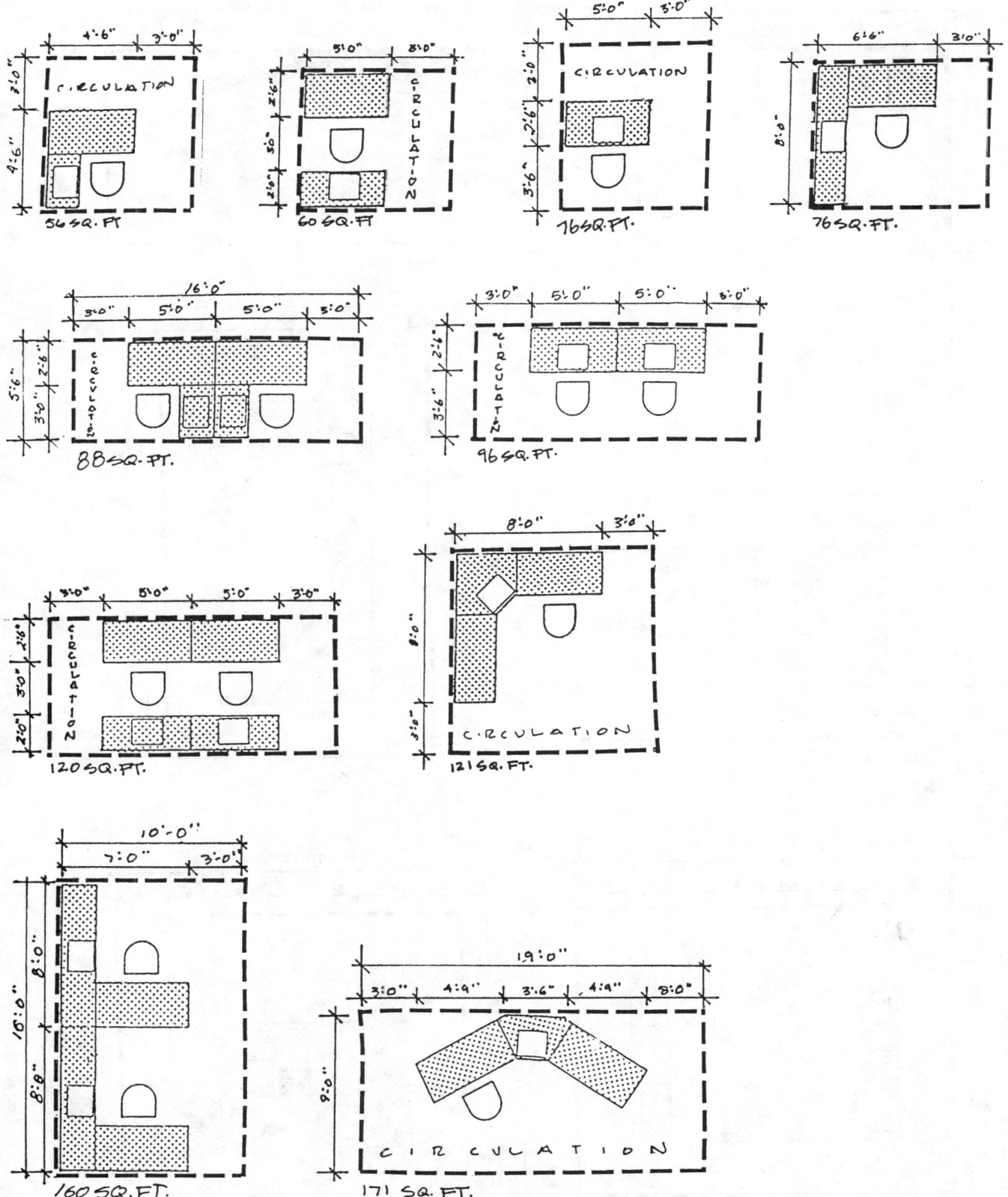

Fig. 3 Depending upon function, the sizes of individual and multiple workstations vary dramatically. Size of worksurface, length and depth of return, chair size, and circulation patterns all influence the gross square footage requirements.

GENERAL OFFICES AND MULTIPLE WORKSTATIONS

Planning Data: Multiple Workstations

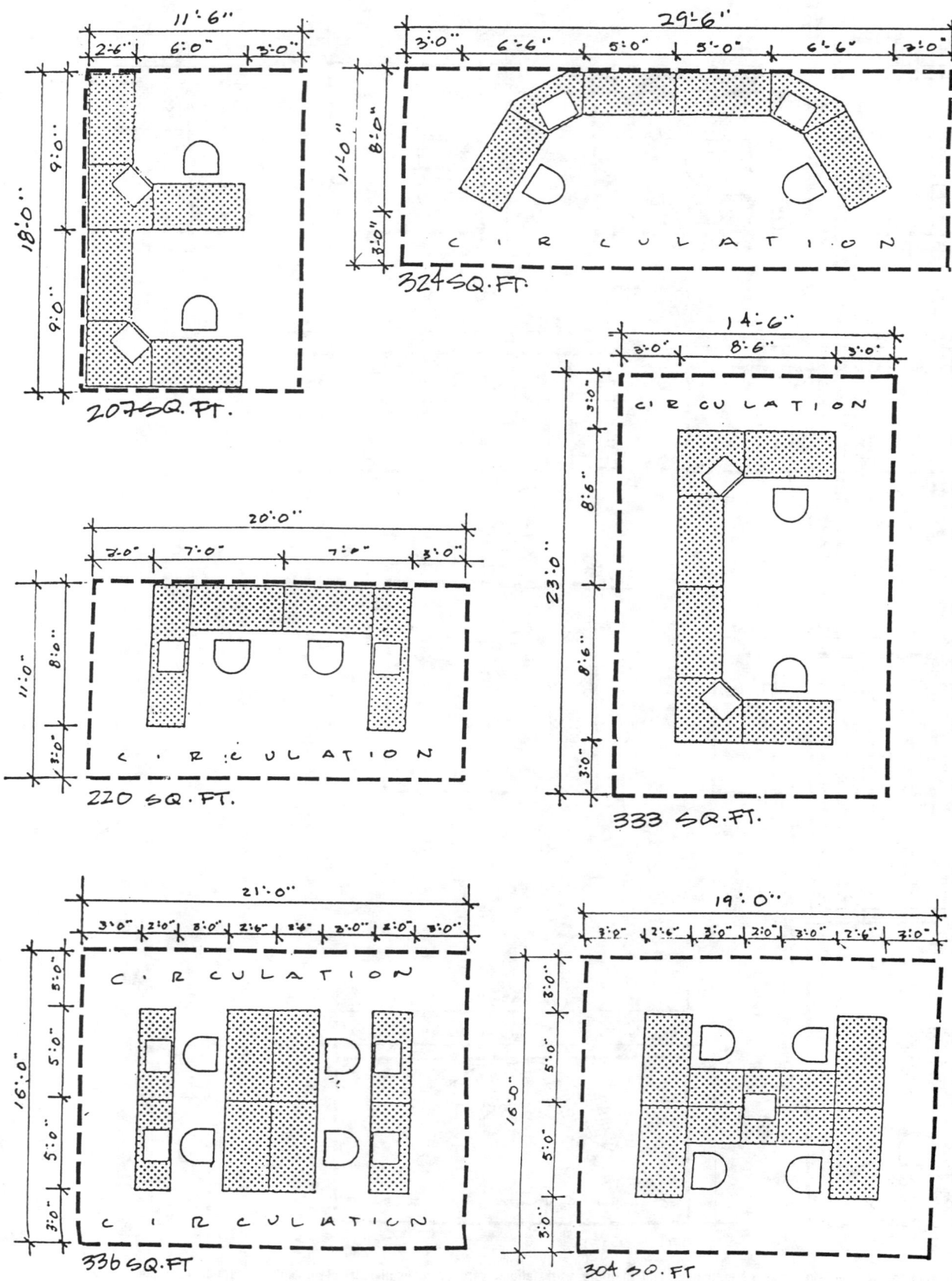

Fig. 4 Floating or free-standing workstations tend to utilize more floor area than workstations placed against a wall or sharing the same wall panel. Clustering of workstations will ultimately result in the use of less floor area, but at the expense of major ergonomic considerations. Decisions relative to both acoustical privacy and personal space are often sacrificed in the name of economy.

GENERAL OFFICES AND MULTIPLE WORKSTATIONS
Planning Data: Multiple Workstations

Multiple workstations can result in efficient utilization of space and sharing of expensive computer terminals and equipment. If use of computer terminals is intensive, individual CRTs should be provided. Figures 5, 6, and 7 each show eight workstations, yet the setups range in area from 448 to 1012 ft². Furniture size, function, and ergonomic considerations all affect setup.

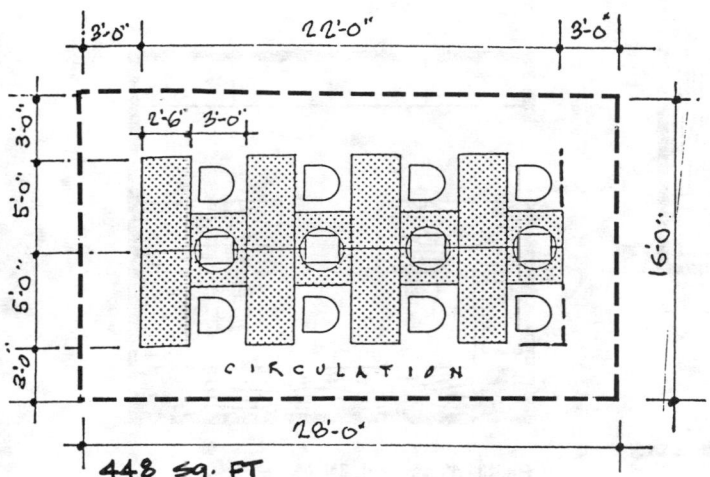

448 SQ. FT

Fig. 5

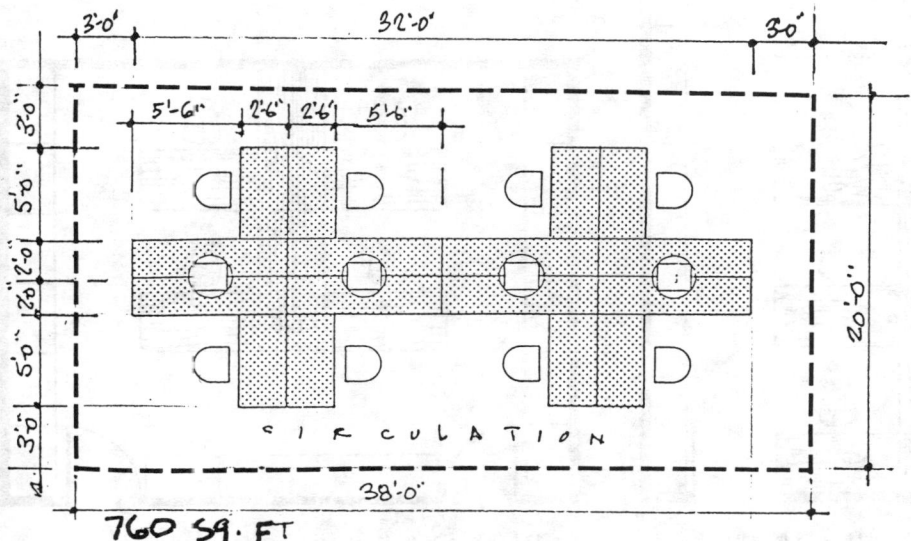

760 SQ. FT

Fig. 6

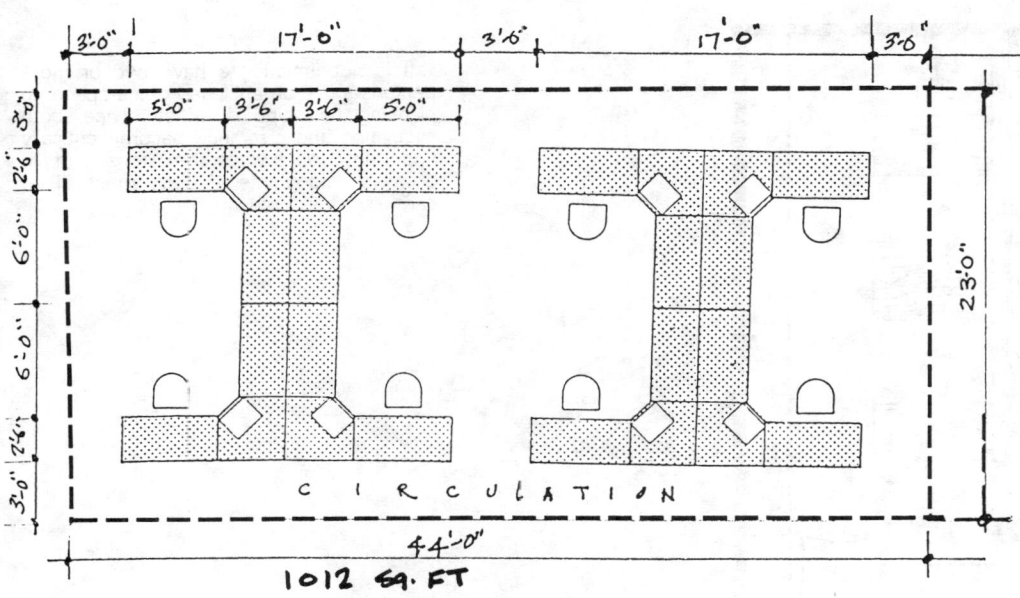

1012 SQ. FT

Fig. 7

GENERAL OFFICES AND MULTIPLE WORKSTATIONS

Planning Data: Office Layout

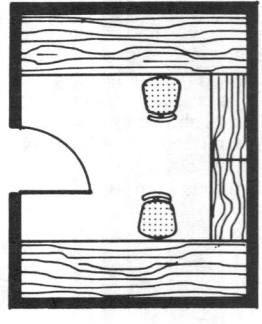

Fig. 8   9 ft × 12 ft, 108 ft².

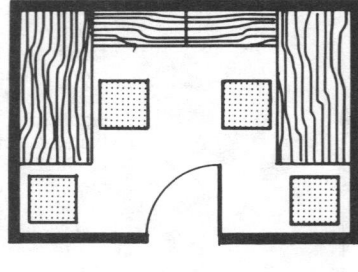

Fig. 9   9 ft × 14 ft, 126 ft².

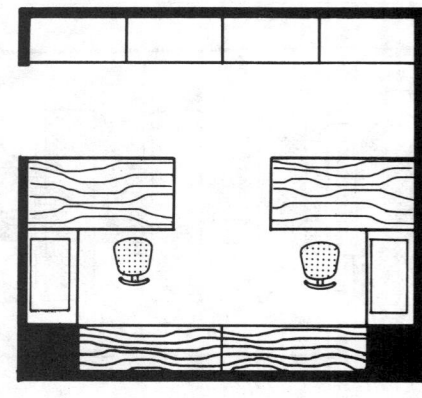

Fig. 10   15 ft × 16 ft, 240 ft².

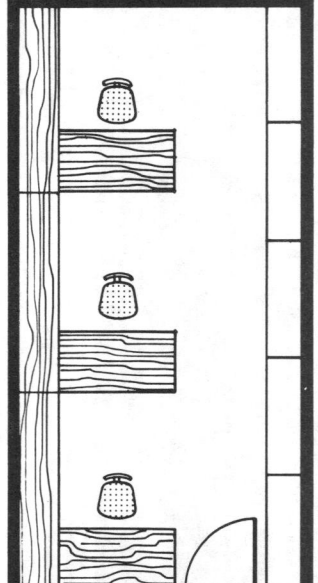

Fig. 11   12 ft × 25 ft, 300 ft².

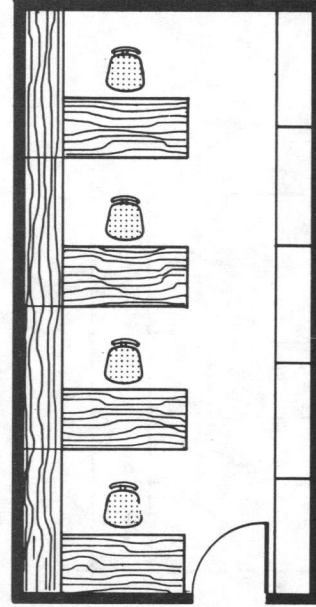

Fig. 12   12 ft × 25 ft, 300 ft².

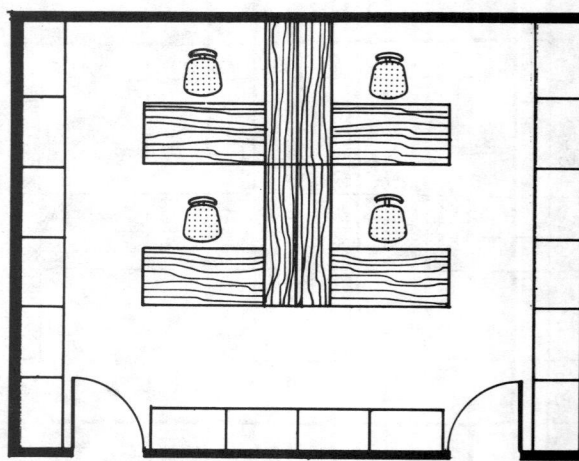

Fig. 13   18 ft × 25 ft, 414 ft².

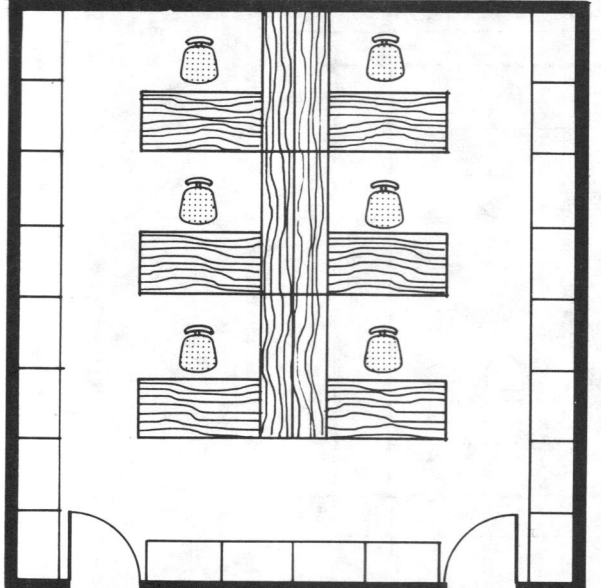

Fig. 14   24 ft × 23 ft, 552 ft².

It is not unusual to have two or more persons share an enclosed office space. In planning this type of office space, both circulation and clearance become critically important. Door swings, the extension of file drawers, and points of entry must all be carefully considered.

The design of the private office requires a knowledge of the basic dimensional requirements and clearances of the executive workstation and, where applicable, of visitor seating accommodations. In certain instances where various aspects of the office interior are customized and/or built into the construction, a knowledge of architectural woodwork detailing is also desirable.

This page and the following pages include the necessary planning criteria required, as well as details of certain customized components.

Executive workstation and/or desk size and configuration can be customized depending on desired image, scale, and ambience. Desks are also available in generally accepted standard sizes. It is these standard desks that are most used in the design of the private office. Figure 1 illustrates the range of desk dimensions, chair dimensions, and clearances involved.

Many private executive offices are being designed with desks that do not conform

with the basic rectangular shape. Such a situation is illustrated in Fig. 2, which shows a circular executive desk. Such a desk is often selected if the executive in question plans to hold conferences within the office and prefers the psychology of having either visitors or employees gather around the worksurface in an egalitarian fashion. While a minimum desk size of 48 in, or 121.9 cm, is shown, this dimension is also influenced by the number of side chairs to be grouped around the desk.

A circular executive desk must be supported by supplementary credenza or file storage within easy reach of the executive chair. Side arm reach relative to the work/activity zone must always be studied carefully.

Figure 3 illustrates a typical circular lounge grouping found within an executive office. Providing for the appropriate leg clearance of 12 to 18 in, or 30.5 to 45.7 cm, is also determined by the sitting zone requirements. Buttock-knee length must also be considered.

	in	cm
A	30–39	76.2–99.1
B	66–84	167.6–213.4
C	21–28	53.3–71.1
D	24–28	61.0–71.1
E	23–29	58.4–73.7
F	42 min.	106.7 min.
G	105–130	266.7–330.2
H	30–45	76.2–114.3
I	33–43	83.8–109.2
J	10–14	25.4–35.6
K	6–16	15.2–40.6
L	20–26	50.8–66.0
M	12–15	30.5–38.1
N	117–148	297.2–375.9
O	45–61	114.3–154.9
P	30–45	76.2–114.3
Q	12–18	30.5–45.7
R	29–30	73.7–76.2
S	22–32	55.9–81.3

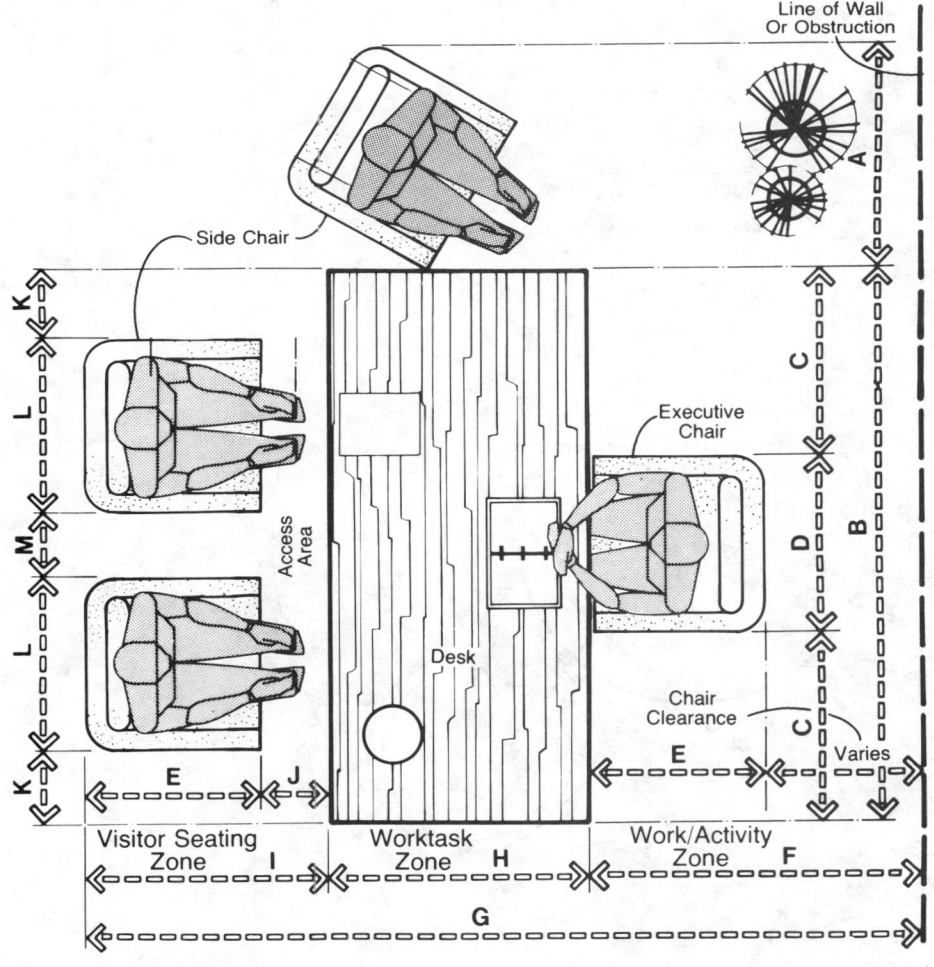

Fig. 1 Executive desk/visitor seating.

PRIVATE OFFICES

Executive Workstation

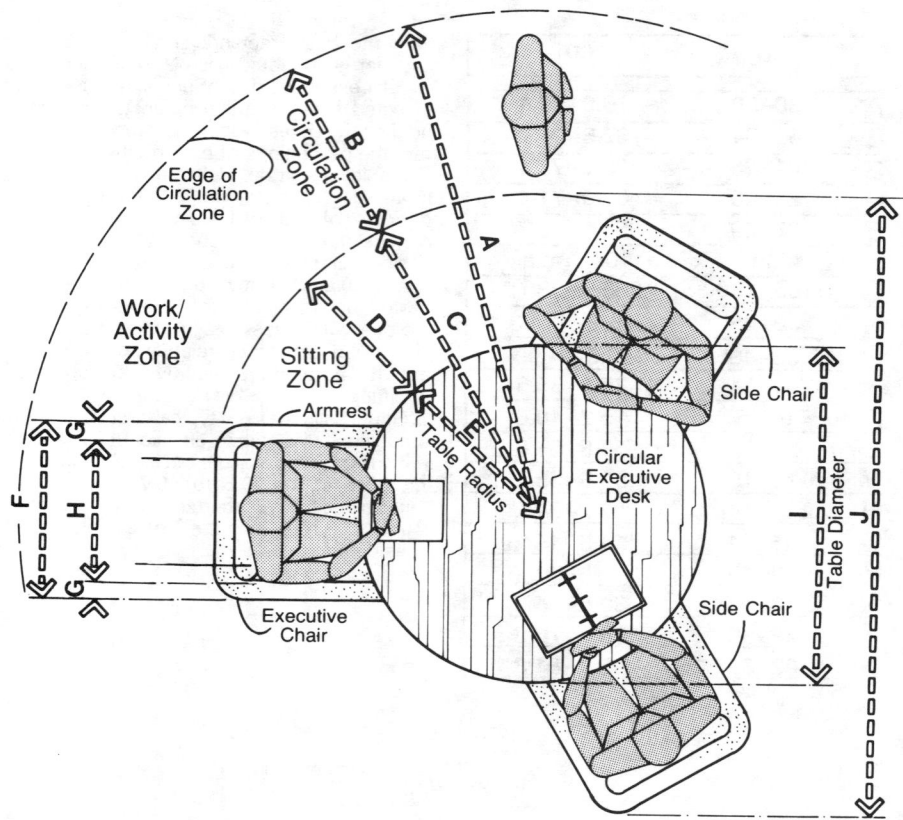

Fig. 2   Circular executive desk.

	in	cm
A	77–88	195.6–223.5
B	30	76.2
C	46–58	116.8–147.3
D	22–28	55.9–71.1
E	24–30	61.0–91.4
F	24–28	61.0–71.1
G	2–3	5.1–7.6
H	20–22	50.8–55.9
I	48–60	121.9–152.4
J	92–116	233.7–294.6
K	36–42	91.4–106.7
L	6–9	15.2–22.9
M	24	61.0
N	42–60	106.7–152.4
O	36–48	91.4–121.9
P	57–78	144.8–198.1
Q	33–48	83.8–121.9
R	12–18	30.5–45.7
S	21–30	53.3–76.2
T	24–32	61.0–81.3

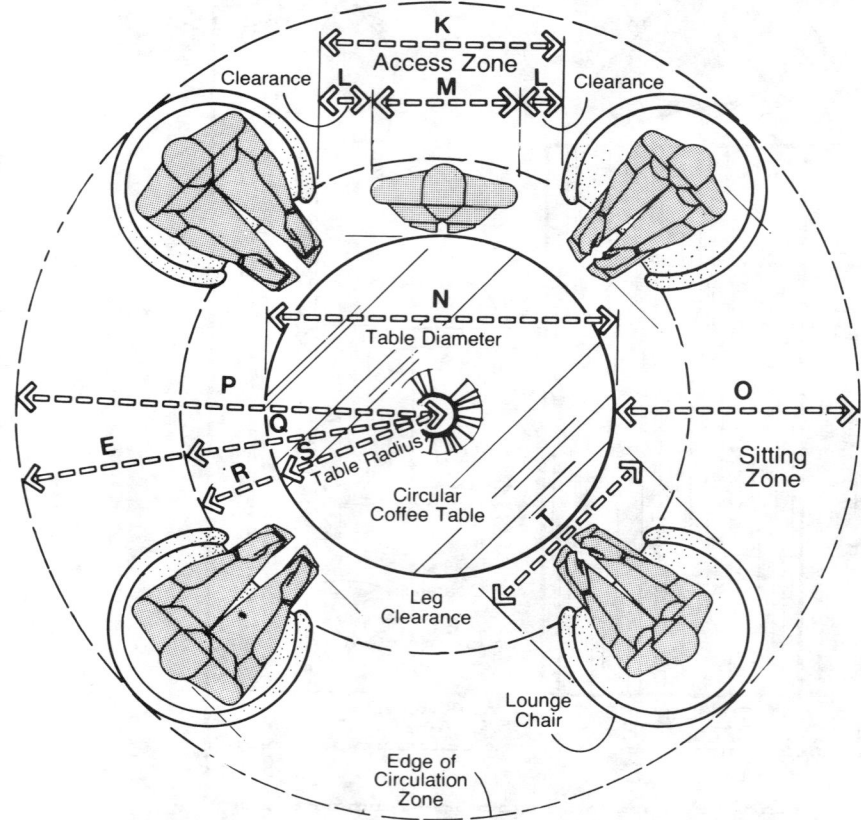

Fig. 3   Circular lounge grouping.

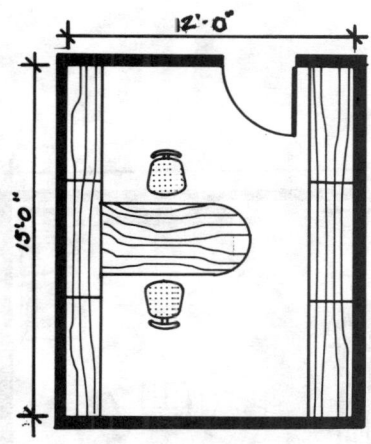

Fig. 4   12 ft × 15 ft, 180 ft².

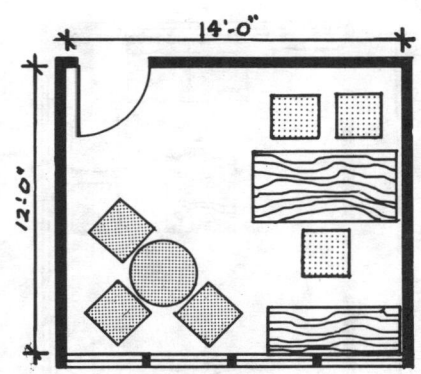

Fig. 5   14 ft × 12 ft, 168 ft².

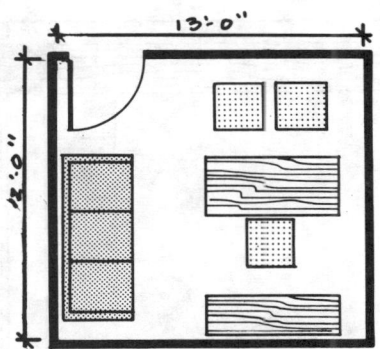

Fig. 6   13 ft × 12 ft, 156 ft².

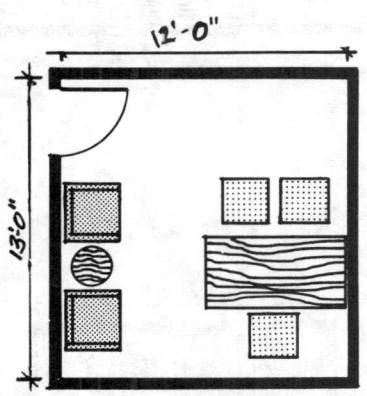

Fig. 7   12 ft × 13 ft, 156 ft².

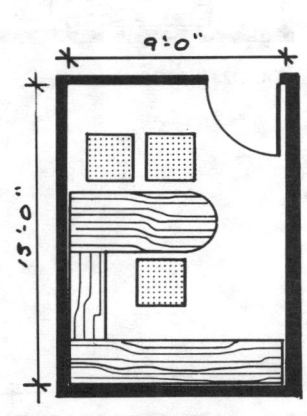

Fig. 8   9 ft × 15 ft, 135 ft².

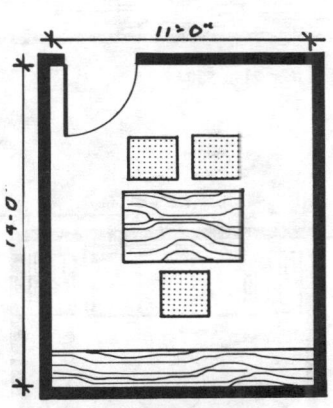

Fig. 9   11 ft × 14 ft, 154 ft².

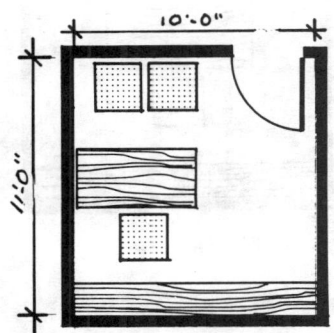

Fig. 10   10 ft × 11 ft, 110 ft².

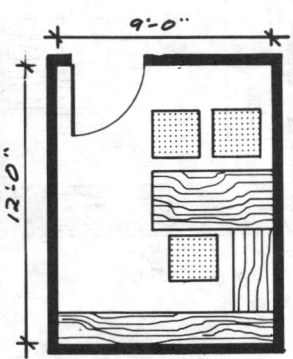

Fig. 11   9 ft × 12 ft, 108 ft².

PRIVATE OFFICES

Planning Data: Typical Room Arrangements

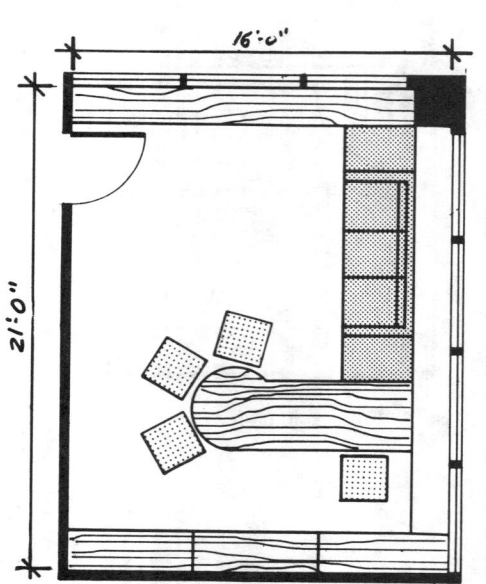

Fig. 12 16 ft × 21 ft, 336 ft².

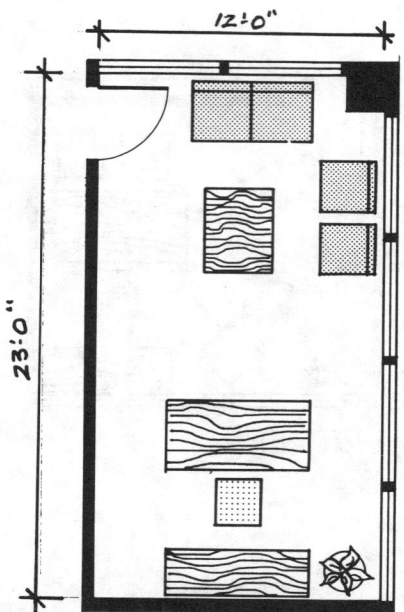

Fig. 13 12 ft × 23 ft, 276 ft².

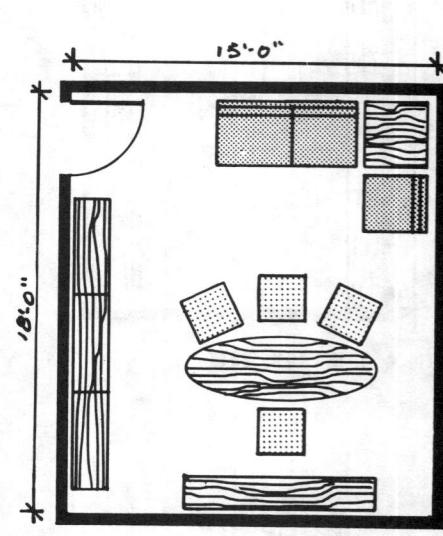

Fig. 14 15 ft × 18 ft, 270 ft².

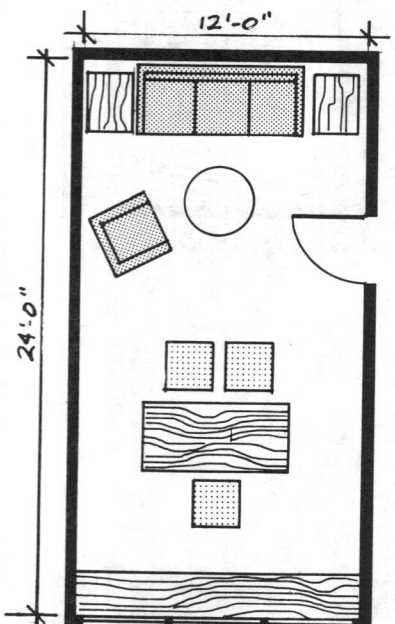

Fig. 15 12 ft × 24 ft, 288 ft².

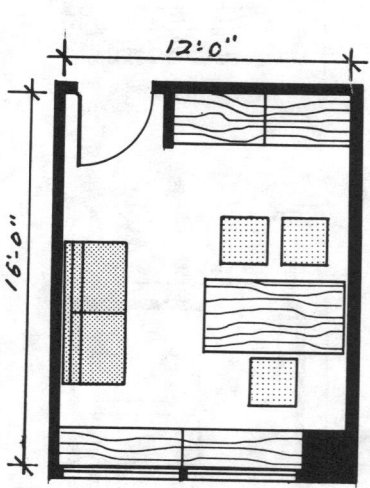

Fig. 16 12 ft × 16 ft, 192 ft².

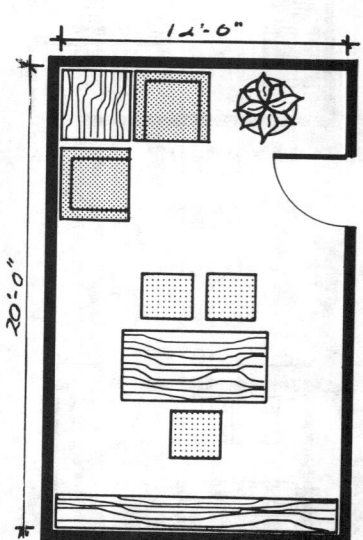

Fig. 17 12 ft × 20 ft, 240 ft².

The private offices illustrated in Figs. 12 to 17 reflect middle to senior management functional, as well as status, requirements. Each office layout should be carefully reviewed with the client to ensure that all programmatic functions have been met. Offices of this size do not easily accommodate an independent conference function.

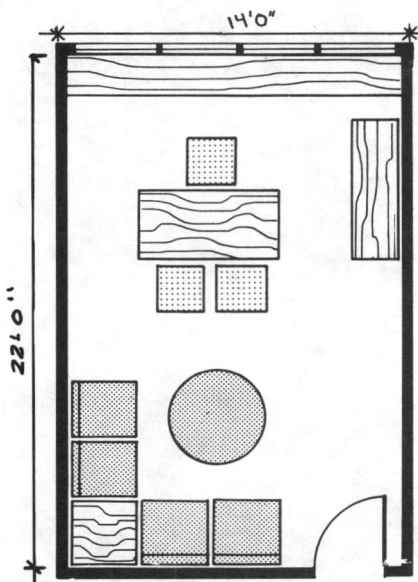

Fig. 18   14 ft × 22 ft, 308 ft².

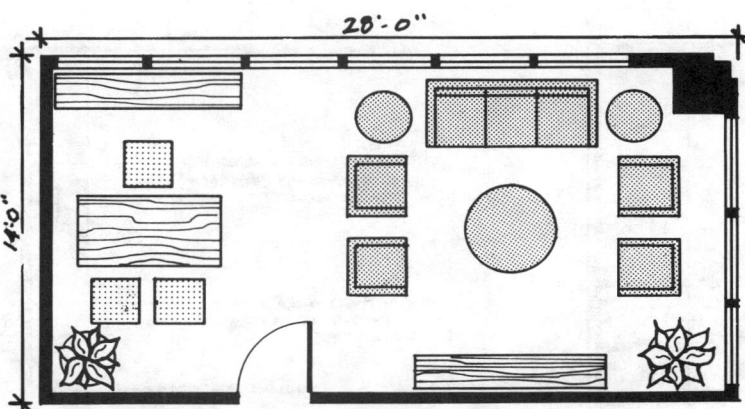

Fig. 19   14 ft × 28 ft, 392 ft².

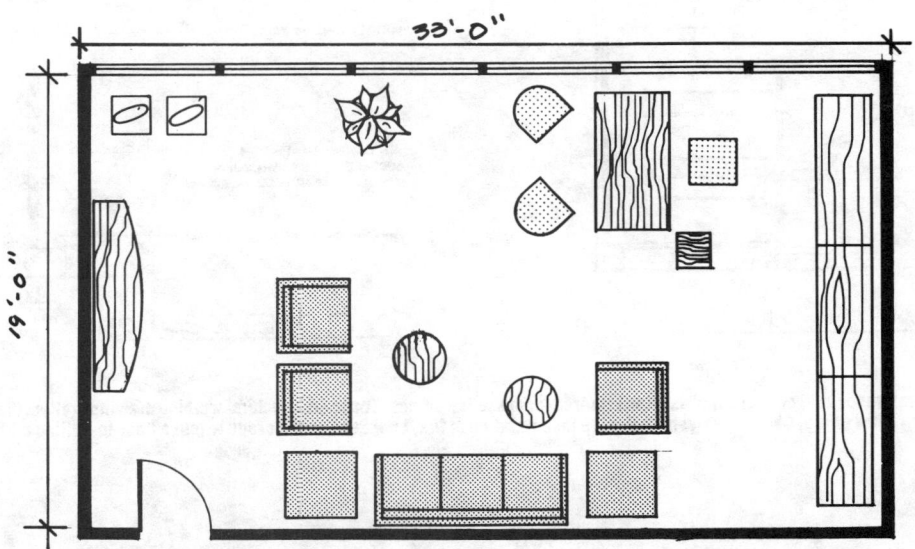

Fig. 20   19 ft × 33 ft, 627 ft².

PRIVATE OFFICES

Wall Unit Details

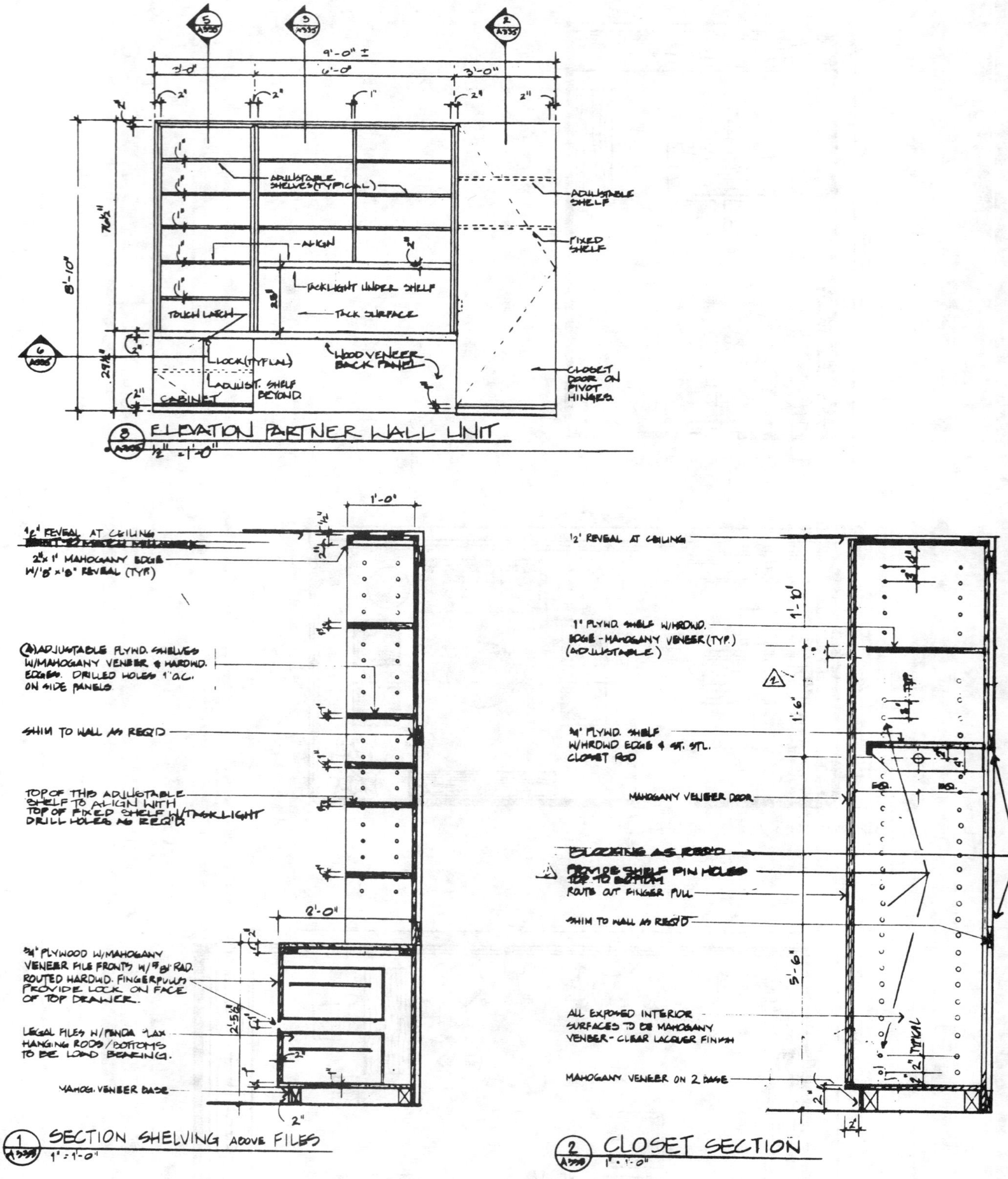

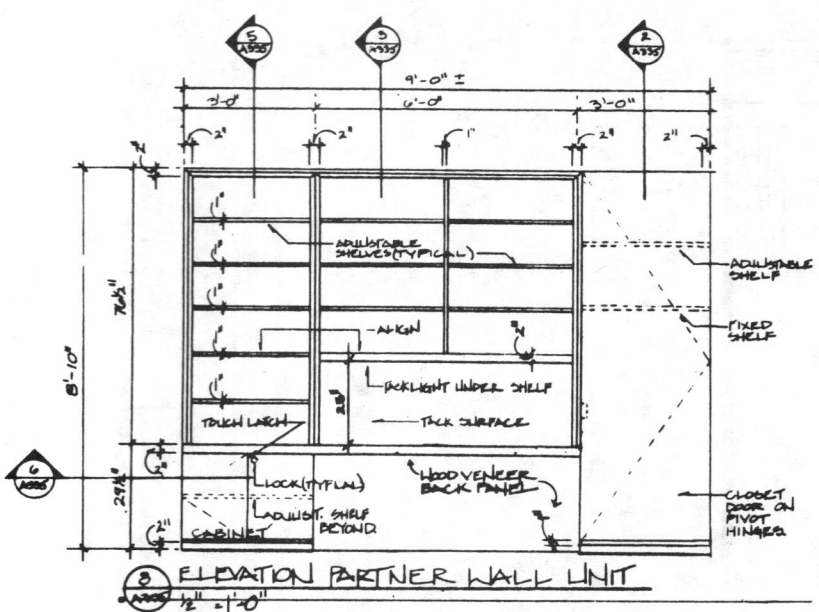

Fig. 21 Custom architectural woodwork, or "built-ins," is often required for executive offices. These architectural working drawings reflect the custom design of a storage wall for a partner in a law office. Careful analysis shows the incorporation of file, book, and coat storage within a floor-to-ceiling mahogany wood unit.

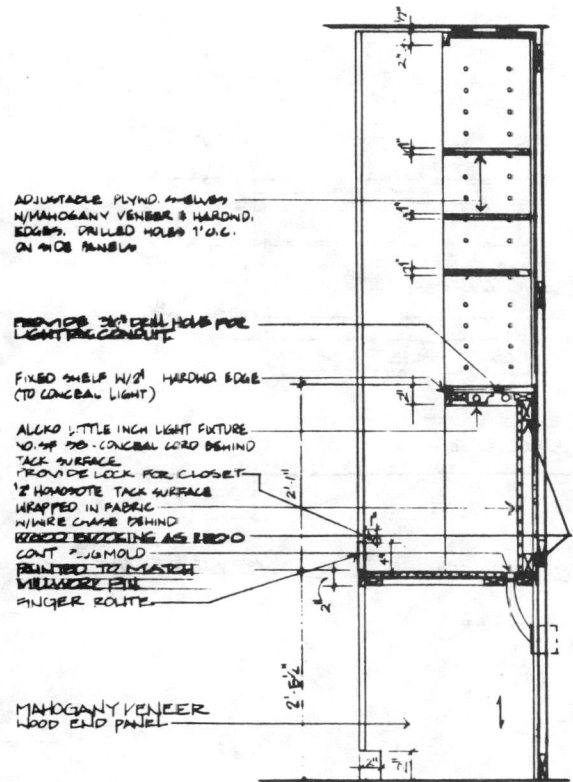

ADJUSTABLE PLYWD. SHELVES
W/MAHOGANY VENEER & HARDWD.
EDGES. DRILLED HOLES 1" O.C.
ON SIDE PANELS

PROVIDE 3½"Ø DRILL HOLE FOR
LIGHTING CONDUIT

FIXED SHELF W/2" HARDWD. EDGE
(TO CONCEAL LIGHT)

ALCO LITTLE INCH LIGHT FIXTURE
NO. 5# 5B - CONCEAL CORD BEHIND
TACK SURFACE
PROVIDE LOCK FOR CLOSET
½" HOMASOTE TACK SURFACE
WRAPPED IN FABRIC
W/WIRE CHASE BEHIND
WOOD BLOCKING AS REQD
CONT. ½" J&MOLD
PAINTED TO MATCH
MILLWORK FIN.
FINGER ROUTE

MAHOGANY VENEER
WOOD END PANEL

③ SECTION WALL UNIT
Ⓐ A399 1" = 1'-0"

½" REVEAL AT CEILING (TYP.)

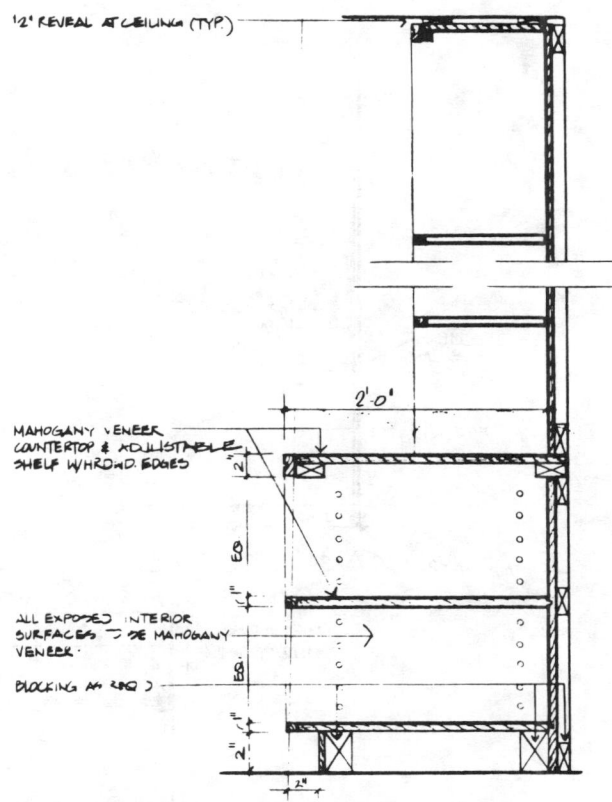

2'-0"

MAHOGANY VENEER
COUNTERTOP & ADJUSTABLE
SHELF W/HRDWD. EDGES

ALL EXPOSED INTERIOR
SURFACES TO BE MAHOGANY
VENEER

BLOCKING AS REQD

④ SECTION OPEN SHELVING UNIT
Ⓐ A399 1½" = 1'-0"

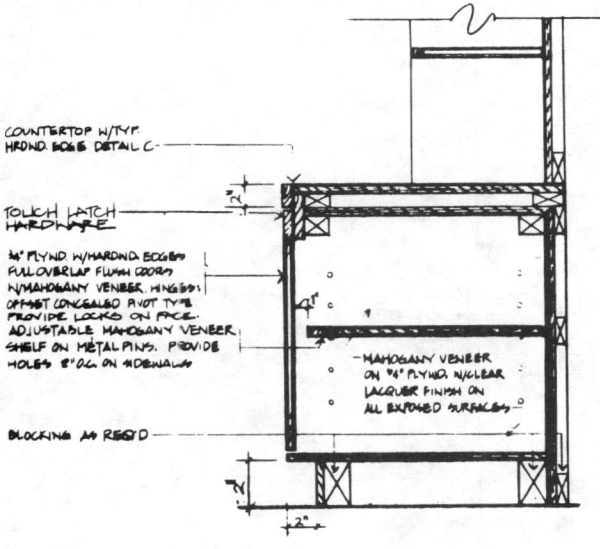

COUNTERTOP W/TYP.
HRDWD. EDGE DETAIL C

TOUCH LATCH
HARDWARE

¾" PLYWD W/HARDWD. EDGES
FULL OVERLAP FLUSH DOORS
W/MAHOGANY VENEER. HINGES
OFFSET CONCEALED PIVOT TYPE
PROVIDE LOCKS ON FACE
ADJUSTABLE MAHOGANY VENEER
SHELF ON METAL PINS. PROVIDE
HOLES 8" O.C. ON SIDEWALLS

MAHOGANY VENEER
ON ¾" PLYWD. NUCLEAR
LACQUER FINISH ON
ALL EXPOSED SURFACES

BLOCKING AS REQD

⑤ SECTION THRU BASE CABINET
Ⓐ A399 1½" = 1'-0"

Fig. 22 These details represent typical vertical sections taken through various storage components for the partner wall unit shown in Fig. 21. Careful attention must be given to integration of electronic equipment, electrical wiring, and task lighting.

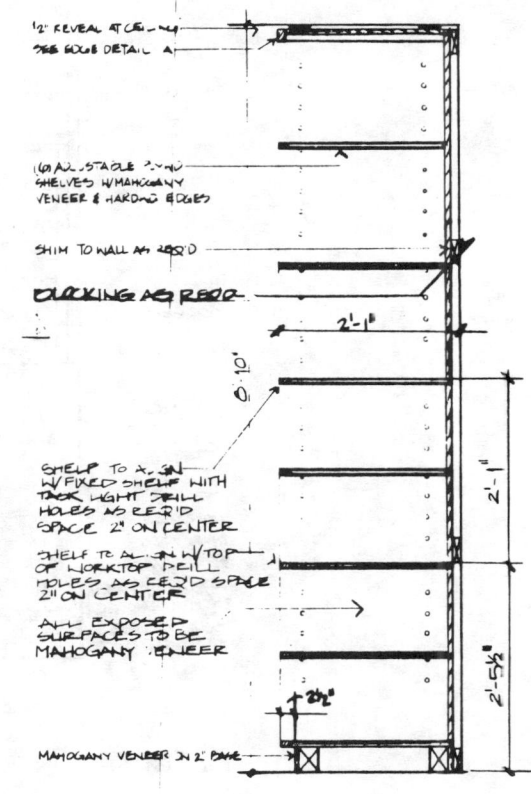

½" REVEAL AT CEILING
SEE EDGE DETAIL A

(6) ADJUSTABLE PLYWD.
SHELVES W/MAHOGANY
VENEER & HARDWD EDGES

SHIM TO WALL AS REQD

BLOCKING AS REQD

2'-1"

0'-10"

SHELF TO ALIGN
W/FIXED SHELF WITH
TACK LIGHT DRILL
HOLES AS REQD
SPACE 2" ON CENTER

SHELF TO ALIGN W/TOP
OF WORKTOP DRILL
HOLES AS REQD SPACE
2" ON CENTER

ALL EXPOSED
SURFACES TO BE
MAHOGANY VENEER

2'-1"

2'-5½"

2½"

MAHOGANY VENEER ON 2" BASE

⑦ SECTION - UNIT SPECIAL
Ⓐ A399 1" = 1'-0"

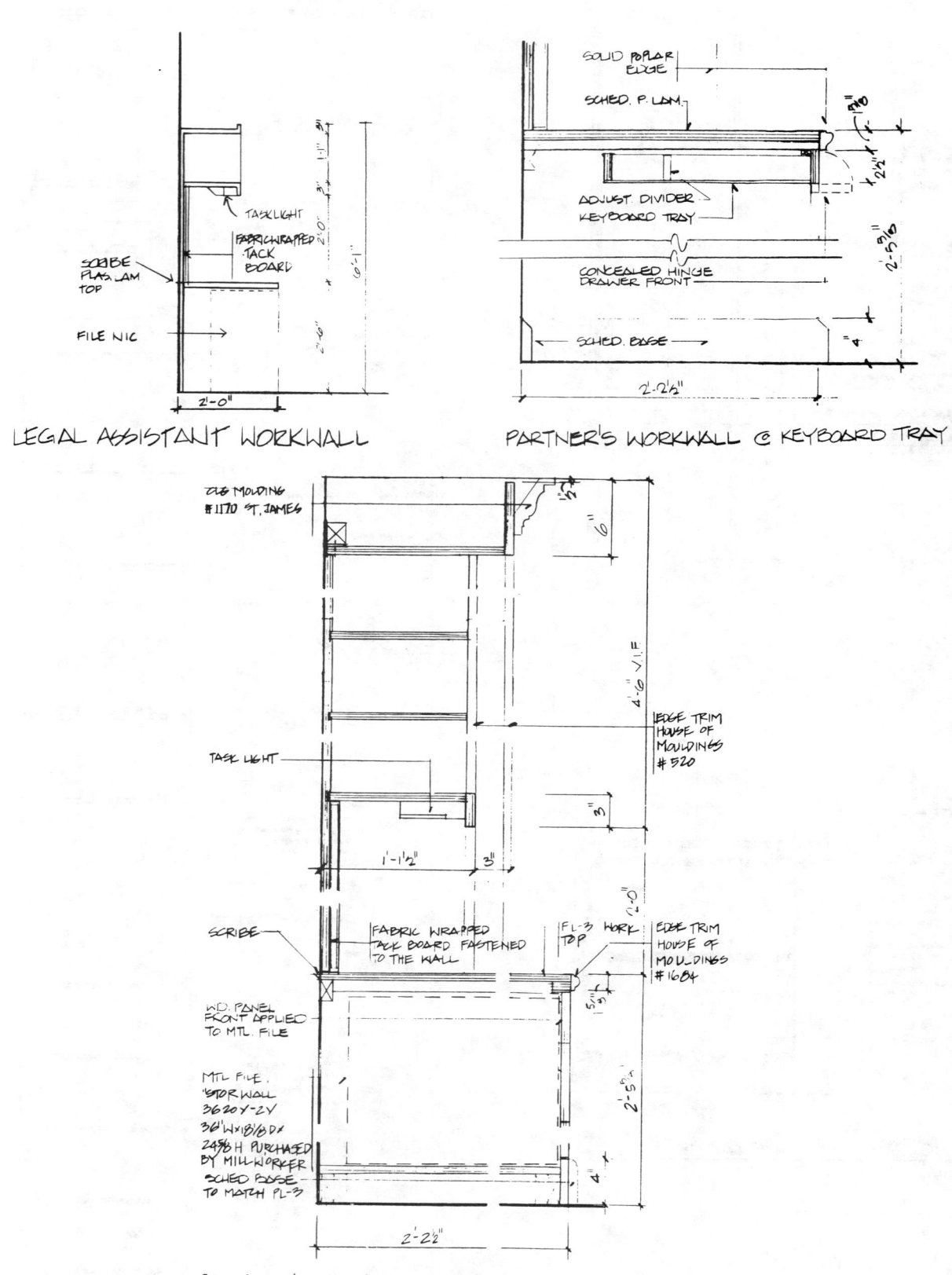

LEGAL ASSISTANT WORKWALL

PARTNER'S WORKWALL @ KEYBOARD TRAY

PARTNER'S WORKWALL

Fig. 23 In many instances, the utilization of standard wood moldings can enhance the overall appearance of an otherwise relatively simple workwall unit. Other cost-saving devices illustrated here are the application of a wood panel to a standard metal file and the use of a fabric-wrapped tack board. The incorporation of an undercabinet task light is almost always required.

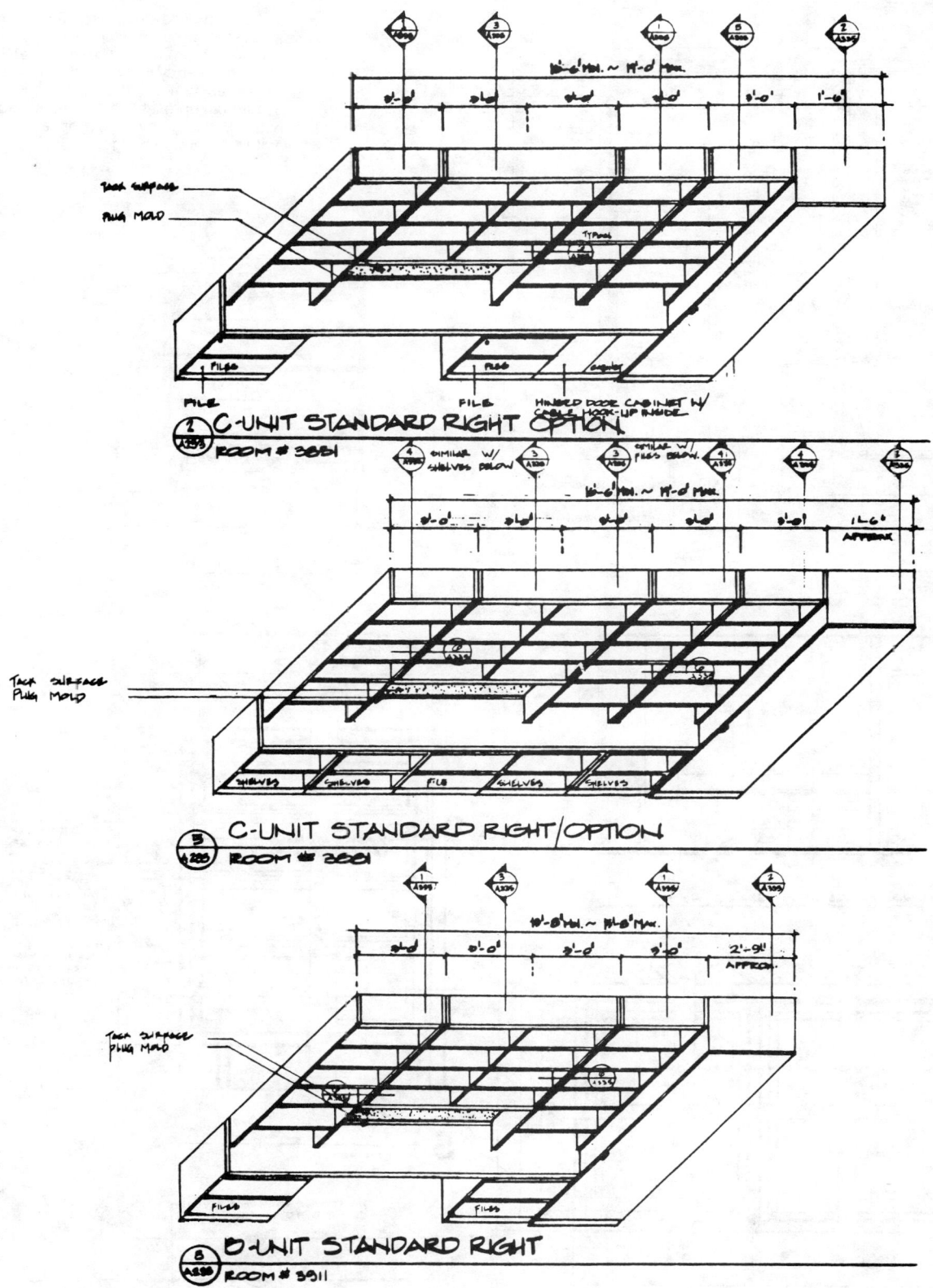

Fig. 24 These plan oblique drawings provide detailed design information to both client and architectural woodwork contractor. These drawings are particularly helpful when the office project for which these wall units are intended consists of many offices, and each office is to be customized within certain constraints.

PRIVATE OFFICES
Credenzas

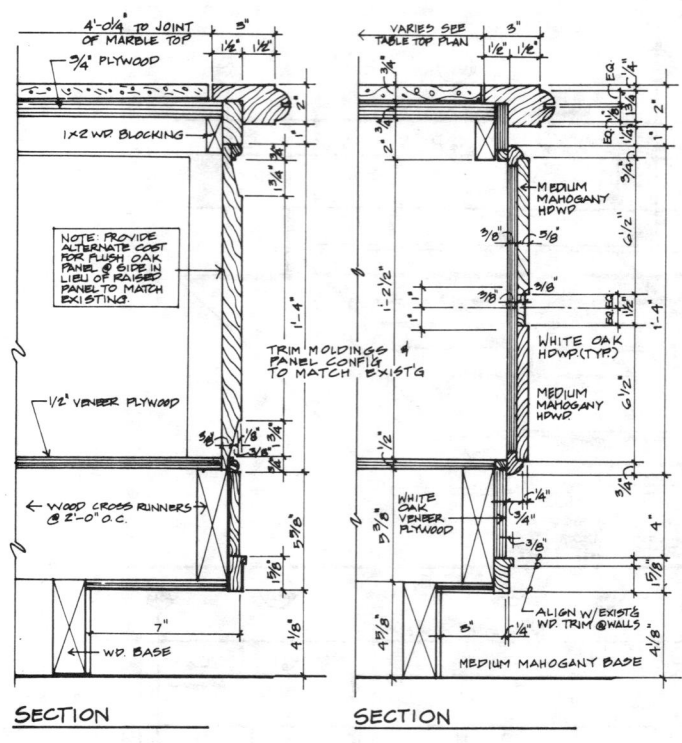

Many private offices require the detailing of custom credenzas and storage units. The sophistication and complexity of such details can significantly influence the budget for the space as well as the time of installation. Figure 25 represents a "high-end" approach, while Fig. 26 is more appropriate for offices with a moderate budget.

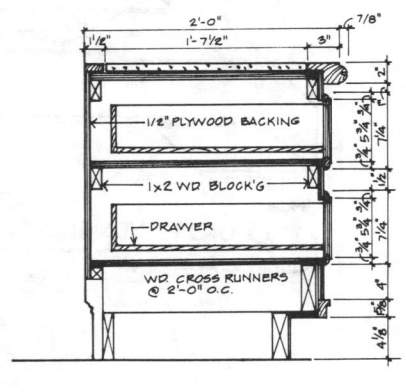

SECTION

SECTION

SECTION

Fig. 25

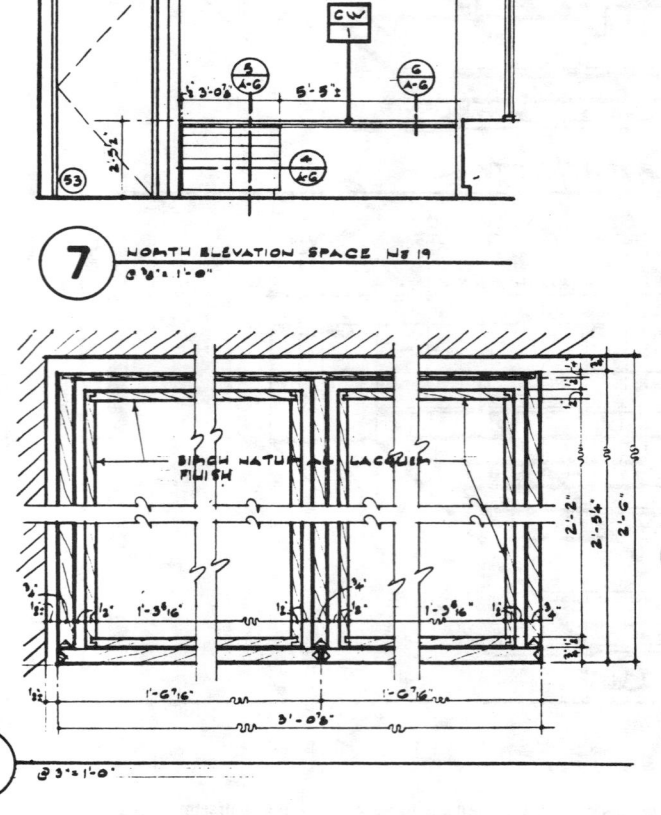

New electronic technologies, together with the advent and proliferation of the microcomputer and the availability of inexpensive packaged software, have changed the complexion of the office workplace. The ergonomic considerations related to this new work environment have necessitated a re-evaluation of the traditional interface between the seated office worker and his or her workplace. It is essential that the design of this electronic workstation be responsive to human factors in order to avoid physical discomfort for the user. The location of the keyboard, angle of the visual display terminal, adjustability of the chair, field of vision, provisions for back support, and height of the seat above the floor are a few of the considerations in the design process.

This page and the following pages provide a variety of anthropometric and ergonomic planning data and details for use as reference in the design of the electronic workstation.

Figure 1 illustrates guidelines for use in establishing preliminary design assumptions for a workstation display console. Since the types of displays and the nature of the tasks associated with those displays can vary considerably, Fig. 1 cannot be taken too literally. The configuration shown, however, is fairly representational. Certain basic factors should be noted anthropometrically. The use of an adjustable chair will permit the eye height of the seated viewer to be raised or lowered to view the display, as may be required depending on body size. An adjustment range between 15 and 18 in, or 38.1 and 45.7 cm, should be adequate to accommodate the eye height sitting requirements of about 90 percent of all viewers. Adjustability, however, will be of little value if the vertical distance between the underside of the desk and the floor is insufficient to accommodate the knee height and thigh clearance when the seat is adjusted to the appropriate position. If such distance is not less than 26.5 in, or 67.3 cm, the majority of viewers will be accommodated.

The location of the top of the display should align with the standard sight line for optimum viewing conditions. Since the eye and the head can rotate within certain limitations and, in so doing, increase the area that can be scanned, displays can be located above the standard sight line when absolutely necessary. It should also be noted that the more perpendicular the normal sight line is to the display plane, the greater the viewing comfort. Accordingly, consideration should be given to sloping the display plane since the normal sight line is about 15° below the horizontal.

Stature is the vertical distance from the floor to the top of the head, measured while the subject stands erect, looking straight ahead.

Elbow height is the distance measured vertically from the floor to the depression formed at the elbow where the forearm meets the upper arm.

Eye height is the vertical distance from the floor to the inner corner of the eye, measured with the subject looking straight ahead and standing erect.

Sitting height erect is the vertical distance from the sitting surface to the top of the head with the subject sitting erect.

Sitting height normal is the vertical distance from the sitting surface to the top of the head, measured with the subject sitting relaxed.

Eye height is the vertical distance from the inner corner of the eye to the sitting surface.

Shoulder height is the distance taken vertically from the sitting surface to a point on the shoulder midway between the neck and acromion.

Shoulder breadth is the maximum horizontal distance across the deltoid muscles.

Elbow to elbow is the distance across the lateral surfaces of the elbows measured with elbows flexed and resting lightly against the body with the forearms extended horizontally.

Hip breadth is the breadth of the body as measured across the widest portion of the hips. Note that a hip breadth measurement can also be taken with the subject in a standing position, in which case the definition would be the maximum breadth of the lower torso.

Elbow rest height is the height from the top of the sitting surface to the bottom of the tip of the elbow.

Thigh clearance is the distance taken vertically from a sitting surface to the top of the thigh at the point where the thigh and the abdomen intersect.

Knee height is the vertical distance from the floor to the midpoint of the kneecap.

Popliteal height is the distance, taken vertically, from the floor to the underside of the portion of the thigh just behind the knee while the subject is seated with body erect. The knees and ankles are usually perpendicular, with the bottom of the thigh and the back of the knees barely touching the sitting surface.

Buttock-popliteal length is the horizontal distance from the rearmost surface of the buttock to the back of the lower leg.

Buttock-knee length is the horizontal distance from the rearmost surface of the buttocks to the front of the kneecaps.

Buttock-toe length is the horizontal distance from the rearmost surface of the buttocks to the tip of the toe.

Buttock-heel length is the horizontal distance from the base of the heel to a wall against which the subject sits erect with his leg maximally extended forward along the sitting surface. This is sometimes referred to as buttock-leg length.

Vertical reach is the height above the sitting surface of the tip of the middle finger when the arm, hand, and fingers are extended vertically.

Vertical grip reach is usually measured from the floor to the top of a bar grasped in the right hand while the subject stands erect and the hand within which the bar is grasped is raised as high as it can be conveniently without experiencing discomfort or strain.

Side arm reach is the distance from the center line of the body to the outside surface of a bar grasped in the right hand while the subject stands erect and the arm is conveniently outstretched horizontally without experiencing discomfort or strain.

Thumb tip reach is the distance from the wall to the tip of the thumb measured with the subject's shoulders against the wall, his arm extended forward, and his index finger touching the tip of his thumb.

Maximum body depth is the horizontal distance between the most anterior point on the body to the most posterior. Anterior points are usually located on the chest or abdomen while the posterior points are usually found in the buttock or shoulder region.

Maximum body breadth is the maximum distance, including arms, across the body.

	in	cm
A	16–18	40.6–45.7
B	16 min.	40.6 min.
C	18 min.	45.7 min.
D	15–18 adjust.	38.1–45.7
E	26.5 min.	67.3 min.
F	30	76.2

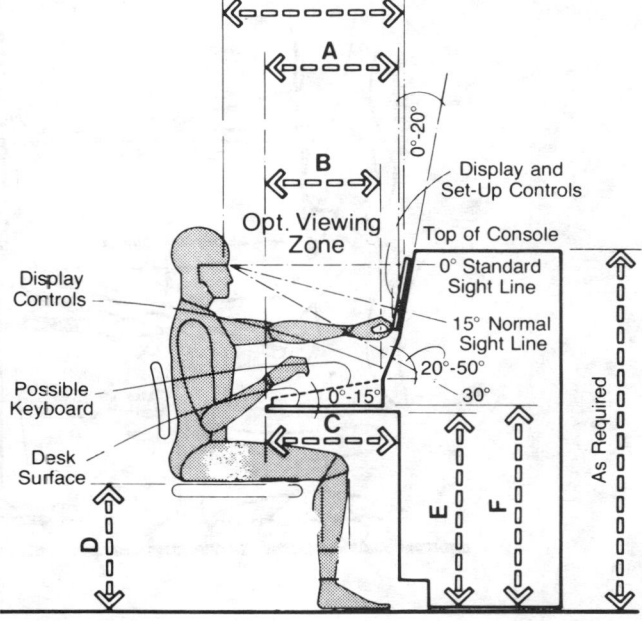

Fig. 1

ELECTRONIC WORKSTATIONS
Planning Data: Anthropometrics

■ Both the work surface and the display monitors must be lowered and raised as a unit with 31.8 cm of travel.

■ The work surface must be tilted anywhere between a horizontal position to 35° below horizontal. The work surface, at its lowest setting and with a 10° tilted angle, as is common in use, must be 63.5 cm in height at its front edge.

■ The work surface must raise to a horizontal height of 104 cm, accommodating a majority of people in a standing position.

■ The monitor screens must be tiltable to any position between 15° forward of vertical and 15° back. This lets the user adjust the screen to avoid reflective glare, and it accommodates various working positions of different lines of sight.

■ Adjustment controls designed for hand operation must be located within the operator's extended reach envelope.

■ All surfaces must have matte or dull finishes. This reduces the likelihood of reflective glare.

■ The workstation must be compact and relatively easy to move through a standard 81-cm doorway.

■ No structural components shall exist which inhibit the workstation's operation by users in wheelchairs, ensuring a barrier-free workstation.

■ Service personnel must have easy access to electrical components.

■ The digitizing surface must accommodate standard European and American D size drawings.

■ Screen depth of view must allow alphanumeric characters to be viewed at an angle between 20 and 28 arc minutes.

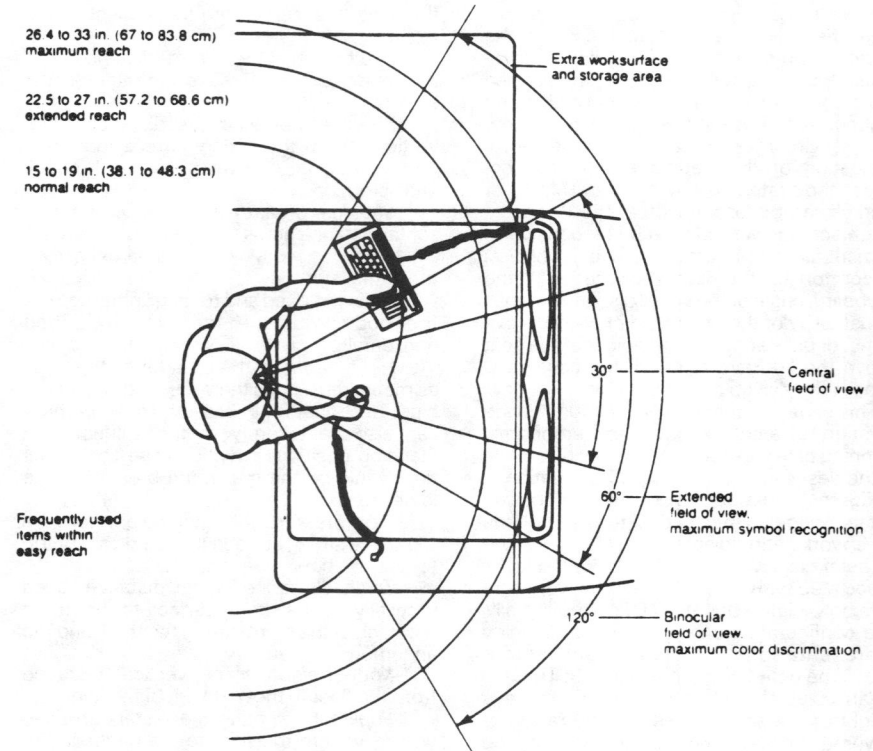

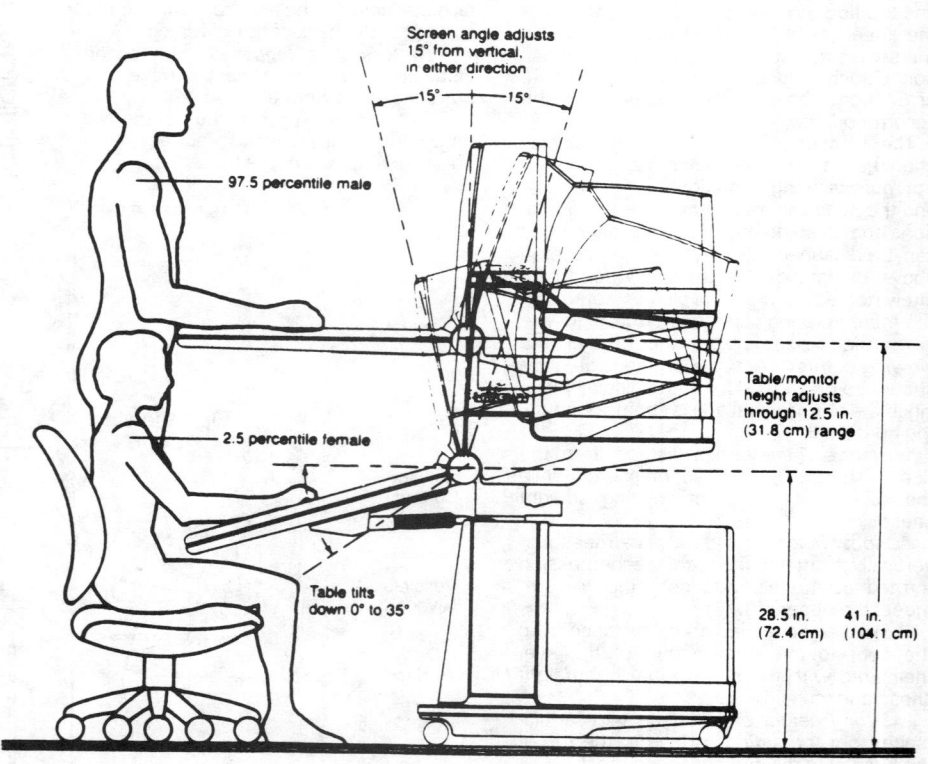

The Automated Task. *Square footage workstation standards for the automated task are also developed primarily according to task profile, equipment, conferencing, and privacy requirements.*

Open
No requirement of equipment or task for privacy, concentration

Screened
Privacy required for reading, working, thinking, calculating, meetings, confidential phone calls, elimination of visual and acoustical distractions

Task Profile: Data Retrieval.
□ Paper, material, or information processed, analyzed, and/or maintained.
□ Multiple reference sources may be used on a task.
□ Reference materials used frequently.
□ Limited volume of supplies and permanent records kept at the workspace.
□ Electronic equipment may be used for easy reference, retrieval, keeping records current, and maintaining data and records.
□ Additional equipment such as microfilm viewers may be required.
□ Ability to see and hear co-workers may be desirable.
□ Tasks may also require screening for concentration.

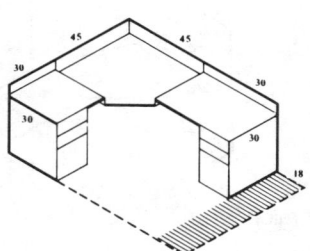 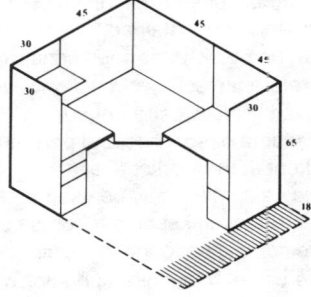

No	Guest chair
45 x 45	Primary work surface
30 x 45	Secondary work surface
(76 x 114 cm)	
3–4	File drawers
0–2	Shelves

56 sq. ft.

Task Profile: Shared Tasks.
□ Paper, material, or information processed, analzyed, and/or maintained.
□ More than one task may be performed concurrently.
□ More than one operator uses same equipment.
□ Multiple reference sources may be used on a task.
□ Reference materials used may be used frequently.
□ Electronic equipment may be used for easy reference, inputting/maintaining data and records, retrieval, keeping records current.
□ Storage requirements vary according to task.

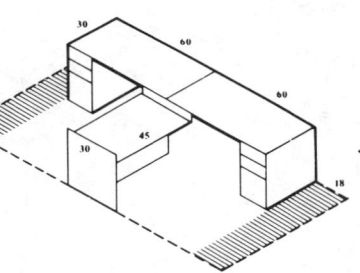

No	Guest chair
30 x 45	Primary work surface
30 x 60	Secondary work surface
(76 x 152 cm)	
1–2	File drawers
0–4	Shelves

81 sq. ft.

Task Profile: Administrative Specialist/Secretarial.
□ Paper, material, or information processed, analyzed, and/or maintained.
□ More than one task may be performed concurrently.
□ Multiple reference sources may be used on a task.
□ Reference materials used frequently.
□ Electronic equipment may be used for easy reference, retrieval, keeping records current, inputting/maintaining data and records.
□ If supervising, ability to see subordinates may be desirable to direct activities.
□ If monitoring, visual access may be desirable.
□ Moderate amount of storage required at the workspace, that is, casework, client accounts, supplies.

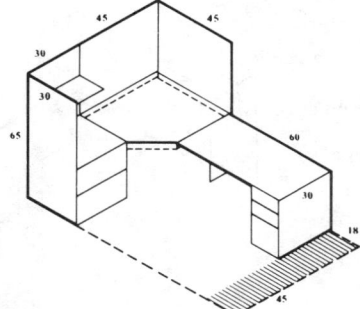 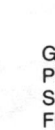 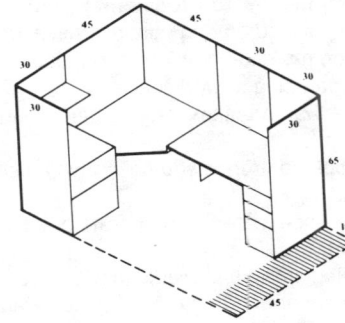

No	Guest chair
45 x 45	Primary work surface
30 x 60	Secondary work surface
3–4	File drawers
1–2	Shelves

64 sq. ft.

The Automated Task	Open	Screened
	No requirement of equipment or task for privacy, concentration	Privacy required for reading, working, thinking, calculating, meetings, confidential phone calls, elimination of visual and acoustical distractions

Task Profile: Administrative Specialist/Secretarial (+ Guest).

- Paper, material, or information processed, analyzed, and/or maintained.
- More than one task performed concurrently.
- Multiple reference sources used on a task.
- Reference materials used frequently.
- Limited volume of supplies and permanent records kept at the workspace.
- Electronic equipment may be used for easy reference, retrieval, keeping records current
- Tasks are complex enough to require concentration.
- Extensive use of telephone and additional equipment such as desk-top printer and micro-film viewer may be required.
- Need to see and hear co-workers is secondary priority.
- Limited conferencing required at workspace.
- If supervising, ability to see subordinates may be desirable to direct activities.
- If monitoring, visual access may be desirable.

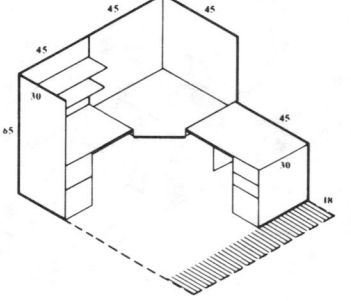

1	Guest chair
45 x 45	Primary work surface
30 x 60	Secondary work surface
3–4	File drawers
1–2	Shelves

80 sq. ft.

Task Profile: Word Processing.

- Time divided among administrative, processing paper, material, or information.
- More than one task may be performed concurrently.
- Multiple reference sources may be used on a task.
- Reference materials moderate but used frequently.
- Limited storage primarily for supplies.
- Ability to see and hear co-workers or subordinates is desirable.
- Typewriter and/or electronic equipment may be used to expedite processing and administrative tasks, for example, VDT, printer, transcriber, OCR, microfilm viewer, separate disk drives.

No	Guest chair
45 x 45	Primary work surface
(114 x 114 cm)	
30 x 45	Secondary work surface
(76 x 114 cm)	
3–4	File drawers
1–2	Shelves

67 sq. ft.

Task Profile: Word Processing (+ Guest).

- Time divided among administrative, processing paper, material, or information, and limited conferencing at workspace.
- More than one task may be performed concurrently.
- Multiple reference sources may be used on a task.
- Reference materials moderate but used frequently.
- Limited storage primarily for supplies.
- Typewriter and/or electronic equipment (VDT, printer, and so on) may be used to expedite processing and administrative tasks.
- Tasks are complex enough to require concentration for analysis, or heavy equipment operations require acoustical screening.
- Work surface needed for organization of work.

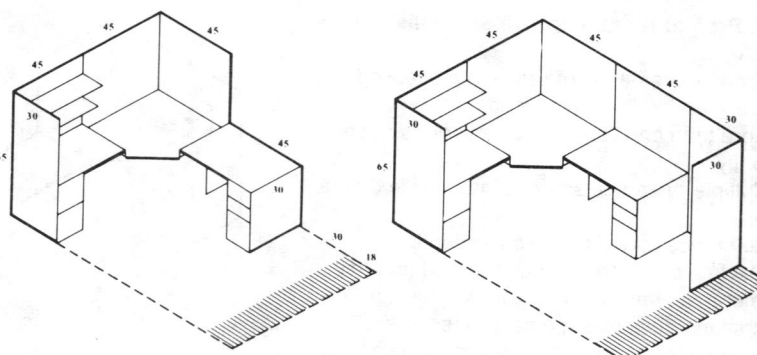

1	Guest chair
45 x 45	Primary work surface
30 x 45	Secondary work surface
3–4	File drawers
1–2	Shelves

86 sq. ft.

The Automated Task	**Open** No requirement of equipment or task for privacy, concentration	**Screened** Privacy required for reading, working, thinking, calculating, meetings, confidential phone calls, elimination of visual and acoustical distractions

Task Profile: Technical/Systems Analyst/Programmer.

- Time divided among administrative, processing paper, material, or information, and limited conferencing at workspace.
- More than one task may be performed concurrently.
- Multiple reference sources may be used on a task.
- Reference materials may be extensive and used frequently.
- Ability to see and hear co-workers or subordinates desirable.
- Typewriter and electronic equipment (VDT, printer, and so on) may be used to expedite processing and administrative tasks.
- Moderate to extensive amount of storage required at the workspace for manuals, binders, computer printouts, coding sheets, supplies, permanent files, reference materials.

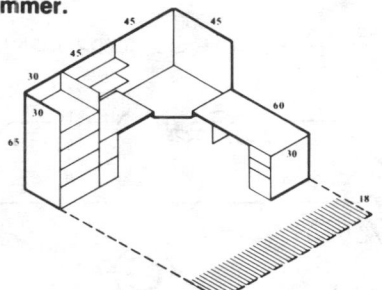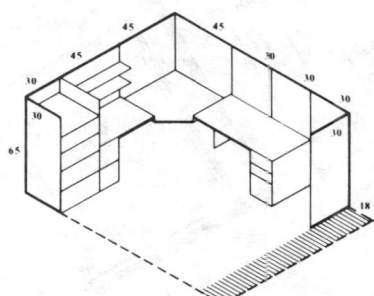

1	Guest chair
45 x 45	Primary work surface
30 x 60	Secondary work surface
(76 x 152 cm)	
6–8	File drawers
3–5	Shelves

128 sq. ft.

Task Profile: Administrative/Managerial.

- Extensive conferencing at individual workspace.
- Analysis of reports, computerized materials, and so on.
- Varied tasks or projects performed simultaneously on an ongoing basis.
- Large amounts of storage extensively used.
- Storage for client/project files, reference manuals, documentation, correspondence.
- Telephone used extensively.
- Supervision of subordinates almost universal.
- Electronic equipment accommodation is secondary priority, used primarily for communication/electronic mail, scheduling.

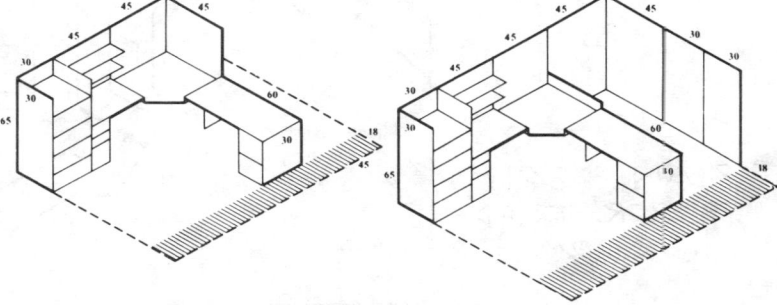

2	Guest chair
45 x 45	Primary work surface
30 x 60	Secondary work surface
(76 x 152 cm)	
5–8	File drawers
3–5	Shelves

154 sq. ft.

Task Profile: Administrative/Total Enclosure.

- Extensive conferencing at individual workspace.
- Analysis of reports, computerized materials, and so on.
- Varied tasks on projects performed simultaneously on an ongoing basis.
- Large amounts of storage extensively used.
- Storage for client/project files, reference manuals, documentation, correspondence.
- Telephone used extensively.
- Supervision of subordinates almost universal.
- Electronic equipment accommodation is secondary priority, used primarily for communication/electronic mail, scheduling.
- Subject matter of job responsibilities requires confidentiality.

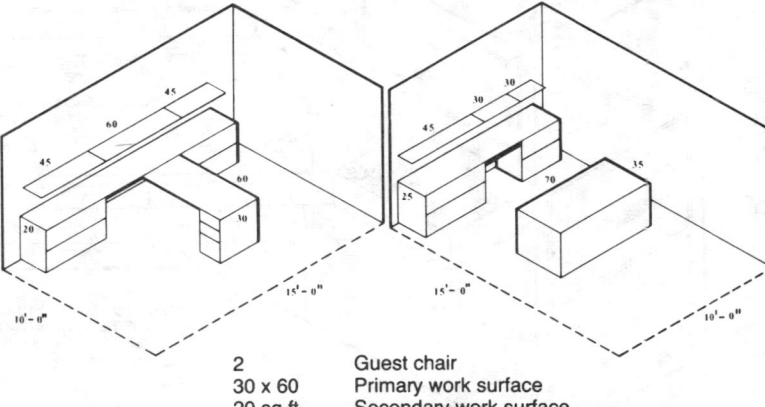

2	Guest chair
30 x 60	Primary work surface
20 sq ft	Secondary work surface
(15 sq m)	
5–8	File drawers
3–5	Shelves

150 sq. ft.

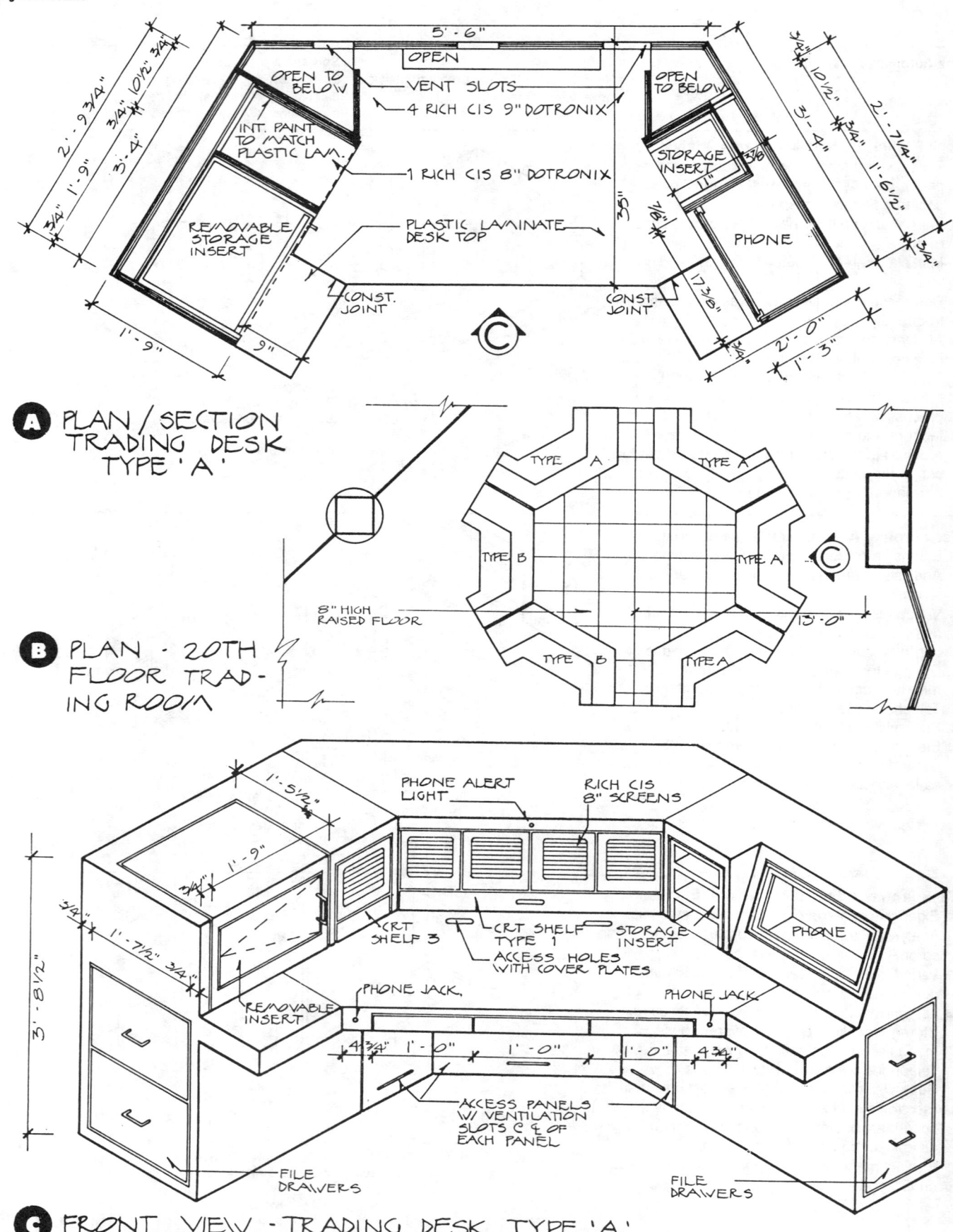

A PLAN / SECTION TRADING DESK TYPE 'A'

B PLAN · 20TH FLOOR TRADING ROOM

C FRONT VIEW - TRADING DESK TYPE 'A'

Fig. 2 Technologically and electronically complex trading desks must be ergonomically correct in every respect. With little, if any, margin for error when designing and detailing multiple workstations of this type, a full-size mockup is always required.

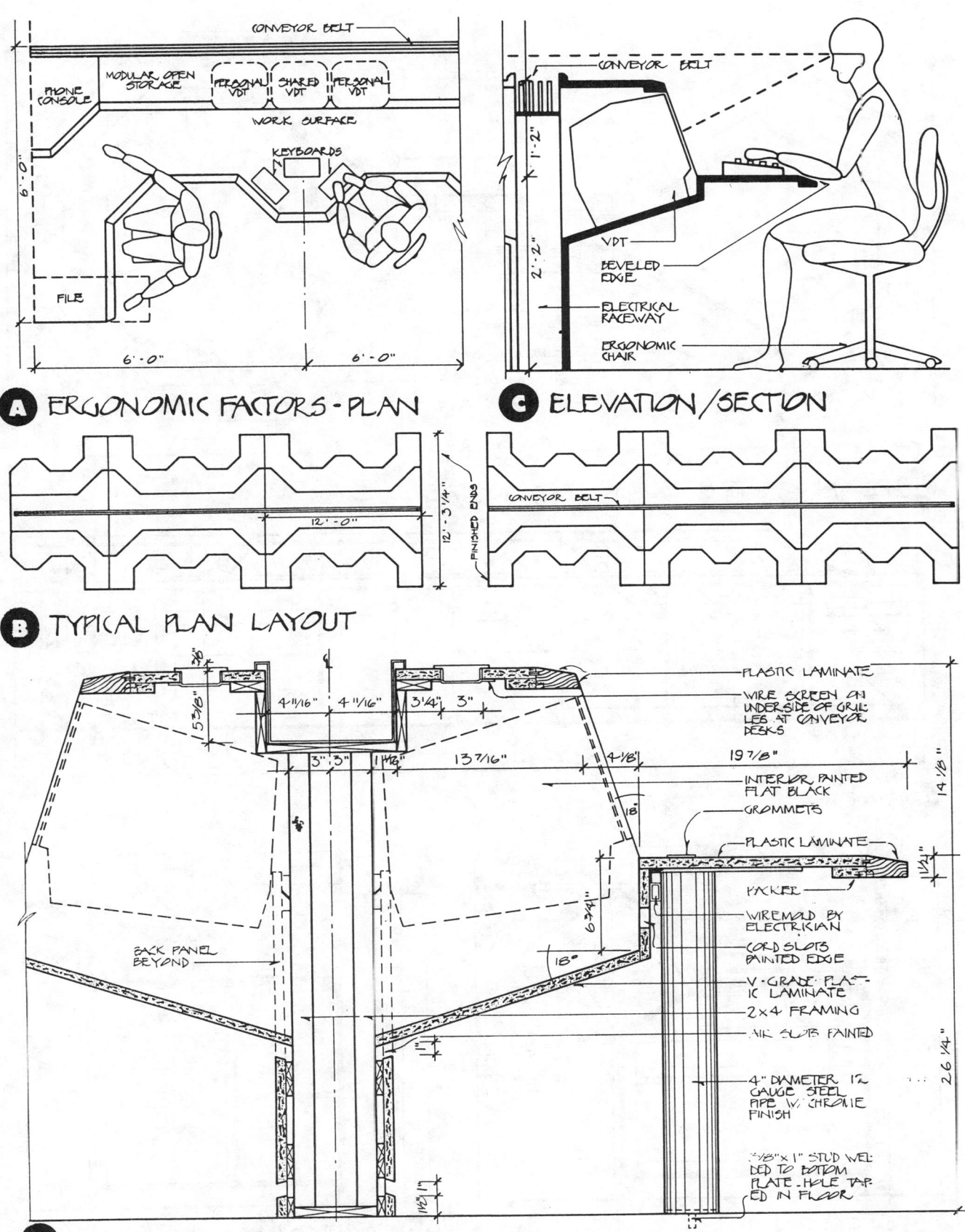

A **ERGONOMIC FACTORS - PLAN**

C **ELEVATION / SECTION**

B **TYPICAL PLAN LAYOUT**

DD **SECTION THRU TYPICAL DESK**

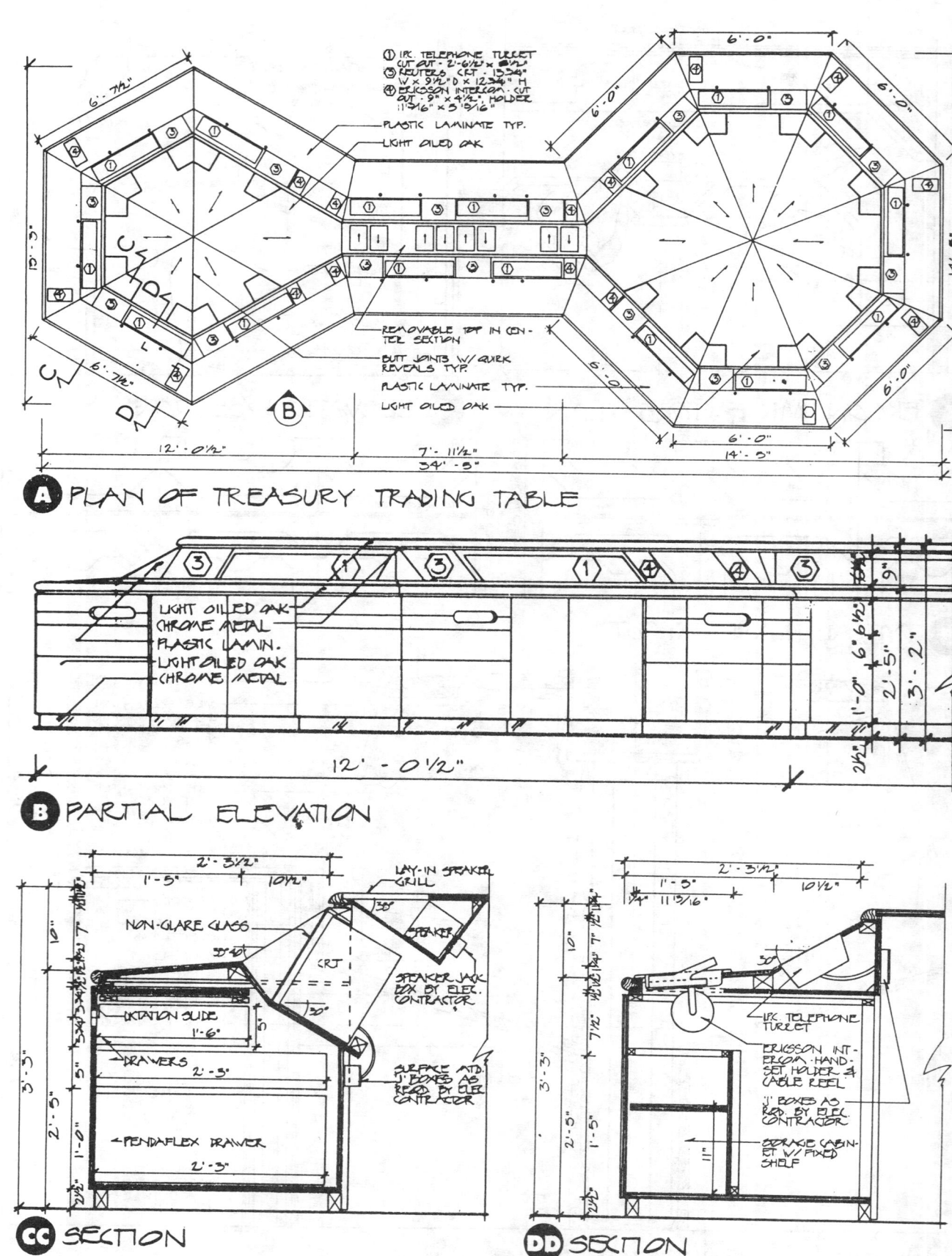

① IPC. TELEPHONE TURRET
  CUT OUT · 2'-6½" × 8½"
② REUTERS CRT · 13¾"
  W × 9½" D × 12¾" H
④ ERICSSON INTERCOM · CUT
  OUT · 9" × 4½" · HOLDER
  11⁷⁄₁₆" × 5⁹⁄₁₆"

PLASTIC LAMINATE TYP.

LIGHT OILED OAK

REMOVABLE TOP IN CEN-
TER SECTION

BUTT JOINTS W/ QUIRK
REVEALS TYP.

PLASTIC LAMINATE TYP.

LIGHT OILED OAK

Ⓐ PLAN OF TREASURY TRADING TABLE

LIGHT OILED OAK
CHROME METAL
PLASTIC LAMIN.
LIGHT OILED OAK
CHROME METAL

Ⓑ PARTIAL ELEVATION

LAY-IN SPEAKER
GRILL

NON-GLARE GLASS

SPEAKER

CRT

SPEAKER JACK
BOX BY ELEC.
CONTRACTOR

STATION SLIDE
1'-6"

DRAWERS
2'-5"

SURFACE MTD.
'J' BOXES AS
REQ'D. BY ELEC.
CONTRACTOR

PENDAFLEX DRAWER
2'-3"

ⒸⒸ SECTION

IPC TELEPHONE
TURRET

ERICSSON INT-
ERCOM · HAND-
SET, HOLDER &
CABLE REEL

'J' BOXES AS
REQ'D. BY ELEC.
CONTRACTOR

STORAGE CABIN-
ET W/ FIXED
SHELF

ⒹⒹ SECTION

248

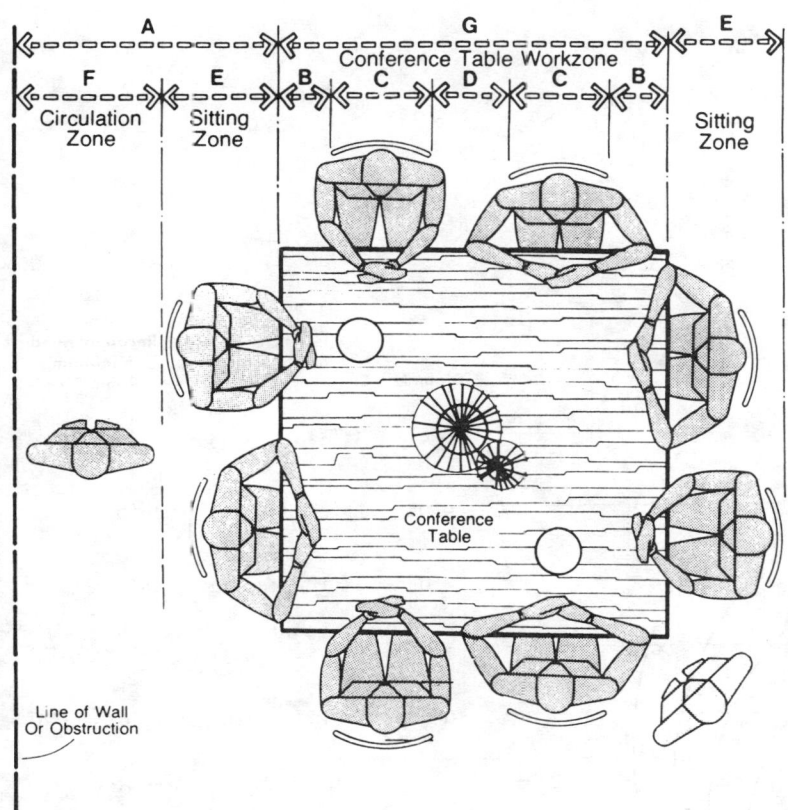

Fig. 1 Square conference table.

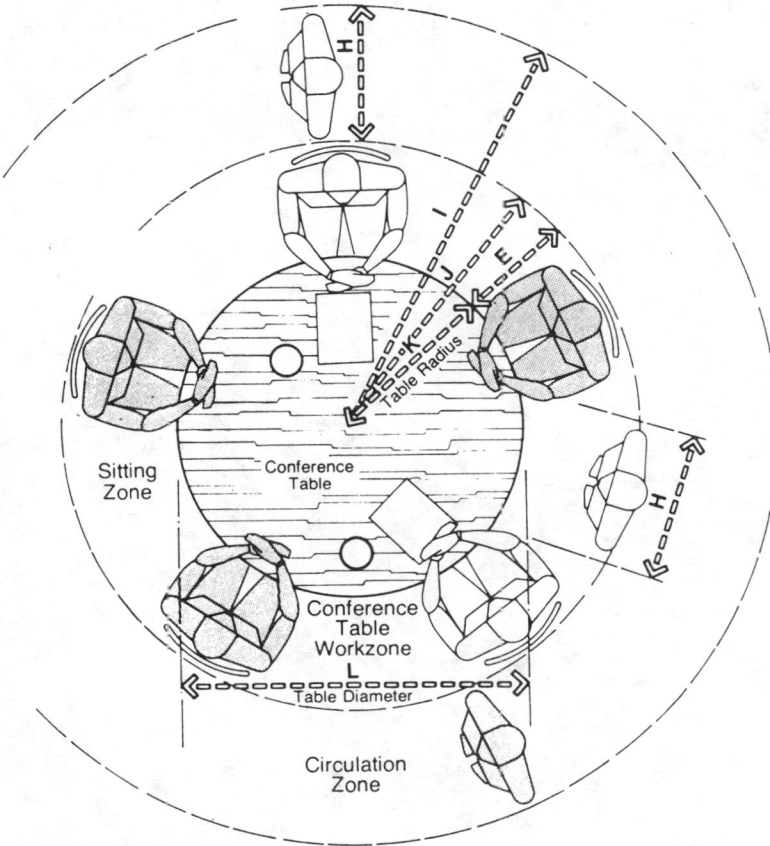

Fig. 2 Circular conference table.

Consideration must be given to clearances and circulation around the larger conference table, as indicated in Figs. 1 and 2. A minimum of 48 in, or 121.9 cm, is suggested from the edge of the table to the wall or nearest obstruction. This dimension under ordinary circumstance allows for a circulation zone beyond the sitting zone of 30 to 36 in, or 76.2 to 91.4 cm, based upon a maximum body breadth measurement of the larger person. The greater dimension is recommended to allow for the chair in a pulled-out position.

The actual dimensions of the conference table are a function of the number of people to be seated. The square table illustrated in Fig. 1 provides for eight people, with each side ranging from 54 to 60 in, or 137.2 to 152.4 cm. The larger dimension is more appropriate to accommodate people of larger body size and to allow for a more generous work zone for each person. This translates into 30 in, or 76.2 cm, per person, which constitutes a comfortable perimeter allocation. The circular table shown in Fig. 2 comfortably accommodates five people while allowing for a 30-in, or 76.2-cm, access zone between chairs. To accommodate both sitting zone and circulation zone, a space with a radius ranging from 72 to 81 in, or 182.9 to 205.7 cm, must be provided.

	in	cm
A	48–60	121.9–152.4
B	4–6	10.2–15.2
C	20–24	50.8–61.0
D	6–10	15.2–25.4
E	18–24	45.7–61.0
F	30–36	76.2–91.4
G	54–60	137.2–152.4
H	30	76.2
I	72–81	182.9–205.7
J	42–51	106.7–129.5
K	24–27	61.0–68.6
L	48–54	121.9–137.2

CONFERENCE ROOMS
Planning Data: Table Sizes and Seating Capacities

Round conference tables offer the advantages of intimacy, "equality," and compactness. On the other hand, if status is an issue, or if one wall within the space is an audiovisual wall, this table shape can be less than satisfactory. The same problems can arise with a square conference table. In both instances, however, the total seating around each table shape must be viewed in the context of chair size, chair spacing, and tasks to be performed at the table.

ROUND TABLES

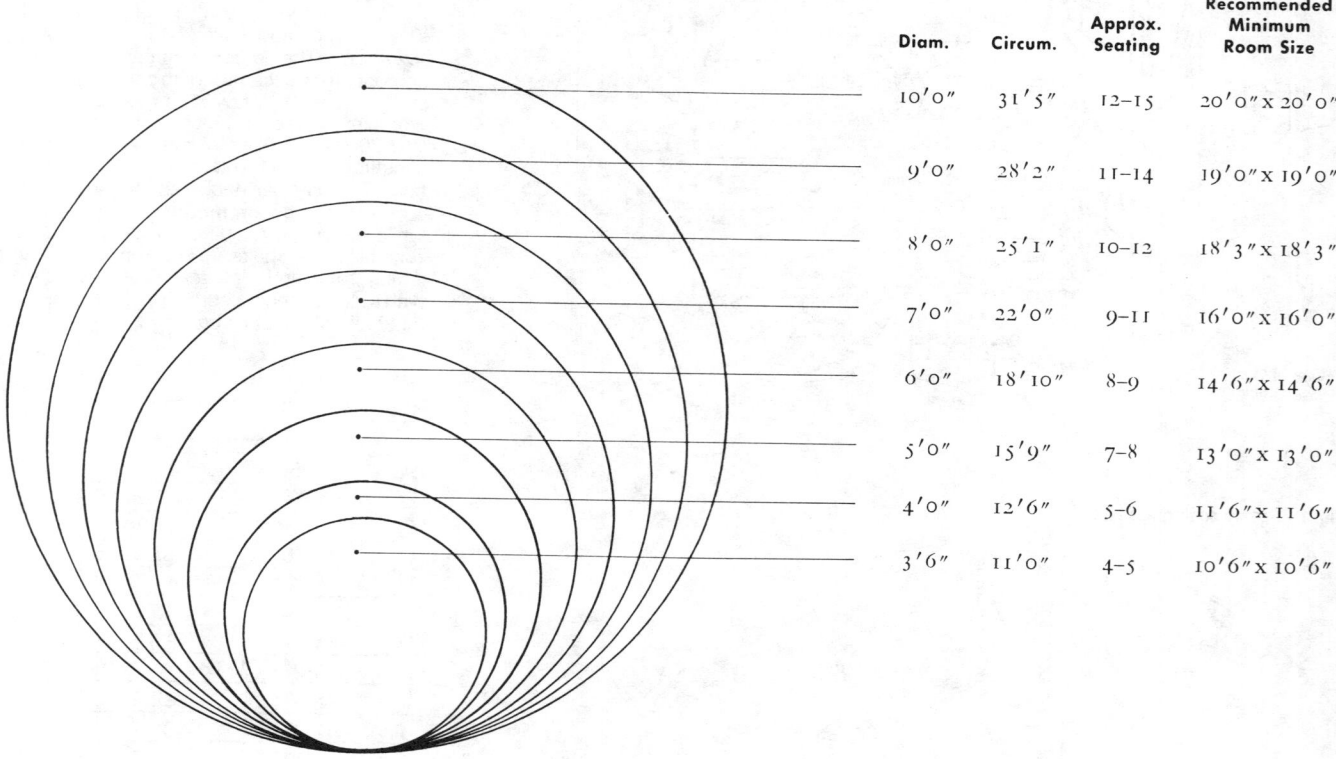

Diam.	Circum.	Approx. Seating	Recommended Minimum Room Size
10′0″	31′5″	12–15	20′0″ x 20′0″
9′0″	28′2″	11–14	19′0″ x 19′0″
8′0″	25′1″	10–12	18′3″ x 18′3″
7′0″	22′0″	9–11	16′0″ x 16′0″
6′0″	18′10″	8–9	14′6″ x 14′6″
5′0″	15′9″	7–8	13′0″ x 13′0″
4′0″	12′6″	5–6	11′6″ x 11′6″
3′6″	11′0″	4–5	10′6″ x 10′6″

SQUARE TABLES

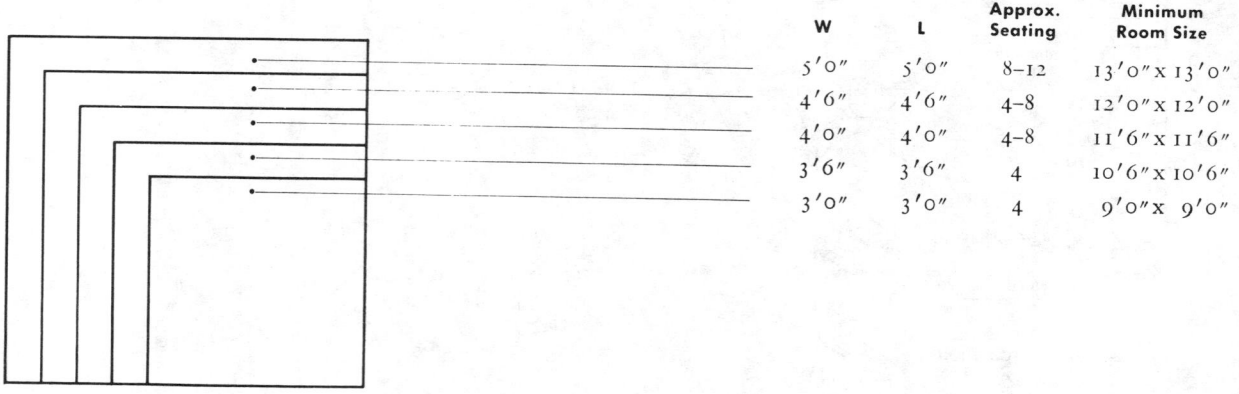

W	L	Approx. Seating	Recommended Minimum Room Size
5′0″	5′0″	8–12	13′0″ x 13′0″
4′6″	4′6″	4–8	12′0″ x 12′0″
4′0″	4′0″	4–8	11′6″ x 11′6″
3′6″	3′6″	4	10′6″ x 10′6″
3′0″	3′0″	4	9′0″ x 9′0″

Rectangular and boat-shaped conference tables lend themselves toward formal settings where status and hierarchy are important. Both table shapes are also more suitable in a room where an audiovisual wall is placed at one end of the space, or where speakers are making presentations. The boat-shaped table also offers greater visibility of others seated at the table, as well as ease of circulation around its perimeter.

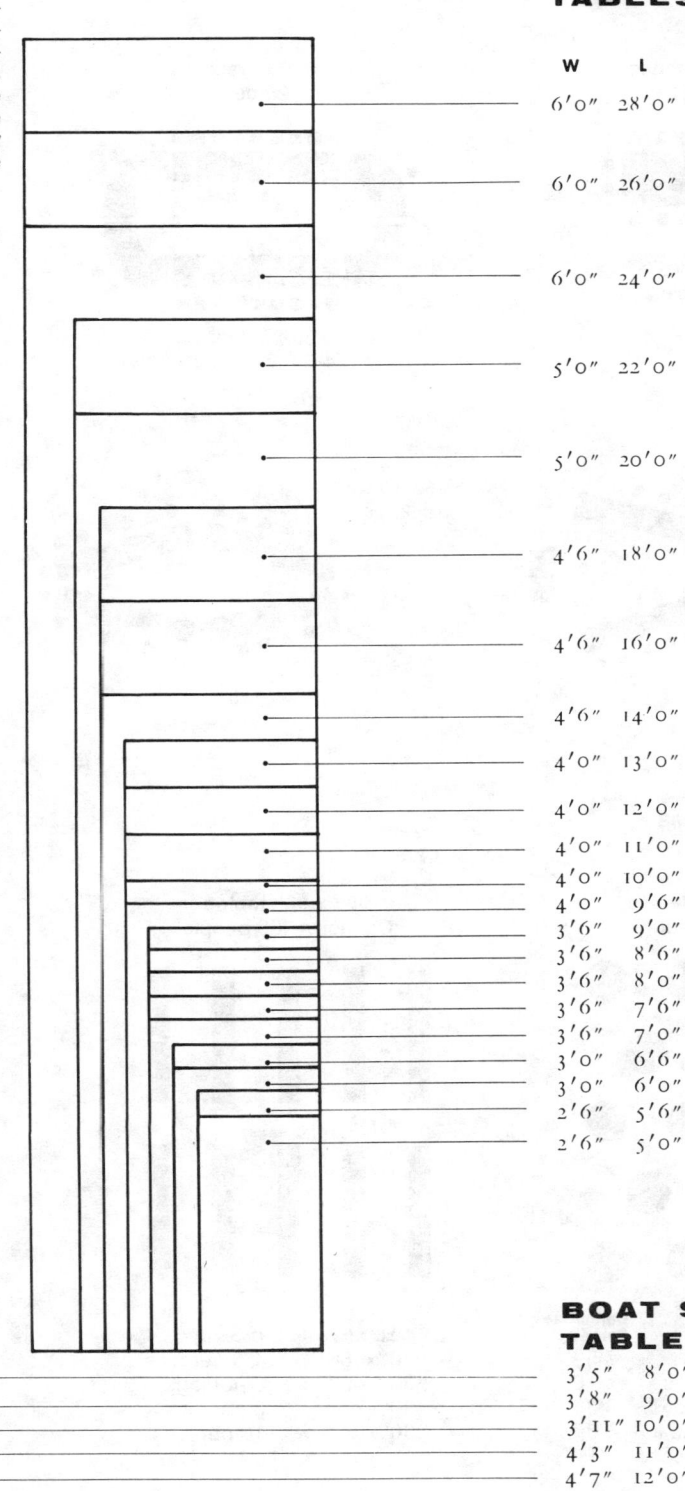

RECTANGULAR TABLES

W	L	Approx. Seating	Recommended Minimum Room Size
6'0"	28'0"	28–30	18'0" x 40'0"
6'0"	26'0"	26–28	18'0" x 38'0"
6'0"	24'0"	24–26	18'0" x 36'0"
5'0"	22'0"	22–24	15'0" x 32'0"
5'0"	20'0"	20–22	15'0" x 30'0"
4'6"	18'0"	18–20	13'6" x 27'0"
4'6"	16'0"	16–18	13'6" x 25'0"
4'6"	14'0"	14–16	13'6" x 23'0"
4'0"	13'0"	12–14	12'0" x 21'0"
4'0"	12'0"	12–14	12'0" x 20'0"
4'0"	11'0"	10–12	12'0" x 19'0"
4'0"	10'0"	10–12	12'0" x 17'0"
4'0"	9'6"	8–10	12'0" x 16'6"
3'6"	9'0"	8–10	10'6" x 16'0"
3'6"	8'6"	8–10	10'6" x 15'6"
3'6"	8'0"	8–10	10'6" x 15'0"
3'6"	7'6"	6–8	10'6" x 14'6"
3'6"	7'0"	6–8	10'6" x 14'0"
3'0"	6'6"	6–8	10'0" x 13'6"
3'0"	6'0"	6–8	10'0" x 13'0"
2'6"	5'6"	4–6	9'0" x 12'6"
2'6"	5'0"	4–6	9'0" x 12'0"

BOAT SHAPED TABLES

W	L	Approx. Seating	Recommended Minimum Room Size
3'5"	8'0"	8–10	10'0" x 15'0"
3'8"	9'0"	8–10	11'0" x 16'0"
3'11"	10'0"	10–12	12'0" x 17'0"
4'3"	11'0"	10–12	13'0" x 19'0"
4'7"	12'0"	12–14	14'0" x 21'0"
4'11"	14'0"	14–16	15'0" x 23'0"
5'3"	16'0"	16–18	16'0" x 26'0"
5'7"	18'0"	20–22	17'0" x 29'0"
6'0"	20'0"	20–24	18'0" x 32'0"

CONFERENCE ROOMS

Planning Data: Table Sizes and Seating Capacities

CONFERENCE/MEETING ROOMS

Solid Conference
For 20 people

4-30"x72" tables
2-30"x 60" tables

Race Track
For 26 people

6-30"x72" tables
4-30" wide crescents

Trapezoid/Round
For 12 people

6-30"x30"x30"x 60" tables

V-Shape
For 20 people

Boat Shape
For 28 people

BANQUET ROOMS

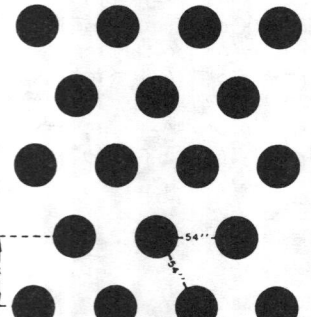

60" diameter tables
Capacity: 180 people

Table Size	Capacity	Centerline Spread
48" dia.	6 persons	7'5"
54" dia.	6-8 persons	7'10"
60" dia.	8-10 persons	8'3"
66" dia.	10 persons	8'8"
72" dia.	10-12 persons	9'1"

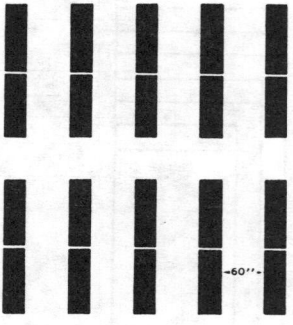

30" x 96" tables
Capacity: 180 people

Table Size	Capacity
30"x48"	4-6 persons
30"x60"	6 persons
30"x72"	8 persons
30"x96"	10 persons

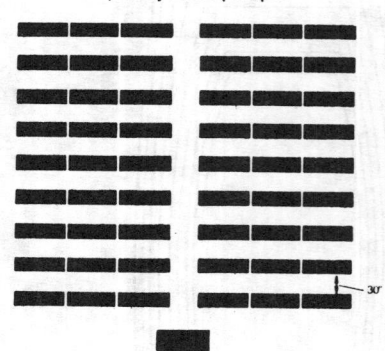

18" x 72" classroom style tables
Capacity: 162 people

Table Size	Capacity
18"x60"	2 persons
18"x72"	3 persons
18"x96"	4 persons

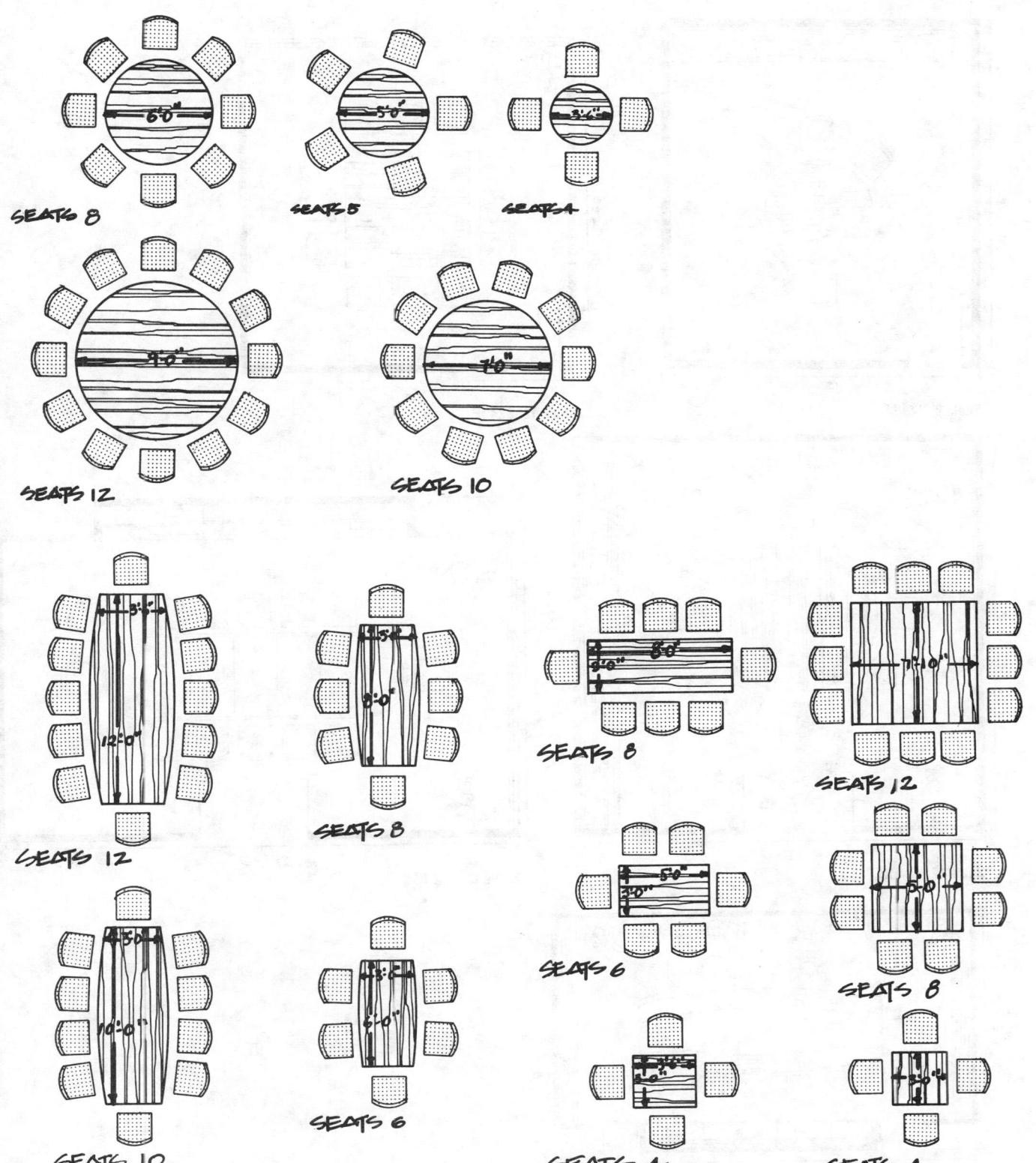

Fig. 3 These conference tables are useful in making initial space planning allocations.

CONFERENCE ROOMS

Planning Data: Table Sizes and Seating Capacities

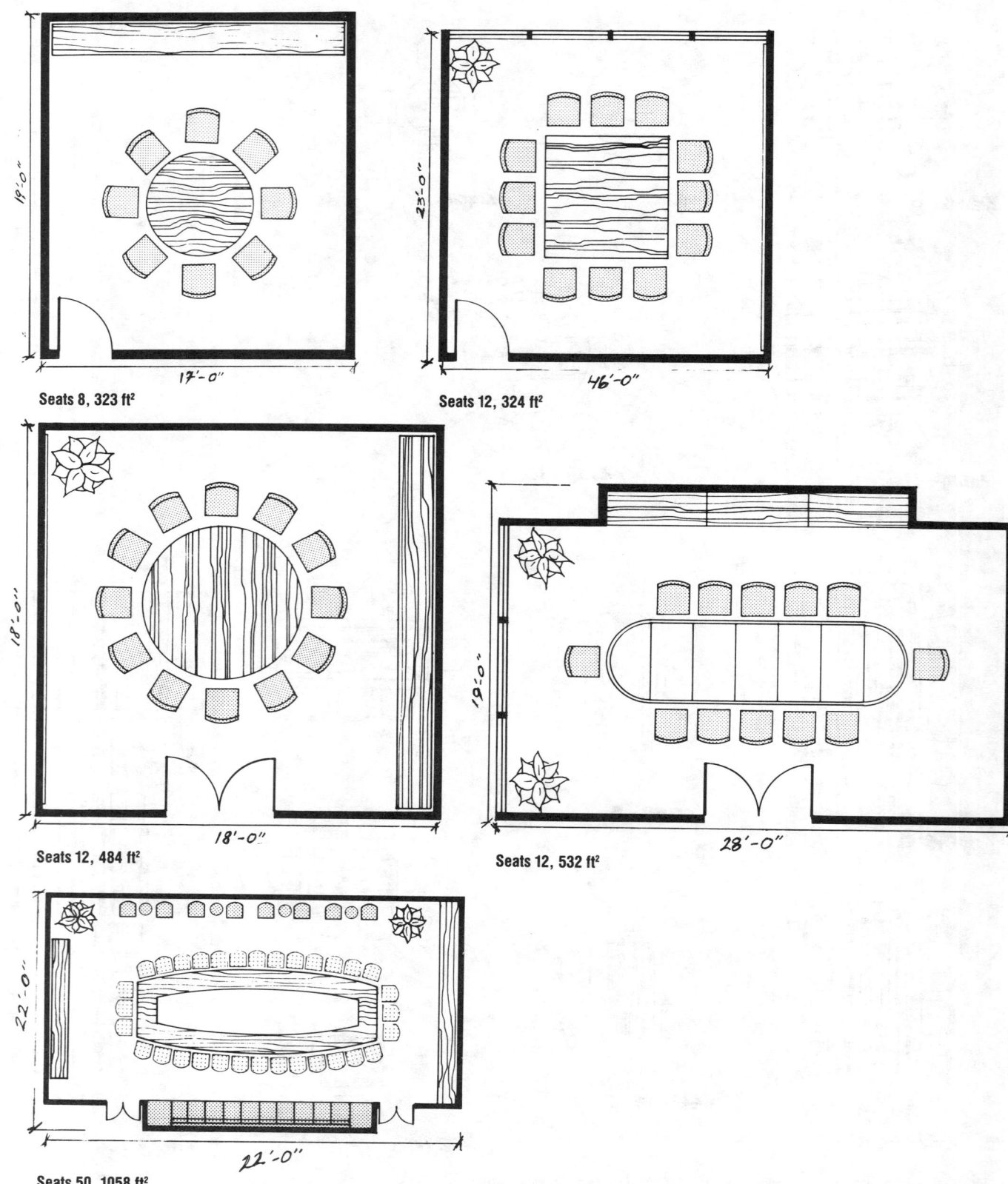

Seats 8, 323 ft²

Seats 12, 324 ft²

Seats 12, 484 ft²

Seats 12, 532 ft²

Seats 50, 1058 ft²

Fig. 4   These drawings provide the designer with a variety of conference room sizes, table shapes, floor areas, and seating capacities. They are useful in client discussions and in making preliminary area allocations. Chair size and circulation areas behind the chairs will, of course, cause overall dimensions to vary.

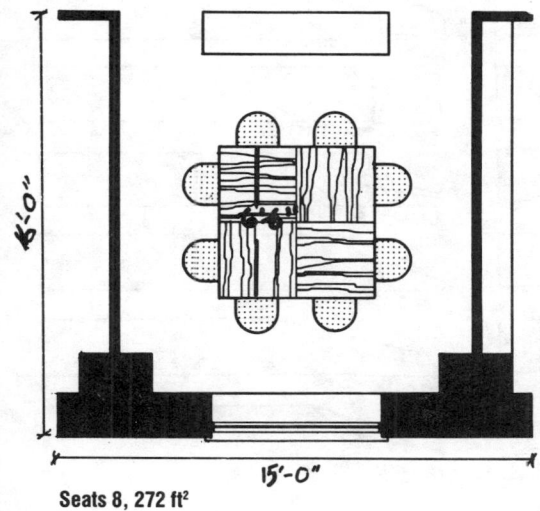

Seats 8, 272 ft²

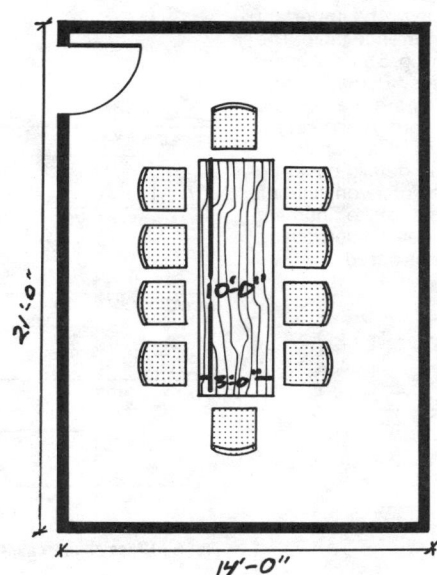

Seats 10, 294 ft²

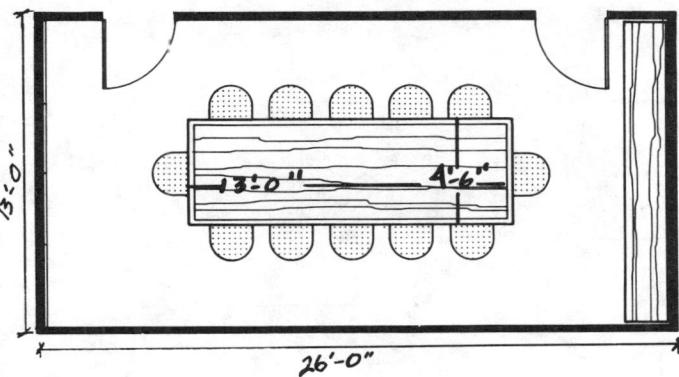

Seats 12, 338 ft²

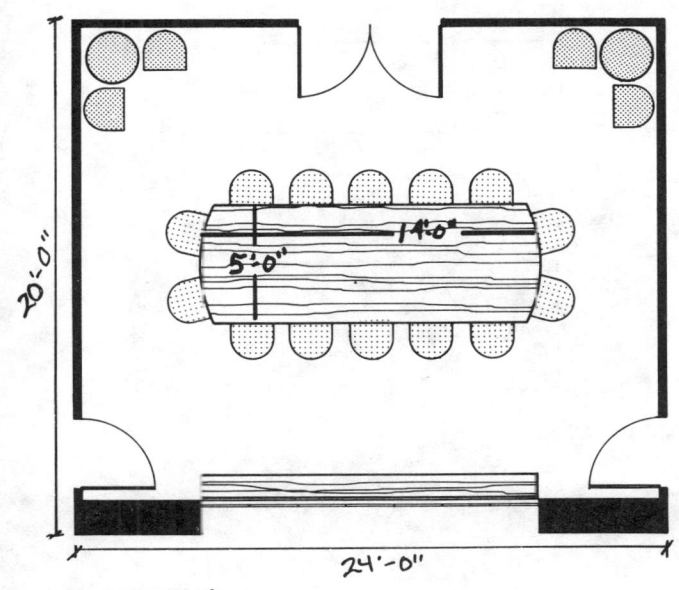

Seats 18, 480 ft²

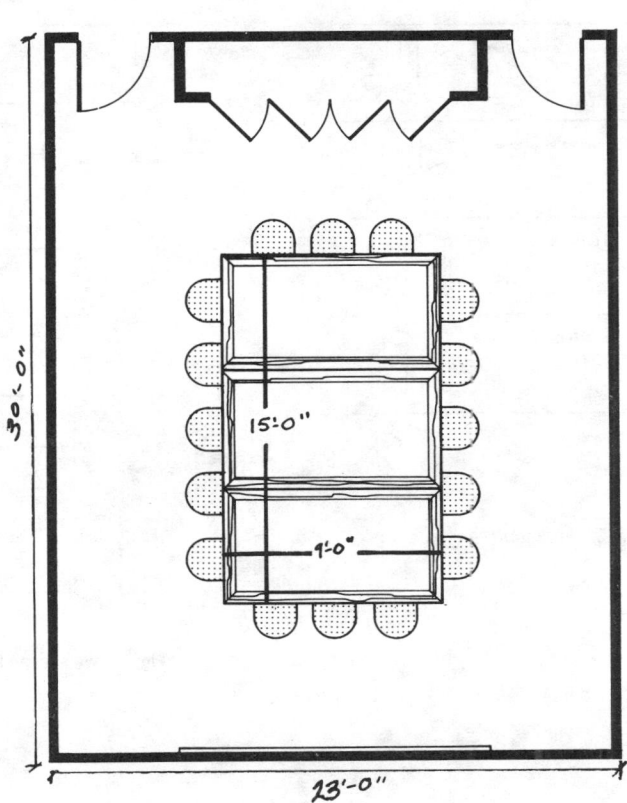

Seats 16, 690 ft²

CONFERENCE ROOMS

Table Base and Edge Treatments

It is important for the designer to understand and appreciate some of the important details that make up a conference table. The base treatments shown in Fig. 5 are but a few of the myriad possibilities. Perhaps even more important to consider are the finished edges of glass and wood conference tables, representative details of which are shown in Figs. 6 and 7. Other edge details could be made of marble, granite, or even leather. Fingers, hands, and arms make intimate contact with these edge details, something that should be carefully considered.

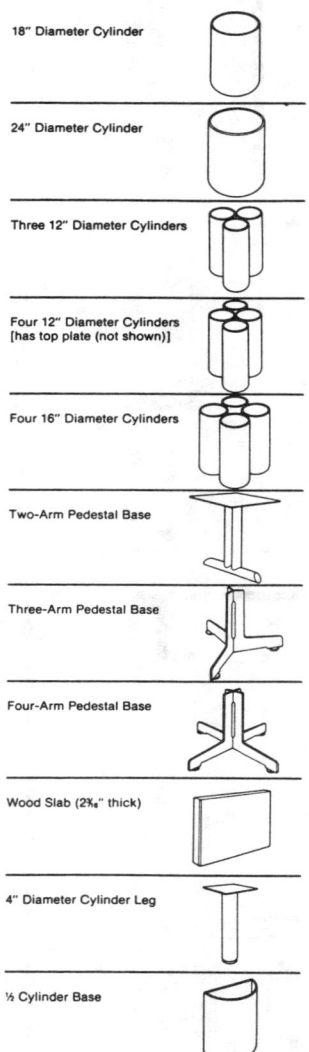

Fig. 5   Base treatment.

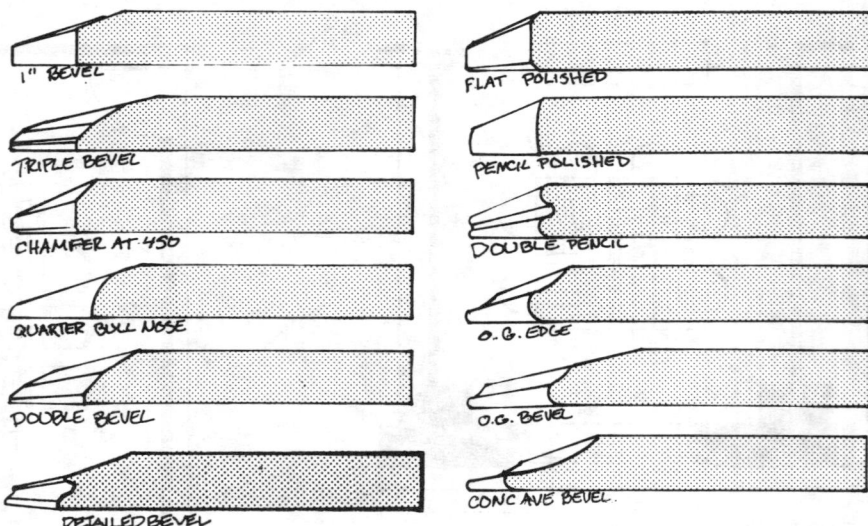

Fig. 6   Glass edge treatment.

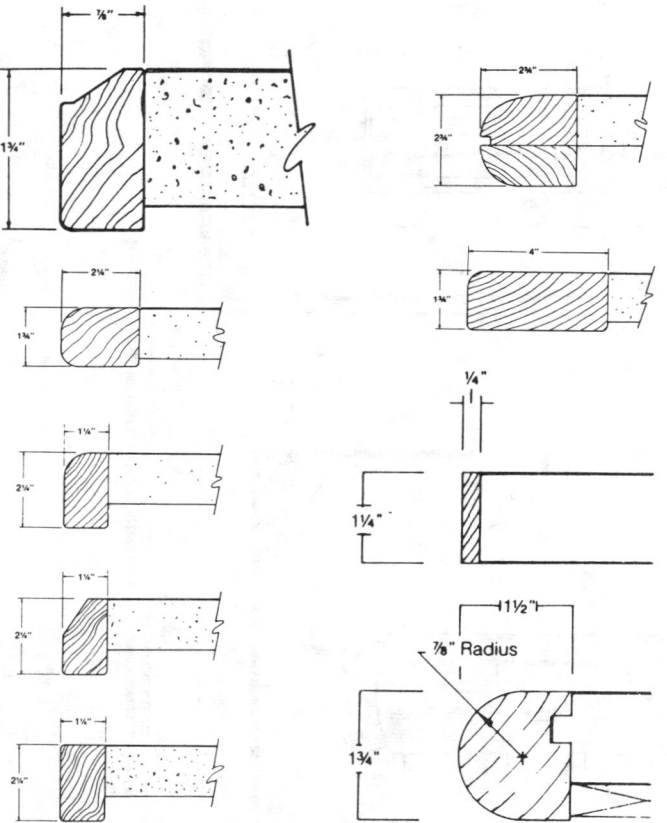

Fig. 7   Wood edge treatment.

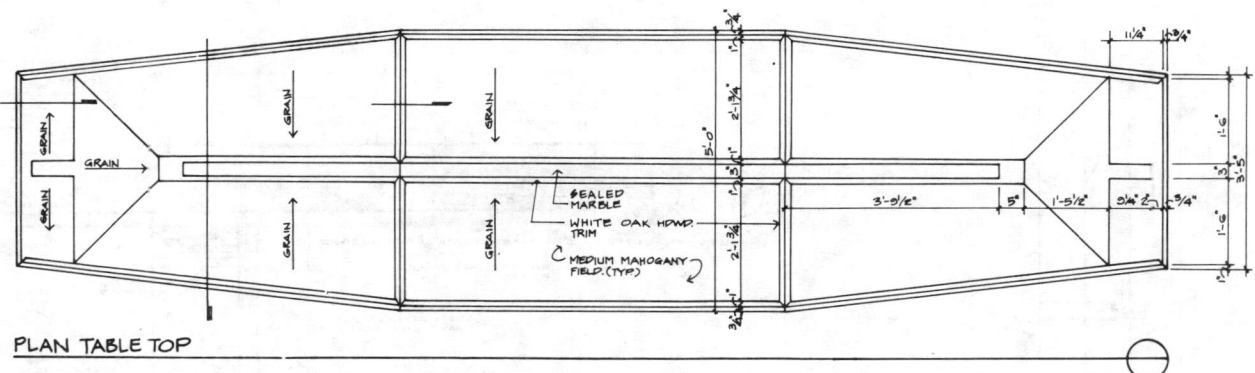

PLAN TABLE TOP

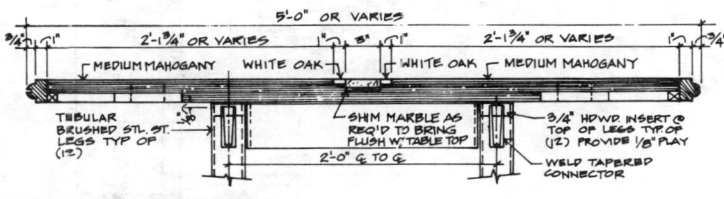

Medium Mahogany **White Oak** **White Oak** **Medium Mahogany**

SECTION TABLE TOP

NOTE! FOR WELDED TAPERED CONN. PREPARE SUBSTRATE AS REQ'D FOR WELDING. CLEAN & DRESS WELDS AS REQ'D.

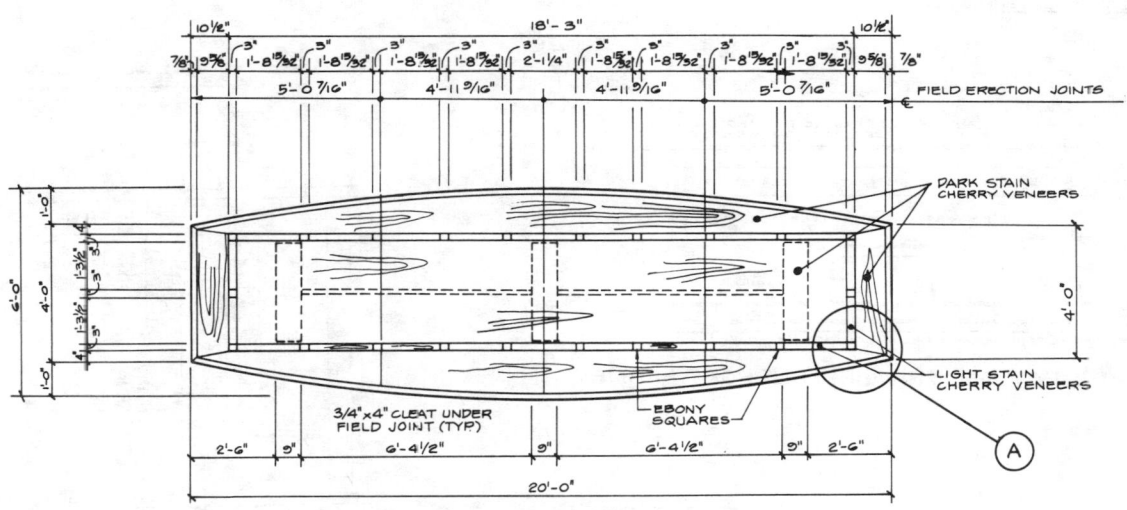

PLAN-CONFERENCE TABLE

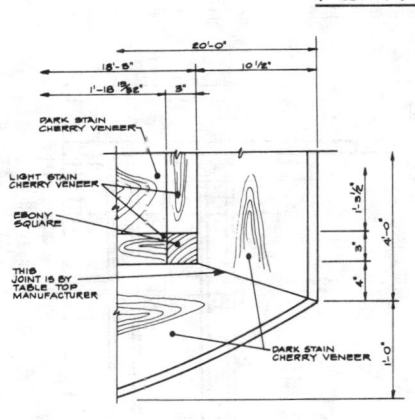

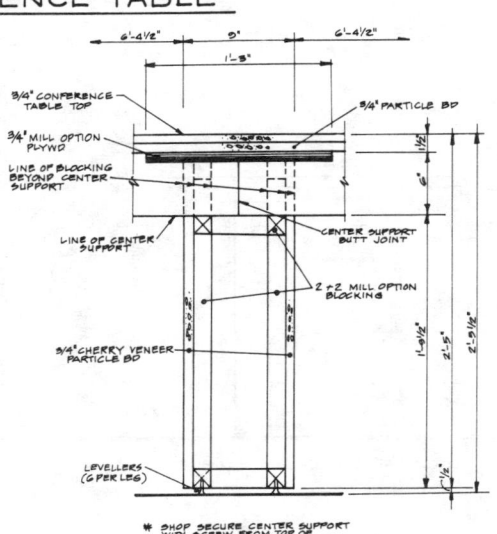

SECTION

CONFERENCE ROOMS
Conference Table Details

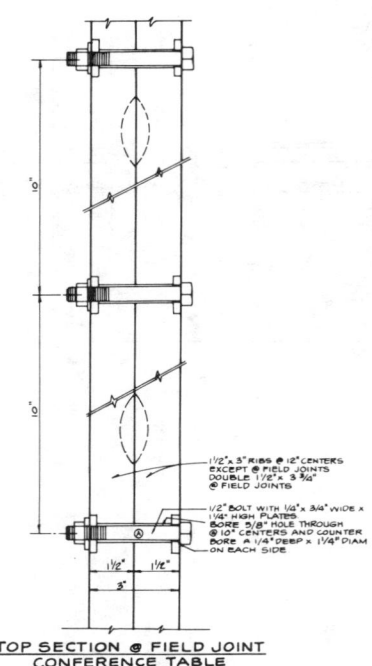

TOP SECTION @ FIELD JOINT
CONFERENCE TABLE

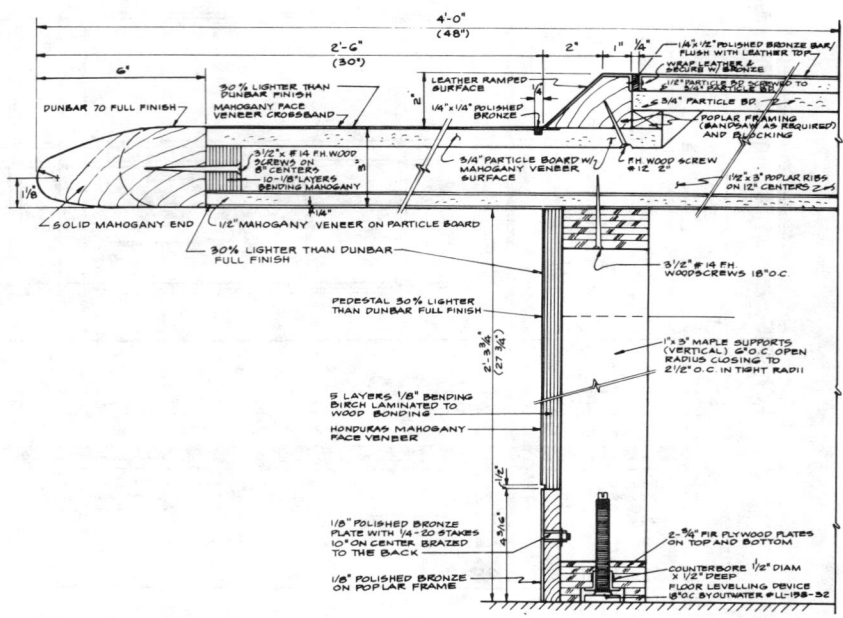

TYPICAL SECTION CONFERENCE TABLE

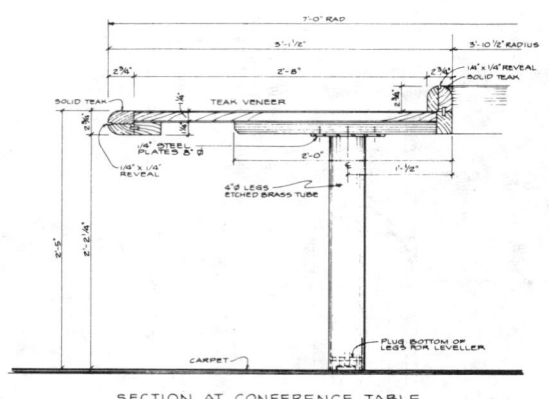

SECTION THROUGH SUPPORT FRAME

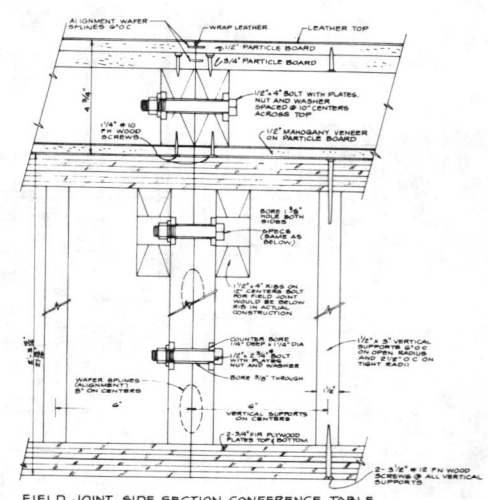

FIELD JOINT SIDE SECTION CONFERENCE TABLE

SECTION AT CONFERENCE TABLE

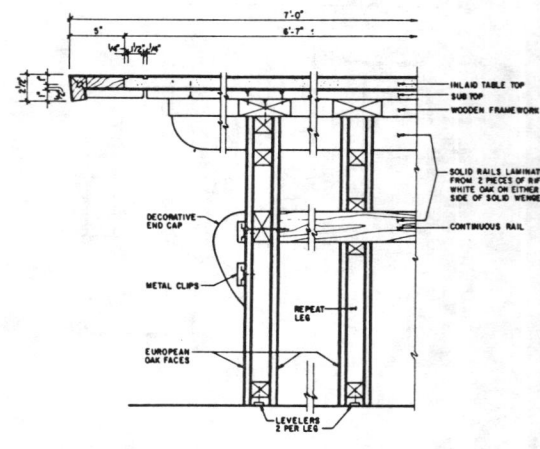

SECTION AT CONFERENCE TABLE

Custom credenza units are often designed to complement the details of a conference table. They serve multiple functions, including storage, incorporation of electronic media equipment, display, and as a work surface. In addition, architectural woodwork is used to enclose existing convector covers and to frame window openings. It is important for the designer to consider providing ease of access to the heating and air-handling elements behind the woodwork, as well as allowing the appropriate flow of air.

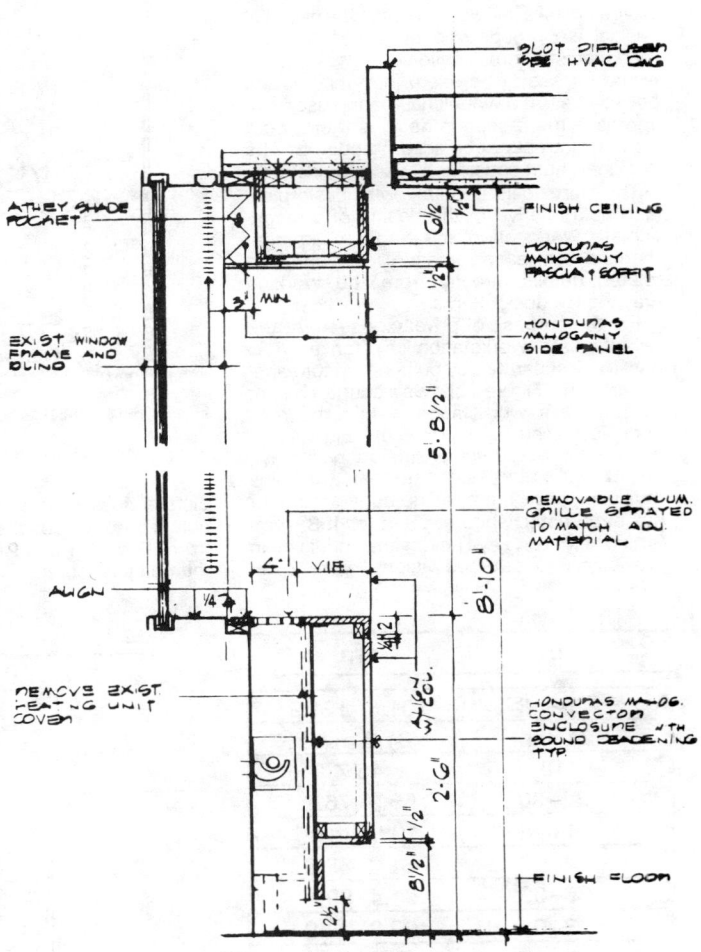

TYP. SECTION THRU CONF CENTER CREDENZA

SECTION THRU MILLWORK HEATING UNIT ENCLOSURE

RECEPTION AREAS

Planning Data: Receptionist's Workstation

Proper design of the reception area is critical in communicating an organization's desired corporate image. Reception spaces are both the first and last areas with which the visitor interacts and, accordingly, have considerable visual impact in communicating that image.

Not only must the reception space look attractive, but it must function properly as well. The two most important planning elements in this regard are the visitor's seating area and the receptionist's workstation or desk.

While most of the examples in this part are drawn from corporate interiors, the designer is urged to take into consideration the needs of special user groups who must interact with a receptionist. If small children are to communicate (or see or be seen), how high is the privacy wall? If a wheelchair-bound user is to approach the reception desk, is there room for the footrests to be accommodated? The designer must consider all user populations.

This part deals primarily with basic planning data relative to the design of a receptionist's workstation and furniture arrangements of the seating areas. Also included are related details directly from the working drawings of design firms.

For the purpose of privacy or security, the receptionist's workstation is often an area physically separated by built-in furniture and/or partitions. Figure 1 shows a counter height receptionist's workstation. While the relationship of worksurface to seat height is key, other anthropometric considerations are eye height and sitting height normal. The minimum height of the opening above the floor has been established at 78 in, or 198.1 cm. Sitting height and eye height are significant in providing unobstructed vision. Figure 2 de-

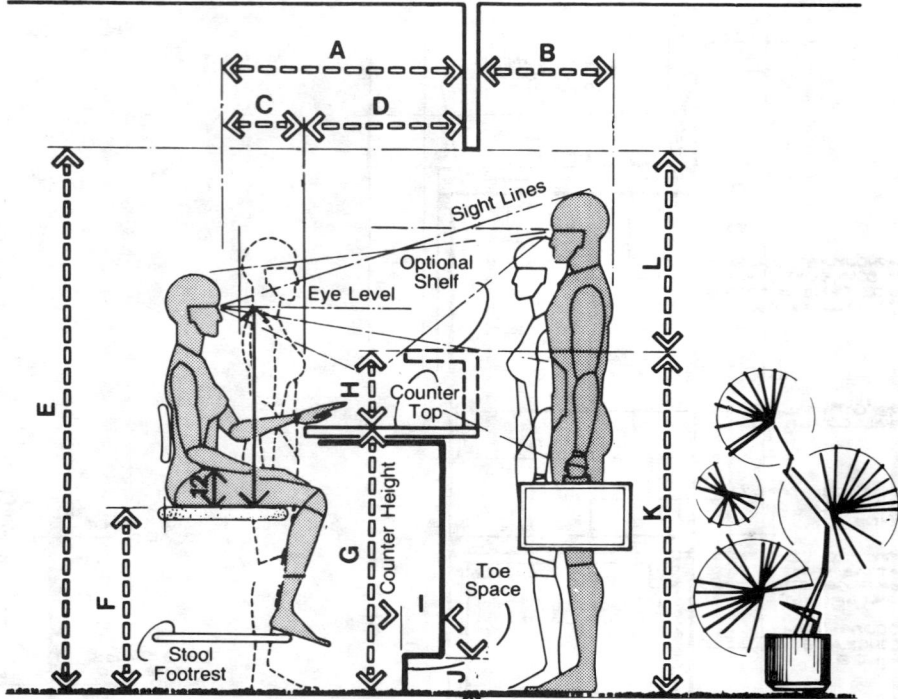

Fig. 1   Receptionist's workstation/counter height.

picts a desk height receptionist's workstation. The depth of the worksurface ranges from 26 to 30 in, or 66 to 76.2 cm, allowing for thumb tip reach required for the exchange of papers and packages. Both Figs. 1 and 2 show in broken line an added counter top element often provided for security or as a visual screen of the work surface top.

	in	cm
A	40–48	101.6–121.9
B	24 min.	61.0 min.
C	18	45.7
D	22–30	55.9–76.2
E	78 min.	198.1 min.
F	24–27	61.0–68.6
G	36–39	91.4–99.1
H	8–9	20.3–22.9
I	2–4	5.1–10.2
J	4	10.2
K	44–48	111.8–121.9
L	34 min.	86.4 min.
M	44–48	111.8–121.9
N	54	137.2
O	26–30	66.0–76.2
P	24	61.0
Q	30	76.2
R	15–18	38.1–45.7
S	29–30	73.7–76.2
T	10–12	25.4–30.5
U	6–9	15.2–22.9
V	39–42	99.1–106.7

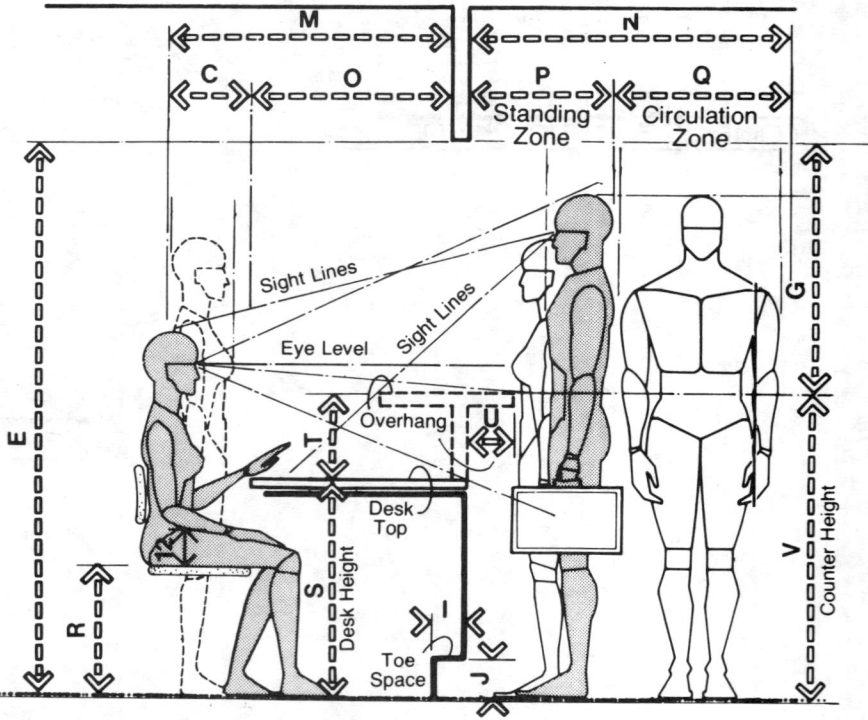

Fig. 2   Receptionist's workstation/desk height.

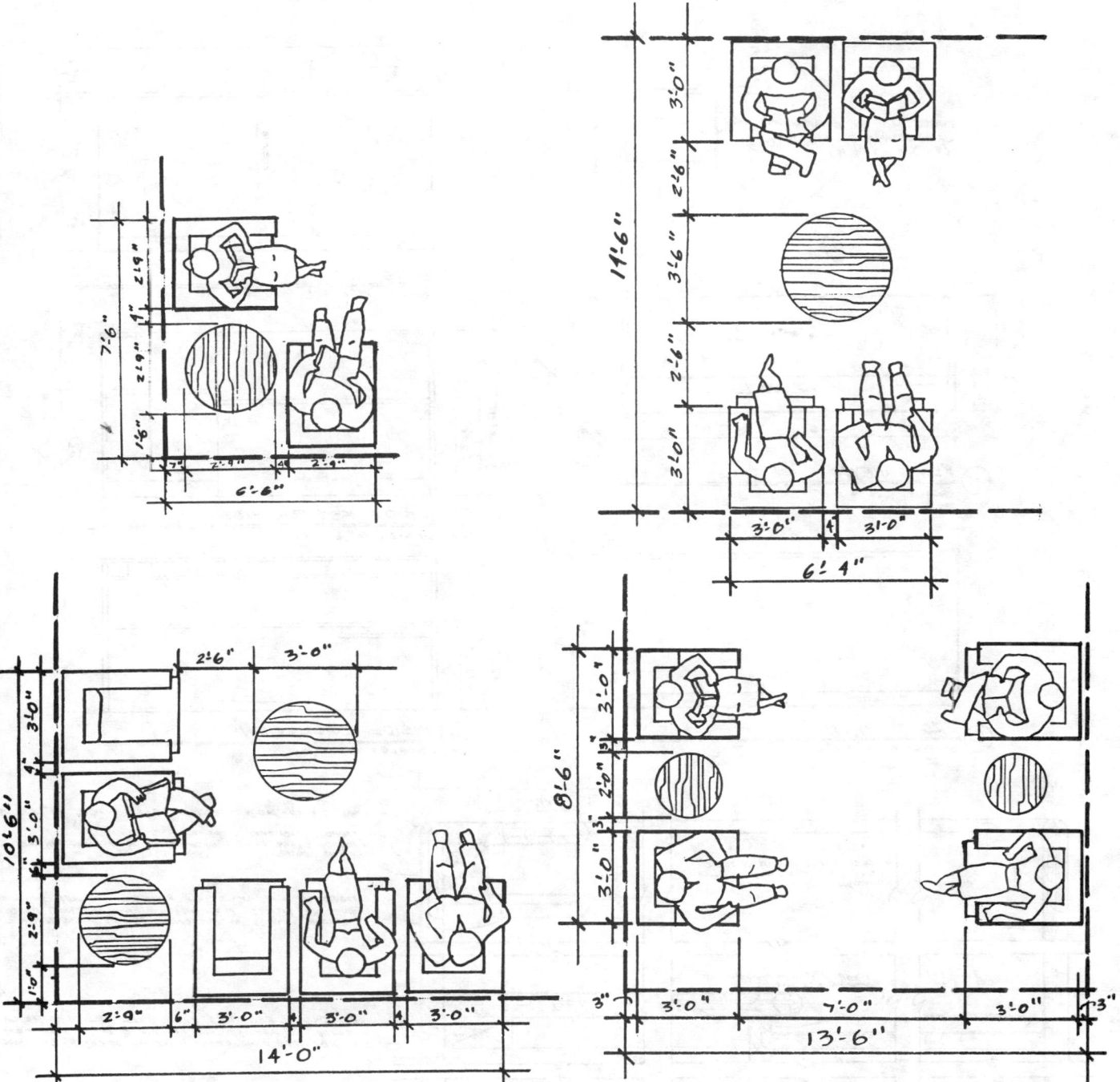

Fig. 3 The seating arrangements illustrated here provide some typical conditions that the designer must address. Individual seats are preferred over sofas. Corner seating arrangements must always consider leg clearance. Circulation between low tables and the edges of chairs must be adequate to allow for the legs of persons seated in the chairs. Convenient locations for side tables, so that magazines, ashtrays, artwork, or portable lighting can be placed on them, are important.

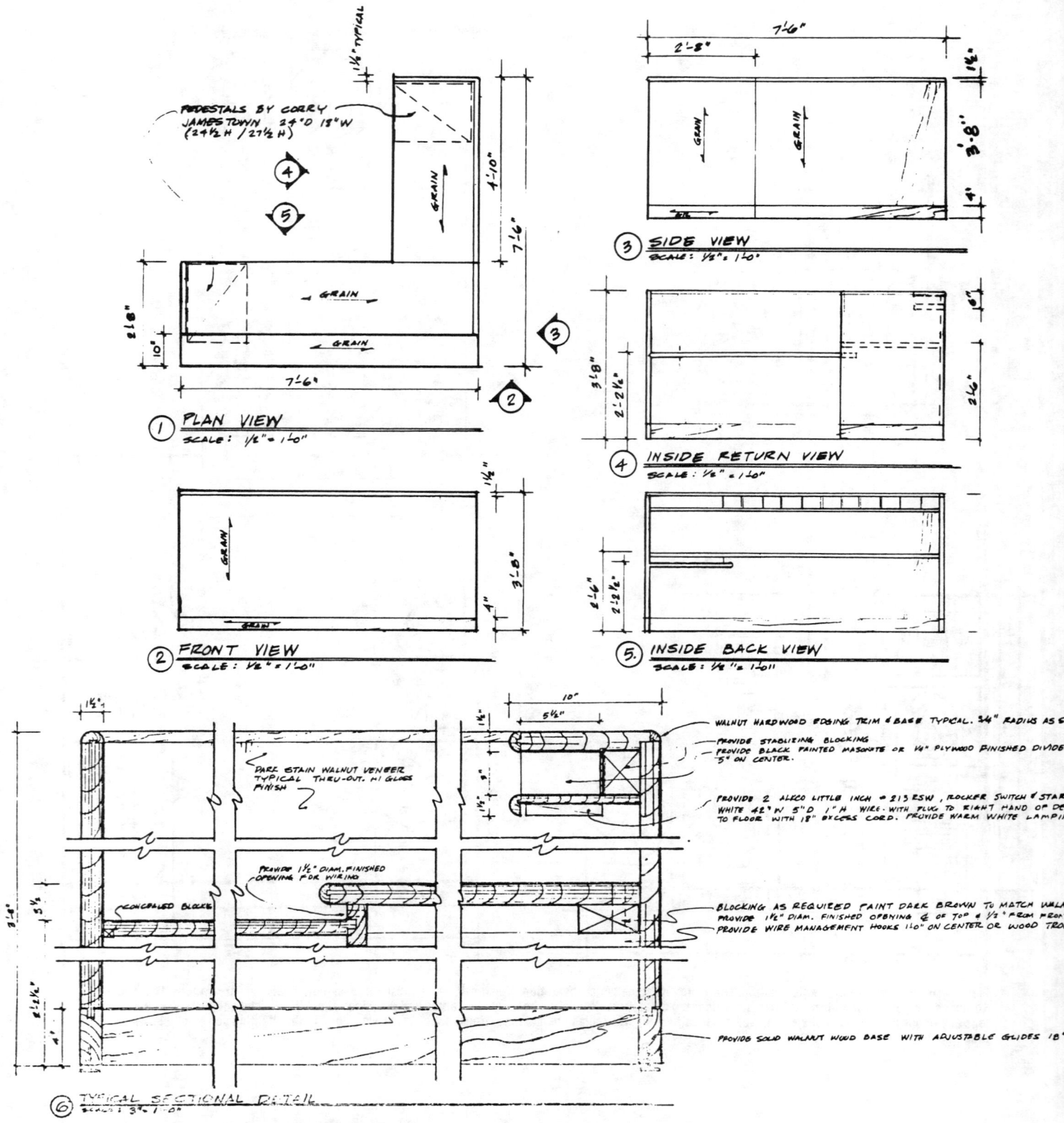

Fig. 4   Depending upon the size of an office, a reception desk can be either relatively simple and small in scale, or relatively complex and large in scale, sometimes staffed by two or more persons. The reception desk illustrated here shows a typical L-shaped unit with 44-in-high privacy panel. Reception desks of this type can either be custom designed or purchased from a manufacturer.

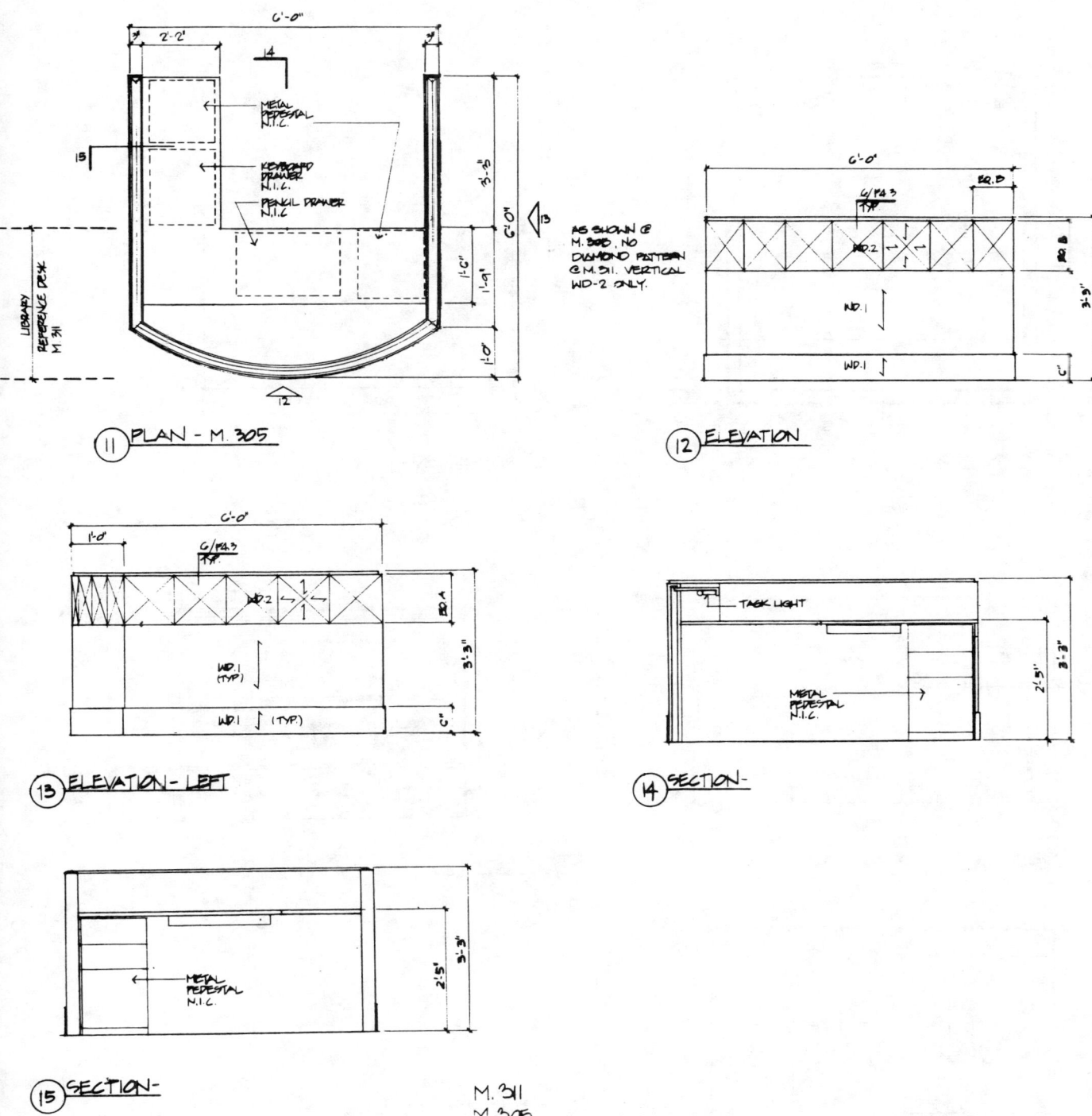

⑪ PLAN - M. 305

⑫ ELEVATION

⑬ ELEVATION - LEFT

⑭ SECTION-

⑮ SECTION-

M. 311
M. 305

Fig. 5   More privacy can be achieved in the design of a reception desk when there is enclosure on three sides, as is shown here. When designing custom reception desks, it is important to fully understand the tasks that the person working there will be asked to perform, in order to provide for adequate storage, work surfaces at the appropriate height, the incorporation of electronic equipment, and task lighting.

RECEPTION AREAS
Reception Desk Details

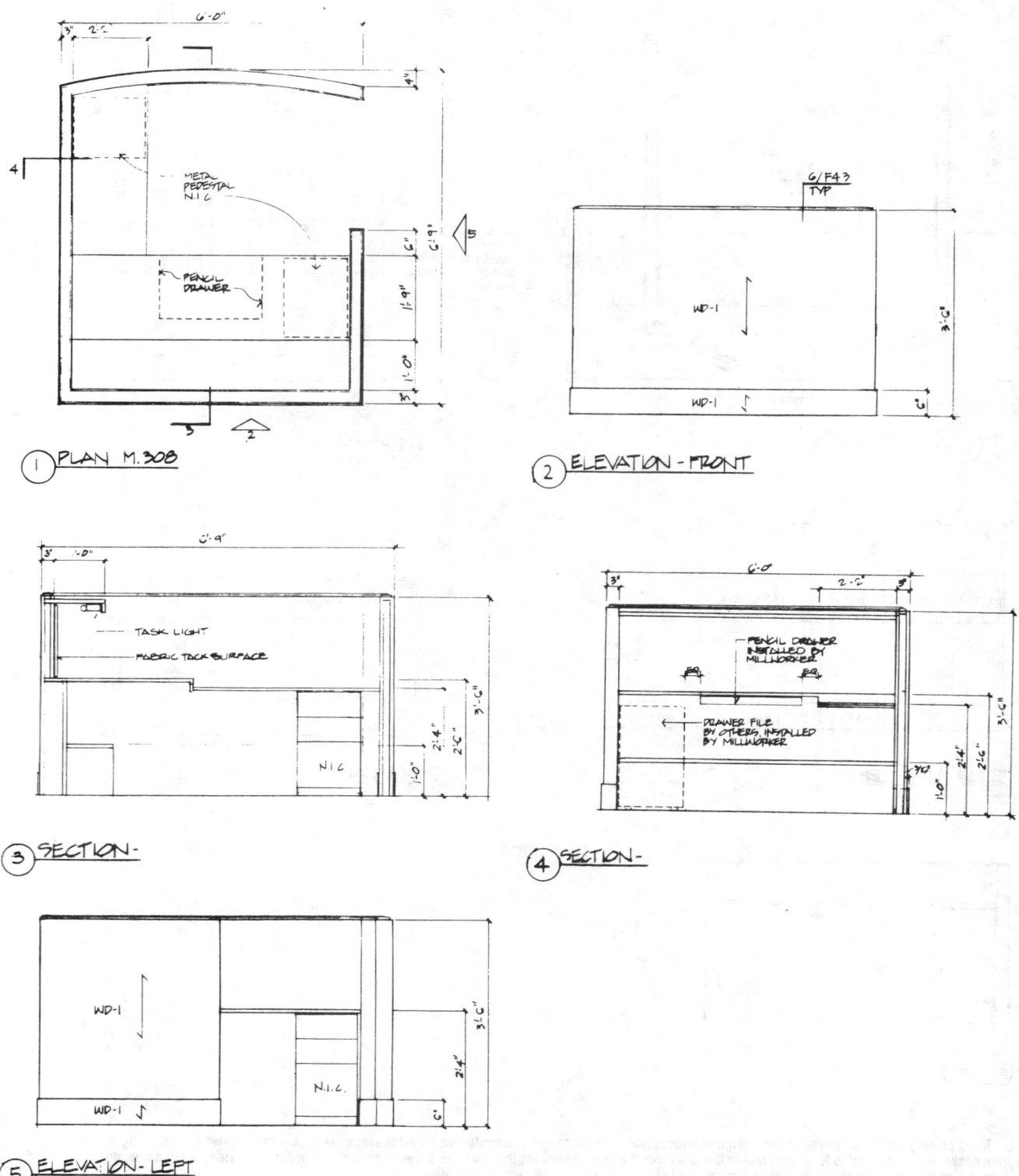

Fig. 6 The reception desk shown here is designed in order to provide privacy on three sides with partial privacy on the fourth side. In this example, a right-hand typing return has been provided. Careful consideration should always be given to the height and placement of task lighting in order to ensure that the surface or task below is being lit properly. Many designers do not give this adequate thought. Overall costs of custom-designed reception desks can be reduced by integrating standard metal file compoments into the architectural woodwork.

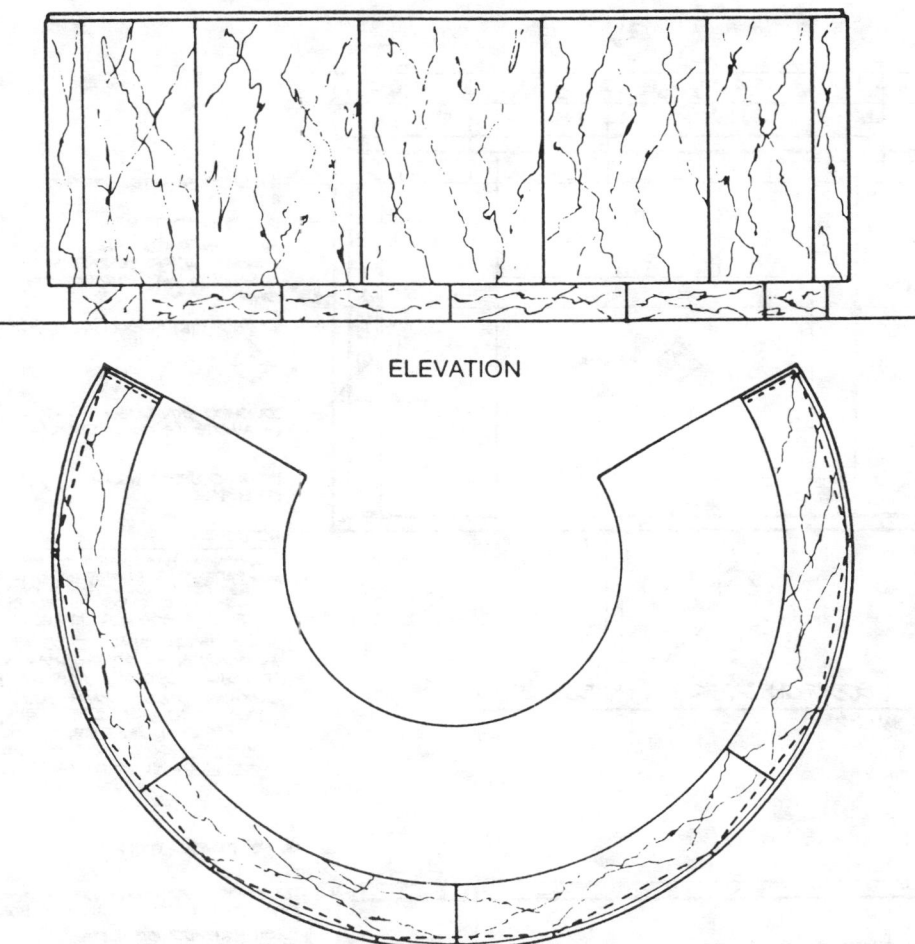

ELEVATION

PLAN RECEPTION DESK

½" = 1'-0"

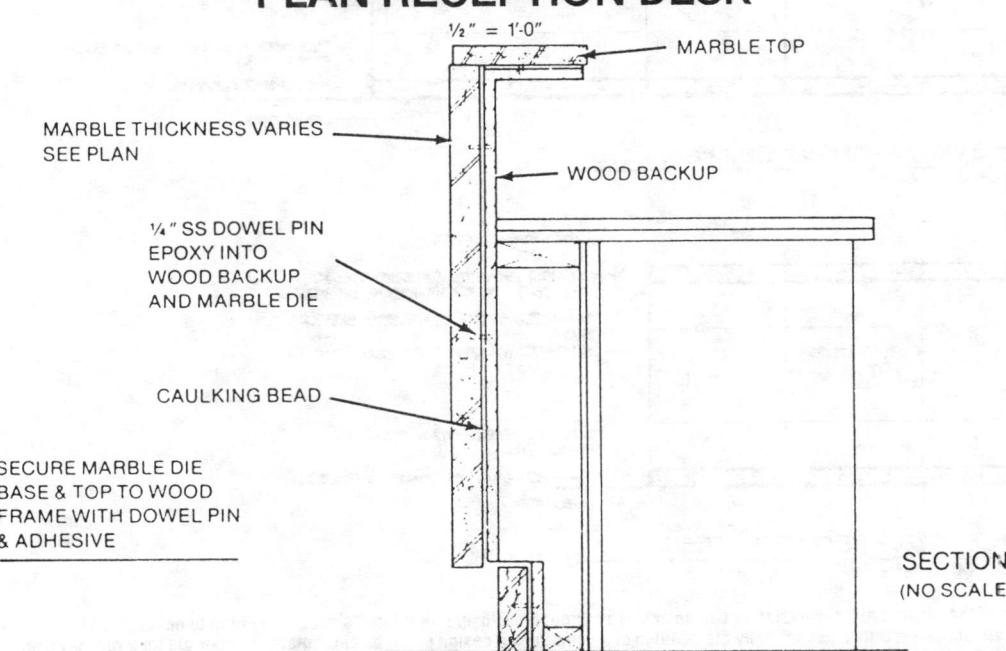

MARBLE TOP

MARBLE THICKNESS VARIES
SEE PLAN

WOOD BACKUP

¼" SS DOWEL PIN
EPOXY INTO
WOOD BACKUP
AND MARBLE DIE

CAULKING BEAD

SECURE MARBLE DIE
BASE & TOP TO WOOD
FRAME WITH DOWEL PIN
& ADHESIVE

SECTION
(NO SCALE)

Fig. 7 A larger reception desk can accommodate work surfaces on three sides, as shown here. With this type of configuration, however, the designer must be concerned with the orientation of the open side. As with all custom reception desks, the designer must anticipate the integration of wiring and electronic equipment within the architectural woodwork.

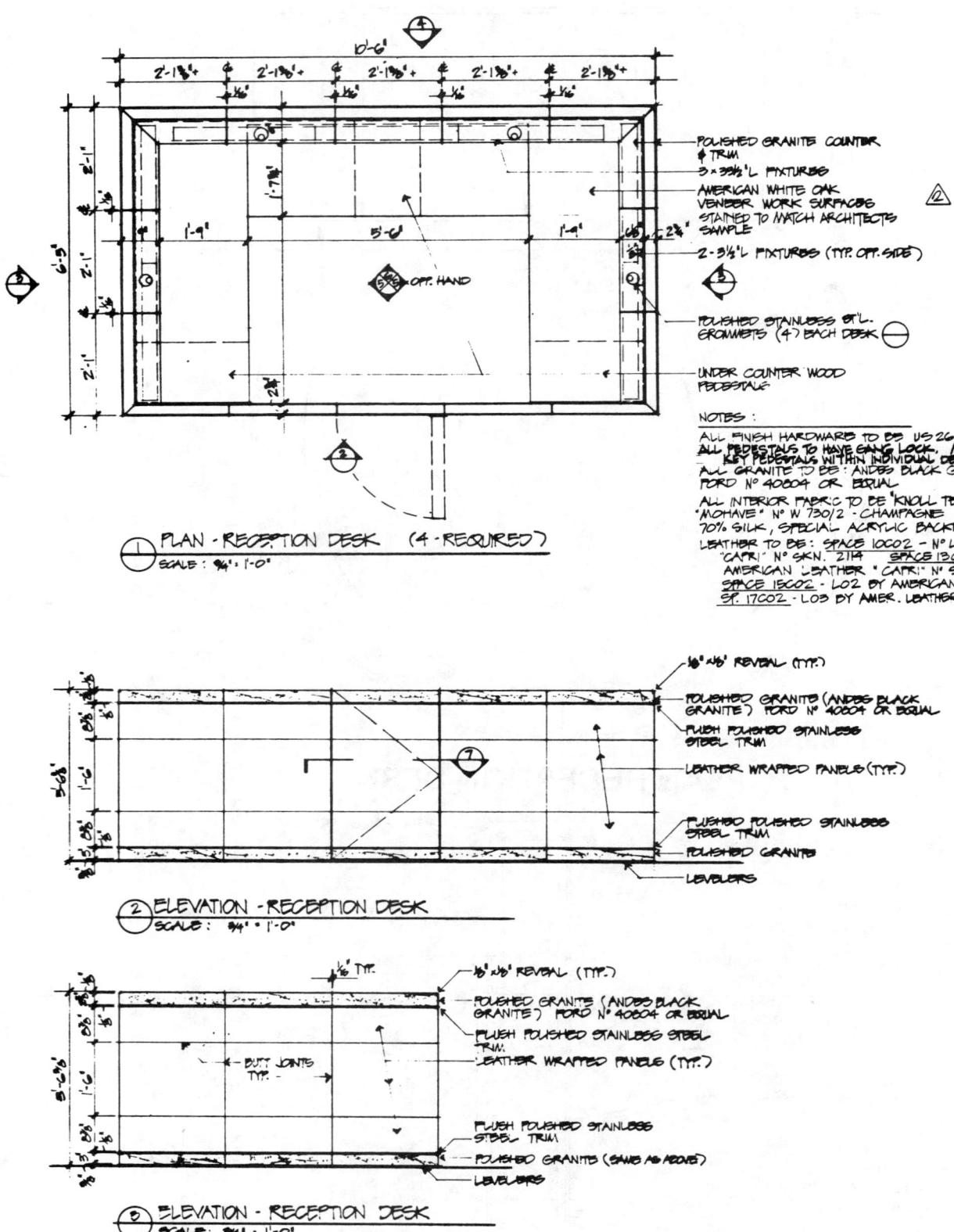

Fig. 8 Total privacy of the receptionist's workstation can be achieved through enclosure on all four sides. In addition to enhancing visual privacy, such a design can also provide added security and control by the addition of a door. Such a design might be particularly appropriate for a reception area where the designer might wish to control access by children.

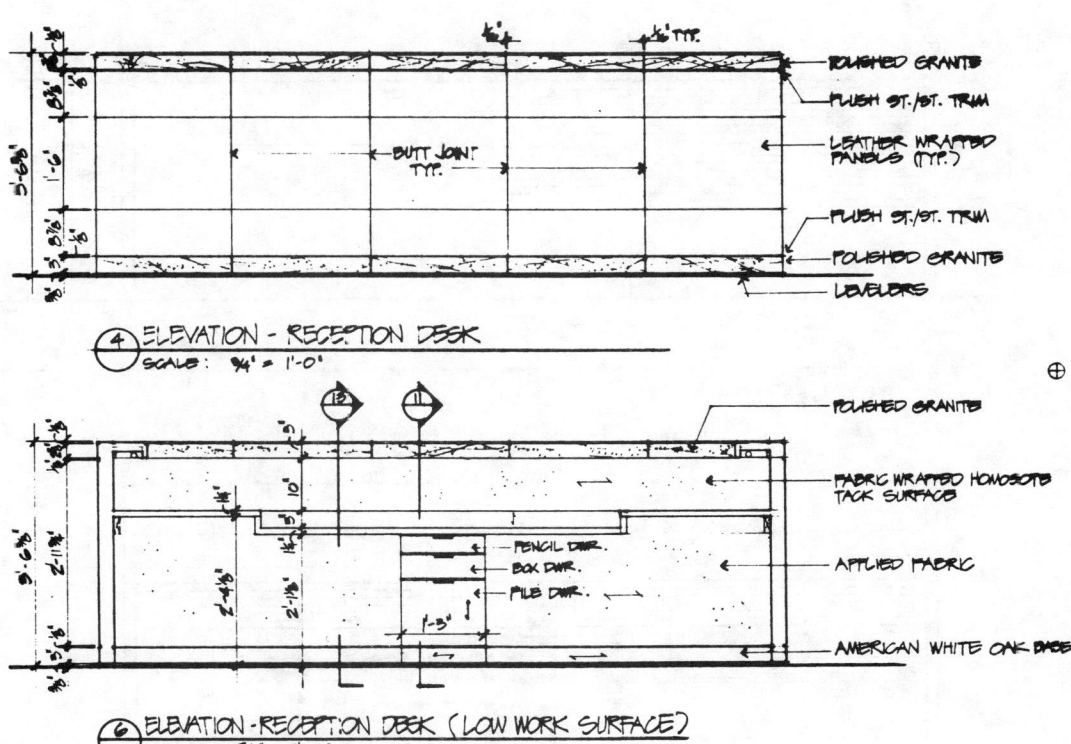

④ ELEVATION - RECEPTION DESK
SCALE: 3/4" = 1'-0"

POLISHED GRANITE
FLUSH ST./ST. TRIM
LEATHER WRAPPED PANELS (TYP.)
FLUSH ST./ST. TRIM
POLISHED GRANITE
LEVELERS

BUTT JOINT TYP.

⑥ ELEVATION - RECEPTION DESK (LOW WORK SURFACE)
SCALE: 3/4" = 1'-0"

POLISHED GRANITE
FABRIC WRAPPED HOMOSOTE TACK SURFACE
APPLIED FABRIC
AMERICAN WHITE OAK BASE

PENCIL DWR.
BOX DWR.
FILE DWR.

⑤ ELEVATION - RECEPTION DESK (WORK SURFACE)
SCALE: 3/4" = 1'-0"

POLISHED GRANITE
FABRIC WRAPPED HOMOSOTE TACK SURFACE
APPLIED FABRIC
AMERICAN WHITE OAK BASE

PENCIL DWR.
BOX DWR.
FILE DWR.

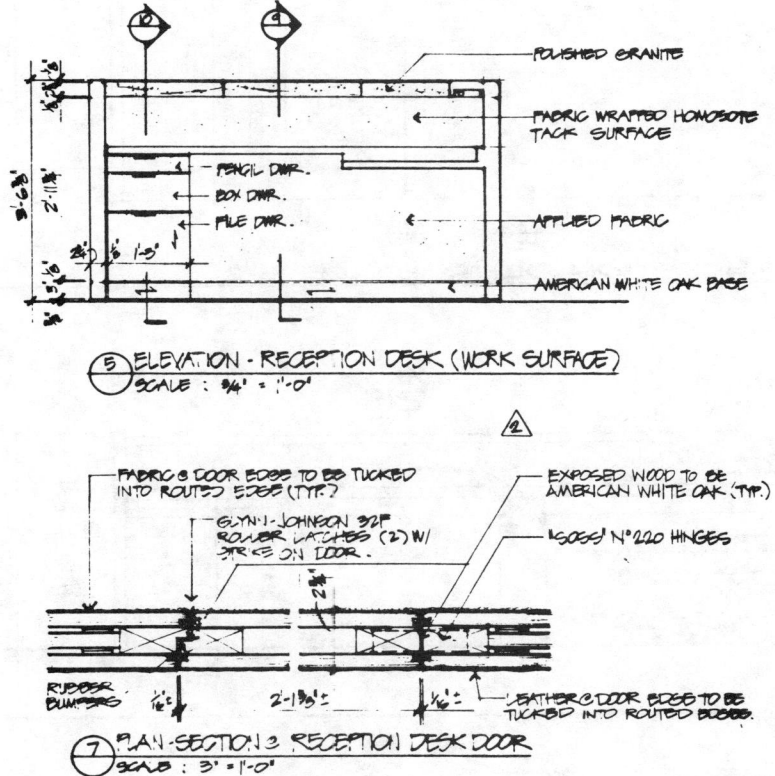

FABRIC & DOOR EDGE TO BE TUCKED INTO ROUTED EDGE (TYP.)
GLYN-JOHNSON 32F ROLLER LATCHES (2) W/ STRIKE ON DOOR.
EXPOSED WOOD TO BE AMERICAN WHITE OAK (TYP.)
SOSS N°220 HINGES
RUBBER BUMPERS
LEATHER & DOOR EDGE TO BE TUCKED INTO ROUTED EDGE.

⑦ PLAN-SECTION @ RECEPTION DESK DOOR
SCALE: 3" = 1'-0"

Fig. 8 *(Continued)*

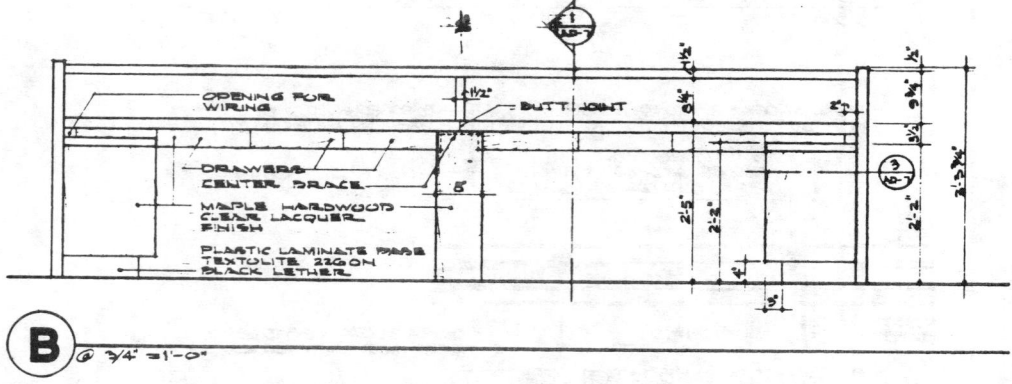

Ⓐ @ 3/4" = 1'-0"

LAMINATED MAPLE

CARPET

Ⓐ AD-7

12'-0"

6'-0" 6'-0"

1/2" Ø HOLE
CENTER BRACE

LAMINATED MAPLE

BUTT JOINT

Ⓢ AD-7

LAMINATED MAPLE

Ⓒ AD-7

Ⓑ AD-7

Ⓛ AD-7

Ⓐ AD-7

PLAN OF RECEPTION DESK SPACE 15-2
@ 3/4" = 1'-0"

Ⓑ @ 3/4" = 1'-0"

OPENING FOR
WIRING

BUTT JOINT

DRAWERS
CENTER BRACE

MAPLE HARDWOOD
CLEAR LACQUER
FINISH

PLASTIC LAMINATE BASE
TEXTOLITE 22GON
BLACK LETHER

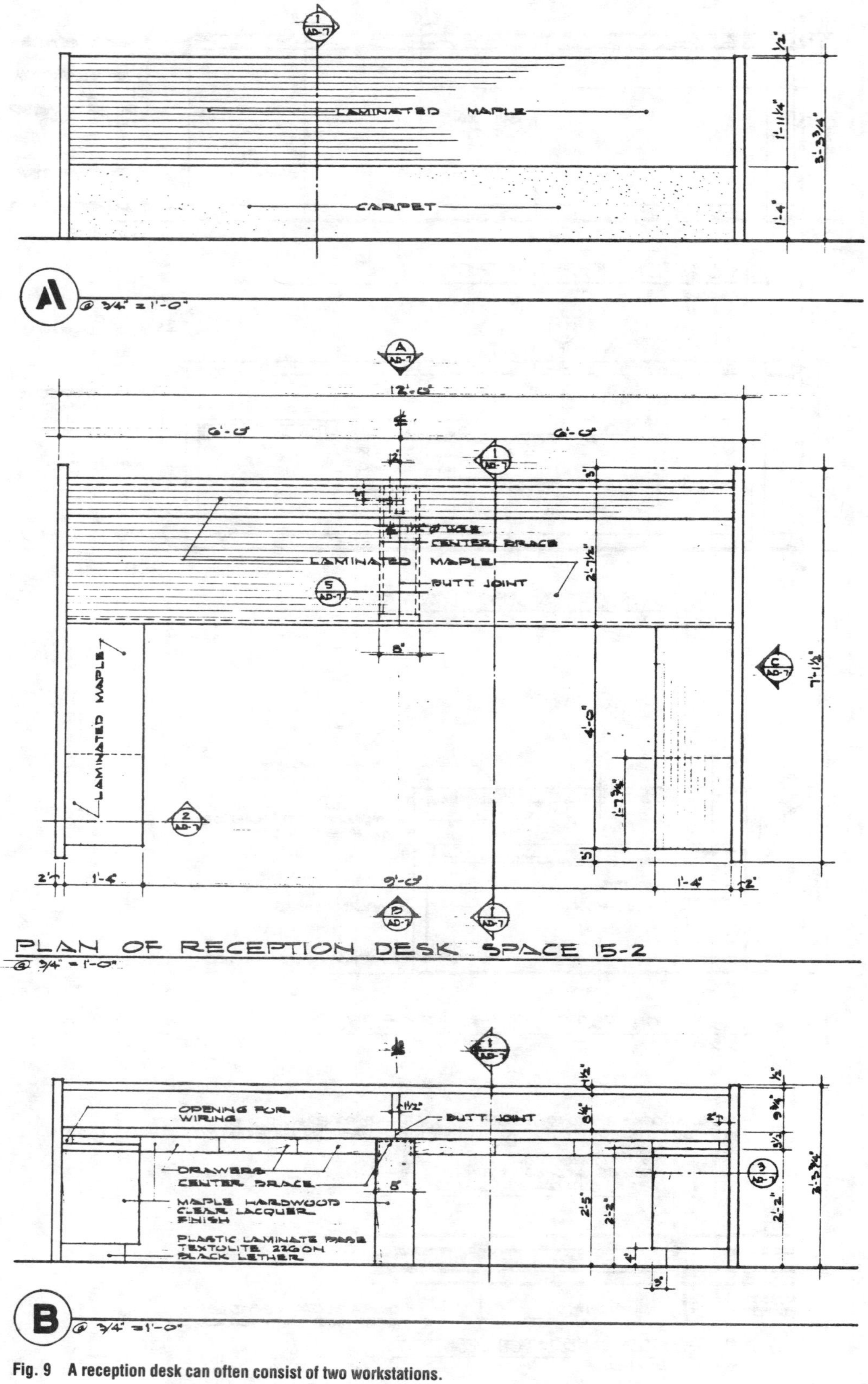

Fig. 9   A reception desk can often consist of two workstations.

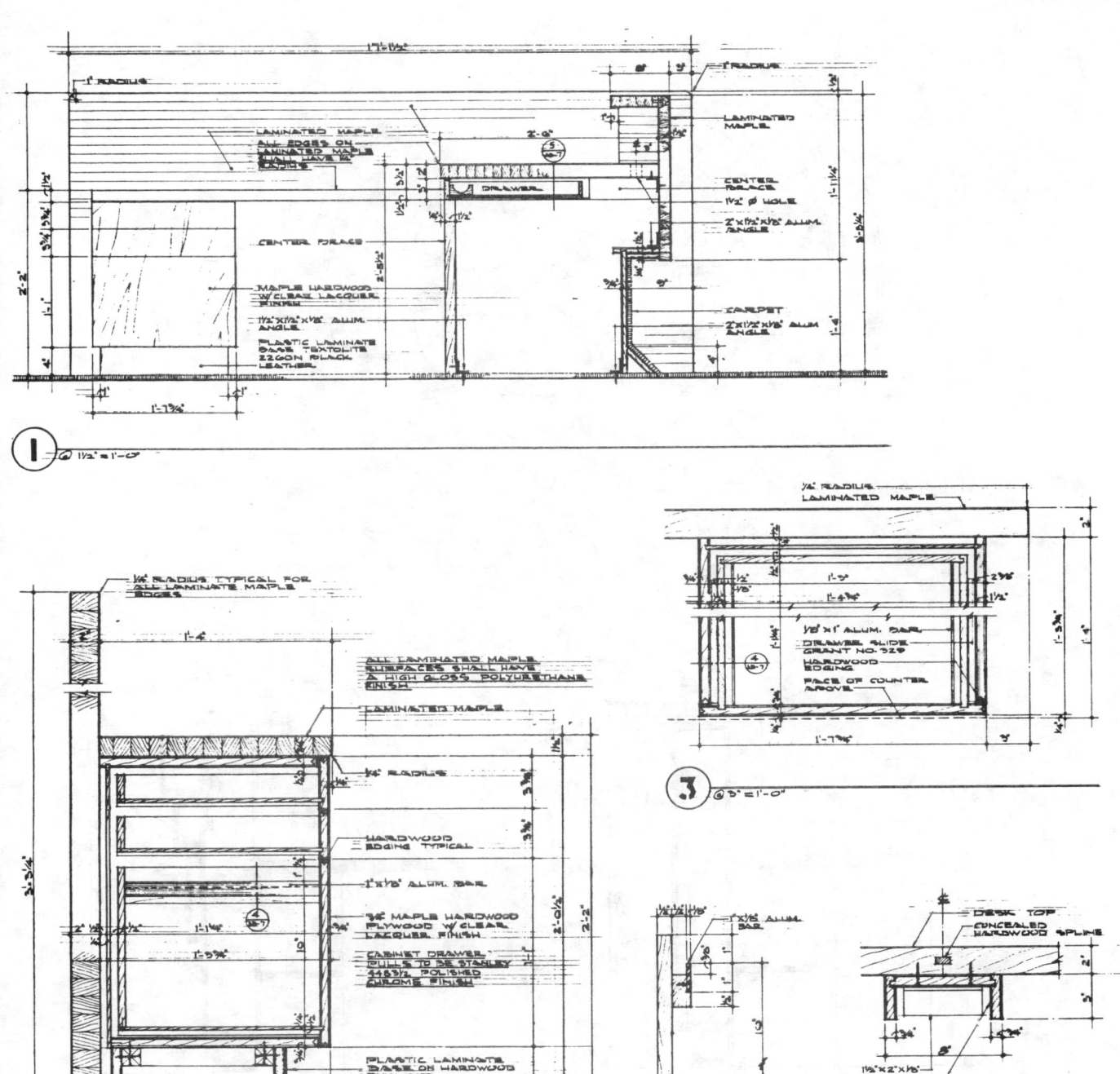

Fig. 9 *(Continued)*

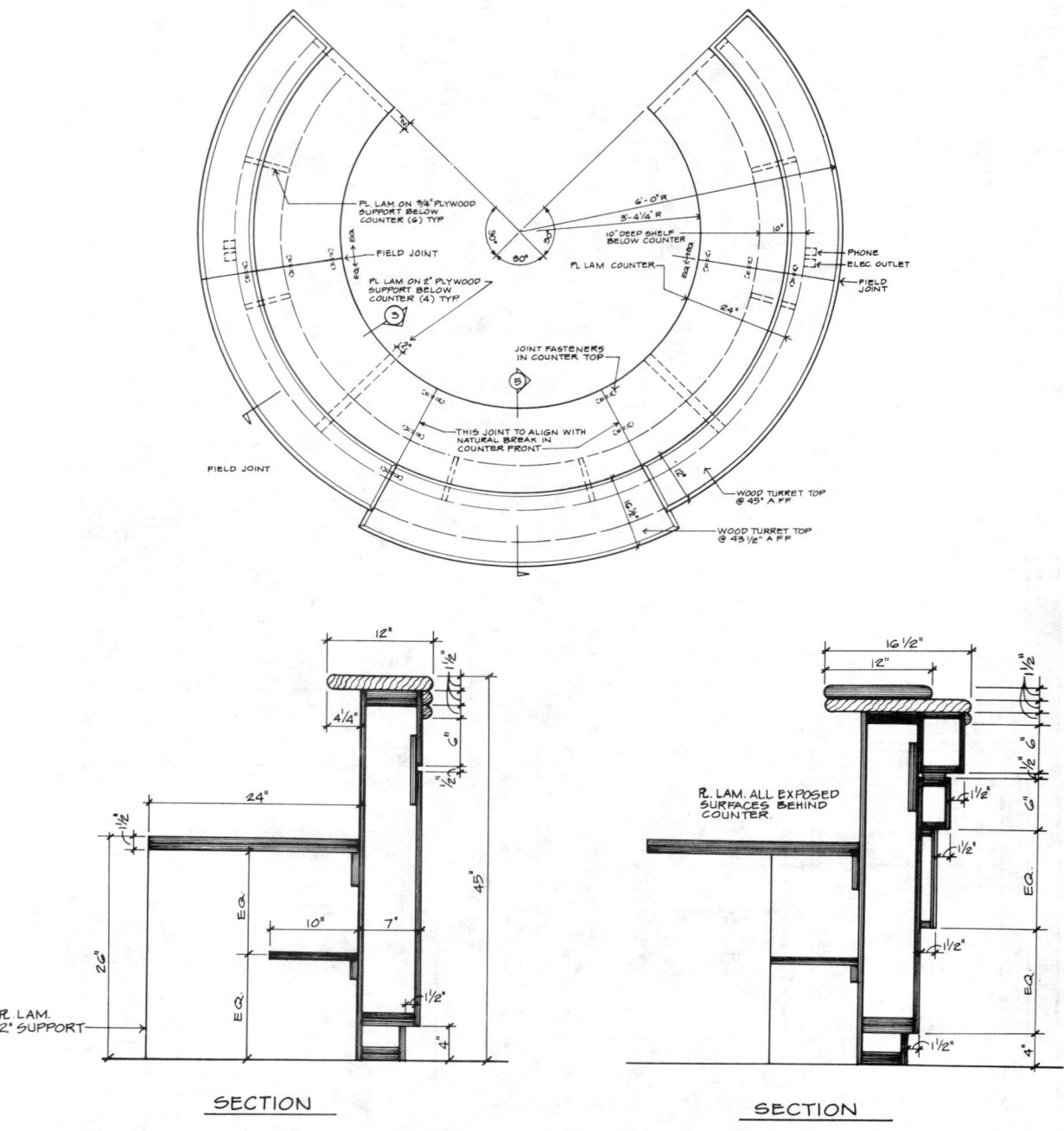

SECTION

SECTION

Fig. 10 A circular reception desk can make a bold and sophisticated corporate statement. The designer is cautioned, however, to carefully analyze the minimum radius required for chair movement. Custom built-in files and drawers, if also curved, can become costly and sometimes impractical.

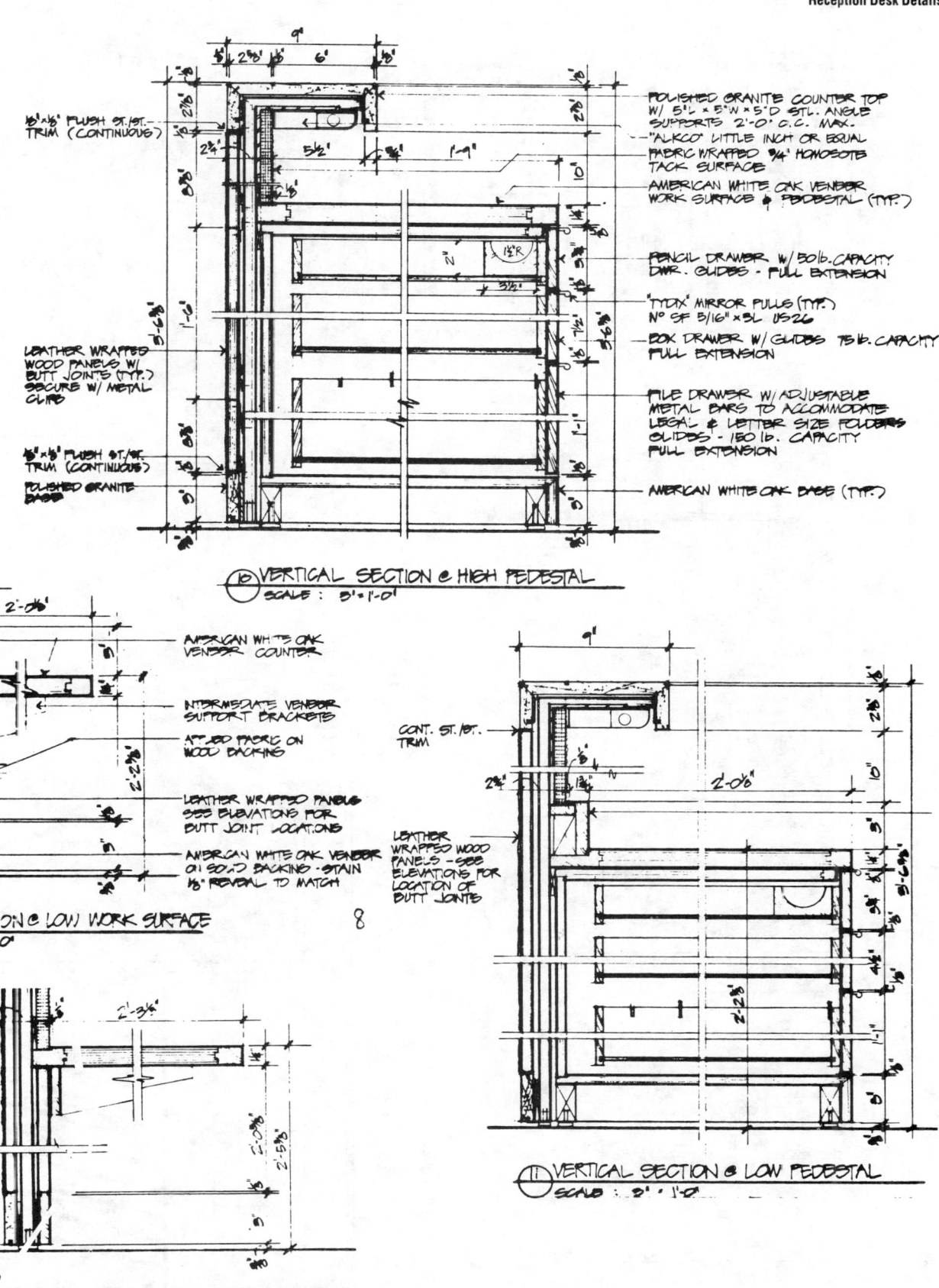

Fig. 11 A fully detailed reception desk will require many large-scale vertical sections to explain the various storage, drawer, work surface, lighting, and electrical requirements. Examples of such details are shown here.

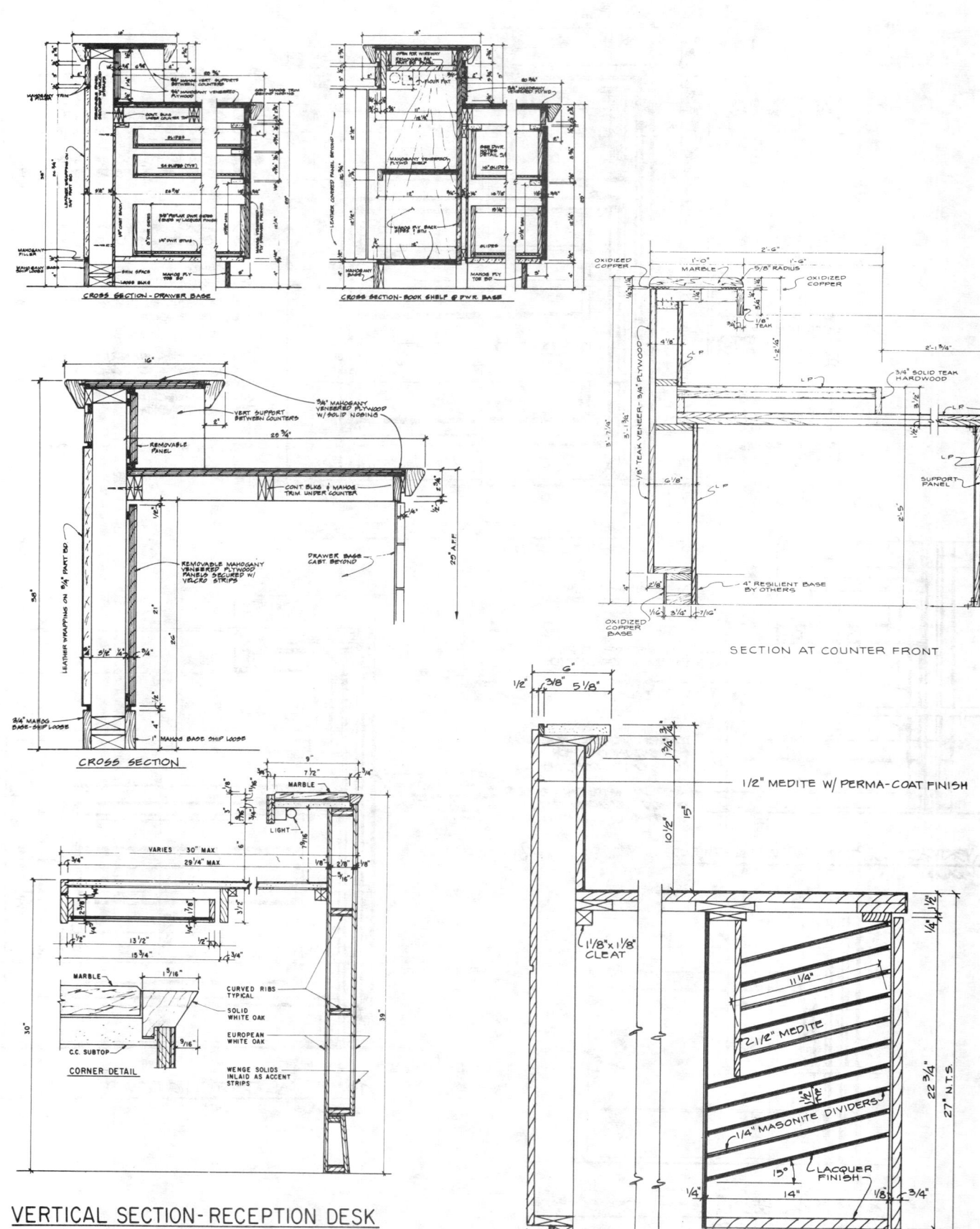

CROSS SECTION - DRAWER BASE

CROSS SECTION - BOOK SHELF @ PWR BASE

CROSS SECTION

SECTION AT COUNTER FRONT

CORNER DETAIL

VERTICAL SECTION - RECEPTION DESK

SECTION OF COUNTER @ STATIONARY FILE

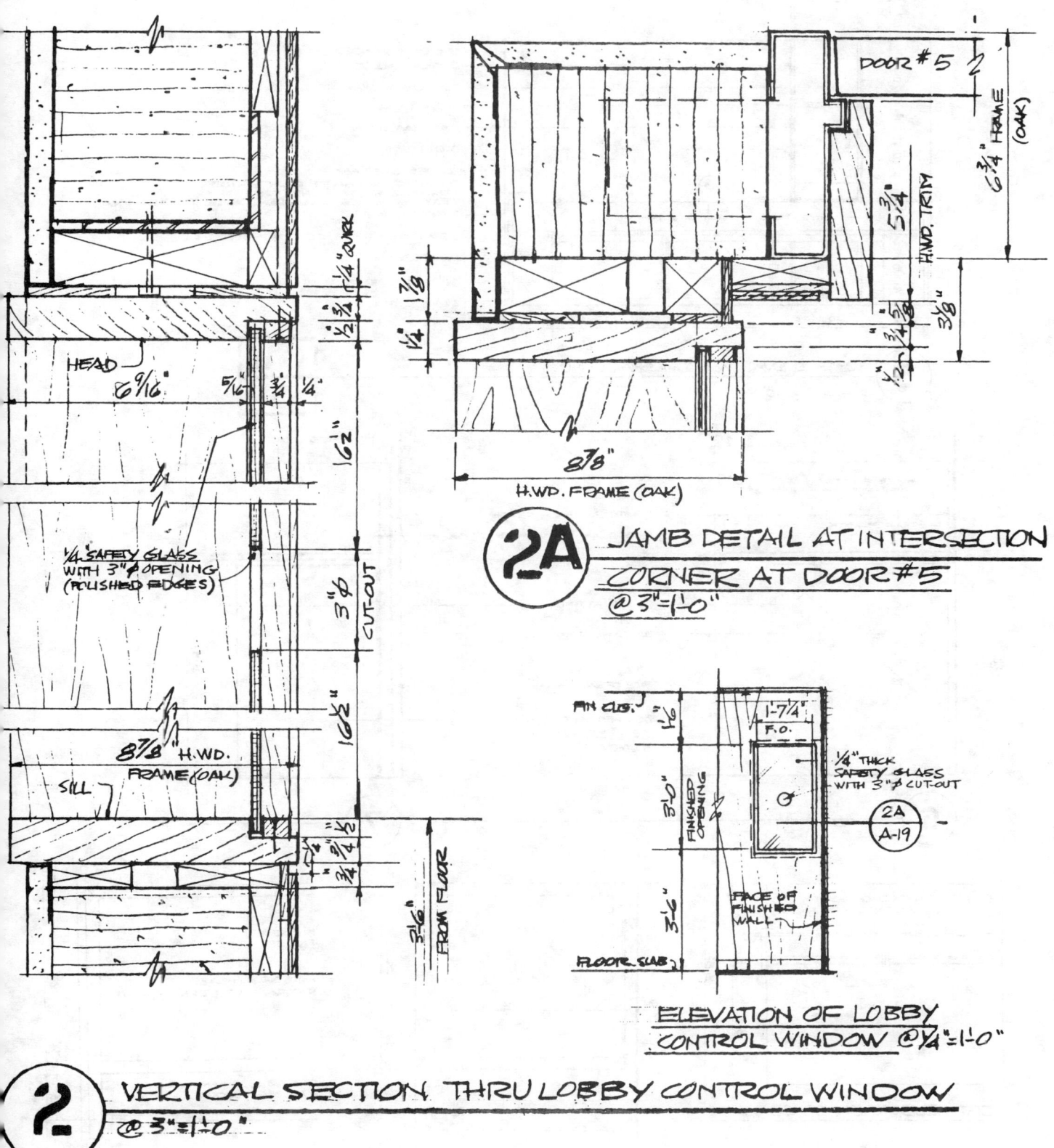

HEAD 6 9/16" 5/16" 3/4" 1/4"

1/4" SAFETY GLASS WITH 3"∅ OPENING (POLISHED EDGES)

8 7/8" H.WD. FRAME (OAK)

SILL

1/4 QUIRK
1/2" 2 3/4"
6 1/2"
3 ∅ CUT-OUT
6 1/2"
2 1/4" 3/4" 4 1/2"
2'-6" FROM FLOOR

DOOR #5

6 3/4" FRAME (OAK)

H.WD. TRIM 5 1/4" 3/4"
3 3/8"
1 7/8"
1/4"
8 7/8"

H.WD. FRAME (OAK)

(2A) **JAMB DETAIL AT INTERSECTION CORNER AT DOOR #5**
@ 3" = 1'-0"

FIN. CLG. 1'-0"
1-7/4" F.O.
5'-0" FINISHED OPENING
1/4" THICK SAFETY GLASS WITH 3"∅ CUT-OUT
(2A) A-19
3'-6"
FACE OF FINISHED WALL
FLOOR SLAB

ELEVATION OF LOBBY CONTROL WINDOW @ 1/4" = 1'-0"

(2) **VERTICAL SECTION THRU LOBBY CONTROL WINDOW**
@ 3" = 1'-0"

Fig. 12   A receptionist's workstation need not be freestanding within a reception area, where security and privacy are of critical importance. A receptionist may be located on the opposite side of a glass partition as shown here. Such a solution is often suggested when the receptionist performs multiple tasks such as typing and answering phones.

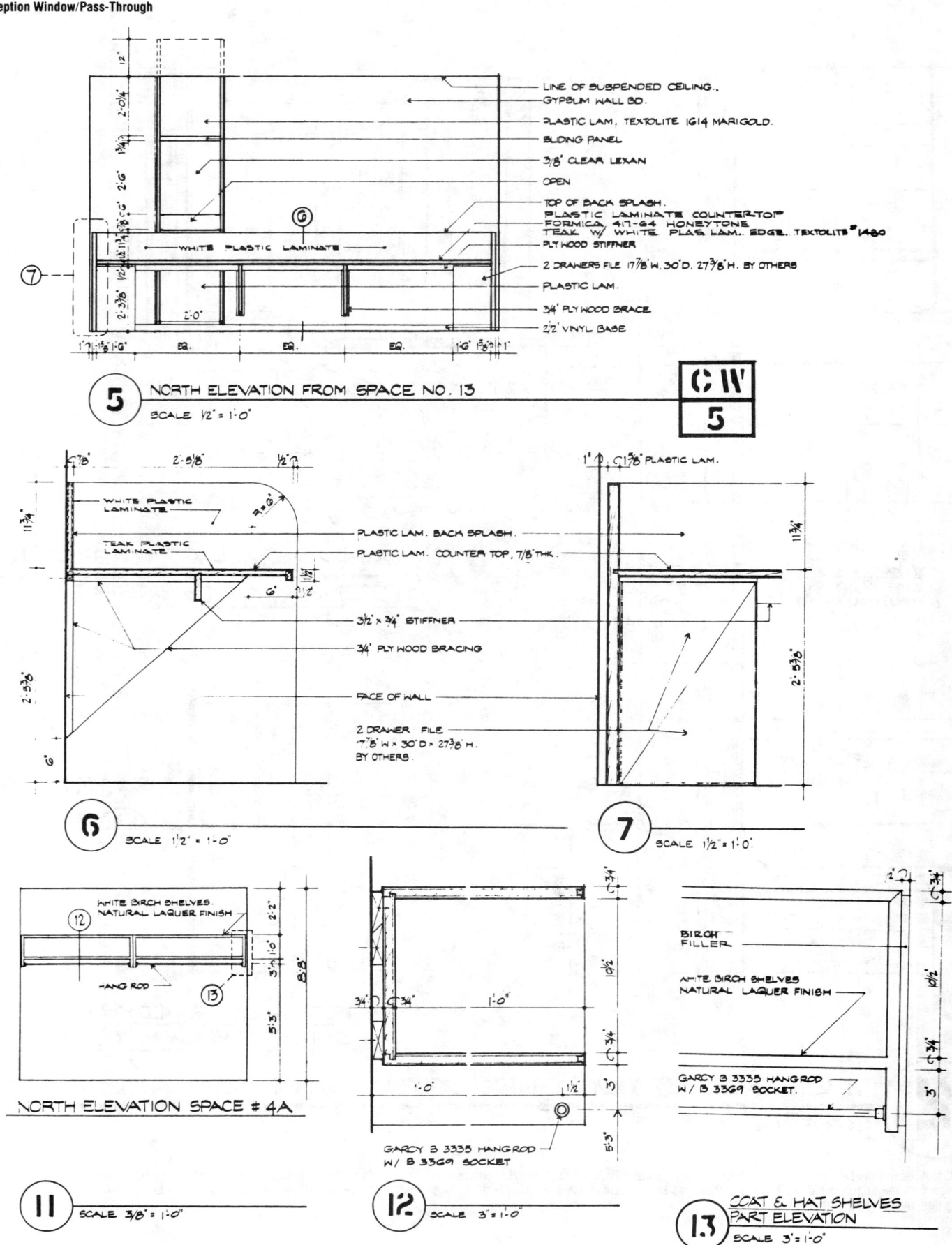

LINE OF SUSPENDED CEILING.
GYPSUM WALL BD.
PLASTIC LAM. TEXTOLITE 1614 MARIGOLD.
SLIDING PANEL
3/8" CLEAR LEXAN
OPEN
TOP OF BACK SPLASH.
PLASTIC LAMINATE COUNTER-TOP
FORMICA, 417-64 HONEYTONE
TEAK W/ WHITE PLAS LAM. EDGE. TEXTOLITE #1480
PLYWOOD STIFFNER
2 DRAWERS FILE 17 7/8" W, 30" D. 27 7/8" H. BY OTHERS
PLASTIC LAM.
3/4" PLYWOOD BRACE
2 1/2" VINYL BASE

WHITE PLASTIC LAMINATE

2'-0"

(5) NORTH ELEVATION FROM SPACE NO. 13
SCALE 1/2" = 1'-0"

CW
5

WHITE PLASTIC LAMINATE
TEAK PLASTIC LAMINATE

PLASTIC LAM. BACK SPLASH.
PLASTIC LAM. COUNTER TOP, 7/8" THK.

3 1/2" x 3/4" STIFFNER
3/4" PLYWOOD BRACING

FACE OF WALL

2 DRAWER FILE
17.8" W x 30" D x 27 7/8" H.
BY OTHERS.

PLASTIC LAM.

(6) SCALE 1 1/2" = 1'-0"

(7) SCALE 1 1/2" = 1'-0".

WHITE BIRCH SHELVES.
NATURAL LAQUER FINISH
(12)
HANG ROD
(13)

NORTH ELEVATION SPACE # 4A

(11) SCALE 3/8" = 1'-0"

GARCY B 3335 HANGROD
W/ B 3369 SOCKET

(12) SCALE 3" = 1'-0"

BIRCH FILLER

WHITE BIRCH SHELVES
NATURAL LAQUER FINISH

GARCY B 3335 HANGROD
W/ B 3369 SOCKET.

COAT & HAT SHELVES
PART ELEVATION
(13) SCALE 3" = 1'-0"

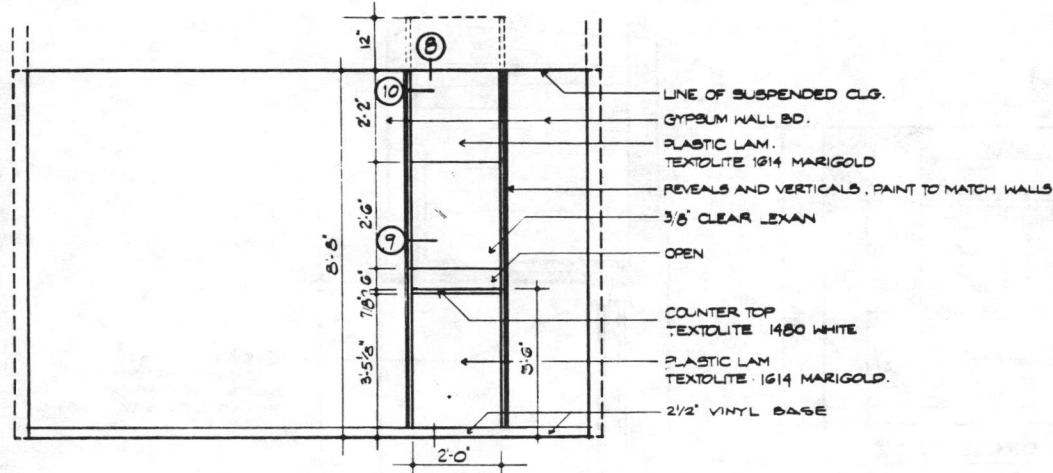

LINE OF SUSPENDED CLG.
GYPSUM WALL BD.
PLASTIC LAM.
TEXTOLITE 1614 MARIGOLD
REVEALS AND VERTICALS, PAINT TO MATCH WALLS
3/8" CLEAR LEXAN
OPEN
COUNTER TOP
TEXTOLITE 1480 WHITE
PLASTIC LAM
TEXTOLITE 1614 MARIGOLD.
2 1/2" VINYL BASE

④ SOUTH ELEVATION FROM SPACE NO. 14
SCALE 1/2" = 1'-0"

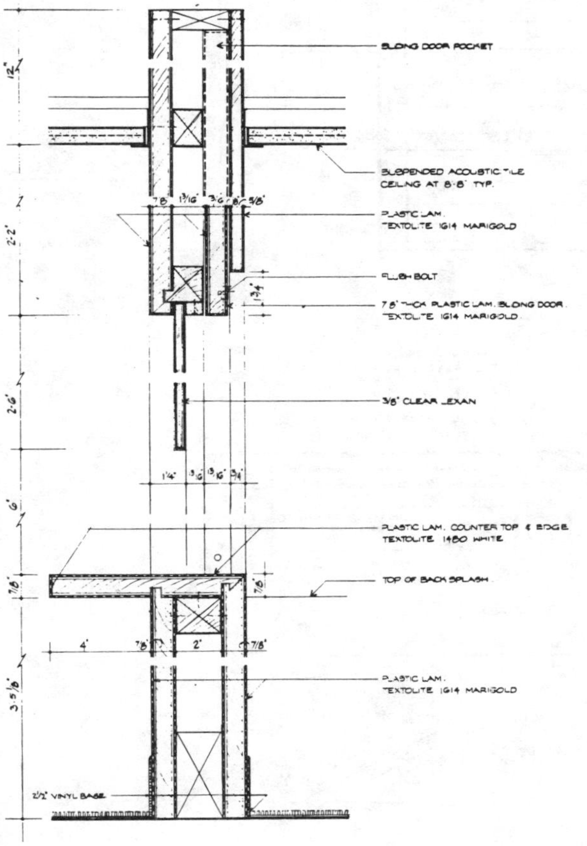

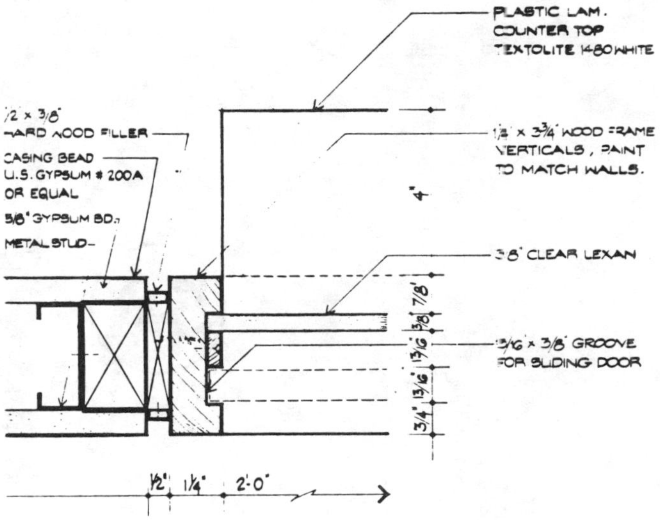

SLIDING DOOR POCKET

SUSPENDED ACOUSTIC TILE
CEILING AT 8'-8" TYP.

PLASTIC LAM.
TEXTOLITE 1614 MARIGOLD

FLUSH BOLT

7/8" THICK PLASTIC LAM. SLIDING DOOR
TEXTOLITE 1614 MARIGOLD.

3/8" CLEAR LEXAN

PLASTIC LAM. COUNTER TOP & EDGE
TEXTOLITE 1480 WHITE

TOP OF BACK SPLASH

PLASTIC LAM.
TEXTOLITE 1614 MARIGOLD

2 1/2" VINYL BASE

PLASTIC LAM.
COUNTER TOP
TEXTOLITE 1480 WHITE

1/2 x 3/8"
HARD WOOD FILLER

CASING BEAD
U.S. GYPSUM # 200A
OR EQUAL

5/8" GYPSUM BD.

METAL STUD

1/2 x 3 3/4" WOOD FRAME
VERTICALS, PAINT
TO MATCH WALLS.

3/8" CLEAR LEXAN

3/16 x 3/8" GROOVE
FOR SLIDING DOOR

4"

⑨ SCALE : HALF FULL SIZE

1/2 x 3/8"
HARD WOOD FILLER

1/4" x 3 3/4" VERTICALS

1/8" x 1/8" QUIRK

PLASTIC LAM.

7/8" SLIDING DOOR
PLASTIC LAM.
TEXTOLITE 1614
MARIGOLD

1/8" x 1/4" QUIRK

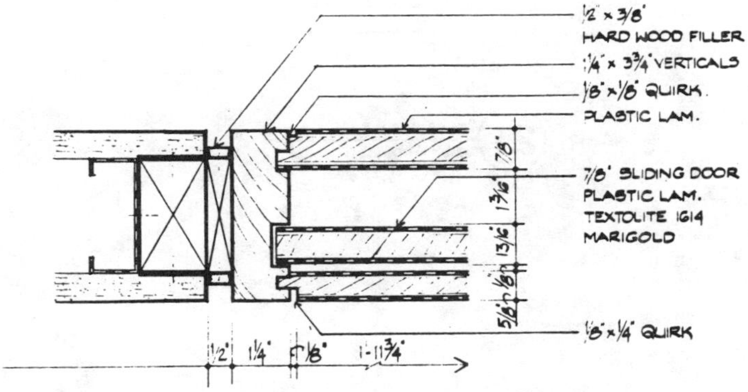

⑩ SCALE : HALF FULL SIZE.

Fig. 12 *(Continued)*

275

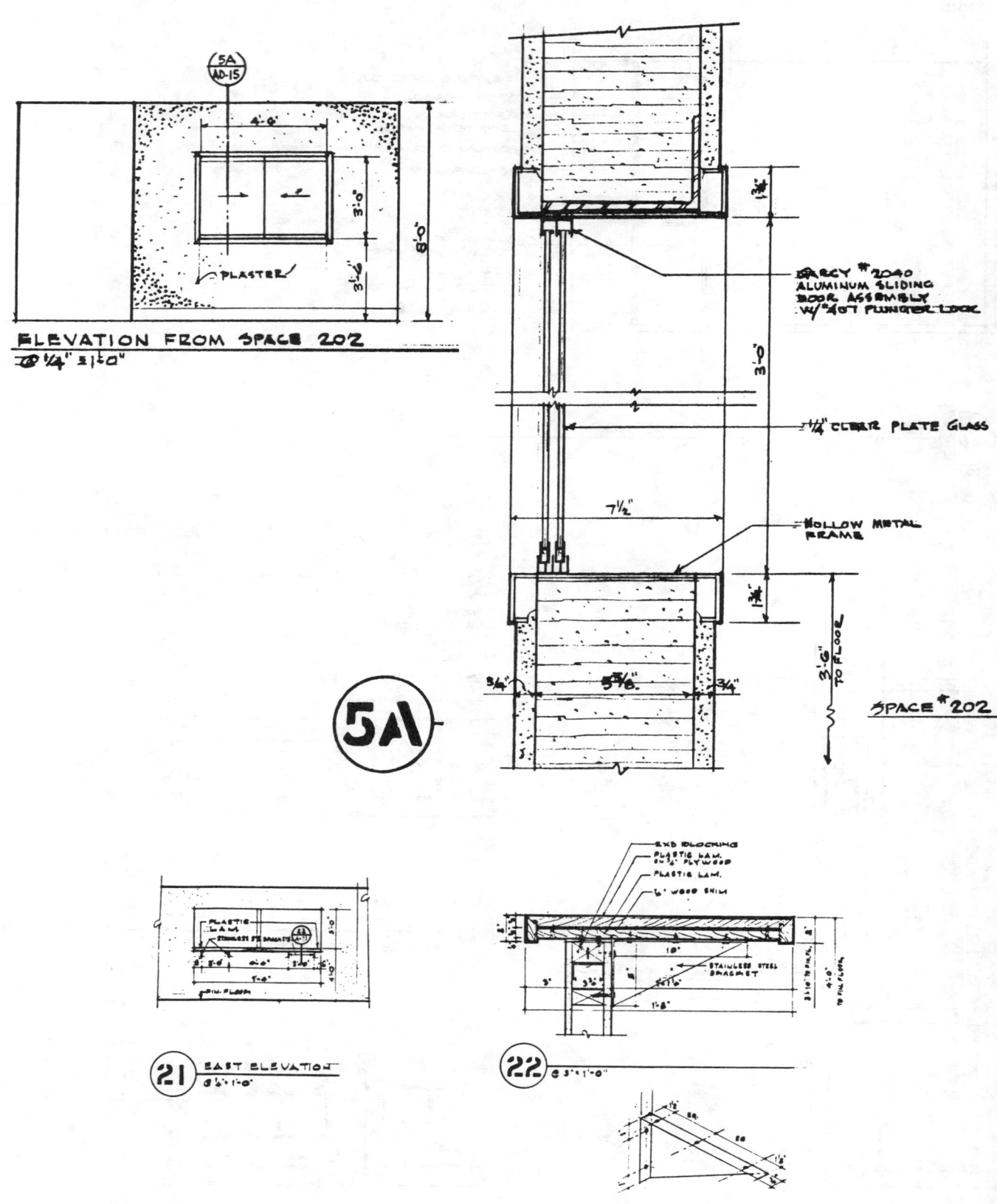

ELEVATION FROM SPACE 202

(21) EAST ELEVATION

(22)

ISOMETRIC OF STAINLESS STEEL BRACKET

Fig. 12 *(Continued)*

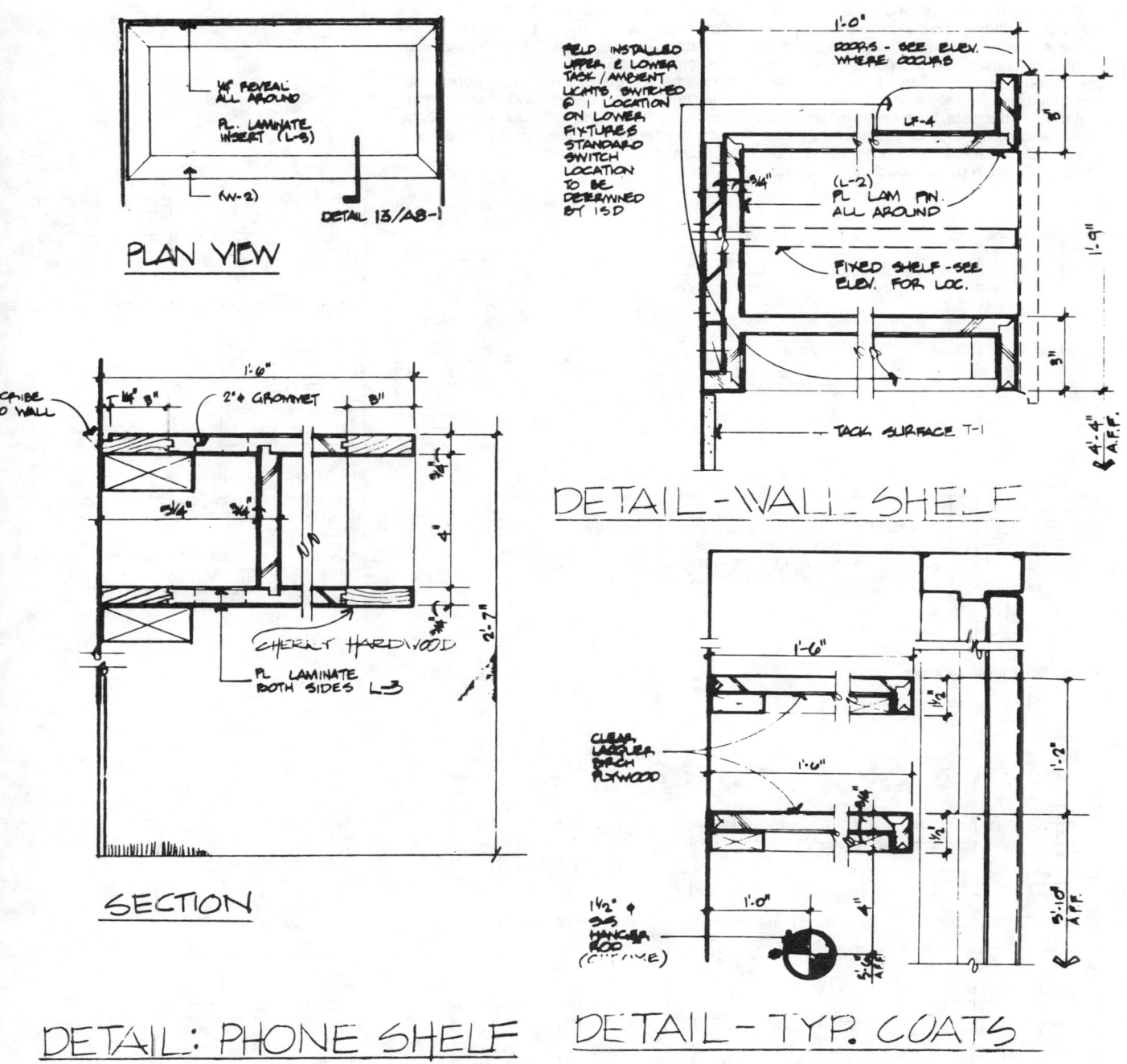

PLAN VIEW

¼" REVEAL ALL AROUND

PL. LAMINATE INSERT (L-3)

(W-2)

DETAIL 13/A8-1

SECTION

SCRIBE TO WALL

1'-6"

¼" 3"

2"Ø GROMMET

3"

3/4"

¾"

4"

CHERRY HARDWOOD

PL LAMINATE BOTH SIDES L-3

2'-7"

DETAIL - WALL SHELF

1'-0"

FIELD INSTALLED UPPER & LOWER TASK/AMBIENT LIGHTS, SWITCHED @ 1 LOCATION ON LOWER FIXTURES STANDARD SWITCH LOCATION TO BE DETERMINED BY ISD

ROD/S - SEE ELEV. WHERE OCCURS

LF-4

(L-2) PL LAM FIN. ALL AROUND

FIXED SHELF - SEE ELEV. FOR LOC.

¾"

5"

1'-9"

5"

4'-4" A.F.F.

TACK SURFACE T-1

DETAIL: PHONE SHELF

DETAIL - TYP. COATS

CLEAR LACQUER BIRCH PLYWOOD

1'-6"

1'-6"

1'-0"

1½"

1½"

4"

1'-2"

5'-10" A.F.F.

1½" Ø S.S. HANGER ROD (CHROME)

Fig. 13   While the reception desk is typically the major element to be designed and detailed for a reception area, other custom-designed components must also be carefully considered. A phone shelf, a wall shelf, a coat hanging area, and a work surface are often items that must be carefully designed and detailed.

FURNITURE, FURNISHINGS, AND EQUIPMENT

`Desks and Seating

Furniture, furnishings, and equipment are the basic building blocks in the design of office spaces. The illustrations and dimensional data contained in this part are based on the product lines available from particular manufacturers.

Although the data, to a great extent, are fairly standard throughout the industry, there will be some variations according to manufacturer. Accordingly, although the information presented is adequate for preliminary planning purposes, the designer is cautioned to reconcile preliminary assumptions with the actual dimensional data of the manufacturer whose product is ultimately specified.

Included in the data provided in this part are examples of filing cabinets, storage cabinets, conference tables, desks, and electronic media.

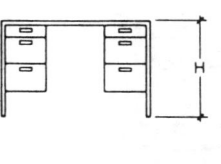
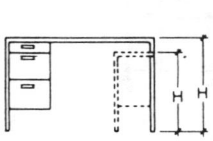
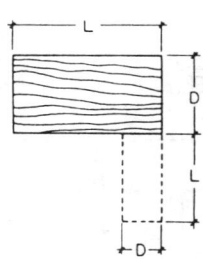

DESK DIMENSIONS

	DESKS				RETURNS	
	DOUBLE PEDESTAL		SINGLE PEDESTAL		FOR EXECUTIVE DESK RETURNS ARE AVAILABLE AT SAME HEIGHT AS DESK	
	STANDARD	RANGE	STANDARD	RANGE	STANDARD	RANGE
D	2'-6"	2'-0"–3'-3"	2'-6"	2'-0"–3'-3"	1'-6"	1'-3"–1'-8"
H	2'-5"	2'-4"–2'-6"	2'-5"	2'-4"–2'-6"	2'-2"	2'-1"–2'-3"
L	5'-0"	4'-6"–7'-0"	5'-0'	3'-9"–7'-0"	3'-0"	2'-0"–5'-0"

DESKS-SINGLE OR DOUBLE PEDESTAL

WORK TABLES ARE OF SIMILAR DIMENSIONS.
FOR EXECUTIVE DESKS WITH RETURNS, RETURNS ARE AVAILABLE AT THE SAME HEIGHT AS THE DESK SURFACE.
A MINIMUM CLEAR WIDTH OF 22" SHOULD BE PROVIDED FOR KNEE ROOM, 24" IS NORMAL.

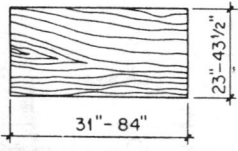

VARIOUS DRAWER ARRANGEMENTS FOR PEDESTALS

ARTIST AND DRAFTING DESKS OR TABLES

PEDESTALS FOR SECRETARIAL RETURNS WILL BE REDUCED IN HEIGHT THE EQUIVALENT OF ONE PENCIL DRAWER.

STANDARD SIZE ENGINEERING OR ARCHITECTURAL DRAFTING TABLES ARE
37 1/2"x 43 1/2 "D x 60"-72"-84"W x 37"H.

Fig. 1   Office planning: desks — sizes.

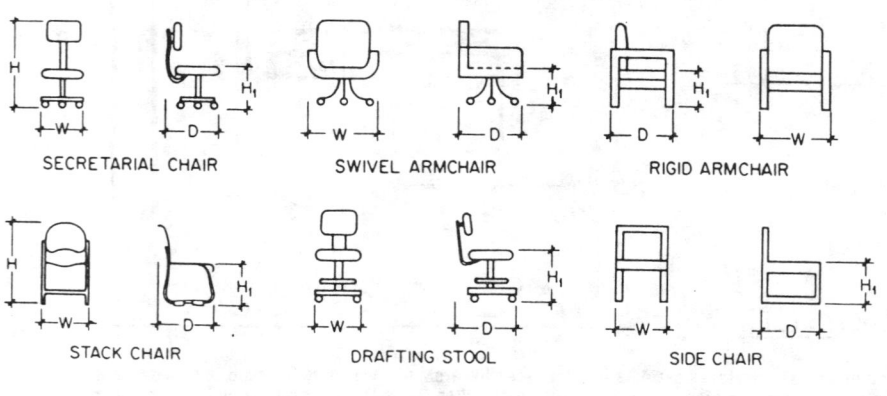

SECRETARIAL CHAIR   SWIVEL ARMCHAIR   RIGID ARMCHAIR   LOUNGE CHAIR

STACK CHAIR   DRAFTING STOOL   SIDE CHAIR   SOFA

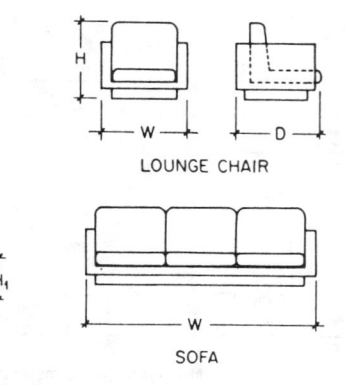

CHAIR DIMENSIONS

	SECRETARIAL		SWIVEL ARMCHAIR		RIGID ARMCHAIR		STACK CHAIR		RIGID AND ADJUSTABLE DRAFTING STOOL		SIDE CHAIR	
	STD.	RANGE	STD.	RANGE	STD.	RANGE	STD.	RANGE	STD.	RANGE	STD.	RANGE
W	1'-5"	1'-4"–1'-8"	2'-4"	1'-8"–2'-6"	1'-10"	1'-6"–2'-3"	1'-9"	1'-6"–1'-11"	1'-6"	1'-5"–2'-0"	1'-8"	1'-4"–2'-0"
D	1'-7 1/2"	1'-6–2'-0"	2'-3"	1'-8"–2'-6"	1'-10"	1'-7"–2'-8"	1'-9"	1'-7"–1'-10"	1'-8"	1'-6"–2'-0"	1'-10"	1'-6–2'-8"
H	2'-6"	2'-5"–2'-10"	2'-9"	2'-6" 3'-0"	2'-6"	2'-4"–2'-10"	2'-6"	2'-4"–2'-9"	3'-0"	2'-11"–3'-6"	2'-6"	2'-4"–2'-10"
H_1	1'-5"	1'-4"–1'-8"	1'-5"	1'-4"–1'-10"	1'-6"	1'-4"–1'-7"	1'-5"	1'-5"–1'-6"	2'-4"	1'-5"–2'-10"	1'-6"	1'-5"–1'-7"

LOUNGE CHAIR AND SOFA DIMENSIONS

	LOUNGE CHAIR		SOFA
	STD.	RANGE	
W	2'-6"	2'-6"–3'-4"	D, H AND H_1 SIMILAR
D	2'-7"	2'-2"–3'-4"	2 SEATS-5'-0"–6'-7"
H	2'-6"	2'-1"–3'-4"	3 SEATS-6'-0"–7'-6"
H_1	1'-3"	1'-0"–1'-6"	4 SEATS -7'-8"–9'-0"

Fig. 2   Office planning: seating — sizes.

**operator
sled base**

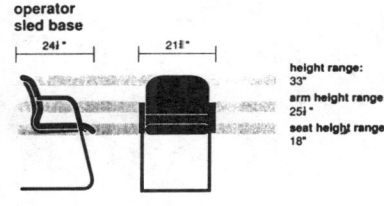

height range:
33"
arm height range:
25½"
seat height range:
18"

operator stool

height range:
39½"-46½" pneumatic
39½"-46½" vecmatic
arm height range:
31"-38½" pneumatic
31"-38½" vecmatic
seat height range:
22½"-29½" pneumatic
22½"-29½" vecmatic

operator

height range:
33"-37" pneumatic
33"-37" vecmatic
34" fixed
seat height range:
16½"-20½" pneumatic
16½"-20½" vecmatic
17½" fixed

operator

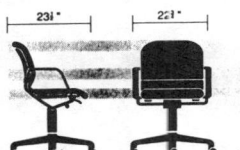

height range:
33"-37" pneumatic
33"-37" vecmatic
34" fixed
arm height range:
25½"-29½" pneumatic
25½"-29½" vecmatic
26" fixed
seat height range:
16½"-20½" pneumatic
16½"-20½" vecmatic
17½" fixed

mid-manager

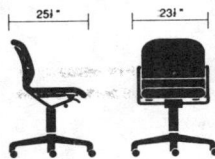

height range:
33½"-37½" pneumatic
33½"-37½" vecmatic
34½" fixed
seat height range:
17"-21" pneumatic
17"-21" vecmatic
17½" fixed

**mid-manager
sled base**

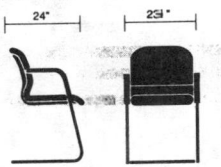

height:
33"
arm height:
25½"
seat height:
18½"

mid-manager

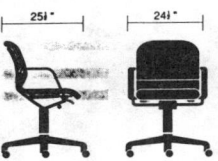

height range:
33½"-37½" pneumatic
33½"-37½" vecmatic
34½" fixed
arm height range:
25½"-29½" pneumatic
25½"-29½" vecmatic
25½" fixed
seat height range:
17"-21" pneumatic
17"-21" vecmatic
17½" fixed

**high back
mid-manager**

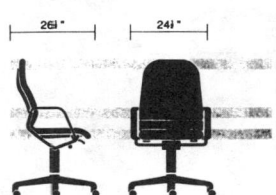

height range:
39½"-43½" pneumatic
39½"-43½" vecmatic
arm height range:
25½"-29½" pneumatic
25½"-29½" vecmatic
seat height range:
17"-21" pneumatic
17"-21" vecmatic
45 pounds
Shipped Set-Up

**manager
sled base**

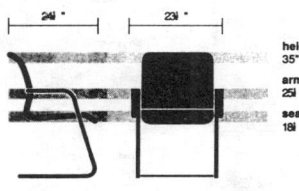

height:
35"
arm height:
25½"
seat height:
18"

**executive
manager
sled bases**

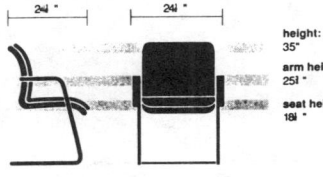

height:
35"
arm height:
25½"
seat height:
18"

**manager
high back**

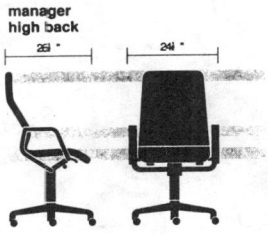

height range:
42"-46" pneumatic
42"-46" vecmatic
arm height range:
25½"-29½" pneumatic
25½"-29½" vecmatic
seat height range:
17½"-21½" pneumatic
17½"-21½" vecmatic

**grand class
manager
sled bases**

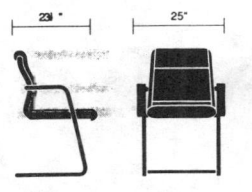

height:
33½"
arm height:
25"
seat height:
18½"

manager

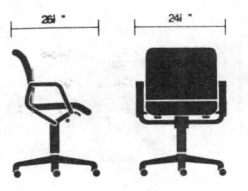

height range:
34½"-39½" pneumatic
34½"-39½" vecmatic
35" fixed
arm height range:
25½"-29½" pneumatic
25½"-29½" vecmatic
26" fixed
seat height range:
17½"-21½" pneumatic
17½"-21½" vecmatic
18" fixed

**grand class
manager**

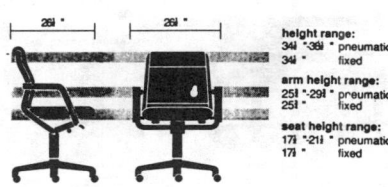

height range:
34½"-39½" pneumatic
34½" fixed
arm height range:
25½"-29½" pneumatic
25½" fixed
seat height range:
17½"-21½" pneumatic
17½" fixed

executive

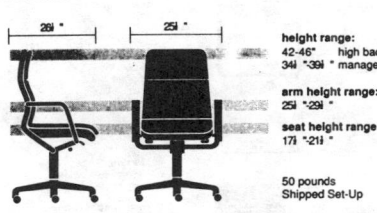

height range:
42-46" high back
34½"-39½" manager
arm height range:
25½"-29½"
seat height range:
17½"-21½"
50 pounds
Shipped Set-Up

**grand class
high back**

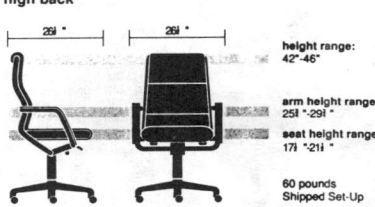

height range:
42"-46"
arm height range:
25½"-29½"
seat height range:
17½"-21½"
60 pounds
Shipped Set-Up

Chair types are often associated with certain generic job titles. The designer, however, is cautioned not to make assumptions as to chair selection without a thorough understanding of the tasks the individual is to perform. Ergonomic considerations are to be carefully reviewed in order to select a chair with appropriate attributes, i.e., seat height, adjustability, back and arm support, firmness, etc. Overall chair size must be understood within the context of available clearances and workstation configuration.

FURNITURE, FURNISHINGS, AND EQUIPMENT

Chairs

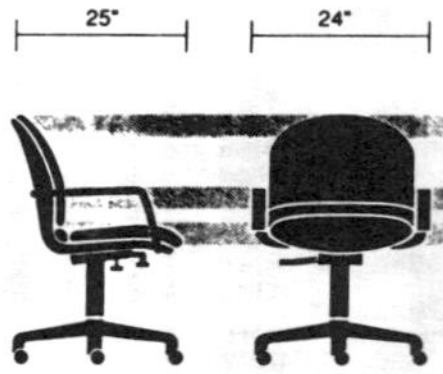

height range:
33ł"-37ł" pneumatic
31"-35" vecmatic
33" fixed
arm height range:
24ł"-28ł" pneumatic
22ł"-26ł" vecmatic
24ł" fixed
seat height range:
18"-22" pneumatic
16"-20" vecma'
18" fixed

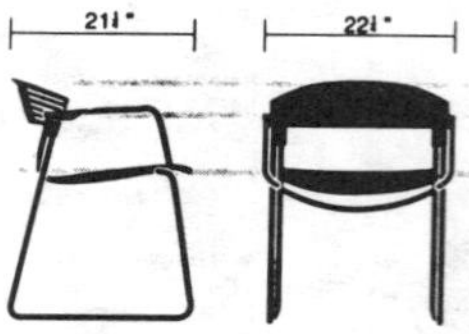

height:
29ł"
arm height:
25ł"
seat height:
17ł"

15 pounds
Shipped Set-Up

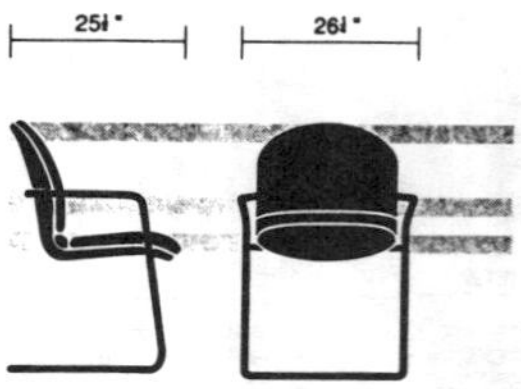

height range:
33ł"
arm height range:
25"
seat height range:
18ł"

43 pounds
Shipped Set-Up

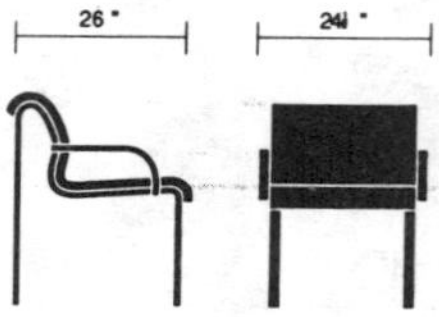

height:
31"
arm height:
25"
seat height:
19"

36 pounds
Shipped Set-Up

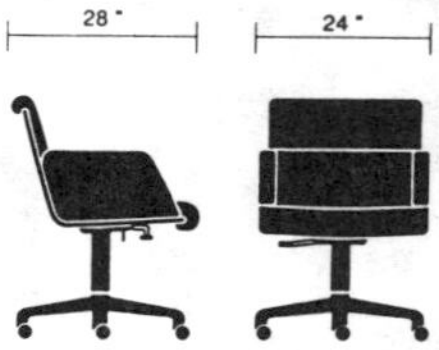

height range:
41"-45" high back
33ł"-37" mid back
arm height range:
24ł"-28"
seat height range:
18ł"-21ł"

67 pounds
Shipped Set-Up

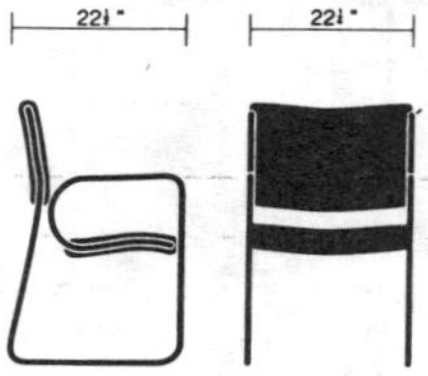

height range:
33ł"
arm height range:
25ł"
seat height range:
17ł"

height range:
41ł" - 44ł" high back
37ł" - 40ł" mid back
35" - 38ł" low back
arm height range:
25ł" - 29"
seat height range:
17ł" - 20ł"

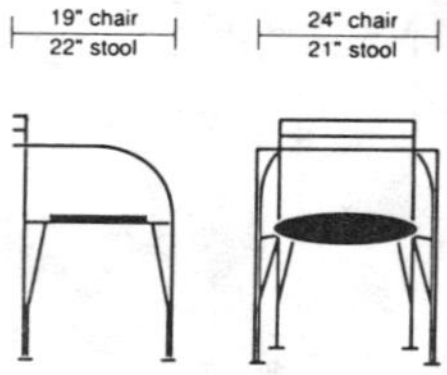

height:
30" chair
33ł" stool
arm height:
26"
seat height:
17ł" chair
30" stool

21 pounds
Shipped Set-Up

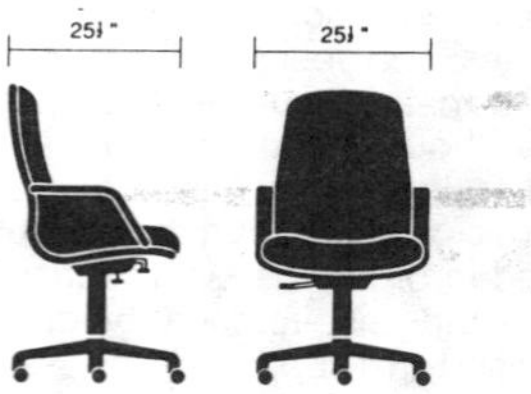

height range:
41ł" - 44ł" high back
37ł" - 40ł" mid back

arm height range:
26" - 29ł"

seat height range:
17ł" - 20ł"

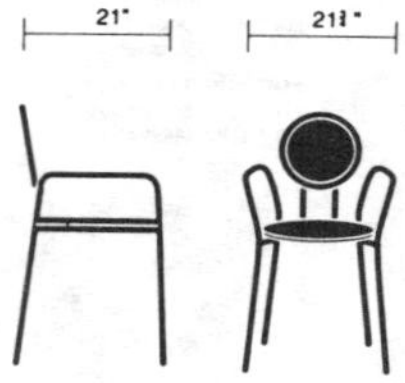

height:
33ł"
arm height:
25ł"
seat height:
17ł"

20 pounds
Shipped Set-l

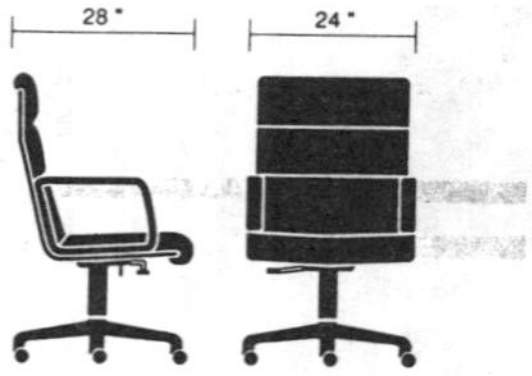

height range:
41"-45" high back
33ł"-37" mid back

arm height range:
24ł"-28"
seat height range:
18ł"-21ł"

67 pounds
Shipped Set-Up

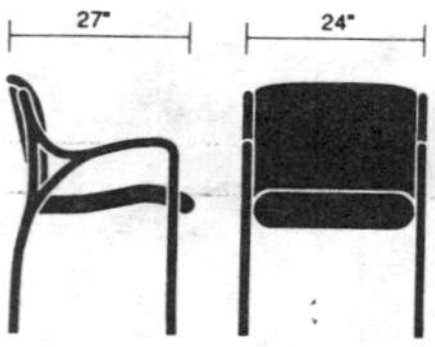

height:
32"
arm height:
25"
seat height:
17ł"

height range:
42ł"-45ł" high back
38ł"-41ł" mid back
arm height range:
24ł"-27ł"
seat height range:
18ł"-21ł"
64 pounds
Shipped Set-Up

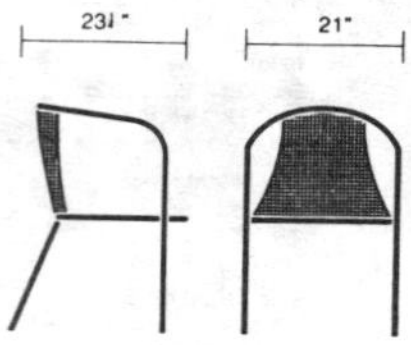

height:
28"
seat height:
16ł"

Executive Chairs

**Tilt-Swivel Chair
with Casters**

Option: CA

**Non-Swivel Lounge
Chair**

Swivel Lounge Chair

**Non-Swivel Lounge
Arm Chair**

Swivel Lounge Arm Chair

**Tilt-Swivel Reclining
Arm Chair**

Ottoman

Lounge

Non-Swivel Lounge Chair

Swivel Lounge Chair

**Non-Swivel Lounge
Armchair**

Swivel Lounge Armchair

**Tilt-Swivel Reclining
Armchair**

Ottoman

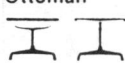

Straight Module

Side/Pull-up Chairs

Non-Swivel Side Chair

Swivel Side Chair

Non-Swivel Arm Chair

Swivel Arm Chair

**Tilt-Swivel Arm Chair
with Glides**

**Tilt-Swivel Arm Chair
with Casters**

Option: CA

Executive Chairs

**Tilt-Swivel Chair
with Glides**

Lounge Chair

Ottoman

**Lounge Chair
and Ottoman**

Eames™ Chaise

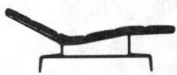

Sofa Compact

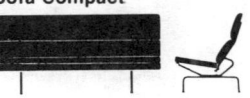

Nelson Sling Sofa

Eames Executive Lounge Chairs

**Executive Swivel
Lounge Chair**

**Adjustable Executive
Tilt-Swivel Lounge Chair**

Adjustable Tilt-Swivel

FURNITURE, FURNISHINGS, AND EQUIPMENT

Reception and Lounge Seating

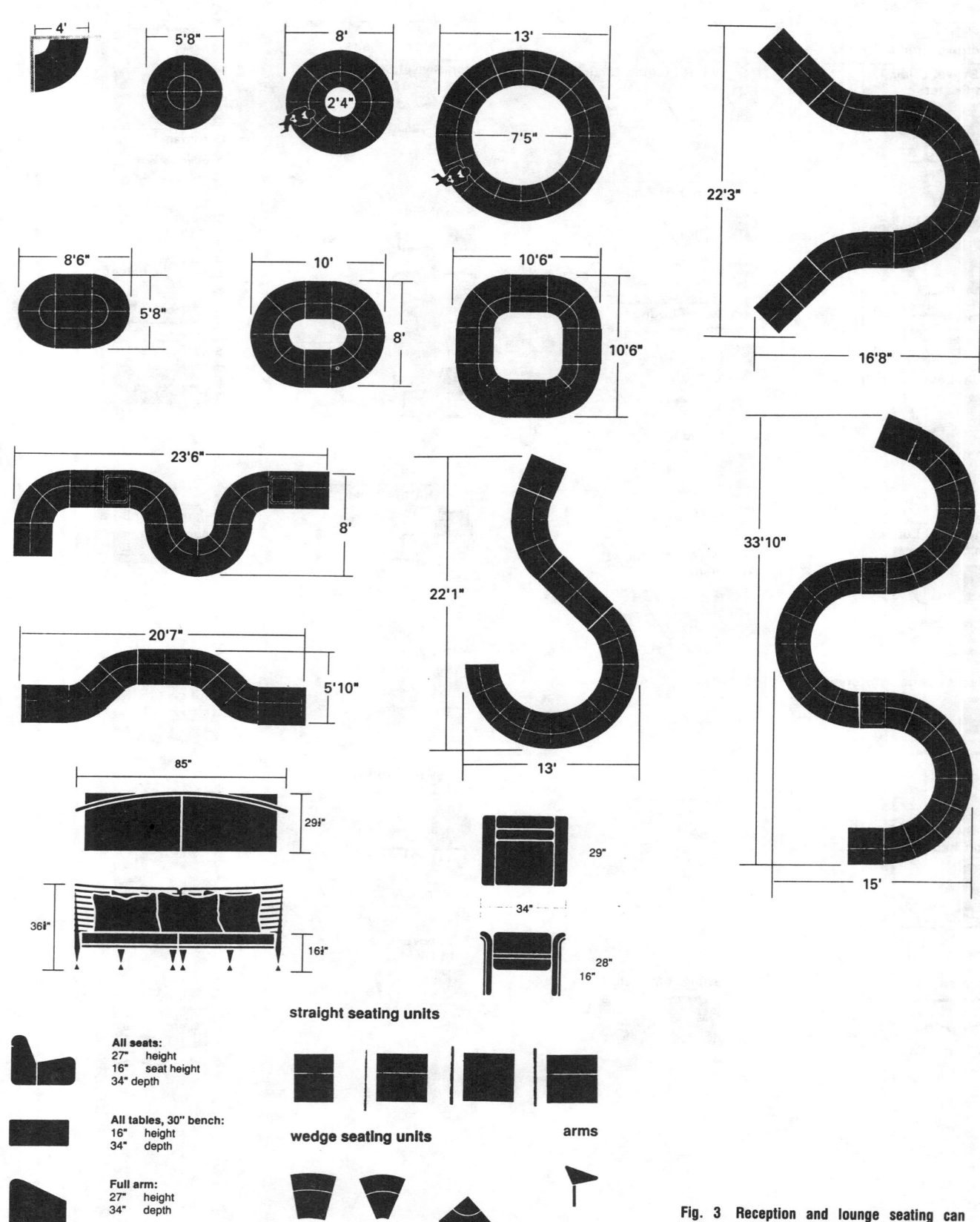

straight seating units

wedge seating units

arms

All seats:
27" height
16" seat height
34" depth

All tables, 30" bench:
16" height
34" depth

Full arm:
27" height
34" depth

Fig. 3 Reception and lounge seating can assume various sizes, shapes, and configurations. Modular seating units can offer a custom built-in look, and can often incorporate table and storage components. Overall sizes will vary from manufacturer to manufacturer.

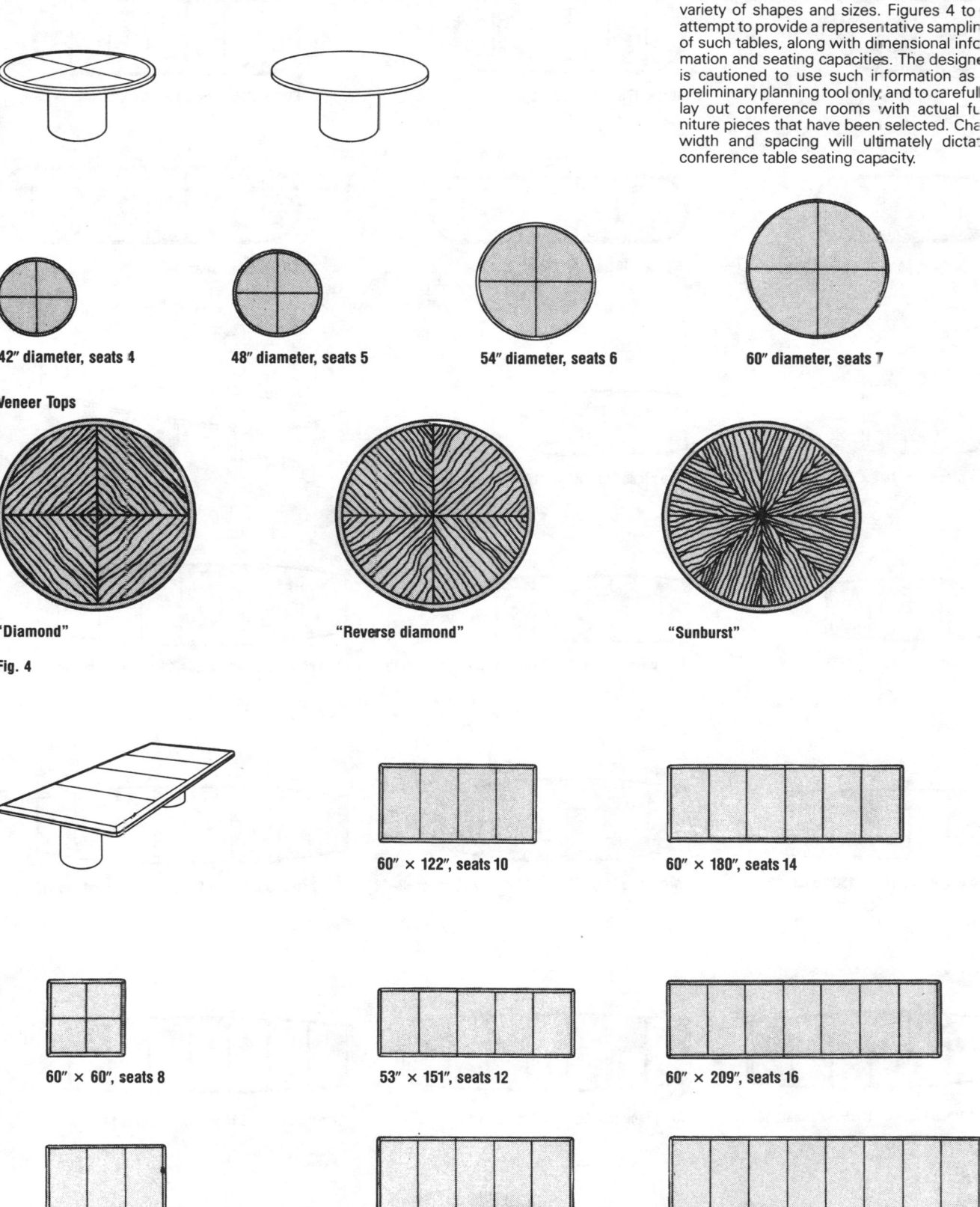

Conference tables come in an infinite variety of shapes and sizes. Figures 4 to 6 attempt to provide a representative sampling of such tables, along with dimensional information and seating capacities. The designer is cautioned to use such information as a preliminary planning tool only, and to carefully lay out conference rooms with actual furniture pieces that have been selected. Chair width and spacing will ultimately dictate conference table seating capacity.

42" diameter, seats 4

48" diameter, seats 5

54" diameter, seats 6

60" diameter, seats 7

Veneer Tops

"Diamond"

"Reverse diamond"

"Sunburst"

Fig. 4

60" × 122", seats 10

60" × 180", seats 14

60" × 60", seats 8

53" × 151", seats 12

60" × 209", seats 16

53" × 93", seats 8

60" × 151", seats 12

60" × 238", seats 18

Fig. 5

FURNITURE, FURNISHINGS, AND EQUIPMENT
Conference Tables

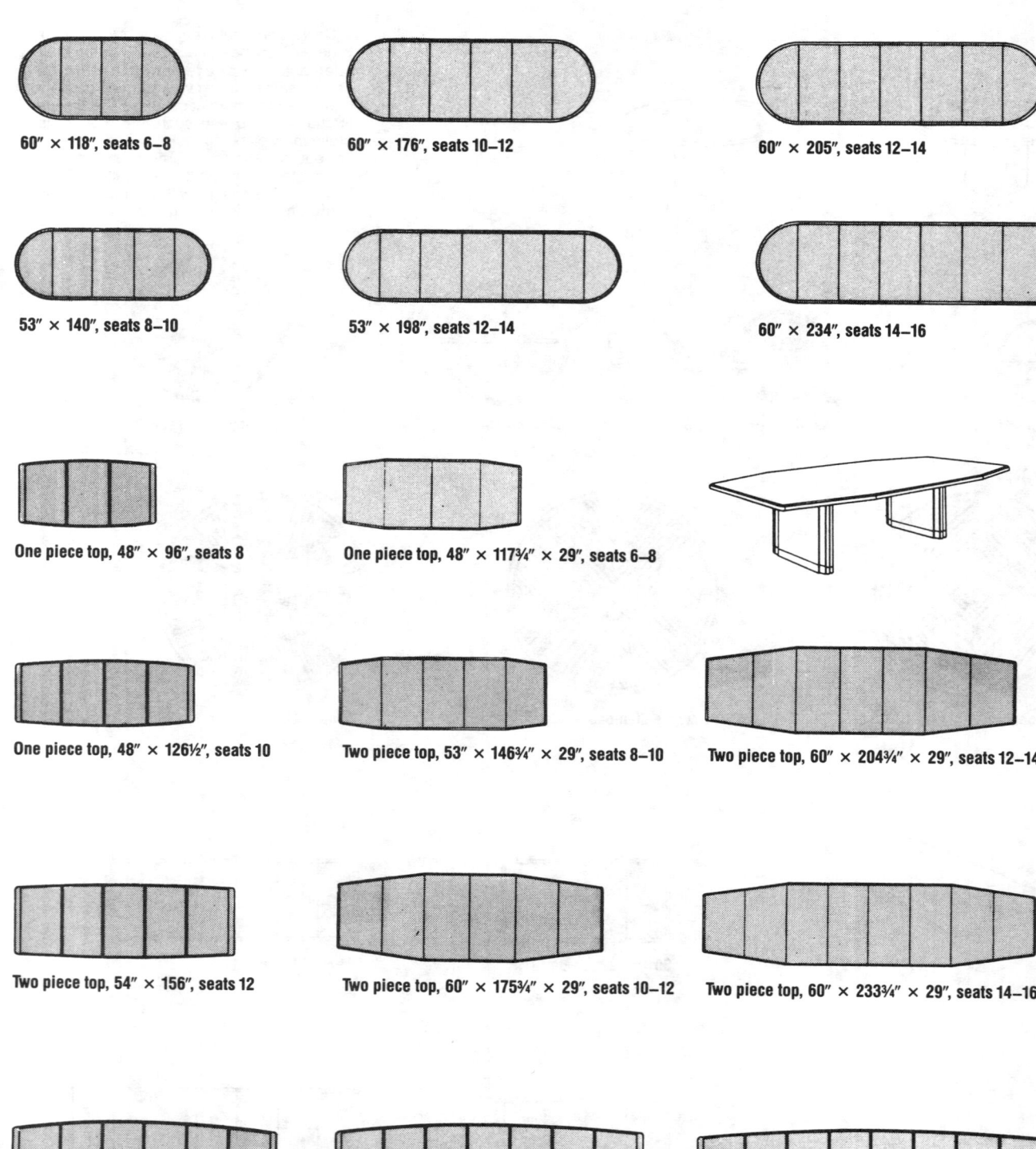

60″ × 118″, seats 6–8

60″ × 176″, seats 10–12

60″ × 205″, seats 12–14

53″ × 140″, seats 8–10

53″ × 198″, seats 12–14

60″ × 234″, seats 14–16

One piece top, 48″ × 96″, seats 8

One piece top, 48″ × 117¾″ × 29″, seats 6–8

One piece top, 48″ × 126½″, seats 10

Two piece top, 53″ × 146¾″ × 29″, seats 8–10

Two piece top, 60″ × 204¾″ × 29″, seats 12–14

Two piece top, 54″ × 156″, seats 12

Two piece top, 60″ × 175¾″ × 29″, seats 10–12

Two piece top, 60″ × 233¾″ × 29″, seats 14–16

Two piece top, 60″ × 185¾″, seats 14

Two piece top, 60″ × 216″, seats 16

Two piece top, 60″ × 245¼″, seats 18

Fig. 6

TABLE 1 Vertical File Cabinets

Description	Cabinet height		Outside dimensions		
			Depth	Width	Height
	58⅝"	Letter	28⁹⁄₁₆"	14⅞"	58⅜"
		Legal	28⁹⁄₁₆"	17⅞"	58⅜"
	52⅜"	Letter	28⁹⁄₁₆"	14⅞"	52⅜"
		Legal	28⁹⁄₁₆"	17⅞"	52⅜"
		Card	28⁹⁄₁₆"	14⅞"	52⅜"
	41¼"	Letter	28⁹⁄₁₆"	14⅞"	41¼"
		Legal	28⁹⁄₁₆"	17⅞"	41¼"
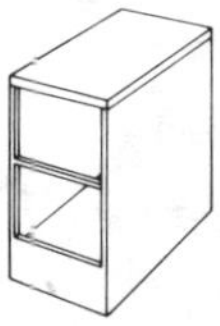	29⅜"	Letter	30"	14⅞"	29⅜"
		Legal	30"	17⅞"	29⅜"
	27⅜"	Letter	30"	14⅞"	27⅞"
		Legal	30"	17⅞"	27⅞"

Standard vertical file cabinets are usually designed to accommodate standard height drawers and half-height file insert drawers (optional). Cabinets are available in letter-size widths (14⅞") and legal-size widths (17⅛"). Vertical file drawers are usually 12" high and accommodate front-to-back filing.

Standard cabinets are available in four heights: five-drawer (58⅝"), four-drawer (52⅜"), three drawer (41¼"), and two-drawer (29⅜" or 27⅜"). The depths of the three-, four-, and five-drawer cabinets are 28⁹⁄₁₆", while the depth of the 2-drawer cabinets is 30". Table 1 lists these dimensional data. It should be noted that although adequate for preliminary planning purposes, the data are based on Steelcase cabinets.

Guidelines for Customizing Vertical Files

Depending on the manufacturer, vertical file cabinets can be customized. Usually two half-height file insert drawers may be substituted for a 12-in-high drawer in any or all positions. Table 2 indicates the dimensions and linear capacities of such insert drawers, while Fig. 7 illustrates basic guidelines for customizing.

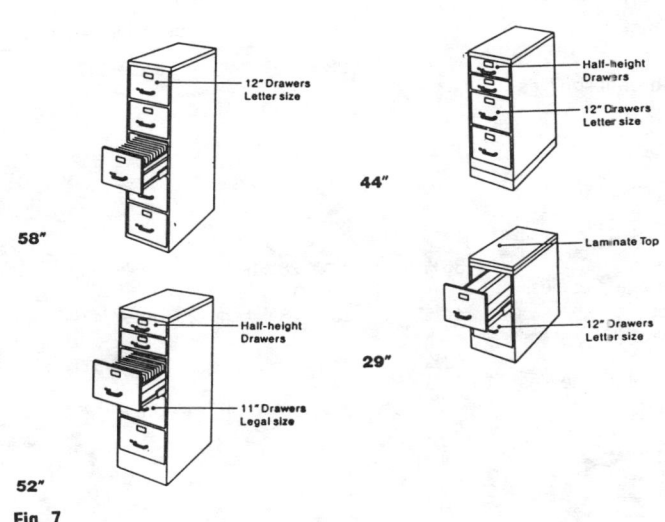

Fig. 7

FURNITURE, FURNISHINGS, AND EQUIPMENT
Vertical File Drawers; Overfile Cabinets; Roll-Away Carts

TABLE 2   Vertical File Insert Drawers

Description	Inside dimensions			Linear capacity
	Depth	Width	Height	
Half-height (3x5 or 4x6 cards) 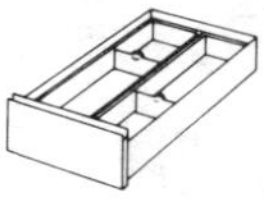	26⅞″	6″(2)	4⅜″	53⅞″* (2 rows)
Half-height (checks)	26⅞″*	10¾″	4⅜″	26⅞″
Half-height (cash)	8¼″	3¼″	1⅞″	Bills
	8½″	11½″	1⅞″	Storage
	4⅜″	2¼″	1¾″	Coin tray
Half-height (box)	26⅞″	12¼″	4¾″	26⅞″ front-to-back
				12¼″ side-to-side
Half-height (microfilm)	26¼″*	4″(3)	4⅜″	80¾″* (3 compartments)
Full height (letter size)	26⅞″*	6″(2)	10⅛″	53⅞″* (2 compartments)
Full height (letter size)	26⅞″*	4″(3)	10⅛″	80¾″* (3 compartments)
Full height (box)	26⅞″	15¼″	4¾″	—
Full height (3x5 cards)	26⅞″*	5″(3)	4½″	80¾″* (3 compartments)
Full height (4x6 cards)	26⅞″*	6¼″(2)	4⅜″	53⅞″ (2 compartments)
Full height (legal size)	26⅞″*	7½″(2)	10⅛″	See style no. C
Full height (legal size)	26⅞″*	5″(3)	10⅛″	See style no. D

*Deduct ⅝″ when compressor is used.

TABLE 3   Drawers, Overfile Cabinets, and Roll-Away File Cart

Description	Width	Inside dimensions			Linear capacity
		Depth	Width	Height	
12″ Letter-size drawer 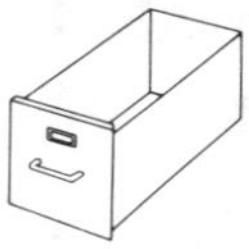	—	27⅜″	12¼″	10½″	27⅜″ front-to-back*
12″ Legal-size drawer 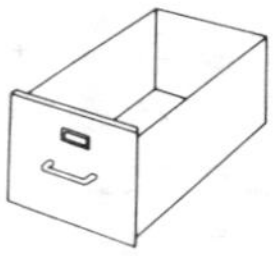	—	27⅜″	15¼″	10½″	27⅜″ front-to-back

Description	Width	Outside/inside dimensions			Linear capacity
Overfile cabinet Fits over two letter-size files 	29¾″	28⅝″/28½″†	29¾″/27⅞″	28⅛″/25⅜″	55¾″ side-to-side on 2 shelves (1 adj., ¾″ thick)
Overfile cabinet Fits over two legal-size files	35¾″	28⅝″/28½″†	35¾″/33⅞″	28⅛″/25⅜″	67¾″ side-to-side on 2 shelves (1 adj., ¾″ thick)
Overfile cabinet Fits over three letter size files	44⅝″	28⅝″/28½″†	44⅝″/42¾″	28⅛″/25⅜″	85½″ side-to-side on 2 shelves (1 adj., ¾″ thick)
Overfile cabinet Fits over three legal-size files	53⅝″	28⅝″/28½″†	53⅝″/51¾″	28⅛″/25⅜″	103½″ side-to-side on 2 shelves (1 adj., ¾″ thick)
Roll-away file cart		30¼″/28″	15⅛″/12⅛″	22⅞″/13⅜″	25″ Letter/legal

*Deduct ⅝″ when compressor is used.
†Deduct 1½″ when ordered with sliding doors.

TABLE 4   Lateral File Cabinets

Description (cabinet inside height)	Cabinet width	Outside/inside dimensions		
		Depth	Width	Height
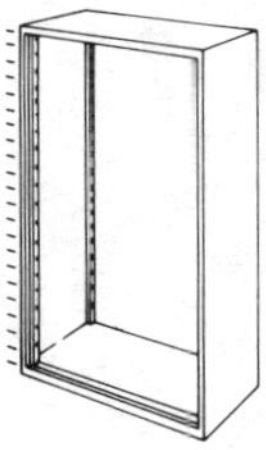 60″	30″	18″/17⅛″*	30″/28½″	64⅝″/60″
	36″	18″/17⅛″*	36″/34½″	64⅝″/60″
	42″	18″/17⅛″*	42″/40½″	64⅝″/60″
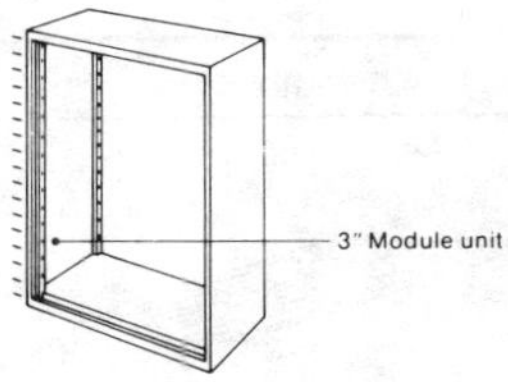 48″	30″	18″/17⅛″*	30″/28½″	52⅜″/48″
	36″	18″/17⅛″*	36″/34½″	52⅜″/48″
	42″	18″/17⅛″*	42″/40½″	52⅜″/48″
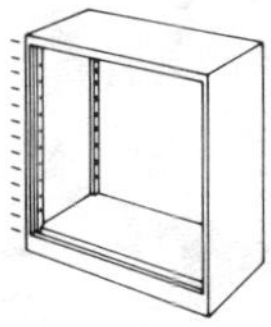 36″	30″	18″/17⅛″*	30″/28½″	41¼″/36″
	36″	18″/17⅛″*	36″/34½″	41¼″/36″
	42″	18″/17⅛″*	42″/40½″	41¼″/36″
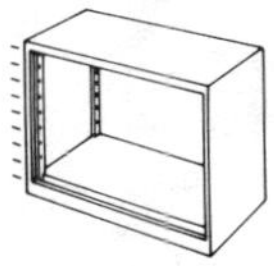 24″	30″	18″/17⅛″*	30″/28½″	28¼″/24″
	36″	18″/17⅛″*	36″/34½″	28¼″/24″
	42″	18″/17⅛″*	42″/40½″	28¼″/24″

3″ Module unit (label pointing to 48″ cabinet illustration)

Loaded Weights											
Cabinet inside height											
Description	24″			36″			48″			60″		
Cabinet width	30″	36″	42″	30″	36″	42″	30″	36″	42″	30″	36″	42″
Loaded weight in pounds	285	336	391	401	475	553	524	645	720	610	725	843

*Deduct ⅝″ when compressor is used.

24″

36″

48″

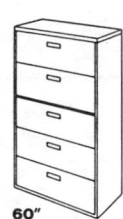
60″

Standard lateral file cabinets are usually available in three widths — 30″, 36″, and 42″ — and with 12″-high drawers or roll-out shelves. Some cabinets are designed on a 3″ module to accommodate 3″-, 6″-, 9″-, 12″-, and 15″-high drawers and shelves.

Ganging hardware is usually included with each file cabinet. Cabinets should be ganged with adjacent files or bolted to the floor. Counterbalance weights should be used for single-application files.

Table 4 shows the outside and inside dimensions of four lateral file cabinets, and their loaded floor weights based on 12″-high drawers filled to capacity.

It should be noted that the dimensional data and load factors are based on Steelcase cabinets. Although these data are adequate for preliminary planning purposes, it is essential that the data of the equipment being specified are verified with its manufacturer.

FURNITURE, FURNISHINGS, AND EQUIPMENT
Lateral File Cabinets

Filing Arrangements

Most lateral file drawers are designed for filing both letter-size and legal-size documents, in addition to EDP printouts. Lateral file drawers can usually accommodate materials in a front-to-back (F to B) arrangement or in a side-to-side (S to S) arrangement. In some instances a combination of the two is possible. The actual capacity in linear inches for each arrangement and for each particular drawer or shelf has been calculated and is shown in the "Linear capacity" column in Tables 2, 3, 6, 7 and 8. It should be noted that the dimensional data in Table 5 are based on Steelcase drawers.

TABLE 5   Filing Arrangements

Description	30" width	36" width	42" width
Letter/legal, 12" drawer			

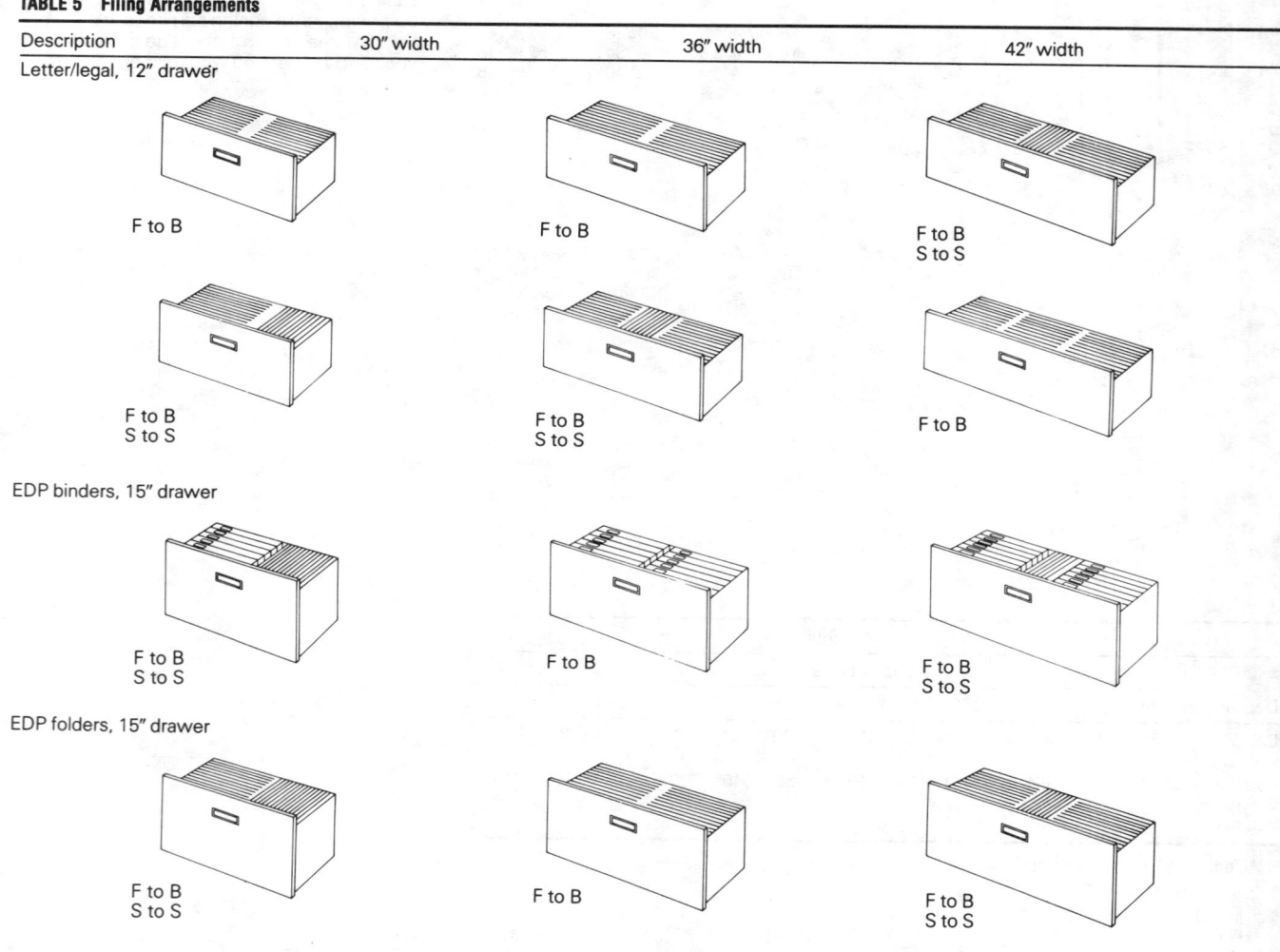

	30" width	36" width	42" width
Letter/legal, 12" drawer	F to B	F to B	F to B / S to S
	F to B / S to S	F to B / S to S	F to B
EDP binders, 15" drawer	F to B / S to S	F to B	F to B / S to S
EDP folders, 15" drawer	F to B / S to S	F to B	F to B / S to S

TABLE 6   Drawers, Shelves, Add-On Cabinets

Description	File cabinet width	Style no.	Outside/inside dimensions			Linear capacity
			Depth	Width	Height	
12" legal fixed shelf with door	30"		16½"	28½"	10½"*	28½" side-to-side
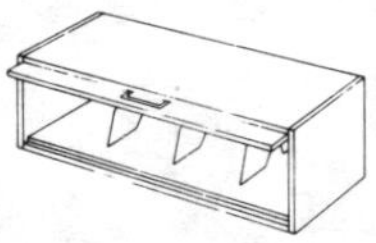	36"		16½"	34½"	10½"*	34½" S to S
	42"		16½"	40½"	10½"*	40½" S to S
15" legal fixed shelf with door	30"		16½"	28½"	13½"	28½" S to S
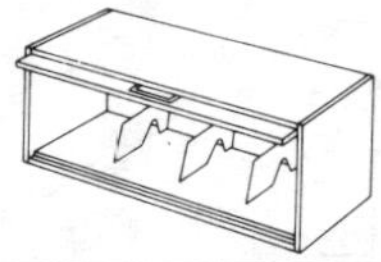	36"		16½"	34½"	13½"	34½" S to S
	42"		16½"	40½"	13½"	40½" S to S
Center hook filing hanger bar	30"		17"	28½"	10⅝" (12" high door) 12¾" (15" high door)	28½" S to S 28½" S to S
	36"		17"	34½"	10⅝" (12" high door) 12¾" (15" high door)	34½" S to S 34½" S to S
	42"		17"	40½"	10⅝" (12" high door) 12¾" (15" high door)	40½" S to S 40½" S to S
T-bar	30"		17"	28½"	10¼" (12" high door) 12⅜" (15" high door)	28½" S to S 28½" S to S
	36"		17"	34½"	10¼" (12" high door) 12¾" (15" high door)	34½" S to S 34½" S to S
	42"		17"	40½"	10¼" (12" high door) 12⅜" (15" high door)	40½" S to S 40½" S to S
Wire tape rack	30"		17"	28½"	7⅛" (9" high door) 10⅛" (12" high door) 13⅛" (15" high door)	28½" S to S 28½" S to S 28½" S to S
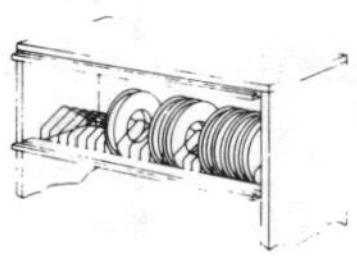	36"		17"	34½"	7⅛" (9" high door) 10⅛" (12" high door) 13⅛" (15" high door)	34½" S to S 34½" S to S 34½" S to S
	42"		17"	40½"	7⅛" (9" high door) 10⅛" (12" high door) 13⅛" (15" high door)	40½" S to S 40½" S to S 40½" S to S
Add-on cabinet	30"	830-610	18"/16⅜"*	30"/28⅛"	15¾"/13⅛"	28⅛" S to S
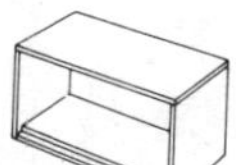	36"	836-610	18"/16⅜"*	36"/34⅛"	15¾"/13⅛"	34⅛" S to S
	42"	842-610	18"/16⅜"*	42"/40⅛"	15¾"/13⅛"	40⅛" S to S
	30"	830-710	18"/16⅜"*	30"/28⅛"	28⅛"/25⅛"	28⅛" S to S
	36"	836-710	18"/16⅜"*	36"/34⅛"	28⅛"/25⅛"	34⅛" S to S
	42"	842-710	18"/16⅜"*	42"/40⅛"	28⅛"/25⅛"	40⅛" S to S

*Deduct ⅝" when compressor is used.

FURNITURE, FURNISHINGS, AND EQUIPMENT

Storage Cabinets

Standard cabinets often provide a fast, flexible, and economical solution to many storage problems. Table 7 provides dimensional data and capacities for four typical cabinet types. These cabinets are manufactured by Steelcase. The dimensions of cabinets of other manufacturers will differ somewhat. The data in Table 7, however, are adequate for preliminary planning purposes.

TABLE 7   Storage Cabinets

Description	Outside/inside dimensions			Linear capacity
	Depth	Width	Height	
Storage cabinet	18"/17"	36"/33⅛"	41¼"/35⅝"	99½" side-to-side on 3 shelves (2 adj., 1" thick)
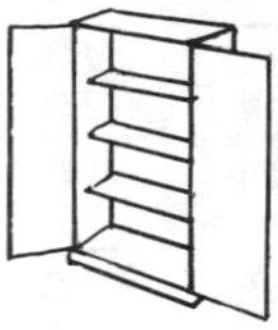	18"/17"	36"/33⅛"	52⅜"/46⅜"	99½" S to S on 3 shelves (2 adj., 1" thick)
	18"/17"	36"/33⅛"	64⅝"/58¾"	132¾" S to S on 4 shelves (3 adj., 1" thick)
	18"/17"	36"/33⅛"	80½"/74½"	165⅞" S to S on 5 shelves (4 adj., 1" thick)
	24"/23"	36"/33⅛"	64⅝"/58¾"	132¾" S to S on 4 shelves (3 adj., 1" thick)
	24"/23"	36"/33⅛"	80½"/74½"	165⅞" S to S on 5 shelves (4 adj., 1" thick)
Wardrobe cabinet	18"/17"	36"/33⅛"	52⅜"/46⅜"	Not for filing
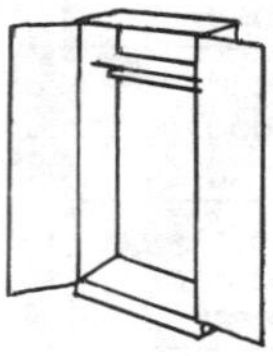	18"/17"	36"/33⅛"	64⅝"/58¾"	Not for filing
	18"/17"	36"/33⅛"	80½"/74½"	Not for filing
	24"/23"	36"/33⅛"	64⅝"/58¾"	Not for filing
	24"/23"	36"/33⅛"	80½"/74½"	Not for filing
Wardrobe/storage cabinet	18"/17"	36"/33⅛"	52⅜"/46⅜"	43¼" S to S on 3 shelves (2 adj., 1" thick)
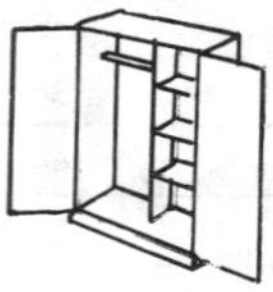	18"/17"	36"/33⅛"	64⅝"/58¾"	58" S to S on 4 shelves (3 adj., 1" thick)
	18"/17"	36"/33⅛"	80½"/74½"	58" S to S on 4 shelves (3 adj., 1" thick)
	24"/23"	36"/33⅛"	64⅝"/58¾"	58" S to S on 4 shelves (3 adj., 1" thick)
	24"/23"	36"/33⅛"	80½"/74½"	58" S to S on 4 shelves (3 adj., 1" thick)
Wardrobe	18"/16⅝"	18"/15⅛"	41⅛"/35⅞"	15⅛" on bar
	18"/16⅝"	18"/15½"	52¼"/47"	15½" on bar
	18"/16⅝"	18"/15⅛"	64½"/59¼"	15⅛" on bar

TABLE 8   Interior Card Trays

(For use in vertical or lateral files)

Description	Style No.	Inside dimensions			Linear capacity
		Depth	Width	Height	
3 x 5 card 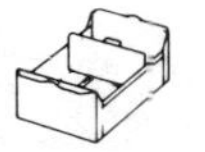	4335	11⅞"	5"	3¼"	10¼"
3 x 5 card	4337M	14⅞"	5"	3¼"	13¼"
5 x 8 card 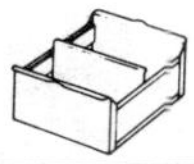	4355	11⅞"	8⅛"	4¾"	11¼"
5 x 8 card	4357	14⅞"	8⅛"	4¾"	13¼"
4 x 6 card 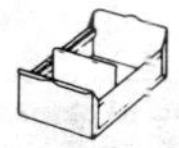	800-TN-46	12"	6⅛"	4⅜"	11⅜"
4 x 6 card	800-TW-46	15"	6⅛"	4⅜"	14⅜"
Tab card 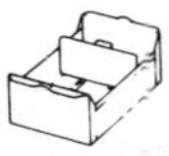	7201	11⅞"	7½"	3⅝"	10⅜"
Tab card	7204	14⅞"	7½"	3⅝"	13⅜"
Coin and bill 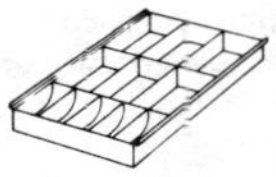	4388	8¼" / 5⅞"	3⅛" / 11¹/₁₂"	1⅞" / 1⅞"	* †
Coin and bill	4389	7⅞" / 2⅜"	3¾" / 2¼"	1⅞" / 1¾"	* †

		Number of card trays accommodated per 6"-high drawer or shelf			
		4337M	800TW46‡	4357	7204M
6" high shelves/drawers 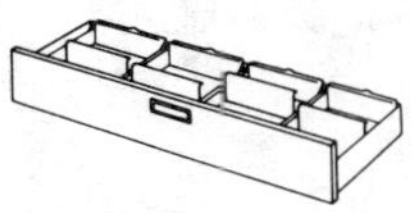	842 DWDV-6	7	5	4	5
	842 SWDV-6	7	5	—	5
	836 DWDV-6	6	4	3	4
	836 SWDV-6	6	4	—	4
	830 DWDV-6	5	3	3	3
	830 SWDV-6	5	3	3	3
	830 SWDV-3	5	3	—	3

*Dimensions of each of 6 bill compartments.
†Dimensions of each of 5 coin compartments.
‡Card trays cannot be installed in 6"-high shelf located directly below a door. Use 3"-high shelf and refer to guidelines.

FURNITURE, FURNISHINGS, AND EQUIPMENT
Storage Components Glossary

Lower storage/Lateral file
Free-standing wall- or panel-mounted files with width dimension greater than depth dimension.

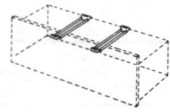

Rails
Mount in lateral file for drawer suspended filing, front-to-back or side-to-side.

Media compartment kit
Can be retrofit or factory assembled to 800/900 Series 6" roll-out shelf. Provides dividers and partitions adjustable for storing a variety of media-cassettes, mini-cassettes, cart-ridges, floppy disks, and more.

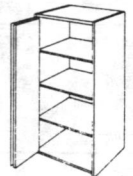

Storage cabinet
Storage for general supplies. Available in 2, 3, or 4 adjustable shelves.

Mobile pedestal
Supports drawers in several combinations and has casters for mobility.

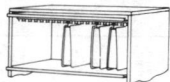

T-bar filing for bound printouts
Accepts EDP printouts in T-bar type binders.

Overfile cabinet
For use above lateral or vertical files. Sliding door, lock, and shelf-modifier options.

Vertical file
Letter- or legal-size filing cabinet with depth dimension greater than width dimension. For front-to-back filing only.

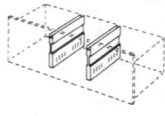

Partition
A double metal wall that mounts into a lateral file drawer to divide drawer.

Vertical file drawer
6" high and 12" high drawers for letter or legal-size filing cabinets.

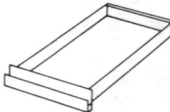

Personal drawer
For personal items. An adjustable divider is included. 3" high.

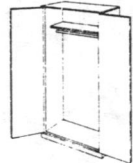

Wardrobe
Provides full-width coat rod for hanging clothes mounted beneath full-width shelf.

Pull-out keyboard shelf
Attaches beneath work-surface for computer keyboard support and storage.

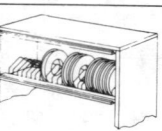

Wire tape racks
Racks can be freestanding or built-in to lateral files for storage of magnetic tapes and disk cart-ridges on edge. Dividers can be positioned to accommodate media of different thicknesses.

FURNITURE, FURNISHINGS, AND EQUIPMENT
Storage Components Glossary

Bookcase
Units have adjustable shelves which can accommodate rows of standard ring binders and other bound materials.

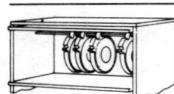

Center hook filing hanging bar
Accepts printouts and magnetic tape reels with center hooks.

Combination wardrobe and storage cabinet
Units are divided – space for hanging clothes and two or three vertically adjustable shelves.

Compressor
A spring-loaded plate that supports file material. Can be moved and locked in position. Used in vertical and lateral file drawers, pedestal file drawers and card trays.

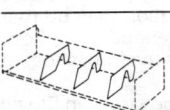

Divider
Metal plate used to separate and support file material. For lateral file and pedestal file drawers, fixed and roll-out shelves.

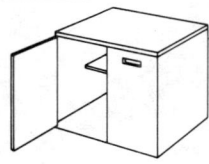

Double-door storage cabinet
For miscellaneous storage below worksurface. Includes one adjustable shelf and two swing-arm doors.

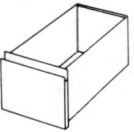

File drawer
For letter- or legal-size documents 12" and 15" high. 15" high drawers can also be used for computer printouts. For front-to-back or side-to-side or combination filing.

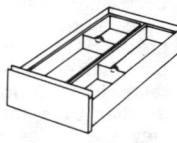

File insert drawers
For use in vertical files instead of card trays.

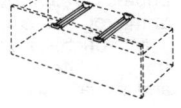

Hanging folder frame
A metal rod mounted in lateral and vertical files for suspended file material. Can be mounted on partitions for front-to-back filing.

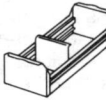

Interior card trays
Portable trays in various sizes for common card sizes: 3 x 5, 4 x 6, etc. Compressor included.

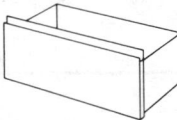

Later file drawer
3" tray drawer, 6" card drawer, and 9", 12" and 15" high file drawers. Letter or legal-size filing. Dividers, three sway blocks, compressor, hanging folder frames, rails, or partitions available.

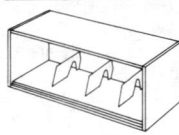

Lateral file fixed shelf
12" or 15" high shelves with or without doors and with three dividers.

Lateral file posting shelf
Metal pull-out shelf option on 48" and 60" interior height lateral files. When not specified, the space will be filled by a posting shelf filler.

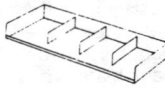

Lateral file roll-out shelf
3", 6", 12", and 15" high shelves extend for accessibility.

Lateral file workshelf
3" high roll-out workshelf with laminate surface.

FURNITURE, FURNISHINGS, AND EQUIPMENT
Electronic Media Storage

Microfiche

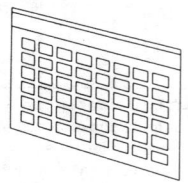

4" x 6"

Description Microfiche is a 4" x 6" film transparency containing multiple rows of greatly reduced page images of any written, printed or graphic material. Image reductions range from 13 up to several hundred times smaller than the originals. A microfiche viewer enlarges the images so that they are readable. Labeling information is written or printed on a narrow strip along the long edge at the top of the microfiche.

Microfiche may be stored in interior card trays, in lateral file 6"-high roll-out shelves, and in a lateral file media compartment.

Microfilm

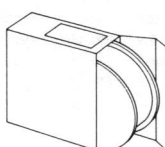

1" x 4" diameter reel
(1¼" x 4¼" x 4¼" box)

Description Microfilm is roll photographic film on a reel or in a square cartridge that contains images of pages of written, graphic or printed material reduced hundreds of times. A microfilm viewer enlarges the images so that they are readable. Microfilm on a reel is kept in a square plastic or cardboard box for protection and ease of handling. Microfilm is most conveniently stored on edge. Labeling is placed on one of the edges of the reel or box.

Microfilm may be stored in the lateral file media compartment kit, in an interior card tray, and in lateral file 6"-high drawers or shelves.

Print-out Paper

Description Print-out paper, also known as continuous form data processing paper, is used in almost all computer printers and some word processing equipment. The most common types are recognizable by:

- Small "pin-feed" holes along both edges which are used by the printer to grip and advance the paper.
- Green or grey-shaded stripes across the paper which serve to organize the printed information.

After printing, the print-out may exist in a "fan-folded" stack or it may be "burst," i.e., separated into individual sheets along the perforations that exist at the fold lines.

If the print-out consists of a significant number of sheets, it may be "bound" for easier handling. Fan-folded printouts *must* be bound along the top or long edge. Print-outs that have been burst may be bound along *either* the long edge *or* the short edge. The binding may consist of only a narrow metal or plastic clamp or it may be include a stiff plastic or fiberboard cover. Frequently the binding may include hooks at both ends so the print-out may be hung from two rails like a hanging file folder. Other hooks may be used to suspend it from special bars or rails.

Identification information may be marked on one of the edges (depending on how the print-out is stored) or on the front sheet of the binding cover.

Print-out paper may be stored in Steelcase lateral and vertical files depending on the paper size. Check the file which will accommodate your paper. Boxed paper can be stored in storage cabinets.

Cartridges

⅝" x 4" x 6" (cartridge)
⅞" x 4¼" x 6¼" (cartridge in case)

Description Cartridges have ¼" wide magnetic tape loaded into a reel-to-reel cartridge generally made of clear plastic with metal back plate. They look similar to an oversize recording cassette. Cartridges come in and are sometimes stored in a "flip-open" plastic or cardboard box. Labels or identification information are located on the long edge or on the side along the long edge of the cartridge or the box.

Cartridges may be stored in interior card trays or in a media compartment kit in lateral file 6"-high drawers or shelves.

Cassettes

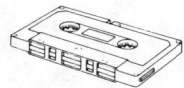

Standard Cassette Case
1¹/₁₆" x 2¾" x 4⁵/₁₆"

Mini Cassette Case
⁷/₁₆" x 1½" x 2⁷/₈"

Description Cassettes are available in "standard" and "mini" sizes and consist of magnetic tape loaded into a reel-to-reel configuration in a plastic case. Standard cassettes for electronic equipment are identical in size and appearance to those used for home recording. Cassettes may be used in microcomputers and in word processing or dictation equipment. They come in and are frequently stored in a flip-open plastic case. Labels or identification information may be located on the long edge or side of the cassette or its case.

Cassettes may be stored in a lateral file media compartment kit.

Disk Cartridges

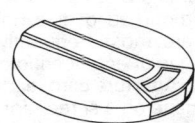

1" x 10" diameter
3" x 10" diameter
1" x 15" diameter
3" x 15" diameter

Description Disk cartridges are round plastic cases which contain a series of rotating platters (or disks) on which data is magnetically recorded. The number of platters in a case varies with the height of the case. In use, the entire case is inserted in a computer disk drive unit where recording arms, which read/record information, enter the case through a slot with a spring door.

Disk cartridges are flat in appearance with an elongated Y-shaped protrusion on the top. They can be stored flat or on edge.

Labels for identification are usually located on the edge of the disk cartridge. Frequently disk cartridges have to be stored in a temperature/humidity controlled environment.

Disk cartridges may be stored in lateral file 6"-high roll-out shelves, storage cabinets, and bookcases.

Disk Packs

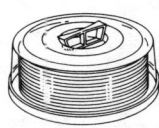

7" x 10" diameter
7" x 15" diameter

Description Disk packs are round plastic cases which contain a series of rotating platters (or disks) on which data is magnetically recorded. The number of platters in a unit varies with the height of the plastic case. In use, the entire case is inserted in a computer disk drive unit where recording arms, to read/record information, enter the case through a slot with a spring door. Disk packs are flat on the bottom and upright with the handle on top. Identification is generally located on the edge of the disk pack. These units should be stored in a temperature/humidity controlled environment. Disk packs *must not* be stored one on another.

Disk packs may be stored in storage cabinets, bookcases, and on 3"- and 6"-high lateral file shelves.

Floppy (Flexible) Disks

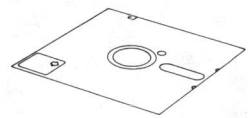

8" x 8"
5¼" x 5¼"
3½" x 3½"

Description Floppy disks, also called diskettes or flexible disks, are small record-like disks each permanently enclosed in a square, stiff paper envelope. They are used to magnetically record information in all types of small computer and word processing equipment. Labels are placed on the paper envelope.

Floppy disks may be stored in 12"-high lateral file drawers and shelves.

FURNITURE, FURNISHINGS, AND EQUIPMENT
Electronic Media Storage

Laser Disks

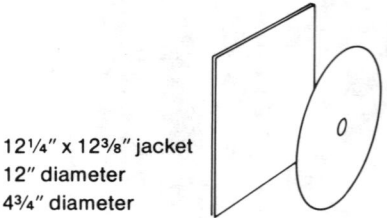

12¼" x 12⅜" jacket
12" diameter
4¾" diameter

Description Laser disks look like long-play record albums complete with a paper protective sleeve. Data are stored and retrieved by laser beam.

Laser disks may be stored in 15"-high lateral file drawers and shelves.

Magnetic, Tab, and Aperture Cards

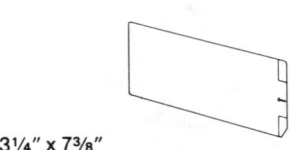

3¼" x 7⅜"

Description Magnetic cards, also known as mag cards, are a tab-size black plastic card with magnetic material coated on one or both sides. The cards are used to record or reproduce information in word processing equipment. In some cases one or more of the cards will be kept in a paper envelope. Identifying information will be marked on the face of the envelope.

Tab cards, also known as keypunch cards, are 80 column cards or punch cards with small holes in them to represent bits of data. Although they may be stored in a workstation or central storage area, they are usually used and produced in a mainframe computer room or keypunch department, and are stored in specially separated decks. The decks are most frequently identified by markings across the edges of the cards.

Aperture cards are tab cards with a piece of microfilm mounted over a hole in their center. They are most frequently used for microfilm images of engineering or architectural drawings. Aperture card reader/printers enlarge the image on a screen for reference and, if required, reproduce a full-sized copy of the drawing. Identifying information is printed in a narrow band along the top (long edge) of the card.

These cards may be stored in interior card trays and in lateral file 6"-high drawers and roll-out shelves.

Magnetic Tape Reels

1" x 7½" diameter
1" x 8½" diameter
1" x 10½" diameter
1" x 15" diameter

Description Magnetic tape is typically ½" wide and loaded on reels of varying diameters. A flexible plastic strip locks around the outside of the reel to protect the tape and prevent unraveling when it is not in use. This media is used in large tape drive units that are generally found only in computer rooms. The long-term storage of magnetic tapes is subject to strict temperature and humidity requirements to prevent damage. Tapes are labeled both on the side and on the flexible strip that is placed around the edge of the reel. They can be stored flat or on edge. For flat storage, handle like disk cartridges.

Magnetic tape reels may be stored in the lateral file add-on cabinets, storage cabinets, or in free-standing wire racks on lateral file shelves.

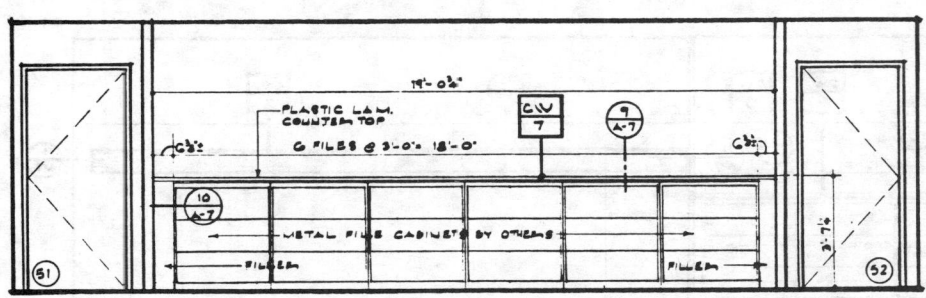

(6) NORTH ELEVATION SPACE No 18
@ 3/8" = 1'-0"

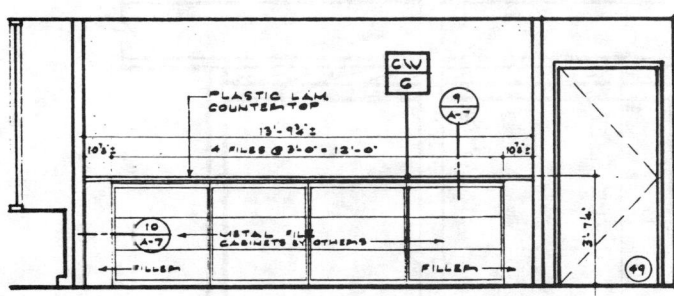

(4) NORTH ELEVATION SPACE No. 16
@ 3/8" = 1'-0"

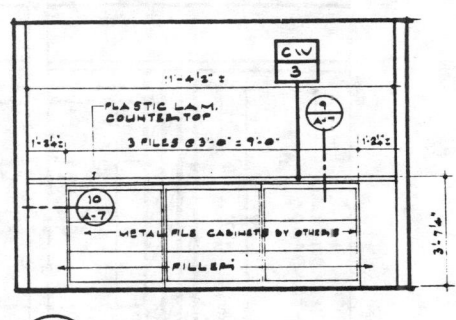

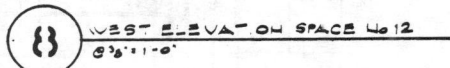

(8) WEST ELEVATION SPACE No 12
@ 3/8" = 1'-0"

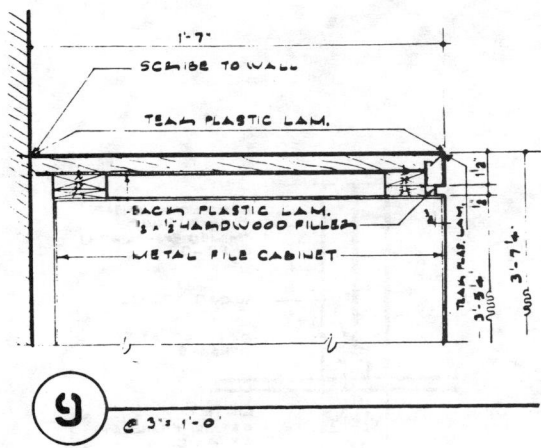

(9) @ 3" = 1'-0"

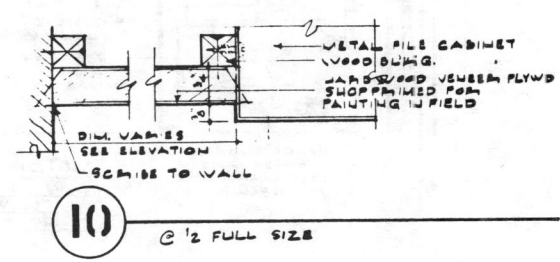

(10) @ 1/2 FULL SIZE

297

FURNITURE, FURNISHINGS, AND EQUIPMENT
File Countertop with Shelf Light

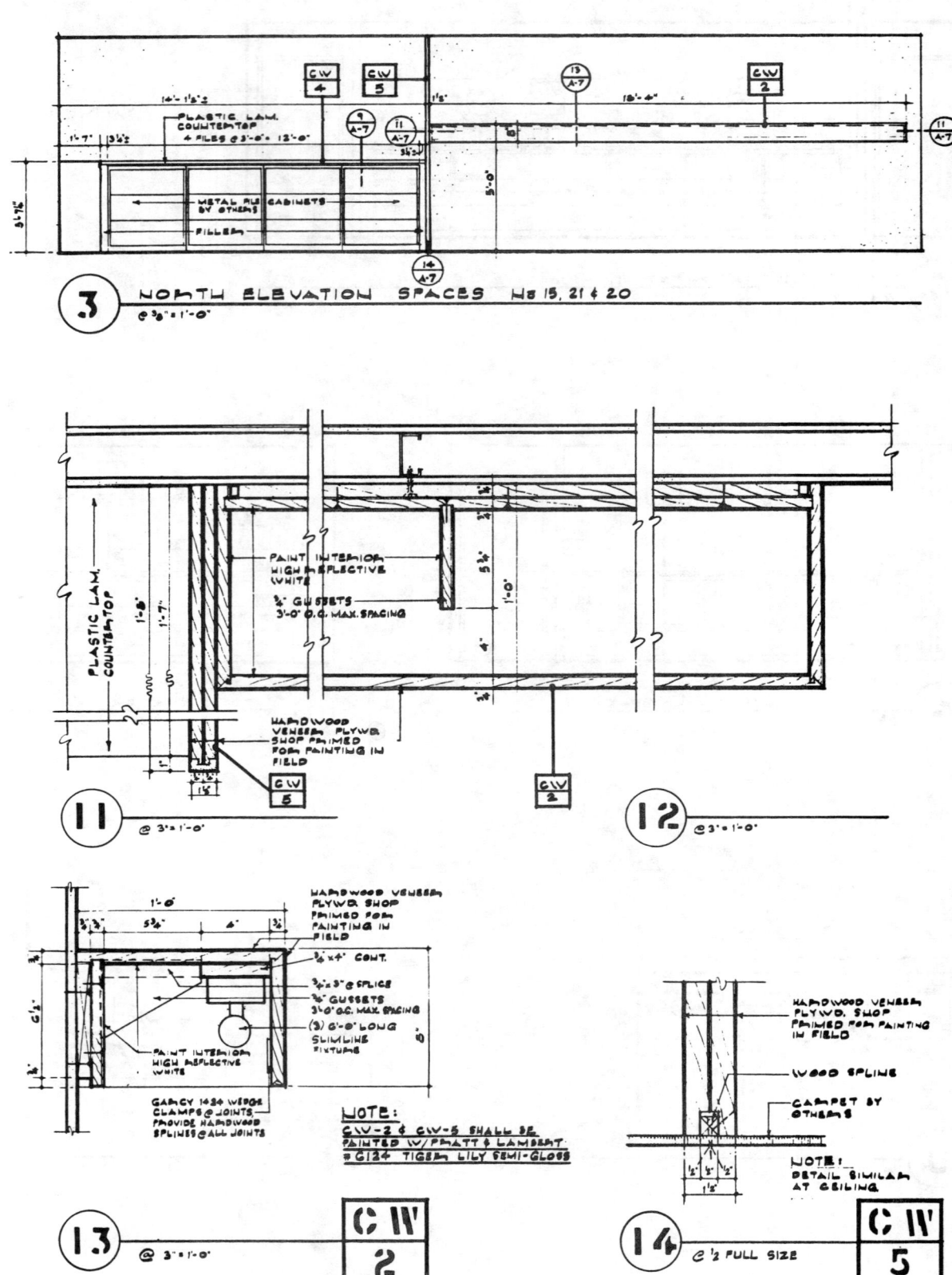

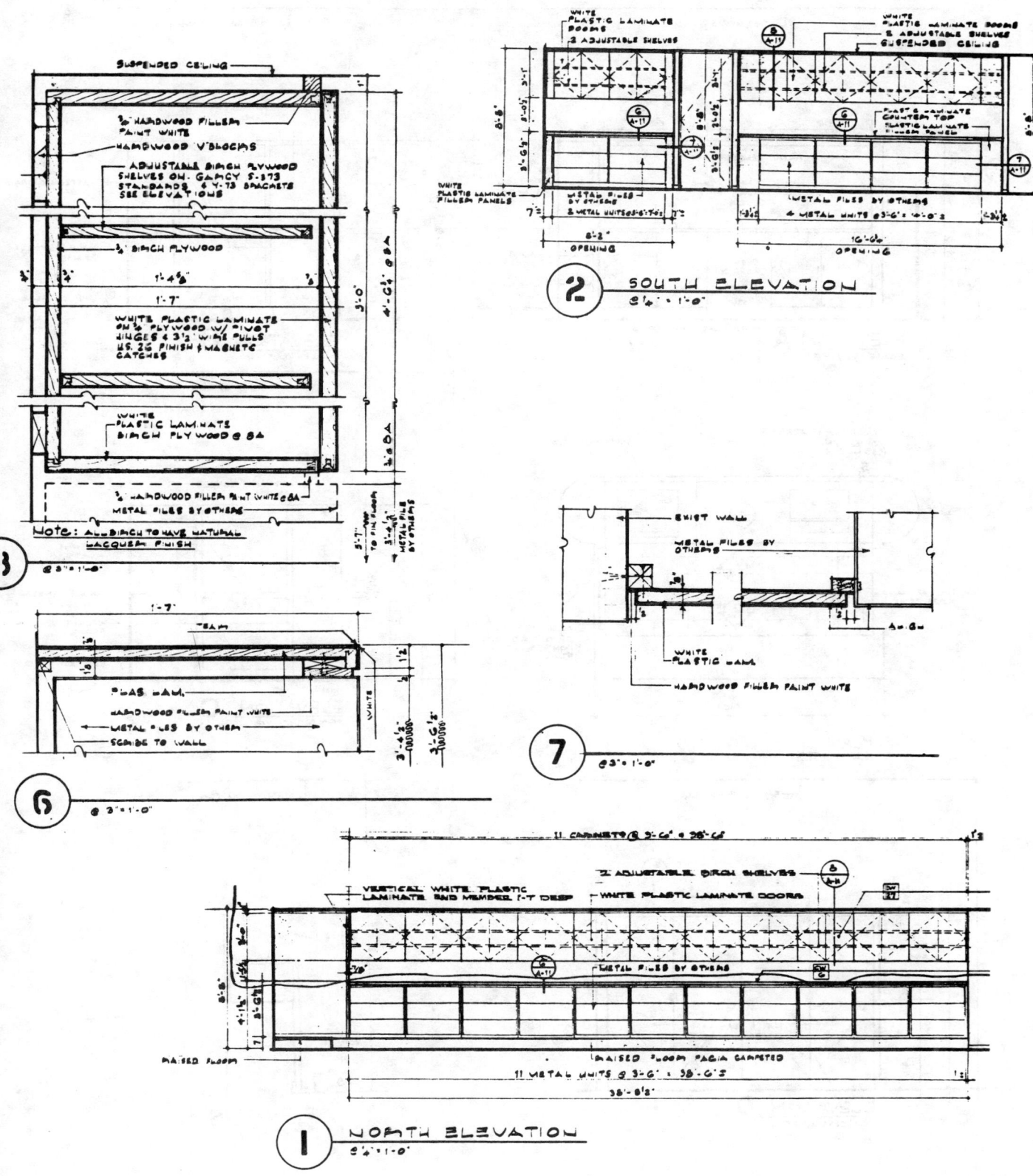

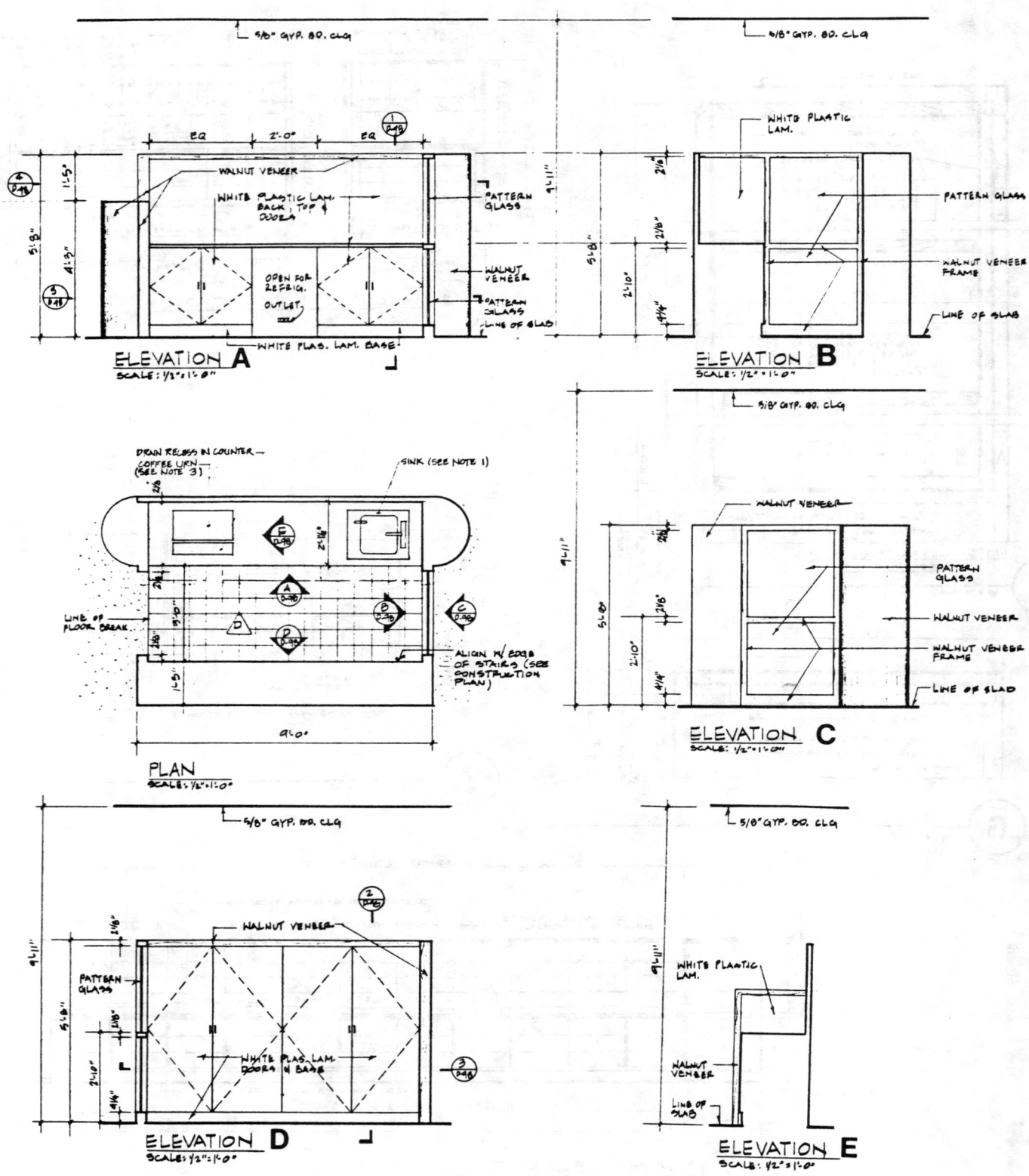

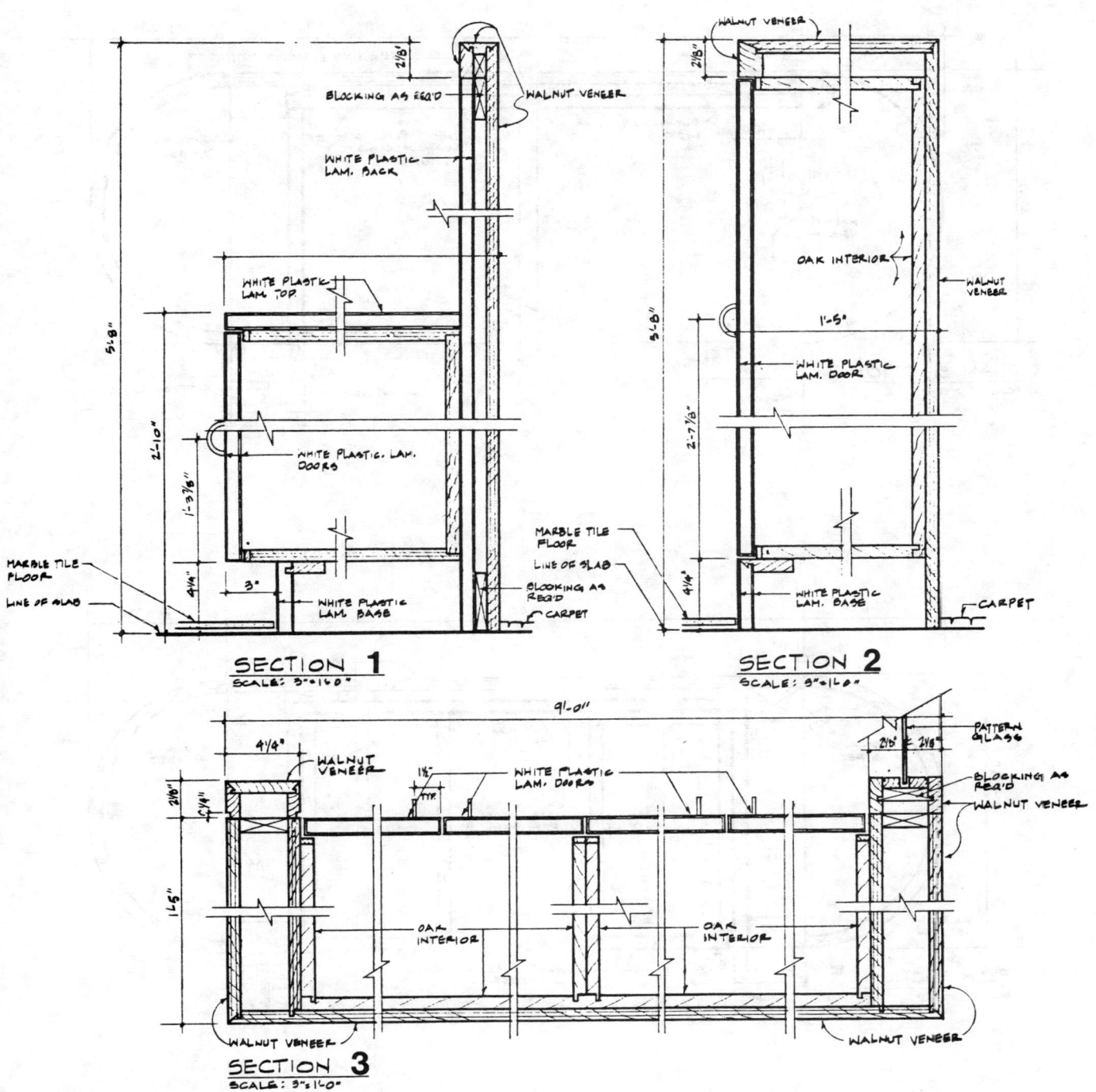

SECTION 1
SCALE: 3"=1'0"

BLOCKING AS REQ'D
WALNUT VENEER
WHITE PLASTIC LAM. BACK
WHITE PLASTIC LAM. TOP
WHITE PLASTIC LAM. DOORS
MARBLE TILE FLOOR
LINE OF SLAB
WHITE PLASTIC LAM. BASE
MARBLE TILE FLOOR
LINE OF SLAB
BLOCKING AS REQ'D
CARPET

SECTION 2
SCALE: 3"=1'0"

WALNUT VENEER
OAK INTERIOR
WALNUT VENEER
WHITE PLASTIC LAM. DOOR
WHITE PLASTIC LAM. BASE
CARPET

SECTION 3
SCALE: 3"=1'0"

WALNUT VENEER
WHITE PLASTIC LAM. DOORS
PATTERN GLASS
BLOCKING AS REQ'D
WALNUT VENEER
OAK INTERIOR
OAK INTERIOR
WALNUT VENEER
WALNUT VENEER

FURNITURE, FURNISHINGS, AND EQUIPMENT
Office Pantry

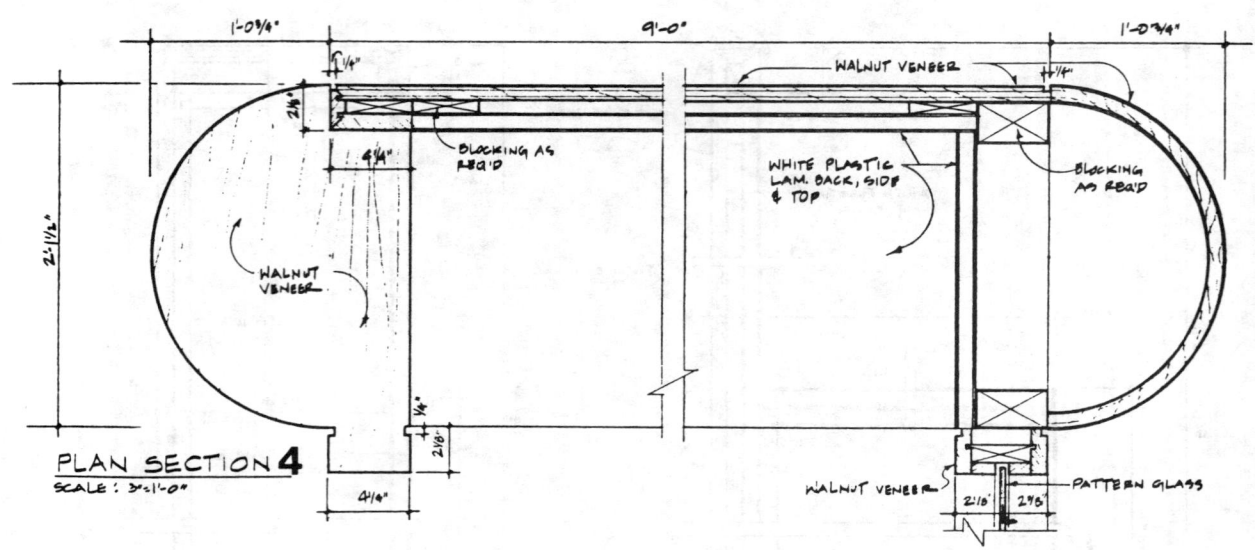

PLAN SECTION **4**
SCALE: 3"=1'-0"

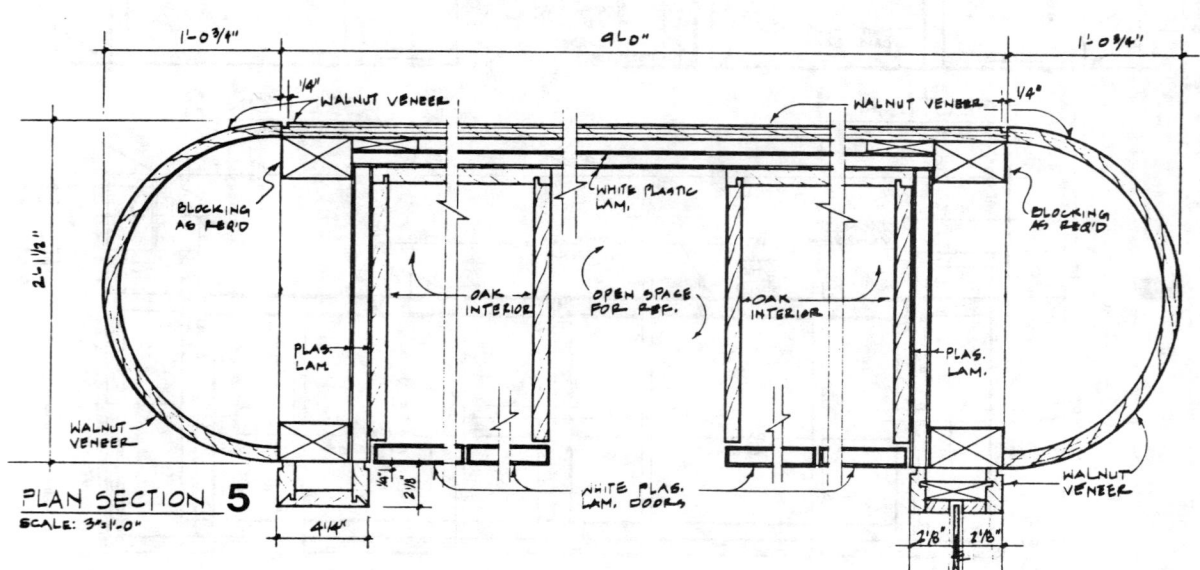

PLAN SECTION **5**
SCALE: 3"=1'-0"

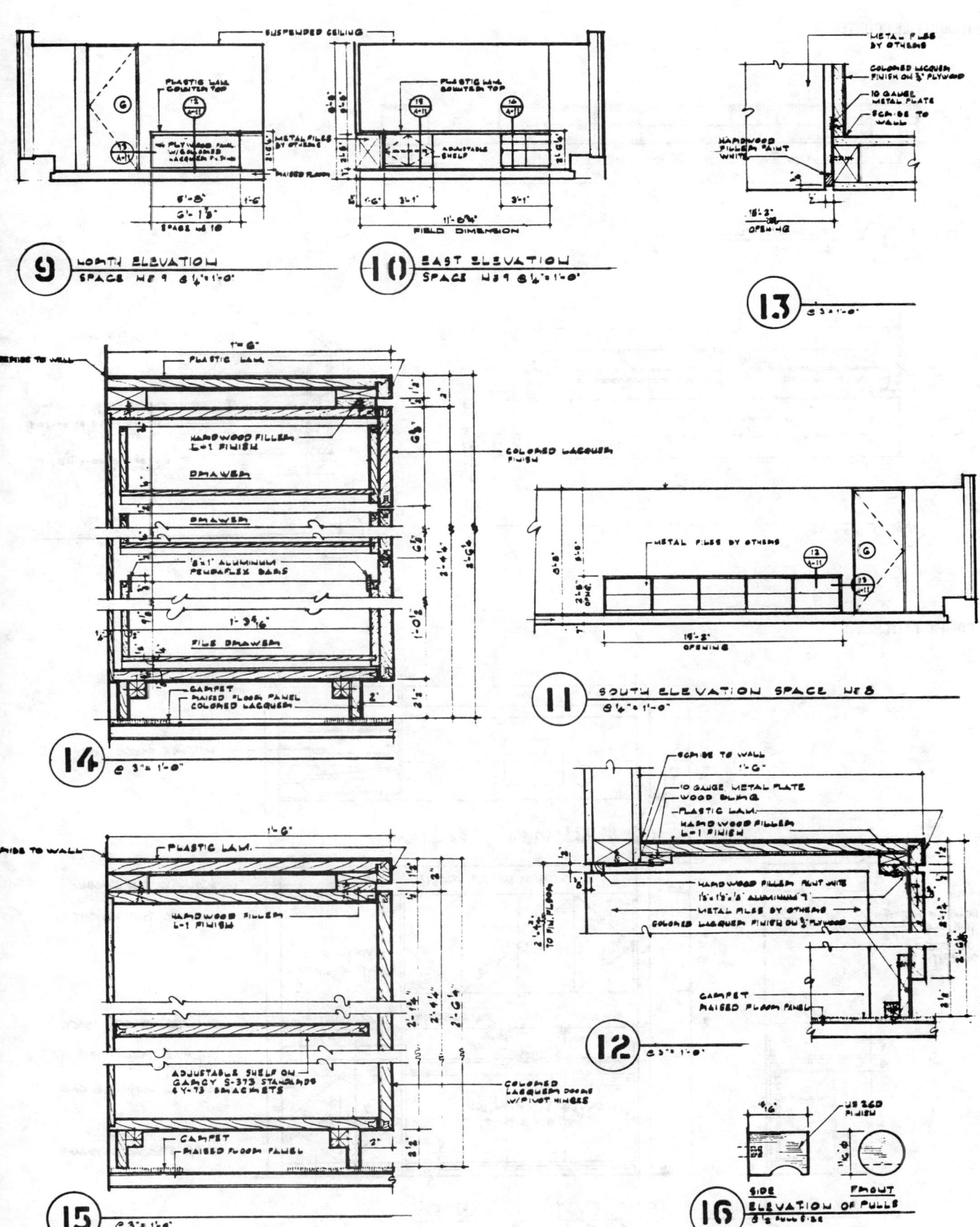

FURNITURE, FURNISHINGS, AND EQUIPMENT
Island File Counter; Compact Kitchen

ISLAND FILE COUNTER

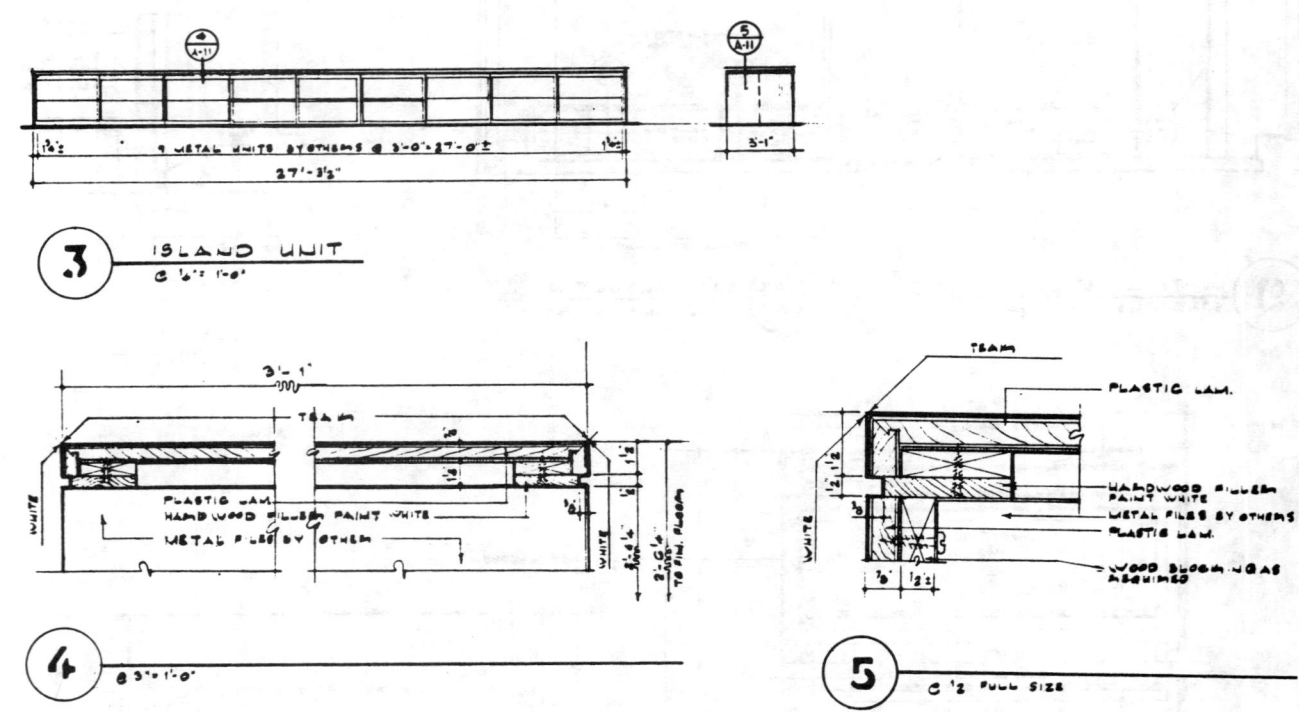

COMPACT KITCHEN

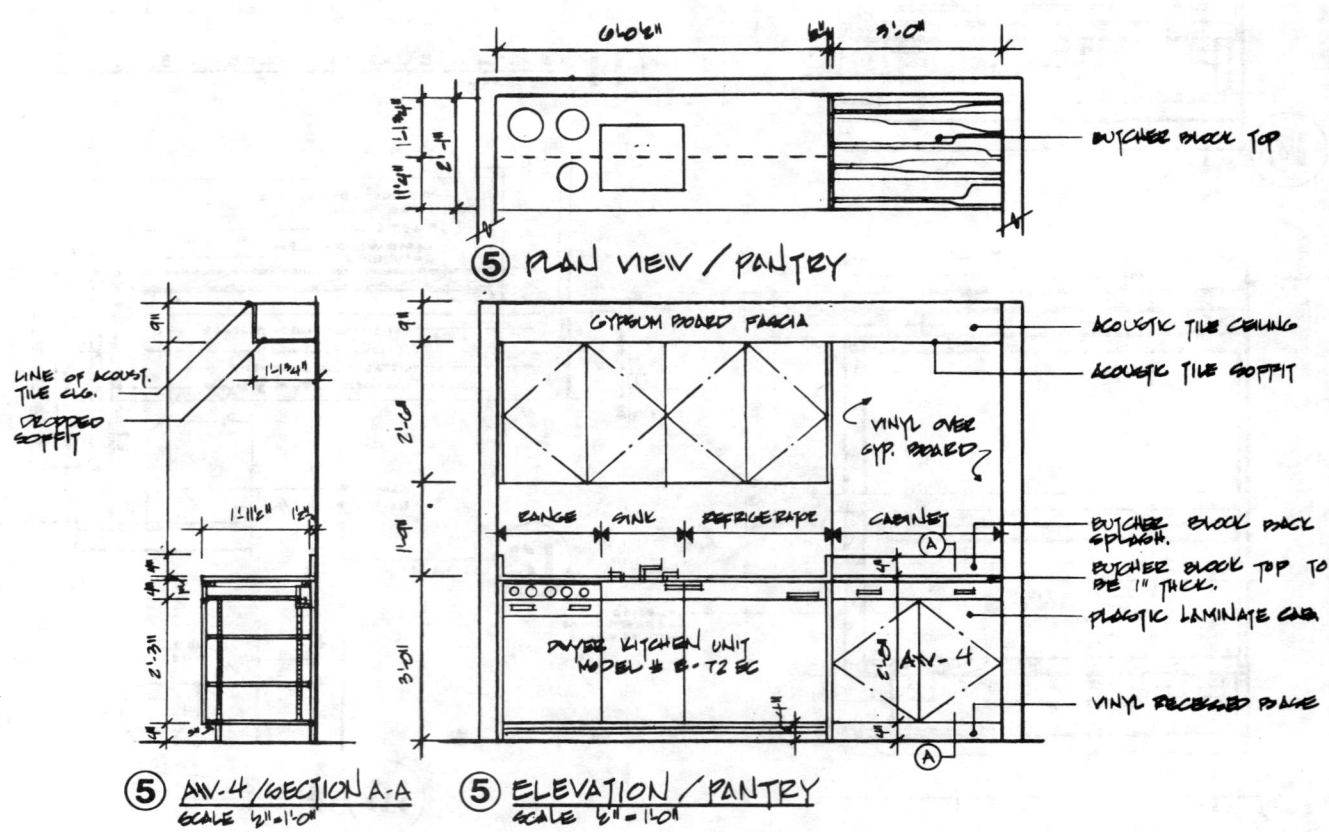

Hospitality Spaces

The basic components of any restaurant interior are the chair and the table. Depending upon restaurant type, menu, service, table setting, furniture selection, and degree of intimacy required, table size and overall chair space requirements can, and should, vary greatly. A restaurant that encourages rapid turnover of customers will normally provide smaller table top and chair sizes. On the other hand, those restaurants that encourage limited turnover and emphasize the wining and dining experience will typically provide larger table top sizes and larger, more comfortable chairs, with greater distance between table groupings.

There is no agreement among even the most experienced restauranteurs and restaurant designers as to what the optimal table and chair dimensions should be. In addition, many other design factors will influence the final decision, including circulation and egress, accessibility standards, methods of service, and the overall dimensions of any given space.

Figures 1 to 19 provide the designer with restaurant planning standards that have been developed by many experienced architects and interior designers. These drawings not only show the various individual table and chair arrangements, but provide the designer with groupings of these arrangements, as well as an indication of overall size, floor area, and number of persons accommodated. These arrangements, however, should only be utilized for preliminary planning information.

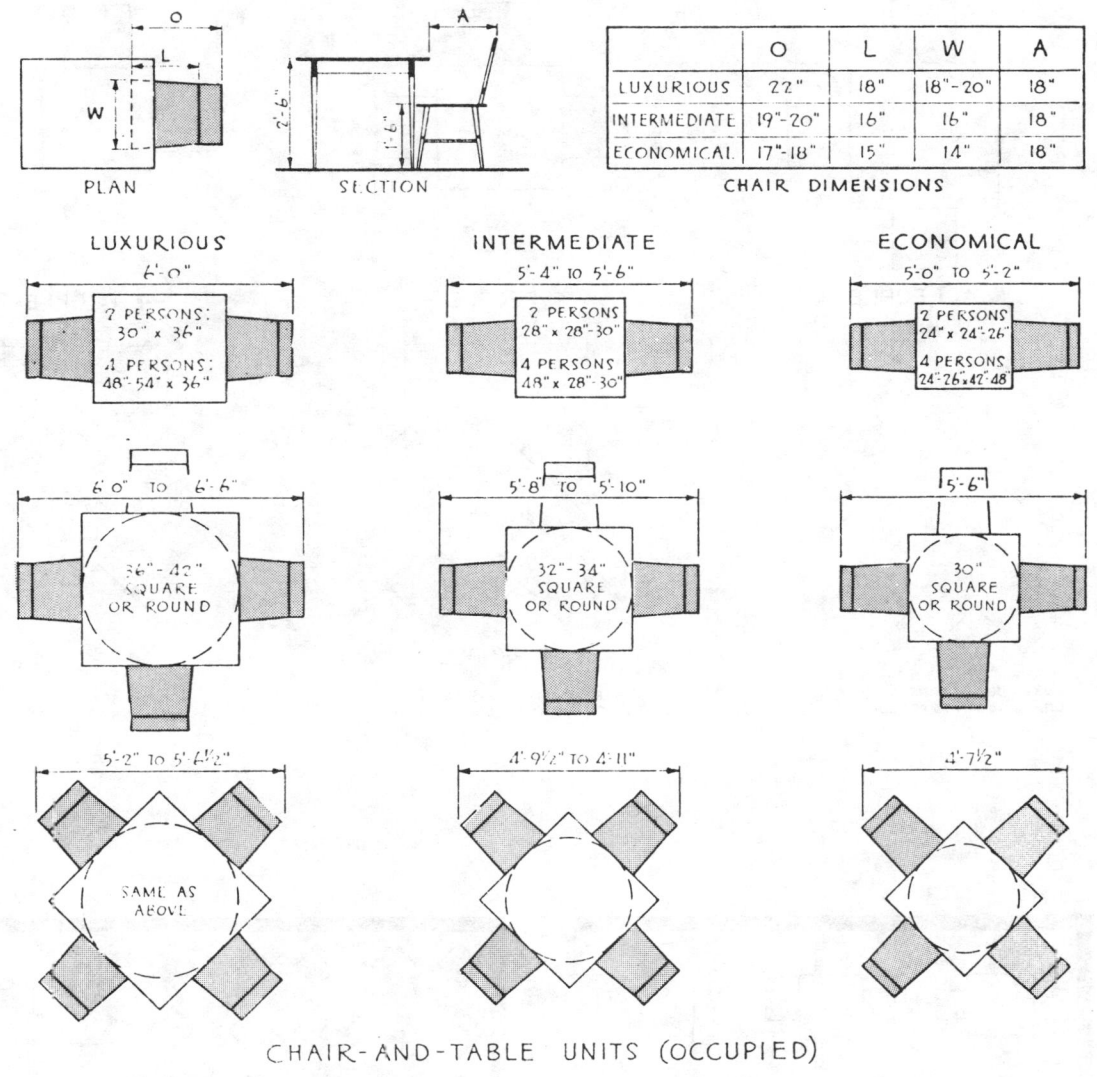

	O	L	W	A
LUXURIOUS	22"	18"	18"-20"	18"
INTERMEDIATE	19"-20"	16"	16"	18"
ECONOMICAL	17"-18"	15"	14"	18"

CHAIR DIMENSIONS

CHAIR-AND-TABLE UNITS (OCCUPIED)

AISLE WIDTHS: FOR PUBLIC CIRCULATION: 36" MINIMUM CLEAR WIDTH | FOR SERVICE ONLY: 24" MIN. BETWEEN CHAIR BACKS | FOR MAIN ENTRANCE: LARGE AS POSSIBLE

Fig. 1

RESTAURANTS

Types and Sizes of Table Arrangements

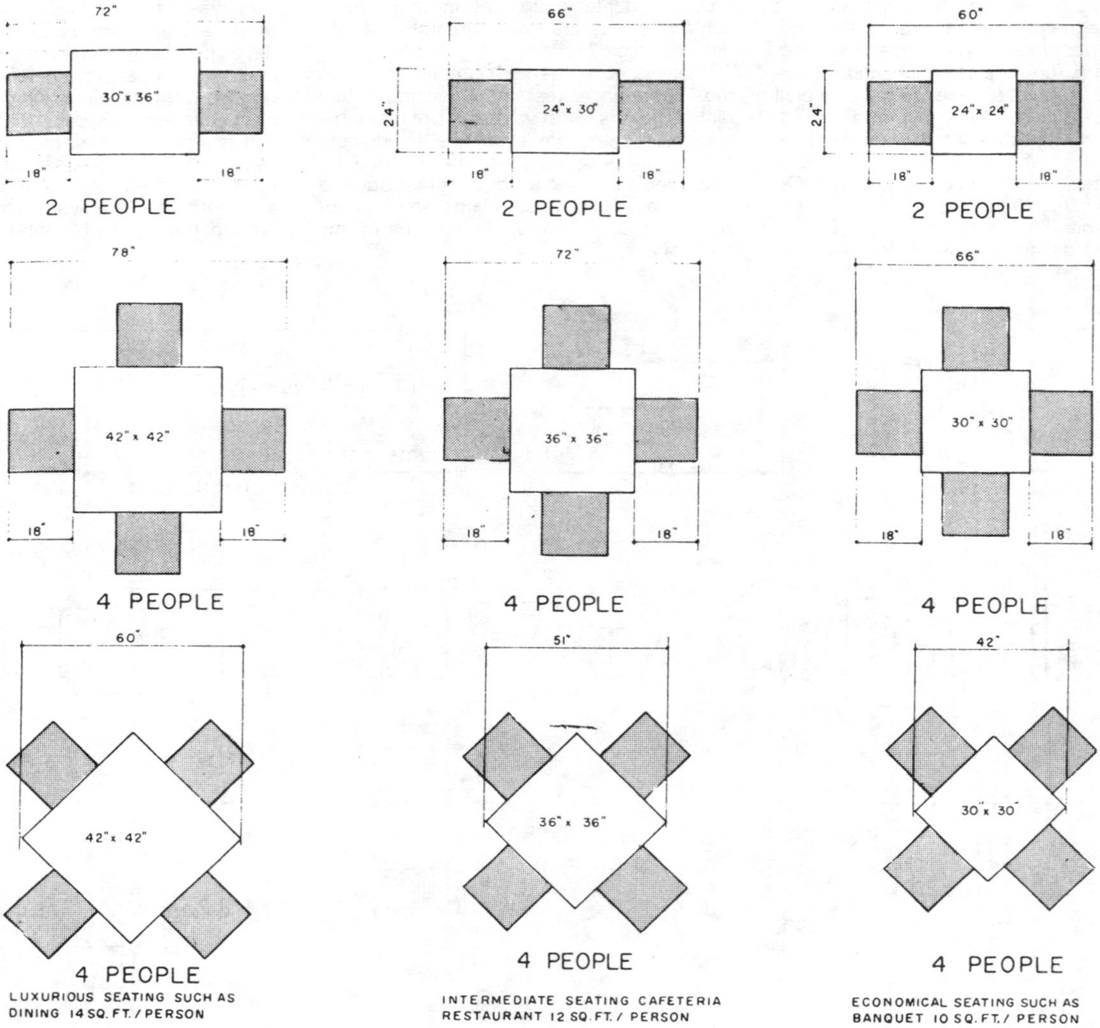

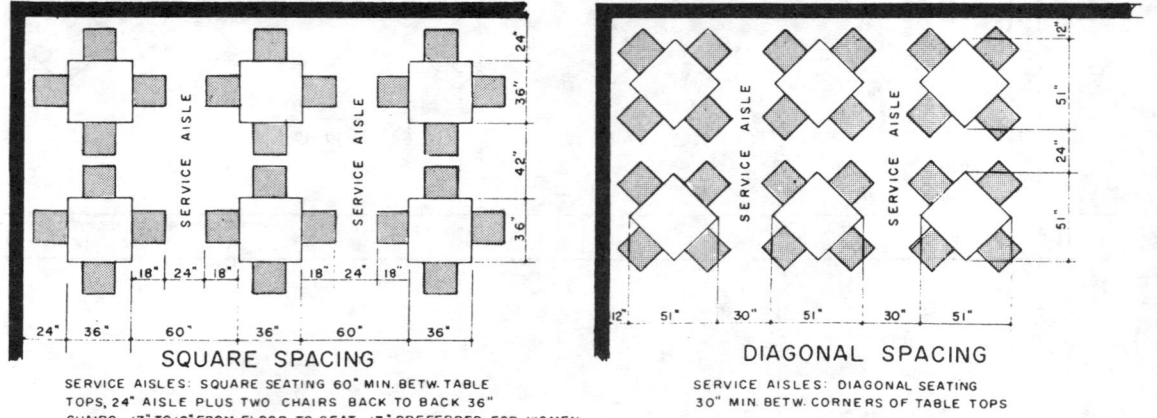

72"
30"x 36"
18"
18"
2 PEOPLE
66"
24"
24"x 30"
18"
18"
2 PEOPLE
60"
24"
24"x 24"
18"
18"
2 PEOPLE
78"
42"x 42"
18"
18"
4 PEOPLE
72"
36"x 36"
18"
18"
4 PEOPLE
66"
30"x 30"
18"
18"
4 PEOPLE
60"
42"x 42"
4 PEOPLE
LUXURIOUS SEATING SUCH AS DINING 14 SQ. FT. / PERSON
51"
36"x 36"
4 PEOPLE
INTERMEDIATE SEATING CAFETERIA RESTAURANT 12 SQ. FT. / PERSON
42"
30"x 30"
4 PEOPLE
ECONOMICAL SEATING SUCH AS BANQUET 10 SQ. FT. / PERSON

SERVICE AISLE
SERVICE AISLE
24"
36"
42"
36"
18"
24"
18"
18"
24"
18"
24"
36"
60"
36"
60"
36"
SERVICE AISLE
SERVICE AISLE
12"
51"
24"
51"
12"
51"
30"
51"
30"
51"

SQUARE SPACING

SERVICE AISLES: SQUARE SEATING 60" MIN. BETW. TABLE TOPS, 24" AISLE PLUS TWO CHAIRS BACK TO BACK 36"
CHAIRS: 17" TO 18" FROM FLOOR TO SEAT, 17" PREFERRED FOR WOMEN
TABLES: 29" TO 30" HIGH

DIAGONAL SPACING

SERVICE AISLES: DIAGONAL SEATING 30" MIN. BETW. CORNERS OF TABLE TOPS

Fig. 2

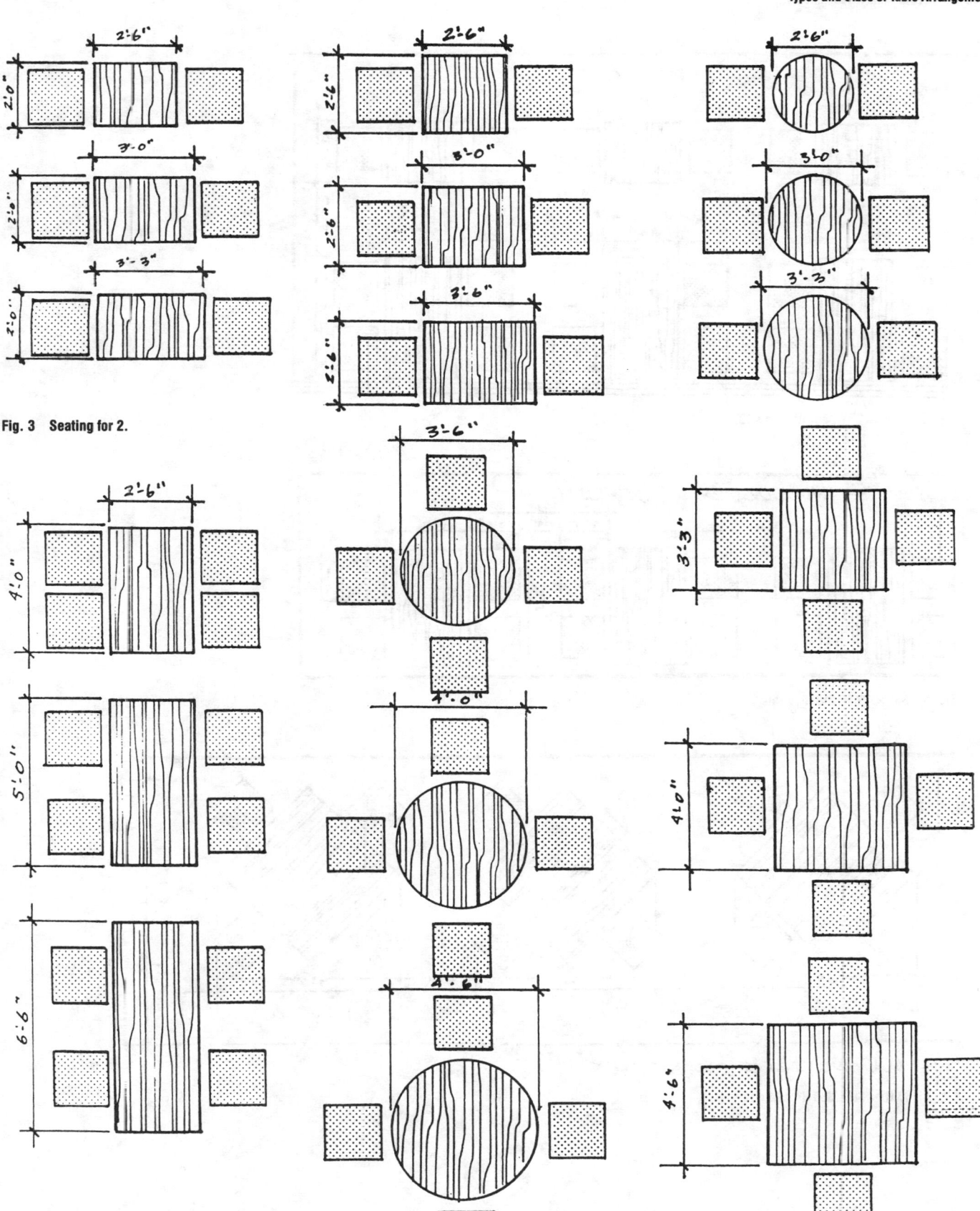

Fig. 3   Seating for 2.

Fig. 4   Seating for 4.

RESTAURANTS
Types and Sizes of Table Arrangements

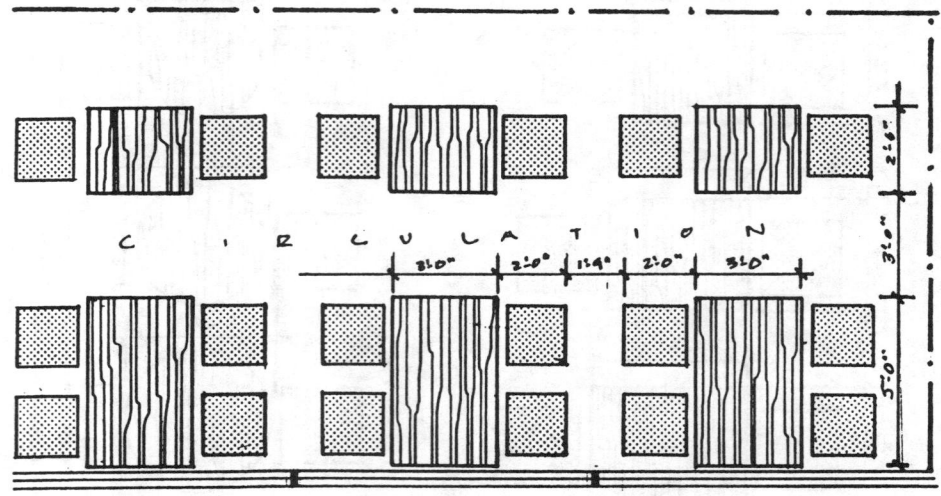

Fig. 5   13 ft × 27 ft, 351 ft², seats 18.

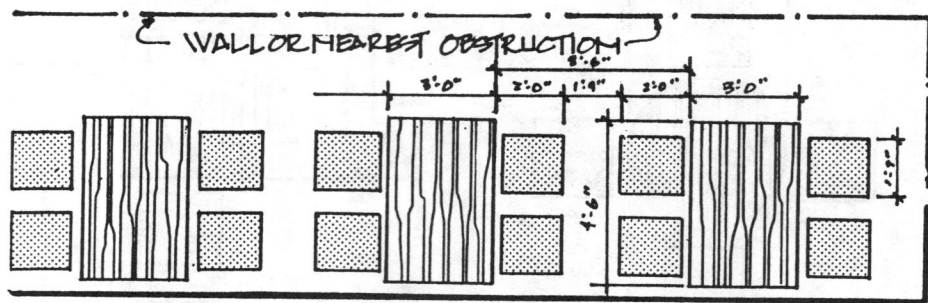

Fig. 6   8 ft × 27 ft, 216 ft², seats 12.

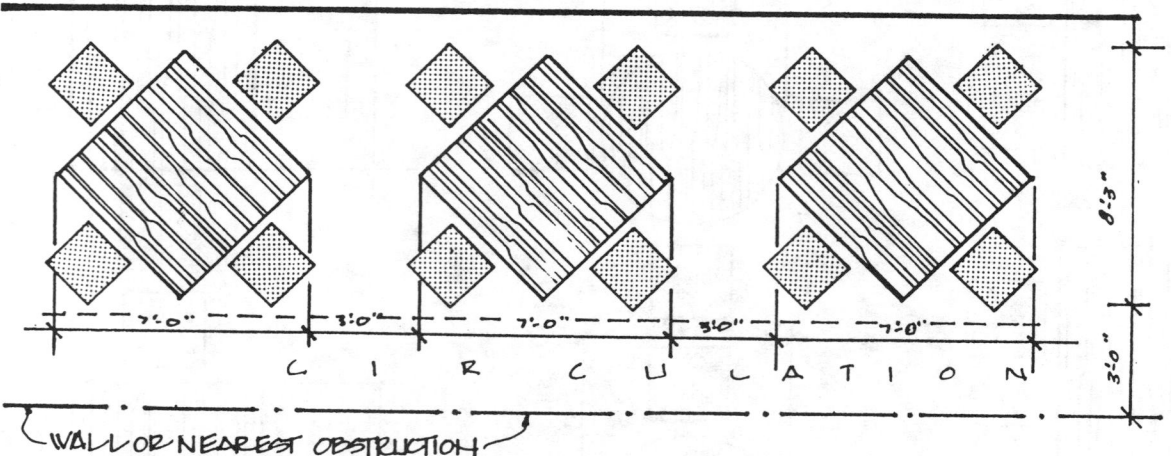

Fig. 7   33 ft × 11 ft, 363 ft², seats 12.

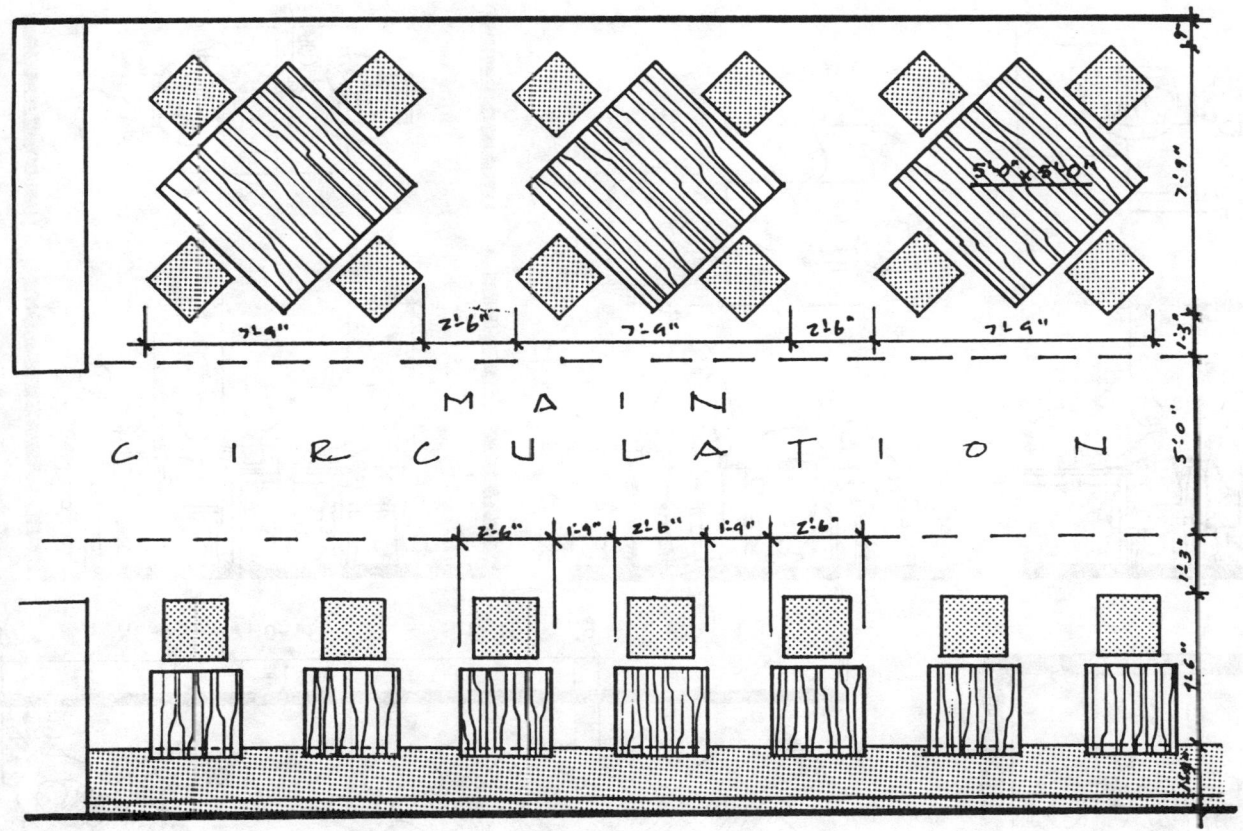

Fig. 8   33 ft × 22 ft, 726 ft², seats 26.

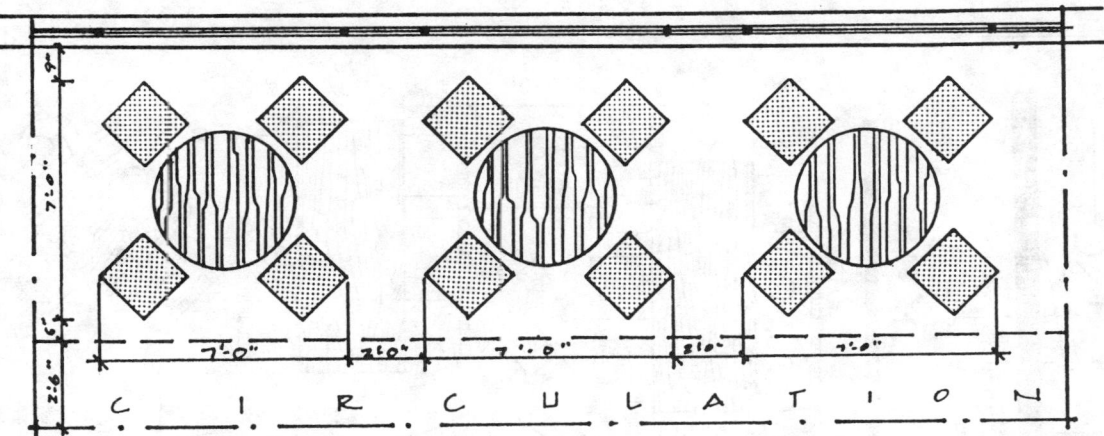

Fig. 9   11 ft × 28 ft, 308 ft², seats 12.

RESTAURANTS

Tables: Design Criteria

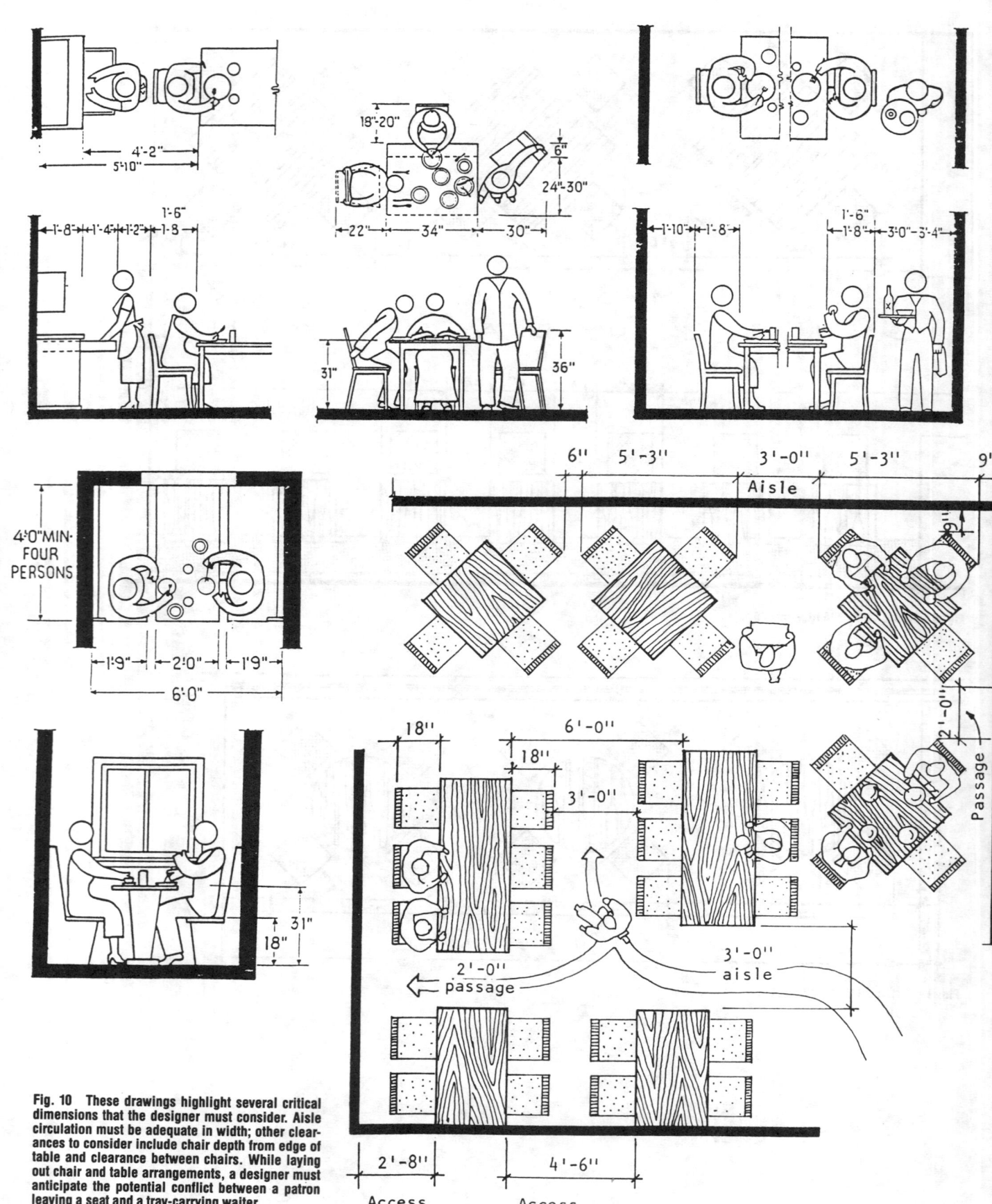

Fig. 10 These drawings highlight several critical dimensions that the designer must consider. Aisle circulation must be adequate in width; other clearances to consider include chair depth from edge of table and clearance between chairs. While laying out chair and table arrangements, a designer must anticipate the potential conflict between a patron leaving a seat and a tray-carrying waiter.

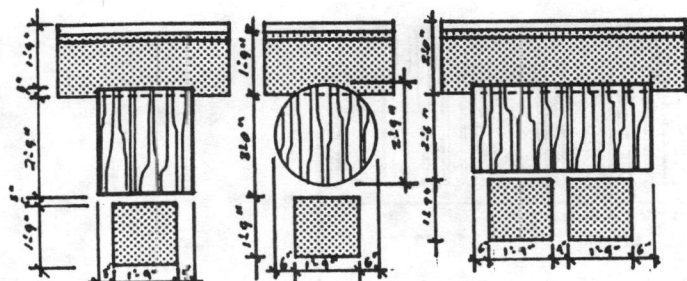

Fig. 11 Mixed banquette seating.

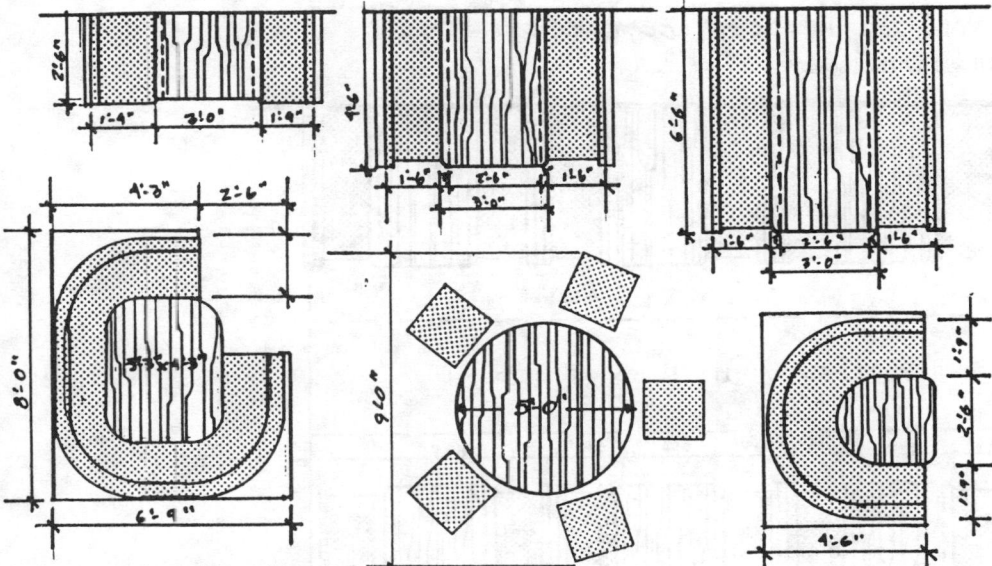

Fig. 12 Banquettes for 2, 4, and 6 persons.

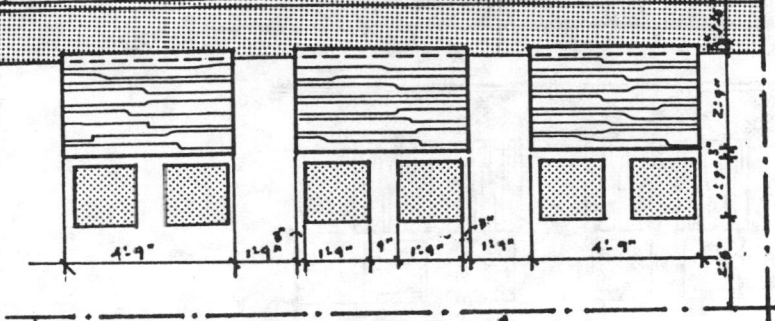

Fig. 13 21 ft × 9 ft, 189 ft², seats 12.

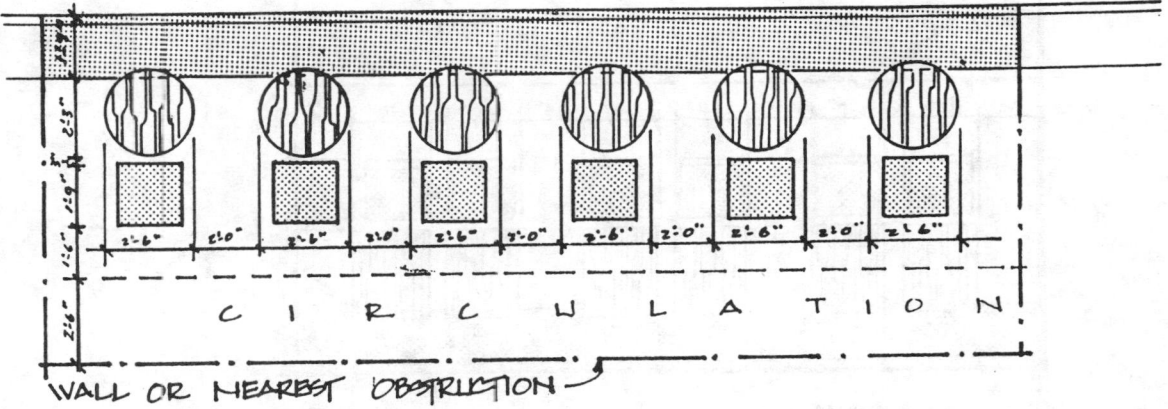

Fig. 14 27 ft × 10 ft, 270 ft², seats 12.

RESTAURANTS

Types and Sizes of Banquette Arrangements

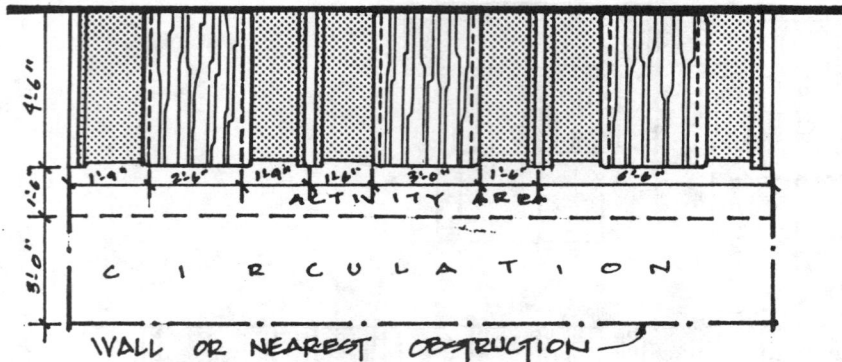

Fig. 15   19 ft × 9 ft, 171 ft², seats 12.

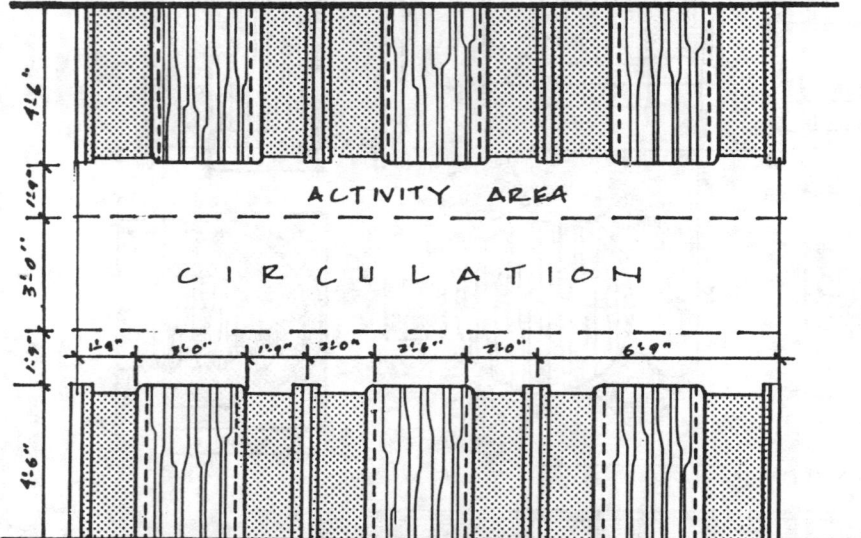

Fig. 16   19 ft × 15 ft, 285 ft², seats 24.

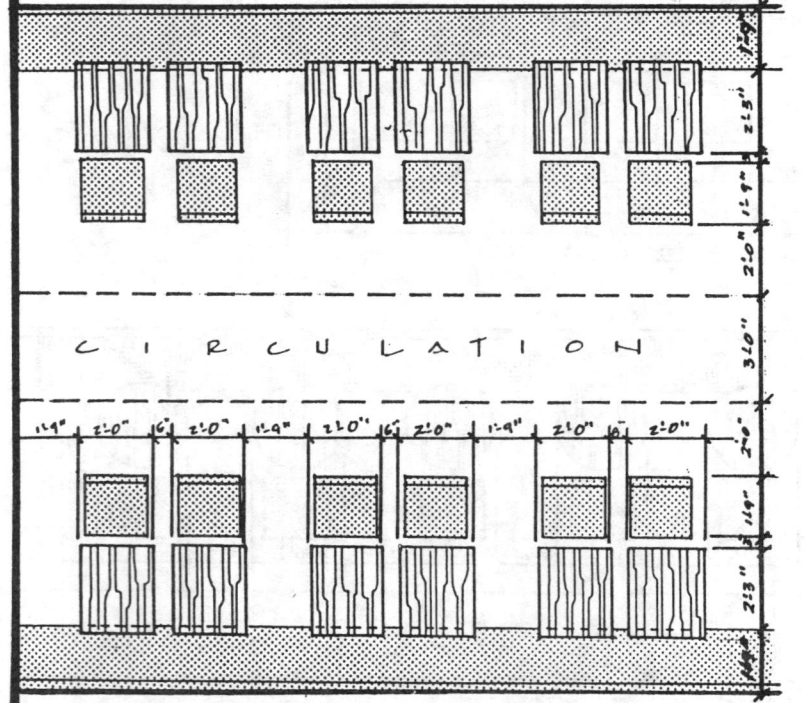

Fig. 17   21 ft × 19 ft, 400 ft², seats 24.

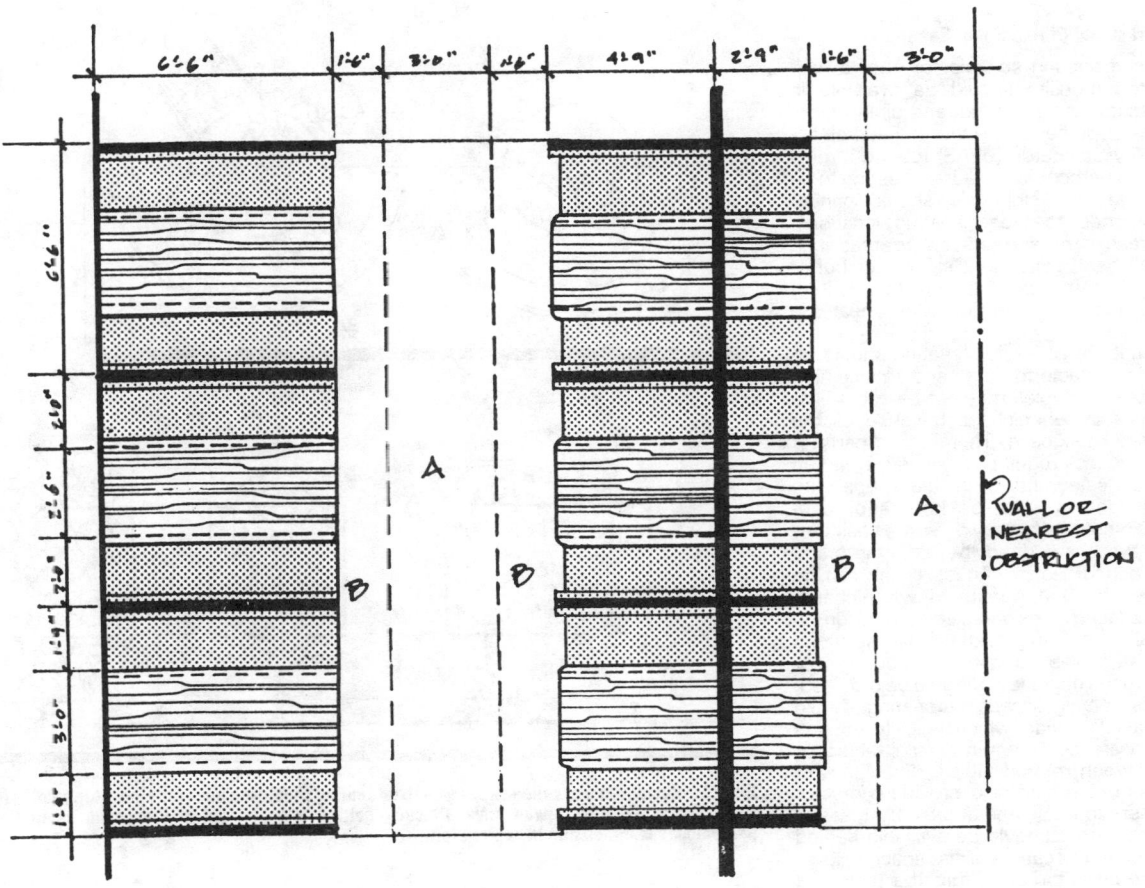

Fig. 18   24 ft × 20 ft, 480 ft², seats 36. A = main circulation, B = activity zone.

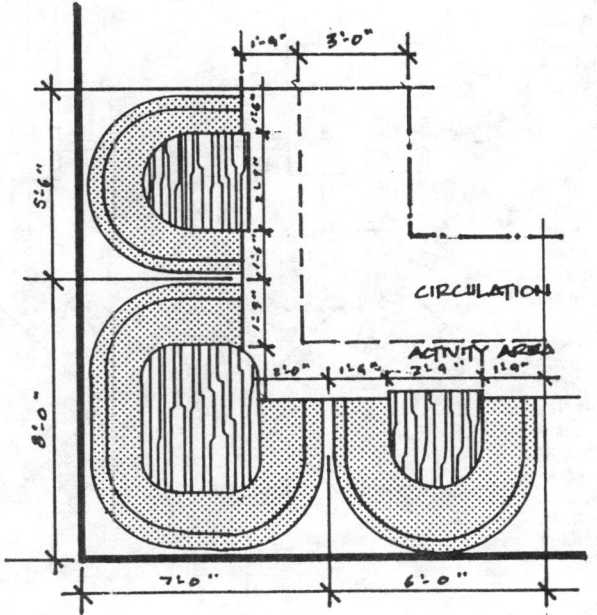

Fig. 19   13 ft × 13 ft, 169 ft², seats 16.

RESTAURANTS

Dining Room Seating

Restaurant and Dining Room Seating

Dispersed seating suitable for guests with restricted mobility should be available in restaurants, coffee shops, and dining facilities. As a guide, the Uniform Federal Accessibility Standards (UFAS) require a minimum of 5 percent of restaurant seating to be accessible. Accessible aisles should connect the entrance to these seating locations, public restrooms, and self-service areas such as salad bars, condiment stands, or buffet tables. Comfortable seating for waiting should be available to customers near the entrance.

A variety of accessible seating should be available, suitable for large and small dining groups. Small tables may not be accessible to guests in wheelchairs because of the restricted kneespace. Therefore, a party of one or two may require a table usually set up for four. Restaurants or coffee shops with built-in seating, such as booths or banquettes, should also provide some chairs for guests who have difficulty getting into and out of bench seating. These chairs can be removed to seat guests in wheelchairs. Where seating areas are raised on platforms, accessible seating and similar services should be available on the main-floor level or a ramp to the upper level should be provided.

Aisles serving accessible seating should be at least 3'0" wide, which typically requires a 6'0" clearance between parallel tables, or 4'6" between rotated tables. (See Fig. 21.) Aisle widths should also provide room for customers to be seated at tables. At least a 2'6" clear space should be available behind each seating location. This space allows chairs to be withdrawn from the table and staff to assist guests reposition chairs close to the table.

For wheelchair seating, a 3'0" to 3'6" aisle is necessary, depending on the width of the kneespace. (See Fig. 25.) Wheelchairs positioned at tables project approximately 5" further into aisles than most chairs. To allow guests with restricted mobility to turn around, seating arrangements should also include a 5'0" diameter circle or T-shaped clear area at dead-end aisles.

Dining Tables and Chairs

Accessible seating locations should allow guests with restricted mobility to dine with ambulatory customers. Tables should provide kneespace for customers in wheelchairs, and dining chairs should be coordinated to provide comfortable seating at the same table height.

Dining room chairs should be stable to maintain balance as guests seat themselves, and comfortable to sit in during dinner. Chairs should be light and easy to reposition. The seat should have a slight slant to the rear to transfer body weight to the back of the chair. However, an exaggerated incline makes it difficult to rise. The seat should be approximately 16" deep and at least 16" wide to allow space for customers to reposition themselves during the meal. Padding or cushions on the chair seat should be firm, and the chair back should also be slightly inclined to the rear. To help guests sit and rise, dining chairs should have armrests 7" to 8" above the front edge of the seat. (See Fig. 22.) Supports or cross-bracing should not

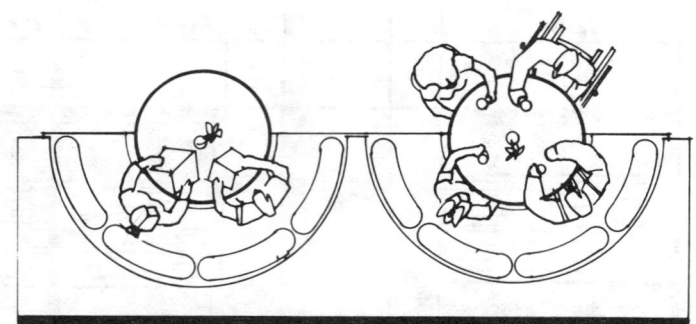

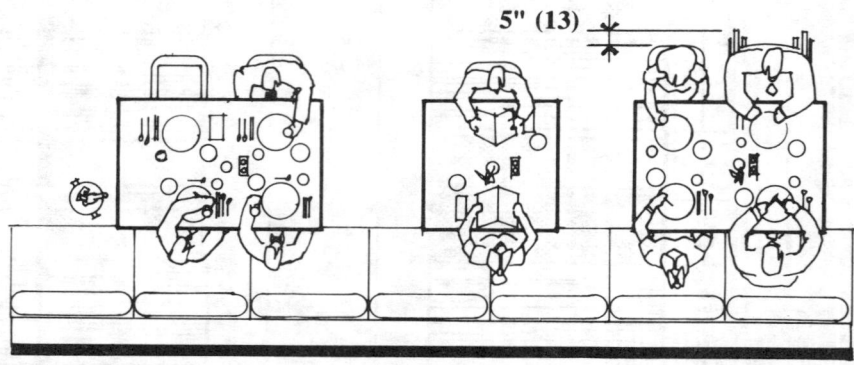

Fig. 20 Restaurants or coffee shops with fixed seating should include some movable seating for guests in wheelchairs and guests who have difficulty getting into and out of the bench seating. Number in parentheses is dimension in centimeters.

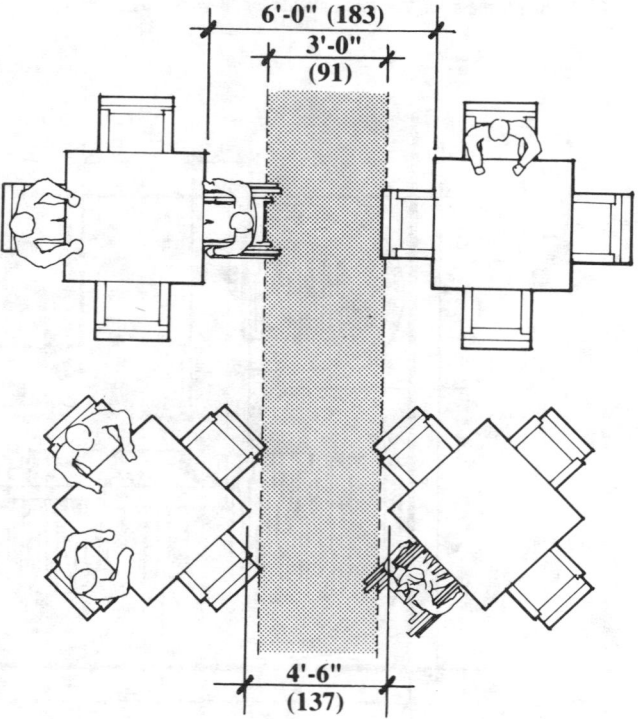

Fig. 21 Aisles serving accessible seating should provide a path at least 3'0" wide for passage and clear space for guests to seat themselves at tables. Numbers in parentheses are dimensions in centimeters.

interfere with kickspace below the seat, so the feet can be positioned to rise. The front edge of the chair seat should be low enough to allow the feet to rest on the floor, but not so low that it is difficult to rise. This is determined by the lower leg length (popliteal height) which varies between 15" and 20" for most adults.

The height of the chair seat should be 10½" to 11½" below the top of the table. Common seat heights vary between 14" and 18". Because the height of wheelchair seats is typically 19", a relatively high chair seat is necessary to coordinate with the table height. A chair with an 18" high seat is comfortable for most ambulatory guests and closely approximates the height of a wheelchair seat.

Dining room tables should have a stable surface at a convenient height and kneespace and legroom below the tabletop for customers in wheelchairs. Narrow table configurations allow face-to-face seating, which reduces the distance between diners, making conversation easier and table lighting more effective. For safety, the corners and edges of the top should be rounded.

Full-height wheelchair kneespace is 2'6", which requires tabletops to be at least 2'7" above the floor, too high for most seating. Many wheelchairs now provide adjustable or two-tier armrests, which allow customers to sit close to tables in a kneespace only 2'3" high. To provide this kneespace, the tabletop (without an apron) should be 2'4½" to 2'5" above the floor. This is 11" to 11½" above the chair seat, 10½" to 11" above the seat of wheelchairs, and convenient for both. This kneespace also permits the armrests of chairs to pass below the tabletop so seated customers can draw close. This combination of tables and chairs is suitable for the majority of wheelchair users and most ambulatory guests.

Footroom is important for customers with wheelchairs or leg braces. The footrests of wheelchairs are 2½" to 3" above the ground and angled slightly forward, which requires 1'7" of footroom, measured from the edge of the tabletop. The outside width of footrests is only 1'6", but 2'6" of side-to-side clearance is necessary to maneuver into position beneath the table. To provide kneespace, table legs should be at least 2'6" apart, and the tabletop, for face-to-face seating, should be 3'6" wide. Pedestalbase tables should have low, tapered bases and a minimum diameter of 3'6", although 4'0" is preferred.

A portable raised leaf should be available to modify tables for customers in wheelchairs with high armrests. The leaf should be approximately the size of a place setting, 1'4" by 2'0", and secured to the underside of an accessible table with clamps. The raised leaf should project 6" beyond the edge of the table and provide 2'6" clearance above the floor. (See Fig. 24.)

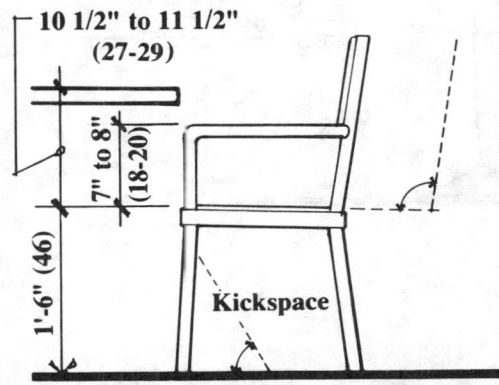

Fig. 22 Dining room chairs should have a seat 10½" to 11½" below the top of the table and armrests 7" to 8" above the seat. To coordinate with an accessible table, the seat height should be 18". Numbers in parentheses are dimensions in centimeters.

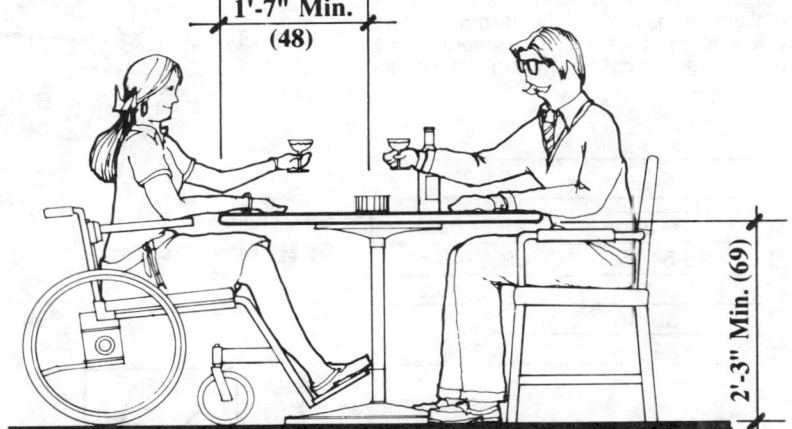

Fig. 23 Accessible tables should provide kneespace at least a 2'3" high by 2'6" wide with 1'7" of footroom. To increase the kneespace height, a raised portable leaf can be provided. (See Fig. 24.) Numbers in parentheses are dimensions in centimeters.

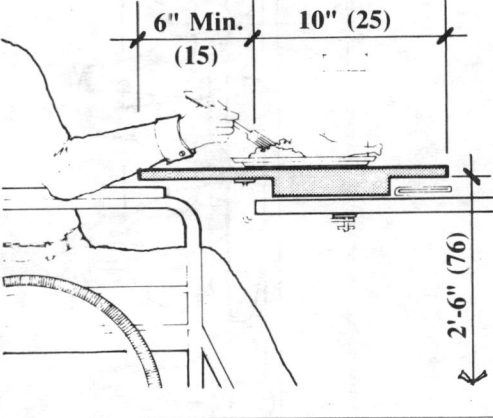

Kneespace Width	Clearance
2'-6" (minimum)	3'-6"
3'-0" or greater	3'-0"

Fig. 24 A portable raised leaf can be provided for accessible tables to accommodate customers in wheelchairs with high armrests. Numbers in parentheses are dimensions in centimeters.

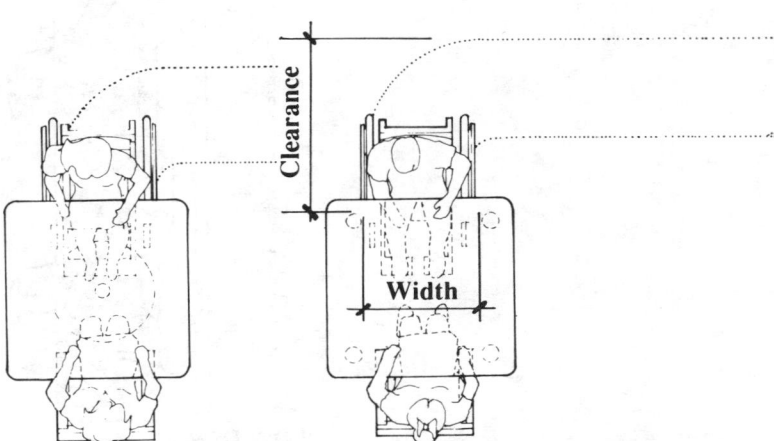

Fig. 25 The necessary maneuvering room required to access a kneespace depends on its width.

RESTAURANTS

Banquettes: Design Criteria

Figure 27 shows the basic dimensions for the design of banquette seating. The lack of armrests makes it difficult to define seat boundaries. The user, therefore, tends to establish a territory by assuming a desired sitting posture and placing personal articles next to him or her, such as a briefcase, purse, or package. Since the nature of this type of seating can permit some form of body contact, hidden dimensions and personal space also play an important part in how close the users sharing the banquette will sit.

Because of the many hidden psychological factors involved, the actual efficiency of this seating type in terms of capacity is questionable. Figure 27 indicates two possible seating situations, each dictated by the anthropometrics involved. One arrangement is based on the premise that the user's elbows will be extended, possibly in conjunction with some activity, such as reading, or simply as an attempt to stake out additional territory, as would be the case in the strategic positioning of some personal article on the seat. In this situation it would be reasonable to assume that each user would take up about 30 in, or 76.2 cm, of space. The other diagram shows a more compact seating arrangement. Figure 26 shows a section through a typical banquette.

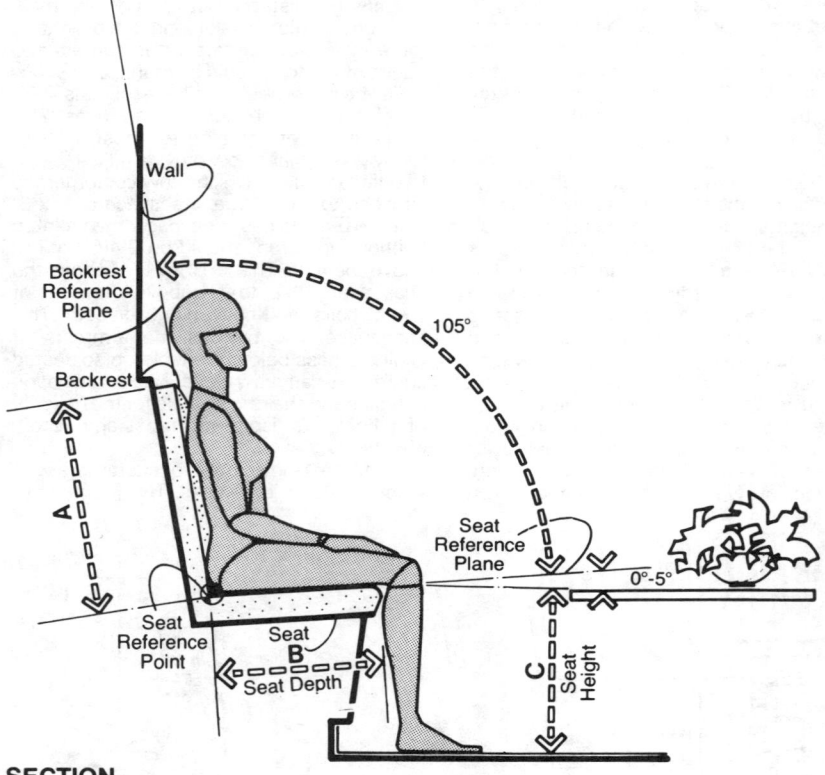

SECTION

Fig. 26   Banquette seating.

	in	cm
A	18–24	45.7–61.0
B	15.5–16	39.4–40.6
C	16–17	40.6–43.2
D	30	76.2
E	24	61.0

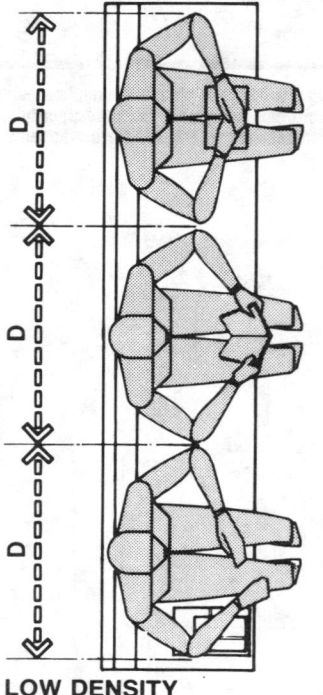

LOW DENSITY

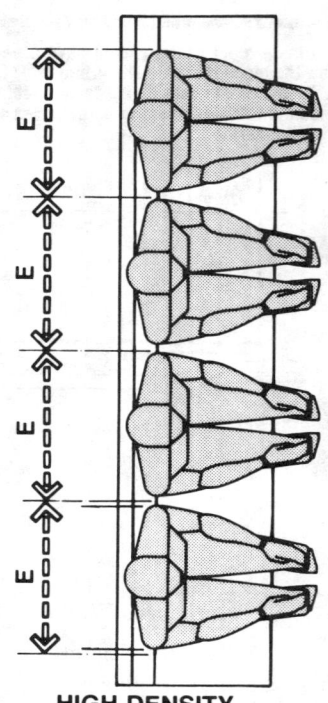

HIGH DENSITY

Fig. 27   Banquette seating.

Banquette seating provides the designer with one of the few opportunities to custom design restaurant seating. While there can be a great variety of aesthetic solutions achieved through use of various materials, ergonomic considerations must be analyzed carefully. Specific attention should be given to depth of seat, slope of seat and back, height of back, and relationship of seat height to table height.

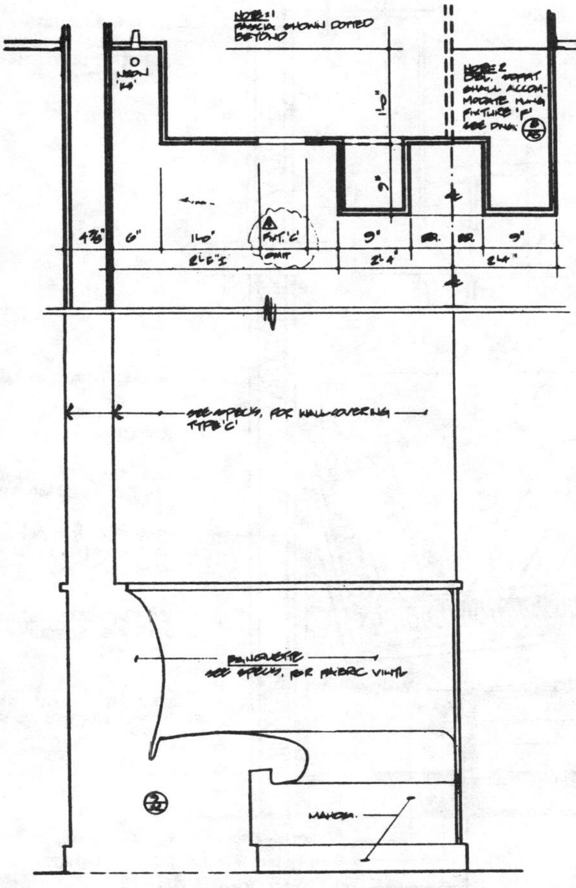

FASCIA/SOFFIT DETL @ REAR BANQUETTE · DINING 10·
SCALE · 1½"=1'-0"

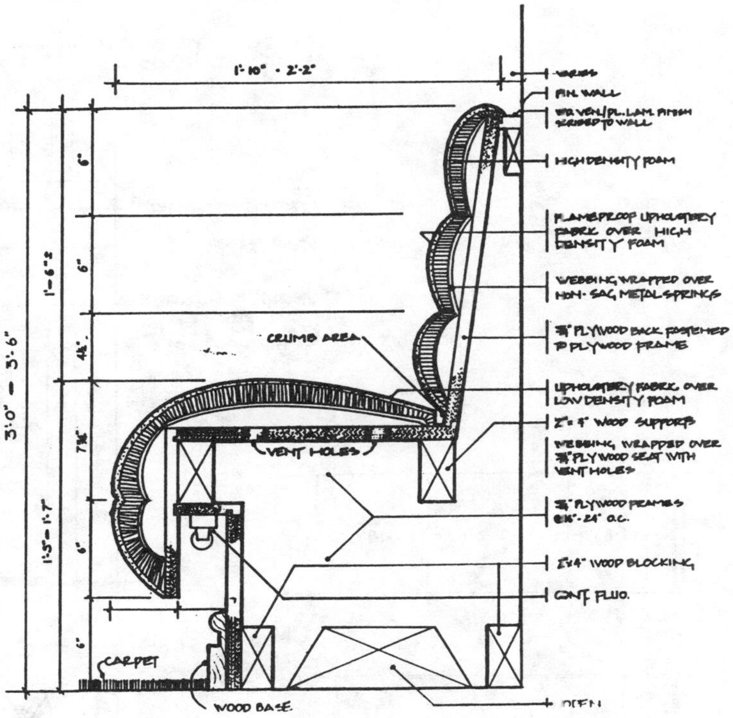

TYPICAL BANQUETTE DETAIL
SCALE · 1½"=1'-0"

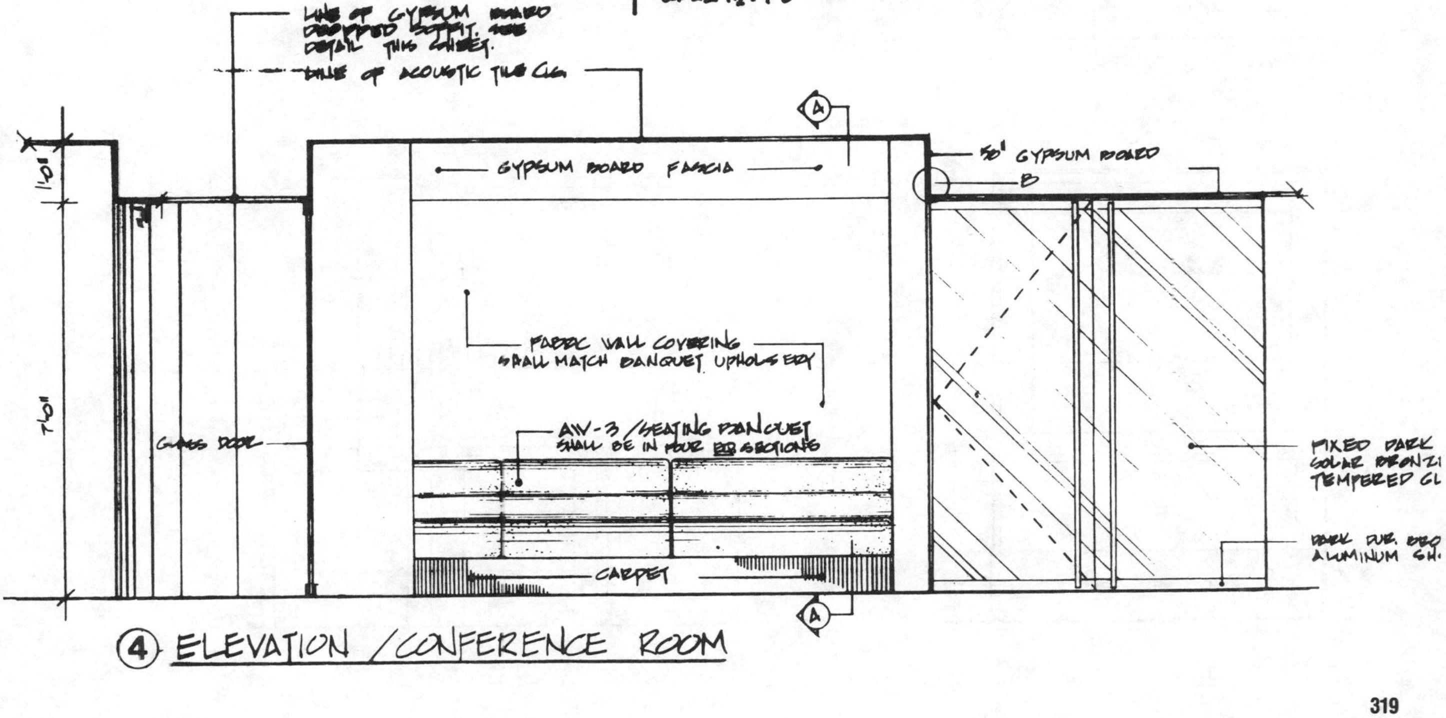

④ ELEVATION / CONFERENCE ROOM

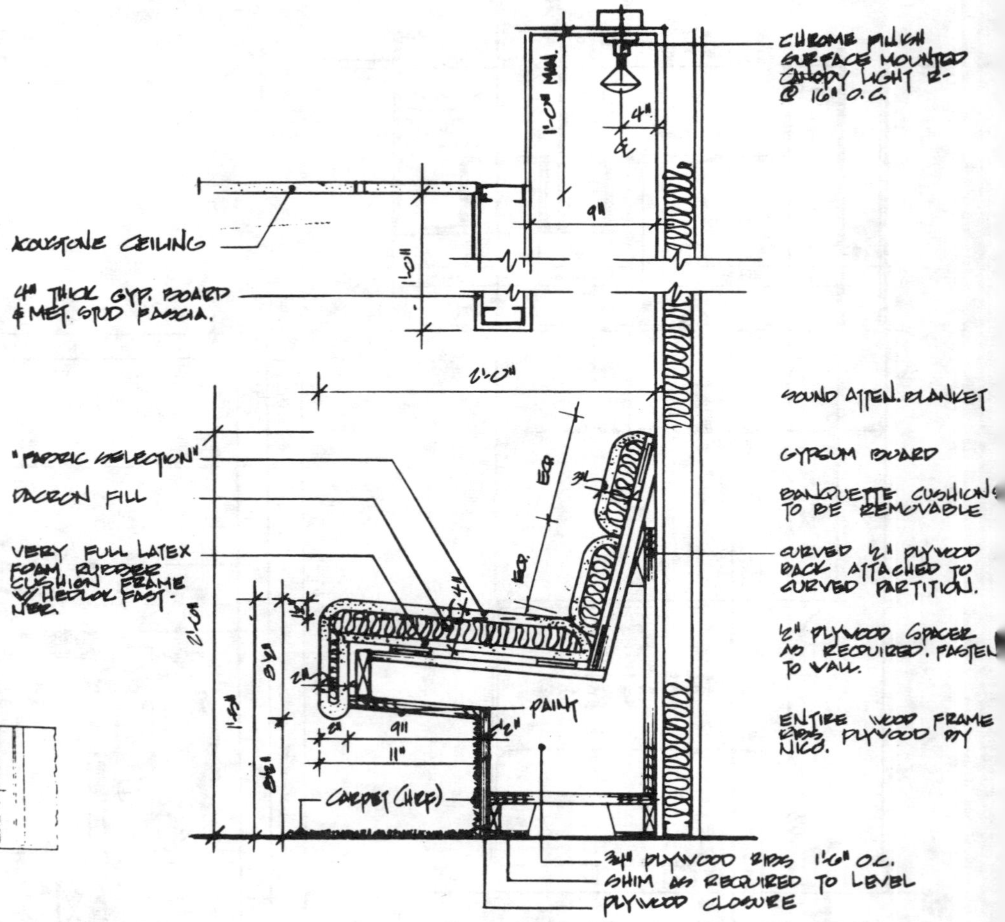

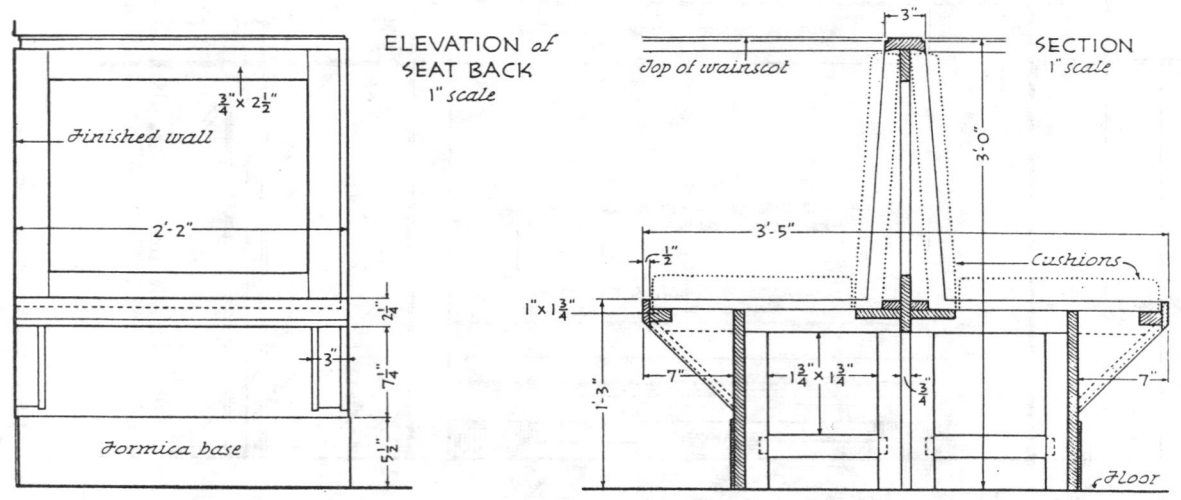

CHROME FINISH SURFACE MOUNTED CANOPY LIGHT R- @ 16" O.C.

ACOUSTONE CEILING

4" THICK GYP. BOARD & MET. STUD FASCIA.

SOUND ATTEN. BLANKET

GYPSUM BOARD

BANQUETTE CUSHION TO BE REMOVABLE

CURVED 1/2" PLYWOOD BACK ATTACHED TO CURVED PARTITION.

1/2" PLYWOOD SPACER AS REQUIRED. FASTEN TO WALL.

ENTIRE WOOD FRAME SPEC. PLYWOOD BY NIC.

"FABRIC SELECTION"

DACRON FILL

VERY FULL LATEX FOAM RUBBER CUSHION FRAME W/VELCRO FAST-NER.

PAINT

CARPET (CHEF)

3/4" PLYWOOD RIBS 1'-6" O.C.
SHIM AS REQUIRED TO LEVEL
PLYWOOD CLOSURE

④ AIV-3 / SECTION THRU BANQUETTE

SCALE 1½" = 1'-0"

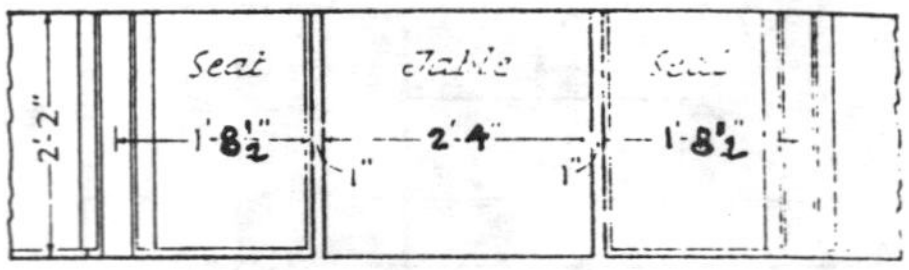

PLAN of SEATS 3/8" scale

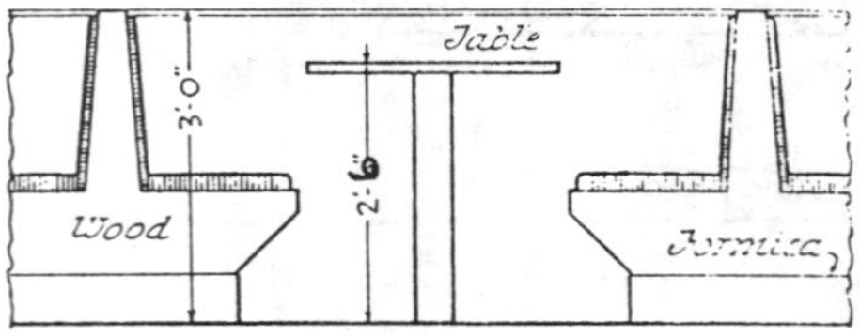

Seat Table Seat
2'-2"
1'-8½" 2'-4" 1'-8½"

ELEVATION of SEATS

Table
3'-0"
2'-6"
Wood   Formica

ELEVATION of SEAT BACK
1" scale

Finished wall

2'-2"
3/4" x 2½"

Formica base

SECTION
1" scale

Top of wainscot

3"
3'-0"
Cushions
3'-5"
1"
1" x 1¾"
1'-3"
7"
1¾" x 1¾"
7"
Floor

Banquette seating can be detailed relatively simply, as Figs. 28 to 30 suggest. The simplest form of banquette seating may take the form of a plywood seating platform with a removable seat cushion, or a box cushion seat and back support. Such seating is appropriate in fast food or quick turnover restaurant operations.

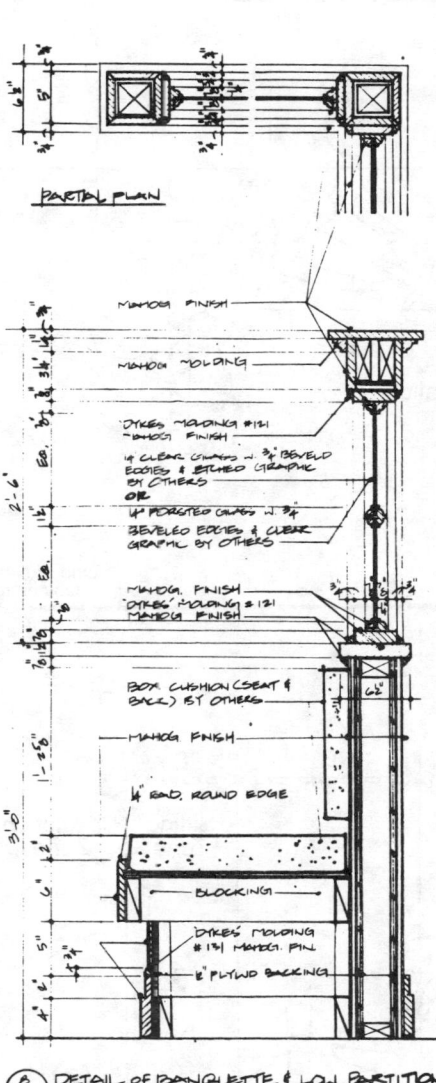

Fig. 28

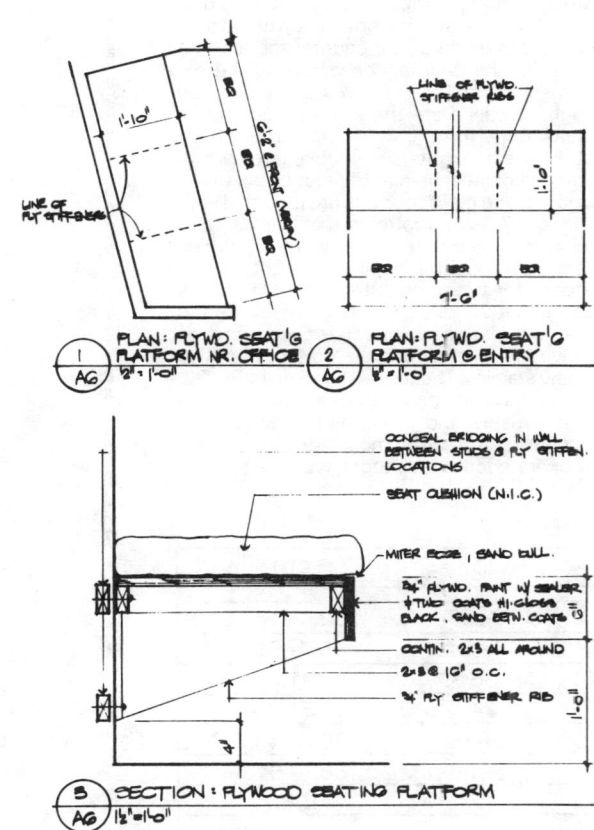

Fig. 29

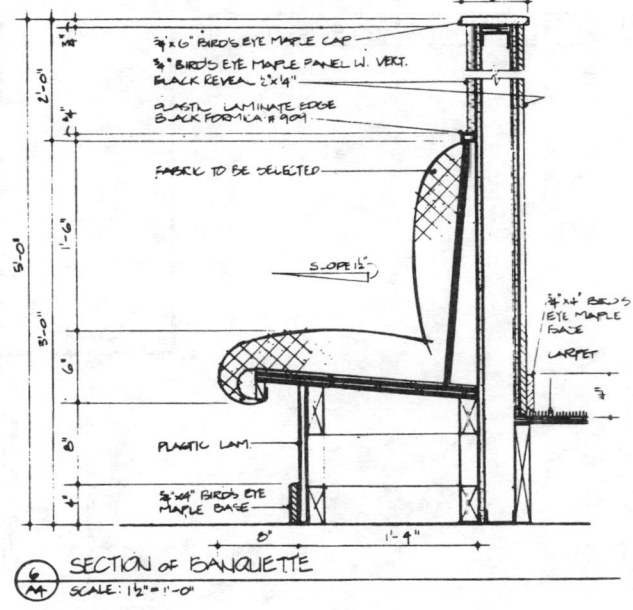

Fig. 30

RESTAURANTS

Lunch Counters: Design Criteria

Figure 31 shows some of the basic clearances required for a typical counter: 36 in, or 91.4 cm, for workspace behind the counter; 18 to 24 in, or 45.7 to 61 cm, for the counter top; and 60 to 66 in, or 152.4 to 167.6 cm, between the front face of the counter and the nearest obstruction. Figure 32 shows a section through the counter and back counter. Most counters are about 42 in, or 106.7 cm, in height. The clearance from the top of the seat to the underside of the counter top and the depth of the counter top overhang are extremely important. Buttock-knee length and thigh clearance are the key anthropometric measurements to consider for proper body fit. Footrest heights should take into consideration popliteal height. In most cases this is ignored, and 42-in counters are provided with 7-in, or 17.8-cm, footrests that are 23 in, or 58.4 cm, below the seat surface, which cannot work. The popliteal height of the larger user, based on 99th percentile data, is only about 20 in, or 50.8 cm. Therefore, the feet dangle unsupported several inches above the footrest and the body is deprived of any stability. The footrest shown in Fig. 32, although higher, only serves a portion of the seated users and is intended primarily for standing patrons. The most logical solution is a separate footrest, integral with the stool.

	in	cm
A	60–66	152.4–167.6
B	18–24	45.7–61.0
C	36	91.4
D	24	61.0
E	12–18	30.5–45.7
F	35–36	88.9–91.4
G	42	106.7
H	30–31	76.2–78.7
I	11–12	27.9–30.5
J	10	25.4
K	12–13	30.5–33.0

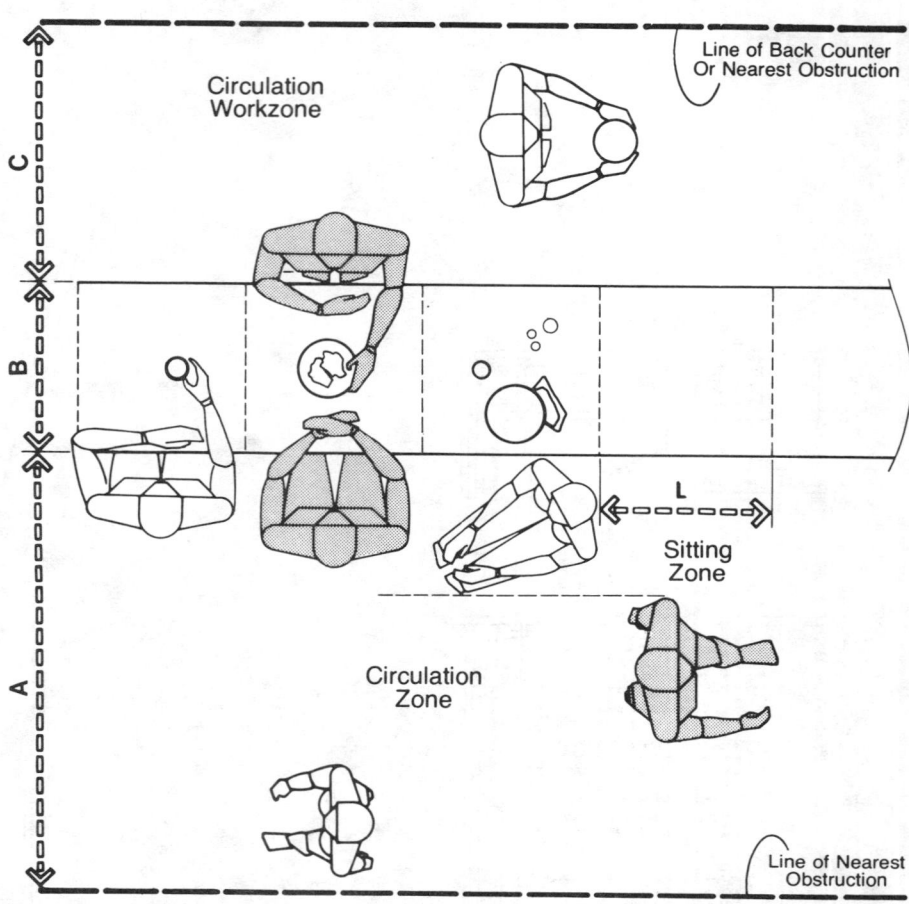

Fig. 31   Lunch counter.

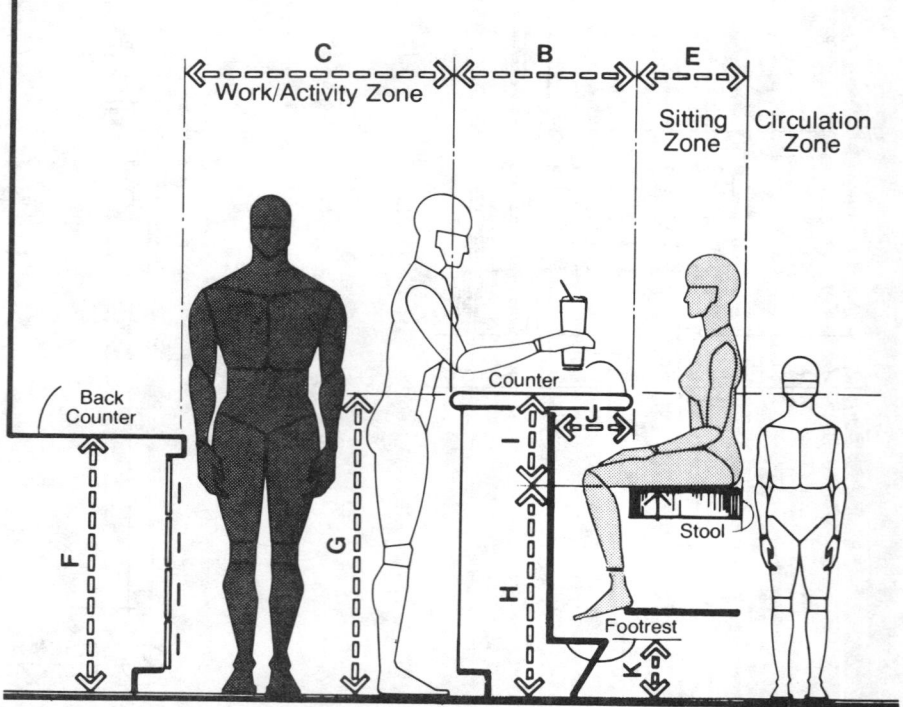

Fig. 32   Lunch counter.

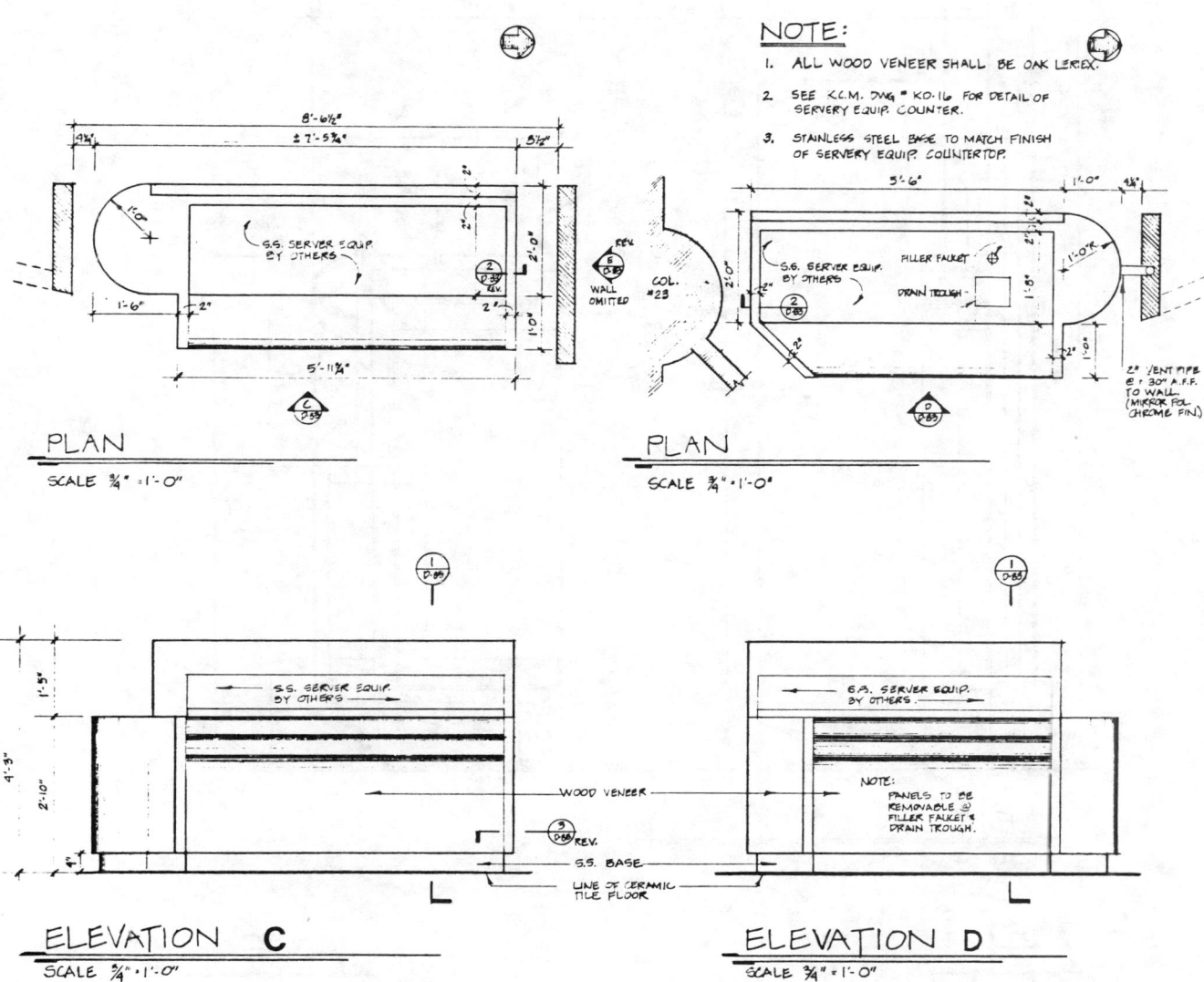

NOTE:

1. ALL WOOD VENEER SHALL BE OAK LEREX.

2. SEE K.C.M. DWG # KO·16 FOR DETAIL OF SERVERY EQUIP. COUNTER.

3. STAINLESS STEEL BASE TO MATCH FINISH OF SERVERY EQUIP. COUNTERTOP.

PLAN
SCALE ¾" = 1'-0"

PLAN
SCALE ¾" = 1'-0"

ELEVATION C
SCALE ¾" = 1'-0"

ELEVATION D
SCALE ¾" = 1'-0"

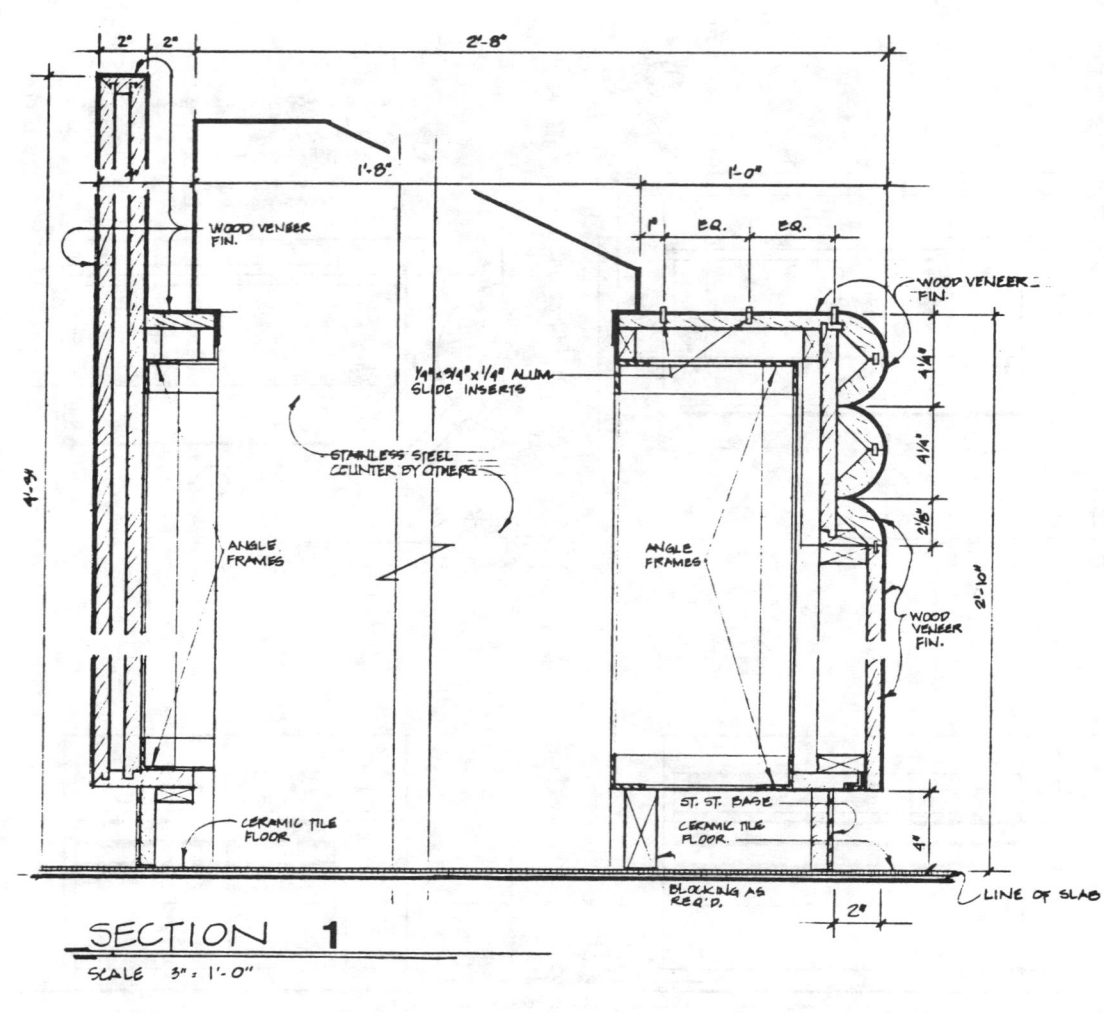

SECTION **1**

SCALE 3" = 1'-0"

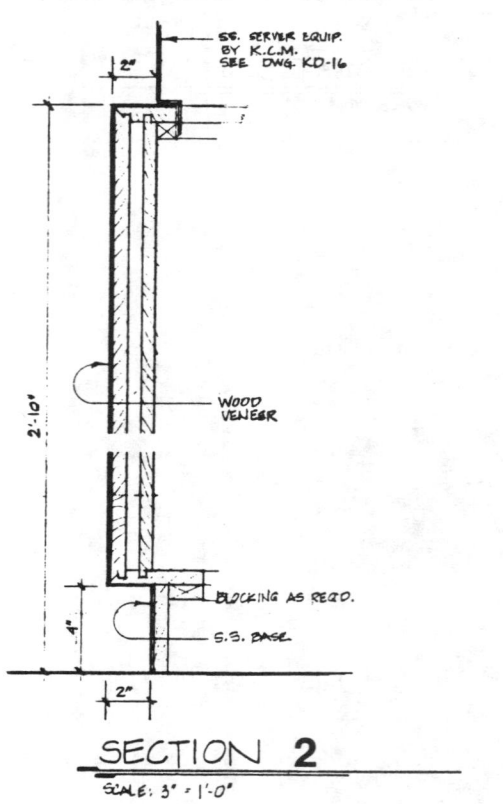

SECTION **2**

SCALE: 3" = 1'-0"

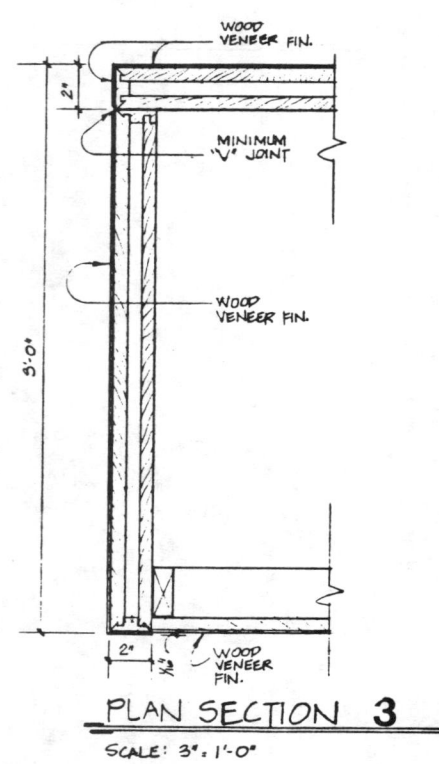

PLAN SECTION **3**

SCALE: 3" = 1'-0"

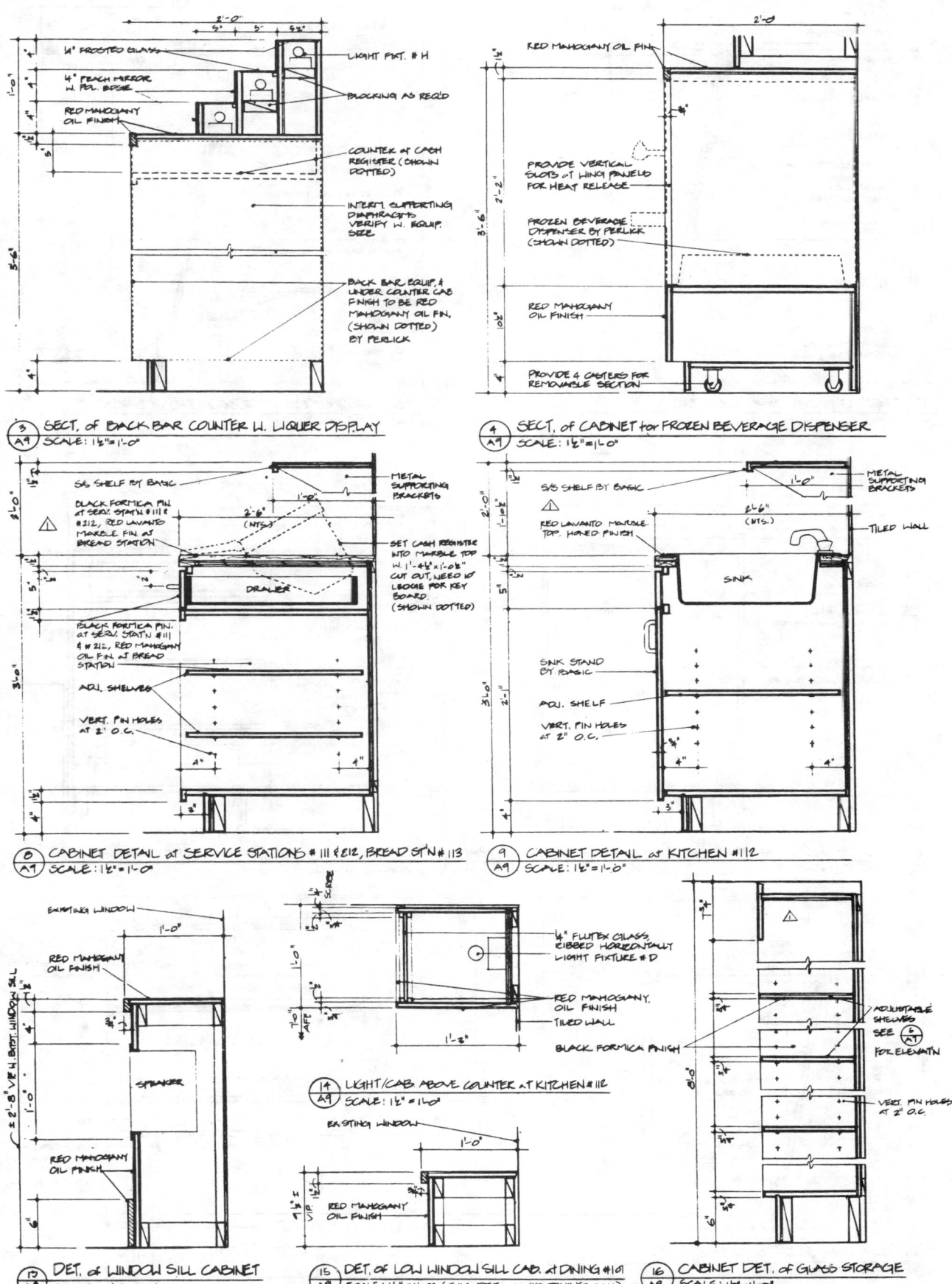

3 SECT. of BACK BAR COUNTER W. LIQUER DISPLAY
A9 SCALE: 1½"=1'-0"

Labels (detail 3):
- ¼" FROSTED GLASS
- LIGHT FIXT. # H
- ¼" PEACH MIRROR W. POL. EDGE
- BLOCKING AS REQ'D
- RED MAHOGANY OIL FINISH
- COUNTER at CASH REGISTER (SHOWN DOTTED)
- INTERM' SUPPORTING DIAPHRAGMS VERIFY W. EQUIP. SIZE
- BACK BAR EQUIP. & UNDER COUNTER CAB FINISH TO BE RED MAHOGANY OIL FIN. (SHOWN DOTTED) BY PERLICK

4 SECT. of CABINET for FROZEN BEVERAGE DISPENSER
A9 SCALE: 1½"=1'-0"

Labels (detail 4):
- RED MAHOGANY OIL FIN
- PROVIDE VERTICAL SLOTS at WING PANELS FOR HEAT RELEASE
- FROZEN BEVERAGE DISPENSER BY PERLICK (SHOWN DOTTED)
- RED MAHOGANY OIL FINISH
- PROVIDE 4 CASTERS FOR REMOVABLE SECTION

8 CABINET DETAIL at SERVICE STATIONS # 111 & 212, BREAD ST'N # 113
A9 SCALE: 1½"=1'-0"

Labels (detail 8):
- S/S SHELF BY BASIC
- METAL SUPPORTING BRACKETS
- BLACK FORMICA FIN at SERV. STAT'N #111 & #212, RED LAVANTO MARBLE FIN at BREAD STATION
- SET CASH REGISTER INTO MARBLE TOP W. 1'-4½"x1'-0½" CUT OUT, NEED 10" LEDGE FOR KEY BOARD. (SHOWN DOTTED)
- DRAWER
- BLACK FORMICA FIN. at SERV. STAT'N #111 & 212, RED MAHOGANY OIL FIN at BREAD STATION
- ADJ. SHELVES
- VERT. PIN HOLES at 2' O.C.

9 CABINET DETAIL at KITCHEN #112
A9 SCALE: 1½"=1'-0"

Labels (detail 9):
- S/S SHELF BY BASIC
- METAL SUPPORTING BRACKETS
- TILED WALL
- RED LAVANTO MARBLE TOP, HONED FINISH
- SINK
- SINK STAND BY BASIC
- ADJ. SHELF
- VERT. PIN HOLES at 2' O.C.

13 DET. of WINDOW SILL CABINET
A9 SCALE: 1½"=1'-0"

Labels (detail 13):
- EXISTING WINDOW
- RED MAHOGANY OIL FINISH
- SPEAKER
- RED MAHOGANY OIL FINISH

14 LIGHT/CAB ABOVE COUNTER at KITCHEN #112
A9 SCALE: 1½"=1'-0"

Labels (detail 14):
- ¼" FLUTEX GLASS, RIBBED HORIZONTALLY
- LIGHT FIXTURE # D
- RED MAHOGANY OIL FINISH
- TILED WALL
- BLACK FORMICA FINISH

15 DET. of LOW WINDOW SILL CAB. at DINING #101
A9 SCALE: 1½"=1'-0" (SIM. DET. at VIP DINING #211)

Labels (detail 15):
- EXISTING WINDOW
- RED MAHOGANY OIL FINISH

16 CABINET DET. of GLASS STORAGE
A9 SCALE: 1½"=1'-0"

Labels (detail 16):
- ADJUSTABLE SHELVES SEE 6 AT FOR ELEVATN
- VERT. PIN HOLES at 2" O.C.

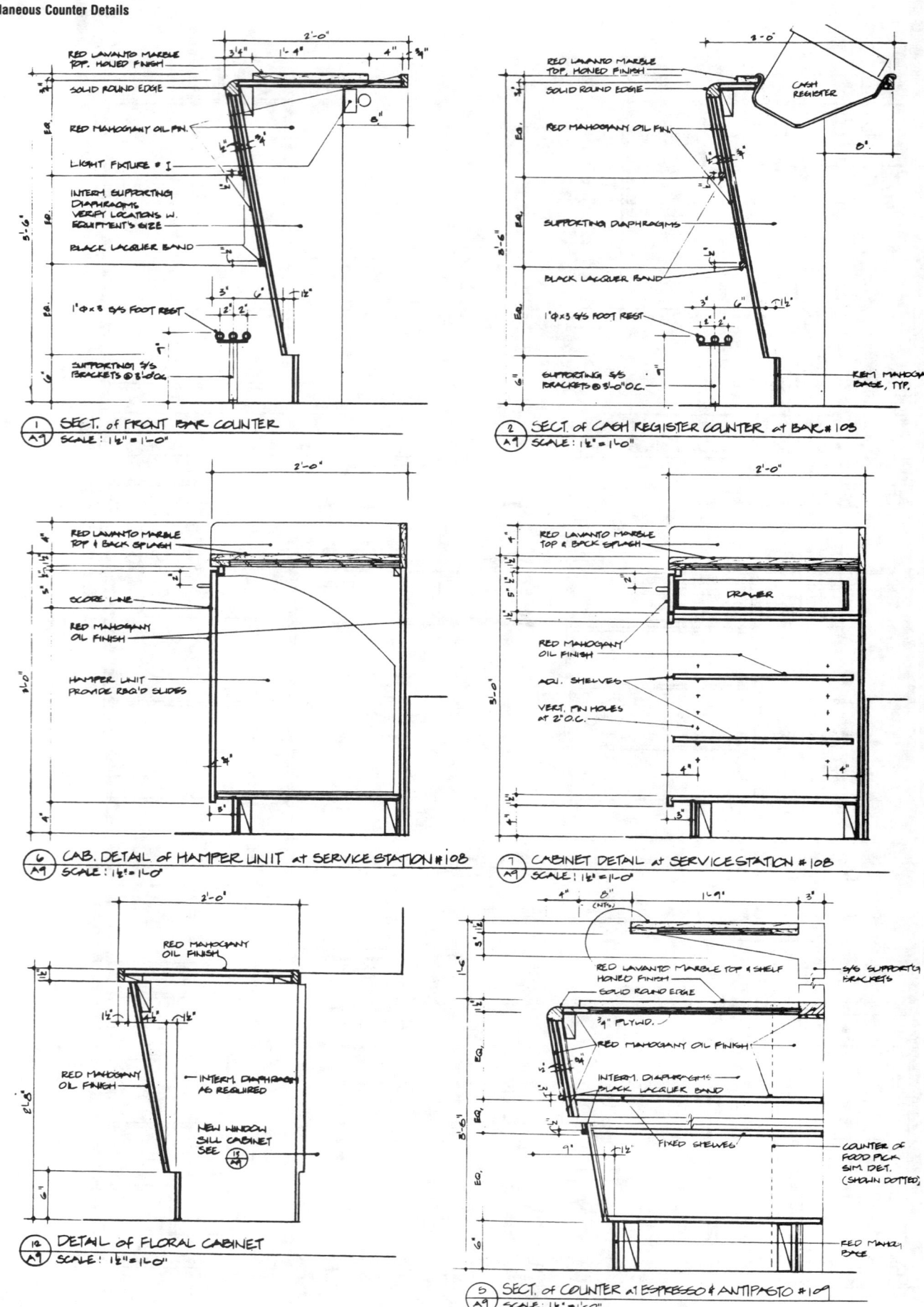

1 SECT. of FRONT BAR COUNTER
A9   SCALE: 1½" = 1'-0"

2 SECT. of CASH REGISTER COUNTER at BAR #103
A9   SCALE: 1½" = 1'-0"

6 CAB. DETAIL of HAMPER UNIT at SERVICE STATION #108
A9   SCALE: 1½" = 1'-0"

7 CABINET DETAIL at SERVICE STATION #108
A9   SCALE: 1½" = 1'-0"

12 DETAIL of FLORAL CABINET
A9   SCALE: 1½" = 1'-0"

5 SECT. of COUNTER at ESPRESSO & ANTIPASTO #109
A9   SCALE: 1½" = 1'-0"

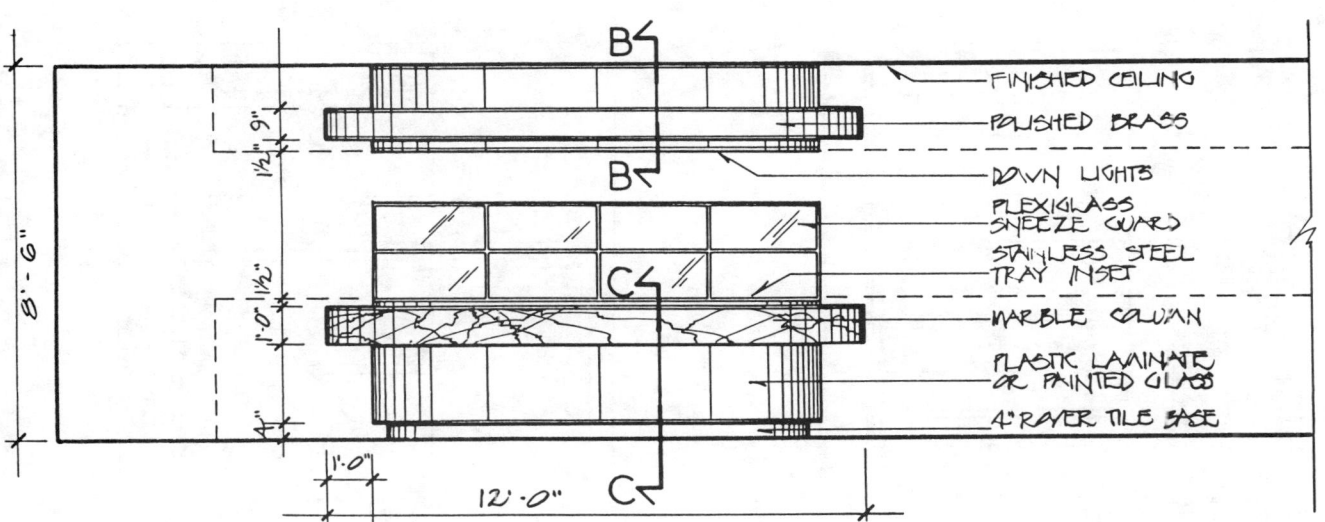

- FINISHED CEILING
- POLISHED BRASS
- DOWN LIGHTS
- PLEXIGLASS SNEEZE GUARD
- STAINLESS STEEL TRAY INSET
- MARBLE COLUMN
- PLASTIC LAMINATE OR PAINTED GLASS
- 4" ROVER TILE BASE

8'-6"

1'-2" 9"

1'-0 1/2"

4"

1'-0"

12'-0"

A ELEVATION OF SERVING ISLAND

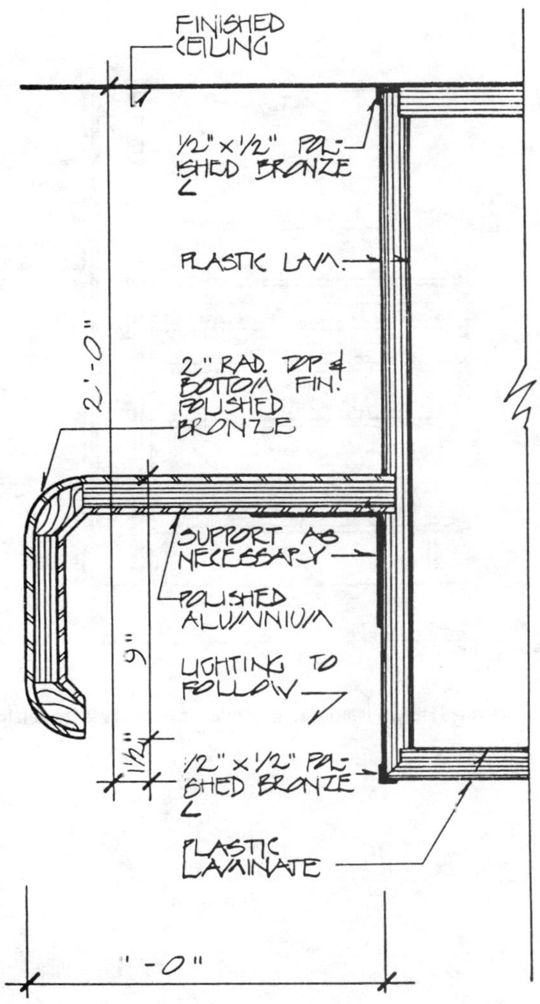

FINISHED CEILING

1/2" x 1/2" POLISHED BRONZE L

PLASTIC LAM.

2" RAD. TOP & BOTTOM FIN. POLISHED BRONZE

SUPPORT AS NECESSARY

POLISHED ALUMINIUM

LIGHTING TO FOLLOW

1/2" x 1/2" POLISHED BRONZE L

PLASTIC LAMINATE

2'-0"

9"

1/2"

1'-0"

BB SECTION THRU HOOD

PLEXIGLASS SNEEZE GUARD SUPPORTS TO BE 1/2" DIAM POL. BRONZE

PLASTIC LAMINATE

1/2" TYP.

2" 2" 2" 2" 2"

1/2"

POL BRONZE

PLASTIC LAM.

MARBLE TO HAVE 2" RAD TOP & BOTTOM MARBLE TO BE BONDED TO PLYWOOD SUPPORT AS NECESSARY

1 2" x 1/2" POL. BRONZE L

ROVER TILE BASE

1'-0"

2'-0"

4"

4"

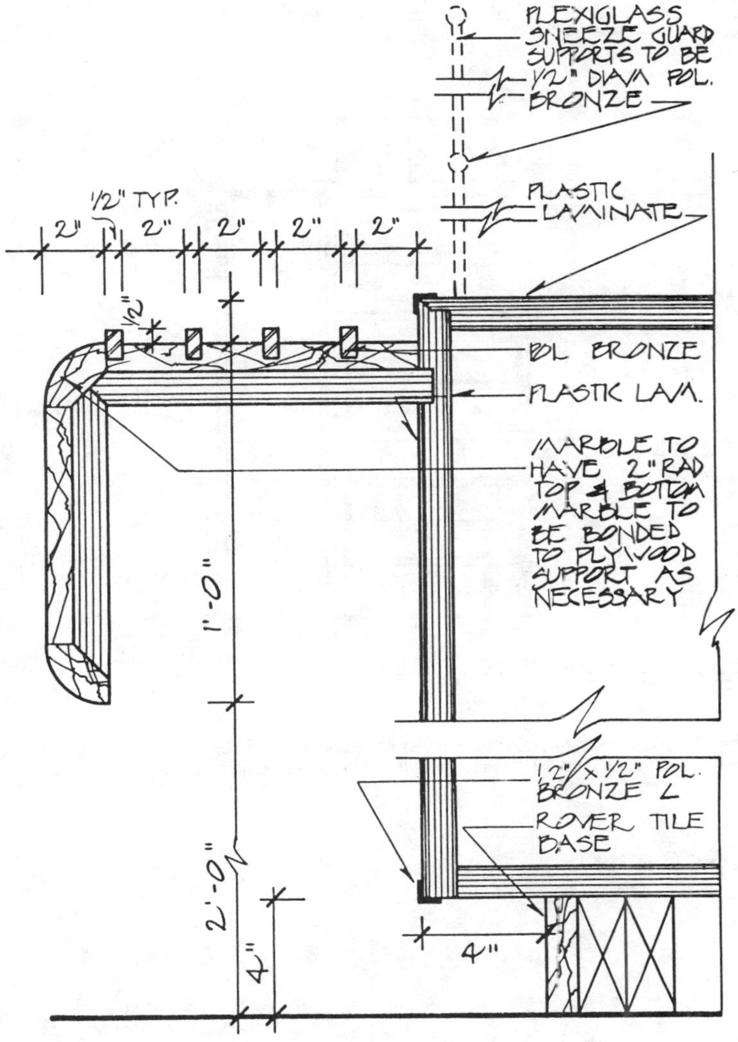

CC SECTION THRU SERVING COUNTER

RESTAURANTS

Waiter Station/Host Counter Details

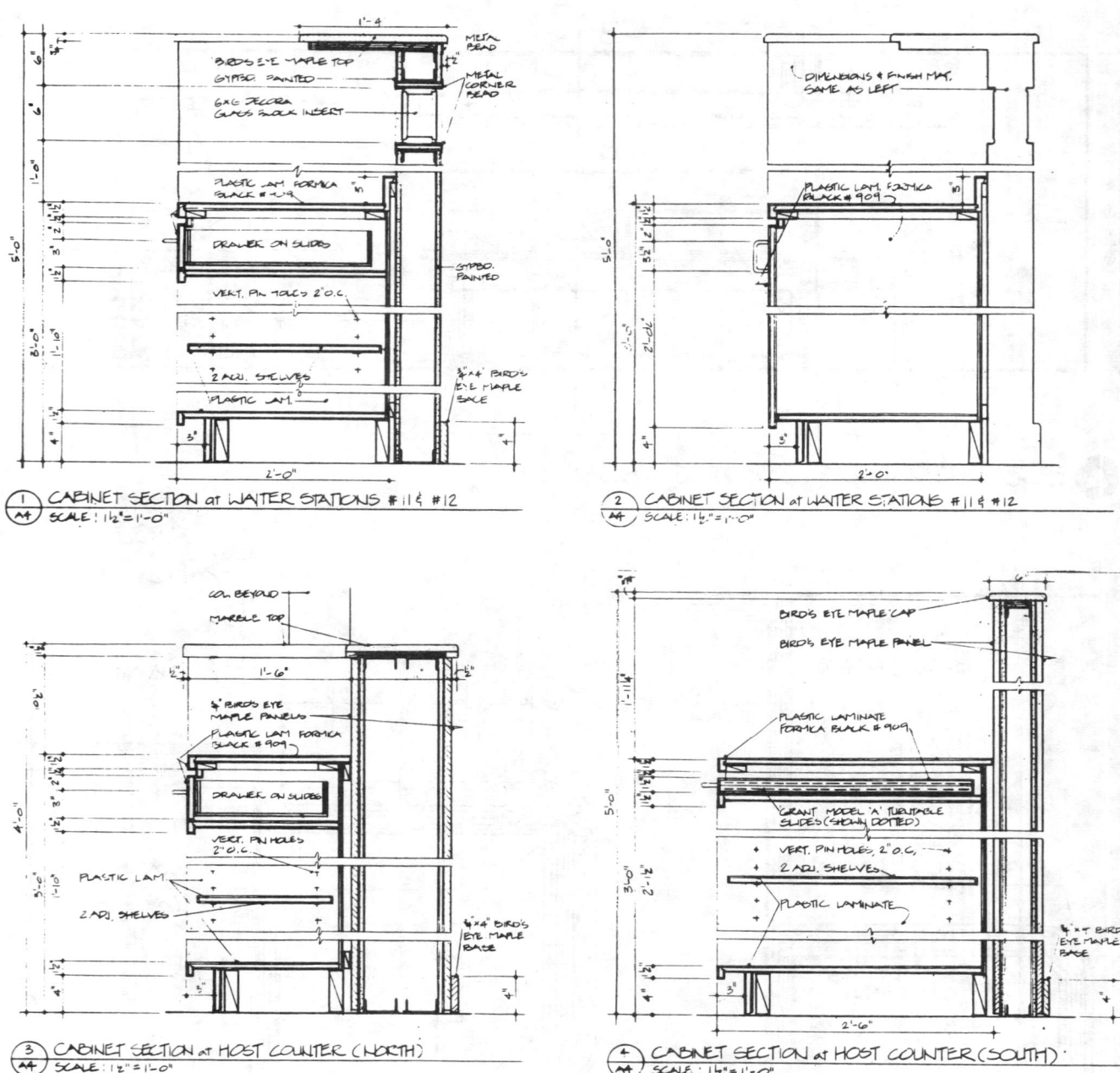

Fig. 33 Waiter stations and host/hostess counters can be designed as freestanding elements or integrated into the interior architecture, as shown by these details. Special attention must be given to specific drawer and storage requirements.

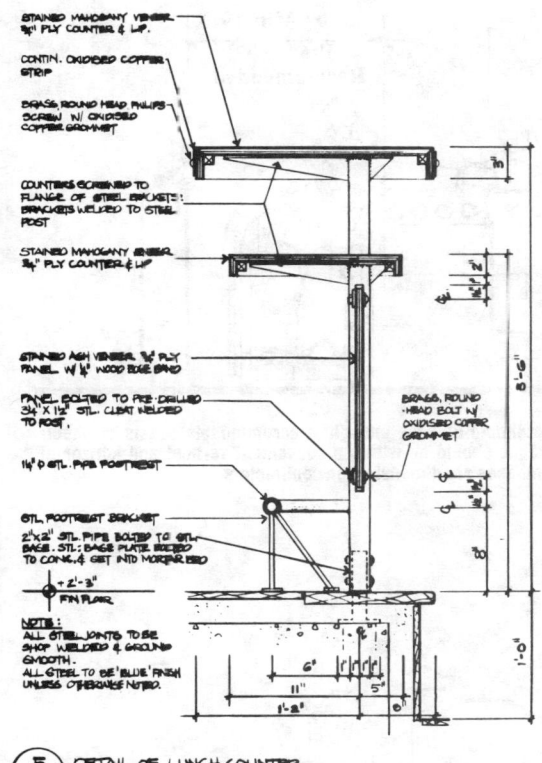

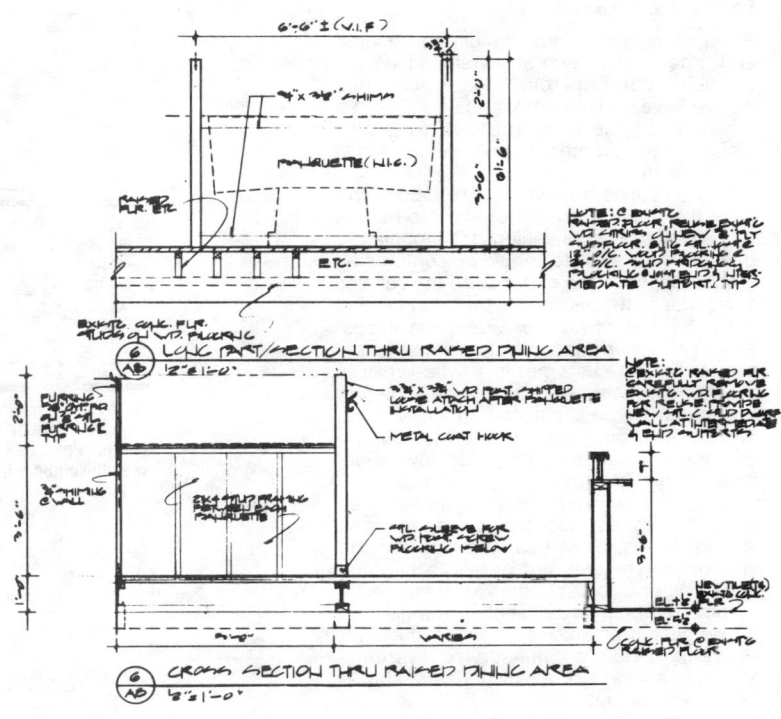

5 DETAIL OF LUNCH COUNTER
A15 1½" = 1'-0"

6 LONG PART/SECTION THRU RAISED DINING AREA
AB ½" = 1'-0"

6 CROSS SECTION THRU RAISED DINING AREA
AB ½" = 1'-0"

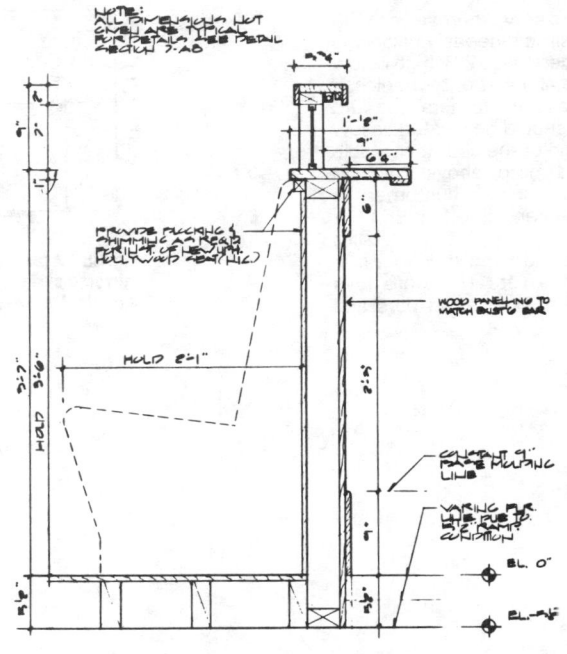

10 SECTION @ CURVED SEAT IN SHUFFLE BD. AREA
AB 1½" = 1'-0"

RESTAURANTS

Wheelchair Accessibility to Self-Service Areas

Self-Service Areas

Salad bars, buffet lines, condiment stands, and other self-service areas should be accessible. Cafeteria or food-service lines should have a minimum width of 3'0", but a width of 3'6" is recommended to permit ambulatory customers to pass customers in wheelchairs.

The tray slide should be 2'10" above the floor, the maximum height for customers in wheelchairs and convenient for ambulatory guests. The tray slide should be continuous, if possible, from the entrance to the cashier. Tray slides restrict access to the counters and therefore should not be wider than necessary (1'0" recommended). In this instance, the reach of a customer in a wheelchair is extended if the wheelchair can be angled or positioned perpendicular to the tray slide. This is possible if the lower face of the counter is recessed to provide low knee-space. (See Fig. 34.)

For guests with a limited range-of-motion, food, beverages, utensils, or other items should be displayed near the edge of the counter where they are easier to see and reach. When duplicate items are displayed, a vertical rather than horizontal arrangement allows customers to select items at the most convenient height. Self-service systems, such as beverage or ice-dispensers, should be easy to operate without fine hand function. Instructions and price information should be prominently displayed in large clear lettering.

Salad bars and buffets should provide a 3'0"-wide clear space for access on all sides and plate slides, or areas to temporarily set plates, at a maximum height of 2'10". This permits customers to serve themselves with one hand, without simultaneously balancing the plate or bowl. Kneespace 2'3" high below the counter or table allows front wheelchair approach, to increase customers' forward reach. Condiments should be located as low and close to the edge of the counter or table as practical. A tilted mirror above the food display at salad bars also aids customers in wheelchairs and children. (See Fig. 35.) For some customers with restricted mobility, poor balance, or limited hand function, it is more difficult to carry a plate. Therefore trays should be available at both salad bars and buffets.

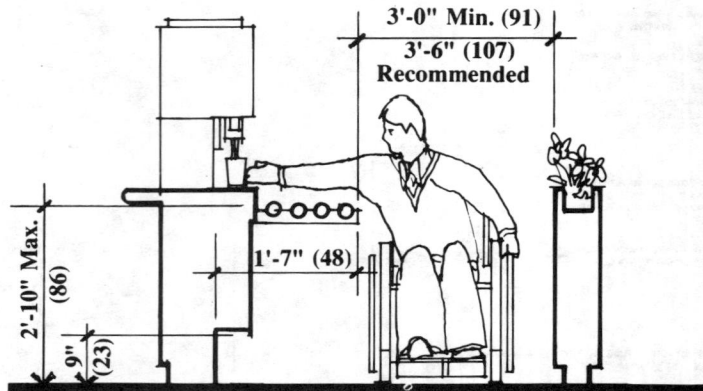

Fig. 34 Cafeteria lines should be wide enough to accommodate guests in wheelchairs. Food and beverages should be within a convenient vertical and horizontal reach. Numbers in parentheses are dimensions in centimeters.

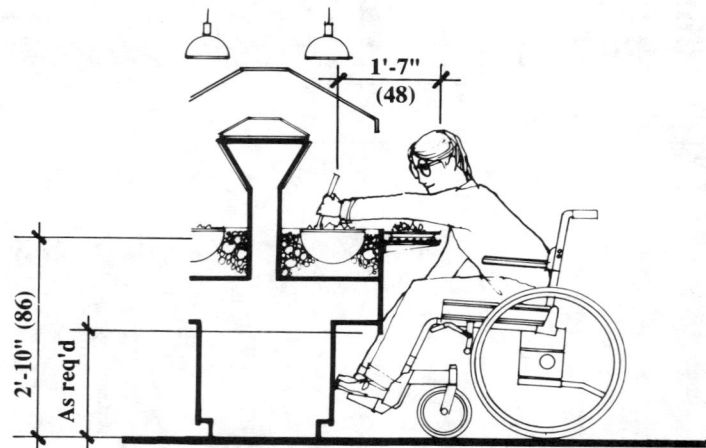

Fig. 35 A plate slide is recommended at salad bars and a kneespace at the counter. A mirrored surface above the bar is a further aid to guests in wheelchairs. Numbers in parentheses are dimensions in centimeters.

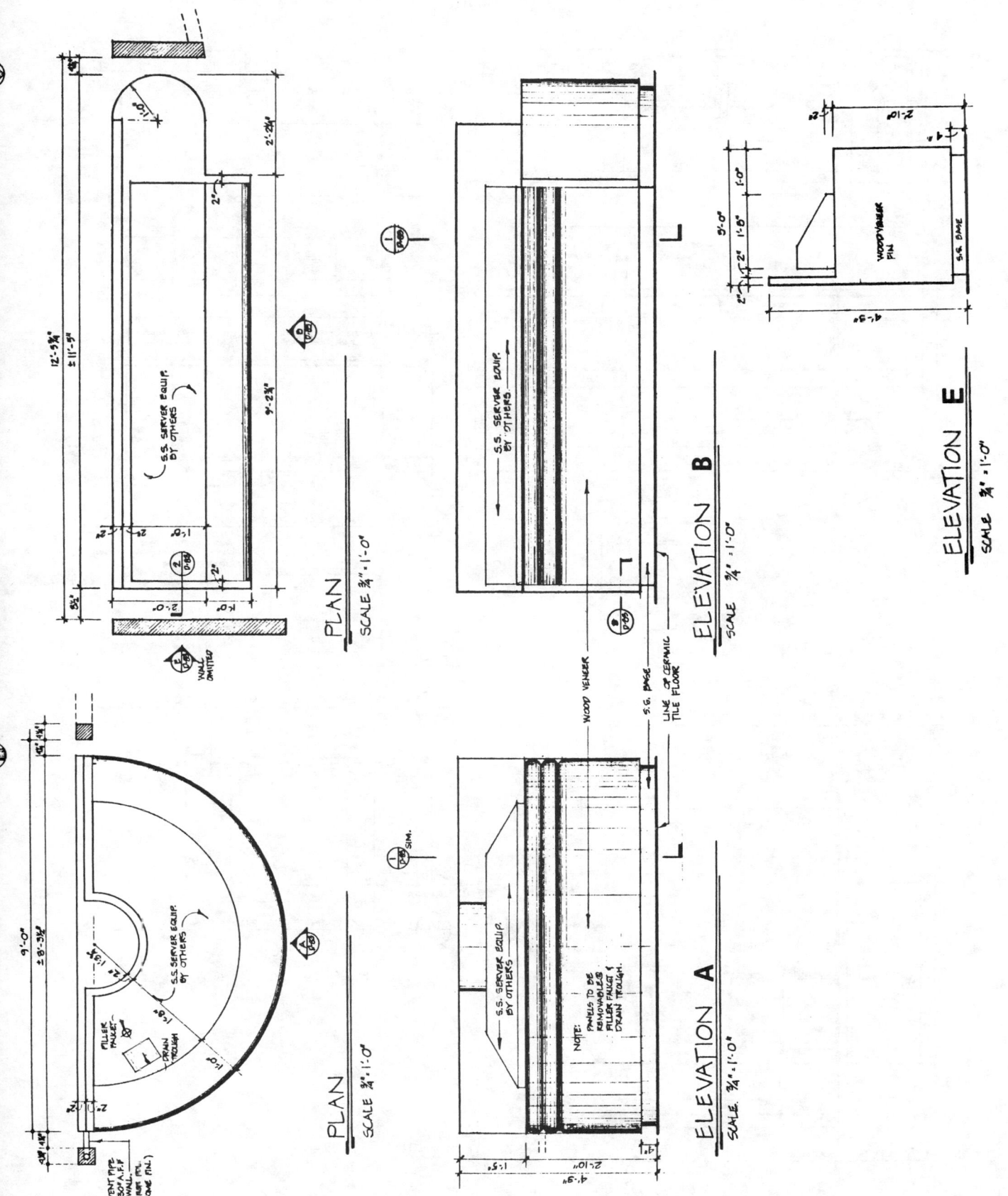

PLAN
SCALE ¾" = 1'-0"

PLAN
SCALE ¾" = 1'-0"

ELEVATION A
SCALE ¾" = 1'-0"

ELEVATION B
SCALE ¾" = 1'-0"

ELEVATION E
SCALE ¾" = 1'-0"

S.S. SERVER EQUIP.
BY OTHERS

NOTE: PANELS TO BE
REMOVABLE
FILLER FAUCET &
DRAIN TROUGH.

WOOD VENEER

S.G. BASE

LINE OF CERAMIC
TILE FLOOR

WOOD VENEER
FIN.

S.S. BASE

RESTAURANTS

Lunch Counters: Cashier Station

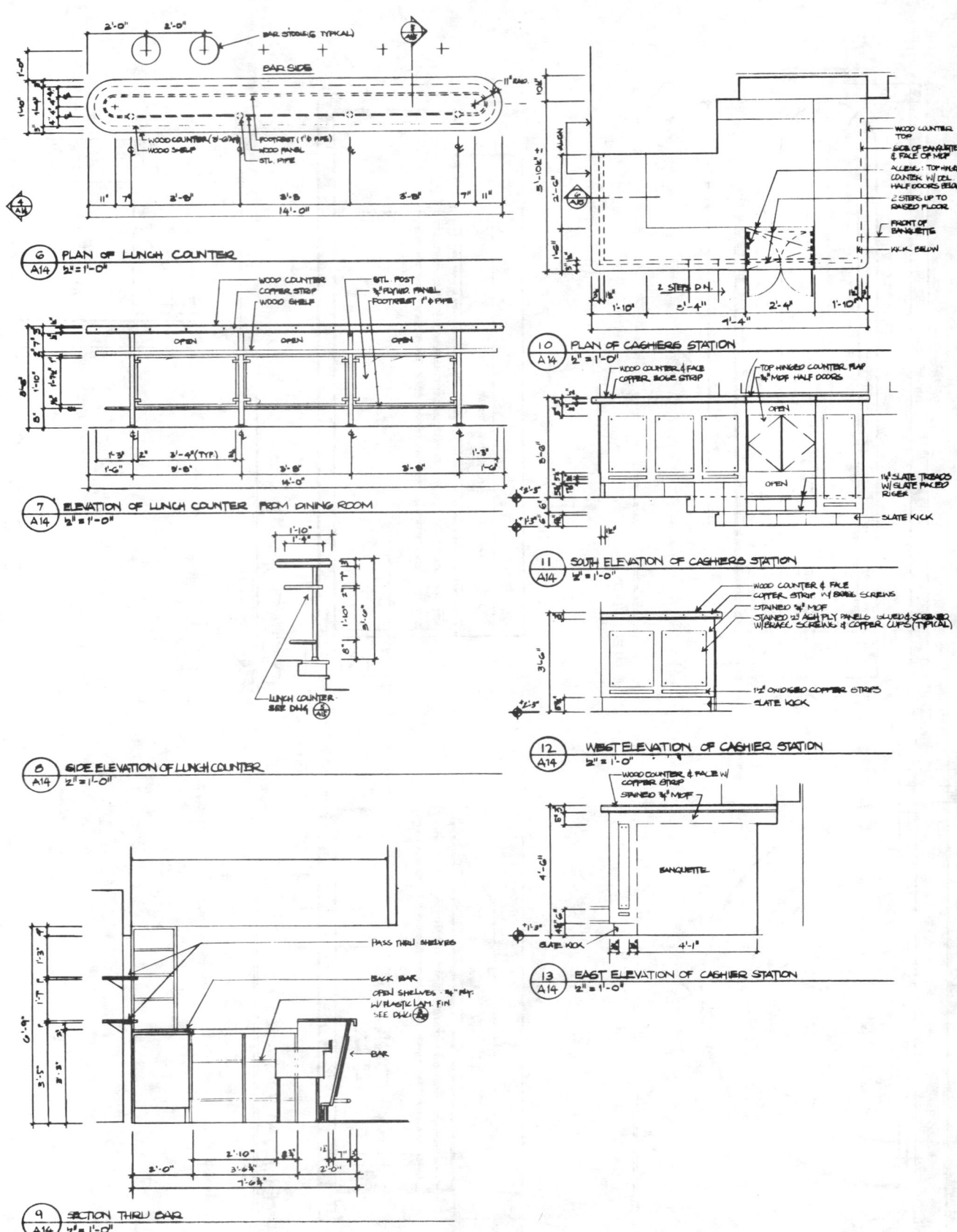

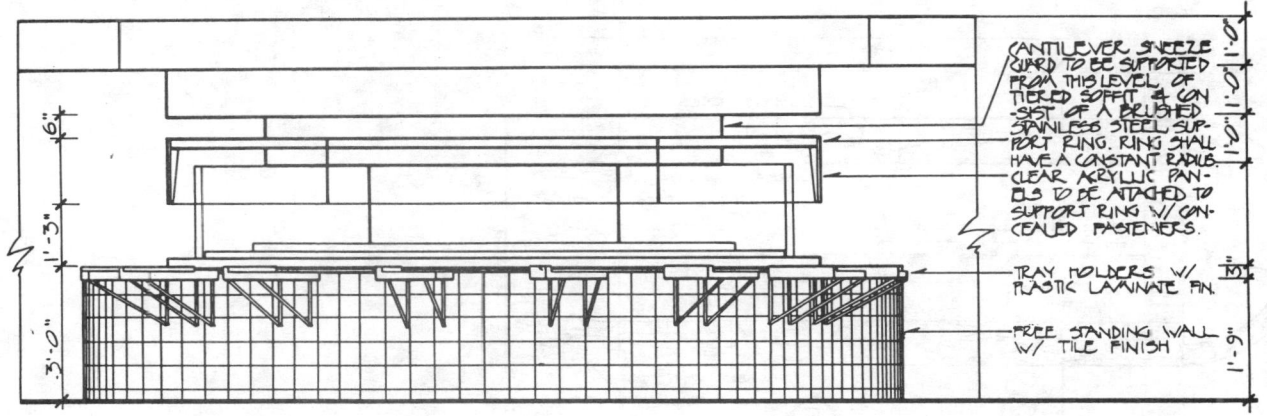

CANTILEVER SNEEZE GUARD TO BE SUPPORTED FROM THIS LEVEL OF TIERED SOFFIT & CONSIST OF A BRUSHED STAINLESS STEEL SUPPORT RING. RING SHALL HAVE A CONSTANT RADIUS. CLEAR ACRYLIC PANELS TO BE ATTACHED TO SUPPORT RING W/ CONCEALED FASTENERS.

TRAY HOLDERS W/ PLASTIC LAMINATE FIN.

FREE STANDING WALL W/ TILE FINISH

6"

1'-3"

3'-0"

1'-0"

1'-0"

1'-0"

3"

1'-9"

Ⓐ ELEVATION OF TYPICAL 'ROTARY SERVING' UNIT

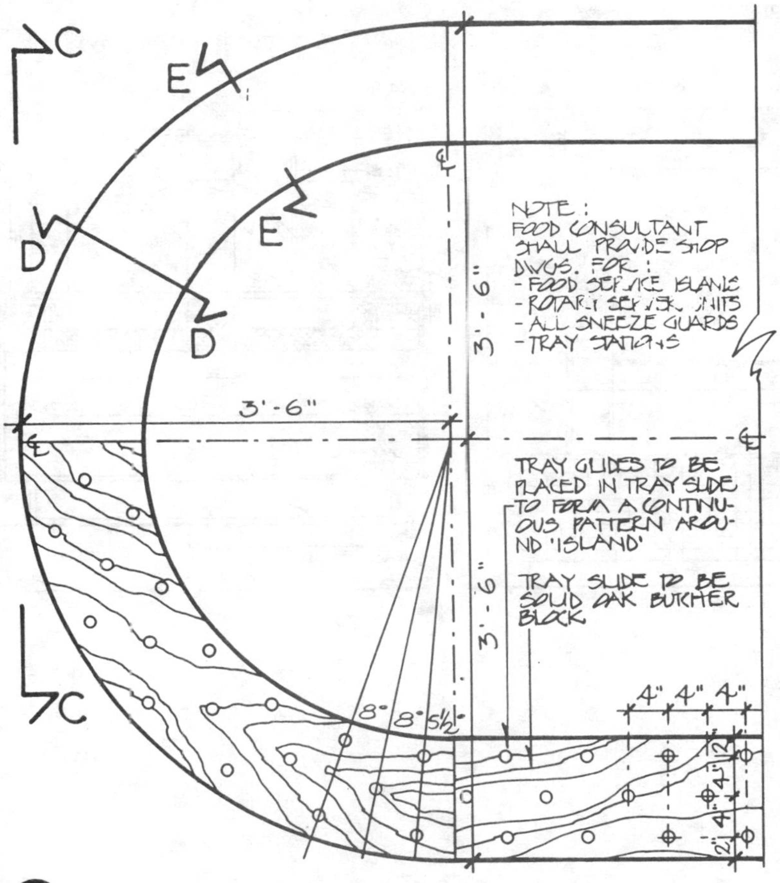

C

E

E

D

D

C

3'-6"

3'-6"

3'-6"

NOTE:
FOOD CONSULTANT SHALL PROVIDE SHOP DWGS. FOR:
- FOOD SERVICE ISLANDS
- ROTARY SERVER UNITS
- ALL SNEEZE GUARDS
- TRAY STATIONS

TRAY GLIDES TO BE PLACED IN TRAY SLIDE TO FORM A CONTINUOUS PATTERN AROUND 'ISLAND'

TRAY SLIDE TO BE SOLID OAK BUTCHER BLOCK

8" 8" 5½"

4" 4" 4"

Ⓑ PARTIAL PLAN OF TYPICAL 'ISLAND'

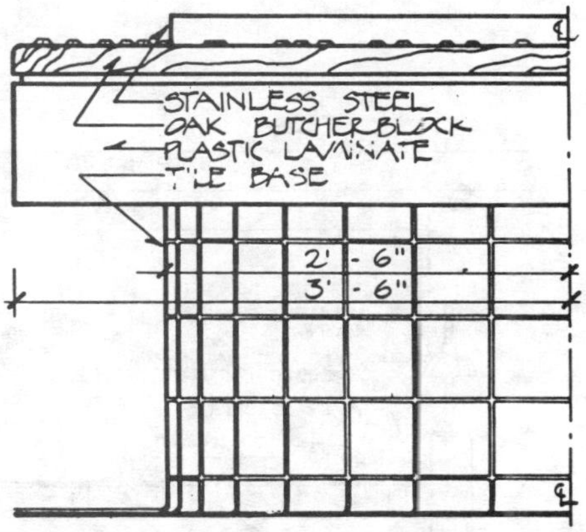

STAINLESS STEEL
OAK BUTCHER BLOCK
PLASTIC LAMINATE
TILE BASE

2'-6"

3'-6"

Ⓒ PARTIAL ELEVATION

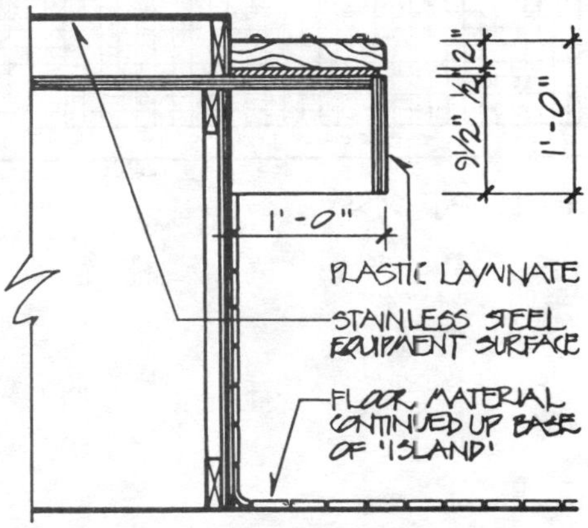

9½" ½"

1'-0"

1'-0"

PLASTIC LAMINATE

STAINLESS STEEL EQUIPMENT SURFACE

FLOOR MATERIAL CONTINUED UP BASE OF 'ISLAND'

ⒹⒹ SECTION OF TRAY SLIDE

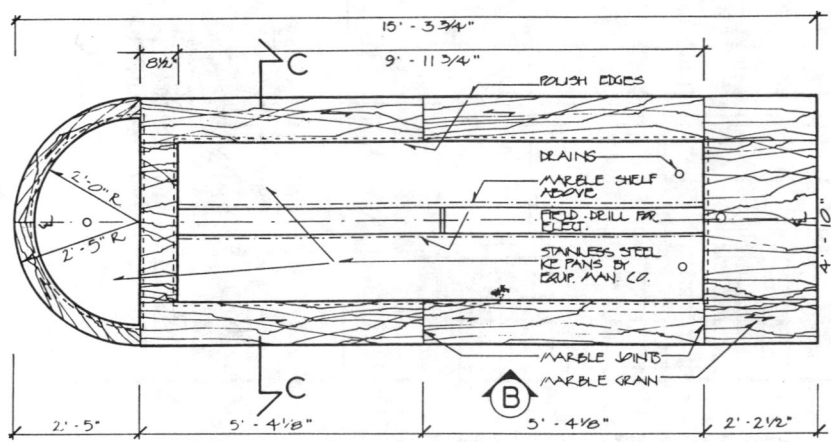

15' - 3 3/4"
8 1/2"
C
9' - 11 3/4"
POLISH EDGES
DRAINS
2'- 0" R
MARBLE SHELF
ABOVE
FIELD DRILL FOR
ELECT.
2' - 5" R
STAINLESS STEEL
KE PANS BY
EQUIP. MAN. CO.
C
MARBLE JOINTS
B
MARBLE GRAIN
2' - 5"
5' - 4 1/8"
5' - 4 1/8"
2' - 2 1/2"

A PLAN AT MARBLE COUNTER

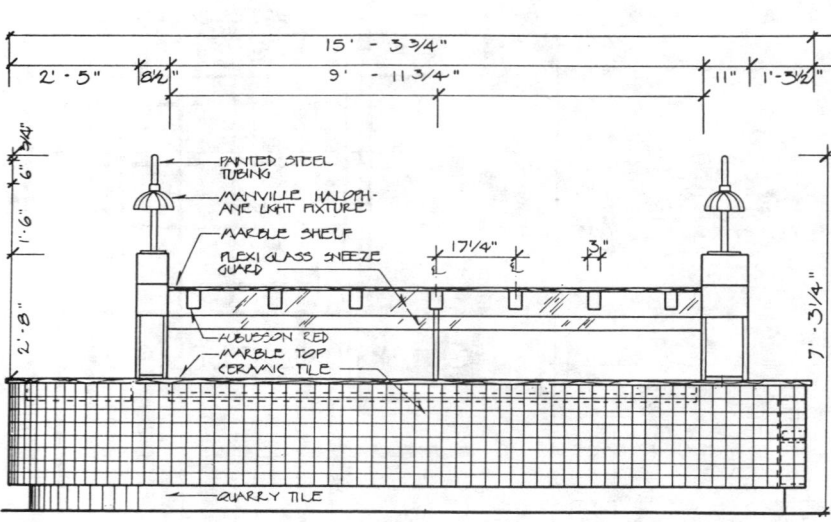

15' - 3 3/4"
2' - 5"
8 1/2"
9' - 11 3/4"
11"
1'-3 1/2"
PAINTED STEEL
TUBING
MANVILLE HALOPH-
ANE LIGHT FIXTURE
MARBLE SHELF
PLEXI GLASS SNEEZE
GUARD
17 1/4"
AUBUSSON RED
MARBLE TOP
CERAMIC TILE
QUARRY TILE
7' - 3 3/4"

B ELEVATION

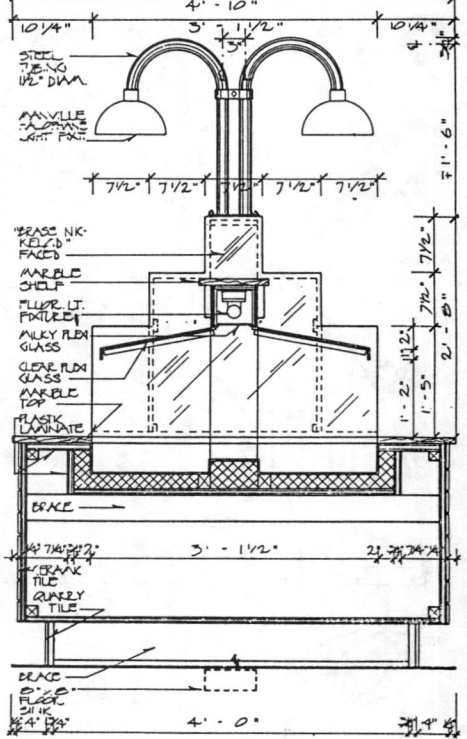

4' - 10"
10 1/4"
3' - 11 1/2"
10 1/4"
STEEL
TUBING
1/2" DIAM
MANVILLE
HALOPH-
ANE LIGHT FIX.
7 1/2" 7 1/2" 7 1/2" 7 1/2"
"BRASS NK.
KELS'D"
FACES
MARBLE
SHELF
FLUOR. LT.
FIXTURE
MILKY PLEXI
GLASS
CLEAR PLEXI
GLASS
MARBLE
TOP
PLASTIC
LAMINATE
BRACE
CERAMIC
TILE
QUARRY
TILE
3' - 1 1/2"
BRACE
EDGE
FLOOR
TILE
4' - 0"

CC SECTION

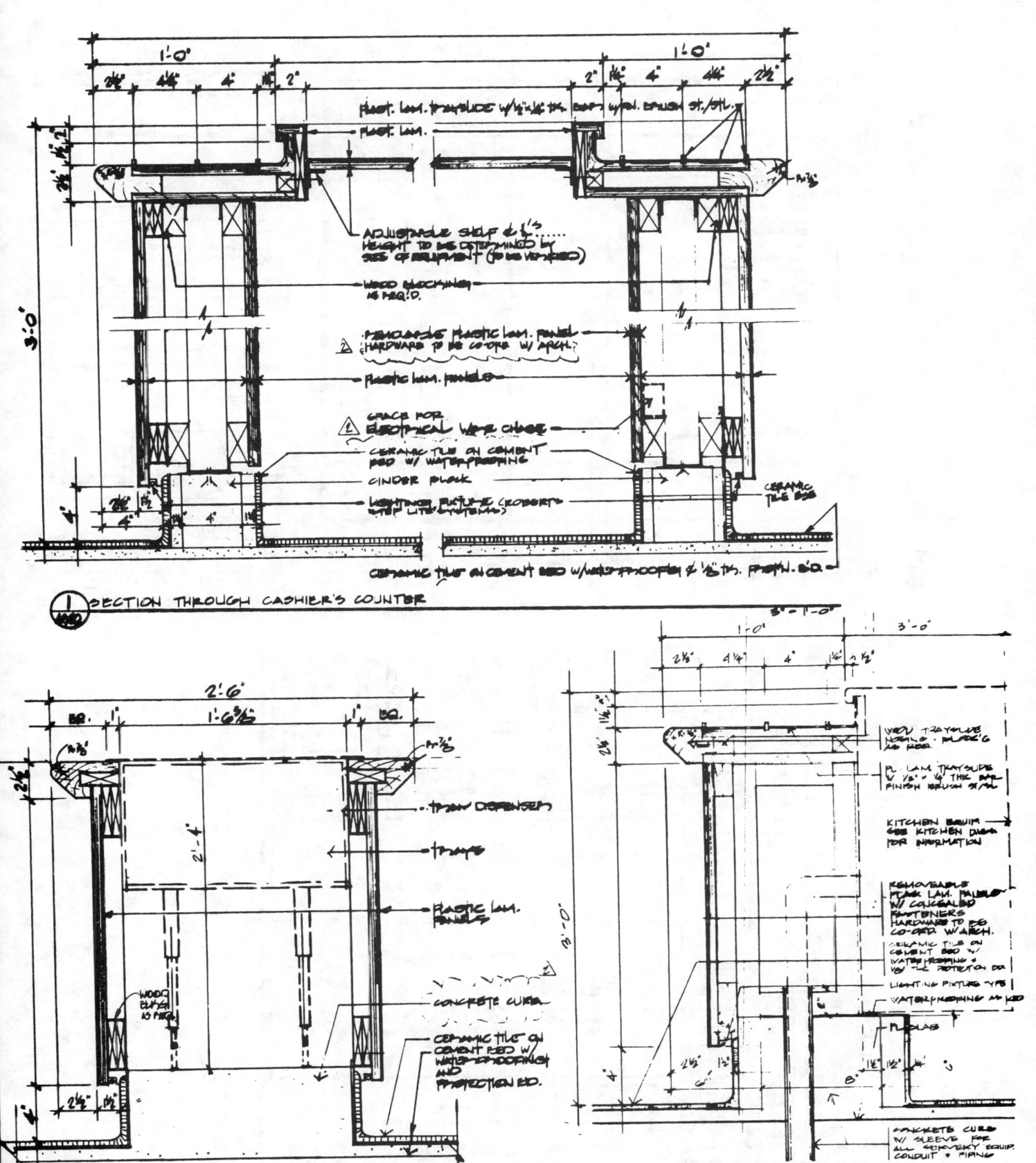

1 SECTION THROUGH CASHIER'S COUNTER

2 SECTION THROUGH TRAY PICK-UP COUNTER

3 SECTION DETAIL - SERVERY TRAYSLIDE

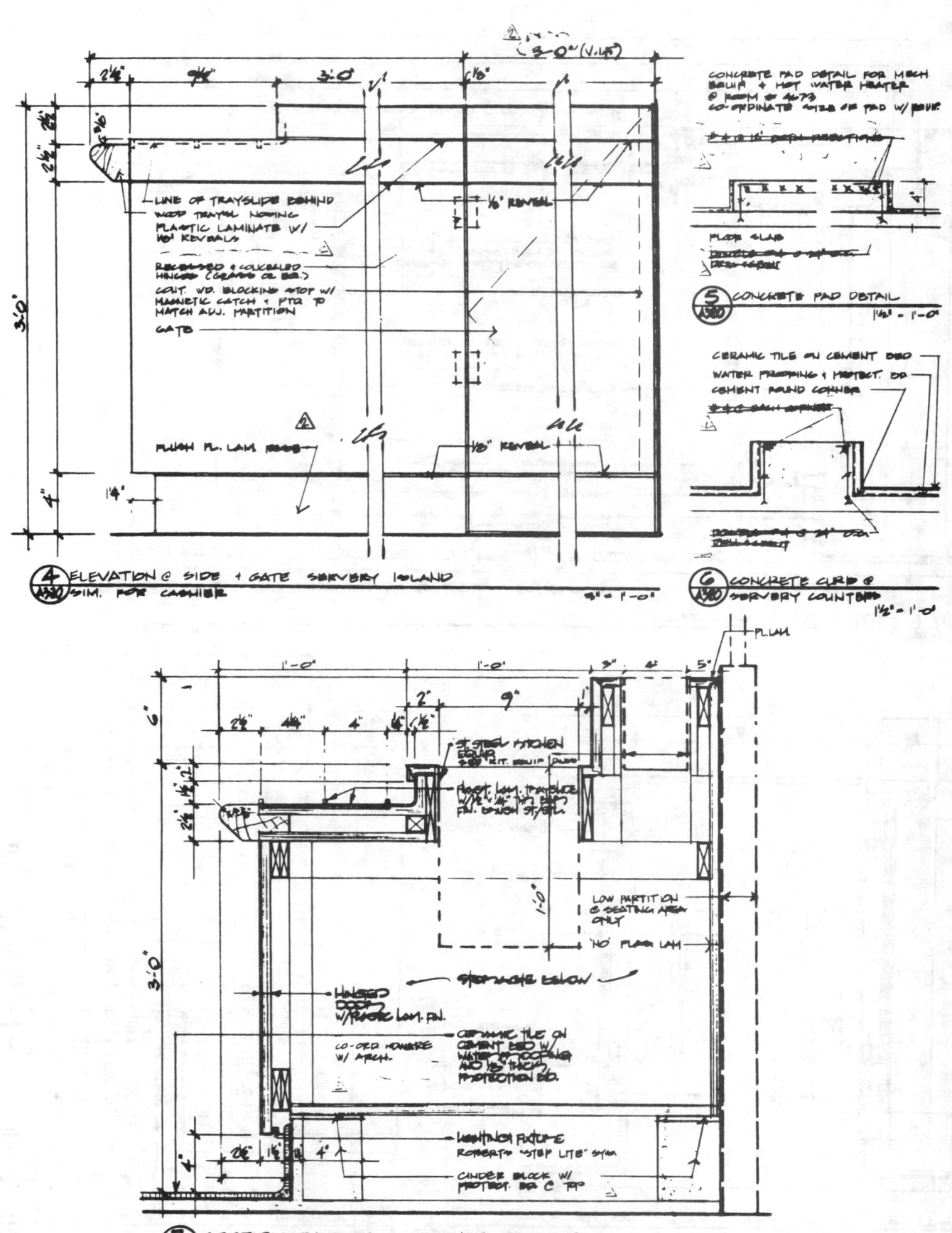

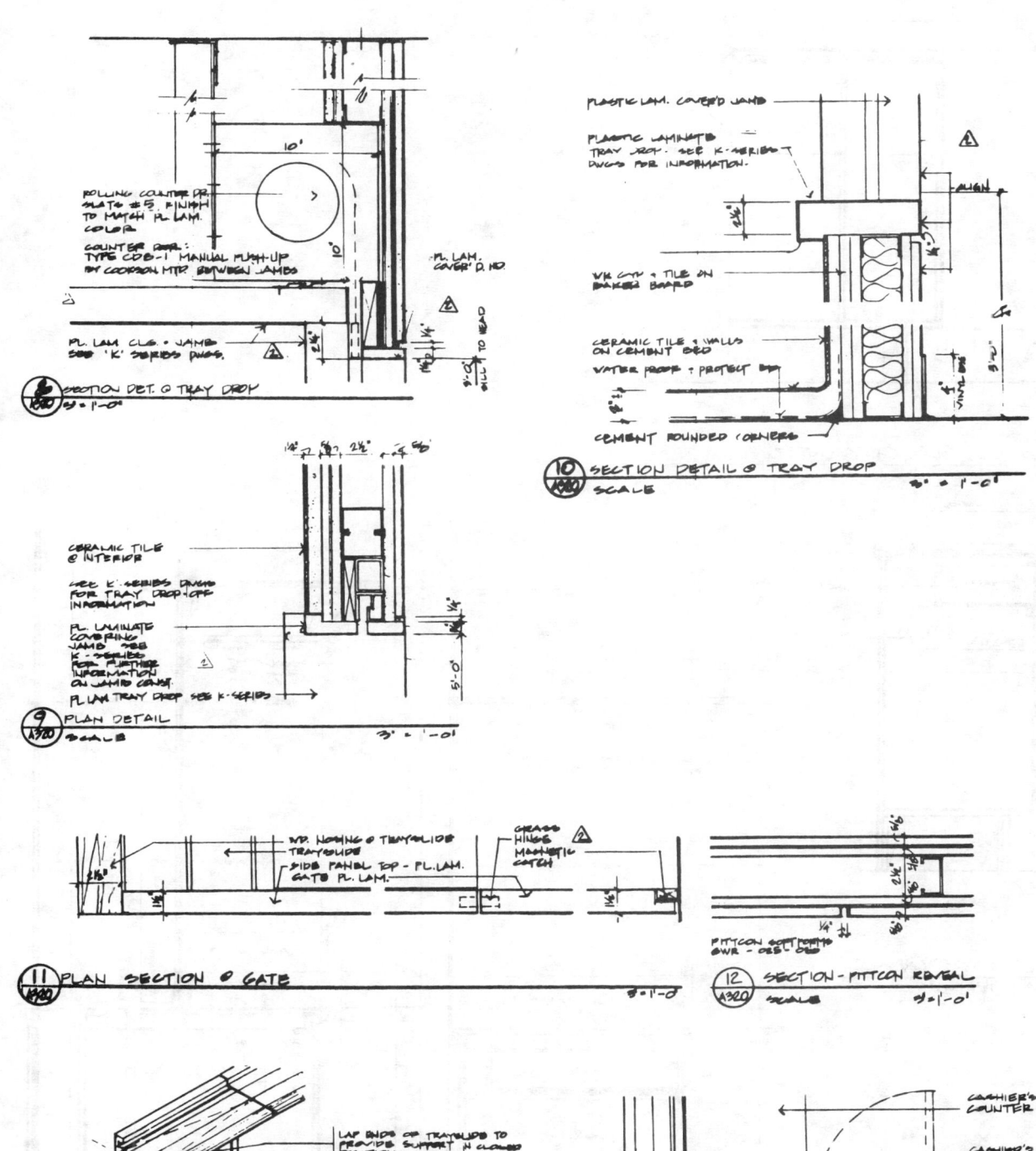

ROLLING COUNTER DR.
SLATS #5. FINISH
TO MATCH PL.LAM.
COLOR.

COUNTER DR:
TYPE CD8-1 MANUAL PUSH-UP
BY COOKSON MTR. BETWEEN JAMBS

PL. LAM.
COVER'D. HD.

PL. LAM. CLG. JAMB
SEE 'K' SERIES DWGS.

SECTION DET. @ TRAY DROP

PLASTIC LAM. COVER'D JAMB

PLASTIC LAMINATE
TRAY DROP. SEE K-SERIES
DWGS FOR INFORMATION.

WK. GYP. + TILE ON
BAKER BOARD

CERAMIC TILE + WALLS
ON CEMENT BED

WATER PROOF + PROTECT BED

CEMENT ROUNDED CORNERS

ALIGN

10 SECTION DETAIL @ TRAY DROP
SCALE   3" = 1'-0"

CERAMIC TILE
@ INTERIOR

SEE K-SERIES DWGS
FOR TRAY DROP-OFF
INFORMATION

PL. LAMINATE
COVERING
JAMB   SEE
K-SERIES
FOR FURTHER
INFORMATION
ON JAMB CONST.

PL. LAM TRAY DROP SEE K-SERIES

9 PLAN DETAIL
SCALE   3" = 1'-0"

WD. HOUSING @ TRAYSLIDE
TRAYSLIDE
SIDE PANEL TOP - PL. LAM.
GATE PL. LAM.

GRASS
HINGE
MAGNETIC
CATCH

11 PLAN SECTION @ GATE
3"=1'-0"

PITTCON SOFT FORMED
GWR - DEL. 555

12 SECTION - PITTCON REVEAL
SCALE   3"=1'-0"

LAP ENDS OF TRAYSLIDE TO
PROVIDE SUPPORT IN CLOSED
POSITION

WOOD HOUSING + WOOD END
CERAMIC TILE FACE (TYP)
NOTE:
ALL END PIECES TO BE
PLASTIC LAMINATE - PL.?
UNLESS OTHERWISE NOTED

OPEN @ POSS

CASHIER'S ADJ
COUNTER

CASHIER'S GATE
2 PIECES - DOOR +
LIFT-UP TRAYSLIDE

15 AXONOMETRIC + PLAN   CASHIER'S GATE
SCALE   1½" = 1'-0"

RESTAURANTS
Service Counter; Host Cabinet; Waiter's Station; Trash Counter

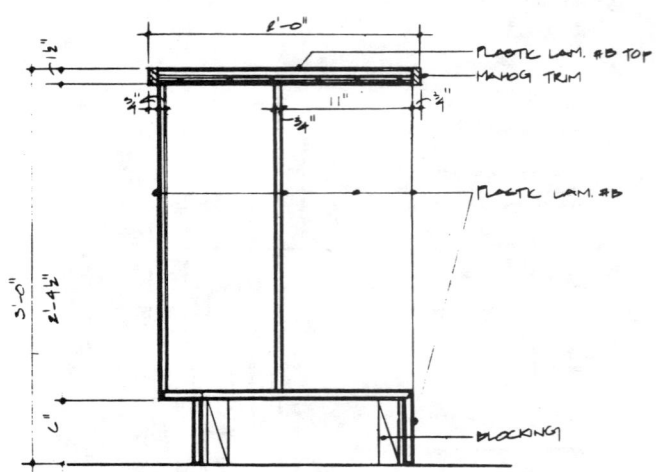

1'-0"

PLASTIC LAM. #B TOP
MAHOG. TRIM

PLASTIC LAM. #B

5'-0"
2'-4½"

2"

BLOCKING

⑤ SECTION thru SERVICE COUNTER
A11   SCALE : 1½"=1'-0"

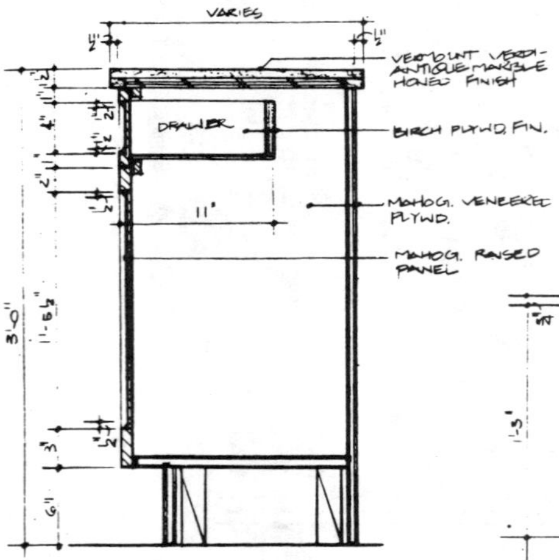

VARIES

VERDULINT VERD-
ANTIQUE MARBLE
HONED FINISH

DRAWER

BIRCH PLYWD. FIN.

11"

MAHOG. VENEERED
PLYWD.

MAHOG. RAISED
PANEL

3'-0"

3"

6"

⑯ SECT. of HOST CABINET
A11   SCALE : 1½"=1'-0"

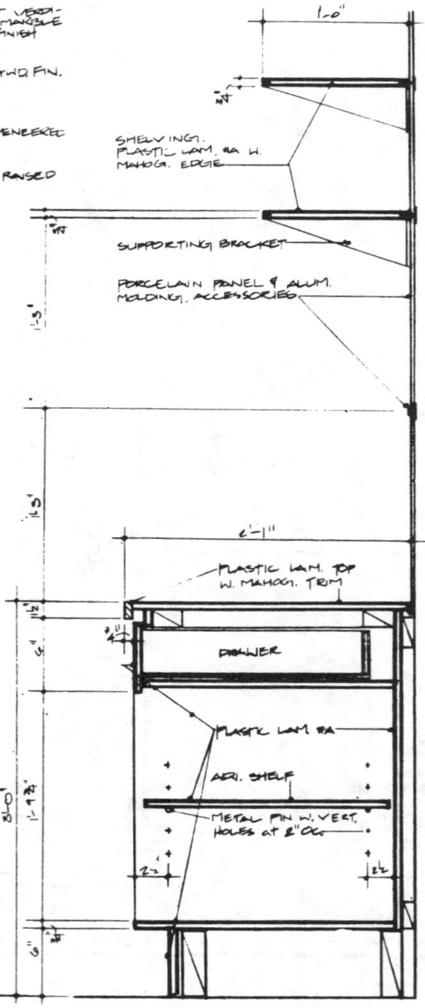

1'-0"

SHELVING,
PLASTIC LAM. #A W.
MAHOG. EDGE

SUPPORTING BRACKET

PORCELAIN PANEL & ALUM.
MOLDING, ACCESSORIES

1'-3"

1'-3"

5'-10"

2'-1"

PLASTIC LAM. TOP
W. MAHOG. TRIM

DRAWER

PLASTIC LAM. #A

ADJ. SHELF

METAL PIN W. VERT.
HOLES at 2"OC

5'-0"
1'-7½"

2"

6"

⑱ TYP. WAITER'S STATION CABINET
A11   SCALE : 1½"=1'-0"

3"
5"

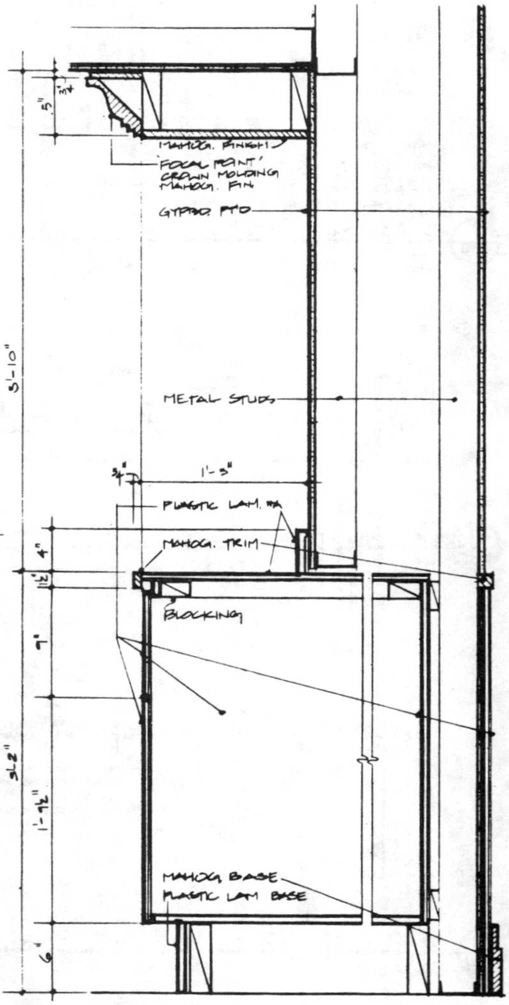

MAHOG. FINISH

'FOCAL POINT'
CROWN MOLDING
MAHOG. FIN

GYP.BD. PT'D

METAL STUDS

1'-3"

3"
4"

PLASTIC LAM. #A

MAHOG. TRIM

BLOCKING

7"

3'-2"
1'-7½"

MAHOG BASE
PLASTIC LAM BASE

6"

⑲ SECT. of TRASH COUNTER CABINET
A11   SCALE : 1½"=1'-0"

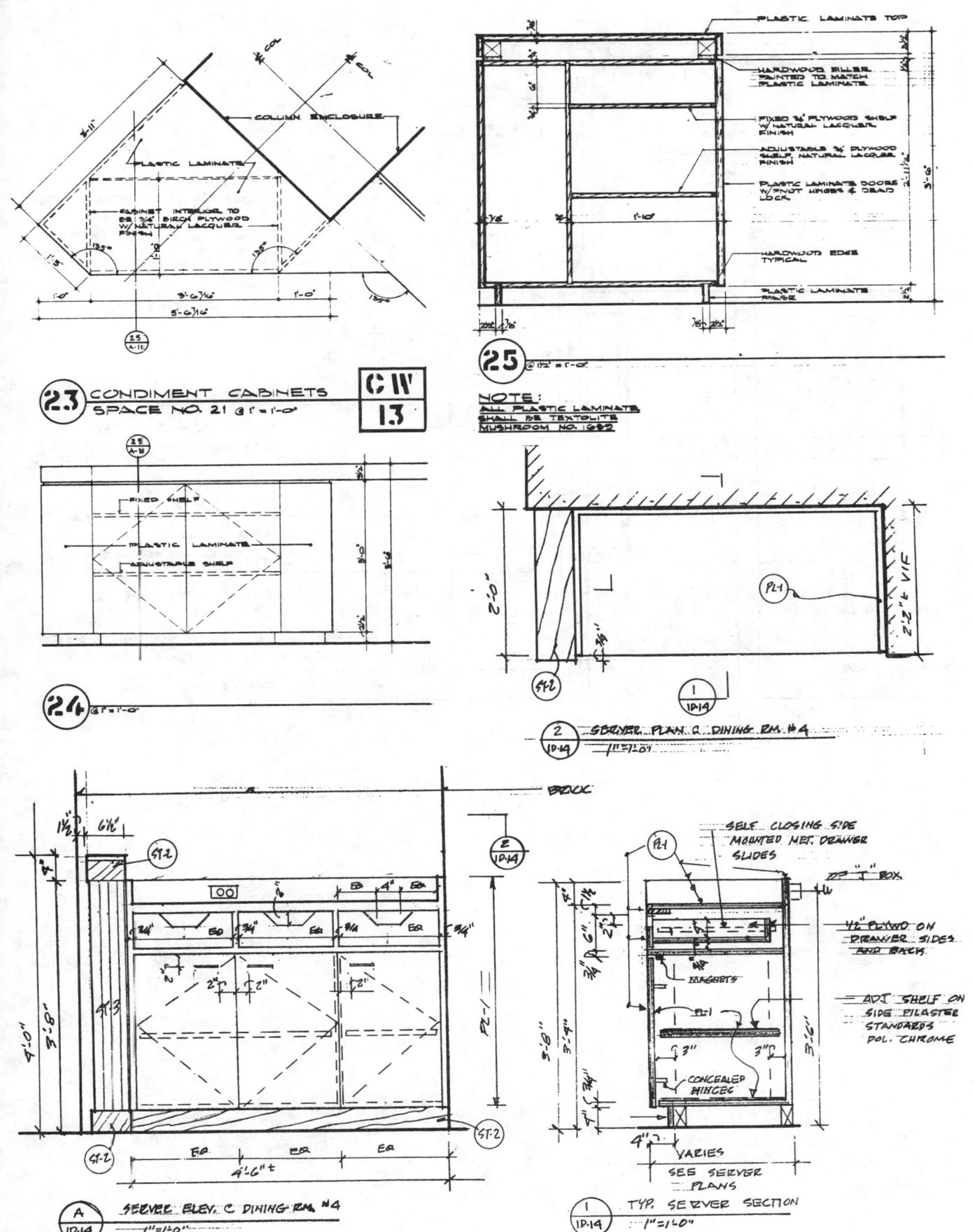

(23) CONDIMENT CABINETS
SPACE NO. 21 @1"=1'-0"

CW
13

NOTE:
ALL PLASTIC LAMINATE
SHALL BE TEXTOLITE
MUSHROOM NO. 1692

(24) @1"=1'-0"

(2/10-14) SERVER PLAN @ DINING RM. #4   1"=1'-0"

(A/10-14) SERVER ELEV. @ DINING RM. #4   1"=1'-0"

(1/10-14) TYP. SERVER SECTION   1"=1'-0"

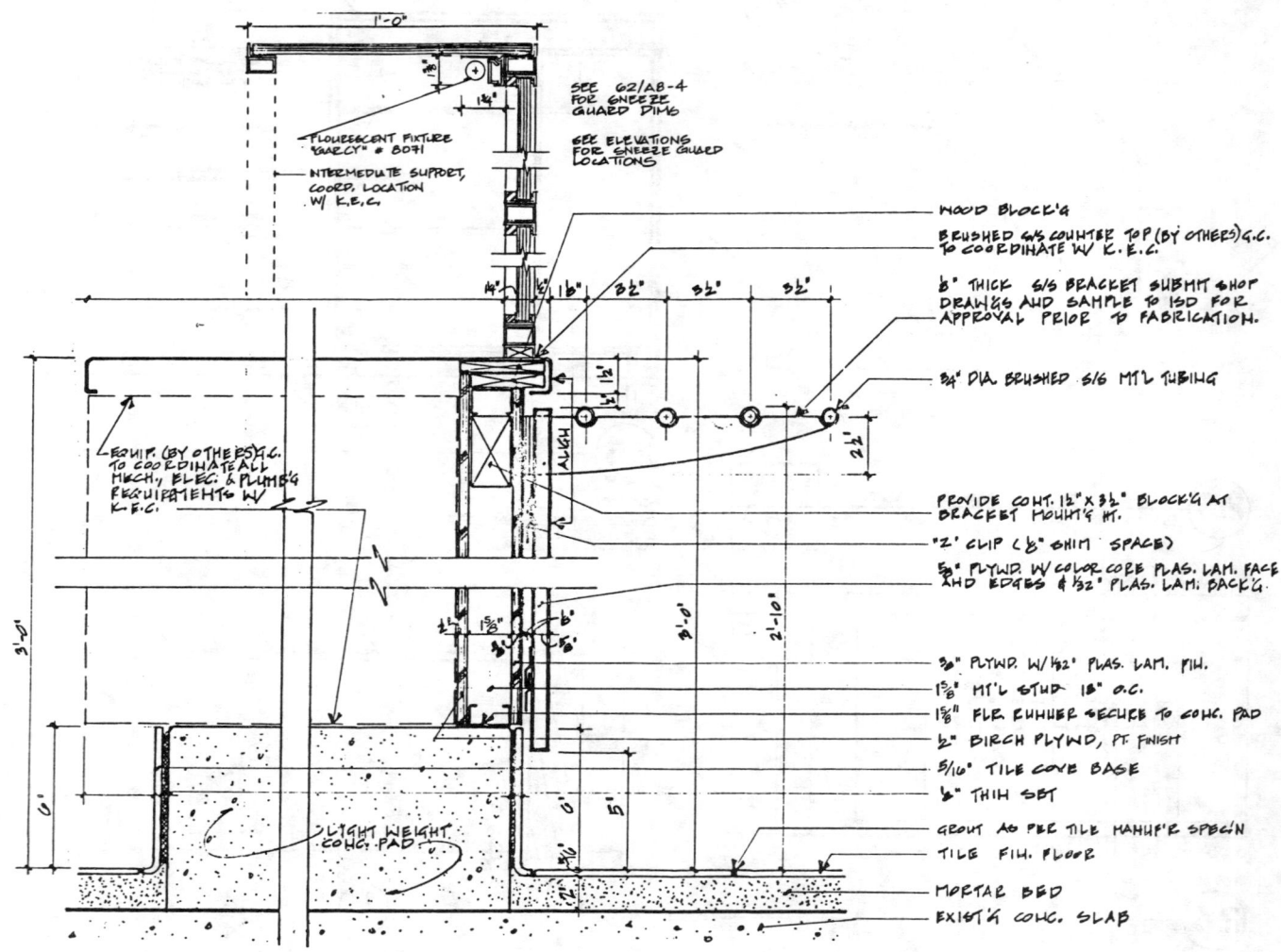

SEE 62/A8-4
FOR GNEEZE
GUARD DIMS

SEE ELEVATIONS
FOR GNEEZE GUARD
LOCATIONS

FLOURESCENT FIXTURE
"MARCY" # 8071

INTERMEDIATE SUPPORT,
COORD. LOCATION
W/ K.E.C.

EQUIP. (BY OTHERS) G.C.
TO COORDINATE ALL
MECH., ELEC. & PLUMB'G
REQUIREMENTS W/
K.E.C.

LIGHT WEIGHT
CONC. PAD

WOOD BLOCK'G

BRUSHED S/S COUNTER TOP (BY OTHERS) G.C.
TO COORDINATE W/ K.E.C.

8" THICK S/S BRACKET SUBMIT SHOP
DRAWINGS AND SAMPLE TO ISD FOR
APPROVAL PRIOR TO FABRICATION.

3/4" DIA BRUSHED S/S MT'L TUBING

PROVIDE CONT. 1½" X 3½" BLOCK'G AT
BRACKET MOUNT'G HT.

"Z" CLIP (⅛" SHIM SPACE)

⅝" PLYWD. W/ COLOR CORE PLAS. LAM. FACE
AND EDGES & 1/32" PLAS. LAM. BACK'G

¾" PLYWD. W/ 1/32" PLAS. LAM. FIN.

1⅝" MT'L STUD 18" O.C.

1⅝" FLR. RUNNER SECURE TO CONC. PAD

½" BIRCH PLYWD, PT. FINISH

5/16" TILE COVE BASE

½" THIN SET

GROUT AS PER TILE MANUF'R SPEC'N

TILE FIN. FLOOR

MORTAR BED

EXIST'G CONC. SLAB

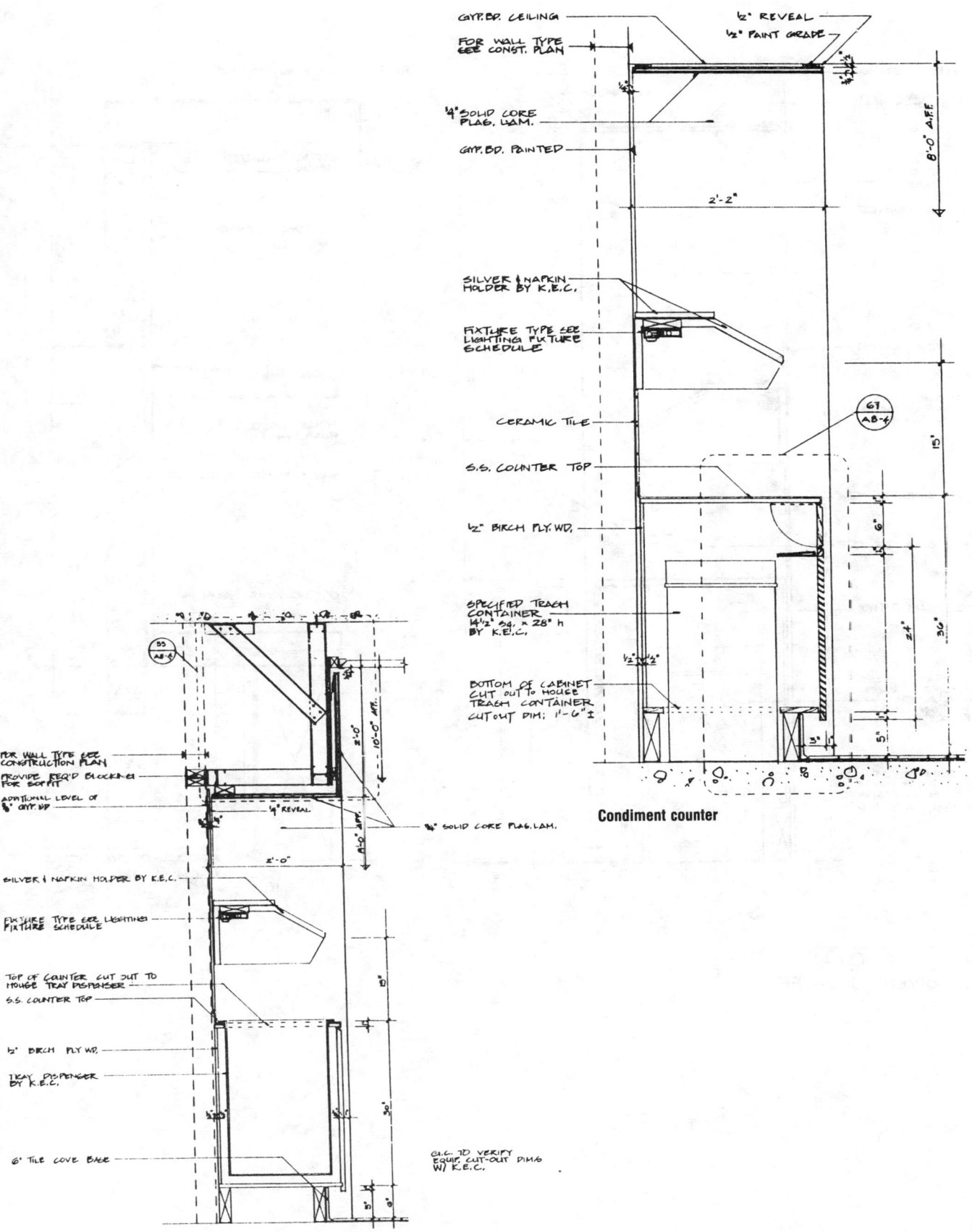

GYP. BD. CEILING

½" REVEAL

½" PAINT GRADE

FOR WALL TYPE
SEE CONST. PLAN

8'-0" A.F.F.

¼" SOLID CORE
PLAS. LAM.

GYP. BD. PAINTED

2'-2"

SILVER & NAPKIN
HOLDER BY K.E.C.

FIXTURE TYPE SEE
LIGHTING FIXTURE
SCHEDULE

67
AB-6

CERAMIC TILE

15'

S.S. COUNTER TOP

6"

½" BIRCH PLY. WD.

SPECIFIED TRASH
CONTAINER
14½" SQ. × 28" h
BY K.E.C.

24"

36"

BOTTOM OF CABINET
CUT OUT TO HOUSE
TRASH CONTAINER
CUTOUT DIM; 1'-6" ±

½" 1½"

5"

3"

5"

Condiment counter

55
AB-6

2'-0" MTL.

10'-0" MTL.

4½" MTL.

FOR WALL TYPE SEE
CONSTRUCTION PLAN

PROVIDE REQ'D BLOCKING
FOR SOFFIT

ADDITIONAL LEVEL OF
⅝" GYP. BD

¼" REVEAL

¾" SOLID CORE PLAS.LAM.

2'-0"

SILVER & NAPKIN HOLDER BY K.E.C.

FIXTURE TYPE SEE LIGHTING
FIXTURE SCHEDULE

TOP OF COUNTER CUT OUT TO
HOUSE TRAY DISPENSER

10"

S.S. COUNTER TOP

½" BIRCH PLY. WD.

TRAY DISPENSER
BY K.E.C.

30"

6" TILE COVE BASE

5"

G.C. TO VERIFY
EQUIP. CUT-OUT DIMS
W/ K.E.C.

Section at tray pick-up

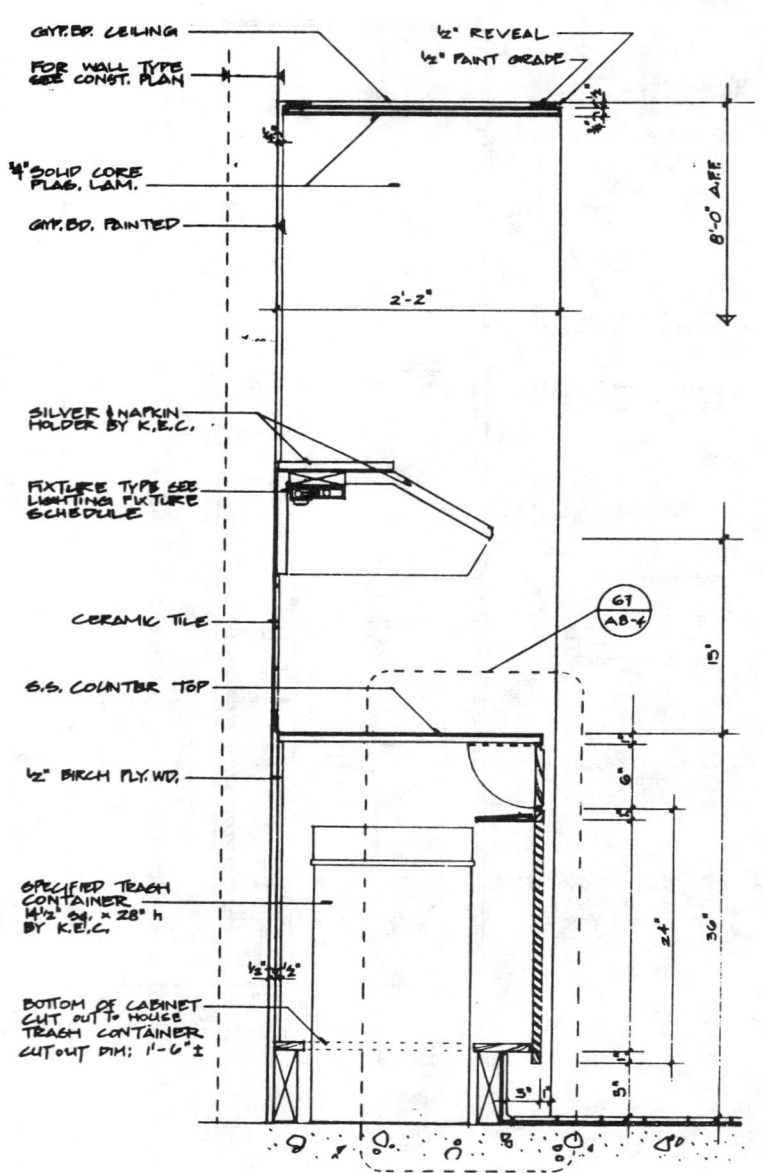

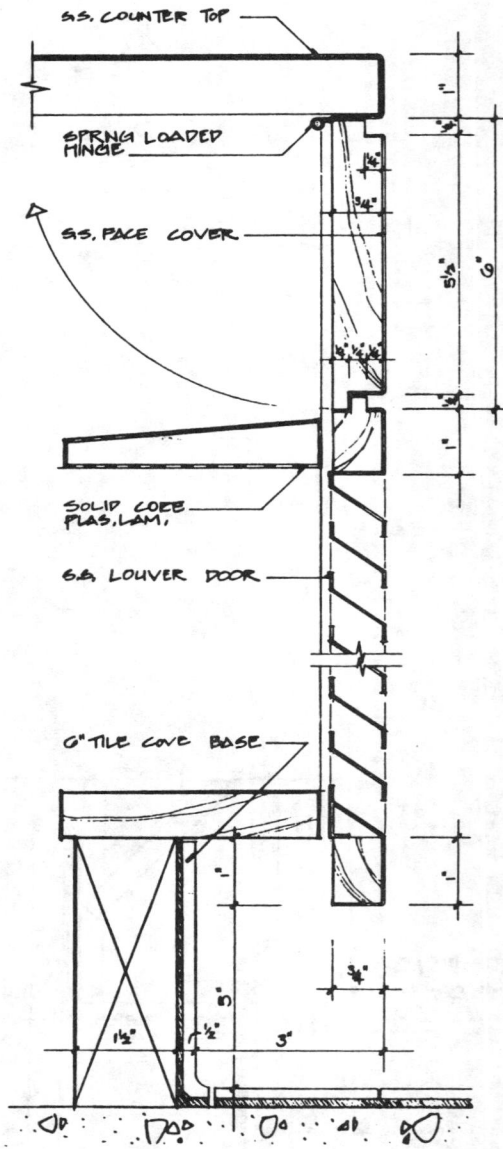

DETAIL SECTION AT CONDIMENT COUNTER

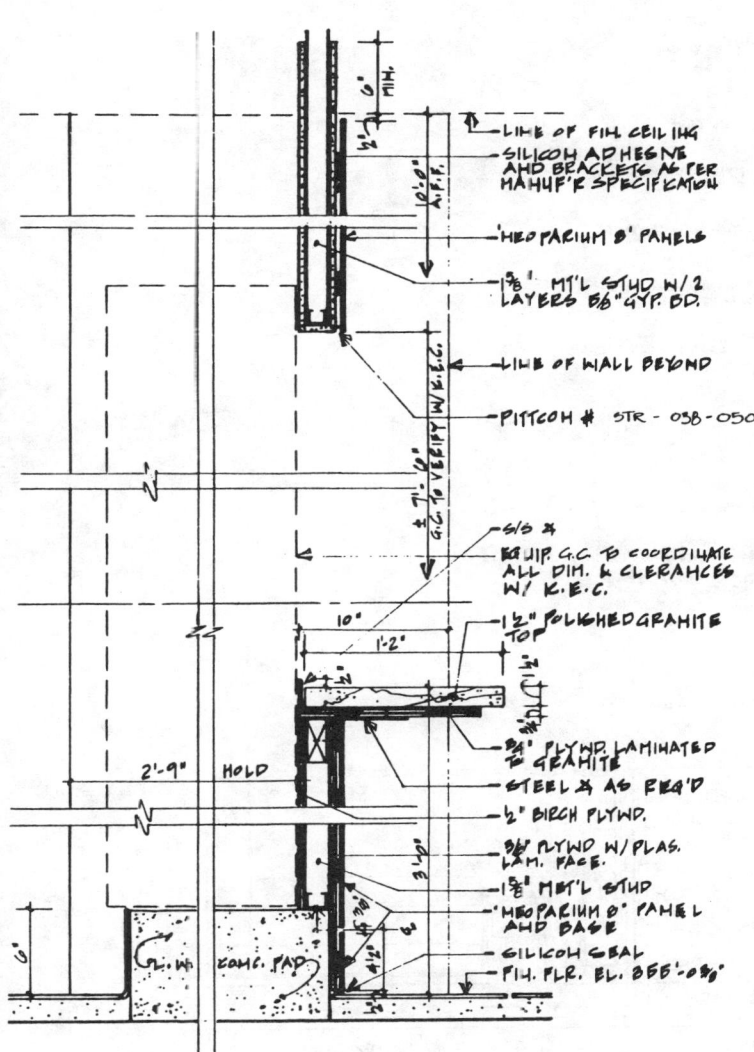

SECTION AT STONE COUNTERS

Labels (left diagram):
- LINE OF FIN. CEILING
- SILICON ADHESIVE AND BRACKETS AS PER MANUF'R SPECIFICATION
- 'NEOPARIUM B' PANELS
- 1⅝" MT'L STUD W/2 LAYERS ⅝" GYP. BD.
- LINE OF WALL BEYOND
- PITTCON # STR - 03B - 050
- S/S &
- EQUIP G.C. TO COORDINATE ALL DIM. & CLEARANCES W/ K.E.C.
- 1½" POLISHED GRANITE TOP
- ¾" PLYWD. LAMINATED TO GRANITE
- STEEL & AS REQ'D
- ½" BIRCH PLYWD.
- ¾" PLYWD W/ PLAS. LAM. FACE
- 1⅝" MET'L STUD
- 'NEOPARIUM B' PANEL AND BASE
- SILICON SEAL
- FIN. FLR. EL. 355'-0¾"
- 2'-9" HOLD
- CONC. PAD
- 10"
- 1'-2"

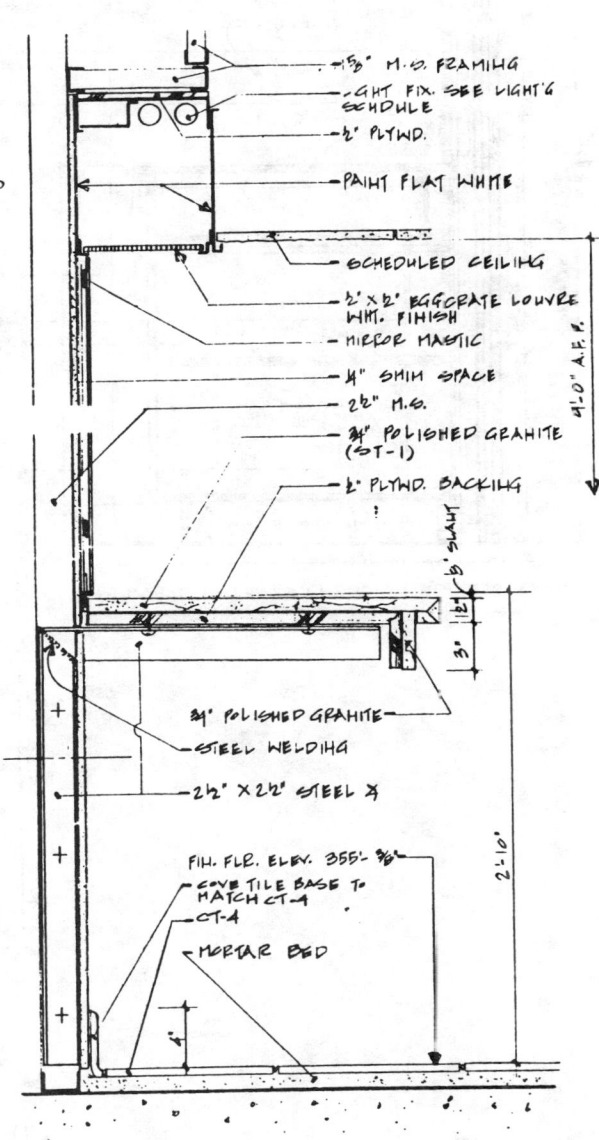

VERT. SECTION AT
SALAD BAR / GRANITE COUNTER

Labels (right diagram):
- 1⅝" M.S. FRAMING
- LIGHT FIX. SEE LIGHT'G SCHEDULE
- ½" PLYWD.
- PAINT FLAT WHITE
- SCHEDULED CEILING
- 2' X 2' EGGCRATE LOUVRE WHT. FINISH
- MIRROR MASTIC
- ¼" SHIM SPACE
- 2½" M.S.
- ¾" POLISHED GRANITE (ST-1)
- ½" PLYWD. BACKING
- ¾" POLISHED GRANITE
- STEEL WELDING
- 2½" X 2½" STEEL &
- FIN. FLR. ELEV. 355'-⅜"
- COVE TILE BASE TO MATCH CT-A
- CT-A
- MORTAR BED
- 4'-0" A.F.F.
- 2'-10"

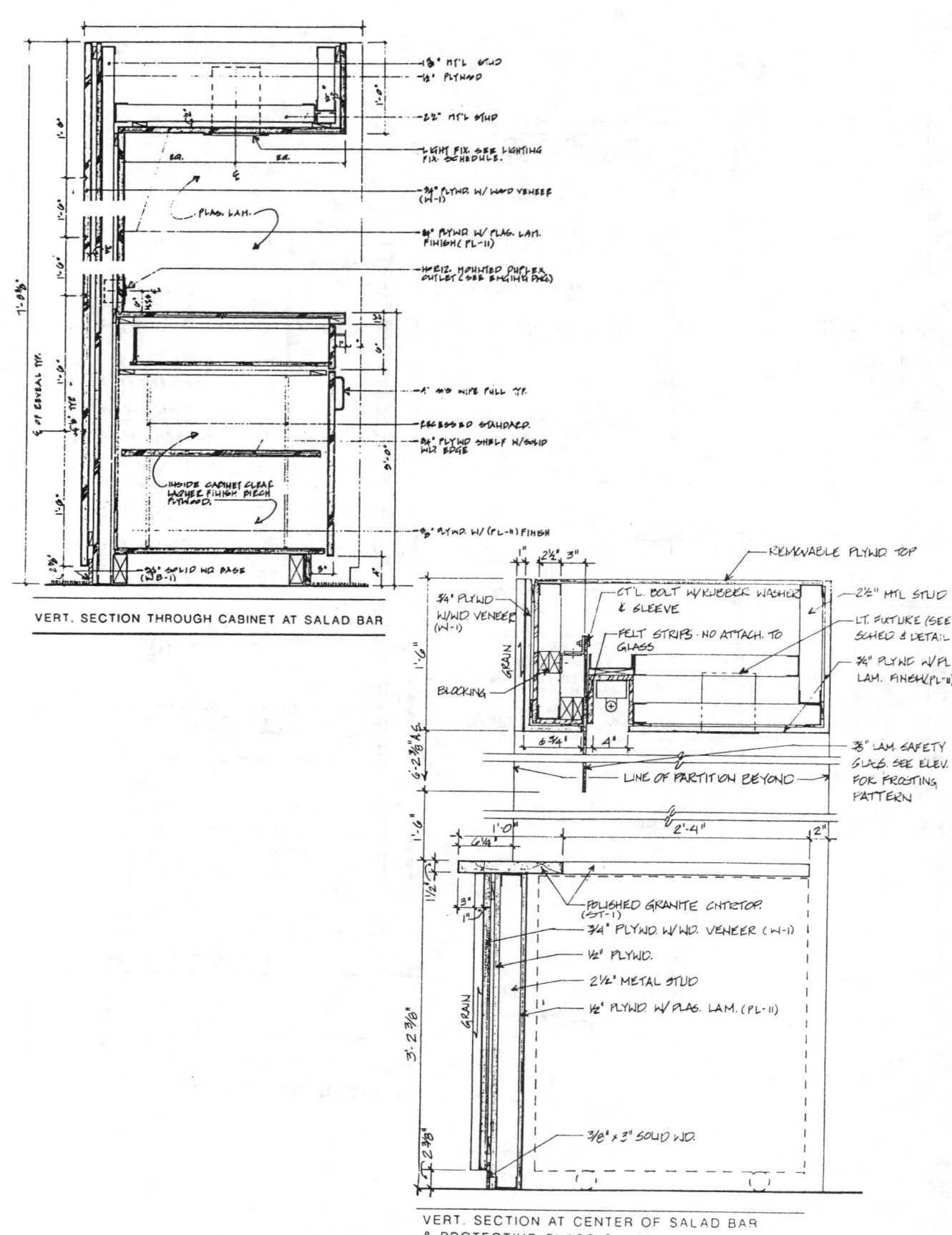

VERT. SECTION THROUGH CABINET AT SALAD BAR

VERT. SECTION AT CENTER OF SALAD BAR
& PROTECTIVE GLASS GUARD

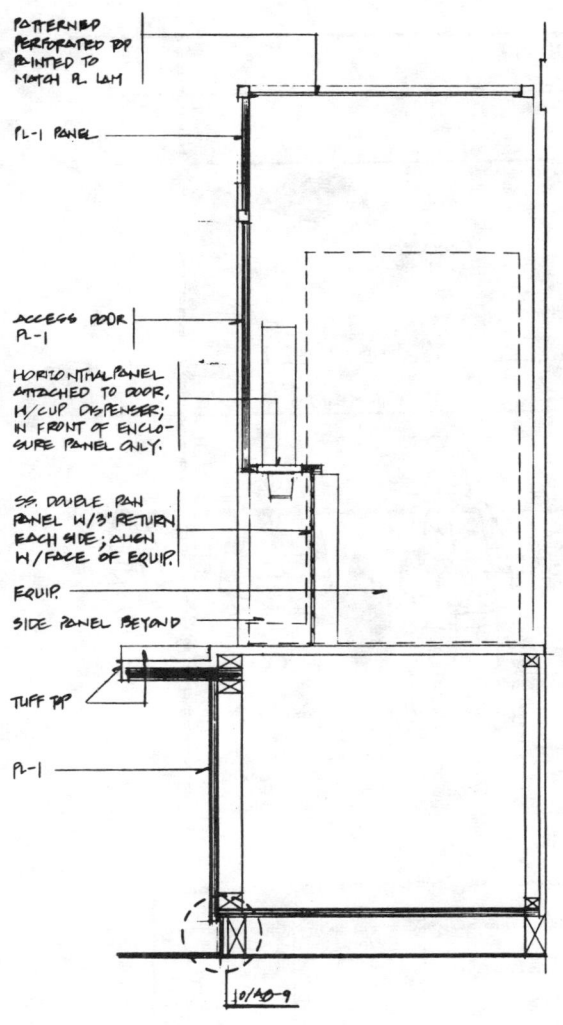

PATTERNED
PERFORATED PP
PAINTED TO
MATCH PL. LAM

PL-1 PANEL

ACCESS DOOR
PL-1

HORIZONTAL PANEL
ATTACHED TO DOOR,
W/CUP DISPENSER;
IN FRONT OF ENCLO-
SURE PANEL ONLY.

SS. DOUBLE PAN
PANEL W/3" RETURN
EACH SIDE; ALIGN
W/FACE OF EQUIP.

EQUIP.

SIDE PANEL BEYOND

TUFF PP

PL-1

10/A0-9

__COLD BEVERAGE & DESSERT STAND__

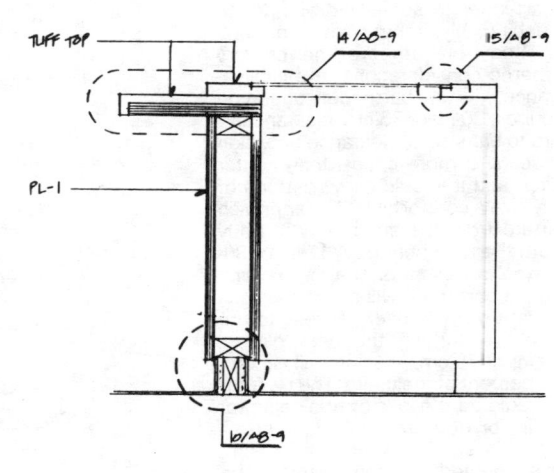

TUFF TOP

14/A0-9   15/A0-9

PL-1

10/A0-9

__HOT FOOD STAND__

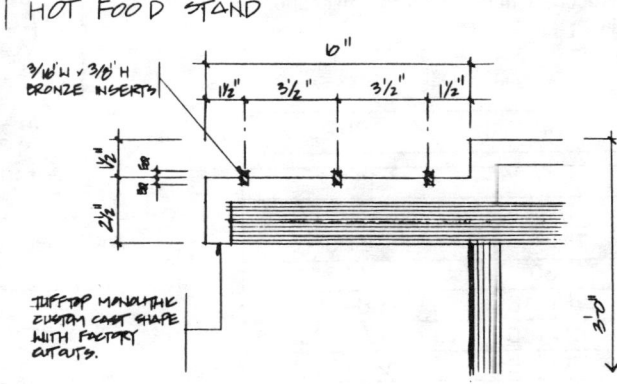

3/16" W x 3/8" H
BRONZE INSERTS

6"

1½"   3½"   3½"   1½"

TUFFTOP MONOLITHIC
CUSTOM CAST SHAPE
WITH FACTORY
CUTOUTS.

3'-0"

__TRAY SLIDE__

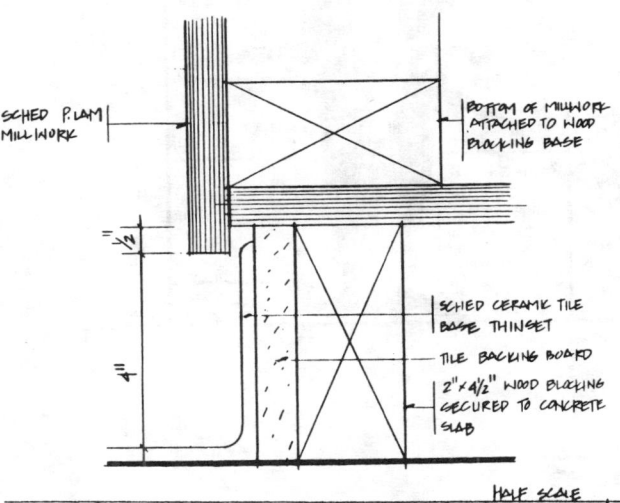

SCHED P.LAM
MILLWORK

BOTTOM OF MILLWORK
ATTACHED TO WOOD
BLOCKING BASE

SCHED CERAMIC TILE
BASE THINSET

TILE BACKING BOARD

2" x 4½" WOOD BLOCKING
SECURED TO CONCRETE
SLAB

HALF SCALE

__TYPICAL BASE DETAIL @ SERVERY MILLWORK__ | 10

BARS

Bar Section Details

The distance between bar and backbar should allow adequate workspace. A minimum of 36 in, or 90 cm, should provide space for one bartender to serve and another to circulate behind. Maximum body depth and maximum body breadth are the primary anthropometric considerations in establishing clearance. A one-bartender operation would require a 30-in, or 75-cm, clearance.

In regard to bar stools, clearance between the stool seats is more critical than center line spacing, and it should allow patrons of larger body size a comfortable side approach and departure from the stool without body contact with the next person. A 12-in, or 30-cm wide stool on 24-in, or 61-cm, centers, which is quite common, will allow only less than 5 percent of male users access to the stool without disturbing the next patron, while a 30-in, or 75-cm, spacing will accommodate 95 percent of the users. The tradeoff however, would be the loss of two seats for every 120 in, or 300 cm, of bar length. A spacing of 12-in stools on 28-in, or 70-cm, centers is suggested as a compromise. The ultimate decision is an individual one and must reconcile human factors with economic viability.

	in	cm
A	54	137.2
B	18–24	45.7–61.0
C	24	61.0
D	30	76.2
E	16–18	40.6–45.7
F	24–30	61.0–76.2
G	30–36	76.2–91.4
H	28–38	71.1–96.5
I	100–128	254.0–325.1
J	42–45	106.7–114.3
K	11–12	27.9–30.5
L	6–7	15.2–17.8
M	7–9	17.8–22.9
N	6–9	15.2–22.9
O	22–26	55.9–66.0
P	60–69	152.4–175.3
Q	36–42	91.4–106.7

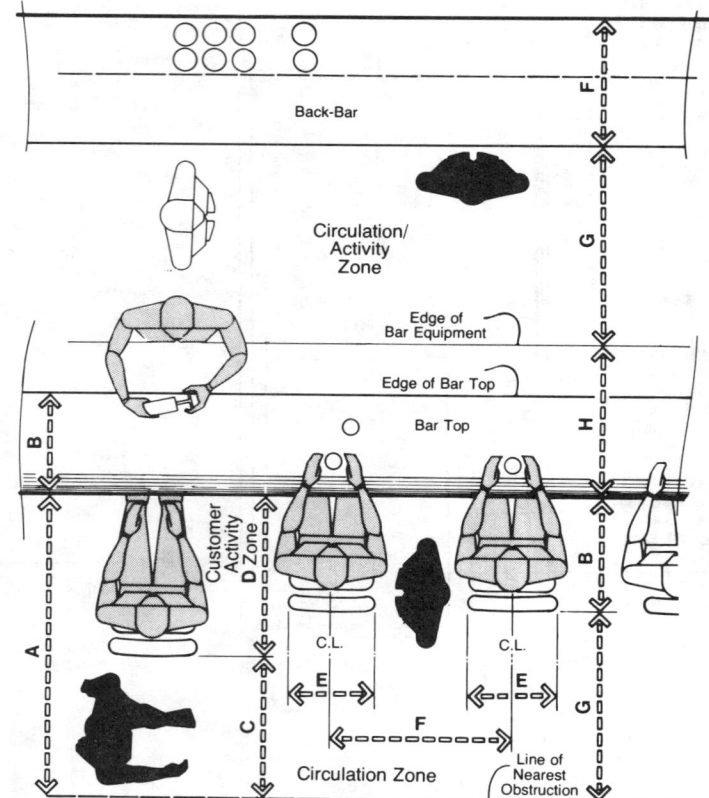

BAR AND BACK-BAR

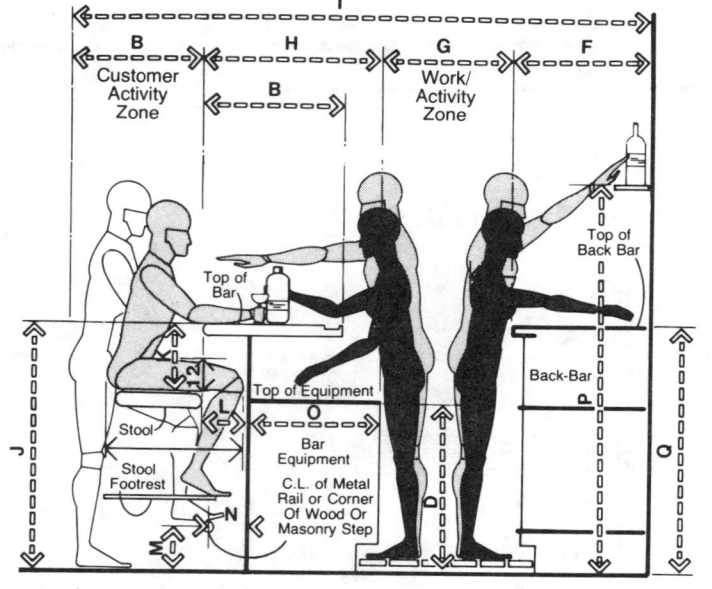

BAR / SECTION

Fig. 1

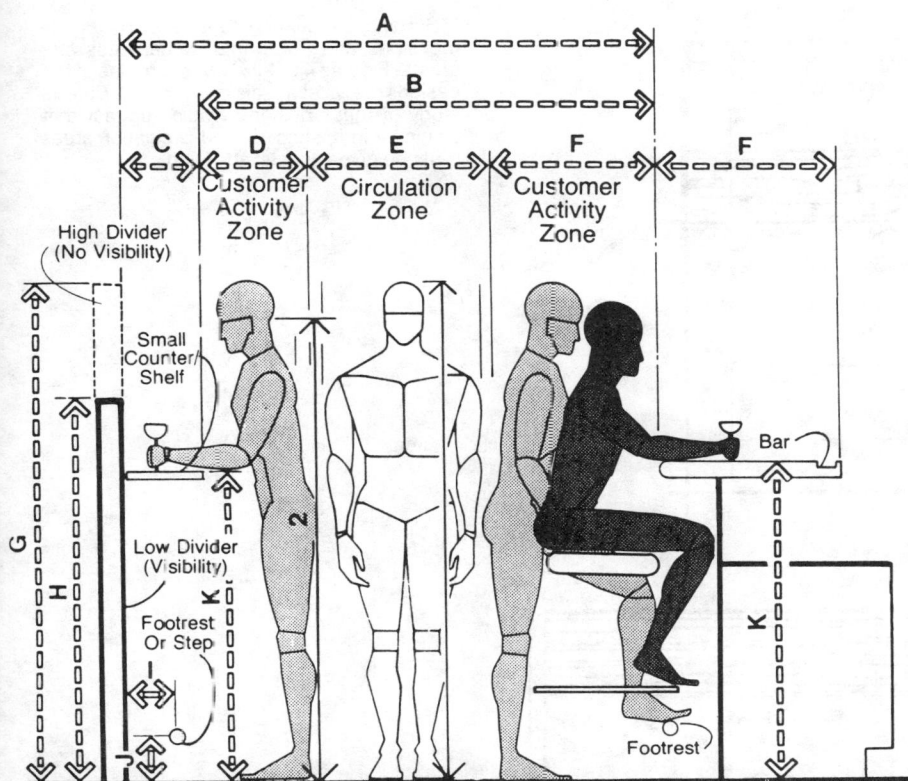

Fig. 2 Bar/clearances public side.

To ensure proper circulation and interface, adequate clearances in front of the bar are illustrated in Fig. 2. A customer activity zone of 18 to 24 in, or 45.7 to 61.0 cm, should be provided to allow for seating, standing, and access, in addition to a general circulation zone of at least 30 in, or 76.2 cm. If a supplementary drinking surface or shelf is provided, a smaller activity zone of 18 in is suggested in front of the shelf. The shelf can be 10 to 12 in, or 25.4 to 30.5 cm, deep. Figure 3 shows suggested clearances for 18 or 24 in cocktail tables.

	in	cm
A	76–84	193.0–213.4
B	66–72	167.6–182.9
C	10–12	25.4–30.5
D	18	45.7
E	30	76.2
F	18–24	45.7–61.0
G	76	193.0
H	54–56	137.2–142.2
I	6–9	15.2–22.9
J	7–9	17.8–22.9
K	42–45	106.7–114.3
L	24	61.0
M	29–33	73.7–83.8
N	32–36	81.3–91.4

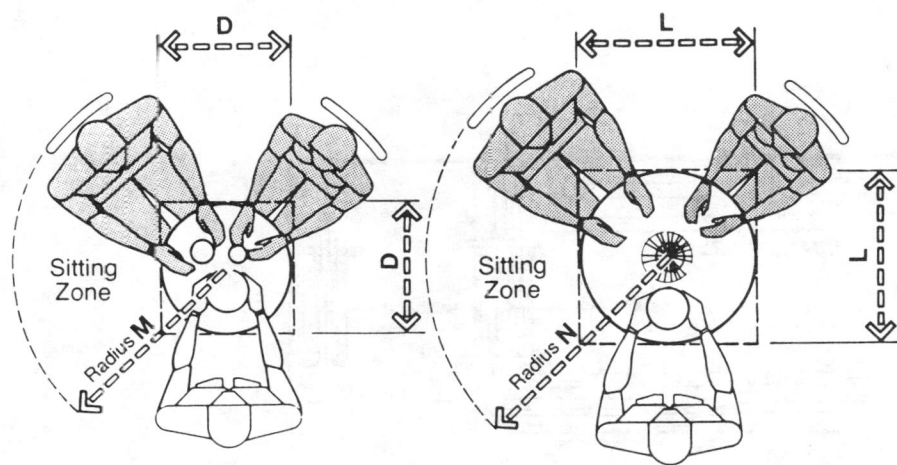

Fig. 3 Cocktail tables/seating for two.

BARS

Bar Shapes: Planning Criteria

Bar shapes, seating capacities, overall dimensions, and "footprints" of bar areas vary greatly. Figures 4 to 22 show examples of bar designs drawn at a scale of ¼" = 1'0". Careful study of these designs would suggest that seating width, spacing, and circulation areas must be given special attention.

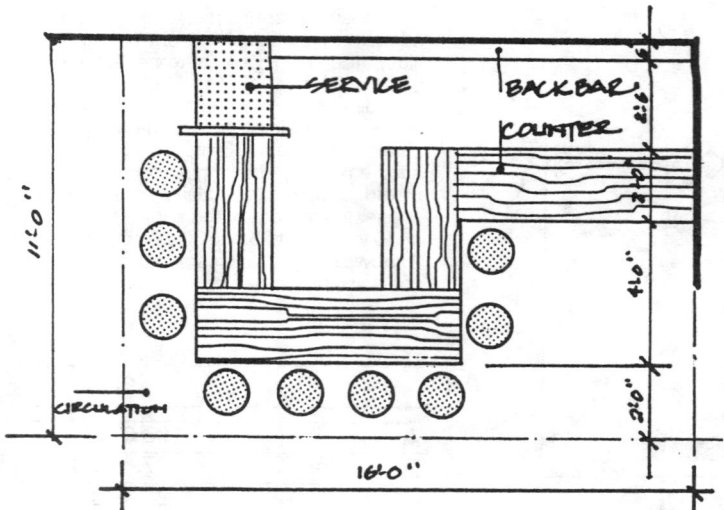

Fig. 4 U shape: 16 ft × 11 ft, 176 ft², seats 9.

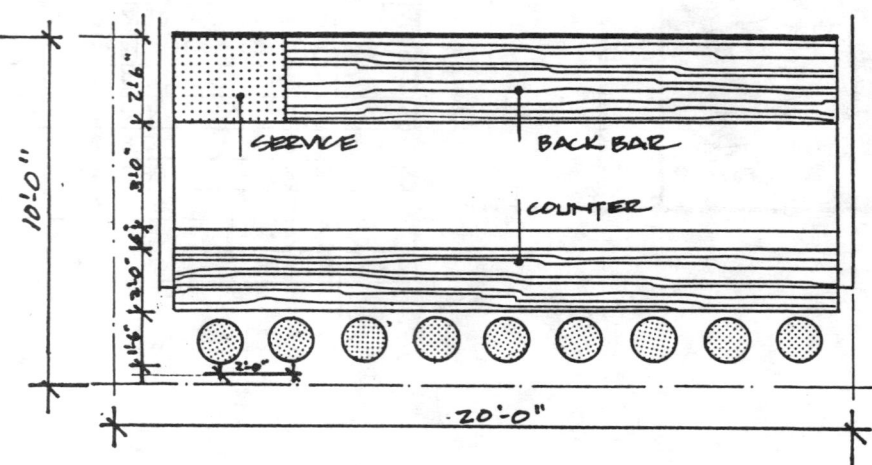

Fig. 5 Straight/enclosed: 20 ft × 10 ft, 200 ft², seats 9.

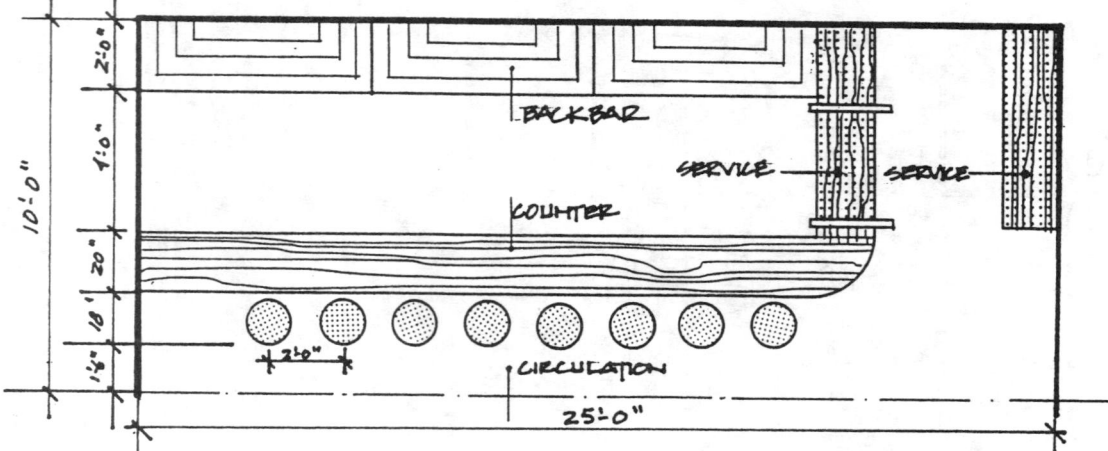

Fig. 6 Straight bar: 25 ft × 10 ft, 250 ft², seats 8.

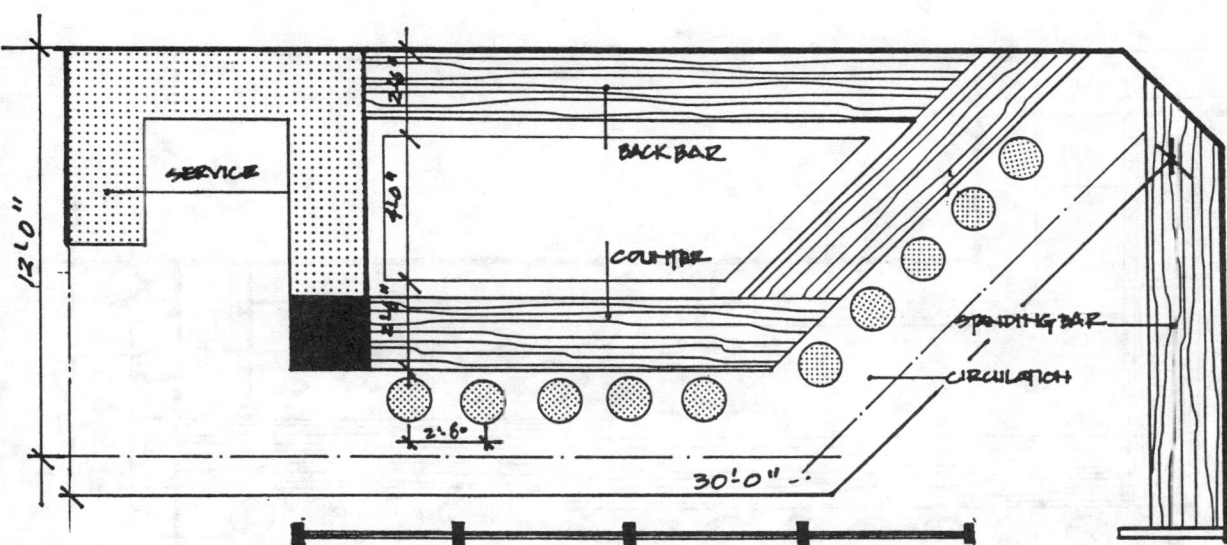

Fig. 7 Angular: 30 ft × 12 ft, 320 ft², seats 10.

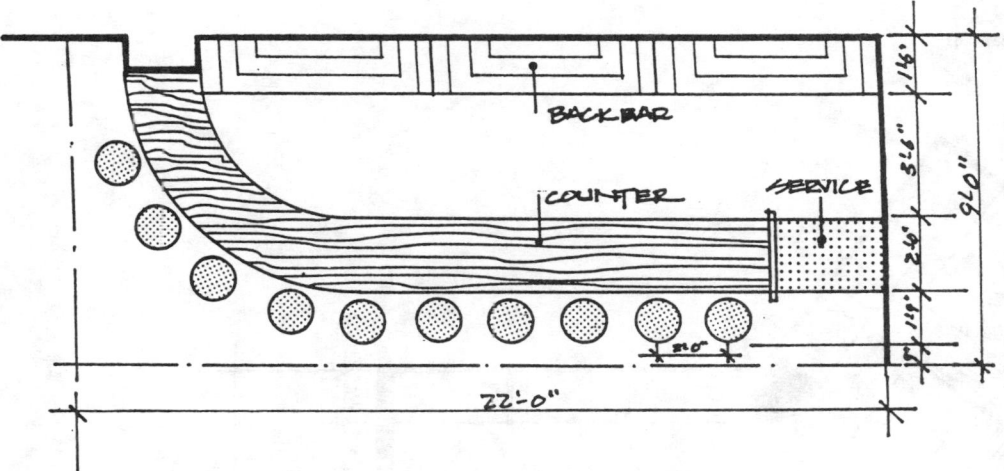

Fig. 8 Enclosed/rounded end: 22 ft × 9 ft, 198 ft², seats 10.

BARS

Bar Shapes: Planning Criteria

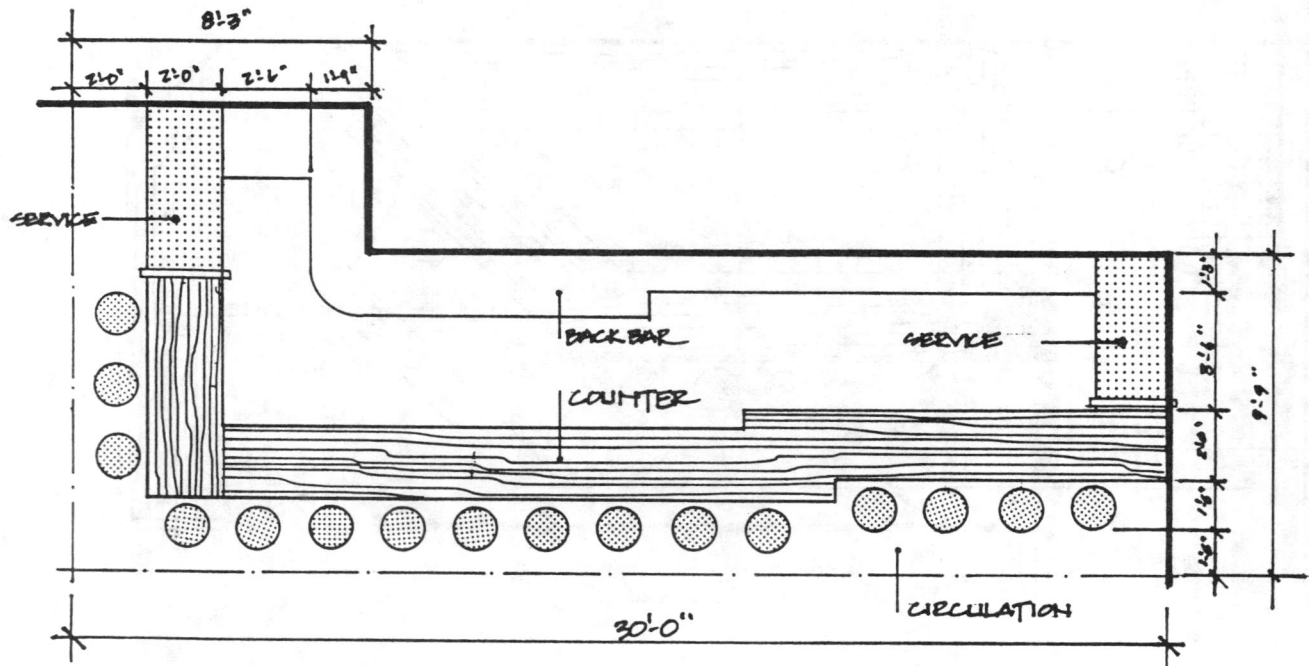

Fig. 9 L shape: 30 ft × 13 ft, 390 ft², seats 15.

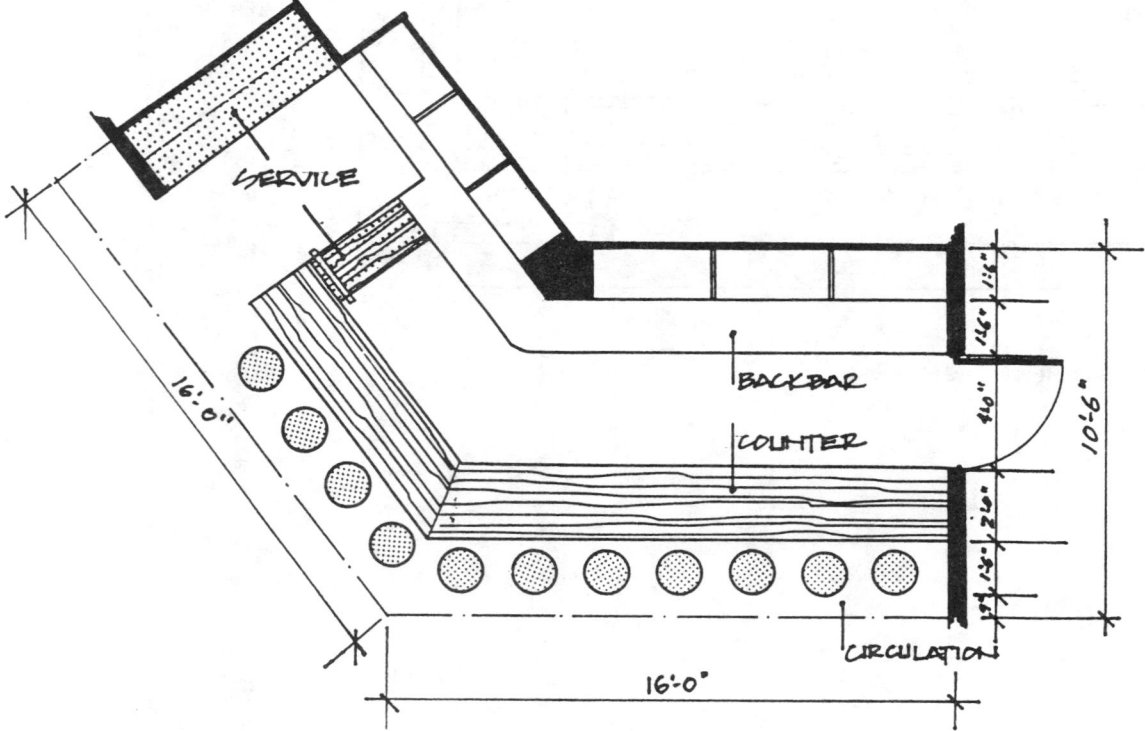

Fig. 10 Angular: 16 ft × 16 ft, 256 ft², seats 11.

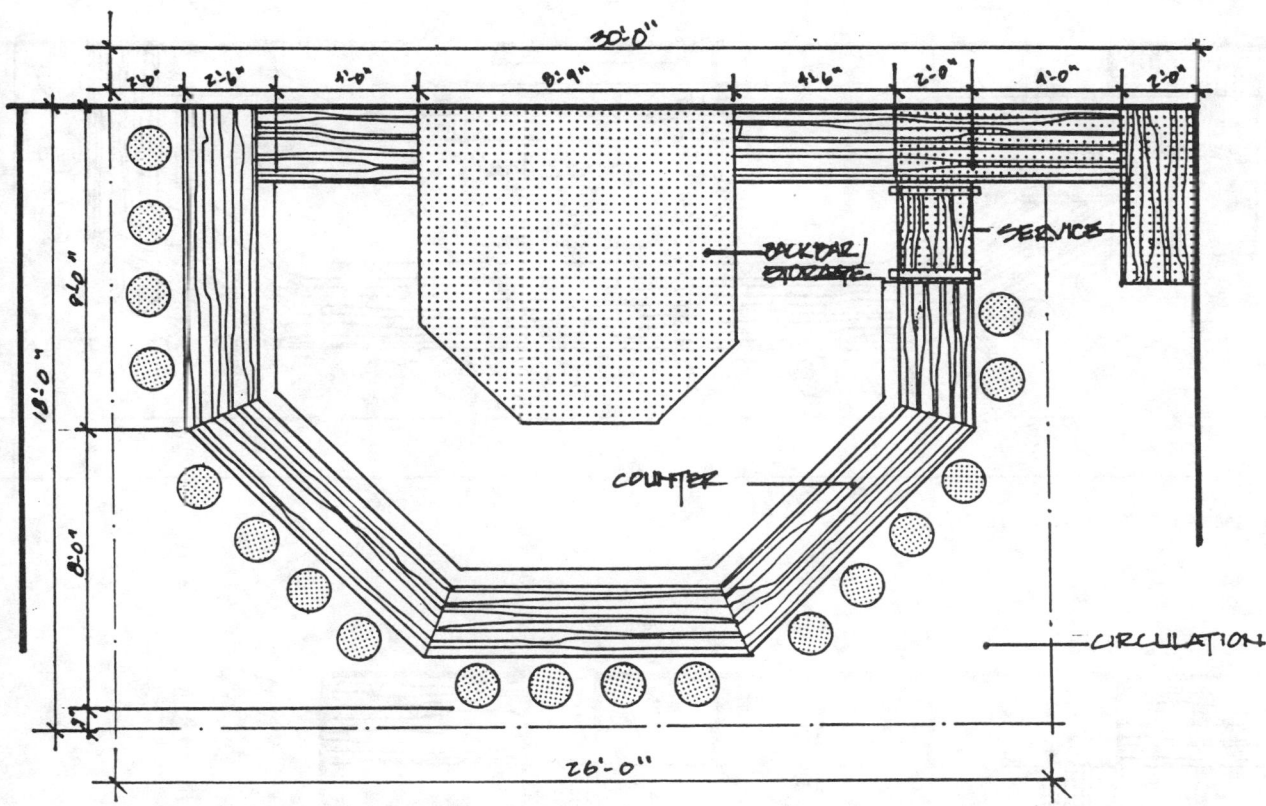

Fig. 11 Octagon/partial: 26 ft × 18 ft, 468 ft², seats 16.

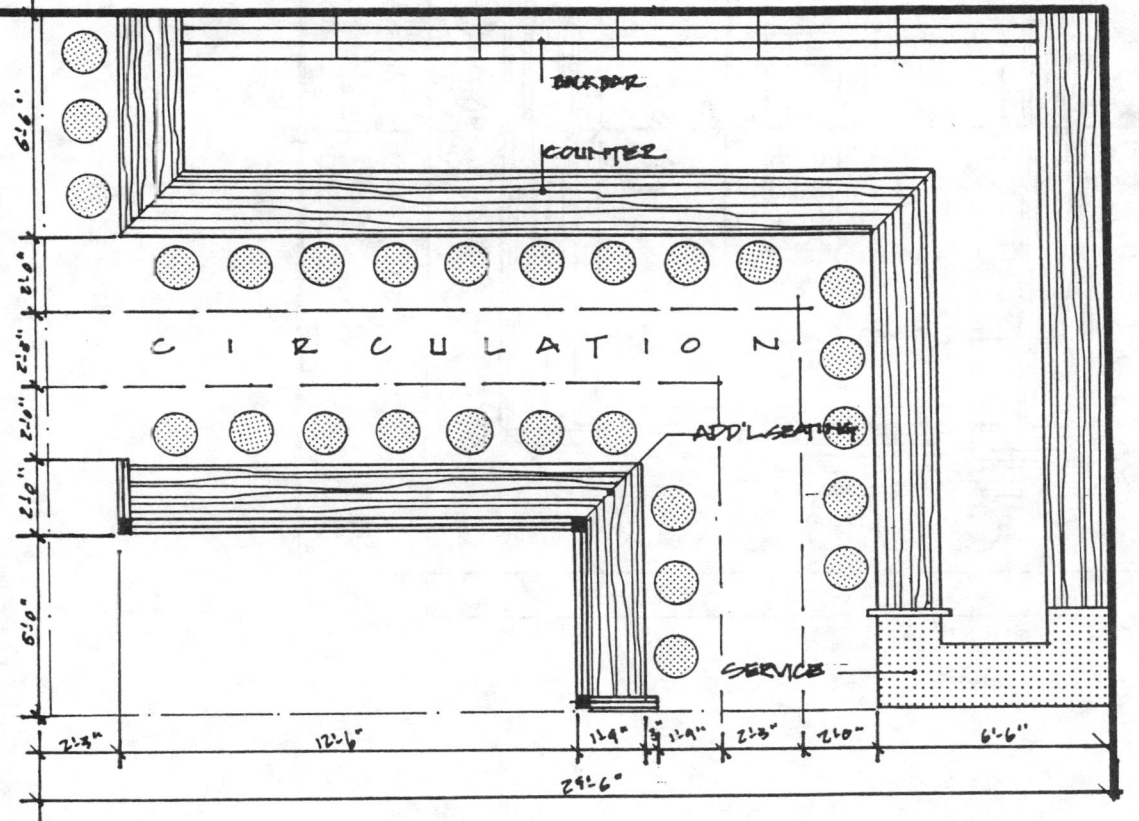

Fig. 12 L shape: 27 ft × 20 ft, 510 ft². Bar seating, 17; additional seating, 10.

BARS

Bar Shapes: Planning Criteria

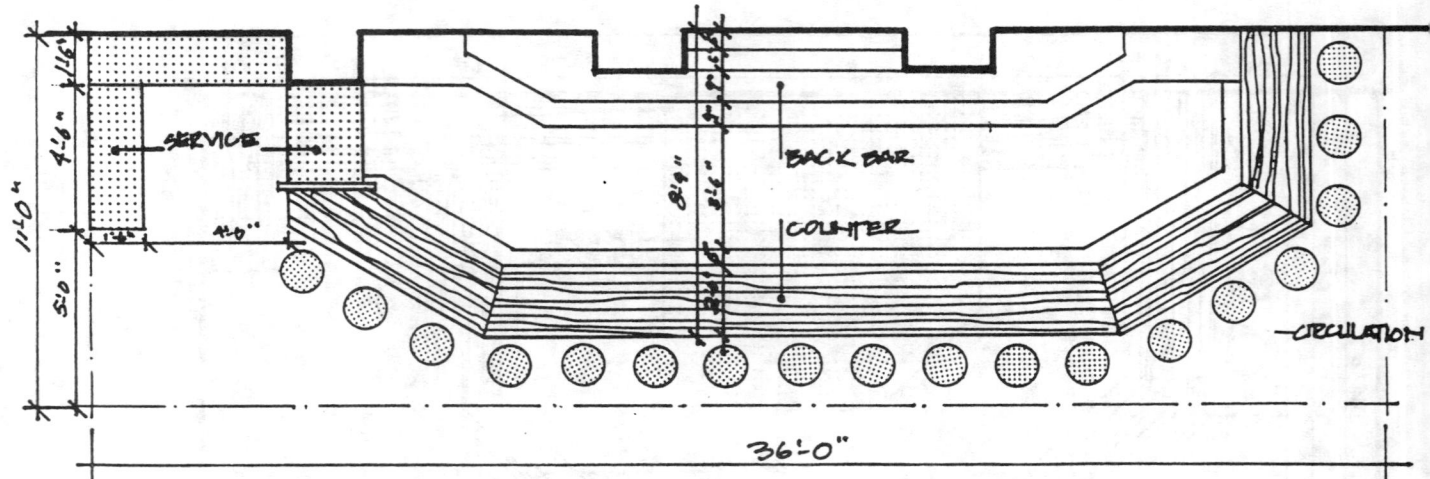

Fig. 13   Polygon: 36 ft × 11 ft, 396 ft², seats 18.

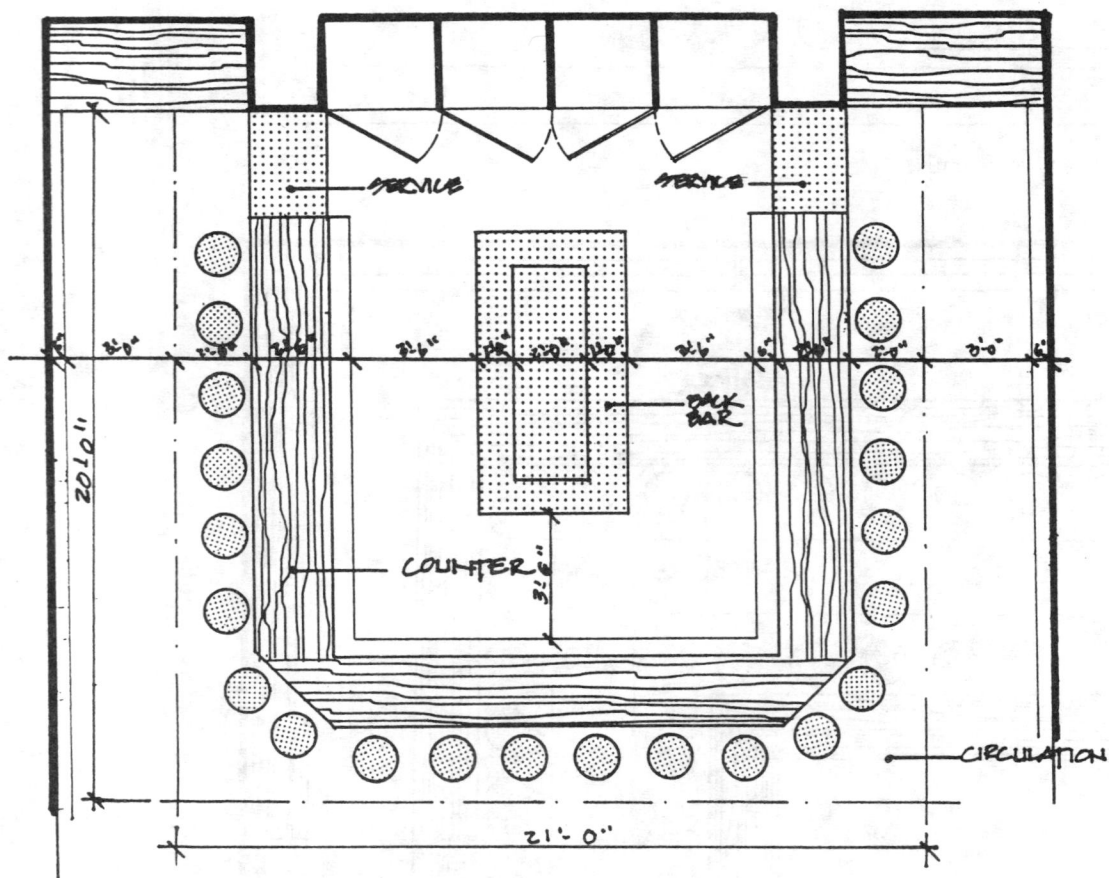

Fig. 14   U shape: 21 ft × 20 ft, 420 ft², seats 22.

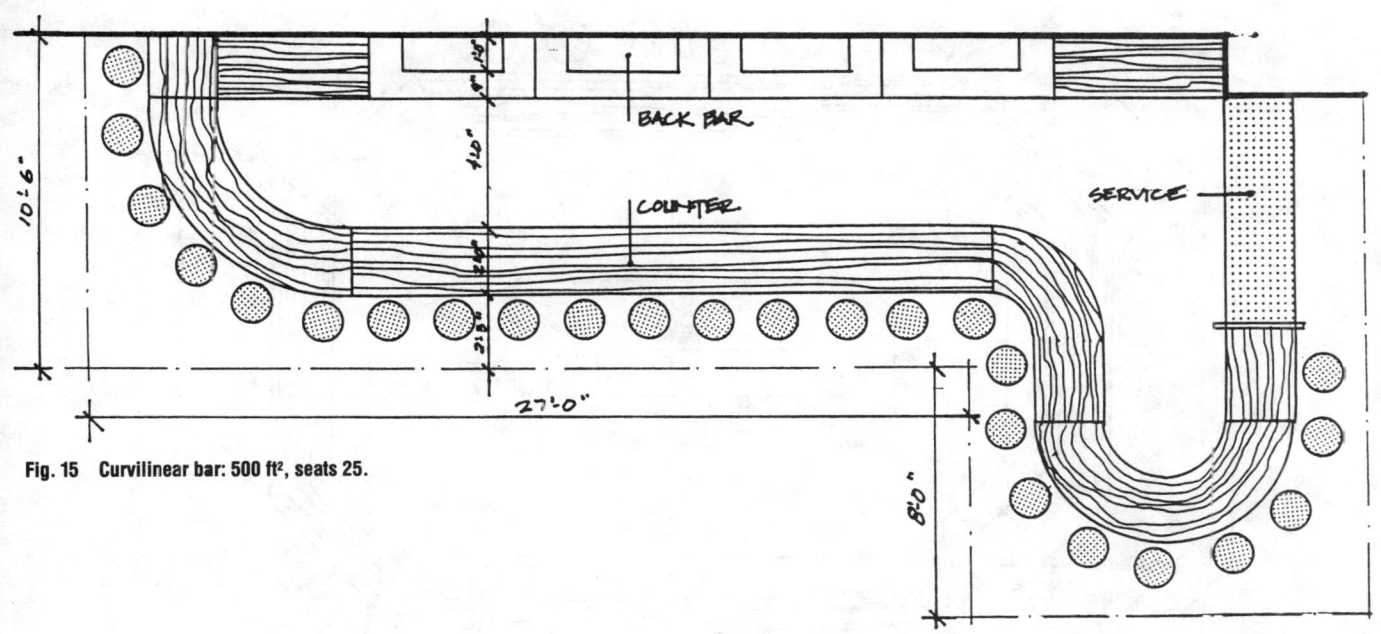

Fig. 15 Curvilinear bar: 500 ft², seats 25.

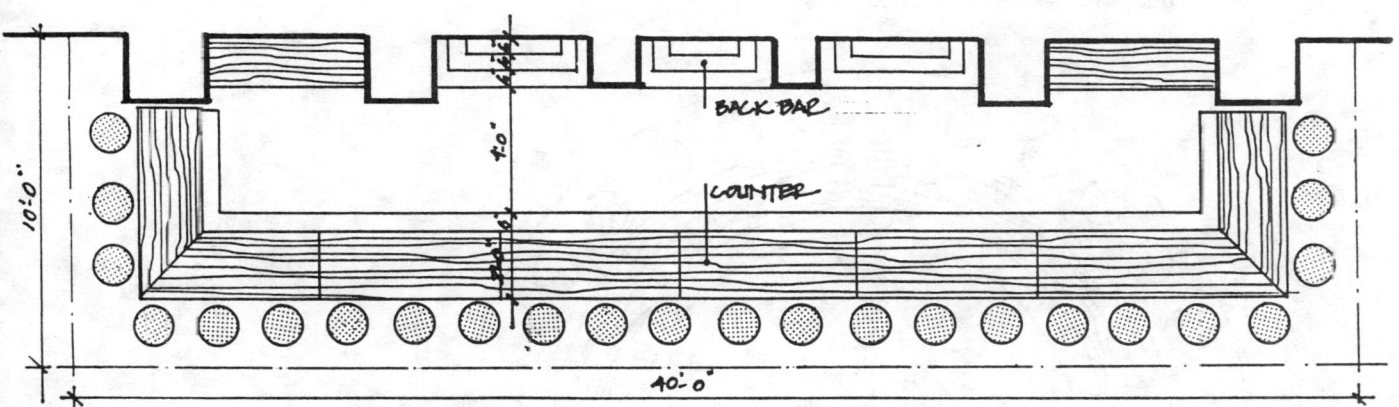

Fig. 16 Straight bar: 40 ft × 10 ft, 400 ft², seats 24.

BARS

Bar Shapes: Planning Criteria

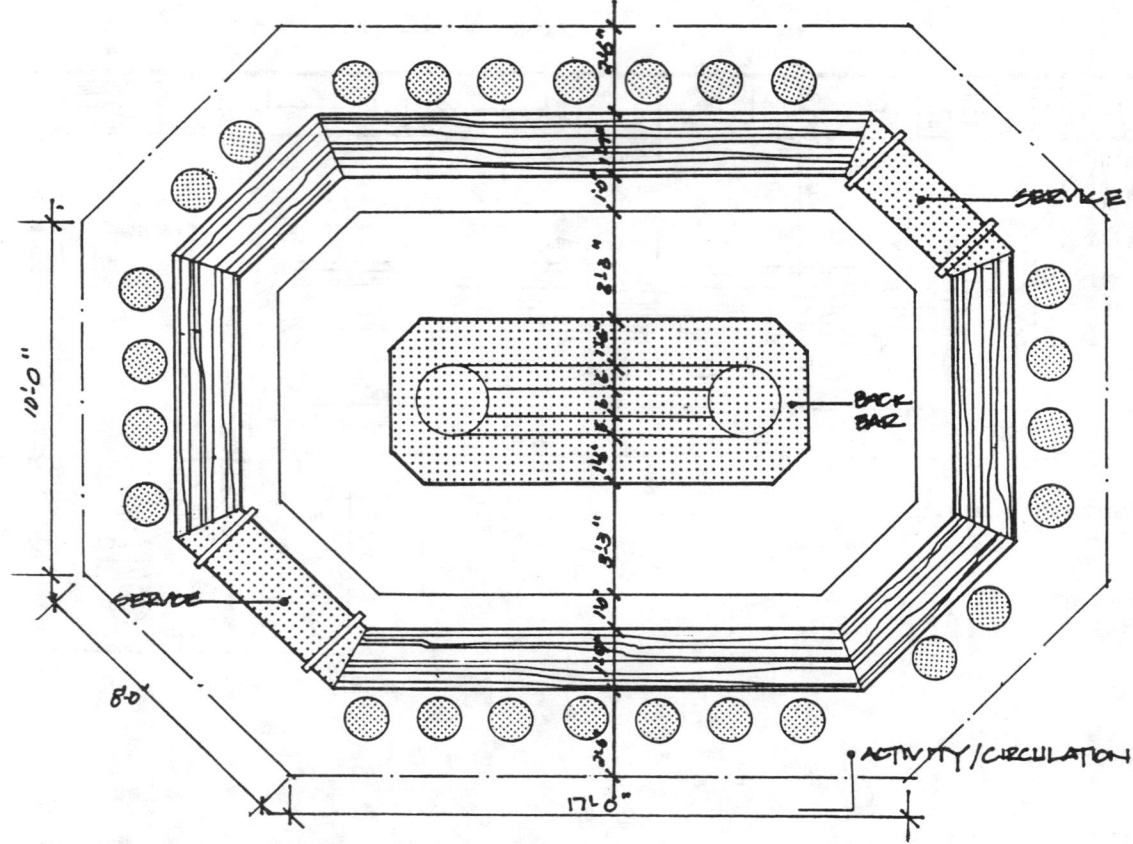

Fig. 17 Octagon/freestanding: 28 ft × 21 ft, 558 ft².

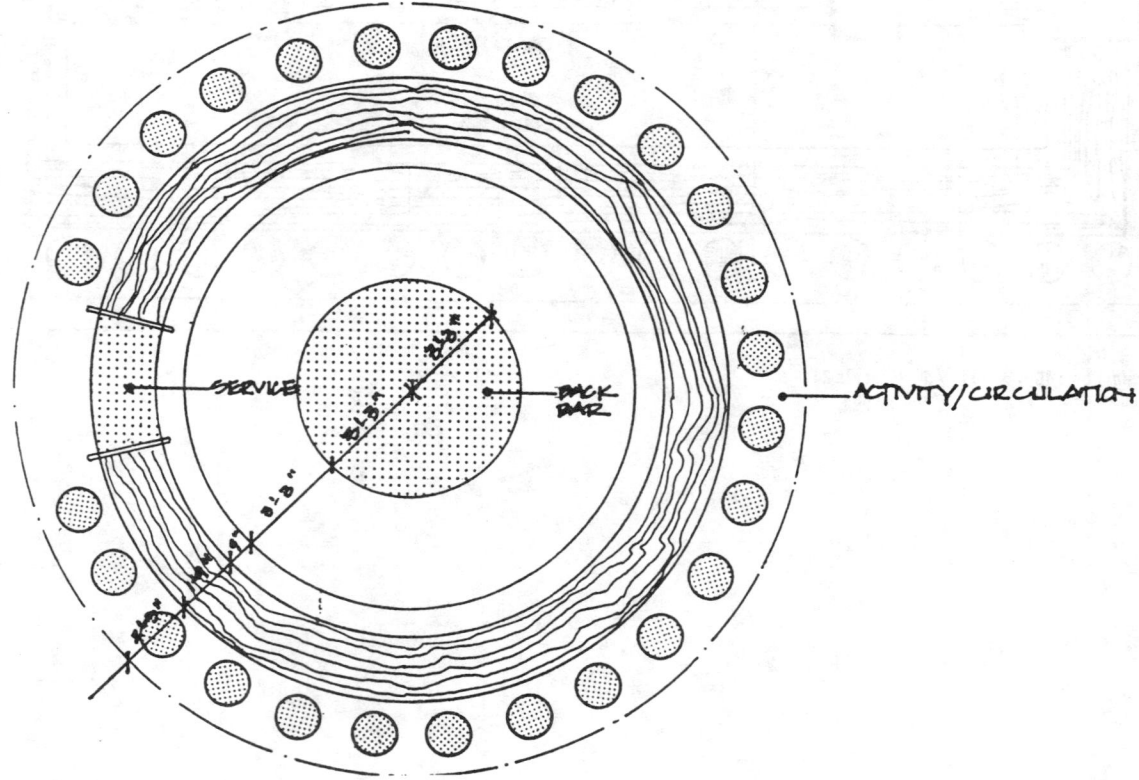

Fig. 18 Circular/freestanding: 22 ft × 22 ft, 334 ft², seats 26.

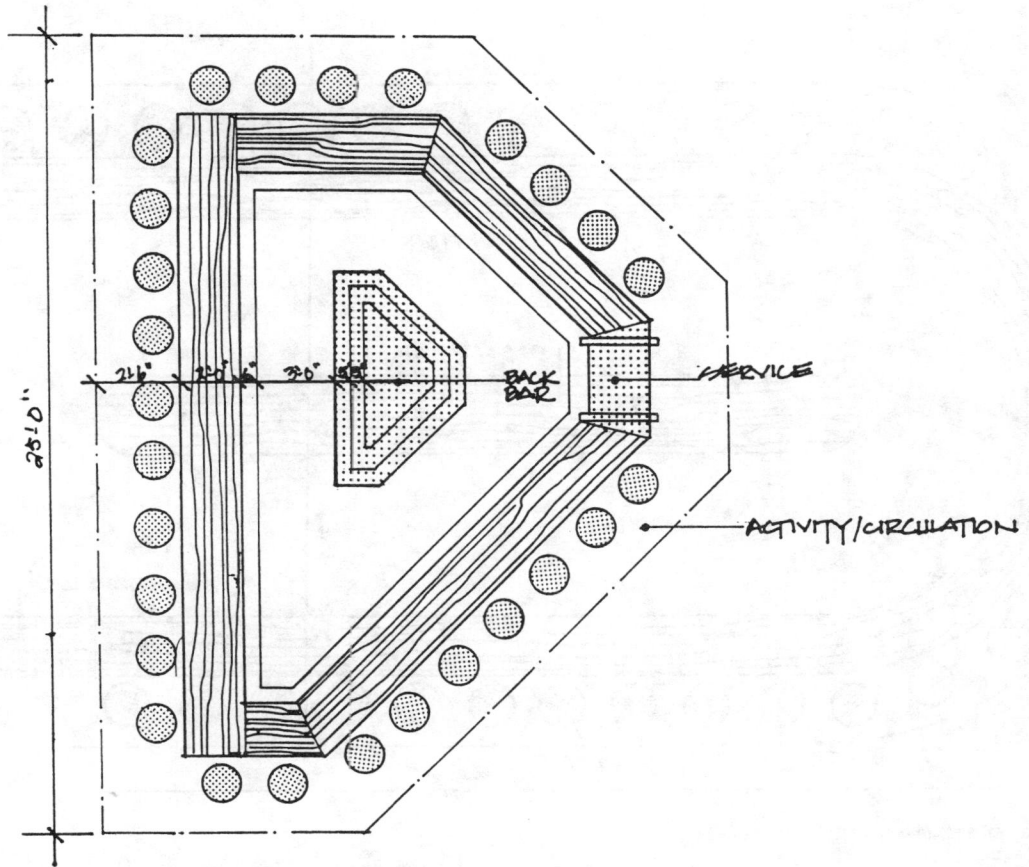

Fig. 19 Polygon irregular: 20 ft × 25 ft, 360 ft², seats 27.

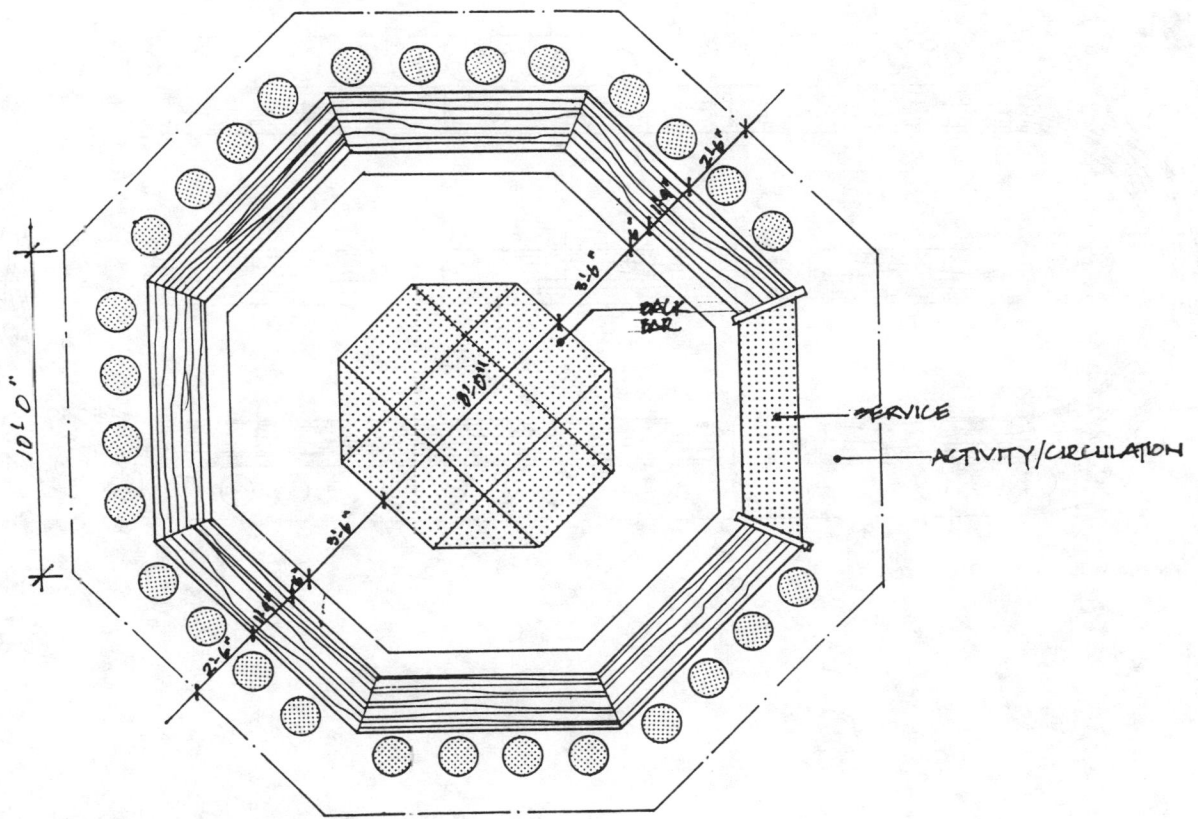

Fig. 20 Octagon: 25 ft × 25 ft, 429 ft², seats 28.

BARS
Bar Shapes: Planning Criteria

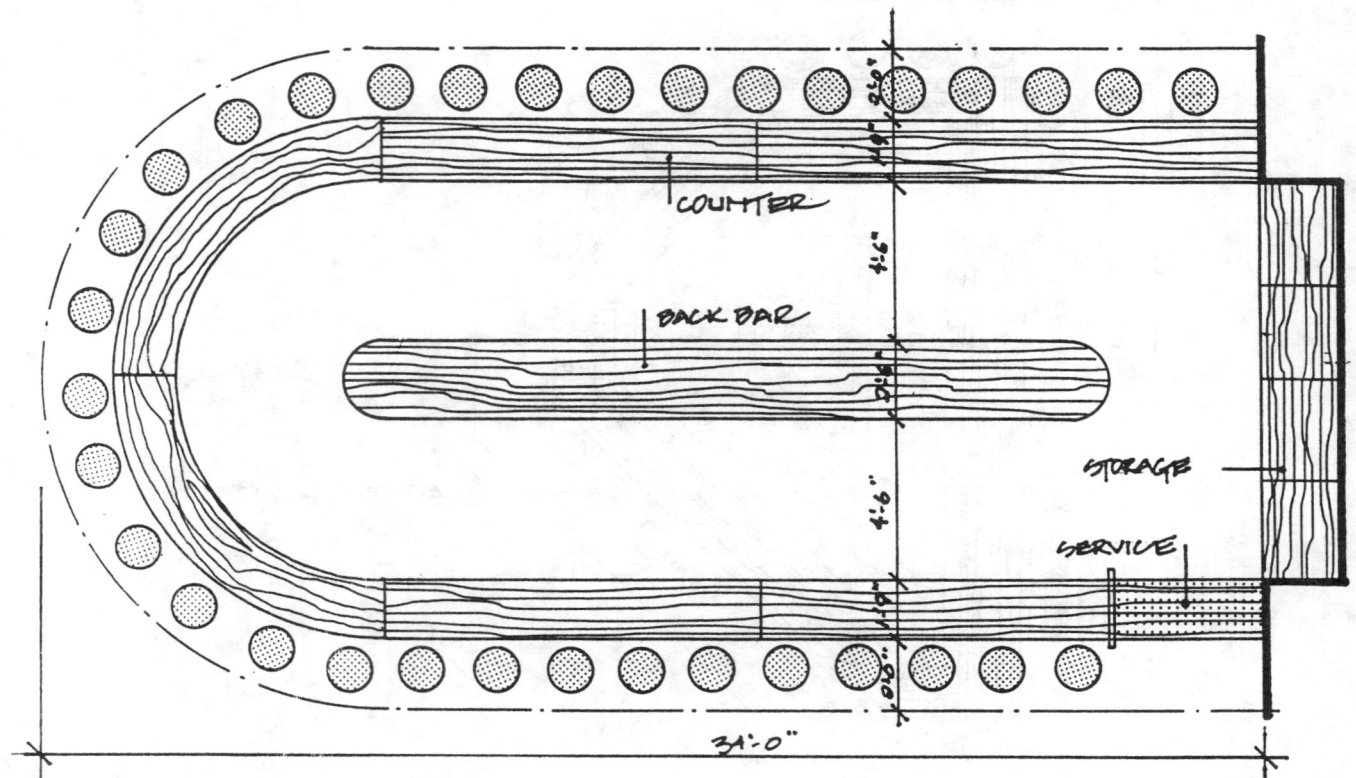

COUNTER

BACK BAR

STORAGE

SERVICE

Fig. 21   Horseshoe/oval end: 34 ft × 19 ft, 546 ft², seats 34.

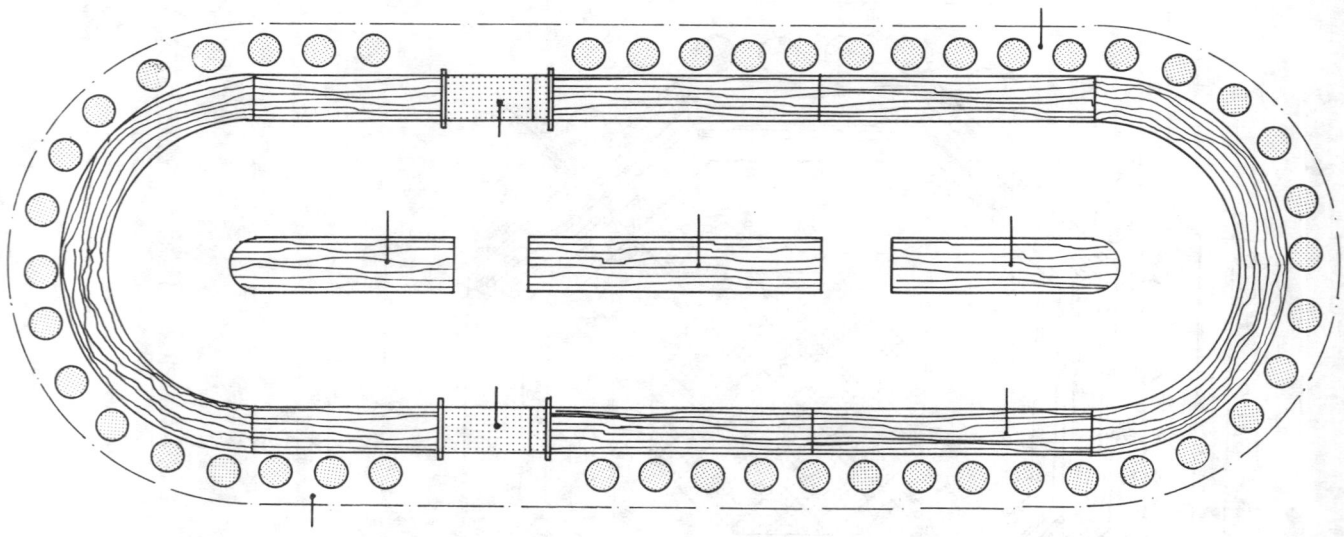

Fig. 22   Racetrack: 50 ft × 19 ft, 750 ft², seats 48.

The detailing of bars and backbars can vary from the very simple and basic to the complicated and intricate. Figures 23 to 40 provide the designer with selected examples of working drawings from some of the most experienced restaurant and hospitality design firms in the world. Careful review of these drawings would suggest that overall dimensions and clearances vary from detail to detail. In that regard, individual requirements based upon bar type and the hospitality area serviced must be given careful consideration. In addition, local building codes and health codes must be consulted.

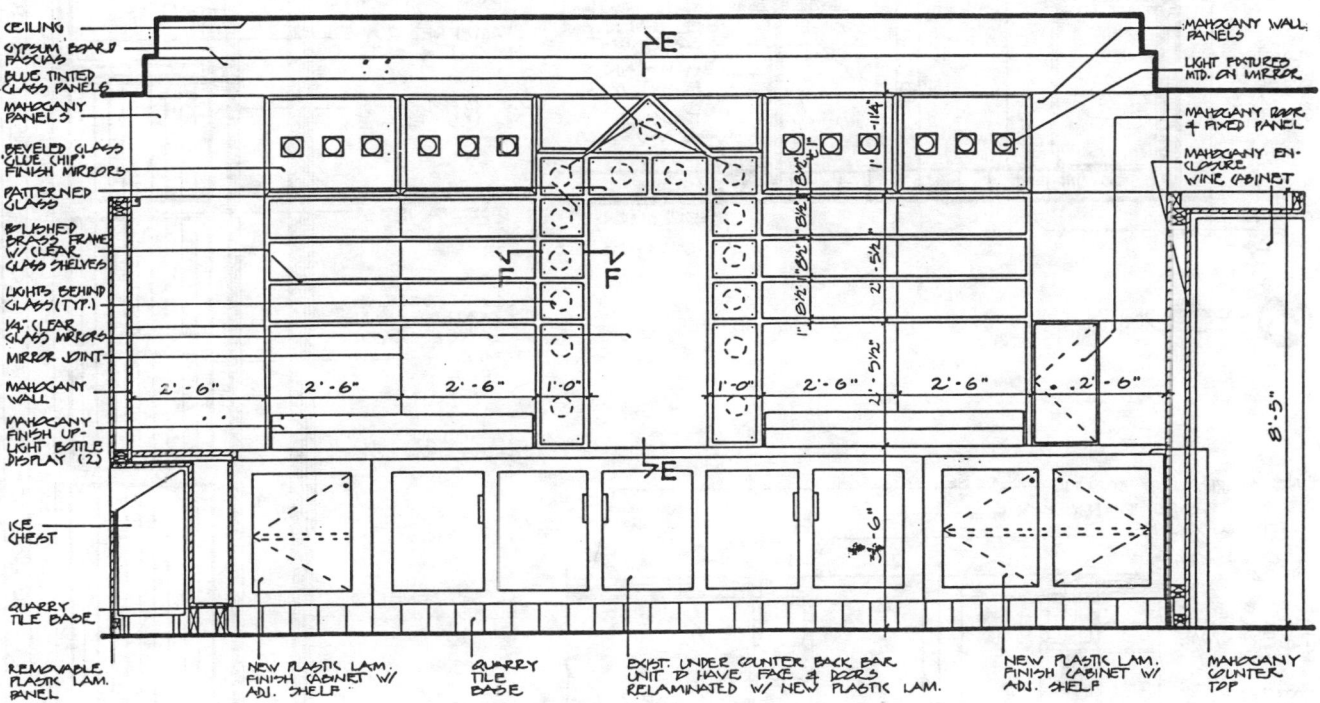

B ELEVATION

Fig. 23

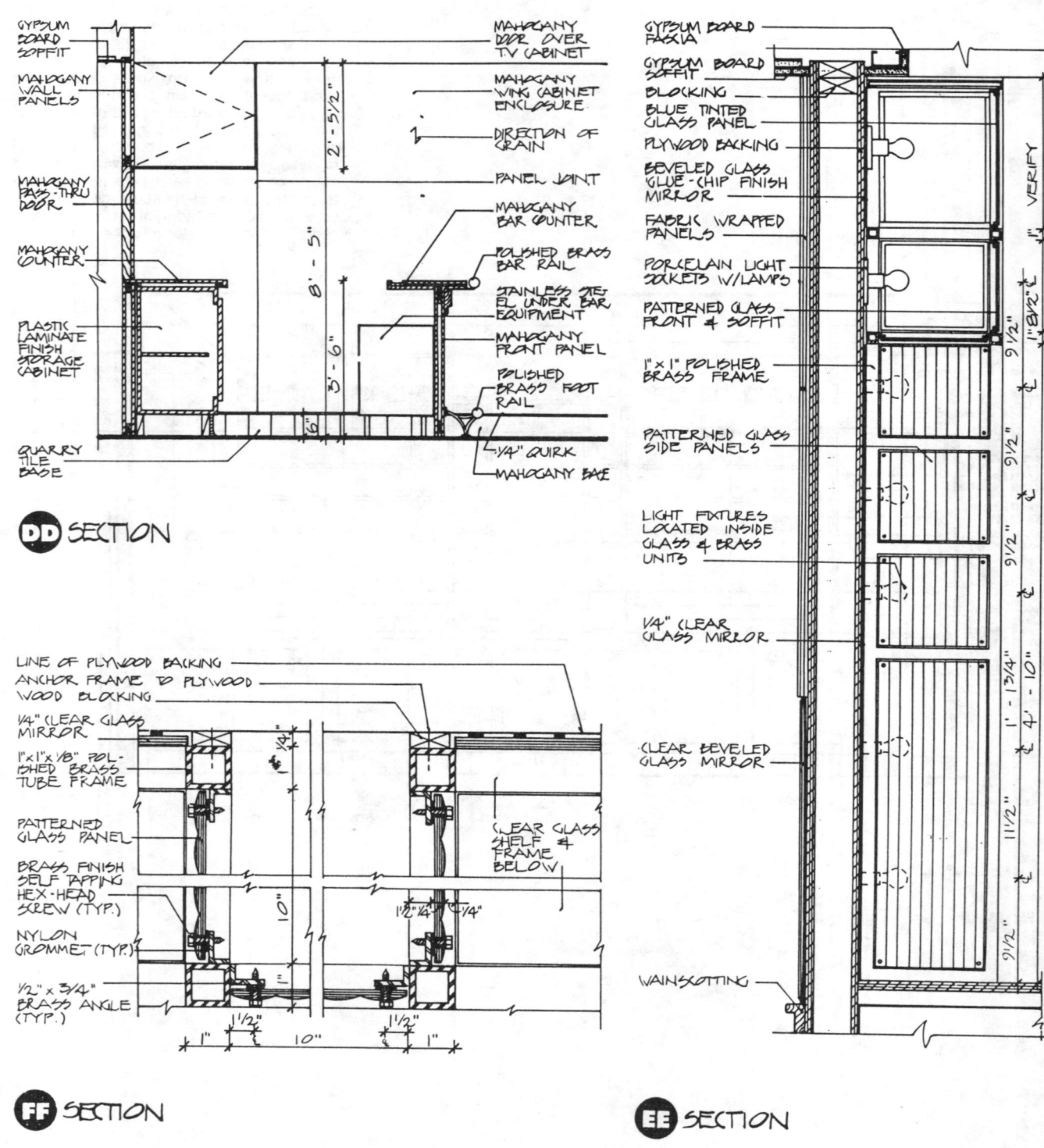

GYPSUM
BOARD
SOFFIT

MAHOGANY
WALL
PANELS

MAHOGANY
PASS-THRU
DOOR

MAHOGANY
COUNTER

PLASTIC
LAMINATE
FINISH
STORAGE
CABINET

QUARRY
TILE
BASE

MAHOGANY
DOOR OVER
T.V. CABINET

MAHOGANY
WING CABINET
ENCLOSURE

DIRECTION OF
GRAIN

PANEL JOINT

MAHOGANY
BAR COUNTER

POLISHED BRASS
BAR RAIL

STAINLESS STEEL UNDER BAR
EQUIPMENT

MAHOGANY
FRONT PANEL

POLISHED
BRASS FOOT
RAIL

1/4" QUIRK

MAHOGANY BASE

2'-5 1/2"

8'-5"

3'-6"

6"

DD SECTION

LINE OF PLYWOOD BACKING
ANCHOR FRAME TO PLYWOOD
WOOD BLOCKING

1/4" CLEAR GLASS
MIRROR

1"x1"x1/8" POLISHED BRASS
TUBE FRAME

PATTERNED
GLASS PANEL

BRASS FINISH
SELF TAPPING
HEX-HEAD
SCREW (TYP.)

NYLON
GROMMET (TYP.)

1/2" x 3/4"
BRASS ANGLE
(TYP.)

CLEAR GLASS
SHELF &
FRAME
BELOW

10"

1 1/2" 1/4" 1/4"

1" 1 1/2" 10" 1 1/2" 1"

FF SECTION

GYPSUM BOARD
FASCIA

GYPSUM BOARD
SOFFIT

BLOCKING

BLUE TINTED
GLASS PANEL

PLYWOOD BACKING

BEVELED GLASS
GLUE-CHIP FINISH
MIRROR

FABRIC WRAPPED
PANELS

PORCELAIN LIGHT
SOCKETS W/LAMPS

PATTERNED GLASS
FRONT & SOFFIT

1"x1" POLISHED
BRASS FRAME

PATTERNED GLASS
SIDE PANELS

LIGHT FIXTURES
LOCATED INSIDE
GLASS & BRASS
UNITS

1/4" CLEAR
GLASS MIRROR

CLEAR BEVELED
GLASS MIRROR

WAINSCOTTING

VERIFY

8 1/2"

9 1/2"

9 1/2"

9 1/2"

9 1/2"

11 1/2"

1'-13/4"

4'-10"

EE SECTION

Fig. 23 *(Continued)*

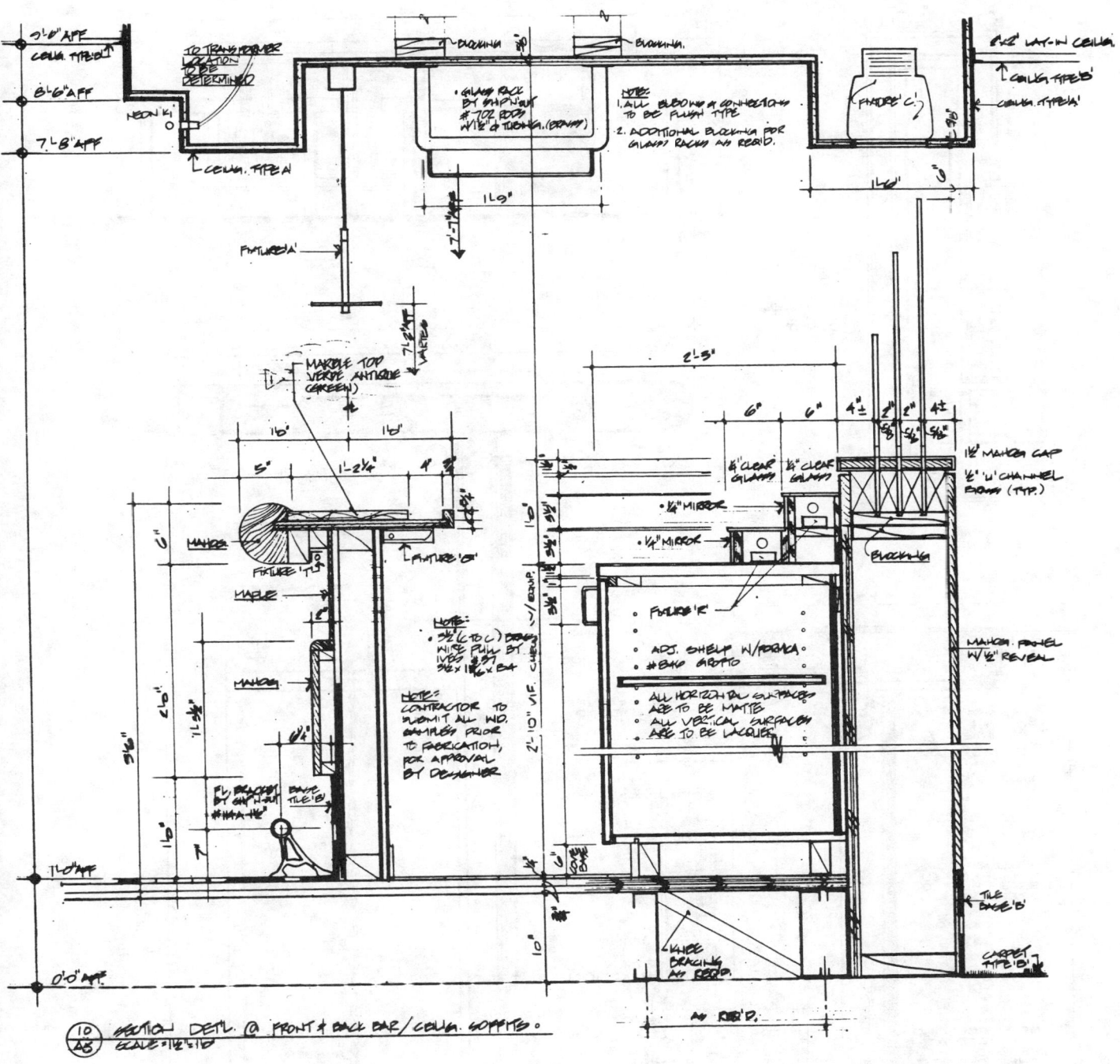

Fig. 24

BARS

Bar Plans, Elevations, and Sections

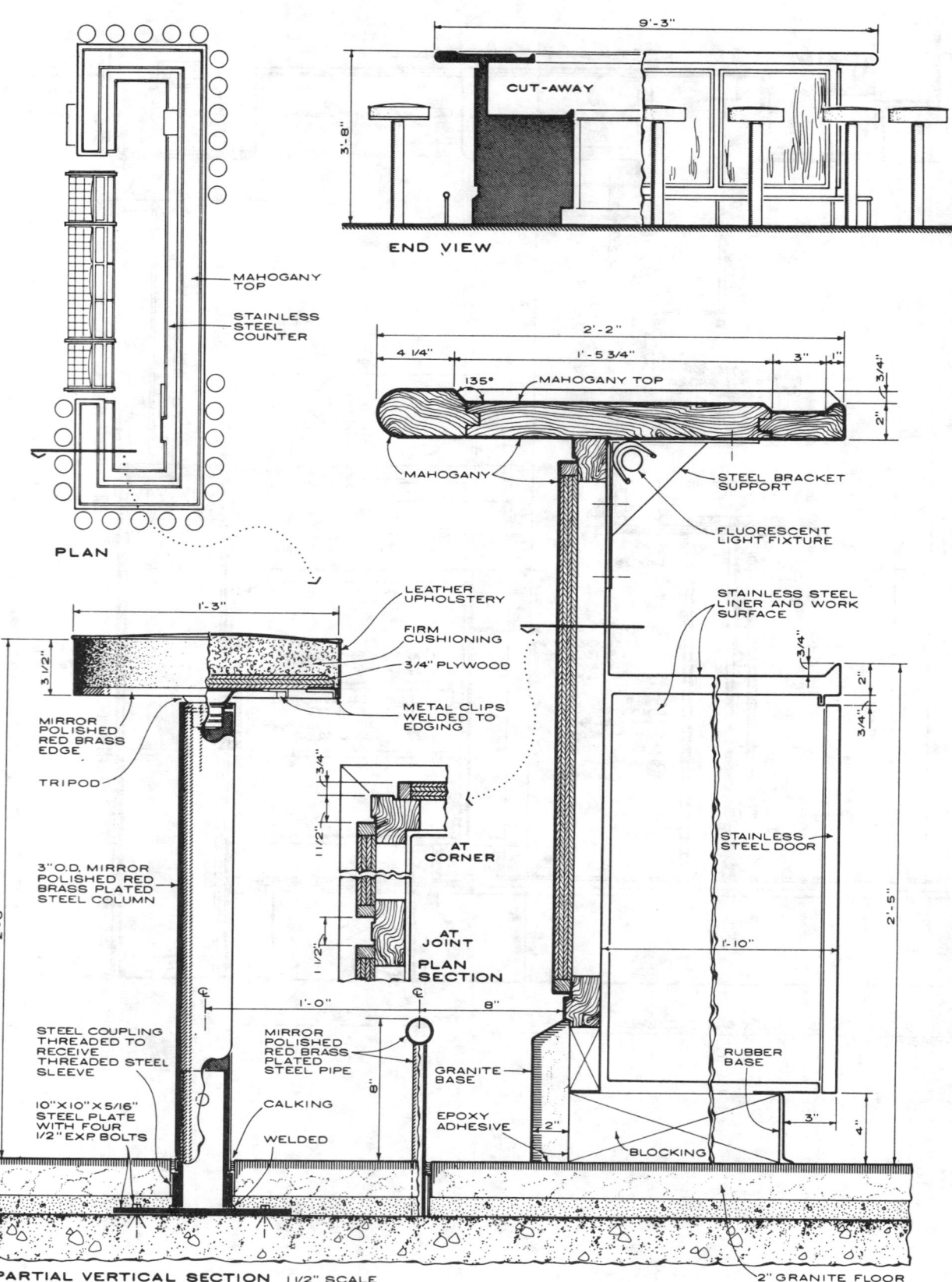

CUT-AWAY

9'-3"

3'-8"

END VIEW

MAHOGANY TOP

STAINLESS STEEL COUNTER

PLAN

2'-2"

4 1/4"   1'-5 3/4"   3"   1"

135°   MAHOGANY TOP

3/4"

2"

MAHOGANY

STEEL BRACKET SUPPORT

FLUORESCENT LIGHT FIXTURE

STAINLESS STEEL LINER AND WORK SURFACE

3/4"

2"

3/4"

LEATHER UPHOLSTERY

FIRM CUSHIONING

3/4" PLYWOOD

METAL CLIPS WELDED TO EDGING

1'-3"

3 1/2"

MIRROR POLISHED RED BRASS EDGE

TRIPOD

3/4"

1 1/2"

AT CORNER

1 1/2"

AT JOINT

PLAN SECTION

STAINLESS STEEL DOOR

2'-6"

3" O.D. MIRROR POLISHED RED BRASS PLATED STEEL COLUMN

1'-0"

8"

8"

1'-10"

2'-5"

STEEL COUPLING THREADED TO RECEIVE THREADED STEEL SLEEVE

MIRROR POLISHED RED BRASS PLATED STEEL PIPE

GRANITE BASE

RUBBER BASE

10"X10"X5/16" STEEL PLATE WITH FOUR 1/2" EXP BOLTS

CALKING

WELDED

EPOXY ADHESIVE

2"

BLOCKING

3"

4"

2" GRANITE FLOOR

PARTIAL VERTICAL SECTION 1 1/2" SCALE

Fig. 25

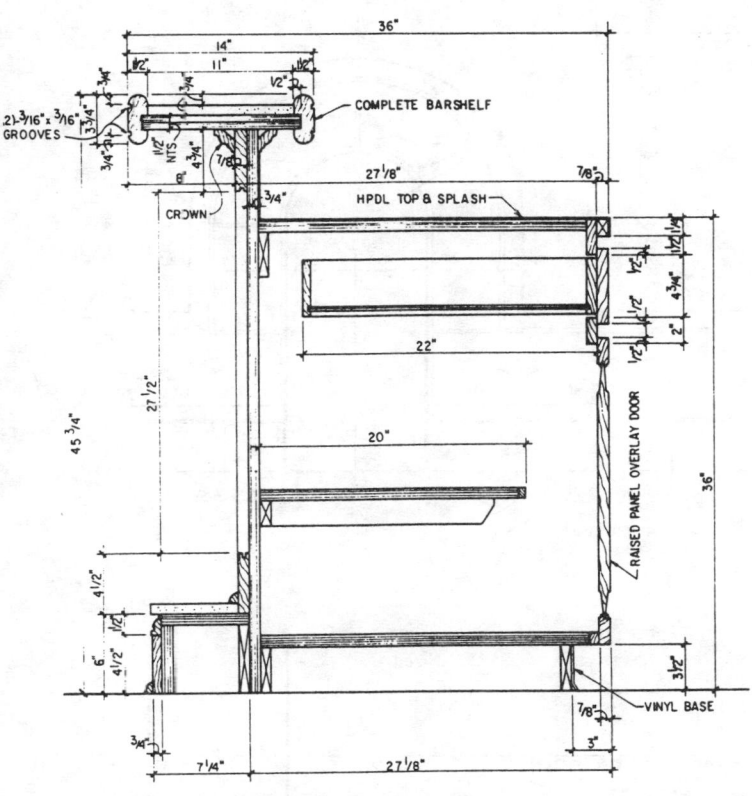

SECTION THRU BAR CABINET

Labels visible: COMPLETE BARSHELF, GROOVES, CROWN, HPDL TOP & SPLASH, RAISED PANEL OVERLAY DOOR, VINYL BASE

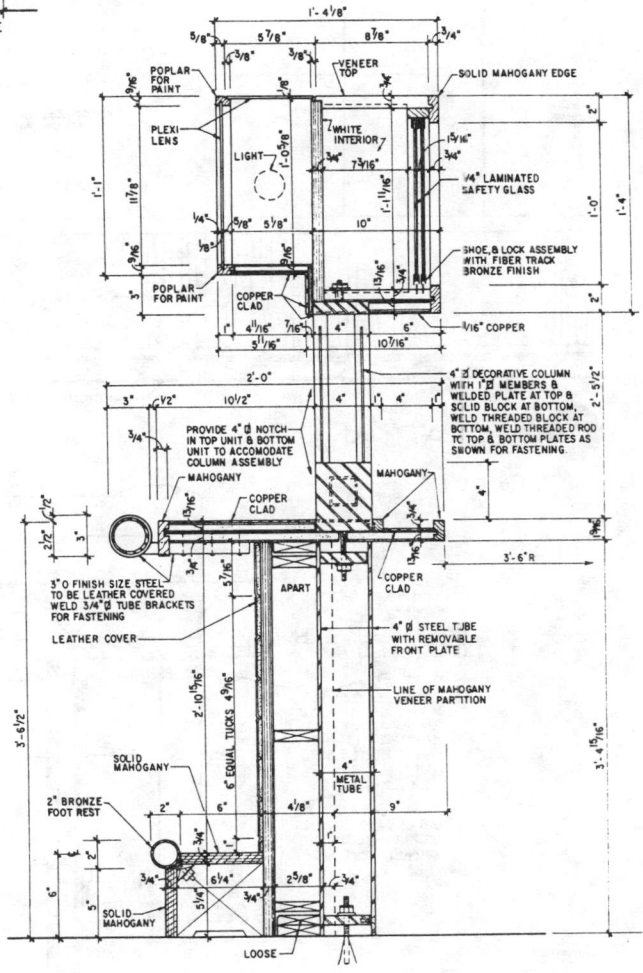

VERTICAL SECTION
AT METAL POST AND LIGHT BOX

Labels visible: POPLAR FOR PAINT, PLEXI LENS, LIGHT, WHITE INTERIOR, VENEER TOP, SOLID MAHOGANY EDGE, 1/4" LAMINATED SAFETY GLASS, SHOE & LOCK ASSEMBLY WITH FIBER TRACK BRONZE FINISH, 1/16" COPPER, COPPER CLAD, 4" Ø DECORATIVE COLUMN WITH 1" Ø MEMBERS & WELDED PLATE AT TOP & SOLID BLOCK AT BOTTOM, WELD THREADED BLOCK AT BOTTOM, WELD THREADED ROD TO TOP & BOTTOM PLATES AS SHOWN FOR FASTENING, PROVIDE 4" Ø NOTCH IN TOP UNIT & BOTTOM UNIT TO ACCOMODATE COLUMN ASSEMBLY, MAHOGANY, COPPER CLAD, 3" Ø FINISH SIZE STEEL TO BE LEATHER COVERED WELD 3/4" Ø TUBE BRACKETS FOR FASTENING, LEATHER COVER, 4" Ø STEEL TUBE WITH REMOVABLE FRONT PLATE, LINE OF MAHOGANY VENEER PARTITION, SOLID MAHOGANY, 2" BRONZE FOOT REST, 6 EQUAL TUCKS, METAL TUBE, SOLID MAHOGANY, APART, LOOSE

Fig. 26

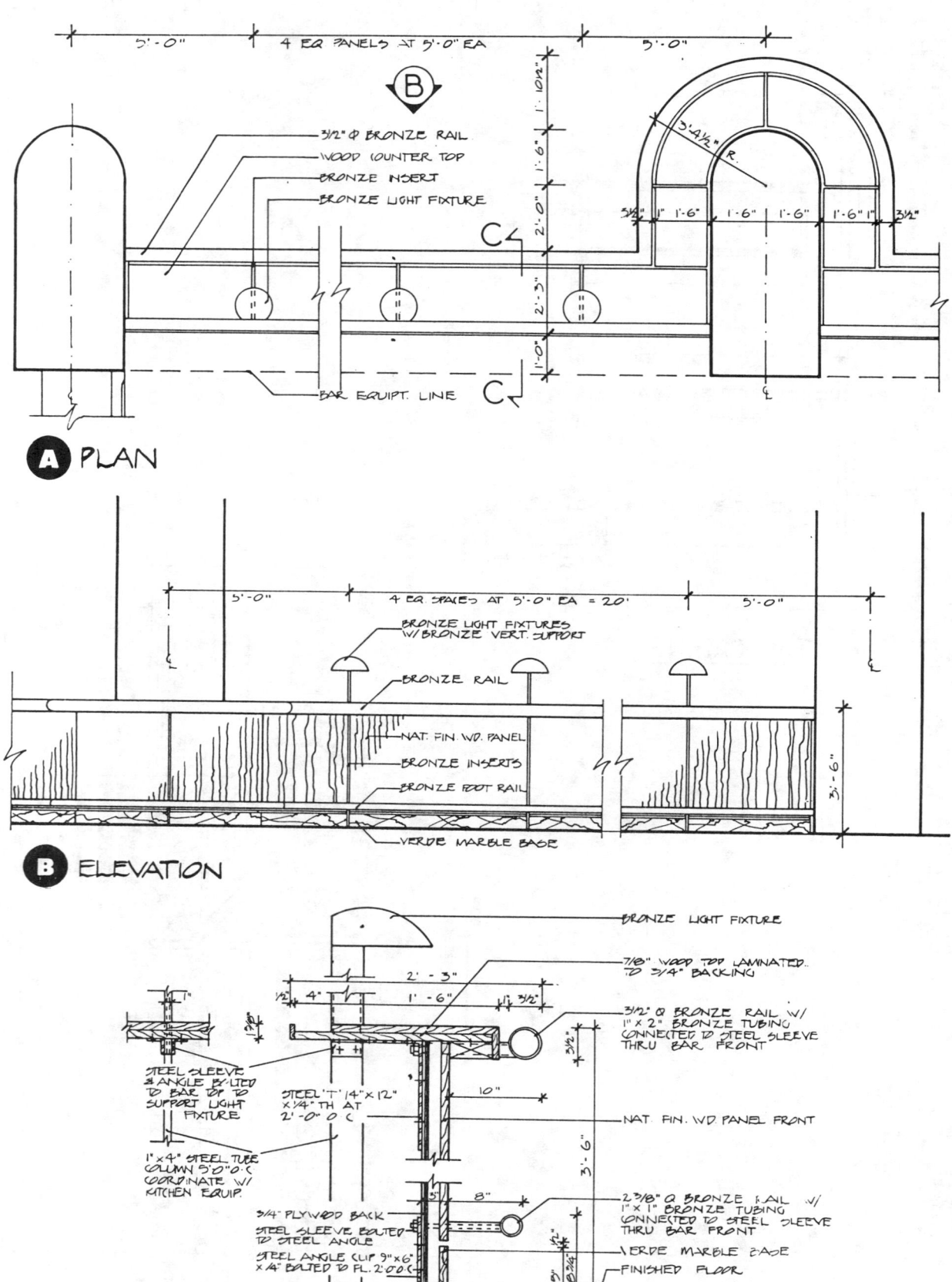

5'-0"   4 EQ. PANELS AT 5'-0" EA.   5'-0"

B

3½" Ø BRONZE RAIL
WOOD COUNTER TOP
BRONZE INSERT
BRONZE LIGHT FIXTURE

3'-4½" R.

5½" 1" 1'-6" 1'-6" 1'-6" 1'-6" 1" 3½"

1'-10½" 1'-6" 2'-0" 2'-3" 1'-0"

BAR EQUIPT. LINE

C

A PLAN

5'-0"   4 EQ. SPACES AT 5'-0" EA = 20'   5'-0"

BRONZE LIGHT FIXTURES
W/ BRONZE VERT. SUPPORT

BRONZE RAIL

NAT. FIN. WD. PANEL

BRONZE INSERTS

BRONZE FOOT RAIL

3'-6"

VERDE MARBLE BASE

B ELEVATION

BRONZE LIGHT FIXTURE

7/8" WOOD TOP LAMINATED
TO ¾" BACKING

2'-3"

1'-6"

½" 4"   1½ 3½"

3½" Ø BRONZE RAIL W/
1" X 2" BRONZE TUBING
CONNECTED TO STEEL SLEEVE
THRU BAR FRONT

STEEL SLEEVE
& ANGLE BOLTED
TO BAR TOP TO
SUPPORT LIGHT
FIXTURE

STEEL 'T' 14" X 12"
X ¼" TH AT
2'-0" O.C.

10"

NAT. FIN. WD. PANEL FRONT

3'-6"

1" X 4" STEEL TUBE
COLUMN 5'-0" O.C.
COORDINATE W/
KITCHEN EQUIP.

¾" PLYWOOD BACK

5"   8"

2⅜" Ø BRONZE RAIL W/
1" X 1" BRONZE TUBING
CONNECTED TO STEEL SLEEVE
THRU BAR FRONT

STEEL SLEEVE BOLTED
TO STEEL ANGLE

STEEL ANGLE CLIP 9" X 6"
X ¼" BOLTED TO FL. 2'-0" O.C.

VERDE MARBLE BASE

FINISHED FLOOR

CC ELEVATION

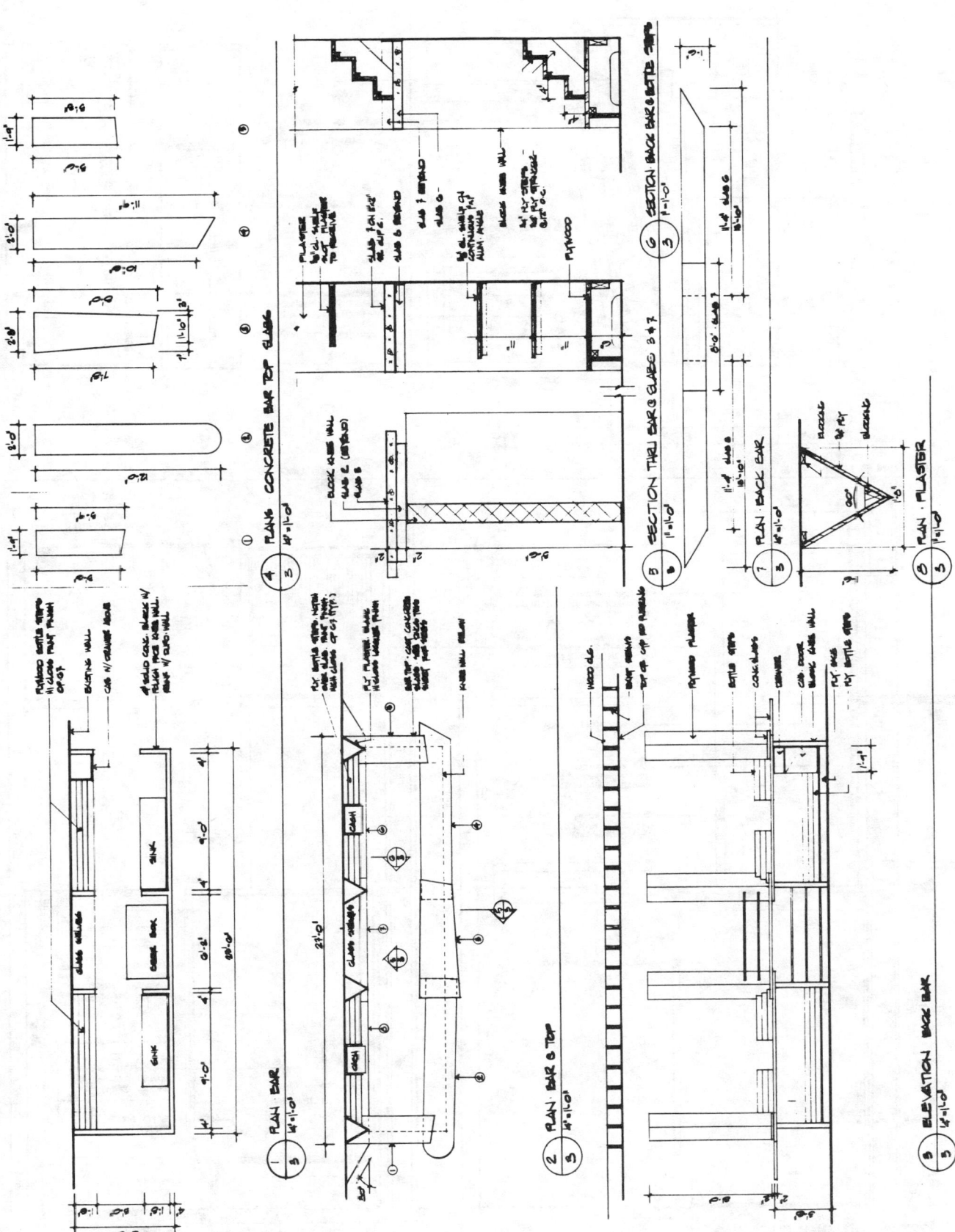

Fig. 28

BARS

Bar Plans, Elevations, and Sections

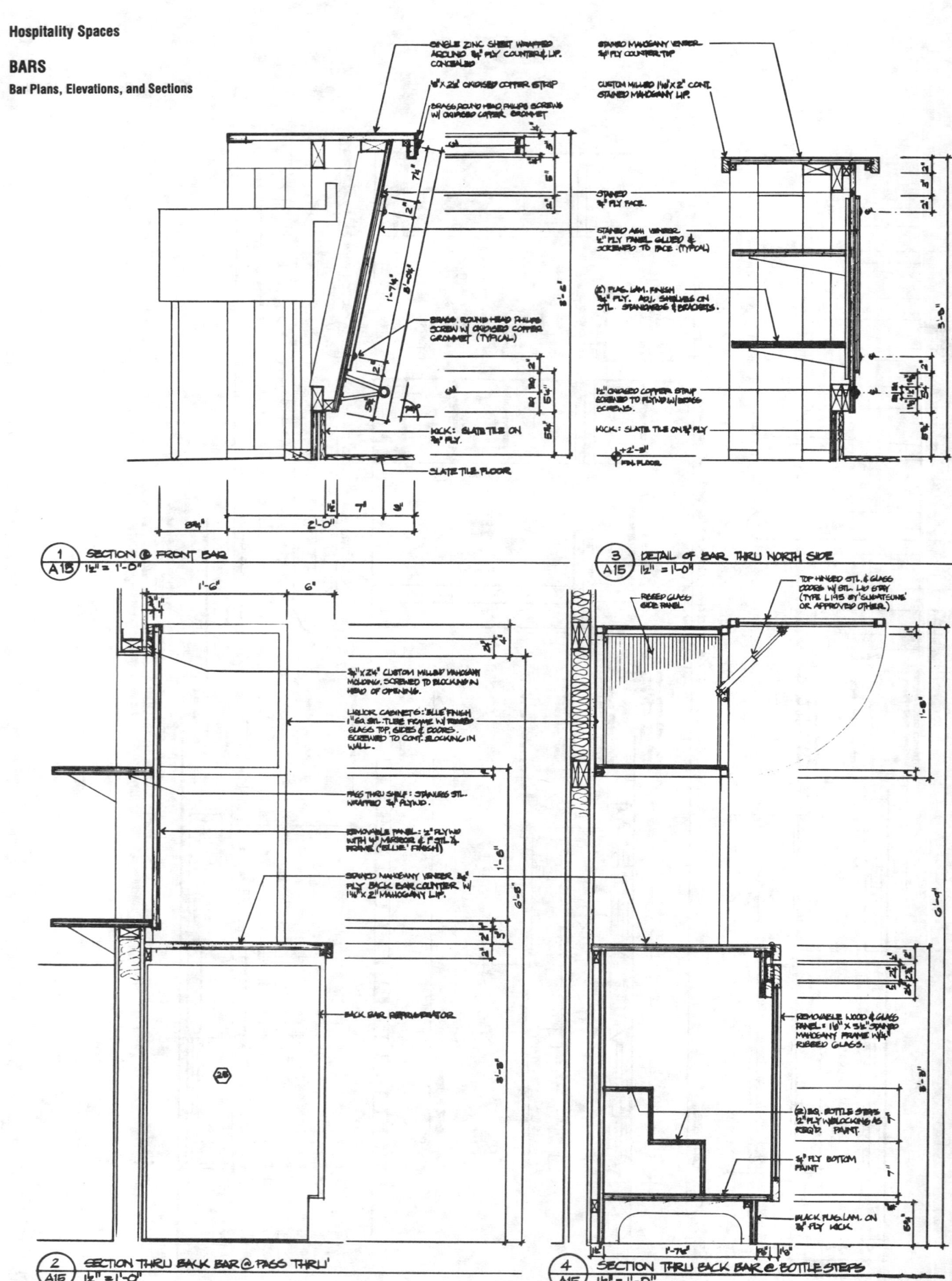

1   SECTION @ FRONT BAR
A15   1½" = 1'-0"

3   DETAIL OF BAR THRU NORTH SIDE
A15   1½" = 1'-0"

2   SECTION THRU BACK BAR @ PASS THRU'
A15   1½" = 1'-0"

4   SECTION THRU BACK BAR @ BOTTLE STEPS
A15   1½" = 1'-0"

Fig. 29

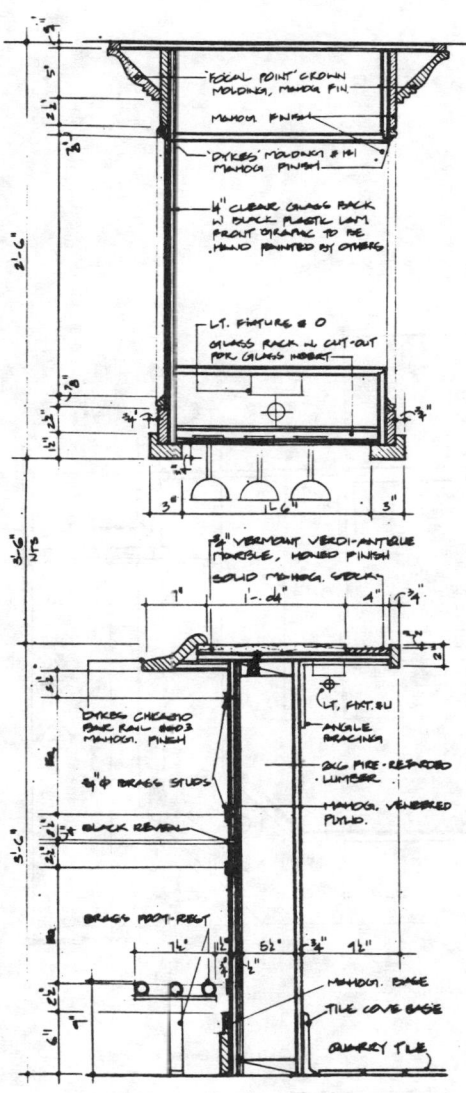

"FOCAL POINT" CROWN MOLDING, MAHOG. FIN.

MAHOG. FINISH

"DYKES" MOLDING # 141 MAHOG. FINISH

¼" CLEAR GLASS BACK W/ BLACK PLASTIC LAM FRONT GRAPHIC TO BE HAND PAINTED BY OTHERS

LT. FIXTURE @ O

GLASS RACK W/ CUT-OUT FOR GLASS INSERT

¾" VERMONT VERDI-ANTIQUE MARBLE, HONED FINISH

SOLID MAHOG. DECK

DYKES CHICAGO BAR RAIL #103 MAHOG. FINISH

¾"Ø BRASS STUDS

BLACK REVEAL

BRASS FOOT-REST

LT. FIXT. @ U

ANGLE BRACING

2x6 FIRE-RETARDED LUMBER

MAHOG. VENEERED PLYWD.

MAHOG. BASE

TILE COVE BASE

QUARRY TILE

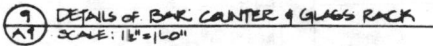

9 / A9 DETAILS OF BAR COUNTER & GLASS RACK
SCALE: 1½"=1'-0"

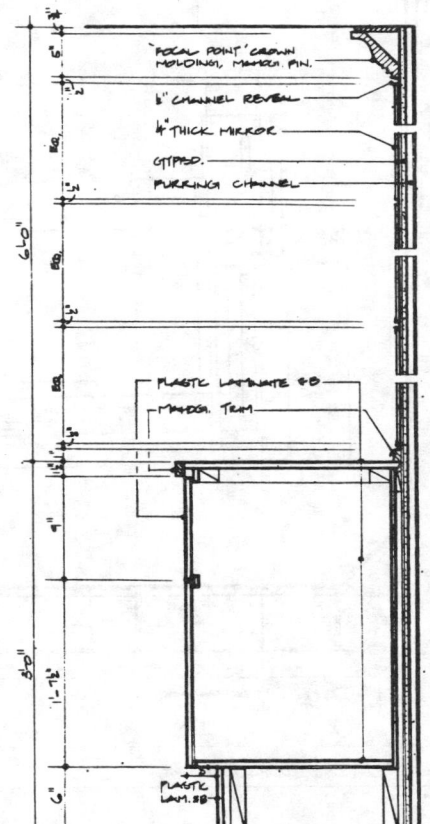

"FOCAL POINT" CROWN MOLDING, MAHOG. FIN.

½" CHANNEL REVEAL

¼" THICK MIRROR

GYPSD.

FURRING CHANNEL

PLASTIC LAMINATE #B

MAHOG. TRIM

PLASTIC LAM. #B

10 / A9 SECTION OF SERVING COUNTER # 104
SCALE: 1½"=1'-0"

Fig. 30

BARS

Bar Plans, Elevations, and Sections

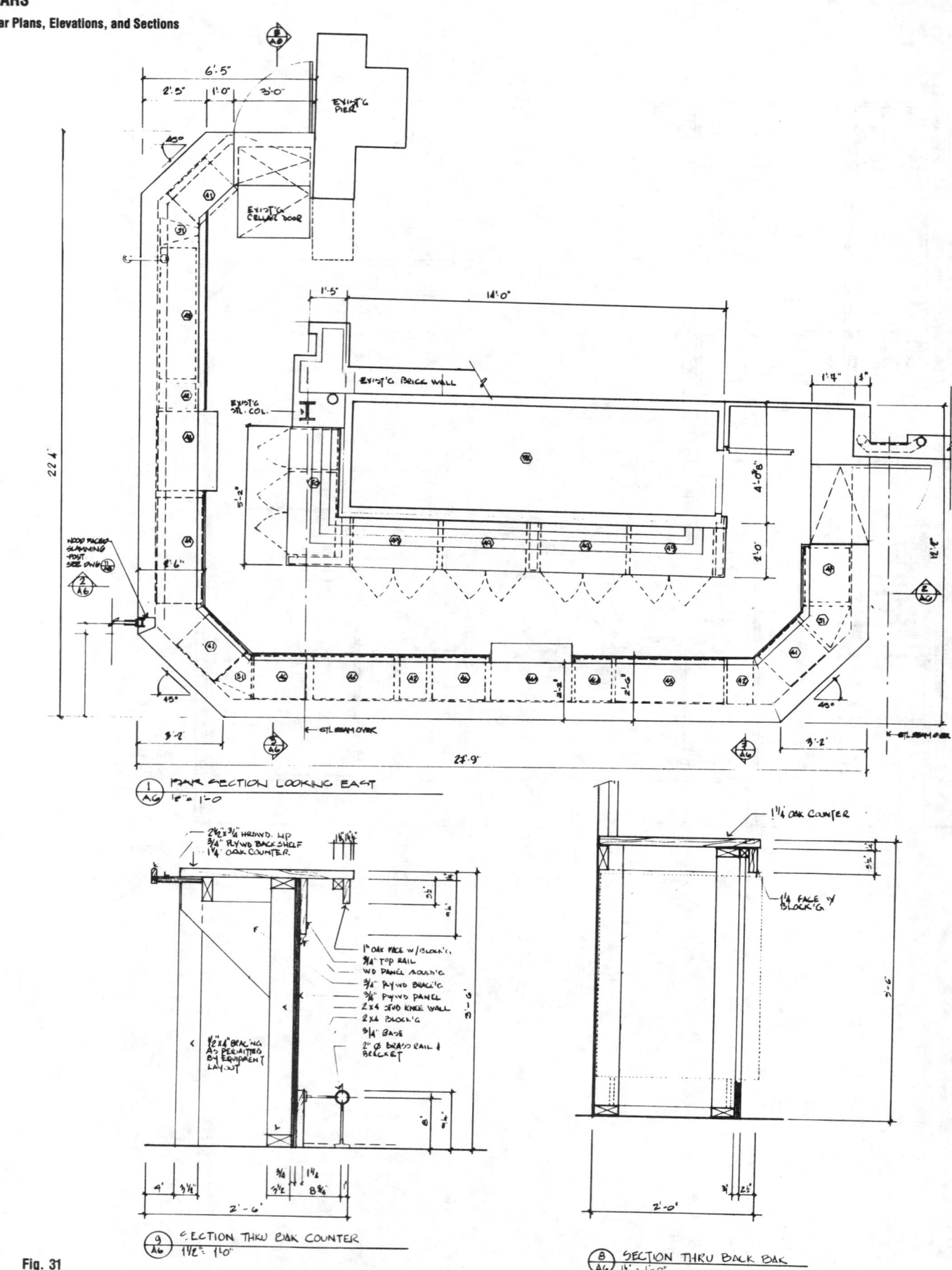

Fig. 31

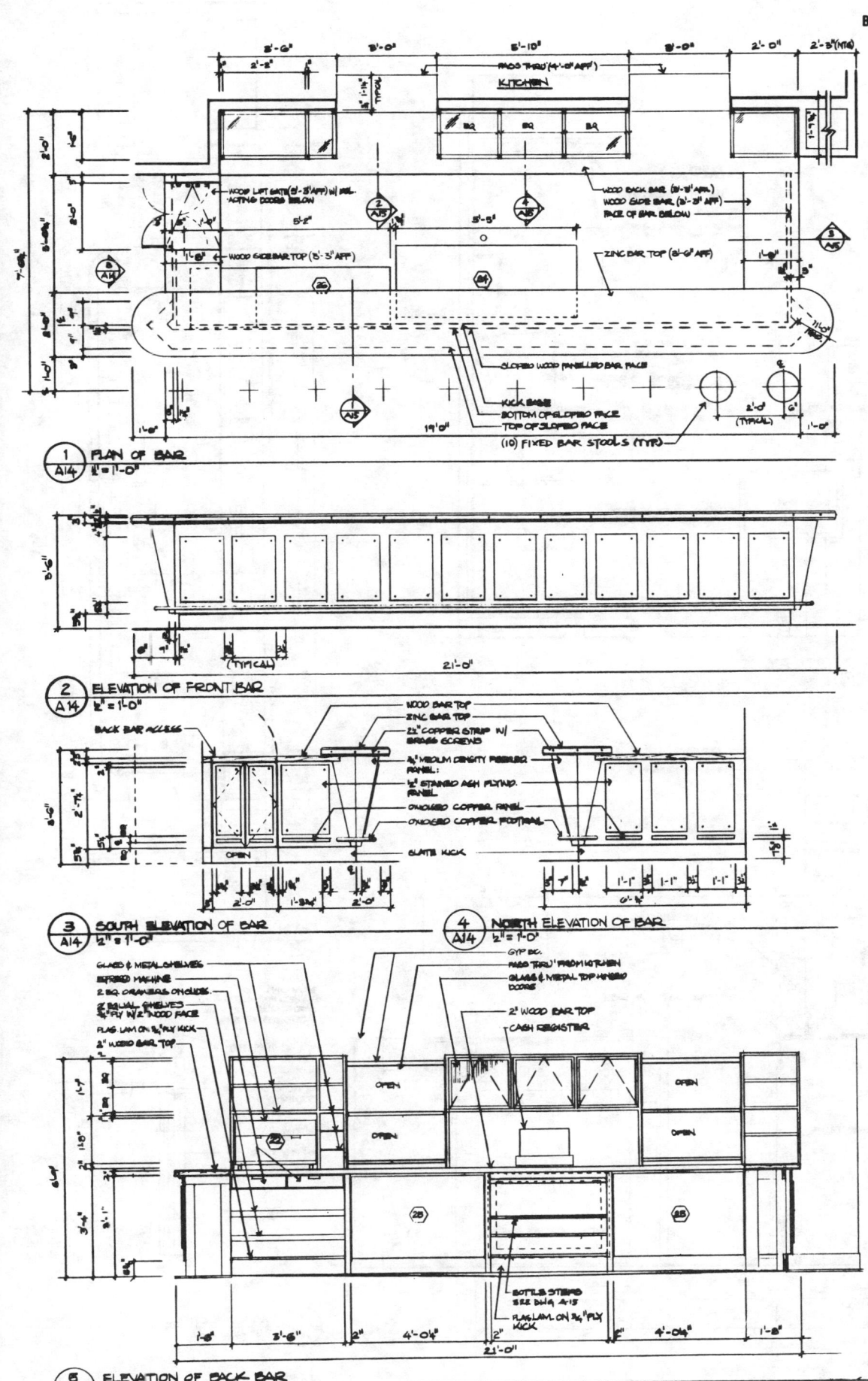

BARS
Bar Section Details

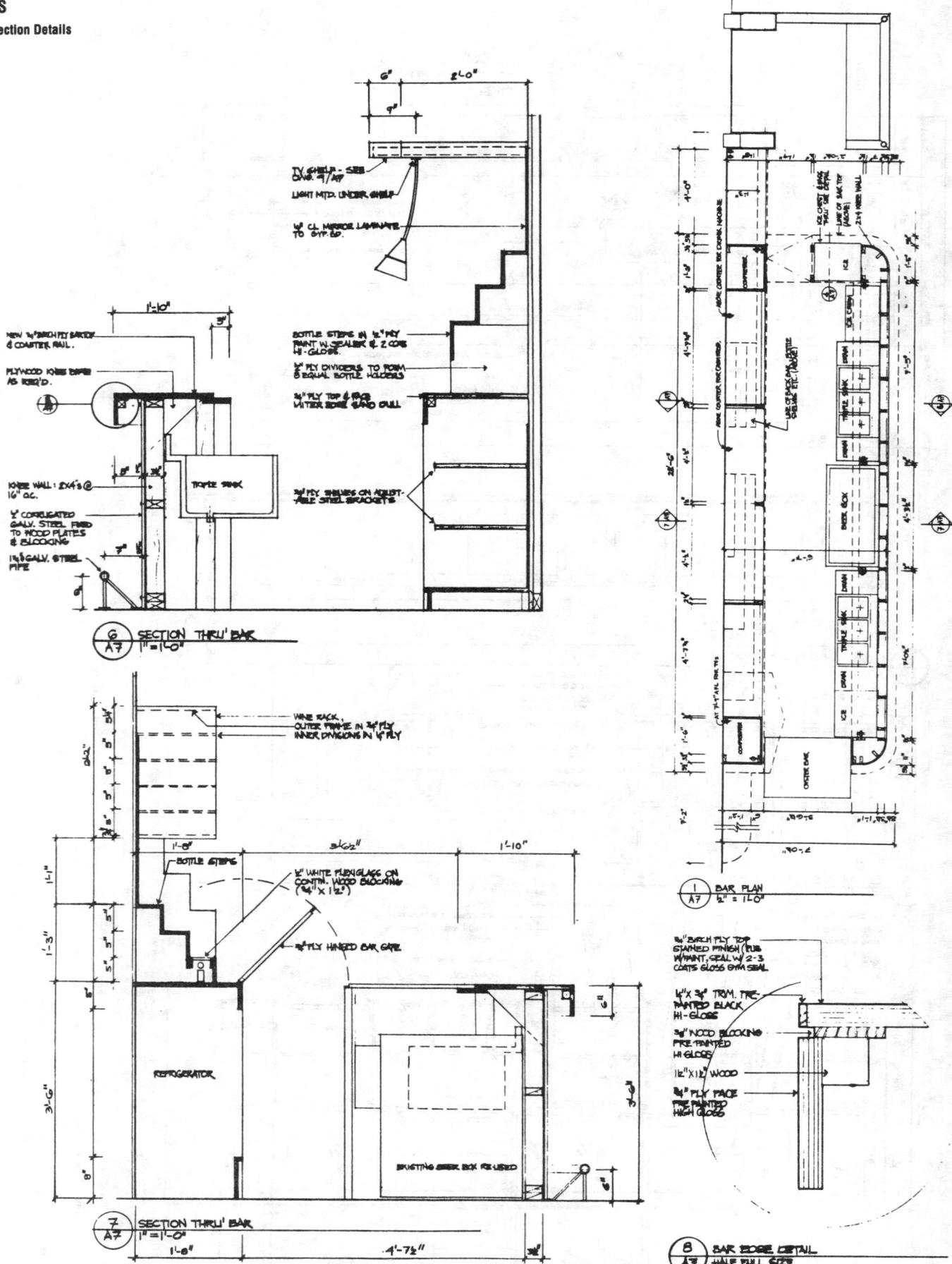

Fig. 33

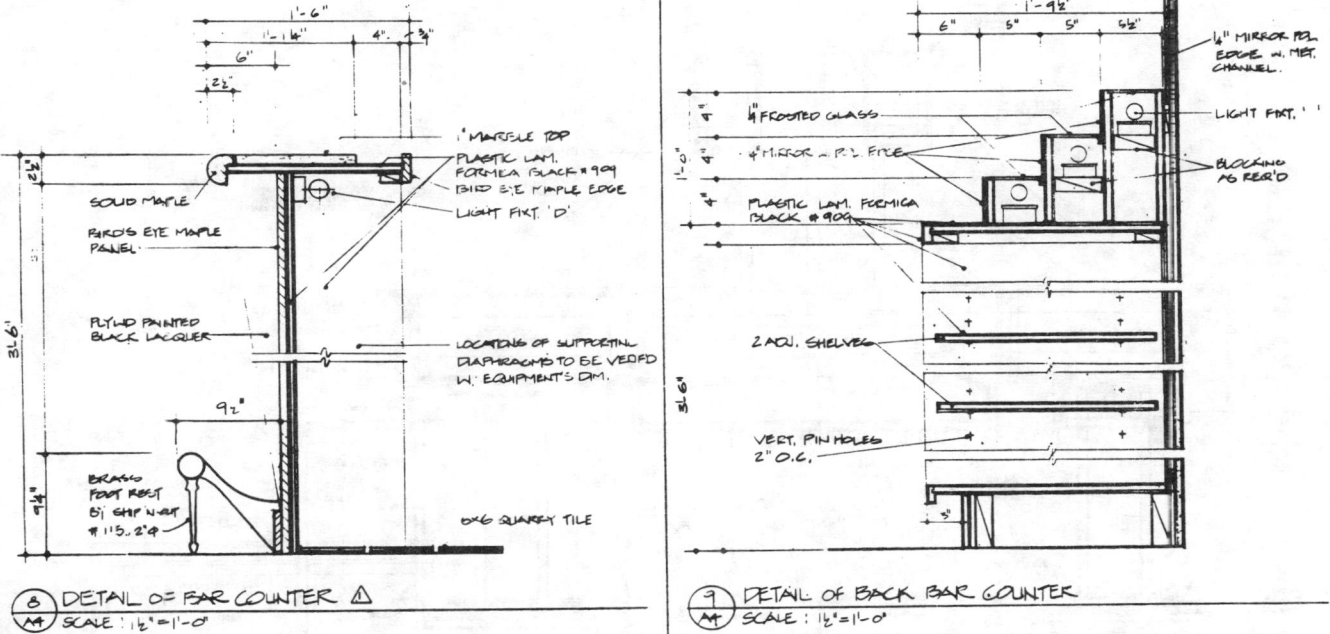

Fig. 34

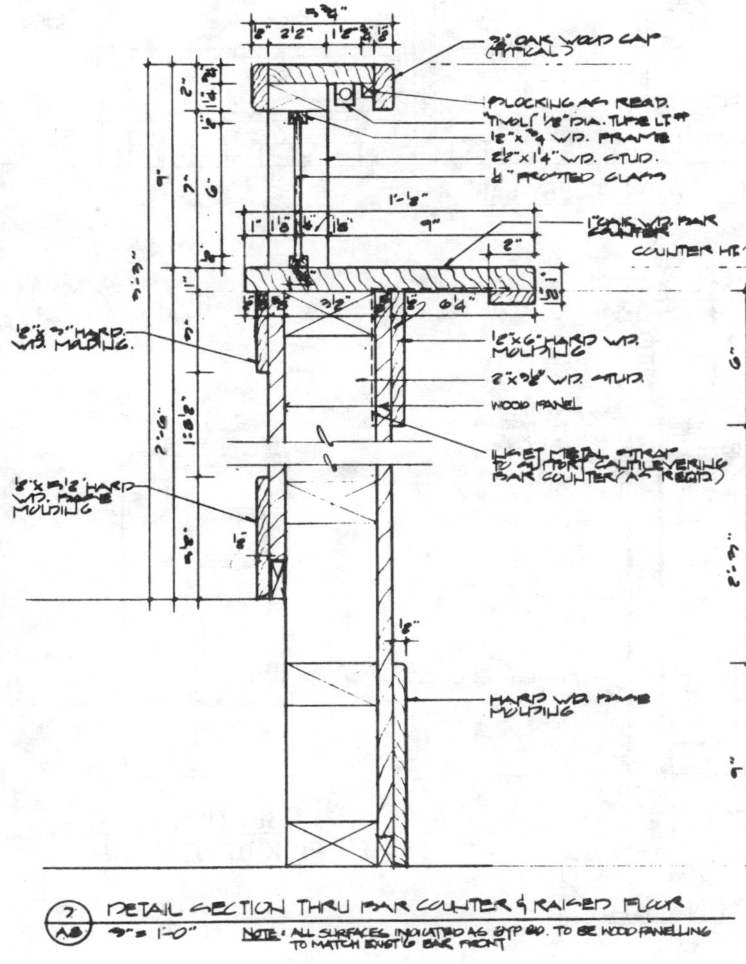

1'-6"
6"
2½"
1½" 4" ¾"

1' MARBLE TOP
PLASTIC LAM.
FORMICA BLACK #909
BIRD EYE MAPLE EDGE

SOLID MAPLE

LIGHT FIXT. 'D'

BIRD'S EYE MAPLE
PANEL

PLYWD PAINTED
BLACK LACQUER

LOCATION OF SUPPORTING
DIAPHRAGMS TO BE VERFD
W. EQUIPMENT'S DIM.

9½"

BRASS
FOOT REST
BY SHIP N OUT
#115, 2"Ø

6x6 QUARRY TILE

31'-6"

⑧/M4 DETAIL OF BAR COUNTER △
SCALE : 1½"=1'-0"

1'-9½"
6" 5" 5½"

⅛" MIRROR POL
EDGE W. MET.
CHANNEL.

LIGHT FIXT.

¼" FROSTED GLASS

¼" MIRROR W. P.L. FACE

BLOCKING
AS REQ'D

PLASTIC LAM. FORMICA
BLACK #909

2 ADJ. SHELVES

VERT. PIN HOLES
2" O.C.

3"

31'-6"

⑨/M4 DETAIL OF BACK BAR COUNTER
SCALE : 1½"=1'-0"

3½" OAK WD CAP
(TYPICAL)

BLOCKING AS REQD.

TIVOLI ⅛" DIA. TUBE LT #

1½"x ¾ WD. FRAME

2⅝"x1¼" WD. STUD.

⅛" FROSTED GLASS

1¾"x5 WD. BAR
COUNTER HT.

1½"x6" HARD WD
MOULDING

2"x3⅝" WD. STUD

WOOD PANEL

LIGHT MET. STRAP
TO SUPPORT CANTILEVERING
BAR COUNTER (AS REQ'D)

1½"x5⅛" HARD
WD. FRAME
MOULDING

HARD WD FRAME
MOULDING

②/AB DETAIL SECTION THRU BAR COUNTER & RAISED FLOOR
3"=1'-0"

NOTE : ALL SURFACES INDICATED AS GYP BD. TO BE WOOD PANELLING
TO MATCH BRUSHD BAR FRONT

Fig. 35

24" OVERALL WITH SANDSTONE
23½"
21½"
2"
4"
¼" SPACE 17¼"

¾" SANDSTONE
½" EXT. A-C FIR PLYWOOD

¼" SETTING
SPACE

⅜" RAD-TYPICAL
AT TOP AND BOTTOM

¾" SANDSTONE

¾" EXT A-C
FIR PLYWOOD

WHITE OAK

1"x 4" BLOCKING

4" BLOCK WALL

11¾"

14½"

¾" PLYWOOD WITH
RIFT CUT W OAK
FACE VENEERS

WHITE OAK
PANEL MOULDING

3"

28½"

31"

1½"x 8" BASE

6"

12" (TYP.)

40½" TO TOP OF 4" BLOCK WALL

SECTION AT BAR

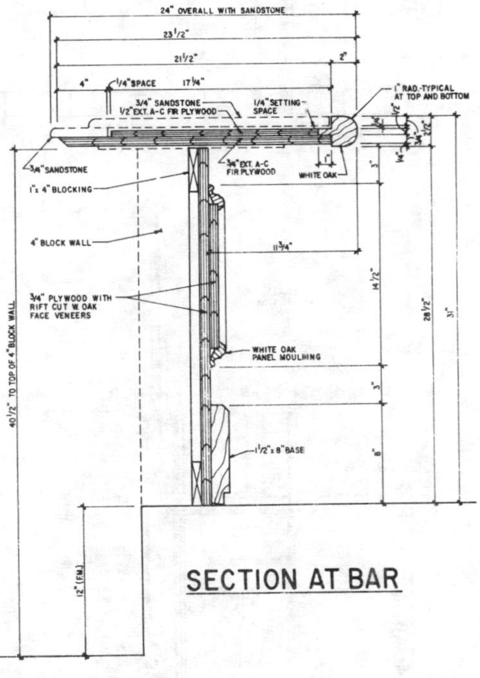

Fig. 36

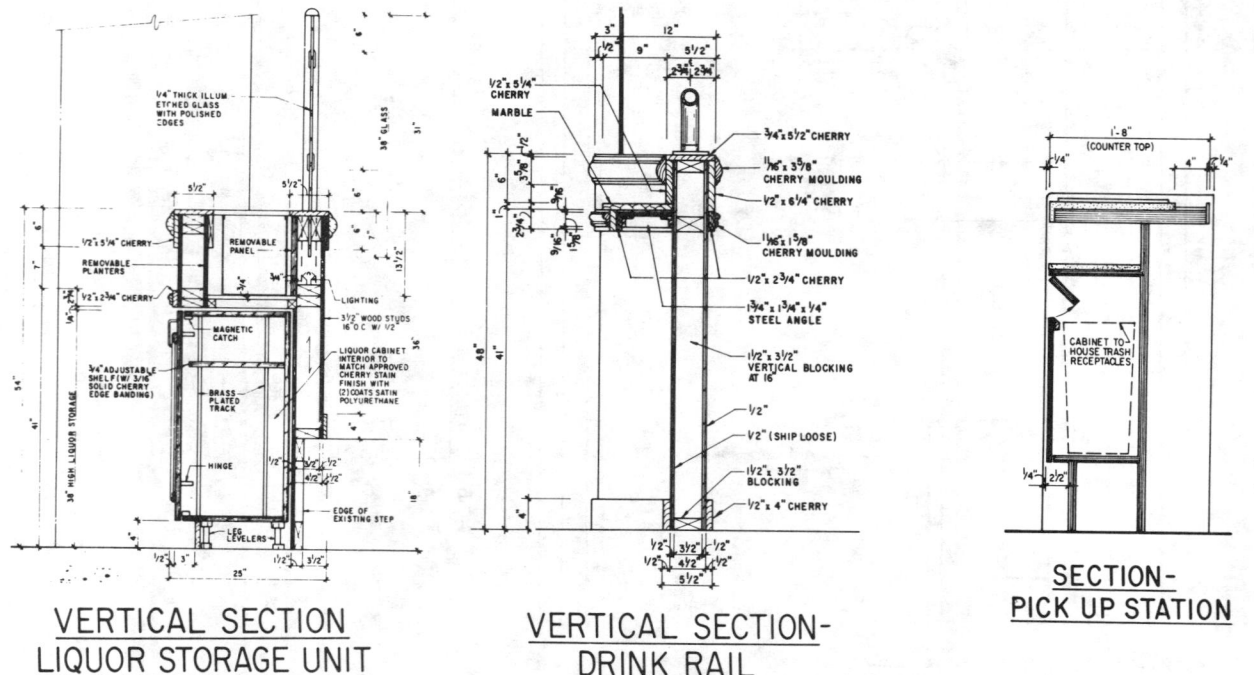

NOTE: ALL FRAMING MEMBERS AT CANOPY SHALL BE STAMPED CONSTRUCTION GRADE FIRE RETARDANT STRUCTURAL LUMBER.

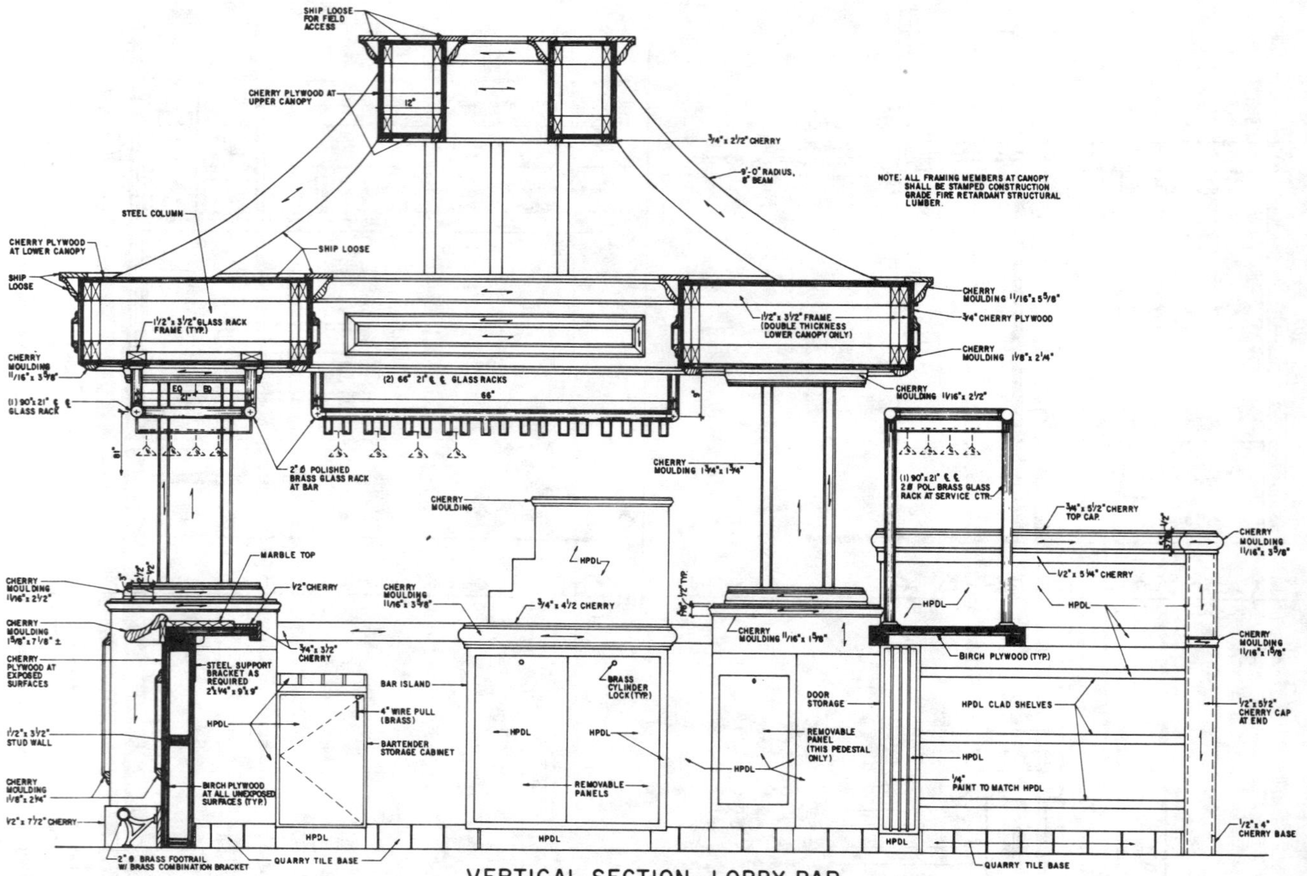

VERTICAL SECTION-LOBBY BAR

VERTICAL SECTION LIQUOR STORAGE UNIT

VERTICAL SECTION- DRINK RAIL

SECTION- PICK UP STATION

Fig. 37

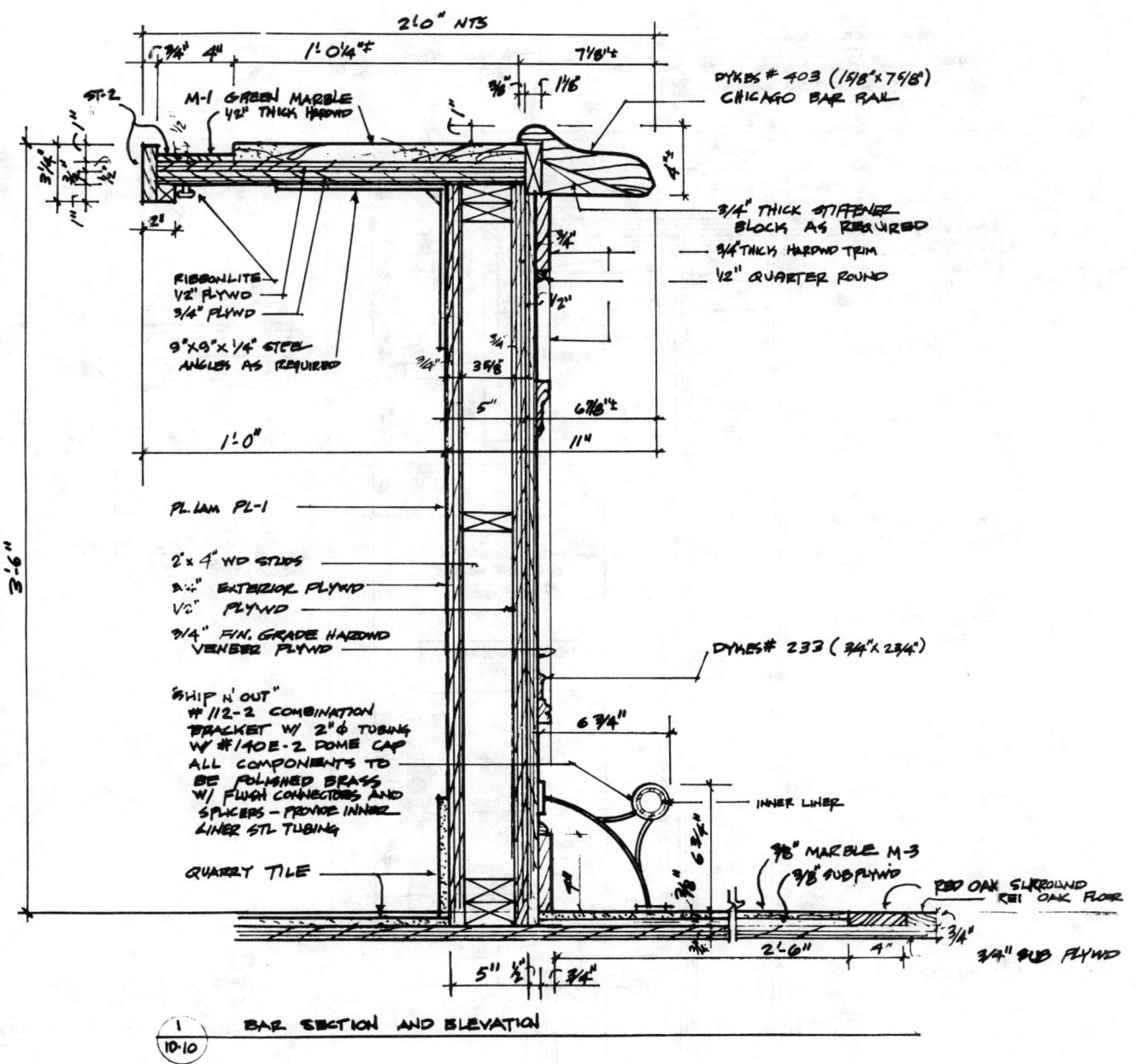

2'0" NTS

3/4" 4" 1'-0 1/4"± 7 1/8"±

3/8" 1 1/8"

ST-2

M-1 GREEN MARBLE
1/2" THICK HARDWD

DYKES # 403 (1 1/8"×7 5/8")
CHICAGO BAR RAIL

3/4" THICK STIFFENER
BLOCK AS REQUIRED

3/4" THICK HARDWD TRIM

1/2" QUARTER ROUND

RIBBONLITE
1/2" PLYWD
3/4" PLYWD

9"×9"×1/4" STEEL
ANGLES AS REQUIRED

3/4"

3 5/8"

6 1/2"

1'-0"

5" 6 7/8"±

11" 1"

PL. LAM PL-1

2"×4" WD STUDS

3/4" EXTERIOR PLYWD

1/2" PLYWD

3/4" FIN. GRADE HARDWD
VENEER PLYWD

DYKES # 233 (3/4"×2 3/4")

6 3/4"

"SHIP N' OUT"
112-2 COMBINATION
BRACKET W/ 2"Ø TUBING
W/ # 140 E-2 DOME CAP
ALL COMPONENTS TO
BE POLISHED BRASS
W/ FLUSH CONNECTORS AND
SPACERS - PROVIDE INNER
LINER STL TUBING

INNER LINER

6 1/2"

QUARRY TILE

3/8" MARBLE M-3
3/8" SUBPLYWD

RED OAK SURROUND
RED OAK FLOOR

3/4"

2'-6" 4"

3/4" SUB PLYWD

5" 1/2" 3/4"

3'-6"

(1 / 10-10) BAR SECTION AND ELEVATION

Fig. 38

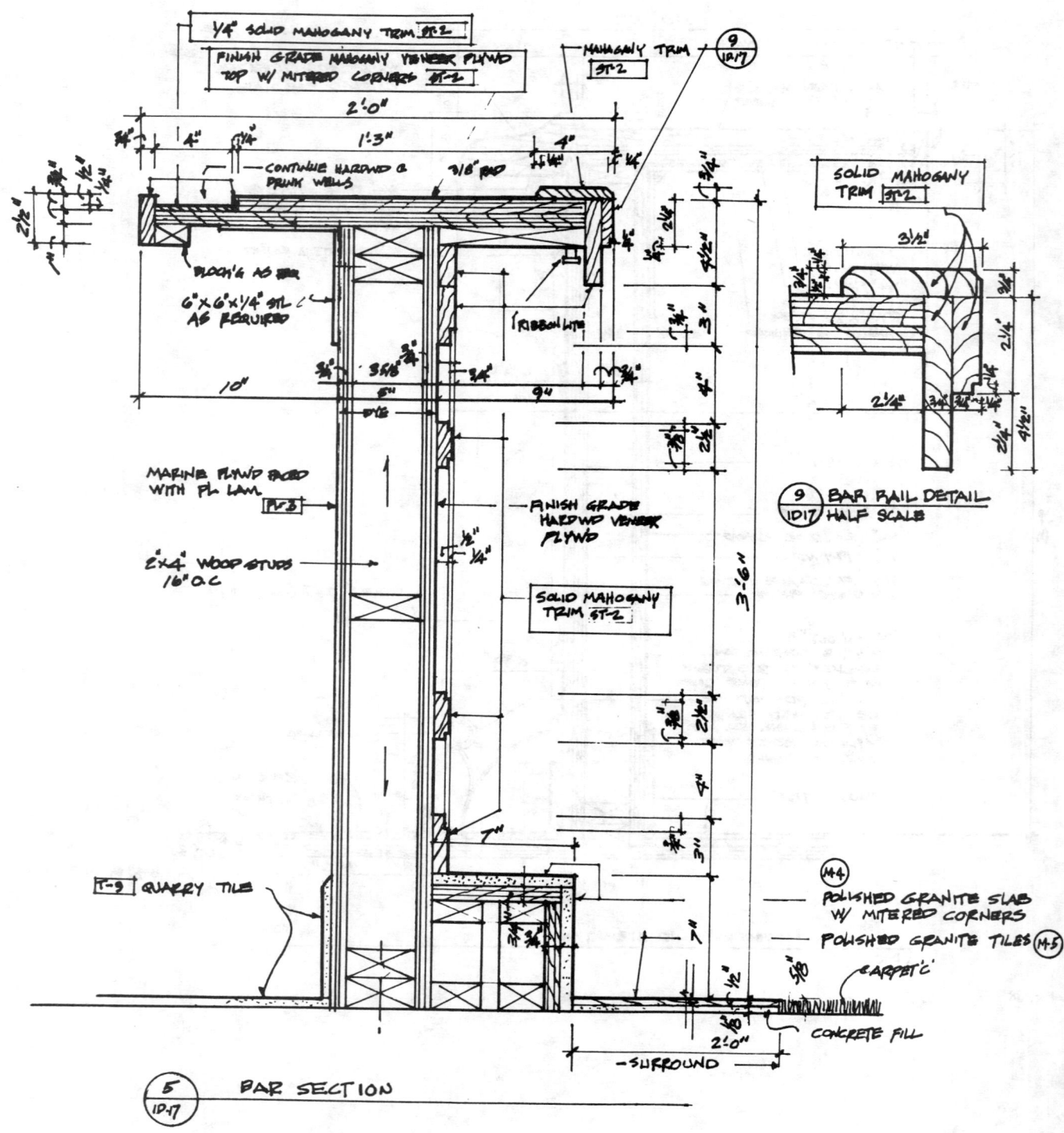

¼" SOLID MAHOGANY TRIM ST-2

FINISH GRADE MAHOGANY VENEER PLYWD TOP W/ MITERED CORNERS ST-2

MAHOGANY TRIM ST-2

9 1D17

2'-0"

1'-3"

4"

CONTINUE HARDWD @ DRINK WELLS

3/8" RAD

RIBBON LITE

BLOCK'G AS REQ

6"x6"x¼" STL L AS REQUIRED

SOLID MAHOGANY TRIM ST-2

10"

MARINE PLYWD FACED WITH PL LAM   PL-3

FINISH GRADE HARDWD VENEER PLYWD

2"x4" WOOD STUDS 16" OC

SOLID MAHOGANY TRIM ST-2

3'-6"

SOLID MAHOGANY TRIM ST-2

3½"

2¼"

2¼"

3½"

4½"

9 1D17   BAR RAIL DETAIL   HALF SCALE

T-9 QUARRY TILE

M-4   POLISHED GRANITE SLAB W/ MITERED CORNERS

POLISHED GRANITE TILES M-5

CARPET C

CONCRETE FILL

2'-0"

SURROUND

7"

5 1D17   BAR SECTION

Fig. 39

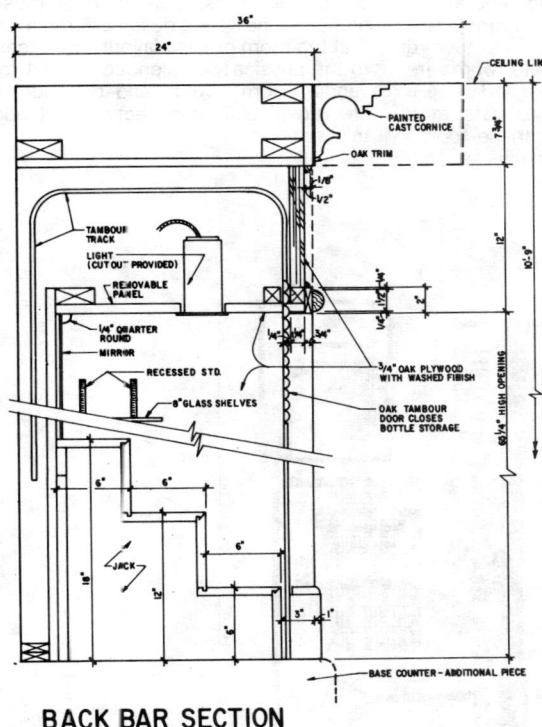

BACK BAR SECTION

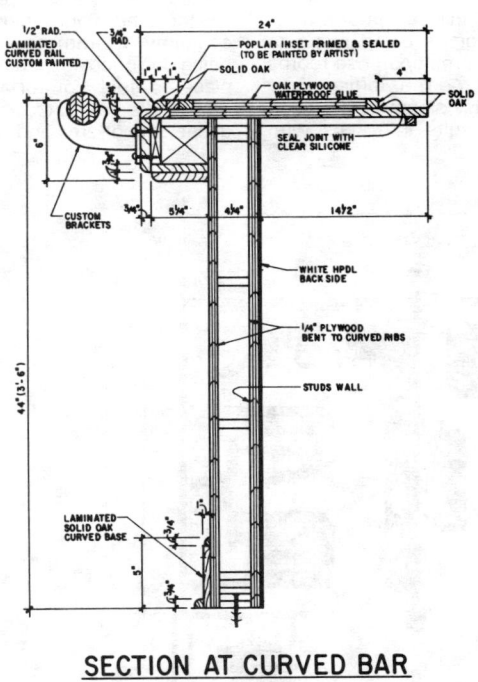

SECTION AT CURVED BAR

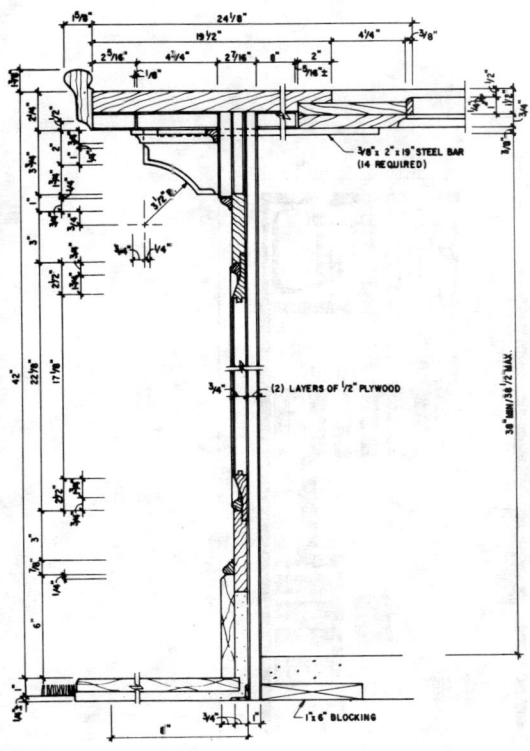

VERTICAL SECTION AT BAR

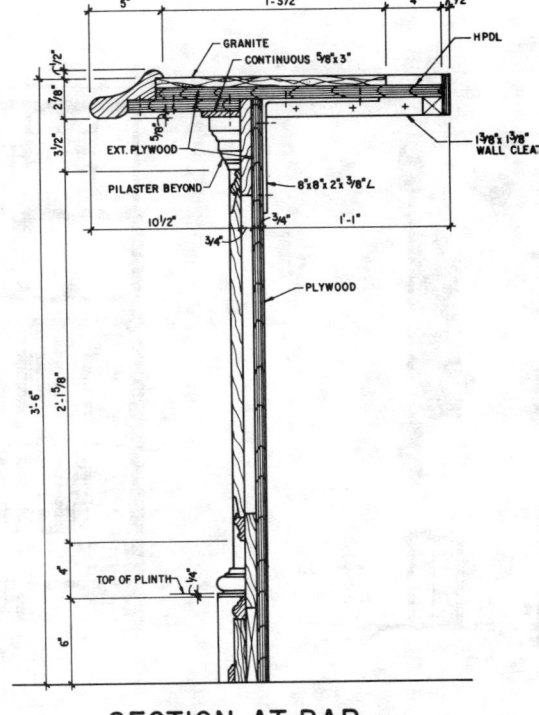

SECTION AT BAR

Fig. 40

HOTELS

Guestroom Plans

It is interesting to note how trends in hotel design have headed off in two directions, especially in regard to the design of rooms. On one hand, an effort is being made to provide more luxurious multipurpose rooms and suites. The hotel room as office away from work or as fantasy sleeping/relaxation environment often results in rooms with work areas, living rooms, and hot tubs, just to name a few of the more popular amenities. On the other hand, there is a trend toward economy accommodations. Hotel rooms are being designed as a place to rest and sleep, a place to feel comfortable and safe at a reasonable cost. Accordingly, these rooms use less floor area and provide less second-ary or frill items. With both of these ap-proaches, however, designers must ensure that the room or suite layouts are accessible to the physically challenged. In that regard, various room layouts and bathroom plans are provided in this section that address this issue.

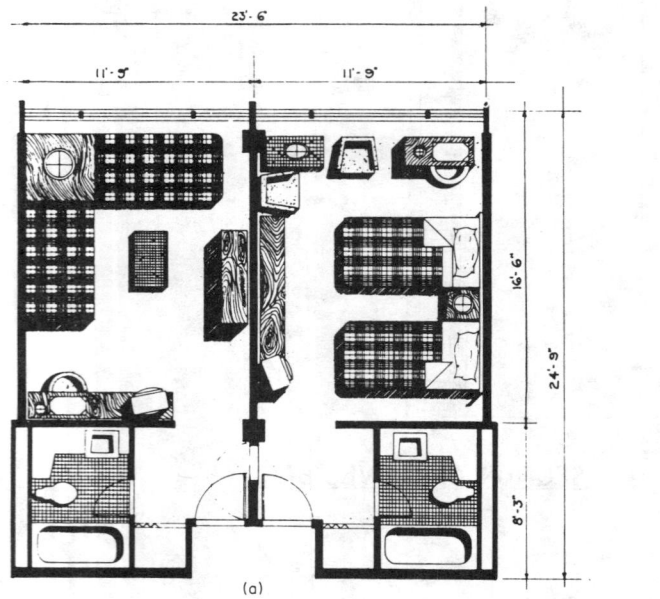

(a)

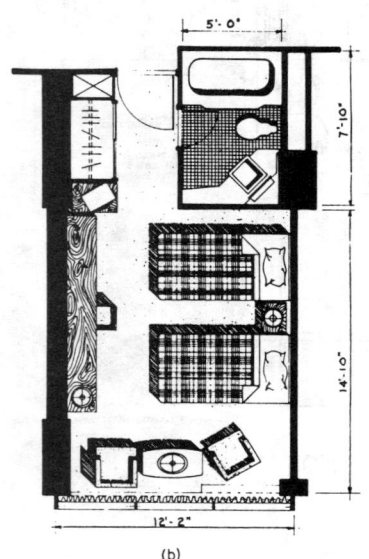

(b)

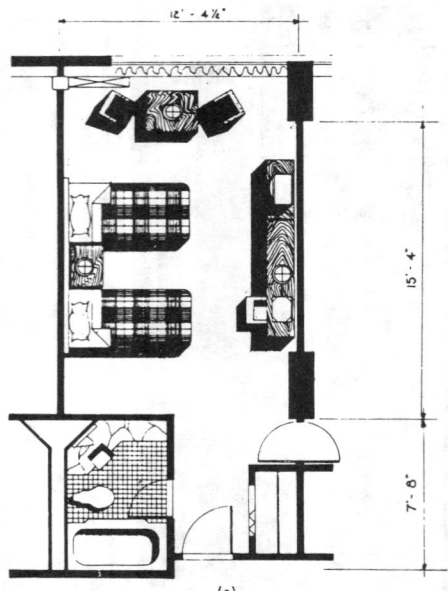

(c)

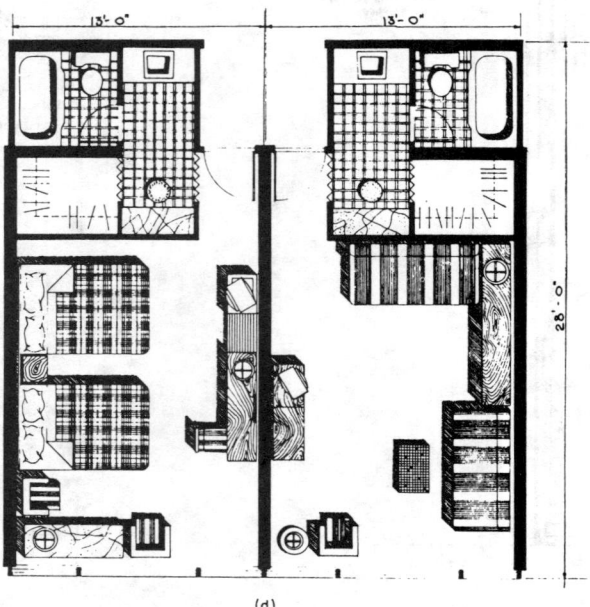

(d)

Fig. 1 *(a)* **Uris Brothers Hotel, New York.** *(b)* **Americana Hotel, New York, typical tower room.** *(c)* **Loews N.Y. Motel, typical room.** *(d)* **Causeway Inn, Tampa, Florida.**

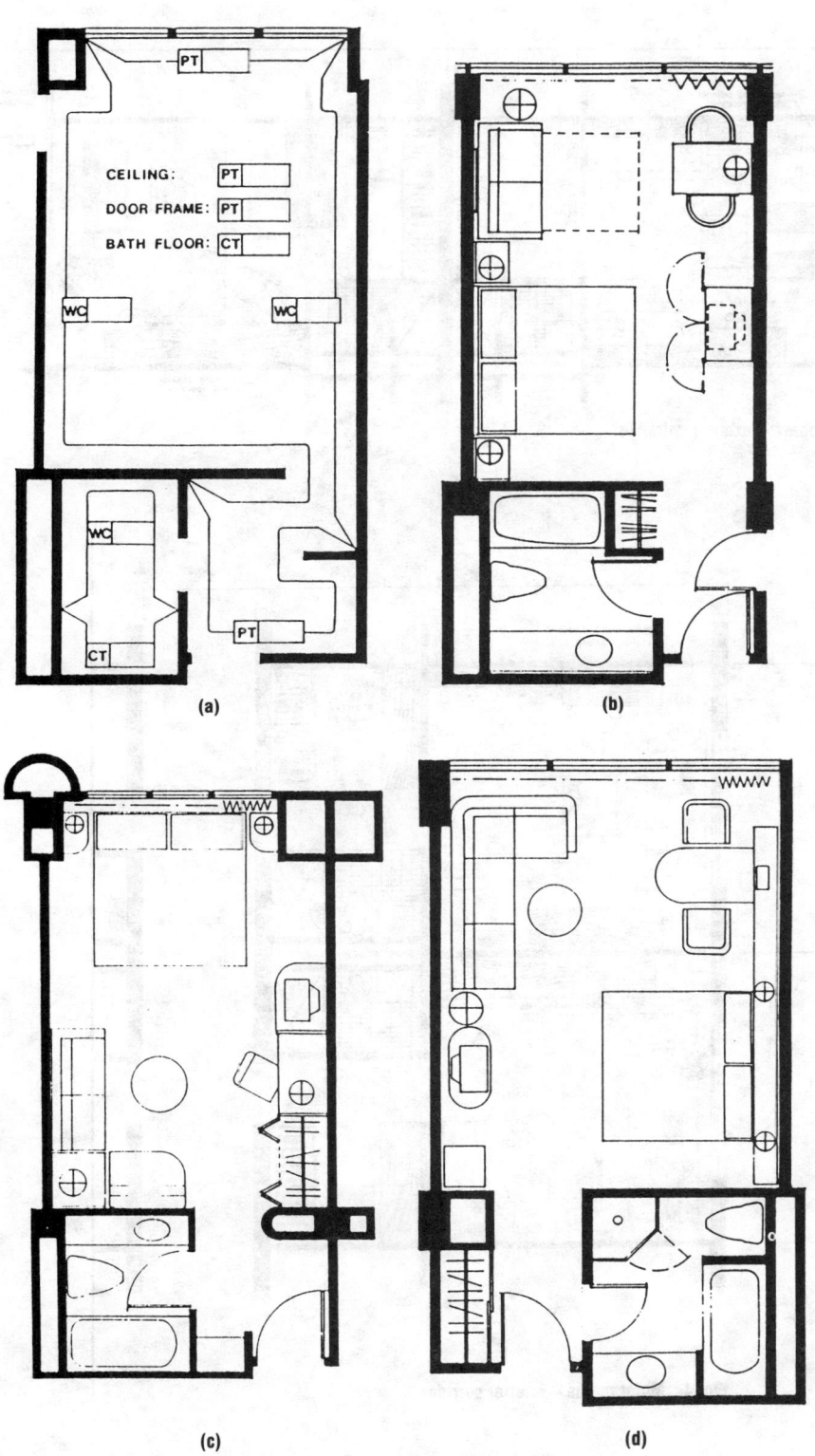

Fig. 2   Guestroom plans. *(a)* Typical double-double finishes plan: vinyl wallcovering (WC), paint
(P), carpet (C), ceramic tile *(CT)* identified and keyed to legend. *(b)* King-studio (Holiday Inn):
standard layout with armoire unit and large lounge area including a convertible sofa. *(c)* Reversed
layout (Sheraton, Washington, D.C.): unusual room with bed placed in front of window and lounge
area near bathroom. *(d)* Luxury king room (Sheraton Grande, Los Angeles): oversized room with
shelf/ledge in place of headboard, large desk surface, and lounge area; four-fixture bathroom.

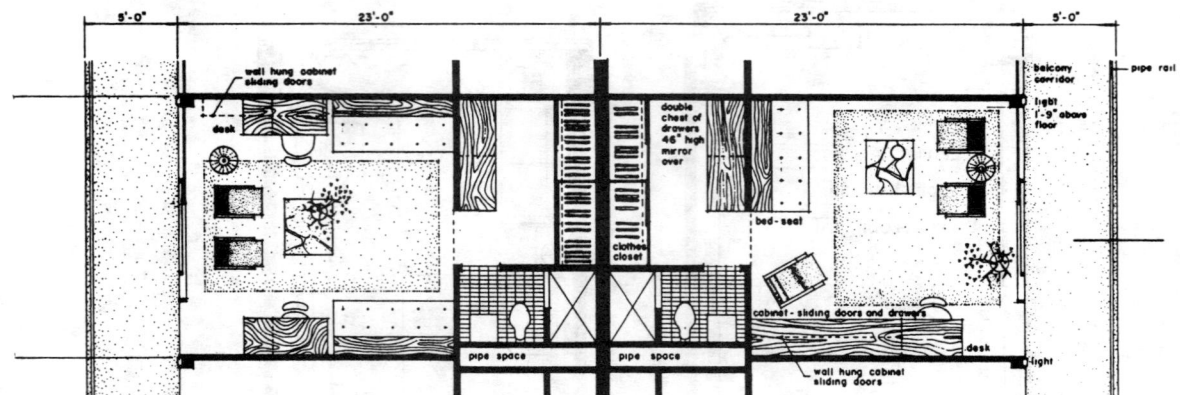

Fig. 3   Motel rooms — exterior entrance.

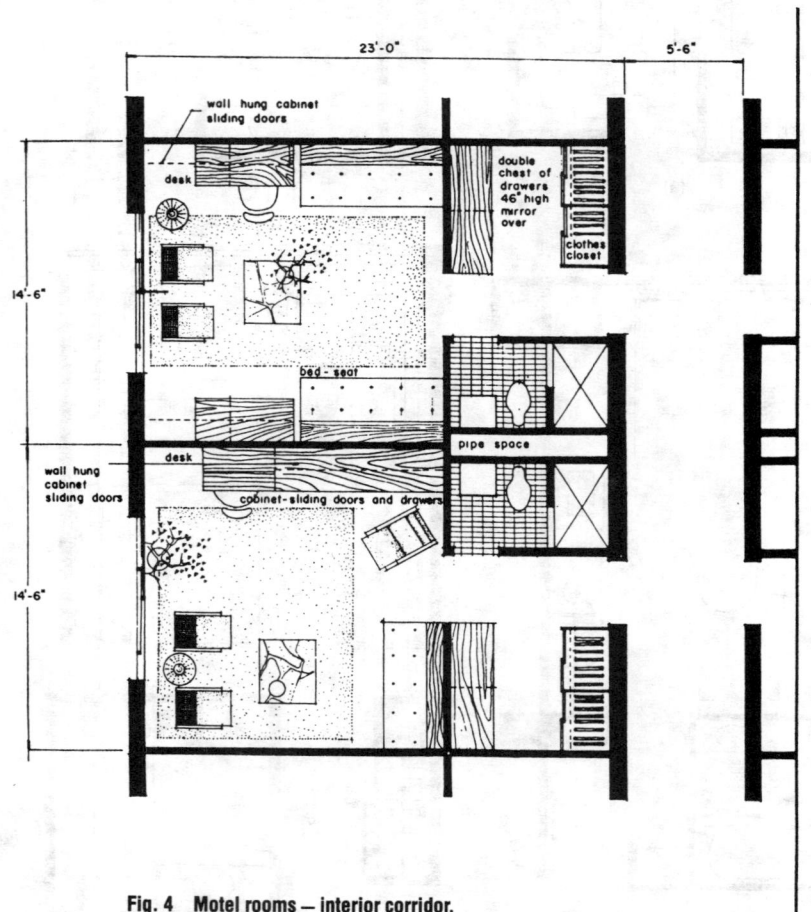

Fig. 4   Motel rooms — interior corridor.

Guestroom Plans

Accessible guestrooms have design features and floor plans that provide the maneuvering clearances for guests with limited mobility. Figures 5 to 9 show sample plans of guestrooms and bathrooms with the required:

■ Widths and clearances at the entry, connecting, closet, and bathroom doors

■ Maneuvering space in front of the closet, in the sleeping area, and within the bathroom

■ Clearances to use and transfer to fixtures in the bathroom

■ Clearances to open dresser drawers, to maneuver into kneespace at the desk, and to access the bed, bedside table, windows, blinds, and thermostat

Clearances may depend on the design of specific furnishings. The width of the access aisle at the bed is determined by the design of the bedside table. Access to dressers is determined by the width of the drawer. The maneuvering space to turn into the desk is determined by the width of the kneespace.

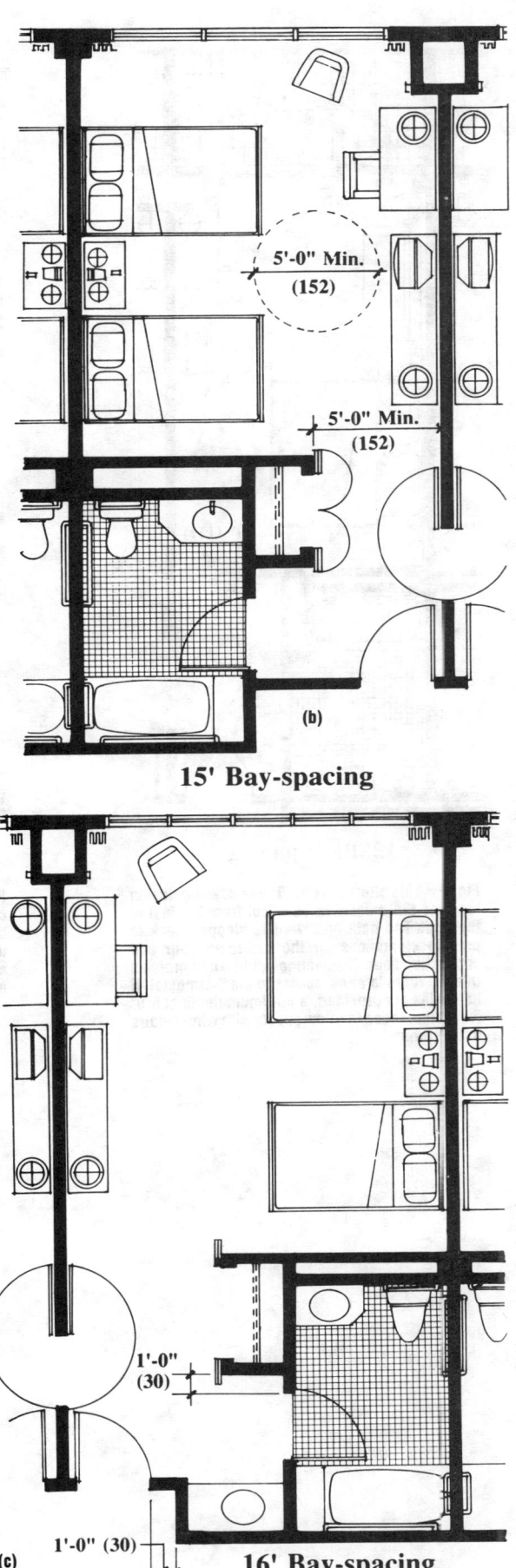

5'-0" Min. (152)

5'-0" Min. (152)

(b)

15' Bay-spacing

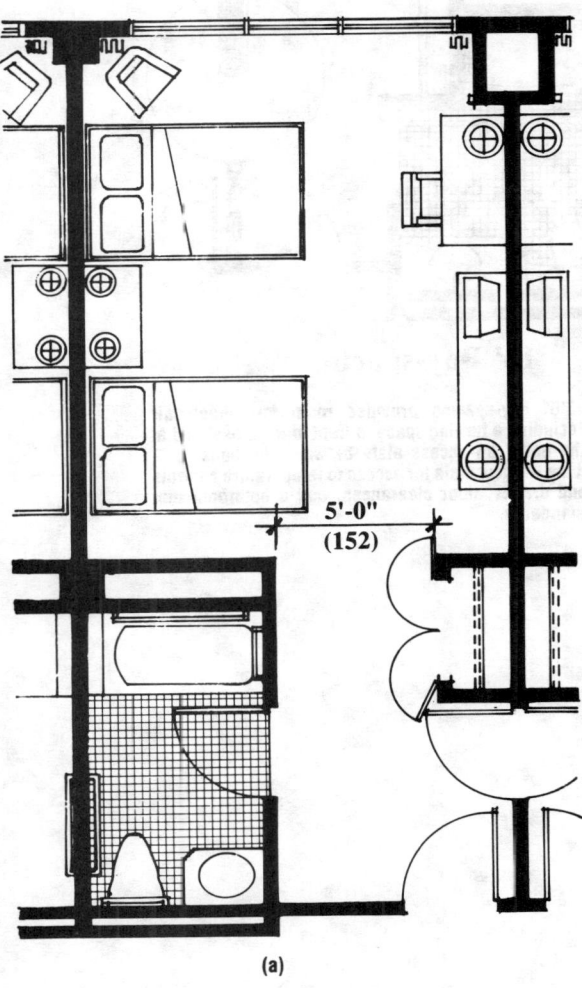

5'-0" (152)

(a)

14' Bay-spacing

Fig. 5   Bay-spacings of (a) 14', (b) 15', and (c) 16' can easily accommodate guests with restricted mobility.

1'-0" (30)

1'-0" (30)

(c)

16' Bay-spacing

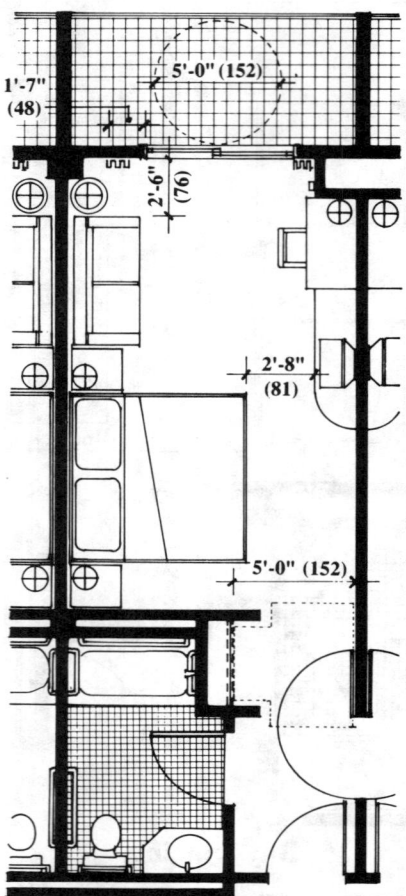

12' Bay-spacing

Fig. 6 This alternative 12'0" bay-spacing design requires the dresser to be offset from the foot of the bed. The bathroom wall is stepped back to provide clearances for the bathroom door and connecting door. The heating/cooling unit projects into the room to allow access to the thermostat. If balconies are provided, a minimum depth of 5'0" is recommended to allow guests with wheelchairs to turn around.

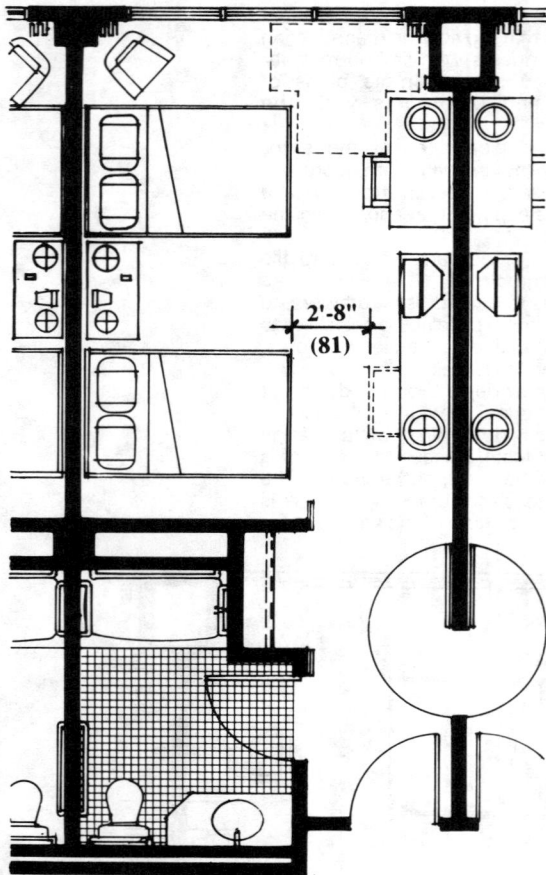

13' Bay-spacing

Fig. 7 A 13'0" bay-spacing provides room for wheelchair clearances, including a turning space in front of the closet and at the foot of the beds, an access aisle between the beds, a T-turnaround at the window aisle for access to temperature controls and blinds and drapes, door clearances, and a bathroom that meets ANSI standards.

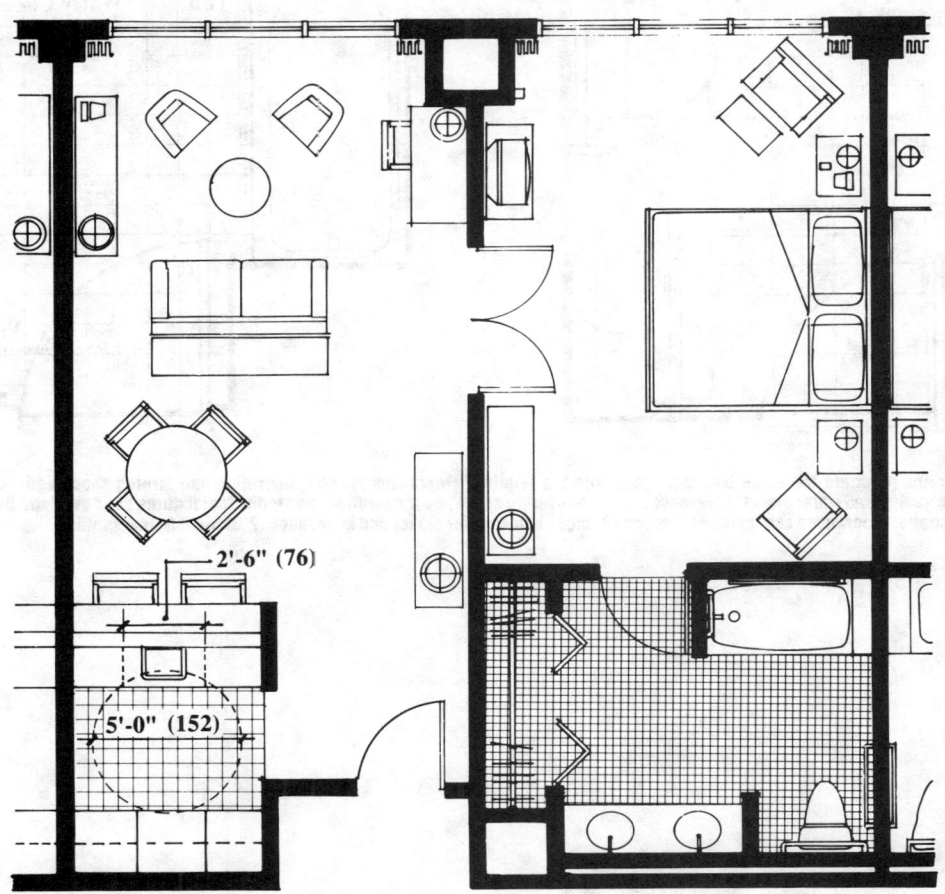

2'-6" (76)

5'-0" (152)

Suite with 14' Bay-spacing

Fig. 8 Accessible suites should meet the same requirements for accessible guestrooms and guest baths. Because suites are usually more generous in terms of space, providing accessibility is less difficult. If a small kitchenette is included, a kneespace 2'3" high should be provided below the sink. A countertop height of 2'10" (2" lower than standard) is suitable for both ambulatory guests and guests in wheelchairs. A pull-out lapboard at a height of 2'6" provides a workspace for guests in wheelchairs. The kitchenette should include a 5'0" turning space.

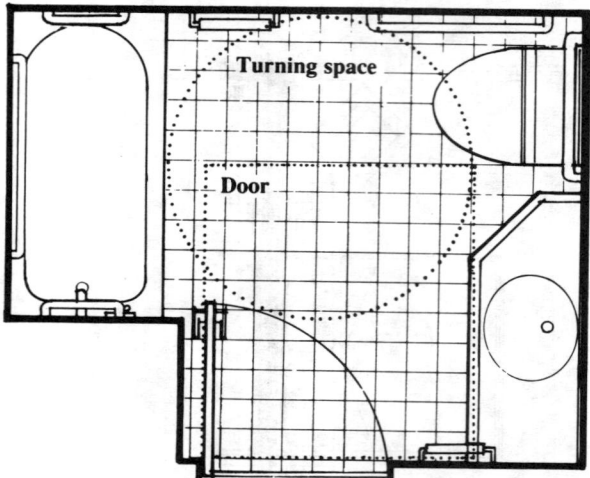
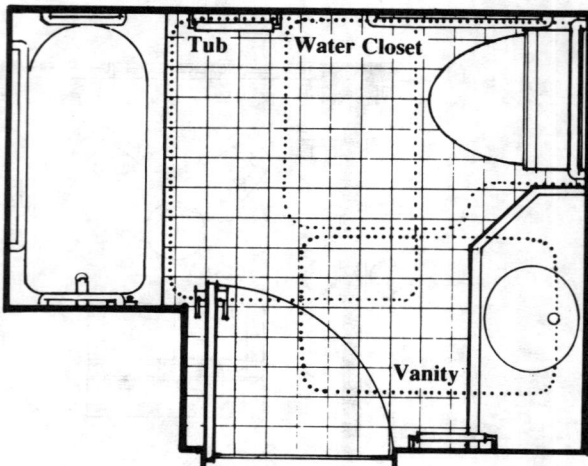

Fig. 9 These two diagrams illustrate the same bathroom plan with the required clearances for door operation and turning space and access to each fixture, including the tub/shower, vanity, and water closet. Clearances for maneuvering space, door operation, and individual fixtures can "overlap." Because of the vertical characteristics of wheelchairs, clearances can include toespace (9″ high) below water closet and kneespace (2′3″ high) below vanities.

The hotel registration desk serves as both a symbol of hospitality for the arriving guest and the operational nerve center for the hotel. With the advent of electronic check-in procedures, credit cards, and computer-aided management, the registration desk has become a sophisticated electronic workstation not unlike a trading table or an airline reservations desk. At the same time, this electronic data processing capability is meant to be maintained at low visibility for reasons of hotel image and confidentiality. Accordingly, the designer must be able to project the appropriate hospitality image while at the same time integrating all of the required technologies. Figures 10 to 13 show examples of architectural working drawings and details that meet many of these requirements.

The design of a front desk or registration desk can take many forms and be constructed with a variety of materials. Regardless of the design vocabulary used or architectural style, certain important design considerations must be observed.

1. The number of persons actively staffing the counterlike facility will dictate both the width and overall depth of the front desk. It is suggested that between 5–7 ft be allocated per staff workstation and that one workstation be allocated for every 125–150 rooms. For every additional 125–150 rooms, an additional workstation should be provided. Peak check-in/check-out loads could require even more staff workstations.

2. The front desk should be easily accessible from and to the main hotel entrance. "Easily accessible" strongly implies clear visibility.

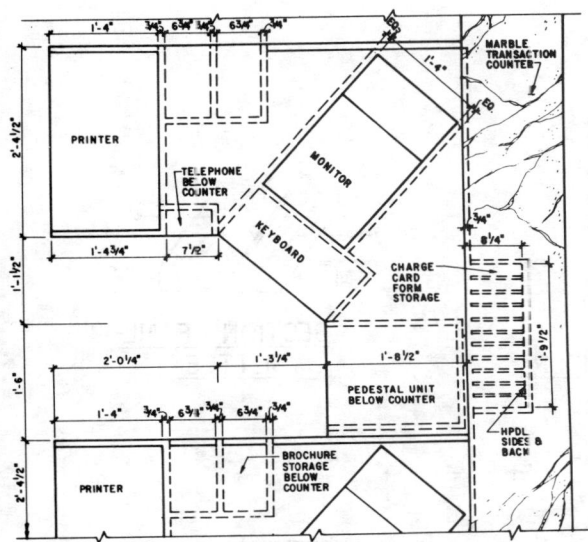

ENLARGED PARTIAL PLAN
REGISTRATION COUNTER
GRAND FLORIDIAN HOTEL

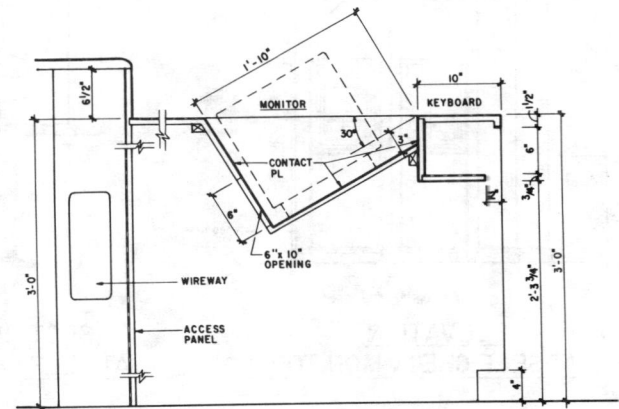

SECTION AT REGISTRATION DESK
GRAND FLORIDIAN HOTEL

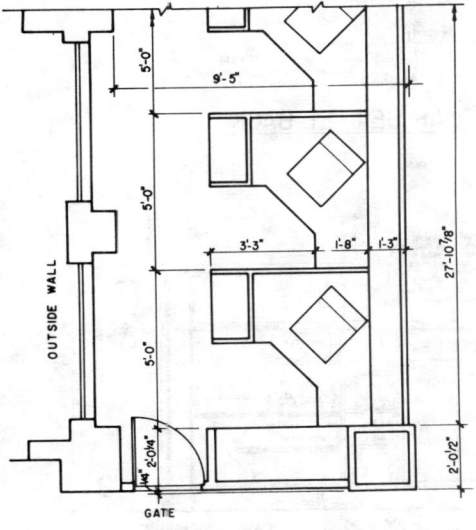

PARTIAL PLAN
REGISTRATION COUNTER
GRAND FLORIDIAN HOTEL

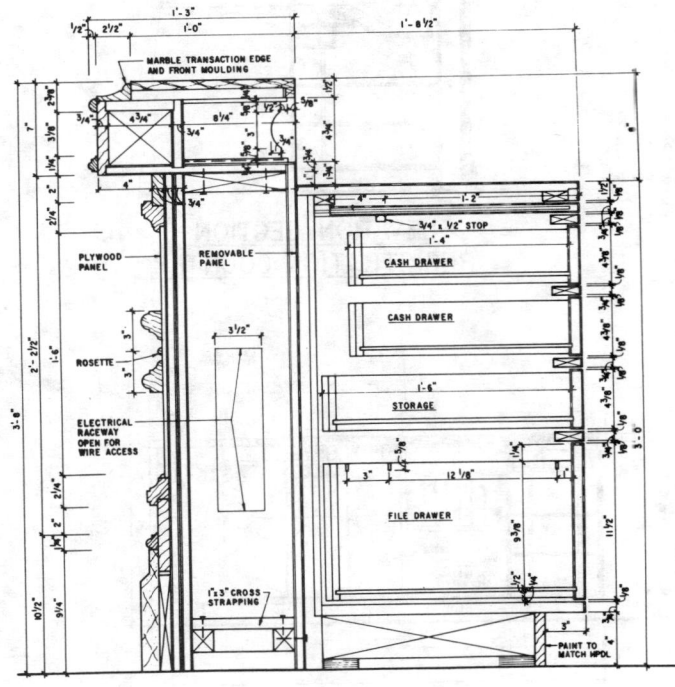

SECTION AT COUNTER
GRAND FLORIDIAN HOTEL

Fig. 10

HOTELS
Registration Desk

3. Elevators servicing the hotel guest rooms should be readily visible from the front desk. This is not always feasible in extremely large hotels.

4. The front desk should be designed in such a way as to take into consideration the various users it will accommodate. Special attention should be given to the fact that hotel guests may be physically challenged or chairbound. The overall height, writing sur- faces, and overhangs should be designed to accommodate a hotel guest seated in a wheelchair.

5. The basic front desk design should avoid, wherever possible, visual obstructions that block sightlines or create blind spots. Accordingly, columns and high walls should be avoided.

6. Equipment and custom elements that are typically incorporated within the front desk include computer monitors/CRTs with keyboards and printer, room racks, reserva- tion racks, information racks, room status displays, mail drawers, key drawers, alpha guest listings, message-waiting display, credit card imprinters, fax and telex, guest/ employee paging system, automatic wake- up system, electric receptacles, cable chases, alarm systems, and file and cash drawers.

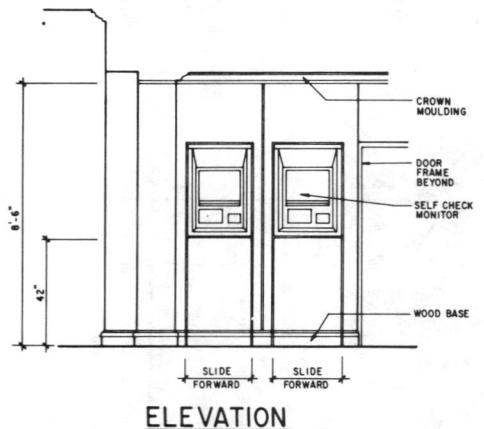

ELEVATION
AT SELF CHECK MONITOR

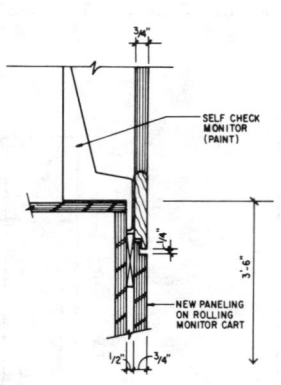

SECTION DETAIL
AT SELF CHECK MONITOR

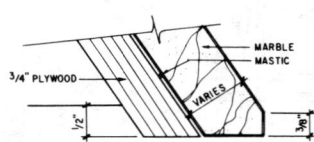

SECTION DETAIL-
SETTEE

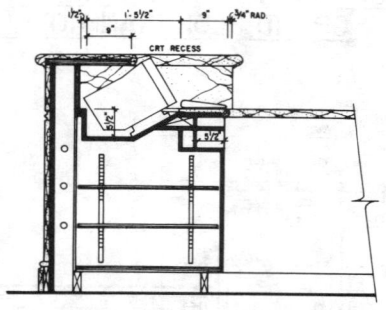

ELEVATION / SECTION -
REGISTRATION COUNTER

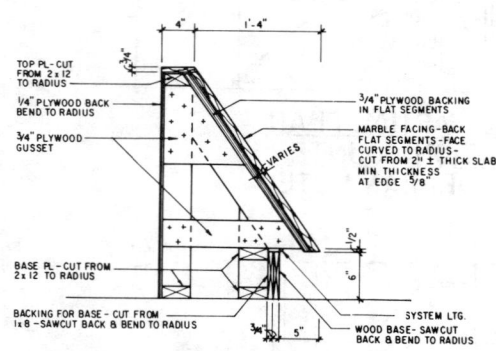

SECTION-CIRCULAR SETTEE BACK

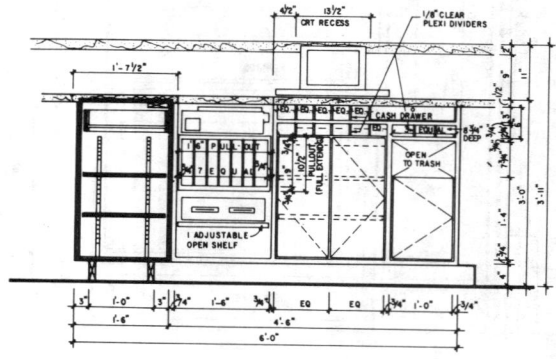

ELEVATION-REGISTRATION COUNTER

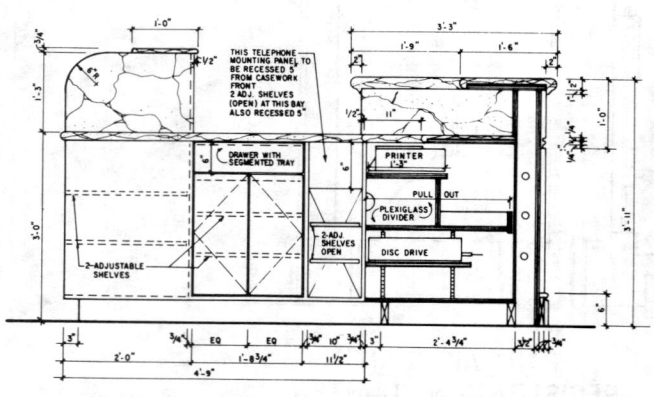

ELEVATION / SECTION-REGISTRATION COUNTER

Fig. 11

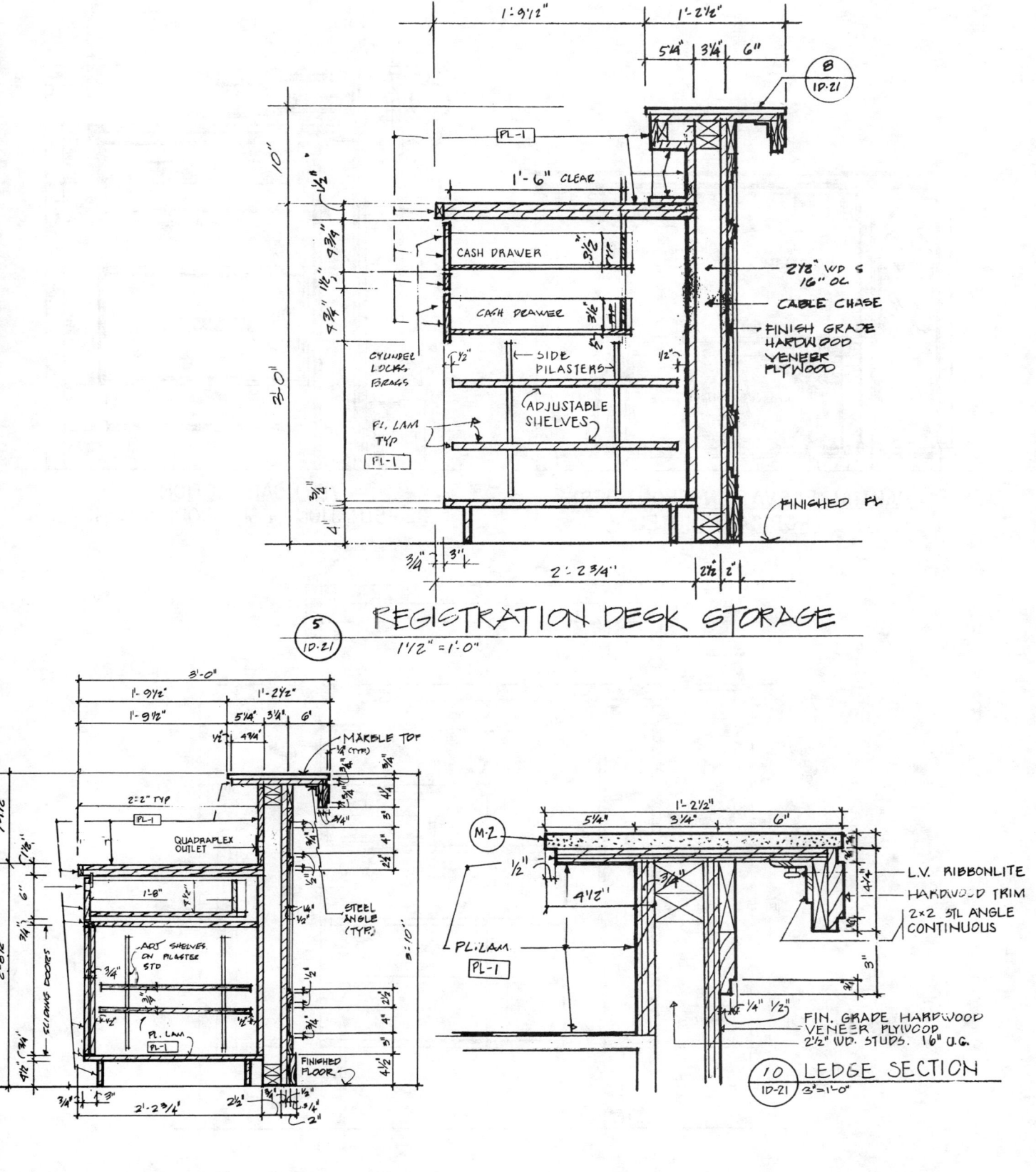

5 (ID·21) REGISTRATION DESK STORAGE 1½" = 1'-0"

1 (ID·21) RECEPTION DESK STORAGE SCALE: 1½" = 1'-0"

10 (ID·21) LEDGE SECTION 3" = 1'-0"

Fig. 12

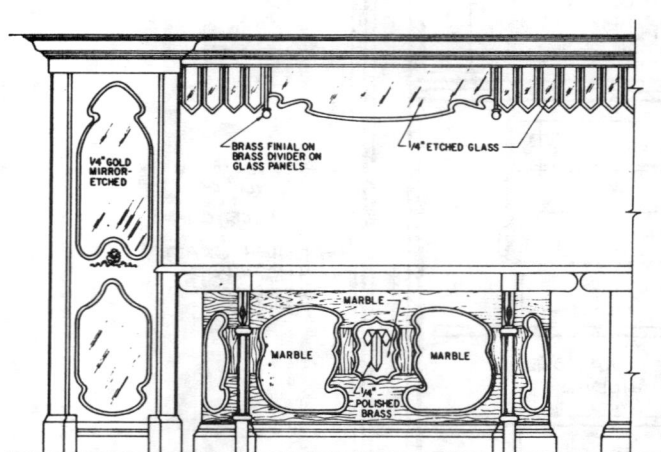

**PARTIAL ELEVATION - FRONT DESK
TROPICANA HOTEL**

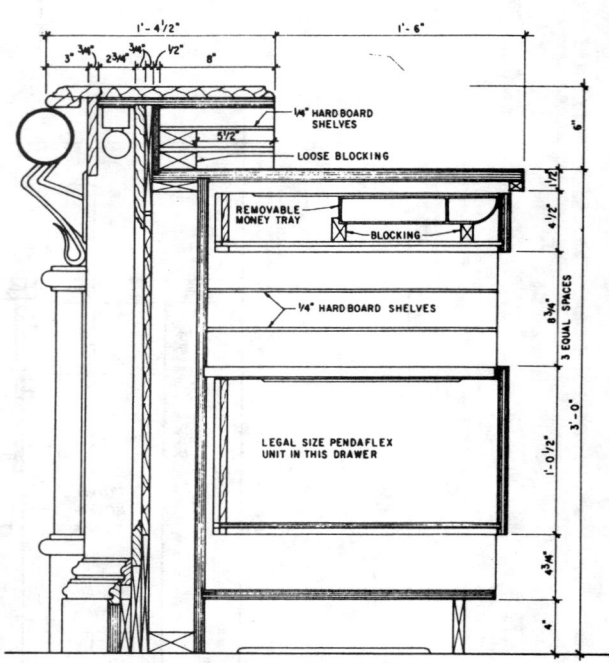

**VERTICAL SECTION
REGISTRATION DESK TROPICANA HOTEL**

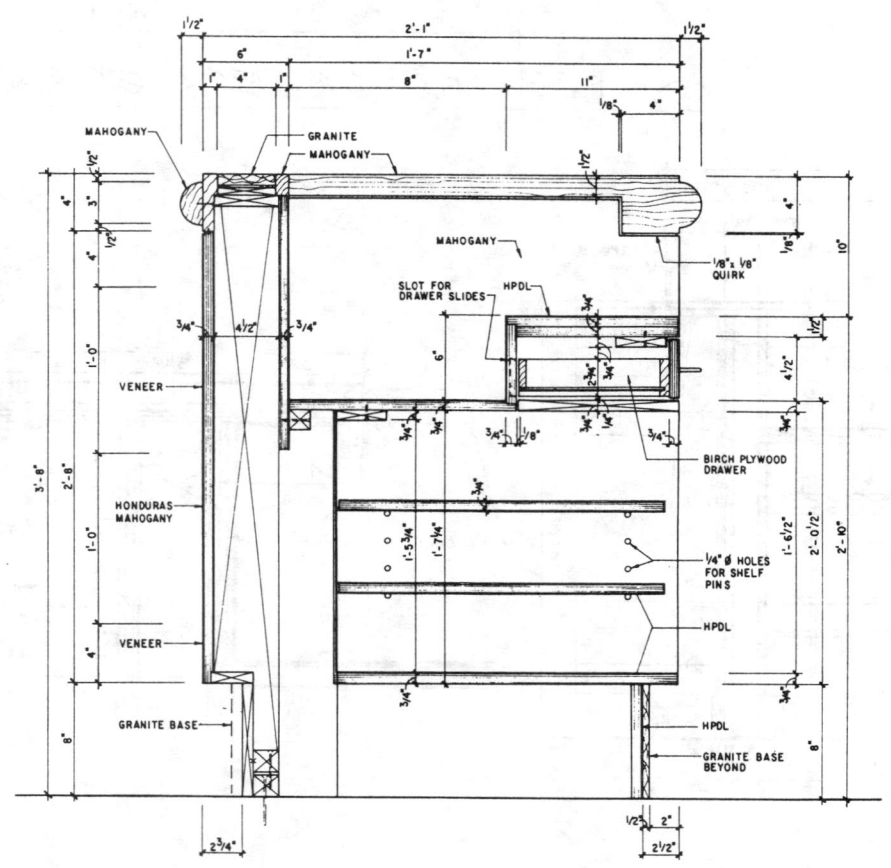

VERTICAL SECTION AT RECEPTION DESK

Fig. 13

384

Retail Spaces

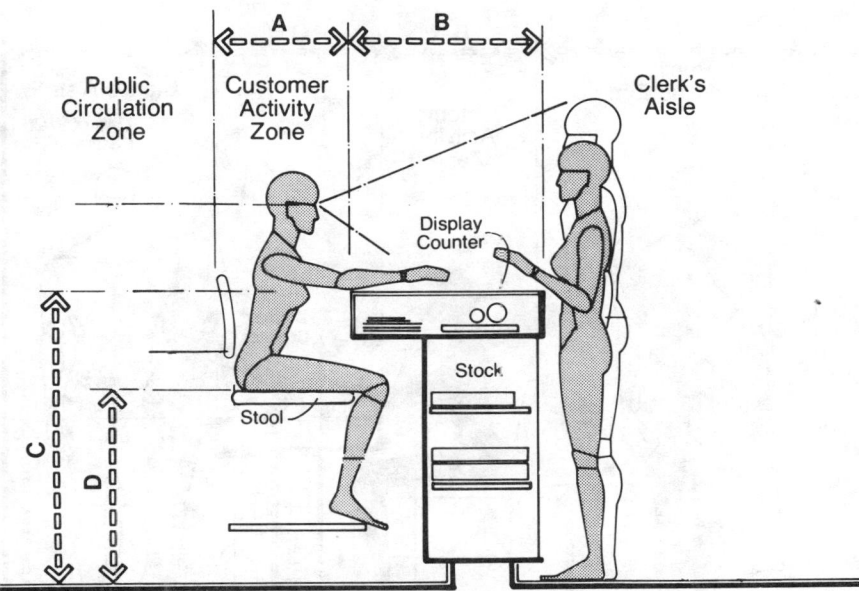

Fig. 1   Seated customer/high counter height.

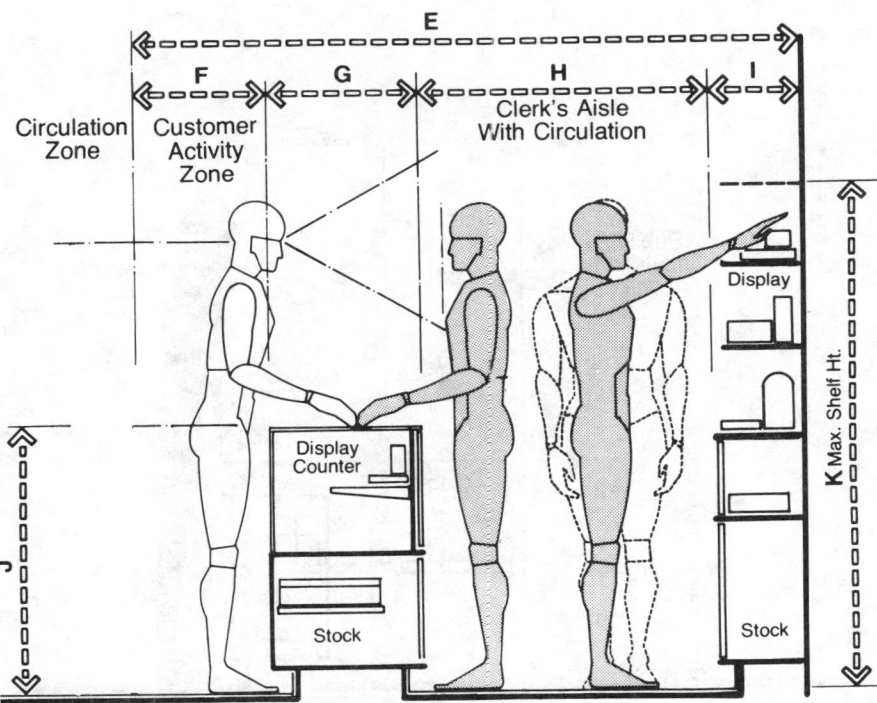

Fig. 2   Typical sales area/standing customer.

The essential function of retail spaces is to display and sell merchandise. The design of these spaces involves the manipulation and coordination of architectural, interior design, and merchandising elements as necessary to meet the programmatic needs of the client. It is critical that the space in which the customer and store personnel function is of the highest quality. Ensuring this quality requires a knowledge of the planning and design of the various interior components that constitute the building blocks of retail spaces.

Figure 1 shows the clearances involved for a 42-in, or 106.7-cm, high counter to service a seated user. By filling the recess with an additional display, however, the counter can also be used exclusively as a typical sales counter. It should be noted, however, that although sometimes used for special display situations, such a counter height is not recommended. Both the customer and the sales clerk of smaller body size would find coping with such a height uncomfortable anthropometrically, particularly when one considers that the counter would be higher than the elbow height of slightly over 5 percent of the population. From a merchandising viewpoint, where customer convenience is of paramount importance, it would be unwise to exceed 39 to 40 in, or 99 to 101.6 cm, as a counter height. In addition, the smaller sales clerk forced to tend such a counter for extended periods of time could be subjected to severe backaches and pains. Getting on and off a high stool for elderly and disabled people or those of smaller body size can be not only difficult, but hazardous. Figure 2 illustrates the clearances for a typical sales counter.

	in	cm
A	26–30	66.0–76.2
B	18–24	45.7–61.0
C	42	106.7
D	28	71.1
E	84–112	213.4–284.5
F	18	45.7
G	18–24	45.7–61.0
H	30–48	76.2–121.9
I	18–22	45.7–55.9
J	35–38	88.9–96.5
K	72	182.9

Figure 3 shows the clearances required for a medium height display counter. The suggested seat height of 21 to 22 in, or 53.3 to 55.8 cm, requires a footrest for the seated customer. The counter height shown will allow the display to be viewed by both the seated customer and the standing sales clerk. The customer activity zone allows adequate space for the chair. Knee height, buttock-knee length, popliteal height, and eye height sitting are all significant human dimensions to consider in the design of counters to be used by a seated customer.

Figure 4 shows a low 30-in, or 76.2-cm, display counter also for use by a seated customer. The anthropometric considerations are the same. Although the counter height is responsive to the anthropometric requirements of the seated customer, it is less than ideal for the standing clerk. For the standing user's optimum comfort, the counter height should be about 2 or 3 in, or 5 to 7.6 cm, below elbow height. This will allow a person to handle objects comfortably on the counter surface or use the counter as support for his or her arms. The 30-in height is too low to permit such use.

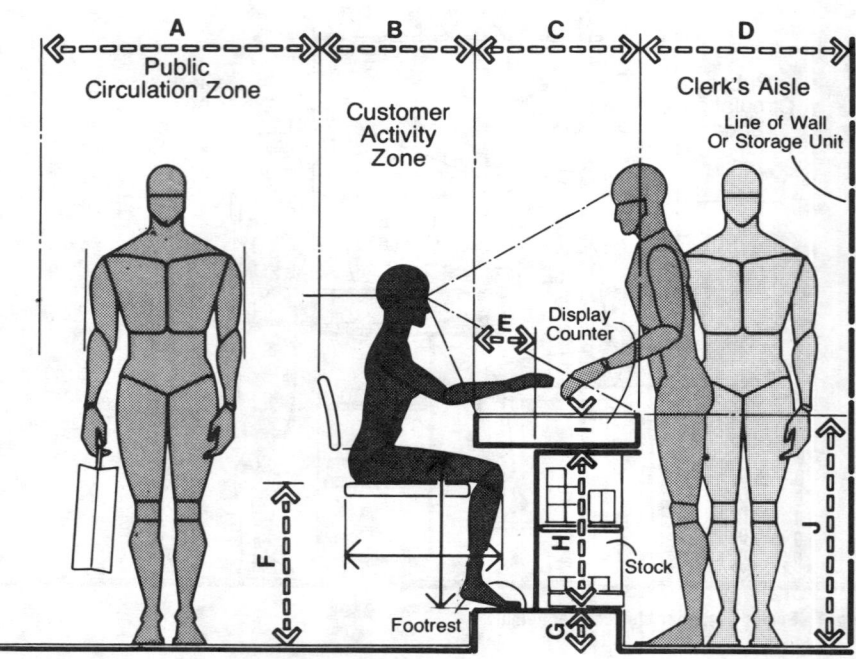

Fig. 3 Seated customer/desirable counter height.

	in	cm
A	36	91.4
B	26–30	66.0–76.2
C	18–24	45.7–61.0
D	30 min.	76.2 min.
E	10	25.4
F	21–22	53.3–55.9
G	5	12.7
H	23–25	58.4–63.5
I	4–6	10.2–15.2
J	34–36	86.4–91.4
K	30	76.2
L	16–17	40.6–43.2

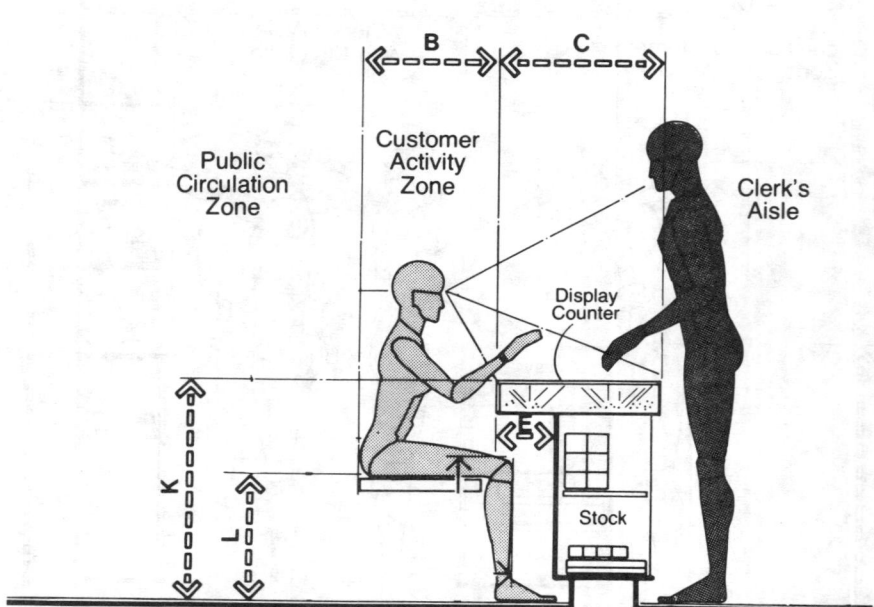

Fig. 4 Seated customer/low counter height.

Shelving is probably used more than any other single interior component for the storage and/or display of merchandise. Not only must the merchandise be within reach anthropometrically, but it must be fairly visible as well. The heights established must therefore be responsive to vertical grip reach dimensions as well as to eye height. In establishing height limits, the body size data of the smaller person should be used. Since in retail spaces, departments may cater exclusively to members of one sex or the other, two sets of data are presented. One is based on the body size of the smaller female and the other on the body size of the smaller male. The suggested heights reflect a compromise between reach requirements and visibility requirements.

Figure 6 illustrates the clearances involved in hanging-type merchandise cases. Rod heights should be related not only to human reach limitations, but in certain cases to the sizes of the merchandise displayed. There is usually no conflict in respect to garments.

	in	cm
A	48 max.	121.9 max.
B	30–36	76.2–91.4
C	51 min.	129.5 min.
D	66	167.6
E	72	182.9
F	84–96	213.4–243.8
G	20–26	50.8–66.0
H	28–30	71.1–76.2
I	18–24	45.7–61.0
J	18 min.	45.7 min.
K	72 max.	182.9 max.
L	4	10.2
M	42	106.7
N	26 min.	66.0 min.

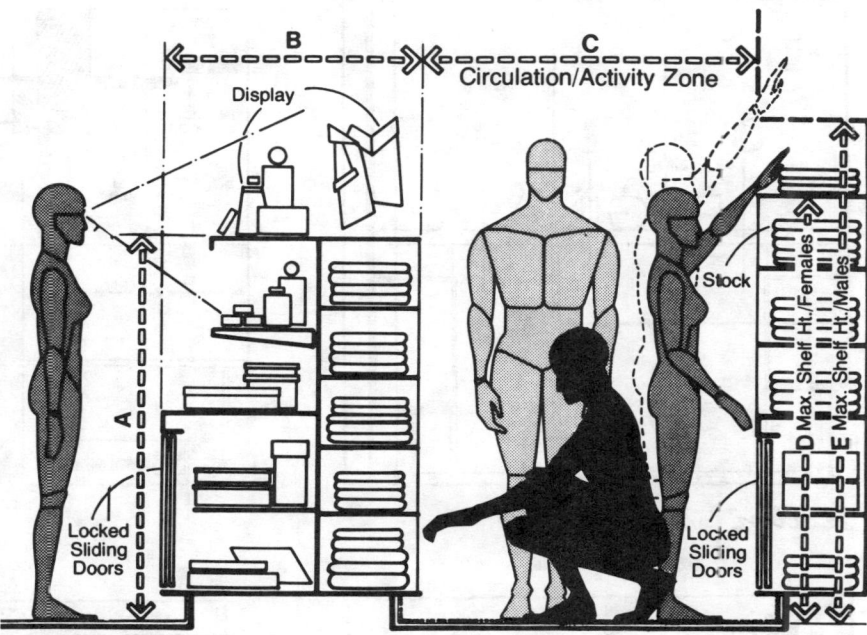

Fig. 5　Typical merchandise cases.

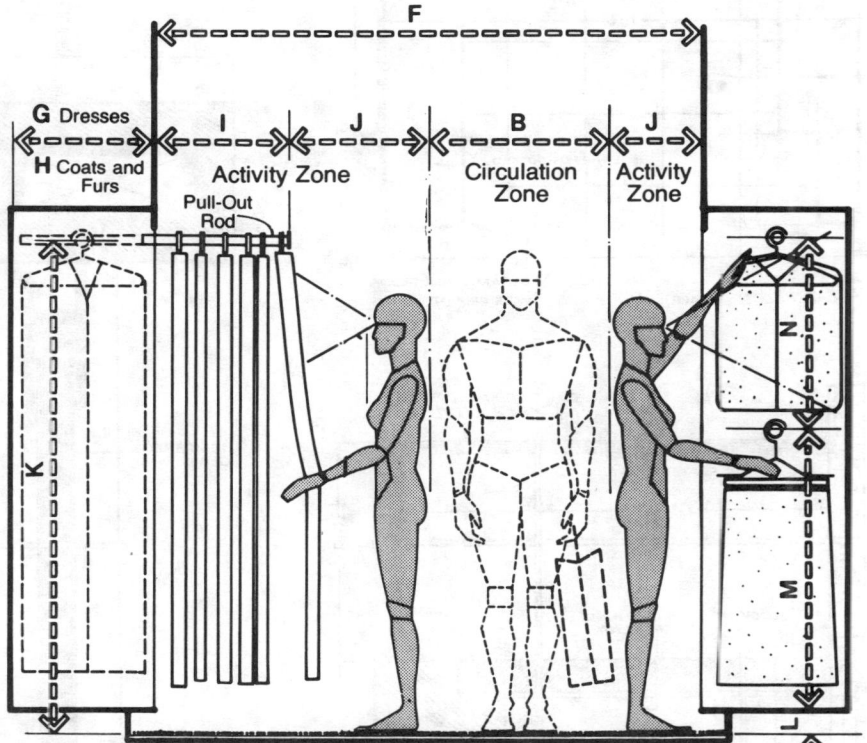

Fig. 6　Hanging merchandise cases.

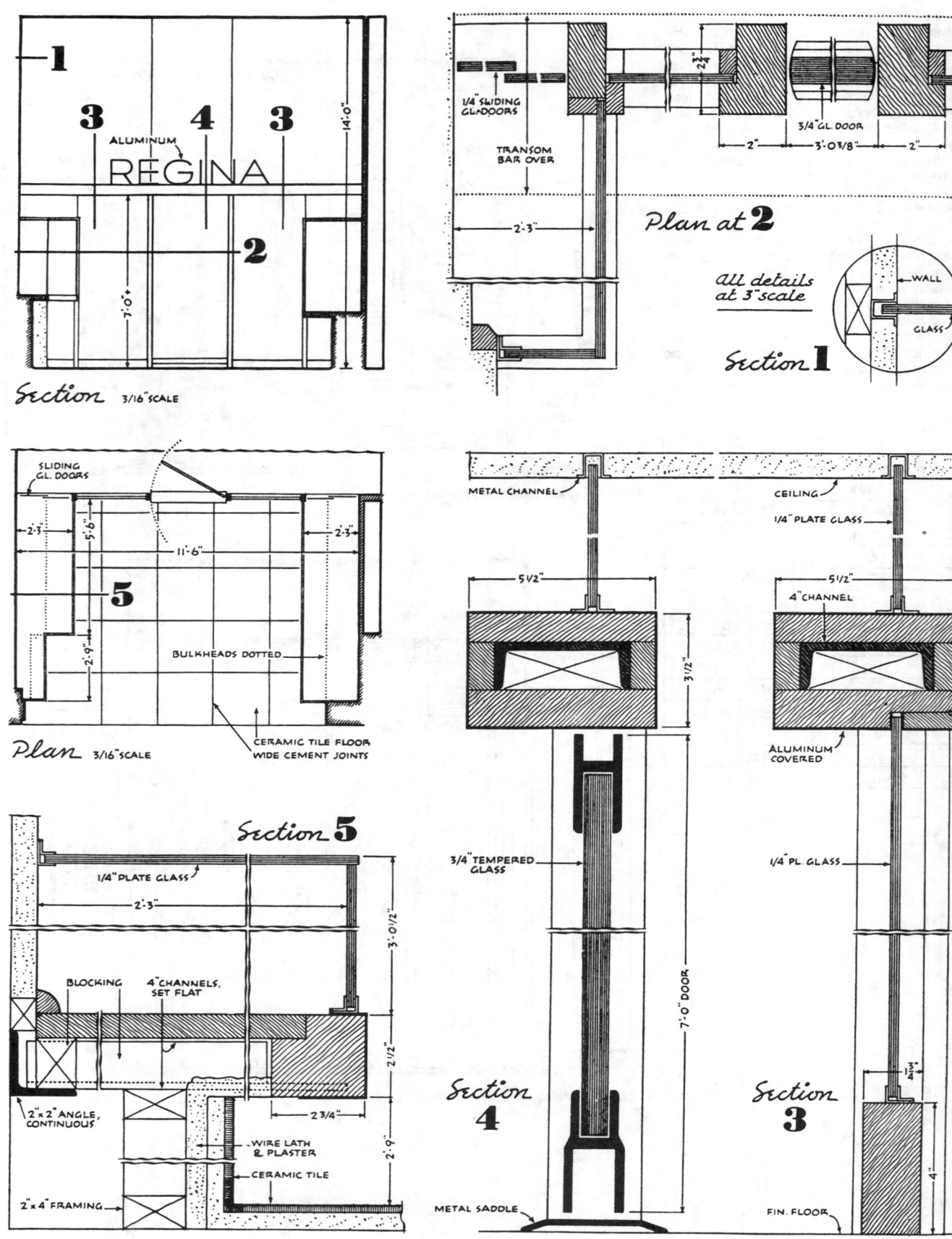

1/4" SLIDING GL. DOORS

TRANSOM BAR OVER

3/4" GL. DOOR

2" | 3'-0 3/8" | 2"

2 3/4"

2'-3"

Plan at **2**

All details at 3" scale

WALL

GLASS

Section **1**

ALUMINUM

REGINA

14'-0"

7'-0"

Section 3/16" SCALE

SLIDING GL. DOORS

2'-3"

5'-6"

11'-6"

2'-3"

2'-9"

BULKHEADS DOTTED

5

CERAMIC TILE FLOOR WIDE CEMENT JOINTS

Plan 3/16" SCALE

Section **5**

1/4" PLATE GLASS

2'-3"

3'-0 1/2"

BLOCKING

4" CHANNELS, SET FLAT

2 1/2"

2" x 2" ANGLE, CONTINUOUS

2 3/4"

2'-9"

WIRE LATH & PLASTER

CERAMIC TILE

2" x 4" FRAMING

METAL CHANNEL

5 1/2"

3 1/2"

3/4" TEMPERED GLASS

7'-0" DOOR

Section **4**

METAL SADDLE

CEILING

1/4" PLATE GLASS

5 1/2"

4" CHANNEL

ALUMINUM COVERED

1/4" PL. GLASS

Section **3**

4"

FIN. FLOOR

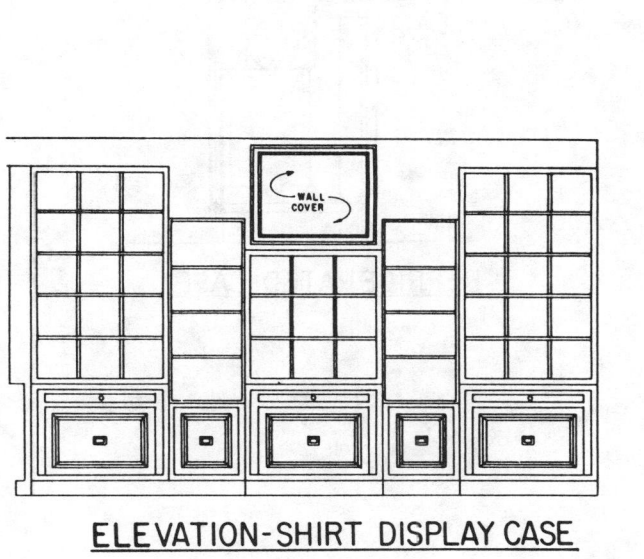

ELEVATION-SHIRT DISPLAY CASE

VERTICAL SECTION
SHIRT DISPLAY

VERTICAL SECTION
JEWELRY SHOWCASE

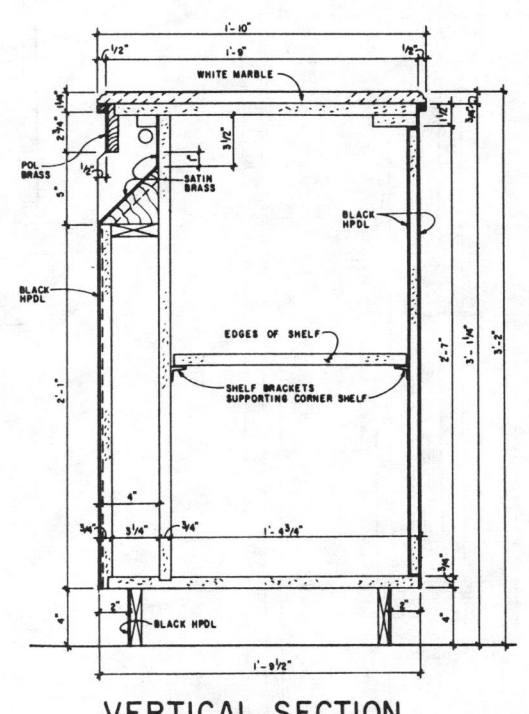

VERTICAL SECTION
COSMETIC DISPLAY

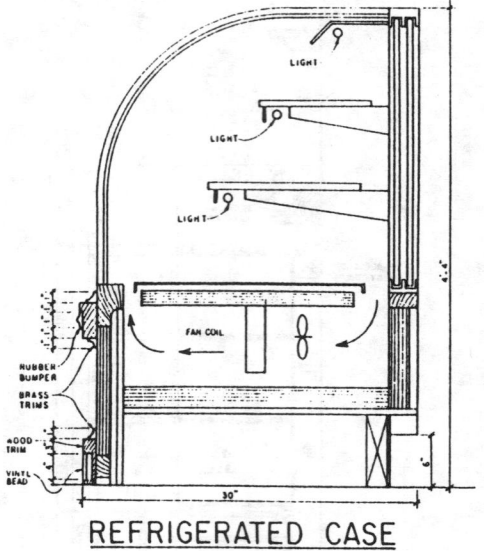

REFRIGERATED CASE

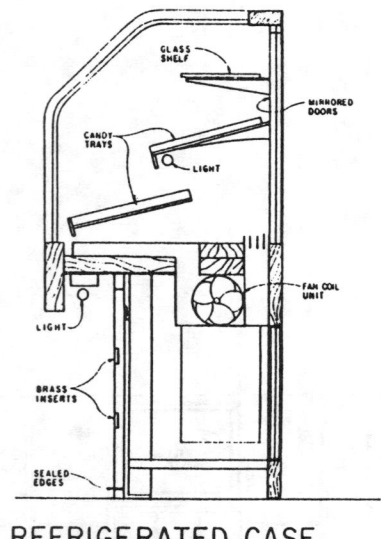

REFRIGERATED CASE

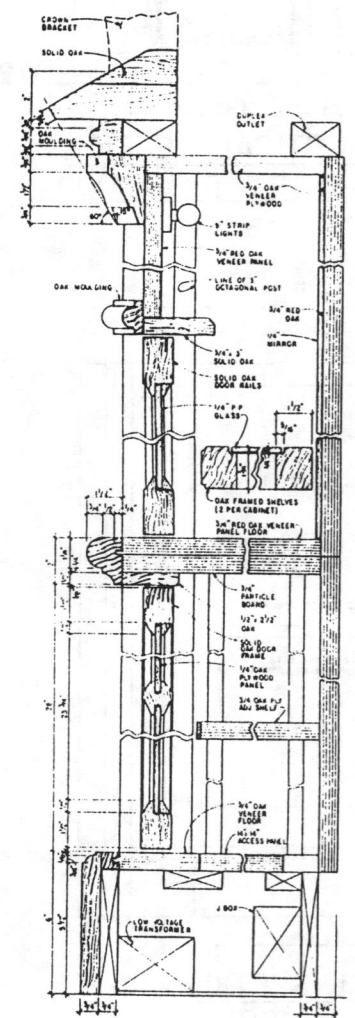

CROSS SECTION-DISPLAY CABINET

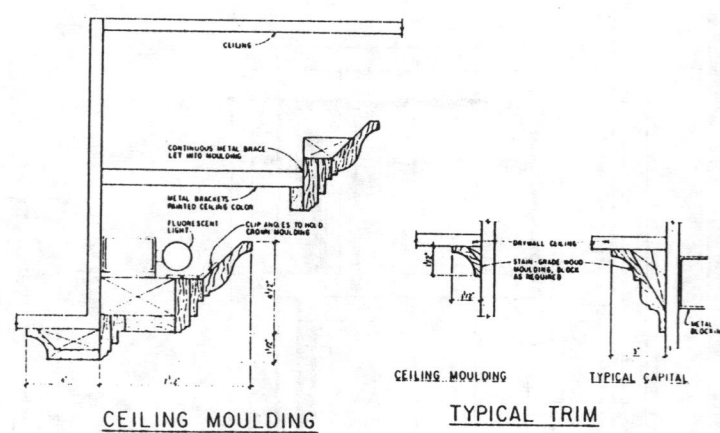

CEILING MOULDING   TYPICAL TRIM

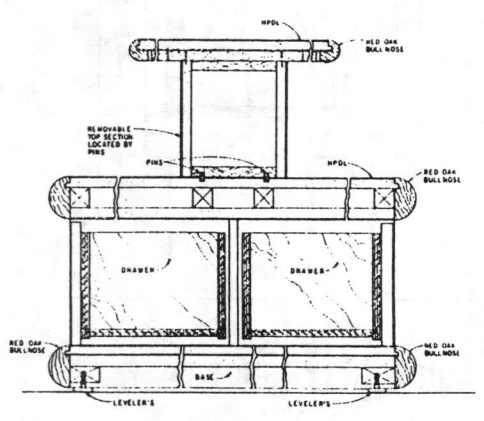

ISLAND DISPLAY

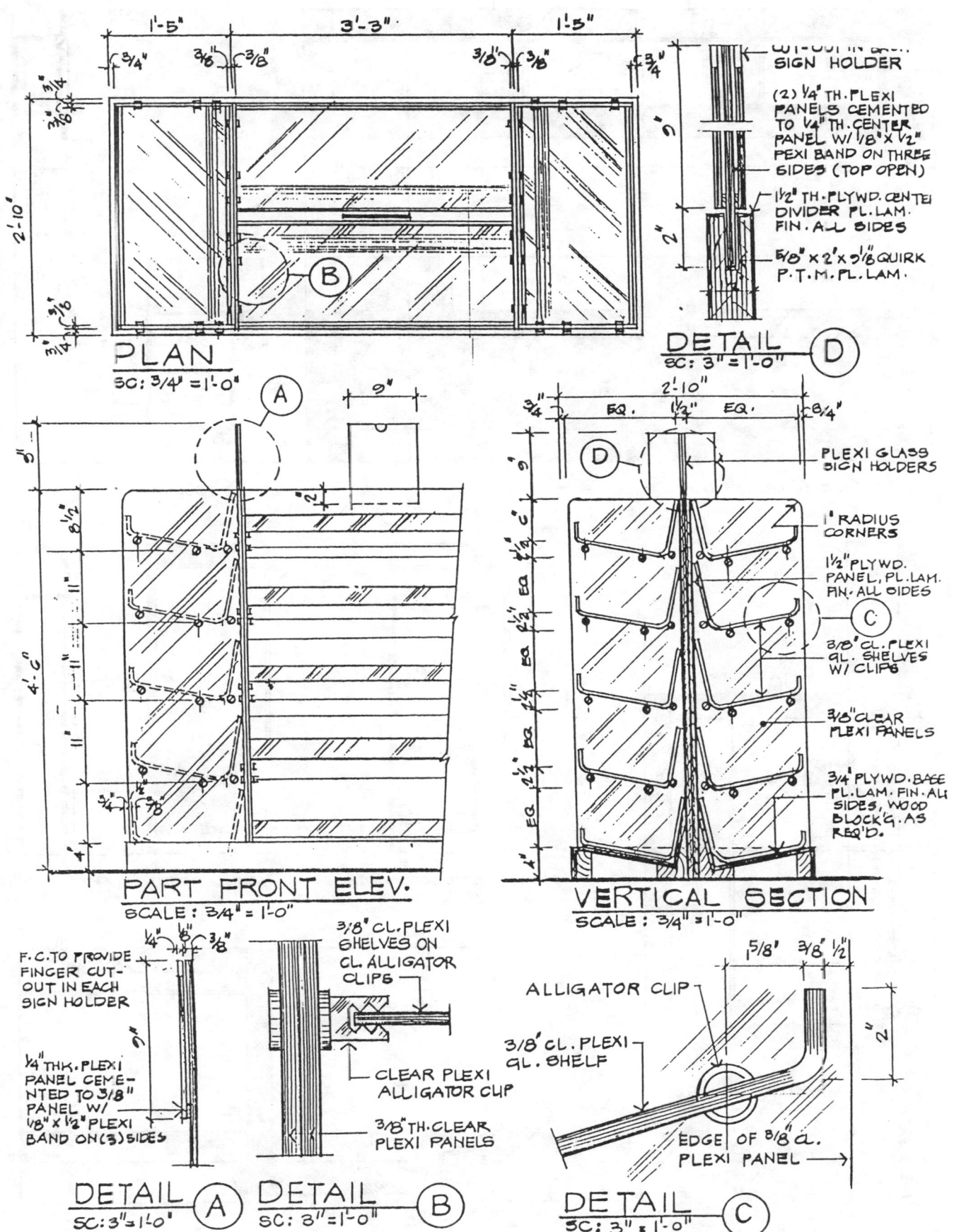

1'-5"   3'-3"   1'-5"

3/4" 3/8" 3/8"   3/8" 3/8"   3/4"

2'-10"

PLAN
SC: 3/4" = 1'-0"

B

CUT-OUT IN BASE
SIGN HOLDER

(2) 1/4" TH. PLEXI
PANELS CEMENTED
TO 1/4" TH. CENTER
PANEL W/ 1/8" X 1/2"
PLEXI BAND ON THREE
SIDES (TOP OPEN)

1 1/2" TH. PLYWD. CENTER
DIVIDER PL. LAM.
FIN. ALL SIDES

5/8" X 2' X 5 1/8" QUIRK
P. T. M. PL. LAM.

DETAIL
SC: 3" = 1'-0"   D

9"

A

4'-6"

3/4" 7/8"

4"

PART FRONT ELEV.
SCALE: 3/4" = 1'-0"

D

2'-10"
3/4" EQ. 1 1/2" EQ. 3/4"

PLEXI GLASS
SIGN HOLDERS

1" RADIUS
CORNERS

1 1/2" PLYWD.
PANEL, PL. LAM.
FIN. ALL SIDES

C

3/8" CL. PLEXI
GL. SHELVES
W/ CLIPS

3/8" CLEAR
PLEXI PANELS

3/4" PLYWD. BASE
PL. LAM. FIN. ALL
SIDES, WOOD
BLOCK'G. AS
REQ'D.

VERTICAL SECTION
SCALE: 3/4" = 1'-0"

F. C. TO PROVIDE
FINGER CUT-
OUT IN EACH
SIGN HOLDER

1/4" 3/8" 3/8"

1/4" THK. PLEXI
PANEL CEMEN-
TED TO 3/8"
PANEL W/
1/8" X 1/2" PLEXI
BAND ON (3) SIDES

DETAIL   A
SC: 3" = 1'-0"

3/8" CL. PLEXI
SHELVES ON
CL. ALLIGATOR
CLIPS

CLEAR PLEXI
ALLIGATOR CLIP

3/8" TH. CLEAR
PLEXI PANELS

DETAIL   B
SC: 3" = 1'-0"

ALLIGATOR CLIP

1 5/8" 3/8" 1/2"

2"

3/8" CL. PLEXI
GL. SHELF

EDGE OF 3/8" CL.
PLEXI PANEL

DETAIL   C
SC: 3" = 1'-0"

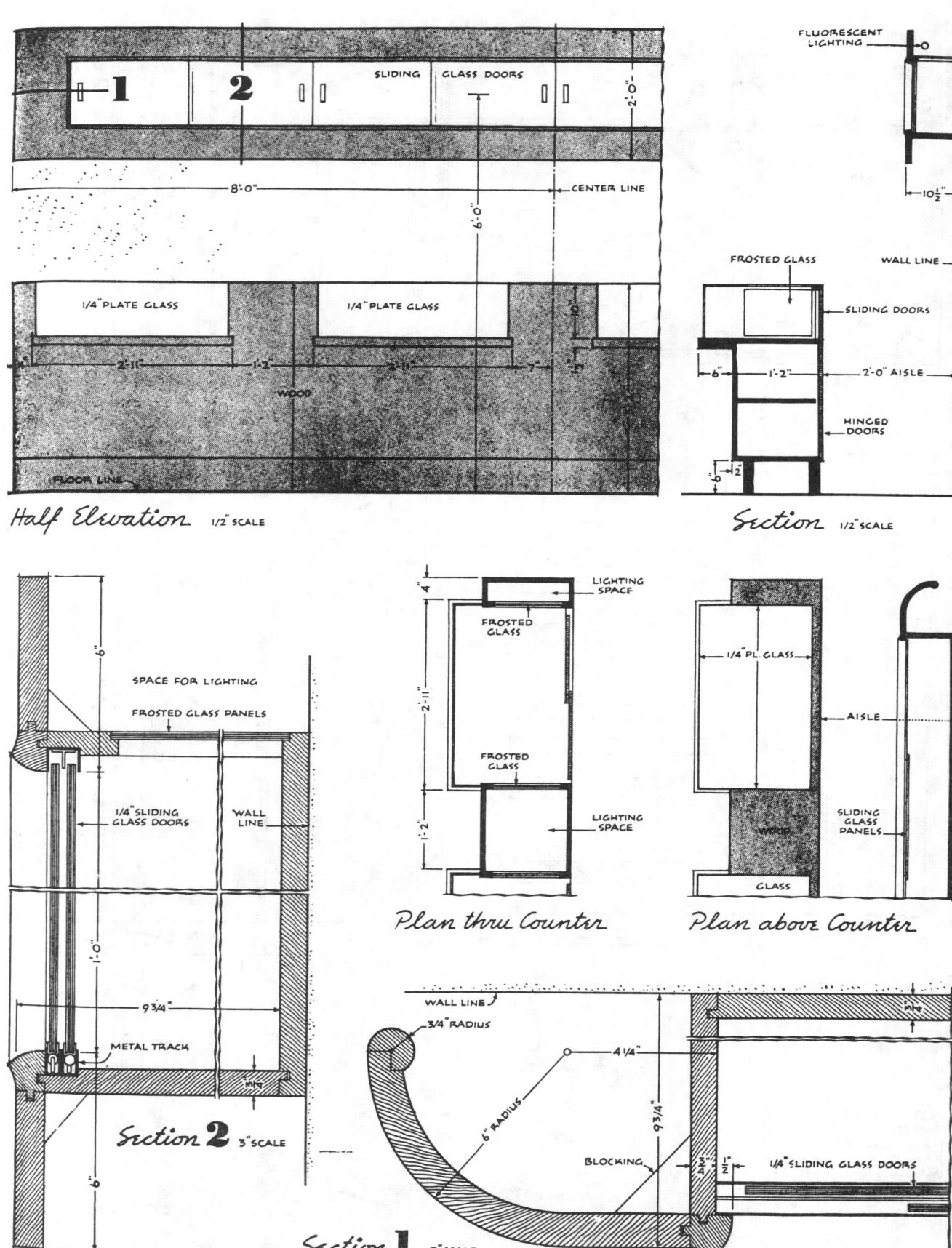

Half Elevation 1/2" SCALE

Section 1/2" SCALE

Section 2 3" SCALE

Plan thru Counter

Plan above Counter

Section 1 3" SCALE

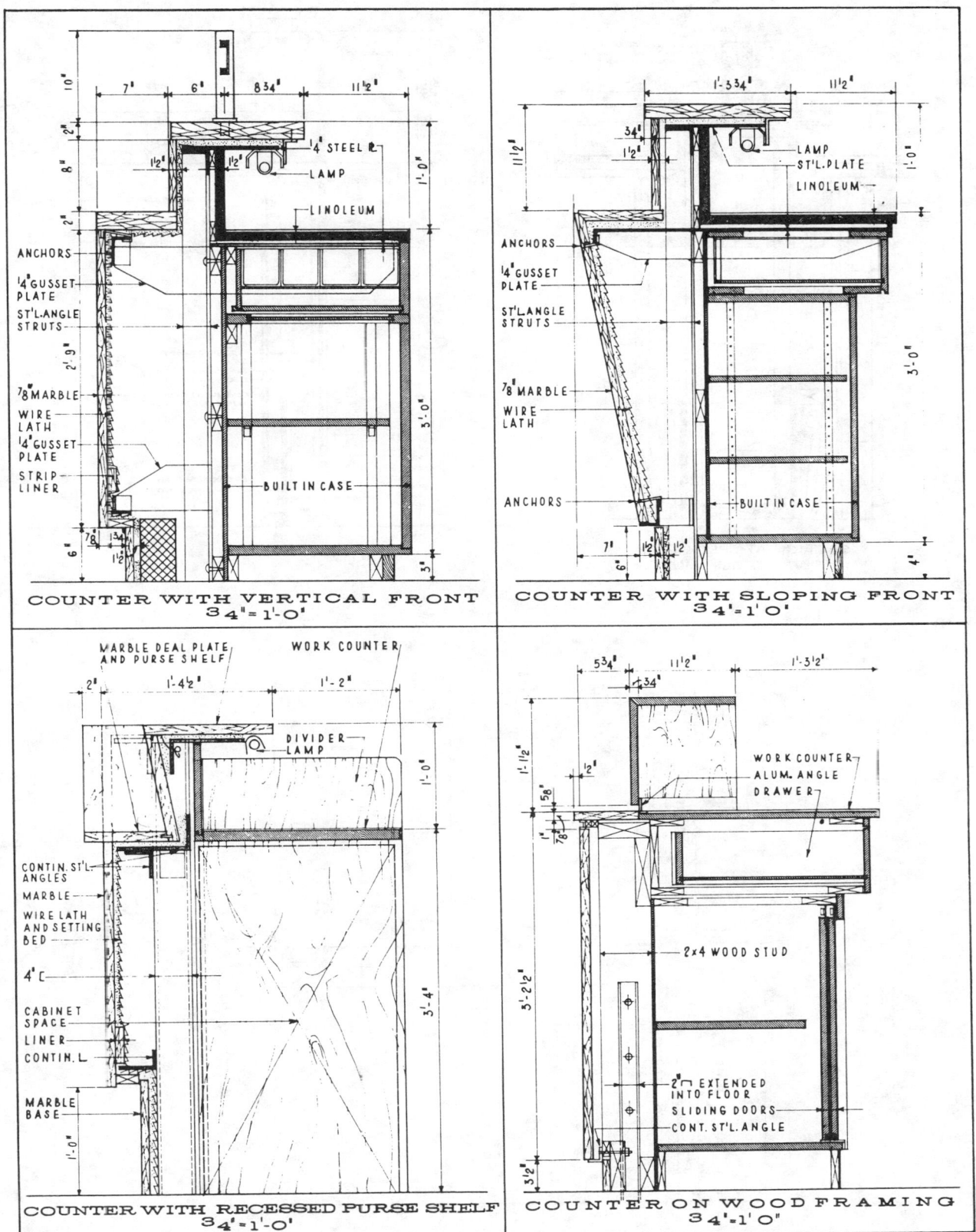

COUNTER WITH VERTICAL FRONT
3 4" = 1'-0'

COUNTER WITH SLOPING FRONT
3 4"=1' 0'

COUNTER WITH RECESSED PURSE SHELF
3 4"=1'-0'

COUNTER ON WOOD FRAMING
3 4'=1' 0"

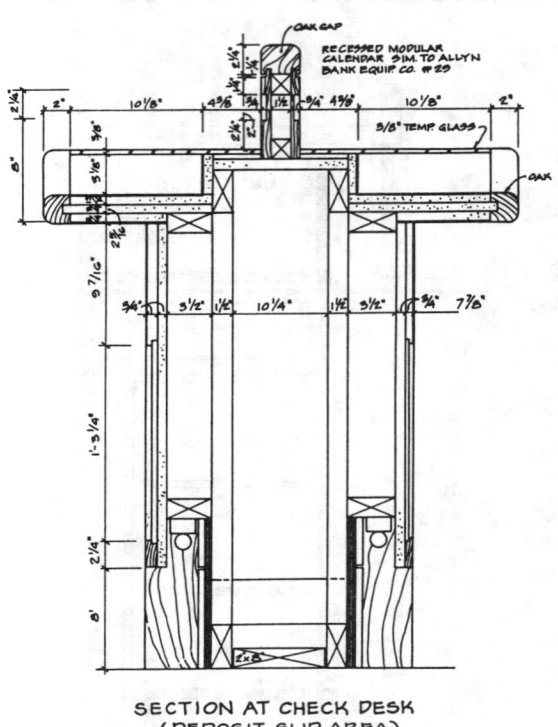

SECTION AT CHECK DESK
(DEPOSIT SLIP AREA)

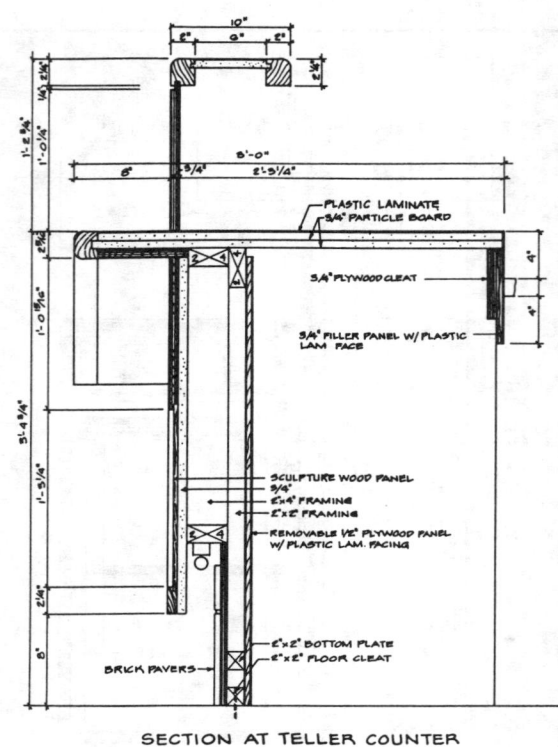

SECTION AT TELLER COUNTER

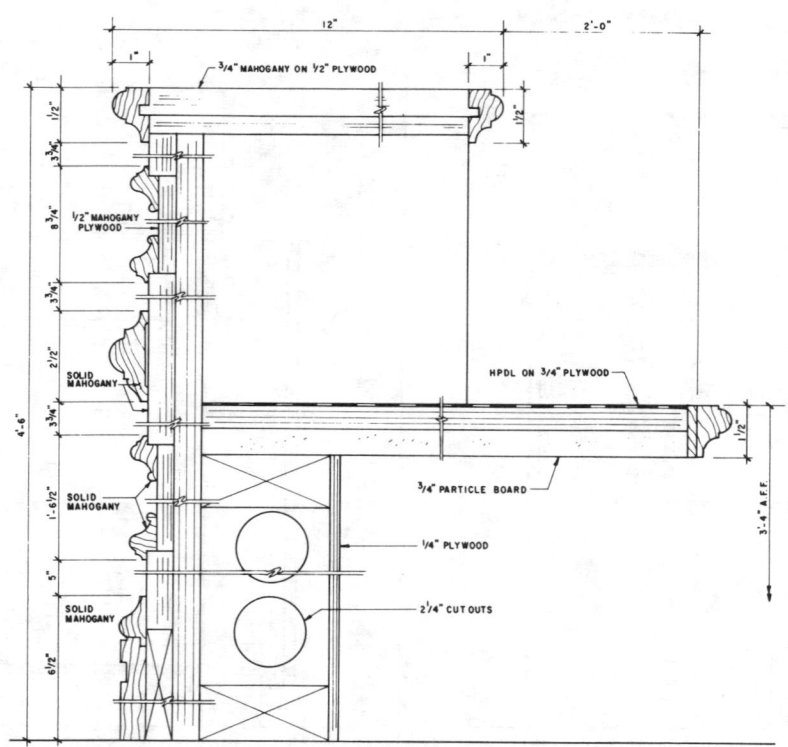

VERTICAL SECTION AT TELLERS COUNTER

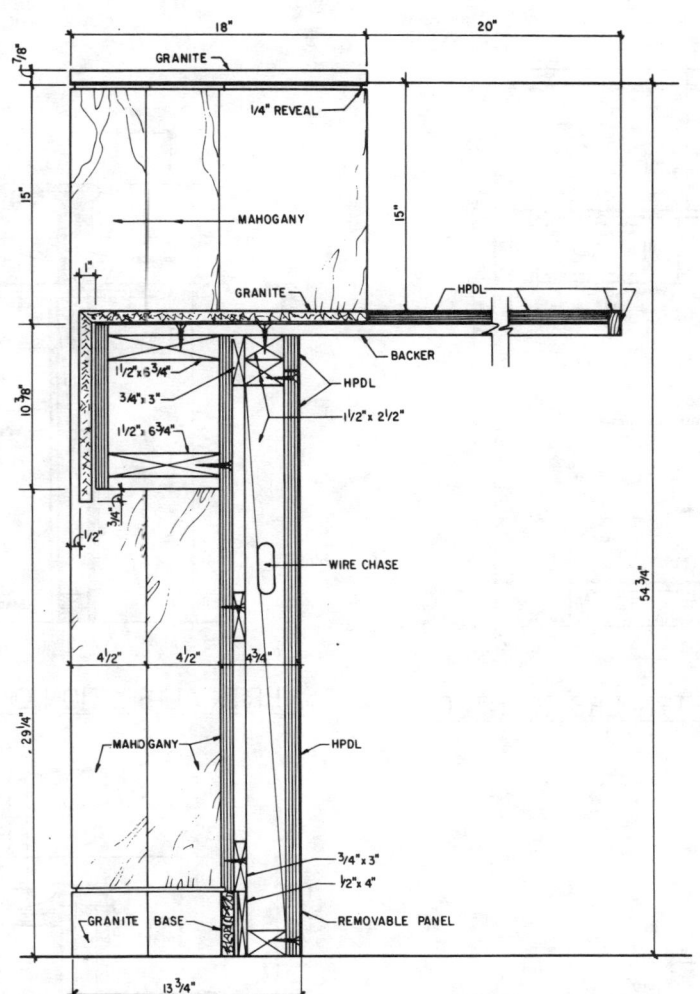

VERTICAL SECTION-TELLERS UNITS

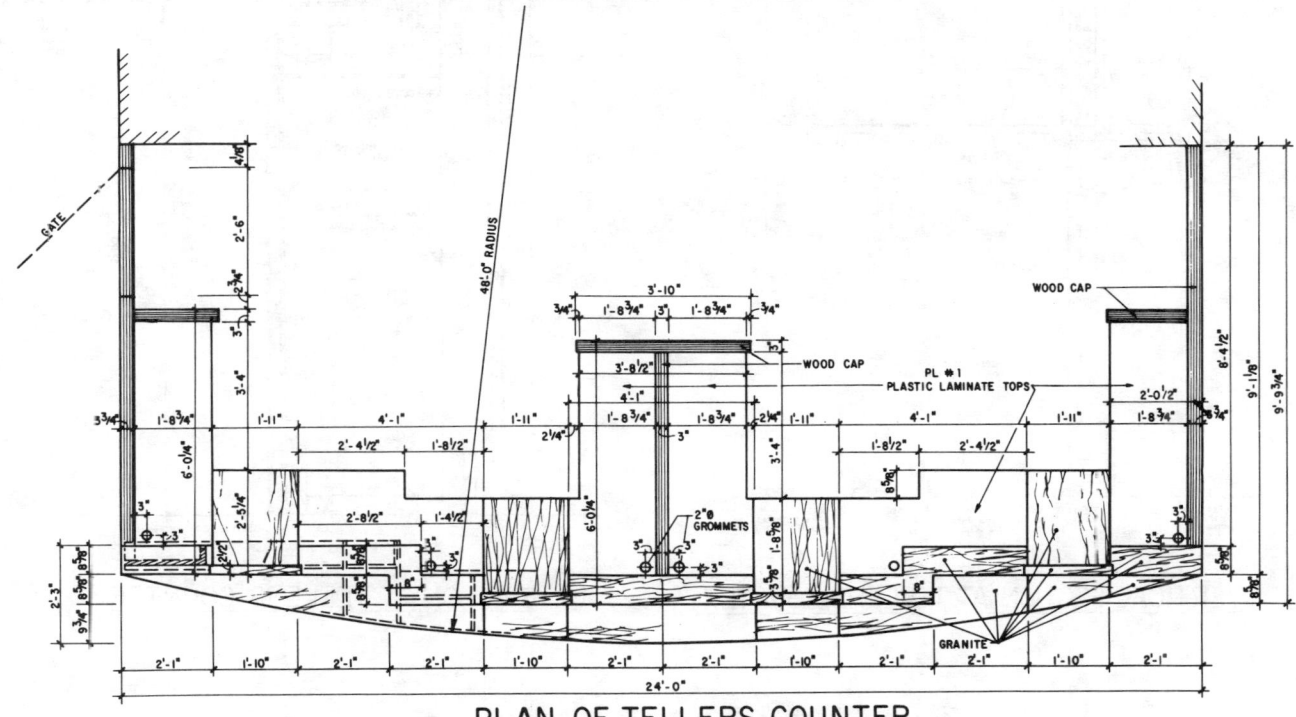

PLAN OF TELLERS COUNTER

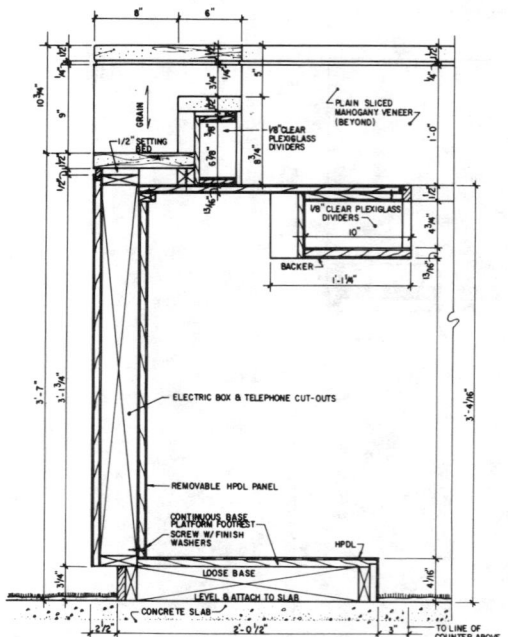

VERTICAL SECTION-TELLERS COUNTER

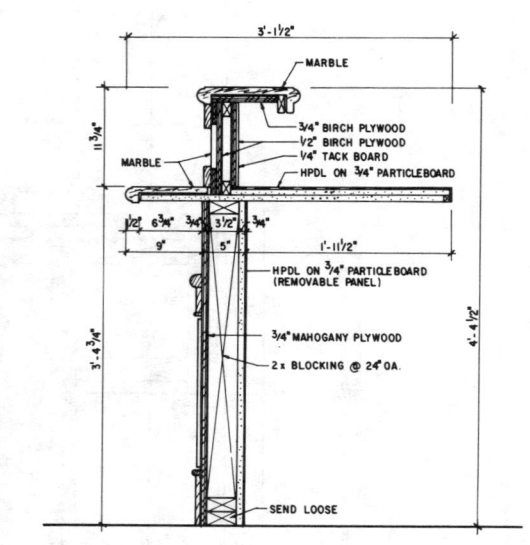

VERTICAL SECTION OF TELLERS COUNTER

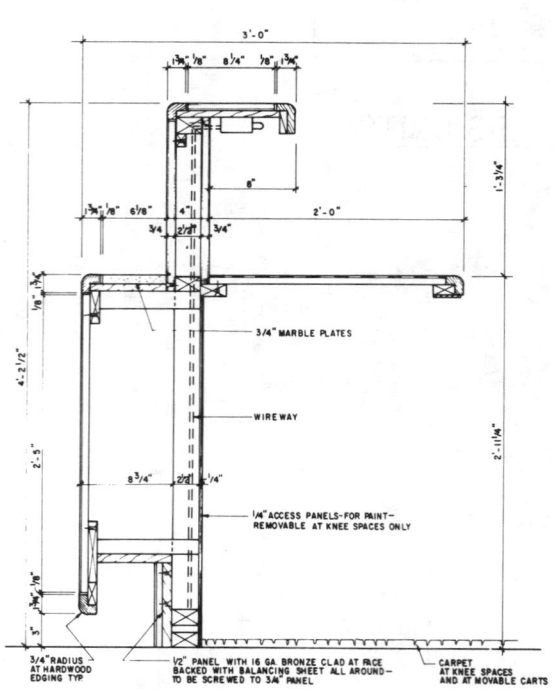

VERTICAL SECTION AT TELLERS COUNTER

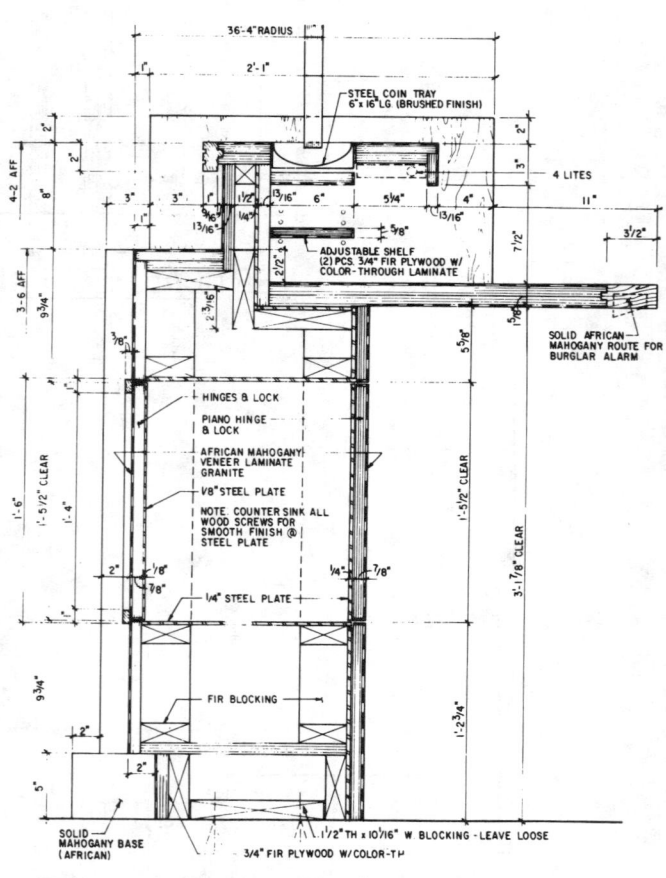

SECTION AT TELLERS COUNTER

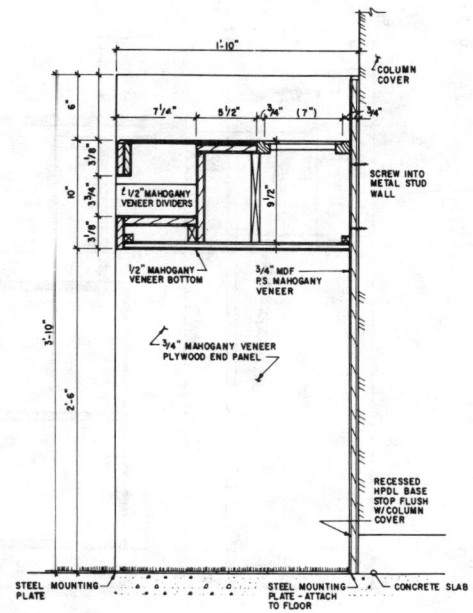

VERTICAL SECTION AT CHECK STAND

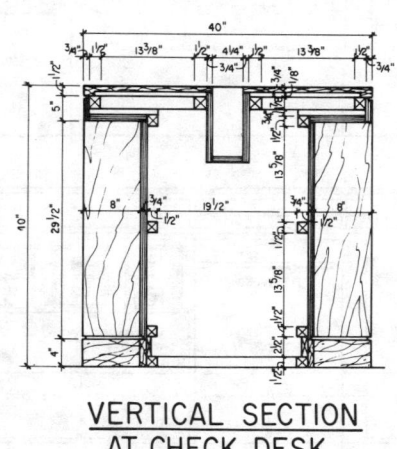

VERTICAL SECTION AT CHECK DESK

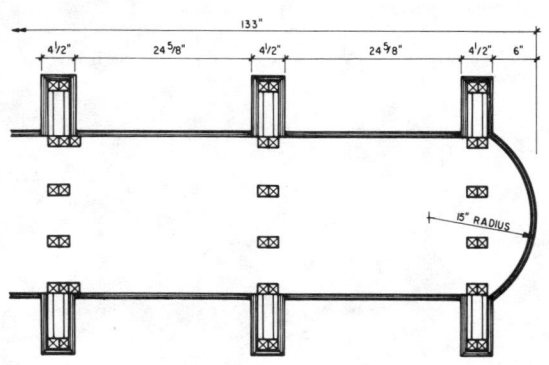

HALF PLAN THRU CHECK DESK

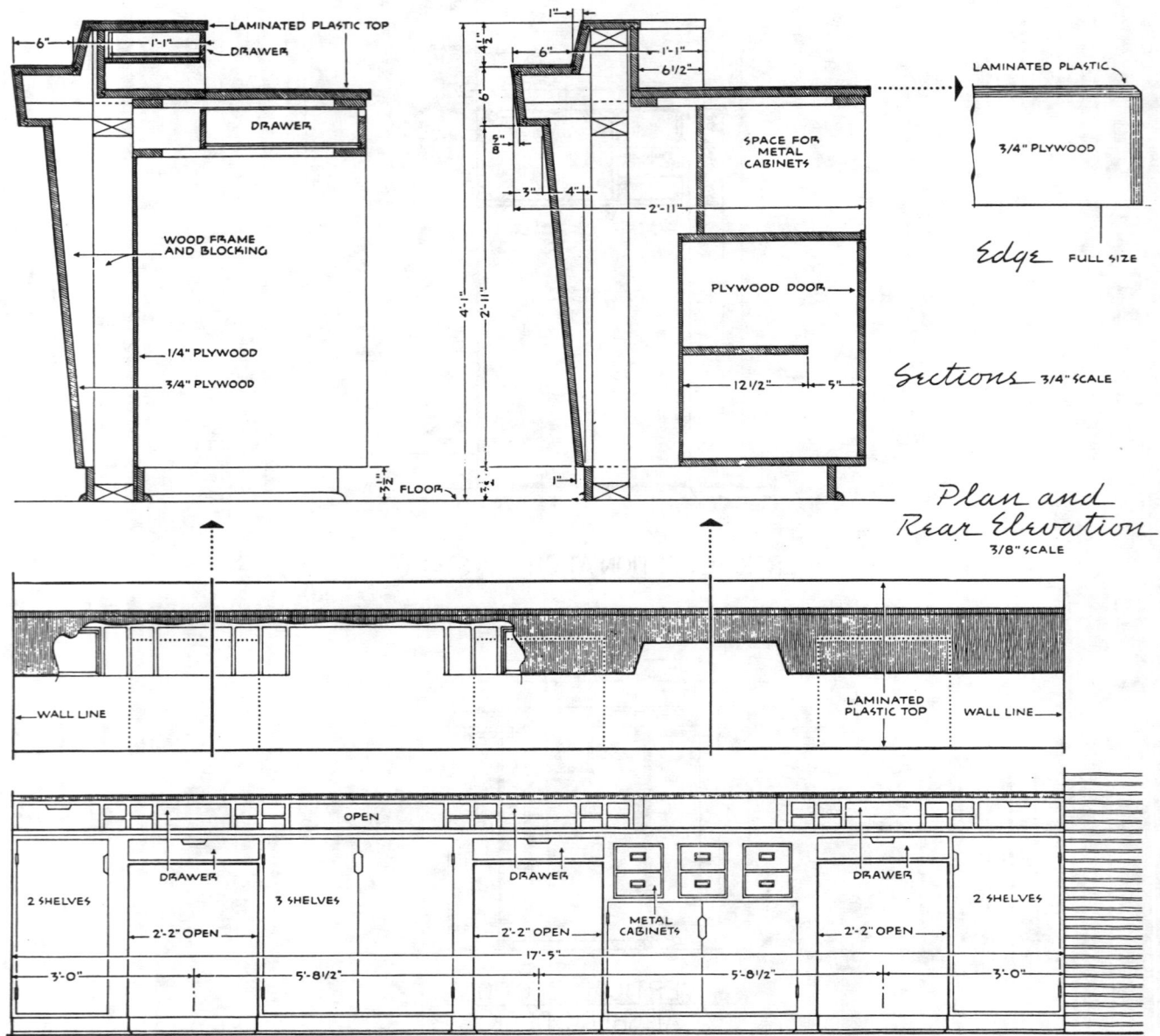

LAMINATED PLASTIC TOP

DRAWER

6"

1'-1"

DRAWER

WOOD FRAME
AND BLOCKING

1/4" PLYWOOD

3/4" PLYWOOD

3½"

FLOOR

4'-1"

2'-11"

1"

1'-1"

6"

4½"

6"

5"
⅝

3"   4"

6½"

2'-11"

SPACE FOR
METAL
CABINETS

PLYWOOD DOOR

12½"   5"

1"

LAMINATED PLASTIC

3/4" PLYWOOD

Edge   FULL SIZE

Sections 3/4" SCALE

*Plan and
Rear Elevation*
3/8" SCALE

WALL LINE

LAMINATED
PLASTIC TOP   WALL LINE

OPEN

2 SHELVES

DRAWER

3 SHELVES

2'-2" OPEN

3'-0"

5'-8½"

DRAWER

2'-2" OPEN

17'-5"

METAL
CABINETS

5'-8½"

DRAWER

2'-2" OPEN

2 SHELVES

3'-0"

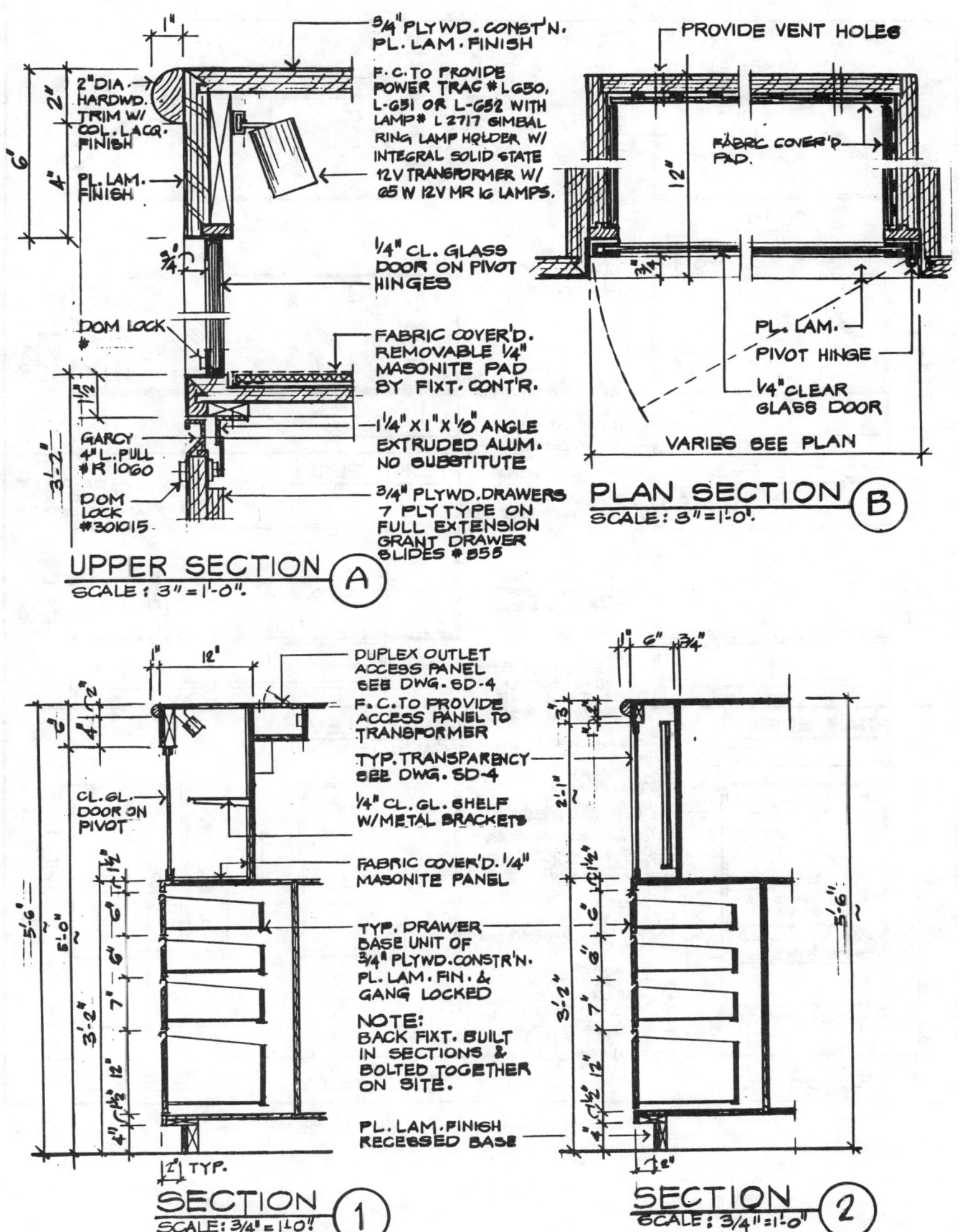

3/4" PLYWD. CONST'N.
PL. LAM. FINISH

F.C. TO PROVIDE
POWER TRAC # L-G50,
L-G51 OR L-G52 WITH
LAMP # L 2717 GIMBAL
RING LAMP HOLDER W/
INTEGRAL SOLID STATE
12V TRANSFORMER W/
Q5 W 12V MR 16 LAMPS.

1/4" CL. GLASS
DOOR ON PIVOT
HINGES

FABRIC COVER'D.
REMOVABLE 1/4"
MASONITE PAD
BY FIXT. CONT'R.

1 1/4" X 1" X 1/8" ANGLE
EXTRUDED ALUM.
NO SUBSTITUTE

3/4" PLYWD. DRAWERS
7 PLY TYPE ON
FULL EXTENSION
GRANT DRAWER
SLIDES # 555

2" DIA.
HARDWD.
TRIM W/
COL. LACQ.
FINISH

PL. LAM.
FINISH

DOM LOCK
#

GARCY
4" L. PULL
R 1060

DOM
LOCK
301015

UPPER SECTION (A)
SCALE: 3" = 1'-0".

PROVIDE VENT HOLES

FABRIC COVER'D
PAD.

PL. LAM.

PIVOT HINGE

1/4" CLEAR
GLASS DOOR

VARIES SEE PLAN

PLAN SECTION (B)
SCALE: 3" = 1'-0".

DUPLEX OUTLET
ACCESS PANEL
SEE DWG. SD-4

F.C. TO PROVIDE
ACCESS PANEL TO
TRANSFORMER

TYP. TRANSPARENCY
SEE DWG. SD-4

1/4" CL. GL. SHELF
W/ METAL BRACKETS

FABRIC COVER'D. 1/4"
MASONITE PANEL

TYP. DRAWER
BASE UNIT OF
3/4" PLYWD. CONSTR'N.
PL. LAM. FIN. &
GANG LOCKED

NOTE:
BACK FIXT. BUILT
IN SECTIONS &
BOLTED TOGETHER
ON SITE.

PL. LAM. FINISH
RECESSED BASE

CL. GL.
DOOR ON
PIVOT

1" TYP.

SECTION (1)
SCALE: 3/4" = 1'-0".

SECTION (2)
SCALE: 3/4" = 1'-0".

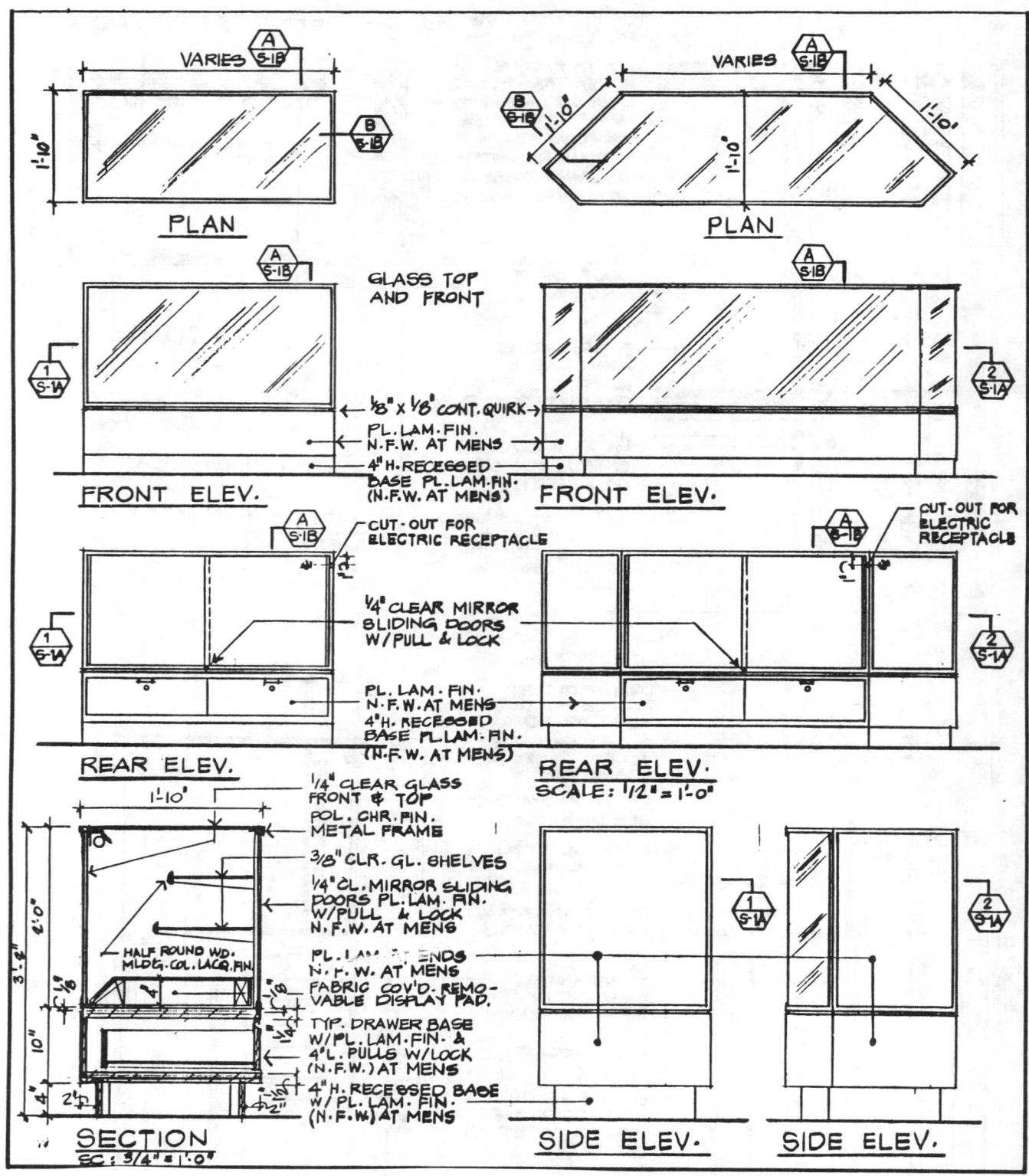

PLAN

PLAN

GLASS TOP
AND FRONT

FRONT ELEV.

FRONT ELEV.

1/8" x 1/8" CONT. QUIRK

PL. LAM. FIN.
N.F.W. AT MENS

4" H. RECESSED
BASE PL. LAM. FIN.
(N.F.W. AT MENS)

REAR ELEV.

REAR ELEV.
SCALE: 1/2" = 1'-0"

CUT-OUT FOR
ELECTRIC RECEPTACLE

CUT-OUT FOR
ELECTRIC RECEPTACLE

1/4" CLEAR MIRROR
SLIDING DOORS
W/PULL & LOCK

PL. LAM. FIN.
N.F.W. AT MENS
4" H. RECESSED
BASE PL. LAM. FIN.
(N.F.W. AT MENS)

1/4" CLEAR GLASS
FRONT & TOP
POL. CHR. FIN.
METAL FRAME

3/8" CLR. GL. SHELVES

1/4" CL. MIRROR SLIDING
DOORS PL. LAM. FIN.
W/PULL & LOCK
N.F.W. AT MENS

HALF ROUND WD.
MLDG. COL. LACQ. FIN.

PL. LAM. AT ENDS
N.F.W. AT MENS
FABRIC COV'D. REMO-
VABLE DISPLAY PAD.

TYP. DRAWER BASE
W/PL. LAM. FIN. &
4"L. PULLS W/LOCK
(N.F.W.) AT MENS

4" H. RECESSED BASE
W/PL. LAM. FIN.
(N.F.W) AT MENS

SECTION
SC: 3/4" = 1'-0"

SIDE ELEV.

SIDE ELEV.

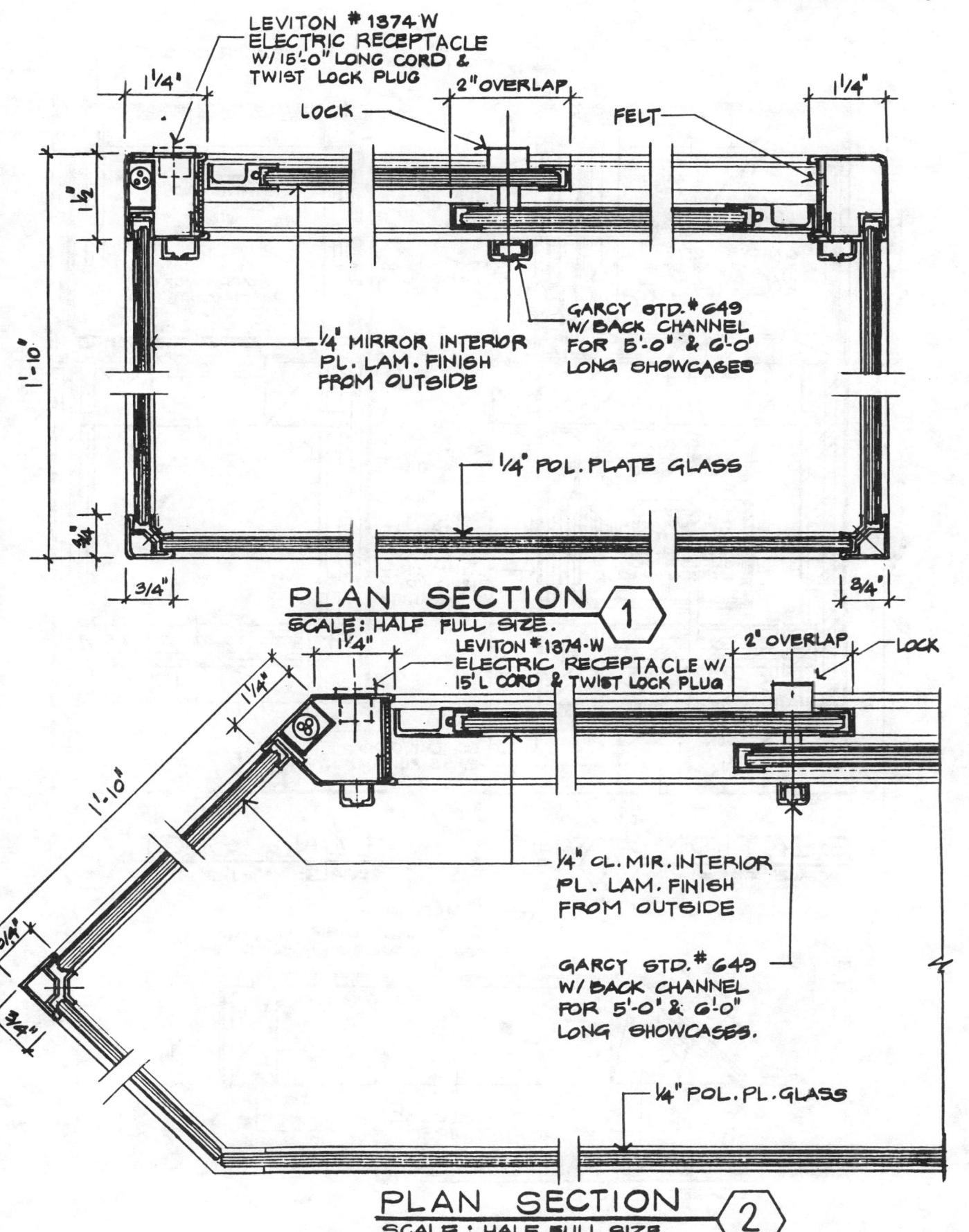

LEVITON #1374·W
ELECTRIC RECEPTACLE
W/15'-0" LONG CORD &
TWIST LOCK PLUG

1¼"

LOCK

2" OVERLAP

FELT

1¼"

1½"

1'-10"

¼" MIRROR INTERIOR
PL. LAM. FINISH
FROM OUTSIDE

GARCY STD. #649
W/ BACK CHANNEL
FOR 5'-0" & 6'-0"
LONG SHOWCASES

¼" POL. PLATE GLASS

¾"

3/4"

3/4"

PLAN SECTION ①
SCALE: HALF FULL SIZE.

1¼"

LEVITON #1374·W
ELECTRIC RECEPTACLE W/
15'L CORD & TWIST LOCK PLUG

2' OVERLAP

LOCK

1¼"

1'-10"

¼" CL. MIR. INTERIOR
PL. LAM. FINISH
FROM OUTSIDE

GARCY STD. #649
W/ BACK CHANNEL
FOR 5'-0" & 6'-0"
LONG SHOWCASES.

3/4"

3/4"

¼" POL. PL. GLASS

PLAN SECTION ②
SCALE: HALF FULL SIZE.

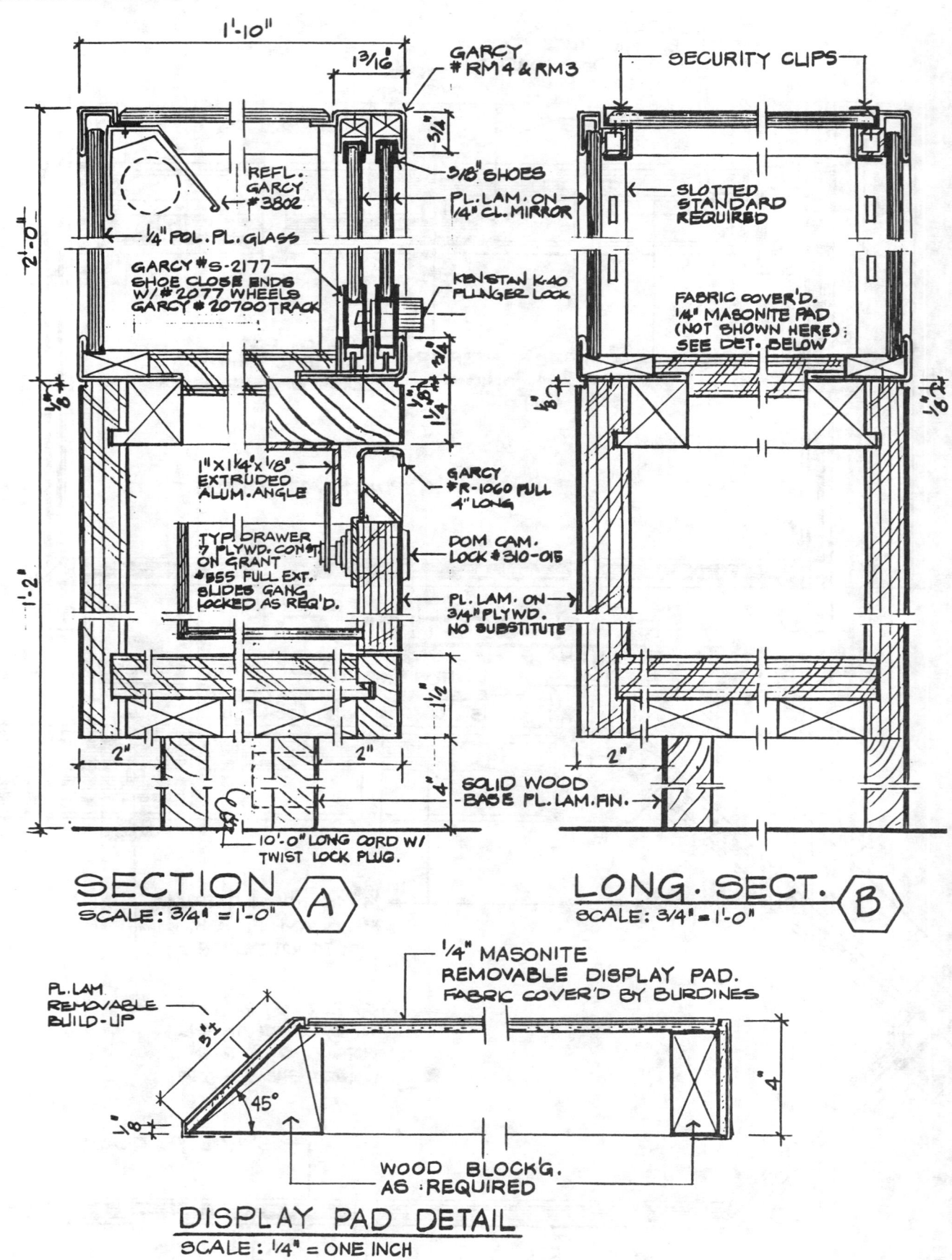

1'-10"

1³/₁₆"

GARCY
#RM4 & RM3

3¼"

3/8" SHOES

REFL.
GARCY
#3802

PL. LAM. ON
¼" CL. MIRROR

¼" POL. PL. GLASS

2'-0"

GARCY #S-2177
SHOE CLOSE ENDS
W/ #2077 WHEELS
GARCY #20700 TRACK

KENSTAN K-40
PLUNGER LOCK

SECURITY CLIPS

SLOTTED
STANDARD
REQUIRED

FABRIC COVER'D.
¼" MASONITE PAD
(NOT SHOWN HERE);
SEE DET. BELOW

1" x 1¼" x ⅛"
EXTRUDED
ALUM. ANGLE

GARCY
#R-1060 FULL
4" LONG

TYP. DRAWER
7 PLYWD. CONST.
ON GRANT
#355 FULL EXT.
SLIDES GANG
LOCKED AS REQ'D.

DOM CAM.
LOCK #310-015

PL. LAM. ON
¾" PLYWD.
NO SUBSTITUTE

1'-2"

½"

2"   2"

4"

SOLID WOOD
BASE PL. LAM. FIN.

2"

10'-0" LONG CORD W/
TWIST LOCK PLUG.

SECTION — A
SCALE: 3/4" = 1'-0"

LONG. SECT. — B
SCALE: 3/4" = 1'-0"

PL. LAM.
REMOVABLE
BUILD-UP

¼" MASONITE
REMOVABLE DISPLAY PAD.
FABRIC COVER'D BY BURDINES

45°

4"

WOOD BLOCK'G.
AS REQUIRED

DISPLAY PAD DETAIL
SCALE: ¼" = ONE INCH

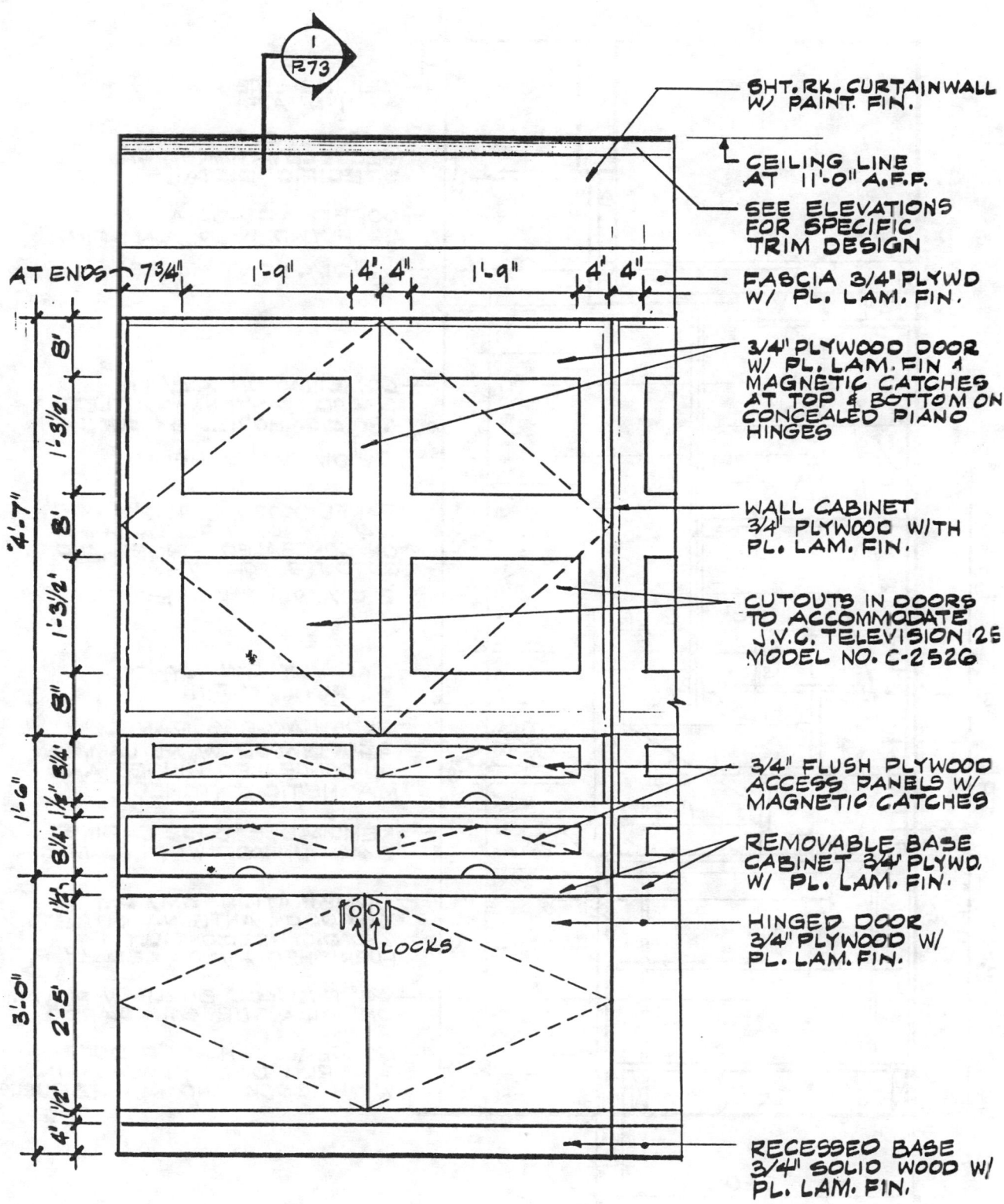

1
R-73

SHT. RK. CURTAIN WALL
W/ PAINT. FIN.

CEILING LINE
AT 11'-0" A.F.F.

SEE ELEVATIONS
FOR SPECIFIC
TRIM DESIGN

AT ENDS 7 3/4"   1'-9"   4' 4"   1'-9"   4' 4"

FASCIA 3/4" PLYWD
W/ PL. LAM. FIN.

3/4" PLYWOOD DOOR
W/ PL. LAM. FIN &
MAGNETIC CATCHES
AT TOP & BOTTOM ON
CONCEALED PIANO
HINGES

WALL CABINET
3/4" PLYWOOD WITH
PL. LAM. FIN.

CUTOUTS IN DOORS
TO ACCOMMODATE
J.V.C. TELEVISION 25
MODEL NO. C-252G

3/4" FLUSH PLYWOOD
ACCESS PANELS W/
MAGNETIC CATCHES

REMOVABLE BASE
CABINET 3/4" PLYWD.
W/ PL. LAM. FIN.

HINGED DOOR
3/4" PLYWOOD W/
PL. LAM. FIN.

RECESSED BASE
3/4" SOLID WOOD W/
PL. LAM. FIN.

LOCKS

ELEVATION
SCALE: 3/4" = 1'-0"

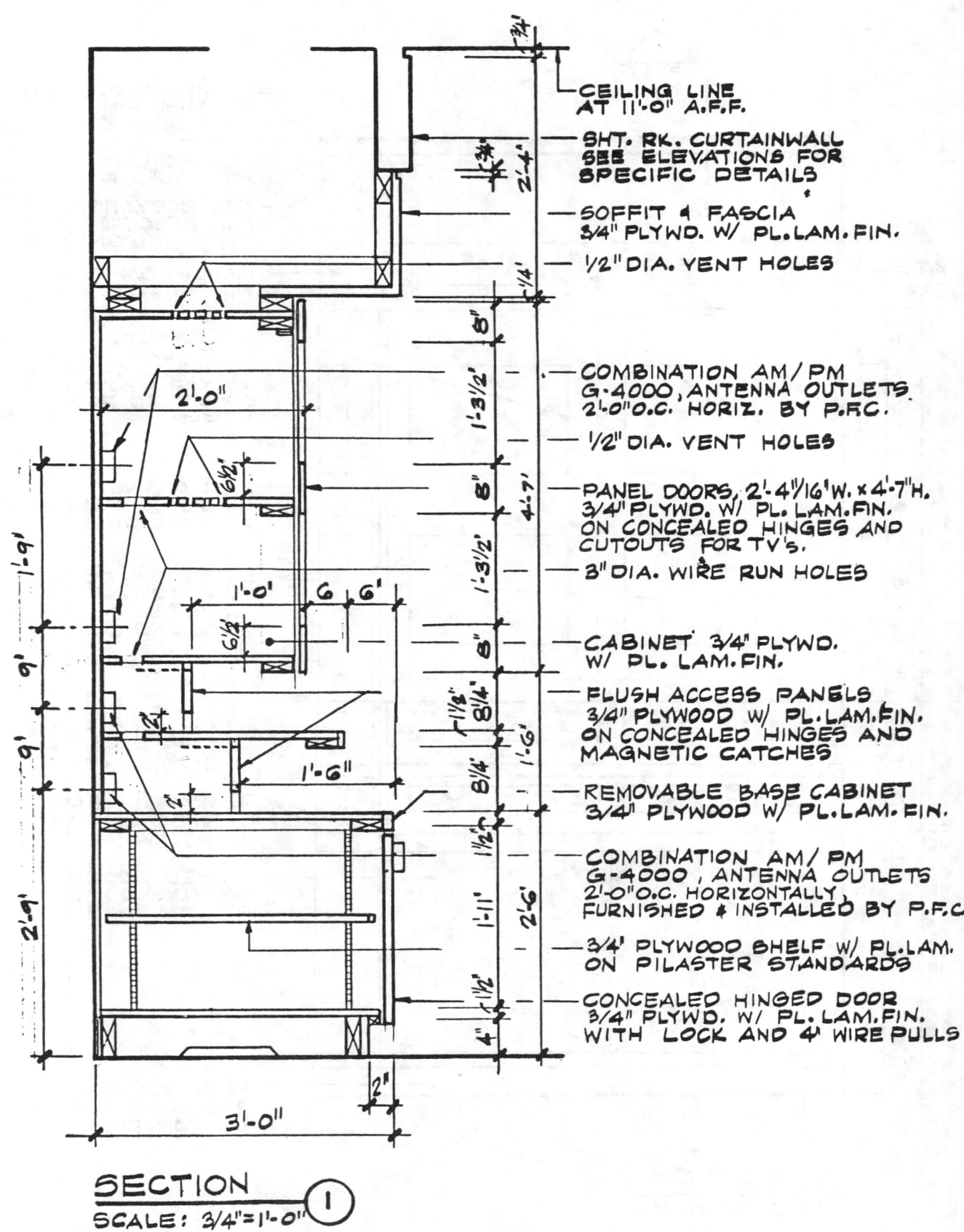

CEILING LINE
AT 11'-0" A.F.F.

SHT. RK. CURTAINWALL
SEE ELEVATIONS FOR
SPECIFIC DETAILS

SOFFIT & FASCIA
3/4" PLYWD. W/ PL.LAM.FIN.

1/2" DIA. VENT HOLES

COMBINATION AM/PM
G-4000, ANTENNA OUTLETS
2'-0" O.C. HORIZ. BY P.F.C.

1/2" DIA. VENT HOLES

PANEL DOORS, 2'-4 11/16" W. x 4'-7" H.
3/4" PLYWD. W/ PL. LAM.FIN.
ON CONCEALED HINGES AND
CUTOUTS FOR TV's.

3" DIA. WIRE RUN HOLES

CABINET 3/4" PLYWD.
W/ PL. LAM.FIN.

FLUSH ACCESS PANELS
3/4" PLYWOOD W/ PL.LAM.FIN.
ON CONCEALED HINGES AND
MAGNETIC CATCHES

REMOVABLE BASE CABINET
3/4" PLYWOOD W/ PL.LAM.FIN.

COMBINATION AM/PM
G-4000, ANTENNA OUTLETS
2'-0" O.C. HORIZONTALLY,
FURNISHED & INSTALLED BY P.F.C.

3/4" PLYWOOD SHELF W/ PL.LAM.
ON PILASTER STANDARDS

CONCEALED HINGED DOOR
3/4" PLYWD. W/ PL. LAM.FIN.
WITH LOCK AND 4" WIRE PULLS

SECTION
SCALE: 3/4" = 1'-0" ①

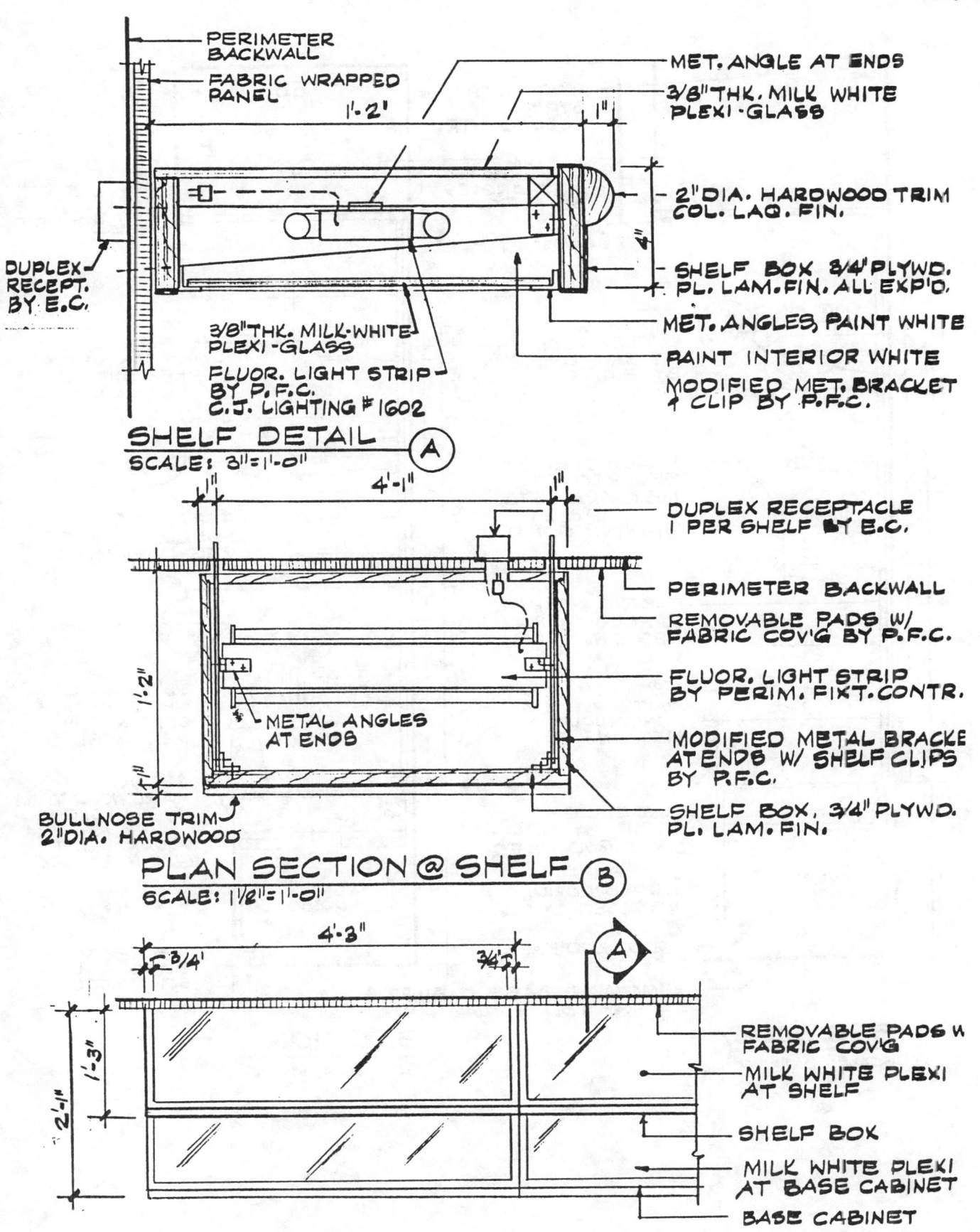

PERIMETER
BACKWALL

FABRIC WRAPPED
PANEL

1'-2"

1"

MET. ANGLE AT ENDS

3/8"THK. MILK WHITE
PLEXI-GLASS

2"DIA. HARDWOOD TRIM
COL. LAQ. FIN.

4"

SHELF BOX 3/4"PLYWD.
PL. LAM.FIN. ALL EXP'D.

MET. ANGLES, PAINT WHITE

PAINT INTERIOR WHITE

MODIFIED MET. BRACKET
& CLIP BY P.F.C.

DUPLEX
RECEPT.
BY E.C.

3/8"THK. MILK-WHITE
PLEXI-GLASS

FLUOR. LIGHT STRIP
BY P.F.C.
C.J. LIGHTING #1602

SHELF DETAIL (A)
SCALE: 3"=1'-0"

4'-1"

1"
1"

DUPLEX RECEPTACLE
1 PER SHELF BY E.C.

PERIMETER BACKWALL

REMOVABLE PADS W/
FABRIC COV'G BY P.F.C.

FLUOR. LIGHT STRIP
BY PERIM. FIXT.CONTR.

1'-2"

METAL ANGLES
AT ENDS

MODIFIED METAL BRACKE
AT ENDS W/ SHELF CLIPS
BY P.F.C.

1"

SHELF BOX, 3/4" PLYWD.
PL. LAM. FIN.

BULLNOSE TRIM
2"DIA. HARDWOOD

PLAN SECTION @ SHELF (B)
SCALE: 1 1/2"=1'-0"

4'-3"

3/4"

3/4"

(A)

1'-3"

2'-1"

REMOVABLE PADS W
FABRIC COV'G

MILK WHITE PLEXI
AT SHELF

SHELF BOX

MILK WHITE PLEXI
AT BASE CABINET

BASE CABINET

PLAN WHERE SHELVES ABUTT
SCALE: 3/4"=1'-0"

407

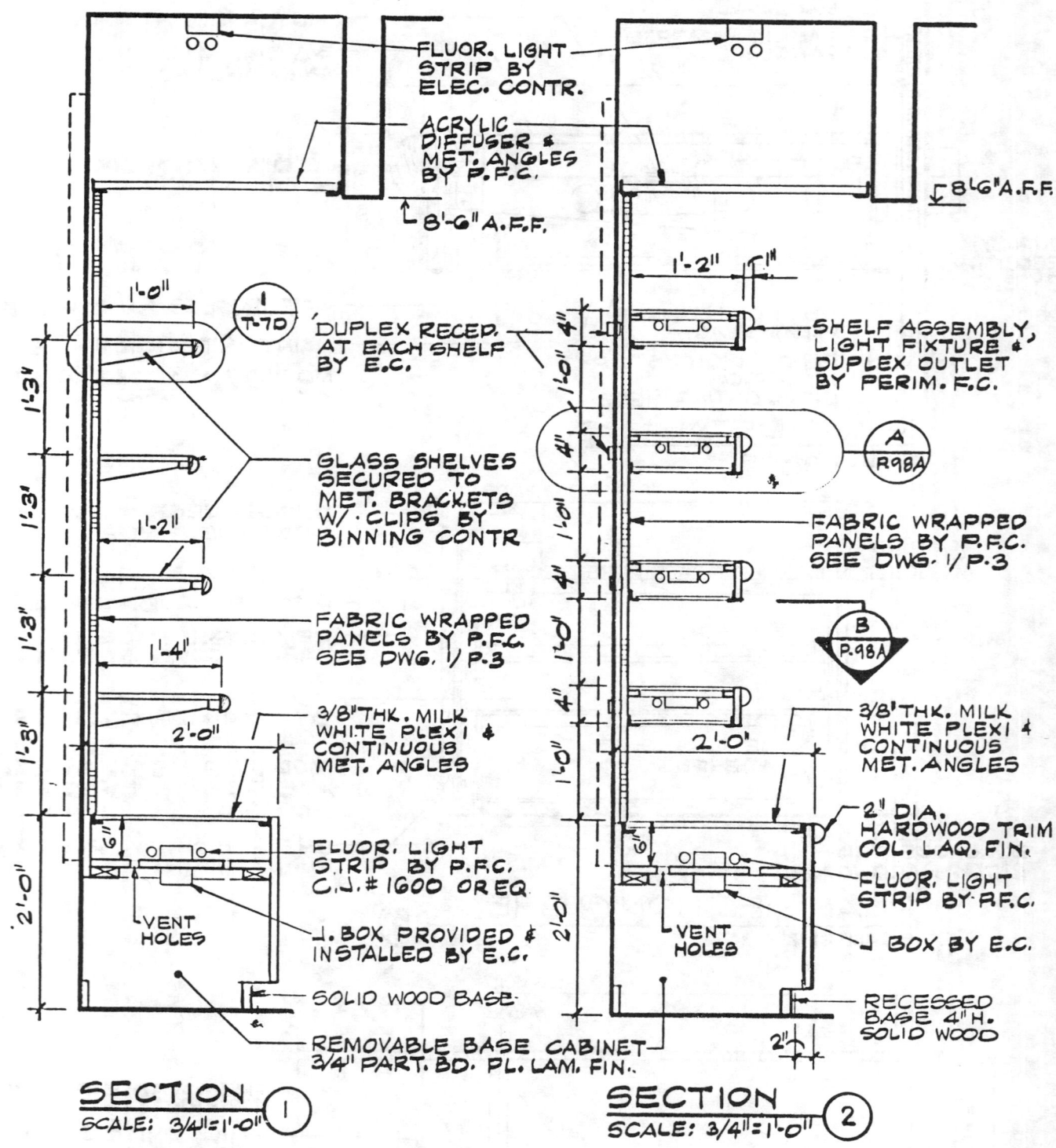

FLUOR. LIGHT STRIP BY ELEC. CONTR.

ACRYLIC DIFFUSER & MET. ANGLES BY P.F.C.

8'-6" A.F.F.

8'-6" A.F.F.

SECTION 1

1'-0"

1 T-70

DUPLEX RECED. AT EACH SHELF BY E.C.

GLASS SHELVES SECURED TO MET. BRACKETS W/ CLIPS BY BINNING CONTR.

1'-2"

FABRIC WRAPPED PANELS BY P.F.C. SEE DWG. 1/P-3

1'-4"

2'-0"

3/8" THK. MILK WHITE PLEXI & CONTINUOUS MET. ANGLES

1'-3"

1'-3"

1'-3"

1'-3"

6"

VENT HOLES

FLUOR. LIGHT STRIP BY P.F.C. C.J. #1600 OR EQ.

J. BOX PROVIDED & INSTALLED BY E.C.

SOLID WOOD BASE

2'-0"

REMOVABLE BASE CABINET 3/4" PART. BD. PL. LAM. FIN.

SECTION 1
SCALE: 3/4"=1'-0"

SECTION 2

1'-2"   1"

4"

1'-0"

SHELF ASSEMBLY, LIGHT FIXTURE & DUPLEX OUTLET BY PERIM. F.C.

4"

A R98A

1'-0"

FABRIC WRAPPED PANELS BY P.F.C. SEE DWG. 1/P-3

4"

1'-0"

B P.98A

4"

1'-0"

2'-0"

3/8" THK. MILK WHITE PLEXI & CONTINUOUS MET. ANGLES

6"

VENT HOLES

2" DIA. HARDWOOD TRIM COL. LAQ. FIN.

FLUOR. LIGHT STRIP BY P.F.C.

J. BOX BY E.C.

RECESSED BASE 4" H. SOLID WOOD

2'-0"

2"

SECTION 2
SCALE: 3/4"=1'-0"

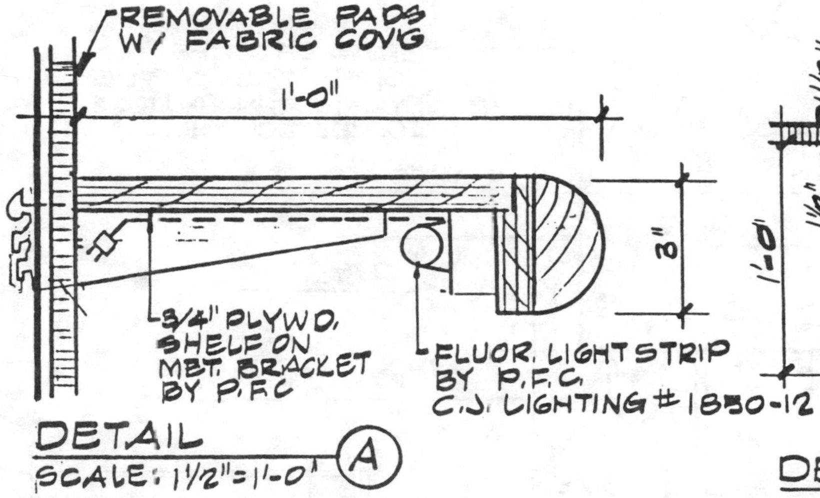

REMOVABLE PADS
W/ FABRIC COV'G

1'-0"

3"

3/4" PLYWD.
SHELF ON
MET. BRACKET
BY P.F.C.

FLUOR. LIGHT STRIP
BY P.F.C.
C.J. LIGHTING #1850-12

DETAIL
SCALE: 1 1/2"=1'-0"   Ⓐ

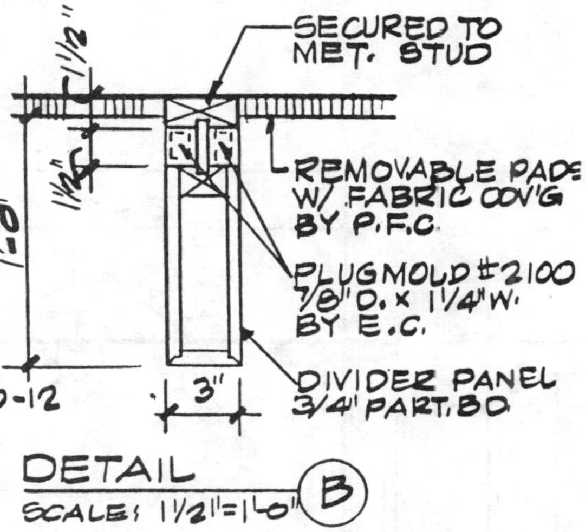

SECURED TO
MET. STUD

1 1/2"

1'-0"

3"

REMOVABLE PADS
W/ FABRIC COV'G
BY P.F.C.

PLUGMOLD #2100
7/8" D. x 1 1/4" W.
BY E.C.

DIVIDER PANEL
3/4" PART. BD.

DETAIL
SCALE: 1 1/2"=1'-0"   Ⓑ

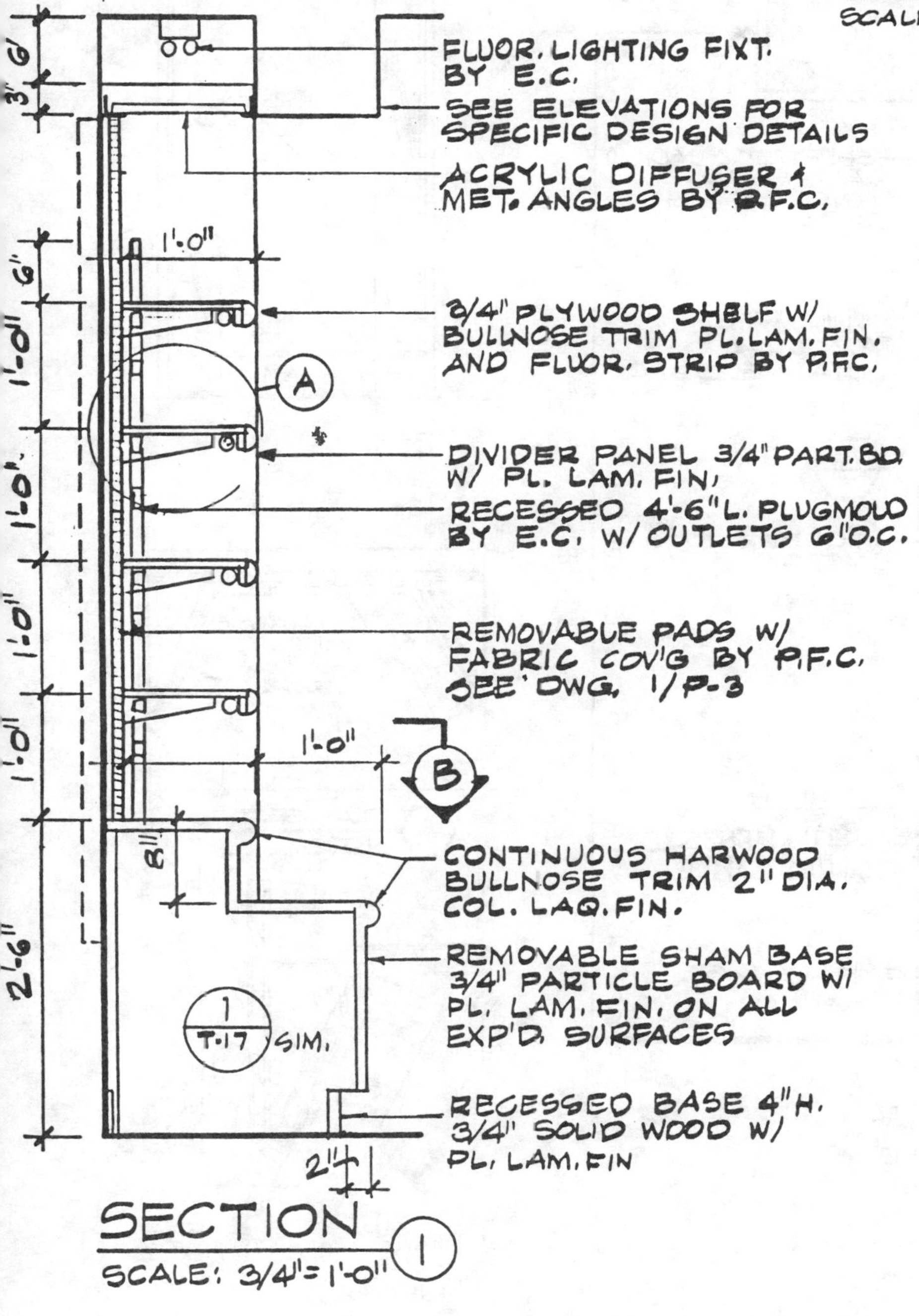

FLUOR. LIGHTING FIXT.
BY E.C.

SEE ELEVATIONS FOR
SPECIFIC DESIGN DETAILS

ACRYLIC DIFFUSER &
MET. ANGLES BY P.F.C.

3/4" PLYWOOD SHELF W/
BULLNOSE TRIM PL. LAM. FIN.
AND FLUOR. STRIP BY P.F.C.

DIVIDER PANEL 3/4" PART. BD.
W/ PL. LAM. FIN.

RECESSED 4'-6" L. PLUGMOLD
BY E.C. W/ OUTLETS 6" O.C.

REMOVABLE PADS W/
FABRIC COV'G BY P.F.C.
SEE DWG. 1/P-3

CONTINUOUS HARWOOD
BULLNOSE TRIM 2" DIA.
COL. LAQ. FIN.

REMOVABLE SHAM BASE
3/4" PARTICLE BOARD W/
PL. LAM. FIN. ON ALL
EXP'D. SURFACES

RECESSED BASE 4" H.
3/4" SOLID WOOD W/
PL. LAM. FIN.

3'-6"
6"
1'-0"
1'-0"
1'-0"
1'-0"
8"
2'-6"
2 1/4"

1'-0"

1'-0"

Ⓐ

Ⓑ

①
T-17 SIM.

SECTION
SCALE: 3/4"=1'-0"   ①

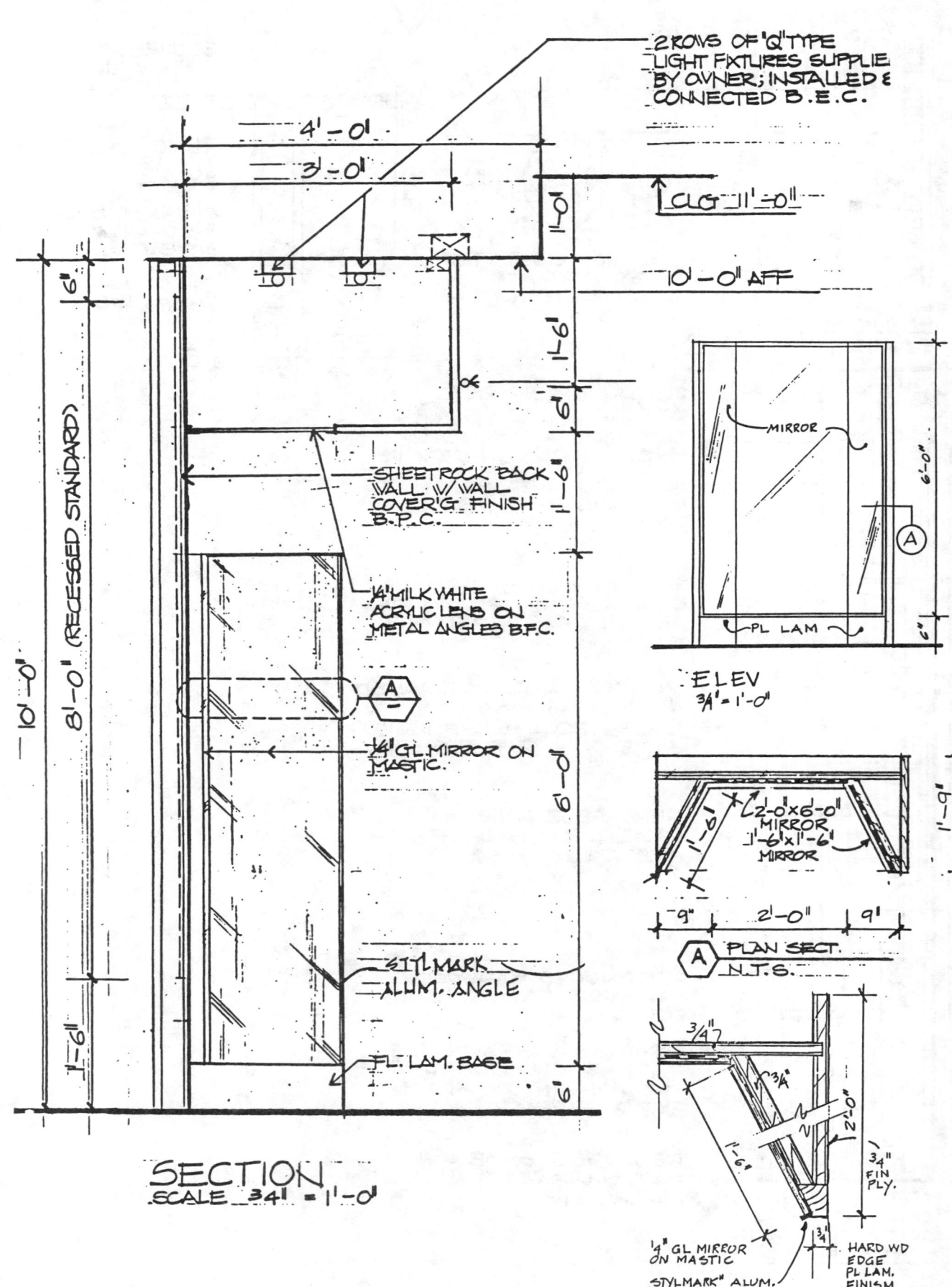

2 ROWS OF 'Q' TYPE LIGHT FIXTURES SUPPLIED BY OWNER; INSTALLED & CONNECTED B.E.C.

CLG 11'-0"

10'-0" AFF

4'-0"

3'-0"

6"

1'-0"

1'-6"

6"

6"

6'-0"

10'-0"

8'-0" (RECESSED STANDARD)

1'-6"

6"

SHEETROCK BACK WALL W/ WALL COVER'G. FINISH B.P.C.

1/4" MILK WHITE ACRYLIC LENS ON METAL ANGLES B.F.C.

1/4" GL. MIRROR ON MASTIC.

STYLMARK ALUM. ANGLE

PL. LAM. BASE

SECTION
SCALE 3/4" = 1'-0"

MIRROR

PL LAM

6'-0"

6"

ELEV
3/4" = 1'-0"

2'-0" x 6'-0" MIRROR
1'-6" x 1'-6" MIRROR

1'-0"

1'-9"

9" | 2'-0" | 9"

(A) **PLAN SECT.**
N.T.S.

3/4"

3/4"

2'-0"

1'-6"

3/4" FIN. PLY.

3/4"

1/4" GL. MIRROR ON MASTIC.

"STYLMARK" ALUM. ANGLE # 120059

HARD WD EDGE PL. LAM. FINISH.

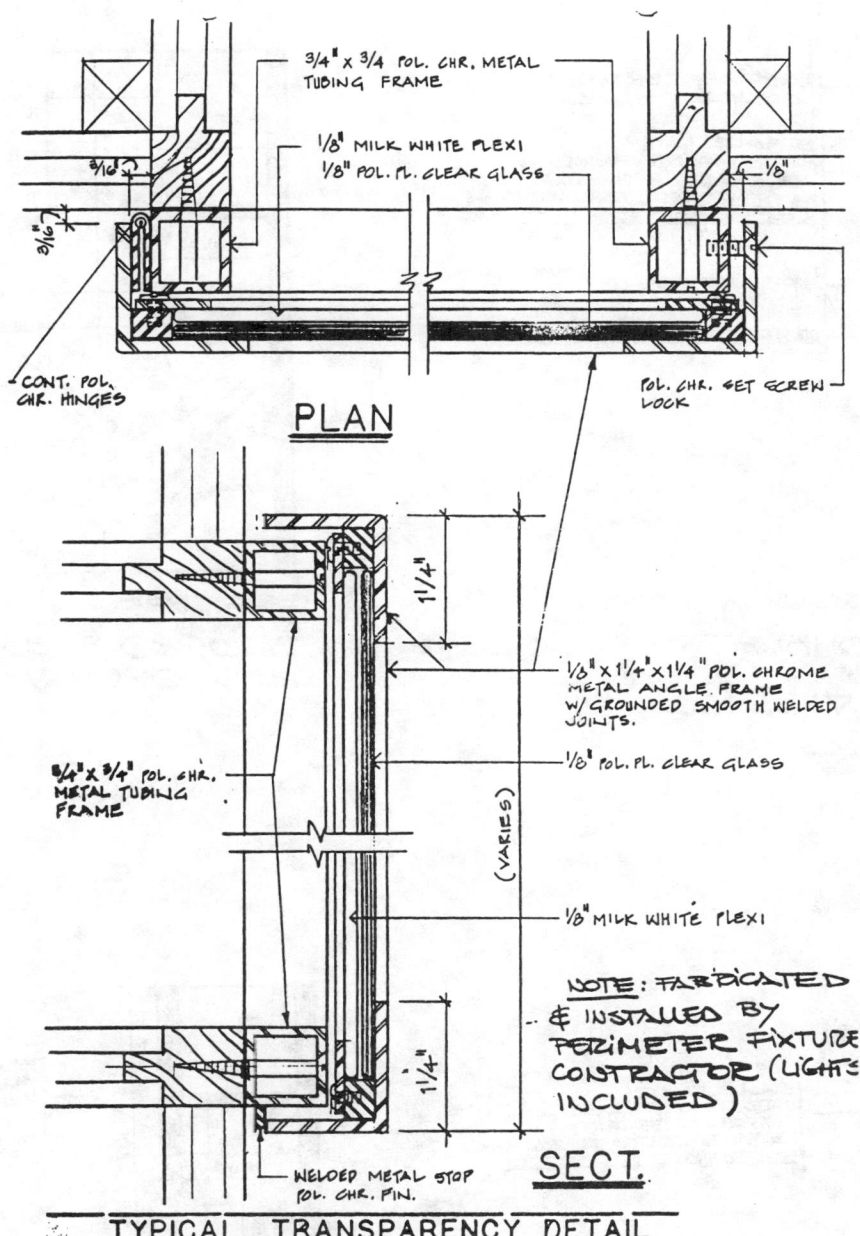

3/4" X 3/4 POL. CHR. METAL TUBING FRAME

1/8" MILK WHITE PLEXI
1/8" POL. PL. CLEAR GLASS

CONT. POL. CHR. HINGES

POL. CHR. SET SCREW LOCK

PLAN

3/4" X 3/4" POL. CHR. METAL TUBING FRAME

1 1/4"

1/8" X 1 1/4" X 1 1/4" POL. CHROME METAL ANGLE FRAME W/ GROUNDED SMOOTH WELDED JOINTS.

1/8" POL. PL. CLEAR GLASS

(VARIES)

1/8" MILK WHITE PLEXI

NOTE: FABRICATED & INSTALLED BY PERIMETER FIXTURE CONTRACTOR (LIGHTS INCLUDED)

1 1/4"

WELDED METAL STOP POL. CHR. FIN.

SECT.

TYPICAL TRANSPARENCY DETAIL

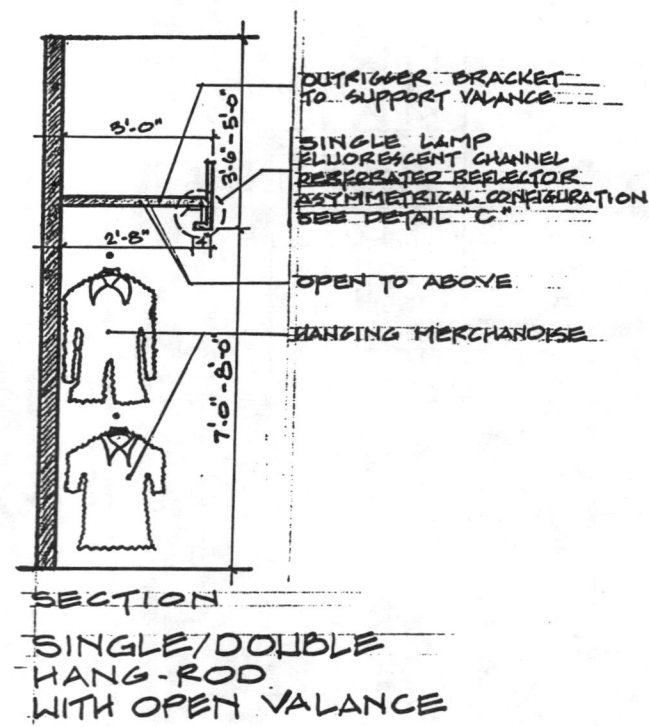

SINGLE/DOUBLE
HANG-ROD
WITH OPEN VALANCE

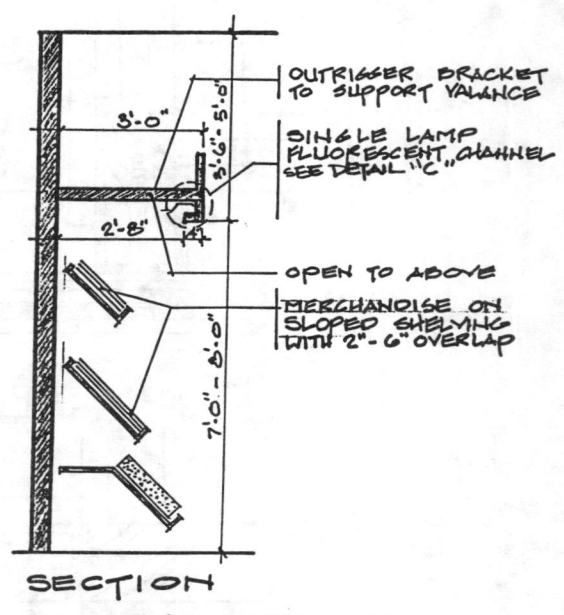

SLOPED SHELVING
WITH OPEN VALANCE

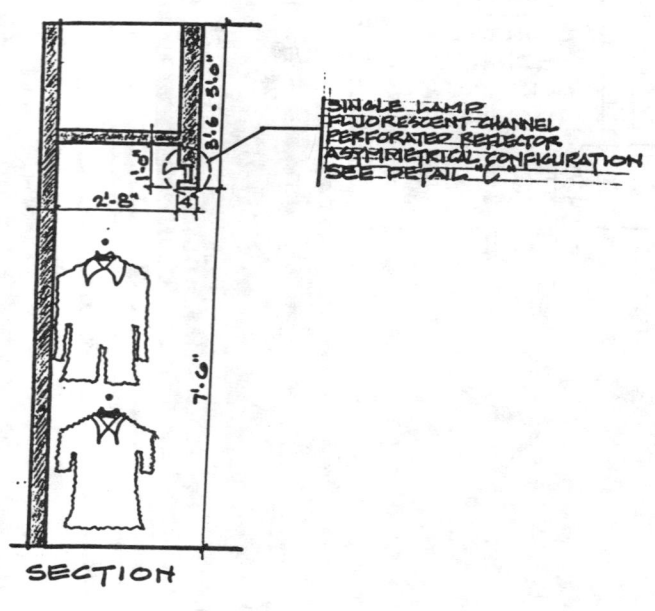

SINGLE/DOUBLE
HANG-ROD

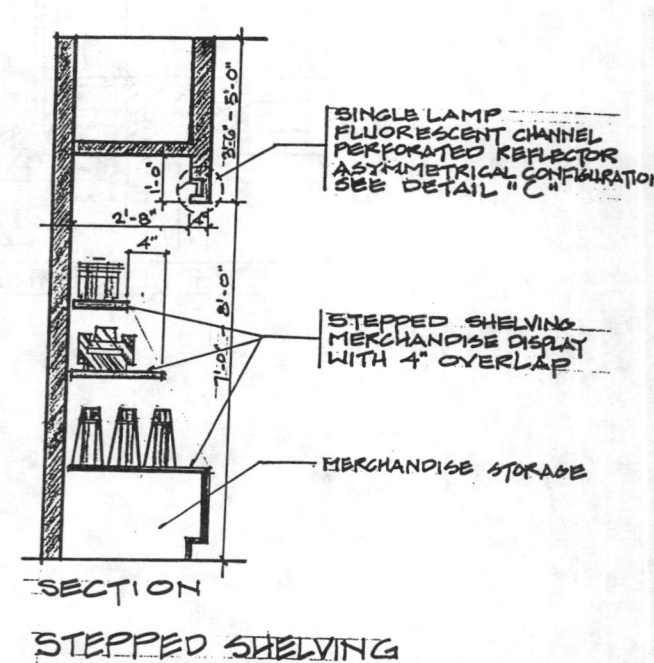

STEPPED SHELVING
MERCHANDISE DISPLAY

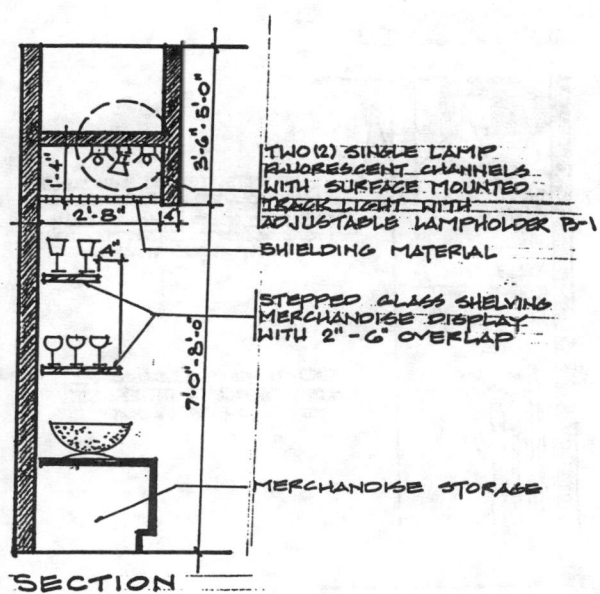

SECTION

STEPPED SHELVING
MERCHANDISE DISPLAY

TWO (2) SINGLE LAMP
FLUORESCENT CHANNELS
WITH SURFACE MOUNTED
TRACK LIGHT WITH
ADJUSTABLE LAMPHOLDER B-1

SHIELDING MATERIAL

STEPPED GLASS SHELVING
MERCHANDISE DISPLAY
WITH 2"-6" OVERLAP

MERCHANDISE STORAGE

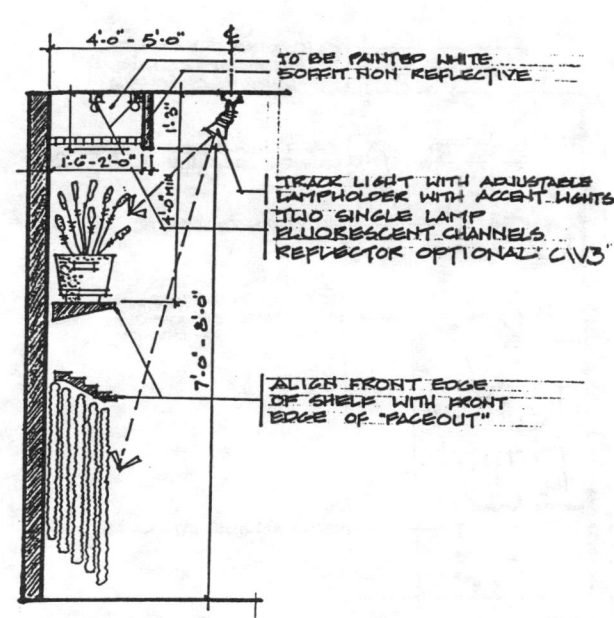

SECTION

FEATURE WALL DISPLAY
WITH ILLUMINATED
SOFFIT AND ACCENT LIGHT

TO BE PAINTED WHITE
SOFFIT NON REFLECTIVE

TRACK LIGHT WITH ADJUSTABLE
LAMPHOLDER WITH ACCENT LIGHTS
TWO SINGLE LAMP
FLUORESCENT CHANNELS
REFLECTOR OPTIONAL C/V3

ALIGN FRONT EDGE
OF SHELF WITH FRONT
EDGE OF "FACEOUT"

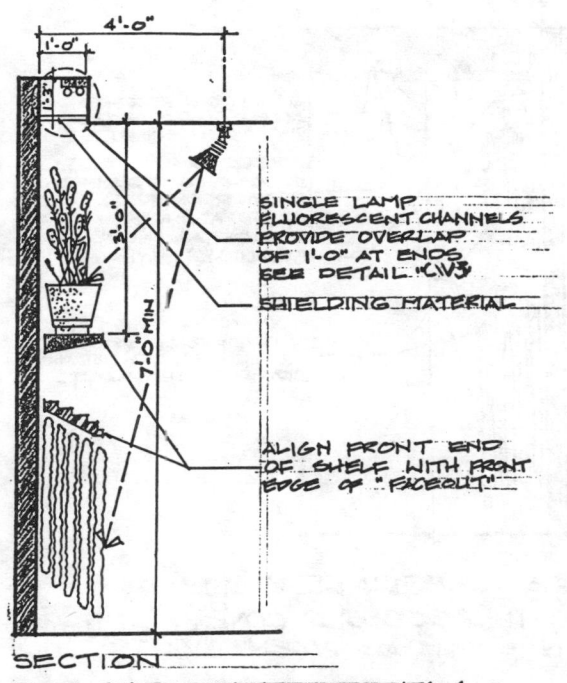

SECTION

FEATURE WALL DISPLAY
WITH RECESSED COVE
IN SOFFIT AND TRACK LIGHT

SINGLE LAMP
FLUORESCENT CHANNELS
PROVIDE OVERLAP
OF 1'-0" AT ENDS
SEE DETAIL "C/V3

SHIELDING MATERIAL

ALIGN FRONT END
OF SHELF WITH FRONT
EDGE OF "FACEOUT"

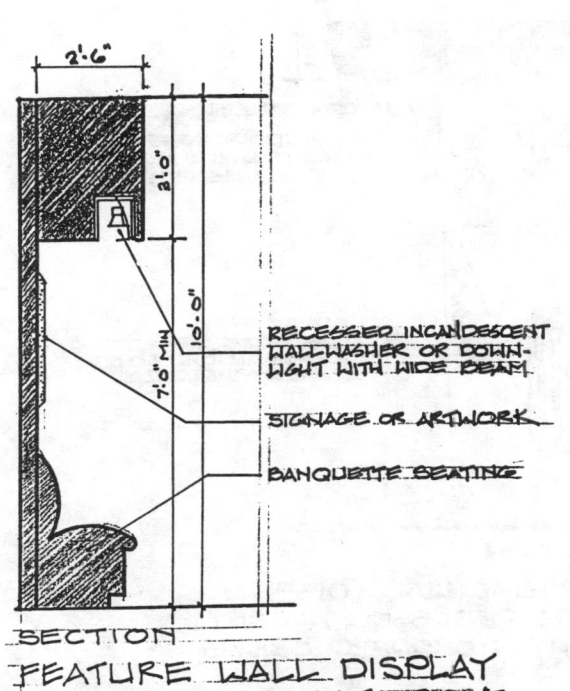

SECTION

FEATURE WALL DISPLAY
DROPPED SOFFIT ABOVE
BANQUETTE SEATING

RECESSED INCANDESCENT
WALLWASHER OR DOWN-
LIGHT WITH WIDE BEAM

SIGNAGE OR ARTWORK

BANQUETTE SEATING

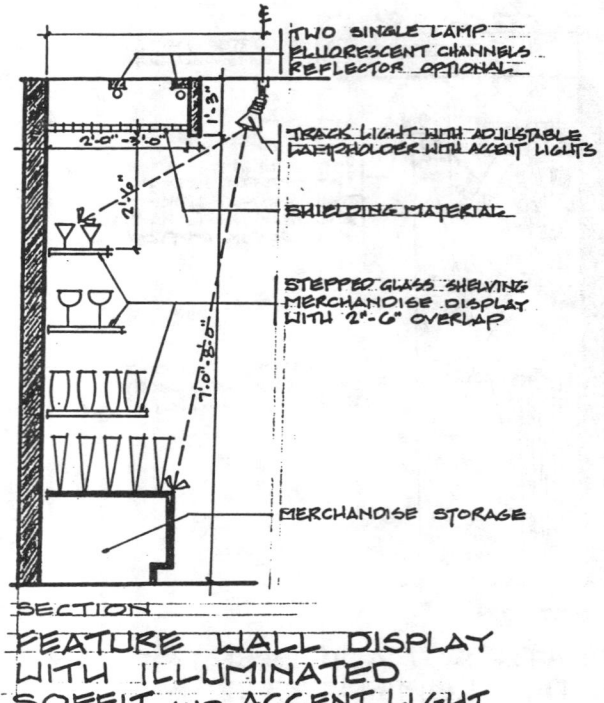

TWO SINGLE LAMP FLUORESCENT CHANNELS REFLECTOR OPTIONAL

TRACK LIGHT WITH ADJUSTABLE LAMPHOLDER WITH ACCENT LIGHTS

SHIELDING MATERIAL

STEPPED GLASS SHELVING MERCHANDISE DISPLAY WITH 2"-6" OVERLAP

MERCHANDISE STORAGE

SECTION

FEATURE WALL DISPLAY WITH ILLUMINATED SOFFIT and ACCENT LIGHT

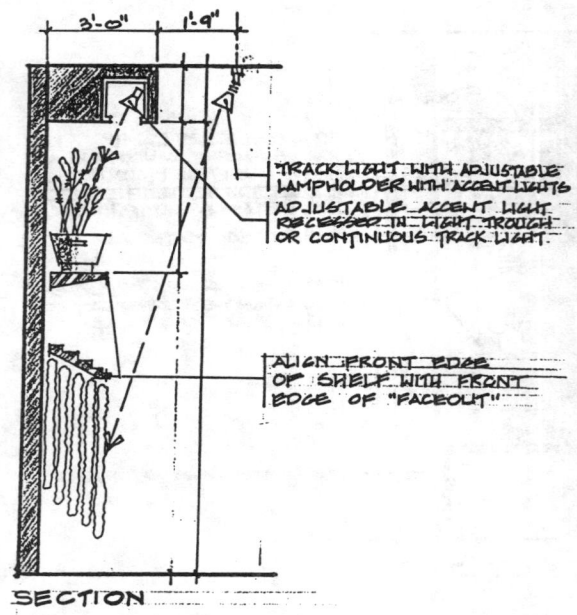

TRACK LIGHT WITH ADJUSTABLE LAMPHOLDER WITH ACCENT LIGHTS

ADJUSTABLE ACCENT LIGHT RECESSED IN LIGHT TROUGH OR CONTINUOUS TRACK LIGHT

ALIGN FRONT EDGE OF SHELF WITH FRONT EDGE OF "FACEOUT"

SECTION

FEATURE WALL DISPLAY WITH RECESSED LIGHT TROUGH and ACCENT LIGHT

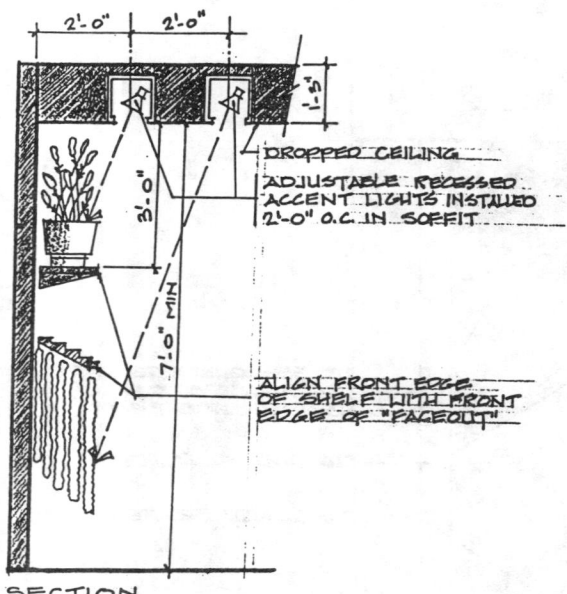

DROPPED CEILING

ADJUSTABLE RECESSED ACCENT LIGHTS INSTALLED 2'-0" O.C. IN SOFFIT

ALIGN FRONT EDGE OF SHELF WITH FRONT EDGE OF "FACEOUT"

SECTION

FEATURE WALL DISPLAY WITH RECESSED ACCENT LIGHT IN DROPPED CEILING

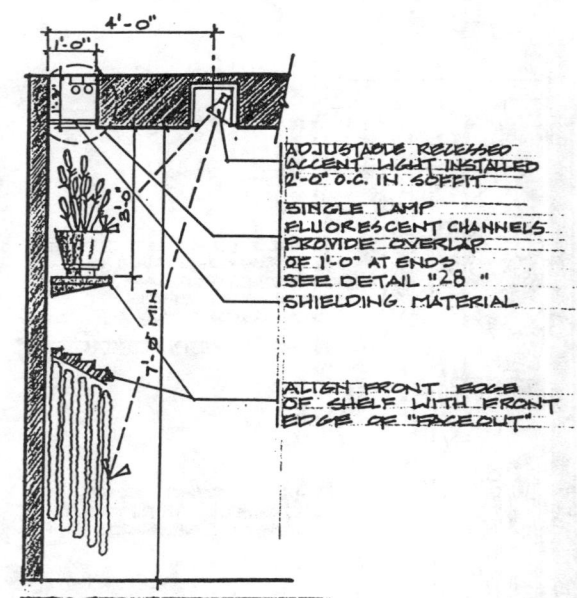

ADJUSTABLE RECESSED ACCENT LIGHT INSTALLED 2'-0" O.C. IN SOFFIT

SINGLE LAMP FLUORESCENT CHANNELS PROVIDE OVERLAP OF 1'-0" AT ENDS SEE DETAIL "28"

SHIELDING MATERIAL

ALIGN FRONT EDGE OF SHELF WITH FRONT EDGE OF "FACEOUT"

SECTION

FEATURE WALL DISPLAY WITH RECESSED COVE IN SOFFIT and ACCENT LIGHT

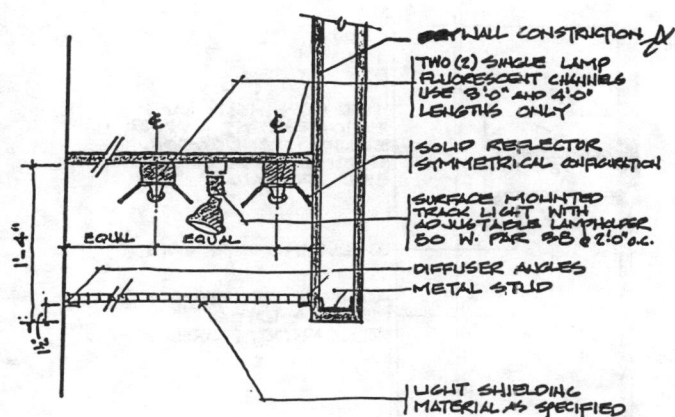

- DRYWALL CONSTRUCTION
- TWO (2) SINGLE LAMP FLUORESCENT CHANNELS USE 3'-0" AND 4'-0" LENGTHS ONLY
- SOLID REFLECTOR SYMMETRICAL CONFIGURATION
- SURFACE MOUNTED TRACK LIGHT WITH ADJUSTABLE LAMPHOLDER 50 W. PAR 38 @ 2'-0" O.C.
- DIFFUSER ANGLES
- METAL STUD
- LIGHT SHIELDING MATERIAL AS SPECIFIED

EQUAL   EQUAL

1'-4"

SHIELDED VALANCE WITH TWO (2) SINGLE LAMP FLUORESCENT CHANNELS AND TRACK LIGHT WITH INCANDESCENT "CURTAIN WALL" TYPE

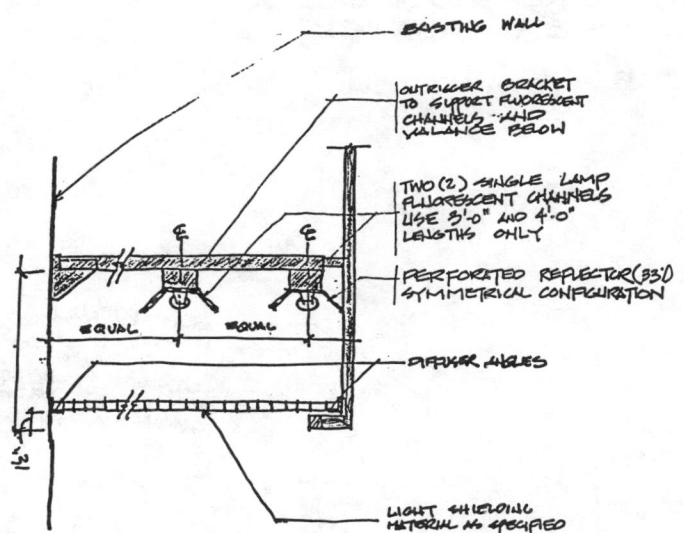

- EXISTING WALL
- OUTRIGGER BRACKET TO SUPPORT FLUORESCENT CHANNELS AND VALANCE BELOW
- TWO (2) SINGLE LAMP FLUORESCENT CHANNELS USE 3'-0" AND 4'-0" LENGTHS ONLY
- PERFORATED REFLECTOR (33%) SYMMETRICAL CONFIGURATION
- DIFFUSER ANGLES
- LIGHT SHIELDING MATERIAL AS SPECIFIED

EQUAL   EQUAL

SHIELDED VALANCE WITH TWO (2) SINGLE LAMP FLUORESCENT CHANNELS

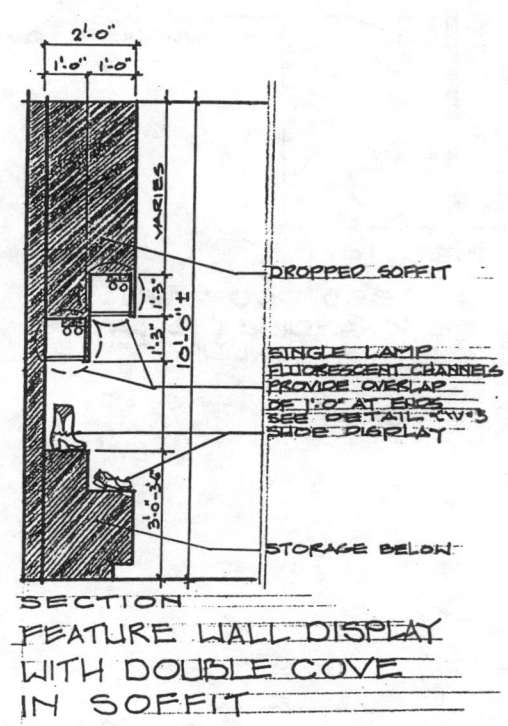

2'-0"
1'-0" 1'-0"

VARIES

1'-0" ±
1'-3"

3'-6"-5'6"

- DROPPED SOFFIT
- SINGLE LAMP FLUORESCENT CHANNELS PROVIDE OVERLAP OF 1'-0" AT ENDS SEE DETAIL "W-3" SHOE DISPLAY
- STORAGE BELOW

SECTION

FEATURE WALL DISPLAY WITH DOUBLE COVE IN SOFFIT

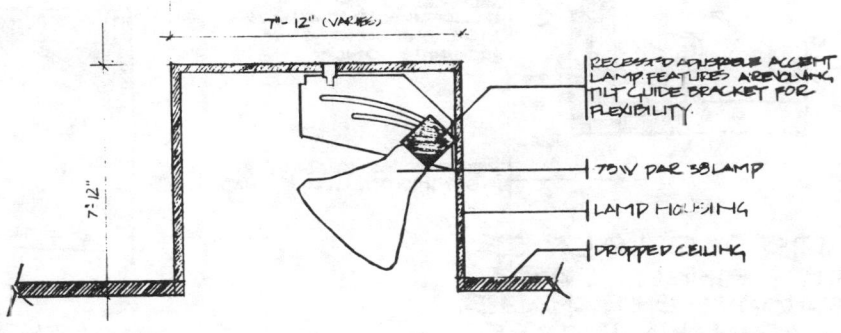

7" - 12" (VARIES)

7"-12"

- RECESSED ADJUSTABLE ACCENT LAMP FEATURES A REVOLVING TILT GUIDE BRACKET FOR FLEXIBILITY.
- 75 W PAR 38 LAMP
- LAMP HOUSING
- DROPPED CEILING

RECESSED ADJUSTABLE ACCENT LIGHT

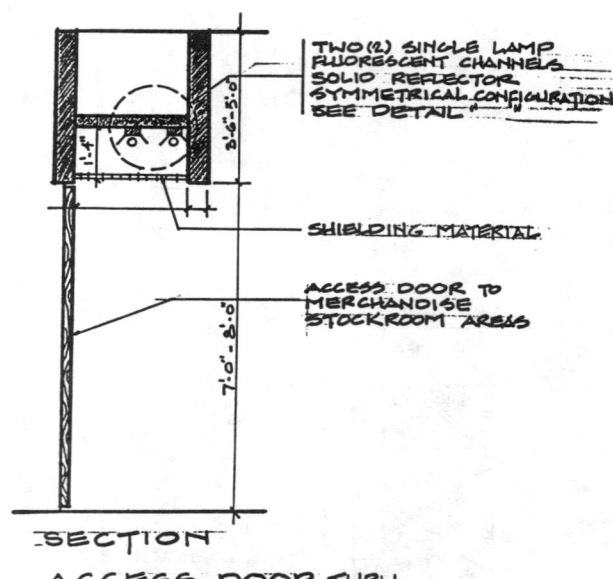

TWO (2) SINGLE LAMP
FLUORESCENT CHANNELS
SOLID REFLECTOR
SYMMETRICAL CONFIGURATION
SEE DETAIL "

SHIELDING MATERIAL

ACCESS DOOR TO
MERCHANDISE
STOCKROOM AREAS

SECTION
ACCESS DOOR THRU
MERCHANDISE DISPLAY
"CURTAIN WALL"

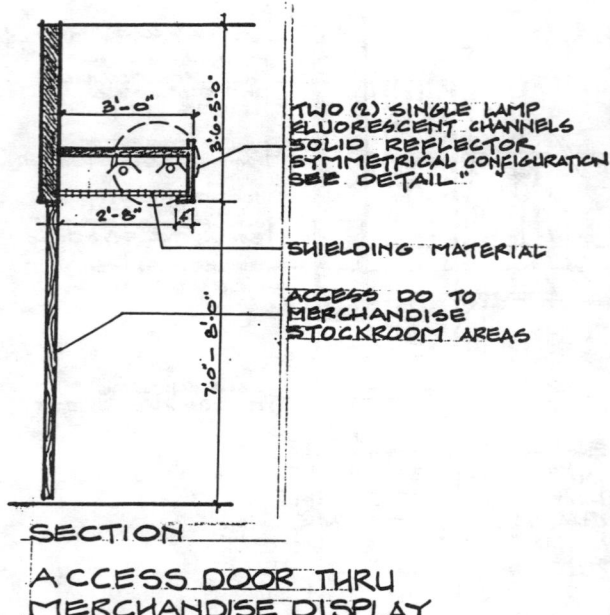

TWO (2) SINGLE LAMP
FLUORESCENT CHANNELS
SOLID REFLECTOR
SYMMETRICAL CONFIGURATION
SEE DETAIL "

SHIELDING MATERIAL

ACCESS DO TO
MERCHANDISE
STOCKROOM AREAS

SECTION
ACCESS DOOR THRU
MERCHANDISE DISPLAY
"OPEN VALANCE"

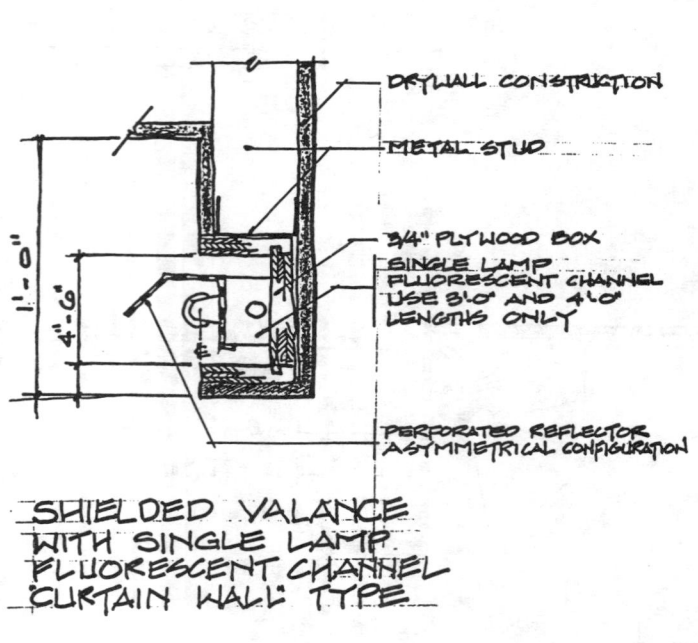

DRYWALL CONSTRUCTION

METAL STUD

3/4" PLYWOOD BOX
SINGLE LAMP
FLUORESCENT CHANNEL
USE 3'-0" AND 4'-0"
LENGTHS ONLY

PERFORATED REFLECTOR
ASYMMETRICAL CONFIGURATION

SHIELDED VALANCE
WITH SINGLE LAMP
FLUORESCENT CHANNEL
"CURTAIN WALL" TYPE

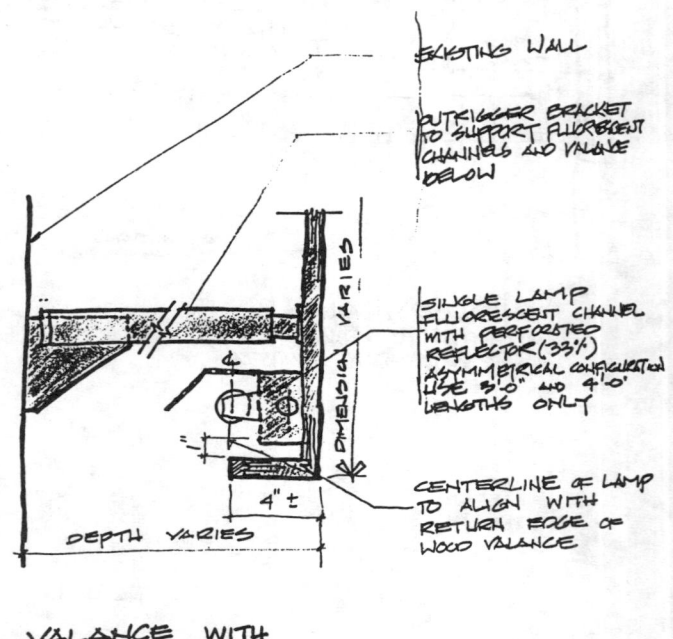

EXISTING WALL

OUTRIGGER BRACKET
TO SUPPORT FLUORESCENT
CHANNELS AND VALANCE
BELOW

SINGLE LAMP
FLUORESCENT CHANNEL
WITH PERFORATED
REFLECTOR (33%)
ASYMMETRICAL CONFIGURATION
USE 3'-0" AND 4'-0"
LENGTHS ONLY

CENTERLINE OF LAMP
TO ALIGN WITH
RETURN EDGE OF
WOOD VALANCE

DEPTH VARIES

VALANCE WITH
SINGLE LAMP
FLUORESCENT CHANNEL

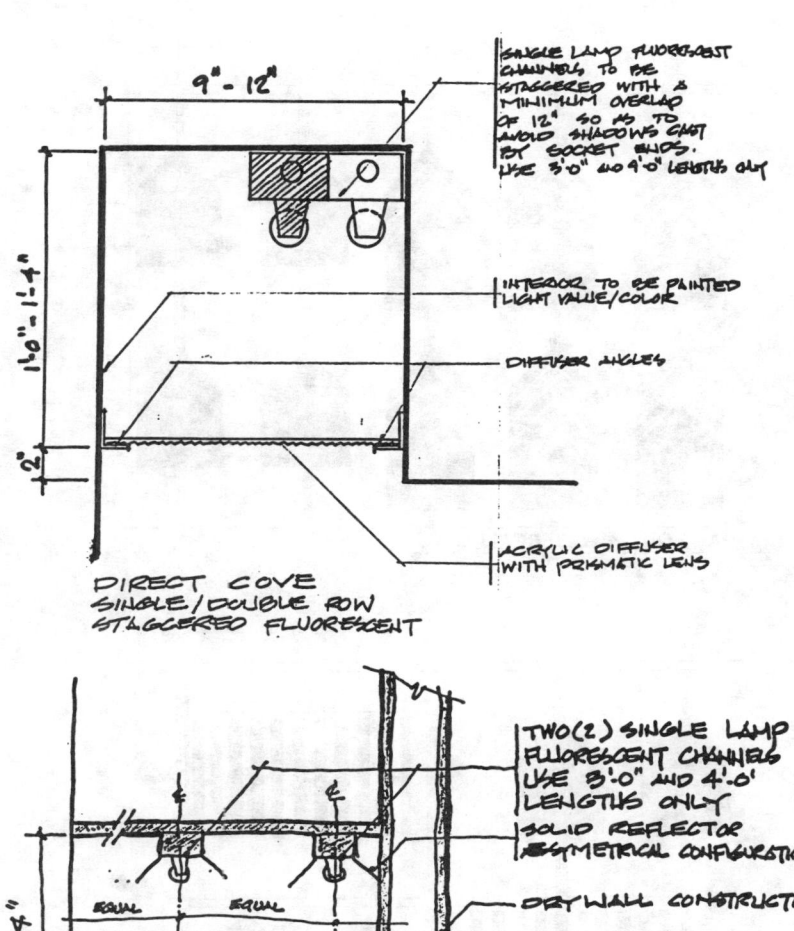

SINGLE LAMP FLUORESCENT
CHANNELS TO BE
STAGGERED WITH A
MINIMUM OVERLAP
OF 12" SO AS TO
AVOID SHADOWS CAST
BY SOCKET ENDS.
USE 3'-0" AND 4'-0" LENGTHS ONLY

INTERIOR TO BE PAINTED
LIGHT VALUE/COLOR

DIFFUSER ANGLES

ACRYLIC DIFFUSER
WITH PRISMATIC LENS

DIRECT COVE
SINGLE/DOUBLE ROW
STAGGERED FLUORESCENT

TWO (2) SINGLE LAMP
FLUORESCENT CHANNELS
USE 3'-0" AND 4'-0"
LENGTHS ONLY
SOLID REFLECTOR
A-SYMETRICAL CONFIGURATION

DRYWALL CONSTRUCTION

DIFFUSER ANGLES
METAL STUD

LIGHT SHIELDING
MATERIAL AS SPECIFIED

SHIELDED VALANCE
WITH TWO (2) SINGLE
LAMP FLUORESCENT CHANNELS
"CURTAIN WALL" TYPE

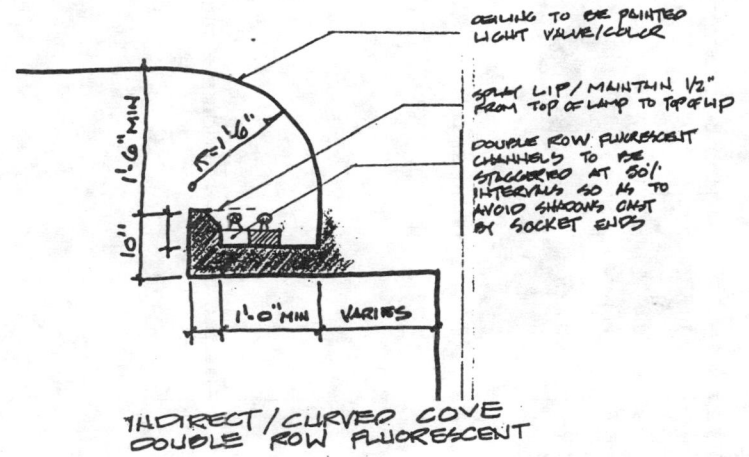

CEILING TO BE PAINTED
LIGHT VALUE/COLOR

SPLAY LIP/MAINTAIN 1/2"
FROM TOP OF LAMP TO TOP OF LIP

DOUBLE ROW FLUORESCENT
CHANNELS TO BE
STAGGERED AT 50/:
INTERVALS SO AS TO
AVOID SHADOWS CAST
BY SOCKET ENDS

INDIRECT/CURVED COVE
DOUBLE ROW FLUORESCENT

417

DEPARTMENT STORES
Wall Display Systems

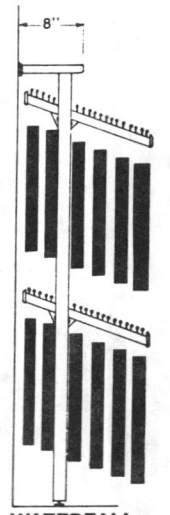

WATERFALL
Average Quantity of
Garments Per Post: 48

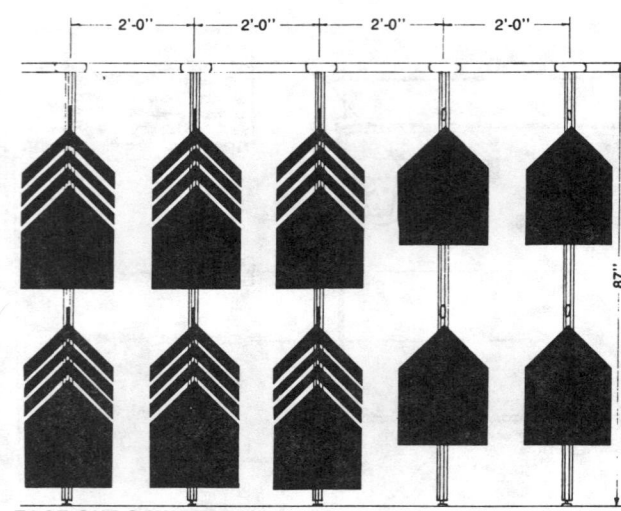

FACE OUT & WATERFALL

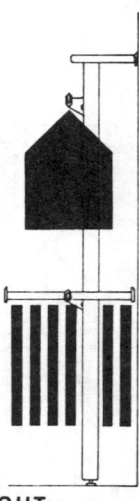

FACE OUT
Average Quantity of
Garments Per Post: 46

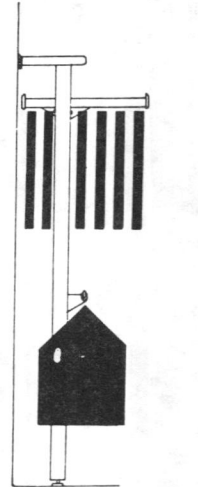

**POST FACE OUT WITH
STRAIGHT HANGING**
Average Quantity of
Garments Per 4'-0" Section: 94

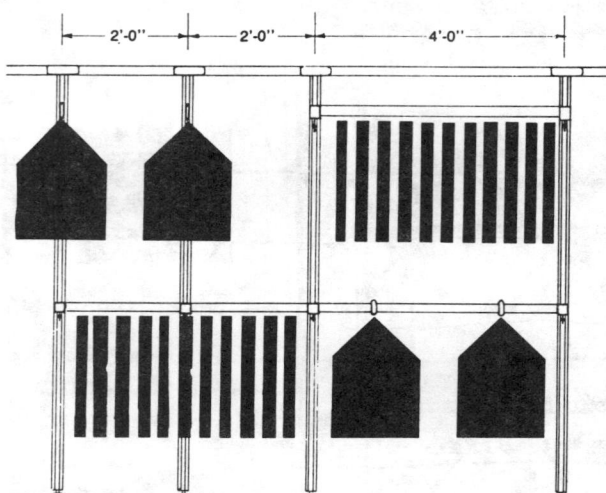

STRAIGHT HANGING & FACE OUT

**STRAIGHT
WITH HANGRAIL FACE OUT**
Average Quantity of Garments
Per 4'-0" Section: 96

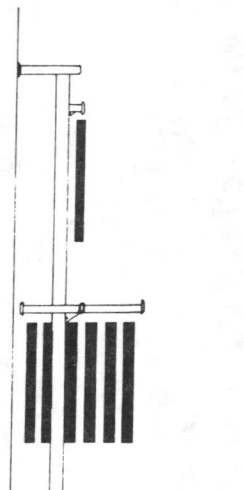

FACE OUT WITH DISPLAY
Average Quantity of Garments
Per 4'-0" Section: 49

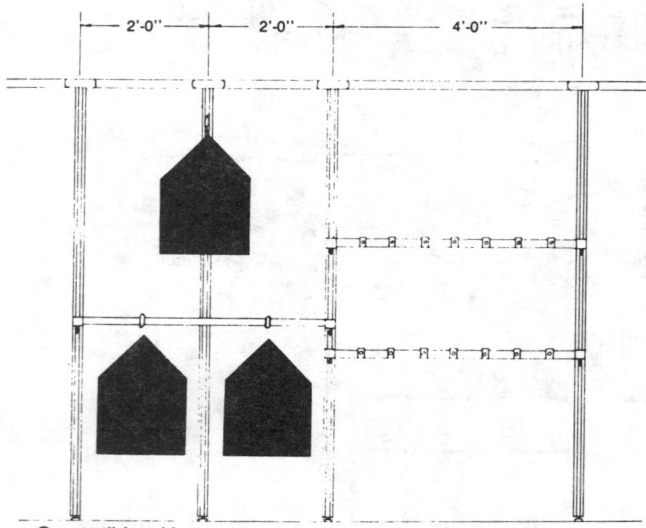

• Compatible with
   universal ½" slotting
• Unique new oval hangrail

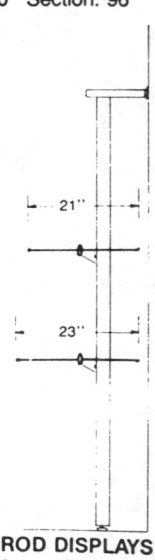

ROD DISPLAYS
6 or 7 Rods Per
4'-0" Section

- Design continuity from wall to floor carries theme throughout the department or the store
- Designed for high volume merchandising
- Flexible merchandising
- Designed to be compatible with other Pam International Systems

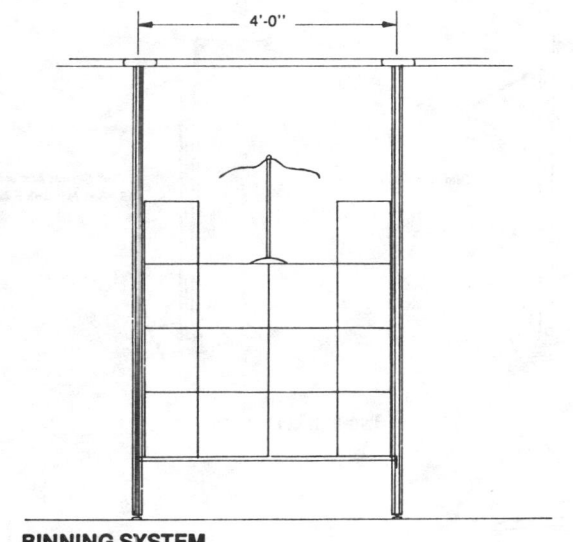

BINNING SYSTEM

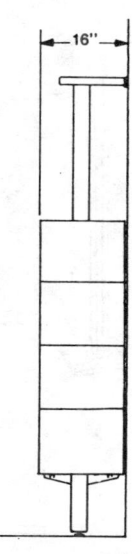

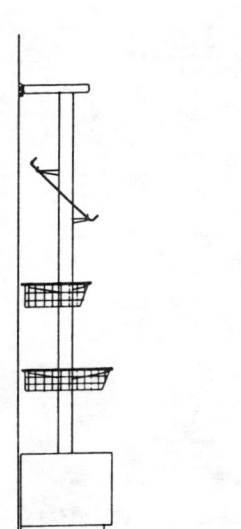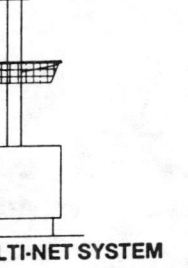

MULTI-NET SYSTEM

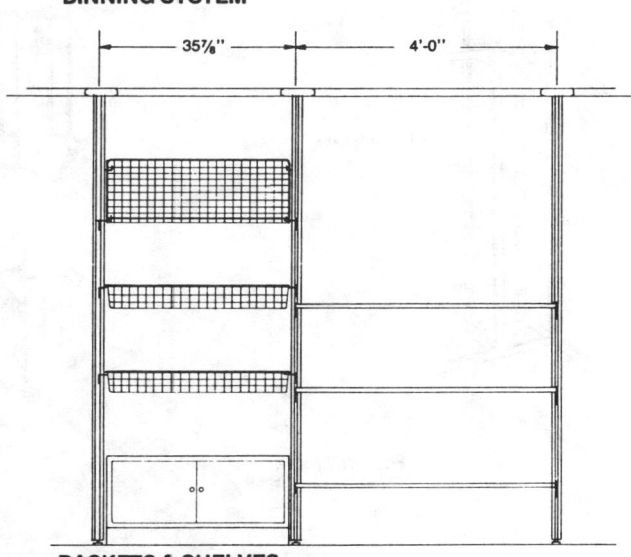

BASKETS & SHELVES

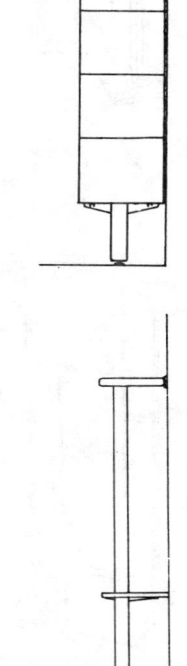

WOOD OR GLASS SHELVES

MULTI-NET PANELS

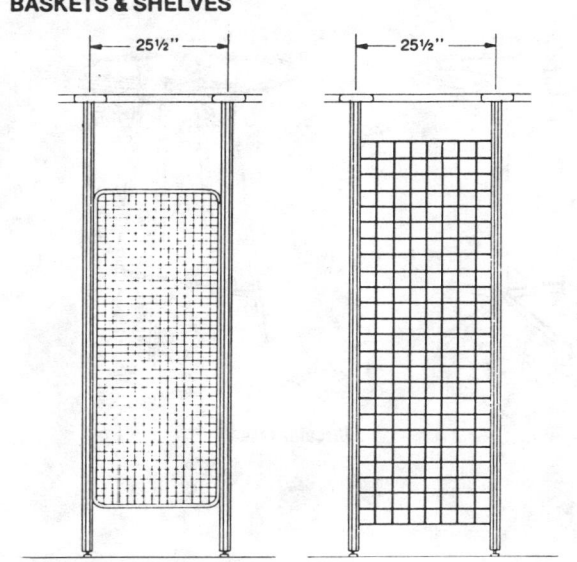

MESH PANEL SYSTEMS

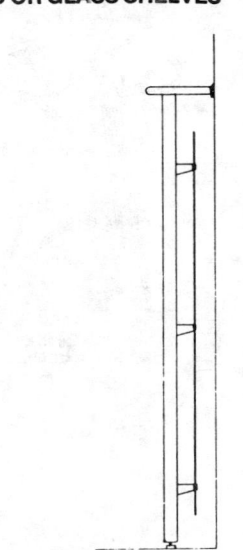

GRID WALL PANELS

- All Multiples/Systems 2™ upright posts are engineered with easily changeable post covers (Pat. Pend.)
- All metal components are coated with a durable, long lasting, baked on epoxy powder finish.

DEPARTMENT STORES
Rack Display Systems

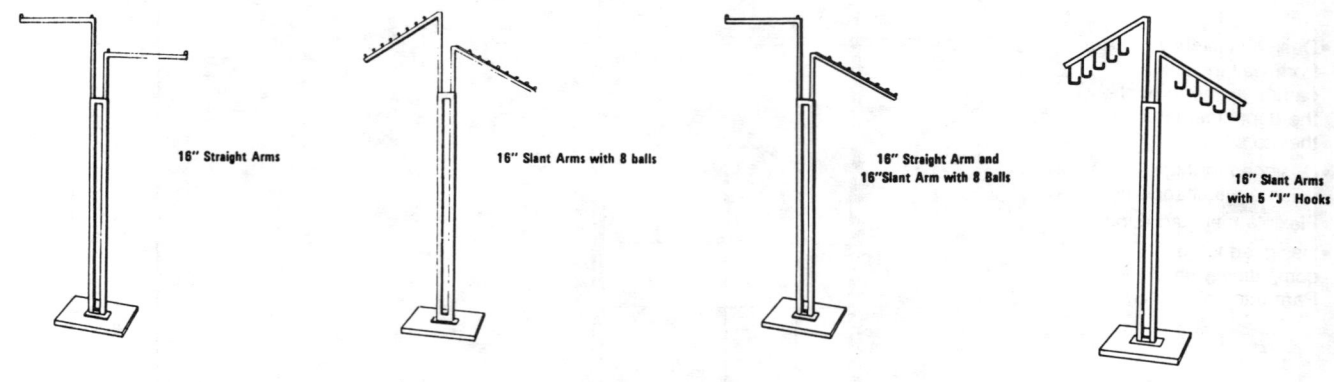

16" Straight Arms

16" Slant Arms with 8 balls

16" Straight Arm and
16"Slant Arm with 8 Balls

16" Slant Arms
with 5 "J" Hooks

Two-arm costumers

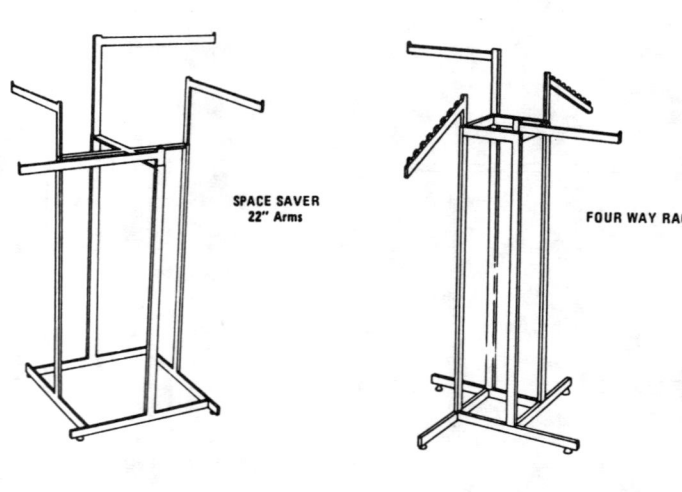

SPACE SAVER
22" Arms

FOUR WAY RACK

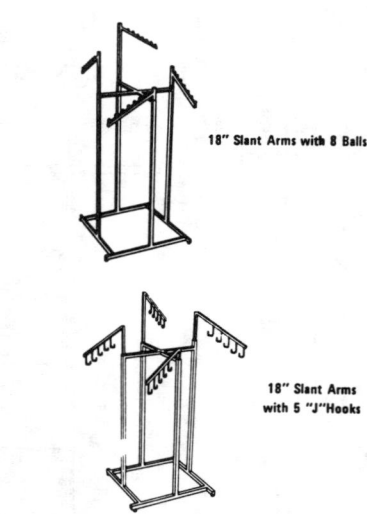

18" Slant Arms with 8 Balls

18" Slant Arms
with 5 "J"Hooks

Four-way racks

Rectangular Hangrail

36" Dia.
42" Dia.

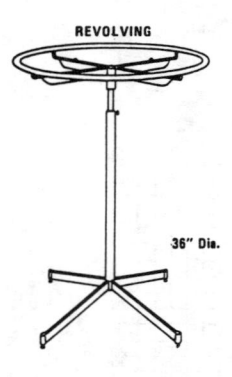

REVOLVING

36" Dia.

1¼" Dia. Hangrail

36" Dia.
42" Dia.

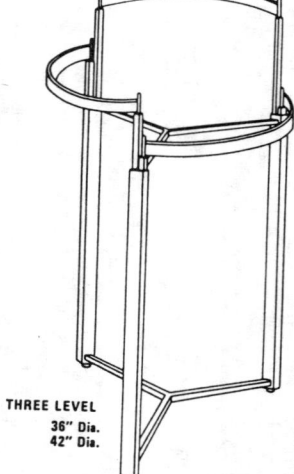

Circular racks

THREE LEVEL
36" Dia.
42" Dia.

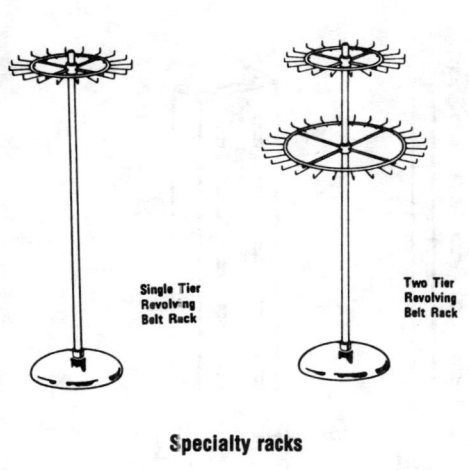

Single Tier Revolving Belt Rack

Two Tier Revolving Belt Rack

Specialty racks

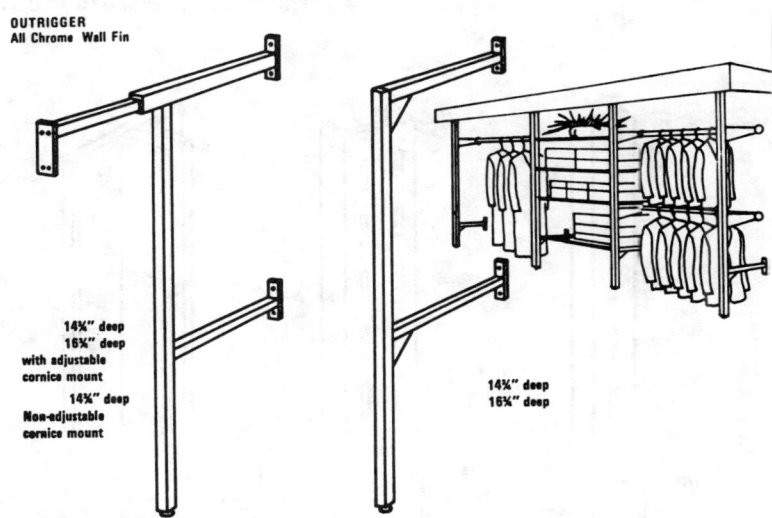

OUTRIGGER
All Chrome Wall Fin

14⅜" deep
16¾" deep
with adjustable cornice mount

14⅜" deep
Non-adjustable cornice mount

14⅜" deep
16¾" deep

Outriggers, wall fins

60" Long

Double Hangrail

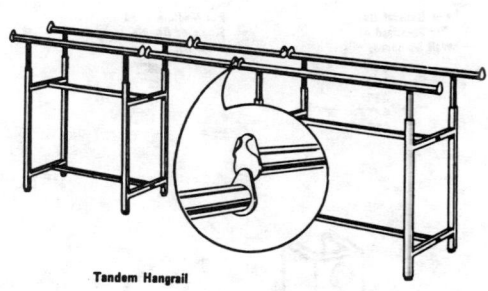

Tandem Hangrail

Rectangular racks

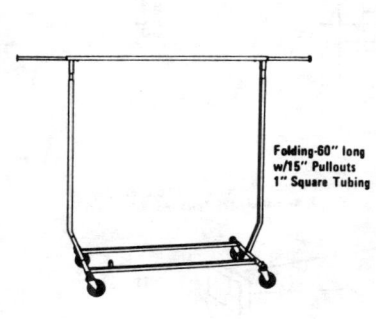

Folding-60" long w/15" Pullouts 1" Square Tubing

**60" Long
All 1" Square Tubing   12" Pullout**

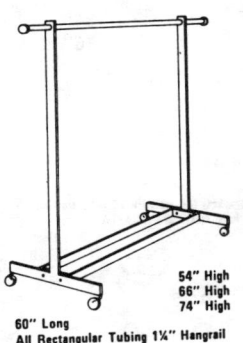

**60" Long
All Rectangular Tubing 1¼" Hangrail**

54" High
66" High
74" High

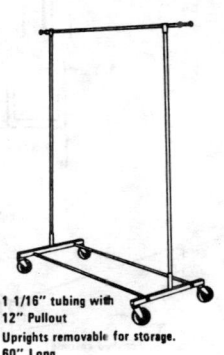

1 1/16" tubing with 12" Pullout
Uprights removable for storage.
60" Long

Rolling racks

MEDIUM DUTY-½" SLOTS 1" O.C.

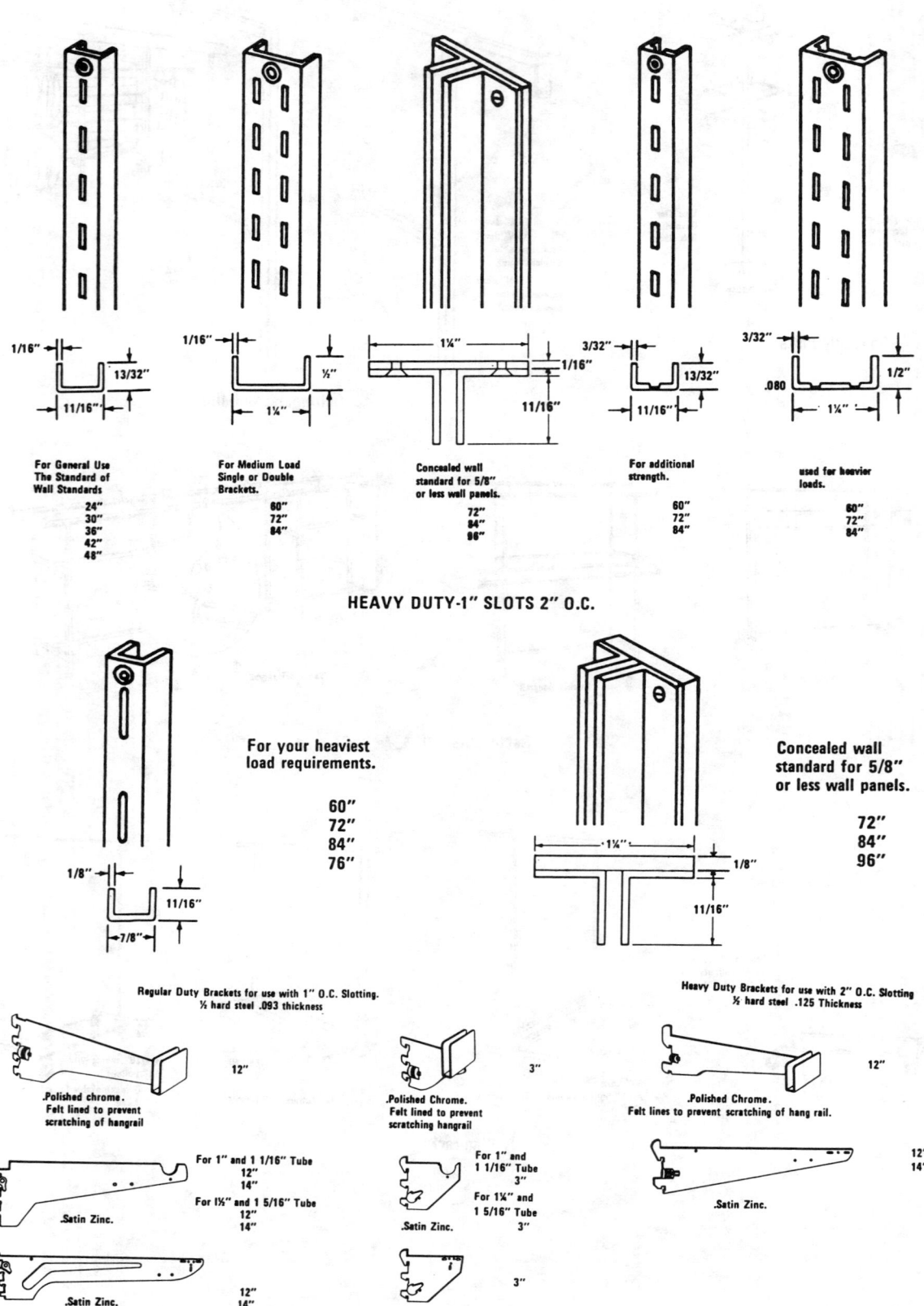

1/16" 13/32" 11/16"	1/16" ½" 1¼"	1¼" 1/16" 11/16"	3/32" 13/32" 11/16"	3/32" .080 ½" 1¼"
For General Use The Standard of Wall Standards 24" 30" 36" 42" 48"	For Medium Load Single or Double Brackets. 60" 72" 84"	Concealed wall standard for 5/8" or less wall panels. 72" 84" 96"	For additional strength. 60" 72" 84"	used for heavier loads. 60" 72" 84"

HEAVY DUTY-1" SLOTS 2" O.C.

For your heaviest load requirements.

60"
72"
84"
76"

1/8"   11/16"   7/8"

Concealed wall standard for 5/8" or less wall panels.

72"
84"
96"

1¼"   1/8"   11/16"

Regular Duty Brackets for use with 1" O.C. Slotting.
½ hard steel .093 thickness

Heavy Duty Brackets for use with 2" O.C. Slotting
½ hard steel .125 Thickness

.Polished chrome.
Felt lined to prevent
scratching of hangrail   12"

.Polished Chrome.
Felt lined to prevent
scratching hangrail   3"

.Polished Chrome.
Felt lines to prevent scratching of hang rail.   12"

For 1" and 1 1/16" Tube
12"
14"
For 1½" and 1 5/16" Tube
12"
14"
.Satin Zinc.

For 1" and
1 1/16" Tube
3"
For 1¼" and
1 5/16" Tube
3"
.Satin Zinc.

12"
14"
.Satin Zinc.

.Satin Zinc.   12"
14"

.Satin Zinc.   3"

Public Restrooms, Toilets, and Coatrooms

TABLE 1   Minimum Number of Plumbing Fixtures Required by Building Occupancy Type*

Type of building occupancy	Type of fixture					
	Water closets	Urinals	Lavatories	Bathtubs or showers	Drinking fountains	Other fixtures
Assembly — places of worship†	1 for ea. sex for ea. 150 persons	Urinals may be provided in toilet rooms in lieu of water closets but for not more than ½ of the required number of water closets	1			
Assembly — other than places of worship (including but not limited to auditoriums, theaters, convention halls) and all spaces classified as F-4	No. of persons / No of fixtures for each sex 1-100 — 1 101-200 — 2 201-300 — 3 301-400 — 4 Over 400, add 1 fixture for ea. sex for ea. additional 200 persons	Urinals may be provided in toilet rooms in lieu of water closets but for not more than ½ of the required number of water closets	No. of persons / No. of fixtures 1-200 — 1 201-400 — 2 401-750 — 3 Over 750, add 1 fixture for ea. 500 persons		1 for ea. 1,000 persons except that there shall be at least 1 fixture at each assembly floor level or tier	Where motion picture projection booths contain more than 2 projectors, at least 1 water closet and 1 lavatory shall be provided on the same level and within 20 ft. of the booth
Dormitories — school or labor, also institutional	1 for ea. sex for ea. 8 persons	Urinals may be provided in toilet rooms in lieu of water closets but for not more than ½ of the required number of water closets	1 for ea. 12 persons	1 for ea. 8 persons; for women's dormitories, 1 bathtub shall be substituted for 1 shower at the ratio of 1 for ea. 30 women		Laundry trays — 1 for ea. 50 persons
Single room occupancies for sleeping accommodations only	1 for ea. 6 persons		1 for ea. 6 persons	1 for ea. 6 persons		
Dwellings — one- and two-family	1 for each dwelling unit		1 for each dwelling unit	1 for each dwelling unit		Kitchen sink — 1 for each dwelling unit
Public buildings, offices, business mercantile, storage; warehouses, factories and institutional employees‡	No. of persons each sex / No. of fixtures 1-15 — 1 16-35 — 2 36-55 — 3 56-80 — 4 81-110 — 5 111-150 — 6 1 fixture for ea. additional 40 persons	Urinals may be provided in toilet rooms in lieu of water closets but for not more than ½ of the required number of water closets when more than 35 persons	No. of persons / No. of fixtures 1-20 — 1 21-40 — 2 41-60 — 3 61-90 — 4 91-125 — 5 1 fixture for ea. additional 45 persons		1 for ea. 75 persons	
Public bathing	1 fixture for ea. sex for ea. 30 persons	Urinals may be provided in toilet rooms in lieu of water closets but for not more than ½ of the required number of water closets	1/60	1/40		
Schools: Elementary Secondary	1 fixture for ea. sex for ea. 35 students	Urinals may be provided in toilet rooms in lieu of water closets but for not more than ½ of the required number of water closets	1/50 pupils 1/50 pupils Over 300 pupils: 1/100 pupils	In gym or pool shower rooms, ⅓ pupils of a largest class using pool at any one time	1/50 persons but at least 1 per floor	
Workers' portable facilities	1/30 workers	1/30 workers			At least 1 per floor equivalent for ea. 100 workmen	
Industrial — foundries only	No. of persons / No. of fixtures 1-10 — 1 11-25 — 2 26-50 — 3 51-80 — 4 81-125 — 5 1 additional fixture for each additional 45 persons	Where more than 10 men are employed: No. of men / No. of urinals 11-29 — 1 30-79 — 2 1 additional fixture for each additional 80 males Urinals may be provided in toilet rooms in lieu of water closets but for not more than ½ of the required number of water closets	No. of persons / No. of fixtures 1-8 — 1 9-16 — 2 17-30 — 3 31-45 — 4 46-65 — 5 1 additional fixture for each additional 25 persons	1 shower for each 15 persons exposed to excessive heat or occupational hazard from poisonous, infectious, or irritating material	1 for ea. 75 persons	
						Other fixtures
Kitchens for public or employees dining			1 lavatory for the personal use of kitchen employees			One machine or a 3-compartment sink for the effective washing and sanitizing of all cutlery, dishes and glasses before re-use
Dwellings — multiple or apartment	1 for each dwelling unit or apartment		1 for each dwelling unit or apartment	1 for each dwelling unit or apartment		Kitchen sink — 1 for each dwelling unit or apartment. Within each dwelling unit, not designed for use by transients, one laundry tray or automatic laundry washing machine; or in a readily accessible location within a general laundry room. 1 two-compartment tray for each 10 dwelling units or 1 automatic laundry washing machine for each 20 dwelling units.

*The population used in determining the number of fixtures required shall be based on the number of people to occupy the space but in no case shall the population be less than that determined by allowing 125 sq. ft. of net floor area per person.

†Such facilities may be in adjacent buildings under the same ownership or control, and shall be accessible during periods when the assembly space is occupied.

‡Facilities for employees in a storage building or warehouse may be located in an adjacent building, under the same ownership, where the maximum distance of travel from the working space to the toilet facilities does not exceed 500 ft. horizontally.

RESTROOMS AND TOILETS
Plumbing Fixture and Accessory Heights

While Fig. 1 provides specific vertical dimensions of both plumbing fixtures and accessories, the designer is cautioned that every plumbing fixture and accessory must be carefully analyzed in light of the users to be served. Plumbing contractors will follow the manufacturer's recommendations or their own standards unless the designer provides this information on the working drawings. In large-scale projects, it is suggested that the designer carefully provide all fixture mounting heights on all interior elevations or on a separate diagramatic drawing, such as is shown in Fig. 1.

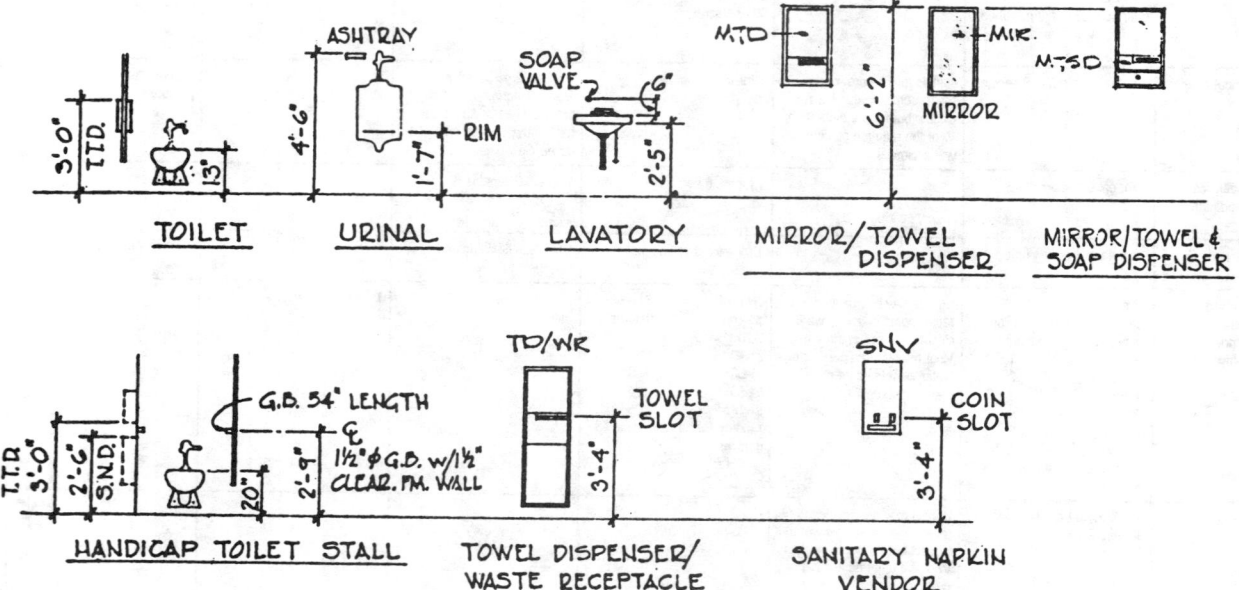

Fig. 1 Fixture heights.

Handicapped Washrooms

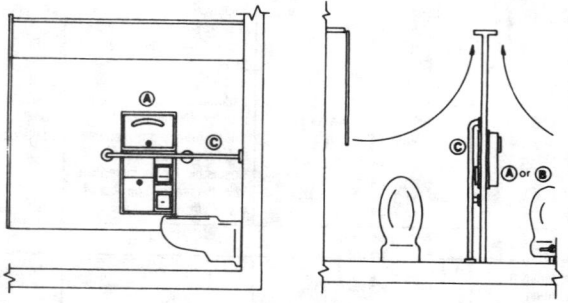

Fig. 2 Suggested mounting heights for various bathroom accessories.

Partition Mounted Units

Fig. 3 Typical back to back male/female washroom stalls using partition mounted units to accommodate a handicapped stall and one standard stall. If room permits, grab bars should be placed on all three sides, resulting in a "U"-shaped configuration. Most codes require toilet stall doors to open outward.

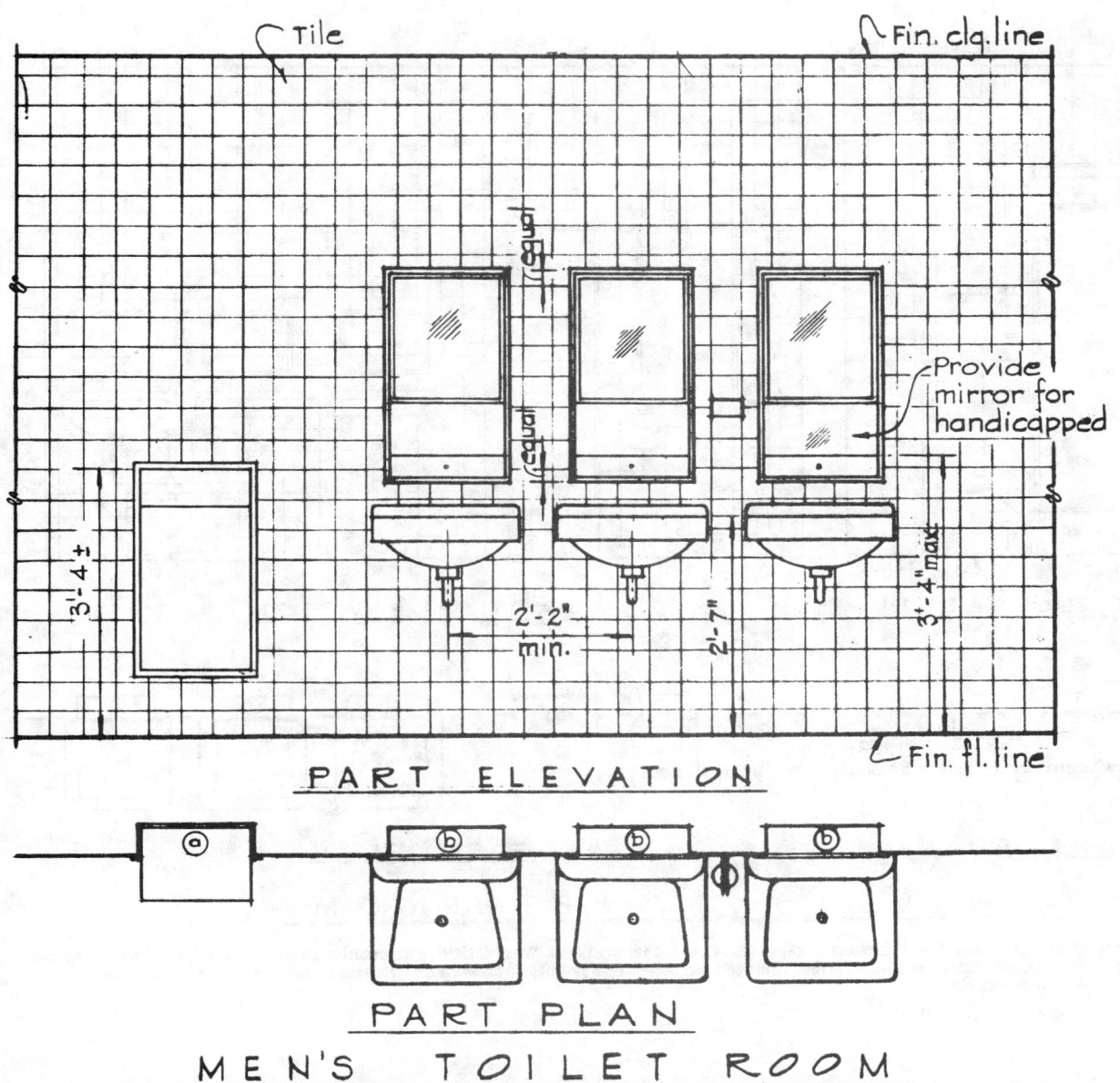

Tile

Fin. clg. line

equal

equal

Provide mirror for handicapped

3'-4"±

2'-2" min.

2'-7"

3'-4" max.

Fin. fl. line

PART ELEVATION

(a)   (b)   (b)   (b)

PART PLAN

MEN'S TOILET ROOM

Fig. 4 This drawing of a part plan and part elevation of a men's toilet room demonstrates how mounting heights of plumbing fixtures and accessories are indicated. In addition, spacing of plumbing fixtures is indicated by use of a horizontal dimension from centerline to centerline of the lavatories. Many designers prefer to show horizontal dimensions on the plan. a = recessed waste receptacle, b = recessed towel dispenser and soap dispenser with shelf.

RESTROOMS AND TOILETS

Plumbing Fixture and Accessory Heights

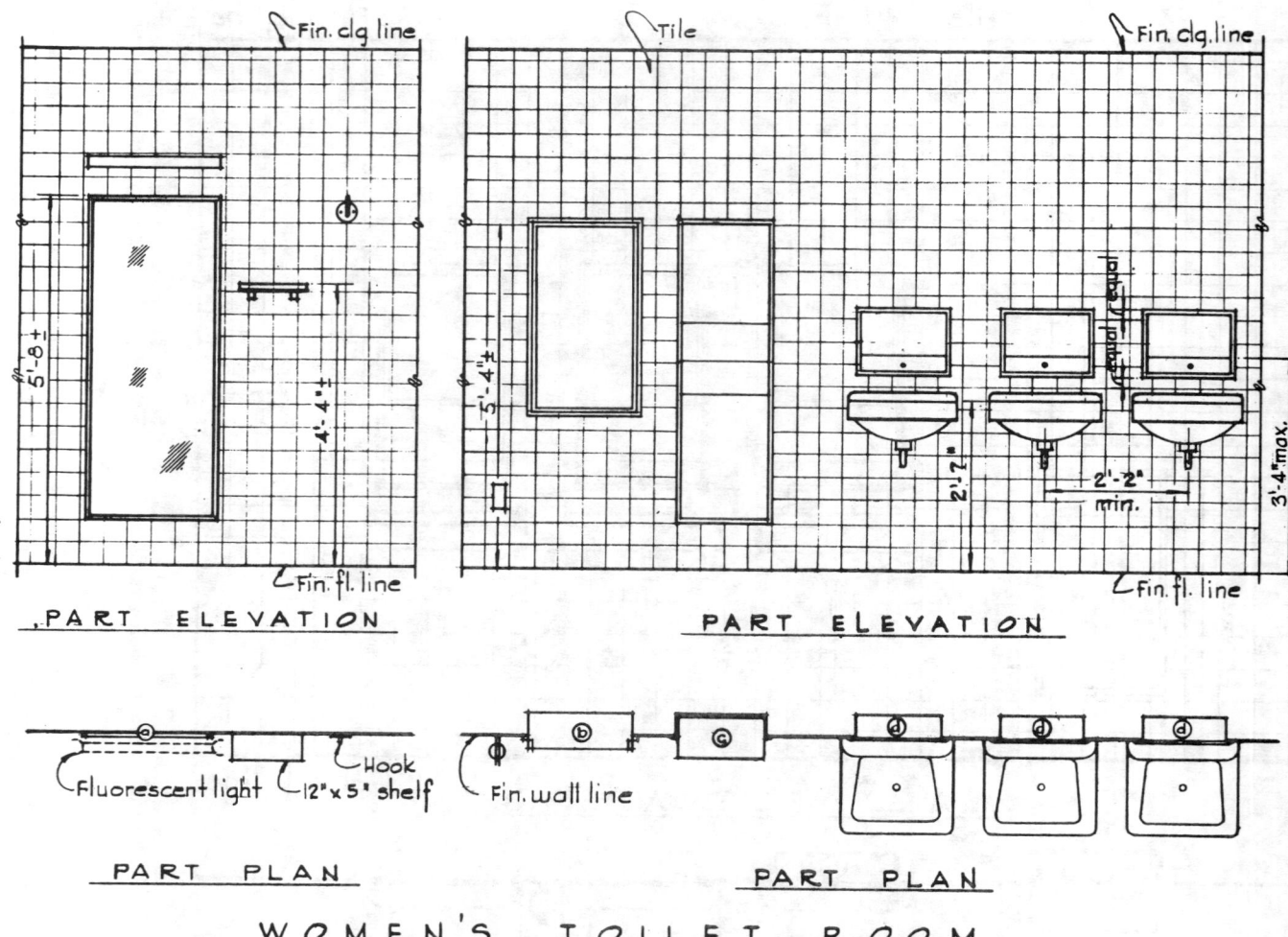

PART ELEVATION

PART ELEVATION

Fluorescent light   Hook   12" x 5" shelf

Fin. wall line

PART PLAN

PART PLAN

WOMEN'S TOILET ROOM

Fig. 5 Mounting heights or vertical dimensions are always taken from the finished floor. When installing accessories on tile walls, the tile module and dimensions should be taken into consideration. a = full length mirror, b = recessed feminine napkin dispenser, c = recessed towel cabinet and waste receptacle, d = recessed soap dispenser with shelf.

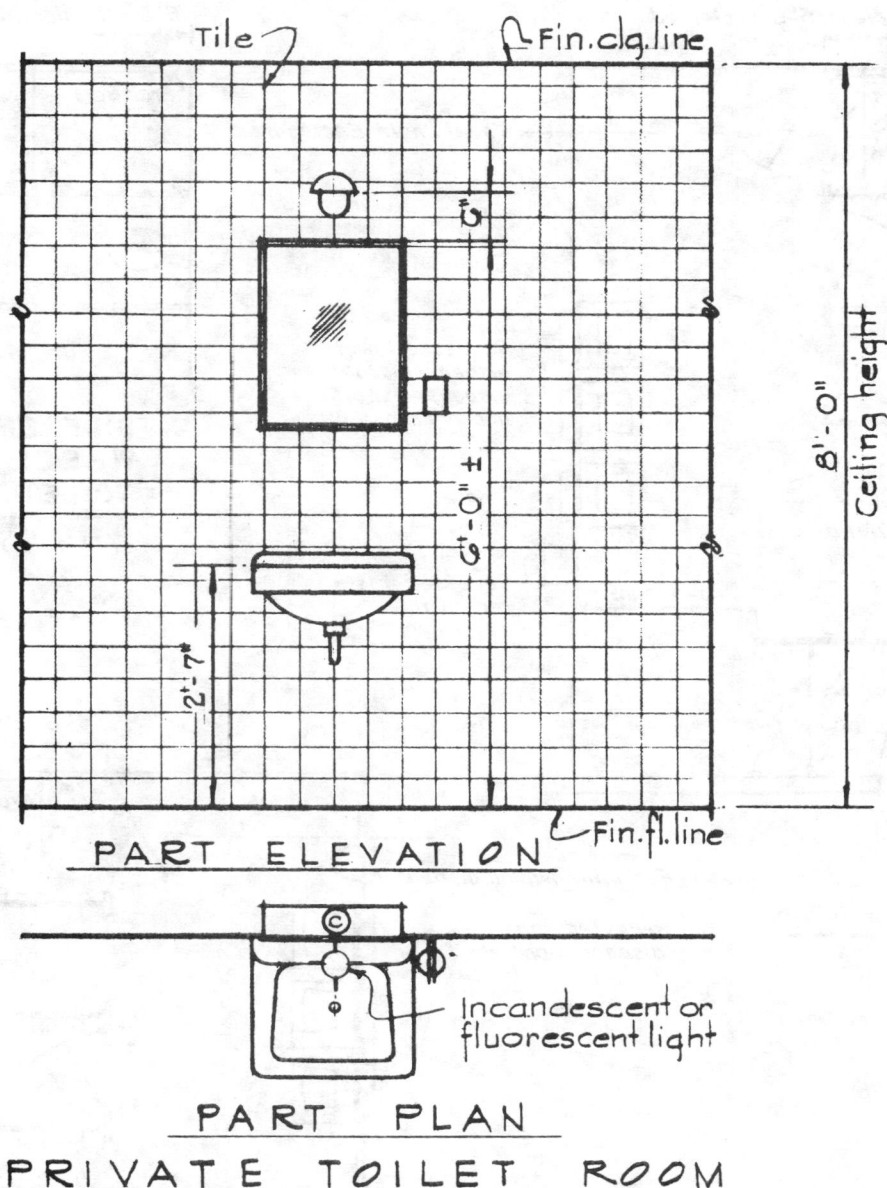

PART ELEVATION

Incandescent or fluorescent light

PART PLAN

PRIVATE TOILET ROOM

Fig. 6 The mounting heights of plumbing fixtures and accessories for a private toilet are, in many instances, determined by the physical characteristics of the primary user. A person 6'6" tall might require the mounting height of a lavatory, mirror, or shower head to be higher than usual. Note that any electrical outlets near a lavatory or shower must be specified with a ground fault interrupter. c = first aid cabinet and medicine cabinet.

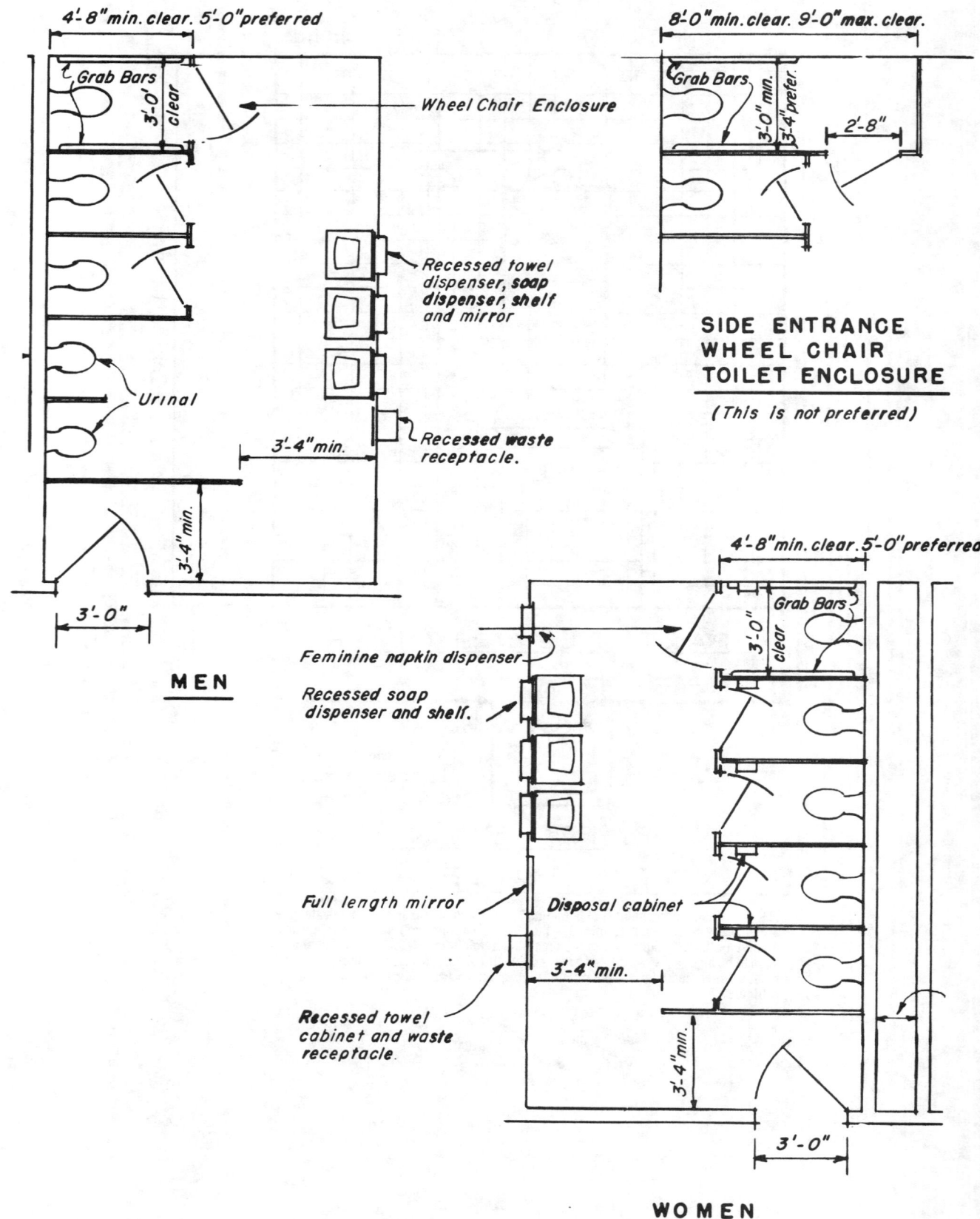

4'-8" min. clear. 5'-0" preferred

Grab Bars

3'-0' clear

Wheel Chair Enclosure

Recessed towel dispenser, soap dispenser, shelf and mirror

Urinal

3'-4" min.

Recessed waste receptacle.

3'-4" min.

3'-0"

MEN

8'-0" min. clear. 9'-0" max. clear.

Grab Bars

3'-0" min. 3'-4" prefer.

2'-8"

SIDE ENTRANCE WHEEL CHAIR TOILET ENCLOSURE

(This is not preferred)

Feminine napkin dispenser

Recessed soap dispenser and shelf.

Full length mirror

Disposal cabinet

Recessed towel cabinet and waste receptacle.

4'-8" min. clear. 5'-0" preferred

Grab Bars

3'-0" clear

3'-4" min.

3'-4" min.

3'-0"

WOMEN

Fig. 7 These drawings show minimum dimensions both for toilet enclosures and between partitions and walls. These layouts are recommendations provided by the General Services Administration, but they may not be in conformity with other codes or desired bathroom layouts, especially in regard to accessibility. Remember, too, that codes provide minimum, not optimal, standards.

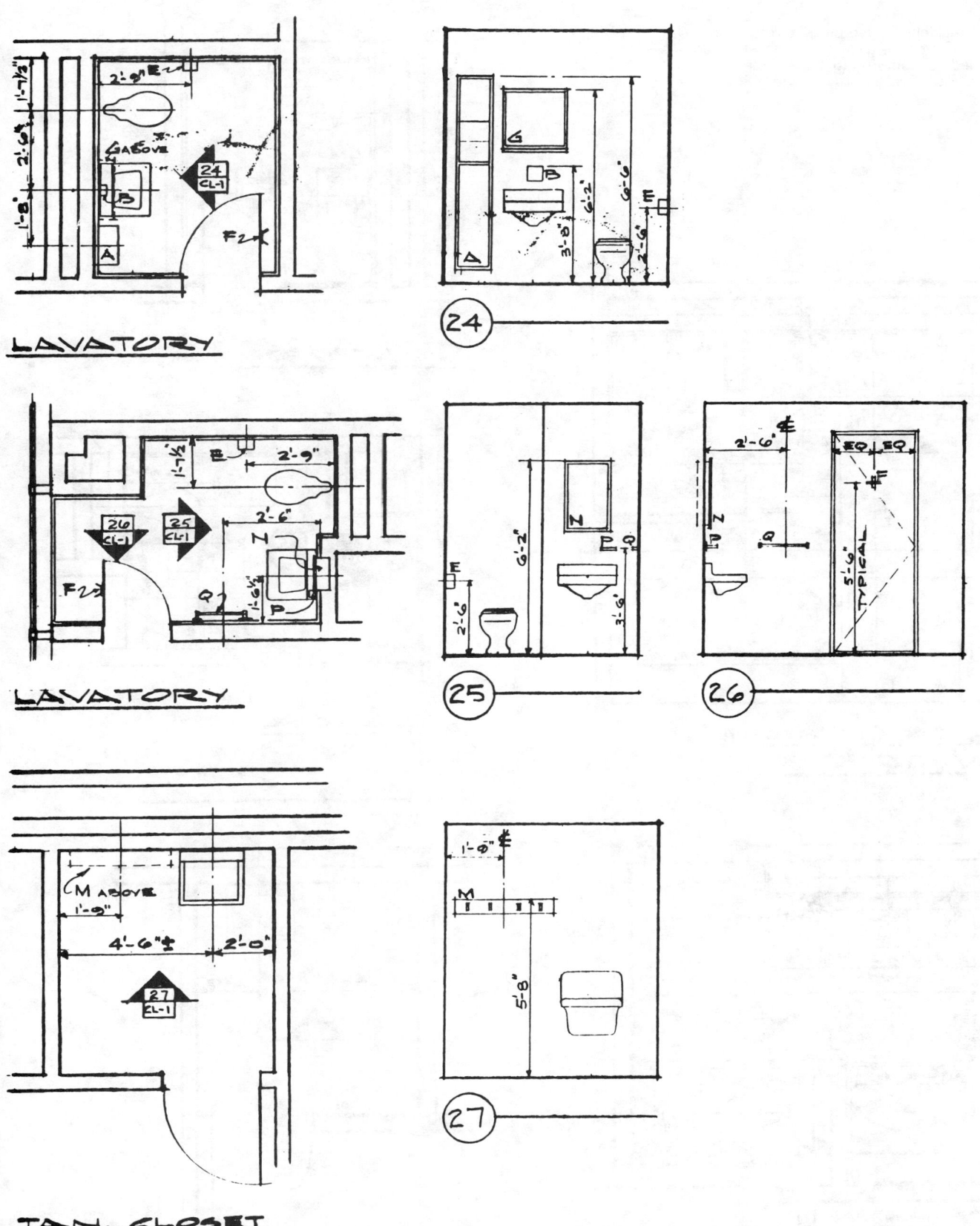

LAVATORY

LAVATORY

JAN. CLOSET

Fig. 8 These working drawings provide both vertical and horizontal dimensions for placement of plumbing fixtures and accessories. Note that accessories are identified or "called out" through the use of letters, which would be coordinated with either a legend or a schedule.

RESTROOMS AND TOILETS

Plans

In multiple-fixtured public toilets, at least one watercloset and lavatory must be designed to conform to barrier-free or accessibility standards.

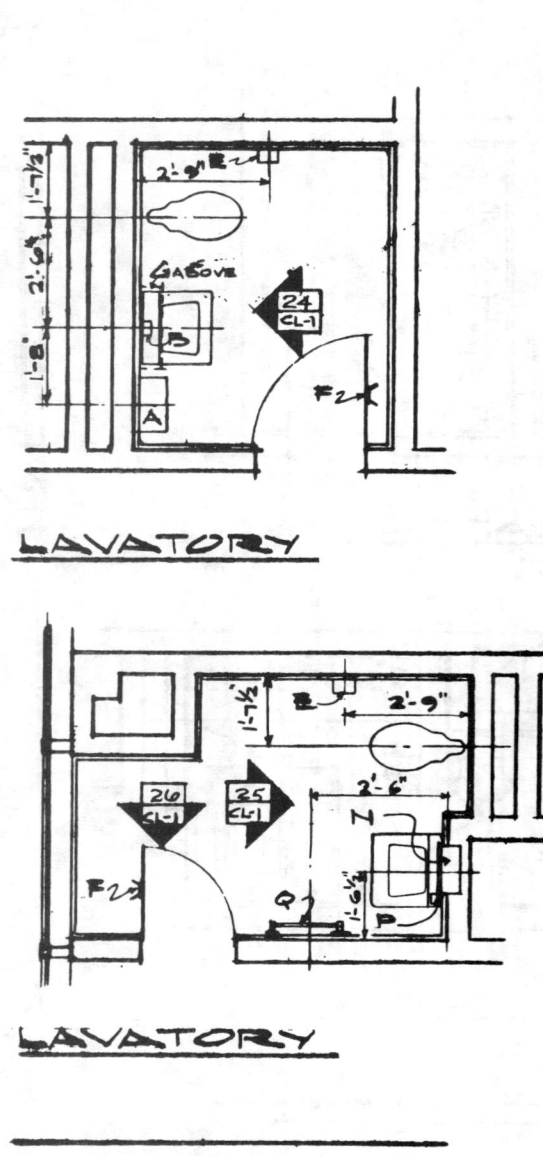

LAVATORY

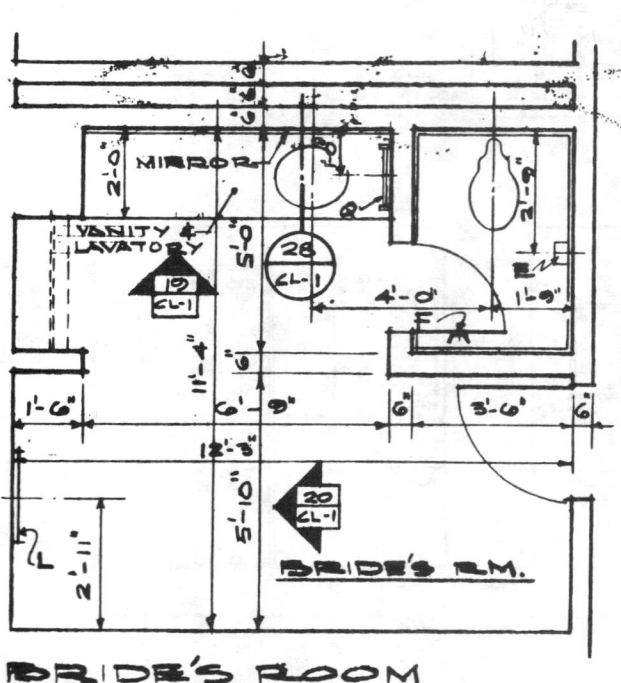

BRIDE'S ROOM
LAVATORY

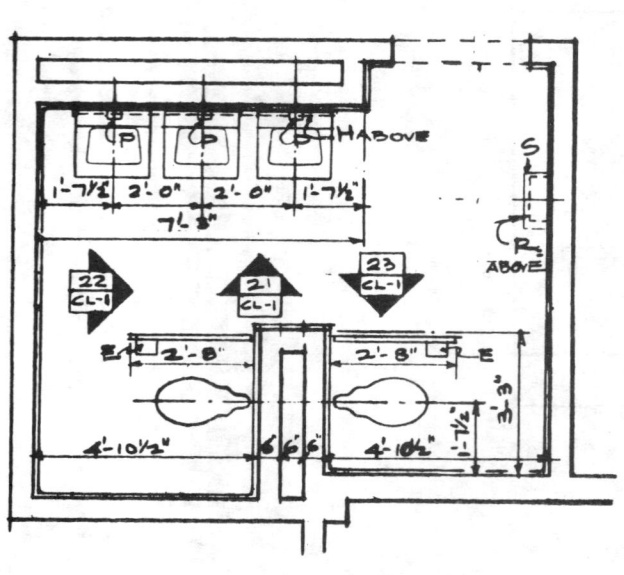

LAVATORY

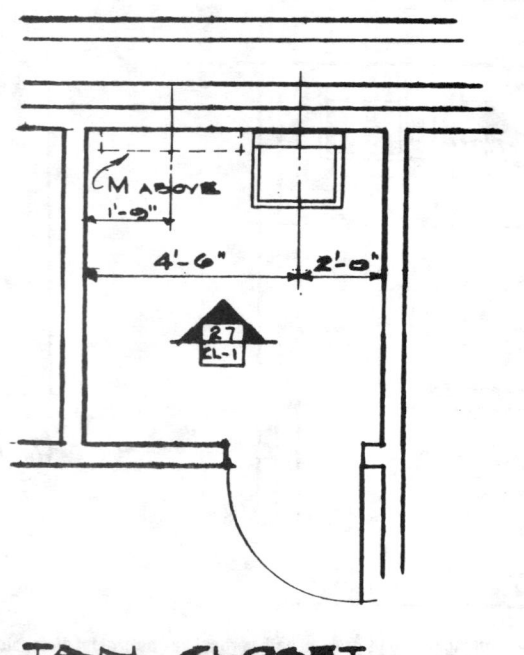

LAVATORY

JAN. CLOSET

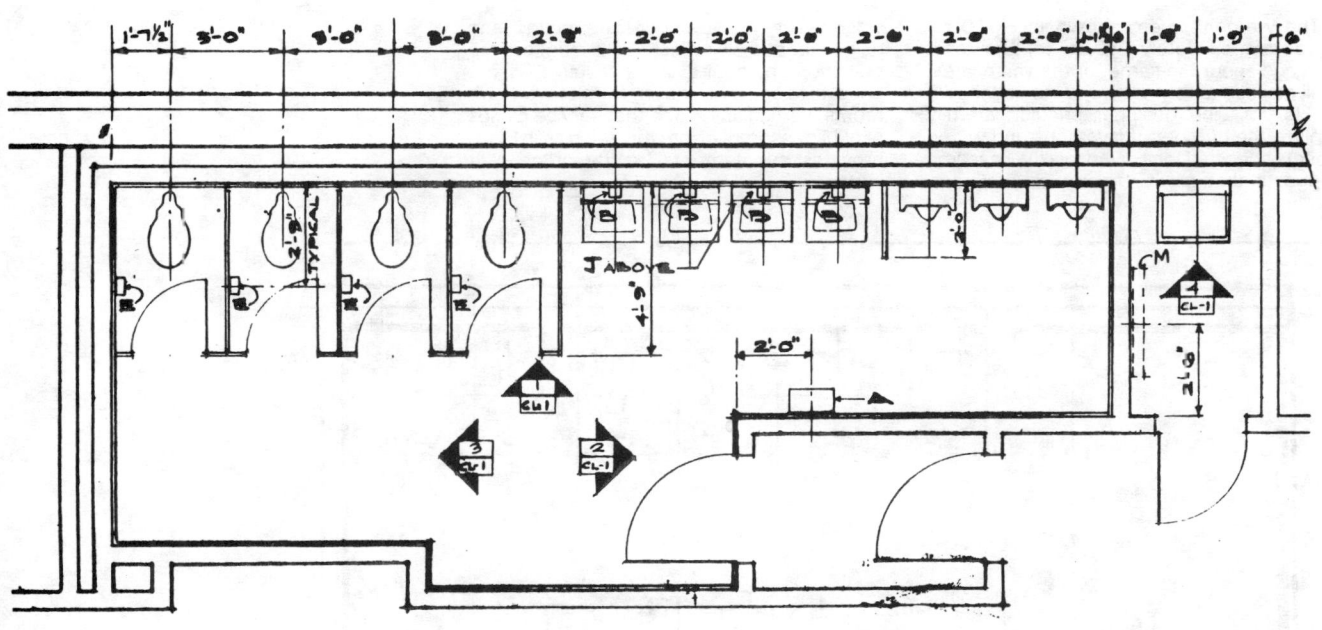

MENS TOILET

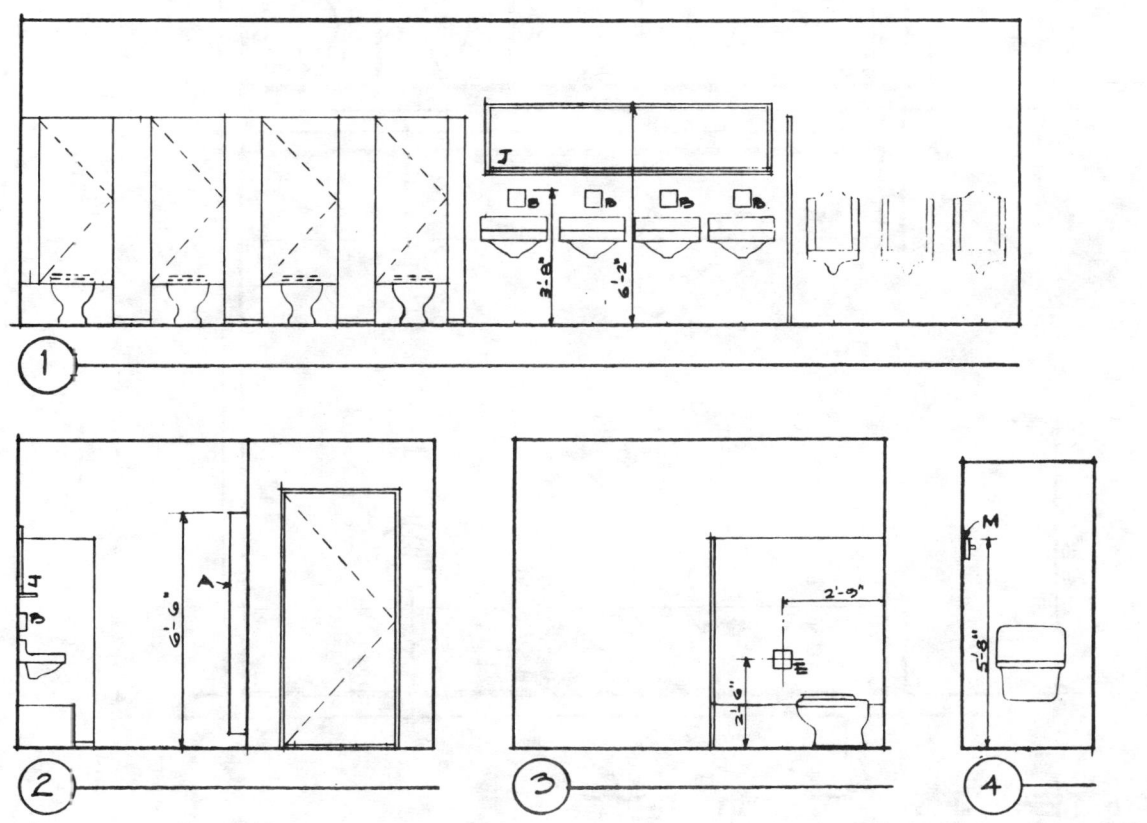

RESTROOMS AND TOILETS

Plans and Elevations

The women's room shown in Fig. 9 requires approximately 250 ft² for the toilet area and about the same for the vanity area. Wall elevations for the two areas are shown in Fig. 10. The designer should carefully analyze the number of lavatories and water-closets specified for a given facility. Research suggests that most "fixture counts" provided by city or state codes are too low and do not adequately reflect the amount of time that women require. As a result, it is not unusual to see long lines in front of women's rooms, particularly those that service places of public assembly. Note that the plan in Fig. 9 provides supplemental vanity or counter surfaces.

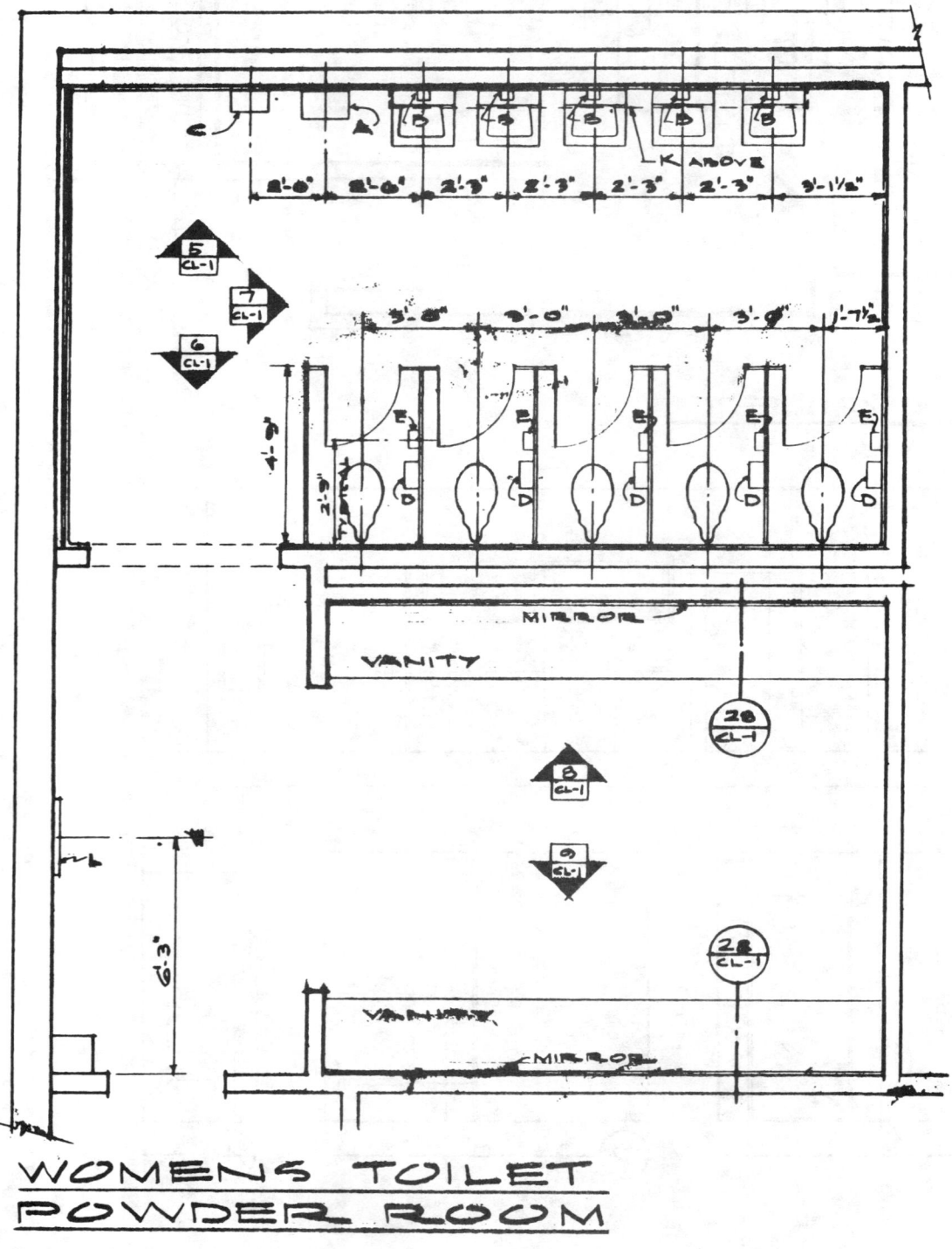

WOMENS TOILET
POWDER ROOM

Fig. 9

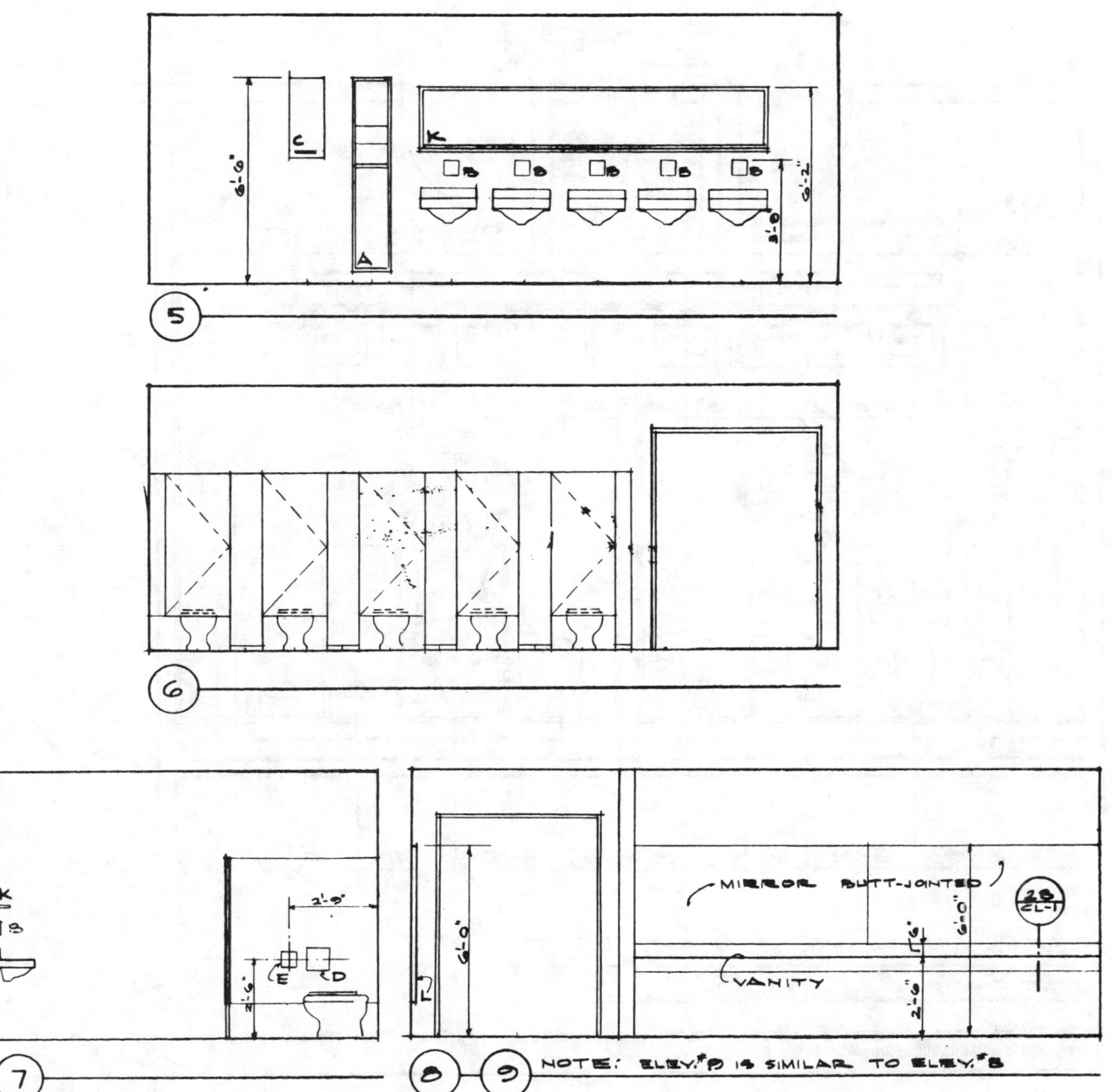

Fig. 10   Wall elevations for the women's room plan in Fig. 9.

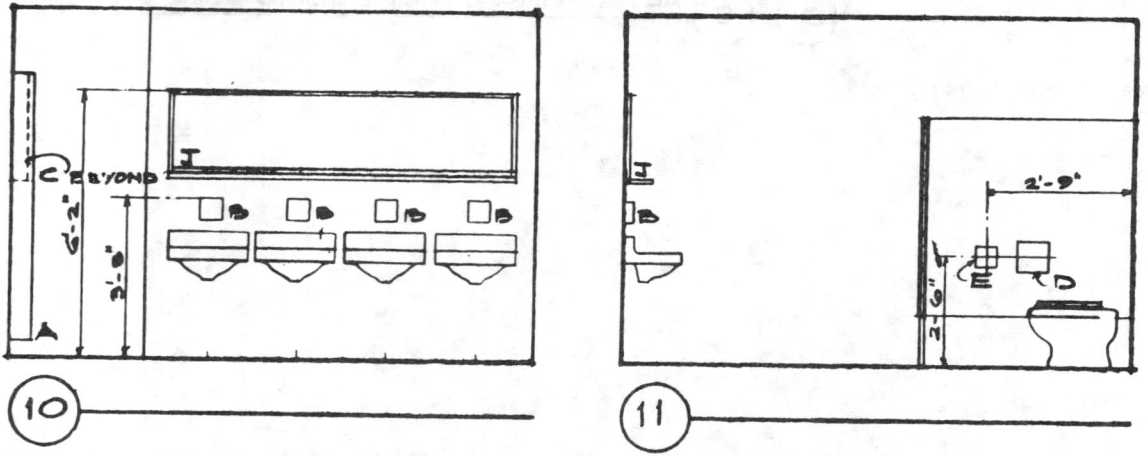

WOMENS TOILET
MENS TOILET

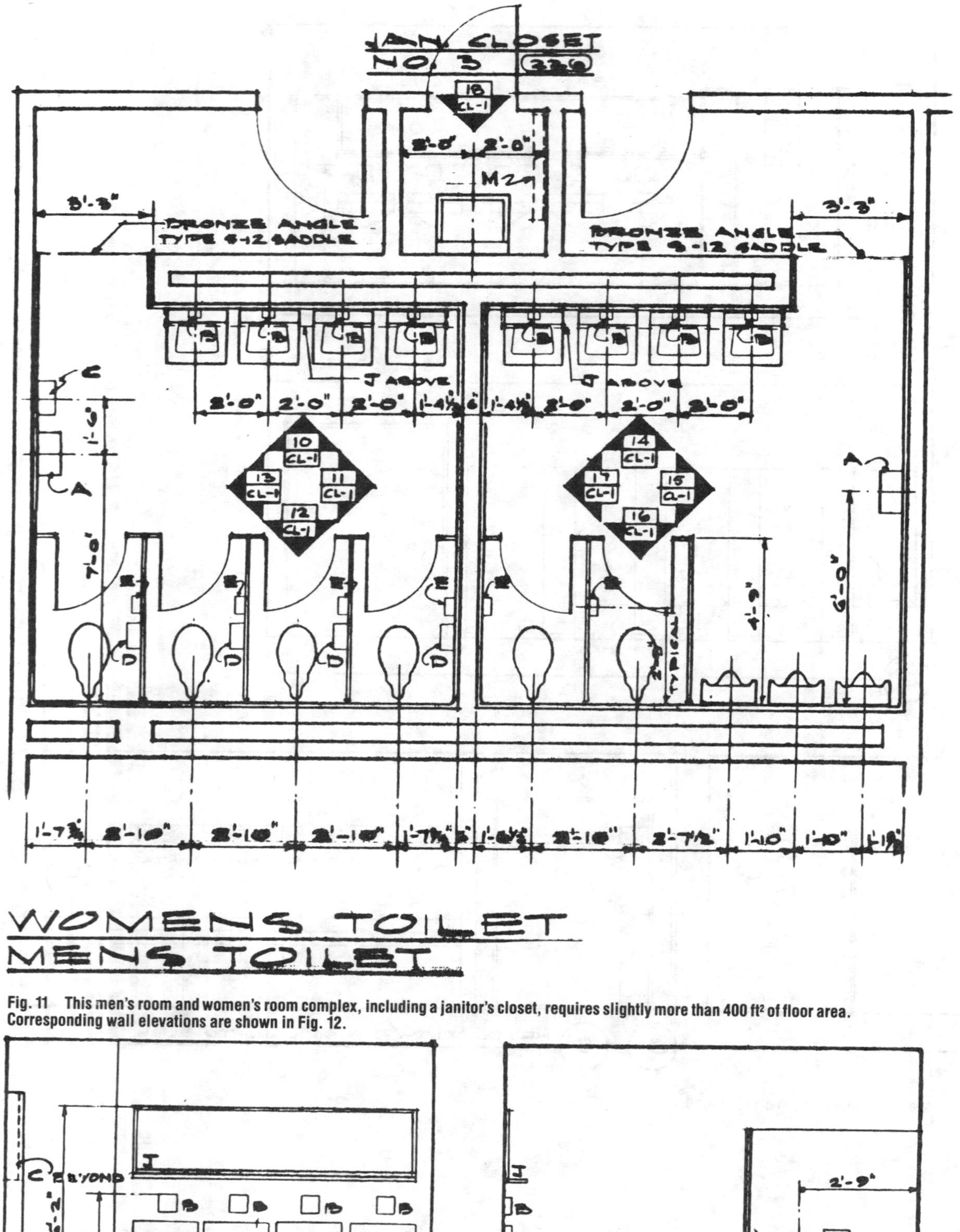

Fig. 11 This men's room and women's room complex, including a janitor's closet, requires slightly more than 400 ft² of floor area. Corresponding wall elevations are shown in Fig. 12.

436   **Fig. 12** Wall elevations for the men's room and women's room complex shown in Fig. 11.

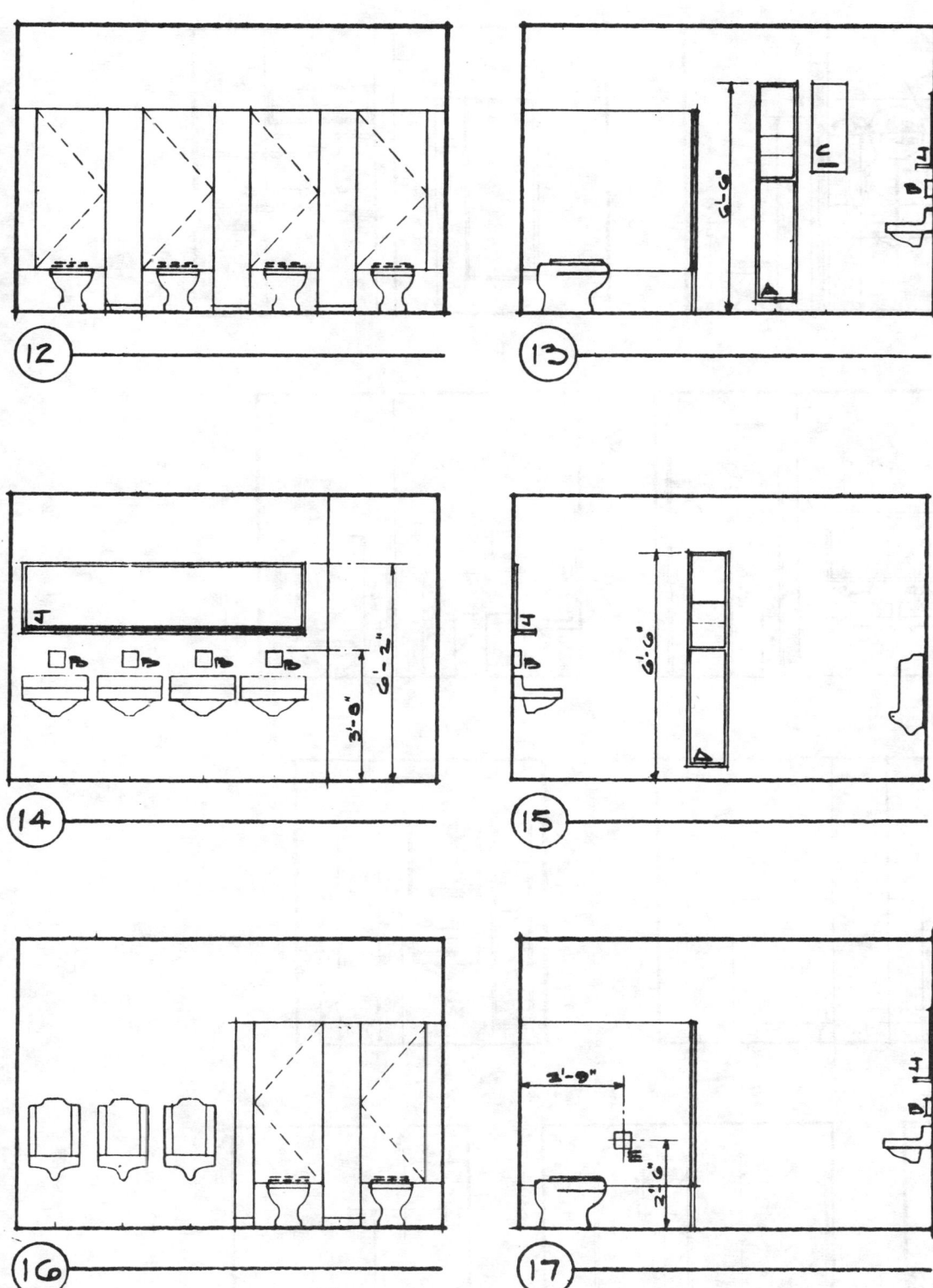

Fig. 12   *(Continued)*

RESTROOMS AND TOILETS
Miscellaneous Elevations

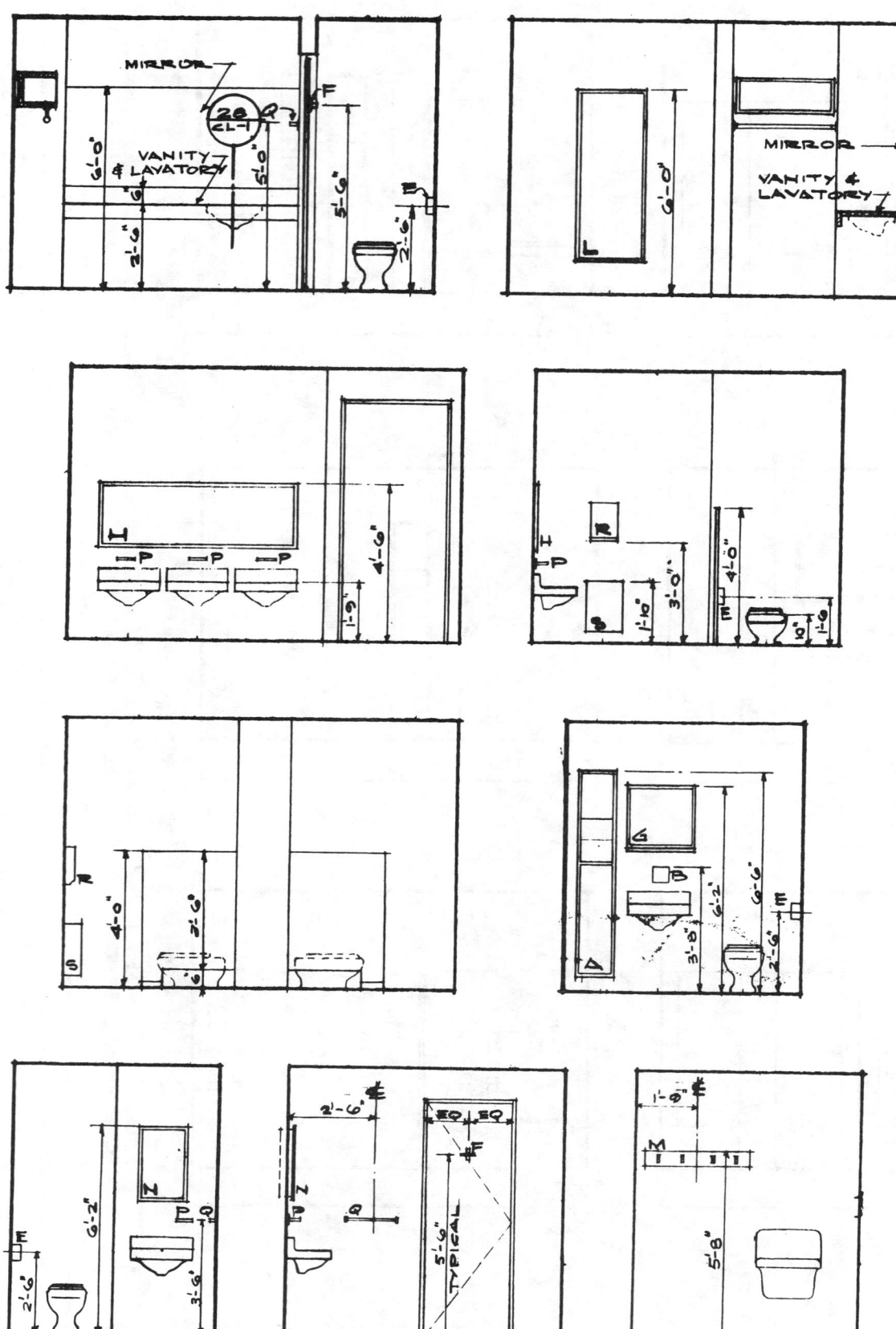

Fig. 13   These drawings show how some designers indicate the heights of certain fixtures and bathroom accessories.

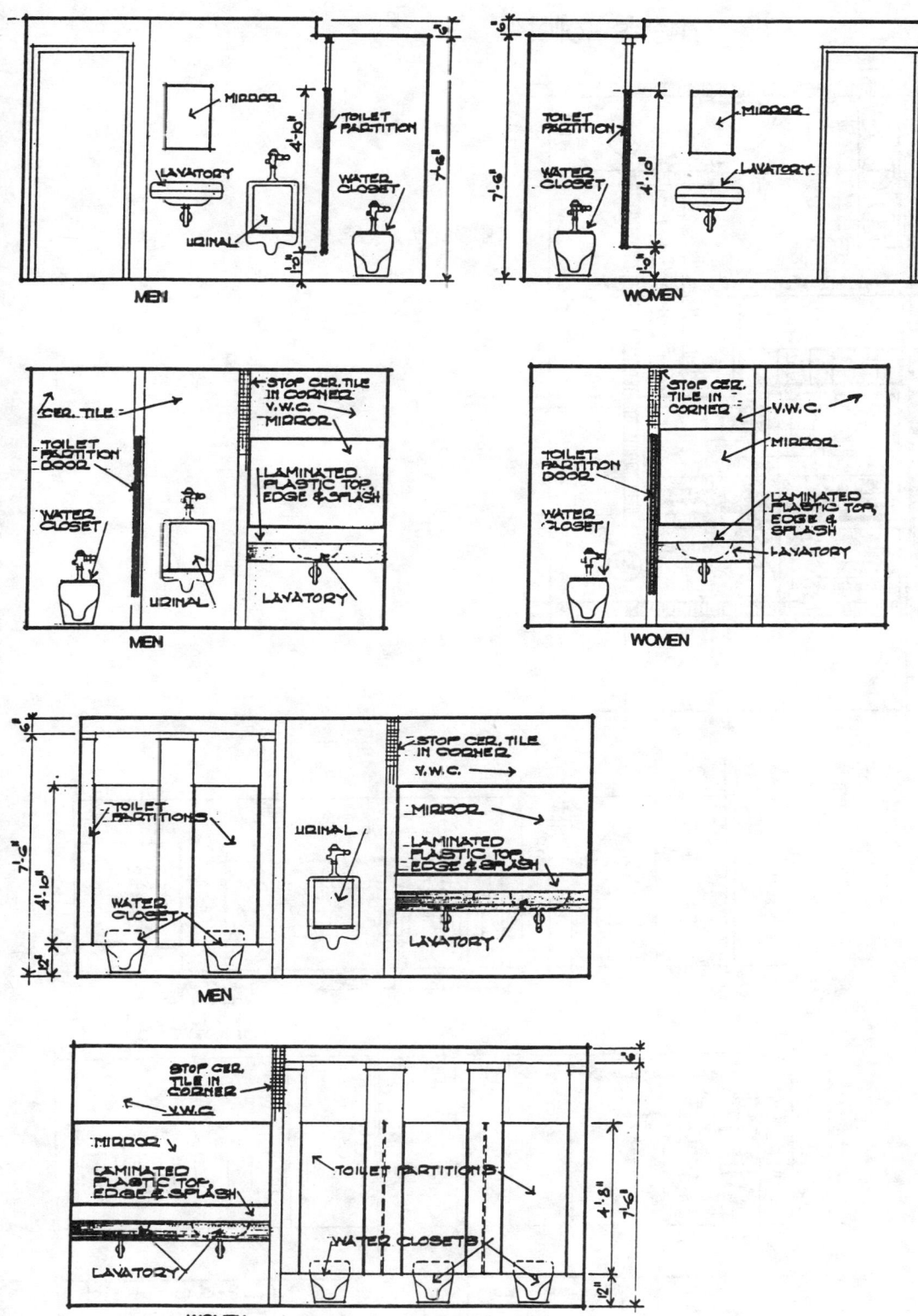

MEN

WOMEN

MEN

WOMEN

MEN

WOMEN

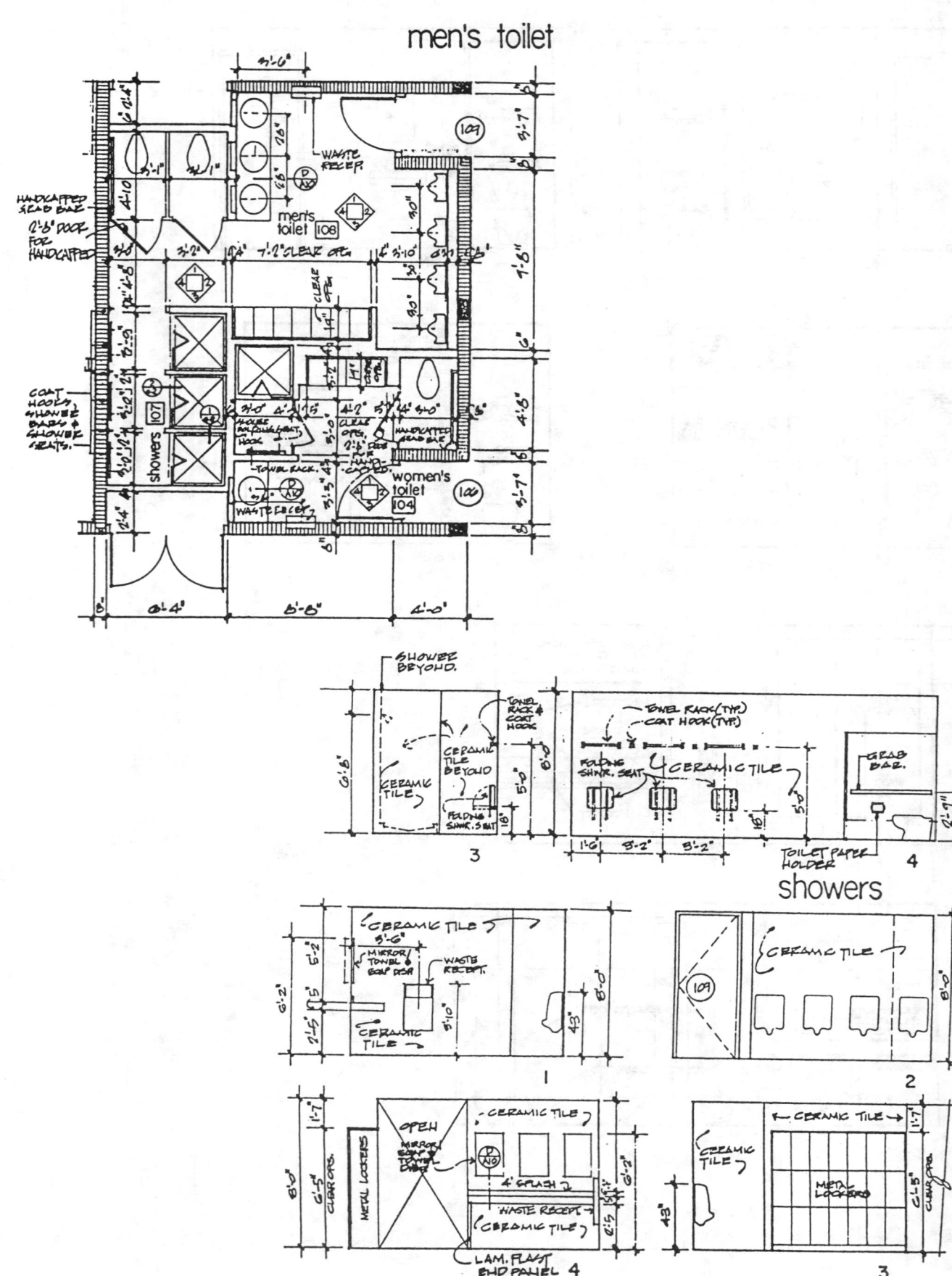

men's toilet

showers

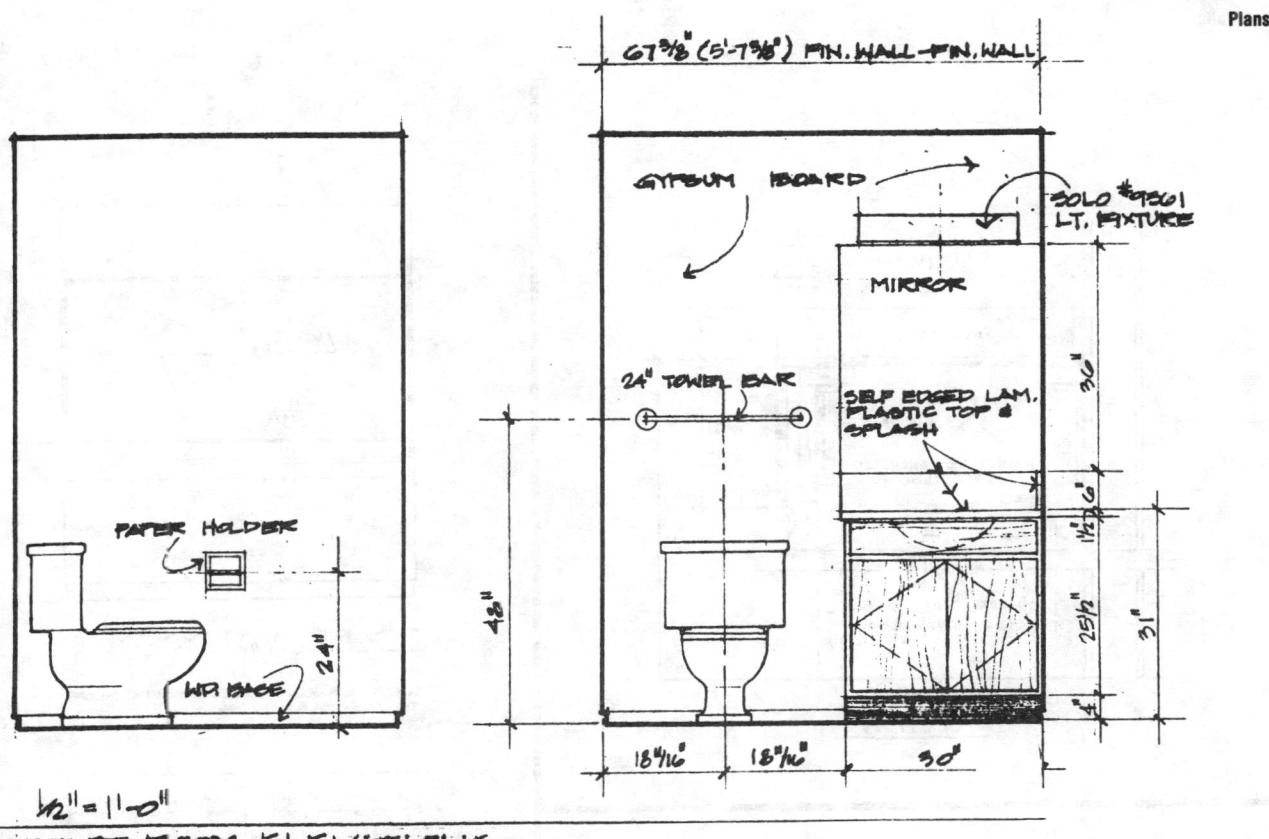

67⅜" (5'-7⅜") FIN. WALL - FIN. WALL

GYPSUM BOARD

SOLO #9361 LT. FIXTURE

MIRROR

24" TOWEL BAR

SELF EDGED LAM. PLASTIC TOP & SPLASH

PAPER HOLDER

48"

24"

WD. BASE

18⁴⁄₁₆" 18⁴⁄₁₆" 30"

36"

6'

25½"

31"

4"

½" = 1'-0"

TOILET ROOM ELEVATIONS

Fig. 14 Detailed large-scale wall elevations such as this are required to show materials, accessory mounting heights, the coordination and placement of plumbing fixtures, and even manufacturer's model numbers.

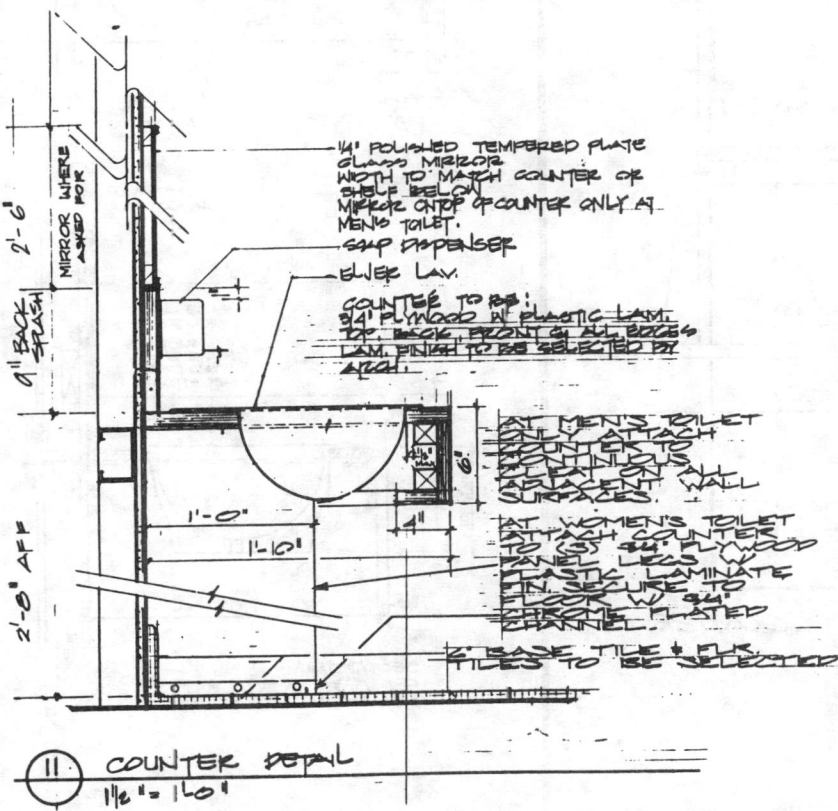

¼" POLISHED TEMPERED PLATE GLASS MIRROR WIDTH TO MATCH COUNTER OR SHELF BELOW. MIRROR ON TOP OF COUNTER ONLY AT MEN'S TOILET.

SOAP DISPENSER

ELJER LAV.

COUNTER TO BE: ¾" PLYWOOD W/ PLASTIC LAM. TOP, BACK, FRONT & ALL EDGES. LAM. FINISH TO BE SELECTED BY ARCH.

2'-6"

9" BACK SPLASH

MIRROR WHERE ASKED FOR

6"

1'-0"

1'-10"

4"

2'-0" AFF

AT MEN'S TOILET ONLY ATTACH COUNTER TO ALUMINUM'S ADJACENT WALL SURFACES.

AT WOMEN'S TOILET ATTACH COUNTER TO (3) ¾" PLYWOOD PANEL LEGS W/ PLASTIC LAMINATE FIN. SECURE TO FLOOR W/ ¾" CHROME PLATED CHANNEL.

6" BASE TILE & FLR. TILES TO BE SELECTED.

⑪ COUNTER DETAIL
1½" = 1'-0"

Fig. 15 The large-scale counter detail shown here provides all the information needed to construct this essential bathroom element. Not only are the construction details carefully defined and described, but all the other design relationships are clearly shown. Note the relationships of the mirror, soap dispenser, and lavatory to the plastic laminate counter. Other lavatory counter details are shown in Figs. 16 to 19.

RESTROOMS AND TOILETS

Lavatory Counter Details

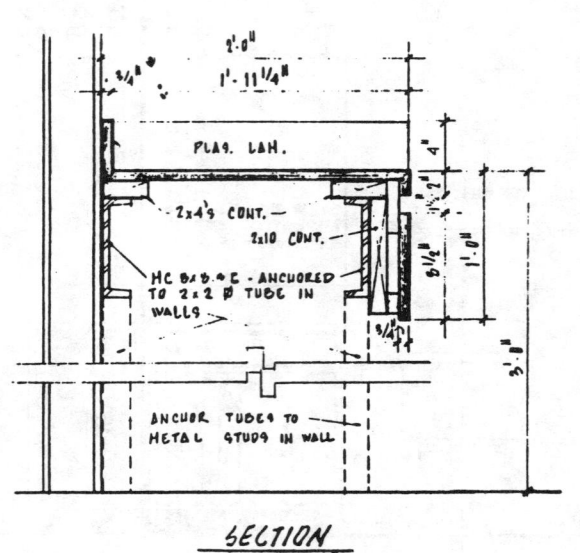

SECTION

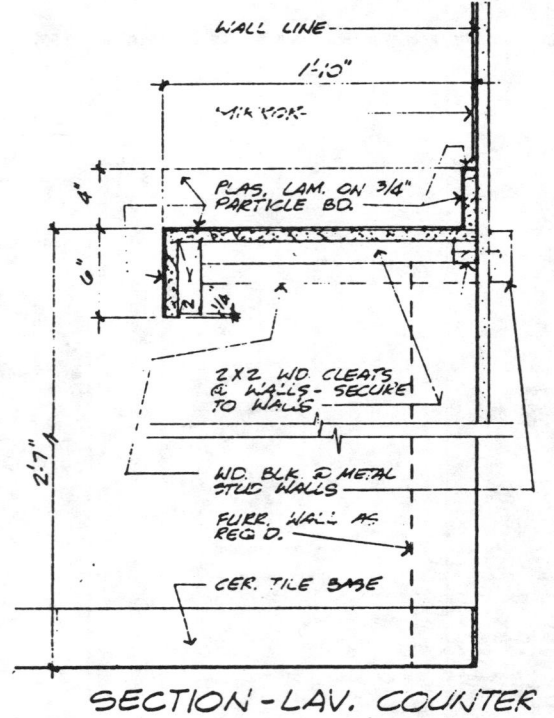

SECTION - LAV. COUNTER

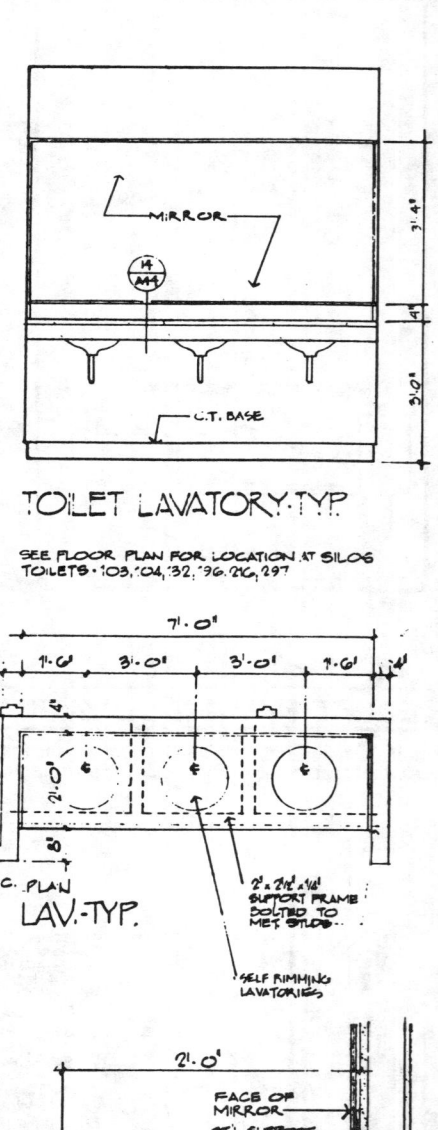

TOILET LAVATORY · TYP.

SEE FLOOR PLAN FOR LOCATION AT SILOS
TOILETS · 103, 104, 132, 196, 216, 297

LAV. · TYP.

SECT./DETAIL
SILO LAVATORIES

Fig. 16

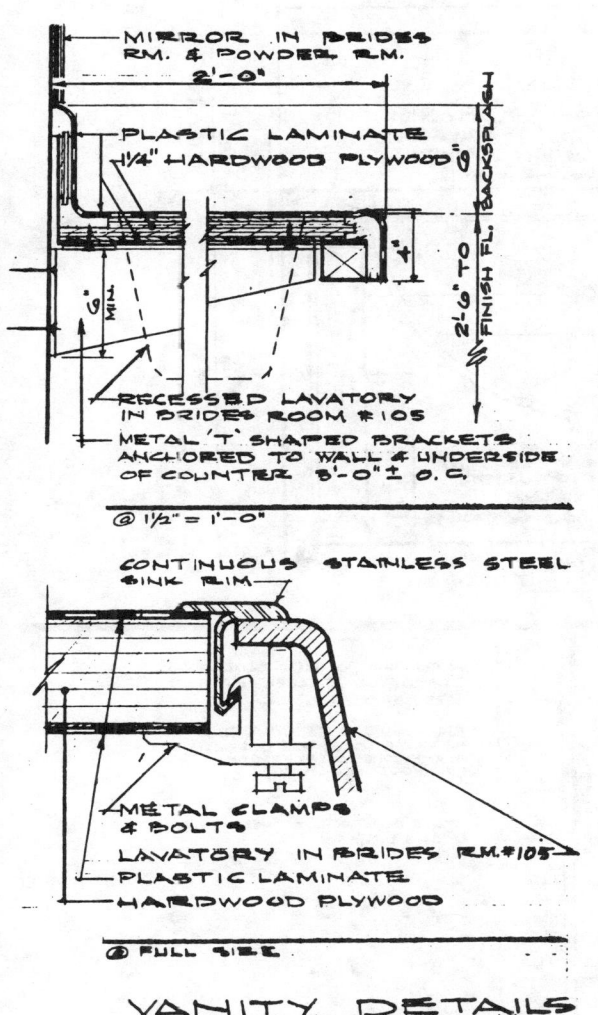

MIRROR IN BRIDES RM. & POWDER RM.

2'-0"

PLASTIC LAMINATE
1¼" HARDWOOD PLYWOOD

FINISH FL. BACKSPLASH

2'-6" TO

RECESSED LAVATORY IN BRIDES ROOM #105

METAL 'T' SHAPED BRACKETS ANCHORED TO WALL & UNDERSIDE OF COUNTER 3'-0" ± O.C.

@ 1½" = 1'-0"

CONTINUOUS STAINLESS STEEL SINK RIM

METAL CLAMPS & BOLTS

LAVATORY IN BRIDES RM. #105

PLASTIC LAMINATE

HARDWOOD PLYWOOD

@ FULL SIZE

VANITY DETAILS

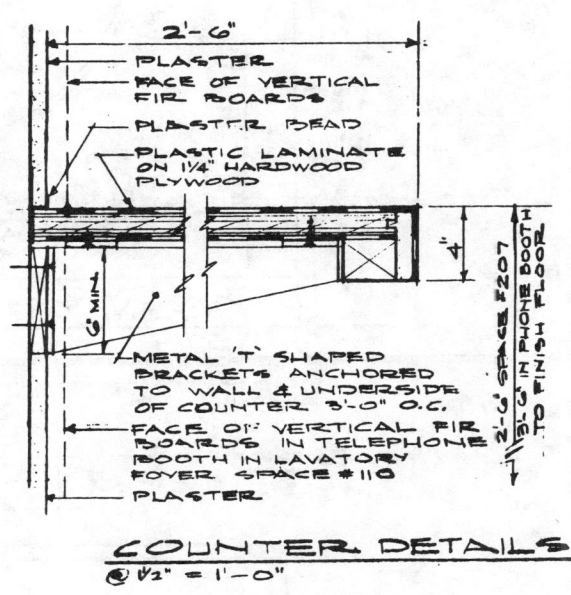

2'-6"

PLASTER

FACE OF VERTICAL FIR BOARDS

PLASTER BEAD

PLASTIC LAMINATE ON 1¼" HARDWOOD PLYWOOD

2'-6" SPACE #207

3'-0" IN PHONE BOOTH TO FINISH FLOOR

METAL 'T' SHAPED BRACKETS ANCHORED TO WALL & UNDERSIDE OF COUNTER 3'-0" O.C.

FACE OF VERTICAL FIR BOARDS IN TELEPHONE BOOTH IN LAVATORY FOYER SPACE #110

PLASTER

COUNTER DETAILS
@ 1½" = 1'-0"

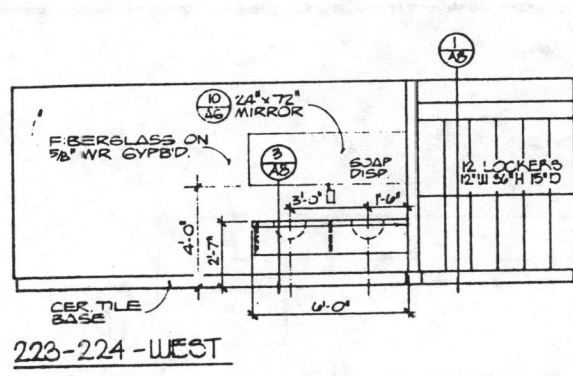

24"x72" MIRROR

FIBERGLASS ON ⅝" W.R. GYP.B'D.

SOAP DISP.

12 LOCKERS 12"W 72"H 15"D

4'-0"

CER. TILE BASE

6'-0"

223-224-WEST

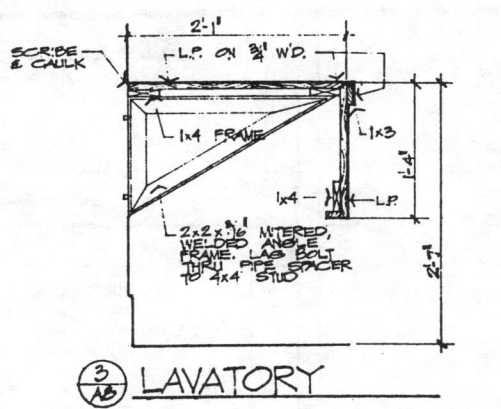

2'-1"

SCRIBE & CAULK

L.P. ON ¾" W'D.

1x4 FRAME

1x3

1x4

L.P.

1'-4"

2'-7"

2x2x¼" MITERED, WELDED ANGLE FRAME. LAG BOLT THRU PIPE SPACER TO 4x4 STUD

LAVATORY

Fig. 17

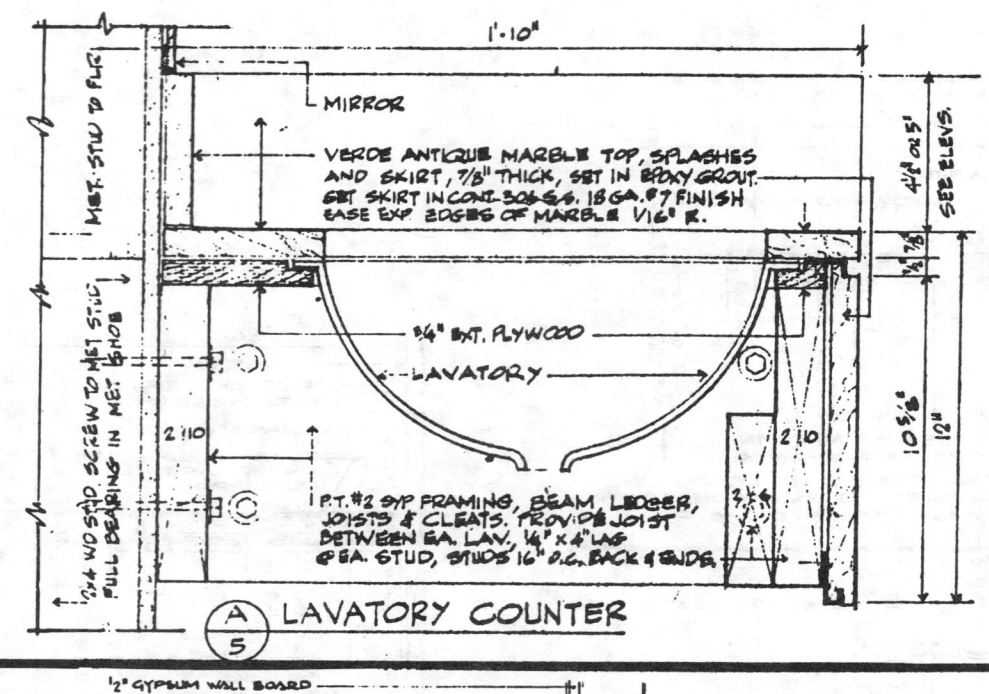

VERDE ANTIQUE MARBLE TOP, SPLASHES
AND SKIRT, 7/8" THICK, SET IN EPOXY GROUT.
SET SKIRT IN CONT. 304 S.S. 18 GA. #7 FINISH
EASE EXP. EDGES OF MARBLE 1/16" R.

MIRROR

3/4" EXT. PLYWOOD

LAVATORY

P.T. #2 SYP FRAMING, BEAM, LEDGER,
JOISTS & CLEATS. PROVIDE JOIST
BETWEEN EA. LAV. 1/4" X 4" LAG
@ EA. STUD, STUDS 16" O.C. BACK & ENDS.

MET. STUD TO FLG.

#14 WD STUD SCREW TO MET STUD
FULL BEARING IN MET BRDS.

2 10

2 10

3 6

1'-10"

4/8 OR 5'

SEE ELEVS.

1/8 7/8

10 5/8"

12"

A / 5 LAVATORY COUNTER

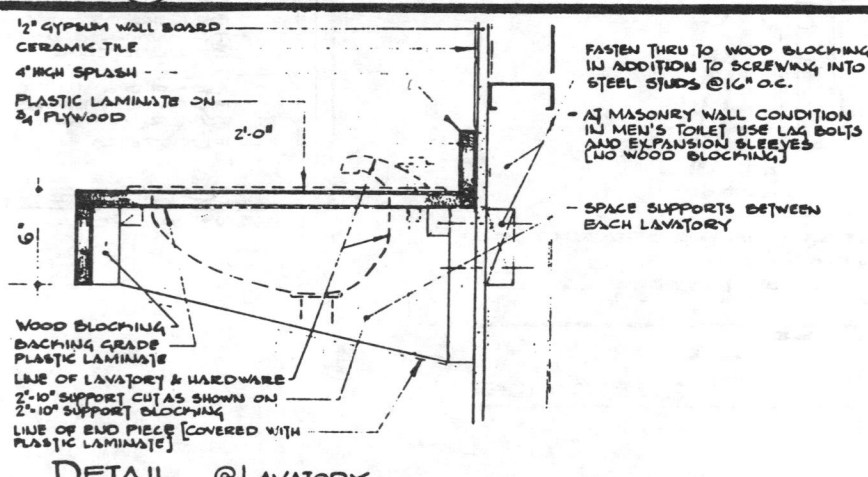

1/2" GYPSUM WALL BOARD
CERAMIC TILE
4" HIGH SPLASH
PLASTIC LAMINATE ON
3/4" PLYWOOD

2'-0"

6"

WOOD BLOCKING
BACKING GRADE
PLASTIC LAMINATE
LINE OF LAVATORY & HARDWARE
2'-10" SUPPORT CUT AS SHOWN ON
2'-10" SUPPORT BLOCKING
LINE OF END PIECE [COVERED WITH
PLASTIC LAMINATE]

FASTEN THRU TO WOOD BLOCKING
IN ADDITION TO SCREWING INTO
STEEL STUDS @ 16" O.C.

AT MASONRY WALL CONDITION
IN MEN'S TOILET USE LAG BOLTS
AND EXPANSION SLEEVES
[NO WOOD BLOCKING]

SPACE SUPPORTS BETWEEN
EACH LAVATORY

DETAIL @ LAVATORY

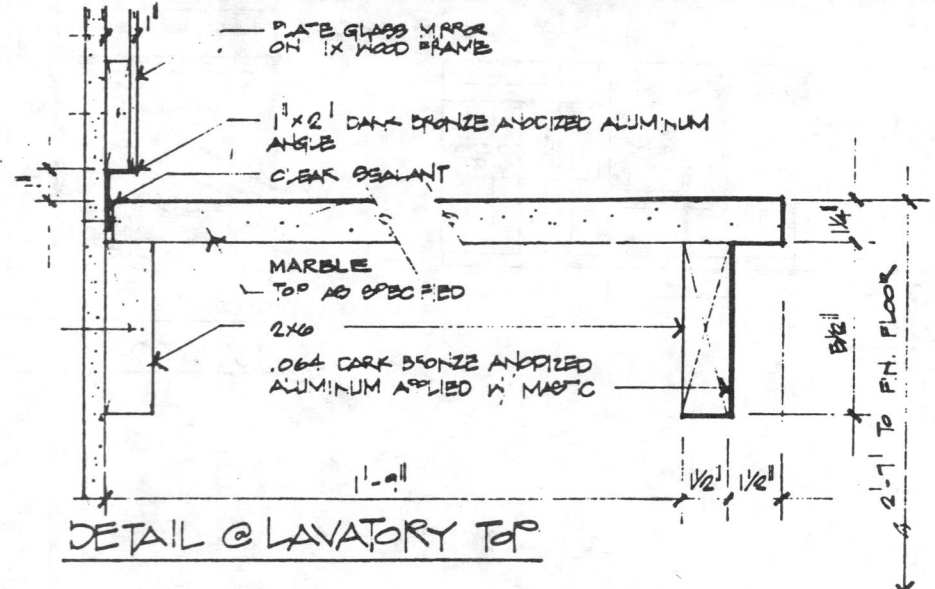

PLATE GLASS MIRROR
ON 1X WOOD FRAME

1" X 2" DARK BRONZE ANODIZED ALUMINUM
ANGLE

CLEAR SEALANT

MARBLE
TOP AS SPECIFIED

2X6

.064 DARK BRONZE ANODIZED
ALUMINUM APPLIED IN MASTIC

1 1/4"

8 3/8"

1'-9"

1/2" 1 1/8"

2'-7" TO FIN. FLOOR

DETAIL @ LAVATORY TOP

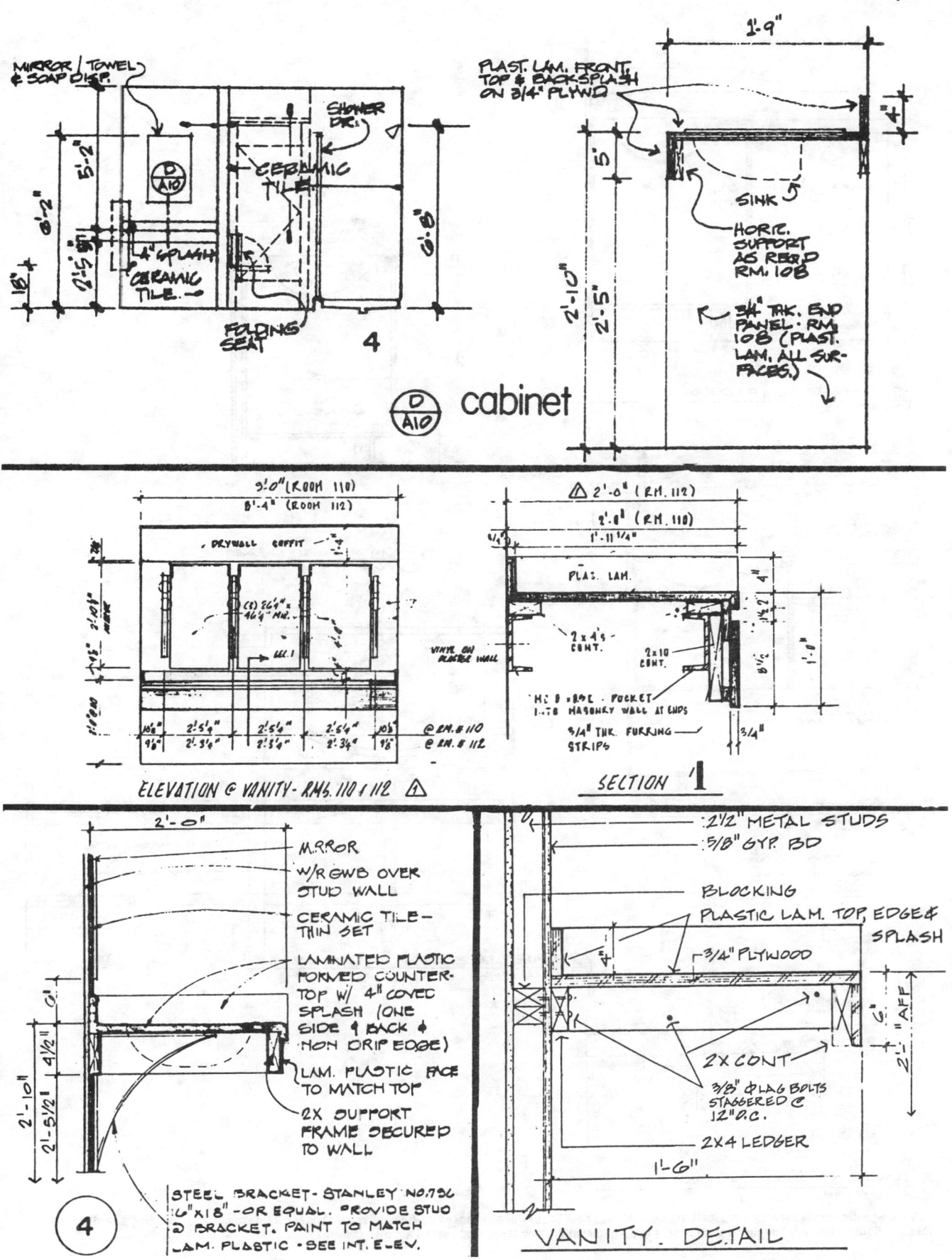

MIRROR / TOWEL & SOAP DISP.

SHOWER DR.

CERAMIC TILE

D / A10

5'-2"

6'-2"

2'-5"

18"

4" SPLASH CERAMIC TILE.

6'-8"

FOLDING SEAT

4

D / A10 cabinet

PLAST. LAM. FRONT, TOP & BACKSPLASH ON 3/4" PLYWD

1'-9"

4"

5"

SINK

HORIZ. SUPPORT AS REQ'D RM. 108

2'-10"

2'-5"

3/4" THK. END PANEL RM. 108 (PLAST. LAM. ALL SUR-FACES.)

3'-0" (ROOM 110)
8'-4" (ROOM 112)

DRYWALL COFFIT

(8) 26'/4" x 46'/4" MIR.

VINYL ON PLASTER WALL

SEL. 1

10'8" 2'-5'/4" 2'-5'/4" 2'-5'/4" 10'8"   @ RM. # 110
9'8" 2'-3'/4" 2'-3'/4" 2'-3'/4" 9'8"   @ RM. # 112

ELEVATION @ VANITY - RMS. 110 & 112

2'-0" (RM. 112)
2'-0" (RM. 110)
1'-11 1/4"

PLAS. LAM.

4"

2 x 4's CONT.

2 x 10 CONT.

8'/2"

3/4"

HI & BSE. POCKET INTO MASONRY WALL AT ENDS

3/4" THK. FURRING STRIPS

SECTION 1

2'-0"

MIRROR W/R GWB OVER STUD WALL

CERAMIC TILE - THIN SET

LAMINATED PLASTIC FORMED COUNTER-TOP W/ 4" COVED SPLASH (ONE SIDE & BACK & NON DRIP EDGE)

LAM. PLASTIC FACE TO MATCH TOP

2X SUPPORT FRAME SECURED TO WALL

6'

4 1/2"

2'-10"

2'-5 1/2"

4

STEEL BRACKET - STANLEY NO. 796 6" X 18" - OR EQUAL. PROVIDE STUD @ BRACKET. PAINT TO MATCH LAM. PLASTIC - SEE INT. E-EV.

2 1/2" METAL STUDS
5/8" GYP. BD

BLOCKING
PLASTIC LAM. TOP, EDGE & SPLASH

3/4" PLYWOOD

6"

2'-1" AFF

2X CONT

3/8" Ø LAG BOLTS STAGGERED @ 12" O.C.

2X4 LEDGER

1'-6"

VANITY DETAIL

Fig. 19

445

RESTROOMS AND TOILETS
Lavatory Cabinet Details

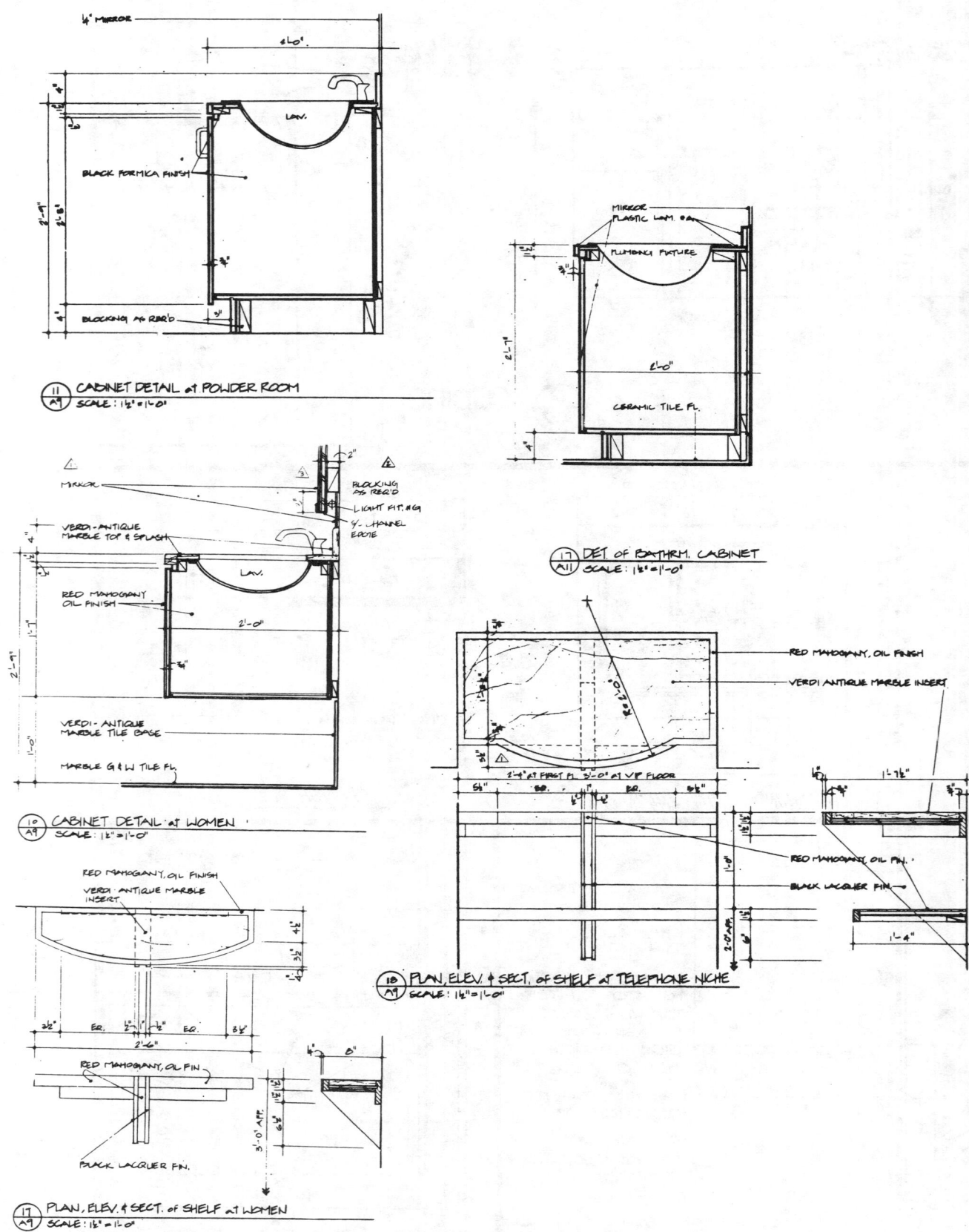

Fig. 20   Elegantly detailed lavatory cabinets are shown here. Note the use of an exposed oil-finished red mahogany frame or edge surrounding a verdi antique marble top. Complementary telephone shelf details in plan, elevation, and large-scale detail are also shown.

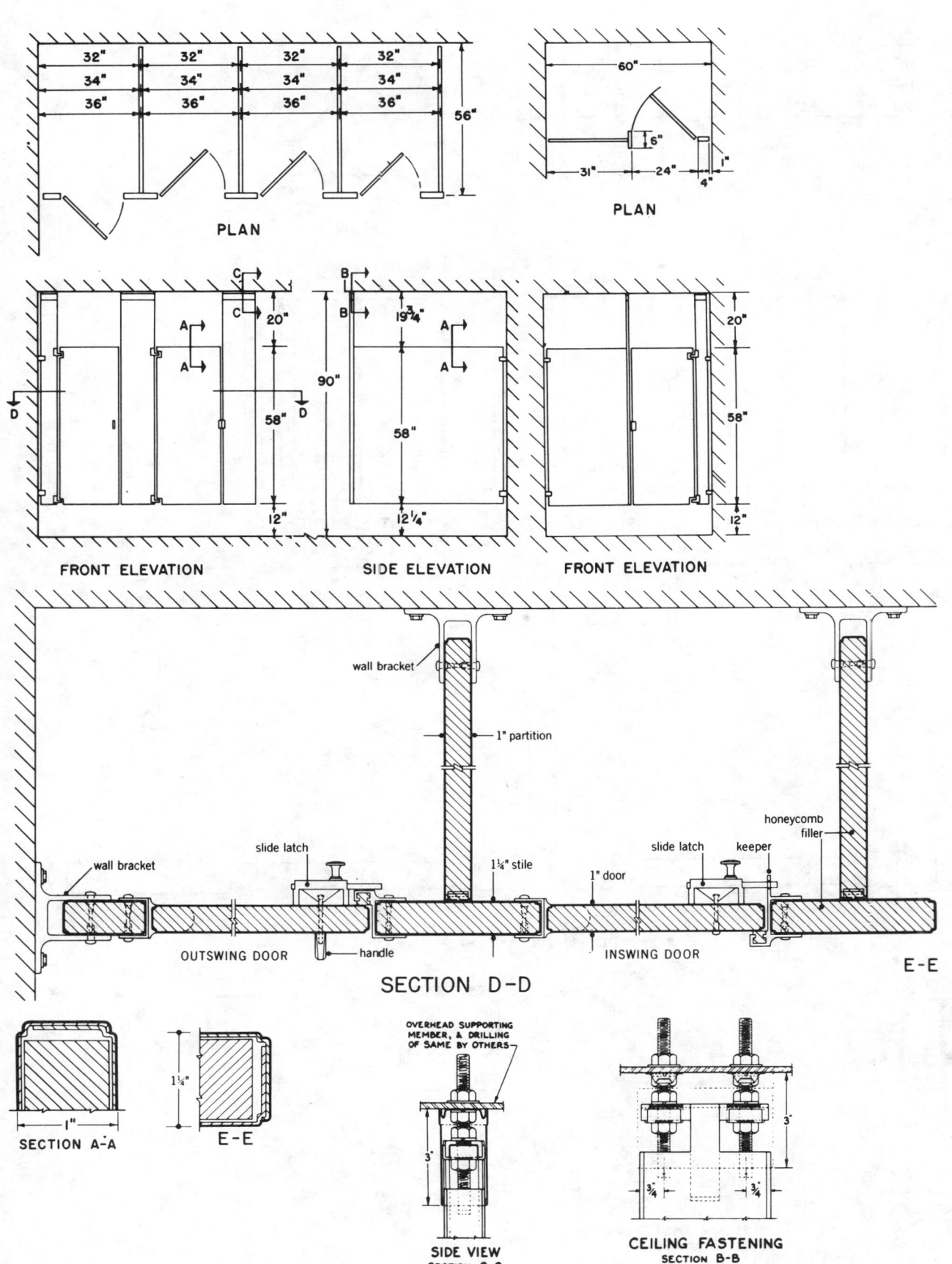

PLAN

PLAN

FRONT ELEVATION

SIDE ELEVATION

FRONT ELEVATION

wall bracket

1" partition

honeycomb filler

wall bracket

slide latch

1¼" stile

slide latch

keeper

1" door

OUTSWING DOOR

handle

INSWING DOOR

E-E

SECTION D-D

SECTION A-A

E-E

OVERHEAD SUPPORTING MEMBER, & DRILLING OF SAME BY OTHERS

SIDE VIEW
SECTION C-C

CEILING FASTENING
SECTION B-B

Fig. 21

RESTROOMS AND TOILETS

Toilet Stall Details

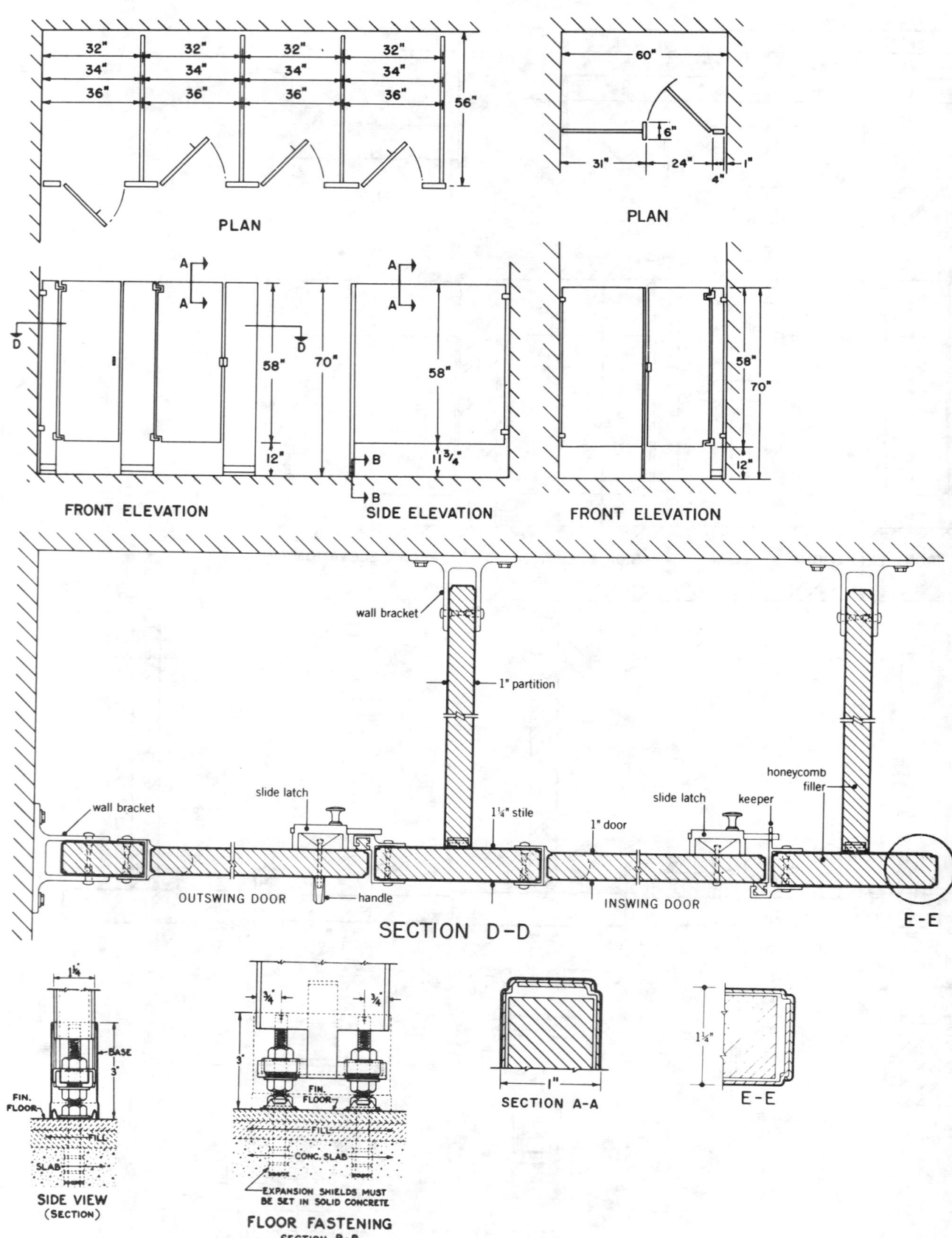

Fig. 22

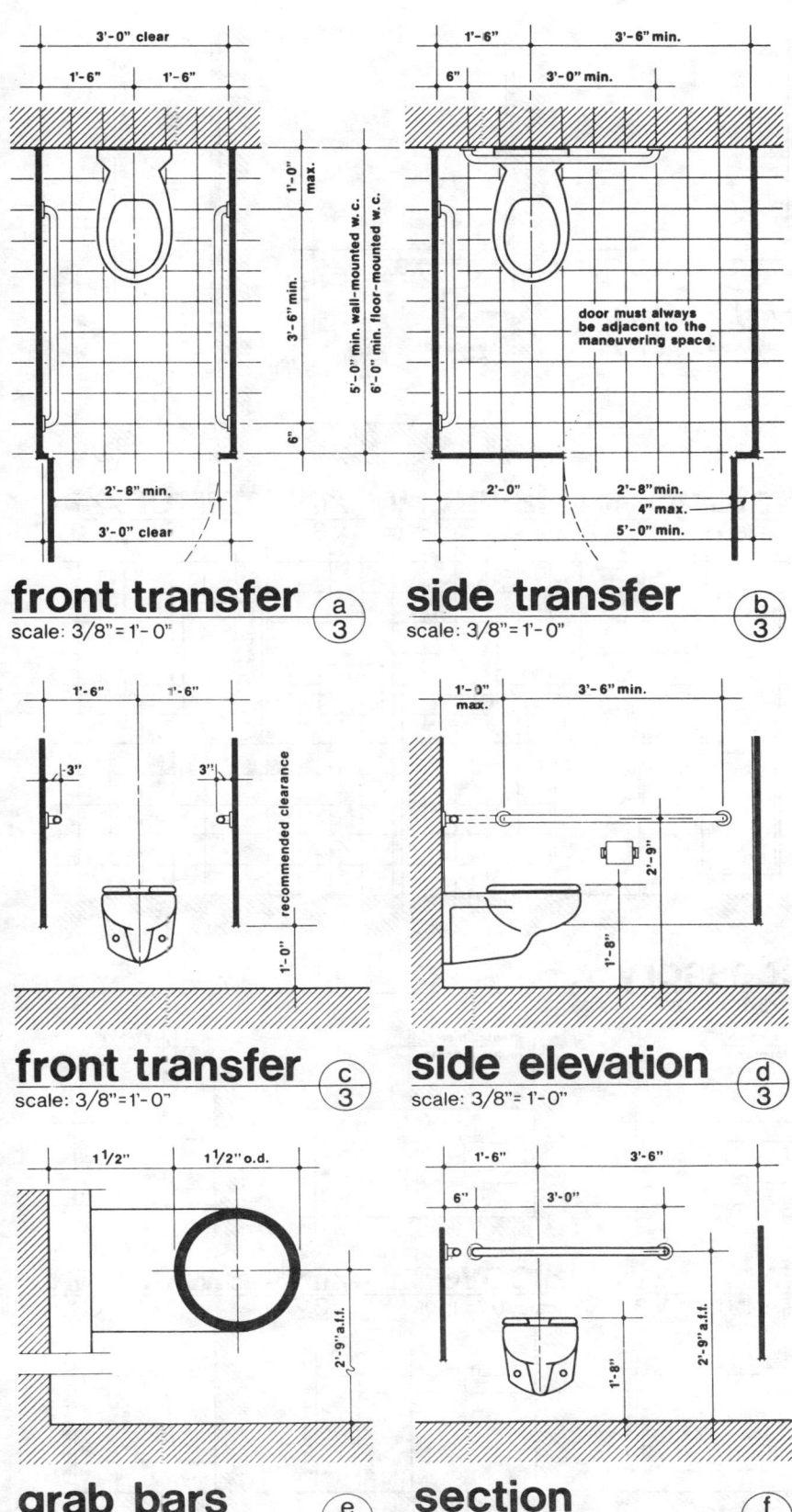

front transfer (a/3)
scale: 3/8"=1'-0"

side transfer (b/3)
scale: 3/8"=1'-0"

front transfer (c/3)
scale: 3/8"=1'-0"

side elevation (d/3)
scale: 3/8"=1'-0"

grab bars (e/3)
scale: half

section (f/3)
scale: 3/8"=1'-0"

TOILET AND RESTROOM DESIGN

The design data contained on the following pages are intended to illustrate functional accessibility concepts. Some examples illustrate minimum federal requirements, while others are culled from among the various state standards. Designers are cautioned to consult local standards in their respective jurisdictions.

The current minimum federal standard is ANSI A117.1-1986, published by the American National Standards Institute, Inc. It specifies a stall typified by detail a/3. This "front transfer" type stall requires a watercloset mounted at 1'8" a.f.f., preferably wall hung. Stall doors must be outswinging.

Because a significant portion of people using wheelchairs cannot transfer in this manner, the side transfer stall (b/3) has been developed. Clear stall dimensions and seat heights vary somewhat with jurisdiction. Most standards that address side transfer stalls require lower seat heights with 15"–17" mounting heights being typical.

We recommend locking devices for doors that do not require twisting and grasping motions, avoidance of foot operated flush valves, installation of ceiling or wall-hung partitions as practical, and avoidance of curtains in lieu of doors.

Federal standards mandate grab bars of 1½" o.d. The bars must be securely mounted 1½" clear from the wall or partition. This mounting distance is critical, as it provides a "cradle" for a forearm during transfer or if a user loses her or his grip.

RESTROOMS AND TOILETS
Wheelchair Accessible Design

Lavatories need not be specialized designs to be accessible. Utilization of clearances shown will do much to make lavatories accessible. Because persons with loss of sensation in their legs cannot feel pain (and because they heal at a slower rate), hot water lines and drains must be insulated. Also, under several state codes, faucets are required to be lever, blade, or multi-arm handle operated.

Single lever controls are preferable. Spring-operated faucets must have time delay devices.

At least one mirror must be located with the reflecting surface mounted at 3'4" a.f.f. (3'2" or lower preferable). Where possible, full-length mirrors are preferable.

At least one of each type of toilet accessory must also be located at 3'4" a.f.f. or less. Note that this dimension is measured to the highest control required for operation. Controls that require twisting and grasping motions should be avoided.

Because people that use wheelchairs require increased fluid intake, drinking fountains become more than convenience items. While there is not space here to address all configurations, the following concerns are typical to all: controls should be operable without the need for precise grasping; the faucet should not direct spray away from the user and must be located as near the front edge as practical; the units must be free of sharp edges and corners and overhead obstructions.

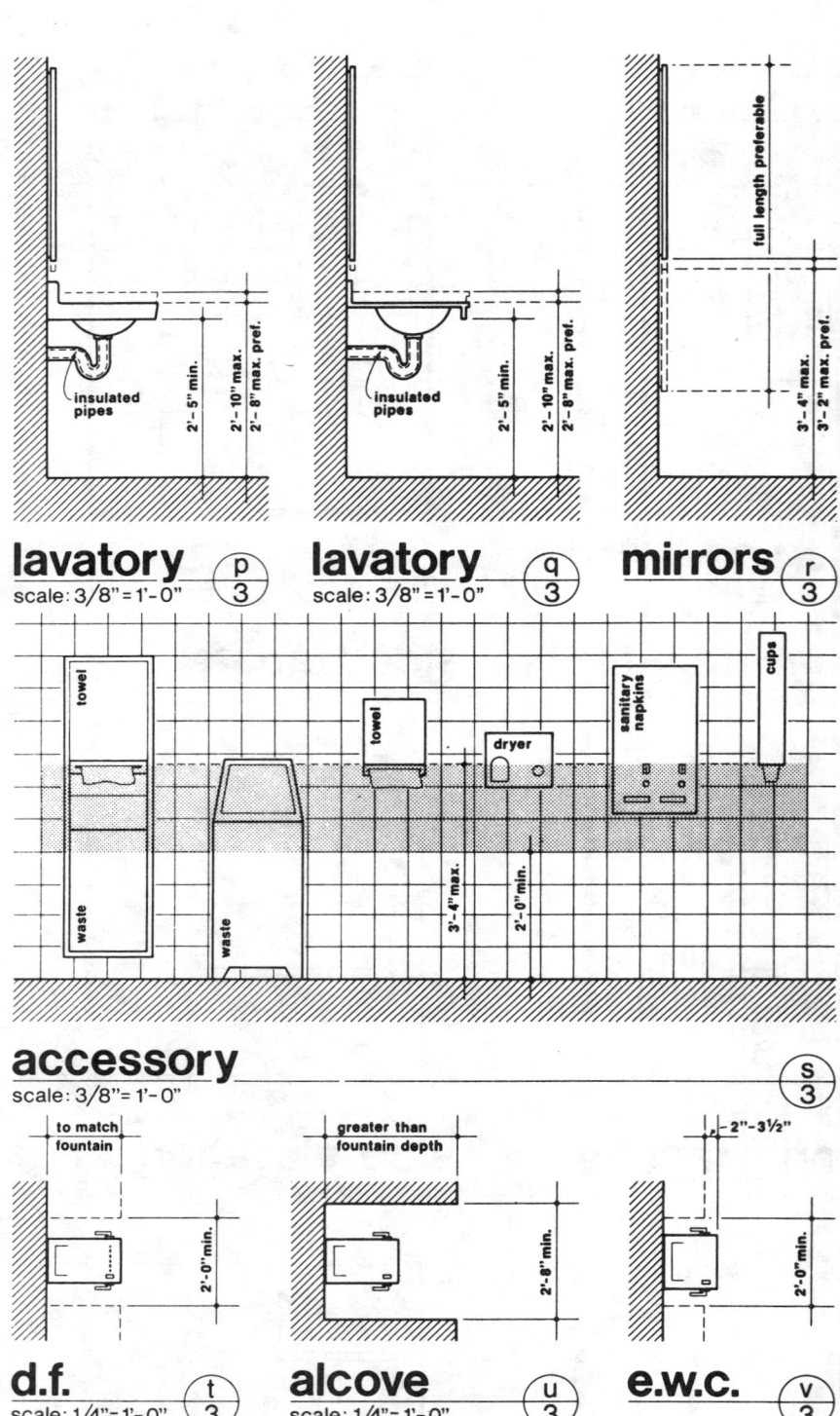

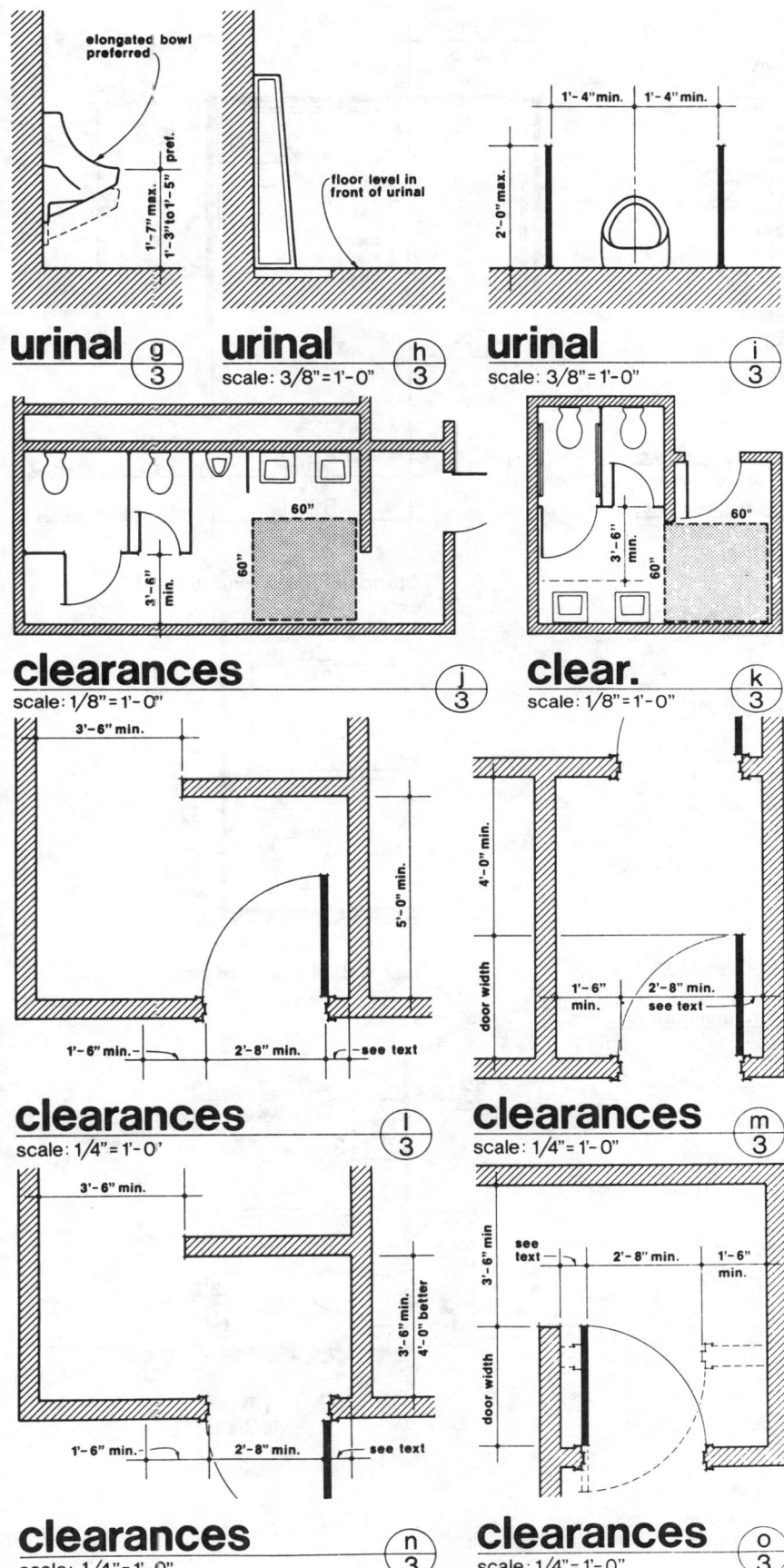

urinal (g/3)

urinal (h/3)
scale: 3/8"=1'-0"

urinal (i/3)
scale: 3/8"=1'-0"

elongated bowl preferred

1'-7" max.
1'-3" to 1'-5" pref.

floor level in front of urinal

1'-4" min. 1'-4" min.

2'-0" max.

clearances (j/3)
scale: 1/8"=1'-0"

clear. (k/3)
scale: 1/8"=1'-0"

60"

60"

3'-6" min.

3'-6" min.

60"

clearances (l/3)
scale: 1/4"=1'-0'

clearances (m/3)
scale: 1/4"=1'-0"

3'-6" min.

5'-0" min.

1'-6" min.   2'-8" min.   see text

4'-0" min.

door width

1'-6" min.   2'-8" min.
see text

clearances (n/3)
scale: 1/4"=1'-0"

clearances (o/3)
scale: 1/4"=1'-0"

3'-6" min.

3'-6" min.
4'-0" better

1'-6" min.   2'-8" min.   see text

see text

3'-6" min

2'-8" min.   1'-6" min.

door width

Urinals, if provided, should have elongated bowls with the opening of the basin located at 19" a.f.f. or less, or mounted level with the main floor. Many state standards specify maximum mounting heights of 15"–16" a.f.f. These lower dimensions are preferable.

The toilet room itself should provide a clear floor area with minimum dimensions of 60" x 60" to facilitate maneuvering wheelchairs. Additionally, provide a minimum of 3'6" clearance in front of accessible toilet stalls to facilitate entry.

Similarly, adequate clearances must be provided at entrances. The spaces shown in details l/3 to o/3 represent typical dimensions specified in state codes. Note, however, that federal and many state standards require 12" clear jamb areas adjoining both sides of all doors. A clearance of 18" or more on the strike side of a door is more effective. In vestibules having doors in series, there must be space for a wheelchair to clear one door prior to opening another.

RESTROOMS AND TOILETS
Wheelchair Accessible Design

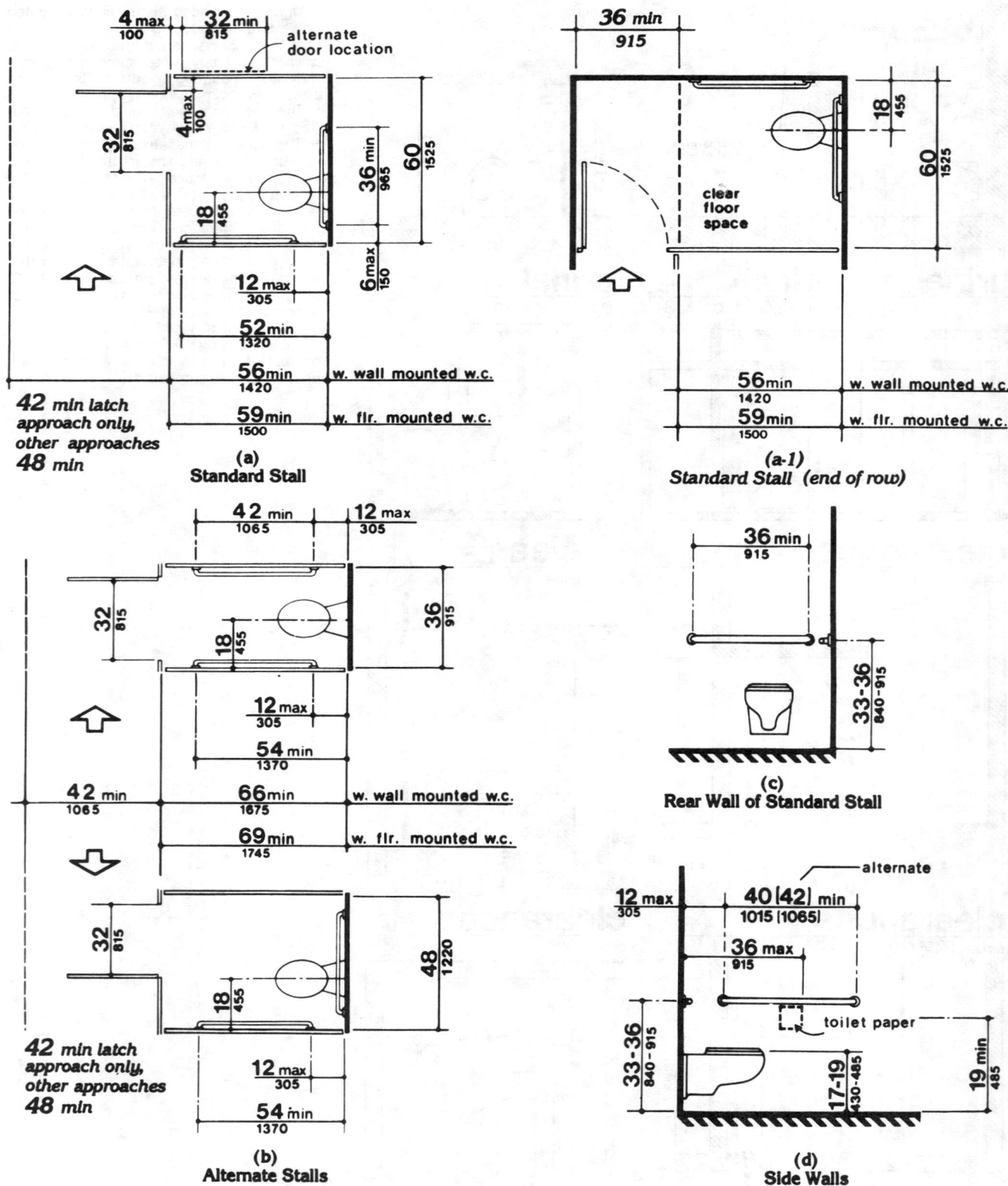

Fig. 23   Toilet stalls.

In Figs. 24 to 30, various generic toilet accessories and grab bar configurations are illustrated. While most manufacturers have similar accessories and grab bars within their catalogs, overall dimensions and methods of installation vary greatly. Placement of accessories in relationship to plumbing fixtures, door swings, and interior circulation is to be carefully studied by the designer.

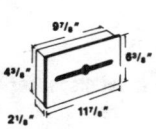

Facial tissue dispenser

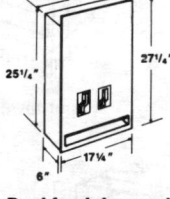

Dual feminine napkin/ tampon vendor

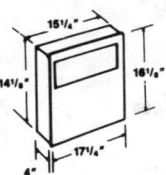

Sanitary napkin disposal

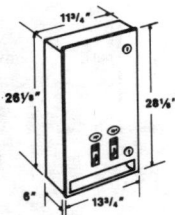

Dual feminine napkin/ tampon vendor

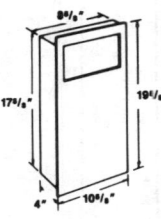

Sanitary napkin disposal

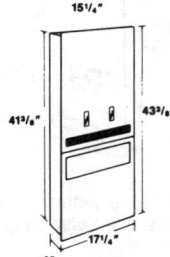

Recessed dual napkin/tampon dispenser and disposal

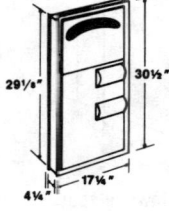

Recessed seat cover and toilet tissue dispenser

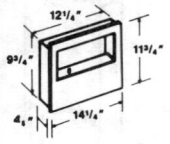

Wall urn ash tray

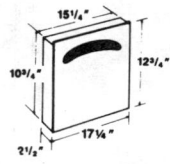

Toilet seat cover dispenser

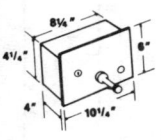

Liquid soap dispenser

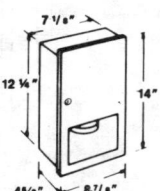

Recessed powdered soap dispenser

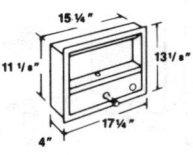

Recessed horizontal soap dispenser and shelf

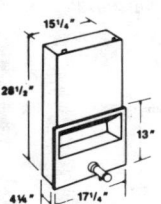

All-purpose unit with concealed towel cabinet

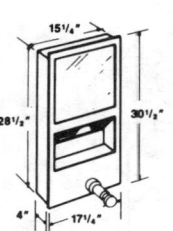

Multipurpose unit with mirror, shelf, towel, and liquid soap dispensers

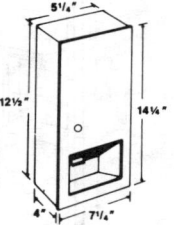

Disposal valve soap gun

Fig. 24

RESTROOMS AND TOILETS
Toilet Accessories

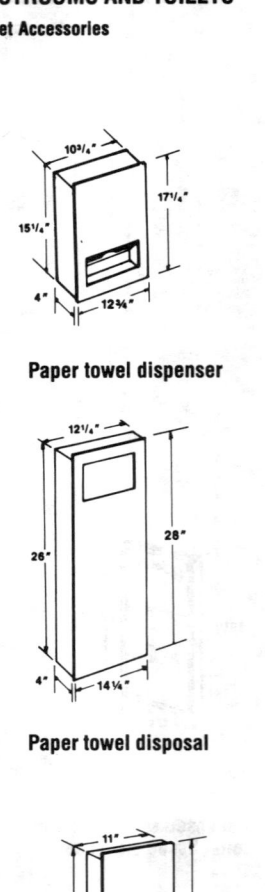

Paper towel dispenser

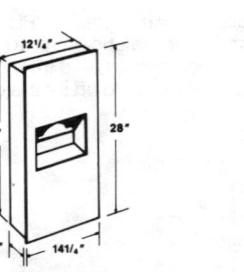

**Paper towel dispenser
and disposal**

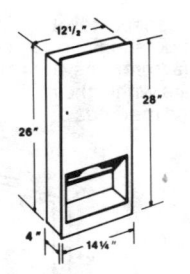

Paper towel dispenser

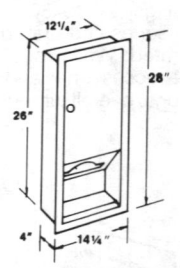

Paper towel dispenser

Paper towel dispenser

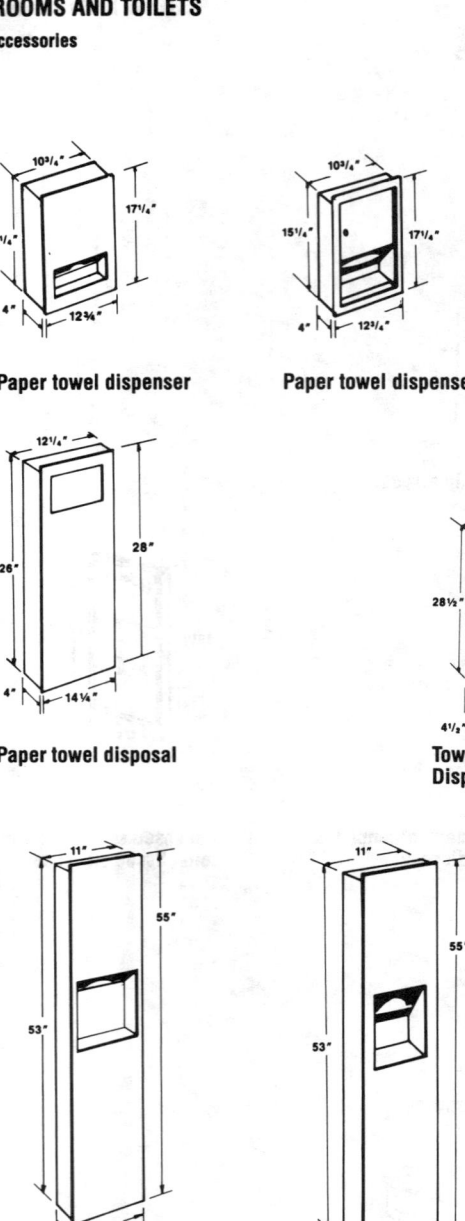

Paper towel disposal

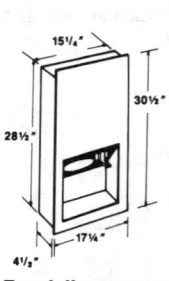

**Towel dispenser and
Disposa-Valve soap gun**

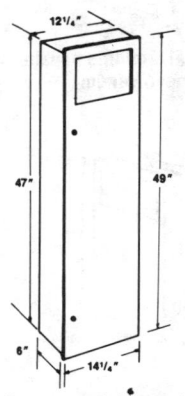

Paper towel disposal

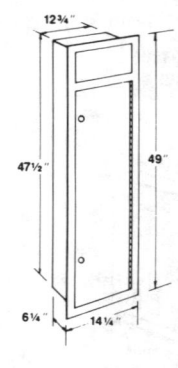

Paper towel disposal

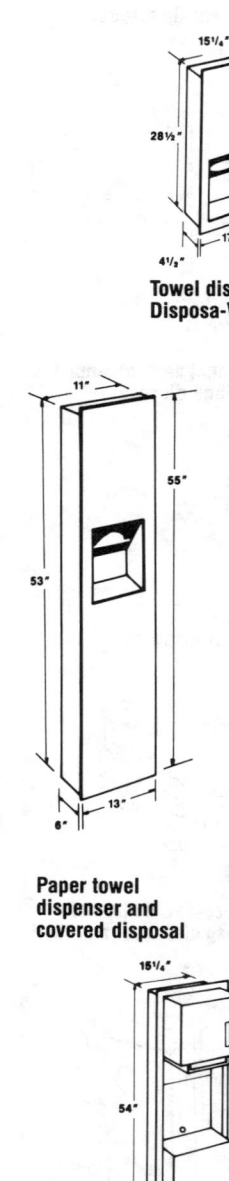

**Paper towel
dispenser and
disposal**

**Paper towel
dispenser and
covered disposal**

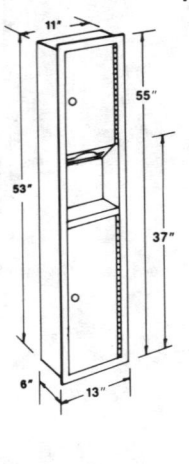

**Paper towel
dispenser and
disposal**

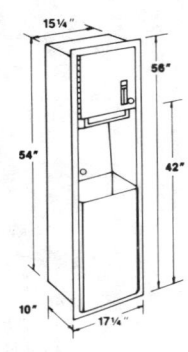

**Roll paper towel
dispenser and
disposal**

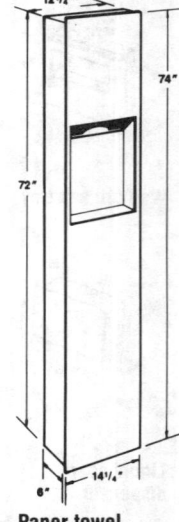

**Paper towel
dispenser and
disposal**

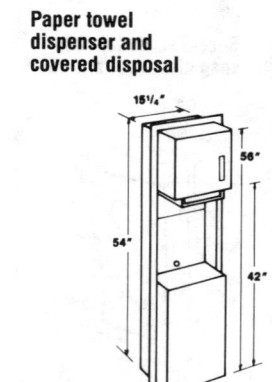

**Roll paper towel dispenser
and disposal**

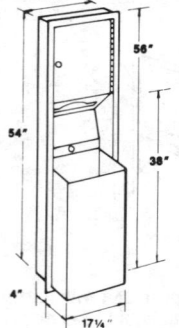

**Paper towel
dispenser
and disposal**

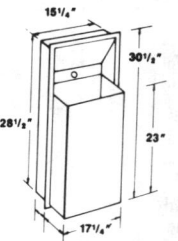

Semirecessed waste receptacle

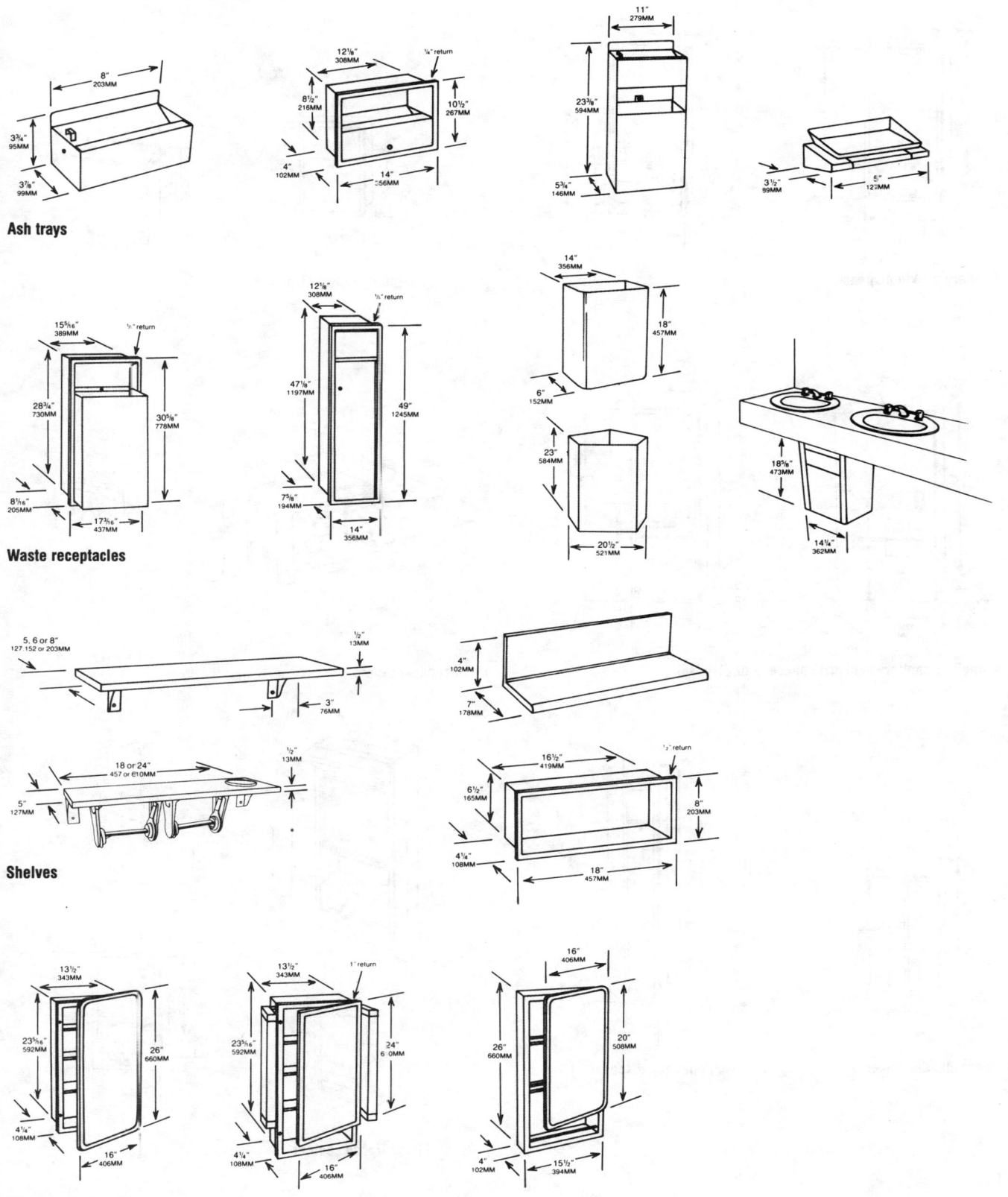

Ash trays

Waste receptacles

Shelves

Medicine cabinets

Fig. 26

RESTROOMS AND TOILETS

Toilet Accessories

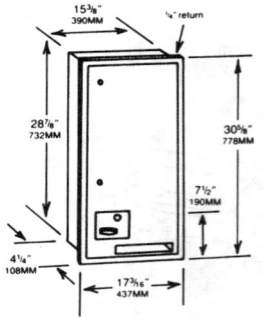

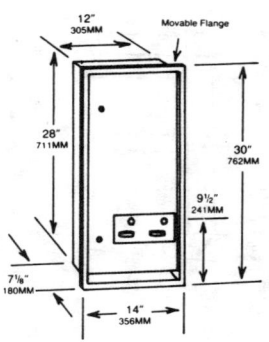

Sanitary napkin dispensers

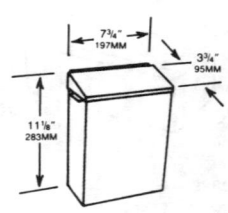

Sanitary napkin disposals

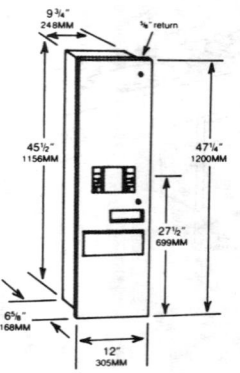

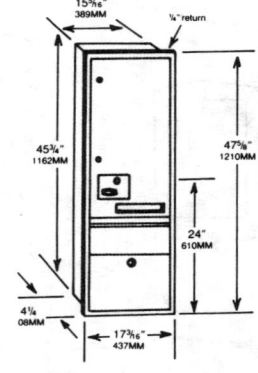

Combined sanitary napkin dispenser and disposal

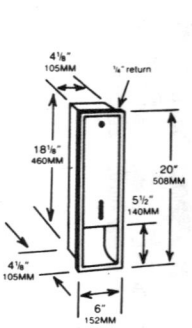

Paper cup dispenser

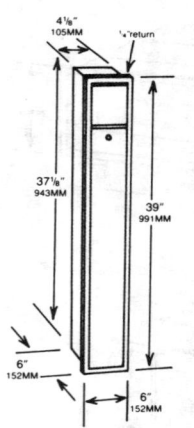

Paper cup disposal

Hand and hair dryers

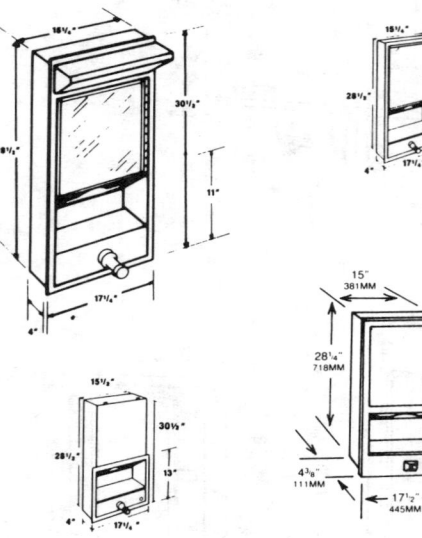

Multipurpose cabinet

Fig. 27

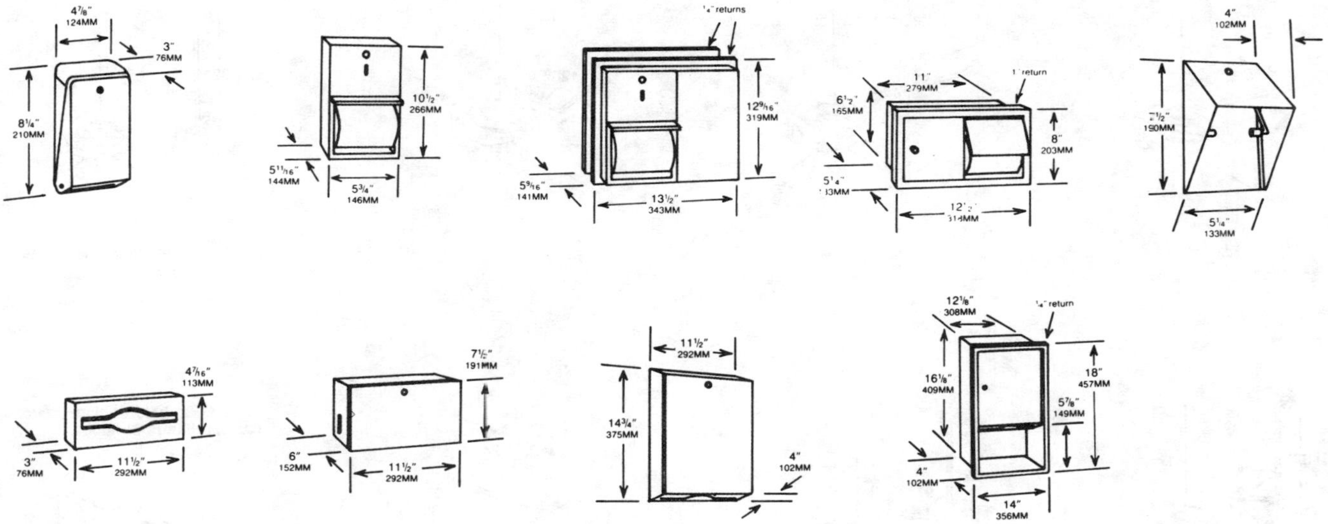

Toilet tissue dispensers

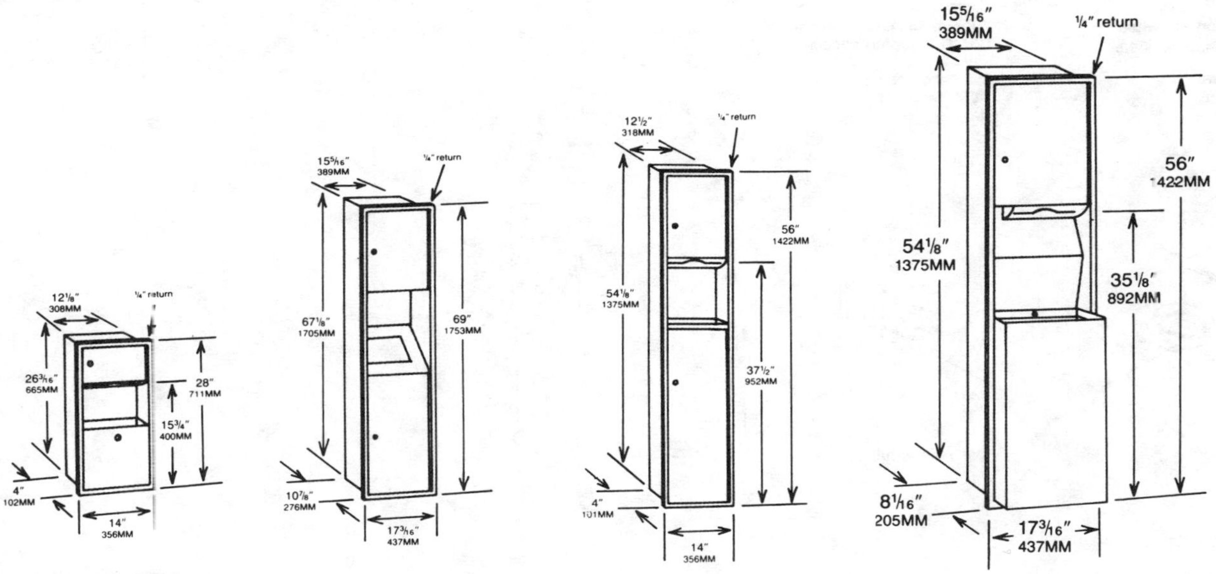

Paper towel dispensers

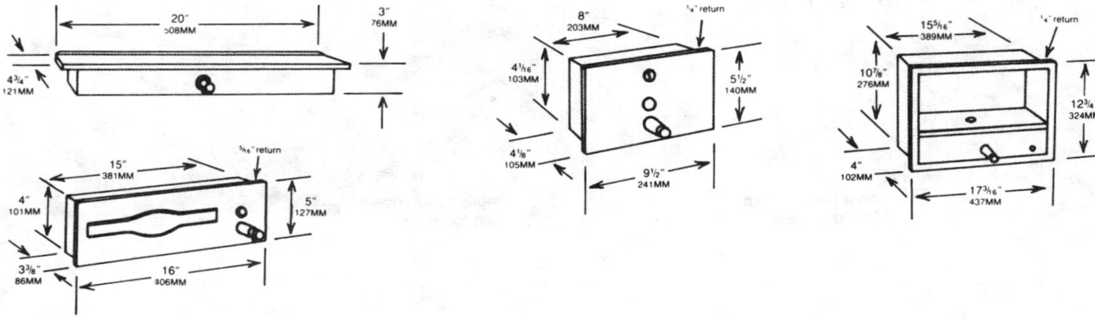

Soap dispensers

Fig. 28

RESTROOMS AND TOILETS
Grab Bar Configurations

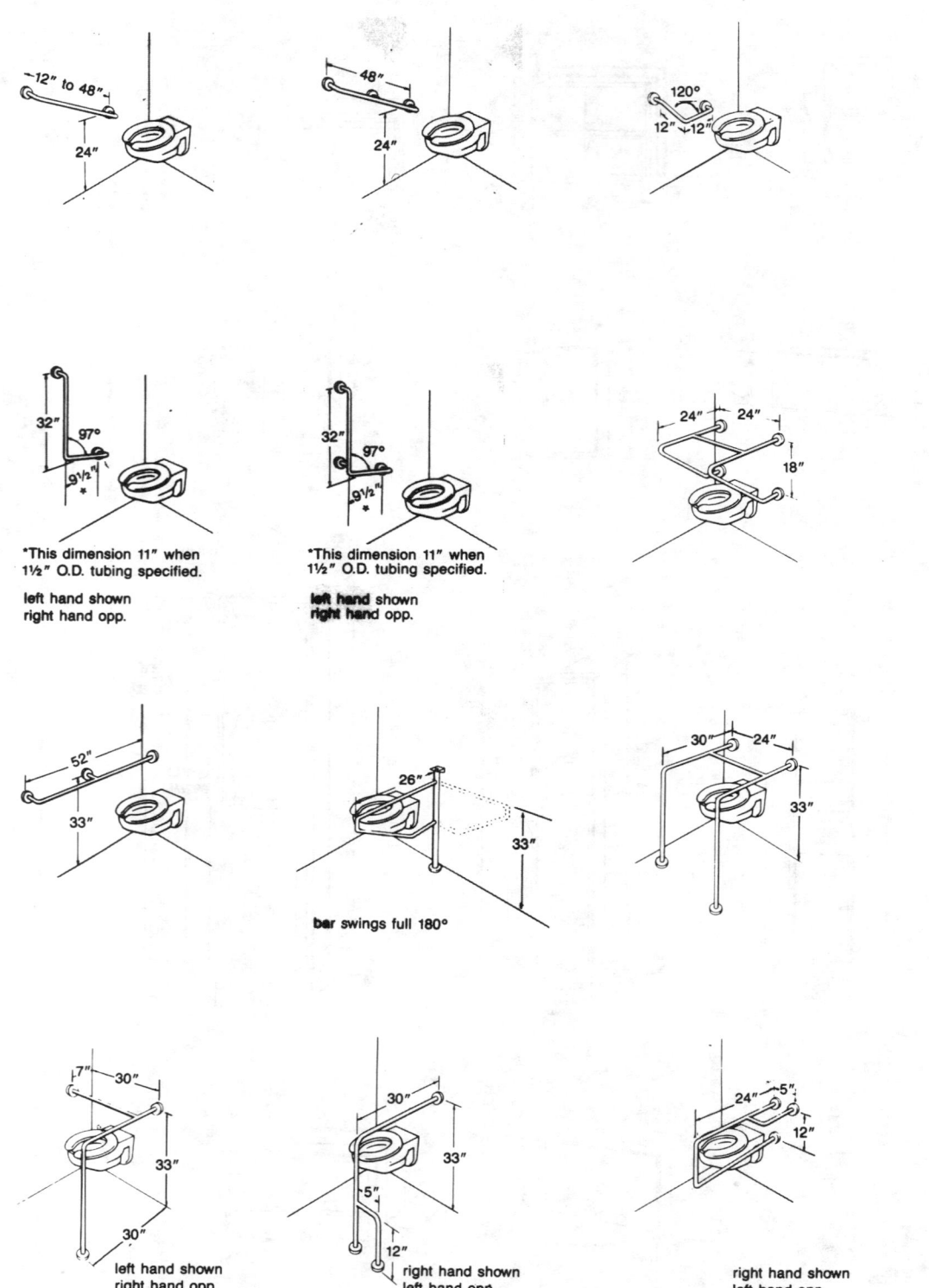

~12" to 48"

24"

48"

24"

120°
12" 12"

32"
16"
24"

left hand shown
right hand opp.

32" 97°
9½"
*

*This dimension 11" when
1½" O.D. tubing specified.

left hand shown
right hand opp.

32" 97°
9½"
*

*This dimension 11" when
1½" O.D. tubing specified.

left hand shown
right hand opp.

24" 24"
18"

Projects 3" below finished floor,
has slip flange at floor.

33"
30"

52"
33"

26"
33"

bar swings full 180°

30" 24"
33"

7" 30"
33"
30"

left hand shown
right hand opp.

30"
33"
5"
12"

right hand shown
left hand opp.

24" 5"
12"

right hand shown
left hand opp.

Fig. 29

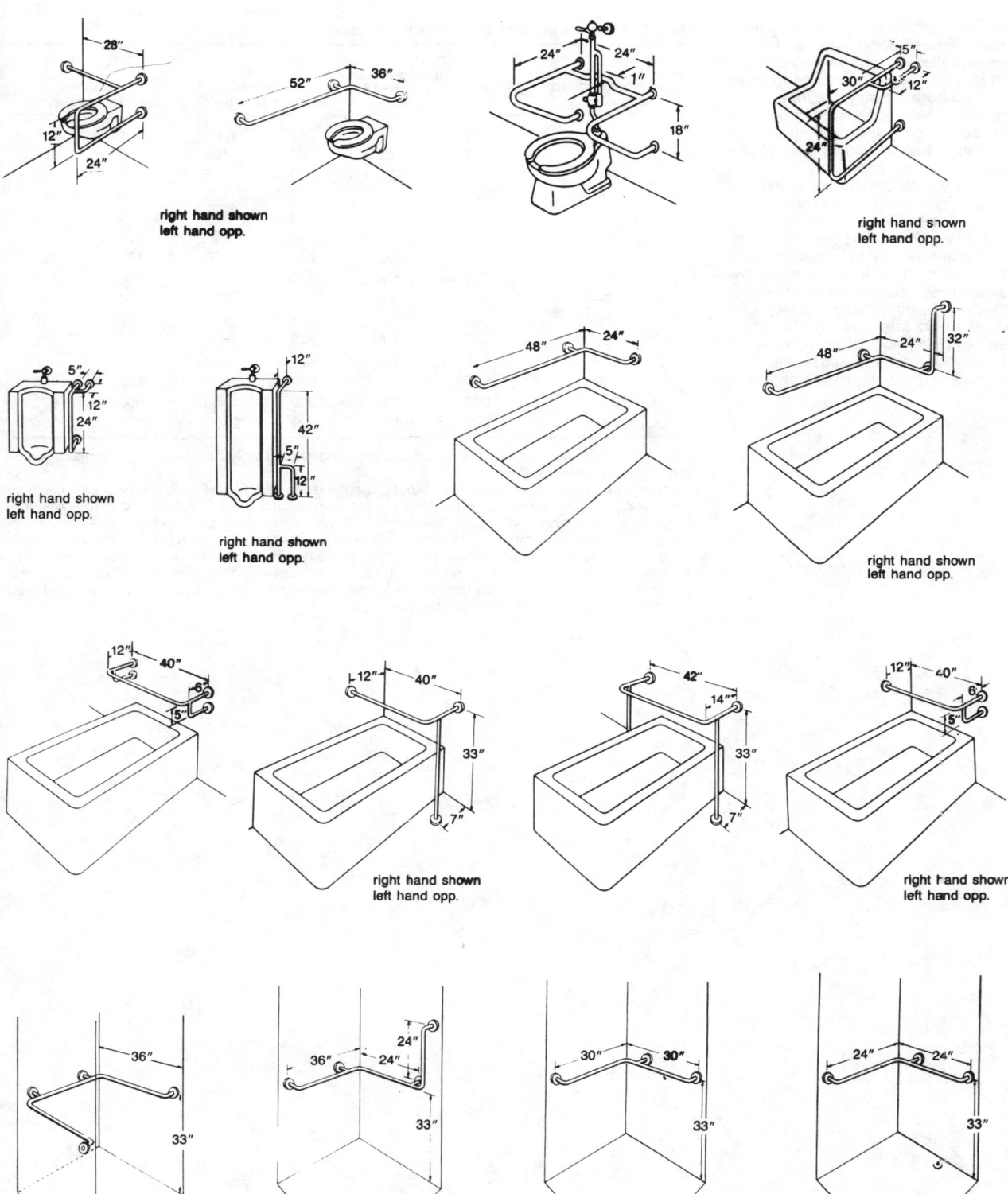

right hand shown
left hand opp.

right hand shown
left hand opp.

right hand shown
left hand opp.

right hand shown
left hand opp.

right hand shown
left hand opp.

right hand shown
left hand opp.

right hand shown
left hand opp.

right hand shown
left hand opp.

36″ from side wall to side wall

right hand shown
left hand opp.

Fig. 30

459

COATROOMS

Floor Area Requirements

Coatrooms typically fall into two categories: those that are self-service and those that are controlled by one or more attendants. The latter category of coatroom can be more compact because only one, or perhaps two, attendants have access to the coats. A self-service coatroom must have more space between rows of coats so that several persons can enter and get their coats.

Self-service coatrooms are susceptible to theft of property, particularly expensive outerwear. Therefore, it is desirable that these coatrooms be visible to someone at all times, such as a maitre d' in a restaurant or a receptionist in an office. In those situations where a supervised self-service coatroom is inappropriate or cannot be provided, self-service keyed locks offer a viable alternative. In addition to being able to provide secure coat storage, lockers can also store briefcases, packages, or other encumbrances.

TABLE 1 Floor Area Requirements for Public Coatrooms

Number of coats (capacity)	Floor area (with attendant)		Floor area (without attendant)		Floor area (electric conveyor)	
	Min	Max				
50	35	50	40	60	N/A	N/A
100	65	85	80	100	80	100
150	90	120	110	145	110	125
200	125	150	150	180	140	150
250	150	190	180	230	100	110
300	180	225	215	270	125	140
350	200	260	240	300	135	150
400	225	275	270	330	150	160
450	260	320	310	370	160	175
500	300	365	425	430	175	190
750	450	500	540	600	250	275
1000	600	650	720	780	325	350
1500	800	900	950	1080	450	480
2000	1000	1250	1200	1500	600	675
3000	1600	1850	1900	2200	1000	1150

Note: The above floor areas are approximate and should only be used for preliminary space planning requirements.

Since the number of coats per linear foot of hanging can vary from 4 to 8, the floor area can vary dramatically. A lightweight overcoat, for example, can measure 1–1.5 inches in width. A medium weight to heavyweight coat might measure from 2 to 4 inches. A fur coat might require a minimum of 4–6 in. The designer must consider the overall size of coatroom based upon the following critical factors: (1) geographic location/climate; (2) attendants required or not required; (3) aisle clearance; (4) peak entry/exit loads for coat retrieval; (5) assumed garment thickness or garments per linear foot; (6) linear feet of counter surface and overhead shelving; and (7) other storage components, i.e., hats, umbrellas, briefcases, packages, etc.

Three basic types of manufactured or prefabricated coat storage units are shown in Figs. 1 to 3. Exact coat storage capacities are provided by the manufacturer. All units can be customized to suit various room configurations. Note the adjoining counter space to speed operations. Coat capacities relative to length are listed in Table 2.

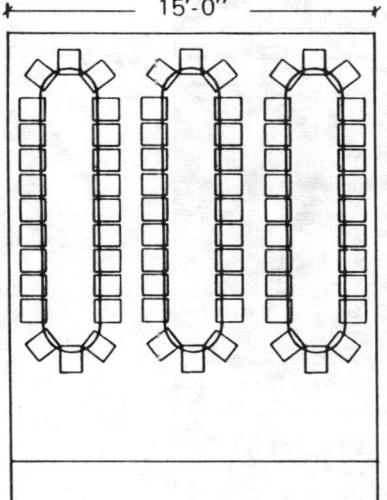
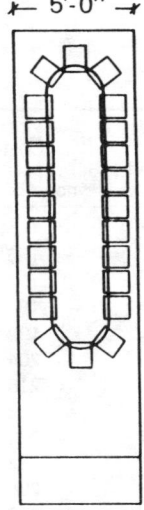

Fig. 1   Electric carousel coat storage.

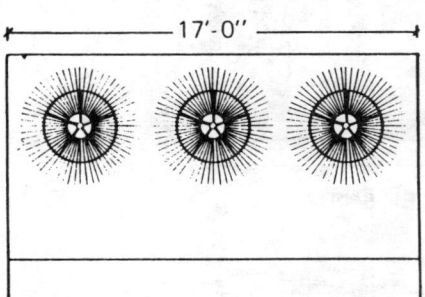
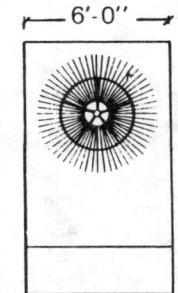

Fig. 2   Rotating reels coat storage.

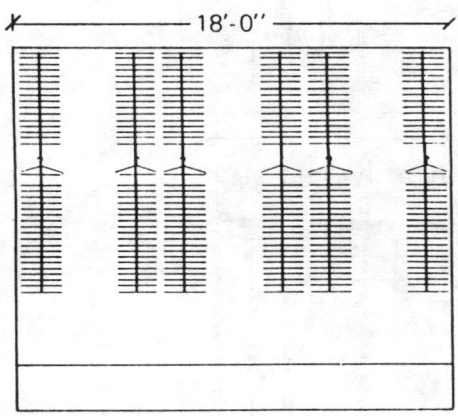
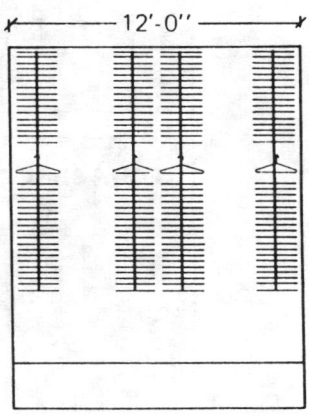
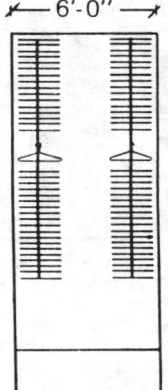

Fig. 3   Stationary coat storage.

COATROOMS
Electric Checkroom Systems

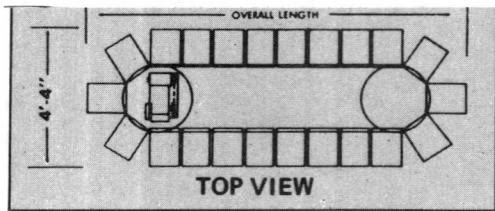

Fig. 4

TABLE 2

Overall length with garments*	Length of hanging capacity	Coat capacity: no. of slots†
7′ 5″	13′ 0″	144
7′11½″	14′ 1″	156
8′ 6″	15′ 2″	168
9′ 1″	16′ 3″	180
9′ 7″	17′ 4″	192
10′ 1½″	18′ 5″	204
10′ 8″	19′ 6″	216
11′ 2½″	20′ 7″	228
11′ 9″	21′ 8″	240
12′ 3½″	22′ 9″	252
12′10″	23′10″	264
13′ 4½″	24′11″	276
13′11″	26′ 0″	288
14′ 5½″	27′ 1″	300
15′ 0″	28′ 2″	312
15′ 6½″	29′ 3″	324
16′ 1″	30′ 4″	336
16′ 7½″	31′ 5″	348
17′ 2″	32′ 6″	360
17′ 8½″	33′ 7″	372
18′ 3″	34′ 8″	384
18′ 9½″	35′ 9″	396
19′ 4″	36′10″	408
19′10½″	37′11″	420
20′ 5″	39′ 0″	432
20′11½″	40′ 1″	444
21′ 6″	41′ 2″	456
22′ 0½″	42′ 3″	468
22′ 7″	43′ 4″	480
23′ 1½″	44′ 5″	492
23′ 8″	45′ 6″	504
24′ 2½″	46′ 7″	516
24′ 9″	47′ 8″	528
25′ 3½″	48′ 9″	540
25′10″	49′10″	552
26′ 4½″	50′11″	564
26′11″	52′ 0″	576
27′ 5½″	53′ 1″	588
28′ 0″	54′ 2″	600

*Add 4″ minimum clearance to each end and each side when adjacent to walls, columns, obstructions, or other machines.

†This provides 1.1″ per coat. In areas or facilities where bulky coats are customary, the actual capacity may be reduced one-third.

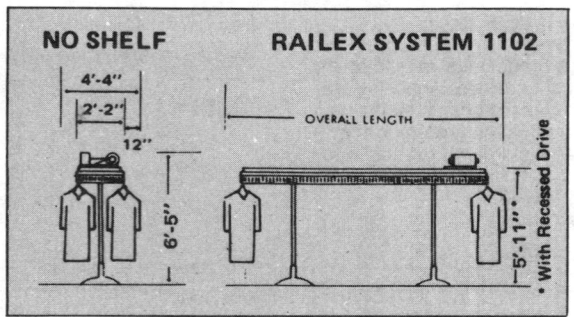

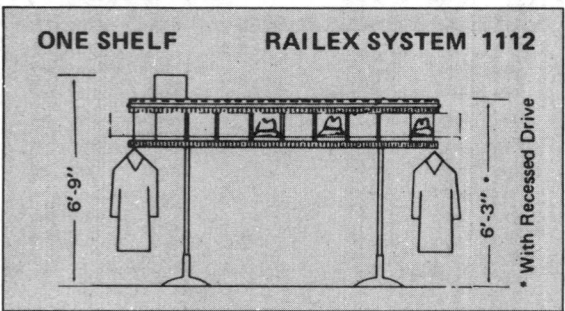

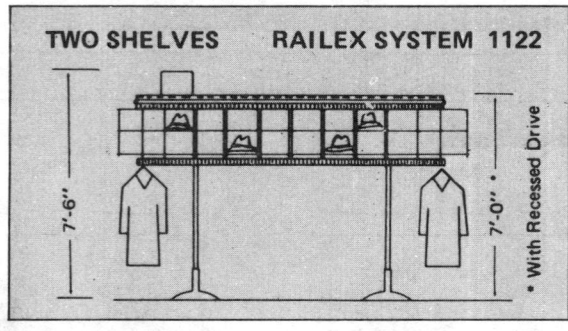

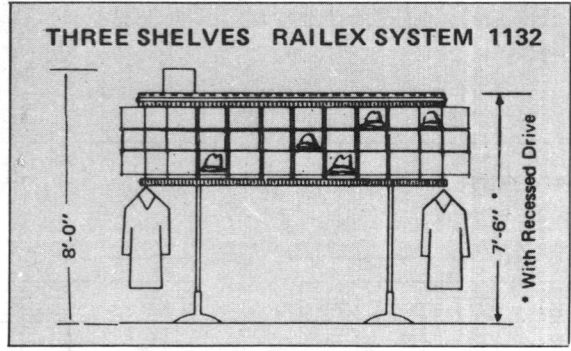

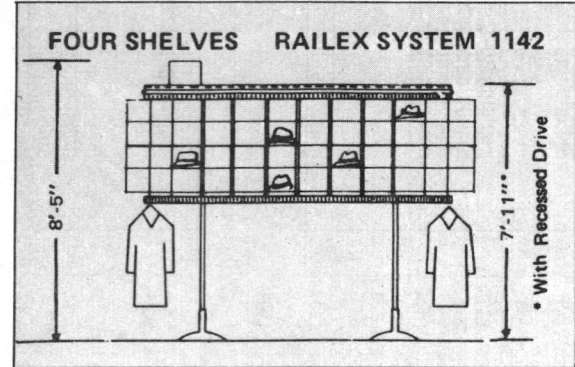

Fig. 5

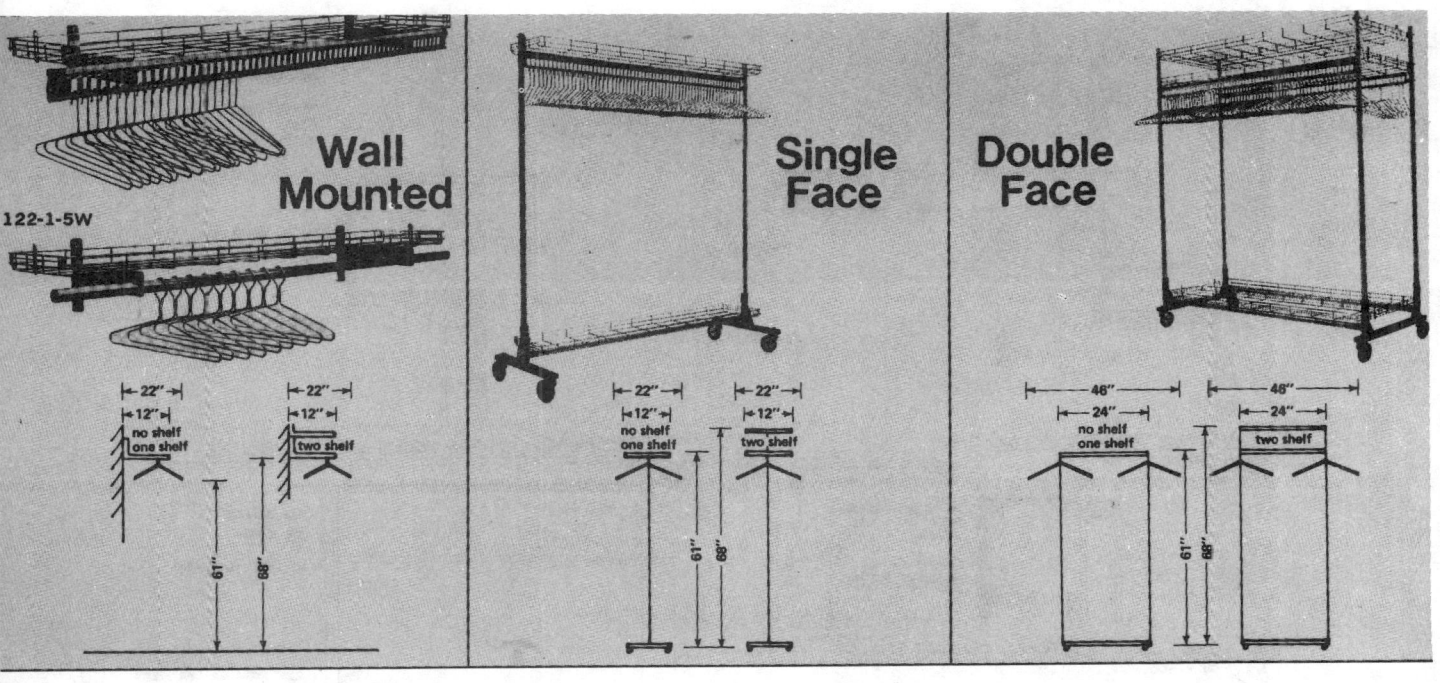

	Length	Number of Coats	Number of Shelves
Wall Mounted	3'-0"	36	0 1 2
	4'-0"	48	0 1 2
	5'-0"	60	0 1 2
Single Face	3'-4"	36	0 1 2
	4'-4"	48	0 1 2
	5'-4"	60	0 1 2
Double Face	3'-4"	72	0 1 2
	4'-4"	96	0 1 2
	5'-4"	120	0 1 2

COATROOMS
Coatroom Plans, Elevations, and Sections

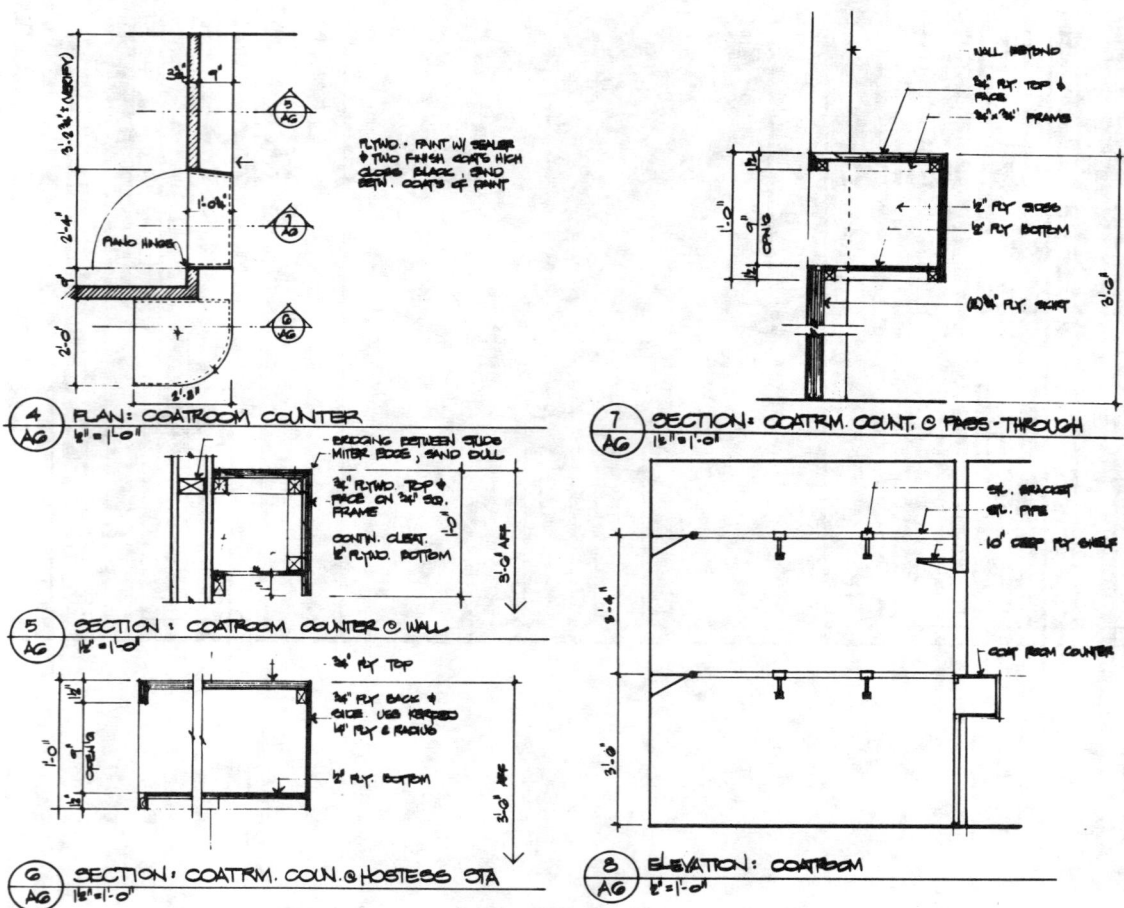

Fig. 6   A typical coatroom configuration will often consist of a counter with an access door plus the required shelves and hang rods. The overall size of the coatroom will vary with the number and types of coats to be stored. In high-volume coatroom situations, the design should provide appropriate counter space for those persons working behind the counter.

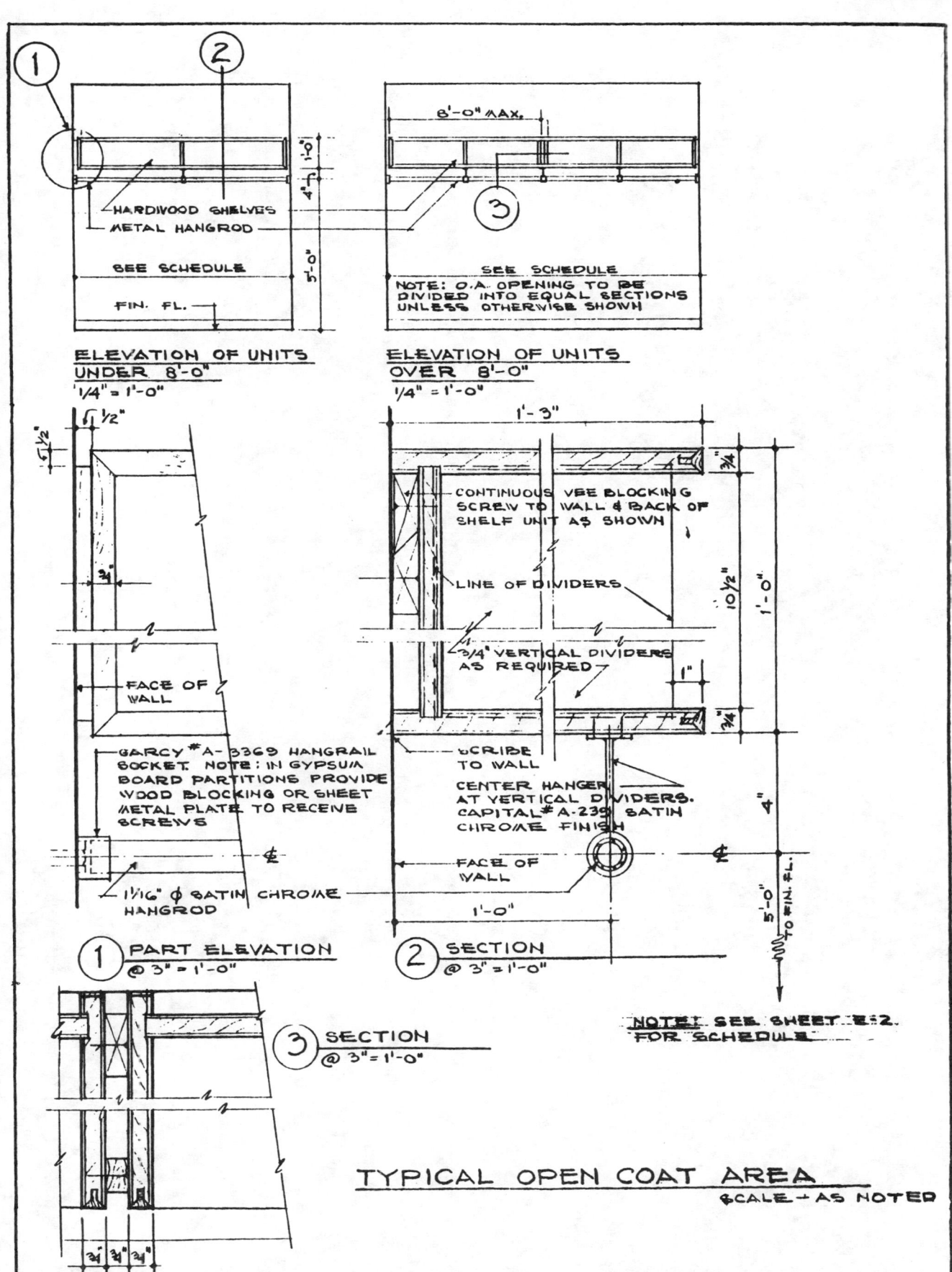

① ②

HARDWOOD SHELVES
METAL HANGROD

SEE SCHEDULE

FIN. FL.

ELEVATION OF UNITS UNDER 8'-0"
1/4" = 1'-0"

8'-0" MAX.

③

SEE SCHEDULE

NOTE: O.A. OPENING TO BE DIVIDED INTO EQUAL SECTIONS UNLESS OTHERWISE SHOWN

ELEVATION OF UNITS OVER 8'-0"
1/4" = 1'-0"

FACE OF WALL

GARCY #A-3369 HANGRAIL SOCKET. NOTE: IN GYPSUM BOARD PARTITIONS PROVIDE WOOD BLOCKING OR SHEET METAL PLATE TO RECEIVE SCREWS

1 1/16" Ø SATIN CHROME HANGROD

① **PART ELEVATION**
@ 3" = 1'-0"

1'-3"

CONTINUOUS VEE BLOCKING SCREW TO WALL & BACK OF SHELF UNIT AS SHOWN

LINE OF DIVIDERS

3/4" VERTICAL DIVIDERS AS REQUIRED

SCRIBE TO WALL

CENTER HANGER AT VERTICAL DIVIDERS. CAPITAL #A-239 SATIN CHROME FINISH

FACE OF WALL

1'-0"

② **SECTION**
@ 3" = 1'-0"

③ **SECTION**
@ 3" = 1'-0"

NOTE: SEE SHEET 2-2 FOR SCHEDULE

TYPICAL OPEN COAT AREA
SCALE — AS NOTED

Construction Details and Finishes

Selecting the appropriate partition or wall type is both a science and an art. In fact, there are so many options available to the designer that it is not unusual to refer to the partition or wall as a system, a combination of framing, sheathing, and finish elements, all working together to meet aesthetic, functional, code, and economic requirements.

In that regard, this section explores the great variety of wall and partition types, examining all of their characteristics with the exception of load bearing capacity and cost of labor and materials. With respect to load bearing or structural capacities, while many of the wall and partition types are able to carry superimposed loads, it is not the intent of this book to discuss structural issues. With respect to cost, too many factors and variables make this a topic that is difficult to analyze with any precision.

Information on both traditional and contemporary partitions and wall types is provided. Many traditional materials and methods of construction, such as solid gypsum plaster and plaster on clay tile, are cited, thus providing information to the designer who is redesigning or altering older structures.

A large portion of this section is devoted to the detailing of contemporary partition systems. In addition to providing examples of partition types, these pages place great emphasis on the detailing of unusual interface conditions that many designers often leave to the contractor to work out in the field. It should be noted that most, if not all, of these details have been selected from the working drawings of outstanding architectural and interior design firms.

While general information has also been provided about acoustics, sound transmission, and fire ratings of various walls and partitions, the designer is cautioned to verify all such information with manufacturers' certified test results, as well as with those building and fire codes having jurisdiction. It also should be noted that while test results may demonstrate a certain fire rating or sound transmission classification, it is important to determine if the results have been accepted by the local building or fire department.

It is often necessary to apply a finish to a wall or partition. Again, both traditional and contemporary methods to apply wood paneling, ceramic tile, and stone are clearly illustrated through the use of architectural details.

Finally, walls and partitions must ultimately meet floors and ceilings, and, of course, have doors and openings penetrate them. While some examples are provided in this section, the designer will also find important information in the sections Floors and Floor Finishes; Doors; and Ceilings, which follow.

PARTITIONS AND WALL FINISHES
Characteristics of Interior Partitions

DRAWING AND DESCRIPTION	FIRE-RATING	SOIL AND DAMAGE RESISTANCE	ACOUSTICS	REMARKS	COST COMPARISON
4 inch face brick, tooled joints; Actual thickness, 3⅝ inches; Weight, 40 lbs. per square foot of wall surface	Incombustible, with one hour fire-rating	Good	Very good; transmission loss, 45 decibels	Low maintenance, but limited flexibility; a good-looking wall, but poor light reflection	installation cost / maintenance and insurance cost for 20 years
4 inch concrete block, tooled joints, two coats of paint on each side; Actual thickness, 3⅝ inches; Weight, 30 lbs. per square foot	Incombustible, with one hour fire-rating	Good	Good; transmission loss, 40 decibels	Inexpensive; attractive if constructed neatly; frequently used for corridors, gyms, assembly rooms, etc.; no flexibility	
4 inch cinder block, ¾ inch layer of plaster on each side, 2 coats of paint on each side; Actual thickness, 5¼ inches; Weight, 30 lbs. per square foot	Incombustible, with two hour fire-rating	Poor	Good; transmission loss, 43 decibels	A smooth, dense finish; a good light reflector if painted a light color; no flexibility	
3 inch cinder block, ¾ inch layer of plaster on each side, 2 coats of paint on each side; Thickness, 4½ inches; Weight, 21 lbs. per square foot	Incombustible, with two hour fire-rating	Poor	Good; transmission loss, 39 decibels	A smooth, dense finish; a good light reflector if painted a light color; no flexibility	
4 inch structural facing tile, glazed on each side; Actual thickness, 3¾ inches; Weight, 40 lbs. per square foot	Incombustible, with a fire-rating of less than one hour	Very good	Good; transmission loss, 35 decibels	Used well in classrooms, corridors, also in toilets and showers; care must be taken with the design to avoid bright reflectivity; no flexibility	
4 inch concrete block, 2 coats of vinyl plastic spray over entire surface of each side; Actual thickness, 3¾ inches; Weight, 38 lbs. per square foot	Incombustible, with one hour fire-rating	Good	Good; transmission loss, 40 decibels	Sleek finish, but no flexibility	
2 by 4 inch wood studs, spaced 16 inches apart; metal lath and plaster, 2 coats of paint on each side; Thickness, 4¾ inches; Weight, 20 lbs. per square foot	Combustible	Poor	Good; transmission loss, 39 decibels	Good light reflector, not much flexibility	

W-1 — WOOD STUDS - 16" O.C. 3/8" 3-PLY PLYWOOD NAILED BOTH SIDES

W-2 — WOOD STUDS - 16" O.C., METAL LATH, GYPSUM SCRATCH & BROWN, WHITE FINISH BOTH SIDES

W-3 — WOOD STUDS - 16" O.C. 1/2" FIBERBOARD, JOINTS FILLED, BOTH SIDES

W-4 — SAME AS W-3, WITH 1/2" SCRATCH, BROWN & WHITE, GYPSUM BOTH SIDES

W-5 — 2" x 4" WOOD STUDS, STAGGERED, 8" O.C. 2"x 6" STUD AT EDGES 1/2" FIBERBOARD NAILED BOTH SIDES

W-6 — SAME AS W-5, WITH 1/2" SCRATCH, BROWN, & WHITE GYPSUM, BOTH SIDES

W-7 — WOOD STUDS - 16" O.C., GYPSUM LATH, ATTACHED WITH STIFF CLIPS 3/8" SCRATCH, BROWN, WHITE GYPSUM PLASTER BOTH SIDES

W-8 — SAME AS W-7, EXCEPT ATTACHED WITH SPRING CLIPS 1/2" PLASTER BOTH SIDES.

W-9 — 2" SOLID GYPSUM PLASTER ON PERFORATED GYP LATH, 3/4" CHANNEL STUDS, SMOOTH WHITE BOTH SIDES

W-10 — 2" SOLID GYPSUM PLASTER SAME AS W-9 EXCEPT EXPANDED METAL LATH

W-11 — 2 1/2" SOLID GYPSUM PLASTER SAME AS W-10

W-12 — 3" METAL STUDS - 16" O.C., METAL LATH, 1/2" SCRATCH, BROWN, WHITE GYPSUM PLASTER BOTH SIDES

W-13 — TWO PANELS, NOT JOINED; 3/4" CHANNEL STUDS, EXPANDED METAL LATH, SCRATCH, BROWN & WHITE GYPSUM PLASTER BOTH SIDES FACE TO FACE = 10"

W-14 — SAME AS W-13, EXCEPT FACE TO FACE = 4 1/2"

W-15 — 3" x 12" x 30" GYPSUM TILE 1/2" BROWN, WHITE GYPSUM PLASTER BOTH SIDES

W-16 — 3" x 12" x 30" GYPSUM TILE, RESILIENT CLIP, METAL LATH, 3 COATS GYPSUM PLASTER, 2 COATS GYPSUM PLASTER ON TILE, OTHER SIDE (WHITE FIN. BOTH SIDES)

W-17 — 4" BRICK PARTITION, 1/2" BROWN, WHITE FINISH GYPSUM PLASTER BOTH SIDES

W-18 — SAME AS W-17, EXCEPT 8" BRICK PANEL

W-19 — SAME AS W-17, EXCEPT ONE LAYER OF BRICK LAID ON EDGE

W-20 — BRICK LAID ON EDGE, 1" x 2" FURRING, WIRED, & GYPSUM LATH PLUS 1/2" BROWN & WHITE GYPSUM PLASTER BOTH SIDES.

W-21 — 3" x 12" x 12" - 3 CELL CLAY TILE, 1/2" BROWN & WHITE GYPSUM PLASTER BOTH SIDES.

W-22 — ANOTHER PANEL BUILT AS NEARLY LIKE W-21 AS POSSIBLE

W-23 — SAME AS W-21 EXCEPT 4" x 12" x 12" 3-CELL TILE

W-24 — SAME AS W-21 EXCEPT 6" x 12" x 12" 3-CELL TILE

W-25 — SAME AS W-21 EXCEPT 8" x 12" x 12" 3-CELL TILE

W-26 — DOUBLE CLAY TILE: 3 3/4" x 12" x 12" 8" x 12" x 12", 1/2" BROWN AND WHITE GYPSUM PLASTER BOTH SIDES

W-27 — DOUBLE PARTITION WITH AIR SPACE. TWO WALLS OF 3" x 12" x 12" 3-CELL CLAY TILE 1" FLAXLINUM BUTTED TIGHT BETWEEN TILE. NO PLASTER. 1" x 4" FLAXLINUM STRIP AT BOTTOM, SIDES & TOP OF ONE PARTITION

W-28 — PUMICE & PORTLAND CEMENT 2-CELL TILE 4" x 8" x 16" NO PLASTER (VERY POROUS)

W-29 — SAME AS W-28, BUT 1/2" GYPSUM PLASTER ON ONE SIDE ONLY

W-30 — SAME AS W-28, BUT 1/2" GYPSUM PLASTER ON BOTH SIDES

W-31 — GLASS BRICK 3 3/4" x 4 7/8" x 8"

PARTITIONS AND WALL FINISHES

Partition and Wall Types

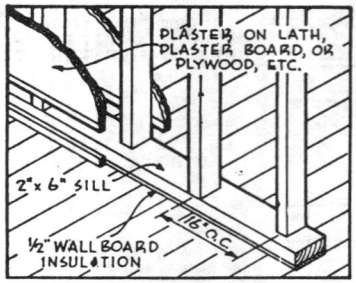

SOUND CONTROL BY
STAGGERED STUDS

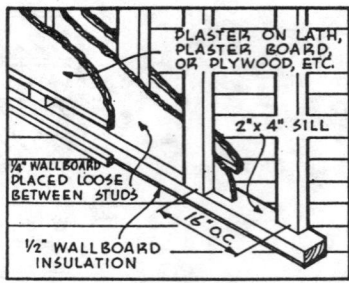

SOUND CONTROL-STAGGERED
STUDS AND WALL BOARD

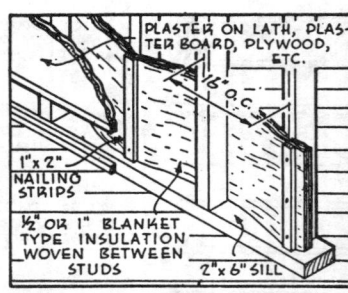

SOUND CONTROL-STAGGERED
STUDS AND BLANKET CENTER

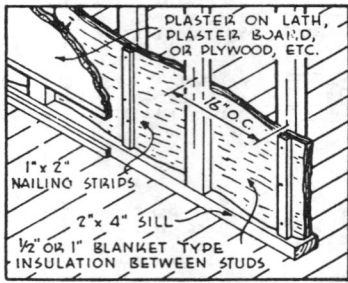

SOUND CONTROL-SIDEWISE
STUDS AND BLANKET CENTER

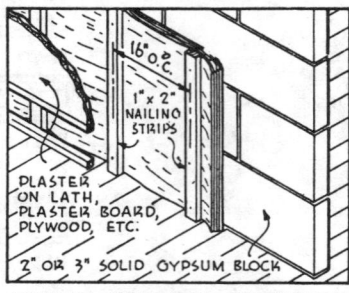

SOUND CONTROL-BLANKET
OVER GYPSUM BLOCK

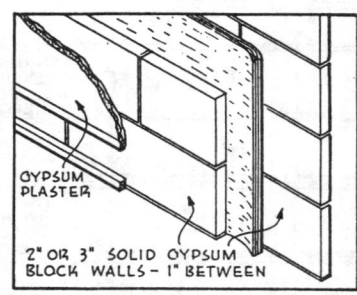

SOUND CONTROL-BLANKET
BETWEEN GYPSUM BLOCK

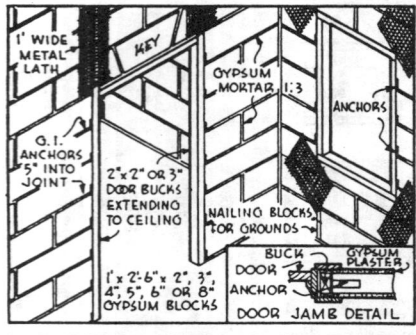

GYPSUM SOLID OR HOLLOW
PARTITION TILE-1

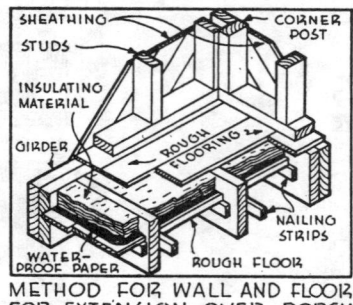

METHOD FOR WALL AND FLOOR
FOR EXTENSION OVER PORCH

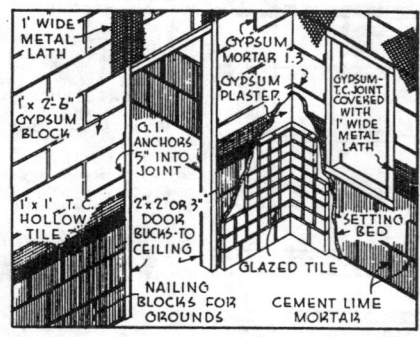

TERRA COTTA BLOCK PARTITION
TO HEIGHT OF GLAZED TILE

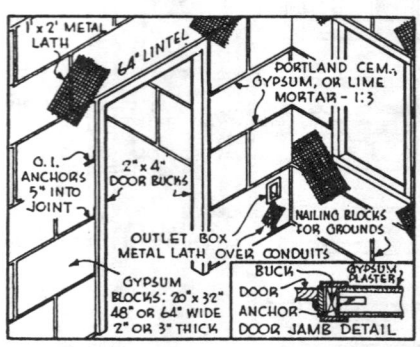

GYPSUM SOLID OR HOLLOW
PARTITION TILE-2

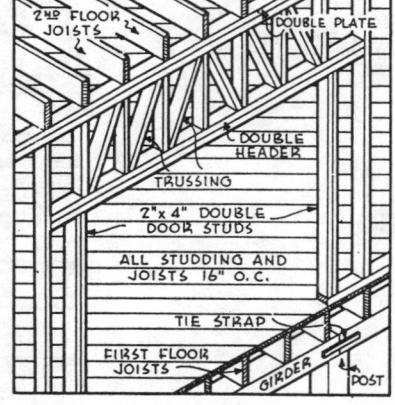

FRAMING FOR WIDE OPENING
ABOVE SUB-STRUCTURE

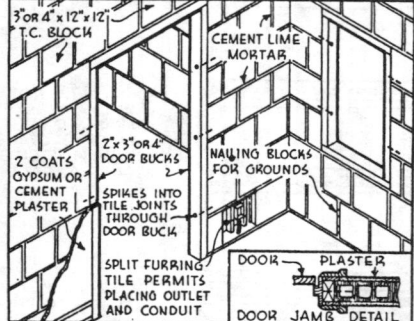

TERRA COTTA HOLLOW
PARTITION TILE

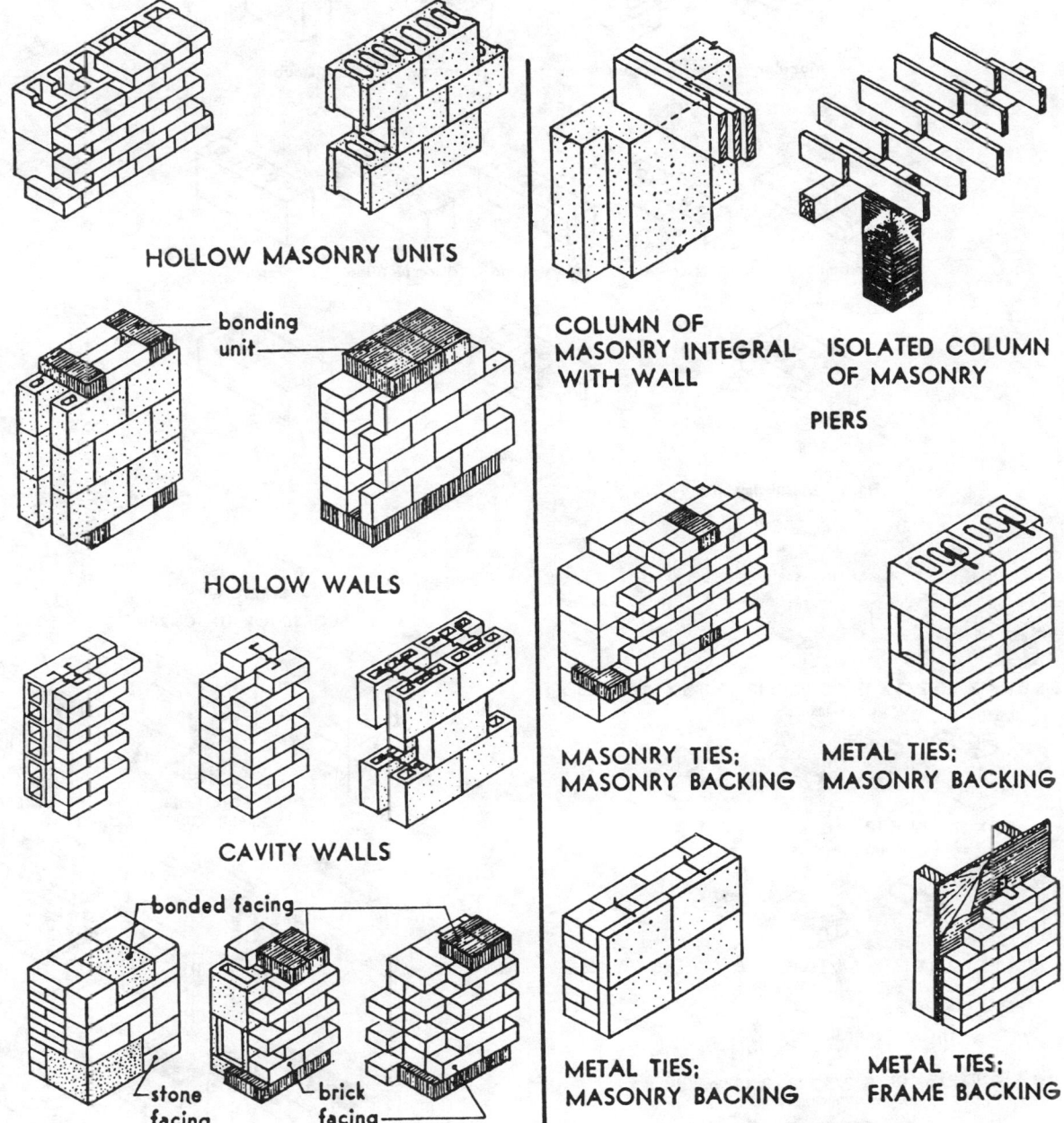

HOLLOW MASONRY UNITS

bonding unit

HOLLOW WALLS

CAVITY WALLS

bonded facing

stone facing

brick facing

FACED WALLS

COLUMN OF MASONRY INTEGRAL WITH WALL

ISOLATED COLUMN OF MASONRY

PIERS

MASONRY TIES; MASONRY BACKING

METAL TIES; MASONRY BACKING

METAL TIES; MASONRY BACKING

METAL TIES; FRAME BACKING

VENEERED WALLS

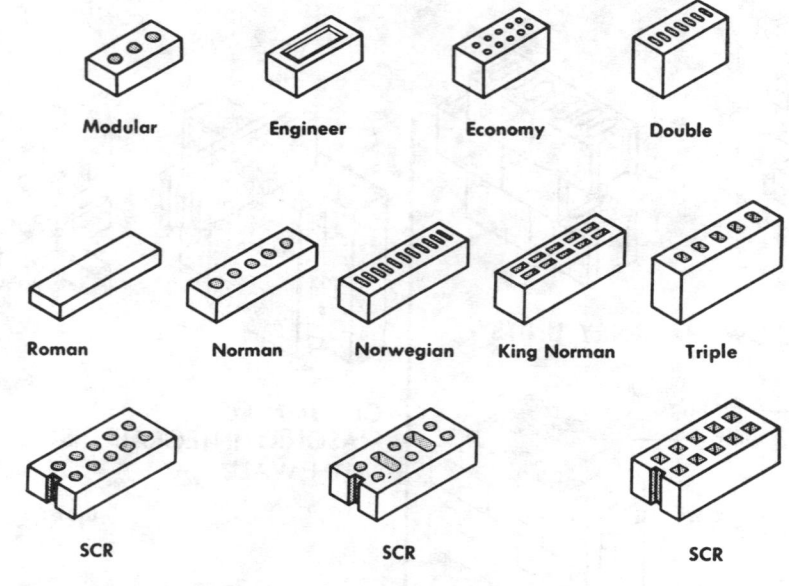

Fig. 1 Typical clay brick.

Fig. 2 Structural clay tile.

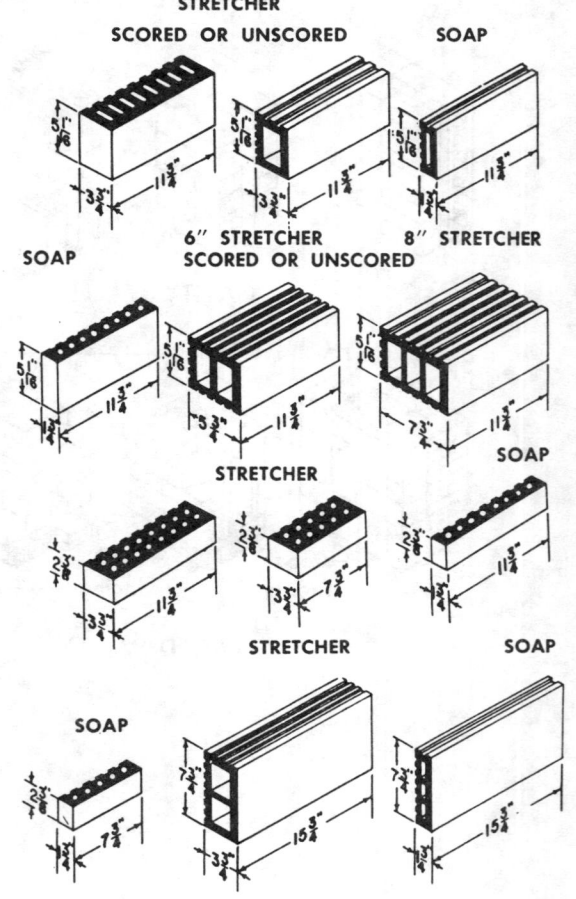

Fig. 3 Structural facing tile.

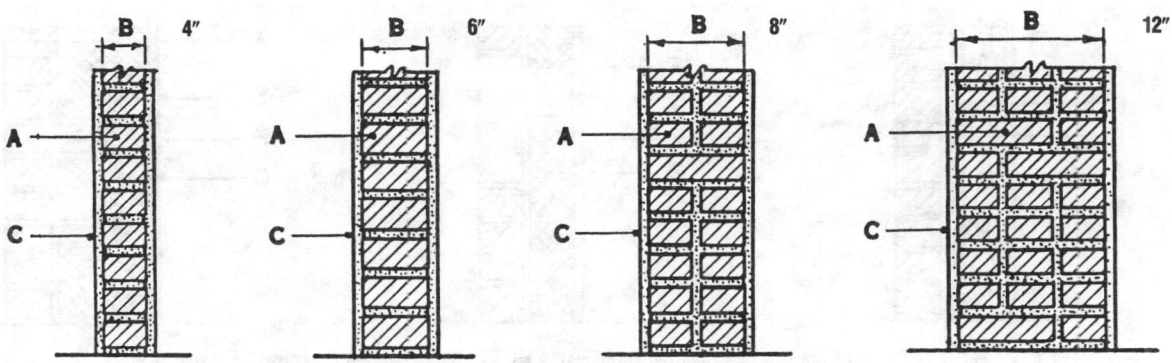

Fig. 4   Solid brick: bearing or nonbearing (sections). A = brick, B = nominal wall thickness, C = finish.

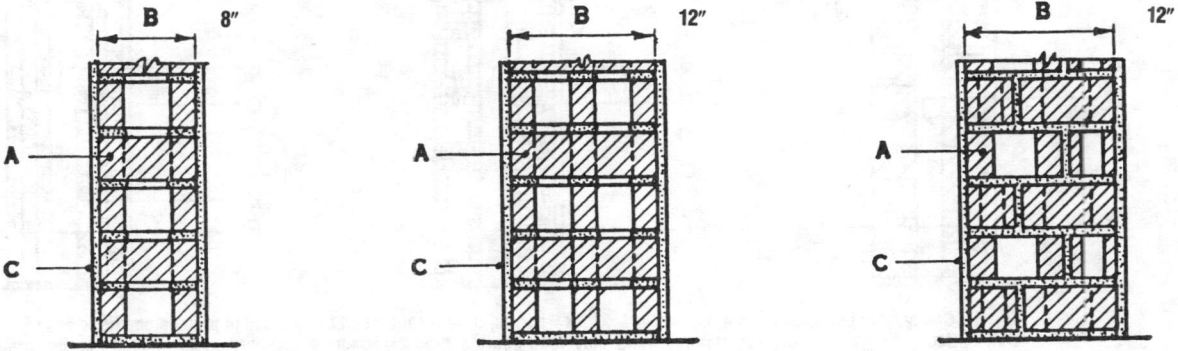

Fig. 5   Hollow brick units: bearing or nonbearing (sections). A = brick, B = nominal wall thickness, C = finish.

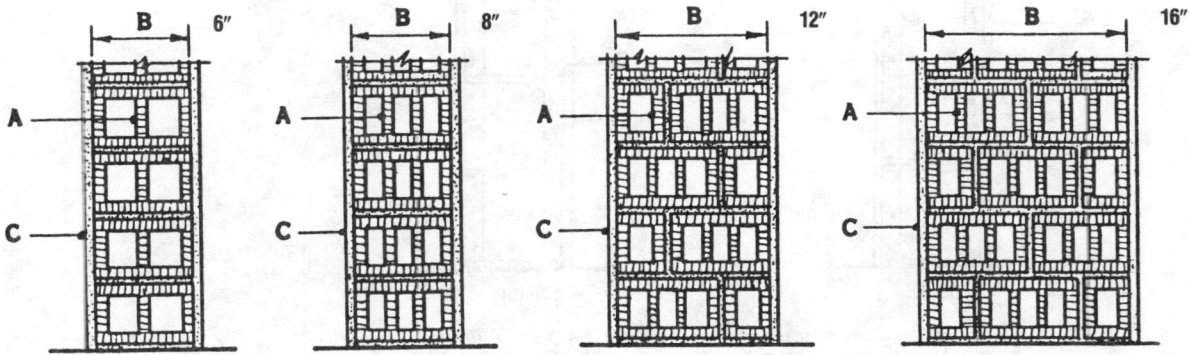

Fig. 6   Structural clay tile: bearing (sections). A = structural clay tile, B = nominal wall thickness, C = finish.

PARTITIONS AND WALL FINISHES

Types of Masonry

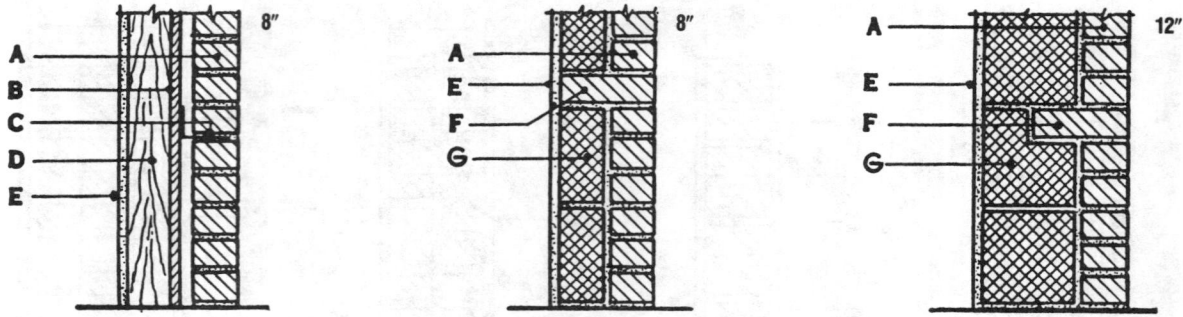

Fig. 7 Faced or veneered construction: bearing (sections). A = brick; B = sheathing; C = corrosion-resistant metal ties spaced 24 in on centers, vertically and horizontally; D = wood or steel studs; E = plaster or gypsum wallboard; F = masonry bond; G = masonry backing unit.

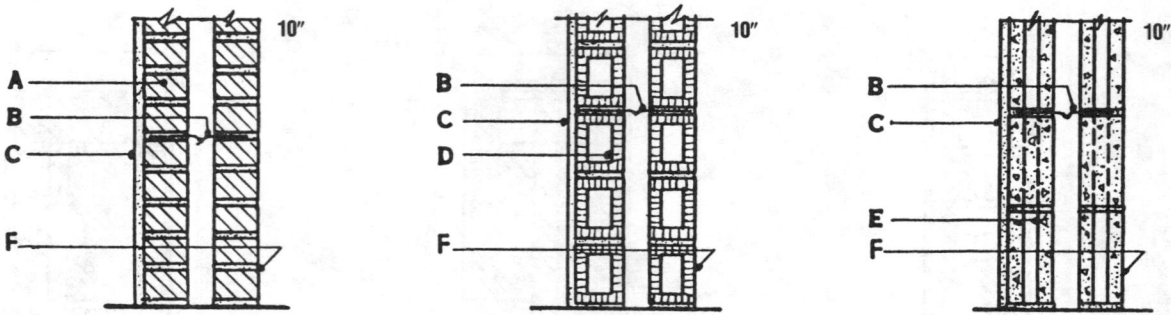

Fig. 8 Cavity type: bearing (sections). A = clay brick, B = corrosion-resistant metal ties spaced to provide one tie to each 3 ft² of wall surface, C = gypsum plaster, D = structural clay load-bearing tile, E = concrete masonry units of load-bearing grade, F = exterior face of wall.

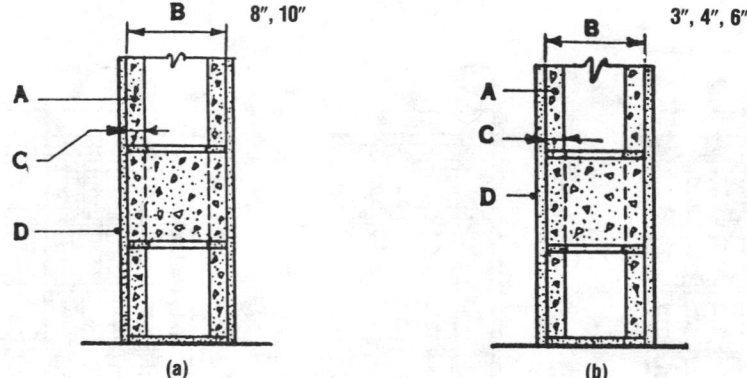

Fig. 9 Hollow concrete masonry units (sections). (a) Bearing, (b) Non-bearing. A = concrete masonry units conforming to ASTM, *Standard Specifications for Hollow Load-Bearing Concrete Masonry Units;* B = nominal wall thickness, C = nominal shell thickness, D = gypsum plaster.

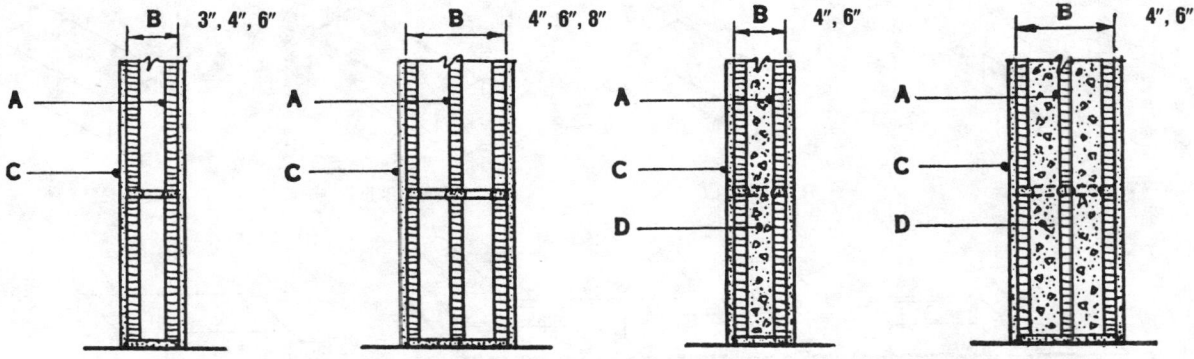

Fig. 10 Structural clay tile: nonbearing (sections). A = structural clay tile, B = nominal wall thickness, C = finish, D = fill.

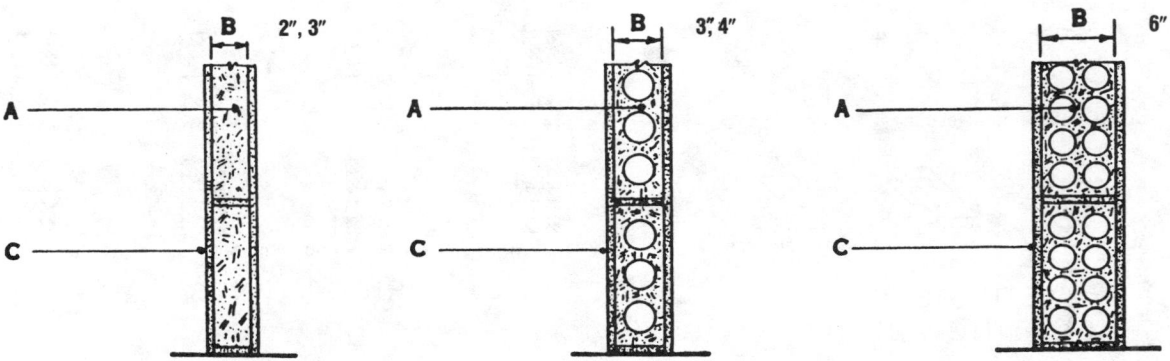

Fig. 11 Gypsum tile or block: nonbearing (sections). A = gypsum block, B = nominal wall thickness, C = finish.

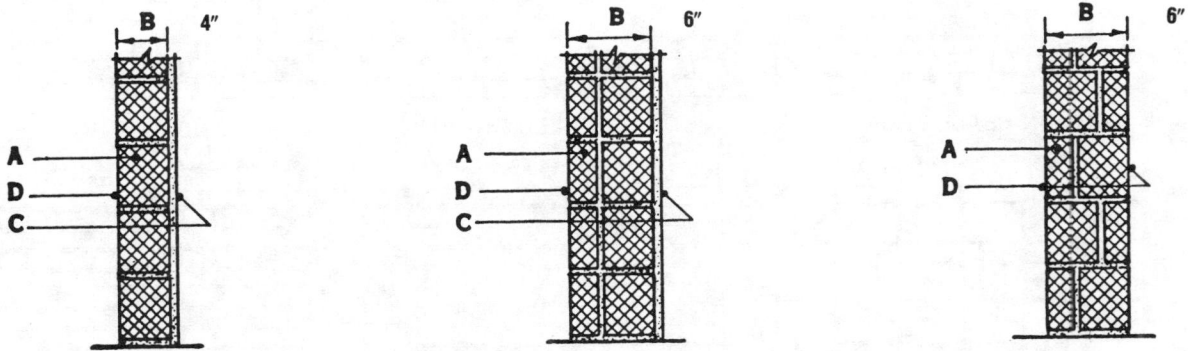

Fig. 12 Structural clay facing tile: nonbearing (sections). A = clay tile, B = nominal wall thickness, C = plaster, D = glazed or smooth-surfaced side of tile.

PARTITIONS AND WALL FINISHES

Brick Types and Bonds

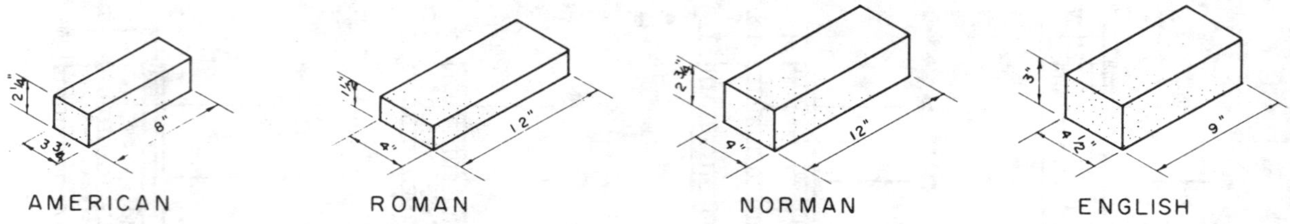

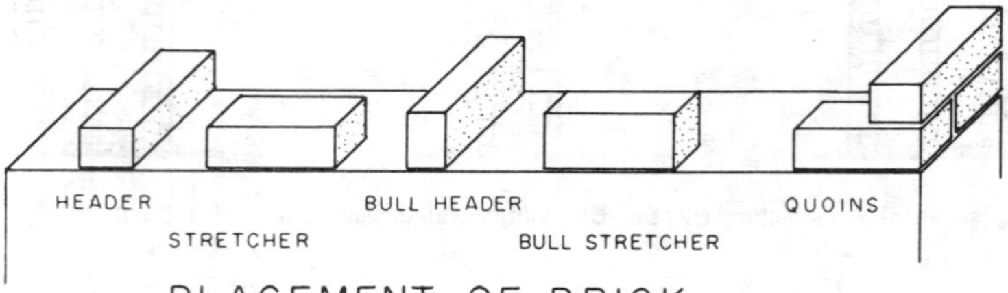

2¼"
3¾"
8"
AMERICAN
1½"
4"
12"
ROMAN
2¾"
4"
12"
NORMAN
3"
4½"
9"
ENGLISH

HEADER
STRETCHER
BULL HEADER
BULL STRETCHER
QUOINS

PLACEMENT OF BRICK

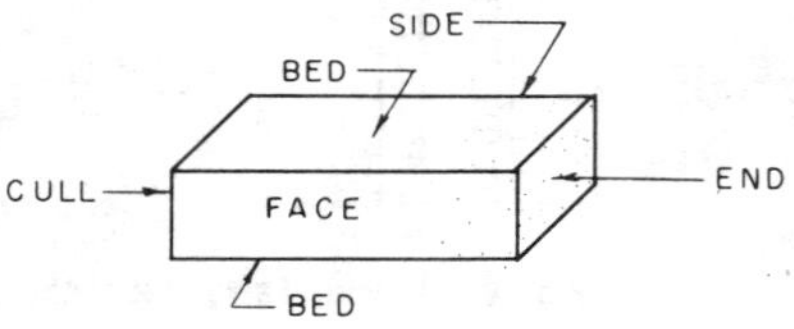

SIDE
BED
CULL
FACE
END
BED

SIX FACES OF BRICK

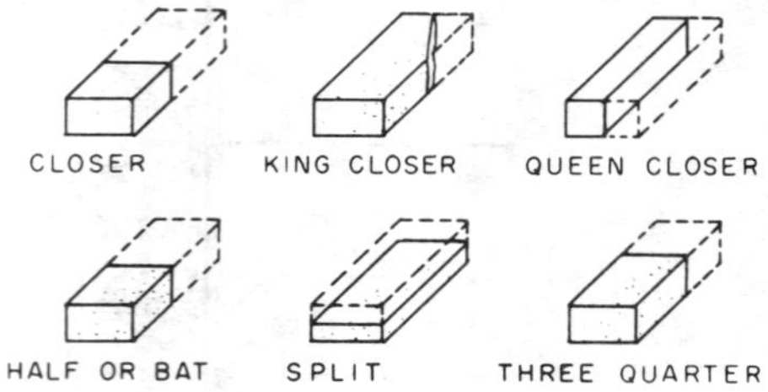

CLOSER
KING CLOSER
QUEEN CLOSER
HALF OR BAT
SPLIT
THREE QUARTER

METHODS OF CUTTING BRICK

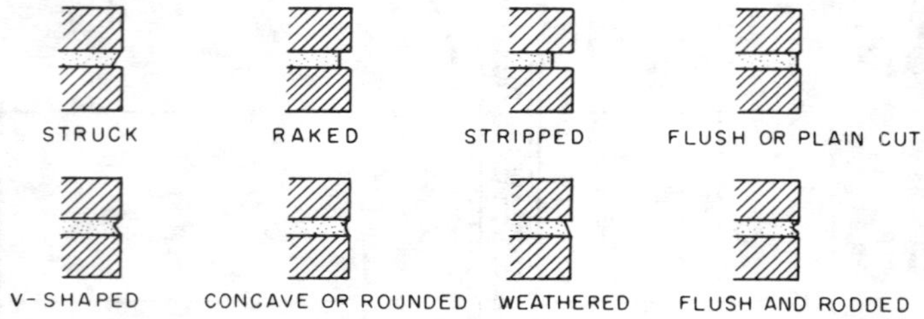

STRUCK
RAKED
STRIPPED
FLUSH OR PLAIN CUT
V-SHAPED
CONCAVE OR ROUNDED
WEATHERED
FLUSH AND RODDED

BRICK JOINTS

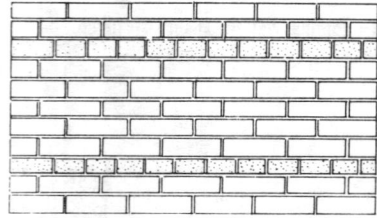

COMMON HEADER BOND
HEADER COURSE EVERY 6TH COURSE
7.88 BRICK PER SQ. FT.

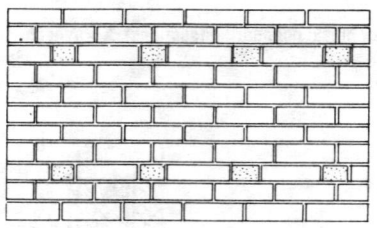

COMMON FLEMISH BOND
ALTERNATE FULL HEADERS EVERY 6TH COURSE
7.15 BRICK PER SQ. FT.

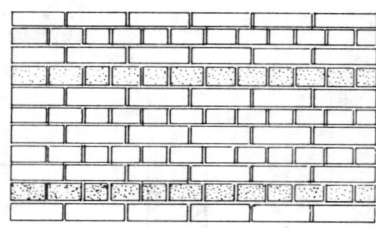

ENGLISH BOND
HEADER EVERY 6TH COURSE - HALF BRICK USED FOR HEADER COURSE EXCEPT EVERY 6TH
7.88 BRICK PER SQ. FT.

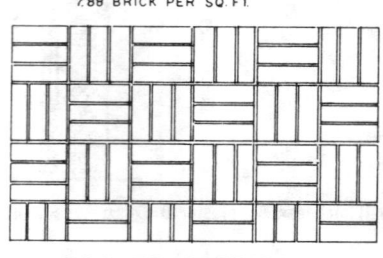

BASKET PATTERN
6.75 BRICK PER SQ. FT.

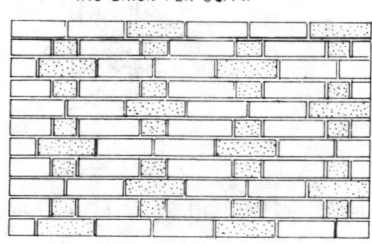

FLEMISH CROSS BOND
ALTERNATE FULL HEADER EVERY 6TH COURSE
7.15 BRICK PER SQ. FT.

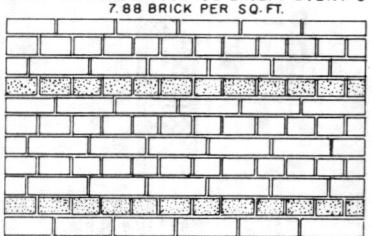

ENGLISH CROSS BOND
CONTINUOUS FULL HEADERS EVERY 6TH COURSE
7.88 BRICK PER SQ. FT.

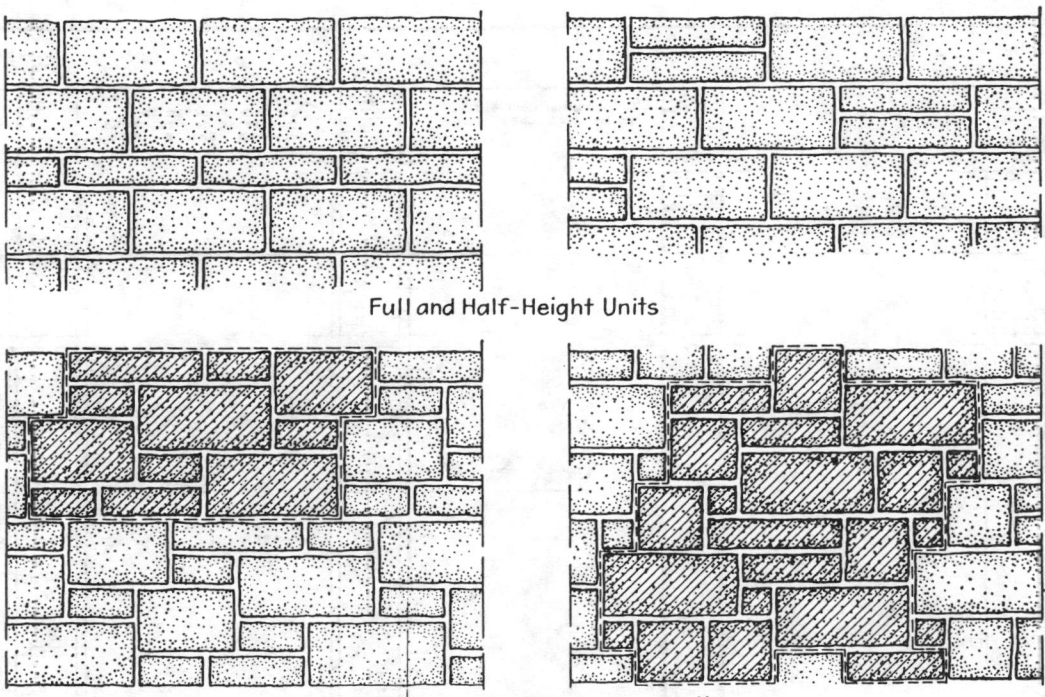

Full and Half-Height Units

Full, Half and Fractional Size Units

Fig. 13   Designs of standard-size hollow concrete-masonry units.

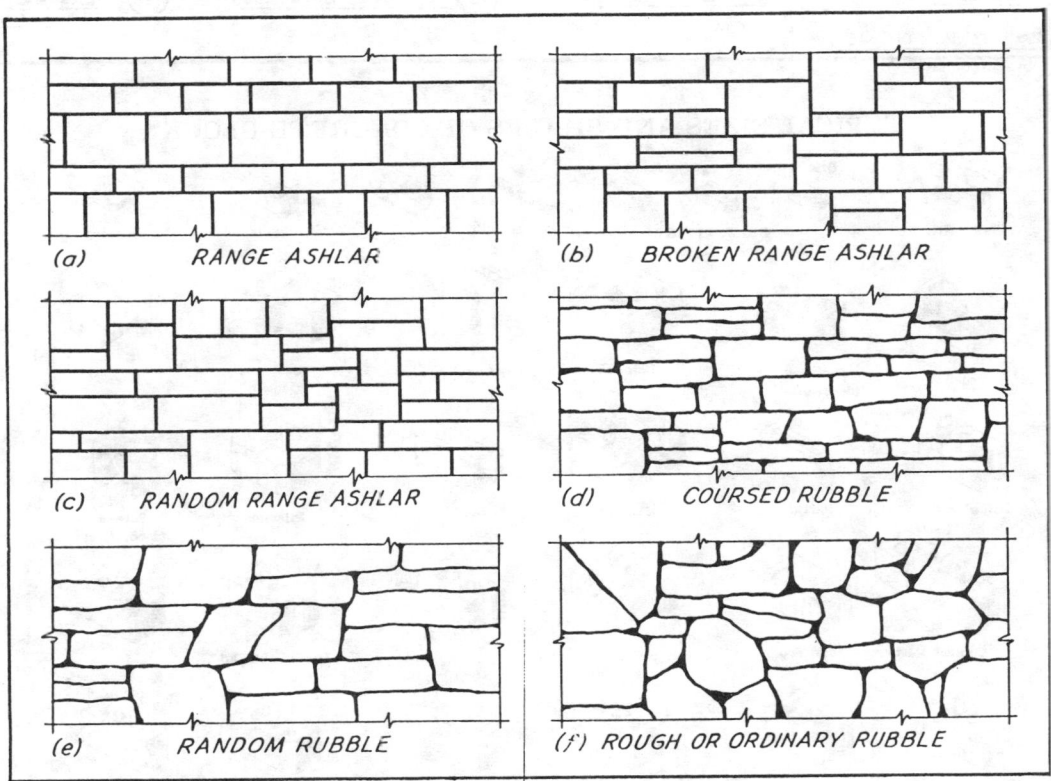

(a)   RANGE ASHLAR

(b)   BROKEN RANGE ASHLAR

(c)   RANDOM RANGE ASHLAR

(d)   COURSED RUBBLE

(e)   RANDOM RUBBLE

(f)   ROUGH OR ORDINARY RUBBLE

Fig. 14   Stone ashlar and rubble masonry.

PARTITIONS AND WALL FINISHES
Masonry Partitions

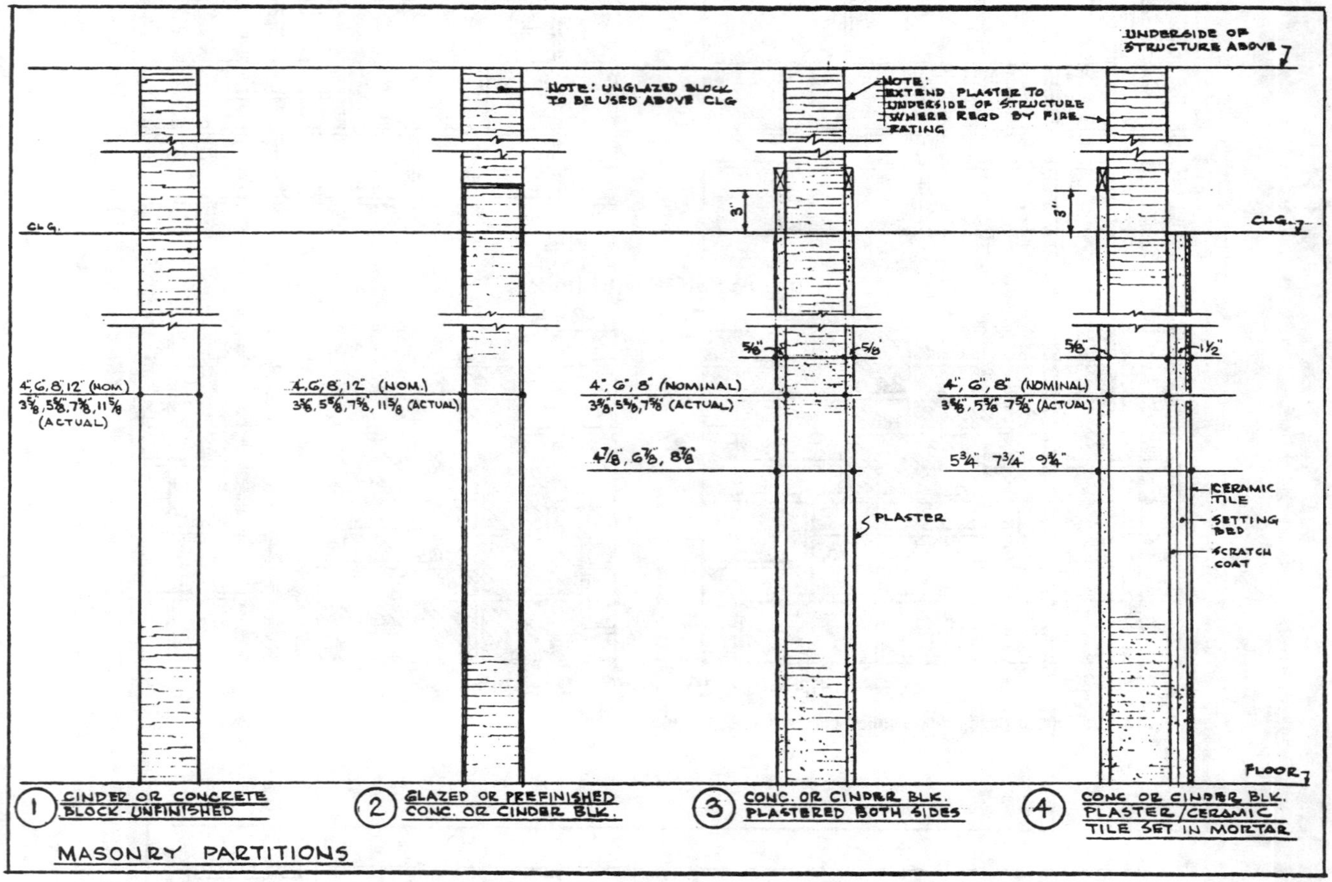

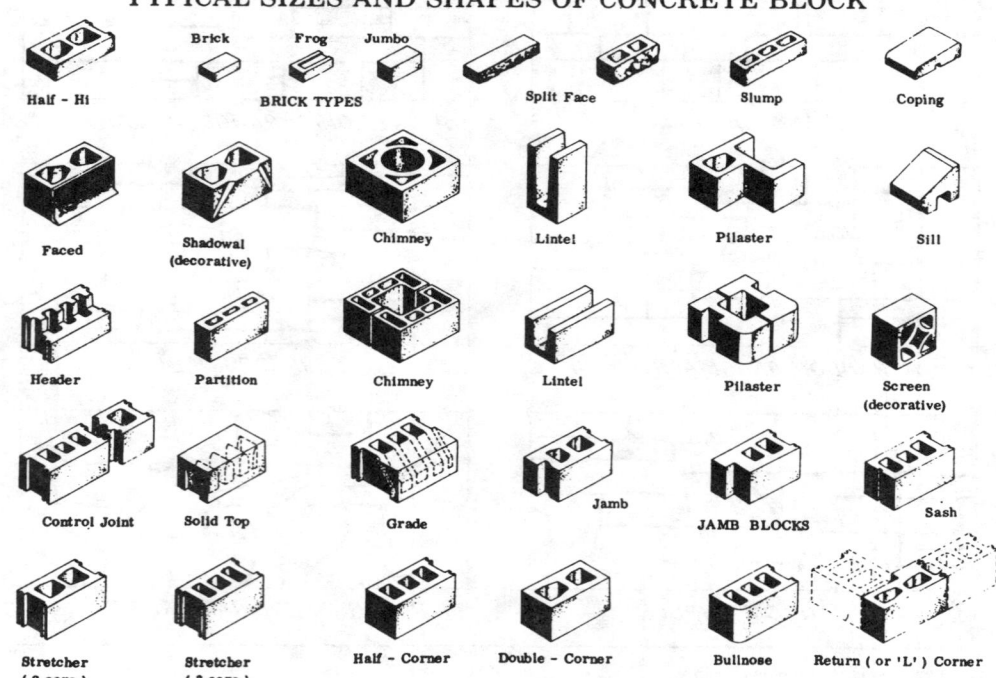

NOTE: UNGLAZED BLOCK TO BE USED ABOVE CLG

NOTE: EXTEND PLASTER TO UNDERSIDE OF STRUCTURE WHERE REQD BY FIRE RATING

UNDERSIDE OF STRUCTURE ABOVE

CLG.

CLG.

4,6,8,12 (NOM)
3⅝,5⅝,7⅝,11⅝ (ACTUAL)

4,6,8,12 (NOM.)
3⅝,5⅝,7⅝,11⅝ (ACTUAL)

4", 6", 8" (NOMINAL)
3⅝,5⅝,7⅝ (ACTUAL)

4", 6", 8" (NOMINAL)
3⅝,5⅝ 7⅝ (ACTUAL)

4⅞, 6⅞, 8⅞

5¾ 7¾ 9¾

PLASTER

CERAMIC TILE
SETTING BED
SCRATCH COAT

FLOOR

(1) CINDER OR CONCRETE BLOCK - UNFINISHED

(2) GLAZED OR PREFINISHED CONC. OR CINDER BLK.

(3) CONC. OR CINDER BLK. PLASTERED BOTH SIDES

(4) CONC OR CINDER BLK. PLASTER/CERAMIC TILE SET IN MORTAR

MASONRY PARTITIONS

TYPICAL SIZES AND SHAPES OF CONCRETE BLOCK

Half - Hi

Brick   Frog   Jumbo
BRICK TYPES

Split Face

Slump

Coping

Faced

Shadowal (decorative)

Chimney

Lintel

Pilaster

Sill

Header

Partition

Chimney

Lintel

Pilaster

Screen (decorative)

Control Joint

Solid Top

Grade

Jamb

JAMB BLOCKS

Sash

Stretcher (2 core)

Stretcher (3 core)

Half - Corner

Double - Corner

Bullnose

Return (or 'L') Corner

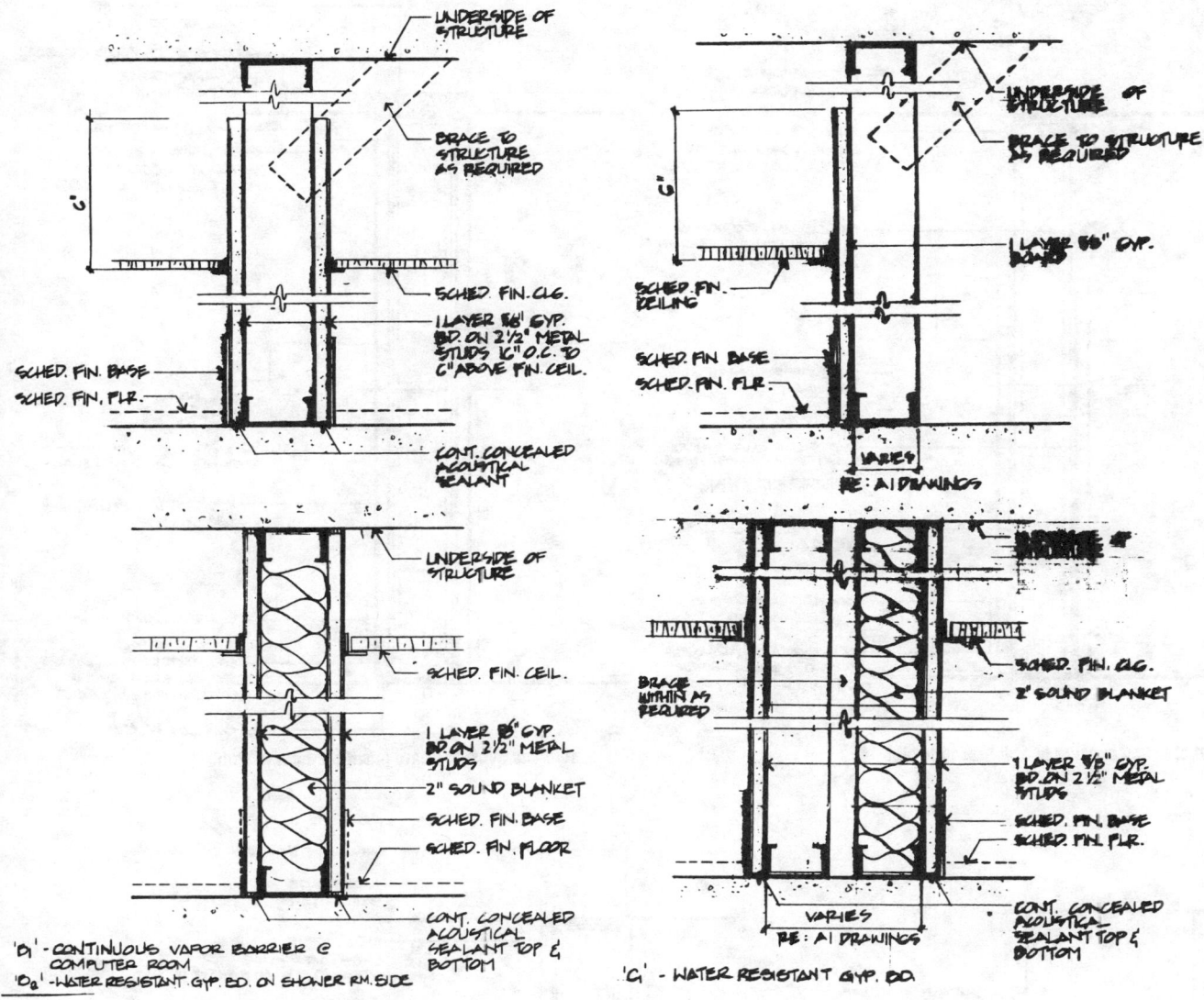

UNDERSIDE OF STRUCTURE

BRACE TO STRUCTURE AS REQUIRED

6"

SCHED. FIN. CLG.

1 LAYER 5/8" GYP. BD. ON 2 1/2" METAL STUDS 16" O.C. TO 6" ABOVE FIN. CEIL.

SCHED. FIN. BASE

SCHED. FIN. FLR.

CONT. CONCEALED ACOUSTICAL SEALANT

UNDERSIDE OF STRUCTURE

BRACE TO STRUCTURE AS REQUIRED

6"

1 LAYER 5/8" GYP. BOARD

SCHED. FIN. CEILING

SCHED. FIN. BASE

SCHED. FIN. FLR.

VARIES
RE: A1 DRAWINGS

UNDERSIDE OF STRUCTURE

SCHED. FIN. CEIL.

1 LAYER 5/8" GYP. BD. ON 2 1/2" METAL STUDS

2" SOUND BLANKET

SCHED. FIN. BASE

SCHED. FIN. FLOOR

CONT. CONCEALED ACOUSTICAL SEALANT TOP & BOTTOM

UNDERSIDE OF STRUCTURE

BRACE WITHIN AS REQUIRED

SCHED. FIN. CLG.

2" SOUND BLANKET

1 LAYER 5/8" GYP. BD. ON 2 1/2" METAL STUDS

SCHED. FIN. BASE
SCHED. FIN. FLR.

VARIES
RE: A1 DRAWINGS

CONT. CONCEALED ACOUSTICAL SEALANT TOP & BOTTOM

'D₁' - CONTINUOUS VAPOR BARRIER @ COMPUTER ROOM
'D₂' - WATER RESISTANT GYP. BD. ON SHOWER RM. SIDE

ACOUSTICAL PARTITION

'C' - WATER RESISTANT GYP. BD.

PARTITIONS AND WALL FINISHES
Metal Stud and Gypsum Board

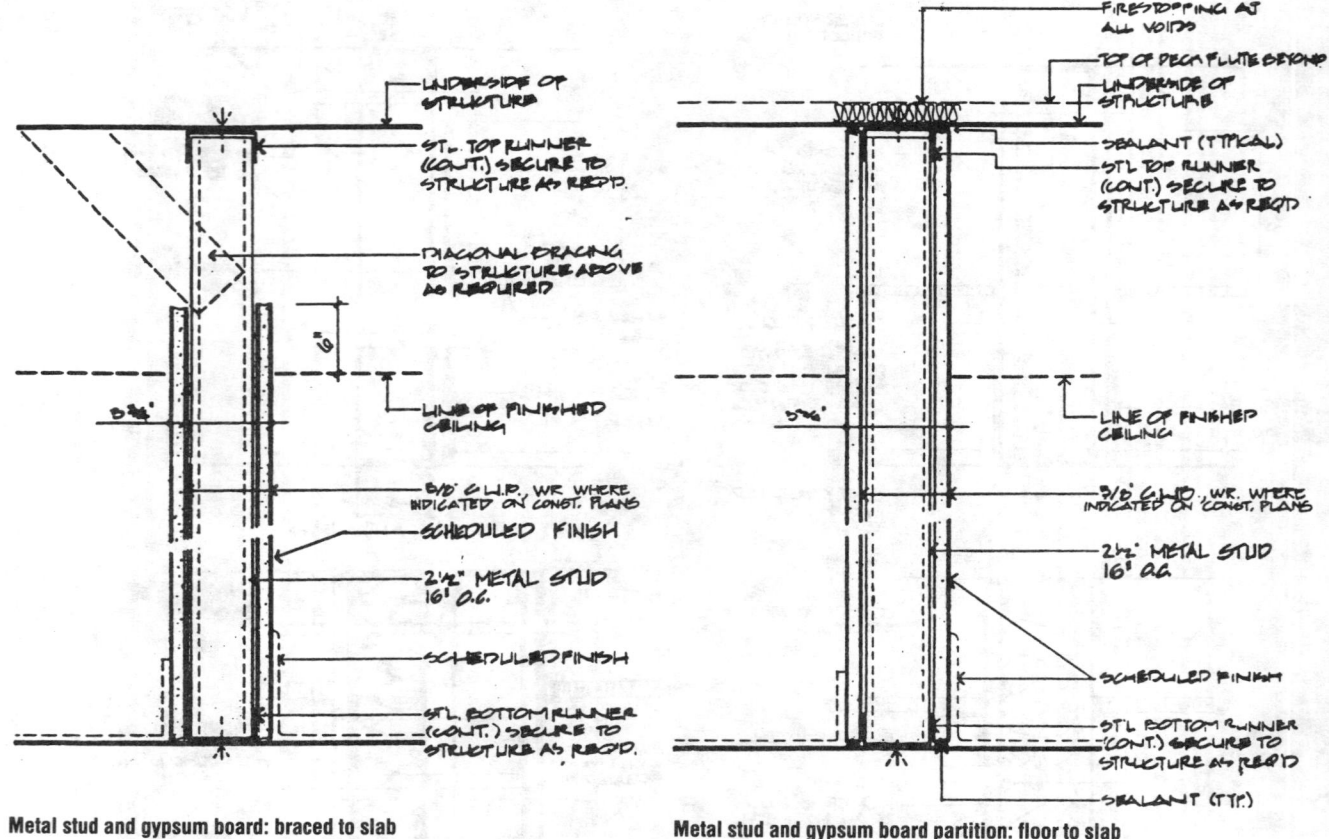

Metal stud and gypsum board: braced to slab

Metal stud and gypsum board partition: floor to slab

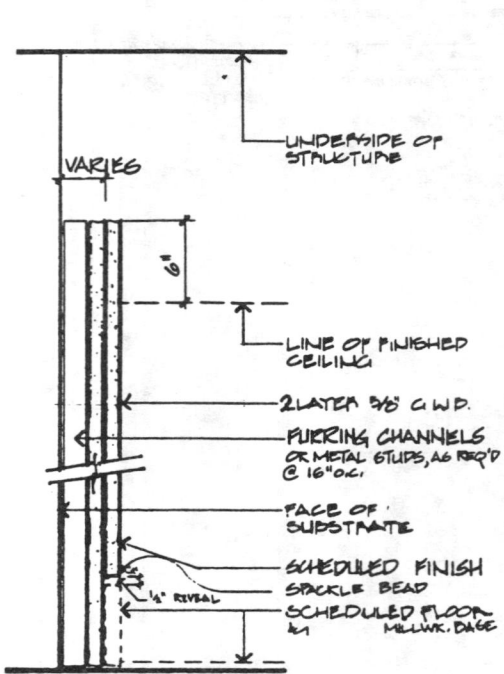

Metal channels and gypsum board: wall furring

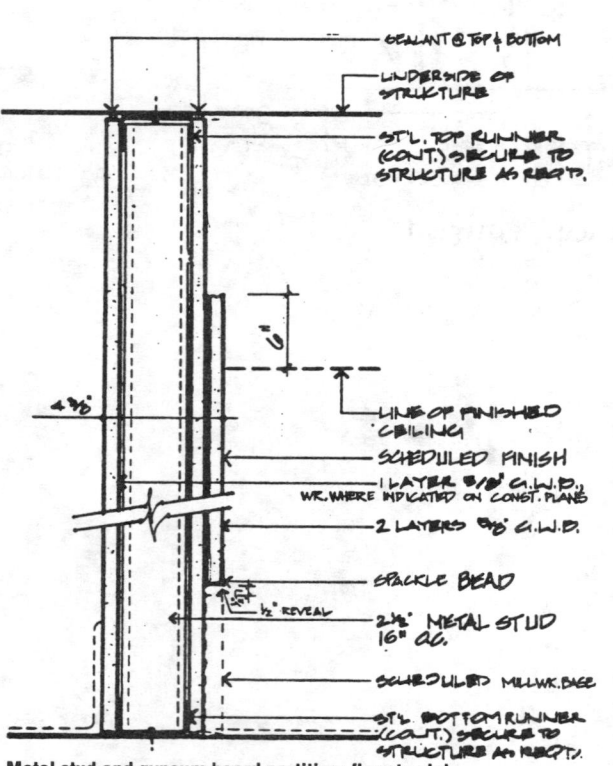

Metal stud and gypsum board partition: floor to slab

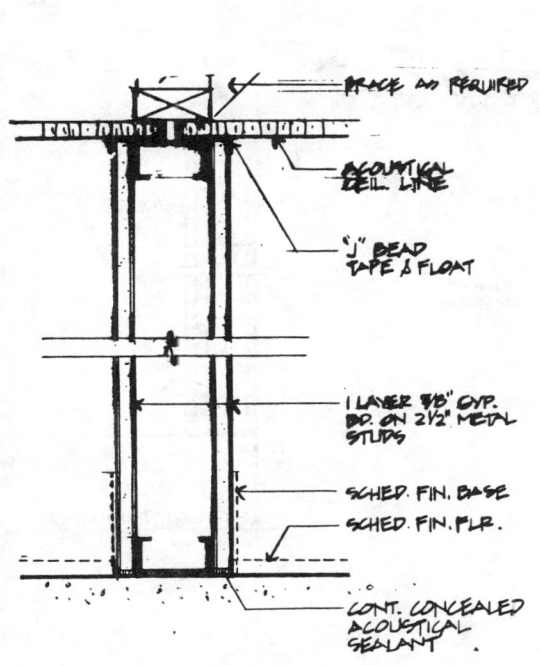

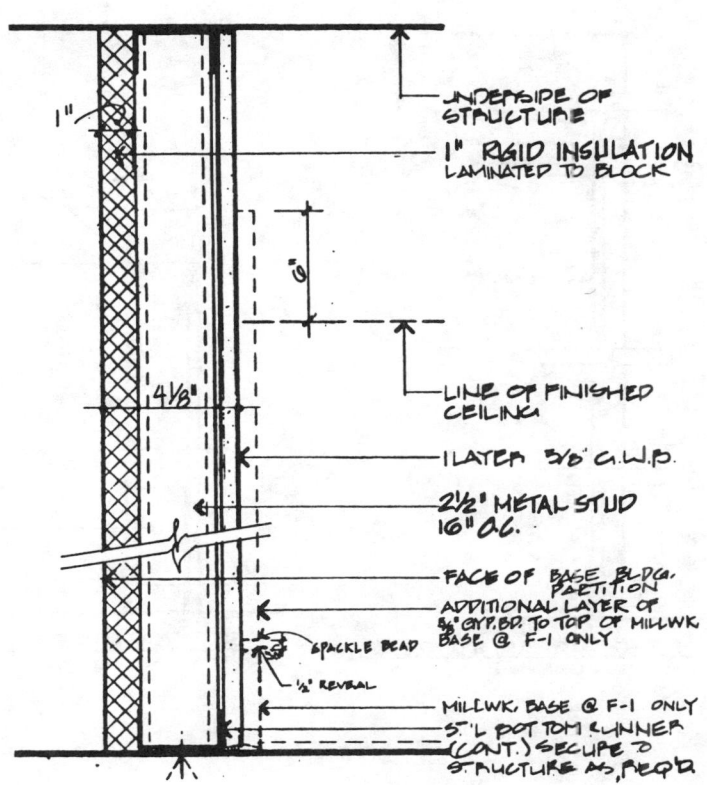

Metal stud and gypsum board: underside of ceiling

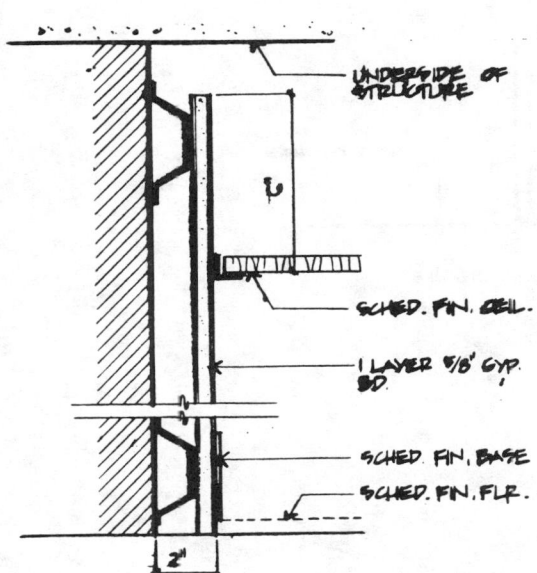

Metal channels and gypsum board: wall furring

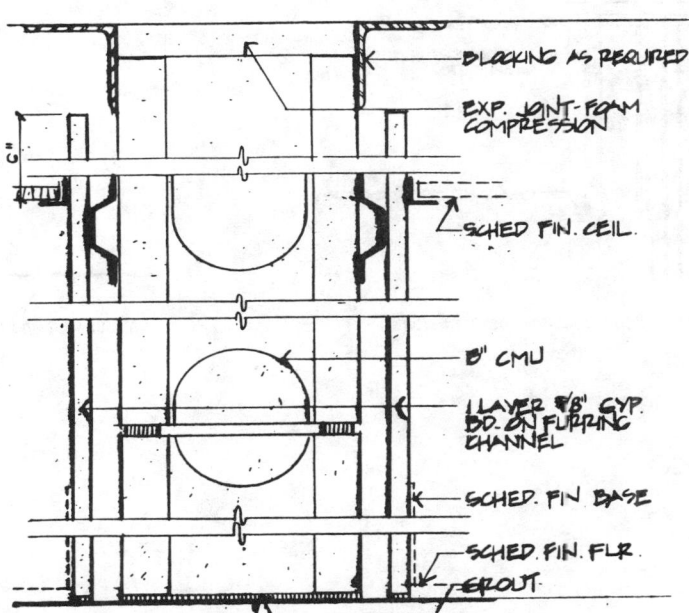

Construction Details and Finishes

PARTITIONS AND WALL FINISHES
Metal Stud and Gypsum Board

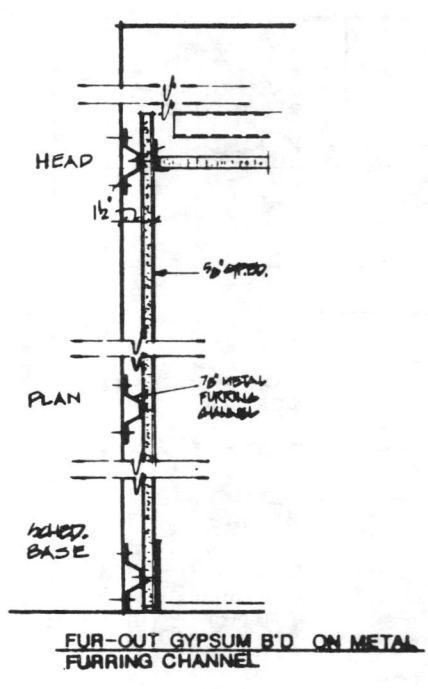

FUR-OUT GYPSUM B'D ON METAL
FURRING CHANNEL

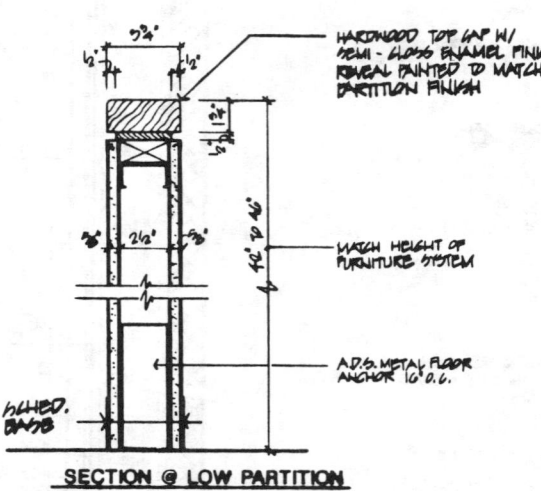

SECTION @ LOW PARTITION

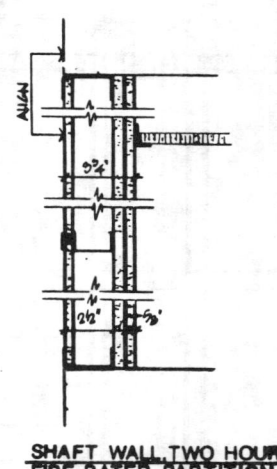

SHAFT WALL, TWO HOUR
FIRE RATED PARTITION

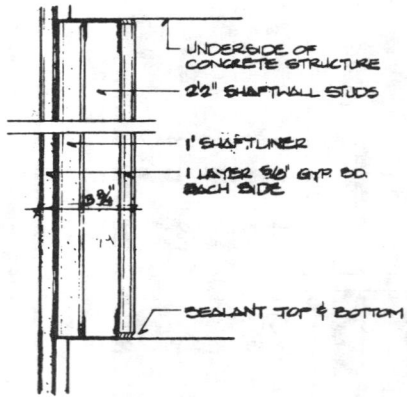

Metal stud and gypsum board: shaftwall

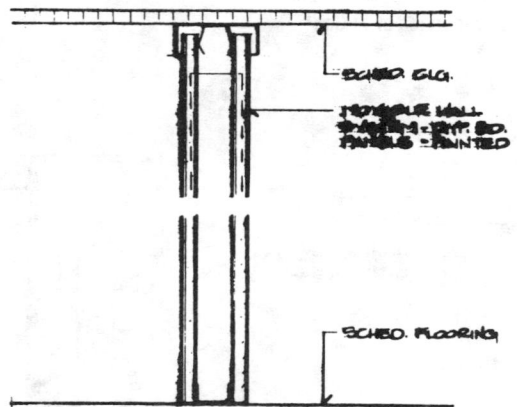

Metal stud and gypsum board: movable

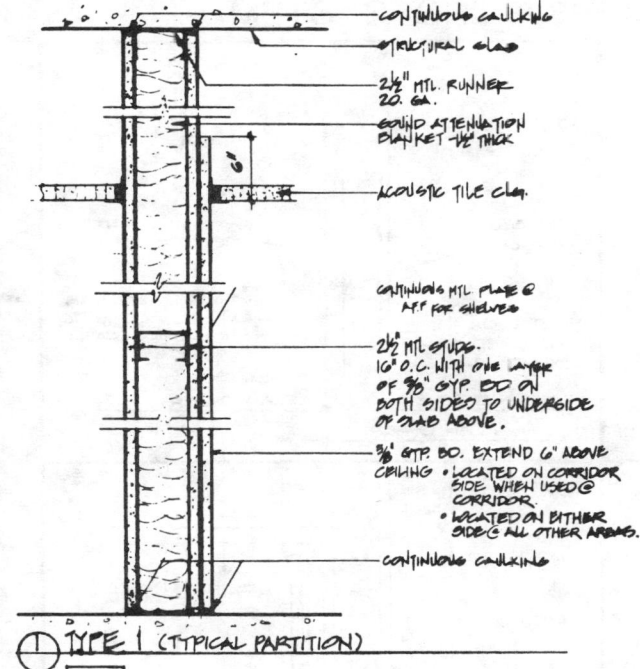

CONTINUOUS CAULKING
STRUCTURAL SLAB
2½" MTL. RUNNER 20. GA.
SOUND ATTENUATION BLANKET-1½" THICK
ACOUSTIC TILE CLG.
CONTINUOUS MTL. PLATE @ A.F.F. FOR SHELVES
2½" MTL. STUDS. 16" O.C. WITH ONE LAYER OF ⅝" GYP. BD. ON BOTH SIDES TO UNDERSIDE OF SLAB ABOVE.
⅝" GYP. BD. EXTEND 6" ABOVE CEILING
• LOCATED ON CORRIDOR SIDE WHEN USED @ CORRIDOR.
• LOCATED ON EITHER SIDE @ ALL OTHER AREAS.
CONTINUOUS CAULKING

① TYPE 1 (TYPICAL PARTITION)

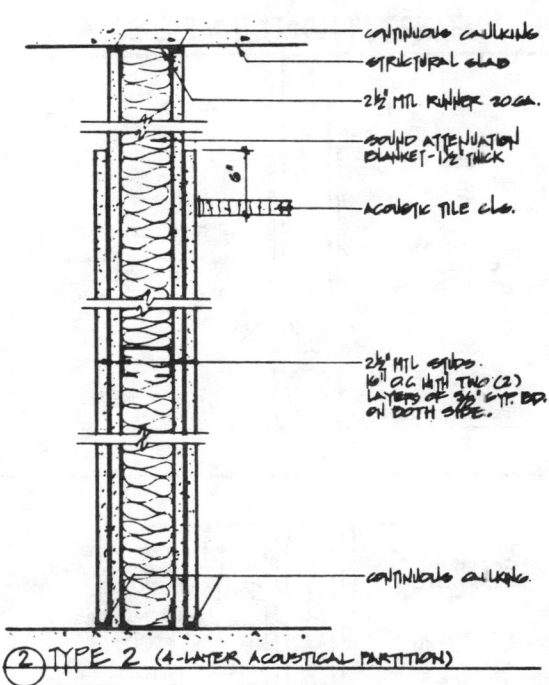

CONTINUOUS CAULKING
STRUCTURAL SLAB
2½" MTL. RUNNER 20 GA.
SOUND ATTENUATION BLANKET-1½" THICK
ACOUSTIC TILE CLG.
2½" MTL. STUDS. 16" O.C. WITH TWO (2) LAYERS OF ⅝" GYP. BD. ON BOTH SIDE.
CONTINUOUS CAULKING.

② TYPE 2 (4-LAYER ACOUSTICAL PARTITION)

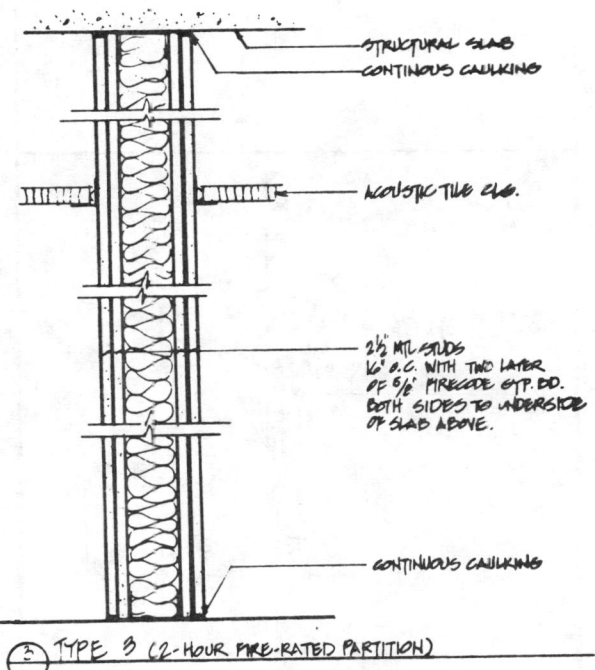

STRUCTURAL SLAB
CONTINUOUS CAULKING
ACOUSTIC TILE CLG.
2½" MTL. STUDS 16" O.C. WITH TWO LAYER OF ⅝" FIRECODE GYP. BD. BOTH SIDES TO UNDERSIDE OF SLAB ABOVE.
CONTINUOUS CAULKING

③ TYPE 3 (2-HOUR FIRE-RATED PARTITION)

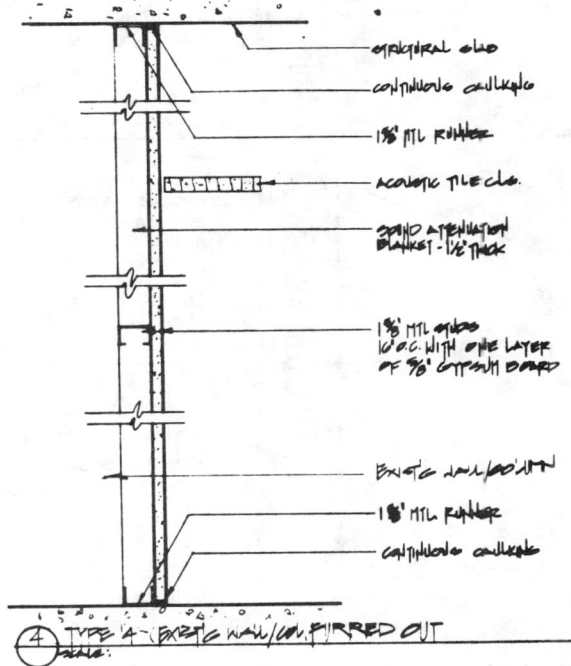

STRUCTURAL SLAB
CONTINUOUS CAULKING
1⅝" MTL. RUNNER
ACOUSTIC TILE CLG.
SOUND ATTENUATION BLANKET-1½" THICK
1⅝" MTL. STUDS 16" O.C. WITH ONE LAYER OF ⅝" GYPSUM BOARD
EXIST'G WALL/COLUMN
1⅝" MTL. RUNNER
CONTINUOUS CAULKING

④ TYPE 4 - EXIST'G WALL/COL. FURRED OUT
SCALE:

PARTITIONS AND WALL FINISHES
Metal Stud and Gypsum Board

PARTITION TYPES AND DIMENSIONING SYSTEM

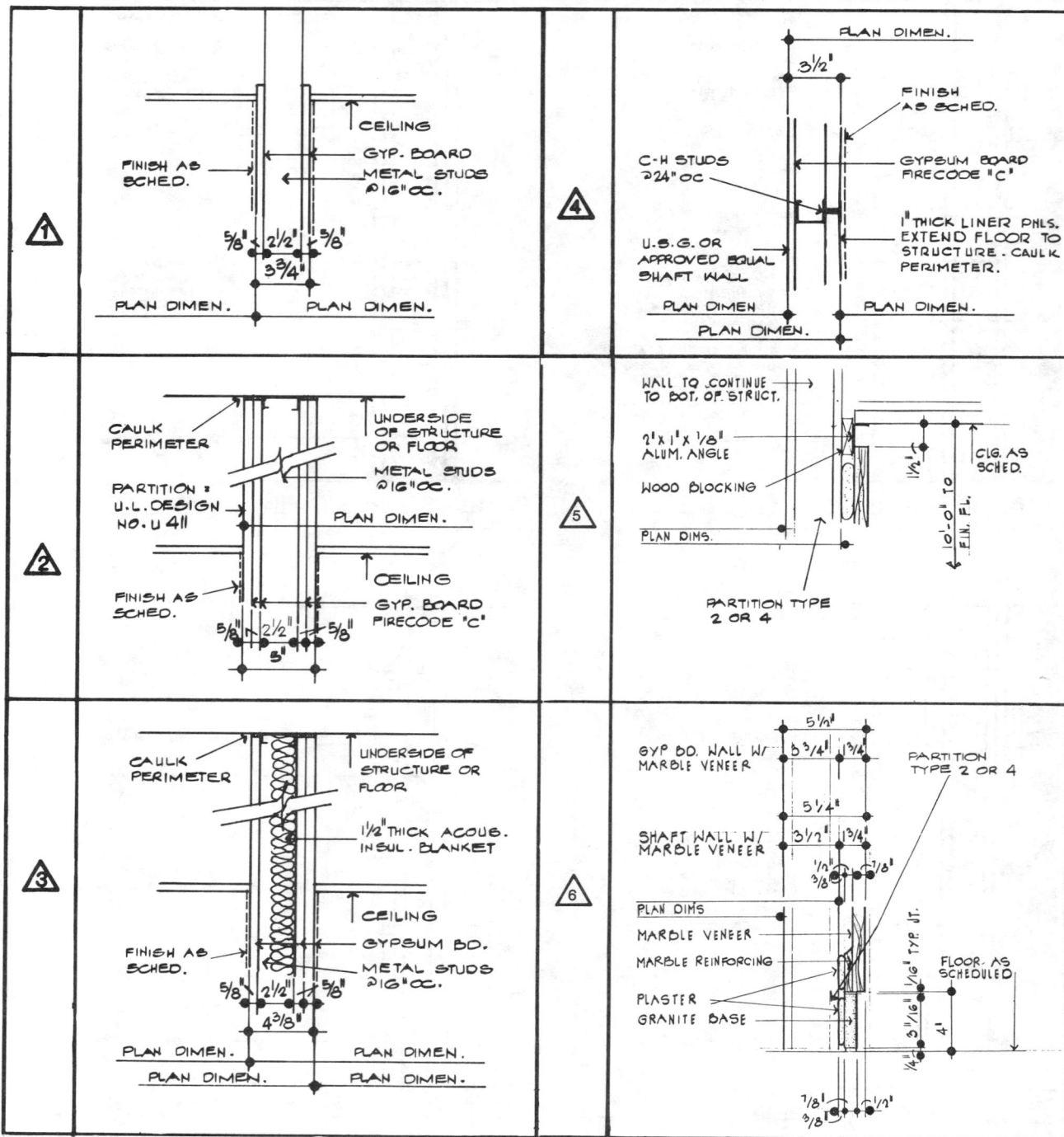

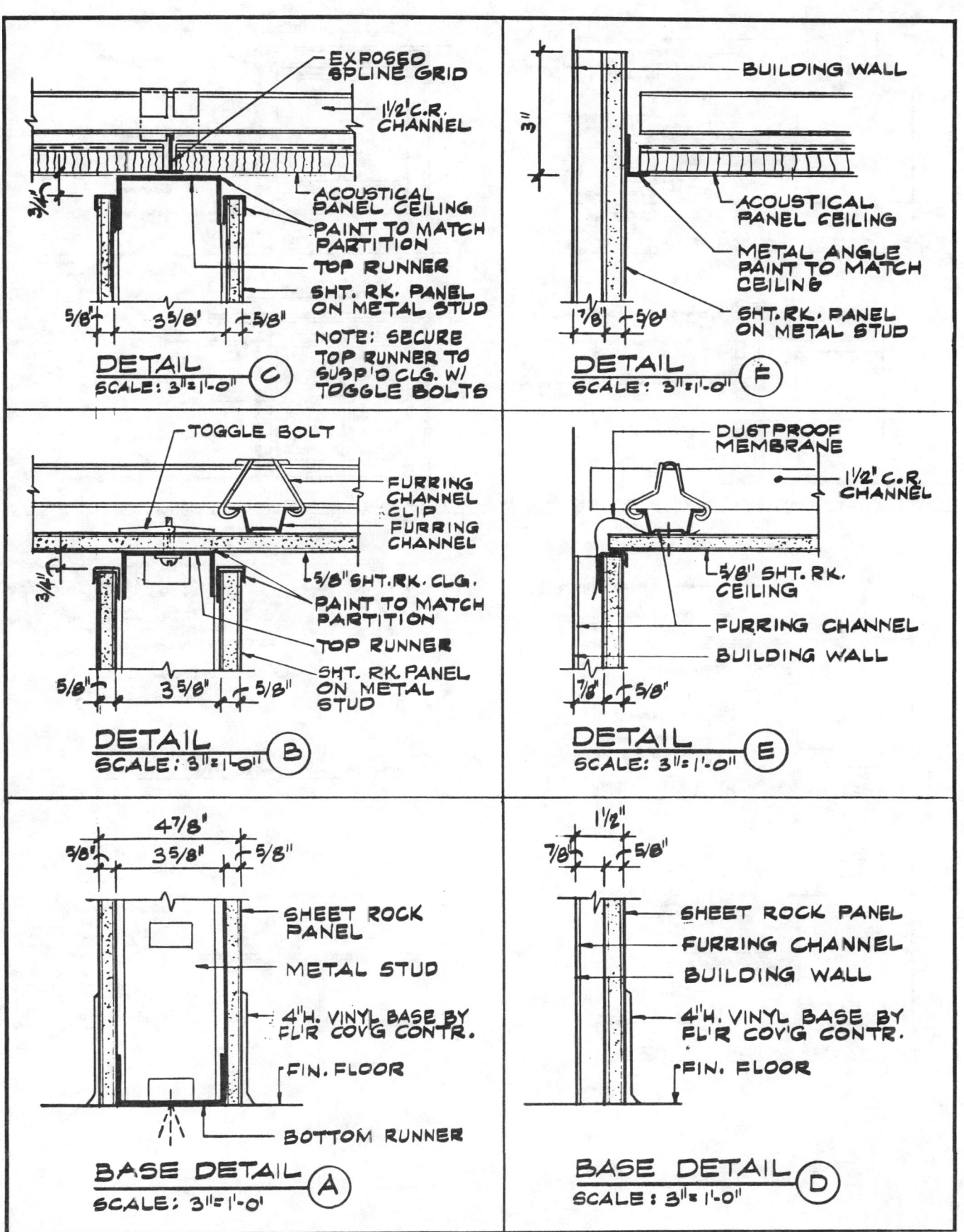

EXPOSED SPLINE GRID

1 1/2' C.R. CHANNEL

ACOUSTICAL PANEL CEILING

PAINT TO MATCH PARTITION

TOP RUNNER

SHT. RK. PANEL ON METAL STUD

NOTE: SECURE TOP RUNNER TO SUSP'D CLG. W/ TOGGLE BOLTS

5/8" 3 5/8' 5/8"

DETAIL C
SCALE: 3"=1'-0"

BUILDING WALL

3"

ACOUSTICAL PANEL CEILING

METAL ANGLE PAINT TO MATCH CEILING

SHT. RK. PANEL ON METAL STUD

7/8' 5/8'

DETAIL F
SCALE: 3"=1'-0"

TOGGLE BOLT

FURRING CHANNEL CLIP

FURRING CHANNEL

5/8"SHT.RK. CLG.

PAINT TO MATCH PARTITION

TOP RUNNER

SHT. RK. PANEL ON METAL STUD

3/4"

5/8"C 3 5/8" 5/8"

DETAIL B
SCALE: 3"=1'-0"

DUSTPROOF MEMBRANE

1 1/2' C.R. CHANNEL

5/8" SHT. RK. CEILING

FURRING CHANNEL

BUILDING WALL

7/8' 5/8"

DETAIL E
SCALE: 3"=1'-0"

4 7/8"

3 5/8"

5/8" 5/8"

SHEET ROCK PANEL

METAL STUD

4"H. VINYL BASE BY FL'R COV'G CONTR.

FIN. FLOOR

BOTTOM RUNNER

BASE DETAIL A
SCALE: 3"=1'-0"

1 1/2"

7/8' 5/8"

SHEET ROCK PANEL

FURRING CHANNEL

BUILDING WALL

4"H. VINYL BASE BY FL'R COV'G CONTR.

FIN. FLOOR

BASE DETAIL D
SCALE: 3"=1'-0"

PARTITIONS AND WALL FINISHES
Metal Stud and Gypsum Board Details

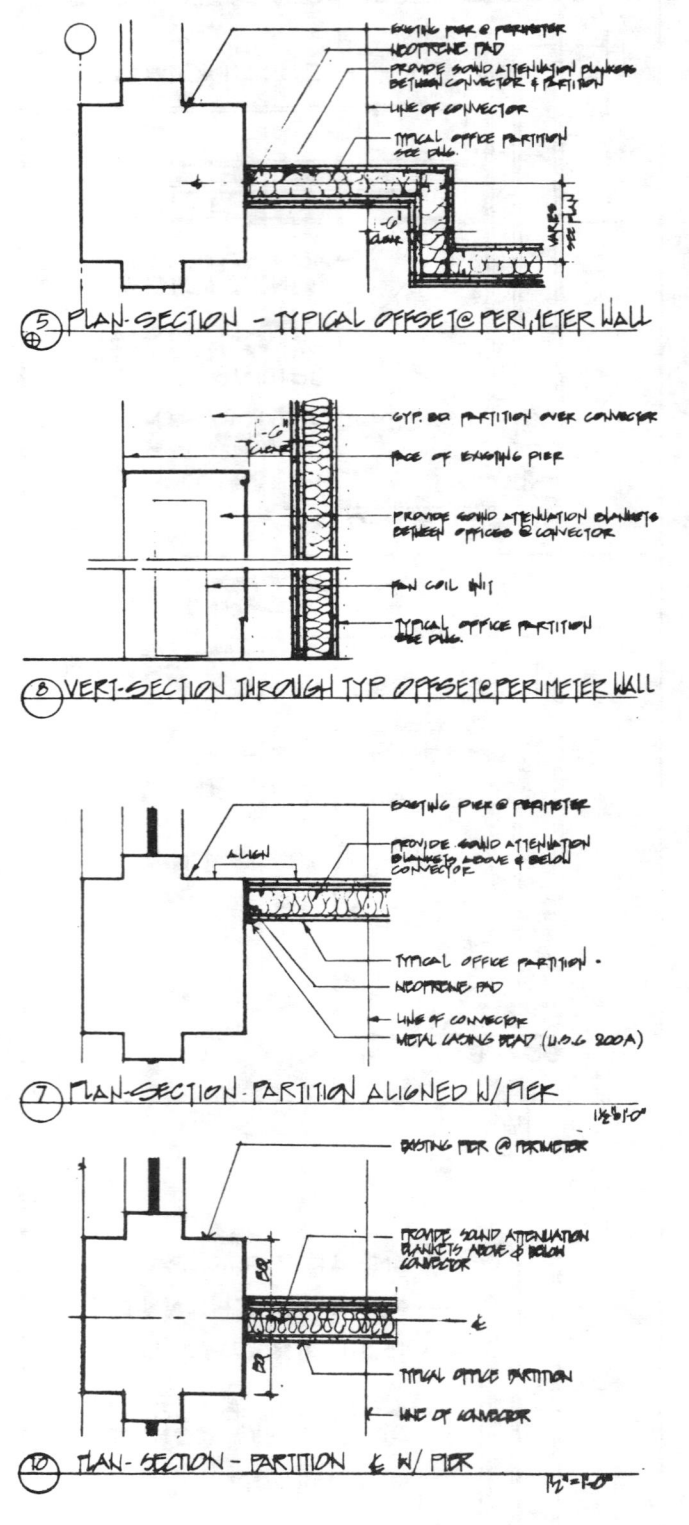

⑤ PLAN-SECTION - TYPICAL OFFSET @ PERIMETER WALL

⑧ VERT-SECTION THROUGH TYP. OFFSET @ PERIMETER WALL

⑦ PLAN-SECTION-PARTITION ALIGNED W/ PIER

⑩ PLAN-SECTION - PARTITION ℄ W/ PIER

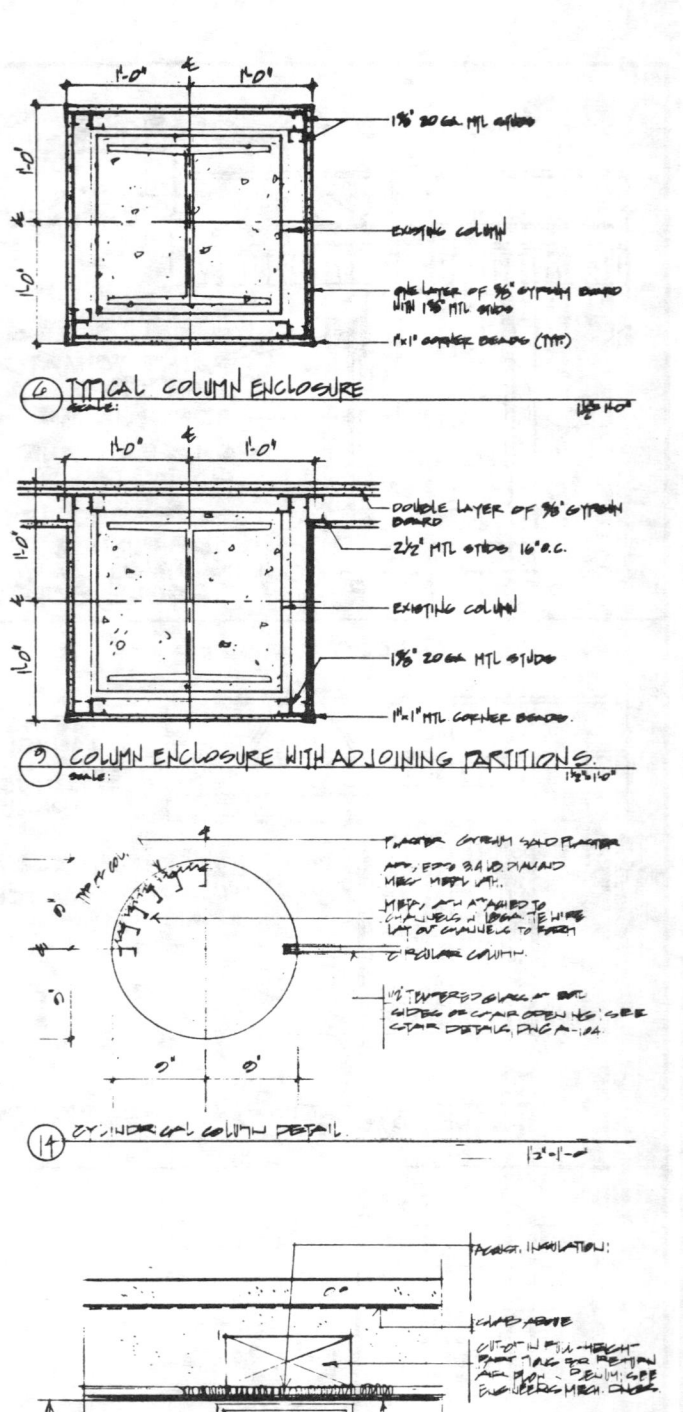

⑥ TYPICAL COLUMN ENCLOSURE

⑨ COLUMN ENCLOSURE WITH ADJOINING PARTITIONS.

⑭ CYLINDRICAL COLUMN DETAIL

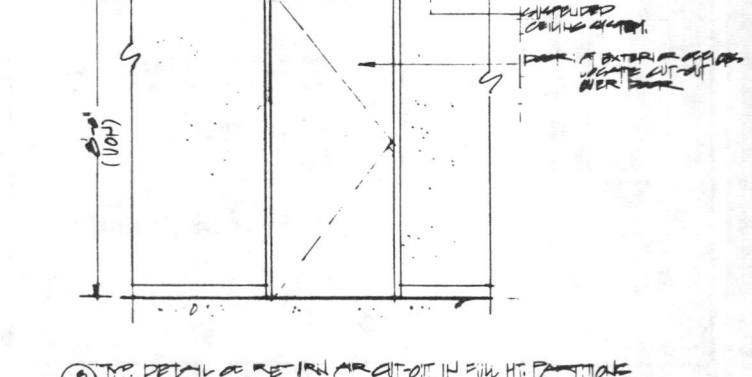

⑨ TYP. DETAIL OF RETURN AIR CUT-OUT IN FULL HT. PARTITION

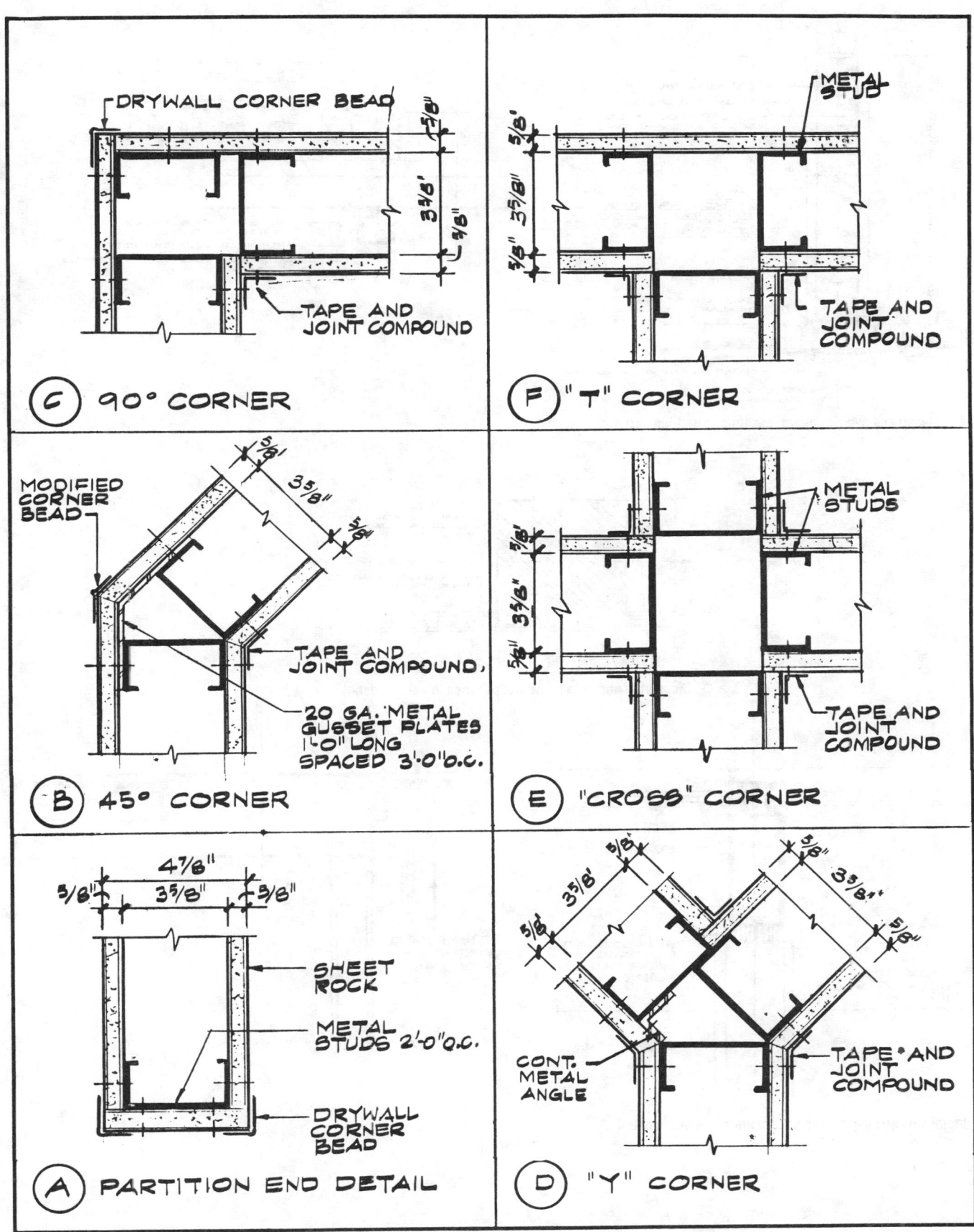

C 90° CORNER

- DRYWALL CORNER BEAD
- 5/8"
- 3 5/8"
- 5/8"
- TAPE AND JOINT COMPOUND

F "T" CORNER

- METAL STUD
- 5/8"
- 3 5/8"
- 5/8"
- TAPE AND JOINT COMPOUND

B 45° CORNER

- MODIFIED CORNER BEAD
- 5/8"
- 3 5/8"
- 5/8"
- TAPE AND JOINT COMPOUND
- 20 GA. METAL GUSSET PLATES 1'-0" LONG SPACED 3'-0" O.C.

E "CROSS" CORNER

- METAL STUDS
- 5/8"
- 3 5/8"
- 5/8"
- TAPE AND JOINT COMPOUND

A PARTITION END DETAIL

- 4 7/8"
- 5/8" 3 5/8" 5/8"
- SHEET ROCK
- METAL STUDS 2'-0" O.C.
- DRYWALL CORNER BEAD

D "Y" CORNER

- 5/8"
- 3 5/8"
- 5/8"
- 3 5/8"
- 5/8"
- CONT. METAL ANGLE
- TAPE AND JOINT COMPOUND

PARTITIONS AND WALL FINISHES

Metal Stud and Gypsum Board: Partition Conditions

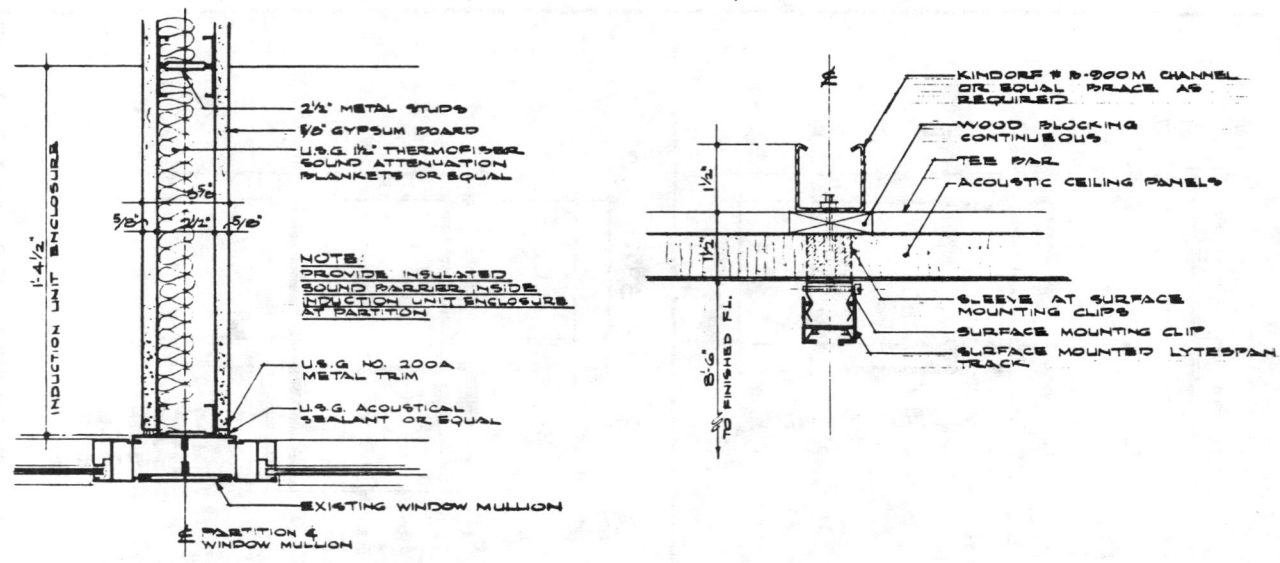

Metal stud and gypsum board: partition to mullion detail

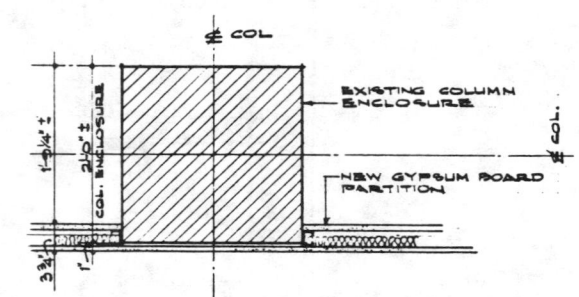

Metal stud and gypsum board: partition to column detail

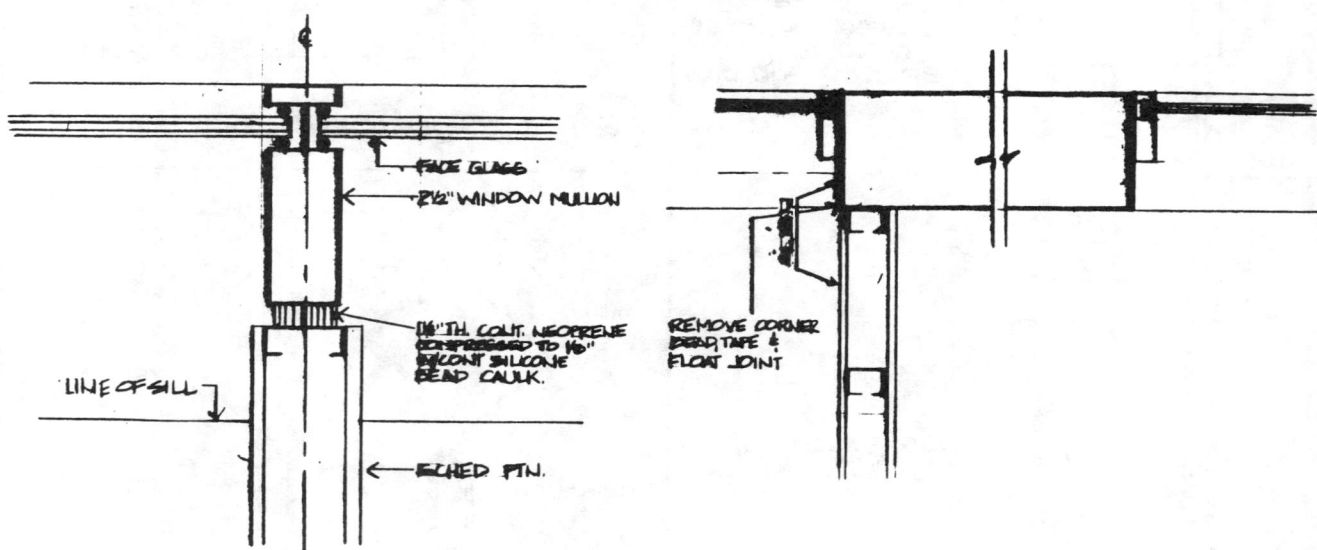

Metal stud and gypsum board: partition to mullion detail

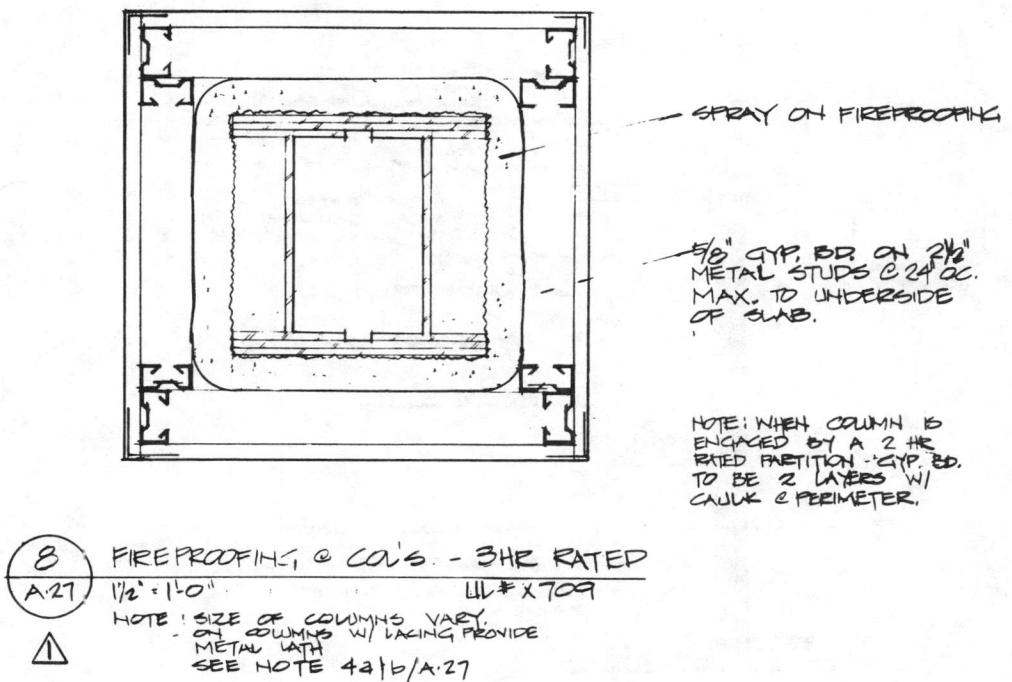

- SPRAY ON FIREPROOFING

- 5/8" GYP. BD. ON 2½"
METAL STUDS @ 24" O.C.
MAX. TO UNDERSIDE
OF SLAB.

NOTE: WHEN COLUMN IS
ENGAGED BY A 2 HR
RATED PARTITION - GYP. BD.
TO BE 2 LAYERS W/
CAULK @ PERIMETER.

⑧ FIREPROOFING @ COL'S. - 3HR RATED
A.27   1½" = 1'-0"   UL# X 709
⚠   NOTE: SIZE OF COLUMNS VARY.
        - ON COLUMNS W/ LACING PROVIDE
        METAL LATH
        SEE NOTE 4a|b/A.27

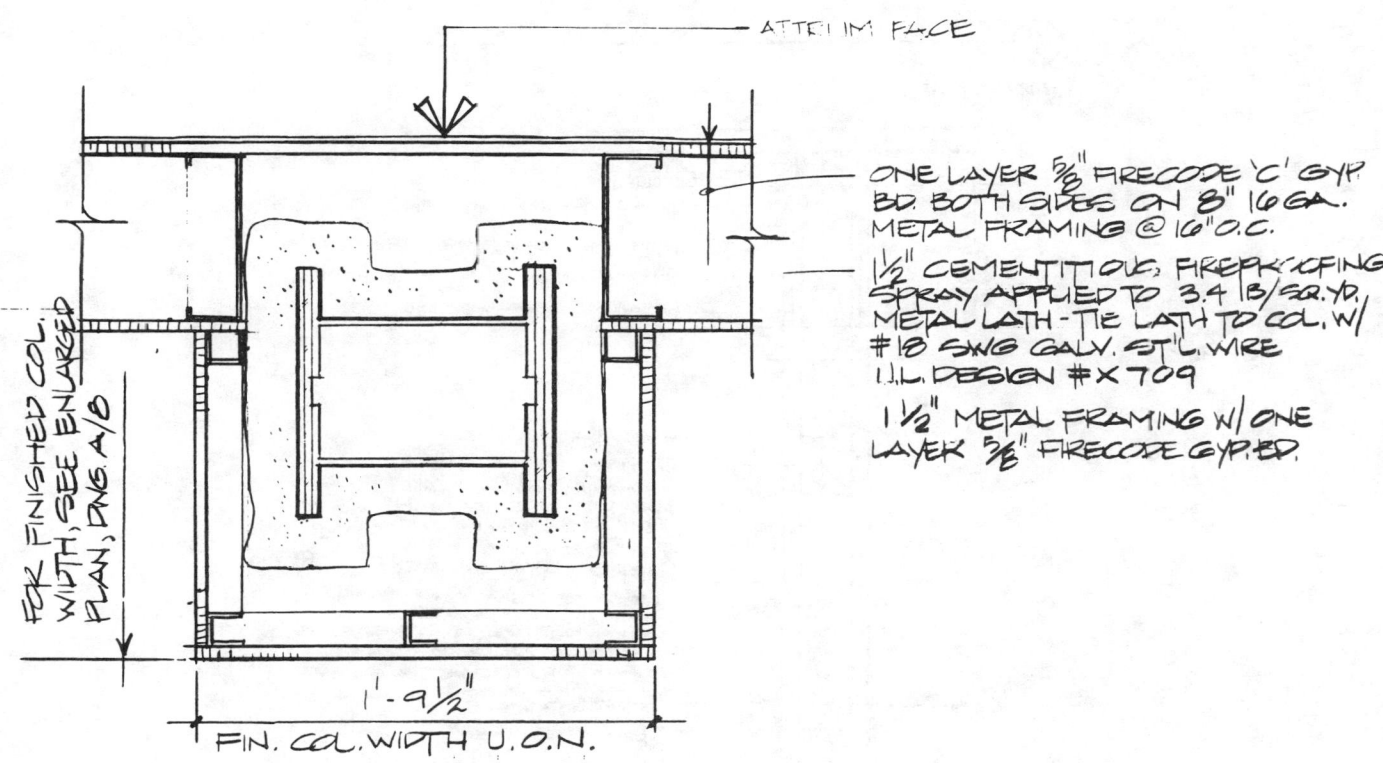

- ATRIUM FACE

- ONE LAYER 5/8" FIRECODE 'C' GYP.
BD. BOTH SIDES ON 8" 16 GA.
METAL FRAMING @ 16" O.C.

- 1½" CEMENTITIOUS FIREPROOFING
SPRAY APPLIED TO 3.4 LB/SQ.YD.
METAL LATH - TIE LATH TO COL. W/
#18 SWG GALV. ST'L. WIRE
U.L. DESIGN # X 709

- 1½" METAL FRAMING W/ ONE
LAYER 5/8" FIRECODE GYP. BD.

FOR FINISHED COL.
WIDTH, SEE ENLARGED
PLAN, DWG. A/B

1'-9½"

FIN. COL. WIDTH U.O.N.

⑨ TYPICAL COL. FIREPROOFING @
A.27 PERIMETER OF ATRIUM

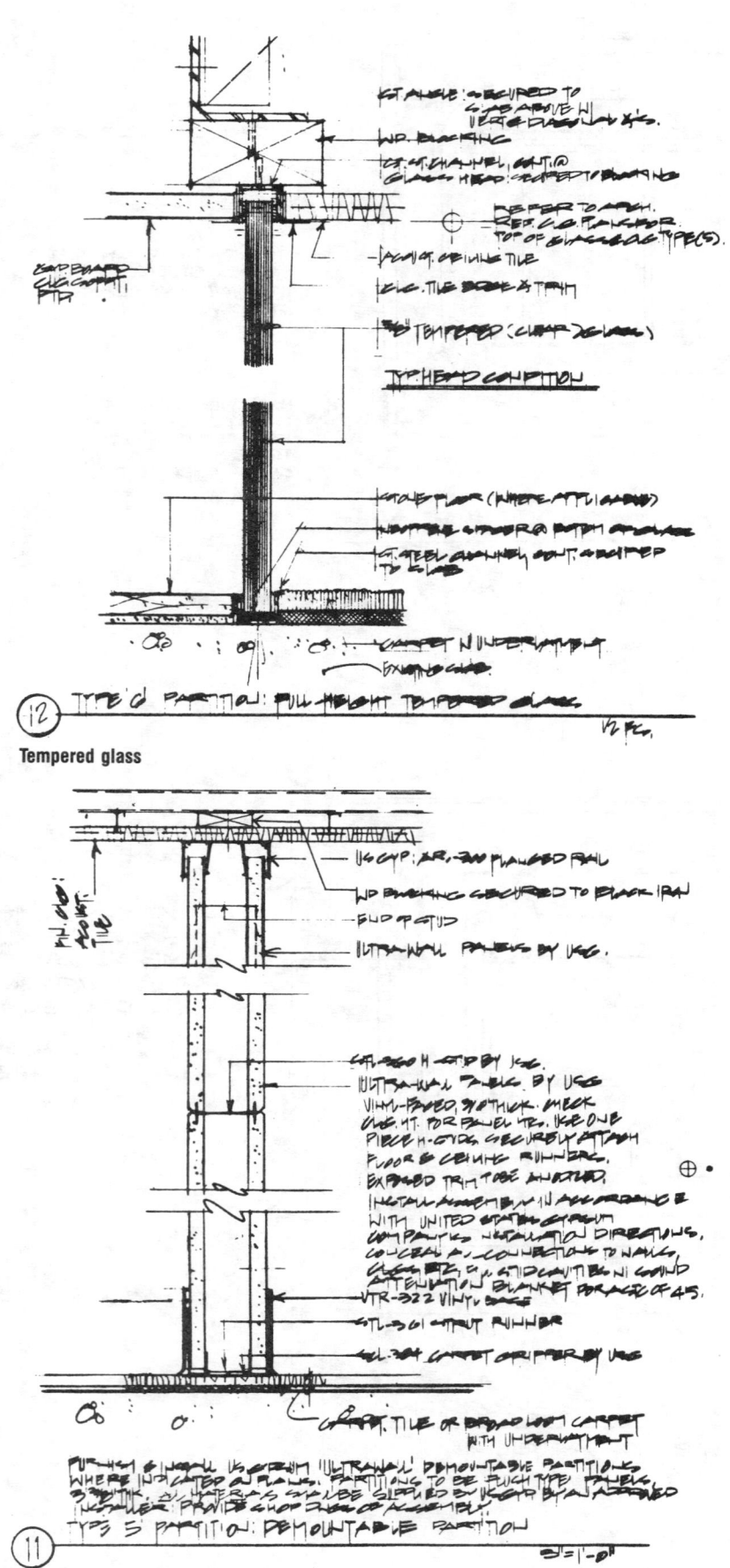

Tempered glass

Demountable

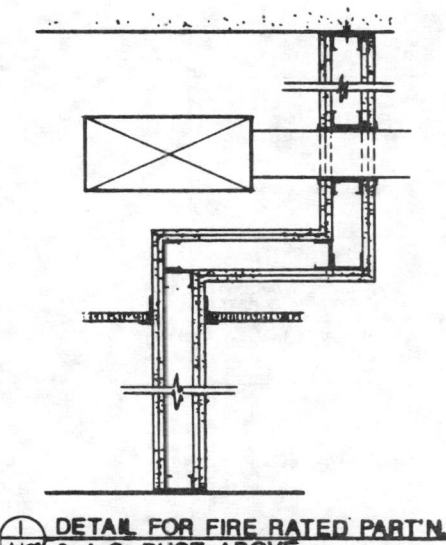

① DETAIL FOR FIRE RATED PART'N
   & A.C. DUCT ABOVE

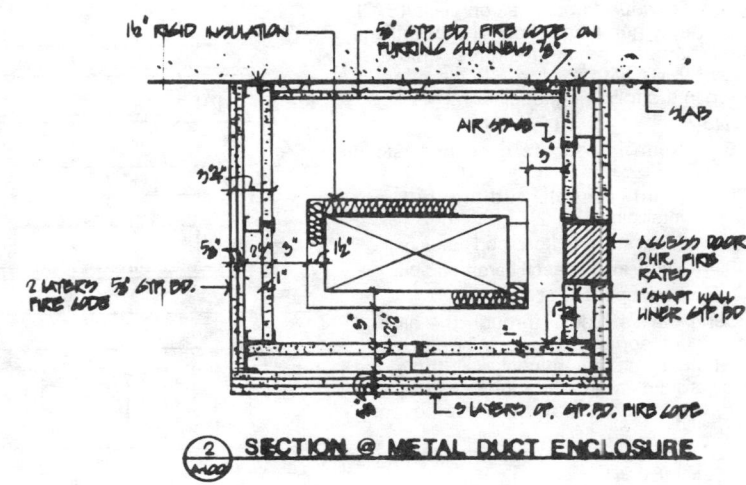

② SECTION @ METAL DUCT ENCLOSURE

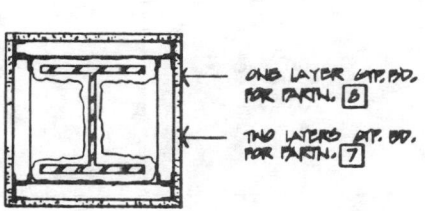

③ COLUMN FURRING

- ONE LAYER GYP. BD. FOR PART'N. ⑥
- TWO LAYERS GYP. BD. FOR PART'N. ⑦

NOTES:
1. DUCT ENCLOSURE TO EXTEND FOR 20' DISTANCE FROM FAN ROOM
2. MAINTAIN ½" MIN. CLEARANCE BETWEEN DUCT AND 1⅝" METAL STUDS.

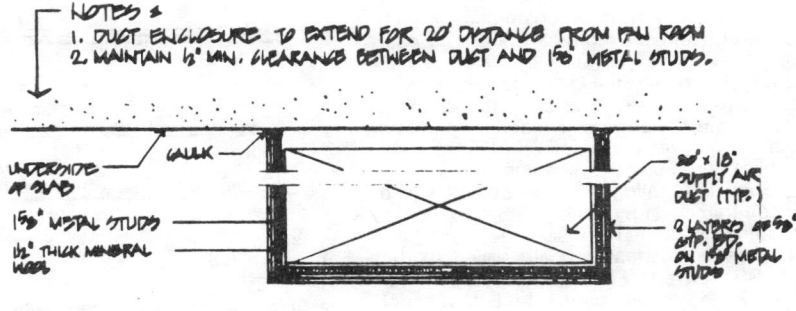

④ SECTION AT SUPPLY AIR DUCT ENCLOSURE

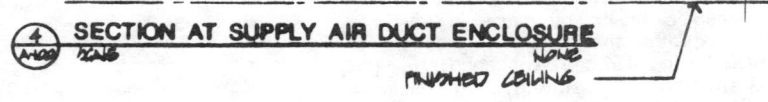

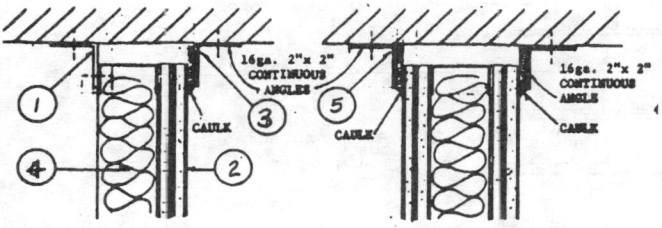

SEQUENCE OF CONSTRUCTION

STEP ① FASTEN TEMPORARY 2" x 2" ANGLE TO SLAB. FASTEN TOP RUNNER OF PARTITION TO TEMPORARY ANGLE AND ERECT STUDS. (MAINTAIN 1" AIR SPACE BETWEEN RUNNER AND SLAB.)

STEP ② APPLY GYPSUM BOARD LAYER(S) TO ONE SIDE OF STUDS.

STEP ③ FASTEN 2" x 2" CONTINUOUS ANGLE (WITH ¼" FELT GLUED TO SIDE) TO SLAB ONLY (DO NOT SECURE STUDS TO THIS ANGLE).

STEP ④ INSTALL USG SAB MINERAL WOOL BETWEEN STUDS.

STEP ⑤ REMOVE TEMPORARY ANGLE AND REPLACE WITH 2" x 2" CONTINUOUS ANGLE (WITH ¼" FELT GLUED TO SIDE). FASTEN THIS ANGLE TO SLAB ONLY.

⑤ "SOFT" TERMINATION OF PARTITIONS

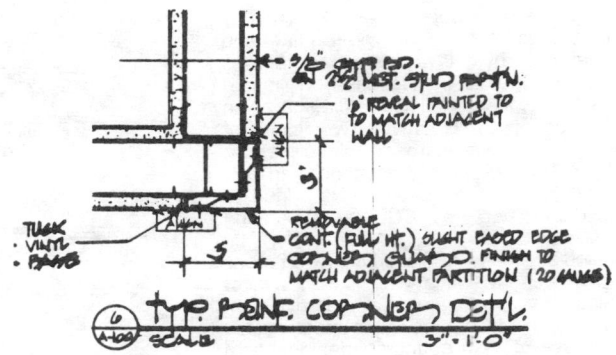

⑥ TYP. PHONE CORNER DET'L.

PARTITIONS AND WALL FINISHES

Sound Insulation and Transmission

The resistance of a building element, such as a wall, to the passage of airborne sound is rated by its *sound transmission class* (STC). Thus, the higher the number, the better the sound barrier. The approximate effectiveness of walls with varying STC numbers is shown in the following tabulation:

STC No.	Effectiveness
25	Normal speech can be understood quite easily
35	Loud speech audible but not intelligible
45	Must strain to hear loud speech
48	Some loud speech barely audible
50	Loud speech not audible

Sound travels readily through the air and also through some materials. When airborne sound strikes a conventional wall, the studs act as sound conductors unless they are separated in some way from the covering material.

Wall Construction

As the preceding STC tabulation shows, a wall providing sufficient resistance to airborne sound transfer likely has an STC rating of 45 or greater. Thus, in construction of such a wall between the rooms of a house, its cost as related to the STC rating should be considered. As shown in Fig. 5, details *A*, with gypsum wallboard, and *B*, with plastered wall, are those commonly used for partition walls. However, the hypothetical rating of 45 cannot be obtained in this construction.

Good STC ratings can be obtained in a wood-frame wall by using the combination of materials shown in Fig. 5D and E. One-half-inch sound-deadening board nailed to the studs, followed by a lamination of ½-in gypsum wallboard, will provide an STC value of 46 at a relatively low cost. A slightly better rating can be obtained by using ⅝-in gypsum wallboard rather than ½-in. A very satisfactory STC rating of 52 can be obtained by using resilient clips to fasten gypsum backer boards to the studs, followed by adhesive-laminated ½-in fiberboard (Fig. 5E). This method further isolates the wall covering from the framing.

A similar isolation system consists of resilient channels nailed horizontally to 2- by 4-in studs spaced 16 in on center. Channels are spaced 24 in apart vertically and ⅝-in gypsum wallboard is screwed to the channels. An STC rating of 47 is thus obtained at a moderately low cost.

Thus use of a double wall, which may consist of a 2 by 6 or wider plate and staggered 2- by 4-in studs, is sometimes desirable. One-half-inch gypsum wallboard on each side of this wall (Fig. 6A) results in an STC value of 45. However, two layers of ⅝-in gypsum wallboard add little, if any, additional sound-transfer resistance (Fig. 6B). When 1½-in blanket insulation is added to this construction (Fig. 6C), the STC rating increases to 49. This insulation may be installed as shown or placed between studs on one wall. A single wall with 3½ in of insulation will show a marked improvement over an open stud space and is low in cost.

The use of ½-in sound-deadening board and a lamination of gypsum wallboard in the double wall will result in an STC rating of 50 (Fig. 6D). The addition of blanket insulation to this combination will likely provide an even higher value, perhaps 53 or 54.

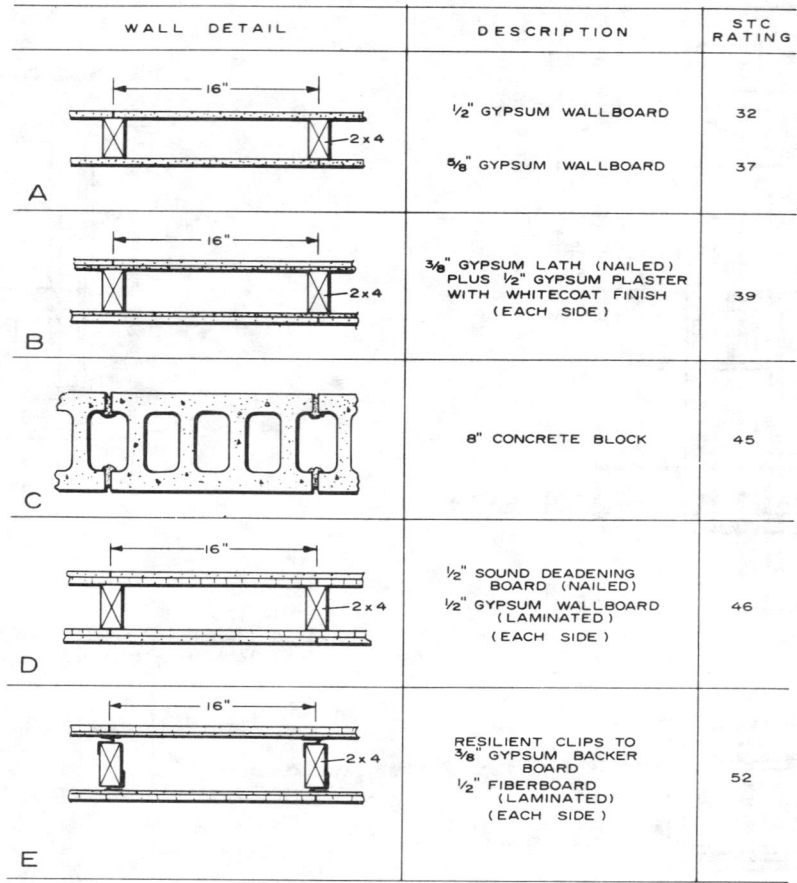

WALL DETAIL	DESCRIPTION	STC RATING
A	½" GYPSUM WALLBOARD	32
	⅝" GYPSUM WALLBOARD	37
B	⅜" GYPSUM LATH (NAILED) PLUS ½" GYPSUM PLASTER WITH WHITECOAT FINISH (EACH SIDE)	39
C	8" CONCRETE BLOCK	45
D	½" SOUND DEADENING BOARD (NAILED) ½" GYPSUM WALLBOARD (LAMINATED) (EACH SIDE)	46
E	RESILIENT CLIPS TO ⅜" GYPSUM BACKER BOARD ½" FIBERBOARD (LAMINATED) (EACH SIDE)	52

Fig. 5   Sound insulation of single walls.

WALL DETAIL	DESCRIPTION	STC RATING
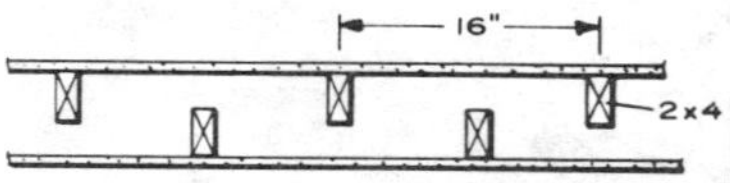 A	½" GYPSUM WALLBOARD	45
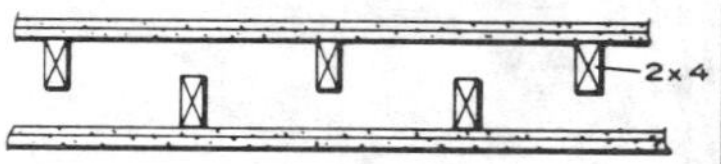 B	⅝" GYPSUM WALLBOARD (DOUBLE LAYER EACH SIDE)	45
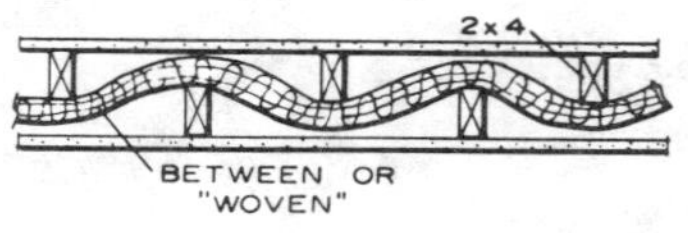 C	½" GYPSUM WALLBOARD 1½" FIBROUS INSULATION BETWEEN OR "WOVEN"	49
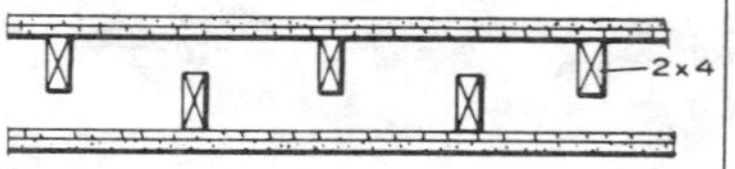 D	½" SOUND DEADENING BOARD (NAILED) ½" GYPSUM WALLBOARD (LAMINATED)	50

Fig. 6   Sound insulation of double walls.

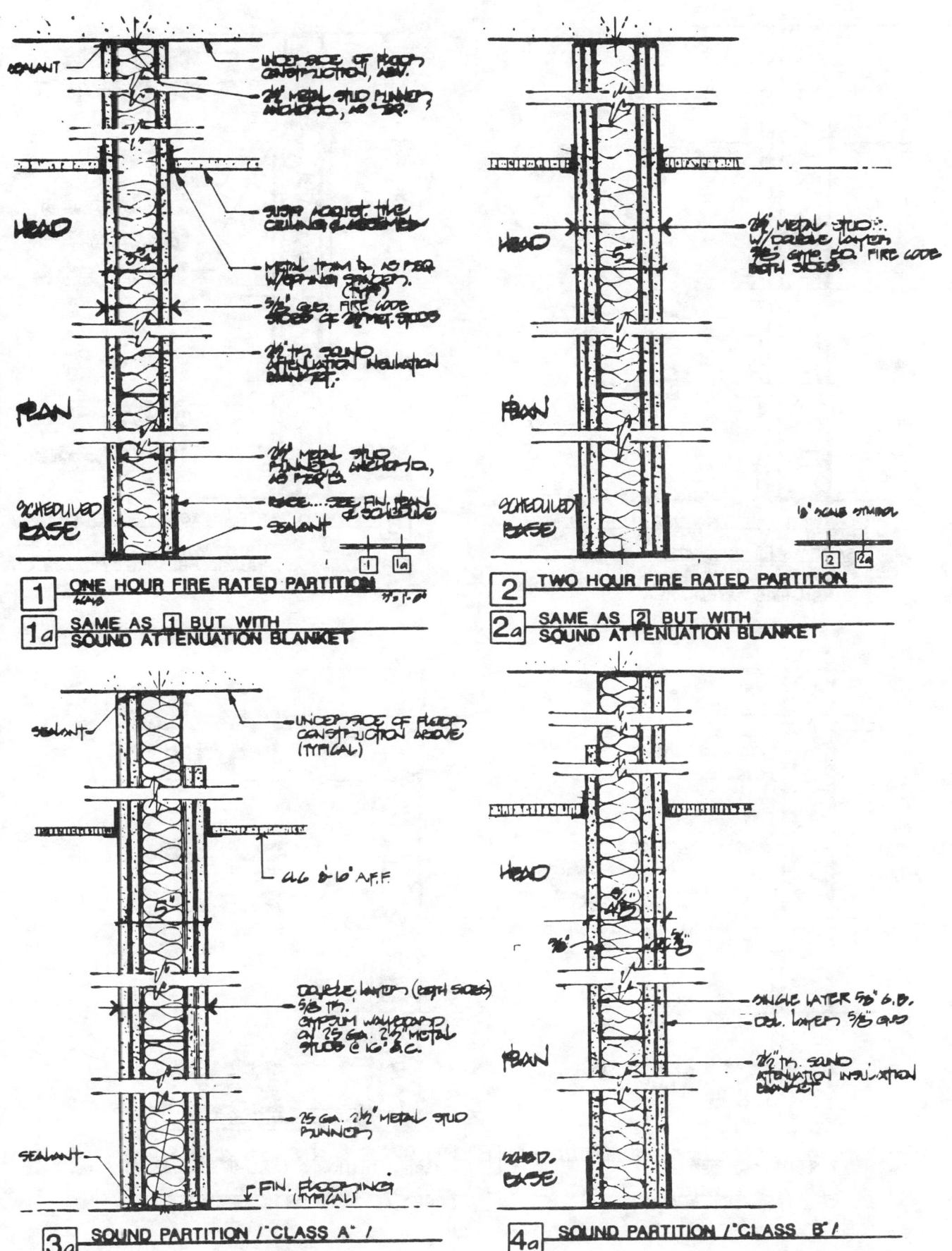

SEALANT

UNDERSIDE OF FLOOR CONSTRUCTION, ABV.

2½" METAL STUD RUNNER, ANCHORED, AS REQ.

HEAD

SUSP. ACOUST. TILE CEILING ASSEMBLY

METAL TRIM @ AS REQ. W/OPENING SPACE (TYP.)

5/8" GYP. FIRE CODE STUDS @ 24 MET. STUDS

2½" TH. SOUND ATTENUATION INSULATION BLANKET

PLAN

2½" METAL STUD RUNNER, ANCHORED, AS PER PL.

SCHEDULED BASE

BASE....SEE FIN. PLAN & SCHEDULE

SEALANT

1 ONE HOUR FIRE RATED PARTITION
HEAD

1a SAME AS **1** BUT WITH SOUND ATTENUATION BLANKET

HEAD

2½" METAL STUD W/ DOUBLE LAYER 5/8" GYP. BD. FIRE CODE BOTH SIDES.

PLAN

SCHEDULED BASE

½" SCALE SYMBOL

2 TWO HOUR FIRE RATED PARTITION

2a SAME AS **2** BUT WITH SOUND ATTENUATION BLANKET

SEALANT

UNDERSIDE OF FLOOR CONSTRUCTION ABOVE (TYPICAL)

CLG 8'-10' A.F.F.

DOUBLE LAYER (BOTH SIDES) 5/8" TH. GYPSUM WALLBOARD ON 25 GA. 2½" METAL STUDS @ 16' O.C.

25 GA. 2½" METAL STUD RUNNER

SEALANT

FIN. FLOORING (TYPICAL)

3a SOUND PARTITION /"CLASS A"/

HEAD

PLAN

SINGLE LAYER 5/8" G.B. ADD. LAYER 5/8" GYP.B.

2½" TH. SOUND ATTENUATION INSULATION BLANKET

SCHED. BASE

4a SOUND PARTITION /"CLASS B"/

PARTITIONS AND WALL FINISHES
Acoustical and Fire-Rated Metal Stud and Gypsum Board

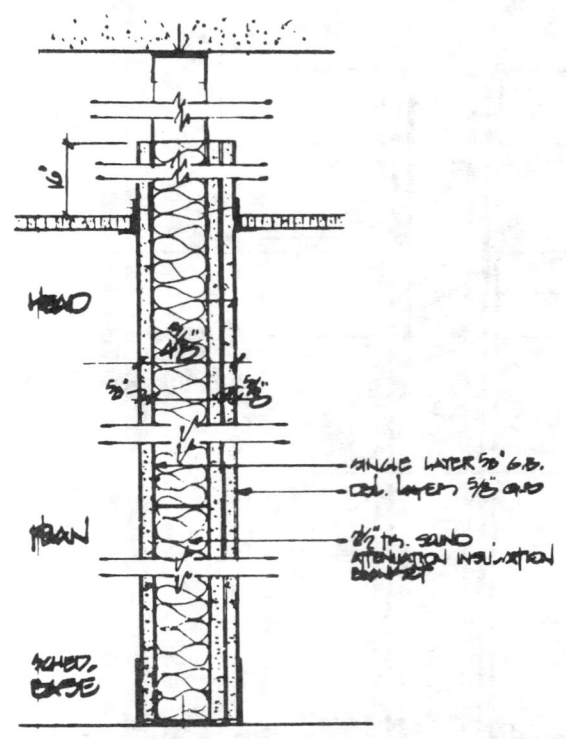

HEAD

PLAN

SCHED.
BASE

SINGLE LAYER 5/8" G.B.
DBL. LAYER 5/8" GYPD

2½" TH. SOUND
ATTENUATION INSULATION
BLANKET

5 DRYWALL PARTITION, USE TO ALIGN WITH
PARTITION **2** @ NON-FIRE RATED AREA

5a SAME AS **5** BUT WITH
SOUND ATTENUATION BLANKET
USE TO ALIGN WITH PARTITION **2a** & **3a**
@ NON-FIRE RATED AREA

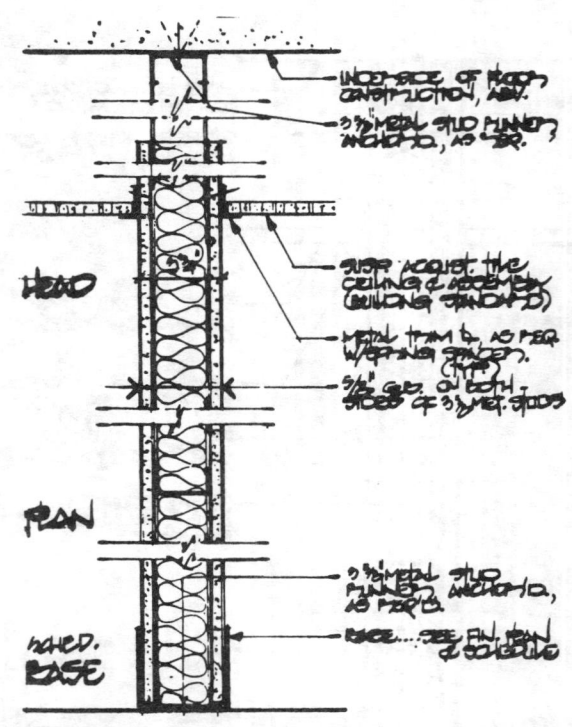

HEAD

PLAN

SCHED.
BASE

UNDERSIDE OF FLOOR
CONSTRUCTION, ABV.

2½" METAL STUD RUNNER
ANCHOR'D, AS REQ.

SUSP. ACOUST. TILE
CEILING & ASSEMBLY
(BUILDING STANDARD)

METAL TRIM D. AS REQ.
W/ STRIPPING SPACERS (TYP.)

5/8" G.B. ON BOTH
SIDES OF 3½" MET. STUDS

2½" METAL STUD
RUNNER ANCHOR'D,
AS REQ'D.

BASE....SEE FIN. PLAN
& SCHEDULE

6 DRYWALL PARTITION TO 6" ABOVE CEILING

6a SAME AS **6** BUT WITH
SOUND ATTENUATION BLANKET / "CLASS C"

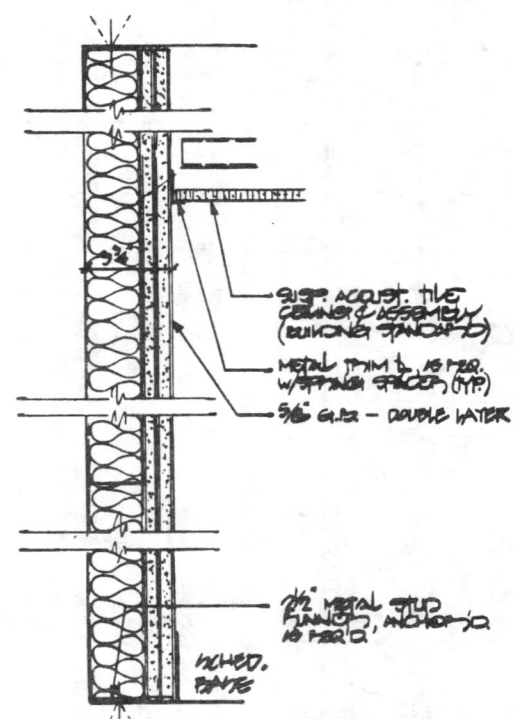

SUSP. ACOUST. TILE
CEILING & ASSEMBLY
(BUILDING STANDARD)

METAL TRIM D. AS REQ.
W/ STRIPPING SPACERS (TYP.)

5/8" G.B. — DOUBLE LAYER

2½" METAL STUD
RUNNER, ANCHOR'D
AS REQ'D.

SCHED.
BASE

7 FUR-OUT PARTITION / USE WITH PARTITIONS
2 @ COLUMN ENCLOSURE

7a SAME AS **7** BUT WITH
SOUND ATTENUATION BLANKET

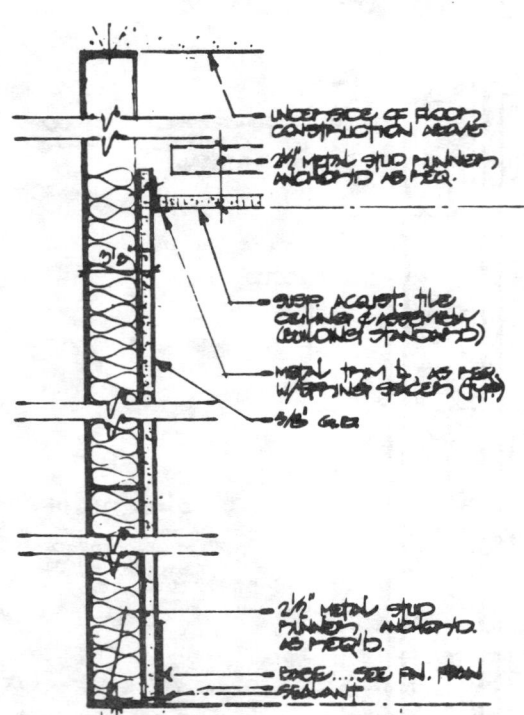

UNDERSIDE OF FLOOR
CONSTRUCTION ABOVE

2½" METAL STUD RUNNER
ANCHOR'D AS REQ.

SUSP. ACOUST. TILE
CEILING & ASSEMBLY
(BUILDING STANDARD)

METAL TRIM D. AS REQ.
W/ STRIPPING SPACERS (TYP.)

5/8" G.B.

2½" METAL STUD
RUNNER, ANCHOR'D
AS REQ'D.

BASE....SEE FIN. PLAN
SEALANT

8 FUR-OUT GYPSUM B'D. ON METAL STUDS,
CHASE PARTITION & COLUMN ENCLOSURE

8a SAME AS **8** BUT WITH
SOUND ATTENUATION BLANKET

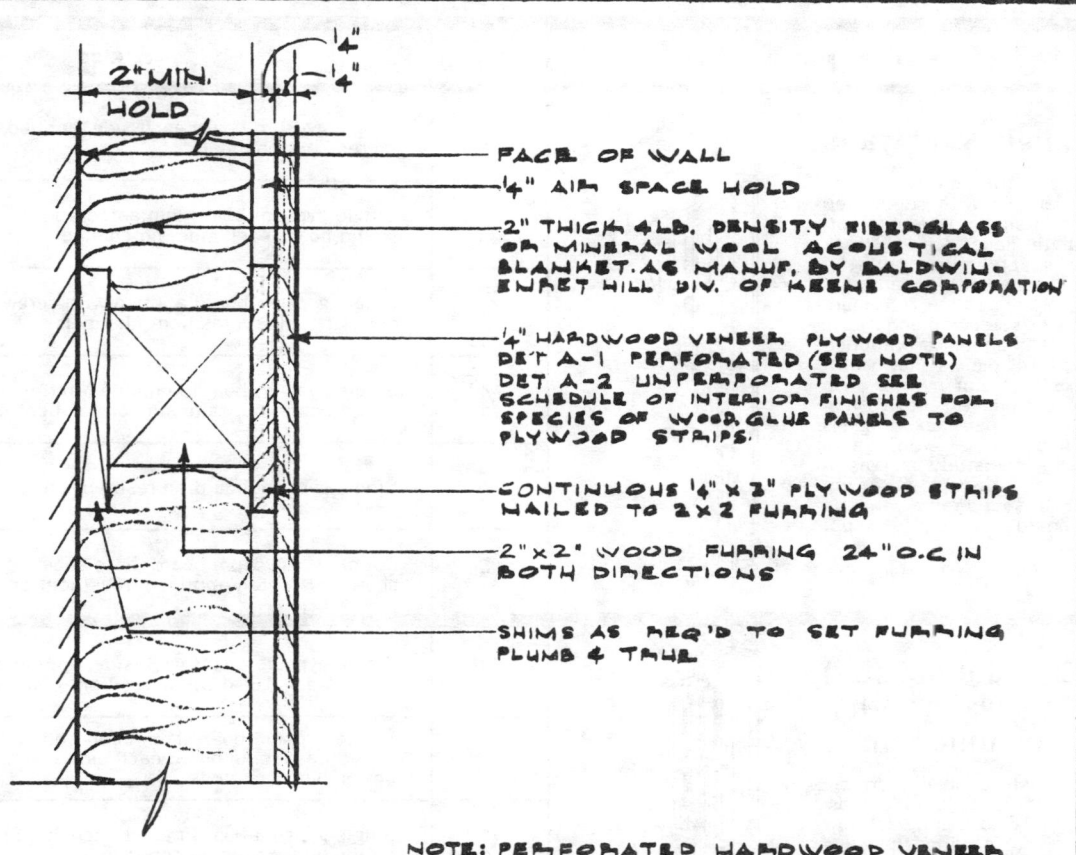

FACE OF WALL

¼" AIR SPACE HOLD

2" THICK 4LB. DENSITY FIBERGLASS OR MINERAL WOOL ACOUSTICAL BLANKET. AS MANUF. BY BALDWIN-EHRET HILL DIV. OF KEENE CORPORATION

¼" HARDWOOD VENEER PLYWOOD PANELS DET A-1 PERFORATED (SEE NOTE) DET A-2 UNPERFORATED SEE SCHEDULE OF INTERIOR FINISHES FOR SPECIES OF WOOD. GLUE PANELS TO PLYWOOD STRIPS.

CONTINUOUS ¼" X 3" PLYWOOD STRIPS NAILED TO 2×2 FURRING

2"×2" WOOD FURRING 24" O.C IN BOTH DIRECTIONS

SHIMS AS REQ'D TO SET FURRING PLUMB & TRUE

NOTE: PERFORATED HARDWOOD VENEER PANELS SHALL HAVE ³⁄₁₆" DIA. HOLES ½" O.C. HOLES SHALL BE DRILLED NOT PUNCHED OPEN AREA TO BE AT LEAST 11%

(A-1) PERFORATED HARDWOOD VENEER PLYWOOD FINISH

(A-2) UNPERFORATED HARDWOOD VENEER PLYWOOD FINISH

ACOUSTIC WALL TREATMENT DETAILS

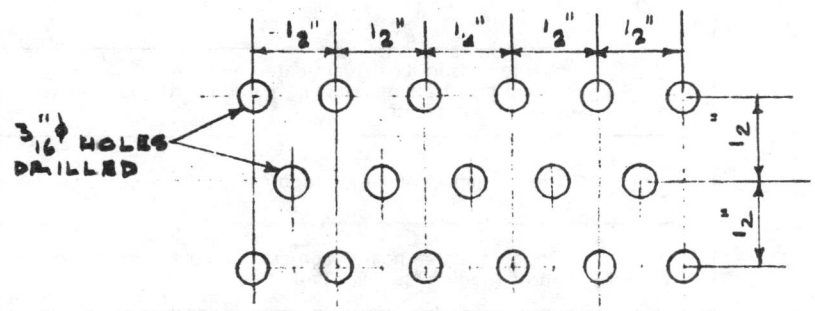

³⁄₁₆"⌀ HOLES DRILLED

PATTERN FOR PERFORATED PLYWOOD

wood frame partition systems for sound control

PARTITION SYSTEM	WALL NUMBER	WALL FACE	STC
single stud walls Basic construction is 2" x 4" studs 16" o.c. with double top plate and single or double bottom plate. Faces are ⅝" thick fire resistive type gypsum board applied, taped and finished in accordance with manufacturer's recommendations. Resilient channels are applied to studs 24" o.c. as shown with a ½"x3" gypsum nailing strip at the bottom. Absorptive material is paper-backed glass fiber or mineral wool batts stapled in the stud space as illustrated. Sound deadening board is sound-rated organic fiber board with a 15-18 pcf density. **no. 3**	1	Single gypsum board each side, applied with screws; no resilient channels	34
	2	Single gypsum board laminated and nailed[2] over sound board each side; no channels	45
	3	Single gypsum board applied with screws 1 side; opposite side on resilient channels	50
	4	Single gypsum board laminated and nailed[2] over sound board, opposite side on resilient channels	52
	5	Single gypsum board on resilient channels each side	53
	6	Double ½" gypsum board, base sheet vertical; face sheet horizontal; applied on resilient channels one side	59
double stud walls with a common plate Basic construction is a double row of 2"x3" or 2"x4" studs, each row 16" o.c. and each row aligned with an opposite edge of the 2"x6" top and bottom plates. The rows of studs are offset 2" to 8" to prevent any chance contact. Other details and materials are as described for single stud walls. **no. 11**	7	Single gypsum board each side, applied with screws (2x3 studs—16" o.c.); no resilient channels	49
	8[1]	Single gypsum board laminated and nailed[2] over sound deadening board each side (2x4 studs—16" o.c.); no resilient channels	49
	9[1]	Single gypsum board nailed one side. Single gypsum on resilient channels opposite	50
	10	Single gypsum board laminated and nailed[2] over sound deadening board 1 side. Single gypsum board on resilient channels opposite (2x3 studs—16" o.c.)	53
	11	Double gypsum board (½" over ⅝") nailed one side; single gypsum board on resilient channels opposite (2x4 studs—24" o.c.)	56
double stud walls on separate plates Basic construction is a double wall of 2"x3" studs on separate plates about 1" apart. Studs of each frame are 16" o.c. with the studs in one frame offset 2" to 8" from those of the other. Other details and materials are as described for single stud walls. **no. 13**	12	Single gypsum board each side applied with screws	51
	13	Single gypsum board laminated and nailed[2] over sound board each side	53
	14	Same as wall 13	60
	15	Single gypsum board laminated and nailed[2] over sound board 1 side; single gypsum board on resilient channels opposite	58
	16	Double gypsum board; nailed each side	51
	17	Double gypsum board each side; outer layer laminated and nailed[2]; base layer nailed	59
	18	Double gypsum board laminated and nailed[2] one side. Single gypsum board on resilient channels opposite	57

[1] Design No. 5—1 Hr. combustible (bearing wall) Underwriters' Lab, Inc. (10)
[2] Face laminated vertically with three 6-inch wide strips of construction adhesive and nailed with about half the usual number of nails.

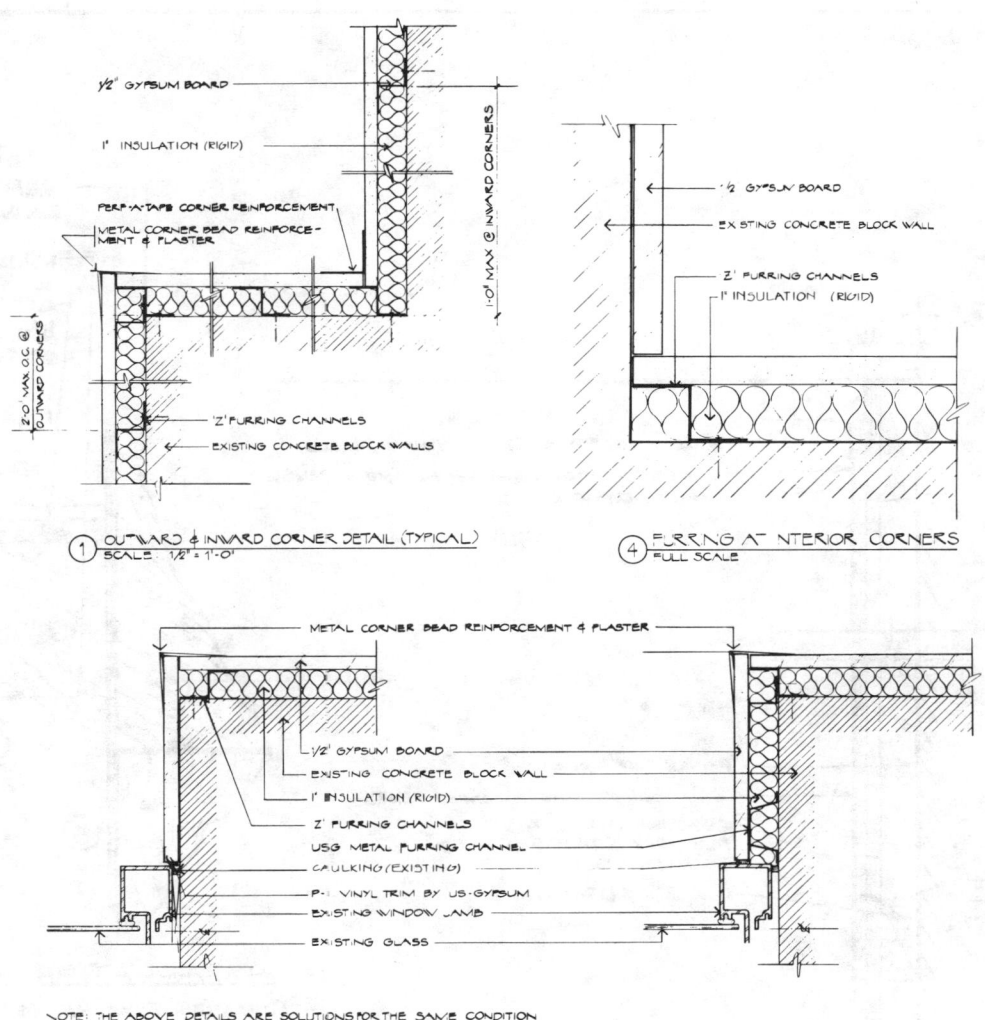

1. OUTWARD & INWARD CORNER DETAIL (TYPICAL)
SCALE: 1/2" = 1'-0"

- 1/2" GYPSUM BOARD
- 1" INSULATION (RIGID)
- PERF-A-TAPE CORNER REINFORCEMENT
- METAL CORNER BEAD REINFORCEMENT & PLASTER
- 'Z' FURRING CHANNELS
- EXISTING CONCRETE BLOCK WALLS
- 1'-0" MAX @ INWARD CORNERS
- 2'-0" MAX O.C. @ OUTWARD CORNERS

4. FURRING AT INTERIOR CORNERS
FULL SCALE

- 1/2" GYPSUM BOARD
- EXISTING CONCRETE BLOCK WALL
- Z' FURRING CHANNELS
- 1" INSULATION (RIGID)

- METAL CORNER BEAD REINFORCEMENT & PLASTER
- 1/2" GYPSUM BOARD
- EXISTING CONCRETE BLOCK WALL
- 1" INSULATION (RIGID)
- Z' FURRING CHANNELS
- USG METAL FURRING CHANNEL
- CAULKING (EXISTING)
- P-1 VINYL TRIM BY US-GYPSUM
- EXISTING WINDOW JAMB
- EXISTING GLASS

NOTE: THE ABOVE DETAILS ARE SOLUTIONS FOR THE SAME CONDITION

2. FURRING AT WINDOW JAMB
SCALE: 1/2" = 1'-0"

3. FURRING AT WINDOW JAMB
SCALE: 1/2" = 1'-0"

Metal "Z" furring and gypsum board: exterior walls

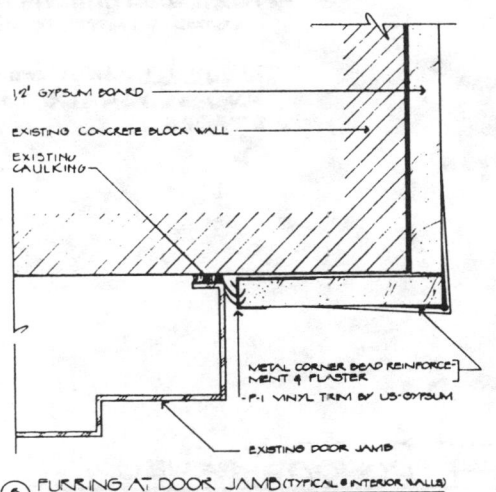

- 1/2" GYPSUM BOARD
- EXISTING CONCRETE BLOCK WALL
- EXISTING CAULKING
- METAL CORNER BEAD REINFORCEMENT & PLASTER
- P-1 VINYL TRIM BY US-GYPSUM
- EXISTING DOOR JAMB

5. FURRING AT DOOR JAMB (TYPICAL @ INTERIOR WALLS)
FULL SCALE

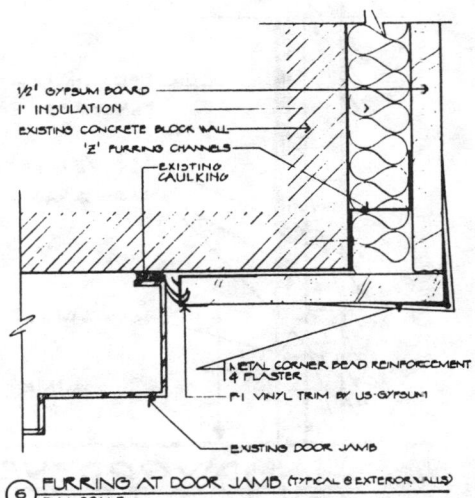

- 1/2" GYPSUM BOARD
- 1" INSULATION
- EXISTING CONCRETE BLOCK WALL
- 'Z' FURRING CHANNELS
- EXISTING CAULKING
- METAL CORNER BEAD REINFORCEMENT & PLASTER
- P-1 VINYL TRIM BY US-GYPSUM
- EXISTING DOOR JAMB

6. FURRING AT DOOR JAMB (TYPICAL @ EXTERIOR WALLS)
FULL SCALE

Metal "Z" furring and gypsum board: door jamb details

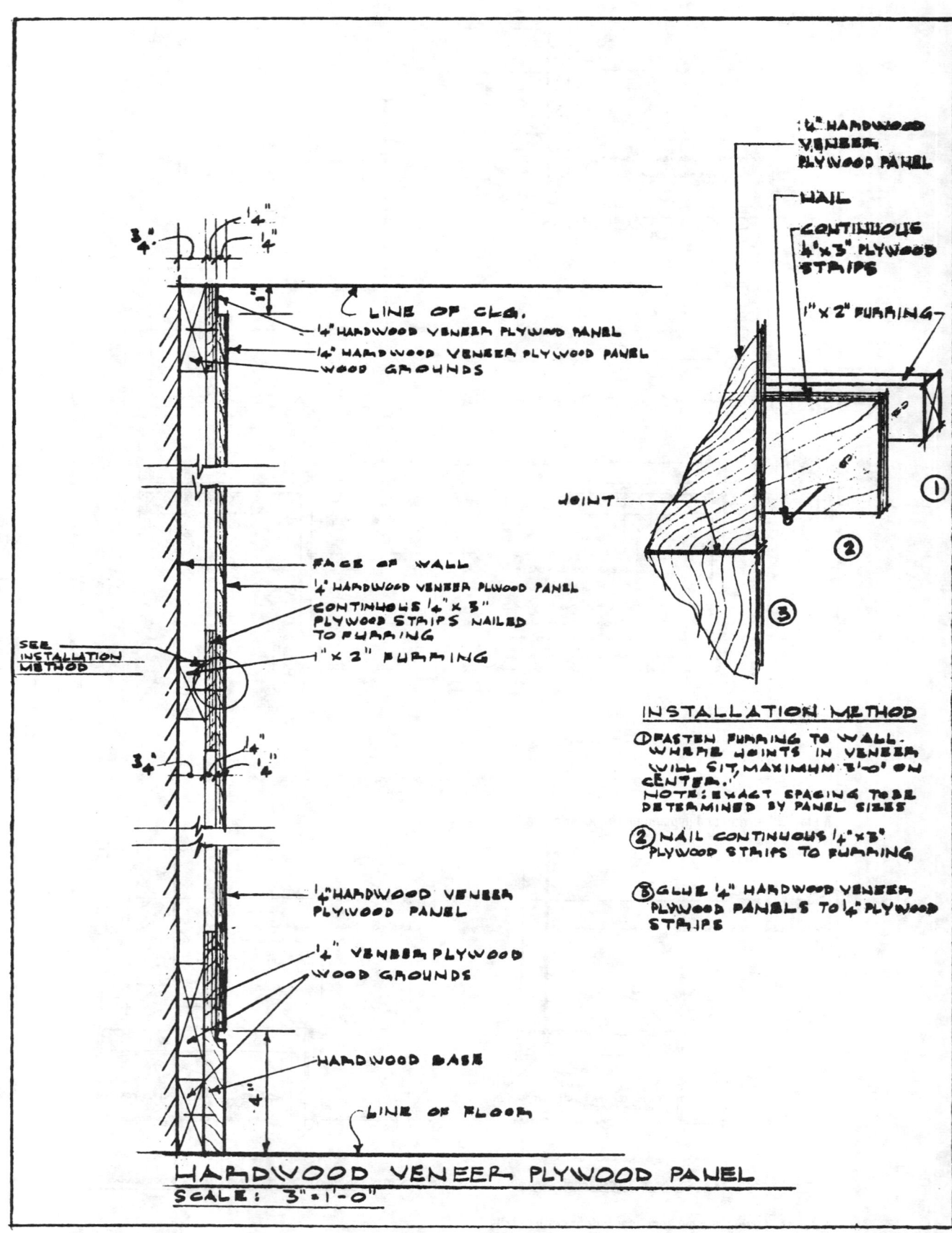

¼" HARDWOOD
VENEER
PLYWOOD PANEL

NAIL

CONTINUOUS
¼"×3" PLYWOOD
STRIPS

1"×2" FURRING

LINE OF CLG.
¼" HARDWOOD VENEER PLYWOOD PANEL
¼" HARDWOOD VENEER PLYWOOD PANEL
WOOD GROUNDS

JOINT

FACE OF WALL
¼" HARDWOOD VENEER PLYWOOD PANEL
CONTINUOUS ¼"×3"
PLYWOOD STRIPS NAILED
TO FURRING
1"×2" FURRING

SEE
INSTALLATION
METHOD

INSTALLATION METHOD

① FASTEN FURRING TO WALL
WHERE JOINTS IN VENEER
WILL SIT, MAXIMUM 3'-0" ON
CENTER.
NOTE: EXACT SPACING TO BE
DETERMINED BY PANEL SIZES

② NAIL CONTINUOUS ¼"×3"
PLYWOOD STRIPS TO FURRING

③ GLUE ¼" HARDWOOD VENEER
PLYWOOD PANELS TO ¼" PLYWOOD
STRIPS

¼" HARDWOOD VENEER
PLYWOOD PANEL

¼" VENEER PLYWOOD
WOOD GROUNDS

HARDWOOD BASE

LINE OF FLOOR

HARDWOOD VENEER PLYWOOD PANEL
SCALE: 3" = 1'-0"

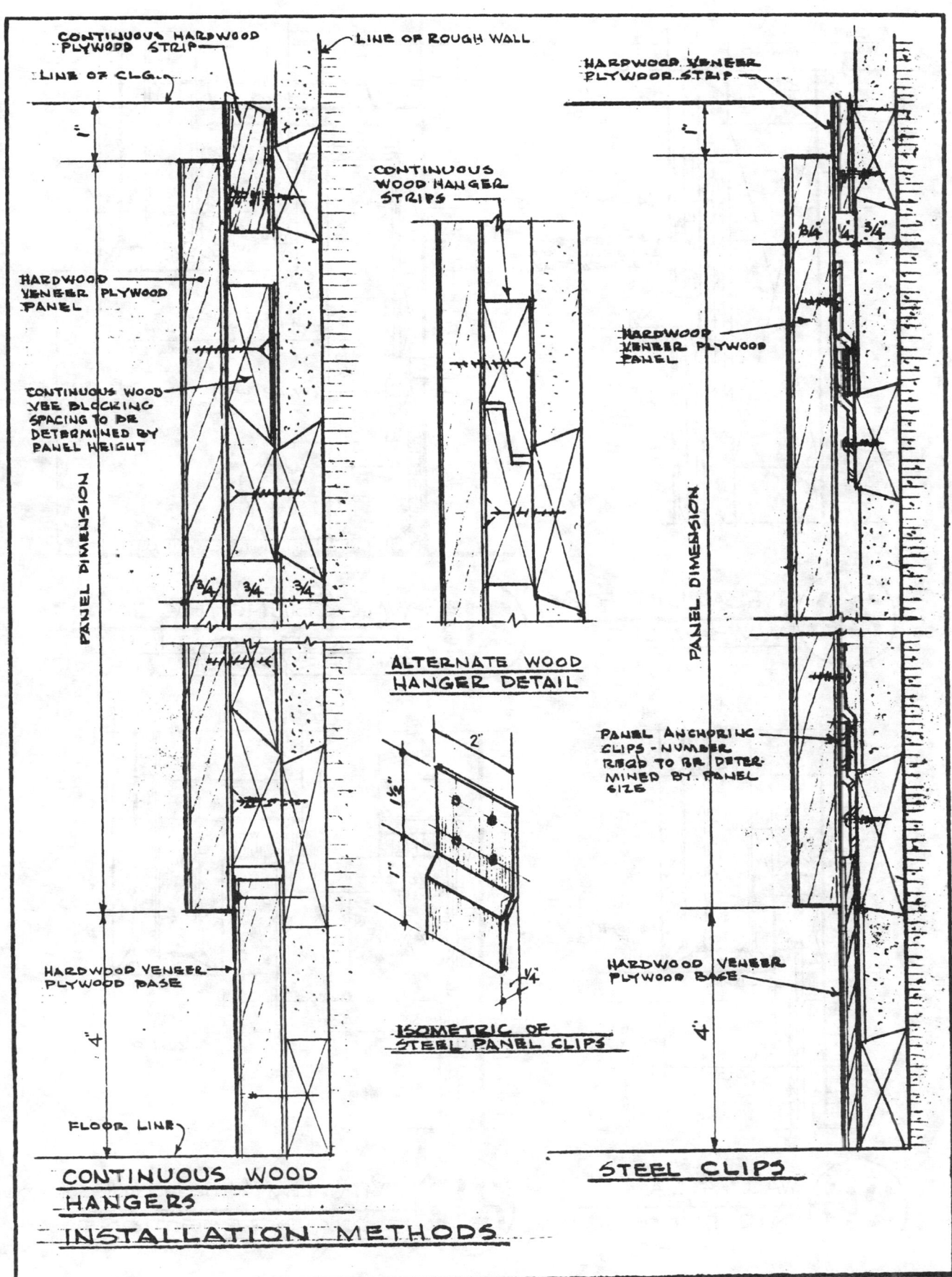

CONTINUOUS HARDWOOD PLYWOOD STRIP

LINE OF CLG.

LINE OF ROUGH WALL

HARDWOOD VENEER PLYWOOD STRIP

HARDWOOD VENEER PLYWOOD PANEL

CONTINUOUS WOOD HANGER STRIPS

HARDWOOD VENEER PLYWOOD PANEL

CONTINUOUS WOOD VEE BLOCKING SPACING TO BE DETERMINED BY PANEL HEIGHT

PANEL DIMENSION

3/4" 3/4" 3/4"

3/4 1/4 3/4

ALTERNATE WOOD HANGER DETAIL

PANEL DIMENSION

PANEL ANCHORING CLIPS - NUMBER REQ'D TO BE DETERMINED BY PANEL SIZE

HARDWOOD VENEER PLYWOOD BASE

2"

1 1/2"

1"

1/4"

ISOMETRIC OF STEEL PANEL CLIPS

HARDWOOD VENEER PLYWOOD BASE

4"

4"

FLOOR LINE

CONTINUOUS WOOD HANGERS

STEEL CLIPS

INSTALLATION METHODS

PARTITIONS AND WALL FINISHES

Wood Wall Paneling Details and Conditions

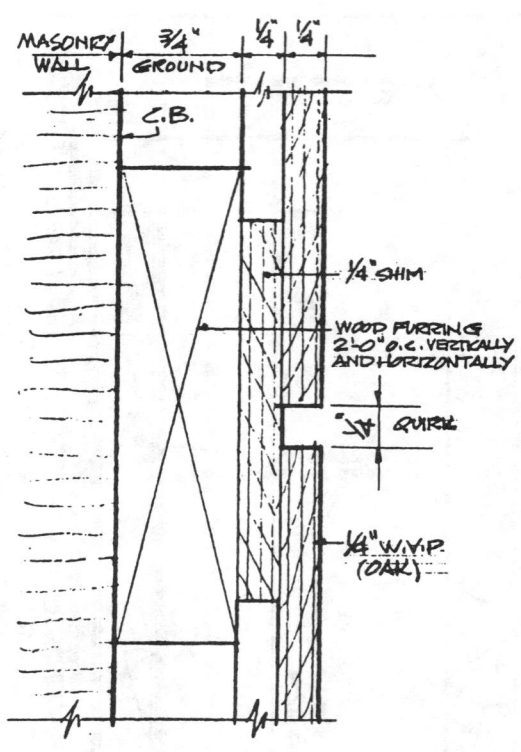

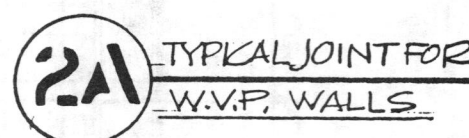

2A — TYPICAL JOINT FOR W.V.P. WALLS

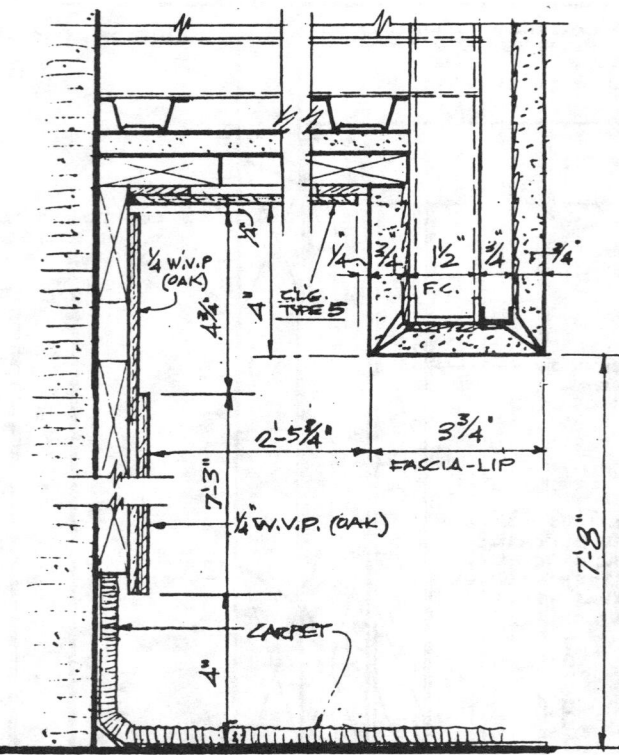

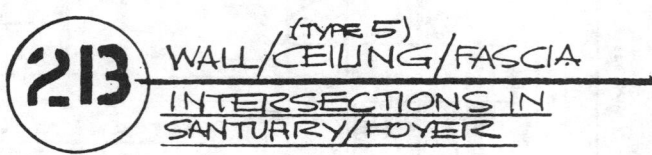

2B — (TYPE 5) WALL/CEILING/FASCIA INTERSECTIONS IN SANTUARY/FOYER

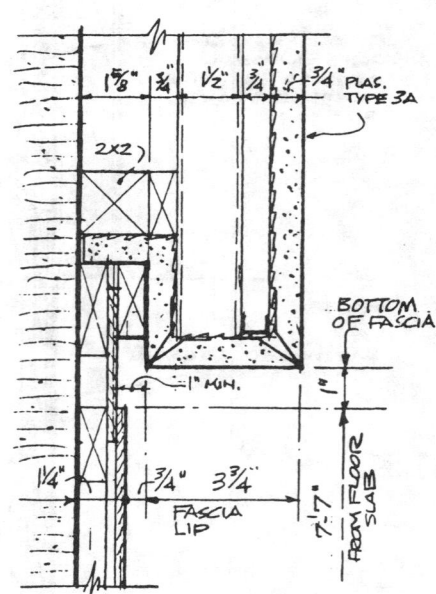

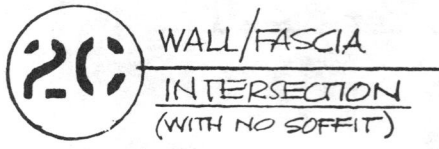

2C — WALL/FASCIA INTERSECTION (WITH NO SOFFIT)

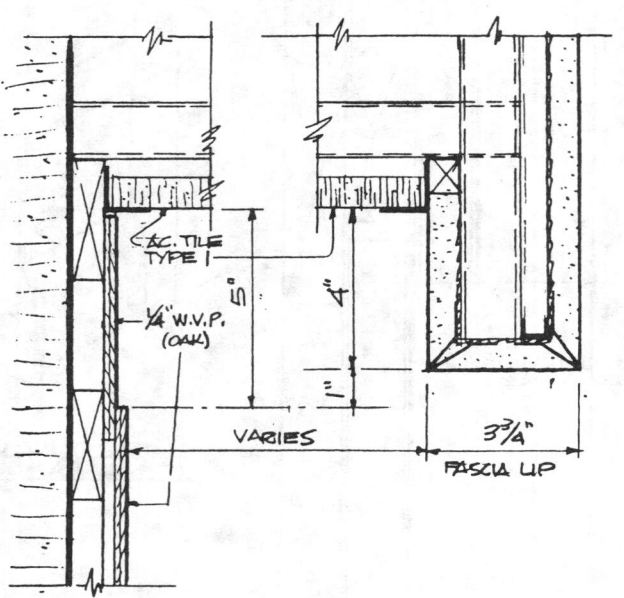

2D — W.V.P. WALL / AC. TILE (TYPE 1) CEILING/ FASCIA INTERSECTIONS

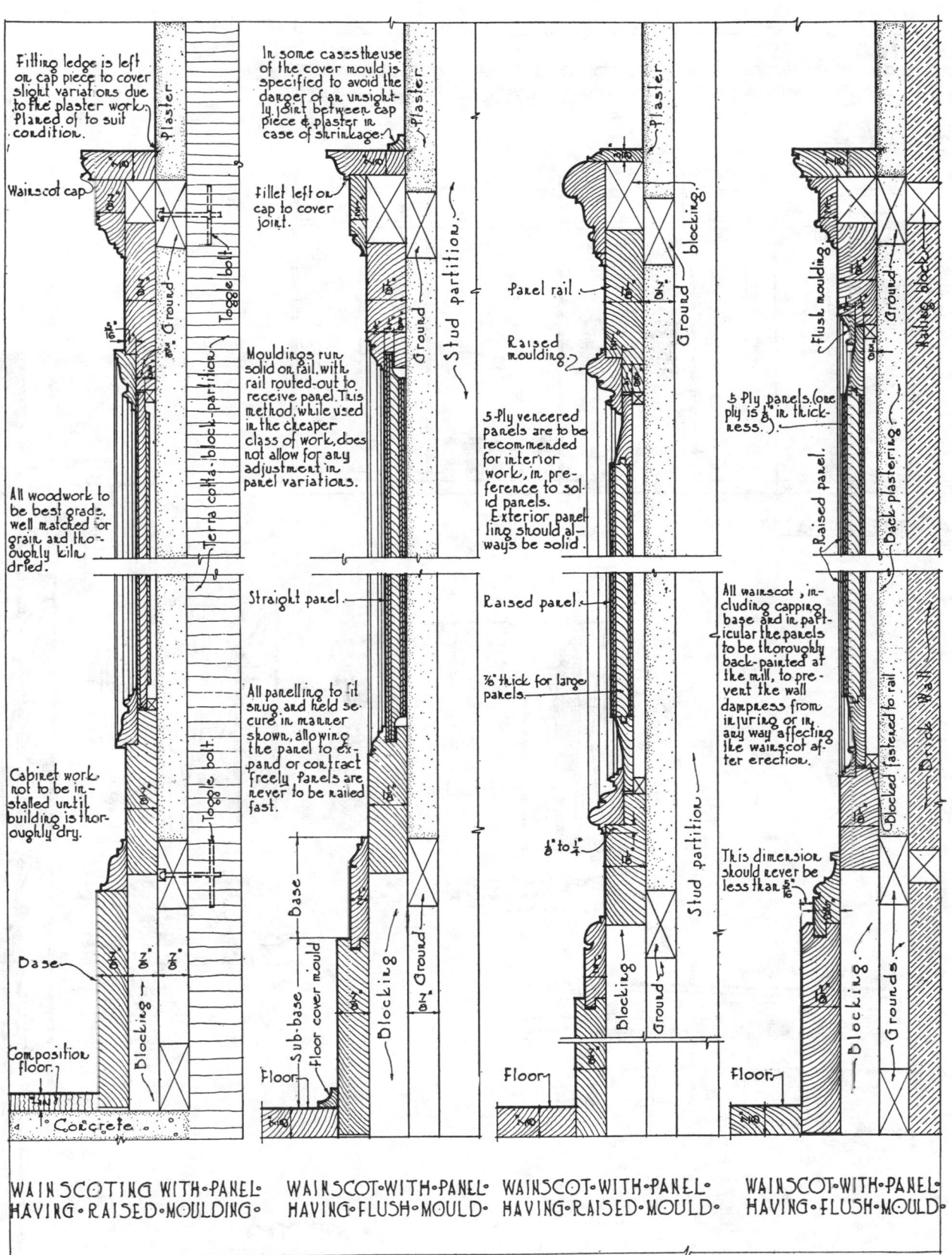

Fitting ledge is left on cap piece to cover slight variations due to the plaster work. Planed off to suit condition.

Wainscot cap

All woodwork to be best grade, well matched for grain and thoroughly kiln dried.

Cabinet work not to be installed until building is thoroughly dry.

Base

Composition floor.

Concrete

Plaster

Ground

Terra cotta block partition.

Toggle bolt.

Toggle bolt.

Blocking

In some cases the use of the cover mould is specified to avoid the danger of an unsightly joint between cap piece & plaster in case of shrinkage.

Fillet left on cap to cover joint.

Mouldings run solid on rail, with rail routed out to receive panel. This method, while used in the cheaper class of work, does not allow for any adjustment in panel variations.

Straight panel.

All panelling to fit snug and held secure in manner shown, allowing the panel to expand or contract freely panels are never to be nailed fast.

Base

Sub-base

Floor cover mould

Floor

Plaster

Ground

Stud partition.

Blocking

Ground

Panel rail.

Raised moulding.

5-Ply veneered panels are to be recommended for interior work, in preference to solid panels. Exterior panelling should always be solid.

Raised panel.

⅞" thick for large panels.

⅜" to ¼"

Floor

Plaster

Ground

Blocking

Stud partition.

Flush moulding.

5 Ply panels (one ply is ⅛" in thickness).

Raised panel.

Back-plastering.

All wainscot, including capping base and in particular the panels to be thoroughly back-painted at the mill, to prevent the wall dampness from injuring or in any way affecting the wainscot after erection.

This dimension should never be less than ⅛".

Plaster

Ground

Furring block

Brick wall.

Blocked fastened to rail.

Blocking

Grounds.

Floor

WAINSCOTING·WITH·PANEL· HAVING·RAISED·MOULDING. **WAINSCOT·WITH·PANEL· HAVING·FLUSH·MOULD.** **WAINSCOT·WITH·PANEL· HAVING·RAISED·MOULD.** **WAINSCOT·WITH·PANEL· HAVING·FLUSH·MOULD.**

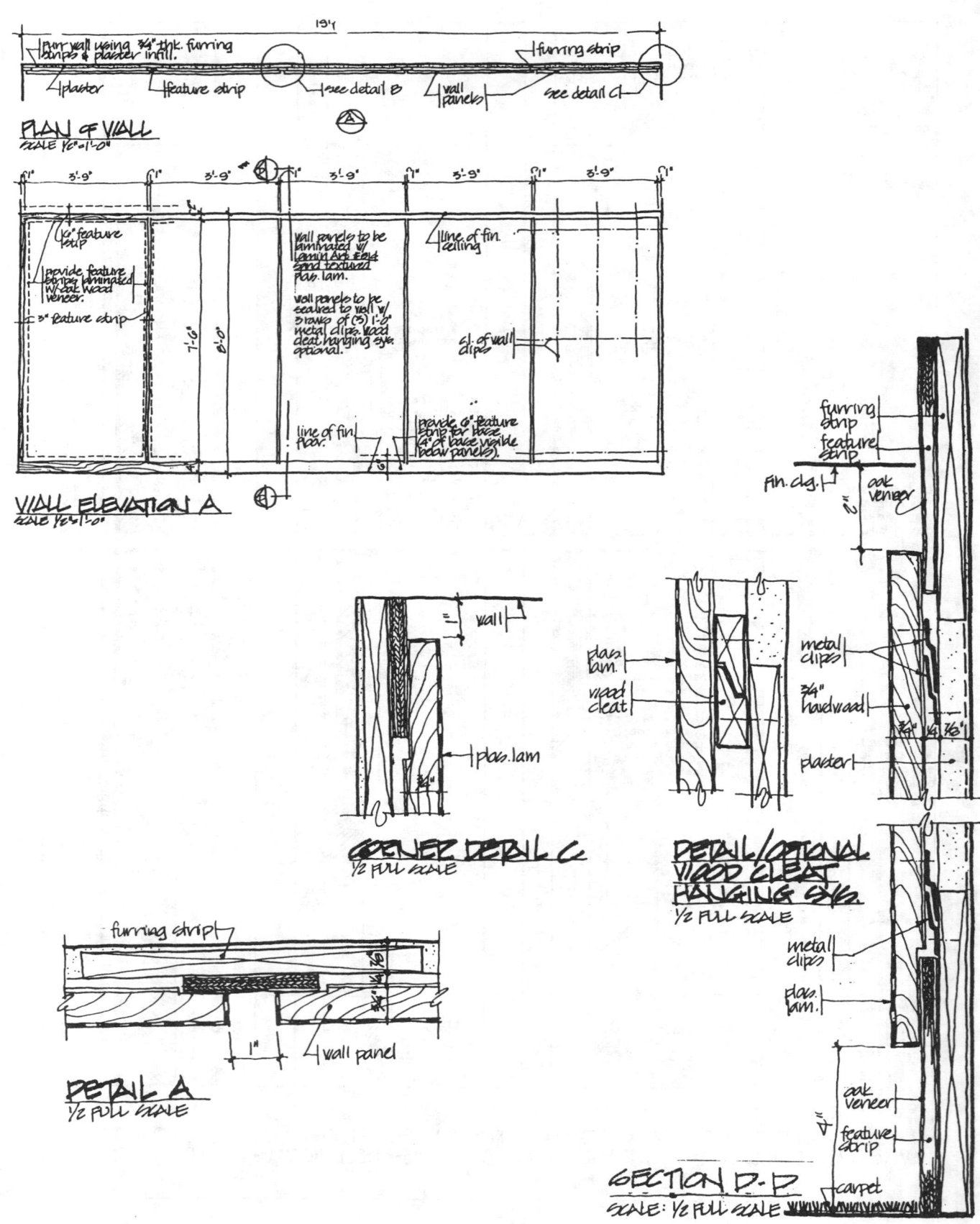

PLAN OF WALL
SCALE 1/6"=1'-0"

WALL ELEVATION A
SCALE 1/2"=1'-0"

CORNER DETAIL C
1/2 FULL SCALE

DETAIL/OPTIONAL WOOD CLEAT HANGING SYS.
1/2 FULL SCALE

DETAIL A
1/2 FULL SCALE

SECTION D-D
SCALE: 1/2 FULL SCALE

Wood Studs or Furring
Cement Mortar

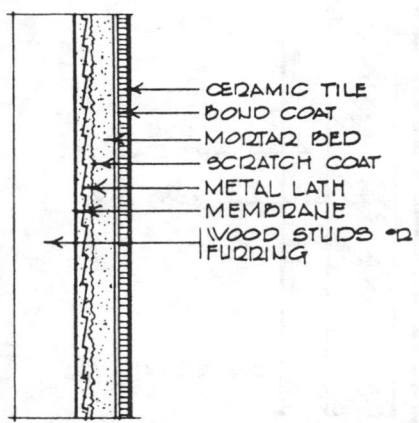

- CERAMIC TILE
- BOND COAT
- MORTAR BED
- SCRATCH COAT
- METAL LATH
- MEMBRANE
- WOOD STUDS OR FURRING

Recommended uses
- over dry, well-braced wood studs or furring
- preferred method of installation over wood studs in showers and tub enclosures

Metal Studs
Cement Mortar

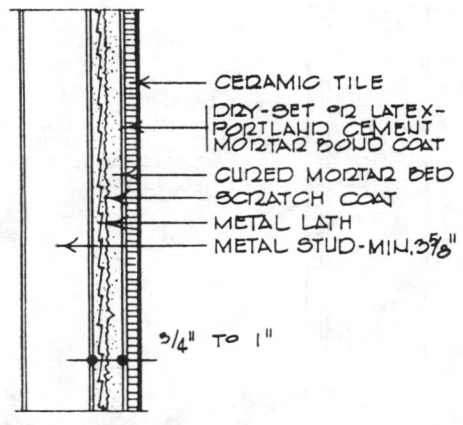

- CERAMIC TILE
- DRY-SET OR LATEX-PORTLAND CEMENT MORTAR BOND COAT
- CURED MORTAR BED
- SCRATCH COAT
- METAL LATH
- METAL STUD-MIN. 3⅝"
- ¾" TO 1"

Recommended use
- over metal studs

Gypsum Board
Organic Adhesive

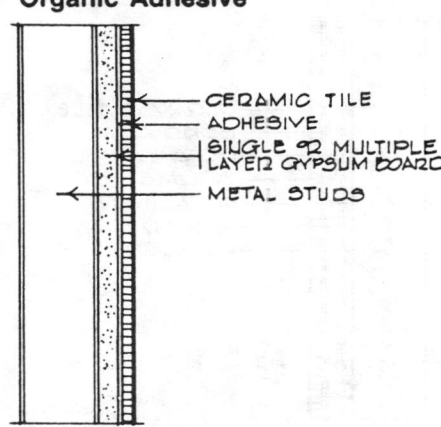

- CERAMIC TILE
- ADHESIVE
- SINGLE OR MULTIPLE LAYER GYPSUM BOARD
- METAL STUDS

Recommended uses
- over gypsum board screwed to metal studs, single or double layer installed in accordance with GA-216
- where a gypsum board, non-load-bearing partition is desired with durable, low-maintenance finish
- for fire-resistant, sound-insulated, ceramic-tiled walls (fire-resistance and sound-insulation ratings calculated on partitions before tiling)
- for dry areas in schools, institutions, and commercial buildings

Wood or Metal Studs
Gypsum Board
Dry-Set Mortar or Latex
Portland Cement Mortar

- CERAMIC TILE
- DRY-SET OR LATEX-PORTLAND CEMENT MORTAR BOND COAT
- GYPSUM BOARD
- WOOD OR METAL STUDS

Recommended uses
- dry interiors over gypsum wall board
- for dry areas in schools, institutions, and commercial buildings

Glass Mesh Mortar Unit
Dry-Set Mortar or Latex
Portland Cement Mortar

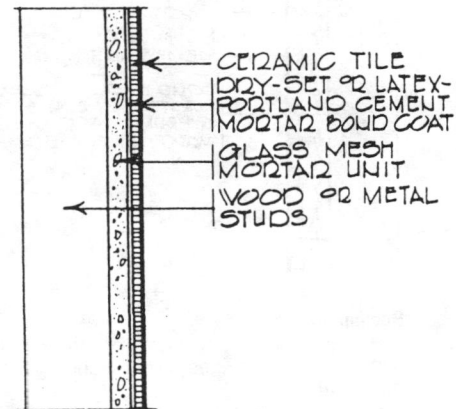

- CERAMIC TILE
- DRY-SET OR LATEX-PORTLAND CEMENT MORTAR BOND COAT
- GLASS MESH MORTAR UNIT
- WOOD OR METAL STUDS

Recommended uses
- in wet areas
- over dry, well-braced wood studs or furring
- over well-braced metal studs

Masonry

Cement Mortar

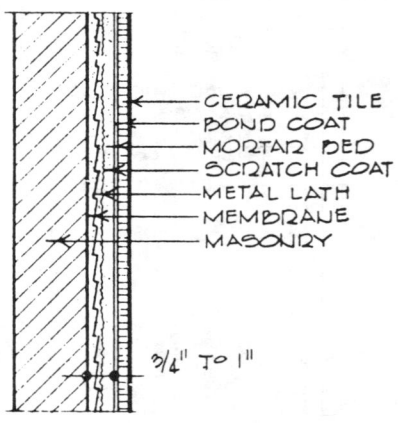

3/4" TO 1"

- CERAMIC TILE
- BOND COAT
- MORTAR BED
- SCRATCH COAT
- METAL LATH
- MEMBRANE
- MASONRY

Recommended use
- over masonry or concrete on exteriors

Dry-Set Mortar or Latex-Portland Cement Mortar

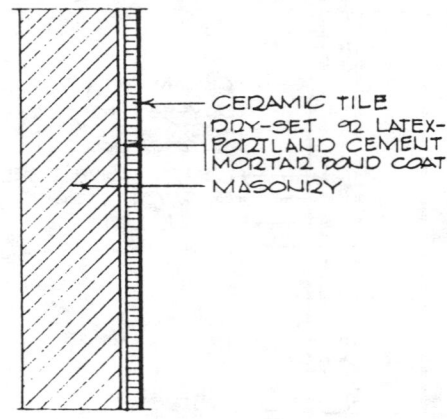

- CERAMIC TILE
- DRY-SET OR LATEX-PORTLAND CEMENT MORTAR BOND COAT
- MASONRY

Recommended use
- over clean, sound, dimensionally stable masonry or concrete

Masonry or Concrete

Cement Mortar Bonded

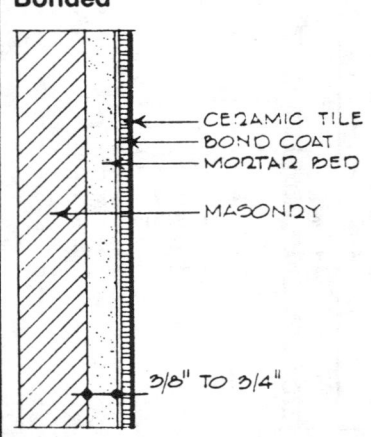

3/8" TO 3/4"

- CERAMIC TILE
- BOND COAT
- MORTAR BED
- MASONRY

Recommended use
- over clean sound, dimensionally stable masonry or concrete

Cement Mortar

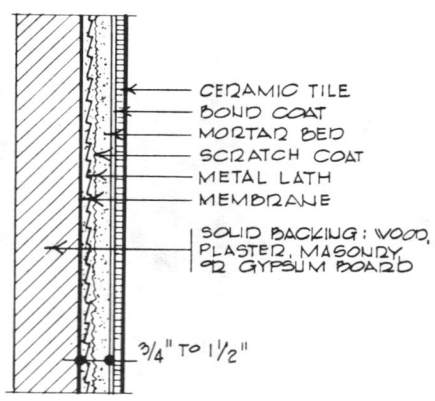

3/4" TO 1 1/2"

- CERAMIC TILE
- BOND COAT
- MORTAR BED
- SCRATCH COAT
- METAL LATH
- MEMBRANE
- SOLID BACKING: WOOD, PLASTER, MASONRY, OR GYPSUM BOARD

Recommended uses
- over masonry, plaster, or other solid backing that provides firm anchorage for metal lath
- ideal for remodeling or on surfaces that present bonding problems

One Coat Method

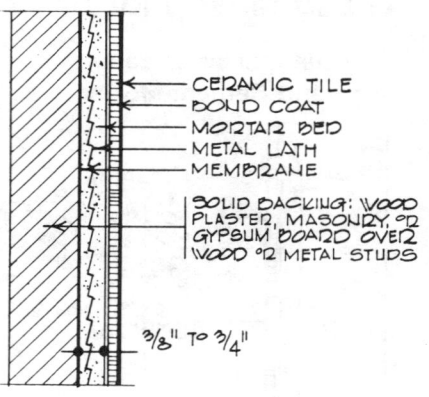

3/8" TO 3/4"

- CERAMIC TILE
- BOND COAT
- MORTAR BED
- METAL LATH
- MEMBRANE
- SOLID BACKING: WOOD PLASTER, MASONRY, OR GYPSUM BOARD OVER WOOD OR METAL STUDS

Recommended uses
- over masonry, plaster, or other solid backing that provides firm anchorage for metal lath
- ideal for remodeling or on surfaces that present bonding problems
- ideal for remodeling where space limitations exist
- preferred method of applying tile over gypsum plaster or gypsum board in showers and tub enclosures

Solid Backing

Organic Adhesive

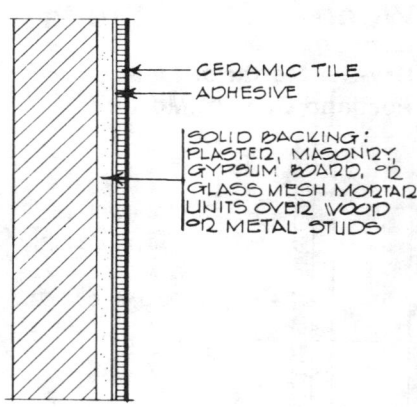

- CERAMIC TILE
- ADHESIVE
- SOLID BACKING: PLASTER, MASONRY, GYPSUM BOARD, OR GLASS MESH MORTAR UNITS OVER WOOD OR METAL STUDS

Recommended use
- interiors over gypsum board, plaster, dimensionally stable masonry, or other smooth surfaces

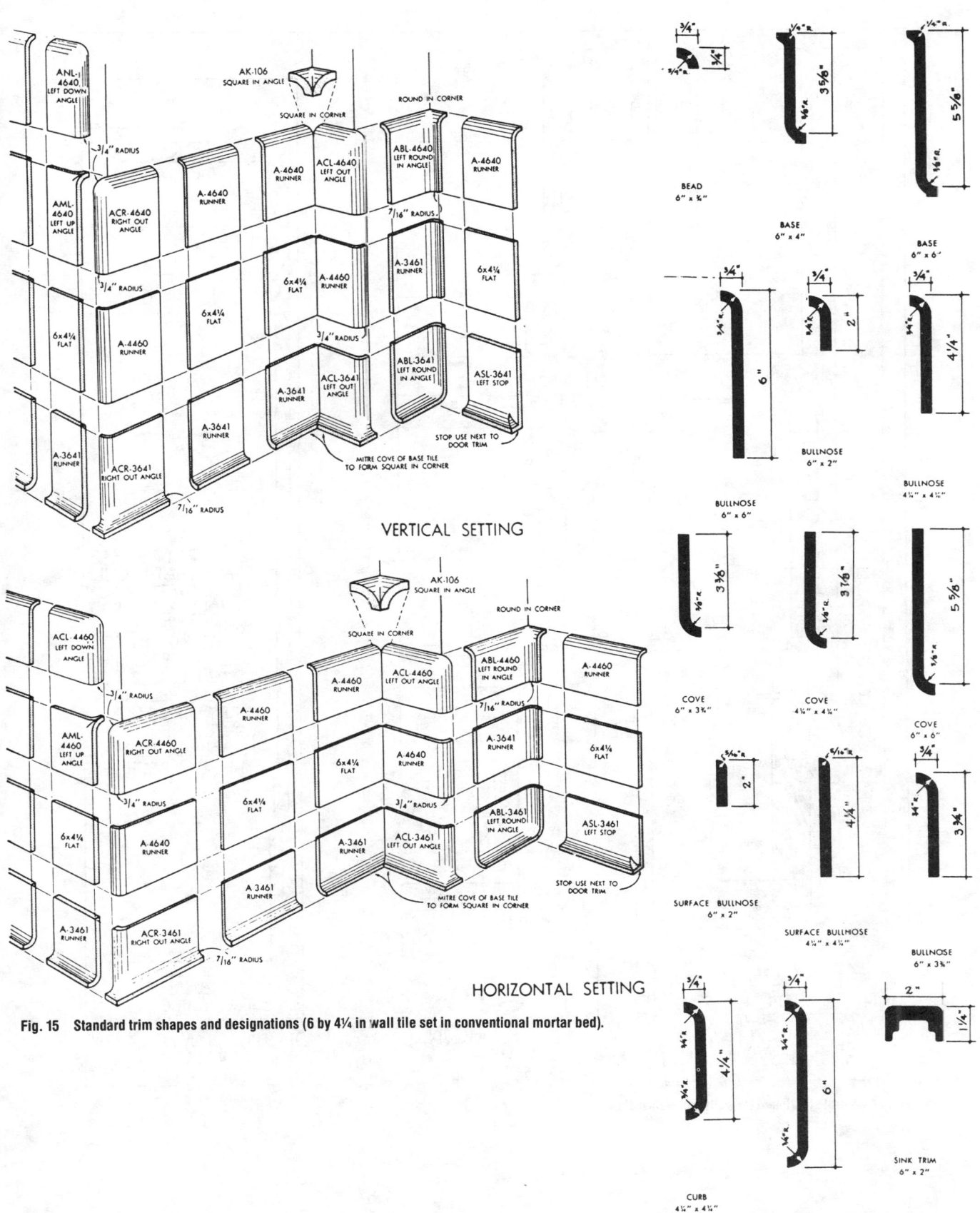

Fig. 15 Standard trim shapes and designations (6 by 4¼ in wall tile set in conventional mortar bed).

Fig. 16 Standard trim shapes and sizes.

PARTITIONS AND WALL FINISHES

Marble Veneer Wall Finishes

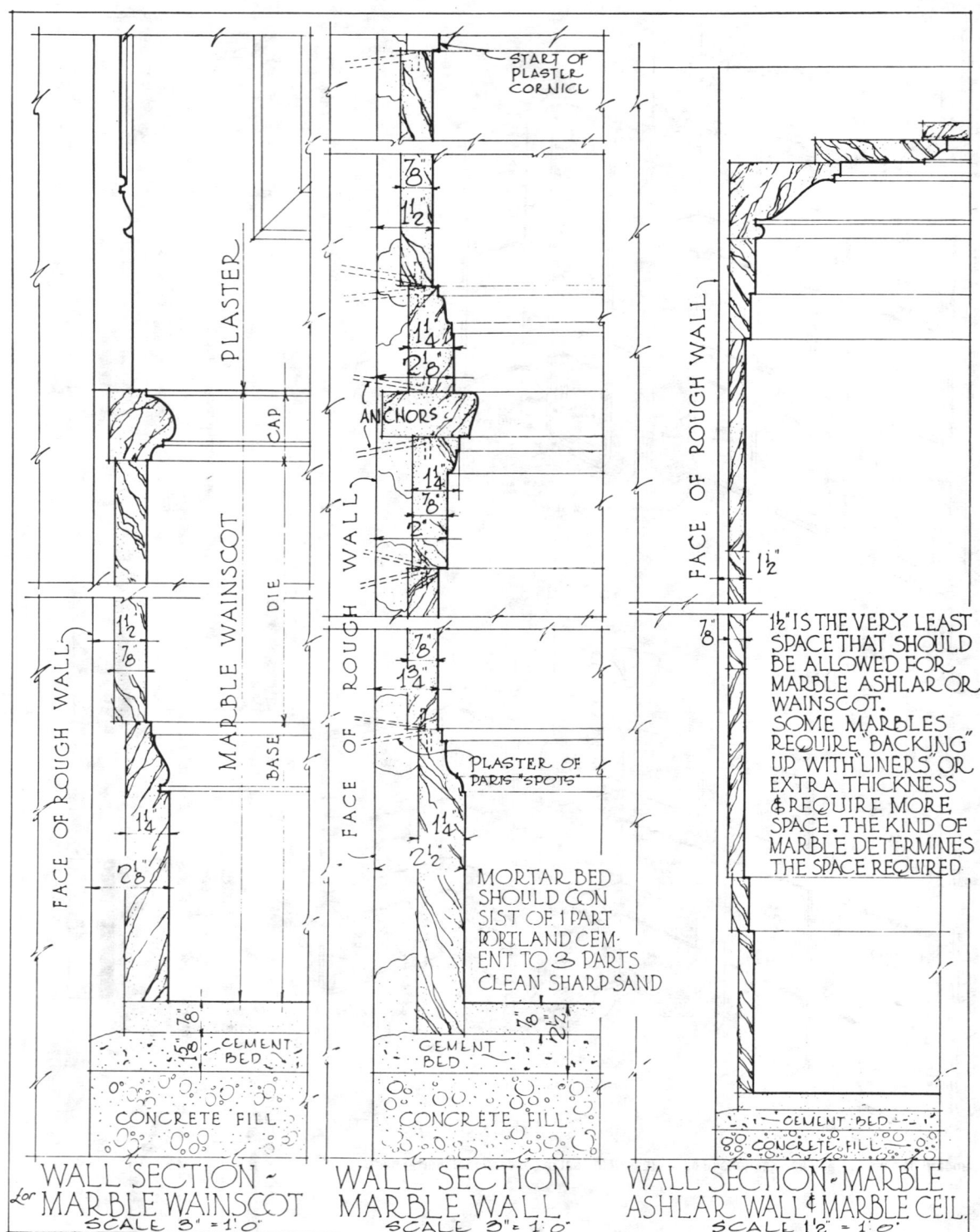

Fig. 17 Marble treatment for walls and wainscots.

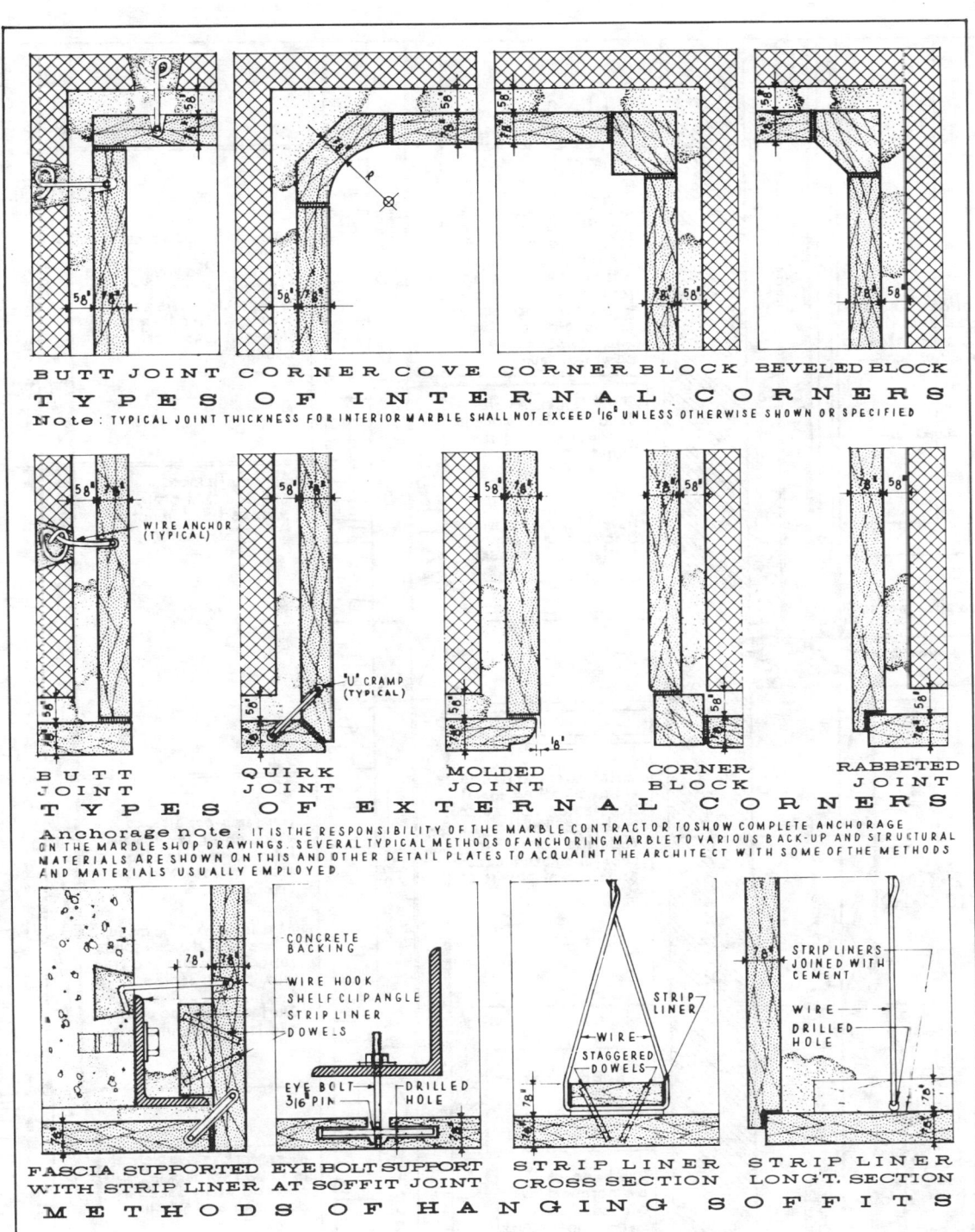

BUTT JOINT   CORNER COVE   CORNER BLOCK   BEVELED BLOCK
TYPES OF INTERNAL CORNERS
Note: TYPICAL JOINT THICKNESS FOR INTERIOR MARBLE SHALL NOT EXCEED 1/16" UNLESS OTHERWISE SHOWN OR SPECIFIED

BUTT JOINT   QUIRK JOINT   MOLDED JOINT   CORNER BLOCK   RABBETED JOINT
TYPES OF EXTERNAL CORNERS

Anchorage note: IT IS THE RESPONSIBILITY OF THE MARBLE CONTRACTOR TO SHOW COMPLETE ANCHORAGE ON THE MARBLE SHOP DRAWINGS. SEVERAL TYPICAL METHODS OF ANCHORING MARBLE TO VARIOUS BACK-UP AND STRUCTURAL MATERIALS ARE SHOWN ON THIS AND OTHER DETAIL PLATES TO ACQUAINT THE ARCHITECT WITH SOME OF THE METHODS AND MATERIALS USUALLY EMPLOYED

FASCIA SUPPORTED WITH STRIP LINER   EYE BOLT SUPPORT AT SOFFIT JOINT   STRIP LINER CROSS SECTION   STRIP LINER LONG'T. SECTION
METHODS OF HANGING SOFFITS

Fig. 18 Anchorage details.

PARTITIONS AND WALL FINISHES

Marble and Travertine Veneer Wall Finishes

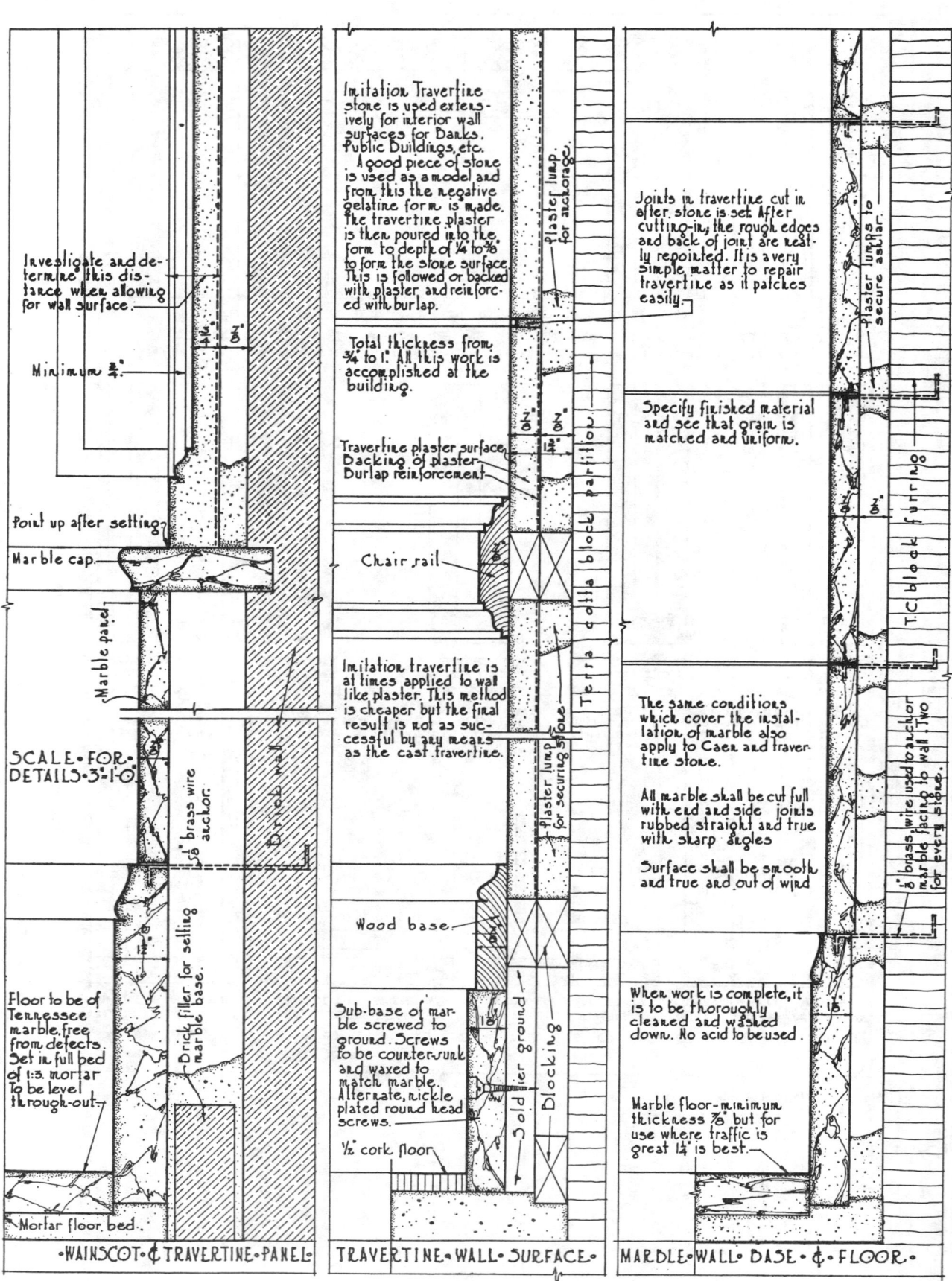

Investigate and determine this distance when allowing for wall surface.

Minimum ¾".

Point up after setting.

Marble cap.

Marble panel.

SCALE·FOR·
DETAILS·3"·1'-0".

⅛" brass wire anchor.

Floor to be of Tennessee marble, free from defects. Set in full bed of 1:3 mortar to be level through-out.

Brick filler for setting marble base.

Brick wall.

Mortar floor bed.

·WAINSCOT·&·TRAVERTINE·PANEL·

Imitation Travertine stone is used extensively for interior wall surfaces for banks, public buildings, etc.
A good piece of stone is used as a model and from this the negative gelatine form is made. The travertine plaster is then poured into the form to depth of ¼ to ⅜" to form the stone surface. This is followed or backed with plaster and reinforced with burlap.

Total thickness from ¾ to 1". All this work is accomplished at the building.

Travertine plaster surface.
Backing of plaster.
Burlap reinforcement.

Chair rail.

Imitation travertine is at times applied to wall like plaster. This method is cheaper but the final result is not as successful by any means as the cast travertine.

Wood base.

Sub-base of marble screwed to ground. Screws to be counter-sunk and waxed to match marble. Alternate, nickle plated round head screws.

½" cork floor.

Plaster lump for anchorage.

Plaster lump for securing stone.

Terra cotta block partition.

Soldier ground.

Blocking.

TRAVERTINE·WALL·SURFACE·

Joints in travertine cut in after stone is set. After cutting-in, the rough edges and back of joint are neatly repointed. It is a very simple matter to repair travertine as it patches easily.

Specify finished material and see that grain is matched and uniform.

The same conditions which cover the installation of marble also apply to Caen and travertine stone.

All marble shall be cut full with end and side joints rubbed straight and true with sharp angles.

Surface shall be smooth and true and out of wind.

When work is complete, it is to be thoroughly cleaned and washed down. No acid to be used.

Marble floor - minimum thickness ⅞" but for use where traffic is great 1¼" is best.

Plaster lumps to secure ashlar.

T.C. block furring.

⅛" brass wire used to anchor marble facing to wall two for every stone.

MARBLE·WALL·BASE·&·FLOOR·

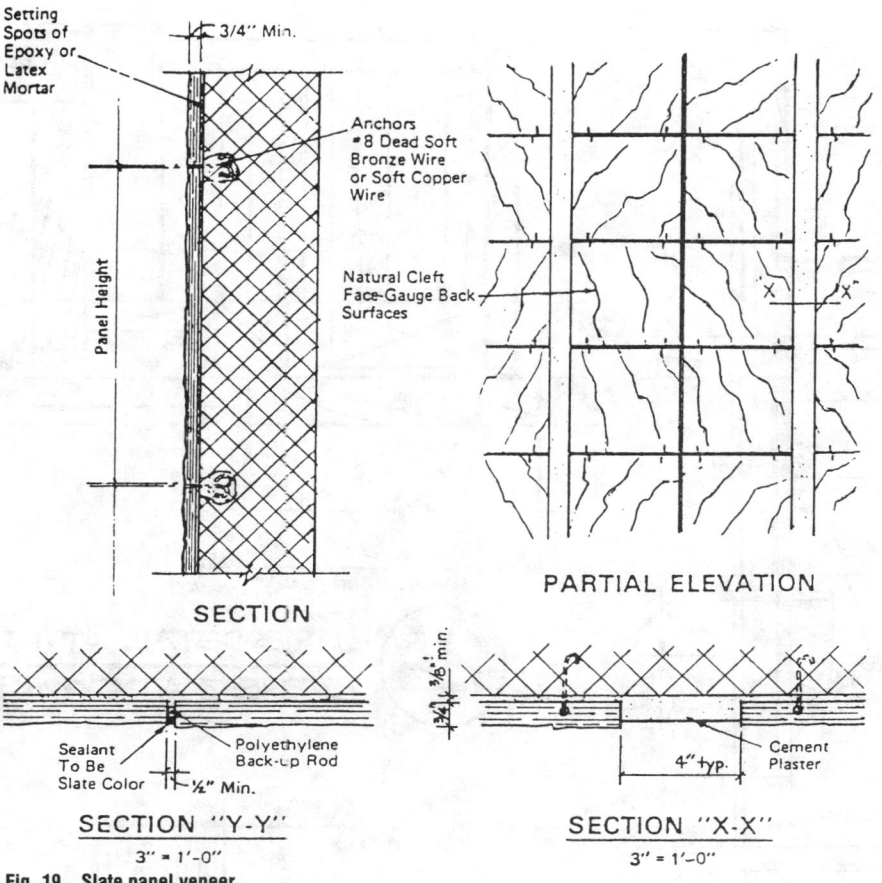

Setting Spots of Epoxy or Latex Mortar

3/4" Min.

Anchors #8 Dead Soft Bronze Wire or Soft Copper Wire

Natural Cleft Face-Gauge Back Surfaces

Panel Height

SECTION

PARTIAL ELEVATION

Sealant To Be Slate Color

Polyethylene Back-up Rod

1/2" Min.

SECTION "Y-Y"
3" = 1'-0"

3/8" min.

Cement Plaster

4" typ.

SECTION "X-X"
3" = 1'-0"

Fig. 19   Slate panel veneer.

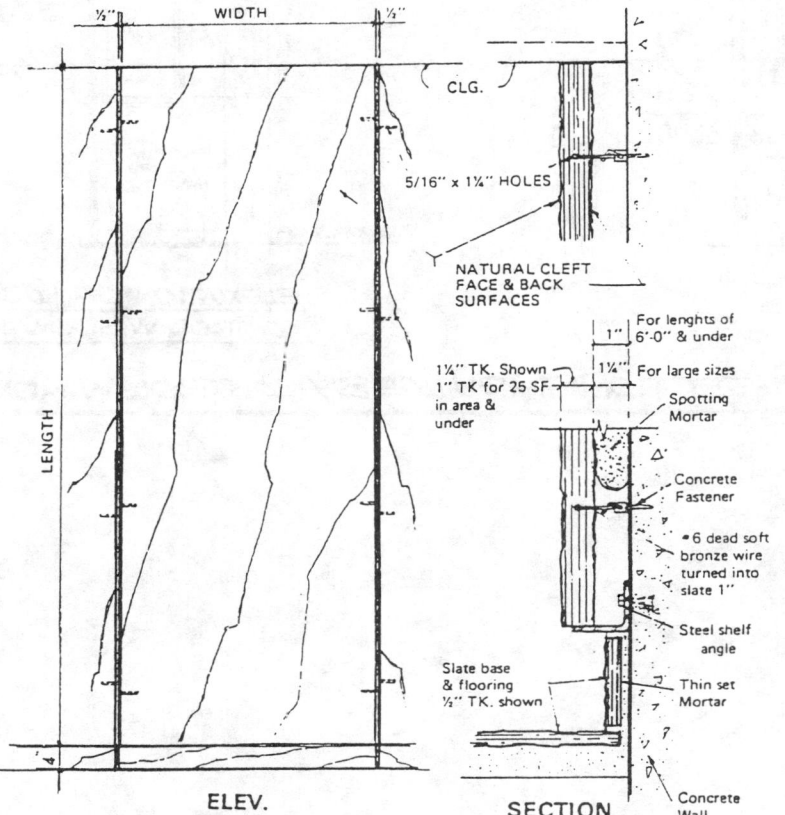

1/2"   WIDTH   1/2"

CLG.

5/16" x 1¼" HOLES

NATURAL CLEFT FACE & BACK SURFACES

LENGTH

For lenghts of 6'-0" & under
1"

1¼"   For large sizes

1¼" TK. Shown
1" TK for 25 SF in area & under

Spotting Mortar

Concrete Fastener

#6 dead soft bronze wire turned into slate 1"

Steel shelf angle

Slate base & flooring ½" TK. shown

Thin set Mortar

Concrete Wall

ELEV.

SECTION

Fig. 20   Slate panels applied to concrete wall.

PARTITIONS AND WALL FINISHES

Reception and Pass-Through Windows

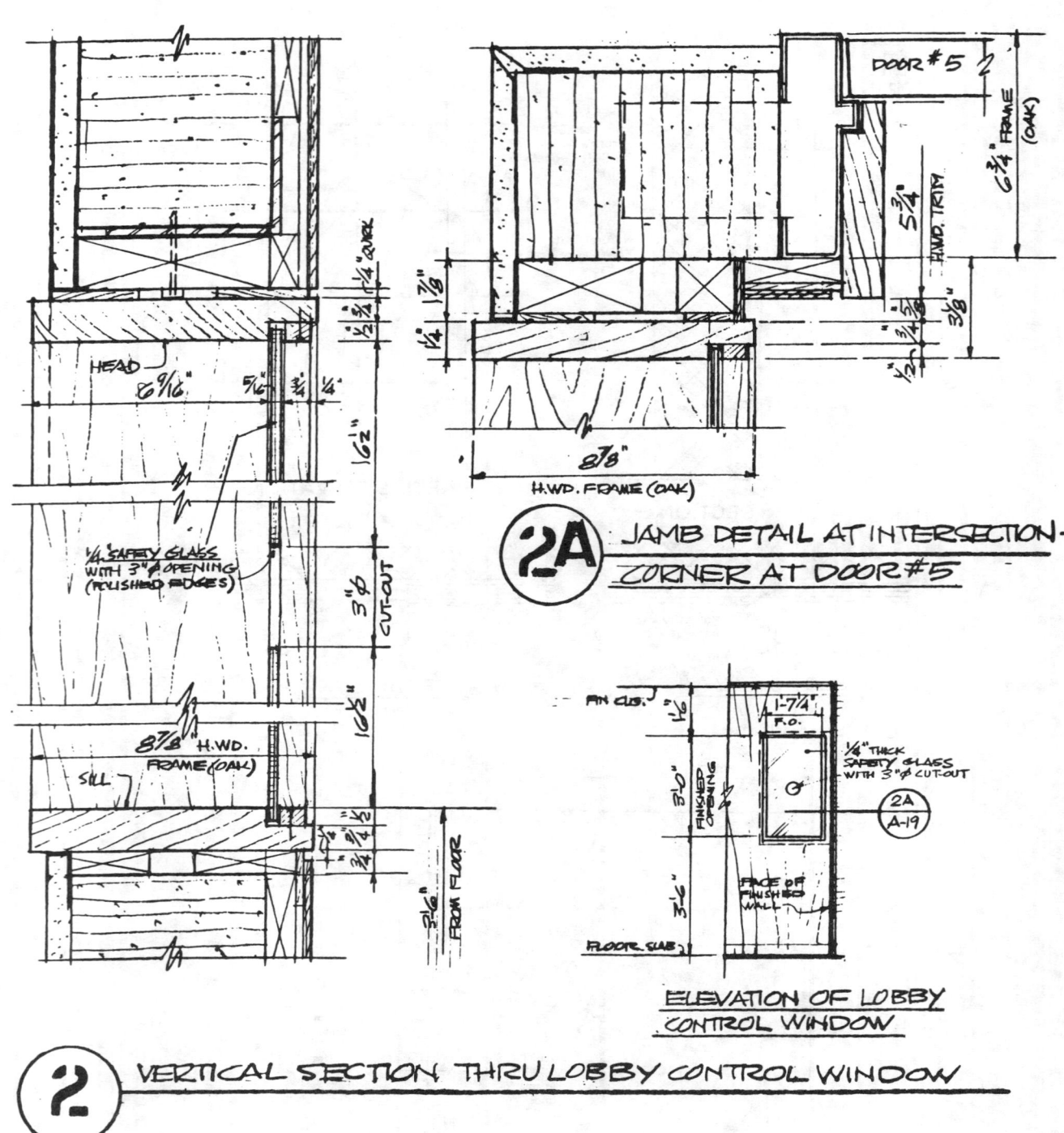

HEAD

6 9/16"   5/16"   3/4"   1/4"

1 3/4" QUIRK

1 3/4" 1/2"

16 1/2"

1/4 SAFETY GLASS
WITH 3"ø OPENING
(POLISHED EDGES)

3"ø
CUT-OUT

16 1/2"

8 7/8" H.WD.
FRAME (OAK)

SILL

3 1/2" 2 1/2"
1/4"
3/4"

3 1/2"
FROM FLOOR

DOOR #5

6 3/4" FRAME (OAK)

5 1/4"   H.WD. TRIM

7/8"   1 3/4"   3/8"

1/4"   1/2" 3/4"

1/2"

8 7/8"

H.WD. FRAME (OAK)

2A JAMB DETAIL AT INTERSECTION-
CORNER AT DOOR #5

FIN CLG.

1/2"

1-7 1/4"
F.O.

1/8" THICK
SAFETY GLASS
WITH 3"ø CUT-OUT

3'-0"
FINISHED OPENING

2A
A-19

FACE OF
FINISHED
WALL

3'-6"

FLOOR SLAB

ELEVATION OF LOBBY
CONTROL WINDOW

2 VERTICAL SECTION THRU LOBBY CONTROL WINDOW

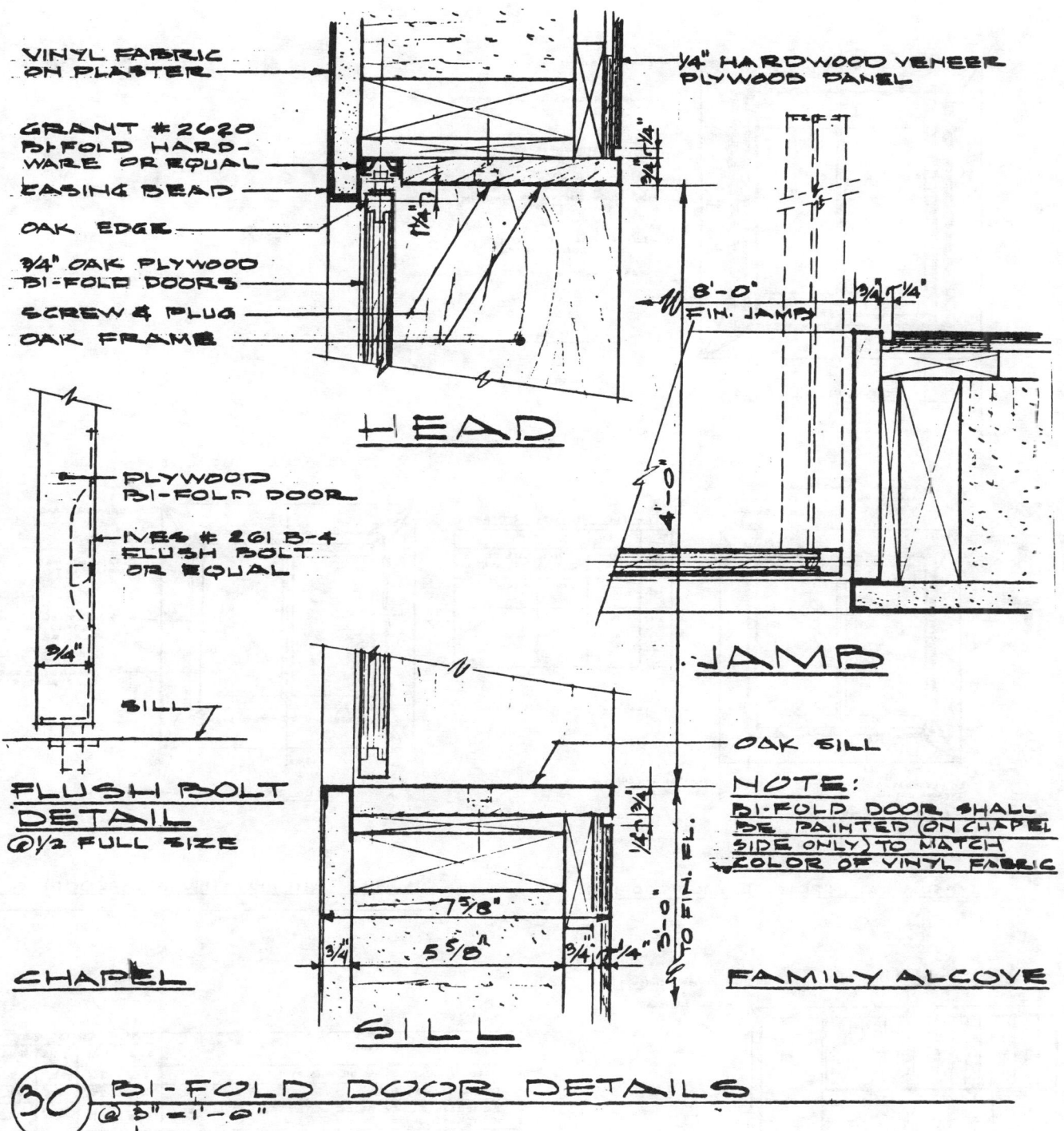

VINYL FABRIC
ON PLASTER

GRANT #2620
BI-FOLD HARD-
WARE OR EQUAL

CASING BEAD

OAK EDGE

3/4" OAK PLYWOOD
BI-FOLD DOORS

SCREW & PLUG

OAK FRAME

1/4" HARDWOOD VENEER
PLYWOOD PANEL

HEAD

PLYWOOD
BI-FOLD DOOR

IVES # 261 B-4
FLUSH BOLT
OR EQUAL

SILL

3/4"

FLUSH BOLT
DETAIL
@ 1/2 FULL SIZE

8'-0"
FIN. JAMB

JAMB

OAK SILL

NOTE:
BI-FOLD DOOR SHALL
BE PAINTED (ON CHAPEL
SIDE ONLY) TO MATCH
COLOR OF VINYL FABRIC

7 5/8"

5 5/8"

3/4"   3/4" 1/4"

CHAPEL

FAMILY ALCOVE

SILL

30 BI-FOLD DOOR DETAILS
@ 3"=1'-0"

PARTITIONS AND WALL FINISHES

Column Fireproofing Details

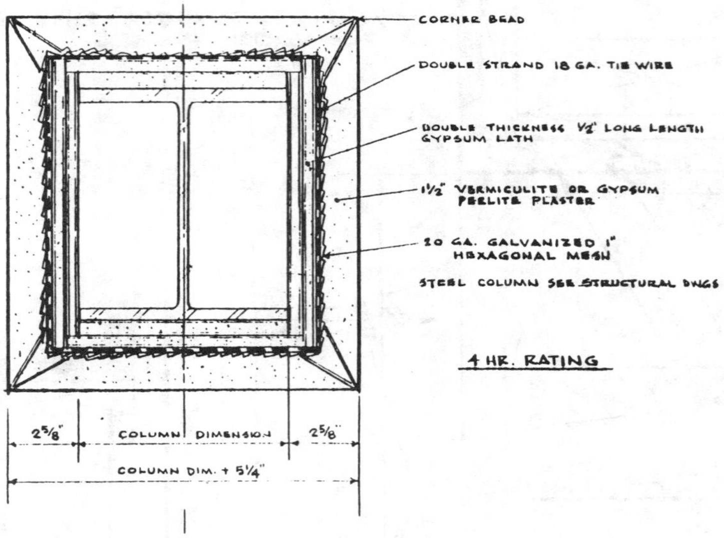
CORNER BEAD
DOUBLE STRAND 18 GA. TIE WIRE
DOUBLE THICKNESS 1/2" LONG LENGTH GYPSUM LATH
1 1/2" VERMICULITE OR GYPSUM PERLITE PLASTER
20 GA. GALVANIZED 1" HEXAGONAL MESH
STEEL COLUMN SEE STRUCTURAL DWGS
4 HR. RATING
2 5/8"
COLUMN DIMENSION
2 5/8"
COLUMN DIM. + 5 1/4"

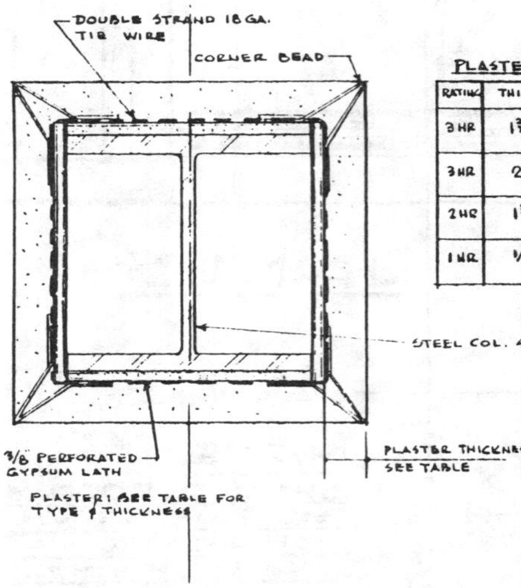
DOUBLE STRAND 18 GA. TIE WIRE
CORNER BEAD
STEEL COL. SEE STRUCTURAL DWGS
3/8 PERFORATED GYPSUM LATH
PLASTER THICKNESS SEE TABLE
PLASTER: SEE TABLE FOR TYPE & THICKNESS

PLASTER THICKNESS & TYPE

RATING	THICK.	TYPE
3 HR	1 3/8"	VERMICULITE OR GYPSUM PERLITE
3 HR	2"	GYPSUM SAND
2 HR	1 3/8"	↓
1 HR	1/2"	↓

GYPSUM LATH & PLASTER FIREPROOFING

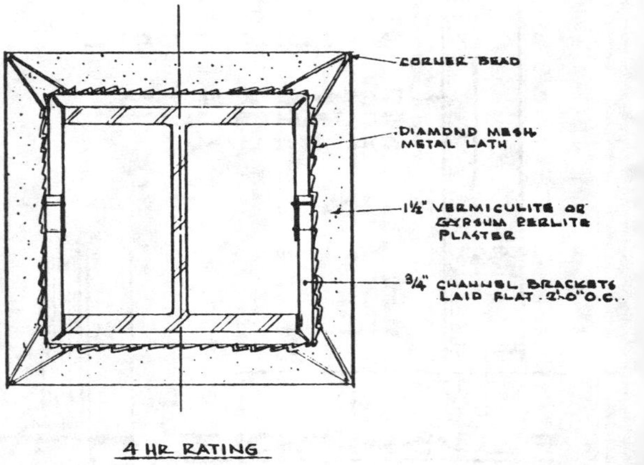
CORNER BEAD
DIAMOND MESH METAL LATH
1 1/2" VERMICULITE OR GYPSUM PERLITE PLASTER
3/4" CHANNEL BRACKETS LAID FLAT 2'-0" O.C.
4 HR RATING

METAL LATH & PLASTER FIREPROOFING

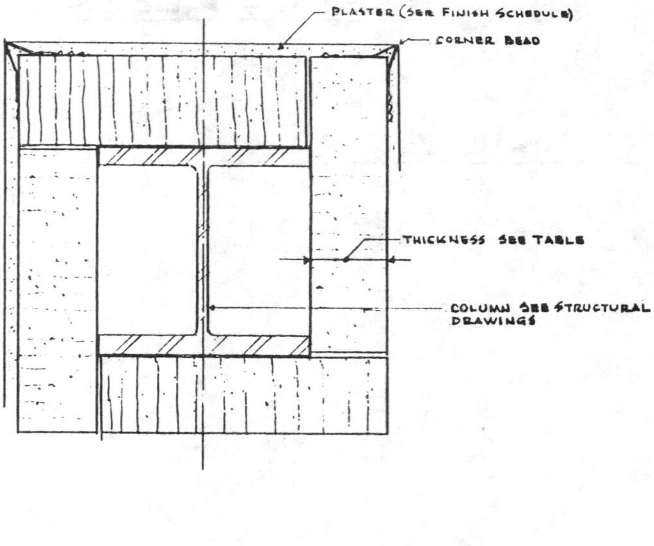
PLASTER (SEE FINISH SCHEDULE)
CORNER BEAD
THICKNESS SEE TABLE
COLUMN SEE STRUCTURAL DRAWINGS

MATERIAL	THICKNESS IN INCHES			
	1 HR	2 HR	3 HR	4 HR
BRICK (BURNED CLAY OR SHALE)	2 1/4"	2 1/4"	3 3/4"	3 3/4"
BRICK (SAND LIME)	2 1/4"	2 1/4"	3 3/4"	3 3/4"
CONCRETE BLOCK, BRICK, OR TILE EXCEPT CINDER CONCRETE UNITS	2 1/4"	2 1/4"	3 3/4"	3 3/4"
HOLLOW CINDER OR CONCRETE BLOCK & TILE HAVING A COMPRESSIVE STRENGTH OF AT LEAST 700#/SQ IN. OF GROSS AREA	1 1/2"	2"	2"	2 1/2"
SOLID GYPSUM BLOCK PROVIDED THAT TO OBTAIN 4 HR RATING, BLOCKS SHALL BE PLASTERED WITH AT LEAST 1/2" GYPSUM PLASTER	1"	1 1/2"	2"	2"
HOLLOW OR SOLID BURNED CLAY TILE OR COMBINATION OF TILE & CONCRETE	1 1/2"	2"	2"	2 1/2"
HOLLOW GYPSUM BLOCK, PROVIDED THAT TO OBTAIN A 4 HR. RATING, BLOCKS SHALL BE PLASTERED WITH AT LEAST 1/2" GYPSUM PLASTER	3"	3"	3"	3"

MASONRY FIREPROOFING

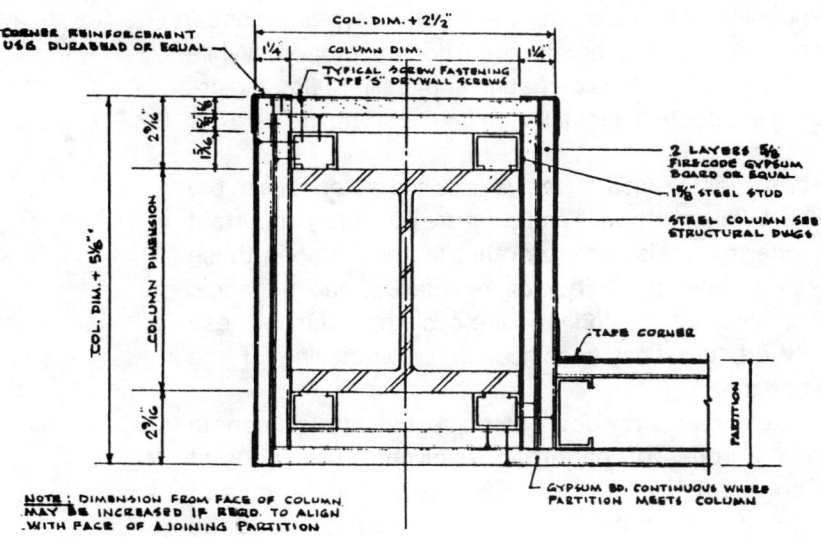

COL. DIM. + 2½"
COLUMN DIM.
1¼ · 1¼

CORNER REINFORCEMENT
USG DURABEAD OR EQUAL

TYPICAL SCREW FASTENING
TYPE "S" DRYWALL SCREWS

2 LAYERS 5/8"
FIRECODE GYPSUM
BOARD OR EQUAL

1 5/8" STEEL STUD

STEEL COLUMN SEE
STRUCTURAL DWGS

TAPE CORNER

PARTITION

GYPSUM BD. CONTINUOUS WHERE
PARTITION MEETS COLUMN

COL. DIM. + 5½"

COLUMN DIMENSION

2 9/16"

2 9/16"

NOTE: DIMENSION FROM FACE OF COLUMN
MAY BE INCREASED IF REQD. TO ALIGN
WITH FACE OF ADJOINING PARTITION

GYPSUM BOARD FIREPROOFING — 2 HR. RATING

FOR 3 HR. RATING ADD 1 ADDITIONAL LAYER OF 5/8" FIRECODE GYPSUM BOARD
1½ HR RATING 3 LAYERS OF GYPSUM BD. (STANDARD)
1 HR. RATING 2 " " " "

SCALE: 3" = 1'-0"

PLASTER THICKNESS FROM
FACE OF LATH

EXPANDED
CORNER BEAD

METAL LATH
SEE TABLE
FOR TYPE

VERMICULITE
OR PERLITE
PLASTER SEE
TABLE FOR
THICKNESS

COLUMN

RATING	PLASTER THICK.	LATH
1 HR.	5/8"	3.4# DIAMOND MESH METAL LATH
2 HR.	1"	3.4# SELF FURRING DIAMOND MESH METAL LATH
3 HR.	1 3/8"	
4 HR.	1¼"	

NOTE: N.Y.C. CODE - 4 HR RATING MAY
BE OBTAINED WITH 1" VERMICULITE
PLASTER ON S.F. LATH & BACKFILL
OF LOOSE VERMICULITE

VERMICULITE OR GYPSUM PERLITE FIREPROOFING

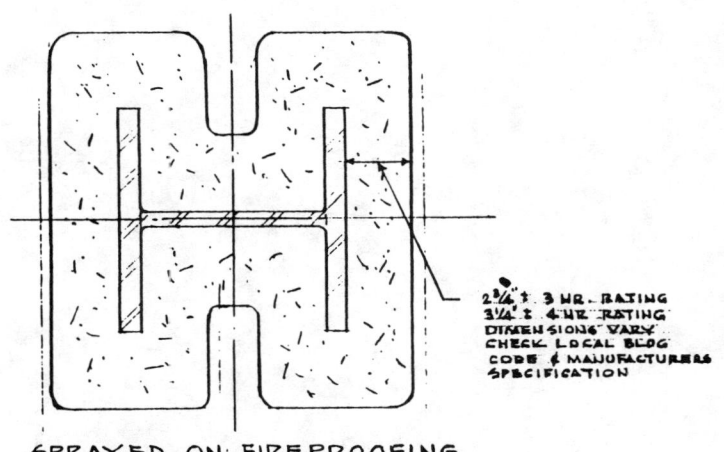

2 3/4" ± 3 HR. RATING
3¼" ± 4 HR. RATING
DIMENSIONS VARY
CHECK LOCAL BLDG
CODE & MANUFACTURERS
SPECIFICATION

SPRAYED ON FIREPROOFING

The designer must be familiar with the great variety of floor types, finishes, and patterns in order to specify and detail architectural flooring properly. While some examples of "soft finishes" such as carpeting and resilient flooring are shown, this section explores in depth the installation and detailing of "hard" or architectural finishes.

It is important for the designer to research the various characteristics of the floor finish being specified. While aesthetics and color are obviously important considerations, the designer must also analyze other factors. Among these factors are wear resistance and durability, soil resistance, maintenance, resiliency, flammability, costs of installation, and life cycle cost. Once these factors have been analyzed, the final specification and detailing of the architectural finish must be developed.

Examples of standard patterns are provided, but the designer must become familiar with the infinite number of pattern possibilities. The inherent limitations of materials control their sizes and thicknesses. The patterns of certain materials are dictated by both the thickness of the material and the weight or "dead load" of the material superimposed upon the structure. For example, a large pattern of marble or granite will necessitate a slab of material that will weigh much more per square foot than that of a smaller pattern. This greater weight might have structural consequences, as well as make floor transitions more significant.

Transitions between flooring materials, particularly under doors or at entrances, and transitions between flooring and walls are some of the key material interfaces that have to be detailed. Again, this section provides such information using both traditional and contemporary approaches.

Finally, a portion of this section is devoted to the detailing of raised computer room floors. While not traditionally a floor finish, raised computer room floors seem appropriate for this section. While generic architectural details are provided, the designer should always develop final details in conjunction with the manufacturer(s) being specified.

FLOORS AND FLOOR FINISHES
Typical Characteristics of Floor Finishes

DRAWING AND DESCRIPTION	WEAR RESISTANCE	SOIL RESISTANCE, CLEANING AND MAINTENANCE	RESILIENCY	REMARKS	COST COMPARISON
⅛ inch hardened cement finish on concrete slab	Good	Poor; frequent cleaning needed; must be refinished every ten years	Very hard	Cement base costs little, is too hard a floor to be comfortable; infrequently used in classrooms, sometimes used in corridors, shops and inexpensive toilet rooms	installation cost maintenance and insurance cost for 20 years
¾ inch terrazzo finish, with ¾ inch cement underbed on a concrete slab	Very good	Very good; needs cleaning once a week with detergent and water	Very hard	Terrazzo base is easy to clean and sanitary, but not resilient and sometimes noisy; seldom used in classrooms, often used in corridors, vestibules, toilets and shower rooms	
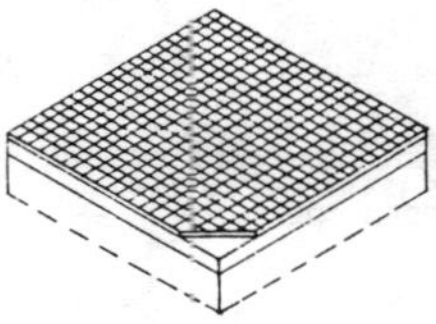 Ceramic mosaic tile, ¾ inch setting bed on concrete slab	Very good	Very good	Very hard	Used in toilet rooms, showers, food service areas, but seldom used in classrooms	
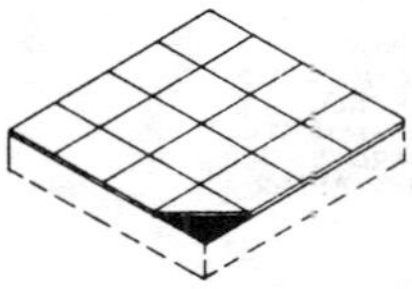 ⅛ inch asphalt tile finish installed in mastic on concrete slab	Poor, usually needs replacing every ten years	Fair; must be cleaned and waxed once a week	Fair	Low first cost; finish requires careful maintenance	
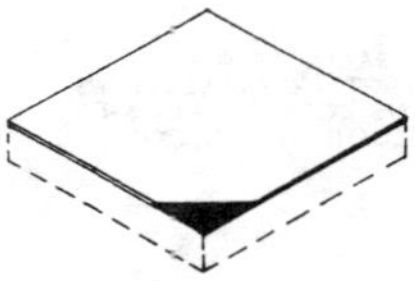 ⅛ inch linoleum finish installed in mastic on concrete slab	Good	Fair; must be cleaned and waxed once a week	Fair	Serviceable; a sanitary floor for classrooms, corridors, assembly and administration rooms	
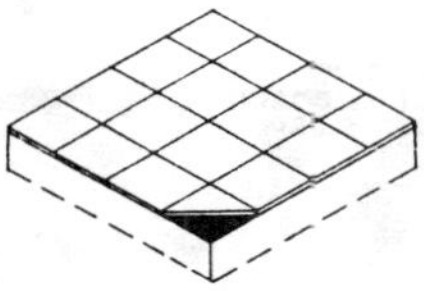 ⅛ inch cork tile floor installed in mastic on concrete slab	Good	Fair; needs frequent cleaning and waxing	Very good	Used primarily in libraries and kindergartens; floor is subject to indentations by chair legs; acoustically good	
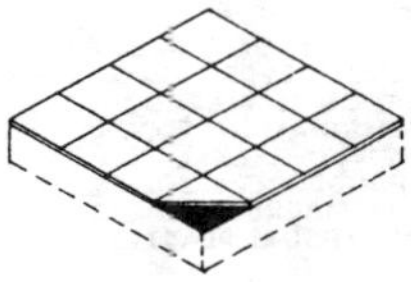 ⅛ inch rubber tile finish installed in mastic on concrete slab	Good	Fair; needs cleaning and waxing once a week	Very good	Subject to slight indentation by chair legs	
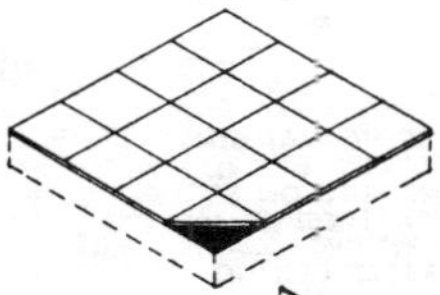 ⅛ inch vinyl tile finish installed in mastic on concrete slab	Good	Fair; needs a weekly cleaning and waxing	Very good	Subject to indentation	
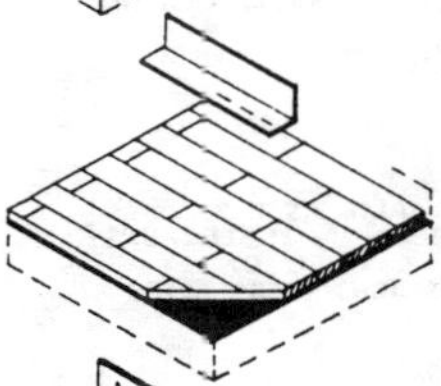 25/32 inch maple strip flooring set in ⅛ inch hot asphalt mastic on concrete slab	Very good	Good; requires monthly cleaning with steelwool and a wax finish	Fair	Steel angles necessary to cover expansion joint; used in gymnasiums and playrooms; not suitable for damp areas or climates	
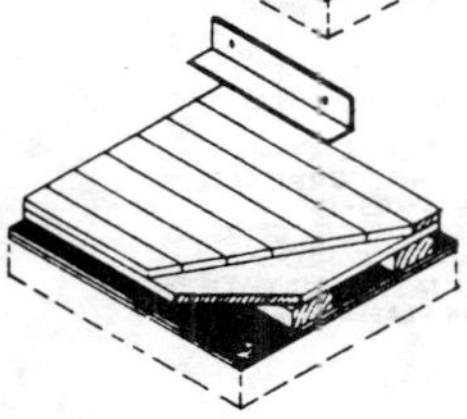 25/32 inch maple finish; 1 by 4 inch cypress subfloor laid diagonally; 2 by 6 inch cypress sleepers, 12 inches apart, set in two ⅛ inch layers of hot asphalt mastic	Very good	Good; requires a monthly cleaning with steelwool and a wax finish; sand and re-finish every 2 years	Excellent	A deluxe gymnasium floor	

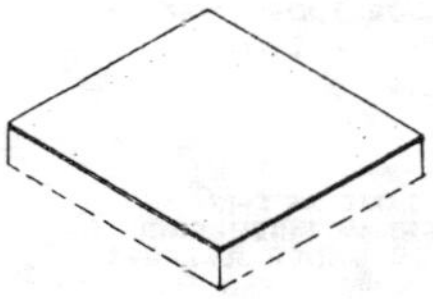

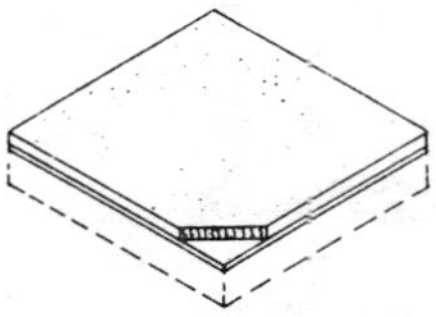

FLOORS AND FLOOR FINISHES

Floor Construction Details

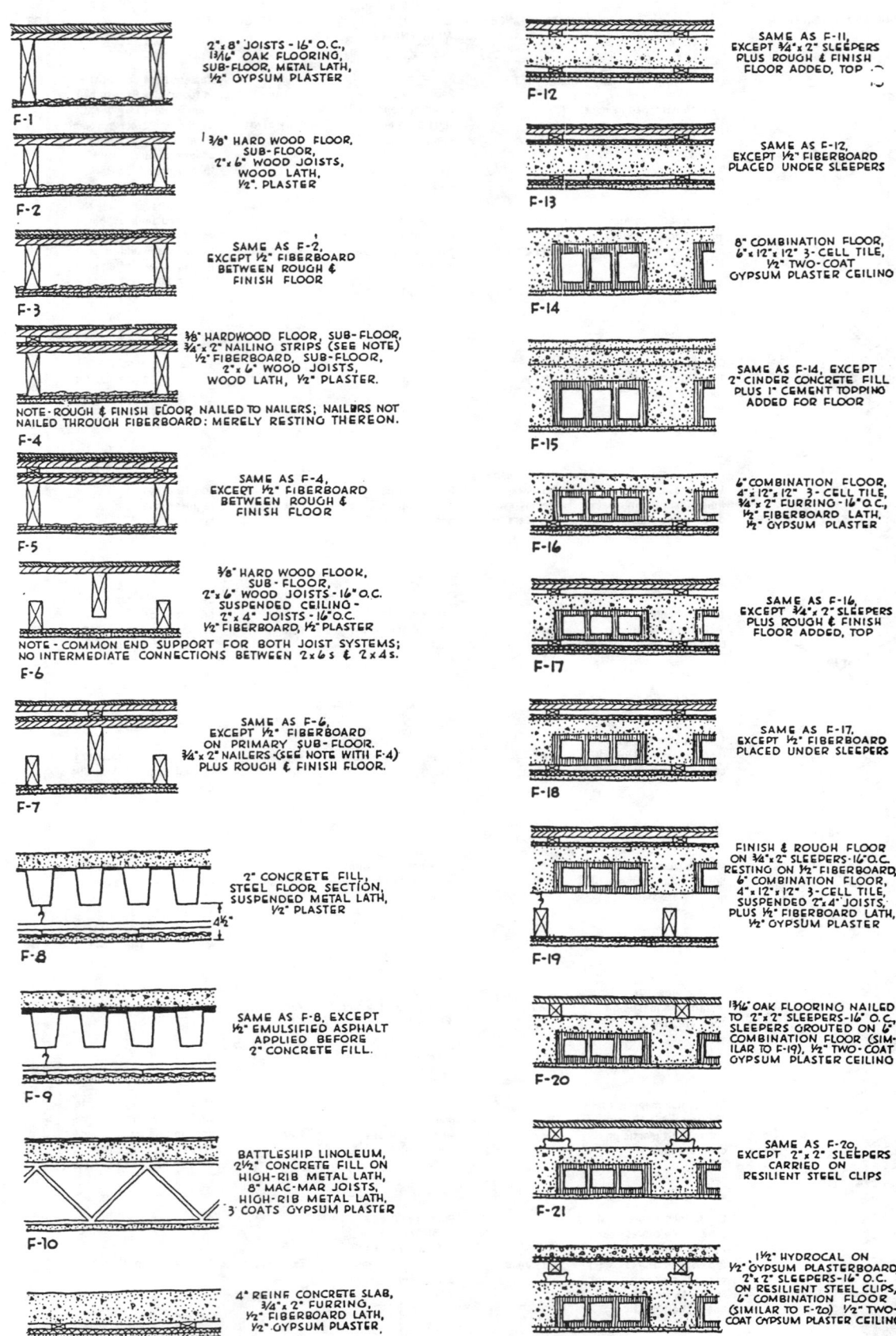

F-1
2" x 8" JOISTS - 16" O.C.,
1 13/16" OAK FLOORING,
SUB-FLOOR, METAL LATH,
½" GYPSUM PLASTER

F-2
1 3/8" HARD WOOD FLOOR,
SUB-FLOOR,
2" x 6" WOOD JOISTS,
WOOD LATH,
½" PLASTER

F-3
SAME AS F-2,
EXCEPT ½" FIBERBOARD
BETWEEN ROUGH &
FINISH FLOOR

F-4
3/8" HARDWOOD FLOOR, SUB-FLOOR,
¾" x 2" NAILING STRIPS (SEE NOTE)
½" FIBERBOARD, SUB-FLOOR,
2" x 6" WOOD JOISTS,
WOOD LATH, ½" PLASTER.
NOTE - ROUGH & FINISH FLOOR NAILED TO NAILERS; NAILERS NOT
NAILED THROUGH FIBERBOARD; MERELY RESTING THEREON.

F-5
SAME AS F-4,
EXCEPT ½" FIBERBOARD
BETWEEN ROUGH &
FINISH FLOOR

F-6
3/8" HARD WOOD FLOOR,
SUB-FLOOR,
2" x 6" WOOD JOISTS - 16" O.C.
SUSPENDED CEILING -
2" x 4" JOISTS - 16" O.C.
½" FIBERBOARD, ½" PLASTER
NOTE - COMMON END SUPPORT FOR BOTH JOIST SYSTEMS;
NO INTERMEDIATE CONNECTIONS BETWEEN 2x6s & 2x4s.

F-7
SAME AS F-6,
EXCEPT ½" FIBERBOARD
ON PRIMARY SUB-FLOOR.
¾" x 2" NAILERS (SEE NOTE WITH F-4)
PLUS ROUGH & FINISH FLOOR.

F-8
2" CONCRETE FILL,
STEEL FLOOR SECTION,
SUSPENDED METAL LATH,
½" PLASTER

F-9
SAME AS F-8, EXCEPT
½" EMULSIFIED ASPHALT
APPLIED BEFORE
2" CONCRETE FILL.

F-10
BATTLESHIP LINOLEUM,
2½" CONCRETE FILL ON
HIGH-RIB METAL LATH,
8" MAC-MAR JOISTS,
HIGH-RIB METAL LATH,
3 COATS GYPSUM PLASTER

F-11
4" REINF. CONCRETE SLAB,
¾" x 2" FURRING,
½" FIBERBOARD LATH,
½" GYPSUM PLASTER

F-12
SAME AS F-11,
EXCEPT ¾" x 2" SLEEPERS
PLUS ROUGH & FINISH
FLOOR ADDED, TOP

F-13
SAME AS F-12,
EXCEPT ½" FIBERBOARD
PLACED UNDER SLEEPERS

F-14
8" COMBINATION FLOOR,
6" x 12" x 12" 3-CELL TILE,
½" TWO-COAT
GYPSUM PLASTER CEILING

F-15
SAME AS F-14, EXCEPT
2" CINDER CONCRETE FILL
PLUS 1" CEMENT TOPPING
ADDED FOR FLOOR

F-16
6" COMBINATION FLOOR,
4" x 12" x 12" 3-CELL TILE,
¾" x 2" FURRING - 16" O.C.,
½" FIBERBOARD LATH,
½" GYPSUM PLASTER

F-17
SAME AS F-16,
EXCEPT ¾" x 2" SLEEPERS
PLUS ROUGH & FINISH
FLOOR ADDED, TOP

F-18
SAME AS F-17,
EXCEPT ½" FIBERBOARD
PLACED UNDER SLEEPERS

F-19
FINISH & ROUGH FLOOR
ON ¾" x 2" SLEEPERS - 16" O.C.
RESTING ON ½" FIBERBOARD,
6" COMBINATION FLOOR,
4" x 12" x 12" 3-CELL TILE,
SUSPENDED 2" x 4" JOISTS,
PLUS ½" FIBERBOARD LATH,
½" GYPSUM PLASTER

F-20
1 13/16" OAK FLOORING NAILED
TO 2" x 2" SLEEPERS - 16" O.C.
SLEEPERS GROUTED ON 6"
COMBINATION FLOOR (SIMILAR TO F-19), ½" TWO-COAT
GYPSUM PLASTER CEILING

F-21
SAME AS F-20,
EXCEPT 2" x 2" SLEEPERS
CARRIED ON
RESILIENT STEEL CLIPS

F-22
1½" HYDROCAL ON
½" GYPSUM PLASTERBOARD,
2" x 2" SLEEPERS - 16" O.C.
ON RESILIENT STEEL CLIPS,
6" COMBINATION FLOOR
(SIMILAR TO F-20), ½" TWO-
COAT GYPSUM PLASTER CEILING

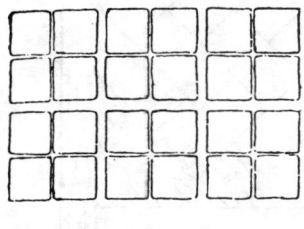

By groups of four squares as a unit separated by wider joints, the scale is increased.

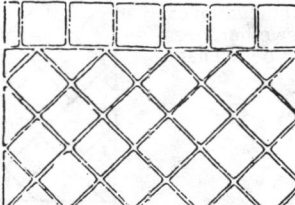

A diagonal pattern of square tiles is emphasized by a border.

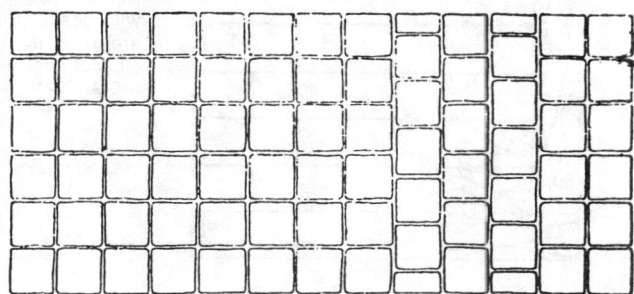

By a few rows of broken joints, an effect of border is produced in a field of square tiles.

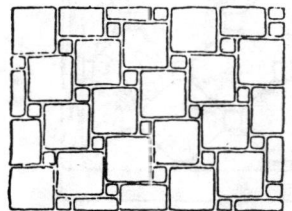

When the small squares are less than one-quarter of the area of the large squares, the pattern runs off at the side.

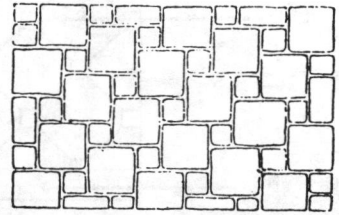

When the small squares are one quarter of the area of the large squares, the pattern has more repose.

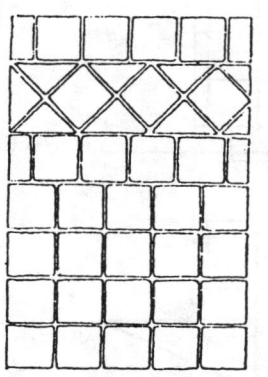

By breaking joints in one course, the border is made wide.

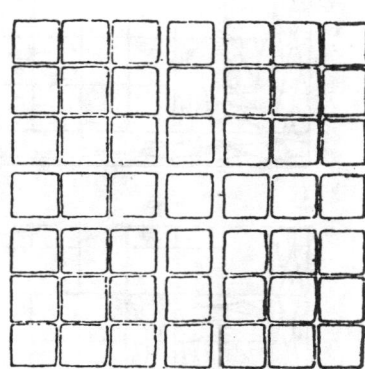

An arrangement adapted to large rooms.

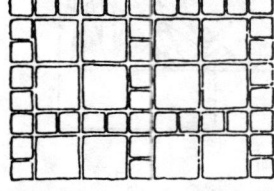

Another way to increase the scale with small tiles.

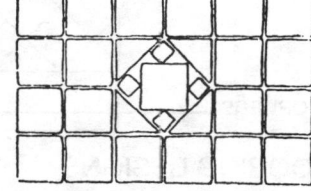

A decorative pattern that can be made on the job.

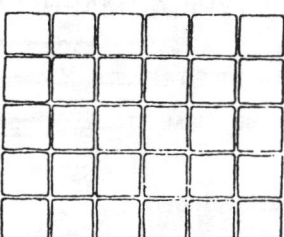

The simplest floor of square tiles is interesting if the joints are in scale.

When square tiles are laid with broken joints, long lines in one direction are the result.

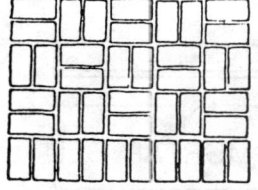

When double squares are laid "basket pattern," the necessary allowance for joints adds interest.

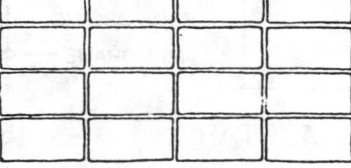

A good pattern for corridors.

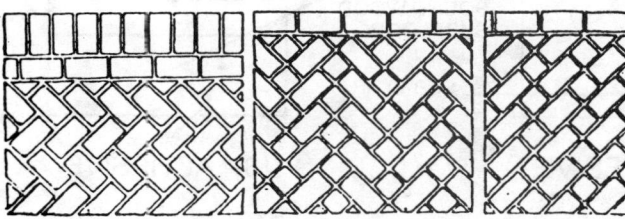

Varieties of "herringbone."

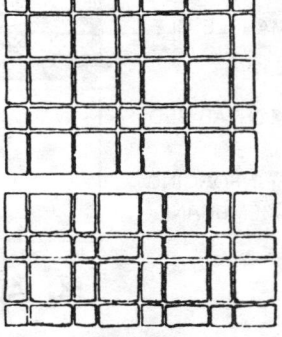

Two combinations suggesting plaids.

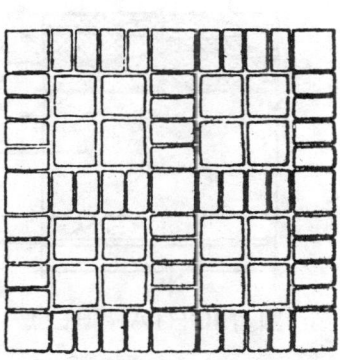

A simple device for a panel or a floor for a large room.

519

FLOORS AND FLOOR FINISHES
Marble Floor Patterns and Details

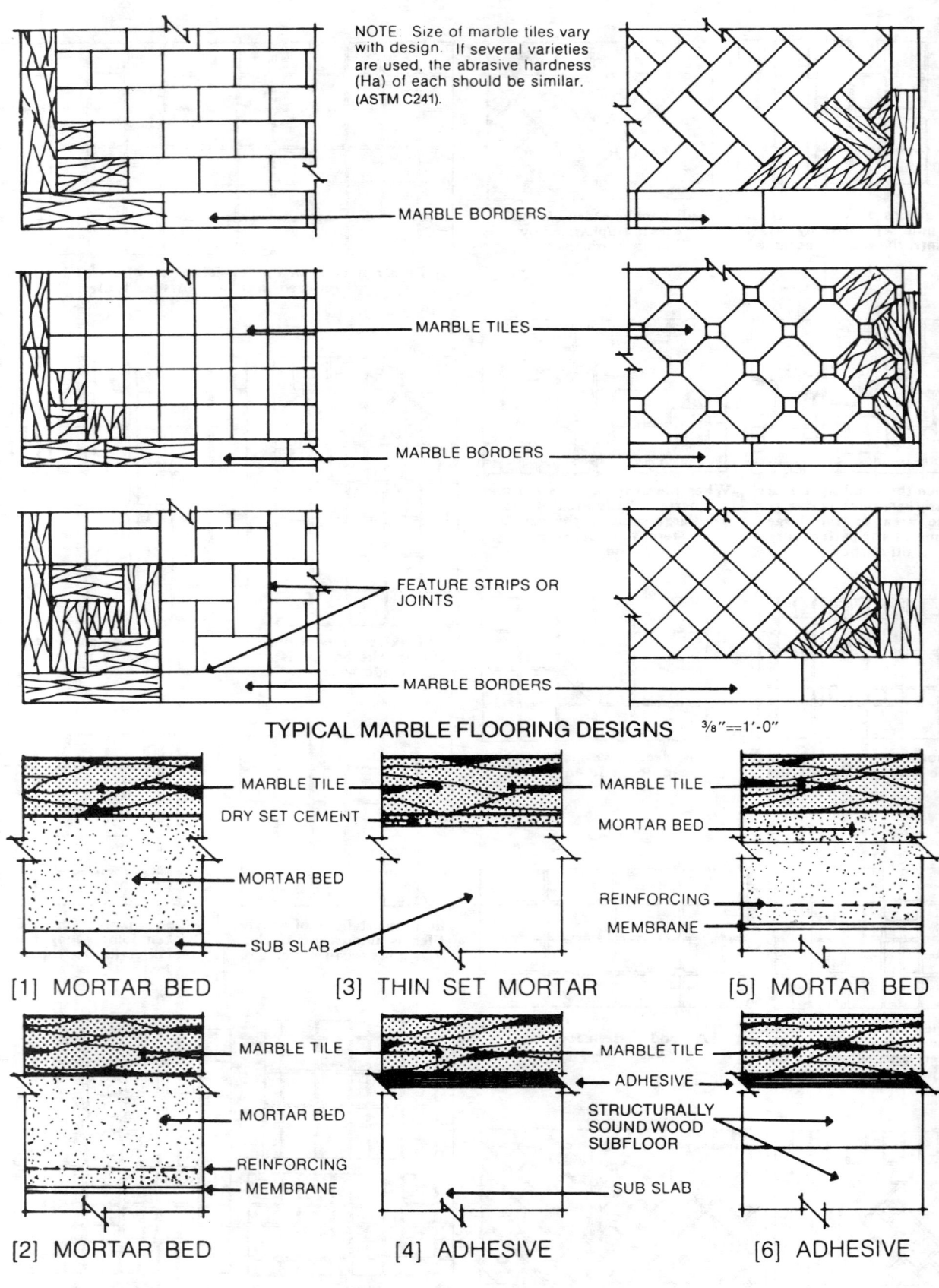

NOTE: Size of marble tiles vary with design. If several varieties are used, the abrasive hardness (Ha) of each should be similar. (ASTM C241).

MARBLE BORDERS

MARBLE TILES

MARBLE BORDERS

FEATURE STRIPS OR JOINTS

MARBLE BORDERS

TYPICAL MARBLE FLOORING DESIGNS   ⅜"=1'-0"

MARBLE TILE
DRY SET CEMENT
MORTAR BED
SUB SLAB

MARBLE TILE
MORTAR BED
REINFORCING
MEMBRANE

[1] MORTAR BED   **[3] THIN SET MORTAR**   **[5] MORTAR BED**

MARBLE TILE
MORTAR BED
REINFORCING
MEMBRANE

MARBLE TILE
ADHESIVE
SUB SLAB

MARBLE TILE
ADHESIVE
STRUCTURALLY SOUND WOOD SUBFLOOR

[2] MORTAR BED   **[4] ADHESIVE**   **[6] ADHESIVE**

METHODS OF INSTALLATION   HALF SIZE

Fig. 1   Marble flooring details.

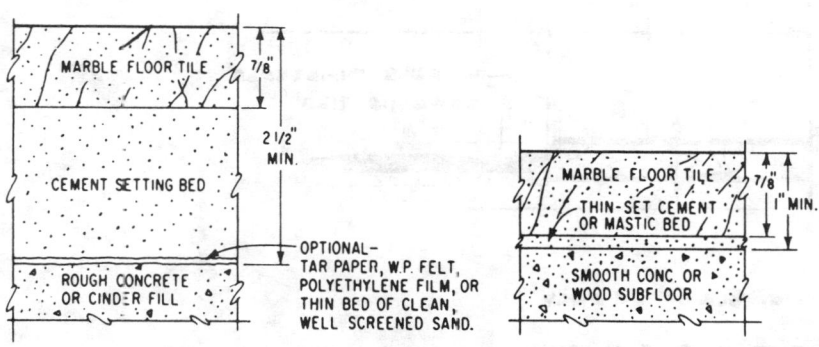

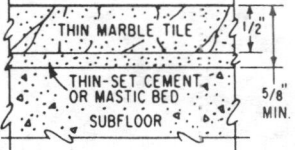

c. Thin marble tile, preferred method

a. Standard floor tile, preferred method   b. Standard floor tile, thin-set method

d. Thin marble tile, thin-set method

Fig. 2   Marble floor setting methods.

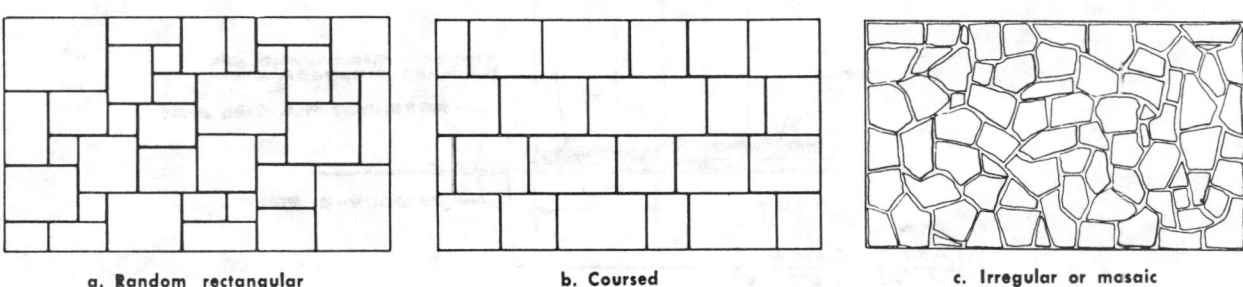

a. Random rectangular   b. Coursed   c. Irregular or mosaic

Fig. 3   Flagging patterns.

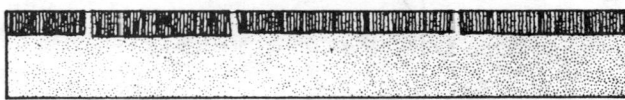

a. On sand bed

Flagging 1 to 1½ in.
Sand bed 4 in.

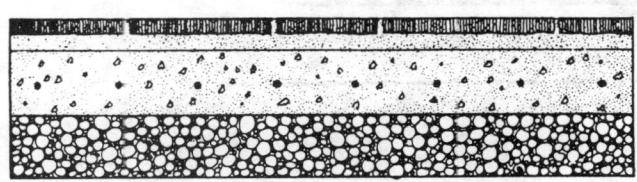

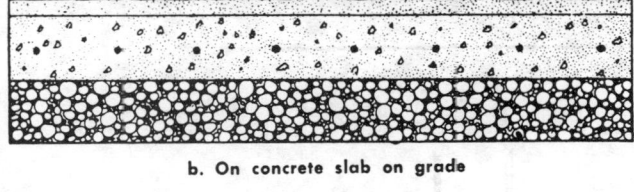

b. On concrete slab on grade

Flagging ¾ to 1 in.
Setting bed 1 to 1½ in.
Reinforced concrete slab 4 in.
Gravel or cinders 4 in.

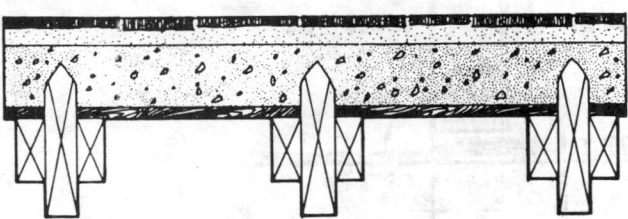

c. On wood joist construction

Flagging ¾ to 1 in.
Setting bed 1 to 1½ in.
Reinforced concrete slab 4 in.
Wood subfloor ¾ in.

Fig. 4   Flagstone setting methods.

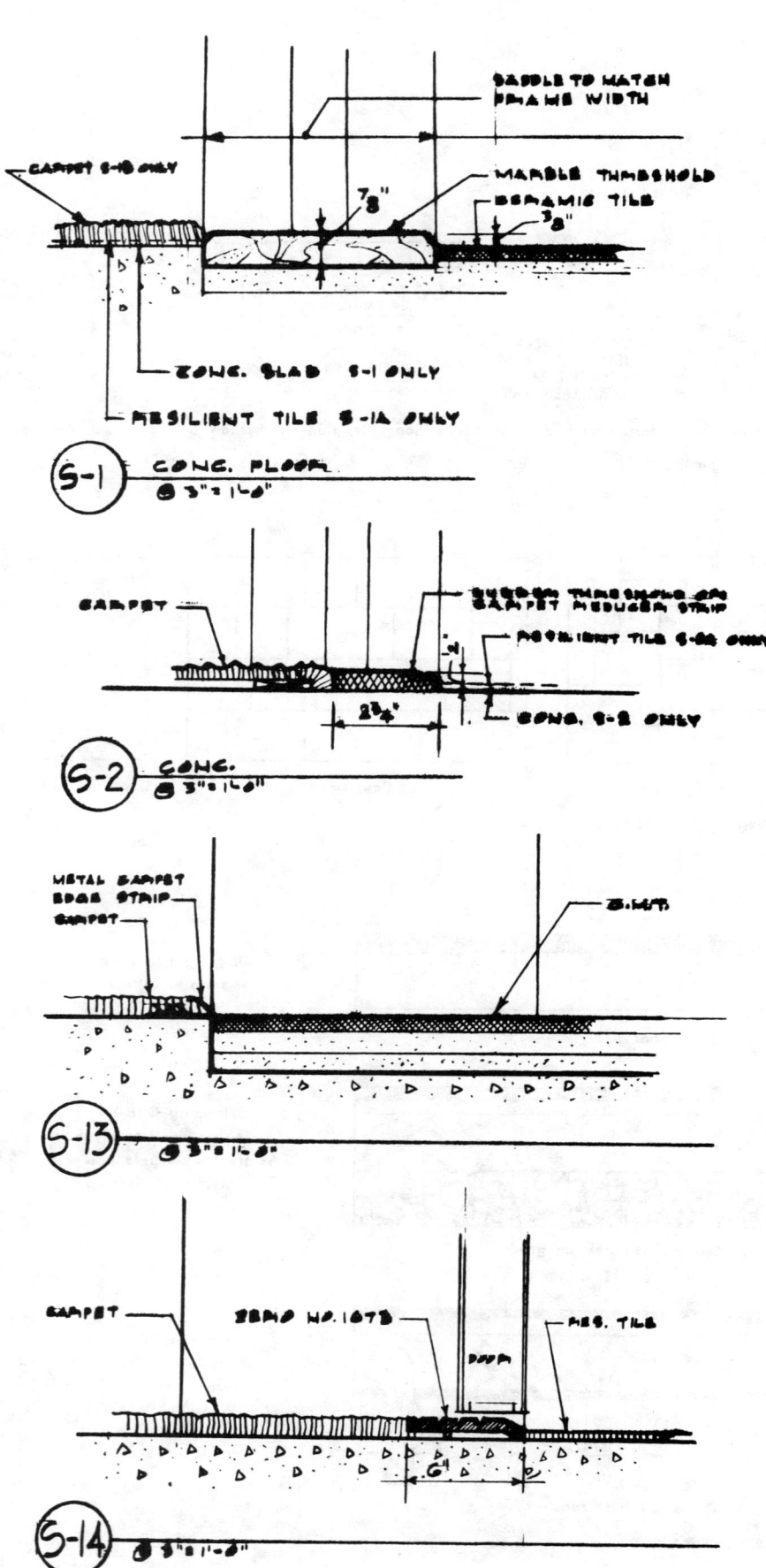

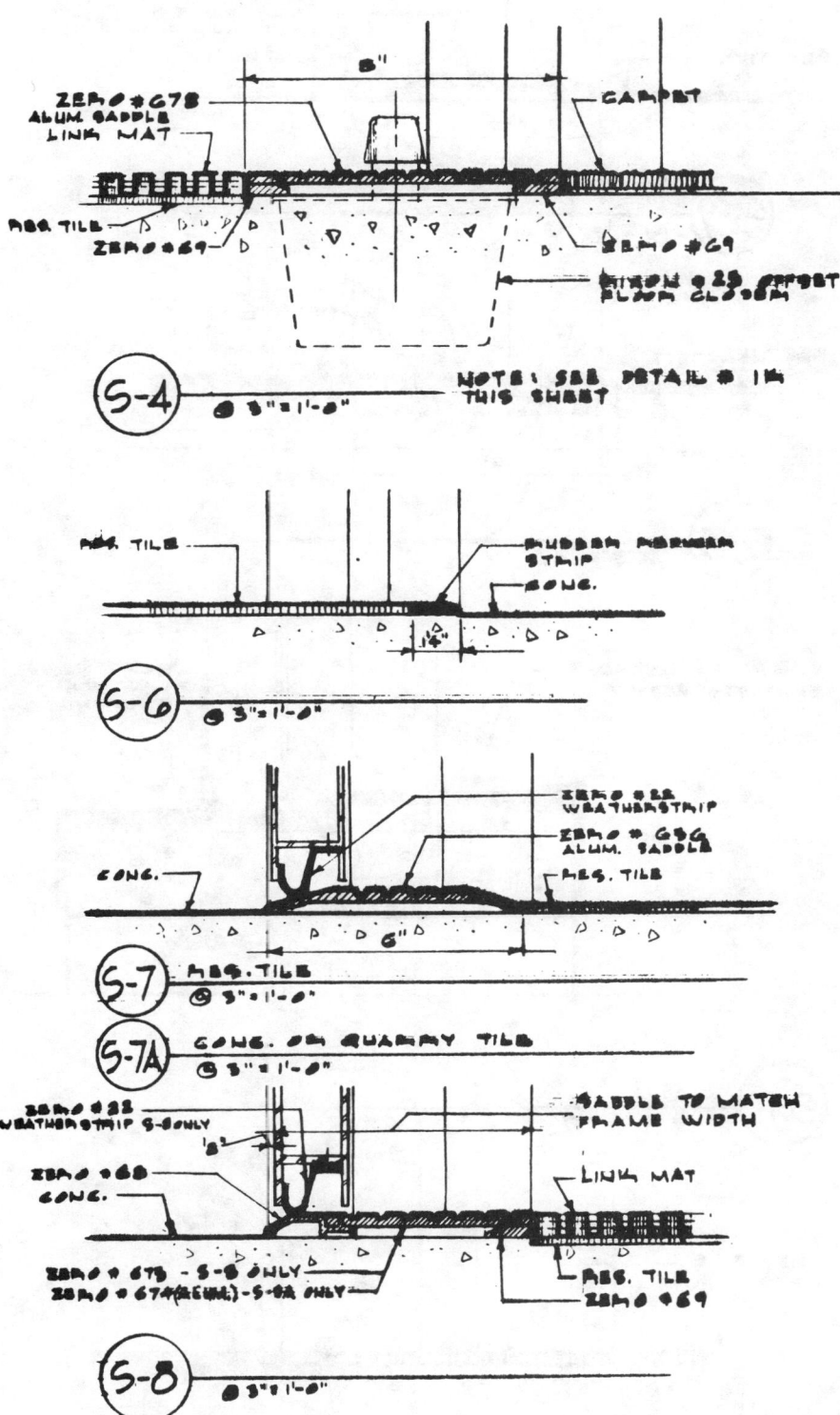

FLOORS AND FLOOR FINISHES
Saddles/Floor Transitions

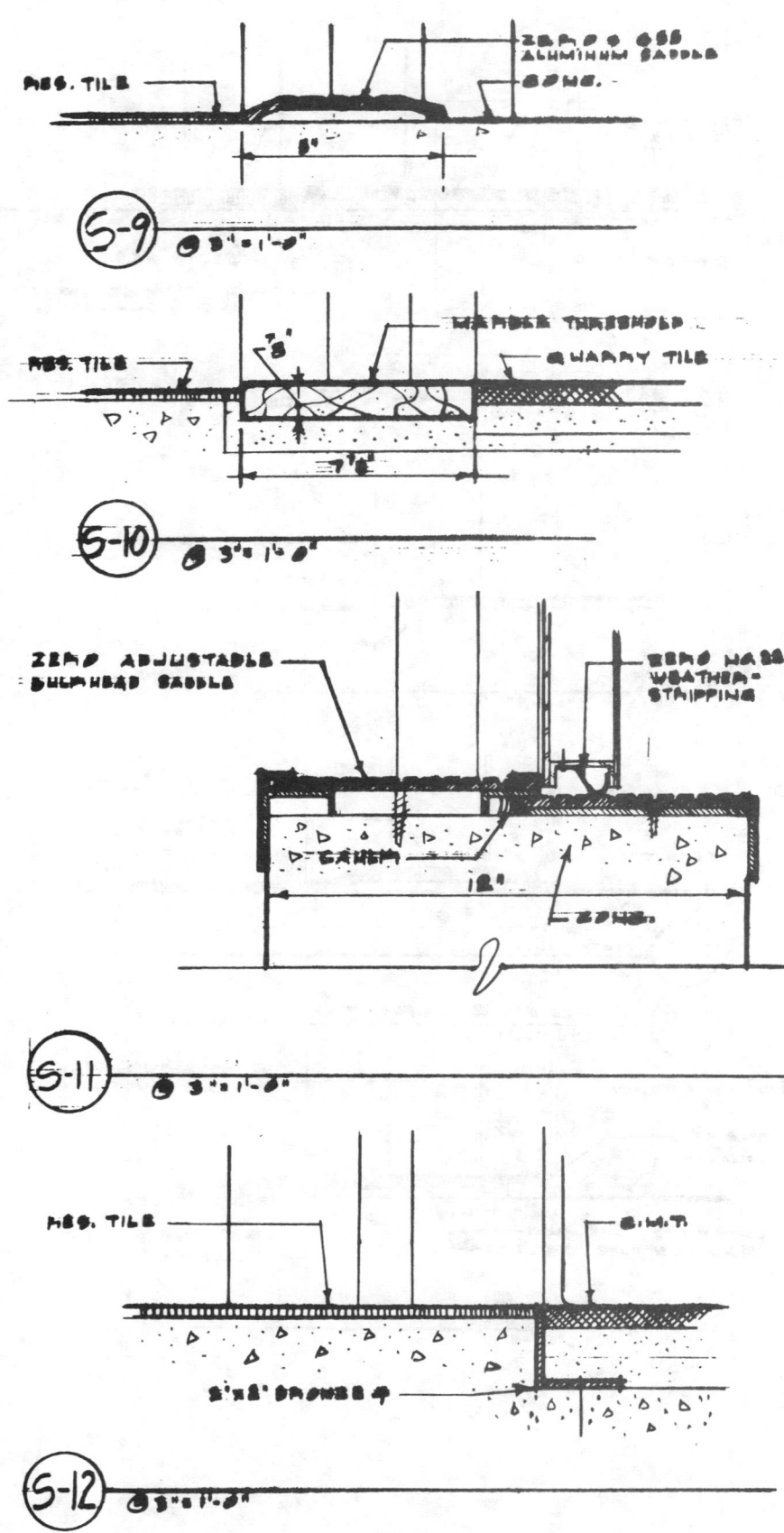

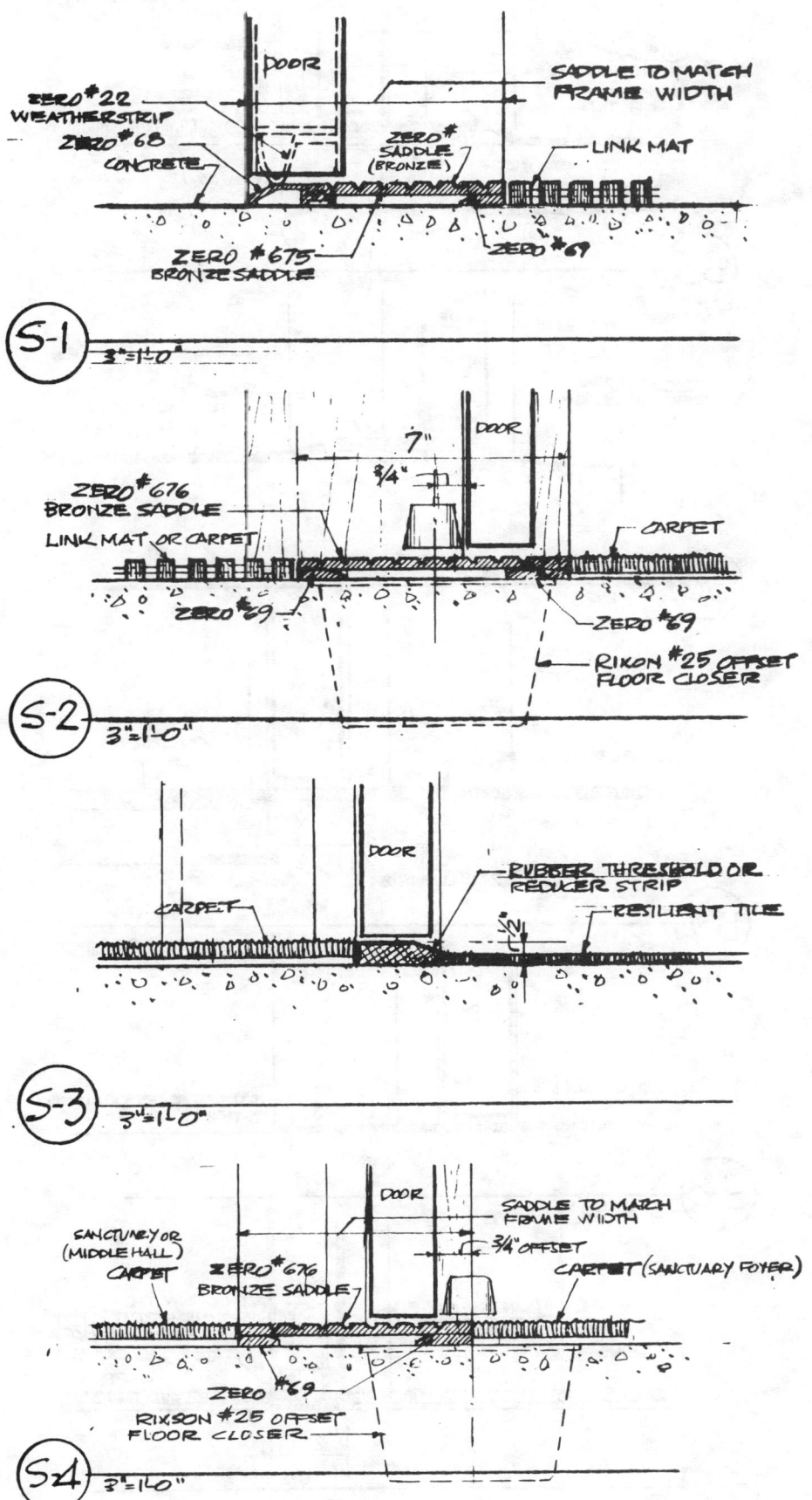

S-1 3"=1'-0"

ZERO #22 WEATHERSTRIP
ZERO #68
CONCRETE
DOOR
SADDLE TO MATCH FRAME WIDTH
ZERO # SADDLE (BRONZE)
LINK MAT
ZERO #675 BRONZE SADDLE
ZERO #69

S-2 3"=1'-0"

ZERO #676 BRONZE SADDLE
LINK MAT OR CARPET
7"
3/4"
DOOR
CARPET
ZERO #69
ZERO #69
RIXON #25 OFFSET FLOOR CLOSER

S-3 3"=1'-0"

CARPET
DOOR
RUBBER THRESHOLD OR REDUCER STRIP
RESILIENT TILE

S-4 3"=1'-0"

SANCTUARY OR (MIDDLE HALL) CARPET
ZERO #676 BRONZE SADDLE
DOOR
SADDLE TO MATCH FRAME WIDTH
3/4" OFFSET
CARPET (SANCTUARY FOYER)
ZERO #69
RIXSON #25 OFFSET FLOOR CLOSER

FLOORS AND FLOOR FINISHES
Door Saddles

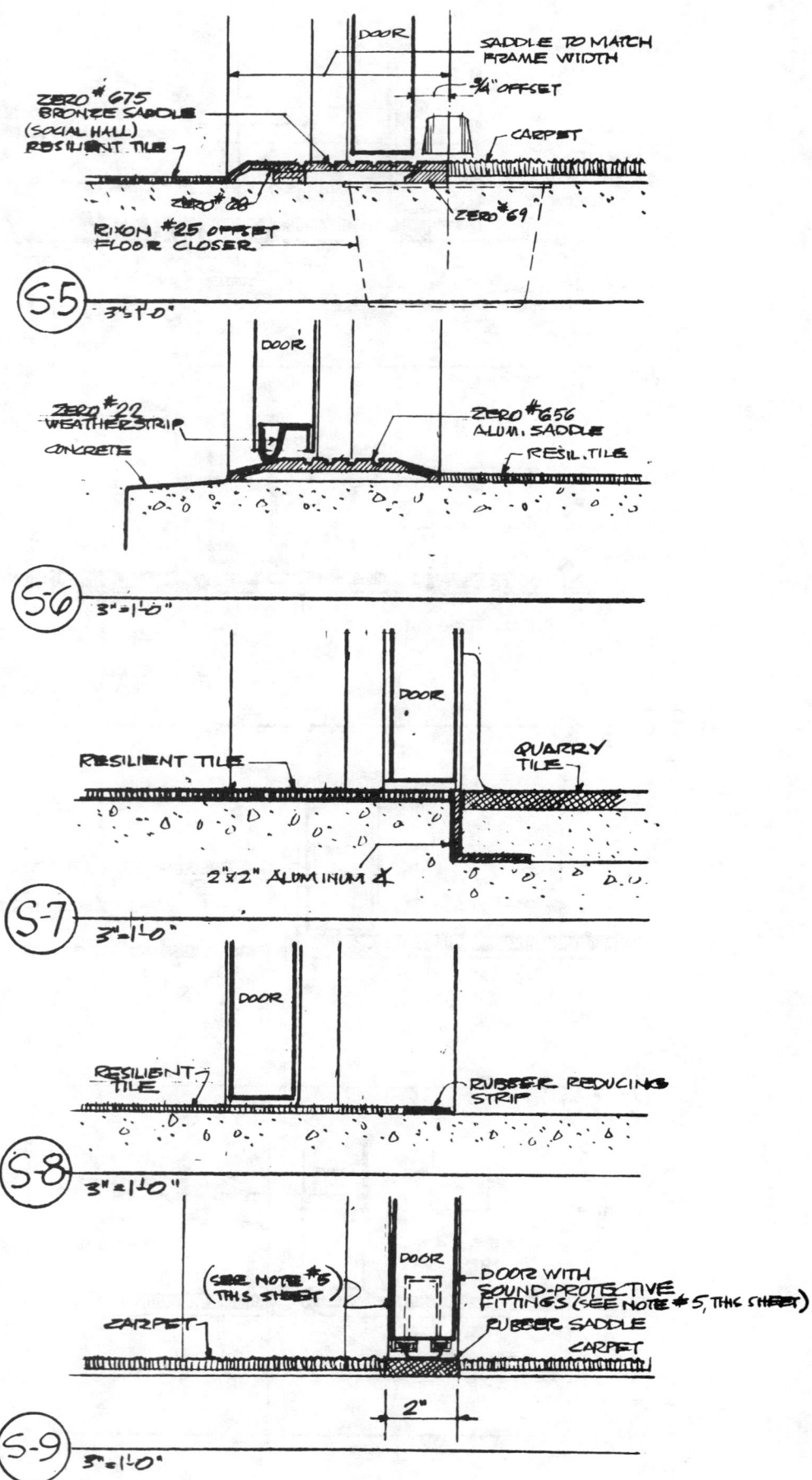

ZERO #675
BRONZE SADDLE
(SOCIAL HALL)
RESILIENT TILE

DOOR

SADDLE TO MATCH
FRAME WIDTH

¾" OFFSET

CARPET

ZERO #08

ZERO #69

RIXON #25 OFFSET
FLOOR CLOSER

(S-5) 3"=1'-0"

DOOR

ZERO #22
WEATHER STRIP

CONCRETE

ZERO #656
ALUM. SADDLE

RESIL. TILE

(S-6) 3"=1'-0"

RESILIENT TILE

DOOR

QUARRY
TILE

2"x2" ALUMINUM ¢

(S-7) 3"=1'-0"

DOOR

RESILIENT
TILE

RUBBER REDUCING
STRIP

(S-8) 3"=1'-0"

(SEE NOTE #5
THIS SHEET)

CARPET

DOOR

DOOR WITH
SOUND-PROTECTIVE
FITTINGS (SEE NOTE #5, THIS SHEET)

RUBBER SADDLE

CARPET

2"

(S-9) 3"=1'-0"

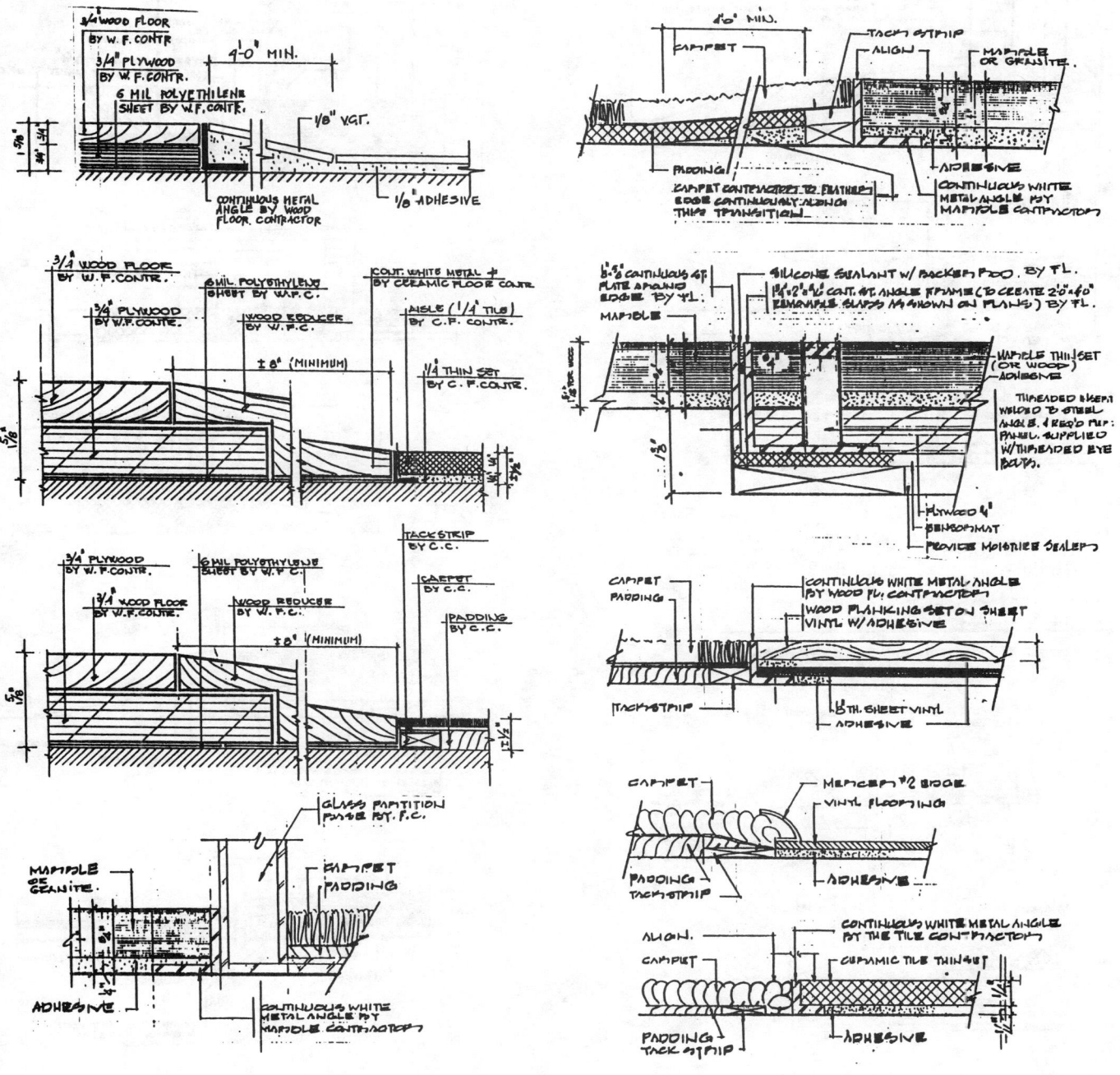

FLOORS AND FLOOR FINISHES

Saddles/Floor Transitions

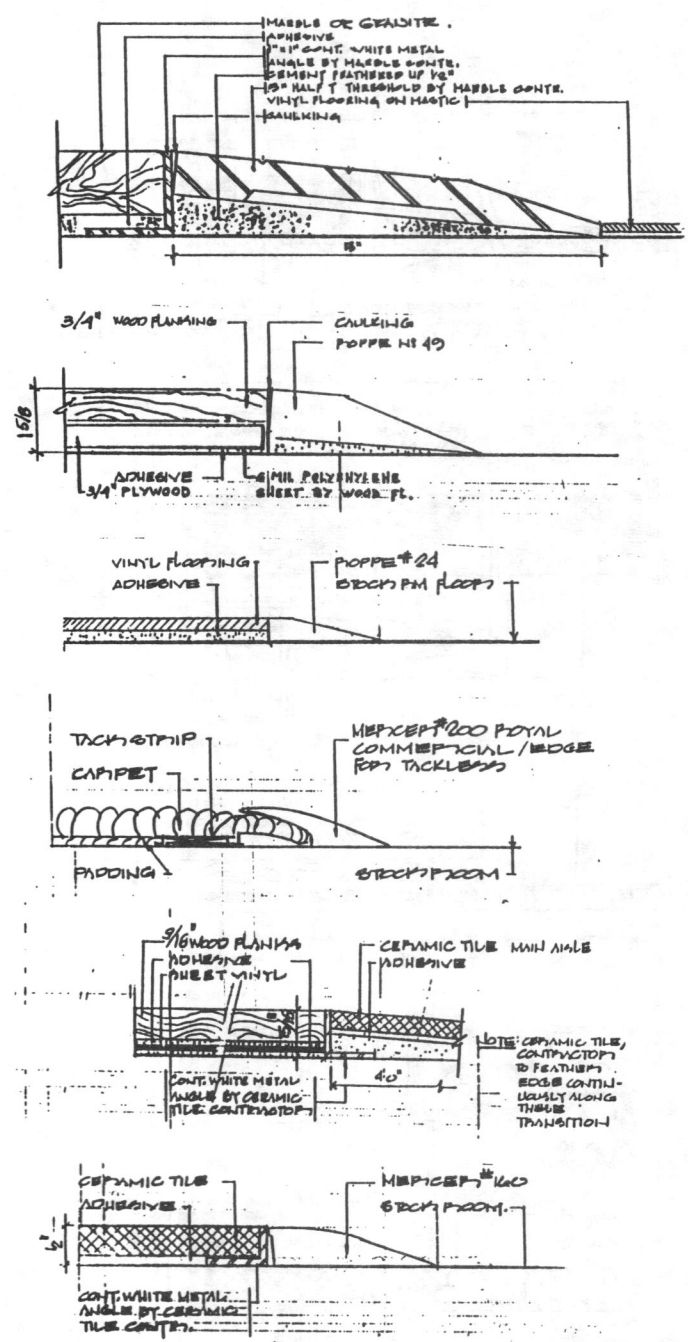

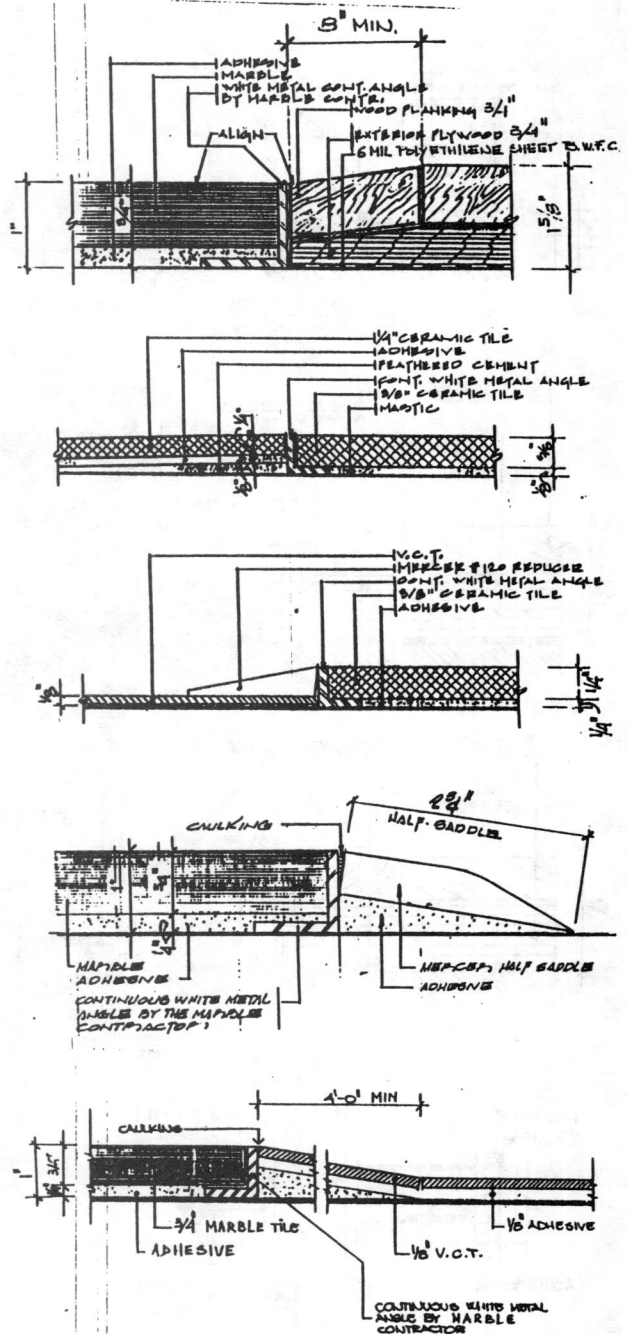

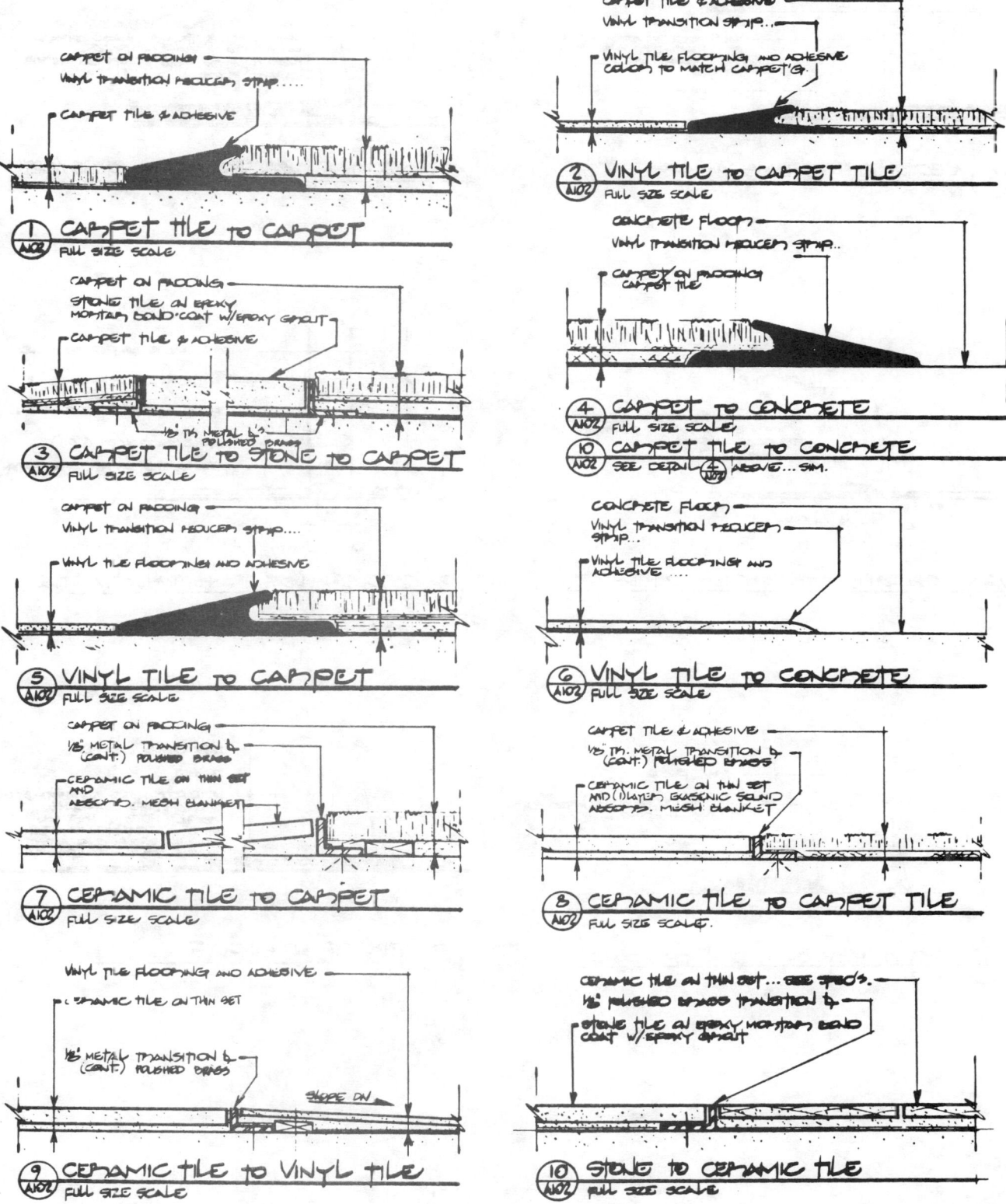

1. CARPET TILE TO CARPET — FULL SIZE SCALE
- CARPET ON PADDING
- VINYL TRANSITION REDUCER STRIP
- CARPET TILE & ADHESIVE

2. VINYL TILE TO CARPET TILE — FULL SIZE SCALE
- CARPET TILE & ADHESIVE
- VINYL TRANSITION STRIP
- VINYL TILE FLOORING AND ADHESIVE COLOR TO MATCH CARPET'G

3. CARPET TILE TO STONE TO CARPET — FULL SIZE SCALE
- CARPET ON PADDING
- STONE TILE ON EPOXY MORTAR BOND COAT W/EPOXY GROUT
- CARPET TILE & ADHESIVE
- 1/8" TH METAL L'S POLISHED BRASS

4. CARPET TO CONCRETE — FULL SIZE SCALE
- CONCRETE FLOOR
- VINYL TRANSITION REDUCER STRIP
- CARPET ON PADDING / CARPET TILE

10. CARPET TILE TO CONCRETE — SEE DETAIL 4 ABOVE... SIM.

5. VINYL TILE TO CARPET — FULL SIZE SCALE
- CARPET ON PADDING
- VINYL TRANSITION REDUCER STRIP
- VINYL TILE FLOORING AND ADHESIVE

6. VINYL TILE TO CONCRETE — FULL SIZE SCALE
- CONCRETE FLOOR
- VINYL TRANSITION REDUCER STRIP
- VINYL TILE FLOORING AND ADHESIVE

7. CERAMIC TILE TO CARPET — FULL SIZE SCALE
- CARPET ON PADDING
- 1/8" METAL TRANSITION & (CONT.) POLISHED BRASS
- CERAMIC TILE ON THIN SET AND ACOUSTIC MESH BLANKET

8. CERAMIC TILE TO CARPET TILE — FULL SIZE SCALE
- CARPET TILE & ADHESIVE
- 1/8" TH. METAL TRANSITION & (CONT.) POLISHED BRASS
- CERAMIC TILE ON THIN SET AND (1) LAYER ACOUSTIC SOUND ABSORPTS. MESH BLANKET

9. CERAMIC TILE TO VINYL TILE — FULL SIZE SCALE
- VINYL TILE FLOORING AND ADHESIVE
- CERAMIC TILE ON THIN SET
- 1/8" METAL TRANSITION & (CONT.) POLISHED BRASS
- SLOPE DN

10. STONE TO CERAMIC TILE — FULL SIZE SCALE
- CERAMIC TILE ON THIN SET... SEE SPEC's.
- 1/8" POLISHED BRASS TRANSITION &
- STONE TILE ON EPOXY MORTAR BOND COAT W/EPOXY GROUT

FLOORS AND FLOOR FINISHES

Floor Finish Transition Details

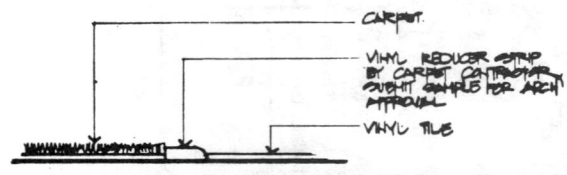

CARPET.

VINYL REDUCER STRIP BY CARPET CONTRACTOR SUBMIT SAMPLE FOR ARCH' APPROVAL

VINYL TILE

② SECTION @ FLOOR TRANSITION/ CARPET/VAT
N.T.S.

GRANITE TILE FLOOR. SEE STONE SPEC'
ALUM. & EDGE TRIM. BY GENERAL CONTRACTOR COORDINATE W/ STONE CONTRACTOR.
FLASH PATCH AS REQ'D. BY CPT CONTRACTOR.
CARPET FLOORING.

① SECTION @ FLOOR TRANSITION. STONE/CPT'
1/2 F.S.

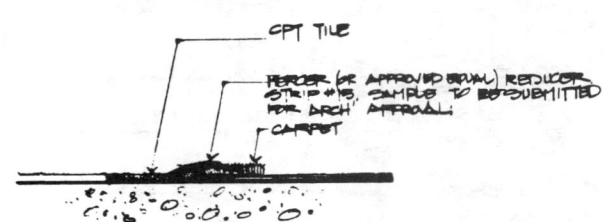

CPT TILE

MERCER (OR APPROVED EQUAL) REDUCER STRIP #15. SAMPLE TO BE SUBMITTED FOR ARCH' APPROVAL.

CARPET

④ SECTION @ FLOOR TRANSITION CPT'TILE/CPT'
NTS

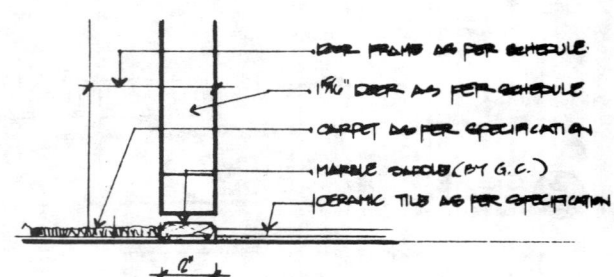

DOOR FRAME AS PER SCHEDULE.

1¾" DOOR AS PER SCHEDULE

CARPET AS PER SPECIFICATION

MARBLE SADDLE (BY G.C.)

CERAMIC TILE AS PER SPECIFICATION

③ SECT' @ FLOOR TRANSITION: CPT/C.TILE.
3"=1'-0"

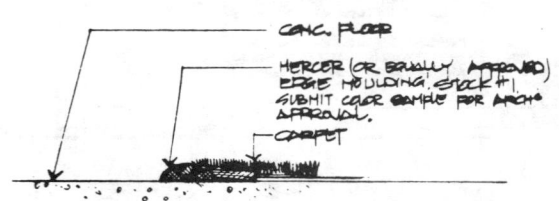

CONC. FLOOR

MERCER (OR EQUALLY APPROVED) EDGE MOULDING. STOCK #1. SUBMIT COLOR SAMPLE FOR ARCH' APPROVAL.

CARPET

⑥ SECT' @ FLOOR TRANSITION. CPT/CONC.
NTS.

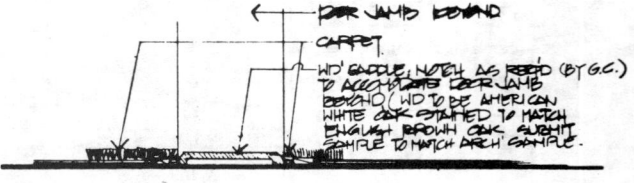

DOOR JAMB BEYOND

CARPET.

WD' SADDLE. NOTCH AS REQ'D (BY G.C.) TO ACCOMMODATE DOOR JAMB BEYOND. WD TO BE AMERICAN WHITE OAK STAINED TO MATCH ENGLISH BROWN OAK. SUBMIT SAMPLE TO MATCH ARCH' SAMPLE.

⑤ SECT' @ WD SADDLE.
NTS.

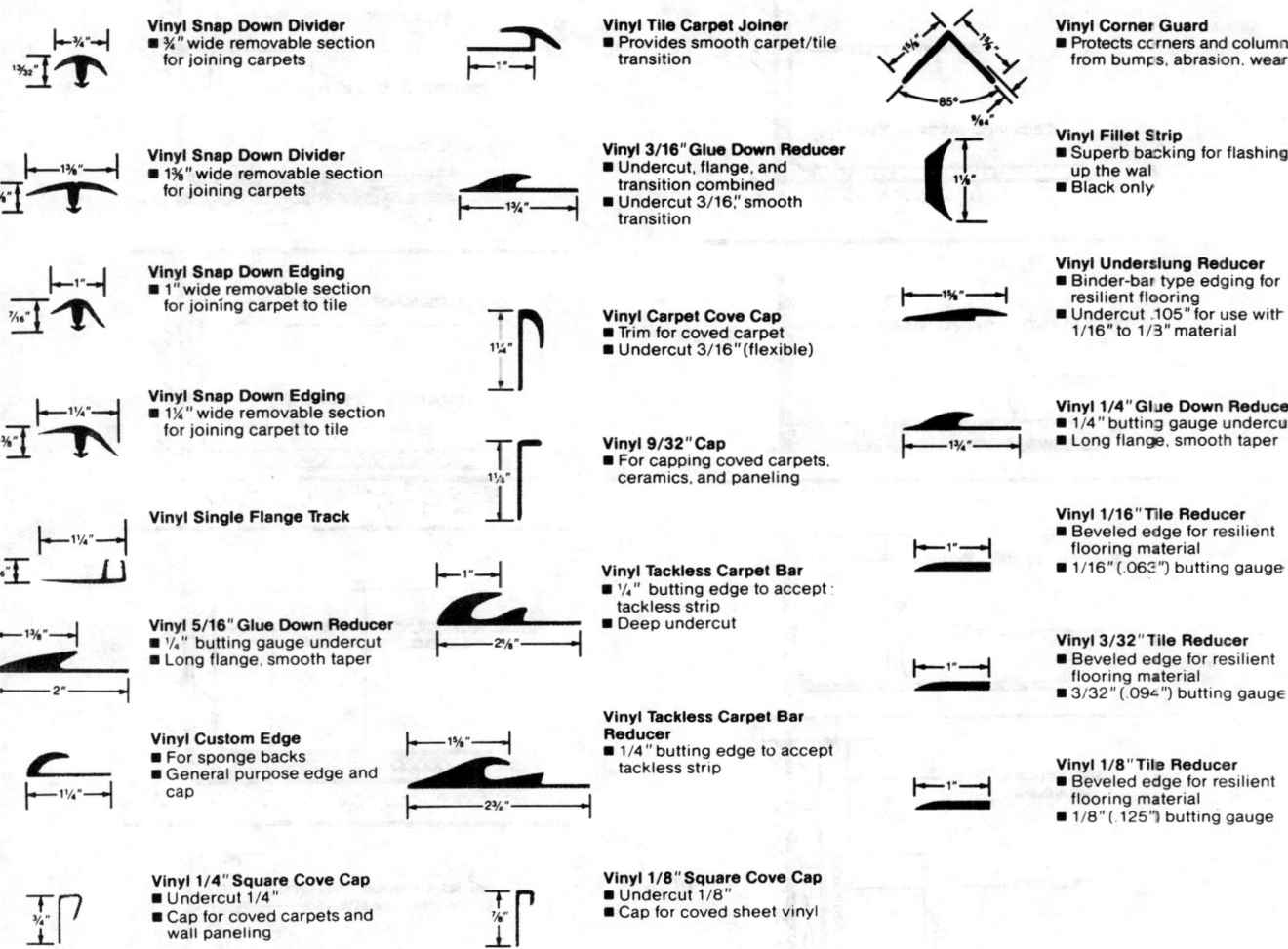

Vinyl Snap Down Divider
- ¾" wide removable section for joining carpets

Vinyl Snap Down Divider
- 1⅜" wide removable section for joining carpets

Vinyl Snap Down Edging
- 1" wide removable section for joining carpet to tile

Vinyl Snap Down Edging
- 1¼" wide removable section for joining carpet to tile

Vinyl Single Flange Track

Vinyl 5/16" Glue Down Reducer
- ¼" butting gauge undercut
- Long flange, smooth taper

Vinyl Custom Edge
- For sponge backs
- General purpose edge and cap

Vinyl 1/4" Square Cove Cap
- Undercut 1/4"
- Cap for coved carpets and wall paneling

Vinyl Tile Carpet Joiner
- Provides smooth carpet/tile transition

Vinyl 3/16" Glue Down Reducer
- Undercut, flange, and transition combined
- Undercut 3/16" smooth transition

Vinyl Carpet Cove Cap
- Trim for coved carpet
- Undercut 3/16" (flexible)

Vinyl 9/32" Cap
- For capping coved carpets, ceramics, and paneling

Vinyl Tackless Carpet Bar
- ¼" butting edge to accept tackless strip
- Deep undercut

Vinyl Tackless Carpet Bar Reducer
- 1/4" butting edge to accept tackless strip

Vinyl 1/8" Square Cove Cap
- Undercut 1/8"
- Cap for coved sheet vinyl

Vinyl Corner Guard
- Protects corners and columns from bumps, abrasion, wear

Vinyl Fillet Strip
- Superb backing for flashing up the wall
- Black only

Vinyl Underslung Reducer
- Binder-bar type edging for resilient flooring
- Undercut .105" for use with 1/16" to 1/3" material

Vinyl 1/4" Glue Down Reducer
- 1/4" butting gauge undercut
- Long flange, smooth taper

Vinyl 1/16" Tile Reducer
- Beveled edge for resilient flooring material
- 1/16" (.063") butting gauge

Vinyl 3/32" Tile Reducer
- Beveled edge for resilient flooring material
- 3/32" (.094") butting gauge

Vinyl 1/8" Tile Reducer
- Beveled edge for resilient flooring material
- 1/8" (.125") butting gauge

FLOORS AND FLOOR FINISHES

Base Details

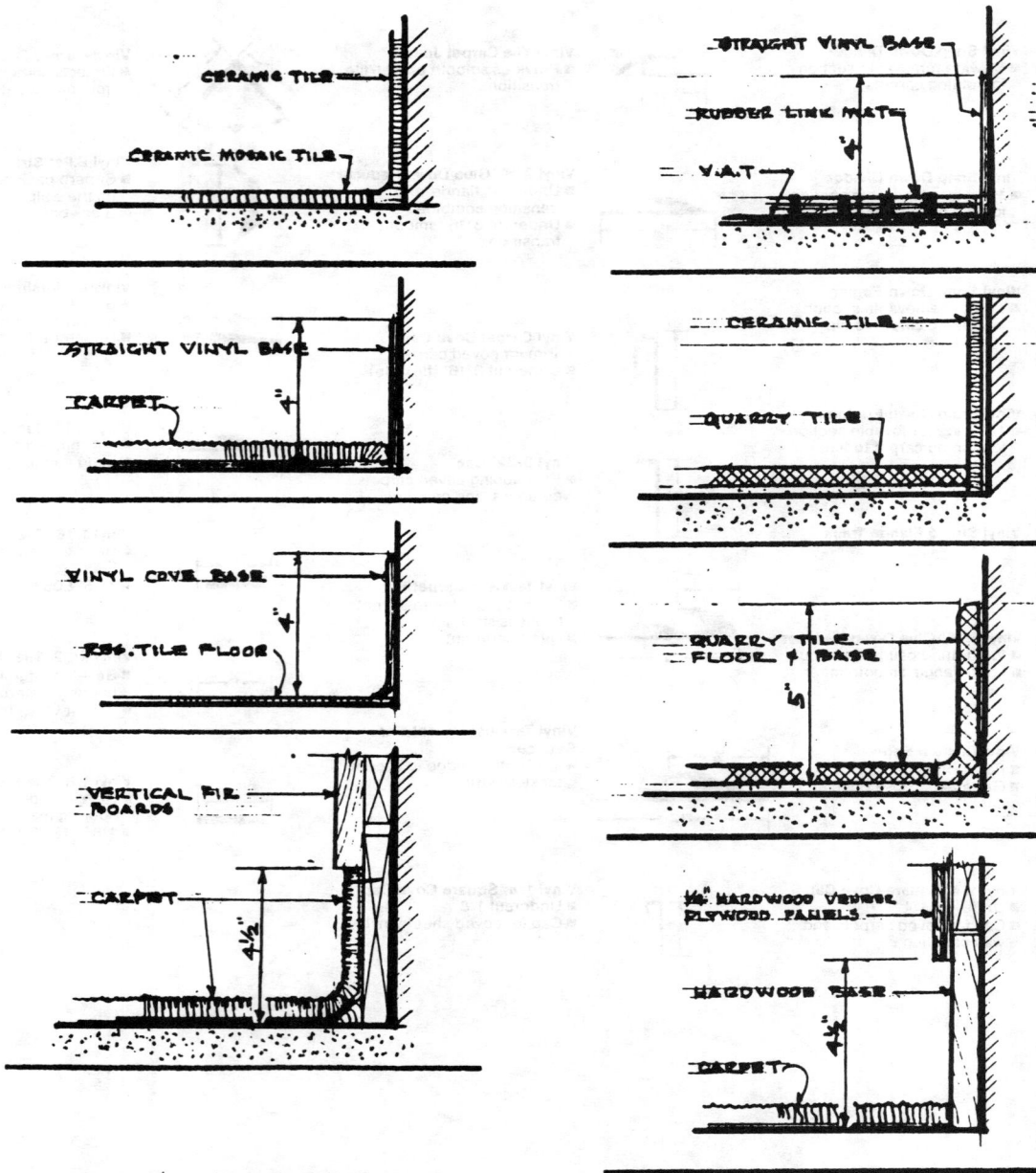

CERAMIC TILE

CERAMIC MOSAIC TILE

STRAIGHT VINYL BASE

RUBBER LINK MAT

V.A.T.

STRAIGHT VINYL BASE

CARPET

CERAMIC TILE

QUARRY TILE

VINYL COVE BASE

RES. TILE FLOOR

QUARRY TILE
FLOOR & BASE

VERTICAL FIR
BOARDS

CARPET

4½"

½" HARDWOOD VENEER
PLYWOOD PANELS

HARDWOOD BASE

4½"

CARPET

BASE TYPES

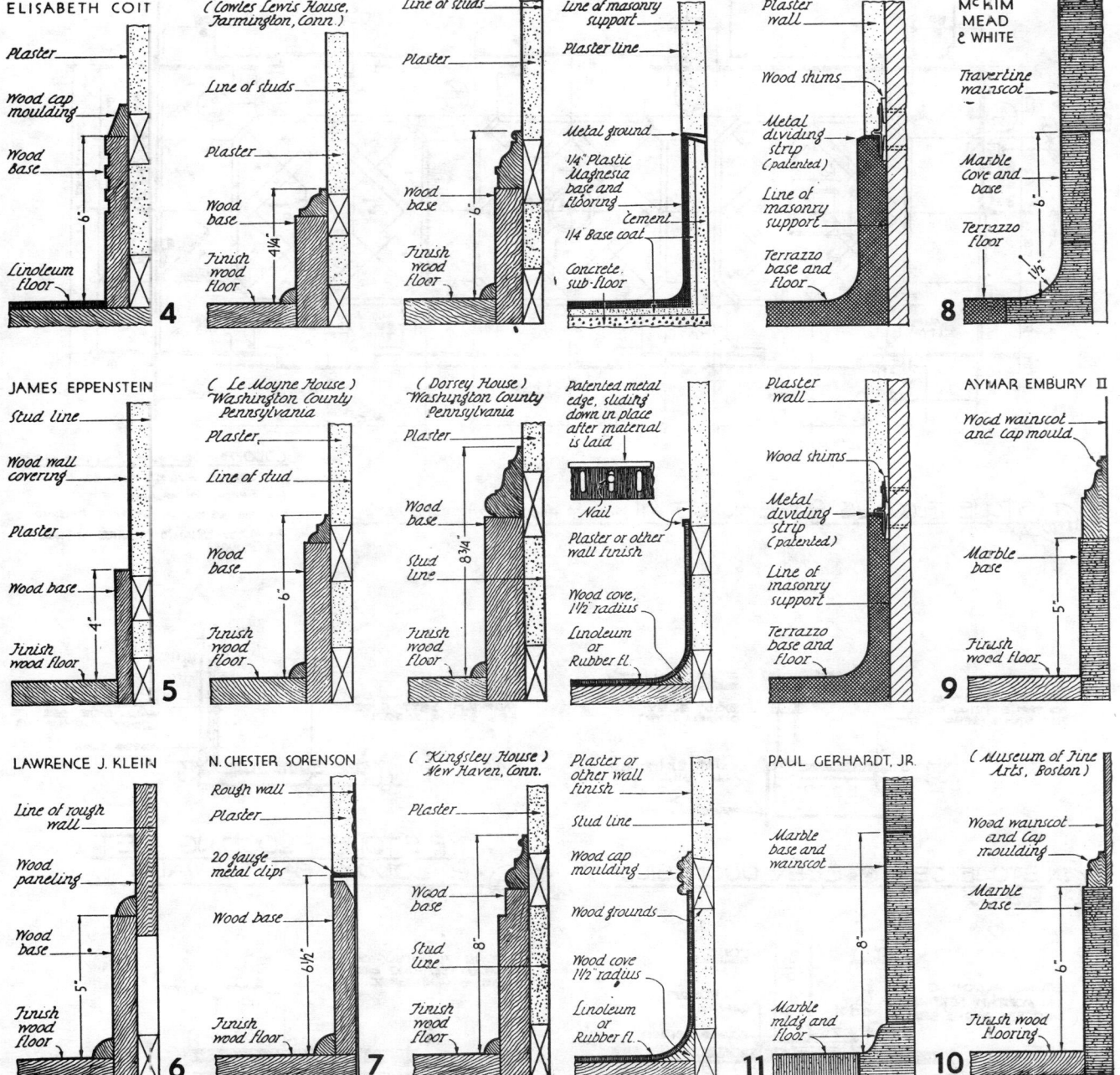

ELISABETH COIT
Plaster
Wood cap moulding
Wood Base
6"
Linoleum floor
4

(Cowles Lewis House, Farmington, Conn.)
Line of studs
Plaster
Wood base
4¼"
Finish wood floor

Line of studs
Plaster
Wood base
6"
Finish wood floor

Line of masonry support
Plaster line
Metal ground
¼" Plastic Magnesia base and flooring
Cement
¼ Base coat
Concrete sub-floor

Plaster wall
Wood shims
Metal dividing strip (patented)
Line of masonry support
Terrazzo base and floor

McKIM MEAD & WHITE
Travertine wainscot
Marble Cove and base
6"
Terrazzo floor
1½"
8

JAMES EPPENSTEIN
Stud line
Wood wall covering
Plaster
Wood base
4"
Finish wood floor
5

(Le Moyne House) Washington County Pennsylvania
Plaster
Line of stud
Wood base
6"
Finish wood floor

(Dorsey House) Washington County Pennsylvania
Plaster
Wood base
Stud line
8¾"
Finish wood floor

Patented metal edge, sliding down in place after material is laid
Nail
Plaster or other wall finish
Wood cove, 1½ radius
Linoleum or Rubber fl.

Plaster wall
Wood shims
Metal dividing strip (patented)
Line of masonry support
Terrazzo base and floor

AYMAR EMBURY II
Wood wainscot and cap mould
Marble base
5"
Finish wood floor
9

LAWRENCE J. KLEIN
Line of rough wall
Wood paneling
Wood base
5"
Finish wood floor
6

N. CHESTER SORENSON
Rough wall
Plaster
20 gauge metal clips
Wood base
6½"
Finish wood floor
7

(Kingsley House) New Haven, Conn.
Plaster
Wood base
Stud line
8"
Finish wood floor

Plaster or other wall finish
Stud line
Wood cap moulding
Wood grounds
Wood cove 1½"radius
Linoleum or Rubber fl.

PAUL GERHARDT, JR.
Marble base and wainscot
8"
Marble mldg and floor
11

(Museum of Fine Arts, Boston)
Wood wainscot and cap moulding
Marble base
6"
Finish wood flooring
10

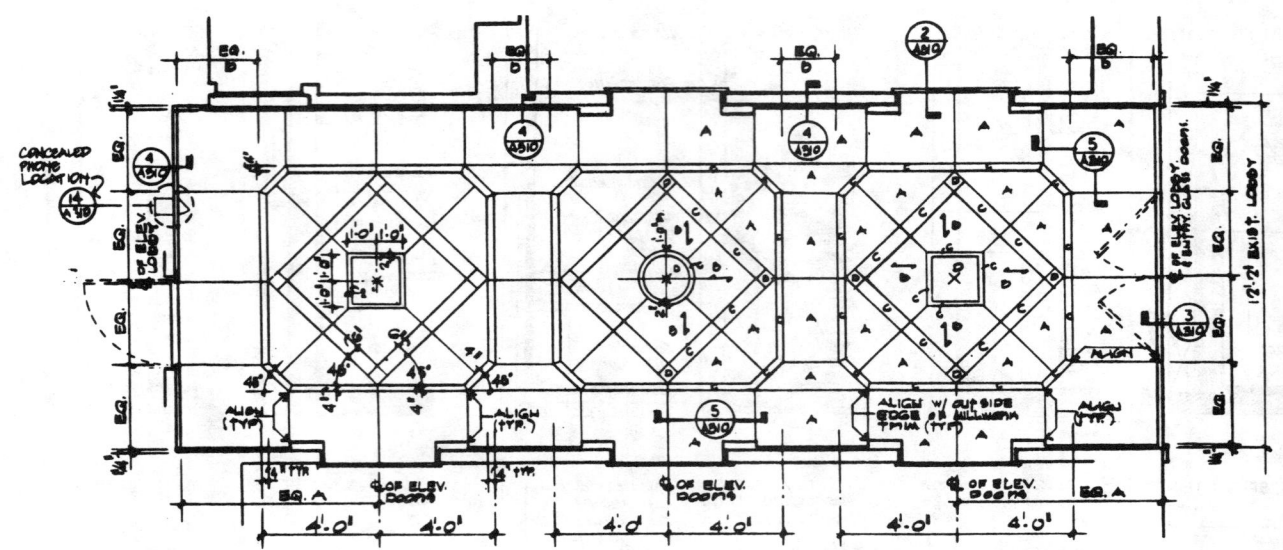

COLONS SEE SPEC. ON DWG A-20
A - VENDE AVEM POLISHED
B - CIPPOLINO POLISHED
C - ANDES BLACK GRANITE POLISHED
D - NOSSO LEVANTO POLISHED WITHOUT GRAIN

(1) STONE FLOORING PATTERN DETAIL   TYP. FLOORS 37TH THRU 45TH FL.
A510 1/4" = 1'-0"

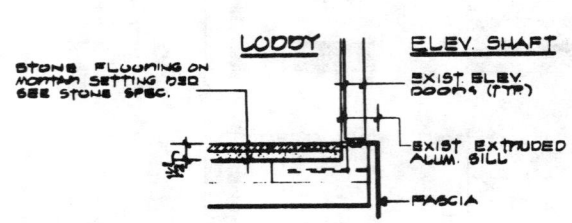

LOBBY   ELEV. SHAFT

STONE FLOORING ON MORTAR SETTING BED SEE STONE SPEC.

EXIST ELEV. DOORS (TYP)

EXIST EXTRUDED ALUM. SILL

FASCIA

(2) STONE DET. @ ELEV. DOOR SILL
A510 1/2" = 1'-0"

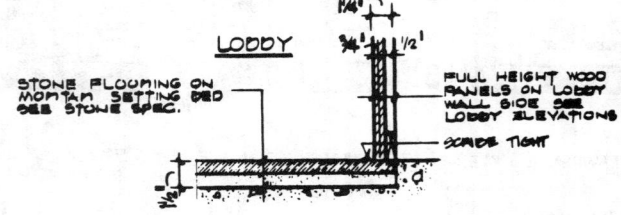

LOBBY

STONE FLOORING ON MORTAR SETTING BED SEE STONE SPEC.

FULL HEIGHT WOOD PANELS ON LOBBY WALL SIDE SEE LOBBY ELEVATIONS

SCRIBE TIGHT

(4) TYP STONE FLOORING DET.
@ LOBBY PANEL WALL
A510 3" = 1'-0"

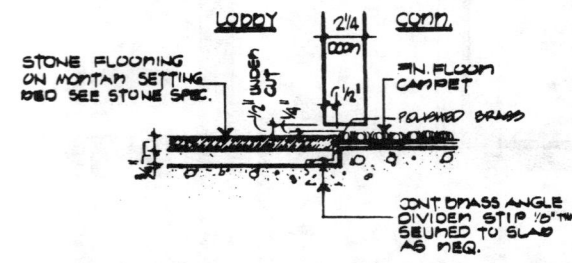

LOBBY   CORR.

STONE FLOORING ON MORTAR SETTING BED SEE STONE SPEC.

FIN. FLOOR CARPET

POLISHED BRASS

JOINT BRASS ANGLE DIVIDER STRIP 1/8" THK. SECURED TO SLAB AS REQ.

(3) STONE FLOORING DET. @ ENTRY DOORS
A510 3" = 1'-0"

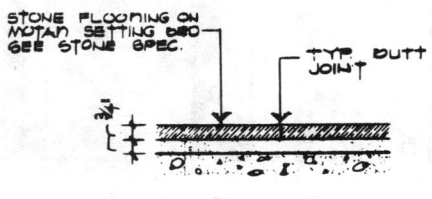

STONE FLOORING ON MORTAR SETTING BED SEE STONE SPEC.

TYP BUTT JOINT

(5) TYP STONE BUTT JOINT DETAIL
A510 3" = 1'-0"

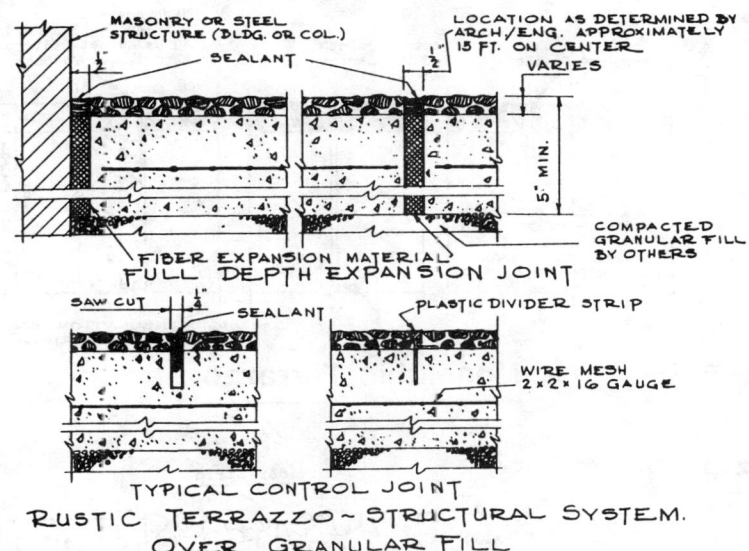

FULL DEPTH EXPANSION JOINT

TYPICAL CONTROL JOINT

RUSTIC TERRAZZO ~ STRUCTURAL SYSTEM.
OVER GRANULAR FILL

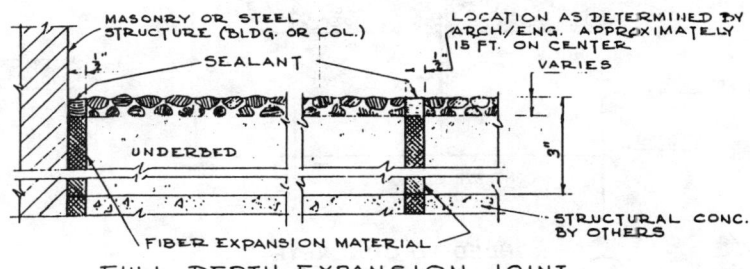

FULL DEPTH EXPANSION JOINT

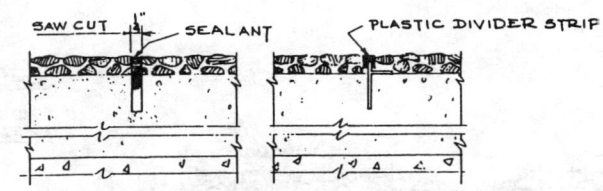

TYPICAL CONTROL JOINT

RUSTIC TERRAZZO ~ BONDED SYSTEM WITH
SETTING BED ~ OVER STRUCTURAL CONCRETE

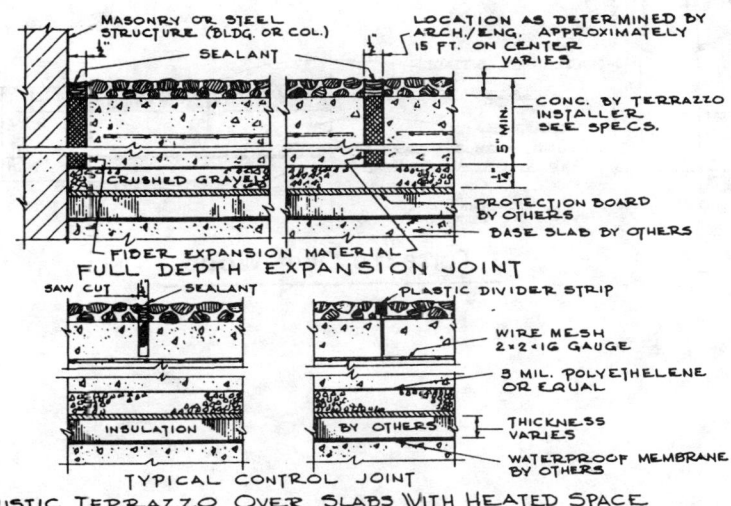

FULL DEPTH EXPANSION JOINT

TYPICAL CONTROL JOINT

RUSTIC TERRAZZO OVER SLABS WITH HEATED SPACE
BELOW & OVER INSULATED & WATERPROOFED SLABS

FLOORS AND FLOOR FINISHES

Terrazzo Floor Construction Details

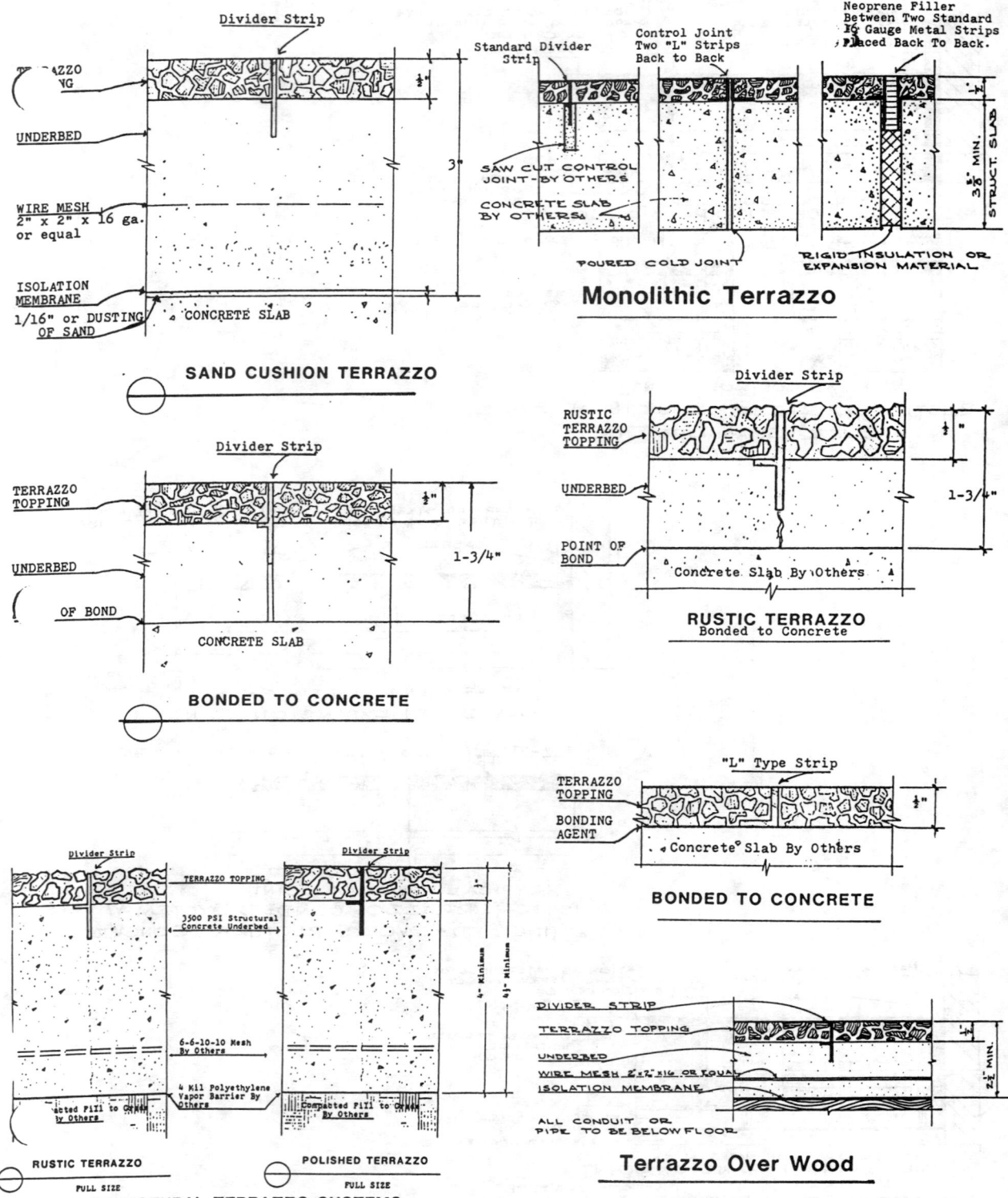

SAND CUSHION TERRAZZO

BONDED TO CONCRETE

STRUCTURAL TERRAZZO SYSTEMS

Monolithic Terrazzo

RUSTIC TERRAZZO
Bonded to Concrete

BONDED TO CONCRETE

Terrazzo Over Wood

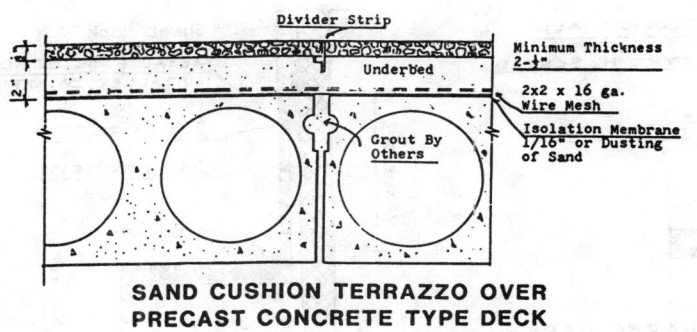

SAND CUSHION TERRAZZO OVER PRECAST CONCRETE TYPE DECK

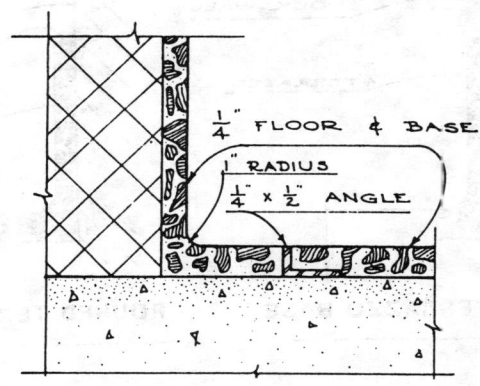

EPOXY, POLYESTER, TERRAZZO FLOOR & BASE

Fig.5

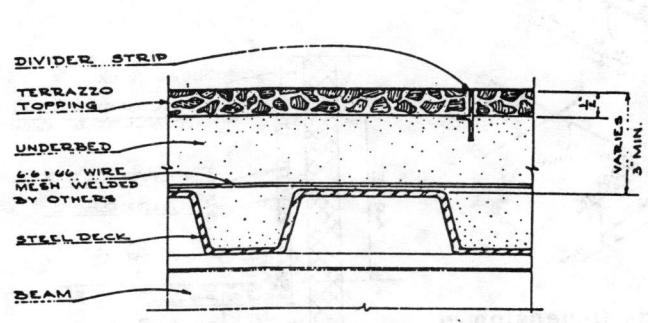

TERRAZZO OVER CORRUGATED METAL TYPE FLOOR

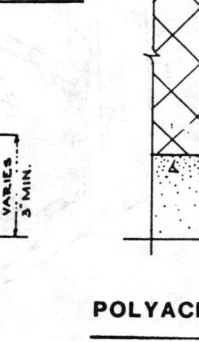

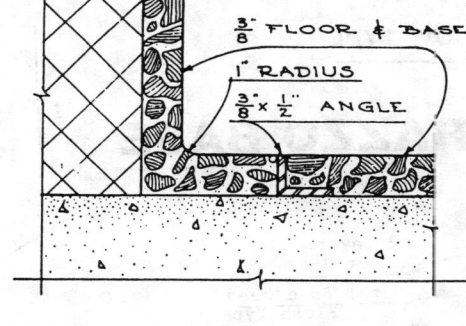

POLYACRYLATE TERRAZZO FLOOR & BASE

TERRAZZO OVER CELL TYPE FLOOR

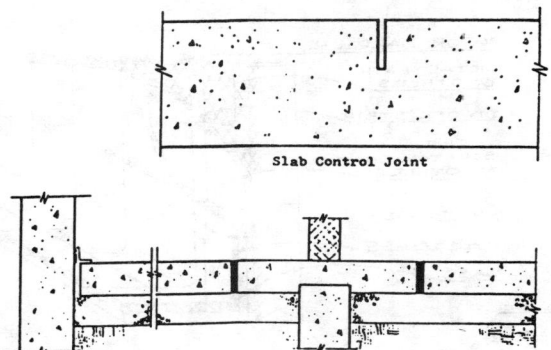

Slab Control Joint

Isolation Joint

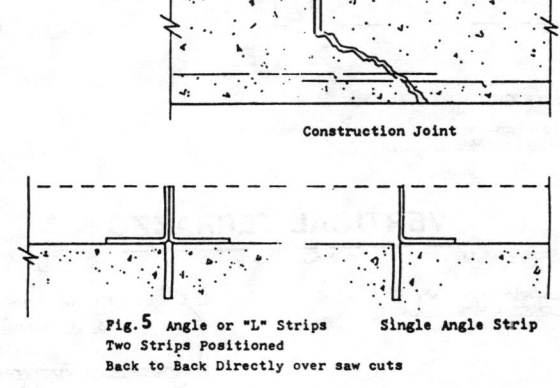

Construction Joint

Fig.5 Angle or "L" Strips   Single Angle Strip
Two Strips Positioned
Back to Back Directly over saw cuts

FLOORS AND FLOOR FINISHES

Terrazzo Base Details

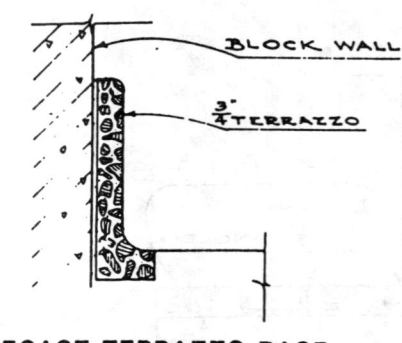

PRECAST TERRAZZO BASE

BLOCK WALL

¾" TERRAZZO

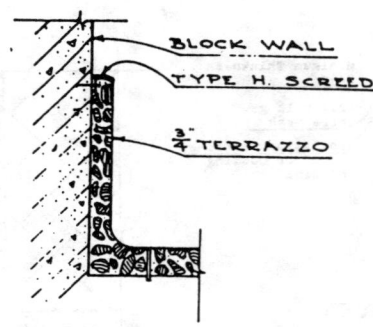

POURED TERRAZZO BASE

BLOCK WALL

TYPE H. SCREED

¾" TERRAZZO

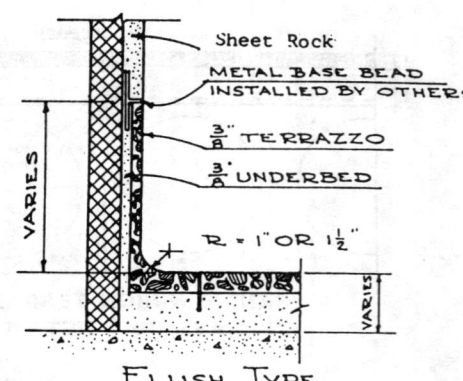

Sheet Rock

METAL BASE BEAD INSTALLED BY OTHERS

⅜" TERRAZZO

⅜" UNDERBED

R = 1" OR 1½"

VARIES

FLUSH TYPE

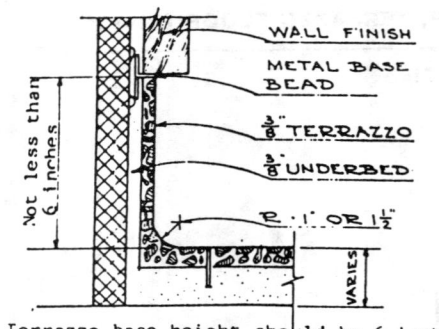

WALL FINISH

METAL BASE BEAD

⅜" TERRAZZO

⅜" UNDERBED

R = 1" OR 1½"

Not less than 6 inches

The Terrazzo base height should be 6 inches or more to use this detail.

SHADOW TYPE

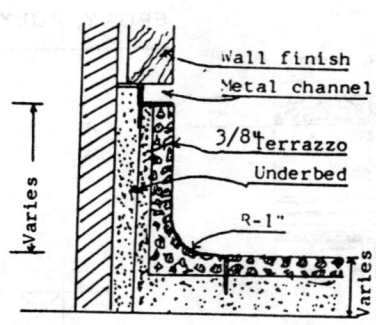

Wall finish

Metal channel

3/8" Terrazzo

Underbed

R = 1"

Varies

RE-VEAL TYPE

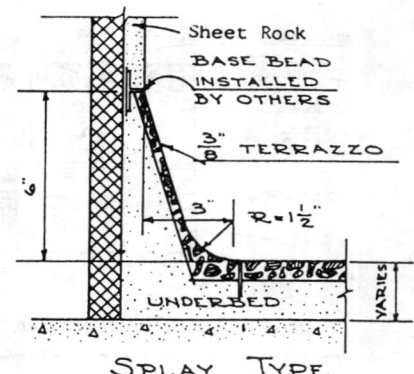

Sheet Rock

BASE BEAD INSTALLED BY OTHERS

⅜" TERRAZZO

3"

R = 1½"

6"

UNDERBED

SPLAY TYPE

TERRAZZO BASE

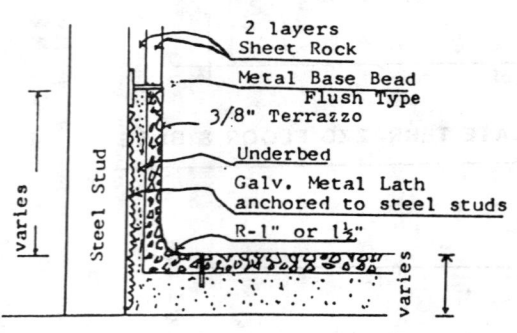

2 layers Sheet Rock

Metal Base Bead Flush Type

3/8" Terrazzo

Underbed

Galv. Metal Lath anchored to steel studs

R = 1" or 1½"

Varies

Steel Stud

Varies

Note: Provide Dimension in Space Indicated "Varies"

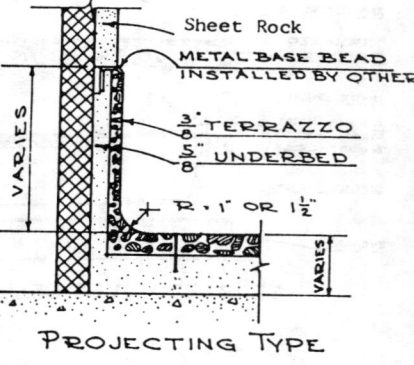

Sheet Rock

METAL BASE BEAD INSTALLED BY OTHERS

⅜" TERRAZZO

⅝" UNDERBED

R = 1" OR 1½"

VARIES

PROJECTING TYPE

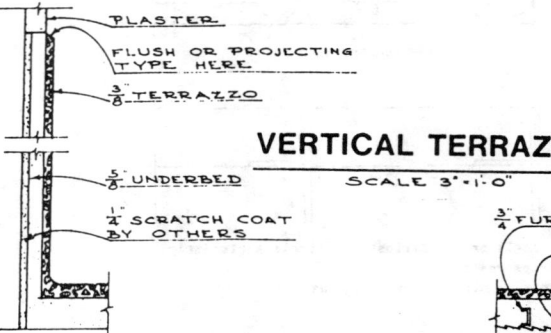

PLASTER

FLUSH OR PROJECTING TYPE HERE

⅜" TERRAZZO

⅝" UNDERBED

¼" SCRATCH COAT BY OTHERS

Varies

VERTICAL TERRAZZO

SCALE 3" = 1'-0"

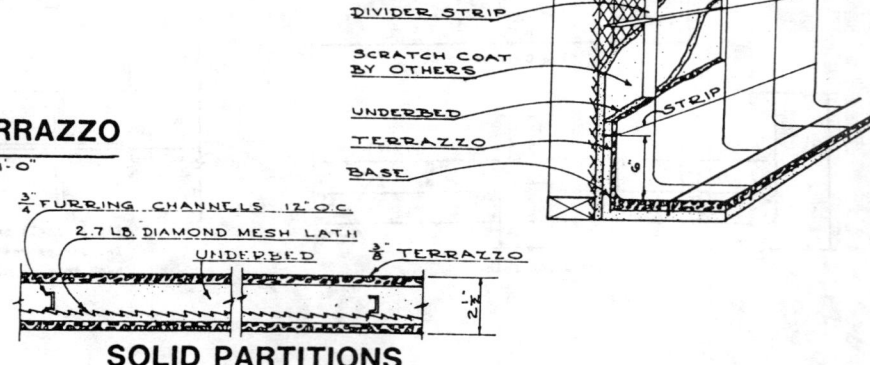

VAPOR BARRIER

METAL LATH BY OTHERS

DIVIDER STRIP

SCRATCH COAT BY OTHERS

UNDERBED

TERRAZZO

BASE

STRIP

6"

¾" FURRING CHANNELS 12" O.C.

2.7 LB. DIAMOND MESH LATH

UNDERBED

⅜" TERRAZZO

2¼"

SOLID PARTITIONS

SCALE 3" = 1'-0"

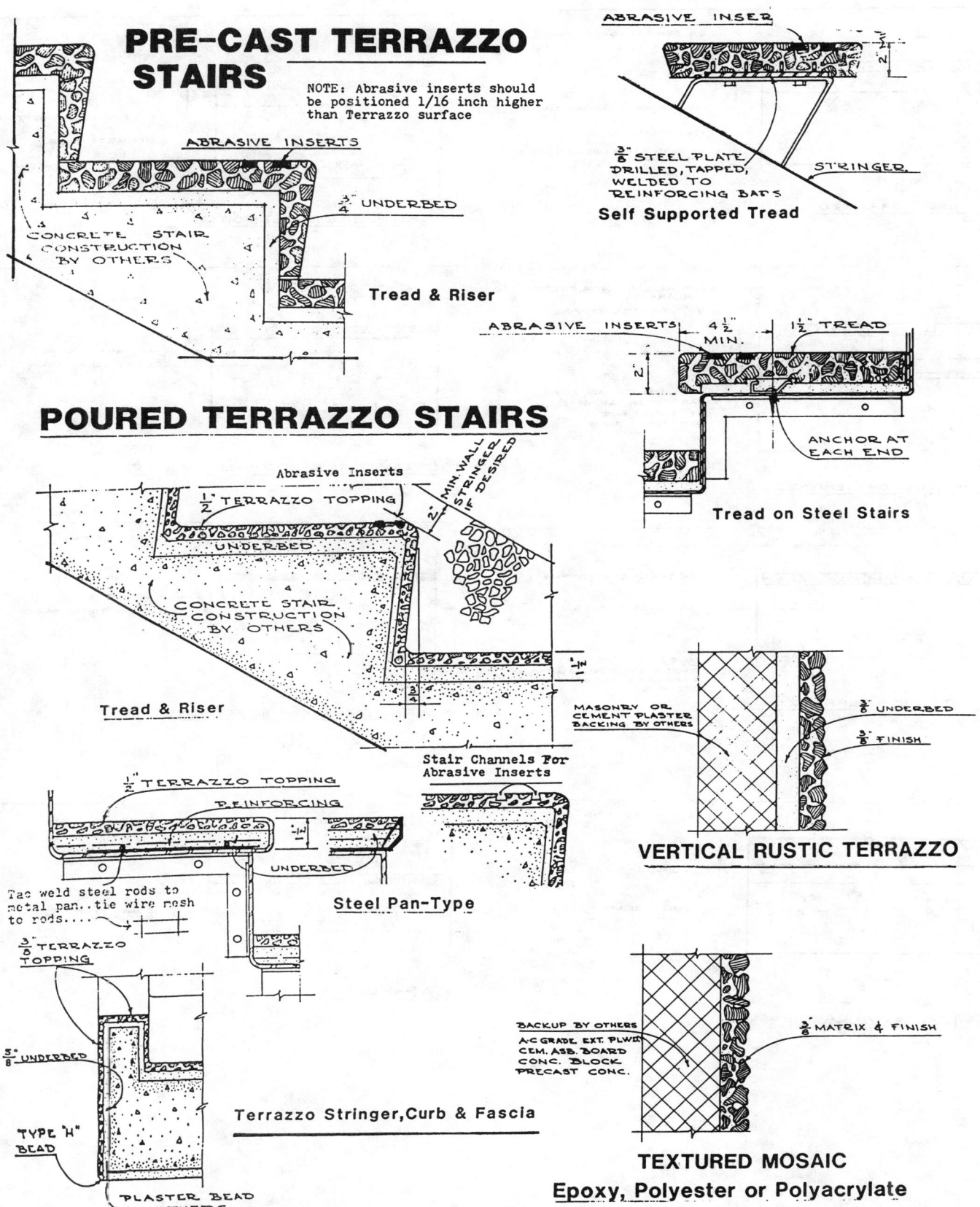

PRE-CAST TERRAZZO STAIRS

NOTE: Abrasive inserts should be positioned 1/16 inch higher than Terrazzo surface

ABRASIVE INSERTS

3/4 UNDERBED

CONCRETE STAIR CONSTRUCTION BY OTHERS

Tread & Riser

ABRASIVE INSERT

3/8 STEEL PLATE DRILLED, TAPPED, WELDED TO REINFORCING BARS

STRINGER

Self Supported Tread

POURED TERRAZZO STAIRS

Abrasive Inserts

1/2 TERRAZZO TOPPING

UNDERBED

CONCRETE STAIR CONSTRUCTION BY OTHERS

Tread & Riser

2" MIN. WALL STRINGER IF DESIRED

3/4

Stair Channels For Abrasive Inserts

ABRASIVE INSERTS 4 1/2" MIN. 1 1/2" TREAD

2"

ANCHOR AT EACH END

Tread on Steel Stairs

1/2 TERRAZZO TOPPING

REINFORCING

UNDERBED

Tac weld steel rods to metal pan..tie wire mesh to rods....

3/8 TERRAZZO TOPPING

5/8 UNDERBED

TYPE "H" BEAD

PLASTER BEAD BY OTHERS

Steel Pan-Type

Terrazzo Stringer, Curb & Fascia

MASONRY OR CEMENT PLASTER BACKING BY OTHERS

3/8 UNDERBED

3/8 FINISH

VERTICAL RUSTIC TERRAZZO

BACKUP BY OTHERS
A-C GRADE EXT. PLWD
CEM. ASB. BOARD
CONC. BLOCK
PRECAST CONC.

3/8 MATRIX & FINISH

TEXTURED MOSAIC
Epoxy, Polyester or Polyacrylate

FLOORS AND FLOOR FINISHES
Ceramic Tile, Terrazzo, and Brick

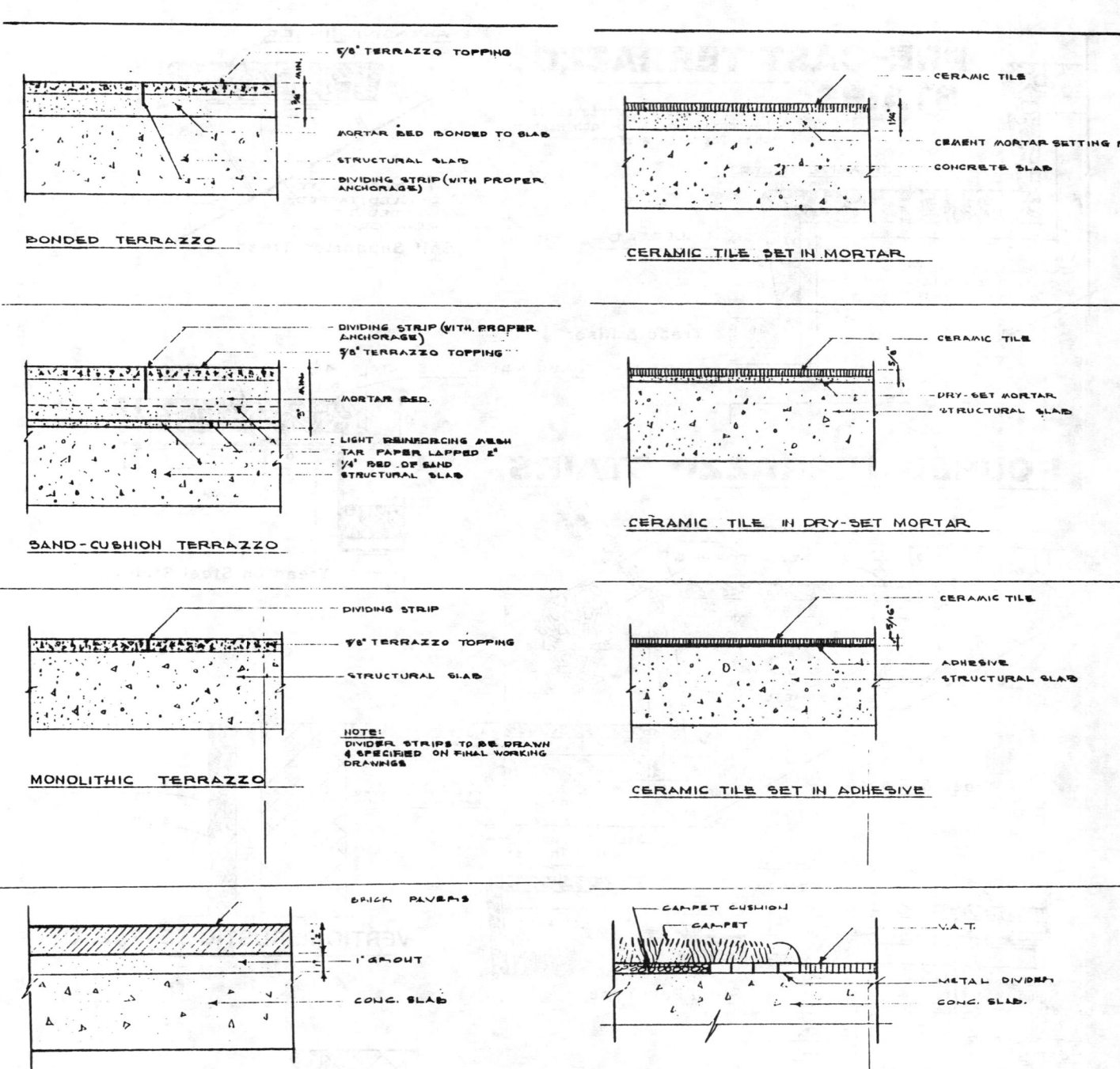

BONDED TERRAZZO

- 5/8" TERRAZZO TOPPING
- MORTAR BED BONDED TO SLAB
- STRUCTURAL SLAB
- DIVIDING STRIP (WITH PROPER ANCHORAGE)

CERAMIC TILE SET IN MORTAR

- CERAMIC TILE
- CEMENT MORTAR SETTING BED
- CONCRETE SLAB

SAND-CUSHION TERRAZZO

- DIVIDING STRIP (WITH PROPER ANCHORAGE)
- 5/8" TERRAZZO TOPPING
- MORTAR BED
- LIGHT REINFORCING MESH
- TAR PAPER LAPPED 2"
- 1/4" BED OF SAND
- STRUCTURAL SLAB

CERAMIC TILE IN DRY-SET MORTAR

- CERAMIC TILE
- DRY-SET MORTAR
- STRUCTURAL SLAB

MONOLITHIC TERRAZZO

- DIVIDING STRIP
- 5/8" TERRAZZO TOPPING
- STRUCTURAL SLAB

NOTE:
DIVIDER STRIPS TO BE DRAWN & SPECIFIED ON FINAL WORKING DRAWINGS

CERAMIC TILE SET IN ADHESIVE

- CERAMIC TILE
- ADHESIVE
- STRUCTURAL SLAB

BRICK PAVERS

- BRICK PAVERS
- 1" GROUT
- CONC. SLAB

CARPET

- CARPET CUSHION
- CARPET
- V.A.T.
- METAL DIVIDER
- CONC. SLAB.

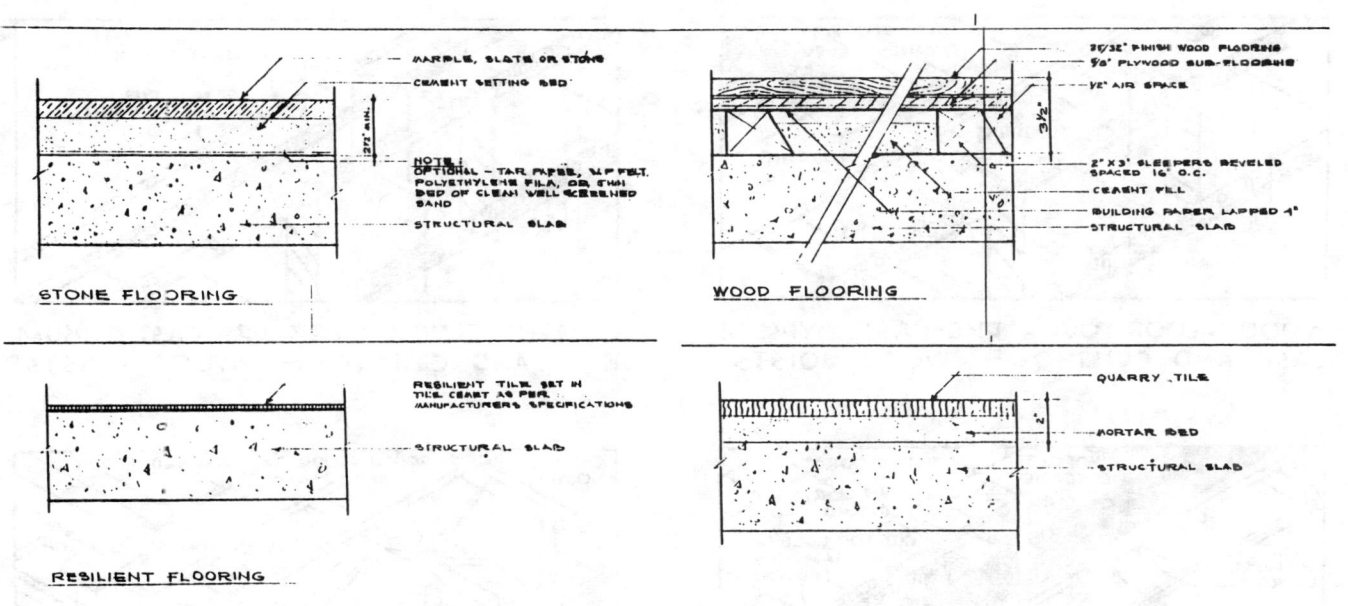

STONE FLOORING

- MARBLE, SLATE OR STONE
- CEMENT SETTING BED
- NOTE: OPTIONAL — TAR PAPER, 15# FELT, POLYETHYLENE FILM, OR THIN BED OF CLEAN WELL SCREENED SAND
- STRUCTURAL SLAB

WOOD FLOORING

- 25/32" FINISH WOOD FLOORING
- 5/8" PLYWOOD SUB-FLOORING
- 1/2" AIR SPACE
- 2"X3" SLEEPERS BEVELED SPACED 16" O.C.
- CEMENT FILL
- BUILDING PAPER LAPPED 4"
- STRUCTURAL SLAB

RESILIENT FLOORING

- RESILIENT TILE SET IN TILE CEMENT AS PER MANUFACTURERS SPECIFICATIONS
- STRUCTURAL SLAB

QUARRY TILE

- QUARRY TILE
- MORTAR BED
- STRUCTURAL SLAB

MORTAR BED METHOD

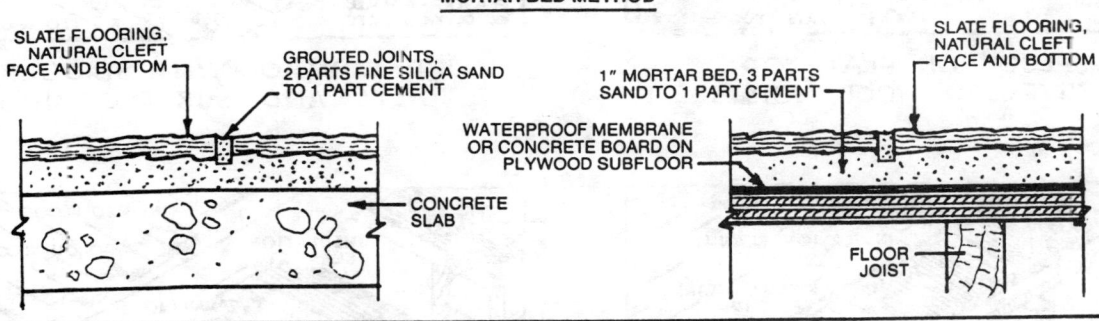

- SLATE FLOORING, NATURAL CLEFT FACE AND BOTTOM
- GROUTED JOINTS, 2 PARTS FINE SILICA SAND TO 1 PART CEMENT
- CONCRETE SLAB
- 1" MORTAR BED, 3 PARTS SAND TO 1 PART CEMENT
- WATERPROOF MEMBRANE OR CONCRETE BOARD ON PLYWOOD SUBFLOOR
- SLATE FLOORING, NATURAL CLEFT FACE AND BOTTOM
- FLOOR JOIST

THINSET METHOD

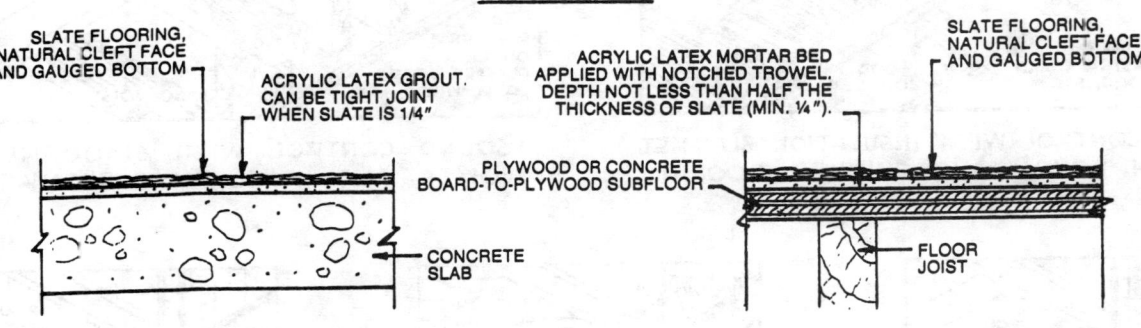

- SLATE FLOORING, NATURAL CLEFT FACE AND GAUGED BOTTOM
- ACRYLIC LATEX GROUT. CAN BE TIGHT JOINT WHEN SLATE IS 1/4"
- CONCRETE SLAB
- ACRYLIC LATEX MORTAR BED APPLIED WITH NOTCHED TROWEL. DEPTH NOT LESS THAN HALF THE THICKNESS OF SLATE (MIN. 1/4").
- PLYWOOD OR CONCRETE BOARD-TO-PLYWOOD SUBFLOOR
- SLATE FLOORING, NATURAL CLEFT FACE AND GAUGED BOTTOM
- FLOOR JOIST

FLOORS AND FLOOR FINISHES

Wood Floor Construction Details

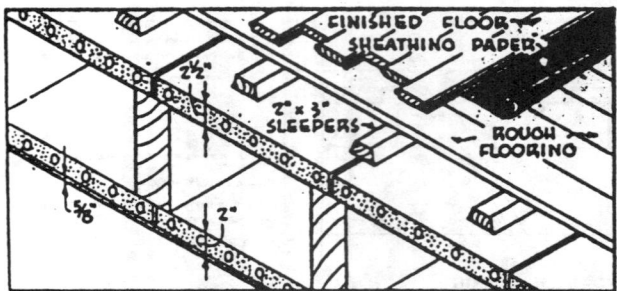

WOOD FLOOR OVER PRE-CAST GYPSUM
BASE AND CEILING — WOOD JOISTS

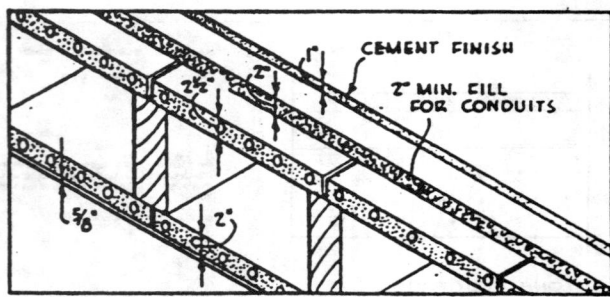

CEMENT FLOOR OVER PRE-CAST GYPSUM
BASE AND CEILING — WOOD JOISTS

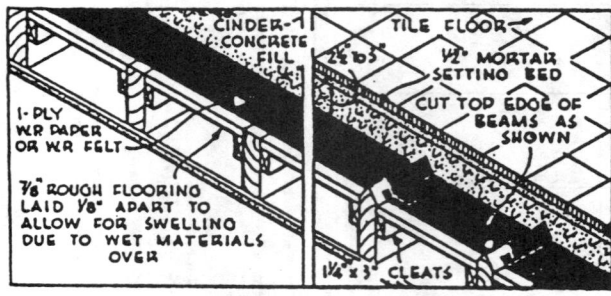

TILE FLOOR ON FLAT-TOP
AND BEVELLED WOOD JOISTS

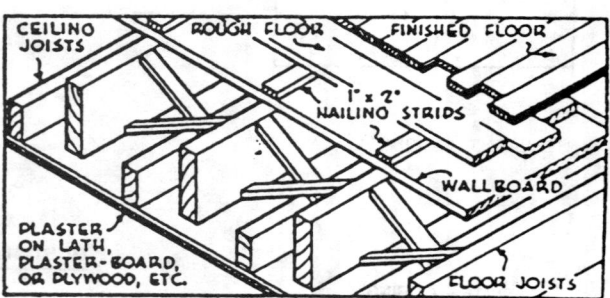

SOUND-CONTROL WITH STAGGERED
JOISTS AND SUB-FLOORING

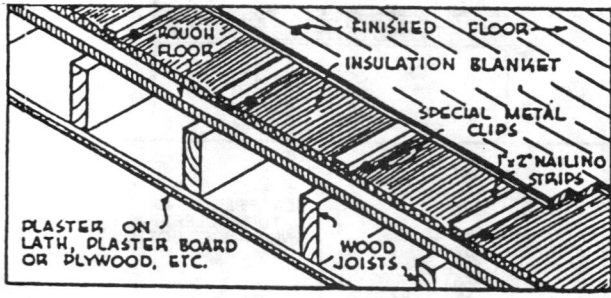

SOUND-CONTROL WITH INSULATION BLANKET
BETWEEN ROUGH AND FINISHED FLOORING

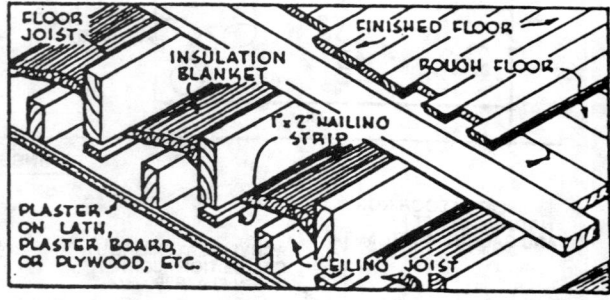

SOUND-CONTROL WITH STAGGERED
JOISTS AND INSULATION BLANKET

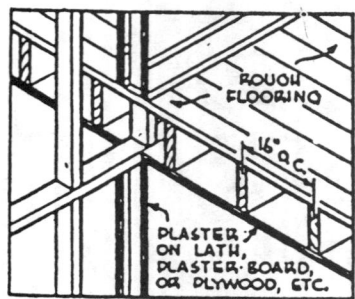

PARTITION OVER PARTITION
PARALLEL WITH JOISTS

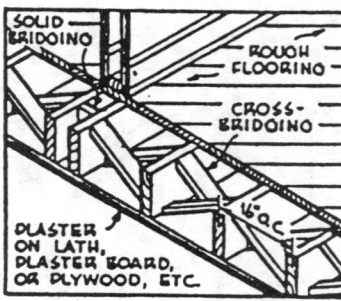

PARTITION NOT OVER PART-
ITION — ON DOUBLE JOISTS

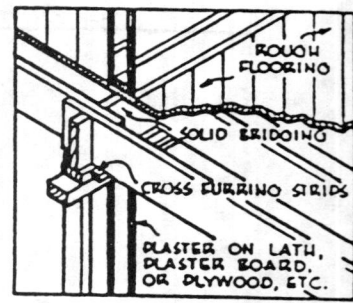

PARTITION OVER PARTITION
AT RIGHT ANGLES TO JOISTS

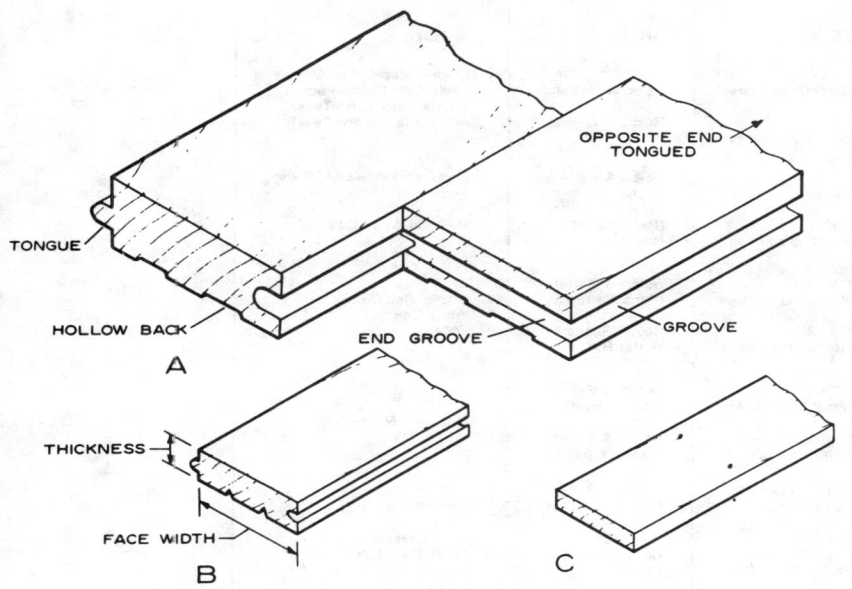

Fig. 6 Types of strip flooring: *A*, side- and end-matched — $^{25}/_{32}$-in; *B*, thin flooring strips — matched; *C*, thin flooring strips — square-edged.

Perhaps the most widely used pattern is a $^{25}/_{32}$- by $2\frac{1}{4}$-in *strip flooring*. These strips are laid lengthwise in a room and normally at right angles to the floor joists. Some type of a subfloor of diagonal boards or plywood is normally used under the finish floor. Strip flooring of this type is tongued-and-grooved and end-matched (Fig. 6). Strips are random length and may vary from 2 to 16 ft or more. End-matched strip flooring in $^{25}/_{32}$-in thickness is generally hollow backed (Fig. 6*A*). The face is slightly wider than the bottom so that tight joints result when flooring is laid. The tongue fits tightly into the groove to prevent movement and floor "squeaks." All of these details are designed to provide beautiful finished floors that require a minimum of maintenance.

Another matched pattern may be obtained in $^3/_8$- by 2-in size (Fig. 6*B*). This is commonly used for remodeling work or when subfloor is edge-blocked or thick enough to provide very little deflection under loads

Square-edged strip flooring (Fig. 6*C*) might also be used occasionally. It is usually $^3/_8$ by 2 inches in size and is laid up over a substantial subfloor. Facenailing is required for this type.

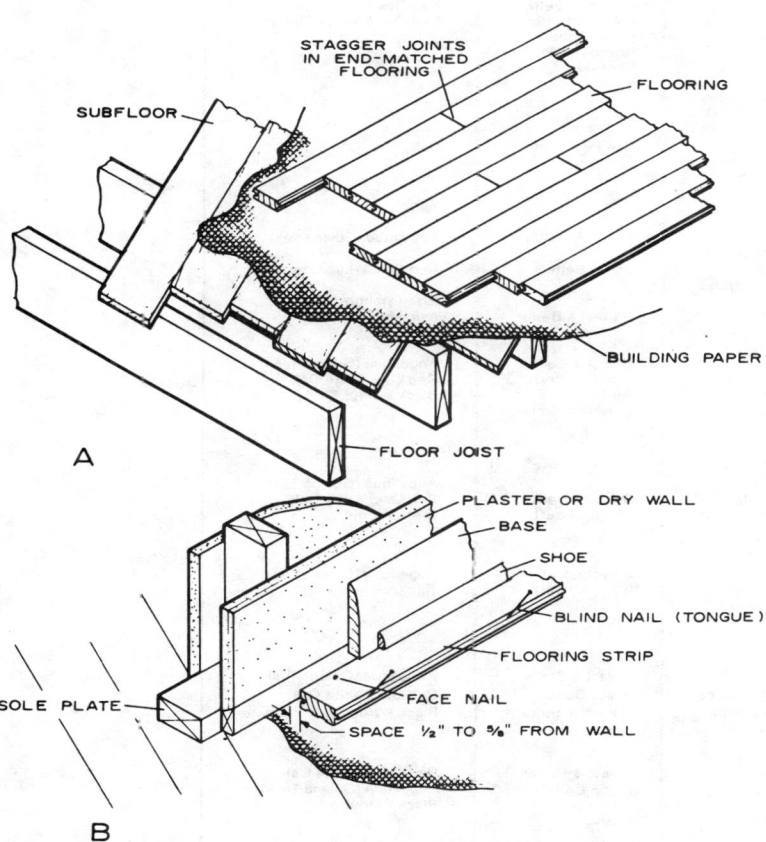

Fig. 7 Application of strip flooring: *A*, general application; *B*, starting strip.

FLOORS AND FLOOR FINISHES
Wood Parquet Floor Patterns

PRODUCT DESCRIPTION AND PATTERN	'PANEL SIZE	GRADE	*SPECIES
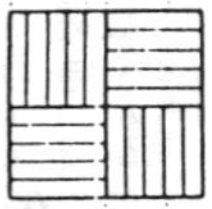 STANDARD Pattern Unfinished—paper-faced	5/16" x 19" x 19" 16 equal alternating squares	Select & Better	Cherry, Maple, Red Oak, White Oak, Cedar, Pecan, Walnut, Rhodesian Teak, Angelique (Guiana Teak)
	5/16" x 12" x 12" 4 equal alternating squares	Rustic	
STANDARD Pattern Unfinished—WebBack or Mesh-Back	5/16" x 19" x 19" 16 equal alternating squares	Select & Better Rustic Select & Better	Red Oak, White Oak, Pecan Pecan
	5/16" x 11" x 11" 4 equal alternating squares	(Par & Better) Rustic	Red and White Oak
STANDARD Pattern Unfinished—WebBack (For Industrial Use)	5/16" x 19" x 19" 16 equal alternating squares	Select & Better (Par & Better)	Maple, Red Oak White Oak Pecan
	9/16" x 19" x 19" 16 equal alternating squares	Select Rustic & Better Rustic	
STANDARD Pattern Unfinished WebBack (For Industrial Use)	11/16" x 11" x 11" 4 equal alternating squares	Select & Better (Par & Better)	Red Oak, Maple White Oak
	¾" x 12-11/16" x 12-11/16" 4 equal alternating squares	Select & Better (Rustic & Better)	
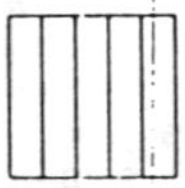 STANDARD Pattern Factory-Finished and Unfinished (Available in various colors)	5/16" x 6-11/32" x 6-11/32" 5/16" x 2" x 12" (slats) 5/16" x 6" x 6" 5/16" x 6⅜" x 6⅜" 5/16" x 6½" x 6½" individual unit	Select & Better Natural & Better Fireside Rustic Cabin & Better Cabin	Oak, Walnut Pecan, Maple White Oak, Ash
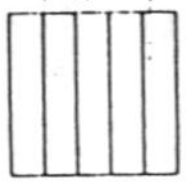 STANDARD Pattern Factory-Finished Foam-Back Tile	5/16" x 6½" x 6½" individual units . . . ⅛" foam, 2 lb. density	Natural & Better Cabin & Better Cabin	Oak, Pecan Maple
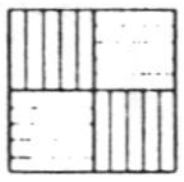 ANTIQUE TEXTURED (Factory-Finished and Unfinished)—Kerfsawn Various colors available	5/16" x 6" x 6" individual squares 5/16" x 6⅜" x 6⅜" individual squares 5/16" x 6½" x 6½" individual squares 5/16" x 11" x 11" 4 equal alternating squares	Select Natural & Better Select & Better (Par & Better) Rustic Fireside	Red Oak & White Oak Red Oak & White Oak
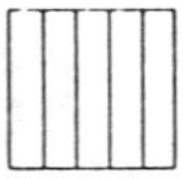 ANTIQUE TEXTURED (Factory-Finished and Unfinished)—Wire brushed Various colors available	5/16" x 6⅜" x 6⅜" 5/16" x 6½" x 6½" individual squares	Natural & Better Cabin	Oak
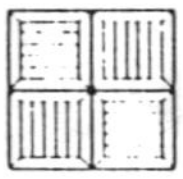 MONTICELLO Pattern Unfinished—Paper-Faced— Pre-Finished, Mesh-Back	5/16" x 6" x 6" individual squares used with 5/16" x ⅞" x 8" pickets 5/16" x 13¼" x 13¼" 4 equal alternating squares 5/16" x 13⅛" x 13⅛" (Factory Finished)	Select & Better (Par & Better) Rustic Natural & Better	Angelique (Guiana Teak) Red Oak, White Oak Black Walnut Ash, Maple
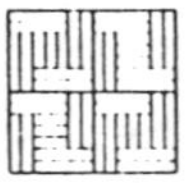 HADDON HALL Pattern Unfinished—Paper-Faced— Pre-Finished, Mesh-Back	5/16" x 14¼" x 14¼" 5/16" x 13¼" x 13¼" 4 equal squares 5/16" x 13⅛" x 13⅛" (Factory Finished)	Select & Better (Par & Better) Rustic Natural & Better	Angelique (Guiana Teak) Red Oak, White Oak Black Walnut
 HERRINGBONE Pattern Unfinished—Paper-Faced	5/16" x 2" x 12" individual slats 5/16" x 14⅛" x 18⅛" (Approximate overall) 2 - "V" shape courses wide and 11 slats long	Select & Better (Par & Better)	Angelique (Guiana Teak) Red Oak, White Oak Black Walnut
 SAXONY Pattern Unfinished—Paper-Faced	5/16" x 19" x 19" 4 equal squares on diagonal and 8 equal half squares	Select & Better (Par & Better)	Angelique (Guiana Teak) Red Oak, White Oak
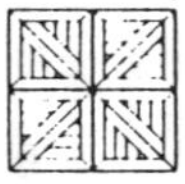 CANTERBURY Pattern Unfinished—Paper-Faced Pre-Finished, Mesh-Back	5/16" x 13¼" x 13¼" 4 equal alternating squares with diagonal center slats 5/16" x 13⅛" x 13⅛"	Select & Better (Par & Better) Natural & Better	Angelique (Guiana Teak) Red Oak, White Oak Black Walnut
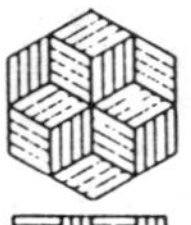 RHOMBS Pattern Unfinished—Paper-Faced	Hexagonal Shape 5/16" x 15⅛" x 15⅛" 12 equal Rhomboids	Select & Better (Par & Better) Rustic	Red Oak & White Oak Angelique (Guiana Teak) Black Walnut
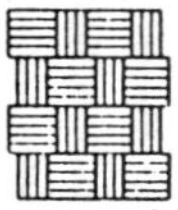 BASKET WEAVE Pattern Unfinished—Paper-Faced	5/16" x 15-1/5" x 19" 4 runs of 3 slats and 5 slats alternating	Select & Better (Par & Better)	Angelique (Guiana Teak) Red Oak, White Oak Black Walnut
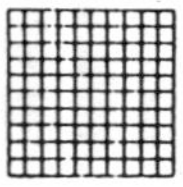 ITALIAN & DOMINO Pattern Unfinished—Paper-Faced	5/16" x 19" x 19" 400 equal size pieces butt-jointed	Select & Better (Par & Better)	Black Walnut Angelique (Guiana Teak) Maple, Red Oak White Oak

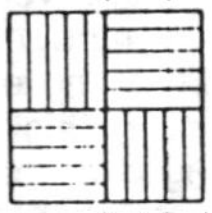

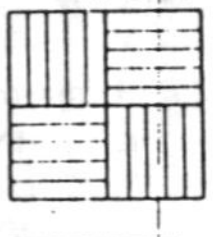

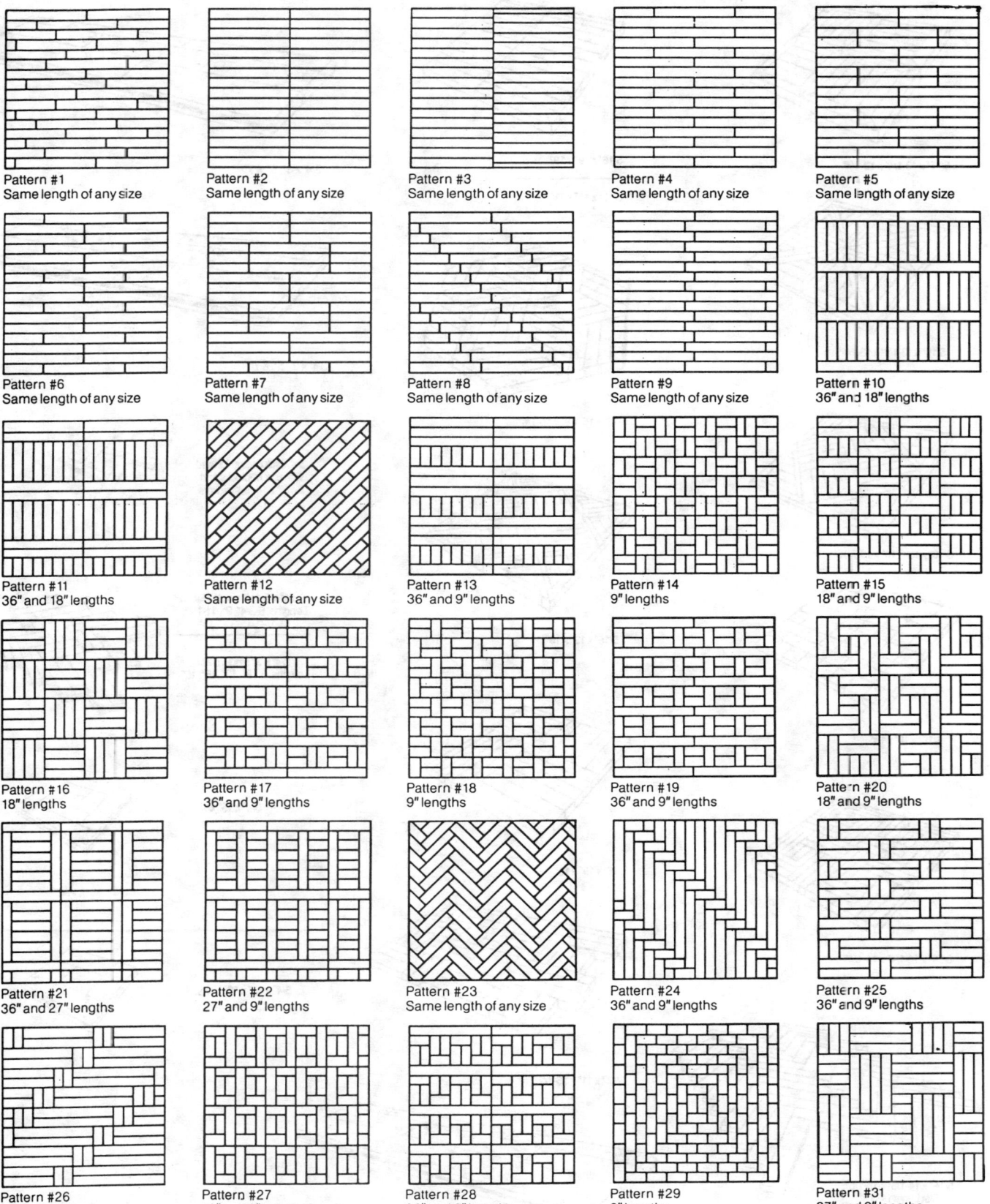

Pattern #1
Same length of any size

Pattern #2
Same length of any size

Pattern #3
Same length of any size

Pattern #4
Same length of any size

Pattern #5
Same length of any size

Pattern #6
Same length of any size

Pattern #7
Same length of any size

Pattern #8
Same length of any size

Pattern #9
Same length of any size

Pattern #10
36" and 18" lengths

Pattern #11
36" and 18" lengths

Pattern #12
Same length of any size

Pattern #13
36" and 9" lengths

Pattern #14
9" lengths

Pattern #15
18" and 9" lengths

Pattern #16
18" lengths

Pattern #17
36" and 9" lengths

Pattern #18
9" lengths

Pattern #19
36" and 9" lengths

Pattern #20
18" and 9" lengths

Pattern #21
36" and 27" lengths

Pattern #22
27" and 9" lengths

Pattern #23
Same length of any size

Pattern #24
36" and 9" lengths

Pattern #25
36" and 9" lengths

Pattern #26
36" and 9" lengths

Pattern #27
18" and 9" lengths

Pattern #28
36" and 9" lengths

Pattern #29
9" lengths

Pattern #31
27" and 9" lengths

FLOORS AND FLOOR FINISHES
Wood Parquet and Plank Floor Patterns

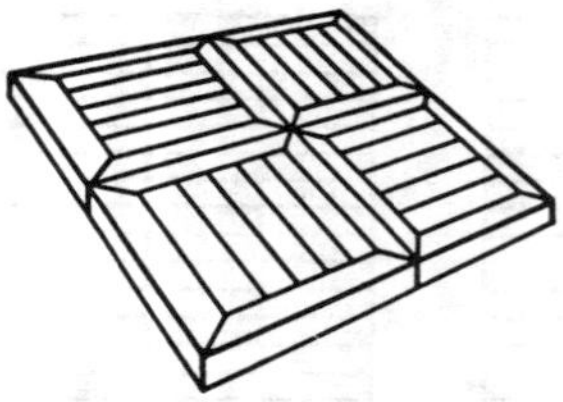

5/16" x 13-1/4" x 13-1/4"

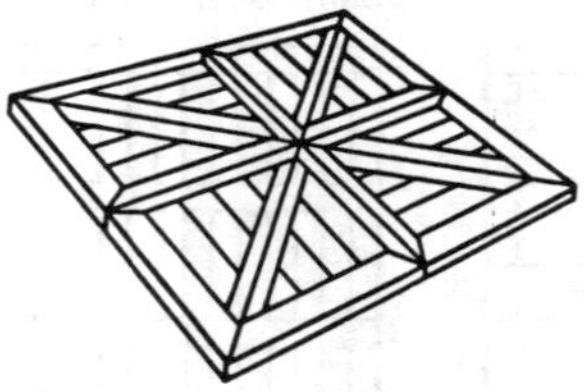

5/16" x 19" x 19"

————————

5/16" x 11" x 11"

3/4" x 3", 5", & 7"

5/16" x 13-1/4" x 13-1/4"

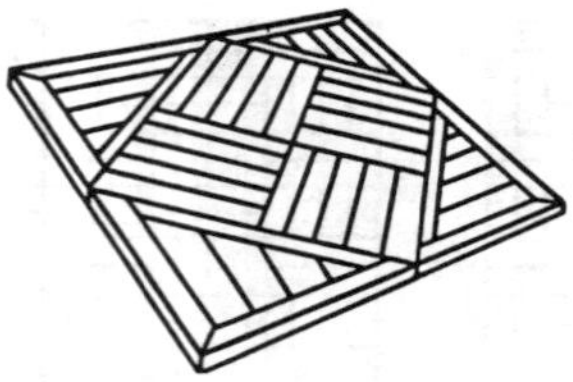

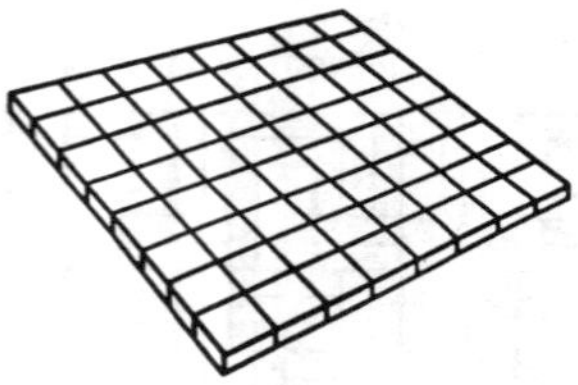

5/16" x 15-1/8" x 15-1/8"

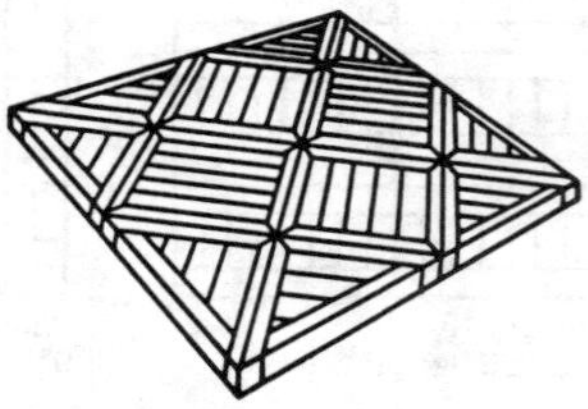

3/4" x 3", 5", & 7""

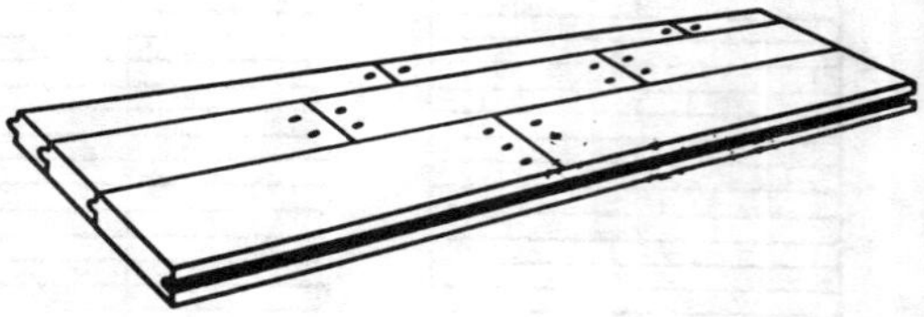

5/16" x 13-7/16" x 13-7/16"

3/4" thick design formed with 6" x 6" blocks and 2-1/4" x 14-1/4" pickets

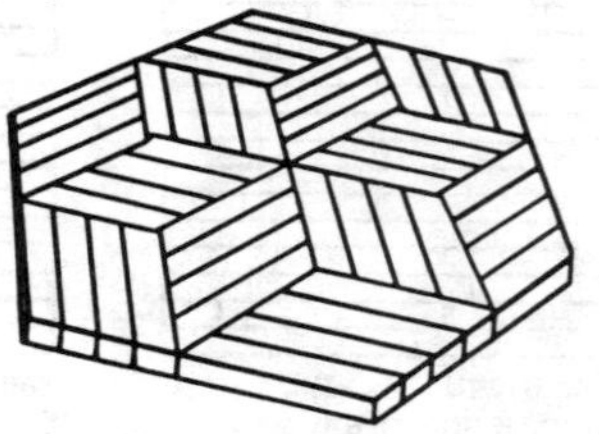

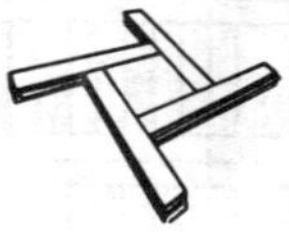

5/16" x 19" x 19"

5/16" x 18" x 18"

3/4" x 2-1/4" single slat. Lengths: 6-3/4", 9", 11-1/4", 13-1/2", 15-3/4", 18"

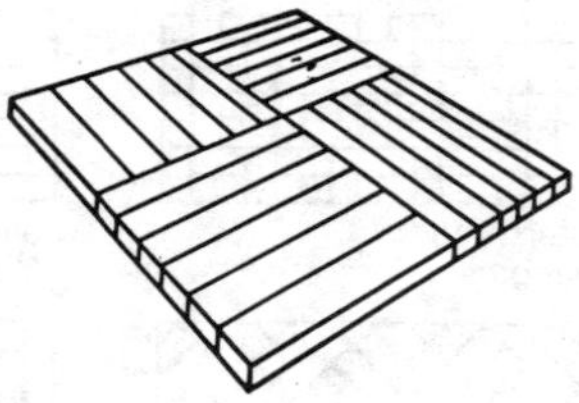

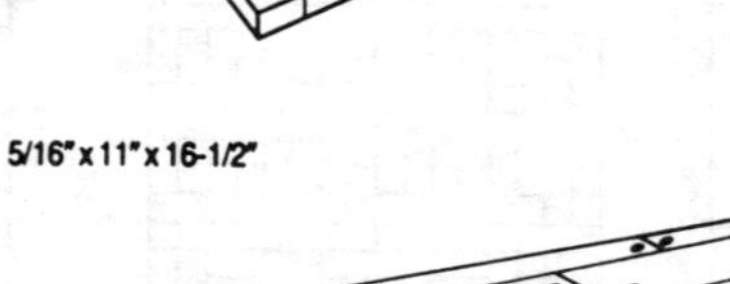

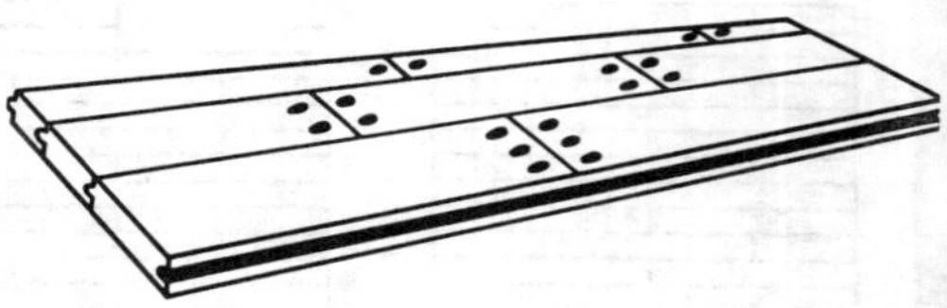

3/4" x 3" single slat. Lengths: 6", 9", 12", 15", 18"

5/16" x 19" x 19"

3/4" x 15" x 15"

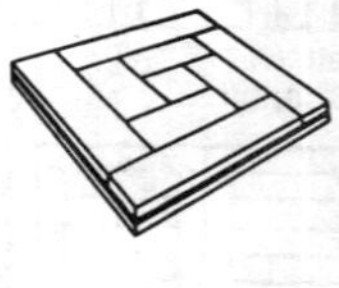

5/16" x 14-1/4" x 14-1/4"

————————

3/4" x 16" x 16" Units

5/16" x 11" x 16-1/2"

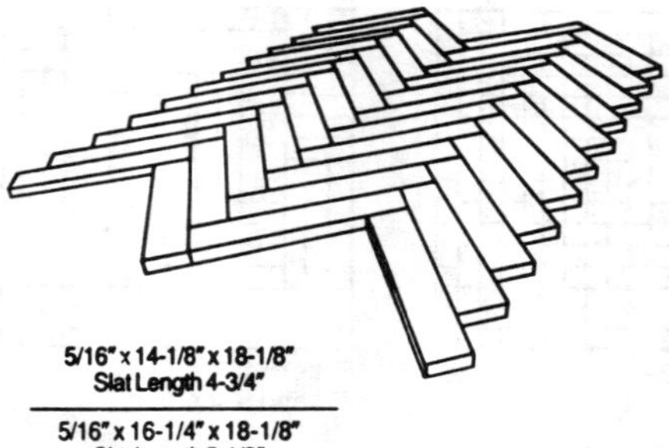

5/16" x 14-1/8" x 18-1/8"
Slat Length 4-3/4"

————————

5/16" x 16-1/4" x 18-1/8"
Slat Length 5-1/2"

3/4" x 3", 5", & 7"

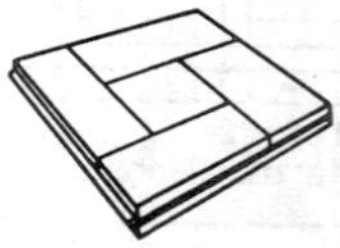

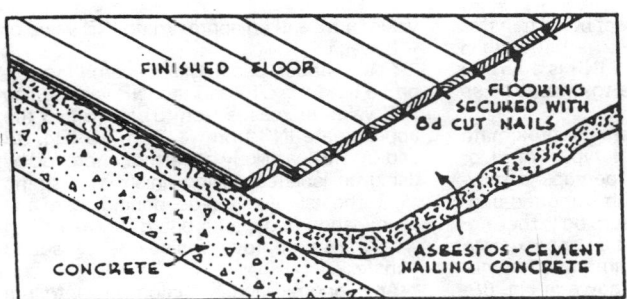

WOOD FLOOR OVER CONCRETE
WITH UNDERLAYER OF NAILING CONCRETE

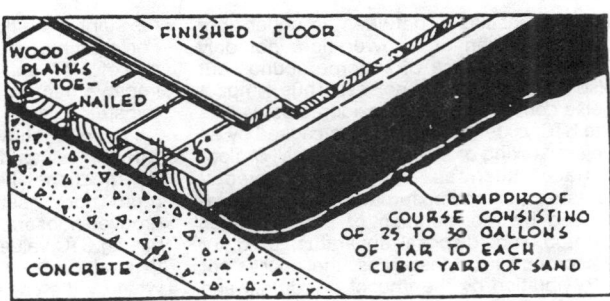

WOOD FLOOR
OVER CONCRETE

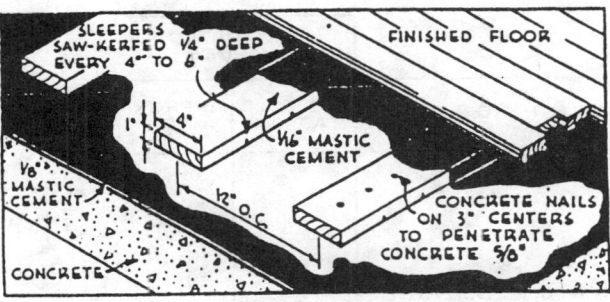

FINISHED FLOOR DIRECTLY ON SLEEPERS
SET IN MASTIC CEMENT & NAILED TO CONCRETE

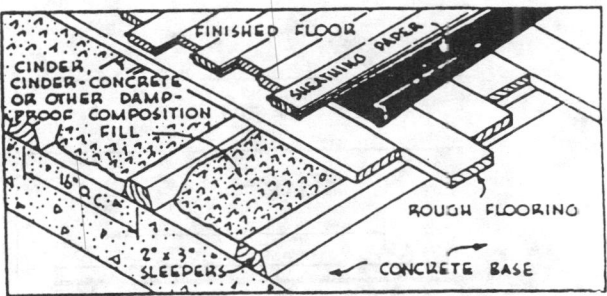

WOOD FLOOR OVER CONCRETE
WITH SUB-BASE OF SLEEPERS & SLEEPER FILL

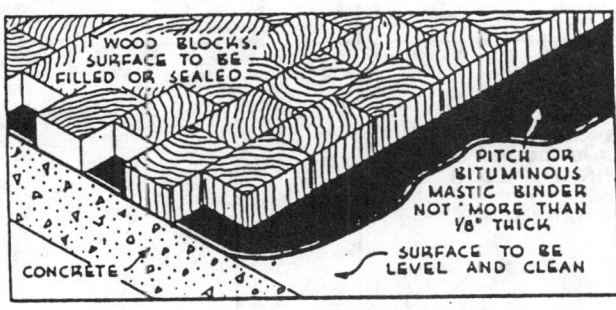

WOOD BLOCK FLOOR
OVER CONCRETE

WOOD FLOOR
OVER CONCRETE IN MASTIC

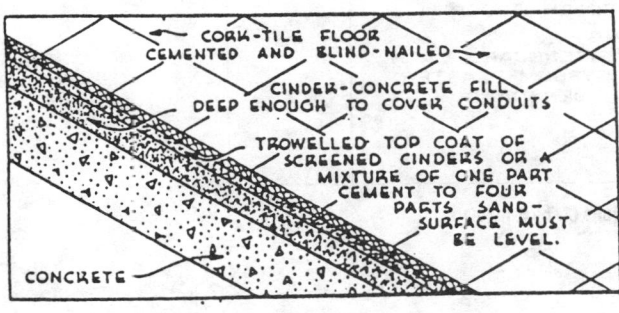

CORK TILE FLOOR
OVER CONCRETE

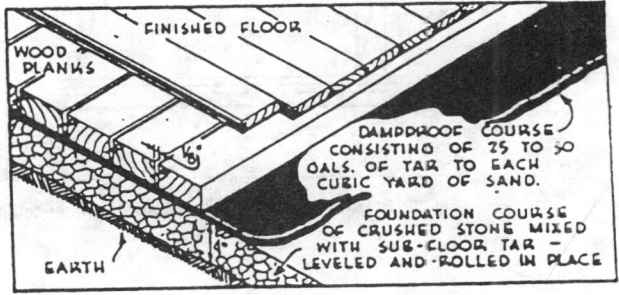

WOOD FLOOR
APPLIED OVER EARTH

FLOORS AND FLOOR FINISHES

Floor Construction Sound Insulation

Sound insulation between an upper floor and the ceiling of a lower floor not only involves resistance of airborne sounds but also that of impact noises. Thus, impact noise control must be considered as well as the STC value. Impact noise is caused by an object striking or sliding along a wall or floor surface, such as by dropped objects, footsteps, or moving furniture. It may also be caused by the vibration of a dishwasher, bathtub, food-disposal apparatus, or other equipment. In all instances, the floor is set into vibration by the impact or contact and sound is radiated from both sides of the floor.

A method of measuring impact noise has been developed and is commonly expressed as the *impact noise ratings (INR)*. The greater the positive value of the INR, the more resistant is the floor to impact noise transfer. For example, an INR of −2 is better than one of −17, and one of +5 INR is a further improvement in resistance to impact noise transfer.

Figure 8 shows STC and approximate INR(db) values for several types of floor constructions. Figure 8A, perhaps a minimum floor assembly with tongued-and-grooved floor and ⅜-in gypsum board ceiling, has an STC value of 30 and an approximate INR value of −18. This is improved somewhat by the construction shown in Fig. 8B, and still further by the combination of materials in Fig. 8C.

The value of isolating the ceiling joists from a gypsum lath and plaster ceiling by means of spring clips is illustrated in Fig. 9A. An STC value of 52 and an approximate INR value of −2 result.

Foam-rubber padding and carpeting improve both the STC and the INR values. The STC value increases from 31 to 45 and the approximate INR from −17 to +5 (Fig. 9B and C). This can likely be further improved by using an isolated ceiling finish with spring clips. The use of sound-deadening board and a lamination of gypsum board for the ceiling would also improve resistance to sound transfer.

An economical construction similar to (but an improvement over) Fig. 9C, with a STC value of 48 and an approximate INR of +18, consists of the following: (a) a pad and carpet over ⅝-in tongued-and-grooved plywood underlayment, (b) 3-in fiberglass insulating

DETAIL	DESCRIPTION	ESTIMATED VALUES	
		STC RATING	APPROX. INR
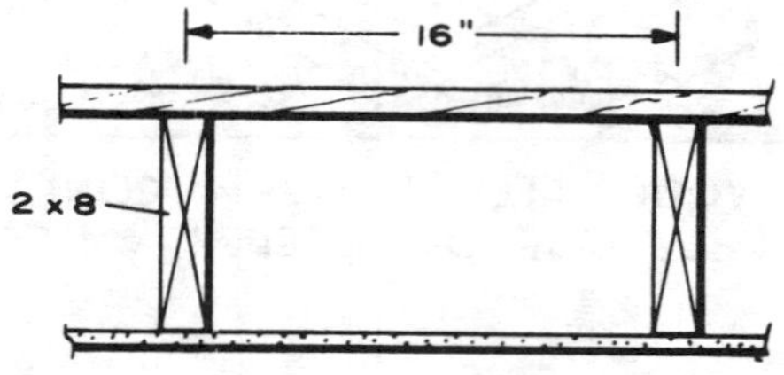 A 2 x 8 16"	FLOOR ⅞" T. & G. FLOORING CEILING ⅜" GYPSUM BOARD	30	−18
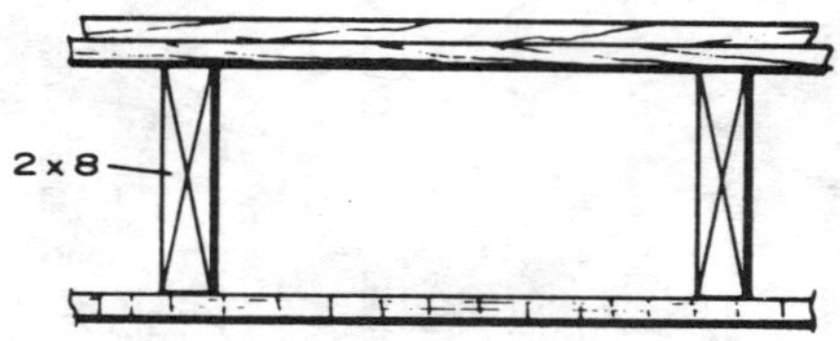 B 2 x 8	FLOOR ¾" SUBFLOOR ¾" FINISH FLOOR CEILING ¾" FIBERBOARD	42	−12
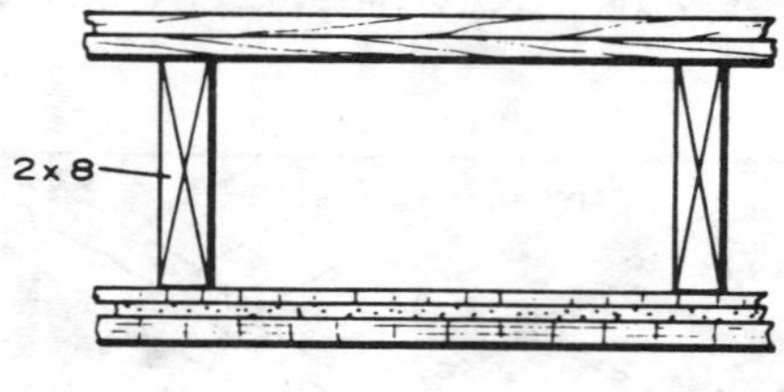 C 2 x 8	FLOOR ¾" SUBFLOOR ¾" FINISH FLOOR CEILING ½" FIBERBOARD LATH ½" GYPSUM PLASTER ¾" FIBERBOARD	45	−4

Fig. 8   Relative impact and sound transfer in floor-ceiling combinations (2- by 8-in joists).

batts between joists, (c) resilient channels spaced 24 in apart across the bottom of the joists, and (d) ⅝-in gypsum board screwed to the bottom of the channels and finished with taped joints.

The use of separate floor joists with staggered ceiling joists below provides reasonable values but adds a good deal to construction costs. Separate joists with insulation between and a soundboard between subfloor and finish provide an STC rating of 53 and an approximate INR value of −3.

Sound absorption Design of the "quiet" house can incorporate another system of sound insulation, namely, sound absorption. Sound-absorbing materials can minimize the

amount of noise by stopping the reflection of sound back into a room. Sound-absorbing materials do not necessarily have resistance to airborne sounds. Perhaps the most commonly used sound-absorbing materials is acoustic tile. Wood fiber or similar materials are used in the manufacture of the tile, which is usually processed to provide some fire resistance and designed with numerous tiny sound traps on the tile surfaces. These may consist of tiny drilled or punched holes, fissured surfaces, or a combination of both.

Acoustic tile is most often used in the ceiling and areas where it is not subjected to excessive mechanical damage, such as above a wall wainscoting. It is normally manufactured in sizes from 12 by 12 to 12 by

48 in. Thicknesses vary from ½ to ¾ in, and the tile is usually factory finished ready for application. Paint or other finishes which fill or cover the tiny holes or fissures for trapping sound will greatly reduce its efficiency.

Acoustic tile may be applied by a number of methods — to existing ceilings or any smooth surface with a mastic adhesive designed specifically for this purpose, or to furring strips nailed to the underside of the ceiling joists. Nailing or stapling tile is the normal application method in this system. It is also used with a mechanical suspension system involving small "H," "Z," or "T" members. Manufacturers' recommendations should be followed in application and finishing.

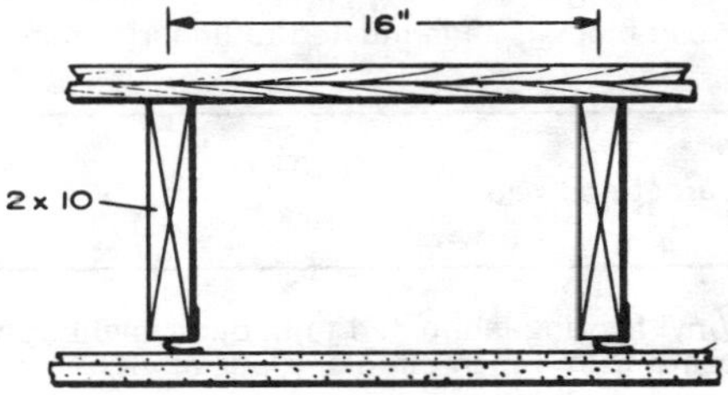

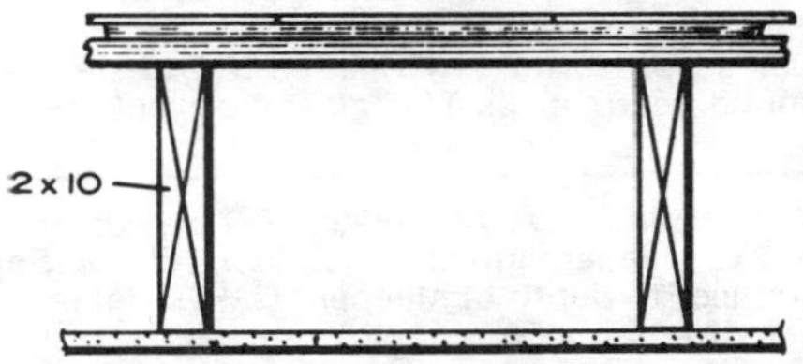

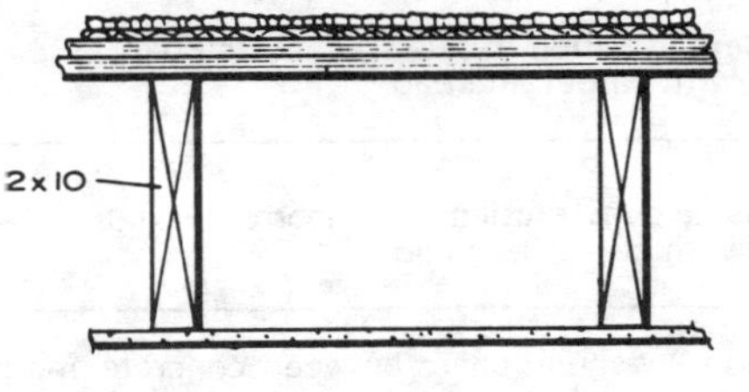

Fig. 9 Relative impact and sound transfer in floor-ceiling combinations (2- by 10-in joists).

FLOORS AND FLOOR FINISHES

Floor Construction Sound Insulation

conventional wood floor joist systems for sound control

FLOOR SYSTEM	FLOOR NUMBER	FLOOR COVERING
conventional CARPET & PAD ⅝" PLYWOOD SUBFLOOR 2 x 8 JOISTS 16" O.C. 3" GLASS FIBER **FLOOR NO. 3** The basic construction is illustrated by floor No. 3 although floors 4 and 5 have 2"x10" joists and ½" subfloor. Except in floor No. 1, the ceiling is fire-resistive type gypsum board applied with screws to resilient channels 24" o.c. Standard carpet is 44-ounce (sq. yd.) gropoint over 40-ounce hair pad.	1	⅛" vinyl asbestos tile on ⅜" plywood underlayment
	2	.075" vinyl sheet on ⅜" plywood underlayment
	3	Carpet and pad directly over subfloor
	4	²⁵⁄₃₂" oak strip floor over subfloor
	5	Carpet and pad added to No. 4
conventional **With Floated Floor Over** ½" UNDERLAYMENT ½" SOUND BOARD ⅝" SUBFLOOR 2 x 10 JOISTS 16" O.C. 3" GLASS FIBER **FLOOR NO. 8** The basic construction is illustrated. Sound deadening board (15-18 p.c.f.) is laid over a ⅝" plywood subfloor, with or without stapling, and ½" T&G underlayment grade plywood glued over the sound board. The ceiling is ⅝" fire-resistive type gypsum board on resilient channels; absorptive material is 3-inch thick glass fiber batts	6	Wood block (⁵⁄₁₆") laminated to underlayment
	7	Carpet and pad
	8	Vinyl flooring laminated to underlayment applied over sound board with 4-inch circular globs of glue
	9	Vinyl covering like 8 with sleepers glued between sound board and underlayment
	10	Oak strip flooring (²⁵⁄₃₂") nailed to 2x3 sleepers glued over sound board strips 1⅞" glass fiber between sleepers
	11	Vinyl flooring (0.07") on ⅝" T&G plywood underlayment glued to 2x2 sleepers glued to subfloor 16" o.c. Sand fill over subfloor to depth of sleepers (1½"). Balance as in basic construction
conventional **With lightweight Concrete or Gypsum Cement Added** 1⅝" LT. WT. CONCRETE ⅝" SUBFLOOR 3" MINERAL WOOL **FLOOR NO. 14** 2 x 10 JOISTS 16" O.C. ⅝" GYPSUM BOARD ON R.C. The basic construction is illustrated by floor No. 14. The floor topping is 1⅝" thick cellular (foamed) concrete (100 p.c.f.). Ceilings are fire-resistive type gypsum board on resilient channels, 24 inches o.c. Absorptive material is 3" thick mineral wool batts. Floor coverings for impact tests are 44-ounce carpet over 40-ounce hair pad or vinyl floor covering, approximately 0.07 inches thick. Note variations from basic construction drawn in plans 12-16.	12	Ceiling nailed to joists; no absorptive material; with carpet and pad...........................
	13	Ceiling nailed to joists; 3" glass fiber with carpet and pad...........................
	14	**Basic construction**—(no floor covering) with carpet and pad...........................
	15	Add ½" sound board between concrete and subfloor with vinyl tile........................... with carpet and pad...........................
	16	Basic construction—but with ¾" thick gypsum concrete in place of 1⅝" thick cellular concrete; ½" gypsum ceiling without floor covering...........................

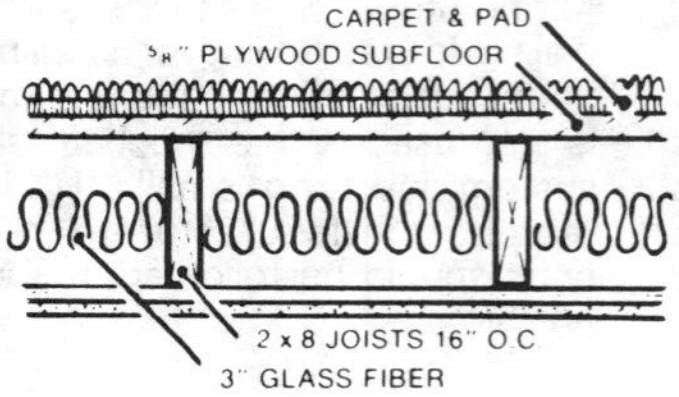

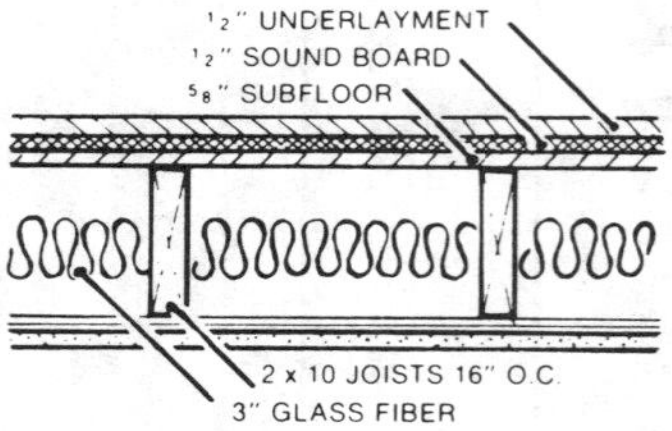

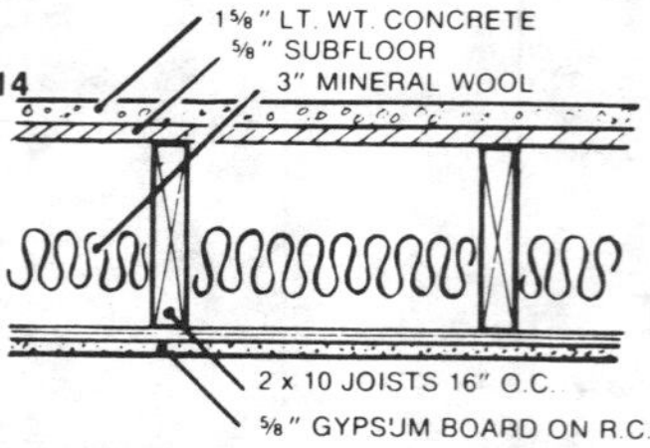

The improved resistance to airborne sound transmission gained by isolating the ceiling with resilient channels and adding absorptive material is evident by comparing floors 2 to 5 with No. 1. A 10-point increase in STC reduces the loudness of transmitted noise by one-half. Improved resistance to impact noise transmission is gained by adding carpet and pad as is evident by comparing floor No. 3 with No. 2 or floor No. 5 with 4. An IIC of 51 is often recommended as an acceptable level of impact insulation.

Standard toe base

No-toe base: Adds a decorative touch to carpeted interiors.

Butt toe base: Engineered to butt precisely to ⅛" floor coverings.

Long toe base: For special applications. Features a onger toe extending 1" to cover wide irregularities between floor and wall.

TABLE 1   Cove Base Specifications

Type	Sizes available		
Standard toe base	2½"	4"	6"
No-toe base	2½"	4"	6"
Butt toe base		4"	6"
Long toe base		4"	

Length: 48"

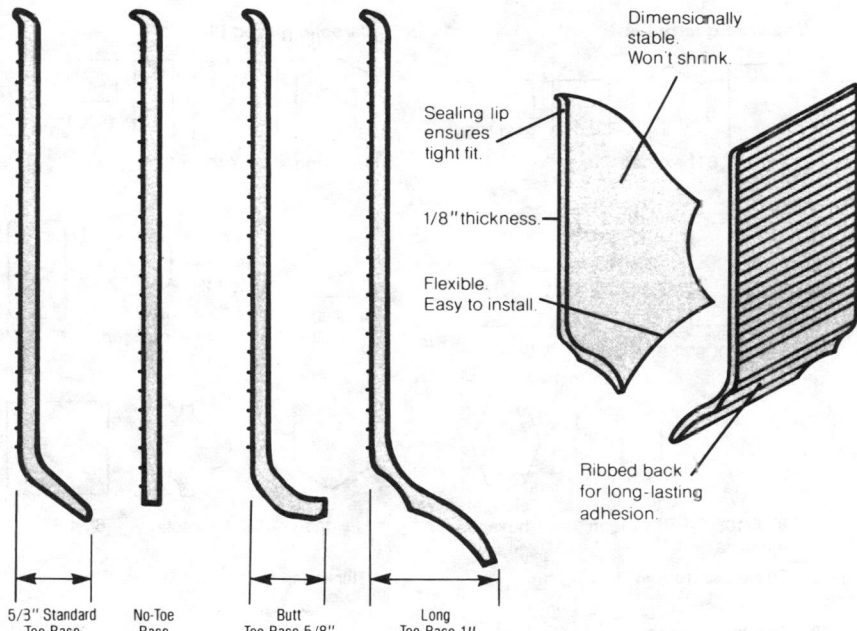

Dimensionally stable. Won't shrink.

Sealing lip ensures tight fit.

1/8" thickness.

Flexible. Easy to install.

Ribbed back for long-lasting adhesion.

5/3" Standard Toe Base

No-Toe Base

Butt Toe Base 5/8"

Long Toe Base 1"

TABLE 2   Corner Specifications

Type	Length of return	Sizes available		
Inside/outside	2¼"	2½"	4"	6"
Underlap outside	3" (with underlap)	4"		
No-toe outside	2¼"	2½"	4"	
Long toe outside	2¼"	4"		

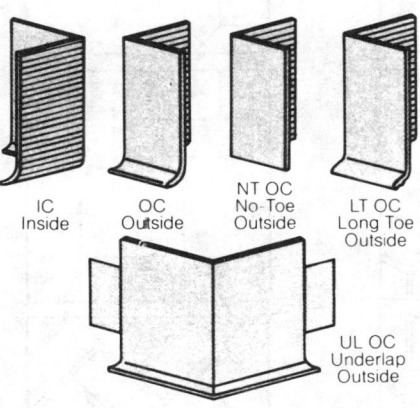

IC Inside

OC Outside

NT OC No-Toe Outside

LT OC Long Toe Outside

UL OC Underlap Outside

FLOORS AND FLOOR FINISHES
Ceramic Tile Patterns

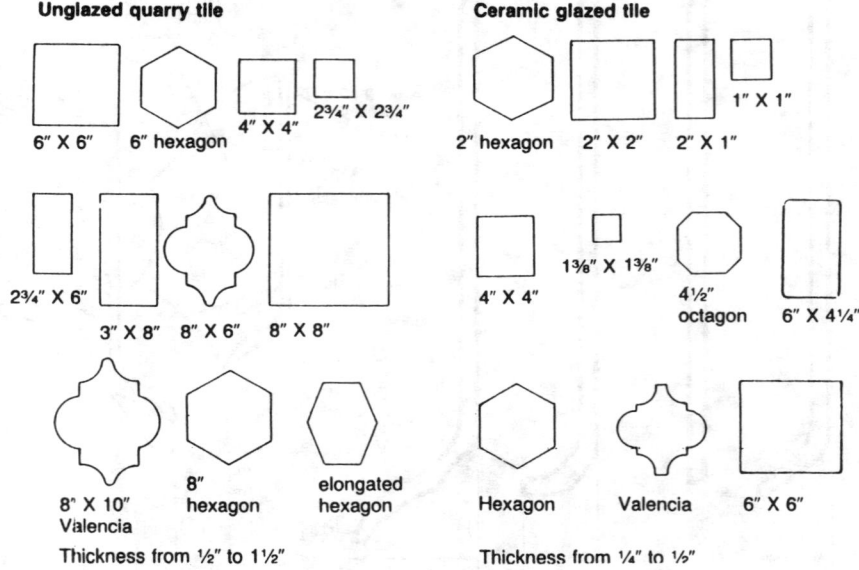

Unglazed quarry tile

6" X 6"   6" hexagon   4" X 4"   2¾" X 2¾"

2¾" X 6"   3" X 8"   8" X 6"   8" X 8"

8" X 10" Valencia   8" hexagon   elongated hexagon

Thickness from ½" to 1½"

Ceramic glazed tile

2" hexagon   2" X 2"   2" X 1"   1" X 1"

4" X 4"   1⅜" X 1⅜"   4½" octagon   6" X 4¼"

Hexagon   Valencia   6" X 6"

Thickness from ¼" to ½"

Fig. 10   Ceramic tile shapes.

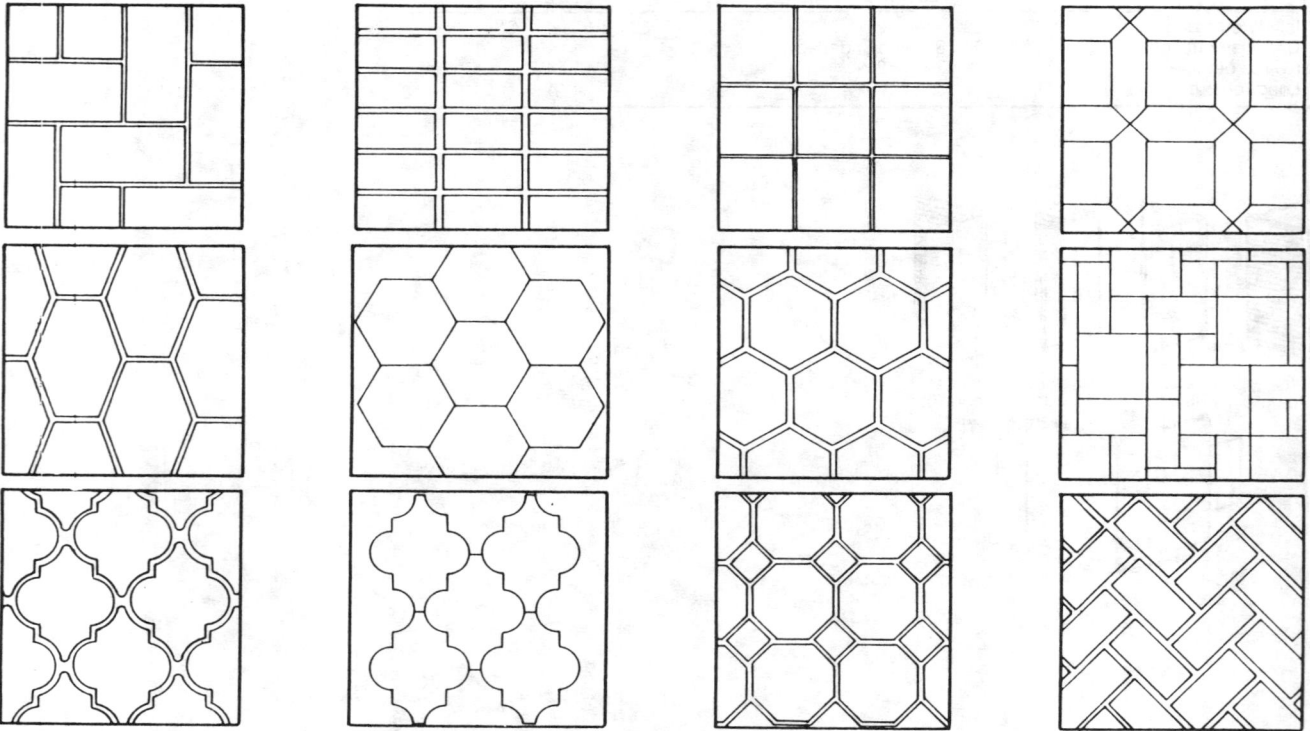

Fig. 11   Ceramic tile patterns.

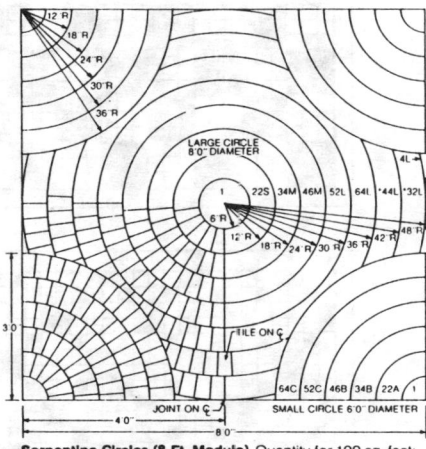

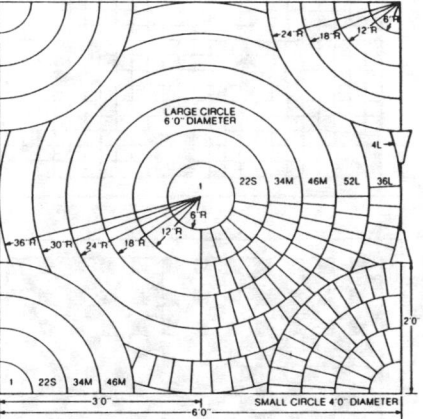

Serpentine Circles (8 Ft. Module) Quantity for 100 sq. feet: 3.2 pcs. circle; 70 pcs. small wedge; 256 pcs. medium wedge; 500 pcs. large wedge

Serpentine Circles (6 Ft. Module) Quantity for 100 sq. feet: 5.7 pcs. circle; 126 pcs. small wedge; 460 pcs. medium wedge; 280 pcs. large wedge

Meandering Serpentine Quantity for 100 sq. feet: 3 pcs circle; 58 pcs. small wedge; 220 pcs. medium wedge; 610 pcs. large wedge

Serpentine Fan Quantity for 100 sq. feet: 106 pcs. small wedge; 290 pcs. medium wedge; 484 pcs. large wedge

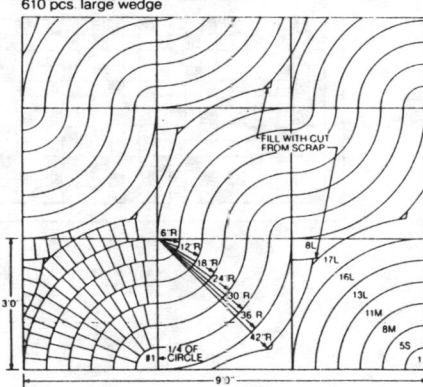

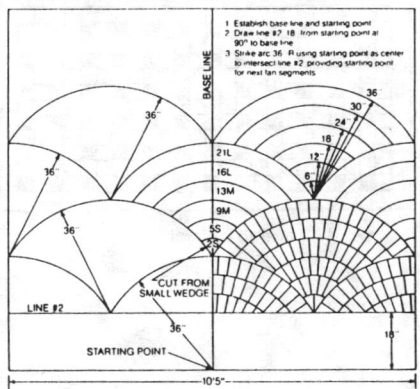

FLOORS AND FLOOR FINISHES
Ceramic Tile Patterns

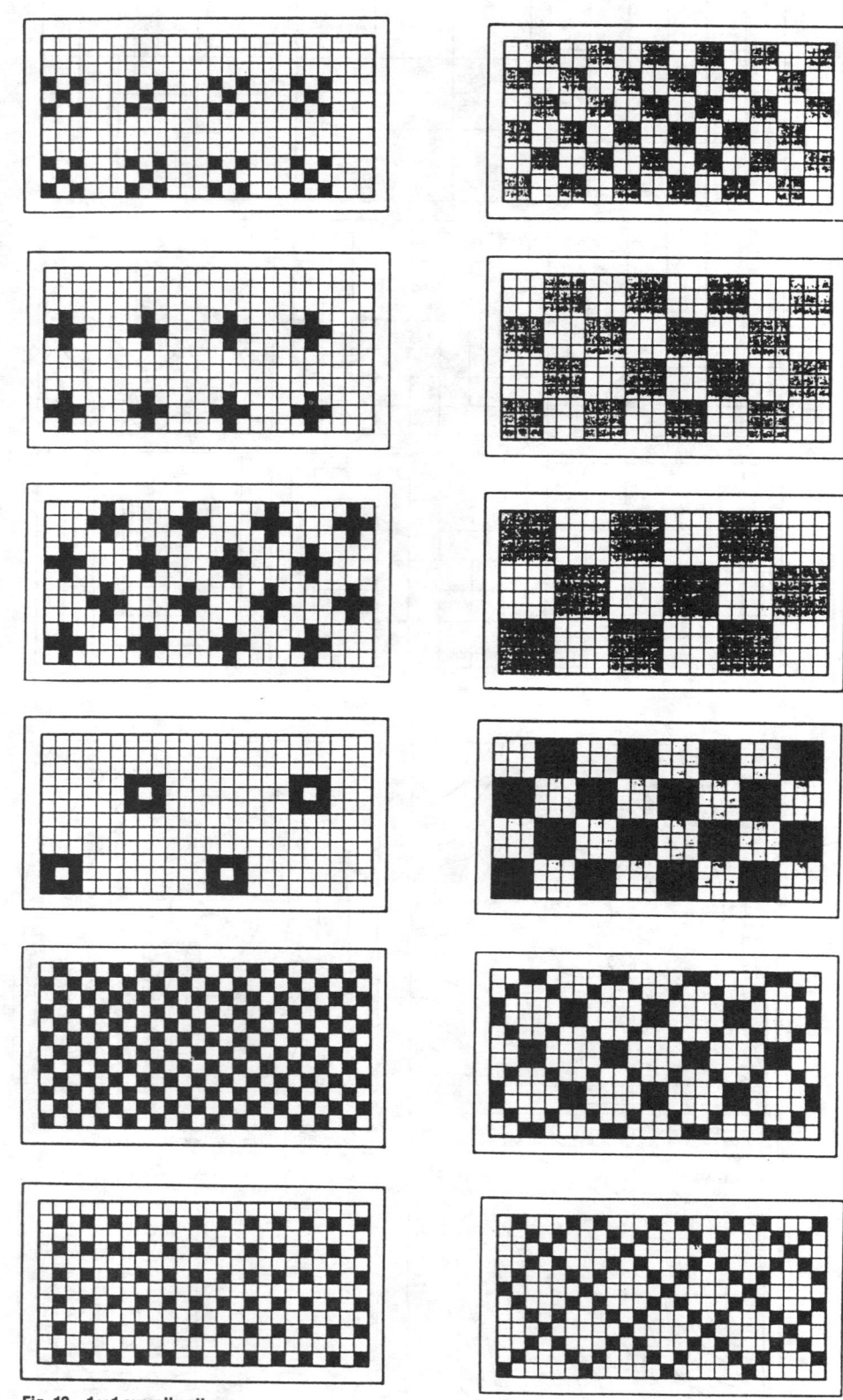

Fig. 12　1×1 overall patterns.

Fig. 13   1×1 six-inch borders.

Fig. 14   1×1 twelve-inch borders.

FLOORS AND FLOOR FINISHES

Ceramic Tile Patterns

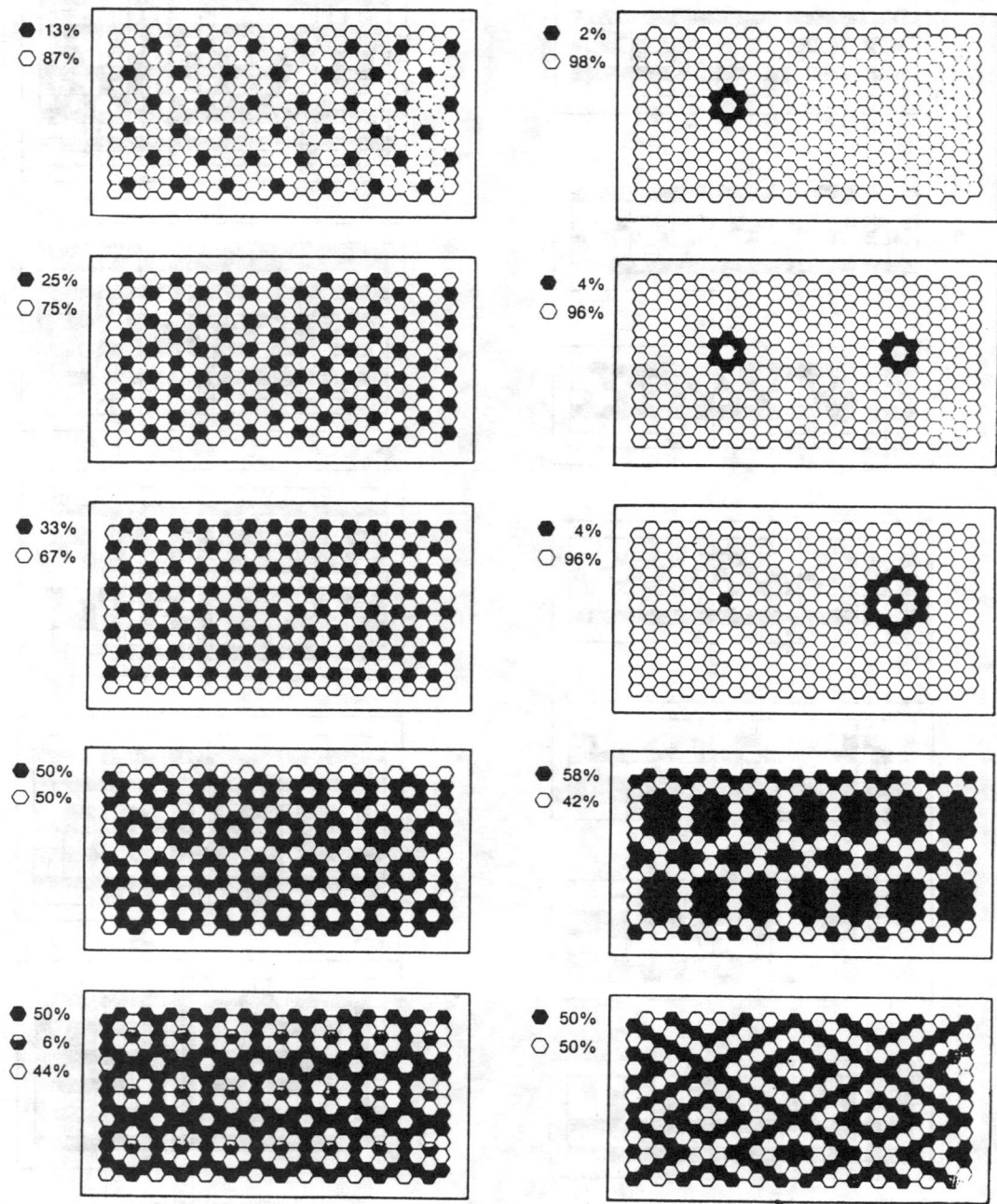

Fig. 15   1″ hex overall patterns. All patterns master-set 12″ × 24″ sheets.

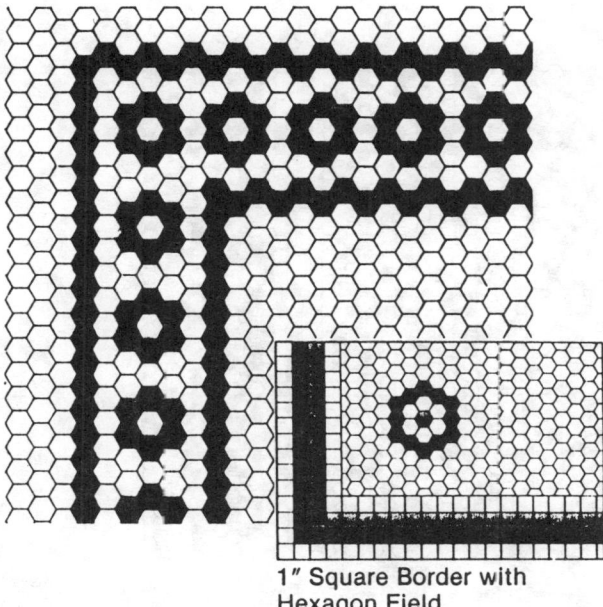

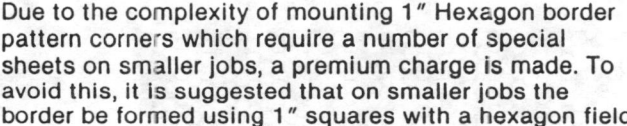

1″ Square Border with
Hexagon Field

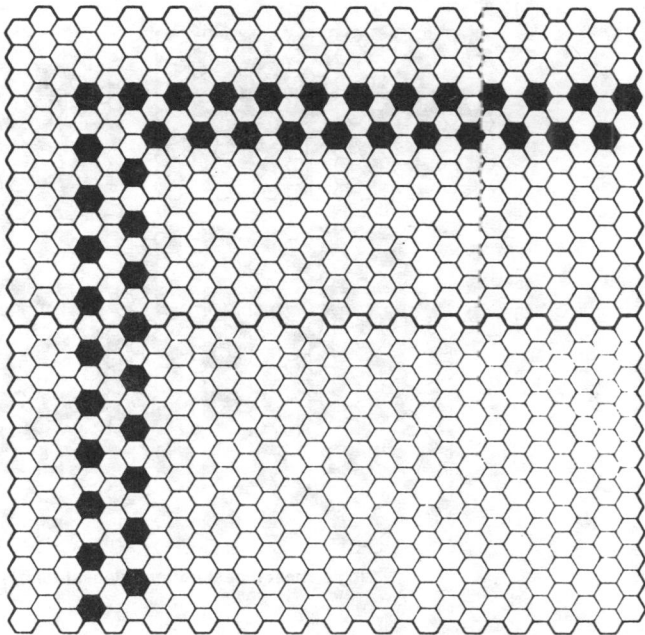

Due to the complexity of mounting 1″ Hexagon border pattern corners which require a number of special sheets on smaller jobs, a premium charge is made. To avoid this, it is suggested that on smaller jobs the border be formed using 1″ squares with a hexagon field.

If a Hexagon border is required, you must provide a plan of the area with dimensions because the Hexagon configuration precludes interchanging sheets. We will provide specific sheets for those areas and setting plans.

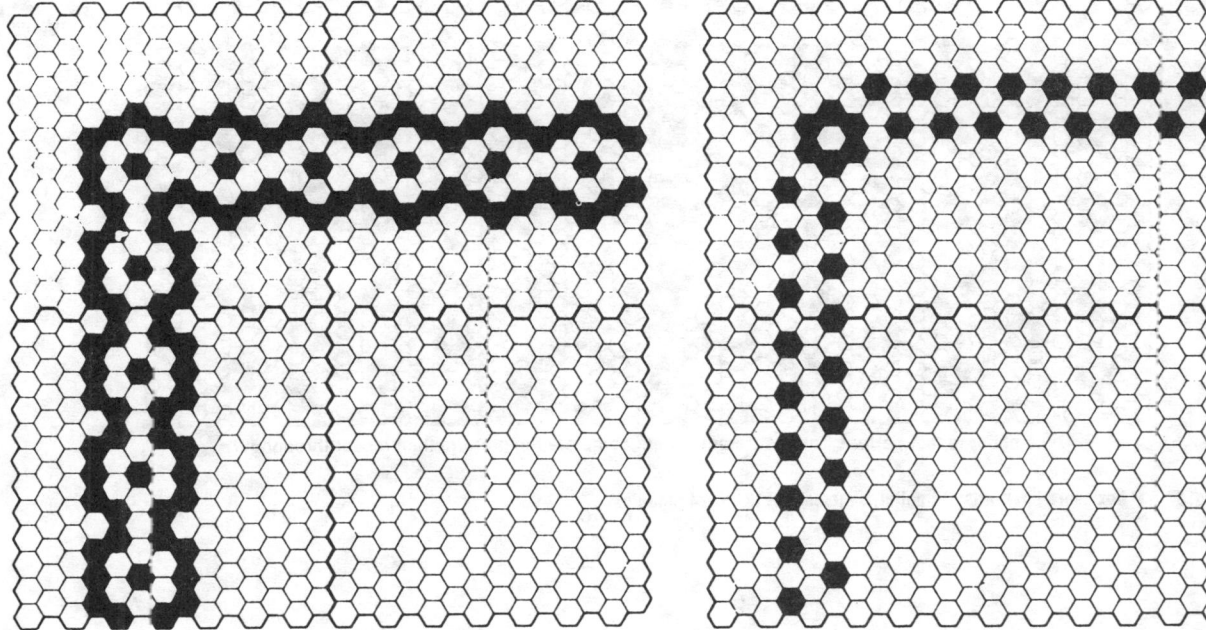

Note that on three of these border patterns a full sheet is used for the corner. Some designs, however, will require a half sheet for the corner as shown in SB-1404. In this case a right and left corner will be on one sheet and the sheet is cut in half before placement.

Fig. 16 1″ hex border patterns. All patterns master-set 12″ × 24″ sheets.

FLOORS AND FLOOR FINISHES
Ceramic Tile Patterns

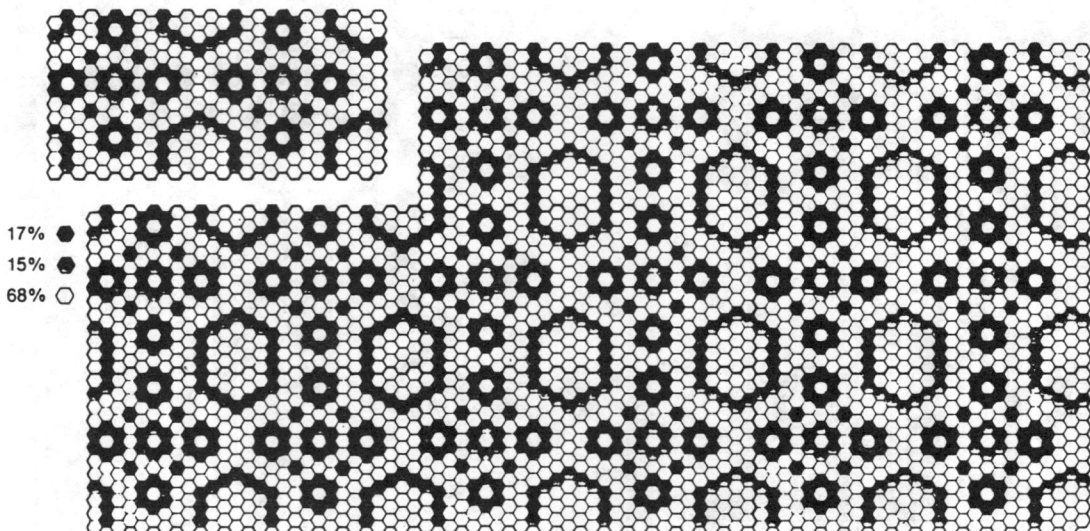

17% ●
15% ●
68% ○

Single sheet repeat pattern. Repeat for overall pattern.

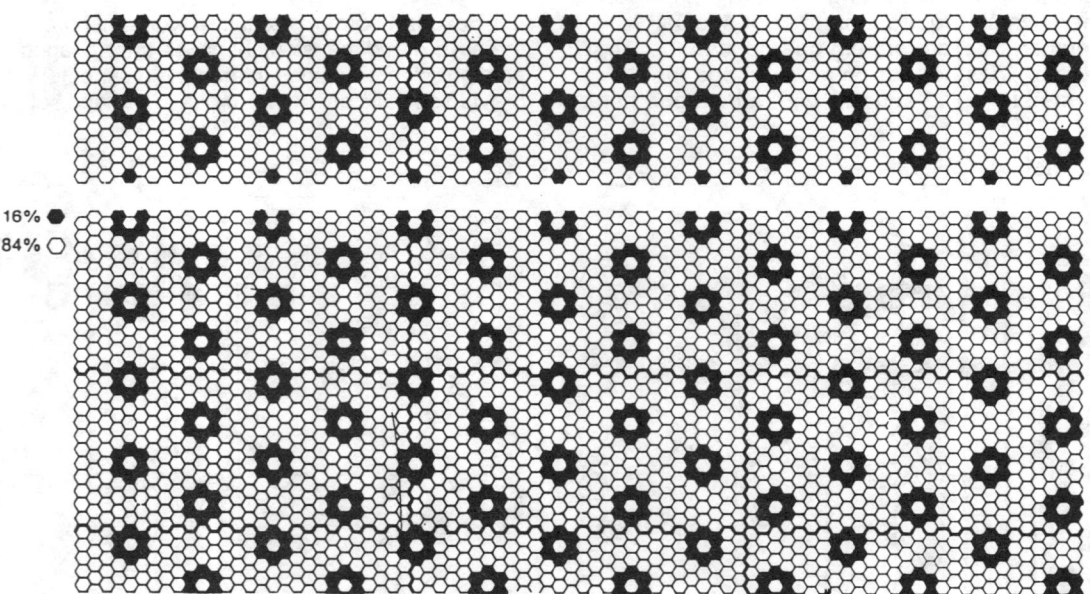

16% ●
84% ○

Three sheet repeat pattern. Three different sheets complete the pattern, then repeat throughout.

Fig. 17 1″ hex overall patterns. All patterns master-set 12″ × 24″ sheets.

FLOORS AND FLOOR FINISHES

Basic Quarry Tile Patterns

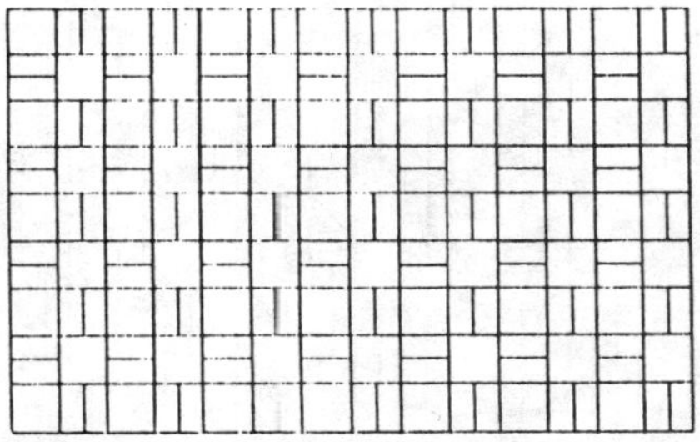

QP-6101 ALTERNATING CHECKERBOARD
Shown: 3⅞" × 8" (50%), 8" × 8" (50%)

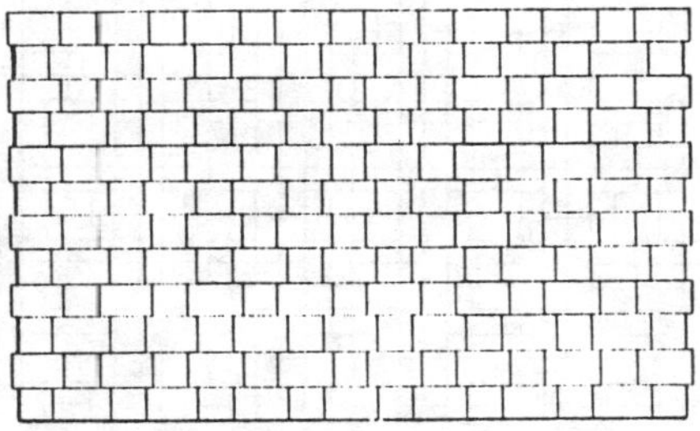

QP-6102 FLEMISH BOND
Shown: 6" × 6" (40%), 6" × 9" (60%)
Also Use: 3⅞" × 3⅞", 3⅞" × 8", or 6" × 6", 6" × 12⅛"

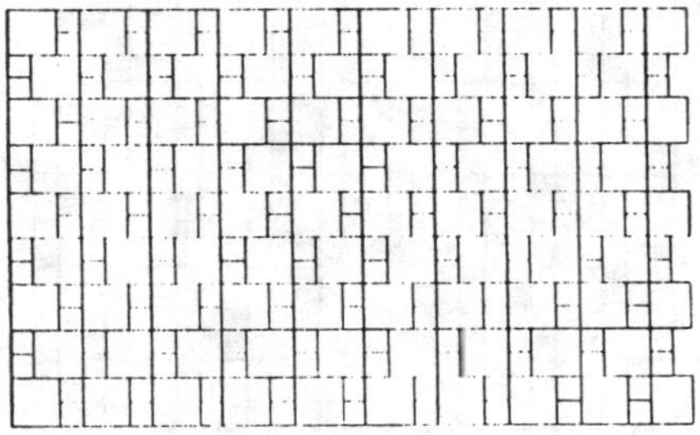

QP-6103 FLEMISH SQUARE BOND
Shown: 3⅞" × 3⅞" (33⅓%), 8" × 8" (66⅔%)

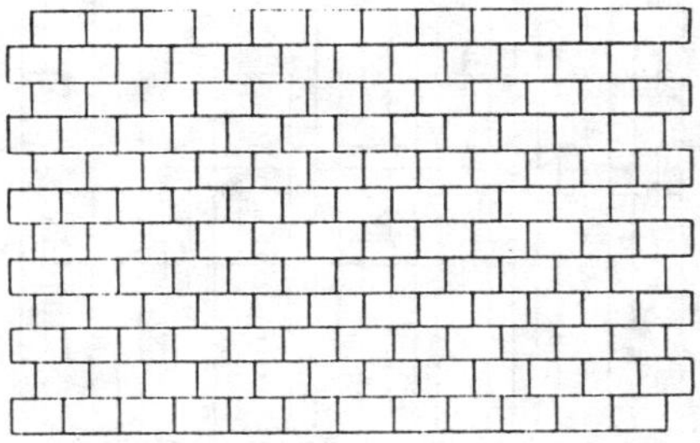

QP-6104 BROKEN JOINT
Shown: 6" × 9" (100%)
Also Use: 3⅞" × 8" or 5" × 12⅛"

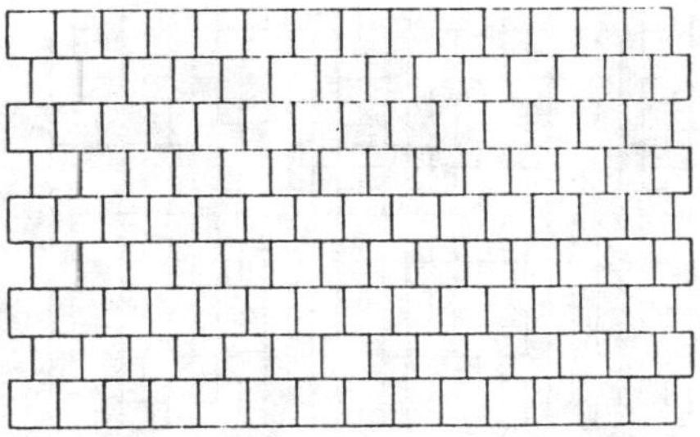

QP-6105 BROKEN JOINT SQUARE
Shown: 8" × 8" (100%)
Also Use: 6" × 6"

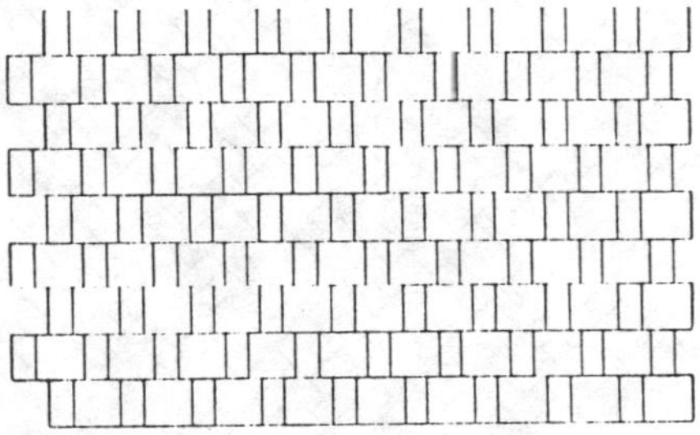

QP-6106 BARRED SQUARE
Shown: 3⅞" × 8" (33⅓%), 8" × 8" (66⅔%)

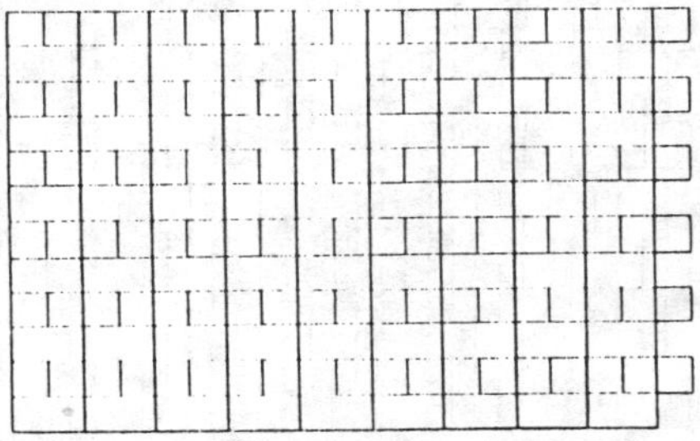

QP-6107 ALTERNATING STRIPE VARIATION
Shown: 6" × 6" (50%), 6" × 12⅛" (50%)
Also Use: 3⅞" × 3⅞" 3⅞" × 8"

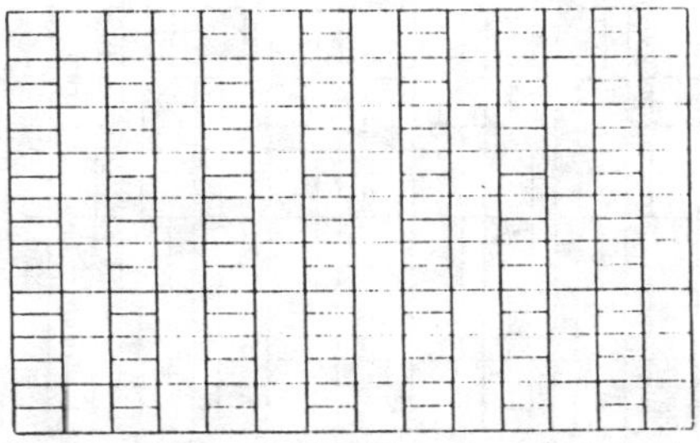

QP-6108 ALTERNATING STRIPE
Shown: 3⅞" × 8" (50%), 8" × 8" (50%)

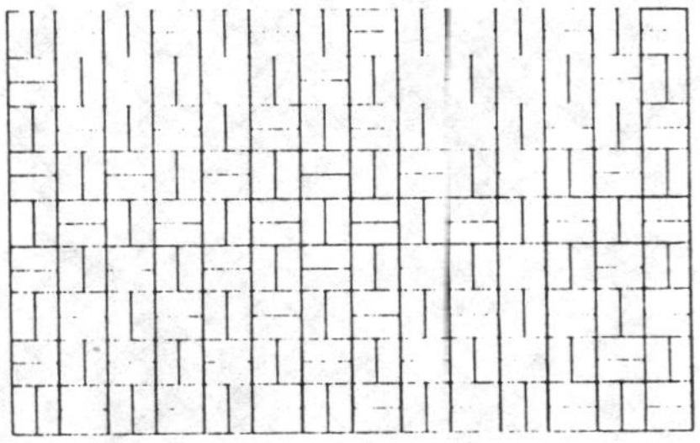

QP-6109 BASKETWEAVE
Shown: 3⅞" × 8" (100%)
Also Use: 6" × 12⅛"

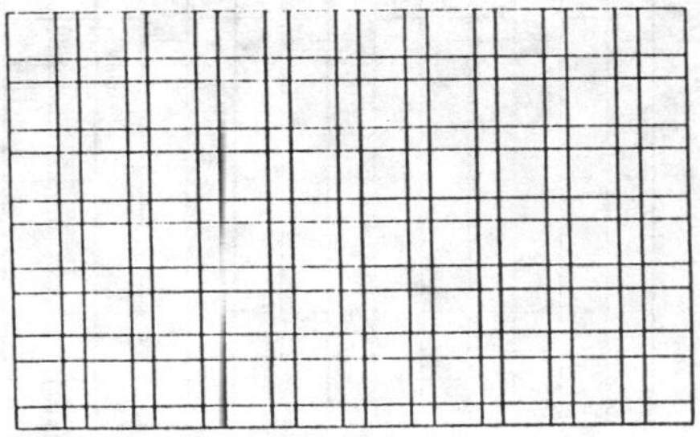

QP-6110 FORMAL RANDOM
Shown: 3⅞" × 3⅞" (11.2%), 3⅞" × 8" (44.4%),
8" × 8" (44.4%)

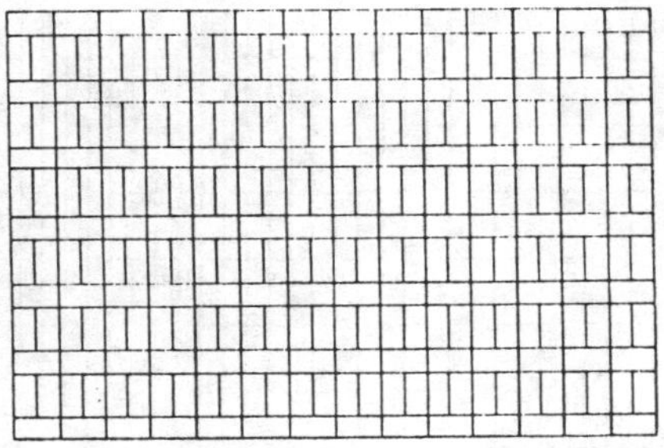

QP-6111 RAILROAD BOND
Shown: 3⅞" × 8" (100%)
Also Use: 6" × 12⅛"

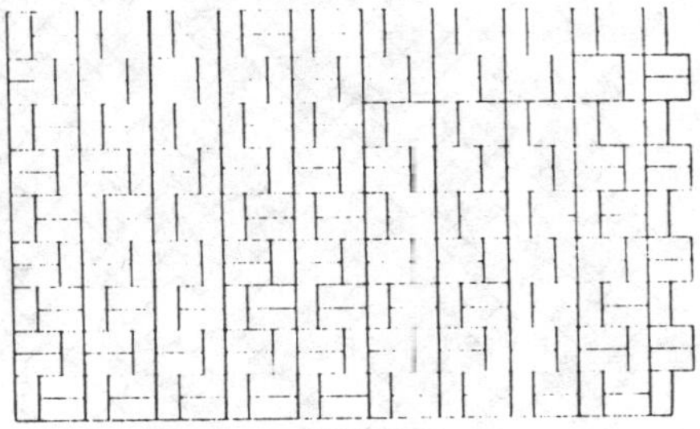

QP-6112 BASKETWEAVE VARIATION
Shown: 3⅞" × 8" (100%)
Also Use: 6" × 12⅛"

FLOORS AND FLOOR FINISHES

Basic Quarry Tile Patterns

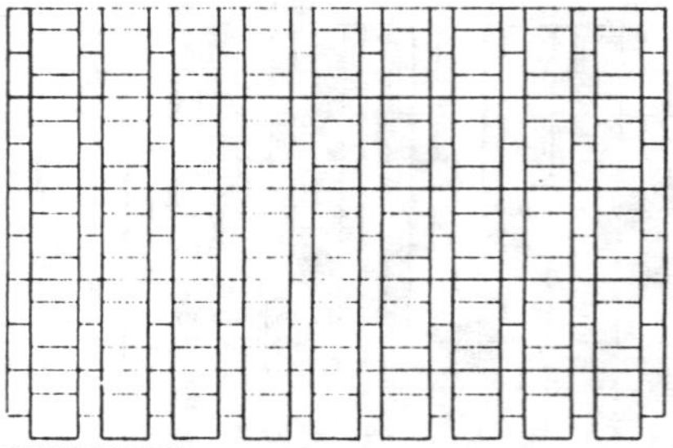

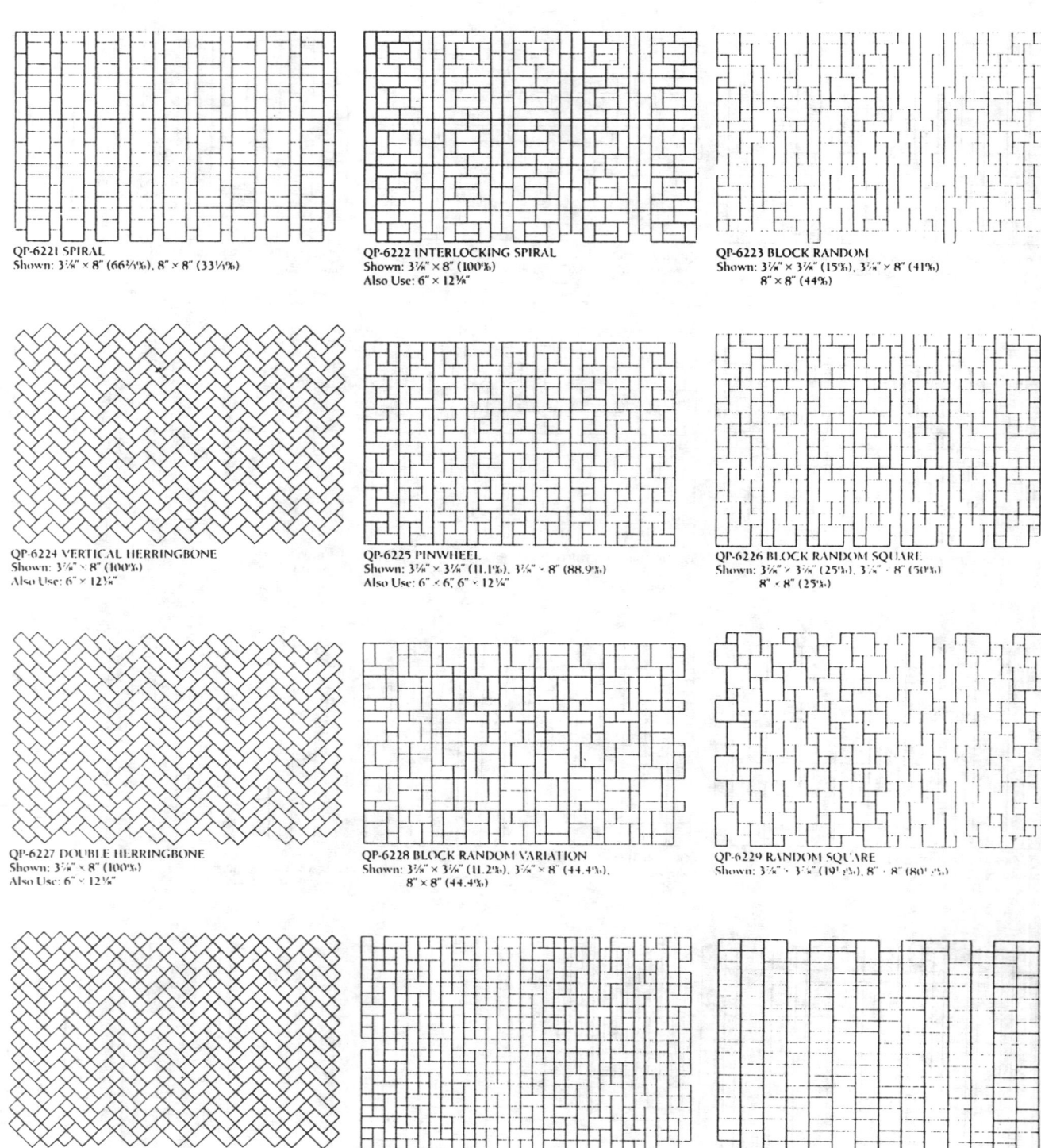

QP-6221 SPIRAL
Shown: 3⅞" × 8" (66⅔%), 8" × 8" (33⅓%)

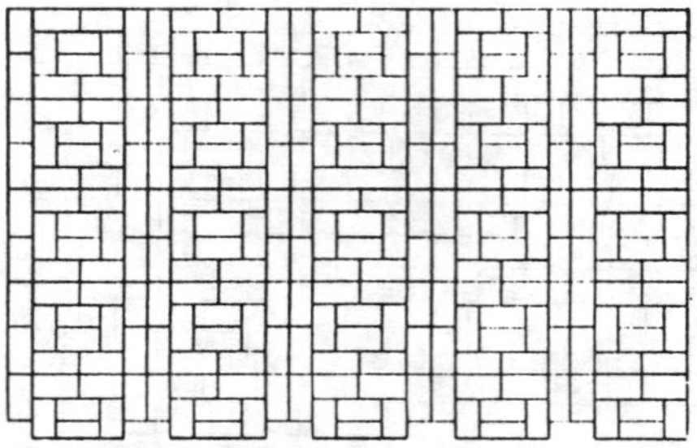

QP-6222 INTERLOCKING SPIRAL
Shown: 3⅞" × 8" (100%)
Also Use: 6" × 12⅛"

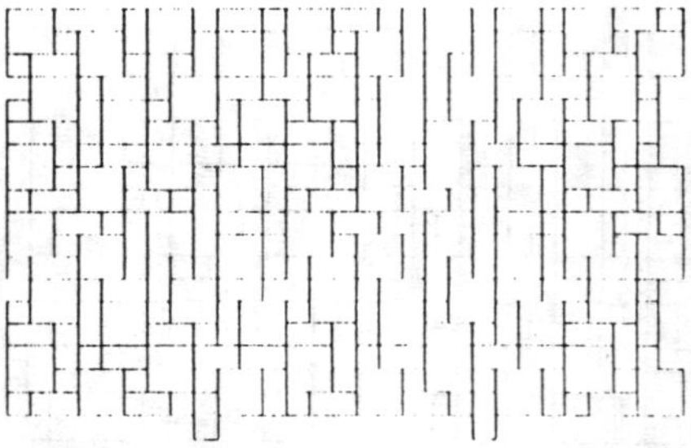

QP-6223 BLOCK RANDOM
Shown: 3⅞" × 3⅞" (15%), 3⅞" × 8" (41%)
8" × 8" (44%)

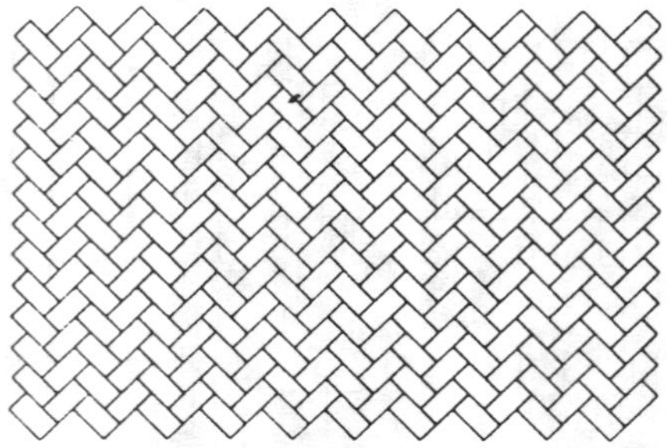

QP-6224 VERTICAL HERRINGBONE
Shown: 3⅞" × 8" (100%)
Also Use: 6" × 12⅛"

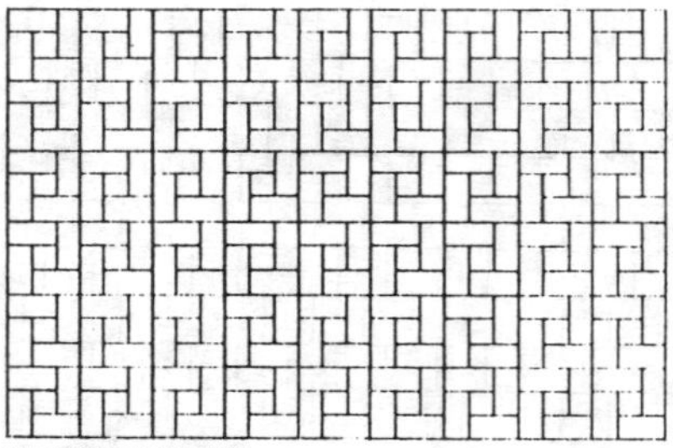

QP-6225 PINWHEEL
Shown: 3⅞" × 3⅞" (11.1%), 3⅞" × 8" (88.9%)
Also Use: 6" × 6", 6" × 12⅛"

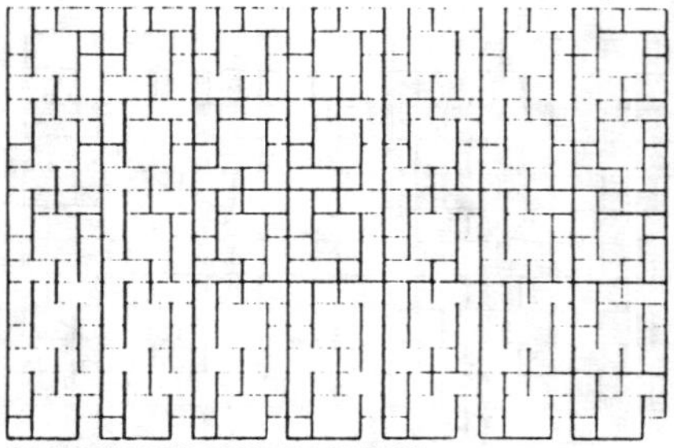

QP-6226 BLOCK RANDOM SQUARE
Shown: 3⅞" × 3⅞" (25%), 3⅞" × 8" (50%)
8" × 8" (25%)

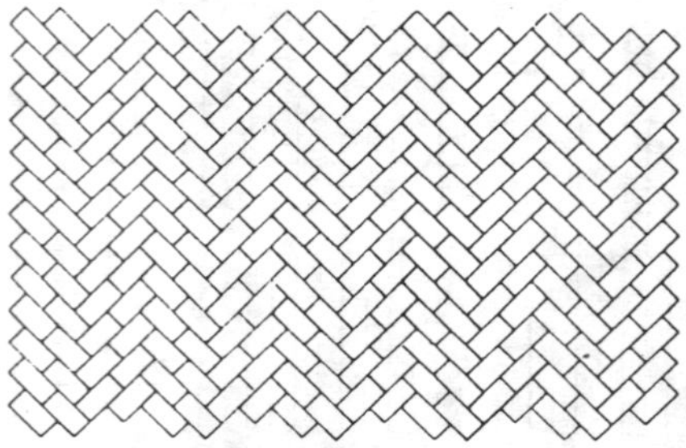

QP-6227 DOUBLE HERRINGBONE
Shown: 3⅞" × 8" (100%)
Also Use: 6" × 12⅛"

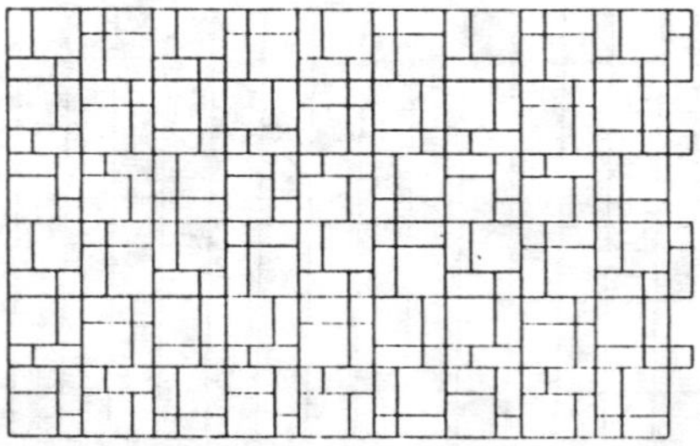

QP-6228 BLOCK RANDOM VARIATION
Shown: 3⅞" × 3⅞" (11.2%), 3⅞" × 8" (44.4%),
8" × 8" (44.4%)

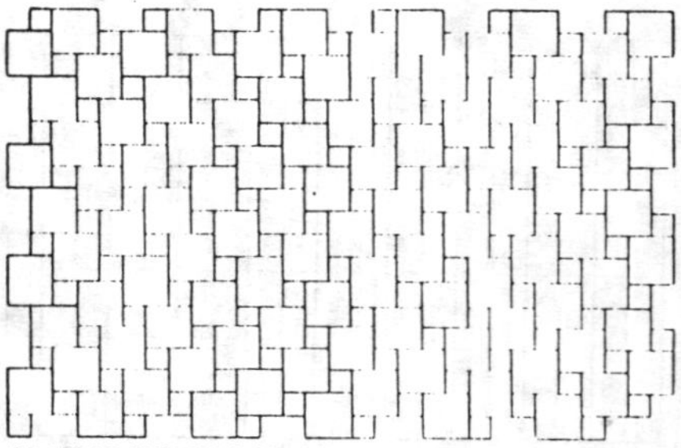

QP-6229 RANDOM SQUARE
Shown: 3⅞" × 3⅞" (19½%), 8" × 8" (80½%)

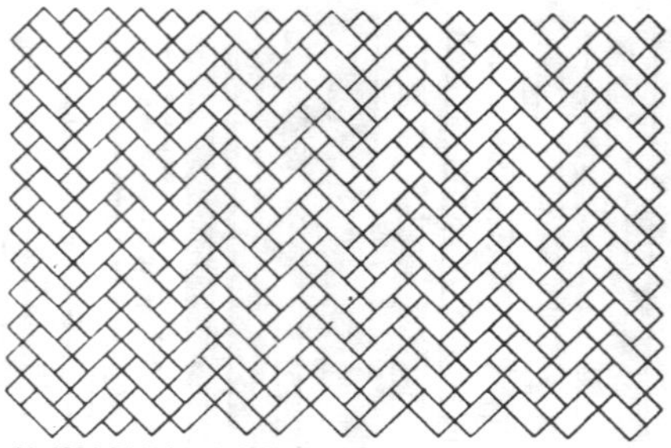

QP-6230 DIAMOND HERRINGBONE
Shown: 3⅞" × 3⅞" (33⅓%), 3⅞" × 8" (66⅔%)
Also Use: 6" × 6", 6" × 12⅛"

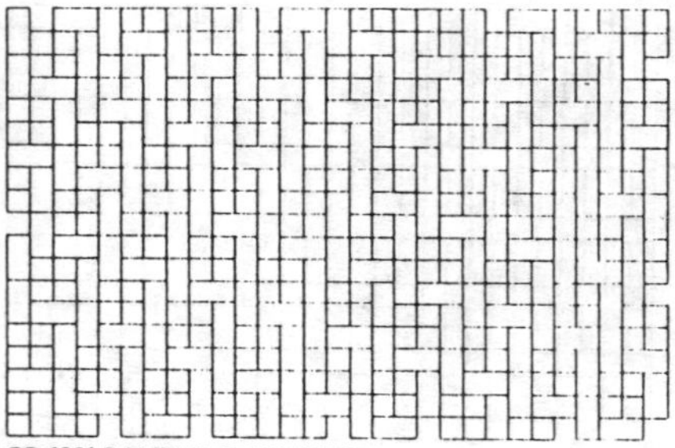

QP-6231 RAMBLING SQUARES
Shown: 3⅞" × 3⅞" (40%), 3⅞" × 8" (60%)
Also Use: 6" × 6", 6" × 12⅛"

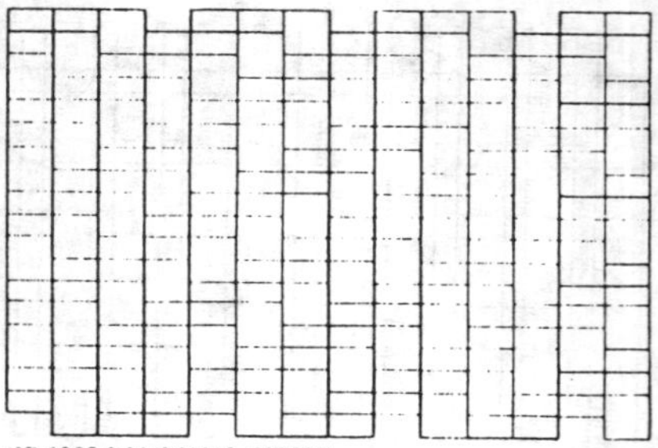

QP-6232 DIAGONAL STRIPE
Shown: 3⅞" × 8" (50%), 8" × 8" (50%)

FLOORS

Wood Subfloor

STAIRS

Cement Mortar

Organic Adhesive

Cement Mortar

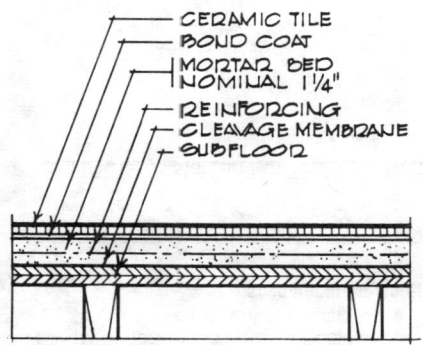

- CERAMIC TILE
- BOND COAT
- MORTAR BED NOMINAL 1¼"
- REINFORCING
- CLEAVAGE MEMBRANE
- SUBFLOOR

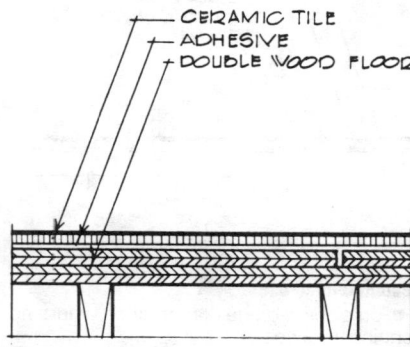

- CERAMIC TILE
- ADHESIVE
- DOUBLE WOOD FLOOR

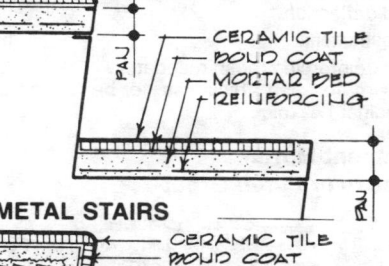

- CERAMIC TILE
- BOND COAT
- MORTAR BED

CONCRETE STAIRS

Recommended use

■ over all wood floors that are structurally sound

Recommended use

■ over wood floors exposed to residential traffic only

- CERAMIC TILE
- BOND COAT
- MORTAR BED
- REINFORCING

METAL STAIRS

Wood Subfloor

Glass Mesh Mortar Units

Epoxy Mortar and Grout

Dry-Set Mortar or Latex-Portland Cement

- CERAMIC TILE
- BOND COAT
- MORTAR BED
- SCRATCH COAT
- METAL LATH
- WATERPROOF MEMBRANE

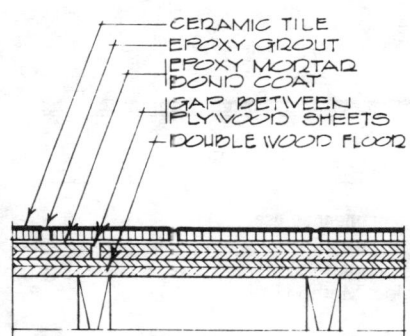

- CERAMIC TILE
- EPOXY GROUT
- EPOXY MORTAR BOND COAT
- GAP BETWEEN PLYWOOD SHEETS
- DOUBLE WOOD FLOOR

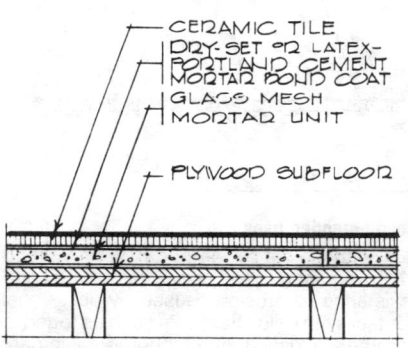

- CERAMIC TILE
- DRY-SET OR LATEX-PORTLAND CEMENT MORTAR BOND COAT
- GLASS MESH MORTAR UNIT
- PLYWOOD SUBFLOOR

WOOD STAIRS ¾" - 1¼"

Recommended uses

■ over wood floors where resistance to foot traffic in better residential, normal commercial, and light institutional use is desired with thin-set construction
■ where water, chemical, and stain resistance is desired
■ for tilework exposed to prolonged high temperatures, use high temperature, chemical resistant epoxy mortar, and grout

Recommended uses

■ over structurally sound plywood where lightweight construction is a factor
■ where water resistance is desired
■ eliminates necessity of recessing subfloor to accommodate portland cement mortar bed

CEILINGS, SOFFITS

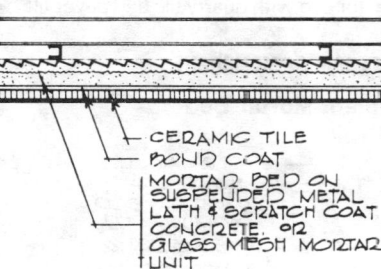

- CERAMIC TILE
- BOND COAT
- MORTAR BED ON SUSPENDED METAL LATH & SCRATCH COAT CONCRETE OR GLASS MESH MORTAR UNIT

Recommended uses

■ over a mortar bed
■ over glass mesh mortar units
■ over clean, sound, dimensionally stable concrete
■ over metal lath attached directly to the bottom of wood joists or trusses; spacing not to exceed 16" on center

FLOORS AND FLOOR FINISHES
Ceramic Tile on Concrete Slab Floor Construction Details

CONCRETE SUBFLOOR

**Cement Mortar
Cleavage Membrane**

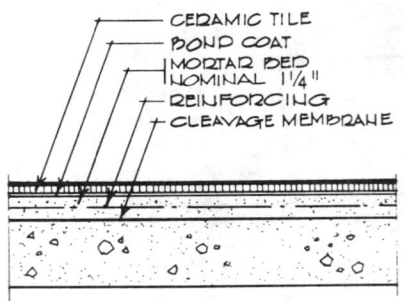

- CERAMIC TILE
- BOND COAT
- MORTAR BED NOMINAL 1¼"
- REINFORCING
- CLEAVAGE MEMBRANE

Recommended use
■ over structural floors subject to bending and deflection

Requirements
■ reinforcing mesh mandatory
■ motor bed thickness to be uniform, nominal 1¼" thick

**Cement Mortar
Epoxy or Furan Grout**

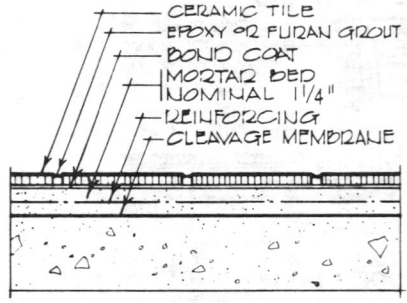

- CERAMIC TILE
- EPOXY OR FURAN GROUT
- BOND COAT
- MORTAR BED NOMINAL 1¼"
- REINFORCING
- CLEAVAGE MEMBRANE

Recommended uses
■ with tile set by Method F111 requiring good stain resistance and resistance to erosion caused by occasional contact with mild chemicals such as found in commercial dining areas, photographic dark rooms, public toilets, public foyers, etc.
■ for use with quarry tile and paver tile

WATERPROOF MEMBRANE

Cement Mortar Bed

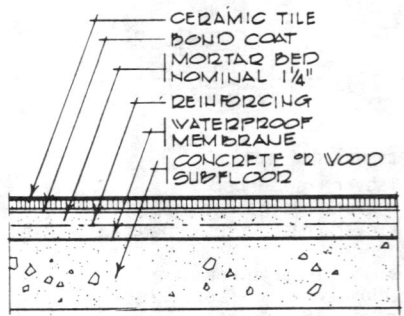

- CERAMIC TILE
- BOND COAT
- MORTAR BED NOMINAL 1¼"
- REINFORCING
- WATERPROOF MEMBRANE
- CONCRETE OR WOOD SUBFLOOR

Recommended use
■ wherever a waterproof interior floor is required in conjunction with ceramic tile installed on a portland cement mortar bed

**Cement Mortar,
Bonded**

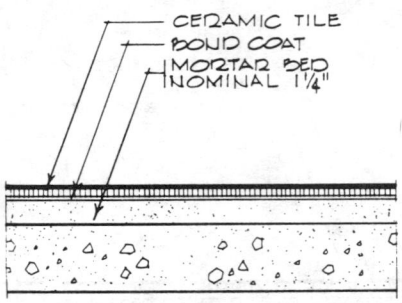

- CERAMIC TILE
- BOND COAT
- MORTAR BED NOMINAL 1¼"

Recommended uses
■ on slab-on-grade construction where no bending stresses occur
■ on properly cured structural slabs where deflection does not exceed 1/360 of span
■ on properly cured structural slabs of limited area

**Dry-Set Mortar,
Epoxy or Furan Grout**

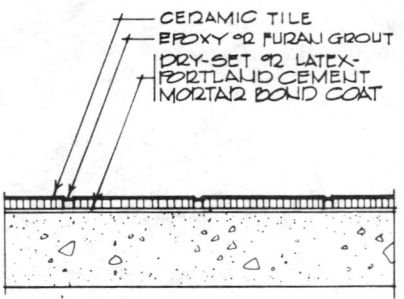

- CERAMIC TILE
- EPOXY OR FURAN GROUT
- DRY-SET OR LATEX-PORTLAND CEMENT MORTAR BOND COAT

Recommended uses
■ with tile set by Method F112 or Method F113 requiring good stain resistance and resistance to erosion caused by occasional contact with mild chemicals such as found in commercial dining areas, photographic dark rooms, public toilets, public foyers, etc.
■ for use with quarry tile and paver tile

Thin-Set

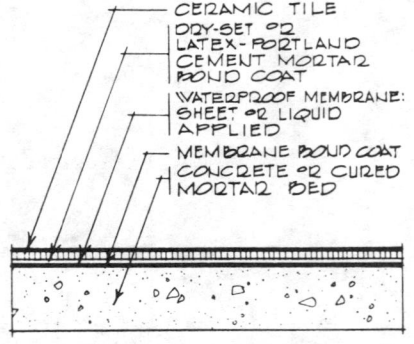

- CERAMIC TILE
- DRY-SET OR LATEX-PORTLAND CEMENT MORTAR BOND COAT
- WATERPROOF MEMBRANE: SHEET OR LIQUID APPLIED
- MEMBRANE BOND COAT
- CONCRETE OR CURED MORTAR BED

Recommended use
■ wherever a waterproof interior floor is required in conjunction with ceramic tile installed in a thin-set method

**Dry-Set Mortar or
Latex-Portland Cement Mortar**

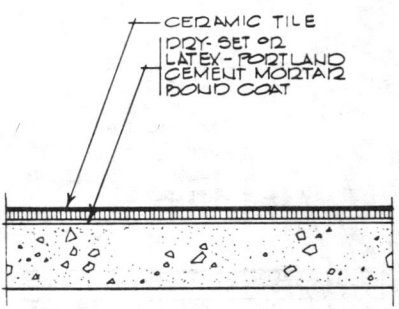

- CERAMIC TILE
- DRY-SET OR LATEX-PORTLAND CEMENT MORTAR BOND COAT

Recommended uses
■ on plane, clean concrete
■ on slab-on-grade construction where no bending stresses occur

**Organic Adhesive or
Epoxy Adhesive**

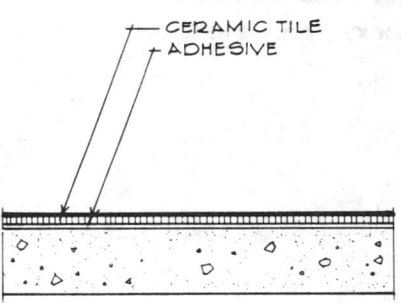

- CERAMIC TILE
- ADHESIVE

Recommended use
■ for use over concrete floors in residential construction only; for heavier service select Method F113

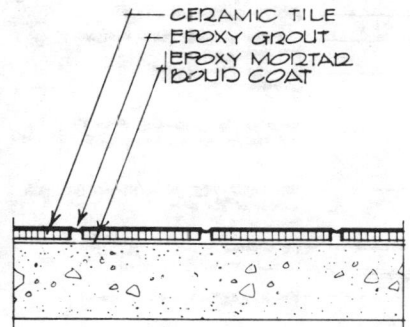

- CERAMIC TILE
- EPOXY GROUT
- EPOXY MORTAR
- BOND COAT

Recommended uses

■ for setting and grouting ceramic mosaics, quarry tile, and paver tile

■ where moderate chemical exposure and severe cleaning methods are used, such as in commercial kitchens, dairies, breweries, food processing plants, etc.

■ for tilework exposed to prolonged high temperatures, use high-temperature, chemical-resistant epoxy mortar and grout

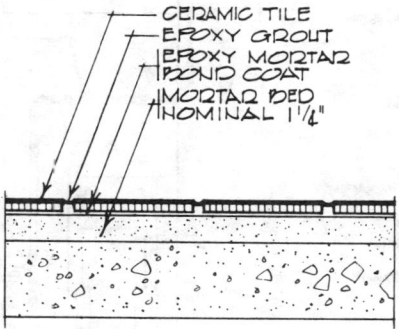

- CERAMIC TILE
- EPOXY GROUT
- EPOXY MORTAR
- BOND COAT
- MORTAR BED NOMINAL 1¼"

Recommended uses

■ where leveling of subfloor is required

■ for setting and grouting ceramic mosaics, quarry tile, and paver tile

■ where moderate chemical exposure and severe cleaning methods are used, such as in commerical kitchens, dairies, breweries, food processing plants, etc.

■ for tilework exposed to prolonged high temperatures, use high-temperature chemical resistant epoxy mortar and grout

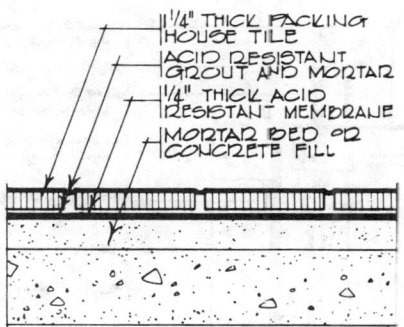

- 1¼" THICK PACKING HOUSE TILE
- ACID RESISTANT GROUT AND MORTAR
- ¼" THICK ACID RESISTANT MEMBRANE
- MORTAR BED OR CONCRETE FILL

Recommended use

■ for setting 1¼" thick packing house tile in areas of continuous or severe chemical exposure where special protection against leakage or damage to concrete subfloor is required

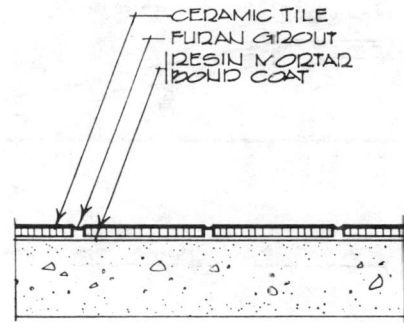

- CERAMIC TILE
- FURAN GROUT
- RESIN MORTAR
- BOND COAT

Recommended uses

■ for setting and grouting quarry tile and paver tile

■ in kitchens, chemical plants, etc.

EXPANSION JOINTS
Vertical and Horizontal

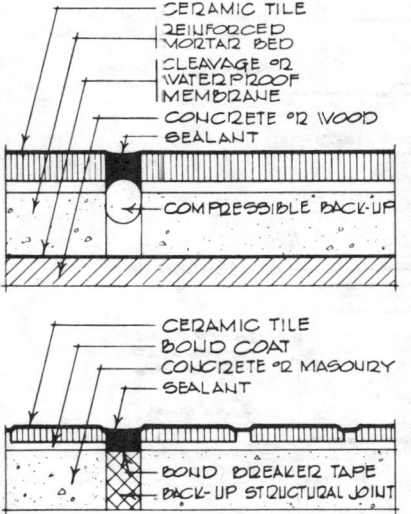

- CERAMIC TILE
- REINFORCED MORTAR BED
- CLEAVAGE OR WATERPROOF MEMBRANE
- CONCRETE OR WOOD
- SEALANT
- COMPRESSIBLE BACK-UP

- CERAMIC TILE
- BOND COAT
- CONCRETE OR MASONRY
- SEALANT
- BOND BREAKER TAPE
- BACK-UP STRUCTURAL JOINT

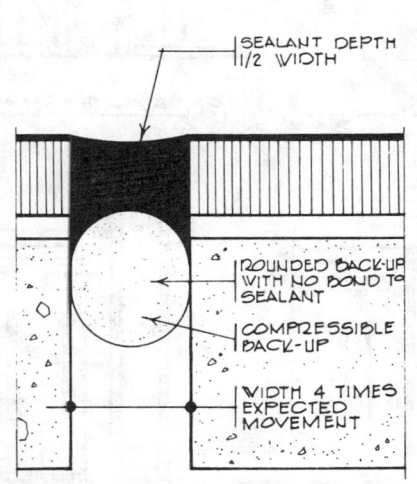

- SEALANT DEPTH 1/2 WIDTH
- ROUNDED BACK-UP WITH NO BOND TO SEALANT
- COMPRESSIBLE BACK-UP
- WIDTH 4 TIMES EXPECTED MOVEMENT

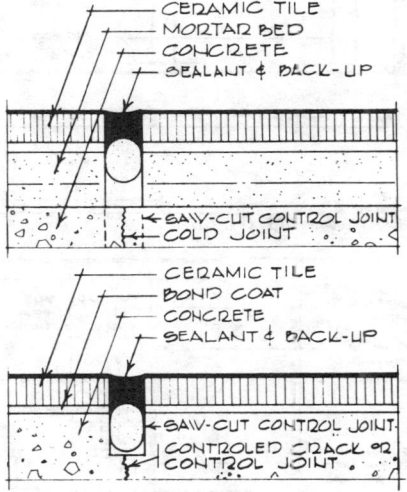

- CERAMIC TILE
- MORTAR BED
- CONCRETE
- SEALANT & BACK-UP
- SAW-CUT CONTROL JOINT
- COLD JOINT

- CERAMIC TILE
- BOND COAT
- CONCRETE
- SEALANT & BACK-UP
- SAW-CUT CONTROL JOINT
- CONTROLED CRACK OR CONTROL JOINT

Use these details for control, contraction, and isolation joints

FLOORS AND FLOOR FINISHES

Raised Computer Room Floors

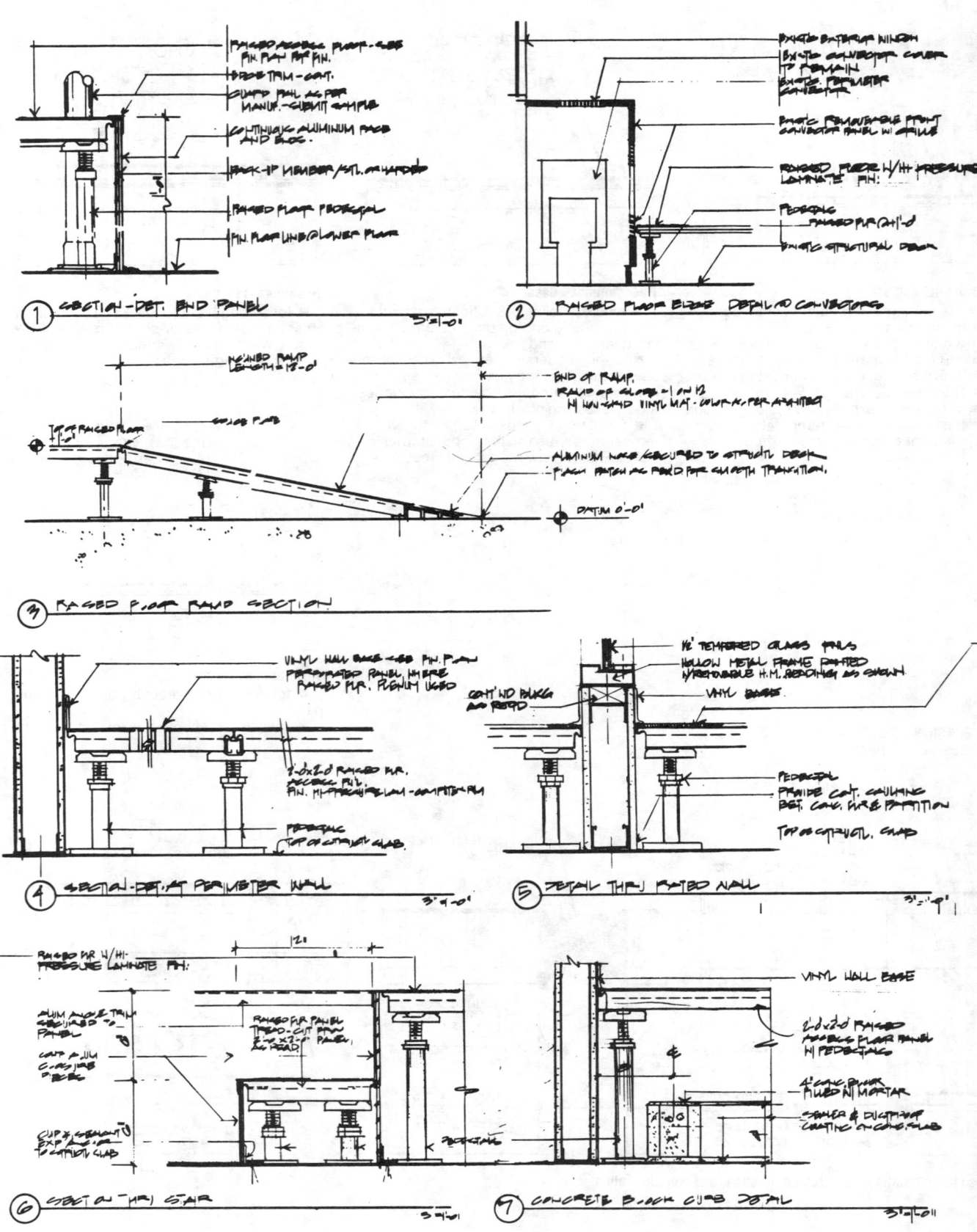

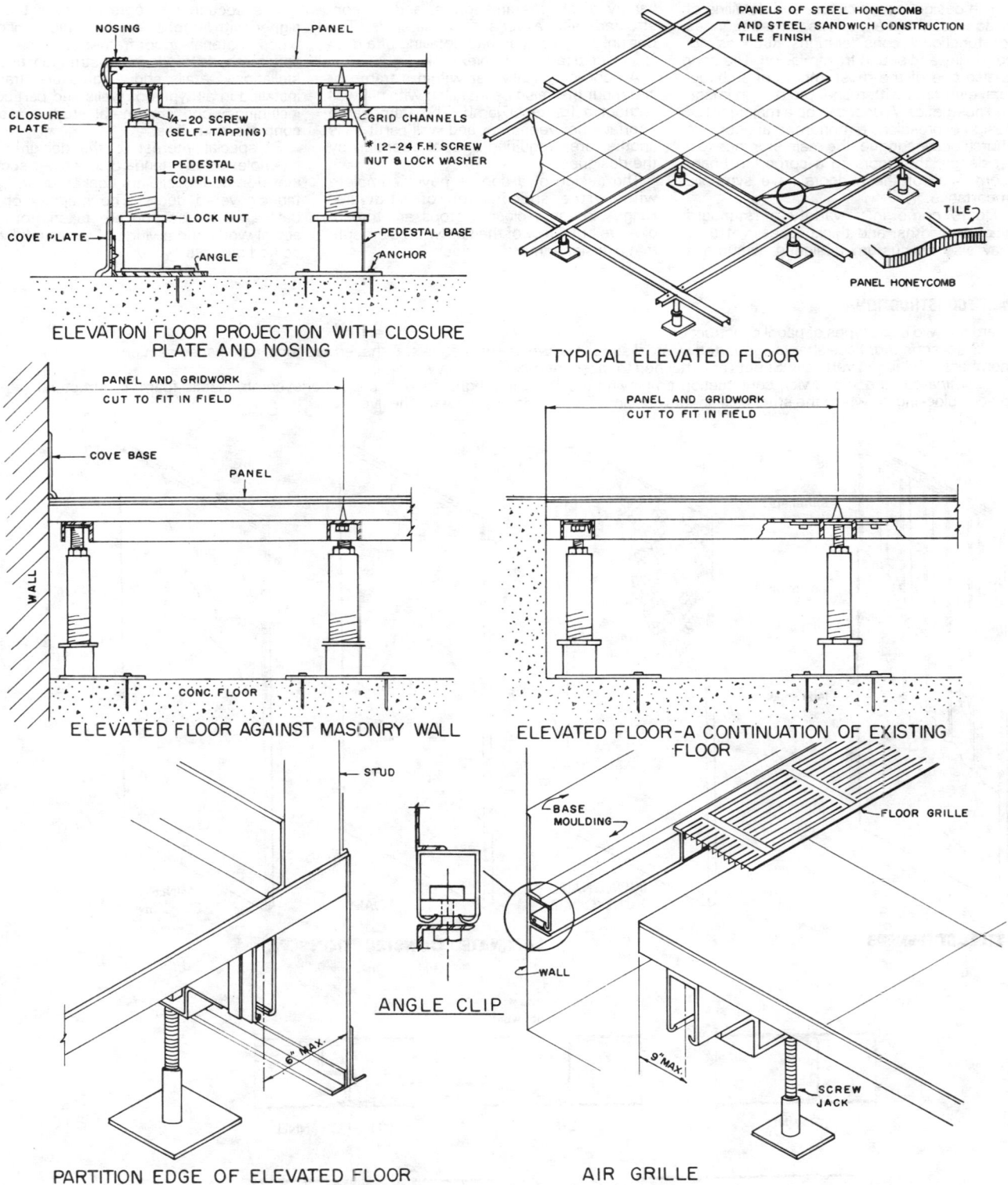

ELEVATION FLOOR PROJECTION WITH CLOSURE
PLATE AND NOSING

TYPICAL ELEVATED FLOOR

ELEVATED FLOOR AGAINST MASONRY WALL

ELEVATED FLOOR-A CONTINUATION OF EXISTING
FLOOR

PARTITION EDGE OF ELEVATED FLOOR

ANGLE CLIP

AIR GRILLE

DOORS

Hollow Metal Door Construction

The design, specification, and detailing of a door can have serious consequences for functional considerations such as accessibility and sound transmission. The door is also one of the most important architectural elements with respect to design image and aesthetics. A door can be a major part of design expression: a monumental door to a church or synagogue, the main entrance to a residence, the doors to a corporate board room — all of these doors have symbolic importance.

Doors come in a variety of standard heights, widths, and thicknesses, yet they may also be custom designed, assume a variety of shapes and forms, and be constructed with a variety of materials. The design, specification, and detailing of a door is, in fact, a rather complex task.

A door is typically set within a frame or jamb, but may also be installed within a wall without a frame or jamb. The frame/jamb interface between door and wall partition is another area requiring special attention by the designer.

The design of a door is never complete without the specification of hardware. Hinges, locksets, closers, stops, and thresholds are but a few of the hardware elements that a designer must consider.

This section on doors provides the designer with extensive information on door types, materials, door frames, and materials and methods of door construction and installation. Details show doors and frames installed in all types of walls and partitions, including wood and metal stud, masonry, concrete, and glass.

Of special interest to the designer are examples of less standard door types such as elevator doors, sliding pocket doors, and fabric-covered doors. The majority of the details in this section are taken from the actual working drawings of successfully executed projects.

PANEL CONSTRUCTION

There are two basic types of panel construction:

Steel stiffened: Face sheets supported by steel stiffeners, which are channels, Z-shaped sections, hat-shaped sections, or similar members, positioned vertically. Sheets are attached to these members by spot welding.

Laminated core: Sandwich construction employing a core of impregnated kraft paper honeycomb, plastic foam, or structural mineral blocking, to which the steel face sheets are laminated, using a structural adhesive.

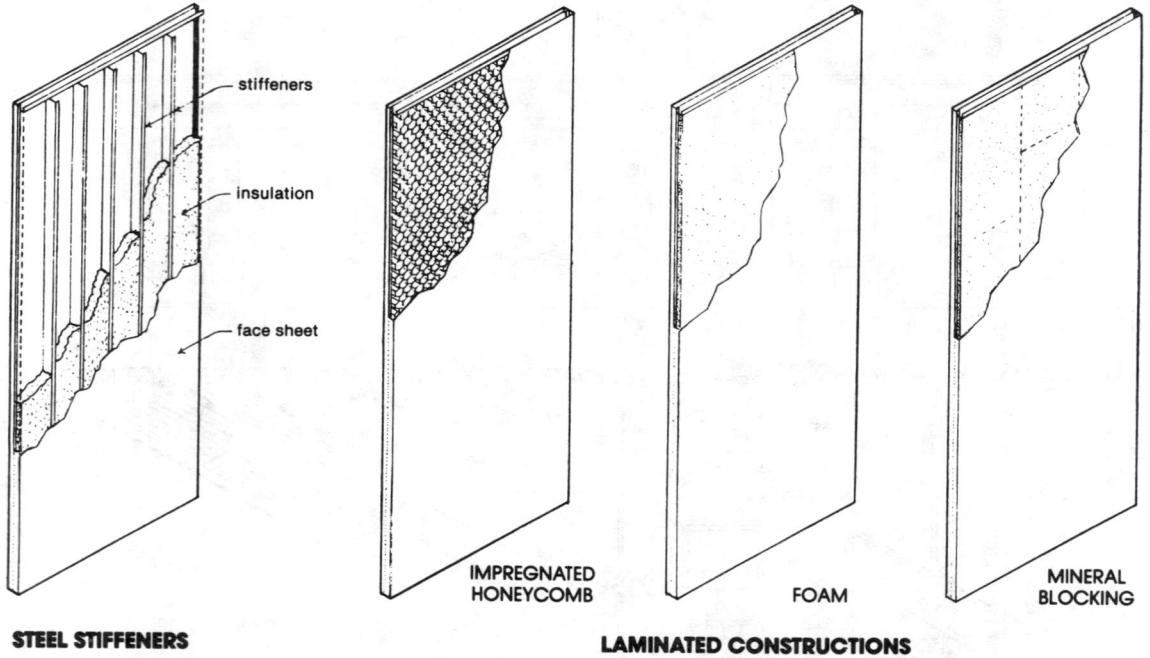

STEEL STIFFENERS

LAMINATED CONSTRUCTIONS

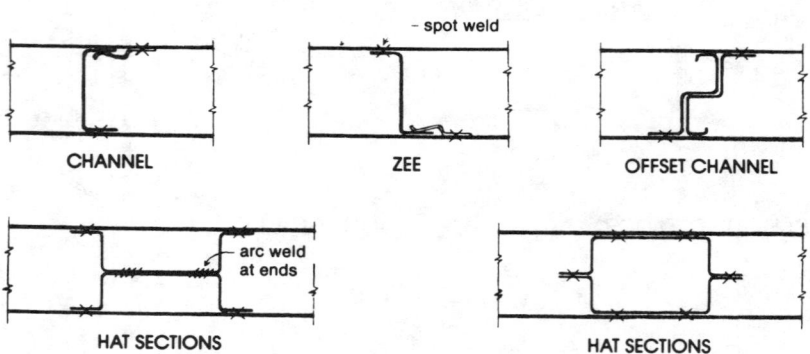

REPRESENTATIVE STIFFENER SECTIONS
Other sections used by some manufacturers

Types of Construction

The four basic types of construction for hollow metal swing doors are illustrated and identified in Fig. 1. The type usually specified in commercial work is the continuously welded edge seam construction, Type A, and it is this type which is the basis of NAAMM Standard HMMA 861.

Most custom hollow metal doors are of the full flush type with continuously welded edges (Type A). When glazed openings, recessed panels, or louvers are to be provided, they are built into the door during fabrication, rather than being cut out of a flush panel door by field modification.

Fire-rated doors may differ in certain details of construction; see NAAMM Standard HMMA 850, Fire-Rated Hollow Metal Doors and Frames.

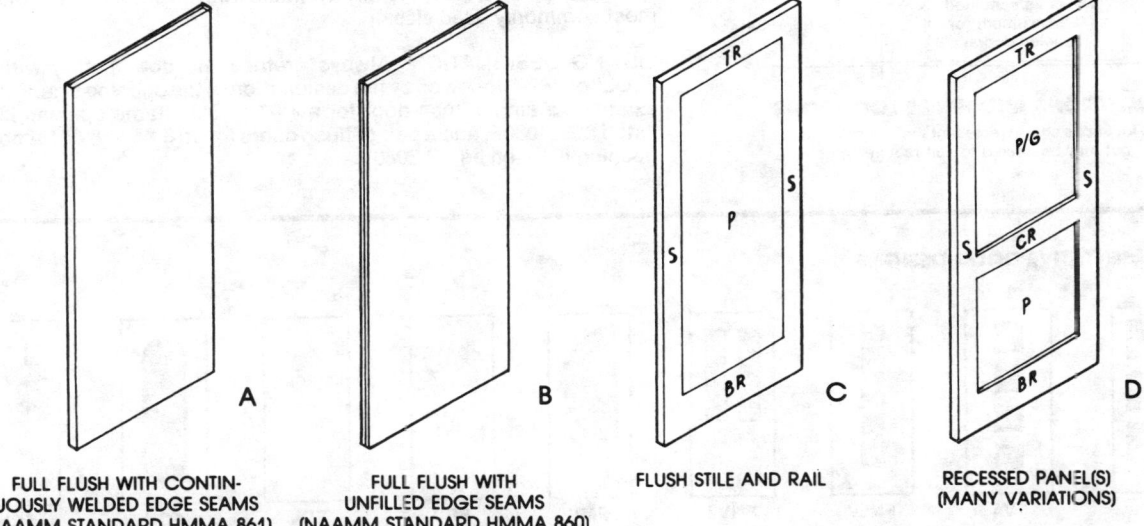

FULL FLUSH WITH CONTIN-
UOUSLY WELDED EDGE SEAMS
(NAAMM STANDARD HMMA 861)

FULL FLUSH WITH
UNFILLED EDGE SEAMS
(NAAMM STANDARD HMMA 860)

FLUSH STILE AND RAIL

RECESSED PANEL(S)
(MANY VARIATIONS)

Fig. 1   The top edge of Types A and B doors may have only an inverted channel (standard construction) or may have an additional closing channel. Types C and D have tubular rails and stiles, with no edge seams. S = stile (hinge stile is stile at edge where hinges or pivots are located; lock stile is stile in which a lock or latch is installed; and meeting stile is stile adjacent to another door, in a pair of doors). TR = top rail. CR = center rail. BR = bottom rail. P = panel. P/G = panel or glass.

DOORS

Hollow Metal Door Types

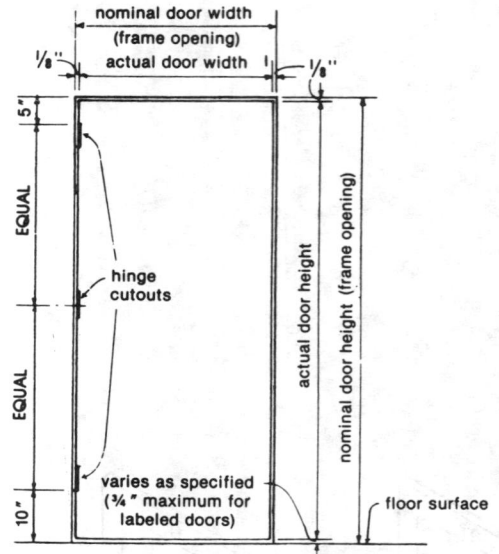

DIMENSIONS AND HINGE LOCATIONS

Hinge locations shown represent the industry standard, but may be altered to suit requirements.

MOST COMMON SIZES FOR 1¾-INCH THICK DOORS*

Width of Opening	Height of Opening				
2'0"	6'8"	7'0"	7'2"	7'10"	8'0"
2'4"	6'8"	7'0"	7'2"	7'10"	8'0"
·2'6"	6'8"	7'0"	7'2"	7'10"	8'0"
2'8"	6'8"	7'0"	7'2"	7'10"	8'0"
3'0"	6'8"	7'0"	7'2"	7'10"	8'0"
3'4"	6'8"	7'0"	7'2"	7'10"	8'0"
3'6"	6'8"	7'0"	7'2"	7'10"	8'0"
3'8"	6'8"	7'0"	7'2"	7'10"	8'0"
4'0"	6'8"	7'0"	7'2"	7'10"	8'0"

*Sizes shown are for single doors only; for pairs of doors, use twice the width indicated.

OTHER DOOR SIZES: The sizes listed are those most commonly used, but custom hollow metal doors are available in any width, height and thickness desired. It is not uncommon to supply them in widths of 5' or more and/or heights of 10' or more. Standard doors, on the other hand, are generally available from inventory only in the most commonly used sizes.

LISTING DESIGNATION: Always preface the door listing with "SGL" or "PR," followed by the designation of the opening size. For example, a single flush door for a 4'0" × 8'0" frame opening is listed SGL 4080F, and a pair of flush doors for an 8'0" × 8'0" frame opening is listed as PR 8080F.

REPRESENTATIVE DOOR DESIGNS

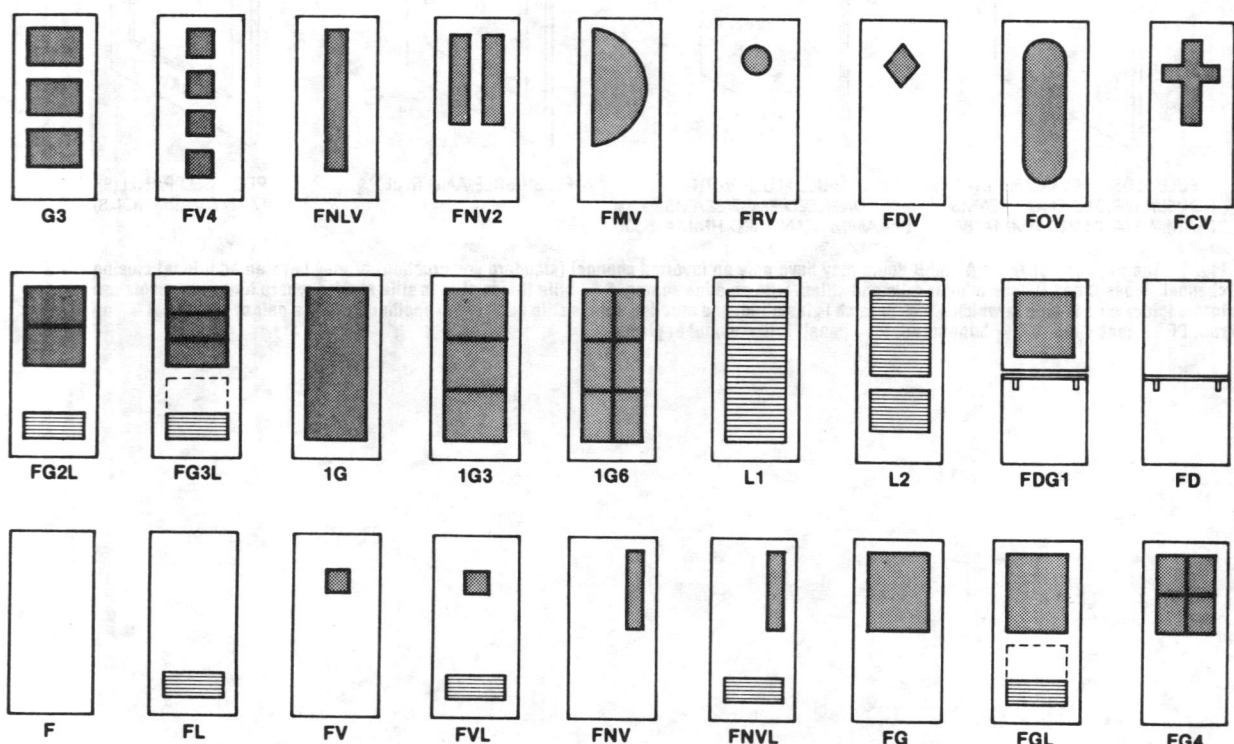

G3 · FV4 · FNLV · FNV2 · FMV · FRV · FDV · FOV · FCV

FG2L · FG3L · 1G · 1G3 · 1G6 · L1 · L2 · FDG1 · FD

F · FL · FV · FVL · FNV · FNVL · FG · FGL · FG4

NOTE: Some manufacturers may use differing designations for some designs

TYPICAL HARDWARE PREPARATION

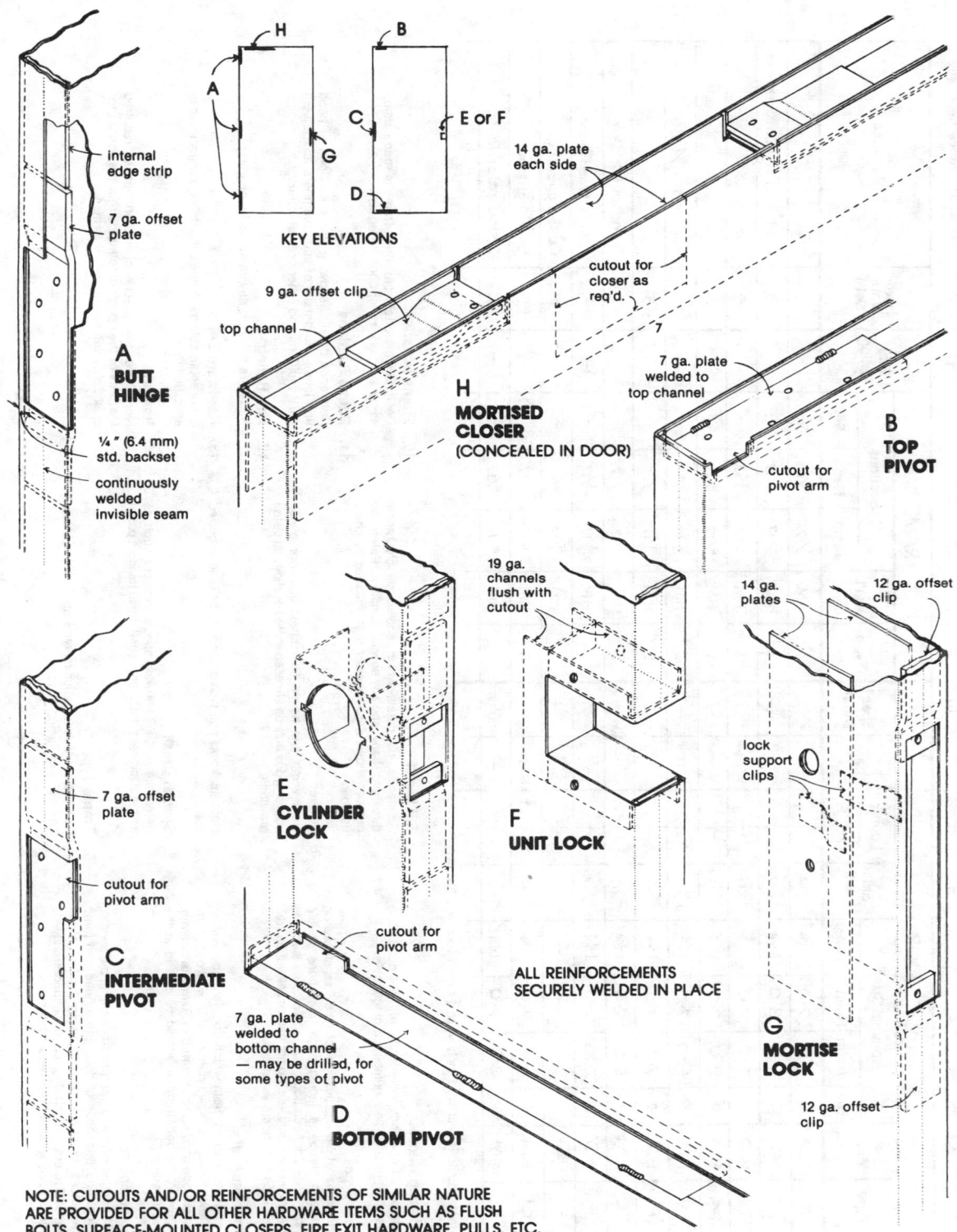

KEY ELEVATIONS

A
BUTT HINGE

internal edge strip

7 ga. offset plate

¼" (6.4 mm) std. backset

continuously welded invisible seam

H
MORTISED CLOSER
(CONCEALED IN DOOR)

14 ga. plate each side

cutout for closer as req'd.

9 ga. offset clip

top channel

B
TOP PIVOT

7 ga. plate welded to top channel

cutout for pivot arm

C
INTERMEDIATE PIVOT

7 ga. offset plate

cutout for pivot arm

E
CYLINDER LOCK

F
UNIT LOCK

19 ga. channels flush with cutout

G
MORTISE LOCK

14 ga. plates

12 ga. offset clip

lock support clips

12 ga. offset clip

ALL REINFORCEMENTS SECURELY WELDED IN PLACE

D
BOTTOM PIVOT

cutout for pivot arm

7 ga. plate welded to bottom channel — may be drilled, for some types of pivot

NOTE: CUTOUTS AND/OR REINFORCEMENTS OF SIMILAR NATURE ARE PROVIDED FOR ALL OTHER HARDWARE ITEMS SUCH AS FLUSH BOLTS, SURFACE-MOUNTED CLOSERS, FIRE EXIT HARDWARE, PULLS, ETC.

DOORS
Hollow Metal Door Schedules

DOOR SCHEDULE

Opening Number	Type	Mat'l.	Nominal Size* No.	Width	Height	Thkns.	Sill Detail	Louver W	Louver H	Glass *	Spec'l Detail	Type	Mat'l.	Sections Jamb	Sections Head	Sections Sill	Fire Rating	Hard-Ware Set	Remarks
		DOOR											FRAME						
101	F	HM	1	3-0	7-0	1 3/4	24/17	-	-	-	-	1	HM	1/17	1/17	-	-	1	-
102	1G	AL	2	6-0	8-0	1 3/4	25/17	-	-	TEMP	-	2	AL	6/17	6/17	-	-	8	Contin. aluminum threshold
103	FGL	WD	1	3-0	7-0	1 3/4	25/17	-	-	1/4" TEMP	28/17	1	HM	1/17	1/17	-	-	4	-
104	FG	HM	1	3-0	7-0	1 3/4	24/17	-	-	1/4" WIRE	-	1	HM	6/17	6/17	-	C	6	-
105	FV	HM	3	4-0	7-0	1 3/4	24/17	-	-	1/4" TEMP	-	5	HM	2/17	2/17	-	-	1	Mullions 16/17
106	F	HM	2	7-0	7-0	1 3/4	29/17	-	-	-	-	2	HM	1/17	1/17	-	A	5	-
107	FL	HM	1	3-0	7-0	1 3/4	24/17	23	12	-	-	2	HM	1/17	1/17	-	-	7	Transom bar 16/17
108	F	WD*	1	2-10	7-0	1 3/4	24/17	-	-	-	28/17	3	HM	3/17	3/17	-	-	4	Plastic faced door
109	-	-	-	-	-	-	-	-	-	-	-	1	HM	5/17	5/17	-	-	-	Cased opening
110	FGL	HM	1	3-0	7-0	1 3/4	26/17	23	20	1/4" TEMP	-	4	HM	1/17	1/17	25, 19/17	-	1	Side light mullion 16/17
111	F	HM	1	3-0	7-0	1 3/4	24/17	-	-	1/4" TEMP	31/17	1	HM	8/17	8/17	-	-	2	Sound retardant

Column numbers are for reference here only
14 ← reference here

*Use metric units if desired; 1 inch = 25.4 mm, 1 foot = 0.305 m.

1. **Opening Number**
Number all openings individually, with the numbering system reflecting floor numbers if practicable.

2. **Door Type**
Use alphabetical designation for types, as shown on elevation views on facing page. Elevations should show door configurations and all features such as louvers, vision lights, etc. Do not use one elevation with dash lines to indicate variations.

3. **Door Material**
Designate material from which door is made: HM = hollow metal; AL = aluminum; WD = wood. * indicates special facing as noted in Remarks column. Type of core construction should be stated in the specifications.

4. **Nominal Size**
List number of doors per framed opening, plus width, height and thickness of door. State head and jamb clearances in specifications, using Hollow Metal Manufacturers Association recommended standards unless special conditions require otherwise.

5. **Sill Detail**
Reference sill detail, which shows sill clearance, threshold if any, and any special condition. Reference number shows detail number first, followed by sheet number.

6. **Louver**
Note width and height (in inches) of louver panel. Louver types may be either specified or shown in detail drawings.

7. **Glass**
Note thickness and type of glass to be used in glazed opening.

8. **Special Detail**
Reference detail(s) showing special features such as astragal (on pair), dutch door shelf, flush transom panel or other.

9. **Frame Type**
Use numerical designation for type, as shown on elevation views on facing page.

10. **Frame Material**
Designate material from which frame is made, using same symbols as for door materials.

11. **Frame Sections**
Reference details, showing frame sections at head and jamb, and details of such members as transom bars, mullions and other special features.

12. **Fire Rating**
State fire rating, if any, required for opening.

13. **Hardware Set**
State applicable hardware set number as described in specifications.

14. **Remarks**
Note here any special characteristics or required features of the opening, to insure that the contractor or supplier will be properly informed.

REPRESENTATIVE DETAILS ACCOMPANYING DOOR SCHEDULE

DOOR TYPES:

FRAME TYPES:

DETAILS:

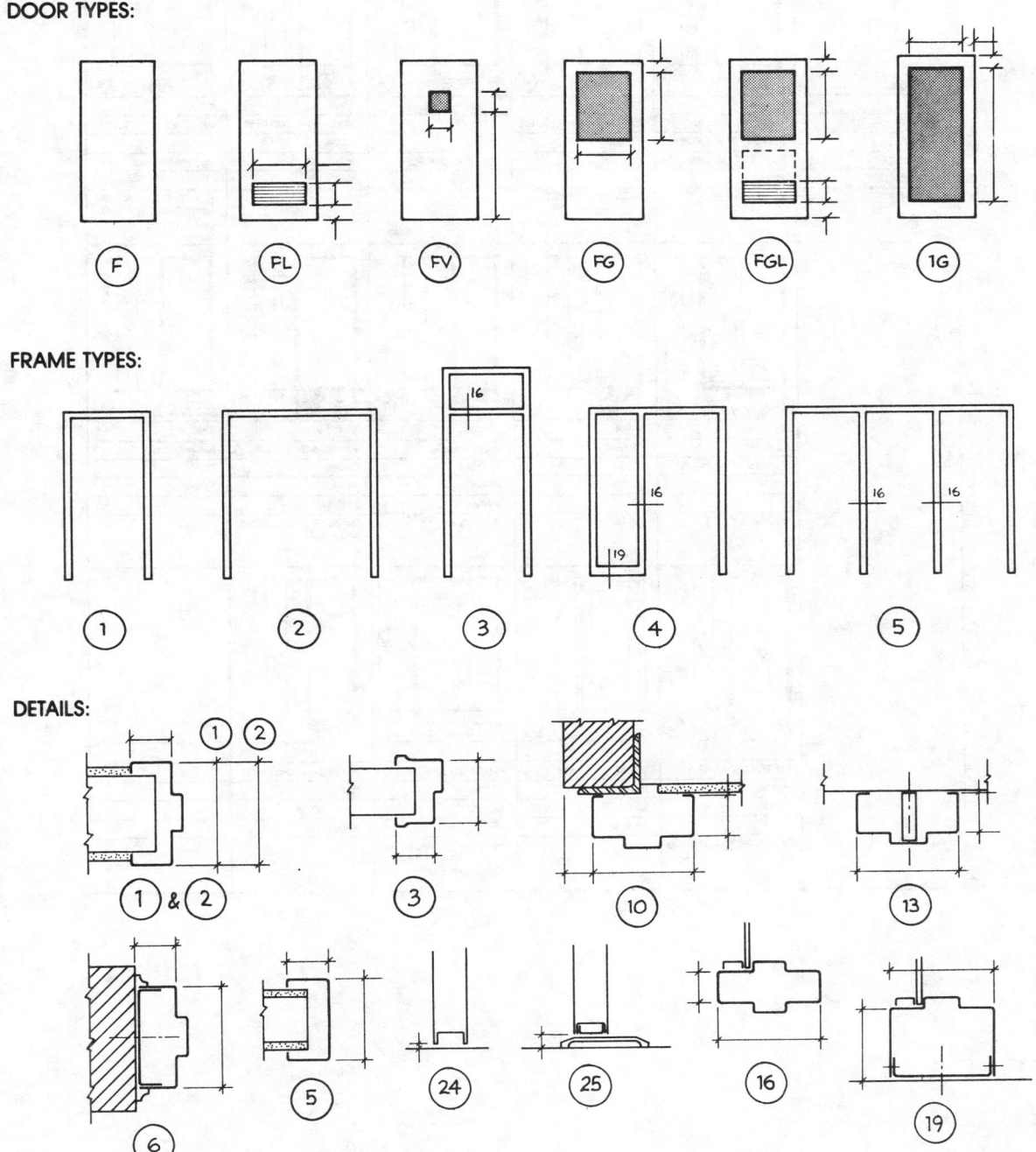

DOORS

Hollow Metal Door Schedules

DOOR SCHEDULE

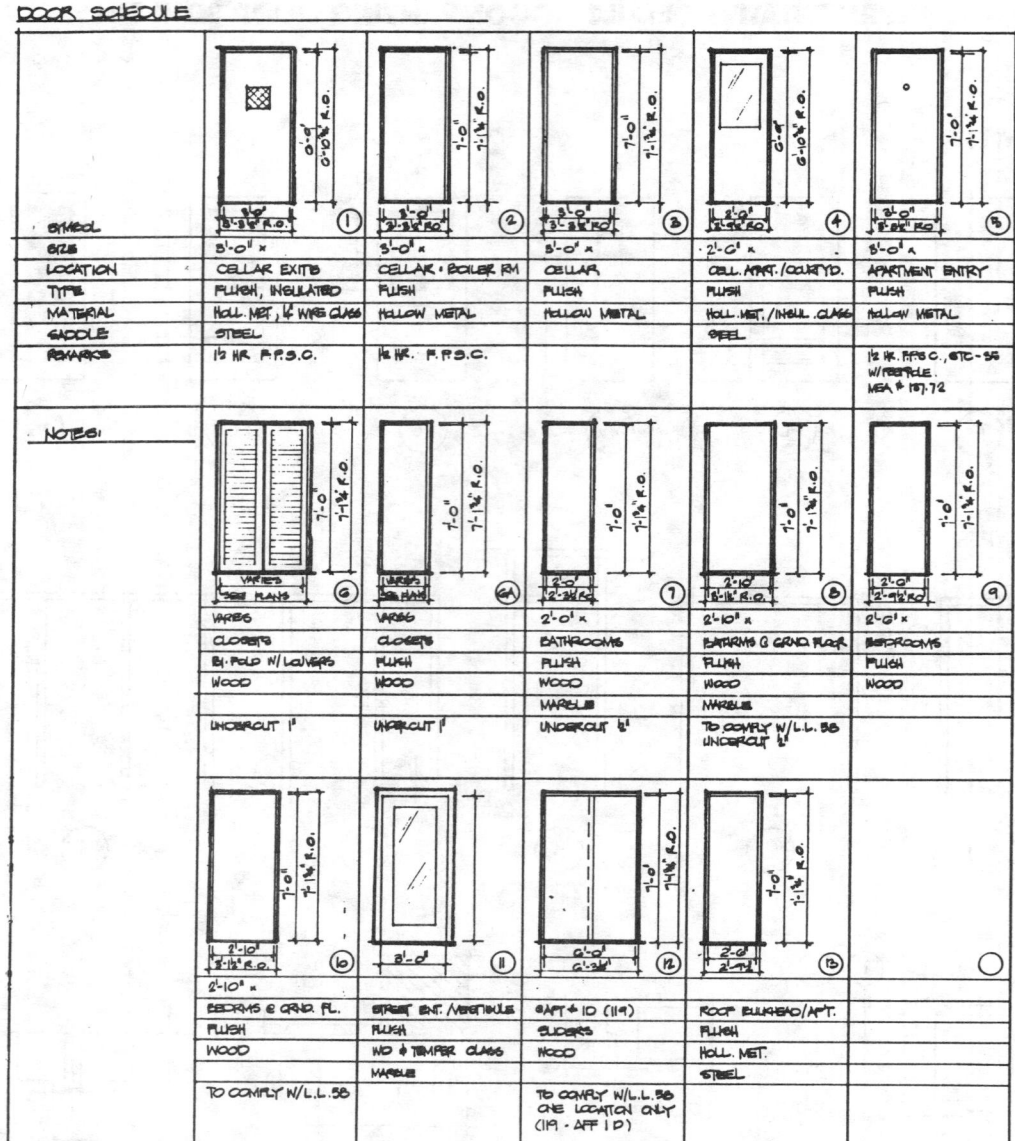

	①	②	③	④	⑤
SYMBOL					
SIZE	3'-0" x	3'-0" x	3'-0" x	2'-6" x	3'-0" x
LOCATION	CELLAR EXITS	CELLAR + BOILER RM	CELLAR	CELL. APT. /COURTYD.	APARTMENT ENTRY
TYPE	FLUSH, INSULATED	FLUSH	FLUSH	FLUSH	FLUSH
MATERIAL	HOLL. MET, ¼" WIRE GLASS	HOLLOW METAL	HOLLOW METAL	HOLL. MET. /INSUL. GLASS	HOLLOW METAL
SADDLE	STEEL			STEEL	
REMARKS	1½ HR. F.P.S.C.	½ HR. F.P.S.C.			1½ HR. F.P.S.C., STC-35 W/ FIREPLACE. MEA # 187-72

NOTES:

	⑥	⑥A	⑦	⑧	⑨
SIZE	VARIES	VARIES	2'-0" x	2'-10" x	2'-6" x
LOCATION	CLOSETS	CLOSETS	BATHROOMS	BATHRMS @ GRND FLOOR	BEDROOMS
TYPE	BI-FOLD W/ LOUVERS	FLUSH	FLUSH	FLUSH	FLUSH
MATERIAL	WOOD	WOOD	WOOD	WOOD	WOOD
SADDLE			MARBLE	MARBLE	
REMARKS	UNDERCUT 1"	UNDERCUT 1"	UNDERCUT ½"	TO COMPLY W/ L.L. 58 UNDERCUT ½"	

	⑩	⑪	⑫	⑬	◯
SIZE	2'-10" x			2'-6" x	
LOCATION	BEDRMS @ GRND. FL.	STREET ENT. /VESTIBULE	6APT # 10 (119)	ROOF BULKHEAD/APT.	
TYPE	FLUSH	FLUSH	SLIDERS	FLUSH	
MATERIAL	WOOD	WD + TEMPER GLASS	WOOD	HOLL. MET.	
SADDLE		MARBLE		STEEL	
REMARKS	TO COMPLY W/ L.L. 58		TO COMPLY W/ L.L. 58 ONE LOCATION ONLY (119 - AFF 1 D)		

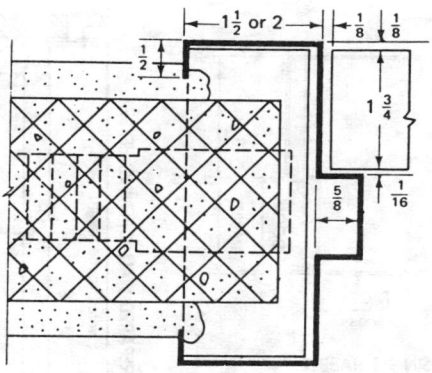

(a) Masonry with plaster, one or both sides

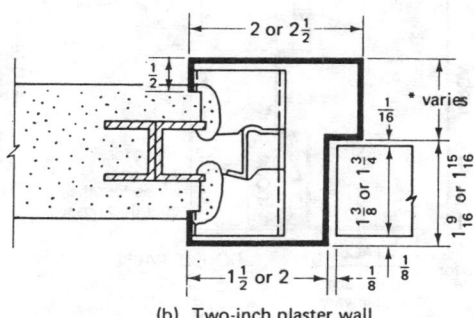

(b) Two-inch plaster wall

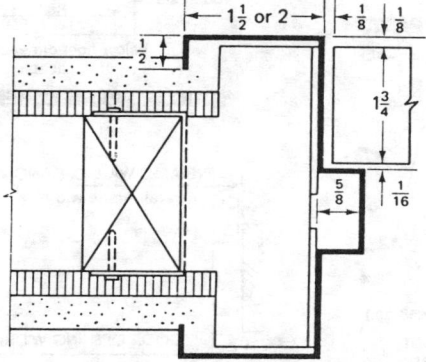

(c) Wood stud and plaster

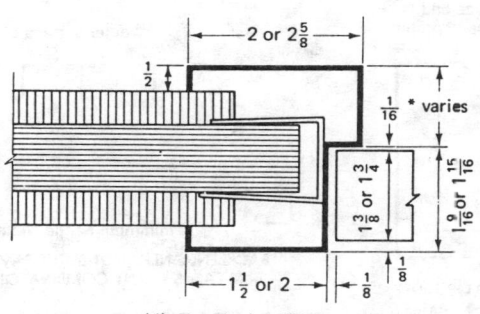

(d) Two-inch solid dry wall

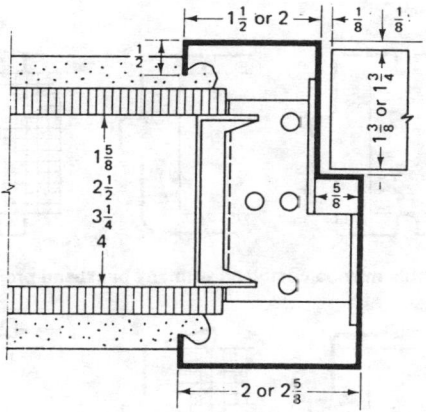

(e) Steel stud and plaster

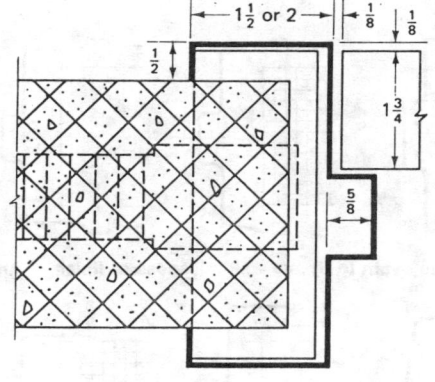

(f) Masonry block. Wrap-around or butt joint

Fig. 2 Typical jamb installations.

DOORS

Hollow Metal Door Frames

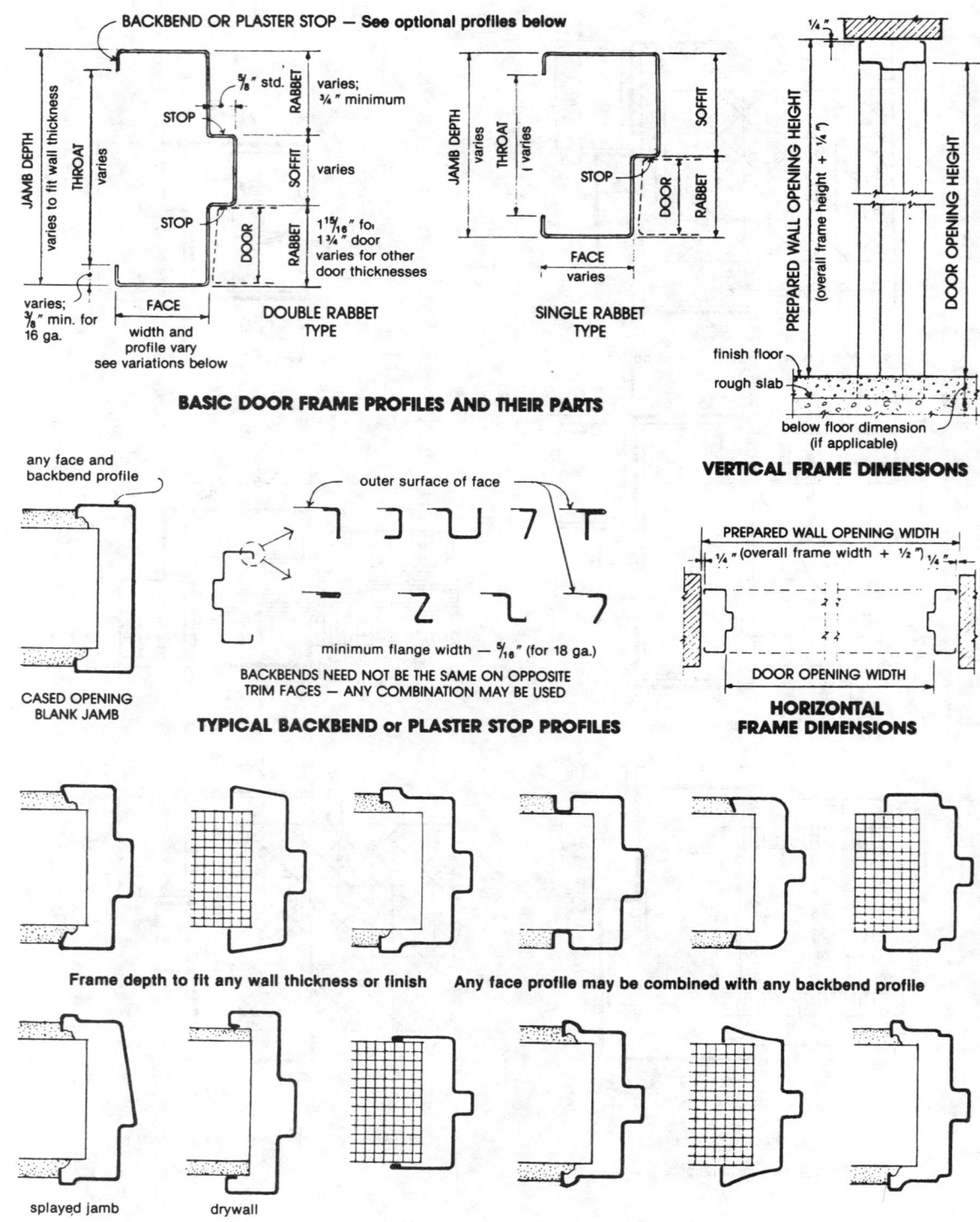

BACKBEND OR PLASTER STOP — See optional profiles below

BASIC DOOR FRAME PROFILES AND THEIR PARTS

DOUBLE RABBET TYPE

SINGLE RABBET TYPE

VERTICAL FRAME DIMENSIONS

CASED OPENING BLANK JAMB

any face and backbend profile

outer surface of face

minimum flange width — ⁵⁄₁₆" (for 18 ga.)

BACKBENDS NEED NOT BE THE SAME ON OPPOSITE TRIM FACES — ANY COMBINATION MAY BE USED

TYPICAL BACKBEND or PLASTER STOP PROFILES

HORIZONTAL FRAME DIMENSIONS

Frame depth to fit any wall thickness or finish   Any face profile may be combined with any backbend profile

splayed jamb   drywall

REPRESENTATIVE FRAME PROFILES

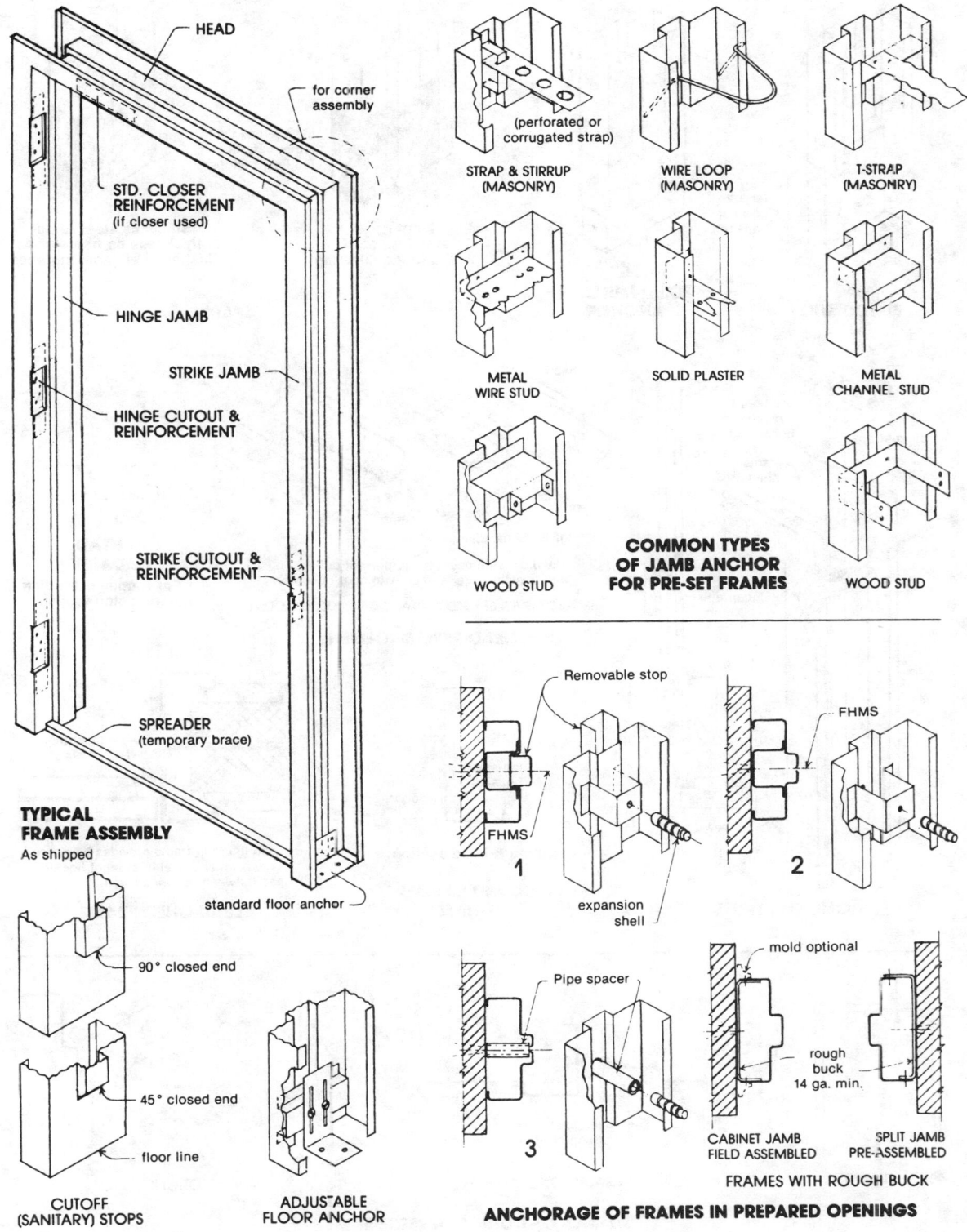

HEAD

for corner assembly

STD. CLOSER REINFORCEMENT (if closer used)

HINGE JAMB

STRIKE JAMB

HINGE CUTOUT & REINFORCEMENT

STRIKE CUTOUT & REINFORCEMENT

SPREADER (temporary brace)

TYPICAL FRAME ASSEMBLY
As shipped

standard floor anchor

90° closed end

45° closed end

floor line

CUTOFF (SANITARY) STOPS

ADJUSTABLE FLOOR ANCHOR

(perforated or corrugated strap)

STRAP & STIRRUP (MASONRY)

WIRE LOOP (MASONRY)

T-STRAP (MASONRY)

METAL WIRE STUD

SOLID PLASTER

METAL CHANNEL STUD

WOOD STUD

COMMON TYPES OF JAMB ANCHOR FOR PRE-SET FRAMES

WOOD STUD

Removable stop

FHMS

FHMS

expansion shell

1

2

Pipe spacer

3

mold optional

rough buck 14 ga. min.

CABINET JAMB FIELD ASSEMBLED

SPLIT JAMB PRE-ASSEMBLED

FRAMES WITH ROUGH BUCK

ANCHORAGE OF FRAMES IN PREPARED OPENINGS

DOORS
Hollow Metal Door Frames

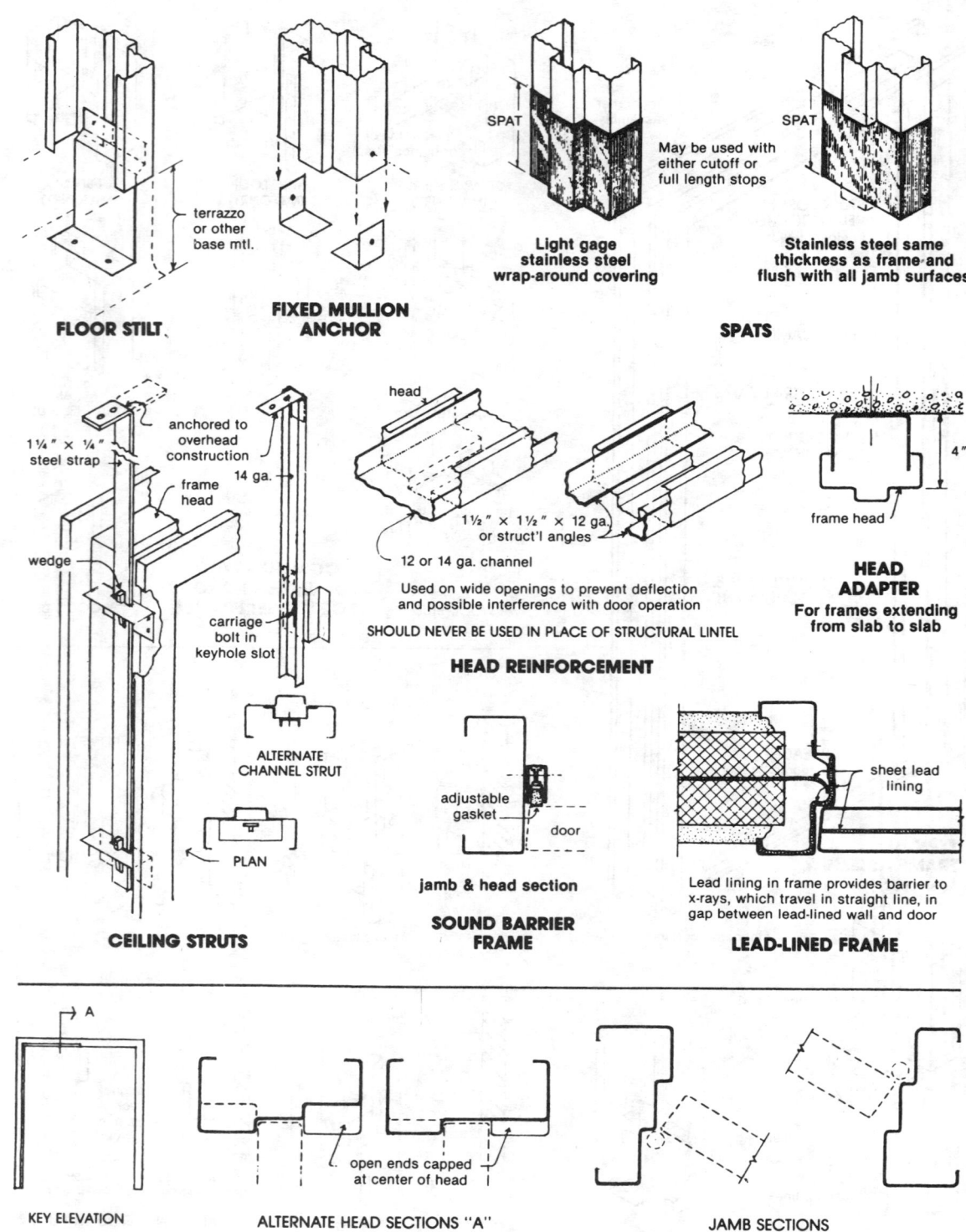

FLOOR STILT

FIXED MULLION ANCHOR

terrazzo or other base mtl.

SPATS

Light gage stainless steel wrap-around covering

May be used with either cutoff or full length stops

Stainless steel same thickness as frame and flush with all jamb surfaces

SPAT

CEILING STRUTS

1¼" × ¼" steel strap

anchored to overhead construction

frame head

14 ga.

wedge

carriage bolt in keyhole slot

ALTERNATE CHANNEL STRUT

PLAN

HEAD REINFORCEMENT

head

1½" × 1½" × 12 ga. or struct'l angles

12 or 14 ga. channel

Used on wide openings to prevent deflection and possible interference with door operation

SHOULD NEVER BE USED IN PLACE OF STRUCTURAL LINTEL

HEAD ADAPTER
For frames extending from slab to slab

4" ±

frame head

SOUND BARRIER FRAME

adjustable gasket

door

jamb & head section

LEAD-LINED FRAME

sheet lead lining

Lead lining in frame provides barrier to x-rays, which travel in straight line, in gap between lead-lined wall and door

A

KEY ELEVATION

ALTERNATE HEAD SECTIONS "A"

open ends capped at center of head

JAMB SECTIONS

DETAILS OF DOUBLE EGRESS FRAME

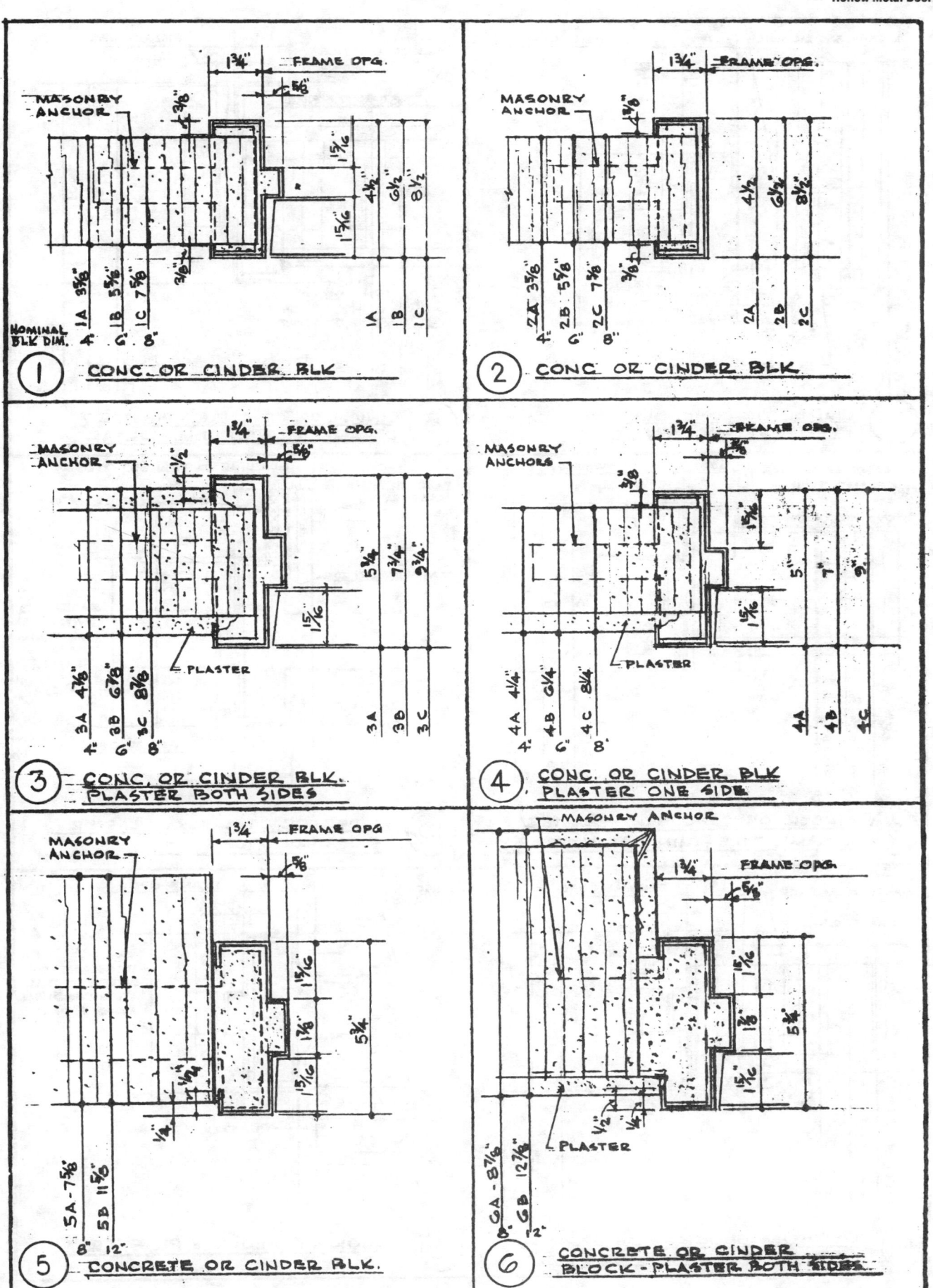

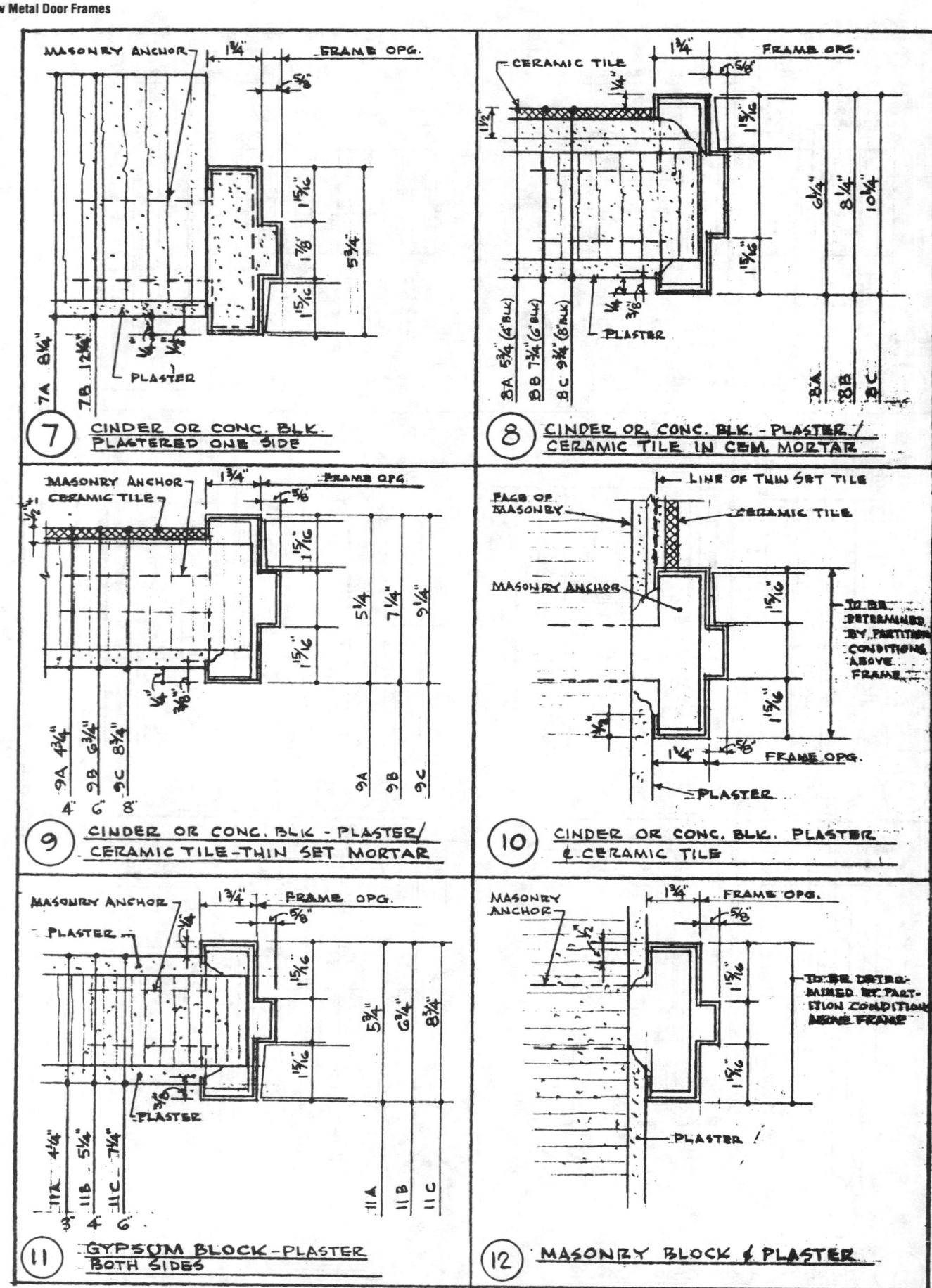

7 — CINDER OR CONC. BLK. PLASTERED ONE SIDE

8 — CINDER OR CONC. BLK. - PLASTER / CERAMIC TILE IN CEM. MORTAR

9 — CINDER OR CONC. BLK. - PLASTER / CERAMIC TILE - THIN SET MORTAR

10 — CINDER OR CONC. BLK. PLASTER & CERAMIC TILE

11 — GYPSUM BLOCK - PLASTER BOTH SIDES

12 — MASONRY BLOCK & PLASTER

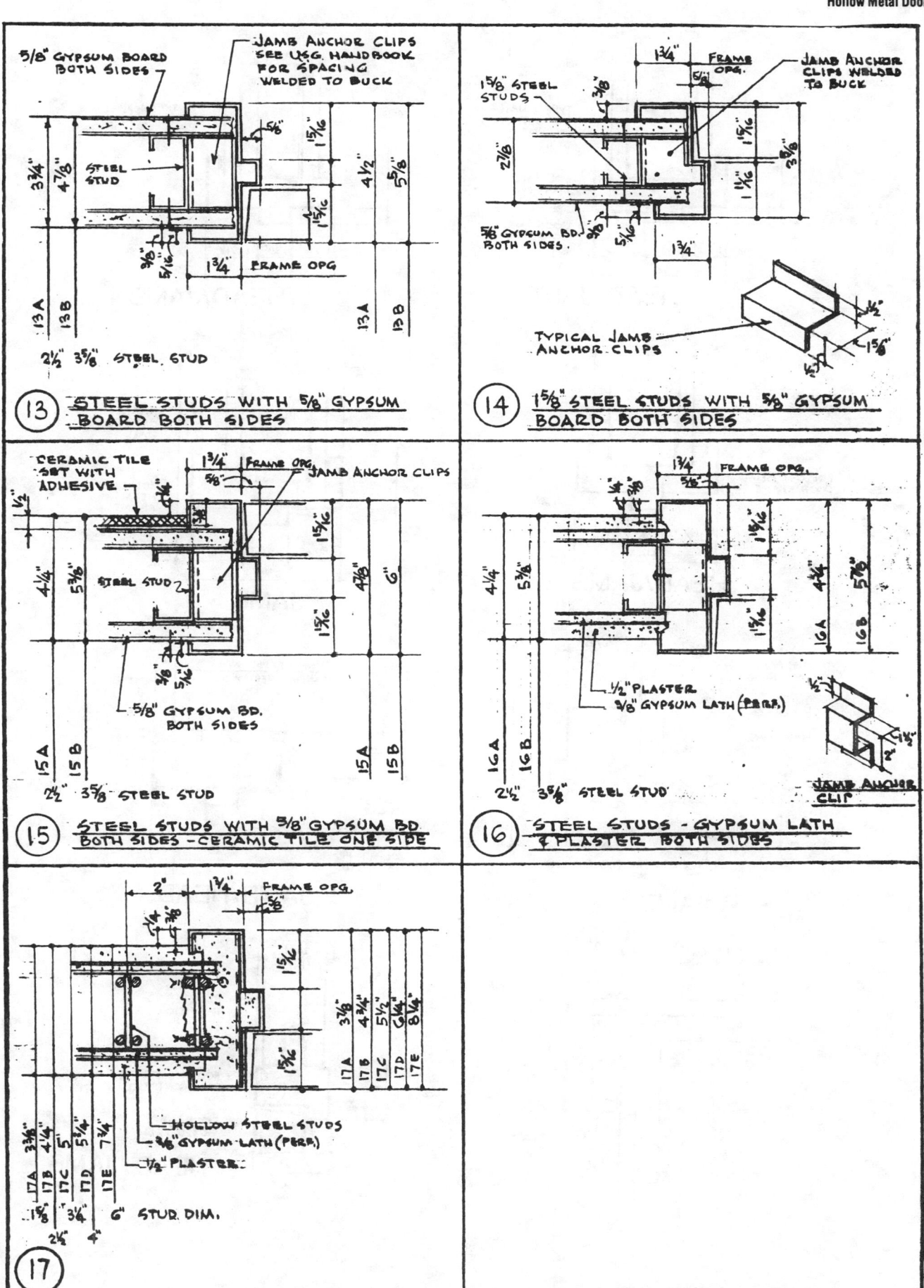

13 STEEL STUDS WITH 5/8" GYPSUM BOARD BOTH SIDES

14 1 5/8" STEEL STUDS WITH 5/8" GYPSUM BOARD BOTH SIDES

15 STEEL STUDS WITH 5/8" GYPSUM BD BOTH SIDES - CERAMIC TILE ONE SIDE

16 STEEL STUDS - GYPSUM LATH & PLASTER BOTH SIDES

17

DOORS
Hollow Metal Door Frames

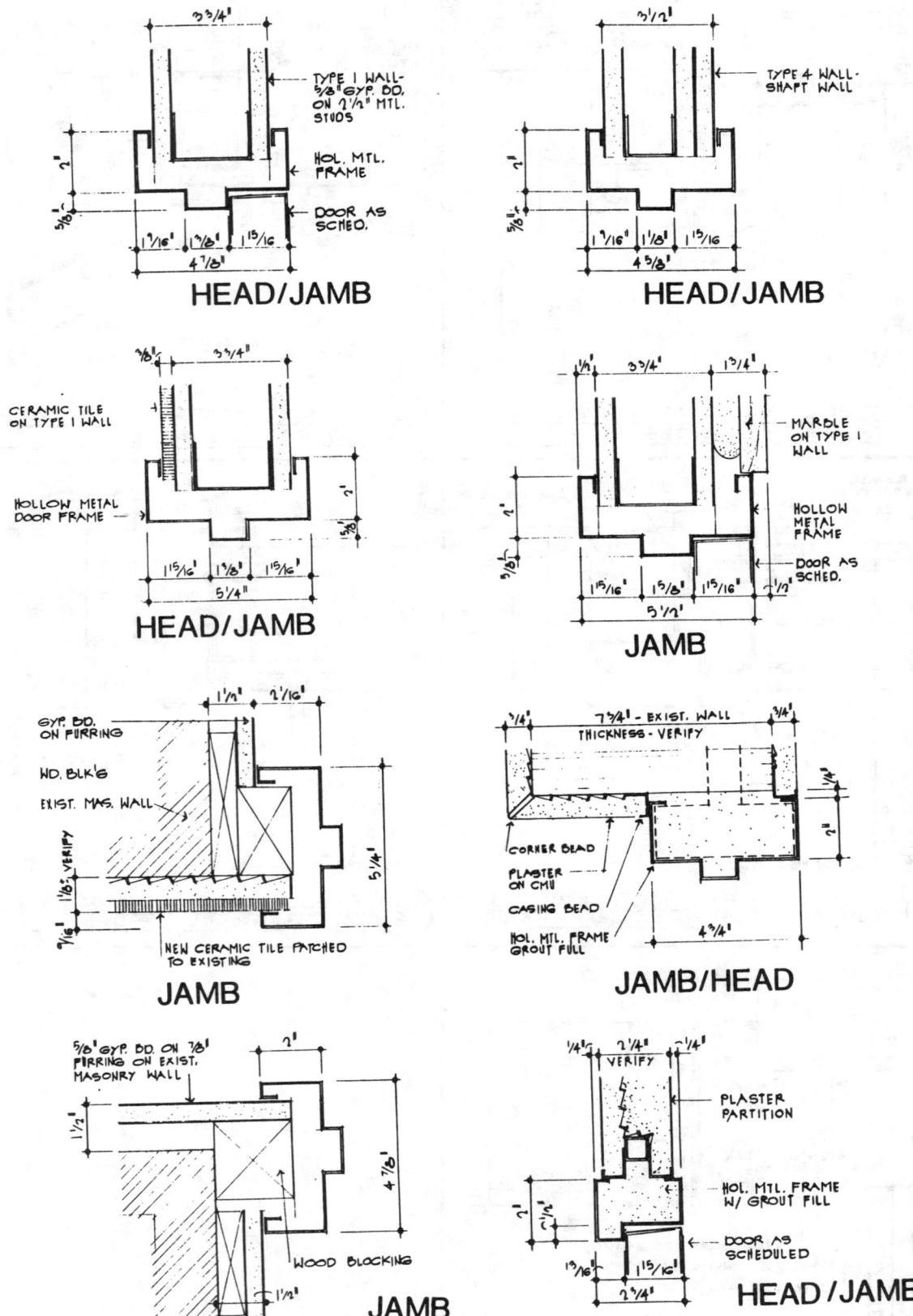

HEAD/JAMB

HEAD/JAMB

HEAD/JAMB

JAMB

JAMB

JAMB/HEAD

JAMB

HEAD/JAMB

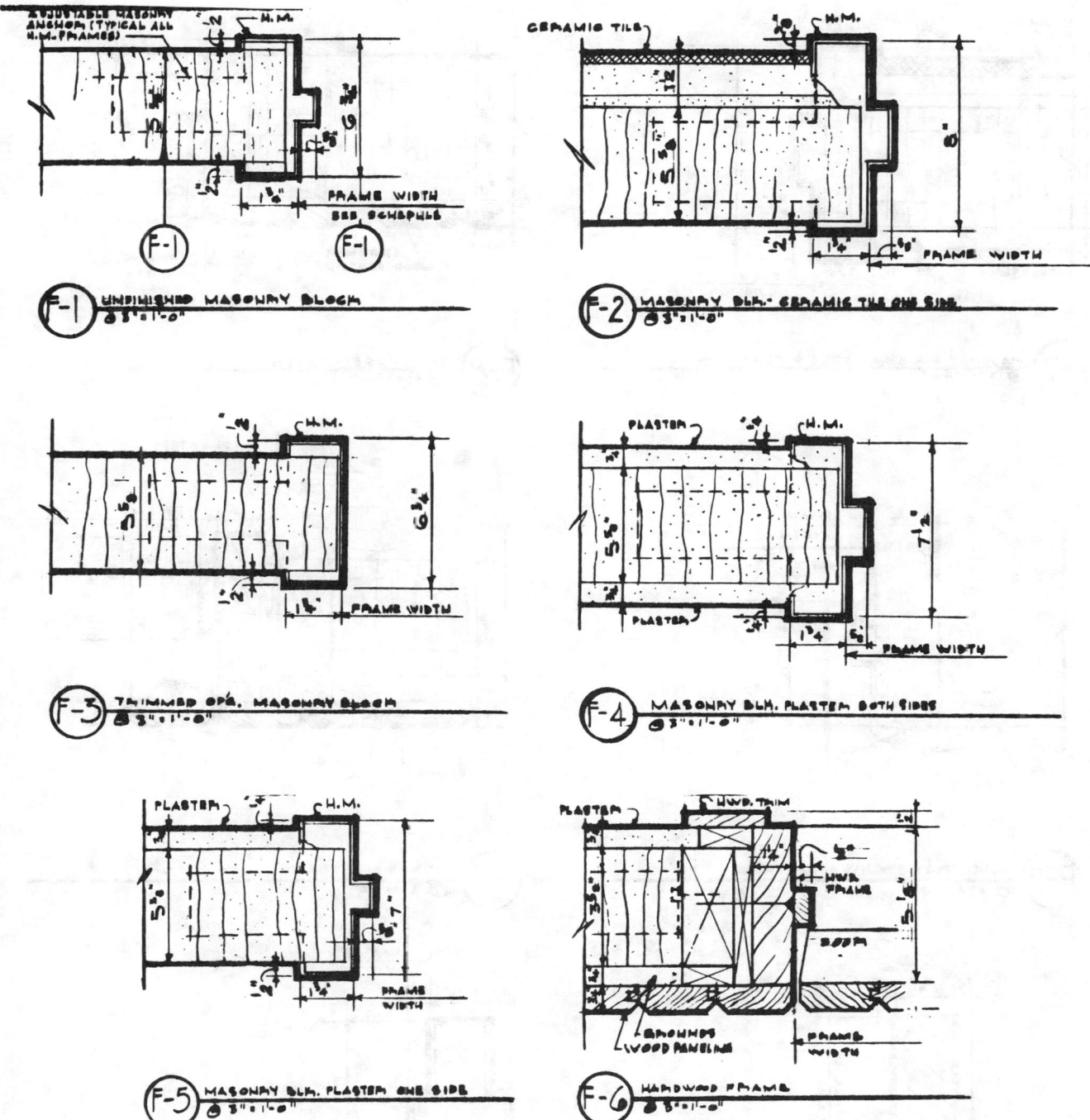

F-1   UNFINISHED MASONRY BLOCK

F-2   MASONRY BLK.- CERAMIC TILE ONE SIDE

F-3   TRIMMED OPG. MASONRY BLOCK

F-4   MASONRY BLK. PLASTER BOTH SIDES

F-5   MASONRY BLK. PLASTER ONE SIDE

F-6   HARDWOOD FRAME

DOORS
Hollow Metal Door Frames

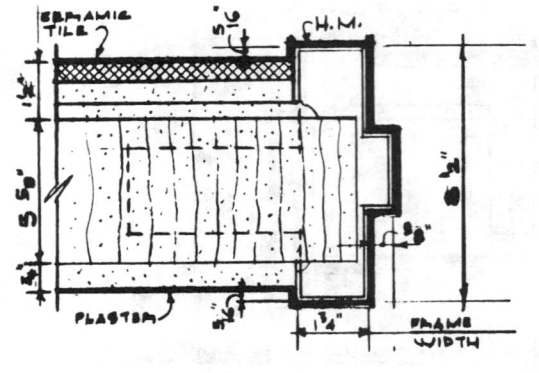

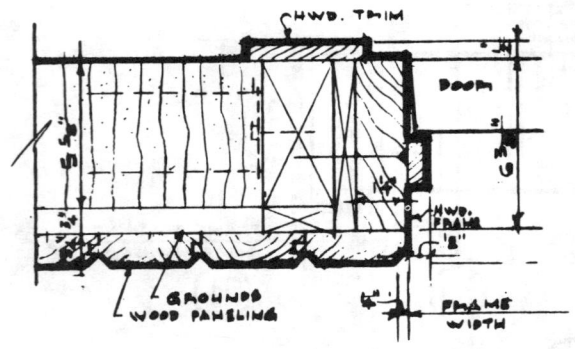

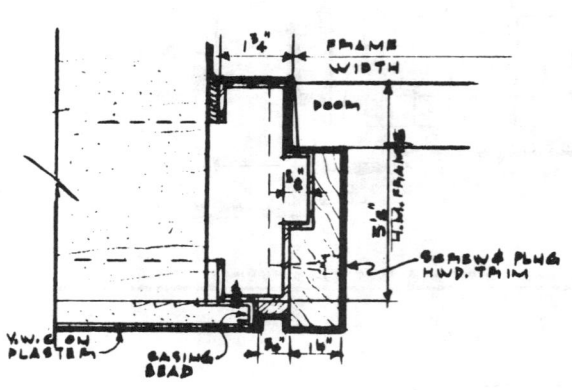

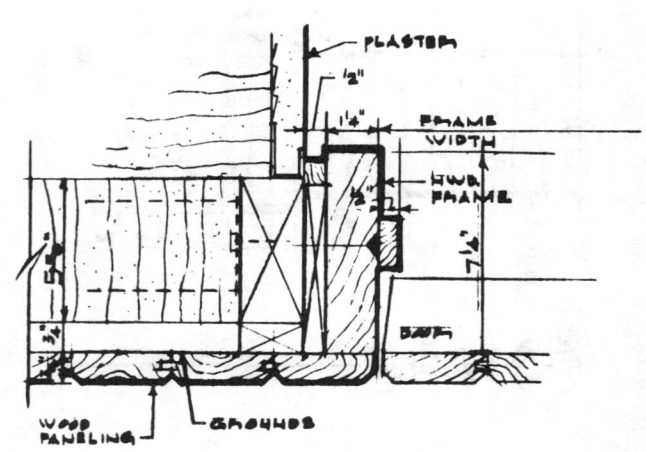

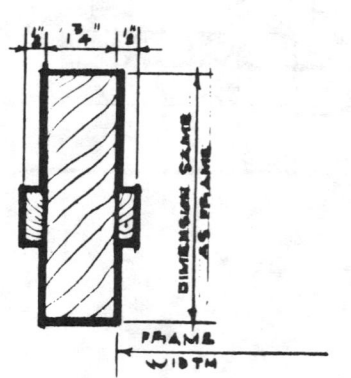

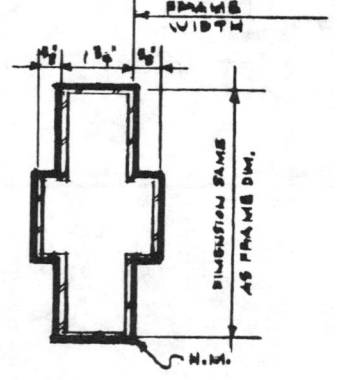

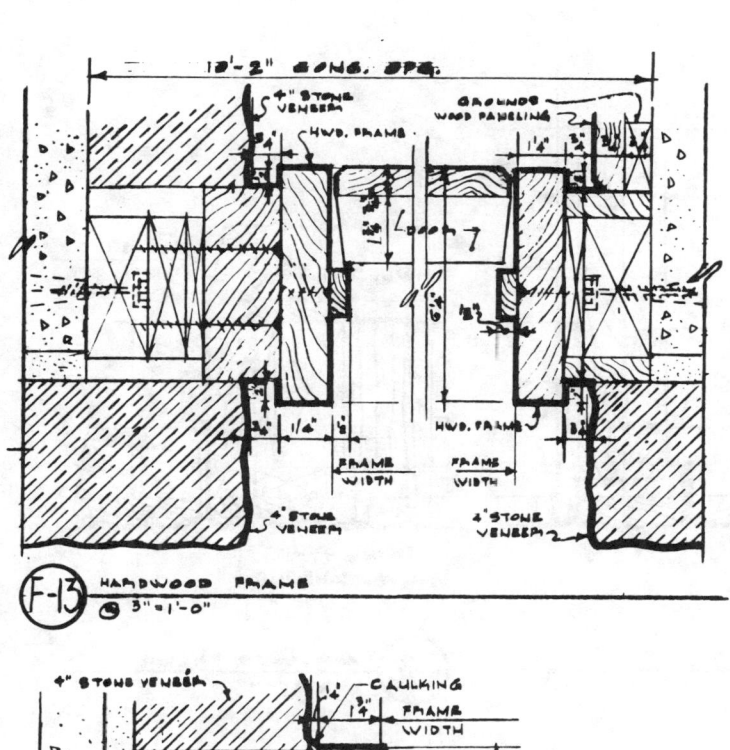

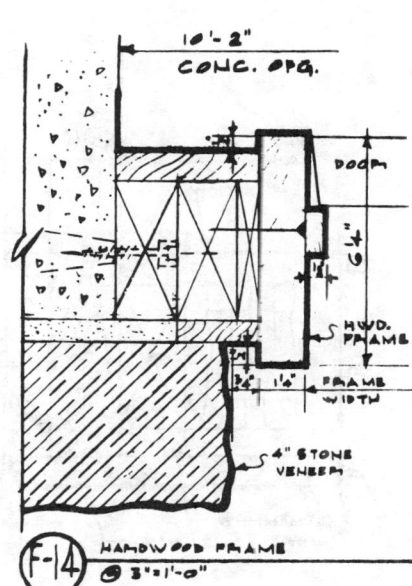

F-13 HARDWOOD FRAME @ 3"=1'-0"

F-14 HARDWOOD FRAME @ 3"=1'-0"

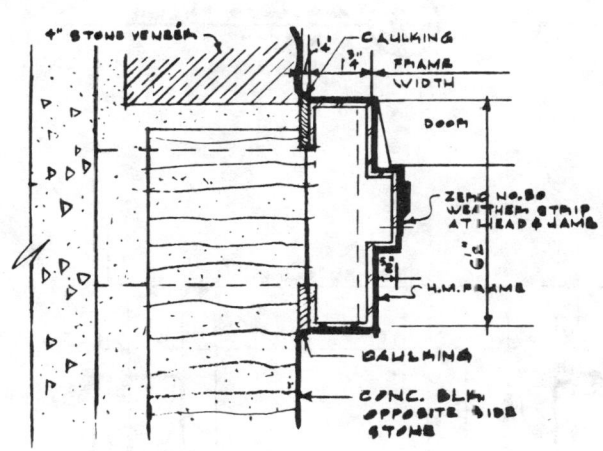

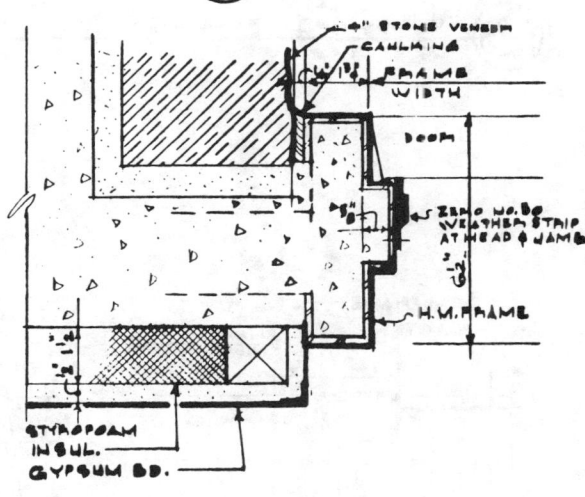

F-15 EXTERIOR HOLLOW METAL FRAME @ 3"=1'-0"

F-16 EXTERIOR HOLLOW METAL FRAME @ 3"=1'-0"

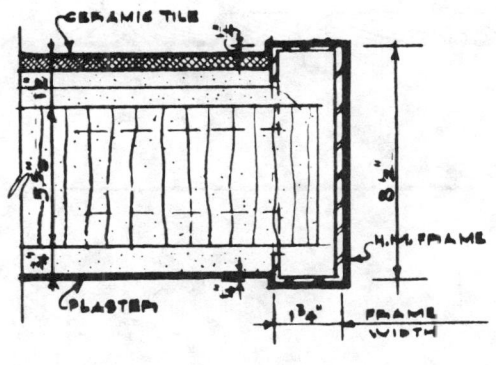

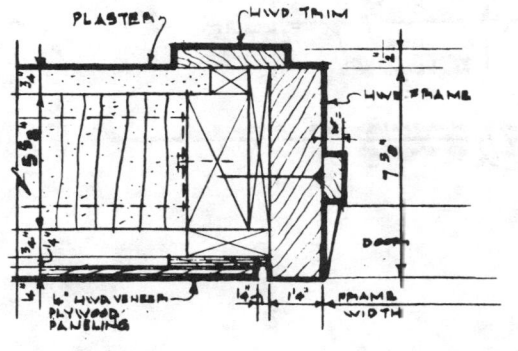

F-17 TRIMMED OPG. MASONRY BLK. CERAMIC TILE & PLASTER @ 3"=1'-0"

F-18 HARDWOOD FRAME @ 3" = 1'-0"

DOORS
Hollow Metal and Wood Door Frames

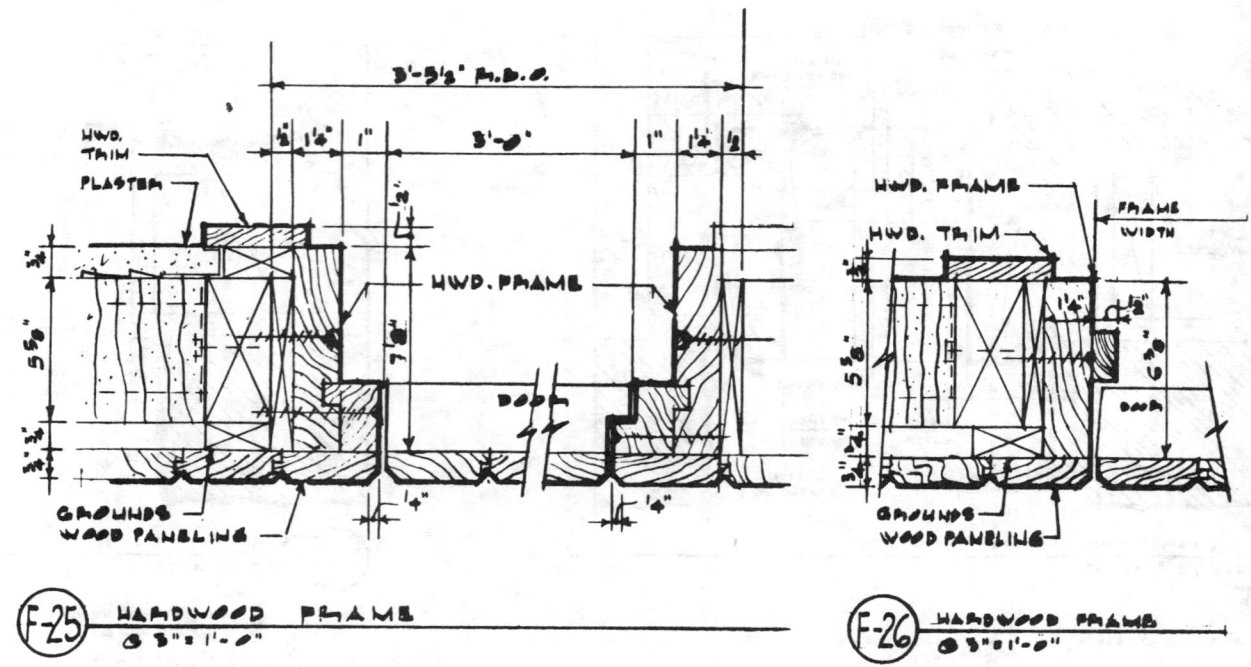

F-25   HARDWOOD FRAME @ 3" = 1'-0"

F-26   HARDWOOD FRAME @ 3" = 1'-0"

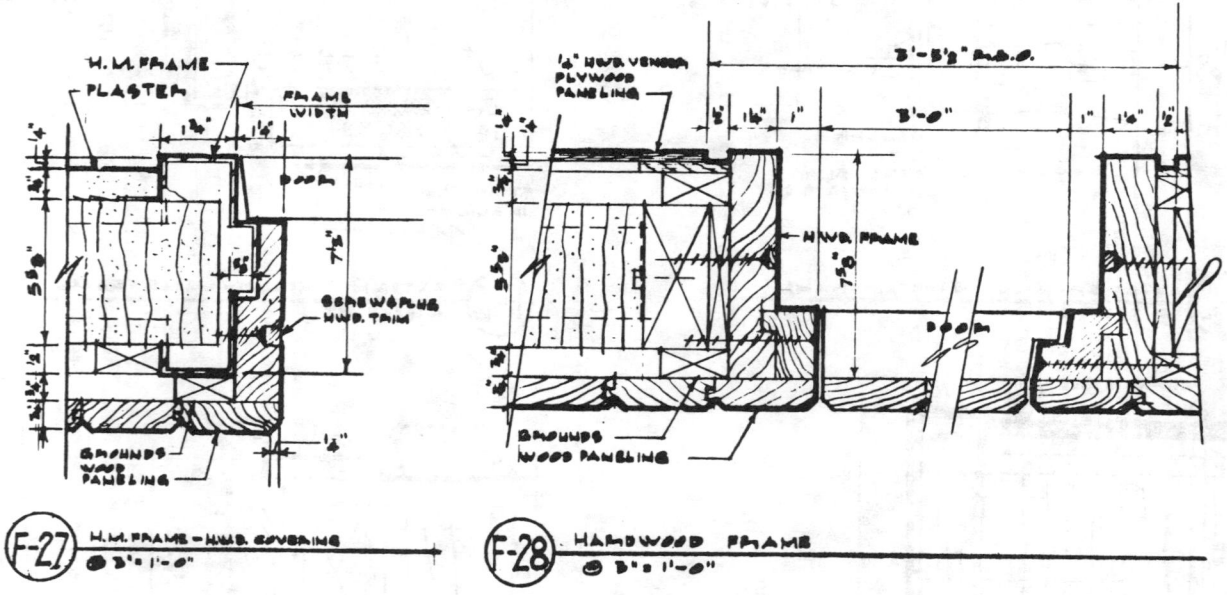

F-27   H.M. FRAME – HWD. COVERING @ 3" = 1'-0"

F-28   HARDWOOD FRAME @ 3" = 1'-0"

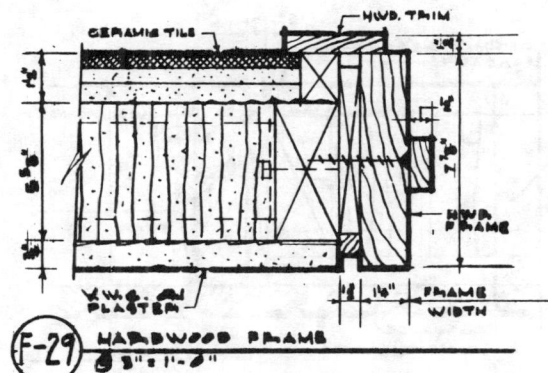

F-29   HARDWOOD FRAME
@ 3" = 1'-0"

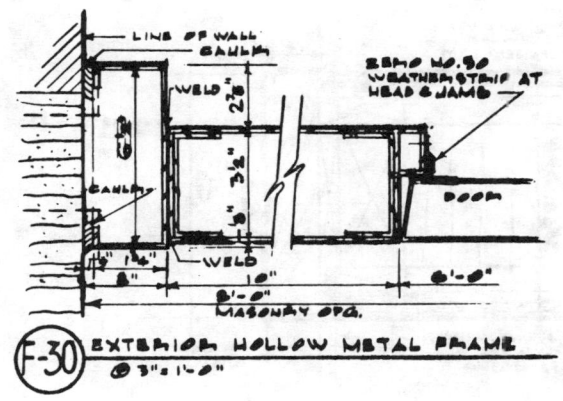

F-30   EXTERIOR HOLLOW METAL FRAME
@ 3" = 1'-0"

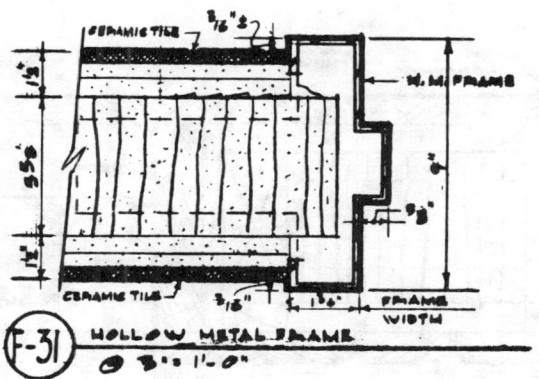

F-31   HOLLOW METAL FRAME
@ 3" = 1'-0"

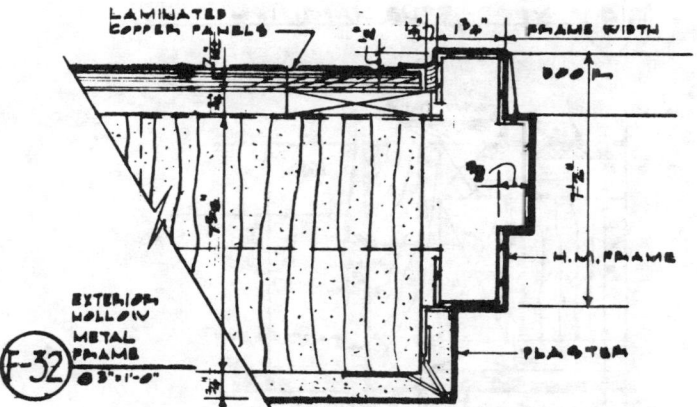

F-32   EXTERIOR HOLLOW METAL FRAME
@ 3" = 1'-0"

DOORS
Hollow Metal and Wood Door Types

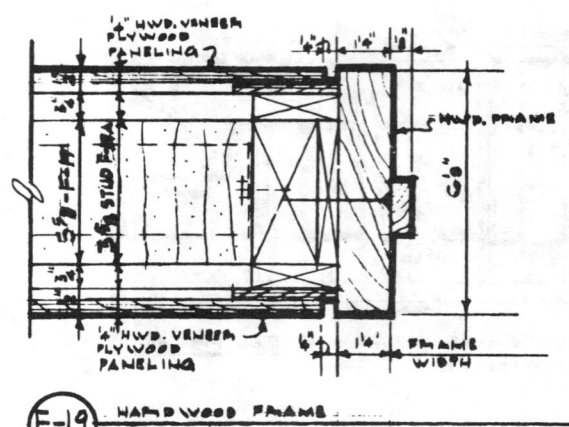

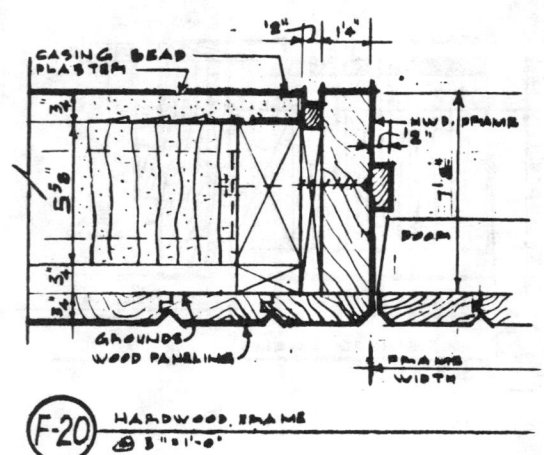

F-19 HARDWOOD FRAME @ 3"=1'-0"

F-19A WOOD STUD PARTITION

F-20 HARDWOOD FRAME @ 3"=1'-0"

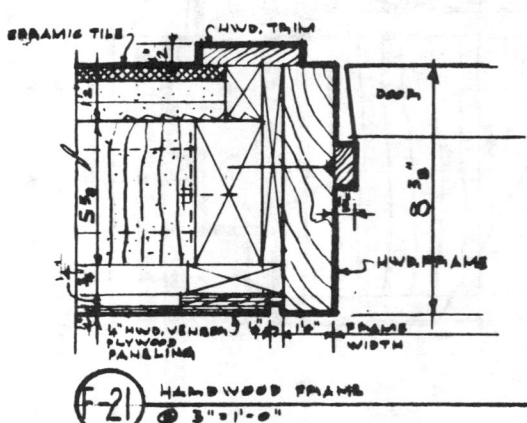

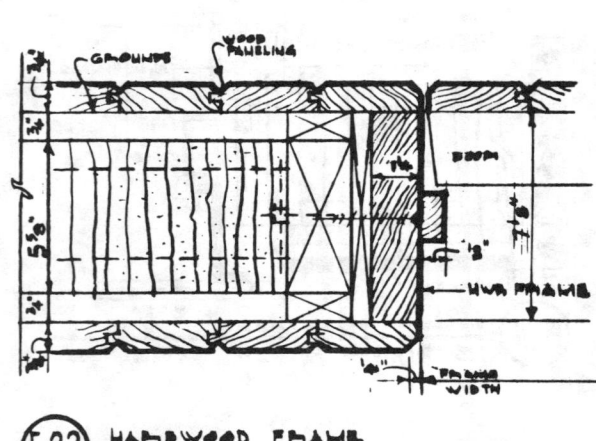

F-21 HARDWOOD FRAME @ 3"=1'-0"

F-22 HARDWOOD FRAME @ 3"=1'-0"

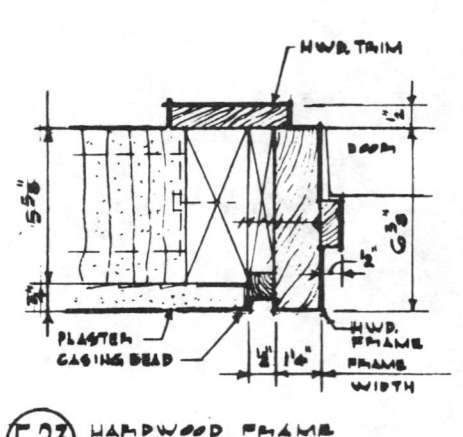

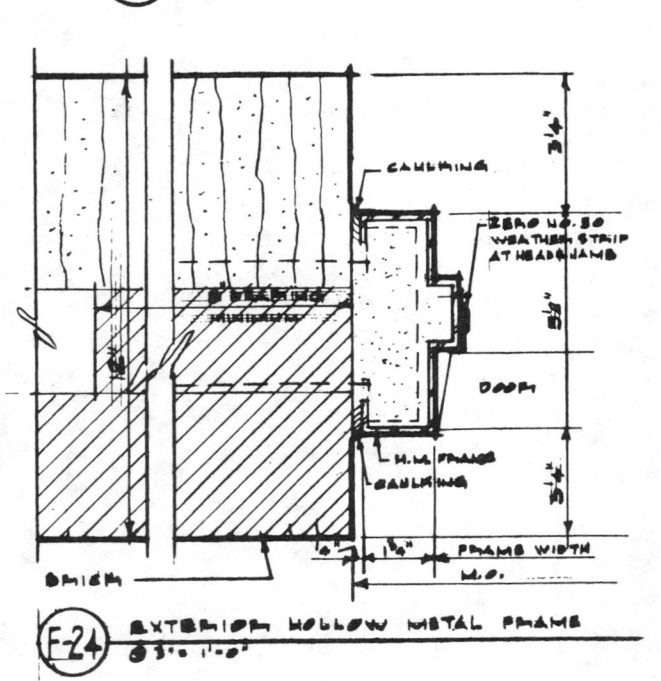

F-23 HARDWOOD FRAME @ 3"=1'-0"

F-24 EXTERIOR HOLLOW METAL FRAME @ 3"=1'-0"

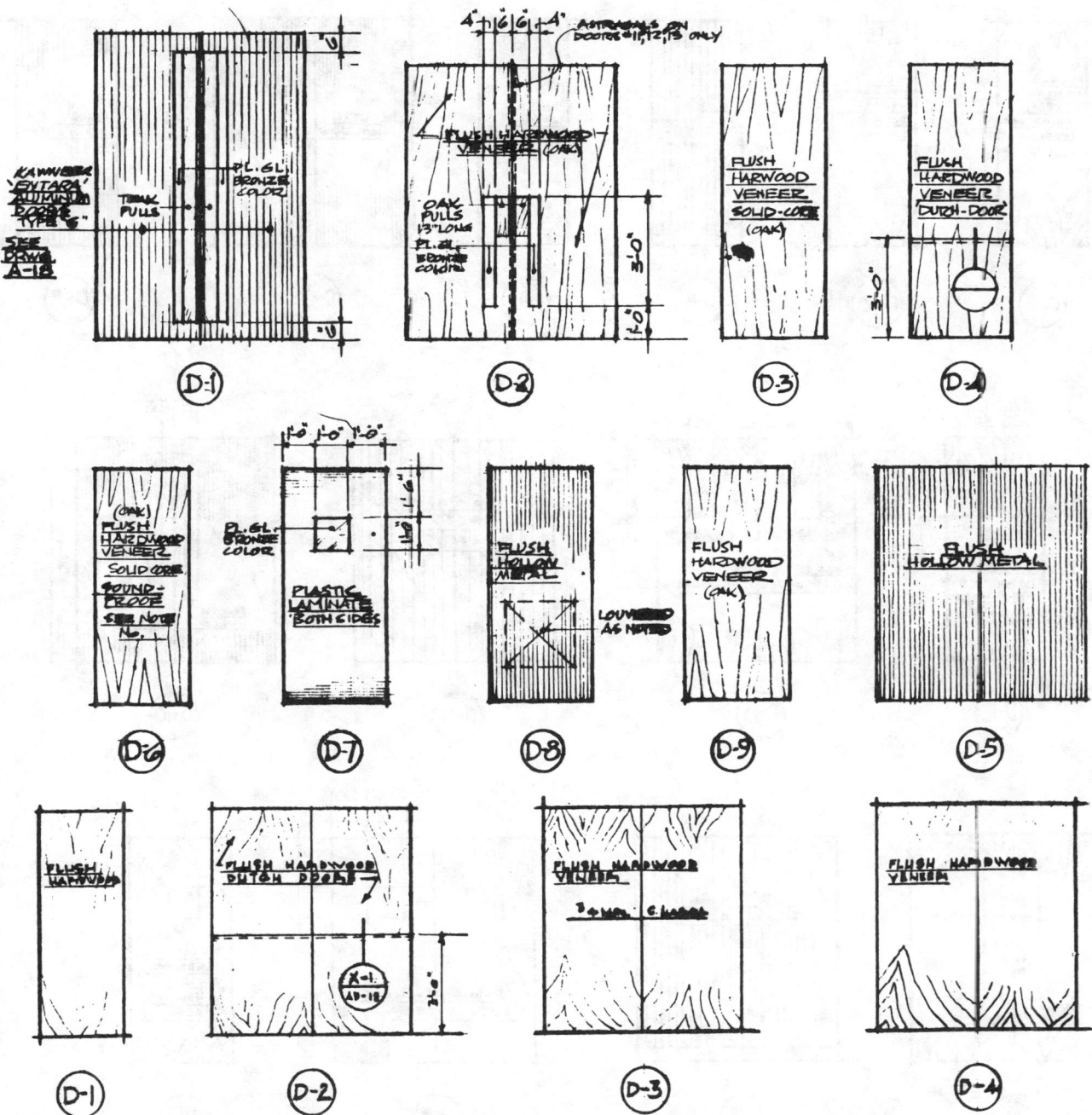

DOORS

Door Types

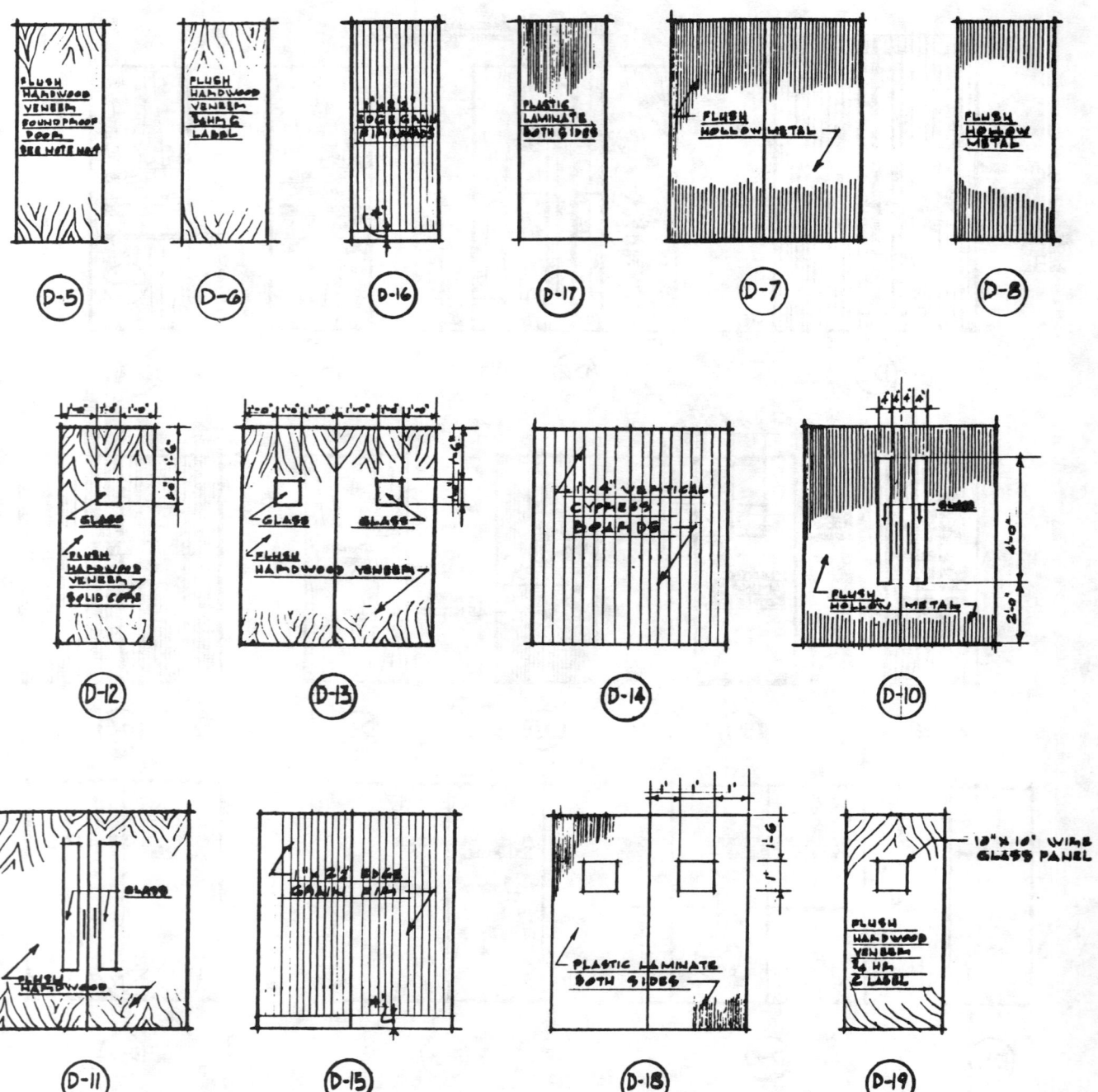

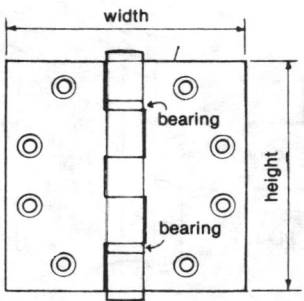

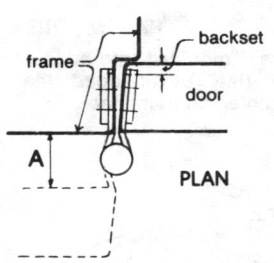

FULL MORTISE BUTT HINGE

Two equal square-edged leaves, one mortised into door edge, the other into frame rabbet.
Two bearings, as shown, on regular weight hinges, four on heavy weight.

Typical Uses:

By far the most common type of hinge for both interior and exterior hollow metal and wood swing doors, in all types of buildings.

Usual Sizes (see NOTE below):

heights — 4½"; 5" for doors over 36" w.
widths — 4½" for 1¾" door and 1½" trim clearance (dimension A); 5" (or more) for thicker doors or larger clearances.

HALF MORTISE BUTT HINGE

One square-edged leaf mortised into door edge; the other leaf, bevel-edged, mounted on face of frame.

Typical Uses:

Used with hollow metal or kalamein doors in structural channel frames, usually in industrial type buildings.

Usual Sizes:

4½", 5" and 6" heights.

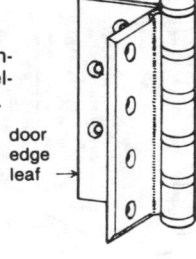

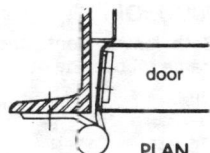

HALF SURFACE BUTT HINGE

One leaf, bevel-edged, mounted on face of door; the other leaf, square-edged, mortised into frame rabbet.

Typical Uses:

Used with hollow metal or kalamein doors in hollow metal frames, usually in industrial buildings. Heavy weight type also used on lead-lined doors.

Usual Sizes: 4½", 5" and 6" heights.

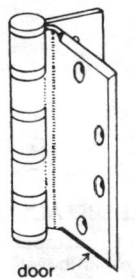

FULL SURFACE BUTT HINGE

Two bevel-edged leaves of differing widths, one surface-mounted on door face, the other on frame face.

Typical Uses:

Used with hollow metal or kalamein doors in structural channel frames, in industrial buildings. Heavy weight type may be used on lead-lined doors.

Usual Sizes: 4½", 5" and 6" heights.

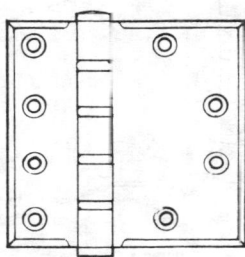

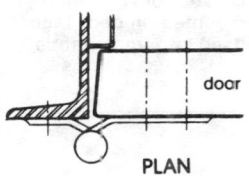

NOTE: Anchor hinges and pivot hinges should be specified for heavy doors and doors with high frequency use, such as entrances to large department stores, office buildings, theaters, banks and schools, or to toilet rooms in schools and airport buildings. Regular weight hinges may be specified for doors with average and low frequency uses such as corridor doors in public buildings and doors in residential buildings.

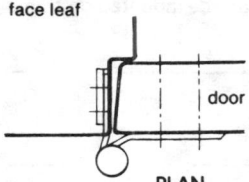

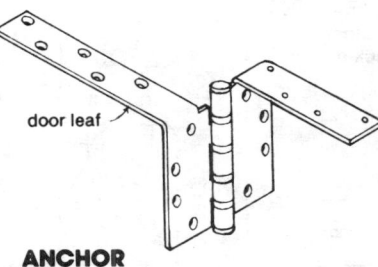

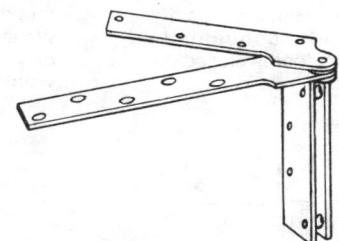

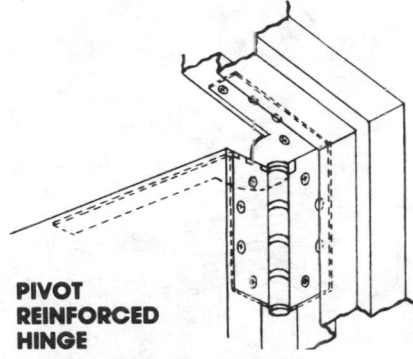

ANCHOR HINGE

Heavy weight hinge with each leaf extended at its top edge and bent to form a flange that fastens to top edge of door and to frame head rabbet. May be used as top hinge on heavy doors and doors having high frequency usage.

THRUST PIVOT UNIT AND HINGE SET

Pivot unit for top of door, with both jamb and top plates for both door and frame. Used, with conventional butt hinges, on wide doors that may be subjected to abnormal abuse. The hinge is almost invisible when door is closed.

PIVOT REINFORCED HINGE

Heavy weight hinge with added pivot on the same pin. Leaves of pivot are interlocked with hinge leaves. Used with conventional butt hinges on doors subject to abnormal abuse, particularly with overhead closers.

DOORS

Hollow Metal Door Hardware: Hinges

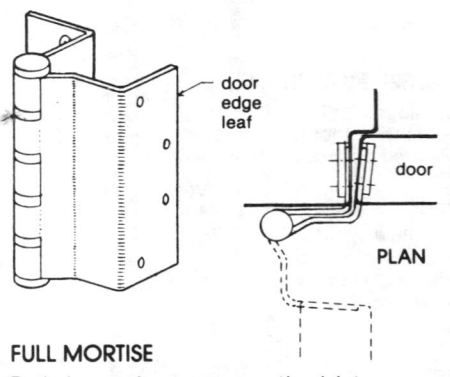

FULL MORTISE

Both leaves bent; one mortised into frame rabbet, the other into door edge.

HOSPITAL "SWING CLEAR" TYPES

These hinges have their pins located approximately 2″ beyond the door edge, providing an unobstructed clear frame opening width when the door is open 90″.

They are used on hospital corridor doors to patients' rooms, operating rooms, emergency rooms, or wherever a completely clear opening is required in hospitals, institutional or public buildings.

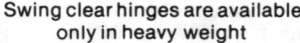

Swing clear hinges are available only in heavy weight

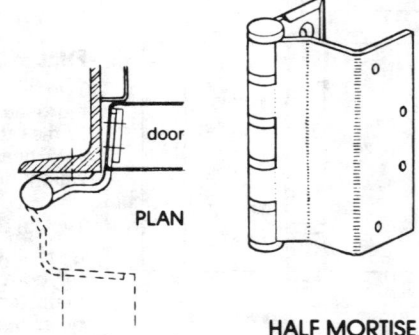

HALF MORTISE

One bent leaf mortised into edge of door, one flat, bevel-edged leaf surface-mounted on frame face.

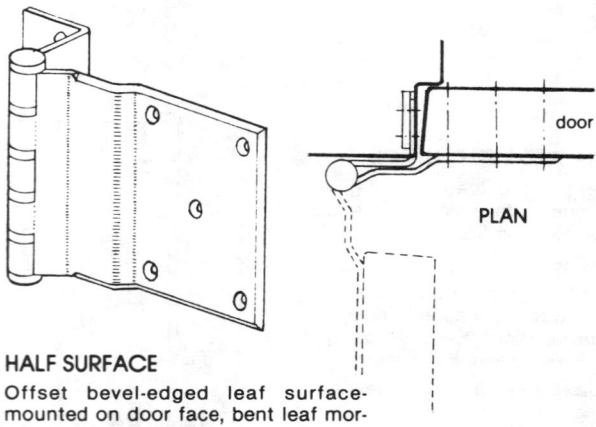

HALF SURFACE

Offset bevel-edged leaf surface-mounted on door face, bent leaf mortised into frame rabbet.

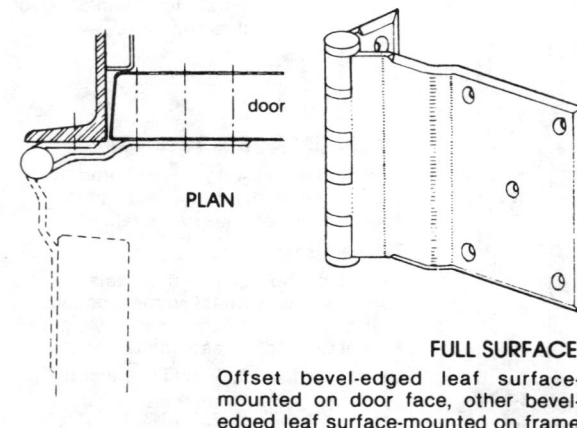

FULL SURFACE

Offset bevel-edged leaf surface-mounted on door face, other bevel-edged leaf surface-mounted on frame face.

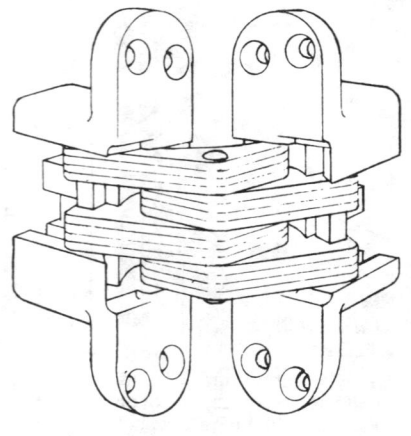

INVISIBLE HINGE

Full mortised, centered on door thickness. Hinge is completely concealed when door is closed.

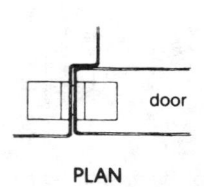

Full mortised; door leaf usually centered on door thickness. When door is closed, only the knuckle is visible.

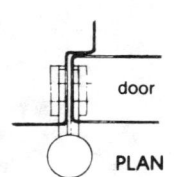

OLIVE KNUCKLE HINGE
(PAUMELLE HINGE SIMILAR)

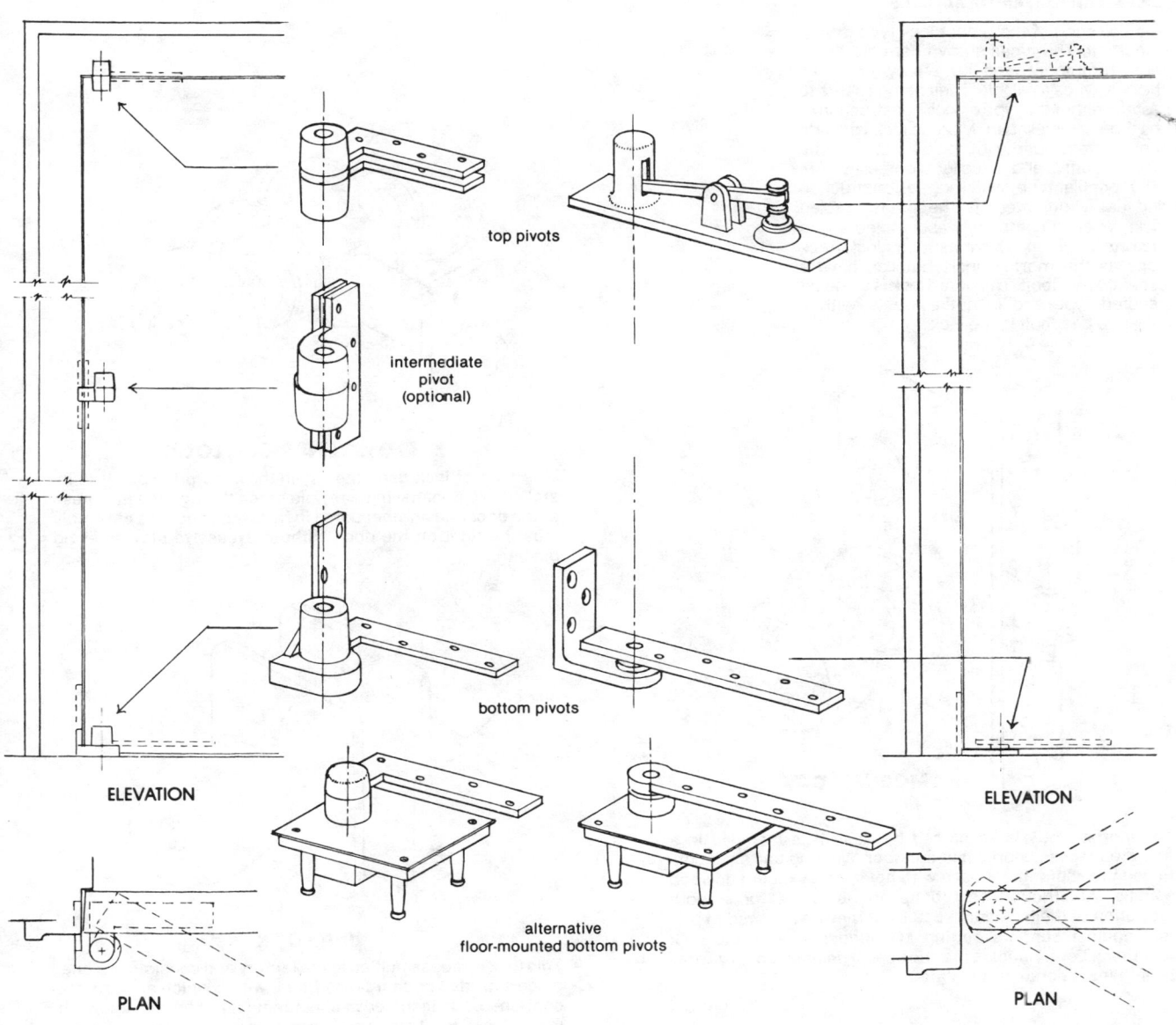

top pivots

intermediate
pivot
(optional)

bottom pivots

alternative
floor-mounted bottom pivots

ELEVATION

PLAN

ELEVATION

PLAN

OFFSET TYPE

Used on single-acting doors only. Need for in-termediate pivot depends upon the size, weight and usage of door; recommendation of hardware manufacturer should be followed. Pivot knuckles visible when door is closed.

CENTER TYPE

Used at top and bottom of double-acting doors only. Pivots are completely invisible when door is closed.

Pivots are stronger and more durable than hinges and are better able to withstand the racking stresses to which doors are subjected. Their use is generally recommended on oversize doors, on heavy doors such as lead-lined doors, and on entrance doors to public buildings such as schools, theaters, banks, store and office buildings.

NOTE: Because of adjustments that must be made during the installation of doors with bottom pivots, it is recommended that reinforcements be fur-nished in blank and that drilling and tapping be done in the field by the con-tractor.

DOORS

LOCKS, LATCHES, AND DEADLOCKS

The selection of the proper lock type is very important. The types shown here are those most commonly used, but are by no means the only types available. Their names serve to identify either the type of lock construction or the type of installation. Mortise locks provide the greatest variety of lock functions, the best security, and excellent durability. Another popular type, with rugged construction and easily operated, is the preassembled lock, which is completely assembled at the factory. It does not have as many lock functions as the mortise lock, but can have a separate deadbolt. The bored lock is the least secured type and is not available with a separate deadbolt in the lock.

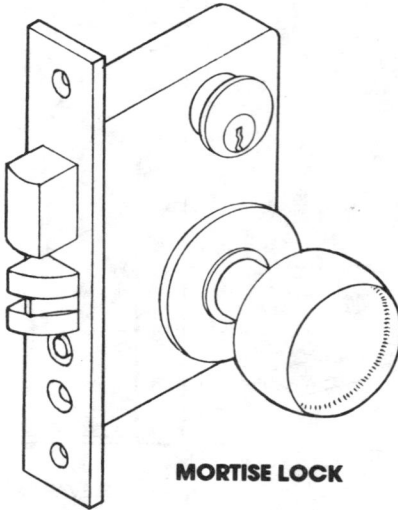

MORTISE LOCK

The mortise lock is so named because it is installed in a prepared recess (mortise) in the door. Working parts are contained in a rectangular case with holes for cylinder and knob spindle. Anti-friction split bolts are available for smooth retraction of the lock bolt. Lock front may be armored to protect against burglars getting at cylinder screws and lock fasteners. Lever handles may be used if desired, and trim may be either sectional or full plate.

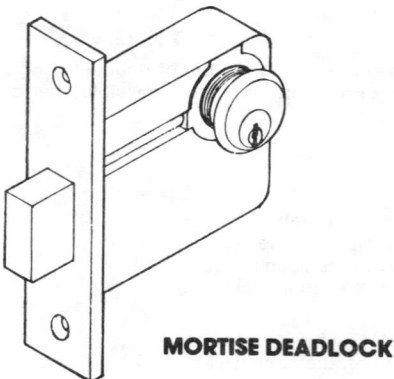

MORTISE DEADLOCK

This is a mortise lock with a deadlock only. (A deadlock is a lock bolt which has no bevel or spring action, and is operated by a key or thumb turn.) It is often used for locking a door having push or pull plates or for providing added security on doors with cylindrical locks.

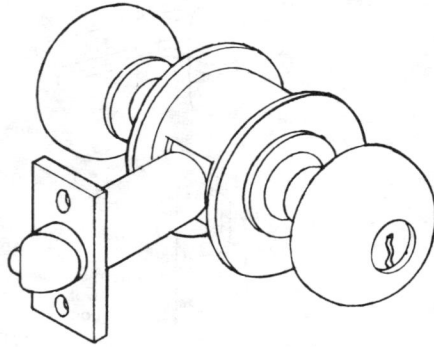

BORED (CYLINDRICAL) LOCK

This type of lock uses the key-in-the-knob principle. It is installed in a door having one hole bored through the thickness of the door and another bored in from the edge. The assembly must be tight on the door, without excessive play, to avoid binding.

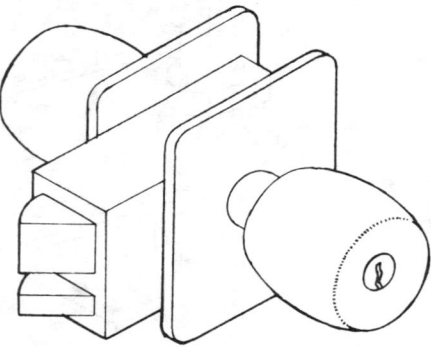

UNIT LOCK

This lock is preassembled in the factory and consists of a one-piece extruded or cast brass frame within which all parts are contained. It is installed in a rectangular reinforced notch cut in the door edge. Lever handles may be used in place of knobs.

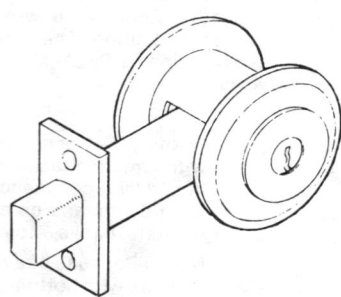

BORED (CYLINDRICAL) DEADLOCK

This is a cylindrical type of lock having a deadbolt only. It fits into the same type of cylindrical cutout as that required for the bored lock.

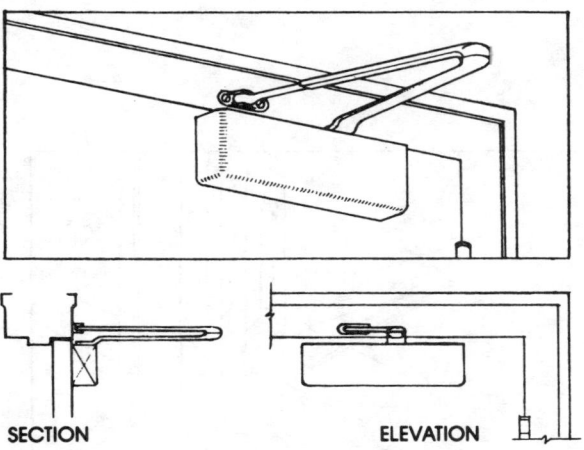

Fig. 3   Surface mounted, on hinge face of door.

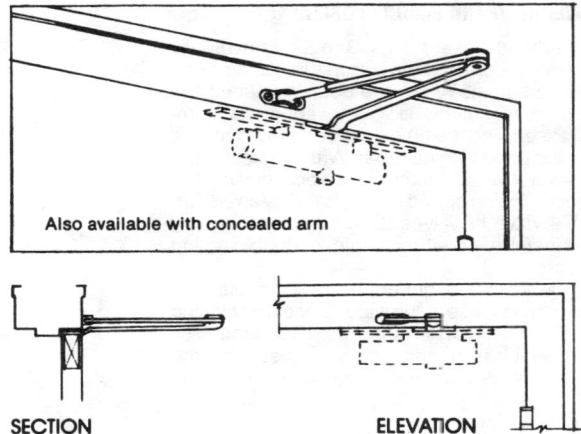

Fig. 4   Concealed in door, with exposed arm.

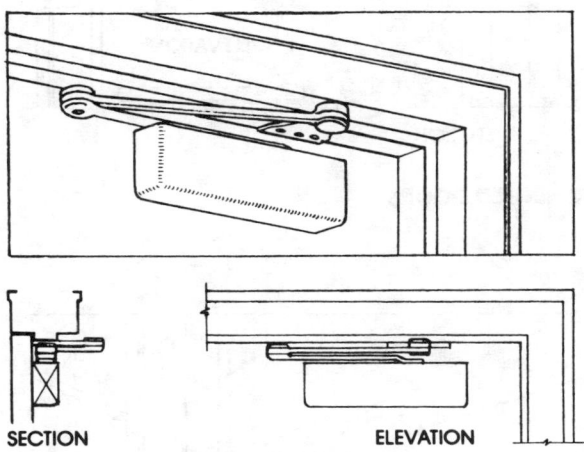

Fig. 5   Surface mounted, on stop face of door.

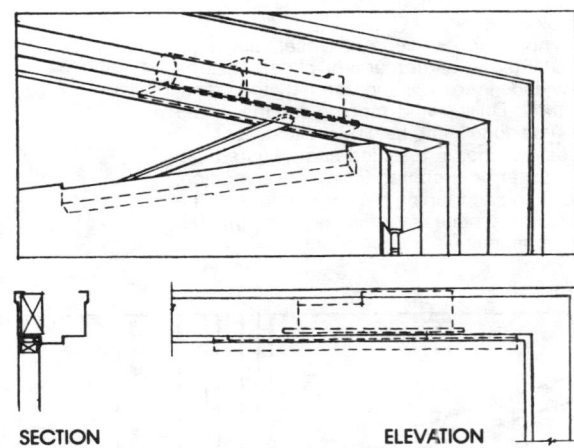

Fig. 6   Concealed in head, with concealed arm.

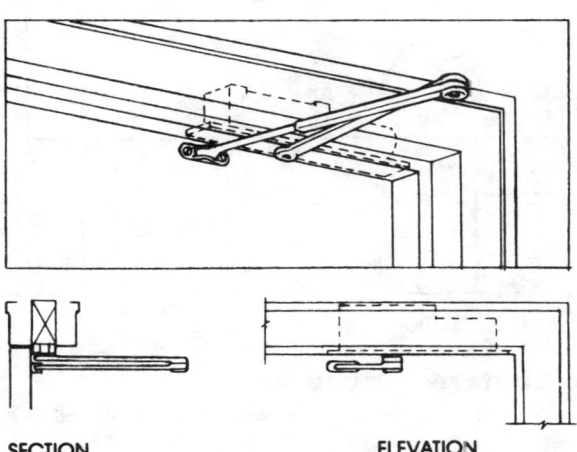

Fig. 7   Concealed in head, with exposed arm.

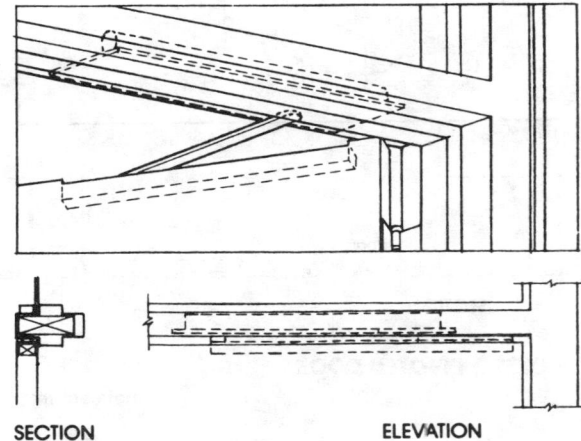

Fig. 8   Concealed in transom bar.

DOORS

Hollow Metal Door Hardware: Floor Closers

OVERHEAD AND FLOOR CLOSERS

Overhead closers (Figs. 3 to 8) are hydraulic devices, containing a piston, fluid chambers, and a spring. When the door is opened the piston is pulled back, the spring is compressed, and the fluid is moved from one side of the piston to the other. With release of the door a reverse action takes place, closing the door. Closing speed is controlled by an adjustable valve or valves. Overhead closers may be installed on either single- or double-acting doors.

Floor closers, generally more durable than overhead closers, provide concealed closing mechanisms often appropriate for doors having a high frequency of use. As shown, the type of closer used depends on whether the door is hung on hinges, offset pivots, or center pivots.

Both overhead and floor closers are available in a range of sizes for various door sizes, locations, and job conditions. The manufacturer's recommendations should always be followed in determining which size and type should be used.

Where surface-mounted closers are specified, internal reinforcement plates shall be provided in the door and frame by the manufacturer. Drilling and tapping for the closer shall be done in the field by the installer. Only after the door is installed and adjusted can the closer be mounted for proper operation. If drilling and tapping have been done at the factory, the necessary field adjustments become difficult if not impossible.

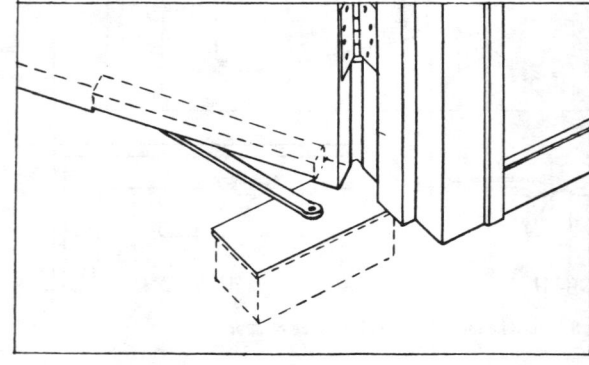

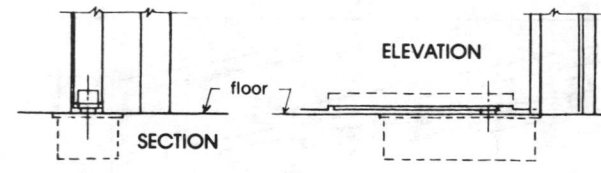

FOR HINGED DOORS

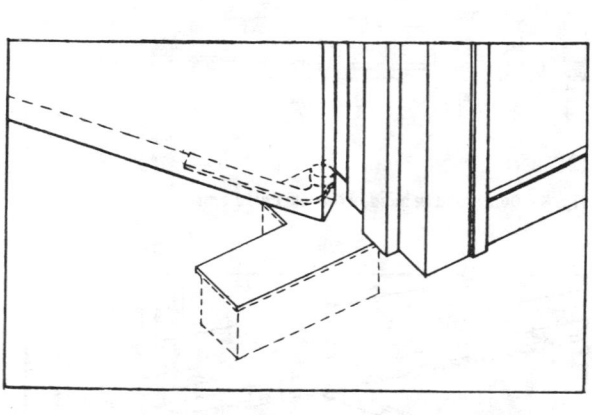

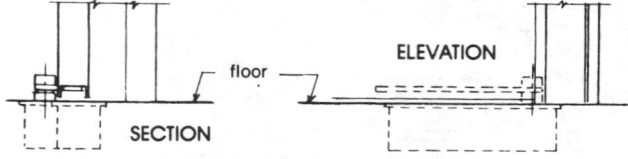

FOR OFFSET PIVOTED DOORS

single acting

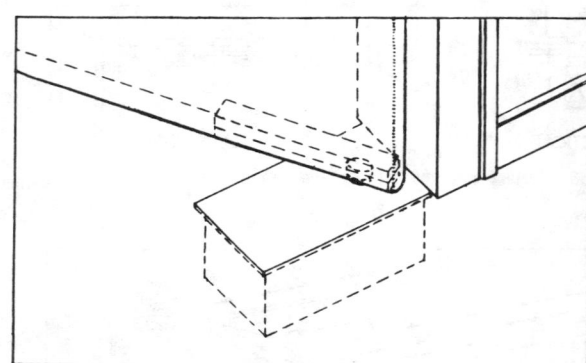

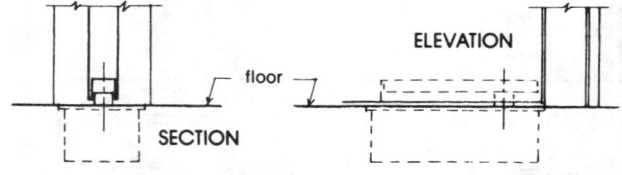

FOR CENTER PIVOTED DOORS

either single or double-acting

PANIC AND FIRE EXIT HARDWARE

Types of Installation

Panic hardware is tested and labeled for casualty only, fire exit hardware for both casualty and fire resistance. Only the latter may be used where fire rated doors are required. Both types are always releasable from the inside by depressing the crash bar. The mortise type (Fig. 9) and the concealed vertical rod type (Fig. 10) are the least conspicuous, and either of these types is readily applicable to custom hollow metal doors.

Rim and mortise types are used on
  Single door
  Active door of pair
  Both doors of pair with mullion
Vertical rod types are used on
  Single door
  Active door of pair
  Both doors of pair

Where rim type (Fig. 11) or exposed vertical rod (Fig. 12) exit devices are specified, internal reinforcement plates shall be provided in the door and frame by the manufacturer. Drilling and tapping for trim and mounting plates shall be done in the field by the installer. The hardware can then be more readily adjusted for best operation.

In preparing the door for a lock, the drilling of three bolt holes (½″ dia. or less) and/or the drilling and tapping for sectional or full trim plates shall be done in the field by the installer and not at the factory. After the lock is installed and adjusted, the trim plate can be applied to suit the final position of the latching device. If thru bolt holes or tapped holes are provided at the factory, this adjustment becomes difficult if not impossible.

The manufacturer shall drill for all function holes, i.e., cylinder, turn piece, and knob.

Door Coordinators

Coordinators (Figs. 13 and 14) are used on pairs of doors having overlapping astragals and closers. When both leaves are open, the coordinator holds the active leaf open until the inactive leaf is closed, preventing interferences of the astragal.

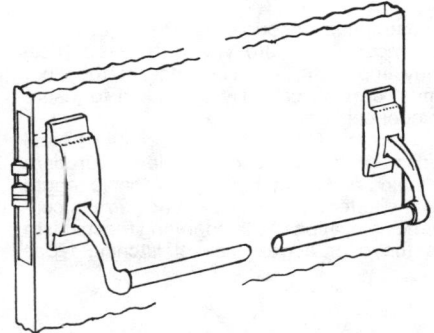

Fig. 9   Mortise type exit device.

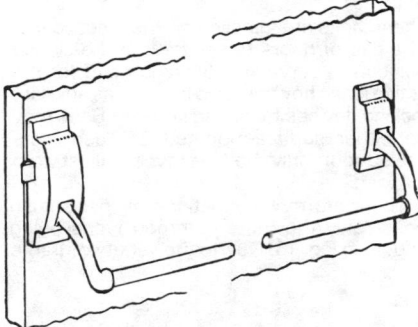

Fig. 11   Rim type exit device.

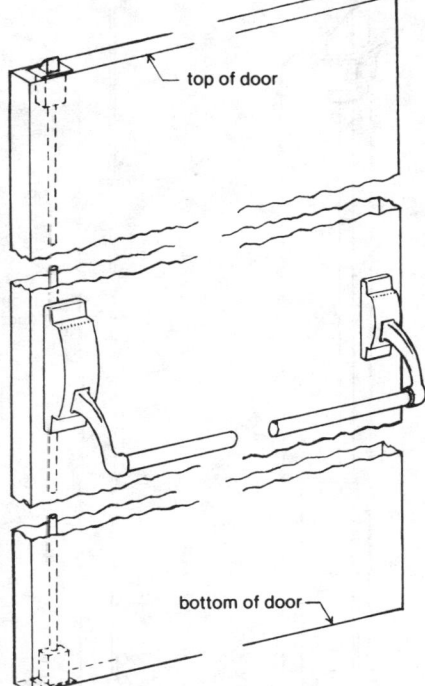

Fig. 10   Concealed vertical rod type exit.

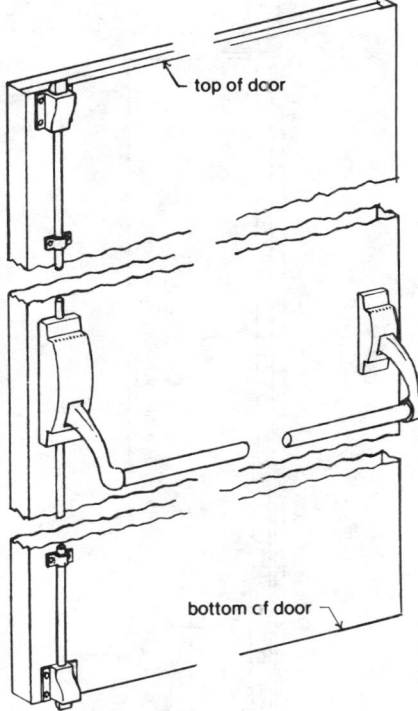

Fig. 12   Exposed vertical rod type exit device.

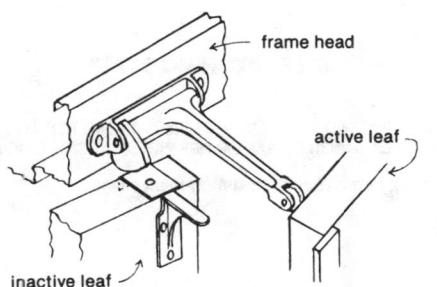

Fig. 13   Surface-mounted type door and coordinator.

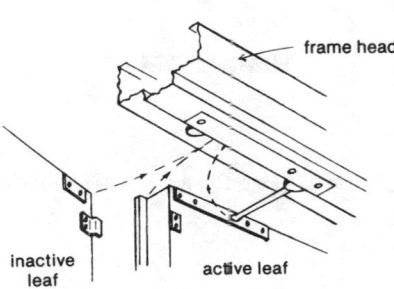

Fig. 14   Mortised type door coordinator.

DOORS

Hollow Metal Door Hardware

FLUSH BOLTS

These bolts are installed on the inactive leaf of a pair of doors to secure it in the closed position to serve as a latching point for the active leaf. They may also be used as auxiliary locking devices for added security. Bolts may be either surface-mounted or flush (concealed rod); only the latter type is illustrated in Fig. 15.

There are many variations of these flush bolts; only the more common types being shown in Fig. 15. Due to the variety of frame construction encountered, the selection of the most appropriate type of strike is particularly important, and clearance at the floor must be very carefully controlled to insure proper engagement.

The manual type (Fig. 15A) requires hand operation of the operating lever for both latching and unlatching. The variable length of the extension rod, however, permits convenient location of the operating mechanism in the door edge. The self-latching types (Fig. 15B and C) latch automatically when the inactive leave is closed, but must be unlatched manually. The automatic type (Fig. 15D) both latches and unlatches automatically when the inactive leaf is closed or opened.

None of these types of flush bolt should be used on doors that are intended to serve as emergency exists. NFPA pamphlet 80 should be consulted for the selection of bolts for fire-rated pairs of doors.

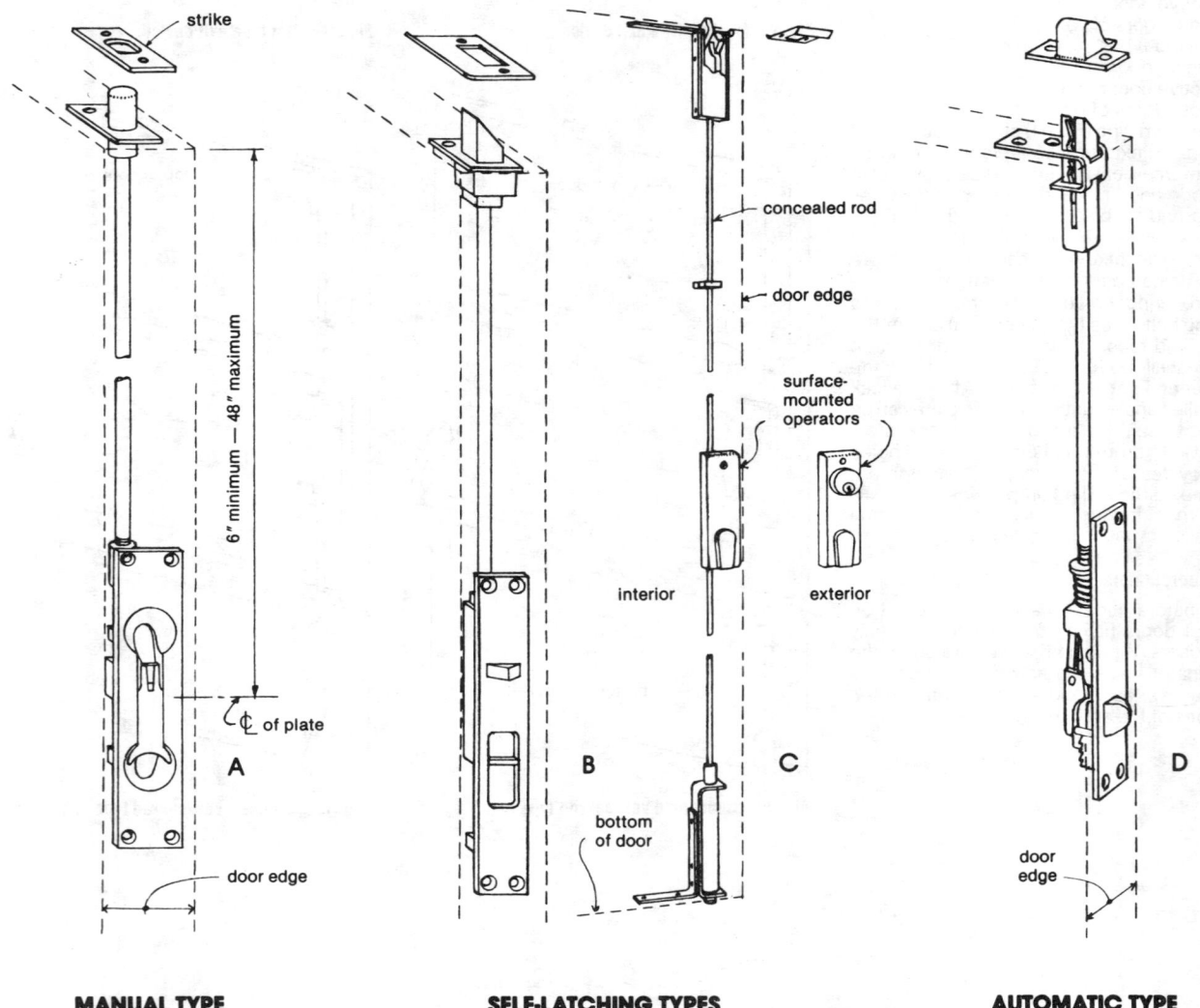

MANUAL TYPE **SELF-LATCHING TYPES** **AUTOMATIC TYPE**

U.L.-APPROVED BOLTS ARE REQUIRED AT BOTH TOP AND
BOTTOM OF INACTIVE LEAF OR FIRE-RATED PAIRS OF DOORS

Fig. 15 Except for Type C, only top bolts are shown; bottom bolts are similar in all cases.

OVERHEAD DOOR HOLDERS

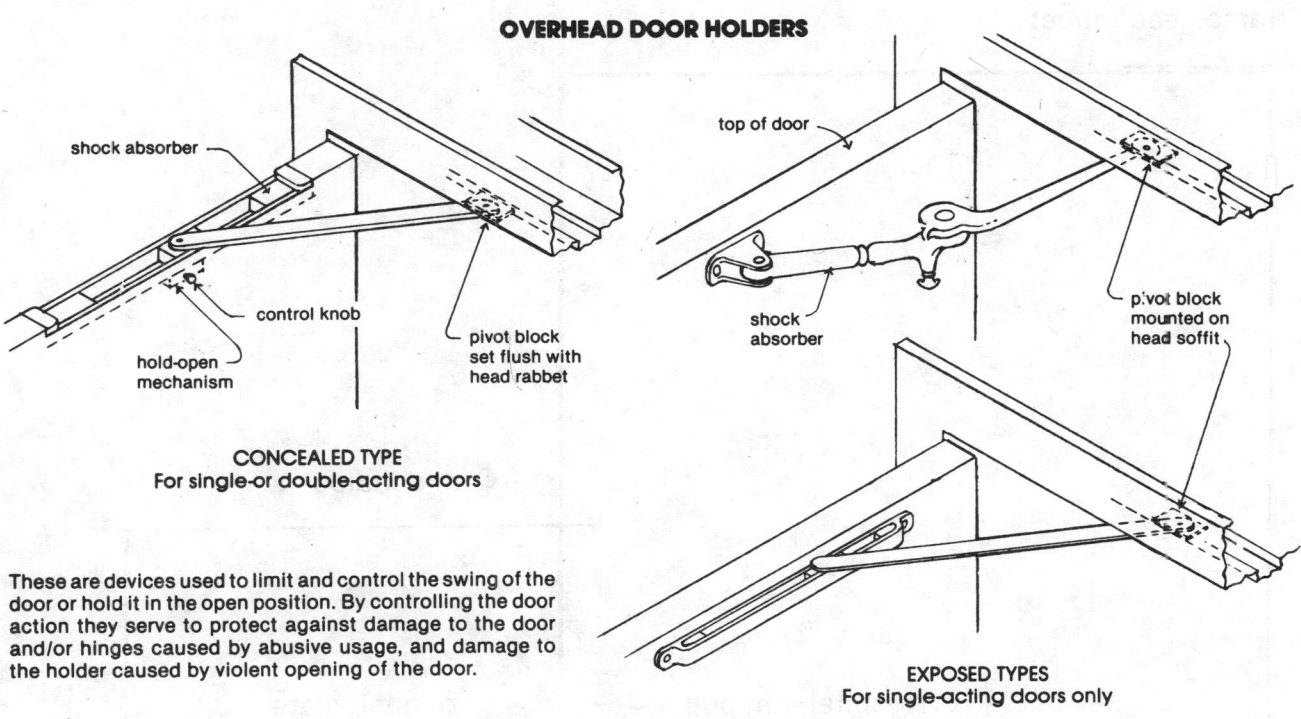

CONCEALED TYPE
For single-or double-acting doors

These are devices used to limit and control the swing of the door or hold it in the open position. By controlling the door action they serve to protect against damage to the door and/or hinges caused by abusive usage, and damage to the holder caused by violent opening of the door.

EXPOSED TYPES
For single-acting doors only

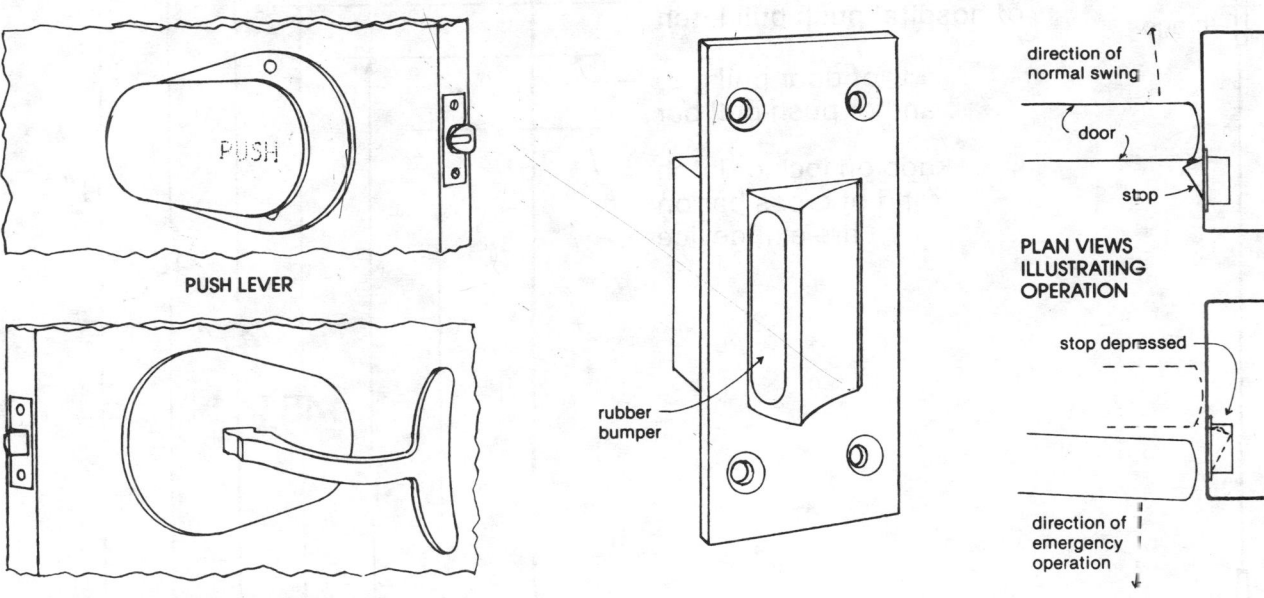

PUSH LEVER

PULL LEVER ON OPPOSITE FACE

HOSPITAL DOOR LATCH

Designed primarily for use in hospitals, on corridor doors leading to patient rooms. May also be used on any door requiring push-pull operation, particularly by forearm or elbow, when hands are engaged in carrying objects.

EMERGENCY DOOR STOP

Intended primarily for use in hospitals, on doors between patient rooms and toilets. This stop permits door to be opened from the stop side in the event that an incapacitated patient should block the normal swing by falling. Door must be hung on center (double-acting) pivots.

DOORS
Hardware Locations

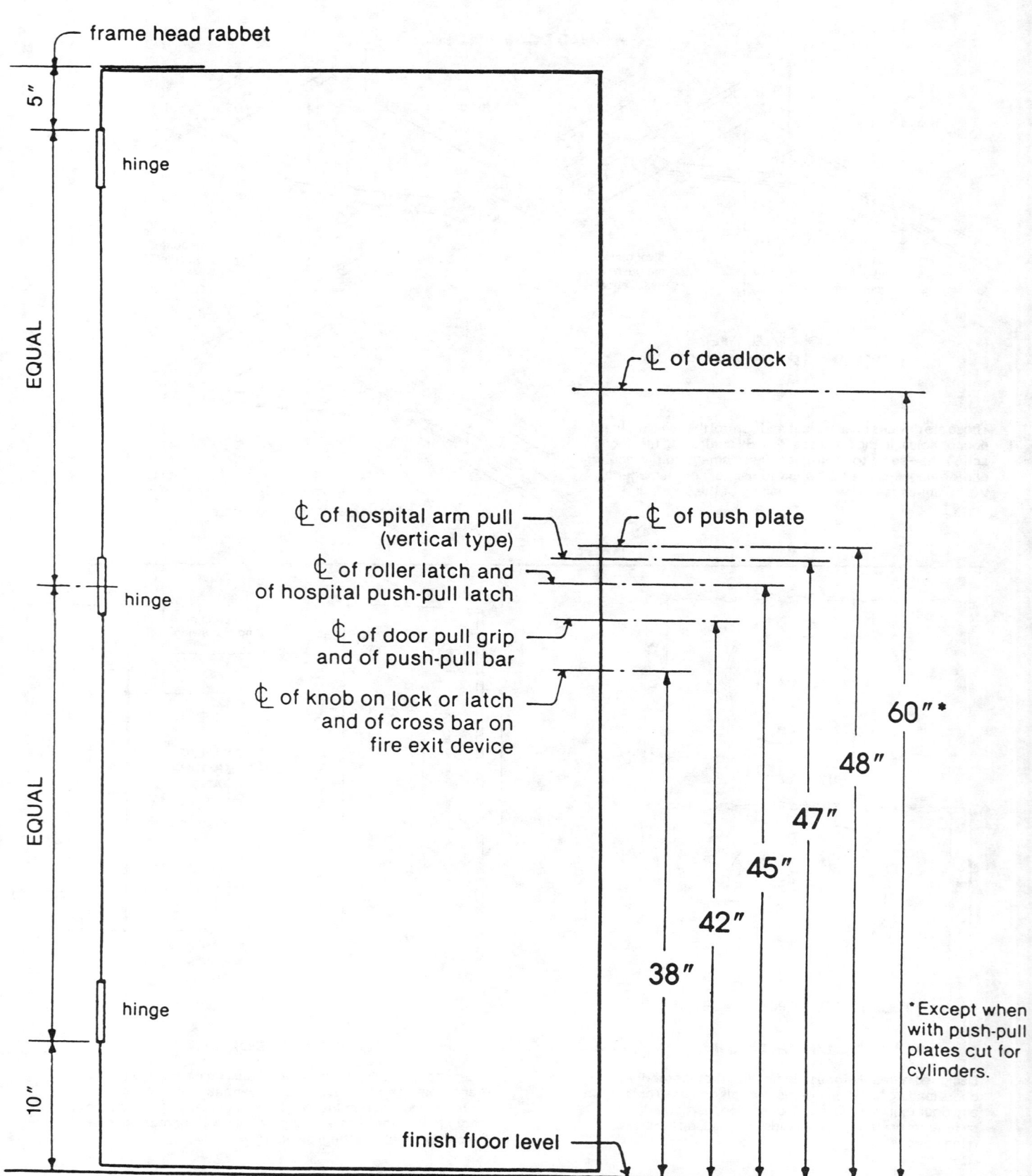

frame head rabbet

5"

hinge

EQUAL

hinge

EQUAL

hinge

10"

finish floor level

₵ of deadlock

₵ of hospital arm pull
(vertical type)

₵ of push plate

₵ of roller latch and
of hospital push-pull latch

₵ of door pull grip
and of push-pull bar

₵ of knob on lock or latch
and of cross bar on
fire exit device

60" *

48"

47"

45"

42"

38"

*Except when
with push-pull
plates cut for
cylinders.

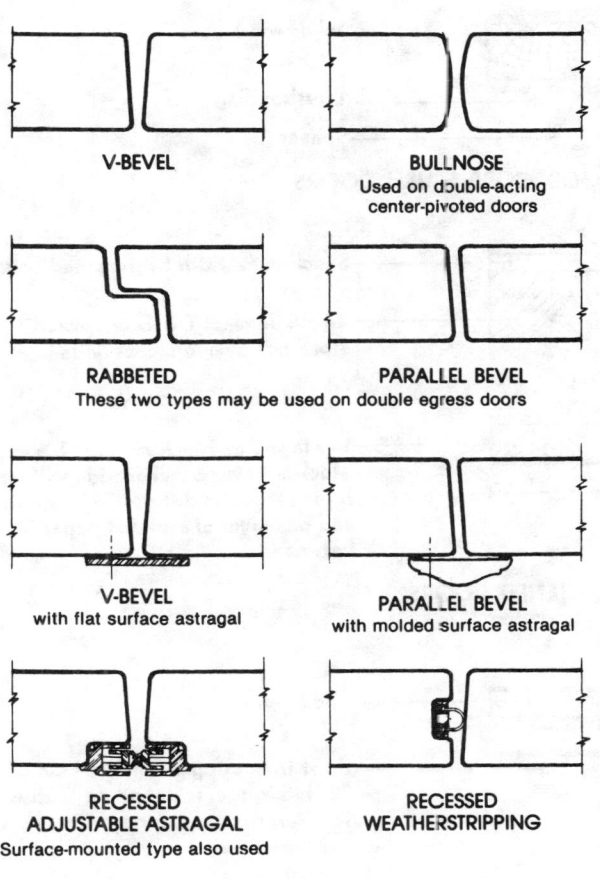

V-BEVEL

BULLNOSE
Used on double-acting
center-pivoted doors

RABBETED

PARALLEL BEVEL
These two types may be used on double egress doors

V-BEVEL
with flat surface astragal

PARALLEL BEVEL
with molded surface astragal

**RECESSED
ADJUSTABLE ASTRAGAL**
Surface-mounted type also used

**RECESSED
WEATHERSTRIPPING**

COMMON MEETING STILE EDGE PROFILES

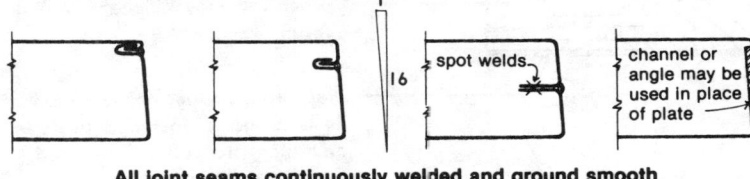

spot welds

channel or
angle may be
used in place
of plate

All joint seams continuously welded and ground smooth

STILE EDGE DETAILS — TYPE A DOORS

HARDWARE REINFORCEMENTS are provided on doors wherever
hardware is to be attached, to insure that it is firmly and securely
fastened.

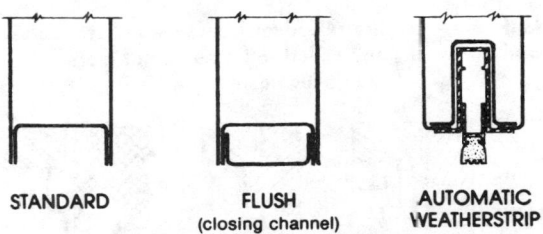

STANDARD

FLUSH
(closing channel)

**AUTOMATIC
WEATHERSTRIP**

Other designs available as required

BOTTOM EDGE DETAILS

sealed
if desired

STANDARD
Inverted channel

**FILLER
CHANNEL**

TOP EDGE DETAILS

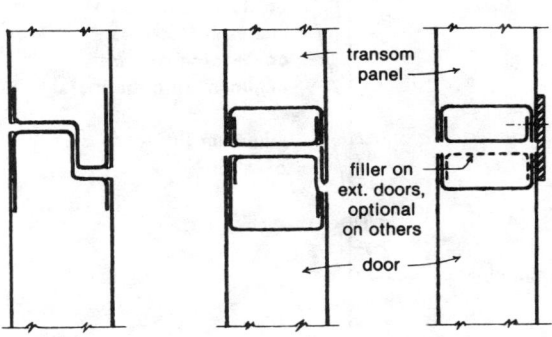

transom
panel

filler on
ext. doors,
optional
on others

door

TOP EDGE DETAILS
WITH FLUSH TRANSOM PANEL ABOVE

DOORS
Fire-Protected Wood Doors

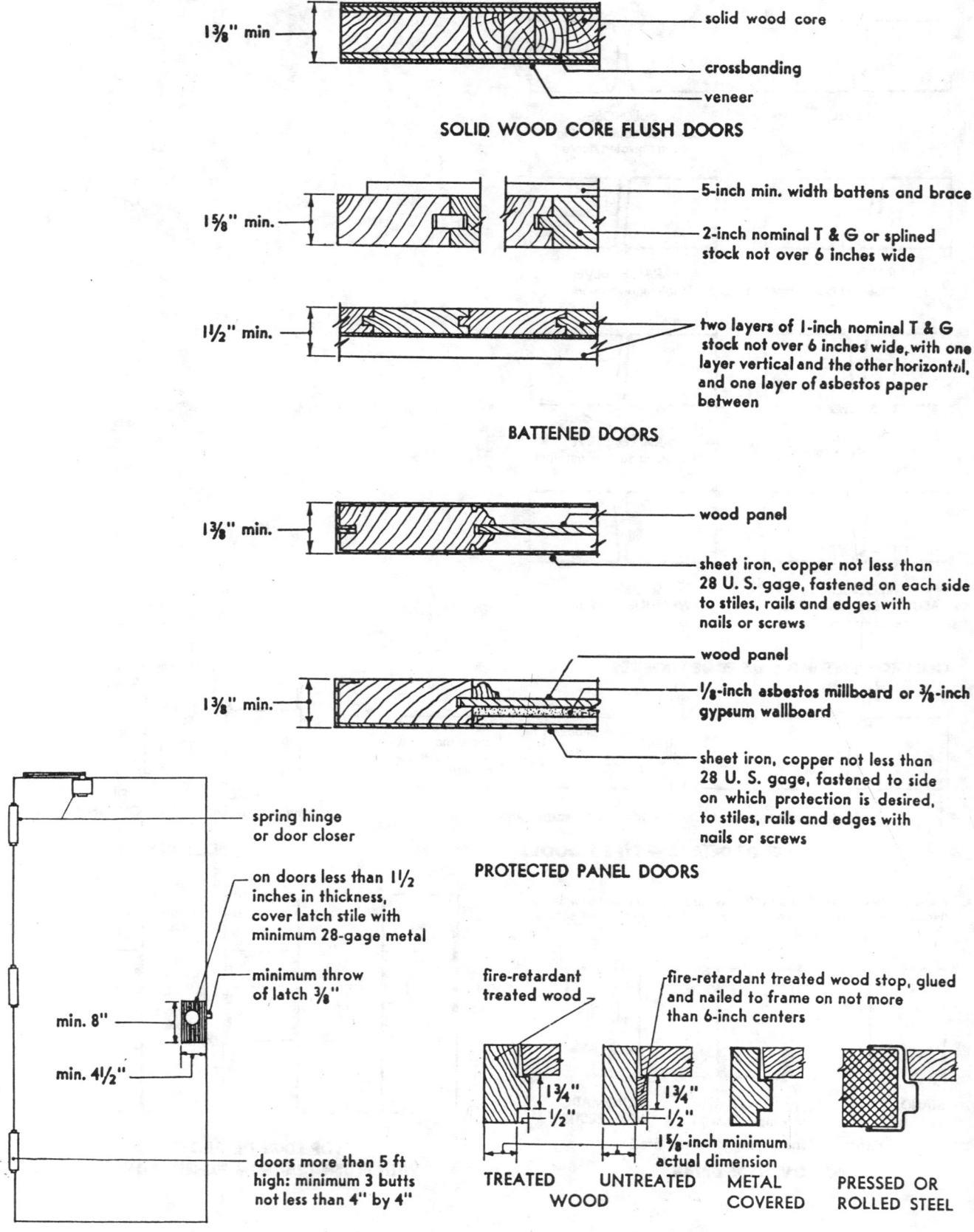

1⅜" min. — solid wood core

crossbanding

veneer

SOLID WOOD CORE FLUSH DOORS

1⅝" min. — 5-inch min. width battens and brace

2-inch nominal T & G or splined stock not over 6 inches wide

1½" min. — two layers of 1-inch nominal T & G stock not over 6 inches wide, with one layer vertical and the other horizontal, and one layer of asbestos paper between

BATTENED DOORS

1⅜" min. — wood panel

sheet iron, copper not less than 28 U. S. gage, fastened on each side to stiles, rails and edges with nails or screws

wood panel

1⅜" min. — ⅛-inch asbestos millboard or ⅜-inch gypsum wallboard

sheet iron, copper not less than 28 U. S. gage, fastened to side on which protection is desired, to stiles, rails and edges with nails or screws

PROTECTED PANEL DOORS

spring hinge or door closer

on doors less than 1½ inches in thickness, cover latch stile with minimum 28-gage metal

minimum throw of latch ⅜"

min. 8"

min. 4½"

doors more than 5 ft high: minimum 3 butts not less than 4" by 4"

fire-retardant treated wood

fire-retardant treated wood stop, glued and nailed to frame on not more than 6-inch centers

1¾"
½"

1¾"
½"

1⅝-inch minimum actual dimension

TREATED WOOD

UNTREATED WOOD

METAL COVERED

PRESSED OR ROLLED STEEL

HARDWARE

FRAMES

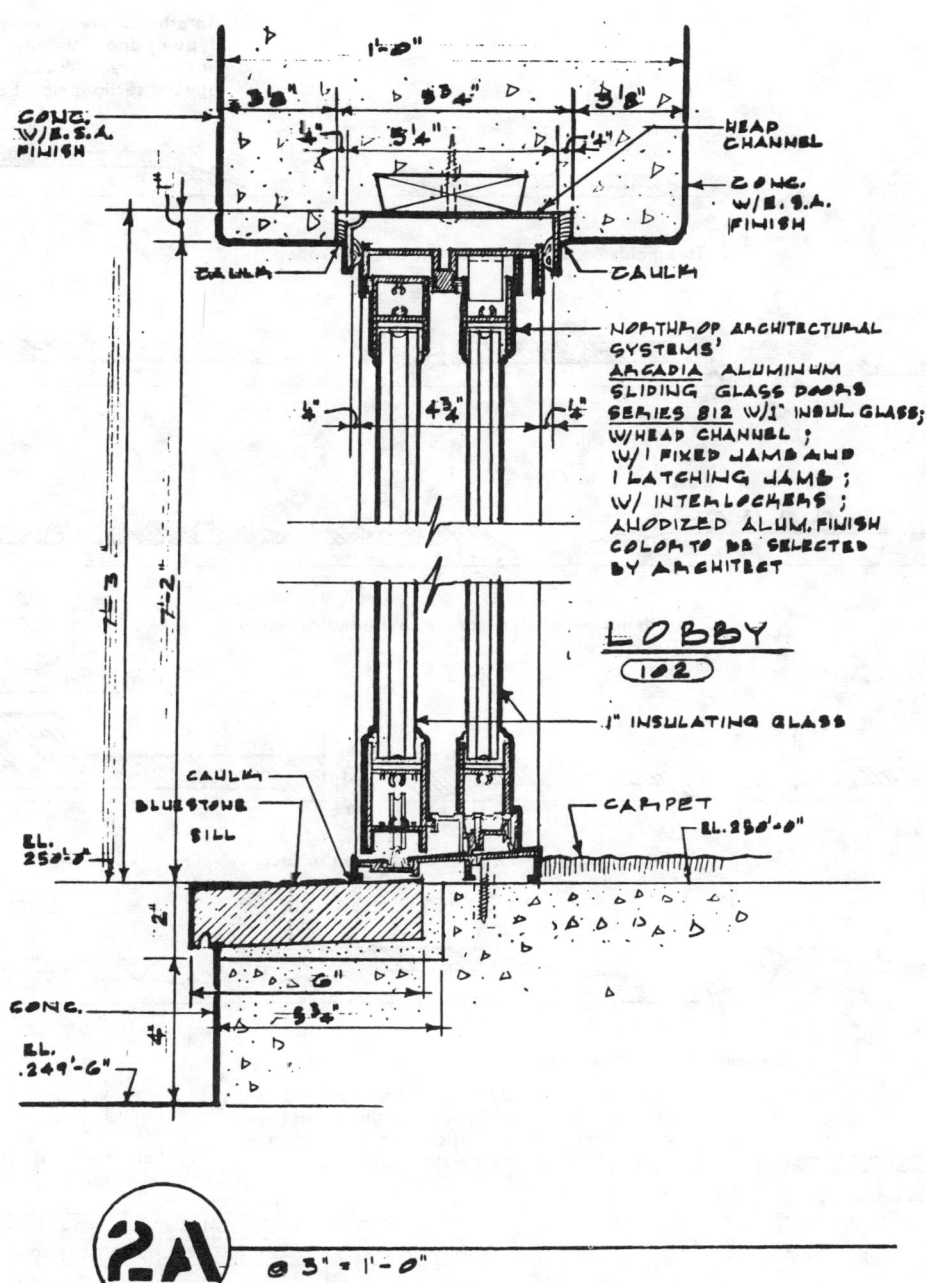

CONC. W/B.S.A. FINISH

HEAD CHANNEL

CONC. W/B.S.A. FINISH

CAULK

CAULK

NORTHROP ARCHITECTURAL SYSTEMS' ARCADIA ALUMINUM SLIDING GLASS DOORS SERIES 812 W/1" INSUL GLASS; W/HEAD CHANNEL; W/ 1 FIXED JAMB AND 1 LATCHING JAMB; W/ INTERLOCKERS; ANODIZED ALUM. FINISH COLOR TO BE SELECTED BY ARCHITECT

LOBBY
(102)

1" INSULATING GLASS

CAULK

BLUESTONE SILL

CARPET

EL. 250'-0"

EL. 250'-8"

CONC.

EL. 249'-6"

2A   @ 3" = 1'-0"

601

DOORS

Thresholds

Thresholds are essential for nearly every type of door. Usually a standard section is satisfactory. Where conditions require, special sections may be designed.

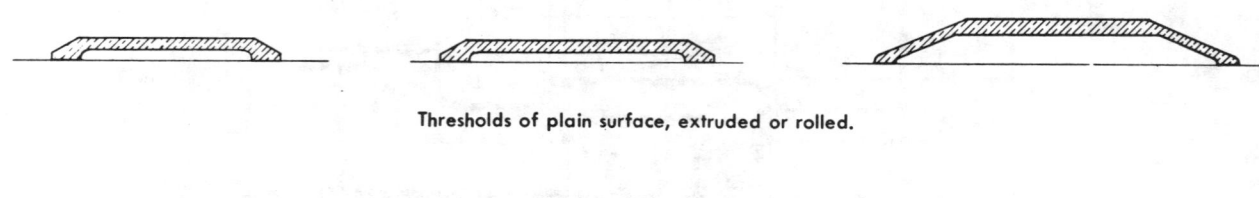

Thresholds of plain surface, extruded or rolled.

Thresholds with fluted surface, extruded or rolled.

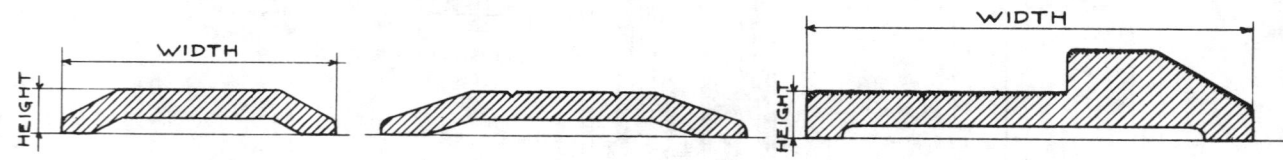

Thresholds cast with plain or abrasive surface.

Thresholds for weather strips.

Holes for fastening not to exceed 12″ o.c. for threshold less than 3″ wide. For thresholds over 3″ fastenings should not exceed 15″ o.c. On wide sills holes may be staggered.

Threshold fastened with screws tapped to steel angle set in floor construction.

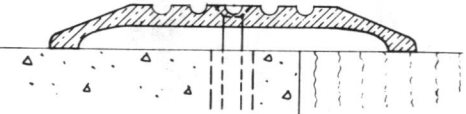

Threshold fastened to wood with wood screws.

Threshold fastened with screw in fibre plug or expansive metal anchor. Floor may be cement, terrazzo or similar construction.

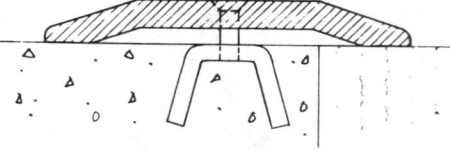

Threshold fastened with screws tapped to clips set in cement.

THRESHOLD SIZES AND METAL								
FIG.	WIDTH	HEIGHT	CAST	STEEL	BRASS	BRONZE	ALUMINUM	NICKEL SILVER
14	2½″	¼″		○	○	○	○	
15	3″	¼″		○	○	○	○	○
16	4″	½″		○	○	○	○	
17	3″	5/16″		○	○	○	○	
18	4″	½″		○	○	○	○	
19	5″	½″		○	○	○	○	
20	6″	5/8″			○	○	○	
21	7½″	½″					○	
22	3″	½″	○					
23	4″	½″	○					
24	5″	½″	○					
25	4 3/16″	5/8″			○	○	○	
26	4″ 5″ 6″	5/8″	○					

Cast metal may be iron, aluminum, bronze, or nickel silver, with or without abrasive surface.

These thresholds are representative of a great many sections produced in various metals, widths, heights, and types of surface. For other sections refer to manufacturers' catalogs.

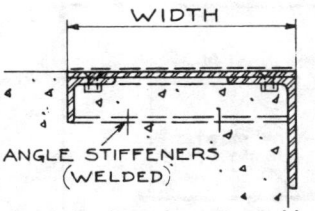

Steel loading door threshold anchored to concrete

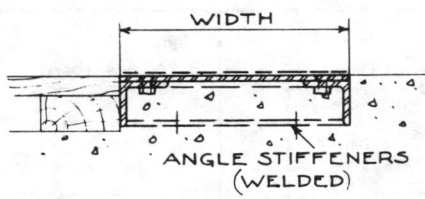

Steel shipping door threshold anchored to concrete

Steel shipping door threshold screwed to floor

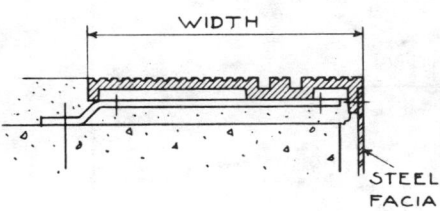

Elevator door threshold for double doors cast with grooves. Surface may be abrasive or plain of cast iron, aluminum or bronze.

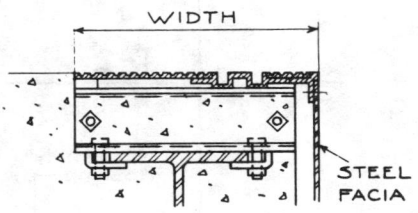

Elevator door threshold for double doors of rolled sections, steel, bronze or aluminum.

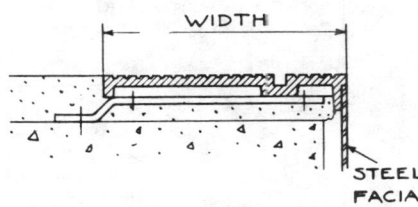

Elevator door threshold for single doors cast with grooves. Surface may be abrasive or plain of cast iron, aluminum or bronze.

Thresholds with concealed steel anchors are usually fastened to anchors with flat head machine screws, the anchors independently fastened to the floor construction.

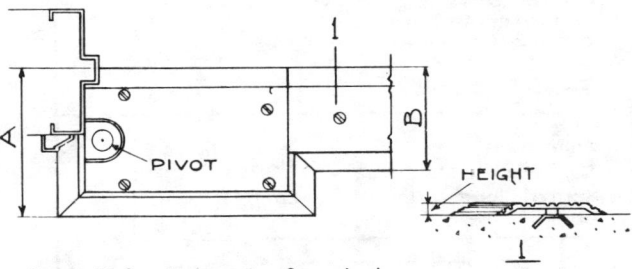

Threshold for single acting floor check.

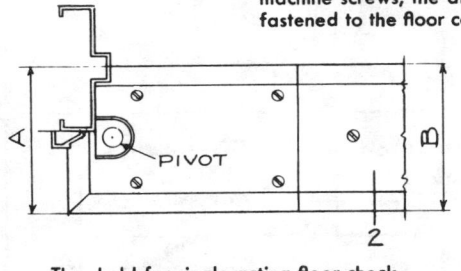

Threshold for single acting floor check.

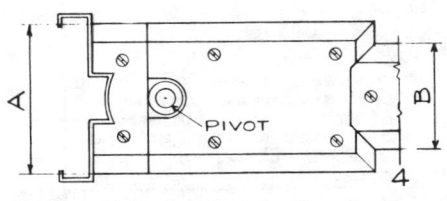

Threshold for double acting floor check.

SCALE 1½"=1'-0"

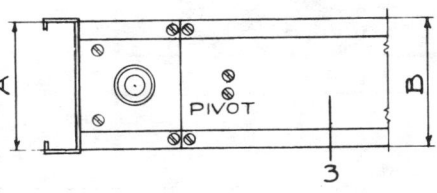

Threshold for double acting floor check.

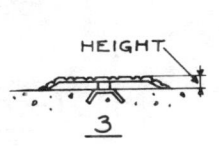

Thresholds for floor checks may be obtained in the same metals and sections as standard thresholds or may be designed to fit special conditions.

All thresholds fitted to floor checks must be designed with removable cover plate.

Screw spacing must fit floor check.

Dimension "A" is determined by type of floor check, usually 5¾", 6¾" or 7¾".

Dimension "B" may be same as "A" or less as specified.

SPECIFY:
Type, location
Width, length
Metal and finish
Show detail of
special requirements

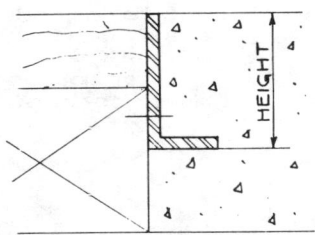

Joint strips, also called dividing strips or division bars, used for separation of floors of different materials, may be of steel or non-ferrous metals. They may be of angles or other sections with anchors attached, or of a patented design.

SCALE ½"=1"

Terrazzo strips for design or pattern work in terrazzo floors are not considered architectural metal.

DOORS

Thresholds and Edging Strips

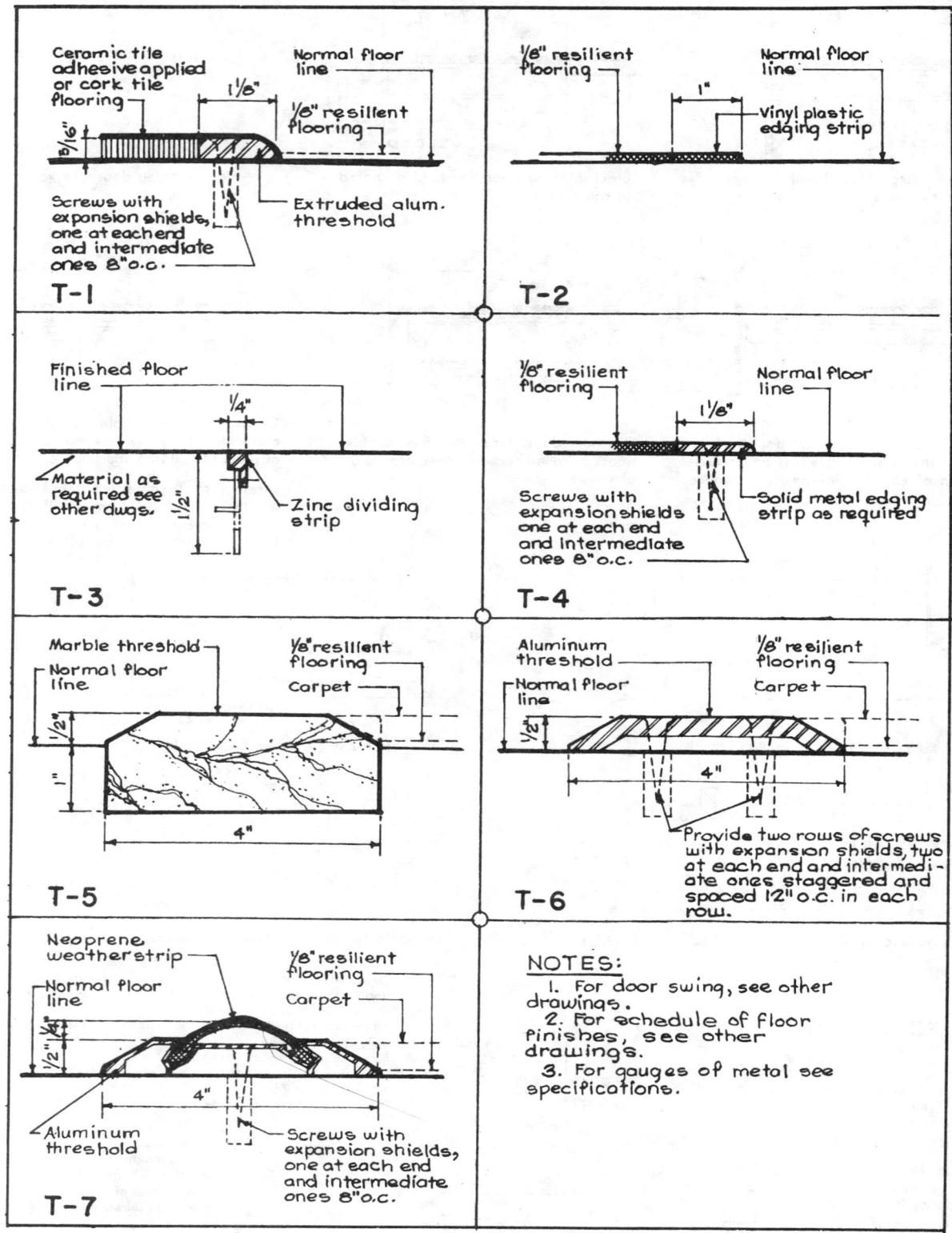

T-1
- Ceramic tile adhesive applied or cork tile flooring
- Normal floor line
- 1⅛"
- ⅛" resilient flooring
- 5/16"
- Screws with expansion shields, one at each end and intermediate ones 8" o.c.
- Extruded alum. threshold

T-2
- ⅛" resilient flooring
- Normal floor line
- 1"
- Vinyl plastic edging strip

T-3
- Finished floor line
- ¼"
- Material as required see other dwgs.
- 1½"
- Zinc dividing strip

T-4
- ⅛" resilient flooring
- Normal floor line
- 1⅛"
- Screws with expansion shields one at each end and intermediate ones 8" o.c.
- Solid metal edging strip as required

T-5
- Marble threshold
- ⅛" resilient flooring
- Normal floor line
- Carpet
- ½"
- 1"
- 4"

T-6
- Aluminum threshold
- ⅛" resilient flooring
- Normal floor line
- Carpet
- ½"
- 4"
- Provide two rows of screws with expansion shields, two at each end and intermediate ones staggered and spaced 12" o.c. in each row.

T-7
- Neoprene weatherstrip
- ⅛" resilient flooring
- Normal floor line
- Carpet
- ½"
- 4"
- Aluminum threshold
- Screws with expansion shields, one at each end and intermediate ones 8" o.c.

NOTES:
1. For door swing, see other drawings.
2. For schedule of floor finishes, see other drawings.
3. For gauges of metal see specifications.

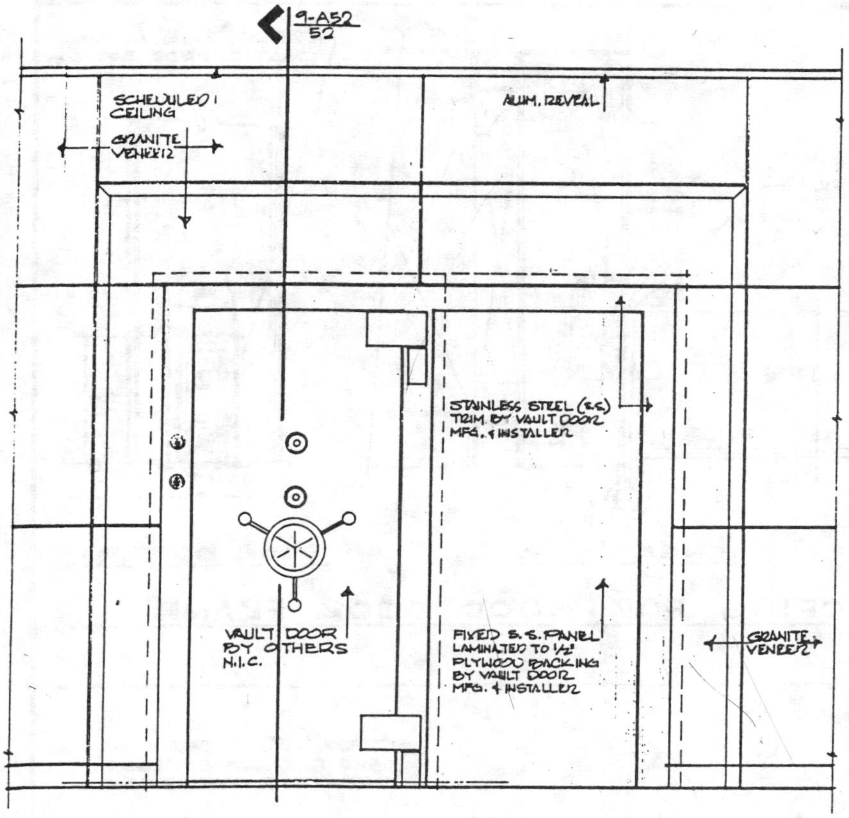

8-A52 ELEVATION

SCHEDULED CEILING

GRANITE VENEER

ALUM. REVEAL

STAINLESS STEEL (S.S.) TRIM BY VAULT DOOR MFG. & INSTALLER

VAULT DOOR BY OTHERS N.I.C.

FIXED S.S. PANEL LAMINATED TO 1/2" PLYWOOD BACKING BY VAULT DOOR MFG. & INSTALLER

GRANITE VENEER

A39   1/2" 1'-0"

9-A52 SECTION

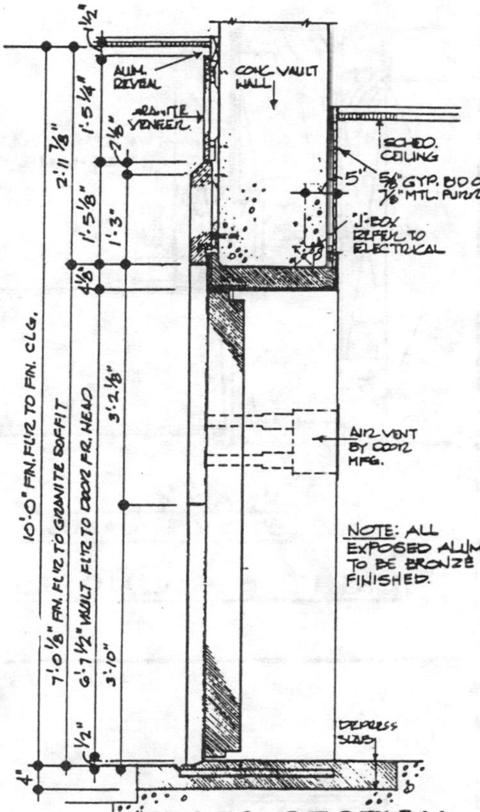

ALUM. REVEAL

CONC. VAULT WALL

GRANITE VENEER

SCHED. CEILING

5/8" GYP. BD ON 7/8" MTL. FURRING

J-BOX REFER TO ELECTRICAL

AIR VENT BY DOOR MFG.

NOTE: ALL EXPOSED ALUM. TO BE BRONZE FINISHED.

10'-0" FIN. FLR. TO FIN. CLG.
7'-0 1/2" FIN. FLR. TO GRANITE SOFFIT
6'-7 1/2" VAULT FLR. TO DOOR FR. HEAD
3'-0"

2'-11 7/8"
1'-5 1/4"
1'-5/8"
1'-3"
4/8"

1/2"
4"

DEPRESS SLAB

A52   1/2" 1'-0"

12-A52 DETAIL

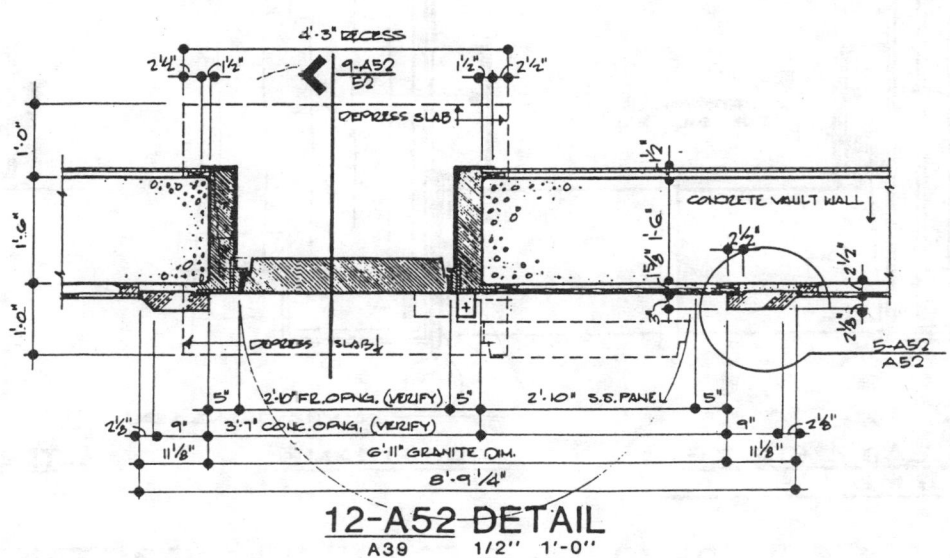

4'-3" RECESS

DEPRESS SLAB

CONCRETE VAULT WALL

1'-0"
1'-6"
1'-0"

DEPRESS SLAB

2 1/4" 6 1/2"   1 1/2" 2 1/2"

1'-6"
5/8"

2 1/2"
2 1/2"
2 5/8"
1 1/2"

5-A52
A52

5"   2'-10" FR. OPNG. (VERIFY)   5"   2'-10" S.S. PANEL   5"
2 5/8" 9"   3'-7" CONC. OPNG. (VERIFY)   9" 2 5/8"
11 5/8"   6'-11" GRANITE DIM.   11 5/8"
8'-9 1/4"

A39   1/2" 1'-0"

DOORS

Light- and Soundproofing of Wood and Hollow Metal Door Frames

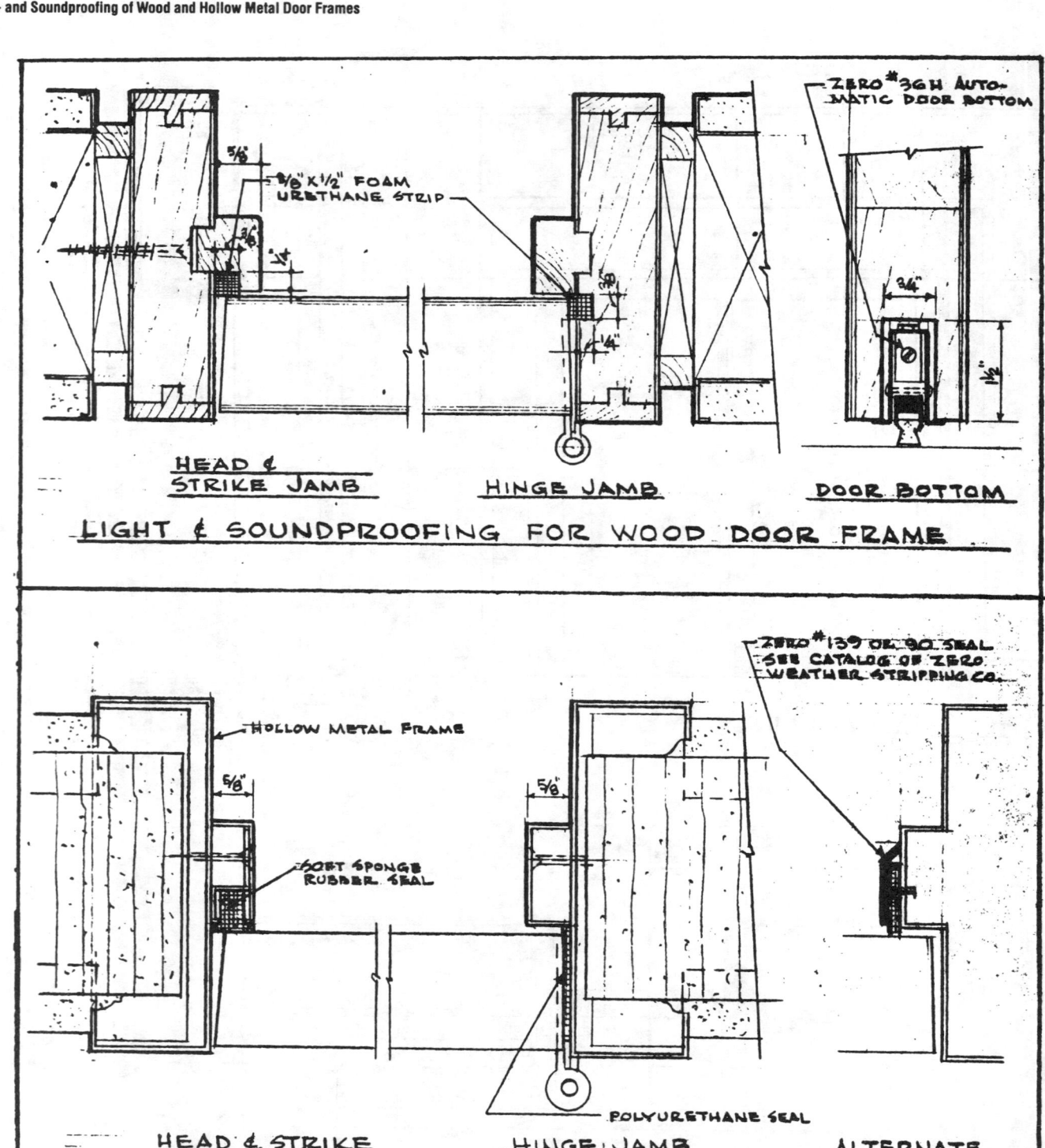

5/8"

3/8" X 1/2" FOAM
URETHANE STRIP

ZERO #36H AUTO-
MATIC DOOR BOTTOM

3/4"

**HEAD &
STRIKE JAMB**   **HINGE JAMB**   **DOOR BOTTOM**

LIGHT & SOUNDPROOFING FOR WOOD DOOR FRAME

HOLLOW METAL FRAME

5/8"

5/8"

SOFT SPONGE
RUBBER SEAL

ZERO #139 OR 90 SEAL
SEE CATALOG OF ZERO
WEATHER STRIPPING CO.

POLYURETHANE SEAL

**HEAD & STRIKE
JAMB**   **HINGE JAMB**   **ALTERNATE**

LIGHT & SOUNDPROOFING FOR HOLLOW METAL FRAME

NOTE: DOOR BOTTOM SIMILAR TO WOOD DOOR ABOVE
FOR SURFACE MOUNTED AUTOMATIC DOOR BOTTOM
USE ZERO #36S

The prime functions of the door frame are to hold the door and its controls in the opening, and to trim the opening. But frames often serve other esthetic or functional purposes also, such as trimming a wall opening having no door, or enclosing glazed areas that provide through-wall visibility or admitting light and/or air. Hollow metal frames, which are strong, sturdy, and durable, serve all such functions economically.

The variety of configurations available in custom hollow metal frames is virtually unlimited. Illustrated in Fig. 16 are some of the more common and representative types.

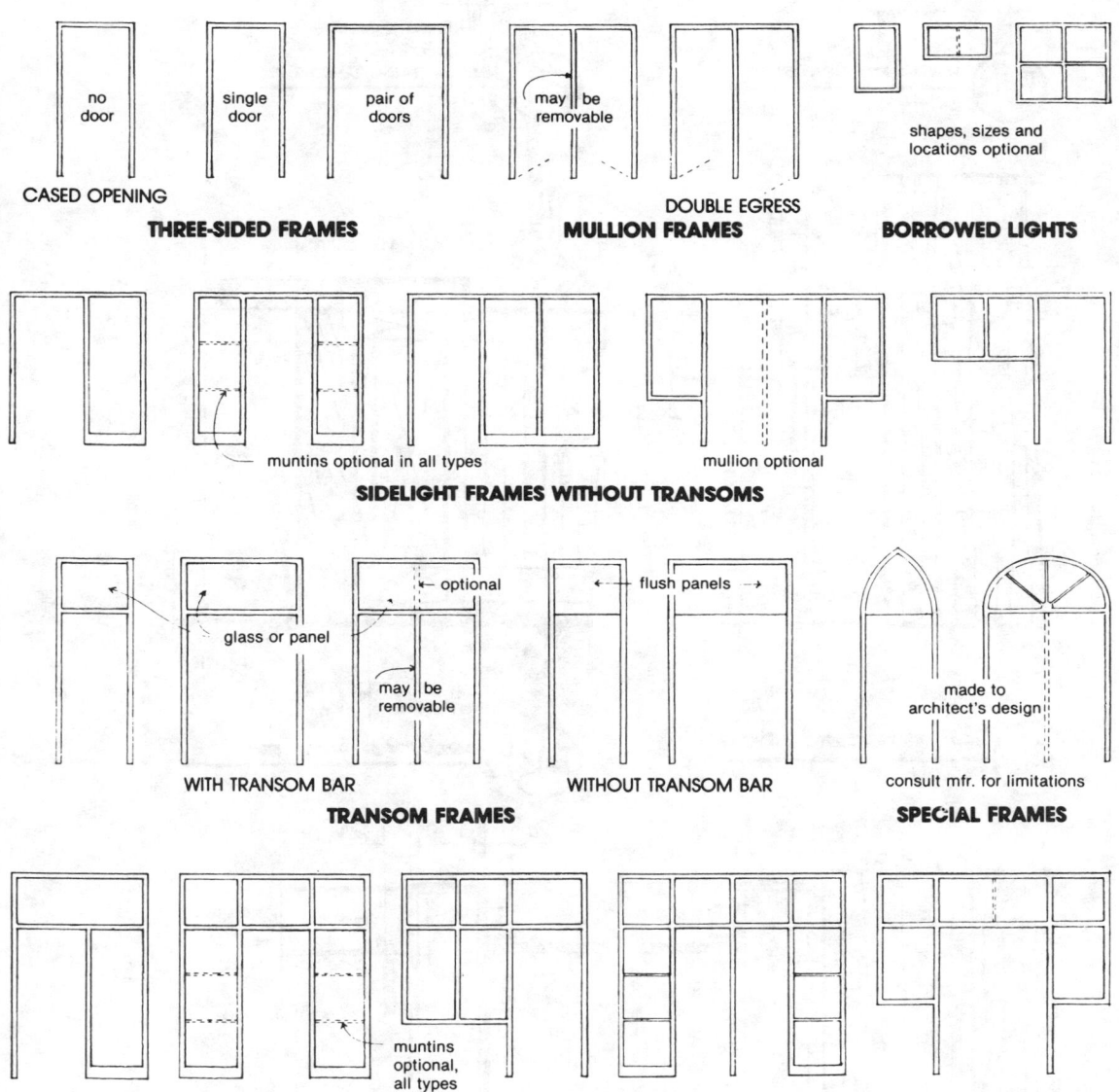

Fig. 16

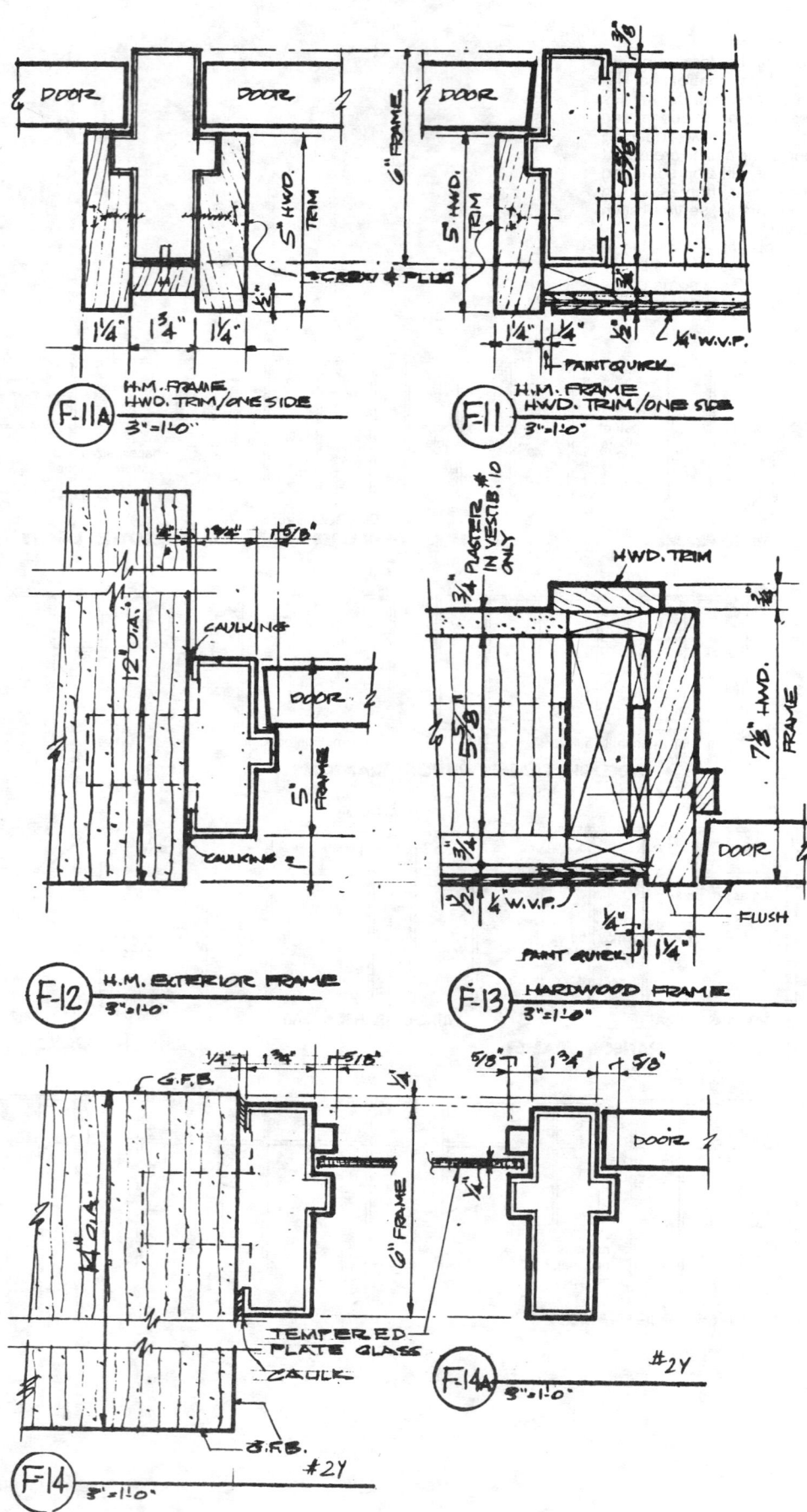

F-11A — H.M. FRAME HWD. TRIM/ONE SIDE — 3"=1'-0"

F-11 — H.M. FRAME HWD. TRIM/ONE SIDE — 3"=1'-0"

F-12 — H.M. EXTERIOR FRAME — 3"=1'-0"

F-13 — HARDWOOD FRAME — 3"=1'-0"

F-14 — 3"=1'-0"   #24

F-14A — 3"=1'-0"   #24

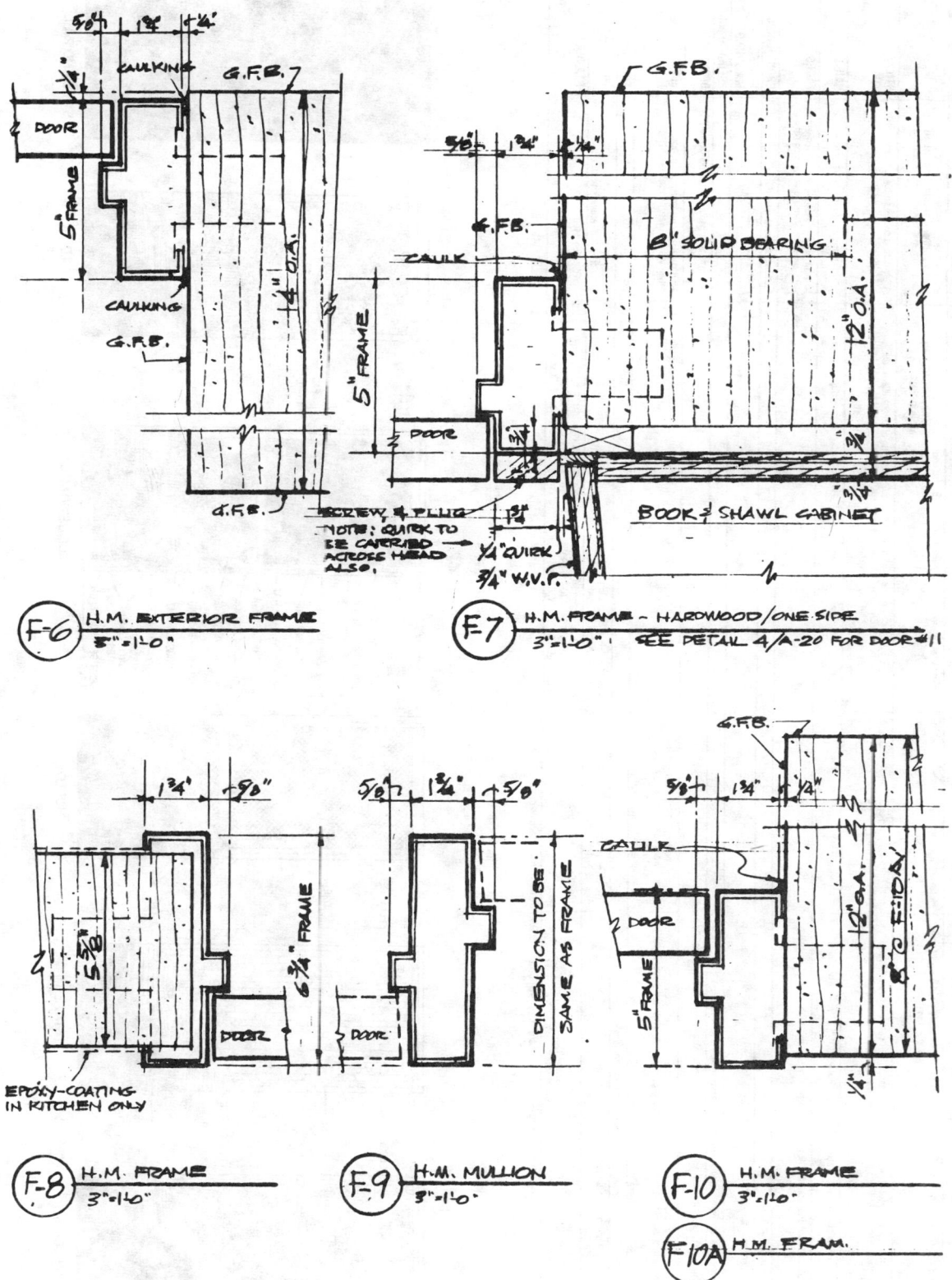

F-6 H.M. EXTERIOR FRAME 3"=1'-0"

F-7 H.M. FRAME - HARDWOOD/ONE SIDE 3"=1'-0" SEE DETAIL 4/A-20 FOR DOOR #11

F-8 H.M. FRAME 3"=1'-0"

F-9 H.M. MULLION 3"=1'-0"

F-10 H.M. FRAME 3"=1'-0"

F-10A H.M. FRAM.

DOORS

Door Types and Construction

	PARTICLE	STAVE	HOLLOW	ACOUSTICAL** STC 31′, 36′, 38′, & 40′	LEAD	STILE AND RAIL	
THICKNESS	1 3/8″, 1 3/4″	1 3/8″, 1 3/4″, 2 1/4″	1 3/8″, 1 3/4″	1 3/4″	1 3/4″ — lead thickness to 3/8″.	1 3/4″, 2 1/4″	THICKNESS
MAX. SIZE	4′ 0″ x 12′ 0″	4′ 0″ x 12′ 0″	4′ 0″ x 12′ 0″	4′ 0″ x 10′ 0″	4′ 0″ x 10′ 0″	4′ 0″ x 12′ 0″	MAX. SIZE
CORE	Mat-formed particle board conforming to ANSI A208.1-1L1.	(21-27 pcf) Low density wood blocks bonded together. One species per core.	Resin impregnated honeycomb — 1/2″ cell.	Special materials and assembly to meet ratings shown.	Divided core. Mat-formed particle board conforming to ANSI A208.1-1M3. Lead over 1/8″ reinforced with lead plugs.	Stiles and rails: Low density wood blocks bonded together & to edgebands. Panels: Mill option, mat-formed particle board or edge-glued lumber core.	CORE
STILES	1 3/8″ face matching or compatible to face veneer, mill option inner-ply. Glued to core. Maximum 5″.	5/8″ matching or compatible to face veneer. Glued to core.	1 1/8″ 2 ply. Matching or compatible to face veneer, mill option inner-ply.	STC 31 — Stave 5/8″, particle 1 3/8″ matching or compatible to face veneer. Glued to core. STC 36, 38, 40 — 2″. Face compatible outer-ply. Glued to core.	1 1/2″ matching or compatible to face veneer. Glued to core.	5/8″ Matching or compatible to face veneer. Glued to stile.	STILES
RAILS	1 3/8″ mill option hardwood glued to core standard. Nominal 2 1/2″, 5″, 8″ and 12″ optional.		2 1/4″ mill option hardwood.	STC 31 — 1 1/8″ mill option hardwood glued to core. STC 36, 38, 40 — 3″.	2 1/2″ mill option hardwood glued to core.	1/2″ edgeband compatible to face veneer. Glued to rail.	RAILS
FACES	All available domestic and foreign veneers. Medium density overlays. High pressure laminates.					All available 1/10″ sliced hardwood veneers on stiles and rails. Standard veneers on panel faces.	FACES
CROSSBANDS	Min. 1/16″ hardwood.					1/30″ mill option hardwood.	CROSSBANDS
VENEER MATCHING	Virtually unlimited in standard veneers, end matching in door and transoms with wood grain plastics.					Limited veneer matching.	VENEER MATCHING
PREMACHINING	Prefitting, mortise for appropriate hardware. No preparation for surface mounted.						PREMACHINING
OPENINGS	Min. 5″ margins edge of door and adjacent hardware cut-outs. Max. opening 40% of door area or 50% of height.					Min. 5″ stiles, minimum 10″ bottom rail, min. 5″ top rail.	OPENINGS
SPECIAL DETAILS	Cut light openings* Install metal and wood louvers, wood beads, and safety glazing. Standard beads or architect's detail at light and louver openings. Applied mouldings. Dutch doors and shelves.		Cut light openings* Install metal and wood louvers, wood beads, and safety glazing. Standard beads or architect's detail at light and louver openings.	Cut light openings* Safety glazing. Standard wood, acoustical and lead lined beads. No applied mouldings. No dutch doors.		Solid sticking or moulding per architect's detail. Wood louvers and safety glazing factory installed.	SPECIAL DETAILS
FINISHING	Gardall II, primed, painted, sealed, oiled or waxed as specified.						FINISHING
WARRANTY	Interior — Life of original installation. Exterior — 2 years.		Interior — 1 year. Exterior — Not recommended.	Interior — Life of original installation. Exterior — Not recommended.		Interior — 2 years. Exterior — Not recommended.	WARRANTY
STANDARDS	NWWDA I.S.-1 AWI Section 1300 PC Federal LLLD581 Type I & II, Class 1	NWWDA I.S.-1 AWI Section 1300 SLC Federal LLLD581 Type I & II, Class1	NWWDA I.S.-1	NWWDA I.S.-1 AWI Section 1300 SR — ASTM E90-70 Federal LLLD581 Type IV, Class 4	NWWDA I.S.-1 AWI-1300-LL and E413-73 Federal LLLD581, Type IV, Class 5	AWI Section 1400 Federal LLLD581, Type III	STANDARDS

*Footnote on openings — Minimum margins per AWI Section 1300. **No rating guaranteed on doors with lites or pairs.

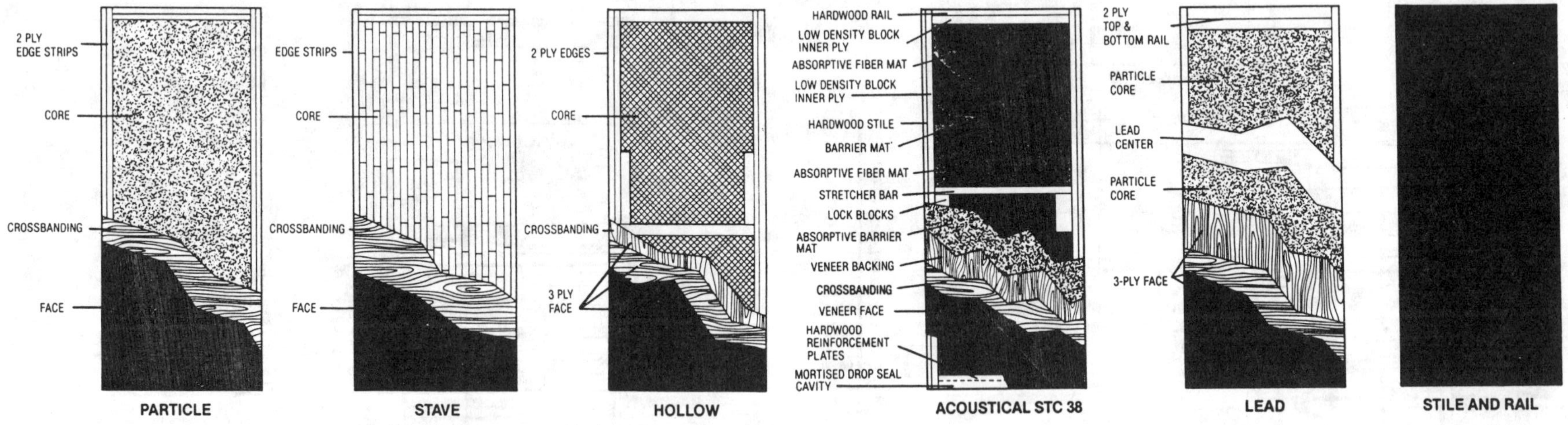
2 PLY EDGE STRIPS
CORE
CROSSBANDING
FACE
PARTICLE
EDGE STRIPS
CORE
CROSSBANDING
FACE
STAVE
2 PLY EDGES
CORE
CROSSBANDING
3 PLY FACE
HOLLOW
HARDWOOD RAIL
LOW DENSITY BLOCK INNER PLY
ABSORPTIVE FIBER MAT
LOW DENSITY BLOCK INNER PLY
HARDWOOD STILE
BARRIER MAT
ABSORPTIVE FIBER MAT
STRETCHER BAR
LOCK BLOCKS
ABSORPTIVE BARRIER MAT
VENEER BACKING
CROSSBANDING
VENEER FACE
HARDWOOD REINFORCEMENT PLATES
MORTISED DROP SEAL CAVITY
ACOUSTICAL STC 38
2 PLY TOP & BOTTOM RAIL
PARTICLE CORE
LEAD CENTER
PARTICLE CORE
3-PLY FACE
LEAD
STILE AND RAIL

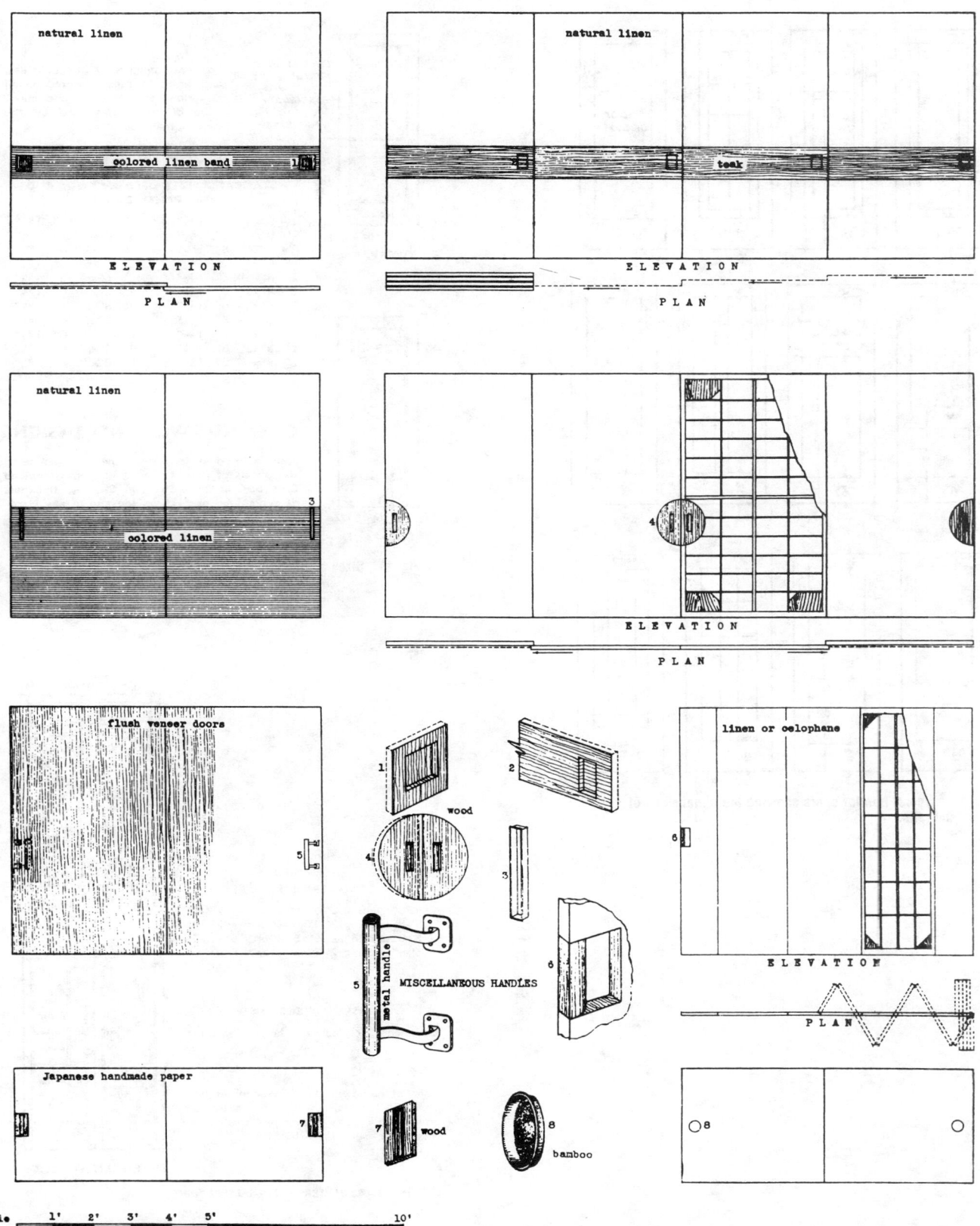

natural linen

colored linen band   1

E L E V A T I O N

P L A N

natural linen

teak

E L E V A T I O N

P L A N

natural linen

colored linen   3

E L E V A T I O N

P L A N

4

E L E V A T I O N

P L A N

flush veneer doors

5

1

2

wood

4

3

5 metal handle

MISCELLANEOUS HANDLES

6

linen or celophane

6

E L E V A T I O N

P L A N

Japanese handmade paper

7

7 wood

8

bamboo

8

scale   1'   2'   3'   4'   5'   10'

DOORS

Door Types

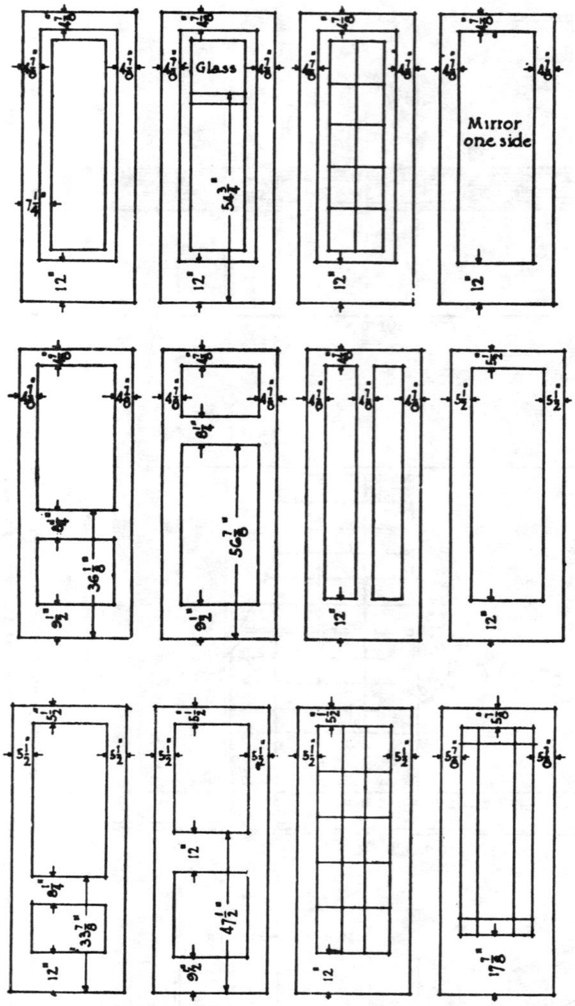
Glass
Mirror one side

Fig. 17 Typical interior doors showing the dimensions of stiles and rails.

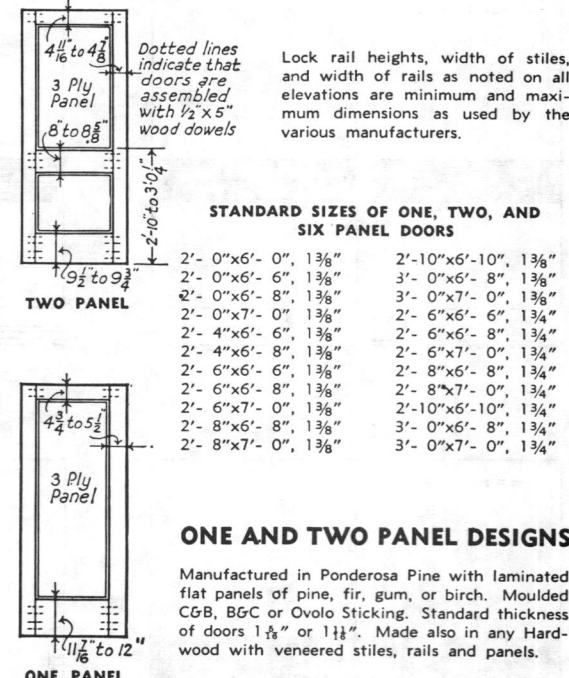

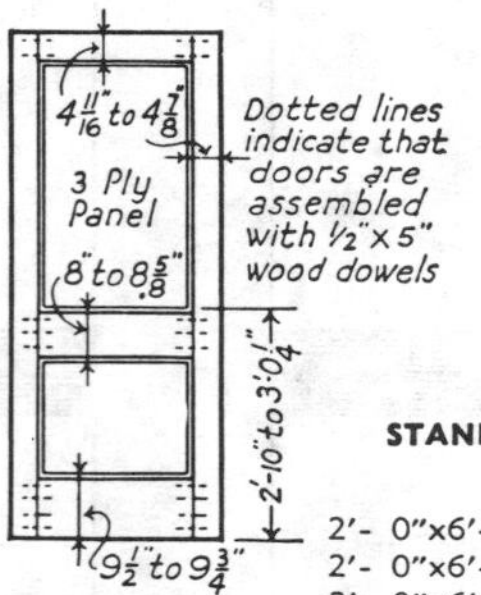
4 11/16" to 4 7/8"
3 Ply Panel
8" to 8 5/8"
Dotted lines indicate that doors are assembled with 1/2"x5" wood dowels
2'-10" to 3'-0 1/4"
9 1/2" to 9 3/4"

TWO PANEL

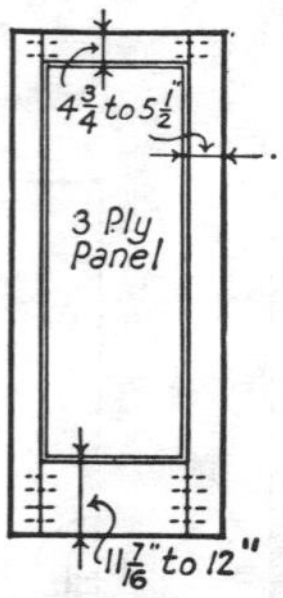
4 3/4 to 5 1/2
3 Ply Panel
11 7/16" to 12"

ONE PANEL

Lock rail heights, width of stiles, and width of rails as noted on all elevations are minimum and maximum dimensions as used by the various manufacturers.

STANDARD SIZES OF ONE, TWO, AND SIX PANEL DOORS

2'- 0"x6'- 0", 1 3/8"	2'-10"x6'-10", 1 3/8"
2'- 0"x6'- 6", 1 3/8"	3'- 0"x6'- 8", 1 3/8"
2'- 0"x6'- 8", 1 3/8"	3'- 0"x7'- 0", 1 3/8"
2'- 0"x7'- 0" 1 3/8"	2'- 6"x6'- 6", 1 3/4"
2'- 4"x6'- 6", 1 3/8"	2'- 6"x6'- 8", 1 3/4"
2'- 4"x6'- 8", 1 3/8"	2'- 6"x7'- 0", 1 3/4"
2'- 6"x6'- 6", 1 3/8"	2'- 8"x6'- 8", 1 3/4"
2'- 6"x6'- 8", 1 3/8"	2'- 8"x7'- 0", 1 3/4"
2'- 6"x7'- 0", 1 3/8"	2'-10"x6'-10", 1 3/4"
2'- 8"x6'- 8", 1 3/8"	3'- 0"x6'- 8", 1 3/4"
2'- 8"x7'- 0", 1 3/8"	3'- 0"x7'- 0", 1 3/4"

ONE AND TWO PANEL DESIGNS

Manufactured in Ponderosa Pine with laminated flat panels of pine, fir, gum, or birch. Moulded C&B, B&C or Ovolo Sticking. Standard thickness of doors 1 3/8" or 1 11/16". Made also in any Hardwood with veneered stiles, rails and panels.

Fig. 18 Sizes of panelled interior doors.

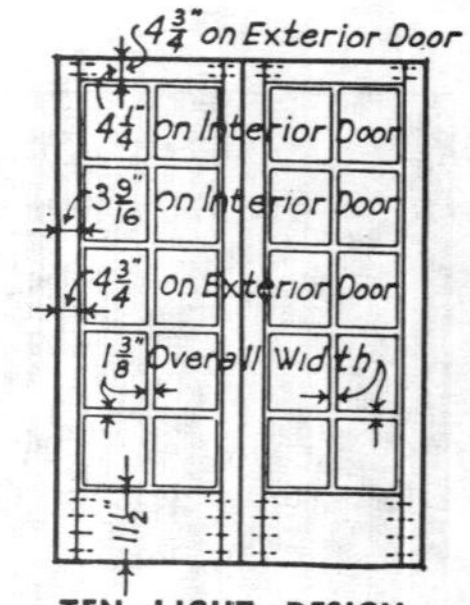
4 3/4" on Exterior Door
4 1/4" On Interior Door
3 9/16" On Interior Door
4 3/4" On Exterior Door
1 3/8" Overall Width
11 1/2

TEN LIGHT DESIGN

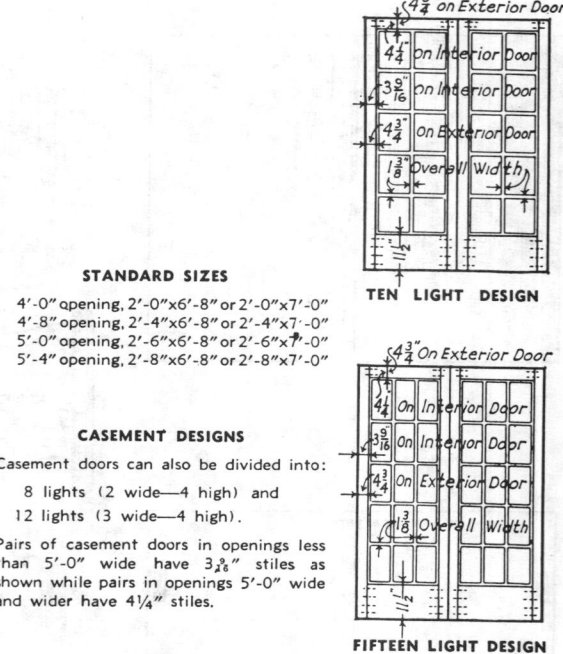

STANDARD SIZES

4'-0" opening, 2'-0"x6'-8" or 2'-0"x7'-0"
4'-8" opening, 2'-4"x6'-8" or 2'-4"x7'-0"
5'-0" opening, 2'-6"x6'-8" or 2'-6"x7'-0"
5'-4" opening, 2'-8"x6'-8" or 2'-8"x7'-0"

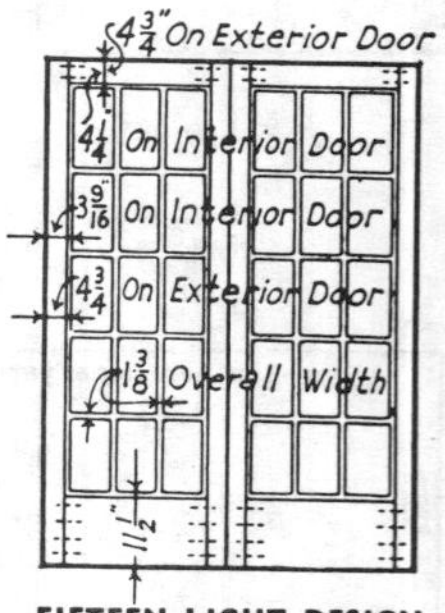
4 3/4" On Exterior Door
4 1/4 On Interior Door
3 9/16 On Interior Door
4 3/4 On Exterior Door
1 3/8 Overall Width
11 1/2

FIFTEEN LIGHT DESIGN

CASEMENT DESIGNS

Casement doors can also be divided into:

8 lights (2 wide—4 high) and

12 lights (3 wide—4 high).

Pairs of casement doors in openings less than 5'-0" wide have 3 9/16" stiles as shown while pairs in openings 5'-0" wide and wider have 4 1/4" stiles.

Fig. 19 Sizes of French or casement doors.

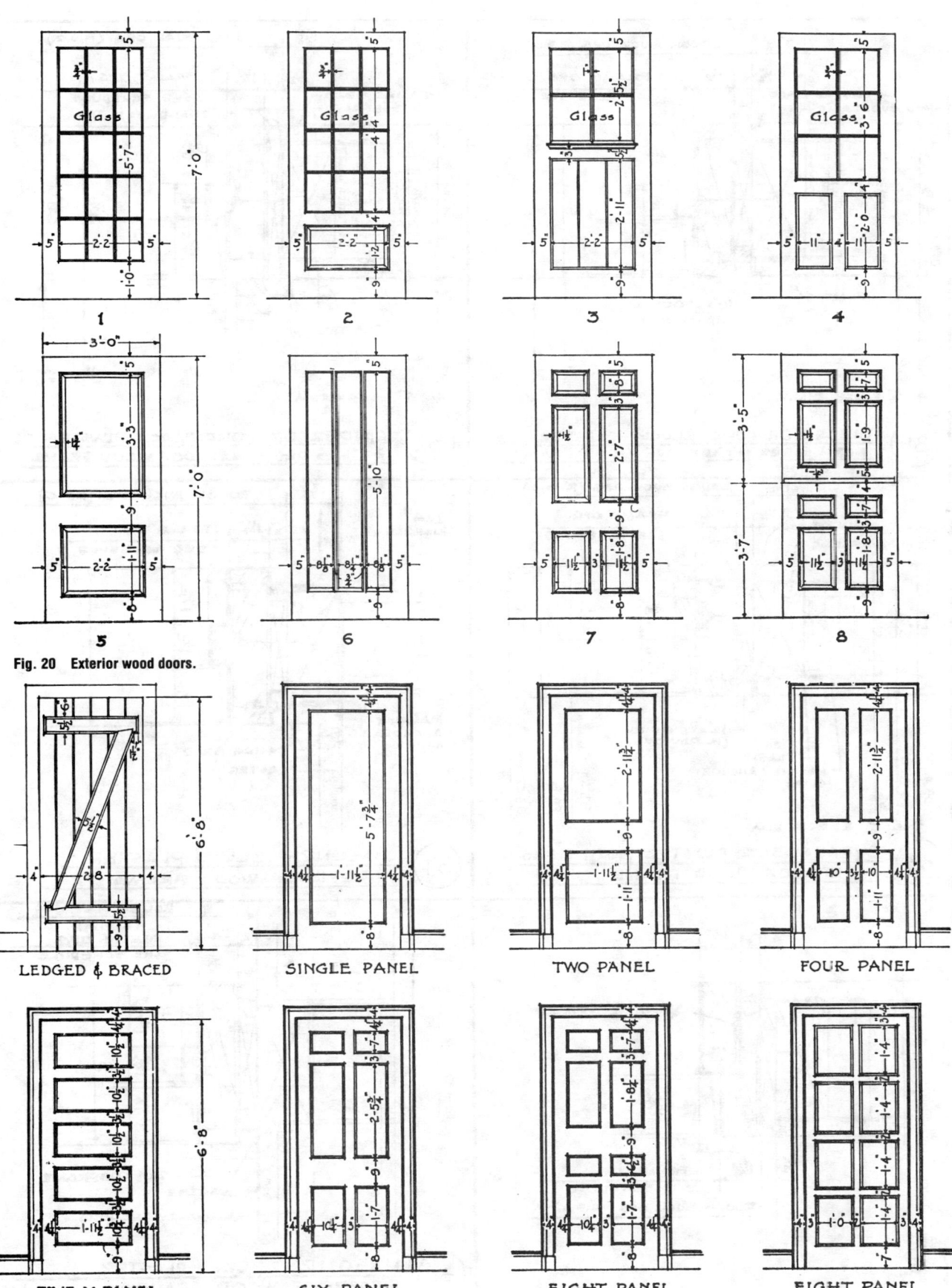

Fig. 20   Exterior wood doors.

Fig. 21   Interior wood doors.

DOORS

Wood Door Frames

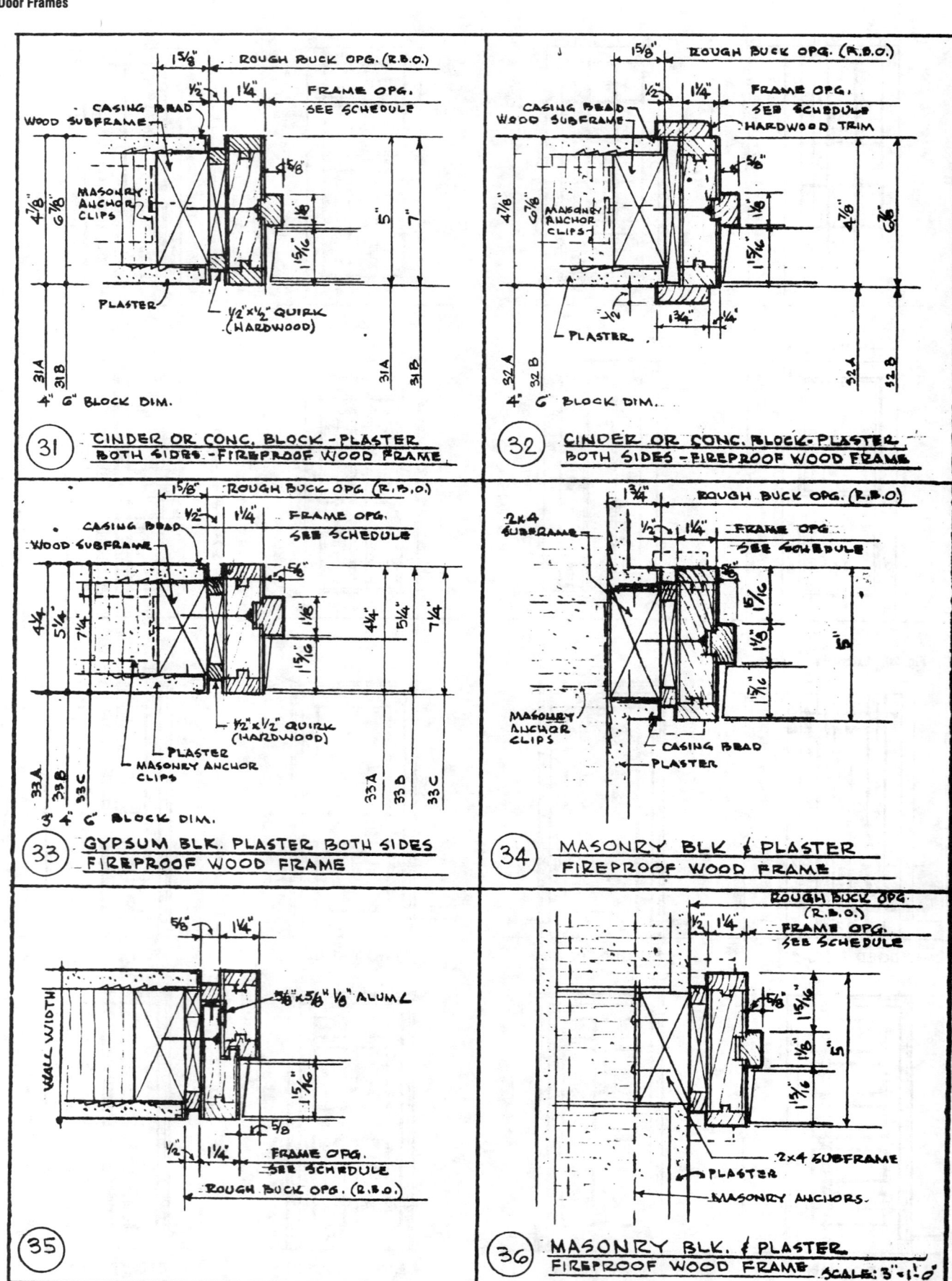

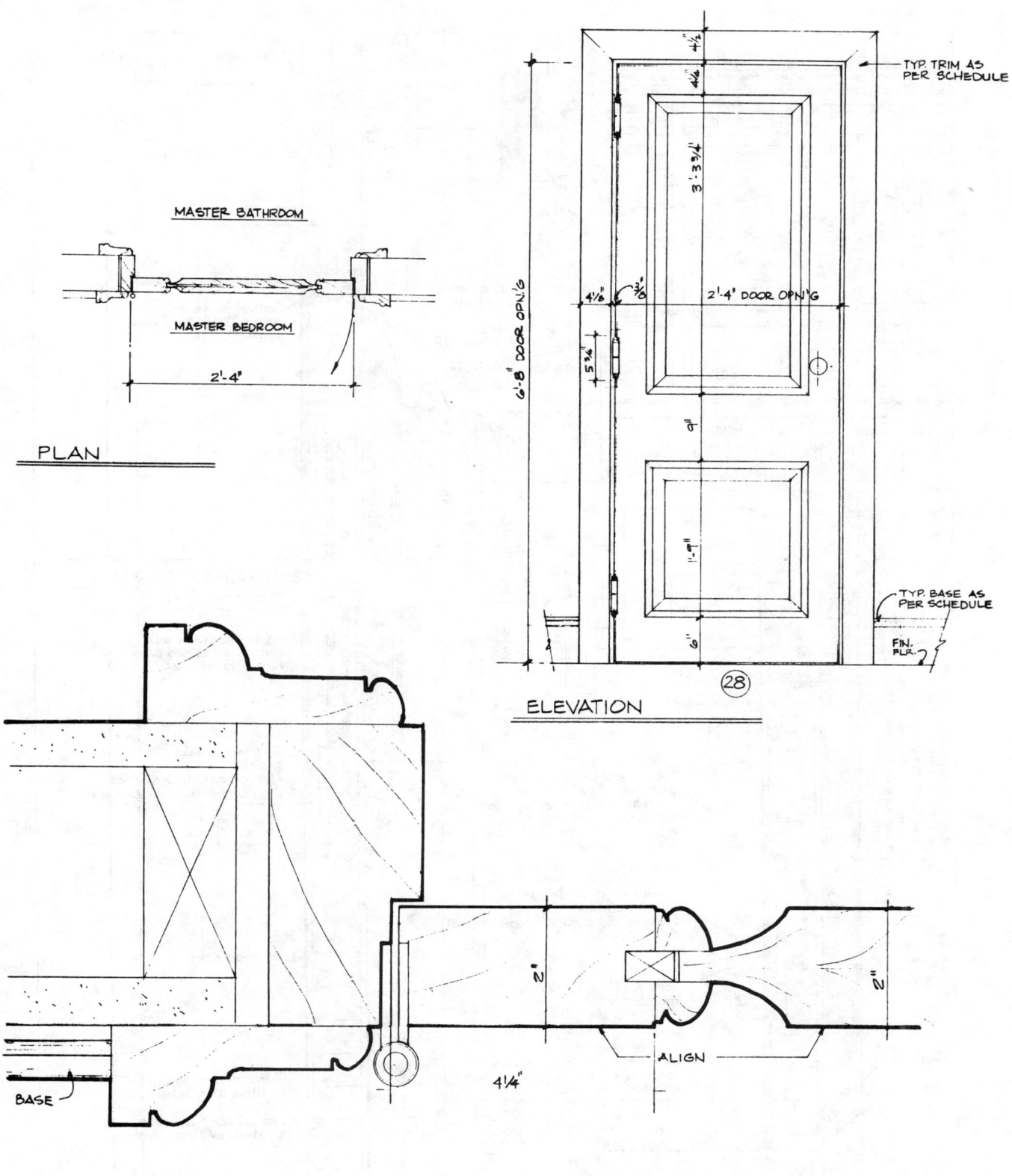

MASTER BATHROOM

MASTER BEDROOM

2'-4"

PLAN

TYP. TRIM AS PER SCHEDULE

6'-8" DOOR OPN'G

4½"

4¼"

3'-3¾"

4⅛" ⅜" 2'-4" DOOR OPN'G

5¾"

9"

1'-9"

6"

TYP. BASE AS PER SCHEDULE

FIN. FLR.

28

ELEVATION

2"

4¼"

2"

ALIGN

BASE

DETAIL @ JAMB
F.S.

DOORS

Secret Door

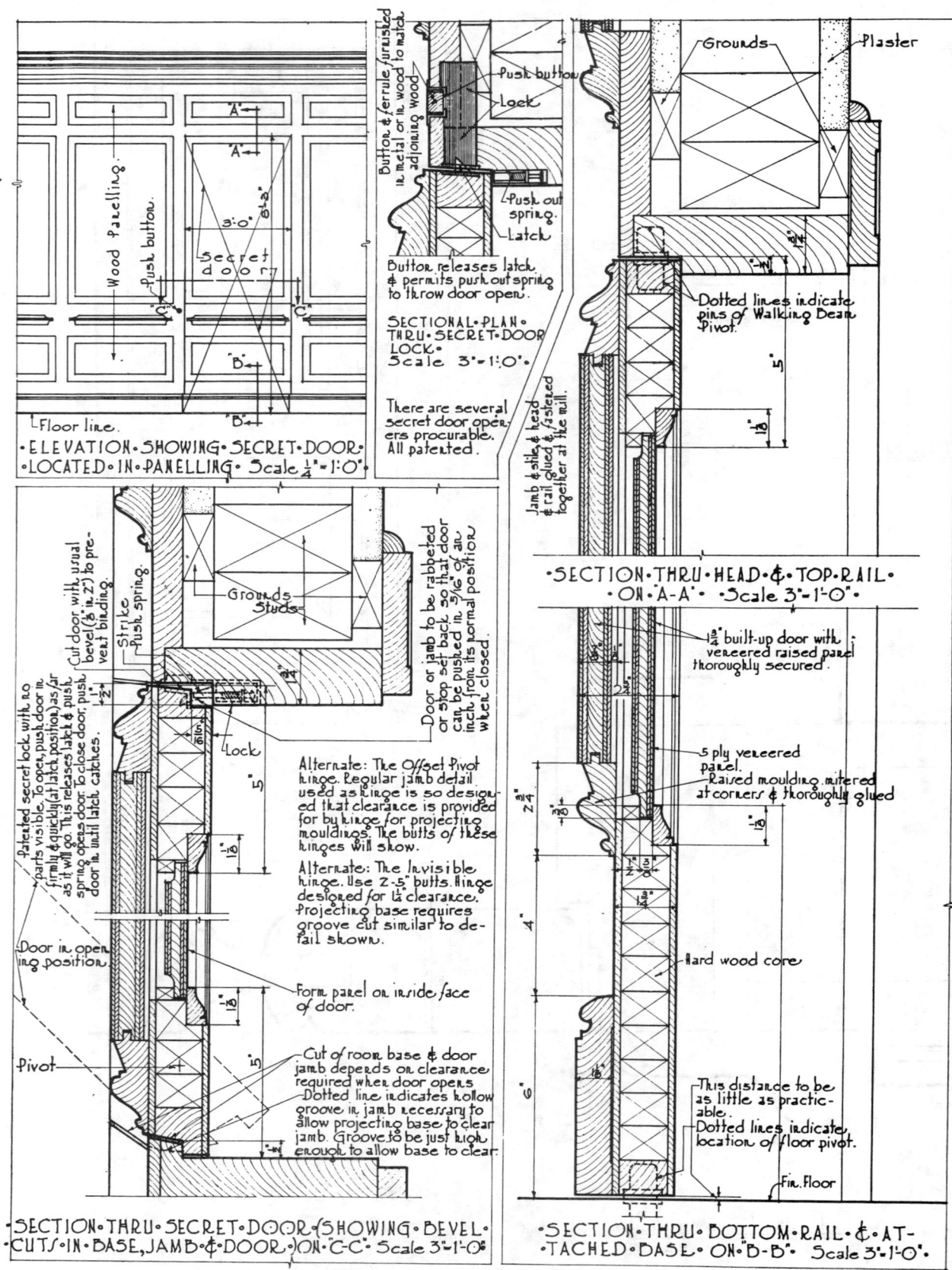

Button & ferrule furnished in metal or in wood to match adjoining wood

Push button

Lock

Push out spring.

Latch

Button releases latch & permits push out spring to throw door open.

SECTIONAL·PLAN· THRU·SECRET·DOOR· LOCK· Scale 3"=1:0"

There are several secret door openers procurable. All patented.

Grounds

Plaster

Dotted lines indicate pins of Walking Beam Pivot.

Jamb & stile, & head & rail glued & fastened together at the mill.

·SECTION·THRU·HEAD·&·TOP·RAIL· ·ON·"A-A"· Scale 3"=1-0"·

1¾" built-up door with veneered raised panel thoroughly secured.

5 ply veneered panel.

Raised moulding mitered at corners & thoroughly glued

Hard wood core

This distance to be as little as practicable. Dotted lines indicate location of floor pivot.

Fin. Floor

·SECTION·THRU·BOTTOM·RAIL·&·AT- ·TACHED·BASE·ON·"B-B"· Scale 3"=1-0"·

Wood Panelling.

Push button.

Secret door

Floor line.

·ELEVATION·SHOWING·SECRET·DOOR· ·LOCATED·IN·PANELLING· Scale ¼"=1:0"·

Grounds Studs

Cut door with usual bevel (⅛ in. 2") to prevent binding.

Strike

Push spring.

Patented secret lock with no parts visible. To open, push door in firmly & quickly (at latch position) as far as it will go. This releases latch & push spring opens door. To close door, push door in until latch catches.

Door or jamb to be rabbeted or stop set back so that door can be pushed in 5/16" of an inch from its normal position when closed.

Lock

Door in opening position.

Pivot

Alternate: The Offset Pivot hinge. Regular jamb detail used as hinge is so designed that clearance is provided for by hinge for projecting mouldings. The butts of these hinges will show.

Alternate: The Invisible hinge. Use 2-5" butts. Hinge designed for 1½" clearance. Projecting base requires groove cut similar to detail shown.

Form panel on inside face of door.

Cut of room base & door jamb depends on clearance required when door opens. Dotted line indicates hollow groove in jamb necessary to allow projecting base to clear jamb. Groove to be just high enough to allow base to clear.

·SECTION·THRU·SECRET·DOOR (SHOWING·BEVEL· ·CUTS·IN·BASE, JAMB·&·DOOR·ON·"C-C"· Scale 3"=1-0"·

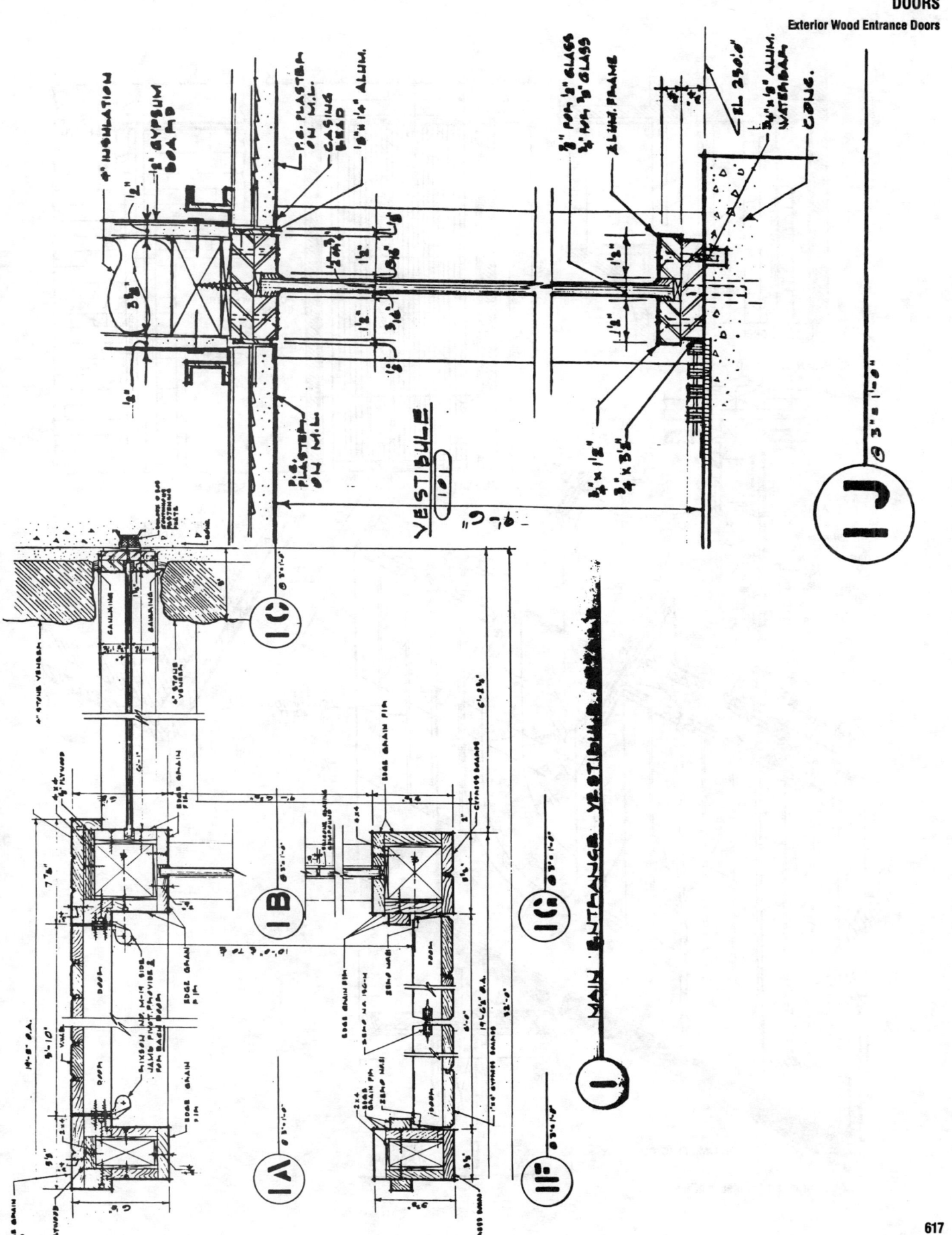

DOORS
Exterior Wood Entrance Doors

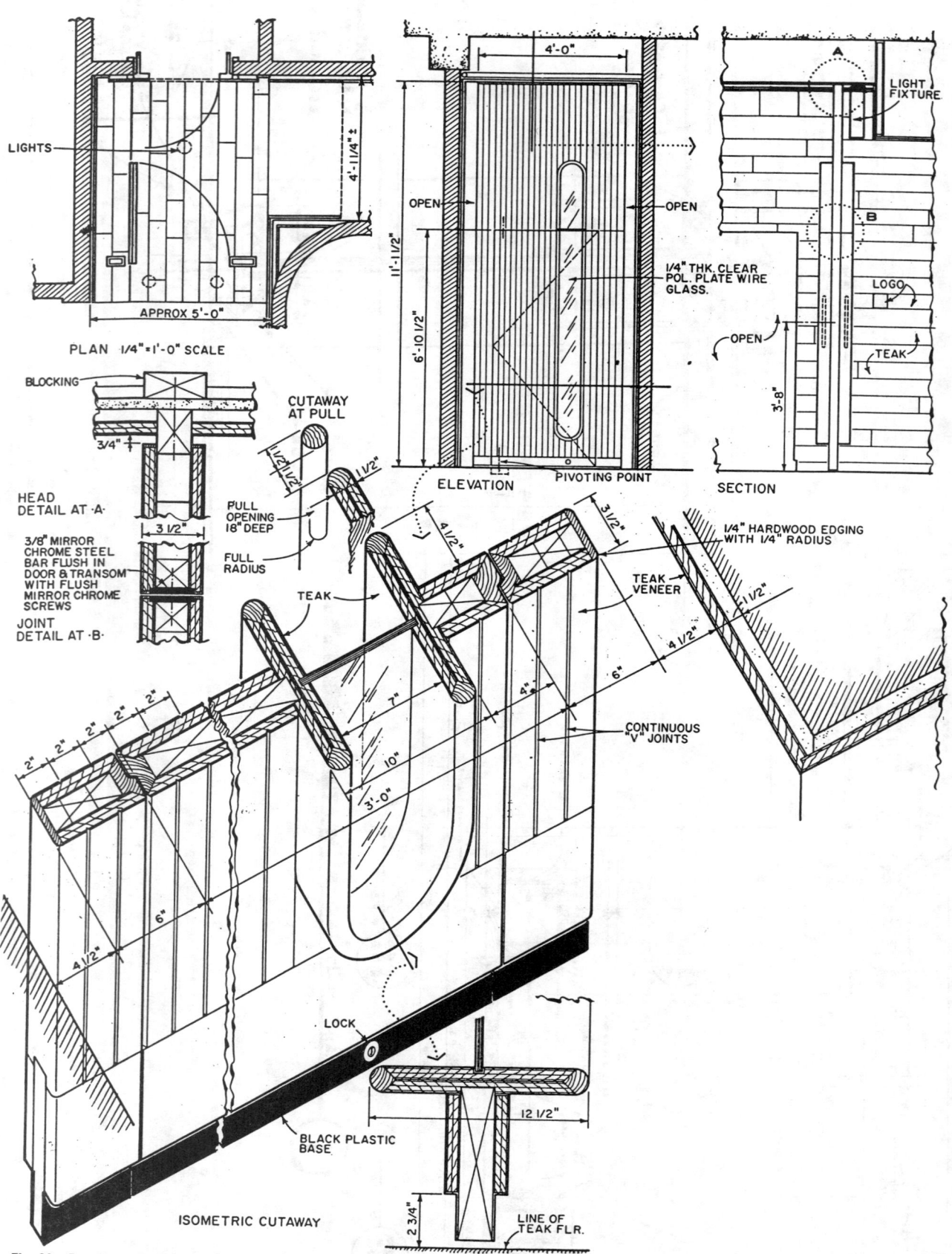

LIGHTS

APPROX 5'-0"

PLAN 1/4"=1'-0" SCALE

BLOCKING

3/4"

HEAD
DETAIL AT ·A·

3/8" MIRROR
CHROME STEEL
BAR FLUSH IN
DOOR & TRANSOM
WITH FLUSH
MIRROR CHROME
SCREWS

JOINT
DETAIL AT ·B·

3 1/2"

CUTAWAY
AT PULL

1/2 1/2

1 1/2"

PULL
OPENING
18" DEEP

FULL
RADIUS

4'-0"

OPEN

OPEN

11'-1 1/2"

6'-10 1/2"

1/4" THK. CLEAR
POL. PLATE WIRE
GLASS.

ELEVATION

PIVOTING POINT

A

LIGHT
FIXTURE

B

OPEN

LOGO

TEAK

3'-8"

SECTION

TEAK

4 1/2"

3 1/2"

TEAK
VENEER

1/4" HARDWOOD EDGING
WITH 1/4" RADIUS

1 1/2"

4 1/2"

6"

CONTINUOUS
"V" JOINTS

2" 2"
2" 2"
2" 2"
2"

7"

10"

3'-0"

4"

6"

4 1/2"

LOCK

BLACK PLASTIC
BASE

12 1/2"

2 3/4"

LINE OF
TEAK FLR.

ISOMETRIC CUTAWAY

Fig. 22   Door for an architect's office.

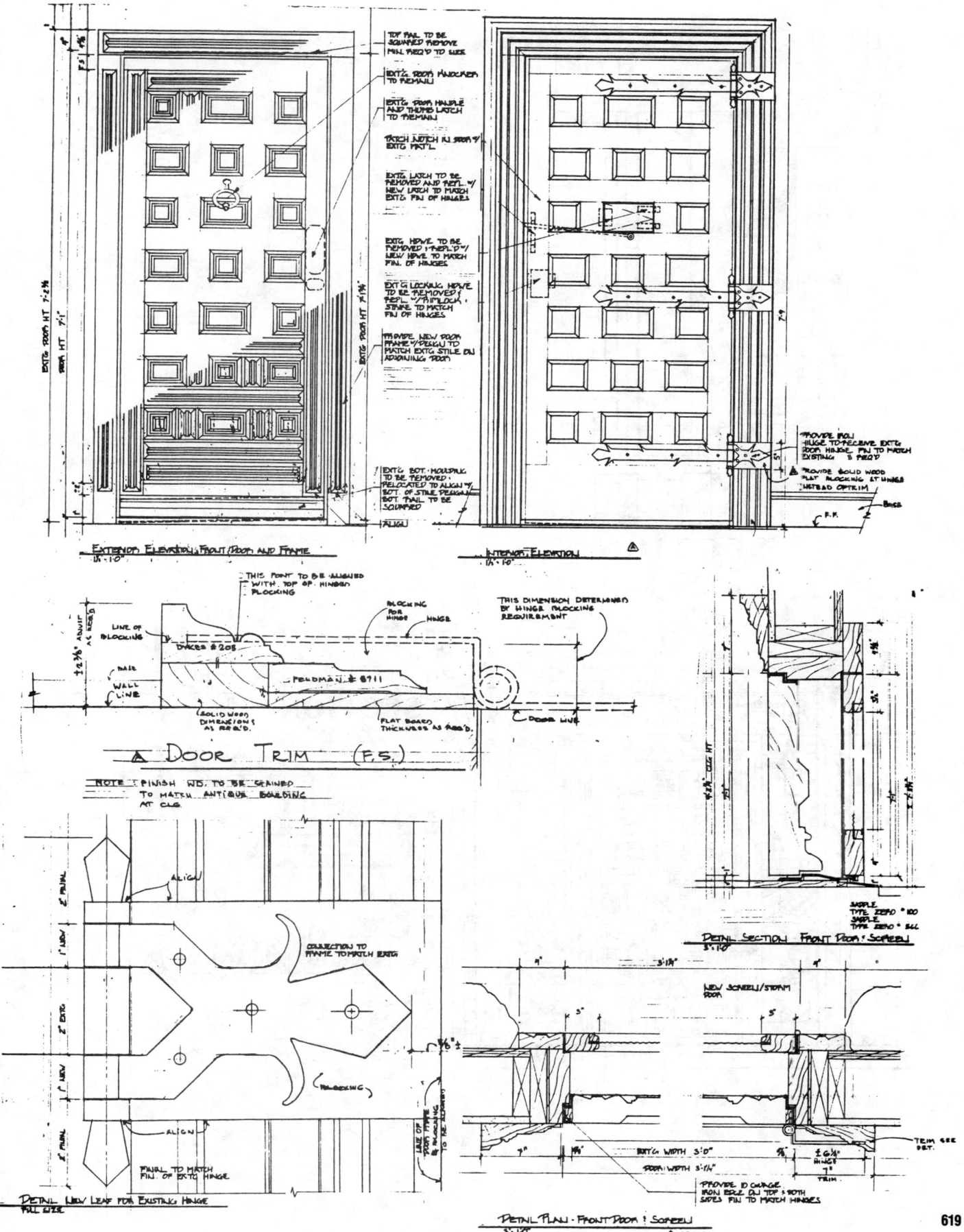

DOORS
Exterior Wood Entrance Doors

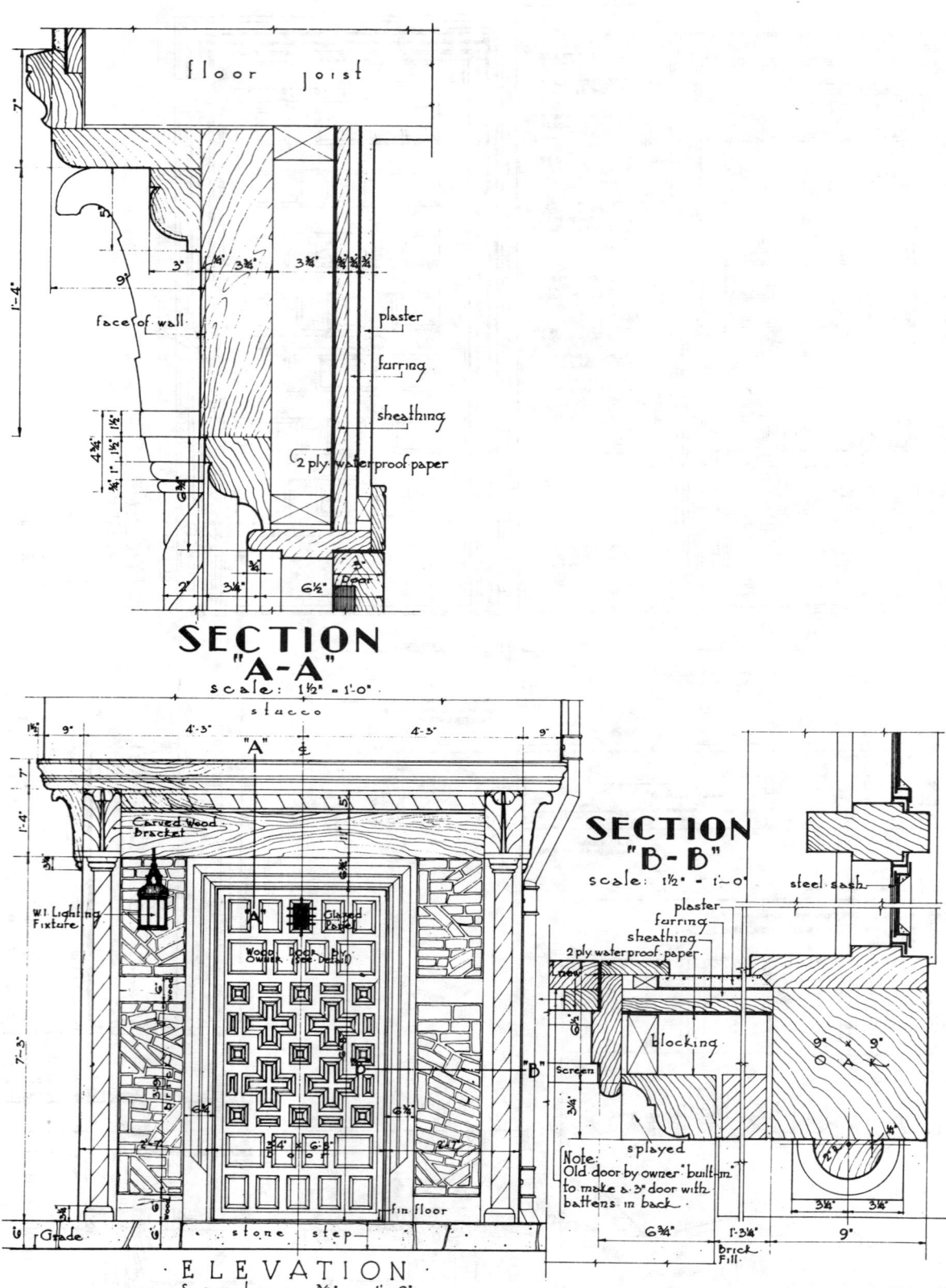

floor joist

face of wall

plaster
furring
sheathing
2 ply waterproof paper

SECTION "A-A"
scale: 1½" = 1'-0"

stucco

"A"

Carved Wood bracket

W.I. Lighting Fixture

Glazed Panel

Wood Door ("A") (See Detail)

fin floor

Grade

stone step

ELEVATION
Scale: ⅜" = 1'-0"

SECTION "B-B"
scale: 1½" = 1'-0"

steel sash

plaster
furring
sheathing
2 ply waterproof paper

blocking

Screen

splayed

9" x 9" OAK

Brick Fill

Note:
Old door by owner: built-in
to make a 3" door with
battens in back

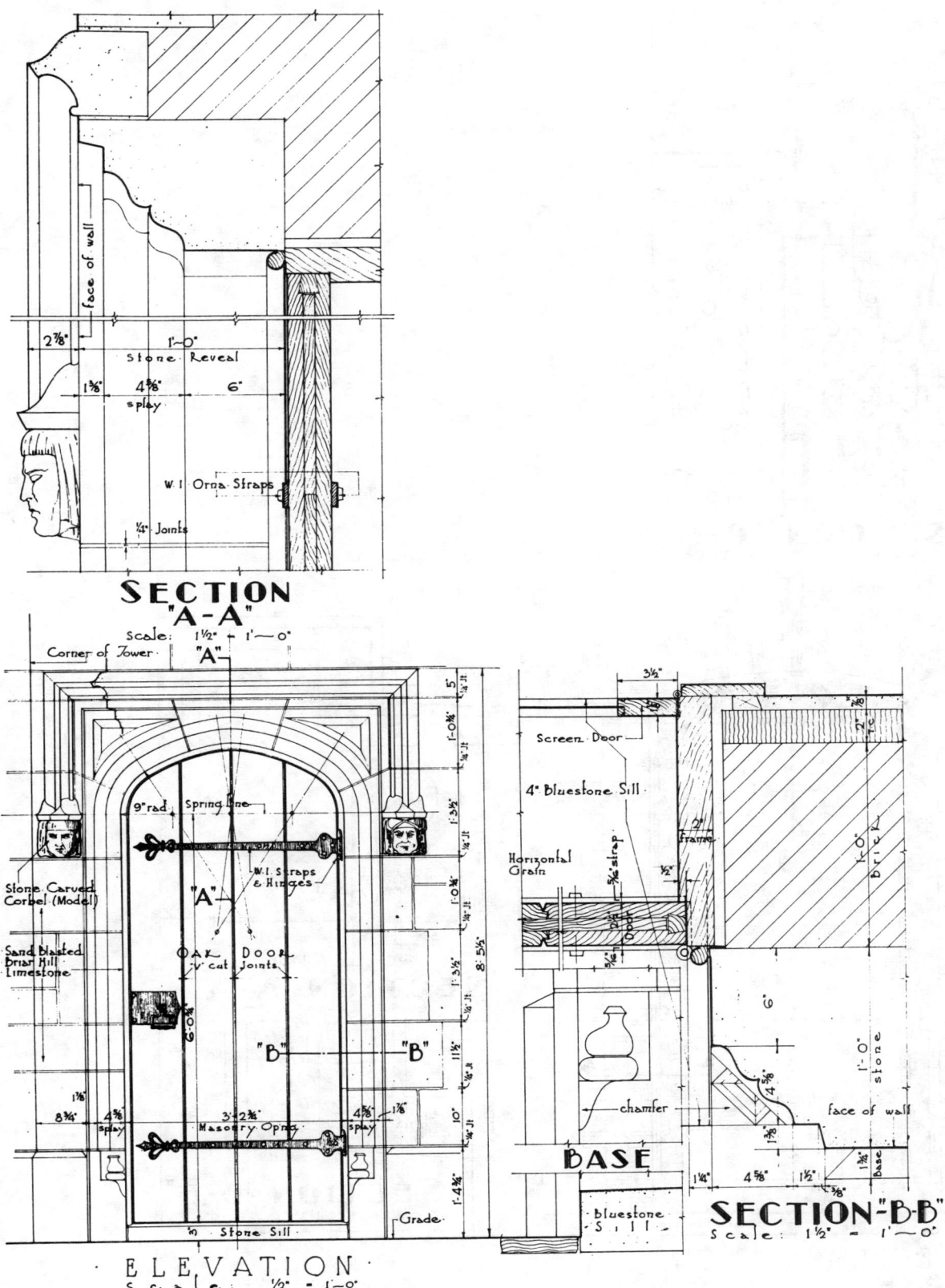

SECTION "A-A"
Scale: 1½" = 1'—0"

face of wall

2⅞"
1'—0"
Stone Reveal
1⅜"
4⅝"
splay
6"

W. I. Orna. Straps

¼" Joints

Corner of Tower   "A"

9" rad.   Spring Line

Stone Carved
Corbel (Model)

"A"

Sand blasted
Briar Hill
Limestone

OAK DOOR
"V" cut Joints

W. I. Straps
& Hinges

"B"   "B"

1⅜"
8¾" 4⅝"
splay

3'-2¾"
Masonry Opng.

4⅝" 1⅜"
splay

Stone Sill   Grade

ELEVATION
scale: ½" = 1'—0"

3½"

Screen Door

4" Bluestone Sill

Horizontal
Grain

chamfer

BASE

bluestone
Sill

2'
frame

½"

6"

1'—0" stone

face of wall

1¼" 4⅝" 1½"
⅜"
Base

1⅜"

SECTION "B-B"
Scale: 1½" = 1'—0"

DOORS

Exterior Wood Entrance Doors

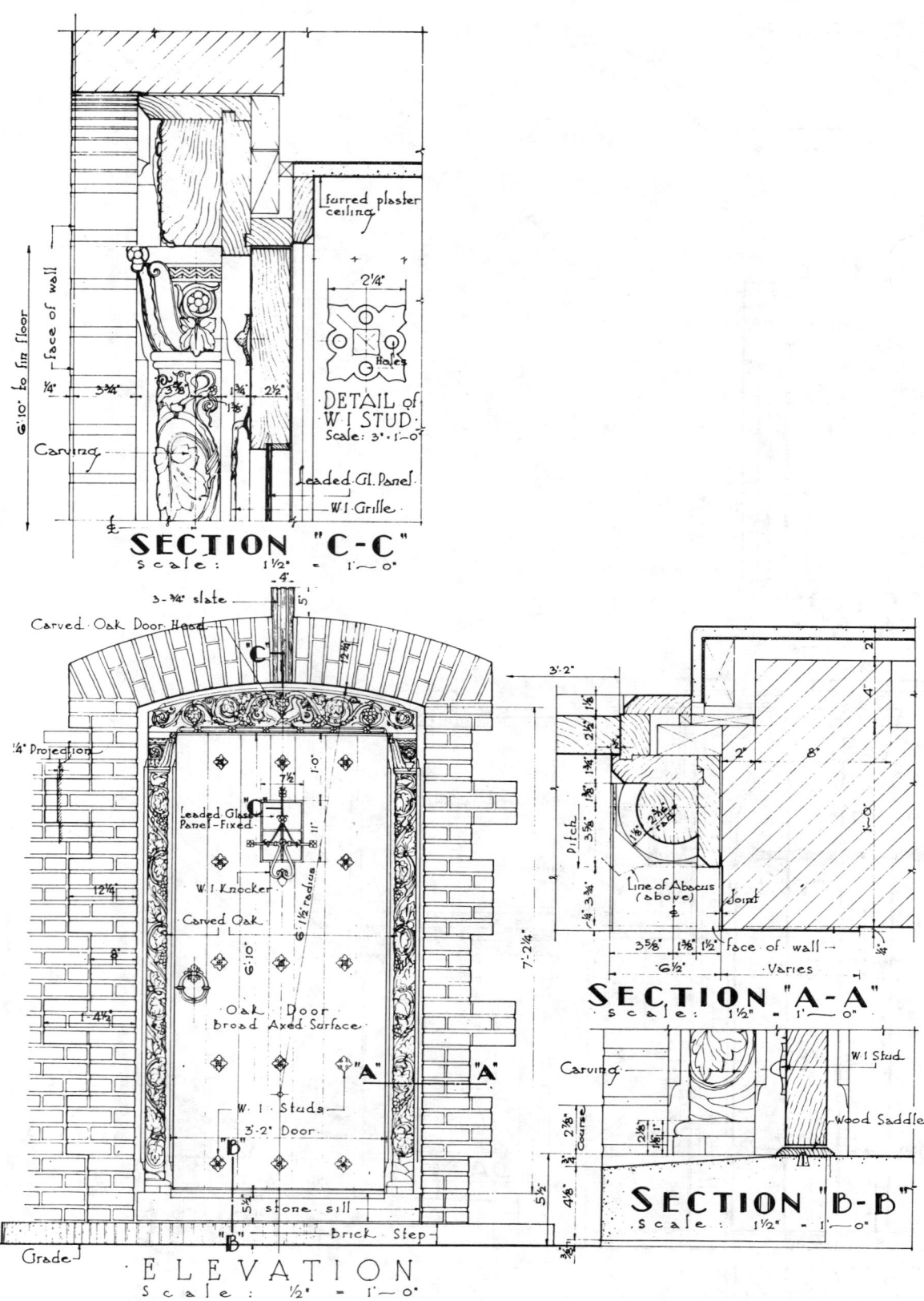

SECTION "C-C"
scale: 1½" = 1'—0"

DETAIL of W.I. STUD.
Scale: 3"=1'—0"

SECTION "A-A"
scale: 1½" = 1'—0"

SECTION "B-B"
scale: 1½" = 1'—0"

ELEVATION
Scale: ½" = 1'—0"

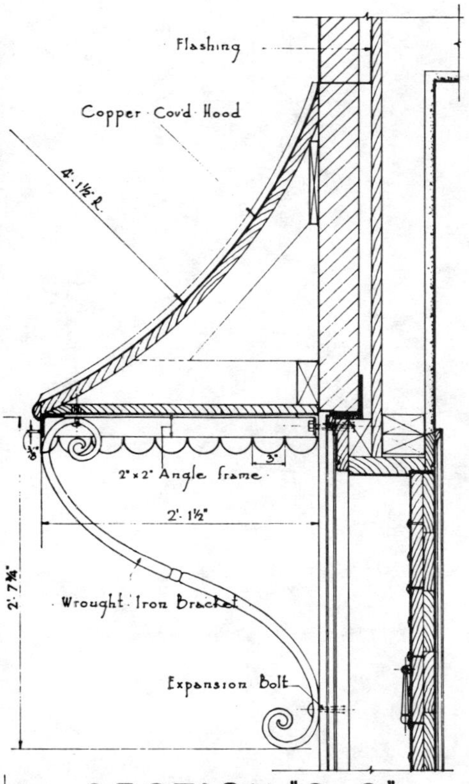
Flashing
Copper Cov'd Hood
4'-1½" R.
2"×2" Angle frame
3"
2'-1½"
2'-7⅝"
Wrought Iron Bracket
Expansion Bolt

SECTION "C-C"
Scale: 3/4" = 1'—0"

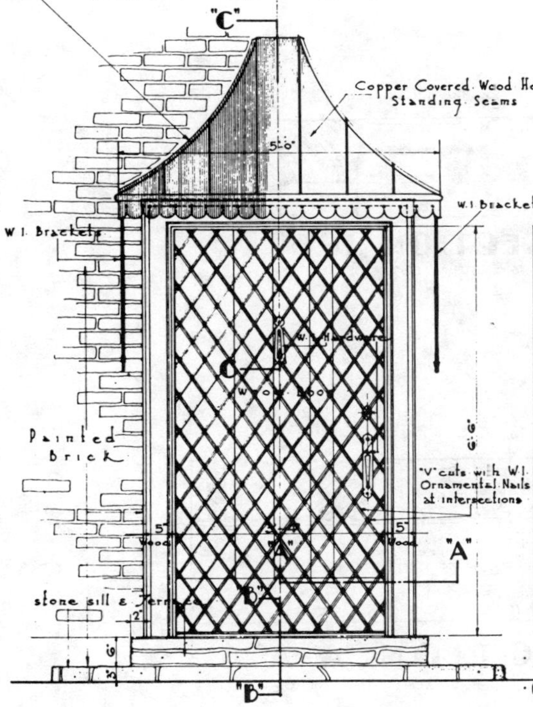
"C"
Copper Covered Wood Hood
Standing Seams
5'-0"
W.I. Bracket
W.I. Brackets
W.I. Hardware
W.I. on Door
Painted Brick
"V" cuts with W.I. Ornamental Nails at intersections
5"
Wood
"A"
stone sill & Terrace
"B"

ELEVATION
Scale: 3/8" = 1'—0"

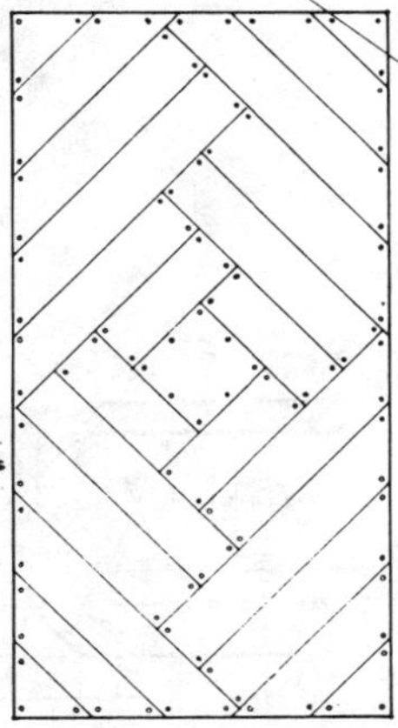

INTERIOR ELEVATION OF DOOR Scale 3/8"=1'-0"

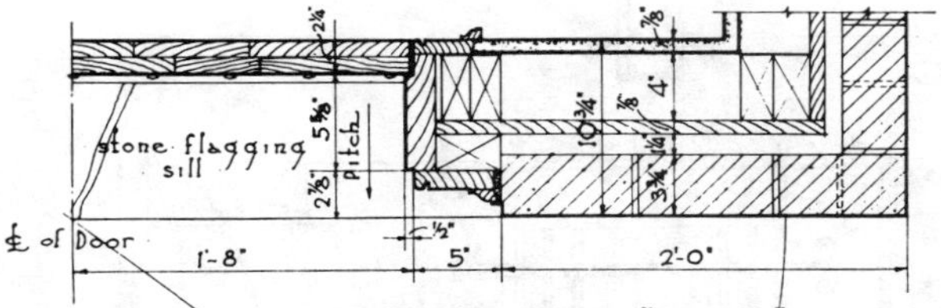
stone flagging sill
pitch
℄ of Door
1'-8"
5"
2'-0"
3'-6" Radius stone flagging

SECTION "A-A"
SCALE: 3/4" = 1'—0"

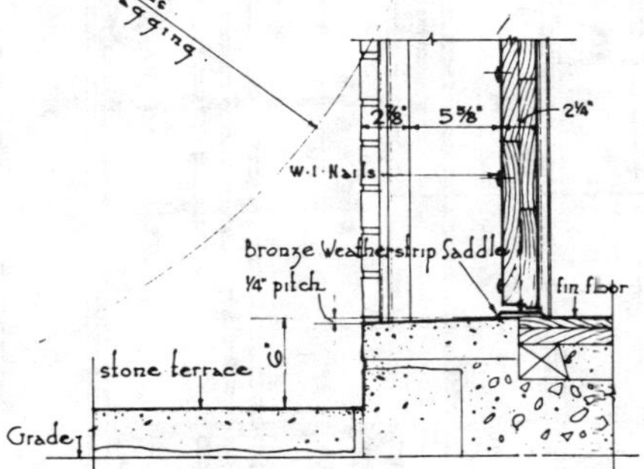
5⅝"
2¼"
W.I. Nails
Bronze Weatherstrip Saddle
¼" pitch
fin floor
stone terrace
Grade

SECTION "B-B"
SCALE: 3/4" = 1'—0"

DOORS

Exterior Wood Entrance Doors

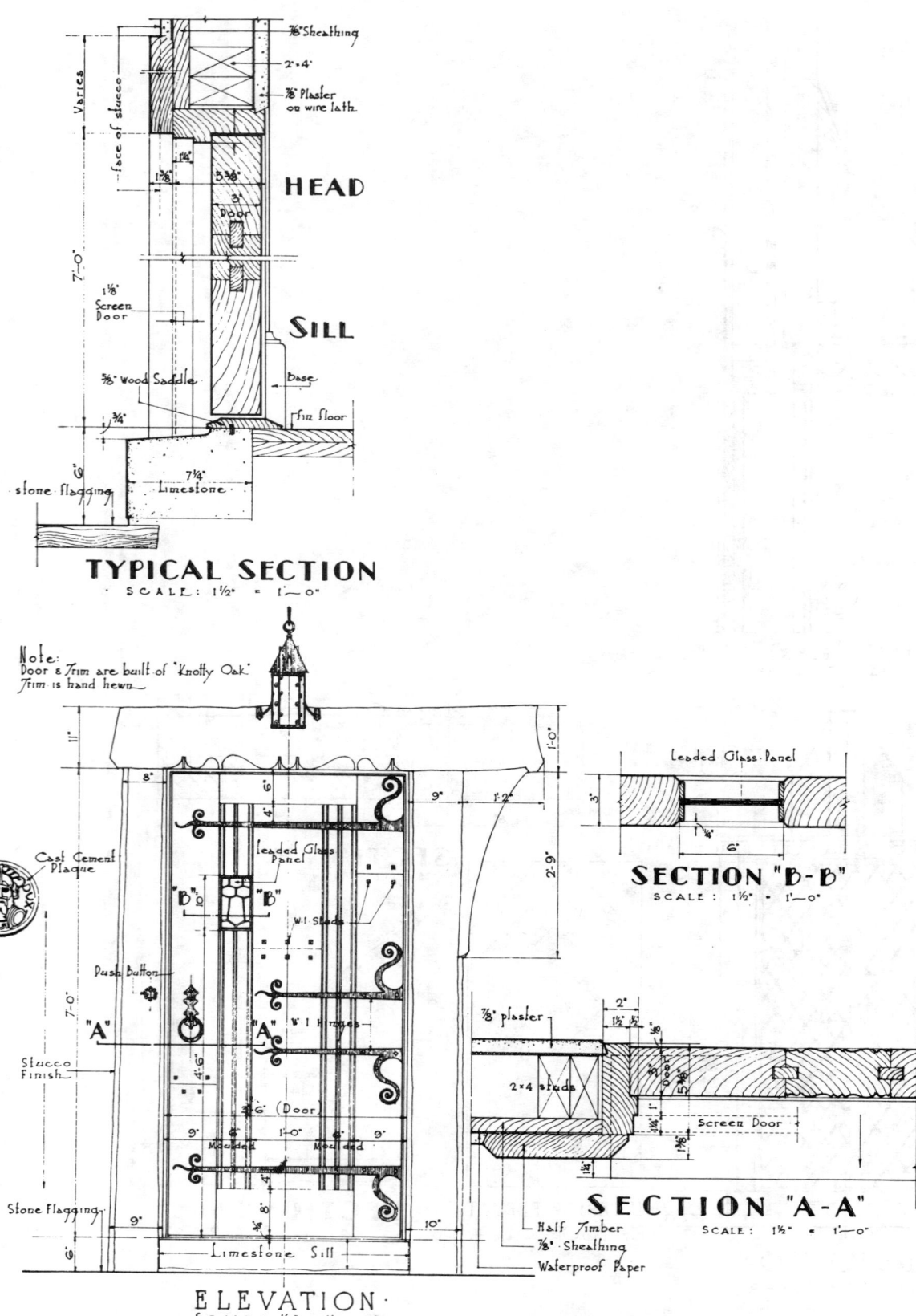

TYPICAL SECTION
SCALE: 1½" = 1'—0"

HEAD

SILL

⅞" Sheathing
2 × 4
⅞" Plaster on wire lath.
face of stucco
Varies
7'-0"
1⅛"
5⅜"
3"
Door
1⅛"
Screen Door
⅜" Wood Saddle
Base
Fin floor
¾"
6"
stone flagging
7¼"
Limestone

Note:
Door & Trim are built of "Knotty Oak"
Trim is hand hewn

SECTION "B-B"
SCALE: 1½" = 1'—0"

Leaded Glass Panel

SECTION "A-A"
SCALE: 1½" = 1'—0"

⅞" plaster
2 × 4 studs
Screen Door
Half Timber
⅞" Sheathing
Waterproof Paper

ELEVATION
SCALE: ½" = 1'—0"

Cast Cement Plaque
Push Button
Stucco Finish
Stone Flagging
Limestone Sill
Leaded Glass Panel
W.I. Studs
W.I. Hinges
Moulded
Moulded

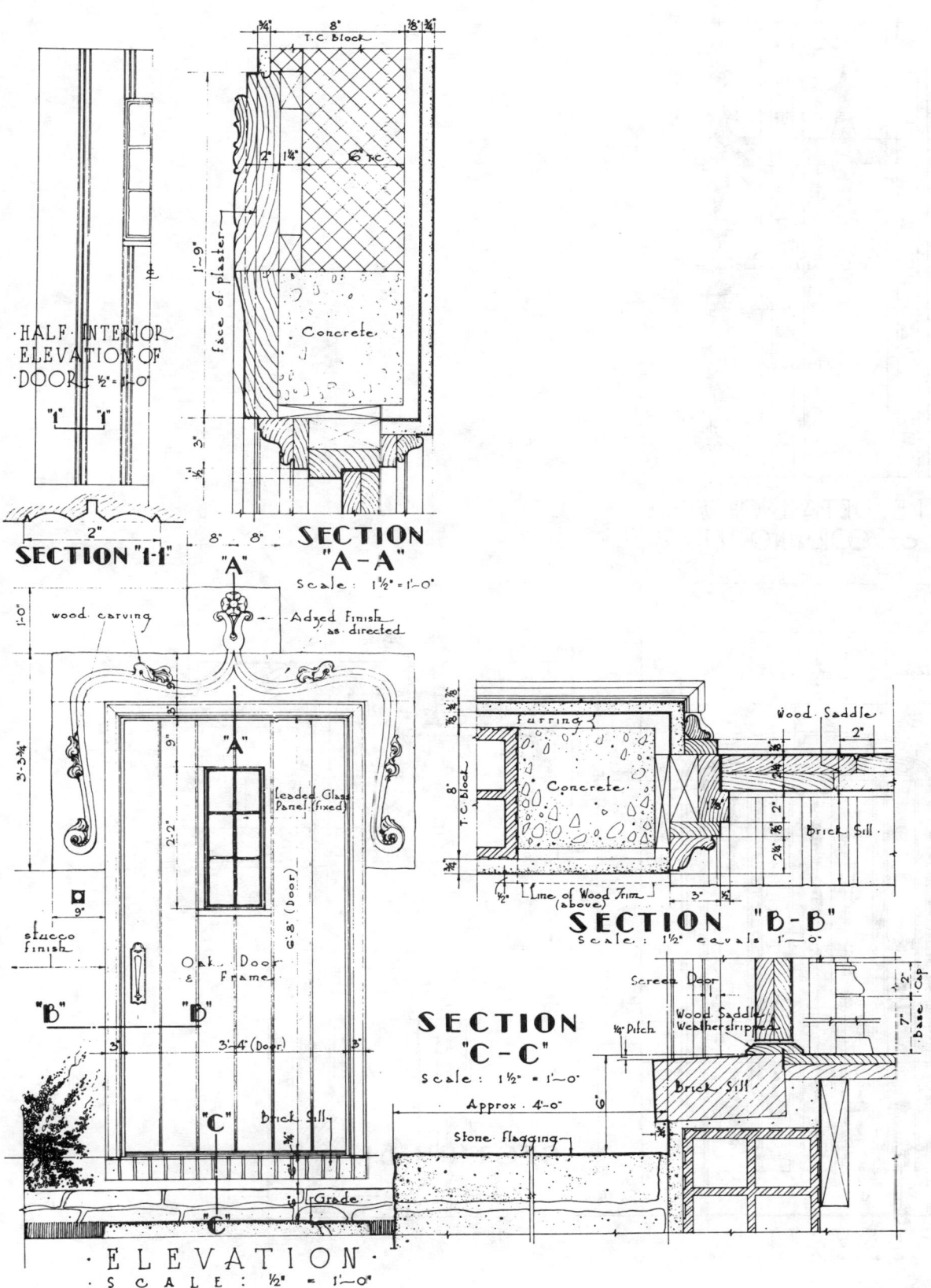

·HALF·INTERIOR·
ELEVATION·OF·
·DOOR· ½"=1'-0"

SECTION "1-1"

T.C. Block

face of plaster

Concrete

SECTION "A-A"
Scale: 1½" = 1'-0"

wood carving

Adzed Finish
as directed

Leaded Glass
Panel (fixed)

stucco finish

Oak Door
& Frame

Brick Sill

·ELEVATION·
·SCALE: ½" = 1'-0"·

furring

T.C. block

Concrete

Line of Wood Trim
(above)

Wood Saddle

Brick Sill

SECTION "B-B"
Scale: 1½" equals 1'-0"

SECTION "C-C"
Scale: 1½" = 1'-0"

Approx 4'-0"

Stone flagging

Screen Door

¼" Pitch

Wood Saddle
Weatherstripped

Brick Sill

Base Cap

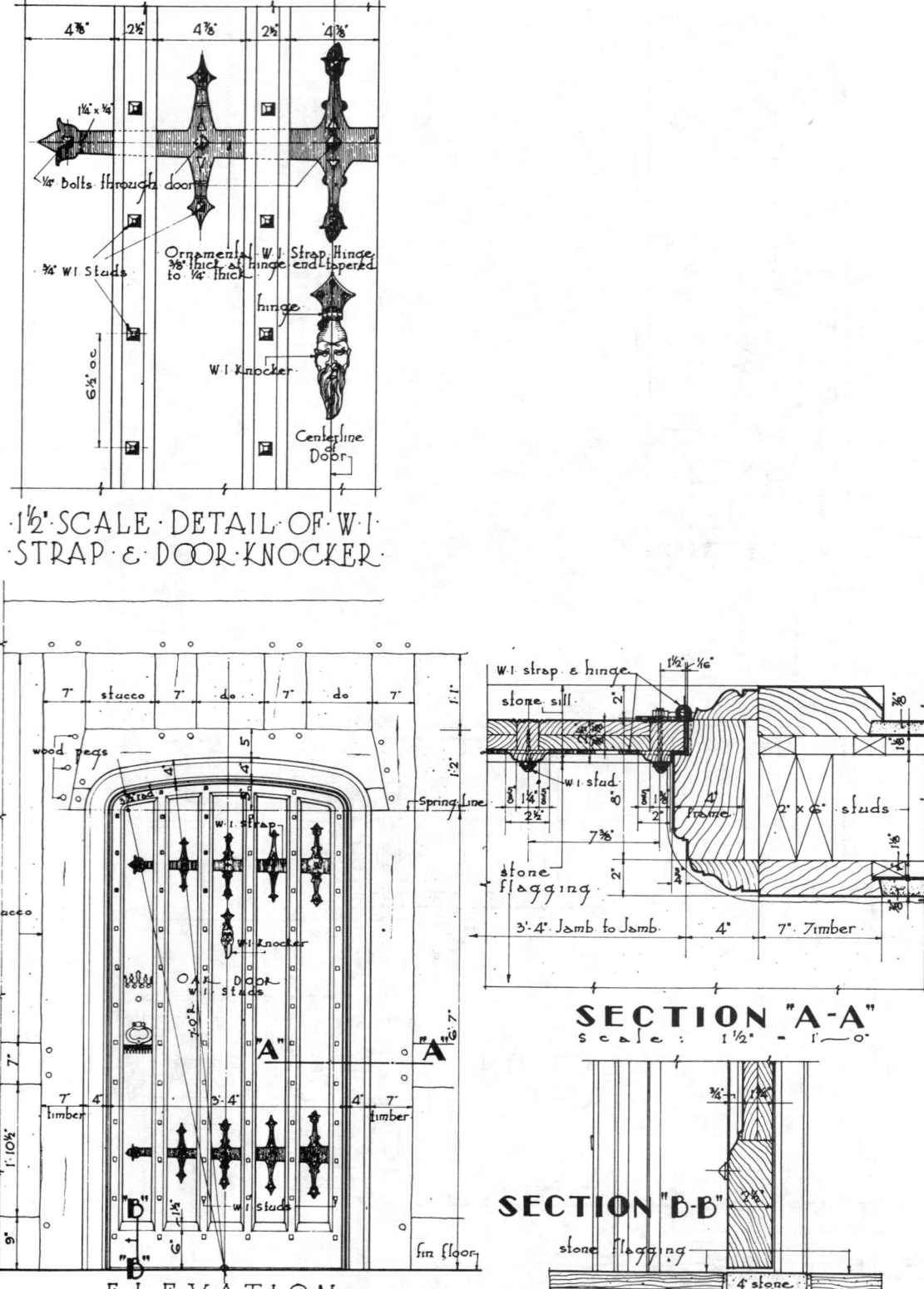

1½" SCALE · DETAIL · OF · W·I·
STRAP · & · DOOR · KNOCKER

ELEVATION
scale: ½" = 1'-0"

SECTION "A-A"
scale: 1½" = 1'-0"

SECTION "B-B"

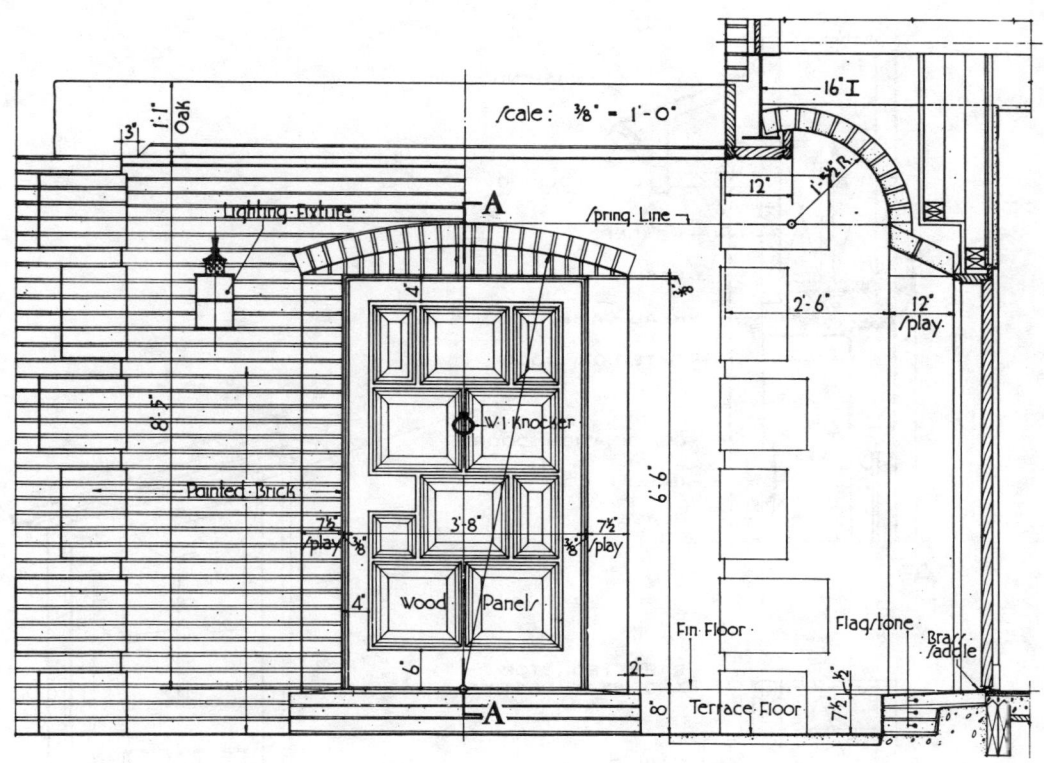

scale: ⅜" = 1'-0"

Oak

1'-1"

3"

Lighting Fixture

A

Spring Line

16" I

12"

1½" R.

2'-6"

12" splay

Painted Brick

8'-5"

W. I. Knocker

7½ splay ⅜"

3'-8"

7½ splay

6'-9"

⅝"

Wood Panels

4"

6"

2"

Fin. Floor

Flagstone

Brass Saddle

8"

7½"

Terrace Floor

A

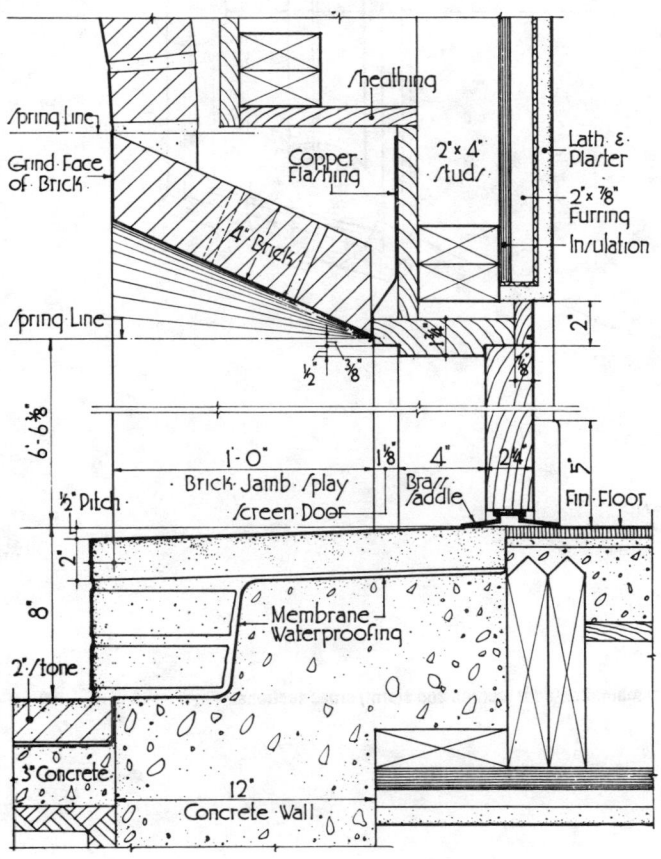

Spring Line

Sheathing

Grind Face of Brick

Copper Flashing

2" x 4" Studs

Lath & Plaster

2" x ⅞" Furring

Insulation

4" Brick

Spring Line

2'

6'-6⅝"

½" ⅜"

1'-0"

1⅛" 4"

2¼"

5"

Brick Jamb splay Screen Door

Brass Saddle

Fin. Floor

½" Pitch

2"

8"

Membrane Waterproofing

2' Stone

3" Concrete

12"

Concrete Wall

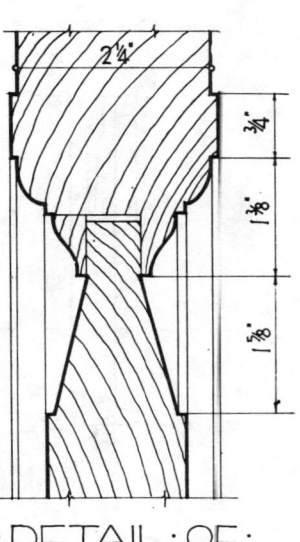

2¼"

¾"

1⅜"

1⅜"

· DETAIL · OF ·
· DOOR · PANEL ·
Scale: Half · Full · Size

627

DOORS

Exterior Wood Entrance Doors

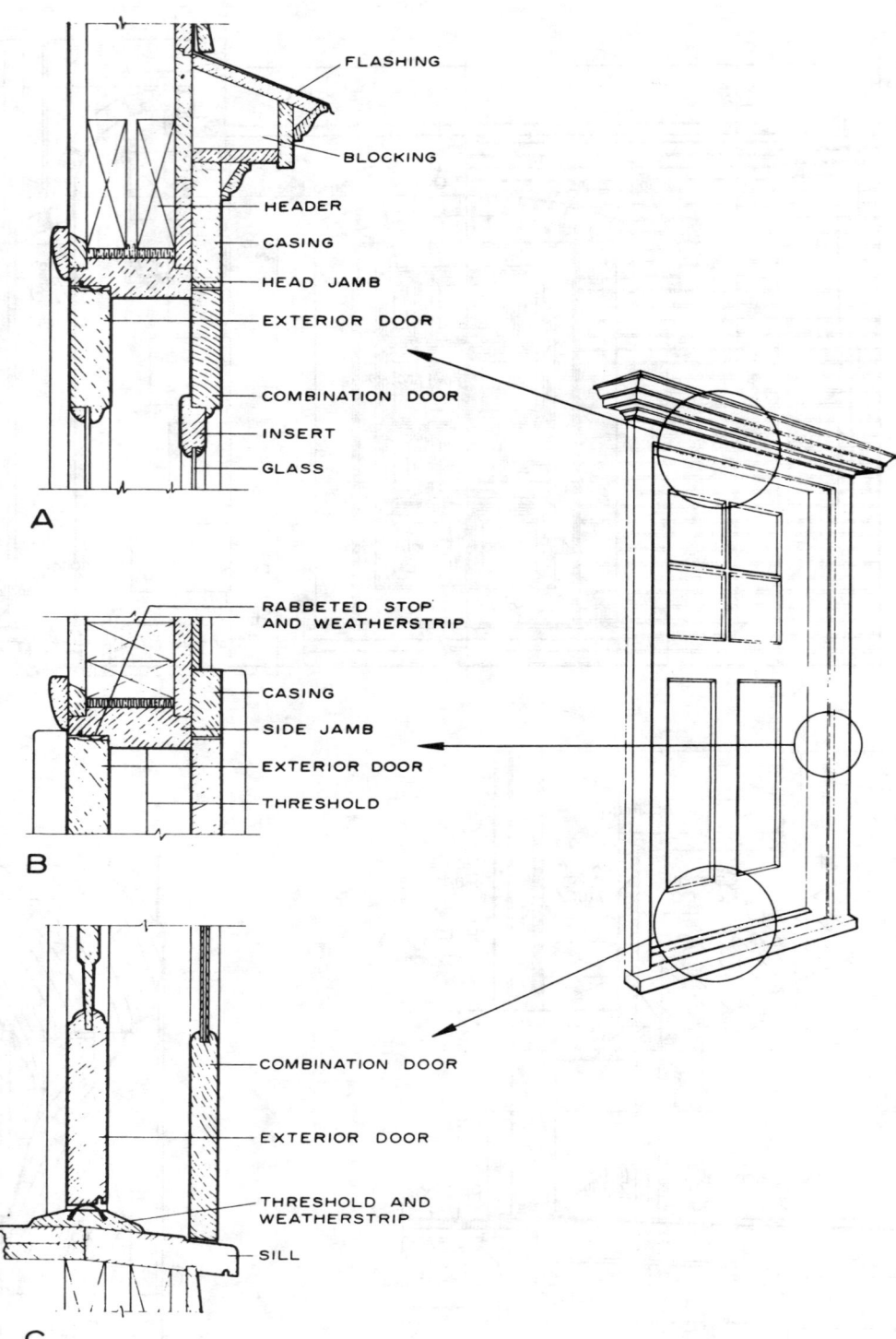

Labels in figure:

A:
- FLASHING
- BLOCKING
- HEADER
- CASING
- HEAD JAMB
- EXTERIOR DOOR
- COMBINATION DOOR
- INSERT
- GLASS

B:
- RABBETED STOP AND WEATHERSTRIP
- CASING
- SIDE JAMB
- EXTERIOR DOOR
- THRESHOLD

C:
- COMBINATION DOOR
- EXTERIOR DOOR
- THRESHOLD AND WEATHERSTRIP
- SILL

Fig. 23   Exterior door and frame. Exterior-door and combination-door (screen and storm) cross sections: *A*, head jamb; *B*, side jamb; *C*, sill.

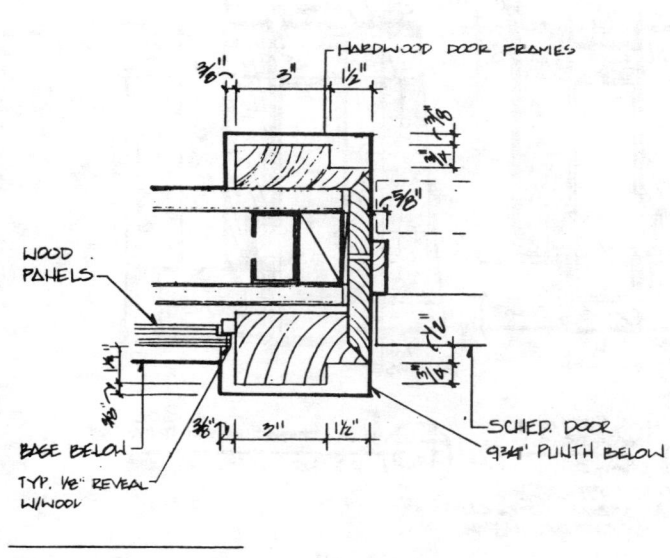

HARDWOOD DOOR FRAMES

WOOD PANELS

BASE BELOW

TYP. ⅛" REVEAL W/WOOD

SCHED. DOOR
9¾" PLINTH BELOW

WOOD DOOR JAMB

Wood clad metal door frames

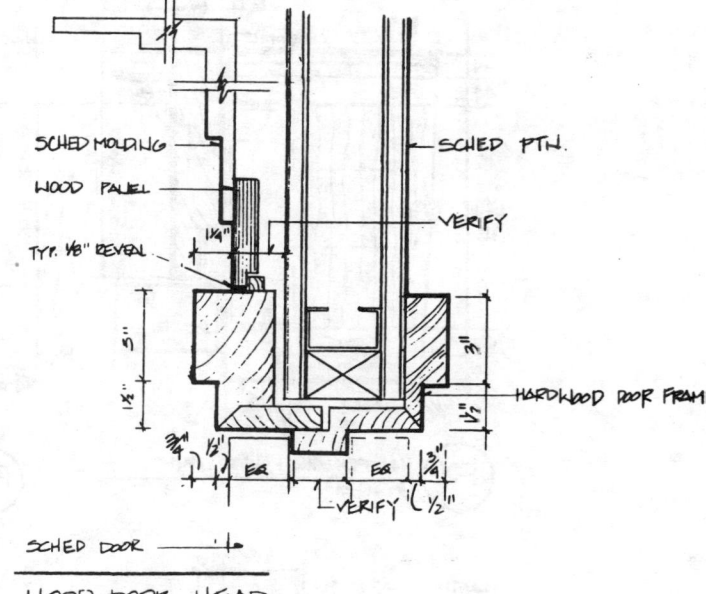

SCHED MOLDING

WOOD PANEL

TYP. ⅛" REVEAL

SCHED PTN.

VERIFY

HARDWOOD DOOR FRAME

SCHED DOOR

VERIFY

WOOD DOOR HEAD

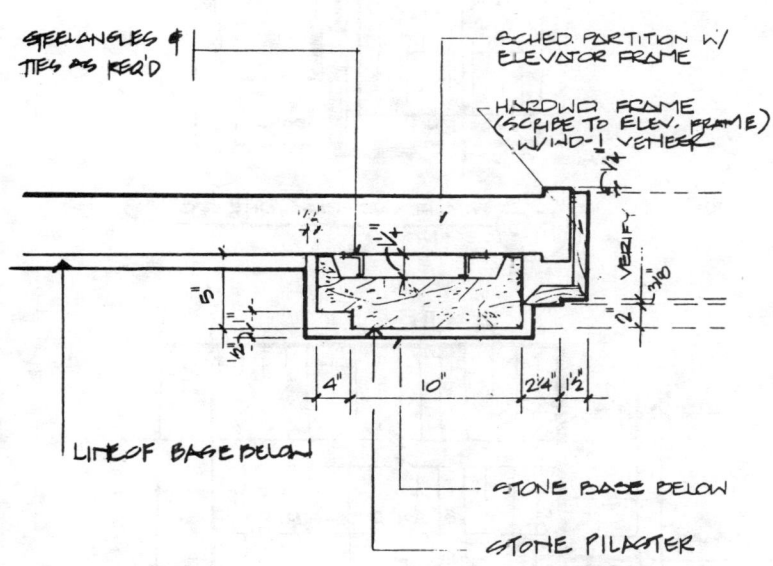

STEEL ANGLES & TIES AS REQ'D

SCHED. PARTITION W/ ELEVATOR FRAME

HARDWD FRAME (SCRIBE TO ELEV. FRAME) W/IND-L VENEER

VERIFY

LINE OF BASE BELOW

STONE BASE BELOW

STONE PILASTER

JAMB @ ELEVATOR

Marble jamb and head details at elevator

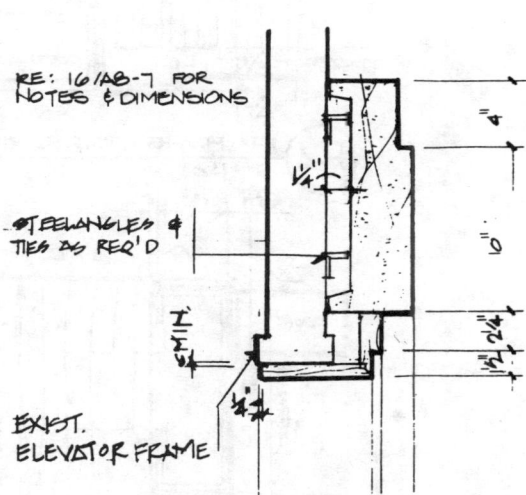

RE: 16/A8-7 FOR NOTES & DIMENSIONS

STEEL ANGLES & TIES AS REQ'D

EXIST. ELEVATOR FRAME

HEAD @ ELEVATOR

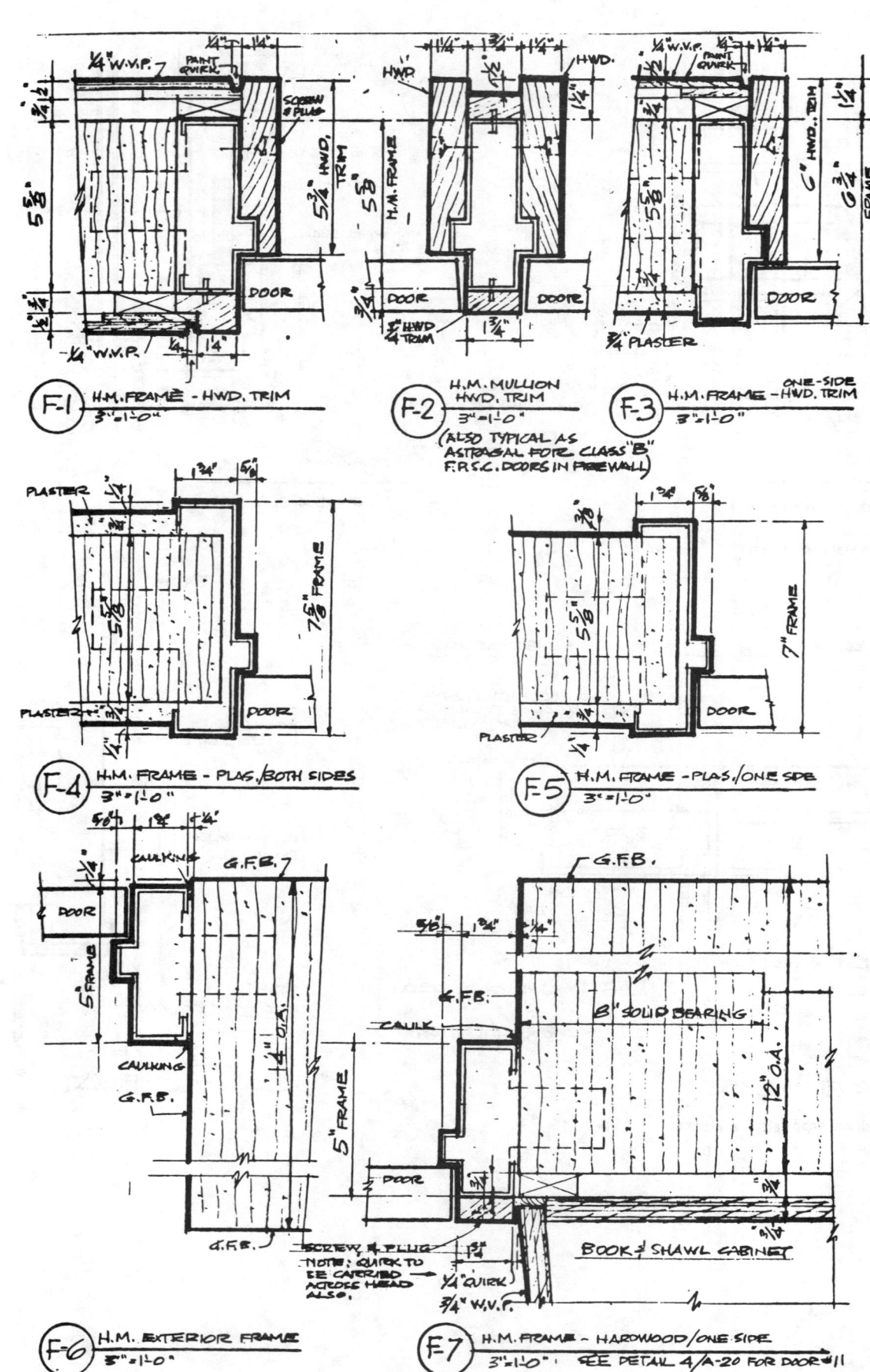

F-1 H.M. FRAME – HWD. TRIM 3"=1'-0"

F-2 H.M. MULLION HWD. TRIM 3"=1'-0" (ALSO TYPICAL AS ASTRAGAL FOR CLASS "B" F.R.S.C. DOORS IN FIREWALL)

F-3 H.M. FRAME – HWD. TRIM ONE-SIDE 3"=1'-0"

F-4 H.M. FRAME – PLAS./BOTH SIDES 3"=1'-0"

F-5 H.M. FRAME – PLAS./ONE SIDE 3"=1'-0"

F-6 H.M. EXTERIOR FRAME 3"=1'-0"

F-7 H.M. FRAME – HARDWOOD/ONE SIDE 3"=1'-0" SEE DETAIL 4/A-20 FOR DOOR #11

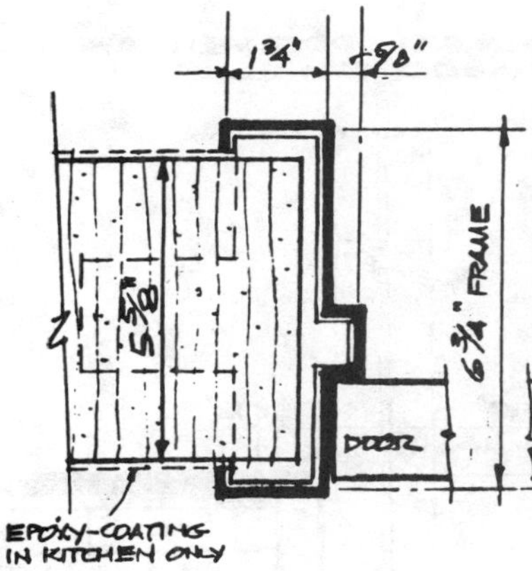

EPOXY COATING
IN KITCHEN ONLY

F-8   H.M. FRAME
       3"=1'-0"

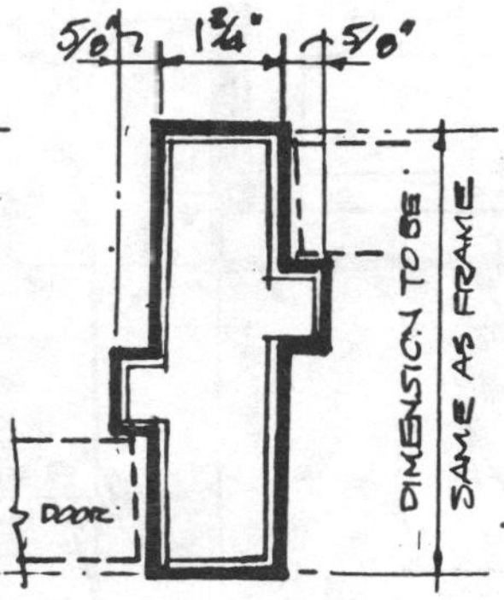

F-9   H.M. MULLION
       3"=1'-0"

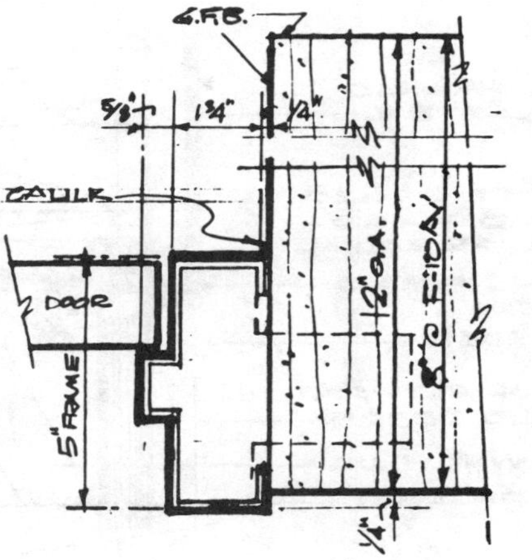

F-10   H.M. FRAME
       3"=1'-0"

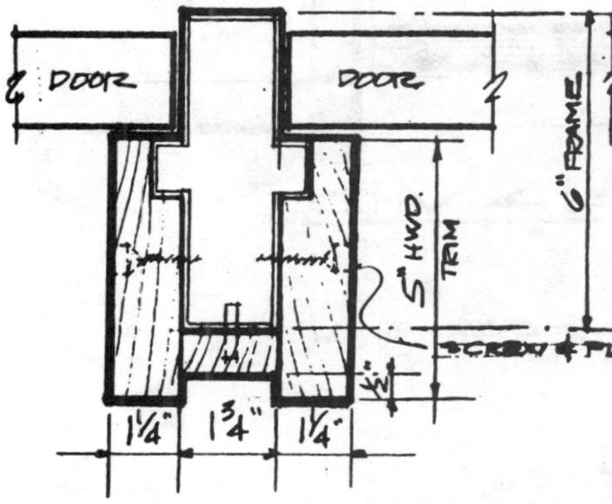

F-11A H.M. FRAME
       HWD. TRIM/ONE SIDE
       3"=1'-0"

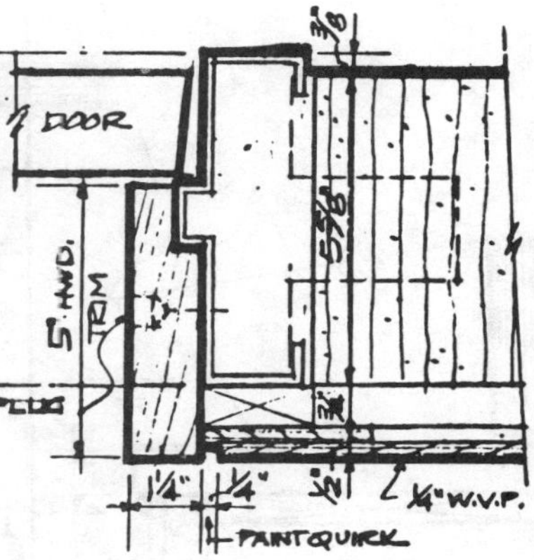

F-11   H.M. FRAME
       HWD. TRIM/ONE SIDE
       3"=1'-0"

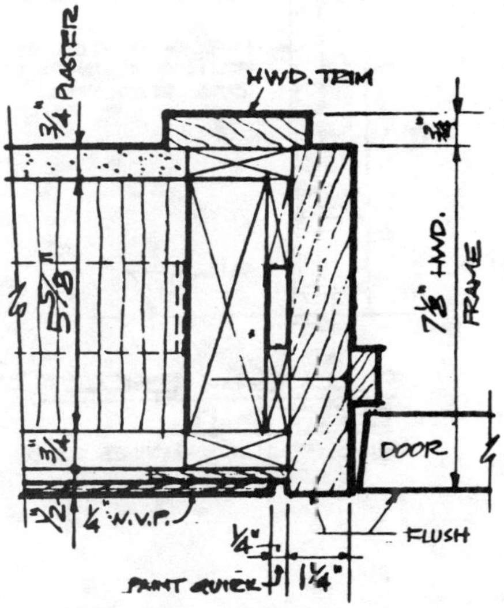

F-13   HARDWOOD FRAME
       3"=1'-0"

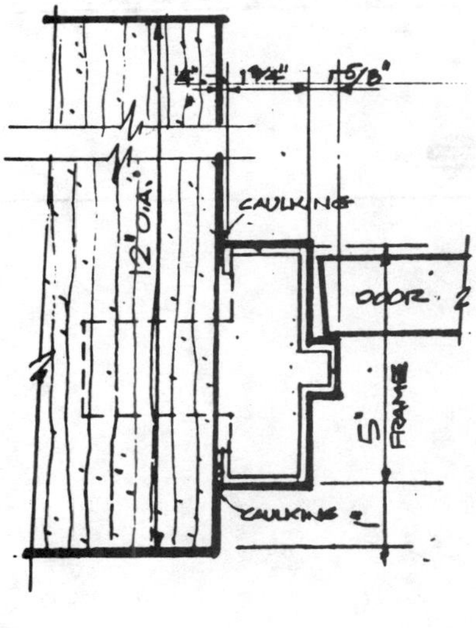

F-12   H.M. EXTERIOR FRAME
       3"=1'-0"

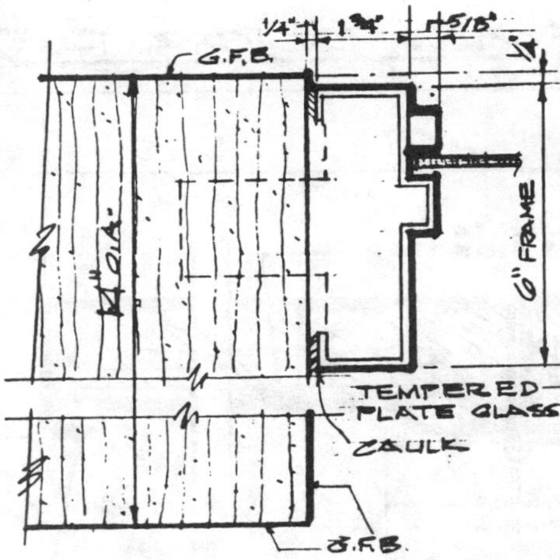

F-14   3"=1'-0"
       #24

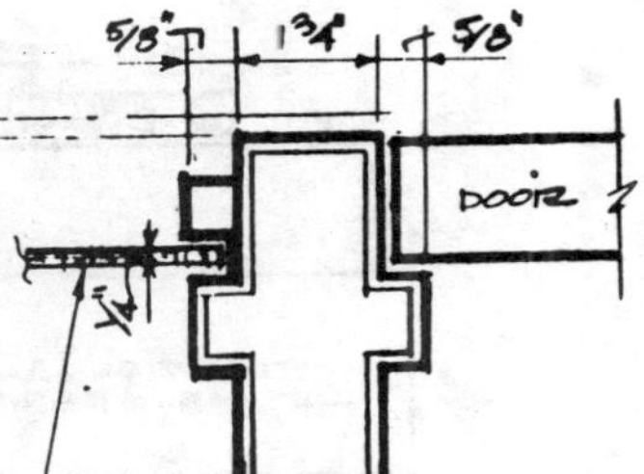

F-14A 3"=1'-0"
       #24

DOORS
Bi-Fold Doors

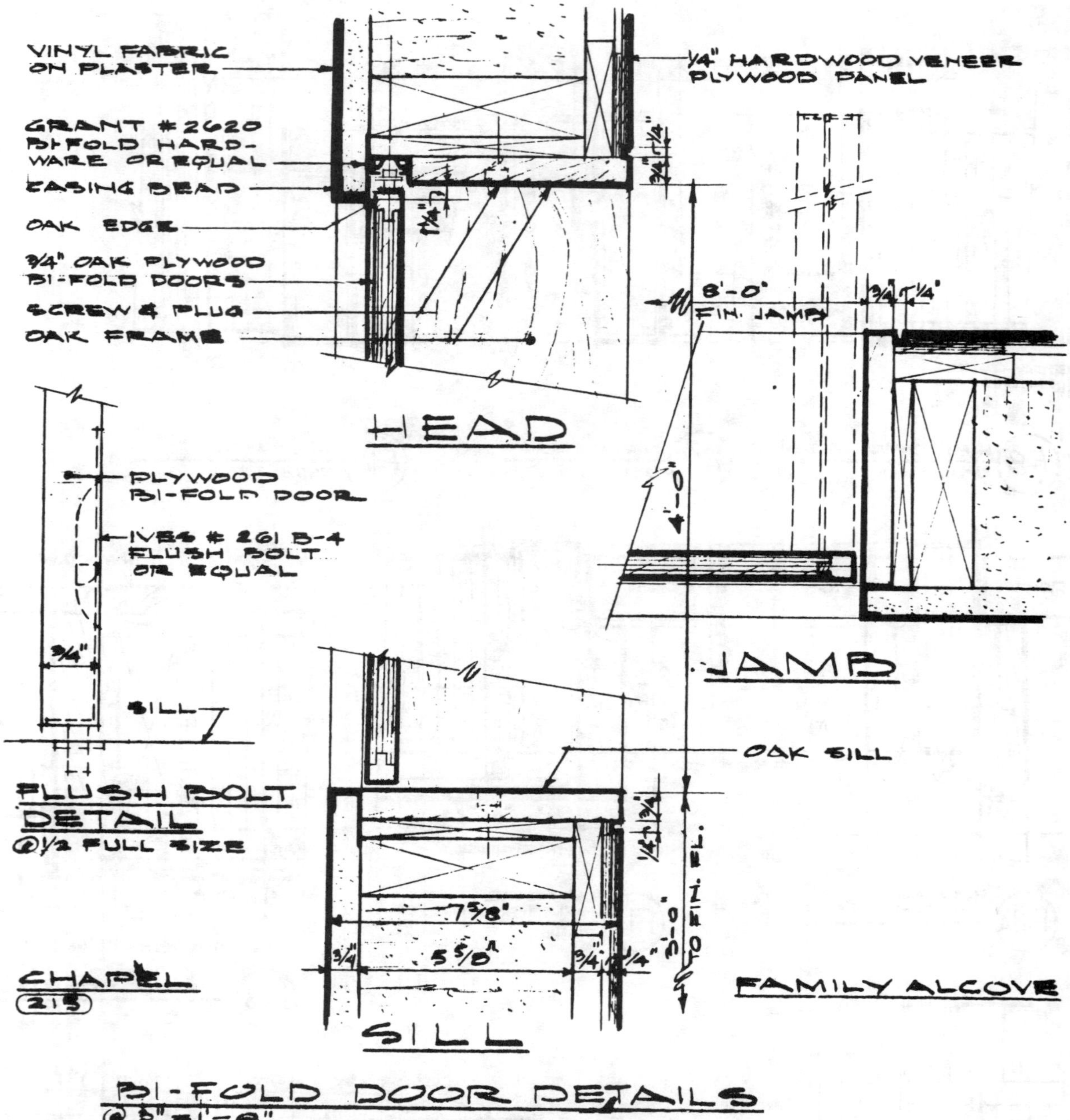

VINYL FABRIC
ON PLASTER

¼" HARDWOOD VENEER
PLYWOOD PANEL

GRANT #2620
BI-FOLD HARD-
WARE OR EQUAL

CASING BEAD

OAK EDGE

¾" OAK PLYWOOD
BI-FOLD DOORS

SCREW & PLUG

OAK FRAME

¾" ¼"

8'-0"
FIN. JAMB

¾" ¼"

__HEAD__

__JAMB__

PLYWOOD
BI-FOLD DOOR

IVES # 261 B-4
FLUSH BOLT
OR EQUAL

¾"

SILL

OAK SILL

__FLUSH BOLT
DETAIL__
@ ½ FULL SIZE

7⅝"

5⅝"

¼" ¾"

¾"

__CHAPEL__
(215)

__SILL__

¼" ¾"

EL.
0'-0"

__FAMILY ALCOVE__

__BI-FOLD DOOR DETAILS__
@ 3" = 1'-0"

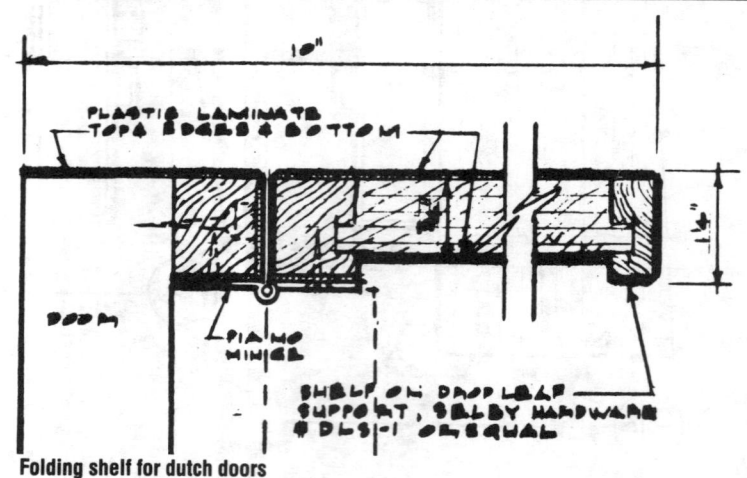

10"

PLASTIC LAMINATE
TOP & EDGES & BOTTOM

1¼"

DOOR

PIANO
HINGE

SHELF ON DROP LEAF
SUPPORT, SELBY HARDWARE
DLS-1 OR EQUAL

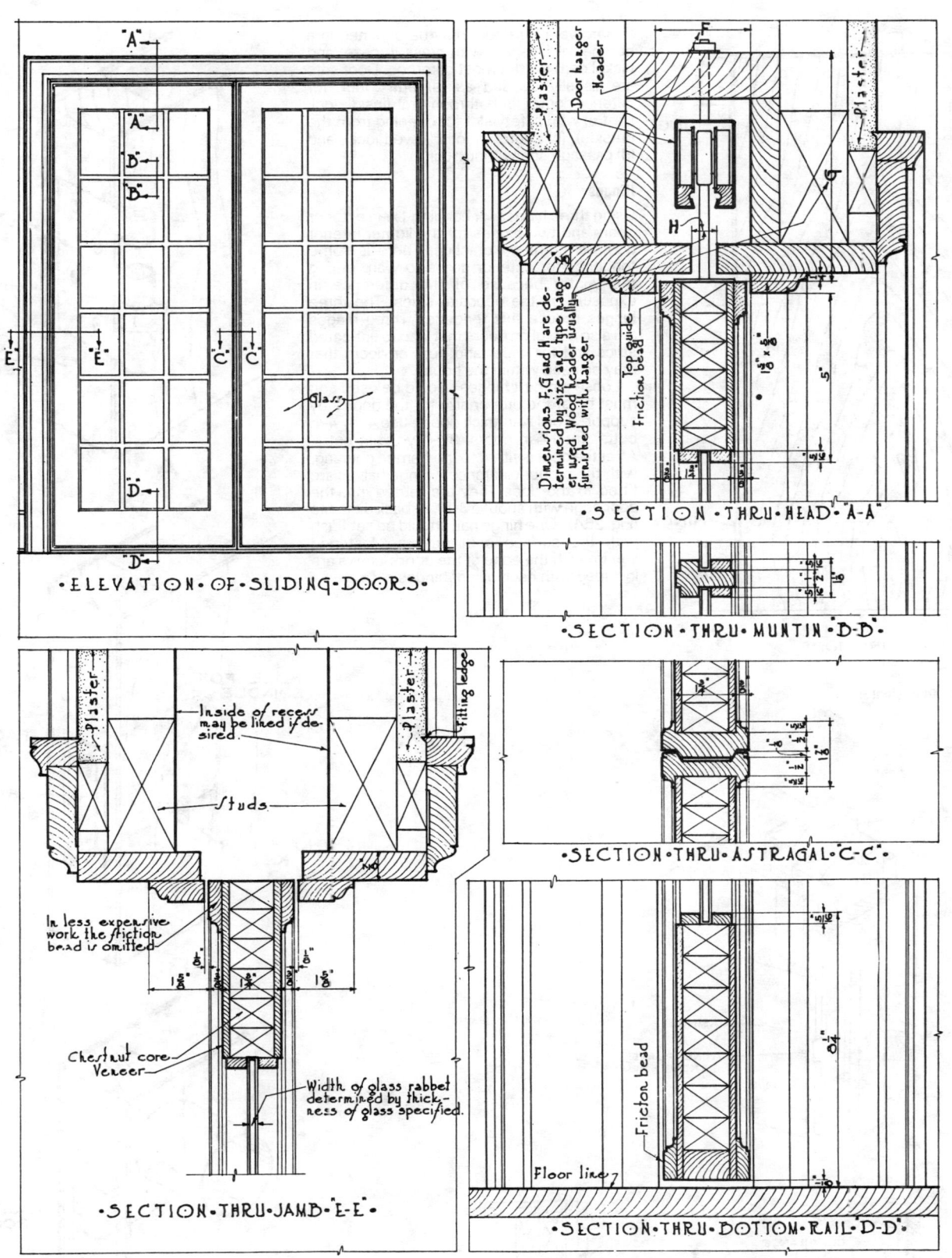

· ELEVATION · OF · SLIDING · DOORS ·

Glass

· SECTION · THRU · HEAD · "A-A" ·

Plaster

Door hanger

Header

Top guide

Friction bead

Dimensions F, G and H are determined by size and type hanger used. Wood header usually furnished with hanger.

· SECTION · THRU · MUNTIN · D-D ·

· SECTION · THRU · ASTRAGAL · C-C ·

Plaster

Fitting ledge

Inside of recess may be lined if desired.

Studs

In less expensive work the friction bead is omitted

Chestnut core Veneer

Width of glass rabbet determined by thickness of glass specified.

· SECTION · THRU · JAMB · "E-E" ·

Friction bead

Floor line

· SECTION · THRU · BOTTOM · RAIL · D-D ·

DOORS
Hardware

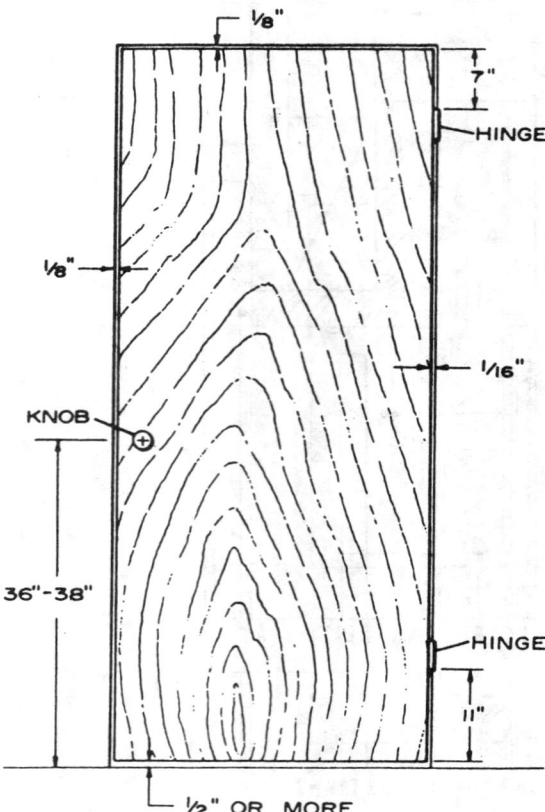

Fig. 24   Door clearances.

Hardware for doors may be obtained in a number of finishes, with brass, bronze, and nickel perhaps the most common. Door sets are usually classed as (a) entry lock for exterior doors, (b) bathroom set (inside lock control with safety slot for opening from the outside), (c) bedroom lock (keyed lock), and (d) passage set (without lock).

Hinges

Using three hinges for hanging 1¾-in exterior doors and two hinges for the lighter interior doors is common practice. There is some tendency for exterior doors to warp during the winter because of the difference in exposure on the opposite sides. The three hinges reduce this tendency. Three hinges are also useful on doors that lead to unheated attics and for wider and heavier doors that may be used within the house.

Loose-pin butt hinges should be used and must be of the proper size for the door they support. For 1¾-in-thick doors, use 4- by 4-in butts; for 1⅜-in doors, 3½- by 3½-in butts. After the door is fitted to the framed opening, with the proper clearances, hinge halves are fitted to the door. They are routed into the door edge with about a 3-16"-in back distance (Fig. 26A). One hinge half should be set flush with the surface and must be fastened square with the edge of the door. Screws are included with each pair of hinges.

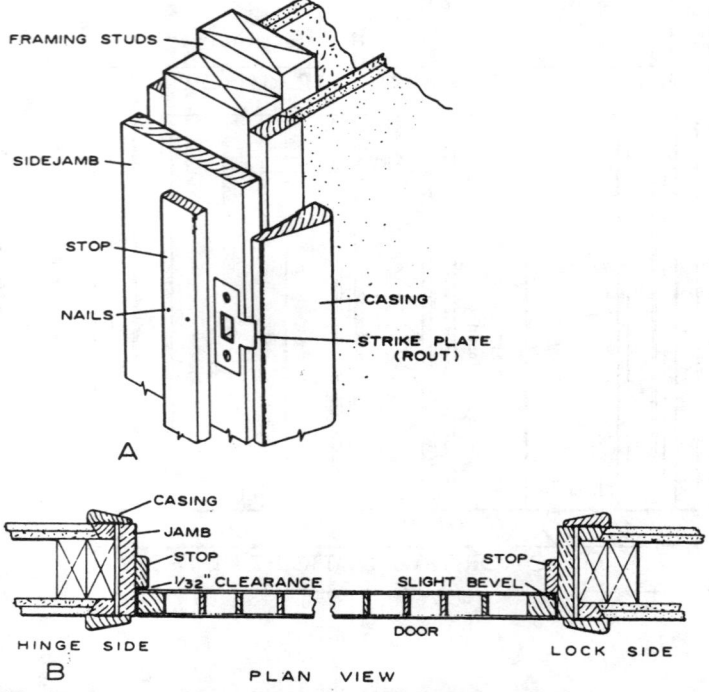

Fig. 25   Door details: A, installation of strike plate; B, location of stops.

Fig. 26   Installation of door hardware: A, hinge; B, mortise lock; C, bored lock set.

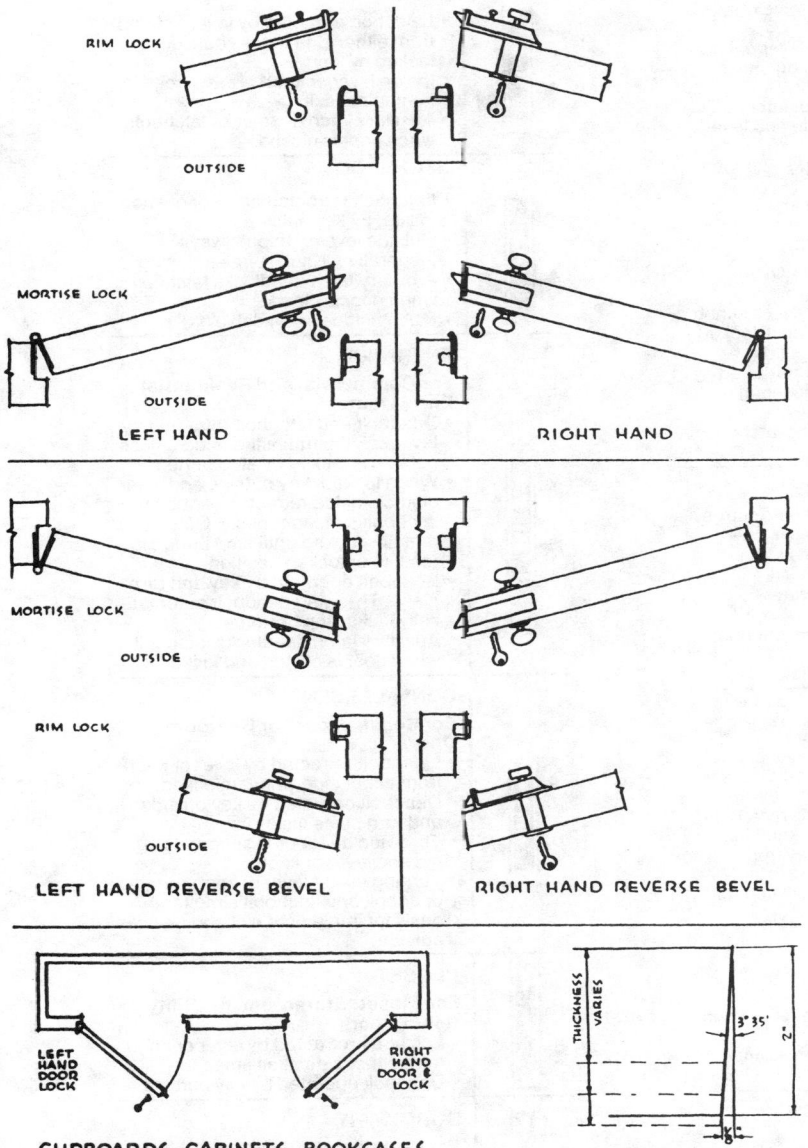

Locks not designated as reversible are made right-hand, left-hand, right-hand reverse bevel, or left-hand reverse bevel.

The hand of a lock is invariably determined from the outside of an entrance door or from the corridor or hall side of a room door. An easy method of determining the hand of a lock is to imagine oneself on that side of the opening from which the lock is controlled or operated by the key. Viewing the opening in this position, note which one of the following is true: (1) If the door swings in and is hinged at your right hand, the lock is right-hand; (2) if hinged at your left hand, the lock is left-hand; (3) if the door swings toward you and is hinged at your right, the lock is right-hand reverse bevel; (4) if hinged at your left hand, the lock is left-hand reverse bevel.

You may find that many locks are marked "reversible," meaning that they are interchangeably right- or left-hand, and in these instances no reference to hand or bevel of lock is necessary. These are locks which operate alike from both sides or locks which can be inverted in order to reverse the locking functions.

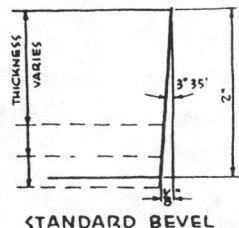

Determination of the hand of mortise or rim locks

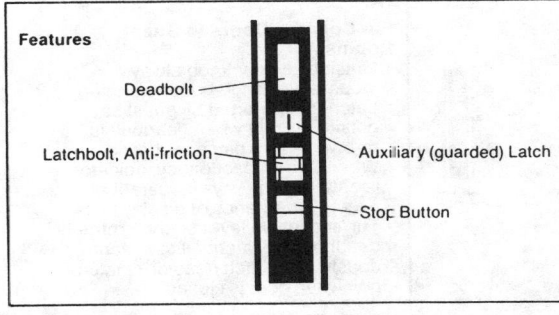

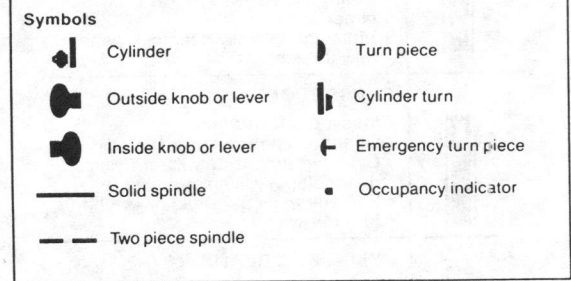

Features of and symbols for door hardware

DOORS

Lock Functions

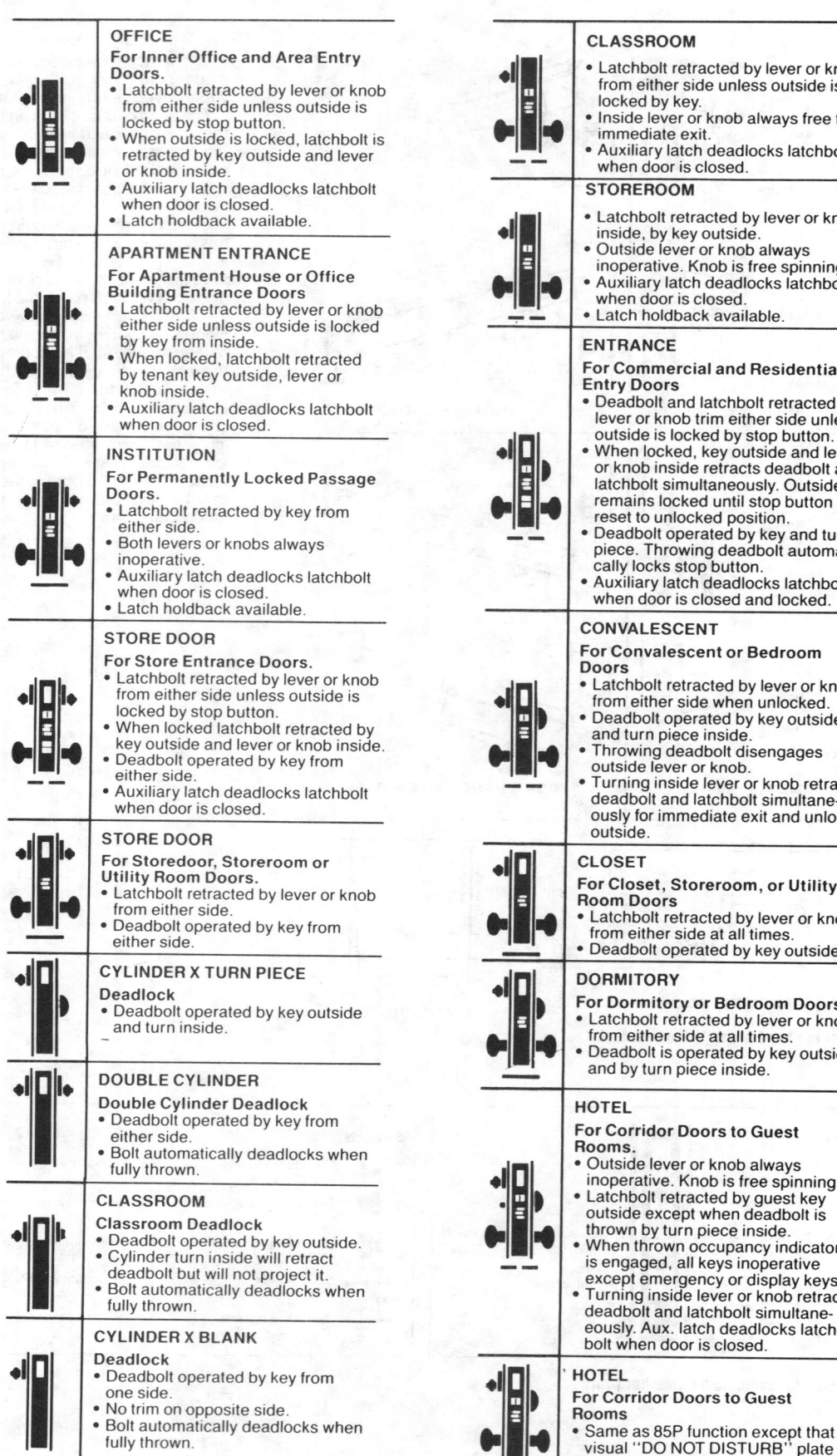

OFFICE

For Inner Office and Area Entry Doors.
- Latchbolt retracted by lever or knob from either side unless outside is locked by stop button.
- When outside is locked, latchbolt is retracted by key outside and lever or knob inside.
- Auxiliary latch deadlocks latchbolt when door is closed.
- Latch holdback available.

APARTMENT ENTRANCE

For Apartment House or Office Building Entrance Doors
- Latchbolt retracted by lever or knob either side unless outside is locked by key from inside.
- When locked, latchbolt retracted by tenant key outside, lever or knob inside.
- Auxiliary latch deadlocks latchbolt when door is closed.

INSTITUTION

For Permanently Locked Passage Doors.
- Latchbolt retracted by key from either side.
- Both levers or knobs always inoperative.
- Auxiliary latch deadlocks latchbolt when door is closed.
- Latch holdback available.

STORE DOOR

For Store Entrance Doors.
- Latchbolt retracted by lever or knob from either side unless outside is locked by stop button.
- When locked latchbolt retracted by key outside and lever or knob inside.
- Deadbolt operated by key from either side.
- Auxiliary latch deadlocks latchbolt when door is closed.

STORE DOOR

For Storedoor, Storeroom or Utility Room Doors.
- Latchbolt retracted by lever or knob from either side.
- Deadbolt operated by key from either side.

CYLINDER X TURN PIECE

Deadlock
- Deadbolt operated by key outside and turn inside.

DOUBLE CYLINDER

Double Cylinder Deadlock
- Deadbolt operated by key from either side.
- Bolt automatically deadlocks when fully thrown.

CLASSROOM

Classroom Deadlock
- Deadbolt operated by key outside.
- Cylinder turn inside will retract deadbolt but will not project it.
- Bolt automatically deadlocks when fully thrown.

CYLINDER X BLANK

Deadlock
- Deadbolt operated by key from one side.
- No trim on opposite side.
- Bolt automatically deadlocks when fully thrown.

CLASSROOM

- Latchbolt retracted by lever or knob from either side unless outside is locked by key.
- Inside lever or knob always free for immediate exit.
- Auxiliary latch deadlocks latchbolt when door is closed.

STOREROOM

- Latchbolt retracted by lever or knob inside, by key outside.
- Outside lever or knob always inoperative. Knob is free spinning.
- Auxiliary latch deadlocks latchbolt when door is closed.
- Latch holdback available.

ENTRANCE

For Commercial and Residential Entry Doors
- Deadbolt and latchbolt retracted by lever or knob trim either side unless outside is locked by stop button.
- When locked, key outside and lever or knob inside retracts deadbolt and latchbolt simultaneously. Outside remains locked until stop button is reset to unlocked position.
- Deadbolt operated by key and turn piece. Throwing deadbolt automatically locks stop button.
- Auxiliary latch deadlocks latchbolt when door is closed and locked.

CONVALESCENT

For Convalescent or Bedroom Doors
- Latchbolt retracted by lever or knob from either side when unlocked.
- Deadbolt operated by key outside and turn piece inside.
- Throwing deadbolt disengages outside lever or knob.
- Turning inside lever or knob retracts deadbolt and latchbolt simultaneously for immediate exit and unlocks outside.

CLOSET

For Closet, Storeroom, or Utility Room Doors
- Latchbolt retracted by lever or knob from either side at all times.
- Deadbolt operated by key outside.

DORMITORY

For Dormitory or Bedroom Doors.
- Latchbolt retracted by lever or knob from either side at all times.
- Deadbolt is operated by key outside and by turn piece inside.

HOTEL

For Corridor Doors to Guest Rooms.
- Outside lever or knob always inoperative. Knob is free spinning.
- Latchbolt retracted by guest key outside except when deadbolt is thrown by turn piece inside.
- When thrown occupancy indicator is engaged, all keys inoperative except emergency or display keys.
- Turning inside lever or knob retracts deadbolt and latchbolt simultaneously. Aux. latch deadlocks latchbolt when door is closed.

HOTEL

For Corridor Doors to Guest Rooms
- Same as 85P function except that visual "DO NOT DISTURB" plate replaces occupancy indicator button.
Available for 1¾" doors and escutcheon trim only.

A. N. S. I. No.	Grade

Non-Keyed Locks — ANSI A156.2 Series 4000

A10S	F75	2
C10S		1
D10S		1
F10N		2

Passage Latch: Both knobs always unlocked

| D12D | F89 | 1 |

Exit Lock: Unlocked by knob inside only. Outside knob always fixed.

| A20S | | |

Closet Latch: Outside knob and inside thumbturn are always unlocked.

| A25D | | |
| D25D | | |

Exit Lock: Blank plate outside. Inside knob always unlocked. (Specify door thickness, 1⅜" or 1¾".)

A30D	F77	2
D30D		1
F30N		2

Patio Lock: Push-button locking. Turning inside knob releases button. Closing door on A & D series also releases button.

A40S	F76	2
C40S		1
D40S		1
F40N		2

Bath/Bedroom Privacy Lock: Push-button locking. Can be opened from outside with small screwdriver or flat narrow tool. Turning inside knob releases push-button. Closing door on A, C and D series also releases button, preventing lock-out.

| A43D | F79 | 2 |

Communicating Lock: Turn button in outer knob locks and unlocks knob and inside thumbturn.

| A44S | | |
| D44S | | |

Hospital Privacy Lock: Push-button locking. Unlocked from outside by turning emergency turn-button. Rotating inside knob or closing door releases inside button.

A. N. S. I. No.	Grade

Dummy Trim

A170		
D170		
F170N		

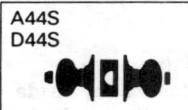

Single Dummy Trim: Single dummy trim for one side of door. Used for door pull or as matching inactive trim.

A. N. S. I. No.	Grade

Keyed Locks — ANSI A156.2 Series 4000

| F51N | F81 | 2 |

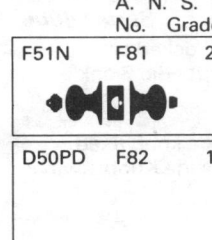

Entrance Lock: Unlocked by key from outside when outer knob is locked by turn-button in inside knob. Inside knob always unlocked.

| D50PD | F82 | 1 |

Entrance/Office Lock: Push button locking. Pushing button locks outside lever until unlocked with key or by turning inside lever.

A53PD	F81	2
C53PD	F82	1
D53PD	F82	1

Entrance Lock: Turn/Push button locking: Pushing and turning button locks outside knob requiring use of key until button is manually unlocked. Push button locking: Pushing button locks outside knob until unlocked by key or by turning inside knob

| A55PD | F92 | 2 |
| D55PD | | 1 |

Service Station Lock: Unlocked by key from outside when outer knob is locked by universal button in inside knob. Closing door releases button. Outside knob may be fixed by rotating universal button.

| D60PD | F88 | 1 |

Vestibule Lock: Unlocked by key from outside when outside knob is locked by key in inside knob. Inside knob is always unlocked.

| D66PD | F91 | 1 |

Store Lock: Key in either knob locks or unlocks both knobs.

A70PD	F84	2
C70PD		1
D70PD		1

Classroom Lock: Outside knob locked and unlocked by key. Inside knob always unlocked.

| D72PD | F80 | 1 |

Communicating Lock: Key in either knob locks or unlocks each knob independently.

| A73PD | F90 | 2 |
| D73PD | | 1 |

Dormitory Lock: Locked or unlocked by key from outside. Push-button locking from inside. Turning inside knob or closing door releases button.

| D76PD | F85 | 1 |

Classroom Hold-Back Lock: Outside knob locked or unlocked by key. Inside knob always unlocked. Latch may be locked in retracted position by key.

DOORS
Lock Functions

A. N. S. I. No. Grade		

Keyed Locks
ANSI A156.2 Series 4000

A79PD		

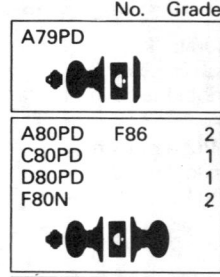

Communicating Lock: Locked or unlocked by key from outside. Blank plate inside.

A80PD	F86	2
C80PD		1
D80PD		1
F80N		2

Storeroom Lock: Outside knob fixed. Entrance by key only. Inside Knob always unlocked.

D82PD	F87	1

Institution Lock: Both knobs fixed. Entrance by key in either knob.

A85PD	F93	2
D85PD		1

Hotel-Motel Lock: Outside knob fixed. Entrance by key only. Push-button in inside knob activates visual occupancy indicator, allowing only emergency masterkey to operate. Rotation of inside spanner-button provides lockout feature by keeping indicator thrown.

A. N. S. I. No. Grade		

Deadbolt Locks ANSI A 156.5

B160N	E2151	2
B460P		1
B560		1

Single Cylinder Deadbolt Lock: Deadbolt thrown or retracted by key from outside or by inside turn unit. Bolt automatically deadlocks when fully thrown.

B162N†	E2141	2
B462P†		1
B562†		1

Double Cylinder Deadbolt Lock: Deadbolt thrown or retracted by key from either side.

B461P	E2161	1

One-Way Deadbolt Lock: Deadbolt thrown or retracted by key only. Blank plate inside.

B463P	E2171	1

Classroom Deadbolt Lock: Deadbolt thrown or retracted by key outside. Inside turn unit will retract bolt only.

B464P		

Cylinder Lock: Deadbolt thrown or retracted by key from one side. No inside trim.

B180	E2191	2
B480		1

Door Bolt: Deadbolt thrown or retracted by turn unit only. No outside trim.

A. N. S. I. No. Grade		

Deadlatch Locks ANSI A156.5

B250PD	E2121	1

Night Latch: Deadlocking latchbolt retracted by key from outside or by inside turn unit. Rotating turn unit and activating hold-back feature keeps latch retracted.

B252PD†	E2111	1

Double Cylinder Deadlatch: Deadlocking latchbolt retracted by key from either side. No hold-back feature.

B270D	E2181	1

Exit Latch: Deadlocking latchbolt retracted by inside turn unit only. No outside trim. Rotating turn unit and activating hold-back feature keeps latch retracted.

Schlage Number	A. N. S. I. No.	Grade
B245S		

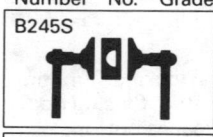

Lever Functions

Lever Passage Latch: For use on passage, closet and doors that do not require locking. Rotating either lever retracts latchbolt. (Specify door hand.)

B281		
B282		

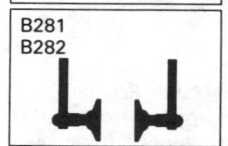

Single Dummy Trim-Double Dummy Trim: For use on single or pairs of doors when fixed turn is required. (Specify door hand.)

A. N. S. I. No. Grade		

Grip Handle Sets

E51PD		

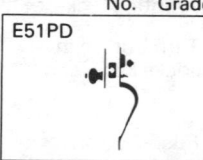

Entrance Lock: Unlocked by key from outside when thumb-piece is locked by inside turn-button.

F160N		

Entrance Lock: Deadbolt thrown or retracted by key from outside or by inside turn unit. Latch retracted by thumbpiece from outside or by inside knob.

F162N†		

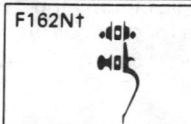

Double Cylinder Entrance Lock: Deadbolt thrown or retracted by key from either side. Latch retracted by thumbpiece from outside or by inside knob.

†CAUTION: Double cylinder locks on residences and any door in any structure which is used for egress are a safety hazard in times of emergency and their use is not recommended. Installation should be in accordance with existing codes only.

Dummy Trim

A. N. S. I. No.	Grade
E193	

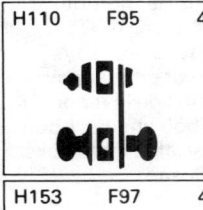

Outside and Inside Dummy Trim: For use as door pull or as dummy trim on an inactive of pair of doors. Fixed thumb-piece and inside knob. Thru bolted dummy cylinder.

A. N. S. I. No.	Grade
F193N	

Outside and Inside Dymmy Trim: For use as door pull or as dummy trim on inactive leaf of pair of doors. Fixed thumbpiece and inside knob. Dummy cylinder with inside plate.

Interconnected Locks   ANSI A156.12

A. N. S. I. No.	Grade
H110	F95	4

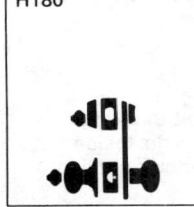

Entrance—Single Locking: Deadbolt thrown or retracted by key in upper lock from outside or by inside turn unit. Latch-bolt retracted by knob from either side. Turning inside knob retracts deadbolt and latchbolt simultaneously for immediate exit.

A. N. S. I. No.	Grade
H153	F97	4

Entrance—Double Locking: Deadbolt thrown or retracted by key in upper lock from outside or by inside turn unit. Dead-latch retracted by key in outer knob when locked by pushing turn-button in inner knob. Outer knob may be fixed in locked position by rotating turn-button. Inside knob retracts deadbolt and deadlatch simultaneously for immediate exit.

A. N. S. I. No.	Grade
H180	

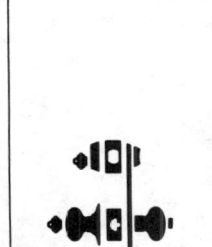

Storeroom Lock: Bolt may be operated by key from outside or by turn unit from inside. Bolt automatically deadlocks when fully thrown. Lock may be opened by key from outside. Inside knob will retract both latch and deadbolt. Latch automatically deadlocks when door is closed, inside knob always free for immediate exit. Outer knob always fixed.

A. N. S. I. No.	Grade
H185	F100	4

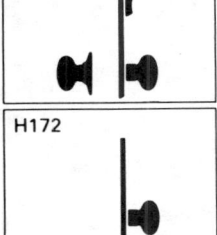

Hotel-Motel Lock: Deadbolt thrown or retracted by key in upper lock from outside or by inside turn unit. Deadlatch retracted by key in outer fixed knob. Push-button in inner knob activates visual occupancy indicator, allowing only emergency masterkey to operate. Rotation of inside spanner-button provides lockout feature by keeping indicator thrown. Turning inside knob retracts deadbolt simultaneously for immediate exit.

Dummy Trim

A. N. S. I. No.	Grade
H170	
H172	

Single Dummy Inside Trim: Snap-on rose and knob. Concealed mounting screws.

Dummy Trim Inside and Outside: Snap-on rose and knobs thru-bolted.

Mortise Locks Non-Keyed   ANSI A156.13   Series 1000

A. N. S. I. No.	Grade
L9010*	F01	1

Passage Latch: Latch bolt retracted by lever or knob from either side at all times.

A. N. S. I. No.	Grade
L9040	F22	1

Bath/Bedroom Privacy Lock: Latchbolt retracted by lever or knob from either side unless outside is locked by inside turn piece. Operating inside lever or knob or closing door unlocks outside lever or knob. To unlock from outside, remove emergency button, insert turn piece (furnished) in access hole and rotate.

A. N. S. I. No.	Grade
L0170	

Single Dummy Trim: Lever or knob on both sides fixed by mounting bar.

A. N. S. I. No.	Grade
L0172*	

Pair Dummy Trim: Lever or knob on both sides fixed by mounting bar.

A. N. S. I. No.	Grade
L9175**	

Single Dummy Trim: Lever or knob on one side fixed. Includes lock chassis and armor front.

A. N. S. I. No.	Grade
L9176**	

Pair Dummy Trim: Lever or knob both sides fixed. Includes lock chassis and armor front.

Keyed Locks

A. N. S. I. No.	Grade
L9050*	F04	1

Office and Inner Entry Lock: Latchbolt retracted by lever or knob from either side unless outside is made inoperative by key outside or by rotating inside turn piece. When outside is locked, latchbolt is retracted by key outside or by lever or knob inside. Outside lever or knob remains locked until thumbturn is returned to vertical or by counter clock-wise rotation of key. Auxiliary latch deadlocks latchbolt when door is closed.

A. N. S. I. No.	Grade
L9060*	F09	1

Apartment Entrance Lock: Latchbolt retracted by lever or knob from either side unless outside is locked by key from inside. When locked, latchbolt retracted by key outside or lever or knob inside. Auxiliary latch deadlocks when door is closed.

A. N. S. I. No.	Grade
L9070*	F05	1

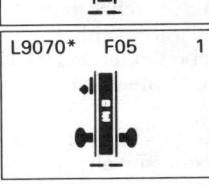

Classroom Lock: Latchbolt retracted by lever or knob from either side unless outside is locked by key. Unlocked from outside by key. Inside lever or knob always free for immediate exit. Auxiliary latch deadlocks latchbolt when door is closed.

**When armored front is required as strike for inactive door, specify L9177 for single or L9178 for pair of dummy trim. Specify door hard.

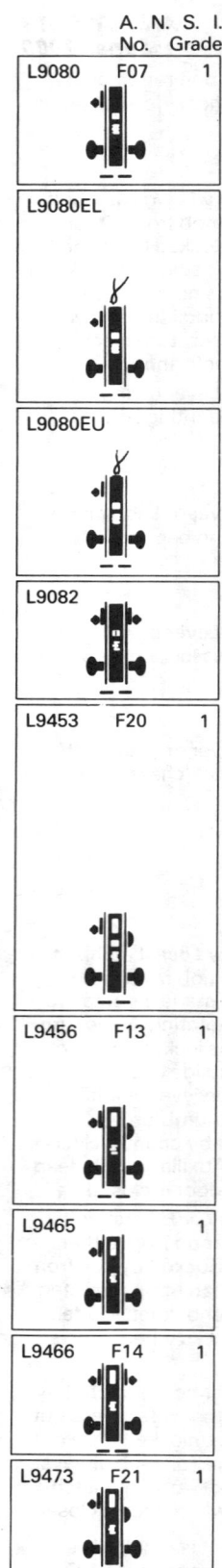

	A. N. S. I.	
	No.	Grade
L9080	F07	1
L9080EL		
L9080EU		
L9082		
L9453	F20	1
L9456	F13	1
L9465		
L9466	F14	1
L9473	F21	1

Keyed Locks

Storeroom Lock: Latchbolt retracted by key outside or by lever or knob inside. Outside lever or knob always inoperative. Auxiliary latch deadlocks latchbolt when door is closed.

Storeroom Lock: Electrically locked. Outside lever or knob continuously locked by 24V AC or DC. Latchbolt retracted by key outside or by lever or knob inside. Switch or power failure allows outside lever or knob to retract latchbolt. Auxiliary latch deadlocks latchbolt when door is closed. Inside lever or knob always free for immediate exit.

Storeroom Lock: Electrically unlocked. Outside lever or knob unlocked by 24V AC or DC. Latchbolt retracted by key outside or lever or knob inside. Auxiliary latch deadlocks latchbolt when door is closed. Inside lever or knob always free for immediate exit.

Institution Lock: Latchbolt retracted by key from either side. Lever or knob on both sides always inoperative. Auxiliary latch deadlocks latchbolt when door is closed.

Entrance Lock: Latchbolt retracted by lever or knob from either side unless outside is locked by 20° rotation of thumbturn. Deadbolt thrown or retracted by 90° rotation of thumbturn. When locked, key outside or lever or knob inside retracts deadbolt and latchbolt simultaneously. Outside lever or knob remains locked until thumbturn is restored to vertical position. Throwing deadbolt automatically locks outside lever or knob. Auxiliary latch deadlocks latchbolt when door is closed.

Dormitory/Exit Lock: Latchbolt retracted by lever or knob from either side. Deadbolt thrown or retracted by key outside or inside thumbturn. Throwing deadbolt locks outside lever or knob. Rotating inside lever or knob simultaneously retracts deadbolt and latchbolt, and unlocks outside lever or knob.

Closet/Storeroom Lock: Latchbolt retracted by lever or knob from either side except when deadbolt is extended. Deadbolt extended or retracted by key outside.

Store/Utility Room Lock: Latchbolt retracted by knob or lever from either side except when deadbolt extended. Deadbolt extended or retracted by key from either side.

Dormitory/Bedroom Lock: Latchbolt retracted by knob or lever from either side except when deadbolt is extended. Deadbolt extended or retracted by key outside or thumbturn inside.

	A. N. S. I.	
	No.	Grade
L9485		
L9486	F15	1

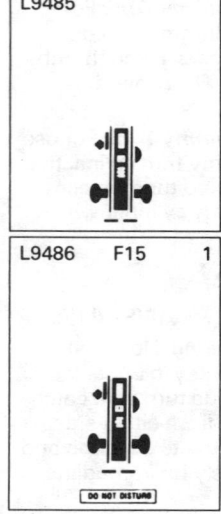

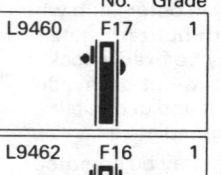

DO NOT DISTURB

Keyed Locks

Hotel Lock: Latchbolt by key outside or by lever or knob inside. Outside lever or knob always fixed. Deadbolt thrown or retracted by inside thumbturn. When deadbolt is thrown, all keys become inoperative except emergency or display keys. Turning inside lever or knob retracts both deadbolt and latchbolt simultaneously. Auxiliary latch deadlocks latchbolt when door is closed.

Hotel Lock: Latchbolt retracted by key outside or by lever or knob inside. Outside lever or knob always fixed. Deadbolt thrown or retracted by inside thumbturn. When deadbolt is thrown, "DO NOT DISTURB" plate is displayed—all keys become inoperative except emergency or display keys. Turning inside lever or knob retracts both deadbolt and latchbolt simultaneously. Auxiliary latch deadlocks latchbolt when door is closed.

	A. N. S. I.	
	No.	Grade
L9460	F17	1
L9462	F16	1
L9463		1
L9464	F18	1

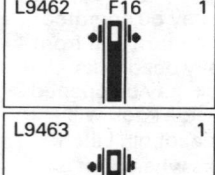

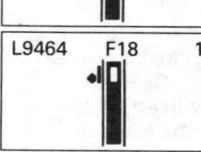

Deadlocks

Cylinder X Thumbturn: Deadbolt thrown or retracted by key outside or thumbturn inside.

Double Cylinder: Deadbolt operated by key from either side.

Classroom Lock: Deadbolt thrown or retracted by key from outside. Inside cylinder turn retracts deadbolt but cannot project it.

Cylinder Lock: Deadbolt thrown or retracted by key from one side. No trim on opposite side.

This section provides the designer with information on both suspended ceilings and ceilings directly attached to the structure above. It starts with a review of generic suspension systems and then provides details and discussion of the various suspended ceiling types.

Large-scale details show how, in addition to standard acoustical tiles, other ceiling materials such as plaster, metal panels, baffles, gypsum board, and wood can be attached to suspension systems. A variety of unusual conditions are also detailed, including curved and vaulted ceilings, wall conditions, light coves, and lighting fixture framing.

The designer is cautioned that in many jurisdictions, suspension systems must attain a higher level of structural integrity than most other architectural elements. For example, wire hangers may not be an acceptable method of suspending channels from the structure above. Rather, steel rods of a minimum diameter or flat bar hangers of a minimum width and thickness may be required. Local or state codes should always be consulted prior to finalizing such details.

In many situations, the ceiling "skin" takes on further importance beyond aesthetic, acoustical, or visual requirements. It can also be used to complete an envelope that provides a fire-resistive rating to the structural members above. Again, it is necessary to thoroughly investigate the building and fire codes that might govern ceiling design.

Acoustical Tile and Lay-in Panel Ceiling Suspension Systems

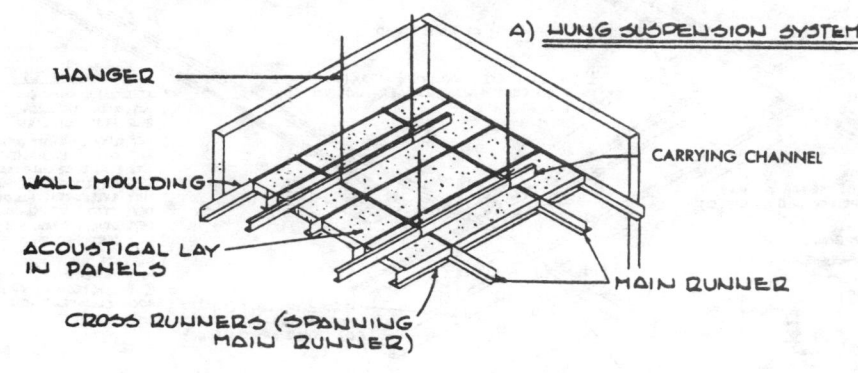

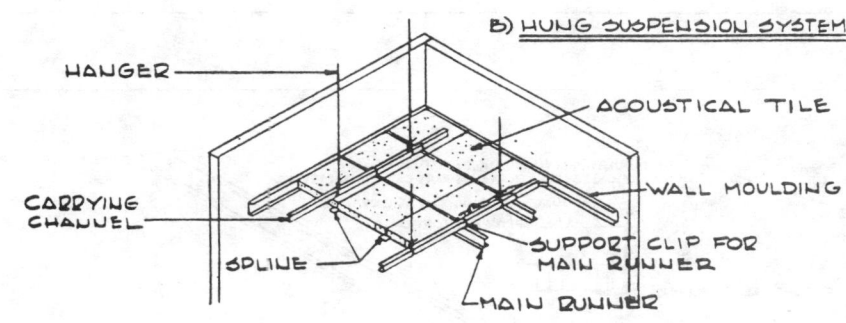

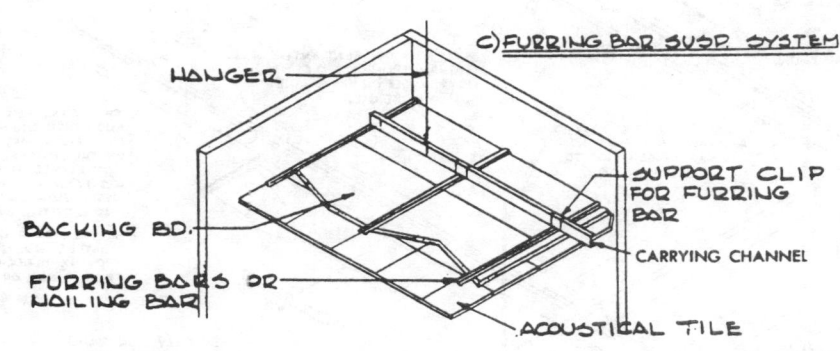

CEILINGS

Suspension System Types

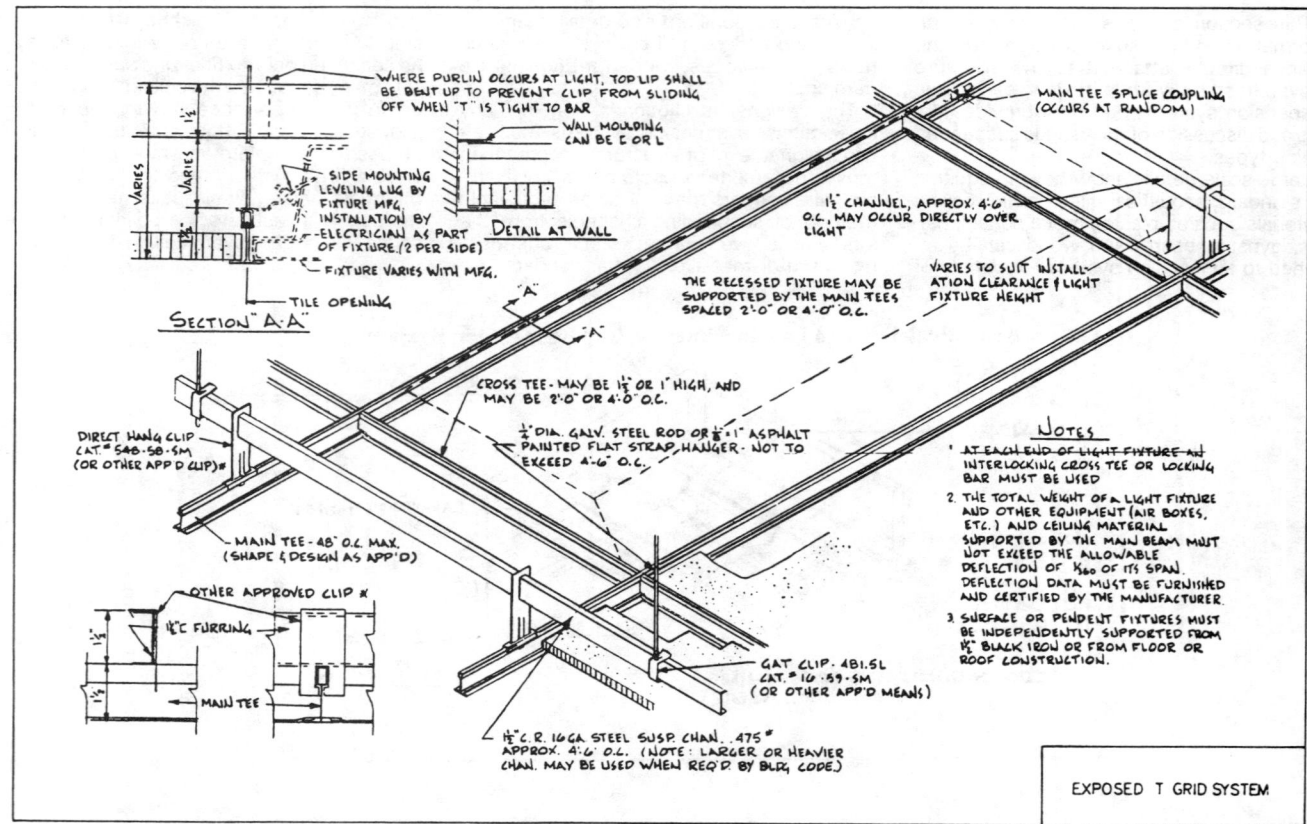

SECTION "A-A"

WHERE PURLIN OCCURS AT LIGHT, TOP LIP SHALL BE BENT UP TO PREVENT CLIP FROM SLIDING OFF WHEN "T" IS TIGHT TO BAR

WALL MOULDING CAN BE C OR L

DETAIL AT WALL

SIDE MOUNTING LEVELING LUG BY FIXTURE MFG. INSTALLATION BY ELECTRICIAN AS PART OF FIXTURE. (2 PER SIDE)

FIXTURE VARIES WITH MFG.

TILE OPENING

VARIES

MAIN TEE SPLICE COUPLING (OCCURS AT RANDOM)

1½ CHANNEL, APPROX. 4'-6" O.C., MAY OCCUR DIRECTLY OVER LIGHT

VARIES TO SUIT INSTALLATION CLEARANCE & LIGHT FIXTURE HEIGHT

THE RECESSED FIXTURE MAY BE SUPPORTED BY THE MAIN TEES SPACED 2'-0" OR 4'-0" O.C.

CROSS TEE - MAY BE 1½" OR 1" HIGH, AND MAY BE 2'-0" OR 4'-0" O.C.

½" DIA. GALV. STEEL ROD OR ⅛" × 1" ASPHALT PAINTED FLAT STRAP HANGER - NOT TO EXCEED 4'-6" O.C.

DIRECT HANG CLIP CAT. #S48-58-SM (OR OTHER APP'D CLIP)

MAIN TEE - 48" O.C. MAX. (SHAPE & DESIGN AS APP'D)

OTHER APPROVED CLIP

1½"C FURRING

MAIN TEE

GAT CLIP 481.5L CAT. #16-59-SM (OR OTHER APP'D MEANS)

1½" C.R. 16GA. STEEL SUSP. CHAN. .475" APPROX. 4'-6" O.C. (NOTE: LARGER OR HEAVIER CHAN. MAY BE USED WHEN REQ'D BY BLDG. CODE.)

NOTES

1. AT EACH END OF LIGHT FIXTURE AN INTERLOCKING CROSS TEE OR LOCKING BAR MUST BE USED

2. THE TOTAL WEIGHT OF A LIGHT FIXTURE AND OTHER EQUIPMENT (AIR BOXES, ETC.) AND CEILING MATERIAL SUPPORTED BY THE MAIN BEAM MUST NOT EXCEED THE ALLOWABLE DEFLECTION OF ⅟360 OF ITS SPAN. DEFLECTION DATA MUST BE FURNISHED AND CERTIFIED BY THE MANUFACTURER

3. SURFACE OR PENDENT FIXTURES MUST BE INDEPENDENTLY SUPPORTED FROM 1½" BLACK IRON OR FROM FLOOR OR ROOF CONSTRUCTION.

EXPOSED T GRID SYSTEM

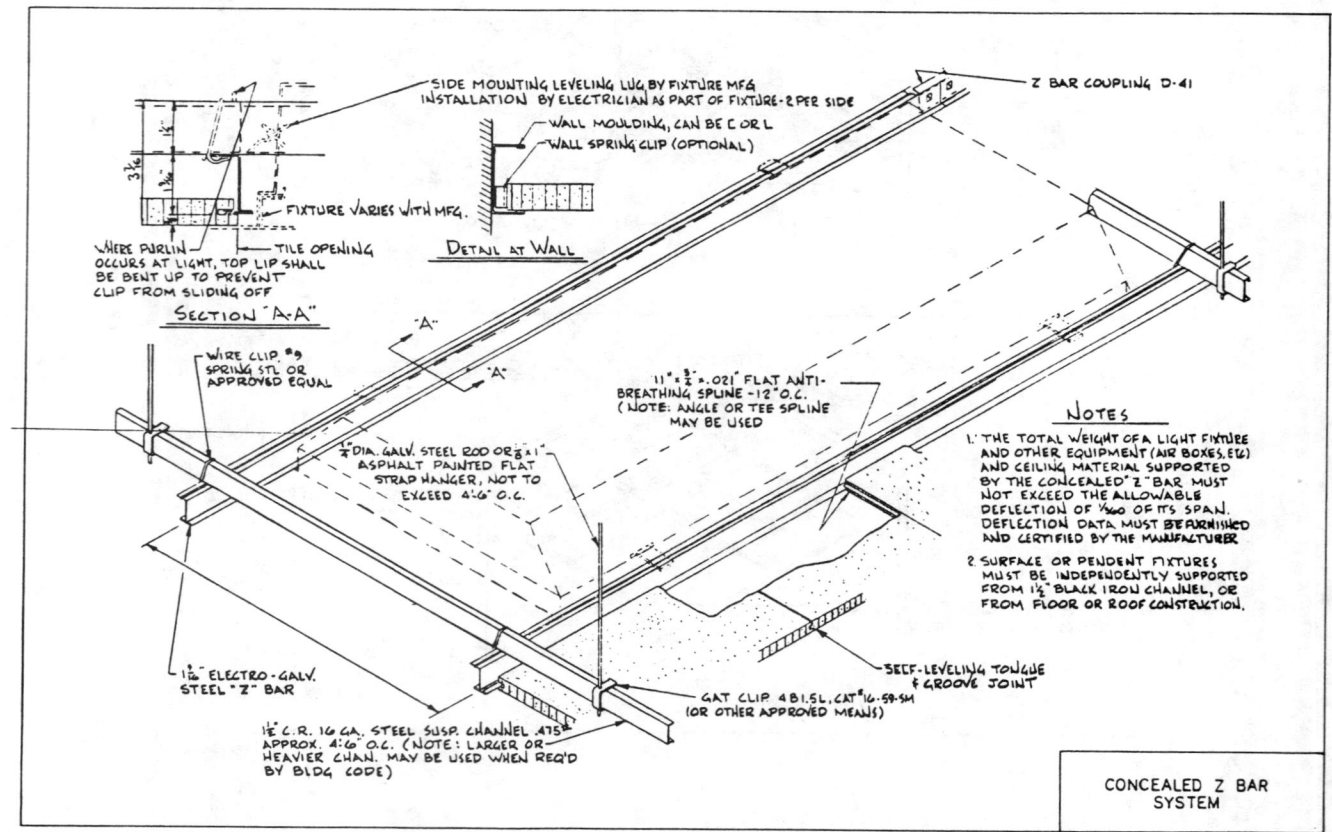

SIDE MOUNTING LEVELING LUG BY FIXTURE MFG. INSTALLATION BY ELECTRICIAN AS PART OF FIXTURE - 2 PER SIDE

WALL MOULDING, CAN BE C OR L

WALL SPRING CLIP (OPTIONAL)

FIXTURE VARIES WITH MFG.

WHERE PURLIN OCCURS AT LIGHT, TOP LIP SHALL BE BENT UP TO PREVENT CLIP FROM SLIDING OFF

TILE OPENING

DETAIL AT WALL

SECTION "A-A"

Z BAR COUPLING D-41

WIRE CLIP #9 SPRING STL. OR APPROVED EQUAL

½" DIA. GALV. STEEL ROD OR ⅛" × 1" ASPHALT PAINTED FLAT STRAP HANGER, NOT TO EXCEED 4'-6" O.C.

11"× ¾"× .021" FLAT ANTI-BREATHING SPLINE -12" O.C. (NOTE: ANGLE OR TEE SPLINE MAY BE USED)

1½" ELECTRO-GALV. STEEL "Z" BAR

1½" C.R. 16 GA. STEEL SUSP. CHANNEL .475" APPROX. 4'-6" O.C. (NOTE: LARGER OR HEAVIER CHAN. MAY BE USED WHEN REQ'D BY BLDG. CODE)

GAT CLIP 481.5L, CAT. #16-59-SM (OR OTHER APPROVED MEANS)

SELF-LEVELING TONGUE & GROOVE JOINT

NOTES

1. THE TOTAL WEIGHT OF A LIGHT FIXTURE AND OTHER EQUIPMENT (AIR BOXES, ETC.) AND CEILING MATERIAL SUPPORTED BY THE CONCEALED "Z" BAR MUST NOT EXCEED THE ALLOWABLE DEFLECTION OF ⅟360 OF ITS SPAN. DEFLECTION DATA MUST BE FURNISHED AND CERTIFIED BY THE MANUFACTURER

2. SURFACE OR PENDENT FIXTURES MUST BE INDEPENDENTLY SUPPORTED FROM 1½" BLACK IRON CHANNEL, OR FROM FLOOR OR ROOF CONSTRUCTION.

CONCEALED Z BAR SYSTEM

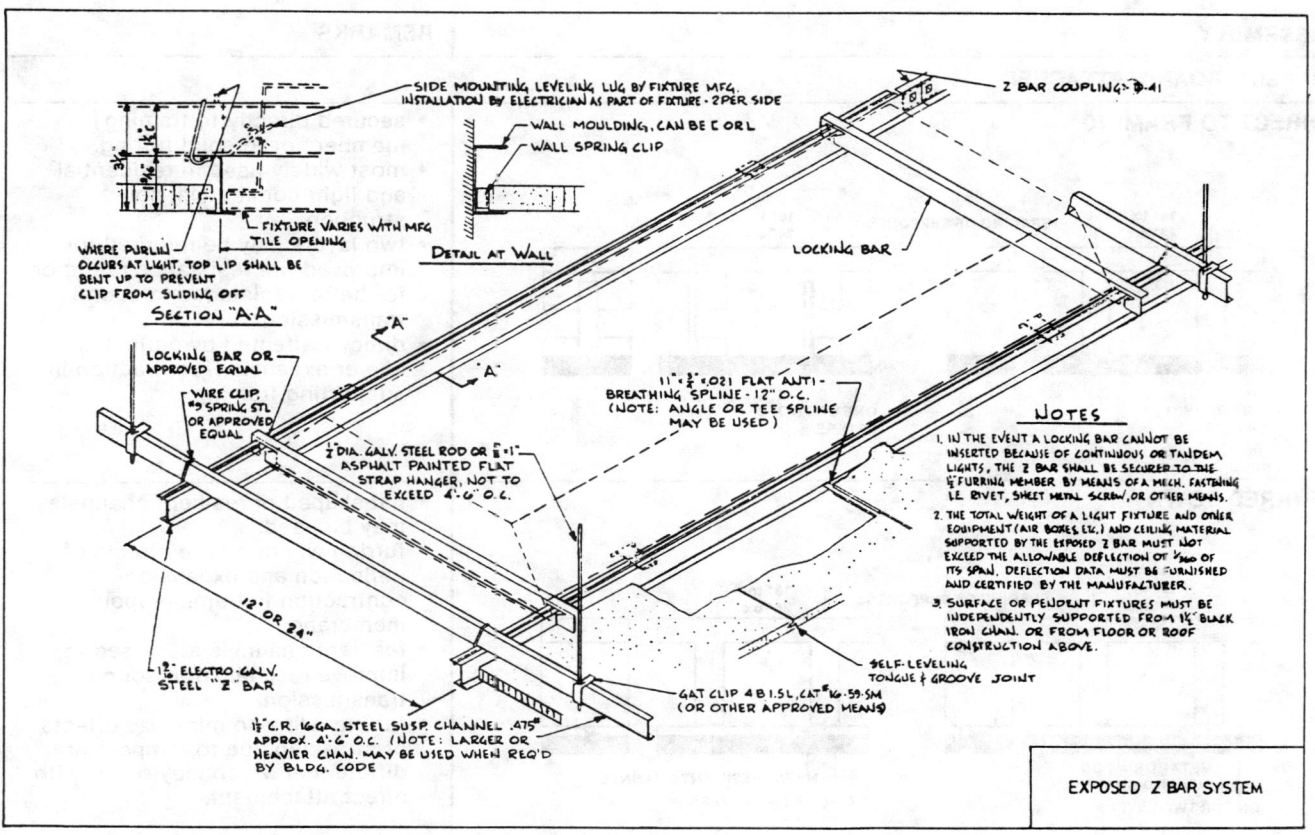

SIDE MOUNTING LEVELING LUG BY FIXTURE MFG.
INSTALLATION BY ELECTRICIAN AS PART OF FIXTURE - 2 PER SIDE

WALL MOULDING, CAN BE C OR L

WALL SPRING CLIP

DETAIL AT WALL

Z BAR COUPLING-B-41

WHERE PURLIN OCCURS AT LIGHT, TOP LIP SHALL BE BENT UP TO PREVENT CLIP FROM SLIDING OFF

FIXTURE VARIES WITH MFG. TILE OPENING

SECTION "A·A"

LOCKING BAR OR APPROVED EQUAL

WIRE CLIP #9 SPRING STL OR APPROVED EQUAL

LOCKING BAR

½" DIA. GALV. STEEL ROD OR ⅜"·1" ASPHALT PAINTED FLAT STRAP HANGER, NOT TO EXCEED 4'·6" O.C.

1"·½"·.021 FLAT ANTI· BREATHING SPLINE - 12" O.C. (NOTE: ANGLE OR TEE SPLINE MAY BE USED)

12" OR 24"

1½" ELECTRO-GALV. STEEL "Z" BAR

1⅝" C.R. 16 GA. STEEL SUSP. CHANNEL .475" APPROX. 4'·6" O.C. (NOTE: LARGER OR HEAVIER CHAN. MAY BE USED WHEN REQ'D BY BLDG. CODE

GAT CLIP 4 B 1.5L, CAT #16·59·SM (OR OTHER APPROVED MEANS)

SELF·LEVELING TONGUE & GROOVE JOINT

NOTES

1. IN THE EVENT A LOCKING BAR CANNOT BE INSERTED BECAUSE OF CONTINUOUS OR TANDEM LIGHTS, THE Z BAR SHALL BE SECURED TO THE 1⅝" FURRING MEMBER BY MEANS OF A MECH. FASTENING I.E. RIVET, SHEET METAL SCREW, OR OTHER MEANS.

2. THE TOTAL WEIGHT OF A LIGHT FIXTURE AND OTHER EQUIPMENT (AIR BOXES ETC.) AND CEILING MATERIAL SUPPORTED BY THE EXPOSED Z BAR MUST NOT EXCEED THE ALLOWABLE DEFLECTION OF 1/360 OF ITS SPAN. DEFLECTION DATA MUST BE FURNISHED AND CERTIFIED BY THE MANUFACTURER.

3. SURFACE OR PENDENT FIXTURES MUST BE INDEPENDENTLY SUPPORTED FROM 1½" BLACK IRON CHAN. OR FROM FLOOR OR ROOF CONSTRUCTION ABOVE.

EXPOSED Z BAR SYSTEM

CEILINGS
Gypsum Board Suspended Ceilings

ASSEMBLY	REMARKS
GYPSUM BOARD, ATTACHED	
DIRECT TO FRAMING 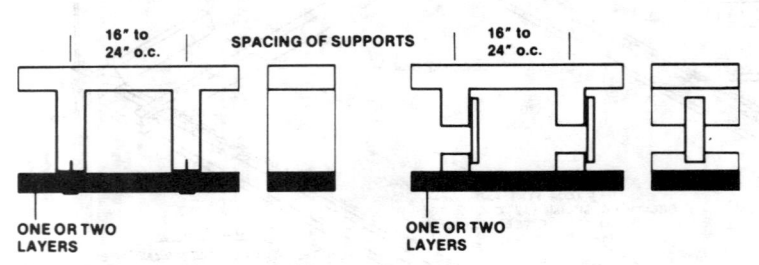	• secured directly to framing members or to solid furring. • most widely used in residential and light commercial construction. • two layers may be required for an improved fire resistance rating or for better resistance to sound transmission. • directly affected by deflection and/or expansion/contraction in supporting framing.
FURRED-DOWN 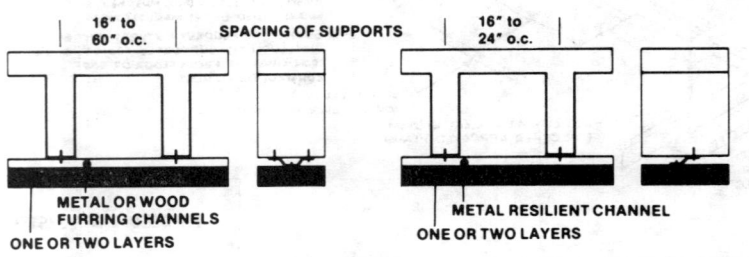	• hat-shaped or resilient channels may be used. • furring will minimize effects of deflection and expansion/ contraction in framing upon membrane. • resilient channels also used to improve resistance to sound transmission. • furring will also minimize effects of streaking due to temperature differential which may occur with direct attachment.
GYPSUM BOARD, SUSPENDED	
PRIMARY SUPPORTS ONLY 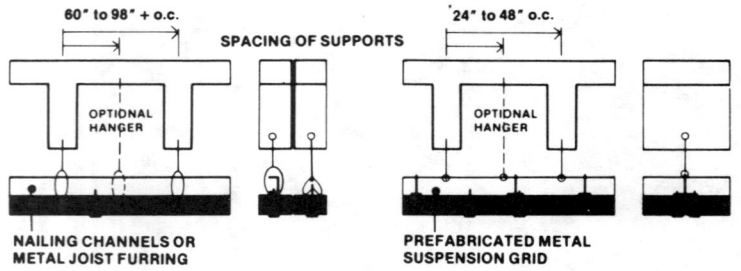	• when framing is spaced more than 24 inches on centers, or when a plenum space for mechanical/electrical service lines is required, a suspension/support system consisting of wood or metal sections or special nailing channels is generally provided. • prefabricated metal suspension systems are available.
PRIMARY AND SECONDARY SUPPORTS 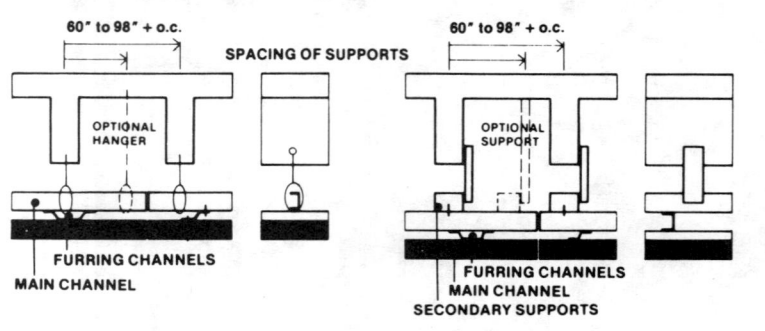	• primary suspension system may also include a secondary system of furring channels used to align the primary system and/or to provide resilient mounting of the membrane. • it is a high cost assembly and not widely used. • resilient furring channels generally used with wood framing.

ASSEMBLY	REMARKS

PLASTER, ATTACHED

DIRECT TO FRAMING

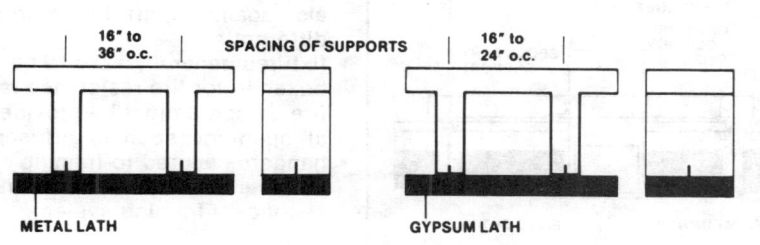

16" to 36" o.c. — SPACING OF SUPPORTS — 16" to 24" o.c.

METAL LATH — GYPSUM LATH

- metal or gypsum lath secured directly to framing.
- membrane will be directly affected by deflection and/or expansion/contraction in supporting framing.
- metal lath may be backed for machine application of plaster.
- fire resistance ratings for different assemblies have been established.

FURRED-DOWN

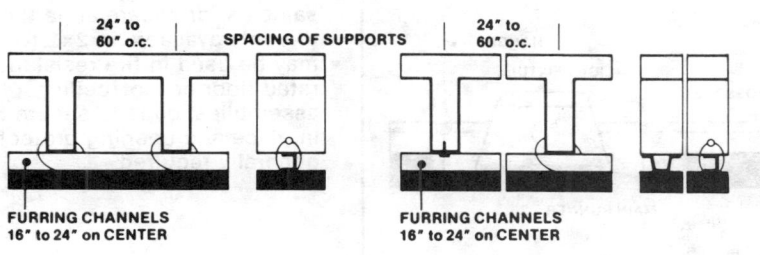

24" to 60" o.c. — SPACING OF SUPPORTS — 24" to 60" o.c.

FURRING CHANNELS 16" to 24" on CENTER — FURRING CHANNELS 16" to 24" on CENTER

- furring channels secured to framing, lath supported by furring.
- furring will minimize effects of deflection and expansion/ contraction upon membrane.
- large areas of membrane should have expansion joints and should not be restrained at the perimeter.
- corners of openings in gypsum lath membranes should have metal lath reinforcing.

PLASTER, SUSPENDED

PRIMARY SUPPORTS ONLY

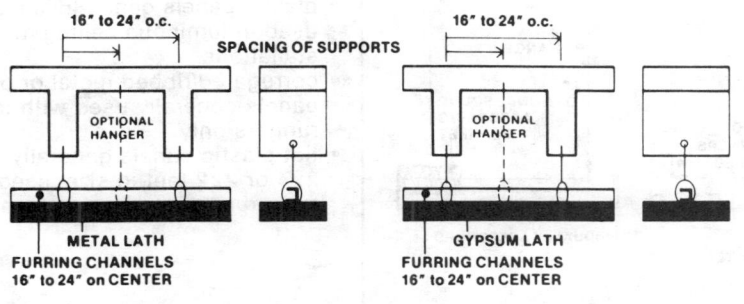

16" to 24" o.c. — SPACING OF SUPPORTS — 16" to 24" o.c.

OPTIONAL HANGER — OPTIONAL HANGER

METAL LATH FURRING CHANNELS 16" to 24" on CENTER — GYPSUM LATH FURRING CHANNELS 16" to 24" on CENTER

- suspended membrane with furring channels only is similar to furred membrane except that furring channels are suspended from, rather than directly attached to, framing members.
- suspension of membrane may be a requirement in some fire resistance rated floor or roof/ceiling assemblies.
- spacing of hangers is quite close and limits the size and/or extent of mechanical/electrical service lines in plenum space.

PRIMARY AND SECONDARY SUPPORTS

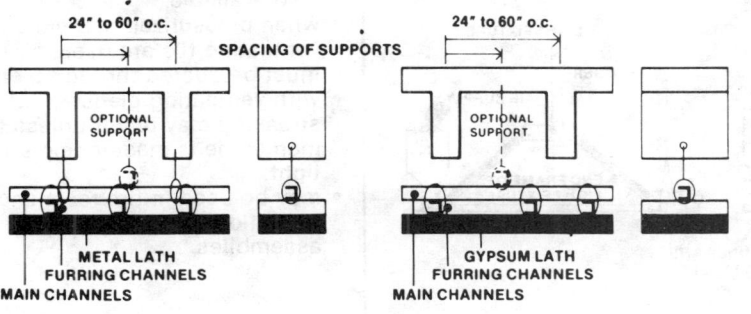

24" to 60" o.c. — SPACING OF SUPPORTS — 24" to 60" o.c.

OPTIONAL SUPPORT — OPTIONAL SUPPORT

METAL LATH FURRING CHANNELS MAIN CHANNELS — GYPSUM LATH FURRING CHANNELS MAIN CHANNELS

- when spacing of framing is wide and/or the number of hangers must be reduced, a primary support system consisting of main carrying channels may be used; the furring channels are then a secondary system, secured to such primary supports.
- for wide hanger spacing, metal joists instead of carrying channels may be used.

CEILINGS
Exposed Grid Suspended Ceilings

ASSEMBLY	REMARKS

EXPOSED GRID: FLAT UNITS

SQUARE EDGE

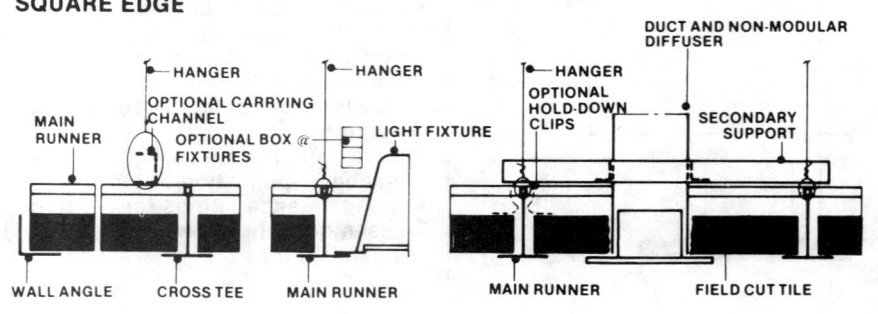

- lay-in panels should be secured in place by clips when assembly requires a fire resistance rating; also against uplift due to pressure differential.
- fixtures generally have to be boxed-in for fire resistance rating; fire dampers must be provided at all openings, such as diffusers.
- hangers secured to framing members, structural deck, or to secondary framing system.

RECESSED EDGE

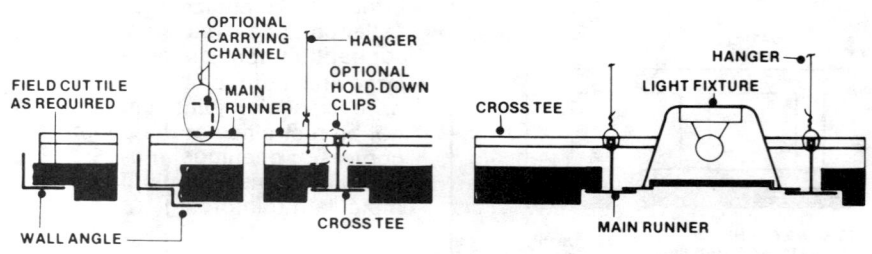

- clearance required for all lay-in panels for tilting them into place.
- suspension system used is the same as for square edge tile, but tile only available in 2x2 foot size.
- may be used in fire resistance-rated floor or roof/ceiling assemblies; clips to secure tiles in place and opening protection generally required.

EXPOSED GRID, SHAPED UNITS

INLAY PANELS, CORRUGATED, RIBBED

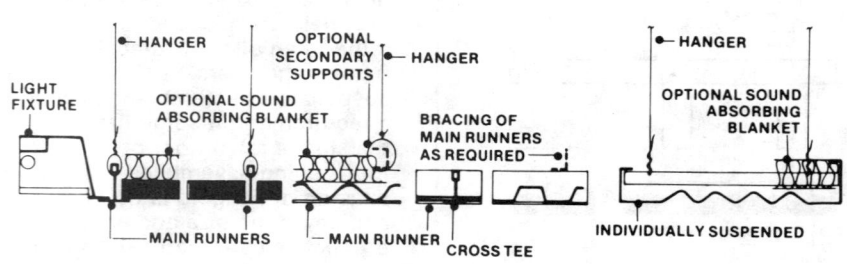

- metal panels generally perforated, with sound absorbing blankets.
- plastic panels generally solid; used in luminous ceiling installations.
- corrugated/ribbed metal or plastic panels generally used with main runners only.
- flat plastic panels generally either 2x4 or 2x2 feet in size, used with main runners and cross tees.

PRE-ASSEMBLED MODULES

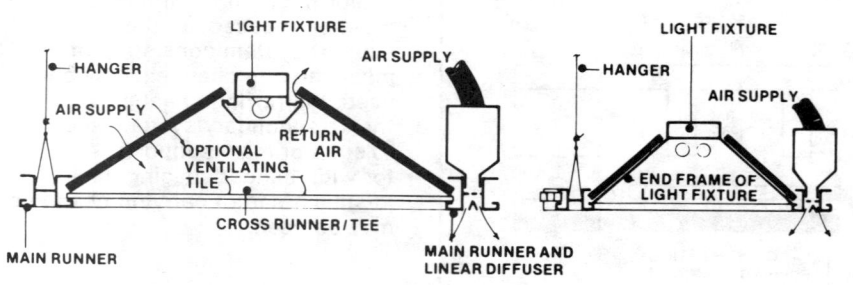

- flat pre-assembled modules are also available.
- when pressurized plenum and ventilating tile are used, air return must be ducted through plenum.
- with ventilating plenum, dirt streaking may result unless the membrane is made completely air tight.
- may be used in fire resistance-rated floor or roof/ceiling assemblies.

ASSEMBLY	REMARKS
CONCEALED GRID, SHAPED UNITS	
### METAL PAN TILE 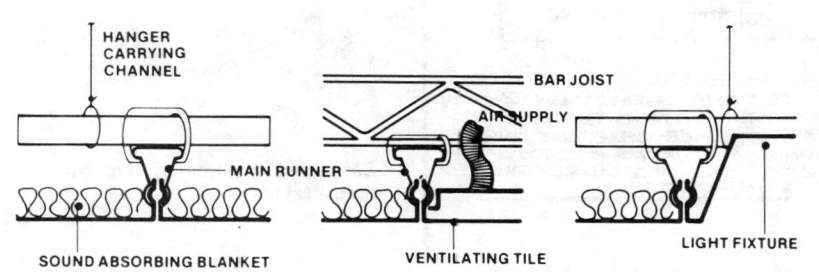	• tile may be repeatedly repainted without loss in sound absorbing characteristics. • heating/cooling piping may be incorporated into the system. • combination lighting/infra-red heating fixtures may be integrated into membrane. • secondary suspension system generally required. • tile may be used for supply/return air.
### LINEAR PANELS 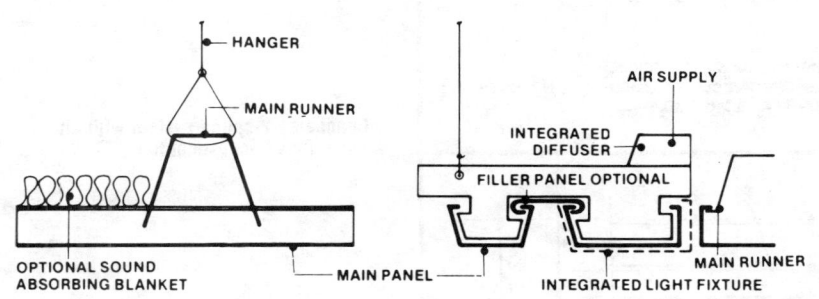	• formed prefinished metal panels in long lengths. • air supply/return and lighting fixtures may be integrated into the system. • may be used outdoors in protected locations, such as large soffits, canopies. • some assemblies may be used as required components in fire resistance rated floor or roof/ceiling assemblies. • membranes may be curved perpendicular to direction of panels.
### BAFFLES 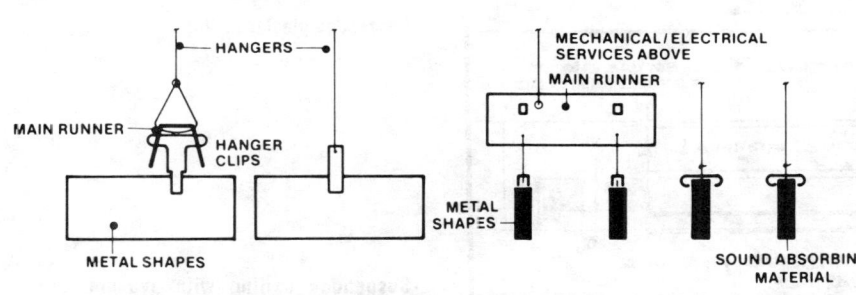	• baffles available in shaped metal, with or without sound absorbent material cores, or in faced sound absorbent material. • various arrangements available, such as linear, radial, hexagonal. • used to: provide additional sound absorption in selected locations; for visual interest, or to conceal mechanical/electrical services.
CONCEALED GRID, FLAT UNITS	
### KERFED EDGE 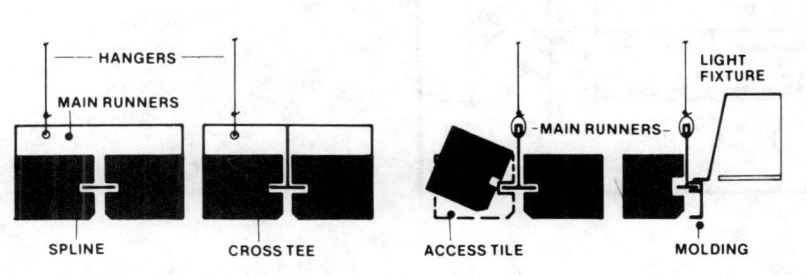	• tile, generally 12 x 12 inches in size with kerfed edges secured in place by main runners in one direction, and cross tees or splines in the other. • secondary supports, such as carrying channels may be used to reduce spacing of hangers to framing system. • may be used as component in fire resistance rated floor or roof/ceiling assemblies. • special panels available to provide access to plenum.

CEILINGS
Suspended Ceiling Types

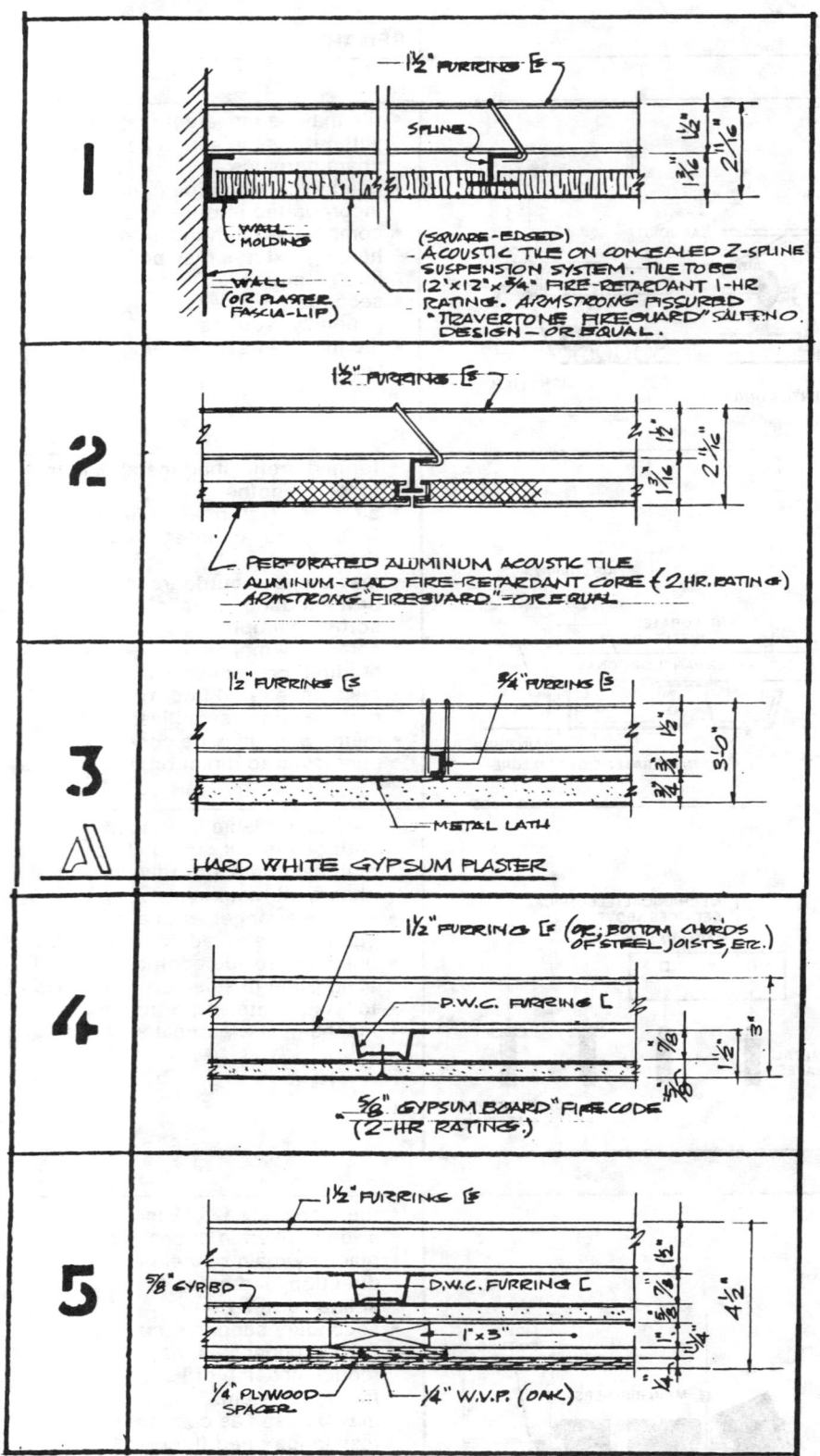

1 — (SQUARE-EDGED) ACOUSTIC TILE ON CONCEALED 2-SPLINE SUSPENSION SYSTEM. TILE TO BE 12"x12"x¾" FIRE-RETARDANT 1-HR RATING. ARMSTRONG FISSURED "TRAVERTONE FIREGUARD" SAME NO. DESIGN — OR EQUAL.

1½" FURRING ⊑ / SPLINE / WALL MOLDING / WALL (OR PLASTER FASCIA-LIP)

Concealed 2-spline system with acoustical tile

2 — PERFORATED ALUMINUM ACOUSTIC TILE ALUMINUM-CLAD FIRE-RETARDANT CORE (2 HR. RATING) ARMSTRONG "FIREGUARD" — OR EQUAL.

1½" FURRING ⊑

Concealed 2-spline system with aluminum-clad acoustical tile

3 — 1½" FURRING ⊑ / ¾" FURRING ⊑ / METAL LATH / HARD WHITE GYPSUM PLASTER

Suspended plaster ceiling

4 — 1½" FURRING ⊑ (OR; BOTTOM CHORDS OF STEEL JOISTS, ETC.) / D.W.C. FURRING ⊏ / ⅝" GYPSUM BOARD "FIRECODE" (2-HR RATING.)

Suspended ceiling with gypsum board

5 — 1½" FURRING ⊑ / ⅝" GYP BD / D.W.C. FURRING ⊏ / 1"x3" / ¼" PLYWOOD SPACER / ¼" W.V.P. (OAK)

Suspended ceiling with plywood finish

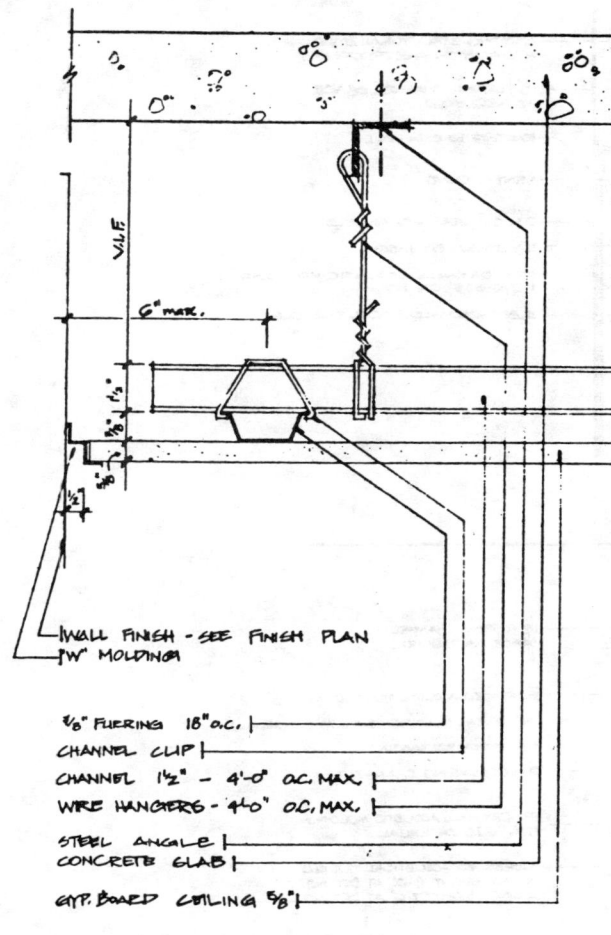

WALL FINISH - SEE FINISH PLAN
"W" MOLDING

⅝" FURRING 18" O.C.
CHANNEL CLIP
CHANNEL 1½" - 4'-0" O.C. MAX.
WIRE HANGERS - 4'-0" O.C. MAX.
STEEL ANGLE
CONCRETE SLAB
GYP. BOARD CEILING ⅝"

TYPICAL HUNG GYP. BOARD
CEILING DETAIL

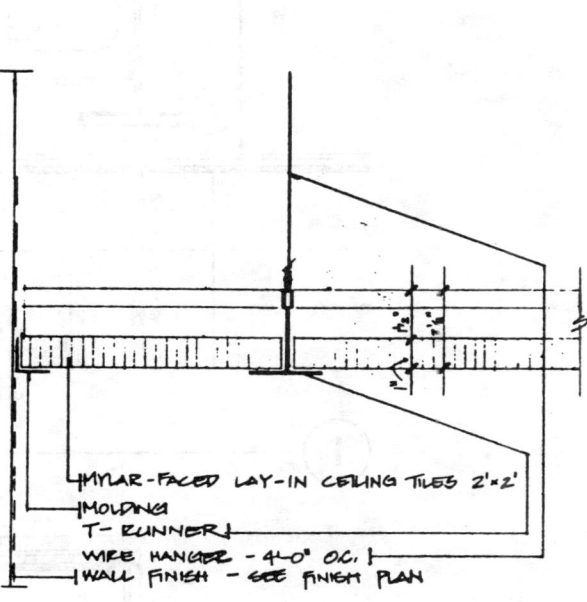

MYLAR-FACED LAY-IN CEILING TILES 2'×2'
MOLDING
T-RUNNER
WIRE HANGER - 4'-0" O.C.
WALL FINISH - SEE FINISH PLAN

TYPICAL LAY-IN TILE
CEILING DETAIL

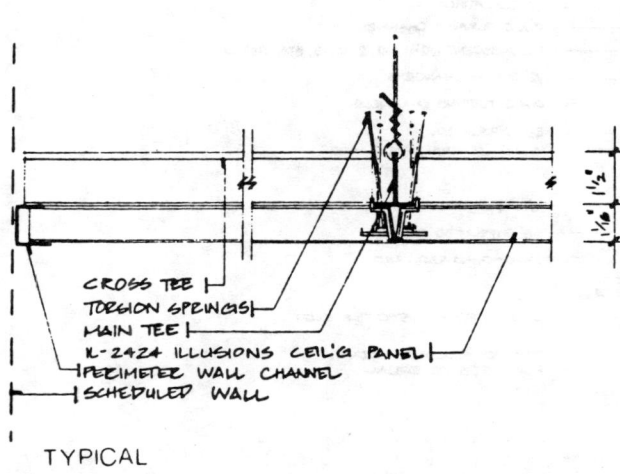

CROSS TEE
TORSION SPRINGS
MAIN TEE
K-2424 ILLUSIONS CEIL'G PANEL
PERIMETER WALL CHANNEL
SCHEDULED WALL

TYPICAL
CEILING DETAIL

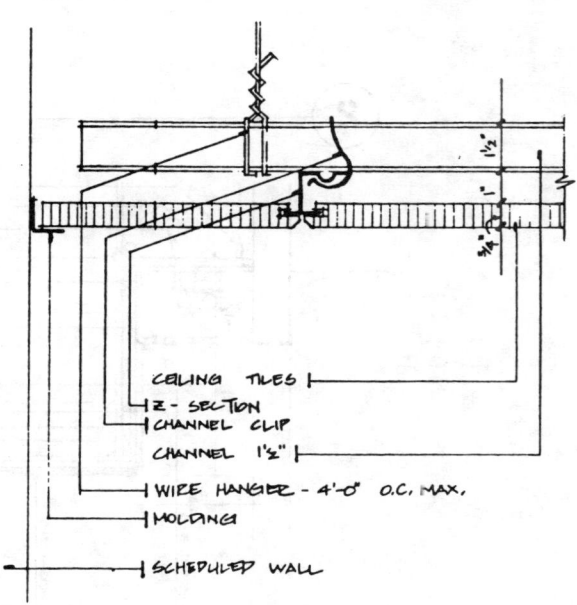

CEILING TILES
Z-SECTION
CHANNEL CLIP
CHANNEL 1½"
WIRE HANGER - 4'-0" O.C. MAX.
MOLDING
SCHEDULED WALL

TYPICAL CONCEALED SPLINE
CEILING DETAIL

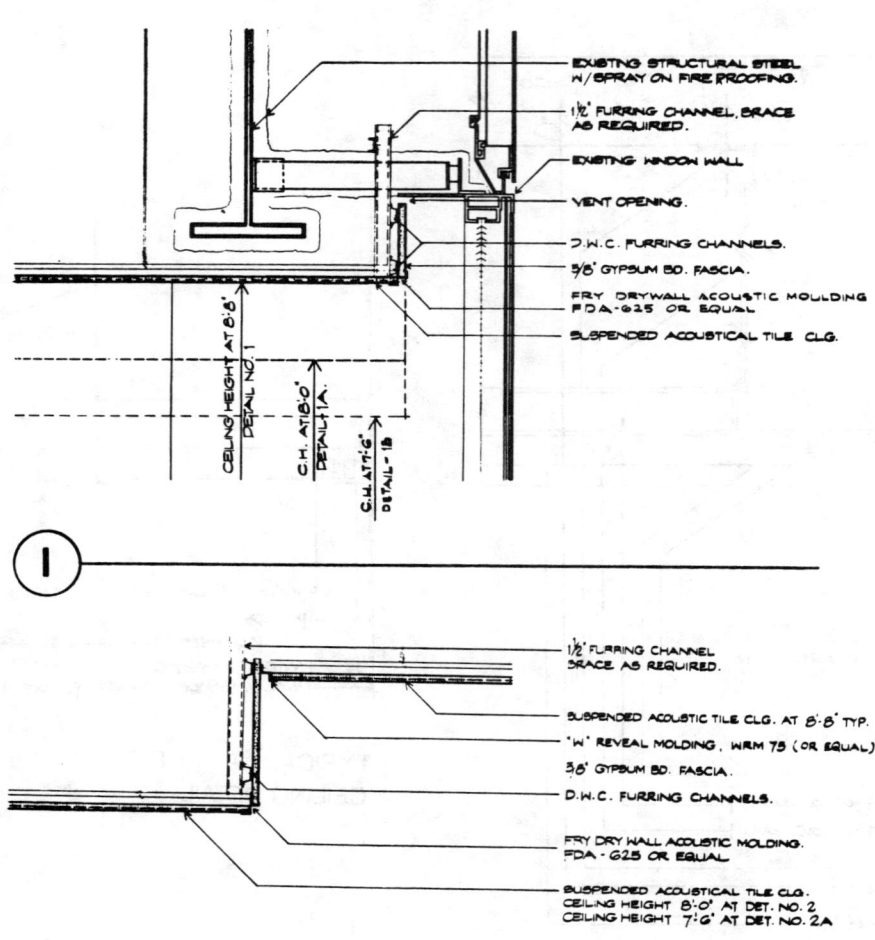

EXISTING STRUCTURAL STEEL W/SPRAY ON FIRE PROOFING.

1½" FURRING CHANNEL, BRACE AS REQUIRED.

EXISTING WINDOW WALL

VENT OPENING.

D.W.C. FURRING CHANNELS.

5/8" GYPSUM BD. FASCIA.

FRY DRYWALL ACOUSTIC MOULDING FDA-G25 OR EQUAL

SUSPENDED ACOUSTICAL TILE CLG.

CEILING HEIGHT AT 8'-8' DETAIL NO.1

C.H. AT 8'-0' DETAIL-1A

C.H. AT 7'-6' DETAIL - 1B

1

1½" FURRING CHANNEL BRACE AS REQUIRED.

SUSPENDED ACOUSTIC TILE CLG. AT 8'-8" TYP.

"W" REVEAL MOLDING, WRM 75 (OR EQUAL)

3/8" GYPSUM BD. FASCIA.

D.W.C. FURRING CHANNELS.

FRY DRY WALL ACOUSTIC MOLDING. FDA - G25 OR EQUAL

SUSPENDED ACOUSTICAL TILE CLG. CEILING HEIGHT 8'-0" AT DET. NO. 2 CEILING HEIGHT 7'-6" AT DET. NO. 2A

2

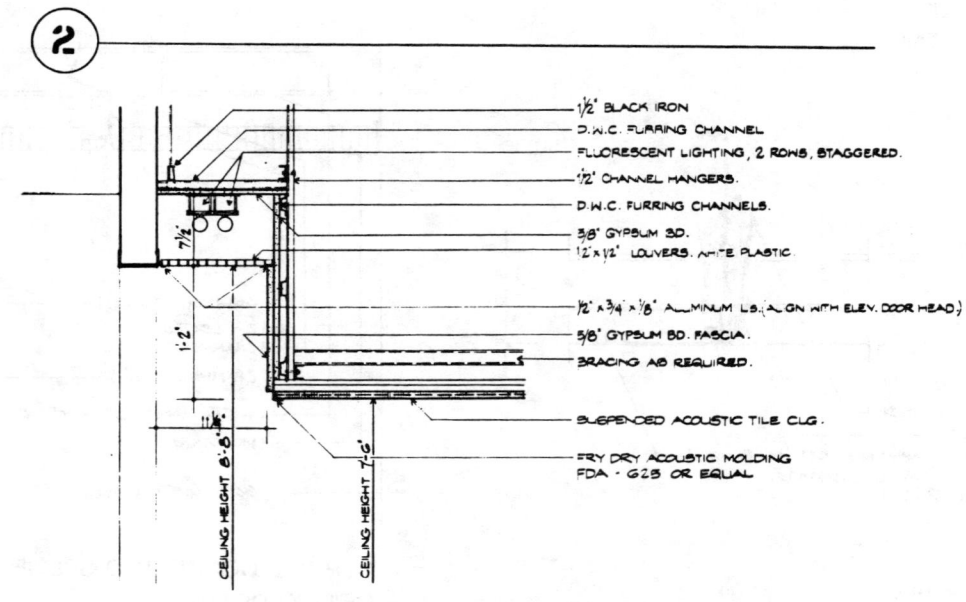

1½" BLACK IRON

D.W.C. FURRING CHANNEL

FLUORESCENT LIGHTING, 2 ROWS, STAGGERED.

½" CHANNEL HANGERS.

D.W.C. FURRING CHANNELS.

3/8" GYPSUM BD.

12"x½" LOUVERS. WHITE PLASTIC.

½" x 3/4" x 1/8" ALUMINUM L.S. (ALIGN WITH ELEV. DOOR HEAD.)

5/8" GYPSUM BD. FASCIA.

BRACING AS REQUIRED.

SUSPENDED ACOUSTIC TILE CLG.

FRY DRY ACOUSTIC MOLDING FDA - G25 OR EQUAL

CEILING HEIGHT 8'-8"

CEILING HEIGHT 7'-6'

3

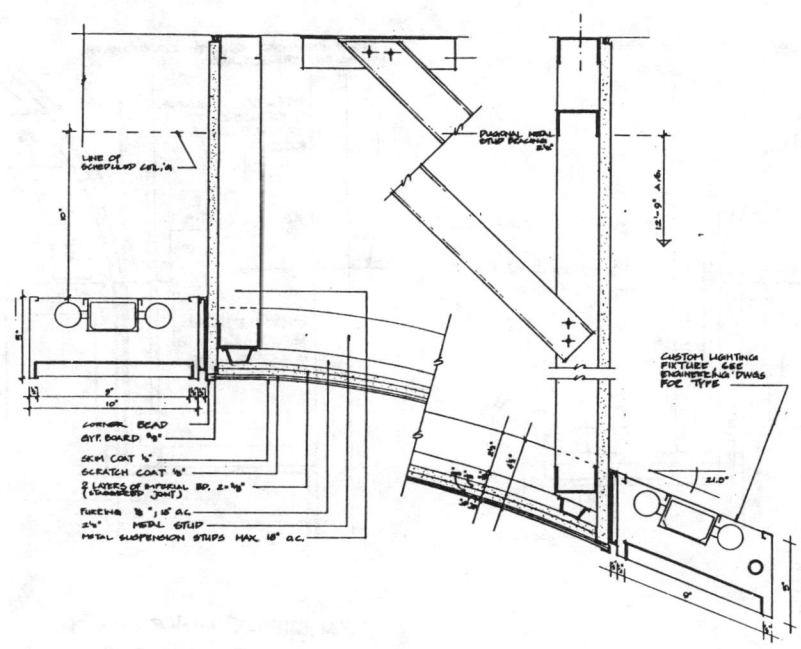

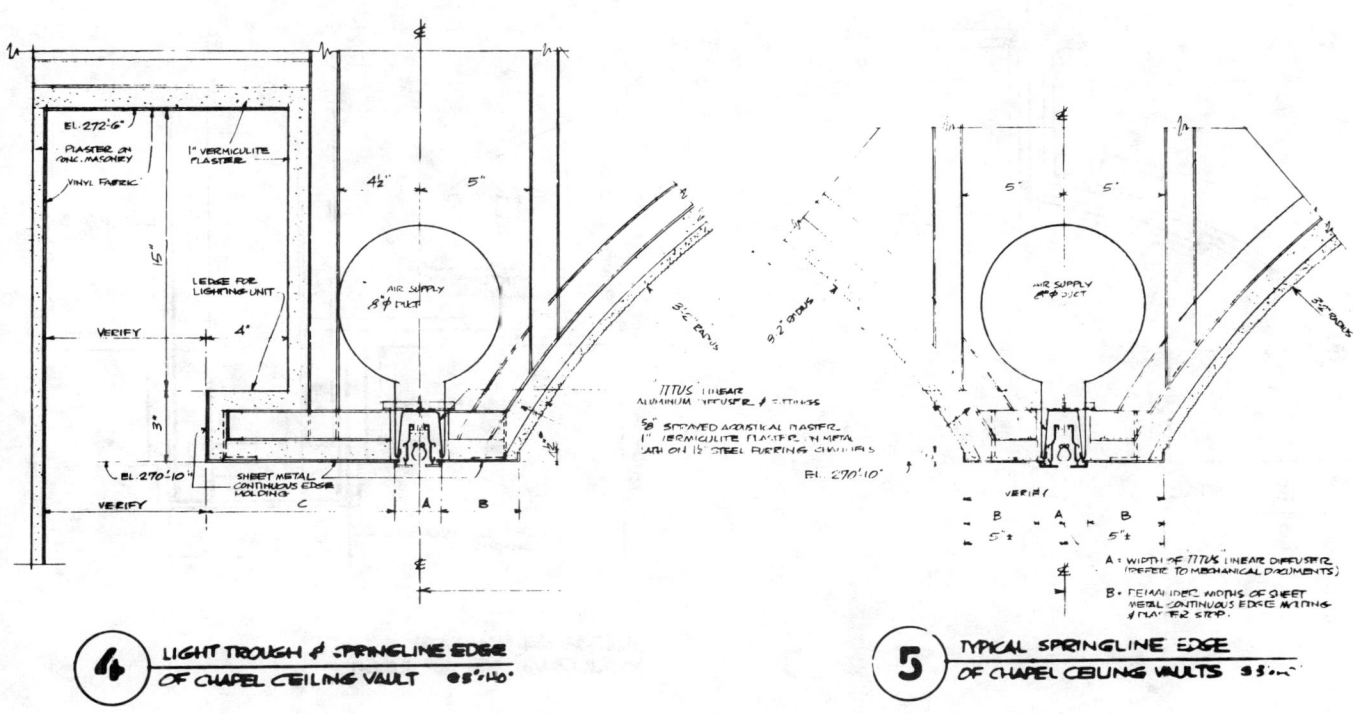

LINE OF
SCHEDULED CEIL'G

DIAGONAL METAL
STUD BRACING 3½"

CUSTOM LIGHTING
FIXTURE SEE
ENGINEERING DWGS
FOR TYPE

21.0°

CORNER BEAD
GYP. BOARD ⅝"
SKIM COAT ½"
SCRATCH COAT ½"
2 LAYERS OF GYP BD. 2×⅝"
(STAGGERED JOINT)
FURRING ⅞"; 16" O.C.
2½" METAL STUD
METAL SUSPENSION STUDS MAX 16" O.C.

EL. 272'-6"

PLASTER ON
CONC. MASONRY

VINYL FABRIC

1" VERMICULITE
PLASTER

LEDGE FOR
LIGHTING UNIT

VERIFY

EL. 270'-10"

VERIFY

SHEET METAL
CONTINUOUS EDGE
MOLDING

4½"   5"

AIR SUPPLY
8 φ DUCT

3½ EA WAY

TITUS LINEAR
ALUMINUM DIFFUSER & FITTINGS

⅝" STRIATED ACOUSTICAL PLASTER
1" VERMICULITE PLASTER ON METAL
LATH ON 1½" STEEL FURRING CHANNELS

EL. 270'-10"

C   A   B

4 LIGHT TROUGH & SPRINGLINE EDGE
      OF CHAPEL CEILING VAULT @ 5'-10"

5'   5'

AIR SUPPLY
8 φ DUCT

3½ EA WAY

9.2 GRADS

VERIFY

B   A   B
5±   5±

A = WIDTH OF TITUS LINEAR DIFFUSER
    (REFER TO MECHANICAL DOCUMENTS)

B = REMAINDER WIDTHS OF SHEET
    METAL CONTINUOUS EDGE MOLDING
    & PLASTER STOP.

5 TYPICAL SPRINGLINE EDGE
      OF CHAPEL CEILING VAULTS 3'-...

CEILINGS
Vaulted Ceiling

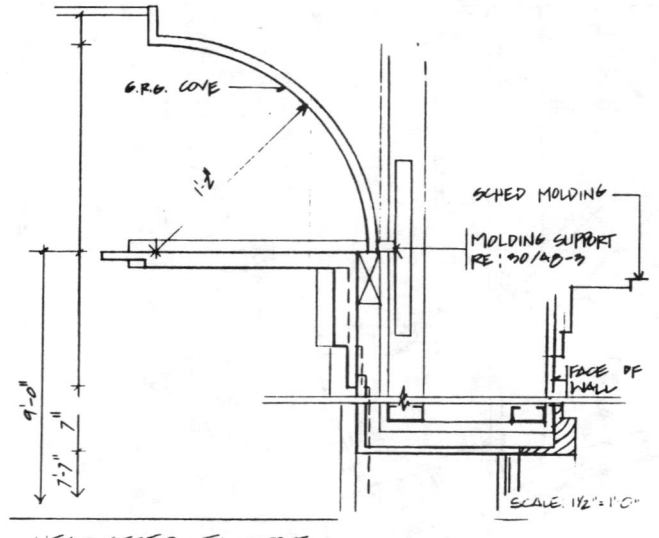

G.R.G. COVE

SCHED MOLDING

MOLDING SUPPORT
RE: 30/AD-3

9'-0"
7"
7'-7"

FACE OF WALL

SCALE: 1½" = 1'-0"

HEAD SECTION THRU PORTAL

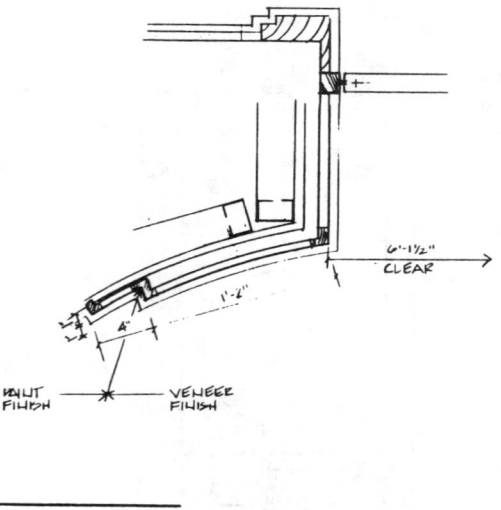

6'-1½" CLEAR

1'-2"

4"

KNUT FINISH   VENEER FINISH

JAMB @ PORTAL

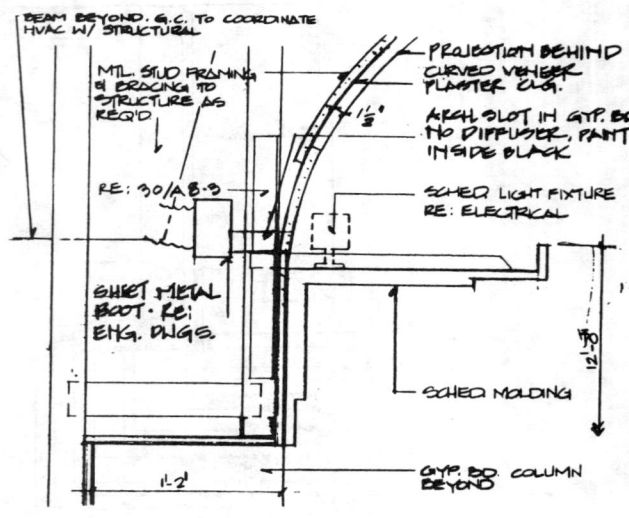

BEAM BEYOND. G.C. TO COORDINATE
HVAC W/ STRUCTURAL

MTL. STUD FRAMING
& BRACING TO
STRUCTURE AS
REQ'D

RE: 30/AB-3

SHEET METAL
BOOT. RE:
ENG. DWGS.

PROJECTION BEHIND
CURVED VENEER
PLASTER CLG.

ARCH SLOT IN GYP. BO.
TO DIFFUSER, PAINT
INSIDE BLACK

SCHED LIGHT FIXTURE
RE: ELECTRICAL

1½"

12'-0"

SCHED MOLDING

GYP. BO. COLUMN
BEYOND

1'-2"

VAULTED CEILING WITH
MOULDING FRAMED
COVE LIGHT

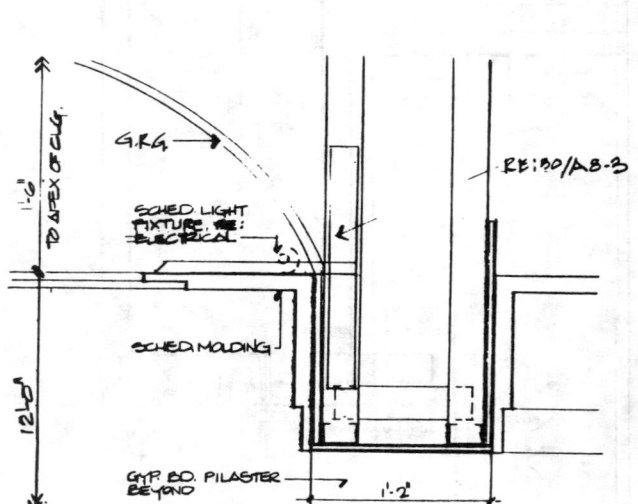

G.R.G.

SCHED LIGHT
FIXTURE. RE:
ELECTRICAL

RE: 30/AB-3

1'-0"
TO APEX OF CLG.

SCHED MOLDING

12'-0"

GYP. BO. PILASTER
BEYOND

1'-2"

VAULTED CEILING WITH
MOULDING FRAMED BEAM

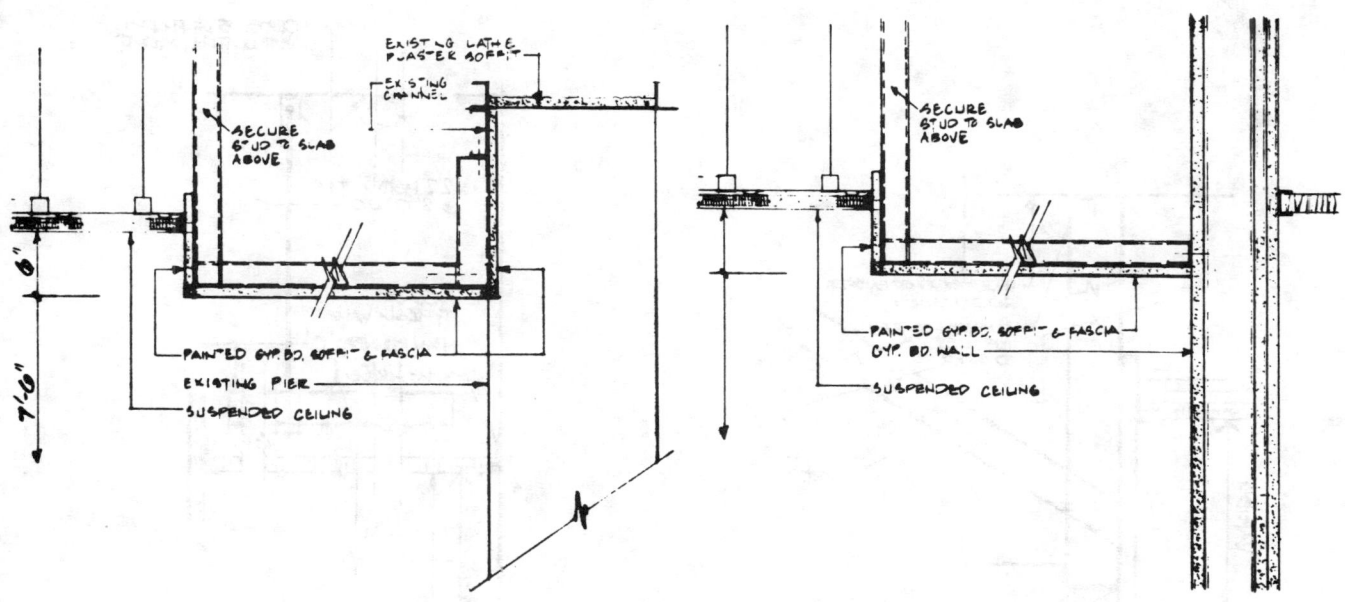

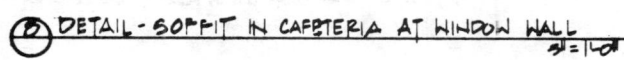

CEILINGS

Miscellaneous Details of Suspended Ceilings

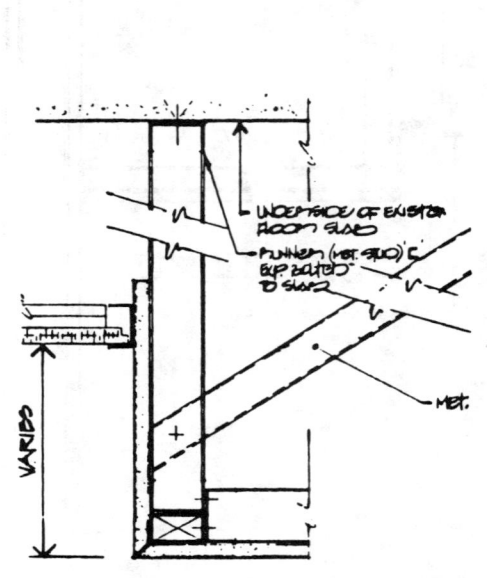

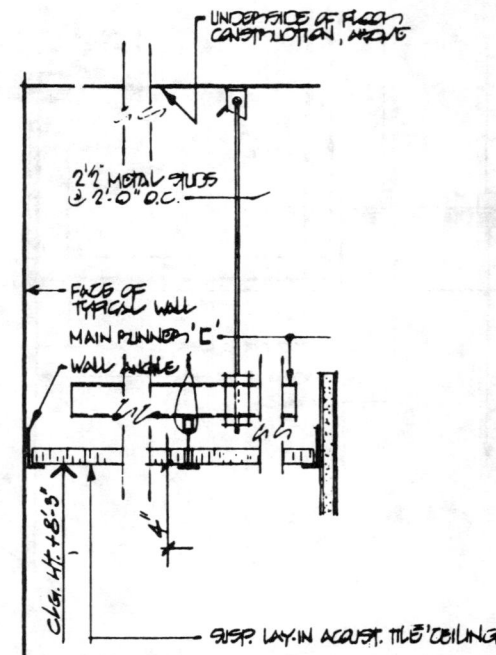

1 SECTION THRU SUSP. CLG.

2 EXPOSED "T" GRID (2'x2')

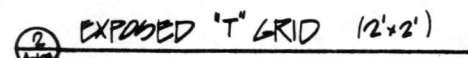

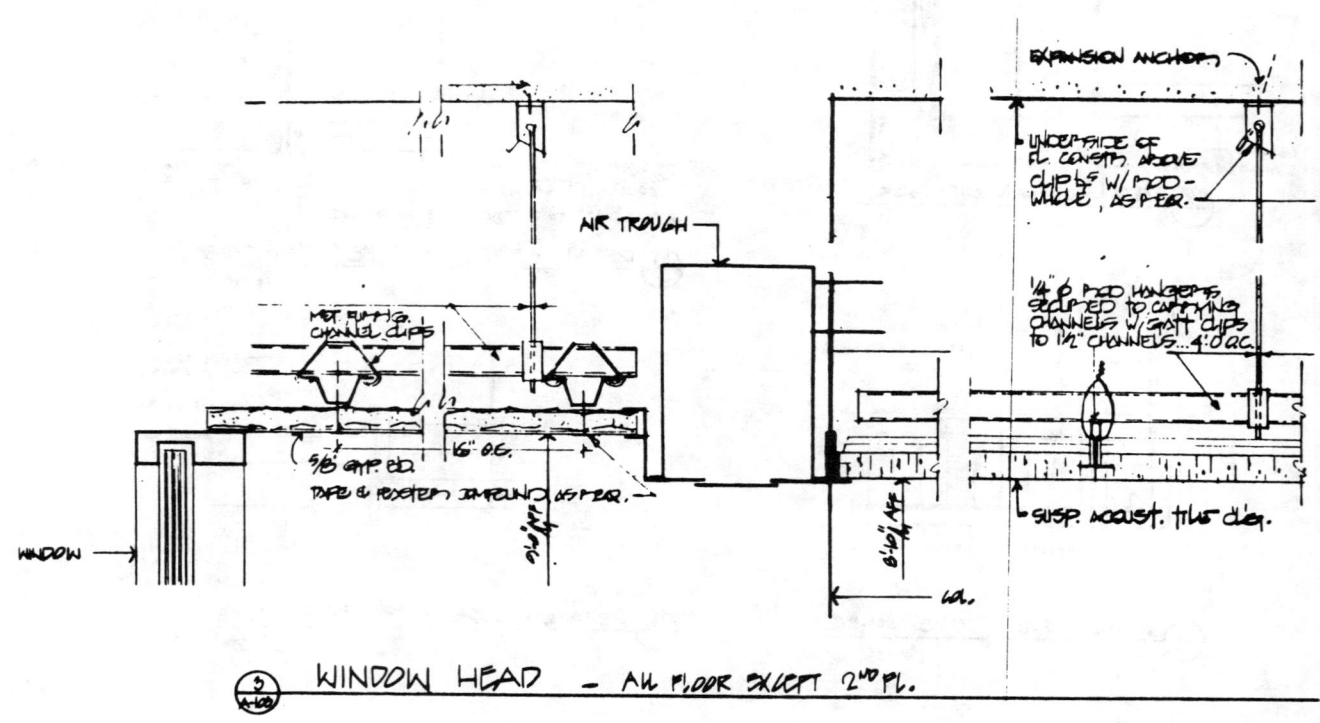

3 WINDOW HEAD - ALL FLOOR EXCEPT 2ND FL.

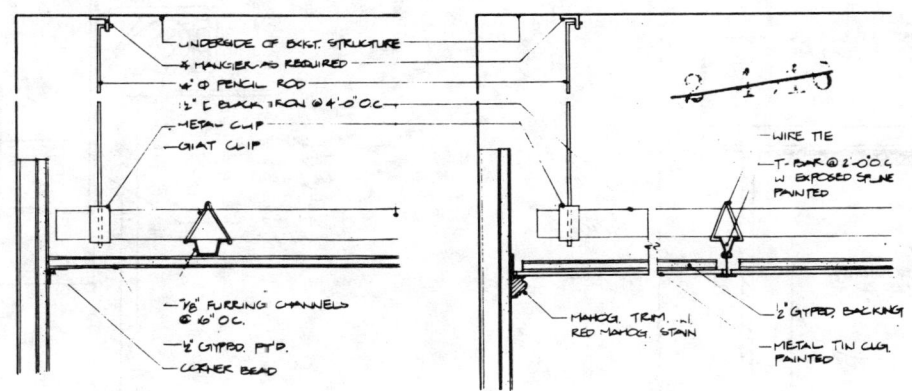

UNDERSIDE OF EXIST. STRUCTURE
& HANGER AS REQUIRED
¼" Ø PENCIL ROD
1½" C BLACK IRON @ 4'-0" O.C.
METAL CLIP
GIAT CLIP

⅞" FURRING CHANNELS @ 6" O.C.
½" GYPBD. PT'D.
CORNER BEAD

WIRE TIE
T-BAR @ 2'-0" O.C. W EXPOSED SPLINE PAINTED

½" GYPBD. BACKING
METAL TIN CLG. PAINTED

MAHOG. TRIM W. RED MAHOG. STAIN

①	GYPBD. CEILING DETAIL
A10	SCALE: 3" = 1'-0"

②	METAL TIN CEILING DETAIL
A10	SCALE: 3" = 1'-0"

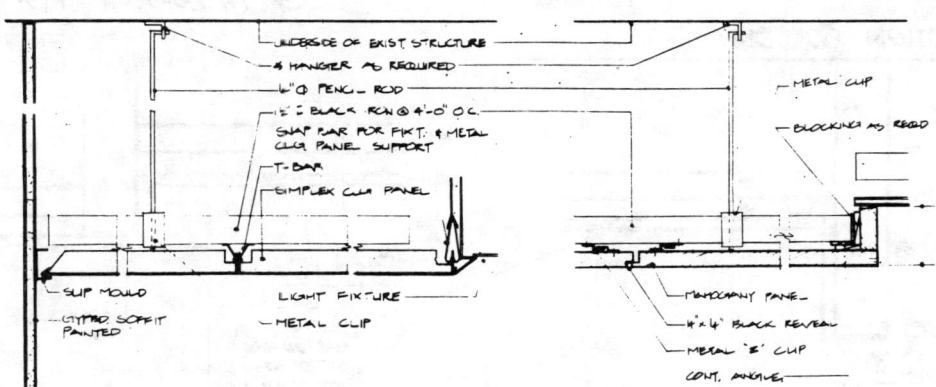

UNDERSIDE OF EXIST. STRUCTURE
& HANGER AS REQUIRED
¼" Ø PENCIL ROD
1½" C BLACK IRON @ 4'-0" O.C.
SNAP BAR FOR FIXT. & METAL CLG. PANEL SUPPORT
T-BAR
SIMPLEX CLG. PANEL

SLIP MOULD
GYPBD. SOFFIT PAINTED
LIGHT FIXTURE
METAL CLIP

METAL CLIP
BLOCKING AS REQ'D

MAHOGANY PANEL
¼" X ¼" BLACK REVEAL
METAL "Z" CLIP
CONT. ANGLE

③	SIMPLEX METAL CEILING DETAIL
A10	SCALE: 3" = 1'-0"

④	MAHOG. PANEL CEILING DETAIL
A10	SCALE: 3" = 1'-0"

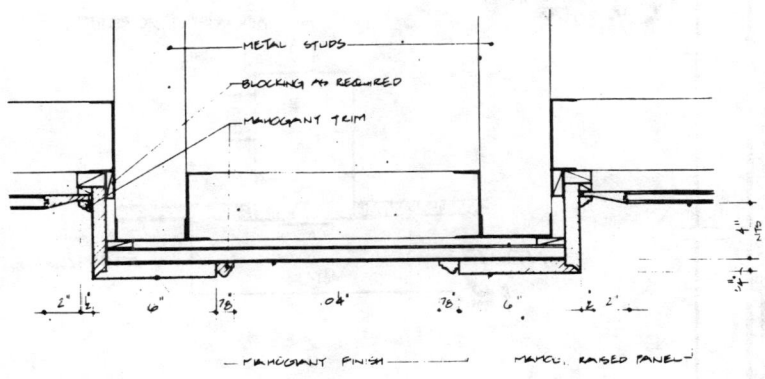

METAL STUDS
BLOCKING AS REQUIRED
MAHOGANY TRIM

2" 1½" 6" 7⅛" 04" 7⅛" 6" 1½" 2"

MAHOGANY FINISH
MAHOG. RAISED PANEL

⑤	DETAIL OF RAISED MAHOGANY PANEL CEILING
A10	SCALE: 3" = 1'-0"

UNDERSIDE OF EXIST. STRUCTURE
& HANGER AS REQUIRED
¼" Ø PENCIL ROD
1½" C BLACK IRON @ 4'-0" O.C.
METAL CLIP
WIRE TIE
T-BAR W EXPOSED SPLINE
ACOUSTIC TILE (2 x 4 LAY-IN)
WALL ANGLE

⑥	ACOUSTICAL TILE CEILING DETAIL
A10	SCALE: 3" = 1'-0"

CEILINGS

Suspended Ceilings: Perimeters and Drops

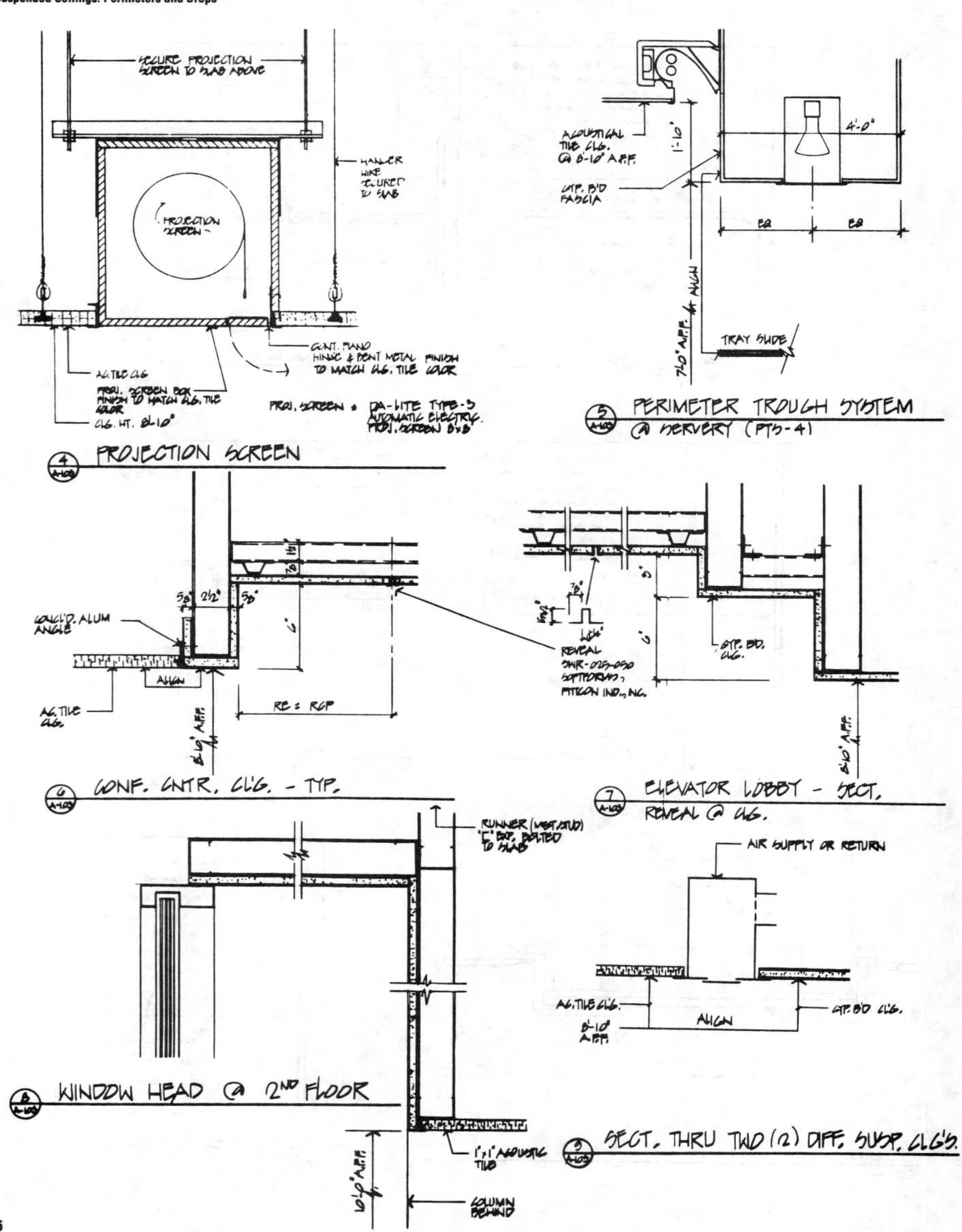

SECURE PROJECTION
SCREEN TO SLAB ABOVE

PROJECTION
SCREEN

HANGER
WIRE
SECURED
TO SLAB

CONT. PIANO
HINGE & BENT METAL FINISH
TO MATCH CLG. TILE COLOR

AC. TILE CLG

PROJ. SCREEN BOX
FINISH TO MATCH CLG. TILE
COLOR

CLG. HT. 8'-10"

PROJ. SCREEN = DA-LITE TYPE-3
AUTOMATIC ELECTRIC
PROJ. SCREEN 8'x8'

④ PROJECTION SCREEN
A-103

ACOUSTICAL
TILE CLG.
@ 8'-10" A.F.F.

GYP. B'D
FASCIA

7'-0" A.F.F. @ MULL

4'-0"

EQ   EQ

TRAY SLIDE

⑤ PERIMETER TROUGH SYSTEM
A-103 @ SERVERY (PT'S-4)

CONC'D. ALUM
ANGLE

AC. TILE
CLG.

5/8" 2½" 5/8"

ALIGN

8'-10" A.F.F.

RE = RCP

REVEAL
SMR-025-050
SOFFORMS,
FITCON IND., INC.

⑥ CONF. CNTR. CLG. - TYP.
A-103

7/8"
1½"

GYP. BD.
CLG.

8'-10" A.F.F.

⑦ ELEVATOR LOBBY - SECT.
A-103 REVEAL @ CLG.

RUNNER (WEST STUD)
"L" EXP. BOLTED
TO SLAB

AIR SUPPLY OR RETURN

AC. TILE CLG.

8'-10"
A.F.F.

ALIGN

GYP. BD CLG.

⑧ WINDOW HEAD @ 2ND FLOOR
A-103

10'-0" A.F.F.

1'x1' ACOUSTIC
TILE

COLUMN
BEHIND

⑨ SECT. THRU TWO (2) DIFF. SUSP. CLG'S.
A-103

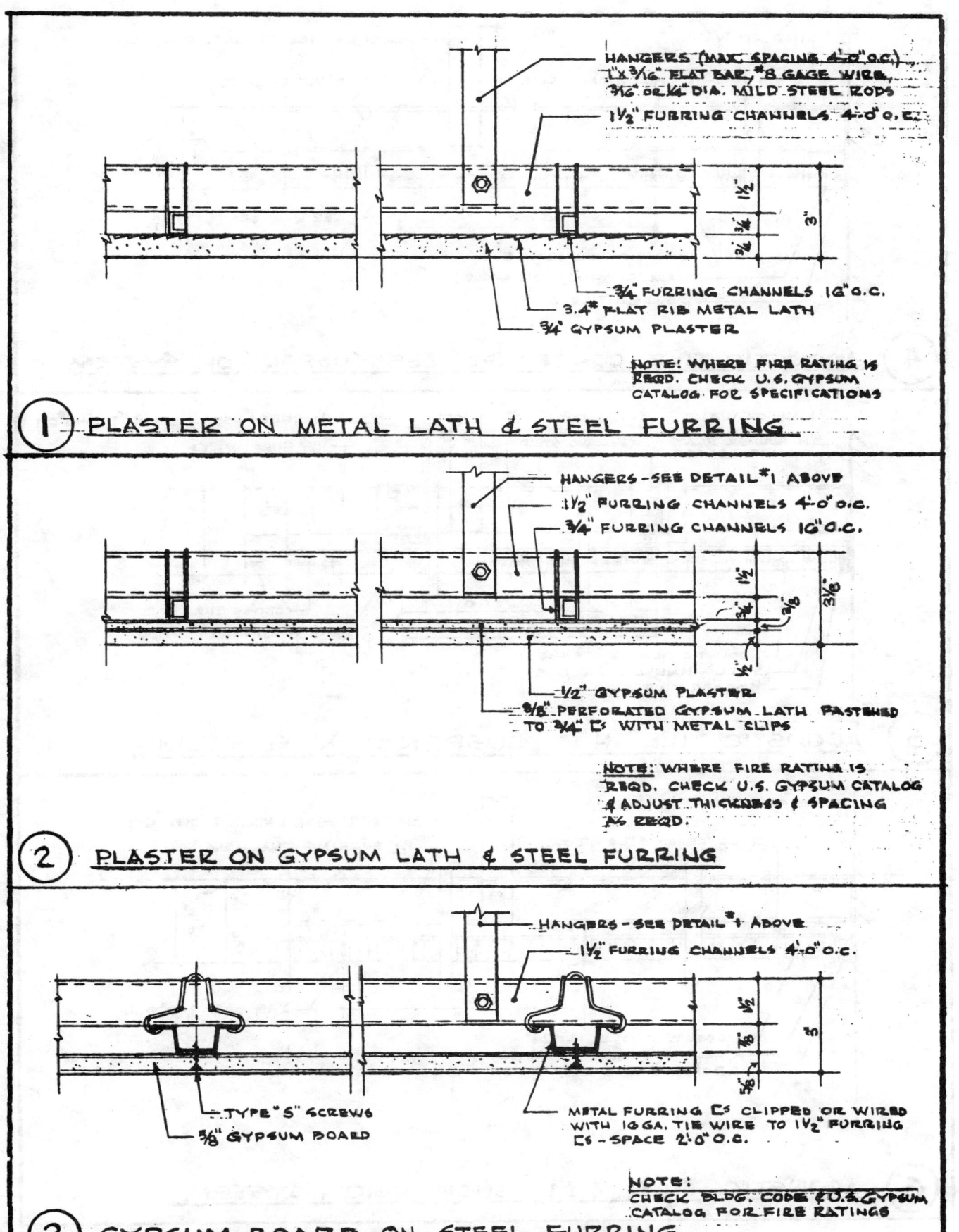

1 PLASTER ON METAL LATH & STEEL FURRING

Labels (detail 1):
- HANGERS (MAX SPACING 4'-0" O.C.) 1"x 3/16" FLAT BAR, #8 GAGE WIRE, 3/16" OR 1/4" DIA. MILD STEEL RODS
- 1 1/2" FURRING CHANNELS 4'-0" O.C.
- 3/4" FURRING CHANNELS 16" O.C.
- 3.4# FLAT RIB METAL LATH
- 3/4" GYPSUM PLASTER
- NOTE: WHERE FIRE RATING IS REQD. CHECK U.S. GYPSUM CATALOG FOR SPECIFICATIONS

2 PLASTER ON GYPSUM LATH & STEEL FURRING

Labels (detail 2):
- HANGERS - SEE DETAIL #1 ABOVE
- 1 1/2" FURRING CHANNELS 4'-0" O.C.
- 3/4" FURRING CHANNELS 16" O.C.
- 1/2" GYPSUM PLASTER
- 3/8" PERFORATED GYPSUM LATH FASTENED TO 3/4" Cs WITH METAL CLIPS
- NOTE: WHERE FIRE RATING IS REQD. CHECK U.S. GYPSUM CATALOG & ADJUST THICKNESS & SPACING AS REQD.

3 GYPSUM BOARD ON STEEL FURRING

Labels (detail 3):
- HANGERS - SEE DETAIL #1 ABOVE
- 1 1/2" FURRING CHANNELS 4'-0" O.C.
- TYPE "S" SCREWS
- 5/8" GYPSUM BOARD
- METAL FURRING Cs CLIPPED OR WIRED WITH 10 GA. TIE WIRE TO 1 1/2" FURRING Cs - SPACE 2'-0" O.C.
- NOTE: CHECK BLDG. CODE & U.S. GYPSUM CATALOG FOR FIRE RATINGS

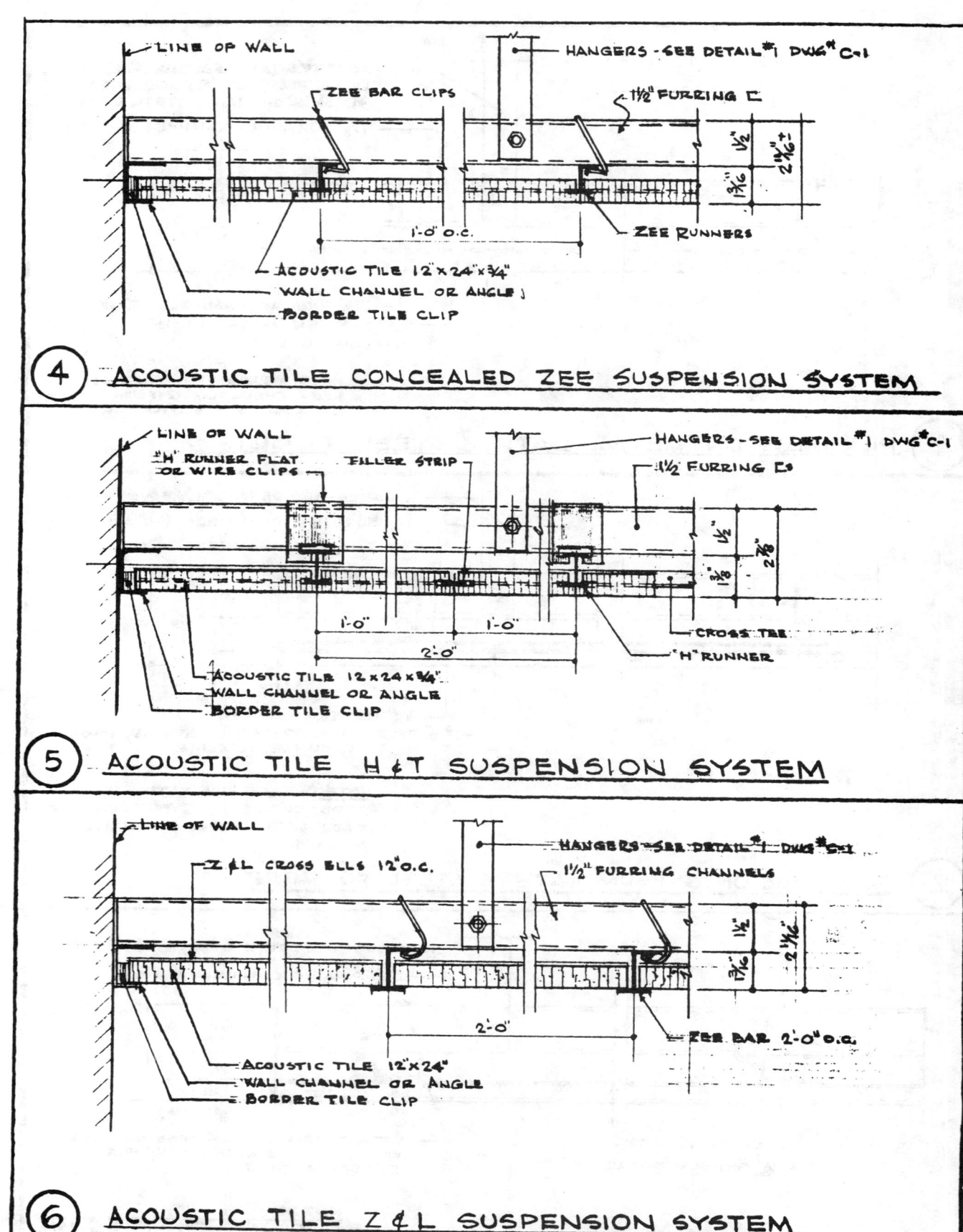

④ ACOUSTIC TILE CONCEALED ZEE SUSPENSION SYSTEM

LINE OF WALL
ZEE BAR CLIPS
HANGERS - SEE DETAIL #1 DWG #C-1
1½" FURRING C
½"
2¼"±
³⁄₁₆"
1'-0" O.C.
ZEE RUNNERS
ACOUSTIC TILE 12"x24"x¾"
WALL CHANNEL OR ANGLE
BORDER TILE CLIP

⑤ ACOUSTIC TILE H & T SUSPENSION SYSTEM

LINE OF WALL
"H" RUNNER FLAT OR WIRE CLIPS
FILLER STRIP
HANGERS - SEE DETAIL #1 DWG #C-1
1½" FURRING C
½"
2⅞"
³⁄₈"
1'-0"
1'-0"
2'-0"
CROSS TEE
"H" RUNNER
ACOUSTIC TILE 12"x24"x¾"
WALL CHANNEL OR ANGLE
BORDER TILE CLIP

⑥ ACOUSTIC TILE Z & L SUSPENSION SYSTEM

LINE OF WALL
Z & L CROSS ELLS 12" O.C.
HANGERS - SEE DETAIL #1 DWG #C-1
1½" FURRING CHANNELS
1½"
2⅛"±
³⁄₁₆"
2'-0"
ZEE BAR 2'-0" O.C.
ACOUSTIC TILE 12"x24"
WALL CHANNEL OR ANGLE
BORDER TILE CLIP

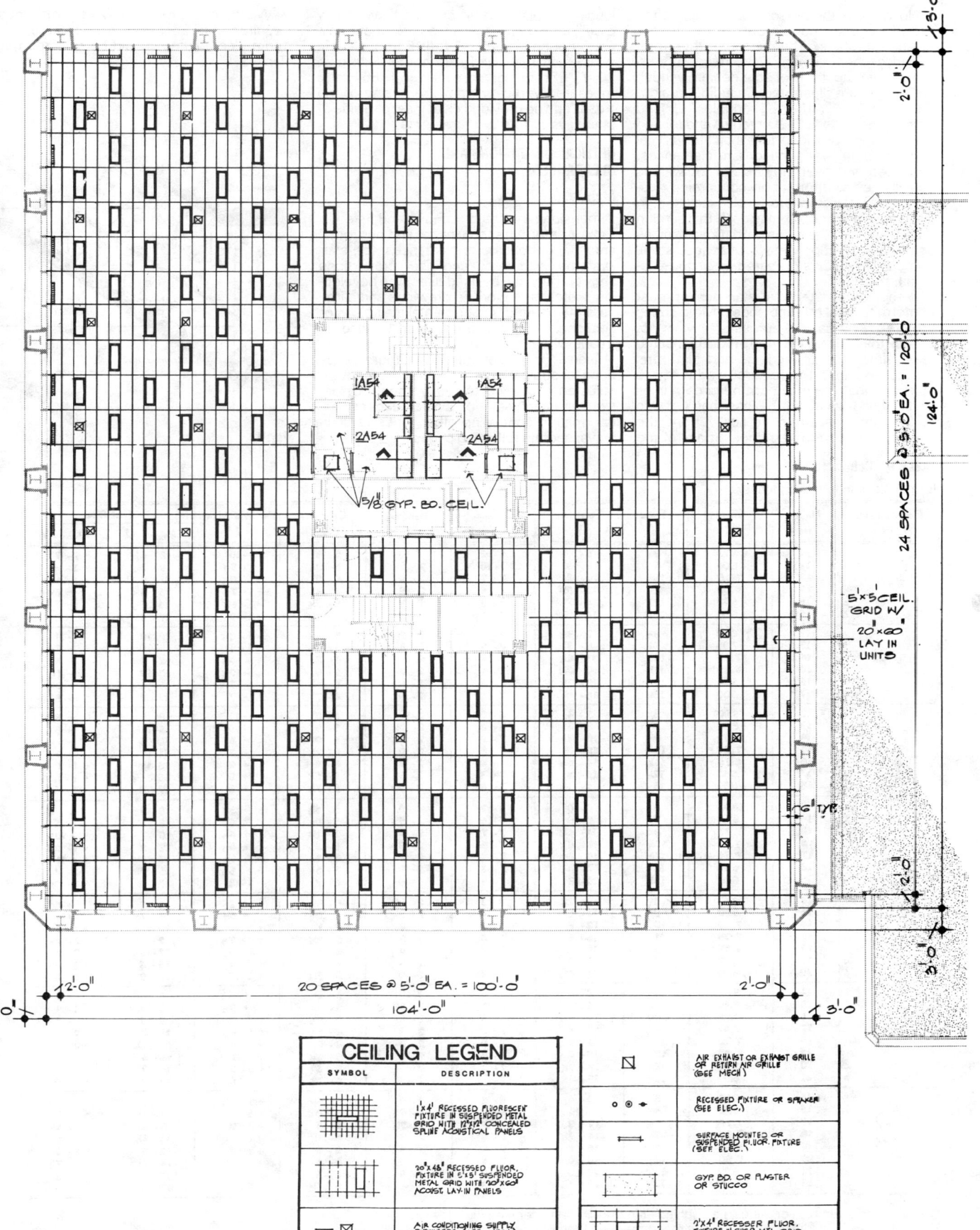

1A54

1A54

2A54

2A54

5/8" GYP. BD. CEIL.

5'x5' CEIL. GRID W/ 20"x60" LAY IN UNITS

6" TYP.

3'-0"

2'-0"

124'-0"

24 SPACES @ 5'-0" EA. = 120'-0"

2'-0"

3'-0"

2'-0"

20 SPACES @ 5'-0" EA. = 100'-0"

2'-0"

104'-0"

3'-0"

3'-0"

CEILING LEGEND	
SYMBOL	DESCRIPTION
	1'x4' RECESSED FLUORESCENT FIXTURE IN SUSPENDED METAL GRID WITH 12"x12" CONCEALED SPLINE ACOUSTICAL PANELS
	20"x48" RECESSED FLUOR. FIXTURE IN 5'x5' SUSPENDED METAL GRID WITH 20"x60" ACOUST. LAY-IN PANELS
	AIR CONDITIONING SUPPLY DIFFUSERS (SEE MECH.)

⊠	AIR EXHAUST OR EXHAUST GRILLE OR RETURN AIR GRILLE (SEE MECH.)
∘ ⊙ ⊕	RECESSED FIXTURE OR SPEAKER (SEE ELEC.)
⊢—⊣	SURFACE MOUNTED OR SUSPENDED FLUOR. FIXTURE (SEE ELEC.)
	GYP. BD. OR PLASTER OR STUCCO
	2'x4' RECESSED FLUOR. FIXTURE IN SUSP. MTL. GRID

STAIRS

Planning Data

Nowhere is the personal safety and comfort of the user more important than in the design of stairs. This section, therefore, provides the planning data necessary to solve most problems of stair design. Various stair types are illustrated, including straight run, long "L," wide "L," double "L," and narrow and wide "U." Stair tables and related diagrams are provided that indicate vertical and horizontal areas, headroom clearances, and tread and riser dimensions for various stair systems. Information concerning nosings, landing widths, etc., is also included. In addition to general planning data, this section includes barrier-free design data as well as actual construction details of wood, steel, and concrete stairs prepared by various design firms.

It should be noted that stair design must conform to local building codes. Most codes require that means-of-egress stairways not be less than 44 in (1118 mm) in width, that the least dimension of landings and platforms not be less than the required width of the stair, and that the minimum headroom in all parts of a stairway not be less than 6 ft 8 in (2032 mm) measured vertically from the tread nosing or from the floor surface of the landing or platform. In one- and two-family dwellings, most codes require that stairways not be less than 3 ft (915 mm) clear in width, and that hand rails not be less than 30 in (762 mm) nor more than 34 in (864 mm) measured vertically from the nosing of the treads and be provided on at least one side of stairways of four or more risers.

CRITICAL DIMENSIONS AND CLEARANCES

Stair Table

Dimensions indicated in Fig. 1 and listed in Table 1 determine the vertical and horizontal areas and headroom clearances for stair systems with tread and riser proportions shown. They can be used directly in developing sketches or working drawings and eliminate the need for experimental stair plans or sections. All dimensions refer to face of treads without nosing.

Tabular data refer only to minimum conditions for straight run stairs. All figures may be adjusted according to requirements of design or stair use. For similar dimensional information controlling other types of stairways, see the following pages.

Widths of stairways may vary with these requirements. For passage of furniture, minimum clear widths should be selected from Table 2.

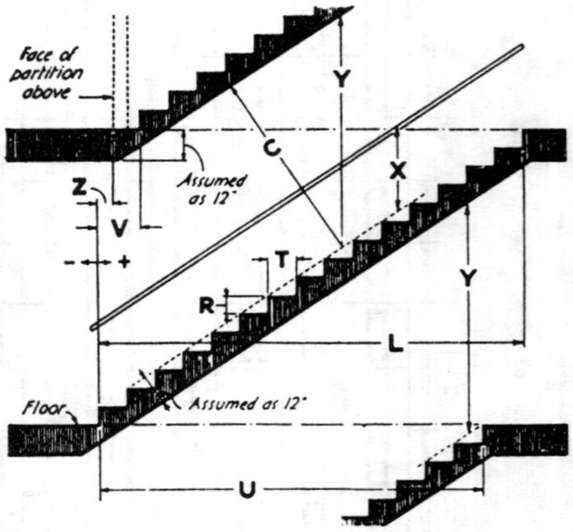

Fig. 1

TABLE 1 Stair Table

(Dimensions in feet and inches)

Floor to Floor Height		No. of Risers	Riser R	Tread T	Total Run L	Min. Headroom Y	Handrail X	Clearance C	Partition Above Z*	First Riser Below - U	First Riser Above - V*
8'-0"	†	11	8.73"	8¼"	6'-10½"	8'- 2"	2'-10"	5'- 8"	– 1'-10"	8'- 6"	– 1'- 7"
	†	12	8.00	9	8- 3	7-10	2- 9½	5-10½	– 1- 8½	9- 7½	– 1- 4
		13	**7.38**	**10½**	**10- 3**	**7- 7**	**2- 9**	**6- 2**	**–1- 8½**	**11- 6**	**– 1- 1½**
		14	**6.86**	**11½**	**12- 5½**	**7- 4**	**2- 9**	**6- 4**	**–1- 7**	**13- 5½**	**– 9½**
	∆	15	6.40	12½	14- 7	7- 3	2- 9	6- 7½	–1- 6½	15- 5½	– 7½
	∆	16	6.00	13½	16-10½	7- 3	2- 9	6- 7½	–1- 9	17- 6	– 8
8'-6"	†	12	8.50	8½	7- 9½	8- 1	2- 9½	5- 8½	– 1- 3½	8-10	–11
	†	13	7.85	9½	9- 3	7- 9	2- 9½	5-10½	– 1- 1	9-10	– 7½
		14	**7.29**	**10½**	**11- 4½**	**7- 6**	**2- 9**	**6- 2**	**–10½**	**12- 9**	**– 4**
		15	**6.80**	**11½**	**13- 8½**	**7- 4**	**2- 9**	**6- 4**	**–10½**	**13-10**	**– 1½**
	∆	16	6.38	12½	15- 7½	7- 3	2- 9	6- 5½	– 7	15- 5½	+ 3½
	∆	17	6.00	13½	18- 0	7- 3	2- 9	6- 7	– 7	17- 8	+ 5
9'-0"	†	12	9.00	8	7- 4	8- 3	2-10	5- 6	–11	8- 1	– 8
	†	13	8.31	8½	8- 6	8- 0	2- 9½	5- 9	– 9	8-11½	– 5
		14	**7.71**	**9½**	**10- 3½**	**7- 9**	**2- 9½**	**6- 0**	**– 6**	**10- 5**	**– ½**
		15	**7.20**	**10½**	**12- 3**	**7- 6**	**2- 9**	**6- 2½**	**– 3**	**11-10**	**+ 4½**
		16	**6.75**	**11¼**	**14- 8¼**	**7- 4**	**2- 9**	**6- 4**	**+ 2**	**13-11**	**+ 1- 0**
	∆	17	6.35	12½	16- 8	7- 3	2- 9	6- 5½	+ 5	15- 5½	+ 1- 4
	∆	18	6.00	13½	19- 1½	7- 3	2- 9	6- 7½	+ 6	17- 8	+ 1- 6
9'-6"	†	13	8.77	8	8- 0	8- 2	2-10	5- 5½	– 3½	8- 2	– ½
	†	14	8.14	9	9- 9	7-10	2- 9½	5- 9½	± 0	9- 5½	+ 5
		15	**7.60**	**9¼**	**11- 4½**	**7- 7**	**2- 9**	**5-11½**	**+ 4½**	**10- 7**	**+10½**
		16	**7.13**	**10¼**	**13- 5¼**	**7- 5**	**2- 9**	**6- 2**	**+ 9½**	**12- 2**	**+ 1- 5½**
		17	**6.71**	**11¼**	**15- 8**	**7- 4**	**2- 9**	**6- 4**	**+1- 1½**	**13-11½**	**+ 1-11**
	∆	18	6.33	12½	17- 8½	7- 3	2- 9	6- 5½	+ 1- 5½	15- 7	+ 2- 4
	∆	19	6.00	13½	20- 3	7- 3	2- 9	6- 8	+ 1- 8	17- 9	+ 2- 7½
10'-0"	†	14	8.57	8½	9- 2½	8- 1	2- 9½	5- 8½	+ 2	8- 8	+ 6
	†	15	8.00	9	10- 6	7-10	2- 9½	5-10½	+ 6½	9- 7	+11
		16	**7.50**	**10**	**12- 6**	**7- 7**	**2- 9**	**6- 1**	**+ 1- 1**	**10-11½**	**+ 1- 6½**
		17	**7.06**	**11**	**14- 8**	**7- 5**	**2- 9**	**6- 2½**	**+ 1- 7½**	**12- 5½**	**+2- 2½**
		18	**6.67**	**12**	**17- 0**	**7- 4**	**2- 9**	**6- 5**	**+2- 0**	**14- 3½**	**+2- 9**
	∆	19	6.32	12½	18- 9	7- 3	2- 9	6- 6	+ 2- 5	15- 8	+ 3- 2½
	∆	20	6.00	13½	21- 4½	7- 3	2- 9	6- 7½	+ 2-10	17- 9	+ 3- 8½
10'-6"	†	14	9.00	8	8- 8	8- 3	2-10	5- 5½	+ 6	8- 0	+ 9
	†	15	8.40	8½	9-11	8- 1	2- 9½	5- 8½	+ 9½	8-10	+ 1- 1
		16	7.88	9¼	11- 6¾	7- 9	2- 9½	5-10½	+ 1- 3½	9-10	+ 1- 8½
		17	**7.41**	**10**	**13- 4**	**7- 7**	**2- 9**	**6- 1**	**+1- 9½**	**11- 0**	**+ 2- 3½**
		18	**7.00**	**11**	**15- 7**	**7- 5**	**2- 9**	**6- 2½**	**+2- 5**	**12- 7½**	**+ 3- 0½**
		19	**6.63**	**12**	**18- 0**	**7- 4**	**2- 9**	**6- 4½**	**+2-11**	**14- 4**	**+ 3- 8½**
	∆	20	6.30	12½	19- 9½	7- 3	2- 9	6- 6	+ 3- 5½	15- 7	+ 4- 3½
	∆	21	6.00	13½	22- 6	7- 3	2- 9	6- 7½	+ 4- 0	17- 9	+ 5- 0
11'-0"	†	15	8.80	8	9- 4	8- 2	2-10	5- 6	+ 1- 0½	8- 1	+ 1- 2½
	†	16	8.25	8¼	10-11¼	8- 0	2- 9½	5-10	+ 1- 5	9- 2½	+ 1- 9
		17	**7.76**	**9½**	**12- 8**	**7- 9**	**2- 9½**	**6- 0**	**+2- 0**	**10- 3½**	**+ 2- 4½**
		18	**7.33**	**10¼**	**14- 6¼**	**7- 6**	**2- 9**	**6- 1½**	**+2- 7½**	**11- 4½**	**+ 3- 1½**
		19	**6.95**	**11**	**16- 6**	**7- 5**	**2- 9**	**6- 3**	**+3- 3**	**12- 8**	**+ 3- 9**
		20	**6.60**	**12**	**19- 0**	**7- 4**	**2- 9**	**6- 5**	**+3-10½**	**14- 5½**	**+ 4- 7½**
	∆	21	6.29	12½	20-10	7- 3	2- 9	6- 6	+ 4- 5	15- 8	+ 5- 3
	∆	22	6.00	13½	23- 7½	7- 3	2- 9	6- 7½	+ 5- 1	17- 8	+ 6- 0

*Dimensions given plus or minus, i.e., behind or in front of first riser (see Fig. 1).

Notes: Figures in boldface indicate stairs recommended for most interiors.
† indicates stairs allowable only for attics and cellars but not recommended.
∆ indicates stairs for exterior or monumental use.

Clearances for Furniture Passage

Width is not always a critical factor of stairway design but is important when the layout involves one or more turns with straight runs. Typical layouts for such stairways include the Long L, Double L, Wide U, Wide L, and Narrow U. (See Fig. 3 for layouts and tabular data on these types.)

Stairways used solely as circulation from floor to floor can be 2'0" wide for comfortable passage of one individual or 3'6" for two, side-by-side. When furniture must be taken up and down, minimum clear widths of straight runs and landings must be carefully selected or corners will constitute obstructions in many instances.

Recommended minimum clear widths as shown in Table 2 are not necessarily the width of stairs, either rough or wall-to-wall. Projections of newels, handrails, or baseboards can obstruct passage of furniture and must be taken into account when determining actual stair widths.

Headroom is also a controlling factor of design. With minimum headroom conditions shown in Table 1, clear widths for furniture passage must be greater in most cases than may be necessary if headroom is unlimited or equal at least to the ceiling heights. This is particularly important at the first riser and at turns, where the under rake of the first stair limits the vertical clearance of the stairway below. Therefore, if stairs must be comparatively narrow and if furniture must be transported over them, headroom, or vertical clearance, must be increased accordingly.

Landing widths may be increased to provide greater turning space for maneuvering furniture. If this is done, minimum clear widths can be proportionately decreased. However, this expedient is not effective unless hallways at either end of the stairway are at least equal to the landing widths. Narrow hallways often offer as great an obstruction to furniture maneuvering as low headroom, narrow runs, or cramped turns.

Open-well stairways give more opportunity to maneuver furniture, since even very bulky but light pieces may often be lifted over rails or newels. In general, a closed-string stair should be wider than an open-string type for the same degree of convenience.

The data in Table 2 reflect safe *average* clearances for transportation of items listed. Dimensions of furniture are subject to wide variations. Consequently, the minimum clear widths recommended here are susceptible to adjustment in certain instances.

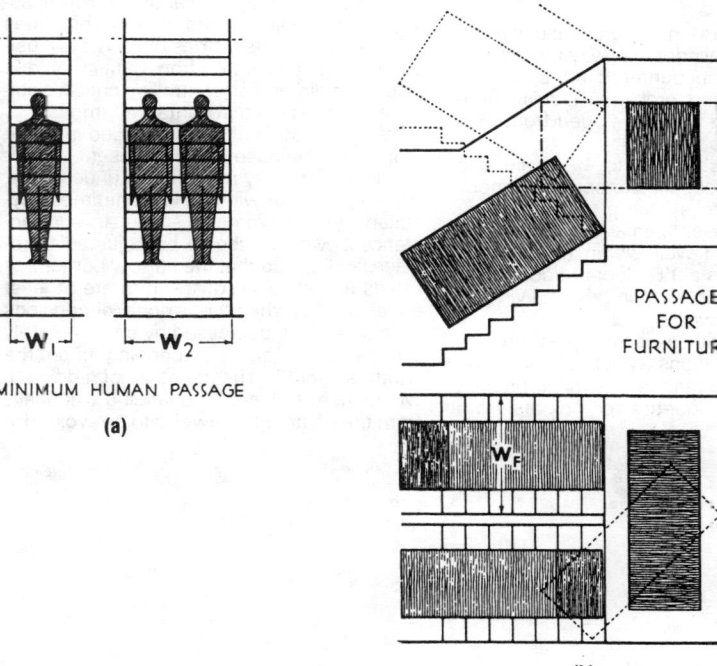

MINIMUM HUMAN PASSAGE

(a)

PASSAGE FOR FURNITURE

(b)

Fig. 2   Minimum stair widths. *(a)* **Stairs designed for comfortable human passage only may be relatively narrow. W₁ may be 2'0" but 2'6" is better. W₂ should be at least 3'6". *(b)* Furniture passage demands greater width. If stair landing is increased or headroom unlimited, W_F may be decreased. See Table 2.**

TABLE 2   Recommended Minimum Clear Widths of Stairs (W_F) for Furniture Movement*

Furniture		Min. Headroom ▲		Unlimited Headroom		
Article	Size	Wide U Type	Narrow U Type	Wide and Narrow U	Narrow U only●	
					Stair	Landing
Double Bed Box Spring	4'-6" x 6'-6" x 8"	3'- 2"	3'- 2"	2'- 3"		
Dressing Table	1'-10"x 4'-0"x 2'-6"	2'- 5"	2'- 5"	2'- 5"		
Bureau	2'-0"x 4'-0"x 3'-0"	2'- 8"	2'- 8"	2'- 8"		
Chiffonier	1'-8"x 3'-4"x 4'-8"	2'- 6"	2'- 6"	2'- 6"		
Chest of Drawers	1'-9"x 3'-4"x 4'-8"	2'- 7"	2'- 7"	2'- 7"		
Divan - Club	3'-6"x 7'-2"x 2'-9"	4'- 8"	4'- 8"	3'- 4"	3'-0"	3'-8"
Divan - Average	3'-0"x 6'-8"x 2'-6"	4'- 4"	4'- 4"	2'-11"		
Piano - Concert Grand	9'-0"x 5'-4"x 1'-8"	4'- 8"	4'- 8"	3'- 2" ■	3'-0" ■	3'-4" ■
Piano - Music Room Grand	7'-3"x 5'-2"x 1'-6"	3'-10"	3'-10"	3'- 0"		
Piano - Drawing Room Grand	6'-9"x 5'-0"x 1'-4"	3'- 6"	3'- 6"	2'-10"		
Piano - Baby Grand	5'-8"x 4'-10"x 1'-2"	3'- 0"	3'- 0"	2'- 8"		
Piano - Standard Upright	2'-2"x 5'-10"x 4'-6"	4'- 0"	3'- 9"	3'- 3"	3'-0"	3'-6"
Highboy - Large	2'-0"x 3'-6"x 7'-6"	4'- 4"	4'- 4"	2'-10"		
Highboy - Average	1'-8"x 3'-4"x 6'-0'	3'- 6"	3'- 6"	2'- 6"		
Secretary - Large	1'-10"x 3'-8"x 7'-2"	4'- 0"	4'- 0"	2'-10"		
Secretary - Average	1'-10"x 3'-0"x 6'-10"	3'-10"	3'-10"	2'- 6"		
Sideboard	1'-9"x 5'-0"x 3'-2"	2'- 6"	2'- 6"	2'- 6"		
Buffet	2'-1"x 3'-3"x 6'-6"	4'- 0"	4'- 0"	2'-10"		
Dresser	1'-9"x 6'-0"x 5'-6"	4'- 4"	3'- 6"	3'- 4"	3'-0"	3'-8"
Table (6 People)	3'-6"x 5'-0"x 2'-6"	3'- 2"	3'- 2"	3'- 2"	3'-0"	3'-4"
Table (8 People)	3'-6"x 7'-0"x 2'-6"	4'- 8"	4'- 4"	3'- 2"	3'-0"	3-4
Table (10 People) Rd.	6'-4" Diam.	4'- 8"	4'- 8"	3'- 0"		
Desk - Slope Top	2'-6"x 3'-8"x 3'-4"	3'- 3"	3'- 2"	3'- 2"	3'-0"	3'-4"
Desk - Flat Top	3'-0"x 5'-6"x 2'-6"	3'- 2"	3'- 0"	3'- 0"		
Desk - Executive's	3'-2"x 6'-0"x 2'-6"	4'- 2"	4'- 2"	3'- 1"	3'-0"	3'-2"
Trunk - Wardrobe	1'-11" x 2'-6"x 3'-7"	2'- 5"	2'- 5"	2'- 5"		

*Clear width between faces of rails, newels, etc., or between rail or newel and finish wall.
Notes: ▲ Headroom limited to minimum for comfortable human passage (see Table 1 and text).
 ● Narrow stairs and wide landings.
 ■ Absolute minimum not recommended (see text).

STAIRS

Planning Data

Purpose

The six diagrams in Fig. 3 represent unit plans for types of nonwinder stairways which are most frequently encountered in the average residential planning problem. Tabular information with each was developed from data contained in Table 1.

Unit plans are drawn to ⅛″ scale and therefore can be supplied directly as a check of stair layouts to sketch plans and elevations. Each represents an average condition with a stair pitch well within the comfort zone. The basis is a 9′6″ floor-to-floor height with 16 risers each 7.13″ in height. Width is 3′0″ from wall to wall.

Tabular data with each unit plan indicate dimensional variations which occur when stairways of substantially similar pitches are planned for floor-to-floor heights from 8 to 11 ft.

Width is the only critical dimension missing from this unit plan information. This varies with requirements of design and stair use and should be selected from data in Table 2. Width is a dimension controlling critical clearances on all stairs that contain a turn.

Winders have not been included in these unit plans because they represent a stair condition generally regarded as undesirable. However, use of winders is sometimes necessary due to cramped space. In such instances, winders should be adjusted to replace landings so that the narrow portions of treads at the inside of the turn are at least equal to ¾″ T. When this is done, dimensions of L_1 and L_2 are decreased by approximately ½T, the exact figure depending upon the width selected. The practice of adding a winder-riser to bisect the landing diagonally from the corner of a newel is to be avoided in all cases for it produces a dangerously narrow step in a particularly undesirable place.

Application of Unit Plans

Diagrammatic data can be used on sketches as a graphic check as noted. Tabular data can be applied to either sketches or working drawings to eliminate the necessity of developing experimental stairway sections to determine run, proportional rise, horizontal and vertical areas, and location of under-rake minimum headroom.

Dimensional data have been confined to a single pitch for all floor-to-floor heights. The pitch indicated is that most generally desirable for human comfort. Data for other pitches listed as tread and riser proportions in Table 1 can be substituted for values of L_1, L_2, and M.

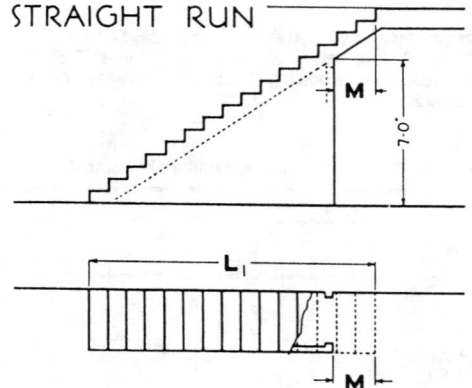

HEIGHT FLOOR TO FLOOR	NO OF RISERS	RISER	TREAD	L_1	M
8′-0″	13	7.38	10¼″	10′-3″	—
8′-6″	14	7.29	10½″	11′-4½″	4½″
9′-0″	15	7.20	10½″	12′-3″	1′-1½″
9′-6″	16	7.13	10¾″	13′-5¼″	1′-11¼″
10′-0″	17	7.06	11″	14′-8″	2′-9½″
10′-6″	18	7.00	11″	15′-7″	3′-7″
11′-0″	19	6.95	11″	16′-6″	4′-5″

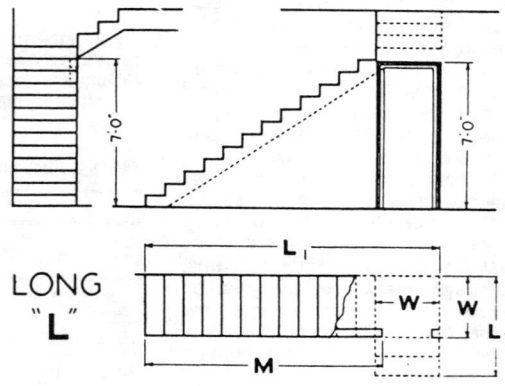

HEIGHT FLOOR TO FLOOR	N° RISERS	RISER	TREAD	N° RISERS	L_1	N° RISERS	L_2	M
8′-0″	13	7.38	10¼″	13	10′-3″ + W	0	W	10′-3″
8′-6″	14	7.29	10½″	13	10′-6″ + W	1	W	10′-6″
9′-0″	15	7.20	10½″	13	10′-6″ + W	2	10½″ + W	10′-6″
9′-6″	16	7.13	10¾″	13	10′-9″ + W	3	1′-9½″ + W	11′-0″
10′-0″	17	7.06	11″	13	11′-0″ + W	4	2′-9″ + W	11′-4″
10′-6″	18	7.00	11″	13	11′-0″ + W	5	3′-8″ + W	11′-5″
11′-0″	19	6.95	11″	13	11′-0″ + W	6	4′-7″ + W	11′-6″

Fig. 3

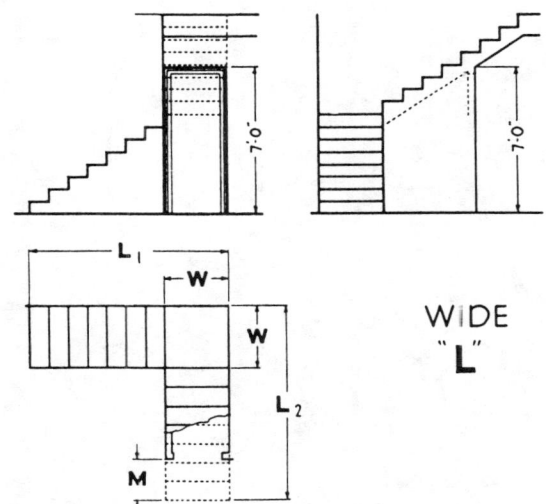

WIDE "L"

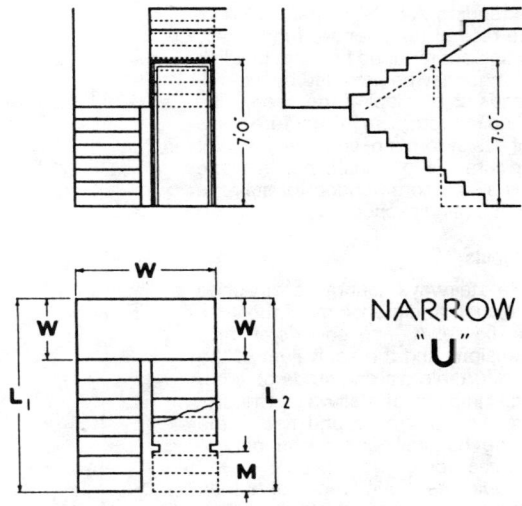

NARROW "U"

HEIGHT FLOOR TO FLOOR	Nº RISERS	RISER	TREAD	Nº RISERS	L_1	Nº RISERS	L_2	M
8'-0"	13	7.38	10¼"	7	5'-1½"+W	6	4'-3¼"+W	—
8'-6"	14	7.29	10½"	7	5'-3"+W	7	5'-3"+W	4½"
9'-0"	15	7.20	10½"	8	6'-1½"+W	7	5'-3"+W	1'-1½"
9'-6"	16	7.13	10¾"	8	6'-3¼"+W	8	6'-3¼"+W	1'-11¼"
10'-0"	17	7.06	11"	9	7'-4"+W	8	6'-5"+W	2'-9½"
10'-6"	18	7.00	11"	9	7'-4"+W	9	7'-4"+W	3'-7"
11'-0"	19	6.95	11"	10	8'-3"+W	9	7'-4"+W	4'-5"

HEIGHT FLOOR TO FLOOR	Nº RISERS	RISER	TREAD	Nº RISERS	L_1	Nº RISERS	L_2	M
8'-0"	13	7.38	10¼"	7	5'-1½"+W	6	4'-3¼"+W	—
8'-6"	14	7.29	10½"	7	5'-3"+W	7	5'-3"+W	4½"
9'-0"	15	7.20	10½"	8	6'-1½"+W	7	5'-3"+W	1'-1½"
9'-6"	16	7.13	10¾"	8	6'-3¼"+W	8	6'-3¼"+W	1'-11¼"
10'-0"	17	7.06	11"	9	7'-4"+W	8	6'-5"+W	2'-9½"
10'-6"	18	7.00	11"	9	7'-4"+W	9	7'-4"+W	3'-7"
11'-0"	19	6.95	11"	10	8'-3"+W	9	7'-4"+W	4'-5"

DOUBLE "L"

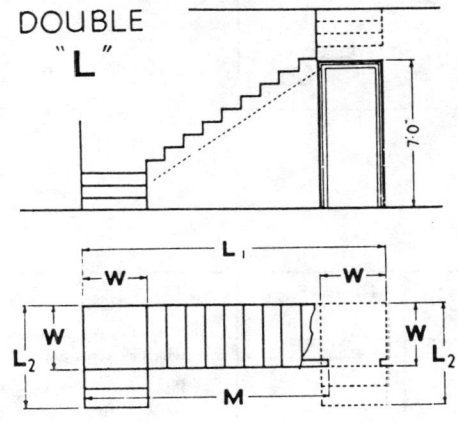

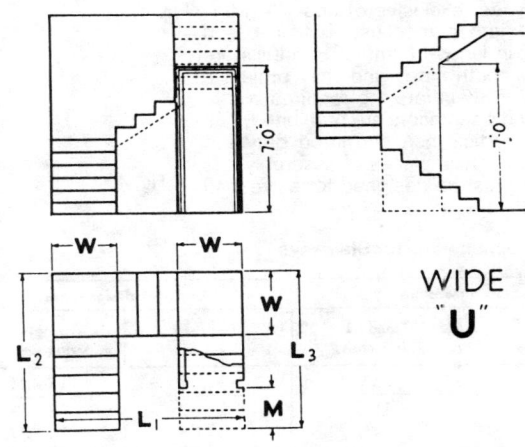

WIDE "U"

HEIGHT FLOOR TO FLOOR	Nº RISERS	RISER	TREAD	Nº RISERS	L_1	Nº RISERS	L_2	M
8'-0"	13	7.38	10¼"	13	10'-3"+2W	0	W	10'-3"+W
8'-6"	14	7.29	10½"	12	9'-7½"+2W	1	W	9'-7½"+W
9'-0"	15	7.20	10½"	11	8'-9"+2W	2	10½"+W	8'-9"+W
9'-6"	16	7.13	10¾"	10	8'-0¾"+2W	3	1'-9½"+W	8'-3¾"+W
10'-0"	17	7.06	11"	9	7'-4"+2W	4	2'-6"+W	7'-8"+W
10'-6"	18	7.00	11"	8	6'-5"+2W	5	3'-8"+W	6'-10"+W
11'-0"	19	6.95	11"	7	5'-6"+2W	6	4'-7"+W	6'-0"+W

HEIGHT FLOOR TO FLOOR	Nº RISERS	RISER	TREAD	Nº RISERS	L_1	Nº RISERS	L_2	Nº RISERS	L_3	M
8'-0"	13	7.38	10¼"	4	2'-6¾"+2W	4	2'-6¾"+W	5	3'-5"+W	—
8'-6"	14	7.29	10½"	4	2'-7½"+2W	5	3'-6"+W	5	3'-6"+W	4½"
9'-0"	15	7.20	10½"	4	2'-7½"+2W	5	3'-6"+W	6	4'-4½"+W	1'-1½"
9'-6"	16	7.13	10¾"	4	2'-8¼"+2W	6	4'-5¾"+W	6	4'-5¾"+W	1'-11¼"
10'-0"	17	7.06	11"	4	2'-9"+2W	6	4'-7"+W	7	5'-6"+W	2'-9½"
10'-6"	18	7.00	11"	4	2'-9"+2W	7	5'-6"+W	7	5'-6"+W	3'-7"
11'-0"	19	6.95	11"	4	2'-9"+2W	7	5'-6"+W	8	6'-5"+W	4'-5"

Fig. 3 *(Continued)*

STAIRS
Layouts and Dimensions

Nosings

Nosings extending ¾ to 1½ in (usually 1¼ in) beyond the face of the riser are functionally necessary and are required by most building codes. Nosings may be provided by extending the treads or by sloping the risers. The latter method is customary in concrete stairs because of easier forming, and in any type of stair where carpet is to be installed. This type of nosing is also recommended for stairs to be used by the handicapped.

Stairway Layouts

Comfortable stairways cannot be designed except in relation to dimensions of the average human figure. As applied to stairways these dimensions and the equivalent of the average comfortable walking stride of about 24 in fix the gradient of stairways, the proportional relation of treads and risers, the height of the handrail, and the minimum necessary headroom.

Figure 4 indicates the influence of human figure dimensions and suggests the desirability of varying ceiling clearances and handrail heights according to variations in stair gradients. These variations are included in Table 3.

Treads and risers in curved stairs should be proportioned on an assumed "line of travel" 18 in from the inner (smaller radius) handrail.

All building codes have strict specifications for stairs which are required exits. The National Building Code of the American Insurance Association and the New York City code both require that treads and risers be proportioned by the formula T × R = 70 to 75, with risers not over 7¾ in high and treads not less than 9 in wide, exclusive of nosings. Minimum stair width for most uses is 44 in, based on two 22-in lanes of traffic. Handrails are required on both sides and may project a maximum of 3½ in into the required width. Winders and open risers are prohibited. The maximum vertical rise permitted between landings is 12 ft; in places of assembly it is 8 ft. Stairs must be designed for a live load of 100 lb/ft².

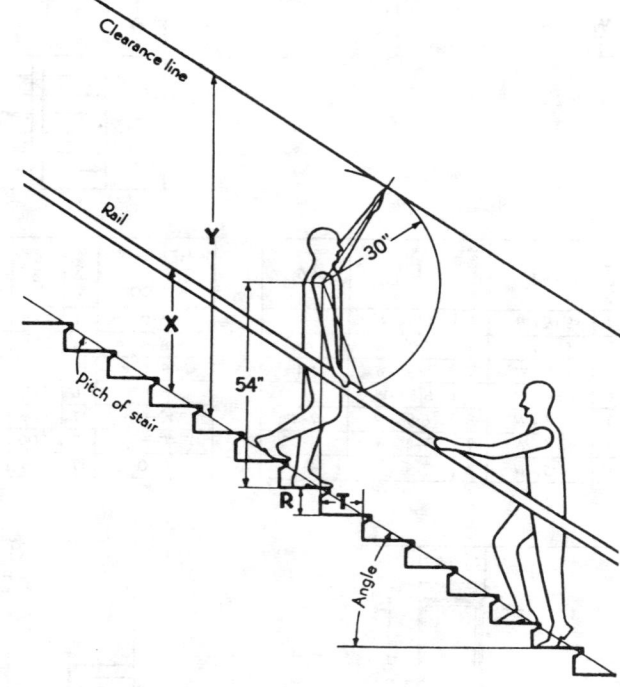

Fig. 4

TABLE 3 Dimensions for Stairways

Step dimensions		Gradient designations		Headroom *	Handrail height	NOTES
Riser **R** in inches	Tread **T** in inches	Per cent grade	Angle in degrees, minutes	**Y** in inches	**X** in inches	
5	16	31.25	17 - 21	85		1. 7" by 11" is the proportion by which all steps are laid out
5¼	15½	33.87	18 - 43		33½	
5½	14¾	37.28	20 - 27	86		2. Risers from 5" to 6½" are suitable for exterior and "grand" interior stairs
5¾	14	41.07	22 - 20			
6	13½	44.44	23 - 58	87		3. Risers from 6⅜" to 7⅜" are most comfortable and most suitable for interior stairs
6¼	13	48.07	25 - 40			
6½	12¼	53.06	27 - 57	88	33	4. Risers for cellar and attic stairs may be up to 9" high
6¾	11¾	57.44	29 - 52			
7	11	63.63	32 - 28	89		5. Width - minimum for single-file travel, 30"
7¼	10½	69.04	34 - 37	90		6. Width - minimum for comfort, 36"
7½	10	75	36 - 52	91		
7¾	9½	81.57	39 - 12	93		7. Width - desirable (for furniture passage etc.), 42"
8	9	88.88	41 - 38	94	33½	
8¼	8¾	97.05	44 - 9	96		8. Consult local building codes on all stair problems
8½	8¾	103.02	45 - 51	97		
8¾	8¼	107.07	46 - 57	98	34	
9	8	112.5	48 - 22	99		

Minimum for head clearance only can be safely taken as 84 in. for all gradients; HUD permits 80 in.

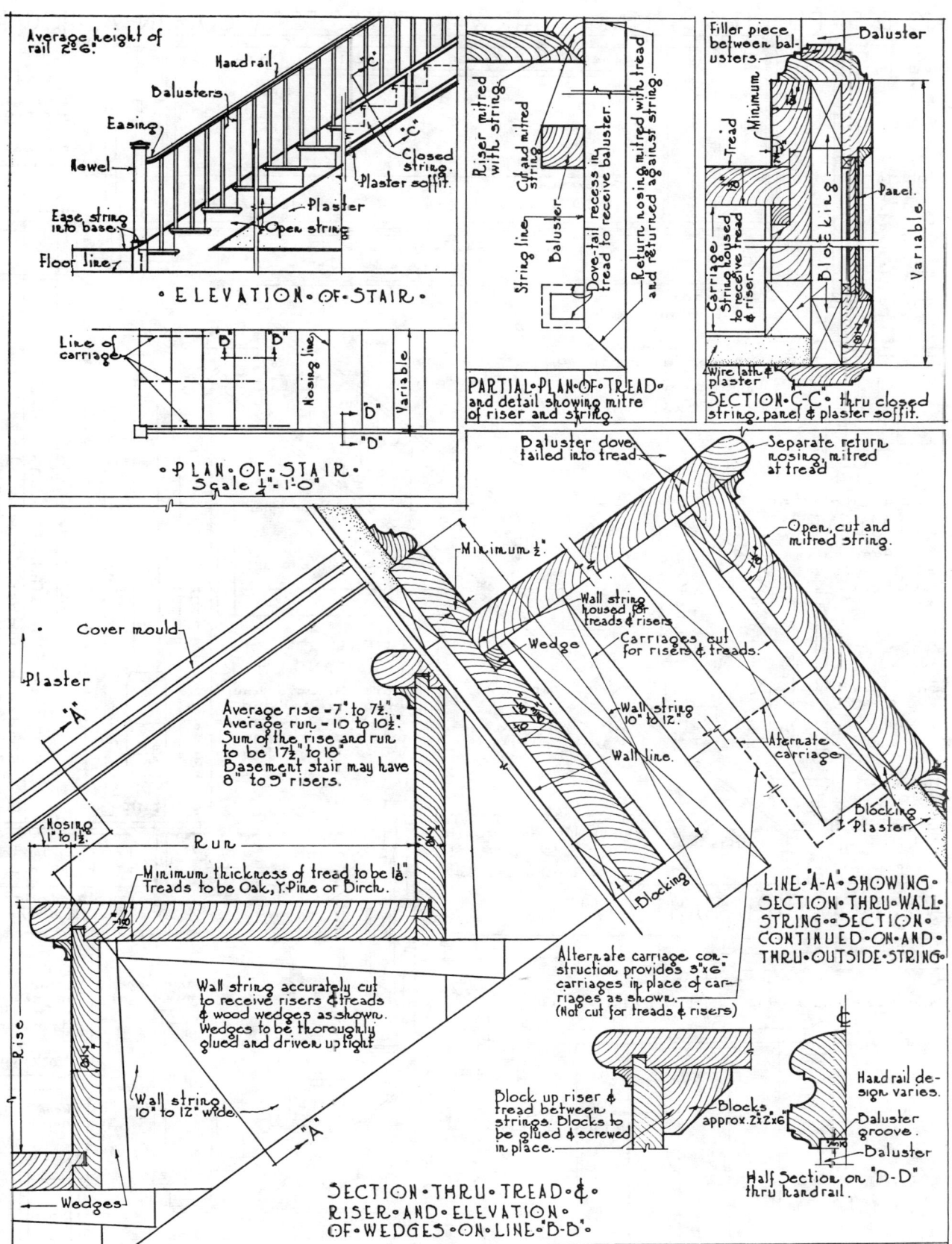

Average height of rail 2'-6".

Handrail

Balusters

Easing

Newel

Ease string into base.

Floor line.

Closed string.

Plaster soffit.

Plaster

Open string

· ELEVATION · OF · STAIR ·

Line of carriage

Nosing line

Variable

· PLAN · OF · STAIR ·
Scale ¼"=1'-0"

Riser mitred with string.

String line

Baluster

Cut and mitred string

Dove-tail recess in tread to receive baluster.

Return nosing mitred with tread and returned against string

PARTIAL · PLAN · OF · TREAD ·
and detail showing mitre of riser and string.

Filler piece between balusters.

Baluster

Tread

Minimum

Carriage String housed to receive tread & riser.

Blocking

Panel.

Variable

Wire lath & plaster

SECTION · C-C · thru closed string, panel & plaster soffit.

Baluster dove tailed into tread

Separate return nosing, mitred at tread

Minimum ½"

Open, cut and mitred string.

Wall string housed for treads & risers

Wedge

Carriages cut for risers & treads.

Wall string 10" to 12".

Wall line.

Alternate carriage

Blocking Plaster

Cover mould

Plaster

'A'

Average rise – 7" to 7½"
Average run – 10" to 10½"
Sum of the rise and run to be 17½" to 18"
Basement stair may have 8" to 9" risers.

Nosing 1" to 1½"

Run

Rise

Minimum thickness of tread to be 1⅛"
Treads to be Oak, Y. Pine or Birch.

Wall string accurately cut to receive risers & treads & wood wedges as shown. Wedges to be thoroughly glued and driven up tight.

Wall string 10" to 12" wide.

Blocking

Alternate carriage construction provides 3"x6" carriages in place of carriages as shown.
(Not cut for treads & risers)

LINE · 'A-A' · SHOWING · SECTION · THRU · WALL · STRING · SECTION · CONTINUED · ON · AND · THRU · OUTSIDE · STRING ·

Block up riser & tread between strings. Blocks to be glued & screwed in place.

Blocks approx. 2"x2"x6"

Handrail design varies.

Baluster groove.

Baluster

Half Section on 'D-D' thru handrail.

'A'

Wedges

SECTION · THRU · TREAD · & · RISER · AND · ELEVATION · OF · WEDGES · ON · LINE · 'B-B' ·

NO. D.5. DETAILS. OF. MAIN. STAIRWAY. TWO. STORY. COLONIAL. HOUSE

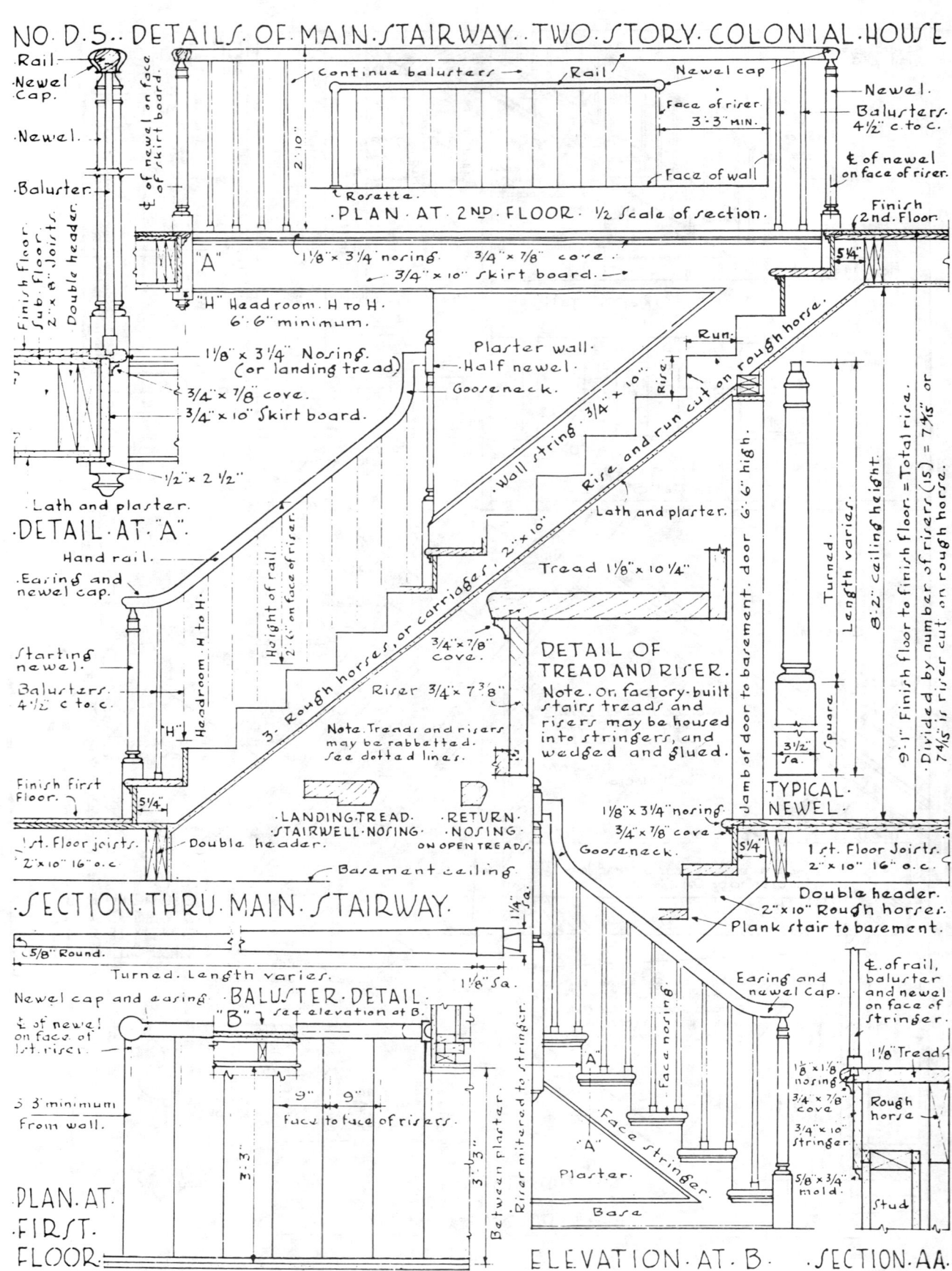

- Rail
- Newel Cap.
- Newel.
- Baluster.

Continue balusters — Rail — Newel cap

℄ of newel on face of skirt board.

2'-0"

Face of riser 3'-3" MIN.

Face of wall

Rosetta.

Newel.
Balusters 4½" c to c.
℄ of newel on face of riser.

Finish 2nd. Floor

PLAN. AT. 2ND. FLOOR. ½ Scale of section.

"A"   1⅛" x 3¼" nosing.   ¾" x ⅞" cove.
¾" x 10" skirt board.

5¼"

Finish Floor
Sub. Floor
2" x 8" Joists.
Double header

"H" Headroom. H to H. 6'-6" minimum.

1⅛" x 3¼" Nosing. (or landing tread)
¾" x ⅞" cove.
¾" x 10" Skirt board.

½" x 2½"

Lath and plaster.

Plaster wall.
Half newel.
Gooseneck.

Wall string ¾" x 10"

Rise and run cut on rough horse.

Run.
Rise.

Lath and plaster.

Jamb of door to basement. door 6'-6" high.

Turned. Length varies.

Square

3½" Sq.

TYPICAL NEWEL.

8'-2" ceiling height.

9'-1" Finish floor to finish Floor = Total rise.
Divided by number of risers (15) = 7⅖" or 7⅘" if riser cut on rough horse.

DETAIL. AT. "A".

- Hand rail.
- Easing and newel cap.
- Starting newel.
- Balusters. 4½" c to c.

Height of rail 2'-6" on face of riser

Headroom. H to H.

"H"

3. Rough horses, or carriages.

Carriages. 2" x 10"

¾" x ⅞" cove.

Tread 1⅛" x 10¼"

Riser ¾" x 7⅜"

Note. Treads and risers may be rabbetted. See dotted lines.

DETAIL OF TREAD AND RISER.

Note. On factory-built stairs treads and risers may be housed into stringers, and wedged and glued.

Finish first Floor.

5¼"

1st. Floor joists. 2" x 10" 16" o.c.
Double header

·LANDING·TREAD·
·STAIRWELL·NOSING·

·RETURN· ·NOSING· ON OPEN TREADS·

Basement ceiling

·SECTION·THRU· MAIN·STAIRWAY.

⅝" Round.

Turned. Length varies.

1⅛" Sq.

Newel cap and easing
℄ of newel on face of 1st. riser.

·BALUSTER· DETAIL "B" see elevation at B.

9" 9"
Face to face of risers.

3'-3" minimum from wall.

3'-3"

3"
3"

¼" Sq.

1⅛" x 3¼" nosing
¾" x ⅞" cove
Gooseneck.

5¼"

1st. Floor Joists. 2" x 10" 16" o.c.

Double header.
2" x 10" Rough horses.
Plank stair to basement.

Easing and newel Cap.

℄ of rail, baluster and newel on face of stringer.

Between plaster.

Riser mitered to stringer.

"A"

Face nosing

Face stringer.

"A"

Plaster.

Base

1⅛" Tread

1⅛" x 1⅛" nosing
¾" x ⅞" cove
¾" x 10" stringer
⅝" x ¾" mold

Rough horse

Stud

·PLAN·AT· ·FIRST· ·FLOOR·

·ELEVATION· AT· B·

·SECTION· AA·

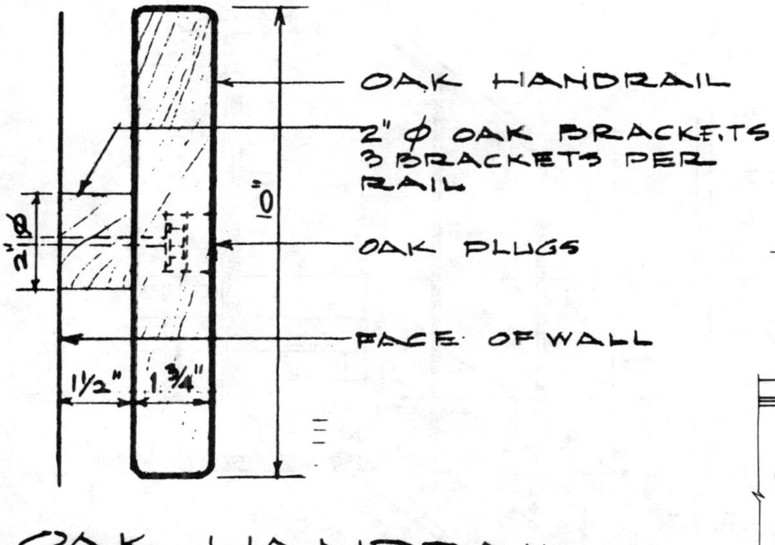

OAK HANDRAIL

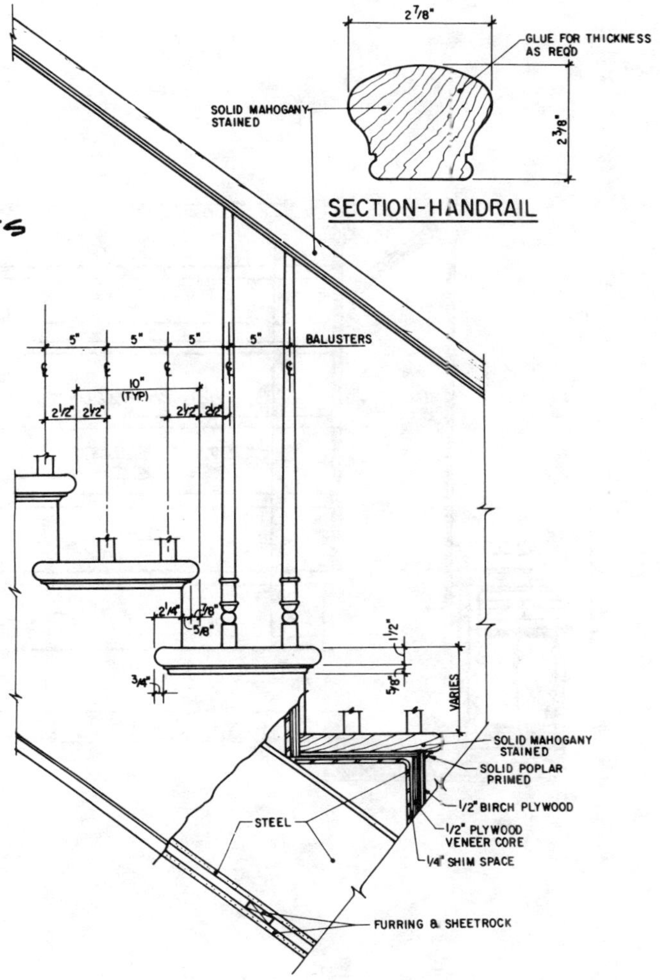

2" ∅ OAK BRACKETS
3 BRACKETS PER
RAIL

OAK PLUGS

FACE OF WALL

OAK HANDRAIL

2 7/8"

GLUE FOR THICKNESS
AS REQD

SOLID MAHOGANY
STAINED

2 7/8"

SECTION-HANDRAIL

5" 5" 5" 5" BALUSTERS

10"
(TYP)

2½" 2½"   2½" 2½"

2¼" 7/8"
5/8"

3/4"

1/2"

5/8"

VARIES

SOLID MAHOGANY
STAINED

SOLID POPLAR
PRIMED

1/2" BIRCH PLYWOOD

1/2" PLYWOOD
VENEER CORE

1/4" SHIM SPACE

STEEL

FURRING & SHEETROCK

PARTIAL ELEVATION STAIR

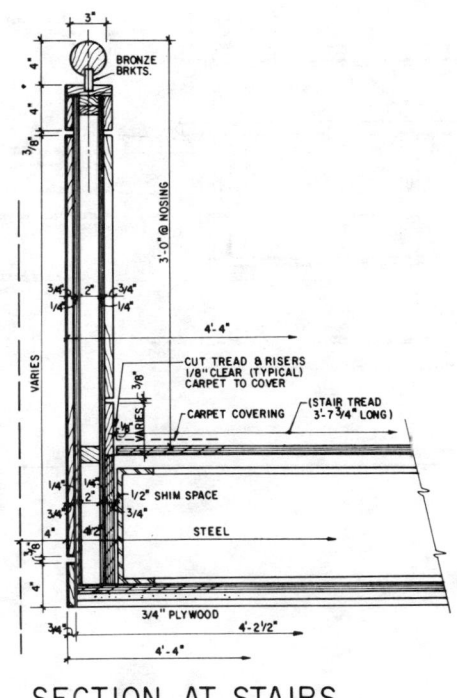

3"

BRONZE
BRKTS.

4" 4" 4"

3/8"

3'-0" @ NOSING

3/4" 2" 3/4"
1/4"   1/4"

VARIES

CUT TREAD & RISERS
1/8" CLEAR (TYPICAL)
CARPET TO COVER

3/8"

4'-4"

CARPET COVERING

(STAIR TREAD
3'-7 3/4" LONG)

VARIES

1/4"
3/4" 2"

1/2" SHIM SPACE

3/4"

STEEL

3/16"

4"

3/4" 4'-2½"

3/4" PLYWOOD 4'-2½"

4'-4"

SECTION AT STAIRS

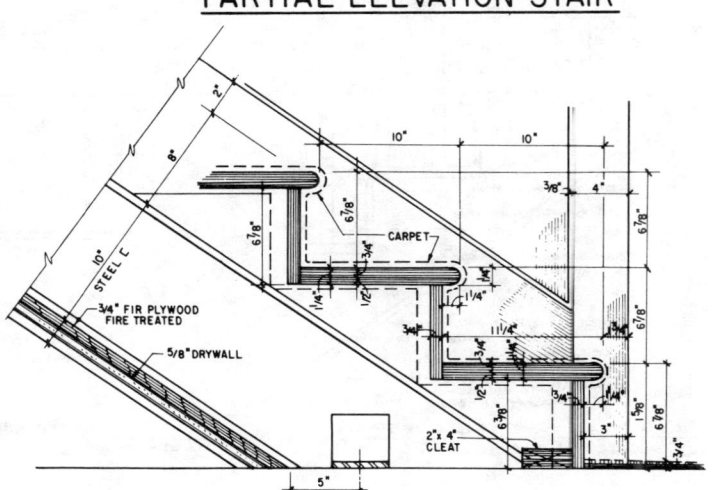

2"

6"

10"

10" 10"

3/8" 4"

6 7/8"

6 7/8"

CARPET

3/4"

1/4"

6 7/8"

STEEL C

10"

3/4" FIR PLYWOOD
FIRE TREATED

5/8" DRYWALL

1/2"

1¼"

3/4"

1¼"

6 7/8"

1/2"

6 7/8"

2" x 4"
CLEAT

1/4"

3"

3/4"

1 5/8"

6 7/8"

5"

TYPICAL SECTION AT STAIRS

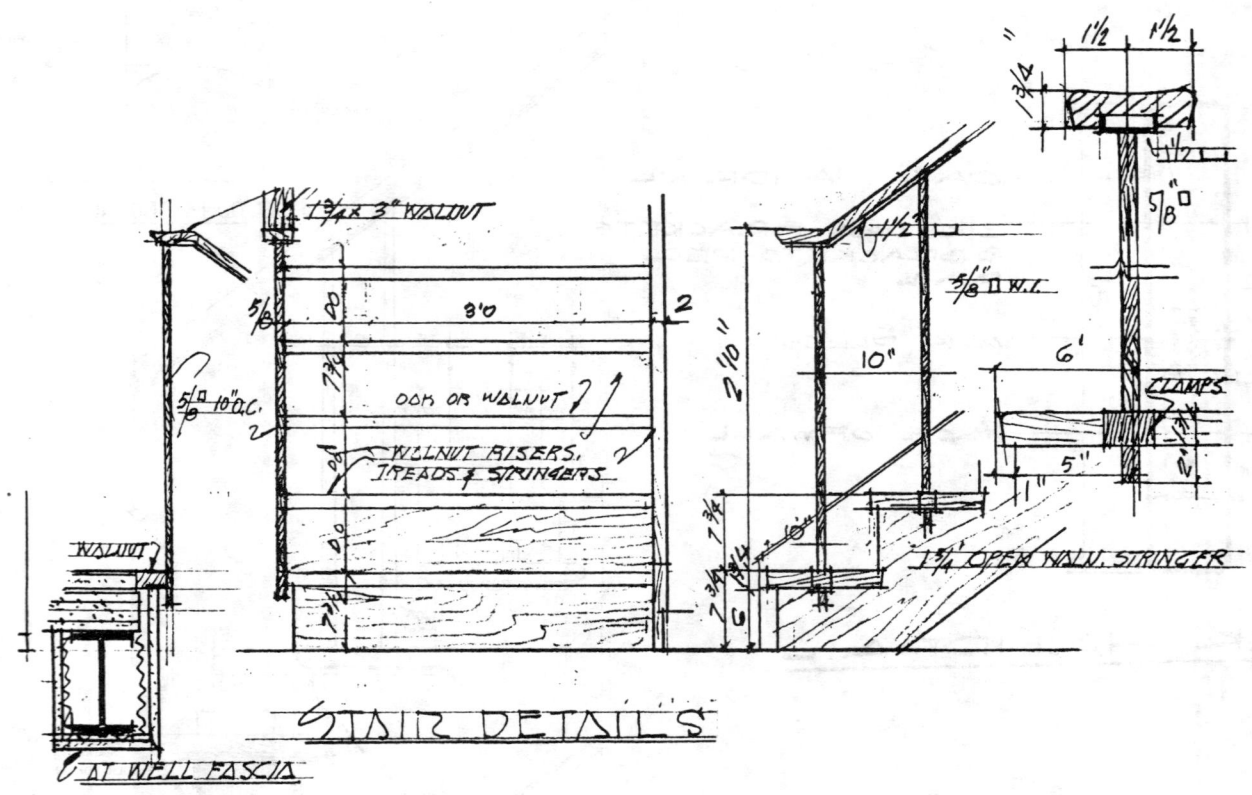

1¾ x 3" WALNUT

3'0

OAK OR WALNUT

WALNUT RISERS,
TREADS & STRINGERS

WALNUT

1¾" OPEN WALN. STRINGER

CLAMPS

STAIR DETAILS

AT WELL FASCIA

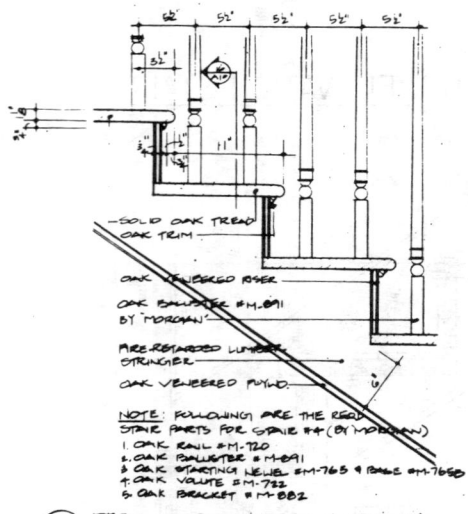

SOLID OAK TREAD
OAK TRIM
OAK VENEERED RISER
OAK BALUSTER #M-891
BY "MORGAN"
FIRE-RETARDED LUMBER
STRINGER
OAK VENEERED PLYWD.

NOTE: FOLLOWING ARE THE REQ'D
STAIR PARTS FOR STAIR #4 (BY MORGAN)
1. OAK RAIL #M-720
2. OAK BALUSTER #M-891
3. OAK STARTING NEWEL #M-763 & BASE #M-765D
4. OAK VOLUTE #M-722
5. OAK BRACKET #M-882

15
A10 DETAIL OF TREAD & RISER AT STAIR #4
SCALE: 3/4" = 1'-0"

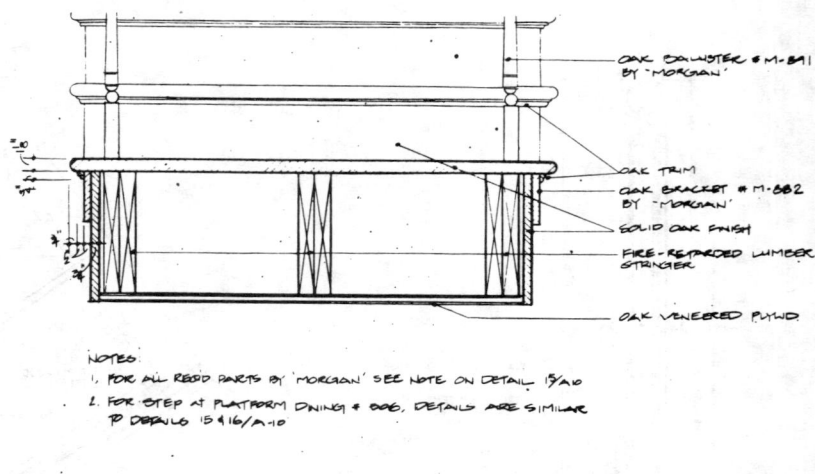

OAK BALUSTER #M-891
BY "MORGAN"

OAK TRIM
OAK BRACKET #M-882
BY "MORGAN"
SOLID OAK FINISH
FIRE-RETARDED LUMBER
STRINGER

OAK VENEERED PLYWD

NOTES:
1. FOR ALL REQ'D PARTS BY "MORGAN" SEE NOTE ON DETAIL 15/A10
2. FOR STEP AT PLATFORM DINING & 006, DETAILS ARE SIMILAR
TO DETAILS 15 & 16/A-10

16
A10 DETAIL OF STRINGER AT STAIR #4
SCALE: 1½" = 1'-0"

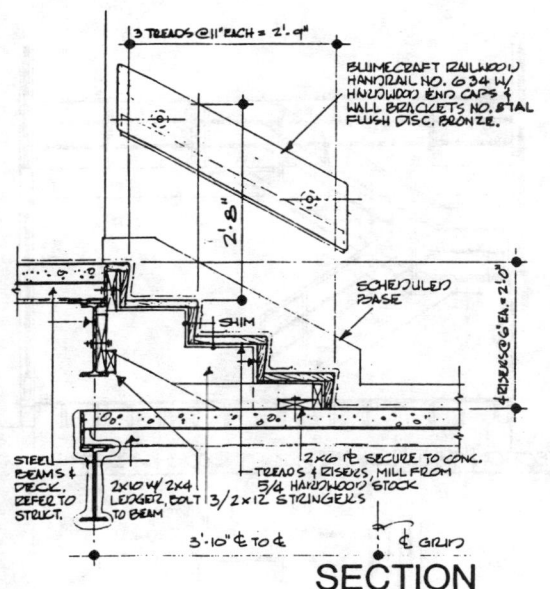

3 TREADS @ 11" EACH = 2'-9"

BLUMECRAFT RAILROAD HANDRAIL NO. 634 W/ HARDWOOD END CAPS & WALL BRACKETS NO. 8 TAL FLUSH DISC. BRONZE.

2'-8"

SCHEDULED BASE

SHIM

4 RISERS @ 6" EA = 2'-0"

STEEL BEAMS & DECK. REFER TO STRUCT.

2×10 W/ 2×4 LEDGER. BOLT TO BEAM

3/2×12 STRINGERS

TREADS & RISERS, MILL FROM 5/4 HARDWOOD STOCK

2×6 PT. SECURE TO CONC.

3'-10" ℄ TO ℄   ℄ GRID

SECTION

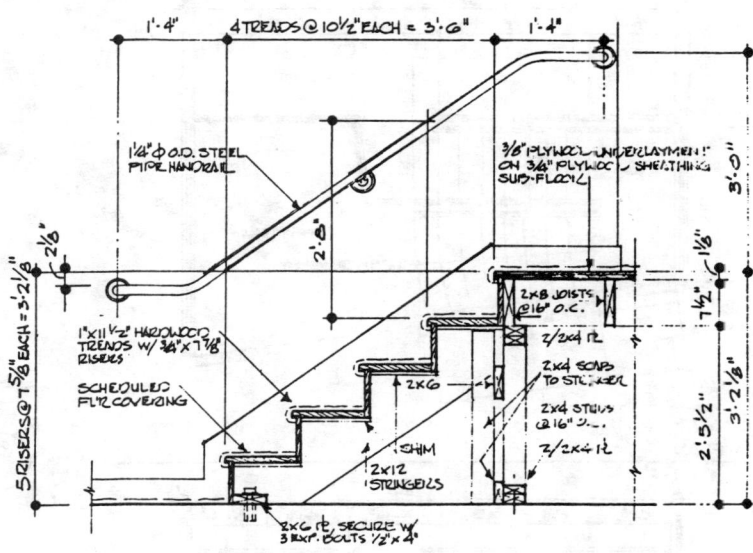

1'-4"   4 TREADS @ 10½" EACH = 3'-6"   1'-4"

1¼" Ø O.D. STEEL PIPE HANDRAIL

3/8" PLYWOOD UNDERLAYMENT ON 3/8" PLYWOOD SHEATHING SUB-FLOOR

2'-8"

2½"

2×8 JOISTS @ 16" O.C.

3/2×4 PT

2×4 SCABS TO STRINGER

2×4 STUDS @ 16" O.C.

3/2×4 PT

2×6

5 RISERS @ 7 5/8" EACH = 3'-2½"

1"×11½" HARDWOOD TREADS W/ 3/4"×7 7/8" RISERS

SCHEDULED FLR COVERING

SHIM

2×12 STRINGERS

7½"   1½"

3'-2½"   2'-5½"   3'-0"

2×6 PT. SECURE W/ 3 EXP. BOLTS ½" × 4"

SECTION

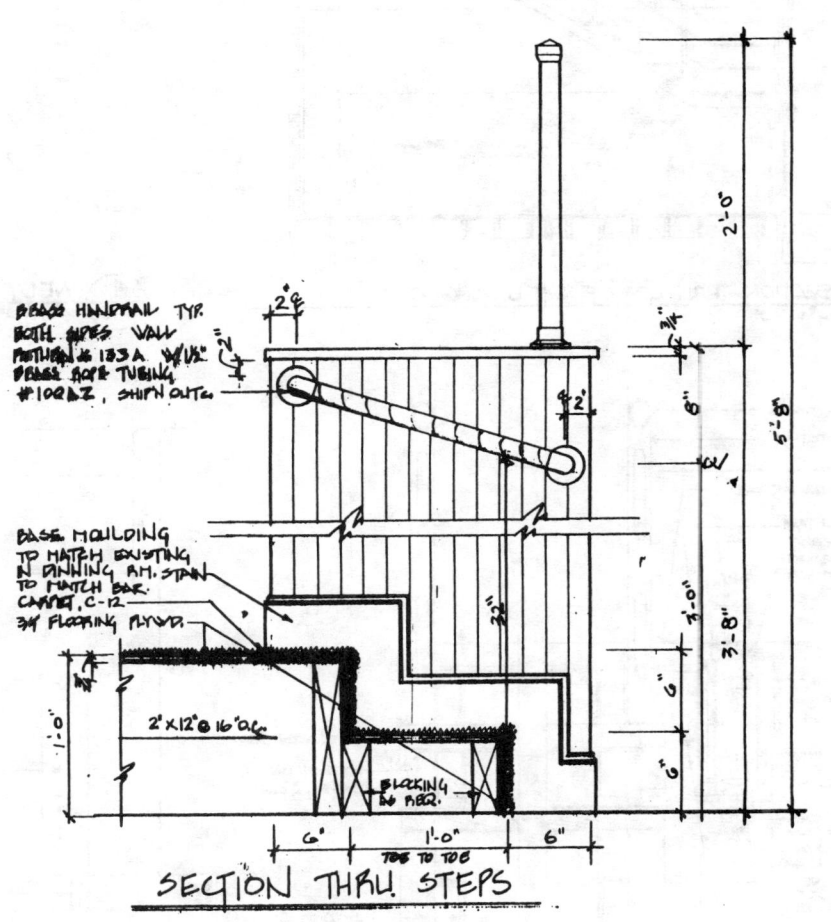

BRASS HANDRAIL TYP. BOTH SIDES WALL MOUNTED # 133 A 3/4"/1½" BRASS ROPE TUBING #102 DZ, SHIP'N OUTS.

BASE MOULDING TO MATCH EXISTING IN DINING RM. STAIN TO MATCH BAR CABINET, C-12

3/4" FLOORING PLYWD.

2"×12" @ 16" O.C.

1'-0"

BLOCKING EA. MBR.

2'-0"   3/4"

8"

5'-8"

7'-0"   3'-8"

6"

6"

2"   2"

6"   1'-0"   6"

TOE TO TOE

SECTION THRU STEPS

STAIRS
Wood and Steel Stairs

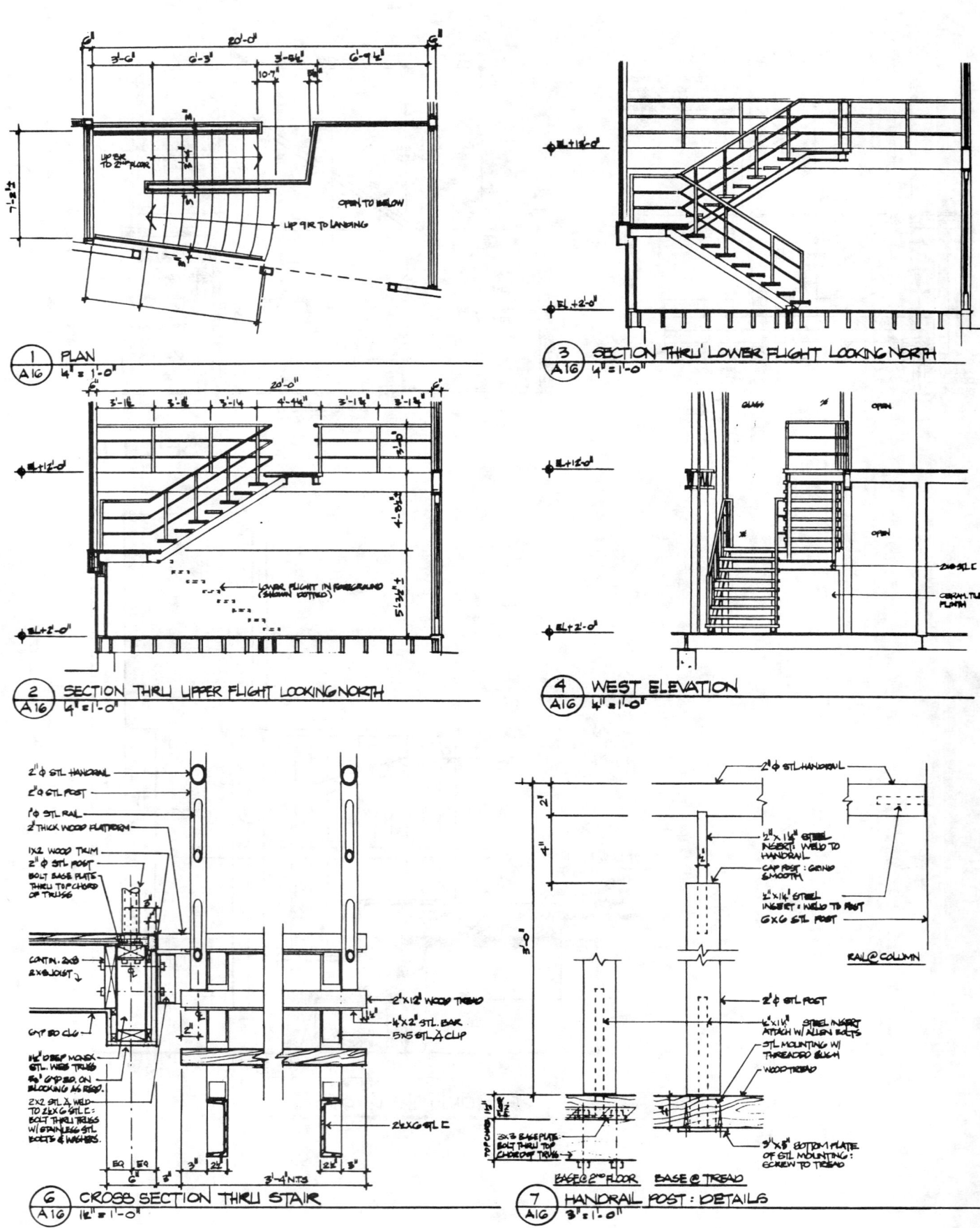

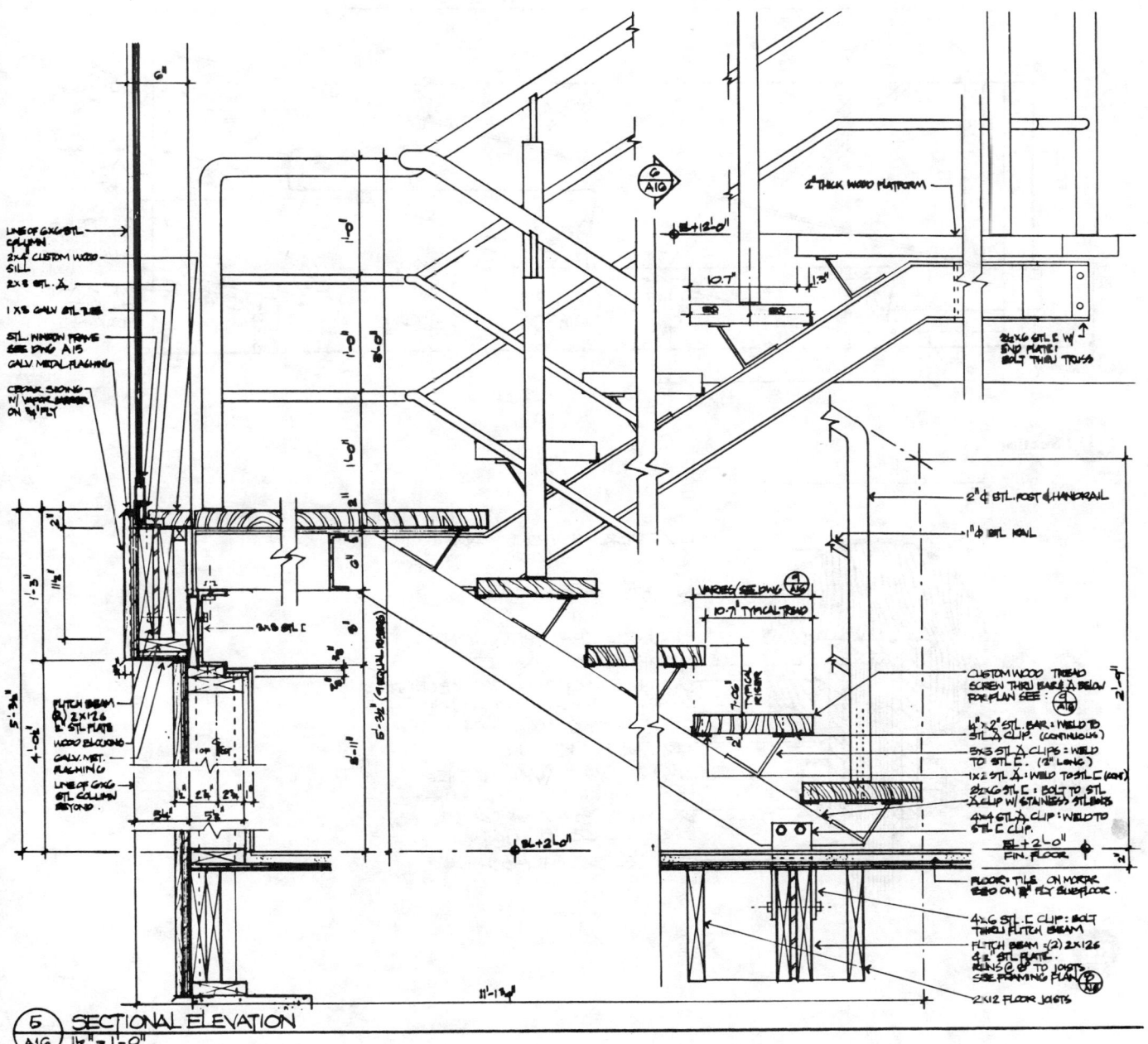

LINE OF 6X6 STL COLUMN
2X8 CUSTOM WOOD SILL
1 X 8 GALV STL. SEE
STL. WINDOW FRAME SEE DWG A15
GALV METAL FLASHING
CEDAR SIDING W/ VAPOR BARRIER ON 3/4" PLY

2" THICK WOOD PLATFORM

EL + 12'-0"

10.7"

2 1/2 X 6 STL. C W/ END PLATE: BOLT THRU TRUSS

2" ∅ STL. POST & HANDRAIL

1" ∅ STL. RAIL

2X8 STL C

VARIES (SEE DWG)
10.7" TYPICAL TREAD

CUSTOM WOOD TREAD SCREW THRU BARS & BELOW FOR PLAN SEE: 4/A16

1/4" X 2" STL. BAR: WELD TO STL C CLIP. (CONTINUOUS)

3X3 STL A CLIPS: WELD TO STL. C. (2" LONG)

1X2 STL A: WELD TO STL C (CONT)

2X6 STL. C: BOLT TO STL A CLIP W/ STAINLESS STL BARS

4X4 STL A CLIP: WELD TO STL C CLIP.

EL + 2'-0"
FIN. FLOOR

FLOOR: TILE ON MORTAR BED ON 3/4" PLY SUBFLOOR.

4X6 STL. C CLIP: BOLT THRU FLITCH BEAM

FLITCH BEAM = (2) 2X12 & 1/4" STL. PLATE. RUNS @ 4' TO JOISTS SEE FRAMING PLAN

2X12 FLOOR JOISTS

FLITCH BEAM (2) 2X12 & 1/4" STL PLATE
WOOD BLOCKING
GALV. MET. FLASHING
LINE OF 6X6 STL COLUMN BEYOND

EL + 2'-0"

11'-1 3/4"

5 / A16 SECTIONAL ELEVATION 1 1/2" = 1'-0"

STAIRS

Concrete Stairs

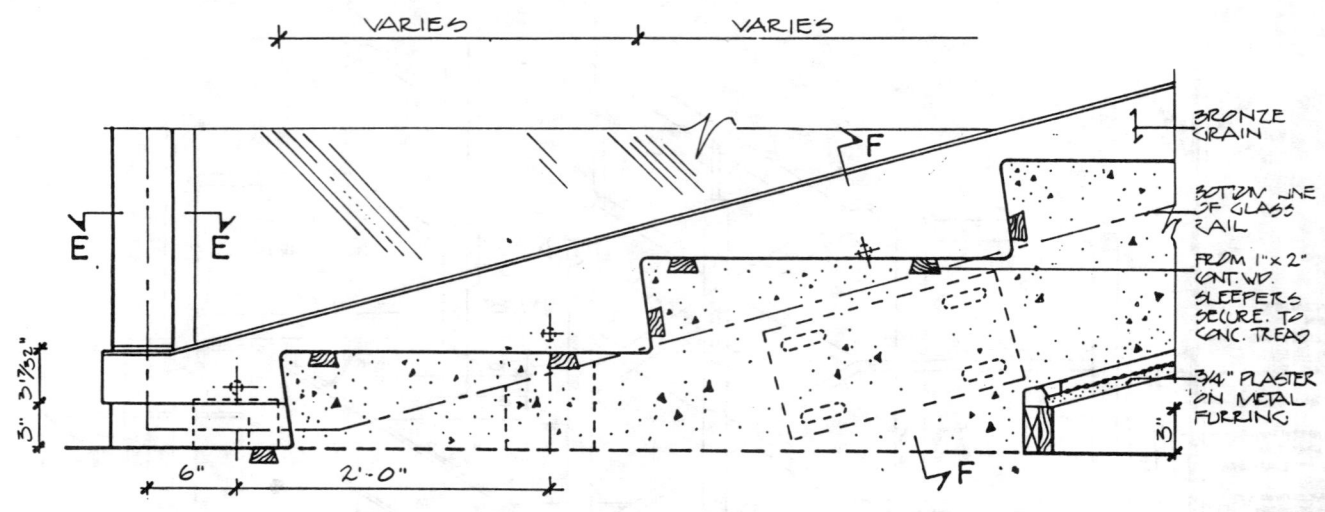

VARIES | VARIES

BRONZE GRAIN

BOTTOM LINE OF GLASS RAIL

FROM 1"×2" CONT. WD. SLEEPERS SECURE. TO CONC. TREAD

3/4" PLASTER ON METAL FURRING

5" 5 7/32"

6" | 2'-0"

3"

DD Section

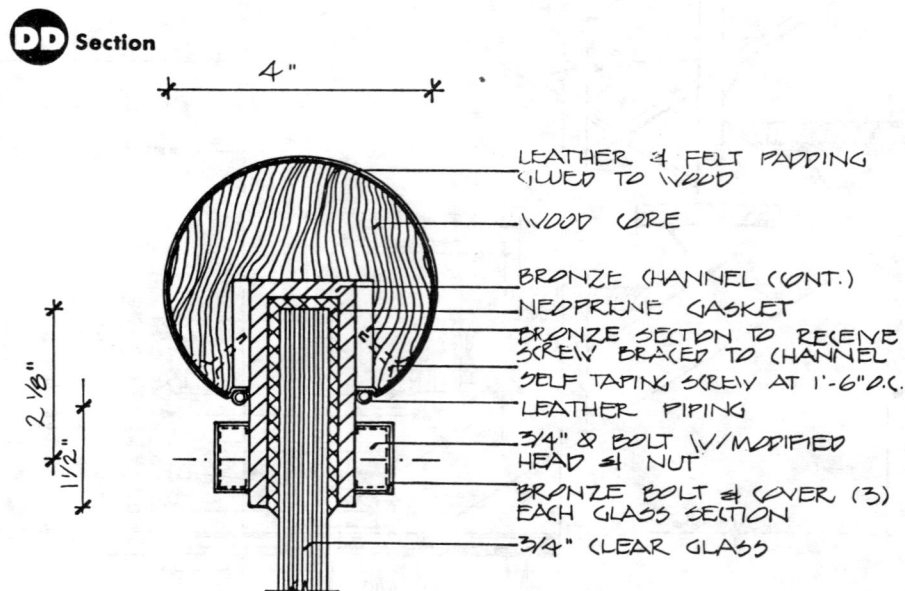

4"

LEATHER & FELT PADDING GLUED TO WOOD

WOOD CORE

BRONZE CHANNEL (CONT.)

NEOPRENE GASKET

BRONZE SECTION TO RECEIVE SCREW BRACED TO CHANNEL

SELF TAPING SCREW AT 1'-6" O.C.

LEATHER PIPING

3/4" Ø BOLT W/MODIFIED HEAD & NUT

BRONZE BOLT & COVER (3) EACH GLASS SECTION

3/4" CLEAR GLASS

2 1/8"
1/2"

EE Section

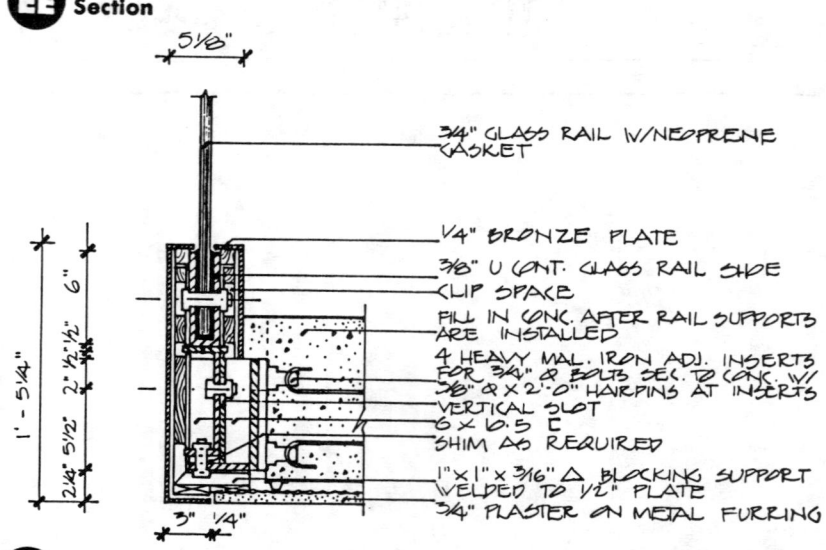

5 1/8"

3/4" GLASS RAIL W/NEOPRENE GASKET

1/4" BRONZE PLATE

3/8" U CONT. GLASS RAIL SHOE

CLIP SPACE

FILL IN CONC. AFTER RAIL SUPPORTS ARE INSTALLED

4 HEAVY MAL. IRON ADJ. INSERTS FOR 3/4" Ø BOLTS SEC. TO CONC. W/ 5/8" Ø × 2'-0" HAIRPINS AT INSERTS

VERTICAL SLOT

6 × 6.5 E

SHIM AS REQUIRED

1"×1"×3/16" ∠ BLOCKING SUPPORT WELDED TO 1/2" PLATE

3/4" PLASTER ON METAL FURRING

6"
2 1/2" 1/2"
1'-5 1/4"
2 1/4" 5 1/2"

3" 1/4"

FF Section

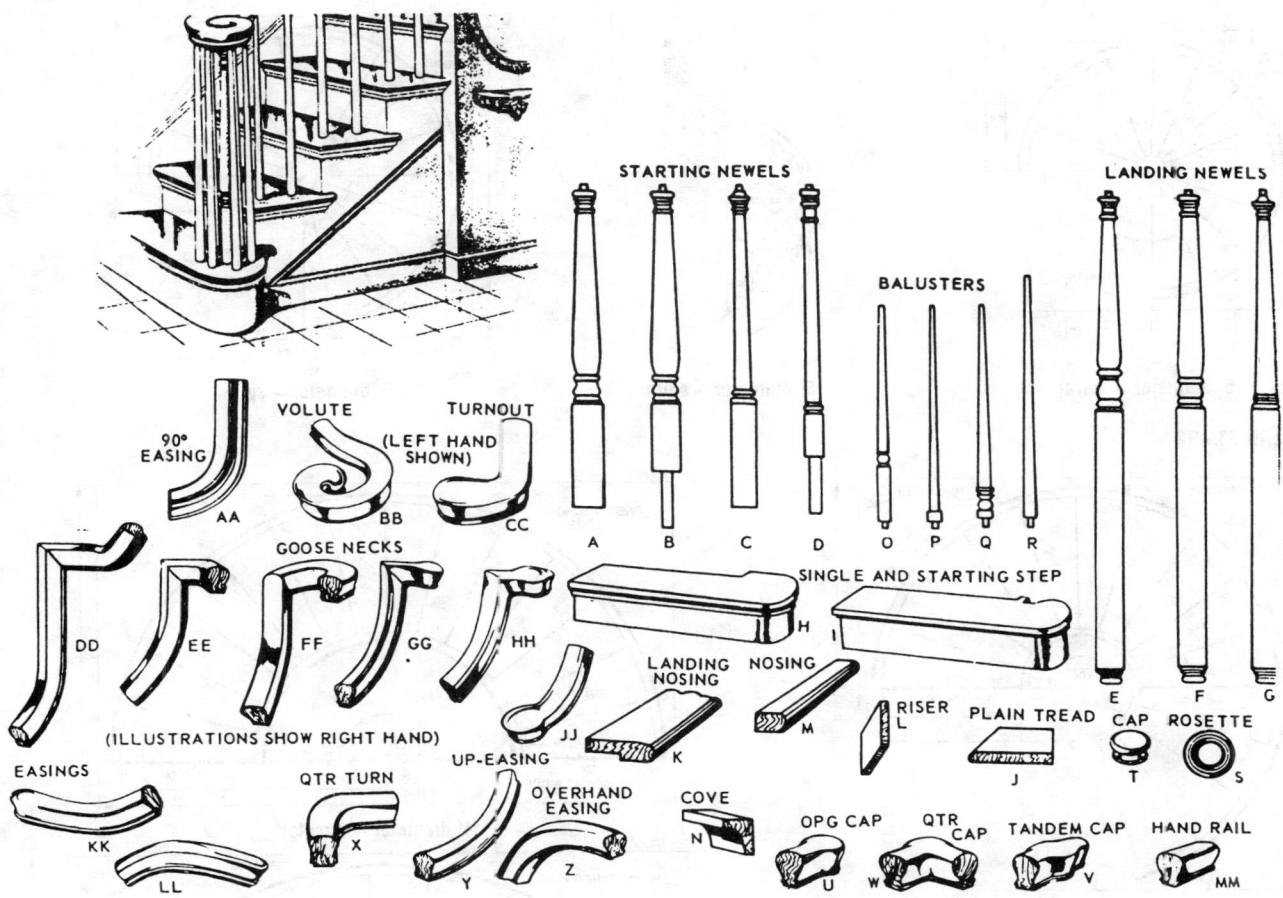

A-D Starting Newels	A	Overhand Easing
E-G Landing Newel	AA	90 degree Up Easing
H-I Starting Step	BB	Volute
J Stair Tread	CC	Turnout
K Landing Tread	DD	Gooseneck 2 Riser
L Risers	EE	Gooseneck 1 Riser
M Return Nosing	FF	Gooseneck 1 Riser Ledge Return
N Stair Cove	GG	Gooseneck Riser with Cap
O-R Turned Balusters	HH	Gooseneck Riser Tandem Cap
S Wall Rosette	JJ	Starting Easing
T Plain Cap	KK	Starting Easing with Return End
U One OPG Newel Cap	MM	Hand Rail
V Tandem Cap		
W Quarter Turn Cap		
X Quarter Turn		
Y Up Easing		

STAIRS

Spiral and Circular Stairs

SPIRAL STAIRS

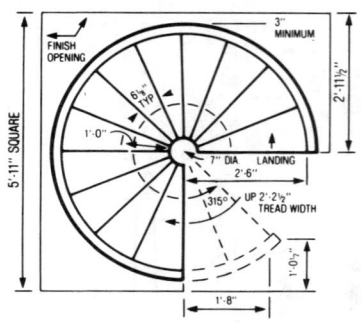

5' diameter — spiral

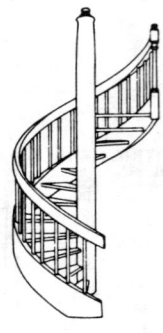

5' diameter — spiral

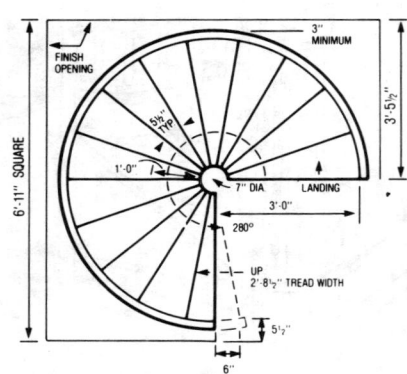

6' diameter — spiral

CIRCULAR STAIRS

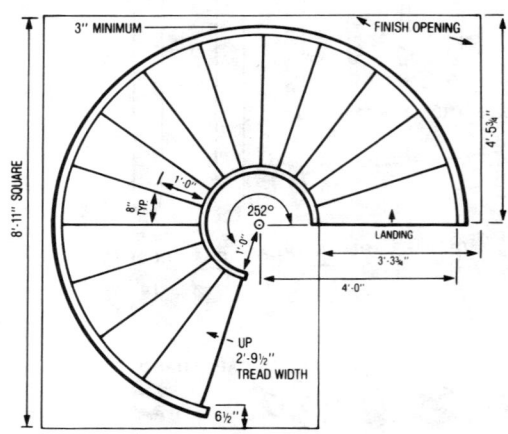

8' diameter — circular

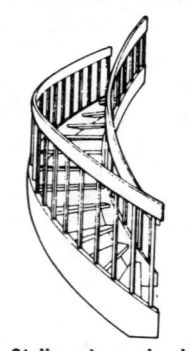

9' diameter — circular

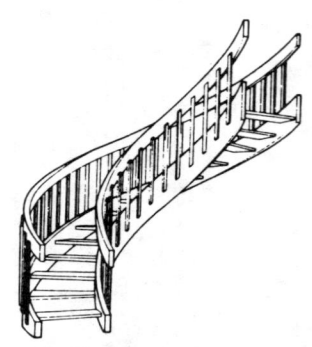

15' diameter — circular

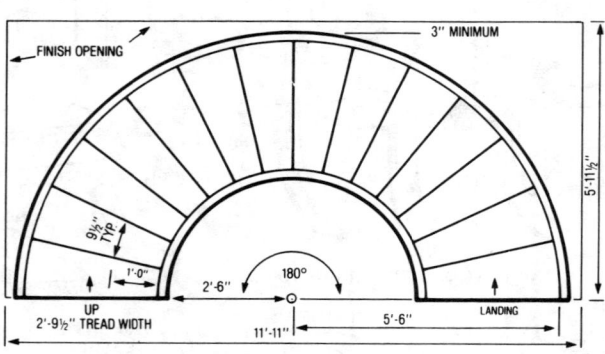

11' diameter — circular

13' diameter — circular

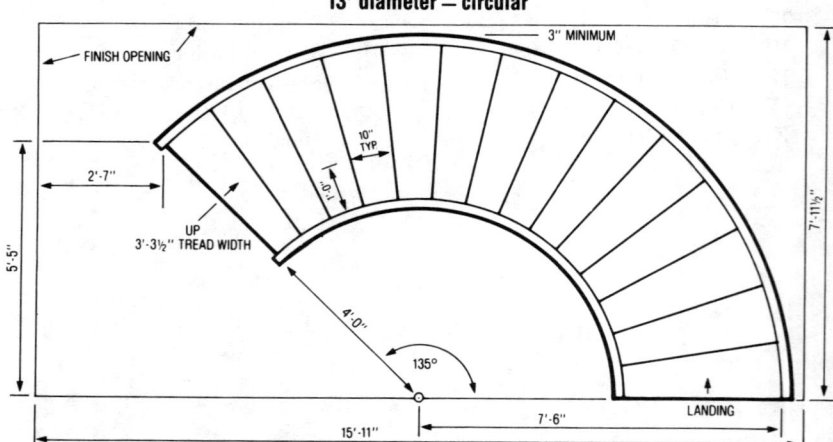

15' diameter — circular

Note: All drawings left-hand turn (looking down).

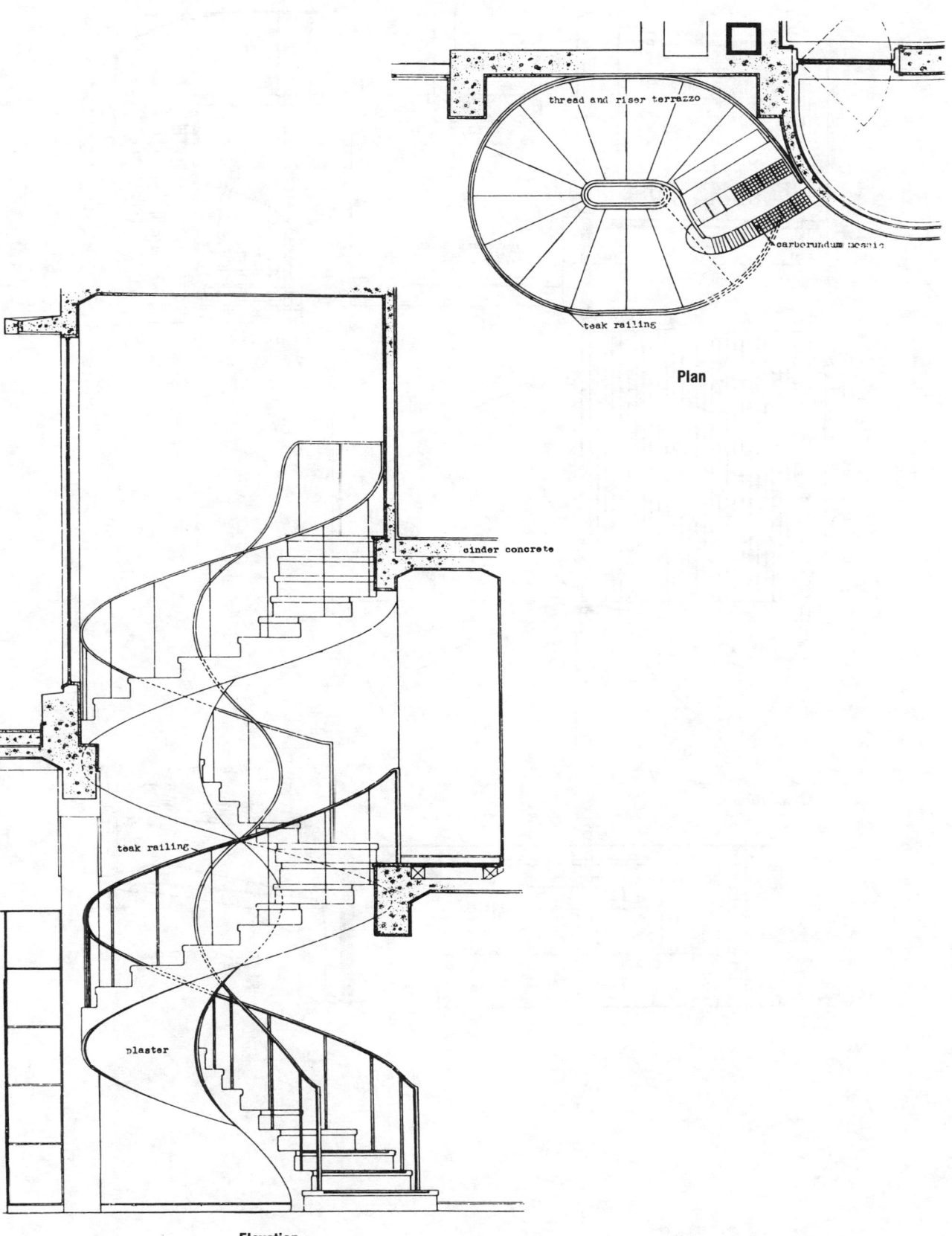

thread and riser terrazzo

carborundum mosaic

teak railing

Plan

cinder concrete

teak railing

plaster

Elevation

STAIRS
Spiral Stairs

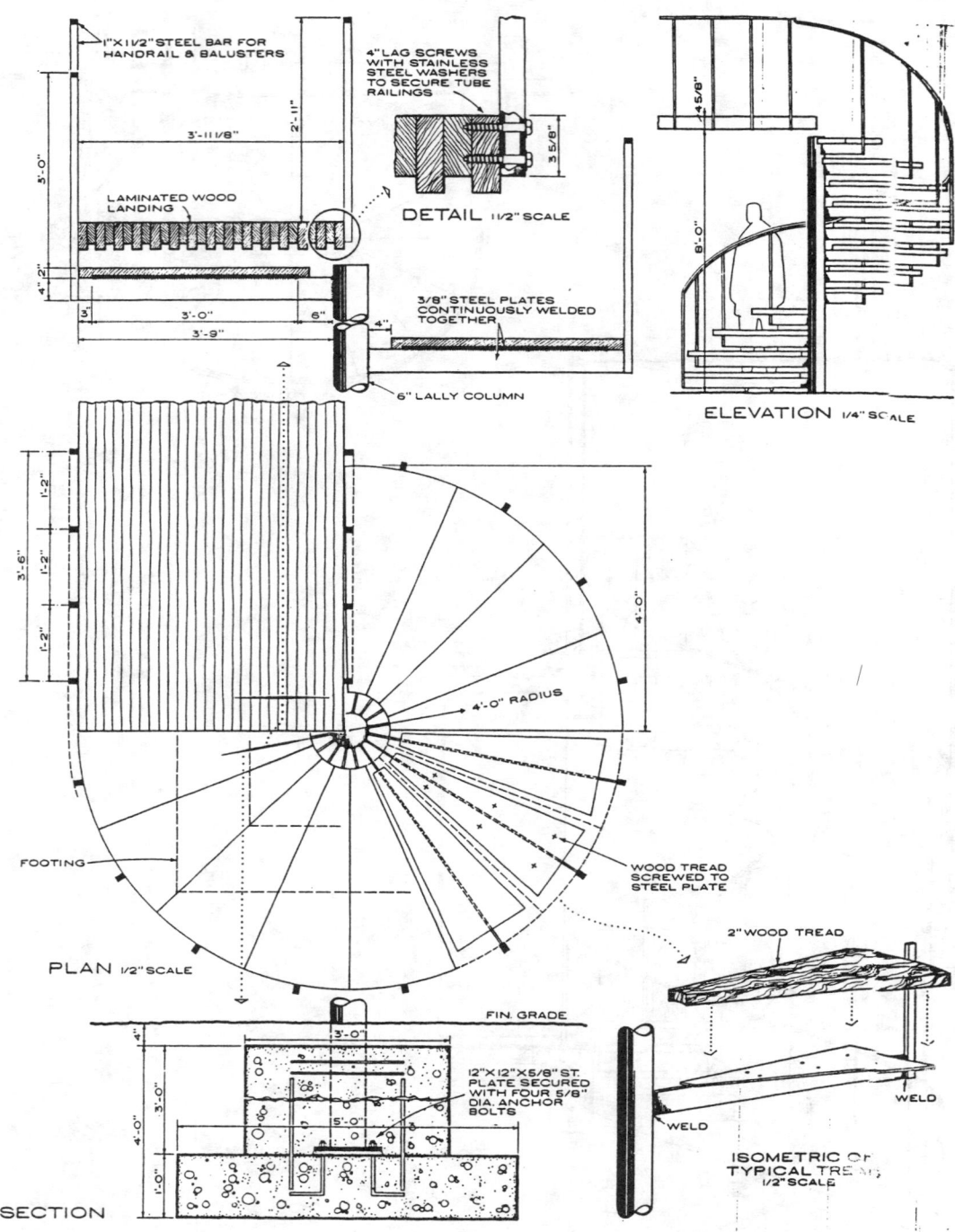

1"X 1 1/2" STEEL BAR FOR HANDRAIL & BALUSTERS

4" LAG SCREWS WITH STAINLESS STEEL WASHERS TO SECURE TUBE RAILINGS

2'-11"

3'-11 1/8"

5'-0"

3 5/8"

DETAIL 1 1/2" SCALE

LAMINATED WOOD LANDING

4'-2"

3"   3'-0"   6"

3'-9"

3/8" STEEL PLATES CONTINUOUSLY WELDED TOGETHER

6" LALLY COLUMN

4 5/8"

8'-0"

ELEVATION 1/4" SCALE

1'-2"

3'-6"

1'-2"

1'-2"

4'-0"

4'-0" RADIUS

FOOTING

WOOD TREAD SCREWED TO STEEL PLATE

2" WOOD TREAD

PLAN 1/2" SCALE

WELD

FIN. GRADE

4"

3'-0"

3'-0"

4'-0"

12"X12"X5/8" ST. PLATE SECURED WITH FOUR 5/8" DIA. ANCHOR BOLTS

5'-0"

1'-0"

SECTION

WELD

ISOMETRIC OF TYPICAL TREAD 1/2" SCALE

Types of Stairs

Four types of stairs are defined: straight stairs, circular stairs, curved stairs, and spiral stairs.

Straight stairs are by far the most common type, representing the bulk of the stair market. Though the term "straight" is self-explanatory, for purposes of classification a straight stair is defined as one in which the stringers are straight members. Straight stairs, unlike stairs of the other three types, may be arranged in several different ways:

Straight run: Either a single flight extending between floors, as shown in Fig. 5A, or a series of two or more flights in the same line, with intermediate platforms between them, as shown in Fig. 5B.

Parallel: Successive flights which parallel each other and are separated only by one or more intermediate platforms, as shown in Fig. 5C.

Angled: Successive flights placed at an angle of other than 180° to each other (often 90°), with an intermediate platform between them, as shown in Fig. 5D or E. The type shown in Fig. 5D is often referred to as a "trussed" stair.

Scissor: A pair of straight run flights paralleling each other in plan and running in opposite directions on opposite sides of a dividing wall, as shown in Fig. 5F.

Circular stairs are stairs which, in plan view, have an open circular form, with a single center of curvature. They may or may not have intermediate platforms between floors.

Curved stairs are stairs which, in plan view, have two or more centers of curvature, being oval, elliptical, or some other compound curved form. They also may or may not have one or more intermediate platforms between floors.

Spiral stairs are stairs with a closed circular form, having uniform sector shaped treads and a supporting center column.

Classes of Stairs

The class designation of stairs, as already noted, is a key to the type of construction, the quality of materials, details and finish and, in most cases, the relative cost. As stairs of all classes are built to meet the same standards of performance in respect to load carrying capacity and safety, these class distinctions *do not represent differences in functional value, but in character and appearance.* It is important to recognize that where function is the prime concern, and esthetics are of minor importance, significant economies can be achieved by specifying one of the less expensive classes.

The following four classes of stairs are listed in order of increasing cost (as a general rule); the general construction characteristics of each class are described.

Industrial class. Stairs of this class are purely functional in character and consequently they are generally the most economical. They are designed for either interior or exterior use, in industrial buildings such as factories and warehouses, or as fire escapes or emergency exitways. They do not include stairs which are integral parts of industrial equipment.

Industrial class stairs are similar in nature to any light steel construction. Hex head bolts are used for most connections, and welds, where used, are not ground. Stringers may be either flat plate or open channels; treads and platforms are usually made of grating or formed of floor plate, and risers are usually open, though in some cases filled pan type treads and steel risers may be used. Railings are usually of either pipe, tubing, or light steel angle construction.

Service class. This class of stairs serves chiefly functional purposes, but is not unattractive in appearance. Service stairs are usually located in enclosed stairwells and provide a secondary or emergency means of travel between floors. In multistoried buildings they are commonly used as egress stairs. They may serve employees, tenants, or the public, and are generally used where economy is a consideration.

Stringers of service stairs are generally the same types as those used on stairs of the industrial class. Treads may be one of several standard types, either filled or formed of floor or tread plate, and risers are either exposed steel or open construction. Railings are typically of pipe construction or a simple bar type with tubular newels, and soffits are usually left exposed. Connections on the underside of the stairs are made with hex head bolts, and only those welds in the travel area are smooth.

Commercial class. Stairs of this class are usually for public use and are of more attractive design than those of the service class. They may be placed in open locations or may be located in closed stairwells or in public, institutional, or commercial buildings.

Stringers for this class of stairs are usually exposed open channel or plate sections. Treads may be any of a number of standard types, and risers are usually exposed steel. Railings vary from ornamental bar or tube construction with metal handrails to simple pipe construction, and soffits may or may not be covered. Exposed bolted connections in areas where appearance is critical are made with countersunk flat or oval head bolts; otherwise, hex head bolts are used. Welds in conspicuous locations are smooth, and all joints are closely fitted.

Architectural class. This classification applies to any of the more elaborate and usually more expensive stairs, those which are designed to be architectural features in a building. They may be wholly custom designed or may represent a combination of standard parts with specially designed elements such as stringers, railings, treads, or platforms. Usually this class of stair has a comparatively low pitch, with relatively low risers and correspondingly wider treads. Architectural metal stairs may be located either in the open or in enclosed stairwells in public, institutional, commercial, or monumental buildings.

The materials, fabrication details, and finishes used in architectural class stairs vary widely, as dictated by the architect's design and specifications. As a general rule, construction joints are made as inconspicuous as possible, exposed welds are smooth, and soffits are covered with some surfacing material. Stringers may be special sections exposed, or may be structural members enclosed in other materials. Railings are of an ornamental type and, like the treads and risers, may be of any construction desired.

General Requirements, All Classes of Stairs

All fixed metal stairs, regardless of class, are of fire-resistant construction and are designed and constructed to carry a minimum live load of 100 pounds per square foot of projected plan area or an alternative concentrated load of 300 pounds applied at the center of any tread span. Railings and handrails are designed and constructed to withstand a minimum force of 200 pounds applied in any direction at any point on the rail.

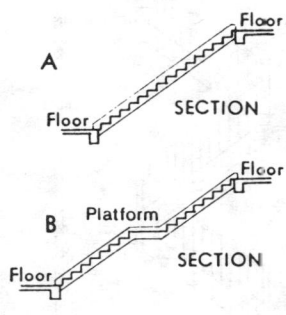

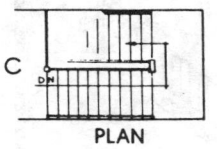

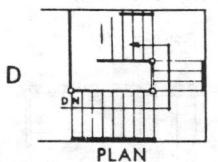

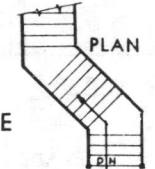

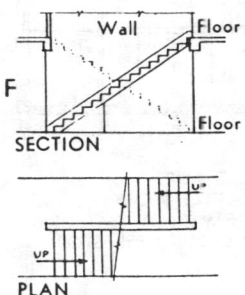

Fig. 5

STAIRS

General Purpose Steel Stairs

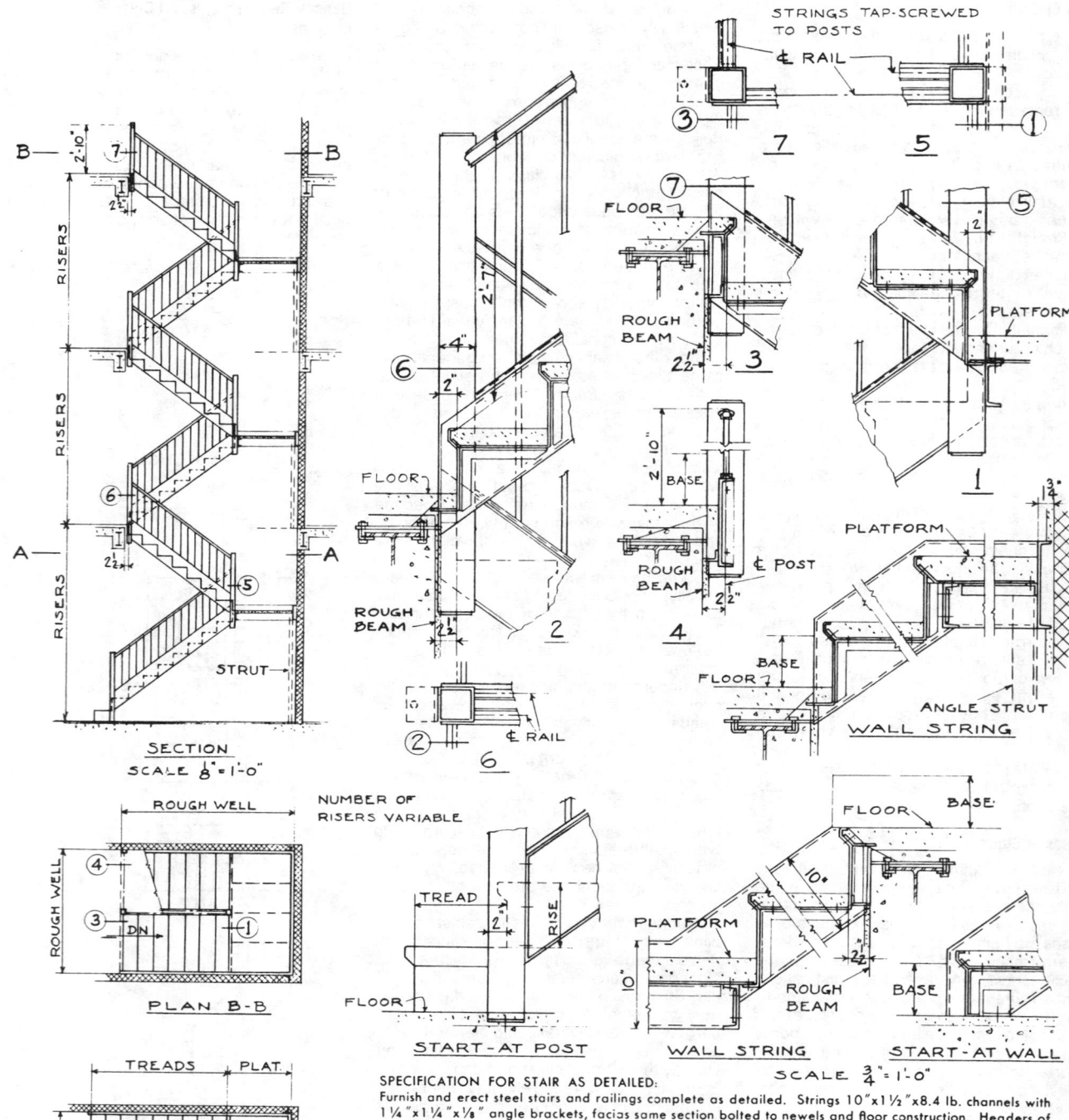

SECTION
SCALE $\frac{1}{8}$"=1'-0"

PLAN B-B

PLAN A-A

LAYOUT FOR:
MULTIPLE STORY
INTERMEDIATE PLATFORM
TWO RUNS PER STORY

NUMBER OF RISERS VARIABLE

START-AT POST

WALL STRING

START-AT WALL

SCALE $\frac{3}{4}$"=1'-0"

STRINGS TAP-SCREWED TO POSTS

WALL STRING

SPECIFICATION FOR STAIR AS DETAILED:
Furnish and erect steel stairs and railings complete as detailed. Strings 10"x1½"x8.4 lb. channels with 1¼"x1¼"x⅛" angle brackets, facias same section bolted to newels and floor construction. Headers of channels bolted or welded to newels and strings. Angle struts placed in wall, bolted to strings and to floor construction. Risers and sub-treads of 14 gauge steel, sub-platforms of 12 gauge steel reinforced with angle or tee stiffeners. Fill, 2" for treads, 3" for platforms, by others. Newels 4" square pipe, railing balusters ½" square spaced 4½" and welded into 1"x½" channels top and bottom with handrail section as shown. All surfaces to be cleaned and painted one shop coat. Shop drawings, to show construction methods and fastenings, are to be approved before fabrication.

ALTERNATE SPECIFICATIONS:
Strings may be channels, flat plates, or formed plates.
Tread Brackets may be other size angles, or bars.
Riser Brackets may be omitted.
Hanger Rods may be used in place of struts.
Sub-Treads, Risers and Sub-Platforms may be heavier gauge.
Newels and **Railings** may be of other construction as designed by architect.
Wall Rails, where required, may have same handrail section as railing.
Prime Coat may be red lead, black graphite, zinc chromate, or other approved paint.

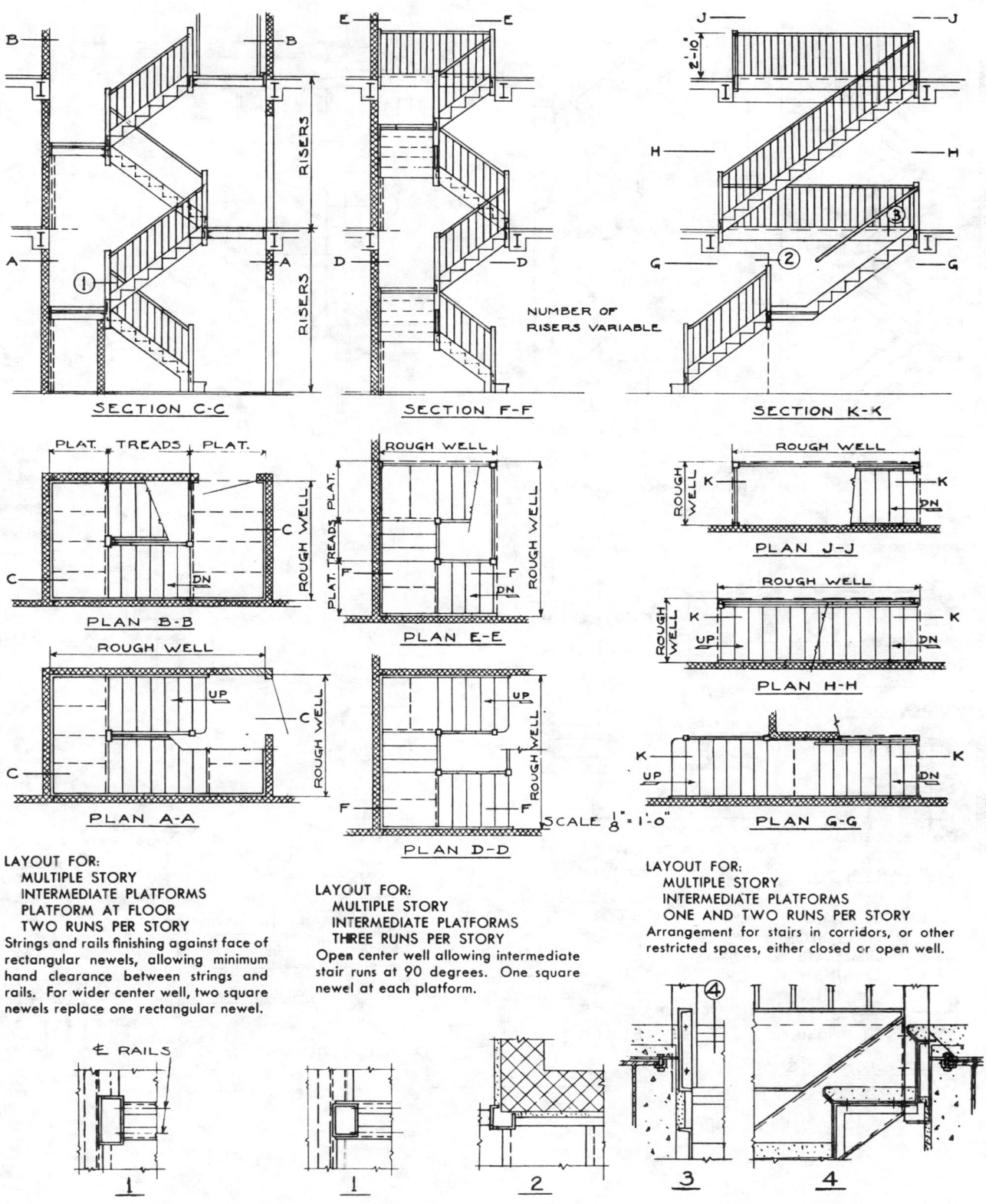

SECTION C-C

SECTION F-F

NUMBER OF
RISERS VARIABLE

SECTION K-K

RISERS

RISERS

PLAT. TREADS PLAT.

ROUGH WELL

PLAN B-B

ROUGH WELL

PLAT. TREADS PLAT.

PLAN E-E

ROUGH WELL

ROUGH WELL

PLAN J-J

ROUGH WELL

ROUGH WELL

UP

DN

PLAN H-H

ROUGH WELL

UP

PLAN A-A

ROUGH WELL

UP

SCALE ⅛"=1'-0"

PLAN D-D

UP

DN

PLAN G-G

LAYOUT FOR:
    MULTIPLE STORY
    INTERMEDIATE PLATFORMS
    PLATFORM AT FLOOR
    TWO RUNS PER STORY
Strings and rails finishing against face of
rectangular newels, allowing minimum
hand clearance between strings and
rails. For wider center well, two square
newels replace one rectangular newel.

LAYOUT FOR:
    MULTIPLE STORY
    INTERMEDIATE PLATFORMS
    THREE RUNS PER STORY
Open center well allowing intermediate
stair runs at 90 degrees. One square
newel at each platform.

LAYOUT FOR:
    MULTIPLE STORY
    INTERMEDIATE PLATFORMS
    ONE AND TWO RUNS PER STORY
Arrangement for stairs in corridors, or other
restricted spaces, either closed or open well.

₵ RAILS

1

1

2

3

4

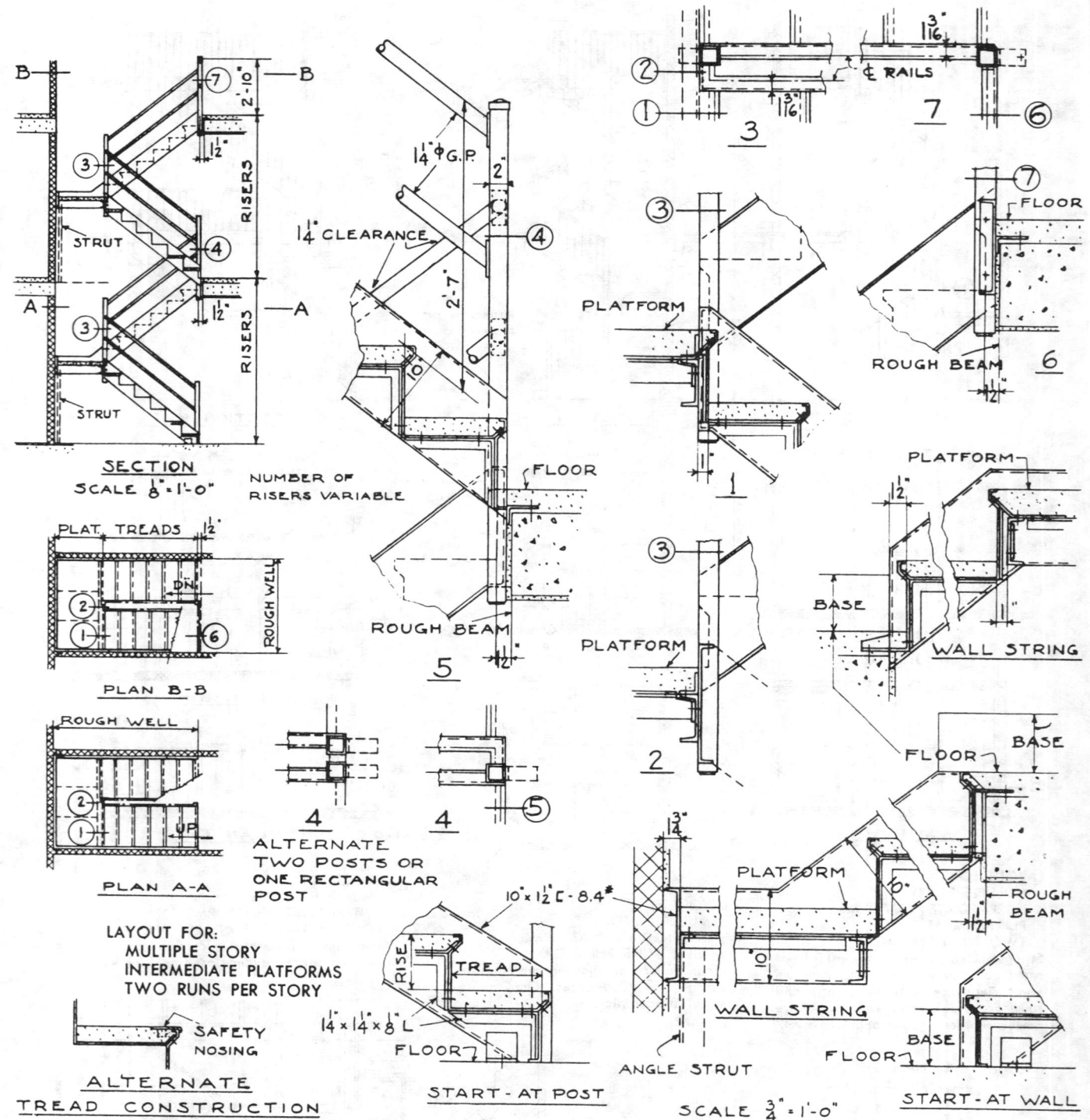

SECTION
SCALE $\frac{1}{8}$"=1'-0"

NUMBER OF RISERS VARIABLE

PLAT. TREADS

PLAN B-B

ROUGH WELL

PLAN A-A

LAYOUT FOR:
MULTIPLE STORY
INTERMEDIATE PLATFORMS
TWO RUNS PER STORY

SAFETY NOSING

ALTERNATE
TREAD CONSTRUCTION

ALTERNATE
TWO POSTS OR
ONE RECTANGULAR
POST

STRUT

RISERS

RISERS

STRUT

ROUGH WELL

DN

UP

$1\frac{1}{4}$" ⌀ G.P.

$1\frac{1}{4}$" CLEARANCE

2'-7"

FLOOR

ROUGH BEAM

℄ RAILS

PLATFORM

PLATFORM

PLATFORM

FLOOR

ROUGH BEAM

PLATFORM

BASE

WALL STRING

FLOOR

BASE

PLATFORM

ROUGH BEAM

BASE

FLOOR

WALL STRING

START-AT WALL

10"×1$\frac{1}{2}$" C - 8.4#

$1\frac{1}{4}$"×1$\frac{1}{4}$"×$\frac{1}{8}$" L

RISE

TREAD

FLOOR

START-AT POST

ANGLE STRUT

SCALE $\frac{3}{4}$"=1'-0"

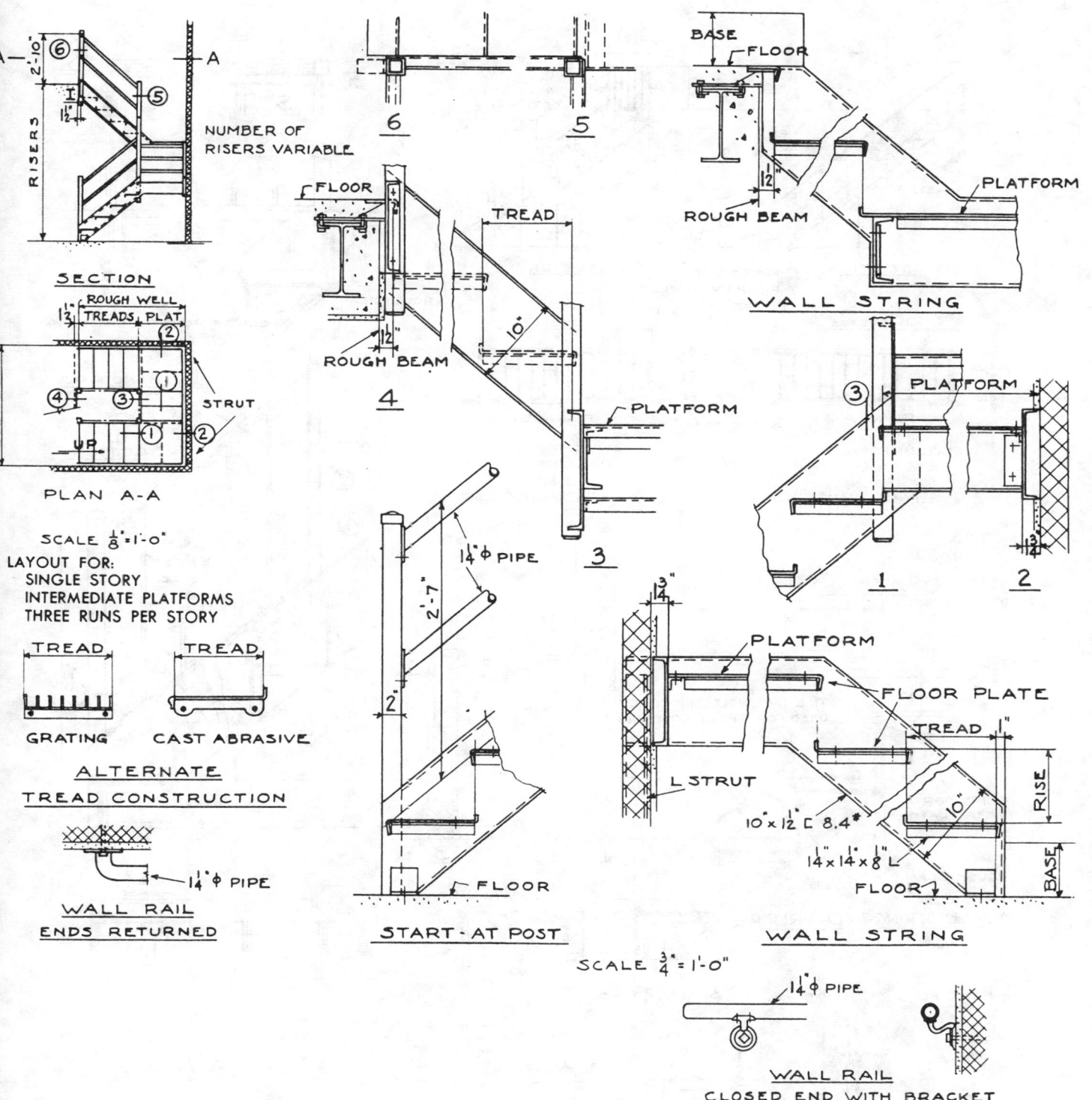

SECTION

NUMBER OF RISERS VARIABLE

PLAN A-A

SCALE $\frac{1}{8}$"=1'-0"

LAYOUT FOR:
SINGLE STORY
INTERMEDIATE PLATFORMS
THREE RUNS PER STORY

TREAD — GRATING

TREAD — CAST ABRASIVE

ALTERNATE TREAD CONSTRUCTION

WALL RAIL
ENDS RETURNED

$1\frac{1}{4}$" φ PIPE

START-AT POST

SCALE $\frac{3}{4}$"=1'-0"

WALL STRING

WALL STRING

$10" \times 12$ ⌶ 8.4#

$1\frac{1}{4}" \times 1\frac{1}{4}" \times \frac{1}{8}"$ L

WALL RAIL
CLOSED END WITH BRACKET

$1\frac{1}{4}$" φ PIPE

STAIRS

Steel Stairs

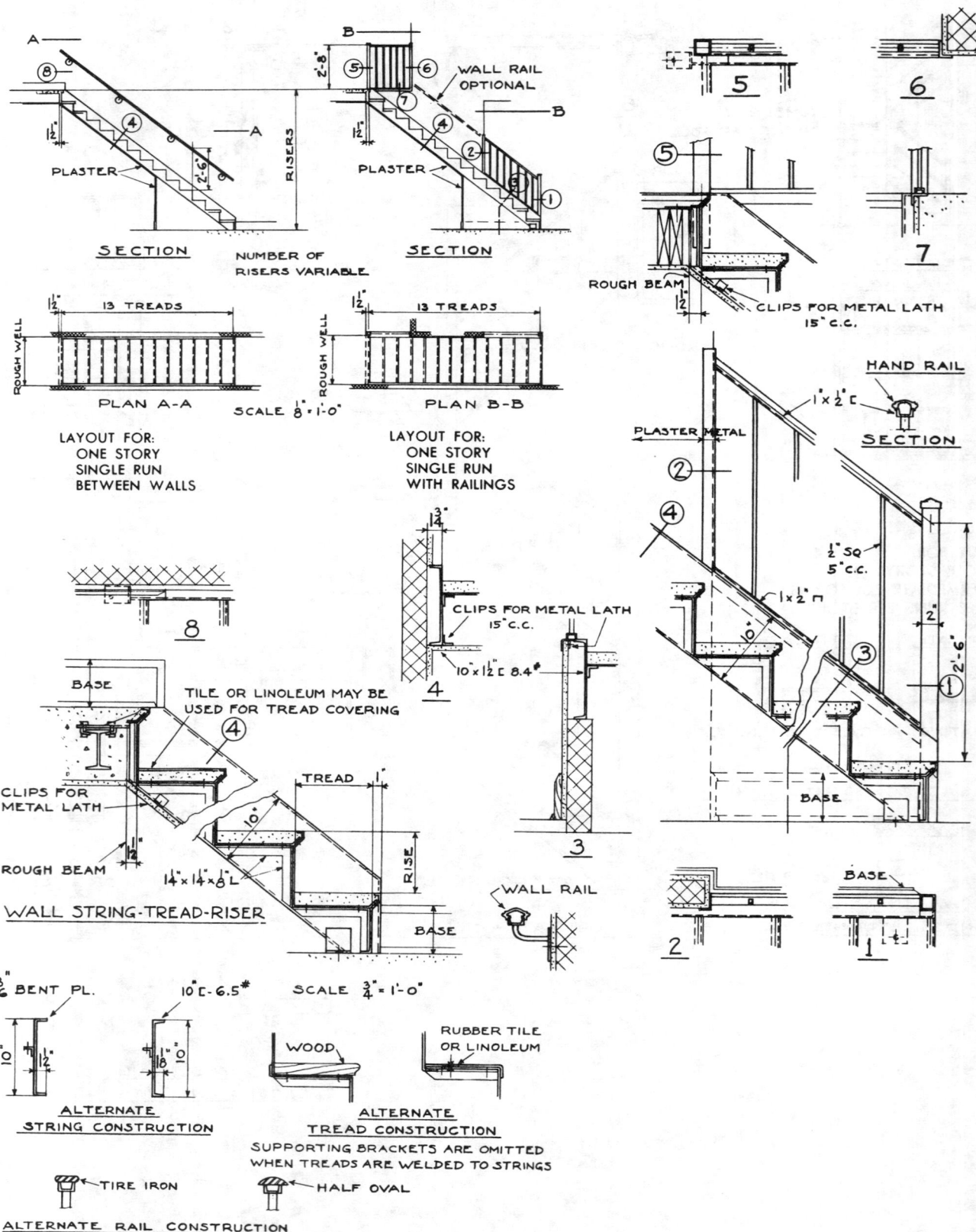

The platform (Fig. 6) is shown constructed with a steel channel, A, of adequate strength to span the well on line X, through Secs. 1, 2, and 3, and supported at both ends by the wall strings. Newel posts rest on this channel through angle clips, around which the platform plate is cut (Sec. 3). Face strings have welded end plates with flathead screws tapped into the newels (Sec. 2).

The two platforms with two intermediate risers (Fig. 7) are shown constructed with the load carried on line Y by string B, post C, and channel D, which are shown bolted together (Secs. 8, 9, and 10) with through bolts. The load is also carried from post C on line Z in the same manner.

The members at post C may be brought together and welded and the post fitted over the connection, or the entire unit welded.

6
5
5
PLATFORM
A
1
2
3
X
TREAD
UP

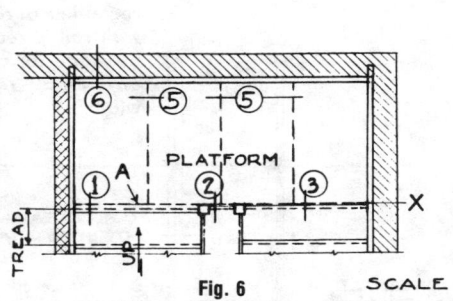

Fig. 6

Plan—One Platform. Load carried on Line X. Wall strings supported on masonry wall.

SCALE $\frac{1}{4}$" = 1'-0"

Y
TREAD
6
ANGLE STRUT
7
5
D
4
5
PLATFORM
PLATFORM
8
7
5
Z
TREAD
4
C
8
UP
B

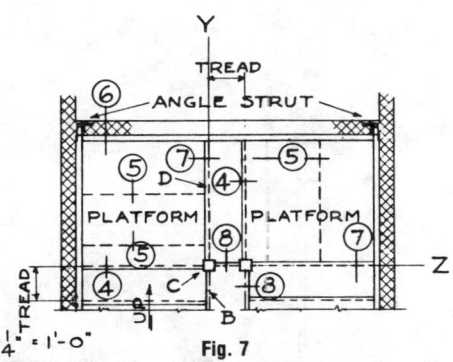

Fig. 7

Plan—Two Platforms with Two Intermediate Risers. Load carried on Line Y and supplemented on Line Z. Wall strings supported by struts.

Stairs are supported by one or more of the following methods, (a) String at floor rests directly on floor construction; (b) String at landing or platform extends into adjacent load-bearing wall; or (c) String at landing or platform is supported by struts extending to the floor below, these being of angles, I-beams or pipes either set in the wall or exposed; or (d) String at landing or platform is supported by rods hung from the floor above, either set in walls or exposed; (e) String paralleling load-bearing wall may have shelf brackets on the back of the strings and set in wall; similar brackets may be used with struts or hanger rods.

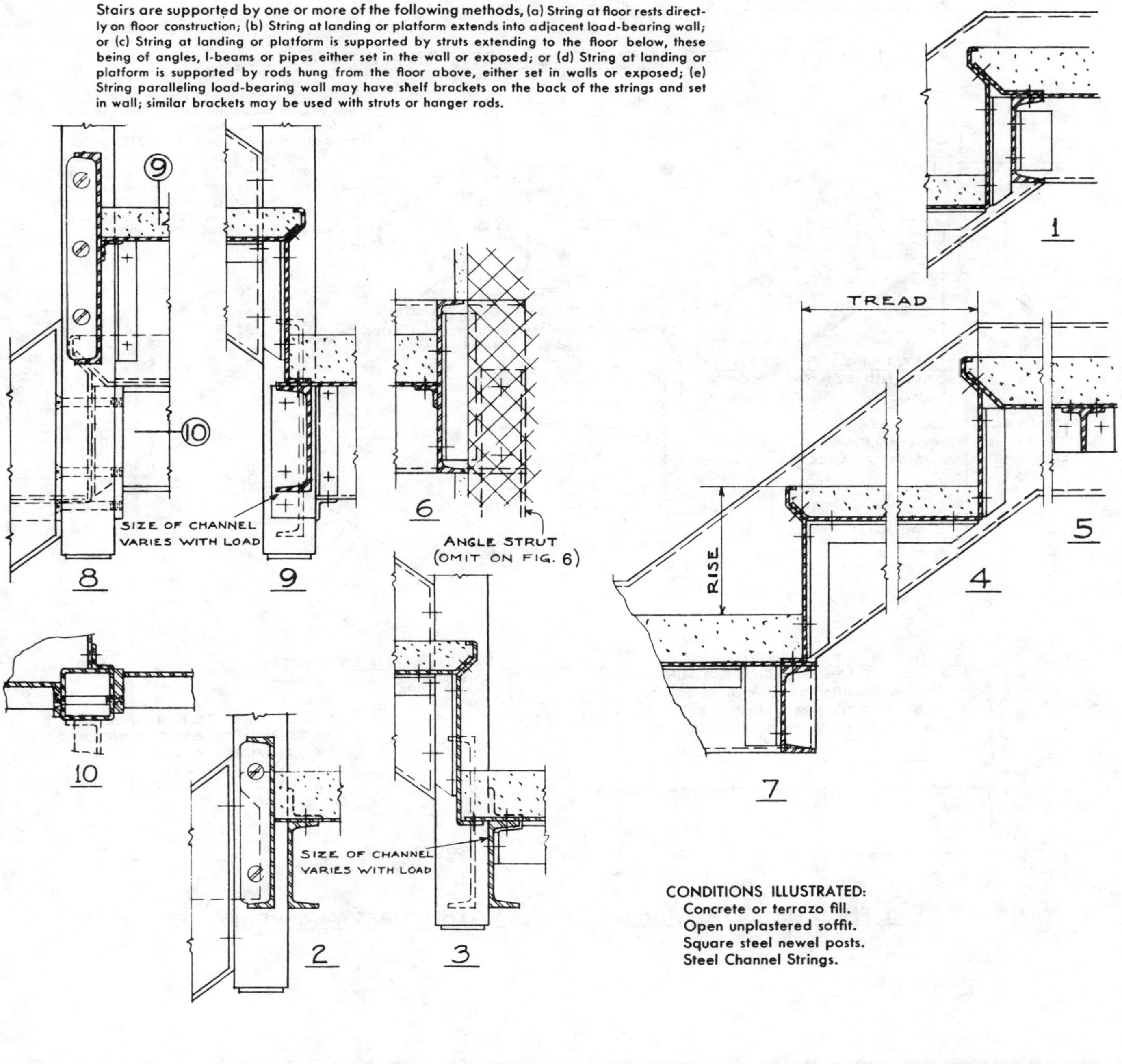

1
9
10
SIZE OF CHANNEL VARIES WITH LOAD
8
9
6
ANGLE STRUT (OMIT ON FIG. 6)
TREAD
RISE
4
5
7
10
SIZE OF CHANNEL VARIES WITH LOAD
2
3

CONDITIONS ILLUSTRATED:
Concrete or terrazo fill.
Open unplastered soffit.
Square steel newel posts.
Steel Channel Strings.

Width of stair is usually considered center line of rail to finished wall. When wall rail is required allowance should be made for clearance to comply with any legal requirements as to net width.

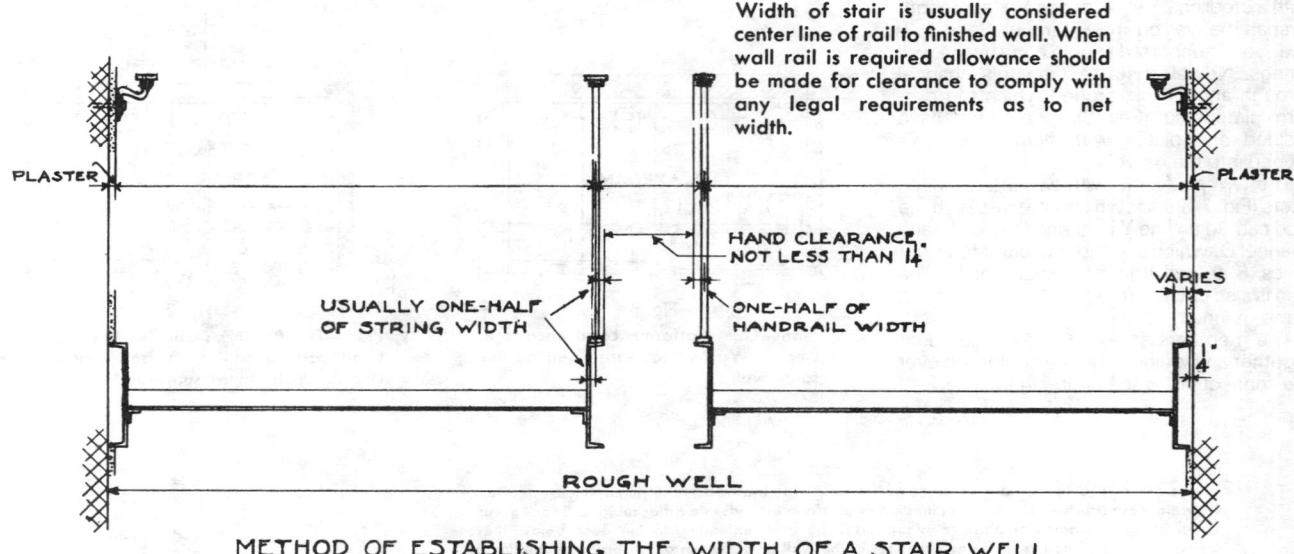

PLASTER

PLASTER

HAND CLEARANCE. NOT LESS THAN 1¼"

USUALLY ONE-HALF OF STRING WIDTH

ONE-HALF OF HANDRAIL WIDTH

VARIES

4"

ROUGH WELL

METHOD OF ESTABLISHING THE WIDTH OF A STAIR WELL

Height of riser and width of tread vary to fit the type of stair and its use. Legal requirements often limit the minimum tread and maximum rise. A tread of 10" and a rise of 7" to 7½" are considered average. Stairs of easy runs are often 10½" to 11" treads with risers under 7". Stairs used exclusively by maintenance and operating men are often constructed with a rise and tread to equal a pitch greater than 40°. Tread width is always face to face of riser.

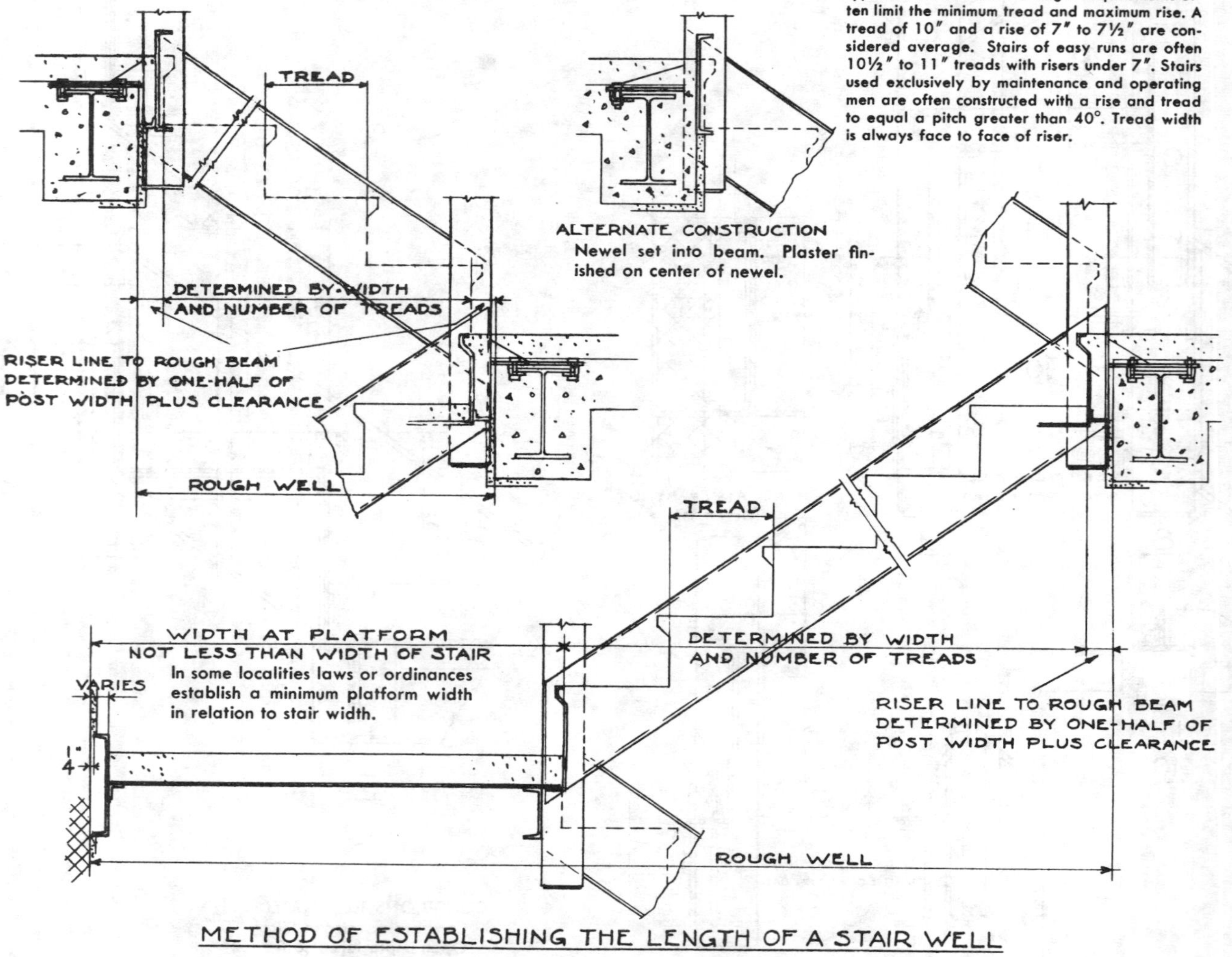

TREAD

DETERMINED BY WIDTH AND NUMBER OF TREADS

RISER LINE TO ROUGH BEAM DETERMINED BY ONE-HALF OF POST WIDTH PLUS CLEARANCE

ROUGH WELL

ALTERNATE CONSTRUCTION
Newel set into beam. Plaster finished on center of newel.

TREAD

DETERMINED BY WIDTH AND NUMBER OF TREADS

RISER LINE TO ROUGH BEAM DETERMINED BY ONE-HALF OF POST WIDTH PLUS CLEARANCE

WIDTH AT PLATFORM NOT LESS THAN WIDTH OF STAIR
In some localities laws or ordinances establish a minimum platform width in relation to stair width.

VARIES

4"

ROUGH WELL

METHOD OF ESTABLISHING THE LENGTH OF A STAIR WELL

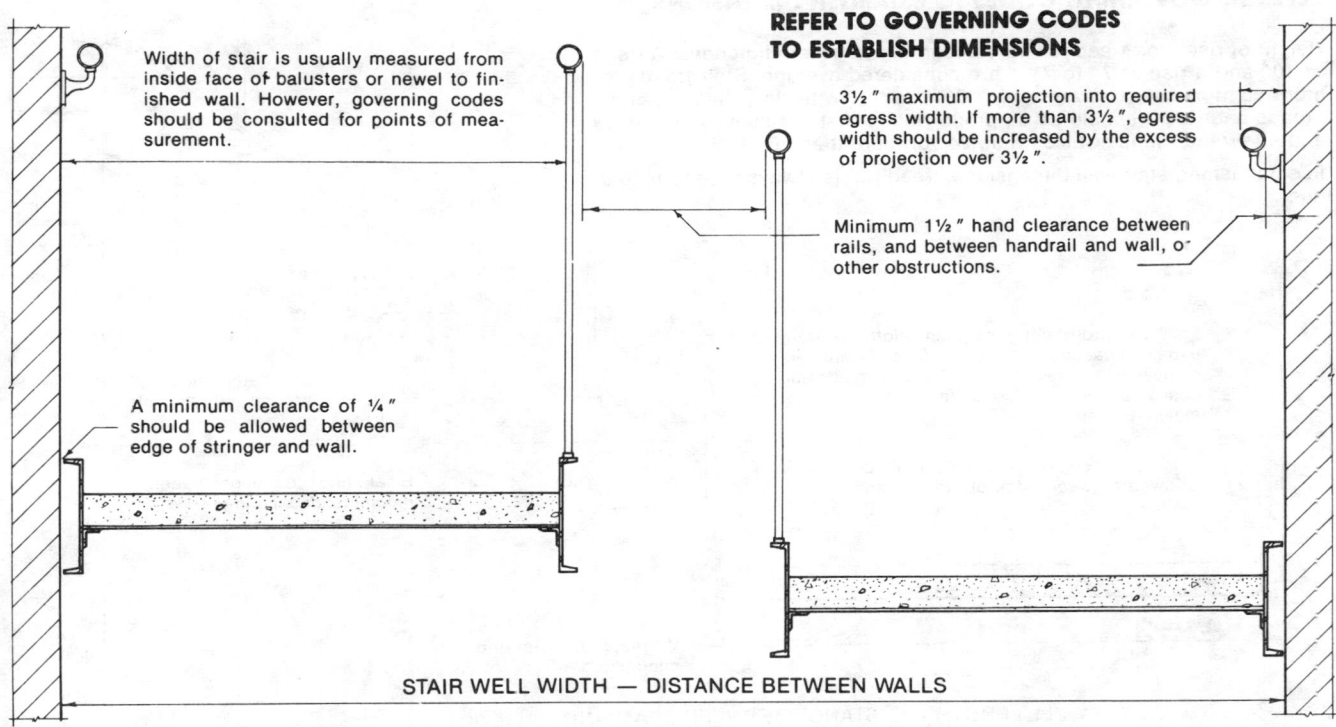

REFER TO GOVERNING CODES TO ESTABLISH DIMENSIONS

Width of stair is usually measured from inside face of balusters or newel to finished wall. However, governing codes should be consulted for points of measurement.

3½″ maximum projection into required egress width. If more than 3½″, egress width should be increased by the excess of projection over 3½″.

Minimum 1½″ hand clearance between rails, and between handrail and wall, or other obstructions.

A minimum clearance of ¼″ should be allowed between edge of stringer and wall.

STAIR WELL WIDTH — DISTANCE BETWEEN WALLS

Minimum code requirements are usually measured from finished wall to finished wall. When establishing rough stair well dimensions, allowance should be made for thicknesses of any finish materials to be applied to the rough walls.

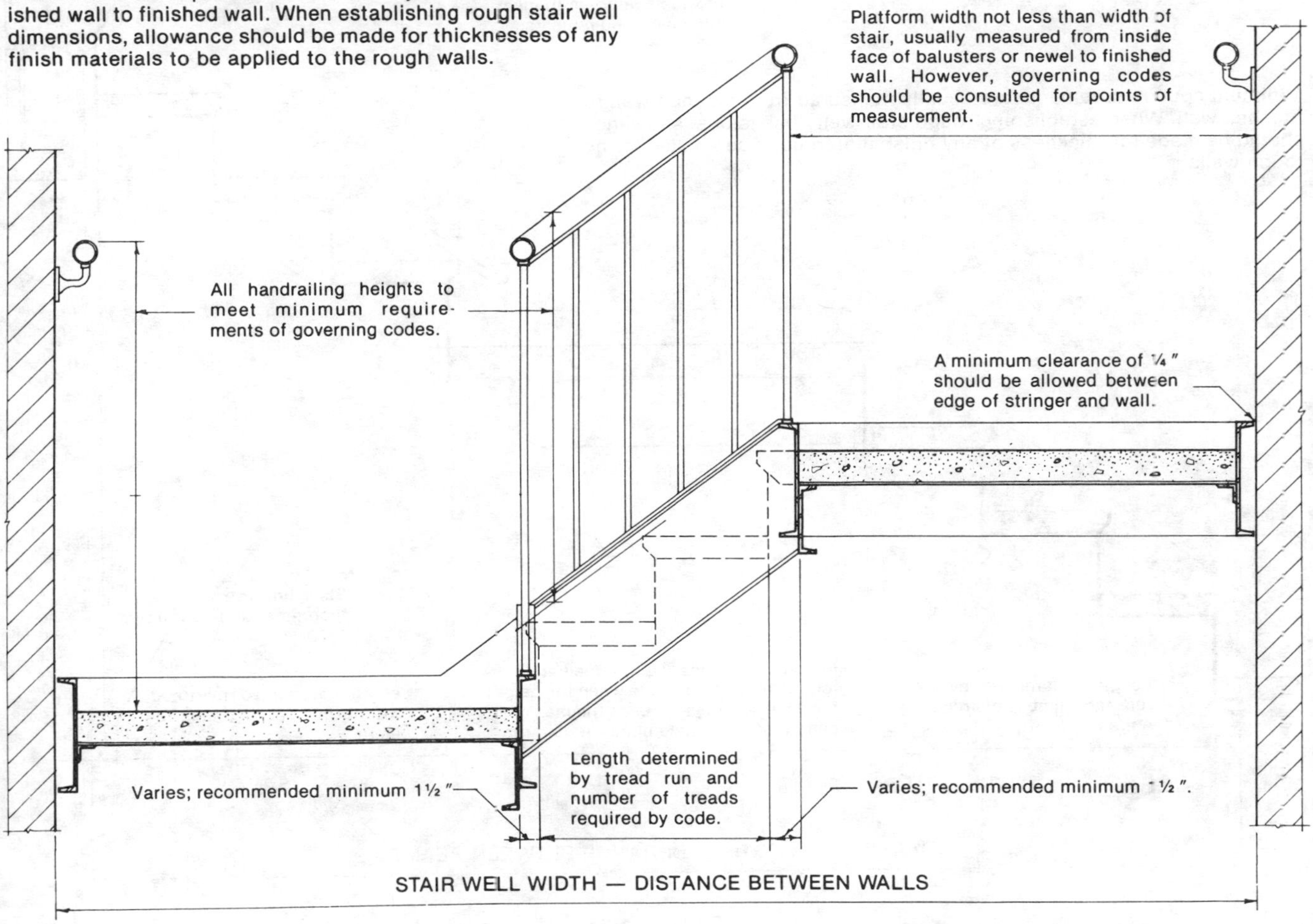

Platform width not less than width of stair, usually measured from inside face of balusters or newel to finished wall. However, governing codes should be consulted for points of measurement.

All handrailing heights to meet minimum requirements of governing codes.

A minimum clearance of ¼″ should be allowed between edge of stringer and wall.

Varies; recommended minimum 1½″.

Length determined by tread run and number of treads required by code.

Varies; recommended minimum 1½″.

STAIR WELL WIDTH — DISTANCE BETWEEN WALLS

STAIRS
Stair Length Dimensions

REFER TO GOVERNING CODES TO ESTABLISH DIMENSIONS

Height of riser and tread run vary according to governing codes. A tread of 10″ and a rise of 7″ to 7½″ are considered average. Stair treads for more comfortable runs are often 10½″ to 11″ with risers less than 7″. Treads and risers should be so proportioned that the sum of two risers and one tread run is not less than 24″ or more than 26″.

In establishing stair well dimensions, tread run is always face to face of riser.

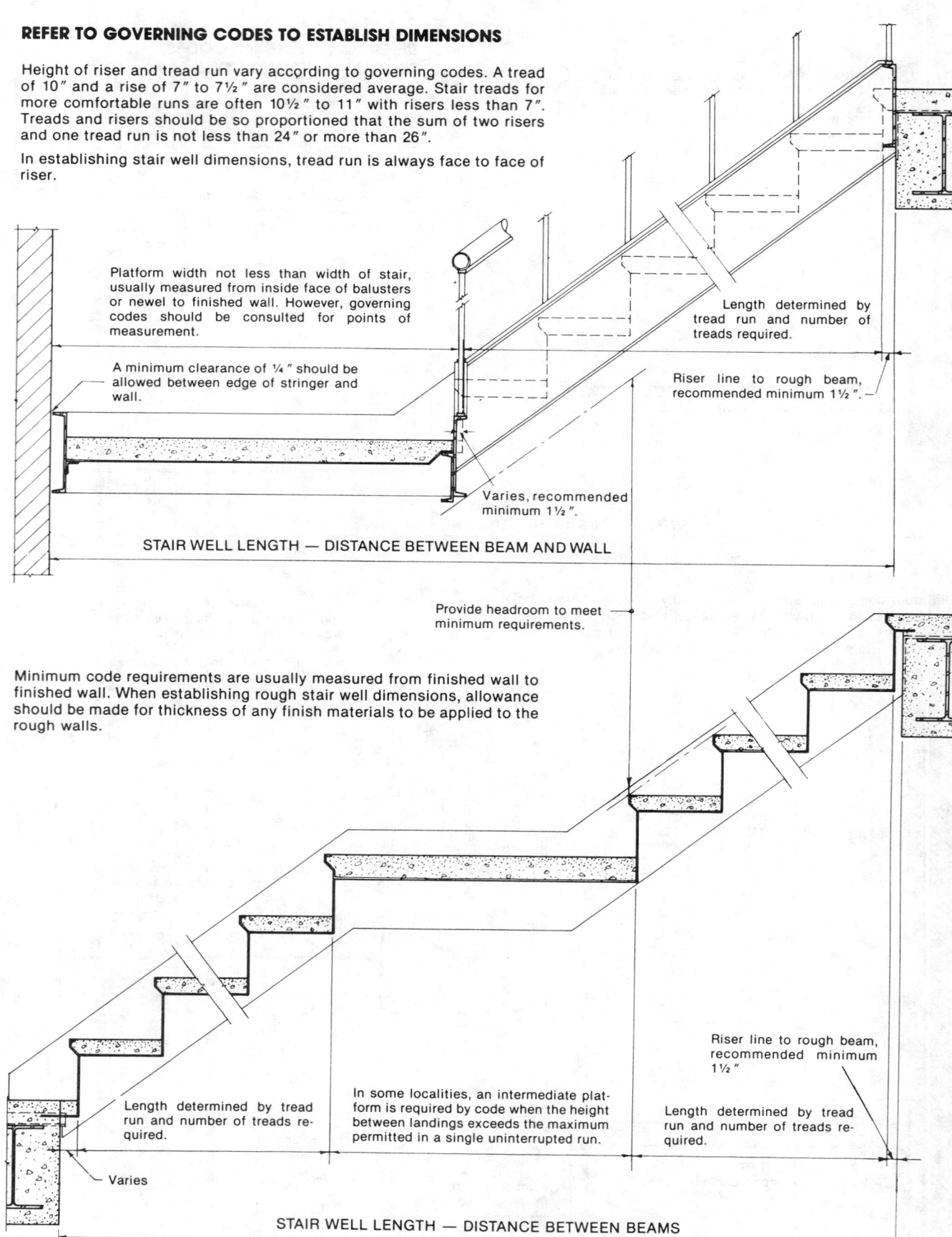

Platform width not less than width of stair, usually measured from inside face of balusters or newel to finished wall. However, governing codes should be consulted for points of measurement.

A minimum clearance of ¼″ should be allowed between edge of stringer and wall.

Length determined by tread run and number of treads required.

Riser line to rough beam, recommended minimum 1½″.

Varies, recommended minimum 1½″.

STAIR WELL LENGTH — DISTANCE BETWEEN BEAM AND WALL

Provide headroom to meet minimum requirements.

Minimum code requirements are usually measured from finished wall to finished wall. When establishing rough stair well dimensions, allowance should be made for thickness of any finish materials to be applied to the rough walls.

Length determined by tread run and number of treads required.

In some localities, an intermediate platform is required by code when the height between landings exceeds the maximum permitted in a single uninterrupted run.

Riser line to rough beam, recommended minimum 1½″

Length determined by tread run and number of treads required.

Varies

STAIR WELL LENGTH — DISTANCE BETWEEN BEAMS

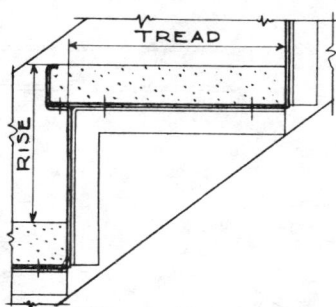

Steel riser and sub tread with formed nosing, angle supporting brackets.

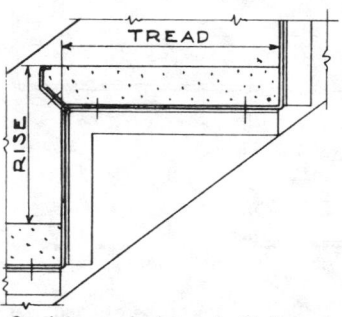

Steel riser and sub tread with formed nosing, angle supporting brackets.

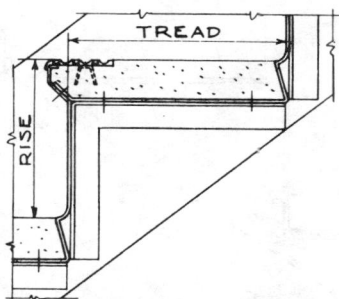

Steel riser and sub tread with lead filled safety nosing, sanitary cove, angle supporting brackets.

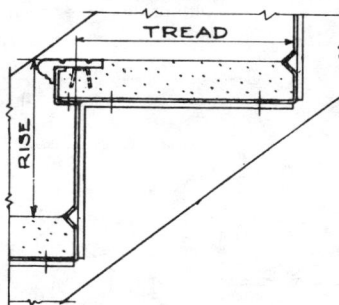

Steel riser and sub tread with abrasive safety nosing, sanitary cove, flat bar supporting brackets.

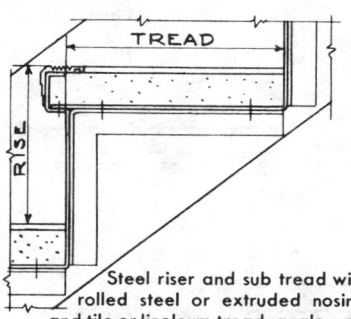

Steel riser and sub tread with rolled steel or extruded nosing and tile or linoleum tread, angle supporting brackets. Other types of safety nosing or tread covering may be used.

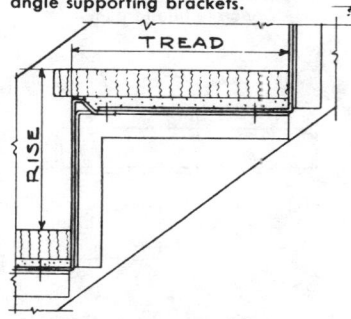

Steel riser and sub tread with marble, or pre-cast tread, angle supporting brackets.

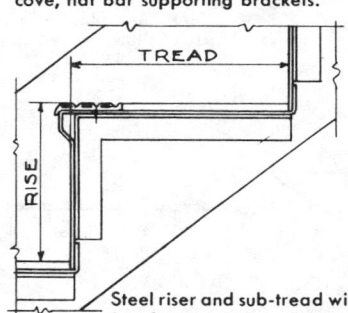

Steel riser and sub-tread with grooved safety nosing and tile or linoleum fill, angle supporting bracket. Other types of safety nosing or tread covering may be used.

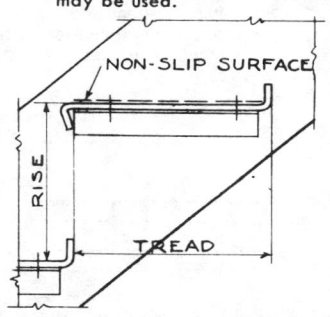

Steel floor plate tread, angle tread bracket, with or without steel riser.

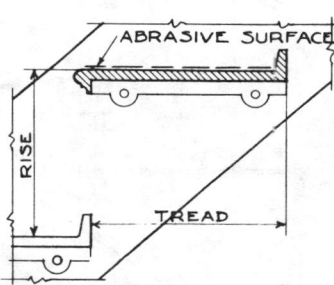

Cast metal abrasive tread, with or without steel riser.

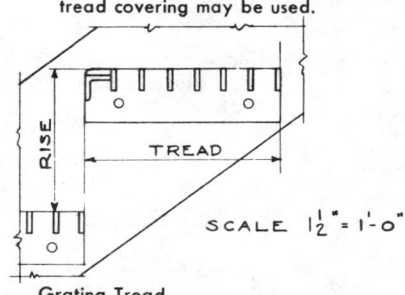

SCALE 1½" = 1'-0"

Grating Tread.

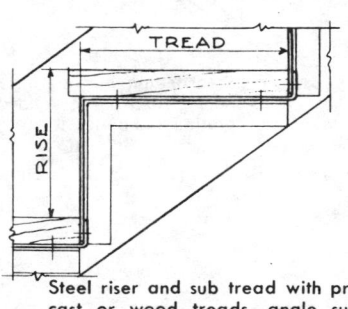

Steel riser and sub tread with pre-cast or wood treads, angle supporting brackets.

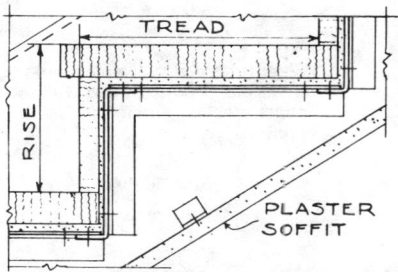

Steel sub-riser and sub tread with marble tread and riser, angle supporting brackets.

Stairs with concrete or terrazzo fill may be constructed with the top of supporting bracket 2" below the tread surface and 3" below the platform surface. These thicknesses may be less for narrow stairs or where use is limited.

Fill is always considered the distance from string bracket to finish tread.

Treads and riser brackets may be 1¼"x1¼"x3/16" or 1/8" angles, welded or riveted to string, or ¼"x1¼" bar welded. Treads and risers are usually bolted to brackets with round head bolts. Cast or grating treads are usually bolted to strings with two 3/8" bolts at each end. Brackets back of risers may be omitted when more economical construction is desired.

STAIRS

Tread Sections

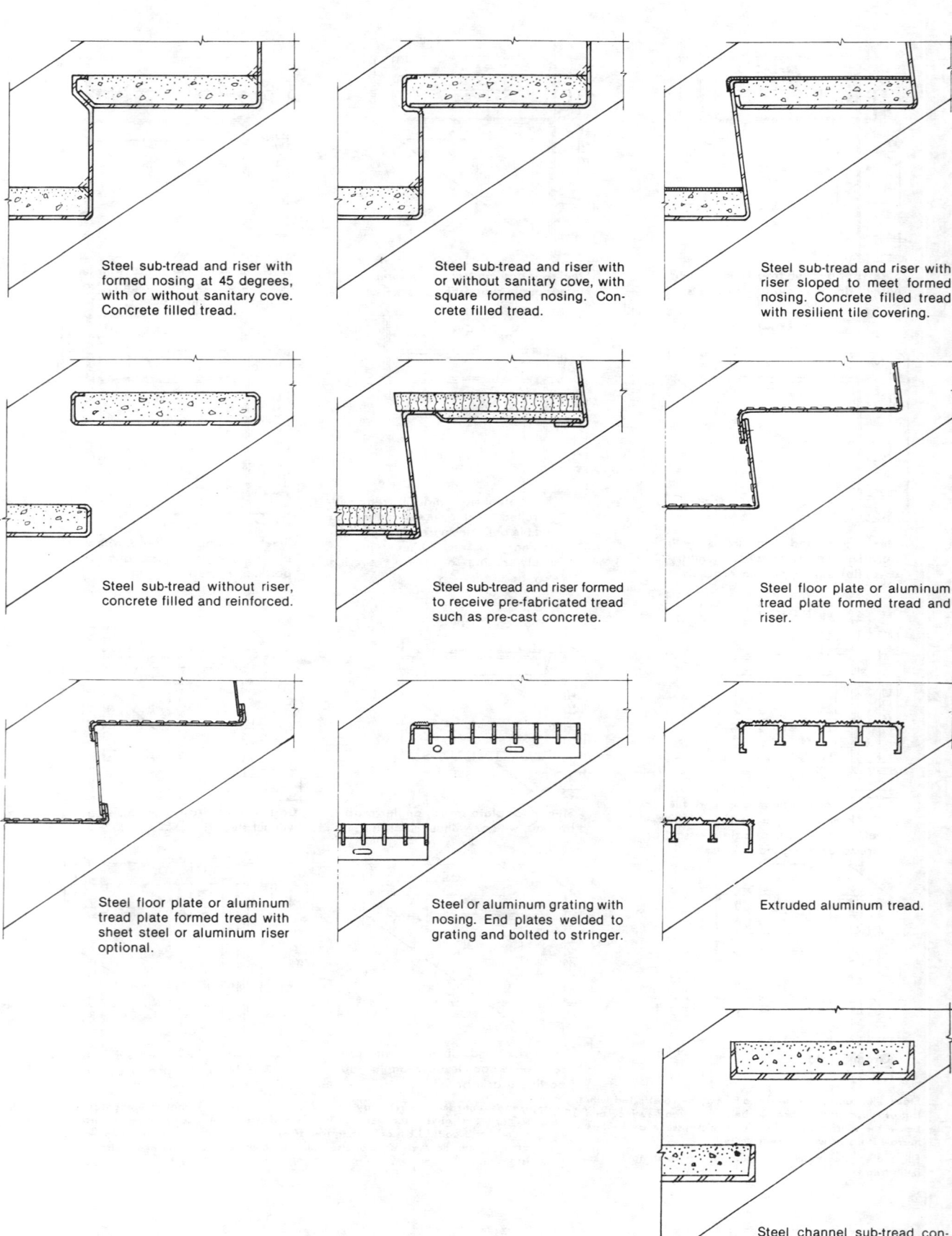

Steel sub-tread and riser with formed nosing at 45 degrees, with or without sanitary cove. Concrete filled tread.

Steel sub-tread and riser with or without sanitary cove, with square formed nosing. Concrete filled tread.

Steel sub-tread and riser with riser sloped to meet formed nosing. Concrete filled tread with resilient tile covering.

Steel sub-tread without riser, concrete filled and reinforced.

Steel sub-tread and riser formed to receive pre-fabricated tread such as pre-cast concrete.

Steel floor plate or aluminum tread plate formed tread and riser.

Steel floor plate or aluminum tread plate formed tread with sheet steel or aluminum riser optional.

Steel or aluminum grating with nosing. End plates welded to grating and bolted to stringer.

Extruded aluminum tread.

Steel channel sub-tread concrete filled.

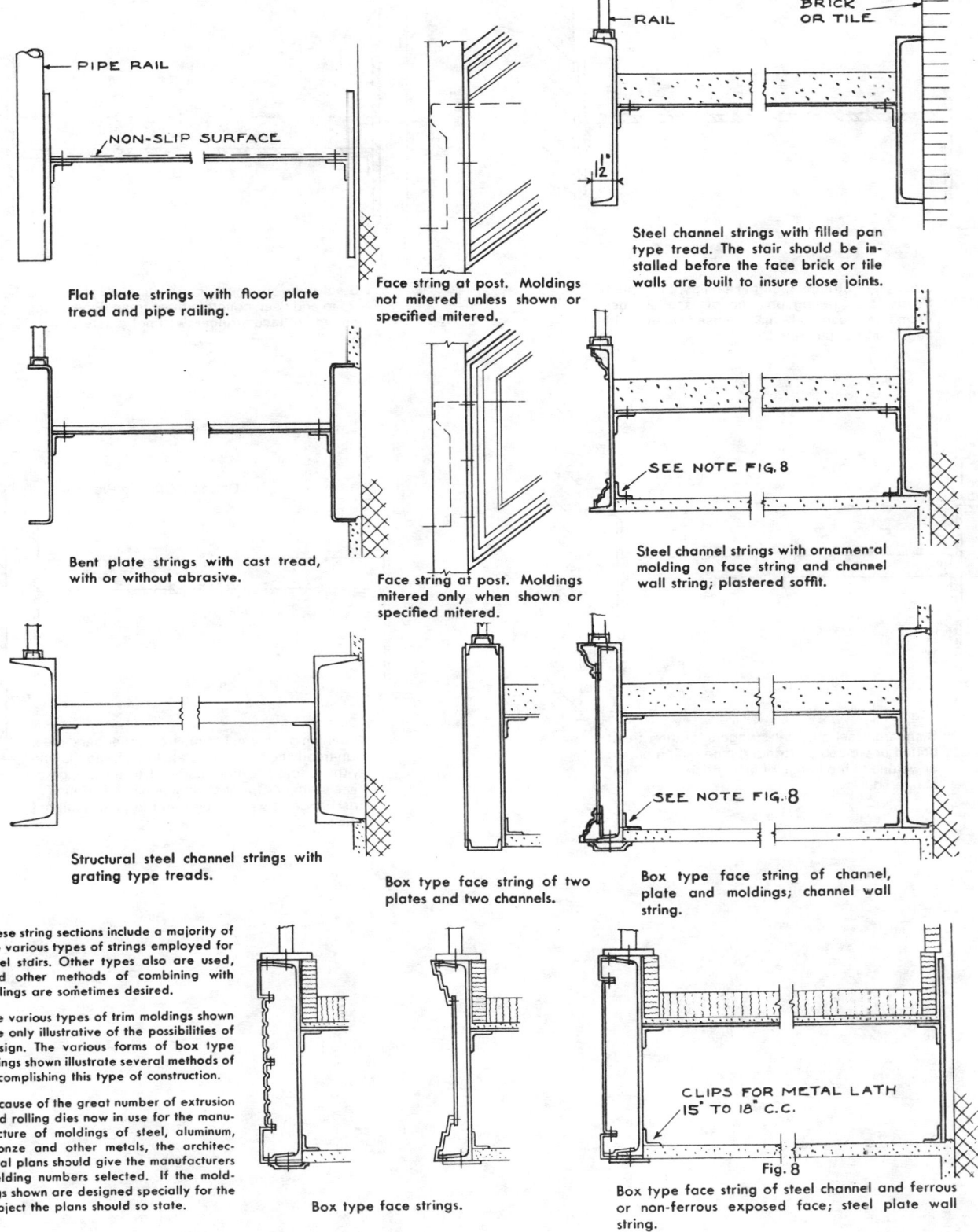

Flat plate strings with floor plate tread and pipe railing.

Face string at post. Moldings not mitered unless shown or specified mitered.

Steel channel strings with filled pan type tread. The stair should be installed before the face brick or tile walls are built to insure close joints.

Bent plate strings with cast tread, with or without abrasive.

Face string at post. Moldings mitered only when shown or specified mitered.

Steel channel strings with ornamental molding on face string and channel wall string; plastered soffit.

Structural steel channel strings with grating type treads.

Box type face string of two plates and two channels.

Box type face string of channel, plate and moldings; channel wall string.

These string sections include a majority of the various types of strings employed for steel stairs. Other types also are used, and other methods of combining with railings are sometimes desired.

The various types of trim moldings shown are only illustrative of the possibilities of design. The various forms of box type strings shown illustrate several methods of accomplishing this type of construction.

Because of the great number of extrusion and rolling dies now in use for the manufacture of moldings of steel, aluminum, bronze and other metals, the architectural plans should give the manufacturers molding numbers selected. If the moldings shown are designed specially for the project the plans should so state.

Box type face strings.

CLIPS FOR METAL LATH 15" TO 18" C.C.

Fig. 8

Box type face string of steel channel and ferrous or non-ferrous exposed face; steel plate wall string.

STAIRS
Stringer Sections

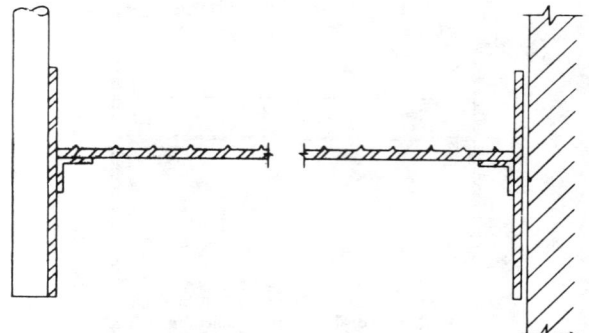

Steel plate stringers, carrier angles, floor plate treads, pipe railing on side of face stringer. Aluminum tread plate may be used when specified. Wall not plastered.

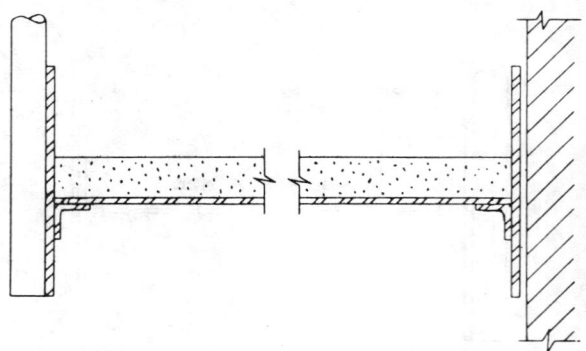

Steel plate stringers, carrier angles, steel sub-tread and riser, concrete filled tread. Pipe railing on side of face stringer, wall not plastered.

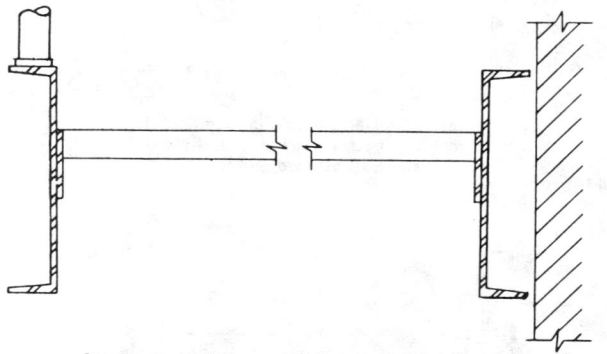

Standard steel channel stringers, grating tread bolted or welded to stringer, pipe railing bolted or welded to top flange of face stringer. Wall not plastered.

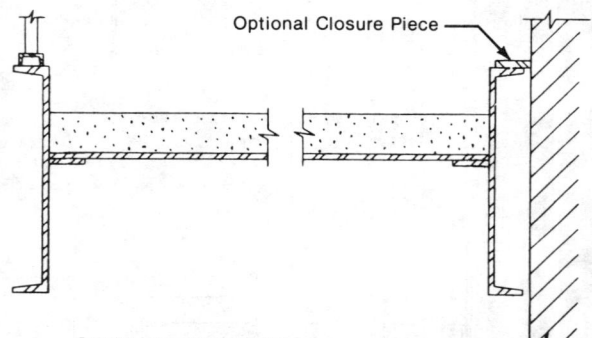

Optional Closure Piece

Steel junior channel stringers, carrier bars, steel sub-tread and riser. Concrete filled tread. Railing with bottom channel fastened to top flange of face stringer. Optional closure piece fastened to top flange of wall stringer in the field. Wall not plastered.

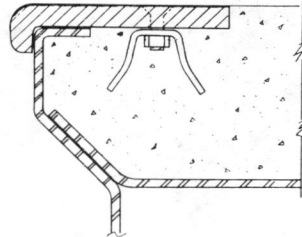

Cast abrasive nosing with short lip, available in iron, bronze or aluminum as specified. Standard drilling with wing anchors, bolts and nuts or drilled as required.

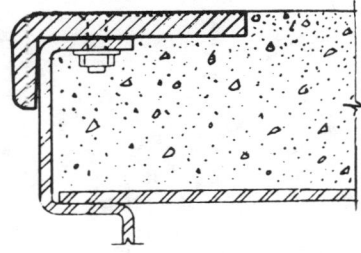

Cast abrasive nosing with deep lip, available in iron, bronze or aluminum as specified. Standard drilling with wing anchors, bolts and nuts or drilled as required.

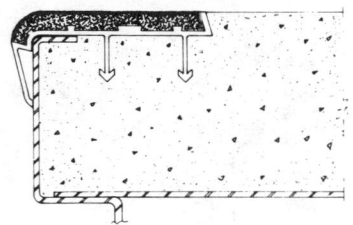

Extruded aluminum base with epoxy top, containing abrasive. Available in colors. Integral anchors for fresh concrete. Also available drilled to specifications without the anchors.

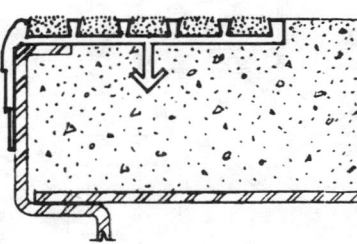

Extruded aluminum or brass with abrasive filled ribs. Concealed integral anchor runs full length of tread. Also available drilled to specifications, without the integral anchor.

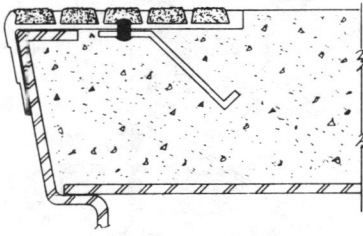

Extruded aluminum with abrasive ribs. Special design for pan stairs with sloped risers. Drilled to specification or furnished with strap anchors or wing anchors.

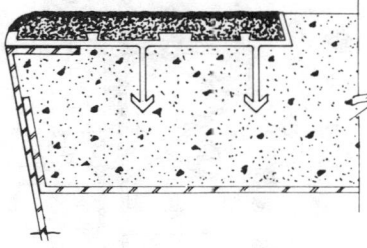

Barrier free design to meet standards for the physically handicapped. Aluminum base with epoxy containing abrasive top. Integral anchors for fresh concrete.

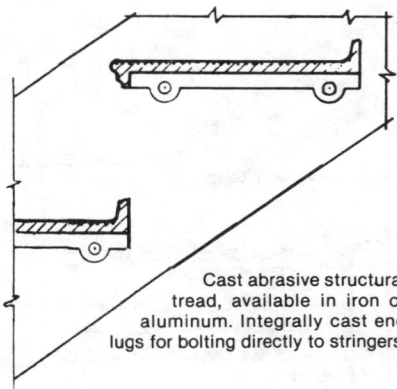

Cast abrasive structural tread, available in iron or aluminum. Integrally cast end lugs for bolting directly to stringers.

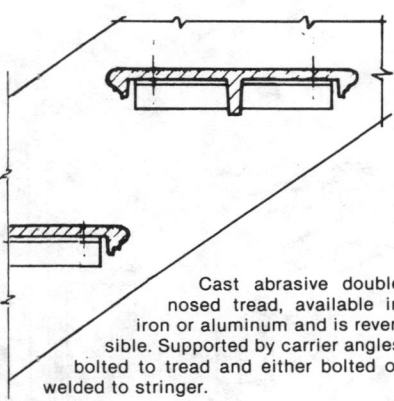

Cast abrasive double nosed tread, available in iron or aluminum and is reversible. Supported by carrier angles bolted to tread and either bolted or welded to stringer.

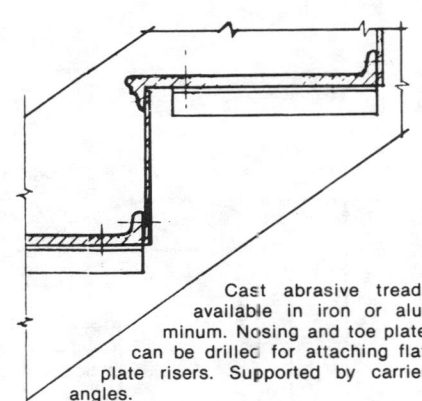

Cast abrasive tread, available in iron or aluminum. Nosing and toe plate can be drilled for attaching flat plate risers. Supported by carrier angles.

691

STAIRS

Handrails

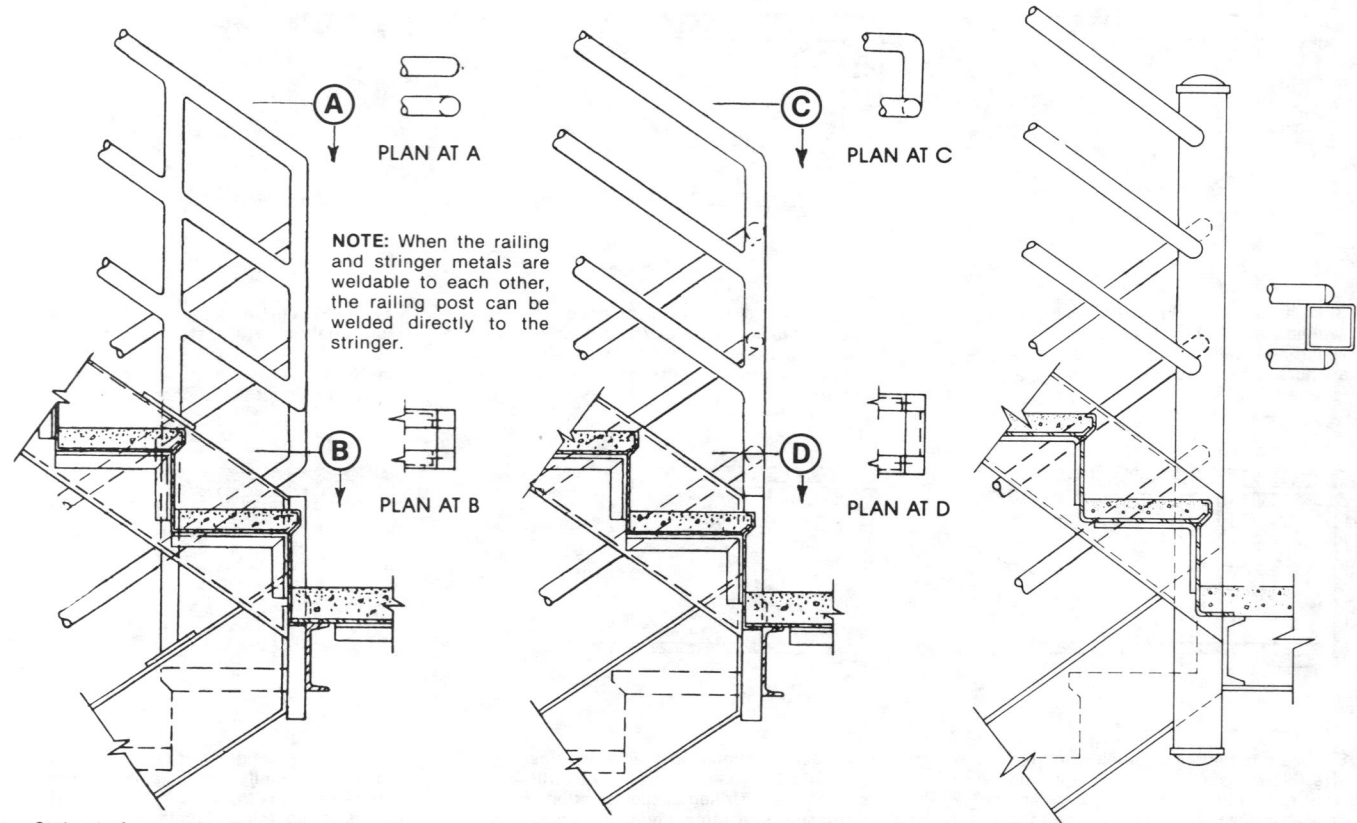

PLAN AT A

NOTE: When the railing and stringer metals are weldable to each other, the railing post can be welded directly to the stringer.

PLAN AT B

PLAN AT C

PLAN AT D

Stair platform or landing with pipe railings, railings not connected, for stairwell having minimum clearance. Short newels, supported on header.

Stair platform or landing with pipe railing, one post at return. Lower rail returned into post, two or more posts used at wide wells. Short newels, supported on header.

Stair platform or landing with rectangular or square newel, pipe railing members capped and welded to newel post.

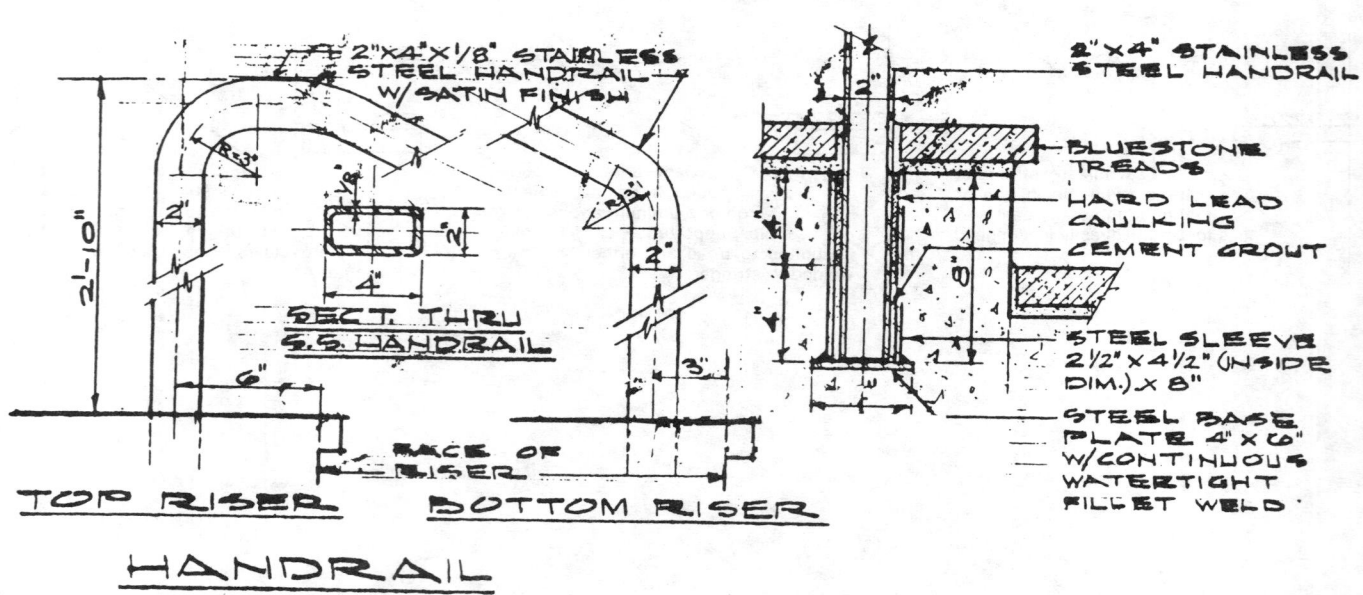

2"x4"x1/8" STAINLESS STEEL HANDRAIL W/ SATIN FINISH

2'-10"

SECT. THRU S.S. HANDRAIL

TOP RISER

FACE OF RISER

BOTTOM RISER

HANDRAIL

2"x4" STAINLESS STEEL HANDRAIL

BLUESTONE TREADS

HARD LEAD CAULKING

CEMENT GROUT

STEEL SLEEVE 2½"x4½" (INSIDE DIM.) x 8"

STEEL BASE PLATE 4"x6" W/CONTINUOUS WATERTIGHT FILLET WELD

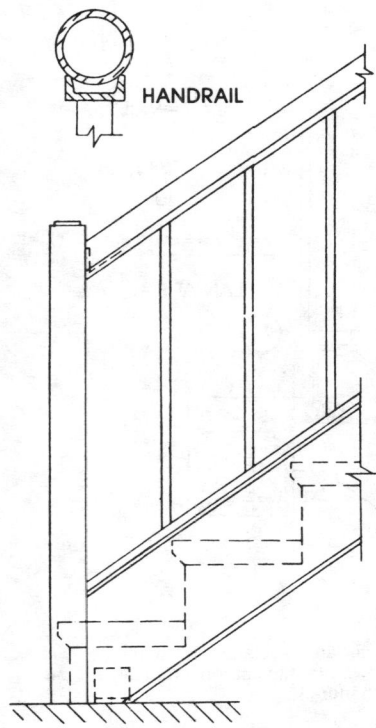

HANDRAIL

Stair start with square newel, baluster type railing with channel top and bottom, pipe handrail.

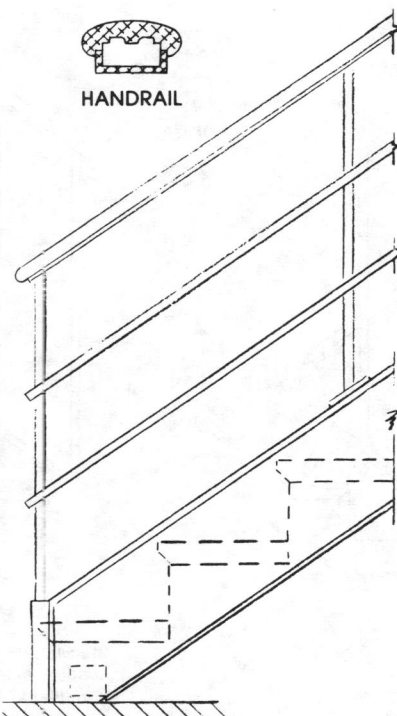

HANDRAIL

Stair start with short newel, parallel bar type railing with end and intermediate posts of square, rectangular or round section, extruded handrail with mitered, forged or cast terminal.

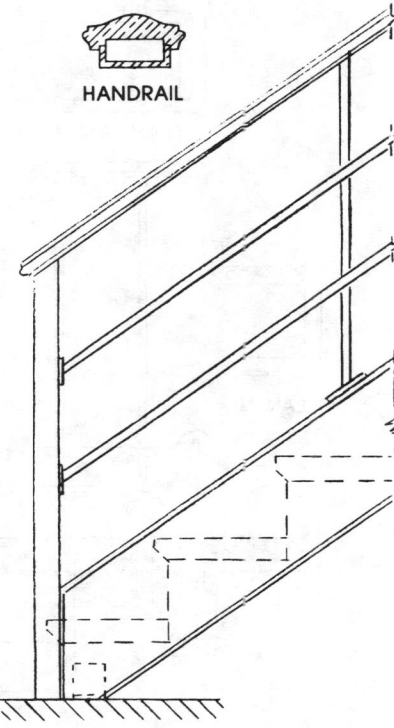

HANDRAIL

Stair start with square newel, parallel bar type railing with intermediate posts of square, rectangular or round section; extruded or rolled handrail section mitered to form cap over newel.

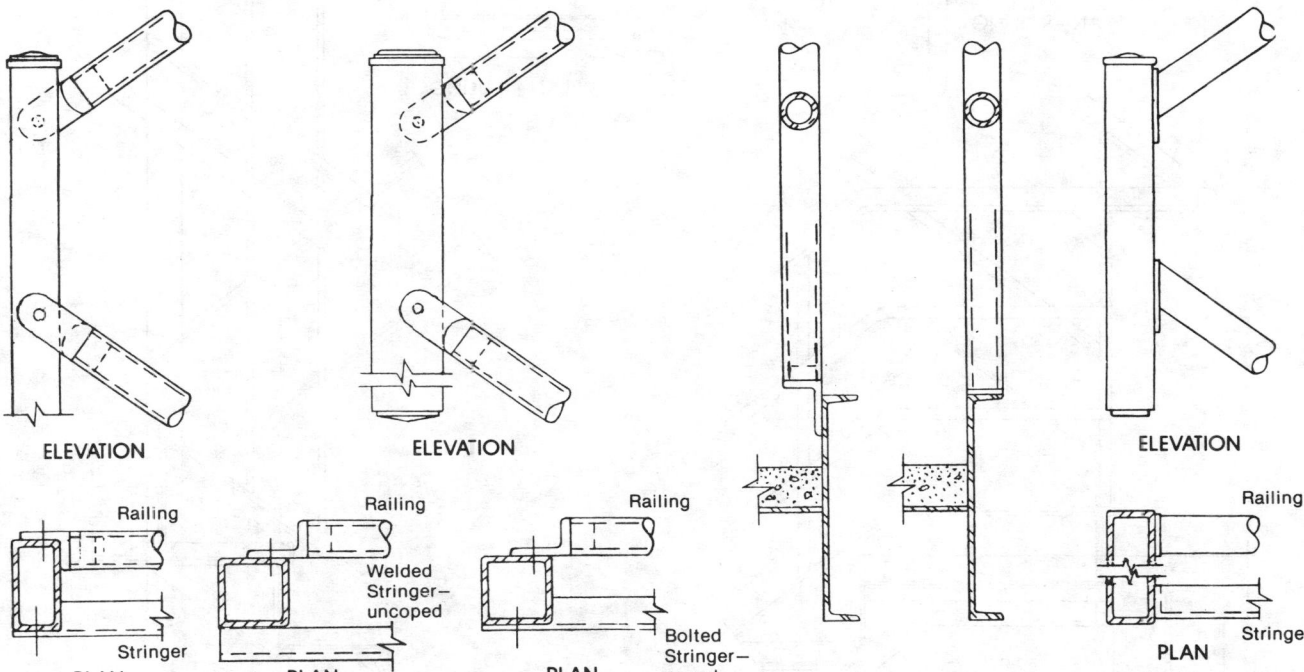

ELEVATION

ELEVATION

ELEVATION

Railing

Railing

Railing

Welded
Stringer—
uncoped

Bolted
Stringer—
coped

Stringer

Railing

Stringer

PLAN

PLAN

PLAN

PLAN

Square or rectangular newel, pipe rail fitted with offset lug to center on stringer.

Square or rectangular newel, pipe rail fitted with offset lug for positioning inside of stringer.

Section showing fastening for intermediate posts to stringers.

Rectangular newel, pipe rail and stringer welded or bolted to face.

STAIRS

Newels and Railings

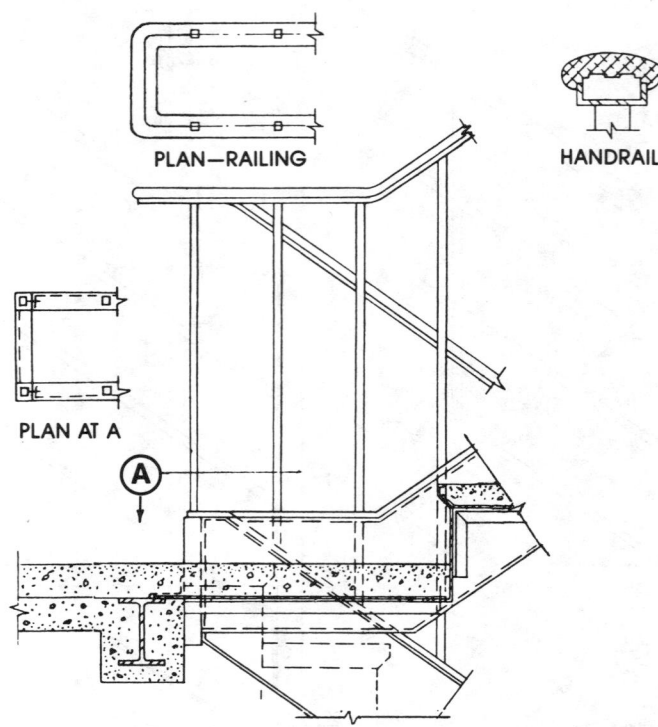

PLAN—RAILING

PLAN AT A

HANDRAIL

Ⓐ

Stair landing with stringers and fascia framed square. Square railing return, end balusters centered on newels and landing extended on up flight to set-back riser.

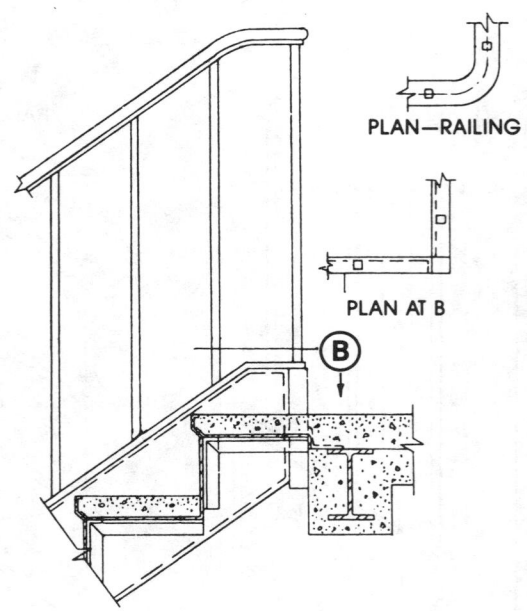

PLAN—RAILING

PLAN AT B

Ⓑ

Stair landing, with stringer and fascia at right angle. Landing extended on down flight to set-forward riser, producing easement in handrail.

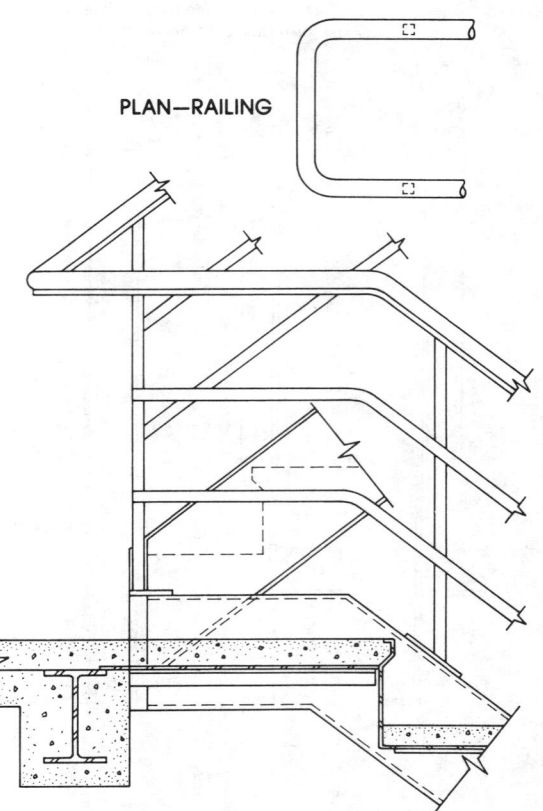

PLAN—RAILING

Stair landing with stringers and fascia framed square. Radius railing return, parallel bar type railing with end balusters centered on newels. Landing extended on down flight to set-forward riser.

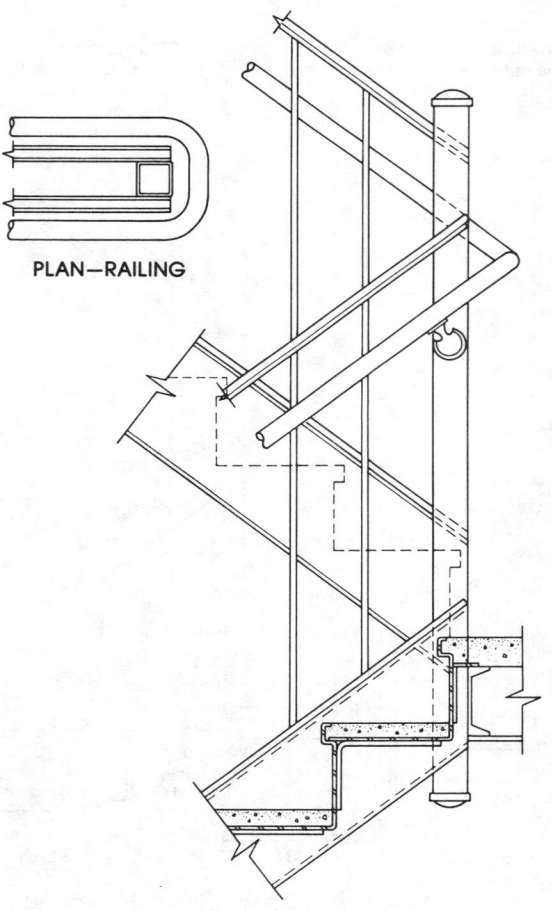

PLAN—RAILING

Stair landing with stringers and fascia framed into full height newel, baluster railing with channel top and bottom. Continuous pipe handrail offset from balusters and newels by brackets.

Figures 9 and 10 indicate typical railings for decks, platforms, balconies, roofs, and similar locations, adapted for residential, apartment, or hotel construction. These railings may be fastened with wood screws or lag bolts to wood, or with expansion bolts to masonry. On roofs or decks the setting of the post bases should be waterproofed.

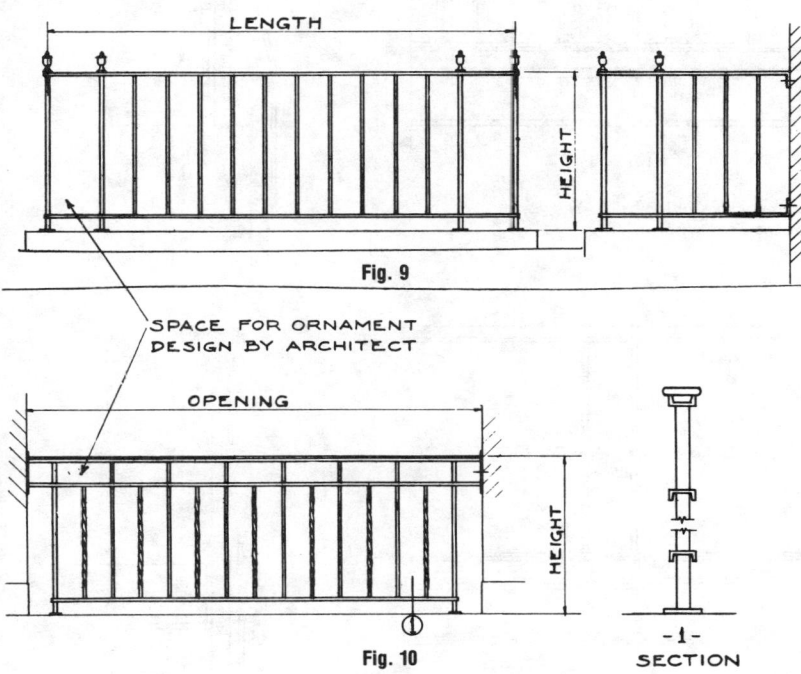

LENGTH

HEIGHT

Fig. 9

SPACE FOR ORNAMENT
DESIGN BY ARCHITECT

OPENING

HEIGHT

Fig. 10

SECTION

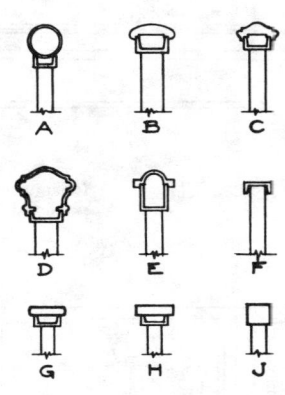

Methods of constructing railing top members.

SCALE $1\frac{1}{2}" = 1'-0"$

TO SPECIFY:
Give locations.
Indicate kind of metal.
Specify finish.
Give sizes of members.
Give height.
Provide scale details of ornaments, finials and bases.

Specify method of fastening, or have fabricator provide fastenings best suited to each condition.

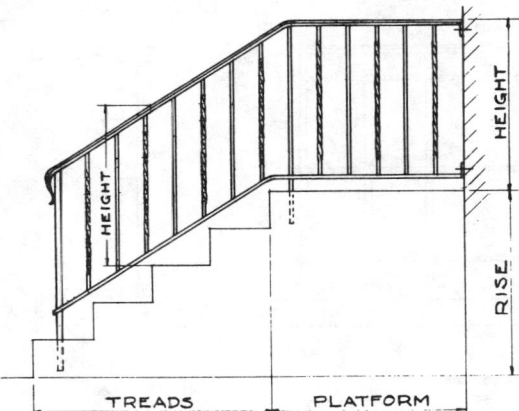

HEIGHT

HEIGHT

RISE

TREADS   PLATFORM

Railing with balusters and bottom longitudinal member supporting balusters. Posts extending into masonry.

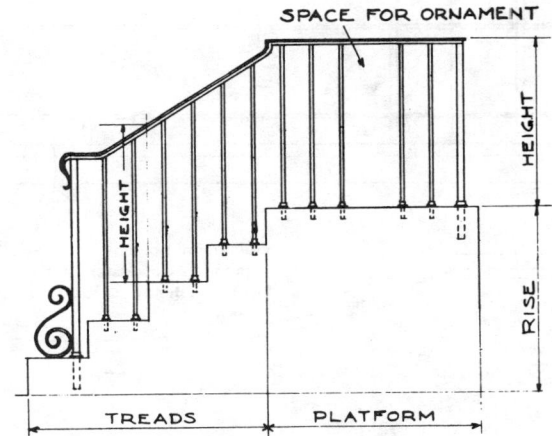

SPACE FOR ORNAMENT

HEIGHT

HEIGHT

RISE

TREADS   PLATFORM

Railing without bottom longitudinal member, each baluster set in masonry and fitted with slip flange or base. Masonry specifications should specify holes.

STAIRS

Ornamental Railings

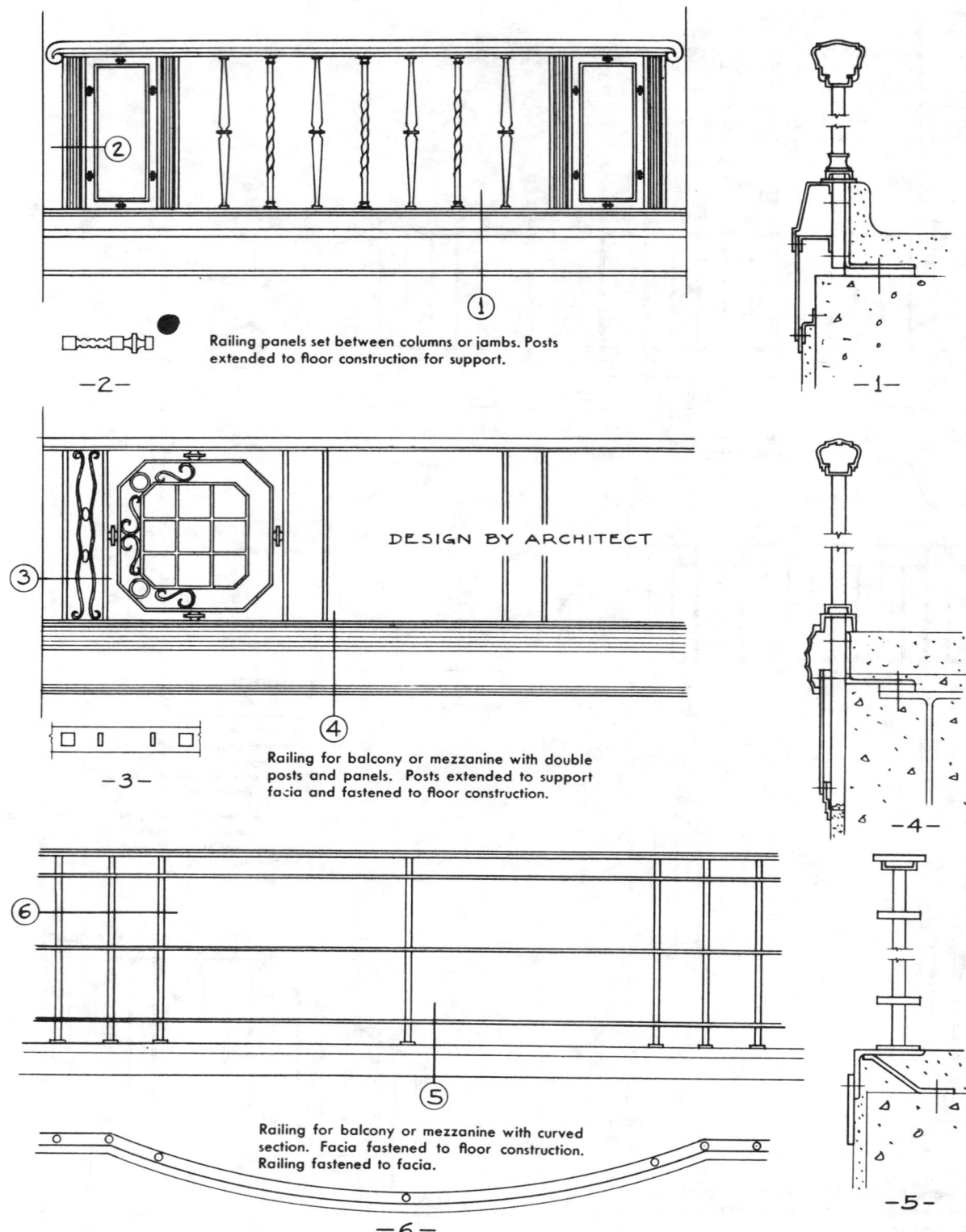

Railing panels set between columns or jambs. Posts extended to floor construction for support.

—2—

—1—

DESIGN BY ARCHITECT

—3—

Railing for balcony or mezzanine with double posts and panels. Posts extended to support facia and fastened to floor construction.

—4—

Railing for balcony or mezzanine with curved section. Facia fastened to floor construction. Railing fastened to facia.

—6—

—5—

Center railings are recommended for wide stairs. They may be a single pipe or tubing railing or they may be designed with double rails and panels of interesting design.

Note: A number of codes require that railings have a level extension beyond the nosings at the floors as indicated in Fig. 11 by dashed lines. This applies to both wall and center railings.

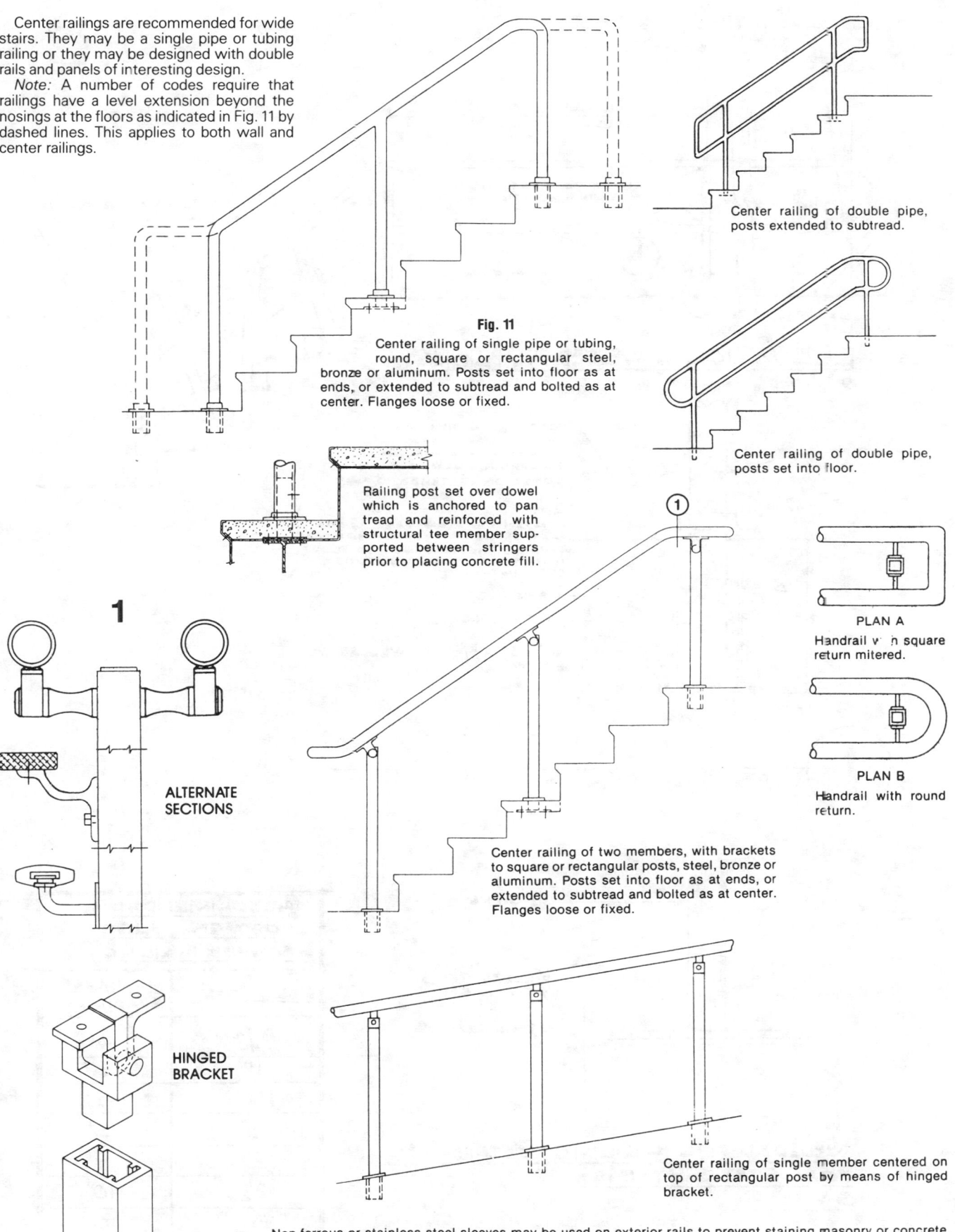

Fig. 11

Center railing of single pipe or tubing, round, square or rectangular steel, bronze or aluminum. Posts set into floor as at ends, or extended to subtread and bolted as at center. Flanges loose or fixed.

Center railing of double pipe, posts extended to subtread.

Center railing of double pipe, posts set into floor.

Railing post set over dowel which is anchored to pan tread and reinforced with structural tee member supported between stringers prior to placing concrete fill.

PLAN A
Handrail with square return mitered.

PLAN B
Handrail with round return.

ALTERNATE SECTIONS

Center railing of two members, with brackets to square or rectangular posts, steel, bronze or aluminum. Posts set into floor as at ends, or extended to subtread and bolted as at center. Flanges loose or fixed.

HINGED BRACKET

Center railing of single member centered on top of rectangular post by means of hinged bracket.

Non-ferrous or stainless steel sleeves may be used on exterior rails to prevent staining masonry or concrete.

STAIRS

Railings

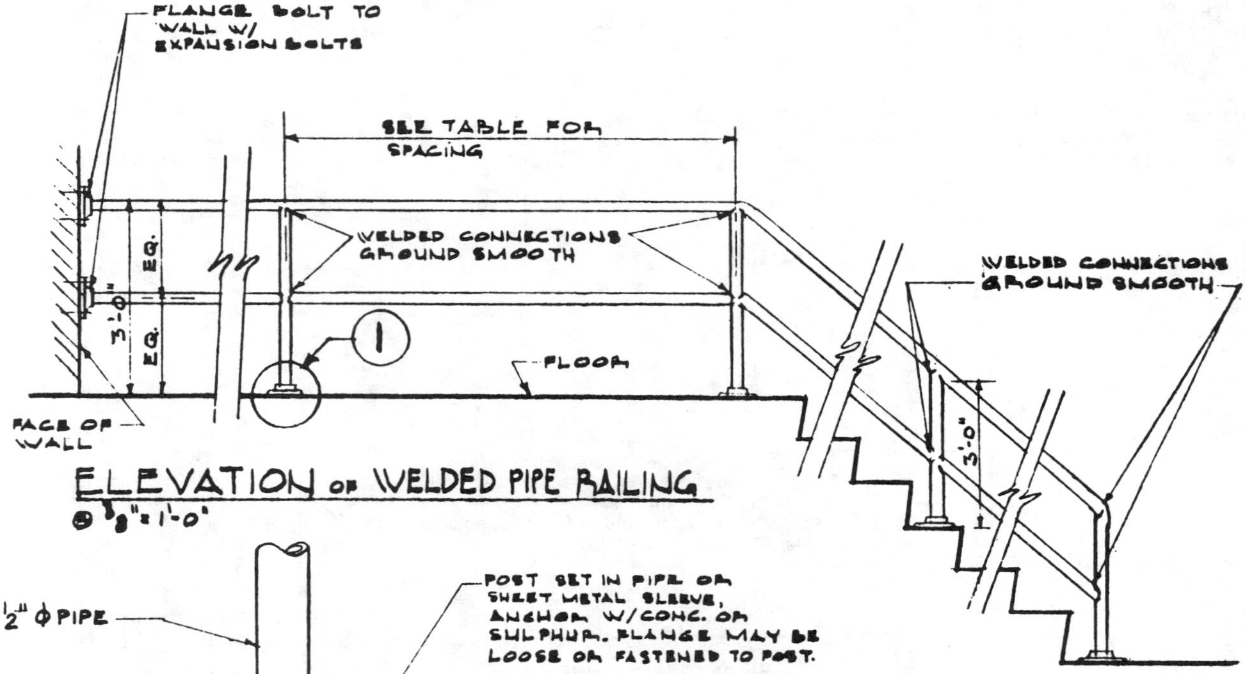

FLANGE BOLT TO WALL W/ EXPANSION BOLTS

SEE TABLE FOR SPACING

WELDED CONNECTIONS GROUND SMOOTH

WELDED CONNECTIONS GROUND SMOOTH

EQ.

3'-0"

EQ.

FLOOR

FACE OF WALL

3'-0"

ELEVATION OF WELDED PIPE RAILING
@ 3/8" = 1'-0"

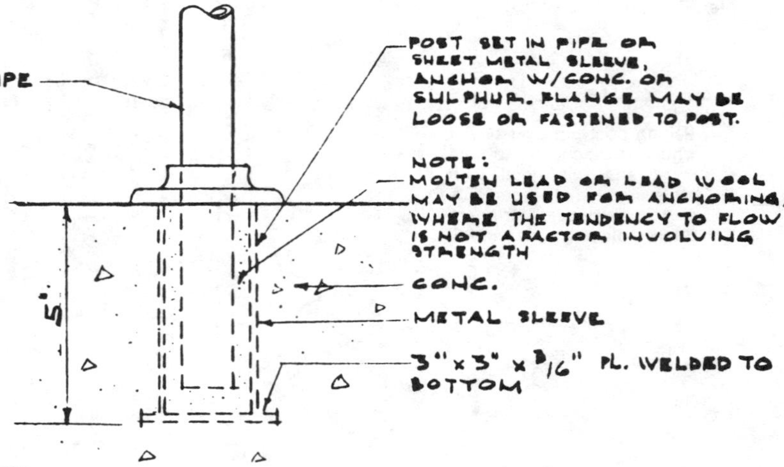

1½" Ø PIPE

POST SET IN PIPE OR SHEET METAL SLEEVE, ANCHOR W/CONC. OR SULPHUR. FLANGE MAY BE LOOSE OR FASTENED TO POST.

NOTE:
MOLTEN LEAD OR LEAD WOOL MAY BE USED FOR ANCHORING, WHERE THE TENDENCY TO FLOW IS NOT A FACTOR INVOLVING STRENGTH

CONC.

METAL SLEEVE

3"x3"x³/16" PL. WELDED TO BOTTOM

5"

1
@ 3" = 1'-0"

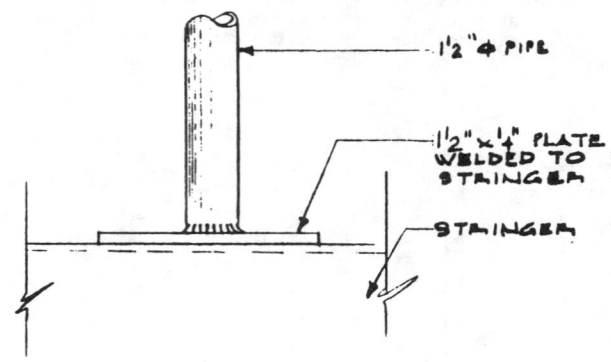

1½" Ø PIPE

1½" x ¼" PLATE WELDED TO STRINGER

STRINGER

WELDED PIPE RAILING DETAIL FOR STEEL STAIRS
@ 3" = 1'-0"

RECOMMENDED POST SPACING FOR PIPE RAILING	
SIZE OF PIPE	MAXIMUM SPACING
¾"	4'
1"	6'
1¼"	7'
1½"	8'
2"	9'
2½"	10'
3"	10'

TYPICAL EXTRUDED ALUMINUM AND BRONZE POST SECTIONS

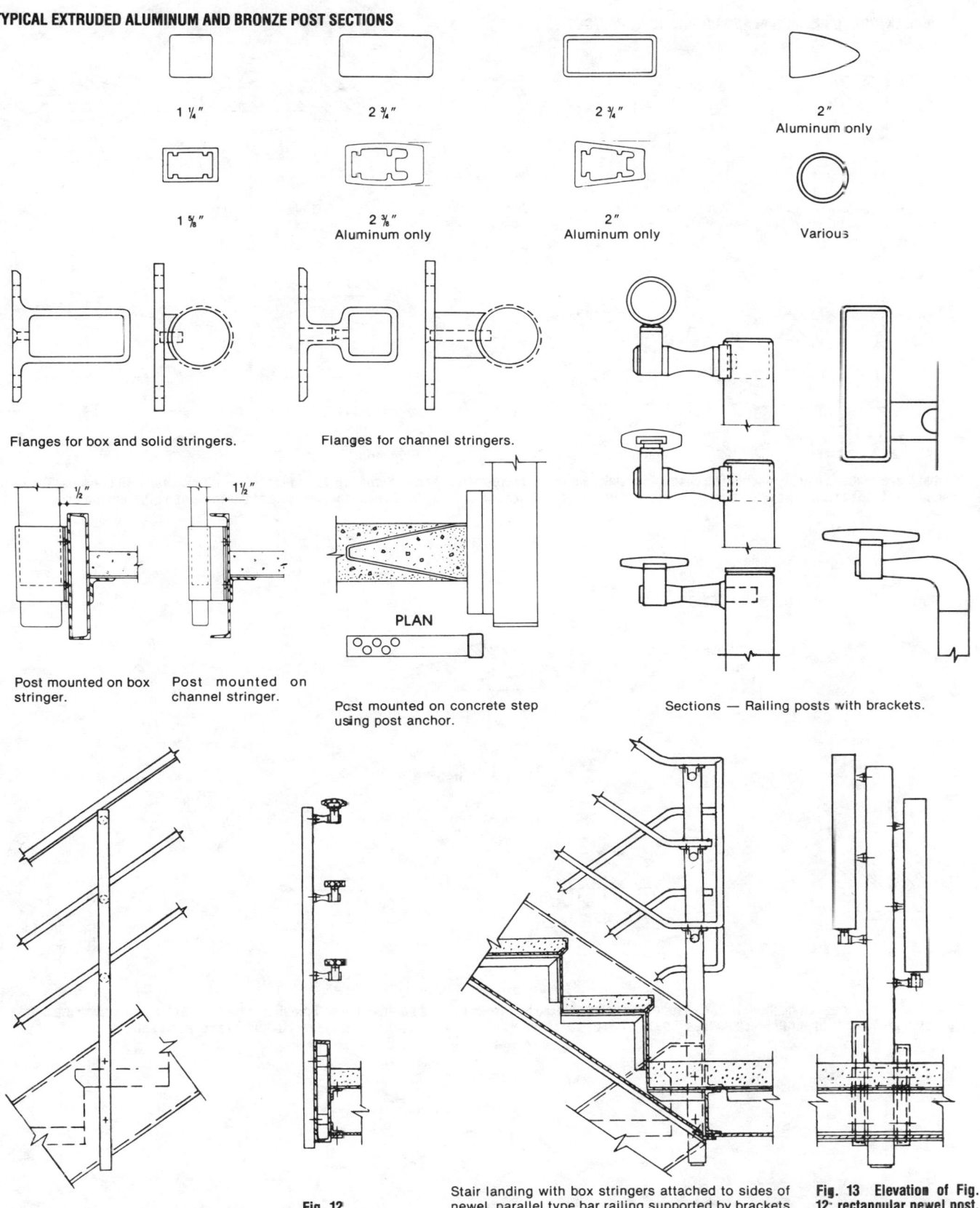

1 ¼"

2 ¾"

2 ¾"

2"
Aluminum only

1 ⅝"

2 ⅜"
Aluminum only

2"
Aluminum only

Various

Flanges for box and solid stringers.

Flanges for channel stringers.

½"

1½"

Post mounted on box stringer.

Post mounted on channel stringer.

PLAN

Post mounted on concrete step using post anchor.

Sections — Railing posts with brackets.

Elevation; intermediate post set on face of box stringer.

Fig. 12

Section; intermediate post set on face of box stringer.

Stair landing with box stringers attached to sides of newel, parallel type bar railing supported by brackets at newels and intermediate posts. Risers offset to allow metal soffits of stair to meet at intersection with soffit of landing. Bottom and top rails must be the same and have symetrical cross section to obtain proper mitered connection.

Fig. 13 Elevation of Fig. 12: rectangular newel post.

STAIRS

Handrail Sections

TYPICAL EXTRUDED ALUMINUM AND BRONZE HANDRAIL SECTIONS

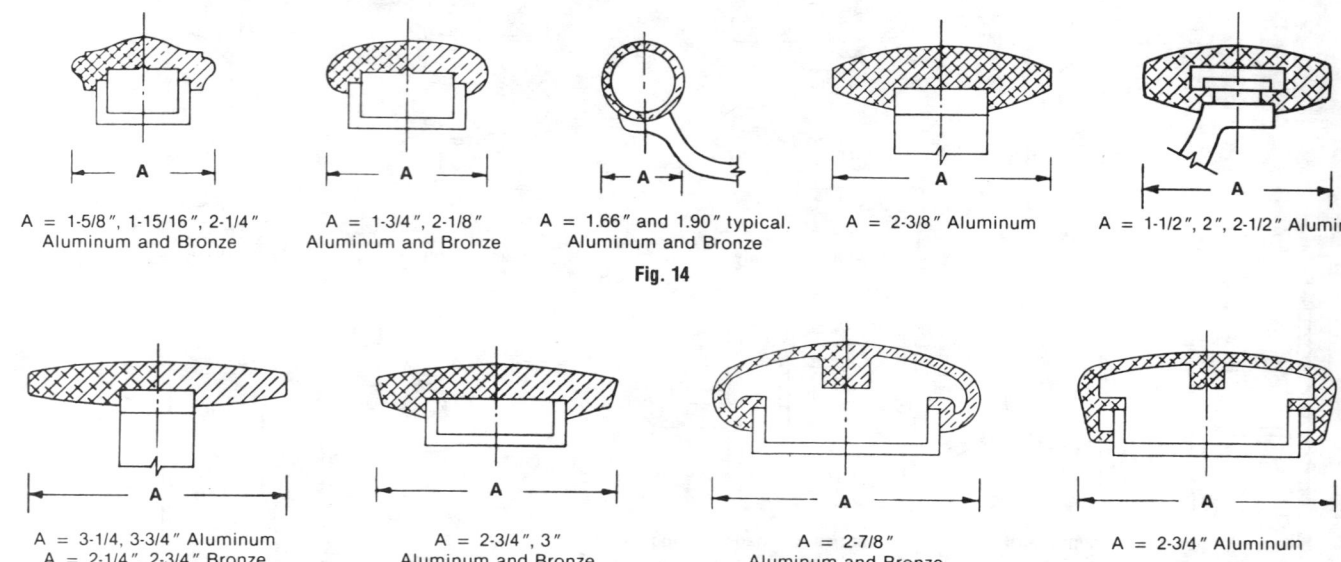

A = 1-5/8″, 1-15/16″, 2-1/4″
Aluminum and Bronze

A = 1-3/4″, 2-1/8″
Aluminum and Bronze

A = 1.66″ and 1.90″ typical.
Aluminum and Bronze

Fig. 14

A = 2-3/8″ Aluminum

A = 1-1/2″, 2″, 2-1/2″ Aluminum

A = 3-1/4, 3-3/4″ Aluminum
A = 2-1/4″, 2-3/4″ Bronze

A = 2-3/4″, 3″
Aluminum and Bronze

A = 2-7/8″
Aluminum and Bronze

A = 2-3/4″ Aluminum

Most of these sections can be mounted on channels or flats, secured by screws from below. Some are designed for mounting on handrail brackets. The use of channels instead of solid bars often simplifies the attachment of baluster and ornaments. The channels may be of the same or a different metal.

TYPICAL ROLLED STEEL HANDRAIL SECTIONS

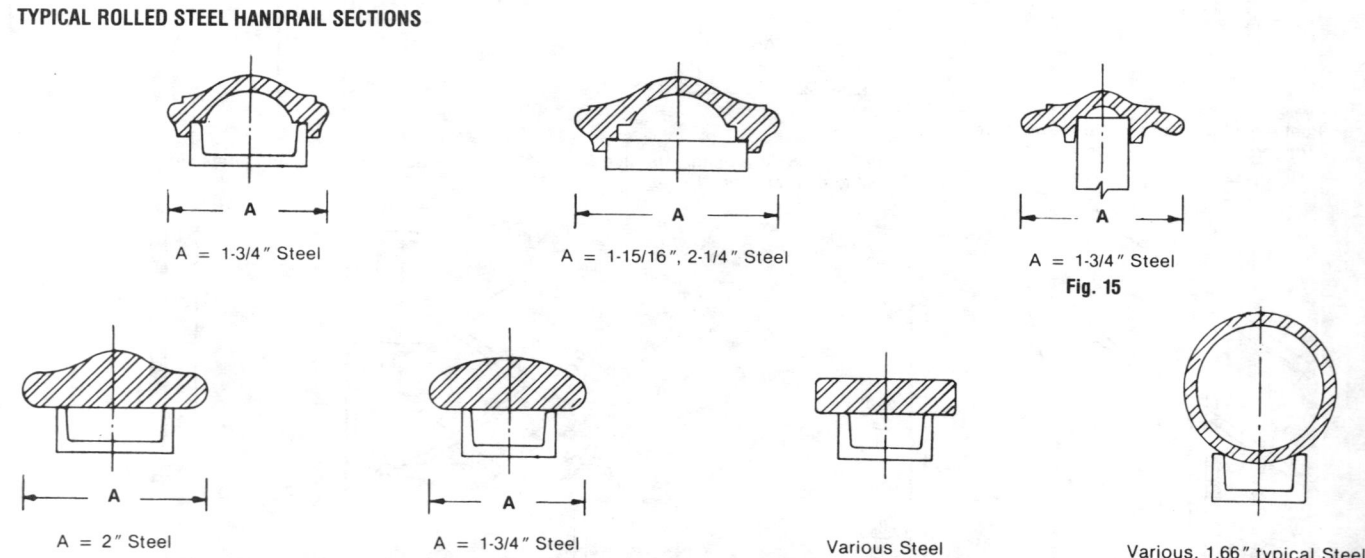

A = 1-3/4″ Steel

A = 1-15/16″, 2-1/4″ Steel

A = 1-3/4″ Steel
Fig. 15

A = 2″ Steel

A = 1-3/4″ Steel

Various Steel

Various, 1.66″ typical Steel

Most of these sections can be mounted on channels or flats, secured by screws or welding from below. Sometimes they are welded directly to the baluster (see Fig. 15) or attached to handrail brackets (see Fig. 14). The use of channels often simplifies the attachment of balusters and ornaments.

REPRESENTATIVE EXTRUDED AND TUBULAR STAINLESS STEEL HANDRAIL SECTIONS

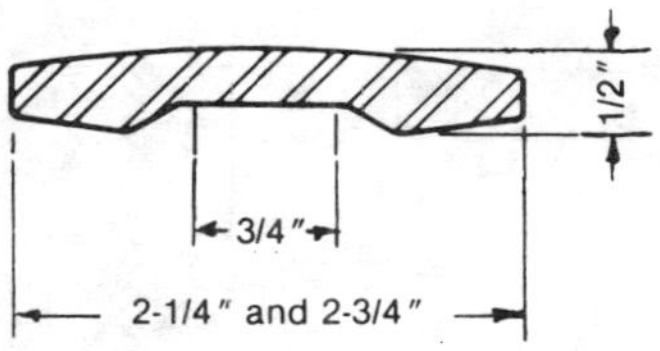

Stainless Steel
Extrusion

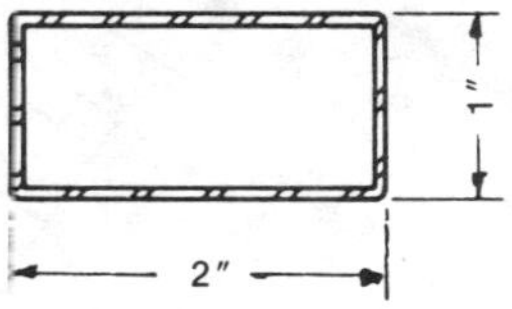

Stainless Steel
(other sizes available)

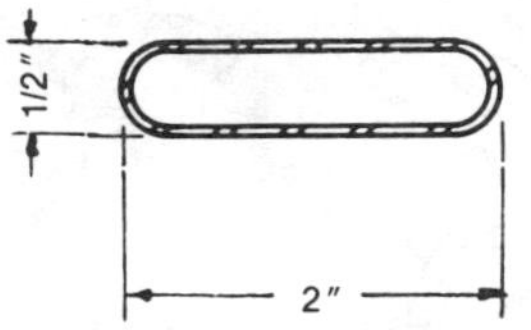

Stainless Steel

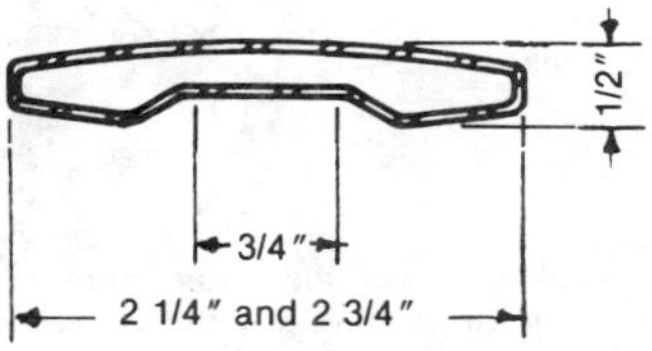

Stainless Steel

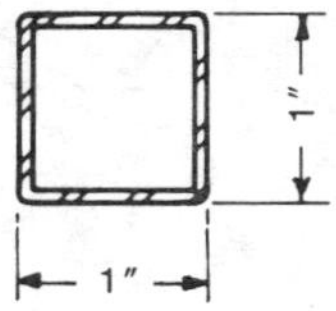

Stainless Steel
(other sizes available)

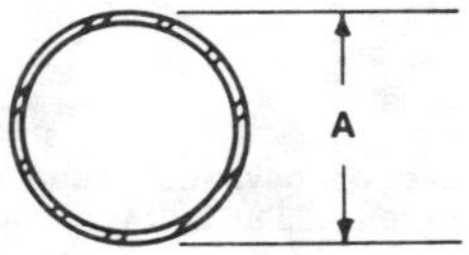

A = Various
1.66" and 1.90" typical

Stainless Steel

Stainless tubular handrail sections usually have a wall thickness of .065".

PLASTIC HANDRAIL COVERINGS

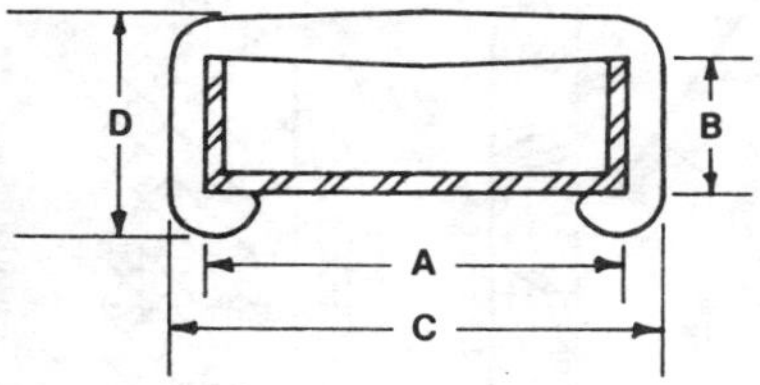

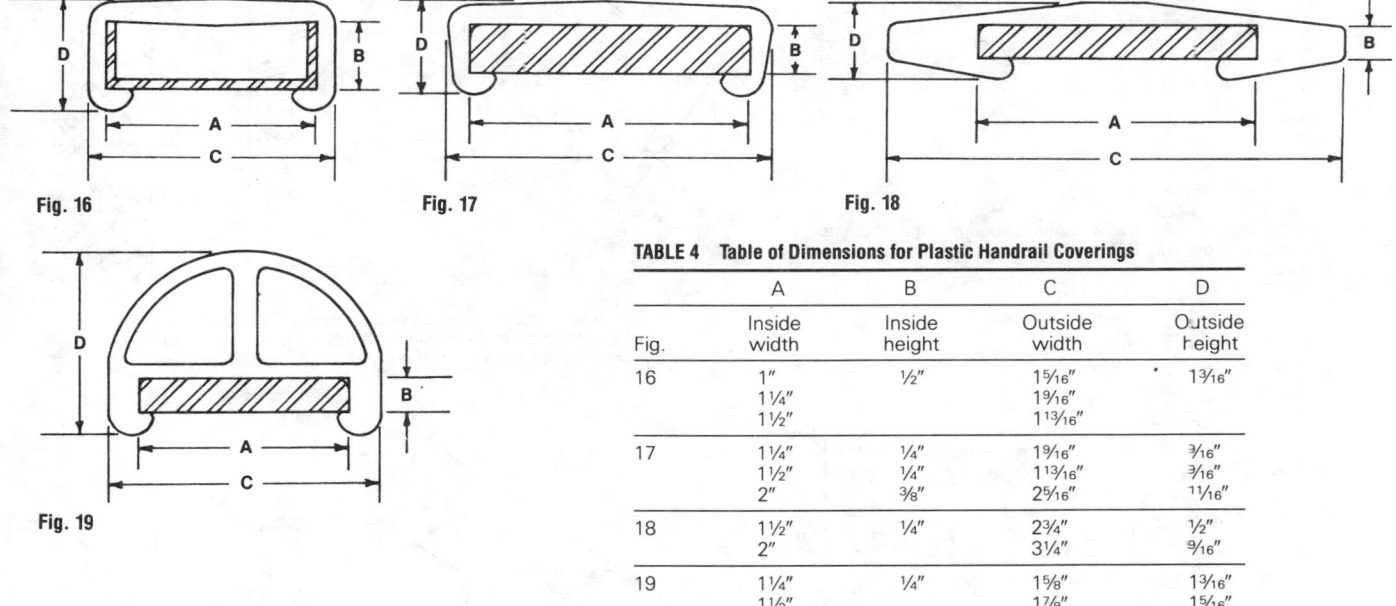

Fig. 16

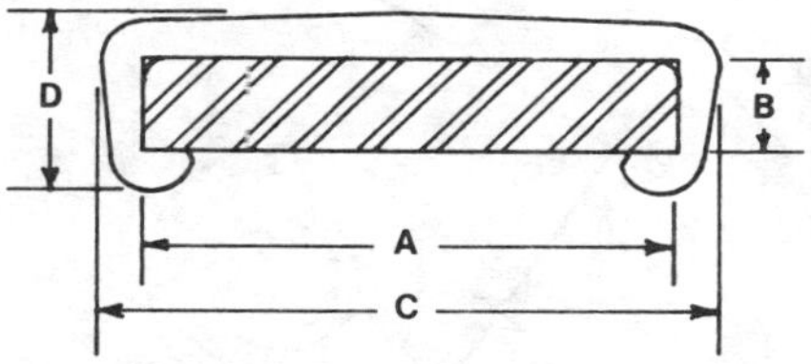

Fig. 17

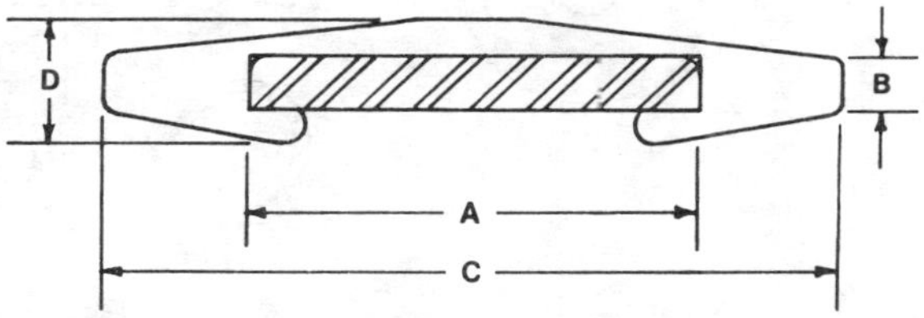

Fig. 18

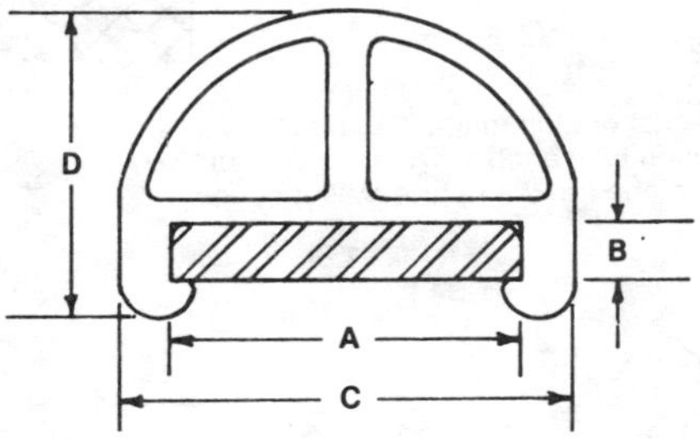

Fig. 19

TABLE 4 Table of Dimensions for Plastic Handrail Coverings

	A	B	C	D
Fig.	Inside width	Inside height	Outside width	Outside height
16	1" 1¼" 1½"	½"	1⁵⁄₁₆" 1⁹⁄₁₆" 1¹³⁄₁₆"	1³⁄₁₆"
17	1¼" 1½" 2"	¼" ¼" ⅜"	1⁹⁄₁₆" 1¹³⁄₁₆" 2⁵⁄₁₆"	³⁄₁₆" ³⁄₁₆" ¹¹⁄₁₆"
18	1½" 2"	¼"	2¾" 3¼"	½" ⁹⁄₁₆"
19	1¼" 1½"	¼"	1⅝" 1⅞"	1³⁄₁₆" 1⁵⁄₁₆"

Caution: Consult manufacturers for fabrication limitations.

General Information

Functional and decorative plastic handrail mouldings of polyvinyl chloride plastics are available in a variety of sizes and profiles, several of which are illustrated in Figs. 16 to 19. Consult suppliers' current literature for variations in details and features.

Plastic handrail mouldings are not structural and require bar, tube, or channel members to support vertical and horizontal loads.

Plastic handrail mouldings are produced in a range of colors from subdued to bright, to suit either formal or informal design situations. The color is integral with the plastic, which is highly resistant to wear, weathering, and corrosion.

The thermoplastic material becomes pliable when heated (not over 165°F), at which time it can be fitted over the support member and conforms to vertical, horizontal, or combined vertical and horizontal curves within certain limitations.

Lateral bends should have a minimum centerline radius of not less than 2 times the width of the plastic section or 2½ to 3 times the width of the support section, whichever is greater. Mitered corners should be used if sharper turns are required.

Combined vertical and horizontal turns can be formed by twisting the moulding.

The material can be joined by thermal welding, and end caps can be shaped using a knife, a file, or abrasives.

The use of a cleaning solution for removing grease and foreign material is recommended, after which a solvent is used for polishing or removing abrasive scratches. Normal cleaning requires only soap and water.

STAIRS

Wall Handrail Brackets

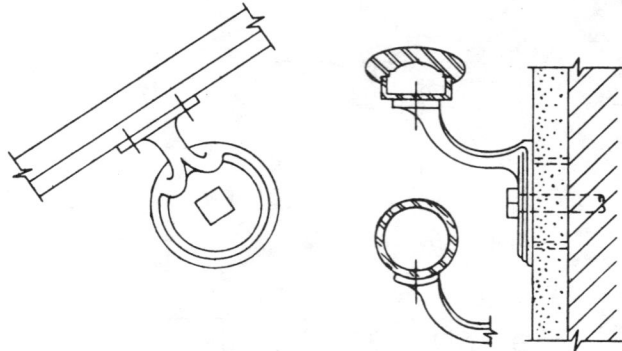

Wall rail bracket of conventional cast design, malleable iron, aluminum or bronze. 3/8″ bolt into wall.

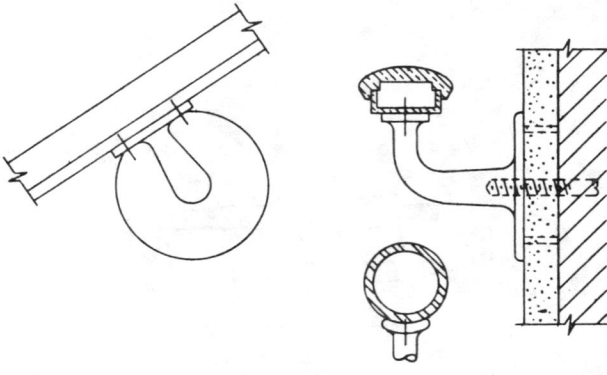

Wall rail bracket of conventional cast design, malleable iron, aluminum or bronze, 3/8″ stud into wall, tapped into arm of bracket.

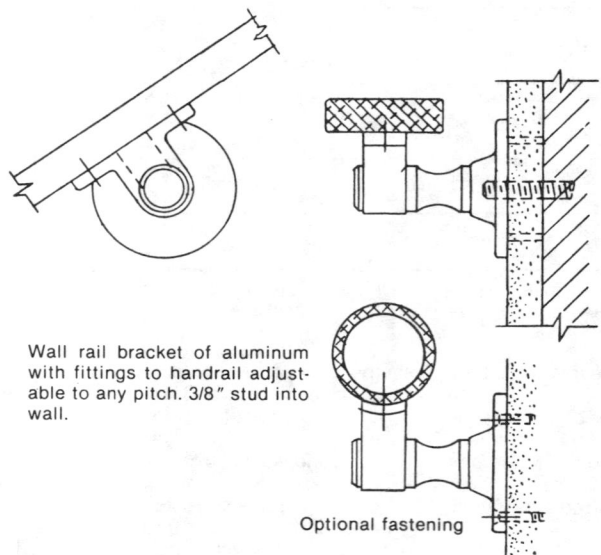

Wall rail bracket of aluminum with fittings to handrail adjustable to any pitch. 3/8″ stud into wall.

Optional fastening

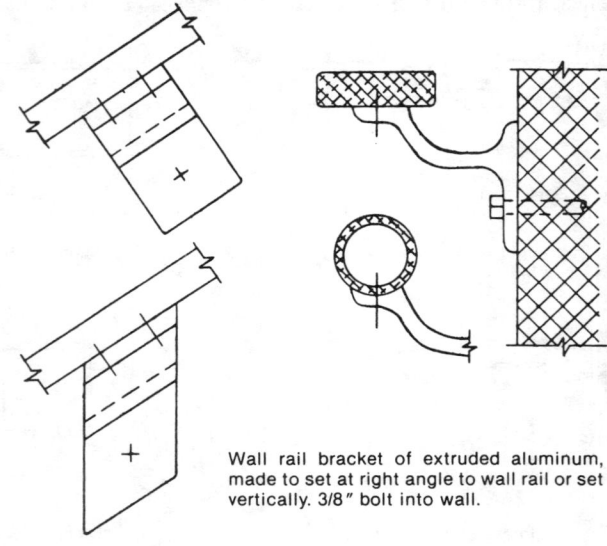

Wall rail bracket of extruded aluminum, made to set at right angle to wall rail or set vertically. 3/8″ bolt into wall.

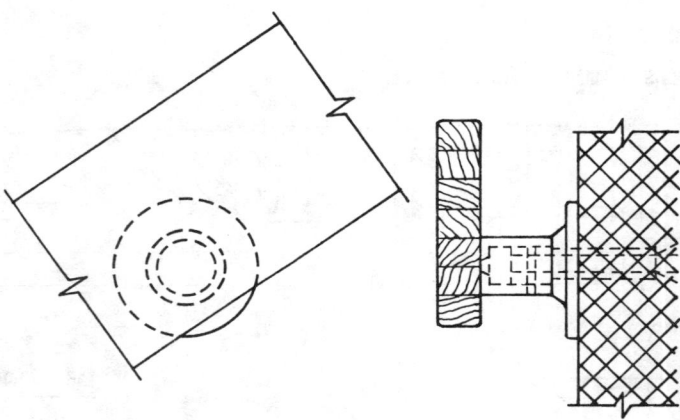

Two-piece wall rail bracket of aluminum. Wall plate bolted into wall through expansion type anchor. Outer sleeve screwed to rail. Outer sleeve fastened to wall plate by set screw.

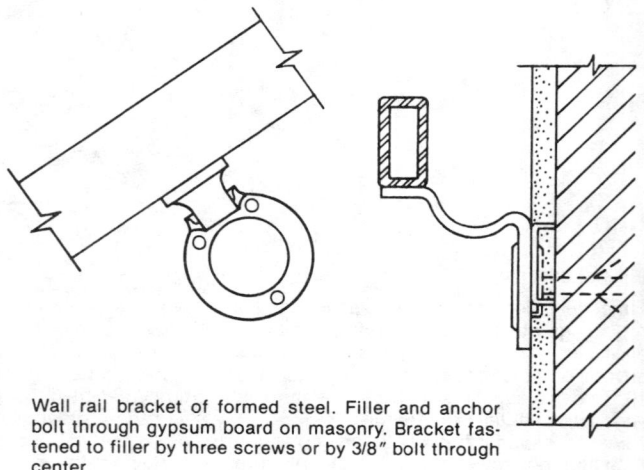

Wall rail bracket of formed steel. Filler and anchor bolt through gypsum board on masonry. Bracket fastened to filler by three screws or by 3/8″ bolt through center.

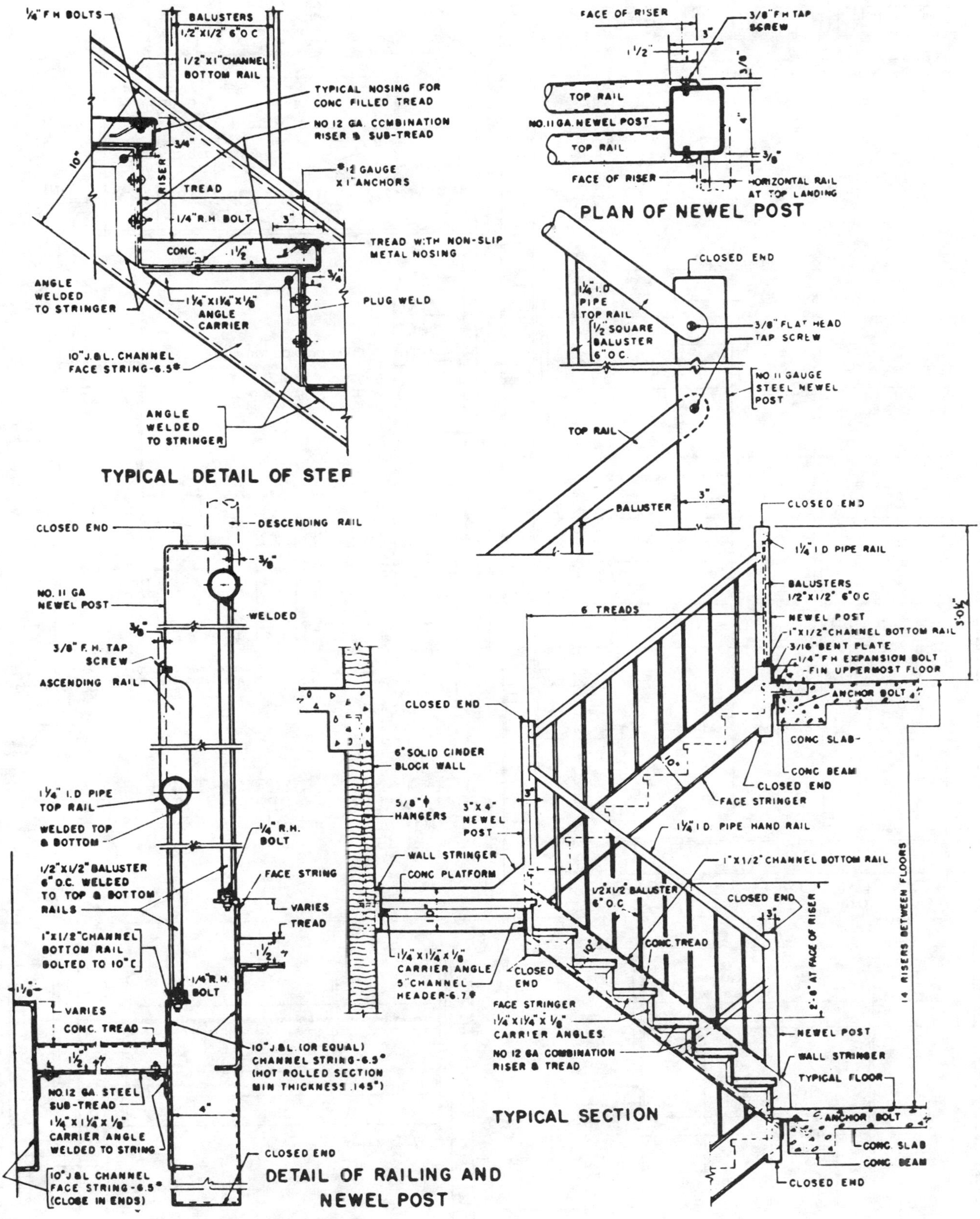
¼" F.H BOLTS
BALUSTERS
1/2"X1/2" 6"O.C
1/2"X1"CHANNEL
BOTTOM RAIL
TYPICAL NOSING FOR
CONC FILLED TREAD
NO 12 GA. COMBINATION
RISER & SUB-TREAD
3/4"
RISER
TREAD
#12 GAUGE
X 1" ANCHORS
1/4" R.H BOLT
3"
10"
CONC.
1½
TREAD WITH NON-SLIP
METAL NOSING
3/4"
ANGLE
WELDED
TO STRINGER
1¼"X1¼"X⅛"
ANGLE
CARRIER
PLUG WELD
10" J.&L. CHANNEL
FACE STRING-6.5#
ANGLE
WELDED
TO STRINGER
TYPICAL DETAIL OF STEP
FACE OF RISER
3/8" F.H TAP
SCREW
3"
1½"
3/8"
TOP RAIL
NO.11 GA. NEWEL POST
4"
TOP RAIL
3/8"
FACE OF RISER
HORIZONTAL RAIL
AT TOP LANDING
PLAN OF NEWEL POST
CLOSED END
1¼" I.D
PIPE
TOP RAIL
½" SQUARE
BALUSTER
6" O.C.
3/8" FLAT HEAD
TAP SCREW
NO 11 GAUGE
STEEL NEWEL
POST
TOP RAIL
3"
BALUSTER
CLOSED END
DESCENDING RAIL
3/8"
NO. 11 GA
NEWEL POST
WELDED
3/8"
3/8" F. H. TAP
SCREW
ASCENDING RAIL
1¼" I.D PIPE
TOP RAIL
WELDED TOP
& BOTTOM
¼" R.H.
BOLT
1/2"X1/2" BALUSTER
6" O.C. WELDED
TO TOP & BOTTOM
RAILS
FACE STRING
VARIES
TREAD
1"X1/2" CHANNEL
BOTTOM RAIL
BOLTED TO 10"[
1½
1/4" R.H.
BOLT
1⅛"
VARIES
CONC. TREAD
1½
NO.12 GA. STEEL
SUB-TREAD
1¼"X1¼"X⅛"
CARRIER ANGLE
WELDED TO STRING
10" J.&L. (OR EQUAL)
CHANNEL STRING-6.5#
(HOT ROLLED SECTION
MIN THICKNESS .145")
4"
10" J.&L. CHANNEL
FACE STRING-6.5#
(CLOSE IN ENDS)
CLOSED END
DETAIL OF RAILING AND
NEWEL POST
6" SOLID CINDER
BLOCK WALL
5/8"φ
HANGERS
3"X4"
NEWEL
POST
CLOSED END
3"
WALL STRINGER
CONC PLATFORM
1¼"X1¼"X⅛"
CARRIER ANGLE
5" CHANNEL
HEADER-6.7#
CLOSED
END
FACE STRINGER
1¼"X1¼"X⅛"
CARRIER ANGLES
NO 12 GA COMBINATION
RISER & TREAD
CLOSED END
1¼" I.D PIPE RAIL
6 TREADS
BALUSTERS
1/2"X1/2" 6"O.C
NEWEL POST
1"X1/2" CHANNEL BOTTOM RAIL
3/16" BENT PLATE
1/4" F.H EXPANSION BOLT
-FIN UPPERMOST FLOOR
3'-0½"
ANCHOR BOLT
CONC SLAB
CONC BEAM
CLOSED END
FACE STRINGER
10"
1¼" I.D. PIPE HAND RAIL
1"X1/2" CHANNEL BOTTOM RAIL
1/2X1/2 BALUSTER
6" O.C
CLOSED END
3"
CONC. TREAD
2'-6" AT FACE OF RISER
14 RISERS BETWEEN FLOORS
NEWEL POST
WALL STRINGER
TYPICAL FLOOR
ANCHOR BOLT
CONC. SLAB
CONC. BEAM
CLOSED END
TYPICAL SECTION

Typical steel stair construction

STAIRS
Steel Stairs

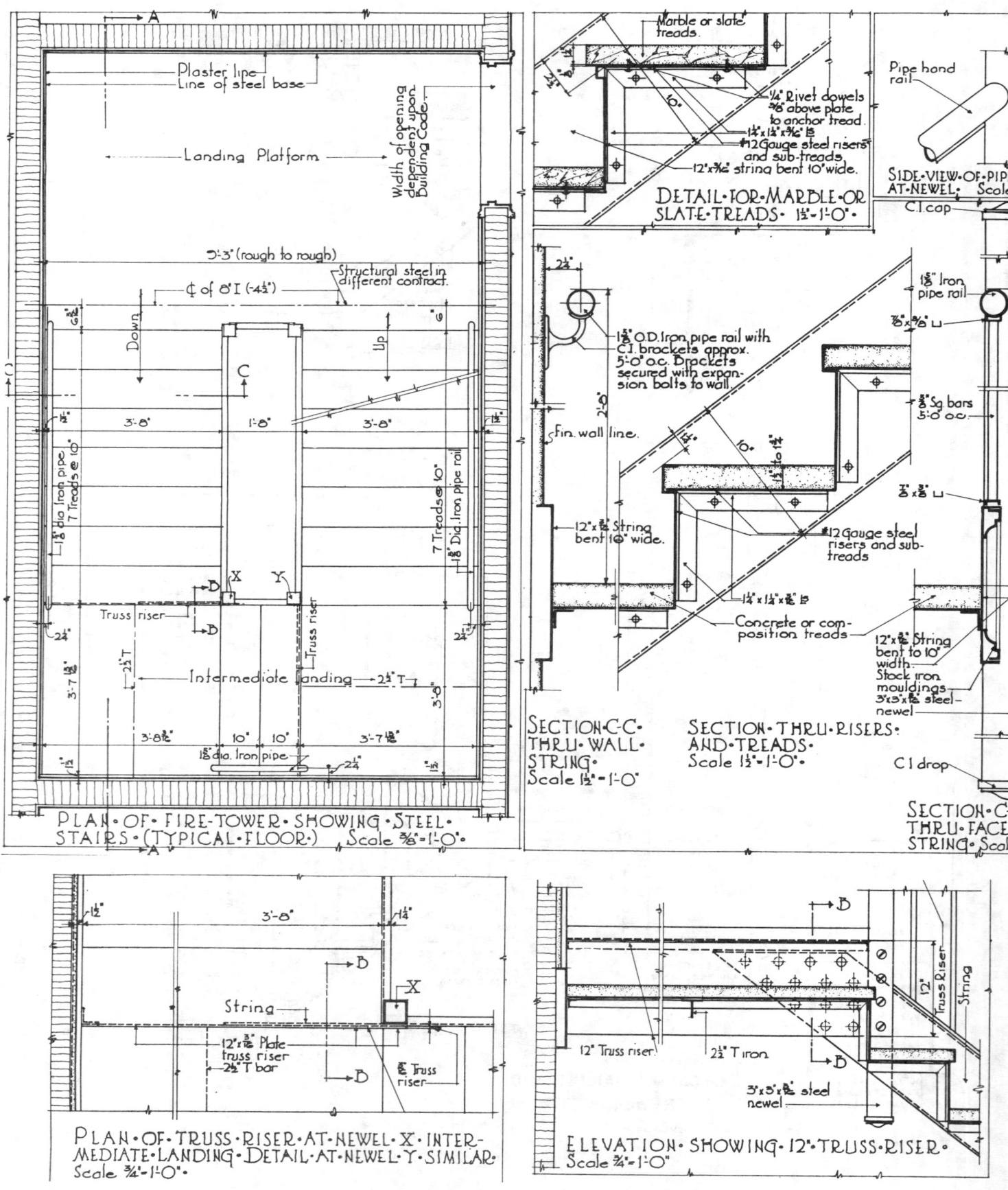

PLAN·OF·FIRE-TOWER·SHOWING·STEEL·
STAIRS·(TYPICAL·FLOOR·)   Scale ⅜"=1'-0"·

DETAIL·FOR·MARBLE·OR
SLATE·TREADS·1½"=1'-0"·

SIDE·VIEW·OF·PIPE·
AT·NEWEL· Scale 1

SECTION·C-C·
THRU·WALL·
STRING·
Scale 1½"=1'-0"·

SECTION·THRU·RISERS·
AND·TREADS·
Scale 1½"=1'-0"·

SECTION·C-C
THRU·FACE·
STRING· Scale

PLAN·OF·TRUSS·RISER·AT·NEWEL·X·INTER-
MEDIATE·LANDING·DETAIL·AT·NEWEL·Y·SIMILAR·
Scale ¾"=1'-0"

ELEVATION·SHOWING·12"·TRUSS·RISER·
Scale ¾"=1'-0"

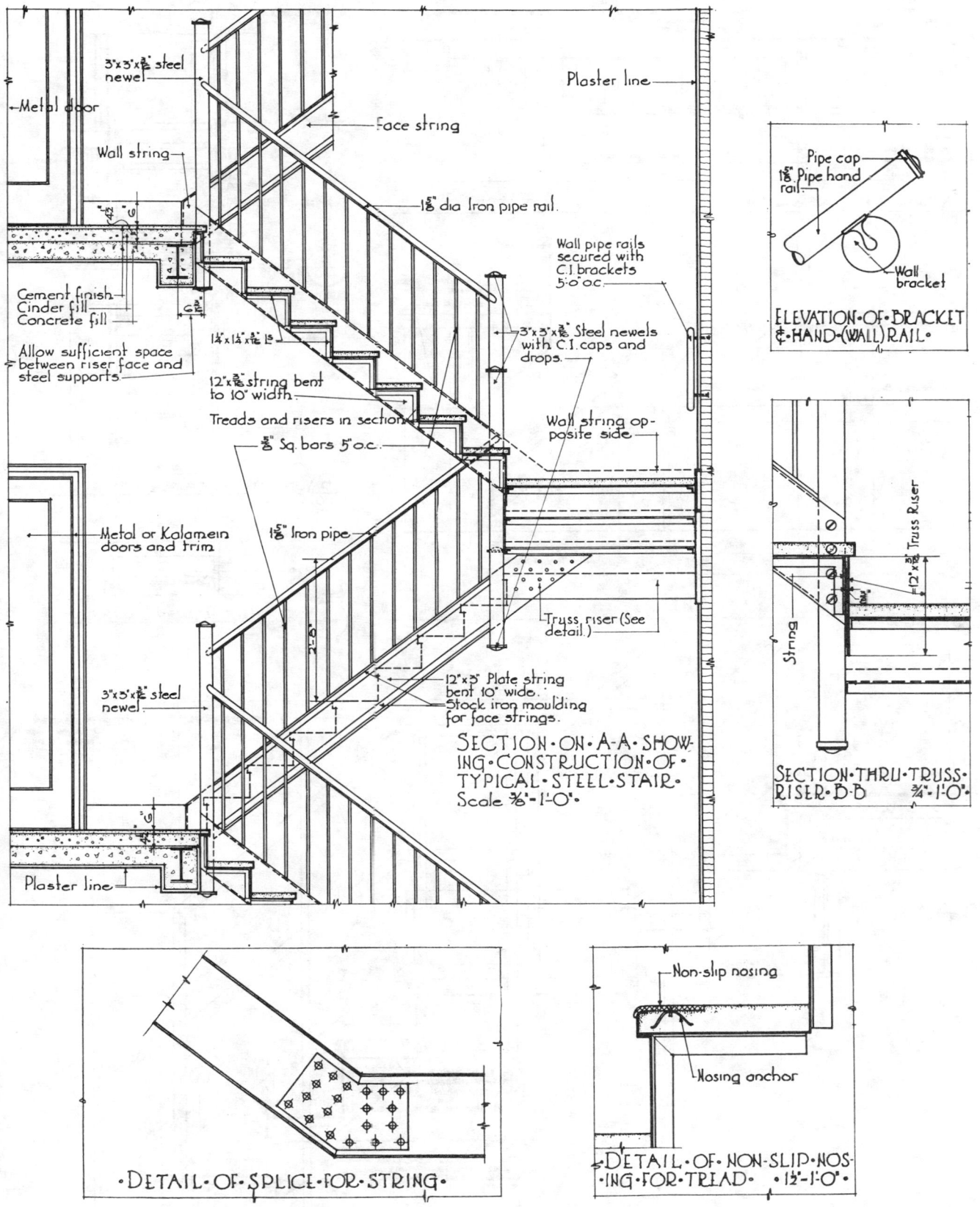

3"x3"x⅜" steel newel

Metal door

Wall string

Cement finish
Cinder fill
Concrete fill

Allow sufficient space between riser face and steel supports

Metal or Kalamein doors and trim

3"x3"x⅜" steel newel

Plaster line

Face string

Plaster line

1⅝" dia Iron pipe rail.

Wall pipe rails secured with C.I. brackets 5'-0" o.c.

3"x3"x⅜" Steel newels with C.I. caps and drops.

Wall string opposite side

1¼"x1¼"x⅜"x1⅝"

12"x⅜" string bent to 10" width

Treads and risers in section

⅝" Sq. bars 5" o.c.

1⅝" Iron pipe

2'-0"

12"x⅜" Plate string bent 10" wide.
Stock iron moulding for face strings.

Truss riser (See detail.)

·SECTION·ON·A-A·SHOW-
ING·CONSTRUCTION·OF·
TYPICAL·STEEL·STAIR·
Scale ⅜"=1'-0".

Pipe cap
1⅝" Pipe hand rail

Wall bracket

·ELEVATION·OF·BRACKET·
& HAND·(WALL)·RAIL·

12"x⅜" Truss Riser

String

SECTION·THRU·TRUSS·
RISER·B-B   ¾"=1'-0"

·DETAIL·OF·SPLICE·FOR·STRING·

Non-slip nosing

Nosing anchor

·DETAIL·OF·NON·SLIP·NOS-
ING·FOR·TREAD·   1½"=1'-0"

STAIRS

Steel Stairs

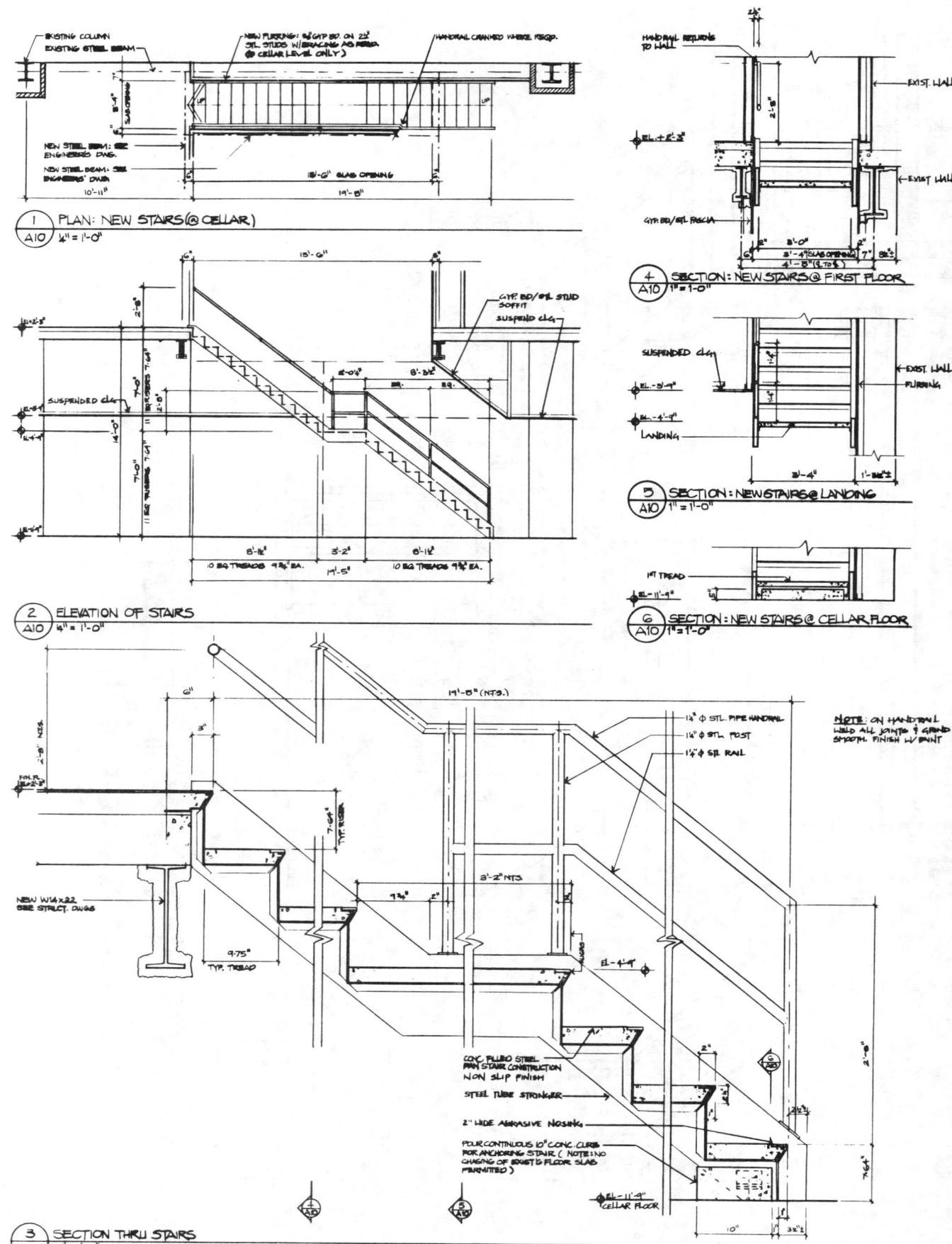

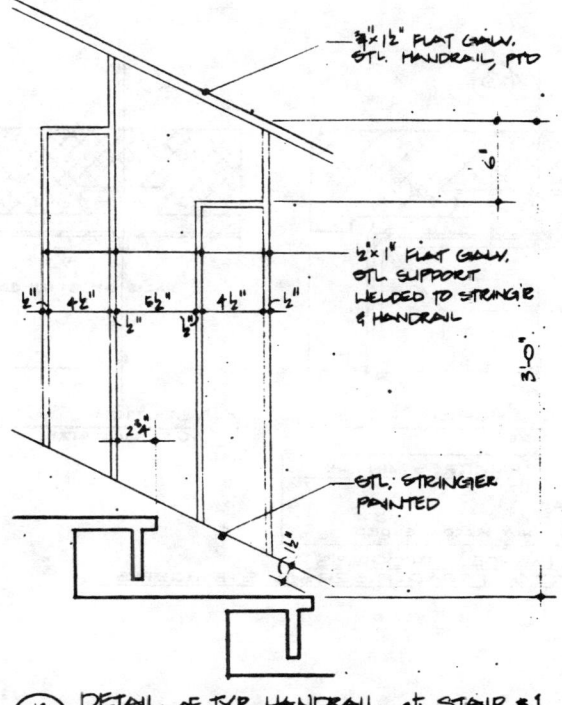

¾"×½" FLAT GALV. STL. HANDRAIL, PT'D

½"×1" FLAT GALV. STL. SUPPORT WELDED TO STRINGER & HANDRAIL

STL. STRINGER PAINTED

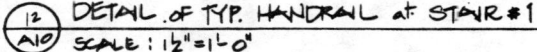

⑫ DETAIL OF TYP. HANDRAIL at STAIR #1
Ⓐ10 SCALE: 1½"=1'-0"

GALV. STL PIPE RAILING, 1½"Ø PAINTED, COLOR#A

GALV. STL PIPE RAILING, 1"Ø PAINTED, COLOR#A

VERT. POST WELDED TO STRINGER

STL. STRINGER W. CLADDING PT'D COLOR #A

NOTE: VERTICAL POST AT DINING & 105 PLATFORM (SHOWN DOTTED)

⑬ DETAIL OF HANDRAIL at STAIR #2
Ⓐ10 SCALE: 1½"=1'-0"

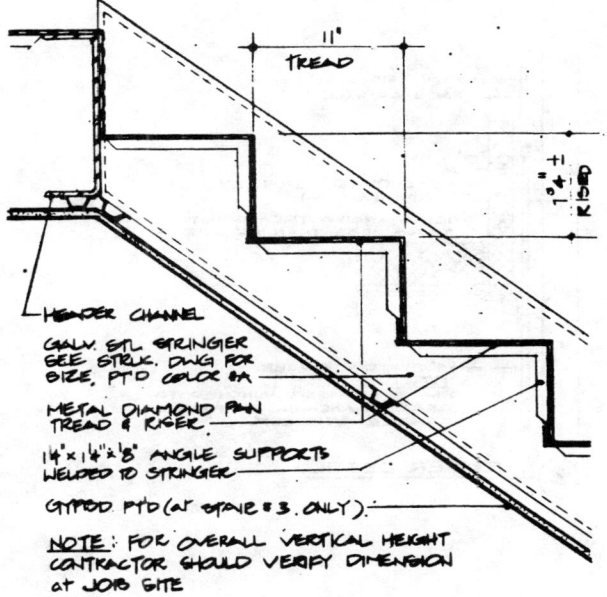

HEADER CHANNEL

GALV. STL. STRINGER SEE STRUC. DWG FOR SIZE, PT'D COLOR #A

METAL DIAMOND PAN TREAD & RISER

1½"×1½"×⅛" ANGLE SUPPORTS WELDED TO STRINGER

GYP'BD. PT'D (at STAIR #3. ONLY)

NOTE: FOR OVERALL VERTICAL HEIGHT CONTRACTOR SHOULD VERIFY DIMENSION at JOB SITE

⑰ DETAIL OF TREAD & RISER at STAIRS #3 & #5
Ⓐ10 SCALE: 1½"=1'-0"

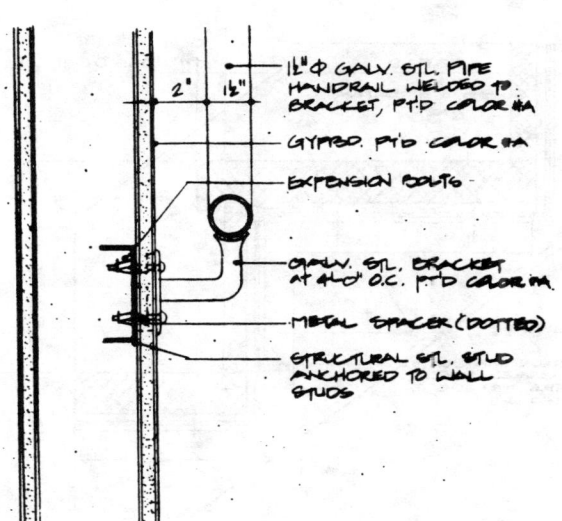

1½"Ø GALV. STL. PIPE HANDRAIL WELDED TO BRACKET, PT'D COLOR #A

GYP'BD. PT'D COLOR #A

EXPANSION BOLTS

GALV. STL. BRACKET AT 4'-0" O.C. PT'D COLOR #A

METAL SPACER (DOTTED)

STRUCTURAL STL. STUD ANCHORED TO WALL STUDS

⑱ DETAIL OF HANDRAIL at STAIRS #3 & #5
Ⓐ10 SCALE: 3"=1'-0"

STAIRS
Steel Stairs

STEEL STAIRS WITH TERRAZZO TREADS

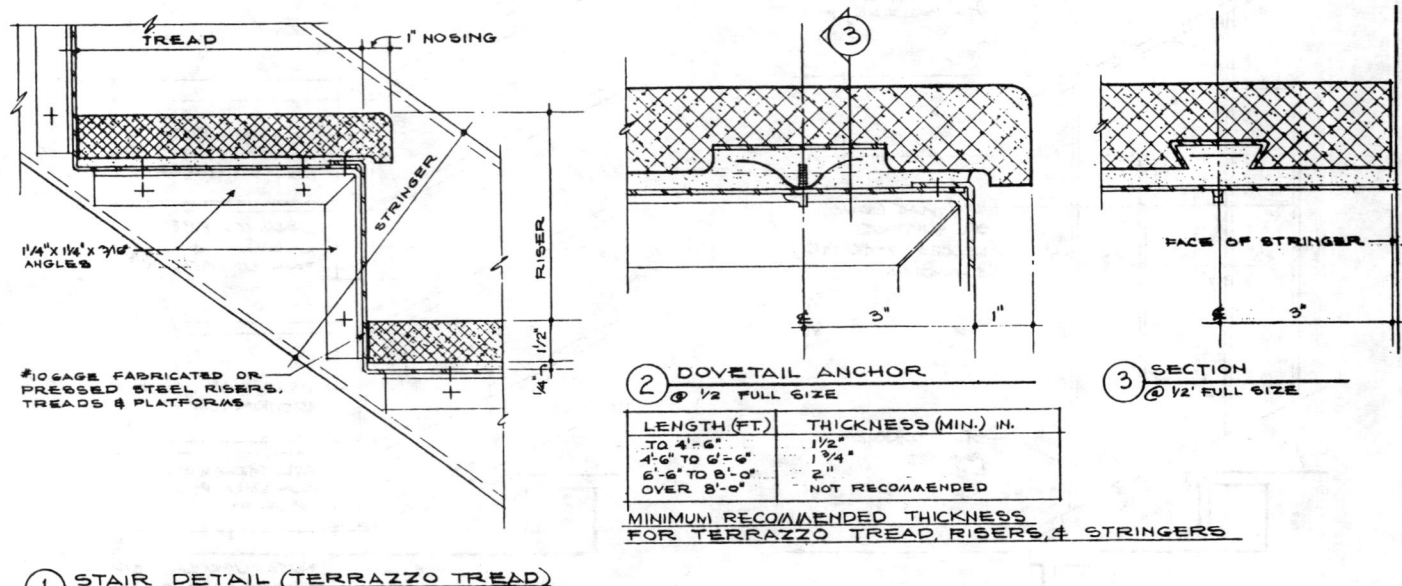

TREAD

1" NOSING

STRINGER

RISER

1¼" X 1¼" X ⅜" ANGLES

#10 GAGE FABRICATED OR PRESSED STEEL RISERS, TREADS & PLATFORMS

¼" 1½"

① STAIR DETAIL (TERRAZZO TREAD)
@ 3" = 1'-0"

③

FACE OF STRINGER

3" 1"

② DOVETAIL ANCHOR
@ ½ FULL SIZE

③ SECTION
@ ½ FULL SIZE

LENGTH (FT.)	THICKNESS (MIN.) IN.
TO 4'-6"	1½"
4'-6" TO 6'-6"	1¾"
6'-6" TO 8'-0"	2"
OVER 8'-0"	NOT RECOMMENDED

MINIMUM RECOMMENDED THICKNESS FOR TERRAZZO TREAD, RISERS, & STRINGERS

STEEL STAIRS WITH TERRAZZO TREADS AND RISERS

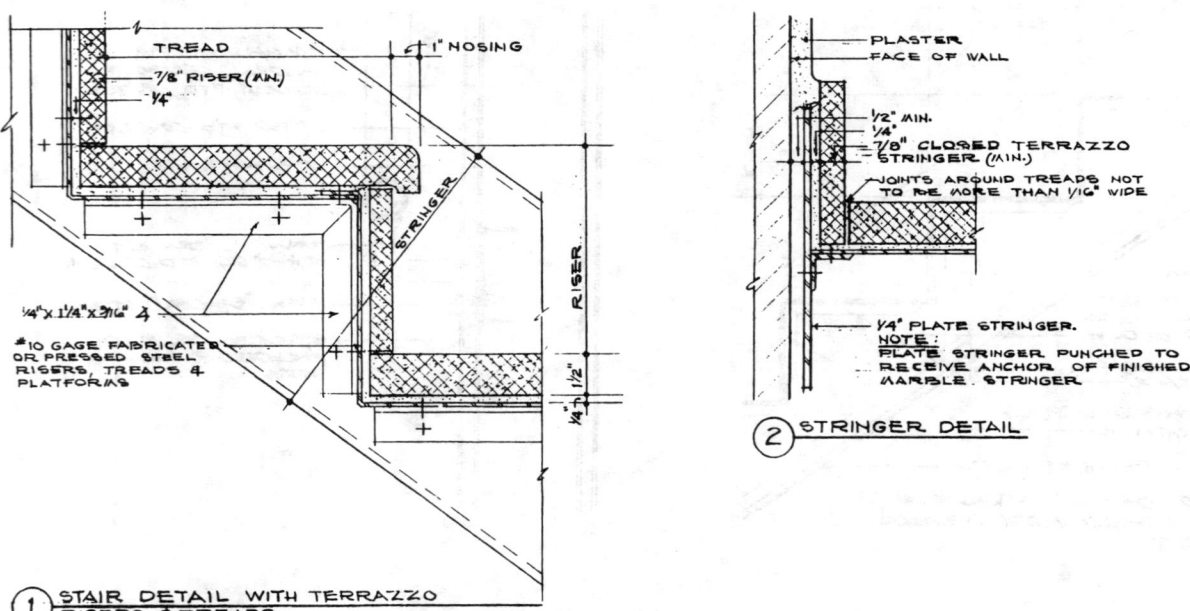

TREAD

1" NOSING

⅞" RISER (MIN.)

¼"

STRINGER

RISER

¼" X 1¼" X ⅜" 4

#10 GAGE FABRICATED OR PRESSED STEEL RISERS, TREADS & PLATFORMS

¼" 1½"

① STAIR DETAIL WITH TERRAZZO RISERS & TREADS

PLASTER
FACE OF WALL

½" MIN.
¼"
⅞" CLOSED TERRAZZO STRINGER (MIN.)

JOINTS AROUND TREADS NOT TO BE MORE THAN 1/16" WIDE

¼" PLATE STRINGER.
NOTE:
PLATE STRINGER PUNCHED TO RECEIVE ANCHOR OF FINISHED MARBLE STRINGER

② STRINGER DETAIL

Construction

Material may be steel, stainless steel, cast iron, or aluminum. Treads are supported in cantilever fashion by the column, each consecutive tread being rotated at a predetermined angle. The platform attaches to the column and is fastened to the floor structure to hold the column secure. The spiral railing is supported by balusters attached to the outer ends of the treads.

Tread Designs

Fabricators provide several standard types and designs of treads and platforms. These include open riser, closed riser, and cantilever types, with surface of checkered plate, abrasive plate, steel grating, or plain surface to receive wood, resilient flooring, carpet, or other covering. Pan type treads to receive concrete or terrazzo fill are also available.

Stair Height

Spiral stairs are adaptable to any height, the height being equal to the distance from finished floor to finished floor.

Stair Diameter

Spiral stairs are available in various diameters from 3'6" to 8'0", normally in 6" increments. A 4'0" diameter is considered minimum for general access purposes; a 5'0" diameter provides a comfortable general purpose stair. Larger diameters are used chiefly for architectural effect. Note that the diameter of the finished well opening should be at least 2" greater than the stair diameter, to provide hand clearance.

Hand of Stairs

Left-hand stairs: User ascends in clockwise direction, with handrail at left.

Right-hand stairs: User ascends in counterclockwise direction, with handrail at right.

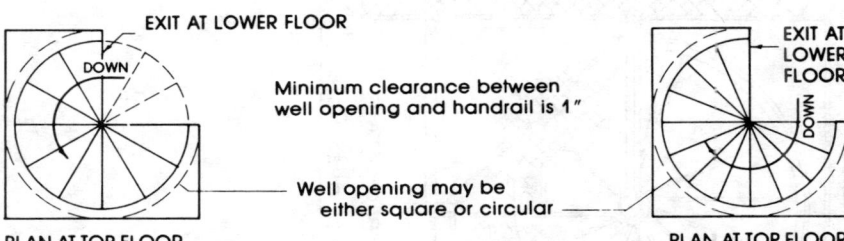

EXIT AT LOWER FLOOR

DOWN

Minimum clearance between well opening and handrail is 1"

Well opening may be either square or circular

EXIT AT LOWER FLOOR

DOWN

PLAN AT TOP FLOOR
Left Hand, 30°. Full Circle

PLAN AT TOP FLOOR
Right Hand, 22½°, ¾ Circle

Fig. 20

TABLE 5 Riser Heights for Various Tread Angles

Tread angle	Min. height of riser*	Treads per ¾ circle	Treads per full circle
30°	8¹⁵⁄₁₆"	9	12
27°	8"	10	13 = 351°
24½°	7⁵⁄₁₆"	11	15 = 367½°
22½°	6¹¹⁄₁₆"	12	16

*Minimum height to attain 6'6" clear headroom using a 90° landing, 2" thick.

TABLE 6 Chart for Selection of Number and Height of Risers

Floor to floor height	Number of risers and height of each in inches								
	10	11	12	13	14	15	16	17	18
7'0"	8.4	7.6	7.0						
7'4"	8.8	8.0	7.3	6.8					
7'8"	9.2	8.4	7.7	7.0					
8'0"	9.6	8.7	8.0	7.4	6.9				
8'2"	9.8	8.9	8.2	7.5	7.0				
8'4"		9.1	8.3	7.7	7.1	6.7			
8'6"		9.3	8.5	7.8	7.3	6.8			
8'8"		9.4	8.7	8.0	7.4	6.9			
8'10"			8.8	8.2	7.6	7.1	6.6		
9'0"			9.0	8.3	7.7	7.2	6.7		
9'2"			9.2	8.5	7.9	7.3	6.9		
9'4"			9.3	8.6	8.0	7.5	7.0		
9'6"				8.8	8.1	7.6	7.1	6.7	
9'8"				9.0	8.3	7.7	7.2	6.8	
9'10"				9.2	8.4	7.9	7.4	6.9	
10'0"				9.3	8.6	8.0	7.5	7.0	6.7
10'2"					8.7	8.1	7.6	7.2	6.8
10'4"					8.9	8.3	7.7	7.3	6.9
10'6"					9.0	8.4	7.9	7.4	7.0
10'8"					9.1	8.5	8.0	7.5	7.1
10'10"						8.6	8.1	7.6	7.2
11'0"						8.7	8.2	7.8	7.3
11'2"						8.9	8.4	7.9	7.4
11'4"						9.0	8.5	8.0	7.6
11'6"							8.6	8.1	7.7
11'8"							8.7	8.2	7.8
12'0"							9.0	8.5	8.0

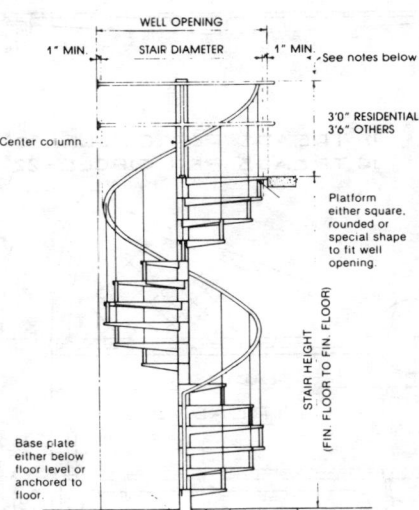

WELL OPENING

1" MIN   STAIR DIAMETER   1" MIN
See notes below

Center column

3'0" RESIDENTIAL
3'6" OTHERS

Platform either square, rounded or special shape to fit well opening.

STAIR HEIGHT
(FIN. FLOOR TO FIN. FLOOR)

Base plate either below floor level or anchored to floor.

TYPICAL ELEVATION — RIGHT HAND OPEN RISER STAIR

STAIRS
Spiral Stairs

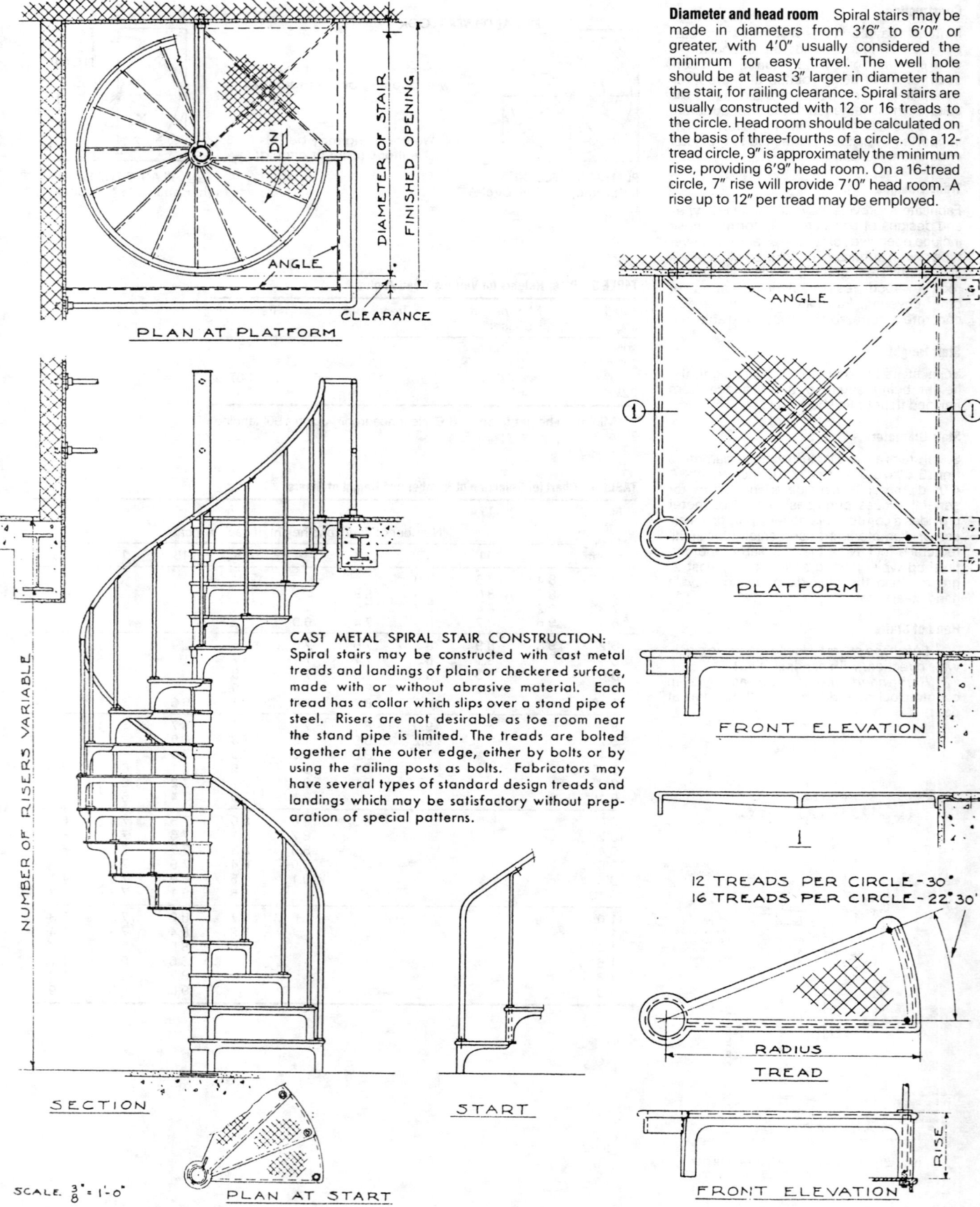

PLAN AT PLATFORM

Diameter and head room   Spiral stairs may be made in diameters from 3'6" to 6'0" or greater, with 4'0" usually considered the minimum for easy travel. The well hole should be at least 3" larger in diameter than the stair, for railing clearance. Spiral stairs are usually constructed with 12 or 16 treads to the circle. Head room should be calculated on the basis of three-fourths of a circle. On a 12-tread circle, 9" is approximately the minimum rise, providing 6'9" head room. On a 16-tread circle, 7" rise will provide 7'0" head room. A rise up to 12" per tread may be employed.

PLATFORM

FRONT ELEVATION

I

12 TREADS PER CIRCLE - 30°
16 TREADS PER CIRCLE - 22° 30'

RADIUS

TREAD

FRONT ELEVATION

RISE

CAST METAL SPIRAL STAIR CONSTRUCTION:
Spiral stairs may be constructed with cast metal treads and landings of plain or checkered surface, made with or without abrasive material. Each tread has a collar which slips over a stand pipe of steel. Risers are not desirable as toe room near the stand pipe is limited. The treads are bolted together at the outer edge, either by bolts or by using the railing posts as bolts. Fabricators may have several types of standard design treads and landings which may be satisfactory without preparation of special patterns.

SECTION

NUMBER OF RISERS VARIABLE

START

PLAN AT START

SCALE. $\frac{3}{8}$" = 1'-0"

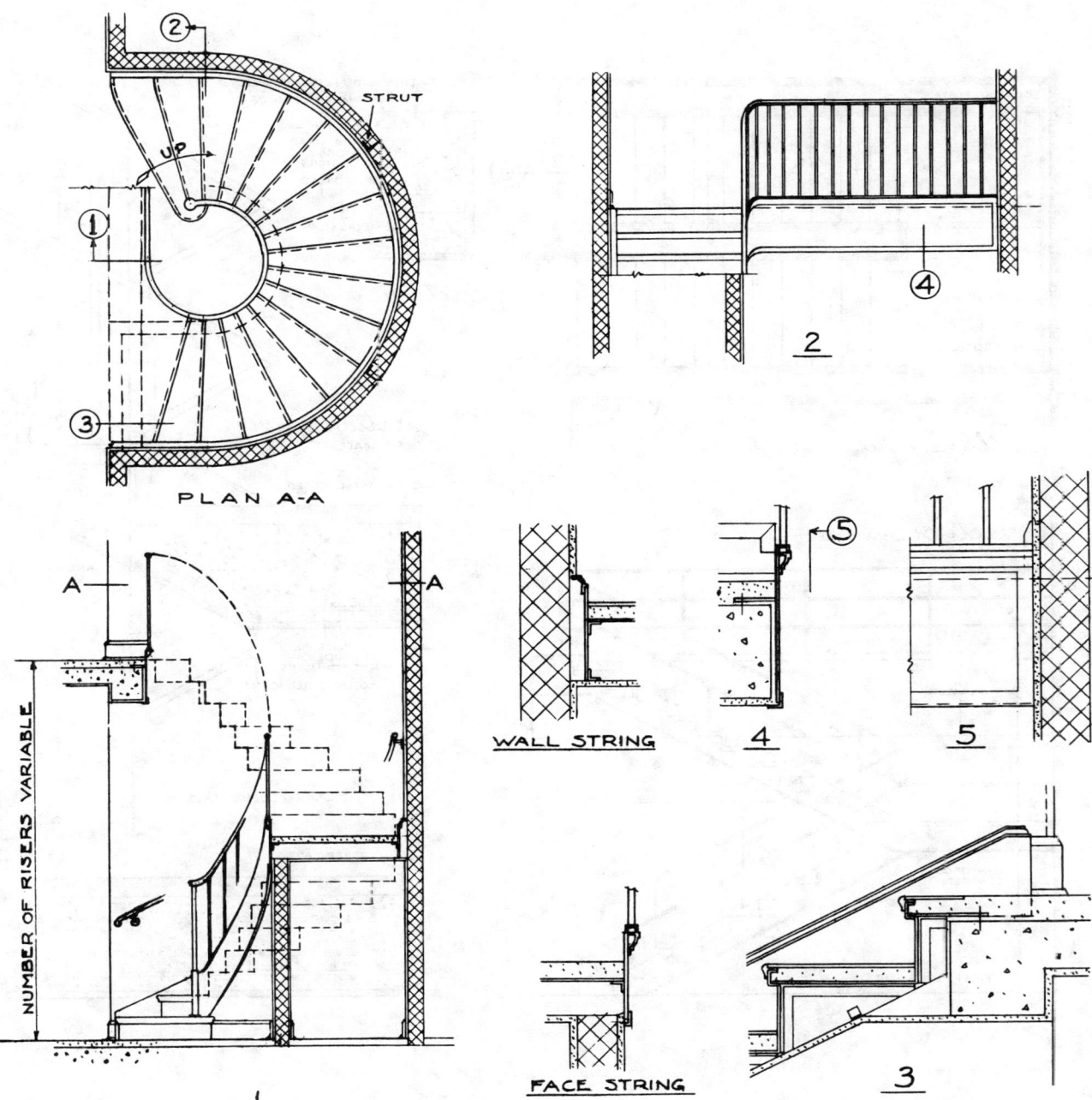

PLAN A-A

STRUT

UP

NUMBER OF RISERS VARIABLE

1

2

WALL STRING

4

5

FACE STRING

3

Circular stairs placed between walls may be built self-supporting at the inner string and be supported by concealed struts or hangers at the outer string. When completely exposed a circular stair may be designed to require few supports between floors.

In constructing a circular stair the overall size of the well and the tread length of the stairs may be adjusted to fit the particular conditions of the structure. Treads should be a minimum width of 8" at a distance 15" out from the inside railing. The treads may be of steel, abrasive cast iron, abrasive nonferrous metal, cement, tile, linoleum, wood, marble or other material.

Landings and platforms may be constructed as part of the stair, and may be supported by beam or cantilever construction. Wall rails and brackets may be constructed with handrail sections matching the railing.

Face strings and railings may be similar to those used on straight stairs but should be designed of shapes adaptable to abrupt curved construction. The small radius to which these are constructed offers possibilities of design that should not be overlooked. Combinations of contrasting metal colors can be effectively employed in such installations.

STAIRS
Concrete Stairs

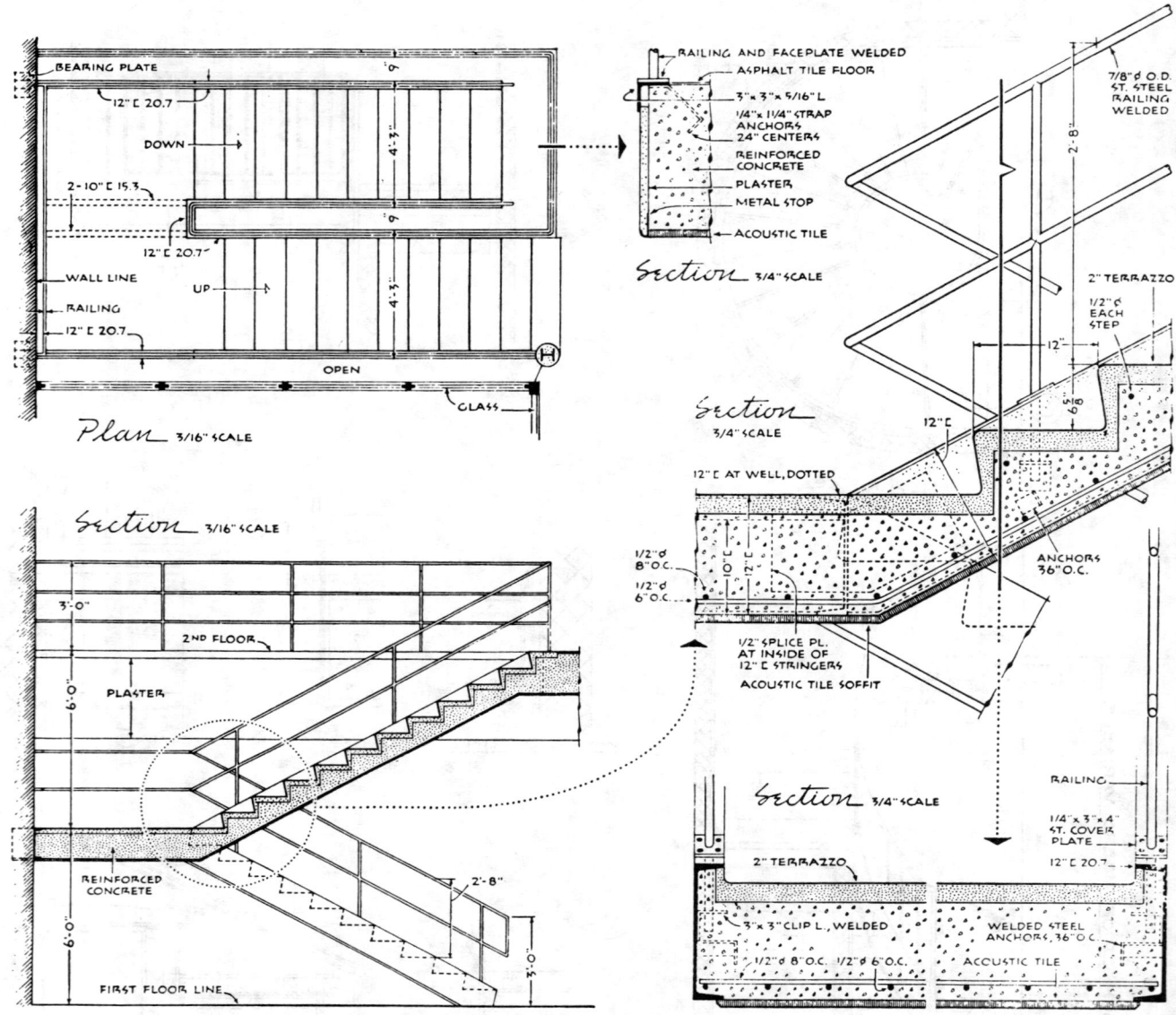

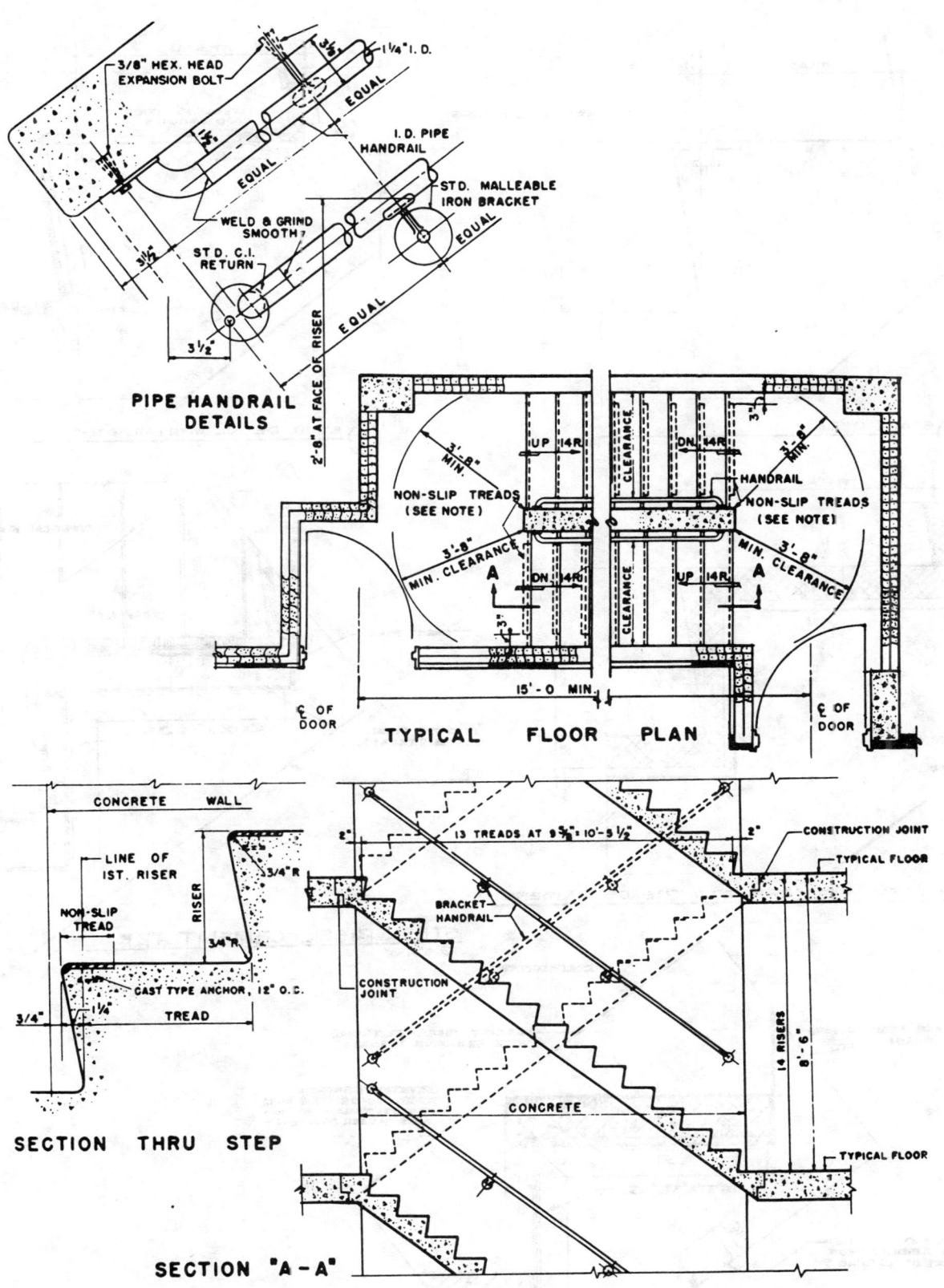

PIPE HANDRAIL DETAILS

3/8" HEX. HEAD EXPANSION BOLT

1¼" I. D.

I. D. PIPE HANDRAIL

STD. MALLEABLE IRON BRACKET

WELD & GRIND SMOOTH

STD. C.I. RETURN

3½

EQUAL

TYPICAL FLOOR PLAN

UP 14R

DN 14R

NON-SLIP TREADS (SEE NOTE)

3'-8" MIN.

3'-8" MIN. CLEARANCE

CLEARANCE

HANDRAIL

DN 14R

UP 14R

A

A

15'-0 MIN.

€ OF DOOR

SECTION THRU STEP

CONCRETE WALL

LINE OF 1ST. RISER

NON-SLIP TREAD

RISER

3/4"R

3/4"R

CAST TYPE ANCHOR, 12" O.C.

3/4"

1¼

TREAD

SECTION "A-A"

13 TREADS AT 9¾"= 10'-5½"

2"

CONSTRUCTION JOINT

TYPICAL FLOOR

BRACKET HANDRAIL

CONSTRUCTION JOINT

CONCRETE

14 RISERS

8'-6"

TYPICAL FLOOR

Typical reinforced concrete scissors stair

STAIRS

Concrete, Steel, and Terrazzo Stairs

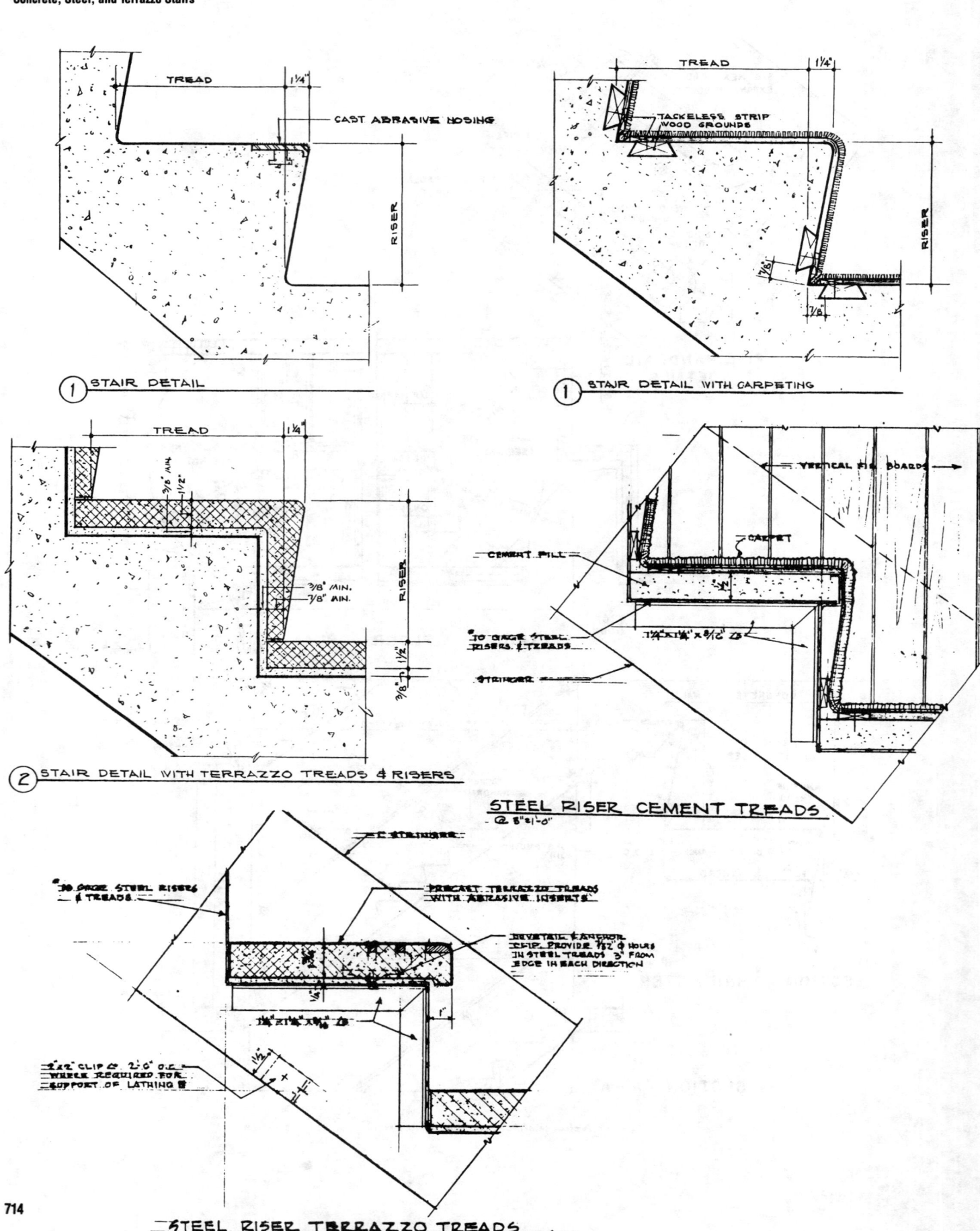

TREAD — 1¼"

CAST ABRASIVE NOSING

RISER

① STAIR DETAIL

TREAD — 1¼"

TACKELESS STRIP
WOOD GROUNDS

⅞"

⅞"

RISER

① STAIR DETAIL WITH CARPETING

TREAD — 1¼"

⅜" MIN.
1½"

⅜" MIN.
⅞" MIN.

RISER

⅜" — 1½"

② STAIR DETAIL WITH TERRAZZO TREADS & RISERS

VERTICAL FIR BOARDS

CARPET

CEMENT FILL

30 GAGE STEEL
RISERS & TREADS

1¼" X 1¼" X 3/16" ∠S

STRINGER

STEEL RISER CEMENT TREADS
@ 8"=1'-0"

C STRINGER

30 GAGE STEEL RISERS
& TREADS

PRECAST TERRAZZO TREADS
WITH ABRASIVE INSERTS

DOVETAIL ANCHOR
CLIP. PROVIDE ½" Ø HOLES
IN STEEL TREADS 3" FROM
EDGE IN EACH DIRECTION

1¼" X 1¼" X 3/16" ∠S

1"

2" X 2" CLIP @ 2'-0" O.C.
WHERE REQUIRED FOR
SUPPORT OF LATHING

STEEL RISER TERRAZZO TREADS
@ 3"=1'-0"

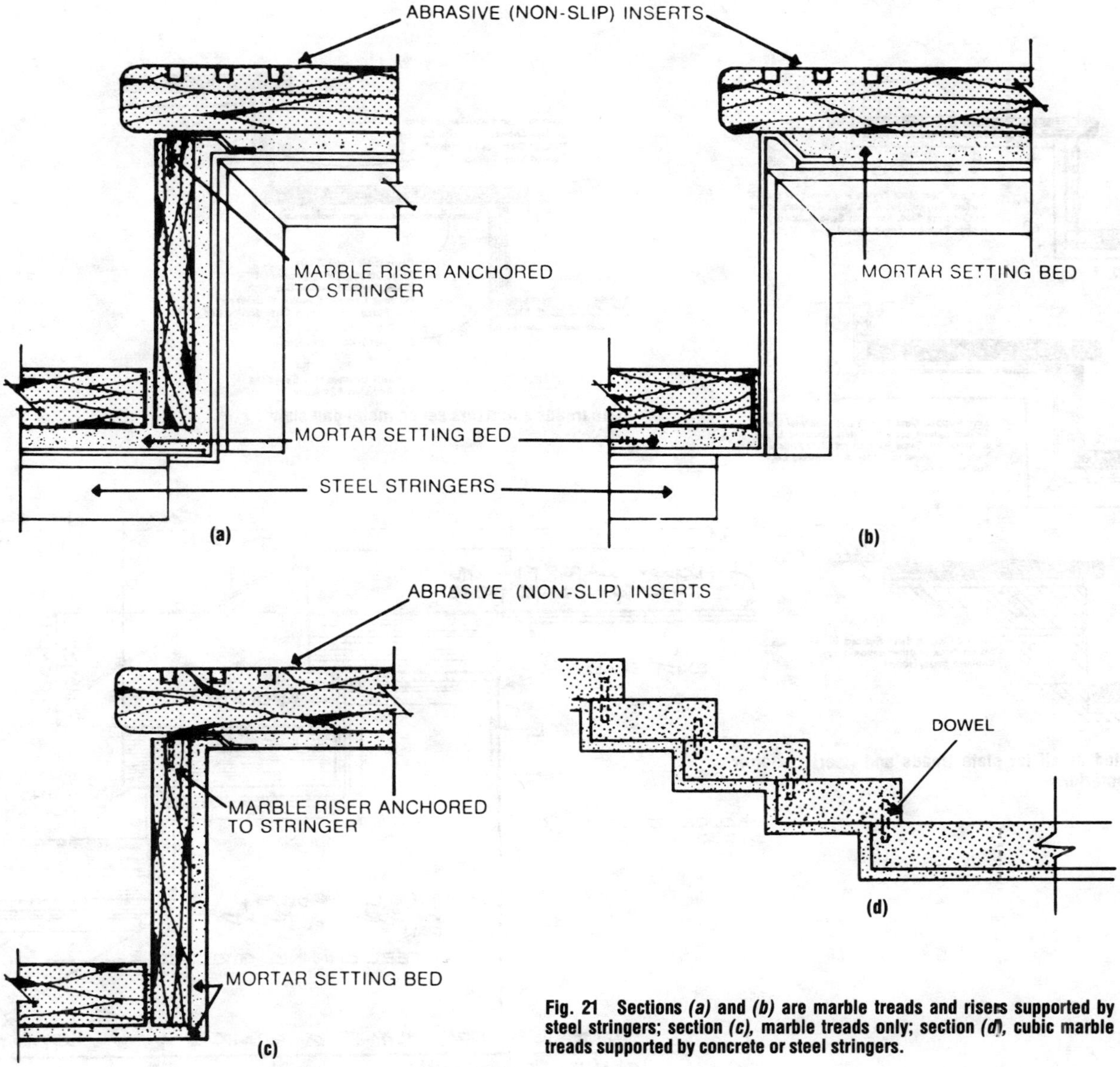

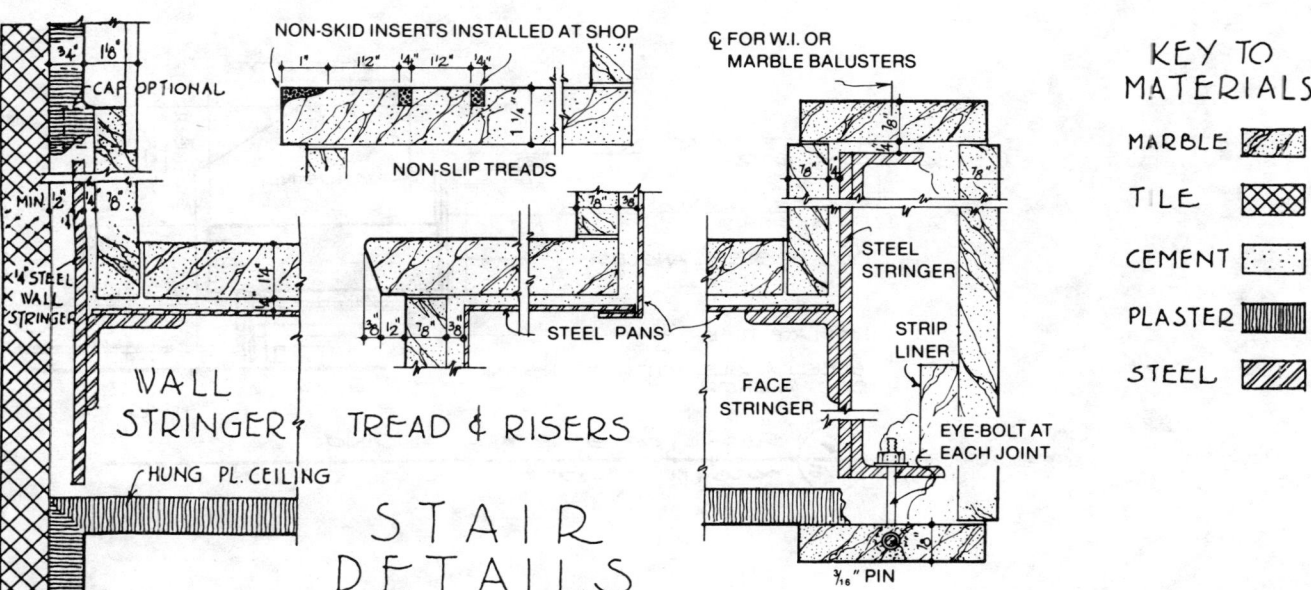

ABRASIVE (NON-SLIP) INSERTS

MARBLE RISER ANCHORED
TO STRINGER

MORTAR SETTING BED

MORTAR SETTING BED

STEEL STRINGERS

(a)

(b)

ABRASIVE (NON-SLIP) INSERTS

MARBLE RISER ANCHORED
TO STRINGER

MORTAR SETTING BED

DOWEL

(c)

(d)

Fig. 21 Sections (a) and (b) are marble treads and risers supported by steel stringers; section (c), marble treads only; section (d), cubic marble treads supported by concrete or steel stringers.

NON-SKID INSERTS INSTALLED AT SHOP

NON-SLIP TREADS

CAP OPTIONAL

MIN

STEEL WALL STRINGER

WALL STRINGER

HUNG PL. CEILING

TREAD & RISERS

STEEL PANS

℄ FOR W.I. OR MARBLE BALUSTERS

STEEL STRINGER

STRIP LINER

FACE STRINGER

EYE-BOLT AT EACH JOINT

PIN

STAIR DETAILS

KEY TO MATERIALS

MARBLE
TILE
CEMENT
PLASTER
STEEL

Fig. 22 Interior marble details.

715

STAIRS

Slate Treads

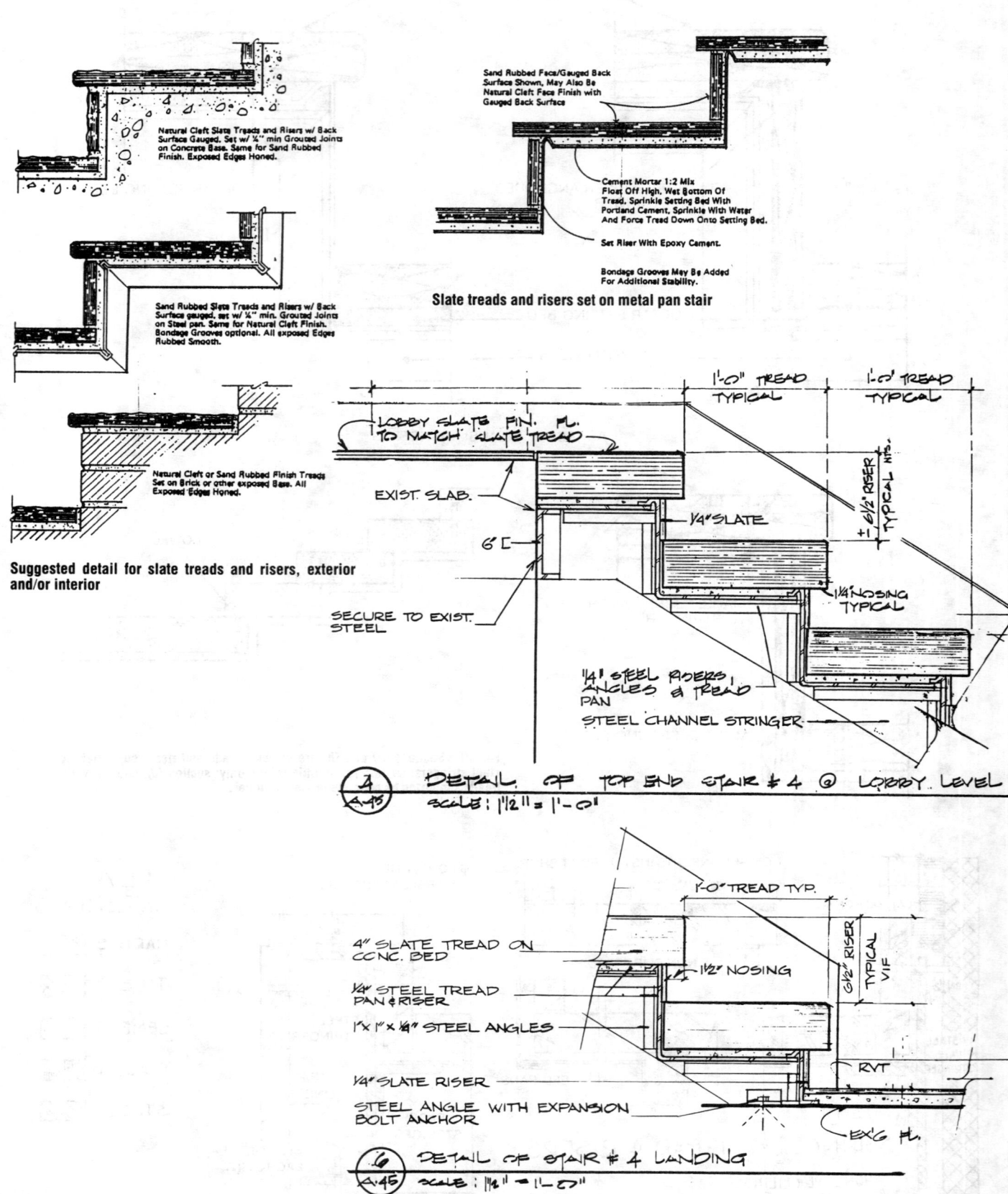

Natural Cleft Slate Treads and Risers w/ Back Surface Gauged. Set w/ ¼" min Grouted Joints on Concrete Base. Same for Sand Rubbed Finish. Exposed Edges Honed.

Sand Rubbed Slate Treads and Risers w/ Back Surface gauged, set w/ ¼" min. Grouted Joints on Steel pan. Same for Natural Cleft Finish. Bondage Grooves optional. All exposed Edges Rubbed Smooth.

Natural Cleft or Sand Rubbed Finish Treads Set on Brick or other exposed Base. All Exposed Edges Honed.

Suggested detail for slate treads and risers, exterior and/or interior

Sand Rubbed Face/Gauged Back Surface Shown. May Also Be Natural Cleft Face Finish with Gauged Back Surface

Cement Mortar 1:2 Mix Float Off High, Wet Bottom Of Tread, Sprinkle Setting Bed With Portland Cement, Sprinkle With Water And Force Tread Down Onto Setting Bed.

Set Riser With Epoxy Cement.

Bondage Grooves May Be Added For Additional Stability.

Slate treads and risers set on metal pan stair

1'-0" TREAD TYPICAL

1'-0" TREAD TYPICAL

6½" RISER TYPICAL HTS.

LOBBY SLATE FIN. FL. TO MATCH SLATE TREAD

EXIST. SLAB.

¼" SLATE

6 C

¼" NOSING TYPICAL

SECURE TO EXIST. STEEL

¼" STEEL RISERS, ANGLES & TREAD PAN

STEEL CHANNEL STRINGER

4 / A·45 DETAIL OF TOP END STAIR #4 @ LOBBY LEVEL
SCALE: 1½" = 1'-0"

1'-0" TREAD TYP.

6½" RISER TYPICAL VIF

4" SLATE TREAD ON CONC. BED

1½" NOSING

¼" STEEL TREAD PAN & RISER

1"x 1" x ⅛" STEEL ANGLES

¼" SLATE RISER

RVT

STEEL ANGLE WITH EXPANSION BOLT ANCHOR

EX'G FL.

6 / A·45 DETAIL OF STAIR #4 LANDING
SCALE: 1½" = 1'-0"

Any potential hazards must be eliminated. Stairs should be "easy going," that is, there must be an appropriate relationship of riser to tread. Treads are of nonslip material which is also extended onto platforms and landings for a distance equal to the width of the stair treads. Double handrails, one higher than the other, are provided on stairs for each line of short or tall pupils. The posts, which support the center handrails of double stairs, are extended high enough above the top handrail to prevent pupils from sliding down.

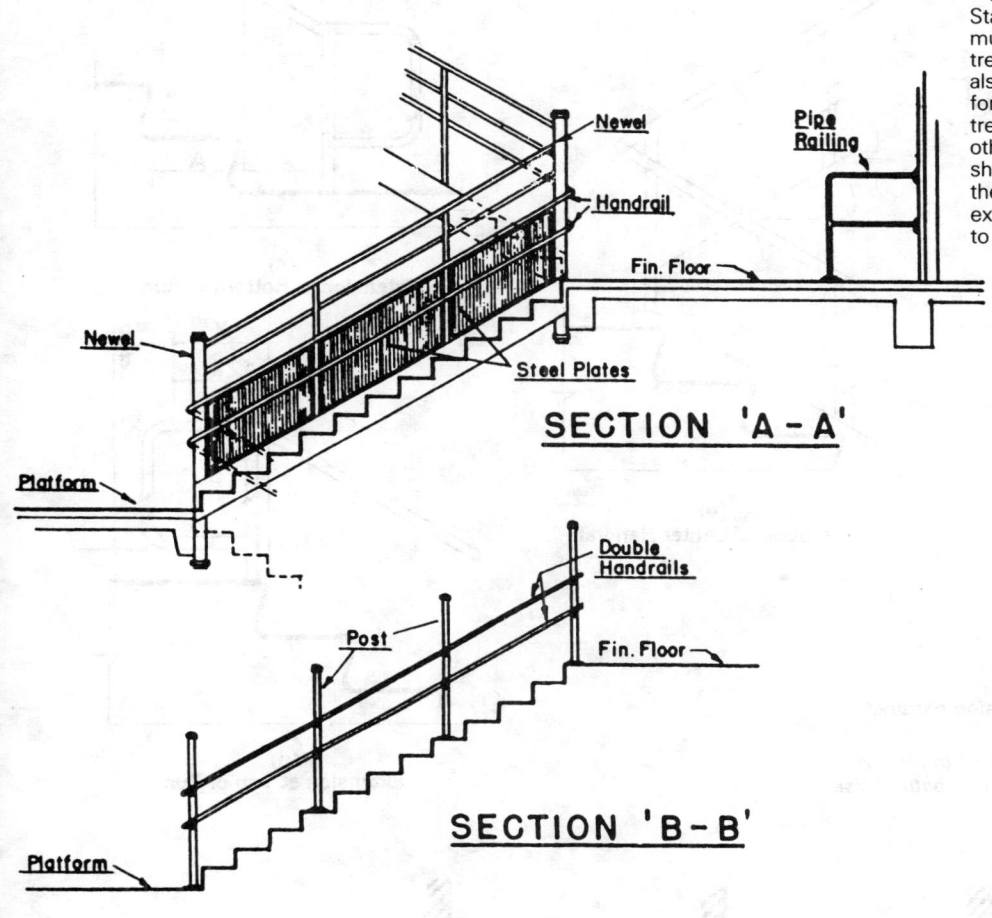

SECTION 'A-A'

SECTION 'B-B'

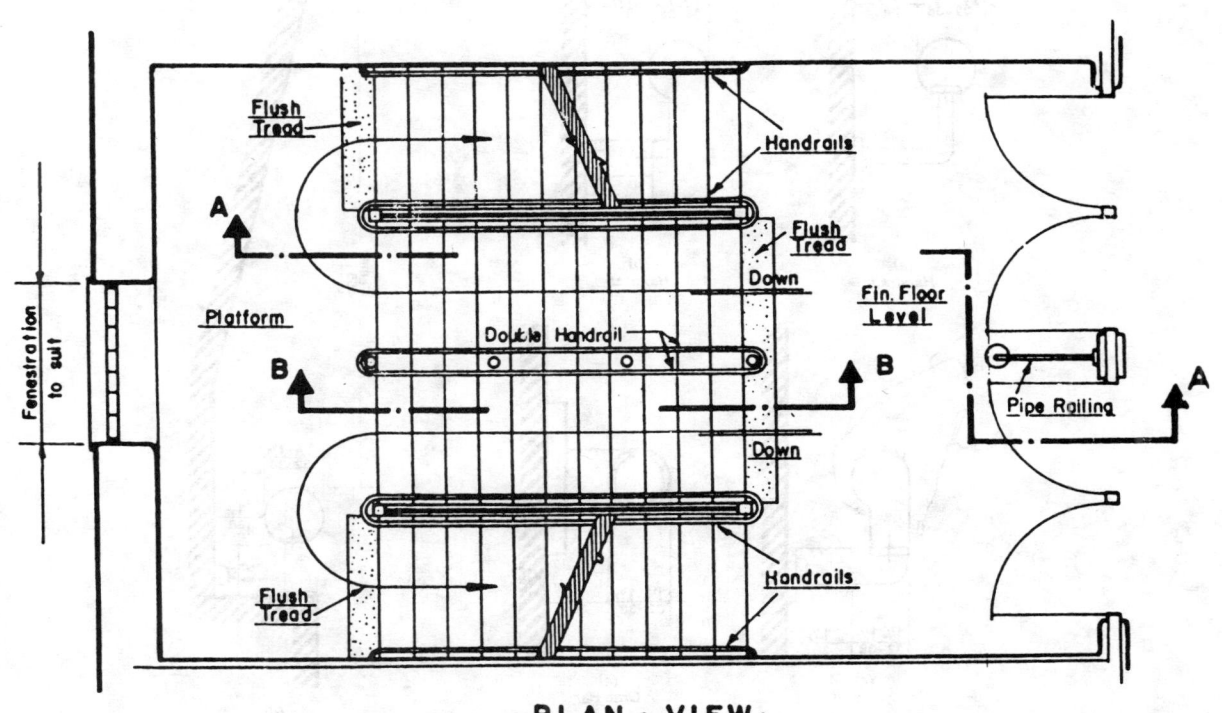

PLAN · VIEW·

STAIRS
Barrier-Free Design Data

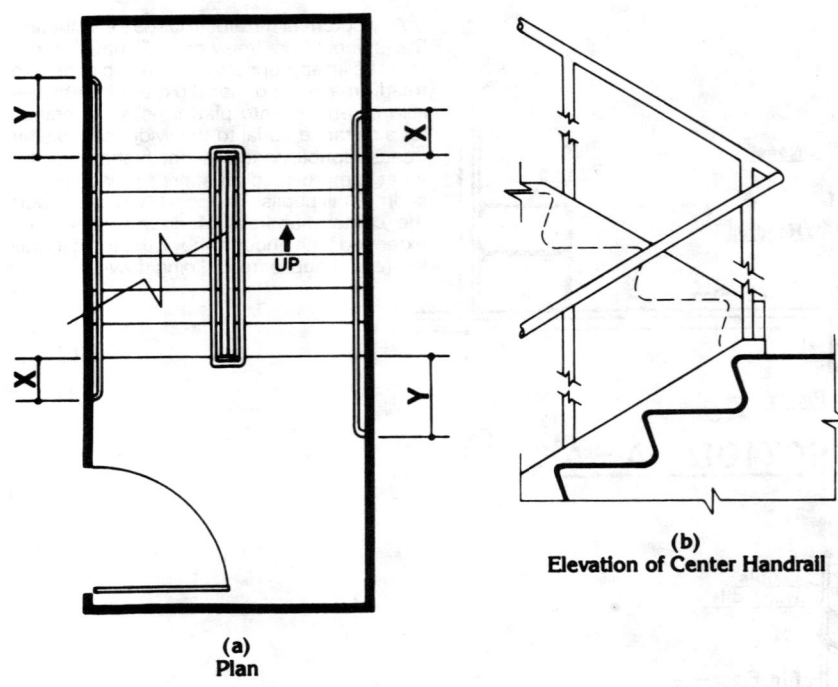

(a)
Plan

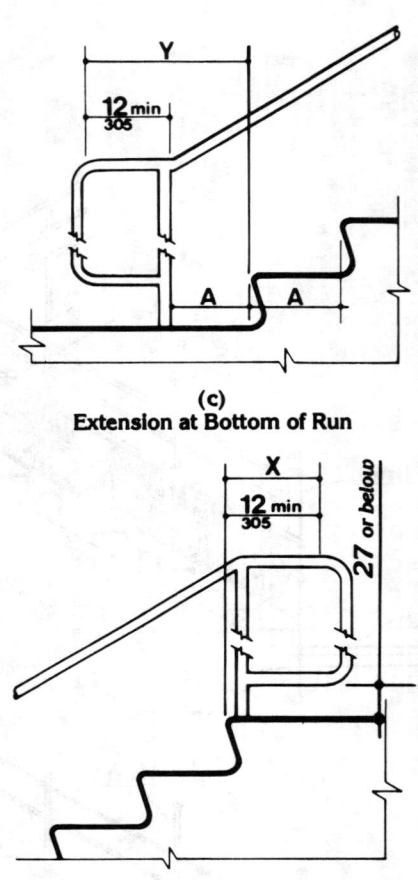

(c)
Extension at Bottom of Run

(d)
Extension at Top of Run

(b)
Elevation of Center Handrail

NOTE:

*X is the 12 in minimum handrail extension required
at each top riser.*

*Y is the minimum handrail extension of 12 in plus the
width of one tread that is required at each bottom riser.*

Fig. 23   Stair handrails.

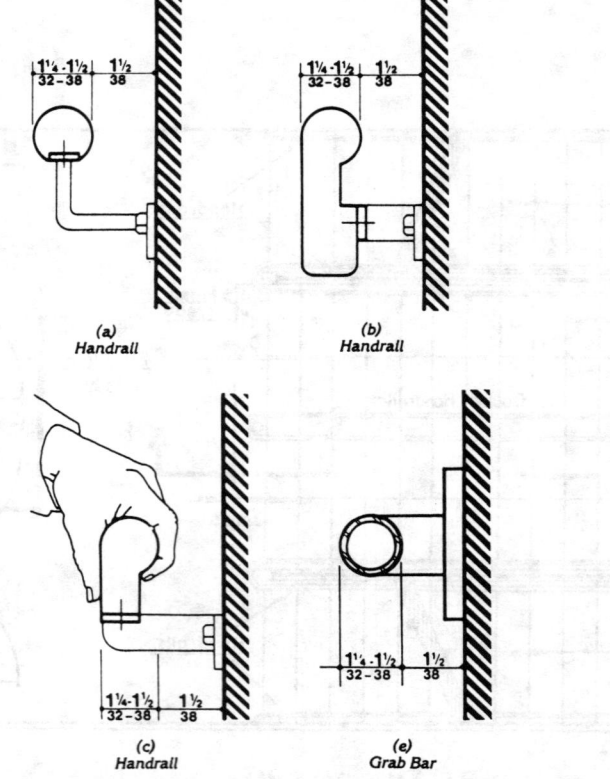

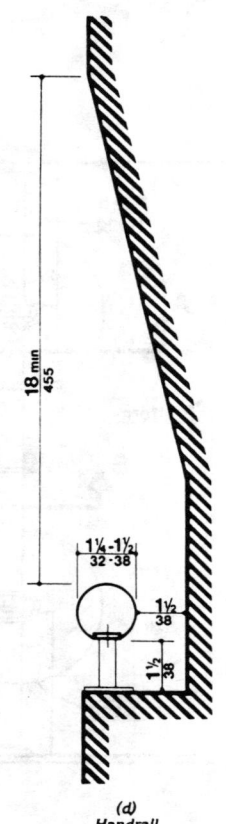

(a)
Handrail

(b)
Handrail

(c)
Handrail

(e)
Grab Bar

(d)
Handrail

Fig. 24   Size and spacing of handrails and grab bars.

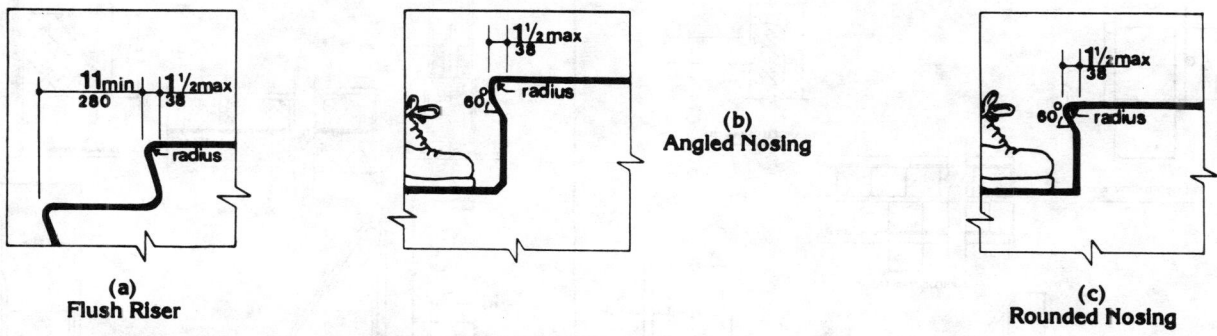

Fig. 25   Usable tread width and examples of acceptable nosings.

(a)
Flush Riser

(b)
Angled Nosing

(c)
Rounded Nosing

Steps and Stairs

Steps and stairs should have nonprotruding nosings so that people with stiff joints, braces, artificial legs, or other leg or stability problems will not catch their toes as they climb.

Handrails should be oval or round with 1½″/4 cm hand clearance between the rails and the wall: 1½″/4 cm clearance will provide ease of grip but will prevent the hand or wrist from slipping between the handrail and the wall if the person loses balance. Handrails should be positioned on both sides of steps and stairs and should extend beyond the first and last steps on at least one side and preferably on both to allow people with long leg braces to pull themselves beyond these points. To guard against falls and to help children, some codes require another, lower handrail.

Steps, stairs, and handrails should not be made of slippery material.

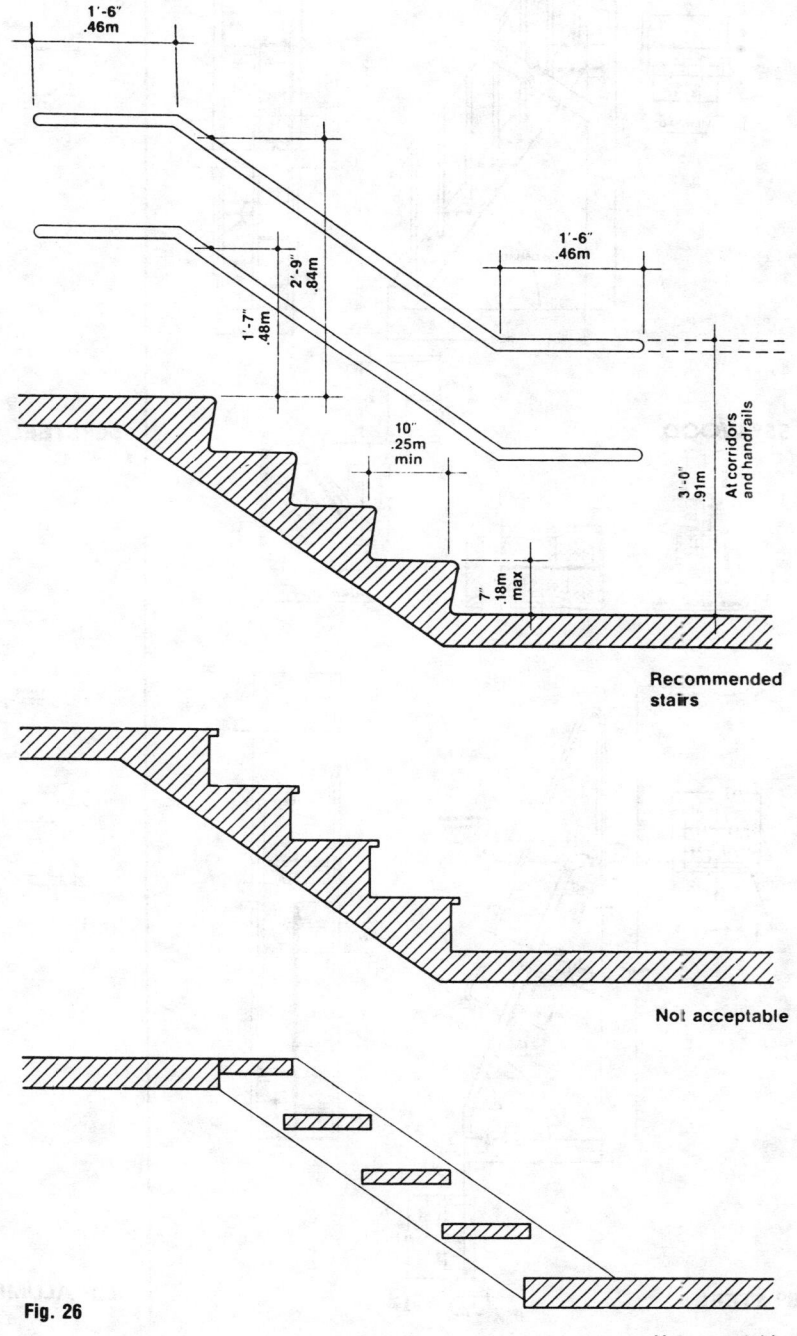

Recommended stairs

Not acceptable

Fig. 26

Not acceptable

STAIRS
Ladders

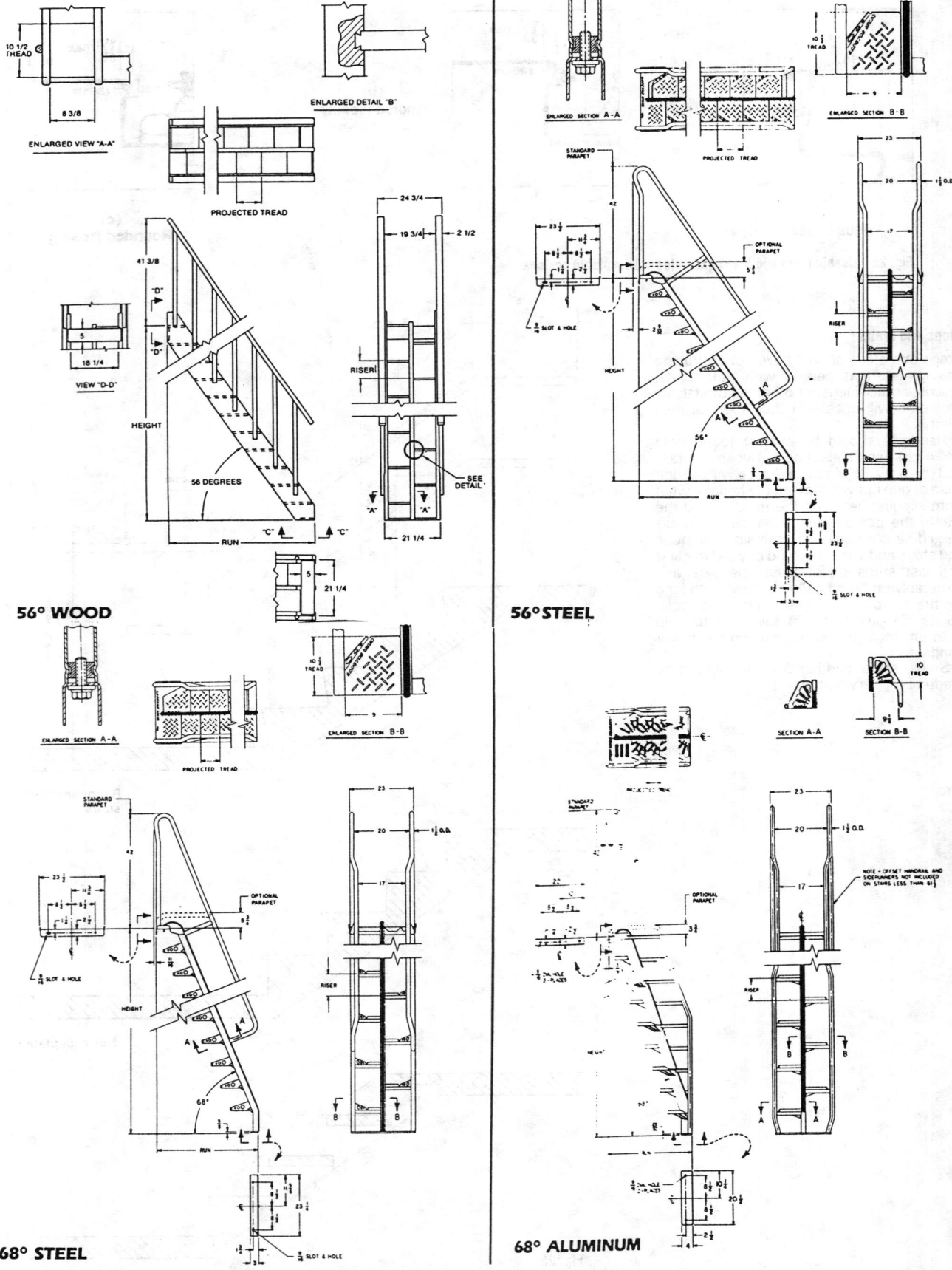

56° WOOD

56° STEEL

68° STEEL

68° ALUMINUM

LADDERS

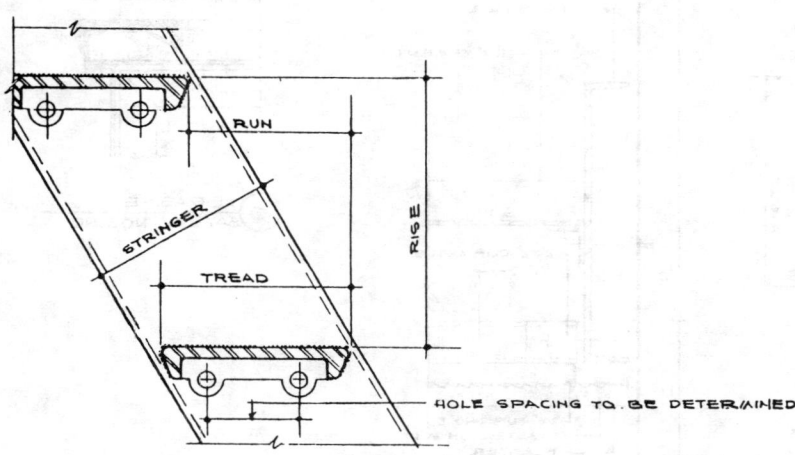

RUN

STRINGER

RISE

TREAD

HOLE SPACING TO BE DETERMINED

① ENGINEERS LADDER WITH CAST ABRASIVE TREADS

RUNG ¾" ROUND BAR

⅜" X 3" FLAT BAR STRINGER

¼" BRACKETS

RUNG SPACING 12"± TO BE DETERMINED

6"

FACE OF WALL

FLOOR

3" X 3" X ⅜" ∠ BRACKET

② VERTICAL LADDER

OPEN STEEL STAIRS

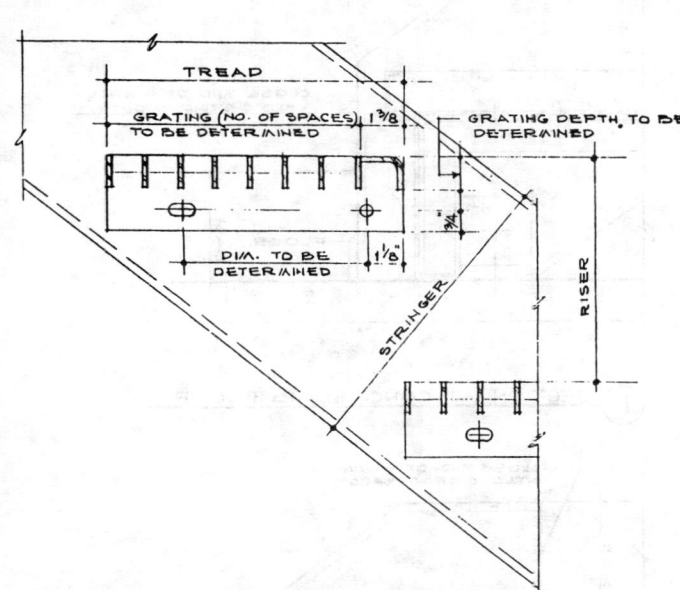

TREAD

GRATING (NO. OF SPACES) 1⅜" TO BE DETERMINED

GRATING DEPTH TO BE DETERMINED

DIM. TO BE DETERMINED

1⅛"

STRINGER

RISER

① STAIR DETAIL (GRATING TREAD)

TREAD

¾"

HOLE SPACING TO BE DETERMINED

② CAST ABRASIVE TREAD

WIDTH OVERALL	CENTER TO CENTER SPACING
5 INCHES	2 INCHE O.C.
6	3
7	3½
8	4
9	5
10	6

STANDARD HOLE SPACING FOR CAST ABRASIVE TREAD

THICKNESS IN INCHES	CAST IRON	CAST ALUMINUM	CAST BRONZE	CAST NICKEL-BRONZE
5/16"	UP TO 6" WIDE	UP TO 8" WIDE	UP TO 8" WIDE	UP TO 8" WIDE
3/8"	12"	18"	18"	18"
7/16"	24"	26"	24"	24"
½"	30"	36"	30"	30"
5/8"	42"	42"	36"	36"

THICKNESS LIMITATIONS FOR VARIOUS WIDTH CASTINGS

STAIRS
Steel Pan Cement-Filled Stairs

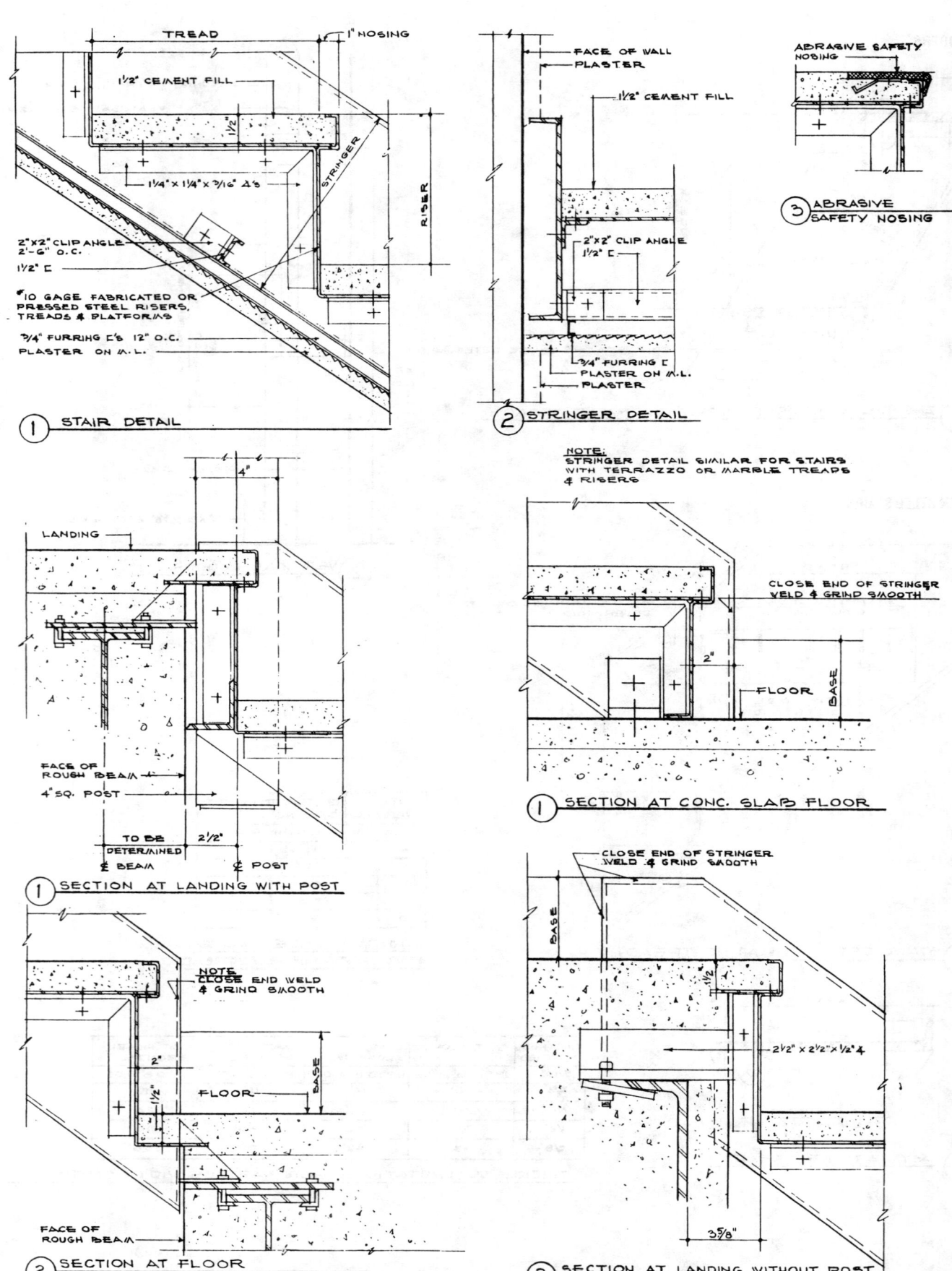

STAIR DETAIL

STRINGER DETAIL

ABRASIVE SAFETY NOSING

NOTE:
STRINGER DETAIL SIMILAR FOR STAIRS
WITH TERRAZZO OR MARBLE TREADS
& RISERS

SECTION AT LANDING WITH POST

SECTION AT CONC. SLAB FLOOR

SECTION AT FLOOR

SECTION AT LANDING WITHOUT POST

Slopes and rise Provide the least practical slope for any ramp or curb ramp subject to the following new construction requirements:

1. Maximum running slope shall not exceed 1:12 (8.3%)
2. Maximum rise for any run shall not exceed 2′6″ (760 mm)

Width Ramps and curb ramps shall have a minimum clear width of 3′0″ (915 mm) exclusive of edge protection or flared sides.

Cross-slope and surface Cross-slope of ramp surfaces shall not exceed 1:48 (¼ in/ft).

rise
ramp surface (running slope)
horizontal projection

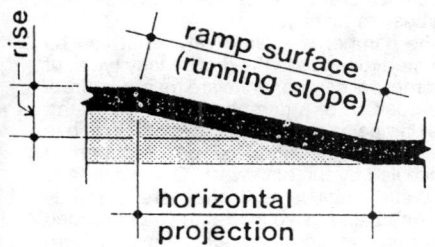

ramp slope

slope	maximum rise		maximum projection	
	in	mm	ft	m
1:12 to < 1:16	30	760	30	9
1:16 to < 1:20	30	760	40	12

maximum rise & projection
new construction

slope	maximum rise		maximum projection	
	in	mm	ft	m
1:10 to 1:8	3	75	2	0.6
1:12 to 1:10	6	150	5	1.5

maximum rise & projection
alterations to existing construction

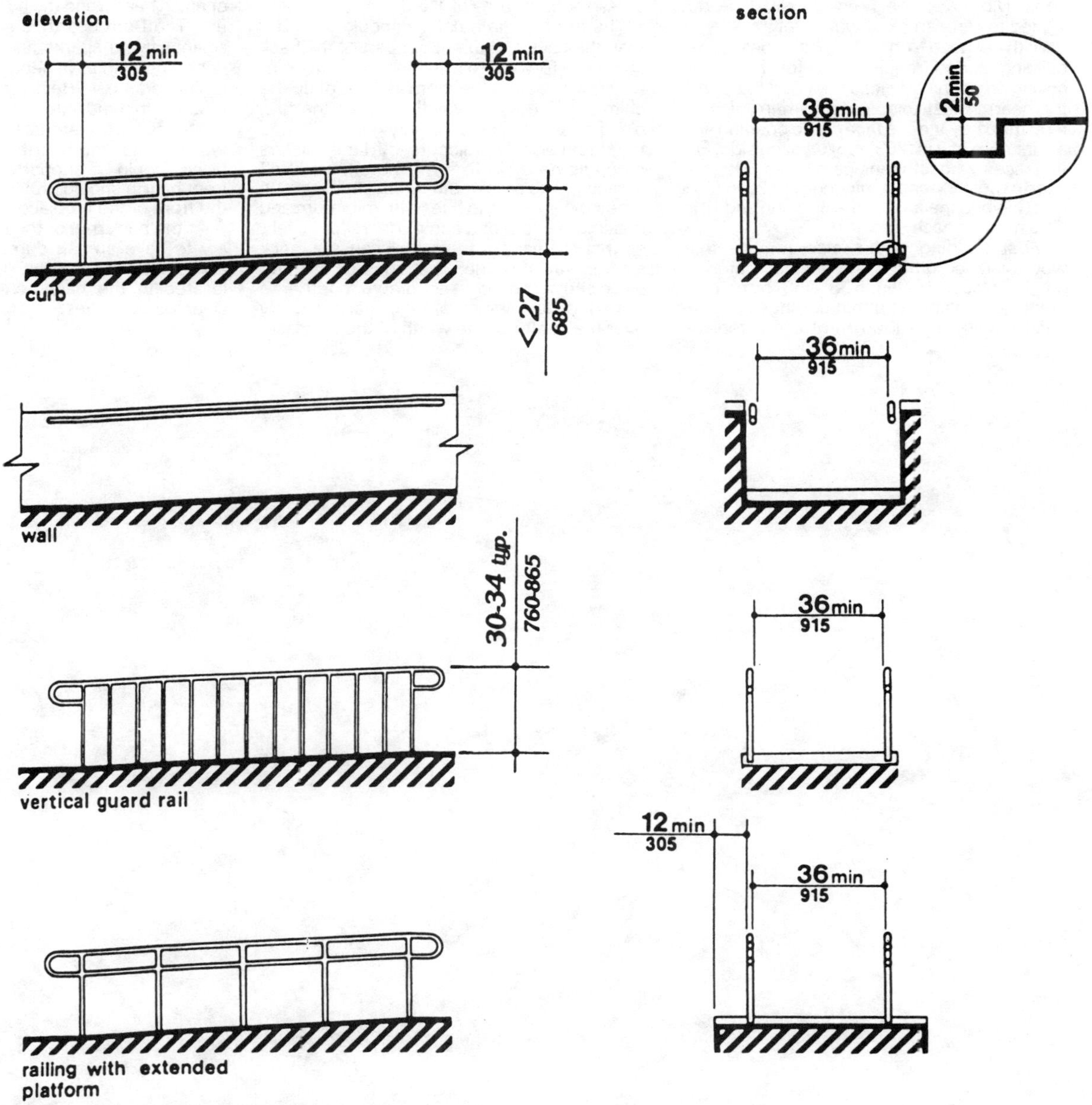

elevation
12 min
305
12 min
305
curb
< 27
685
wall
30-34 typ.
760-865
vertical guard rail
railing with extended platform
section
36 min
915
2 min
50
36 min
915
36 min
915
12 min
305
36 min
915

Fig. 27 Examples of edge protection and handrail extensions.

FIREPLACES

The function of the fireplace today differs dramatically from its role of years ago. Whereas its original function was primarily to provide heat for warmth and/or cooking, today it serves more as a decorative asset and as the focal point of interior spaces and conversational groupings, providing the esthetic pleasure and comfort of firelight.

Of particular interest to the interior designer is the proportion and scale of the fireplace opening, the treatment of wall surfaces surrounding the fireplace, the design of mantel pieces and hearth extensions, and the array of fireplace accessories available. Accordingly, the information contained in this section addresses these considerations. Drawings include elevations, plans, and details of various fireplaces; elevations of a wide selection of prefabricated mantel types; and a sampling of fireplace accessories including andirons, wrought iron fire sets, and log grates. It should be noted that, aside from their decorative aspects, the fireplace and chimney have important structural implications and require special foundations. Moreover, the fireplace must be designed to carry smoke away safely.

With respect to hearth extensions, most building codes require that for fireplaces having an opening of less than 6 ft² (0.56 m²), the hearth must extend a minimum of 16 in (406 mm) beyond the face of the opening and a minimum of 8 in (203 mm) on each side. For fireplaces whose openings exceed 6 ft², the hearth must extend a minimum of 20 in (508 mm) beyond the face of the opening and 12 in (305 mm) on each side.

Most building codes also require that woodwork or other combustible materials not be placed within 6 in (153 mm) of a fireplace opening, and that combustible material within 12 in (305 mm) of a fireplace

opening not project more than ⅛ in for each 1-in distance from such an opening.

Since building codes may vary, it is important that the designer have her or his plans checked for conformance with the applicable local or state codes. Any structural modifications to an existing fireplace and chimney or the design of a new fireplace and chimney should be reviewed by a professional engineer or registered architect.

A fireplace that draws properly can be assured by applying proper principles of design. The size of flue should be adequate and should be based upon the size of the fireplace opening. One rule commonly used is to take one-tenth of the area of the fireplace opening to find the minimum area of the flue. For example, if a fireplace had an opening 3 ft wide by 2 ft 6 in high, it would have an area of 1080 in². One-tenth of 1080 in² equals 108 in². The standard-size flue nearest to this requirement and readily available is a 13- by 13-in flue lining, which has an inside cross-sectional area of 126.56 in². One could also use a 13-in round flue that has a cross-sectional area of 113.0 in².

The front of the fireplace should be wider than the back and the upper part of the back should tilt forward to meet the throat in order to throw heat into the room instead of up the chimney. The arch over the top of the fireplace opening should be only 4 in thick, and the throat should project toward the front as much as possible to form the smoke shelf behind it. The area of the throat should be 1¼ times the area of the flue, with minimum and maximum width of 3 and 4½ in, respectively, so that the narrow throat will cause a quick suction into the flue. The sides of the fireplace above the throat are drawn together to form the flue, which always starts exactly over the center of the width of the fireplace.

The smoke shelf is very necessary to stop back drafts. The depth of the fireplace should be one-half the height of the opening, with a maximum of 24 in. The back should rise one-half the height of the opening before sloping forward and should be two-thirds the opening in width.

The back, sides, and parts of the hearth that are under the fire must be built of heat-resistant materials. Firebrick laid in fire clay is the best combination.

The damper is a large valve that can be adjusted to regulate the draft. Many types of commercial damper units are manufactured. The position of a damper unit is important. The damper is generally set about 8 in above the top of the fireplace opening and is concealed by the brickwork. One advantage of these units is that they are correctly designed and have correctly proportioned throat damper and chamber to provide a form for the masonry and to reduce the risk of failure in the function of the completed fireplace.

The hearth consists of two parts, the front or finish hearth and the back hearth under the fire. The front hearth is simply a precaution against flying sparks and, while it must be noncombustible, it need not resist intense prolonged heat. Because the back hearth must withstand intense heat, it is built of heat-resistant materials. In buildings with wood floors, the hearth in front of the fireplace should be supported on masonry. The front hearth should project at least 16 in from the front of the fireplace.

At the back part of the hearth it is customary to have an ash dump for dropping the ashes into the ash pit, which is generally located in the basement with a door for cleaning out ashes.

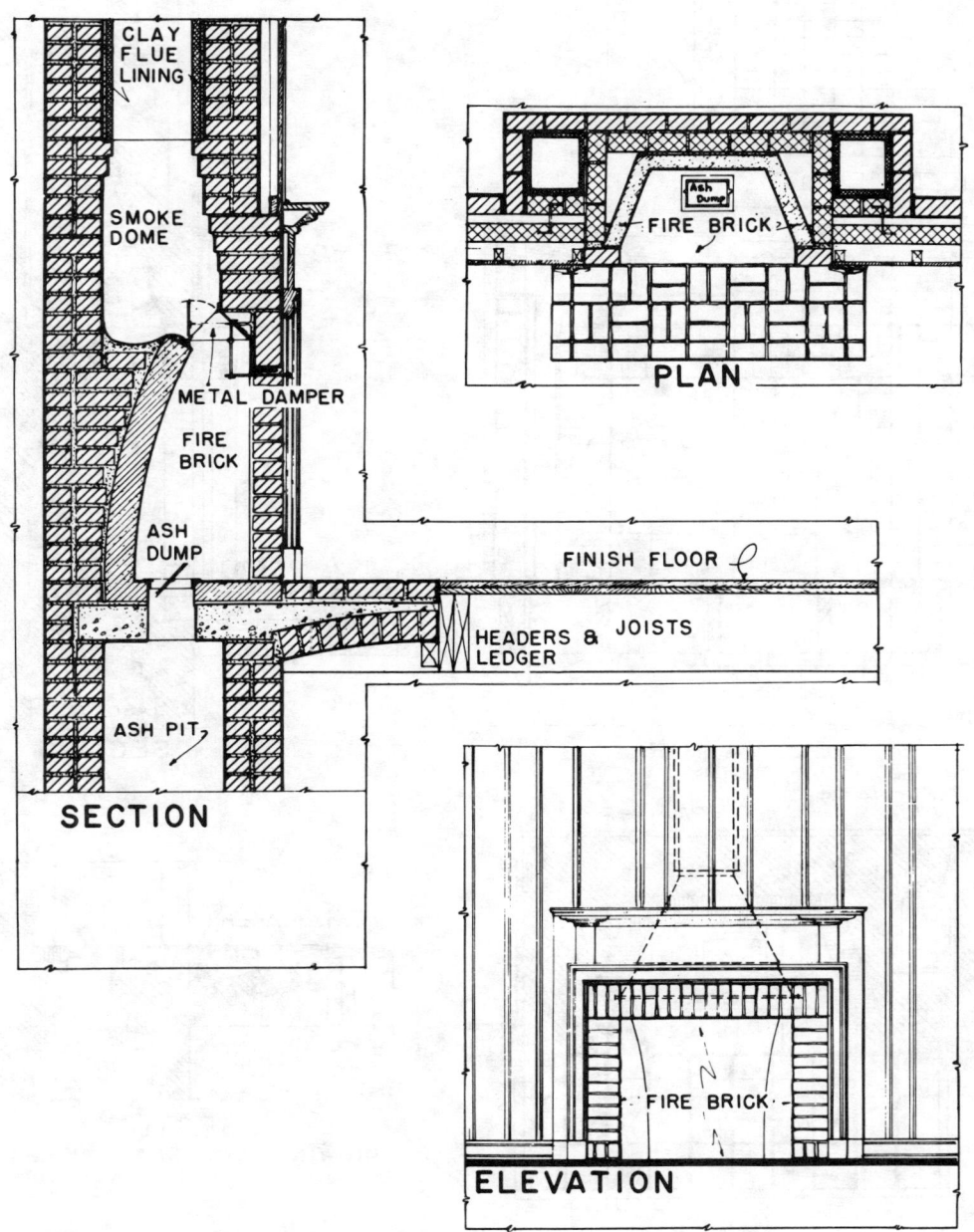

Fig. 1 Construction details of a typical fireplace.

ELEVATION

SECTION

PLAN

SECTION
SHOWING ALTERNATE HEARTH

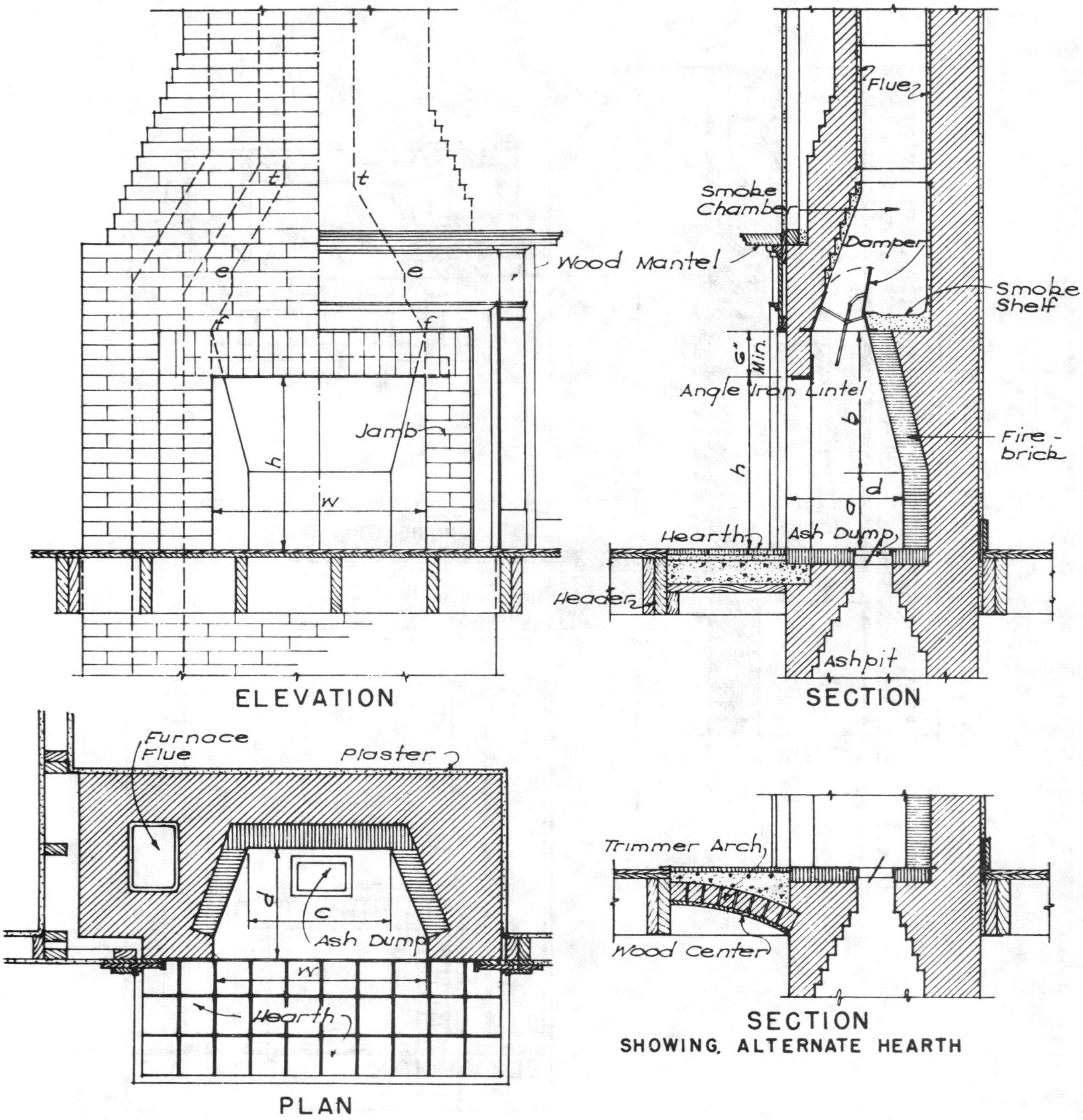

Fig. 2 Construction details of a typical fireplace.

TABLE 1 Recommended Dimensions for Fireplaces and Size of Flue Lining Required
(Letters in column heads refer to Fig. 2; all dimensions in inches)

Size of fireplace opening		Depth, d	Minimum width of back wall, c	Height of vertical back wall, a	Height of inclined back wall, b	Size of flue lining required	
Width, w	Height, h					Standard rectangular (outside dimensions)	Standard round (inside diameter)
24	24	16–18	14	14	16	8½ × 13	10
28	24	16–18	14	14	16	8½ × 13	10
30	28–30	16–18	16	14	18	8½ × 13	10
36	28–30	16–18	22	14	18	8½ × 13	12
42	28–32	16–18	28	14	18	13 × 13	12
48	32	18–20	32	14	24	13 × 13	15
54	36	18–20	36	14	28	13 × 18	15
60	36	18–20	44	14	28	13 × 18	15
54	40	20–22	36	17	29	13 × 18	15
60	40	20–22	42	17	30	18 × 18	18
66	40	20–22	44	17	30	18 × 18	18
72	40	22–28	51	17	30	18 × 18	18

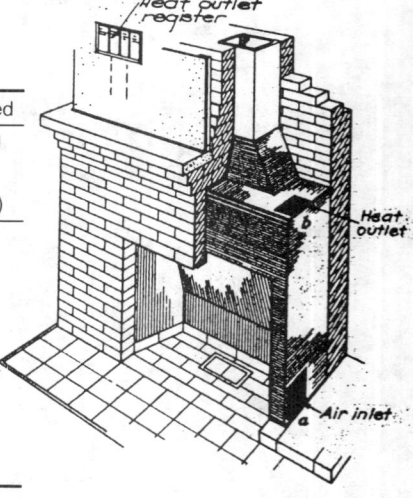

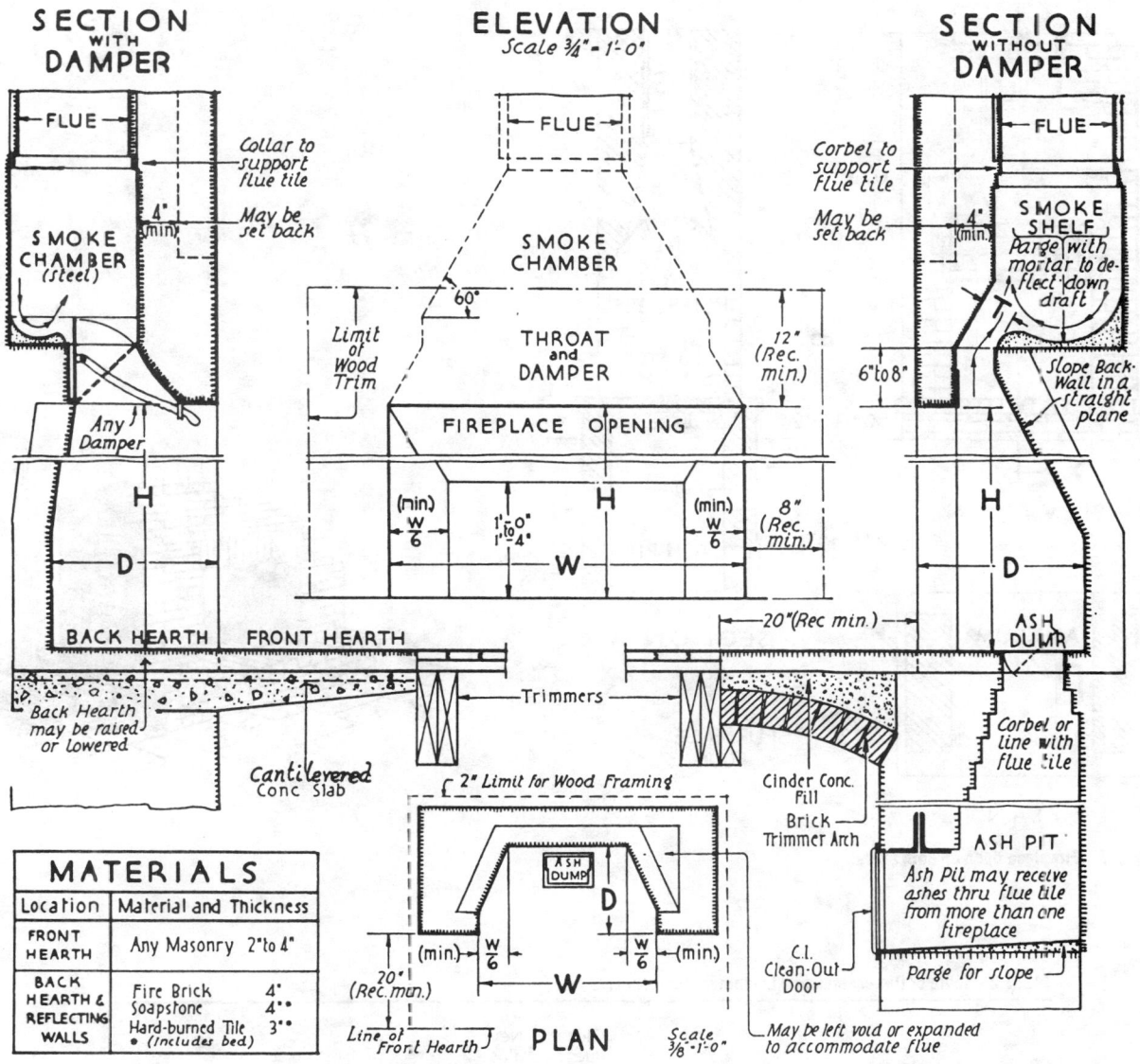

SECTION
WITH
DAMPER

ELEVATION
Scale ¾" = 1'-0"

SECTION
WITHOUT
DAMPER

FLUE

Collar to
support
flue tile

May be
set back

SMOKE
CHAMBER
(steel)

Any Damper

H

D

BACK HEARTH   FRONT HEARTH

Back Hearth
may be raised
or lowered

Cantilevered
Conc Slab

FLUE

SMOKE
CHAMBER

60°

Limit
of
Wood
Trim

THROAT
and
DAMPER

12"
(Rec.
min.)

FIREPLACE OPENING

(min.)
W
6

1'-0"
to
4'-0"

H

(min.)
W
6

8"
(Rec.
min.)

W

20" (Rec min.)

Trimmers

2" Limit for Wood Framing

ASH
DUMP

D

(min.)
W
6

W
6
(min.)

20"
(Rec. min.)

Line of
Front Hearth

PLAN

Scale
⅛" = 1'-0"

FLUE

Corbel to
support
flue tile

May be
set back

4"
(min.)

SMOKE
SHELF

Parge with
mortar to de-
flect down
draft

Slope Back
Wall in a
straight
plane

6" to 8"

H

D

ASH
DUMP

Corbel or
line with
flue tile

Cinder Conc.
Fill

Brick
Trimmer Arch

C.I.
Clean-Out
Door

ASH PIT

Ash Pit may receive
ashes thru flue tile
from more than one
fireplace

Parge for slope

May be left void or expanded
to accommodate flue

MATERIALS

Location	Material and Thickness
FRONT HEARTH	Any Masonry 2" to 4"
BACK HEARTH & REFLECTING WALLS	Fire Brick 4"* Soapstone 4"** Hard-burned Tile 3"** * (Includes bed)

FIREPLACE DIMENSIONS (In Inches)

W	24 to 84
H	⅔ to ¾ W
D	½ to ⅔ H { 16 to 24 (Rec) for Coal 18 to 24 (Rec) for Wood
FLUE (Effective Area)	⅛ WH for unlined flue ⅒ WH for rectangular lining 1/12 WH for circular lining
T (Area)	5/4 to 3/2 FLUE AREA
T (Width)	3" minimum to 4½" maximum

RECOMMENDED FLUE SIZES (In Inches)

FIREPLACE WIDTH W	RECTANGULAR FLUES			EQUIVALENT ROUND	
	Nominal or Outside Dimension	Inside Dimension	Effective Area	Inside Diameter	Effective Area
24	8½ x 8½	7¼ x 7¼	41**	8	50.3**
30 to 34	8½ x 13	7 x 11½	70**	10	78.54**
36 to 44	13 x 13	11¼ x 11¼	99**	12	113.0**
46 to 56	13 x 18	11¼ x 6¼	156**	15	176.7**
58 to 68	18 x 18	15¾ x 5¾	195**	18	254.4**
70 to 84	20 x 24	17 x 21	278**	22	380.13**

FIREPLACES
Through or Two-Way

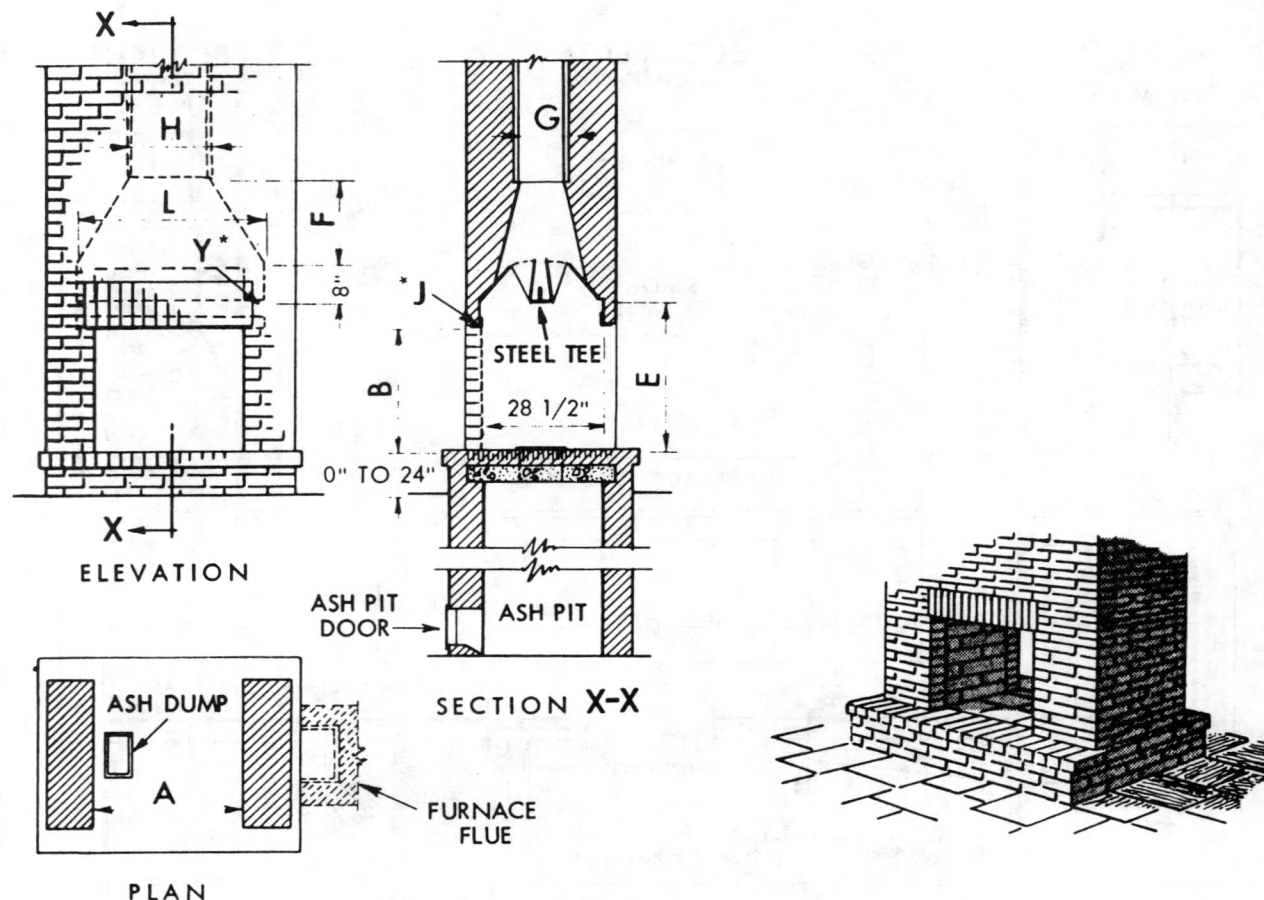

Fig. 3   Fireplace open on both sides.

TABLE 2   Table of Dimensions and Equipment (in inches)

Width of opening, A	Height of opening, B	Damper height, E	Smoke chamber, F	Old flue size		New flue size		Angle (2 req'd),* J	L	Tee	Ash dump	Ash-pit door
				G	H	G	H					
28	24	30	19	13	13	12	16	A-36	36	35	58	12 × 8
32	29	35	21	13	18	16	16	A-40	40	39	58	12 × 8
36	29	35	21	13	18	16	20	A-42	44	43	58	12 × 8
40	29	35	27	18	18	16	20	A-48	48	47	58	12 × 8
48	32	37	32	18	18	20	20	B-54	56	55	58	12 × 8

*Angle sizes: A—3 × 3 × $\frac{3}{16}$; B—3½ × 3½ × ¼".
Note Y from Fig. 3: The damper and the steel T should not be built-in solid at the ends, but given freedom to expand with heat.

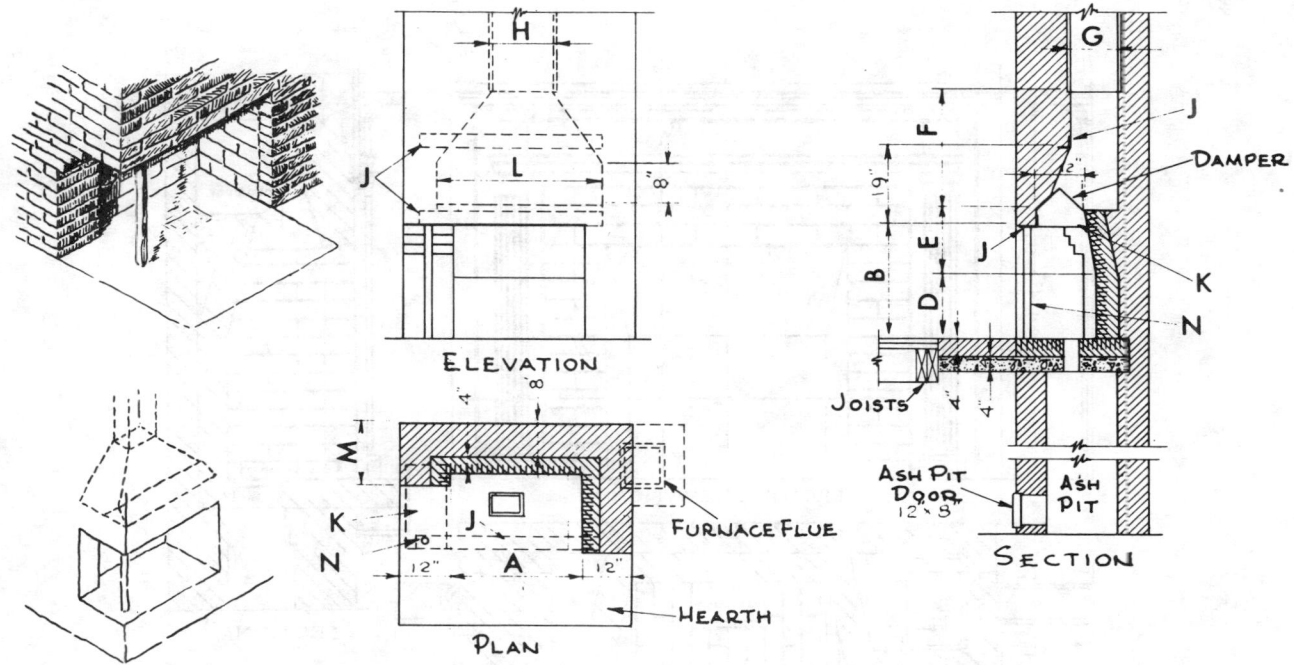

ELEVATION

PLAN

SECTION

TABLE OF DIMENSIONS AND EQUIPMENT (IN INCHES)

A	B	C	D	E	F	OLD FLUE SIZES				NEW FLUE SIZES				L	M	STEEL ANGLE J *	PLATE LINTEL K	CORNER POST N
						IN G	OUT	IN H	OUT	IN G	OUT	IN H	OUT					
28	26½	20	14	20	29¼	11¼	13	11¼	13	10¼	12	10¼	12	36	16	*A-36	11×16	3¢×26½
32	26½	20	14.	20	32	11¼	13	11¼	13	10¼	12	13½	16	40	16	*A-42	11×16	3¢×26½
36	26½	20	14	20	35	11¼	13	11¼	13	10¼	12	13½	16	44	16	*A-48	11×16	3¢×26½
40	29	20	14	20	35	11¼	13	15¾	18	13½	16	13½	16	48	16	*B-54	11×16	3¢×29
48	29	24	14	24	43	11¼	13	15¾	18	13½	16	13½	16	56	20	*B-60	11×16	3¢×29

* ANGLE SIZES　　*A 3×3×³⁄₁₆　　*B 3½×3½×¼

Fig. 4　Corner fireplace.

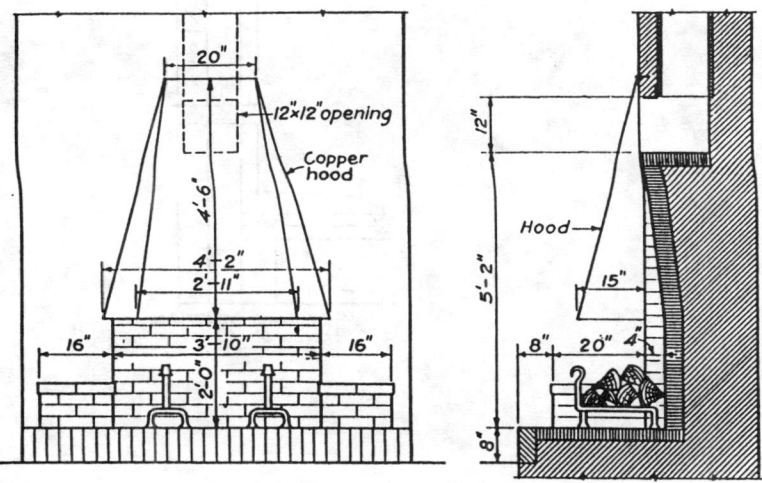

Fig. 5　A shallow fireplace with a copper hood, built as shown, throws out considerable heat after the hood gets hot. The wall should be of fire-resistant masonry.

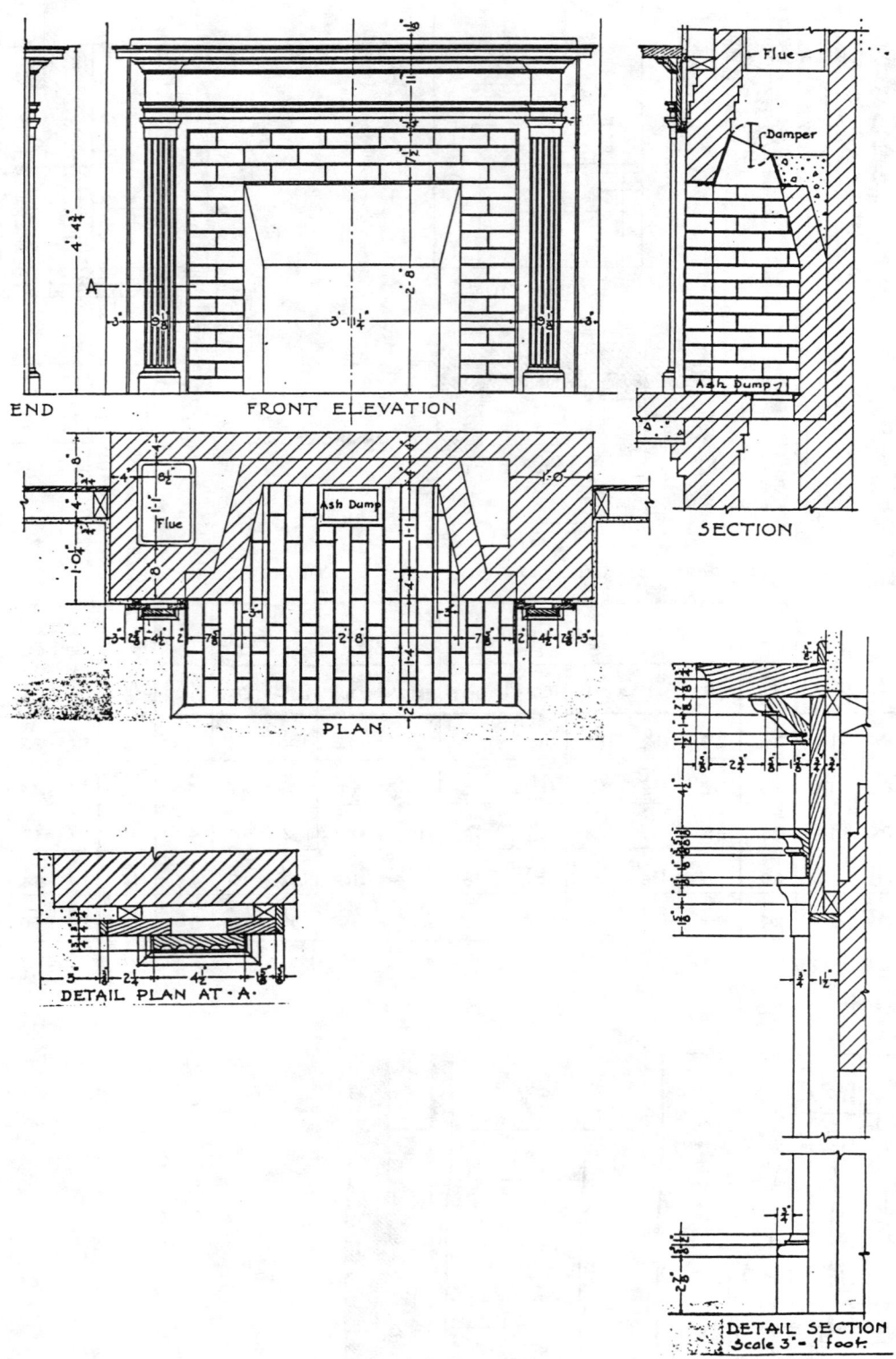

END   FRONT ELEVATION

Flue

Damper

Ash Dump

SECTION

Flue

Ash Dump

PLAN

DETAIL PLAN AT ·A·

DETAIL SECTION
Scale 3" = 1 foot.

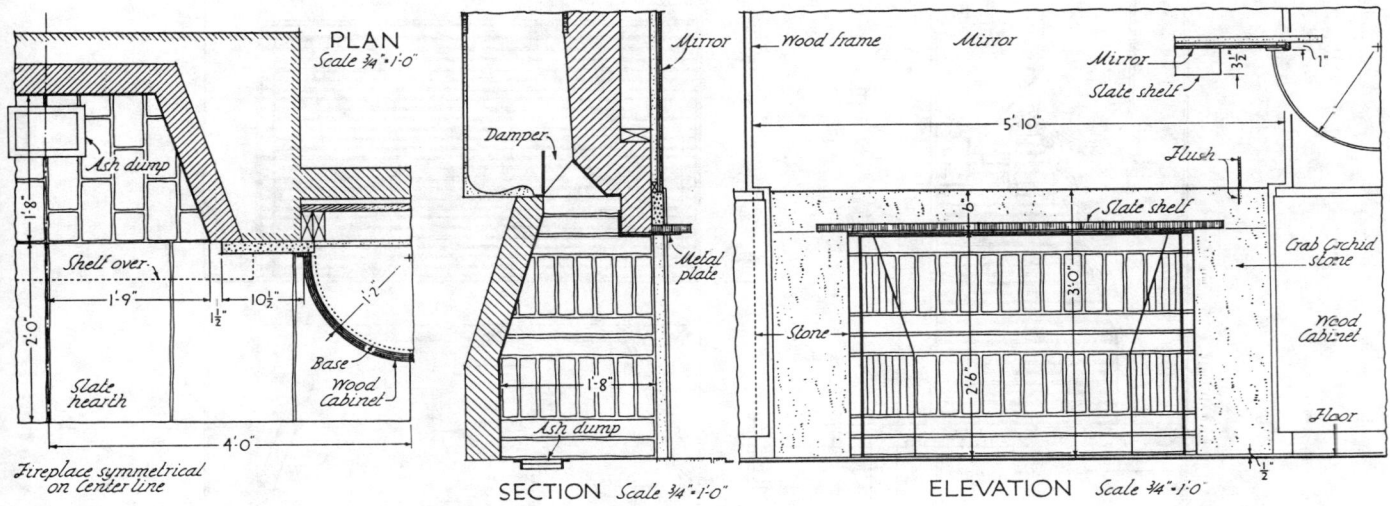

PLAN
Scale ¾"·1·0"

Ash dump

1'-8"

Shelf over
1'-9"   10½"
1½
2'-0"

Slate
hearth   Base
Wood
Cabinet

4'-0"

Fireplace symmetrical
on Center line

Mirror   Wood frame   Mirror

Damper

Mirror
Slate shelf   3½"   1"

Metal
plate   5'-10"

Flush

6"

Slate shelf

Crab Orchid
stone

Stone   3'-0"

2'-6"   Wood
Cabinet

1'-8"

Floor

Ash dump   ½"

SECTION   Scale ¾"·1·0"   ELEVATION   Scale ¾"·1·0"

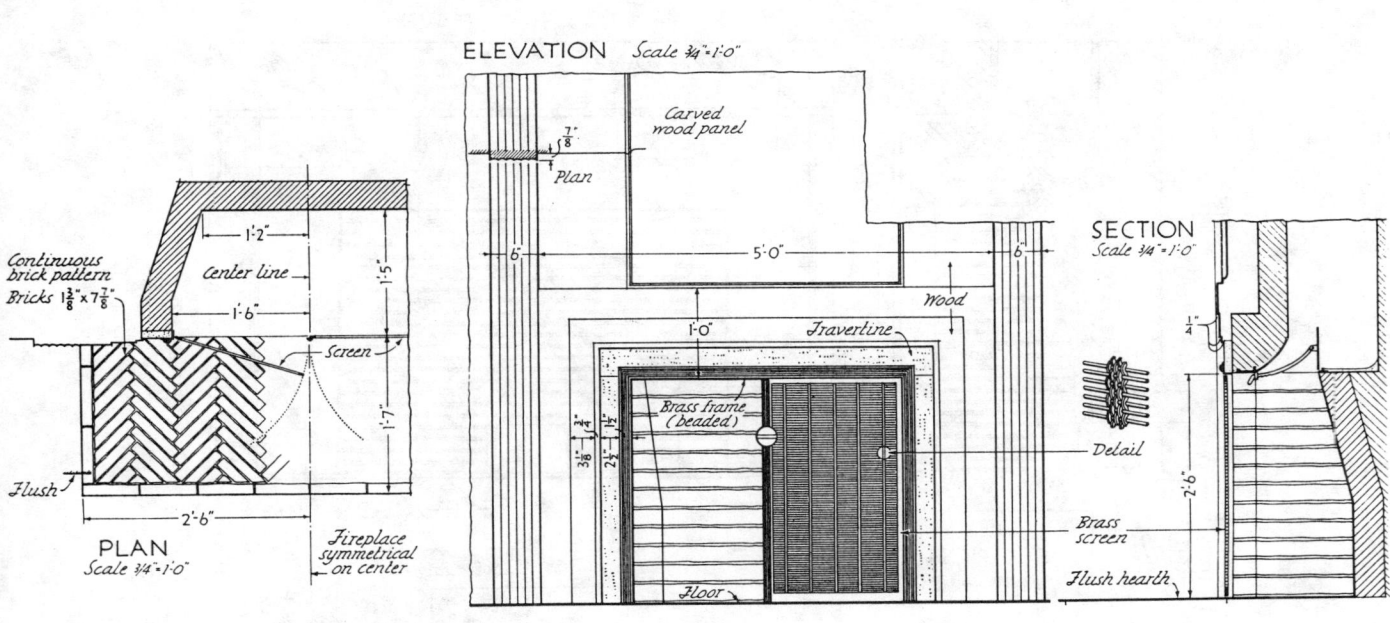

ELEVATION   Scale ¾"·1·0"

Carved
wood panel

7/8"
Plan

Continuous
brick pattern
Bricks 1⅜"×7⅞"

1'-2"
Center line
1'-6"

1'-5"

Screen

6"   5'-0"   6"

Wood

Travertine

1'-0"

Brass frame
(beaded)

SECTION
Scale ¾"·1·0"

1'-7"

Flush

¾"
3/8"
2½"

¼"

Delait

2'-6"

PLAN
Scale ¾"·1·0"

2'-6"

Fireplace
symmetrical
on center

Floor

Brass
screen

Flush hearth

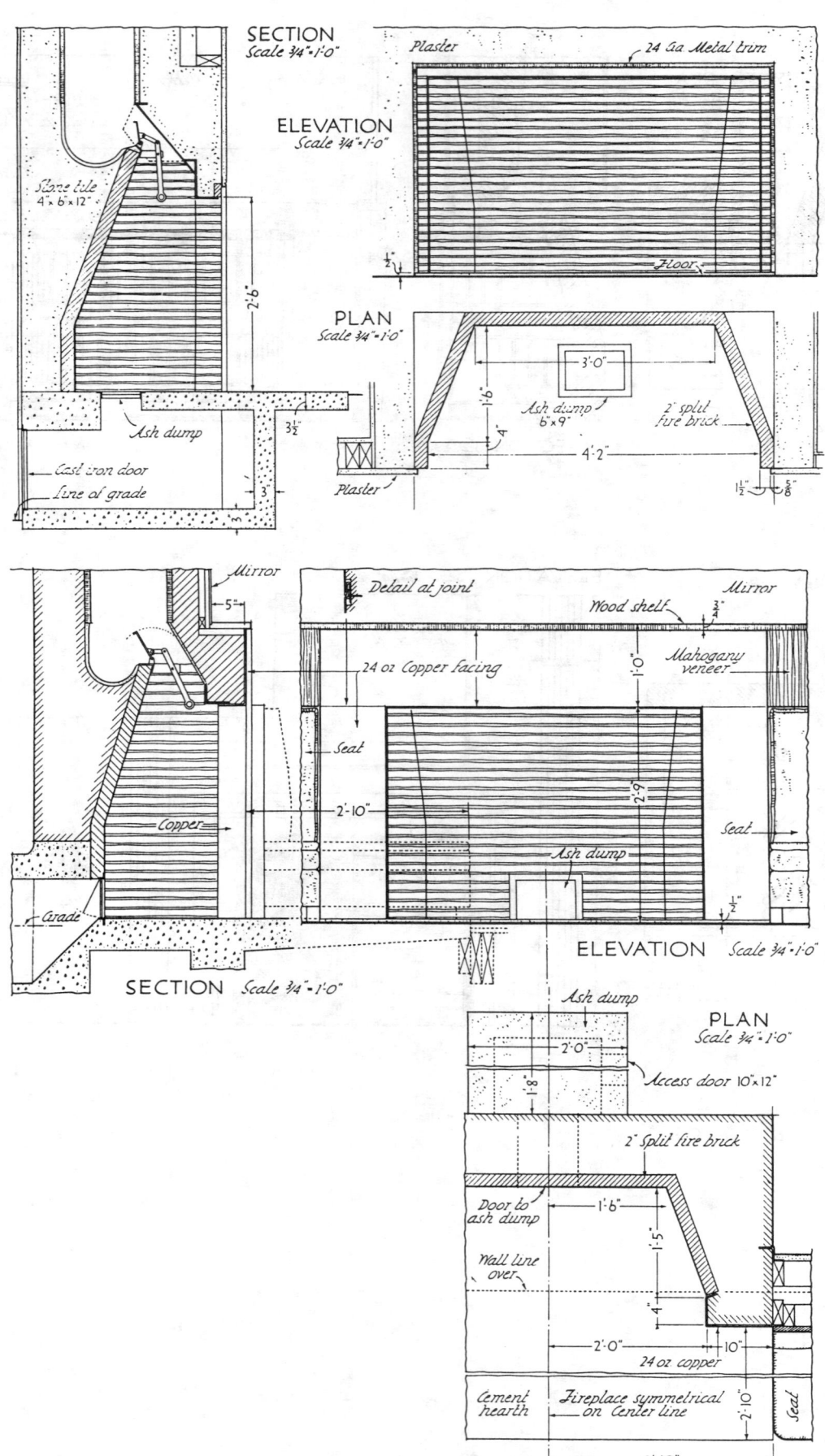

SECTION
Scale ¾"=1'·0"

Stone tile
4" x 6" x 12"

2'·6"

Ash dump

3½"

Cast iron door
Line of grade

3"

ELEVATION
Scale ¾"=1'·0"

Plaster

24 Ga Metal trim

1"

Floor

PLAN
Scale ¾"=1'·0"

1'·6"

Ash dump
6" x 9"

3'·0"

4"

2" split
fire brick

Plaster

4'·2"

1½"

Mirror

5"

Detail at joint

Wood shelf

Mirror

¾"

24 oz Copper facing

1'·0"

Mahogany
veneer

Seat

2'·10"

2'·9"

Copper

Ash dump

Seat

½"

Grade

SECTION   Scale ¾"=1'·0"

ELEVATION   Scale ¾"=1'·0"

Ash dump

PLAN
Scale ¾"=1'·0"

2'·0"

1'·8"

Access door 10" x 12"

2" Split fire brick

Door to
ash dump

1'·6"

1'·5"

Wall line
over

4"

2'·0"

10"

24 oz copper

Cement
hearth

Fireplace symmetrical
on Center line

2'·10"

Seat

2'·10"

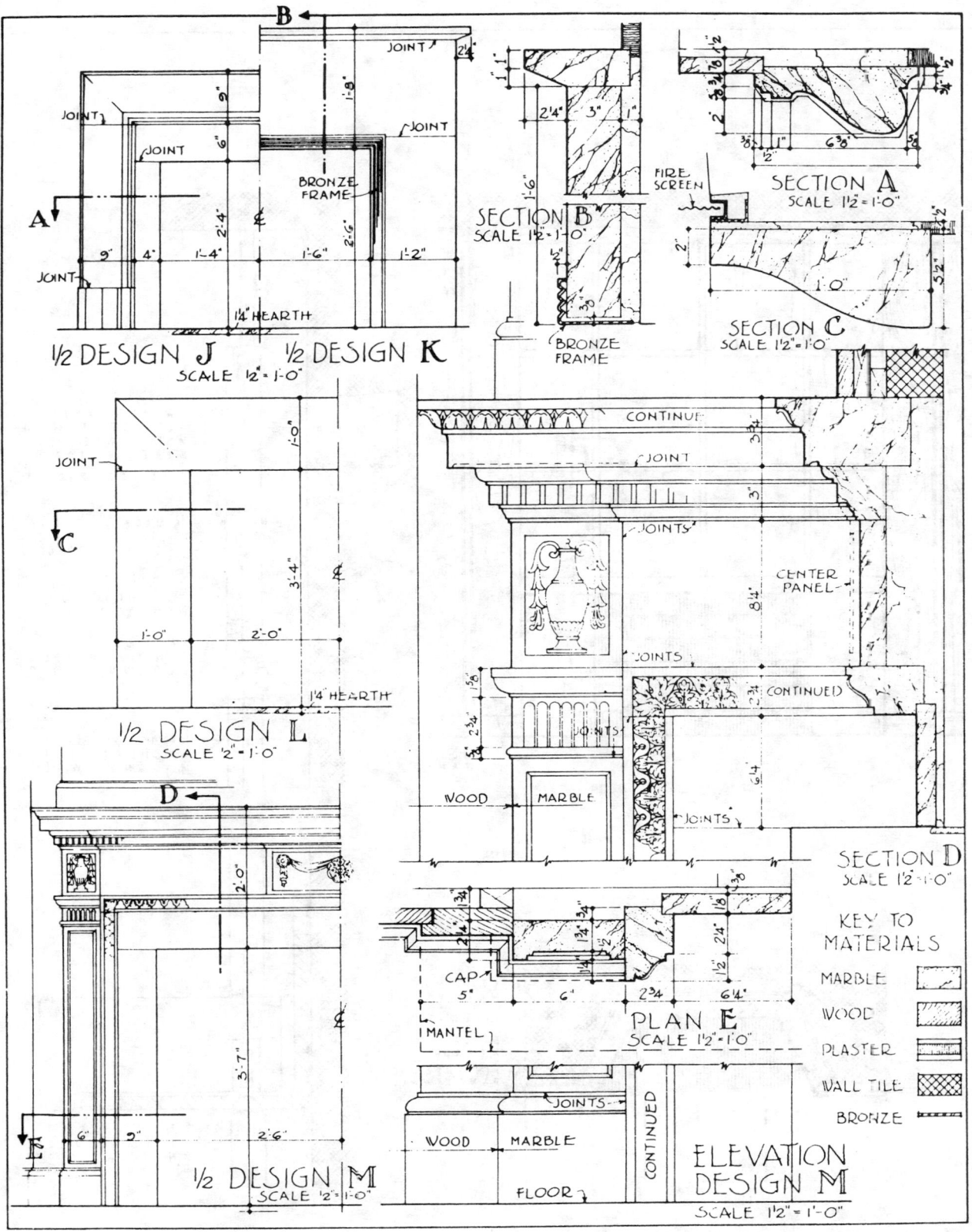

½ DESIGN J ½ DESIGN K
SCALE ½" = 1'-0"

SECTION B
SCALE 1½" = 1'-0"

SECTION A
SCALE 1½" = 1'-0"

SECTION C
SCALE 1½" = 1'-0"

½ DESIGN L
SCALE ½" = 1'-0"

½ DESIGN M
SCALE ½" = 1'-0"

PLAN E
SCALE 1½" = 1'-0"

SECTION D
SCALE 1½" = 1'-0"

KEY TO MATERIALS

MARBLE
WOOD
PLASTER
WALL TILE
BRONZE

ELEVATION DESIGN M
SCALE 1½" = 1'-0"

FIREPLACES
Marble Mantels

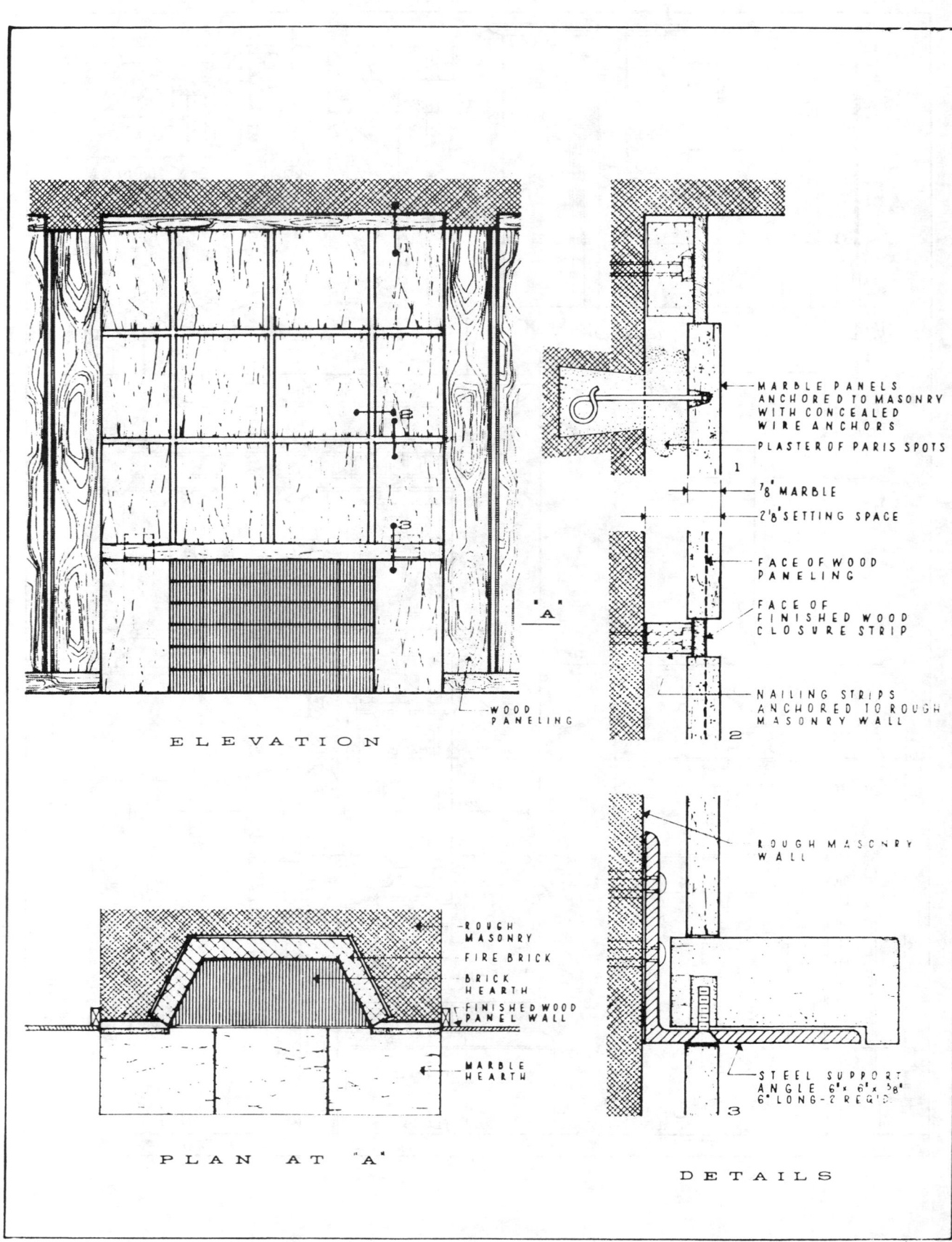

ELEVATION

WOOD
PANELING

MARBLE PANELS
ANCHORED TO MASONRY
WITH CONCEALED
WIRE ANCHORS

PLASTER OF PARIS SPOTS

$\frac{7}{8}$" MARBLE

$2\frac{1}{8}$" SETTING SPACE

FACE OF WOOD
PANELING

FACE OF
FINISHED WOOD
CLOSURE STRIP

NAILING STRIPS
ANCHORED TO ROUGH
MASONRY WALL

1

2

PLAN AT "A"

ROUGH
MASONRY

FIRE BRICK

BRICK
HEARTH

FINISHED WOOD
PANEL WALL

MARBLE
HEARTH

ROUGH MASONRY
WALL

STEEL SUPPORT
ANGLE 6"x 6"x $\frac{5}{8}$"
6" LONG-2 REQ'D

3

DETAILS

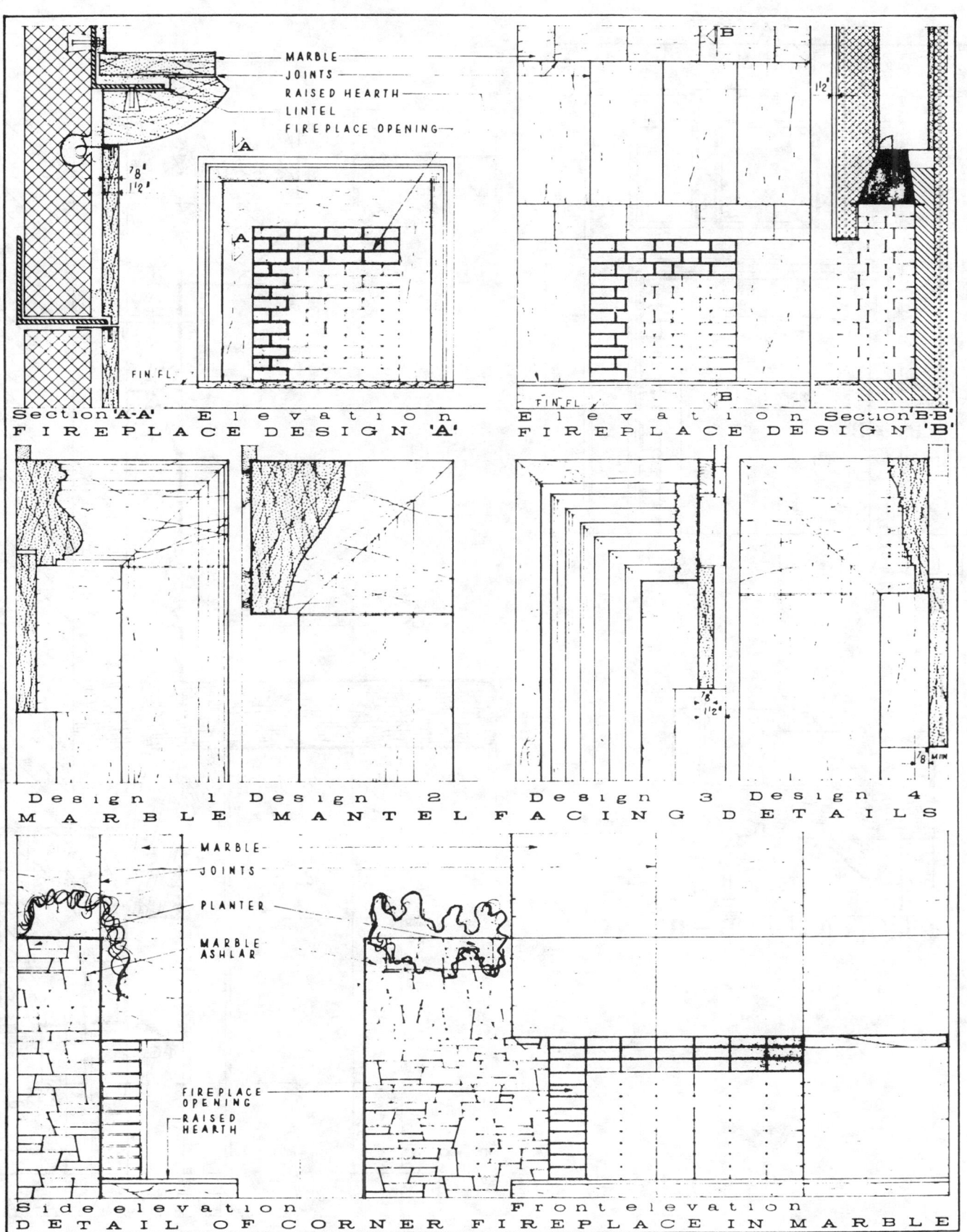

MARBLE
JOINTS
RAISED HEARTH
LINTEL
FIREPLACE OPENING

Section 'A-A' Elevation
FIREPLACE DESIGN 'A'

Elevation Section 'B-B'
FIREPLACE DESIGN 'B'

Design 1 Design 2 Design 3 Design 4
MARBLE MANTEL FACING DETAILS

MARBLE
JOINTS
PLANTER
MARBLE ASHLAR
FIREPLACE OPENING
RAISED HEARTH

Side elevation Front elevation
DETAIL OF CORNER FIREPLACE IN MARBLE

FIREPLACES

Wood Mantels

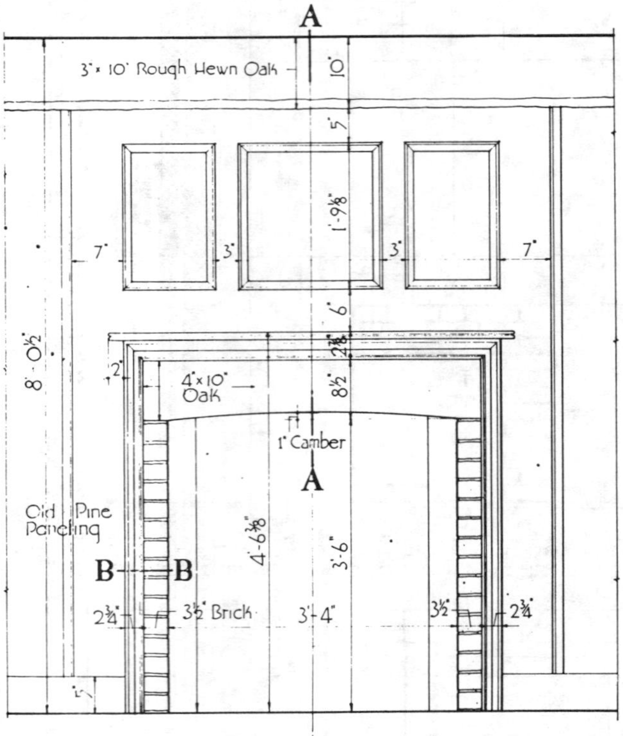
A
3" x 10" Rough Hewn Oak
10"
5"
1'-9⅛"
7"
3"
3"
7"
6"
2⅞"
8'-0½"
2"
4"x10" Oak
8½"
1" Camber
A
Old Pine Paneling
4'-6⅞"
3'-6"
B—B
2¾"
3½" Brick
3'-4"
3½"
2¾"

ELEVATION·

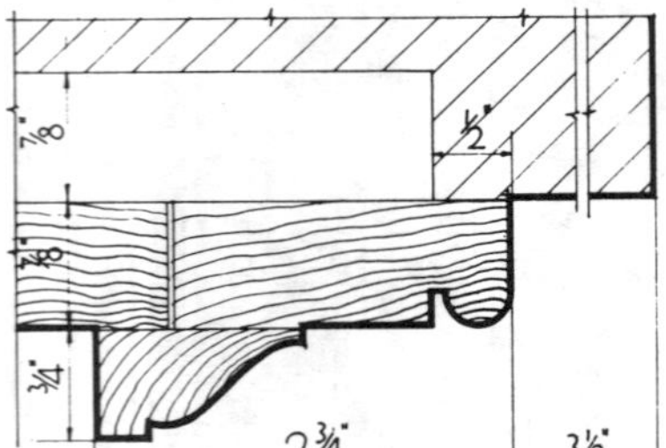
⅞"
½"
⅞"
¾"
2¾"
3½"

·SECTION · B—B

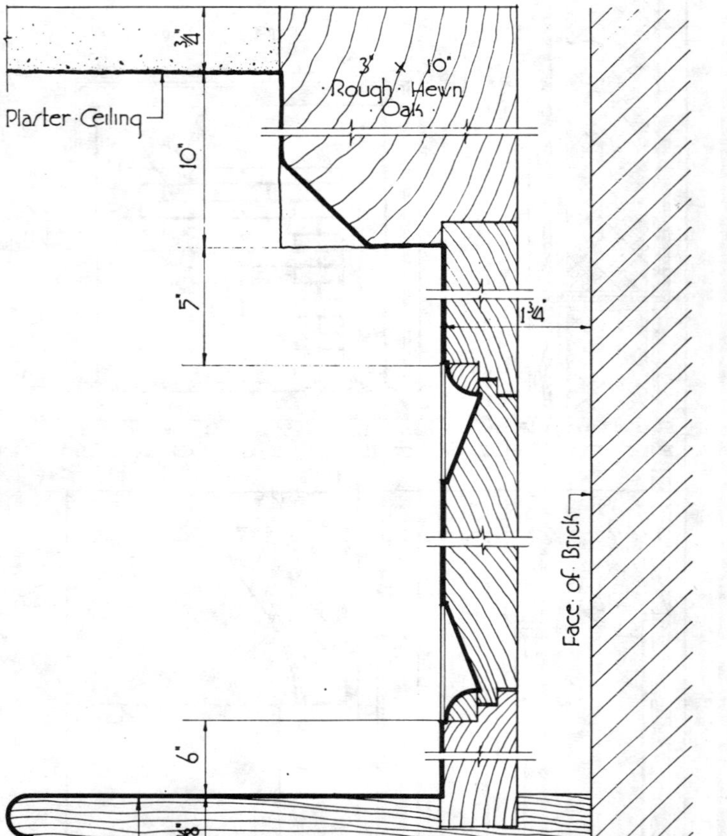
3¼"
3" x 10" Rough Hewn Oak
Plaster·Ceiling
10"
5"
1¾"
Face of Brick
6"
1⅞"
2¼"
⅞"
5" Front
2" Side
4" Oak·Lintel
4'-6⅞"
8½"
1" Camber
Steel & Asbestos Lining
Brick
3'-6"
Fin. Floor

·SECTION·A—A

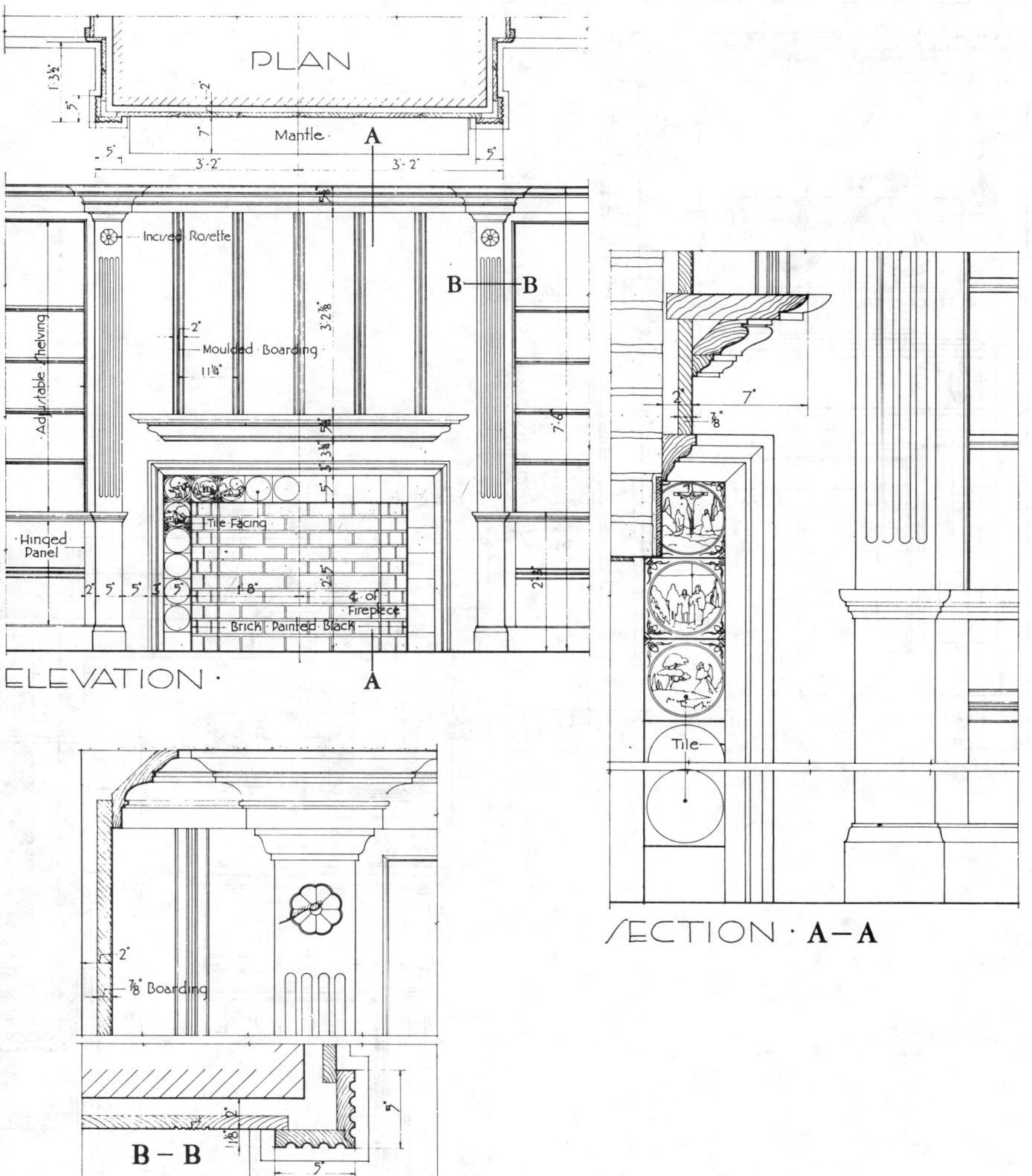

PLAN

Mantle

A

ELEVATION·

Incised Rosette

Adjustable Shelving

2"
Moulded Boarding
11¼"

Tile Facing

Hinged
Panel

1'-8"

Brick Painted Black

¢ of
Fireplace

B — B

2"
⅞" Boarding

SECTION · A-A

Tile Facing

Tile

FIREPLACES
Wood Mantels

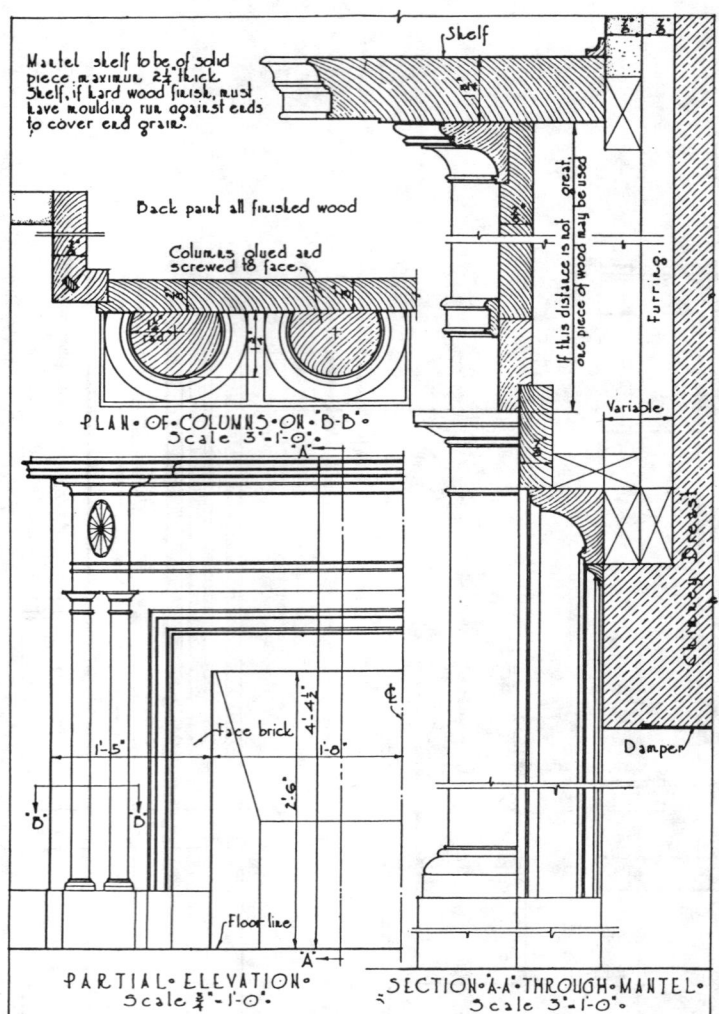

Mantel shelf to be of solid piece, maximum 2¼" thick. Shelf, if hard wood finish, must have moulding run against ends to cover end grain.

Back paint all finished wood

Columns glued and screwed to face.

Shelf

Furring.

If this distance is not great, one piece of wood may be used

Variable

Chimney Breast

PLAN·OF·COLUMNS·ON·B-B·
Scale 3"-1'-0"

Face brick

1'-5"   4'-4½"   1'-0"

2'-6"

Floor line

Damper

PARTIAL·ELEVATION·
Scale ¾"-1'-0"

SECTION·A-A·THROUGH·MANTEL·
Scale 3"-1'-0"

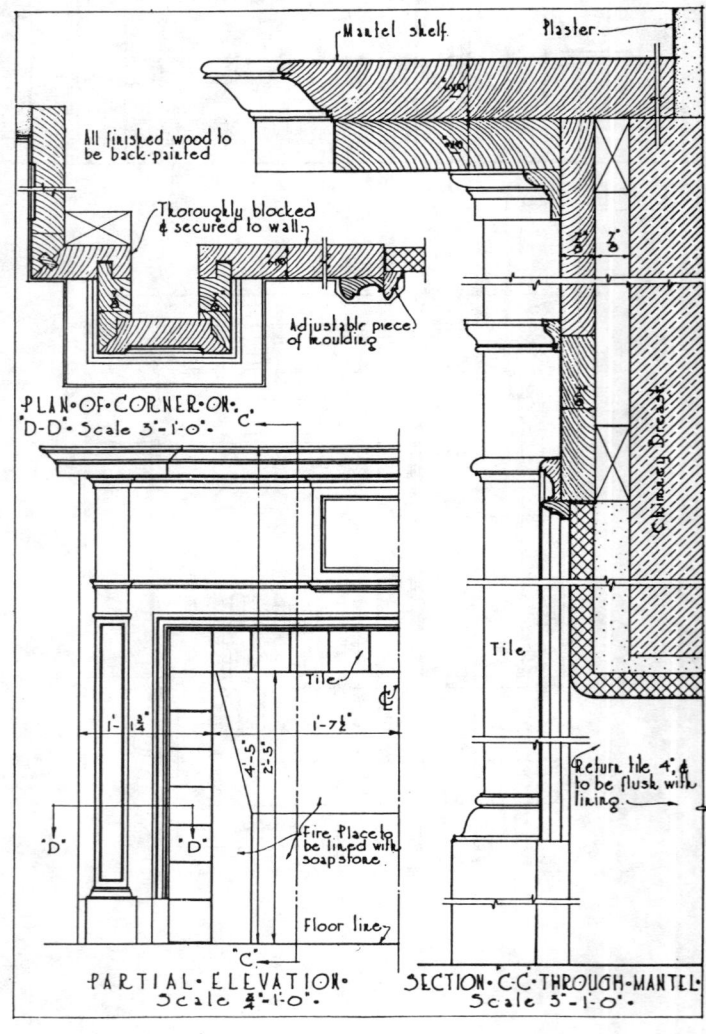

Mantel shelf

Plaster

All finished wood to be back-painted

Thoroughly blocked & secured to wall

Adjustable piece of moulding

Chimney Breast

PLAN·OF·CORNER·ON·
D-D· Scale 3"-1'-0"

Tile

Tile

Return tile 4"; to be flush with lining.

1'-1¾"   1'-7½"

4'-5"   2'-5"

Fire Place to be lined with soapstone.

Floor line

PARTIAL·ELEVATION·
Scale ¾"-1'-0"

SECTION·C-C·THROUGH·MANTEL·
Scale 3"-1'-0"

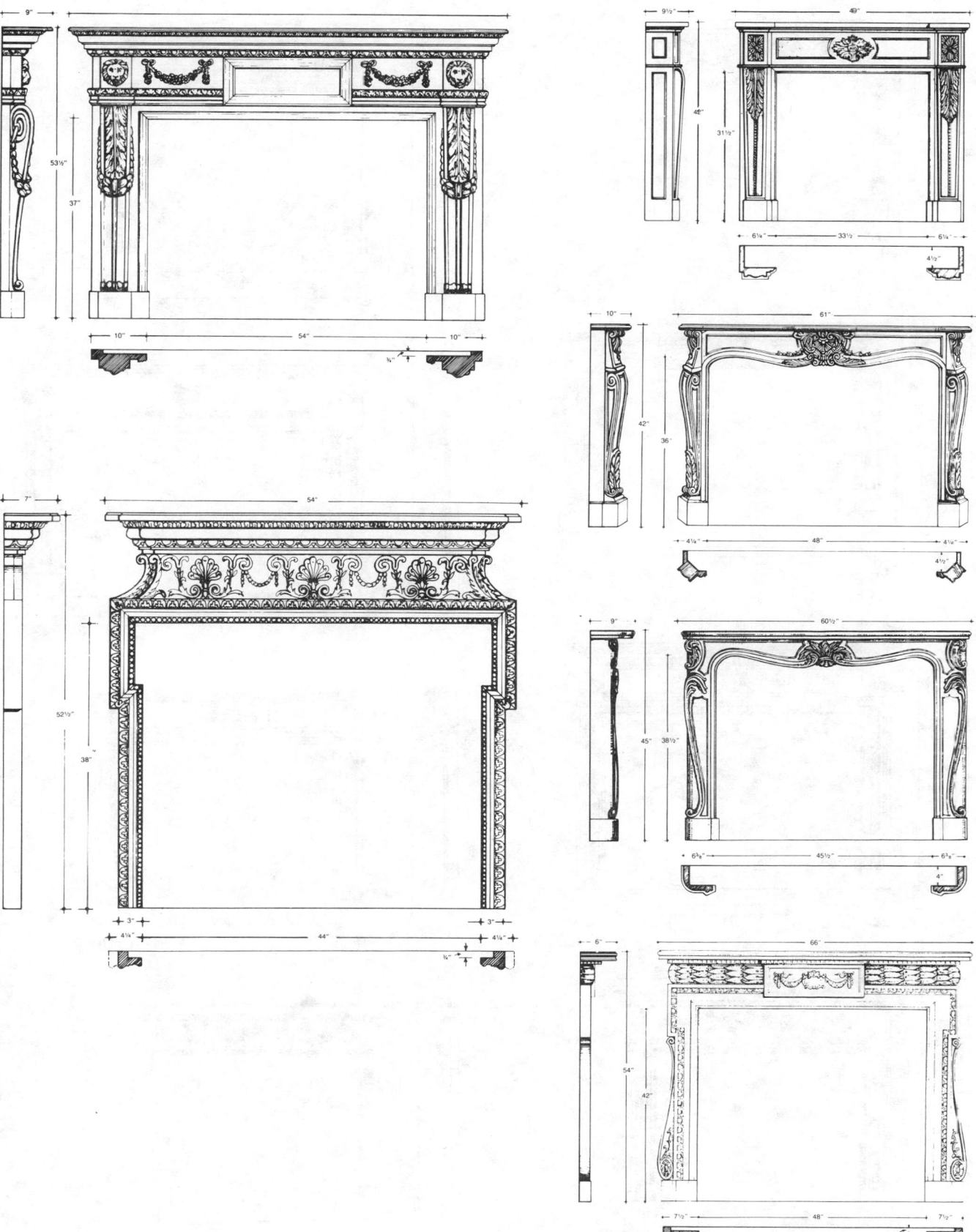

Fig. 6   These wood mantels are readily available.

FIREPLACES
Wood Mantels

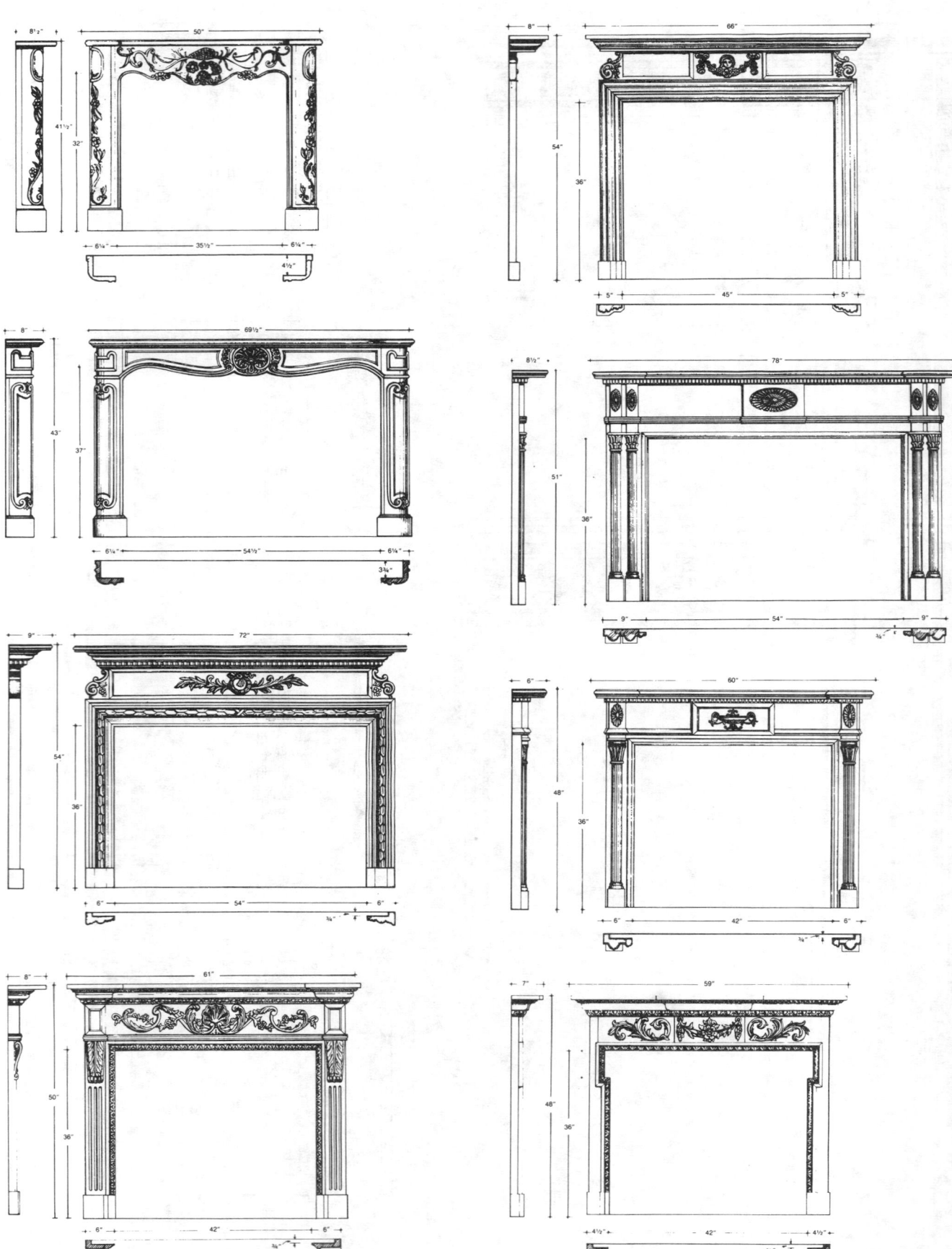

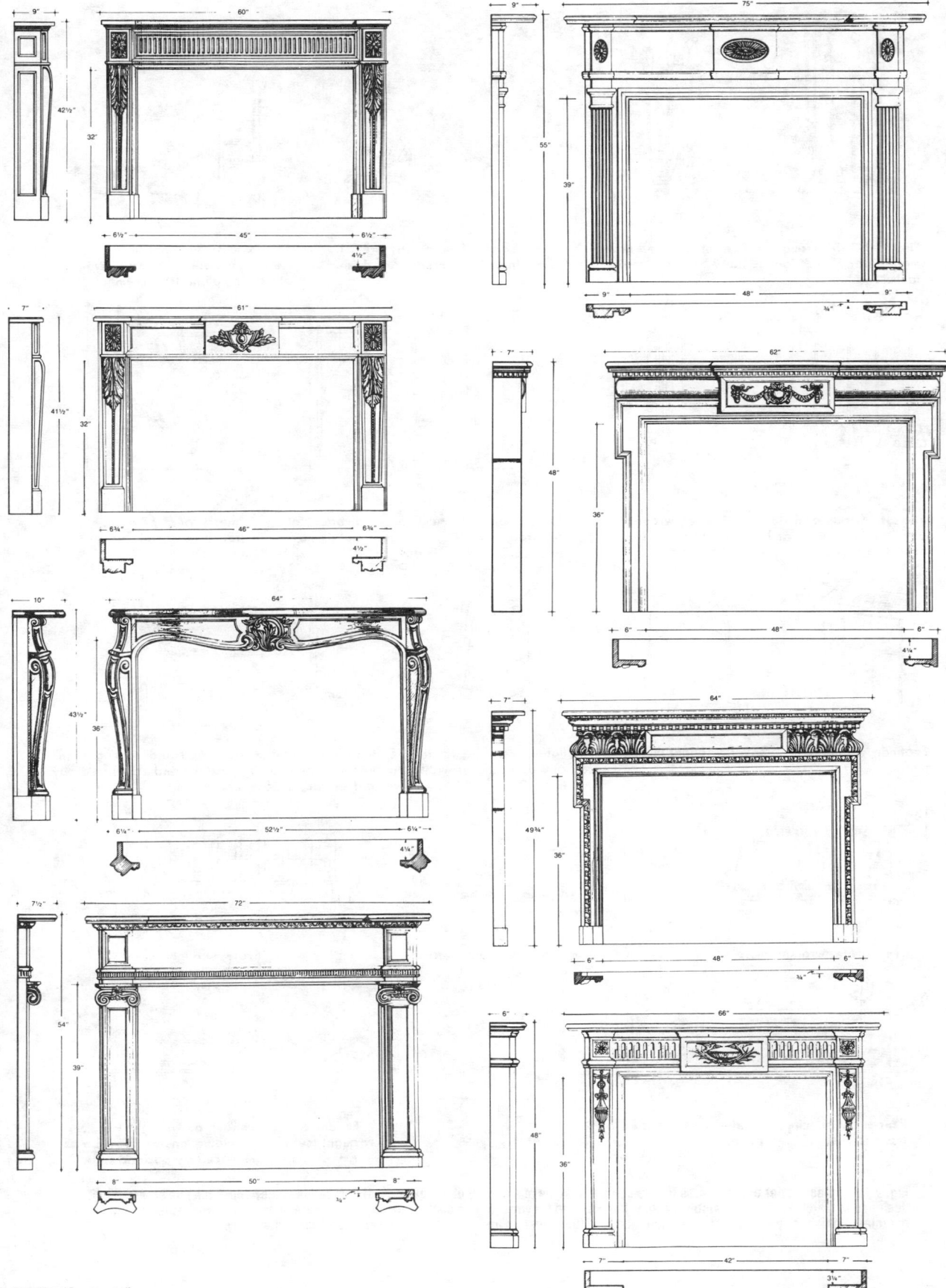

Fig. 6 *(Continued)*

FIREPLACES

Fireplace Accessories

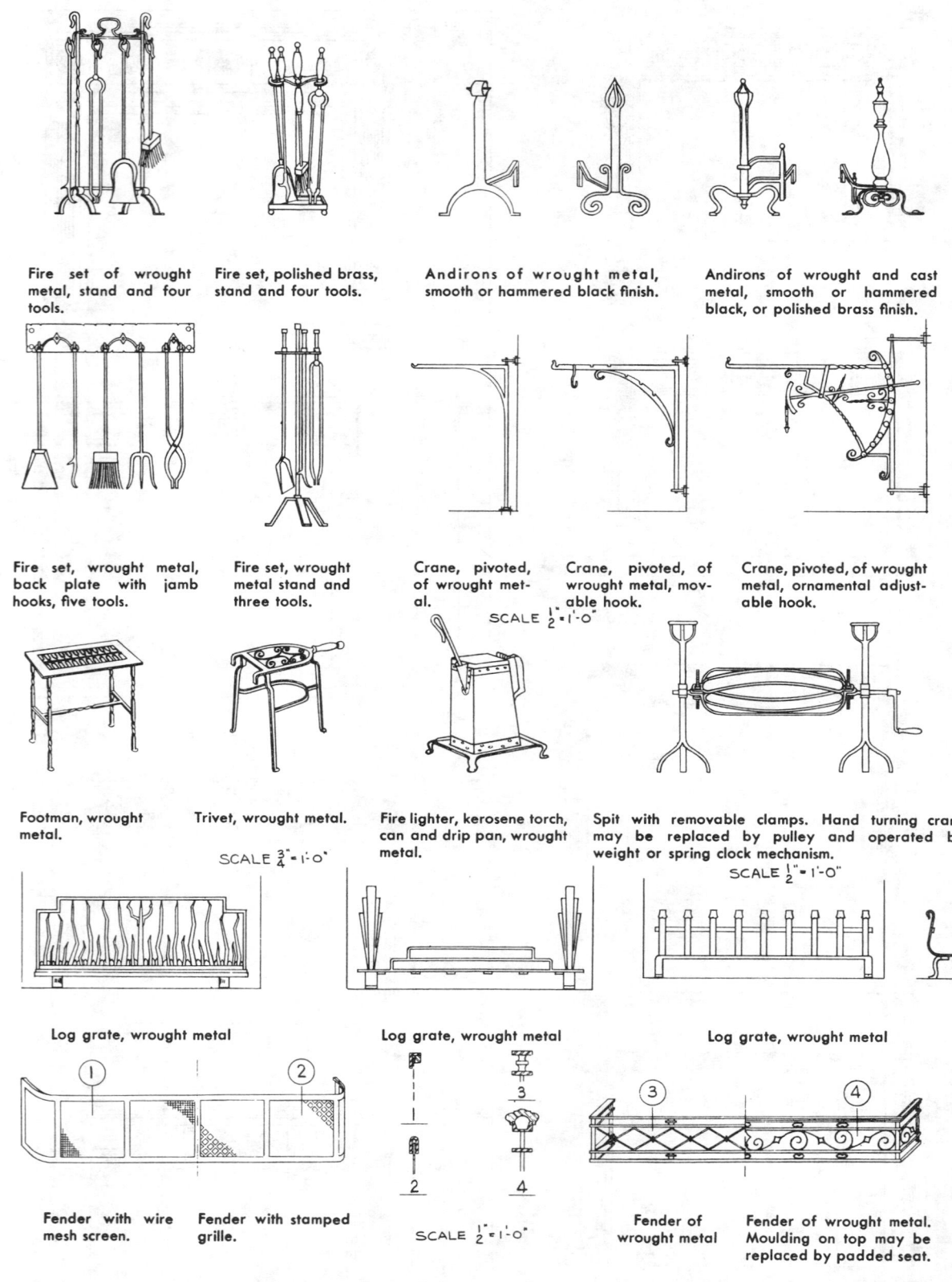

Fire set of wrought metal, stand and four tools.

Fire set, polished brass, stand and four tools.

Andirons of wrought metal, smooth or hammered black finish.

Andirons of wrought and cast metal, smooth or hammered black, or polished brass finish.

Fire set, wrought metal, back plate with jamb hooks, five tools.

Fire set, wrought metal stand and three tools.

Crane, pivoted, of wrought metal.

Crane, pivoted, of wrought metal, movable hook.

SCALE ½" = 1'-0"

Crane, pivoted, of wrought metal, ornamental adjustable hook.

Footman, wrought metal.

Trivet, wrought metal.

SCALE ¾" = 1'-0"

Fire lighter, kerosene torch, can and drip pan, wrought metal.

Spit with removable clamps. Hand turning crank may be replaced by pulley and operated by weight or spring clock mechanism.

SCALE ½" = 1'-0"

Log grate, wrought metal

Log grate, wrought metal

Log grate, wrought metal

Fender with wire mesh screen.

Fender with stamped grille.

SCALE ½" = 1'-0"

Fender of wrought metal

Fender of wrought metal. Moulding on top may be replaced by padded seat.

Fig. 7 Fireplaces offer opportunities for the use and display of a variety of metal items of decorative value. These may be selected or designed to match other material in the room. Metals used for wrought and cast fireplace products are usually cast iron, steel in a dark hammered finish, or polished brass. Combinations of these metals and other metals may be used very effectively.

Although lighting design is a discipline in and of itself, the interior designer and architect must be knowledgeable about the interface between lighting elements and the interior architecture. This section, therefore, focuses primarily on the detailing of this interface. Details from actual contract drawings, prepared by various interior design and architectural firms, are provided for the reader's reference. Among the details are those for valence and cove lighting and for the lighting of stairs, columns, and skylights. This section also provides some basic planning data including illuminance values for residences, offices, stores, and industrial spaces.

Bottom of shade at eye level when seated — approx. 40"-42" off floor.

APPROX. 40"-42"

Exceptions:
Sewing, Piano

Light colored shade should transmit light generously.

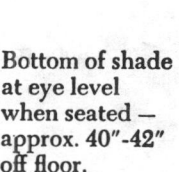

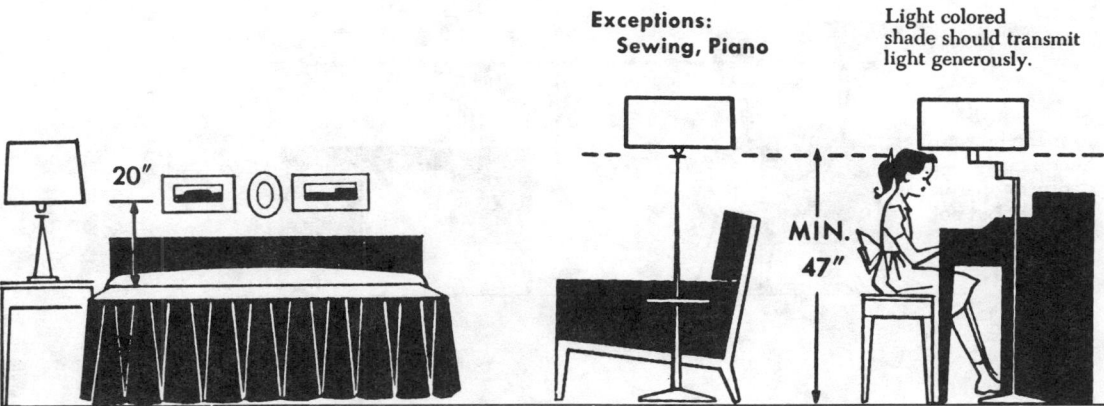

20"

MIN. 47"

Fig. 1   Measuring when the lamp is at the side — when sitting, lying down, or playing the piano.

When bottom of shade is above eye level, lamp stem should be about 10" behind shoulder — near rear corner of chair

MIN. 47"

Fig. 2   Measuring when the lamp is behind — when sitting.

LIGHTING

Planning Data: Minimum Shade Heights

Recommended Minimum Shade Dimensions

LAMP TYPE	Top Dia. "	Depth "	Bottom Dia. "
Sr. Floor	10	10	18
Swing Type	10	10	16
Jr. Floor — Swing Type	10	9	16
Diffuser Type	14	6	16
Bridge	8	8	13
End Table	8	10	16
Diffuser Type	14	6	16
Sr. Table	14	13	16
Wall Lamp	8	8	13
Diffuser Type	4	6	14
Study Type — pair	6	7	10
Make-Up — pair	7	7	9-10
Double Dresser — pair	8	8	12-14

Base Height (measure from table to shade bottom)

+ Table Height
_____

= Seated Eye Height (approx. 40"-42" off floor)

FLOOR LAMPS

Measure from floor to bottom of shade.

SHADES

Measure top and bottom diameters, and depth vertically through center.

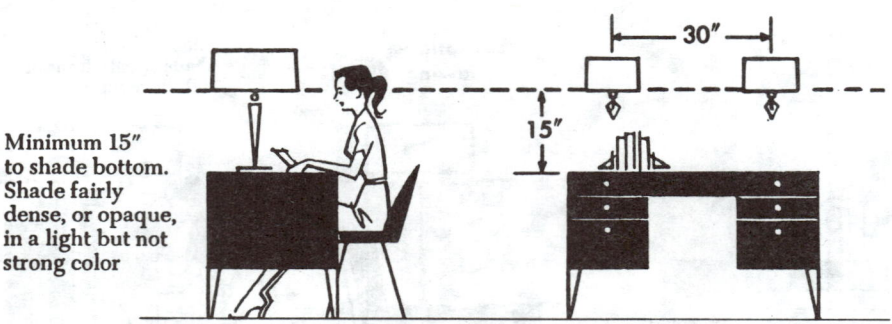

Minimum 15" to shade bottom. Shade fairly dense, or opaque, in a light but not strong color

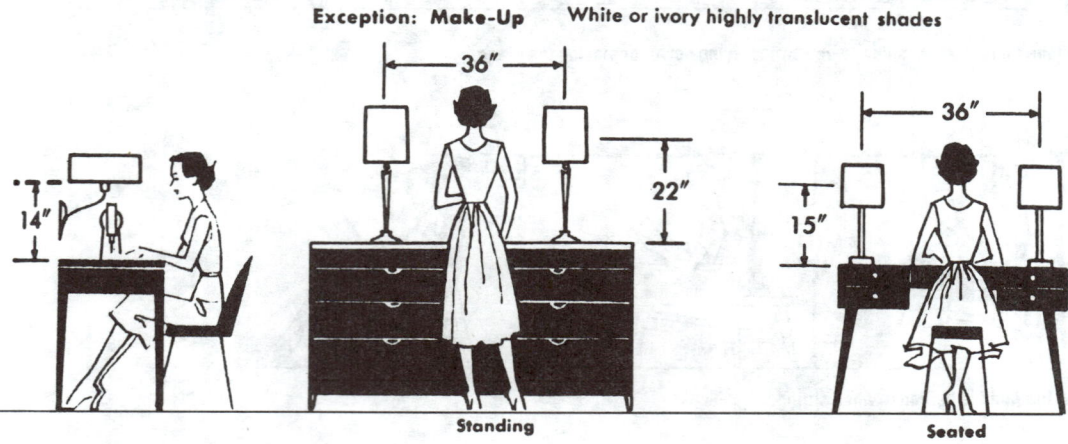

Exception: Make-Up White or ivory highly translucent shades

Standing

Seated

Fig. 3   Measuring when the lamp is in front — when studying, sewing, or grooming oneself.

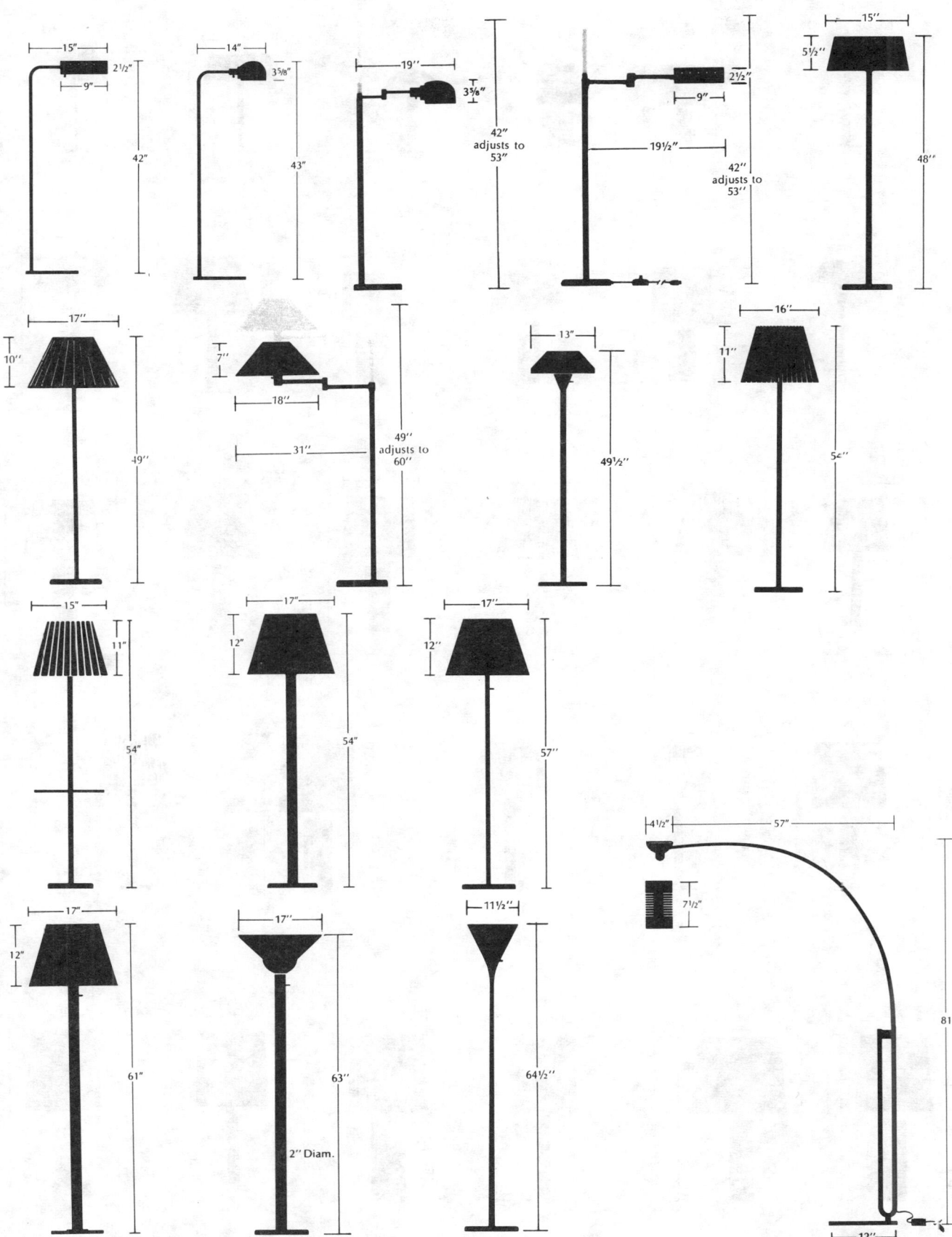

LIGHTING

Table Lamps

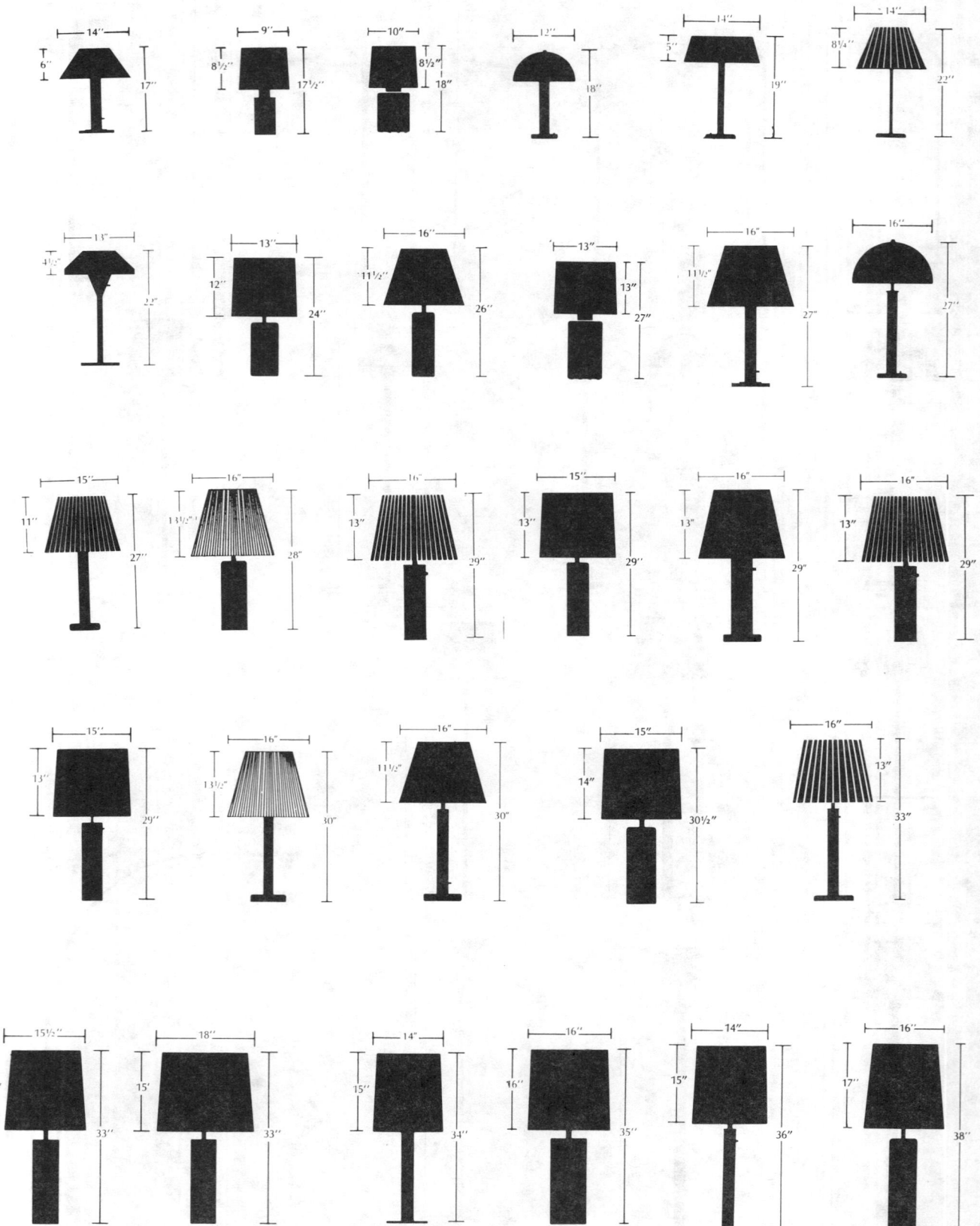

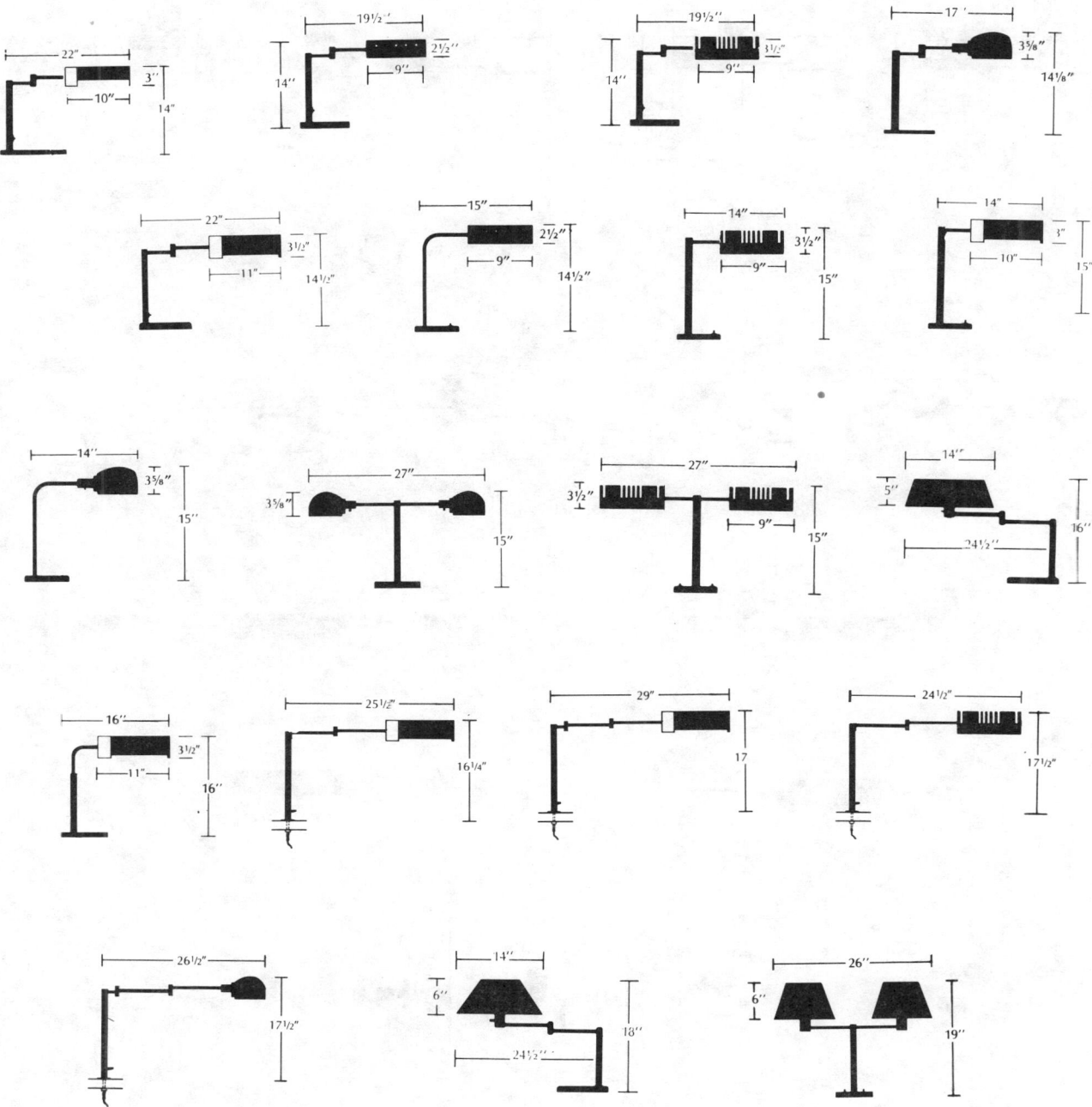

LIGHTING
Wall-Mounted Task Lamps

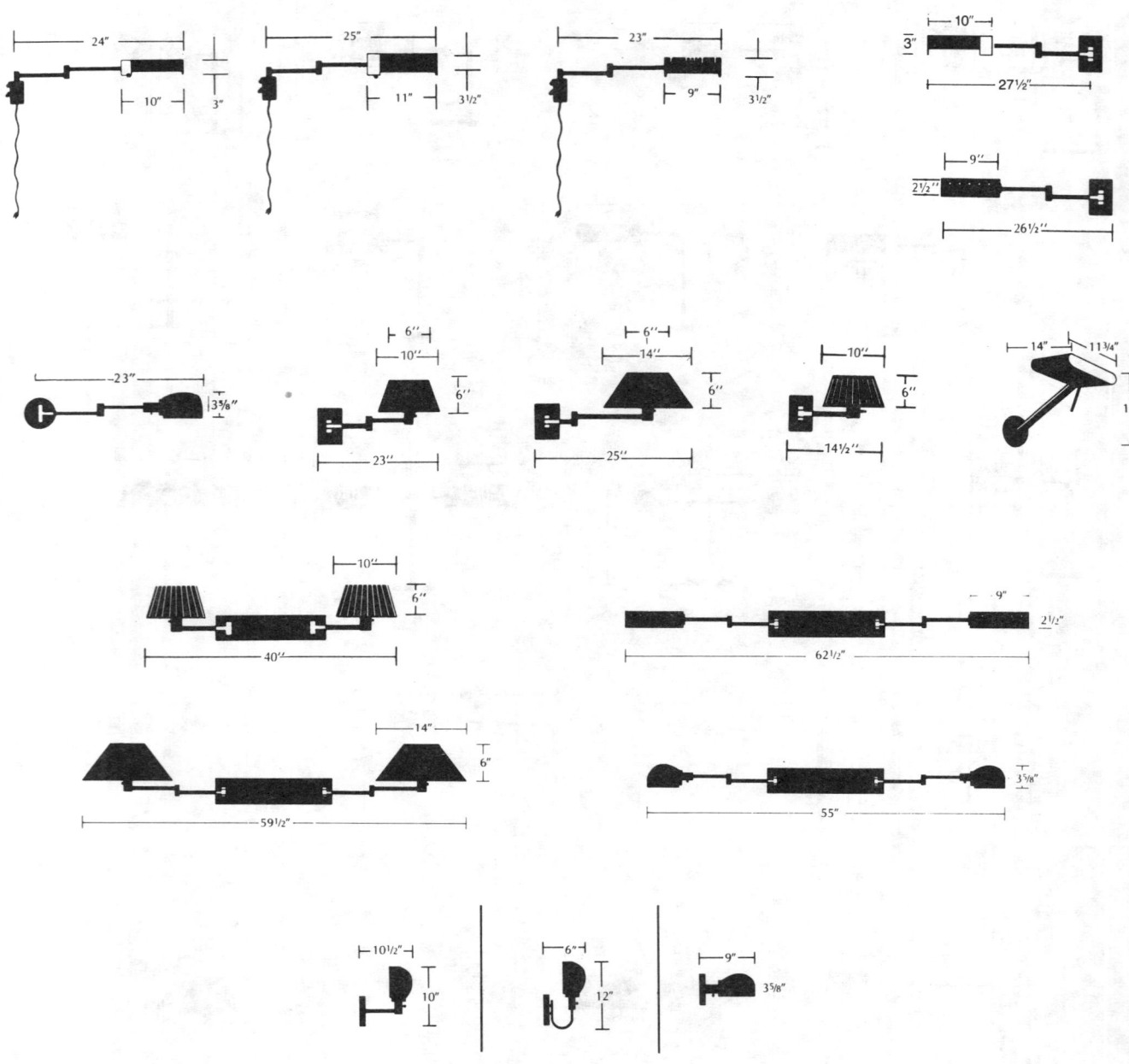

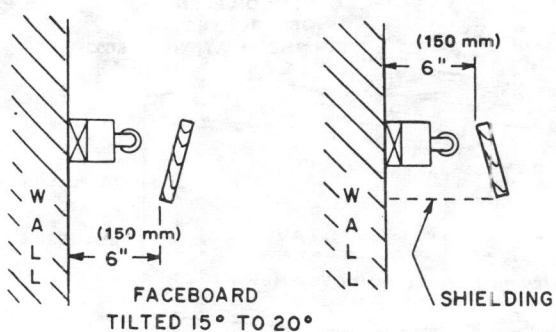

Fig. 4   Valance faceboard may be tilted.

FACEBOARD TILTED 15° TO 20°

SHIELDING

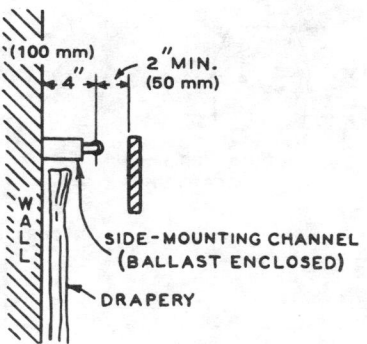

Fig. 5   With side-mounting channels, no extender is necessary.

SIDE-MOUNTING CHANNEL (BALLAST ENCLOSED)

DRAPERY

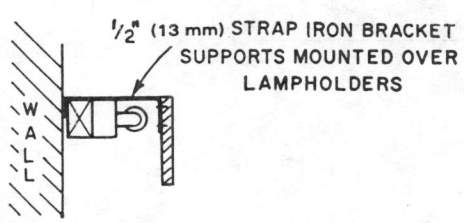

Fig. 6   Intermediate brackets are required to support long faceboards.

½" (13 mm) STRAP IRON BRACKET SUPPORTS MOUNTED OVER LAMPHOLDERS

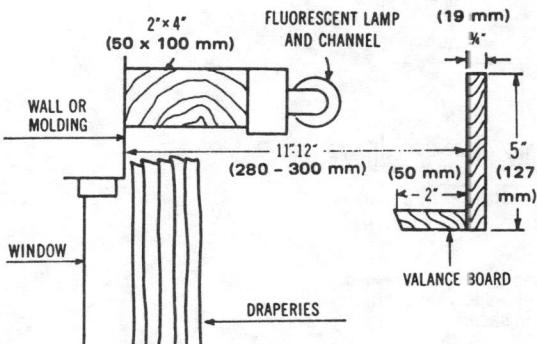

Fig. 7   Variation of valance lighting. (If distance between wall and lamp is increased, light will be distributed more evenly, but shielding may be required at the bottom of the faceboard.)

2" x 4" (50 x 100 mm)   FLUORESCENT LAMP AND CHANNEL   (19 mm) ¾"

WALL OR MOLDING

11"-12" (280 - 300 mm)   (50 mm)   5" (127 mm)   2"

WINDOW

DRAPERIES

VALANCE BOARD

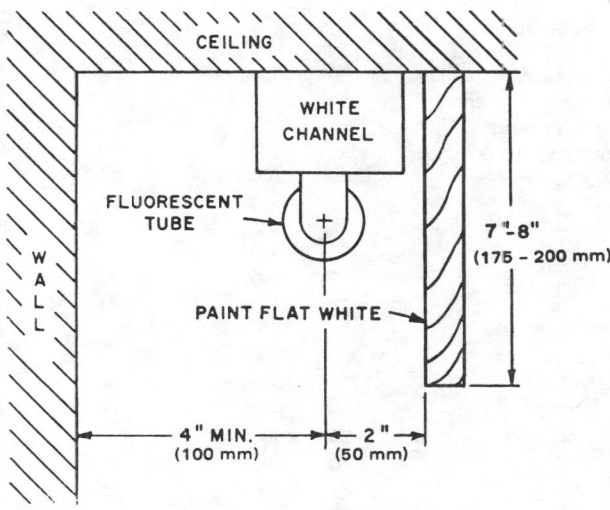

Fig. 8   Minimum dimensions for cornice lighting installation.

CEILING

WHITE CHANNEL

FLUORESCENT TUBE

PAINT FLAT WHITE

7"-8" (175 - 200 mm)

4" MIN. (100 mm)   2" (50 mm)

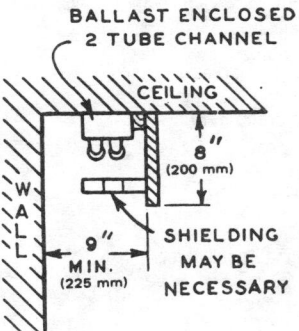

Fig. 9   Cornice lighting with two tubes may require shielding.

BALLAST ENCLOSED 2 TUBE CHANNEL

CEILING

8" (200 mm)

SHIELDING MAY BE NECESSARY

9" MIN. (225 mm)

LIGHTING

Planning Data: Residential Down Lighting

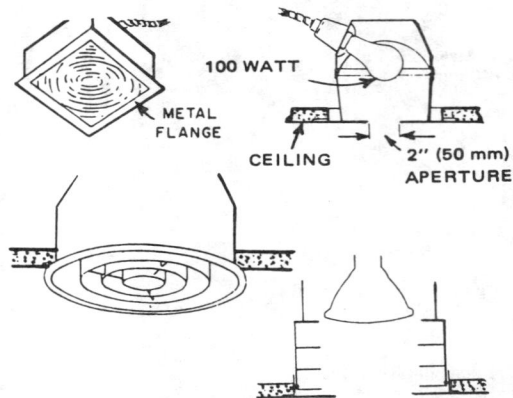

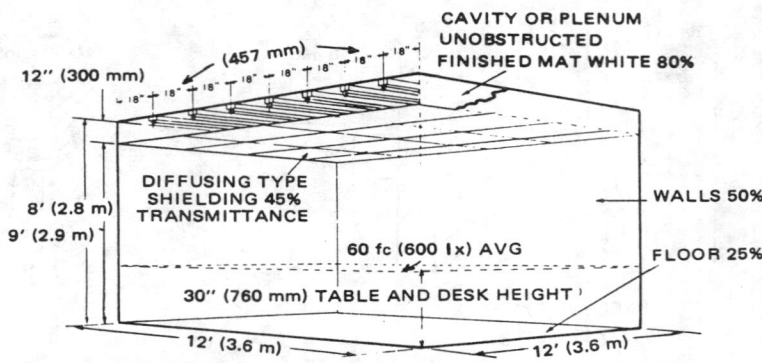

Fig. 15 Basic relationship for the design of luminous panels. [A light level of 60 fc (600 lx) is produced by seven rows of three 40-W fluorescent tubes on 18-in (457 mm) centers. Light distribution and surface luminance are approximately uniform.]

Fig. 10 Common types of downlights.

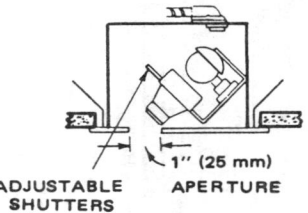

Fig. 11 Pinhole spot, a recessed downlight with adjustable shutters to shape beam pattern.

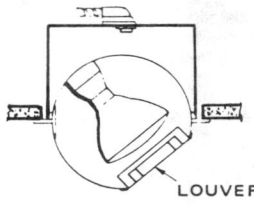

Fig. 12 "Eyeball" semirecessed fully adjustable downlight.

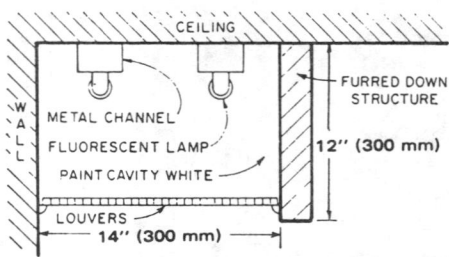

Fig. 13 Luminous panel or soffit lighting, used over a kitchen or bathroom counter.

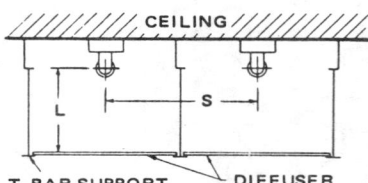

Fig. 14 Critical dimensions for luminous panel and luminous ceiling lighting. (S should not exceed 1½ to 2 times L.)

TABLE 1 Illuminance Values for Residences*

Specific visual tasks	Illuminance	
	Foot-candles	Lux†
Dining	15	150
Grooming, shaving, makeup	50	500
Handcraft		
Ordinary seeing tasks	70	700
Difficult seeing tasks	100	1000
Very difficult seeing tasks	150	1500
Critical seeing tasks	200	2000
Ironing (hand and machine)	50	500
Kitchen duties		
Food preparation and cleaning	150	1500
Serving and other noncritical tasks	50	500
Laundry		
Preparation, sorting, inspection	50	500
Tub area—soaking, tinting	50	500
Washer and dryer areas	30	300
Reading and writing		
Handwriting, reproductions, and poor copies	70	700
Books, magazines, newspapers	30	300
Reading piano or organ scores		
Advanced (substandard size)	150	1500
Advanced	70	700
Simple	30	300
Sewing (hand and machine)		
Dark fabrics	200	2000
Medium fabrics	100	1000
Light fabrics	50	500
Occasional—high contrast	30	300
Study	70	700
Table games	30	300
General lighting		
Conversation, relaxation, entertainment	10	100
Passage areas, for safety	10	100
Areas other than kitchen involving visual tasks	30	300
Kitchen	50	500

*Minimum on the task at all times.
†Lux is an SI unit equal to 0.0929 footcandle.

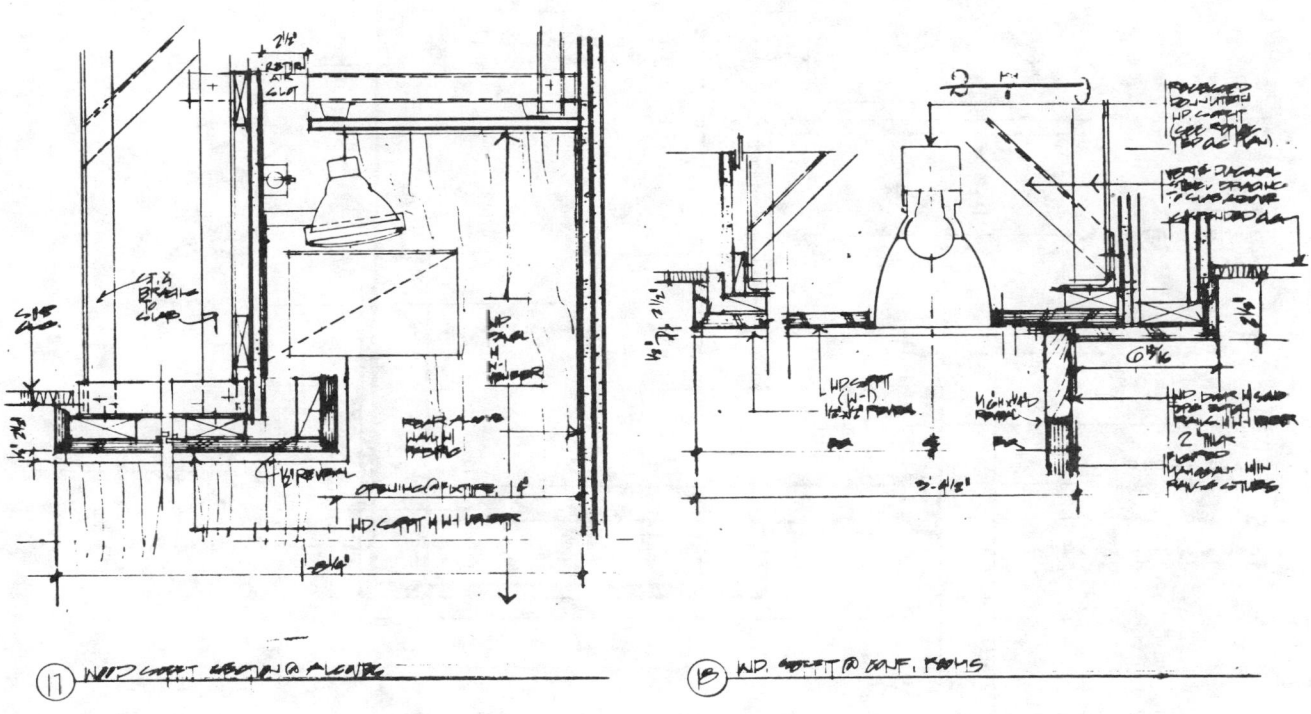

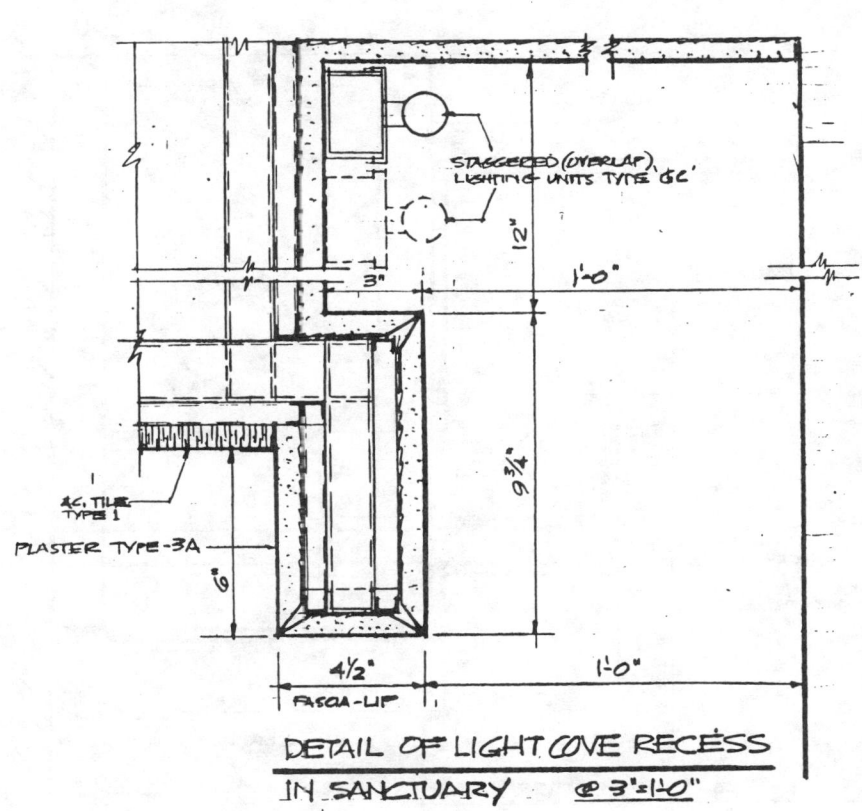

DETAIL OF LIGHT COVE RECESS
IN SANCTUARY @ 3"=1'-0"

LIGHTING
Cove Lighting Details

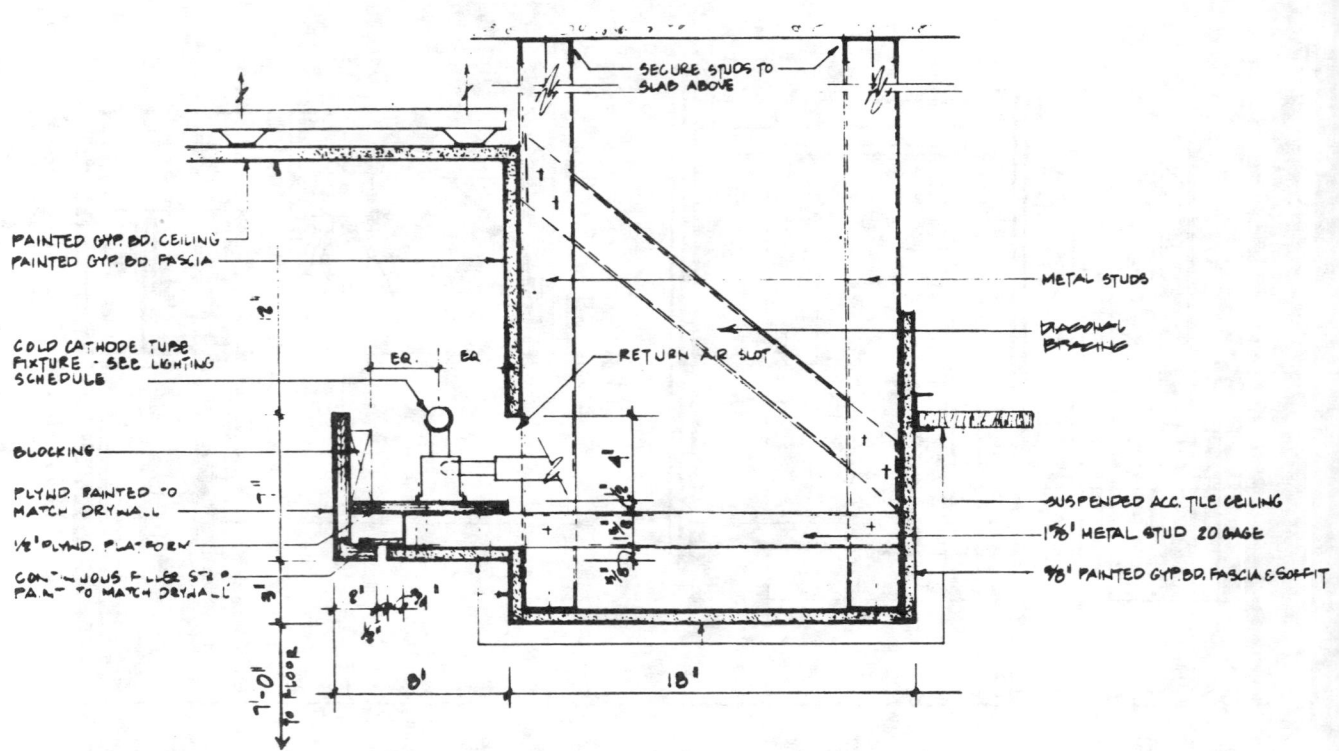

PAINTED GYP. BD. CEILING
PAINTED GYP. BD. FASCIA

COLD CATHODE TUBE
FIXTURE - SEE LIGHTING
SCHEDULE

BLOCKING

PLYWD. PAINTED TO
MATCH DRYWALL

½" PLYWD. PLATFORM

CONTINUOUS FILLER STRIP
PAINT TO MATCH DRYWALL

SECURE STUDS TO
SLAB ABOVE

METAL STUDS

DIAGONAL BRACING

RETURN AIR SLOT

SUSPENDED ACC. TILE CEILING

1⅝" METAL STUD 20 GAGE

⅝" PAINTED GYP. BD. FASCIA & SOFFIT

EQ. EQ

18"

8"

7'-0" TO FLOOR

④ DETAIL - LIGHT COVE @ RECEPTION AREA

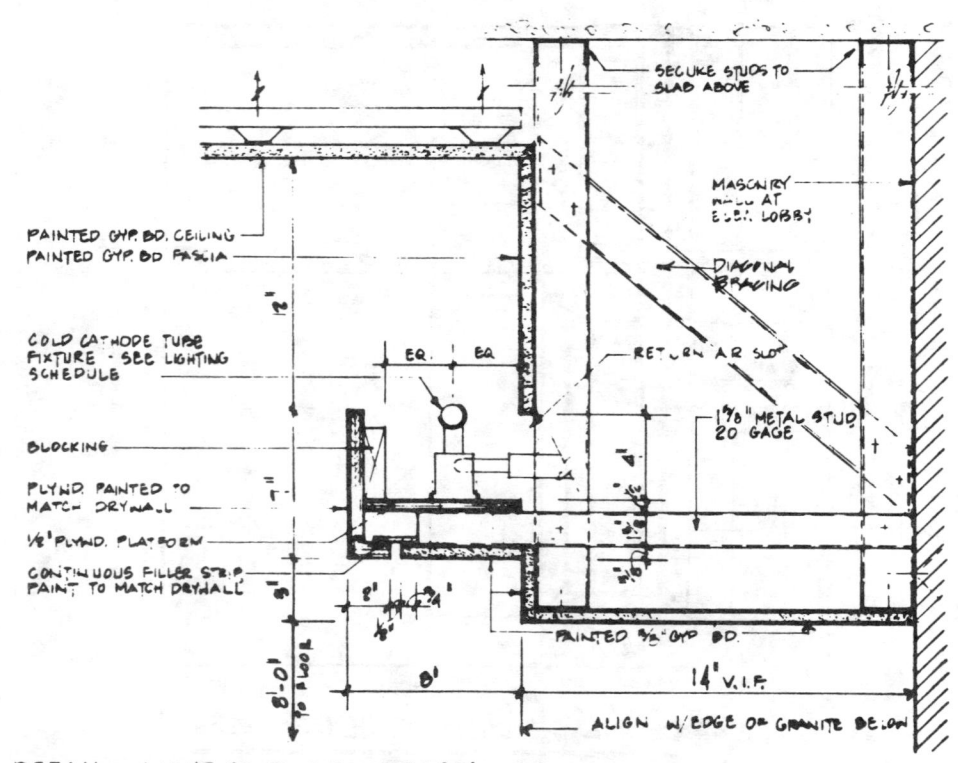

PAINTED GYP. BD. CEILING
PAINTED GYP. BD. FASCIA

COLD CATHODE TUBE
FIXTURE - SEE LIGHTING
SCHEDULE

BLOCKING

PLYWD. PAINTED TO
MATCH DRYWALL

½" PLYWD. PLATFORM

CONTINUOUS FILLER STRIP
PAINT TO MATCH DRYWALL

SECURE STUDS TO
SLAB ABOVE

MASONRY WALL AT
ELEV. LOBBY

DIAGONAL BRACING

RETURN AIR SLOT

1⅝" METAL STUD
20 GAGE

PAINTED ⅝" GYP. BD.

14" V.I.F.

ALIGN W/ EDGE OF GRANITE DESIGN

EQ. EQ

8"

8'-0" TO FLOOR

⑤ DETAIL - LIGHT COVE @ ELEVATOR LOBBY

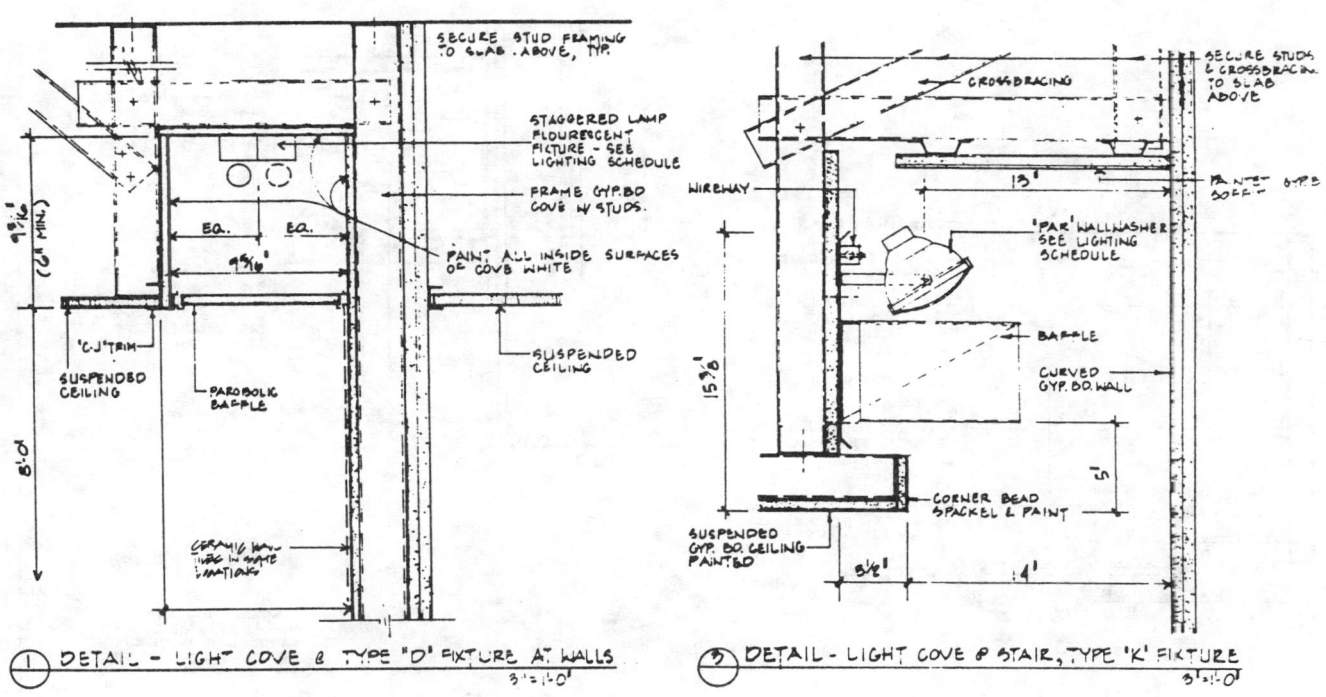

① DETAIL - LIGHT COVE @ TYPE "D" FIXTURE AT WALLS
3"=1'-0"

③ DETAIL - LIGHT COVE @ STAIR, TYPE 'K' FIXTURE
3"=1'-0"

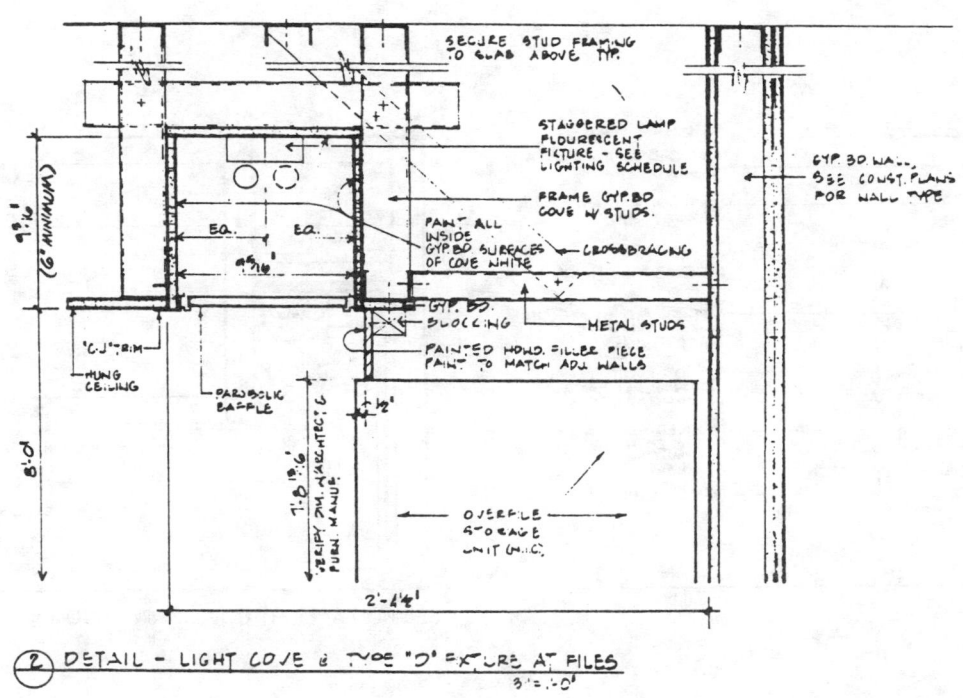

② DETAIL - LIGHT COVE @ TYPE "D" FIXTURE AT FILES
3"=1'-0"

LIGHTING
Cove Lighting Details

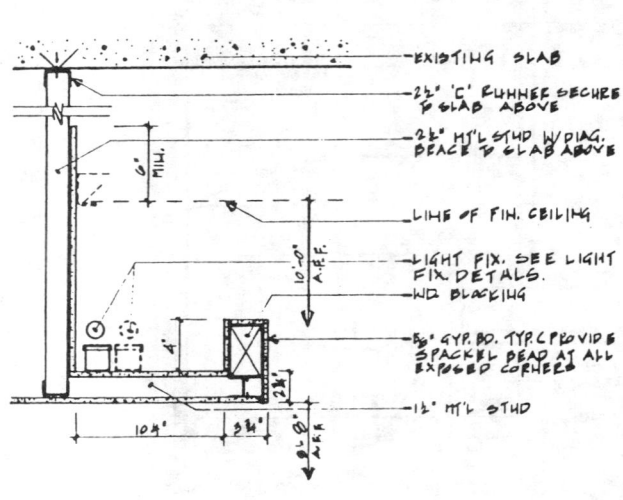

Labels:
- EXISTING SLAB
- 2½" 'C' RUNNER SECURE TO SLAB ABOVE
- 2½" MT'L STUD W/ DIAG. BRACE TO SLAB ABOVE
- LINE OF FIN. CEILING
- LIGHT FIX. SEE LIGHT FIX. DETAILS.
- WD. BLOCKING
- ⅝" GYP. BD. TYP. C PROVIDE SPACKEL BEAD AT ALL EXPOSED CORNERS
- 1½" MT'L STUD

SECTION AT LIGHT COVE

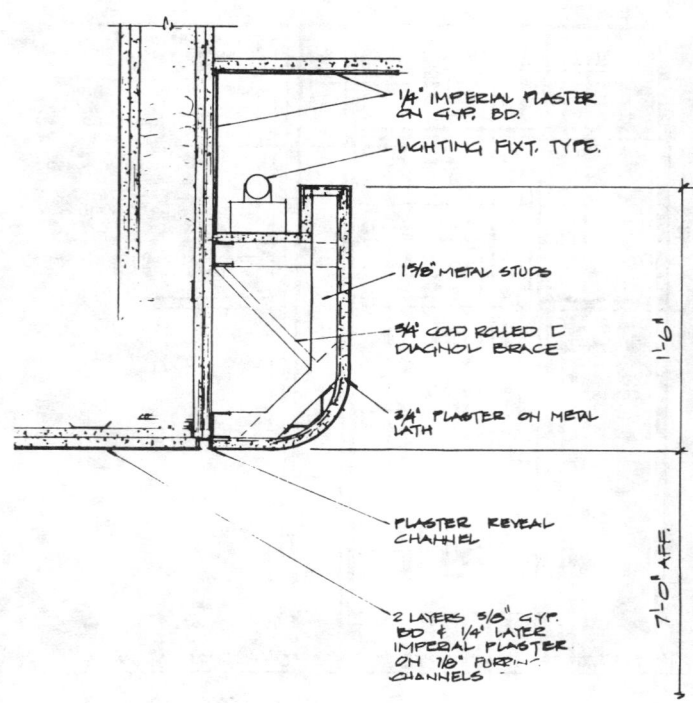

Labels:
- ¼" IMPERIAL PLASTER ON GYP. BD.
- LIGHTING FIXT. TYPE.
- 1⅝" METAL STUDS
- ¾" COLD ROLLED C DIAGNOL BRACE
- ¾" PLASTER ON METAL LATH
- PLASTER REVEAL CHANNEL
- 2 LAYERS ⅝" GYP. BD & ¼" LAYER IMPERIAL PLASTER ON ⅞" FURRIN' CHANNELS

SECTION AT TROUGH AND SOFFIT
1½" = 1'-0"

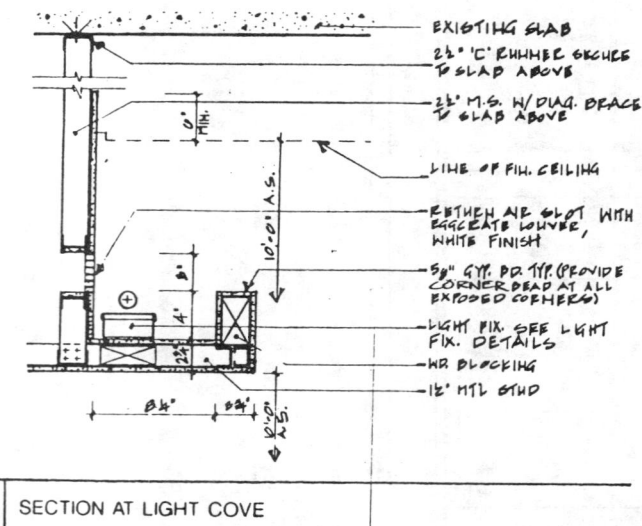

Labels:
- EXISTING SLAB
- 2½" 'C' RUNNER SECURE TO SLAB ABOVE
- 2½" M.S. W/ DIAG. BRACE TO SLAB ABOVE
- LINE OF FIN. CEILING
- RETURN AIR SLOT WITH EGGCRATE LOUVER, WHITE FINISH
- ⅝" GYP. BD. TYP. (PROVIDE CORNER BEAD AT ALL EXPOSED CORNERS)
- LIGHT FIX. SEE LIGHT FIX. DETAILS
- WD. BLOCKING
- 1½" MTL STUD

SECTION AT LIGHT COVE

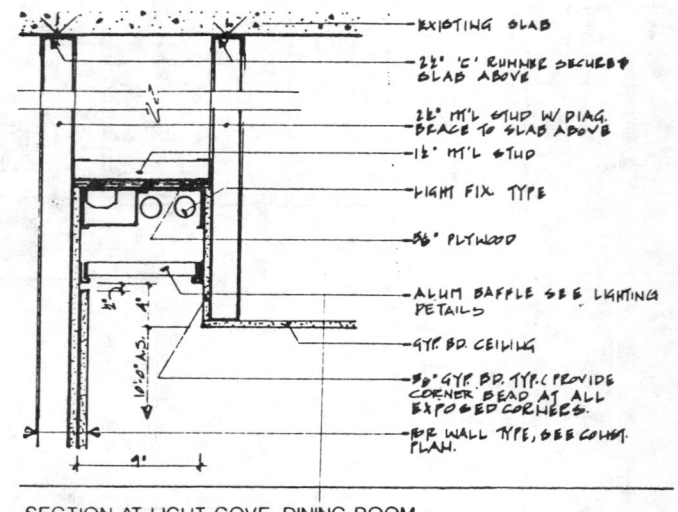

Labels:
- EXISTING SLAB
- 2½" 'C' RUNNER SECURE TO SLAB ABOVE
- 2½" MT'L STUD W/ DIAG. BRACE TO SLAB ABOVE
- 1½" MT'L STUD
- LIGHT FIX TYPE
- ⅝" PLYWOOD
- ALUM BAFFLE SEE LIGHTING DETAILS
- GYP. BD. CEILING
- ⅝" GYP. BD. TYP. C PROVIDE CORNER BEAD AT ALL EXPOSED CORNERS.
- FOR WALL TYPE, SEE CONST. PLAN.

SECTION AT LIGHT COVE, DINING ROOM

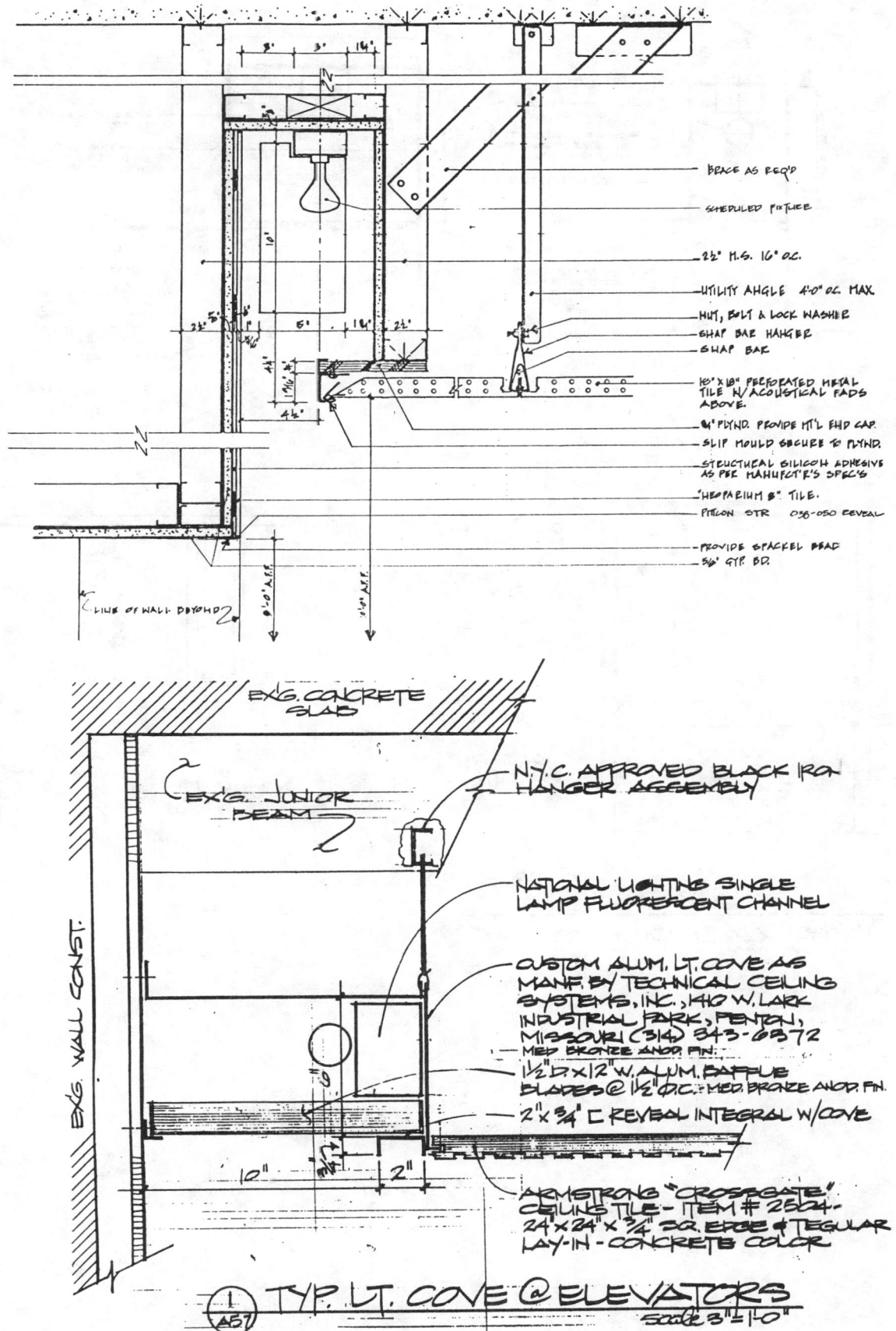

BRACE AS REQ'D

SCHEDULED FIXTURE

2½" M.S. 16" O.C.

UTILITY ANGLE 4'-0" O.C. MAX.

NUT, BOLT & LOCK WASHER
SNAP BAR HANGER
SNAP BAR

18" x 18" PERFORATED METAL TILE W/ ACOUSTICAL PADS ABOVE.

¾" PLYWD. PROVIDE MT'L END CAP.
SLIP MOULD SECURE TO PLYWD.
STRUCTURAL SILICON ADHESIVE AS PER MANUFCT'R'S SPEC'S

"HESPARIUM B" TILE.
PITTCON STR 038-050 REVEAL

PROVIDE SPACKLED BEAD
5⁄8" GYP. BD.

LINE OF WALL BEYOND

EX'G. CONCRETE SLAB

N.Y.C. APPROVED BLACK IRON HANGER ASSEMBLY

EX'G. JUNIOR BEAM

EX'G. WALL CONST.

NATIONAL LIGHTING SINGLE LAMP FLUORESCENT CHANNEL

CUSTOM ALUM. LT. COVE AS MANF. BY TECHNICAL CEILING SYSTEMS, INC., 1410 W. LARK INDUSTRIAL PARK, FENTON, MISSOURI (314) 343-6372
MED BRONZE ANOD. FIN.

1½" D. x 12" W. ALUM. BAFFLE BLADES @ 1½" O.C. MED. BRONZE ANOD. FIN.

2" x ¾" L REVEAL INTEGRAL W/ COVE

ARMSTRONG "CROSSGATE" CEILING TILE - ITEM # 2504 - 24" x 24" x ¾" SQ. EDGE & TEGULAR LAY-IN - CONCRETE COLOR

1 TYP. LT. COVE @ ELEVATORS
A57   Scale 3" = 1'-0"

LIGHTING

Fluorescent Cove Lighting Details

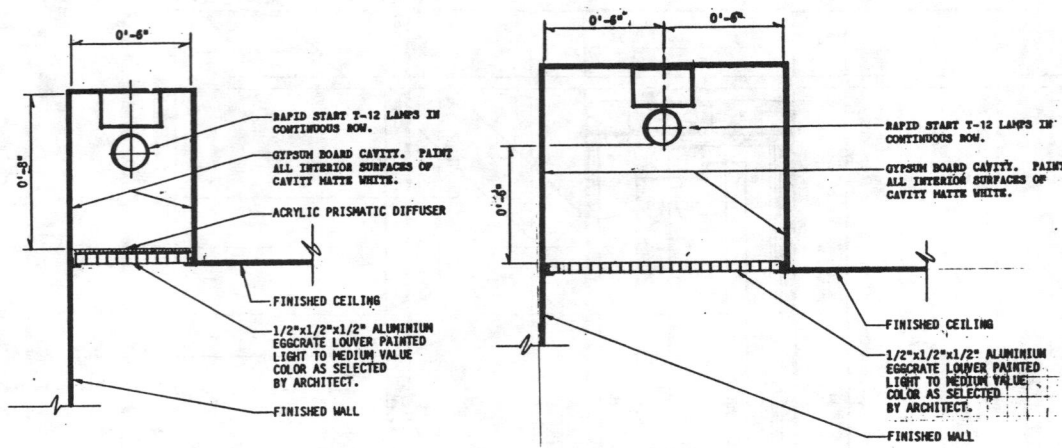

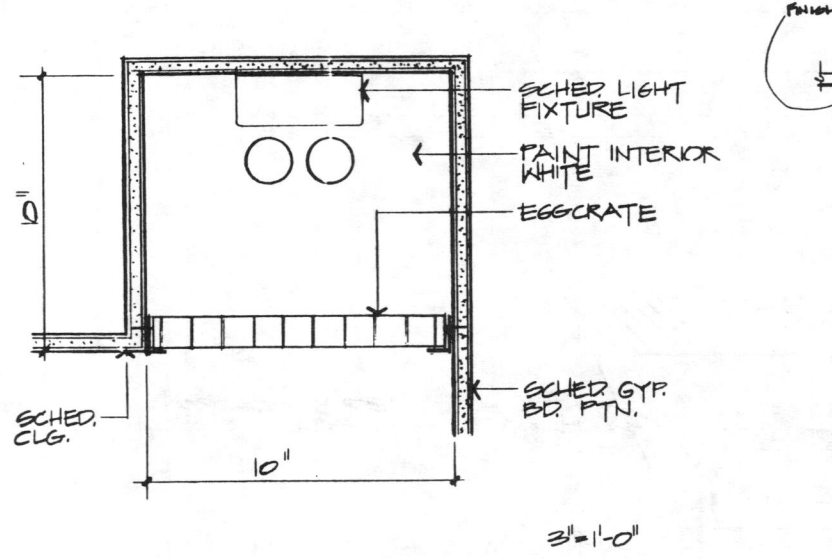

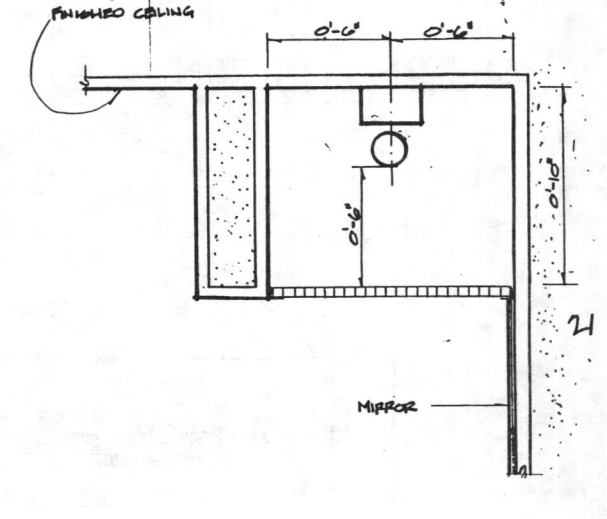

$3" = 1'-0"$

SECTION THRU CONTINUOUS COVE LIGHT

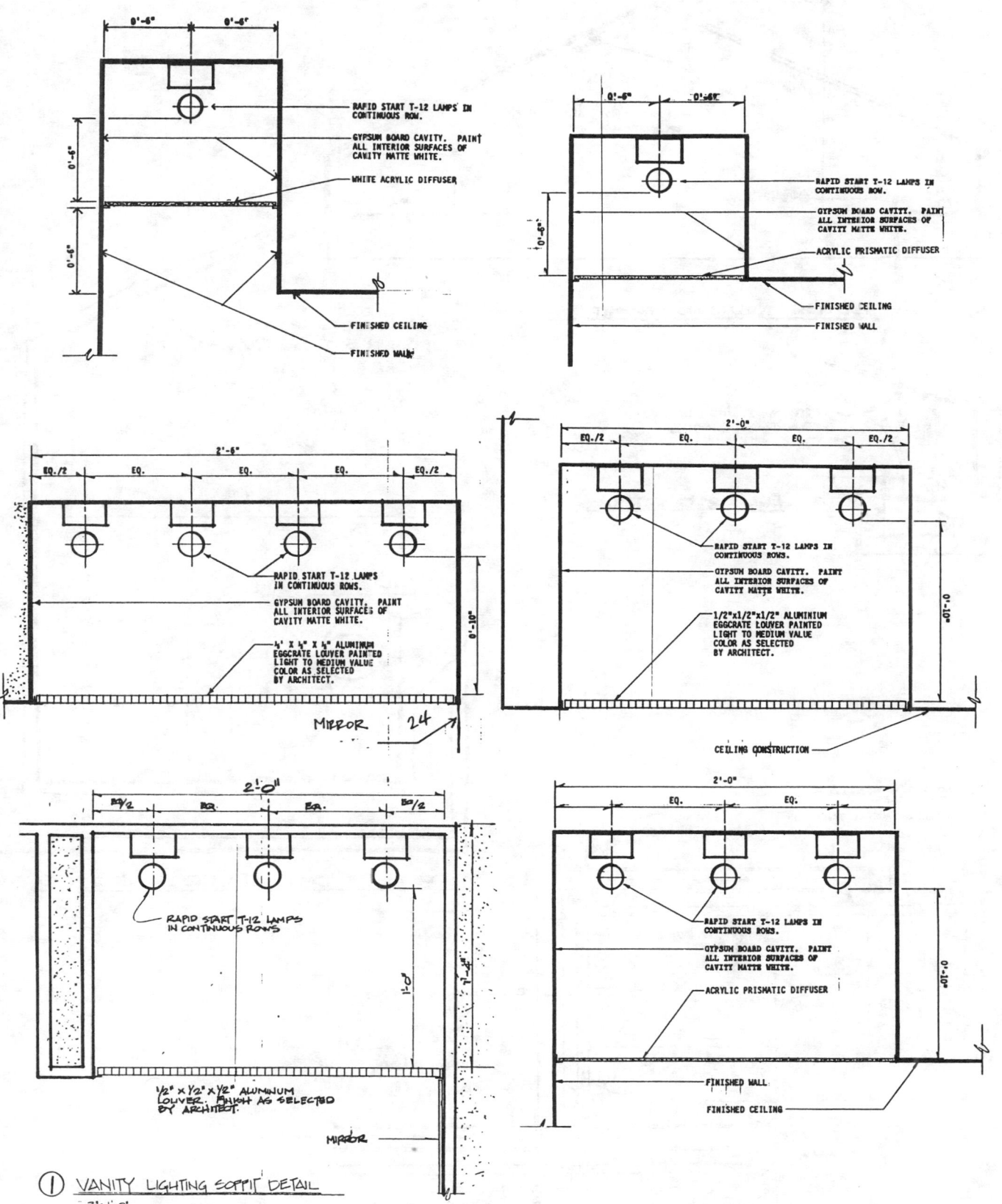

0'-6"   0'-6"

RAPID START T-12 LAMPS IN
CONTINUOUS ROW.

GYPSUM BOARD CAVITY. PAINT
ALL INTERIOR SURFACES OF
CAVITY MATTE WHITE.

WHITE ACRYLIC DIFFUSER

0'-6"

0'-6"

FINISHED CEILING

FINISHED WALL

0'-6"   0'-6"

RAPID START T-12 LAMPS IN
CONTINUOUS ROW.

GYPSUM BOARD CAVITY. PAINT
ALL INTERIOR SURFACES OF
CAVITY MATTE WHITE.

ACRYLIC PRISMATIC DIFFUSER

0'-6"

FINISHED CEILING

FINISHED WALL

2'-6"

EQ./2   EQ.   EQ.   EQ./2

RAPID START T-12 LAMPS
IN CONTINUOUS ROWS.

GYPSUM BOARD CAVITY. PAINT
ALL INTERIOR SURFACES OF
CAVITY MATTE WHITE.

½" X ½" X ½" ALUMINUM
EGGCRATE LOUVER PAINTED
LIGHT TO MEDIUM VALUE
COLOR AS SELECTED
BY ARCHITECT.

0'-10"

MIRROR   24

2'-0"

EQ./2   EQ.   EQ.   EQ./2

RAPID START T-12 LAMPS IN
CONTINUOUS ROWS.

GYPSUM BOARD CAVITY. PAINT
ALL INTERIOR SURFACES OF
CAVITY MATTE WHITE.

1/2"x1/2"x1/2" ALUMINIUM
EGGCRATE LOUVER PAINTED
LIGHT TO MEDIUM VALUE
COLOR AS SELECTED
BY ARCHITECT.

0'-10"

CEILING CONSTRUCTION

2'-0"

EQ./2   EQ.   EQ.   EQ./2

RAPID START T-12 LAMPS
IN CONTINUOUS ROWS

1'-0"

½" X ½" X ½" ALUMINUM
LOUVER. FINISH AS SELECTED
BY ARCHITECT.

MIRROR

① VANITY LIGHTING SOFFIT DETAIL
  3" = 1'-0"

2'-0"

EQ.   EQ.

RAPID START T-12 LAMPS IN
CONTINUOUS ROWS.

GYPSUM BOARD CAVITY. PAINT
ALL INTERIOR SURFACES OF
CAVITY MATTE WHITE.

ACRYLIC PRISMATIC DIFFUSER

0'-10"

FINISHED WALL

FINISHED CEILING

LIGHTING

Fluorescent Cove Lighting Details

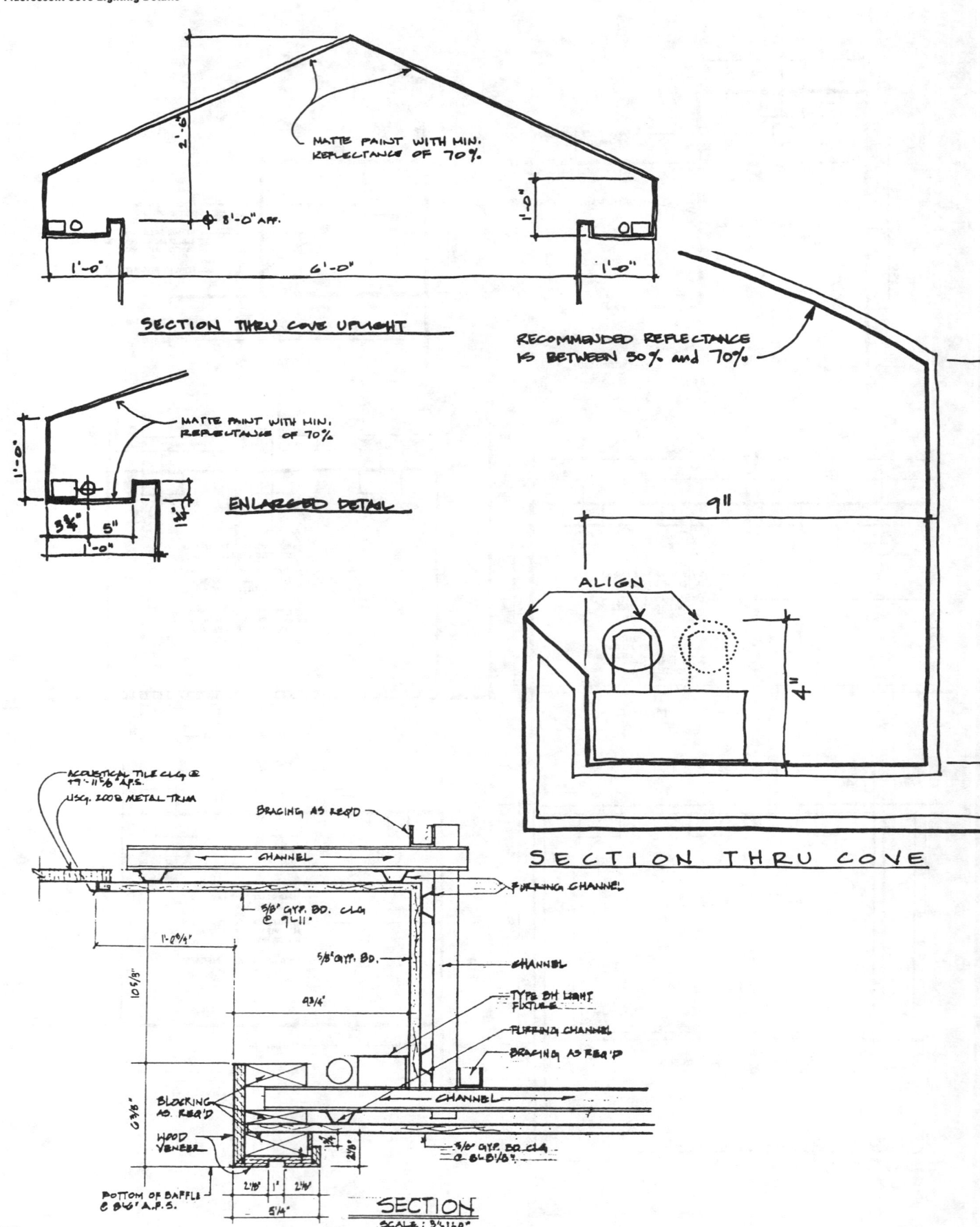

MATTE PAINT WITH MIN.
REFLECTANCE OF 70%.

2'-0"

⊕ 8'-0" A.F.F.

1'-0"   6'-0"   1'-0"

SECTION THRU COVE UPLIGHT

RECOMMENDED REFLECTANCE
IS BETWEEN 50% and 70%

MATTE PAINT WITH MIN.
REFLECTANCE OF 70%

1'-0"

ENLARGED DETAIL

3¼"   5"
1'-0"

9"

ALIGN

4"

SECTION THRU COVE

ACOUSTICAL TILE CLG @
+9'-11⅝" A.F.S.

U.S.G. 200B METAL TRIM

BRACING AS REQ'D

CHANNEL

FURRING CHANNEL

5/8" GYP. BD. CLG
@ 9'-11"

5/8" GYP. BD.

CHANNEL

TYPE BH LIGHT
FIXTURE

FURRING CHANNEL

BRACING AS REQ'D

1'-0⅜"

10⅝"

9¾"

CHANNEL

BLOCKING
AS REQ'D

WOOD
VENEER

6⅜"

5/8" GYP. BD. CLG
@ 8'-6⅛"

BOTTOM OF BAFFLE
@ 8'6' A.F.S.

2⅛" 1" 2⅛"

5¼"

SECTION

SCALE: 3"=1'-0"

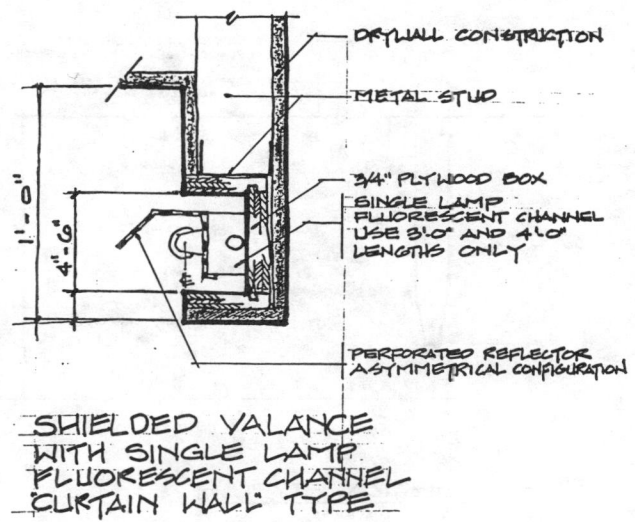

DRYWALL CONSTRUCTION

METAL STUD

3/4" PLYWOOD BOX

SINGLE LAMP FLUORESCENT CHANNEL USE 3'0" AND 4'0" LENGTHS ONLY

PERFORATED REFLECTOR ASYMMETRICAL CONFIGURATION

SHIELDED VALANCE
WITH SINGLE LAMP
FLUORESCENT CHANNEL
"CURTAIN WALL" TYPE

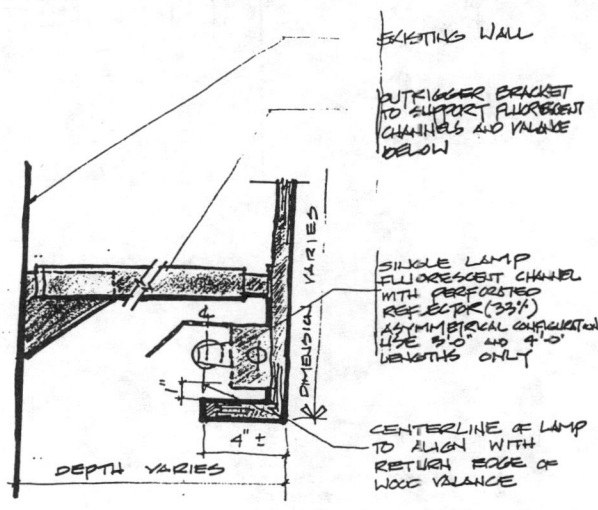

EXISTING WALL

OUTRIGGER BRACKET TO SUPPORT FLUORESCENT CHANNELS AND VALANCE BELOW

SINGLE LAMP FLUORESCENT CHANNEL WITH PERFORATED REFLECTOR (33%) ASYMMETRICAL CONFIGURATION USE 3'0" AND 4'0" LENGTHS ONLY

CENTERLINE OF LAMP TO ALIGN WITH RETURN EDGE OF WOOD VALANCE

DEPTH VARIES

VALANCE WITH
SINGLE LAMP
FLUORESCENT CHANNEL

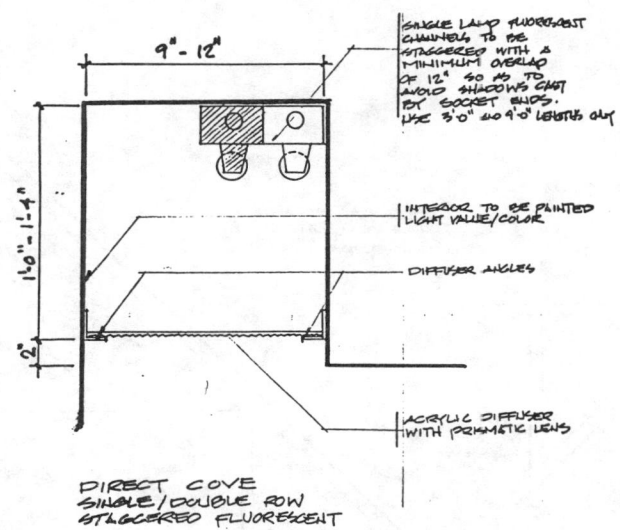

SINGLE LAMP FLUORESCENT CHANNELS TO BE STAGGERED WITH A MINIMUM OVERLAP OF 12" SO AS TO AVOID SHADOWS CAST BY SOCKET ENDS. USE 3'0" AND 4'0" LENGTHS ONLY

INTERIOR TO BE PAINTED LIGHT VALUE/COLOR

DIFFUSER ANGLES

ACRYLIC DIFFUSER WITH PRISMATIC LENS

DIRECT COVE
SINGLE/DOUBLE ROW
STAGGERED FLUORESCENT

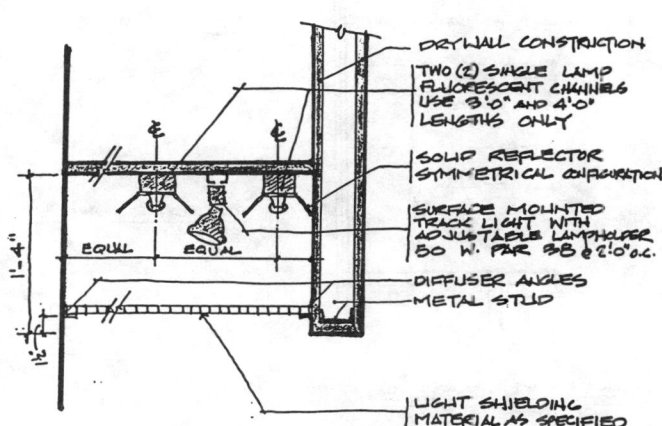

DRYWALL CONSTRUCTION

TWO (2) SINGLE LAMP FLUORESCENT CHANNELS USE 3'0" AND 4'0" LENGTHS ONLY

SOLID REFLECTOR SYMMETRICAL CONFIGURATION

SURFACE MOUNTED TRACK LIGHT WITH ADJUSTABLE LAMPHOLDER 50 W. PAR 38 @ 2'0" O.C.

DIFFUSER ANGLES
METAL STUD

LIGHT SHIELDING MATERIAL AS SPECIFIED

EQUAL   EQUAL

SHIELDED VALANCE
WITH TWO (2) SINGLE
LAMP FLUORESCENT
CHANNELS AND TRACK
LIGHT WITH INCANDESCENT
"CURTAIN WALL" TYPE

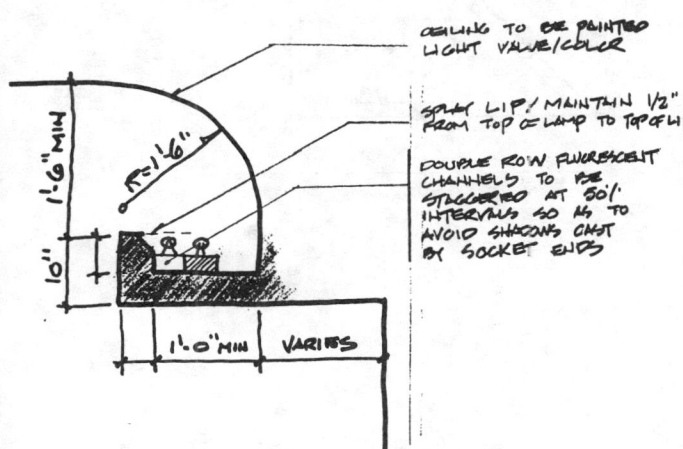

CEILING TO BE PAINTED LIGHT VALUE/COLOR

SPLAY LIP/MAINTAIN 1/2" FROM TOP OF LAMP TO TOP OF LIP

DOUBLE ROW FLUORESCENT CHANNELS TO BE STAGGERED AT 50% INTERVALS SO AS TO AVOID SHADOWS CAST BY SOCKET ENDS

1'-6" MIN
R = 1'-6"
10"
1'-0" MIN   VARIES

INDIRECT/CURVED COVE
DOUBLE ROW FLUORESCENT

LIGHTING

Miscellaneous Lighting Details

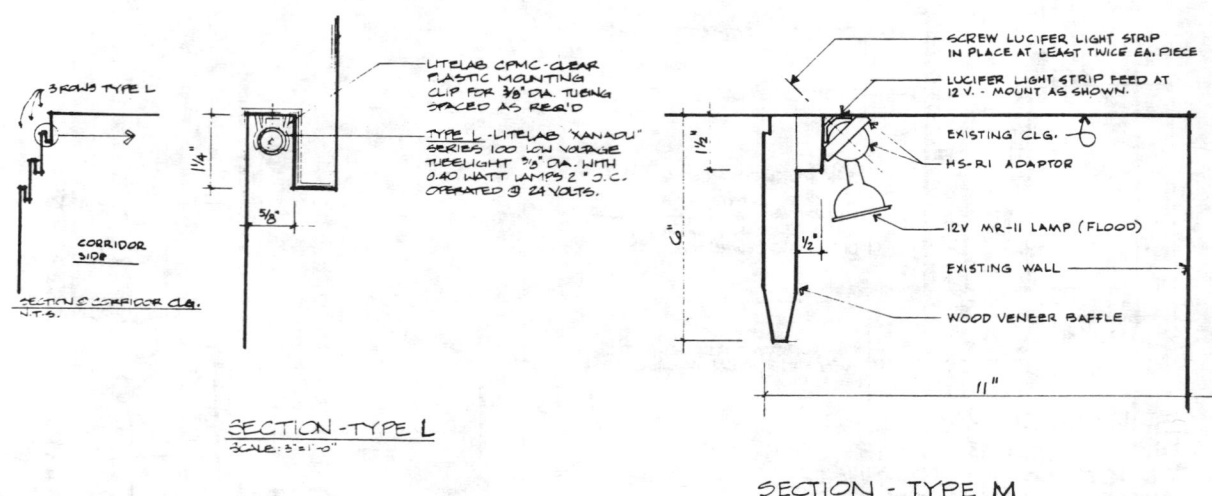

3 ROWS TYPE L

LITELAB CPMC - CLEAR
PLASTIC MOUNTING
CLIP FOR 3/8" DIA. TUBING
SPACED AS REQ'D

TYPE L - LITELAB 'XANADU'
SERIES 100 LOW VOLTAGE
TUBELIGHT 3/8" DIA. WITH
0.40 WATT LAMPS 2" O.C.
OPERATED @ 24 VOLTS.

CORRIDOR
SIDE

1/4"

5/8"

SECTION CORRIDOR CLG.
N.T.S.

SECTION - TYPE L
SCALE : 3" = 1'-0"

SCREW LUCIFER LIGHT STRIP
IN PLACE AT LEAST TWICE EA. PIECE

LUCIFER LIGHT STRIP FEED AT
12 V. - MOUNT AS SHOWN.

EXISTING CLG.

HS-R1 ADAPTOR

12V MR-11 LAMP (FLOOD)

EXISTING WALL

WOOD VENEER BAFFLE

1 1/2"

6"

1/2"

11"

SECTION - TYPE M
SCALE : HALF SIZE

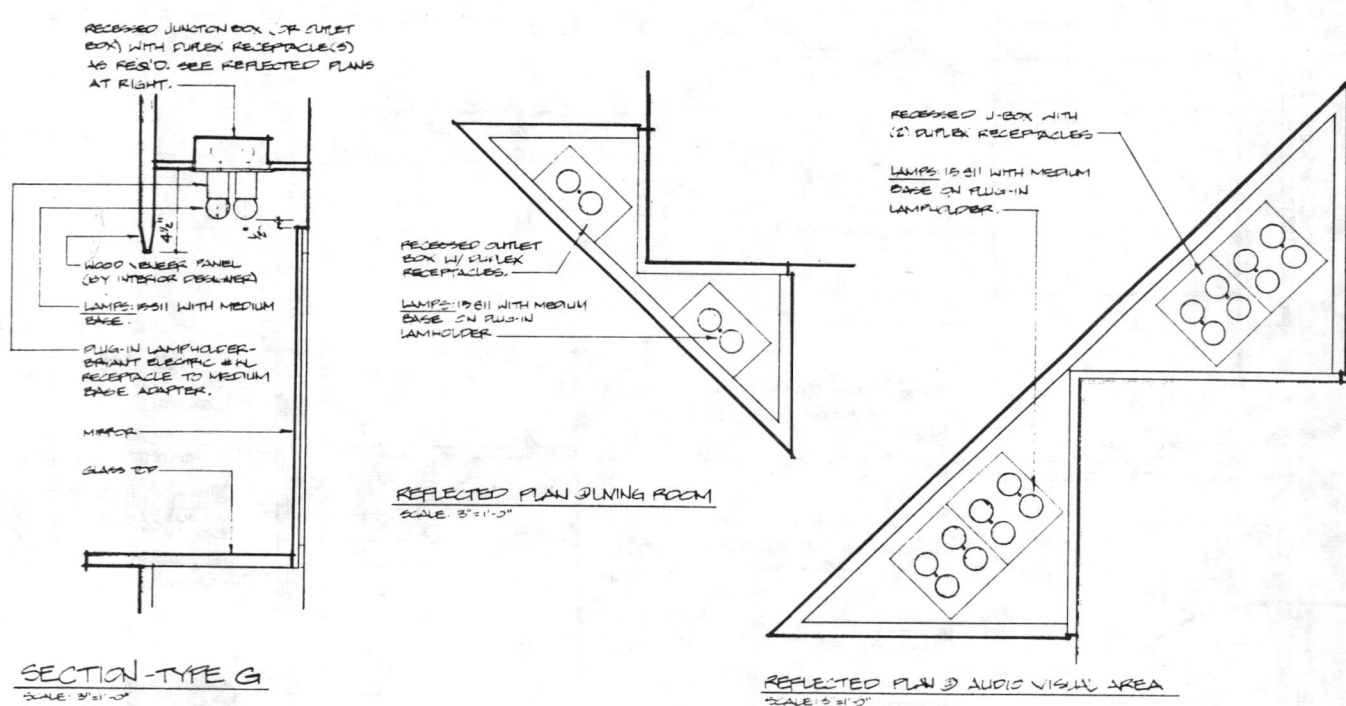

RECESSED JUNCTION BOX (OR OUTLET
BOX) WITH DUPLEX RECEPTACLE(S)
AS REQ'D. SEE REFLECTED PLANS
AT RIGHT.

WOOD VENEER PANEL
(BY INTERIOR DESIGNER)

LAMPS: 15 G11 WITH MEDIUM
BASE.

PLUG-IN LAMPHOLDER -
BRYANT ELECTRIC # N1
RECEPTACLE TO MEDIUM
BASE ADAPTER.

MIRROR

GLASS TOP

4 1/2"

SECTION - TYPE G
SCALE : 3" = 1'-0"

RECESSED OUTLET
BOX W/ DUPLEX
RECEPTACLES.

LAMPS: 15 G11 WITH MEDIUM
BASE ON PLUG-IN
LAMHOLDER

REFLECTED PLAN DINING ROOM
SCALE : 3" = 1'-0"

RECESSED J-BOX WITH
(2) DUPLEX RECEPTACLES

LAMPS: 15 G11 WITH MEDIUM
BASE ON PLUG-IN
LAMHOLDER

REFLECTED PLAN @ AUDIO VISUAL AREA
SCALE : 3" = 1'-0"

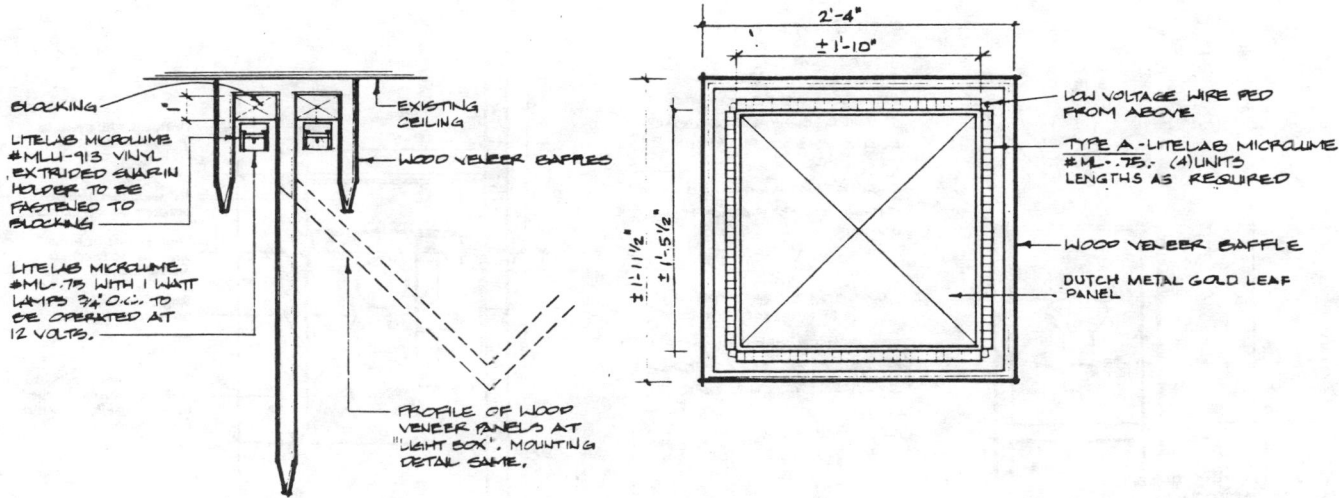

BLOCKING

LITELAB MICROLUME #MLU-913 VINYL EXTRUDED SNAP IN HOLDER TO BE FASTENED TO BLOCKING

LITELAB MICROLUME #ML-.75 WITH I WATT LAMPS 3/4" O.C. TO BE OPERATED AT 12 VOLTS.

EXISTING CEILING

WOOD VENEER BAFFLES

PROFILE OF WOOD VENEER PANELS AT "LIGHT BOX", MOUNTING DETAIL SAME.

2'-4"
± 1'-10"

± 1'-11½"
± 1'-5½"

LOW VOLTAGE WIRE FED FROM ABOVE

TYPE A - LITELAB MICROLUME #ML-.75, (4) UNITS LENGTHS AS REQUIRED

WOOD VENEER BAFFLE

DUTCH METAL GOLD LEAF PANEL

SECTION - TYPE A

REFLECTED PLAN @ LIGHT BOX

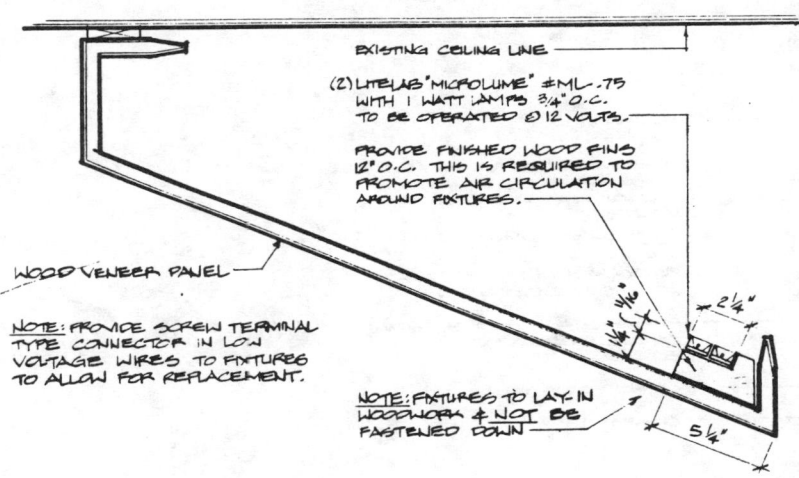

EXISTING CEILING LINE

(2) LITELAB "MICROLUME" #ML-.75 WITH I WATT LAMPS 3/4" O.C. TO BE OPERATED @ 12 VOLTS.

PROVIDE FINISHED WOOD FINS 12" O.C. THIS IS REQUIRED TO PROMOTE AIR CIRCULATION AROUND FIXTURES.

WOOD VENEER PANEL

NOTE: PROVIDE SCREW TERMINAL TYPE CONNECTOR IN LOW VOLTAGE WIRES TO FIXTURES TO ALLOW FOR REPLACEMENT.

NOTE: FIXTURES TO LAY IN WOODWORK & NOT BE FASTENED DOWN

2¼"

5¼"

SECTION - TYPE B

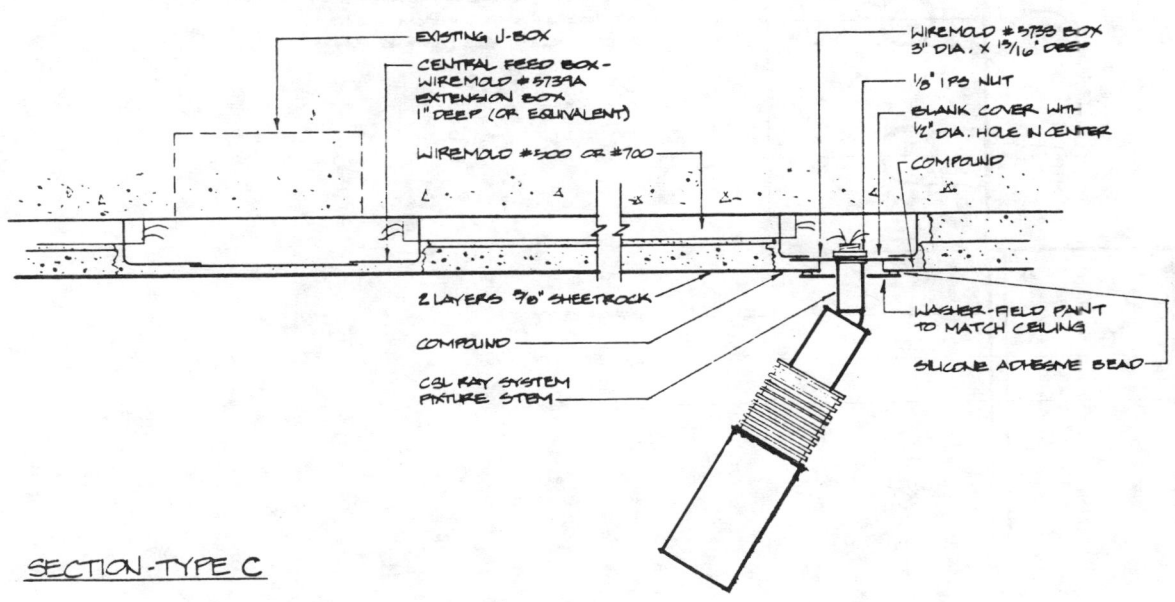

EXISTING J-BOX

CENTRAL FEED BOX - WIREMOLD #5739A EXTENSION BOX 1" DEEP (OR EQUIVALENT)

WIREMOLD #500 OR #700

WIREMOLD #5738 BOX 3" DIA. X 13/16" DEEP

1/8" IPS NUT

BLANK COVER WITH ½" DIA. HOLE IN CENTER

COMPOUND

2 LAYERS 5/8" SHEETROCK

COMPOUND

CSL RAY SYSTEM FIXTURE STEM

WASHER - FIELD PAINT TO MATCH CEILING

SILICONE ADHESIVE BEAD

SECTION - TYPE C

761

LIGHTING

Miscellaneous Lighting Details

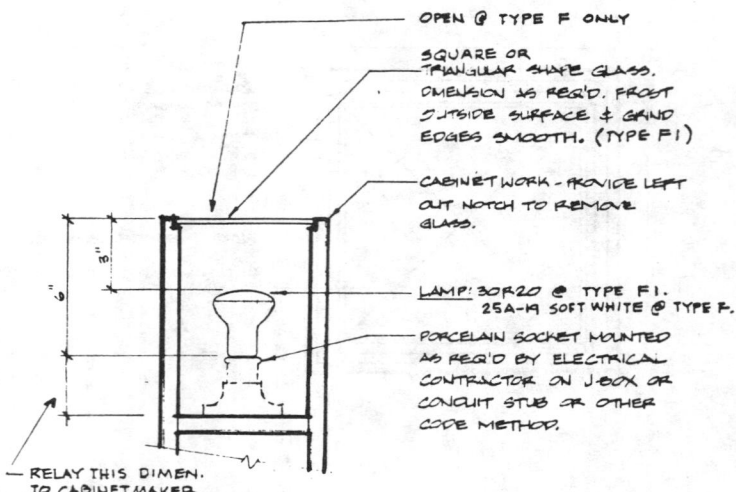

OPEN @ TYPE F ONLY

SQUARE OR TRIANGULAR SHAPE GLASS. DIMENSION AS REQ'D. FROST OUTSIDE SURFACE & GRIND EDGES SMOOTH. (TYPE F1)

CABINET WORK - PROVIDE LEFT OUT NOTCH TO REMOVE GLASS.

LAMP: 30R20 @ TYPE F1. 25A-19 SOFT WHITE @ TYPE F.

PORCELAIN SOCKET MOUNTED AS REQ'D BY ELECTRICAL CONTRACTOR ON J-BOX OR CONDUIT STUB OR OTHER CODE METHOD.

RELAY THIS DIMEN. TO CABINETMAKER

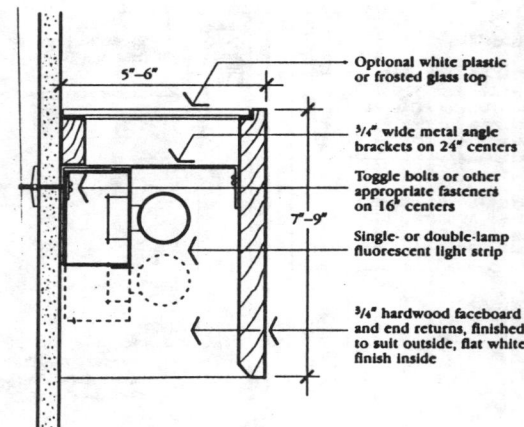

Optional white plastic or frosted glass top

3/4" wide metal angle brackets on 24" centers

Toggle bolts or other appropriate fasteners on 16" centers

Single- or double-lamp fluorescent light strip

3/4" hardwood faceboard and end returns, finished to suit outside, flat white finish inside

5"–6"

7"–9"

Wall bracket cross section

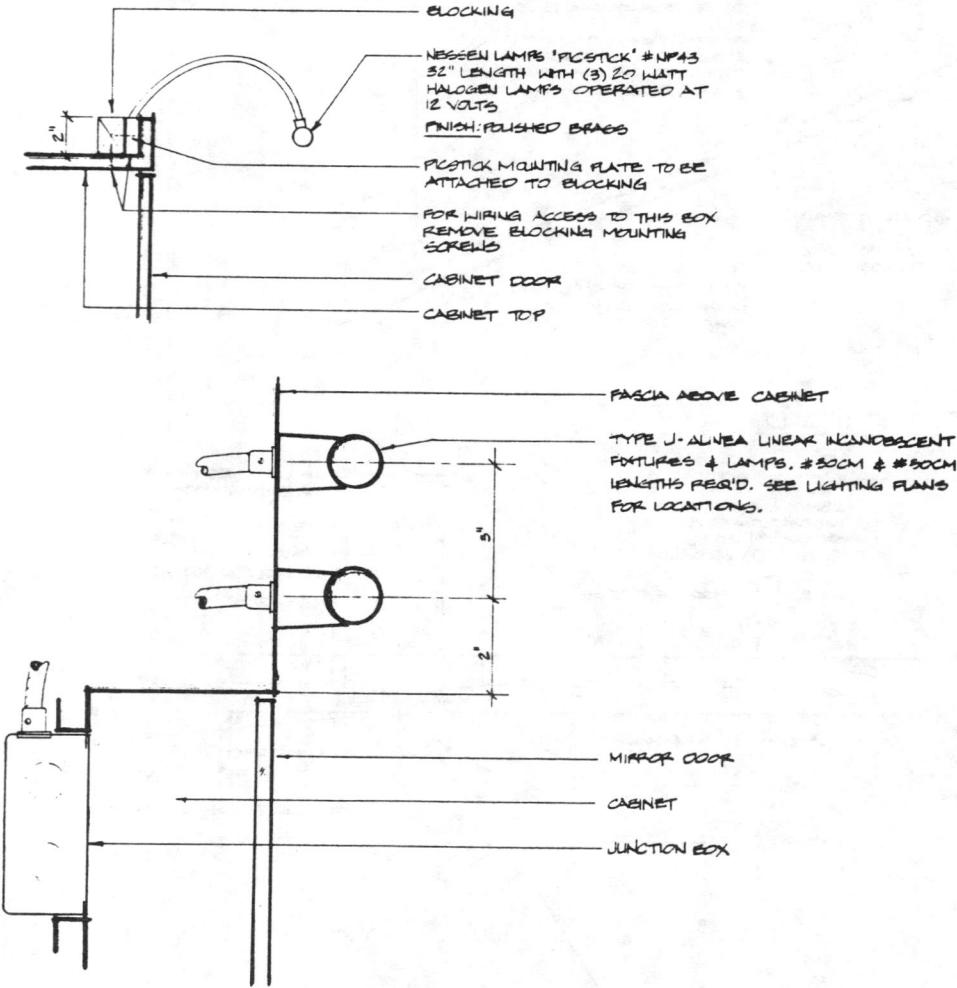

BLOCKING

NESSEN LAMPS 'PICSTICK' #NP43 32" LENGTH WITH (3) 20 WATT HALOGEN LAMPS OPERATED AT 12 VOLTS
FINISH: POLISHED BRASS

PICSTICK MOUNTING PLATE TO BE ATTACHED TO BLOCKING

FOR WIRING ACCESS TO THIS BOX REMOVE BLOCKING MOUNTING SCREWS

CABINET DOOR

CABINET TOP

FASCIA ABOVE CABINET

TYPE J- ALKCO LINEAR INCANDESCENT FIXTURES & LAMPS. #30CM & #30CM LENGTHS REQ'D. SEE LIGHTING PLANS FOR LOCATIONS.

MIRROR DOOR

CABINET

JUNCTION BOX

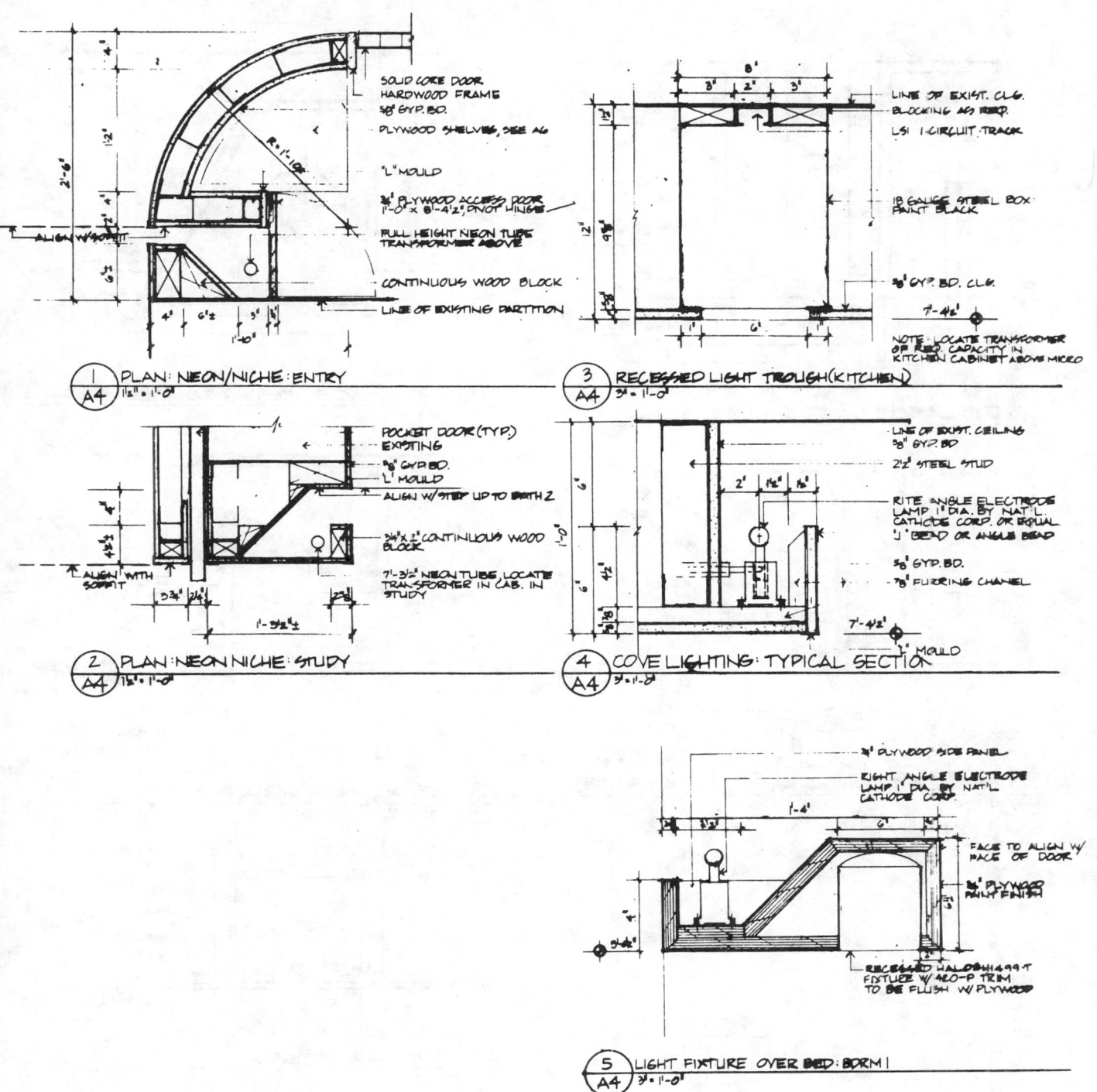

SOLID CORE DOOR
HARDWOOD FRAME
5/8" GYP. BD.

PLYWOOD SHELVES, SEE A6

"L" MOULD

3/4" PLYWOOD ACCESS DOOR
1'-0" x 8'-4 1/2", PIVOT HINGES

FULL HEIGHT NEON TUBE
TRANSFORMER ABOVE

CONTINUOUS WOOD BLOCK

LINE OF EXISTING PARTITION

① PLAN: NEON/NICHE: ENTRY
A4 1 1/2" = 1'-0"

LINE OF EXIST. CLG.
BLOCKING AS REQ.

LSI 1-CIRCUIT TRACK

18 GAUGE STEEL BOX
PAINT BLACK

5/8" GYP. BD. CLG.

7'-4 1/2"

NOTE: LOCATE TRANSFORMER
OF REQ. CAPACITY IN
KITCHEN CABINET ABOVE MICRO

③ RECESSED LIGHT TROUGH (KITCHEN)
A4 3" = 1'-0"

POCKET DOOR (TYP.)
EXISTING

5/8" GYP. BD.
"L" MOULD

ALIGN W/ STEP UP TO BATH 2

3/4" X 2" CONTINUOUS WOOD
BLOCK

7'-3 1/2" NEON TUBE, LOCATE
TRANSFORMER IN CAB. IN
STUDY

② PLAN: NEON NICHE: STUDY
A4 1 1/2" = 1'-0"

LINE OF EXIST. CEILING
5/8" GYP. BD.

2 1/2" STEEL STUD

RITE ANGLE ELECTRODE
LAMP 1" DIA. BY NAT'L.
CATHODE CORP. OR EQUAL
'J' BEND OR ANGLE BEND

5/8" GYP. BD.

7/8" FURRING CHANNEL

7'-4 1/2"

"L" MOULD

④ COVE LIGHTING: TYPICAL SECTION
A4 3" = 1'-0"

3/4" PLYWOOD SIDE PANEL

RIGHT ANGLE ELECTRODE
LAMP 1" DIA. BY NAT'L.
CATHODE CORP.

FACE TO ALIGN W/
FACE OF DOOR

3/4" PLYWOOD
PAINT FINISH

RECESSED HALO #H1499-T
FIXTURE W/ 420-P TRIM
TO BE FLUSH W/ PLYWOOD

⑤ LIGHT FIXTURE OVER BED: BDRM 1
A4 3" = 1'-0"

LIGHTING
Miscellaneous Lighting Details

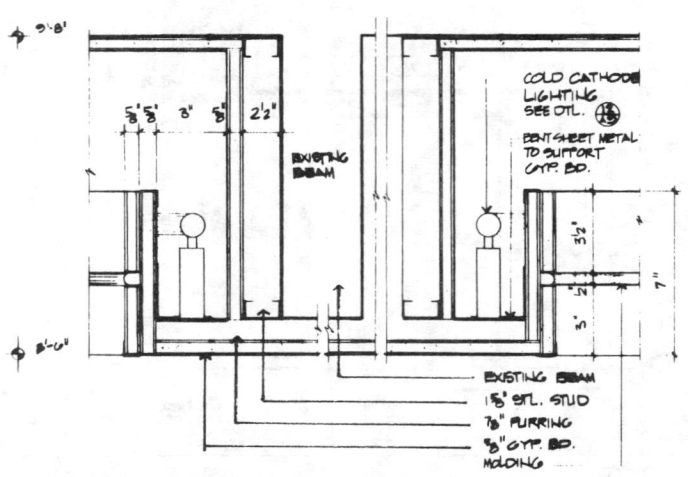

COLD CATHODE
LIGHTING
SEE DTL.

BENT SHEET METAL
TO SUPPORT
GYP. BD.

EXISTING
BEAM

EXISTING BEAM
1⅝" STL. STUD
⅞" FURRING
⅝" GYP. BD.
MOLDING

⑪ DETAIL: COVE LIGHTING IN LIVING ROOM
Ⓐ9 3" = 1'-0"

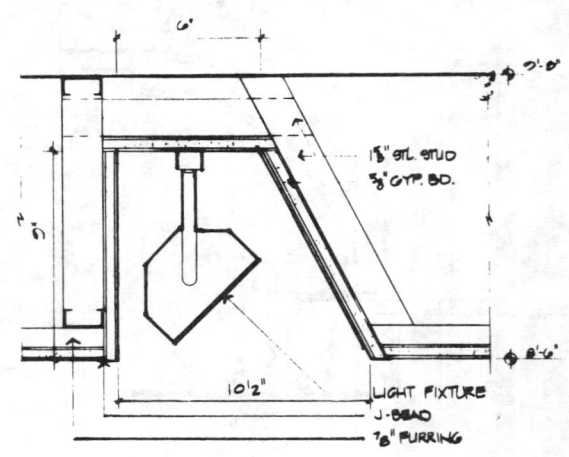

1⅝" STL. STUD
⅝" GYP. BD.

LIGHT FIXTURE
J-BEAD
⅞" FURRING

⑬ DETAIL: COVE LIGHTING @ SLOPED WALL & HALL
Ⓐ9 3" = 1'-0"

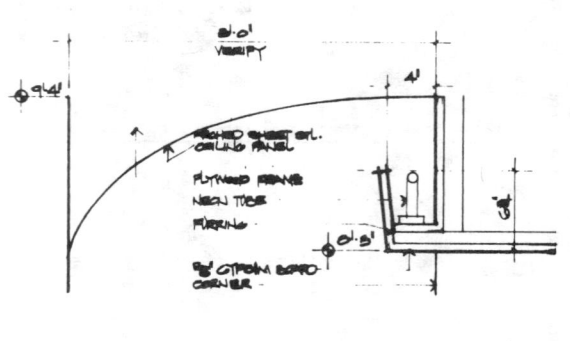

⅝" GYP BD.
1⅝" STL. STUD
COLD CATHODE
LIGHTING

RUBBER
MOLDING

J-BEAD
⅞" FURRING
BENT SHEET METAL TO
SUPPORT GYP. BD.

⑫ DETAIL: COVE LIGHTING IN LIVING, DINING & FAM. RMS.
Ⓐ9 3" = 1'-0"

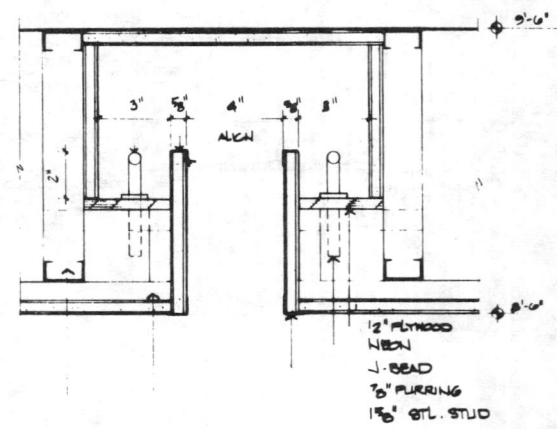

ALIGN

12" PLYWOOD
NEON
J-BEAD
⅞" FURRING
1⅝" STL. STUD

⑭ DETAIL: NEON RECESS @ ENTRY
Ⓐ9 3" = 1'-0"

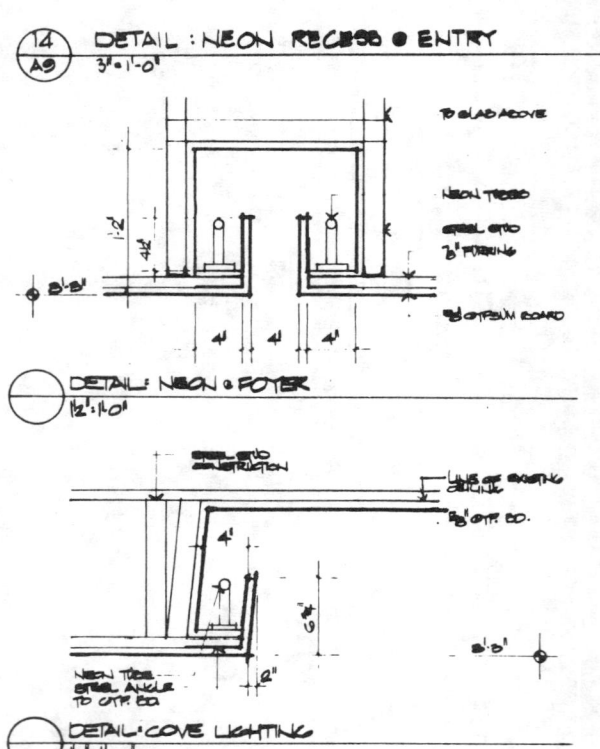

TO SLAB ABOVE
NEON TUBES
STEEL STUD
⅞" FURRING
⅝" GYPSUM BOARD

DETAIL: NEON @ FOYER
1½" = 1'-0"

STEEL STUD
CONSTRUCTION
LINE OF EXISTING
CEILING
⅝" GYP. BD.

NEON TUBE
STEEL ANGLE
TO GYP. BD.

DETAIL: COVE LIGHTING
1½" = 1'-0"

VERIFY

BRAZED SHEET STL.
CEILING PANEL
PLYWOOD FRAME
NEON TUBE
FURRING

⅝" GYPSUM BOARD
CORNER

DETAIL: COVE LIGHT @ BAR
1½" = 1'-0"

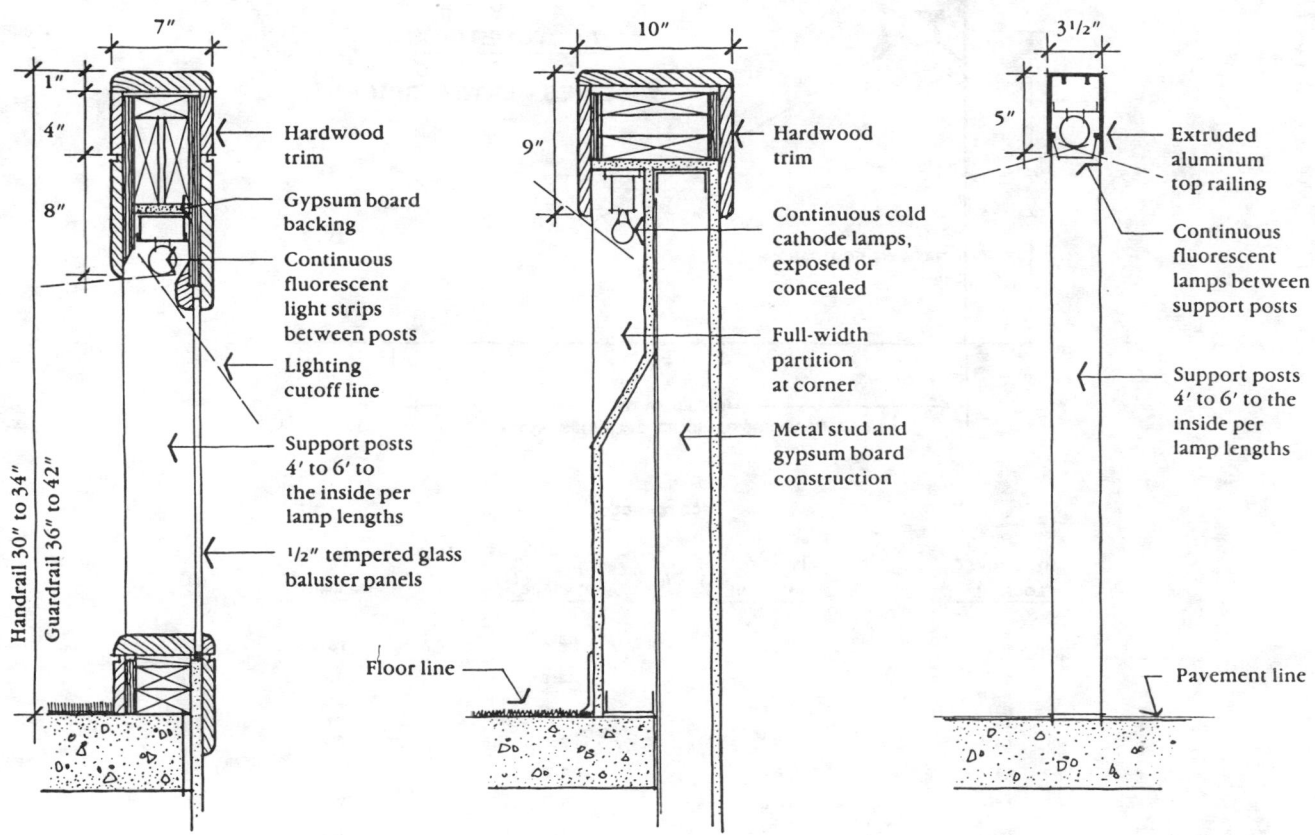

Lighted wood and glass guardrail

Hardwood trim

Gypsum board backing

Continuous fluorescent light strips between posts

Lighting cutoff line

Support posts 4' to 6' to the inside per lamp lengths

1/2" tempered glass baluster panels

Handrail 30" to 34"
Guardrail 36" to 42"

Floor line

Lighted low-partition guardrail

Hardwood trim

Continuous cold cathode lamps, exposed or concealed

Full-width partition at corner

Metal stud and gypsum board construction

Extruded aluminum light rail

Extruded aluminum top railing

Continuous fluorescent lamps between support posts

Support posts 4' to 6' to the inside per lamp lengths

Pavement line

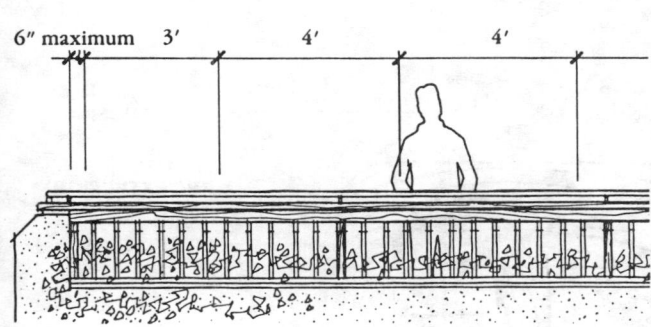

6" maximum   3'   4'   4'

Elevation of lighted guardrail planter demonstrates the use of combined 3-foot and 4-foot fluorescent light strips to achieve overall lengths in 1-foot multiples. To minimize dark areas between lamps, use strips without end caps and install lamps back to back.

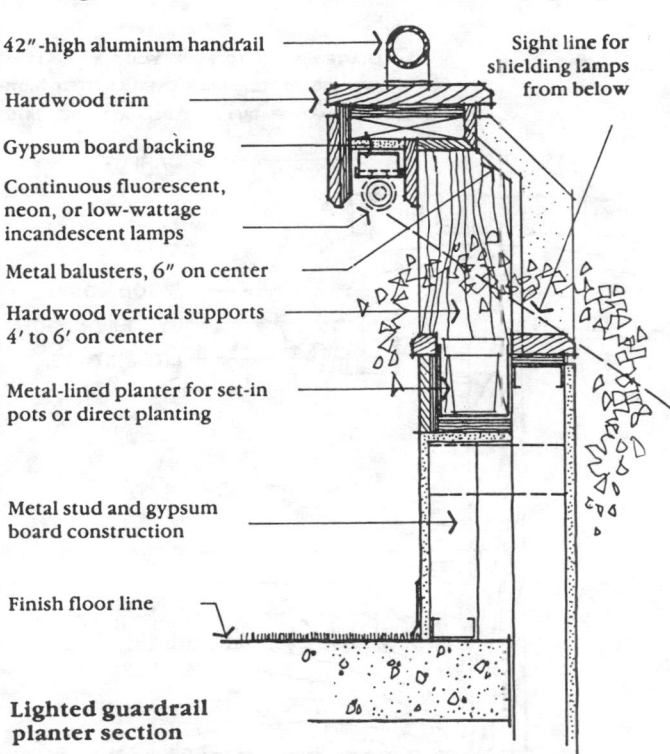

42"-high aluminum handrail

Hardwood trim

Gypsum board backing

Continuous fluorescent, neon, or low-wattage incandescent lamps

Metal balusters, 6" on center

Hardwood vertical supports 4' to 6' on center

Metal-lined planter for set-in pots or direct planting

Metal stud and gypsum board construction

Finish floor line

Sight line for shielding lamps from below

Lighted guardrail planter section

Open circulation areas can be illuminated with lighted railings, as shown in this section of a lighted guardrail planter.

LIGHTING

Stair Lighting Photometrics

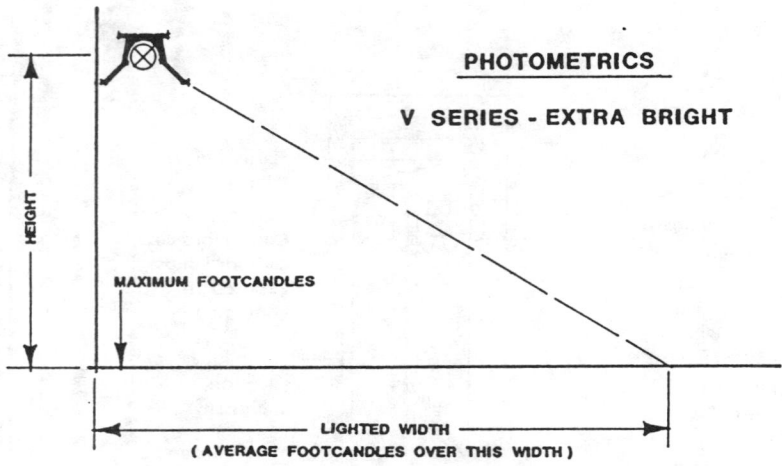

PHOTOMETRICS

V SERIES - EXTRA BRIGHT

FOOTCANDLES

HT. ABOVE FLOOR IN.	LIGHTED WIDTH IN.(1)	AVERAGE(2)	MAXIMUM(3)
6	11	5.0	13.0
8	14	3.8	9.8
10	18	3.0	7.8
12	21	2.5	6.5
18	32	1.7	4.4
24	42	1.3	3.3
30	53	1.0	2.6
36	63	0.8	2.1

NOTES:

1. LIGHTED WIDTH TO POINT FOOTCANDLE LEVEL FALLS TO 10% OF MAXIMUM

2. AVERAGE FOOTCANDLES OVER LIGHTED WIDTH

3. FOOTCANDLES DIRECTLY BELOW LIGHT FIXTURE

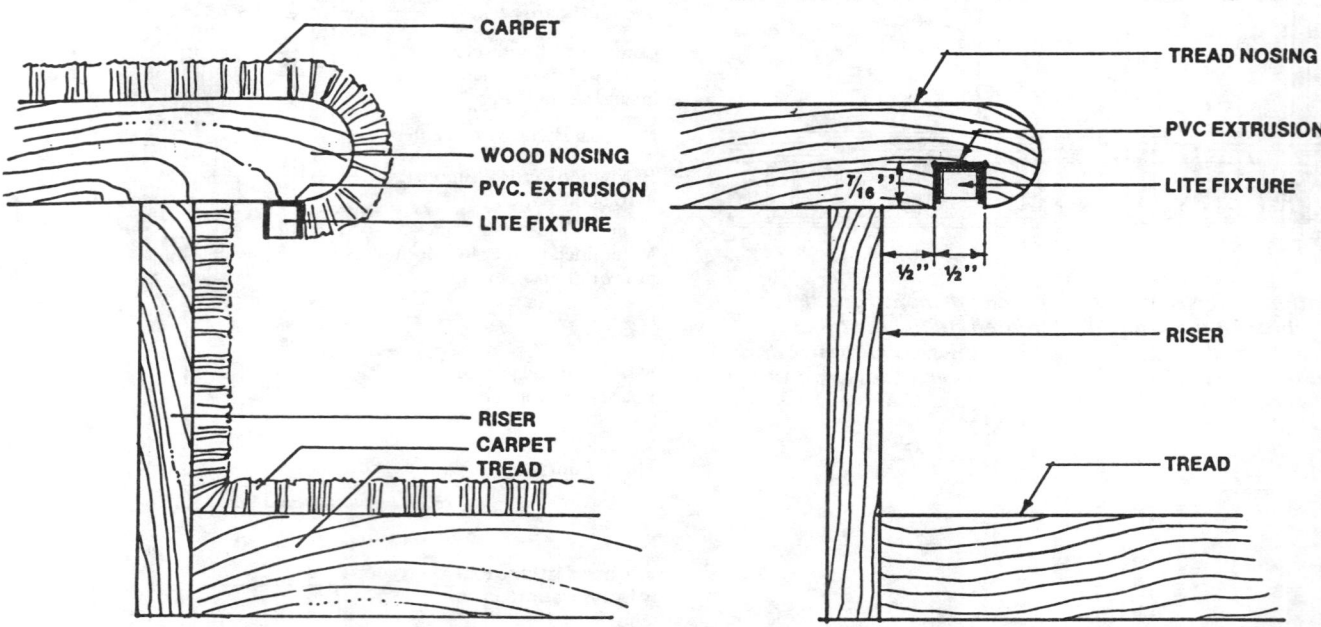

Fig. 16   Surface-mounted step light.   Fig. 17   Recessed step light.

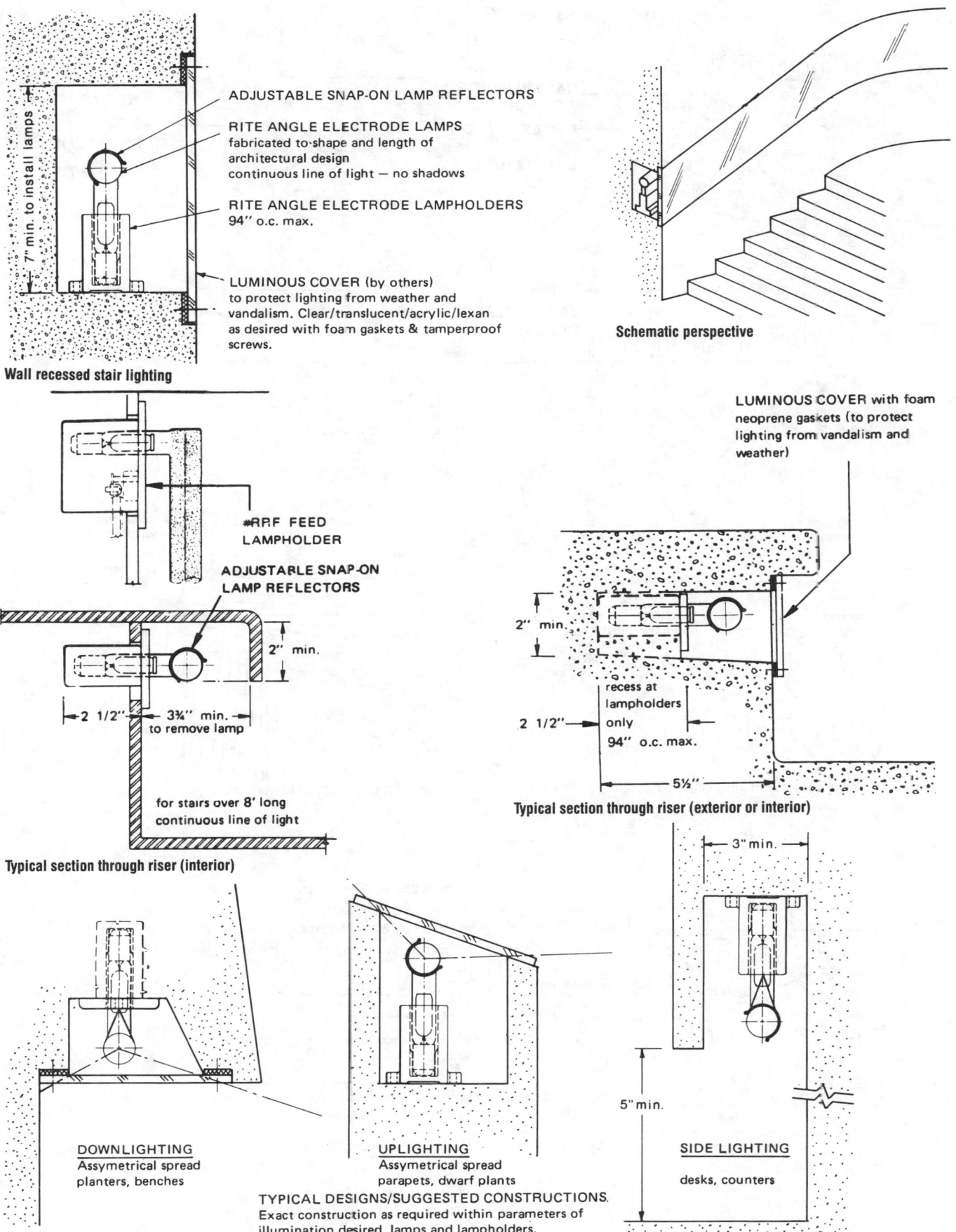

Wall recessed stair lighting

7" min. to install lamps

ADJUSTABLE SNAP-ON LAMP REFLECTORS

RITE ANGLE ELECTRODE LAMPS
fabricated to shape and length of
architectural design
continuous line of light — no shadows

RITE ANGLE ELECTRODE LAMPHOLDERS
94" o.c. max.

LUMINOUS COVER (by others)
to protect lighting from weather and
vandalism. Clear/translucent/acrylic/lexan
as desired with foam gaskets & tamperproof
screws.

Schematic perspective

#RRF FEED
LAMPHOLDER

ADJUSTABLE SNAP-ON
LAMP REFLECTORS

2" min.

2 1/2"   3¾" min.
to remove lamp

for stairs over 8' long
continuous line of light

Typical section through riser (interior)

LUMINOUS COVER with foam
neoprene gaskets (to protect
lighting from vandalism and
weather)

2" min.

recess at
lampholders
only
94" o.c. max.

2 1/2"

5½"

Typical section through riser (exterior or interior)

3" min.

5" min.

DOWNLIGHTING
Assymetrical spread
planters, benches

UPLIGHTING
Assymetrical spread
parapets, dwarf plants

SIDE LIGHTING
desks, counters

TYPICAL DESIGNS/SUGGESTED CONSTRUCTIONS.
Exact construction as required within parameters of
illumination desired, lamps and lampholders.

Alternate stair lighting designs

LIGHTING

Stair Lighting Details

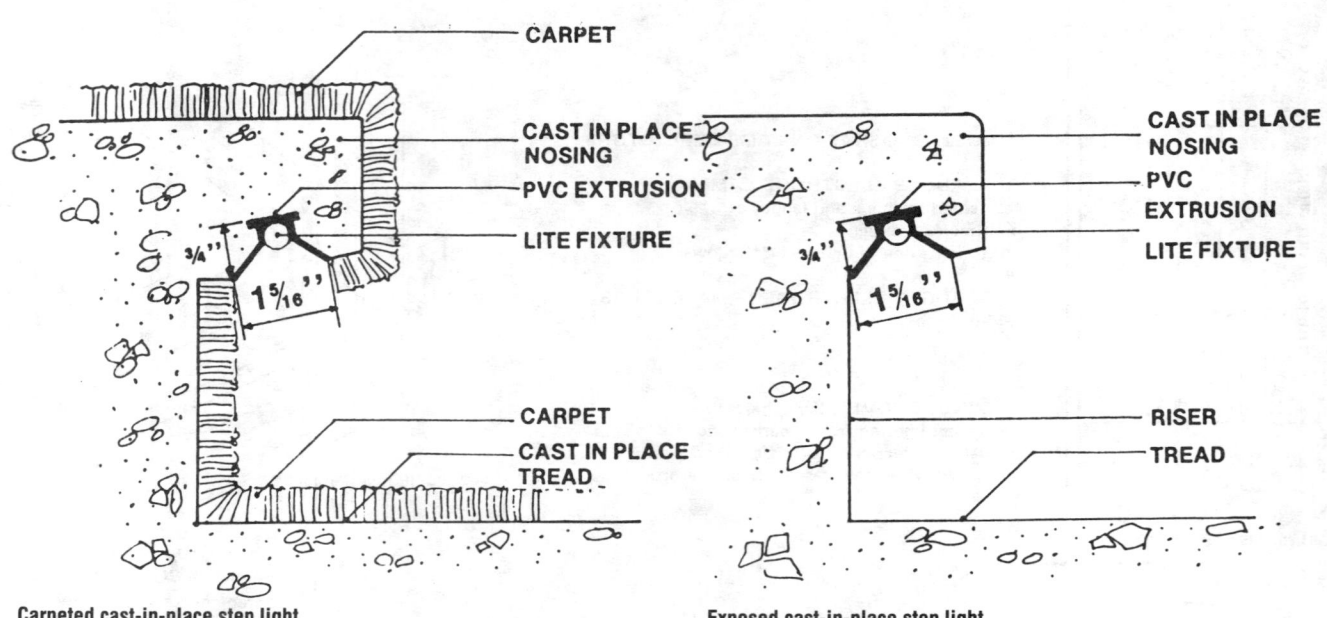

CARPET
CAST IN PLACE NOSING
PVC EXTRUSION
LITE FIXTURE
3/4"
1 5/16"
CARPET
CAST IN PLACE TREAD

CAST IN PLACE NOSING
PVC EXTRUSION
LITE FIXTURE
3/4"
1 5/16"
RISER
TREAD

Carpeted cast-in-place step light

Exposed cast-in-place step light

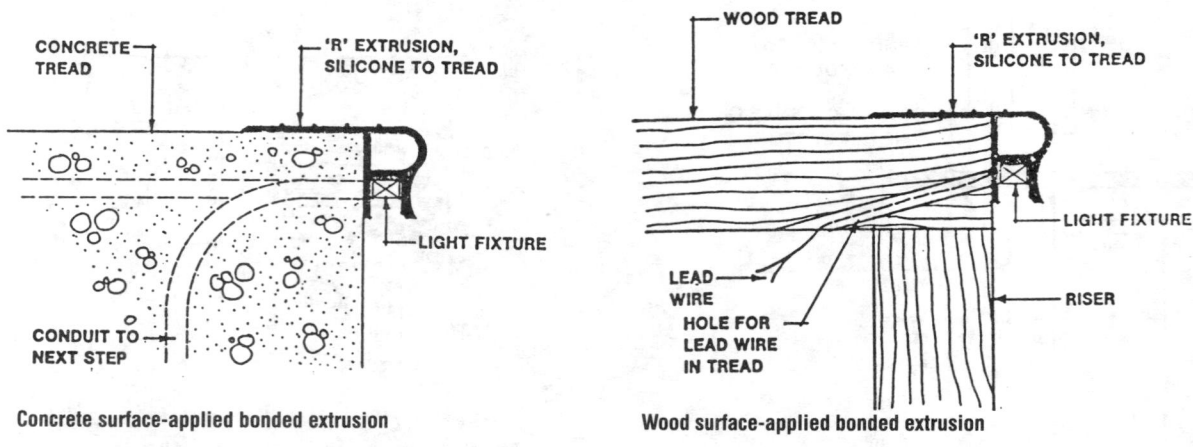

CONCRETE TREAD
'R' EXTRUSION, SILICONE TO TREAD
LIGHT FIXTURE
CONDUIT TO NEXT STEP

WOOD TREAD
'R' EXTRUSION, SILICONE TO TREAD
LIGHT FIXTURE
LEAD WIRE
HOLE FOR LEAD WIRE IN TREAD
RISER

Concrete surface-applied bonded extrusion

Wood surface-applied bonded extrusion

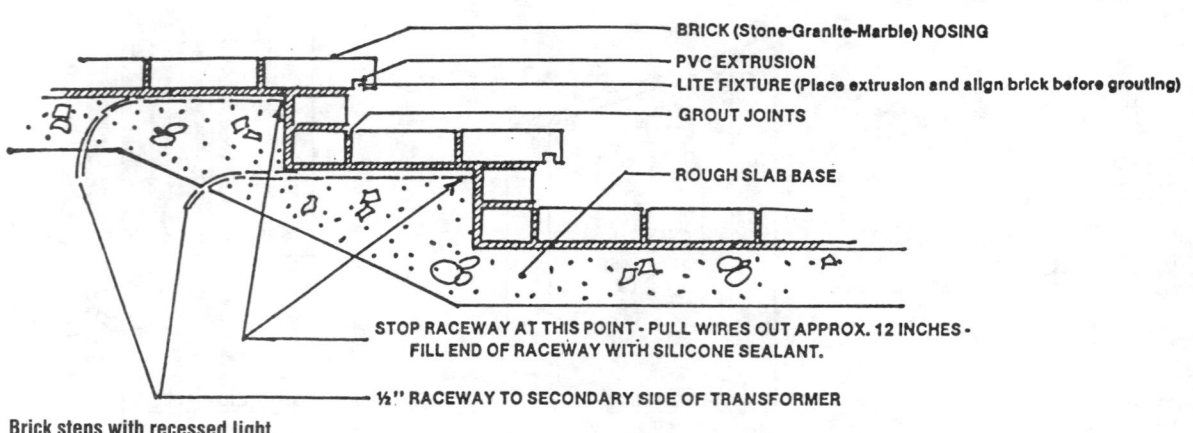

BRICK (Stone-Granite-Marble) NOSING
PVC EXTRUSION
LITE FIXTURE (Place extrusion and align brick before grouting)
GROUT JOINTS
ROUGH SLAB BASE

STOP RACEWAY AT THIS POINT - PULL WIRES OUT APPROX. 12 INCHES - FILL END OF RACEWAY WITH SILICONE SEALANT.

½" RACEWAY TO SECONDARY SIDE OF TRANSFORMER

Brick steps with recessed light

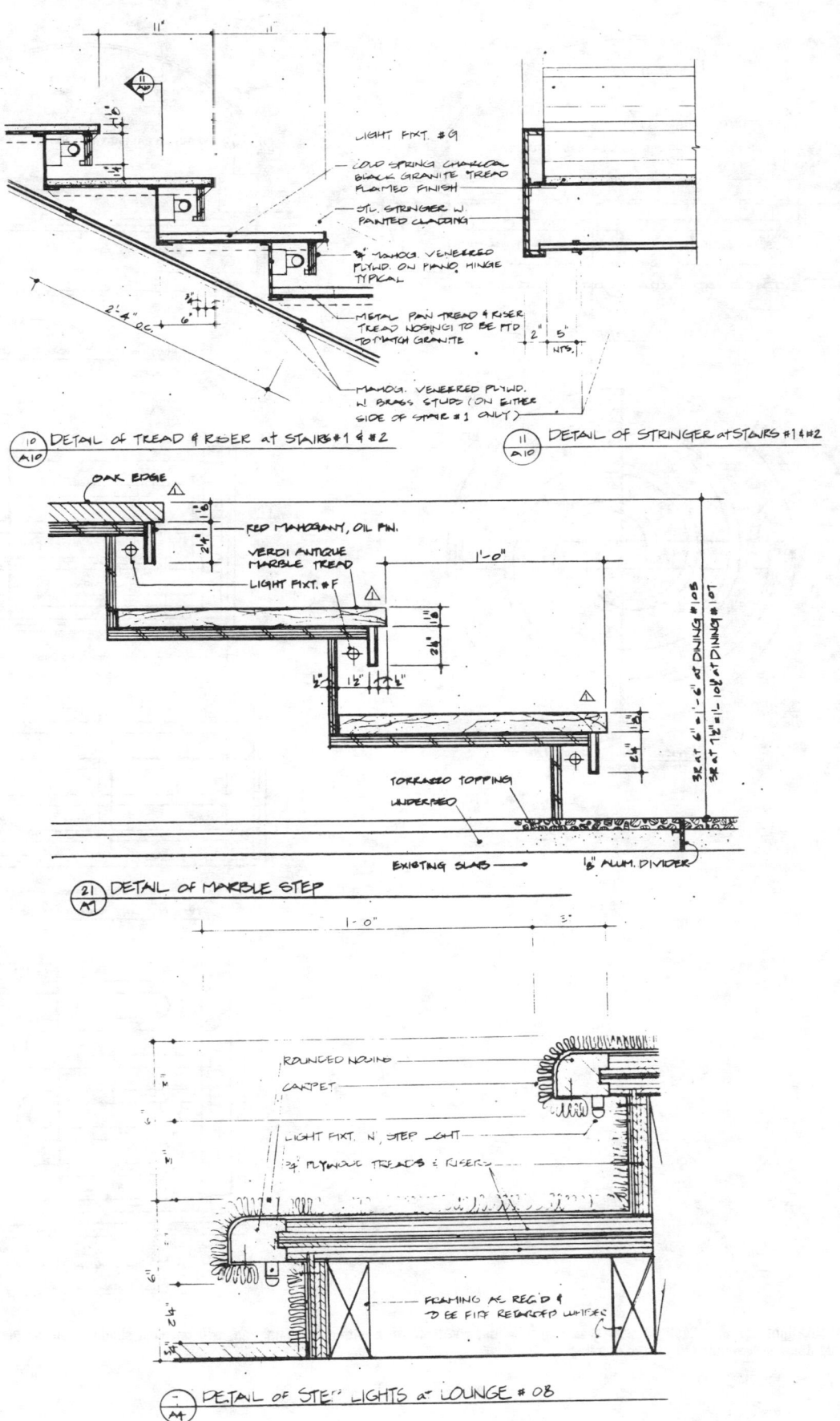

LIGHT FIXT. #9

COLD SPRING CHARCOAL
BLACK GRANITE TREAD
FLAMED FINISH

STL. STRINGER W
PAINTED CLADDING

¾" MAHOG. VENEERED
PLYWD. ON PIANO HINGE
TYPICAL

METAL PAN TREAD & RISER
TREAD NOSING TO BE PTD
TO MATCH GRANITE

MAHOG. VENEERED PLYWD.
W! BRASS STUDS (ON EITHER
SIDE OF STAIR #1 ONLY)

10 / A10   DETAIL OF TREAD & RISER at STAIR #1 & #2

11 / A10   DETAIL OF STRINGER at STAIRS #1 & #2

OAK EDGE

RED MAHOGANY, OIL FIN.

VERDI ANTIQUE
MARBLE TREAD

LIGHT FIXT. #F

TERRAZZO TOPPING
UNDERBED
EXISTING SLAB
⅛" ALUM. DIVIDER

1'-0"

21 / A1   DETAIL OF MARBLE STEP

ROUNDED NOSING
CARPET

LIGHT FIXT. W! STEP LIGHT

¾" PLYWOOD TREADS & RISERS

FRAMING AS REQ'D &
TO BE FIRE RETARD'D WHERE

— / A1   DETAIL OF STEP LIGHTS at LOUNGE #08

LIGHTING

Skylight Lighting Details

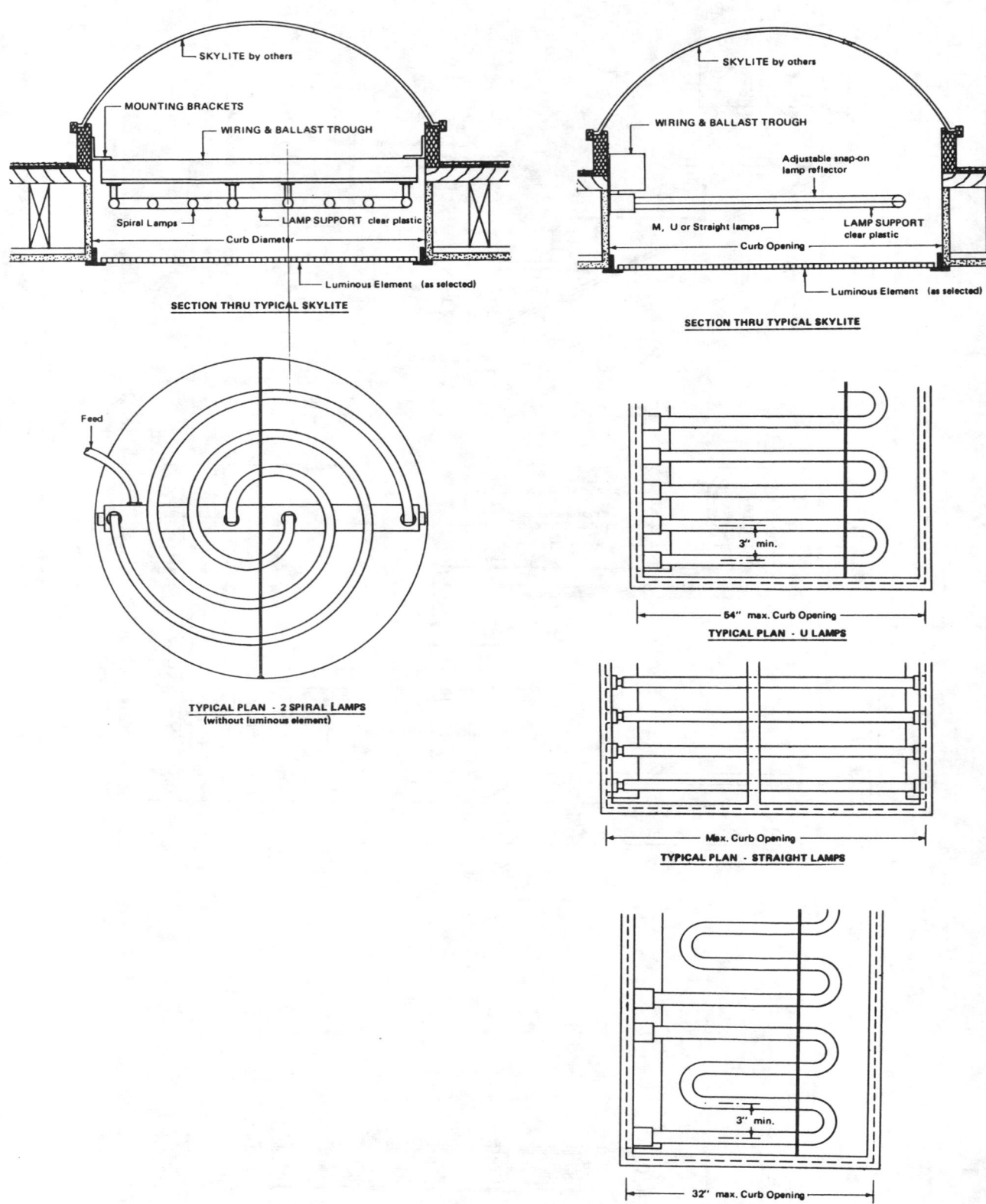

Fig. 18 Skylight lighting. Skylight serves as fixture — does not interfere with natural lighting, will not cast shadows on luminous element. Spiral, M, U, and straight lamps fabricated to fit curb opening.

CL OF EXISTING COL.

2½" X 5" SUPPORTING
ANGLE BRACKETS

LIGHT FIXT. #9
TYP. AT COLUMN

EXISTING COLUMN

FROSTED GLASS

RED MAHOGANY FRAMES
& TRIMS, OIL FINISH

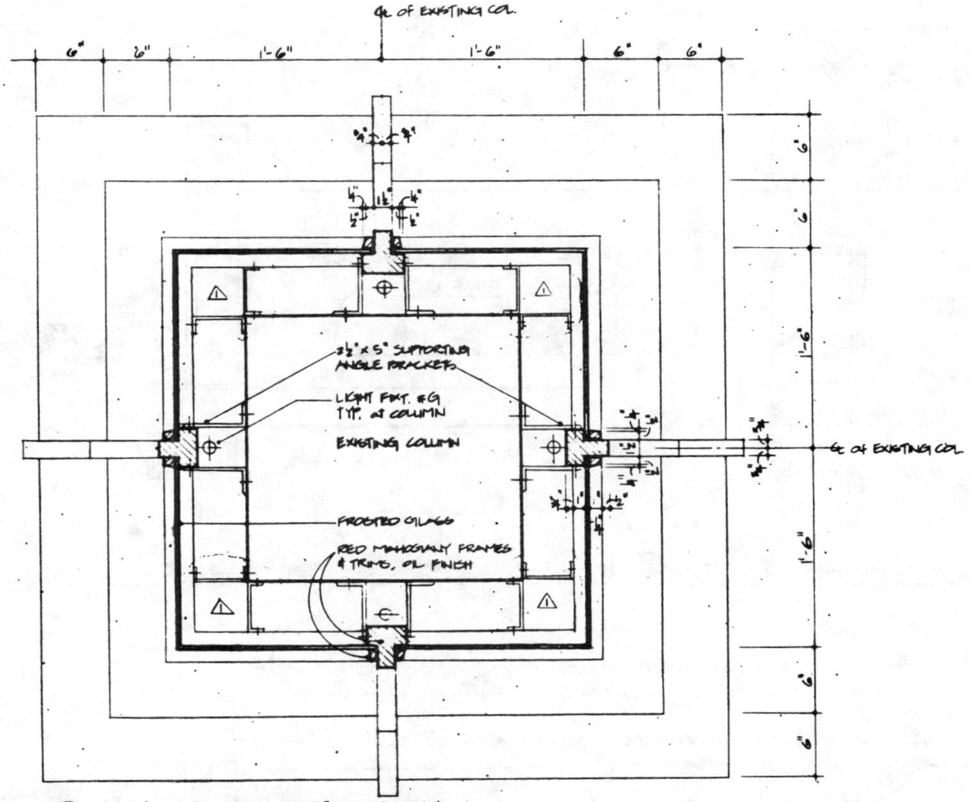

CL OF EXISTING COL

21 PLAN DETAIL OF LIGHTED COLUMN
AB SCALE : 1½" = 1'-0"

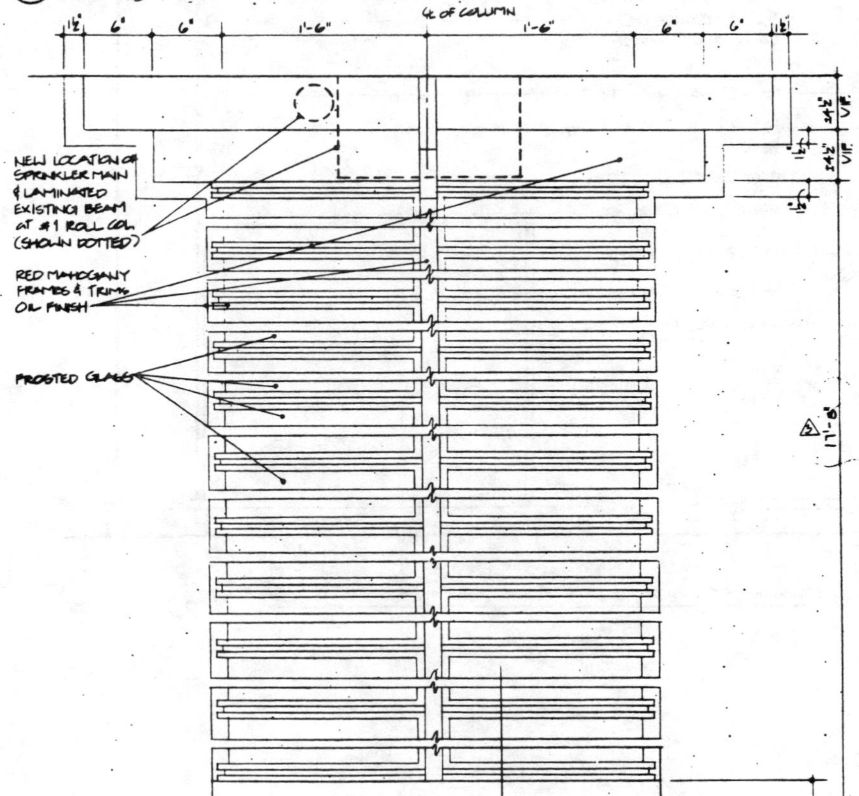

CL OF COLUMN

NEW LOCATION OF
SPRINKLER MAIN
& LAMINATED
EXISTING BEAM
AT #1 ROLL COL.
(SHOWN DOTTED)

RED MAHOGANY OIL FINISH

RED MAHOGANY
FRAMES & TRIMS
OIL FINISH

LIGHT FIXT. #9

¼" FROSTED GLASS

FROSTED GLASS

RED MAHOGANY
FRAMES & TRIMS
OIL FINISH

RED MAHOGANY
OIL FINISH

23
AB

BLOCKING
AS REQUIRED

CABINET

22 ELEVATION OF LIGHTED COLUMN
AB SCALE : 1½" = 1'-0"

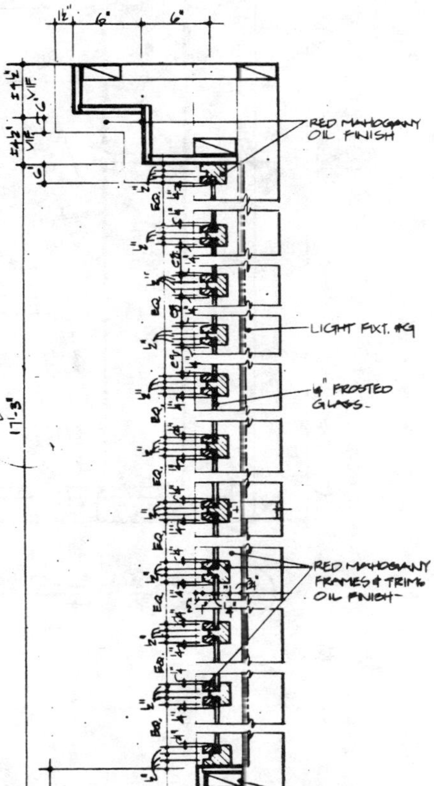

23 SECTION OF LIGHTED COLUMN
AB SCALE : 1½" = 1'-0"

771

LIGHTING

Lighted Column Details

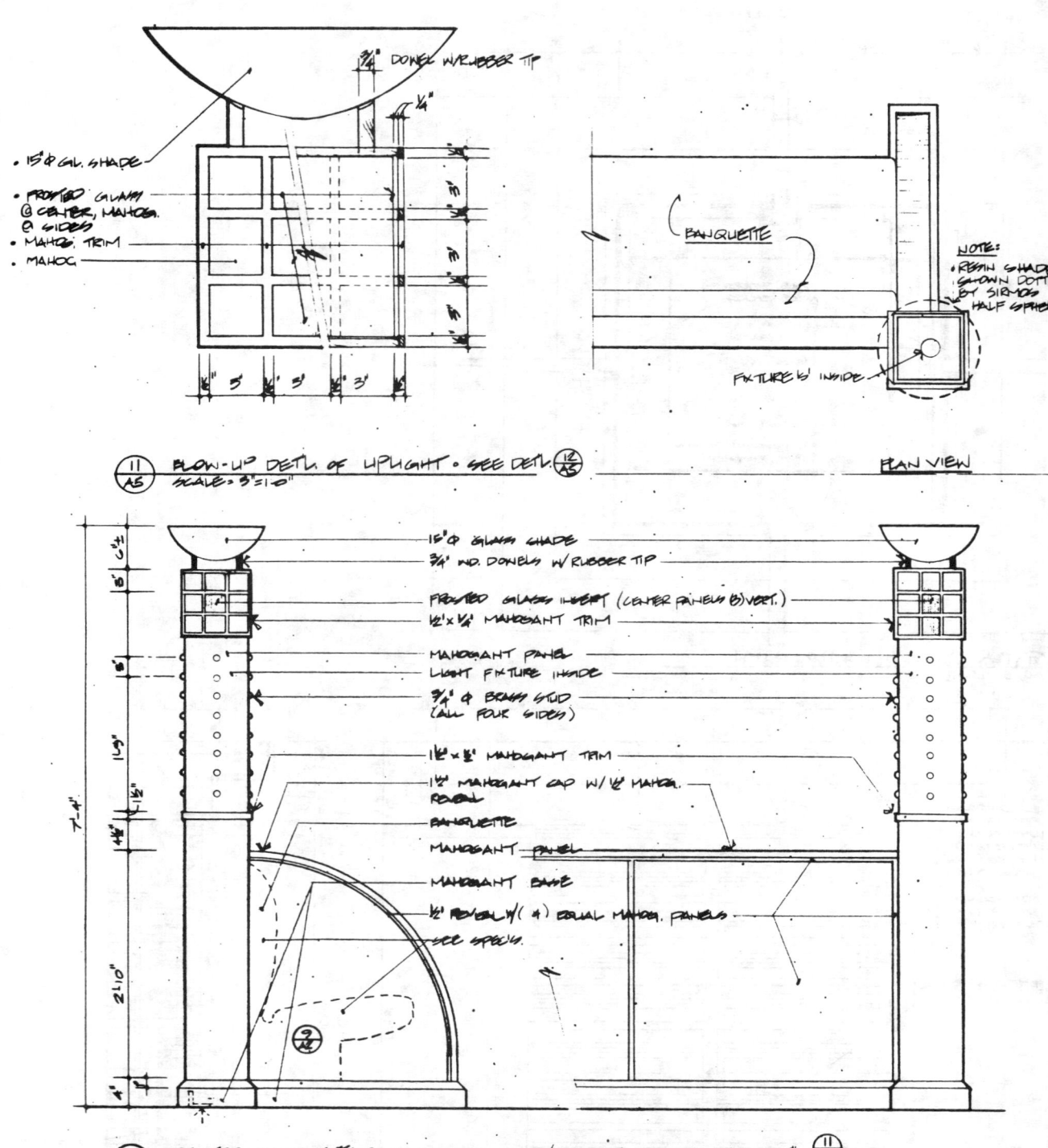

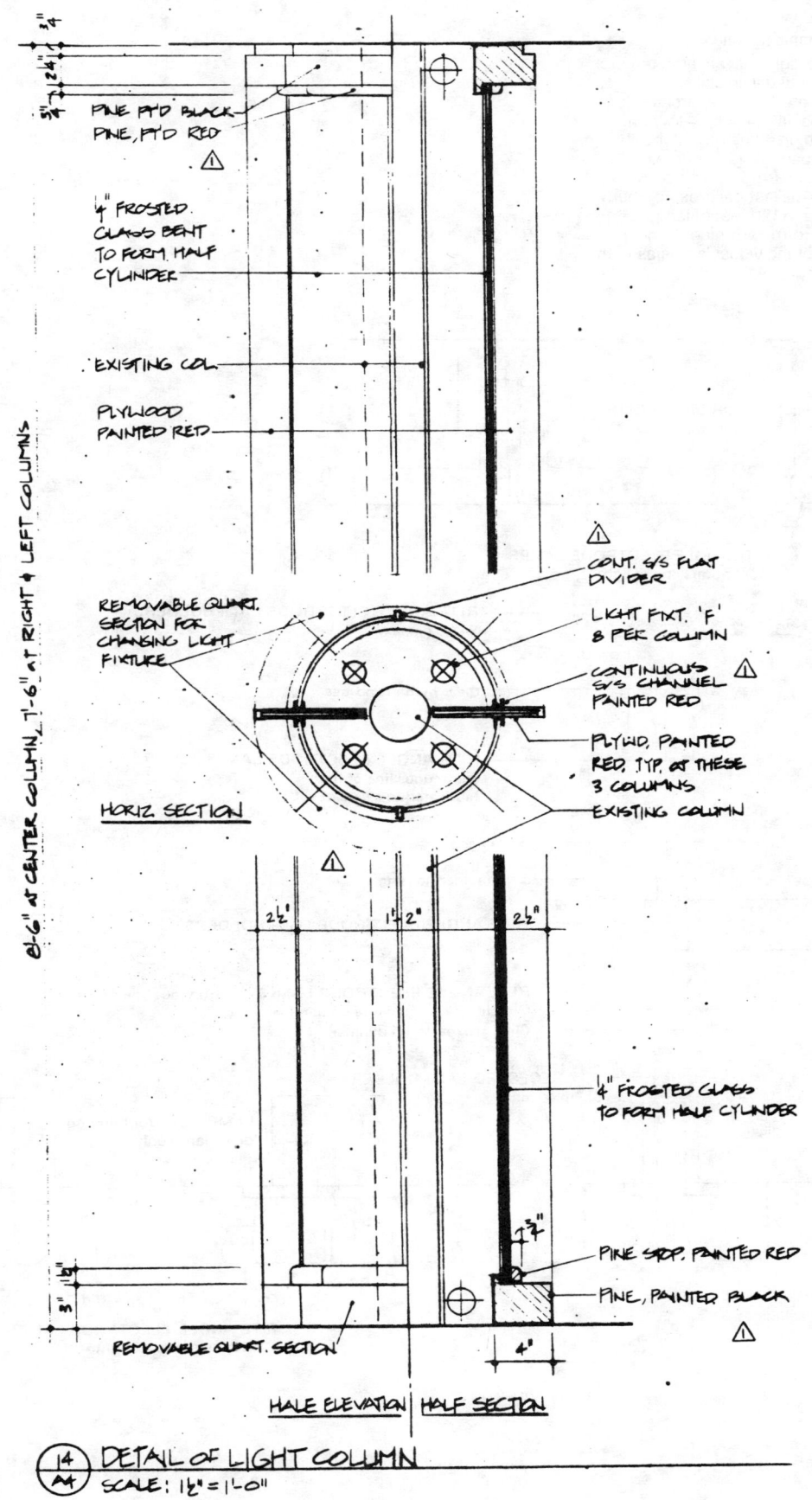

PINE PT'D BLACK
PINE, PT'D RED

⚠

¼" FROSTED.
GLASS BENT
TO FORM HALF
CYLINDER

EXISTING COL.

PLYWOOD
PAINTED RED

8'-6" AT CENTER COLUMN, 7'-6" AT RIGHT & LEFT COLUMNS

REMOVABLE QUART.
SECTION FOR
CHANGING LIGHT
FIXTURE

CONT. S/S FLAT
DIVIDER

⚠

LIGHT FIXT. 'F'
8 PER COLUMN

CONTINUOUS
S/S CHANNEL
PAINTED RED ⚠

PLYWD. PAINTED
RED, TYP. AT THESE
3 COLUMNS

EXISTING COLUMN

HORIZ SECTION

⚠

2½"   1½" 2"   2½"

¼" FROSTED GLASS
TO FORM HALF CYLINDER

1¾"

PINE STOP, PAINTED RED

PINE, PAINTED BLACK

⚠

4"

REMOVABLE QUART. SECTION

HALF ELEVATION | HALF SECTION

⑭ DETAIL OF LIGHT COLUMN
A4 SCALE: 1½"=1'-0"

LIGHTING

Ceiling-Mounted Cold Cathode Lighting Details

Exposed/sculpture lamp lighting

Cold cathode lighting, an architectural lighting tool with unusual flexibility.

Lamps fabricated to the architectural design, continuous line of light — low brightness — no glare — high efficiency — long life — approaches a permanent light source.

Remote transformers — no wiring troughs, ballasts, ballast failures, or hum. Only 2 leads for up to 120 feet of lamps.

Excellent uniform dimming — no premature flickering of individual lamps as with hot cathode lighting.

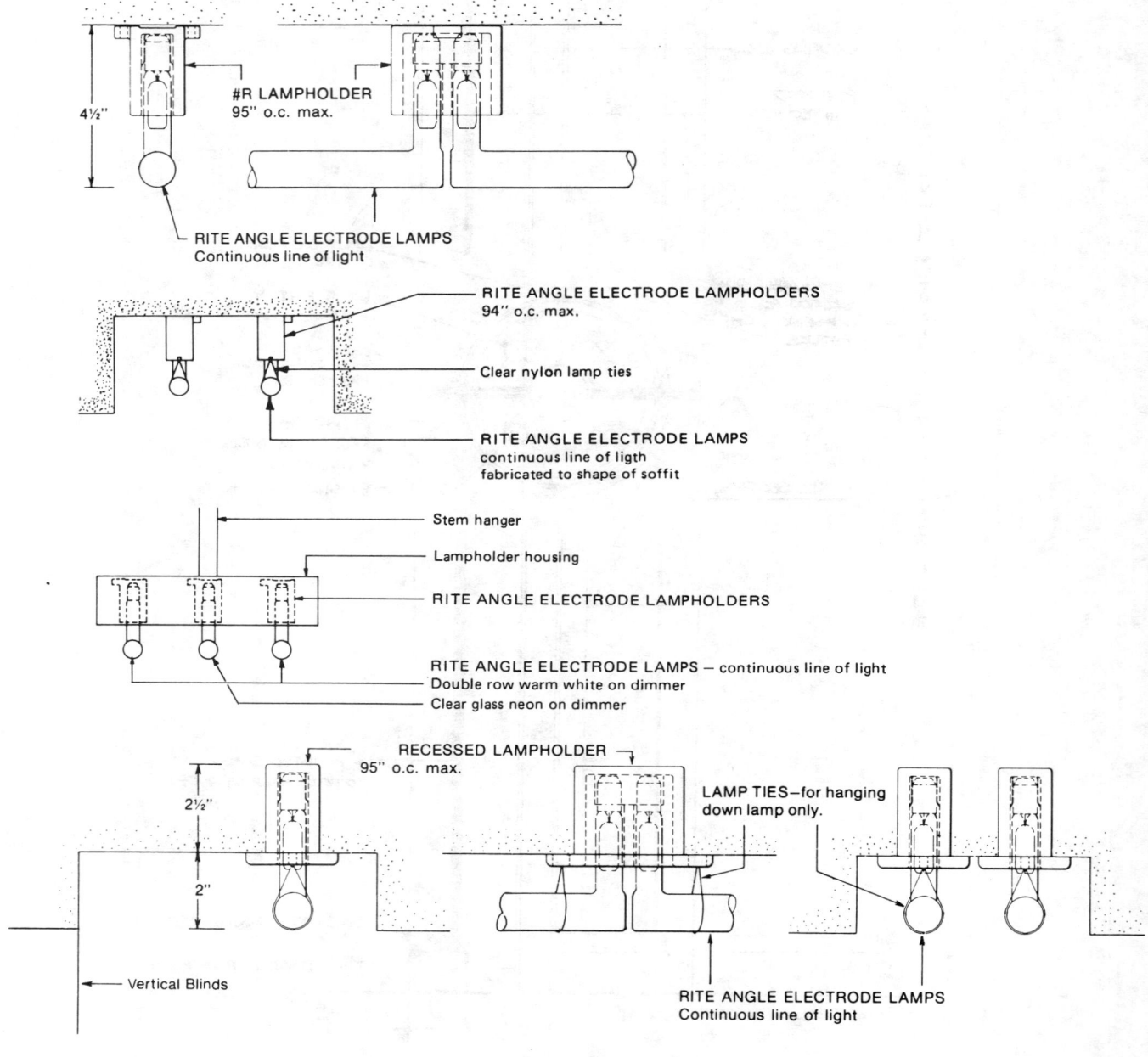

Principal types of lamps for general lighting purposes

Category	Type	Maximum lamp efficacy lm/W	Average life hrs	Characteristic features	Typical application areas
Incandescent Lamps	Normal incandescent lamps and reflector lamps	22	1,000	Easy to install, easy to use; many different versions; instant start; low cost price; reflector lamps allow concentrated light beams	General lighting in the home; decorative lighting; localized lighting; accent and decorative lighting (reflector lamps)
	Halogen	27	2,000	Compact; high light output; white light; easy to install; long life compared with normal incandescent lamps	Accent lighting; floodlighting
Fluorescent Lamps	Tubular	104	20,000	Wide choice of light colors; high lighting levels possible; economical in use	All kinds of commercial and public buildings; streetlighting; home lighting
	SL*	61	10,000	Energy-effective; direct replacement for incandescent lamps	Most applications where incandescent lamps were used before
	PL*	80	10,000	Compact; long life; energy-effective	To create a pleasant atmosphere in social areas, local lighting; signs, security, orientation lighting and general lighting
Gas-Discharge Lamps	Self-ballasted	28	12,000/16,000	Long life; good color rendering; easy to install; better efficacy than incandescent lamps	Direct replacement for incandescent lamps; small industrial and public light projects; plant irradiation
	High pressure mercury	63	24,000 +	High efficacy; long life; reasonable color quality	Residential area lighting; sports grounds; factory lighting
	Metal halide	94	15,000	Very high efficacy combined with excellent color rendering; long life	Floodlighting, especially for color TV; industrial lighting; road lighting; plant irradiation
	High pressure sodium	125	24,000 +	Very high efficacy; extremely long life; good color rendering	Public lighting; floodlighting; industrial lighting; plant irradiation EL: direct replacement for mercury lamps
	Low pressure sodium	200	18,000	Extremely high efficacy; very long life; high visual acuity; poor color rendering: monochromatic light	Many different application areas: wherever energy/cost-effectiveness is important and color is not critical

LIGHTING

Planning Data: Incandescent Bulb Sizes

INCANDESCENT BULBS

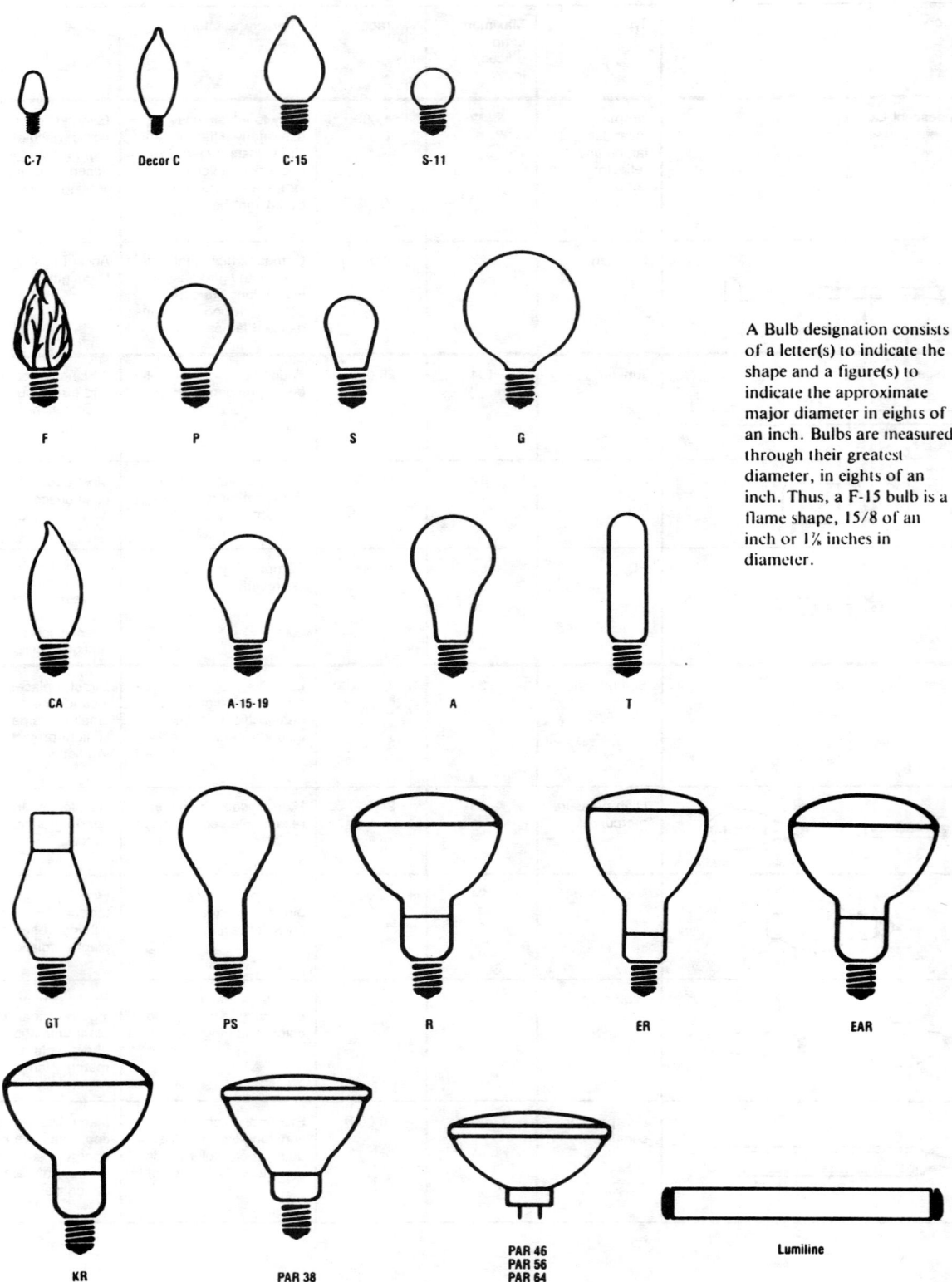

A Bulb designation consists of a letter(s) to indicate the shape and a figure(s) to indicate the approximate major diameter in eights of an inch. Bulbs are measured through their greatest diameter, in eights of an inch. Thus, a F-15 bulb is a flame shape, 15/8 of an inch or 1⅞ inches in diameter.

BASES

Mini-Can Screw
Mini Can

Candelabra
Cand

E-14 Screw European Base

Intermediate
Inter

B-15 Bayonet European Base

B-22 Bayonet European Base

Single Contact Bayonet Candelabra
S C Bay

Double Contact Bayonet Candelabra
D S Bay

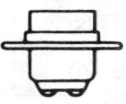
Candelabra Prefocus
S C Pf
D C Pf

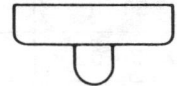
Single Pin
(T 12 Slimline)

Miniature Bipin
Min. Bipin
(T 5 F Lamp)

Single Pin
(T 6 Slimline)

Single Pin
(T 8 Slimline)

Mini Screw
M S.

Screw Terminal
Scr. Term.

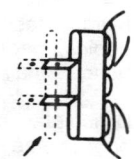
Ext. Mog End Prong **Mogul End Prong**
Mog E Pr

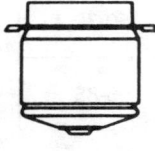
Medium Prefocus
Med Pf

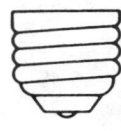
Standard

3 Kon Tact Medium
3 C Med

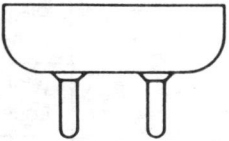
Mogul Bipin
Mog Bipin
(T 17 F Lamp)

Rect RSC Recessed Single Contact

Disc
(Lumiline)

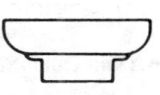
Recessed Dbl Contact
(T 12 F Lamp)

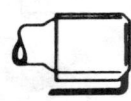
Metal Sleeve

Medium 2 Pin

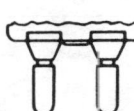
Med Bipcst

Medium Bipin
Med Bipin
(T 8 F Lamp)

Medium Bipin
Med Bipin
(T 12 F Lamp)

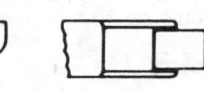
RSC Recessed Single Contact

Mini Can Socket

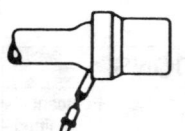
Ceramic Tubular

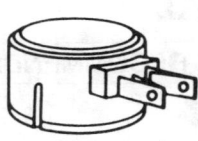
Medium Side Prong

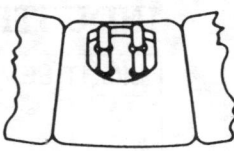
4 Pin
(Circline)

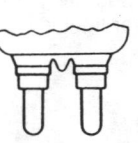
Mogul Bipost
Mog Bip

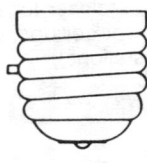
Position Oriented Mogul
Pos Or Mog

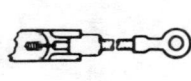
Type Q Axial Lead

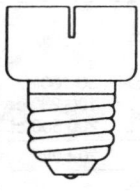
Medium Skirted
Med Skt

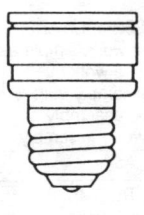
Medium Skirted
Med Skt

Admedium Skirted
Admed

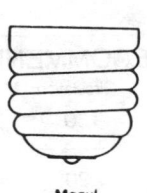
Mogul Prefocus
Mog Pf

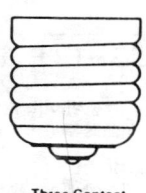
Mogul
Mog

Three Contact Mogul
3 C Mog

OFFICE

LIGHT LEVEL RECOMMENDATIONS

Type of Work	Foot Candles*
Corridors, lobbies	10-15-20
Easy tasks (Typed originals, ball-point pen handwriting, large print)	20-30-50
Medium tasks (Poor copies, medium hard pencil, small print)	50-75-100
Difficult tasks (Very poor copies, hard pencil writing)	100-150-200

*Choose an illuminance value in the mid-range for your type of activity. Then decide upon a specific value (Same, lower, or higher) within that range by considering the age of the workers and the importance of the work.

SELECTING THE PROPER FIXTURE

- Light Output/Efficiency

  The more light, the fewer fixtures needed in new lighting systems and lower operating cost.

- Visual Comfort

  Fixtures should direct light to the task and away from the eyes. The fixture's VCP rating, available from the fixture manufacturer, should be 70 or above.

- Maintainability

  Check ease of lamp replacement, cleanability, and permanence of finishes.

- Fit In Application

  Should look right and cover the area to be lighted (consider smaller fixtures closer together, such as 2 × 2s instead of 2 × 4s, for lower ceilings, or lower light levels or high-panelled work stations).

- Shielding Materials

  Comparison of lighting characteristics for typical 2 × 4 troffer luminaries:

Shielding Material	Efficiency Range (%)	VCP Range
Clear Lens	50-70	55-85
Polarizer	55-60	60-70
Deep Cell Parabolic Louver	45-60	70-85
Diffuser	40-60	40-50
Plastic Louver Panel (45°)	45-55	50-70
White Metal Louver (45°)	35-45	65-85
Parabolic Louver Panel (45°)	40-50	99
Toned Lens	30-60	70-85
Dark Metal Louver	25-40	70-90

STORE

LIGHT LEVEL RECOMMENDATIONS

	Circulation	Merchandising	Feature Displays
High Activity Area (Mass Merchandiser)	30	100	500
Medium (Family Dept. Store)	20	70	300
Low (Boutique. Specialty Stores)	10	30	150

INDUSTRIAL

LIGHT LEVEL RECOMMENDATIONS

	Footcandles Maintained on the Task
GARAGES–SERVICE	
☐ repair	50-100fc
☐ active traffic areas	10-20fc
LOADING PLATFORM	20fc
MACHINE SHOPS AND ASSEMBLY AREAS	
☐ rough bench/machine work, simple assembly	20-50fc
☐ medium bench/machine work, moderately difficult assembly	50-100fc
☐ difficult machine work, assembly	100-200fc
☐ fine bench/machine work, assembly	200-500fc*
RECEIVING & SHIPPING	20-50fc
WAREHOUSES, STORAGE ROOMS	
☐ active-large items/small items, labels	15fc/30fc
☐ inactive	5fc

*Higher illuminance values may be achieved through a combination of supplementary and general lighting.

Architectural Woodwork

INTRODUCTION

Most residential and commercial projects require the design of a certain amount of architectural woodwork. Such woodwork may be in the form of built-in furniture, cabinets, display cases, reception desks, credenzas, work counters, kitchen cabinets, etc. The extent of detail necessary to intelligently communicate and identify the scope and character of required woodwork is an important consideration in the preparation of contract drawings. It is necessary, therefore, that the designer have a knowledge of basic wood joinery and understand how to apply it in the preparation of construction details.

Accordingly, the information in this section can be used as a general guide in the detailing of most woodwork items and addresses four areas of concern. The first deals with basic joinery and typical casework details. This information is fundamental to an understanding of the detailing of woodwork. The typical joints illustrated vary in sophistication and structural integrity and represent the most common methods of joining any two wood members. The casework details are intended to illustrate the construction of routine casework and are divided into three categories: exposed face frame, flush overlay, and reveal overlay. The second area deals with custom woodwork and includes details of woodwork items selected directly from contract drawings contributed by various interior design and architectural firms. This information should prove helpful in providing the reader with a more global perspective of how different firms approach the detailing of some common types of woodwork items and the extent of that detailing. The third area of this section deals with standard cornices and mouldings, and is intended to simply provide the designer with dimensional and design information relative to the many standard items available on the market. Since many woodwork items involve some moveable elements, the fourth area of this section deals with furniture hardware.

Characteristics of Joints

Joints may be divided into four general types: *butted, shiplapped, tongued-and-grooved,* and *mitered.* Used in their simple basic form, none is satisfactory for cabinet work except the tongued-and-grooved type in certain instances. However, when variously combined or when reinforced with gluing and dowels or splines, satisfactory joints can be developed.

Butt joint A simple but weak joint that opens easily and may show end wood when used at angles. Strength and range of use is greatly increased by use of the *mortise and tenon* and *dowels* and even more when a *straight spline* is included. Use of a glued *butterfly spline* with a butt joint produces an extremely strong joint. These variations are widely used to produce large flush surfaces of solid wood or backing for veneers.

Shiplap joint Stronger than a butt joint but subject to opening from shrinkage. Rarely used in a simple form in cabinet work except for door rebates. It is often moulded to conceal shrinkage in quirks or combined as a *miter and shoulder* for corners. Another variation is the *shoulder joint.*

Tongue-and-groove joint A strong joint, widely used for re-entrant angles. Effect of wood shrinkage is concealed when the joint is beaded or otherwise moulded. In expensive cabinet work glued *dovetail* and *multiple tongue-and-groove* are used.

Miter joints are weak and difficult to fit if used alone. Joints with *miter brads* are sufficiently strong for short lengths. Joints made in combination with other forms, as a *tongue-and-groove miter,* are tight and sturdy.

Use of Joints

Use of certain types of joints depends to a large degree upon the type of work and skill involved. The following notes indicate use of joints in various categories, but cannot be regarded as an inclusive check list.

For panels, shelving, etc., or wherever the end of one piece butts against the face of another; *housed joint,* with or without cover mould, or some type of *tongue-and-groove* joint. Omit glue to avoid splitting due to swelling or shrinkage.

For joining stiles and rails: *mortise and tenon,* glued in better work. Dowels may be used or hardwood wedges may be driven and glued into ends of tenons in high grade work.

For re-entrant corners: *shoulder joints* for inexpensive work. *Tongue-and-groove* is sturdier. Both should be glued, are often screwed together, and may be glued to a rough frame.

For external corners: simple *miter* and *quirk and miter* both lack strength. *Miter brads* are practical only for short lengths. *Miter and shoulder* glued and face-screwed or nailed is satisfactory (generally "mil work"). *Miter and spline* is preferable. In high grade work exterior corners are reinforced by gluing to a corner post or short lengths of blocking.

Glued joints: when screws, nails, etc., cannot be used, or when fine work is to be veneered, strength of the joint depends on accuracy of milling and total glue surface. Glue surface may be tremendously increased by using multiple or offset tongues and grooves, by forming miter cuts into waves, multiple shoulders, tongues and grooves, etc. Such work is cabinet work. If done by a reliable cabinet maker, a guarantee should be obtained and joint detail and composition of glue left to him or her.

Mouldings should be applied in continuous lengths if possible. Use simple miter for necessary joints, cope re-entrant angles unless excessively undercut, miter external corners.

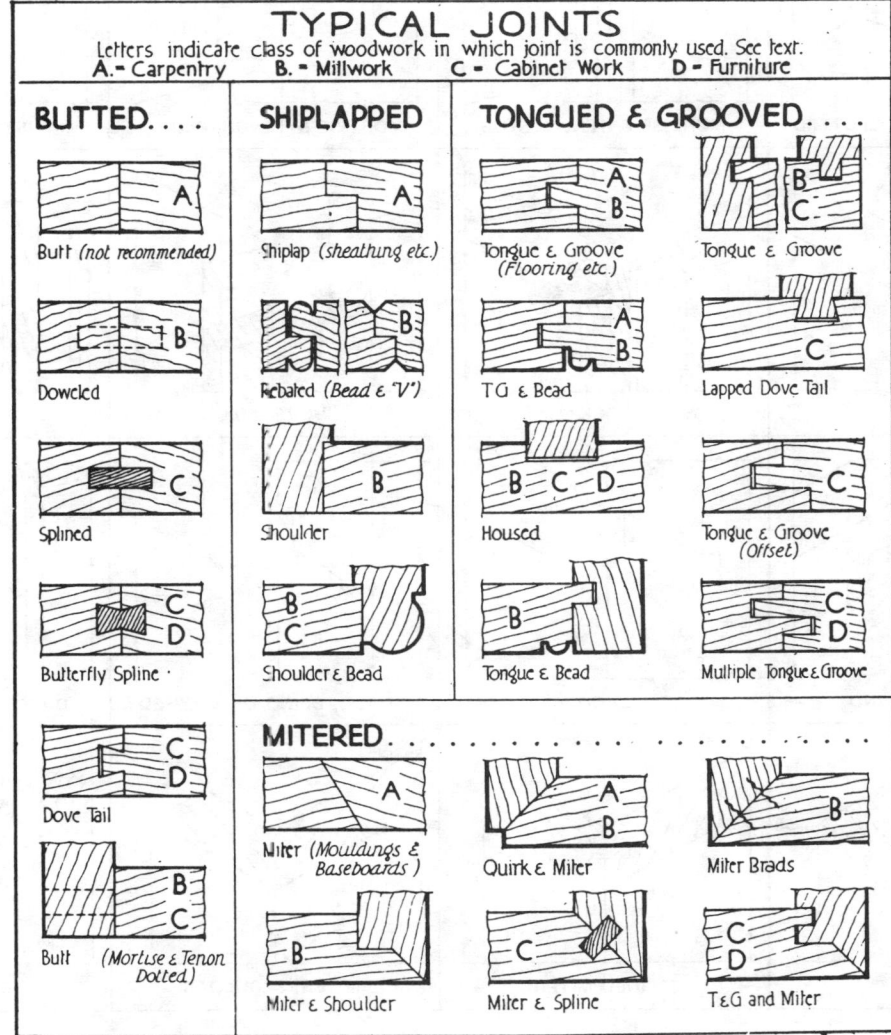

TYPICAL JOINTS
Letters indicate class of woodwork in which joint is commonly used. See text.
A.- Carpentry   B. - Millwork   C - Cabinet Work   D - Furniture

BUTTED....
- Butt (not recommended)
- Dowelled
- Splined
- Butterfly Spline
- Dove Tail
- Butt (Mortise & Tenon Dotted)

SHIPLAPPED
- Shiplap (sheathing etc.)
- Rebated (Bead & 'V')
- Shoulder
- Shoulder & Bead

TONGUED & GROOVED....
- Tongue & Groove (Flooring etc.)
- T G & Bead
- Housed
- Tongue & Bead
- Tongue & Groove
- Lapped Dove Tail
- Tongue & Groove (Offset)
- Multiple Tongue & Groove

MITERED....
- Miter (Mouldings & Baseboards)
- Miter & Shoulder
- Quirk & Miter
- Miter & Spline
- Miter Brads
- T & G and Miter

STANDARD JOINERY AND CASEWORK DETAILS

Typical Joints

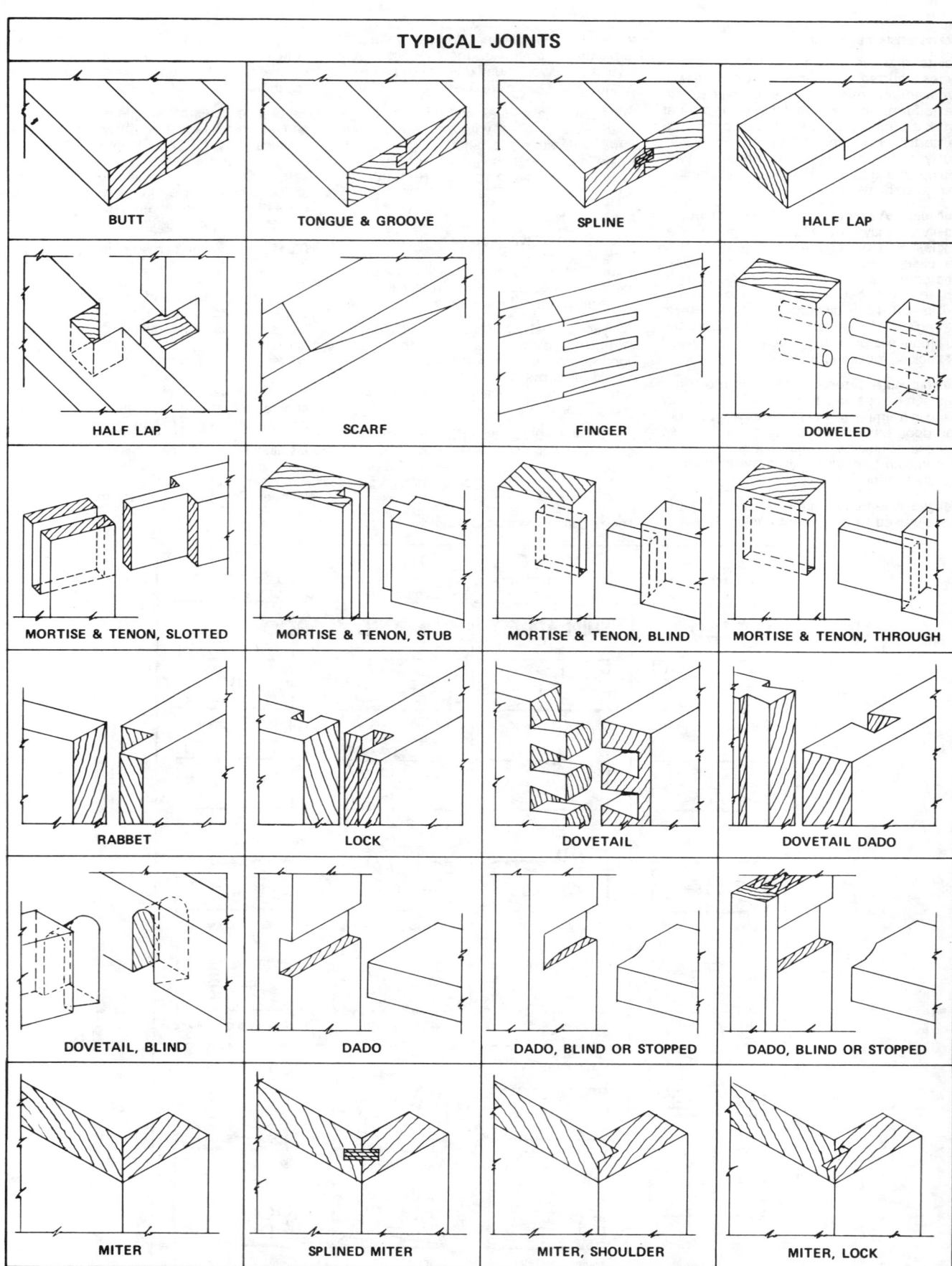

TYPICAL JOINTS

BUTT	TONGUE & GROOVE	SPLINE	HALF LAP
HALF LAP	SCARF	FINGER	DOWELED
MORTISE & TENON, SLOTTED	MORTISE & TENON, STUB	MORTISE & TENON, BLIND	MORTISE & TENON, THROUGH
RABBET	LOCK	DOVETAIL	DOVETAIL DADO
DOVETAIL, BLIND	DADO	DADO, BLIND OR STOPPED	DADO, BLIND OR STOPPED
MITER	SPLINED MITER	MITER, SHOULDER	MITER, LOCK

Terminology

Spline joint Used for gluing plywood in width or length. Since the spline serves to align faces, this joint is also used for items requiring site assembly.

Stub tenon Joinery method for assembling stile and rail type frames that are additionally supported, such as web or skeleton case frames.

Conventional mortise and tenon joint Joinery method for assembling square-edged surfaces such as case face frames.

Dowel joint Alternative joinery method for serving same function as conventional mortise and tenon.

Haunch mortise and tenon joint Joinery method for assembling paneled doors or stile and rail type paneling.

French dovetail joint Method for joining drawer sides to fronts when fronts conceal metal extension slides or overlay the case faces.

Conventional dovetail joint Traditional method for joining drawer sides to fronts or backs. Usually limited to flush or lipped type drawers.

Drawer lock-joint Another joinery method for joining drawer sides to fronts. Usually used for flush type installation but can be adapted to lip or overlay type drawers.

Edge banding Method of concealing plys or inner cores of plywood or particleboard when edges are exposed. Thickness or configuration will vary with manufacturers' practices.

Through dado Conventional joint used for assembly of case body members — dado usually concealed by application of case face frame.

Blind dado Variation of conventional dado with applied edge "stopping" or concealing dado groove. Used when case body edge is exposed.

Stop dado Another method of concealing dado exposure. Applicable when veneer edging or solid lumber is used.

Exposed end detail Illustrates attachment of finished end of case body to front frame using butt joint.

Exposed end detail Illustrates attachment of finished end of case body to front frame using mitered joint.

Paneled door details Joinery techniques when paneled effect is desired. Profiles are optional as is the use of flat or raised panels. Solid lumber raised panels may be used when width does not exceed 10 in. Rim raised panels recommended when widths exceed this dimension or when transparent finish is used.

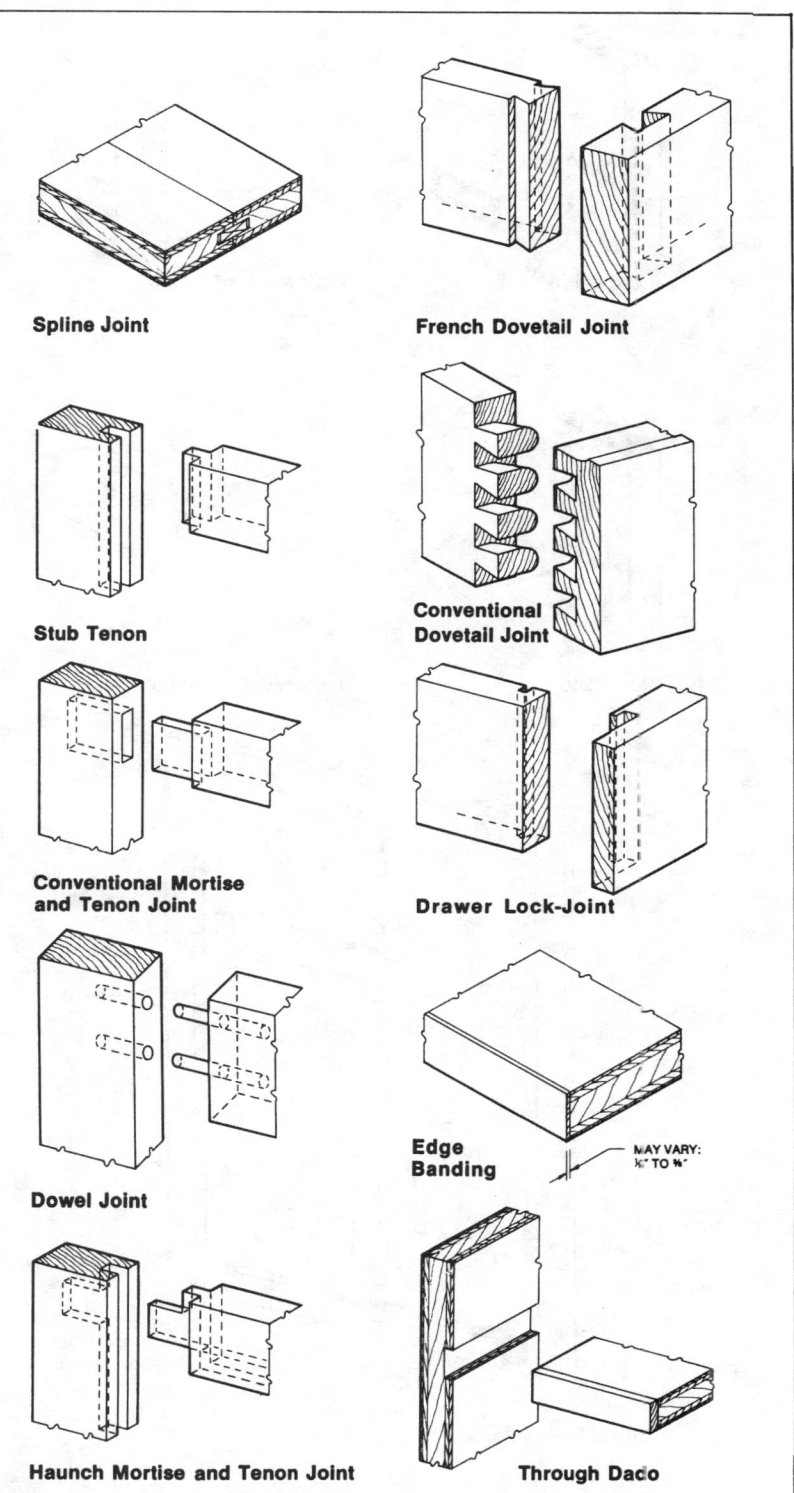

Spline Joint

French Dovetail Joint

Stub Tenon

Conventional Dovetail Joint

Conventional Mortise and Tenon Joint

Drawer Lock-Joint

Dowel Joint

Edge Banding

MAY VARY: ⅛" TO ¾"

Haunch Mortise and Tenon Joint

Through Dado

STANDARD JOINERY AND CASEWORK DETAILS `
Typical Joints

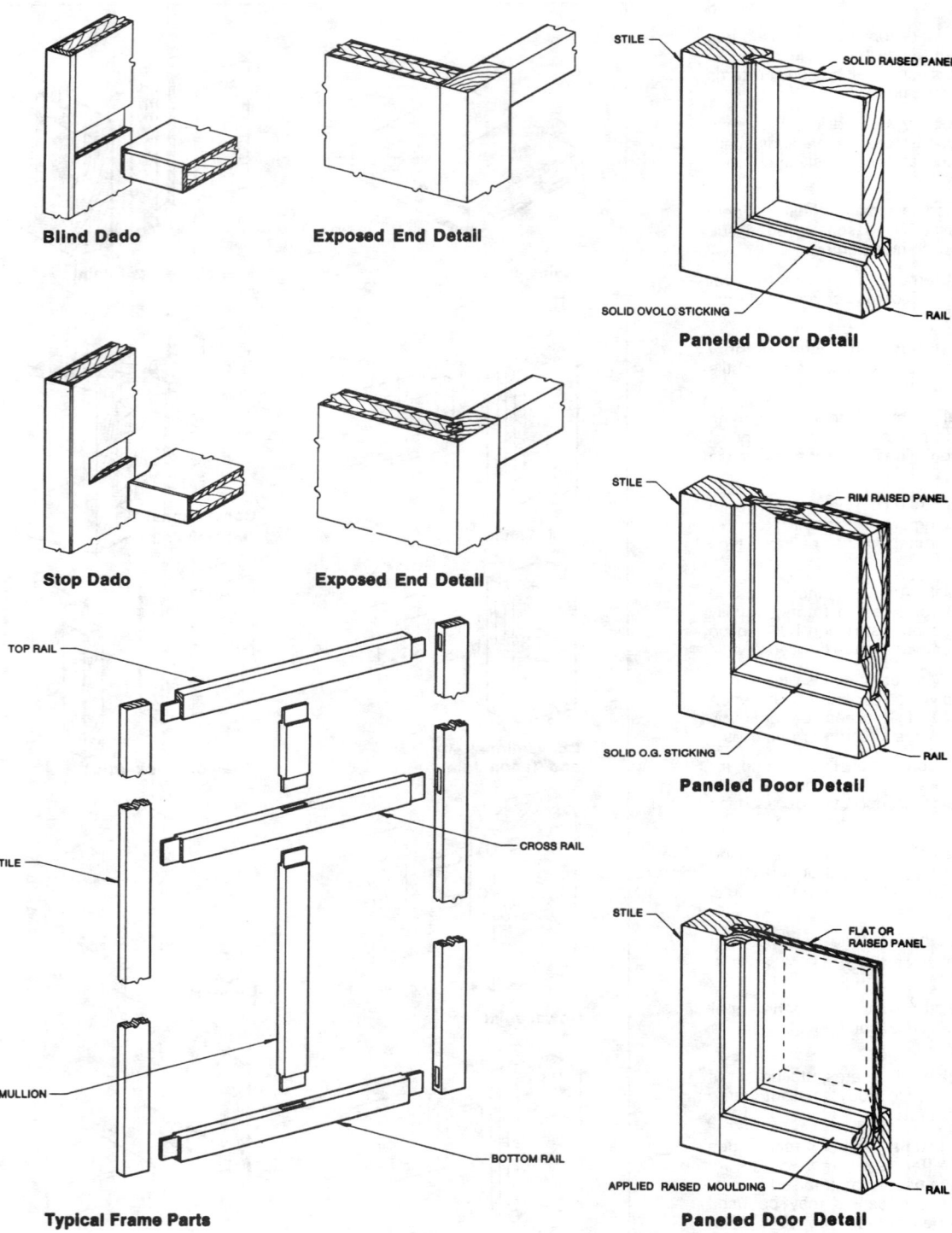

Blind Dado

Exposed End Detail

STILE

SOLID RAISED PANEL

SOLID OVOLO STICKING

RAIL

Paneled Door Detail

Stop Dado

Exposed End Detail

STILE

RIM RAISED PANEL

SOLID O.G. STICKING

RAIL

Paneled Door Detail

TOP RAIL

CROSS RAIL

STILE

MULLION

BOTTOM RAIL

Typical Frame Parts

STILE

FLAT OR RAISED PANEL

APPLIED RAISED MOULDING

RAIL

Paneled Door Detail

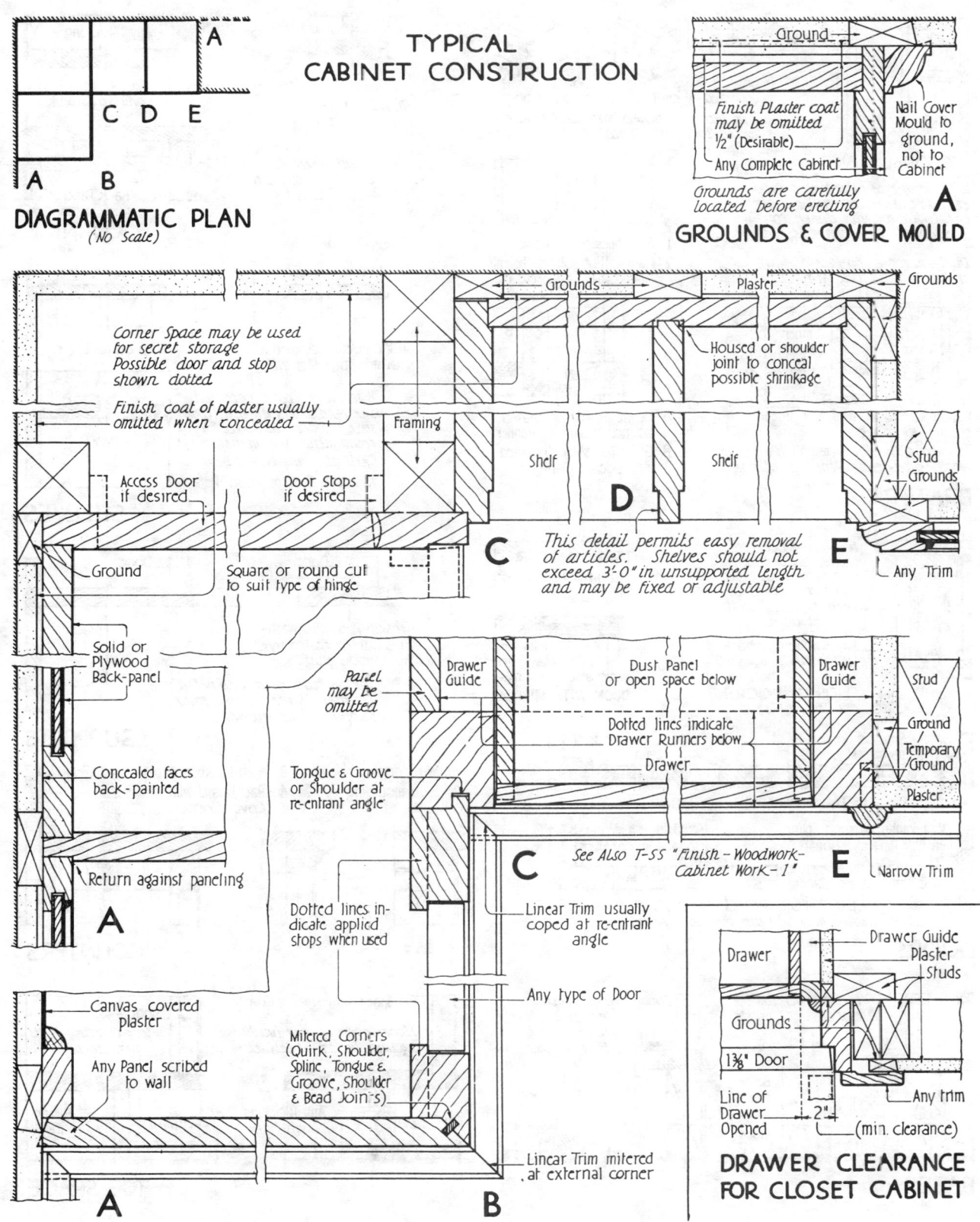

DIAGRAMMATIC PLAN
(No Scale)

A B

C D E

A

TYPICAL CABINET CONSTRUCTION

GROUNDS & COVER MOULD

Finish Plaster coat may be omitted
½" *(Desirable)*

Any Complete Cabinet

Ground

Nail Cover Mould to ground, not to Cabinet

Grounds are carefully located before erecting

A

Corner Space may be used for secret storage Possible door and stop shown dotted

Finish coat of plaster usually omitted when concealed

Grounds   Plaster   Grounds

Housed or shoulder joint to conceal possible shrinkage

Framing

Shelf   Shelf

Stud Grounds

Access Door if desired   Door Stops if desired

Square or round cut to suit type of hinge

Ground

C

D

This detail permits easy removal of articles. Shelves should not exceed 3'-0" in unsupported length and may be fixed or adjustable

E

Any Trim

Solid or Plywood Back-panel

Concealed faces back-painted

Return against paneling

A

Panel may be omitted

Tongue & Groove or Shoulder at re-entrant angle

Drawer Guide

Dust Panel or open space below

Dotted lines indicate Drawer Runners below

Drawer

Drawer Guide

Stud

Ground

Temporary Ground

Plaster

C

See Also T-SS "Finish-Woodwork-Cabinet Work-1"

E

Narrow Trim

Dotted lines indicate applied stops when used

Linear Trim usually coped at re-entrant angle

Any type of Door

Canvas covered plaster

Any Panel scribed to wall

Mitered Corners (Quirk, Shoulder, Spline, Tongue & Groove, Shoulder & Bead Joints)

Linear Trim mitered at external corner

A

B

Drawer

Drawer Guide   Plaster   Studs

Grounds

1⅜" Door

Line of Drawer Opened

2"

(min. clearance)

Any trim

DRAWER CLEARANCE FOR CLOSET CABINET

STANDARD JOINERY AND CASEWORK DETAILS

Cabinet Work

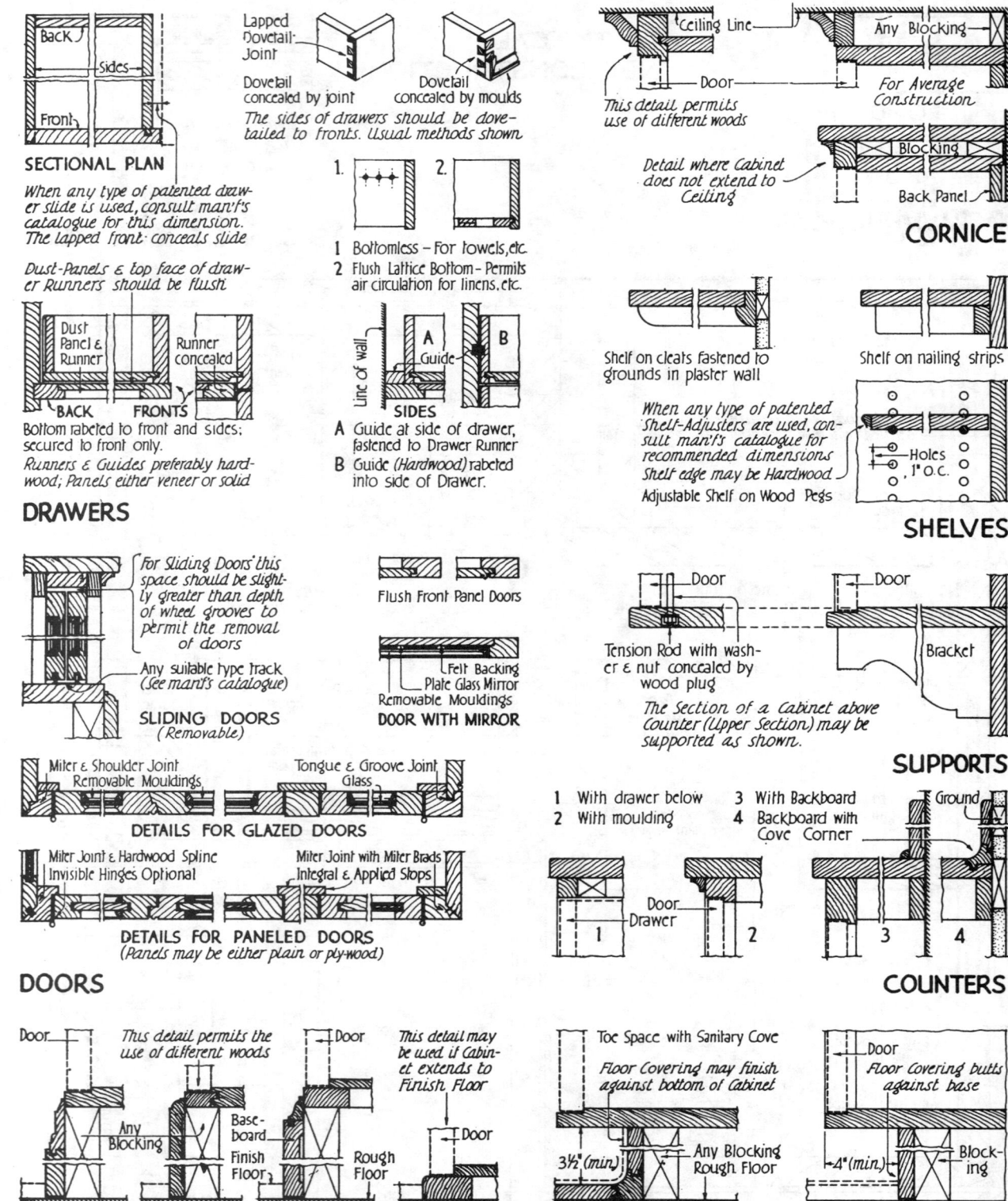

SECTIONAL PLAN

When any type of patented drawer slide is used, consult man'f's catalogue for this dimension. The lapped front conceals slide

Dust-Panels & top face of drawer Runners should be flush

BACK **FRONTS**

Bottom rabeted to front and sides; secured to front only.

Runners & Guides preferably hardwood; Panels either veneer or solid

DRAWERS

Lapped Dovetail Joint

Dovetail concealed by joint

Dovetail concealed by moulds

The sides of drawers should be dovetailed to fronts. Usual methods shown.

1. Bottomless – For towels, etc.
2. Flush Lattice Bottom – Permits air circulation for linens, etc.

SIDES

A Guide at side of drawer, fastened to Drawer Runner

B Guide (*Hardwood*) rabeted into side of Drawer.

For Sliding Doors this space should be slightly greater than depth of wheel grooves to permit the removal of doors

Any suitable type track (See man'f's catalogue)

SLIDING DOORS (Removable)

Flush Front Panel Doors

Felt Backing
Plate Glass Mirror
Removable Mouldings

DOOR WITH MIRROR

Miter & Shoulder Joint
Removable Mouldings

Tongue & Groove Joint
Glass

DETAILS FOR GLAZED DOORS

Miter Joint & Hardwood Spline
Invisible Hinges Optional

Miter Joint with Miter Brads
Integral & Applied Stops

DETAILS FOR PANELED DOORS
(Panels may be either plain or ply-wood)

DOORS

Door
This detail permits the use of different woods

Any Blocking
Baseboard
Finish Floor
Rough Floor

This detail may be used if Cabinet extends to Finish Floor

BASES

Ceiling Line
Door
This detail permits use of different woods

Any Blocking
For Average Construction

Detail where Cabinet does not extend to Ceiling

Blocking
Back Panel

CORNICE

Shelf on cleats fastened to grounds in plaster wall

Shelf on nailing strips

When any type of patented Shelf-Adjusters are used, consult man'f's catalogue for recommended dimensions Shelf edge may be Hardwood

Holes 1" O.C.

Adjustable Shelf on Wood Pegs

SHELVES

Door

Tension Rod with washer & nut concealed by wood plug

Bracket

The Section of a Cabinet above Counter (Upper Section) may be supported as shown.

SUPPORTS

1 With drawer below
2 With moulding
3 With Backboard
4 Backboard with Cove Corner

Ground

Door
Drawer

1 2 3 4

COUNTERS

Toe Space with Sanitary Cove

Floor Covering may finish against bottom of Cabinet

3½" (min)
Any Blocking
Rough Floor

Door
Floor Covering butts against base

4" (min.)
Blocking

TOE SPACE

Purpose

The following information outlines methods of assembly and installation of common cabinet work. Solutions of typical problems are presented without attempting to detail specific cabinets.

Assembly

High-grade cabinet and veneered work is assembled as far as possible at the shop. Joints are glued and blocked, and sometimes secured with finishing nails or screws. Carpentry and millwork are generally put together with finishing nails if of soft wood, or with screws if of hardwood. Hardwood should be drilled to prevent splitting before using nails or screws, and heads should be countersunk and concealed by cover moulds, moulding quirks, or putty, plastic wood, or other filler, colored to match the finish. No nails, screws, or joints should be visible unless they are intentionally incorporated in design.

Shrinkage and warping   effects can be largely eliminated by proper detailing and construction. *Wide flat surfaces* (solid or veneered) should be made up of several narrow strips glued and doweled, splined, or dovetailed together. Cleats may also be screwed or keyed to backs of wide surfaces. *Joints in corners, sheathing, etc.,* should be con- cealed within quirks of moulds (as in moulded tongue-and-groove) or return faces (shoulder joints). *Panels* should be rigidly secured on one side only, and are often left entirely loose. Housed joints, not glued, permit panels to expand and contract without splitting.

Large moulded surfaces   (such as cornices or mantels) should always be shop-assembled and delivered with scribe-moulds (see "Scribing" below) loosely tacked to assembled units.

Installation

All grades of woodwork should be preservative treated or back painted before erection, preferably before delivery to the job. Satisfactory priming coats are aluminum paint or white lead in linseed oil, thinned with turpentine or mineral spirits.

Preparation   On frame walls plaster may be limited to one or two coats, may be recessed between studs, or may be omitted. In the latter case, building paper should be used between woodwork and studs. On masonry, plaster may consist of one or two coats or may be omitted. Masonry surfaces, particularly exterior walls, should be waterproofed or woodwork should be protected by a layer of waterproof paper and should always be furred out. When finish of the interior of cabinets is plaster, either plain or canvas covered, the final coat of plaster is applied after erection of cabinet.

Grounds   of soft wood for attaching cabinet work must be accurately located, are secured directly to framing members or furring, and must be concealed.

Blocking   of rough lumber should be erected for supporting raised floors and large or heavy cabinet work, if it can be concealed. Blocking must be accurately placed and secured with nails.

Shimming   Minor irregularities in blocking, furring, or placement of studs may be corrected by using shims (wedge-shaped pieces of wood, often shingles) to bring completed work to plumb and level lines. Shimming should be concealed.

Scribing   is the practice of fitting edges of cabinet work accurately to all irregularities of finish plaster, masonry, or other abutting surfaces. Wood mouldings, panel frames, or cabinet returns to be scribed should be provided with a beveled edge.

Prefabricated woodwork   is generally delivered knocked down for assembly on the job and is erected similarly to custom-made work. Consult manufacturers' data.

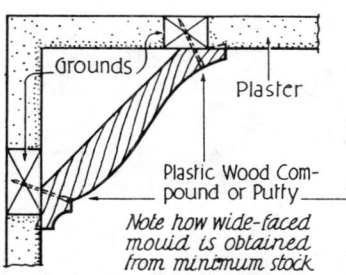

Note how wide-faced mould is obtained from minimum stock

NAILING TO GROUNDS

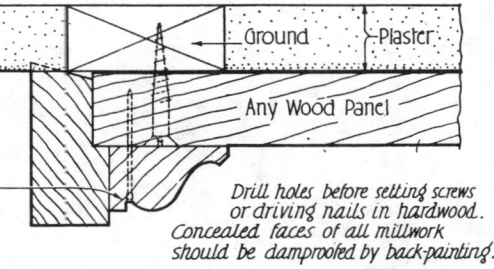

Drill holes before setting screws or driving nails in hardwood. Concealed faces of all millwork should be dampproofed by back-painting.

CONCEALING ATTACHMENT OF HARDWOODS

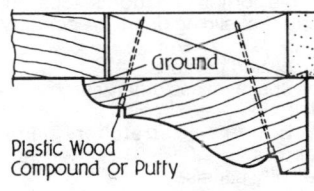

Plastic Wood Compound or Putty

NAILING IN QUIRKS

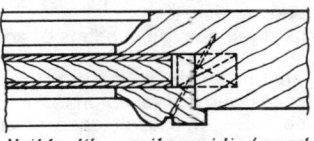

Nail to stiles or rails; avoiding panel

NAILING PANEL MOULD

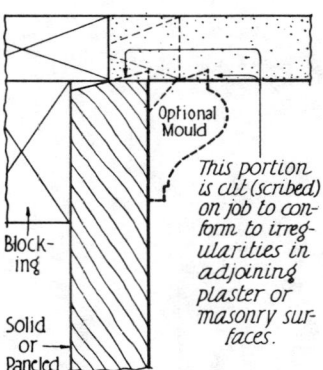

Optional Mould

This portion is cut (scribed) on job to conform to irregularities in adjoining plaster or masonry surfaces.

SCRIBING AGAINST PLASTER OR MASONRY

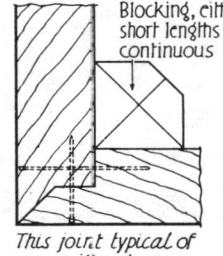

Blocking, either short lengths or continuous

This joint typical of millwork

Nailing & gluing a mortise and shoulder provides a strong, reasonably permanent joint

GLUING AND BLOCKING

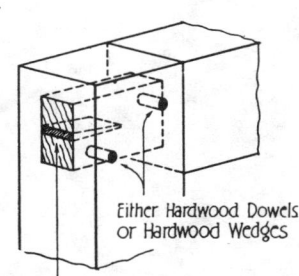

Either Hardwood Dowels or Hardwood Wedges

For wedges, make saw-cut in tenon before assembling. Holes for dowels may be off-set to draw joint tight.

SECURING MORTISE & TENON

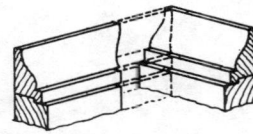

Cope by hand on job unless excessively undercut; if so, use miter. Flat members may be butted or Tongued-and-Grooved

COPING MOULDINGS RE-ENTRANT ANGLE

STANDARD JOINERY AND CASEWORK DETAILS

Plastic-Covered Casework

Casework Definitions

A. Exposed portions
1. All surfaces visible when doors and drawers are closed.
2. Underside of bottoms of cabinets over 4'0" above finished floor.
3. Cabinet tops under 6'0" above finished floor or if over 6'0" and visible from an upper building level or floor.
4. Visible front edges of web frames, ends, divisions, tops, shelves, and hanging stiles.
5. Sloping tops of cabinets that are visible.
6. Visible surfaces in open cabinets or behind glass for premium grade only.
7. Interior faces of hinged doors for premium grade only.
8. Visible portions of bottoms, tops, and ends in front of sliding doors in custom and premium grades only.

B. Semi-exposed portions
1. Shelves.
2. Divisions.
3. Interior face of ends, backs, and bottoms.
4. Drawer sides, subfronts, backs, and bottoms.
5. The underside of bottoms of cabinets between 2'6" and 4'0" above the finished floor.
6. Interior faces of hinged doors, except premium grade.
7. Visible surfaces in open cabinets or behind glass for economy and custom grades and all rooms designated as storage, janitor, closet, or utility.
8. Visible portion of bottoms, tops, and ends in front of sliding doors in economy grade only.

C. Concealed portions
1. Toe space unless otherwise specified.
2. Sleepers.
3. Web frames, stretchers, and solid subtops.
4. Security panels.
5. Underside of bottoms of cabinets less than 2'6" above the finished floor.
6. Flat tops of cabinets 6'0" or more above the finished floor, except if visible from an upper building level.
7. The three nonvisible edges of adjustable shelves.
8. The underside of countertops, knee spaces, and drawer aprons.
9. The faces of cabinet ends of adjoining units that butt together.

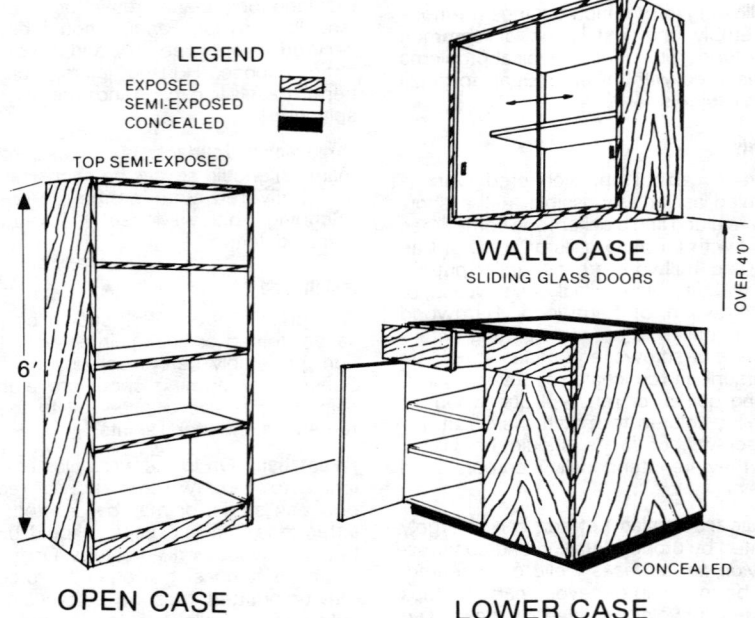

Fig. 1   Inside surfaces of open shelf cabinets and behind glass are considered exposed for premium grade and tops of tall cabinets and upper cabinets 6 ft above the floor that are exposed from upper levels are considered exposed.

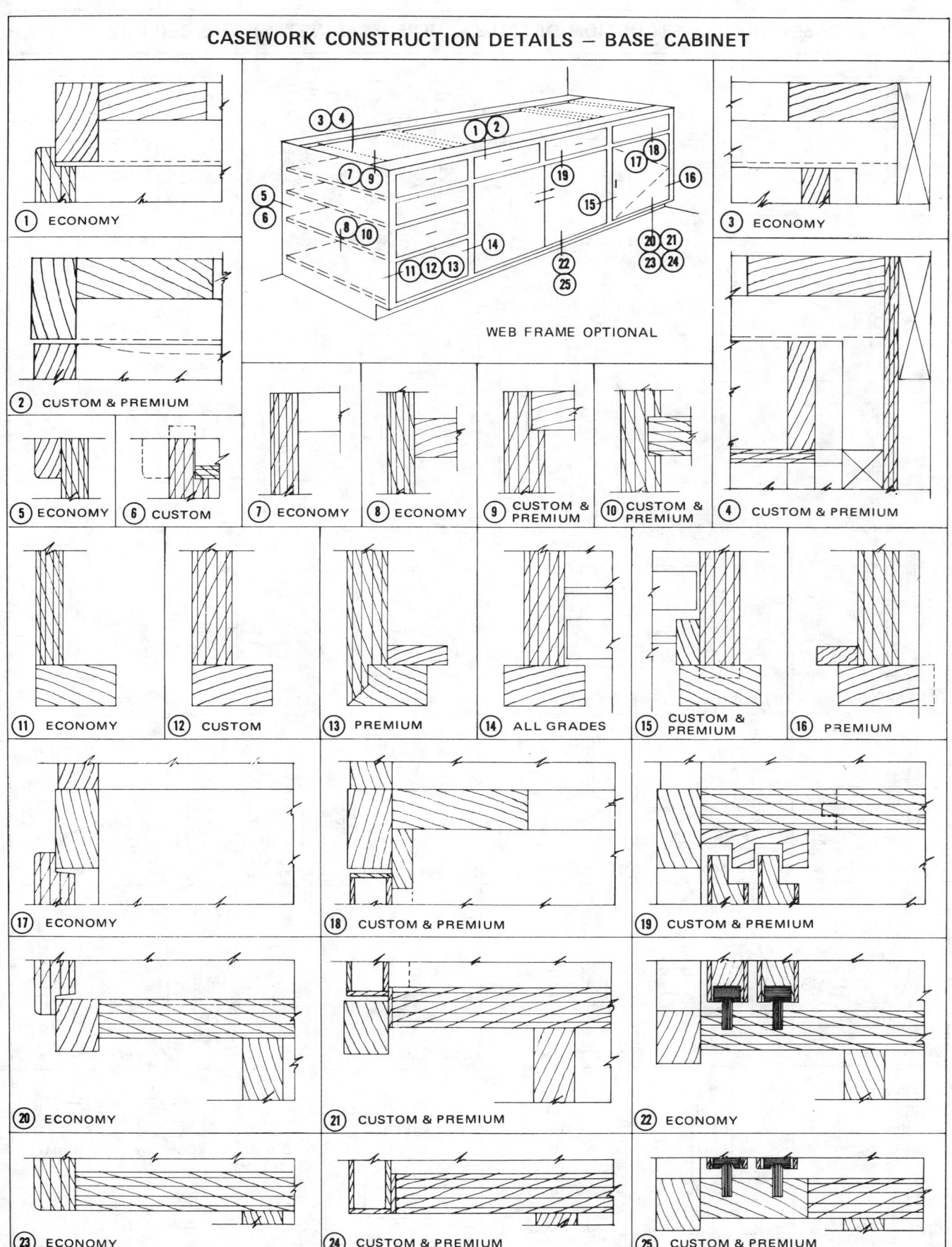

CASEWORK CONSTRUCTION DETAILS — BASE CABINET

WEB FRAME OPTIONAL

1. ECONOMY
2. CUSTOM & PREMIUM
3. ECONOMY
4. CUSTOM & PREMIUM
5. ECONOMY
6. CUSTOM
7. ECONOMY
8. ECONOMY
9. CUSTOM & PREMIUM
10. CUSTOM & PREMIUM
11. ECONOMY
12. CUSTOM
13. PREMIUM
14. ALL GRADES
15. CUSTOM & PREMIUM
16. PREMIUM
17. ECONOMY
18. CUSTOM & PREMIUM
19. CUSTOM & PREMIUM
20. ECONOMY
21. CUSTOM & PREMIUM
22. ECONOMY
23. ECONOMY
24. CUSTOM & PREMIUM
25. CUSTOM & PREMIUM

Fig. 2   Casework construction details — base cabinet

STANDARD JOINERY AND CASEWORK DETAILS

Typical Upper Cabinet Details

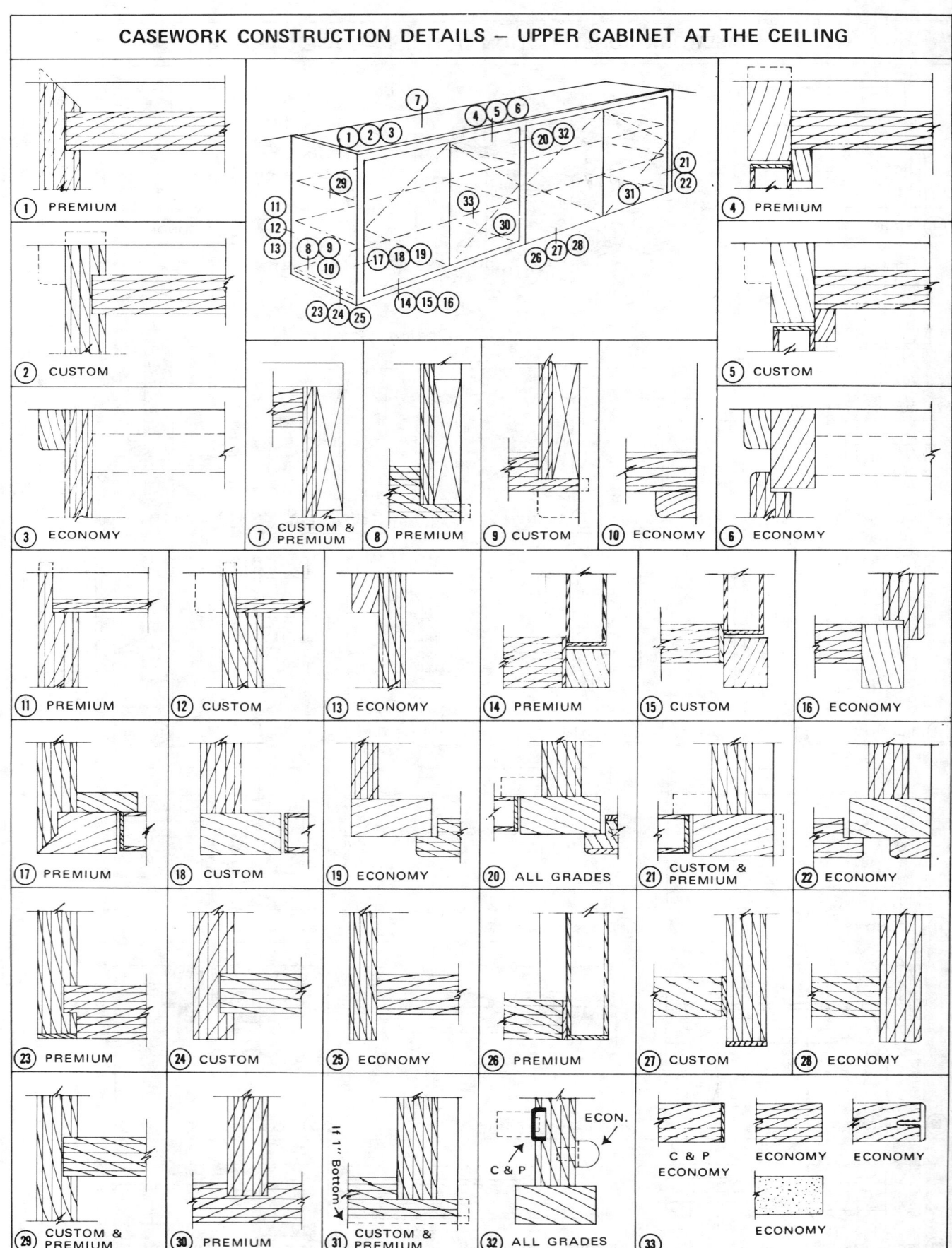

CASEWORK CONSTRUCTION DETAILS — UPPER CABINET AT THE CEILING

1 PREMIUM
2 CUSTOM
3 ECONOMY
4 PREMIUM
5 CUSTOM
6 ECONOMY
7 CUSTOM & PREMIUM
8 PREMIUM
9 CUSTOM
10 ECONOMY
11 PREMIUM
12 CUSTOM
13 ECONOMY
14 PREMIUM
15 CUSTOM
16 ECONOMY
17 PREMIUM
18 CUSTOM
19 ECONOMY
20 ALL GRADES
21 CUSTOM & PREMIUM
22 ECONOMY
23 PREMIUM
24 CUSTOM
25 ECONOMY
26 PREMIUM
27 CUSTOM
28 ECONOMY
29 CUSTOM & PREMIUM
30 PREMIUM
31 CUSTOM & PREMIUM
32 ALL GRADES
33 C & P ECONOMY / ECONOMY / ECONOMY / ECONOMY

If 1" Bottom

ECON.
C & P

Fig. 3   Casework construction details — upper cabinets at the ceiling.

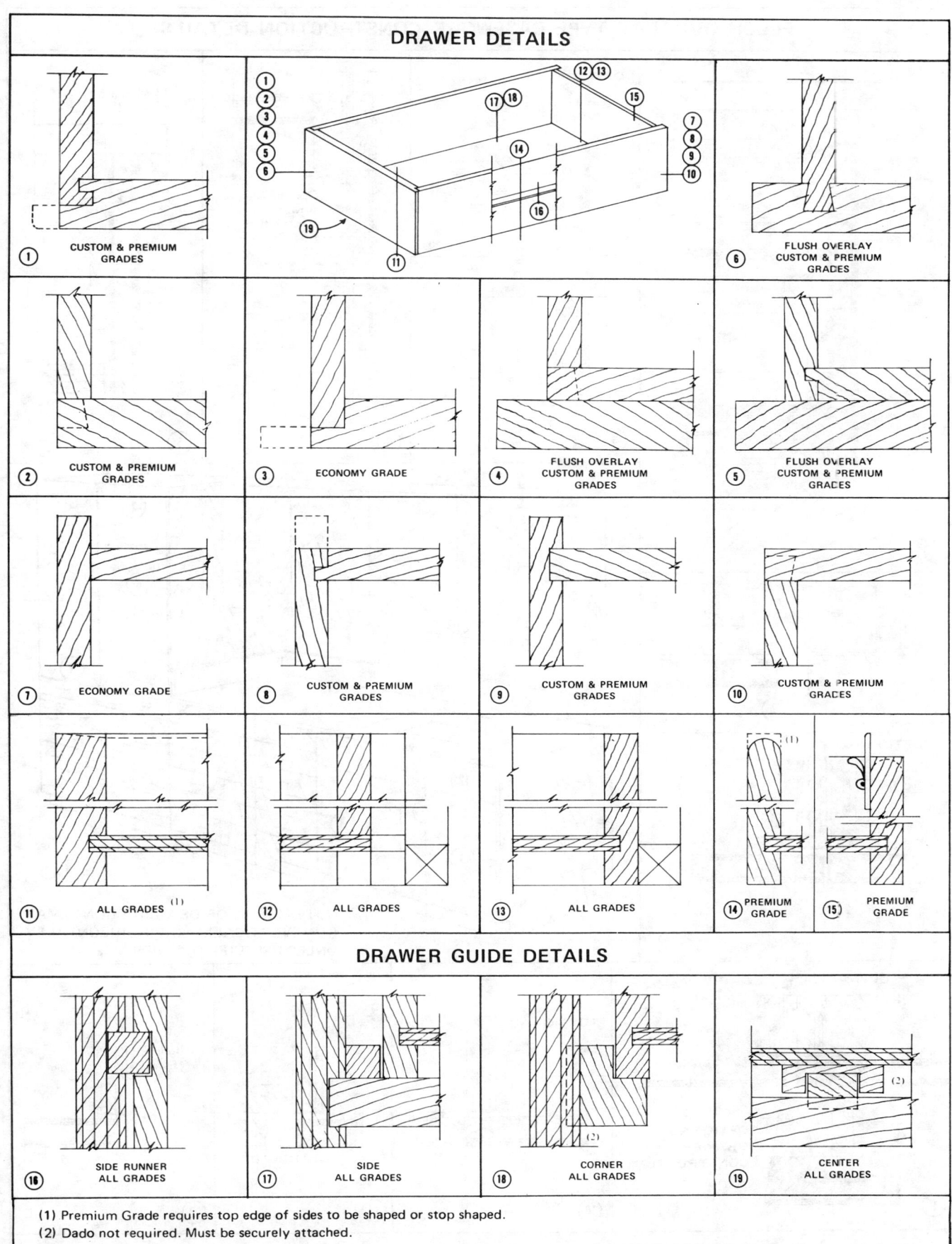

DRAWER DETAILS

① CUSTOM & PREMIUM GRADES

② CUSTOM & PREMIUM GRADES

③ ECONOMY GRADE

④ FLUSH OVERLAY CUSTOM & PREMIUM GRADES

⑤ FLUSH OVERLAY CUSTOM & PREMIUM GRADES

⑥ FLUSH OVERLAY CUSTOM & PREMIUM GRADES

⑦ ECONOMY GRADE

⑧ CUSTOM & PREMIUM GRADES

⑨ CUSTOM & PREMIUM GRADES

⑩ CUSTOM & PREMIUM GRADES

⑪ ALL GRADES (1)

⑫ ALL GRADES

⑬ ALL GRADES

⑭ PREMIUM GRADE

⑮ PREMIUM GRADE

DRAWER GUIDE DETAILS

⑯ SIDE RUNNER ALL GRADES

⑰ SIDE ALL GRADES

⑱ CORNER ALL GRADES

⑲ CENTER ALL GRADES

(1) Premium Grade requires top edge of sides to be shaped or stop shaped.
(2) Dado not required. Must be securely attached.

Fig. 4   Drawer details.

STANDARD JOINERY AND CASEWORK DETAILS

Typical Flush Overlay Casework Construction

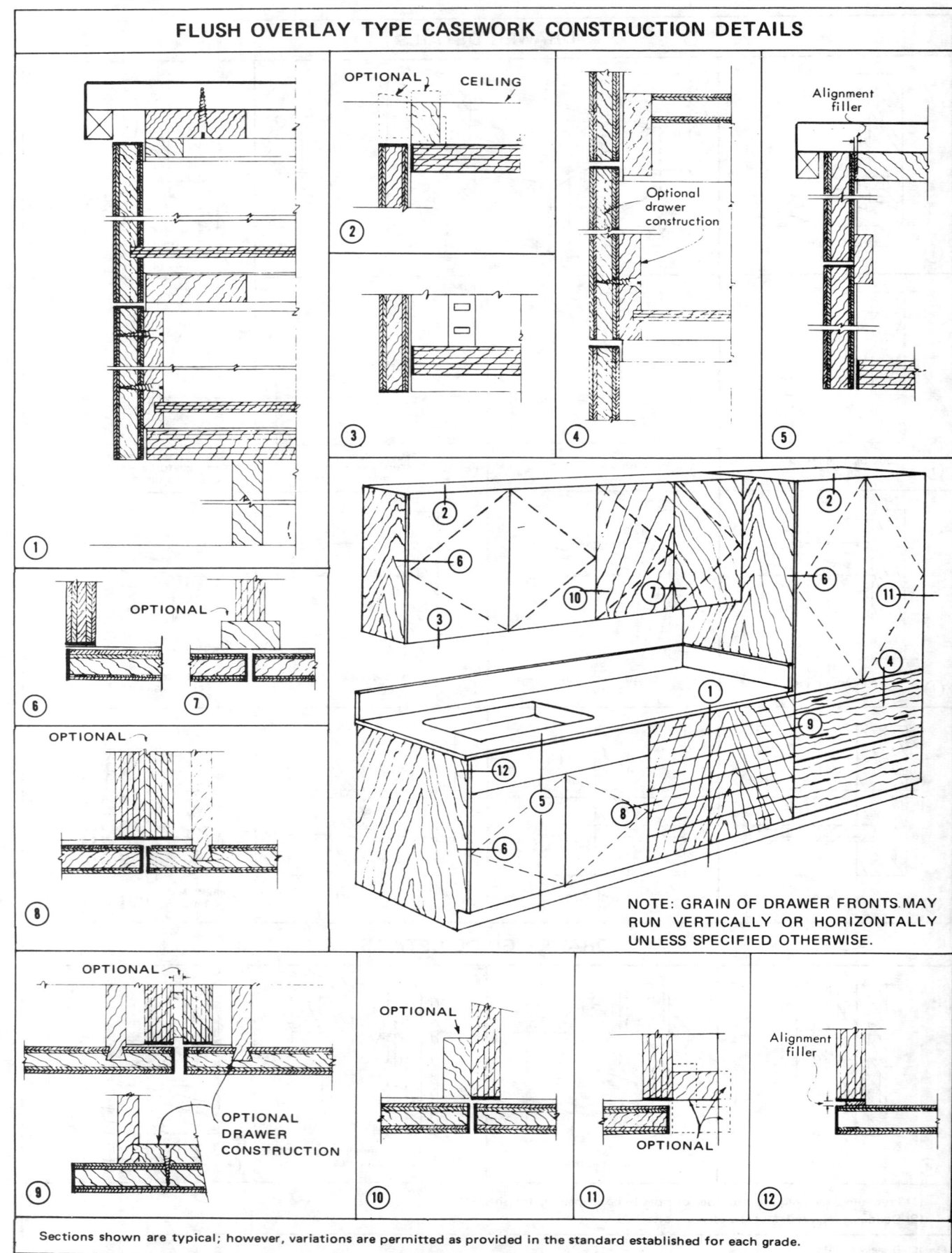

FLUSH OVERLAY TYPE CASEWORK CONSTRUCTION DETAILS

NOTE: GRAIN OF DRAWER FRONTS MAY RUN VERTICALLY OR HORIZONTALLY UNLESS SPECIFIED OTHERWISE.

Sections shown are typical; however, variations are permitted as provided in the standard established for each grade.

Fig. 5 Flush overlay type casework construction details.

ELEVATION

SECTION AT DOORS

SECTION AT DRAWERS

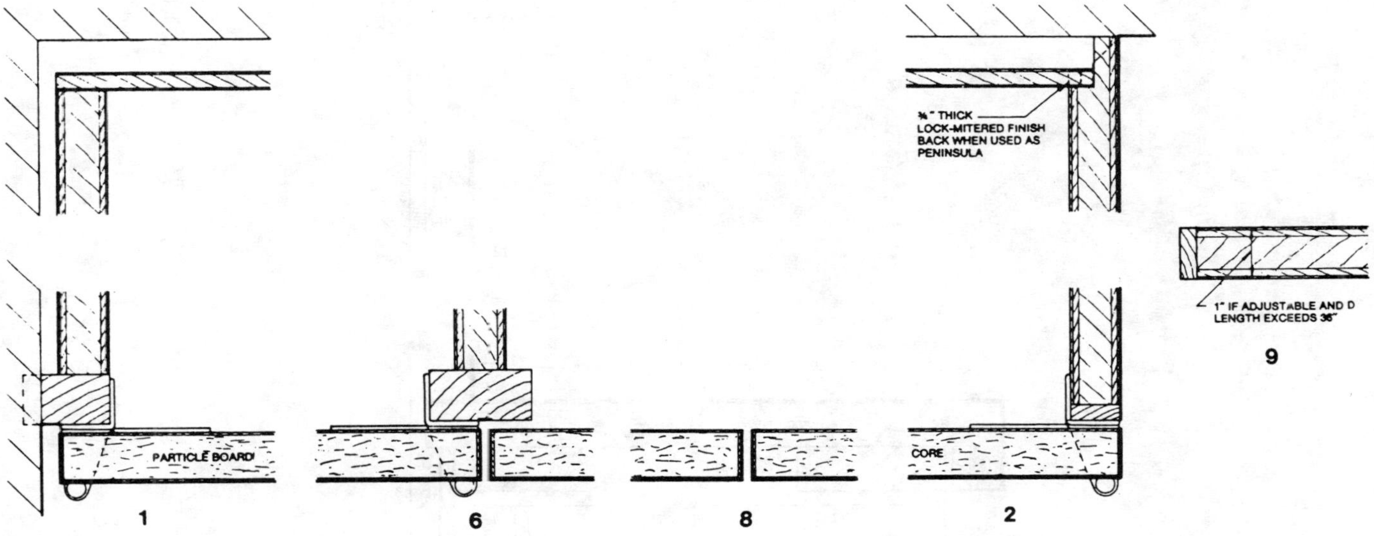

¾" THICK
LOCK-MITERED FINISH
BACK WHEN USED AS
PENINSULA

1" IF ADJUSTABLE AND D
LENGTH EXCEEDS 36"

9

PARTICLE BOARD

1

6

8

CORE

2

SPACE FOR
DRAWER SLIDES
IF REQUIRED
(TYPICAL)

3

4

5

7

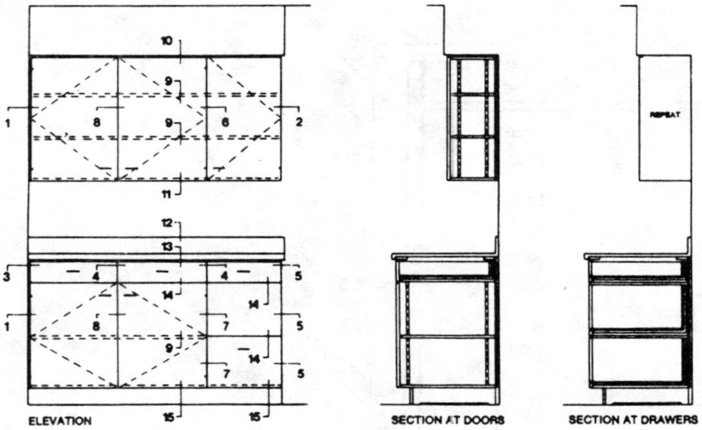

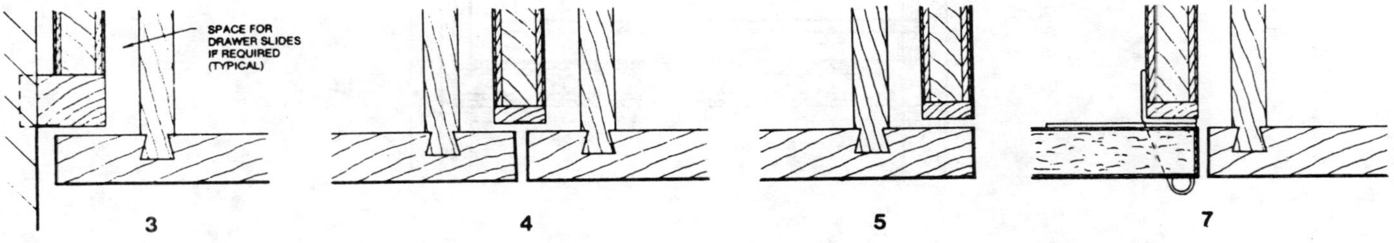

STANDARD JOINERY AND CASEWORK DETAILS

Typical Flush Overlay Casework Construction

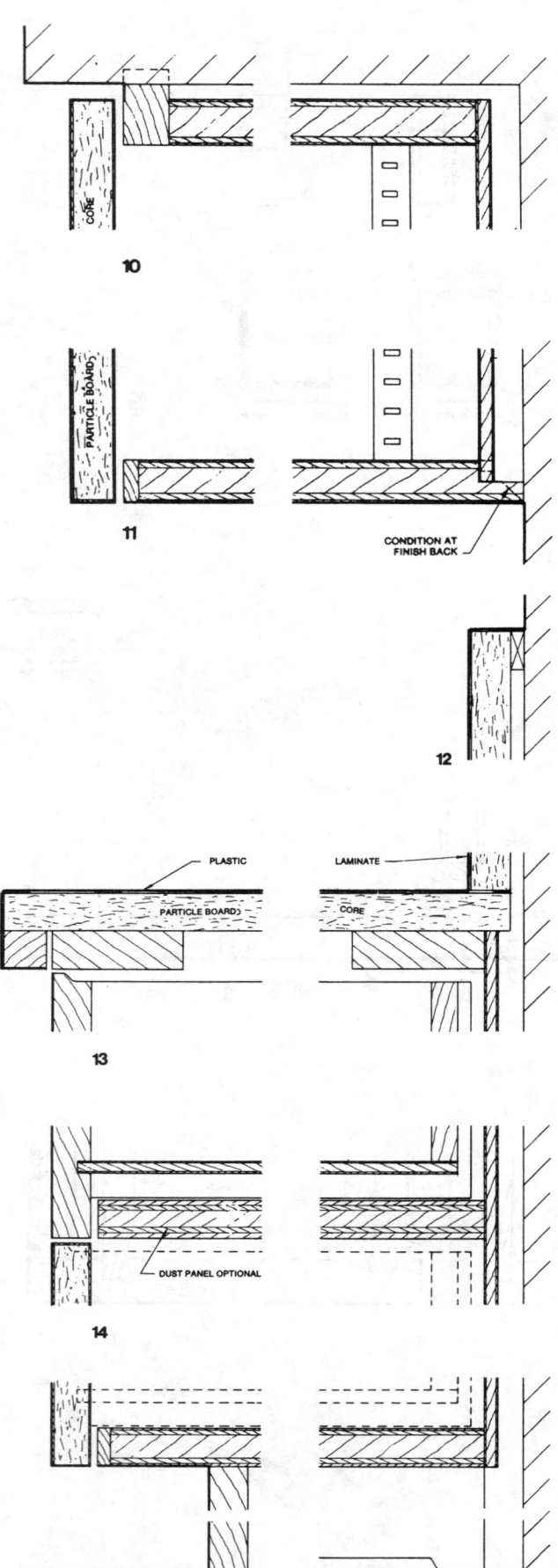

CORE

10

PARTICLE BOARD

11

CONDITION AT
FINISH BACK

12

PLASTIC

LAMINATE

PARTICLE BOARD

CORE

13

DUST PANEL OPTIONAL

14

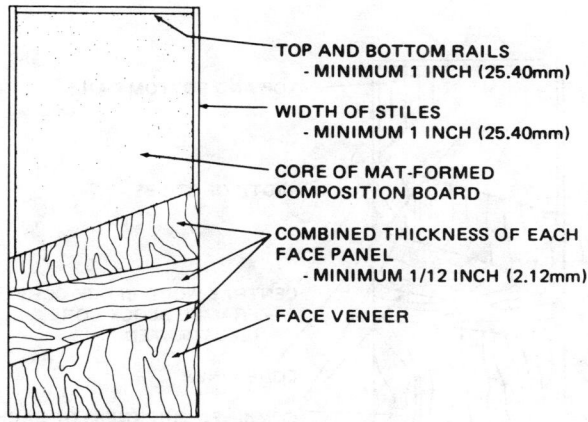

TOP AND BOTTOM RAILS
- MINIMUM 1 INCH (25.40mm)

WIDTH OF STILES
- MINIMUM 1 INCH (25.40mm)

CORE OF MAT-FORMED
COMPOSITION BOARD

COMBINED THICKNESS OF EACH
FACE PANEL
- MINIMUM 1/12 INCH (2.12mm)

FACE VENEER

Fig. 6 Mat-formed wood particleboard core (7-ply construction illustrated).

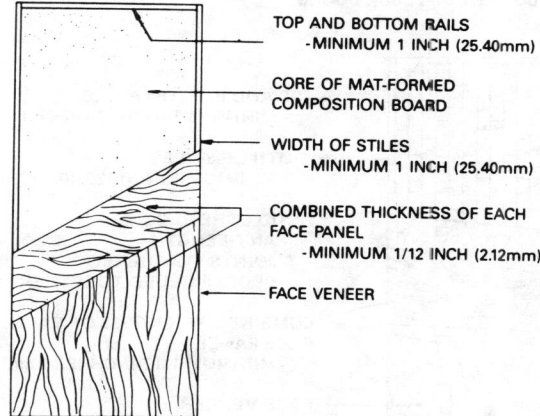

TOP AND BOTTOM RAILS
- MINIMUM 1 INCH (25.40mm)

CORE OF MAT-FORMED
COMPOSITION BOARD

WIDTH OF STILES
- MINIMUM 1 INCH (25.40mm)

COMBINED THICKNESS OF EACH
FACE PANEL
- MINIMUM 1/12 INCH (2.12mm)

FACE VENEER

Fig. 7 Mat-formed wood particleboard core (5-ply construction illustrated).

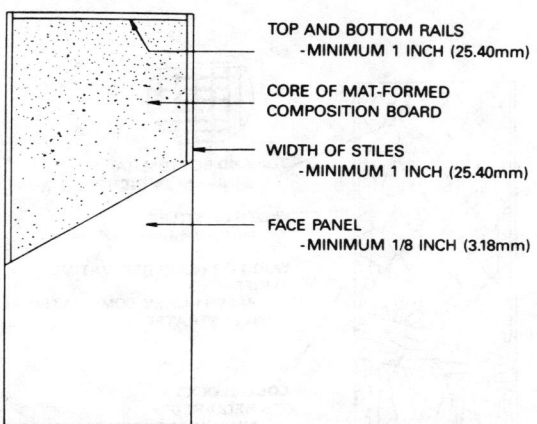

TOP AND BOTTOM RAILS
- MINIMUM 1 INCH (25.40mm)

CORE OF MAT-FORMED
COMPOSITION BOARD

WIDTH OF STILES
- MINIMUM 1 INCH (25.40mm)

FACE PANEL
- MINIMUM 1/8 INCH (3.18mm)

Fig. 8 Mat-formed wood particleboard core (3-ply construction illustrated).

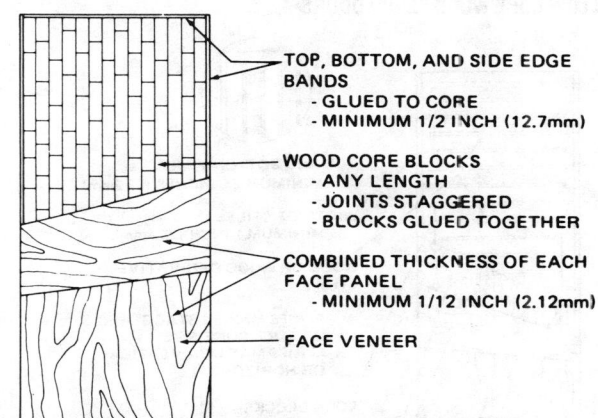

TOP, BOTTOM, AND SIDE EDGE
BANDS
- GLUED TO CORE
- MINIMUM 1/2 INCH (12.7mm)

WOOD CORE BLOCKS
- ANY LENGTH
- JOINTS STAGGERED
- BLOCKS GLUED TOGETHER

COMBINED THICKNESS OF EACH
FACE PANEL
- MINIMUM 1/12 INCH (2.12mm)

FACE VENEER

Fig. 9 Glued block core (5-ply construction illustrated).

STANDARD JOINERY AND CASEWORK DETAILS
Solid Core and Hollow Core Wood Flush Doors

SOLID CORE WOOD FLUSH DOORS

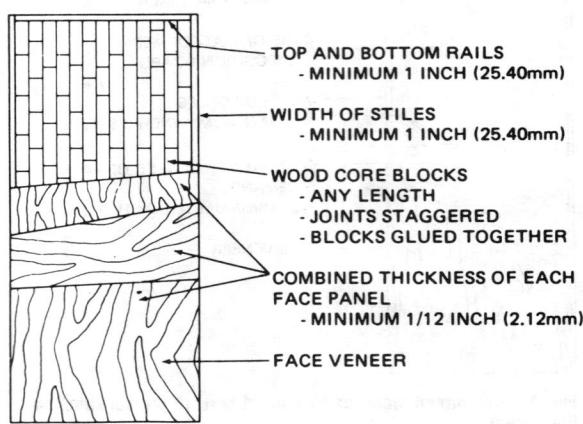

TOP AND BOTTOM RAILS
- MINIMUM 1 INCH (25.40mm)

WIDTH OF STILES
- MINIMUM 1 INCH (25.40mm)

WOOD CORE BLOCKS
- ANY LENGTH
- JOINTS STAGGERED
- BLOCKS GLUED TOGETHER

COMBINED THICKNESS OF EACH
FACE PANEL
- MINIMUM 1/12 INCH (2.12mm)

FACE VENEER

Fig. 10   Framed block glued core (7-ply construction illustrated).

TOP AND BOTTOM RAILS

WIDTH OF STILES

CENTRAL WOOD BLOCK CORE
- FRAMED BLOCK CORE
  ILLUSTRATED

CORE LINER

COMBINED THICKNESS OF EACH
FACE PANEL
- MINIMUM 1/12 INCH (2.12mm)

FACE VENEER

Fig. 11   Wood block lined core (7-ply construction illustrated).

HOLLOW CORE WOOD FLUSH DOORS

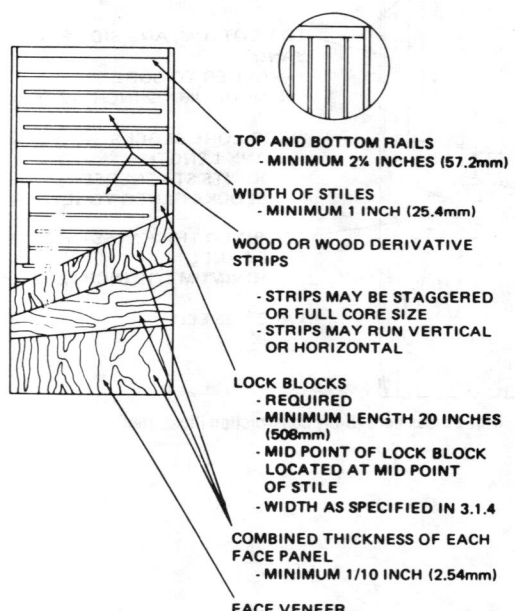

TOP AND BOTTOM RAILS
- MINIMUM 2¼ INCHES (57.2mm)

WIDTH OF STILES
- MINIMUM 1 INCH (25.4mm)

WOOD OR WOOD DERIVATIVE
STRIPS

- STRIPS MAY BE STAGGERED
  OR FULL CORE SIZE
- STRIPS MAY RUN VERTICAL
  OR HORIZONTAL

LOCK BLOCKS
- REQUIRED
- MINIMUM LENGTH 20 INCHES
  (508mm)
- MID POINT OF LOCK BLOCK
  LOCATED AT MID POINT
  OF STILE
- WIDTH AS SPECIFIED IN 3.1.4

COMBINED THICKNESS OF EACH
FACE PANEL
- MINIMUM 1/10 INCH (2.54mm)

FACE VENEER

Fig. 12   Ladder core (7-ply construction illustrated).

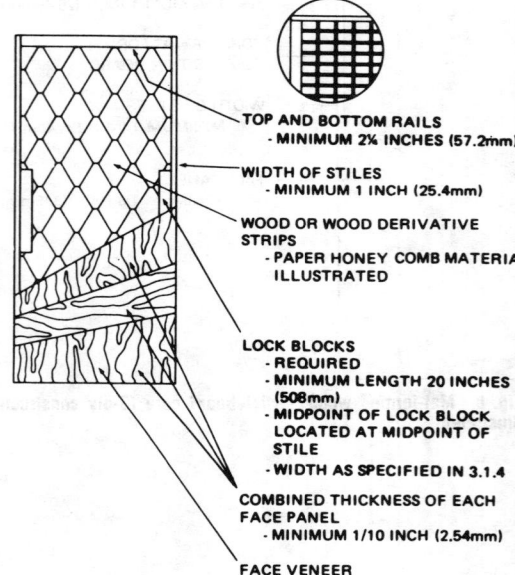

TOP AND BOTTOM RAILS
- MINIMUM 2¼ INCHES (57.2mm)

WIDTH OF STILES
- MINIMUM 1 INCH (25.4mm)

WOOD OR WOOD DERIVATIVE
STRIPS
- PAPER HONEY COMB MATERIAL
  ILLUSTRATED

LOCK BLOCKS
- REQUIRED
- MINIMUM LENGTH 20 INCHES
  (508mm)
- MIDPOINT OF LOCK BLOCK
  LOCATED AT MIDPOINT OF
  STILE
- WIDTH AS SPECIFIED IN 3.1.4

COMBINED THICKNESS OF EACH
FACE PANEL
- MINIMUM 1/10 INCH (2.54mm)

FACE VENEER

Fig. 13   Mesh or cellular core (7-ply construction illustrated).

a. **FLUSH CABINET DOORS. All WIC Grades.**

TYPE "1"
  Veneer / tape banding, 1/16″ maximum.

TYPE "2"
  Solid banding.

TYPE "3" — Medium Density Fiberboard.
  Banding not required for **Economy and Custom Grades.**

  Band required for Premium Grade.

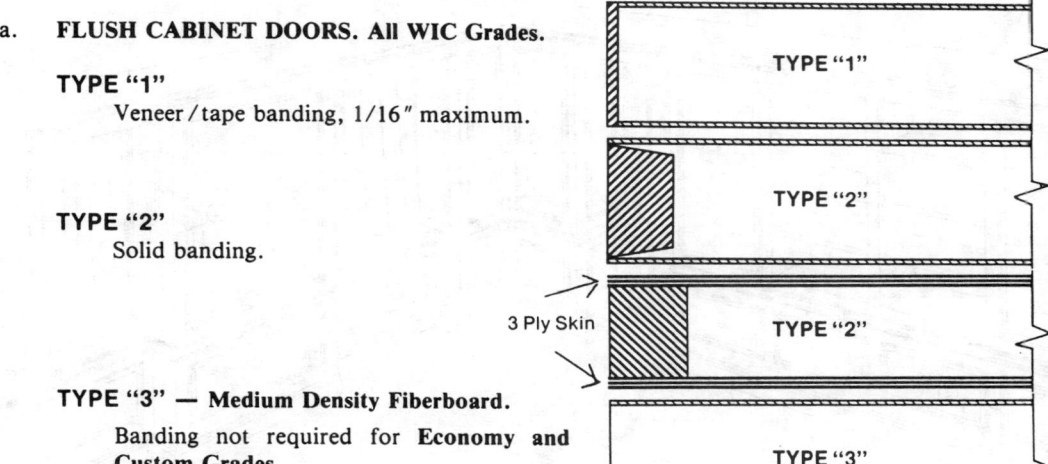

b. **LIPPED CABINET DOORS.**

TYPE "4"
  Veneer / tape banding, 1/16″ maximum, required.

TYPE "5"
  Solid banding.

TYPE "6" — Medium Density Fiberboard.
  Banding not required for **Economy and Custom Grades.**

  Band required for Premium Grade.

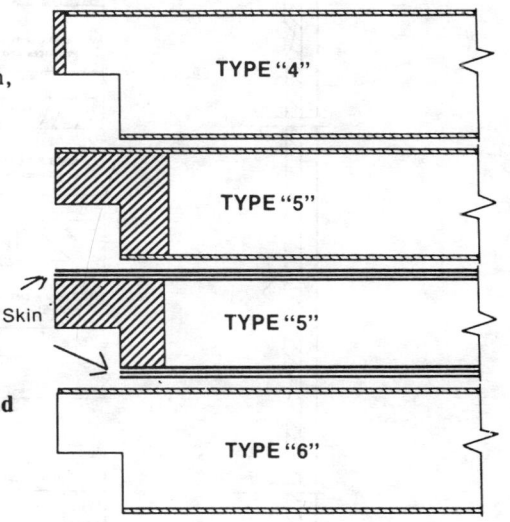

c. **STILE AND RAIL CABINET DOORS. All WIC Grades.**

  TYPE "7", S4S Stop.

  TYPE "8", Solid Stuck.

  TYPE "9", Moulded Stop.

d. **The top and bottom edges of sliding doors do not require an edge band.**

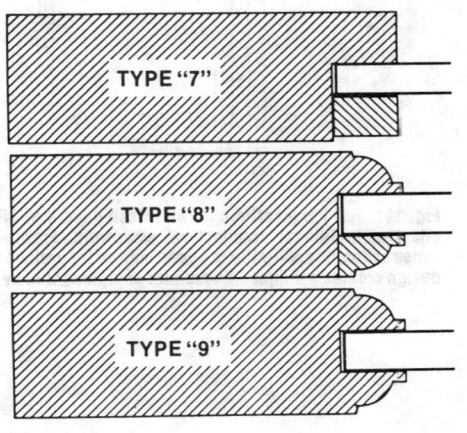

STANDARD JOINERY AND CASEWORK DETAILS

Stile and Rail Joinery Details

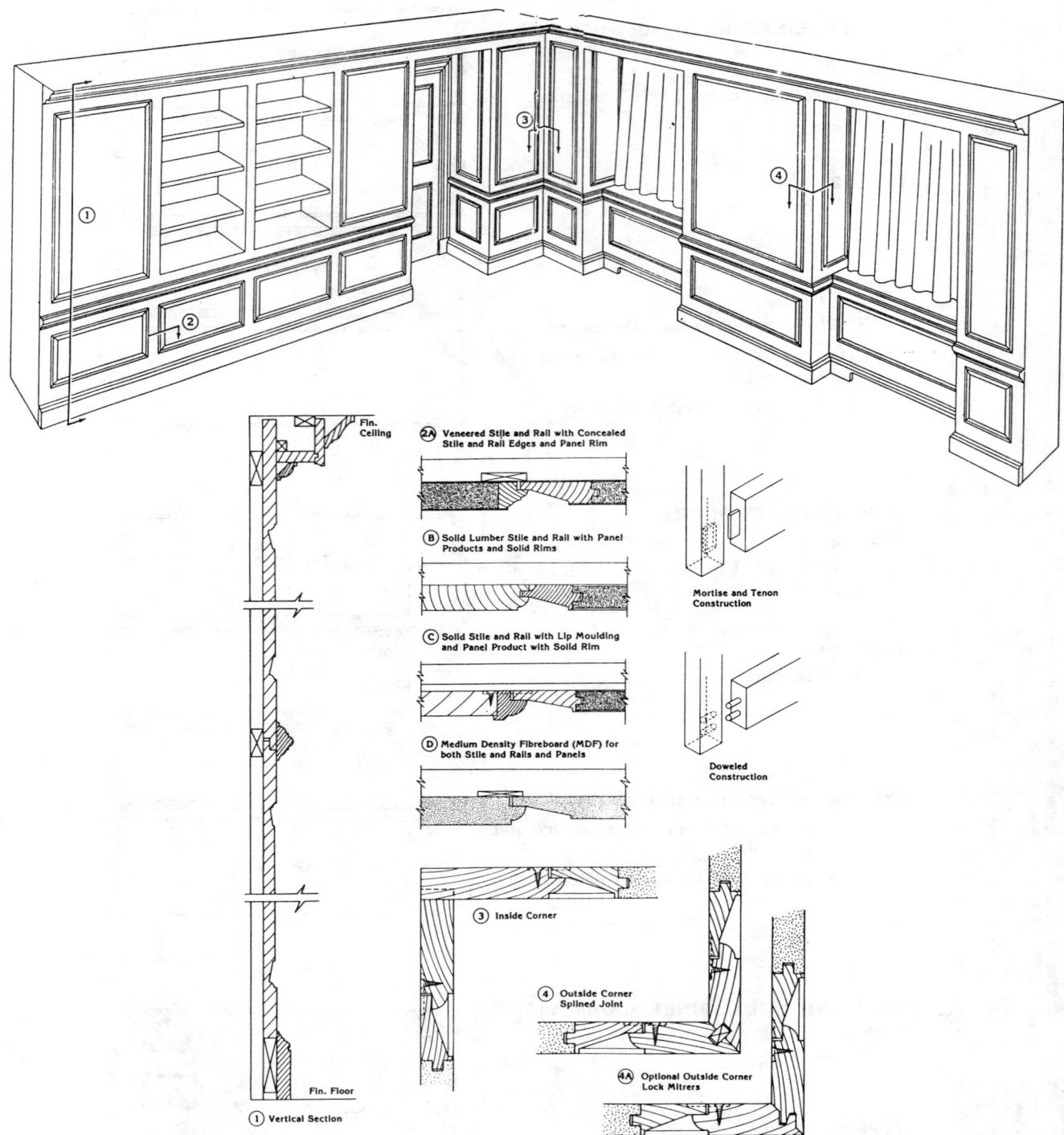

Fin. Ceiling

2A Veneered Stile and Rail with Concealed Stile and Rail Edges and Panel Rim

B Solid Lumber Stile and Rail with Panel Products and Solid Rims

C Solid Stile and Rail with Lip Moulding and Panel Product with Solid Rim

D Medium Density Fibreboard (MDF) for both Stile and Rails and Panels

Mortise and Tenon Construction

Doweled Construction

3 Inside Corner

4 Outside Corner Splined Joint

4A Optional Outside Corner Lock Mitrers

Fin. Floor

1 Vertical Section

Fig. 14 Full-height stile and rail raised paneling. Stile and rail wall paneling accented by raised panels creates a beautiful effect of traditional architectural woodwork. Framed within the stiles and rails and accented by the shadow lines, this construction offers limitless opportunities for various effects through the use of different wood species and veneer cuts. Each design creates a unique atmosphere complimented by the finely proportioned paneling.

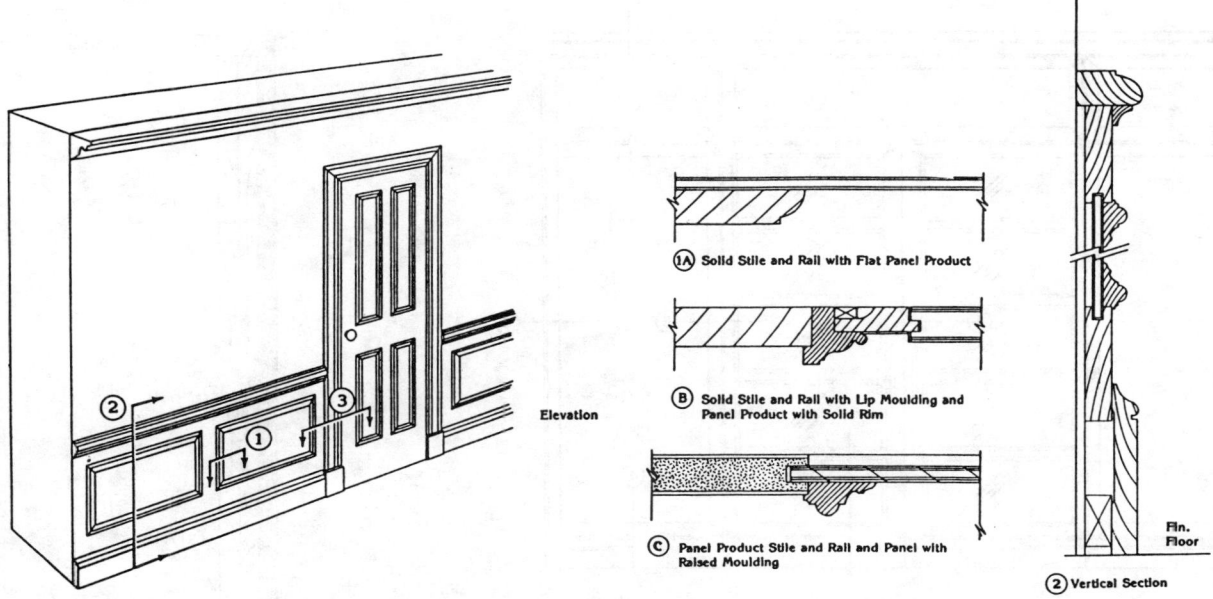

Fig. 15 Flap paneled wainscot. Flat panels set within the frame of the stile and rail create a rich effect of traditional architectural woodwork. Different results can be produced through the use of veneer selections with transparent finish or painted finishes chosen by the architect or designer.

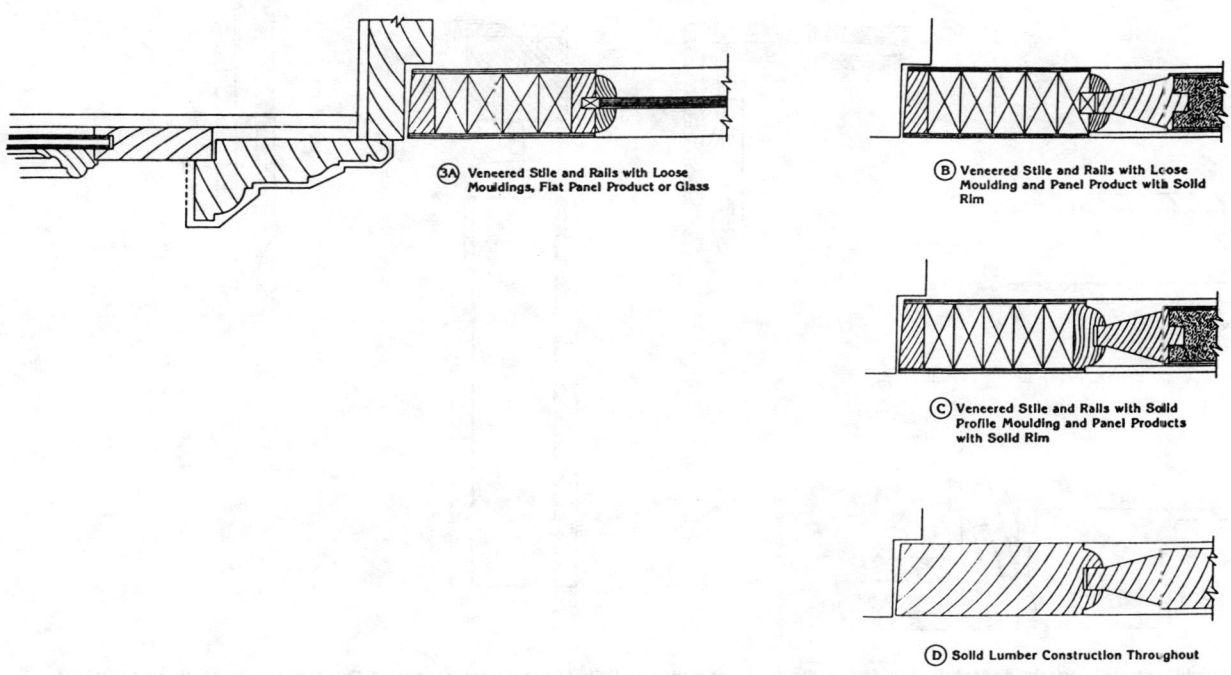

Fig. 16 Paneled doors. Stile and rail doors designed to accent the adjacent wall paneling whether traditional or contemporary, or used alone, beautify an entryway or area.

STANDARD JOINERY AND CASEWORK DETAILS
Raised Paneling

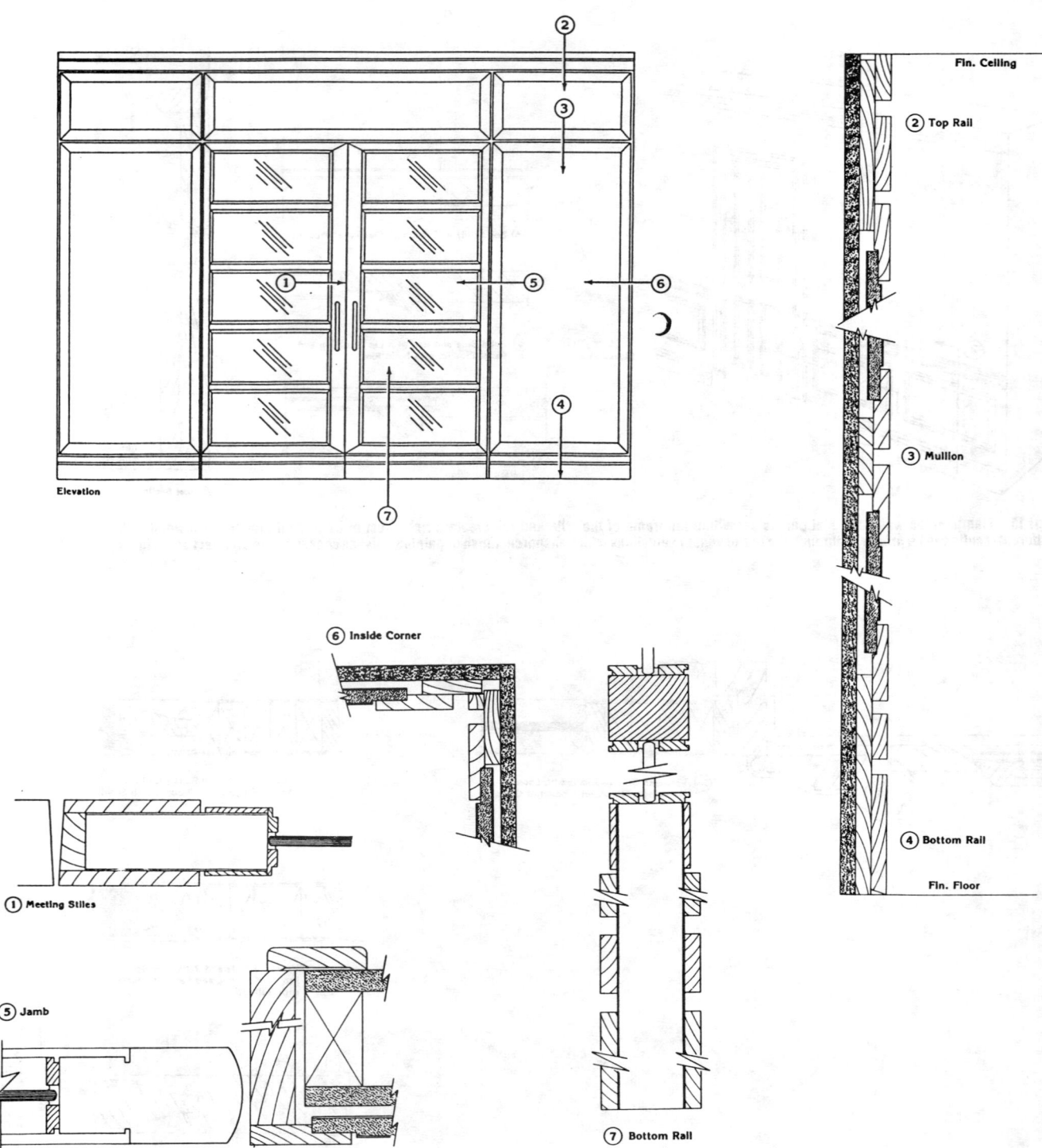

Fig. 17 Full-height contemporary raised paneling. This design, distinguished by its simplicity, is a contemporary expression of the stile and rail construction.

PROFILES OF STOCK STICKING FOR SASH & DOORS

OGEE   OGEE   OGEE

SQUARE   SQUARE   SQUARE

SASH & FRENCH DOORS

B & C   B & C   OVOLO   OVOLO

OGEE   OGEE   SQUARE   SQUARE

PANEL DOORS

STANDARD JOINERY AND CASEWORK DETAILS
Double Hung Windows

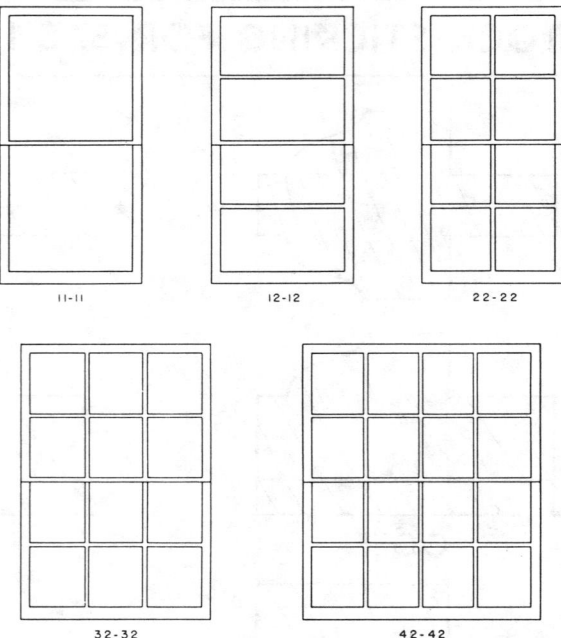

Fig. 18   Double hung windows: stock designs. Standard widths are 1′6″, 2′0″, 2′6″, 3′0″, 3′6″, 4′0″, 4′6″, and 5′0″. Standard heights are 2′0″, 2′6″, 3′0″, 3′6″, 4′0″, 4′6″, 5′1″, 5′6″, and 6′0″. Standard thicknesses are 1⅜″ and 1¾″. Stock thickness is 1⅜″. Standard glazing is s.s.b. glass — not bedded.

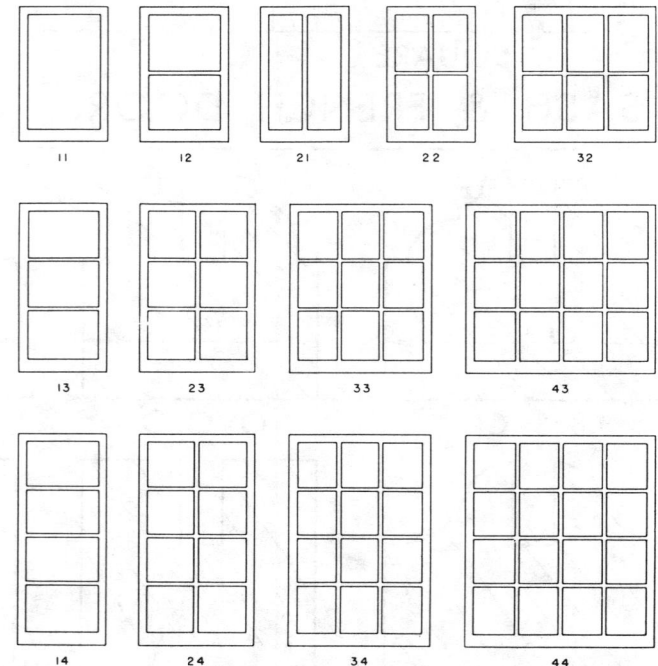

Fig. 19   Single sash: stock designs. Standard widths are 2′0″, 2′6″, 3′0″, 3′6″, 4′0″, 4′6″, 5′0″, 5′6″ and 6′0″. Standard heights are 2′0″, 2′6″, 3′0″, 3′6″, 4′0″, 4′6″, 5′1″, 5′6″, 6′0″, 6′6″, and 7′0″. Standard thicknesses are 1⅜″ and 1¾″. Stock thickness is 1⅜″. Standard glazing is s.s.b. glass — not bedded.

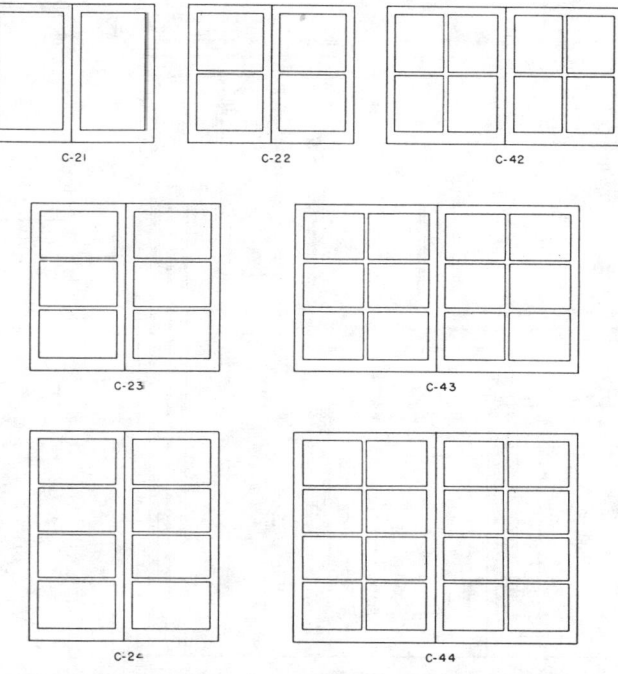

**Fig. 20   Casements in pairs: stock designs. Standard widths are 2'6",
3'0", 3'6", 4'0", 4'6", and 5'0". Standard heights are 2'0", 2'6", 3'0",
3'6", 4'0", 4'6", 5'1", 5'6", and 6'0". Standard thicknesses are 1⅜"
and 1¾". Stock thickness is 1⅜". Standard glazing is s.s.b. glass —
not bedded.**

Fig. 21   Windows and sash: typical diamond light cut-ups.

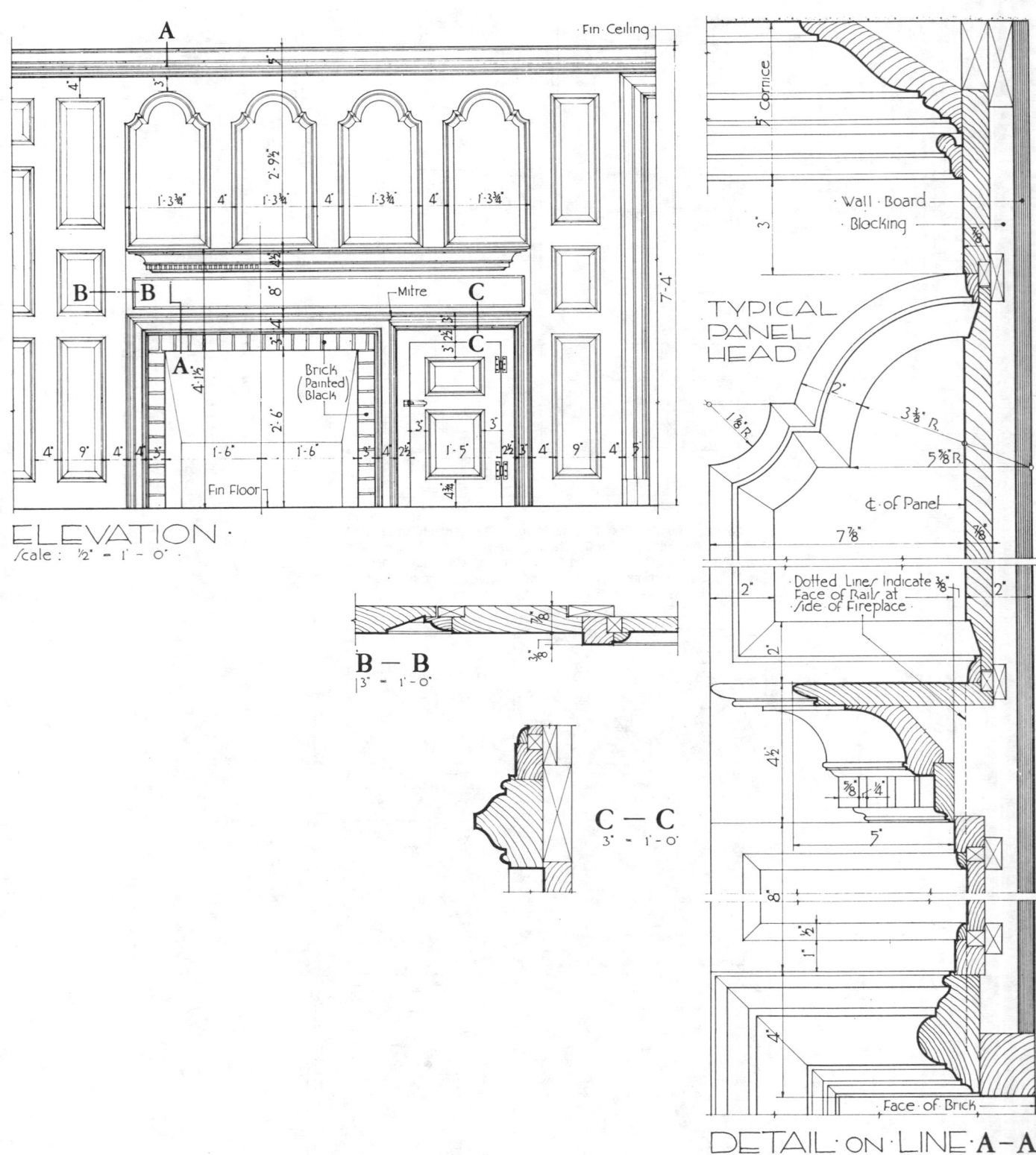

ELEVATION
Scale : ½" = 1'-0"

B – B
3" = 1'-0"

C – C
3" = 1'-0"

TYPICAL PANEL HEAD

DETAIL · ON · LINE · A–A

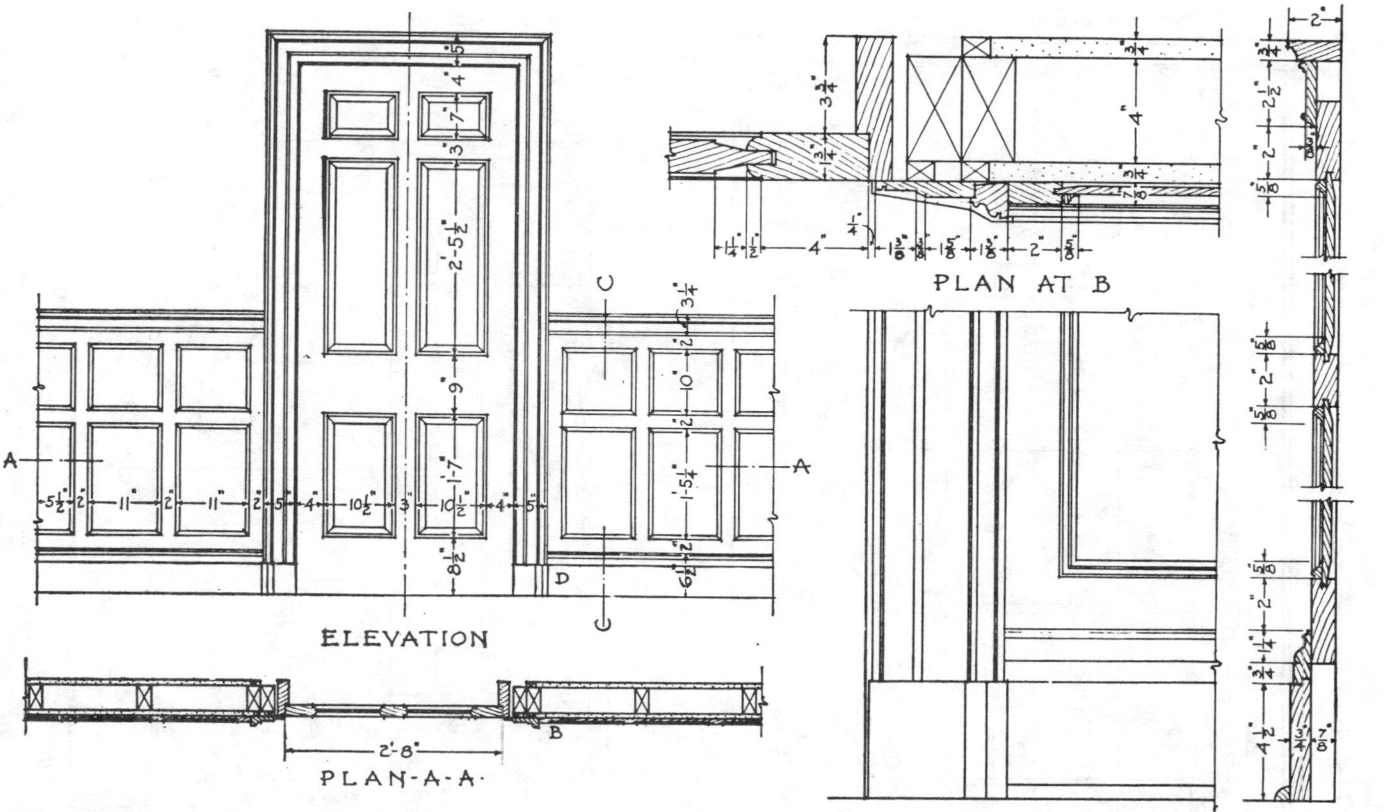

ELEVATION

PLAN·A·A·

PANELED WAINSCOT

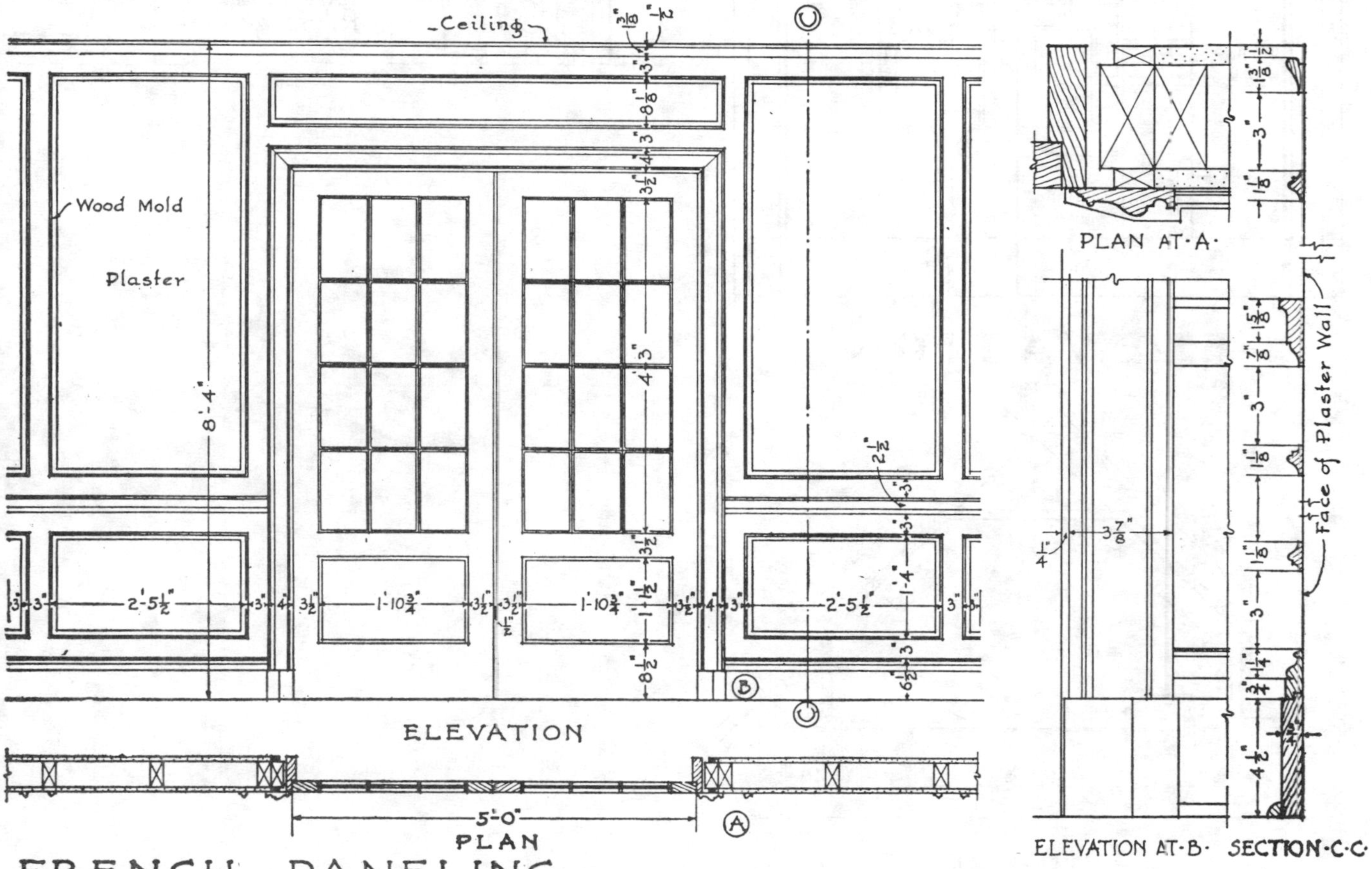

PLAN AT B

ELEVATION AT·D·   SECTION·C·C·

—Ceiling—

Wood Mold

Plaster

8'-4"

ELEVATION

5'-0"

PLAN

FRENCH PANELING

PLAN AT·A·

Face of Plaster Wall

ELEVATION AT·B·   SECTION·C·C·

WOODWORK DETAILS

Corner Cupboard

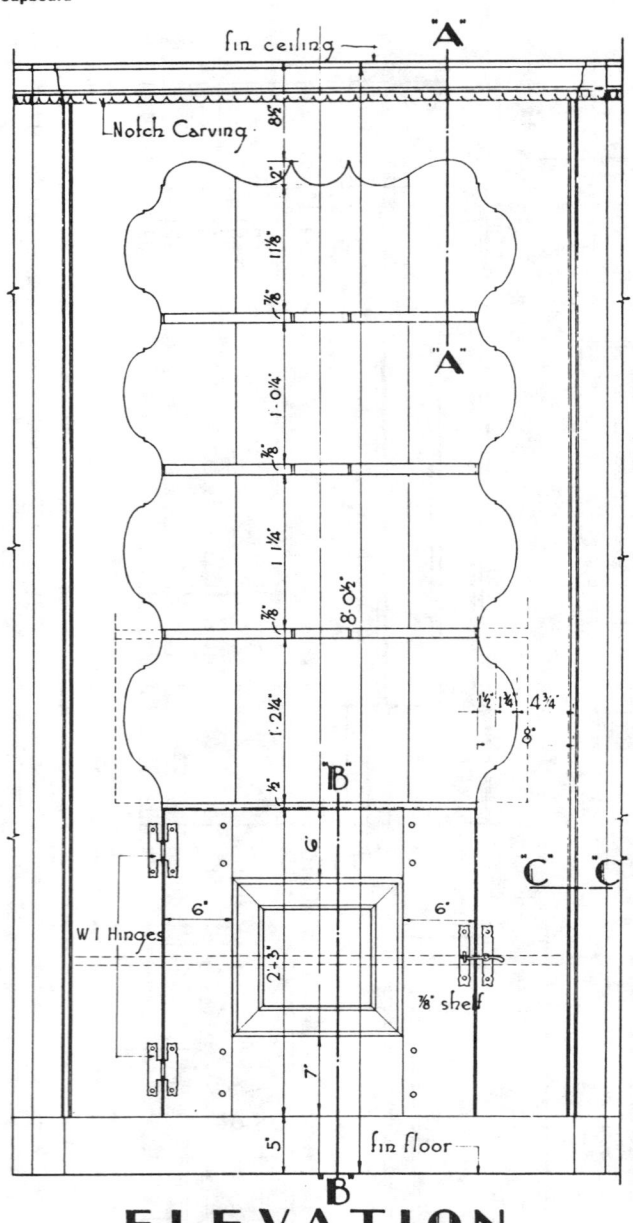

ELEVATION

Scale : ¾" = 1'—0"

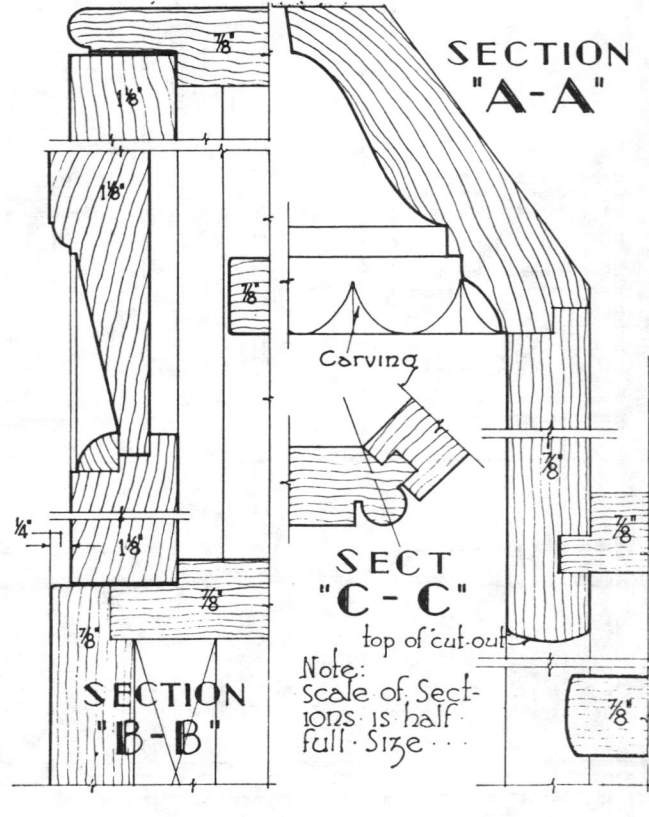

SECTION
"A-A"

Carving

SECT
"C-C"
top of cut-out

Note:
Scale of Sect-
ions is half
full Size . . .

SECTION
"B-B"

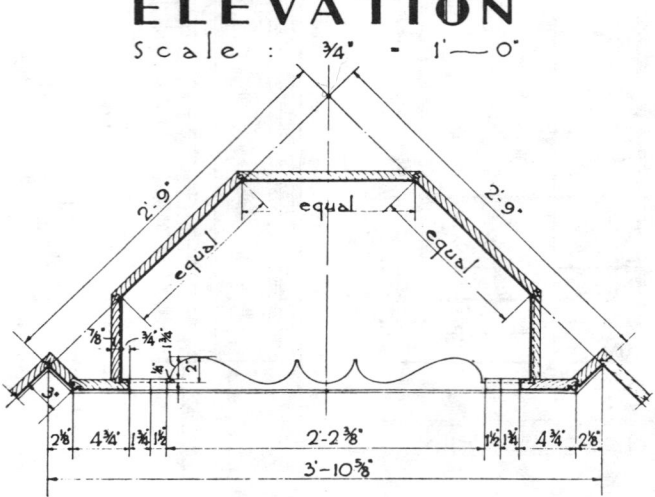

PLAN
¾" = 1'-0"

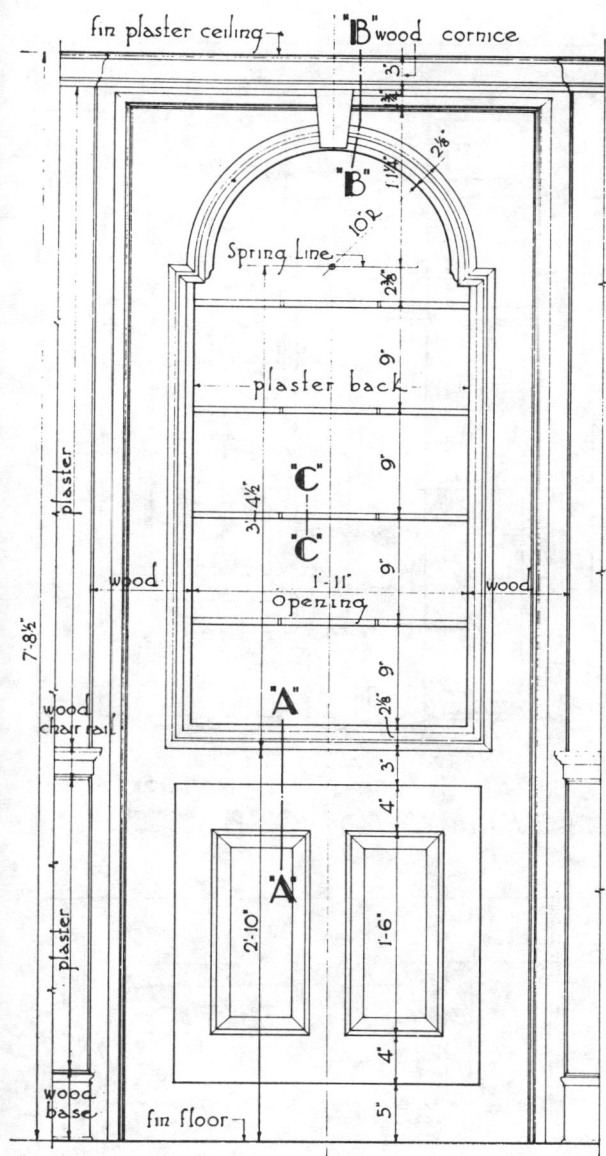

fin plaster ceiling
"B" wood cornice
"B"
Spring Line
10'2
2⅝
11¾
2⅝
plaster back
9"
"C"
9"
"C"
3-4½"
1-11"
Opening
9"
wood
wood
"A"
9"
2⅝
3
"A"
4
2:10"
1-6"
4"
plaster
plaster
wood
chair rail
7-8½"
wood
base
fin floor
5"

ELEVATION
Scale   ¾" = 1'—0'

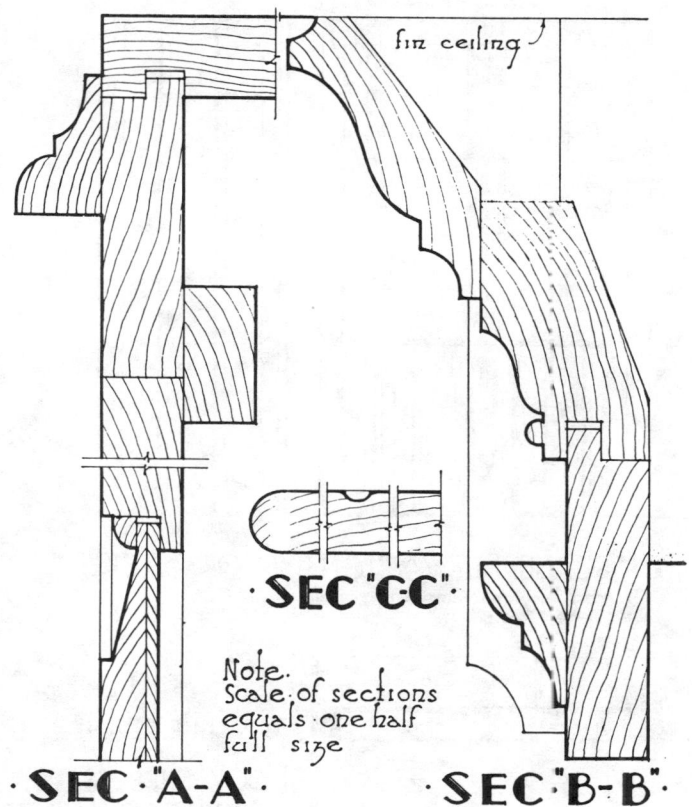

fin ceiling

SEC "CC"

Note.
Scale of sections
equals one half
full size

SEC "A-A"   **SEC "B-B"**

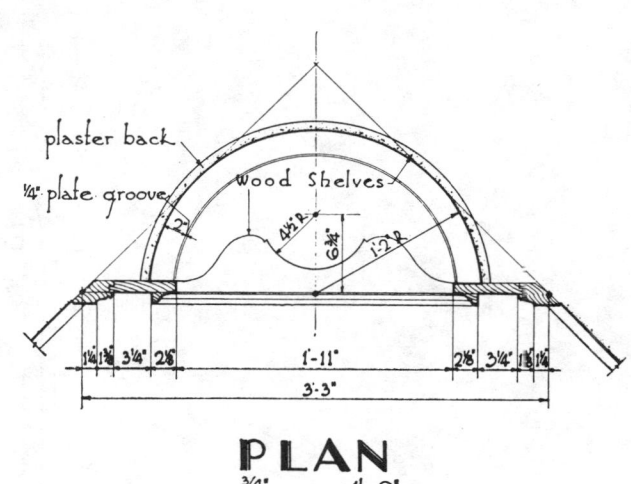

plaster back
¼" plate groove
Wood Shelves
4½" R
6¾"
1-2" R
1¼ 1⅝ 3¾ 2⅝   1-11"   2⅝ 3¾ 1⅝ 1¼
3'-3"

PLAN
¾" - 1'—0'

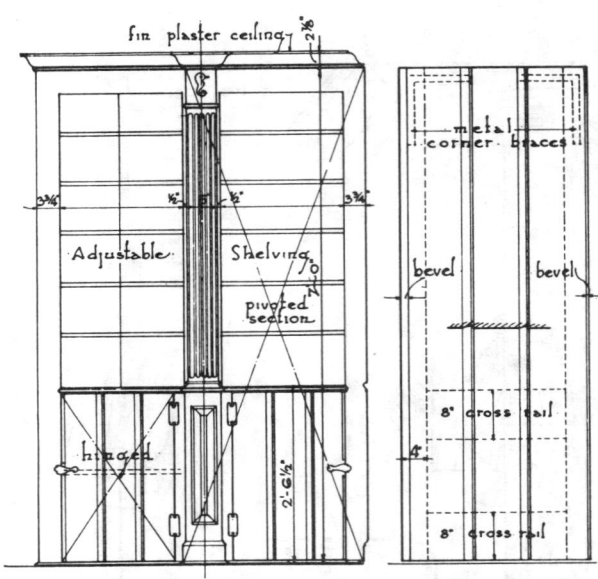

⅜" · SCALE · ELEVATION · DOOR · BACK ·
Showing book shelving and secret
Door to a silver closet ·

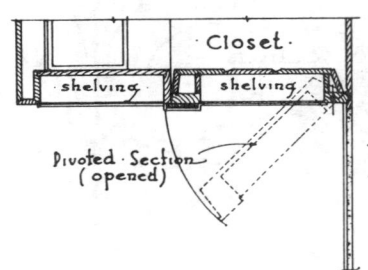

⅜" · SCALE PLAN
of
BOOK · SHELVES ·
& · SECRET · DOOR ·

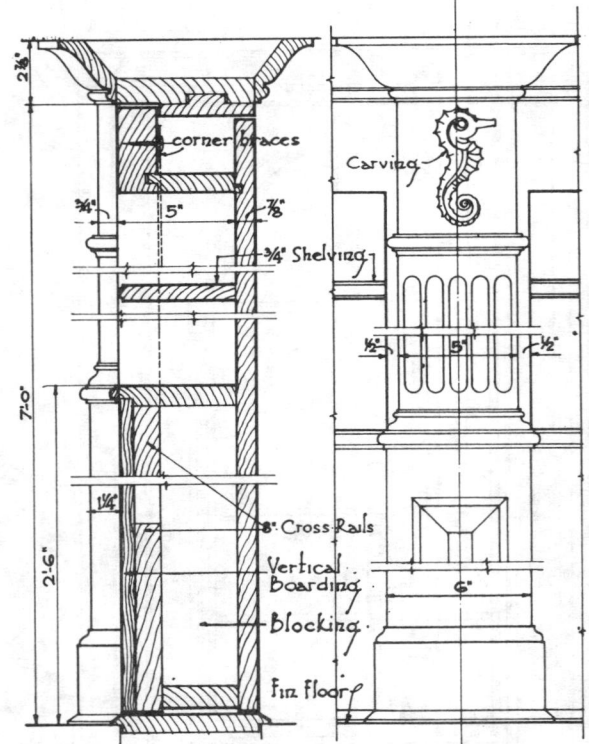

· VERTICAL · SECTION ·   · ELEVATION ·
THROUGH · DOOR ·   OF · PILASTER ·
· Scale: 1½" = 1'–0"

· SECTION · ON · LINE · "A–A" · THRU · SHELVING ·
scale :   1½" = 1'—0"

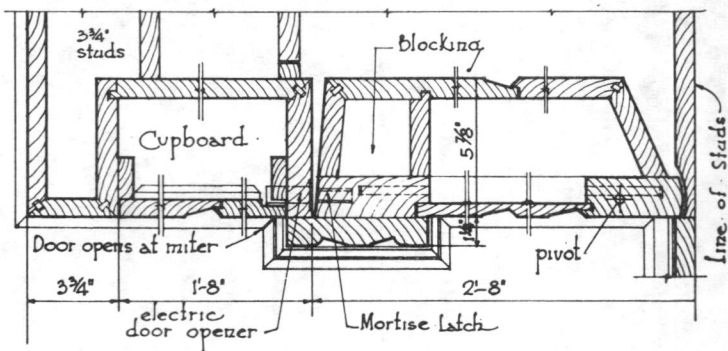

· SECTION · ON · LINE · "B–B" · THRU · CUPBOARD ·
Scale: 1½" ~ 1'—0"

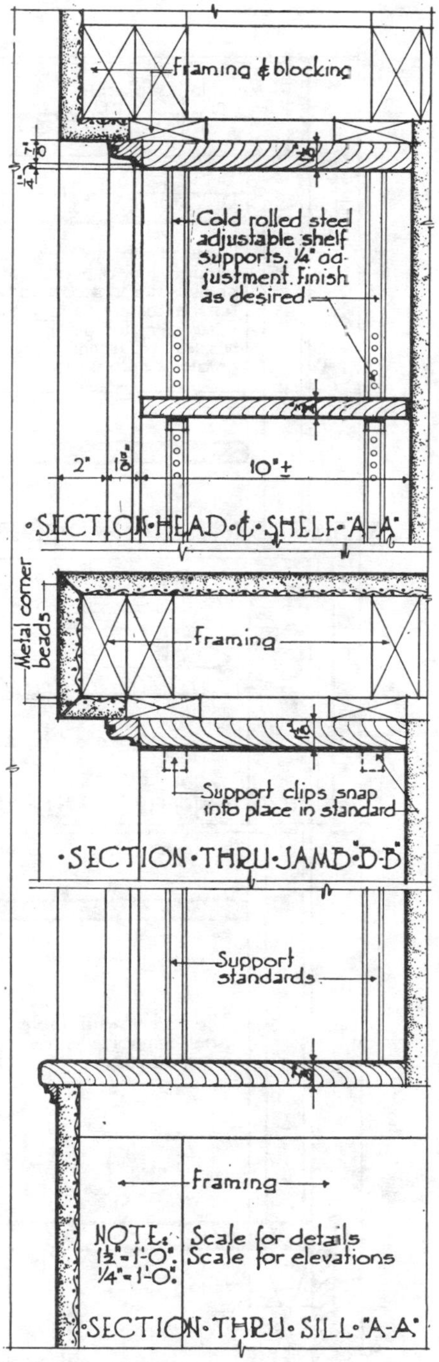

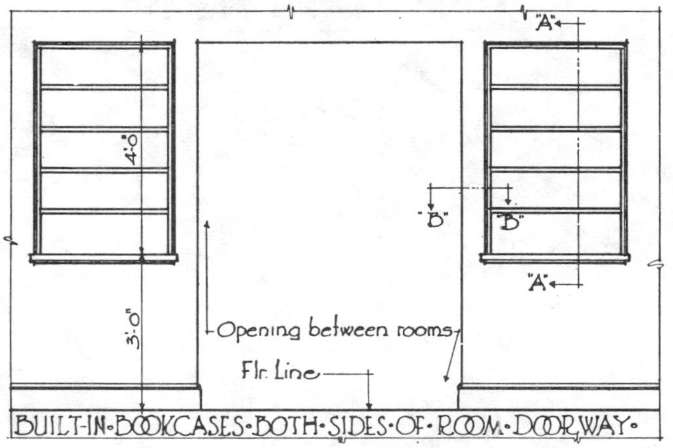

Framing & blocking

Cold rolled steel adjustable shelf supports. 1/4" adjustment. finish as desired.

2" 1 1/8" 10"±

·SECTION·HEAD·&·SHELF·"A-A"·

Metal corner beads

Framing

Support clips snap into place in standard

·SECTION·THRU·JAMB·"D-D"·

Support standards

Framing

NOTE: Scale for details 1 1/2"=1'-0" Scale for elevations 1/4"=1'-0"

·SECTION·THRU·SILL·"A-A"·

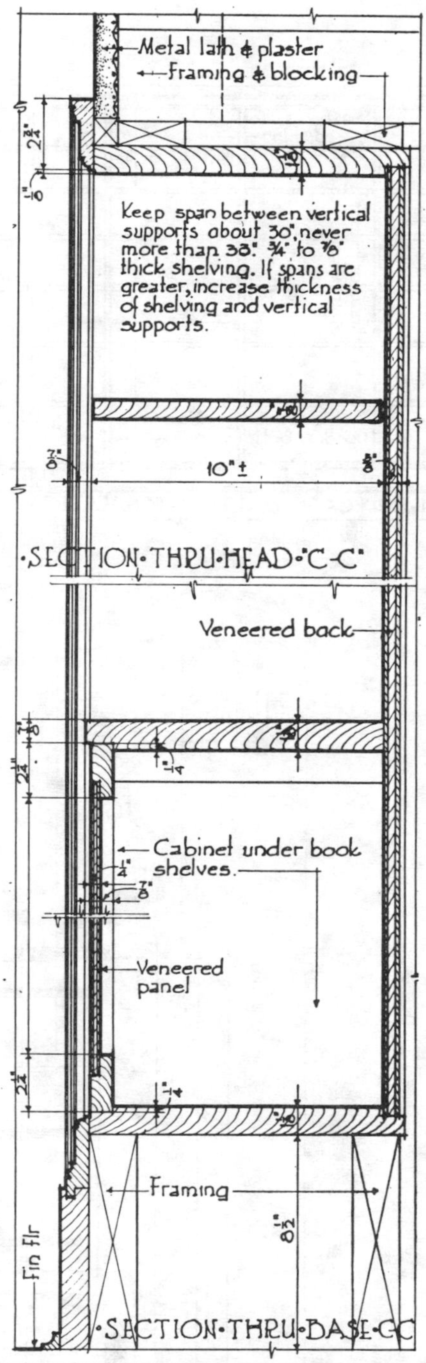

Metal lath & plaster
Framing & blocking

2 1/4"
1"
6"

Keep span between vertical supports about 30", never more than 38". 3/4" to 7/8" thick shelving. If spans are greater, increase thickness of shelving and vertical supports.

6" 10"± 3/8"

·SECTION·THRU·HEAD·"C-C"·

Veneered back

7/8"
2 1/4"
1/4"

Cabinet under book shelves.

1/4"
3/8"

Veneered panel

2 1/4"

1/4"
1/16"

Fin Flr

Framing

8 1/2"

·SECTION·THRU·BASE·"C-C"·

"A"

4'-0"

"D"
"D"

"A"

3'-0"

Opening between rooms

Flr. Line

·BUILT-IN·BOOKCASES·BOTH·SIDES·OF·ROOM·DOORWAY·

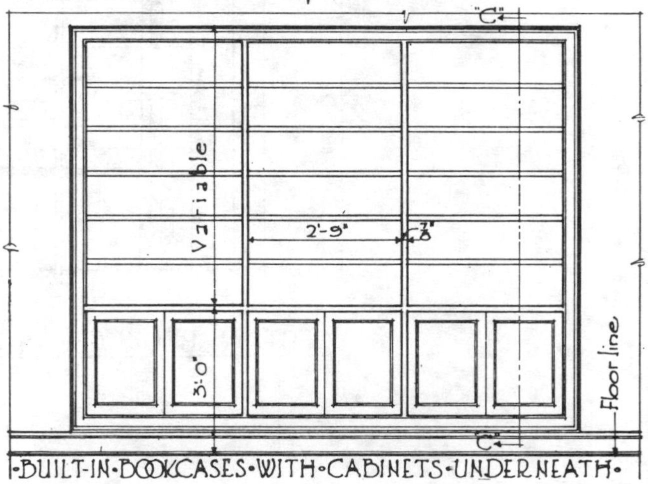

"C"

Variable

2'-9" 7/8"

3'-0"

Floor line

·BUILT-IN·BOOKCASES·WITH·CABINETS·UNDERNEATH·

"C"

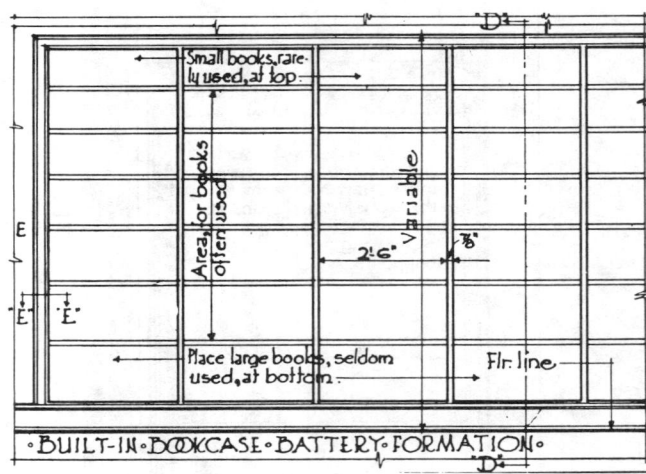

Small books, rarely used, at top

Area, for books often used

Variable

2'-6"

7/8"

Place large books, seldom used, at bottom

Flr. line

E

E'

D

D

·BUILT-IN·BOOKCASE·BATTERY·FORMATION·

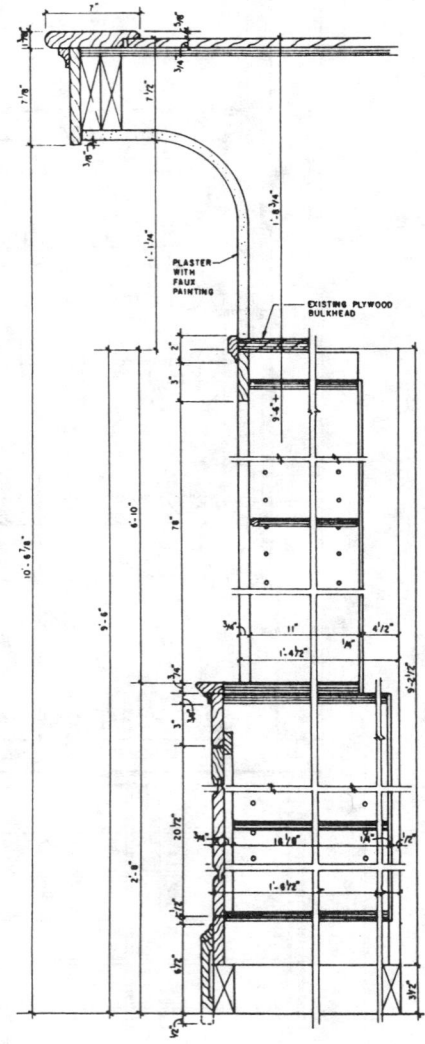

PLASTER WITH FAUX PAINTING

EXISTING PLYWOOD BULKHEAD

SECTION-BOOKCASE UNIT

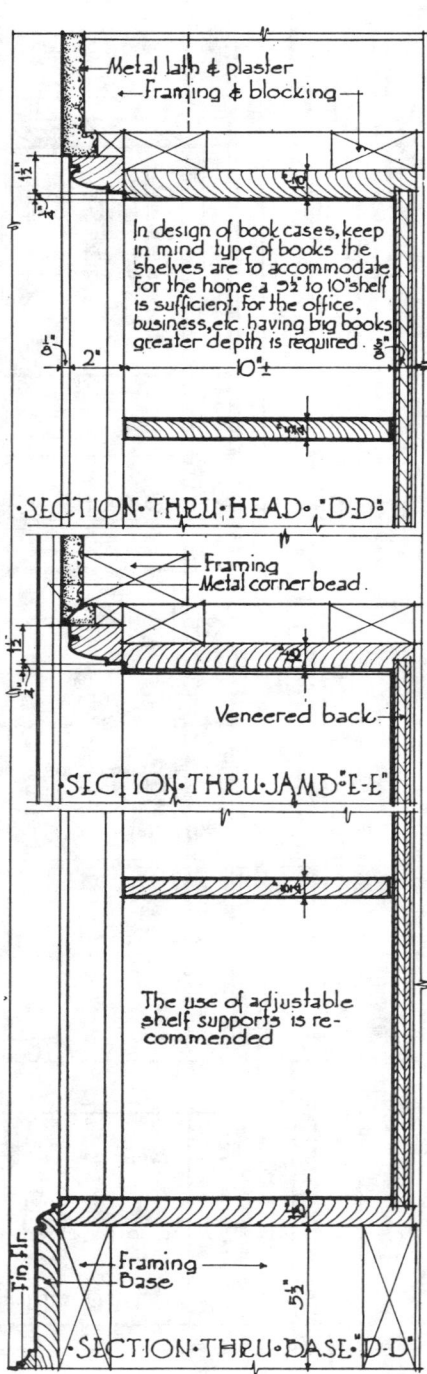

Metal lath & plaster
Framing & blocking

In design of book cases, keep in mind type of books the shelves are to accommodate. For the home a 9½" to 10" shelf is sufficient. For the office, business, etc. having big books greater depth is required.

10"±

·SECTION·THRU·HEAD·"D-D"·

Framing
Metal corner bead.

Veneered back

·SECTION·THRU·JAMB·"E-E"·

The use of adjustable shelf supports is recommended

Fin. Flr.

Framing
Base

5½"

·SECTION·THRU·BASE·"D-D"·

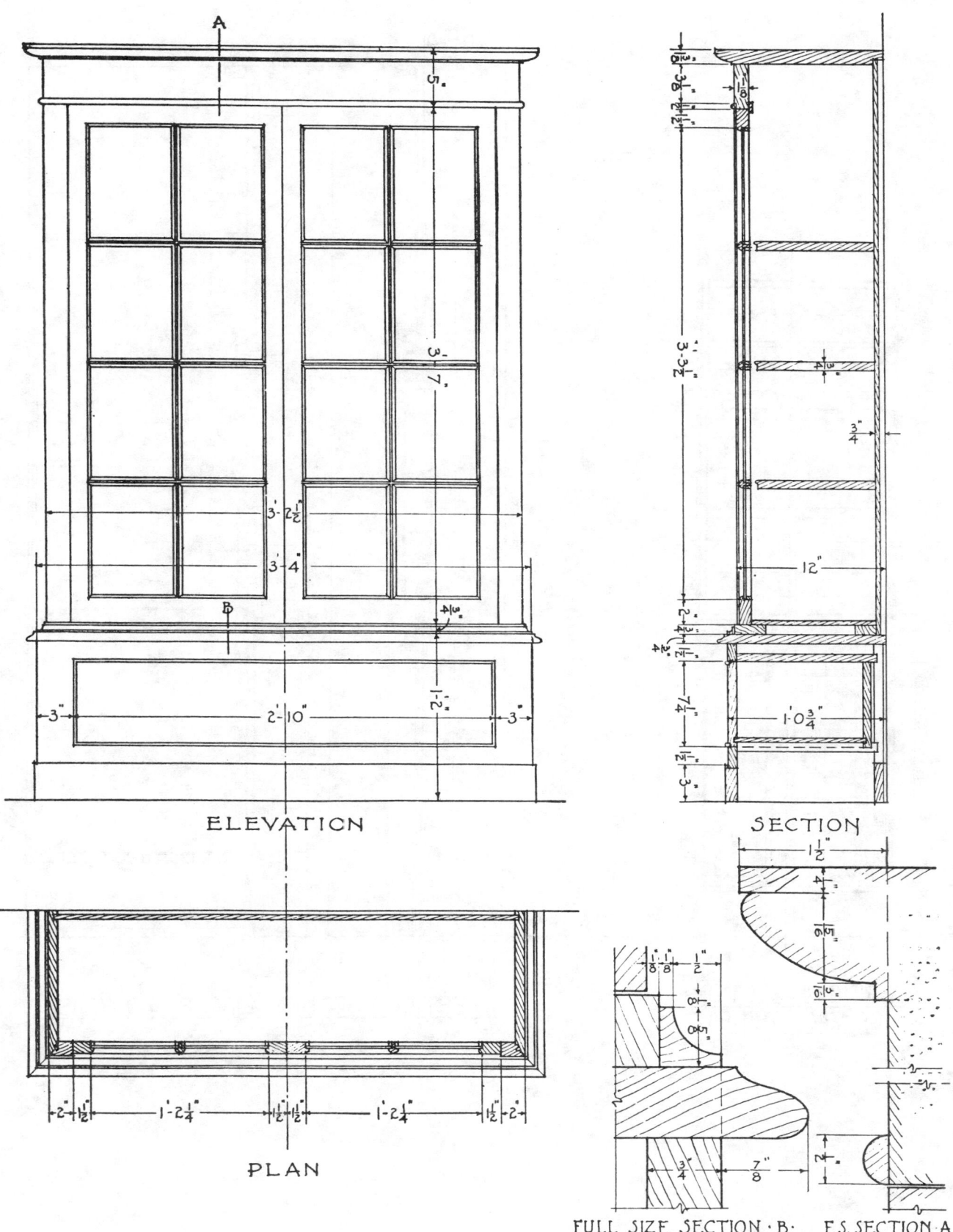

ELEVATION

SECTION

PLAN

FULL SIZE SECTION ·B·

F.S. SECTION A

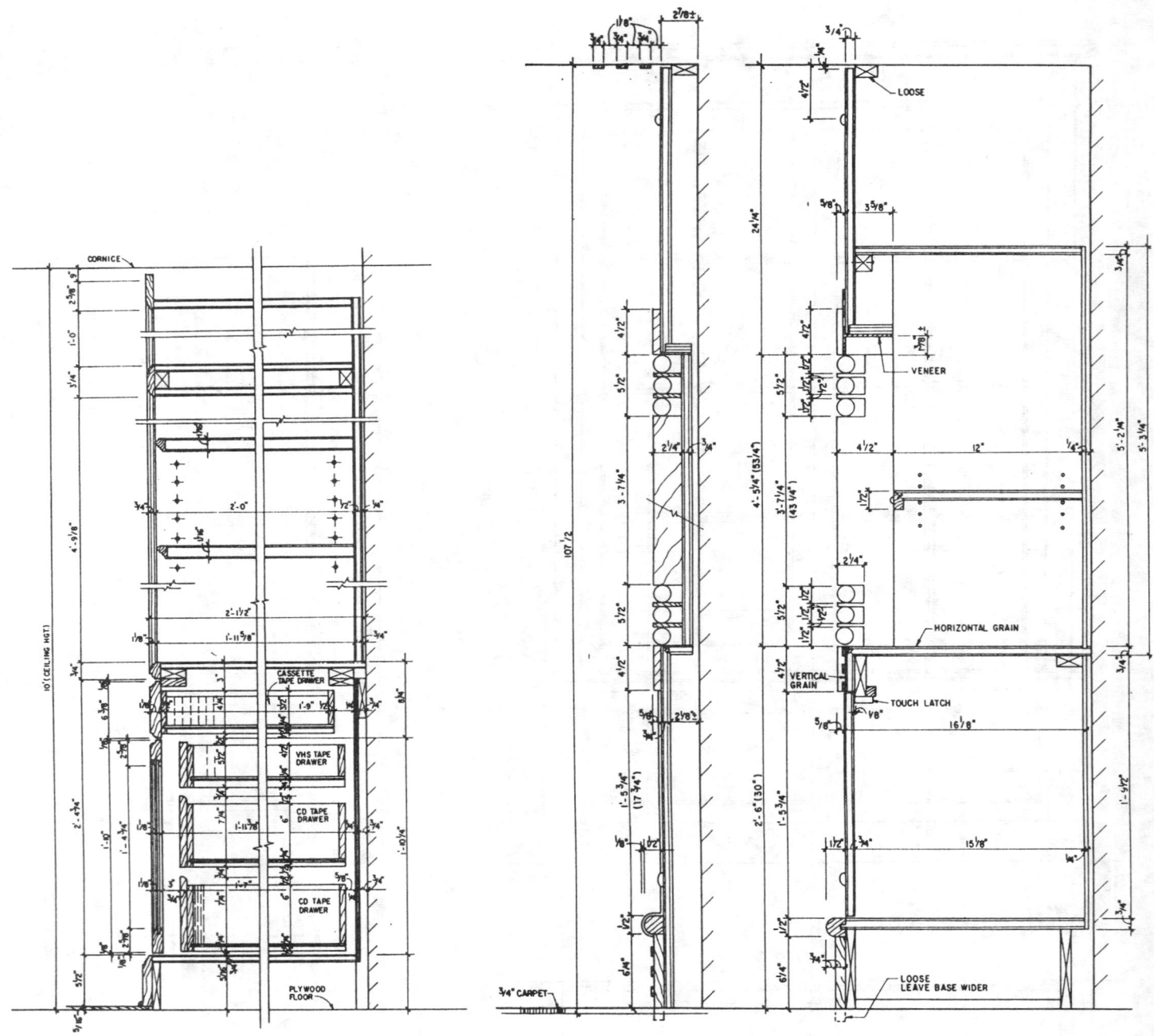

VERTICAL SECTION
LIBRARY CABINETS

VERTICAL SECTION - LIBRARY BOOKCASE

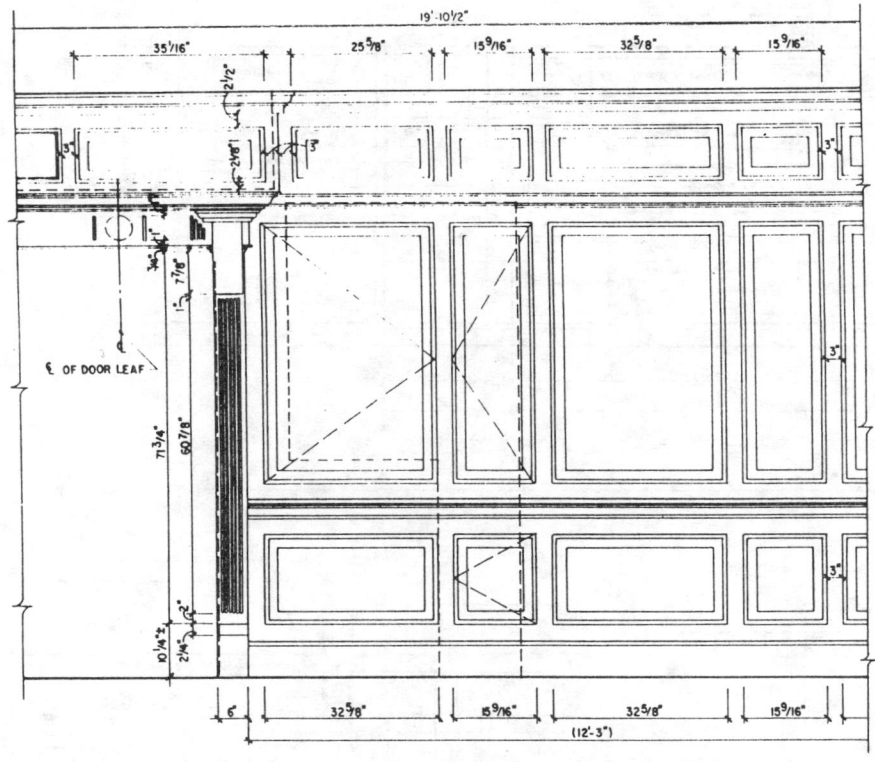

ELEVATION AT BAR

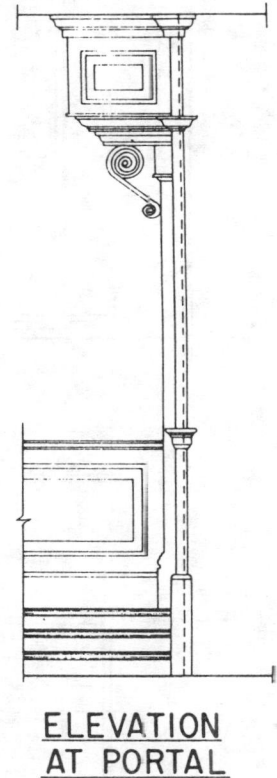

ELEVATION
AT PORTAL

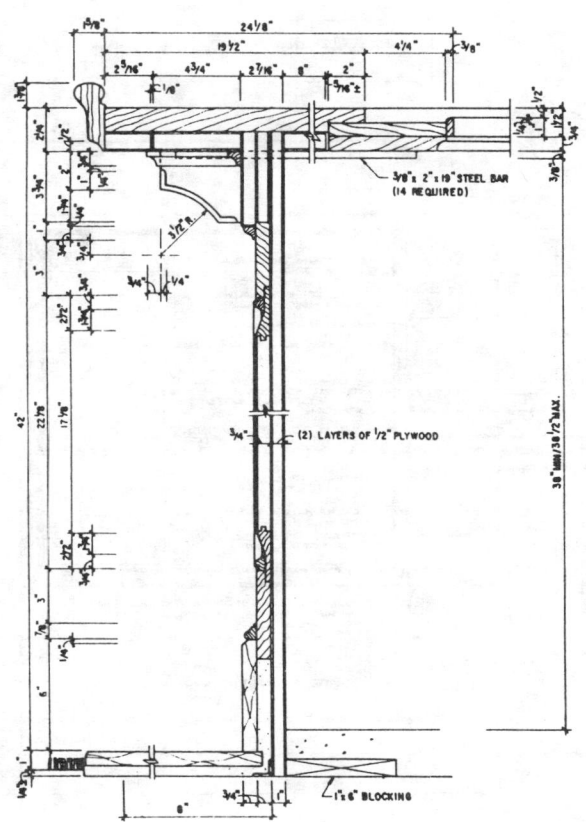

VERTICAL SECTION AT BAR

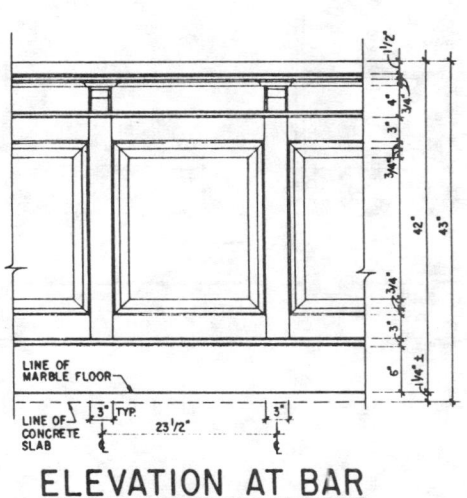

ELEVATION AT BAR

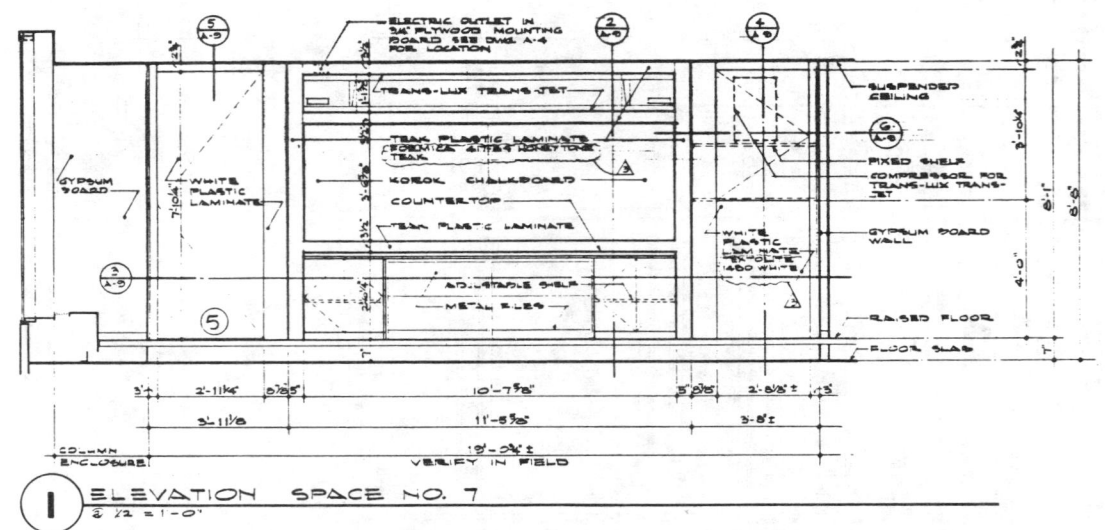

ELECTRIC OUTLET IN ¾" PLYWOOD MOUNTING BOARD SEE DWG A-4 FOR LOCATION

TRANS-LUX TRANS-JET

TEAK PLASTIC LAMINATE (FORMICA 6178-7 HONEY TONE TEAK)

KOROK CHALKBOARD

COUNTERTOP

TEAK PLASTIC LAMINATE

GYPSUM BOARD

WHITE PLASTIC LAMINATE

ADJUSTABLE SHELF

METAL FILES

SUSPENDED CEILING

FIXED SHELF

COMPRESSOR FOR TRANS-LUX TRANS-JET

GYPSUM BOARD WALL

WHITE PLASTIC LAMINATE ISOLITE 1450 WHITE

RAISED FLOOR

FLOOR SLAB

COLUMN ENCLOSURE

VERIFY IN FIELD

1 ELEVATION SPACE NO. 7
½" = 1'-0"

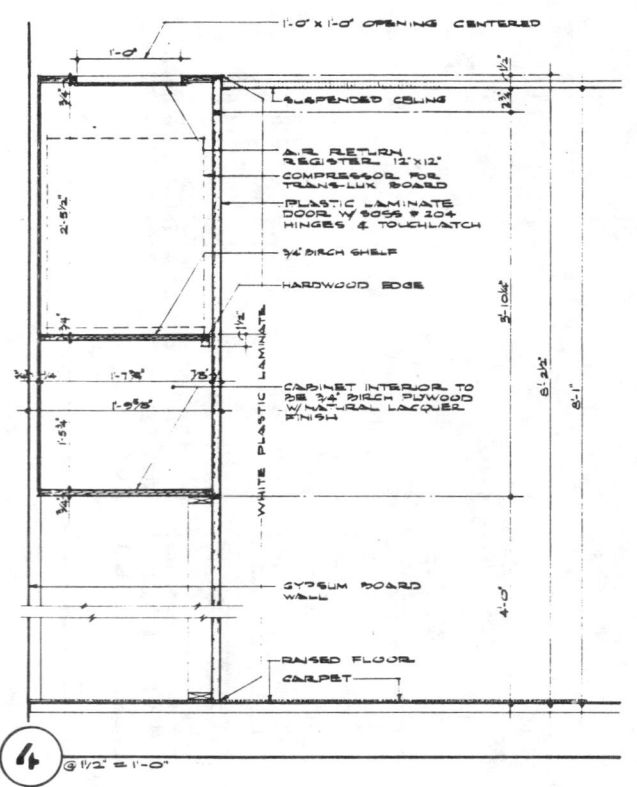

4 @ 1½" = 1'-0"

1'-0" X 1'-0" OPENING CENTERED

SUSPENDED CEILING

AIR RETURN REGISTER 12" X 12"

COMPRESSOR FOR TRANS-LUX BOARD

PLASTIC LAMINATE DOOR W/ SOSS #204 HINGES & TOUCHLATCH

¾" BIRCH SHELF

HARDWOOD EDGE

CABINET INTERIOR TO BE ¾" BIRCH PLYWOOD W/ NATURAL LACQUER FINISH

WHITE PLASTIC LAMINATE

GYPSUM BOARD WALL

RAISED FLOOR

CARPET

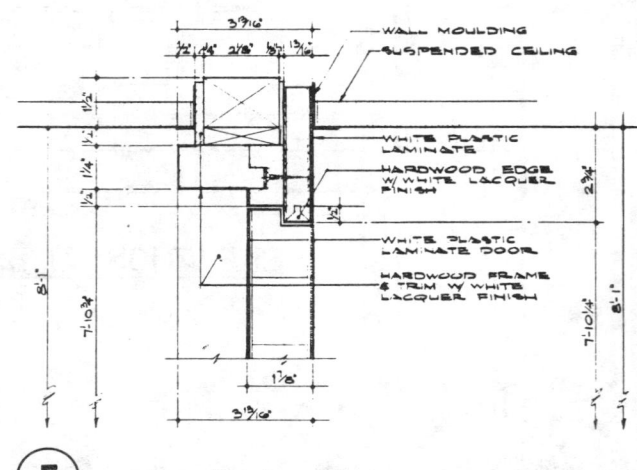

5 @ ½ FULL SIZE

WALL MOULDING

SUSPENDED CEILING

WHITE PLASTIC LAMINATE

HARDWOOD EDGE W/ WHITE LACQUER FINISH

WHITE PLASTIC LAMINATE DOOR

HARDWOOD FRAME & TRIM W/ WHITE LACQUER FINISH

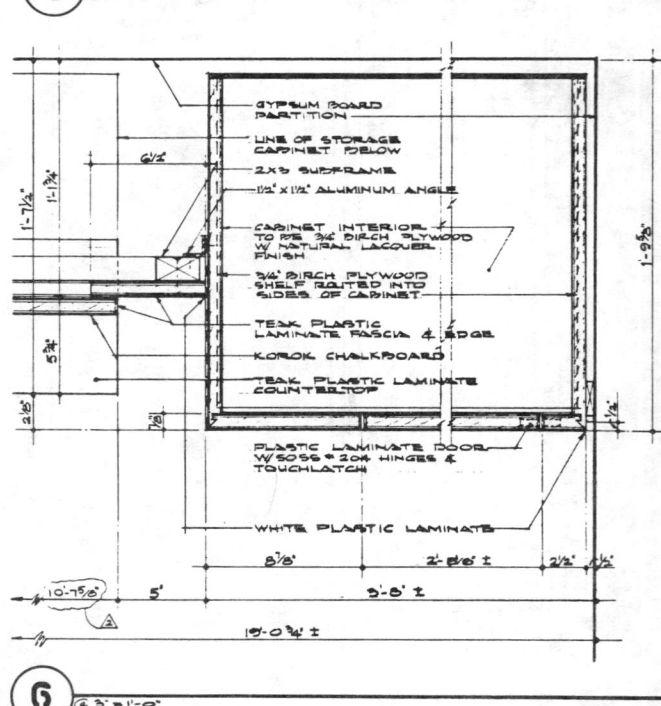

6 @ 3" = 1'-0"

GYPSUM BOARD PARTITION

LINE OF STORAGE CABINET BELOW

2 X 3 SUBFRAME

1½" X 1½" ALUMINUM ANGLE

CABINET INTERIOR TO BE ¾" BIRCH PLYWOOD W/ NATURAL LACQUER FINISH

¾" BIRCH PLYWOOD SHELF ROUTED INTO SIDES OF CABINET

TEAK PLASTIC LAMINATE FASCIA & EDGE

KOROK CHALKBOARD

TEAK PLASTIC LAMINATE COUNTERTOP

PLASTIC LAMINATE DOOR W/ SOSS #204 HINGES & TOUCHLATCH

WHITE PLASTIC LAMINATE

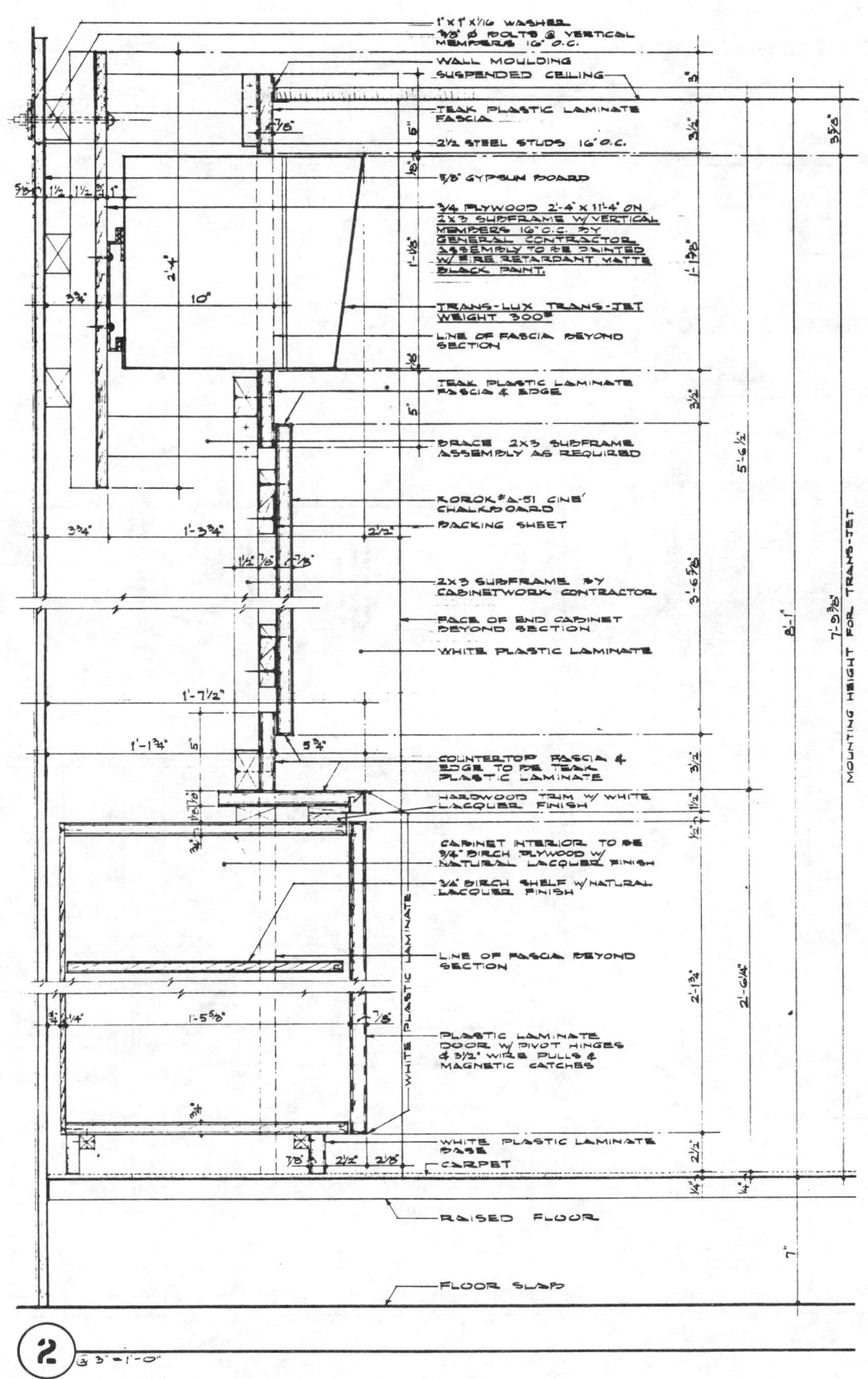

1" X 1" X 1/16 WASHER
3/8" Ø BOLTS @ VERTICAL MEMBERS 16" O.C.

WALL MOULDING
SUSPENDED CEILING

TEAK PLASTIC LAMINATE FASCIA

2 1/2 STEEL STUDS 16" O.C.

5/8" GYPSUM BOARD

3/4 PLYWOOD 2'-4" X 11'-4" ON 2X3 SUBFRAME W/ VERTICAL MEMBERS 16" O.C. BY GENERAL CONTRACTOR. ASSEMBLY TO BE PAINTED W/ FIRE RETARDANT MATTE BLACK PAINT.

TRANS-LUX TRANS-JET WEIGHT 300#

LINE OF FASCIA BEYOND SECTION

TEAK PLASTIC LAMINATE FASCIA & EDGE

BRACE 2X3 SUBFRAME ASSEMBLY AS REQUIRED

KOROK #A-51 CINE' CHALKBOARD

BACKING SHEET

2X3 SUBFRAME BY CABINETWORK CONTRACTOR

FACE OF END CABINET BEYOND SECTION

WHITE PLASTIC LAMINATE

COUNTERTOP FASCIA & EDGE TO BE TEAK PLASTIC LAMINATE

HARDWOOD TRIM W/ WHITE LACQUER FINISH

CABINET INTERIOR TO BE 3/4" BIRCH PLYWOOD W/ NATURAL LACQUER FINISH

3/4" BIRCH SHELF W/ NATURAL LACQUER FINISH

LINE OF FASCIA BEYOND SECTION

PLASTIC LAMINATE DOOR W/ PIVOT HINGES & 3 1/2" WIRE PULLS & MAGNETIC CATCHES

WHITE PLASTIC LAMINATE BASE

CARPET

RAISED FLOOR

FLOOR SLAB

WHITE PLASTIC LAMINATE

MOUNTING HEIGHT FOR TRANS-JET

2 @ 3" = 1'-0"

Fig. 1 (Continued)

WOODWORK DETAILS
Storage Cabinets

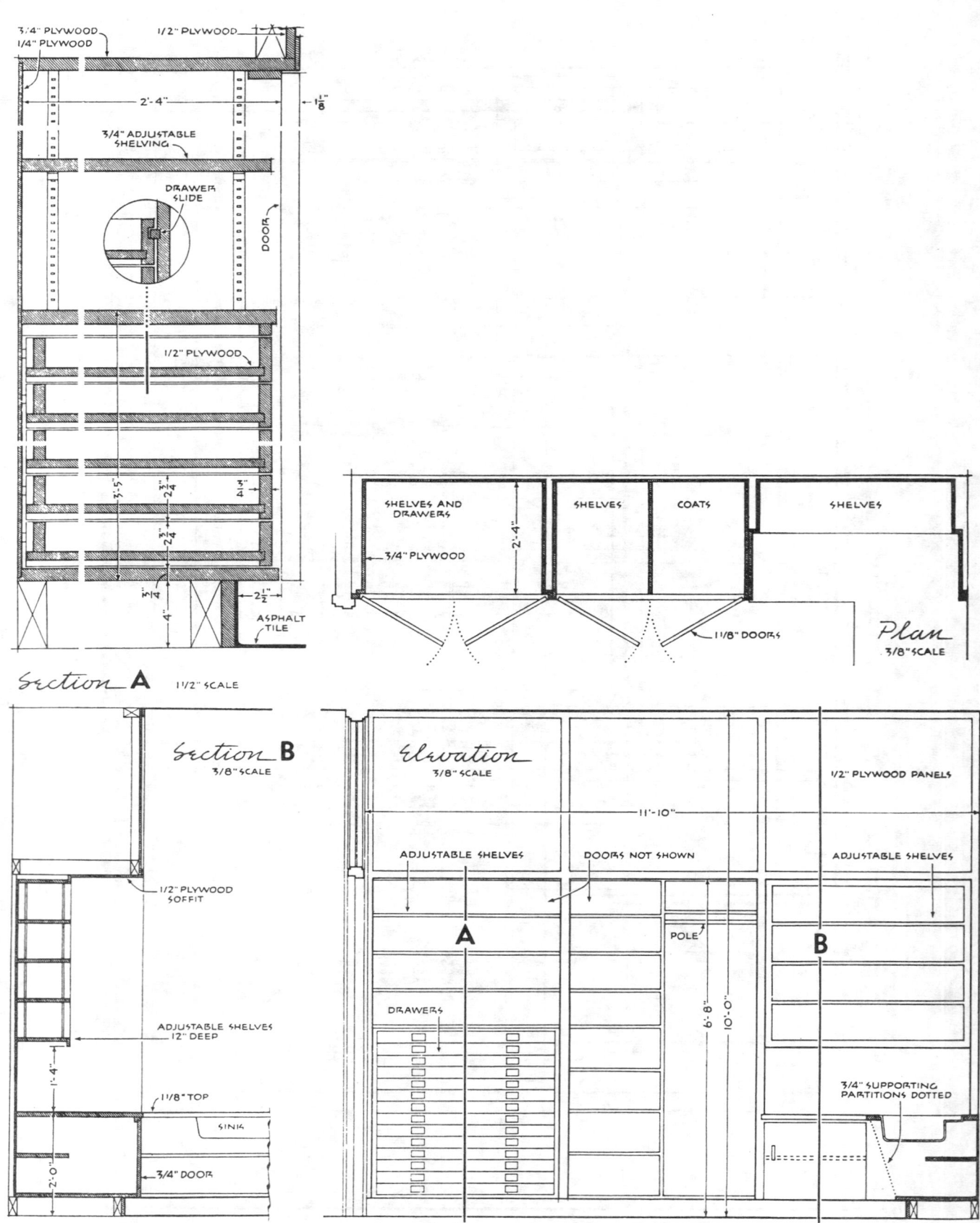

3/4" PLYWOOD
1/4" PLYWOOD
1/2" PLYWOOD

2'-4"

1⅛"

3/4" ADJUSTABLE SHELVING

DRAWER SLIDE

DOOR

1/2" PLYWOOD

3'-5"

2¾"

¾

2¾"

¾

2½"

4"

ASPHALT TILE

Section **A**   1½" SCALE

SHELVES AND DRAWERS

SHELVES

COATS

SHELVES

3/4" PLYWOOD

2'-4"

1⅛" DOORS

Plan
3/8" SCALE

Section **B**
3/8" SCALE

1/2" PLYWOOD SOFFIT

ADJUSTABLE SHELVES 12" DEEP

1'-4"

1⅛" TOP

SINK

2'-0"

3/4" DOOR

Elevation
3/8" SCALE

1/2" PLYWOOD PANELS

11'-10"

ADJUSTABLE SHELVES

DOORS NOT SHOWN

ADJUSTABLE SHELVES

A

POLE

B

6'-8"

10'-0"

DRAWERS

3/4" SUPPORTING PARTITIONS DOTTED

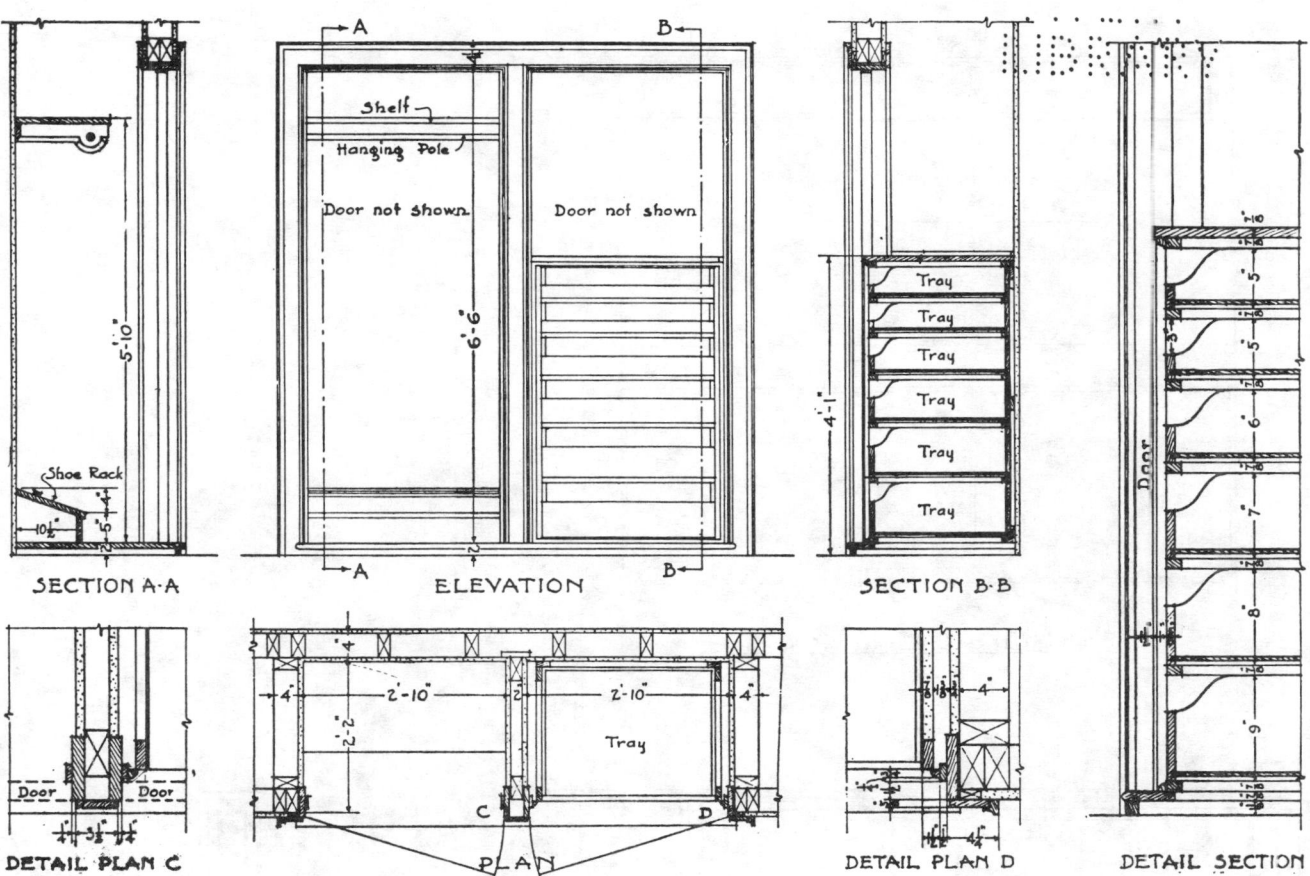

SECTION A·A

ELEVATION

SECTION B·B

DETAIL PLAN C

PLAN

DETAIL PLAN D

DETAIL SECTION

Shelf

Hanging Pole

Door not shown.

Door not shown.

Shoe Rack

Tray

Tray

Tray

Tray

Tray

Tray

Door

Tray

Door

Door

WOODWORK DETAILS
Bar Sink

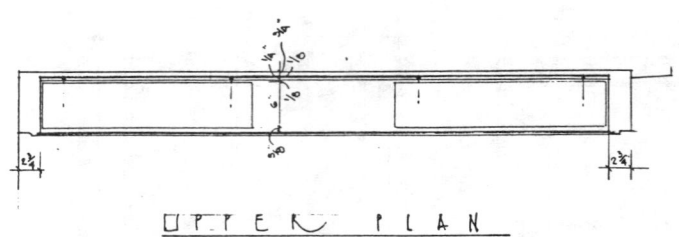

UPPER PLAN

BASE CABINET WIDTH OF WALL AS FAR
AS DOOR TRIM LESS THICKNESS OF
ROOM BASE.

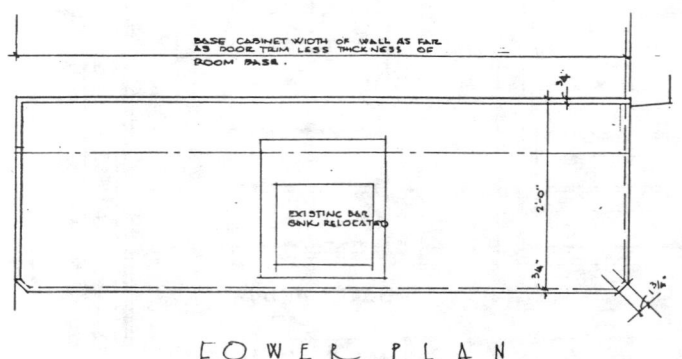

EXISTING BAR
SINK RELOCATED

2'-0"

LOWER PLAN

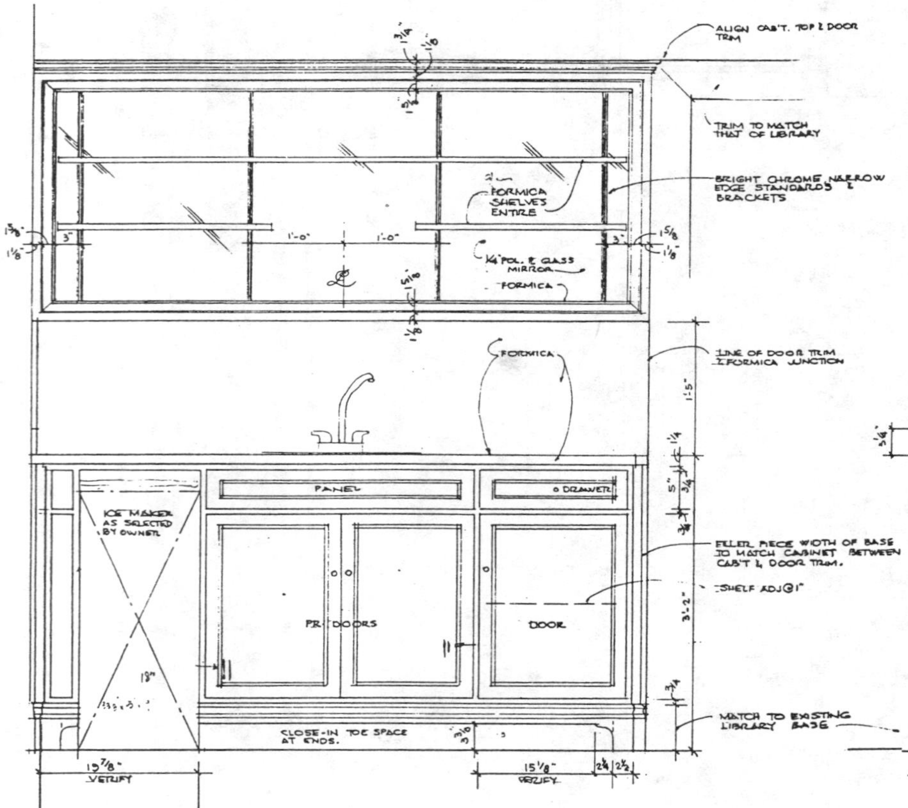

ALIGN CAB'T. TOP & DOOR
TRIM

TRIM TO MATCH
THAT OF LIBRARY

BRIGHT CHROME NARROW
EDGE STANDARDS &
BRACKETS

FORMICA
SHELVES
ENTIRE

1/4" POL. E. GLASS
MIRROR

FORMICA

STILES & RAILS SAME SIZE
FOREWARD OF DOOR TRIM

LINE OF DOOR TRIM

FORMICA

FORMICA

LINE OF DOOR TRIM
& FORMICA JUNCTION

1/2" THICK FILLER PIECE
MATCHING FIN. OF TRIM &

THICKNESS OF DOOR TRIM

STILES (& RAILS) SAME
WIDTH ALL AROUND &
MEASURED HERE FOREWARD
OF DOOR TRIM

ICE MAKER
AS SELECTED
BY OWNER

PANEL

6 DRAWERS

FILLER PIECE WIDTH OF BASE
TO MATCH CABINET BETWEEN
CAB'T & DOOR TRIM.

SHELF ADJ @ 1"

PR. DOORS

DOOR

13"

CLOSE-IN TOE SPACE
AT ENDS.

MATCH TO EXISTING
LIBRARY BASE

15 7/8"
VERIFY

15 1/8"
VERIFY

ELEVATION

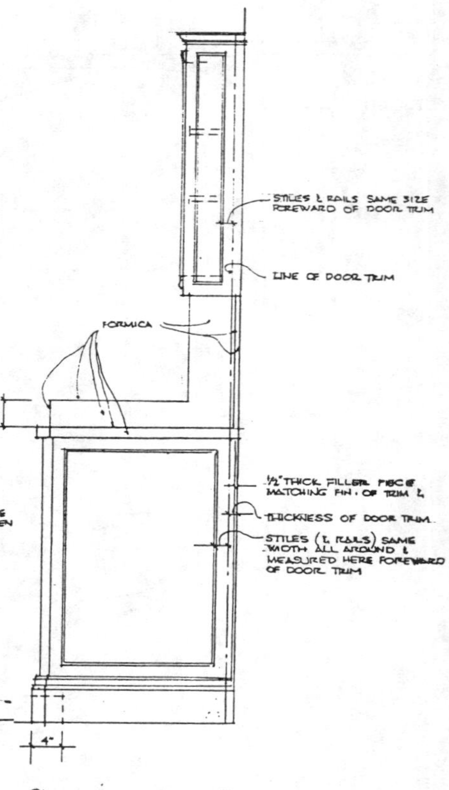

SIDE
ELEVATION

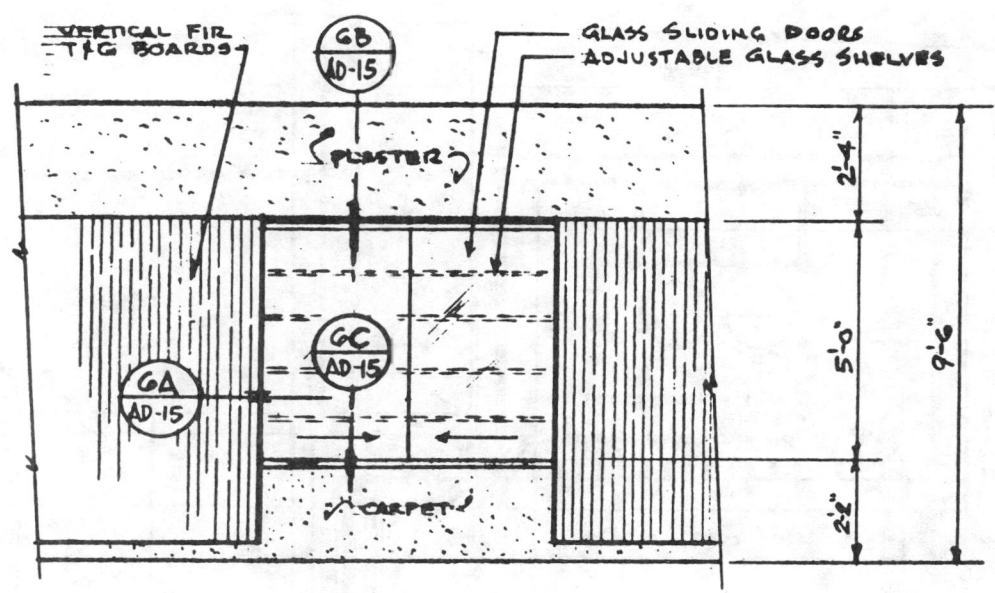

VERTICAL FIR T&G BOARDS

GB / AD-15

PLASTER

GLASS SLIDING DOORS

ADJUSTABLE GLASS SHELVES

2'-4"

9'-6"

5'-0"

GC / AD-15

GA / AD-15

2'-4"

CARPET

ELEVATION OF GIFT DISPLAY CASE

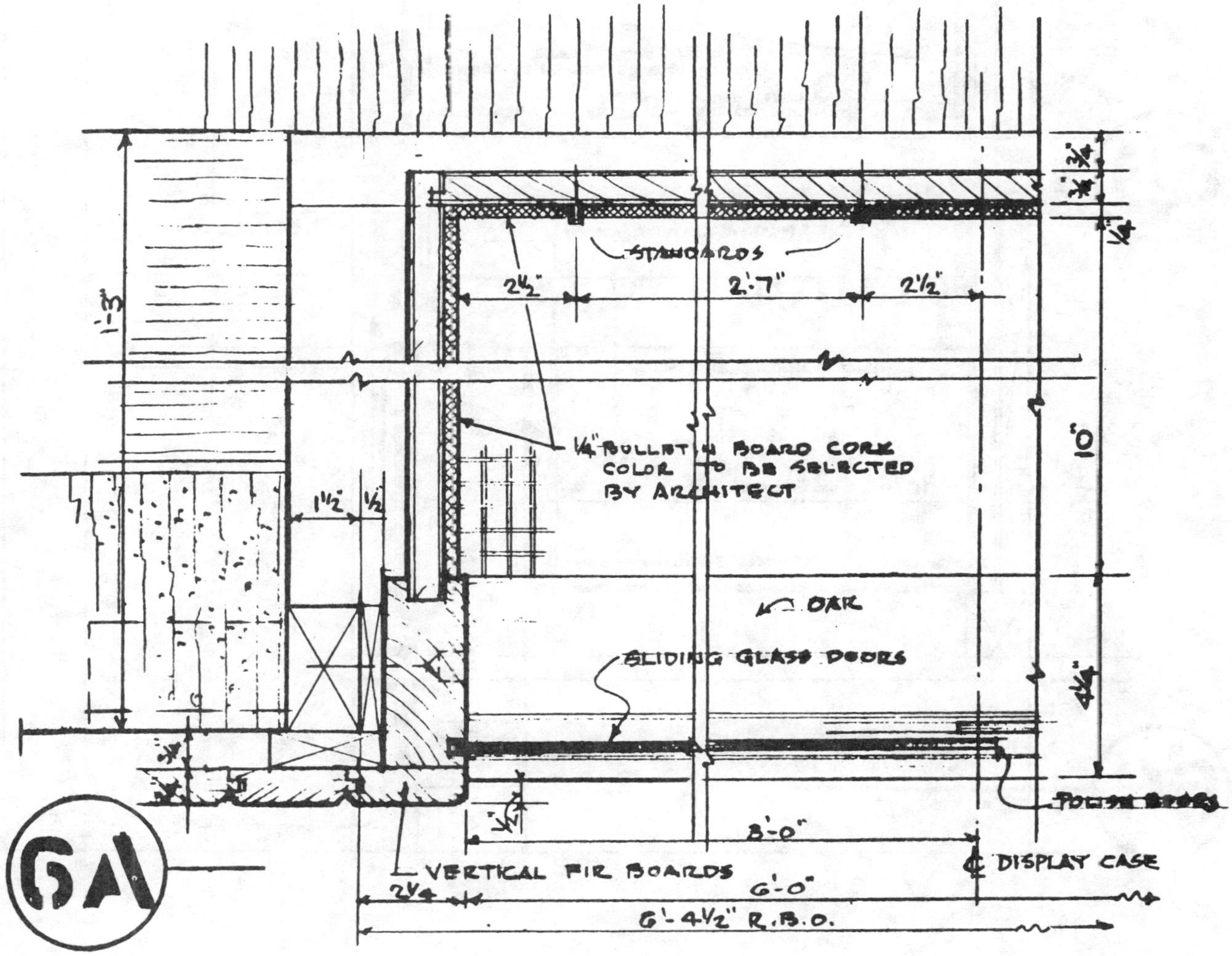

1'-3"

3/4"

STANDARDS

2½"   2'-7"   2½"

¼" BULLETIN BOARD CORK COLOR TO BE SELECTED BY ARCHITECT

1'-0"

1½" ½"

OAK

SLIDING GLASS DOORS

4½"

POLISH BRASS

GA

VERTICAL FIR BOARDS

2¼"   6'-0"

8'-0"

¢ DISPLAY CASE

6'-4½" R.B.O.

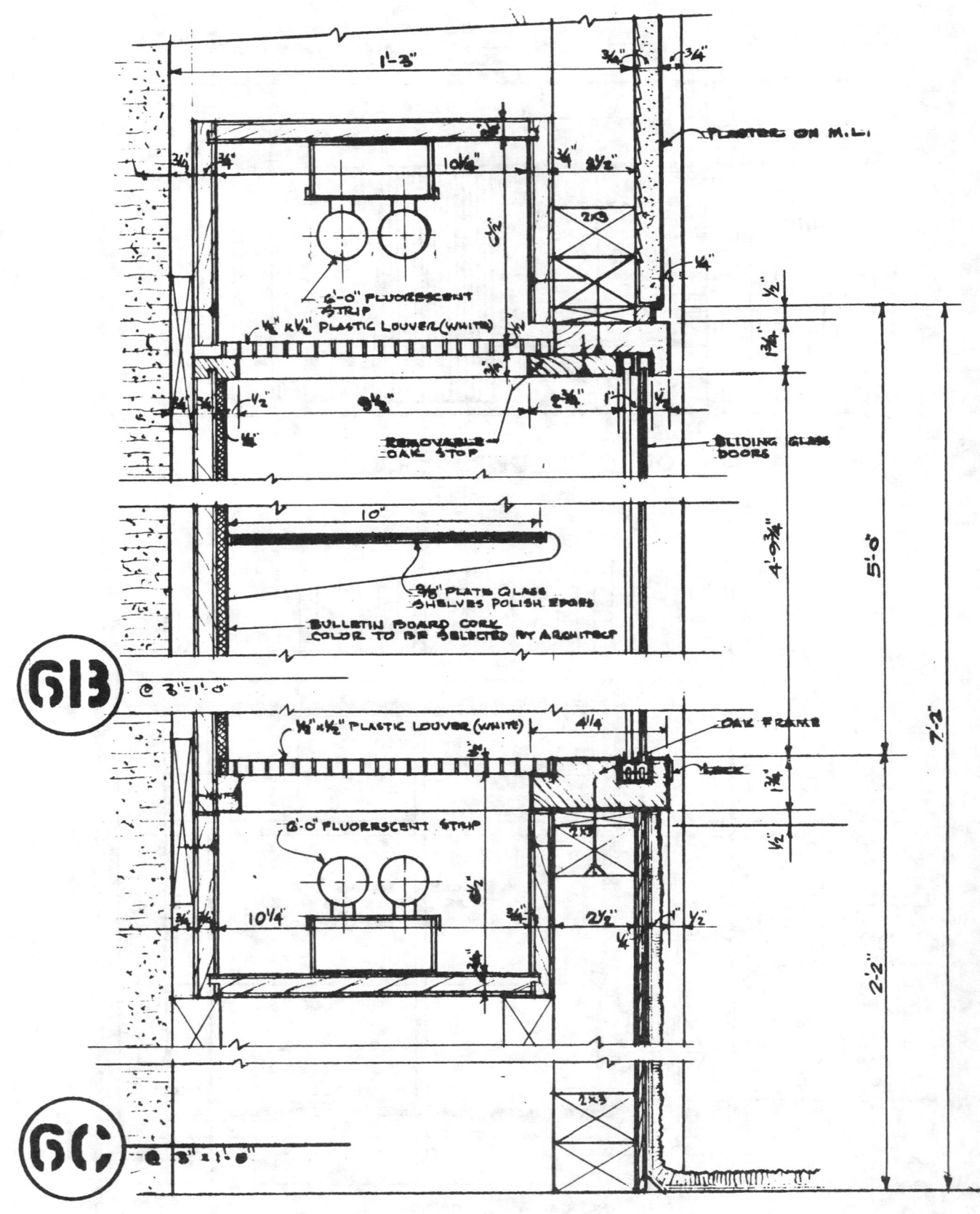

PLASTER ON M.L.

1'-3"

3/4" 3/4"

3/4" 3/4"

10 1/2"

3/4" 2 1/2"

2x3

1/2"

6'-0" FLUORESCENT STRIP

1/2" x 1 1/2" PLASTIC LOUVER (WHITE)

1 3/4"

9 1/4"

1/2"

2 3/4" 1"

REMOVABLE OAK STOP

SLIDING GLASS DOORS

4'-9 3/4"

5'-0"

7'-2"

10"

3/8" PLATE GLASS SHELVES POLISH EDGES

BULLETIN BOARD CORK COLOR TO BE SELECTED BY ARCHITECT

6B @ 3"=1'-0"

1/2" x 1 1/2" PLASTIC LOUVER (WHITE)

4 1/4"

OAK FRAME

1 3/4"

1/2"

6'-0" FLUORESCENT STRIP

2x3

2 1/2" 1" 1/2"

10 1/4"

3/4"

2'-2"

6C @ 3"=1'-0"

2x3

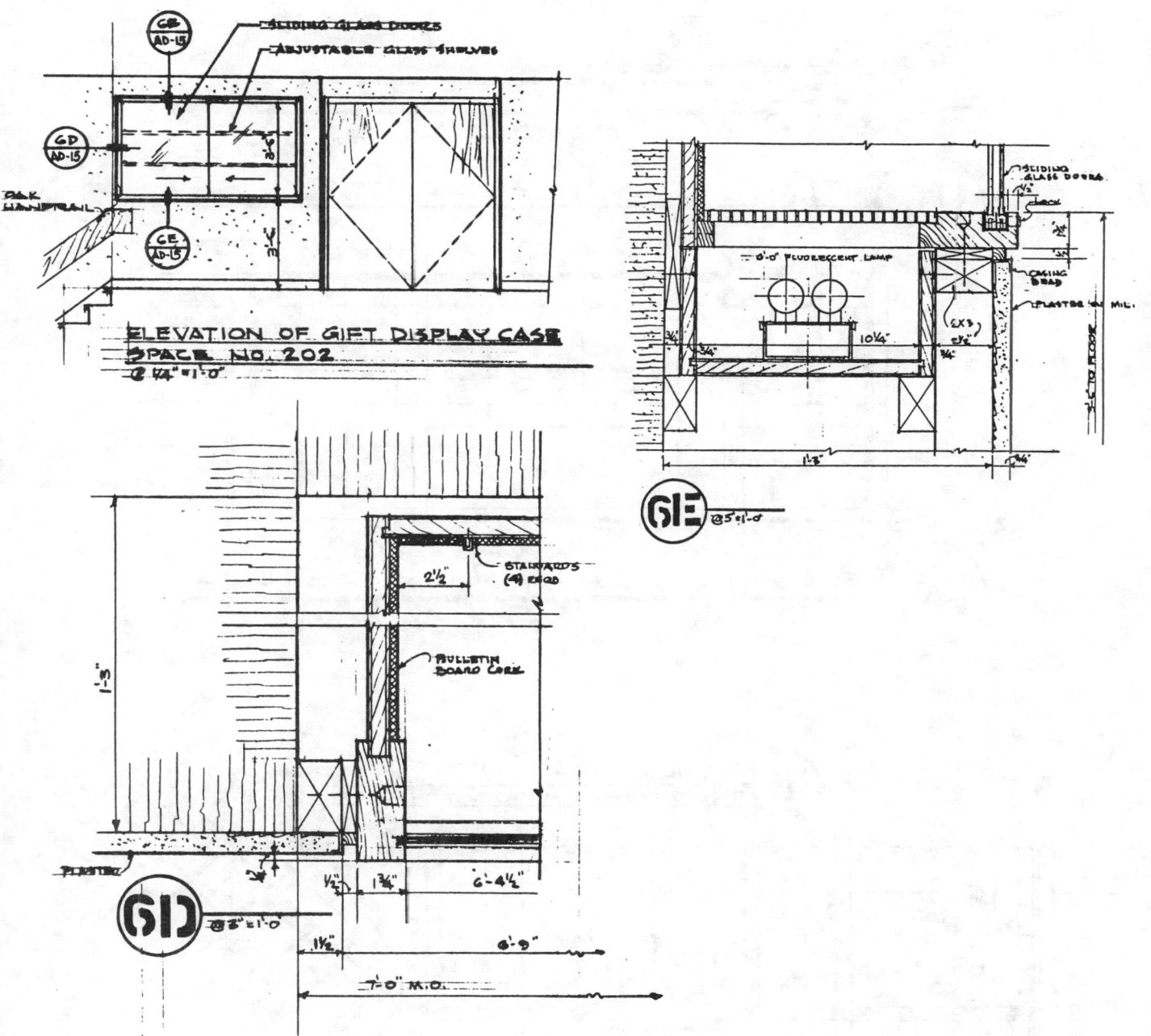

SLIDING GLASS DOORS
ADJUSTABLE GLASS SHELVES

OAK HANDRAIL

ELEVATION OF GIFT DISPLAY CASE
SPACE NO. 202
@ 1/4"=1'-0"

6'-0" FLUORESCENT LAMP

SLIDING GLASS DOORS

CASING BEAD

PLASTER ON METAL

STANDARDS (4) REQD

BULLETIN BOARD CORK

PLASTER

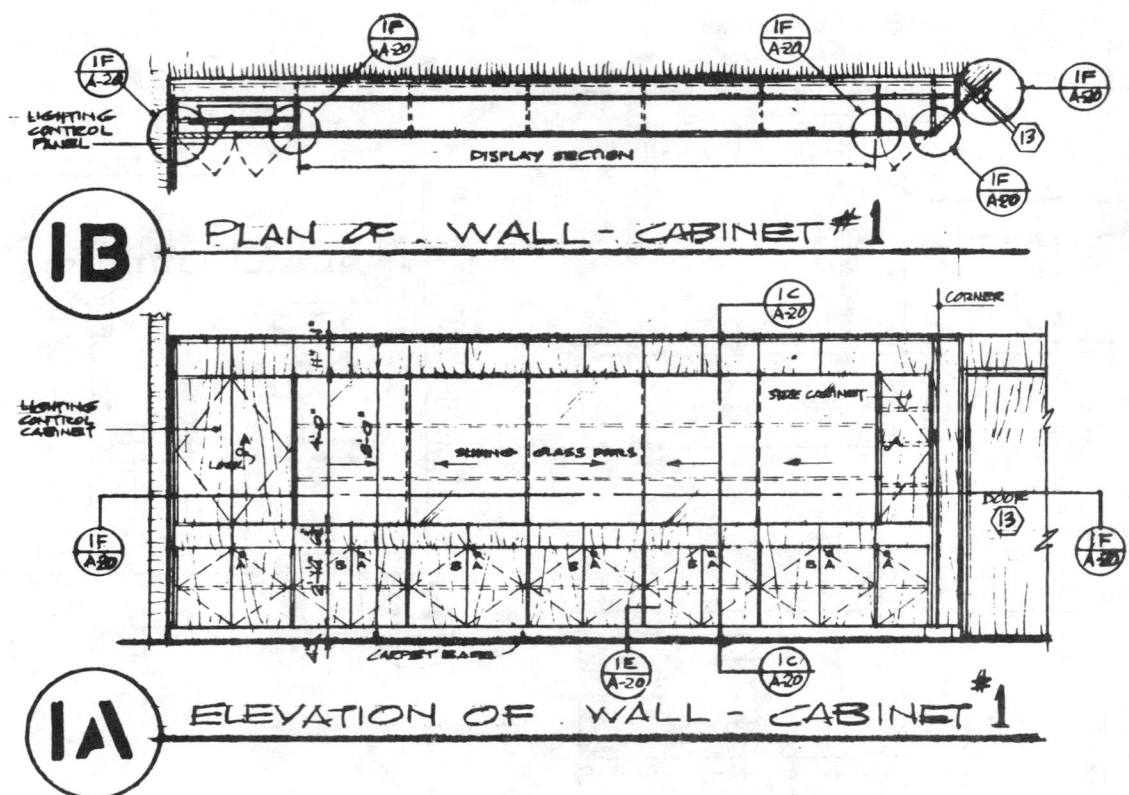

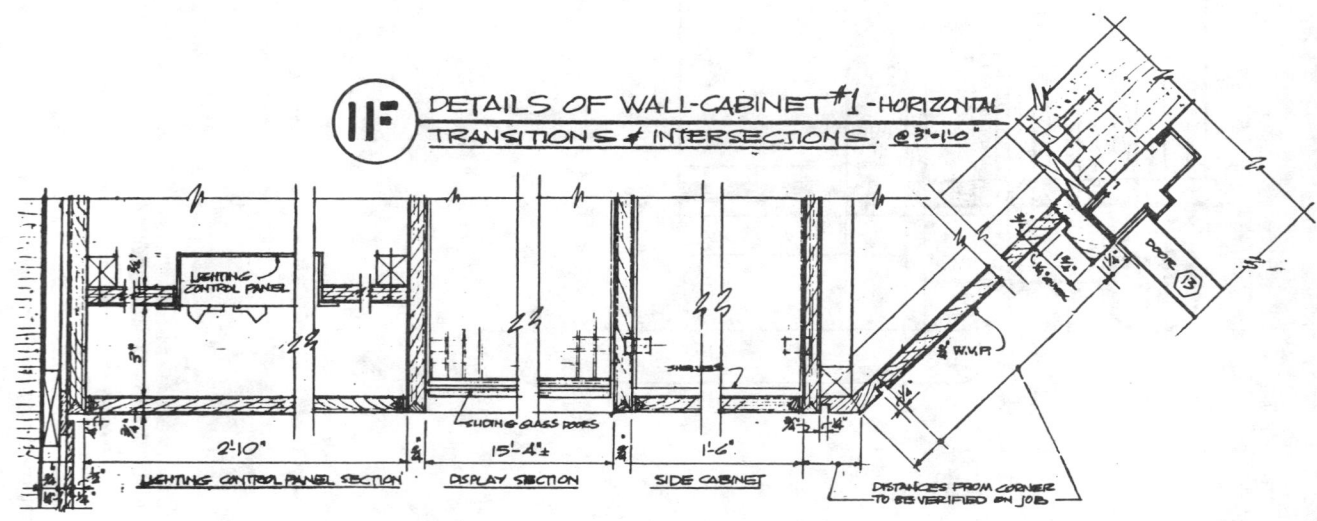

Fig. 2

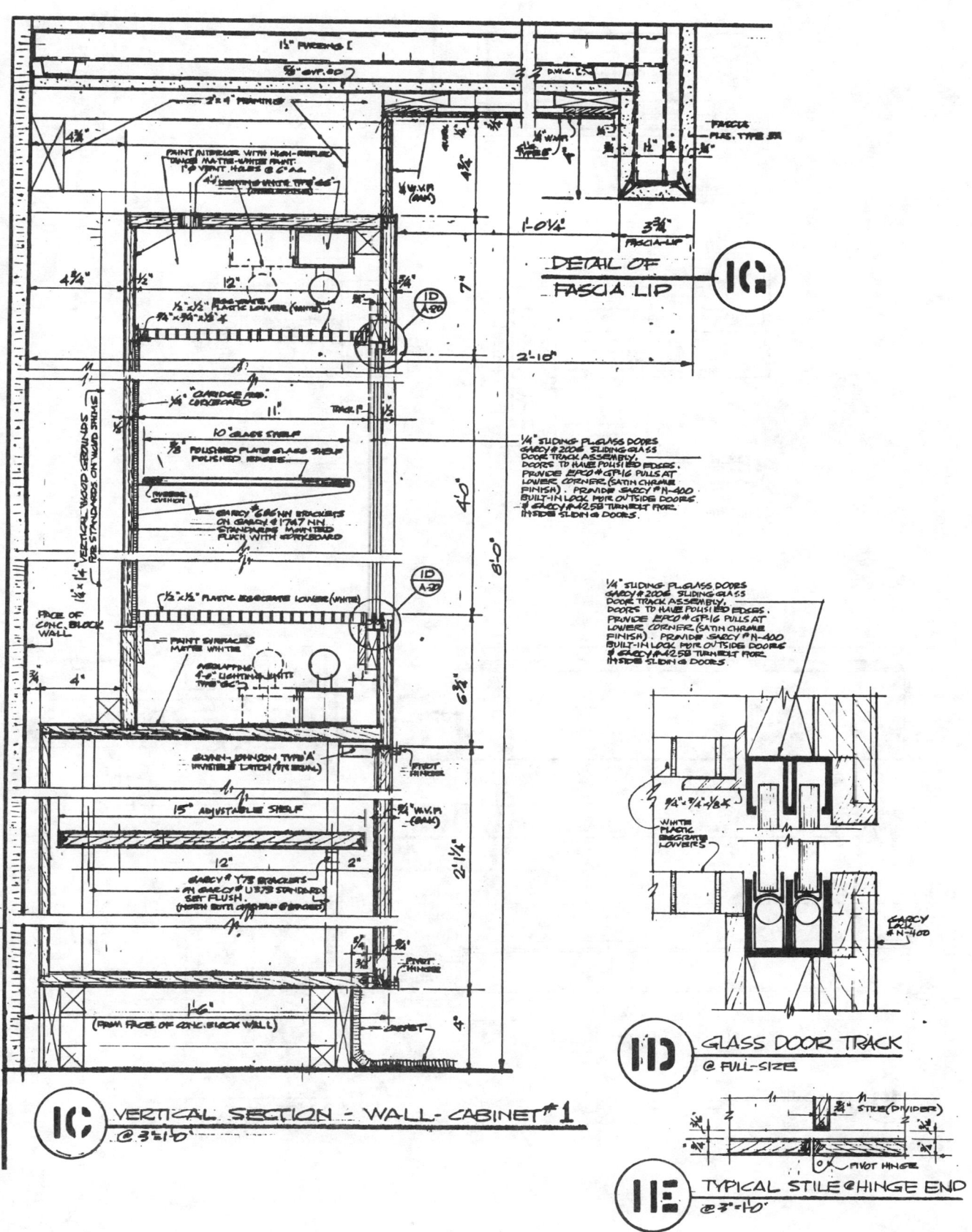

DETAIL OF FASCIA LIP

1G

¼" SLIDING PLGLASS DOORS GARCY #2006 SLIDING GLASS DOOR TRACK ASSEMBLY. DOORS TO HAVE POLISHED EDGES. PROVIDE EPCO #GP-16 PULLS AT LOWER CORNER (SATIN CHROME FINISH). PROVIDE GARCY #N-400 BUILT-IN LOCK FOR OUTSIDE DOORS & GARCY #A-258 TURNBOLT FOR INSIDE SLIDING DOORS.

¼" SLIDING PLGLASS DOORS GARCY #2006 SLIDING GLASS DOOR TRACK ASSEMBLY. DOORS TO HAVE POLISHED EDGES. PROVIDE EPCO #GP-16 PULLS AT LOWER CORNER (SATIN CHROME FINISH). PROVIDE GARCY #N-400 BUILT-IN LOCK FOR OUTSIDE DOORS & GARCY #A-258 TURNBOLT FOR INSIDE SLIDING DOORS.

1C VERTICAL SECTION - WALL-CABINET #1
@ 3"=1'-0"

1D GLASS DOOR TRACK
@ FULL-SIZE

1E TYPICAL STILE @ HINGE END
@ 3"=1'-0"

Fig. 2 (Continued)

823

WOODWORK DETAILS
Work Counter

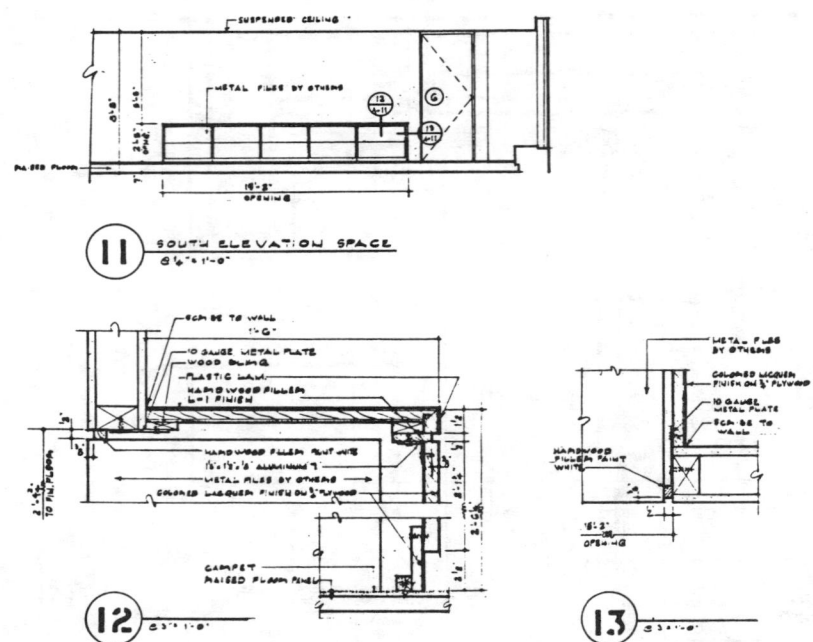

Fig. 3   Countertop.

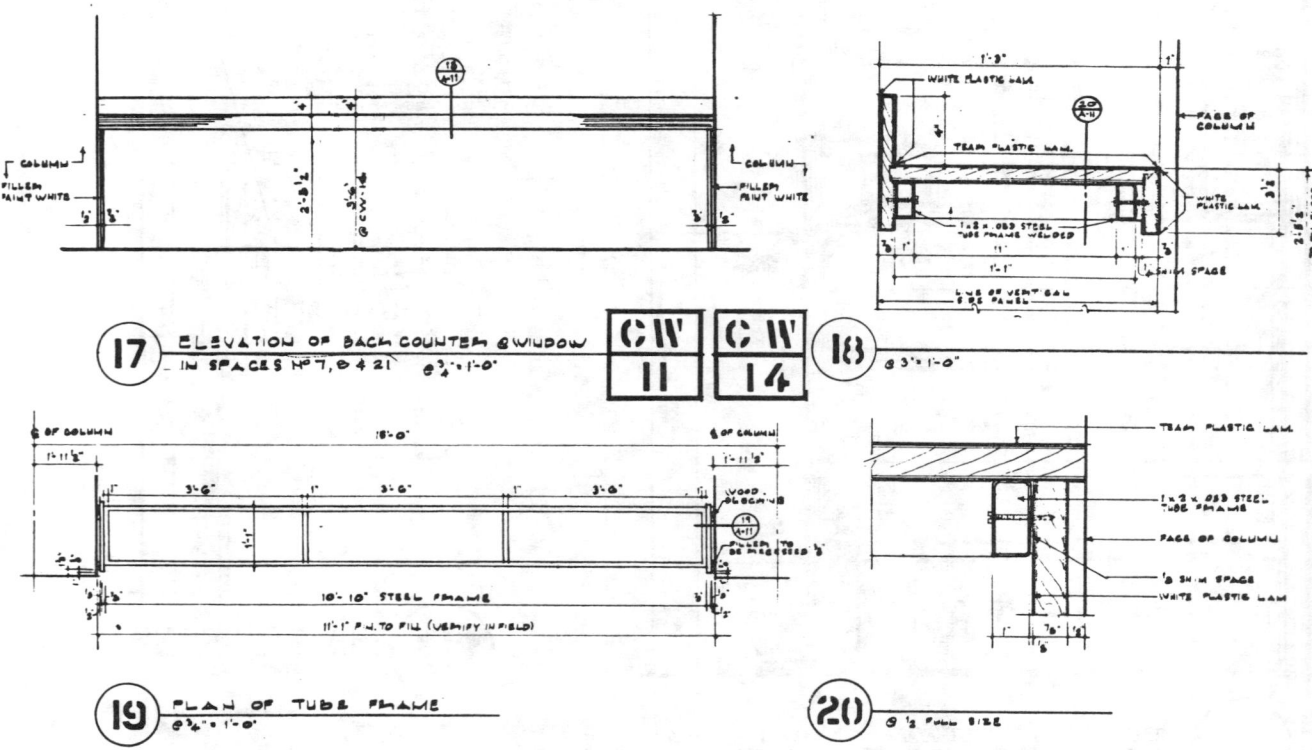

Fig. 4   Back counter.

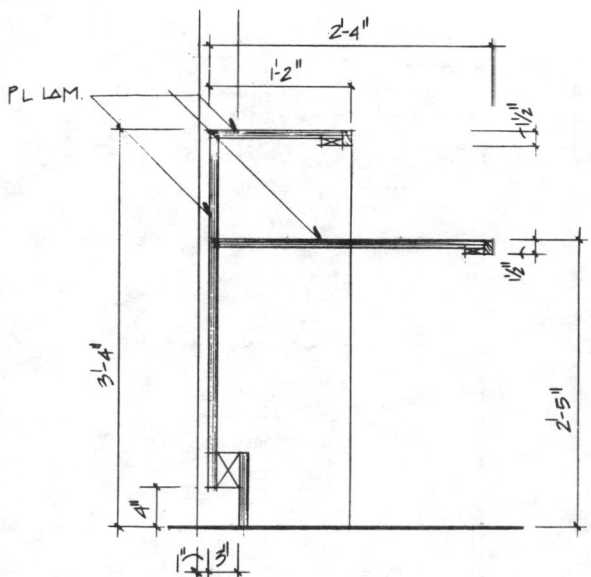

Fig. 5 Word processing counter.

PL LAM.

2'-4"
1'-2"
1½"
3'-4"
½"
2'-5"
4"
½" 3"

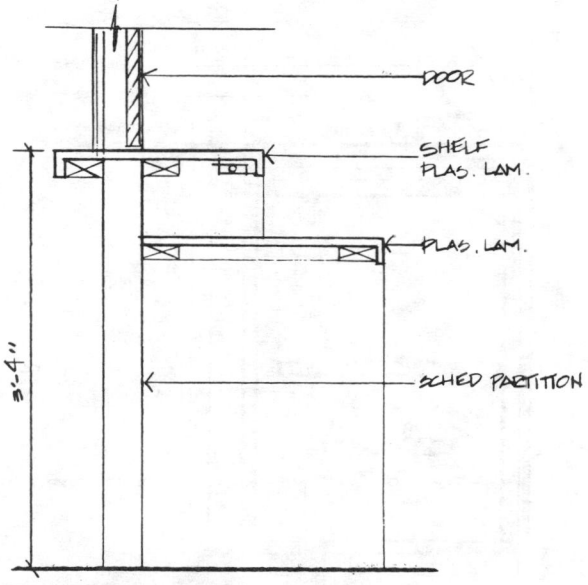

Fig. 6 Cashier counter.

DOOR
SHELF PLAS. LAM.
PLAS. LAM.
SCHED PARTITION
3'-4"

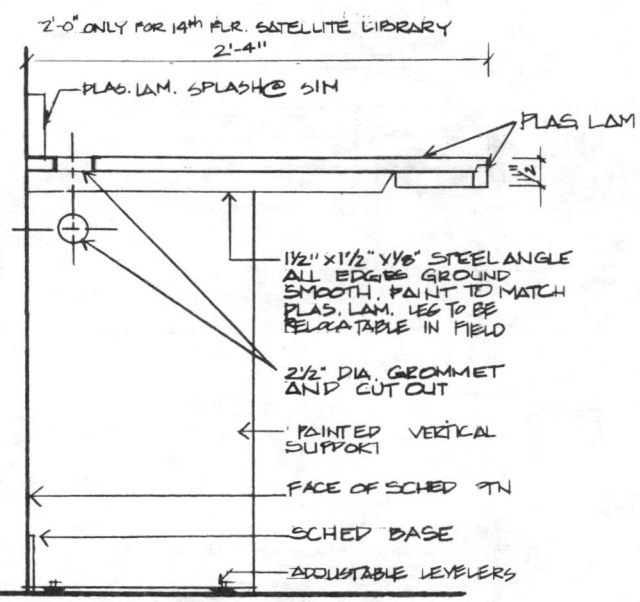

Fig. 7 Base and work counter.

2'-0" ONLY FOR 14th FLR. SATELLITE LIBRARY
2'-4"
PLAS. LAM. SPLASH @ SIM
PLAS LAM
½"
1½" X 1½" X⅛" STEEL ANGLE ALL EDGES GROUND SMOOTH. PAINT TO MATCH PLAS. LAM. LEG TO BE RELOCATABLE IN FIELD
2½" DIA. GROMMET AND CUT OUT
PAINTED VERTICAL SUPPORT
FACE OF SCHED PTN
SCHED BASE
ADJUSTABLE LEVELERS

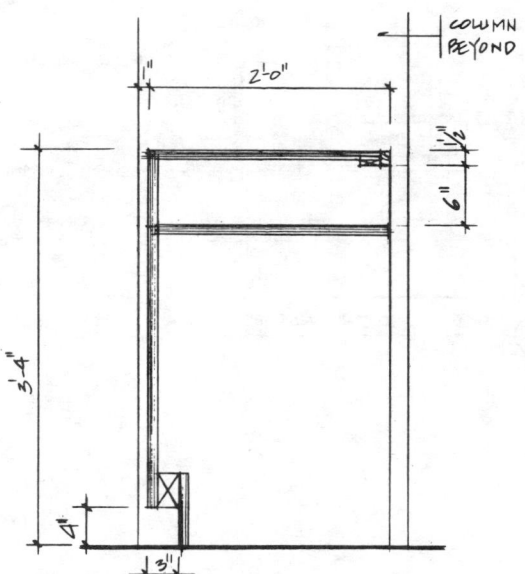

Fig. 8 Walkup counter.

COLUMN BEYOND
1"
2'-0"
1½"
6"
3'-4"
4"
3"

825

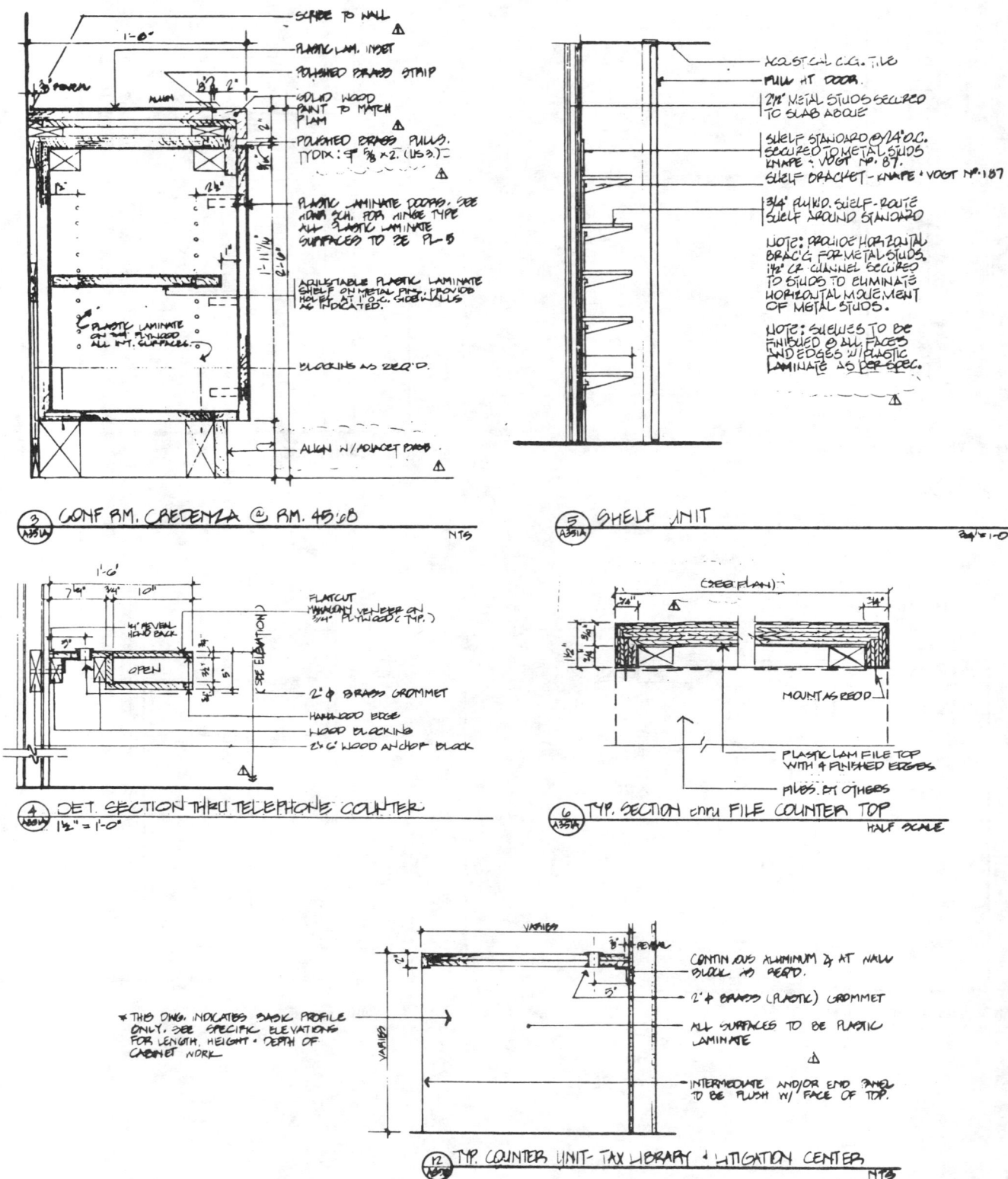

3 CONF RM. CREDENZA @ RM. 45:6B   NTS

SCRIBE TO WALL

PLASTIC LAM. INSET

POLISHED BRASS STRIP

SOLID WOOD PAINT TO MATCH PLAM

POLISHED BRASS PULLS. TYDIX: 5/8 x 2. (US3.)

PLASTIC LAMINATE DOORS. SEE DWR SCH. FOR HINGE TYPE ALL PLASTIC LAMINATE SURFACES TO BE PL-5

ADJUSTABLE PLASTIC LAMINATE SHELF ON METAL PINS. PROVIDE HOLES AT 1" O.C. SIDEWALLS AS INDICATED.

PLASTIC LAMINATE ON 3/4" PLYWOOD ALL INT. SURFACES.

BLOCKING AS REQ'D.

ALIGN W/ ADJACENT DOOR

5 SHELF UNIT   3/4"=1'-0"

ACOUSTICAL C.G. TILE

FULL HT DOOR

2½" METAL STUDS SECURED TO SLAB ABOVE

SHELF STANDARD @ 24'O.C. SECURED TO METAL STUDS KNAPE + VOGT Nº. 87. SHELF BRACKET - KNAPE + VOGT Nº. 187

3/4" PLYWD. SHELF-ROUTE SHELF AROUND STANDARD

NOTE: PROVIDE HORIZONTAL BRAC'G FOR METAL STUDS. 1½" CR CHANNEL SECURED TO STUDS TO ELIMINATE HORIZONTAL MOVEMENT OF METAL STUDS.

NOTE: SHELVES TO BE FINISHED @ ALL FACES AND EDGES W/ PLASTIC LAMINATE AS PER SPEC.

4 DET. SECTION THRU TELEPHONE COUNTER   1½"=1'-0"

FLATCUT MAHOGANY VENEER ON 3/4" PLYWOOD (TYP.)

2" ø BRASS GROMMET

HARDWOOD EDGE

WOOD BLOCKING

2" x 6" WOOD ANCHOR BLOCK

OPEN

6 TYP. SECTION thru FILE COUNTER TOP   HALF SCALE

PLASTIC LAM FILE TOP WITH 4 FINISHED EDGES

FILES BY OTHERS

MOUNT AS REQ'D

12 TYP. COUNTER UNIT- TAX LIBRARY + LITIGATION CENTER   NTS

CONTINUOUS ALUMINUM 3 AT WALL BLOCK AS REQ'D.

2" ø BRASS (PLASTIC) GROMMET

ALL SURFACES TO BE PLASTIC LAMINATE

INTERMEDIATE AND/OR END PANEL TO BE FLUSH W/ FACE OF TOP.

* THIS DWG. INDICATES BASIC PROFILE ONLY. SEE SPECIFIC ELEVATIONS FOR LENGTH, HEIGHT + DEPTH OF CABINET WORK

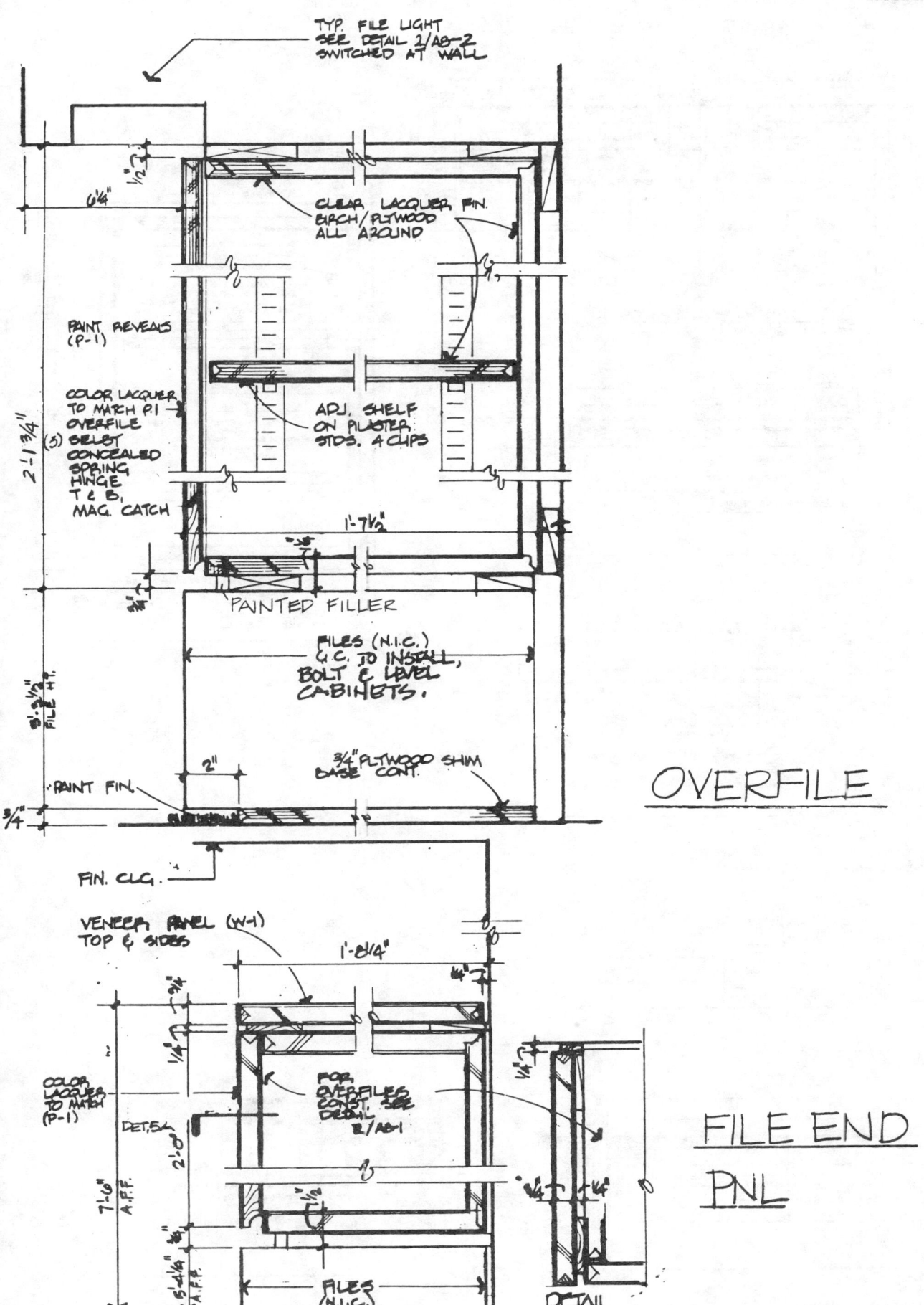

TYP. FILE LIGHT
SEE DETAIL 2/A8-2
SWITCHED AT WALL

6'4"

1/2"

CLEAR LACQUER FIN.
BIRCH/PLYWOOD
ALL AROUND

PAINT REVEALS
(P-1)

COLOR LACQUER
TO MATCH P.1
OVERFILE
(3) SLF/ST
CONCEALED
SPRING
HINGE
T & B,
MAG. CATCH

2'-1 3/4"

ADJ. SHELF
ON PILASTER
STDS. 4 CLIPS

1'-7 1/2"

3/4"

PAINTED FILLER

FILES (N.I.C.)
G.C. TO INSTALL,
BOLT & LEVEL
CABINETS.

3'-2 1/2" FILE HT.

2"

3/4" PLYWOOD SHIM
BASE CONT.

PAINT FIN.

3/4"

OVERFILE

FIN. CLG.

VENEER PANEL (W-1)
TOP & SIDES

1'-8 1/4"

1/4"

COLOR
LACQUER
TO MATCH
(P-1)

DET. 5A

2'-0"

FOR
OVERFILES
CONST. SEE
DETAIL
2/A8-1

7'-0" A.F.F.

FILE END

PNL

5'-4 1/4" A.F.F.

FILES
(N.I.C.)

DETAIL

WOODWORK DETAILS
Overfile Cabinet

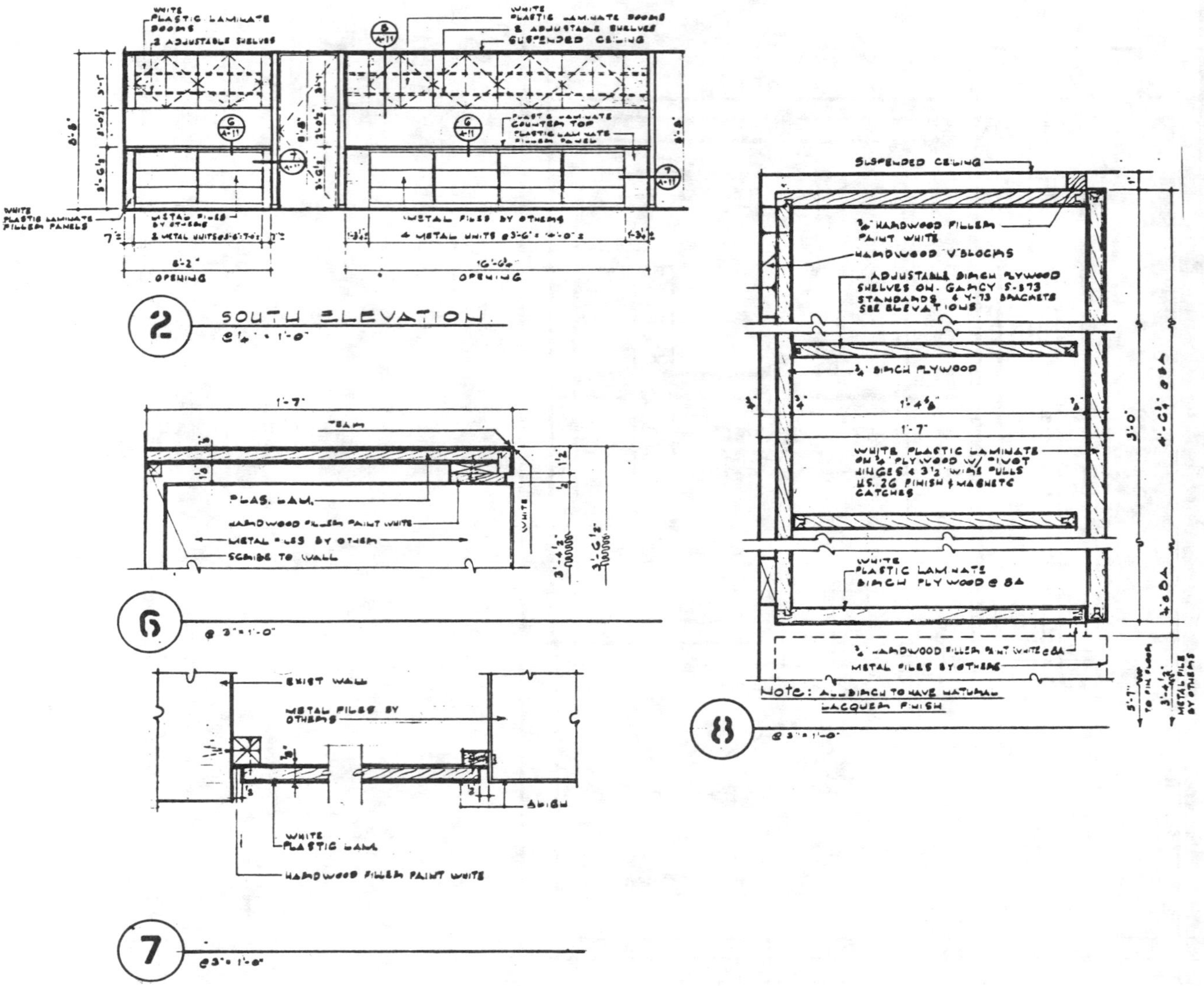

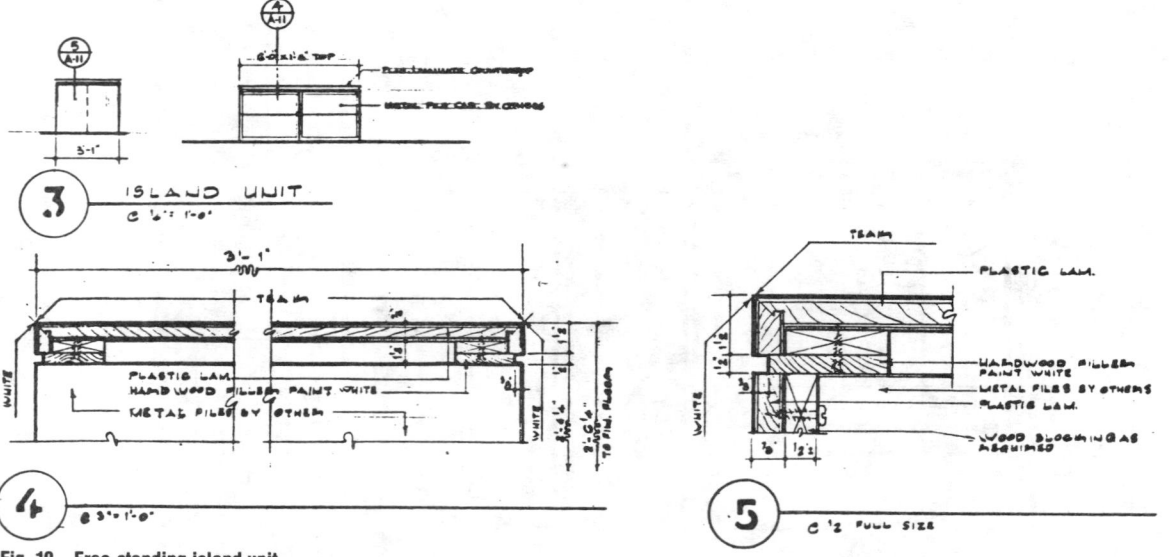

Fig. 9   Wall unit with overhead cabinets.

Fig. 10   Free-standing island unit.

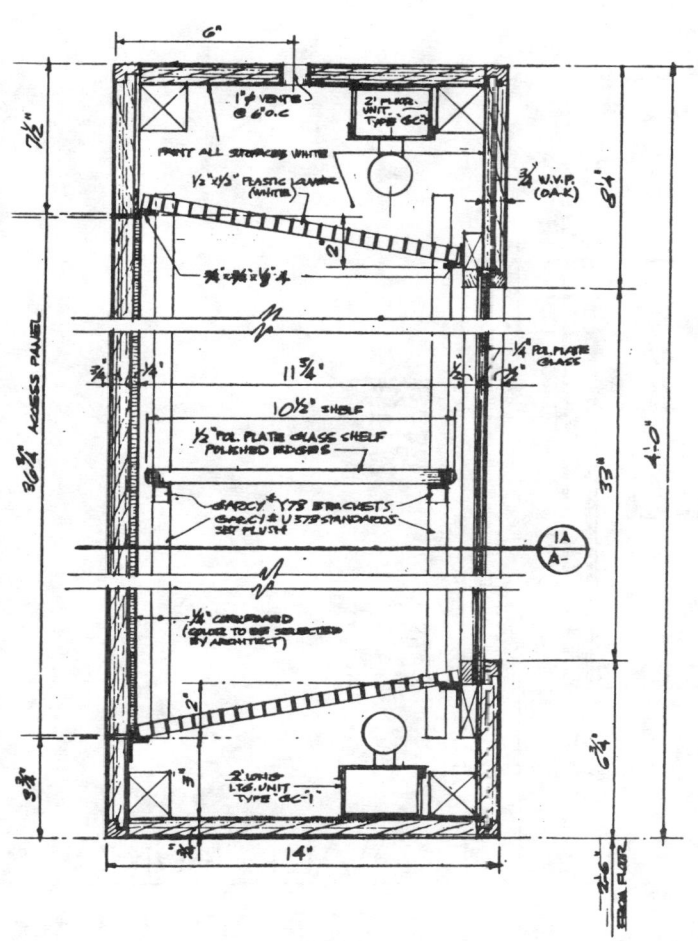

1 **LOBBY DISPLAY CABINET #1**
VERTICAL SECTION @ 3"=1'-0"

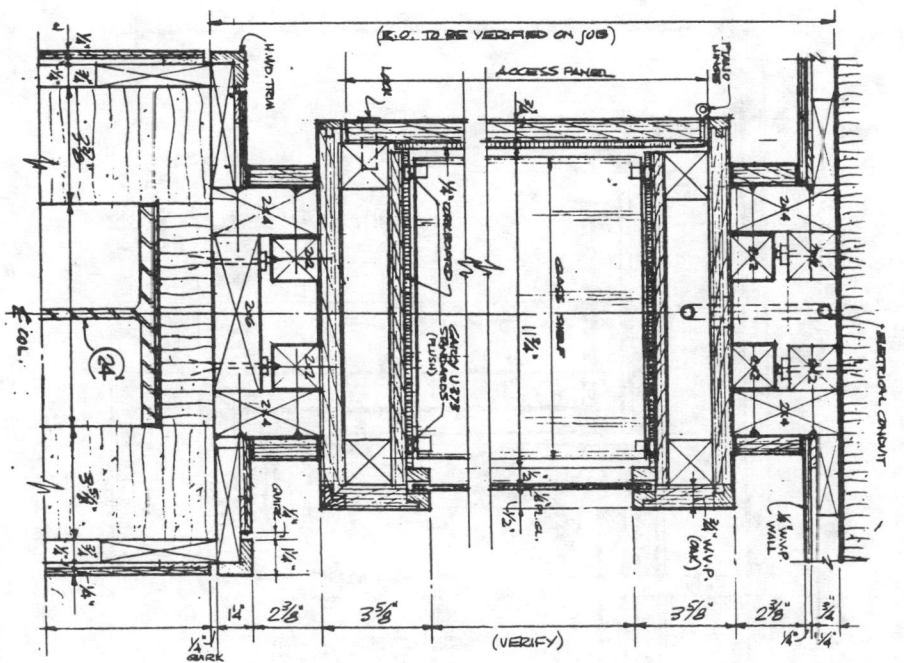

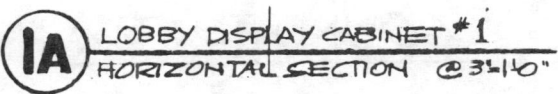

1A **LOBBY DISPLAY CABINET #1**
HORIZONTAL SECTION @ 3"=1'-0"

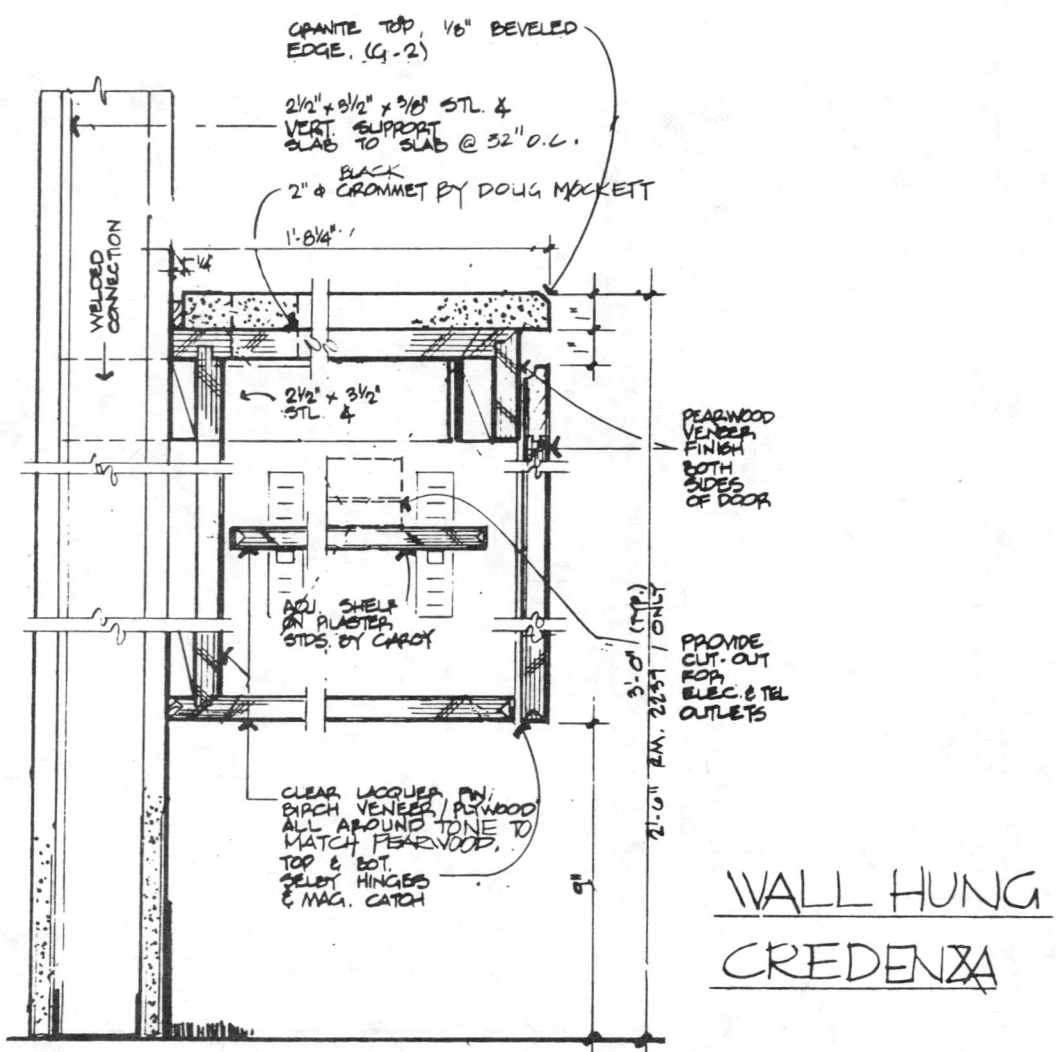

GRANITE TOP, 1/8" BEVELED EDGE. (G-2)

2 1/2" x 3 1/2" x 3/8" STL. 4 VERT. SUPPORT SLAB TO SLAB @ 32" O.C.

BLACK
2" ⌀ GROMMET BY DOUG MOCKETT

1'-8 1/4"

WELDED CONNECTION

2 1/2" x 3 1/2" STL. 4

PEARWOOD VENEER FINISH BOTH SIDES OF DOOR

ADJ. SHELF ON PILASTER STDS. BY CARDY

3'-0" (TYP.) 2'-5" FM. ONLY 21'-0"

PROVIDE CUT-OUT FOR ELEC. & TEL. OUTLETS

CLEAR LACQUER FIN. BIRCH VENEER / PLYWOOD ALL AROUND TONE TO MATCH PEARWOOD, TOP & BOT. SELF HINGES & MAG. CATCH

9"

WALL HUNG
CREDENZA

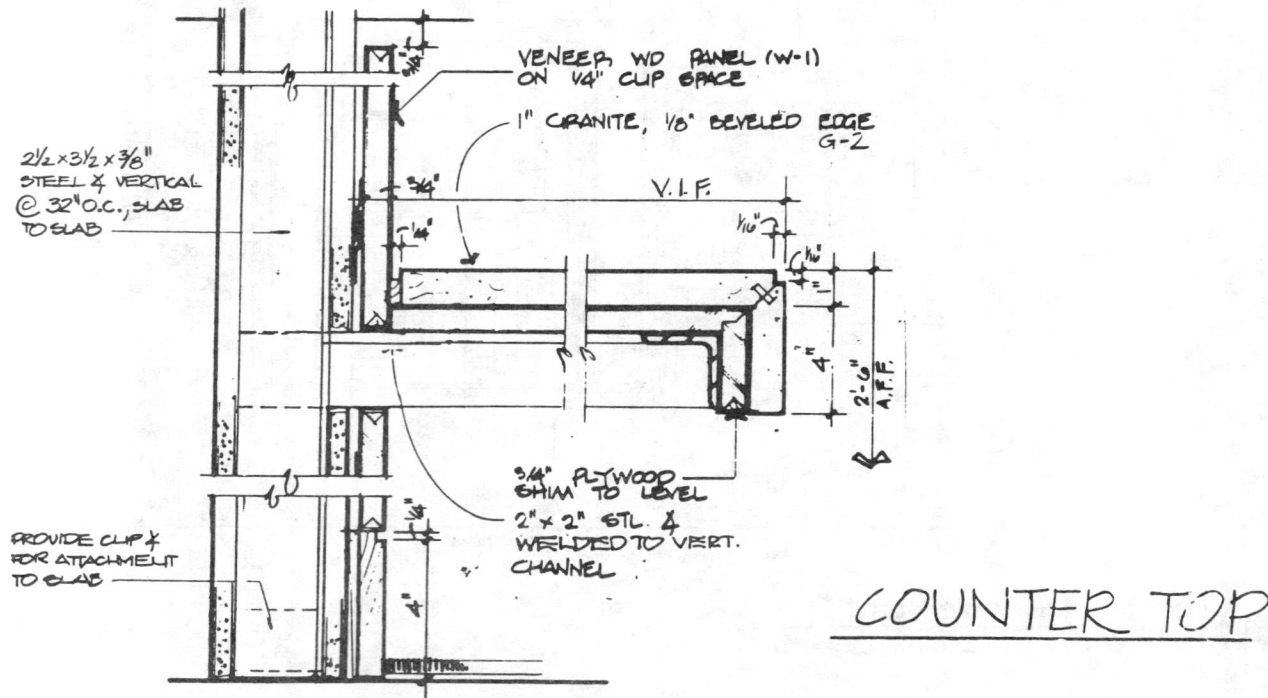

VENEER WD PANEL (W-1) ON 1/4" CLIP SPACE

1" GRANITE, 1/8" BEVELED EDGE G-2

2 1/2 x 3 1/2 x 3/8" STEEL 4 VERTICAL @ 32" O.C., SLAB TO SLAB

3/4"

1/4"

V.I.F.

1/16"

2'-6" A.F.F.

4"

PROVIDE CLIP 4 FOR ATTACHMENT TO SLAB

3/4" PLYWOOD SHIM TO LEVEL

2" x 2" STL. 4 WELDED TO VERT. CHANNEL

COUNTER TOP

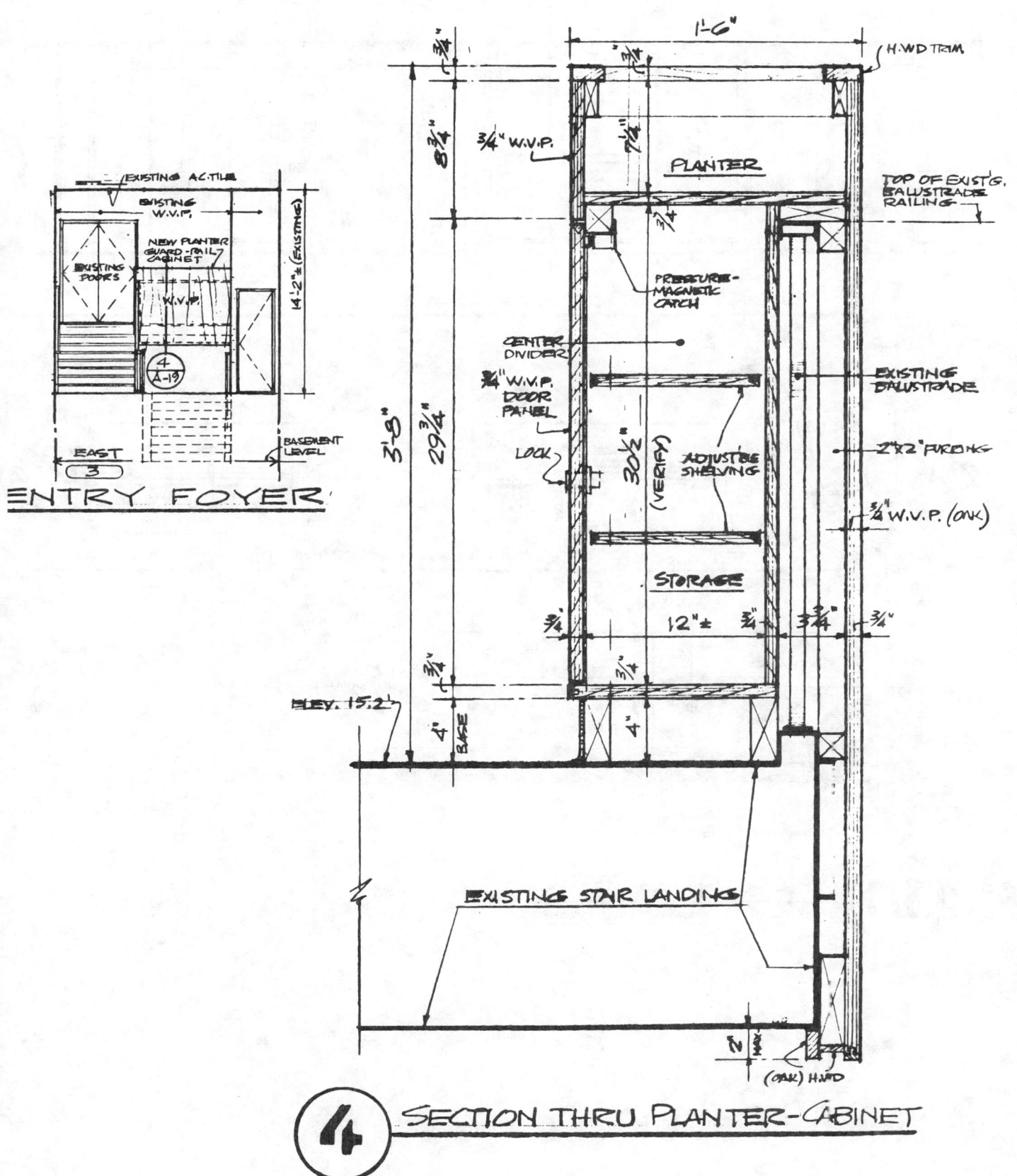

EXISTING A.C. TILE
EXISTING W.V.P.
NEW PLANTER GUARD-RAIL CABINET
EXISTING DOORS
W.V.P.
14'-2"± (EXISTING)
4 A-19
EAST 3
BASEMENT LEVEL

ENTRY FOYER

1'-6"
3/4"
H. WD TRIM
3/4"
8 3/4"
3/4" W.V.P.
PLANTER
TOP OF EXIST'G. BALUSTRADE RAILING
7 1/4"
3/4"
PRESSURE-MAGNETIC CATCH
CENTER DIVIDER
EXISTING BALUSTRADE
3/4" W.V.P. DOOR PANEL
30 1/2" (VERIFY)
ADJUSTABLE SHELVING
2"x2" FURRING
LOCK
3/4" W.V.P. (OAK)
3'-8"
29 3/4"
STORAGE
3/4"
12"±
3/4"
3 3/4"
3/4"
3/4"
3/4"
ELEV. 15.2'
4"
BASE
4"
2"
(OAK) H. WD

EXISTING STAIR LANDING

④ SECTION THRU PLANTER-CABINET

3A
A-20

METAL ASH.

BOOK SHELVES

ACTUAL ELEV.

F-7

SHAWL RODS

DOORS IN OPEN POSITION

13

12

11

CARPET BASE

313 ELEVATIONS OF BOOK & SHAWL CABINETS
@ 1/4"=1'-0"

13'

13

3A
A-20

12

F-7
A-23

12

4
A-

1F
A-20

SHAWL RODS

SHAWL RODS

W.V.

11

4"

6'-0"

4"

4"

6'-0"

VERIFY ON JOB

3C PLAN OF BOOK & SHAWL CABINETS
@ 1/4"=1'-0"

3/4" 3/4" 3/4"

3/4" ROD ABOVE

NOTCHED PLYWOOD PLATE ATTACHED TO PLYWOOD DIVIDER

3/4"Ø SHAWL ROD

2 1/4"

3 1/2"

3/4"

PIVOT HINGES

3/4" W.V.P. DOORS

3D TYPICAL STILE DETAIL
@ 3"=1'-0"   BOOK & SHAWL CABINETS

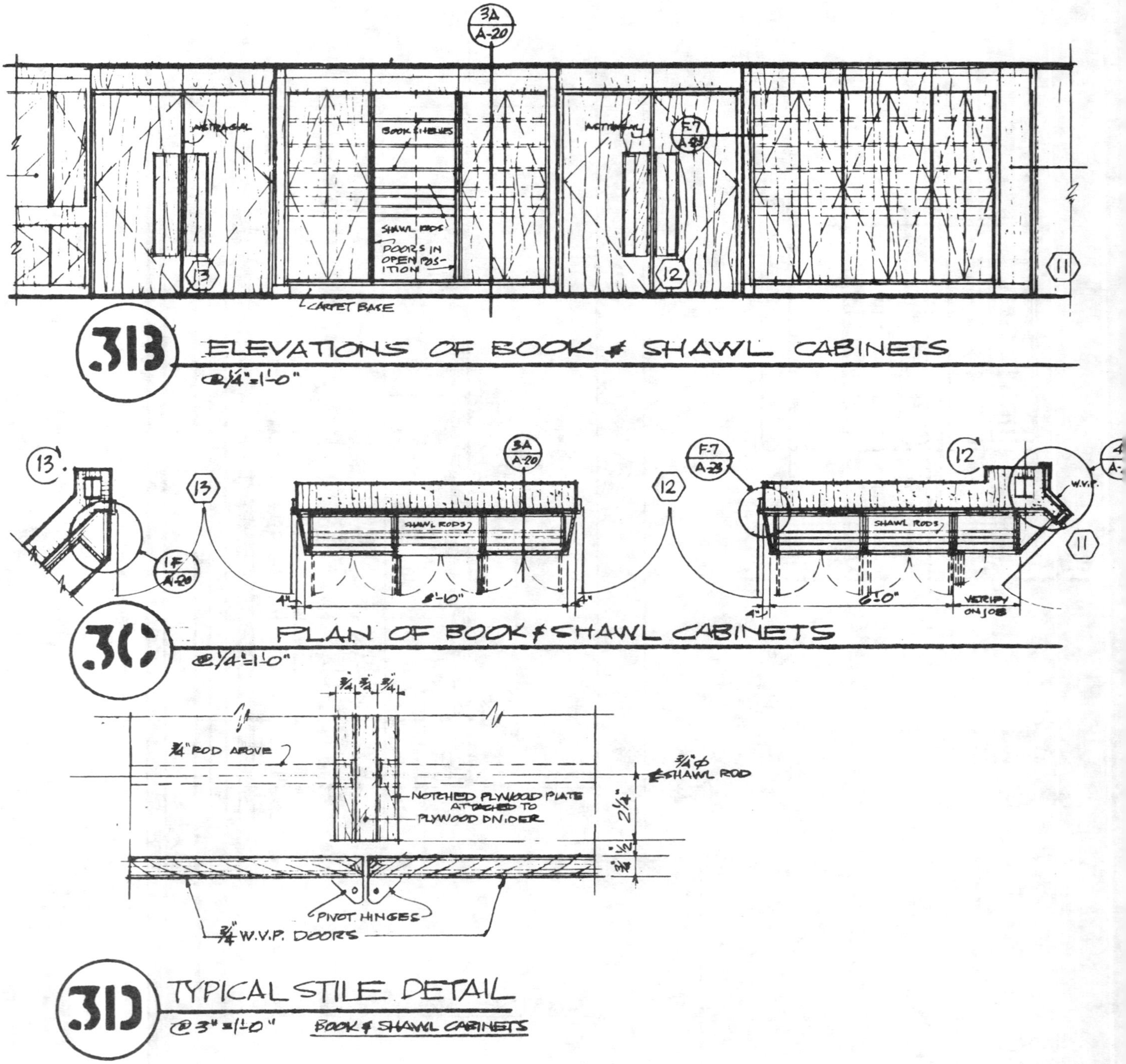

Fig. 11

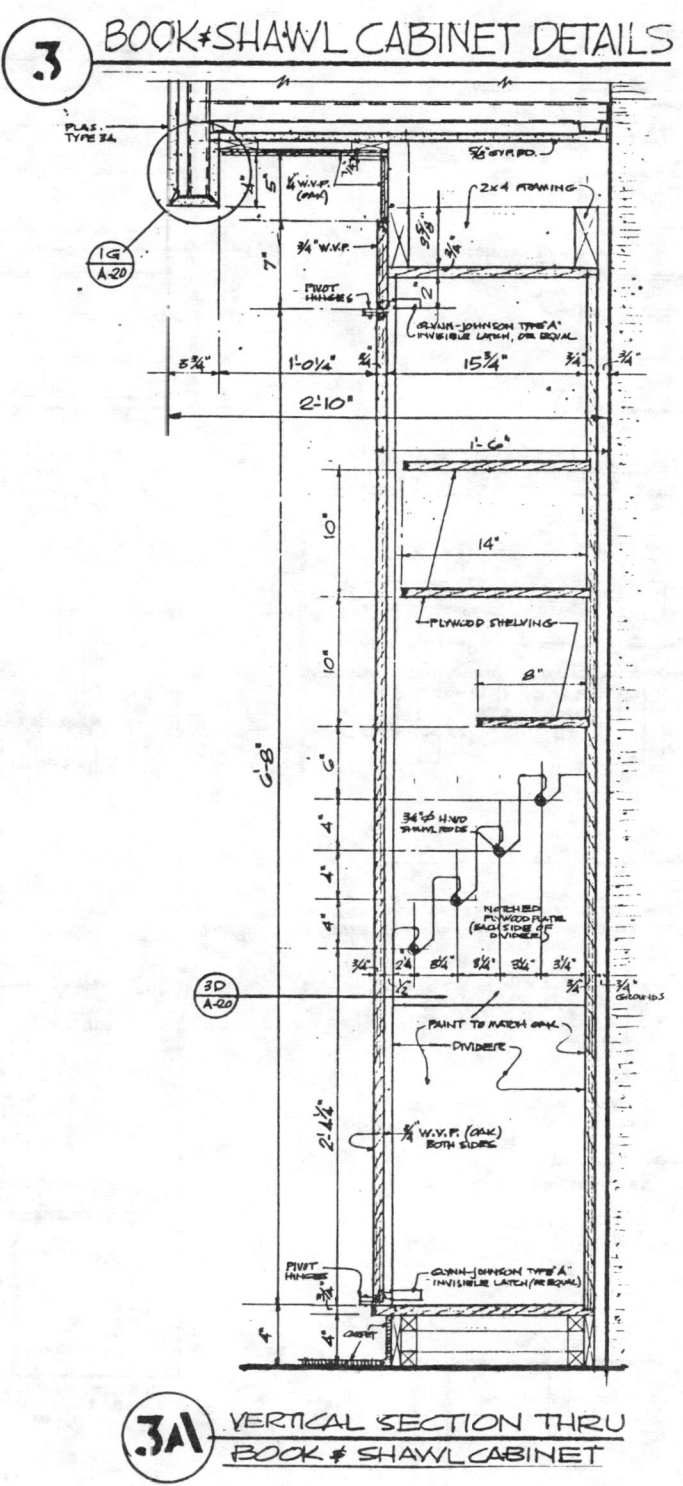

③ BOOK & SHAWL CABINET DETAILS

③A VERTICAL SECTION THRU
BOOK & SHAWL CABINET

Fig. 11 *(Continued)*

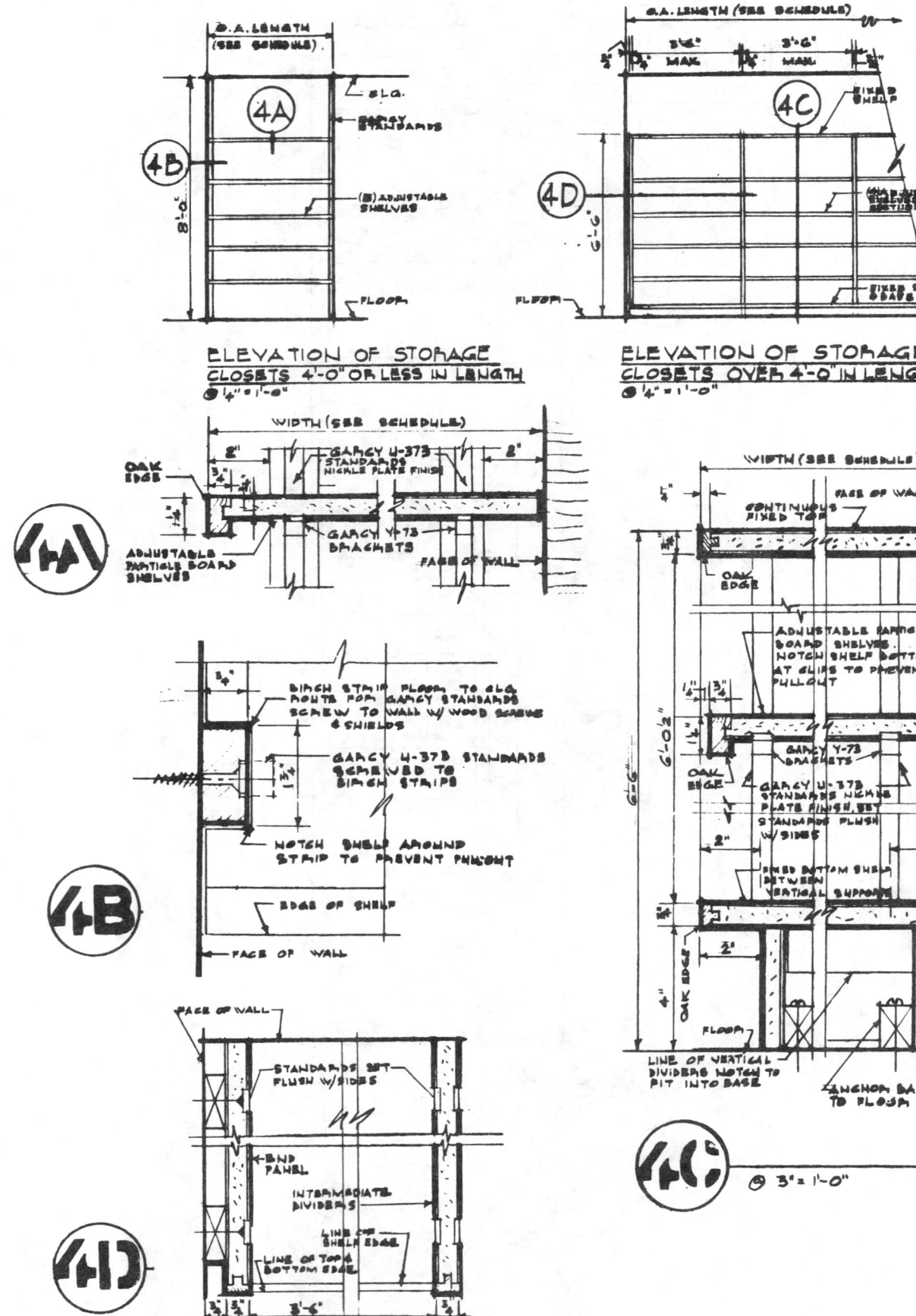

ELEVATION OF STORAGE
CLOSETS 4'-0" OR LESS IN LENGTH
@ ¼" = 1'-0"

ELEVATION OF STORAGE
CLOSETS OVER 4'-0" IN LENGTH
@ ¼" = 1'-0"

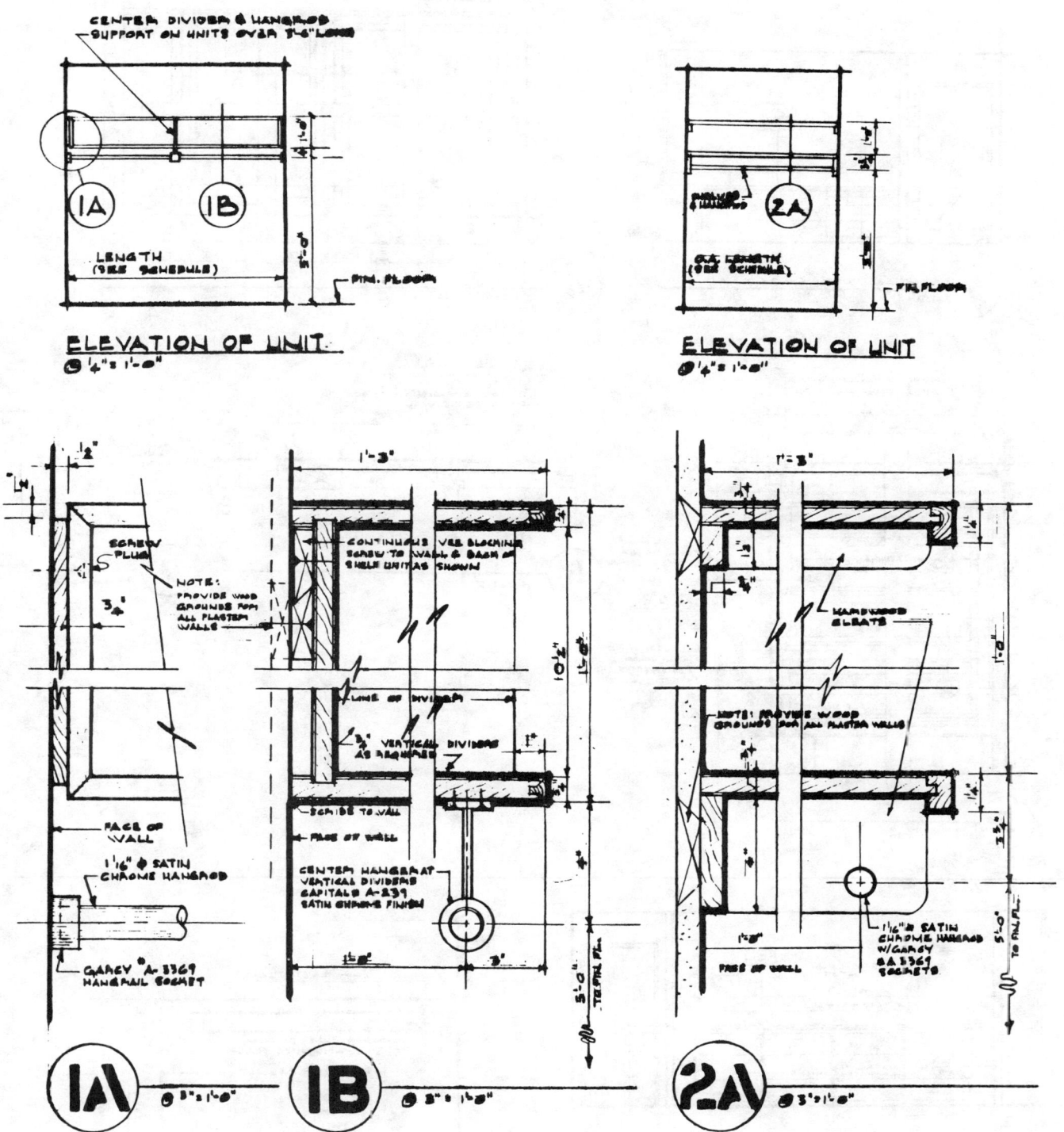

ELEVATION OF UNIT
@ 1/4" = 1'-0"

ELEVATION OF UNIT
@ 1/4" = 1'-0"

WOODWORK DETAILS

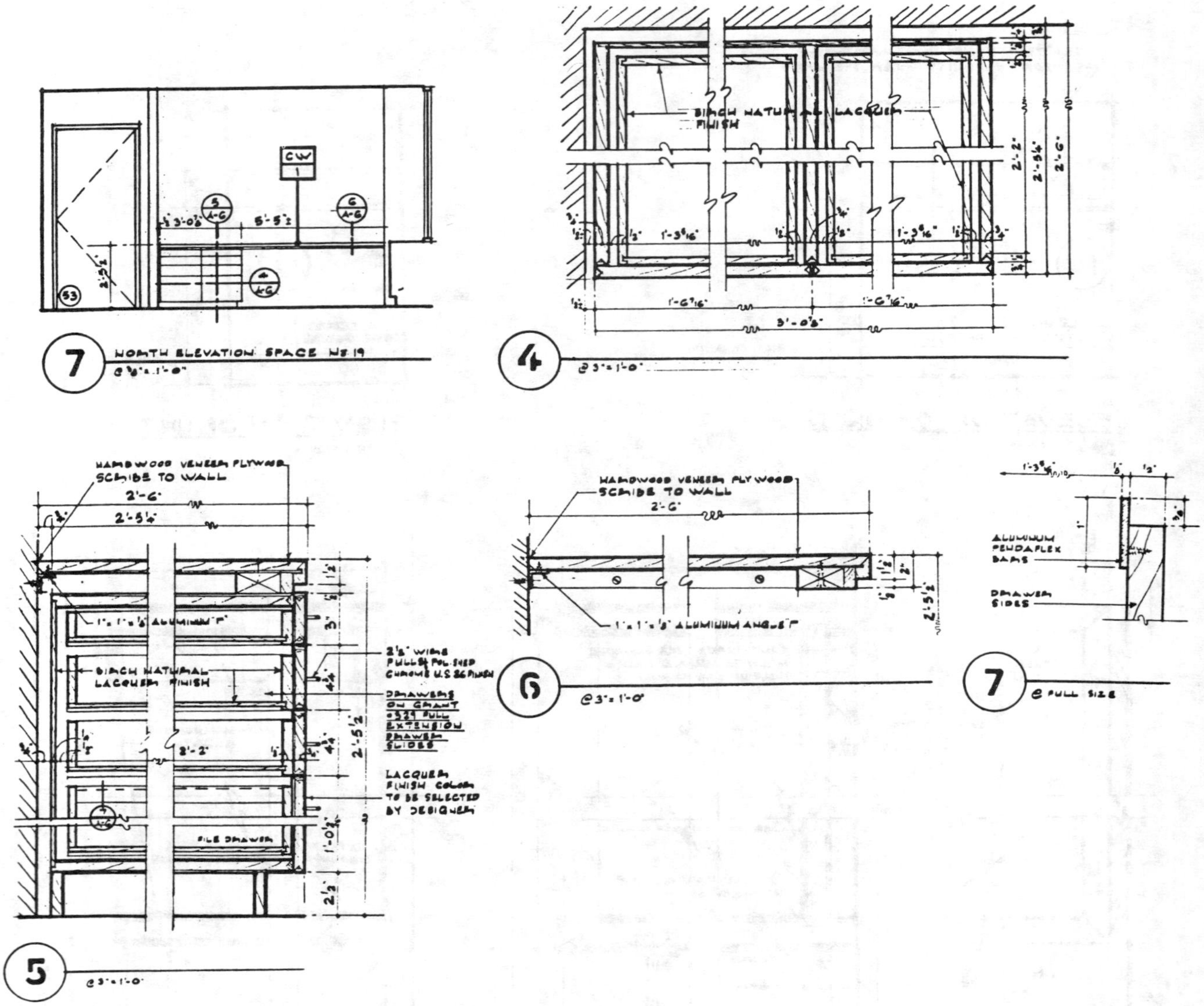

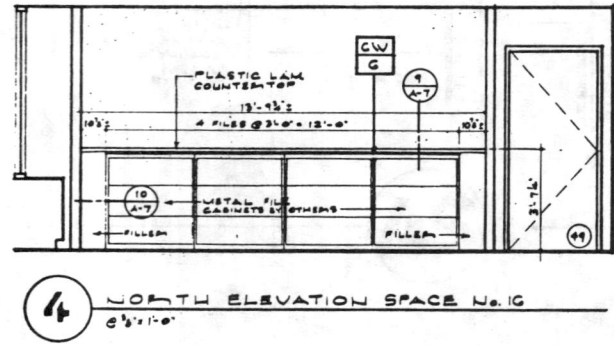

Fig. 12 Credenza.

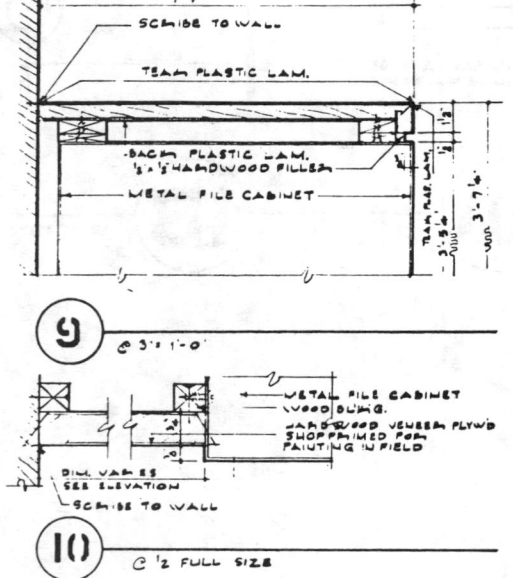

Fig. 13 File countertop.

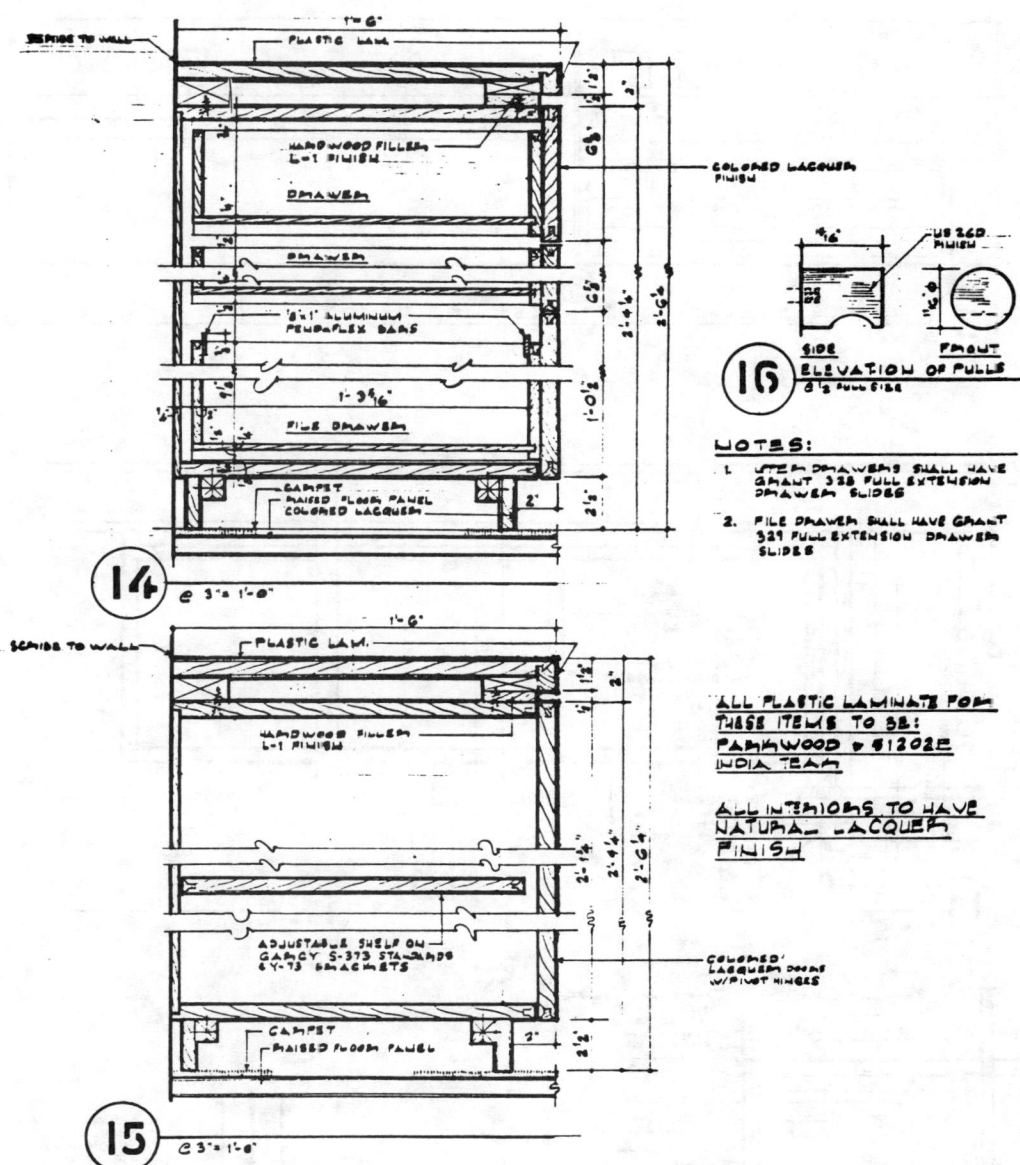

NOTES:

1. STEM DRAWERS SHALL HAVE GRANT 338 FULL EXTENSION DRAWER SLIDES

2. FILE DRAWER SHALL HAVE GRANT 329 FULL EXTENSION DRAWER SLIDES

ALL PLASTIC LAMINATE FOR THESE ITEMS TO BE:
PARKWOOD # 51202E
INDIA TEAK

ALL INTERIORS TO HAVE NATURAL LACQUER FINISH

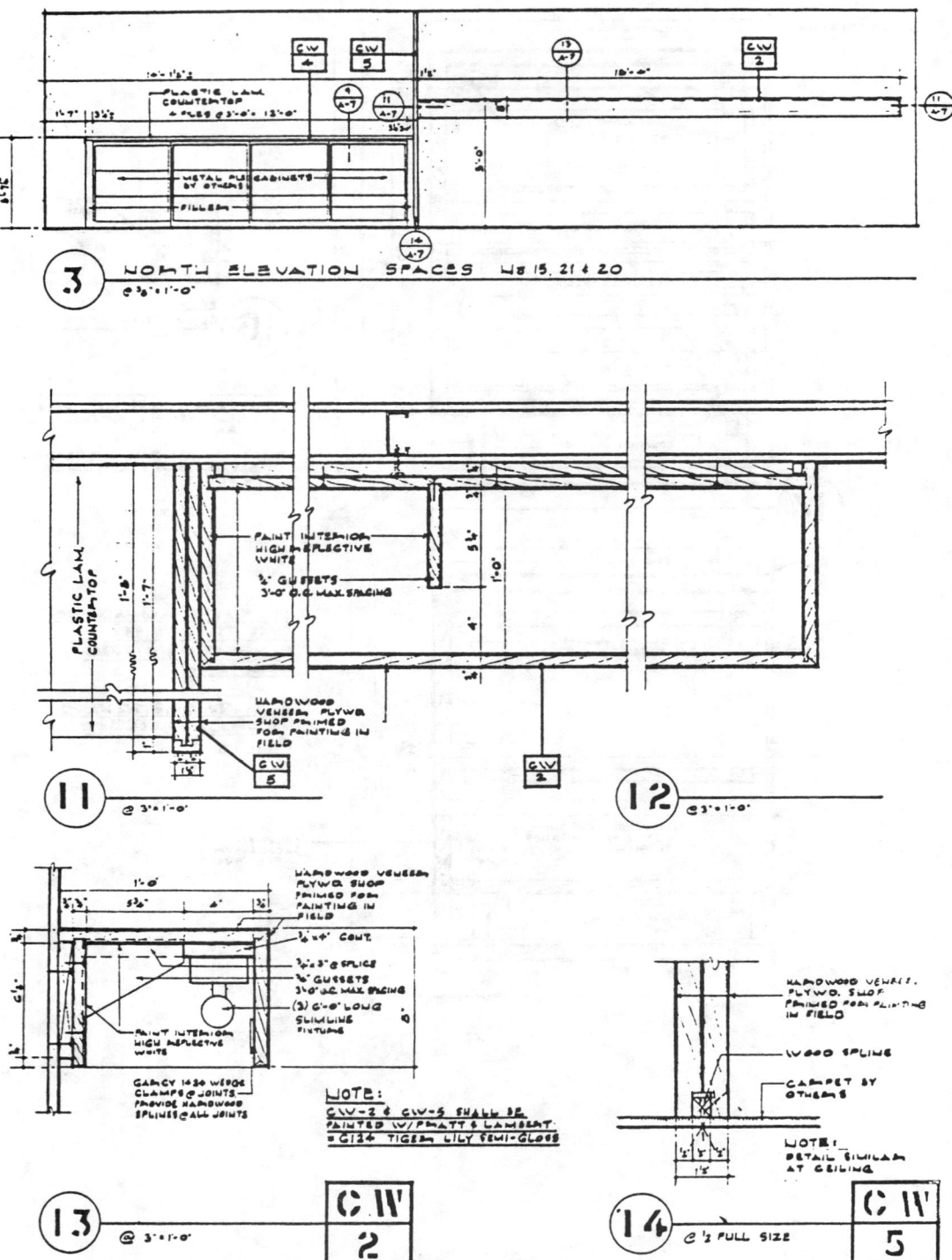

③ NORTH ELEVATION SPACES NS 15, 21 & 20
@ 3/8" = 1'-0"

⑪ @ 3" = 1'-0"

⑫ @ 3" = 1'-0"

NOTE:
CW-2 & CW-5 SHALL BE PAINTED W/PRATT & LAMBERT #6124 TIGER LILY SEMI-GLOSS

⑬ @ 3" = 1'-0"

⑭ @ 1/2 FULL SIZE

NOTE:
DETAIL SIMILAR AT CEILING

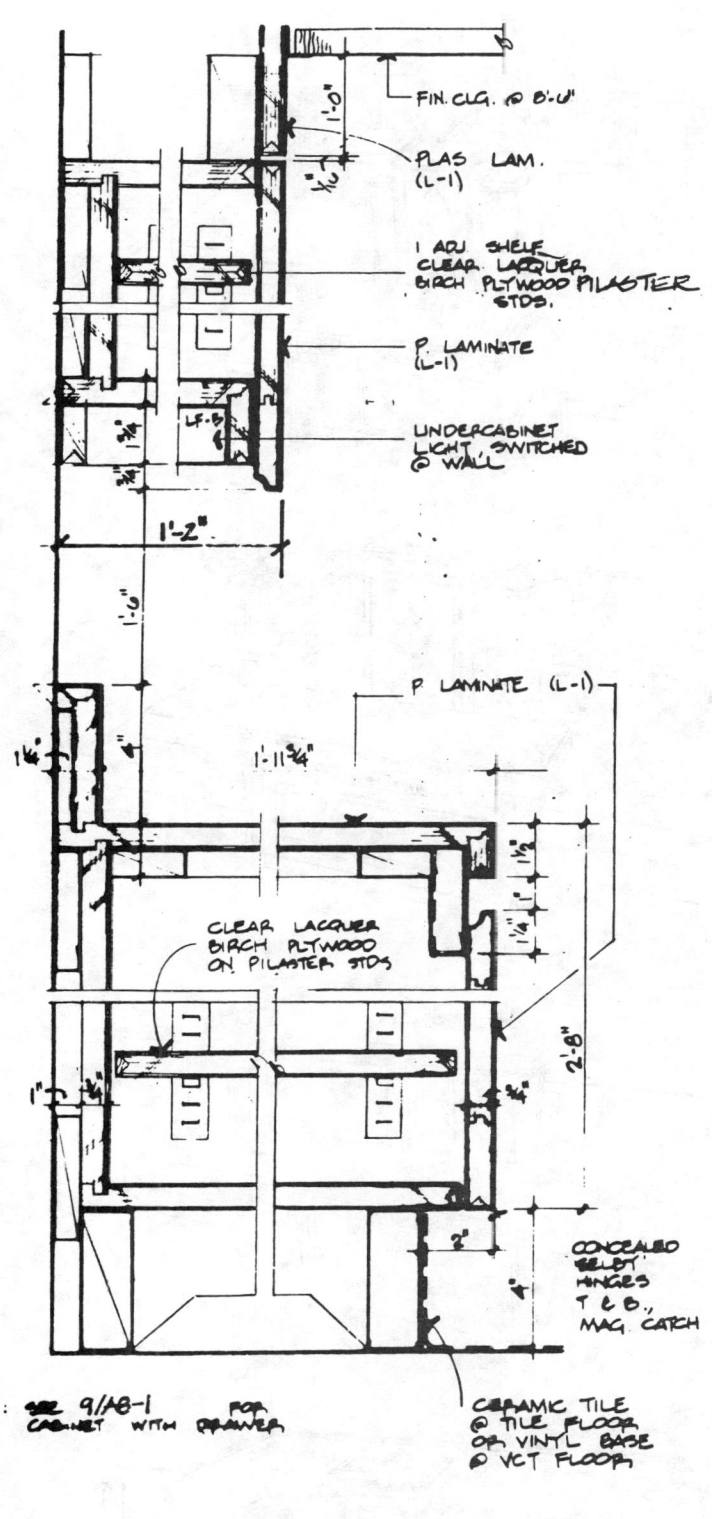

FIN. CLG. @ 8'-0"

PLAS LAM.
(L-1)

1 ADJ SHELF
CLEAR LACQUER
BIRCH PLYWOOD PILASTER
STDS.

P. LAMINATE
(L-1)

UNDERCABINET
LIGHT, SWITCHED
@ WALL

P LAMINATE (L-1)

CLEAR LACQUER
BIRCH PLYWOOD
ON PILASTER STDS

CONCEALED
ELBT
HINGES
T & B,
MAG CATCH

CERAMIC TILE
@ TILE FLOOR
OR VINYL BASE
@ VCT FLOOR

NOTE: SEE 9/A8-1 FOR
CABINET WITH DRAWER

PANTRY CABINETS

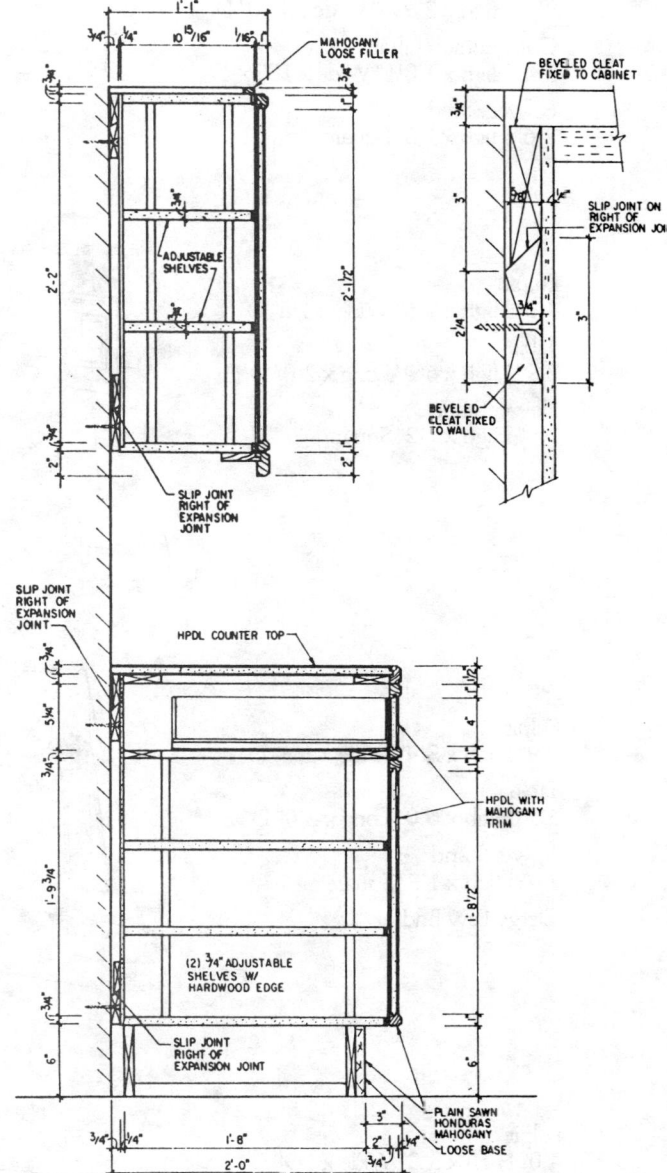

MAHOGANY LOOSE FILLER

ADJUSTABLE SHELVES

SLIP JOINT RIGHT OF EXPANSION JOINT

BEVELED CLEAT FIXED TO CABINET

SLIP JOINT ON RIGHT OF EXPANSION JOINT

BEVELED CLEAT FIXED TO WALL

SLIP JOINT RIGHT OF EXPANSION JOINT

HPDL COUNTER TOP

HPDL WITH MAHOGANY TRIM

(2) 3/4" ADJUSTABLE SHELVES W/ HARDWOOD EDGE

SLIP JOINT RIGHT OF EXPANSION JOINT

PLAIN SAWN HONDURAS MAHOGANY LOOSE BASE

VERTICAL SECTION - PANTRY CABINETS

Pulpit
3′9″ High x 3′6″ Wide x 1′8½″ D

Table
2′7″ High x 5′0″ Long x 2′ D

Center Pulpit Chair
4′ High x 2′2½″ Wide x 1′10″ D

Side Pulpit Chair
3′9″ High x 2′2½″ Wide x 1′10″ D

Communion Chair
3′4″ High x 1′8½″ Wide x 1′7½″ D

Flower Stand
2′6″ High x 1′3″ Square

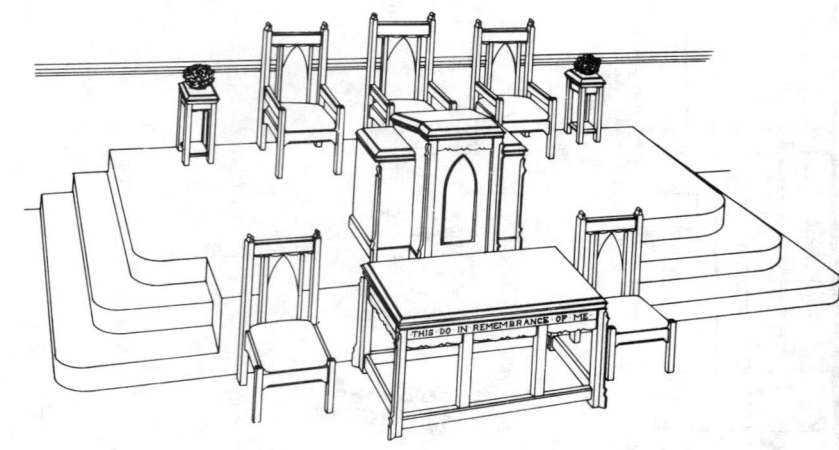

Pulpit
4′0″ High x 3′6″ Wide x 1′8″ D

Table
2′9″ High x 6′0″ Long x 2′0″ D

Flower Stand
2′0″ High x 1′2″ Square

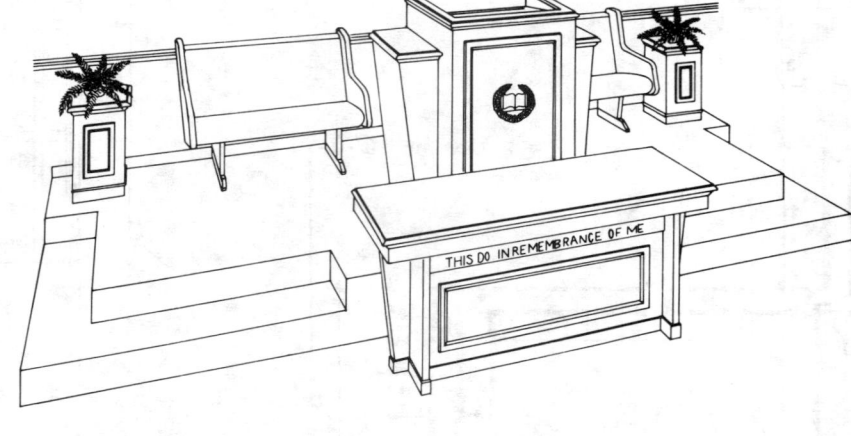

Pulpit
3′9″ High x 3′4″ Wide x 1′8″ D

Table
2′9″ High x 6′0″ Long x 2′0″ D

Flower Stand
2′0″ High x 1′2″ Square

Clergy Pew End

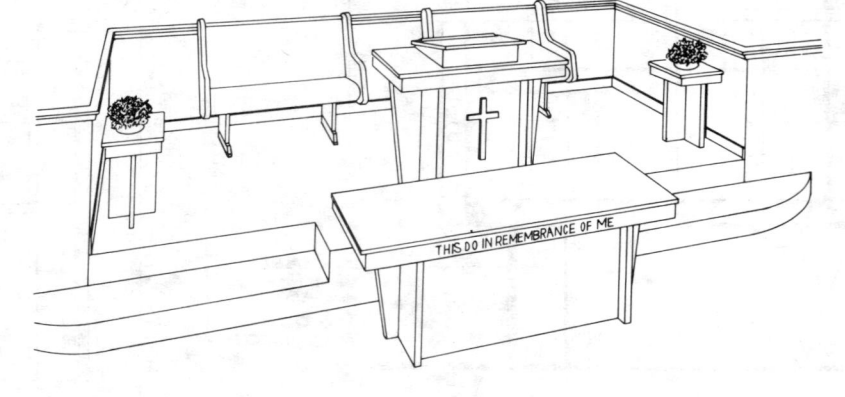

Pulpit
4′0″ High x 3′8″ Wide x 1′9″ D

Table
2′9″ High x 4′6″ Long x 2′0″ D

Flower Stand
2′0″ High x 1′2″ Square

Clergy Pew End

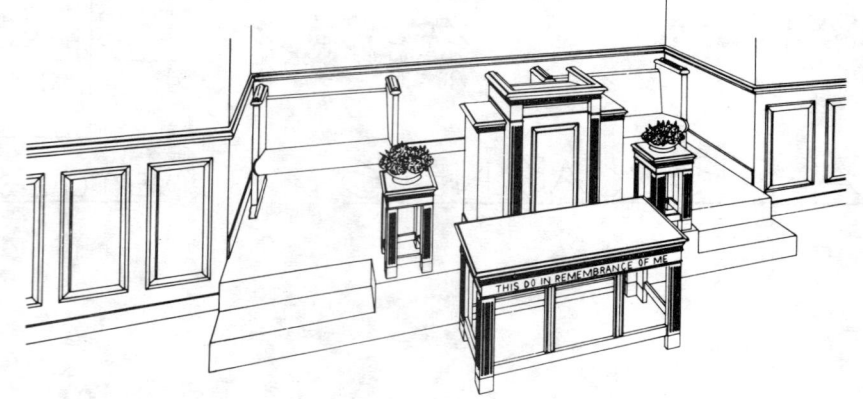

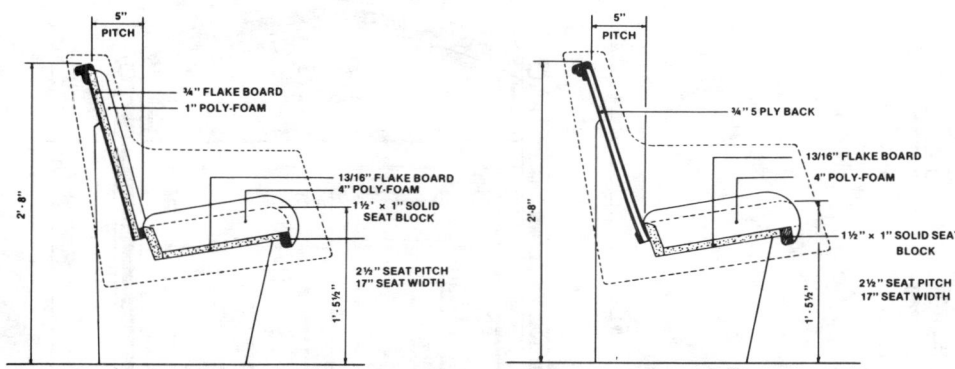

Fig. 15 Fully upholstered seat. All exposed surfaces of the seat and back are fully upholstered.

Cup holder

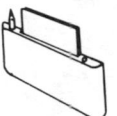

Card and
pencil holder

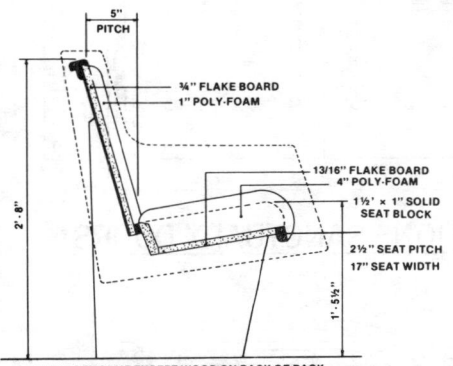

Fig. 16 Combination upholstered/wood seat. An upholstered seat with a wooden back (either solid or veneer laminate).

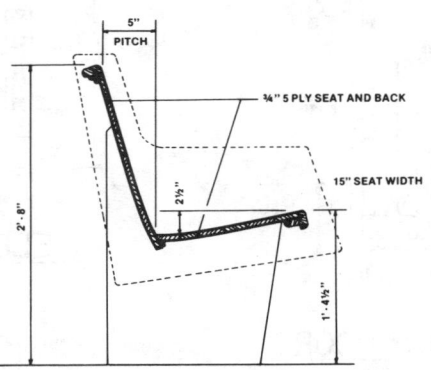

Fig. 17 All wood seat. Either solid wood or veneered seat and back. Generally the most expensive option. Wood seats and back can be contoured for increased comfort.

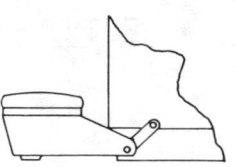

Wood, with bonded foam, upholstered pad

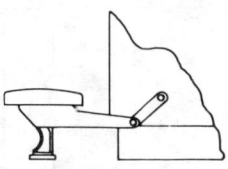

Metal, with bonded foam, upholstered pad

Fig. 18 Pew accessories.

Fig. 19 Screens are adaptable for many uses in the sanctuary. They serve as modesty screens in front of the first row of pews, or they can be adapted for use as communion rails, as choir boxes, or as wainscoating.

WOODWORK DETAILS

Sanctuary Doors and Miscellaneous Details

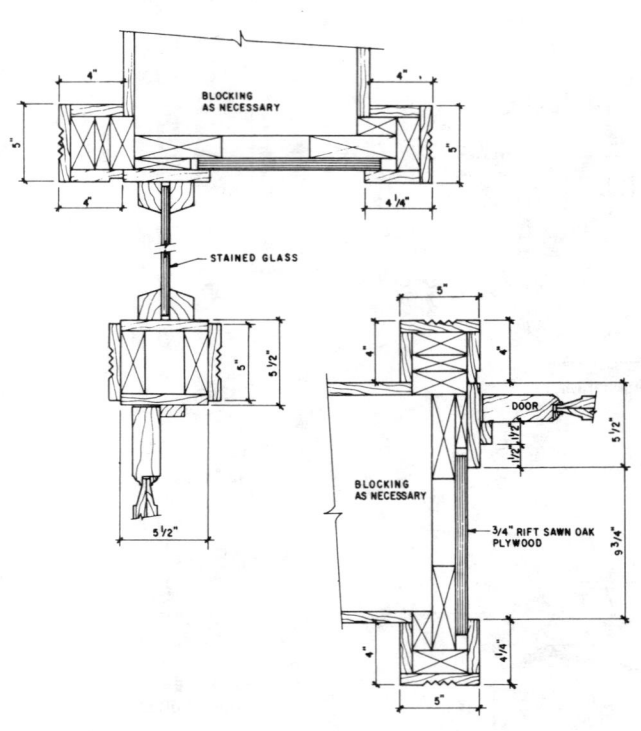

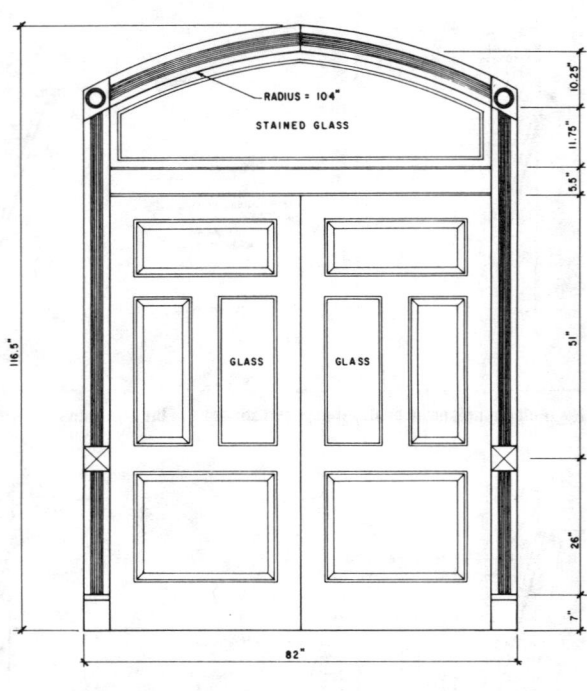

ELEVATION - SANCTUARY DOORS

SECTIONS - SANCTUARY DOORS

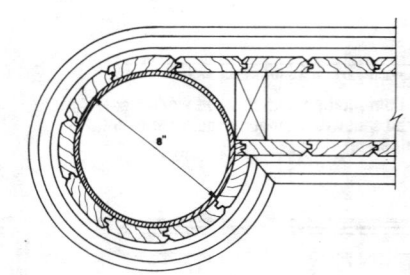

PLAN AT INTERSECTION
OF CHANCEL RAIL AND COLUMN

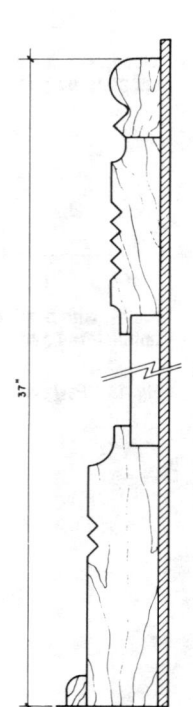

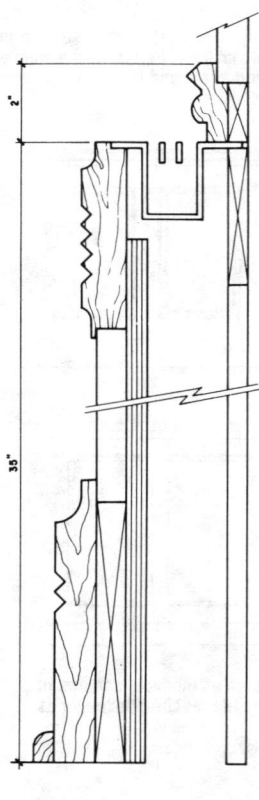

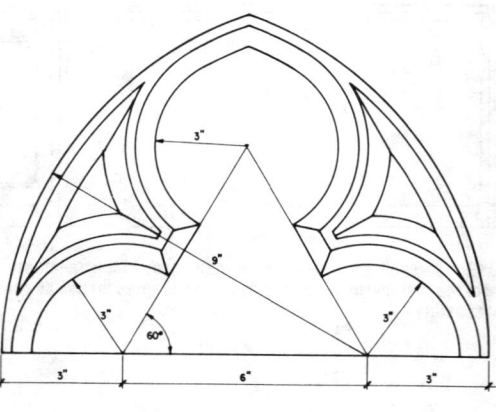

SECTION
AT SANCTUARY COLUMN

SECTION
AT WAINSCOT

TREFOIL LAYOUT

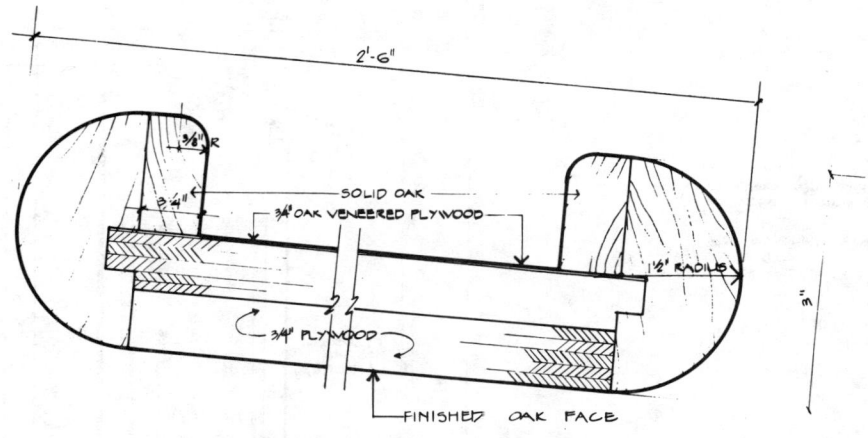

2'-6"

¾" R
3¾"
SOLID OAK
¾" OAK VENEERED PLYWOOD
1½" RADIUS
3"
¾" PLYWOOD
FINISHED OAK FACE

2 FULL SIZE SECTION THRU BIMAH TOP

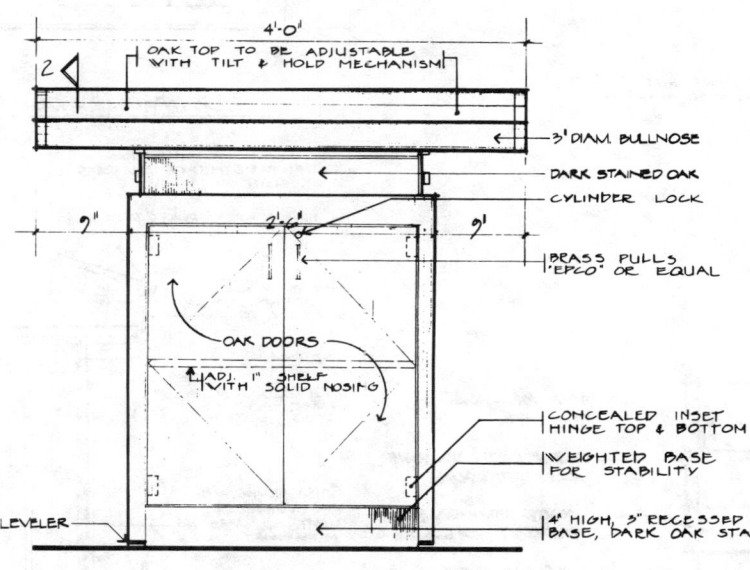

4'-0"

OAK TOP TO BE ADJUSTABLE WITH TILT & HOLD MECHANISM
3' DIAM. BULLNOSE
DARK STAINED OAK
CYLINDER LOCK
2'-6"
2"
9"
BRASS PULLS 'EPCO' OR EQUAL
OAK DOORS
ADJ. 1" SHELF WITH SOLID NOSING
CONCEALED INSET HINGE TOP & BOTTOM
WEIGHTED BASE FOR STABILITY
LEVELER
4" HIGH, 3" RECESSED BASE, DARK OAK STAIN

4 FRONT ELEVATION (EAST SIDE)
SCALE: 1½" = 1'-0"

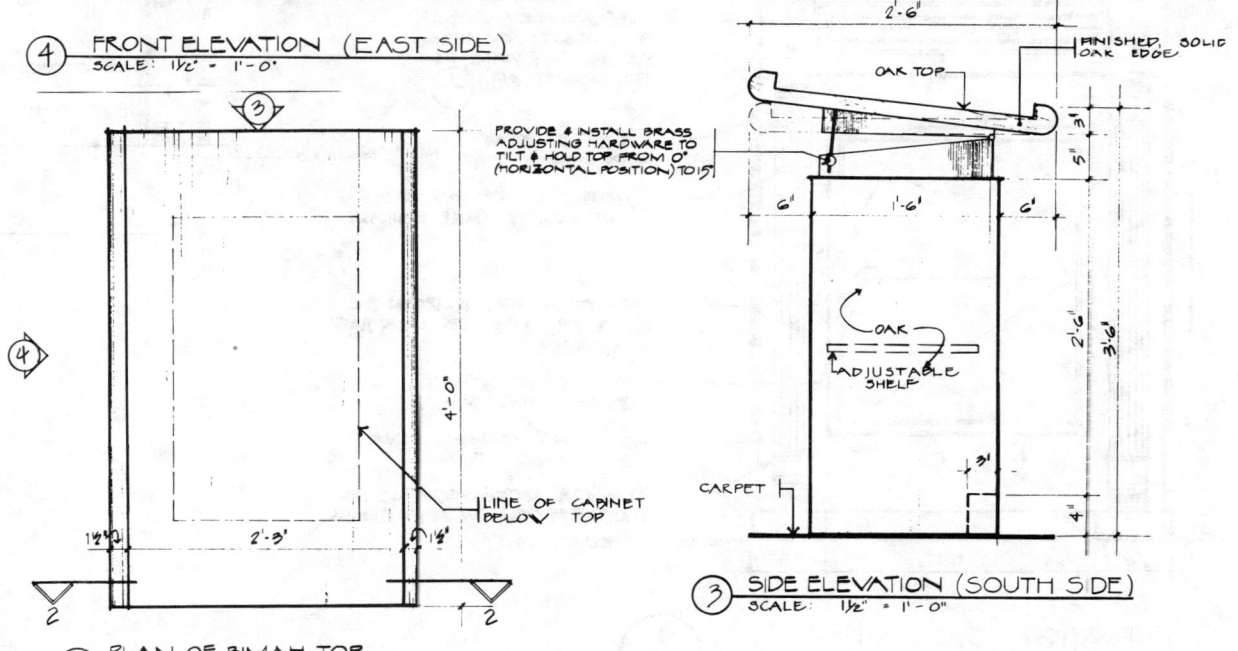

3

4

LINE OF CABINET BELOW TOP

4'-0"

1½" 2'-3" 1½"

1 PLAN OF BIMAH TOP
SCALE: 1½" = 1'-0"

2'-6"
OAK TOP
FINISHED SOLID OAK EDGE
3"
5"
PROVIDE & INSTALL BRASS ADJUSTING HARDWARE TO TILT & HOLD TOP FROM 0° (HORIZONTAL POSITION) TO 15°
6" 1'-6" 6"
OAK ADJUSTABLE SHELF
2'-6"
3'-6"
CARPET
3"
4"

3 SIDE ELEVATION (SOUTH SIDE)
SCALE: 1½" = 1'-0"

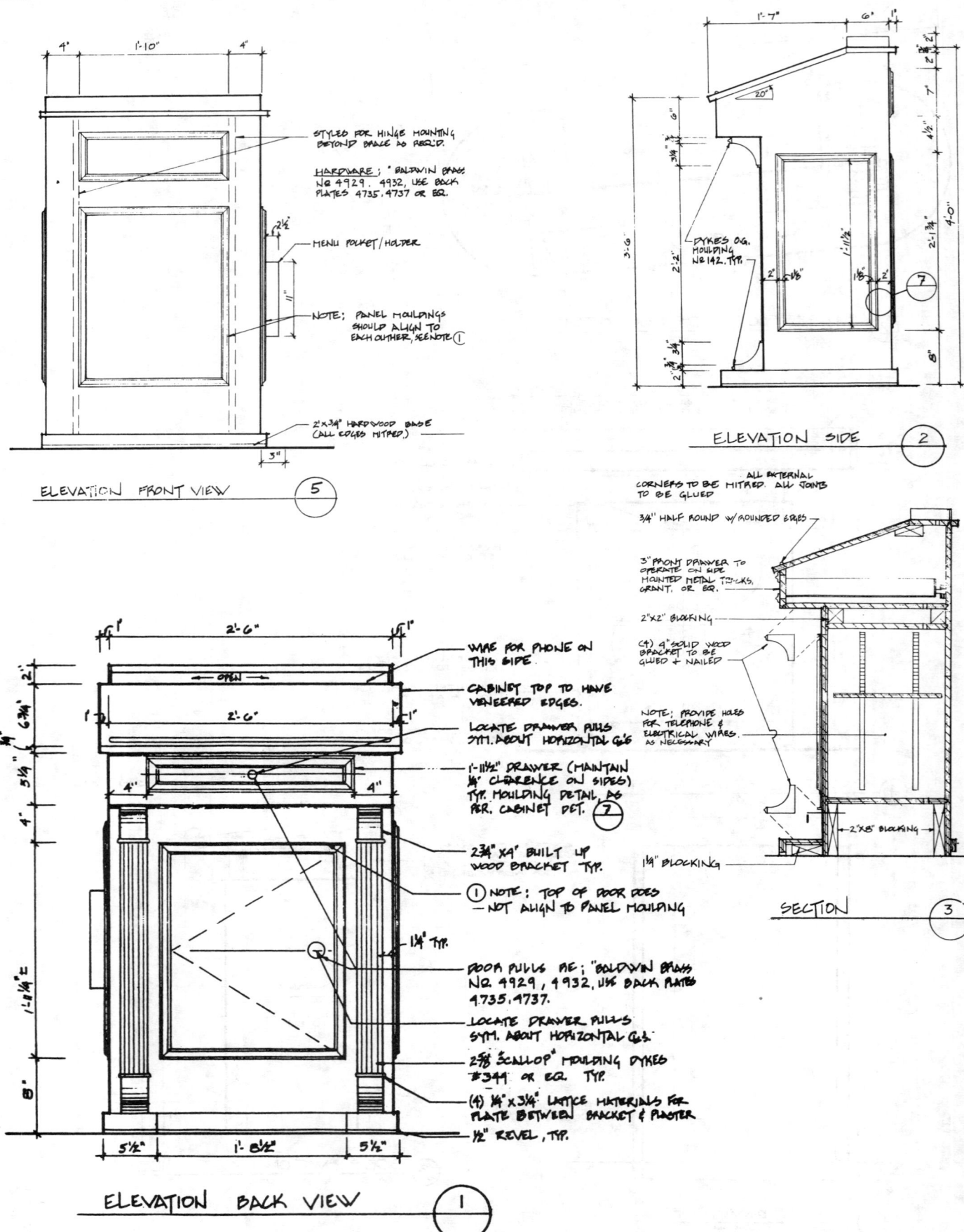

STYLED FOR HINGE MOUNTING BEYOND BRACE AS REQ'D.

HARDWARE; "BALDWIN BRASS No 4929 . 4932 . USE BACK PLATES 4735, 4737 OR EQ.

MENU POCKET/HOLDER

NOTE; PANEL MOULDINGS SHOULD ALIGN TO EACH OTHER, SEE NOTE ①

2"x3¾" HARDWOOD BASE (ALL EDGES MITRED.)

ELEVATION   FRONT VIEW   5

ELEVATION   SIDE   2

DYKES O.G. MOULDING No 142. TYP.

ALL EXTERNAL CORNERS TO BE MITRED. ALL JOINTS TO BE GLUED

¾" HALF ROUND w/ ROUNDED EDGES

3" FRONT DRAWER TO OPERATE ON SIDE MOUNTED METAL TRACKS, GRANT, OR EQ.

2"x2" BLOCKING

(4) 9" SOLID WOOD BRACKET TO BE GLUED & NAILED

NOTE; PROVIDE HOLES FOR TELEPHONE & ELECTRICAL WIRES AS NECESSARY

2"x8" BLOCKING

1¾" BLOCKING

SECTION   3

WIRE FOR PHONE ON THIS SIDE.

CABINET TOP TO HAVE VENEERED EDGES.

LOCATE DRAWER PULLS SYM. ABOUT HORIZONTAL C/L

1'-11½" DRAWER (MAINTAIN ¼" CLEARANCE ON SIDES) TYP. MOULDING DETAIL AS PER CABINET DET. ⑦

2¾" X4" BUILT UP WOOD BRACKET TYP.

① NOTE: TOP OF DOOR DOES NOT ALIGN TO PANEL MOULDING

1¼" TYP.

DOOR PULLS ARE; "BALDWIN BRASS No. 4929, 4932. USE BACK PLATES 4.735. 4737.

LOCATE DRAWER PULLS SYM. ABOUT HORIZONTAL C/L

2⅝" "SCALLOP" MOULDING DYKES #344 OR EQ. TYP.

(4) ¼" X 3¾" LATTICE MATERIALS FOR PLATE BETWEEN BRACKET & PILASTER

½" REVEL, TYP.

OPEN

ELEVATION   BACK VIEW   ①

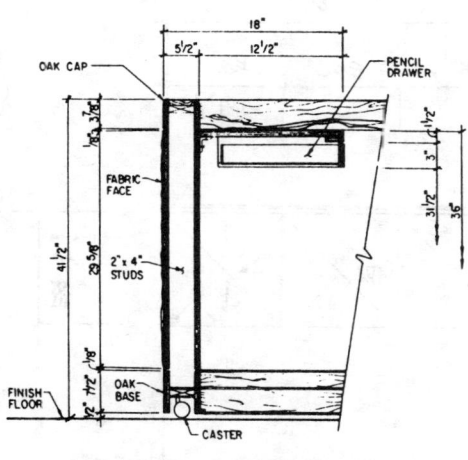

OAK CAP

PENCIL DRAWER

FABRIC FACE

2" x 4" STUDS

FINISH FLOOR

OAK BASE

CASTER

SECTION VIEW THRU LECTERN STANDS

OAK CAPPING

COUNTER TOP W/ 4½" APRON

PENCIL DRAWER

PLAN VIEW OF LECTERN STANDS

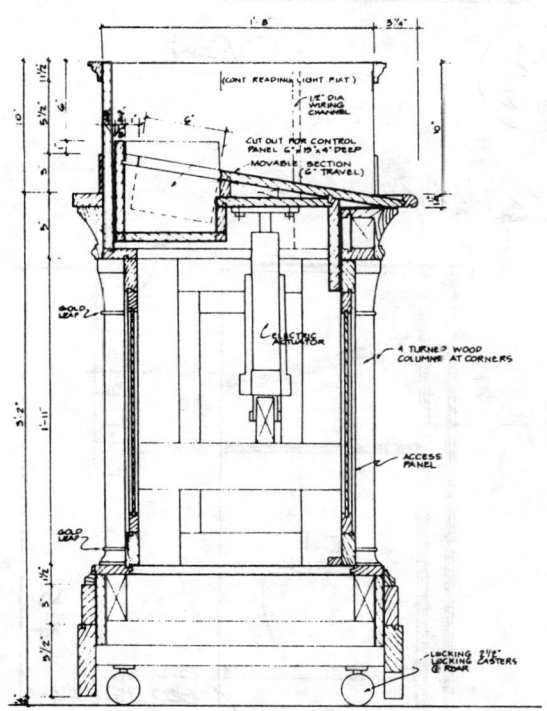

(CONT READING LIGHT FIXT)

1½" DIA WIRING CHANNEL

CUT OUT FOR CONTROL PANEL 6"x 19"x 4" DEEP

MOVABLE SECTION (6" TRAVEL)

GOLD LEAF

ELECTRIC ELEVATOR

4 TURNED WOOD COLUMNS AT CORNERS

ACCESS PANEL

GOLD LEAF

LOCKING CASTERS @ REAR

CROSS SECTION @ PODIUM

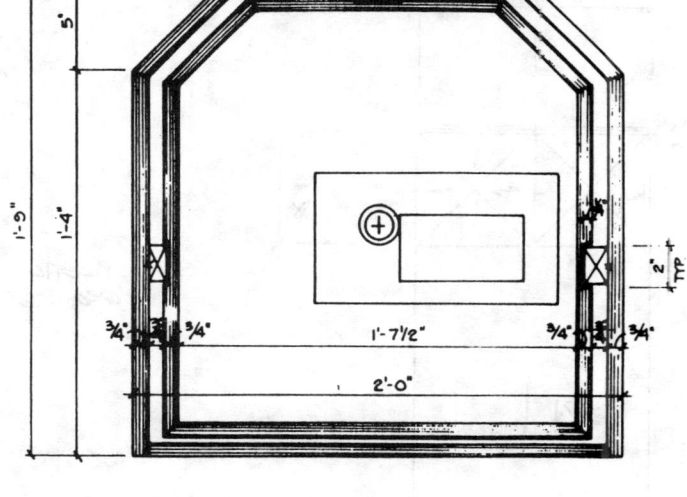

PLAN SECTION

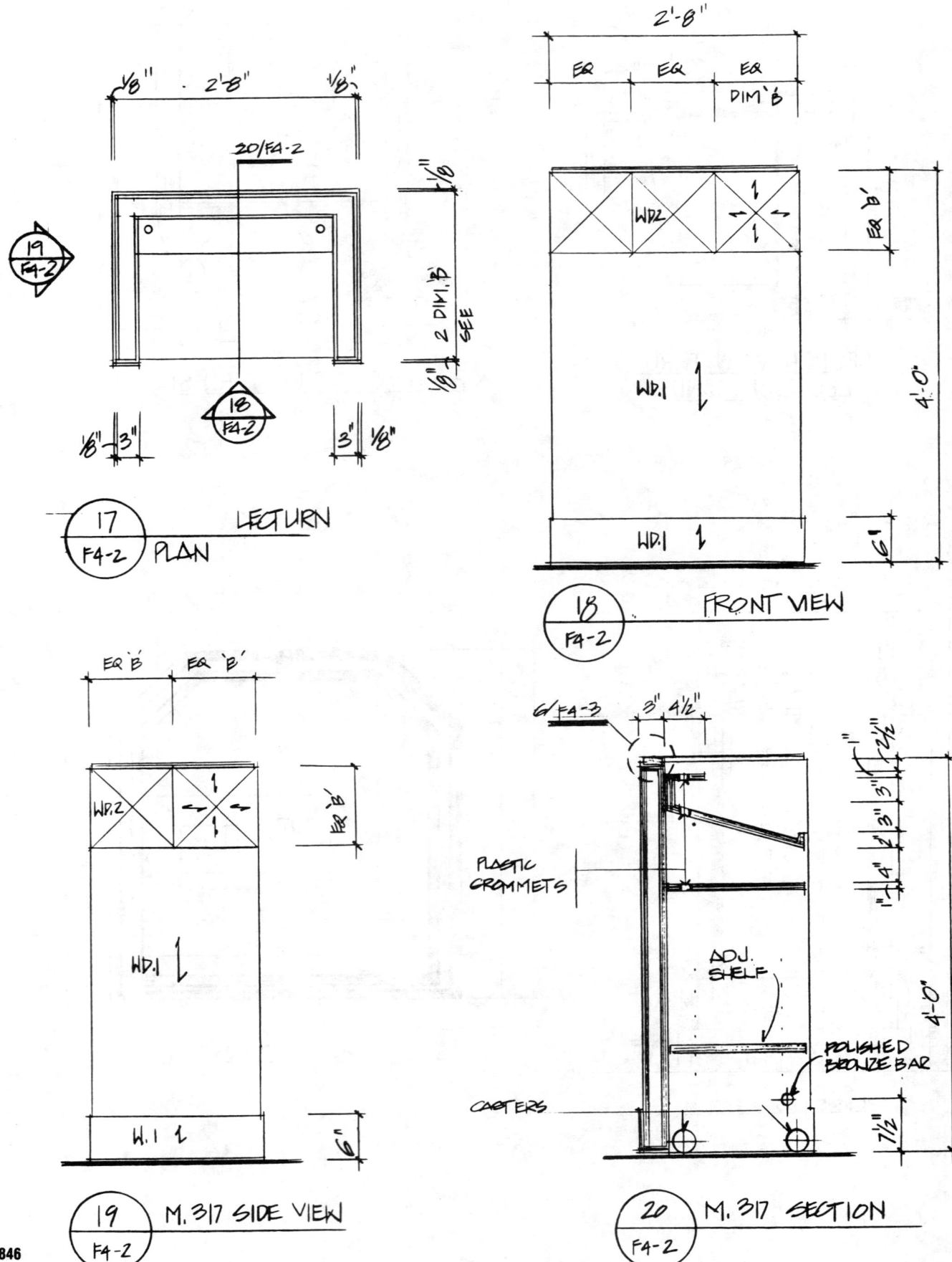

⌀1/8"   2'-8"   1/8"

20/F4-2

19
F4-2

18
F4-2

1/8" 3"   3" 1/8"

1/8" 2 DIM 'B' SEE

17
F4-2   LECTERN PLAN

2'-8"

EQ   EQ   EQ
DIM 'B'

WD2   1 ↕

EQ 'B'

WD.1 ↕

4'-0"

WD.1 ↕

6"

18
F4-2   FRONT VIEW

EQ 'B'   EQ 'B'

WD.2   1 ↕ →

EQ 'B'

WD.1 ↕

W.1 ↕

6"

19
F4-2   M.317 SIDE VIEW

6/F4-3   3" 4½"

PLASTIC GROMMETS

ADJ. SHELF

CASTERS

POLISHED BRONZE BAR

1" 4" 1" 3" 3" 2½"

4'-0"

7½"

20
F4-2   M.317 SECTION

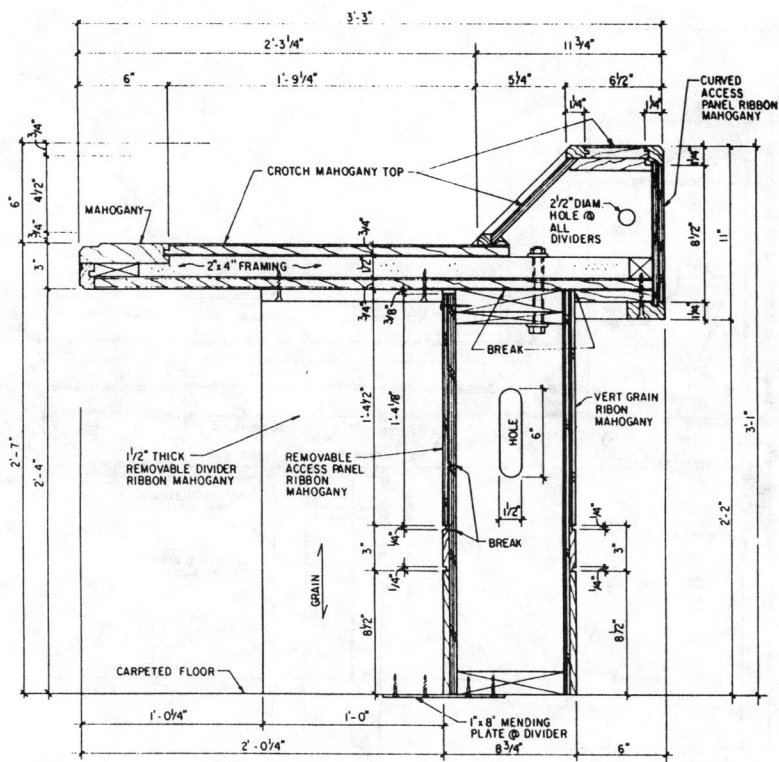

VERTICAL SECTION-BOARDROOM TABLE

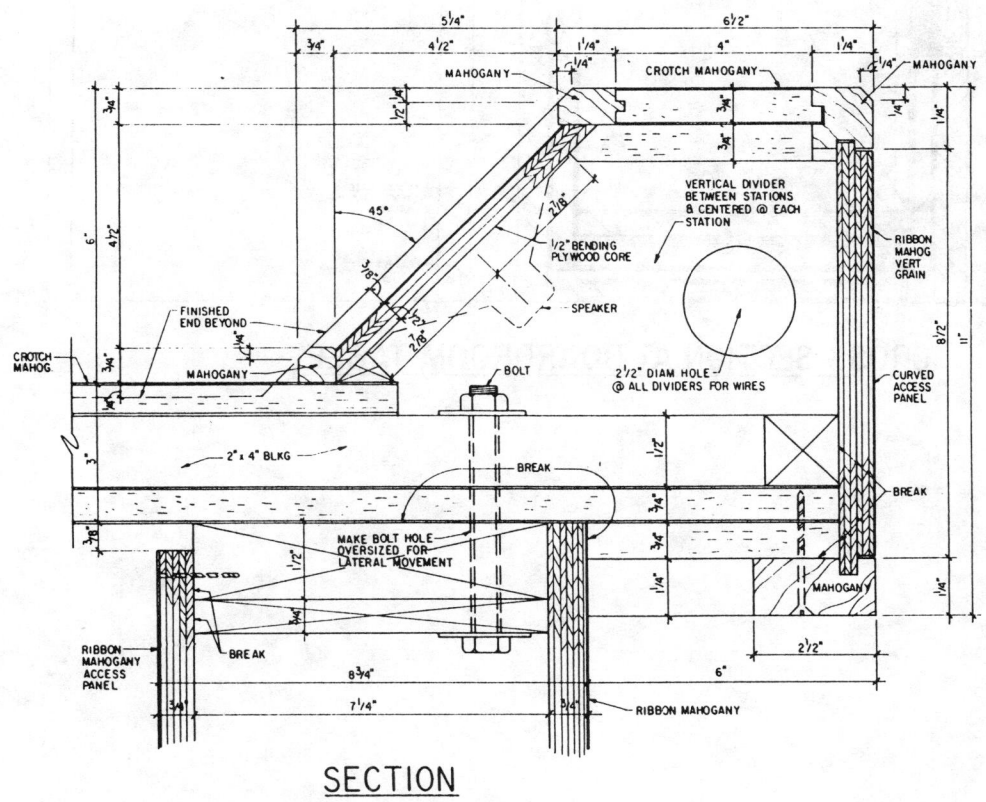

SECTION

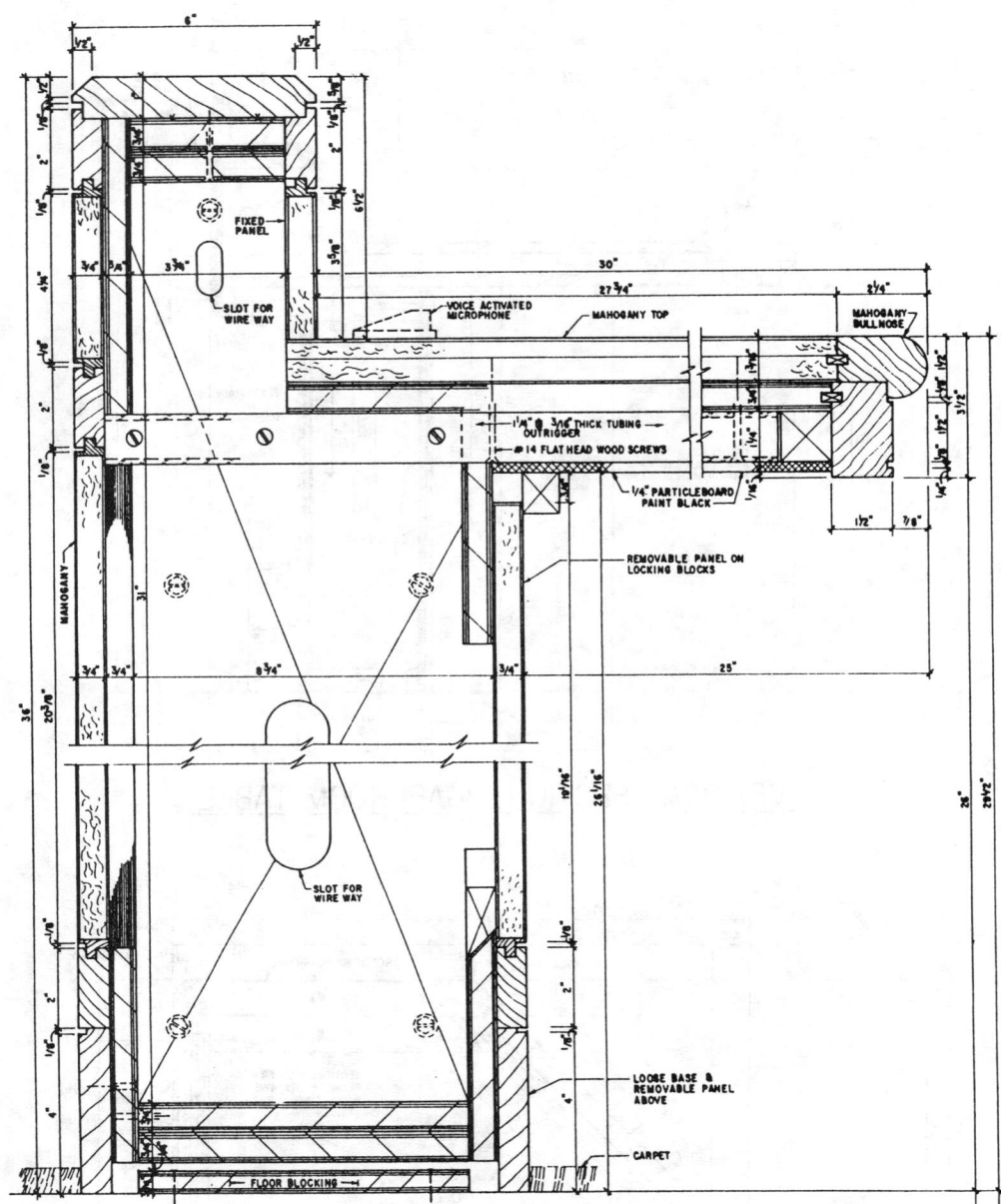

CROSS SECTION AT BOARDROOM TABLE

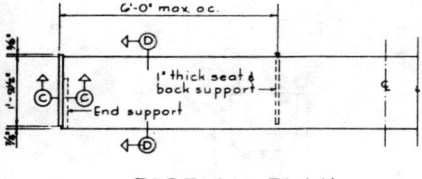

6'-0" max. o.c.

1" thick seat &
back support

End support

PARTIAL PLAN
OF BENCH

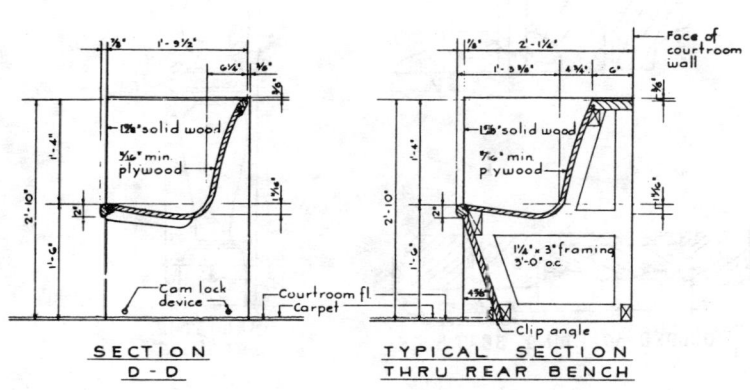

1'-9½"

6½"

1⅝" solid wood

⁷⁄₁₆" min.
plywood

1'-4"

2'-10"

1'-6"

Cam lock
device

SECTION
D-D

Face of
courtroom
wall

2'-1½"

1'-3¾"

4¾"

6"

1⅝" solid wood

⁷⁄₁₆" min
plywood

1¼" x 3" framing
5'-0" o.c.

1'-4"

2'-10"

1'-6"

2"

Courtroom fl.
Carpet

Clip angle

4⅝"

TYPICAL SECTION
THRU REAR BENCH

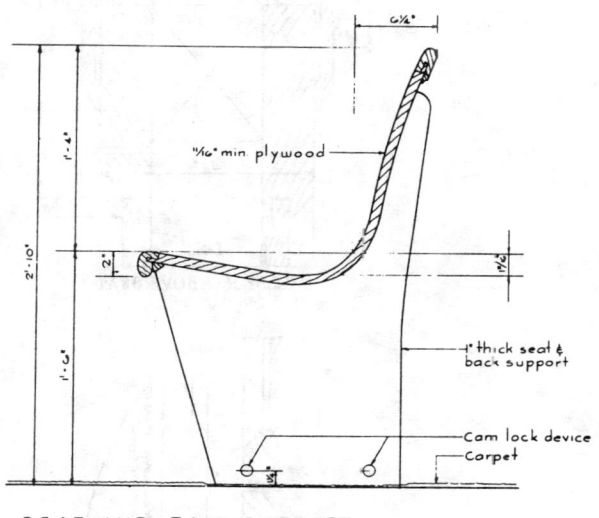

6½"

2'-10"

1'-4"

1'-6"

⁷⁄₁₆" min plywood

2"

1" thick seat &
back support

Cam lock device

Carpet

SEAT AND BACK SUPPORT

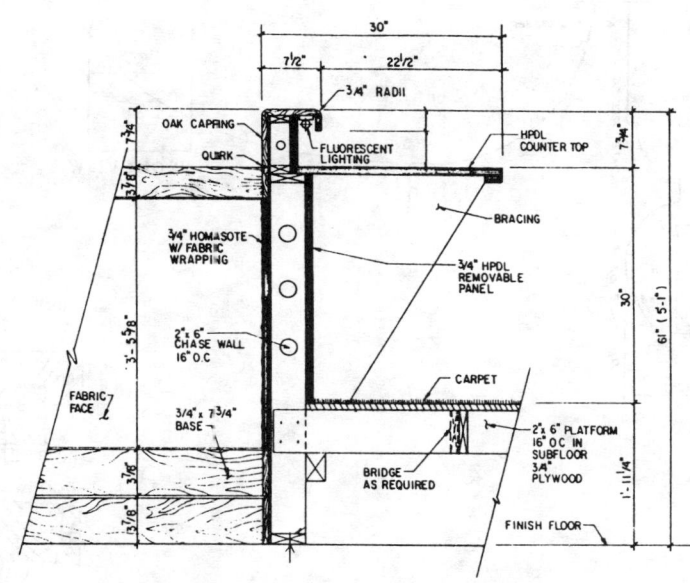

30"

7½"

22½"

3/4" RADII

OAK CAPPING

QUIRK

FLUORESCENT
LIGHTING

HPDL
COUNTER TOP

BRACING

3/4" HOMASOTE
W/ FABRIC
WRAPPING

3/4" HPDL
REMOVABLE
PANEL

2" x 6"
CHASE WALL
16" O.C.

FABRIC
FACE

3/4" x 7¾"
BASE

CARPET

BRIDGE
AS REQUIRED

2" x 6" PLATFORM
16" O.C. IN
SUBFLOOR
3/4"
PLYWOOD

FINISH FLOOR

30"

61' (5'-1")

1'-11¼"

3'-5⅝"

7¾"

3⅝"

3⅝"

3⅝"

SECTION THRU JUDGES BENCH

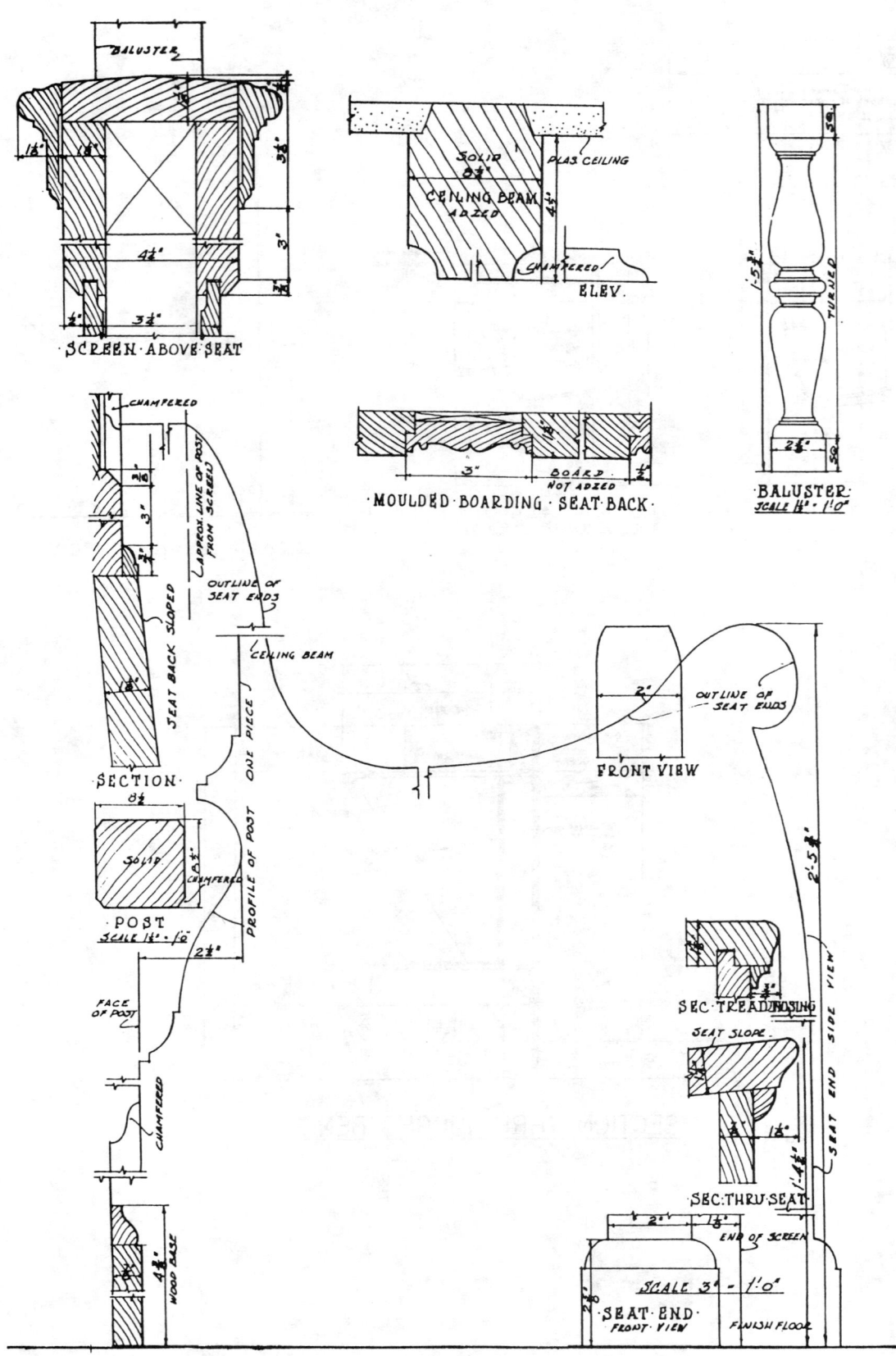

SCREEN·ABOVE·SEAT

ELEV.

MOULDED·BOARDING·SEAT·BACK

BALUSTER
SCALE 1½" = 1'0"

SECTION

POST
SCALE 1½" = 1'0"

FRONT VIEW

SEC·TREAD NOSING

SEC·THRU·SEAT

SEAT·END
FRONT·VIEW

SCALE 3" = 1'0"

DETAIL·OF·STAIR·SCREEN·&·SEAT·MAIN·HALL·

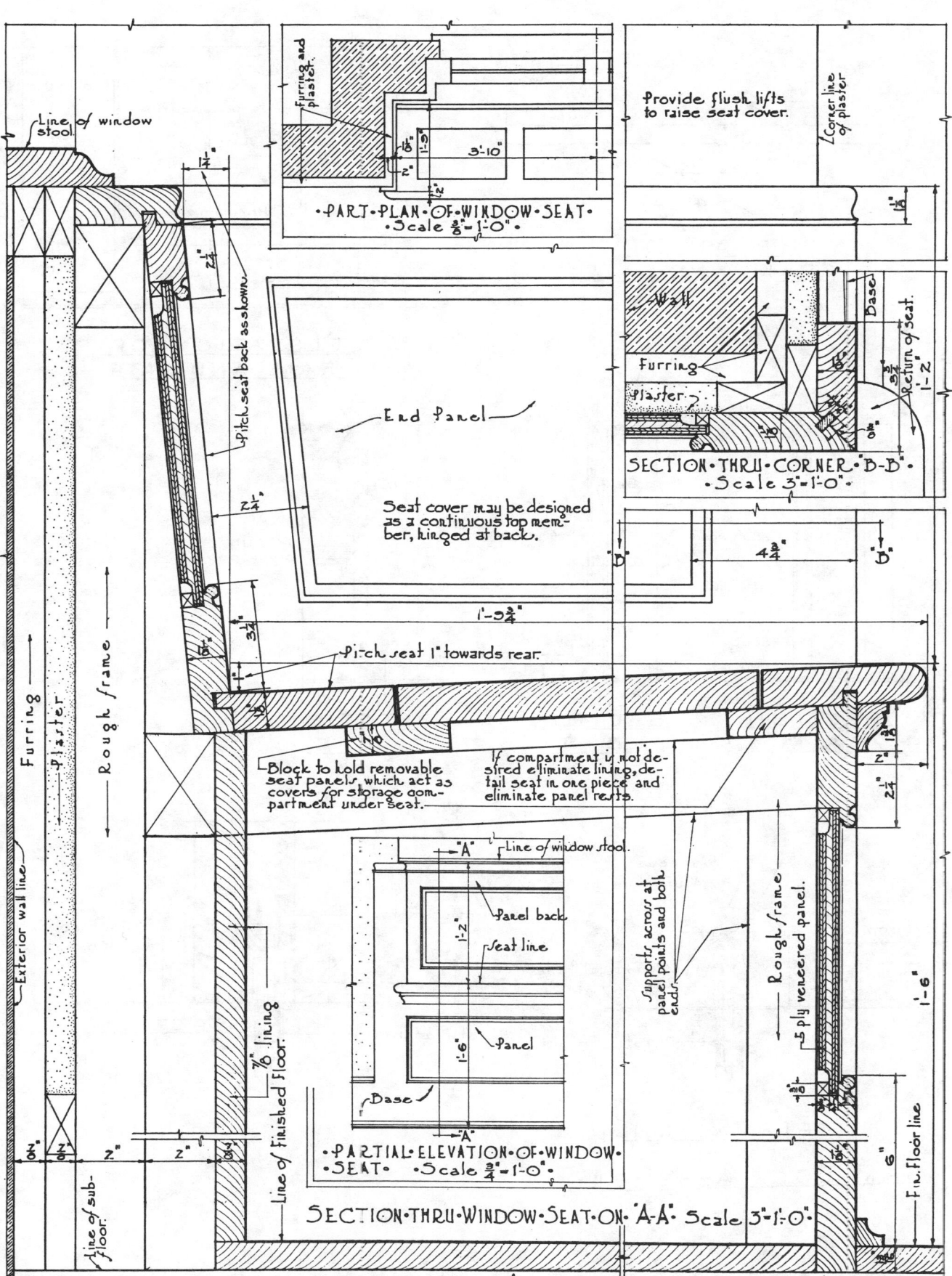

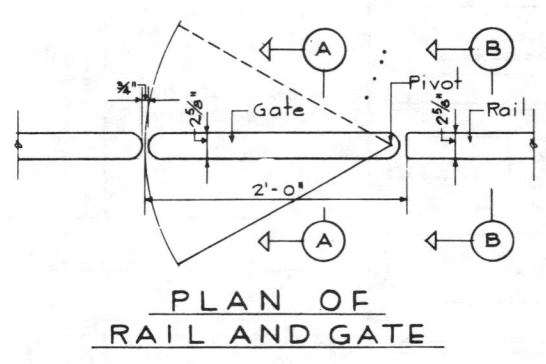

PLAN OF
RAIL AND GATE

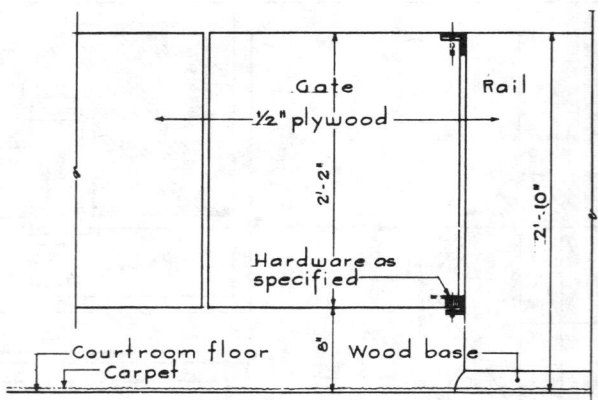

ELEVATION OF
RAIL AND GATE

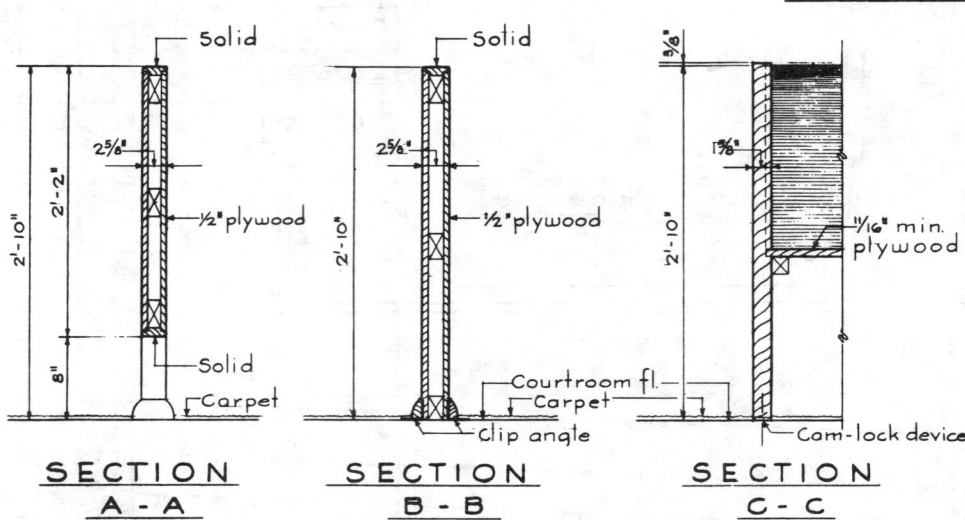

SECTION
A - A

SECTION
B - B

SECTION
C - C

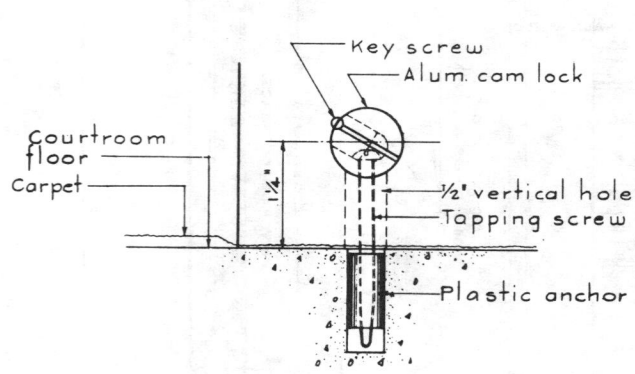

ELEVATION

CAM LOCK ASSEMBLY

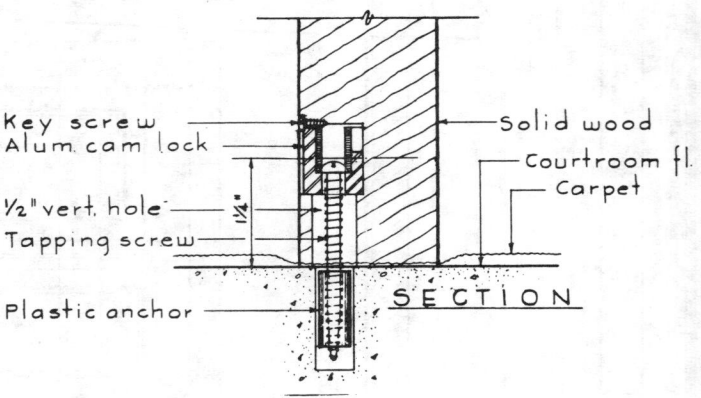

SECTION

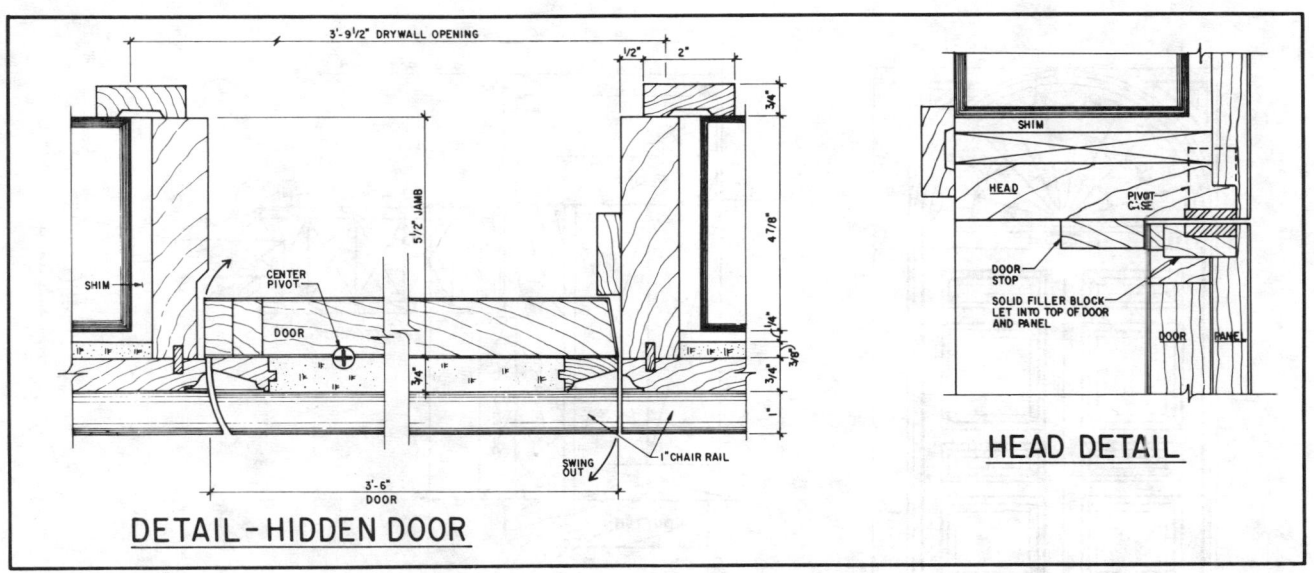

DETAIL-HIDDEN DOOR

HEAD DETAIL

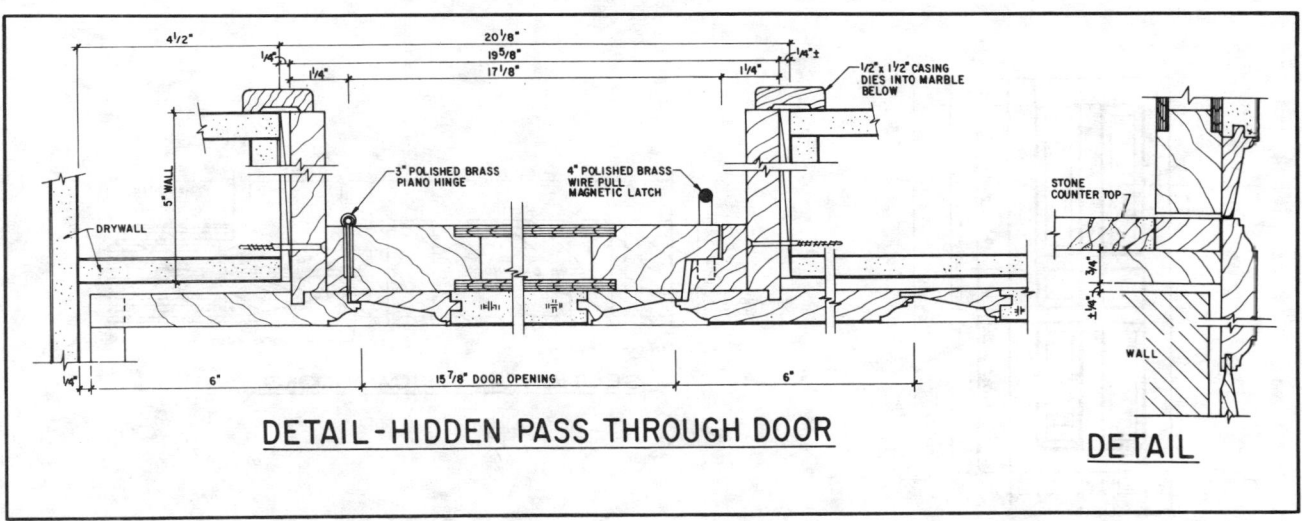

DETAIL-HIDDEN PASS THROUGH DOOR

DETAIL

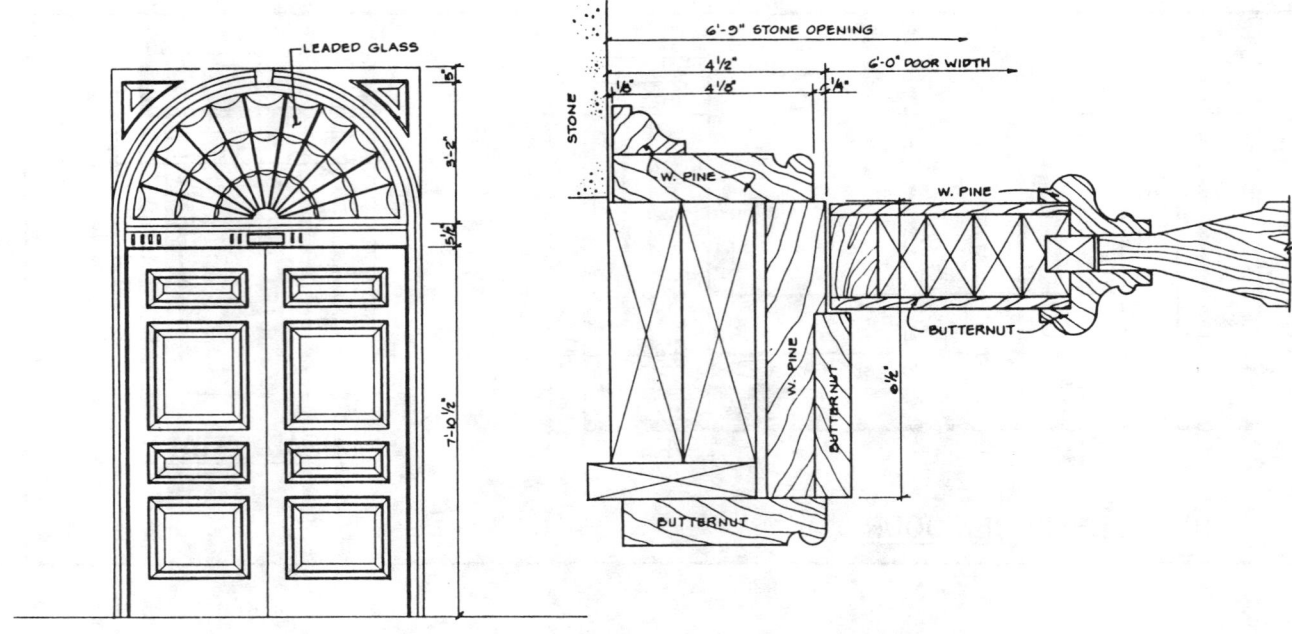

ELEVATION—FRONT ENTRY

JAMB DETAIL AT ENTRY

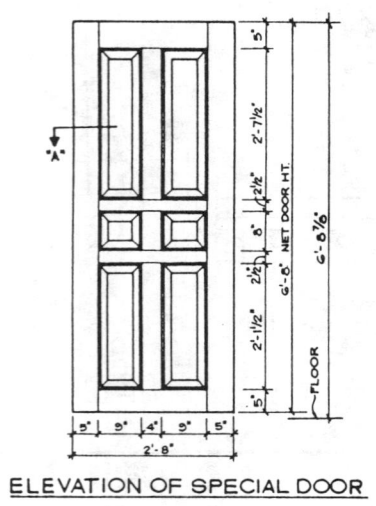

ELEVATION OF SPECIAL DOOR

SECTION "A" TYPICAL DOORS

JAMB DETAIL AND DOOR DETAIL

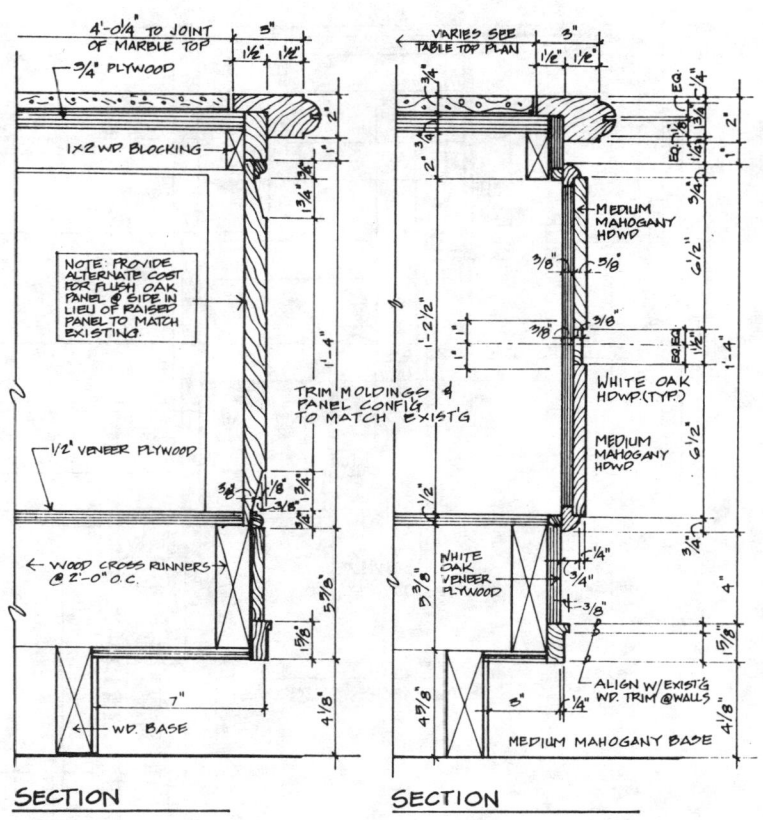

SECTION

SECTION

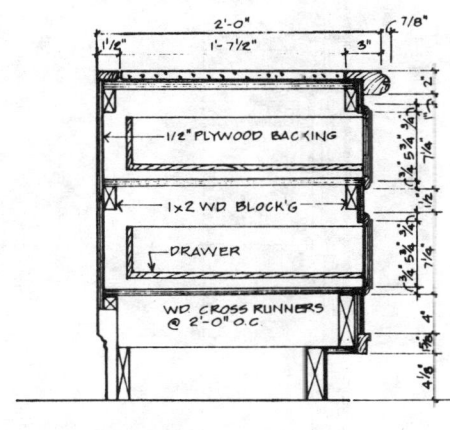

SECTION

CREDENZA

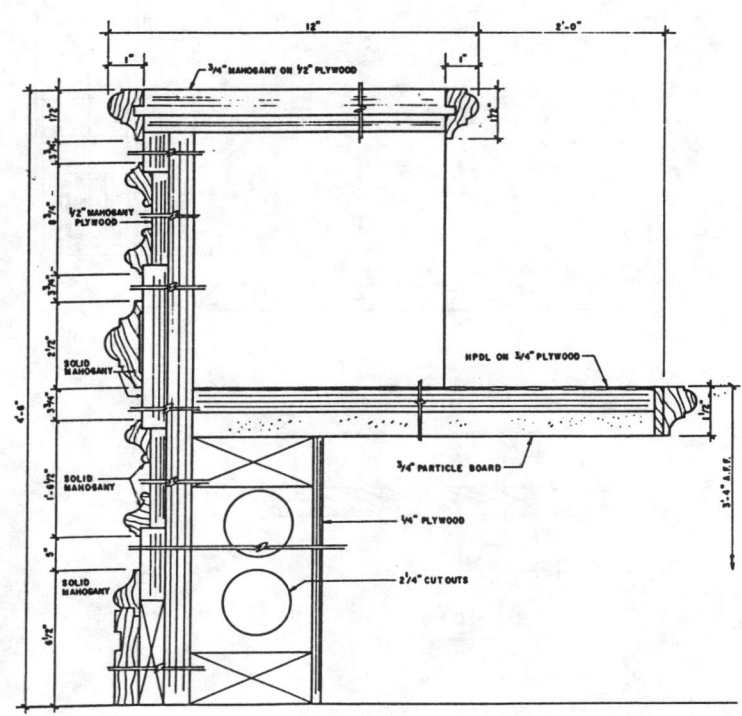

VERTICAL SECTION AT TELLERS COUNTER

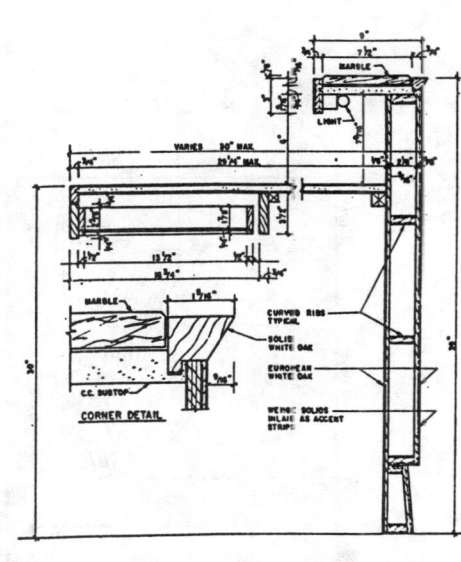

VERTICAL SECTION-RECEPTION DESK

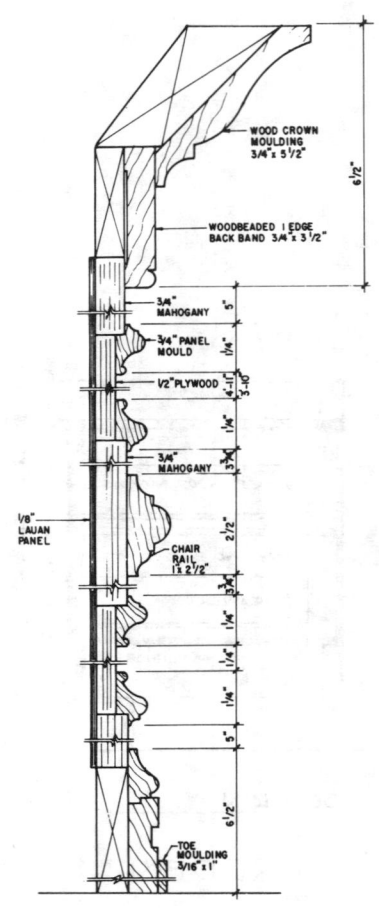

WOOD CROWN
MOULDING
3/4" x 5 1/2"

WOODBEADED I EDGE
BACK BAND 3/4" x 3 1/2"

3/4"
MAHOGANY

3/4" PANEL
MOULD

1/2" PLYWOOD

3/4"
MAHOGANY

1/8"
LAUAN
PANEL

CHAIR
RAIL
1 x 2 1/2"

TOE
MOULDING
3/16" x 1"

TYPICAL TRIM AND CORNICE

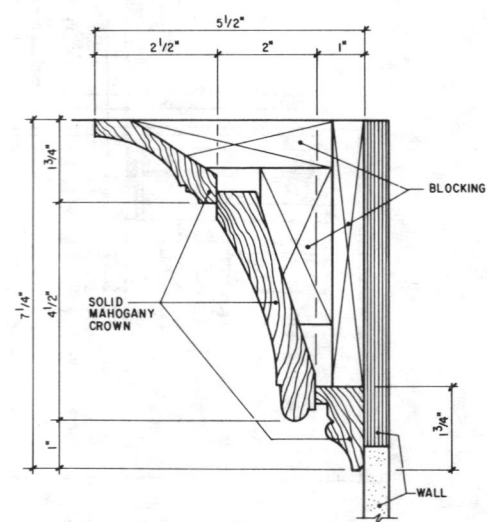

BLOCKING

SOLID
MAHOGANY
CROWN

WALL

SECTION-TYPICAL CEILING MOULDINGS

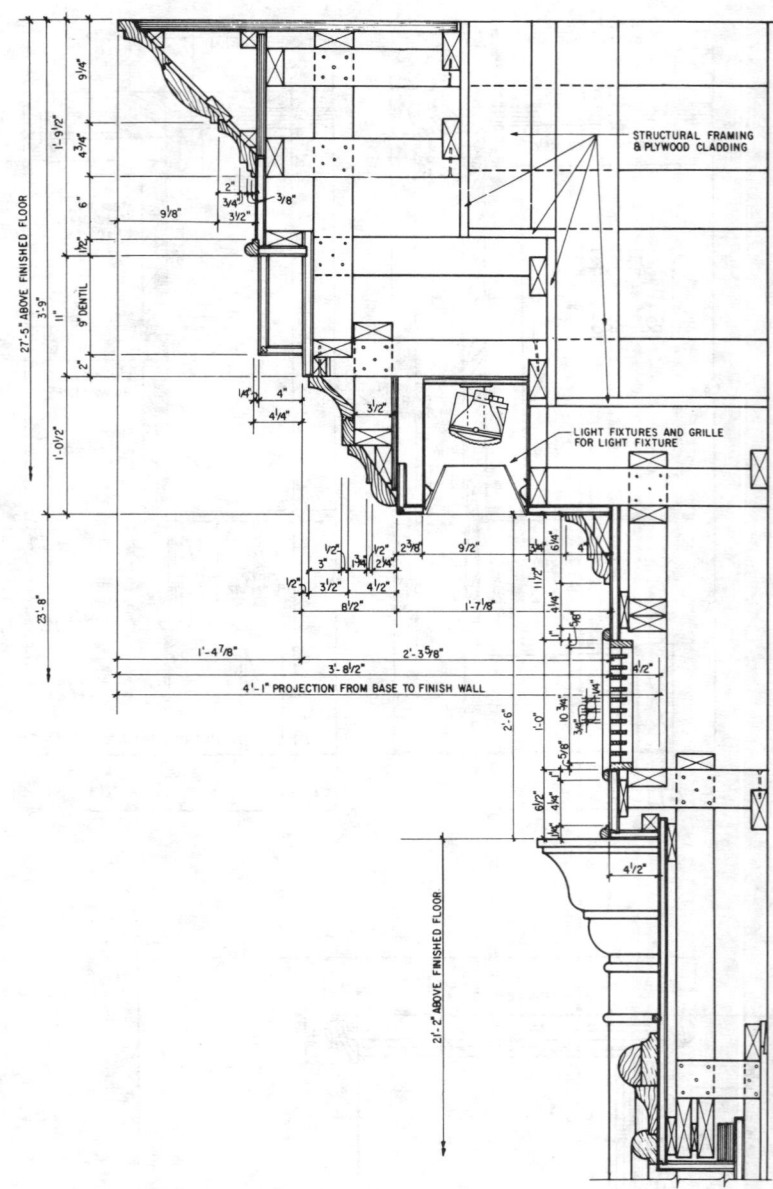

STRUCTURAL FRAMING
& PLYWOOD CLADDING

LIGHT FIXTURES AND GRILLE
FOR LIGHT FIXTURE

4'-1" PROJECTION FROM BASE TO FINISH WALL

SECTION AT ENTABLATURE

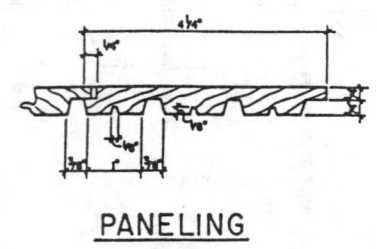

PANELING

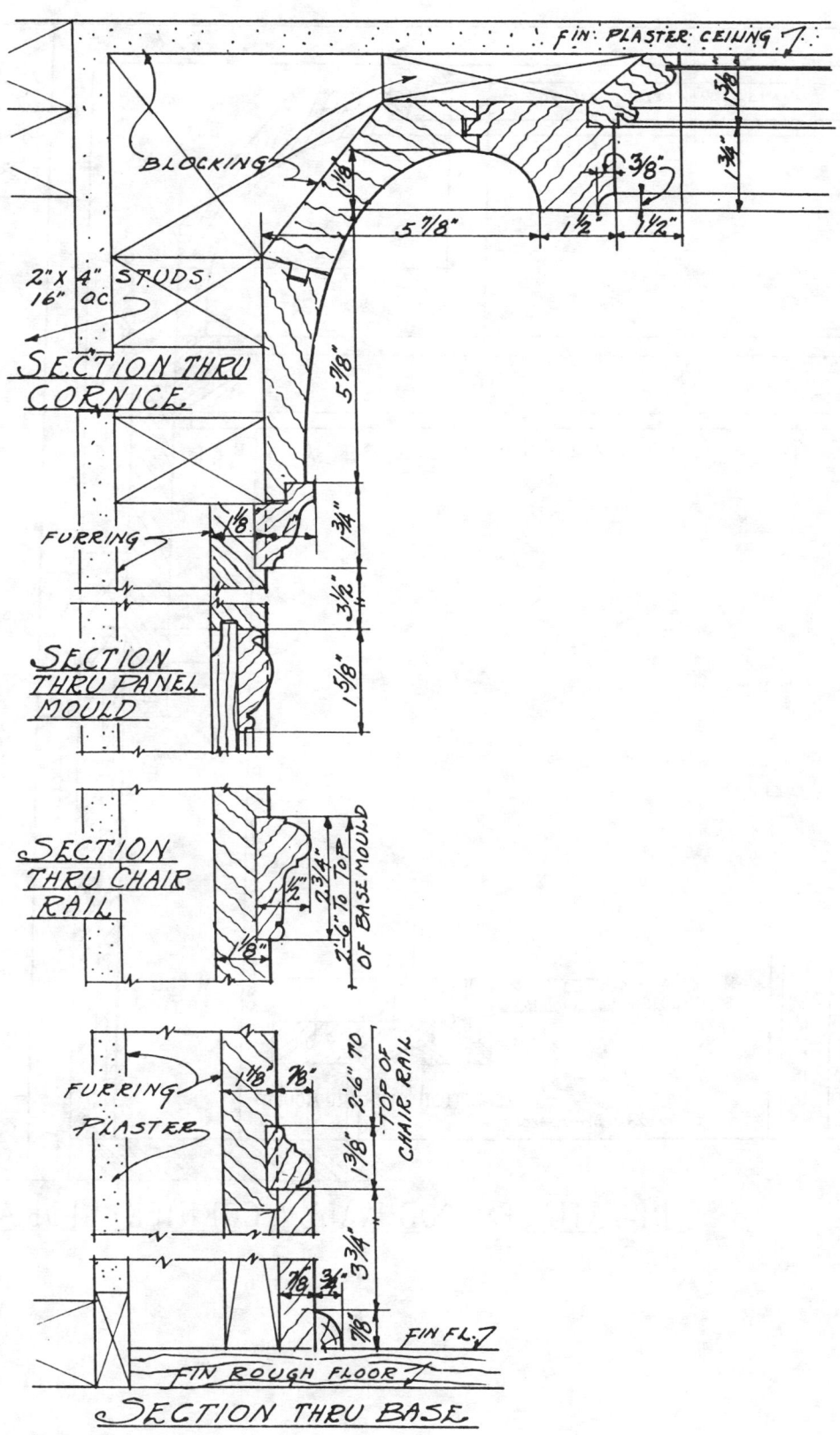

FIN. PLASTER CEILING

BLOCKING

1/8"

5 7/8"

3/8"

3/4"

5/8"

1 1/2"

1 1/2"

2"X 4" STUDS
16" OC

SECTION THRU
CORNICE

5 7/8"

FURRING

1/8"

3/4"

3 1/2"

1 5/8"

SECTION
THRU PANEL
MOULD

2 3/4"

1 1/2"

1/8"

2'-6" TO TOP
OF BASE MOULD

SECTION
THRU CHAIR
RAIL

FURRING

PLASTER

1 1/8"

7/8"

1 3/8"

3/4"

1/8"

3/4"

1/8"

2'-6" TO
TOP OF
CHAIR RAIL

FIN FL.

FIN ROUGH FLOOR

SECTION THRU BASE

DETAIL OF WOOD CORNICE AND PANELING

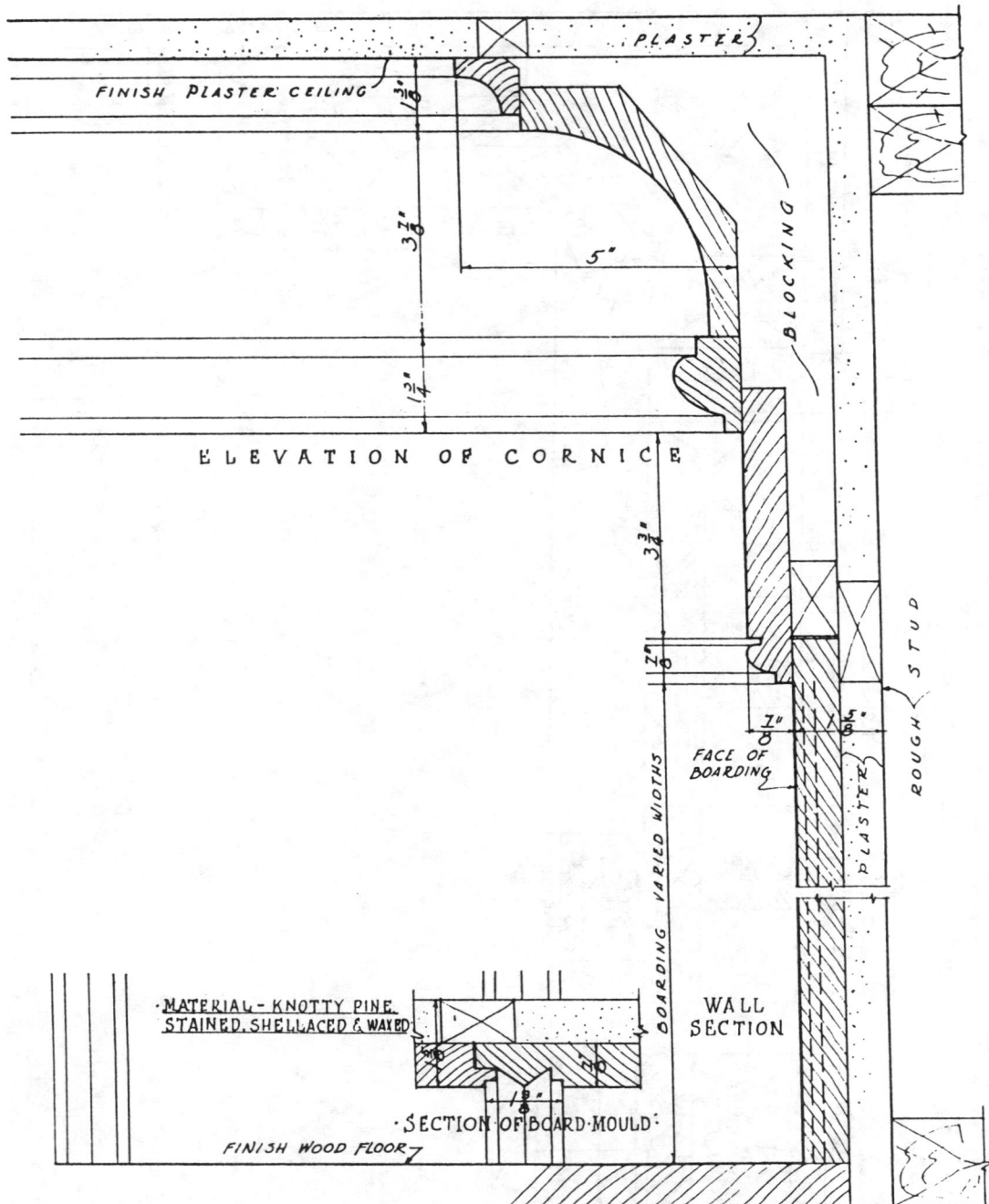

FINISH PLASTER CEILING

PLASTER

BLOCKING

3⅛"

3⅞"

1½"

5"

ELEVATION OF CORNICE

3¾"

5⅞"

ROUGH STUD

7"

⅝"

FACE OF BOARDING

PLASTER

BOARDING VARIED WIDTHS

WALL SECTION

MATERIAL - KNOTTY PINE.
STAINED, SHELLACED & WAXED

SECTION OF BOARD MOULD

FINISH WOOD FLOOR

· DETAIL·OF·WOOD·WALL·&·CORNICE·LIBRARY·

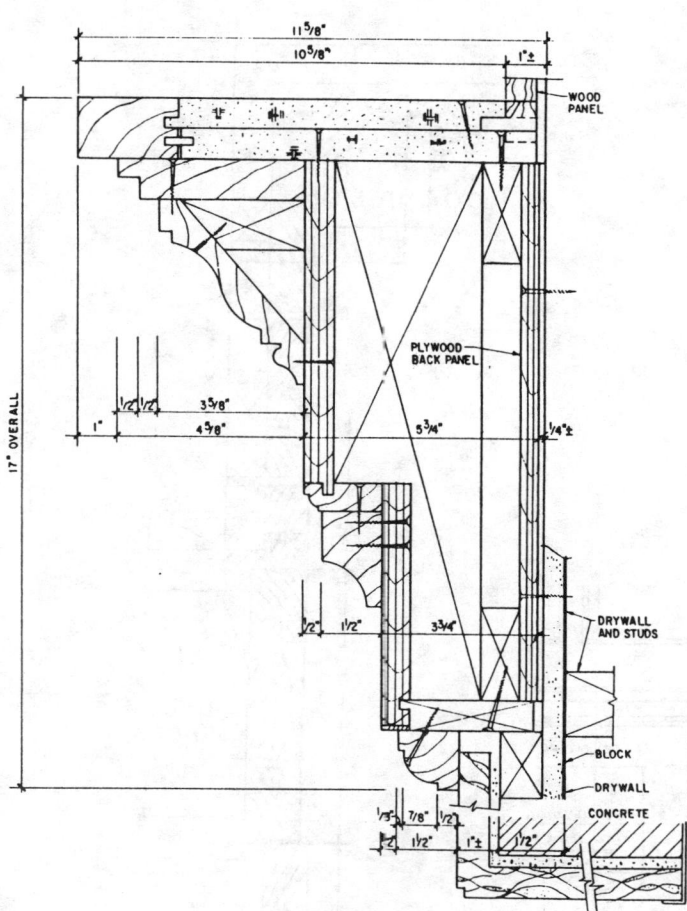

DETAIL-FIREPLACE MANTEL

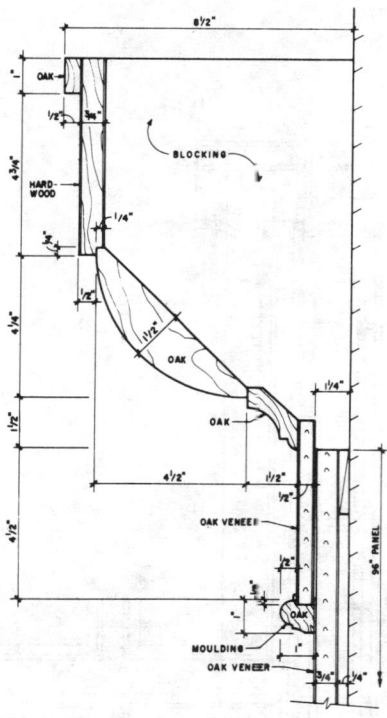

DETAIL AT
COLUMN CAPITAL

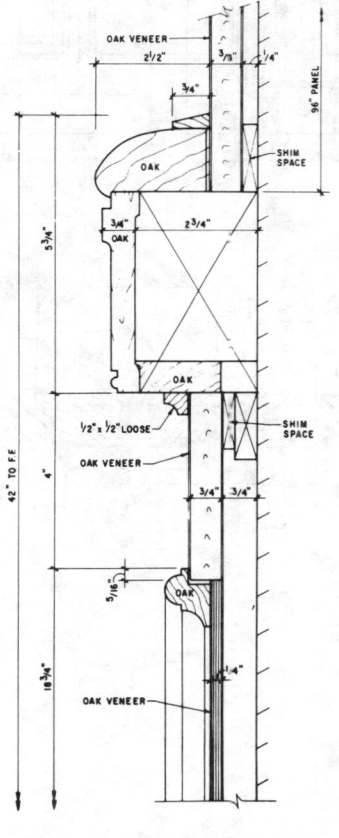

DETAILS AT COLUMN

WOODWORK DETAILS

Detail of Wood-Paneled Wall and Bookcase

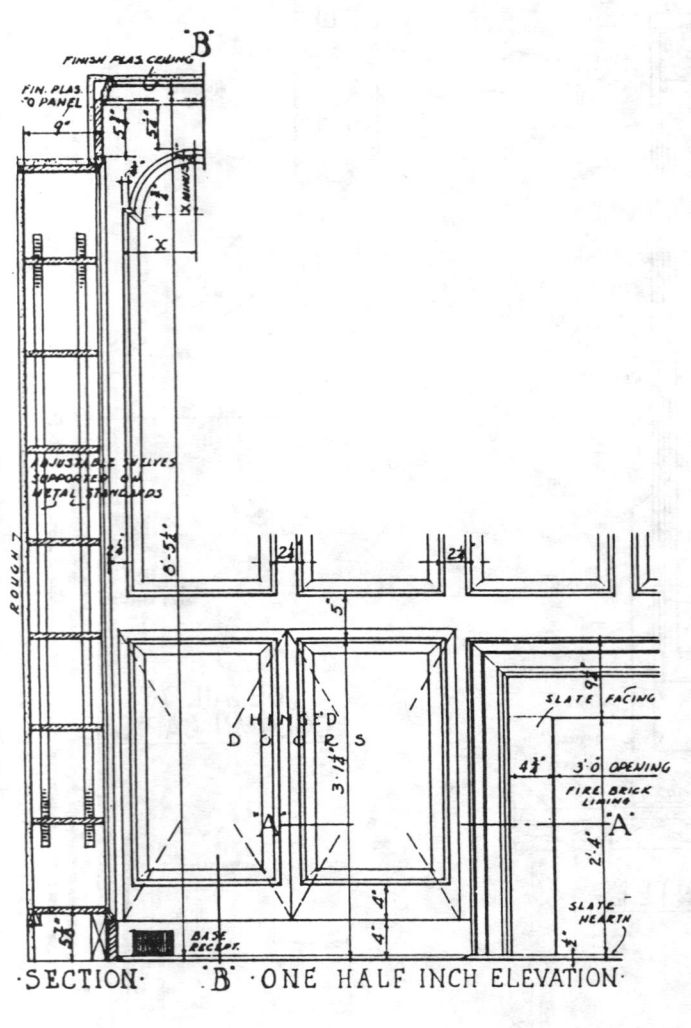

·SECTION· ·B· ONE HALF INCH ELEVATION·

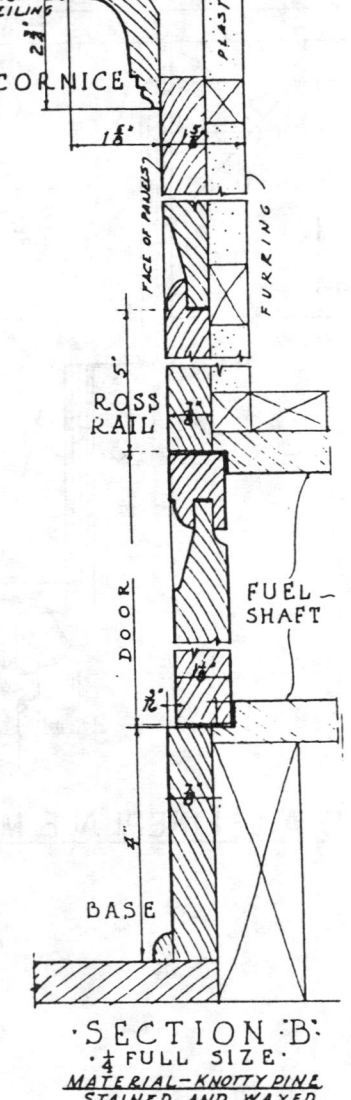

CORNICE

CROSS RAIL

DOOR

FUEL SHAFT

BASE

·SECTION ·B·
¼ FULL SIZE·
MATERIAL—KNOTTY PINE
STAINED AND WAXED·

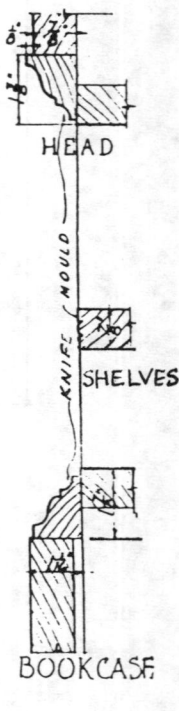

HEAD

SHELVES

BOOKCASE

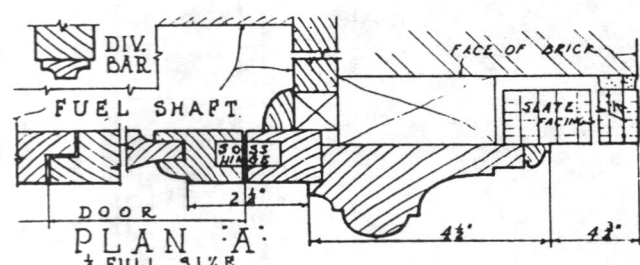

DIV. BAR
FUEL SHAFT
DOOR
PLAN ·A·
¼ FULL SIZE

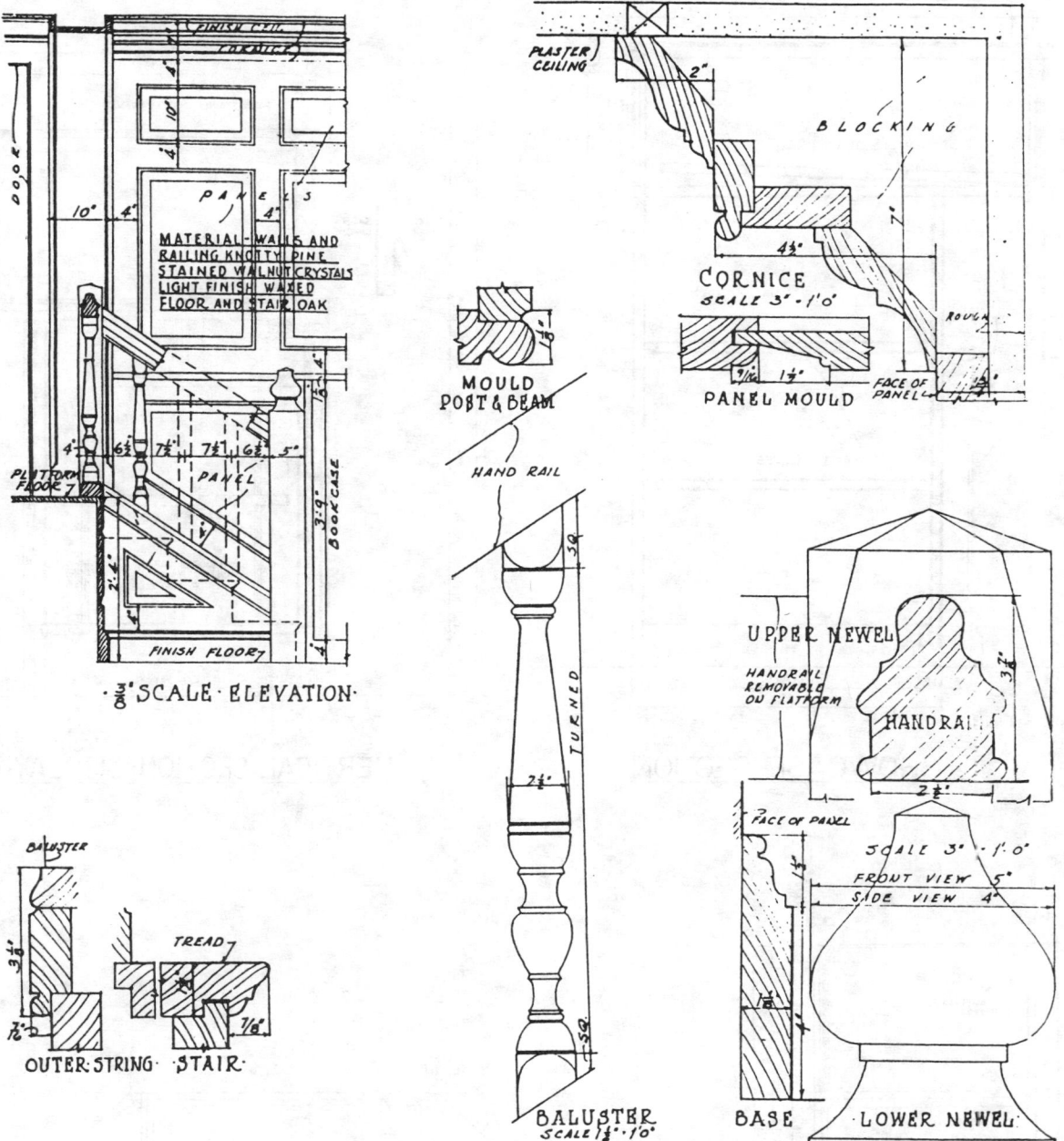

MATERIAL-WALLS AND
RAILING KNOTTY PINE
STAINED WALNUT CRYSTALS
LIGHT FINISH WAXED
FLOOR AND STAIR OAK

PANELS

·3"SCALE·ELEVATION·

MOULD
POST & BEAM

HAND RAIL

BALUSTER
SCALE 1¼"·1'0"

OUTER·STRING   STAIR·

CORNICE
SCALE 3"·1'0"

PANEL MOULD

FACE OF
PANEL

BLOCKING

ROUGH

UPPER NEWEL

HANDRAIL
REMOVABLE
ON PLATFORM

HANDRAIL

FACE OF PANEL

SCALE 3"·1'0"

FRONT VIEW 5"

SIDE VIEW 4"

BASE   LOWER NEWEL

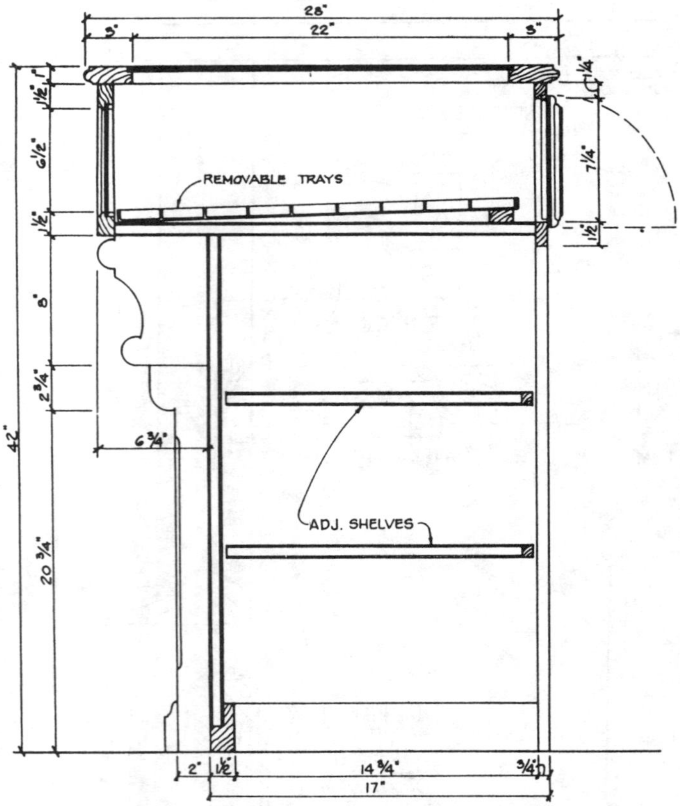

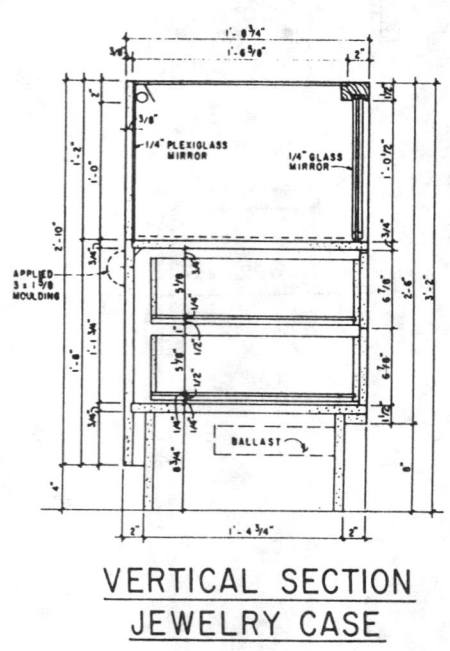

REMOVABLE TRAYS

ADJ. SHELVES

SHOWCASE SECTION

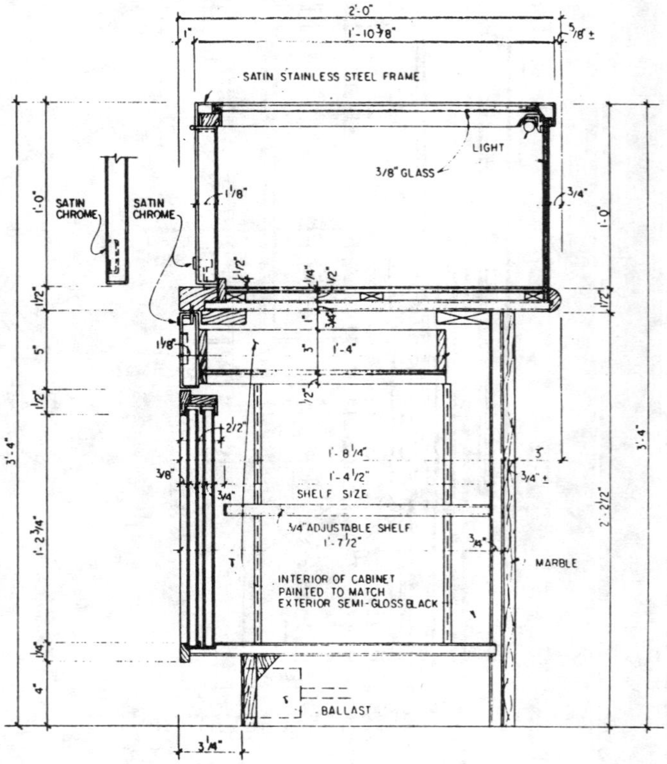

SATIN STAINLESS STEEL FRAME

LIGHT

3/8" GLASS

SATIN CHROME

SATIN CHROME

SHELF SIZE

1/4" ADJUSTABLE SHELF

INTERIOR OF CABINET
PAINTED TO MATCH
EXTERIOR SEMI-GLOSS BLACK

MARBLE

BALLAST

VERTICAL SECTION-DISPLAY CASE

1/4" PLEXIGLASS MIRROR

1/4" GLASS MIRROR

APPLIED 3 x 1 1/8 MOULDING

BALLAST

VERTICAL SECTION
JEWELRY CASE

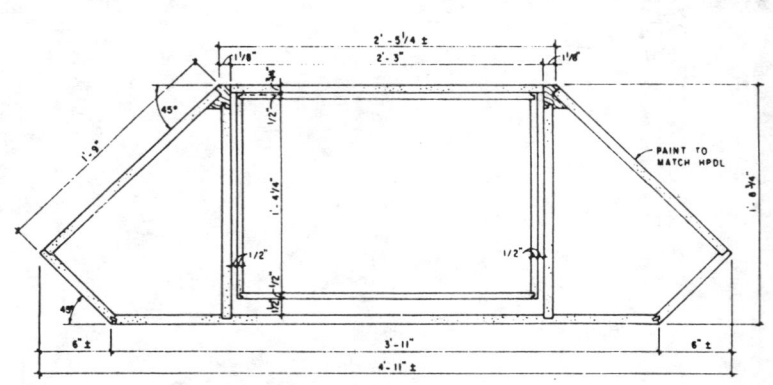

PAINT TO MATCH HPDL

PLAN SECTION JEWELRY CASE

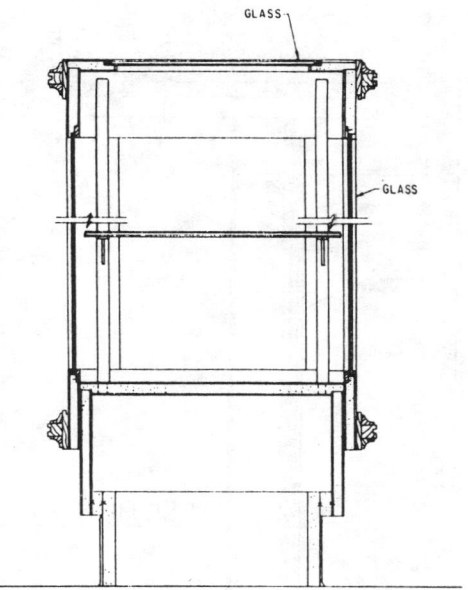

GLASS

GLASS

VERTICAL SECTION
AT DISPLAY CASE

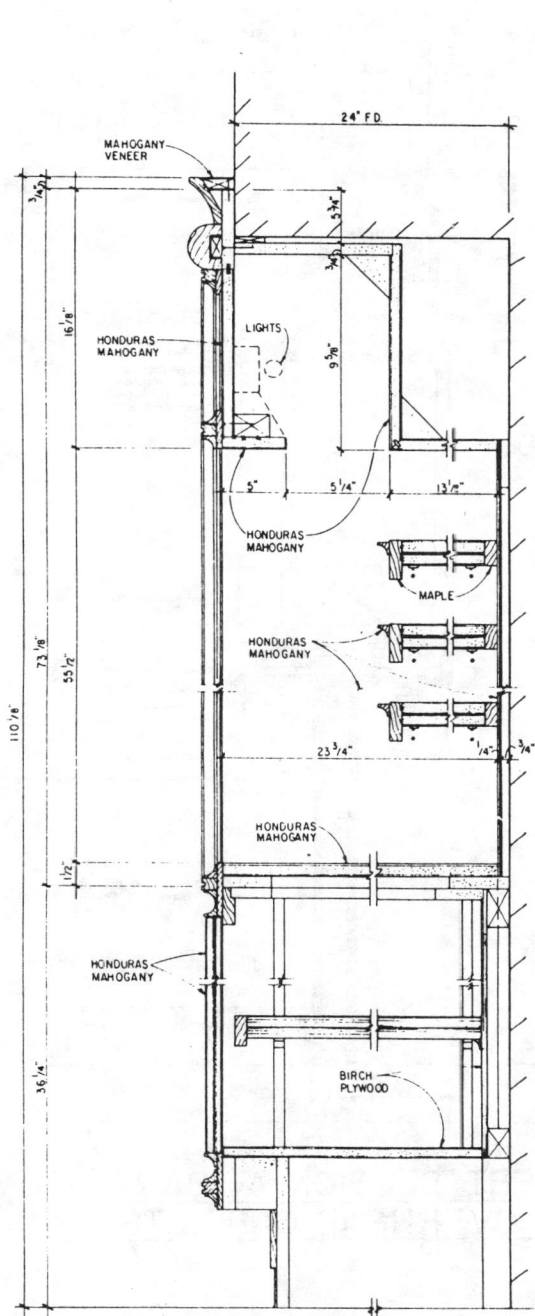

24" F.D.

MAHOGANY
VENEER

HONDURAS
MAHOGANY

LIGHTS

HONDURAS
MAHOGANY

MAPLE

HONDURAS
MAHOGANY

HONDURAS
MAHOGANY

HONDURAS
MAHOGANY

BIRCH
PLYWOOD

TYPICAL VERTICAL SECTION
AT WALL UNIT

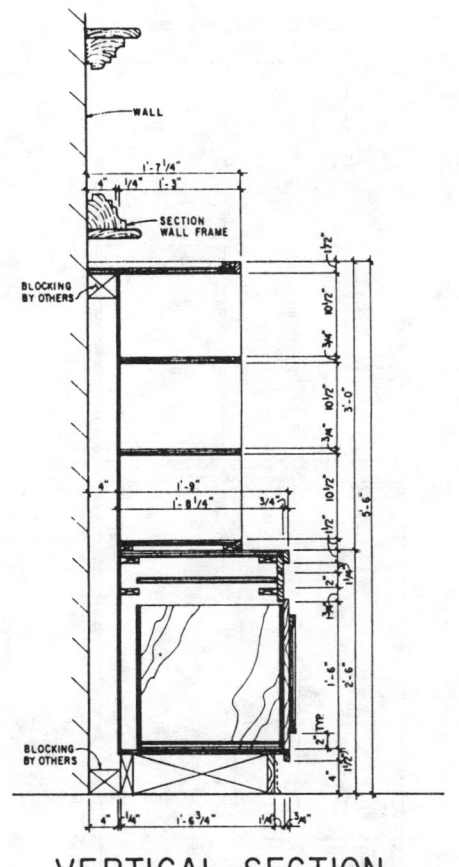

WALL

SECTION
WALL FRAME

BLOCKING
BY OTHERS

BLOCKING
BY OTHERS

VERTICAL SECTION
SHIRT DISPLAY

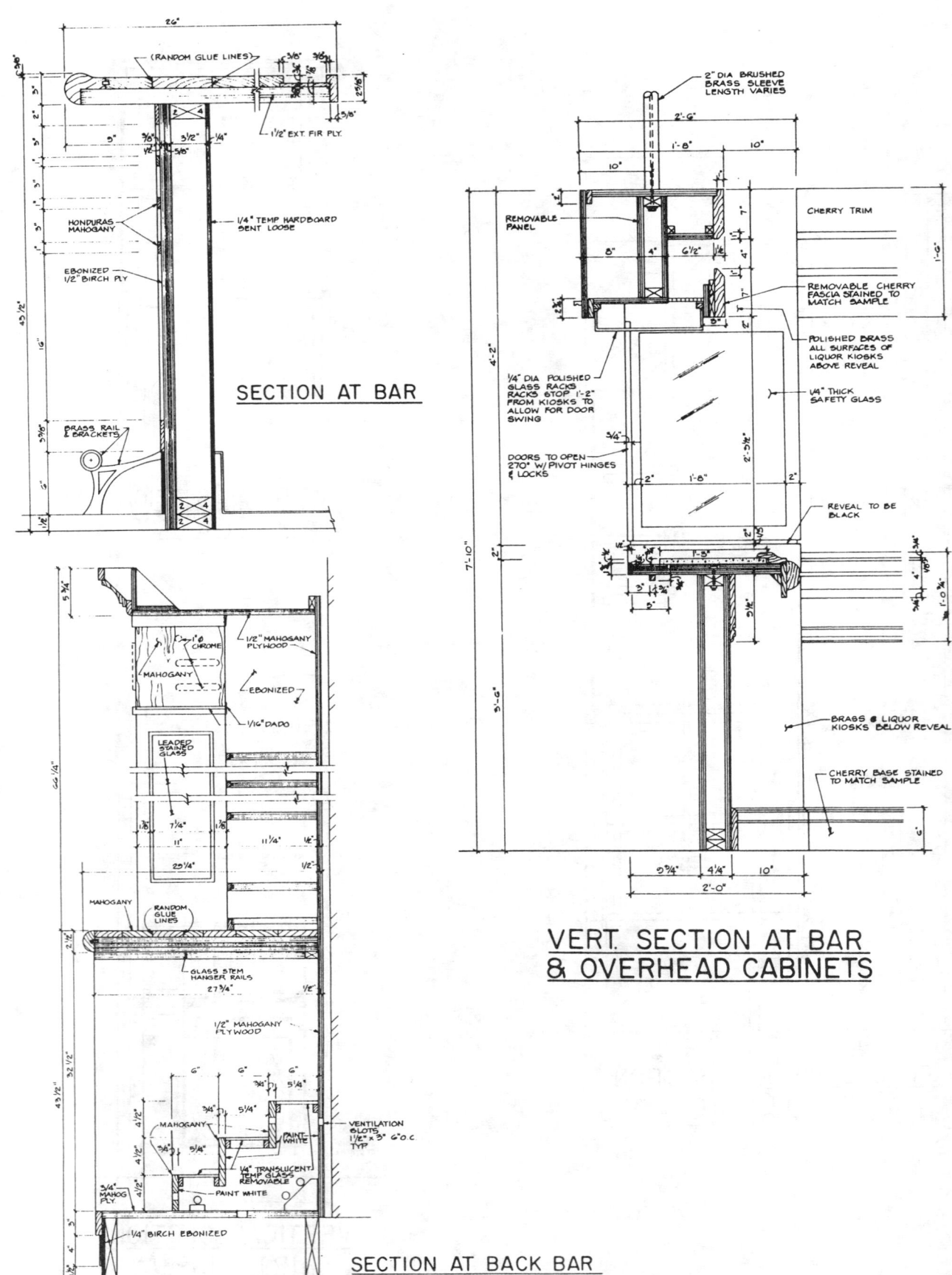

SECTION AT BAR

SECTION AT BACK BAR

VERT. SECTION AT BAR
& OVERHEAD CABINETS

FINISHING MATERIALS

GENERIC TYPE	RECOMMENDED USAGE	CHARACTERISTICS
System #1 Lacquers	For all wood surfaces except medium to heavy acid areas; Interior use.	Good coverage; Easy to apply; Sands easy; Poor water resistance.
Catalyzed Lacquers	For wood surfaces requiring medium acid resistance; Interior use.	Tough wearing surface; Good water resistance; Can be repaired.
System #2 Varnishes	For all wood surfaces; Interior use; Exterior use — spar varnishes.	Good build; Tends to amber with age; Slow drying.
Conversion Varnishes	For all wood surfaces; Some acid resistance; Interior use.	Good build and solids; Can be repaired.
System #3 Polyurethane	For all wood surfaces; Interior use.	Tough surface; Excellent wear and abrasion resistance; Can be repaired.
Catalyzed Polyurethane	For all wood surfaces; High acid resistance; Interior use.	Tough surface; Excellent wear and abrasion resistance; Can be repaired.
System #4 Epoxy	For all wood surfaces; High acid resistance; Interior use.	Very hard surface; Excellent wear and abrasion resistance; Limited pot life; High water resistance.
System #5 Penetrating Oils	For all wood surfaces; Performs well on Oak, Teak, Walnut, etc.	Easy to apply; Makes touch-up easy; Average wear and abrasion qualities; Easy to repair.
System #6 Synthetic Enamels	Most wood and wood product surfaces; Interior use; Most colors available.	Good coverage; Tough wearing; Can be recoated or repaired; Easy to apply.
System #7 Vinyl Lacquer	For all wood products; Interior use; Light acid resistance.	Tough surface; Good wearing; Resists light chemicals.
Catalyzed Vinyl	For all wood products; Interior use; Excellent for residential kitchens, etc.; Better acid resistance.	Tough surface; Good wearing; Repairs not easy.
System #8 Fire Retardant Coatings (Intumescent)	For surfaces of wood products requiring flame spread protection. (See WIC Technical Bulletin No. 423 — Section 19.) Interior use only. UL Rated-UL-723; NFPA-255; and ASTM E-84; Tested for flame spread, fuel contributed, and smoke developed.	Leaching will result if exposed directly to high humidity or direct water. Can be coated with compatible overcoat system or waterproofing materials. Available for transparent and opaque finishes.

CORNICES AND MOULDINGS
Deep Sculpt and Crown Mouldings

Deep Sculpt Mouldings

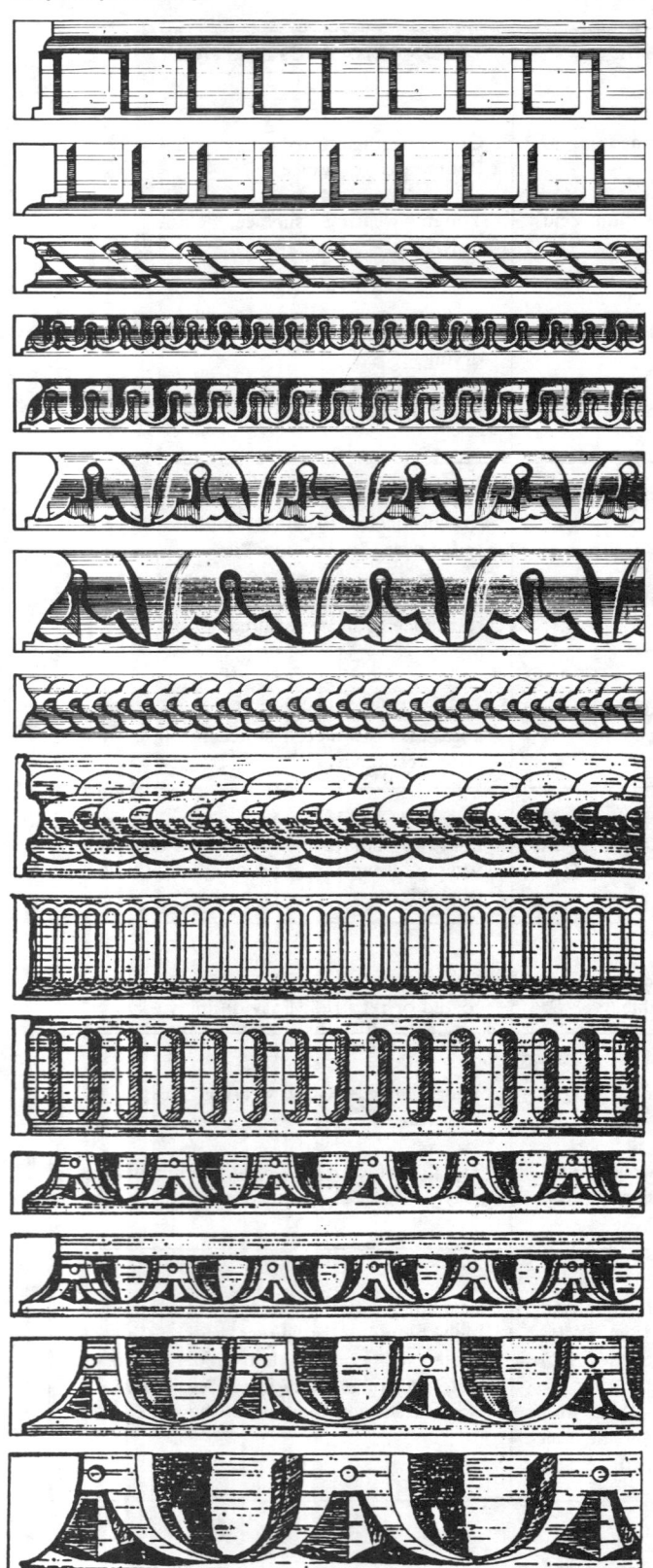

Crown Mouldings

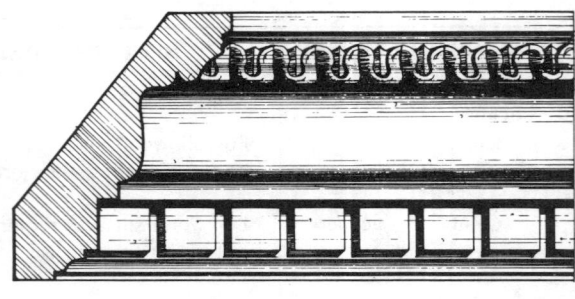

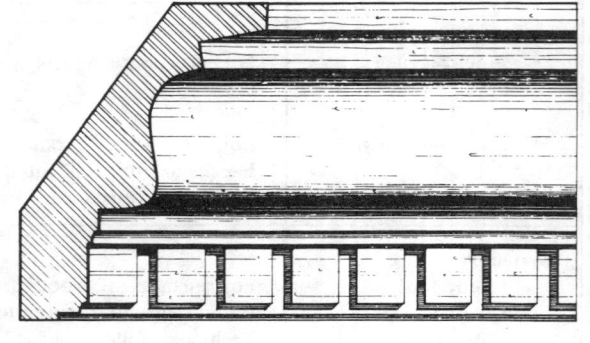

CORNICES AND MOULDINGS
Crown Mouldings

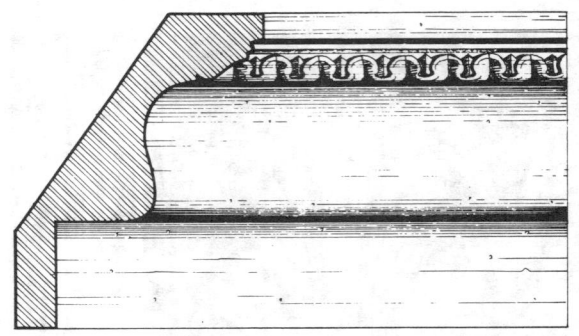
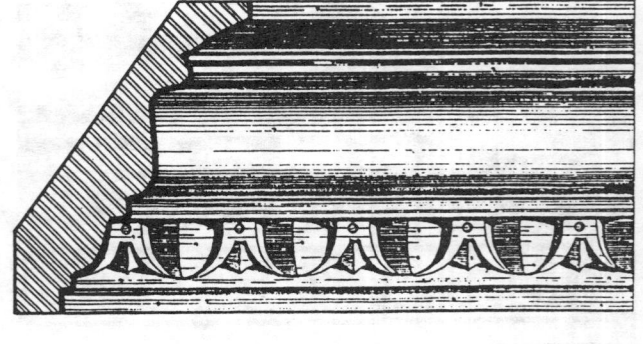
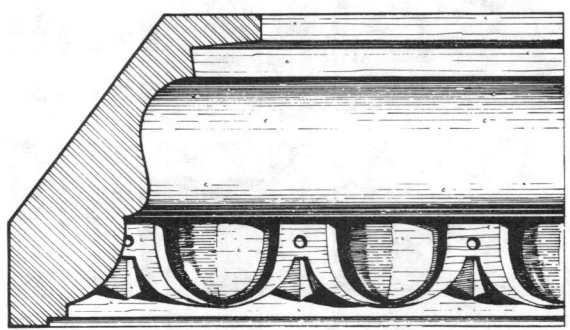
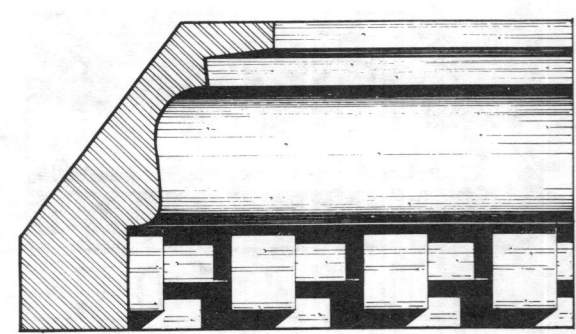
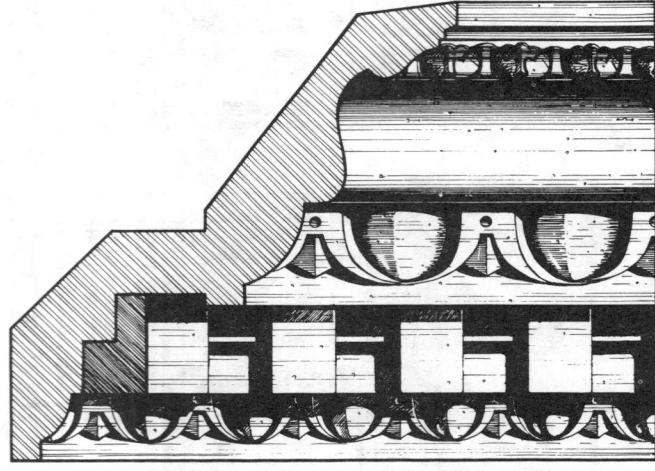
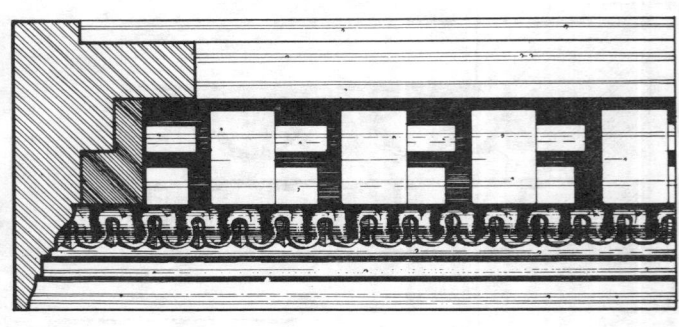
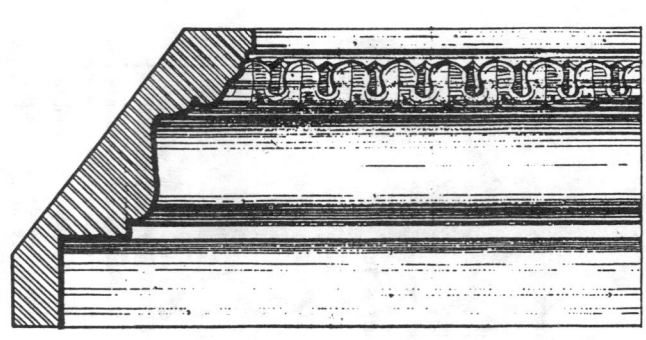

CORNICES AND MOULDINGS

Miscellaneous Mouldings

Chair Rail Mouldings

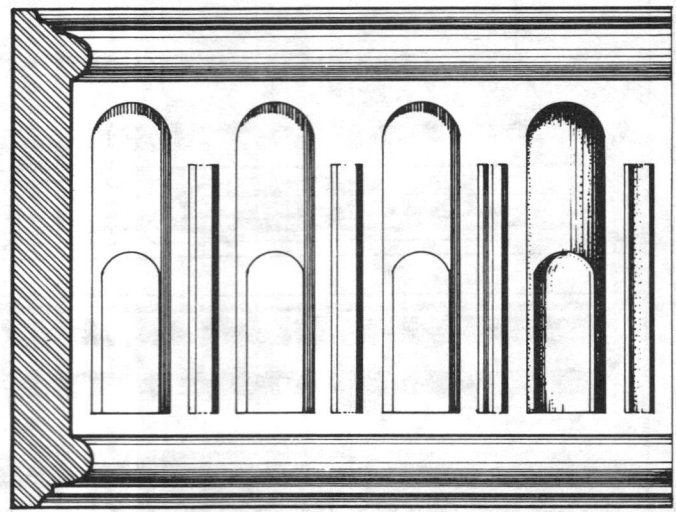

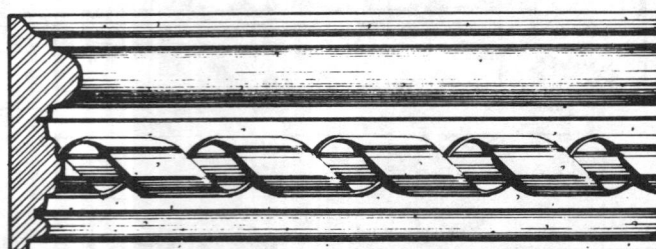

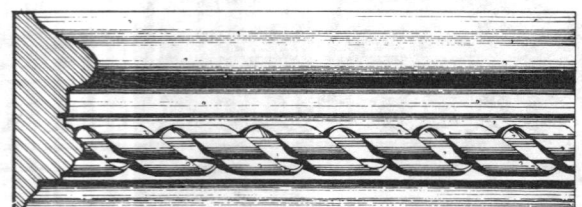

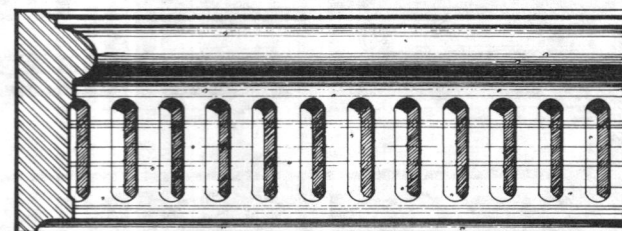

Picture/Mirror Hanging Mouldings

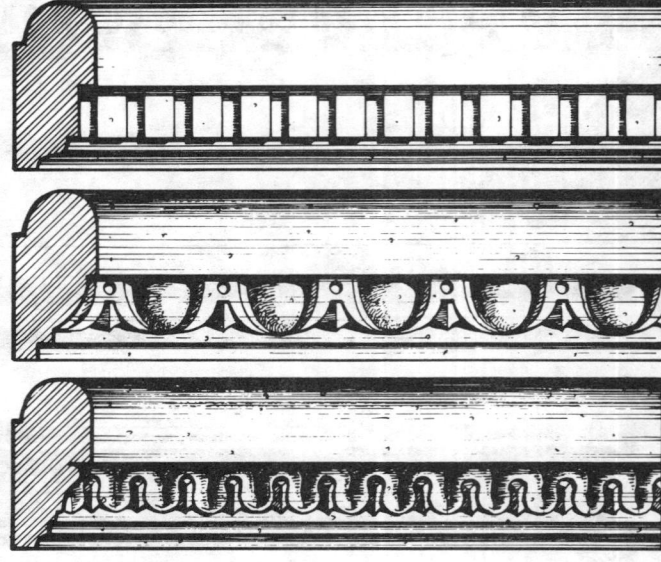

Door Trim Moulding

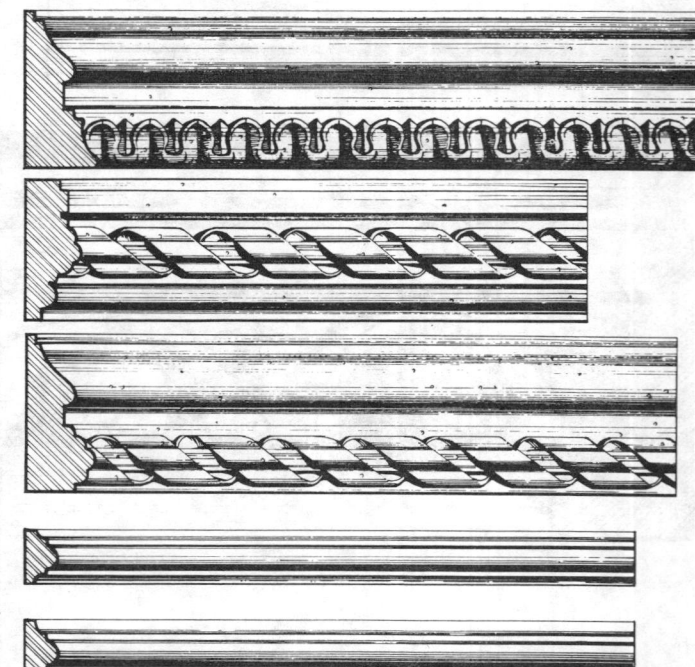

Panel and Trim Mouldings

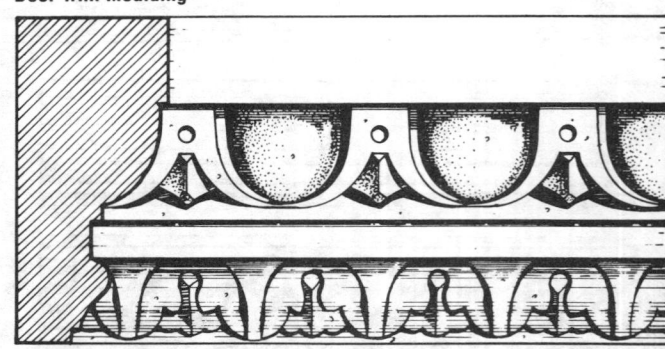

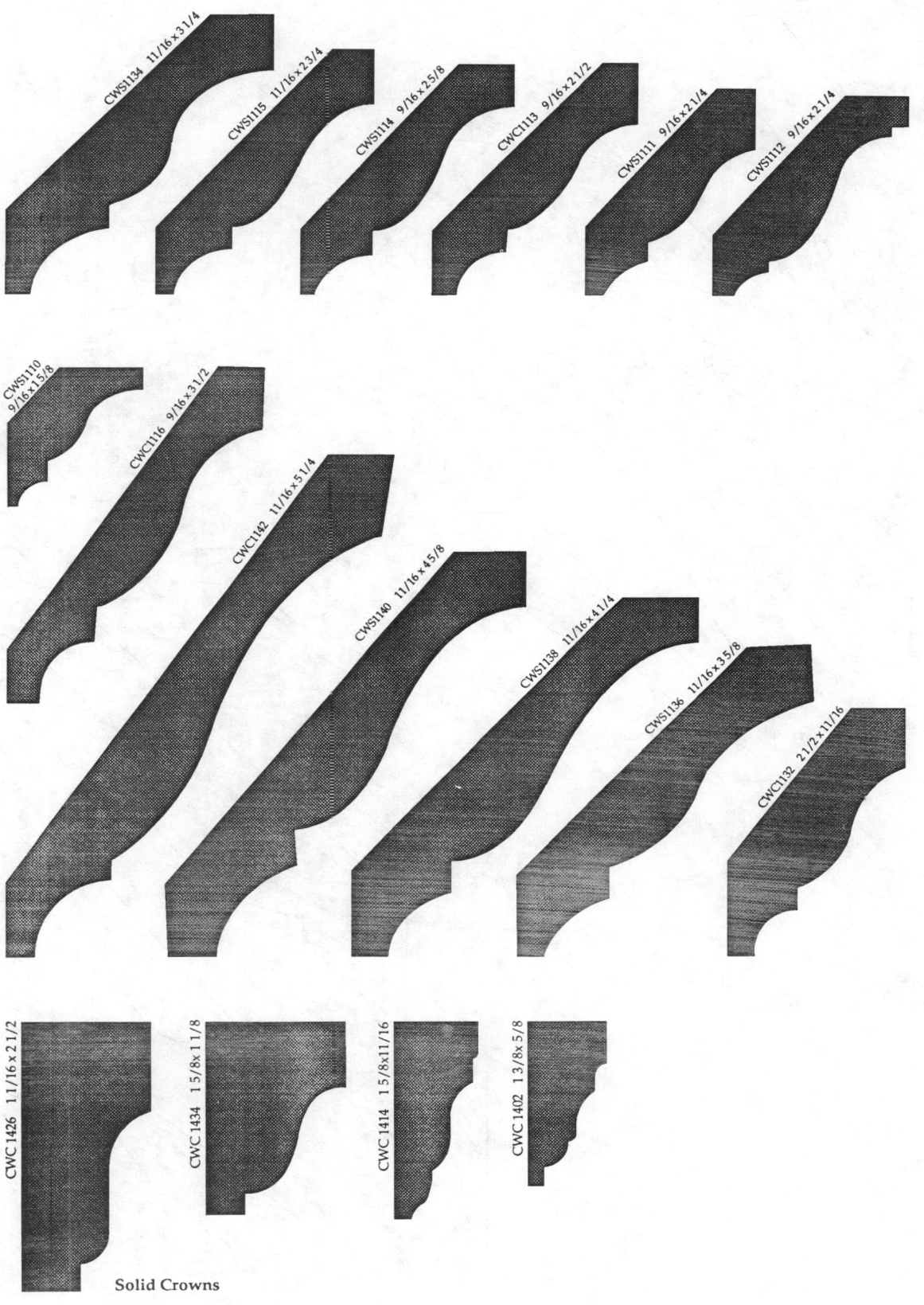

CWS1134 11/16 x 3 1/4

CWS1115 11/16 x 2 3/4

CWS1114 9/16 x 2 5/8

CWC1113 9/16 x 2 1/2

CWS1111 9/16 x 2 1/4

CWS1112 9/16 x 2 1/4

CWS1110 9/16 x 1 5/8

CWC1116 9/16 x 3 1/2

CWC1142 11/16 x 5 1/4

CWS1140 11/16 x 4 5/8

CWS1138 11/16 x 4 1/4

CWS1136 11/16 x 3 5/8

CWC1132 2 1/2 x 11/16

CWC 1426 11/16 x 2 1/2

CWC 1434 1 5/8 x 1 1/8

CWC 1414 1 5/8 x 11/16

CWC 1402 1 3/8 x 5/8

Solid Crowns

CORNICES AND MOULDINGS
Crown Mouldings

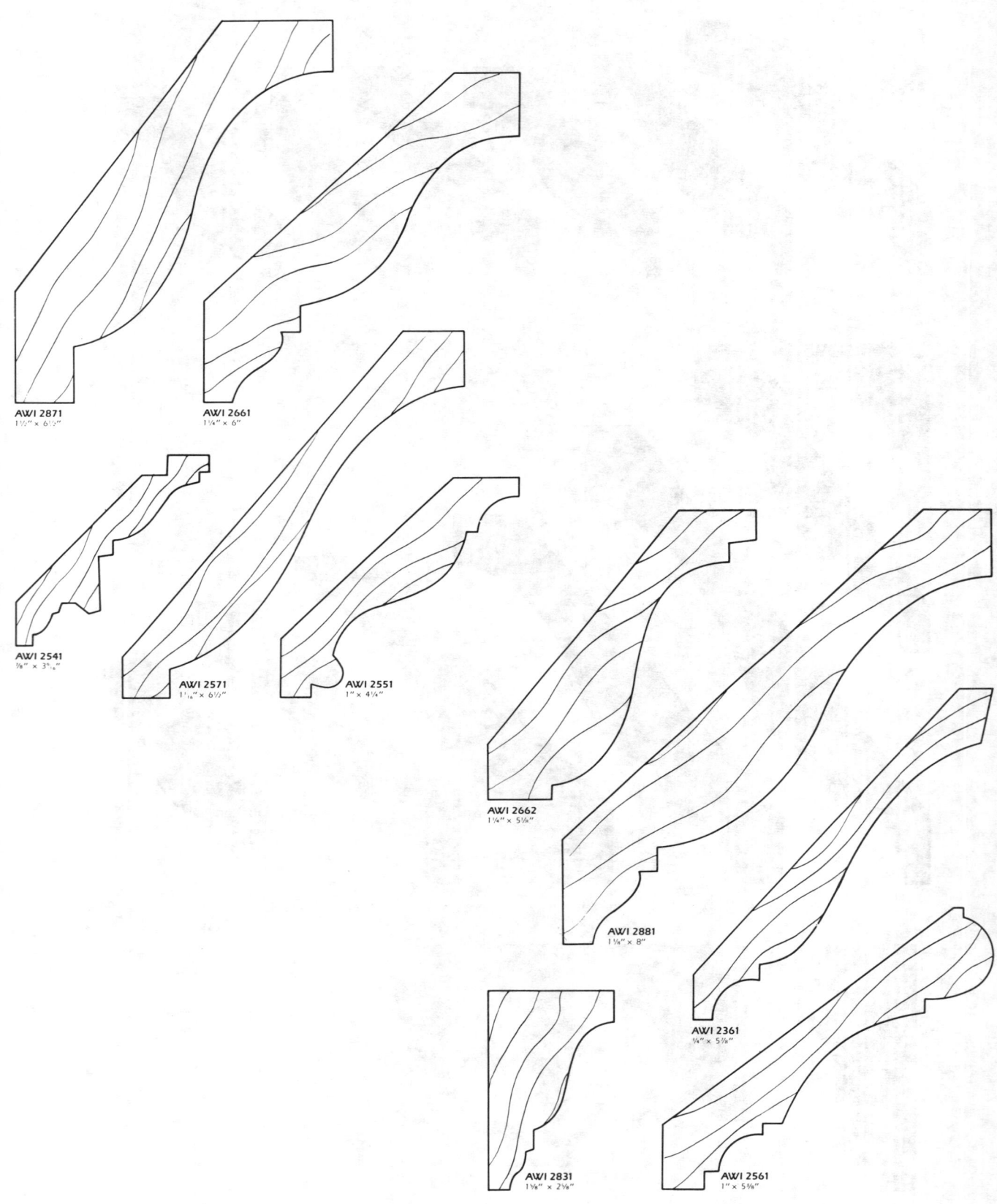

AWI 2871
1½" × 6½"

AWI 2661
1¼" × 6"

AWI 2541
⅝" × 3⁵⁄₁₆"

AWI 2571
1¹⁄₁₆" × 6½"

AWI 2551
1" × 4¼"

AWI 2662
1¼" × 5⅛"

AWI 2881
1⅛" × 8"

AWI 2361
¼" × 5⅞"

AWI 2831
1⅜" × 2⅛"

AWI 2561
1" × 5⅛"

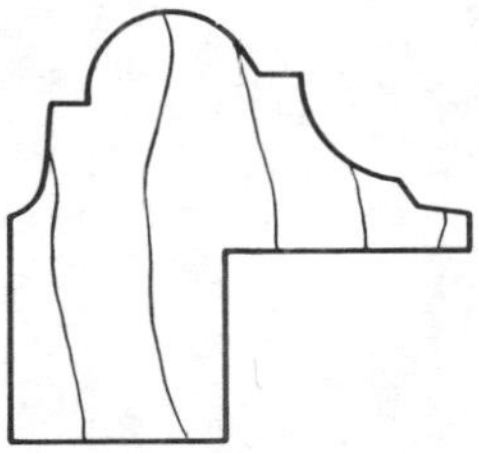

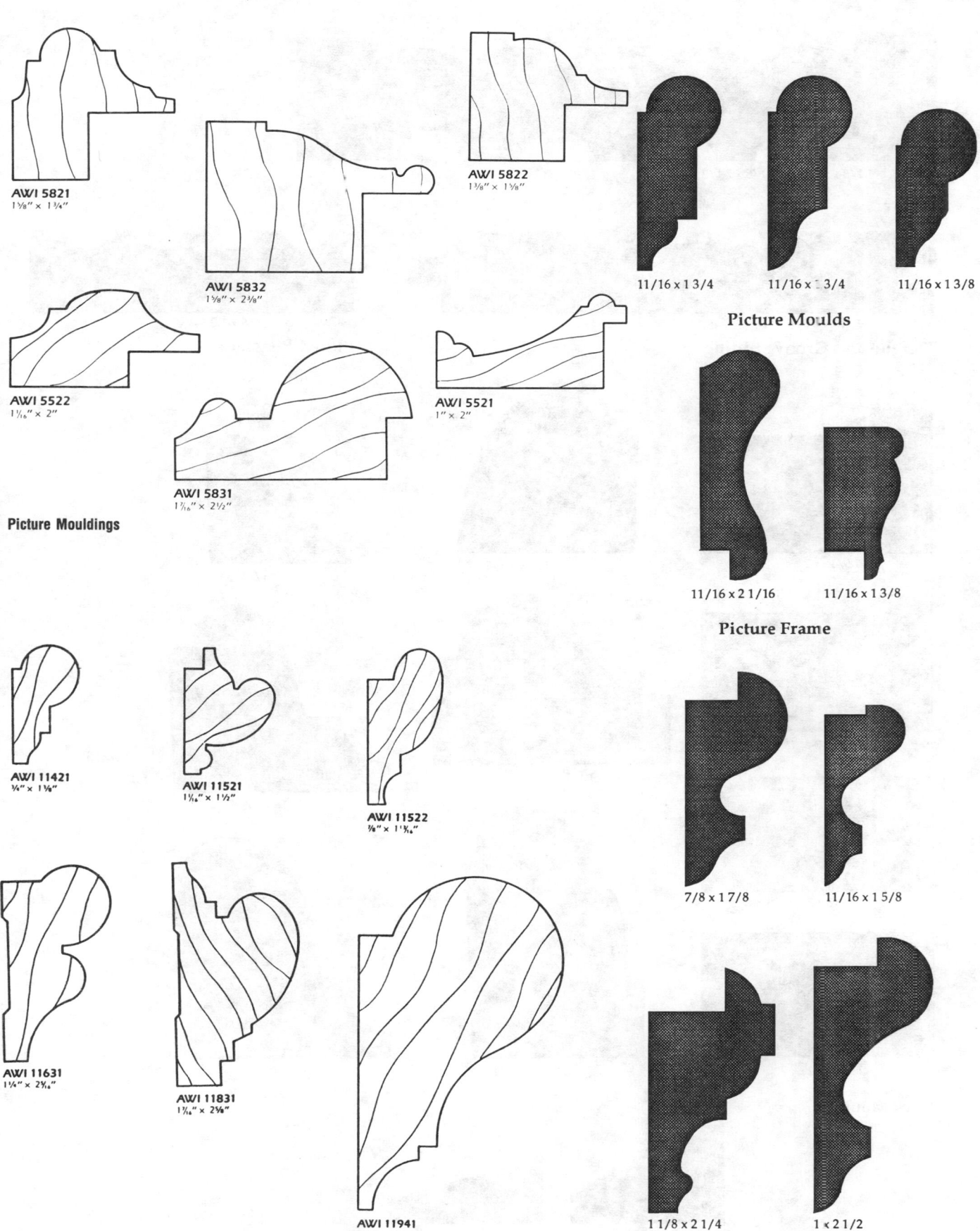

AWI 5821
1 5/8" × 1 3/4"

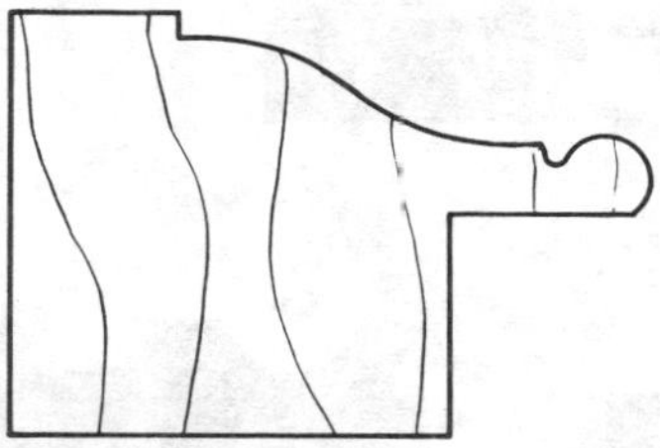

AWI 5832
1 5/8" × 2 3/8"

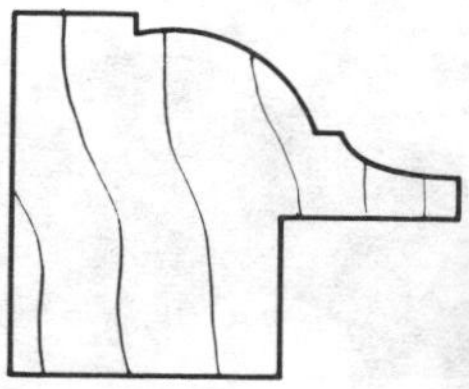

AWI 5822
1 3/8" × 1 5/8"

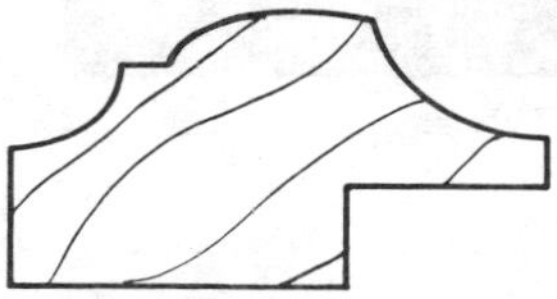

AWI 5522
1 1/16" × 2"

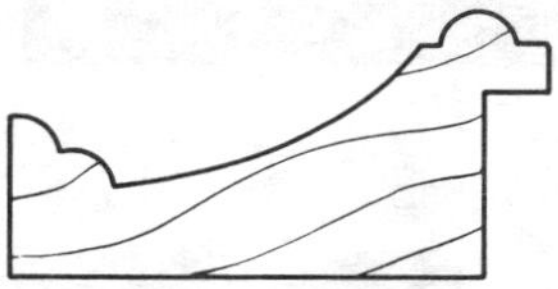

AWI 5521
1" × 2"

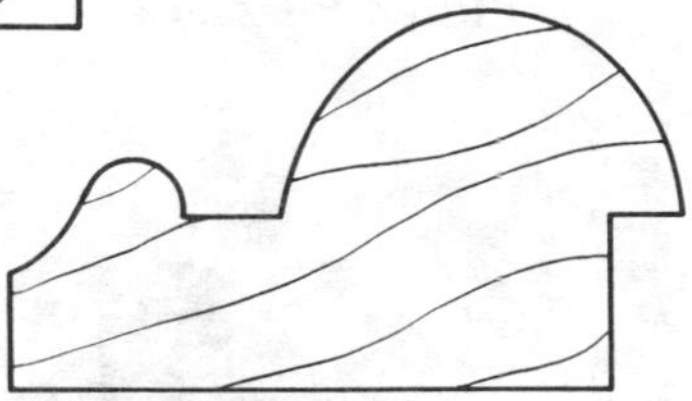

AWI 5831
1 7/16" × 2 1/2"

Picture Mouldings

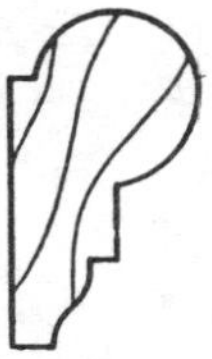

AWI 11421
3/4" × 1 1/8"

AWI 11521
1 1/16" × 1 1/2"

AWI 11522
7/8" × 1 13/16"

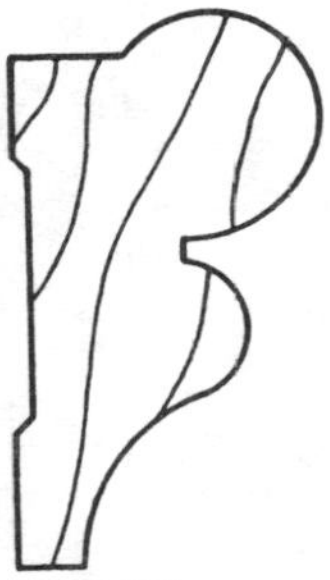

AWI 11631
1 1/4" × 2 3/16"

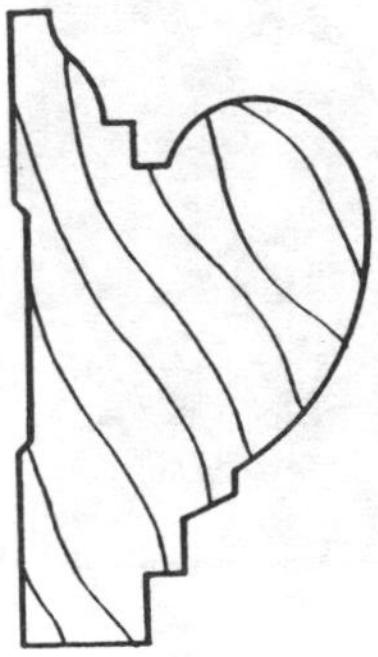

AWI 11831
1 7/16" × 2 5/8"

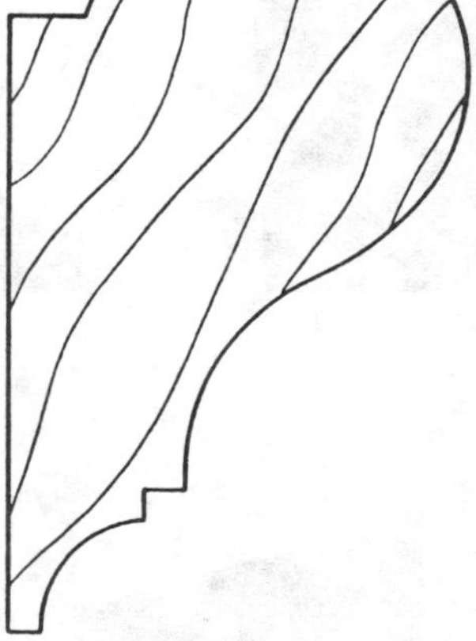

AWI 11941
2 3/8" × 4"

Back Bands

11/16 x 1 3/4

11/16 x 1 3/4

11/16 x 1 3/8

Picture Moulds

11/16 x 2 1/16

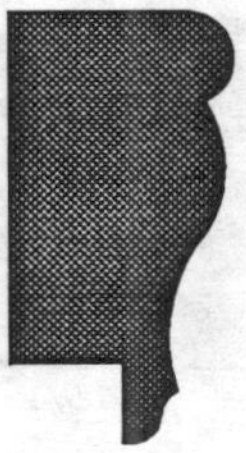

11/16 x 1 3/8

Picture Frame

7/8 x 1 7/8

11/16 x 1 5/8

1 1/8 x 2 1/4

1 x 2 1/2

Step Moulds

CORNICES AND MOULDINGS
Miscellaneous Mouldings

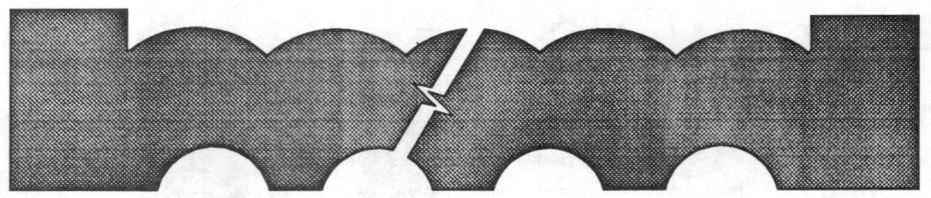

1 1/8 x 5 1/2 & 1 1/8 x 7 1/2

Pilaster

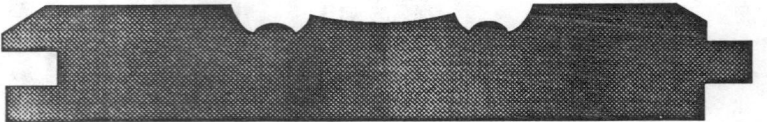

3/16 x 1 3/4

Tongue and Groove Siding

11/16 x 1 3/4

Fluted Pilaster

1 5/16 x 2

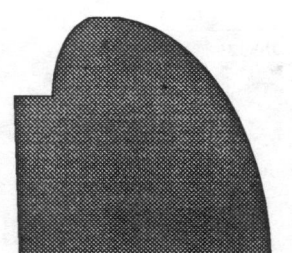

1 5/8 x 1 1/2

1 1/8 x 1 1/4

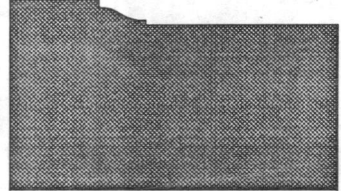

1 1/4 x 2

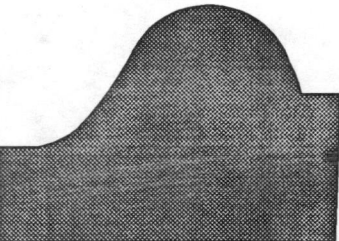

1 1/2 x 2

1 11/16 x 1 7/8

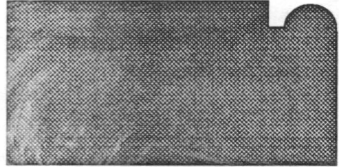

1 1/16 x 2

1 3/32 x 2

Brick Moulds

2 1/4 x 1 1/2

1 7/8 x 2

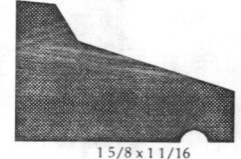

1 5/8 x 1 1/16   11/16 x 1 5/8

Drip Caps

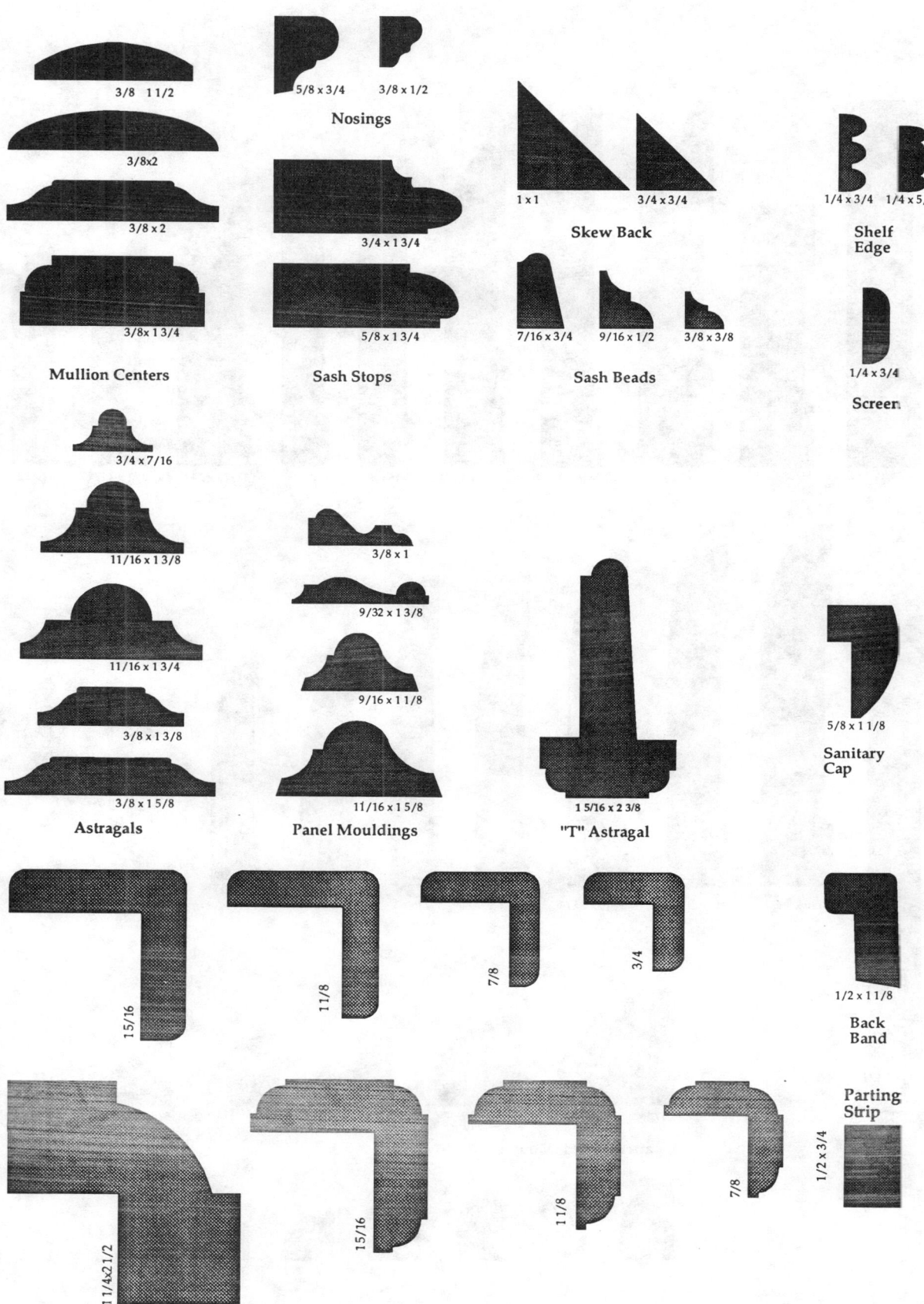

Mullion Centers

3/8 1 1/2

3/8 x 2

3/8 x 2

3/8 x 1 3/4

Nosings

5/8 x 3/4

3/8 x 1/2

Sash Stops

3/4 x 1 3/4

5/8 x 1 3/4

Skew Back

1 x 1

3/4 x 3/4

Sash Beads

7/16 x 3/4

9/16 x 1/2

3/8 x 3/8

Shelf Edge

1/4 x 3/4

1/4 x 5/8

Screen

1/4 x 3/4

Astragals

3/4 x 7/16

11/16 x 1 3/8

11/16 x 1 3/4

3/8 x 1 3/8

3/8 x 1 5/8

Panel Mouldings

3/8 x 1

9/32 x 1 3/8

9/16 x 1 1/8

11/16 x 1 5/8

"T" Astragal

1 5/16 x 2 3/8

Sanitary Cap

5/8 x 1 1/8

15/16

1 1/8

7/8

3/4

Back Band

1/2 x 1 1/8

Parting Strip

1/2 x 3/4

1 1/4 x 2 1/2

15/16

1 1/8

7/8

Cornerguards

875

CORNICES AND MOULDINGS
Base Mouldings

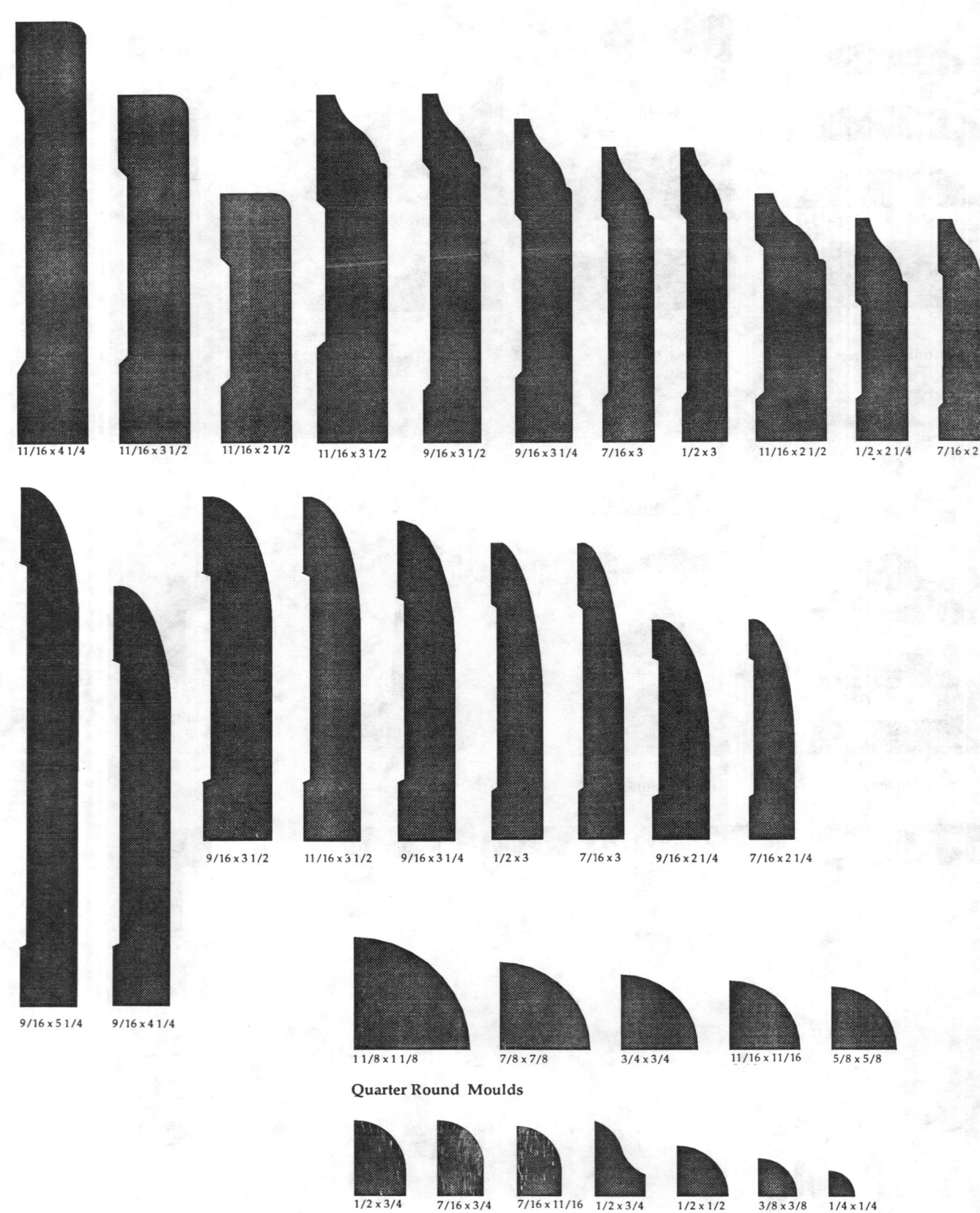

11/16 x 4 1/4 11/16 x 3 1/2 11/16 x 2 1/2 11/16 x 3 1/2 9/16 x 3 1/2 9/16 x 3 1/4 7/16 x 3 1/2 x 3 11/16 x 2 1/2 1/2 x 2 1/4 7/16 x 2 1/

9/16 x 3 1/2 11/16 x 3 1/2 9/16 x 3 1/4 1/2 x 3 7/16 x 3 9/16 x 2 1/4 7/16 x 2 1/4

9/16 x 5 1/4 9/16 x 4 1/4

1 1/8 x 1 1/8 7/8 x 7/8 3/4 x 3/4 11/16 x 11/16 5/8 x 5/8

Quarter Round Moulds

1/2 x 3/4 7/16 x 3/4 7/16 x 11/16 1/2 x 3/4 1/2 x 1/2 3/8 x 3/8 1/4 x 1/4

Base Shoe & Floor Moulds

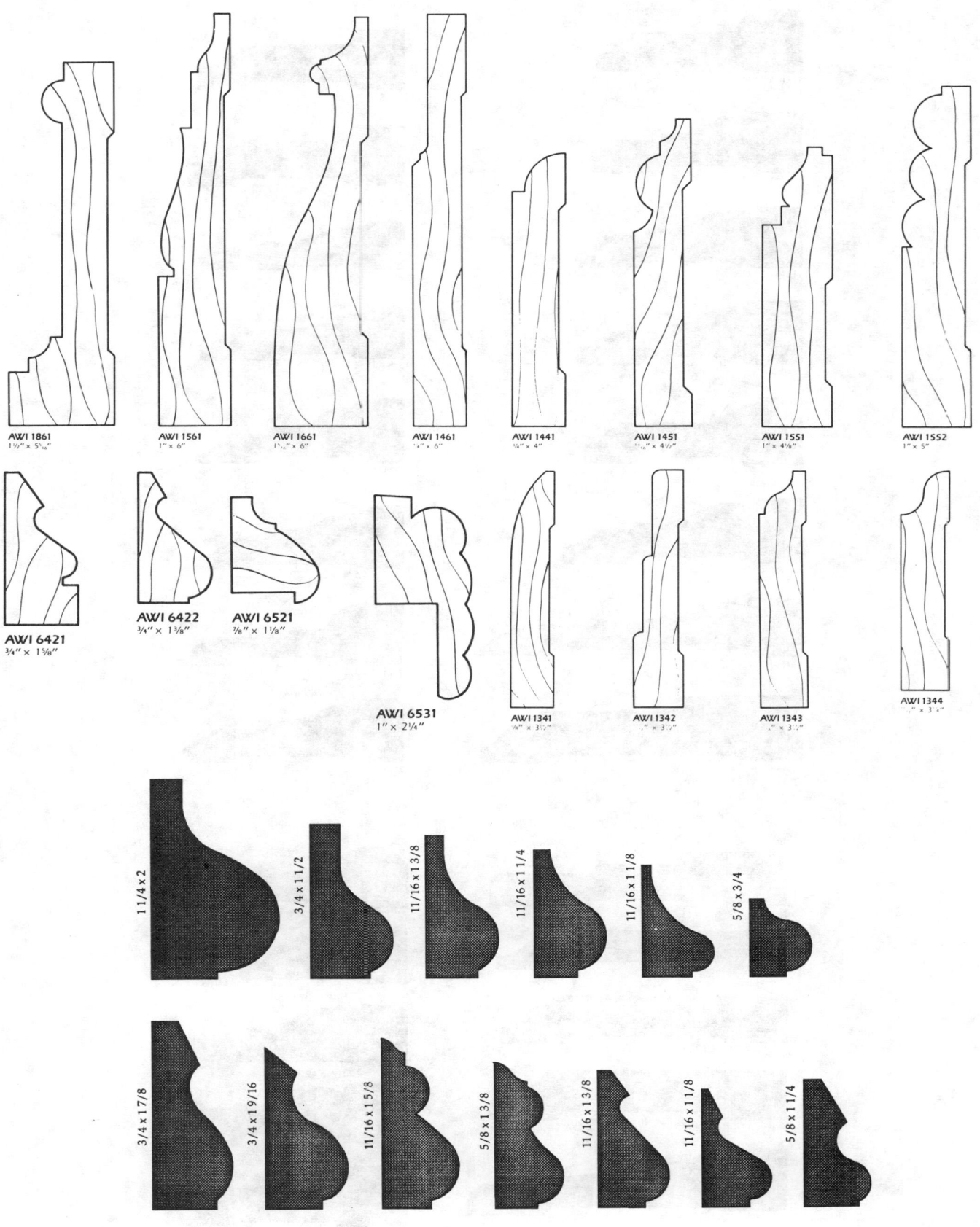

AWI 1861
1½" × 5¾"

AWI 1561
1" × 6"

AWI 1661
1¼" × 6"

AWI 1461
¾" × 6"

AWI 1441
¾" × 4"

AWI 1451
1⅛" × 4½"

AWI 1551
1" × 4⅛"

AWI 1552
1" × 5"

AWI 6421
¾" × 1⅝"

AWI 6422
¾" × 1⅜"

AWI 6521
⅞" × 1⅛"

AWI 6531
1" × 2¼"

AWI 1341
⅞" × 3½"

AWI 1342
⅞" × 3½"

AWI 1343
⅞" × 3½"

AWI 1344
⅞" × 3½"

11/4 x 2

3/4 x 11/2

11/16 x 13/8

11/16 x 11/4

11/16 x 11/8

5/8 x 3/4

3/4 x 17/8

3/4 x 19/16

11/16 x 15/8

5/8 x 13/8

11/16 x 13/8

11/16 x 11/8

5/8 x 11/4

Base Cap Moulds

CORNICES AND MOULDINGS
Casings

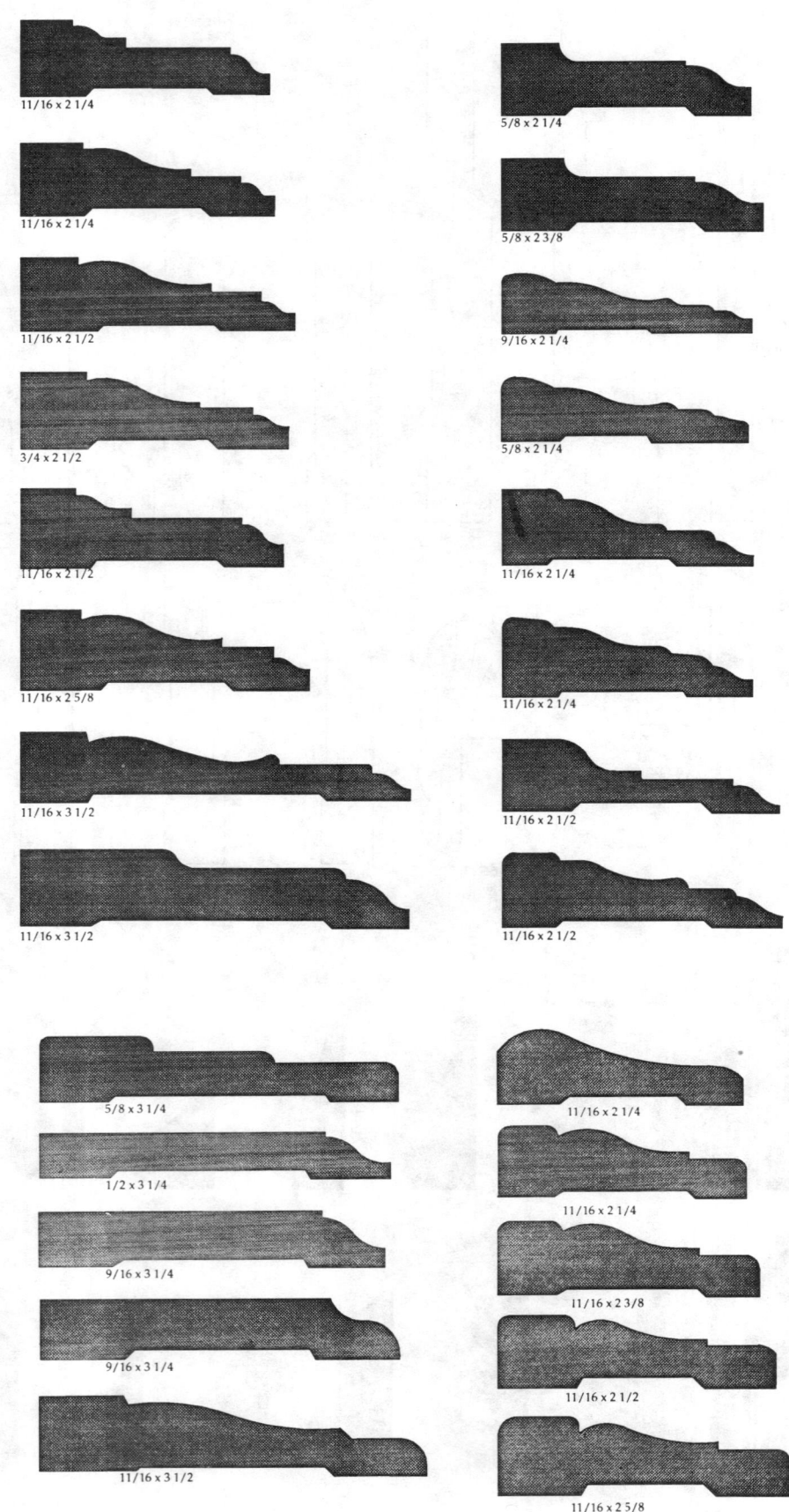

11/16 x 2 1/4

11/16 x 2 1/4

11/16 x 2 1/2

3/4 x 2 1/2

11/16 x 2 1/2

11/16 x 2 5/8

11/16 x 3 1/2

11/16 x 3 1/2

5/8 x 2 1/4

5/8 x 2 3/8

9/16 x 2 1/4

5/8 x 2 1/4

11/16 x 2 1/4

11/16 x 2 1/4

11/16 x 2 1/2

11/16 x 2 1/2

5/8 x 3 1/4

1/2 x 3 1/4

9/16 x 3 1/4

9/16 x 3 1/4

11/16 x 3 1/2

11/16 x 2 1/4

11/16 x 2 1/4

11/16 x 2 3/8

11/16 x 2 1/2

11/16 x 2 5/8

CORNICES AND MOULDINGS

Casings

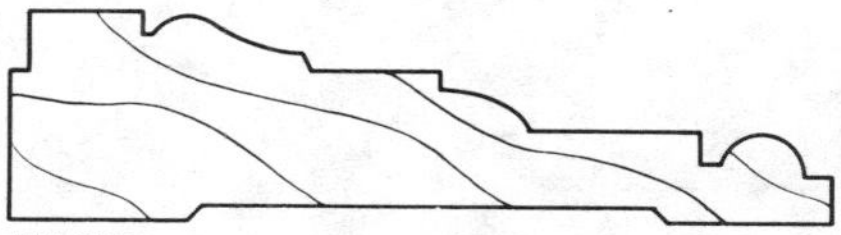
AWI 4551
1 1/16" × 4 1/8"

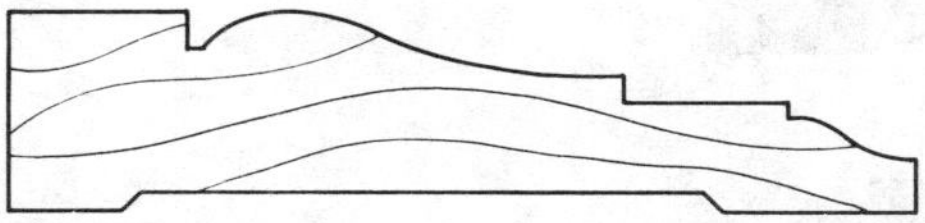
AWI 4552
1" × 4 [illegible]"

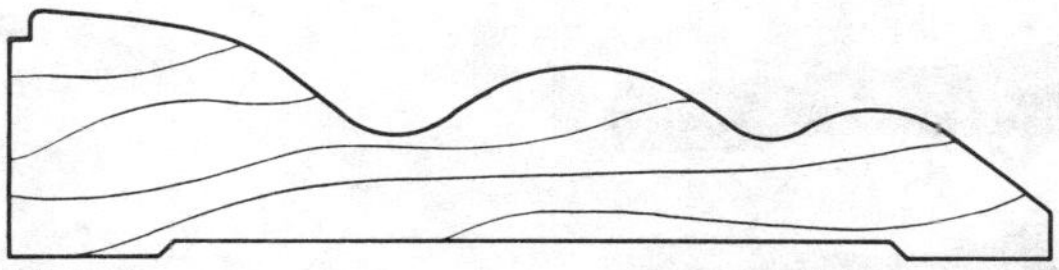
AWI 4661
1 1/4" × 5 3/16"

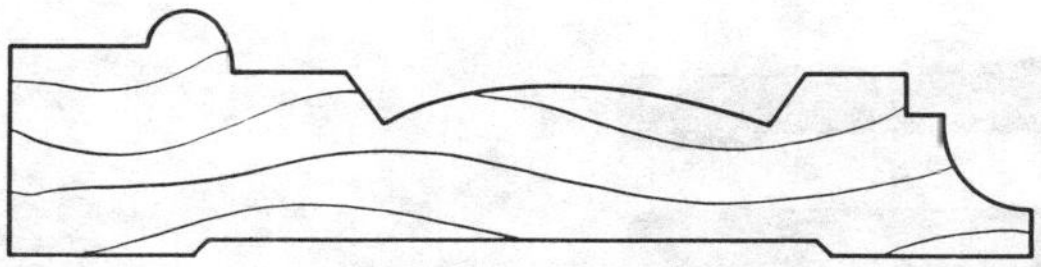
AWI 4662
1 1/4" × 5 1/8"

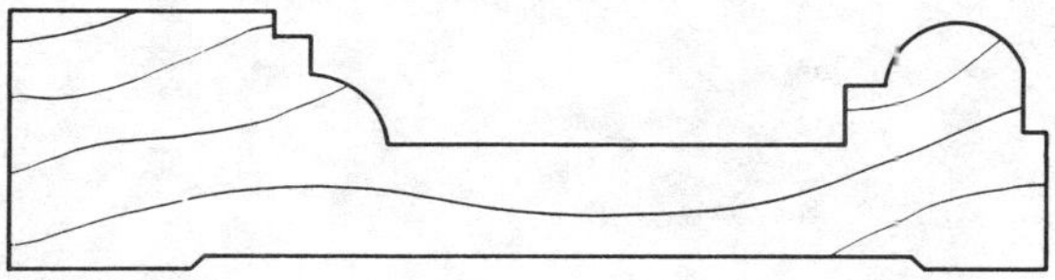
AWI 4861
1 7/16" × 5 7/16"

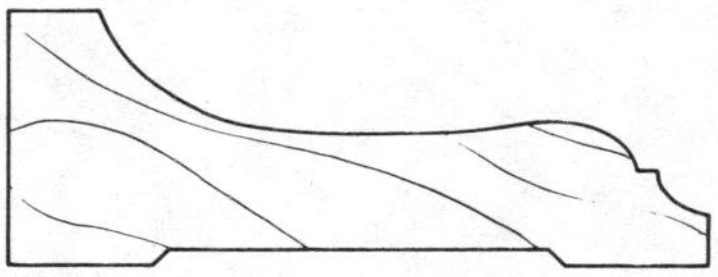
AWI 4641
1[illegible]" × 3[illegible]"

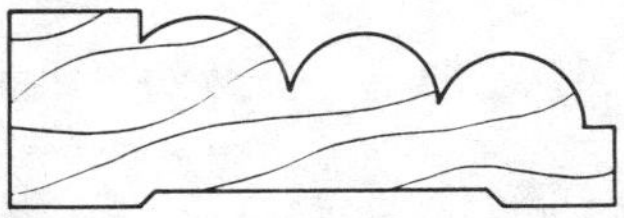
AWI 4531
1" × 3"

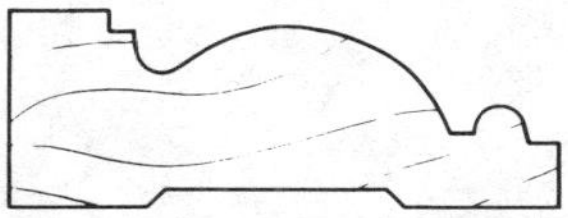
AWI 4532
1" × 2[illegible]"

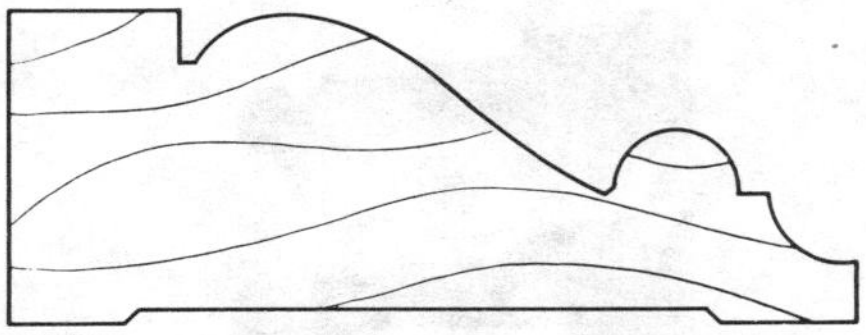
AWI 4851
1 3/8" × 4 1/4"

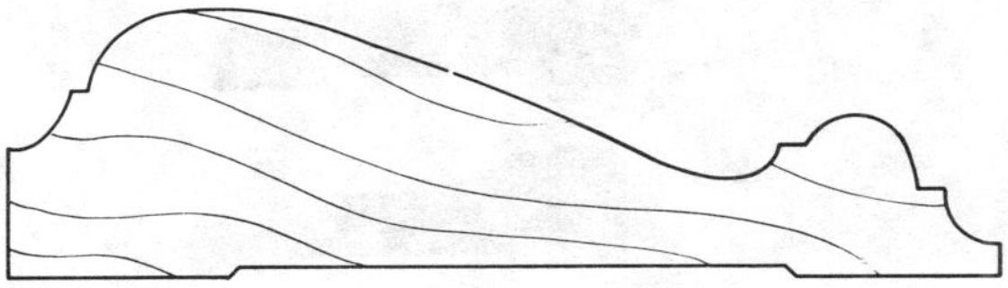
AWI 4862
1[illegible]" × 5 1/2"

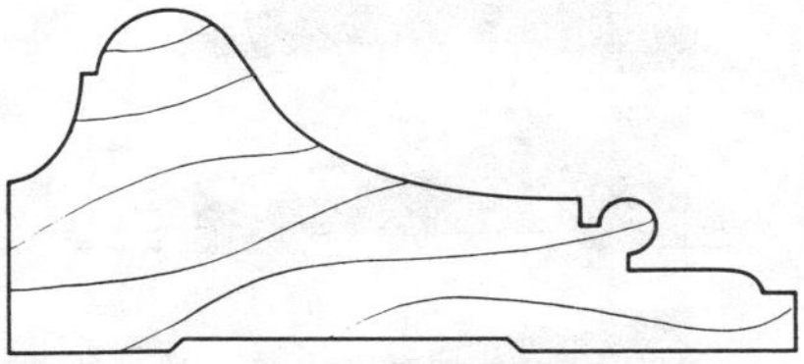
AWI 4842
1[illegible]" × 3 7/8"

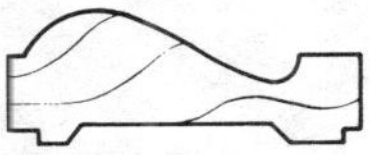
AWI 4321
[illegible]" × 1 3/4"

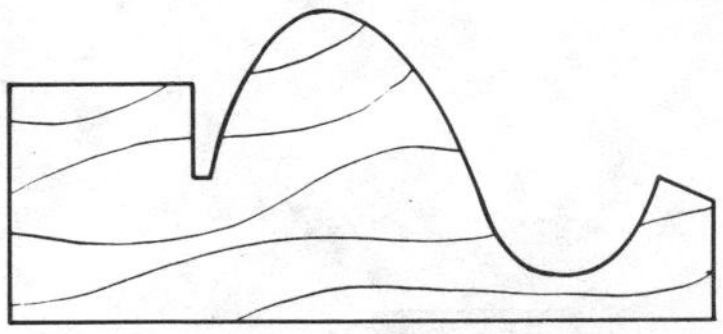
AWI 4841
1 3/8" × 3 1/2"

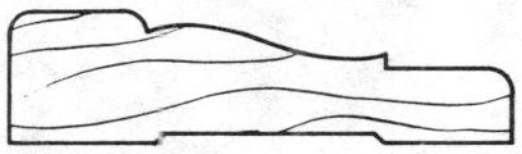
AWI 4332
[illegible]" × 2 1/2"

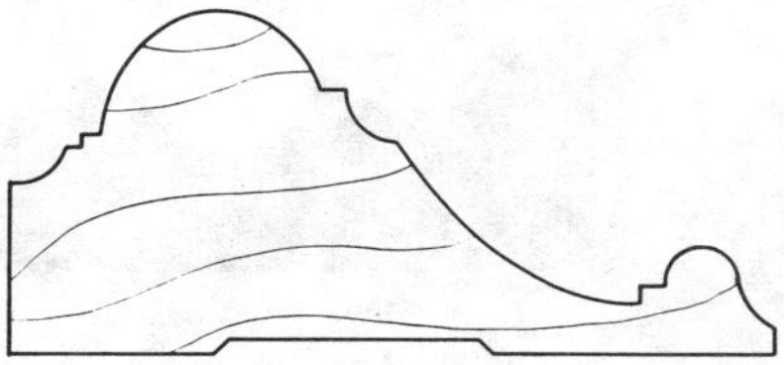
AWI 4842
1 1/4" × 4"

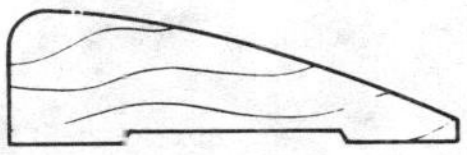
AWI 4331
[illegible]" × 2[illegible]"

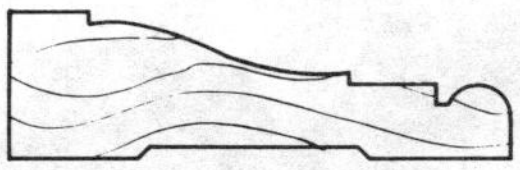
AWI 4431
3/4" × 2[illegible]"

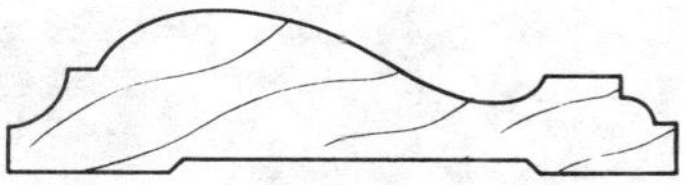
AWI 4441
[illegible]" × 3[illegible]"

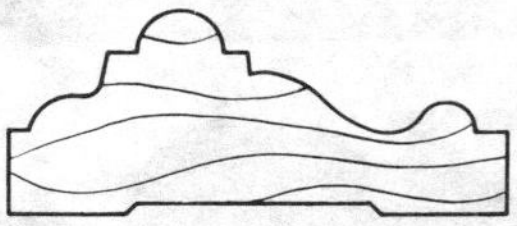
AWI 4533
1[illegible]" × 2[illegible]"

CORNICES AND MOULDINGS

Beaded Casings

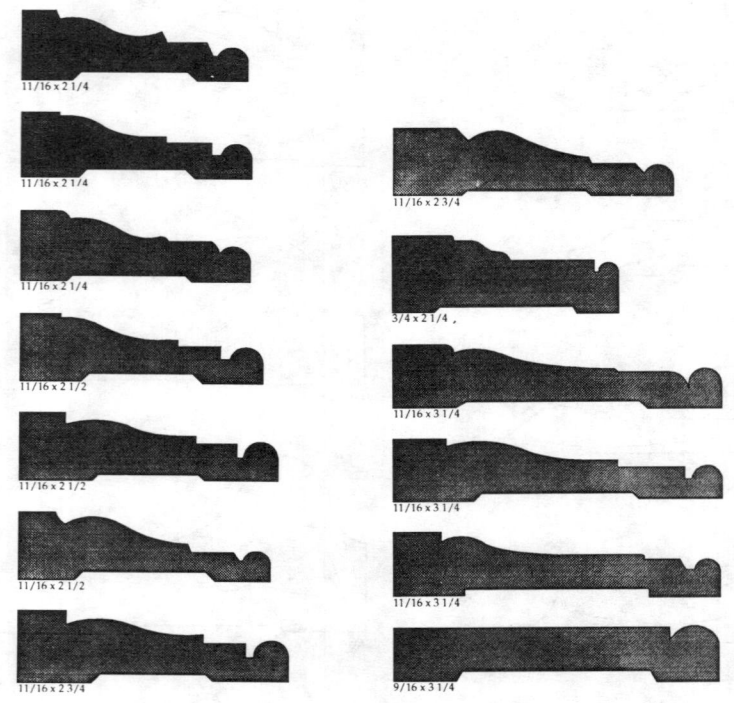

11/16 x 2 1/4

11/16 x 2 1/4

11/16 x 2 1/4

11/16 x 2 1/2

11/16 x 2 1/2

11/16 x 2 1/2

11/16 x 2 3/4

11/16 x 2 3/4

3/4 x 2 1/4

11/16 x 3 1/4

11/16 x 3 1/4

11/16 x 3 1/4

9/16 x 3 1/4

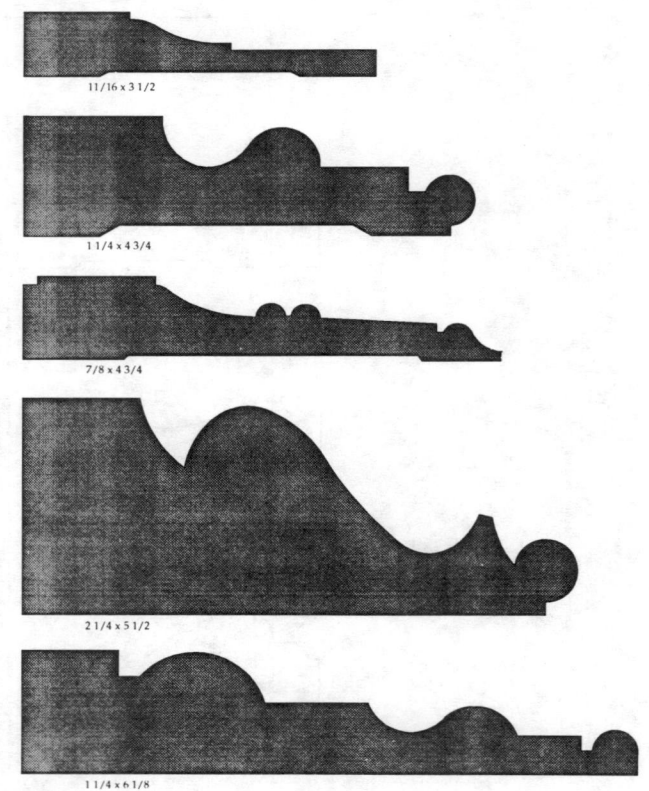

11/16 x 3 1/2

1 1/4 x 4 3/4

7/8 x 4 3/4

2 1/4 x 5 1/2

1 1/4 x 6 1/8

Specialty casings

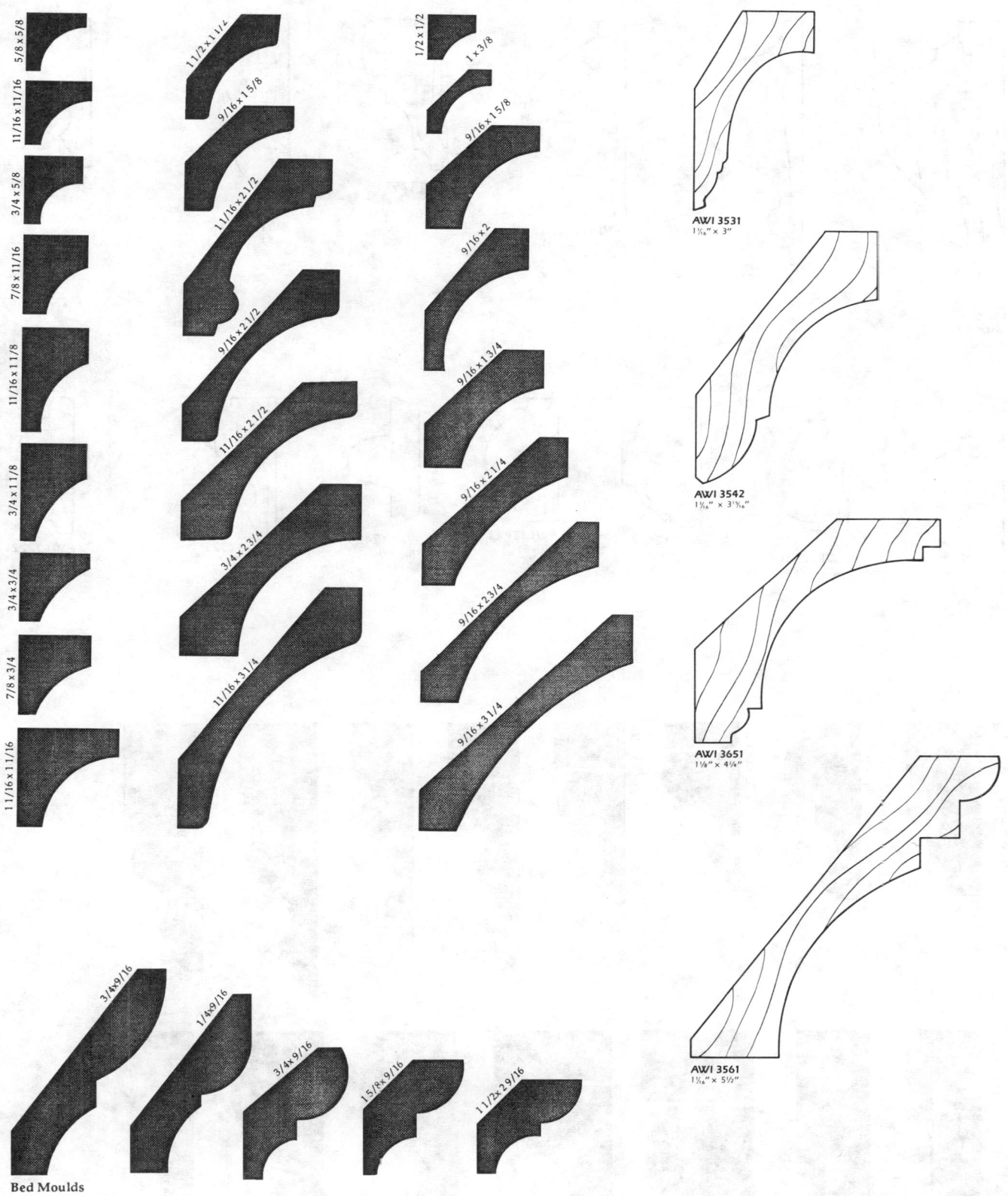

5/8 x 5/8

11/16 x 11/16

3/4 x 5/8

7/8 x 11/16

11/16 x 1 1/8

3/4 x 1 1/8

3/4 x 3/4

7/8 x 3/4

1 1/16 x 1 11/16

1 1/2 x 1 1/4

9/16 x 1 5/8

11/16 x 2 1/2

9/16 x 2 1/2

11/16 x 2 1/2

3/4 x 2 3/4

11/16 x 3 1/4

1/2 x 1/2

1 x 3/8

9/16 x 1 5/8

9/16 x 2

9/16 x 1 3/4

9/16 x 2 1/4

9/16 x 2 3/4

9/16 x 3 1/4

AWI 3531
1 1/16" × 3"

AWI 3542
1 1/16" × 3 1/16"

AWI 3651
1 1/8" × 4 1/4"

AWI 3561
1 1/8" × 5 1/2"

3/4 x 9/16

1/4 x 9/16

3/4 x 9/16

1 5/8 x 9/16

1 1/2 x 2 9/16

Bed Moulds

CORNICES AND MOULDINGS
Panel Mouldings

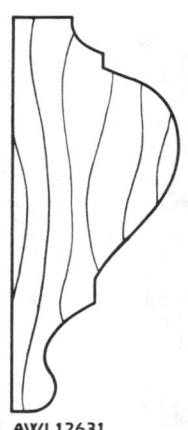

AWI 12631
1¼" × 3"

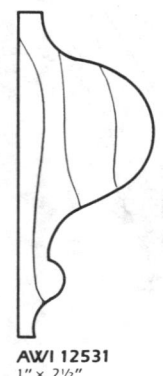

AWI 12531
1" × 2½"

AWI 12522
1" × 2"

AWI 12523
1" × 1½"

AWI 12321
¹¹⁄₁₆" × 1¹⁵⁄₁₆"

AWI 12322
¹¹⁄₁₆" × 1½"

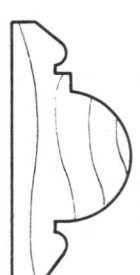

AWI 12521
⅞" × 2"

AWI 12421
1³⁄₁₆" × 1½"

AWI 12422
1³⁄₁₆" × 1⁵⁄₁₆"

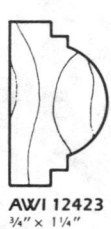

AWI 12423
¾" × 1¼"

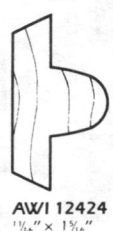

AWI 12424
¹¹⁄₁₆" × 1⁵⁄₁₆"

AWI 12323
¹¹⁄₁₆" × 1⅜"

AWI 12221
⁹⁄₁₆" × 1⅜"

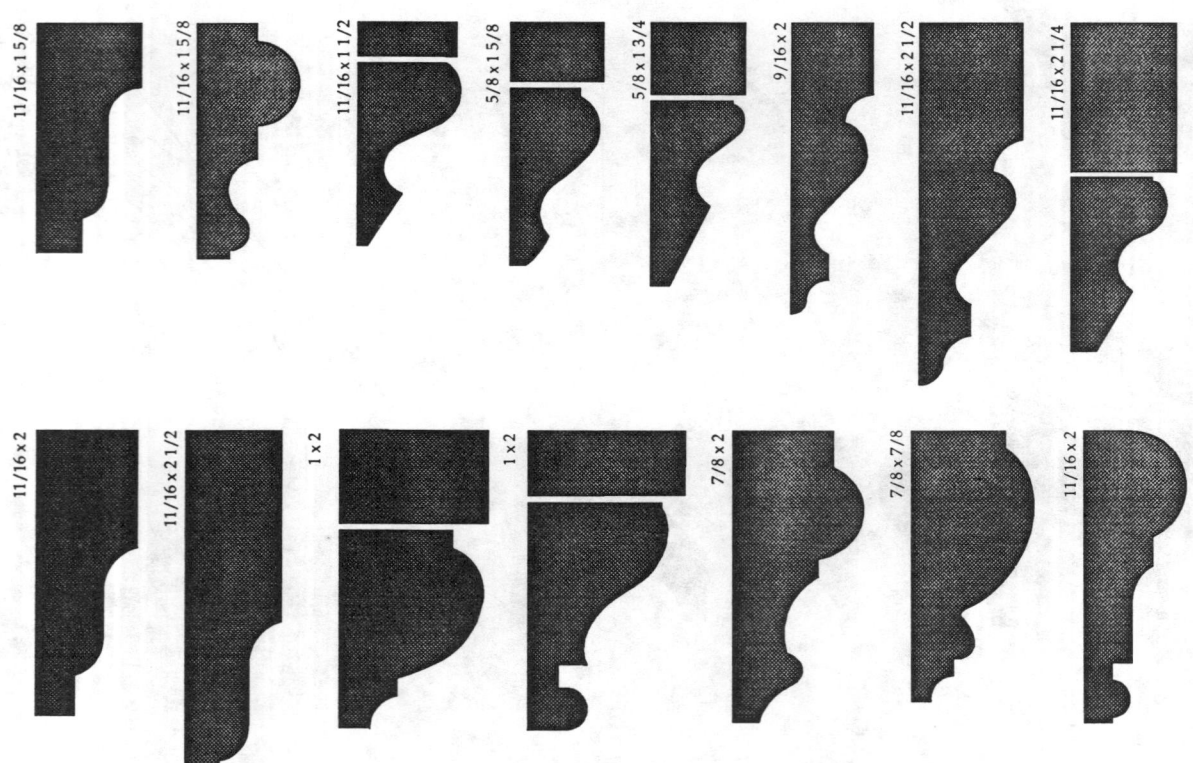

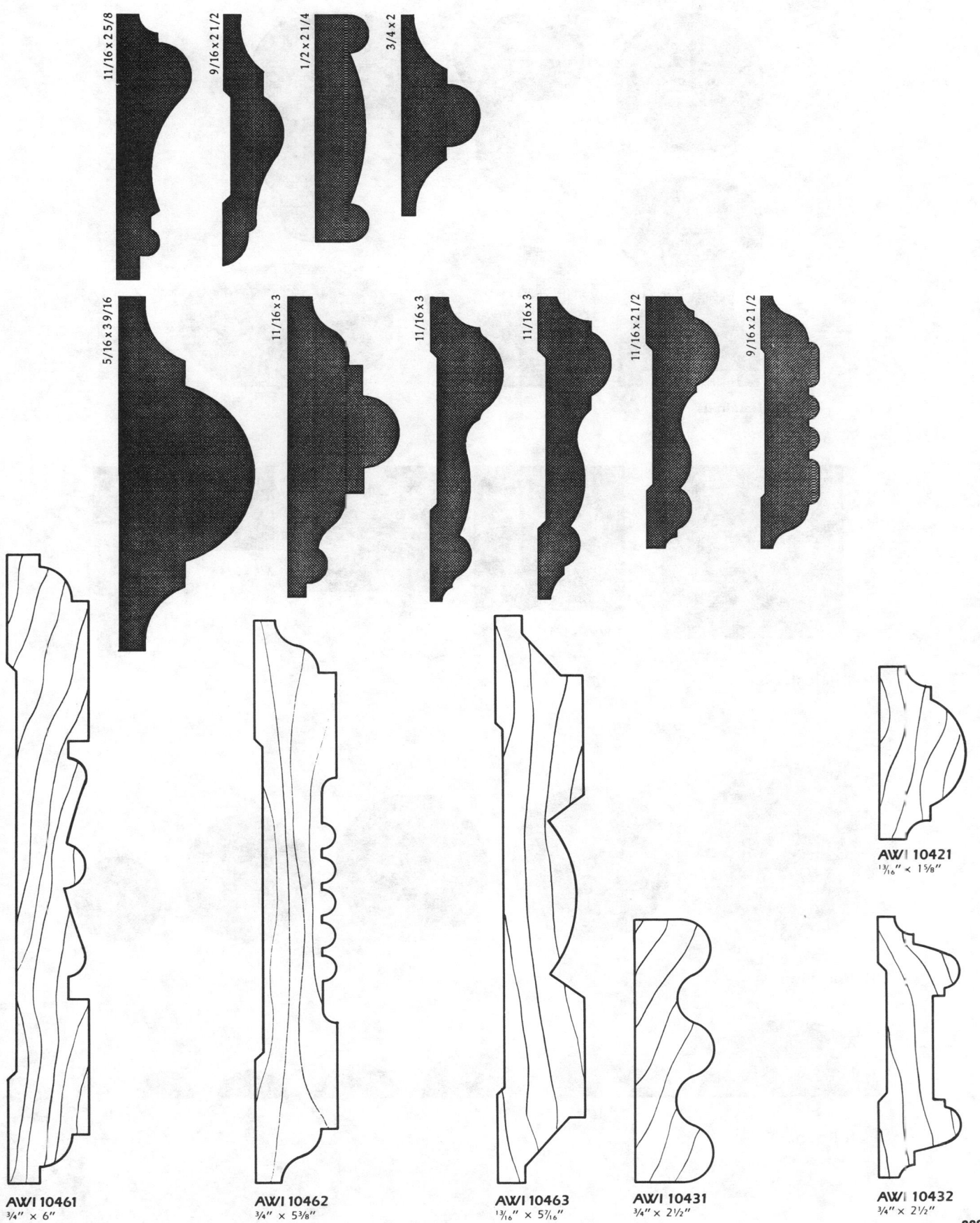

11/16 x 2 5/8

9/16 x 2 1/2

1/2 x 2 1/4

3/4 x 2

5/16 x 3 9/16

11/16 x 3

11/16 x 3

11/16 x 3

11/16 x 2 1/2

9/16 x 2 1/2

AWI 10461
¾" × 6"

AWI 10462
¾" × 5⅜"

AWI 10463
1³⁄₁₆" × 5⁷⁄₁₆"

AWI 10431
¾" × 2½"

AWI 10432
¾" × 2½"

AWI 10421
1³⁄₁₆" × 1⅝"

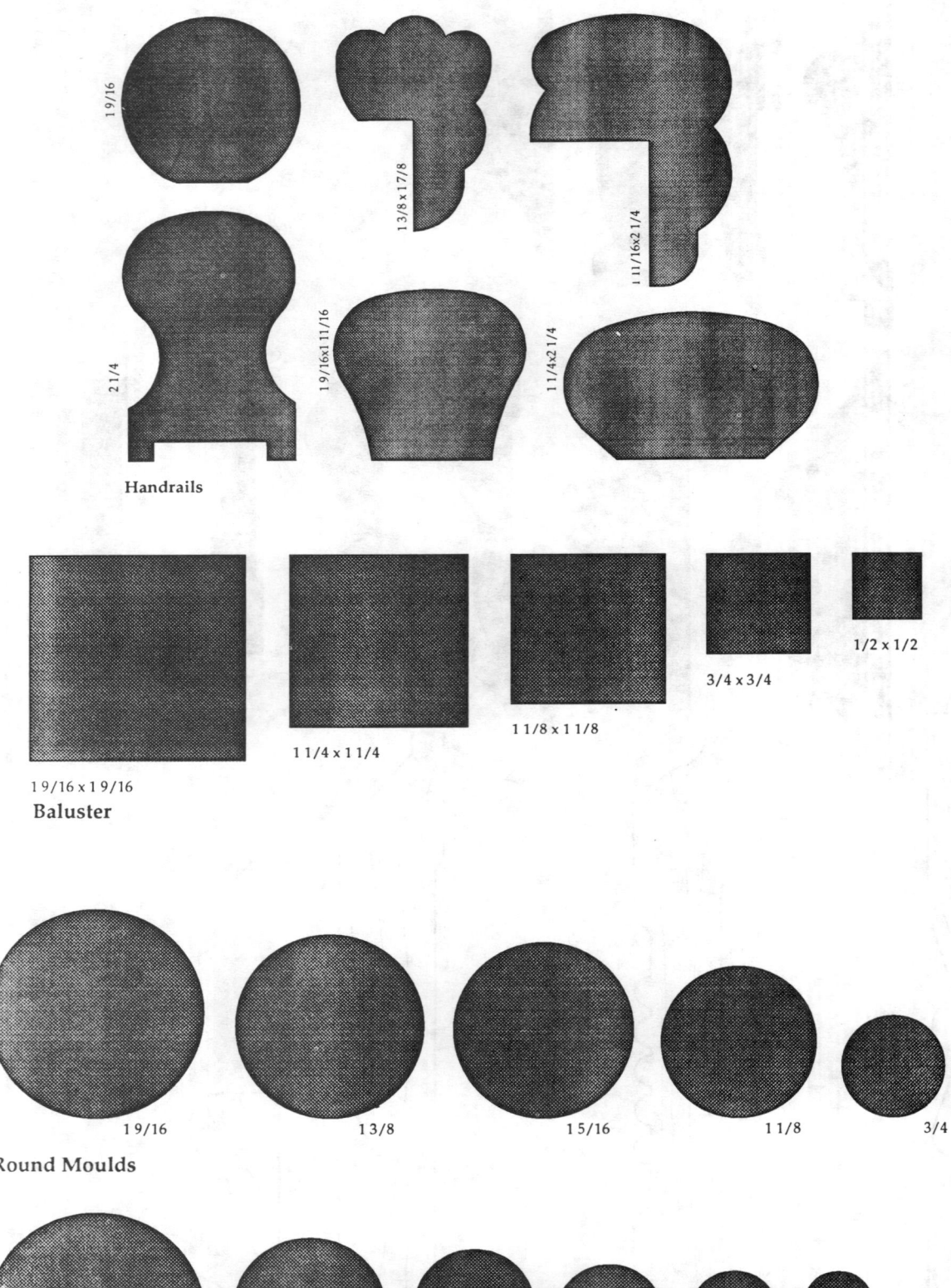

1 9/16

1 3/8 x 1 7/8

1 11/16x2 1/4

2 1/4

1 9/16x1 11/16

1 1/4x2 1/4

Handrails

1 9/16 x 1 9/16

1 1/4 x 1 1/4

1 1/8 x 1 1/8

3/4 x 3/4

1/2 x 1/2

Baluster

1 9/16

1 3/8

1 5/16

1 1/8

3/4

Round Moulds

1 9/16

1 1/8

7/8

3/4

5/8

1/4

Half Rounds

CORNICES AND MOULDINGS

Clam Shell and Stop Mouldings

CLAM SHELL MOULDINGS

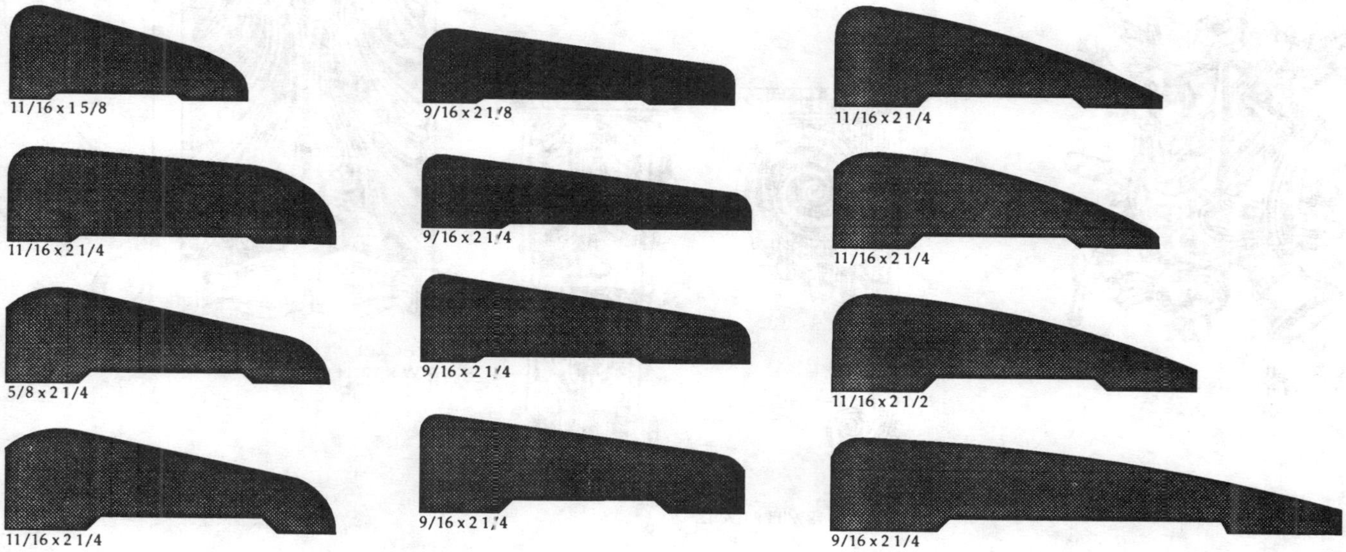
11/16 x 1 5/8
9/16 x 2 1/8
11/16 x 2 1/4
11/16 x 2 1/4
9/16 x 2 1/4
11/16 x 2 1/4
5/8 x 2 1/4
9/16 x 2 1/4
11/16 x 2 1/2
11/16 x 2 1/4
9/16 x 2 1/4
9/16 x 2 1/4

STOP MOULDINGS

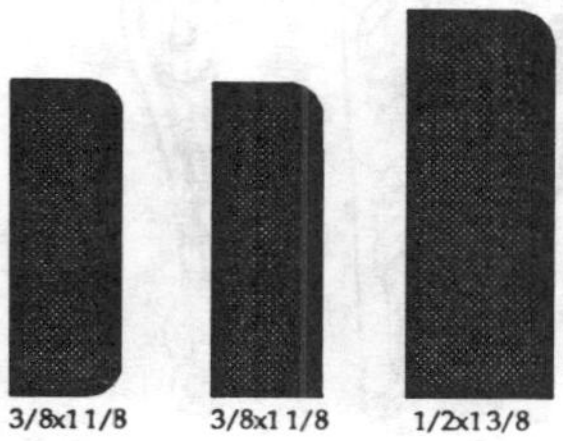
3/8x1 1/8
3/8x1 1/8
1/2x1 3/8

Sanitary

Lattice

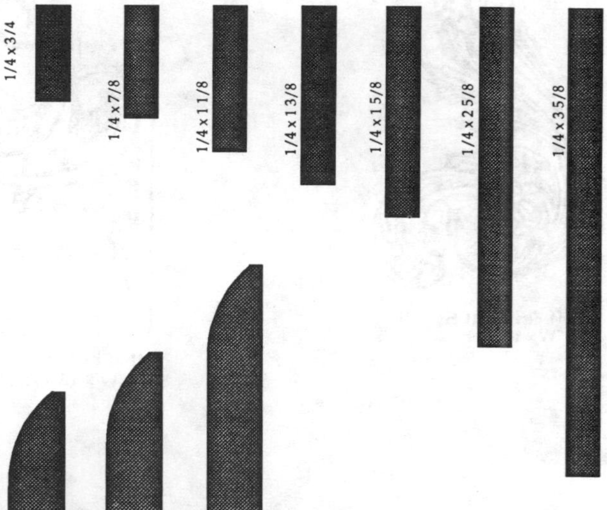
1/4 x 3/4
1/4 x 7/8
1/4 x 1 1/8
1/4 x 1 3/8
1/4 x 1 5/8
1/4 x 2 5/8
1/4 x 3 5/8

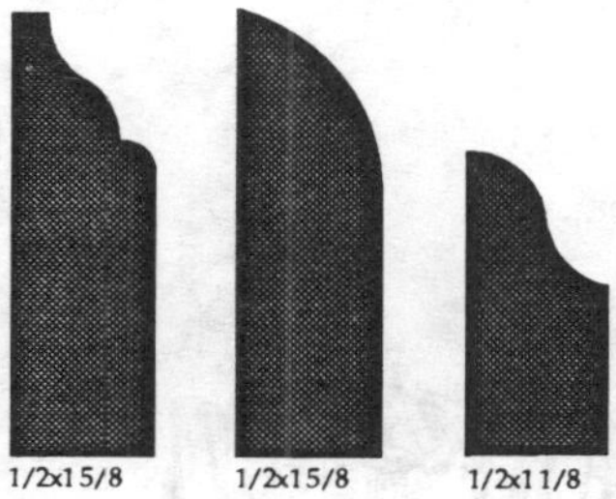
1/2x1 5/8
1/2x1 5/8
1/2x1 1/8

Sash

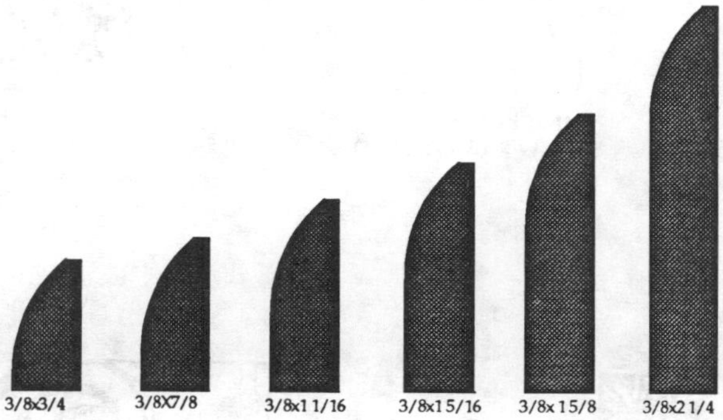
3/8x3/4
3/8X7/8
3/8x1 1/16
3/8x1 5/16
3/8x 1 5/8
3/8x2 1/4

Clam Shell

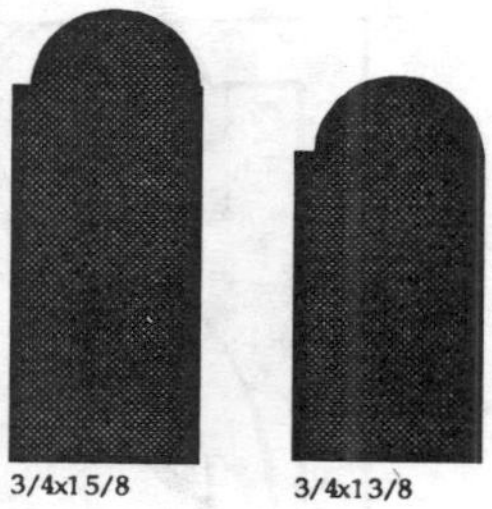
3/4x1 5/8
3/4x1 3/8

Sash

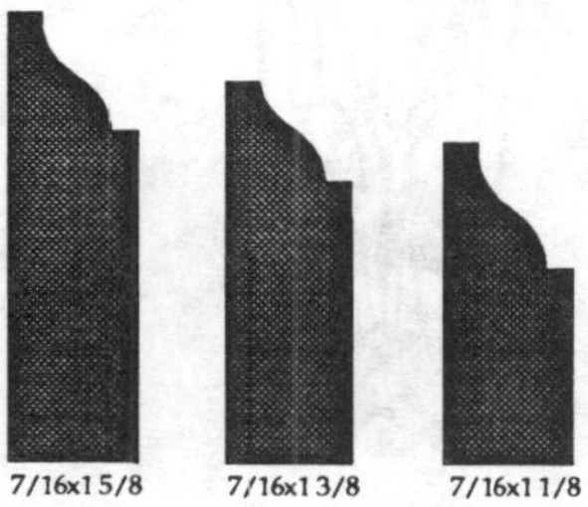
7/16x1 5/8
7/16x1 3/8
7/16x1 1/8

Sash

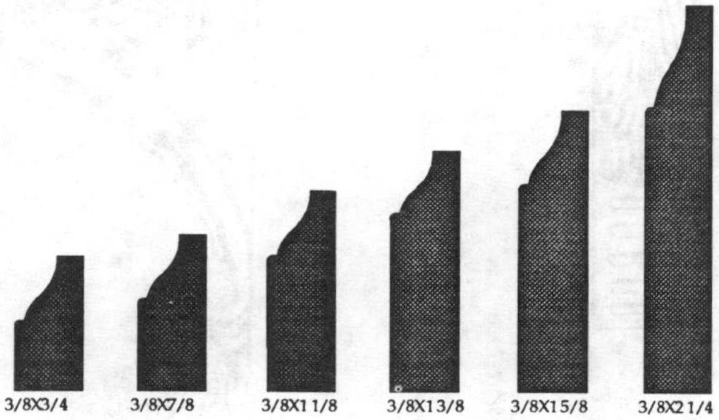
3/8X3/4
3/8X7/8
3/8X1 1/8
3/8X1 3/8
3/8X1 5/8
3/8X2 1/4

Colonial

Flute & Lyre
10½"W x 11"H

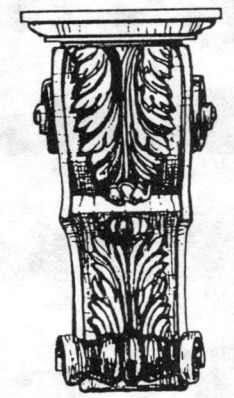

Bracket
6½"W x 12½"H x 5¼"D.

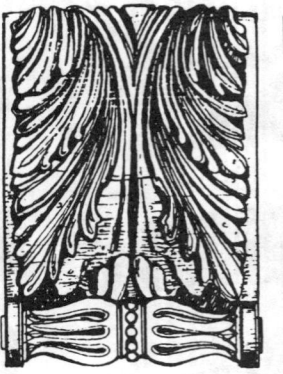

Bracket
8"W x 12"H x 4"D.

Left & Right Scroll
8¼"W x 11½"H

Bracket
4½"W x 13"H x 9½"D.

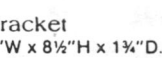

Bracket
4"W x 8½"H x 1¾"D.

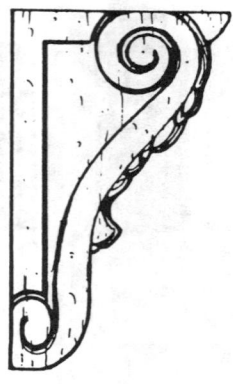

Bracket
2¾"W x 12"H x 7"D

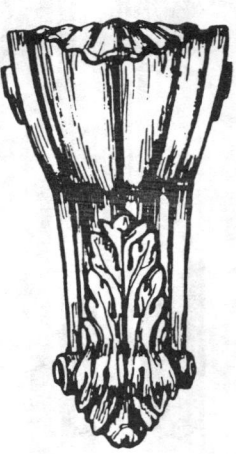

Bracket
7½"W x 14"H x 7½"D

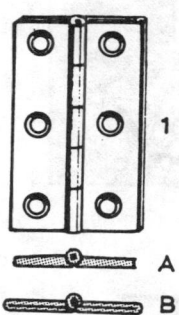

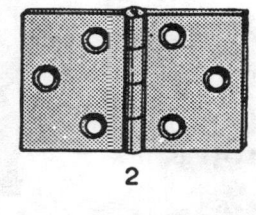

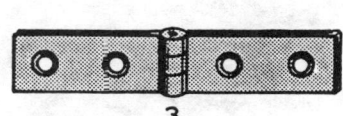

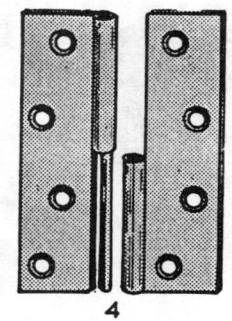

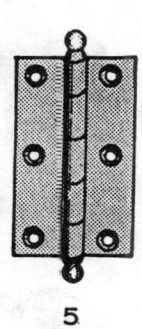

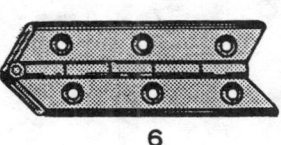

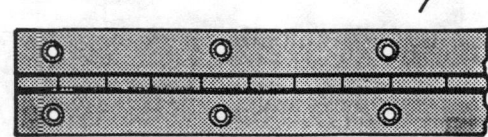

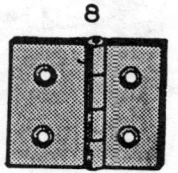

TABLE 1 Butt Hinges

No.	Type	Comments
1	Standard brass butt: A, solid drawn type; B, pressed pattern	General usage
2	Back flap hinge	With wide plates for table leaves and rebated or rabbeted fallflaps
3	Strap hinge	For narrow sections
4	Lift-off butt	For doors which have to be removed from time to time without disturbing setting
5	Loose pin hinge; ball-tipped hinge	Where it is necessary to throw door clear of carcass frame with the whole or the hinge knuckle protruding
6	Stopped hinge	Opens through 90° only for box lids, etc.
7	Piano hinge	Continuous strip form for supporting long lengths; supplied in drilled and countersink or undrilled blanks
8	Clock case hinge	One plate is wider to allow for a projecting door

FURNITURE HARDWARE
Hinges

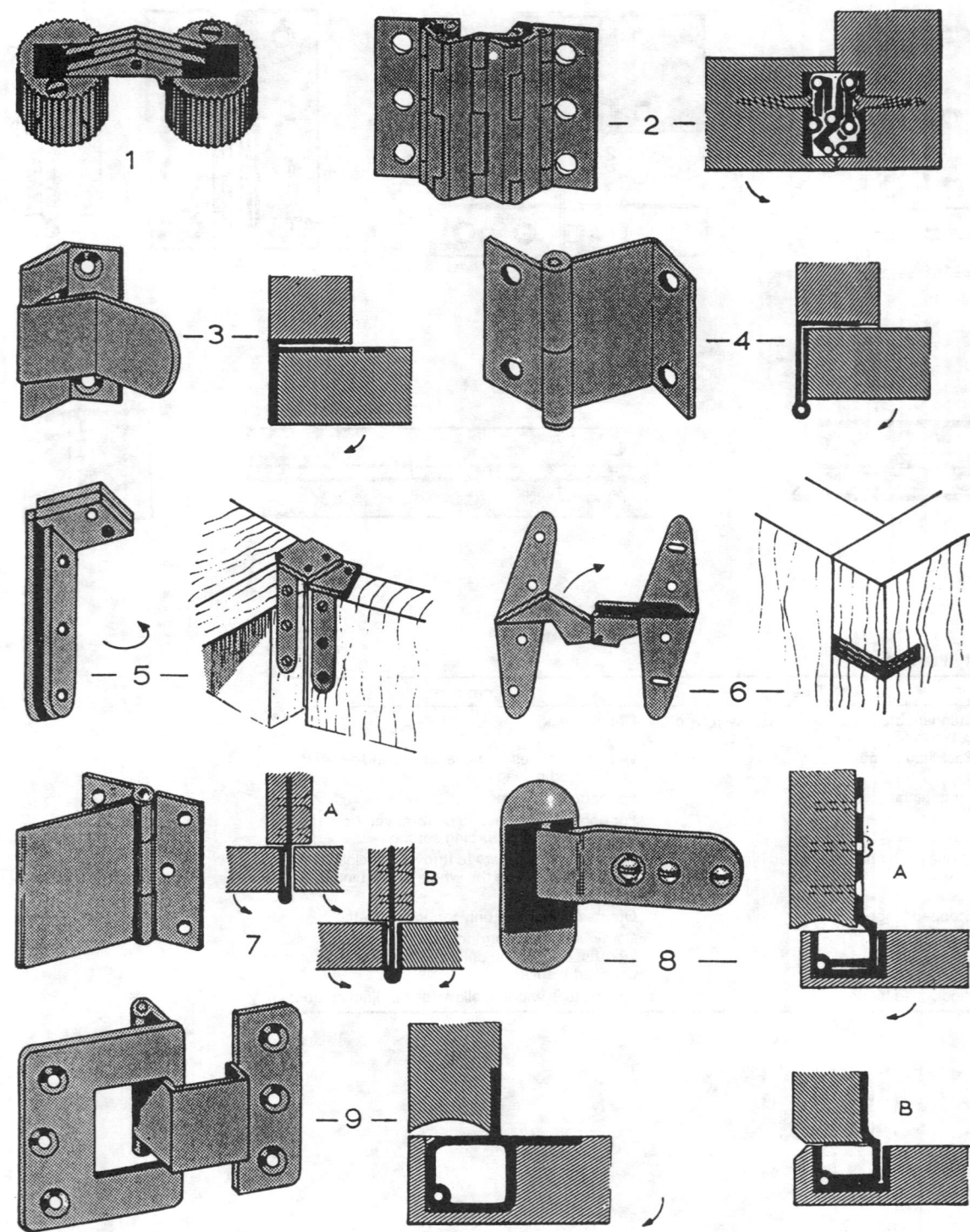

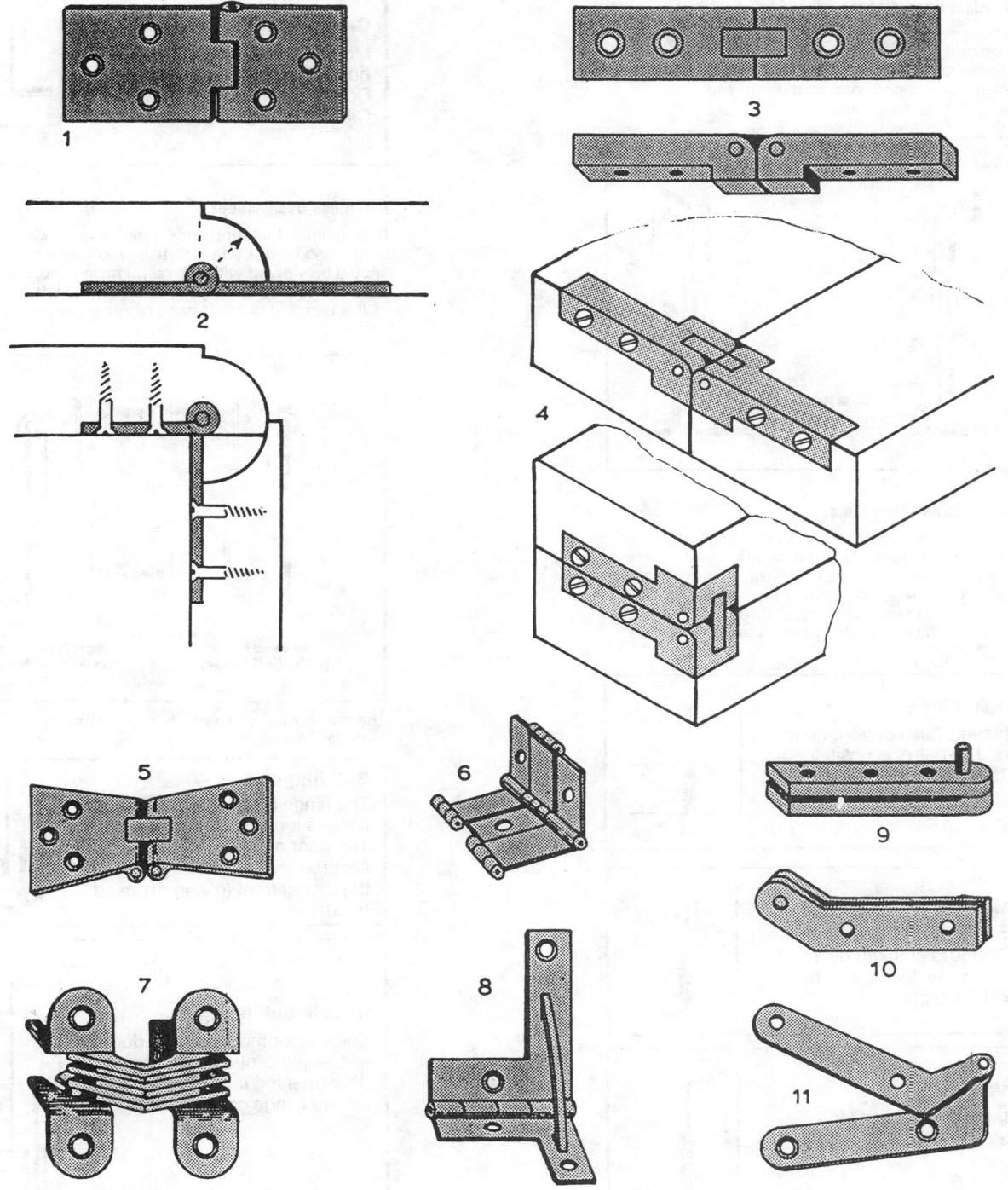

FURNITURE HARDWARE
Hinges

Left- and Right-Hand Hinges

Hinges with screw-mounted flanges should be viewed as if in mounted condition with the countersunk screw holes facing you. If the female flange is uppermost on the left, the hinge is a left-hand hinge and vice versa.

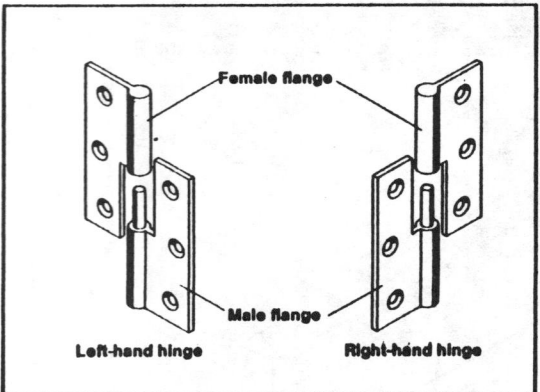

Cranked Hinges and Their Uses

The position of the door relative to the side panel can vary considerably, being decided at the design stage in accordance with the final effect required. A wide variety of hinge types has developed from variations in door mounting methods, which must be coordinated at the design stage.

Straight hinge

For butting, flush or front-hung doors. The barrel is positioned centrally between the two flanges.

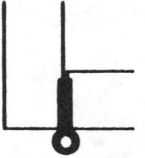

Crank B

Mounting with set-back doors. One flange is cranked by an amount equivalent to the thickness of the material.

Crank C

Similar to crank B but for forward-set doors.

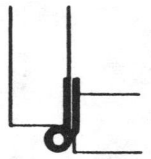

Crank D

Mounting with rebated doors with flanges of non-uniform width (reduced female flanges).

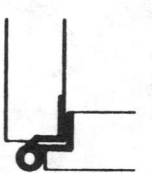

Crank L1

Mounting with butting front-hung doors
Door opening range 270°.
Crank features internal roll.

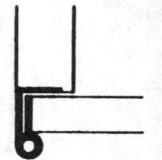

Butt Hinge Designations

Butt hinges for cupboards, windows, and doors, and hinges with mortise-type flanges should be viewed with the barrel facing you. If the female flange is positioned on the left of the barrel, it is a left-hand hinge and vice versa.

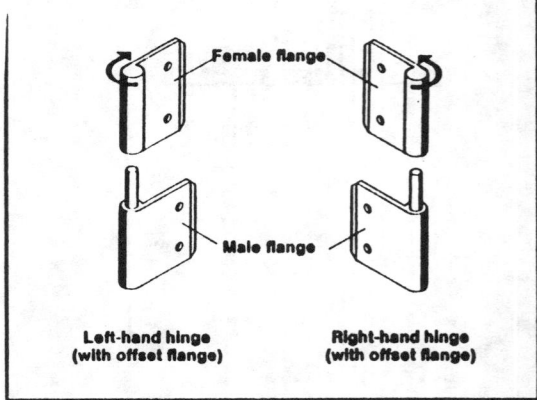

The same rule applies to hinges with symmetrical flanges.

Butt hinge

The hinge is made with offset flanges for mortised mounting. The door-mounted flange is secured with screws or pins from the rear or front (giving exposed heads).

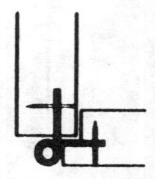

Double butt hinge

Suitable for mounting two doors to a single centre panel. The door opening range is 180° each (centre flange only mortised).

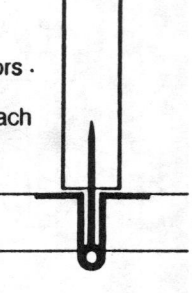

FOLDING TABLE HINGE

Functional diagram

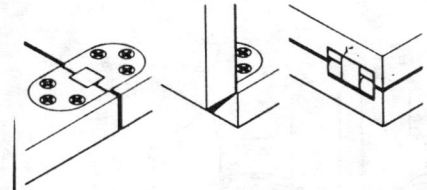

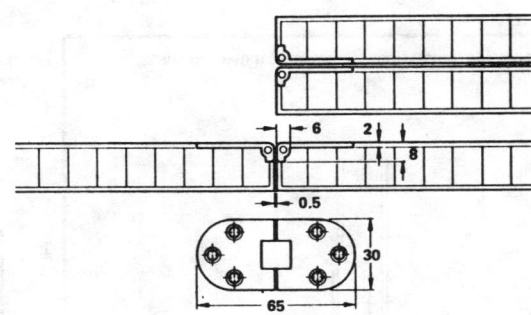

Self-supporting hinge,
for folding and sewing machine tables,
flush-mounted

Functional diagram
(seen from below)

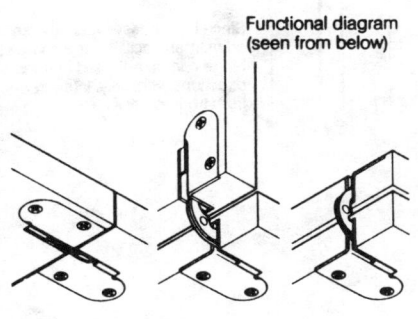

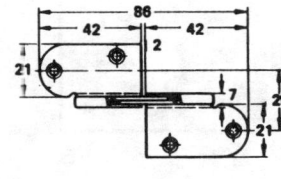

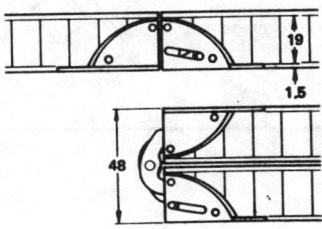

Folding table hinge,
flush-mounted

Functional diagram

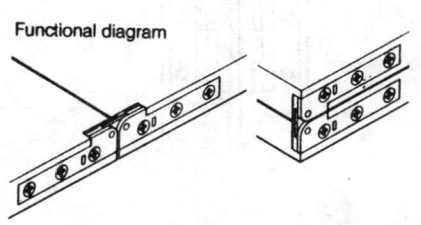

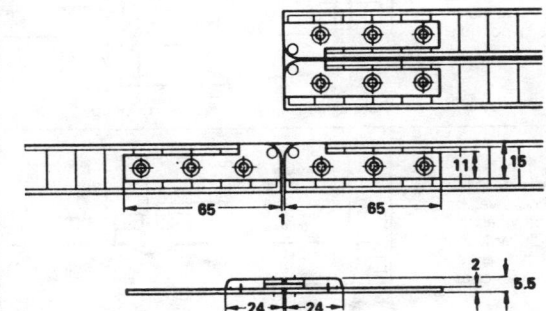

Card table hinge
Two-way table-leaf hinge,
flush-mounted

FLAP HINGES

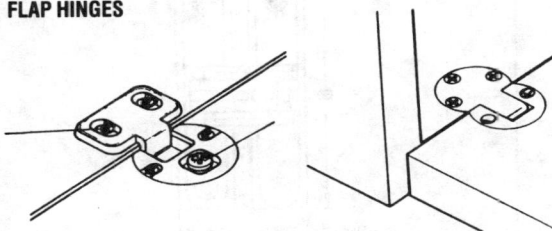

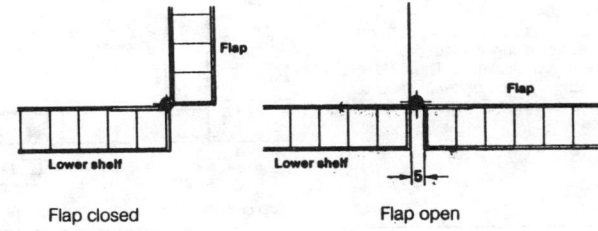

Flap closed   Flap open

Specimen mounting

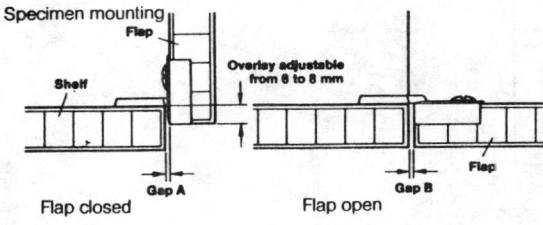

Flap closed   Flap open

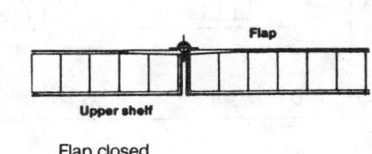

Flap closed

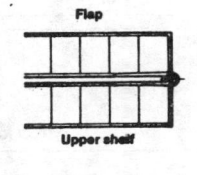

Flap open

Dimensions in mm.

FURNITURE HARDWARE
Mitred and Concealed Hinges

MITRED HINGE

The hinges are suitable for wooden doors and side panels from 16 mm to 22 mm in thickness, chamfered at an angle of 45°.

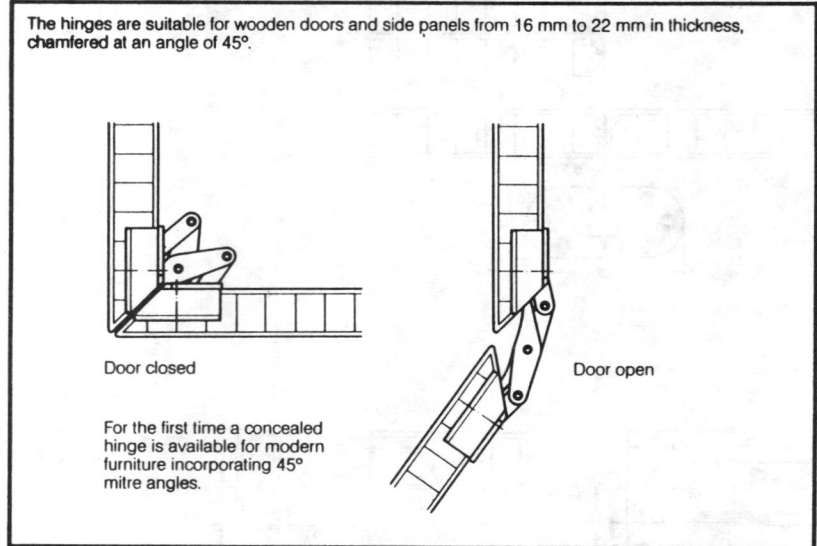

Door closed

Door open

For the first time a concealed hinge is available for modern furniture incorporating 45° mitre angles.

An all-metal mitred hinge, specially designed to enable door and carcase edges to meet at an angle of 45°.

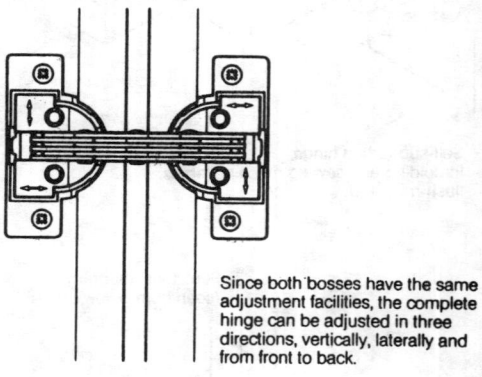

Since both bosses have the same adjustment facilities, the complete hinge can be adjusted in three directions, vertically, laterally and from front to back.

CONCEALED HINGES

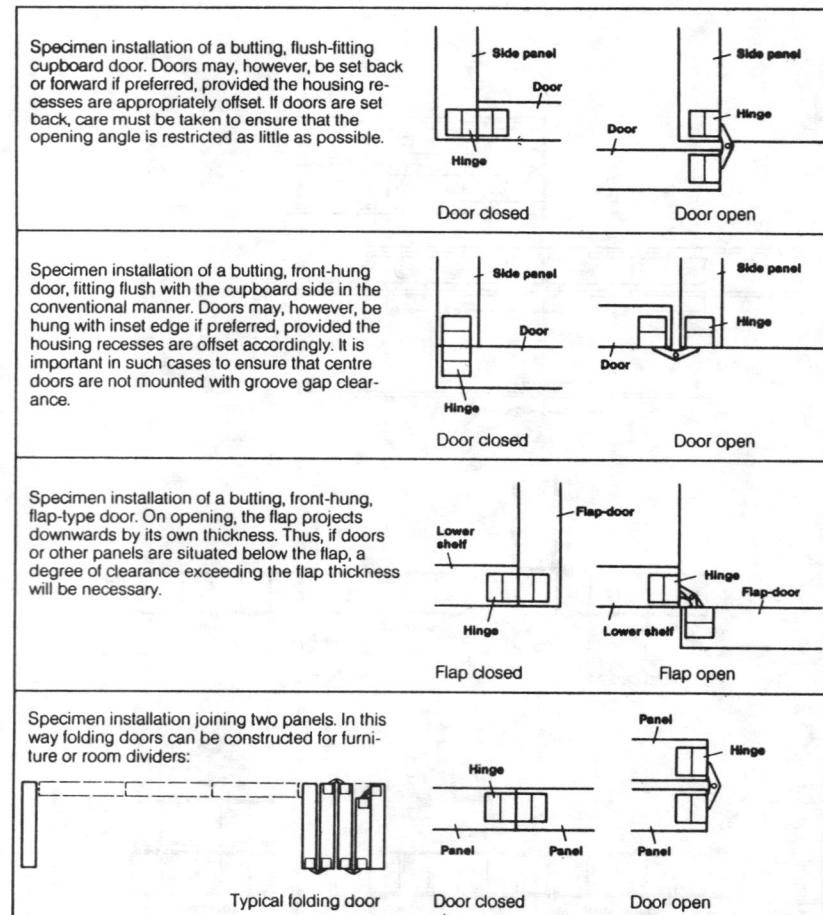

Specimen installation of a butting, flush-fitting cupboard door. Doors may, however, be set back or forward if preferred, provided the housing recesses are appropriately offset. If doors are set back, care must be taken to ensure that the opening angle is restricted as little as possible.

Side panel
Door
Hinge
Door closed

Side panel
Hinge
Door
Door open

Specimen installation of a butting, front-hung door, fitting flush with the cupboard side in the conventional manner. Doors may, however, be hung with inset edge if preferred, provided the housing recesses are offset accordingly. It is important in such cases to ensure that centre doors are not mounted with groove gap clearance.

Side panel
Door
Hinge
Door closed

Side panel
Hinge
Door
Door open

Specimen installation of a butting, front-hung, flap-type door. On opening, the flap projects downwards by its own thickness. Thus, if doors or other panels are situated below the flap, a degree of clearance exceeding the flap thickness will be necessary.

Lower shelf
Hinge
Flap closed

Flap-door
Hinge
Flap-door
Lower shelf
Flap open

Specimen installation joining two panels. In this way folding doors can be constructed for furniture or room dividers:

Typical folding door

Hinge
Panel
Panel
Door closed

Panel
Hinge
Panel
Door open

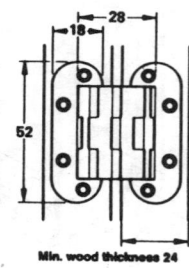

28
18
52
Min. wood thickness 24

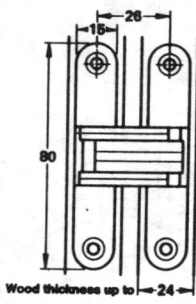

26
15
80
Wood thickness up to 24

Dimensions in mm.

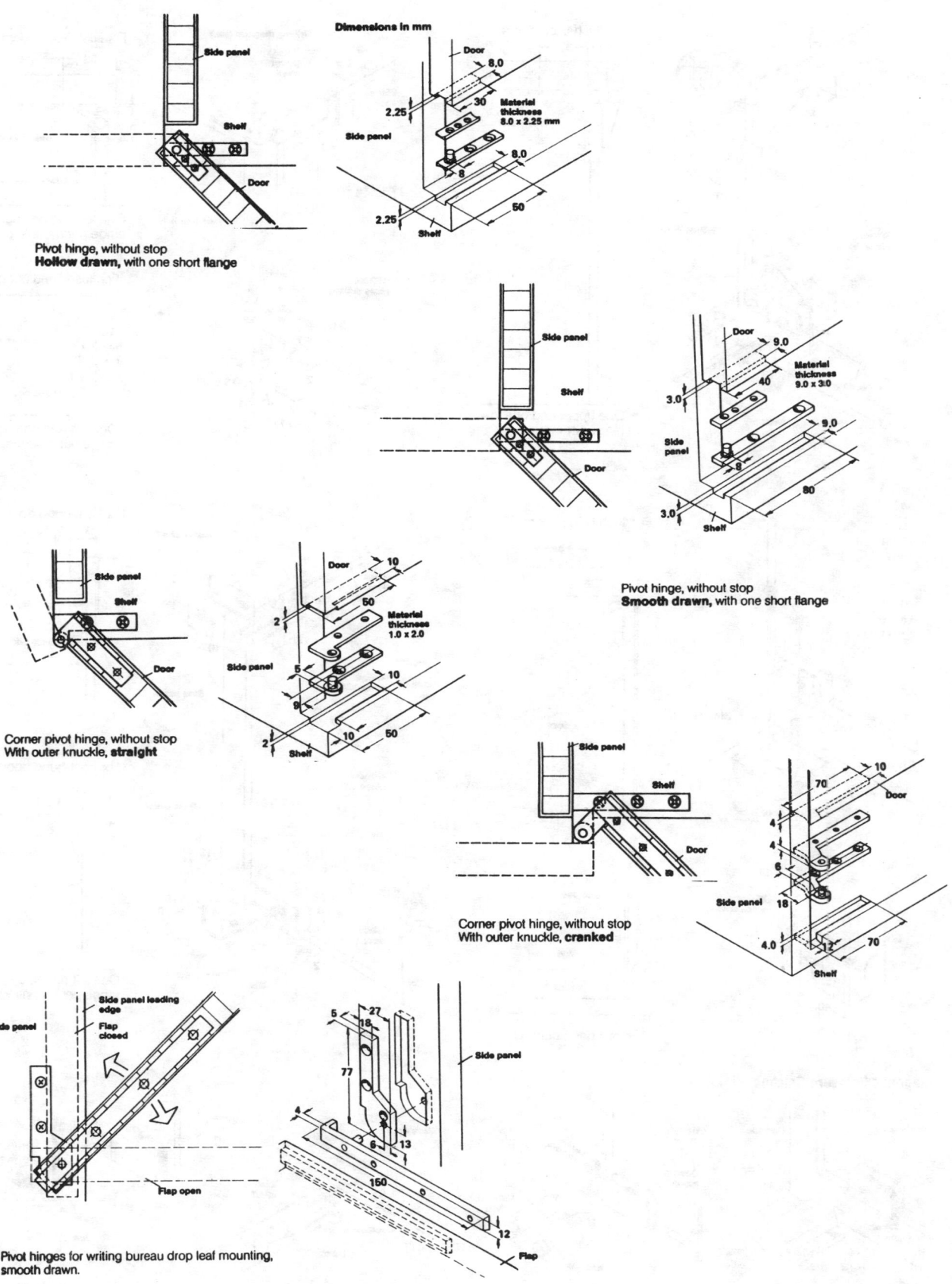

Dimensions in mm

Pivot hinge, without stop
Hollow drawn, with one short flange

Material thickness 8.0 x 2.25 mm

Pivot hinge, without stop
Smooth drawn, with one short flange

Material thickness 9.0 x 3.0

Corner pivot hinge, without stop
With outer knuckle, **straight**

Material thickness 1.0 x 2.0

Corner pivot hinge, without stop
With outer knuckle, **cranked**

Pivot hinges for writing bureau drop leaf mounting,
smooth drawn.

Dimensions in mm.

FURNITURE HARDWARE

Glass Door Hinges

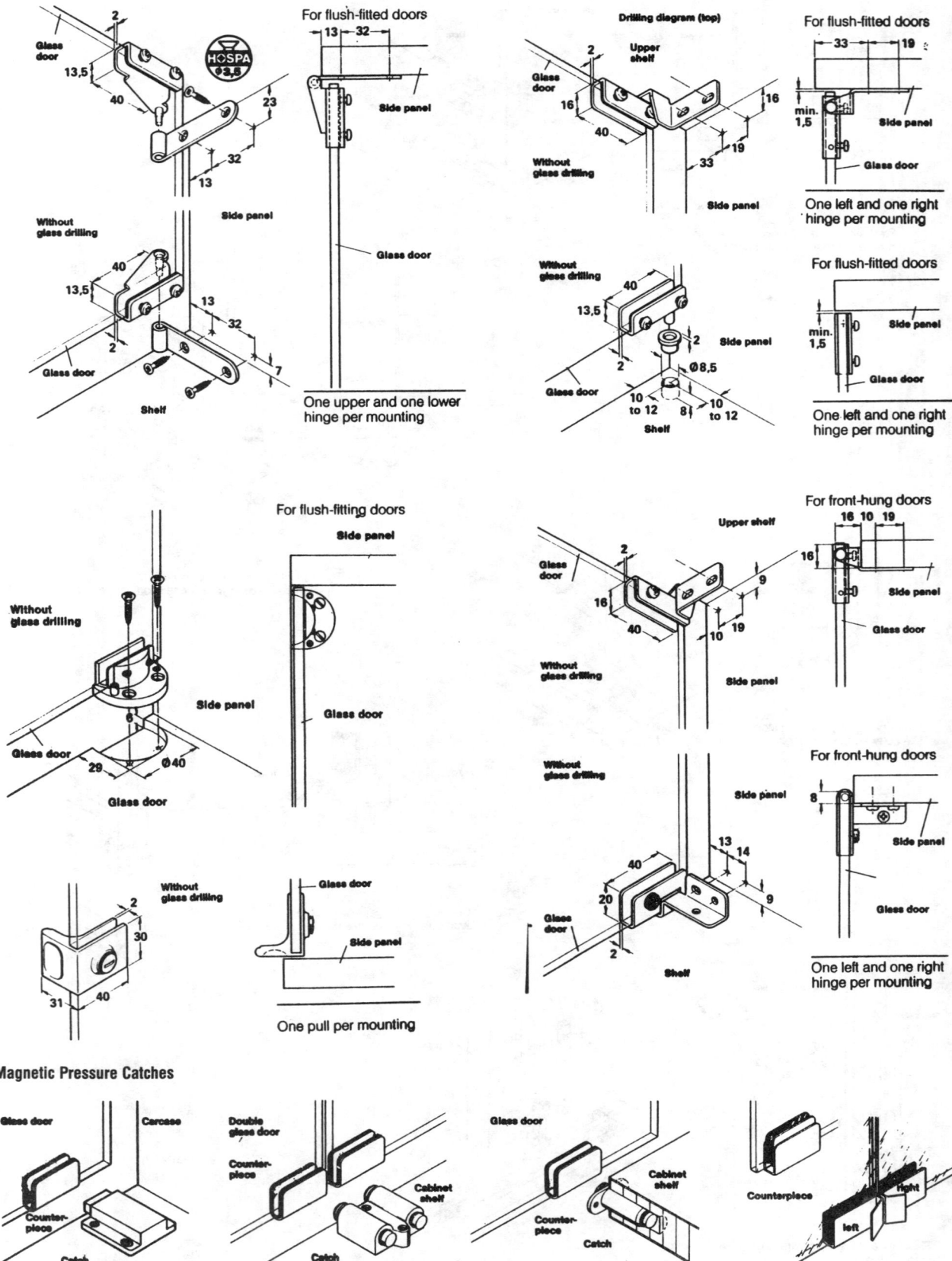

Magnetic Pressure Catches

Dimensions in mm.

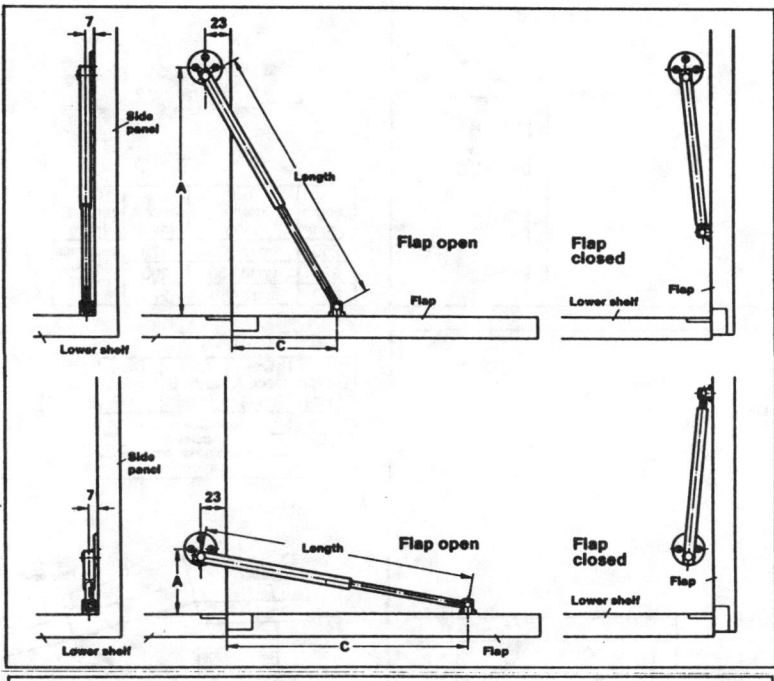

Vertical mounting

Length (mm)	Internal carcase height (mm)	Distance A (mm)	Distance C (mm)
250	300 to 400	240	Determine by trial mounting
325	350 to 450	308	
450	400 to 500	430	

Horizontal mounting

Length (mm)	Internal carcase height (mm)	Distance A (mm)	Distance C (mm)
250	300 to 400	65	Determine by trial mounting
325	350 to 450	100	
450	400 to 500	150	

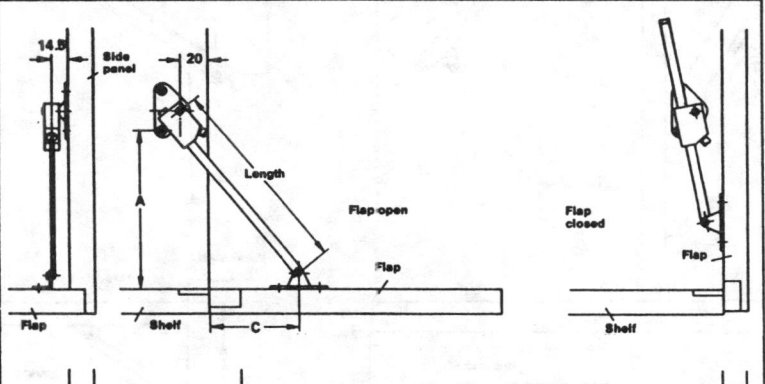

Vertical mounting

Length (mm)	Internal carcase height (mm)	Distance A (mm)	Distance C (mm)
160	250 to 350	127	Determine by trial mounting
190	300 to 400	151	
220	350 to 450	175	
250	400 to 500	198	
280	450 to 550	222	

Horizontal mounting

Length (mm)	Internal carcase height (mm)	Distance A (mm)	Distance C (mm)
160	200 to 300	82	Determine by trial mounting
190	230 to 330	105	
220	260 to 360	127	
250	290 to 430	148	
280	320 to 460	171	

Length (mm)	Internal carcase height (mm)	Distance A (mm)	Distance C (mm)
150	min. 130	70	Determine by trial mounting
200	min. 170	105	
250	min. 210	140	

Dimensions in mm.

FURNITURE HARDWARE

Lid Stays

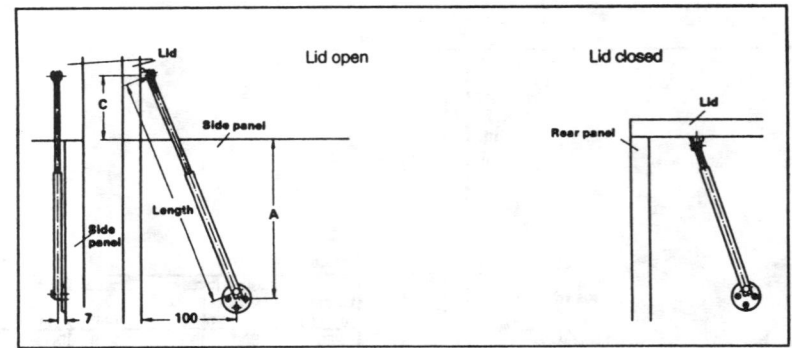

Length (mm)	Lid height (mm)	Distance A (mm)	Distance C (mm)
250	up to 300	170	Determine by trial mounting
325	up to 450	205	
450	over 450	275	

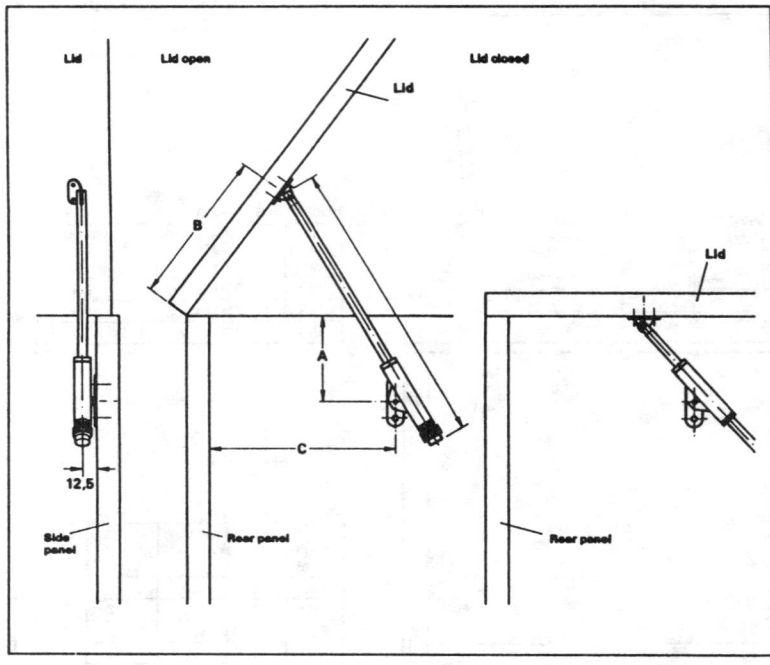

Length (mm)	Distance A (mm)	Distance B (mm)	Distance C (mm)
145	Determine by trial mounting depending on opening angle of lid.		
260			
330			

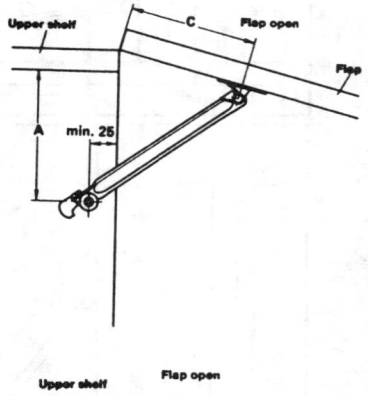

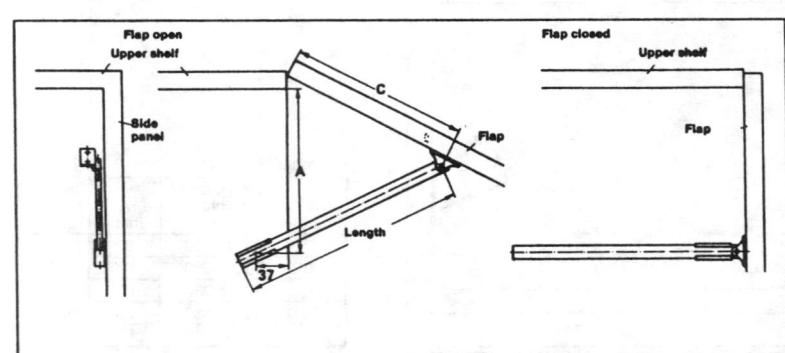

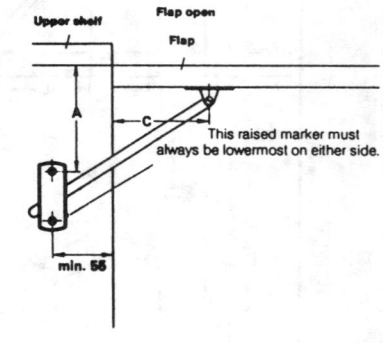

This raised marker must always be lowermost on either side.

Length (mm)	Carcase depth (mm)	Distance A (mm)	Distance C (mm)
200	210	150	Determine by trial mounting
250	260	180	
300	310	230	

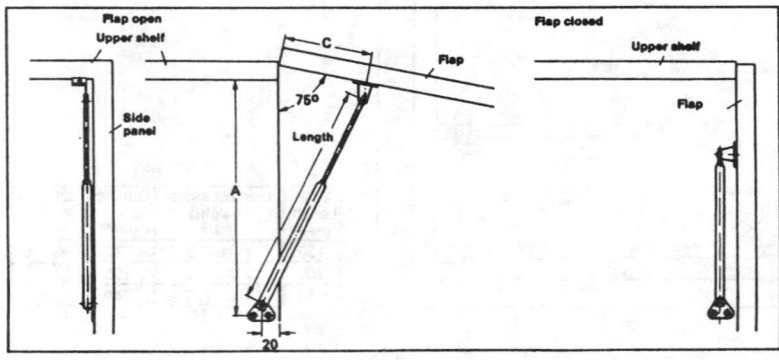

Length (mm)	Distance A (mm)	Distance C (mm)
130	150	Determine by trial mounting
250	260	

Dimensions in mm.

Extension type

Soft-Roller systems are capable of varying degrees of extension, depending on design. Basically, three types are employed:

E — Single extension

The withdrawal distance offered by single extensions is designed to be less than the installation length. Drawers cannot be opened clear of the carcase.

V — Full extension

The full extension model incorporates a pull-out distance as great as, or greater than, the installation length.
Drawers can be opened completely clear of the carcase.

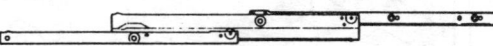

T — Telescopic extension

Telescopic extensions are fully extending systems. Their particular design is such that all the elements travel on a central axis resulting in a particularly neat, space-saving, compact assembly.

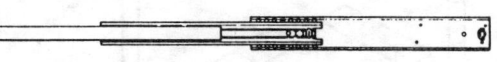

Mounting method

An indication as to how the rails are secured to the drawer or pull-out element.

A — Base mounted

S — Side mounted

N — Groove mounted

T — Shelf mounted

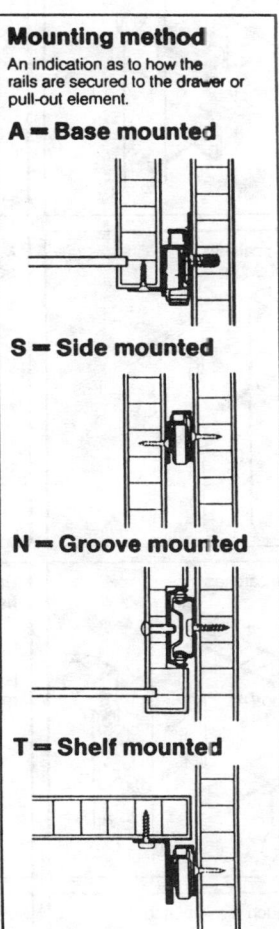

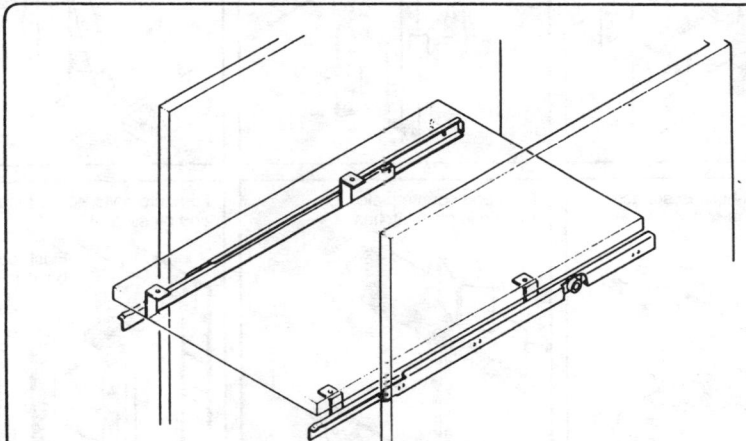

Single extensions with friction bearing mounted nylon rollers

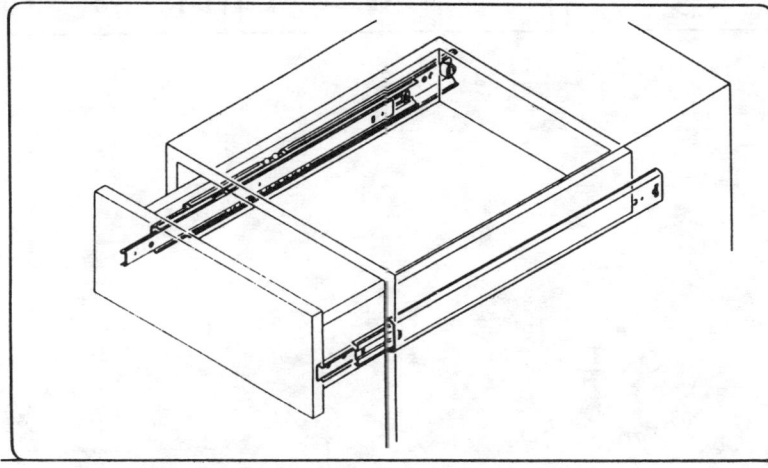

Telescopic extensions guided by means of ball cages

FURNITURE HARDWARE

Magnetic and Spring Catches; Bolts

Magnetic catches,
screw-mounted

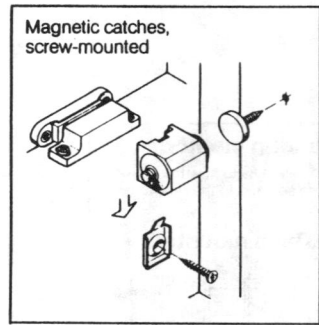

Magnetic catches, mortised

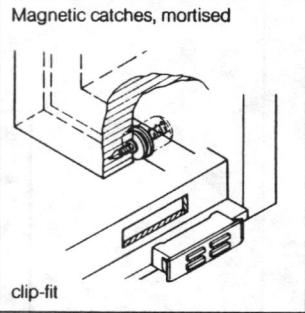

clip-fit

Magnetic catches,
(heat resistant)

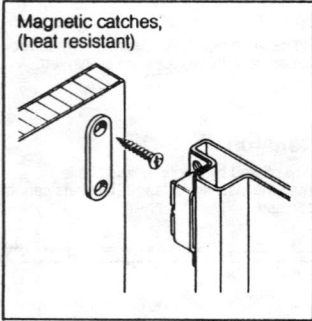

Magnetic catches,
for double doors

Magnetic catches,
for metal doors

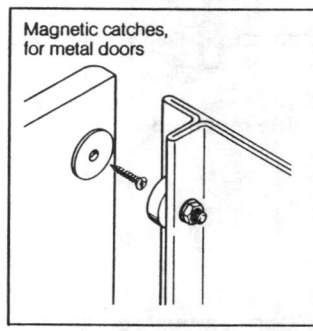

Magnetic catches, for installation in
series-drilled holes

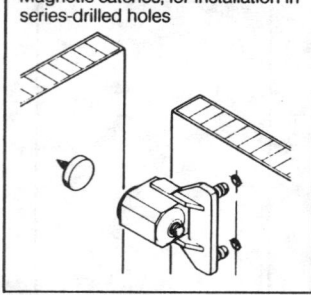

Elbow catches, screw-mounted

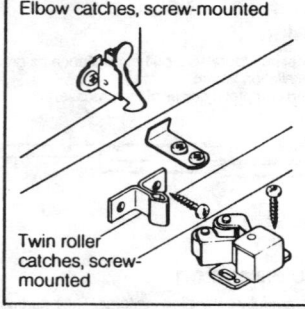

Twin roller
catches, screw-
mounted

Roller catches, screw-mounted

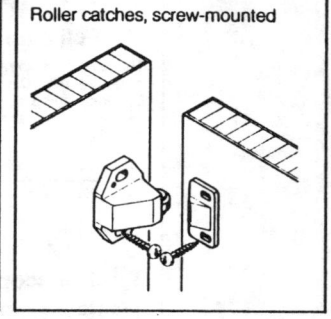

Twin ball catches

Glass door/
shelf catches

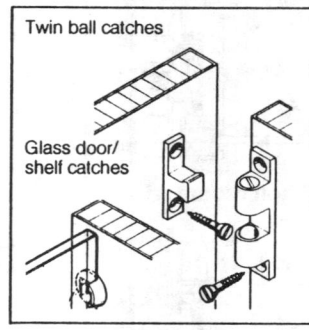

Ball catches, with stop plate or ball
headed screw

Ball catches,
mortised

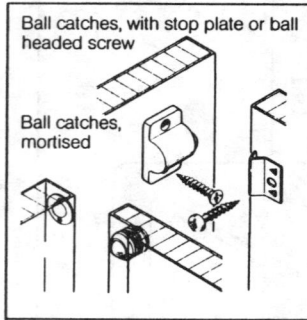

Plinth spring catches, screw-
mounted and press-fit

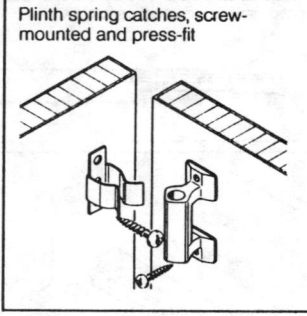

Spring catches, screw-mounted

Flexa-Touch drawer latch

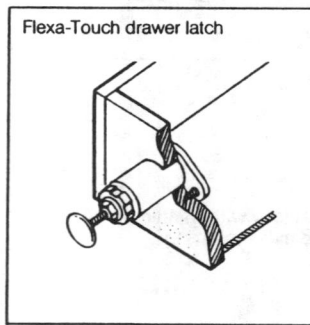

Magnetic push-latches, surface-
mounted or mortised

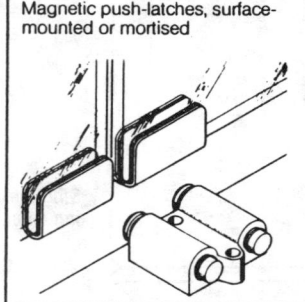

Pulls and counterplates for
magnetic push latches

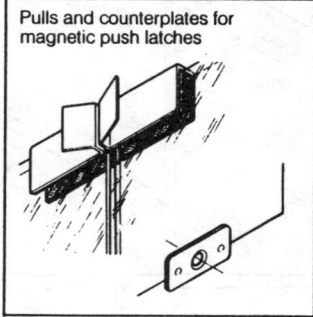

Furniture bolts, screw-mounted
and press-fit

Flush bolts, barrel
bolts, tower bolt

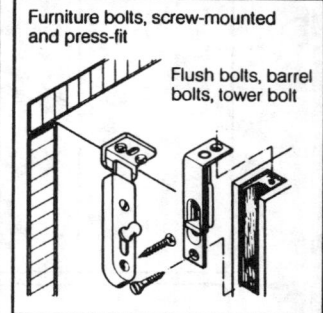

Automatic door bolt

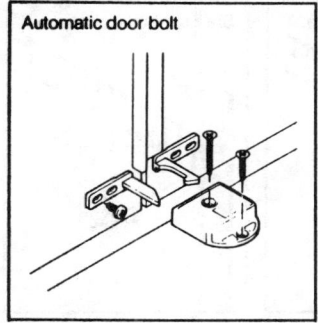

Rim locks

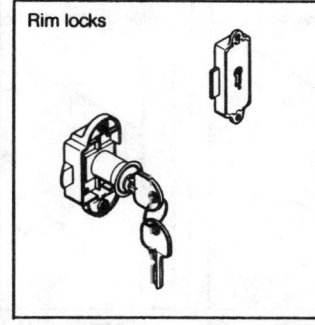

Lever-type rim locks

Inlaid-and
Inlaid flap locks

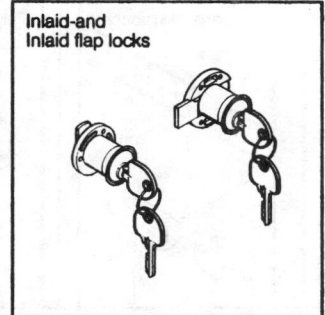

Mortise locks

Sliding door locks
pushbutton cylinders

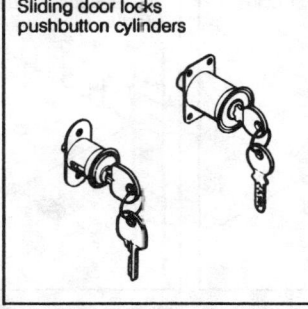

Central locking cylinders

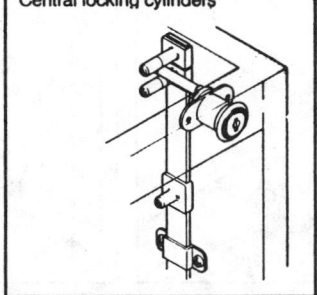

Espagnolette
locks

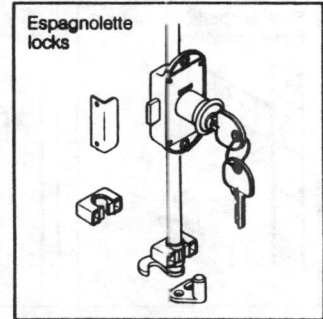

Central locking systems with
anti-tilt mechanism

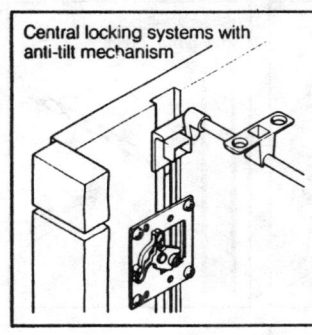

Cylinder modul system

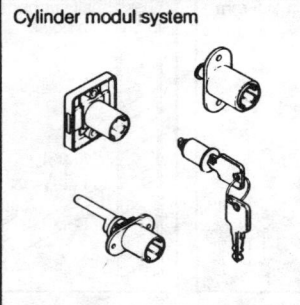

Glass door locks

Lever locks

Locker locks

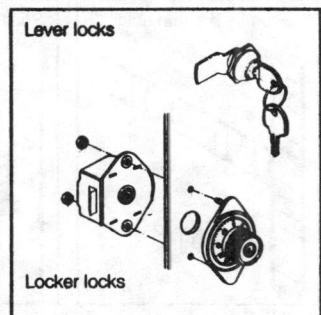

FURNITURE HARDWARE

Shelf Supports

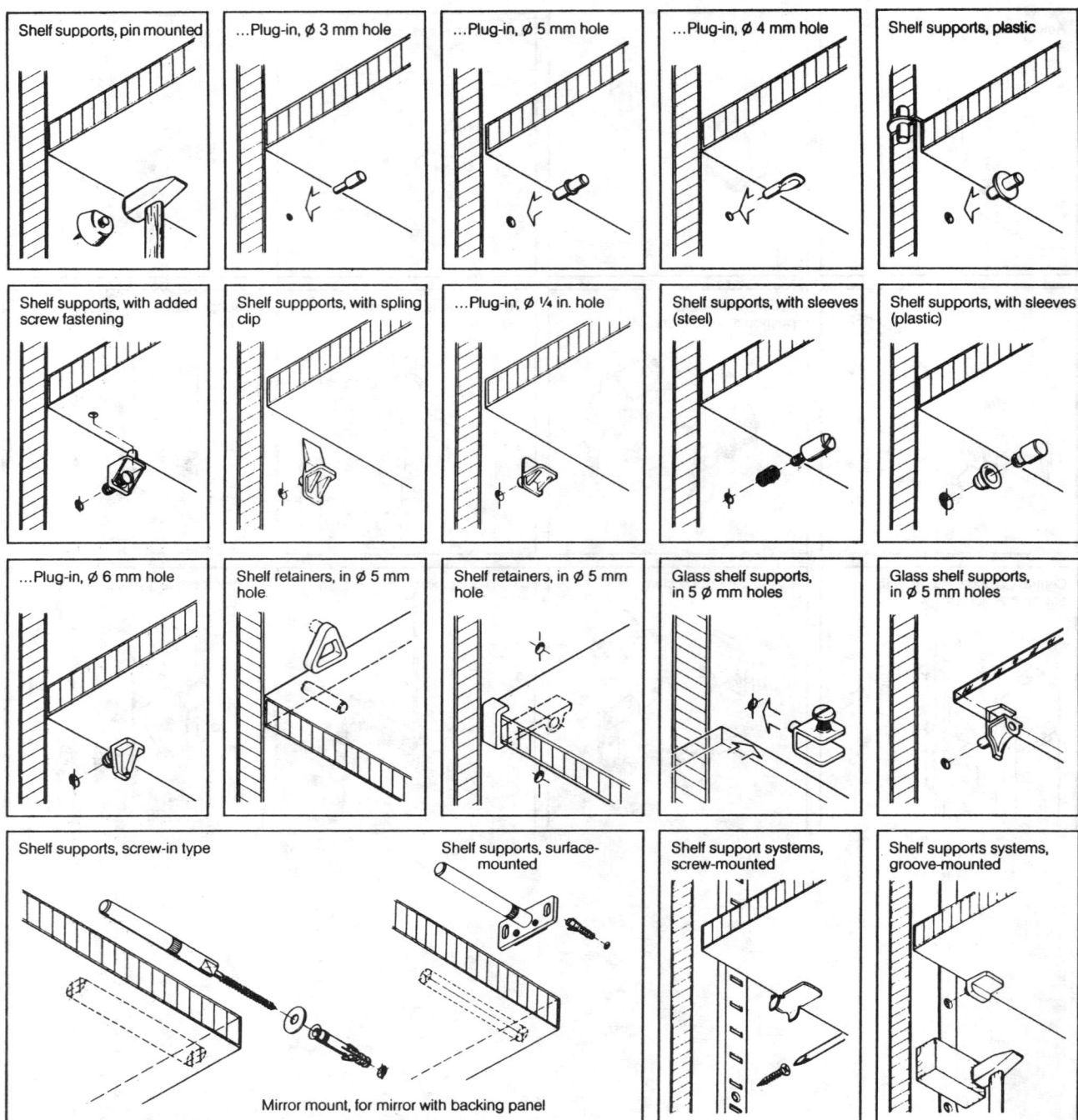

| Shelf supports, pin mounted | ...Plug-in, ∅ 3 mm hole | ...Plug-in, ∅ 5 mm hole | ...Plug-in, ∅ 4 mm hole | Shelf supports, plastic |

| Shelf supports, with added screw fastening | Shelf suppports, with spling clip | ...Plug-in, ∅ ¼ in. hole | Shelf supports, with sleeves (steel) | Shelf supports, with sleeves (plastic) |

| ...Plug-in, ∅ 6 mm hole | Shelf retainers, in ∅ 5 mm hole | Shelf retainers, in ∅ 5 mm hole | Glass shelf supports, in 5 ∅ mm holes | Glass shelf supports, in ∅ 5 mm holes |

| Shelf supports, screw-in type | Shelf supports, surface-mounted | Shelf support systems, screw-mounted | Shelf supports systems, groove-mounted |

Mirror mount, for mirror with backing panel

WARDROBE RAILS AND SUPPORTS

OVA wardrobe rails
and supports

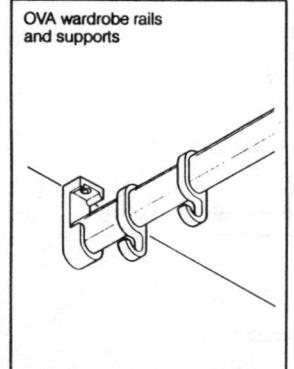

Shoe racks

Universal storage rack
Pull-relief plug

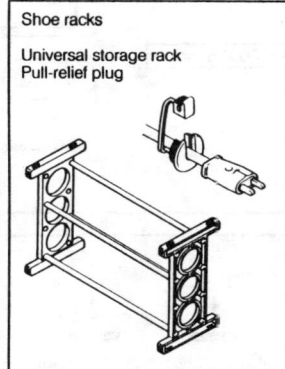

Single and double hooks,
pew hooks

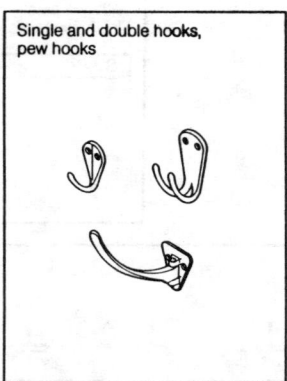

CASTORS AND GLIDES

Twin-Wheel Castors
Audio and
Audio-Stop

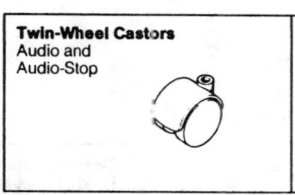

Enclosed Castors

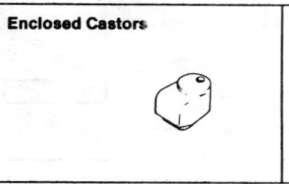

Ø 18 mm, Ø 20 mm,
Ø 25 mm wardrobe rails
and supports

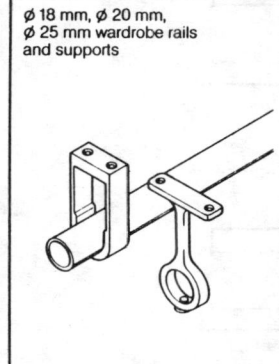

Wardrobe lifts,
hanging rails

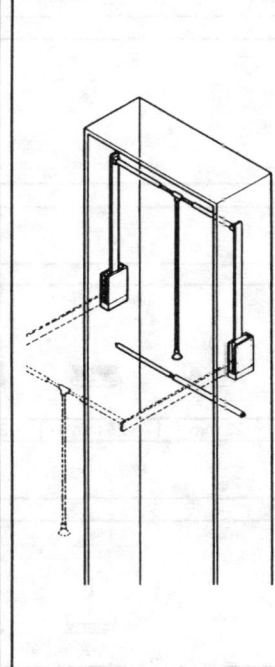

Cloakroom, wall and
ceiling hooks, nylon

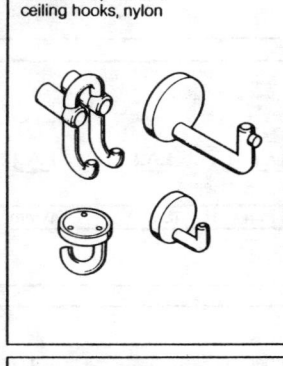

Furniture Glides

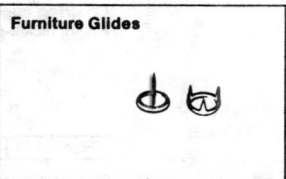

Furniture Glides
Cylindrical

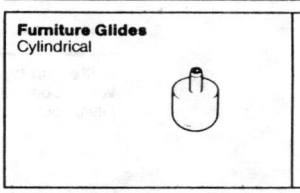

Cloakroom fittings
Thiefproof cloakroom fittings

Nylon tubular rails and coat
hangers

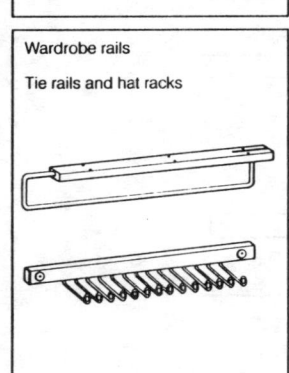

Cloakroom hooks, wood

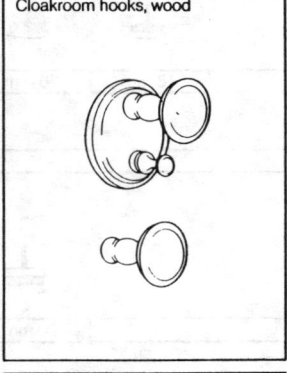

**Furniture Legs
Furniture Glides**

**Bed Box Castors
Ball Castors**

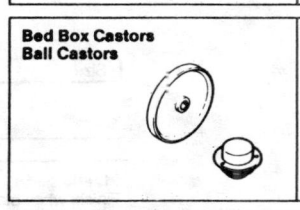

Wardrobe rails

Tie rails and hat racks

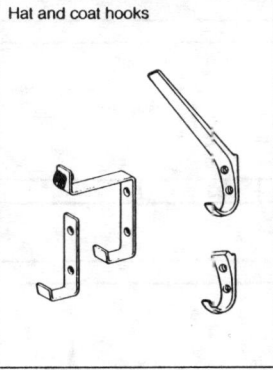

Hat and coat hooks

Wardrobe hanging bars
and rails

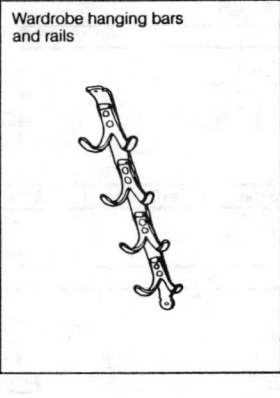

**Coal Box Castors
Light Duty
Swivel Castors**

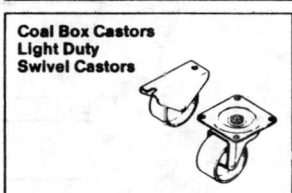

FURNITURE HARDWARE
Furniture Glides

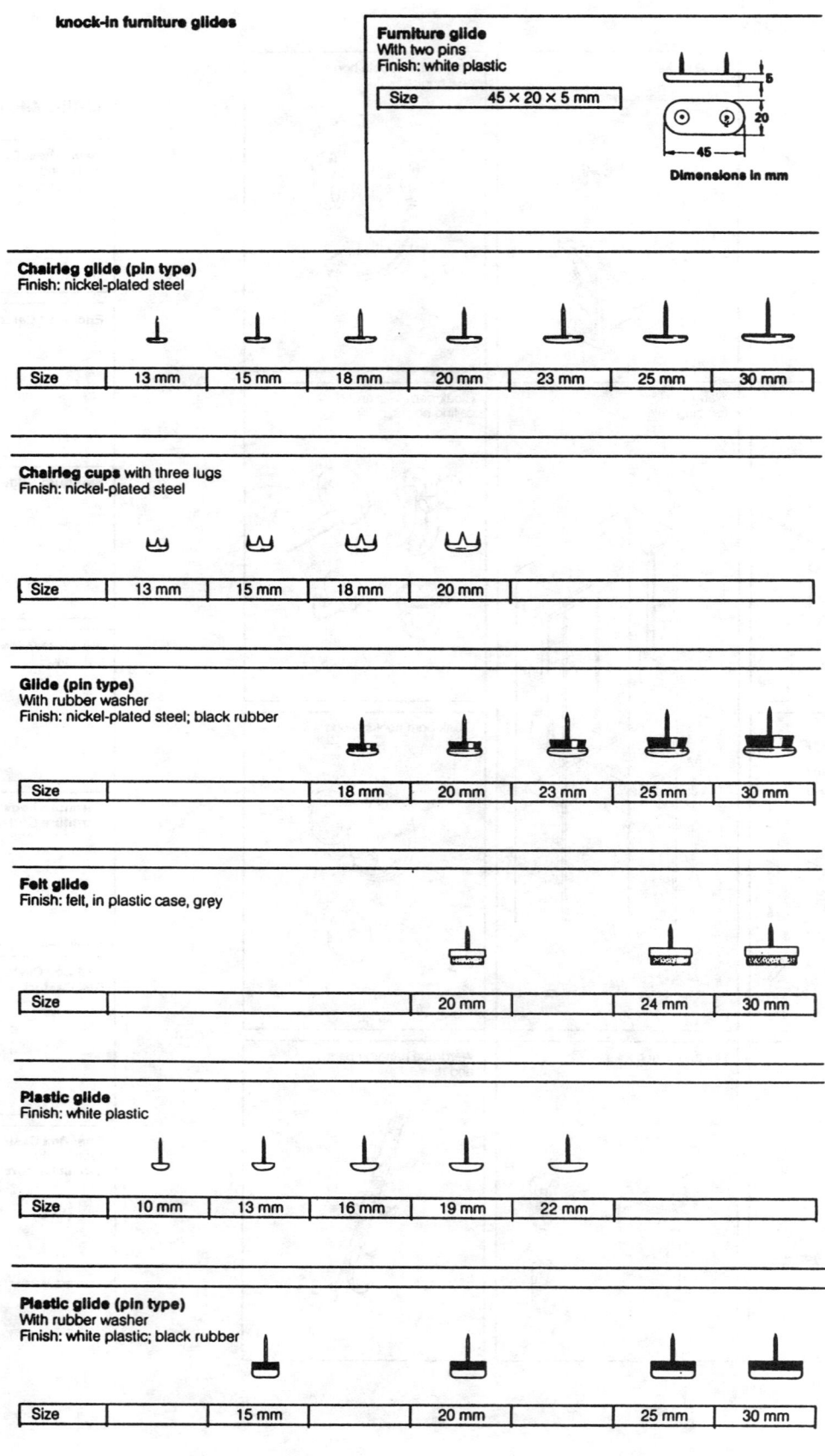

knock-in furniture glides

Furniture glide
With two pins
Finish: white plastic

Size	45 × 20 × 5 mm

Dimensions in mm

Chairleg glide (pin type)
Finish: nickel-plated steel

Size	13 mm	15 mm	18 mm	20 mm	23 mm	25 mm	30 mm

Chairleg cups with three lugs
Finish: nickel-plated steel

Size	13 mm	15 mm	18 mm	20 mm			

Glide (pin type)
With rubber washer
Finish: nickel-plated steel; black rubber

Size		18 mm	20 mm	23 mm	25 mm	30 mm

Felt glide
Finish: felt, in plastic case, grey

Size		20 mm		24 mm	30 mm

Plastic glide
Finish: white plastic

Size	10 mm	13 mm	16 mm	19 mm	22 mm	

Plastic glide (pin type)
With rubber washer
Finish: white plastic; black rubber

Size	15 mm	20 mm	25 mm	30 mm

Specialties

903

In most instances, the design process requires a knowledge of, or at the very least, an awareness of, certain specialized elements that can contribute heavily to the success or failure of a project in terms of aesthetics or function, or both. These elements may take the form of manufactured "off-the-shelf" products or consist of design theories, standards, and guidelines for certain areas of expertise. Accordingly, this section deals with ten such elements, ranging from plantscaping to accessories.

Information can be found concerning the height, spacing, and diameter of indoor trees and floor plants. Also included are planting standards, details, and maintenance information. The section dealing with signage and graphics provides information on signage systems, symbols, mounting heights, and locations. Other sections provide data on audio-visual systems, including projection room layouts and details, and auditorium seating arrangements and sightlines. The section dealing with security includes information on door and window hardware, mailbox rooms, lighting, and security systems. Still other sections provide information on color theory and window treatments, including draperies and curtains, shutters and shades, and rods, holdbacks, and ties.

PLANTSCAPING
Design Guidelines

DESIGNING WITH PLANTS

Any successful design uses plants that are compatible not only in an aesthetic design sense, but also in their growing requirements. No matter how beautiful the design, if neighboring plants are not matched to the correct growing conditions, parts of the design will either deteriorate or require elaborate maintenance. The aesthetic design considerations involve choosing the proper variety of plant textures, heights, and spacing to give the desired effect. The growing considerations involve the proper matching of light intensity, soil, and water, as well as proper container size, to the plant environmental requirements.

Of all the growing conditions, the most important is the light intensity. It is easy to underestimate the amount of available light, since the human eye can easily see in 20 footcandles of light, while even the plant needing the lowest light requires 50 to 75 footcandles to remain healthy. If the light intensity is to be below 100 footcandles, even these "low-light" plants must be slowly acclimatized prior to installation.

No matter if the space to be planted is a small office, a large interior garden, or a cafeteria, the first step is to ascertain the actual level of the existing or planned lighting. To allow maximum creativity in the planting design, the light intensity should be considered in the initial planning stages, especially in large areas such as those in shopping malls or corporate interior gardens. Adding the needed lighting fixtures after the initial electrical installation is often expensive or impossible. In smaller-scale situations, such as offices or homes, extra light fixtures should be added or the plants should be chosen according to the available light. If the plants do not have the proper light intensity, they will die. The lower the light intensity below the minimum needed by the species, the faster they will do so.

Since the light source (incandescent, fluorescent, sun, or other) is not important, but the light intensity is, accurate intensity measurements are essential. For these measurements we recommend the General Electric Model 213 or 214 light meter or its equivalent. The measurements must be made at the level of the plant foliage; they must be made several times a day on several days typical of the location if sunlight is used; and they must take curtains, tinted glass, and other light-shielding devices into account. Only light hitting the top of the leaves is effective. While underlighting with spotlights can create dramatic effects, it does very little to help the plant.

After the light intensity is determined, the plants should be selected from the appropriate light-level group (see Fig. 7), consistent with the design aims. Plants that will be growing near one another should have similar water requirements (also given in Fig. 7). If plants with different watering requirements must be close, they should be kept in their own growing containers so they can be watered separately.

An interior planting designer creates the mood through the interplay of plant texture and plant height, working only with those plants that will live under the predetermined light intensity. Color cannot really be used as a design element, since the average interior light intensity is seldom more than 100 footcandles and brightly colored plants or blooming flowers need up to 1000 footcandles. If flowering plants are used where the lighting conditions are normal, they will generally have to be replaced every few days.

Plant Texture

The good designer will provide for design variety through the clever use of plant texture. The term is used here to describe the general structure, shape, and appearance of the plant, regardless of height. It includes the size, shape, edging, and thickness of the plant's leaves, as well as its overall shape and the arrangement and number of leaves on the plant.

Five general rules concerning texture should be kept in mind.

1. Juxtapose fragmented foliage (such as that of a palm) with solid foliage (say, that of a dracaena).
2. Avoid too much of the same type of foliage (e.g., large flat leaves) in one area, unless a border or hedge effect is desired.
3. An exception to these previous rules on groupings is the palm. Although all palms have similar foliage, they vary slightly in color and interest, so that different types of palms may be planted together.
4. To create interest, mix small-leaved with large-leaved plants, and narrow-leaved with broad-leaved plants.
5. When using plants as specimens, especially as interior design elements in offices or homes, pick the plant with the background fabric, carpet, or wallpaper in mind. For example, a "busy" foliage plant will fight with a "busy" fabric.

Plant Height

Plant height not only determines the scale of the design, but it adds variety to the plant groupings. There are six general rules regarding plant height selection to keep in mind.

1. In the plant grouping, build up with the low plants in front. If the grouping can be seen from all sides, the grouping must be well balanced throughout and built up to the center height.
2. If a plant has canes with no lower foliage, try to place the lower plants in front to conceal the absence of foliage of the taller plants in the rear.
3. Uneven sizes throughout a grouping add more interest than consistent levels of foliage.
4. If a single plant is desired to hide a column or some other object, be sure that the plant height, including its container, is about three-fourths the height of the object to be concealed.
5. Keep the scale of the surroundings in mind when choosing the plant height. A 3-foot plant is fine next to a desk, but a plant of at least 6 feet should be selected if it is to be viewed when entering a room.
6. By convention, interior plant heights are measured from the bottom of the root ball or planter, while exterior plant heights are measured from the top of the root ball. The reason is that interior plants are usually placed in a container or raised planter, and the total available height from floor to ceiling is fixed.

Plant Spacing

Under certain conditions, the plants of an interior landscaping design will grow. Therefore, any possible change in the plant size must be considered by the designer. If the lighting intensity is at or below the recommended level, there will be little or no plant growth and the plant size and relationships will change little over time. If the lighting intensity is well above the required level, there will be plant growth, with different plant species growing at different rates.

Unlike outdoor plants, indoor tropical plants seldom grow outward; most of their growth occurs upward. The main exceptions are the *Ficus* family, the schefflera, and the *Philodendron Selloum,* which will spread somewhat outward. If a full plant design is desired, the required number of plants should be placed close together at the time of installation since future growth will seldom fill in the bare spots.

Even if the light intensity is high enough, before the plant can grow significantly, its root system must be able to expand. Thus, the best way to ensure that the size relationships of the plants do not change is to keep them in their original growing containers and not to replant them into a growing medium. If they are kept in the original containers, they will become pot-bound and future growth will be automatically limited.

Plant material is sold on the basis of height or growing-container size, and one must be familiar with the particular species to know what the spread will be. For each plant species considered here, Fig. 1 lists the height range for each plant in each standard growing-container size and gives a recommended minimum center-to-center plant spacing. This recommended spacing is based on experience with the plant's branching habits and growth patterns and will give a full plant design. If an open or a less full design is called for, the spacing should be increased.

When the plants are to be displayed in individual planters or decorative containers, each plant, still in its growing can, is placed directly into the planter or container, on top of a layer of drainage material of the appropriate depth. However, many standard planters have lips that reduce the interior diameter to less than the overall diameter. This inner diameter should be larger than the growing cans diameter so that the plant can be placed directly into it without being repotted and risking the attendant danger of root damage. To emphasize this requirement, Fig. 2 gives the standard planter diameter needed for each standard size of growing container. The size of the lip changes when a nonstandard type is used. If space is limited, this measurement should be carefully checked.

INDOOR TREES Species	Height Range	Recommended Center-to-Center Plant Spacing	Growing Can Diameter
Fiddle-leaf fig *(Ficus lyrata)*	3- 4 ft	24-36 in	10 in
	4- 6 ft	30-42 in	14 in
	6-11 ft	42 in & up	17 in
Indian laurel *(Ficus retusa)*	5- 7 ft	42-54 in	14 in
	7- 9 ft	48-60 in	17 in
	9-12 ft	60 in & up	22 in
Rubber plant *(Ficus elastica* cv. 'Decora'), tree standard	4-5 ft	48-60 in	10 in
	5-6 ft	54-66 in	12 in
	6-7 ft	60-72 in	14 in
Rubber plant *(Ficus elastica* cv. 'Decora'), bush type	1½-2 ft	12-18 in	6 in
	2 -2½ ft	12-24 in	8 in
	3 -4 ft	24-36 in	10 in
	4 -5 ft	36-48 in	12 in
	4 -5 ft	48-60 in	14 in
Weeping fig *(Ficus benjamina)*	3- 4 ft	24-36 in	10 in
	4- 5 ft	30-42 in	12 in
	5- 7 ft	36-48 in	14 in
	6- 8 ft	48-60 in	17 in
	9-10 ft	60 in & up	22 in
	9-12 ft	60 in & up	28 in
	10-12 ft	72 in & up	36 in
Norfolk Island pine *(Araucaria heterophylla)*	1½-2 ft	18-30 in	6 in
	2 -3 ft	24-36 in	8 in
	3 -5 ft	30-42 in	10 in
	4 -5 ft	36-48 in	12 in
	4 -6 ft	42-54 in	14 in
	6 -7 ft	54-66 in	17 in
Schefflera *(Brassaia actinophylla)*	3- 4 ft	36-48 in	10 in
	4- 5 ft	36-48 in	10 in
	5- 7 ft	55-66 in	14 in
	7- 8 ft	60-72 in	17 in
	8- 9 ft	60 in & up	22 in
	9-12 ft	72 in & up	Metal tubs
FLOOR PLANTS			
Bamboo palm *(Chamaedorea erumpens)*	3-4 ft	30-42 in	10 in
	4-6 ft	36-48 in	12 in
	5-7 ft	42-54 in	14 in
	7-9 ft	48-60 in	17 in
Corn plant *(Dracaena fragrans* cv. 'Massangeana')	1½-2 ft	24-30 in	6 in
	3½-4 ft	24-36 in	10 in
	4½-6 ft	30-42 in	12 in
	5 -7 ft	36-48 in	14 in
Corn plant bush *(Dracaena fragrans* cv. 'Massangeana')	1 -1½ ft	18-24 in	6 in
	1½-2½ ft	18-30 in	8 in
	3 -4 ft	24-36 in	10 in
	4 -5 ft	30-42 in	14 in
	5 -7 ft	36-48 in	17 in
Dwarf date palm *(Phoenix Roebelenii)*	2-3 ft	30-42 in	10 in
	3-4 ft	36-48 in	12 in
	4-5 ft	42-54 in	14 in
	5-6 ft	48-60 in	17 in
	5-6 ft	54-66 in	22 in

Fig. 1 Spacing recommendations.

PLANTSCAPING

Plant Height, Spacing, and Diameter

Species	*Height Range*	*Recommended Center-to-Center Plant Spacing*	*Growing Can Diameter*
Dwarf dragon tree *(Dracaena marginata)*	3-4 ft	24-36 in	10 in
	4-5 ft	30-42 in	12 in
	5-7 ft	36-48 in	14 in
	7-9 ft	48 in & up	17 in
Dwarf schefflera *(Brassaia arboricola)*	1 -1½ ft	18-24 in	6 in
	1½-2½ ft	30-42 in	8 in
	3 -4 ft	36-48 in	10 in
	4 -5 ft	42-54 in	14 in
False aralia *(Dizygotheca elegantissima)*	1½-2 ft	18-30 in	6 in
	3 -4 ft	30-42 in	10 in
	5 -7 ft	36-48 in	14 in
	7 -8 ft	42-54 in	17 in
Green dracaena (*Dracaena deremensis* cv. 'Janet Craig')	1 -1½ ft	18-24 in	6 in
	1½-2½ ft	18-30 in	8 in
	3 -4 ft	24-36 in	10 in
	4 -5 ft	30-42 in	14 in
	5 -7 ft	36-48 in	17 in
Green pleomele *(Dracaena reflexa)*	1½-2 ft	12-18 in	6 in
	3 -4 ft	18-30 in	10 in
	4 -5 ft	30-45 in	14 in
	5 -6 ft	36-48 in	17 in
Kentia palm *(Howea Forsterana)*	3-4 ft	36-48 in	10 in
	4-5 ft	42-54 in	12 in
	5-8 ft	48-60 in	14 in
Lady palm *(Rhapis excelsa)*	3-4 ft	36-48 in	10 in
	4-5 ft	42-54 in	12 in
	5-7 ft	48-60 in	14 in
Mock orange *(Pittosporum Tobira)*	1¼-1½ ft	24-36 in	10 in
	1½-2½ ft	30-42 in	12 in
	2 -3 ft	36-48 in	14 in
Narrow-leaved pleomele *(Dracaena angustifolia honorarii)*	3-4 ft	24-36 in	12 in
	5-6 ft	30-42 in	14 in
	6-7 ft	36-48 in	17 in
Neantha bella palm *(Chamaedorea elegans)*	1 -1½ ft	18-30 in	6 in
	1½-2½ ft	24-36 in	8 in
	2½-3½ ft	30-42 in	10 in
	4 -5 ft	36-48 in	14 in
Ponytail *(Beaucarnea recurvata)*	1½-2 ft	24-36 in	10 in
	2 -3 ft	30-42 in	12 in
	3 -4 ft	36-48 in	14 in
	4 -5 ft	42-54 in	17 in
Reed palm *(Chamaedorea Seifrizii)*	4-6 ft	36-48 in	12 in
	6-7 ft	42-54 in	14 in
	7-9 ft	48-60 in	17 in
Self-heading philodendron *(Philodendron Selloum)*	3 ft	30-42 in	10 in
	4 ft	42-54 in	14 in
	5 ft	54-66 in	17 in
Southern yew (*Podocarpus macrophyllus* var. Maki)	4-5 ft	36-48 in	10 in
	5-6 ft	42-54 in	12 in
	5-6 ft	48-60 in	14 in
	6-7 ft	54-66 in	17 in

Fig. 1 ***(Continued)***

Species	Height Range	Recommended Center-to-Center Plant Spacing	Growing Can Diameter
TABLE OR DESK PLANTS—GROUND COVER			
Boston fern (*Nephrolepis exaltata* cv. 'Bostoniensis')	1 ft	24-30 in	6 in
	1 -1½ ft	30-36 in	8 in
	1½-2 ft	36-42 in	10 in
Common philodendron (*Philodendron scandens oxycardium*)	1 ft	18-24 in	8 in
	1¼-1½ ft	24-30 in	10 in
	1¼-1½ ft	24-36 in	12 in
Chinese evergreen (*Aglaonema commutatum* var. *maculatum*)	1¼-1½ ft	18-24 in	6 in
	1½-2 ft	24-30 in	8 in
	2 -2½ ft	30-36 in	10 in
Dumb cane (*Dieffenbachia maculata* cv. 'Rudolph Roehrs')	1 ft	18-24 in	6 in
	2 ft	24-30 in	8 in
	3 ft	30-36 in	10 in
	3 -3½ ft	36-42 in	12 in
	3½-4 ft	42-48 in	14 in
Golden pothos (*Epipremnum aureum* or *Scindapsus aureus*)	1 ft	12-18 in	6 in
	1 ft	18-24 in	8 in
	1¼-1½ ft	24-30 in	10 in
	1¼-1½ ft	30-36 in	12 in
Grape ivy (*Cissus rhombifolia*)	1 ft	18-24 in	6 in
	1 -1½ ft	18-30 in	8 in
	1¼-1½ ft	24-36 in	10 in
	1¼-1½	24-36 in	12 in
Jade plant (*Crassula argentea*)	1 ft	18-24 in	8 in
	2 ft	24-36 in	10 in
	2 -2½ ft	30-42 in	12 in
	2½-3½ ft	36-48 in	14 in
Prayer plant (*Maranta leuconeura*)	1 ft	18-24 in	8 in
	1 ft	24-30 in	10 in
	1-1½ ft	24-30 in	12 in
Swedish ivy (*Plectranthus australis*)	1 ft	18-24 in	6 in
	1 -1¼ ft	18-30 in	8 in
	1¼-1½ ft	24-36 in	10 in
	1¼-1½ ft	24-36 in	12 in
Wax plant (*Hoya carnosa*)	1 ft	12-18 in	6 in
	1 ft	18-24 in	8 in
	1 ft	24-30 in	10 in
White flag (*Spathiphyllum* cv. 'Clevelandii')	1¼-1½ ft	24-36 in	6 in
	2 -3 ft	30-42 in	8 in
	2½-3½ ft	36-48 in	10 in
	3 -4 ft	48-54 in	14 in
White-striped Dracaena (*Dracaena deremensis* cv. 'Warneckii')	1¼-1½ ft	18-24 in	6 in
	2 ft	24-30 in	8 in
	3 -4 ft	24-36 in	10 in
	4 -5 ft	30-42 in	12 in
	4 -7 ft	36-48 in	14 in
Green dracaena (*Dracaena deremensis* cv. 'Janet Craig')	1 -1½ ft	18-24 in	6 in
	1½-2½ ft	24-30 in	8 in
	3 -4 ft	30-42 in	10 in
Neantha bella palm (*Chamaedorea elegans*)	1 -1½ ft	18-30 in	6 in
	1½-2½ ft	24-36 in	8 in
	2½-3½ ft	30-42 in	10 in
Self-heading philodendron (*Philodendron Selloum*)	1 ft	18-24 in	6 in
	2 ft	24-36 in	8 in
	3 ft	30-42 in	10 in

Plant Growing Container Diameter	Recommended Planter Exterior Diameter
4 in	6 in
6 in	8 in
8 in	10 in
10 in	12 in
11 in	14 in
12 in	14 in
13 in	16 in
14 in	16 in
17 in	18-22 in
22 in	24 in

Fig. 2 Planter selection. These recommendations are based on the fact that most standard planters have either a 1-inch lip or no lip at all. Because the growing cans sometimes have ridges or have become deformed, it is always best to allow for a little extra leeway, even for planters with no lip. Some manufacturers, however, put 2-inch lips on their planters, a possiblity that should be checked. If the planter is an automatic watering type, the inside and outside diameters will be quite different, depending on the manufacturer.

Fig. 1 *(Continued)*

PLANTSCAPING
Design Guidelines

Writing Specifications

The interior landscaping business is very competitive, and a common practice is for the architect or designer to send out the landscaping specifications for bids. Unless the specifications for the job are well-written, however, there are many ways for the contractor to cut corners and still be within the specifications. Consequently, the final installation may not be what the designer had in mind. The lowest bid is not necessarily the best bargain, unless the specifications are very tightly written or unless the architect is dealing with a well-established landscape contractor with a reputation for high-quality work.

The following are some suggested guidelines to use in writing specifications. If they are observed, the bids received will accurately reflect the design requirements of the job.

1. Specify the plant heights within a 6-inch bracket. For example, designate 5 to 5½ feet or 5½ to 6 feet. If the specification were simply "5 to 6 feet," the supplier could use all 5-foot plants, which are considerably less expensive than 6-foot plants.

2. For corn plants, dwarf dragon trees, and the like, specify the number of canes and approximate number of foliage heads, as well as the height. The difference in cost between a two-cane and a three-cane corn plant of the same height is not minor.

3. For reed palms, bamboo palms, and the like, specify the number of stems desired, five to six being medium full.

4. For the green dracaena and white-striped dracaena, list the number of main foliage stems desired. They range from one to three stems.

5. For ficus trees, it should be specified whether the bush style or standard tree style is desired. In the bush style, the plant has multiple stems (ranging from two to five in number) branching out from the base of the plants. The standard tree or "lollipop" style has one main 5- to 6-foot stem with a sheared, ball-shaped foliage head.

6. Small plants should be specified as to single plants or combinations or several plants. Examples are dumb cane, Chinese evergreen, and white flag.

7. If ivy trailers are desired, their length should be specified. The trailers take up to eight months to grow, depending on the length, so the designer must plan for these up to a year before installation. Examples are grape ivy, swedish ivy, golden pothos, common philodendron, and wax plant.

8. Specifications should call for plant cleaning and spraying before installation.

9. Perlite should be specified as the drainage material for both planters and decorative containers. Styrofoam, which is much cheaper, is often used but has little long-term value.

10. The amount of ingredients in large planters (soil mixture, drainage material, soil separator) should be specified, as should the composition of each of the ingredients.

11. If bark chips, moss cover, or other soil coverings are desired, they should be specified.

12. Special attention should be given to the description of specimen plants, including the number of heads, stems, or canes, and any unusual stem structure that is desired. If canes with character (such as angle and peculiarity of growth), tufts of foliage at various heights, or other unusual features are wanted, they should be specifically mentioned.

13. If the landscape contractor will not maintain the plants after installation, provision should be made for a training program for the maintenance crew. Also, the contractor should provide for two weeks' initial maintenance of the plants and replacement of any that fall below specifications during the period.

14. If the landscape contractor is to maintain the plants after the installation (usually the best all-around solution), such an agreement should be reached before the plants are installed and a maintenance contract should be signed. This contract should include a provision for the replacement of any plant that falls below specifications because of faulty maintenance. This stipulation gives the contractor incentive for professional-quality maintenance.

15. If a large garden is planned and the landscape contractor is given design responsibility for it, the contractor should provide a floor plan of the garden for the designer's approval, before the installation.

16. If the architect or designer provides the landscape contractor with a detailed planting floor plan and the contractor finds it impossible to meet all the specifications (because of unavailability of certain species, etc.), the contractor and the designer or architect should agree in writing on any changes.

USE OF INTERIOR PLANTS AND PROCEDURES

The general rule of interior planting design is to vary the plant heights, shapes, and textures to give the desired design feeling consistent with the available light level and planting space. The best way to learn to apply this rule to specific situations is to study successful designs.

Interior planting designs have usually been found to fall into one of two categories: (1) interior gardens, both large and small, such as those seen in residential and hotel lobbies, corporate headquarters reception areas, and enclosed shopping mall public spaces; and (2) open plan or specimen design, like office landscaping designs and designs that use individual plants as living sculptures. In both categories of design, the main requirements to be considered are the available light intensity, the scale of the design, and the client's wishes and budget. After these basic requirements are determined, however, the design considerations are somewhat different for the two types of design.

Interior Gardens

Interior gardens are planting areas, sometimes contained in built-in planters, that have a variety of plants and that convey their design feeling through plant arrangements rather than through individual plant specimens. Small gardens generally contain only a single grouping of plants, act as a single design element, and have uniform lighting and watering requirements throughout. Large gardens have a variety of plant groupings and varying design feelings among the groupings, and they can encompass areas of different lighting and watering requirements. Since any garden conveys its effects through the juxtaposition of different plants, a single dominant plant cannot be considered a garden from the design point of view, even if it is in a built-in planter with ground-cover plants.

In designing any built-in planter, enough planter depth must be provided to allow the root ball or the planting can to be covered with soil and to rest on 4 to 8 inches of drainage material. Since soil and gravel are expensive, it is best not to overdesign the planter, by making it larger than necessary, and not to buy too much soil to fill in between the plants. (For example, a depth of 1½ to 2 feet is usually enough for most small gardens.) Figure 1 lists the size of the growing can for different sizes of plants of each species. The depth of the largest growing can, plus the depth of the drainage material, yields the minimum planter depth for the garden. The volume of the planter minus the total volume of all the growing cans indicates the amount of additional soil and drainage material to be provided.

If the planter is already in place, its depth may limit the size of the plants that may be used. Since soil must reach to the top of the root ball or can, the only way to utilize too shallow a planter is to put the large plant in the center and to build up from the edge inward. The planter must be wide enough to slant the soil gradually so that the slope is not too great.

Small gardens While a garden may be large enough to have only a single design function, that function can be quite varied, provided that the lighting intensity is appropriate. It can serve as a small glen or a space separator, or it can be simply a large decorative planter. The garden can be airy and open or it can be dense and closed. Planter depth of 1½ to 2 feet is usually sufficient.

Also, some small gardens can be designed to be changed with the seasons. Often, flowering plants, such as chrysanthemums or azaleas, are used, but the plants must then be replaced every two weeks. If the seasonal or flowering plant changes are desired, the plants should be left in their containers so that they may be easily moved. Some care should be given to the planter design so that the growing cans are not obvious and do not detract from the arrangement.

Creative additions of volcanic rocks, small ponds, or fountains can be quite attractive and set off and enhance the plants. However, with the usually limited space in the small garden, these additions can produce a crowded or overdone appearance. Overcrowding will give a jungle effect that is rarely desired.

Just as in other design fields, good proportion and good sense will create a pleasing design that is neither overlooked or overbearing.

Large gardens Large gardens are simply larger versions of small gardens, but their very size opens up more design possibilities, since they may be subdivided into related sections. The shape, height, and texture of the planters may be varied from section to section. The plants may be chosen to reflect varying design moods and functions. The lighting and watering requirements may differ between sections. In fact, variety is often necessary for good large-garden design, since a large mass of similar plants or plant groupings will create the impression of a monotonous forest or field.

Because large indoor gardens usually are in areas of high ceilings, the light level must be very carefully considered. Just the presence of windows or skylights does not guarantee enough light. In addition, if the light sources are distant from the plants, the taller plants may effectively block some of the light from reaching the lower plants and foliage.

When large areas are to be planted, there is a tendency to use rocks, pools, gravel, or fountains to cut down the plant costs and simplify the maintenance. Care is essential when using these elements to prevent the plant arrangement from looking bare and sterile.

Large gardens are most commonly used in shopping malls. The skilled designer will take this illumination into account, as well as design the garden to enhance the shopper's view of the stores.

The designer will always remember that large gardens achieve their effectiveness by both the proper variation of plant groupings and the proper variation of plants within the groupings.

Procedures for planting gardens As pointed out earlier, a successful garden needs proper planting, since improper procedures can inflict severe damage. Correct planting involves not only correct technique and design but also correct organization.

The techniques of proper drainage, spacing, and handling will ensure that the plants remain healthy once they are installed. Experienced supervision of the installation staff will be important in this regard, since a large installation of expensive plants is no place for the on-the-job training of the supervisor.

Proper planning and organization will ensure that the plants remain healthy between unloading and planting. If the plants are left on an unheated loading dock or stored in an unlighted or unheated room until they are installed, irreversible damage may occur.

Drainage Overwatering of plants leads to root rot and is often more harmful than underwatering. To minimize this danger, the planter or container should be installed with proper drainage. The simplest technique is to provide a porous reservoir below the planting soil; any excess water will then drain into it from the root ball and be slowly fed back to the soil as the soil dries out.

To prepare the planter or decorative container, the drainage material is poured into the bottom and leveled. The plant growing can be placed on top of the drainage layer and surrounded with more of the drainage material. For the smaller plants (in pots 6 inches or less in diameter), a 1-inch depth of drainage material is usually enough. For the larger plants, a layer of 3 to 4 inches is suggested. For very large gardens, about one-third of the planter depth should be the drainage layer, provided it leaves enough room for the root ball or planting can.

The drainage material can be perlite (a readily available synthetic material) alone or

mixed with small pebbles or gravel. The perlite is suggested since it is porous enough to feed back the excess water to the soil as the soil dries out. If only gravel or pebbles are used, the excess water will sit and stagnate in the reservoir and will not be fed back to the plants.

Even with the proper drainage layer, overwatering is possible if so much excess water is used that it fills up the reservoir. The water level in a small container can be determined by tapping the container at various intervals and listening for the change in sound. In large planted areas, it is wise to provide for "dipstick" readings of the water level. To take such a reading, rigid hollow plastic tubes, with a cloth over their lower ends, are "planted" at intervals along with the plants. The hollow tubes reach from the top of the container to just above the drainage layer and the cloth on the bottom prevents soil or drainage material from entering the tube. A dipstick is lowered into the tube until it touches the cloth. If the stick, upon removal, shows more than ½ inch of water, there is too much water in the bottom of the planter.

If gravel is used as part of the drainage material, it should be ⅜ inch to ½ inch in diameter. Under no circumstances should limestone be used, since it is alkaline and will raise the pH of the water to a level that is too high for most tropical plants.

Soil separator If the plants are removed from their growing cans and replanted in growing soil, it is usually best to use a soil separator between the drainage layer and the planting soil. The separator is a semiporous sheet, often composed of fiberglass wool, which serves to keep the soil from falling into the drainage material. If the separator is not used, soil will clog the drainage material. Fiberglass wool of building material grade should not be used, as it contains chemicals that will damage the plant (Fig. 3).

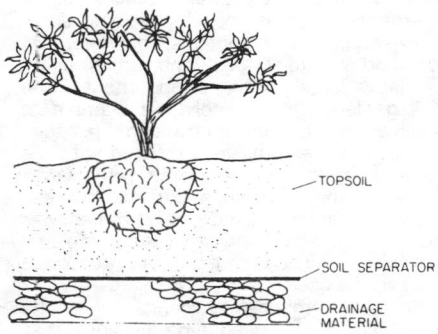

Fig. 3 Soil separation.

Planting medium Because the root systems of tropical plants are much finer than those of outdoor plants, pure topsoil is too heavy and too easily compacted to be used as a planting medium. It will constrict the plant roots and will retain too much water.

For the common tropical plants discussed here, we recommend the use of the foliage plant mix developed by Cornell University. Because it is easiest to calculate the quantity of needed soil in terms of the volume of the planter to be filled, the formula given here is

for 1 cubic yard of soil. For conversion purposes, 1 cubic yard equals 21.7 bushels, 765 liters, or 27 cubic feet.

Sphagnum peat moss: ½ cu yd = 383 lit
Vermiculite #2: ¼ cu yd = 191 lit
Perlite, medium fine: ¼ cu yd = 191 lit
Ground limestone, dolomitic: 0.85 gal = 13.5 cup = 3.2 lit
Superphosphate 20 percent solution: 0.21 gal = 3.4 cup = 0.79 lit
10-10-10 fertilizer: 0.32 gal = 5.1 cup = 1.2 lit
Iron sulphate: 0.11 gal = 1.7 cup = 0.41 lit
Potassium nitrate: 0.11 gal = 1.7 cup = 0.41 lit

While this Cornell foliage plant mix gives the best all-around results a simpler mix that gives good results in most cases is as follows:

⅓ by volume sterilized commercial mix of peat moss and vermiculite
⅓ by volume sterilized topsoil
⅓ by volume perlite

This mix is particularly effective for container planting. If it is to be used in a larger garden planting, such as a shopping mall garden, more perlite should be added for improved drainage.

The peat and topsoil mix is considerably heavier than the Cornell mix and both are heavier wet than dry. If the garden is not situated at grade level, this weight can be an important consideration. Figure 4 gives guidelines to be used in estimating the weight of the planting medium.

Planting organization The basic ingredients for a large planting installation are drainage material, planting medium, soil separator, plant material, material-handling equipment, light, water, and labor. Organization of all these ingredients is important since every one must be ready and available for a successful installation. Arrangements for all these factors should be made ahead of time, and they should be ready and waiting when the plants are delivered.

The amount of interior volume in the planters and containers determines the amount of needed drainage material, soil separator, and planting medium. If detailed blueprints are not available, actually measuring the planters is generally a good way to obtain this volume. The relationship between planting medium, drainage material, and soil separator can be determined using the guidelines of the previous subsection. If the plants are to be left in their cans (as generally recommended), the space between the plants is filled with drainage material. If they are removed from their cans, the space between plants is filled with planting medium. In either case, the amount of volume displaced by the plants is simply the sum of the volume contained in the growing cans. Information for each standard size of growing container is given in Fig. 5.

The installation should not be started unless all lights and water connections are operating, as the plants will need both light and water during the installation — especially the light. If the plants are delivered dry, they should be watered in their cans unless they are to be planted at once and watered immediately after planting. If the plants are removed from their cans and placed into dry planting medium, they and the planting medium should be thoroughly watered immedi-

PLANTSCAPING
Plant Use and Procedures

ately afterward.

Fewer design mistakes will be made if the plants are installed one section at a time, under the direction of a supervisor familiar with the design of the section. If the installation is in an office building, it may be necessary to arrange for a workroom and a freight elevator with access both to the loading dock and the workroom. Depending on the exact arrangements, a crew of four to six workers per supervisor is generally optimum.

It is recommended that each section be planted in the following order. First, leftover building material and other debris are removed from the planting areas. Second, drainage material is added to the proper depth and leveled. Third, the plants, either in or out of their growing containers, are placed on top of the drainage material and the soil separator if present, and arranged according to the design. The spaces between the plants are then filled in with drainage material or planting medium, depending on whether the plants are in or out of their growing containers. If planting medium is used, it should be lightly compacted to prevent its settling later. (If the light intensity is below specifications and periodic replacement of the plants is expected, the plants should be left in their cans.)

After the spaces between the large plants have been filled in, the groundcover, if any, is planted. The use of decorative bark or marble chips on top of the soil is not recommended as they easily mix with the soil and are hard to remove if the plants are replaced.

After all the spaces have been filled, the plants should be thoroughly watered and the maintenance schedule begun. If dry planting medium is used, it should be watered thoroughly several times during the first week to ensure that it is completely wet.

Removing plants from cans or burlap A healthy root system is necessary for the maintenance of a healthy plant. It is the new, very fine, feathery roots that are the most important and also the most easily damaged. This damage is very likely if the soil between the fine roots is dislodged in the course of repotting. Whether the tropical plants are delivered in growing cans or with their roots wrapped in burlap, the root system must be handled with care.

The best procedure for removing a plant from its container is to lean the pot on its side, tap on the container sides and bottom, and carefully slide out the plant. In large container-grown plants (in 17-inch or larger cans), the root system may be held very tightly in the can. In this case, a can cutter, which works on either metal or rubber cans, may be the most gentle way of removing the can. Once the can is removed, the root ball of soil and roots should be scored by making ¼-inch-deep vertical cuts at 3-inch intervals around the root ball from top to bottom. If the can removal and ball scoring are done near the planting site, the exposed root system is subjected to minimum handling.

Very large plants and trees are frequently field-grown rather than container-grown. The root balls of such plants will come wrapped in burlap. When planting them, only the upper half of the burlap should be removed. The lower portion will disintegrate in the soil after the plant is installed.

Planting Bed Material	Dry Weight	Wet Weight
Cornell foliage mix	12 - 18 lb/cu ft	25 - 35 lb/cu ft
Peat/topsoil mix	38 - 42 lb/cu ft	70 - 90 lb/cu ft
Topsoil (loam)	80 - 100 lb/cu ft	100 - 120 lb/cu ft
Gravel	120 - 135 lb/cu ft	120 - 135 lb/cu ft
Sand	95 - 110 lb/cu ft	120 - 130 lb/cu ft

Note: For conversion to metric system: 1 lb = 0.454 kg; 1 cu ft = 0.028 cu m.

Fig. 4 Planting material weight. These figures are the normal weight for each of the materials in both the dry and the wet state. The exact weight depends on the degree of compaction of the material.

Pot Size	Soil Volume	Pot Diameter x Height
6 in	1 gal	6½ in x 6 in
8 in	2 gal	8 in x 7 in
10 in	3 gal	10 in x 9½ in
12 in	4 gal	11 in x 10½ in
14 in	7 gal	13½ in x 12 in
17 in	10 gal	17 in x 16 in
22 in	20 gal	21 in x 17 in
30 in	35 gal	29 in x 17 in
32 in	65 gal	32 in x 22 in
36 in	95 gal	36 in x 24 in

Note: For conversion to different units, use the following factors. 1 gal = .00495 cu yd = .0038 cu m = .134 cu ft = 3.79 lit; 1 in = 2.54 cm.

Fig. 5 Pot-size and volume proportions.

Rock formations and decorative pools Natural elements, such as rock formations, decorative pools, water fountains, and waterfalls, can add an artistic touch and turn an unimaginative large planting arrangement into a full garden. Unfortunately the overuse of such design elements is tempting, since they are usually inexpensive compared with the cost of filling the same area with plants. Provided they are not overused, they can serve as natural sculpture or as the answer for areas with too little light to support plants or where conditions limit the variety of plants that can be used.

In rock formations, volcanic rock is the most commonly used type because it is much lighter than ordinary rock. This weight factor can be of considerable importance when the weight of the garden must be limited. This type of rock is also easy to shape with a hammer and chisel.

Although a large decorative pool or fountain must be custom-designed, there are small fiberglass pools that can be purchased in a variety of sizes and are available in kidney, free-form, or rectangular shapes. They are usually no longer than 6 feet, but they are of a standard 16-inch depth, which is deep enough to accommodate any water plants, recirculating pump, and a filter tray with mat

and gravel. Their high-capacity, low-pressure pumps are usually adequate for small fountains and waterfalls.

If decorative pools are used, some thought might be given to using water plants in them. These plants are very attractive and can be easily grown indoors. As with all plants, different species have different growing and flowering habits. A reputable dealer should be consulted for information.

The use of fish in pools should be carefully studied in light of the plant maintenance requirements. Fertilizer, plant chemicals, and limestone runoff from the planting area may enter the circulating water system and kill the fish. Fish can be an attractive design element, but their maintenance requirements must be considered along with the maintenance requirements of the plants.

Open Plan and Specimen Design

Modern offices are sometimes sterile places in which to work. The introduction of live plants into such an environment is one way of making the space seem less austere and more comfortable without disrupting the integrity of the original design. For windowless offices, plants provide an attractive natural setting appreciated by the occupants. For offices and other windowed areas, the plants provide a transition which makes indoors and outdoors seem to flow together.

In all locations, however, the light intensity must be at the proper level before the plants are introduced. The intensity cannot be taken for granted, since artificial lighting designed for office vision is seldom enough for any but the lowest-light plant species. Even a large window will not provide enough light if it has an overhang or a northern exposure. If the light intensity cannot be directly measured or calculated from detailed ceiling plans, one must assume the worst and use only low-light material. There is sometimes a tendency to use plants to fill in otherwise forgotten spots, such as corners, stairwells, and hallways. Such areas are often poorly lit and no plant will survive there unless additional lighting is installed.

In large areas with barely enough light, the usual design problem is how to arrange the limited number of low-light species so that different areas stand out from one another. Design interest can be accomplished by using different types of foliage (for example, fragmented and solid) in the different areas, varying the plant sizes among the areas or using specimen plants selectively.

Specimen plants usually have fuller foliage or an unusual stem structure and hence appear to be different from other plants of that species. The true specimen plants are more expensive than ordinary plants of the same species, but can solve many a design problem. However, a plant with fuller foliage than most will also require more light than most to maintain the foliage.

If the office has floor-to-ceiling walls, the best design procedure is to select specimen plants that act as living sculptures. Since these plants are used for visual emphasis, the plant height and container size should conform to the scale of the rest of the interior design. The plant texture and container finish should blend with each other and with the wall and floor treatments. The particular plant specimen chosen should have an inherently interesting shape and texture.

If the office area is very large or is designed along an "office landscaping" plan with movable partitions, the plants can become an integral part of the design. They can be used with the partitions as space dividers and are excellent for indicating the importance of the space. They also may be effective in relating widely separated areas with one another. They break the monotony of the partitions with both color and texture. They act as sound absorbers. Also, specimen plants can be used in the office landscaping scheme for visual emphasis.

Planting into individual planters Individual decorative containers are used for individual plants or small plant groupings. The plants are left in their growing containers and placed directly into the decorative planter on top of 4 to 6 inches of perlite as the drainage material. The decorative planter or container must be tall enough to accommodate the growing can and the perlite, and wide enough to accommodate the width of the growing can. The space between the growing can and the inner wall of the planter can be filled with additional perlite. (See Fig. 2 for size-selection guidance.) As a decorative finishing, bark chips or sheet moss may be placed on the surface of the soil in the growing can. This decorative cover can be easily removed if the plant is replaced and it does not mix with the soil as sometimes happens in large gardens.

Removing the plant from the growing can and repotting it directly into the planter is not generally recommended. Replacing the plant, if necessary, is a messy job unless drainage material and soil separator are added to the bottom of the container. Also, once removed from its growing container, the plant may take up to four weeks to adjust fully to its new environment.

CONTAINERS

Decorative Containers: Different Types

A plant container should be more than decorative. Its proper selection is the first element of proper maintenance, since the container must provide the plant roots with sufficient growing room and with adequate drainage.

All small to medium-size plants are received from the grower in growing containers, usually metal cans or rubber tubs. Large plants are either in large growing containers or their root balls are wrapped in burlap. As a rule, these growing cans provide the proper volume of soil for the size of the plant and have a hole in the bottom for drainage. There is seldom any need to remove the plant from its growing container, especially since rough handling of the root system can shock the plant. Only the smaller plants, such as ivy, can be repotted without much disturbance of the root system. If it is absolutely necessary to repot a larger plant, it should be done carefully as outlined earlier, and it should be always into a larger volume of soil, never into a smaller volume.

The decorative container should be chosen so that its inside dimensions are large enough that the plant-growing container can be dropped directly into it. In addition, it should be deep enough for the growing container to rest on at least 2 inches of perlite or other drainage material, and leave about 1 inch between the top of the growing can and the top of the decorative container. Some care must be taken in the choice since the interior dimensions of the decorative container are often not uniformly related to the exterior dimensions. For example, some fiberglass containers have a large lip which limits the size of the growing can that can be dropped directly into them. Also some containers have a large false bottom, which makes the interior depth much less than the outside height.

With these simple size-selection rules in mind, the proper decorative container can be selected using Fig. 6 as a guide. This figure lists the decorative pros and cons of the most common types of containers.

Excess Water in Container

Overwatering of plants is more harmful than underwatering. This problem is most likely to occur when the plants are in individual decorative containers that do not allow the excess water to flow off. To minimize this danger, we have recommended that a plant in a decorative container be double-potted. In the bottom of the decorative container, below the plant growing can, there should be at least 2 inches of perlite or other drainage material to act as a reservoir for excess water. Nevertheless, if the plant is continually overwatered, this reservoir will fill up and lead to root rot because the roots are in a pool of water.

If the plant soil is continually wet to the touch, excess water may be the problem. The water level in the container may be determined by tapping the sides of the container. If the water level indicates excess water, the container is tilted on its side, the plant gently pulled from the container, and the excess water drained from the perlite. If the perlite is completely saturated or appears old, it must be discarded and replaced with new drainage material. If the plant has been sitting in a pool of water for some time, the root ball should be allowed to dry before repotting.

If a very large container or garden has been overwatered and there is no way to drain out the excess water, not really much can be done short of using a small electric pump. One must simply avoid watering the plant or garden at all until the soil has begun to dry out and feels dry to the touch.

PLANTSCAPING
Plant Containers

Automatic Watering Devices

In areas where regular maintenance would be difficult, the use of automatic watering devices can be of considerable help. Even when they are used, however, the plant must be checked periodically to see that the device is working properly, that its water reservoir is full, and that no other maintenance problems have developed.

Automatic watering devices are either external to the container or are built into the planter. The external devices tend to work well only with small plants, and also, they are likely to detract from the design. For these reasons, the built-in type of device is preferred. The planters with this type come in both cylindrical and rectangular shapes and in several colors. The planter has a hollow space within its double-wall sides which serves to hold a three- to four-week water supply, feeding the water to the plant soil by a wick mechanism, sensor, or capillary action. Most types have a float to indicate the amount of water remaining in the reservoir.

Since the soil must be in contact with the wick or capillary tubes for the device to work, the plant must be removed from its original growing can and repotted directly in the planter. As the soil never dries out, the plant must be watched for symptoms of overwatering. Because different plants use water at different rates under different humidity and temperature conditions, a timetable should be kept for each container so the maintenance staff will know when to refill each reservoir.

The use of automatic watering devices will not eliminate maintenance personnel, but it will reduce the number of workers needed. One person can handle many more plants, devoting more time to cleaning and trimming, since the reservoir has to be refilled only every month or so. Occasionally, however, one will find a client who will resist the use of the automatic devices because he or she likes the assurance of seeing a person with a watering can once a week.

The use of the automatic watering devices is expected to increase in the future as more architects and designers become aware of them and convince their clients of their usefulness, and as the manufacturers produce more colors and styles and improve the efficiency of the devices.

Container Type	Pros	Cons
Fiberglass	Large selection of sizes, shapes, and colors. Light weight, easy to move. Some types have casters. Reasonable prices. Many manufacturers.	Easily scratched. Some types have large lips.
Ceramic	Large selection of sizes, shapes, colors, and textures. Rich appearance. Can be put on casters.	Expensive. Easily broken in shipping and handling.
Metal	Large selection of sizes and styles. Rich appearance. Polished or brushed finish.	Expensive.
Baskets, traditional	Good range of styles and textures. Combines well with all furniture styles. Reasonable prices.	Limited sizes. Tend to sag. Need saucer under plant can to prevent water spillage.
Baskets woven around metal	Good texture range. Reasonable prices. Do not sag. Need no saucers. Combine well with all furniture styles.	Sizes limited.
Plastic	Least expensive. Good for table plants. Versatile.	Available mostly in green or white. Sizes largely limited to standard pot sizes. Need saucers underneath. Cheap appearance.
Hanging planters (Heavy; must be used with a rotating hook which can support the weight and allow for easy plant access.)	Available in ceramic, fiberglass, plastic, and metal. Ceramic in various shapes and textures, metal in various finishes. Plastic and fiberglass are inexpensive. All are versatile.	Makes plants susceptible to drafts from heating and air conditioning. Difficult to water without spilling on floor. Metal very expensive. All need inner pot to allow for drainage. Ceramic is porous and presents condensation problem.

Fig. 6 Comparison of container types.

Design Type	Plant Name	Watering Requirements
HIGH-LIGHT PLANTS — 150 FOOTCANDLES AND UP		
T	Fiddle-leaf fig (*Ficus lyrata*)	W
T	Indian laurel (*Ficus retusa*)	W
T	Rubber plant (*Ficus elastica* cv. 'Decora')	W
T	Weeping fig (*Ficus benjamina*)	W
T	Norfolk Island pine (*Araucaria heterophylla*)	LF
T	Schefflera (*Brassaia actinophylla*)	W
FP	Dwarf date palm (*Phoenix Roebelenii*)	LF
FP	Dwarf schefflera (*Brassaia arboricola*)	W
FP	False aralia (*Dizygotheca elegantissima*)	W
FP	Lady palm (*Rhapis excelsa*)	W
FP	Mock orange (*Pittosporum Tobira*)	W
FP	Ponytail (*Beaucarnea recurvata*)	LF
FP	Southern yew (*Podocarpus macrophyllus* var. Maki)	LF
DTP	Jade plant (*Crassula argentea*)	LF
DTP	Swedish ivy (*Plectranthus australis*)	MF
DTP	Wax plant (*Hoya carnosa*)	MF
MEDIUM-LIGHT PLANTS — 100 TO 150 FOOTCANDLES		
T	Indian laurel (*Ficus retusa*)	W
T	Schefflera (*Brassaia actinophylla*)	W
T	Weeping fig (*Ficus benjamina*)	W
FP	Bamboo palm (*Chamaedorea erumpens*)	MF
FP	Corn plant (*Dracaena fragrans* cv. 'Massangeana')	W
FP	Dwarf date palm (*Phoenix Roebelenii*)	LF
FP	Dwarf dragon tree (*Dracaena marginata*)	LF
FP	Dwarf schefflera (*Brassaia arboricola*)	W
FP	Green dracaena (*Dracaena deremensis* cv. 'Janet Craig')	W
FP	Green pleomele (*Dracaena reflexa*)	W
FP	Kentia palm (*Howea Forsterana*)	W
FP	Narrow-leaved pleomele (*Dracaena angustifolia honorail*)	W
FP	Neantha bella palm (*Chamaedorea elegans*)	W
FP	Reed palm (*Chamaedorea Seifrizii*)	MF
FP	Self-heading philodendron (*Philodendron Selloum*)	LF

Design Type	Plant Name	Watering Requirements
DTP	Boston fern (*Nephrolepis exaltata* cv. 'Bostoniensis')	W
DTP	Chinese evergreen (*Aglaonema commutatum* var. maculatum)	LF
DTP	Common philodendron (*Philodendron scandens oxycardium*)	W
DTP	Dumb cane (*Dieffenbachia maculata* cv. 'Rudolph Roehrs')	LF
DTP	Golden pothos (*Epipremnum aureum*)	LF
DTP	Grape ivy (*Cissus rhombifolia*)	W
DTP	Prayer plant (*Maranta leuconeura*)	W
DTP	Swedish ivy (*Plectranthus australis*)	W
DTP	White flag (*Spathiphyllum* cv. 'Clevelandii')	W
DTP	White-striped dracaena (*Dracaena deremensis* cv. 'Warneckii')	W
LOW-LIGHT PLANTS — 50 TO 100 FOOTCANDLES		
FP	Corn plant (*Dracaena fragrans* cv. 'Massangeana')	W
FP	Dwarf dragon tree (*Dracaena marginata*)	LF
FP	Green dracaena (*Dracaena deremensis* cv. 'Janet Craig')	W
FP	Green pleomele (*Dracaena reflexa*)	W
FP	Kentia palm (*Howea Forsterana*)	W
FP	Neantha bella palm (*Chamaedorea elegans*)	W
FP	Reed palm (*Chamaedorea Seifrizii*)	W
FP	Self-heading philodendron (*Philodendron Selloum*)	W
DTP	Chinese evergreen (*Aglaonema commutatum* var. maculatum)	LF
DTP	Common philodendron (*Philodendron scandens oxycardium*)	W
DTP	White Flag (*Spathiphyllum* cv. 'Clevelandii')	W

A Final Word about Lighting Intensity The preceding lighting-intensity recommendations are based on experience and the assumption that these levels will be provided eight hours a day, five days a week, and that the plants have been fully acclimatized. If light can be provided for more hours each day or more days each week, the plant material will look its best for longer periods. On the other hand, often the energy costs of the longer lighting exposure are more than the costs of plant replacement. However, if the plants are not to be maintained by the landscape contractor with a plant replacement guarantee, provision should be made for giving the plants light exposure seven days a week.

Fig. 7   Growing requirements. Design type: T = tree; FP = floor plant; DTP = desk or table plant or ground cover. Watering requirements: W = water weekly; MF = water more frequently, as required; LF = water less frequently, as required.

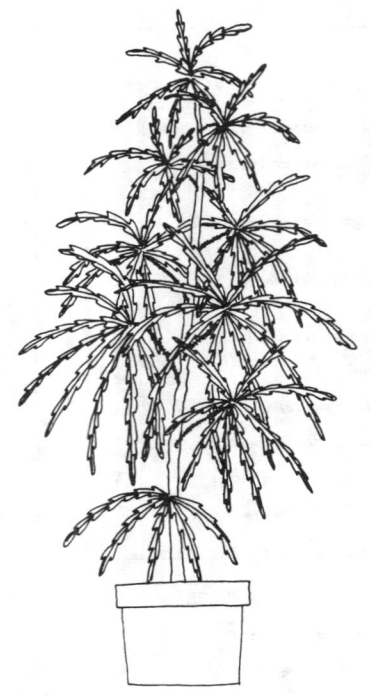

(False) Aralia

A plant of grace and elegance with narrow, ribbonlike, notched leaves of dark green, usually born on slender, single stems. The aralia is attractive if two or three plants are planted together in one pot. It grows very quickly, so prune the stem tips from time to time to prevent the foliage from thinning at the bottom.

Temperature The aralia is tolerant of warm temperatures if there is plenty of humidity.

Light/sun The plant likes a semisunny to semishady window; an east or west window is ideal.

Water/humidity Keep the soil damp but not soggy. The false aralia likes a humid atmosphere. Place your plant on a pebble tray and mist the foliage daily.

Soil The soil should be equal parts loam, sand, and peat moss.

Special care You can rejuvenate leggy plants by drastically cutting the stems back to four to six inches from the pot. Do this in the spring and leave the plant in a sheltered location, being sure to fertilize and water frequently.

African Violet

The African violet, a longtime favorite houseplant, does insist on more care and attention, but its beautiful blossoms make the effort worthwhile.

Temperature African violets are more contented and grow best within a temperature range of 65 to 80 degrees. Be careful that your plants are not in an open window or a draft.

Light/sun The African violet enjoys a place in an east or west window. Direct sun is too strong, unless filtered through a curtain. Excess sun will cause spotting and loss of color, and too little light causes elongated stems and no blooms.

Water/humidity African violets should be watered from the saucer underneath in the morning with *lukewarm* water. Water when the soil begins to dry out. Do not keep it soggy. If the air is dry in your home, place the potted plant in a tray of moistened pebbles.

Soil The soil should be porous for good drainage and should contain ample organic matter such as compost or peat moss. Commercial African violet soil mixture is specially prepared for these plants; however, add sand or perlite to ensure adequate drainage. A plastic pot is less likely to cause the lower leaves to rot where they touch the pot.

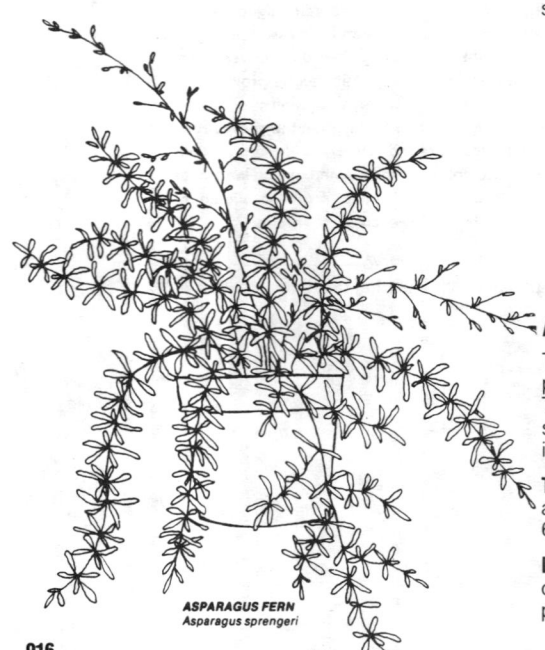

Asparagus Fern — Emerald Feather

The bright feathery green of this delightful plant is best displayed in a hanging container. The long branches drape gracefully and are studded with tiny white flowers that ripen into red-orange berries.

Temperature Asparagus fern is not fussy about temperatures, but prefers a range of 60 to 68 degrees.

Light/sun The bright filtered sun of an east or west window is a good location for this plant.

Water/humidity Soak the soil in the pot thoroughly and allow it to become dry to the touch before rewatering.

Soil A well-drained potting soil or a mixture of equal parts of loam, peat moss, and sand or perlite.

How to start new plants Allow the berries to ripen and when dry sow the seeds they contain. Asparagus fern can usually be grown from seed quite well.

ASPARAGUS FERN
Asparagus sprengeri

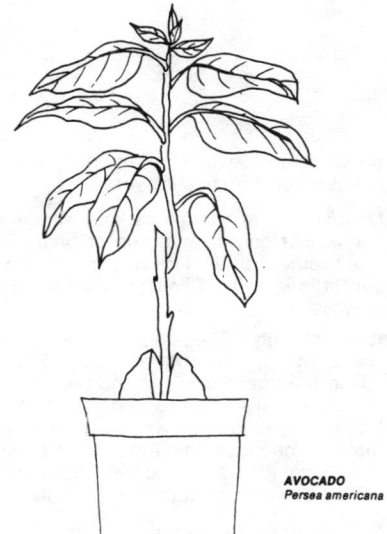

Avocado

The avocado comes easily from seed and is grown for its ornamental foliage. It makes a nice tree for your indoor garden. Allow the plant to reach the desired height and then begin regular pinching to force branching and encourage bushy growth.

Temperature Temperatures between 60 and 70 degrees suit the avocado well.

Light/sun Keep your avocado in bright light but protected from direct sun. Avocados are easily sunburned, especially when they are first moved outside.

Water/humidity Use tepid water and keep the soil moist. Place the plant on a pebble tray to raise the humidity level around it. This plant likes a fair amount of humidity and benefits from regular misting. Any signs of browning or crispness at the tips and along the edges of the leaves means the plant needs more humidity.

Soil Use a mixture consisting of equal parts of sand, loam, and peat moss.

AVOCADO
Persea americana

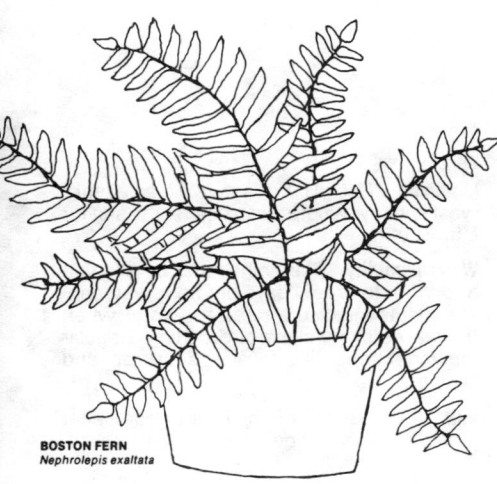

Boston Fern

Exaltant is a good adjective for this family of ferns that can fill a corner with rich green foliage. These ferns are excellent for hanging baskets. Initially the ferns may need a lot of attention until the right combination of environmental factors is achieved, but the effort is well worth it. The leaflets grow on a midrib that is covered with fine brown hairs and vary from smooth-edged to feathery and even ruffled. A mature fern can have fronds ranging in length from two to three feet and two to three inches across.

Temperature With lots and lots of humidity, ferns will do well in house temperatures in the 60 to 70 degree range.

Light/sun Ferns need a location with good bright light, but this means filtered sunlight. *Avoid direct sunlight.*

Water/humidity It is essential that the roots of the ferns never dry out at any time. Soak the soil regularly. Clay pots and hanging baskets can be soaked in a bucket or the sink for half an hour and then drained. The soil should be checked daily to make sure that it is not drying out. Humidity is the most important ingredient to successful fern growing. Place pots of ferns on a pebble tray. Mist the foliage daily with room temperature water.

Soil Ferns need a soil that is loose and easily penetrated by their dense root system. The soil mixture should be rich in peat moss and organic matter with a liberal amount of sand for drainage. A sprinkling of charcoal mixed in the soil helps to keep the soil from becoming sour from the frequent waterings. When potting ferns, place a layer of bits of broken pots or gravel in the bottom of the pot. Ferns do not take kindly to having their roots tampered with, so be careful not to damage them when repotting.

BOSTON FERN
Nephrolepis exaltata

Chinese Evergreen

This beautiful foliage plant has waxy dark green leaves. The leaves grow on a canelike stem and are oblong, tapering to a thin tip. Some of the varieties are variegated with splashes of creamy white or yellow. Under optimal conditions, it will produce a flower spike surrounded by a white spathe. The flower is similar to a calla lilly. The great thing about this plant is that it will adapt to a variety of environments which makes it a good plant for a beginner or a difficult location.

Temperature A range of 60 to 70 degrees suits this plant well.

Light/sun A shady spot, an artificial light, or any other location will suit this plant. The Chinese evergreen is an excellent plant for a north window.

Water/humidity Keep the soil moist but not soggy. To avoid waterlogged soil, allow the surface soil to become dry to the touch before rewatering. The Chinese evergreen can be grown in water. The roots are attractive so a clear glass container shows them off to best advantage. It is important to wash the leaves regularly to keep them dust free.

Soil The soil should be equal parts of garden loam, peat moss, and sand.

CHINESE EVERGREEN
Aglanonema modestum

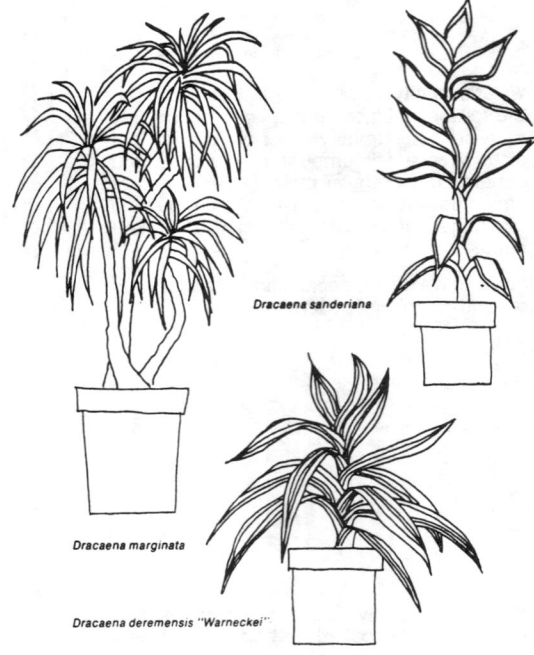

Dracaena sanderiana

Dracaena marginata

Dracaena deremensis "Warneckei"

Dracaenas

There are several varieties of dracaenas which vary in foliage color, variegation, and size. Here are three that are commonly available.

Dracaena deremensis "Warneckei": is a good choice for a location without much light. The gray green foliage is striped with white and gray.

Dracaena marginata: has clusters of narrow deep green leaves edged with red and gray stems strongly marked with leaf scars. This variety will reach a height of five or six feet.

Dracaena sanderiana: resembles a corn plant in the brightness of the green and the size and shape of the leaves with the difference that the leaves are striped with white.

Temperature Moderate household temperatures in the 60 to 70 degree range suit these plants best. It is important to keep plants away from heating vents.

Light/sun The marginata and sanderiana should get only filtered sun or bright light. The Warneckei will fare well in a spot with very little light; it will flourish when more light is available.

Water/humidity These plants all like soil that is kept evenly moist but not soggy. Soak the soil in the pot thoroughly and then rewater when the soil surface feels dry to the touch. Humidity is a must. Brown crispy leaf tips and margins mean too little moisture in the air. It is a good idea to place the dracaenas in pebble trays and mist the foliage daily.

Soil Commercial potting soil is adequate but added drainage material such as sand or perlite is advisable.

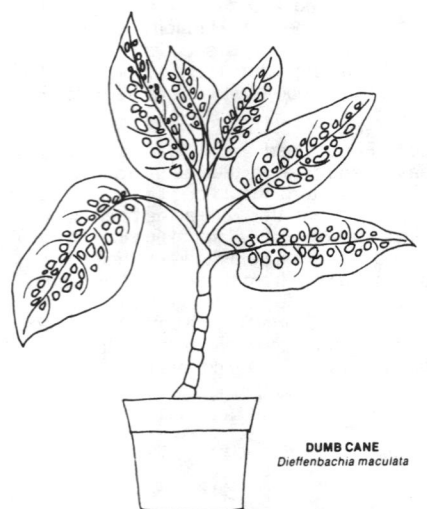

DUMB CANE
Dieffenbachia maculata

Dumb Cane

The cool-looking foliage of this plant is yellow-green, mottled with white. The leaves are pointed ovals that become quite large as the plant matures. The dieffenbachia is known as the "mother-in-law" plant or the dumb cane because when a piece of the stem is placed on the tongue it causes temporary numbness and loss of speech. All joking aside, *this plant is poisonous.*

Temperature The dieffenbachia prefers warm temperatures and will tolerate hot dry places with added humidity.

Light/sun This plant does well in an east or west window where it can bask in the sun for a few hours.

Water/humidity The soil should be allowed to dry out for a few days before rewatering. The plants indicate a need for water when the leaves show signs of dropping. Regular misting keeps the foliage dust-free and luxuriant.

Soil A porous soil of equal parts loam, peat moss, and sand is fine.

GARDENIA
Gardenia radicans floraplena

Gardenia

The gardenia is a handsome foliage plant with intensely fragrant blooms, but it has an extremely temperamental nature. It is a challenging plant to grow successfully indoors. The most frequently available varieties are *Gardenia radicans floraplena,* a low spreading plant with small double flowers, and *Gardenia florida,* which blooms in summer.

Temperature The temperature must be kept above 65 degrees to maintain healthy foliage and flower buds. These plants hate drafts. Loss of flower buds is often due to sudden changes in temperature.

Light/sun The gardenia needs lots of light, but avoid strong sun that might burn the leaves.

Water/humidity The soil must be kept constantly moist without becoming soggy. Submerge the pot in a bucket of lukewarm water and allow it to soak for half an hour or until the soil is moist on the surface. Do not allow the pot to sit in water as that will cause the roots to rot. Gardenias need very high humidity at all times. Place the pot in a tray of moistened pebbles. Mist the foliage daily with tepid water. Leaf or bud drops indicate the air is too dry.

Soil Potting soil should be a mixture of equal parts peat moss, loam and well-decayed manure with sand or perlite added for drainage.

Grape Ivy

Grape ivy is a climber or trailer. The olive colored green leaves look a bit like those of holly without the stiffness or the sharp tips. The leaves form attractive groups of three and are accompanied by furry tendrils.

Temperature The plant is fairly tolerant of a wide temperature range. Increase the amount of humidity as the temperature goes up.

Light/sun Grape ivy will do all right in low light and is often used in low light areas. But it flourishes with bright light or filtered sunlight.

Water/humidity Soak the pot and soil thoroughly and then allow the soil to become dry to the touch before rewatering. Mist frequently and wash the foliage regularly to remove dust and restore the luster of the leaves.

Soil A potting soil that is rich in organic matter is the best. Be sure to add plenty of drainage material to the soil mixture.

GRAPE IVY
Cissus rhombifolia

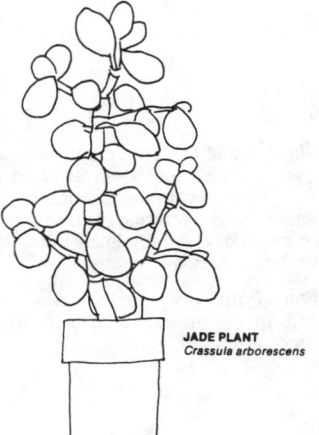

Jade Plant

The jade plant is a tough plant well-suited to the hot dry conditions so prevalent in office and apartment buildings. The rounded leaves are in pairs on the branched treelike stem. A plant that is six to eight years old will produce clusters of lacy-looking star-shaped flowers.

Temperature Temperatures ranging from 65 to 75 degrees are fine. Lower and higher temperature will be tolerated.

Light/sun The jade plant will require full sunlight with shade at midday if possible. A west or south window would be good locations. If you put the plant outside in the summer, place it in a lightly shaded spot.

Water/humidity The soil should remain dry for several days between waterings. The fleshy leaves soak up the soil water and store it for future use. Too much water will cause stem and root rot and certain death.

Soil The jade plant will do well in rich garden soil that has coarse sand or fine bits of broken pots added to it for drainage. Each year give the pot a top dressing of humus. A new pot will be necessary only after about three or four years.

JADE PLANT
Crassula arborescens

Norfolk Island Pine

The delightful symmetry of this evergreen makes it a desirable house plant. The branches grow in tiers of six, each tier representing a year's growth. The bright green needles are soft and pleasant to touch.

Temperature The ideal temperature is between 50 and 60 degrees. High temperatures are tolerated when sufficient humidity is available.

Light/sun The filtered sun of an east or west window is best. Yellowing of the needles might mean too much sun.

Water/humidity Provide the plant with a well-drained soil and pot. Water thoroughly and allow the soil surface to become dry before rewatering. Daily misting is necessary for the warmer temperatures of most houses and offices. A pebble tray will help to add more moisture to the air around the plant.

Soil Garden loam mixed with equal parts of sand and peat moss makes a suitable potting mixture. Repot the Norfolk Island pine only when it has become potbound (the pot is crammed with roots). This would be about every two or three years.

NORFOLK ISLAND PINE
Araucaria excelsa

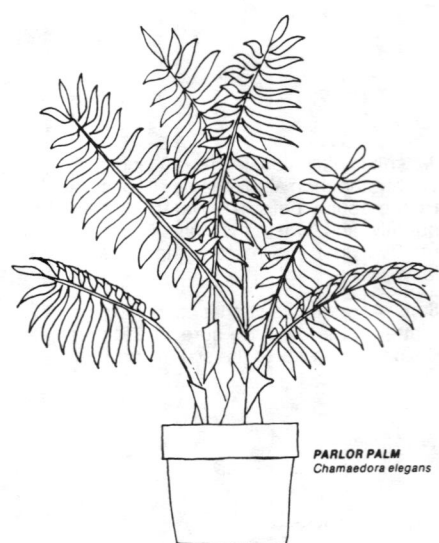

PARLOR PALM
Chamaedora elegans

Parlor Palm

The palm trees are not the easiest plants to grow. However, once you have discovered their basic needs they are a delightful addition to your indoor garden. This palm grows to about four feet tall. It is most attractive when two or three plants are grouped together in a pot. The long feathery fronds grow out of a single stem. Other varieties to try are *C. seifrizii, C. erumpens,* and *C. costarincana.*

Temperature The best growing temperatures for palms range between 60 and 75 degrees.

Light/sun Palms are good plants for locations without much light. They do not like direct sun light.

Water/humidity During the active growing season, between March and October, the palm needs moist soil but it will not tolerate soggy soil. In the winter months, allow the soil to dry on the surface before rewatering. If the foliage shows signs of browning and drying on the tips, it needs more humidity. Misting regularly is recommended to keep the foliage healthy.

Soil The palm needs well-drained soil of equal parts rich garden loam, peat moss, and sand. It will need repotting only every two or three years. It prefers being a bit potbound.

COMMON PHILODENDRON
Philodendron oxycardium

Philodendron

By nature, the philodendron is a climbing plant, but it also trails. It looks best on a bracket beside the window frame, and for good effect must be kept strongly pinched back so that the plant is full of bushy young growth and does not deteriorate into two or three stringlike stems.

Temperature Normal house or office temperatures are fine.

Light/sun The philodendron is quite hardy and robust and will grow almost anywhere. However, it will fare better in a well-lighted area.

Water/humidity The plant should be kept evenly moist and never allowed to dry out. Be certain water does not remain in the saucer after watering. The foliage should be misted daily and the leaves cleaned of accumulated dust.

Soil Potting soil mixed with perlite, vermiculite, or sand and peat moss is recommended.

WINDOWLEAF PHILODRON
Philodendron pertusum "Monstera deliciosa"

Windowleaf Philodendrom

This philodendron has large heart-shaped leaves that are slashed irregularly. It is an enthusiastic climber and needs a piece of bark or totem for support. The aerial roots can be inserted in the soil or encouraged to attach to the totem. Keep the growing tips pinched back so that the plant doesn't get leggy.

Temperature The windowleaf prefers temperatures between 65 and 70 degrees.

Light/sun Bright light is best for this plant. However, avoid putting the plant in a location where the plant would get direct sun.

Water/humidity Soak the plant thoroughly and allow the soil surface to remain dry for a day or two before rewatering. Mist the foliage daily and wash the leaves weekly to remove dust.

Soil A soil mixture of equal parts garden loam, peat moss, and sand is fine.

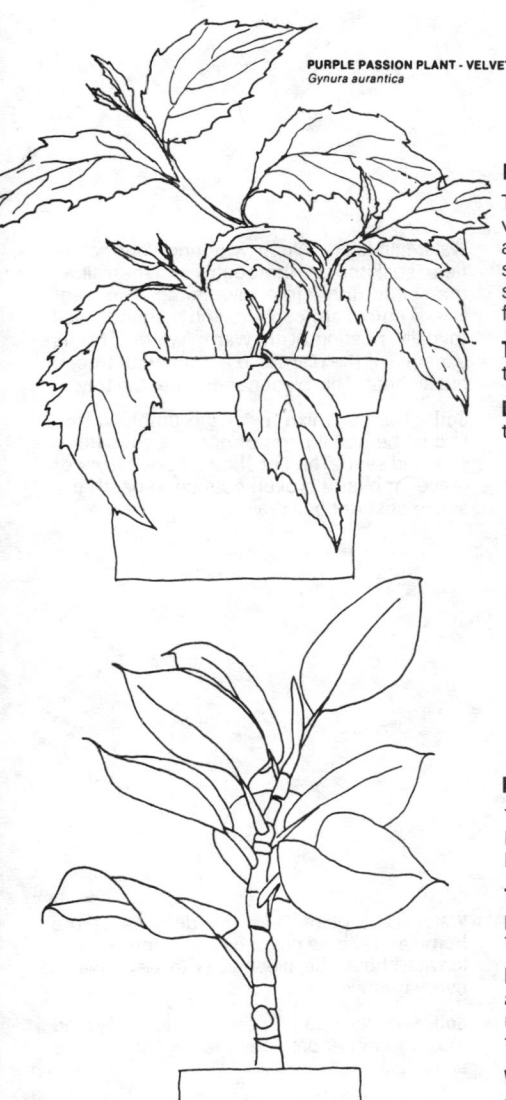

PURPLE PASSION PLANT - VELVET PLANT
Gynura aurantica

Purple Passion Plant — Velvet Plant

The strikingly rich royal purple coloring and velvety texture of the foliage and stems attract many growers. The green leaves and stems are covered with tiny purple hairs. The straggly growth habit is best kept in check by frequent prunning.

Temperature The purple passion plant likes temperatures in the 65 to 70 degree range.

Light/sun Direct or partial sun will promote the color.

Water/humidity It is important that the velvet plant not dry out. Keep the soil evenly moist at all times. A humid atmosphere is important to keep the brilliant color. Mist the foliage frequently and place the pot in a tray of moistened pebbles to raise the humidity.

Soil Use potting soil of equal parts garden loam, peat moss, and sand. This plant will also grow in water.

Rubber Tree Plant

This house plant with dark green glossy leaves can grow to be four feet high with a little care and not too much water.

Temperature Due to its hardy nature, the plant does well in any normal household temperature.

Light/sun The plant will do well in almost any light, but a well-lighted area is best for the rich green foliage characteristic of the rubber tree plant.

Water/humidity Water only when the soil is completely dry all through the pot. You should set the entire pot in a bucket when

watering, so that moisture can penetrate the deepest roots. Clean the leaves every two weeks or so with a damp cloth. Do not artificially shine the leaves as this clogs the plant's pores and does not allow it to breathe!

Soil Soil should be a well-drained mixture of equal parts of sand, peat moss, and garden loam. If pot is plastic or rubber, be sure to provide plenty of drainage material in the bottom of the pot.

RUBBER TREE PLANT
Ficus elastica decora

Wandering Jew

This is a particularly attractive hanging plant. It is hardy and easy to grow with only one special requirement, which is regular pinching to keep it full and bushy. There are several plants called Wandering Jew, distinguished from each other by their different colorings and markings. The illustration is a *Zebrina pendula*. The leaf is a pointed oval with a deep purple underside, and the upperside is dark green striped with pale silvery-green. *Tradescantia fluminensis* has small oval green leaves marked with white, silver and white, or yellow.

Temperature These plants prefer warm temperatures.

Light/sun Bright indirect sunlight keeps the foliage brilliant. Avoid direct sunlight as they are susceptible to sunburn.

Water/humidity Water generously, keeping the soil moist at all times. During the winter months it will not need quite as much water.

Soil This plant grows in a well-drained potting soil, or water.

WANDERING JEW
Zebrina pendula

Schefflera — Umbrella Tree

If you are looking for a tree for your indoor garden, a schefflera is a good choice. It has handsome deep green leaves that radiate out from a long slender stalk rather like the ribs of an umbrella.

Temperature   The umbrella tree does well in a room where the temperature ranges from 55 to 75 degrees.

Light/sun   The schefflera does not like direct sunlight. It grows best in good light from a shaded window.

Water/humidity   When watering your schefflera, soak the pot thoroughly and then allow the soil to dry before rewatering. The plant likes a humid atmosphere and responds well to daily misting with warm water. This is essential if the plant is in a room with forced hot air heat. This plant needs a pebble tray.

Soil   The soil mixture for the umbrella tree should be equal parts of peat moss, garden soil, and sand. The pot should have a layer of gravel or bits of broken pots underneath the soil to ensure good drainage.

SCHEFFLERA - UMBRELLA TREE
Schefflera venulosa

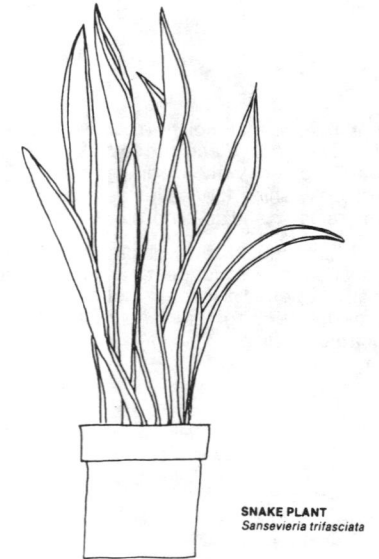

Snake Plant

Seen in many homes and offices, this spikey, banded plant will take almost any abuse.

Temperature   Normal household temperatures are best, *but* do not allow the plant to become suddenly chilled!

Light/sun   The snake plant is a good low light plant but needs sun in order to bloom.

Water   The plant likes the dryness of the home and should never be overwatered. The leaves should be cleaned with clear water every two weeks.

Soil   Garden loam, peat moss, and sand mixed together provides the best soil for the snake plant.

SNAKE PLANT
Sansevieria trifasciata

Spider Plant

With its green and white foliage, the spider plant makes one of the best hanging plants. The graceful trailing runners have plantlets and white star-shaped flowers. There are all-green varieties but the more commonly seen one has a green leaf striped with white.

Temperature   The plant lives best in a warm location.

Light/sun   This lovely plant does very well hanging in indirect sun or a moderately lighted area.

Water/humidity   The spider plant should be allowed to dry out before rewatering. Drying leaf tips usually indicates lack of humidity. To tidy up the plant just snip these off.

Soil   The plant grows contentedly in a rich soil composed of garden loam, sand, and peat moss.

SPIDER PLANT
Chlorophytum elatum vittatum

Zebra Plant
The zebra plant is one of the showiest house plants one can grow. Its spike of waxy yellow flowers and deep shiny green leaves veined in white makes it a striking specimen.

Temperature The zebra plant needs warm temperatures free from drafts.

Light/sun The plant wants bright light but not direct sunlight.

Water/humidity It is important never to allow the soil to dry out. Set the pot in a pebble tray and mist the foliage daily.

Soil The zebra plant likes loose soil consisting of one part garden loam, one part sand or perlite, and two parts peat moss.

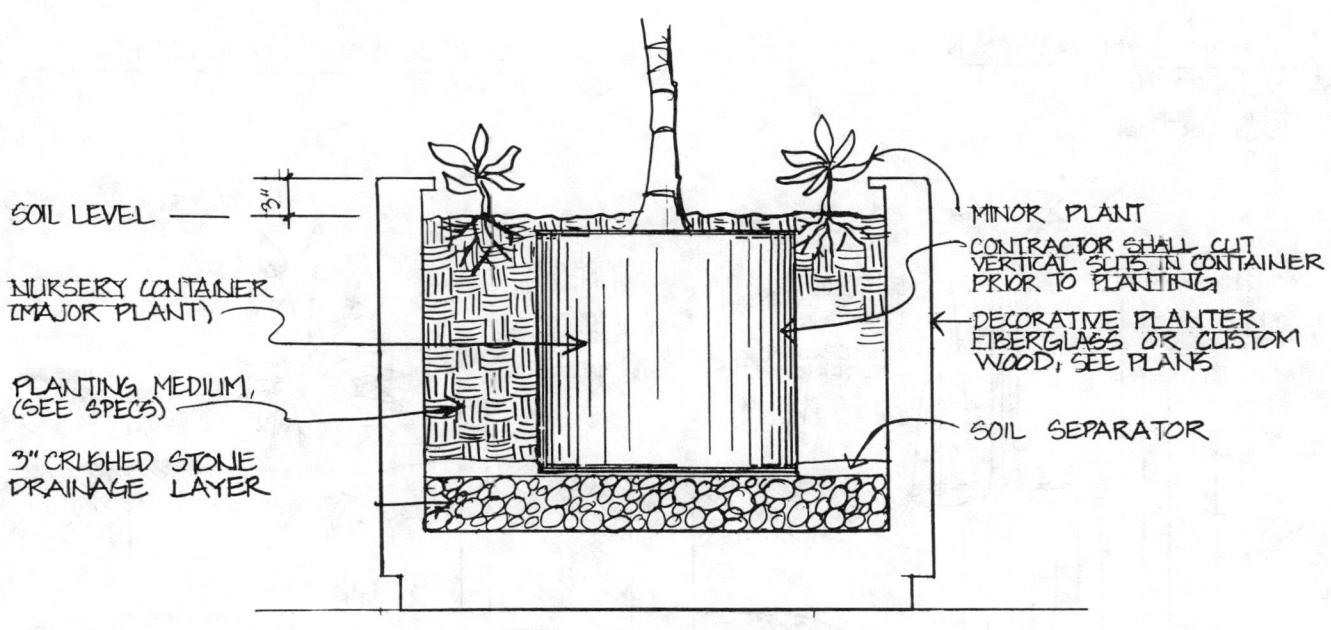

SOIL LEVEL

NURSERY CONTAINER (MAJOR PLANT)

PLANTING MEDIUM, (SEE SPECS)

3" CRUSHED STONE DRAINAGE LAYER

MINOR PLANT

CONTRACTOR SHALL CUT VERTICAL SLITS IN CONTAINER PRIOR TO PLANTING

DECORATIVE PLANTER FIBERGLASS OR CUSTOM WOOD; SEE PLANS

SOIL SEPARATOR

TYPICAL PLANTING DETAIL

PLANTSCAPING

Planting Standards and Details

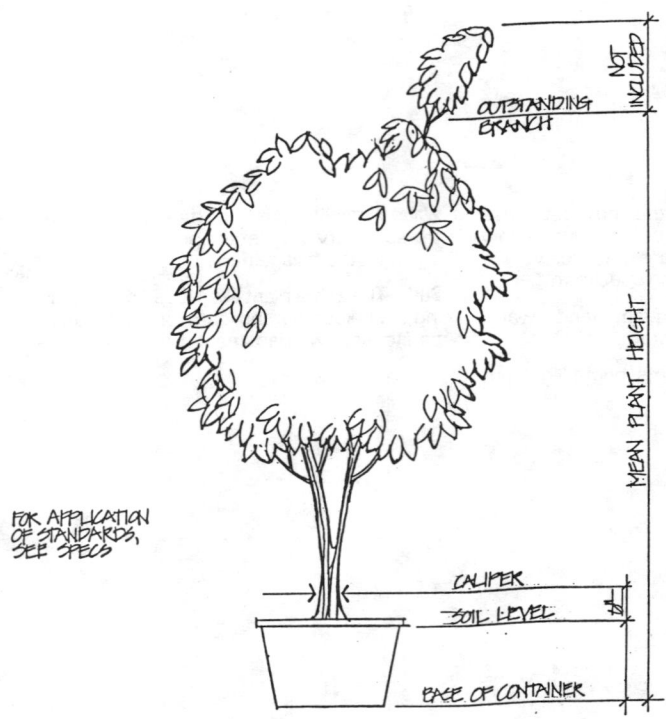

FOR APPLICATION OF STANDARDS, SEE SPECS

OUTSTANDING BRANCH

NOT INCLUDED

MEAN PLANT HEIGHT

CALIPER

SOIL LEVEL

BASE OF CONTAINER

(1) PLANT STANDARDS: OVERALL PLANT HEIGHT
NOT TO SCALE

THIS DETAIL APPLIES TO ALL SHRUBS OVER 5' HIGH

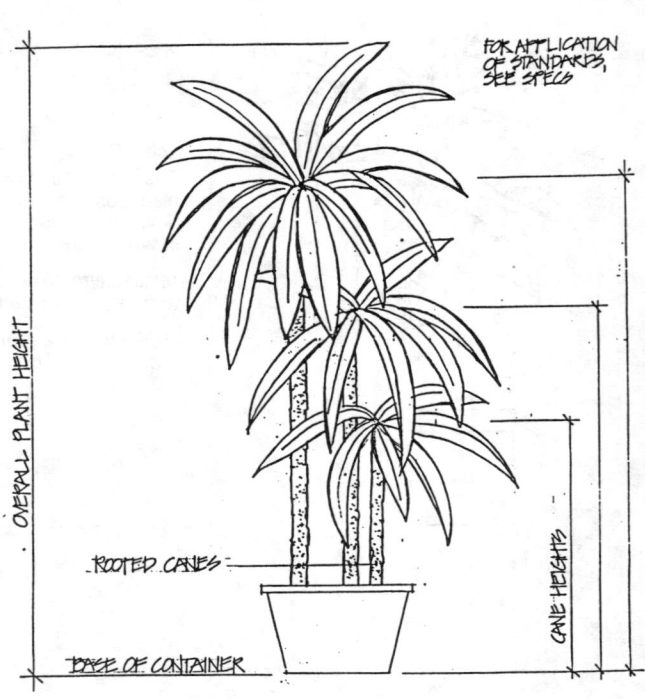

FOR APPLICATION OF STANDARDS, SEE SPECS

OVERALL PLANT HEIGHT

ROOTED CANES

CANE HEIGHTS

BASE OF CONTAINER

(2) PLANT STANDARDS: CANE HEIGHT
NOT TO SCALE

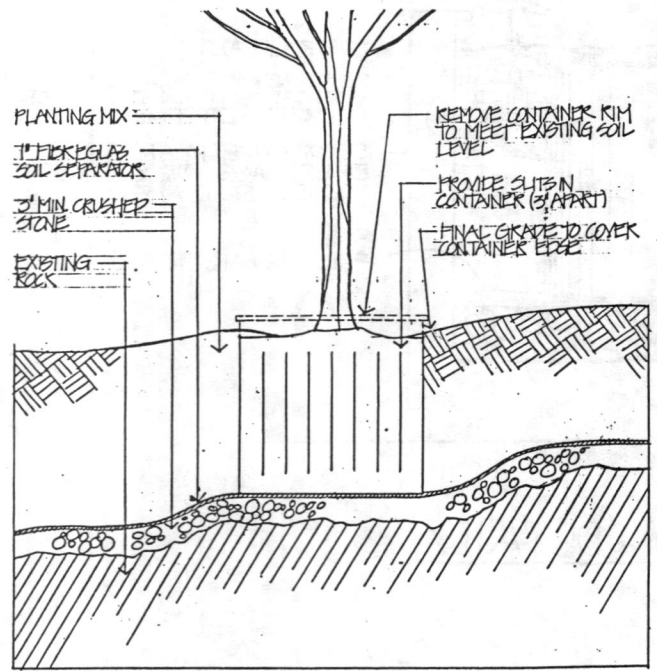

PLANTING MIX

1" FIBERGLAS SOIL SEPARATOR

3" MIN CRUSHED STONE

EXISTING ROCK

REMOVE CONTAINER RIM TO MEET EXISTING SOIL LEVEL

PROVIDE SLITS IN CONTAINER (3" APART)

FINAL GRADE TO COVER CONTAINER EDGE

(3) TREE PLANTING DETAIL
NOT TO SCALE

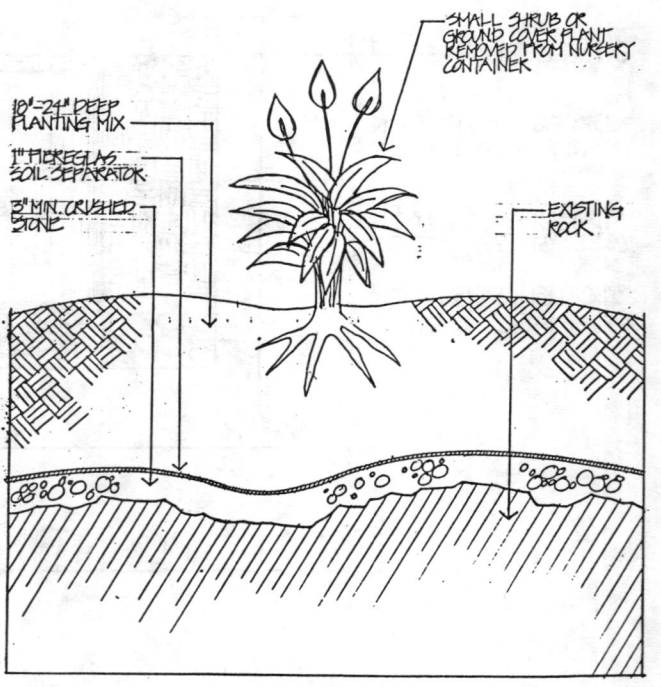

18"-24" DEEP PLANTING MIX

1" FIBERGLAS SOIL SEPARATOR

3" MIN. CRUSHED STONE

SMALL SHRUB OR GROUND COVER PLANT REMOVED FROM NURSERY CONTAINER

EXISTING ROCK

(4) SHRUB PLANTING DETAIL
NOT TO SCALE

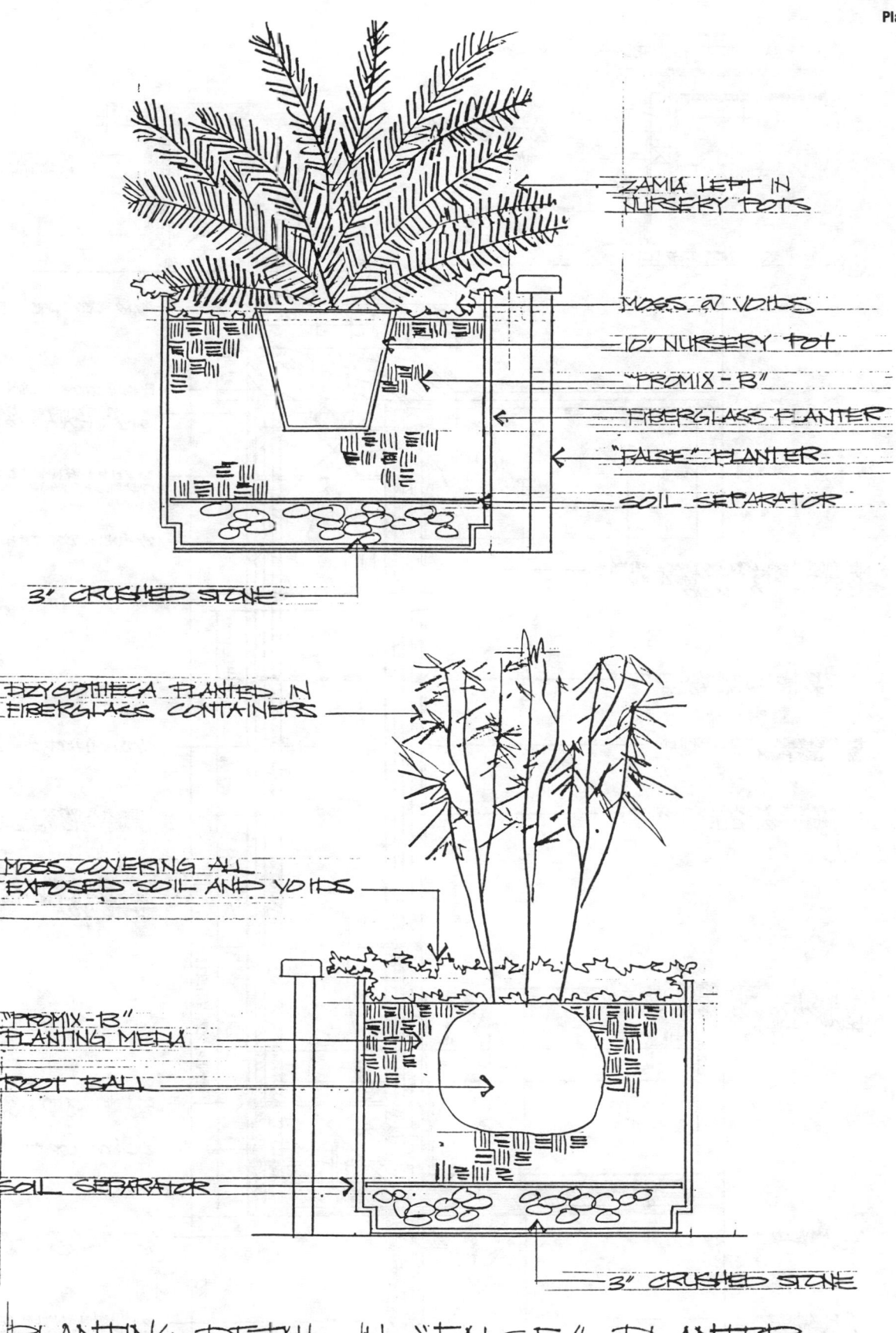

ZAMIA LEFT IN NURSERY POTS

MOSS @ VOIDS

10" NURSERY POT

"PROMIX -B"

FIBERGLASS PLANTER

"FALSE" PLANTER

SOIL SEPARATOR

3" CRUSHED STONE

DIZYGOTHECA PLANTED IN FIBERGLASS CONTAINERS

MOSS COVERING ALL EXPOSED SOIL AND VOIDS

"PROMIX -B" PLANTING MEDIA

ROOT BALL

SOIL SEPARATOR

3" CRUSHED STONE

PLANTING DETAIL IN "FALSE" PLANTER

PLANTSCAPING

Plant Containers

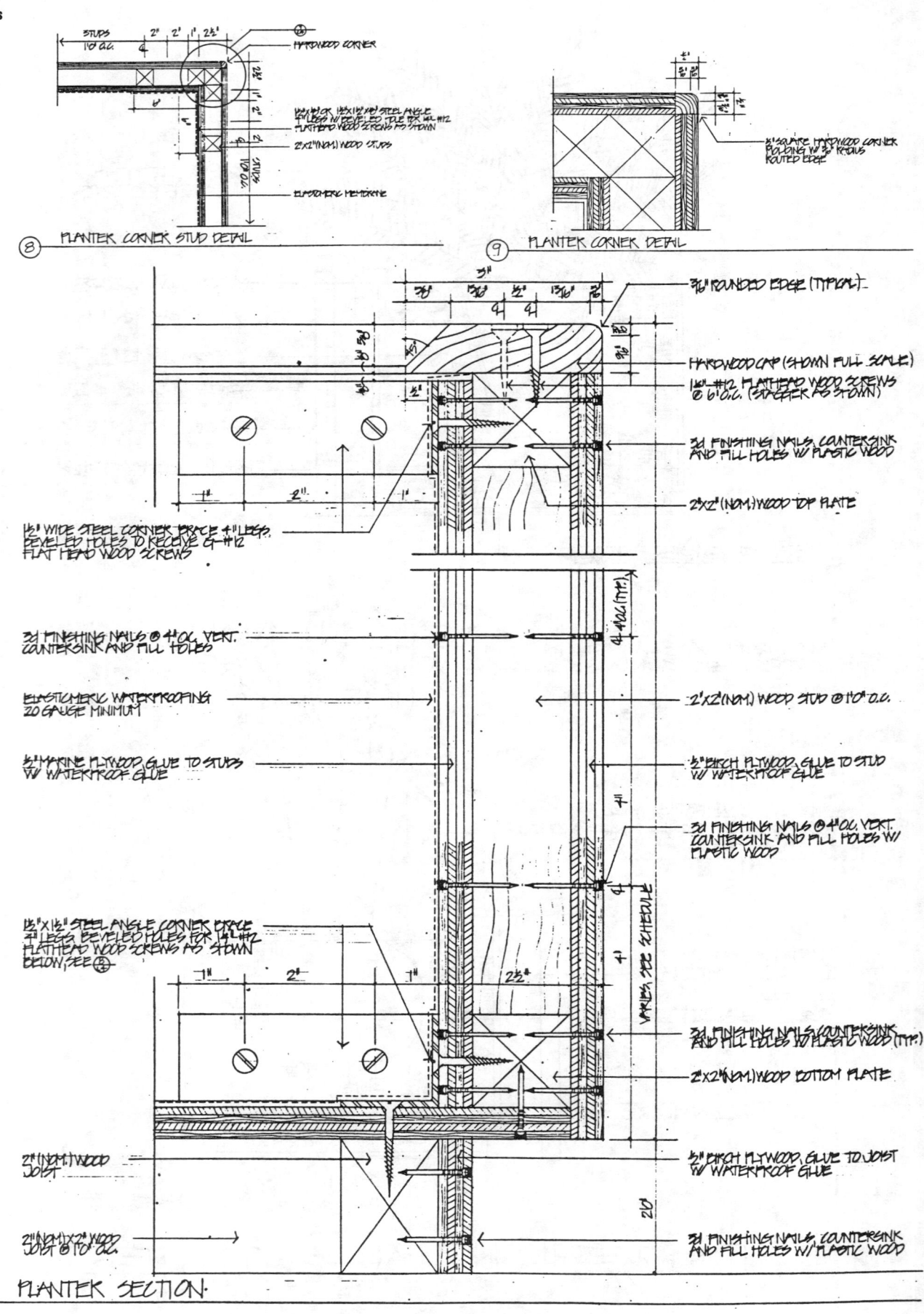

STUDS 1'0" O.C.

HARDWOOD CORNER

1½"×½"×¼" STEEL ANGLE 4" LEGS W/ BEVELED HOLE FOR #12 FLATHEAD WOOD SCREWS AS SHOWN

2"×2"(NOM.) WOOD STUDS

ELASTOMERIC MEMBRANE

⑧ PLANTER CORNER STUD DETAIL

¾" SQUARE HARDWOOD CORNER MOLDING W/ ¾" RADIUS ROUTED EDGE

⑨ PLANTER CORNER DETAIL

3⁄16" ROUNDED EDGE (TYPICAL)

HARDWOOD CAP (SHOWN FULL SCALE)

1¼" #12 FLATHEAD WOOD SCREWS @ 6" O.C. (STAGGER AS SHOWN)

3d FINISHING NAILS, COUNTERSINK AND FILL HOLES W/ PLASTIC WOOD

2"×2"(NOM.) WOOD TOP PLATE

1½" WIDE STEEL CORNER BRACE 4" LEGS, BEVELED HOLES TO RECEIVE 4-#12 FLAT HEAD WOOD SCREWS

3d FINISHING NAILS @ 4" O.C. VERT. COUNTERSINK AND FILL HOLES

ELASTOMERIC WATERPROOFING 20 GAUGE MINIMUM

½" MARINE PLYWOOD GLUE TO STUDS W/ WATERPROOF GLUE

2"×2"(NOM.) WOOD STUD @ 1'0" O.C.

½" BIRCH PLYWOOD, GLUE TO STUD W/ WATERPROOF GLUE

3d FINISHING NAILS @ 4" O.C. VERT. COUNTERSINK AND FILL HOLES W/ PLASTIC WOOD

1½"×1½" STEEL ANGLE CORNER BRACE 4" LEGS BEVELED HOLES FOR 1¼-#12 FLATHEAD WOOD SCREWS AS SHOWN BELOW, SEE ⑧

3d FINISHING NAILS, COUNTERSINK AND FILL HOLES W/ PLASTIC WOOD (TYP.)

2"×2"(NOM.) WOOD BOTTOM PLATE

2"(NOM.) WOOD JOIST

½" BIRCH PLYWOOD, GLUE TO JOIST W/ WATERPROOF GLUE

2"(NOM.)×2" WOOD JOIST @ 1'0" O.C.

3d FINISHING NAILS, COUNTERSINK AND FILL HOLES W/ PLASTIC WOOD

⑦ PLANTER SECTION

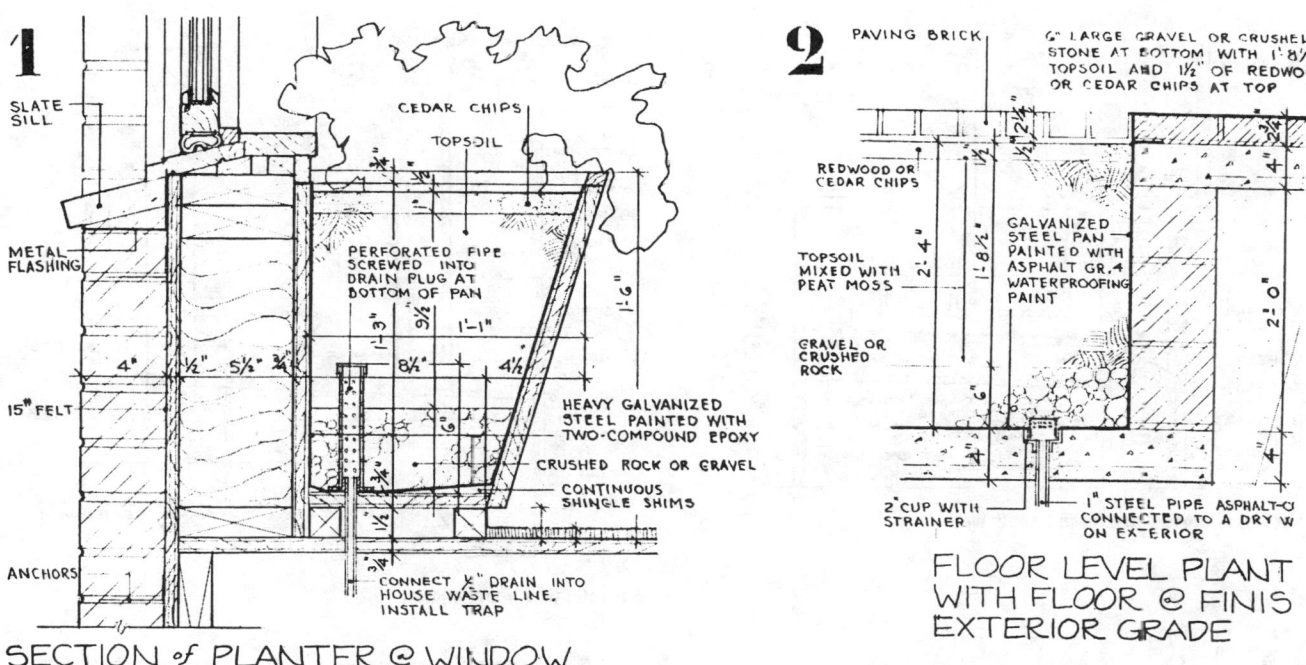

1 SECTION of PLANTER @ WINDOW

SLATE SILL

METAL FLASHING

15" FELT

ANCHORS

CEDAR CHIPS

TOPSOIL

PERFORATED PIPE SCREWED INTO DRAIN PLUG AT BOTTOM OF PAN

HEAVY GALVANIZED STEEL PAINTED WITH TWO-COMPOUND EPOXY

CRUSHED ROCK OR GRAVEL

CONTINUOUS SHINGLE SHIMS

CONNECT ½" DRAIN INTO HOUSE WASTE LINE. INSTALL TRAP

2 FLOOR LEVEL PLANT WITH FLOOR @ FINIS EXTERIOR GRADE

PAVING BRICK

6" LARGE GRAVEL OR CRUSHED STONE AT BOTTOM WITH 1' 8½ TOPSOIL AND 1½" OF REDWOO OR CEDAR CHIPS AT TOP

REDWOOD OR CEDAR CHIPS

TOPSOIL MIXED WITH PEAT MOSS

GRAVEL OR CRUSHED ROCK

GALVANIZED STEEL PAN PAINTED WITH ASPHALT GR. 4 WATERPROOFING PAINT

2" CUP WITH STRAINER

1" STEEL PIPE ASPHALT-C CONNECTED TO A DRY W ON EXTERIOR

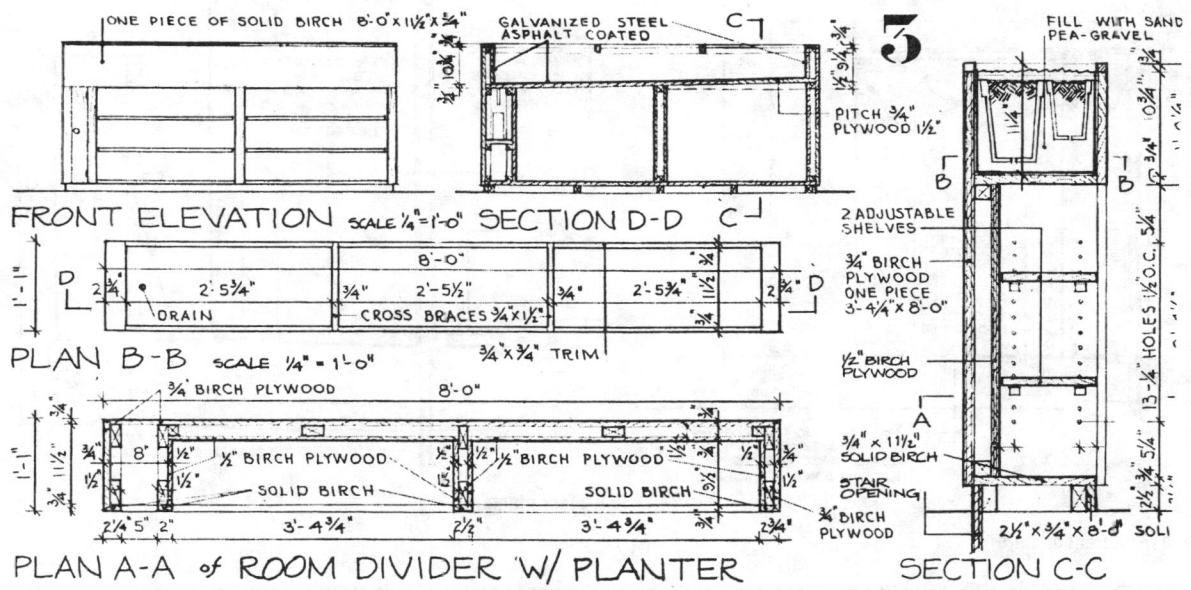

3

ONE PIECE OF SOLID BIRCH 8'-0" X 1½" X ¾"

FRONT ELEVATION SCALE ¼"=1'-0"

GALVANIZED STEEL ASPHALT COATED

SECTION D-D

PITCH ¾" PLYWOOD 1½"

PLAN B-B SCALE ¼" = 1'-0"

2'-5¾" 2'-5½" 2'-5¾"

DRAIN CROSS BRACES ¾"x1½"

¾" x ¾" TRIM

¾" BIRCH PLYWOOD 8'-0"

½" BIRCH PLYWOOD ½" BIRCH PLYWOOD

SOLID BIRCH SOLID BIRCH

3'-4¾" 3'-4¾"

PLAN A-A of ROOM DIVIDER W/ PLANTER

FILL WITH SAND PEA-GRAVEL

2 ADJUSTABLE SHELVES

¾" BIRCH PLYWOOD ONE PIECE 3'-4¼" X 8'-0"

½" BIRCH PLYWOOD

¾" X 11½" SOLID BIRCH

STAIR OPENING

¾" BIRCH PLYWOOD

13-¼" HOLES ½"O.C. 5¾"

SECTION C-C

2½" X ¾" X 8'-0" SOLI

Fig. 8 Detail 1: In this window planter, the plants are placed directly in the earth or growing medium filling the planter and continue to grow and blossom there. The entire planter is contained within a galvanized steel pan with drain. The 6-in-high perforated pipe allows for drainage of excess water over a long period of time before the entire planter has to be cleaned out and started anew. Detail 2: This is a simple floor-level planter where the drainage can easily be connected to the building's drainage system. Here also, plants are installed and grow naturally until a complete planting change is required. Detail 3: A room divider planter for the Ackermann residence, Southampton, New York, consists of a planter-bookcase combination. Here the plants remain in their clay pots and are inserted in the planter with or without gravel or some other type of filler. The entire planter is pitched toward one end, where the drain empties into a small container which catches any extra water.

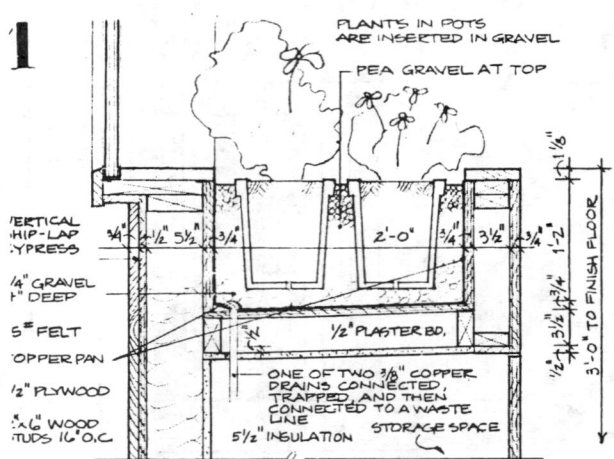

Section of window planter in a south wall

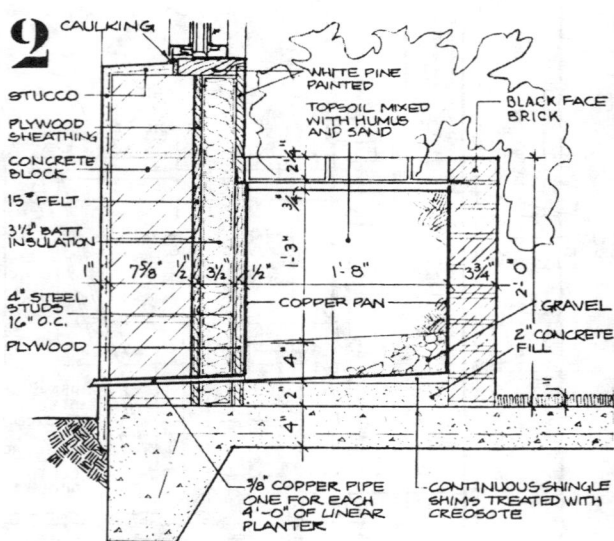

Planter for a warm climate

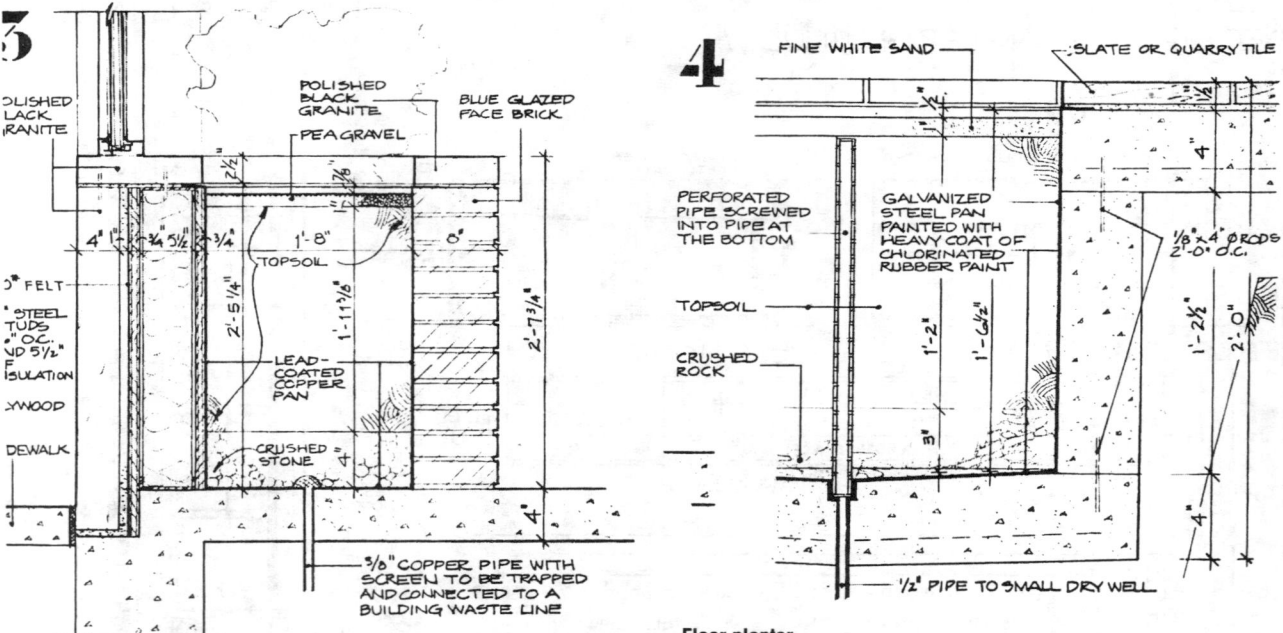

Planter for a restaurant or store

Floor planter

Fig. 9 Detail 1: The plants remain in their own clay pots. The use of pea gravel at top and only 4 in of ¾-in gravel at bottom permits easy changes of the plants. To take care of watering and drainage, the copper pan is simply sloped to one side and two screened drains are connected, trapped, and joined to a waste line. This takes care of any excess water, as it is eliminated by gravity drainage. Detail 2: This planter is for areas where freezing does not occur, and the drainage of excess water can be taken care of by simply extending small pipes directly to the exterior. Detail 3: In this planter the plants remain within the planter and excess water is carried off by a screened pipe at the bottom. Pea gravel is used as a 1-in topping so that odds and ends dropped into the planter can easily be removed. Detail 4: A planter in a commercial lobby or entrance is shown in this detail. The plants are permanently installed and the tall drainage pipe takes care of any top applied water. The white sand at the top is to bring contrast to the colors of the plants.

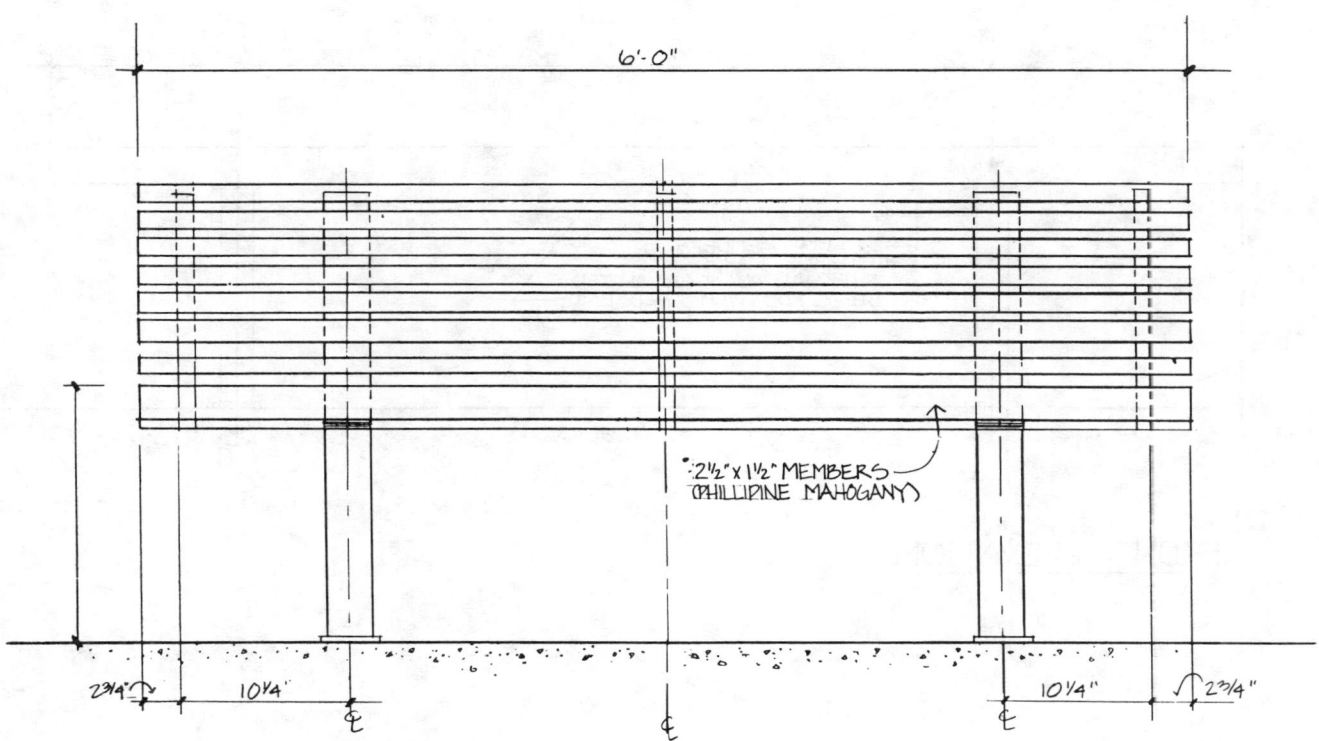

6'-0"

2½" x 1½" MEMBERS
(PHILLIPINE MAHOGANY)

2¾"   10¼"   10¼"   2¾"

FRONT ELEVATION

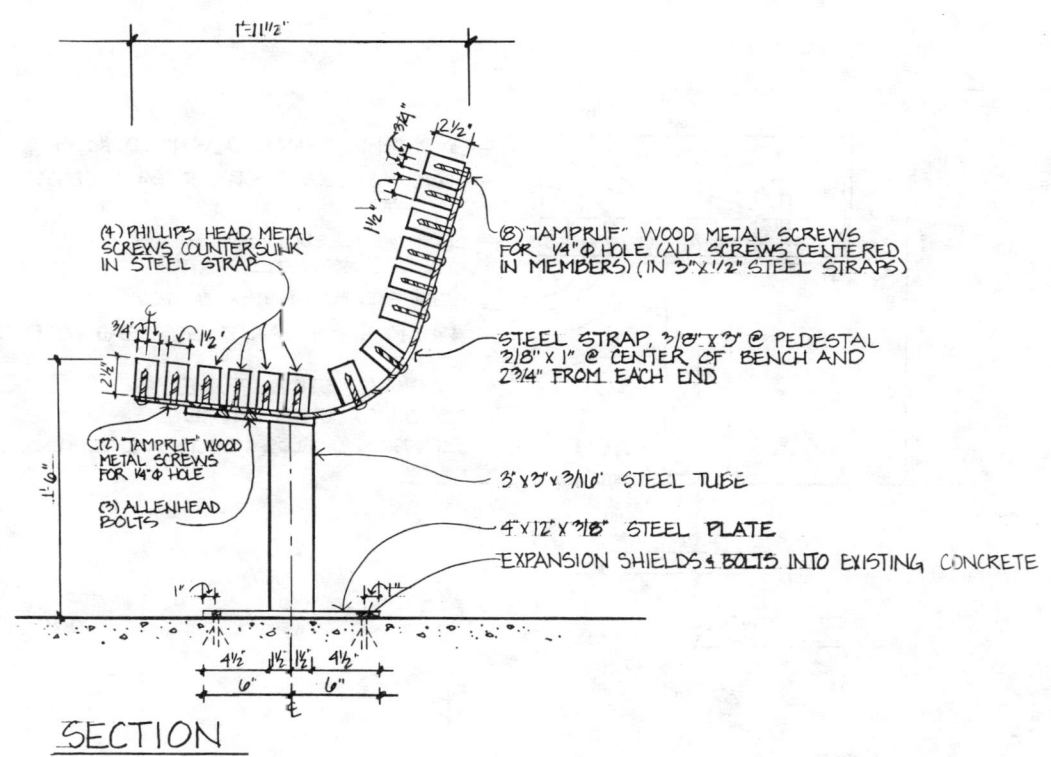

1'-11½"

¾"   2½"

1½"

(4) PHILLIPS HEAD METAL
SCREWS COUNTERSUNK
IN STEEL STRAP

(8) "TAMPRUF" WOOD METAL SCREWS
FOR ¼"Φ HOLE (ALL SCREWS CENTERED
IN MEMBERS) (IN 3"x½" STEEL STRAPS)

¾"   1½"

2½"

STEEL STRAP, 3/8" x 3" @ PEDESTAL
3/8" x 1" @ CENTER OF BENCH AND
2¾" FROM EACH END

(2) "TAMPRUF" WOOD
METAL SCREWS
FOR ¼"Φ HOLE

(3) ALLENHEAD
BOLTS

3"x3"x3/16" STEEL TUBE

4"x12"x3/8" STEEL PLATE

EXPANSION SHIELDS & BOLTS INTO EXISTING CONCRETE

1'-6"

1" ⌀   1¼"

4½"   1½"   1⅛"   4½"

6"   6"

SECTION

929

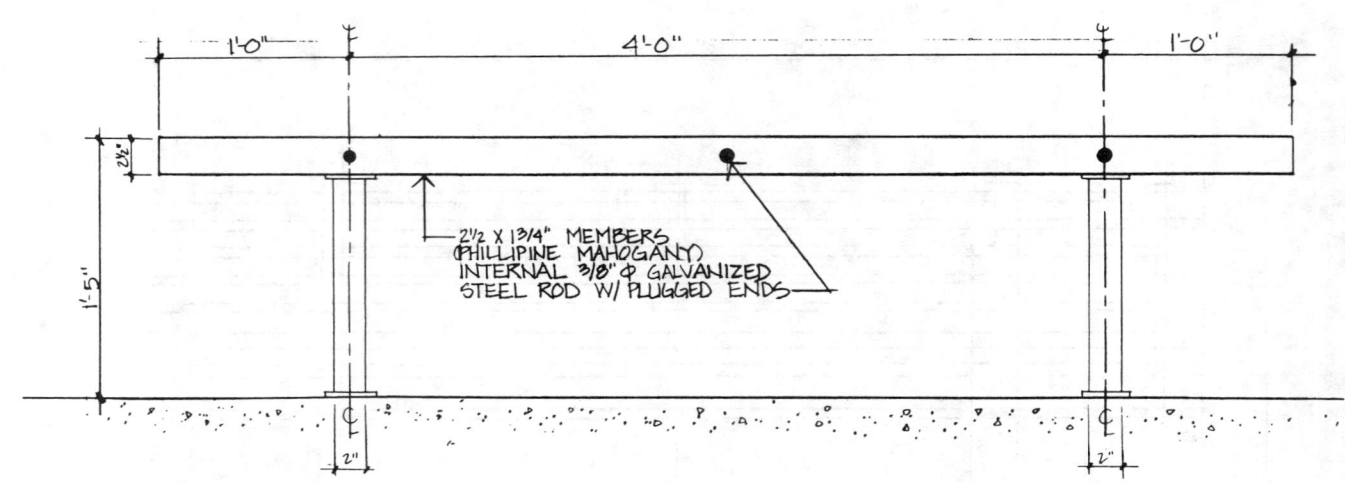

2½ X 1¾" MEMBERS
(PHILLIPINE MAHOGANY)
INTERNAL 3/8" Φ GALVANIZED
STEEL ROD W/ PLUGGED ENDS

FRONT ELEVATION

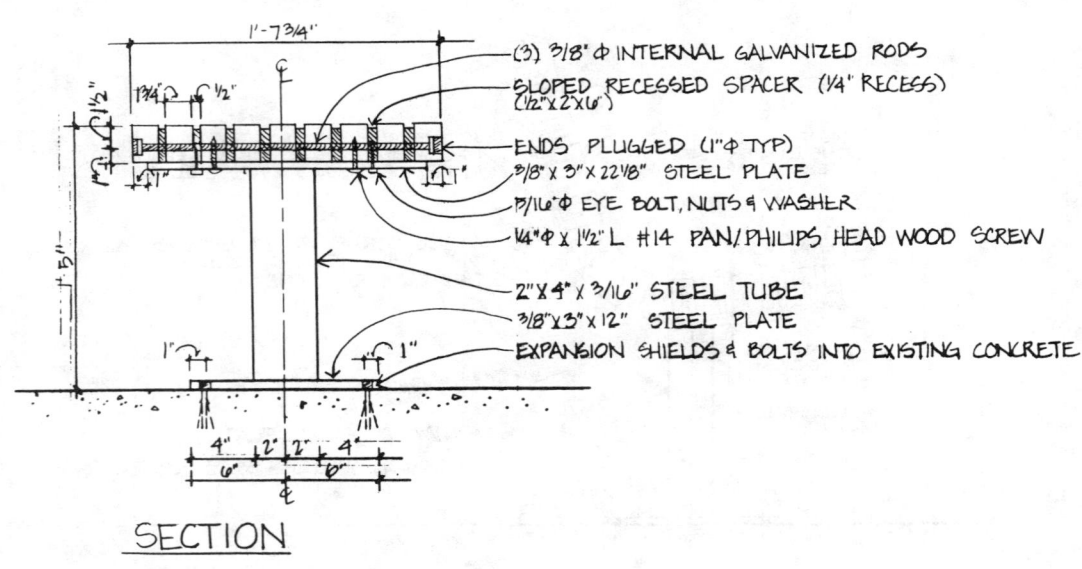

(3) 3/8" Φ INTERNAL GALVANIZED RODS

SLOPED RECESSED SPACER (¼" RECESS)
(½"X 2 X 6")

ENDS PLUGGED (1"Φ TYP)

3/8" X 3" X 22⅛" STEEL PLATE

5/16"Φ EYE BOLT, NUTS & WASHER

¼"Φ X 1½" L #14 PAN/ PHILIPS HEAD WOOD SCREW

2" X 4" X 3/16" STEEL TUBE

3/8" X 3" X 12" STEEL PLATE

EXPANSION SHIELDS & BOLTS INTO EXISTING CONCRETE

SECTION

SIGNAGE SYSTEM DESIGN CRITERIA

Initial consideration should be directed toward determining the basic parameters required in developing the sign system. Each of them merits discussion here.

Performance Requirements

Signs usually must be designed to meet specific performance requirements. The good designer will determine how a system is to perform within given space relationships. The sign system may function entirely on its own merit, or it may be supplemented by staff personnel at major decision-making locations, such as the main lobby and reception areas. Sign devices may become decorative amenities to be featured within the environment, or they may be subtle and low-key elements of minor importance. Supergraphics may be considered in certain areas simply as an art form, or as a functional graphic device presented in large scale for emphasis of context. Certainly, a combination of the two is feasible. These are only several performance considerations that should be addressed prior to the development of the signage system. The designer must evaluate the needs of the client, the unique traffic flow requirements and mounting restrictions dictated by the structure, and the basic performance requirements desired of the signing devices to be utilized.

Usage Considerations

The general nature of the building complex often defines how signs are to be used. They may be given an appearance of being fixed and an integral part of the architecture by the appropriate selection of materials, colors, and mountings, or they may appear changeable and temporary should need so dictate. Some signage requires constant change to properly relate information to people or people to facility, while most sign devices are considered permanent fixtures within a given space. The designer is responsible for determining how signs are to be used most effectively, and at the same time, for enhancing the environment.

Durability Requirements

Prior to the selection of materials for a signing system, durability requirements must be considered. The vast assortment of materials available for signs covers a wide spectrum of durability from soft plastics to metals. The sign copy and background material should be evaluated both individually and jointly when considering durability requirements.

Vandalism Considerations

Signs located in controlled spaces are often free from destructive vandalism; however, in many instances vandalism becomes rampant and uncontrolled. There are no materials that may accurately be labeled "vandal-proof." However, some materials are more vandal-resistant than others. Where vandalism is of prime importance, only materials and graphic techniques engineered to resist destruction should be considered.

Flexibility to Accommodate Changes and Additions

Modern architectural structures are designed to accommodate inner spacial changes to meet tenant needs. Partition systems, prehung door units, room dividers, and modular furniture have ensured ease of change in officescapes. The sign system may also require alterations to preserve continuity. Changes and additions to a sign system should be considered by the designer prior to the selection of materials, graphic techniques, and mounting methods to be used.

Readability Factors

Sign readability is determined by the letter style selected, size of copy, interletter spacing, copy position relevant to background, colors, and angle of observance.

Letter style Letter styles are classified as sanserif and serif. Sanserif letters, such as Helvetica, are more contemporary than serif letters, such as Clarendon (Fig. 1). Each letter style has its own unique personality and flavor. Printers carry alphabets in most letter styles, including lowercase letters as well as uppercase (Fig. 2). Test results indicate that messages starting with an initial uppercase letter and followed by lowercase characters are more recognizable than messages formed with uppercase characters only. Lowercase letters have more "personality" because their shape is varied by ascenders and descenders, resulting in characteristic word forms that are much easier to recognize than all-uppercase word forms. Also, people are more accustomed to reading text in upper- and lowercase than in all uppercase. The proper selection of a particular alphabet should be carefully considered, not only from a legibility point of view, but also from a "personality" standpoint. The letter style should make a concise and meaningful impression in the environment it serves.

Readability Readability is directly related to the size of copy. Visibility studies indicate that 1-inch-high Helvetica Medium, for example, is readable from a distance of 40 feet. Using this as a measure for comparison, 1-inch-high Clarendon style would be readable from a somewhat lesser distance, approximately 25 feet. The distance visibility per 1-inch height may be used as a guideline to determine distance readability for larger letters; that is, 2-inch-high Helvetica Medium will be readable at 80 feet, and 3-inch-high at 120 feet. This direct proportion may be helpful for determining copy (text) sizes for signs used in pedestrian situations. However, the direct proportion may not hold true for vehicular traffic applications where many other factors are involved. The designer must exercise caution after selecting the alphabet and copy size to make certain the lettering will fit properly on the sign background. The sign size should be determined using the longest line of copy and the maximum number of copy lines that may be required.

Letters and line spacing Interletter spacing and interline spacing of copy greatly affect the overall readability of a sign. Message legibility and ease of recognition are increased when proper visual relationships are established between individual characters, words, and lines of copy. Copy with spacing too tight becomes very difficult to read; copy with too open spacing tends to break the message down into fragments (Fig. 3). Proper spacing depends largely on the distance from which the message is to be read. Messages to be read at close distances should employ tighter spacing than messages that will be read at greater distances. Spacing is also affected by the angle at which the message is to be viewed: Greater angles of observance require wider interletter spacing to prevent the characters of the message from appearing to run together.

Copy position The position of copy on the sign background influences the overall readability. Signs on which copy occupies most of the background are not as readable as signs that have sufficient background material surrounding the copy to form a visual barrier separating the message from the environment (Fig. 4 and 5).

Emphasis should be placed on selecting an appropriate sign size to best accommodate the sign message. There are nine basic copy placement positions to be considered in determining the important relationship of copy to sign background. They are: upper left, upper centered, upper right, centered left, centered, centered right, lower left, lower centered, and lower right. Traditionally, the most popular placement selections have been the centered and upper left positions.

Color Color of copy and sign background greatly affect readability. Strong contrasting colors are more readable than less dramatic color combinations. White copy on a black background offers the greatest contrast and readability. Color also influences the apparent relationship between the copy size and the background. For example, white copy on a black field appears larger than black copy on a white field, although letter height, size, and copy position remain the same in both examples (Fig. 6).

Colors in a signage system should also relate harmoniously with the pallet of colors selected for the building and its environment. The designer may choose to select colors that blend with the environment or vibrant primary colors that accent the sign system and perhaps contrast with the architectural color scheme.

Helvetica Medium
Clarendon
Fig. 1

HELVETICA MEDIUM
CLARENDON
Fig. 2

Architectural Signage Systems
Architectural Signage Systems
Architectural Signage Systems
Fig. 3

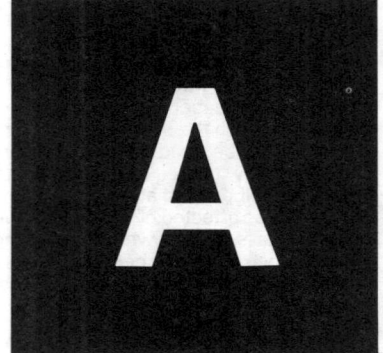

Fig. 4

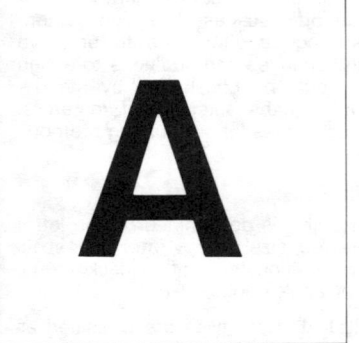

Fig. 5

Fig. 6

The viewing angle The angle of observance is influential in the design of a signage system, since it affects interletter spacing and overall readability. Normally, interior signs are viewed chiefly from a straight-on position; however, exterior signs are frequently seen from more than one angle. Signs to be read from vehicles moving at varying speeds with different angles of observance may require a compromise in letter spacing to best communicate the message.

Multilingual Needs

The jet age is a contributing factor in bringing people together from all over the world to visit and transact business. Transportation terminals and public facilities that may be used by visitors unaccustomed to reading English should employ sign systems that bridge any visual communication gap. Multilingual messages in English and the dominant foreign languages used by visitors may be combined and presented on one sign background. However, sign design and graphic formats become very critical to prevent confusion. A more popular solution involves the use of pictorial symbols as word substitutes. Pictographic signs are bold, recognizable images not bound by language barriers.

Regulatory Considerations

The designer should become aware of regulations governing signs. Federal regulations concerning safety signs are enumerated in Occupational Safety and Health Administration (OSHA) publications. American National Standards Institute (ANSI) publishes standards concerning signage for the physically handicapped. Underwriters' Laboratory (UL) issues standards applicable to illuminated signs. State and local codes contain regulatory information concerning sign sizes, mounting locations and heights, quantities of

signs allowable in various zoning areas, and other restrictions relating to exterior signs. These rules, and those of other regulatory bodies, should be taken under advisement prior to completing a comprehensive signage program.

Need for Illumination

Many signs are required to relate their messages after dark as well as during natural daylight. The careful designer will determine which signs require artificial illumination and decide on the method of illumination. Signs can be externally illuminated by readily available stock fixtures produced by many manufacturers, or they can be internally illuminated. Fluorescent lighting is the most common source of internal illumination, although metal arc lamps, incandescent lamps, and neon are frequently employed.

Need for a Graphics Manual

Many signage programs are developed for institutions that have a continuing need not only to maintain, but also to augment or change, their signage systems. The preparation of a signage manual containing all the information required to create additional signs or components would benefit the client and ensure continuity in the system as changes and additions are made. The designer should determine this potential need and include the manual with other documents developed for the signage program.

SIGN TYPES CATEGORIZED BY FUNCTION

Signage systems should be logically broken down into various types of signs to be utilized on a particular project. Many categories of sign types may be developed, but one of the most conclusive listings is based on function. The following discussion of signage system

components, including sign requirements for specific applications, covers these functions.

Exterior Signs

Exterior sign system components are normally viewed from vehicles or by pedestrians who have parked their vehicles and are walking toward their destination.

Primary identification All architectural projects require some form of identification that is both easily readable and recognizable. A person's first association with a building is the identifying device selected to "label" the structure. The importance of the first impression created by this device should be recognized. A sign that produces an image in keeping with the environment it serves reflects the quality of the people associated with that environment. Major corporations spend large sums of money on corporate identity programs to ensure the visual image presented to the public best reflects corporate philosophy and product desirability. Equal emphasis should be placed upon the image presented by the device employed to identify an architectural structure.

Secondary identification Many complexes containing more than one basic structure require secondary identification signs to properly identify the various elements within the complex. A systems approach to design will provide continuity in the relationship of primary to secondary identification signs.

Vehicular advance notice A system of road signs suitably located in advance of decision-making points will allow vehicular traffic to execute the proper decisions smoothly and safely at the appropriate times.

Vehicular directional Intersections and parking facility entrances are major decision-making locations requiring directional devices to guide drivers toward their destination.

Traffic regulatory and control Vehicular traffic can be systematically controlled by employing signing devices. Traffic codes are usually clear as to what signs are required, where they are to be located, and the height at which they are to be mounted. Usually, colors, sizes, and shapes are standardized by the traffic authorities. Stop, yield, and speed limit signs are representative of this classification of signs.

Instructional Frequently, signs are required to instruct vehicular and pedestrian traffic. These notices must be properly installed in carefully selected locations to be effective. Examples include parking procedures, delivery and service directions, and the like.

Informational Signs are required to present information that is both relevant to the location and important to the viewer. This information may pertain to parking rates, hours of operation, and security, or it may relate to items of interest within the environment.

Decorative Decorative graphics may be employed to enhance the beauty or decor of a particular area; form, color, and design may be utilized to create interest and to become features of the exterior landscape.

Interior Signs

Interior sign system components should assist visitors to travel from the building entrances throughout the complex until they reach their desired destination.

Identification Multiple-occupancy buildings require tenant identification; frequently, buildings with only one tenant will also utilize identification in the main lobby or reception areas to reinforce the corporate signature. Criteria for multiple-tenant signage are very important and should be included in lease documents to provide for visual continuity and architectural harmony. When individuals are allowed to implement their own desires concerning signage, each will attempt to outdo the other, resulting in clutter, confusion, and visual pollution. Signs that are too big, too gaudy, too competitive, and poorly conceived and executed will become commonplace unless controls on tenant identification are established and enforced.

Primary directory Information relevant to one's location within a complex should be clearly enumerated on the primary directory, usually located in a very visible area of the main lobby. Alphabetized listings of tenants, departments, and individuals should be concise and should designate the floor and room numbers. Such directories may be flush or recessed wall mounts, horizontal projected wall mounts, or pedestal or kiosk mounts, and internally illuminated or not, depending upon the ambient lighting conditions.

Elevator lobby floor directory High-rise structures require well-positioned signage that not only identifies each individual floor, but also serves as a secondary directory system for that floor. Frequently, the floor identification, directory, and corridor directional signage may be included in one device. When a visitor exits from an elevator on a chosen floor, a sign showing the floor number and also the direction of the office or room number sought is both helpful and reassuring.

Pictorial "you are here" indicators Pictorial schematic maps may become an integral part of directory systems, or they may be utilized separately as visual aids in depicting one's intended passage through a complex. Hospitals, sports complexes, and transportation centers, are good examples of structure that may require pictorial maps to supplement word messages. Caution will be exercised by the expert designer to keep the pictorial map simple and correctly oriented in the building according to where the viewer is standing, and to evaluate the need of color coding as part of the visual aid. Too frequently, designers employ a complicated color-coded system that becomes very confusing to the viewer that and, in fact, compromises the effectiveness of the system.

Primary directional The maze that often results from interior corridor layouts creates many decision-making points for a visitor. Primary directional signs may be ceiling-mounted, wall-mounted, or floor-mounted as kiosk-type units in open areas. Areas with heavy pedestian traffic should have directional signs located so that people do not obstruct the line of sight to the sign device.

Normally, ceiling-suspended or kiosk-type units are the best choice to enhance visibility.

Secondary directional Directional signs should be considered in locations where traffic flow and corridor layouts do not demand primary directional devices but do require some guidance for direction control. Corridors within suites of offices and corridors that change direction should be considered as decision-making points that may require a secondary directional signage device.

Area identification Specific areas within a complex should be properly identified. These areas may be tenant spaces, divisions, or departments. When occurring along main corridors, they are usually designated by wall-, door-, or transom-mounted devices. Ceiling-suspended signs are a good solution in open office spaces.

Room identification Wall- or door-mounted room identification signs are required to "label" the function of a particular room. Work functions are properly identified within tenant areas, while service and maintenance functions should be suitably designated in most situations.

Desk identification Reception areas may require a sign device located on a desk or counter to identify a particular service or individual rendering assistance to visitors. Such signs may be permanently affixed or removable, and may provide for changeable name inserts.

Personnel identification Persons rendering a service to the public, such as nurses, maintenance personnel, and food service personnel, generally are identified by name badges or pins.

Regulatory and control signs Signs that authorize or prohibit certain functions are required, frequently by law or code, to inform people using the facility. Examples include signs for the handicapped and signs relevant to no smoking areas, elevator capacities, "no entry" areas, fire control, and "authorized personnel only" areas. These signs are usually mounted on doors or their adjacent walls; they may employ colors which deviate from the standard colors used in the comprehensive signage system to emphasize a dangerous situation or the need for caution.

Exits Exit signs are required by codes to designate exits effectively in times of emergency. Supplemental devices are used to give additional information pertaining to a particular exit such as "Emergency Exit Only" and "Alarm Sounds When Door Is Opened." OSHA-approved exit signs are standard items manufactured by many lighting companies, and are generally provided by the electrical contractor.

Information exhibit cases Notices, posters, attractions, and promotional pieces should be contained within an appropriately designed case to control the display of this type of information. Standard units featuring vinyl-covered cork panels housed within extruded aluminum frames with lockable doors are available from many directory manufacturers.

Decorative features Decorative designs may be reproduced on walls as interior features. Reproduction processes include appliqués, painting, and screen printing on location; or mural processes, which are applied much like wall-coverings, may be considered. Doors may also receive supergraphic treatments in which copy may become an integral part of the design.

Dedicatory plaques Building dedication plaques should be carefully conceived and implemented, using materials that reflect favorably upon the talents involved in the realization of the project. Historically, these plaques have been bronze or aluminum castings. However, modern technology has provided photographic methods and photochemical processes which offer the designer a freedom of size, format, letterform, and color not available in the casting operation.

Donor recognition Buildings constructed in part by contributions from donors require special recognition for the donors. Hospitals, performing arts centers, and service institutions rely on gifts to assist in financing buildings, additions, and furnishings, and usually stipulate that donors will be remembered and recognized in some prestigious location in the building. The designer is responsible for establishing controls and developing a system that fulfills promises made by those soliciting funds, while allowing flexibility to expand the system as future needs may dictate. Location selection is very important in the overall effectiveness of the donor recognition signage.

Mechanical, instrumentation, and control system markings Many industrial and mechanical installations require equipment, control, and pipe markings to meet codes, assist maintenance and service personnel, and ensure safety. Often, these locations are not public spaces, and require an industrial, rather than an architectural, approach to signage. Elevator floor-indicator panels, however, should receive special attention and be considered in a comprehensive signage program.

CONCEPTUAL DESIGN OF THE SIGN FACE

Emphasis will not be placed on the graphic design of each sign required in a comprehensive signage program. However, the following considerations will help to ensure continuity, correctness, and aesthetic acceptability.

Alphabet selection An alphabet must be carefully chosen that best exemplifies the graphic image to be portrayed to the public without compromising legibility and performance requirements. More than one alphabet may be selected should need dictate. However, good design practices should be maintained in choosing the family of alphabets to be employed.

Interletter, word, and line spacing Each alphabet has its own "personality" and visual impact; therefore, spacing between characters, words, and lines of copy must be carefully developed to give the best legibility and visual harmony possible (Fig. 8).

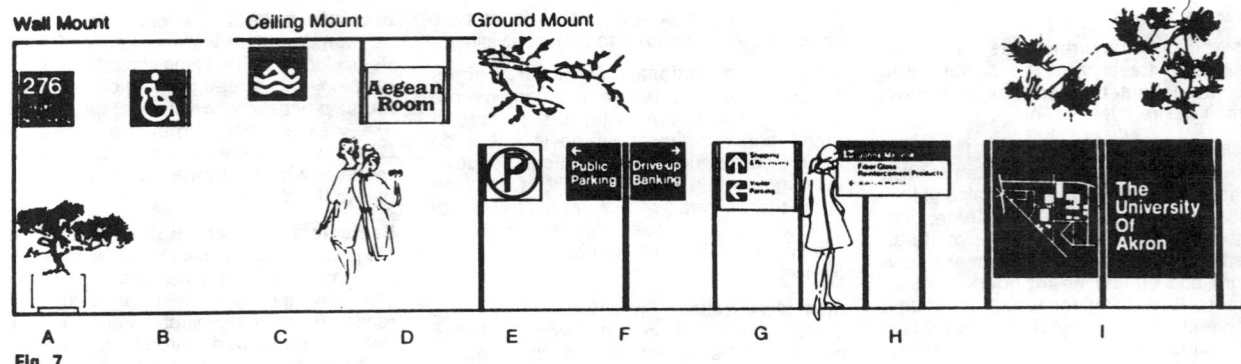

Fig. 7

Architectural Signage Systems
Planning · Design · Implementation

Fig. 8

Fig. 9

These Doors Should Not Be Opened Except During An Emergency

Fig. 10

Emergency Exit Only

Fig. 11

Arrow selection Directional arrows should be designed to reflect the "personality" of the letterform selected. Stroke width and size relationships are important considerations (Fig. 9).

Copy determination The message for each sign must be accurately determined and the copy condensed to the fewest words that will still relay the desired message. Wordy signs are frequently misread or not read at all. The message must be concise, clear, and informative (Fig. 10 and 11).

Copy placement format The placement of copy on a sign face may take one of the nine basic positions or a custom format for special situations (Fig. 12).

Size determination of the sign face After the copy for each sign is in final form, the sign with the greatest amount of copy is selected from each of the sign types utilized and the desired copy height is determined for each type. This height should be based upon the distance from which the sign will be read and the graphic design portrayed. Using this letter height, the message should be laid out with photographic type or transfer lettering to scale, incorporating the copy placement and spacing requirements. The most pleasing shape and size for the message to be contained are then determined, realizing that this particular layout is for the maximum copy required for that particular sign type. A shape and size format should be chosen that works well as a module which can be proprotioned and become applicable to the entire family of

sign types. While this may be ideal, frequently the proportional system is not applicable. An example of each sign type should be drawn to scale and fully dimensioned to serve as a production guide for signs within that type. (Fig. 13).

Color selections Selection is then made of the copy and background colors that offer good contrast and harmoniously blend with the prominent colors in the environment. It is also wise to consider any corporate colors required by the client.

SIGNAGE SYSTEM DEVELOPMENT CHECKLIST

The completed sign schedule, location plans, scaled drawings of typical examples from each sign type, construction or assembly details or both, mounting details, and specifications form the documents required to bid competitively or to negotiate signage projects. Well-prepared documents prevent individual interpretation by vendors and result in comparable competitive bids.

The following systematic approach to the design and development of a comprehensive signage program will serve as a guideline to problem solving, employing the concepts contained in this chapter. This checklist may be expanded or condensed to meet individual project parameters. The basic systematic thought process, however, is applicable to all projects.

1. Develop the signage system design criteria based on:

a. Performance requirements
b. Usage considerations
c. Durability requirements
d. Vandalism considerations
e. Flexibility to accommodate changes and additions
f. Readability factors
g. Multilingual needs
h. Regulatory considerations
i. Need for illumination
j. Need for graphics manual for ongoing implementation and system maintenance

2. Study the traffic flow patterns, determine all sign locations, and draw the location symbols on the site and floor plans.

3. Evaluate and select the sign types required from the following list, categorized by function, that meet the design criteria:

a. Exterior sign types:
Type A – Primary identification
Type B – Secondary identification
Type C – Vehicular advance notice
Type D – Vehicular directional
Type E – Traffic regulatory and control
Type F – Instructional
Type G – Informational
Type H – Decorative

b. Interior sign types:
Type I – Primary identification
Type J – Primary directory
Type K – Elevator lobby floor directories
Type L – Pictorial "You Are Here" indicators
Type M – Primary directional
Type N – Secondary directional

Type O – Area identification
Type P – Room identification
Type Q – Desk identification
Type R – Personnel identification
Type S – Regulatory and control
Type T – Exit
Type U – Information exhibit cases
Type W – Dedicatory
Type X – Donor recognition
Type Y – Mechanical,
    instrumentation, and control
    system markings
Type Z – Other (to be specified by
    designer)

4. Select the best signing devices for each sign type designated above from the following lexicon of signage system components

that most effectively satisfy the design criteria established:
  a. Elevated pylons
  b. Monolithic sign structures
  c. Panel and post assemblies
  d. Illuminated sign cabinets
  e. Directory and informational systems
  f. Die-cut pressure-sensitive lettering
  g. Dimensional graphics
  h. Plaque signage
  i. Environmental graphics
  j. Other (to be defined by the designer)

5. Conceptually design the sign face for each sign type selected, indicating:
  a. Alphabet selection
  b. Interletter, word, and line spacing
  c. Arrow selection

  d. Copy determination
  e. Copy placement format
  f. Size determination of copy and sign
     face
  g. Color selections

6. Complete the location plans by filling in the symbol indicating sign number and type.

7. Prepare scaled drawings of typical examples from each sign type.

8. Prepare the detailed sign schedule.

9. Prepare typical construction and assembly details, mounting details, and engineering drawings for wind loading, foundations, and illumination.

10. Prepare detailed specifications for all materials, techniques, and components required in the system.

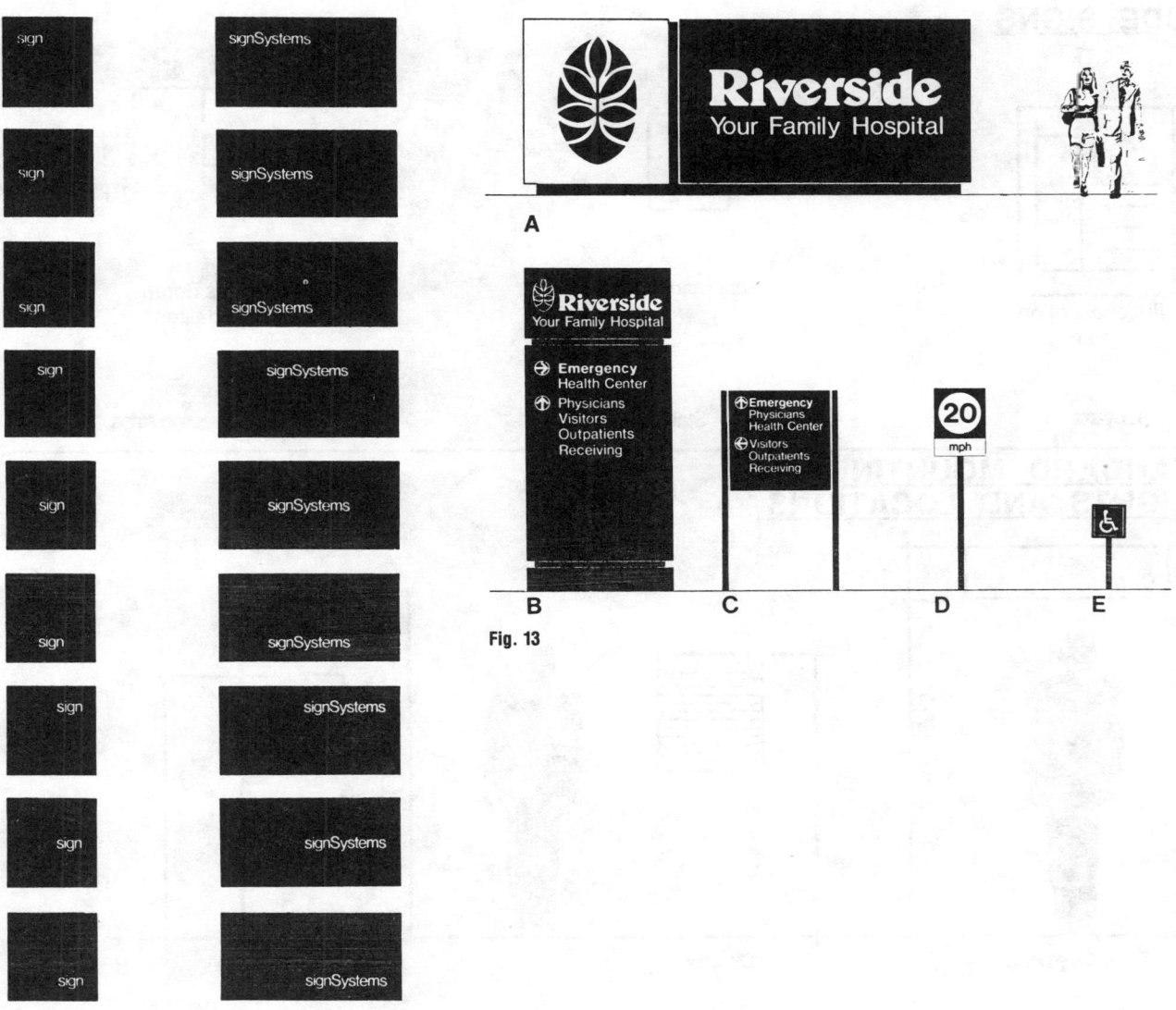

Fig. 12

Fig. 13

SIGNAGE AND GRAPHICS
Standard Sign Type and Mounting Heights

STANDARD SIGN SYSTEM

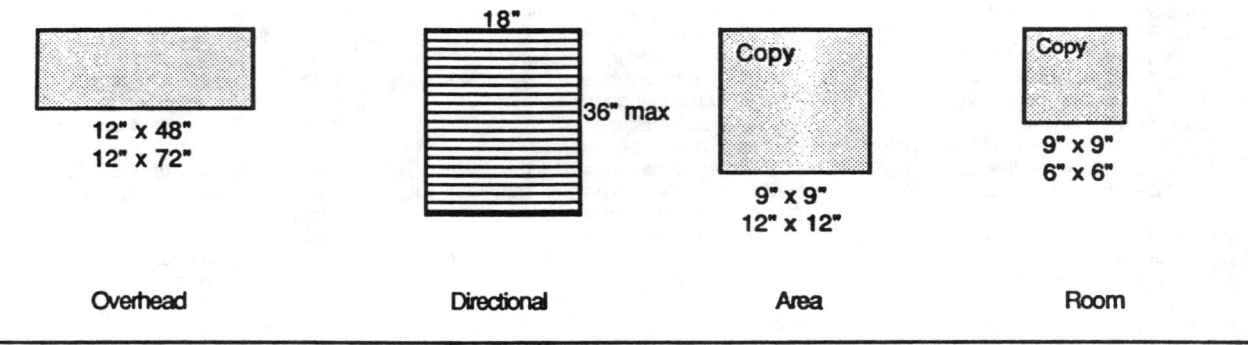

| Overhead | Directional | Area | Room |

12" x 48"
12" x 72"

18"
36" max

Copy
9" x 9"
12" x 12"

Copy
9" x 9"
6" x 6"

CODE SIGNS

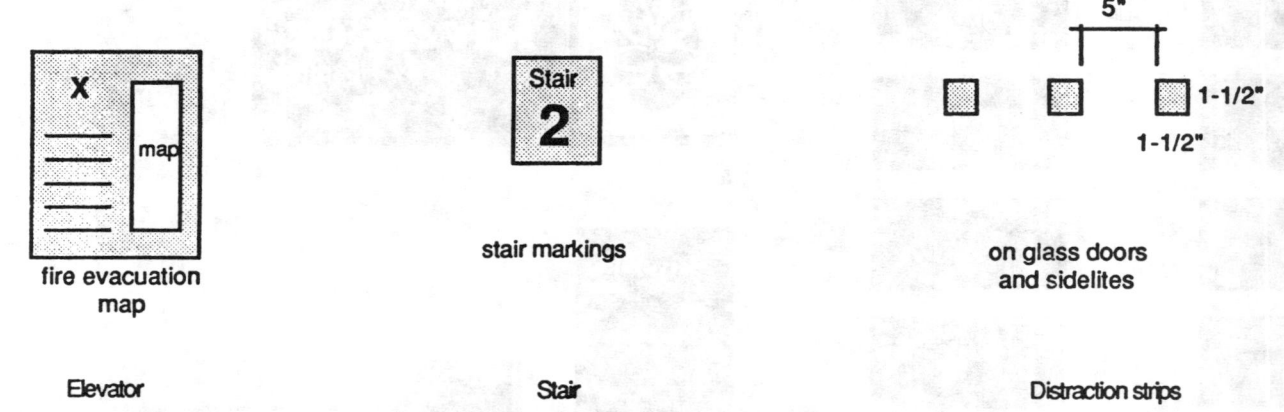

X
map
fire evacuation map

Stair
2
stair markings

5"
1-1/2"
1-1/2"
on glass doors and sidelites

Elevator

Stair

Distraction strips

STANDARD MOUNTING HEIGHTS AND LOCATIONS

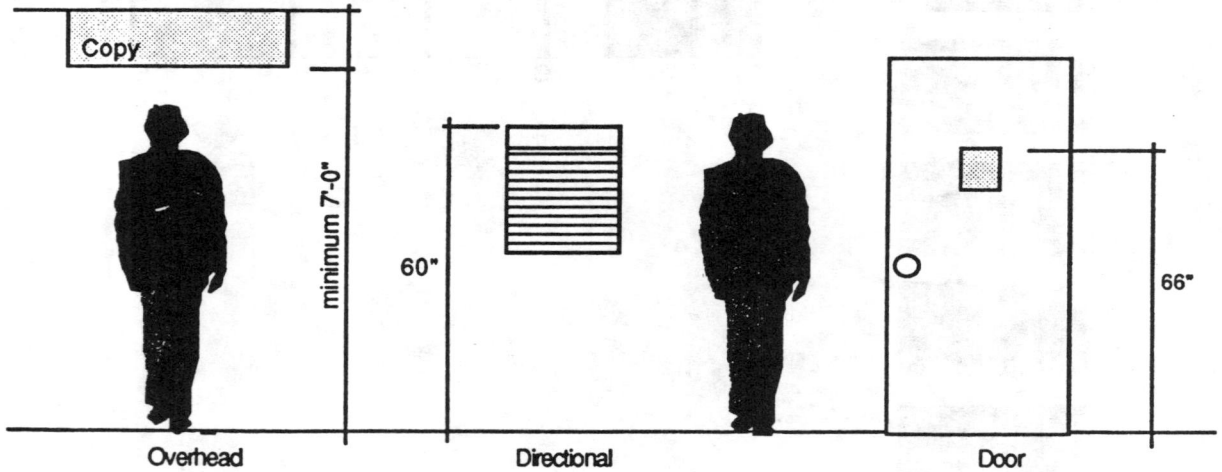

Copy

minimum 7'-0"

60"

66"

Overhead

Directional

Door

Sign Type

DIRECTIONAL (CEILING-HUNG)

Material Choices

MDO board, acrylic

Finishes

Painted, plastic laminate, metal laminate

Graphics

Vinyl die cuts, silkscreen, dimensional applied letters

Standard Mounting Detail

1. Threaded rod: pendant, flush
2. Scissor clip

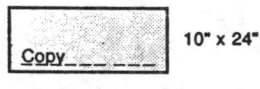

10" x 24"

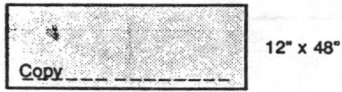

12" x 48"

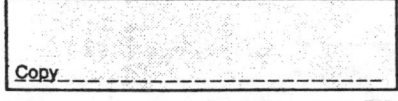

12" x 72"

Standard sizes

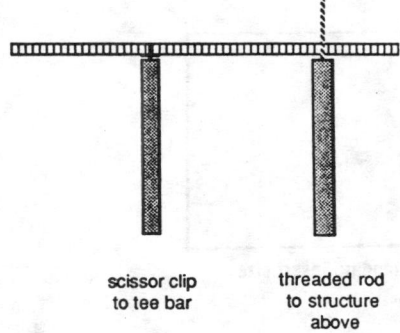

scissor clip to tee bar

threaded rod to structure above

Section

Sign Type

DIRECTIONAL (WALL-MOUNTED)

Material Choices

Acrylic, aluminum, acrylic with metal laminate face

Finishes

Painted acrylic or aluminum, natural aluminum or brass (satin or polished), laminates available in standard laminate finishes

Graphics

Silkscreen, front surface or reverse

Standard Mounting Materials

1. Backpanel: backplate with countersunk screws with shields; magnetic, form, or vinyl tape with adhesive
2. Strips: vinyl tape

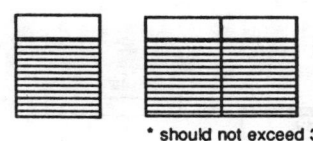

* should not exceed 36" high

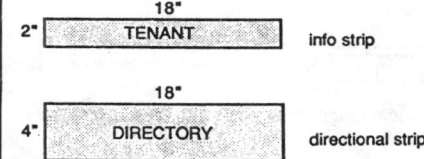

2" 18" TENANT info strip

4" 18" DIRECTORY directional strip

Standard sizes

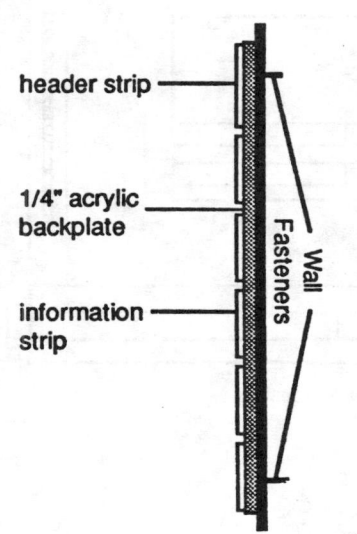

header strip

1/4" acrylic backplate

information strip

Wall Fasteners

Section

Sign Type

AREA DESIGNATION (WALL-MOUNTED)

Material Choices

Acrylic, aluminum, acrylic with metal laminate face

Finishes

Painted acrylic or aluminum, natural aluminum or brass (satin or polished), laminates available in standard laminate finishes

Graphics

Silkscreen, front surface or reverse; vinyl die cuts

Standard Mounting Materials

Vinyl or magnetic tape, foam tape, silastic adhesive

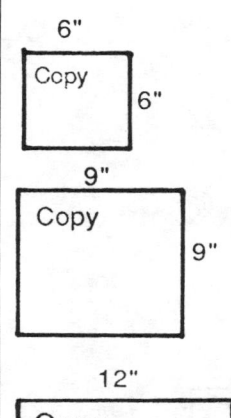

6" Copy 6"

9" Copy 9"

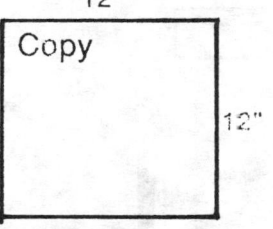

12" Copy 12"

Standard sizes

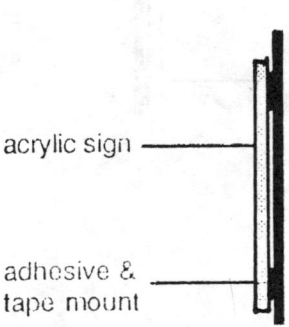

acrylic sign

adhesive & tape mount

Section

SIGNAGE AND GRAPHICS

Sign Type
ROOM IDENTIFIER (WALL-MOUNTED)

Material Choices
Acrylic, aluminum, acrylic with metal laminate face

Finishes
Painted acrylic or aluminum, natural aluminum or brass (satin or polished), laminates available in standard laminate finishes

Graphics
Silkscreen, front surface or reverse

Standard Mounting Materials
Vinyl tape, foam tape, magnetic tape, silastic adhesive

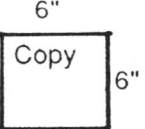

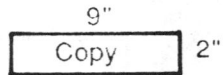

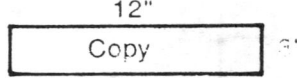

Standard sizes

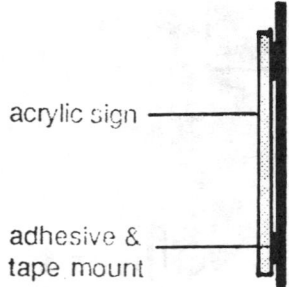

acrylic sign

adhesive & tape mount

Section

Sign Type
ROOM IDENTIFIER, CHANGEABLE MESSAGE (WALL-MOUNTED)

Material Choices
Holder, acrylic; insert, vinyl

Finishes
Painted (surface or subsurface)

Graphics
Silkscreen or vinyl die cuts

Standard Mounting Materials
Vinyl tape, foam tape, silastic adhesive

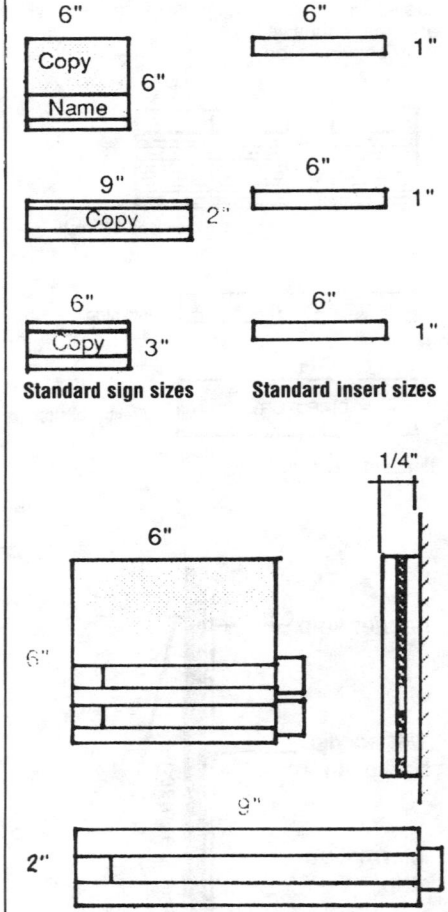

Standard sign sizes   **Standard insert sizes**

Elevation and section

Sign Type
FRAMED PLAQUE SIGNS, WALL-MOUNTED (previous plaque types are insertable into standard frame signs)

Material Choices
Molded acrylic, aluminum, brass

Finishes
Painted, satin, polished

Standard Frame Mounting Materials
1. Frame: screw mount, tape and adhesive
2. Insert: adhesive or magnetic tape, Velcro, magnet

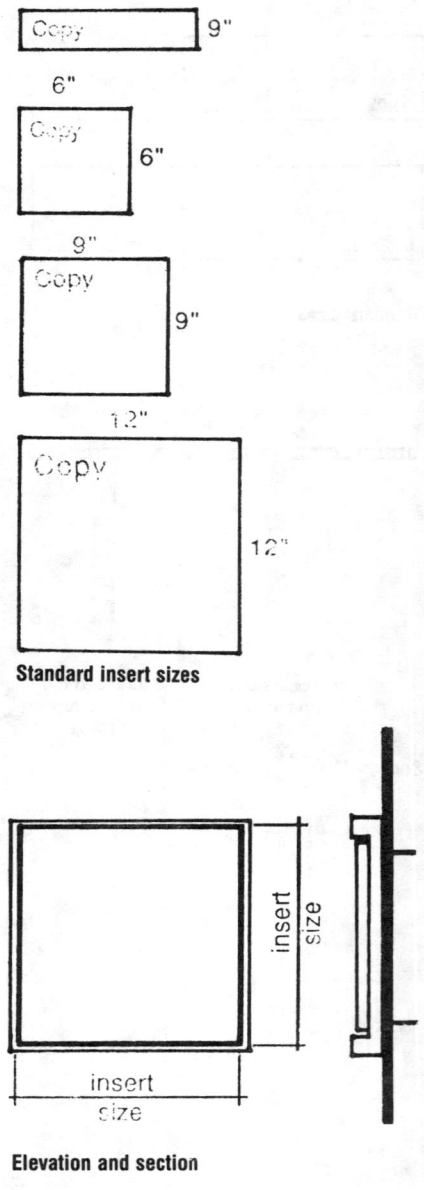

Standard insert sizes

Elevation and section

Sign Type

COUNTERTOP/FLAG MOUNT

Extrusion Material

Aluminum

Insert Material

Acrylic, aluminum, acrylic with metal laminate

Graphics

See area and room plaques

Standard Mounting Details

1. Counter: free-standing with extruded aluminum base
2. Flag mount: countersunk screws and shields

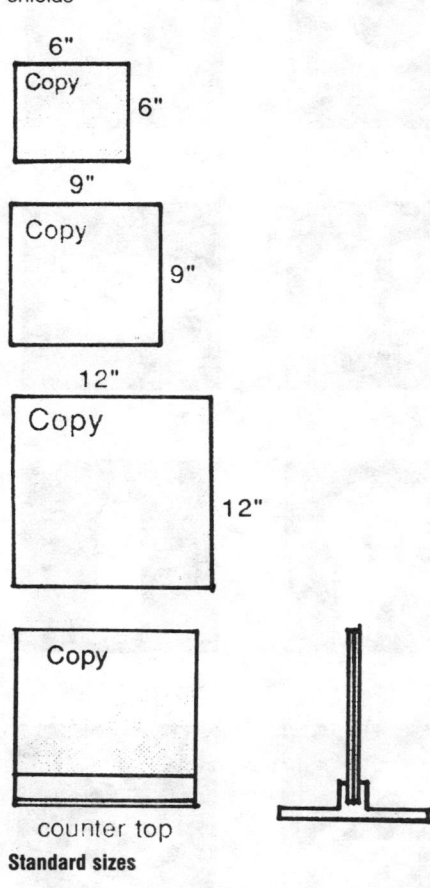

counter top

Standard sizes

Elevation and section

Sign Type

DESKBAR (DESK TOP)

Material Choices

Aluminum, molded acrylic

Finishes

Painted, satin, polished

Graphics

Vinyl die cuts; silkscreen on acrylic plaque, front surface or reverse

Standard Mounting Detail

Free-standing on desks or countertops

2" x 9"

1-5/8" x 9"

Standard sizes

Note: Changeable face available by using acrylic sign plaque.

Sign Type

CUT LETTERS: FLUSH, PROJECTED

Material Choices

Acrylic, acrylic with metal laminate face, brass, aluminum

Finishes

Polished, painted, brushed, sand blasted

Standard Mounting Details

Adhesive mount, flush pin mount, standoff mount

Standard Letter Sizes

Varies from 2" to 18"

Front View

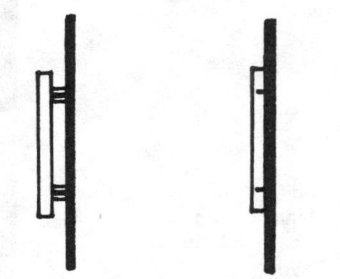

Projected Mount   Flush Mount
(least vandal resistant)

Sections

Medical

Nursing Homes
Medical Complexes
First-Aid Centers

Picto'grafics not shown:
1.516	Parking		1.413	Health
1.372	Playroom		2.531	Warning
1.150	Library or Reading	1.147	Chest

Hospital
Pharmacy
Dental Care
Wheelchair

 1.508

 1.518

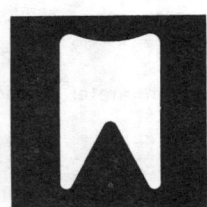 1.184

 1.188

X-Ray
Physiotherapy
General Medicine, Female
General Medicine, Male

 1.146

 1.148

 1.440

 1.450

Coronary Care
Hematology
Urology
Eye

 1.446

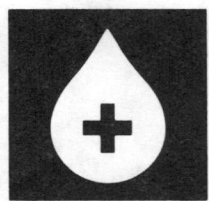 1.417

 1.448

 1.123

Podiatry
Mental Health
Ear, Nose & Throat
Oxygen

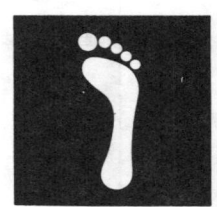 1.129

 1.473

 1.137

 1.368

Shower
Isolation
Nursery
Laboratory

 1.376

 1.411

 1.302

 1.359

Conference
Occupational Therapy
Rehabilitation
Ambulatory Patients

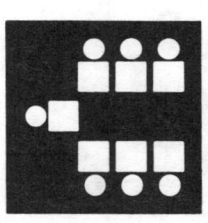 1.406

 1.347

 1.483

 1.152

Commercial

Shopping Centers
Stores & Shops
Eating Facilities
Community Services

Picto'grafics not shown:
1.218	Concrete Mixer	1.226	Flatbed Truck	1.314	Vegetable Produce
1.219	Cushman Vehicle	1.250	Pickup Truck	1.363	Newspaper Vendor
1.222	Dump Truck	1.304	Basket	1.370	Record Store
				1.394	Cooking

Cocktail Lounge
Pub
Coffee Shop
Liquor Store

 1.344

 1.361

 1.360

 1.307

Mens' Furnishings
Furniture
Cinema
Camera Store

 1.352

 1.315

 1.126

 1.338

Gift Shop
Florist
Dress Shop
Shoe Store

 1.339

 1.393

 1.321

 1.375

Restaurant
Soda Fountain
Grocery Store
Tobacco Shop

 1.354

 1.341

 1.337

 1.316

Bookstore
Record Shop
Fuel
Toy Shop

 1.305

 1.455

 1.336

 1.372

Theater
Van
Beauty Salon
Barber Shop

 1.449

 1.290

 1.192

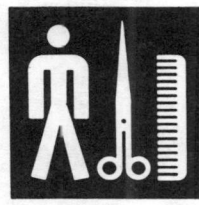 1.149

Travel

Picto'grafics not shown:

1.350   Motel
1.266   Seaplane Base

Airport
Departures
Arrivals
Car Rentals

1.253

1.255

1.254

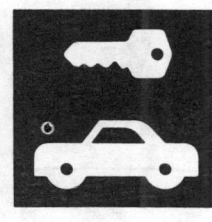

1.202

Bus
Subway
Train
Taxi

1.208

1.268

1.278

1.203

Monorail
Ferry
Cable Car
Automobile

1.239

1.225

1.215

1.201

Lost & Found
Porter
Locker
Fuel

1.310

1.319

1.308

1.336

Baggage Claim
Customs
Immigration
Money Exchange

1.303

1.125

1.464

1.532

Motorcycle
Moving Sidewalk
Lodging
Ice Cubes

1.241

1.145

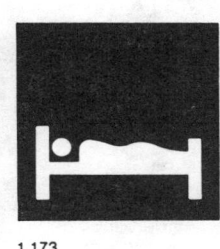

1.173

1.353

SIGNAGE AND GRAPHICS

Travel Symbols

Recreation and Sports

Sports Arenas
Parks
Recreation Facilities
Amusement Parks

Picto'grafics not shown:
1.112 Curling
1.115 Dancing
1.140 LaCrosse

1.138 Hockey
1.183 Tobogganing

1.471 Wintersports
1.387 Outdoor Recreation

Campers
Picnic Area
Midway
Trailer Train

1.276

1.366

1.313

1.185

Water
Swimming
Canoeing
Sailing

1.492

1.177

1.217

1.265

Marina, Boating
Life Preserver
Snowmobiling
Camping

1.401

1.357

1.267

1.385

Judging
Bicycling
Women's/Girl's Toilet
Fishing

1.370

1.211

1.910

1.334

Skiing
Soccer
Ice Skating
Football

1.172

1.176

1.181

1.130

Hunting, Shooting
Golf
Baseball
Tennis, Badminton

1.170

1.133

1.105

1.182

SIGNAGE AND GRAPHICS
Universal Symbols

Universal

	Applicable to any building or facility	Picto'grafics not shown:

Picto'grafics not shown:
1.110 Children
1.144 Man with boy
1.340 Fragile

1.372 Playroom
1.410 Church
1.472 Synagogue
1.469 Police

1.493 Smoke
1.516 Parking
1.488 Keep Dry
1.155 Janitor

Entry
Exit
Ramp up
Ramp down

1.403

1.404

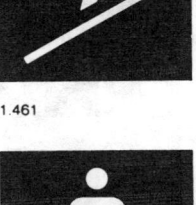
1.461

1.462

Emergency
Women's Toilet
Men's Toilet
Stairs

4.412

1.189

1.143

1.377

Handicapped
No Smoking
Telephone
Escalator

1.188

3.316

1.365

1.328

Elevator
Down
No Parking
Drinking fountain

1.311

1.402B

3.516

1.139

Mail Box
Check Room
Up
No Entry

1.326

1.317

1.402A

3.463

Shower
Waiting Room
Telegraph Office
Information

1.376

1.151

1.327

1.530

International symbol of accessibility

Alternate GOTHIC NO. 3	Futura MEDIUM	Quorum MEDIUM
Americana	**Futura** DEMIBOLD	Romana NORMAL
Americana ITALIC	**Garamond** BOLD	**Schadow** ANTIQUA SEMIBOLD
Aster	Gerstner Program MEDIUM	Serif Gothic REGULAR
Avant Garde GOTHIC MEDIUM	Gill Sans	**Serif Gothic** BOLD
Baker Danmark 2 ˉ	**Harry** FAT	Solitaire BOLD ˉ
Baker Sans MONO REGULAR ˉ	**Hellenic** WIDE	Souvenir LIGHT
Baskerville BOLD ITALIC	Helvetica LIGHT	*Souvenir* MEDIUM ITALIC
Bodoni	Helvetica	**Standard** MEDIUM
Bookman	**Helvetica** MEDIUM	**Stymie** BOLD
Caledonia BOLD ITALIC	Helvetica MEDIUM OUTLINE	Times ROMAN
Caslon BOLD	Horizon MEDIUM	**Times** ROMAN BOLD
Century SCHOOLBOOK	**Karen** BOLD	Trooper ROMAN LIGHT
Century SCHOOLBOOK BOLD	Korinna	**Trooper** ROMAN
Cheltenham MEDIUM	**Korinna** BOLD	Univers 55
Columbus	Lydian	*Univers 56*
COPPERPLATE GOTHIC L GHT	Melior	**Univers 65**
Craw Clarendon BOOK	**Melior** SEMIBOLD	**Univers 67**
Craw Clarendon	MICROGRAMMA NORMAL	Univers 53
Craw Modern	**MICROGRAMMA** BOLD	Univers 63
Delta MEDIUM ⁹	**MICROGRAMMA** BOLD EXTENDED	Univers 55 OUTLINE
Eastern Souvenir MEDIUM ⁹	Modula MEDIUM ˉ	Univers 65 OUTLINE
Eurostile	**News Gothic** BOLD	Univers 83 OUTLINE
Eurostile BOLD	Olive ANTIQUE	Venus MEDIUM
Eurostile EXTENDED	Optima	**Venus** EXTRABOLD
Eurostile BOLD EXTENDED	**Optima** SEMIBOLD	**Venus** EXTRABOLD CONDENSED
Firmin Didot	Palatino	**Venus** BOLD EXTENDED
Folio MEDIUM	**Palatino** SEMIBOLD	**Walbaum** MEDIUM
Folio MEDIUM EXTENDED	**Permanent** MEDIUM	**Weiss** ROMAN EXTRABOLD
Fortuna LIGHT	Perpetua ROMAN	**Windsor**
Franklin Gothic	Plantin	Windsor OUTLINE

Clarendon Medium
abcdefghijklmnopqrstuvwxyz
ABCDEFGHIJKLM
NOPQRSTUVWXYZ
0123456789 !"#$%&'*()"+¢£:?-=;/,.

Optima Regular
abcdefghijklmnopqrstuvwxyz
ABCDEFGHIJKLM
NOPQRSTUVWXYZ
0123456789 !"$%&'()"¢£:?-;/,.

Helvetica Medium
abcdefghijklmnopqrstuvwxyz
ABCDEFGHIJKLM
NOPQRSTUVWXYZ
0123456789 ®!"#$%&'°()"+¢£:?-=;/,.

Times New Roman
abcdefghijklmnopqrstuvwxyz
ABCDEFGHIJKLM
NOPQRSTUVWXYZ
0123456789 !"#$%&'()+e£:?-=;,.

General Symbols Extended

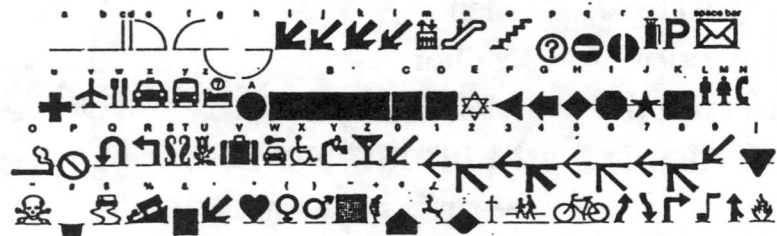

Fig. 14   General type styles with maximum readability. ½" cap height is legible up to 25', ¾"–1" cap height is legible up to 50', 1–2" cap height is legible up to 100'.

DESIGNING THE SYSTEM

The formulation of a communications program is based on the functional requirements delineated in the feasibility study. The presentation modes to be utilized are a part of such a program. They might include slides, films, videotape, and a sound-recording and playback system. The detailed design of the facility includes the selection of basic equipment, possible modification of that equipment, and provision for additional optical elements, as well as the engineering of the electrical control circuitry and the design of the electromechanical devices that may be needed.

The implementation of a proposed A-V system is not merely an exercise in mechanical assembly. It is a highly complex process of logistics that involves specific functional requirements within architectural and economic constraints. Careful engineering and balancing of the alternatives available will generally achieve optimum results.

A large number of variables is encountered in every A-V design problem. As an example, the dimensions of the presentation room have a significant effect on the audience size, the acoustic characteristics, the size of the projected image, the choice of equipment, and the location and the interrelationship of the components.

The A-V consultant who is responsible for the program planning, the design, and the engineering of this complex, multifaceted discipline should be intimately familiar with the problems of fabrication, installation, and operation of such systems. This knowledge will enable the consultant to plan a facility whose execution will not create difficulties and whose construction and operation can be effected without costly changes. However, even when the consultant has experience as an adviser to members of the architectural and engineering professions, the creation of a well-integrated facility is not necessarily assured. His or her work and the completed facilities should be viewed and evaluated.

Optical Aspects

It is of critical importance for an A-V system to have the ability to display bright, sharp images to all viewers and to maintain the stability and consistency of those images in a simple and straightforward manner. The picture quality is a function of a number of factors requiring careful attention during all phases of the project. These include:

■ The quality of the original photography or artwork
■ The density, contrast, and sharpness of the actual material being projected
■ The output intensity of the projector light source
■ The optical characteristics of each projection unit
■ The optical characteristics of the integrated system
■ The ratio of the projection distance to the image size
■ The centering integrity of the light path from the material being projected to its image on the screen
■ The characteristics of the projection screen or other viewing surface

Projection Engineering

Room size Ideally, the dimensions of the viewing room should be an outgrowth of the estimate of the audience size that was established in the original A-V study. In many cases, however, the A-V design engineer must utilize a predetermined space. Given the characteristics of that space, the designer can determine the ideal audience size for each type of seating arrangement, and also ascertain whether a front or rear projection mode is feasible and what the image size should be.

The type of relationship that is desired between the person making the presentation and the audience will determine the seating configuration: theatre, lecture, or conference format. That configuration will in turn dictate the number of viewers that can be comfortably seated for optimum viewing (Fig. 1).

As an illustration, a room 20 feet by 32 feet can accommodate about 49 people in a theatre configuration (Fig. 2); in a lecture arrangement, the audience size would be 24 (Fig. 3); a U-shaped table would seat 18 (Fig. 4); and 15 people could fit comfortably at a conference table (Fig. 5). Circular and multiuse arrangements (Figs. 6 and 7) are additional examples of the relationship of seating configuration and audience size.

Other seating configurations have been devised for other types of communication program modes, each with a direct relationship between room size and audience size. The audience size is also affected by the angle of view between each member of the audience and the screen (Fig. 1).

Whenever the A-V design engineer has the opportunity of establishing the dimensions of the presentation room, he or she should be aware of the important fact that a longer projection throw for a particular image size results in more even light distribution and sharpness as well as a better angle of view. Consequently a larger audience can be accommodated than would be possible using a system with a short projection distance and a narrower angle of view. This question of projection distance applies to both front and rear projection systems. However, as the throw is normally quite short when a rear projection screen is used, this factor of design in rear projection facilities is an extremely critical planning element.

Distortion, sometimes called "keystoning," will result if the viewing surface is not precisely parallel to the plane of the image being projected. Therefore, the light path, which is usually perpendicular to the projected material, must be carefully controlled in relation to the projector and the screen. The size of the audience and the room, as well as the mode of projection, will determine whether the screen will be vertical or at an angle (Fig. 8). Normally, a rear projection screen will permit a vertical viewing surface.

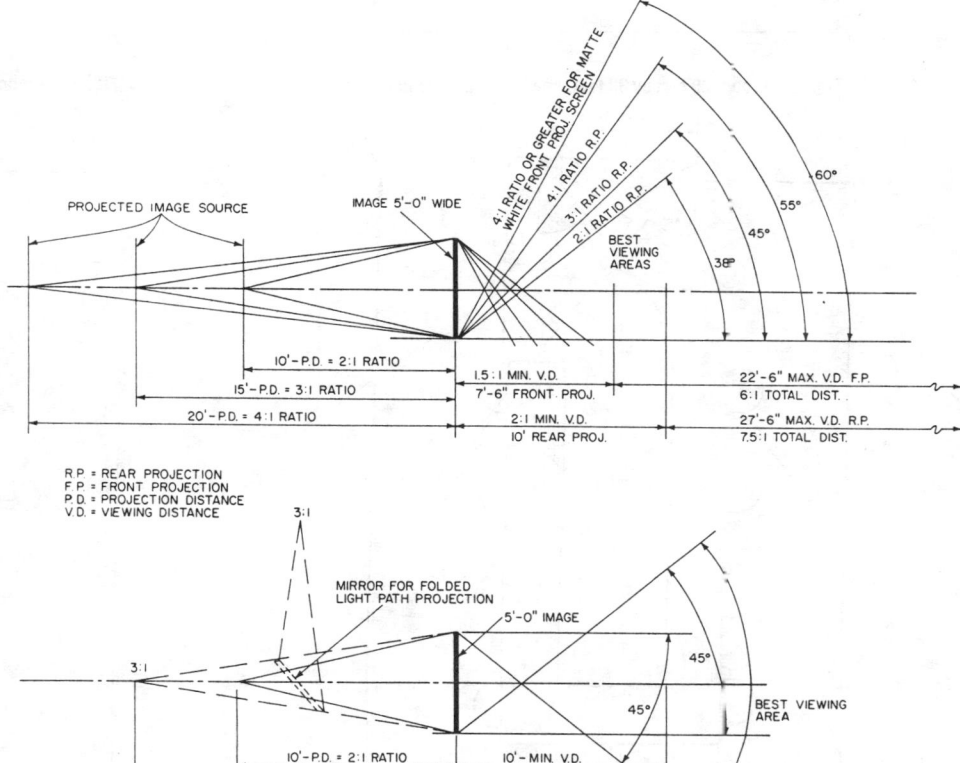

Fig. 1   The interrelationship of projection distance, image size, and viewing area.

AUDIO-VISUAL SYSTEMS

Typical Projection Room Layout and Sightlines

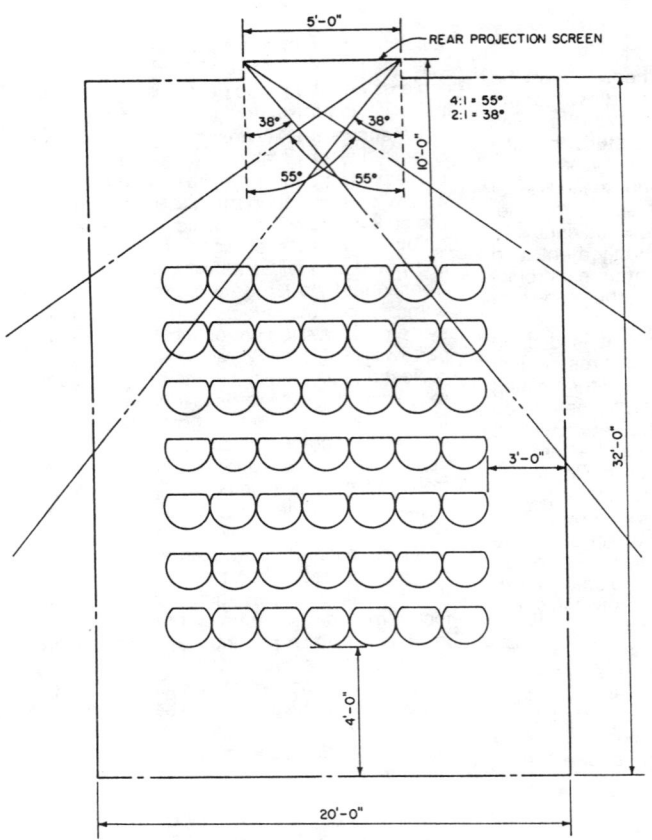

Fig. 2 A room 20 feet by 32 feet, seating 49 people in theatre style.

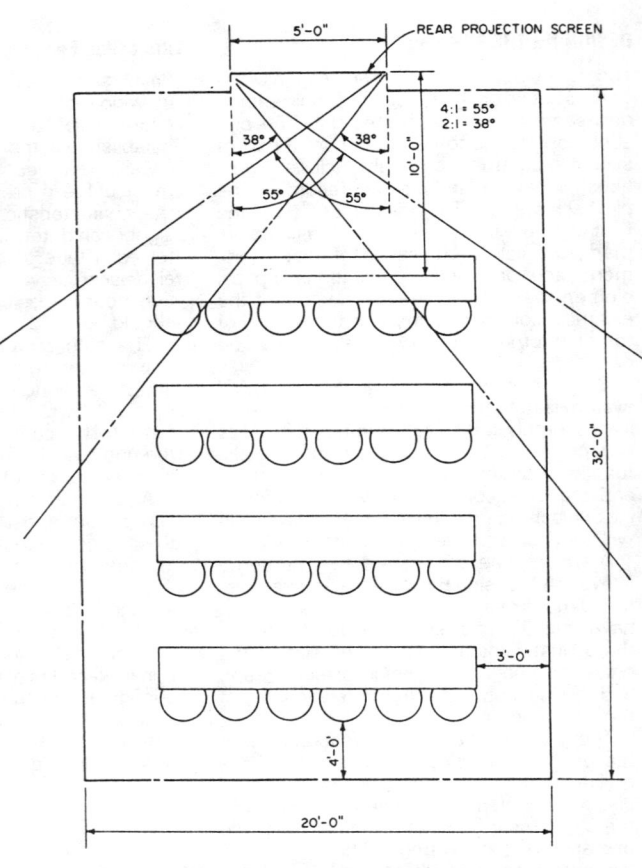

Fig. 3 A room 20 feet by 32 feet, seating 24 people in lecture style.

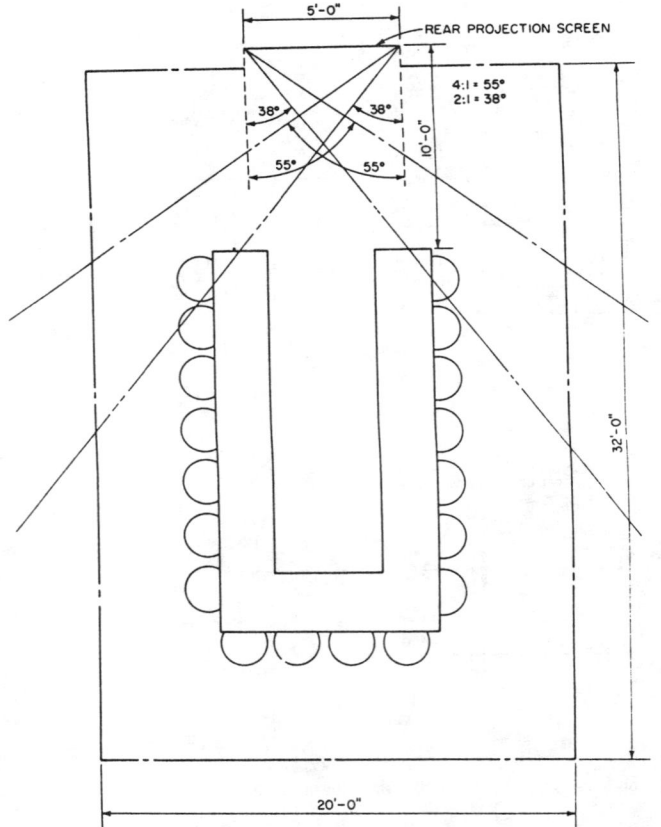

Fig. 4 A room 20 feet by 32 feet, seating 18 people at a U-shaped table.

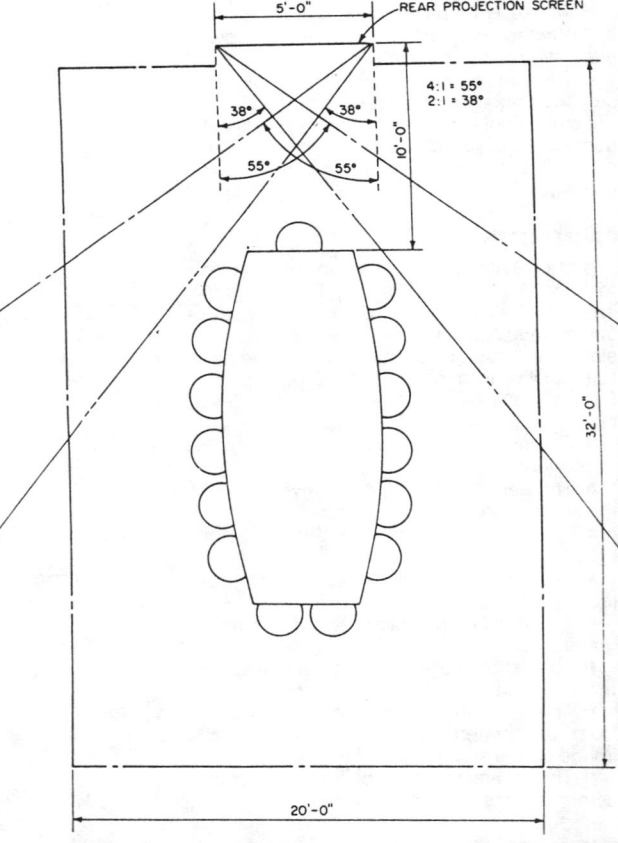

Fig. 5 A room 20 feet by 32 feet, seating 15 people at a boat-shaped conference table.

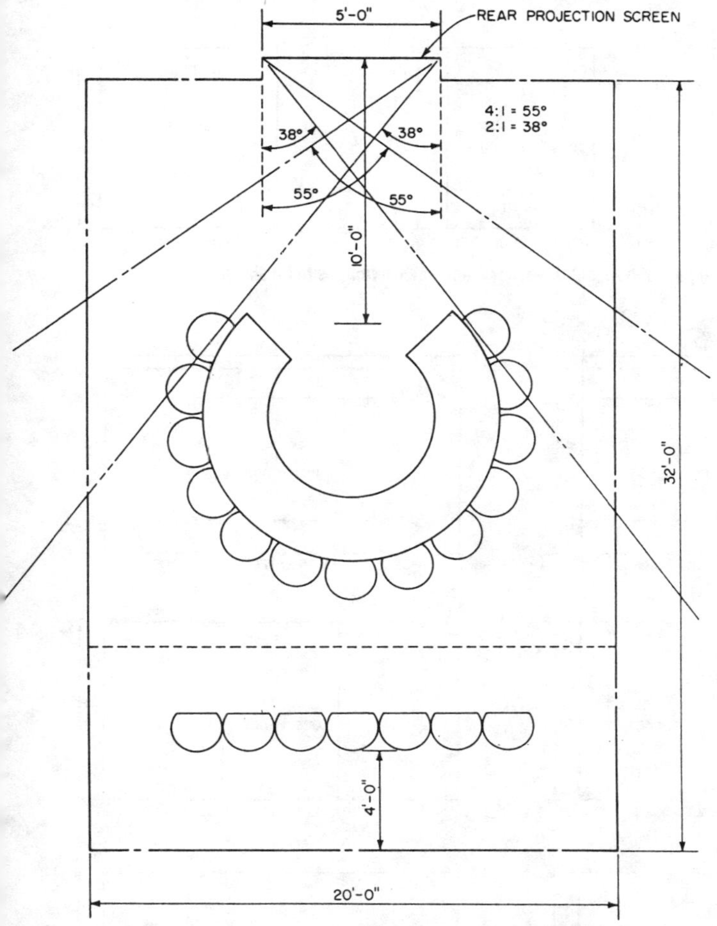

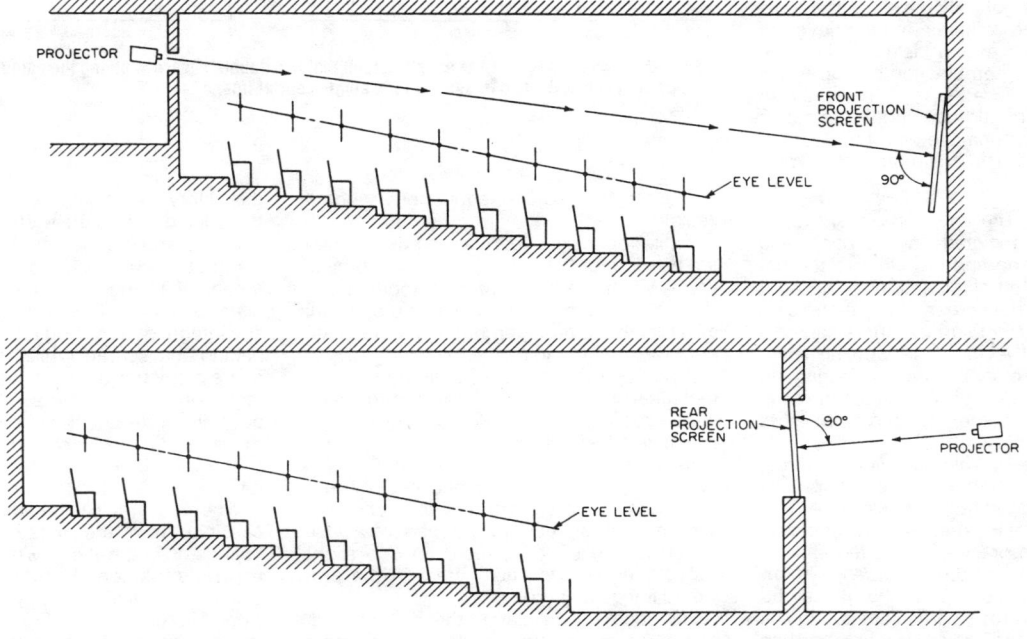

Fig. 6 A room 20 feet by 24 feet, seating 13 people at a circular table. With the depth increased to 32 feet, from 7 to 14 observers can also be accommodated.

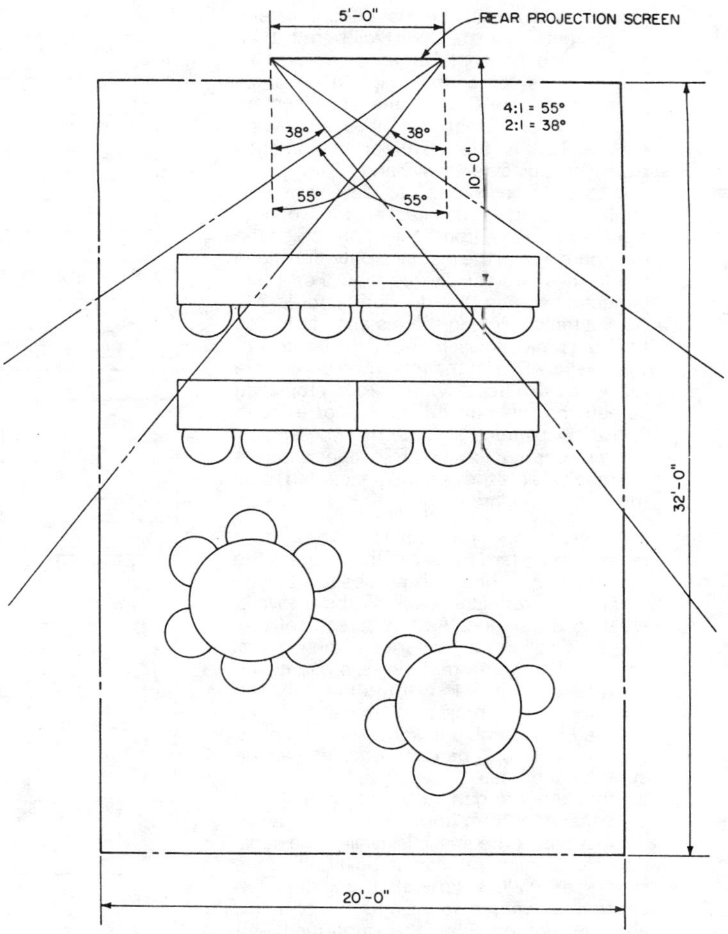

Fig. 7 A modified classroom arrangement including both lecture and separate tables.

Fig. 8 Cross section of a theatre-style auditorium with stepped seating showing both front and rear projection. Note that the projected light beam is perpendicular to the screen in both cases.

AUDIO-VISUAL SYSTEMS
Planning Guideline Summary

Screen image area The most useful screen is one that is square, as it will permit both vertical and horizontal images, as well as square ones, of course (Fig. 9). A single image format will need one such screen, while a dual format will have a viewing surface that is the width of two images placed side by side (Figs. 9 and 10).

It is an easy matter to determine the minimum image size necessary for a room of a given size. For a front projection screen the minimum size is the distance between it and the farthest viewer divided by 6. For a rear projection screen, the division factor is 7.5. As illustration: When the distance between the front projection screen and the last row of viewers, is 45 feet, the minimum image size would be 7.5 feet; with a rear projection screen, the minimum image should be 6 feet. These calculations assume that the original artwork from which the projection materials are made meets the generally accepted basic minimum standards.

Front projection The projector in a front projection system transmits the image in the form of a light beam to an opaque screen where it is reflected back to the viewers, creating the image. As the screen reflects any light falling on its surface, the general light level in the room during a presentation must be extremely low. If the full color and contrast of the projected image is to be retained, the ambient light should be no greater than 0.3 percent of the average screen brightness.

Projectors are generally noisy and should be separated from the audience to avoid distractions. If the space is available, a separate projection booth can be built behind the room's rear wall. Besides insulating the viewers from unwanted sound and light spill, this arrangement provides the opportunity for equipment to remain in place ready for use. There are other possible arrangements when space is constricted (Figs. 11, 12, and 13).

Creating an A-V front projection system that is both aesthetically pleasing and functionally efficient requires a high level of technical expertise and design skill. The results of such a combination can be effective yet unobtrusive. Fig. 16 provides an example of a multimedia front projection system that is compatible with the decor of the room and its formalized seating arrangement.

Rear projection The image in a rear projection system is focused on the back of a translucent screen and is visible to the audience on the other side. Since the light passes through the screen rather than being reflected off its front surface, there can be a reasonable light level in the viewing room during the presentation without affecting the quality of the image. It is only in the immediate vicinity of the screen that the room lights need be dimmed.

As is the case with all projection systems, for minimum distractions the equipment should be separated from the audience. This can be effected by means of a separate projection booth or by an enclosed cabinet within the viewing room. A separate room usually requires more space, but it may be the best solution for a particular situation. A cabinet within the viewing room permits front access to the projectors, enabling the

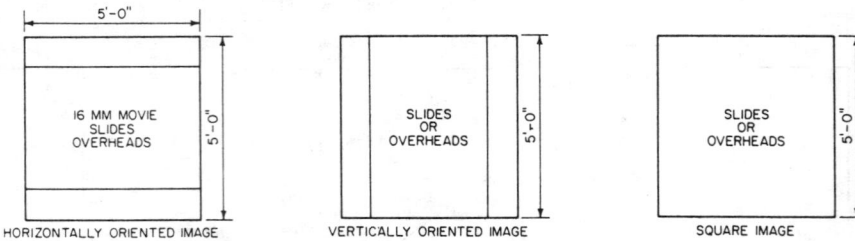

Fig. 9 A square screen will permit horizontal, vertical, and square images to be shown.

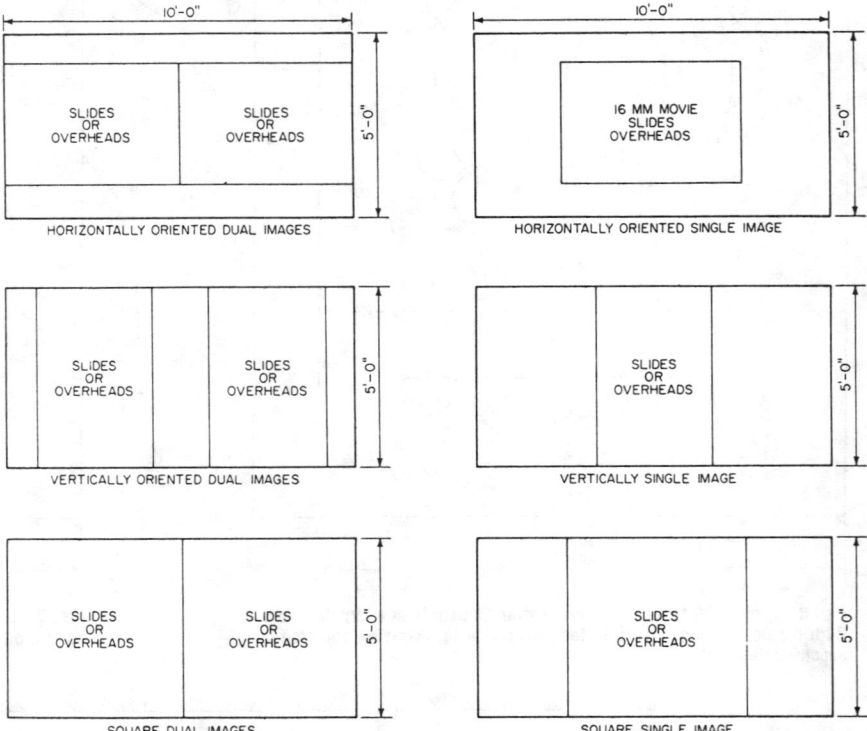

Fig. 10 A dual-image format uses a screen that is a double square — giving the same flexibility of image shape for each of the two images or for a single central image.

presenter to load the equipment without assistance.

While technical expertise and design skill are needed for the creation of a front projection A-V system, they are even more important for a system intended for rear projection, as a rear-mode arrangement has more inherent problems to overcome.

A rear projection system utilizing the indirect deep method in a separate projection booth requires a considerable amount of space. In addition, if more than one projector is used in such a system, either the projectors must be optically aligned each time a change is made (as there is only one true screen axis), or they are permanently positioned a little off axis, resulting in a slight "keystone" or distortion effect in the projected image (Fig. 17).

For good image clarity, the distance between the image source and the screen must be at least twice the picture size. To achieve

this clarity within a limited amount of space, the folded light-path method can be used (Figs. 18 and 19). As the name implies, the light path from the projector is "folded" by means of a large mirror, usually placed some distance away. This arrangement has the advantage of reducing the depth required behind the screen while retaining an adequate projection distance. As a further advantage, several projectors can be aligned in optically true positions by the use of a movable mirror with preset position stops.

The use of the folded light-path method of projection and a movable mirror can also be engineered in a cabinet that is directly accessible from the presentation room for "hands-on" operation by the person making the presentation. Both single-image and side-by-side dual-image systems can be designed in this manner (Figs. 20 and 21).

A great number of variations are possible using the same basic engineering concepts.

These variations can accommodate different functional requirements, spatial limitations, and image-quality parameters. Figures 14, 15, 22, and 23 illustrate some of the possible arrangements. User requirements and job conditions will guide the A-V engineer in the design of a specific system.

The Optical Design Factor

A projection system — of whatever nature — is only as good as the quality of the image on the screen. The clarity, sharpness, resolution, and angle of view that can be expected are a direct result of the thought and care that go into the optical design of the system. The more complex the system becomes, the more critical is the system optics. The need for larger images, sharper images, multiple images, multiple image sources and the existence of physically constraining parameters all add to the conflicting requirements that must be satisfied. And they must be satisfied if an acceptable image quality is to be achieved.

The Sound System

The quality and the functional characteristics of the sound system that is part of an audiovisual facility are as important as the quality and functional characteristics of the optical system. The two aspects of a facility are mutually complementary and the one should not be neglected in relation to the other if the goal of an effective and useful facility is to be attained.

The quality of the sound, as perceived by the listener, will be influenced by such factors as:

The sensitivity of controls
The quality of the amplifiers
The quality of the speakers
The location of the speakers
The elimination of extraneous sounds
The overall acoustical characteristics of the space

The design factors that govern the functional characteristics of the sound system might include the following:

Sound sources: voice, movie sound-track, videotape, audiotape
Telecommunication facilities for outside program sources
Mixing and control requirements
Quantity and placement of speakers
Room size and function: conference room, classroom, auditorium
Provision for flexibility and future expansion

The Remote-Control System

Most people who make informational presentations are not audiovisual specialists. Their primary concern is with the material they are presenting and not with the mechanics of how it is to be presented. As a result, any control devices they may be required to operate should be simple and logical. The presenter should be asked to make only a minimum of effort to determine how to manipulate the controls in order to achieve a desired result. The fewer operations necessary to reach a particular goal, the better. For example, in order for a change to be made from one presentation mode to another, it may be necessary to alter the ambient room lighting, reposition a mirror, turn one machine

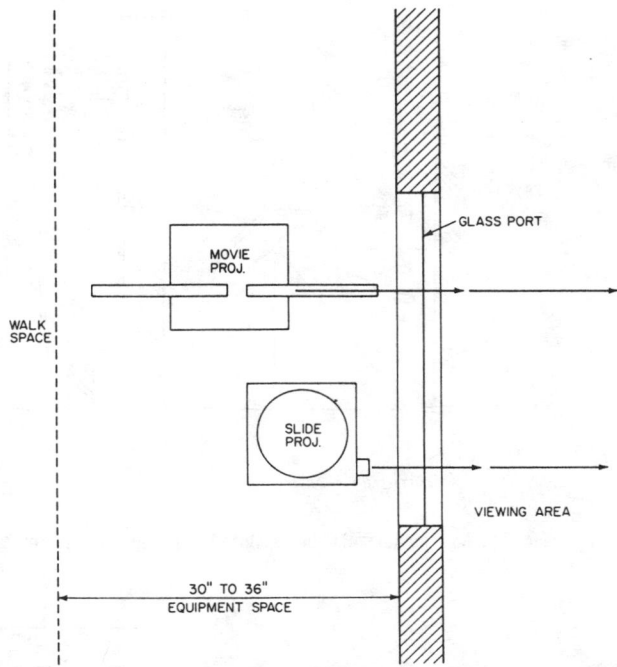

Fig. 11   A typical rear-access equipment arrangement for front projection.

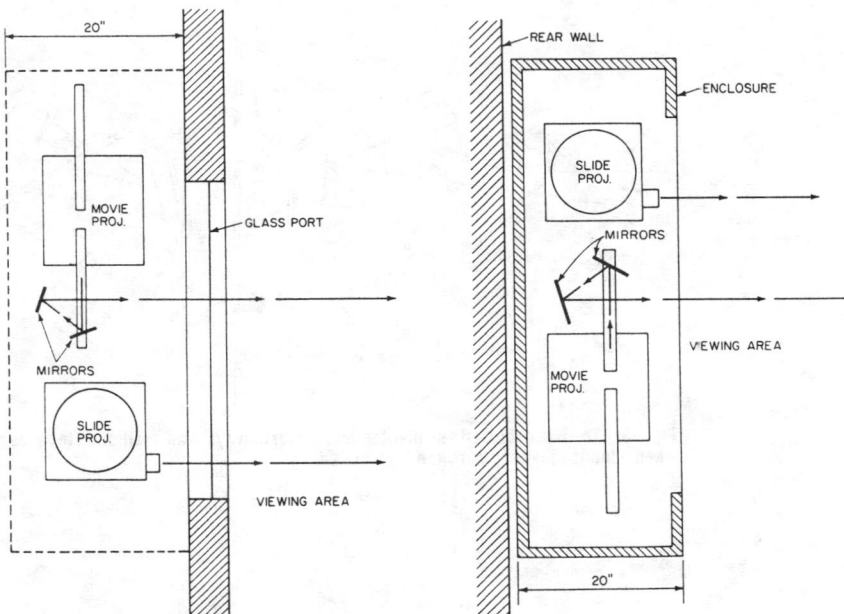

Fig. 12   A rear-access reduced-depth arrangement of equipment for front projection.

Fig. 13   A front-access equipment cabinet for front projection.

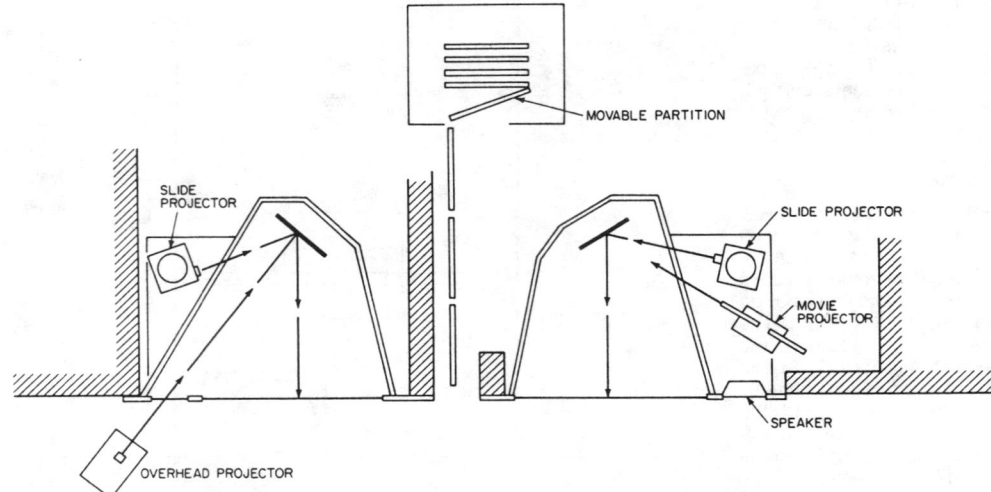

Fig. 14   An arrangement of two enclosed rear projection systems serving a single large room.

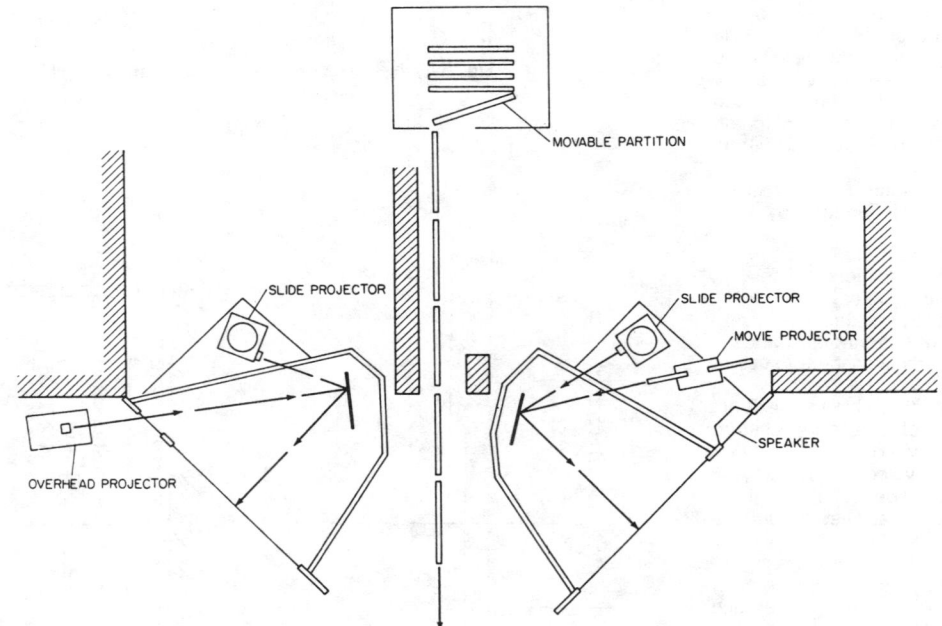

Fig. 15   The two enclosed and pivoted rear projection systems positioned to serve the two separate rooms that are created when a hidden dividing partition is extended.

off and then another on. If all these things can be accomplished merely by flipping one clearly marked switch, the presenter is freed from mechanical distractions and can concentrate full attention on the message being delivered. The location and spacing of the various switches on the panel, as well as the use of nomenclature unmistakable to a nontechnical person, are important parts of the design of a remote-control system that will aid the presenter in the use of the audiovisual facility.

Other considerations that may affect the design of a remote-control system include:

The seating configuration
The room lighting
The number of control points required
The use of a lectern incorporating a control module
The number and type of functions to be controlled
The degree of automation required to meet system objectives

SUMMARY

An audiovisual presentation facility is made up of many components and subsystems which are interdependent and must perform as an integrated unit. Regardless of its size or scope, the A-V system must be conceived, designed, and installed to function as a totality – as a single entity that works with optimum efficiency and effectiveness in an unobtrusive manner.

In order to achieve this goal – that of developing a logical and workable solution to any particular communication problem – careful and detailed preliminary investigations must be made. These will determine the functional requirements that make up the design program. From this program, the space needs for the equipment and for the audience can be established early enough in the development of the project to avoid undesirable procrustean solutions later. The selection, adaptation, manufacture, assembly, and installation of equipment and components should be carefully coordinated to ensure their functional integrity and performance.

Ultimately, a successful audiovisual system is one that serves as a logical and natural extension of the human capabilities of the person using it. It should respond easily and unobtrusively to the communicator's needs, and it should reproduce the material being communicated with the highest possible degree of fidelity.

RECAP

Front Projection

1. Viewing distance factor is 6. (For example, if image size is 5 feet the alphanumerics

would be clear at a maximum distance of 30 feet to a viewer with a 20/40 vision if characters are ¾₁₆ inch on 6- by 9-inch original copy area.)

2. Advantages
   a. Good angle of view
   b. Good for checking laboratory quality of all projectuals
   c. Virtually no apparent falloff to the sides

3. Disadvantages
   a. High ceilings are required to utilize a square screen to accommodate vertical as well as horizontal images.
   b. Distraction occurs when the presenter or viewers interrupt the light beam.
   c. Any ambient light adversely affects image quality. The room must be relatively dark to achieve the desired picture contrast.
   d. An overhead projector cannot be used most effectively.

Rear Projection (Rigid or Flexible Material)

1. Viewing distance factor is 7.5. (For example, if image size is 5 feet the maximum viewing distance would be 37.5 feet.)

2. Advantages
   a. A 20 percent smaller image than is required by front projection permits minimum standards to be met in low-ceilinged rooms.
   b. Can be used in higher ambient light conditions.
   c. No distracting light beam. (Presenter can more comfortably point at details).
   d. In a brighter room, the presenter easily maintains eye contact.
   e. An overhead projector can be used, so that neither it nor the presenter blocks the image from the viewers.

3. Disadvantages
   a. The inherent grain and directional quality of the rear screen eliminate it as a viewing medium to determine laboratory quality of projectuals.
   b. The projection system must be designed to overcome apparent illumination falloff at the sides and improve the angle of view.
   c. Mirrored image is required for proper use.
   d. More space is required than with front projection.
   e. Usually costs more.

Seating

(Plan should permit several arrangements.)

1. A U- or V-table layout provides for best

viewing and viewer/presenter interaction (lowest audience capacity).

2. Conference table (boat-shape or oval) provides good interaction for conferences but not so good as the U- or V-table layout for audiovisual communication.

3. Random seating style (usually with writing tablets) is frequently selected for high-level visitor presentations. It permits larger capacity and creates a more luxurious atmosphere than the two arrangements above.

4. Classroom style (shallow tables parallel to front wall with chairs behind) is the next best method but less conducive to student interraction.
   a. Stepped, curved seating (lecture hall) provides unobstructed viewing.
   b. When classroom style is contemplated, study and programmed-learning carrels should be considered.

5. Auditorium style provides the largest capacity seating and is generally used for large group-orientation and overview types of presentation.

Rear Projection System Factors

1. The physical center of all projector lenses must be in perfect alignment with the physical center of the screen to eliminate any "keystone" effect. (For dissolve mode, 2° off center vertically is permitted.)

2. A front-surface mirror should be used to reverse the image so the equipment can be loaded much as it is for front projection; slides in magazines need not be reversed, and special reversed prints are not needed for motion pictures. The use of a mirror can also extend the projection distance appreciably by folding the light path. Remember, the longer the projection distance, the better the viewing angle. Minimum projection distance should be at least 2 times the image size.

3. The screen-image area should be considered to be square to accommodate vertical and horizontal images unless the system is to be used for a special, limited requirement.

4. Apparent light falloff at the sides can be diminished or eliminated by increasing the projection distance and projector illumination. Another minor contributor is slide density. A dense or underexposed slide reduces the amount of light transmission. This condition increases apparent light falloff.

AUDIO-VISUAL SYSTEMS

Equipment Arrangement

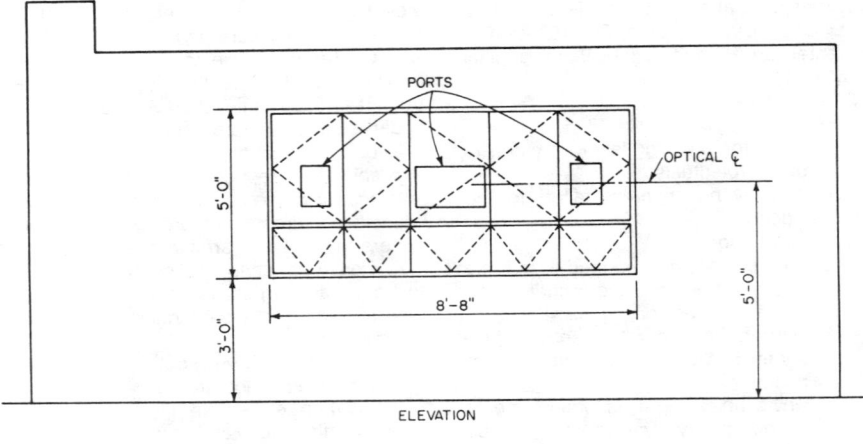

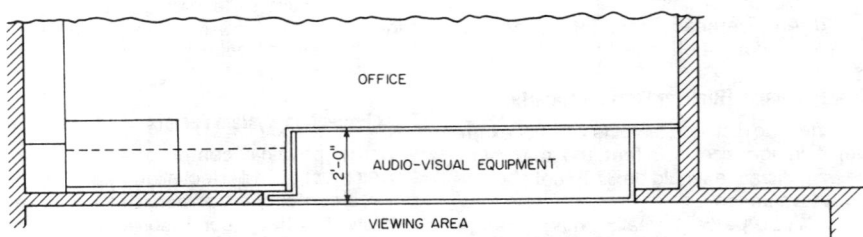

Fig. 16   A custom-designed recessed front-access equipment cabinet for a multi-image front projection system.

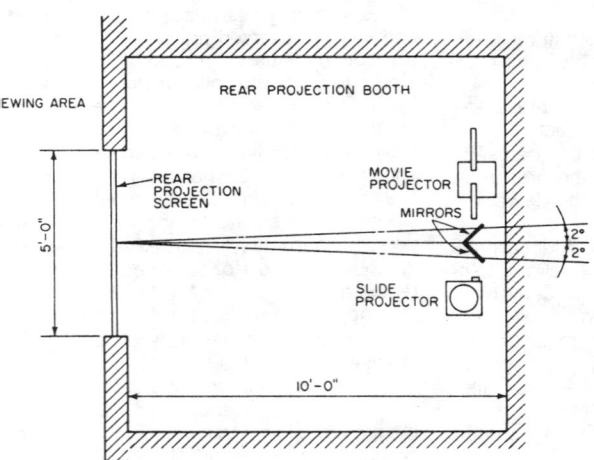

Fig. 17   A deep, indirect-method, rear projection arrangement using the minimum recommended ratio of 2 to 1 between projection distance and image size.

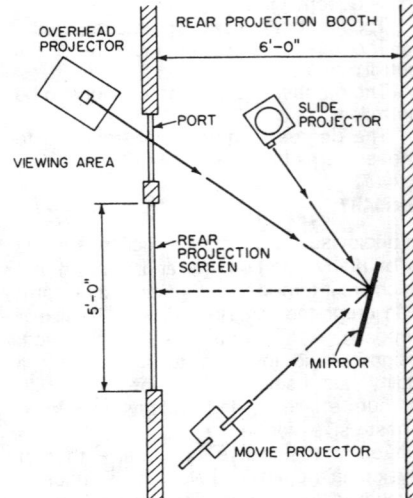

Fig. 19   An indirect rear projection arrangement using the folded-light-path method and the minimum recommended 2 to 1 ratio of projection distance to image size. This permits a flexible equipment arrangement within tight space limitations.

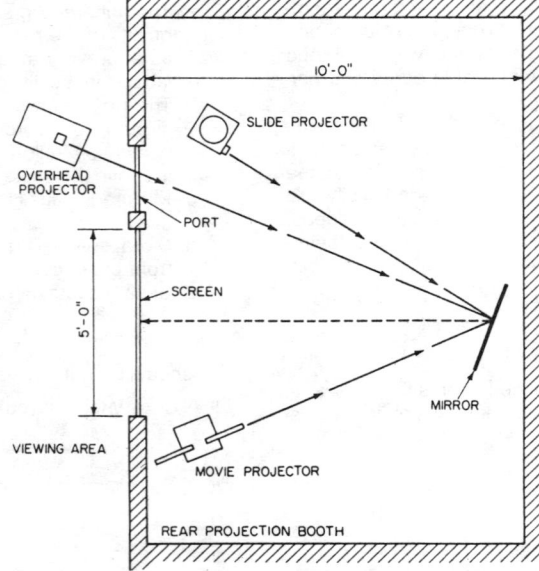

Fig. 18   An indirect rear projection arrangement using the folded-light-path method, resulting in a ratio of 3.5 to 1 within the same depth. This improves the image quality and increases the possible viewing angle as well as allowing rear projection of overhead transparencies with the overhead projector in the presentation room.

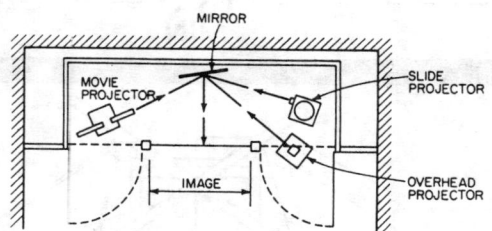

Fig. 20   A front-access rear projection arrangement using the folded-light-path method for single-image presentations.

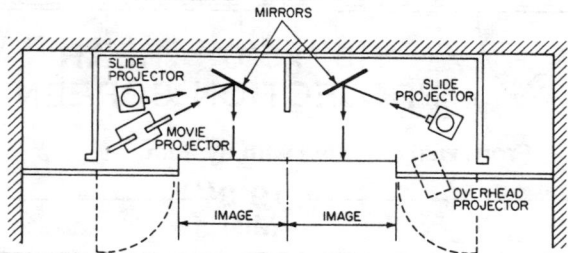

Fig. 21   A front-access rear projection arrangement using the folded-light-path method for dual-image presentations.

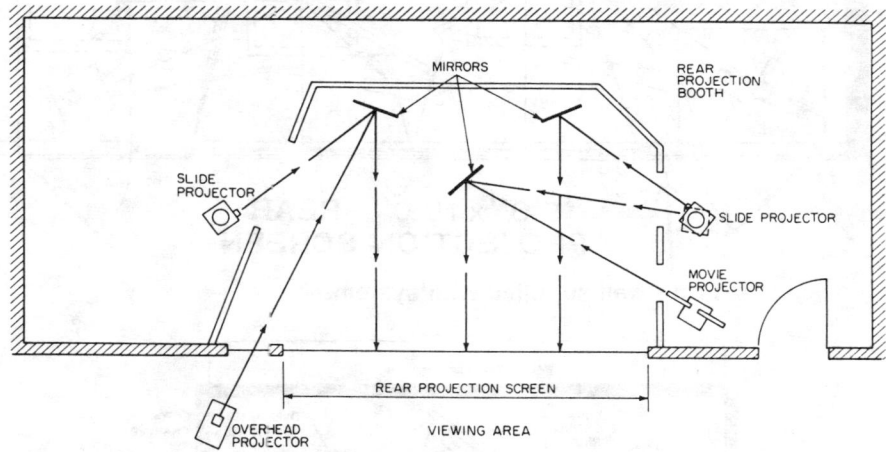

Fig. 22   A rear-access rear projection arrangement using the folded-light-path method for dual-image or single central-image presentations.

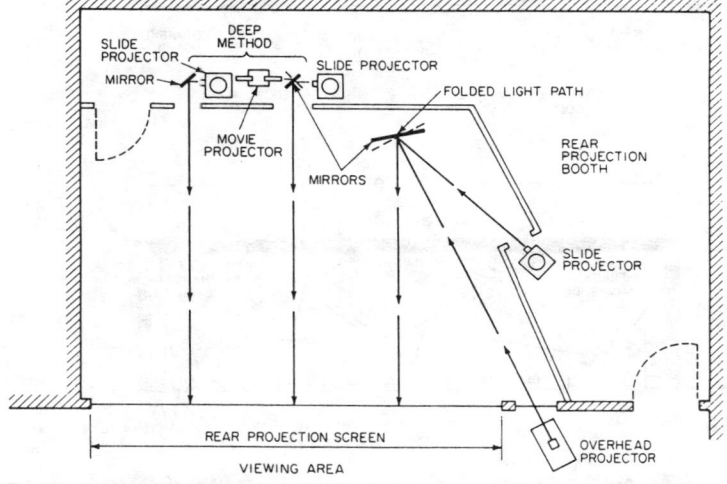

Fig. 23   A rear projection arrangement for dual-image and single central-image presentations utilizing both deep indirect projection and the folded-light-path method.

AUDIO-VISUAL SYSTEMS
Typical Projection Room Layout

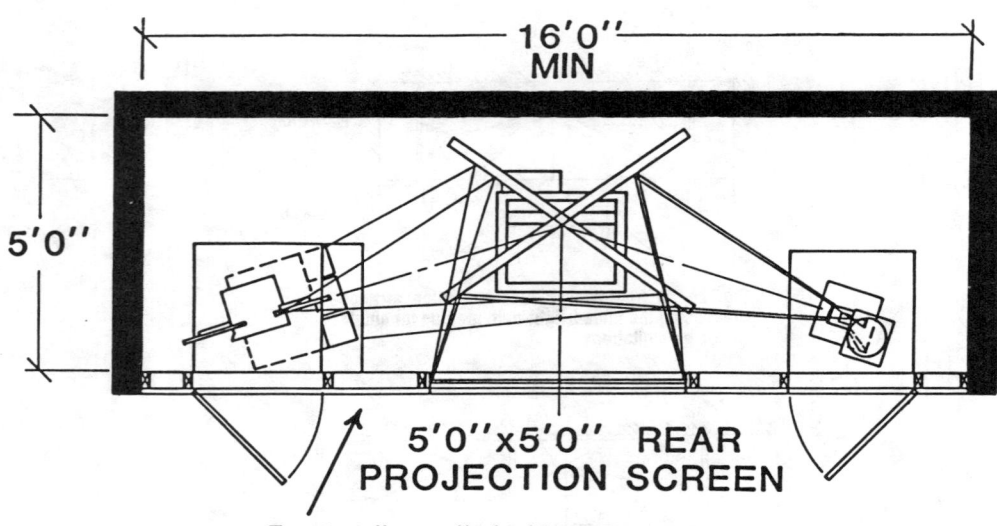

5'0''x5'0'' REAR
PROJECTION SCREEN

Front wall supplied with system.

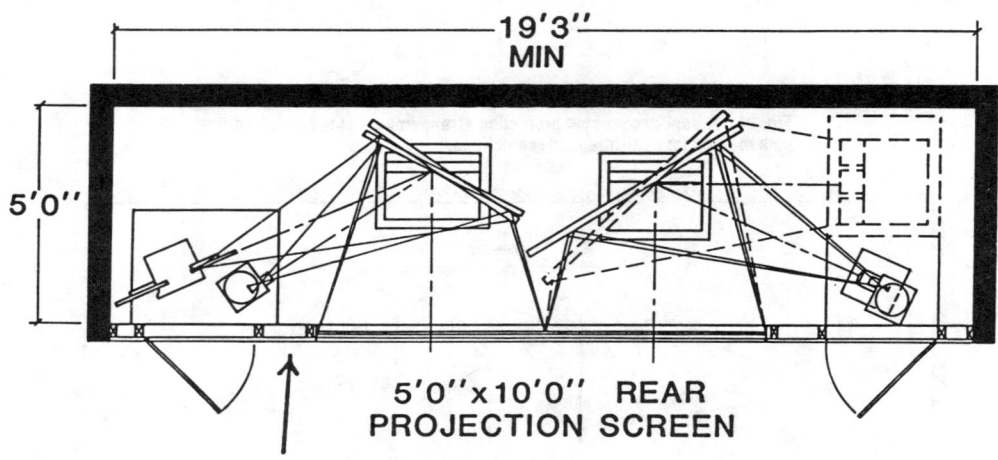

5'0''x10'0'' REAR
PROJECTION SCREEN

Front wall supplied with system.

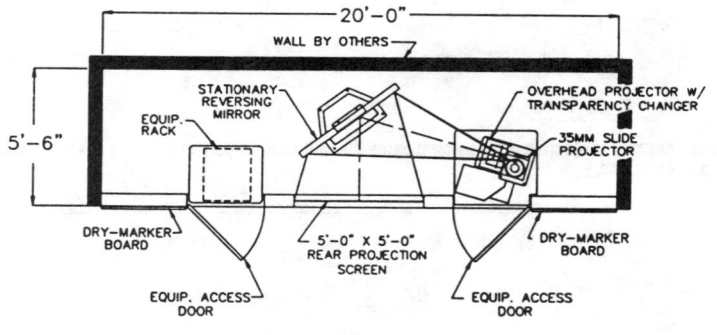

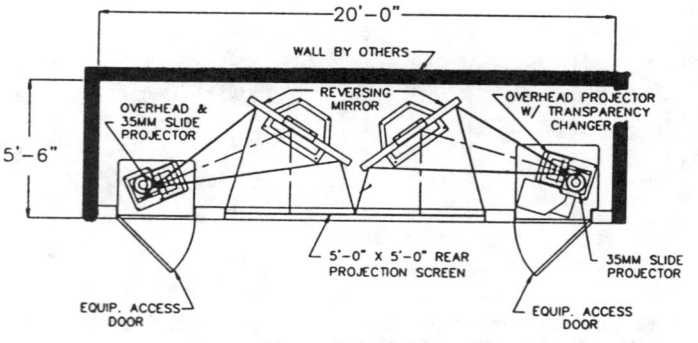

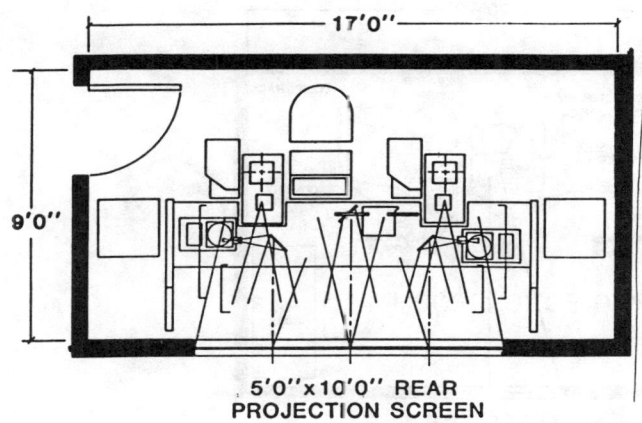

17'0"

9'0"

5'0"x10'0" REAR
PROJECTION SCREEN

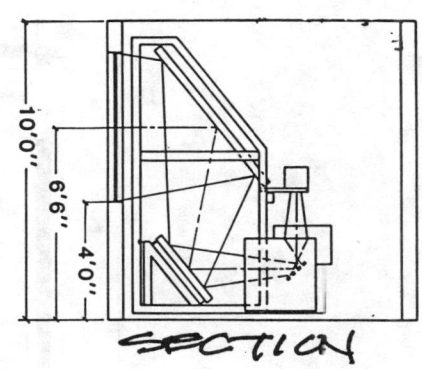

10'0"

6'6"

4'0"

SECTION

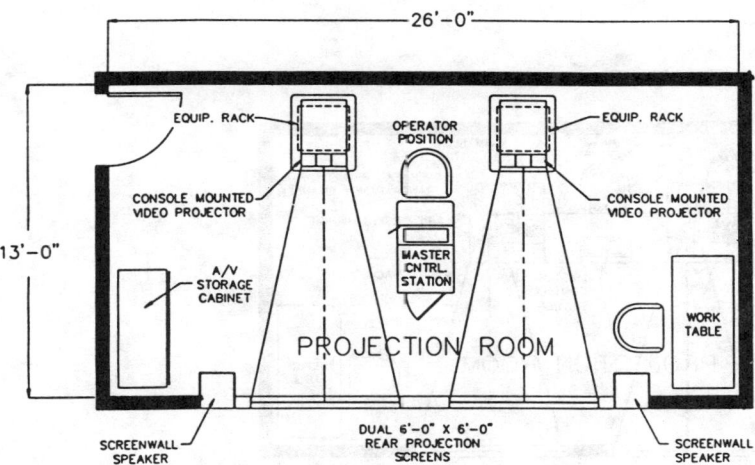

26'-0"

13'-0"

EQUIP. RACK

OPERATOR
POSITION

EQUIP. RACK

CONSOLE MOUNTED
VIDEO PROJECTOR

CONSOLE MOUNTED
VIDEO PROJECTOR

A/V
STORAGE
CABINET

MASTER
CNTRL.
STATION

WORK
TABLE

PROJECTION ROOM

SCREENWALL
SPEAKER

DUAL 6'-0" X 6'-0"
REAR PROJECTION
SCREENS

SCREENWALL
SPEAKER

TYPICAL CONFIGURATION

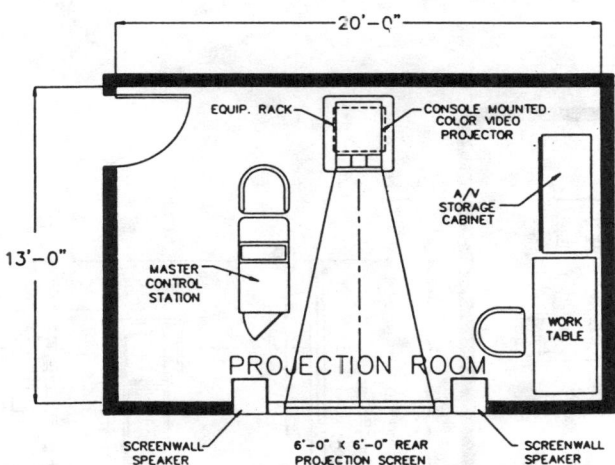

20'-0"

13'-0"

EQUIP. RACK

CONSOLE MOUNTED
COLOR VIDEO
PROJECTOR

A/V
STORAGE
CABINET

MASTER
CONTROL
STATION

WORK
TABLE

PROJECTION ROOM

SCREENWALL
SPEAKER

6'-0" X 6'-0" REAR
PROJECTION SCREEN

SCREENWALL
SPEAKER

TYPICAL CONFIGURATION

AUDIO-VISUAL SYSTEMS
Typical Projection Room Layout

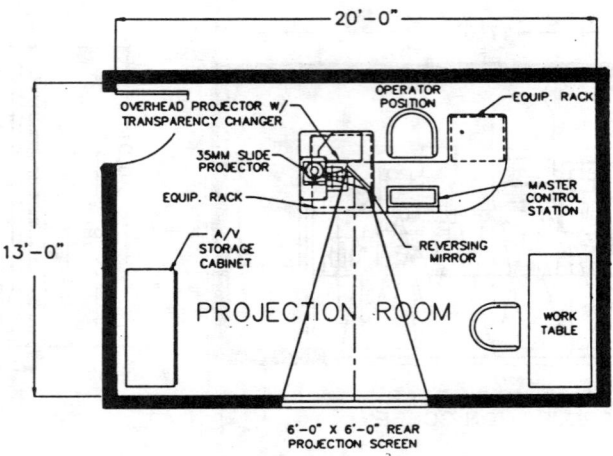

TYPICAL CONFIGURATION

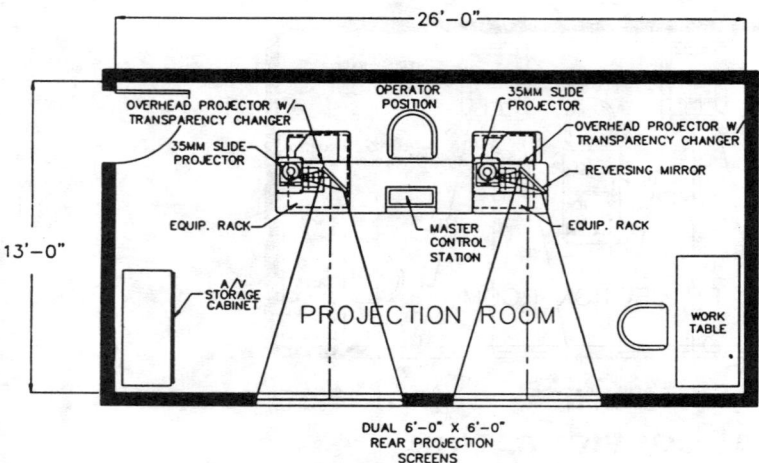

TYPICAL CONFIGURATION

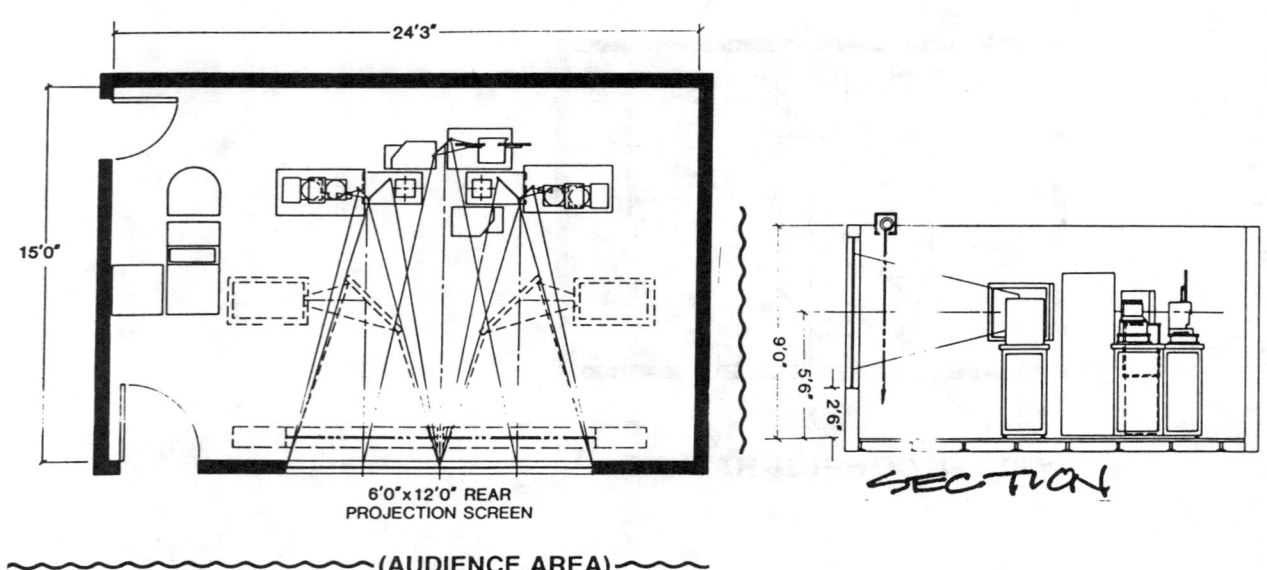

(AUDIENCE AREA)

Sight line studies vary depending on the particular event and seating configuration. The following are some basic design elements. (*Note:* Remember to review and verify slope, riser heights, tread depths, etc., with pertinent national and local code requirements.)

The visibility profile shown in Fig. 1:

Angle A: Shifting position to look between heads in row immediately in front of spectator and over all other heads.

Angle B: Shifting position to look between heads of two rows immediately in front of spectators and over all other heads.

Generally, the variables considered in determining these angles are:

■ 3'8" eye level in the seated position
■ 5" minimum eye clearance
■ Row spacing and row rise

Angle A is commonly used in determining floor slope for auditorium, performing arts or theater type seating configurations. When angle A profile is used in conjunction with a staggered seating arrangement (chairs staggered or alternated in arrangement of sizes opposite every other row) it allows unobstructed view of spectators to a determined focal point at screen on stage. The final analysis is to have all sight lines to intersect the desired focal point (usually 5'6" elevation either at screen or 12'0" back from front of stage).

Angle B is most commonly used in determining riser or stepped applications for gymnasium, arena, or stadium type seating configurations. When the angle B profile is used (generally associated with an aligned seating arrangement) it allows unobstructed view of spectators to a determined focal point at court line or line of play. The final analysis is to have all the critical sight lines to intersect the focal point or line of play at generally a 3'0" elevation.

Legal responsibility lies with the owners and users of equipment in acquiring acceptance with local officals. The following are some basic guidelines.

Standard Seating

1. Row spacing shall provide a clear space of not less than 12" (30.5 cm) from the back of one chair to the front of the most forward projection of the chair directly behind it when measured with the self-rising seat in the up position.

2. Rows of chairs shall not exceed 14 chairs between aisles and exceed seven chairs from an aisle to a row end.

3. Aisles serving 60 seats or less shall be a minimum of 30" (76 cm) wide. Aisles serving more than 60 seats shall be at least 3' (91 cm) wide when serving seats on one side and at least 3'6" (107 cm) wide when serving seats

on both sides. These minimum widths, measured at the point furthest from an exit, cross aisles, or foyer shall be increased 1½" (3.8 cm) for each 5' (152 cm) in length toward the exit, cross aisle, or foyer. Where egress is possible in either direction, aisles shall be uniform in width. Dead end aisles are not allowed over 20'0" (61.0 m) in length.

4. Cross aisles, foyer or exit widths shall be not less than the sum of the required width of the widest aisle plus 50% of the total required width of the remaining aisles that it serves.

Continental Seating

1. Row spacing shall provide a clear space of not less than: 18" (45.7 cm) between rows of 18 chairs or less; 20" (50.8 cm) between rows of 35 chairs or less; 21" (53.3 cm) between rows of 45 chairs or less; 22" (55.9 cm) between rows of 45 chairs or more to a maximum of 100 chairs per row, measured from the back of one chair to the front of the most forward projection of the chair directly behind it with the self-rising seat in the up position.

2. There shall be exits of 66" (168 cm) minimum clear width along each side aisle of the chair rows for each five rows of chairs.

3. Aisles shall not be less than 44" (112 cm) in clear width.

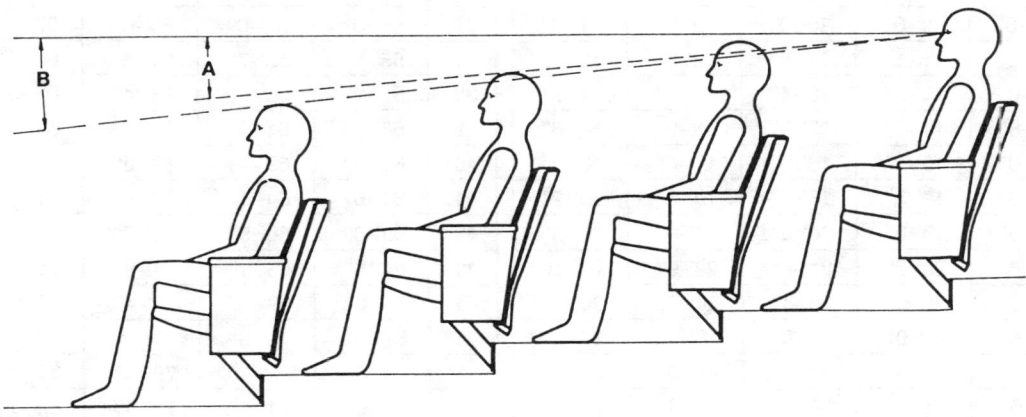

Fig. 1

AUDITORIUM SEATING
Row Length

Row length = ₵ to ₵ + (2A) measured at the Chair Size Line

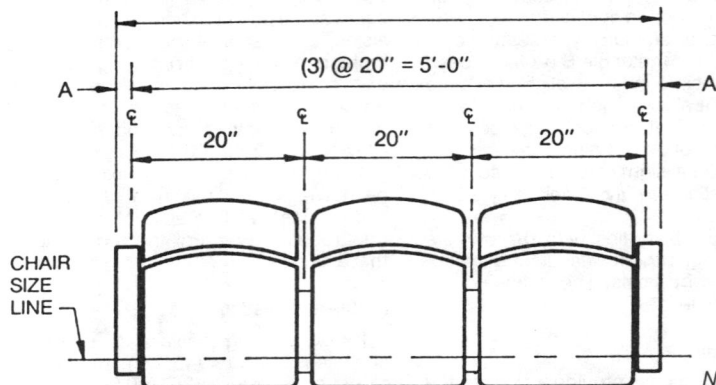

Note: End dim. A varies 2″ to 3″ for end tablet arm applications.

EXAMPLE:
(3) 20″ chairs = 5′-4″ row length.

	DIMENSIONS: Center line to center line (₵ to ₵)										
QTY	**SIZE**					**QTY**	**SIZE**				
	18″	**19″**	**20″**	**21″**	**22″**		**18″**	**19″**	**20″**	**21″**	**22″**
2	3′-0″	3′-2″	3′-4″	3′-6″	3′-8″	32	48′-0″	50′-8″	53′-4″	56′-0″	58′-8″
3	4′-6″	4′-9″	5′-0″	5′-3″	5′-6″	33	49′-6″	52′-3″	55′-0″	57′-9″	60′-6″
4	6′-0″	6′-4″	6′-8″	7′-0″	7′-4″	34	51′-0″	53′-10″	56′-8″	59′-6″	62′-4″
5	7′-6″	7′-11″	8′-4″	8′-9″	9′-2″	35	52′-6″	55′-5″	58′-4″	61′-3″	64′-2″
6	9′-0″	9′-6″	10′-0″	10′-6″	11′-0″	36	54′-0″	57′-0″	60′-0″	63′-0″	66′-0″
7	10′-6″	11′-1″	11′-8″	12′-3″	12′-10″	37	55′-6″	58′-7″	61′-8″	64′-9″	67′-10″
8	12′-0″	12′-8″	13′-4″	14′-0″	14′-8″	38	57′-0″	60′-2″	63′-4″	66′-6″	69′-8″
9	13′-6″	14′-3″	15′-0″	15′-9″	16′-6″	39	58′-6″	61′-9″	65′-0″	68′-3″	71′-6″
10	15′-0″	15′-10″	16′-8″	17′-6″	18′-4″	40	60′-0″	63′-4″	66′-8″	70′-0″	73′-4″
11	16′-6″	17′-5″	18′-4″	19′-3″	20′-2″	41	61′-6″	64′-11″	68′-4″	71′-9″	75′-2″
12	18′-0″	19′-0″	20′-0″	21′-0″	22′-0″	42	63′-0″	66′-6″	70′-0″	73′-6″	77′-0″
13	19′-6″	20′-7″	21′-8″	22′-9″	23′-10″	43	64′-6″	68′-1″	71′-8″	75′-3″	78′-10″
14	21′-0″	22′-2″	23′-4″	24′-6″	25′-8″	44	66′-0″	69′-8″	73′-4″	77′-0″	80′-8″
15	22′-6″	23′-9″	25′-0″	26′-3″	27′-6″	45	67′-6″	71′-3″	75′-0″	78′-9″	82′-6″
16	24′-0″	25′-4″	26′-8″	28′-0″	29′-4″	46	69′-0″	72′-10″	76′-8″	80′-6″	84′-4″
17	25′-6″	26′-11″	28′-4″	29′-9″	31′-2″	47	70′-6″	74′-5″	78′-4″	82′-3″	86′-2″
18	27′-0″	28′-6″	30′-0″	31′-6″	33′-0″	48	72′-0″	76′-0″	80′-0″	84′-0″	88′-0″
19	28′-6″	30′-1″	31′-8″	33′-3″	34′-10″	49	73′-6″	77′-7″	81′-8″	85′-9″	89′-10″
20	30′-0″	31′-8″	33′-4″	35′-0″	36′-8″	50	75′-0″	79′-2″	83′-4″	87′-6″	91′-8″
21	31′-6″	33′-3″	35′-0″	36′-9″	38′-6″	51	76′-6″	80′-9″	85′-0″	89′-3″	93′-6″
22	33′-0″	34′-10″	36′-8″	38′-6″	40′-4″	52	78′-0″	82′-4″	86′-8″	91′-0″	95′-4″
23	34′-6″	36′-5″	38′-4″	40′-3″	42′-2″	53	79′-6″	83′-11″	88′-4″	92′-9″	97′-2″
24	36′-0″	38′-0″	40′-0″	42′-0″	44′-0″	54	81′-0″	85′-6″	90′-0″	94′-6″	99′-0″
25	37′-6″	39′-7″	41′-8″	43′-9″	45′-10″	55	82′-6″	87′-1″	91′-8″	96′-3″	100′-10″
26	39′-0″	41′-2″	43′-4″	45′-6″	47′-8″	56	84′-0″	88′-8″	93′-4″	98′-0″	102′-8″
27	40′-6″	42′-9″	45′-0″	47′-3″	48′-6″	57	85′-6″	90′-3″	95′-0″	99′-9″	104′-6″
28	42′-0″	44′-4″	46′-8″	49′-0″	51′-4″	58	87′-0″	91′-10″	96′-8″	101′-6″	106′-4″
29	43′-6″	45′-11″	48′-4″	50′-9″	53′-2″	59	88′-6″	93′-5″	98′-4″	103′-3″	108′-2″
30	45′-0″	47′-6″	50′-0″	52′-6″	55′-0″	60	90′-0″	95′-0″	100′-0″	105′-0″	110′-0″
31	46′-6″	49′-1″	51′-8″	54′-3″	56′-10″	——	——	——	——	——	——

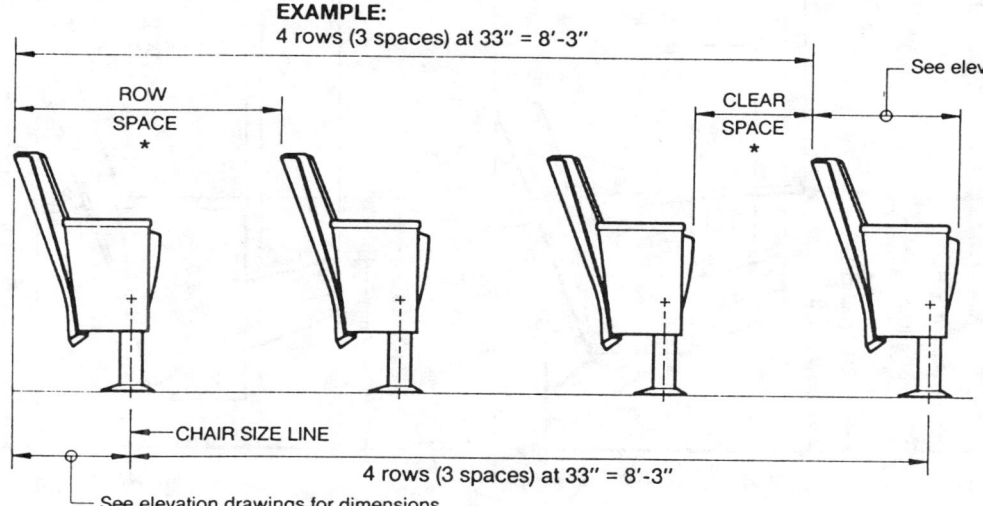

EXAMPLE:
4 rows (3 spaces) at 33" = 8'-3"

ROW SPACE *

CLEAR SPACE *

See elevation drawings for envelope dimensions

CHAIR SIZE LINE

4 rows (3 spaces) at 33" = 8'-3"

See elevation drawings for dimensions

*Notes:
1. Refer to applicable building codes.
2. Spacing varies with tablet arm applications.
3. Row space dimension will be the sum of "clear space" (see building codes) plus "chair envelope" (see chair dimensions) plus any additional space as desired for convenience to permit patron easy access to concessions, restrooms, etc.

Number of seating rows (spaces + 1)	OVERALL SPACING OF CHAIRS (back to back)										
	ROW SPACE DIMENSIONS										
	32"	33"	34"	35"	36"	37"	38"	39"	40"	41"	42"
2	2'-8"	2'-9"	2'-10"	2'-11"	3'-0"	3"-1"	3'-2"	3'-3"	3'-4"	3'-5"	3'-6"
3	5'-4"	5'-6"	5'-8"	5'-10"	6'-0"	6'-2"	6'-4"	6'-6"	6'-8"	6'-10"	7'-0"
4	8'-0"	8'-3"	8'-6"	8'-9"	9'-0"	9'-3"	9'-6"	9'-9"	10'-0"	10'-3"	10'-6"
5	10'-8"	11'-0"	11'-4"	11'-8"	12'-0"	12'-4"	12'-8"	13'-0"	13'-4"	13'-8"	14'-0"
6	13'-4"	13'-9"	14'-2"	14'-7"	15'-0"	15'-5"	15'-10"	16'-3"	16'-8"	17'-1"	17'-6"
7	16'-0"	16'-6"	17'-0"	17'-6"	18'-0"	18'-6"	19'-0"	19'-6"	20'-0"	20'-6"	21'-0"
8	18'-8"	19'-3"	19'-10"	20'-5"	21'-0"	21'-7"	22'-2"	22'-9"	23'-4"	23'-11"	24'-6"
9	21'-4"	22'-0"	22'-8"	23'-4"	24'-0"	24'-8"	25'-4"	26'-0"	26'-8"	27'-4"	28'-0"
10	24'-0"	24'-9"	25'-6"	26'-3"	27'-0"	27'-9"	28'-6"	29'-3"	30'-0"	30'-9"	31'-6"
11	26'-8"	27'-6"	28'-4"	29'-2"	30'-0"	30'-10"	31'-8"	32'-6"	33'-4"	34'-2"	35'-0"
12	29'-4"	30'-3"	31'-2"	32'-1"	33'-0"	33'-11"	34'-10"	35'-9"	36'-8"	37'-7"	38'-6"
13	32'-0"	33'-0"	34'-0"	35'-0"	36'-0"	37'-0"	38'-0"	39'-0"	40'-0"	41'-0"	42'-0"
14	34'-8"	35'-9"	36'-10"	37'-11"	39'-0"	40'-1"	41'-2"	42'-3"	43'-4"	44'-5"	45'-6"
15	37'-4"	38'-6"	39'-8"	40'-10"	42'-0"	43'-2"	44'-4"	45'-6"	46'-8"	47'-10"	49'-0"
16	40'-0"	41'-3"	42'-6"	43'-9"	45'-0"	46'-3"	47'-6"	48'-9"	50'-0"	51'-3"	52'-6"
17	42'-8"	44'-0"	45'-4"	46'-8"	48'-0"	49'-4"	50'-8"	52'-0"	53'-4"	54'-8"	56'-0"
18	45'-4"	46'-9"	48'-2"	49'-7"	51'-0"	52'-5"	53'-10"	55'-3"	56'-8"	58'-1"	59'-6"
19	48'-0"	49'-6"	51'-0"	52'-6"	54'-0"	55'-6"	57'-0"	58'-6"	60'-0"	61'-6"	63'-0"
20	50'-8"	52'-3"	53'-10"	55'-5"	57'-0"	58'-7"	60'-2"	61'-9"	63'-4"	64'-11"	66'-6"
21	53'-4"	55'-0"	56'-8"	58'-4"	60'-0"	61'-8"	63'-4"	65'-0"	66'-8"	68'-4"	70'-0"
22	56'-0"	57'-9"	59'-6"	61'-3"	63'-0"	64'-9"	66'-6"	68'-3"	70'-0"	71'-9"	73'-6"
23	68'-8"	60'-6"	62'-4"	64'-2"	66'-0"	67'-10"	69'-8"	71'-6"	73'-4"	75'-2"	77'-0"
24	61'-4"	63'-3"	65'-2"	67'-1"	69'-0"	70'-11"	72'-10"	74'-9"	76'-8"	78'-7"	80'-6"
25	64'-0"	66'-0"	68'-0"	70'-0"	72'-0"	74'-0"	76'-0"	78'-0"	80'-0"	82'-0"	84'-0"
26	66'-8"	68'-9"	70'-10"	72'-11"	75'-0"	77'-1"	79'-2"	81'-3"	83'-4"	85'-5"	87'-6"
27	69'-4"	71'-6"	73'-8"	75'-10"	78'-0"	80'-2"	82'-4"	84'-6"	86'-8"	88'-10"	91'-0"
28	72'-0"	74'-3"	76'-6"	78'-9"	81'-0"	83'-3"	85'-6"	87'-9"	90'-0"	92'-3"	94'-6"
29	74'-8"	77'-0"	79'-4"	81'-8"	84'-0"	86'-4"	88'-8"	91'-0"	93'-4"	95'-8"	98'-0"
30	77'-4"	79'-9"	82'-2"	84'-7"	87'-0"	89'-5"	91'-10"	94'-3"	96'-8"	99'-1"	101'-6"
31	80'-0"	82'-6"	85'-0"	87'-6"	90'-0"	92'-6"	95'-0"	97'-6"	100'-0"	102'-6"	105'-0"

AUDITORIUM SEATING

Chair Dimensions

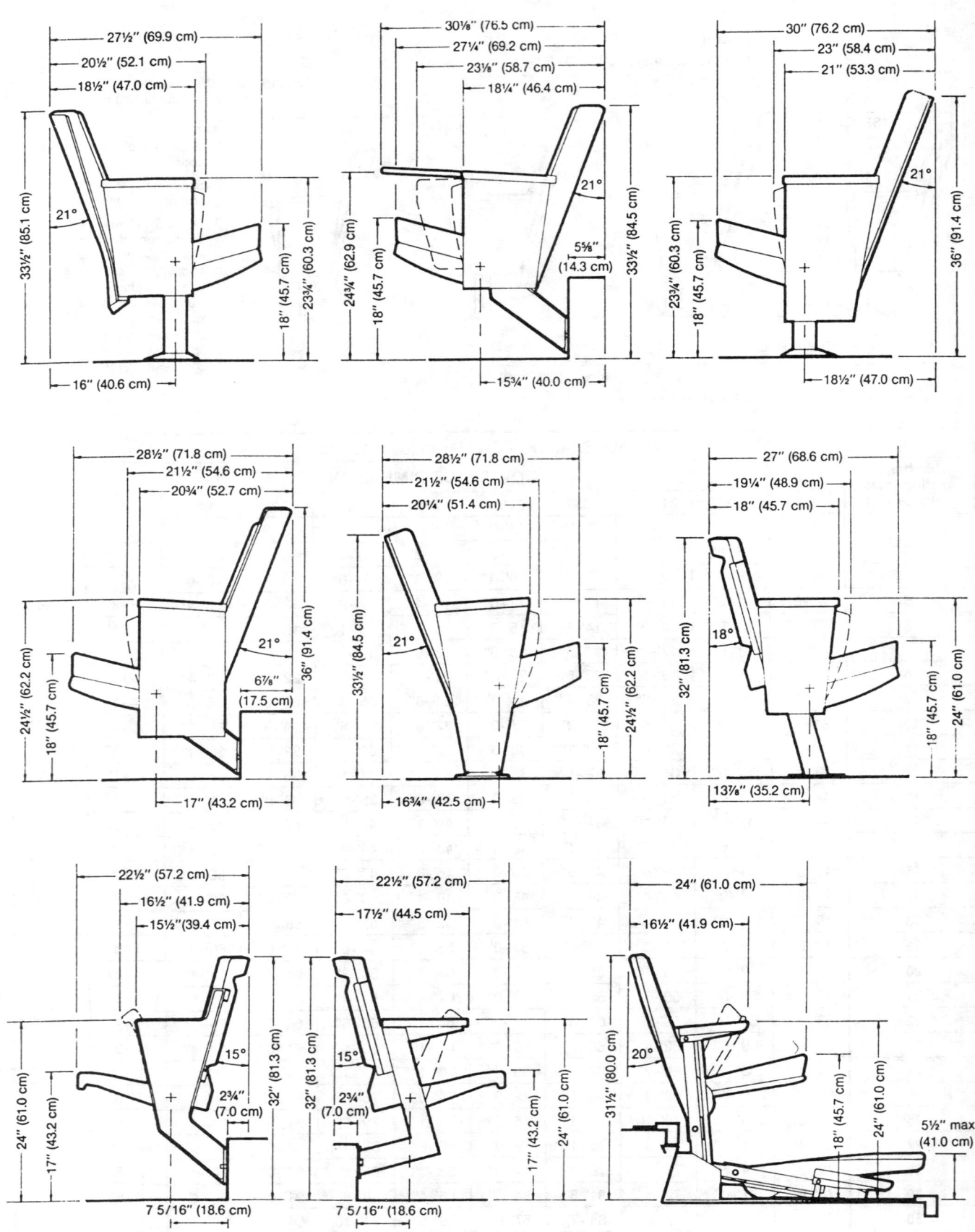

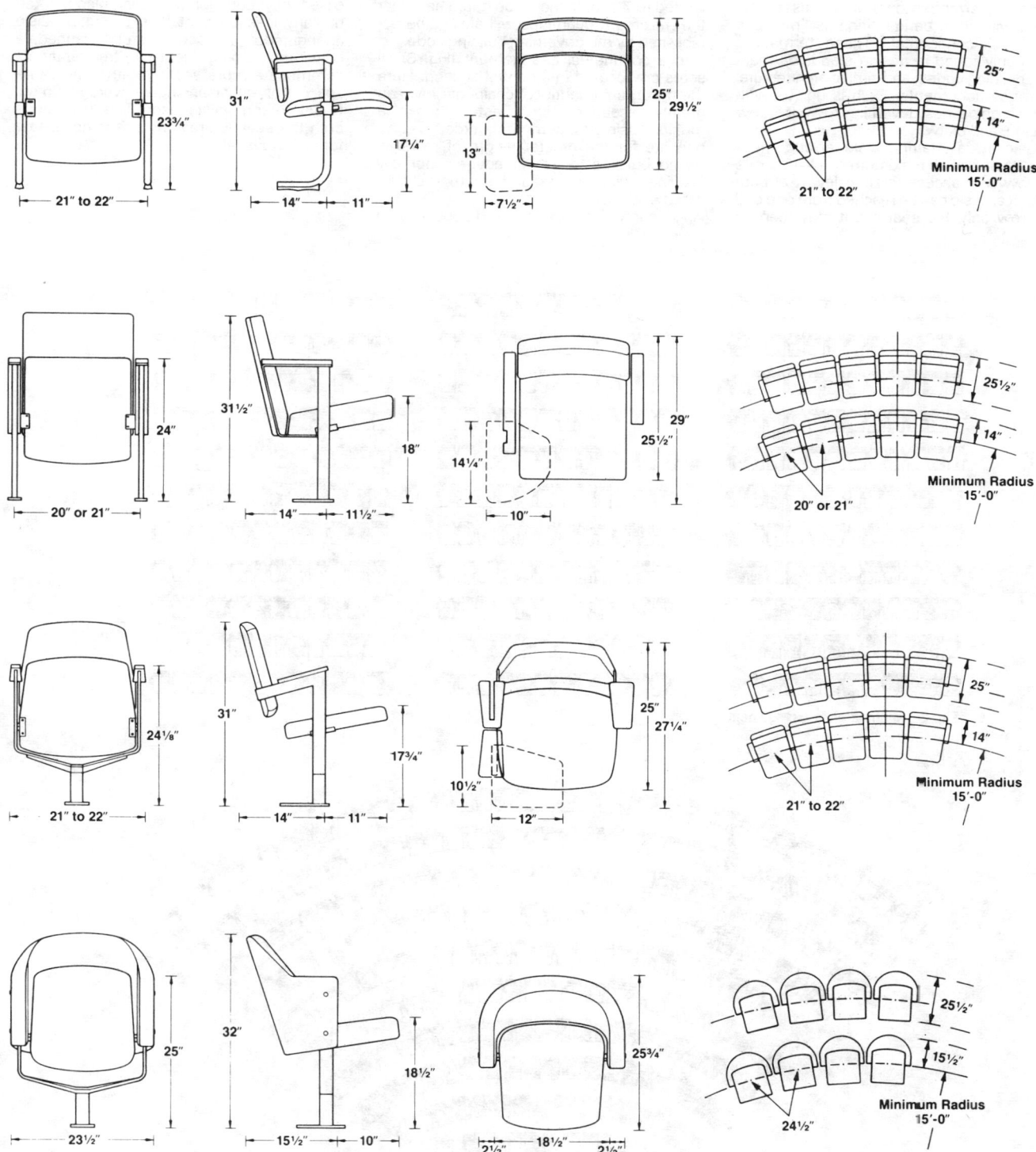

AUDITORIUM SEATING

General Seating Arrangement

Seating arrangements in an assembly space will either be identified as "multiple-aisle" or "continental." These terms are commonly found in design standards manuals, building codes, and similar architectural reference documents. Each is unique with specific guidelines governing row size, row spacing, and exitways.

Basically, a multiple-aisle arrangement (Fig. 2) will have a maximum of 14–16 chairs per row with access to an aisleway at both ends. If an aisle can be reached from one end of a row only, the seat count may then be limited to 7 or 8. It should be noted here that the maximum quantities will always be established by the governing building code.

In a continental arrangement (Fig. 3) all seats are located in a central section. Here the maximum quantity of chairs per row can greatly exceed the limits established in a multiple-aisle arrangement. In order to compensate for the greater length of rows allowed, building codes will require wider row spacing, wider aisles and strategically located exit doors.

Although more space would appear to be called for, a continental seating plan is often not any less efficient than a multiple-aisle arrangement. In fact, carefully planned, a continental arrangement can frequently accommodate more seating within the same space. For early planning an average 7.5 sq. ft. per person may be used. This will include both the seating area and space necessary for aisleways.

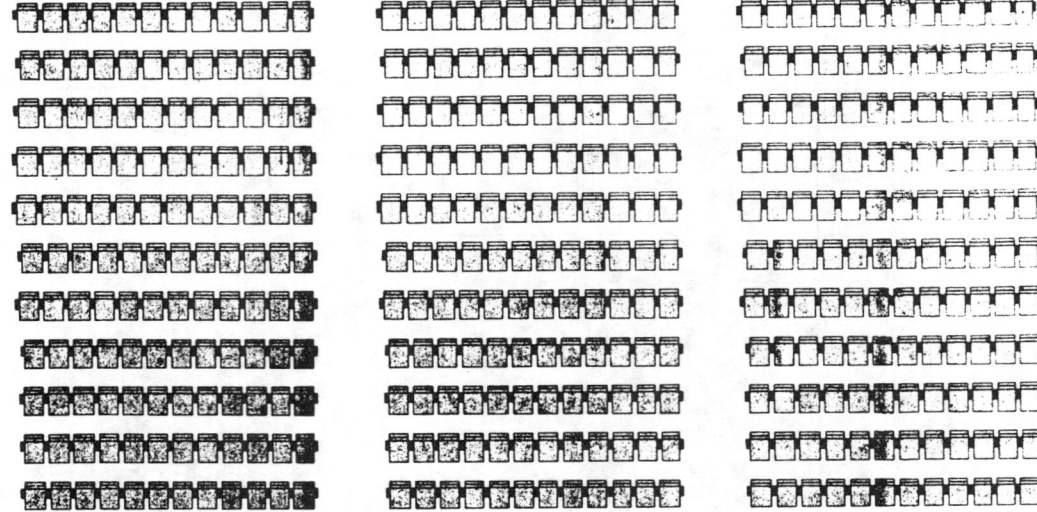

Fig. 2   Multiple-aisle arrangement.

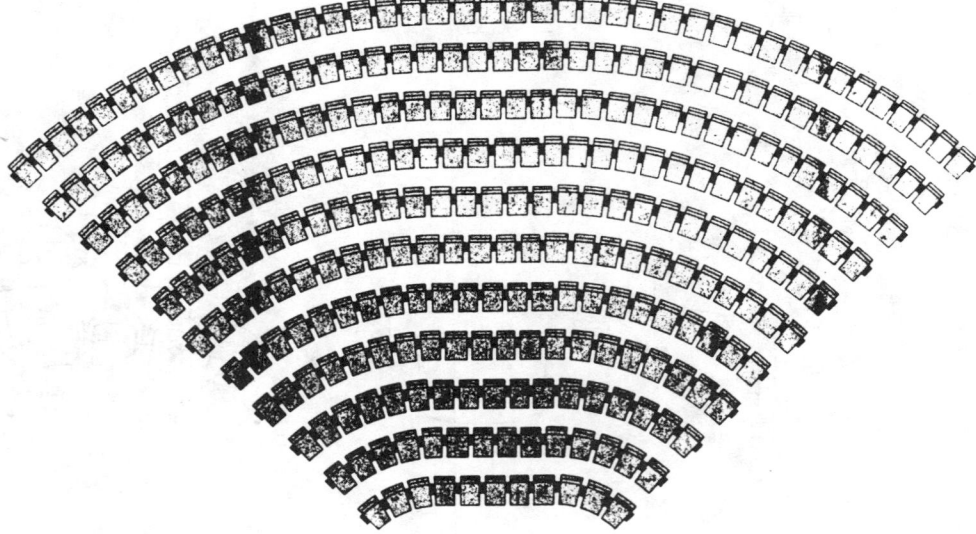

Fig. 3   Continental arrangement.

Design Considerations

1. Layout per applicable building and life safety codes, regulations, and ordinances.

2. Allow sufficient distance between aisles for desired quantity and size of chairs plus end space.

3. Space rows to allow for proper seat to back clear space.

4. Determine radius or straight rows and locate by the chair size line.

5. Allow 1" minimum clearance from either side or rear of chair to any adjacent side wall, end walls, etc.

6. Provide adequate sightlines for either sloping or stepped (riser) floor configurations.

7. Seating area should be free of obstructions.

8. To allow for sufficient aisle illumination: Aisle lights are generally located in the end panel standards at least every other row. Locate aisle light junction box 6" from the standard.

9. Provide adequate floor or riser materials for sound anchorage.

TYPICAL PLAN OF SEATING AND TERMINOLOGY

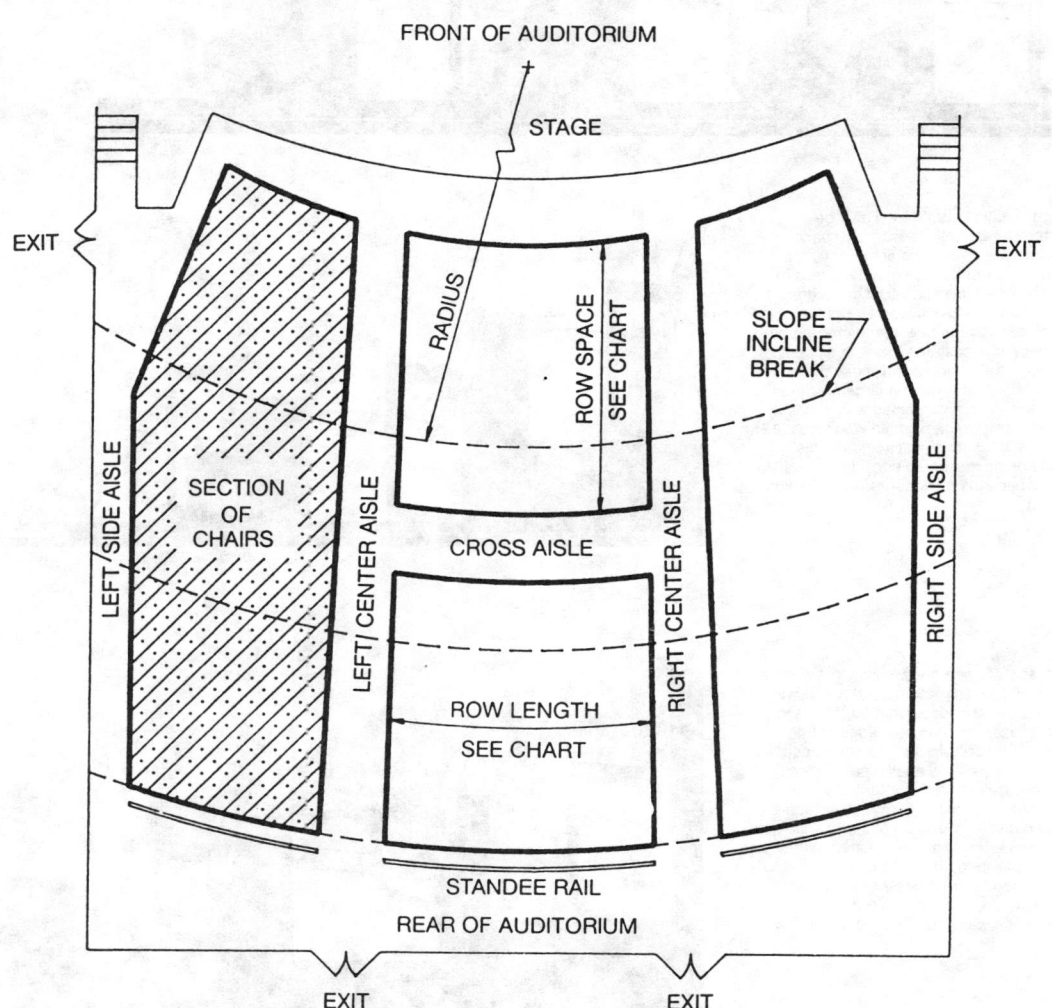

AUDITORIUM SEATING

Row Seating

Seat Widths Seating comfort is initially established by individual chair widths. Available sizes range from 18" to 24", however, all may not be produced by a single manufacturer. The most commonly used chair widths are 20", 21", and 22". It should be noted that these dimensions are nominal, being measured from center to center of the support legs. If seating comfort is a high priority, thought must be given to a particular width and the space taken up by chair arms to determine an actual size. Usually, smaller sizes of 18" and 19" have limited application due to the minimum clear width provided. Typically, all manufacturers size their chairs along an imaginary line which may be referred to as a "datum line", "chair radius line" or a similar name. For accurate planning in an assembly area, this line must be identified so as not to over or underestimate the potential of a row of chairs.

Row Spacing Row spacing or "back to back" spacing of seats is also very important in developing a comfortable assembly area. A minimum dimension occasionally used is 2'-8" (32"). This spacing provides marginal clearance between a seated person's knees and the back of the chair in the next forward row. At the same time, however, it will require that a seated person stand to permit the passage of another individual. As the row spacing is increased to 3'-0" (36"), seating comfort is dramatically improved and passage along a row of seated persons is accomplished with less disruption.

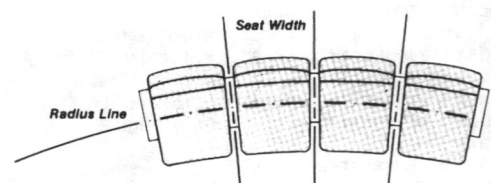

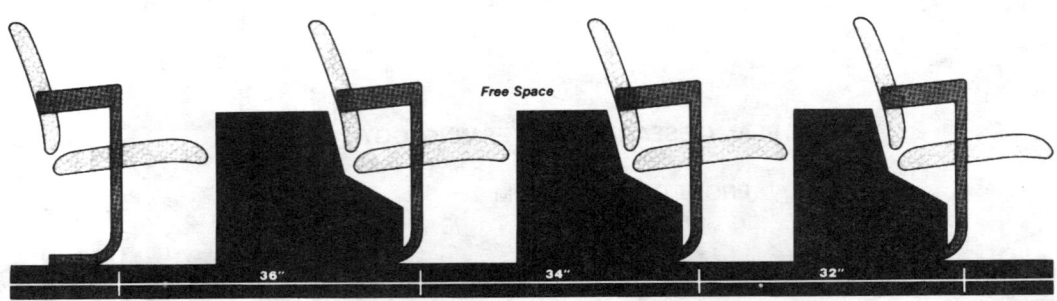

Floor Design Seating comfort will also be affected by the design of the assembly space floor. Flat or less steeply sloped floors will usually allow a person to extend their knees and legs even under minimum row spacing dimensions. Here an individual can take advantage of the open area under a seat and the free space created by the pitched back of a chair. As the floor slope is increased, this "free" space diminishes. The extreme condition exists where a large elevation change between rows is combined with a minimum row spacing. An example would be a 12" high riser and a 32" wide row spacing. At this point, it becomes necessary to consider increasing the back to back dimension to provide more leg room.

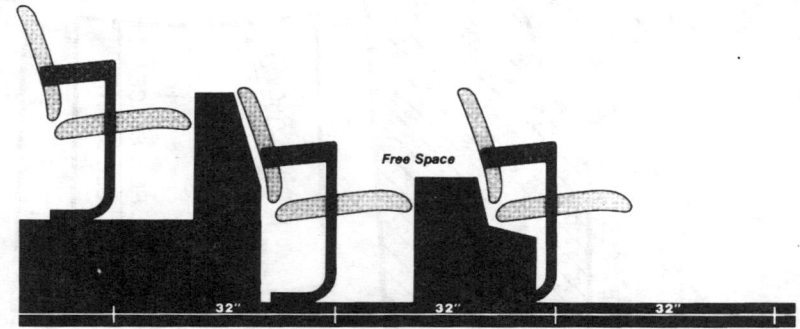

The "free" space under a chair is also lost when a row of seats is located directly behind a low wall. In this case a recommended minimum clearance would be 11" measured from seat edge in the lowered position to face of wall. The back to back dimension of a row of seats abutting a rear wall should also be carefully studied. Normally, the pitched back of a chair will overlap a riser face, automatically reducing the width of that row unless succeeding rows are similarly positioned. Where a rear wall exists the recommended procedure is to increase the dimension of the last row sufficiently to accommodate any overlap plus a minimal space between the wall and top edge of the chair back.

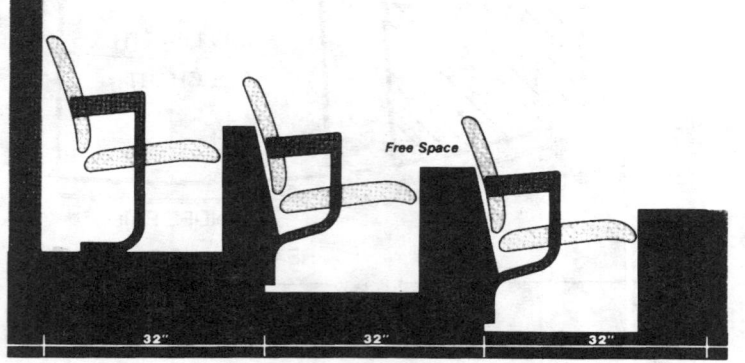

Visibility in an assembly space is a function of seat location. As stated earlier, building codes, comfort guidelines, floor design and the overall form of an assembly space will play a part in seating arrangements. This information combined with a basic understanding of sightline analysis and related planning guidelines can result in achieving an acceptable, if not optimum, level of viewing for spectators.

Perhaps film projection requires the most critical sightline analysis, since poor seat location will result in distorted images. For this activity the seating parameters are established by the screen or image size. An angle of 30° up to 45° measured perpendicular to the far and near edges of the screen can establish a side to side seating limit, while the screen or image height may determine the maximum distance. The minimum dimension or closest recommended seat will also be set by the screen height. (It should be noted that these figures are approximate and apply principally to flat screen projection.)

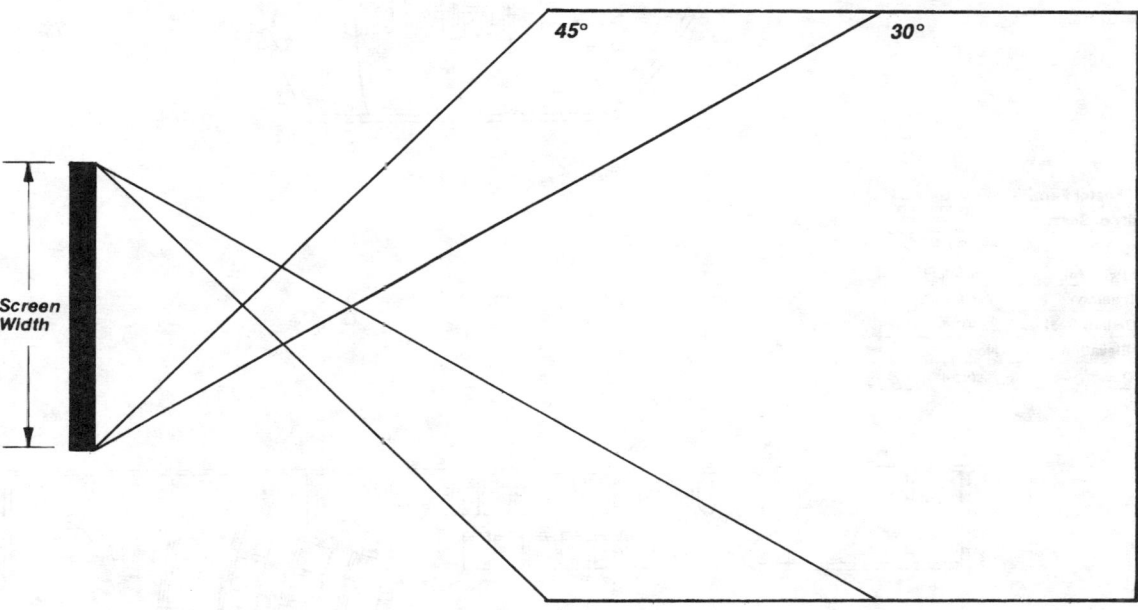

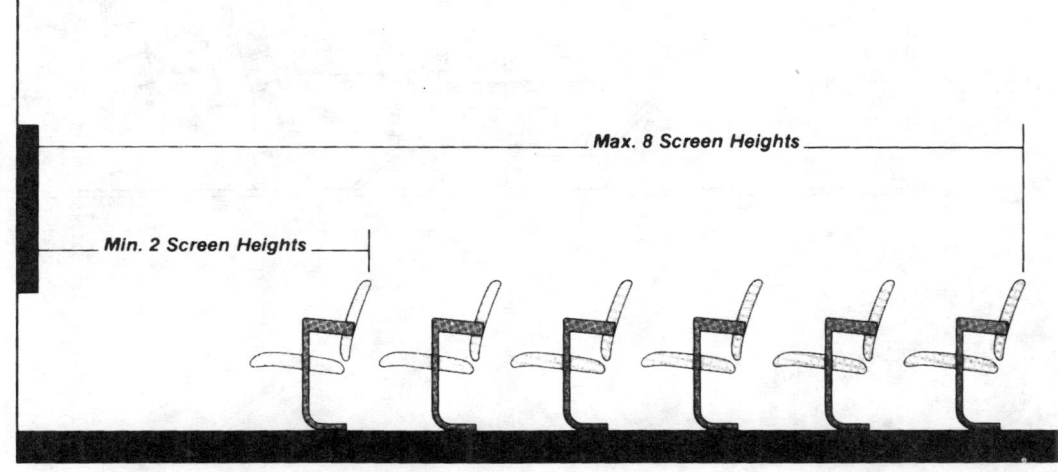

AUDITORIUM SEATING

End Stage; ¾ Arena

Basic Theater Form	End Stage
Quantity of Seats	55
Seating Area	450 Sq. Ft.
Space per Seat	8.23 Sq. Ft.
Row Spacing	2'-9"
Most Distant Seat	22'-0"
Stage Elevation	None
Floor Design	Flat/One Riser 8"

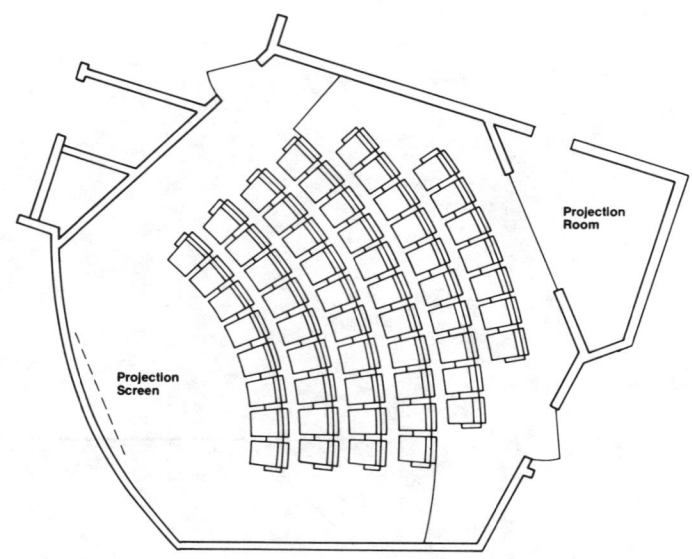

Basic Theater Form	¾ Arena
Quantity of Seats	56
Seating Area	622 Sq. Ft.
Space per Seat	11.1 Sq. Ft.
Row Spacing	3'-3"
Most Distant Seat	32'-0"
Stage Elevation	None
Floor Design	Risers 4"

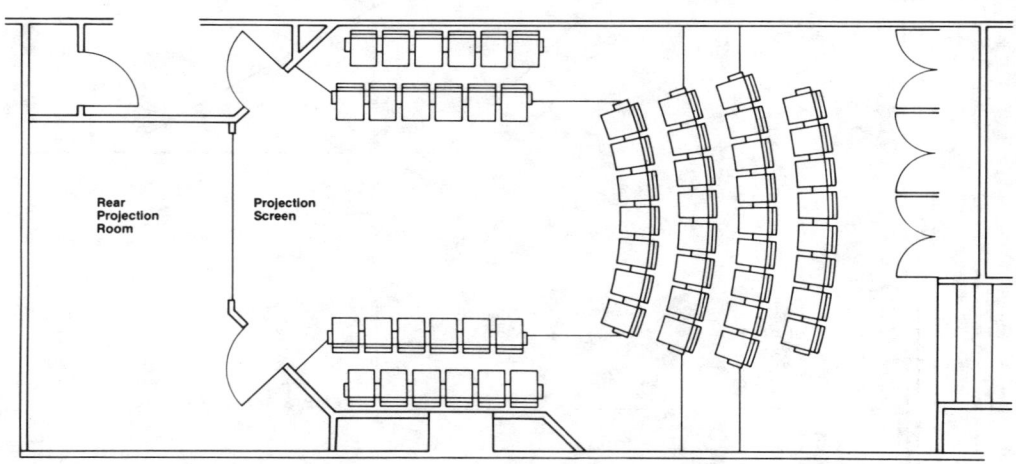

AUDITORIUM SEATING

End Stage

Basic Theater Form	End Stage
Quantity of Seats	80
Seating Area	700 Sq. Ft.
Space per Seat	8.75 Sq. Ft.
Row Spacing	3′-6″
Most Distant Seat	25′-0″
Stage Elevation	3′-6″
Floor Design	Risers 6″

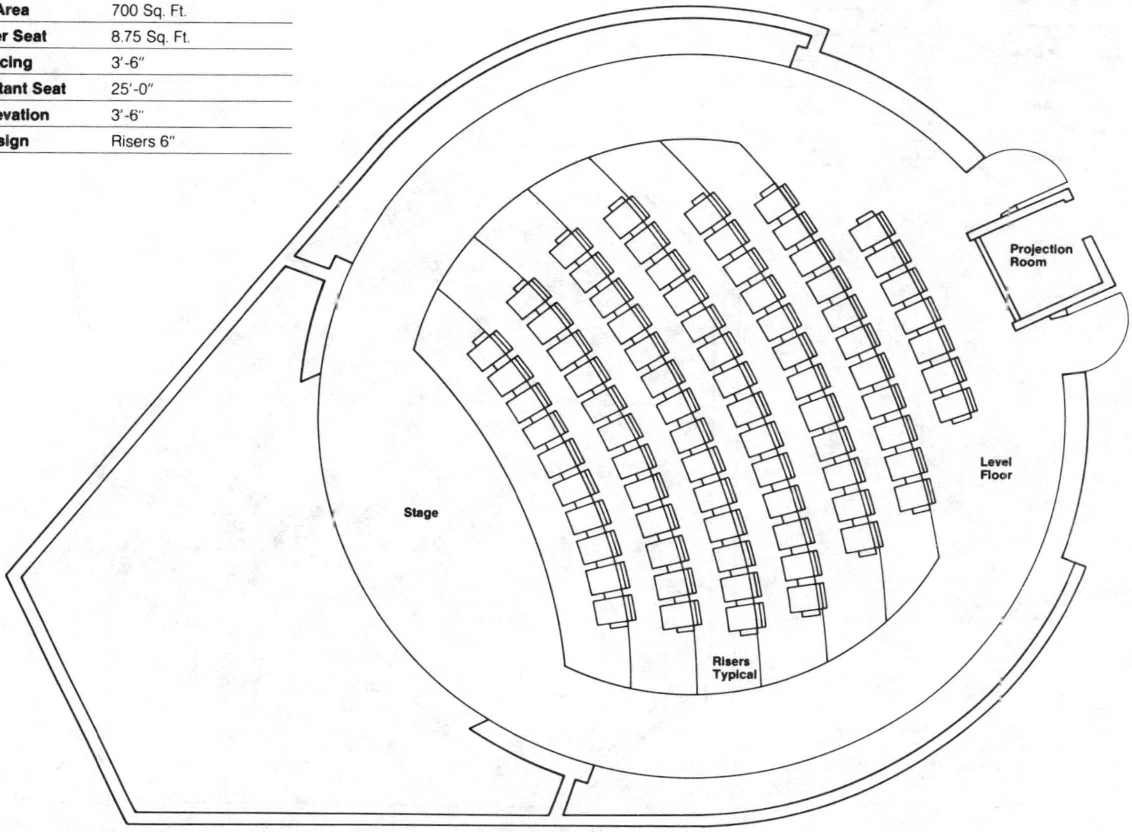

Basic Theater Form	End Stage
Quantity of Seats	92
Seating Area	956 Sq. Ft.
Space per Seat	10.4 Sq. Ft.
Row Spacing	3′-0″
Most Distant Seat	37′-0″
Stage Elevation	12″
Floor Design	Flat

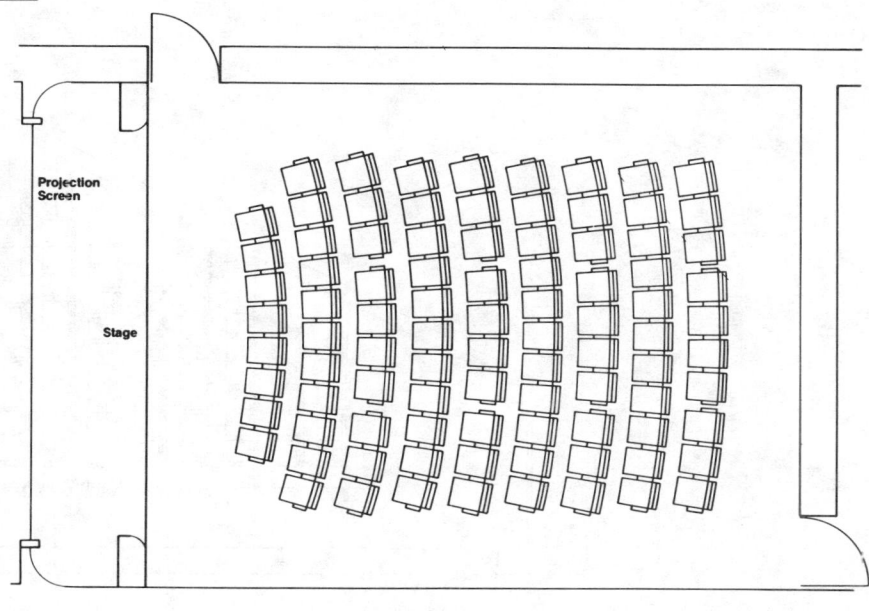

AUDITORIUM SEATING
End Stage

Basic Theater Form	End Stage
Quantity of Seats	99
Seating Area	953 Sq. Ft.
Space per Seat	9.62 Sq. Ft.
Row Spacing	3'-5"
Most Distant Seat	32'-0"
Stage Elevation	12"
Floor Design	Risers 12"

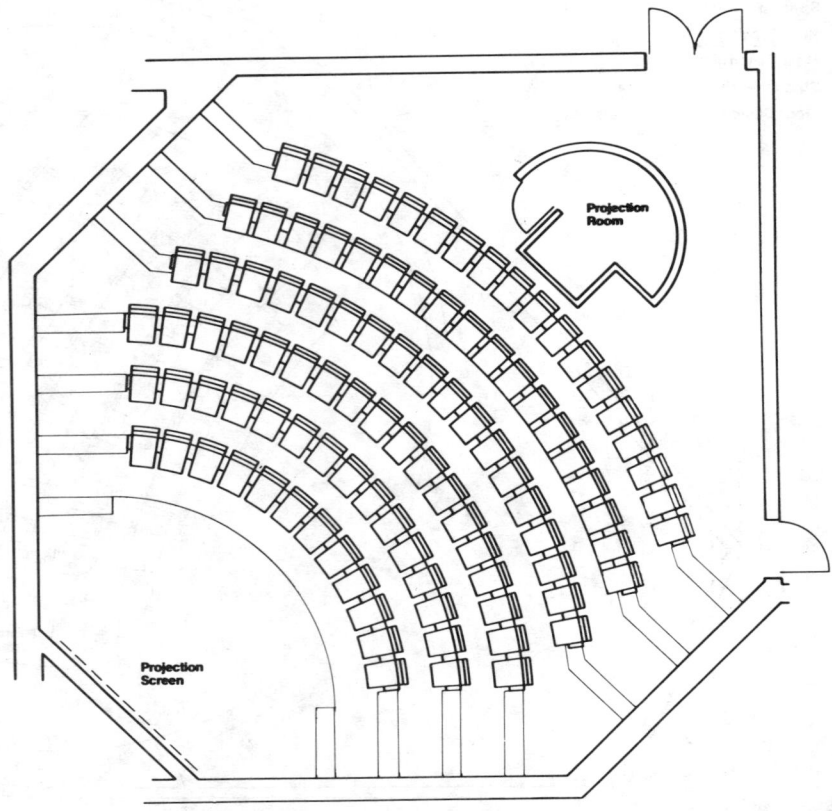

Basic Theater Form	End Stage
Quantity of Seats	105
Seating Area	903 Sq. Ft.
Space per Seat	8.6 Sq. Ft.
Row Spacing	3'-0"
Most Distant Seat	35'-0"
Stage Elevation	5"
Floor Design	Risers 12"

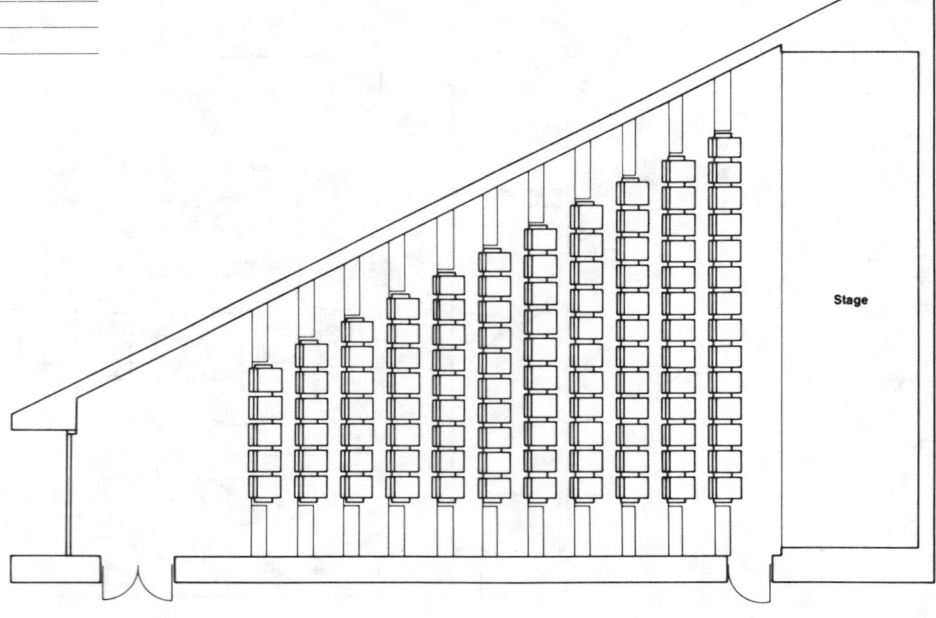

AUDITORIUM SEATING

¾ Arena; End Stage

Basic Theater Form	¾ Arena
Quantity of Seats	108
Seating Area	1200 Sq. Ft.
Space per Seat	11.1 Sq. Ft.
Row Spacing	3′-0″
Most Distant Seat	45′-0″
Stage Elevation	Varies
Floor Design	Risers 12″

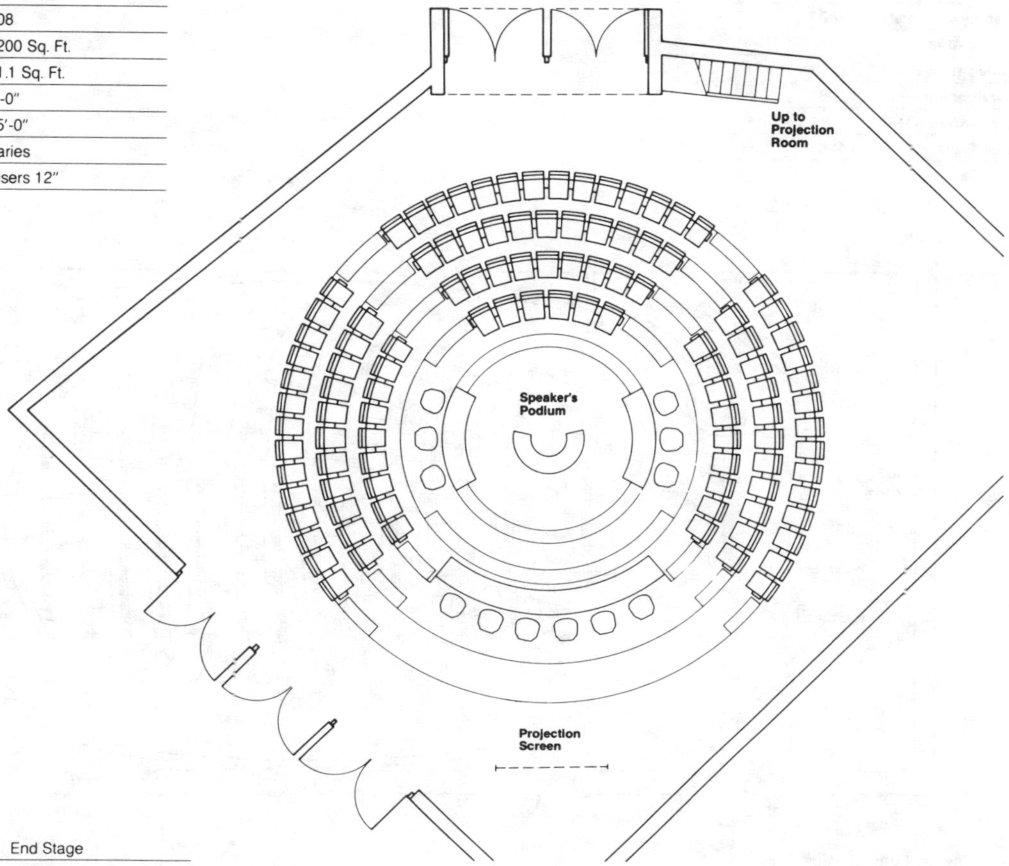

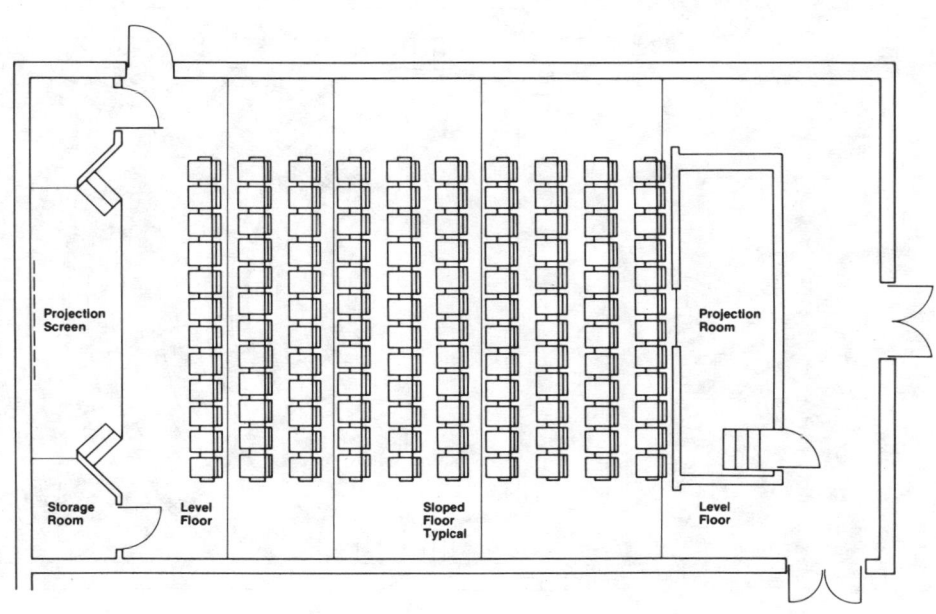

Up to Projection Room
Speaker's Podium
Projection Screen

Basic Theater Form	End Stage
Quantity of Seats	120
Seating Area	1088 Sq. Ft.
Space per Seat	9.1 Sq. Ft.
Row Spacing	3′-3″
Most Distant Seat	41′-0″
Stage Elevation	1′-6″
Floor Design	Iscidomal Slope 2.4°, 4.7°, 7.1°

Projection Screen
Projection Room
Storage Room
Level Floor
Sloped Floor Typical
Level Floor

AUDITORIUM SEATING
End Stage; Wide Fan

Basic Theater Form	End Stage
Quantity of Seats	180
Seating Area	1218 Sq. Ft.
Space per Seat	6.8 Sq. Ft.
Row Spacing	2'-8"
Most Distant Seat	50'-0"
Stage Elevation	1'-6"
Floor Design	Iscidomal Slope
	-1° to 10°

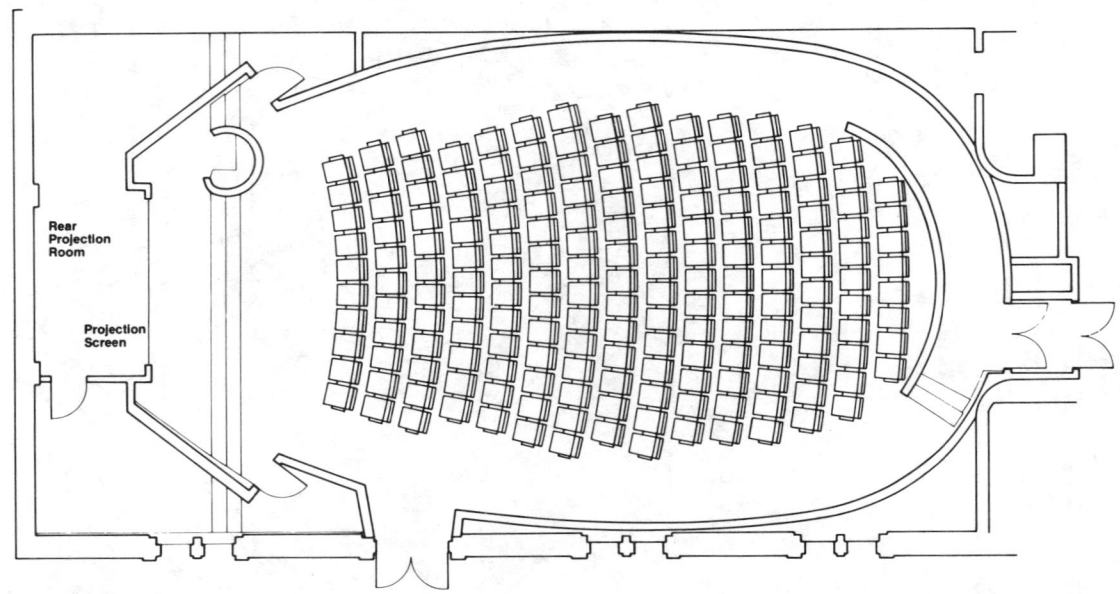

Basic Theater Form	Wide Fan
Quantity of Seats	253
Seating Area	1790 Sq. Ft.
Space per Seat	7.1 Sq. Ft.
Row Spacing	3'-0"
Most Distant Seat	48'-0"
Stage Elevation	None
Floor Design	Risers—Varying
	Height 10½" to 16"

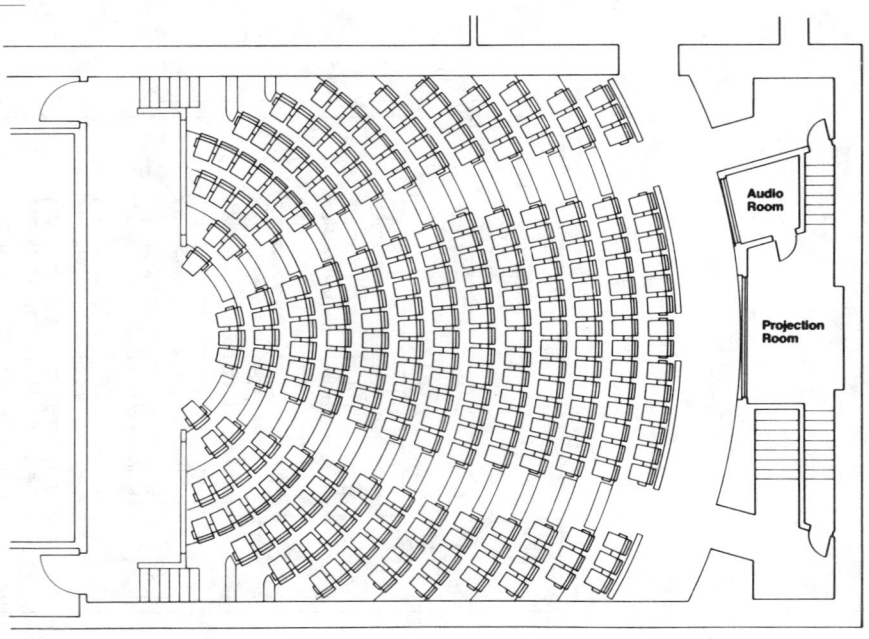

Basic Theater Form	End Stage
Quantity of Seats	430
Seating Area	2586 Sq. Ft.
Space per Seat	6.0 Sq. Ft.
Row Spacing	2'-8¾"
Most Distant Seat	58'-0"
Stage Elevation	2'-6"
Floor Design	Sloped 7.1°

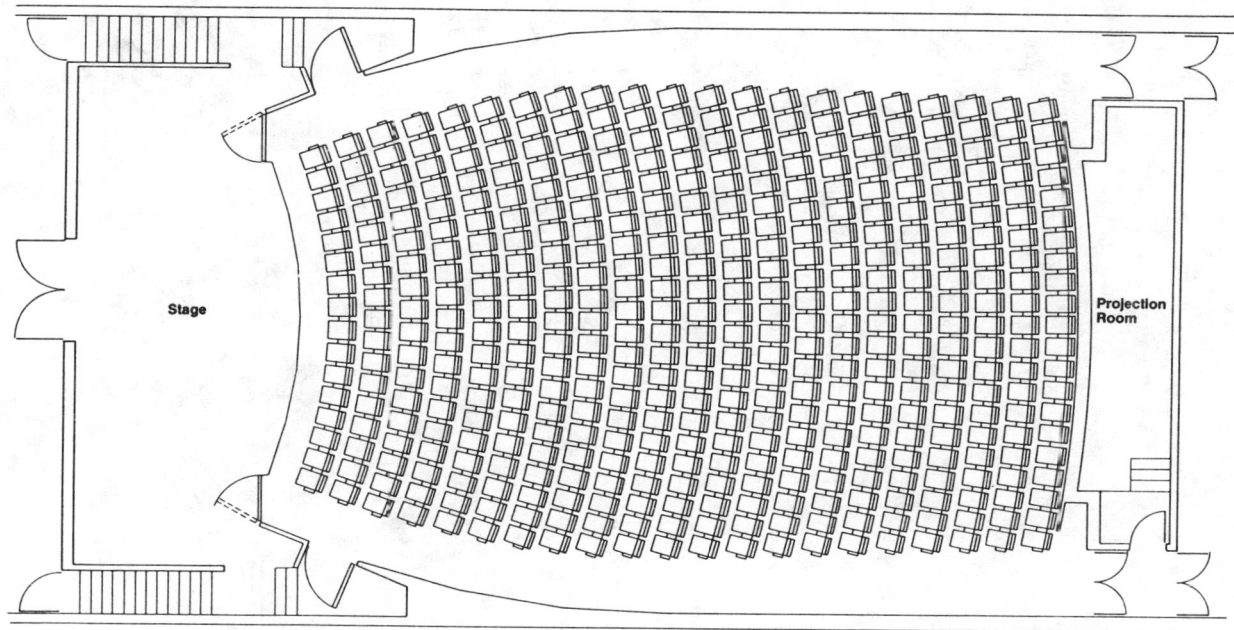

Basic Theater Form	End Stage
Quantity of Seats	224
Seating Area	1660 Sq. Ft.
Space per Seat	7.4 Sq. Ft.
Row Spacing	2'-9"
Most Distant Seat	60'-0"
Stage Elevation	None
Floor Design	Sloped 7.1°/Risers 13¾"

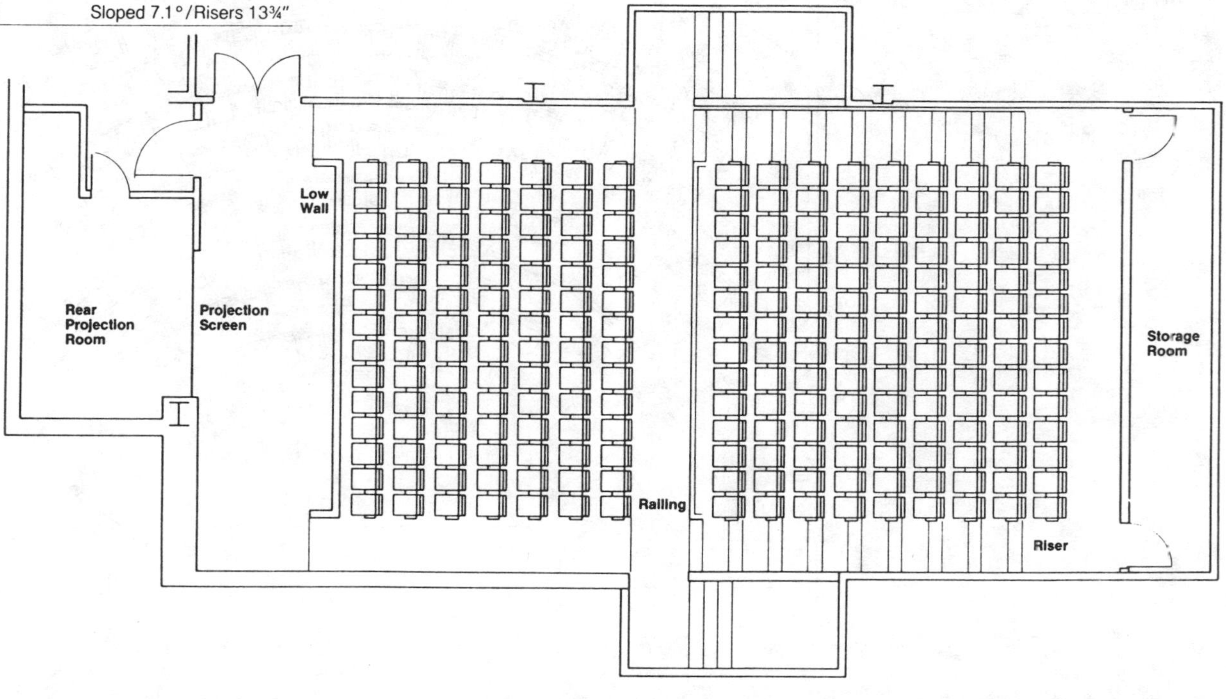

AUDITORIUM SEATING
Wide Fan

Basic Theater Form	Wide Fan
Quantity of Seats	208
Seating Area	1557 Sq. Ft.
Space per Seat	7.5 Sq. Ft.
Row Spacing	2'-8"
Most Distant Seat	48'-0"
Stage Elevation	5"
Floor Design	Risers 14"

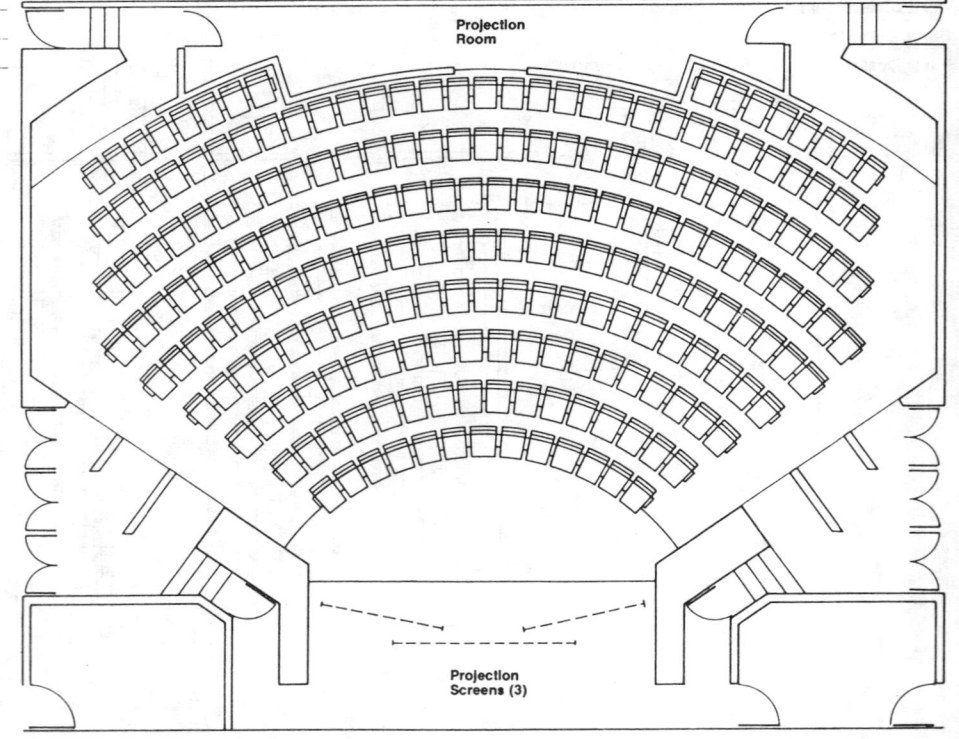

Basic Theater Form	Wide Fan
Quantity of Seats	207
Seating Area	1428 Sq. Ft.
Space per Seat	6.9 Sq. Ft.
Row Spacing	3'-4"
Most Distant Seat	40'-0"
Stage Elevation	2'-3"
Floor Design	Sloped 6.6°

CONTROL OF GROUNDS

Fencing can be a very effective means of limiting access to secondary exits and to vulnerable ground-level dwellings. Fencing functions as a control by requiring entry through a single, limited, highly visible area. The fencing surrounding most single-family homes does not have locked gates. It is intended primarily to protect children, pets, and gardens, and to define the area immediately around the home as the private outdoor space of that household. Any intrusion into the area within the fence is therefore noticeable. As a security measure, such fencing, used symbolically, is of minimal value against premeditated crime, but it does make criminal intent visible and so is an important deterrent.

A conventional use of fencing in multifamily complexes is to limit access to backyards and windows of a housing cluster. On conventional city blocks, backyards of row housing are accessible only through one of the houses. However, in many superblock designs, such backyards are left open to public access. In this situation, addition of a limited amount of fencing can protect a large group of homes (see Fig. 1). This approach can also subdivide the superblock and so create small, natural clusters.

The Lobby

Improving visibility is the most important ingredient in providing a naturally secure lobby. It is crucial that a tenant entering a building be able to see what is going on in the lobby from the outside. Hidden nooks and blind curves provide perfect hiding places. Where such features cannot be removed structurally, the use of mirrors, windows, and improved lighting may ease the situation.

Ideally, a person walking down a path to enter a building should be able to see anyone standing in the lobby and elevator waiting area. In fact, it is often advantageous if the arriving person can see into the elevator from across the lobby.

CONTROL OF INTERIOR PUBLIC SPACES OF MULTIFAMILY DWELLINGS

The most vulnerable locations in multifamily buildings are the interior public spaces: lobbies, elevators, stairwells, and corridors. These are areas open to the public but without the attending surveillance given a public street by passersby and police. The crimes that occur in these interior public spaces are the most fearful types of crimes, involving acts of personal confrontation such as robbery, assault, and rape. Limiting access to these spaces through the use of a doorman or intercom/door lock system can be of substantial benefit.

Lobby visibility discourages a number of different kinds of crime. Crimes of personal confrontation may be deterred primarily because the potential victim can readily perceive and avoid a suspicious person in the lobby. The potential criminal must also fear the possibility that another tenant or the police may be viewing the crime in the well-lit open area.

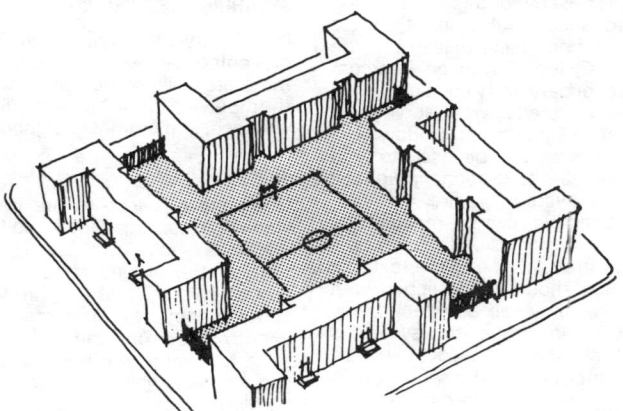

Fig. 1 Use of fencing to define and secure large semiprivate areas.

Mailbox crime — generally the theft of checks — can be deterred when mailboxes are located in a highly protected area of the lobby. This protection can consist of placing the mailboxes behind an intercom or in a locked mailroom. It is essential that the mailboxes be visible from as many different viewpoints as possible. Improved visibility in this context can be a significant deterrent to crime.

Some managers designate an area of the lobby as a legitimate resting place, where chairs and other lounging items are provided. Lounging may aid security, particularly if the building includes a high proportion of elderly. The best locations for such seating are areas with high visibility. Often tenant patrols use this space as a station and provide still another dimension of security.

A bulletin board is an inexpensive device that can improve lobby security by providing a diversion. If, for example, a tenant enters the lobby and sees someone she doesn't recognize waiting for an elevator, she may need a reasonable excuse for not taking the same elevator. The bulletin board provides the tenant with a natural excuse to pause and survey the situation.

The area around the main entry to a multifamily building should be clearly distinguished from the public walkway which leads to it. A person entering through the main door should feel distinctly that he is entering a space controlled by the residents of the building. The main entry should be well lit and clearly visible from outside.

Entry doors should be constructed of a transparent material covering as large an area as possible. In vandalism-prone areas, the main entry doors should be made of unbreakable glass or other similar, very sturdy transparent material. Because of the need for good visibility, replacing glass panels with metal or other material should be avoided. For window walls and doors where the incidence of vandalism is extreme, glass panels less than 2 feet from the ground and higher than 7 feet from the ground may be replaced by solid materials.

Fire Doors and Fire Stairs

Secondary exit doors are the weakest link in security of buildings. An ideal secondary exit door would be one that allows exit but not entrance. Unfortunately, there is no acceptable emergency exit system that allows egress only.

In the design of any security system there is a continuing clash between the need for security against crime and the need for safety in case of fire. Fire doors are frequently used for entry and exit by criminals. Installation of panic hardware and the absence of exterior hardware sometimes prevent criminal use. These measures will not suffice, however, where tenants do not cooperate in avoiding use of secondary exits and ensuring they are kept closed.

To a large extent, the design and location of secondary fire exits determine tenant attitudes about the exits. For example, a building's main entry may face the street, but the parking lot may be to the rear of the building. If the secondary exit is also at the rear and close to this destination, the temptation to use the fire door as an entry or exit will be difficult to resist. Similarly, security is decreased in buildings where the main entries face the interior of the project while the fire doors face the surrounding streets with their parking and shopping facilities. Where the fire exit does not represent any shortcut or improved convenience to the tenant, it is far more likely to remain closed. A securely designed building is one in which the fire door exits to an area that is less convenient or desirable than the area outside the main door.

In cases of persistent breaks in security of secondary exits, it is possible to modify the building plan at the ground level and open a new doorway in a better location. However, this improvement is costly and can only be done where architecturally possible.

Another architectural modification to improve security involves making a fire exit into a legitimate secondary entry and developing a security system that protects both the main and secondary entries. If a fire door exits to a parking area, for example, this modification may be more successful than efforts to prevent tenants from using that exit. If the main entry is equipped with an intercom system, the secondary entry should be similarly equipped and made easily surveillable through the use of lighting and windows.

Other mechanisms can be used to limit access to and prevent circulation through the emergency exit system. A fire exit passageway, for example, can be modified by installing a second door inside the building a short distance from the existing exterior door. Both doors should be equipped with hardware so that they can be opened only from the inside. The point of this system is that it is unlikely that both doors will be propped or jammed open at the same time. A tenant entering an open exterior fire door which leads only to the locked second door will have to exit and use another door. A few experiences of this kind will convince most tenants that it is probably more convenient to go directly through the main entrance. This double-door system generally does not conflict with fire codes.

An extension of this concept is to have the fire door on each floor above ground level openable from the corridor only. Thus, once someone has gone into a stairwell he can only exit at the ground level. This system may be somewhat inconvenient to tenants accustomed to moving easily between floors, but it does create roadblocks for anyone attempting to enter the building from the ground-level exit door.

The improvements outlined above are generally applicable to all dwellings. In buildings which have such security personnel, additional measures are possible.

A doorman or security guard can only be effective if he controls all access to the building, including access through fire doors. In a well-designed building, the doorman can see the fire doors from his position at the main entry. Where this is not possible, an inexpensive and effective solution is to install panic hardware with an alarm, and make sure the doorman can hear and respond to the alarm. Where the doorman or guard has access to closed-circuit TV, this may be used to monitor the fire doors. If the doorman can also be given a device for controlling the secondary door, it becomes very difficult for a criminal to use the fire entry.

Elevators

There are virtually no structural modifications that can improve security within elevators. The only possible improvements are use of mirrors, communication devices, emergency buttons, or an electronic surveillance system.

Security modifications to other areas of a building improve security within the elevator. If the elevator waiting area and the elevator cab are a visible extension of the lobby, the residents are afforded some protection. Similarly, if the fire door and fire stairs are secure, there is less chance of a criminal entering the elevator on an upper floor. In this sense, the safety of the elevator is dependent upon the general security of the building.

SECURING THE DWELLING

Illegal entry into dwelling units is traditionally prevented by use of hardware. However, there are building design features which in themselves limit access, improve surveillance, and promote neighbor recognition.

Windows

Ground-level windows are generally most vulnerable to illegal entry and breakage. (All windows whose lower ledges are less than 7 feet off the ground should be considered ground level.) There are three ways to discourage criminal entry through ground-floor windows: design ground-floor areas which need few windows; house activities on the ground floor which hold no interest to the burglar; and assign the grounds immediately adjacent to the building for the use of the neighboring resident and fence off the grounds for his protection.

Elaborate architectural details — protruding ledges, for example — often increase the vulnerability of lower windows. Fences, garbage containers, and parked cars, when located near windows, are used as stepping stones to an otherwise inaccessible window. Care should be taken to prevent this type of situation.

Most windows above the ground floor are relatively inaccessible, with very important exceptions. Fire escapes make windows accessible. Little can be done to modify fire escapes, except in terms of hardware, because of fire safety and fire codes. One solution is to ensure that the ladder from the lowest fire escape is at least 12 feet above the ground. The ground area under the fire escape should be highly visible.

Another point of entry to the fire escape is the roof, which can be secured with panic hardware and possibly patrolled. The roof also provides possible entry to windows or balconies on the top floor. Therefore, security of the roof is quite essential, particularly to top-floor residents. Other accessible windows are those located diagonally across from a stairwell window. The criminal can open a stairwell window and cross from the stairwell into the units. It is not advisable to board up stairwell windows, as they provide the security of visibility to the stairwell and may have a fire safety function.

Accessible windows are also those located above or near door canopies. Criminals can reach the canopy by climbing onto it from the ground or from a stair or hall window.

Doors

Security of doors, beyond the hardware aspect, depends upon surveillance and neighbor recognition. An experienced burglar needs just a few seconds to enter a locked apartment door equipped with minimal hardware. Within this interval, the crucial factors are: Will the intruder be seen or heard by tenants, will the viewer perceive that the potential criminal is in fact an intruder, and will the viewer respond by calling authorities or in some way challenge the criminal?

Physical design can directly influence the opportunity for surveillance of doors. Corridors that are open to view, either single loaded or with windows, are more easily surveillable by residents and police. Thus the opportunity for the criminal to attempt entry undetected is reduced.

In most single-family homes (detached or row) where the entrance door is on the street, the only means of improving surveillance is to avoid placing trees and shrubs where they hide the doors and windows, and to locate lighting to improve visibility around these openings.

In multiple-family dwellings, the apartment doors, located on interior corridors, are generally difficult to keep under surveillance. Any windows, mirrors, or lighting that allow someone inside an apartment or outside the building to view the hallway and doors can be helpful.

HARDWARE

This section describes hardware devices that secure the individual residential dwelling and the multifamily dwelling. Much of this material is intended to prevent burglary. However, some of the measures, particularly those directed at multifamily dwellings, will also deter forcible entry, robbery, and vandalism.

THE RESIDENTIAL DWELLING

Door Materials

The major security tests of door material are its ability to withstand efforts to force entry by brute strength and its ability to retain securely the locking devices attached. Materials most commonly used for doors are wood, aluminum, steel, and glass, often in combination with hardboard, fiberboard, asbestos, and plastic. The two most common door designs are panel and flush. Panel doors consist of vertical and horizontal members framing rectangular areas in which opaque panels, panes of glass, or louvers are located. Flush doors consist of flat panels running the full height and width of the door. (See Fig. 2.)

Solid-steel flush doors, although most secure, are rarely used except in very high-security areas such as banks and prisons. Steel-clad doors, which are flush doors constructed of 24-gauge sheetmetal facing bonded to a nonresinous, kiln-dried wood interior, provide an optimum weight-strength situation for ordinary residential use. Hollow steel doors (1¾-inch flush type) are satisfactory in multiple-dwelling buildings. Aluminum doors can provide sufficient protection but may be comparatively expensive.

While less strong than steel-clad doors, wood doors can be secure. All exterior wooden doors should be of solid-core construction with a minimum thickness of 1¾ inches. Although flush doors provide better security, if panel doors are desired for aesthetic reasons, the panels should have a minimum ½-inch thickness (see Fig. 3). Both hollow-core wood doors and thin-wood panel doors are unacceptable where security is a factor.

Door Frames

The sides and top of a doorway are provided with a door frame which holds the door in position. The side members of the door frame are called jambs; the top member is called the head (see Fig. 4). The strike is the portion of the jamb which is cut out or drilled out to allow installation of a metal plate, which accepts the latch or bolt from the door lock (see Fig. 5).

Wooden frames provide an unacceptable level of security unless they are at least 2 inches thick. Metal-covered wood frames provide an optimum cost-security investment when used in combination with metal-covered wood doors. If a hollow steel frame is used, the residual air space behind the frame should be filled with a crush-resistant material such as cement grout, especially in the area of the strike (see Fig. 6). This will prevent an intruder from wedging a crowbar between the door and frame and crushing the frame to free the lock.

For doors swinging in, rabbeted jambs should be used. These are jambs containing a metal extension that protrudes beyond the edges of the closed door, thus preventing tampering in the area of the strike (see Fig. 7).

For doors without rabbeted jambs, an L-shaped piece of angle-iron at least 2 feet long, mounted in the area of the strike, gives extra protection (see Fig. 8). The iron acts as a lip which protects the strike from attack.

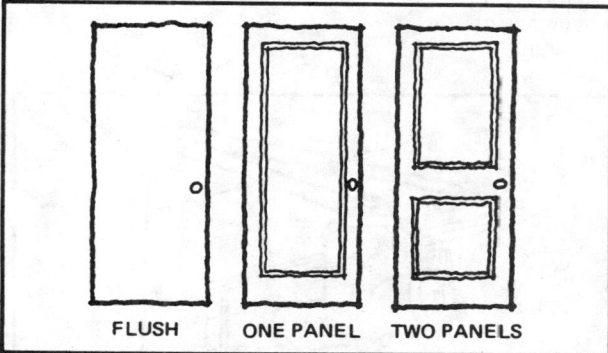

FLUSH   ONE PANEL   TWO PANELS

Fig. 2   Door types.

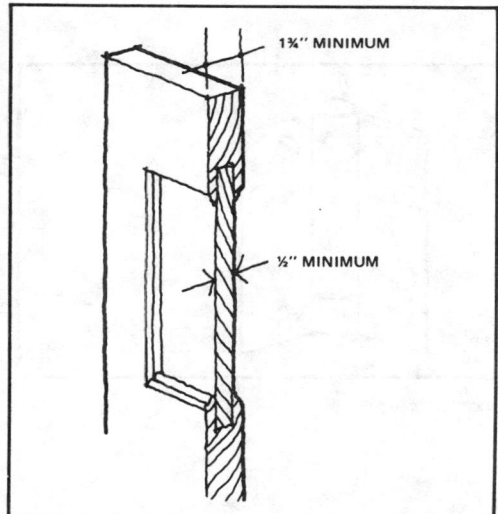

1¾" MINIMUM

½" MINIMUM

Fig. 3   Panel door.

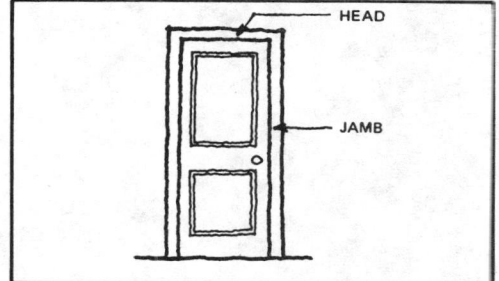

HEAD

JAMB

Fig. 4   Door frame.

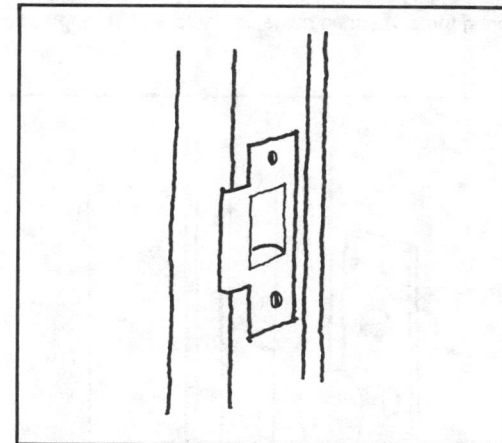

Fig. 5   Door strike.

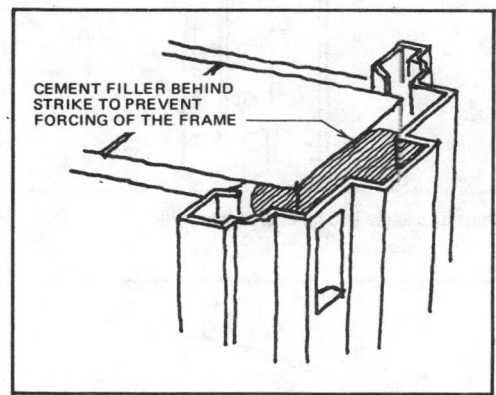

CEMENT FILLER BEHIND STRIKE TO PREVENT FORCING OF THE FRAME

Fig. 6   Hollow metal door frame.

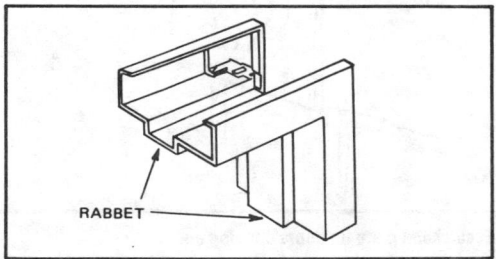

RABBET

Fig. 7   Rabbeted jamb.

For doors opening out, a flat metal plate, called an escutcheon plate, can be mounted to the face of the door in the area of the lock. This plate, which extends beyond the edge of the door and fits flush with the jamb when the door is closed, will protect the lock from attack in the area of the strike (see Fig. 9).

All plates located on the outsides of doors should be attached with tamper-resistant connectors such as round-headed carriage bolts or one-way screws.

Door Hinges and Closers

Spring hinges close the door automatically by using spring force. A spring hinge prevents a criminal from slipping in behind a resident who has neglected to close the door immediately upon entering. Also, spring hinges prevent the resident from leaving the door open when he exits. Door closers (see Fig. 10) serve the same purpose. These are for more heavy duty and are commonly used in lobbies and commercial facilities.

Hinges should be mounted on the inside of the door so that burglars cannot remove the door from the hinges to enter. If hinges must be placed on the outside, they should have nonremovable pins. Pins can be made nonremovable by peening the straight end or by drilling and tapping a machine screw into the middle portion of each pin from the inside of the open hinge (see Fig. 11). Doors with outside hinge pins can also be protected by screwing two screws halfway into the jamb edge of the door. One screw is placed near each hinge, and a receiving hole is drilled into the jamb for each screw. These protruding screws hold the door when it is closed, even if the hinge pins are removed.

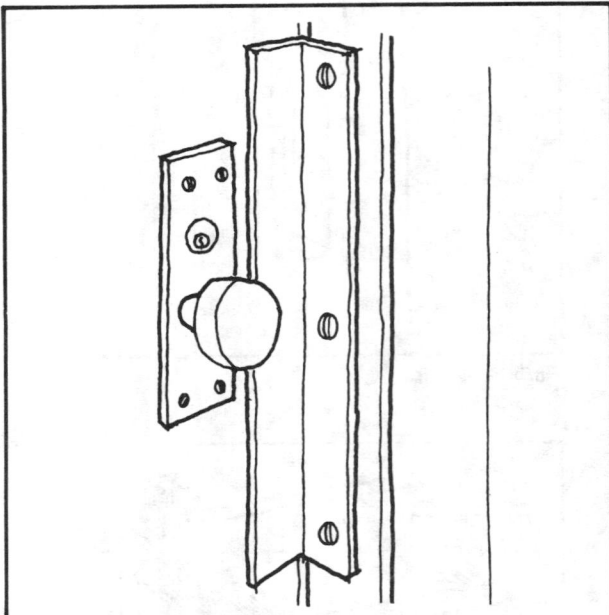

Fig. 8 Protective angle-iron for doors opening in.

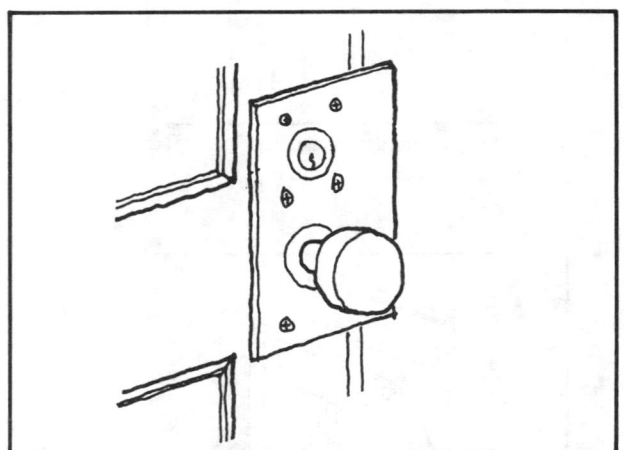

Fig. 9 Escutcheon plate for doors opening out.

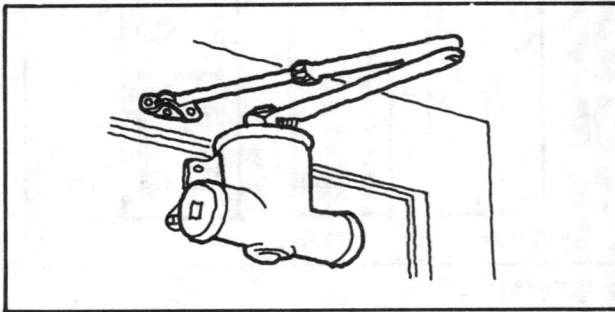

Fig. 10 Door closer.

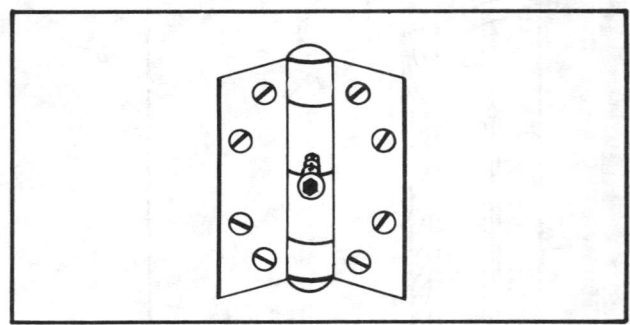

Fig. 11 Nonremovable hinge pin.

Door Locks

Locks must withstand or seriously delay not only a simple forced entry but also sophisticated criminal attack. Locks may also guard against window entry-door exit crimes.

Parts of the a lock are defined as follows:

Cylinder: A cylinder is that part of the lock into which the key is inserted. If the proper key is used, the cylinder will allow the key to turn, thus moving a bolt or latch.

Deadbolt: A deadbolt (or bolt lock) is a heavy metal bar which moves horizontally into the strike of the door jamb, thus locking the two together. It is called a deadbolt because it cannot be pushed back unless the knob is turned by the correct key.

Latch: A latch (or spring lock) is the part of the lock that keeps the door in a closed position by extending into the strike automatically when the door is closed. The latch is most often operated by the doorknob. Most latches can be pushed back by external pressure without having to turn the doorknob.

Deadlatch: In a deadlatch, the latch is positively held in the projected position by an automatic mechanism which is depressed against the strike plate (see Fig. 12).

Strike: The strike is the portion of the jamb where a metal plate has been placed to receive the deadbolt and/or the latch (see Fig. 5).

Stopworks: Stopworks consist of two buttons located under the latch. Pressing the top button in allows the doorknob to turn freely and operate the latch, from both inside and out. Pressing the lower button in allows the inside doorknob to operate the latch, but "freezes" the outside doorknob.

Throw: The throw of a lock is the length (in inches) that the deadbolt extends beyond the face of the lock.

Primary locks

Primary locks operate in conjunction with the latch. There are two major types: mortise locks and cylindrical or bore-in tubular locks (commonly called key-in-the-knob locks).

Mortise locks (see Fig. 13) are more common than key-in-the-knob locks and will provide good security. All mortise locks with latches should contain a deadbolt with at least a 1-inch throw constructed of case-hardened steel, brass or zinc alloy, or bronze. Federal FF-H 106a heavy-duty series 86 mortise locks or 185 latch and 190K modified deadbolts are recommended. The deadbolt and latch should be key-operated from the exterior and operated from the inside by a device not requiring a key.

Mortise locks with latches used in residences should not contain an automatic spring latch with stopworks. Although stopworks prevent the outside knob from being turned, they leave the premises open to easy entry because they do not prevent the latch from being pushed back. An intruder need only insert a credit card into the strike area, push back the spring latch, and open the door (called "loiding" or "shimming" the lock). In locks without stopworks, the deadbolt (which cannot be loided) must be thrown by the key of the resident. Eliminating the stopworks prevents the resident from relying on the stopwork and latch mechanism alone.

Key-in-the-knob locks (see Fig. 14) are less secure than mortise locks. Although inex-

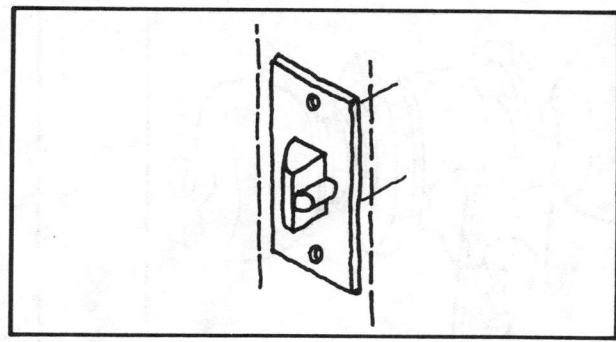

Fig. 12   Deadlatch.

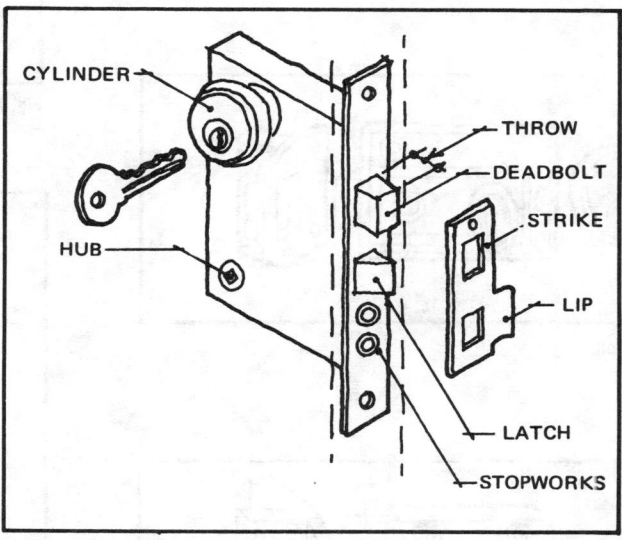

Fig. 13   Mortise lock.

pensive due to easy installation, key-in-the-knob locks can be easily gripped by a tool and twisted until they break. A key-in-the-knob lock can include a deadbolt, at a comparable to slightly higher price than a mortise lock.

Secondary locks

A secondary lock (rim lock) operates independently of the latch. "Secondary" is perhaps a poor name, since this type of lock is essential for good security. Secondary locks are usually mounted above the primary lock at shoulder level. They are operated by a key from the outside, and by a turnbolt from the inside. Both mortise and secondary locks may require keys to open them from inside and outside — useful where access to premises may be gained through a small opening other than the door (window transom), since this will prevent the thief from using the door to remove large objects or to escape.

There are three major types of secondary locks: spring bolt, horizontal deadbolt, and vertical deadbolt. The spring bolt lock operates much the same as the primary door latch. Because the bolt must be spring loaded and bevelled to allow automatic latching, the bolt can be easily opened. A button (slide stop) may be set to deadlock the bolt. However, the button must be set from the

inside and can only be used when another means of egress is available. The spring bolt is not recommended as a secondary lock (see Fig. 15).

Horizontal bolt rim locks operate much the same as deadbolts on primary locks. While horizontal deadbolts afford much better protection than spring bolts, they still can be easily overcome. By inserting a crowbar between the door and the jamb, the intruder can pry them apart to release the bolt from the strike. For this reason, the longer the throw of the deadbolt, the greater protection it affords. However, throws of over 1½ inches may have excessive cantilever. The recommended minimum throw is 1 inch (see Fig. 16).

Vertical bolt deadlocks should be used as secondary locks wherever possible. These utilize two deadbolts that fit vertically into eyeholes or sockets attached to the jamb. This creates a firm bond between the door and the jamb. The vertical bolt deadlock made by Segal is highly recommended, both for its pressed-steel construction and for its ability to hold up under heavy use (see Fig. 17). For additional security, a pick-resistant cylinder should be installed in a good vertical deadbolt body. This combination provides excellent security.

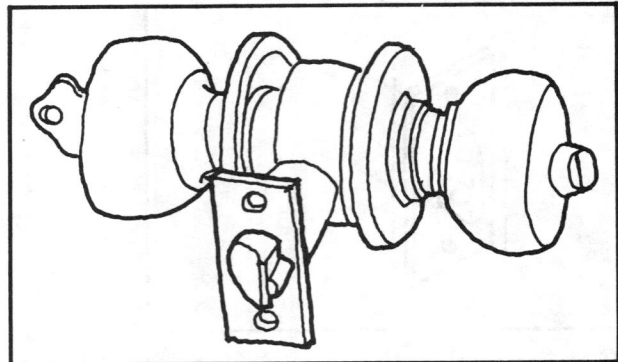

Fig. 14. Key-in-knob lock.

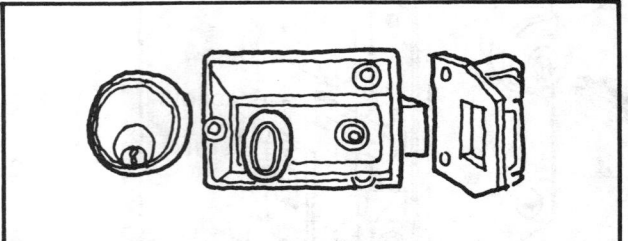

Fig. 15 Spring bolt.

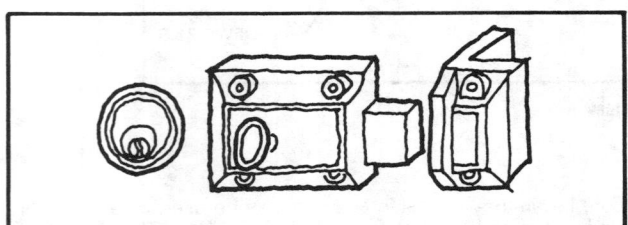

Fig. 16 Horizontal bolt.

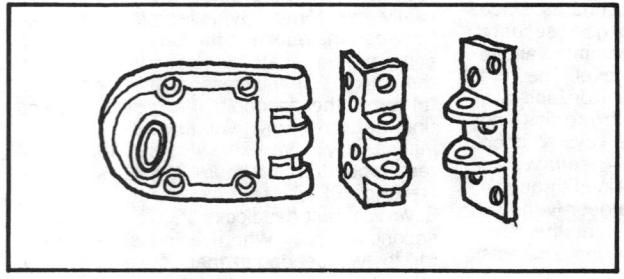

Fig. 17 Vertical bolt.

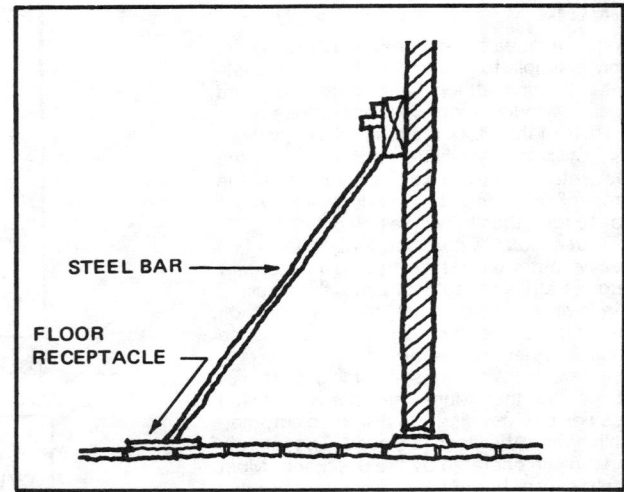

STEEL BAR

FLOOR
RECEPTACLE

Fig. 18 Buttress door lock.

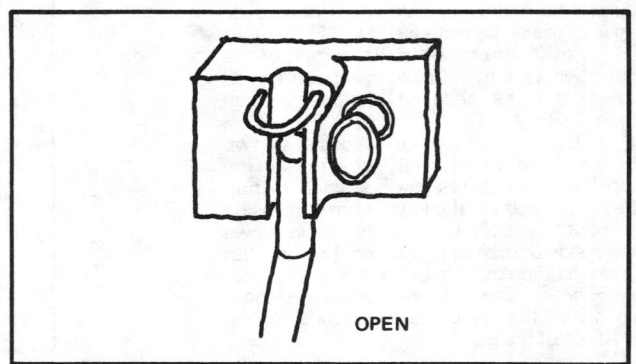

OPEN

Fig. 19 "Magic Eye" lock with thumb turn.

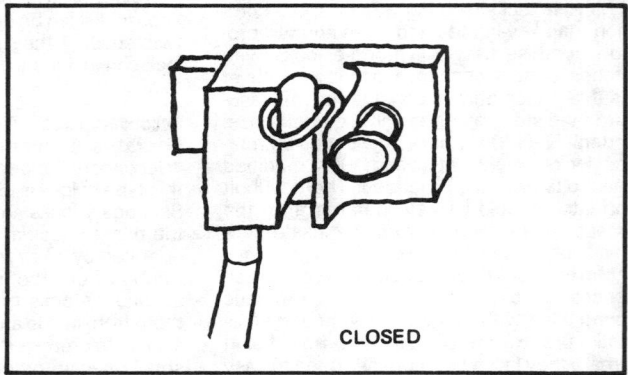

CLOSED

Fig. 20 Buttress door lock with deadbolt.

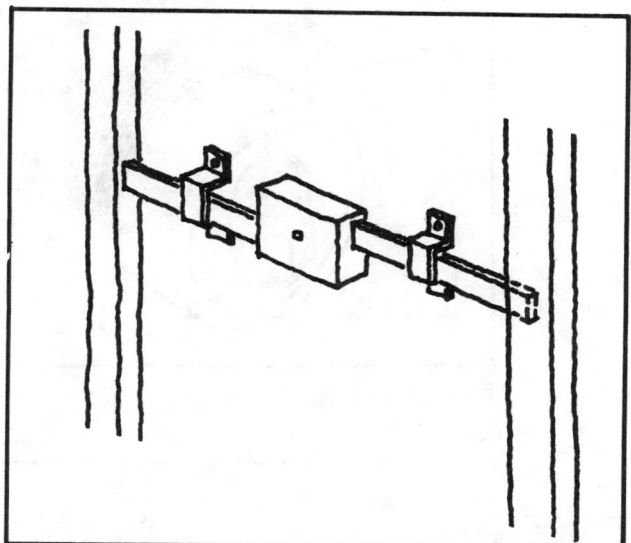

Fig. 21 Double-bar lock.

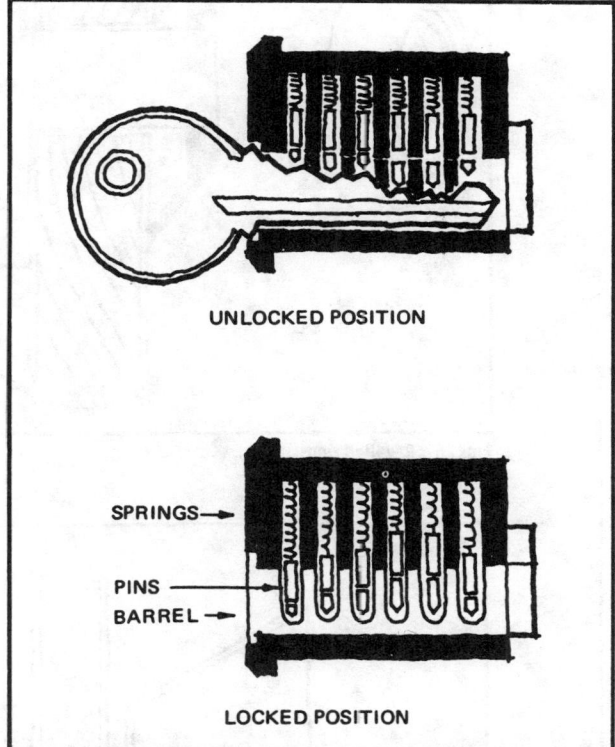

UNLOCKED POSITION

SPRINGS→

PINS→

BARREL→

LOCKED POSITION

Fig. 22 Cylinders.

The locks discussed so far rely on the rigidity of an existing door frame to resist attacks on the lock. Since older buildings may contain weak door frames, a buttress-type door lock is advisable. Locks of this type include a bar set against a plate on the door and into a receptacle in the floor, thus forming a triangular buttress (see Fig. 18). Most of these locks can be operated only by a key from the outside. The Magic Eye Company buttress lock can be operated from the outside by a key and from the inside by a turnbolt to prevent accidental locking (see Fig. 19). One model contains a heavy-duty deadbolt as well as the buttress bar, and affords still further protection (see Fig. 20).

The double-bar lock may also be used to increase the strength of a door, by means of two steel bars that extend up to 2½ inches into each side of the jamb (see Fig. 21). The cylinder is protected on the outside by an escutcheon plate to prevent forcible removal. A pick-resistant cylinder can be installed for added protection. The Fox Police Lock and the Fichet Locking Bar are examples of high-quality double-bar locks.

Cylinders Regardless of the type of lock purchased, the cylinder is critical in providing protection. It must withstand efforts by sophisticated criminals such as lock pick experts.

The cylinder is the part of the lock into which the key is inserted. The most common type of cylinder is the pin tumbler which operates as follows: As the key is inserted, spring-loaded pins are raised to the proper position to allow the barrel and the key to turn; the turning causes the bolt or latch (or both) to move. If the wrong key is used, the pins will line up incorrectly and prevent the barrel from turning (see Fig. 22).

Recently, cylinders have become available which utilize special keyways and keys to make the cylinder pick proof or pick resistant (see Fig. 23). Medeco, Illinois Duo, Sargent, Keso, Eagle Three Star, Mela, Fitchet, and Miracle Magnetic are highly pick resistant. Such cylinders provide improved security, but may require registered keys that can be duplicated only at the factory upon receipt of a signed request. A compromise is the use of a key type whose blank is not available normally, but for which spare blanks are kept for replacements.

Of all cylinders on the market, Medeco has proven most difficult to overcome. Medeco utilizes twisting tumblers operated by a key with angular or criss-cross cuts. Only if the proper key is inserted will the pins twist the exact amount needed to allow the barrel to turn.

If special keyway cylinders are deemed unnecessarily secure or costly (Medeco cylinders cost about two times the next adequate), the cylinder used should be of solid-bar-stock bronze and machined for a tight fit.

The cylinders of a master-key system of locks are constructed so that individual keys fit only one lock, but a single master key can open all locks in the system. Use of a master-key system makes maintenance and other authorized access simpler, but the dangers of improper use of a lost or stolen master key far outweigh the benefits.

From a security standpoint, a cylinder should have at least six pins. This often results in the cylinder being longer than the thickness of the door. In mortise locks (which are recessed into doors), a six-pin cylinder often extends slightly beyond the surface of the door, thus making it susceptible to forcible removal by use of a gripping tool. To prevent use of such a tool, protruding cylinders should be protected by one of the following:

Spinner ring: A hardened steel ring that forms a collar around the cylinder and which spins freely around the cylinder when gripped (see Fig. 24).

Bevelled-ring cylinder guard: A case-hardened steel ring that prevents the cylinder from being gripped by a tool because of its bevelled shape (see Fig. 25). Scotsman makes a flat, very secure, cylinder guard ring.

Escutcheon plate: A metal plate mounted to the door, which covers all of the cylinder except the core (the part where the key is inserted), thus protecting the cylinder from attack. The escutcheon plate should be constructed of malleable cast iron and attached to the door with one-way screws. Machine bolts should not be used to mount escutcheon plates on mortise locks, as the increased pressure can have an adverse effect on the mechanism (see Fig. 26).

Sliding Doors

Sliding doors opening onto a ground-level patio or accessible balcony (on the first floor or top floor, or adjacent to other balconies) should be constructed so the movable section of the door slides on the inside of the fixed portion. Sliding doors should be break resistant (plate glass) and equipped with a vertical-bolt Segal lock (see Fig. 27), which uses a hook-type bolt to grip door and frame together, or a Loxem Sli-door lock that hoods at top and bottom (see Fig. 28).

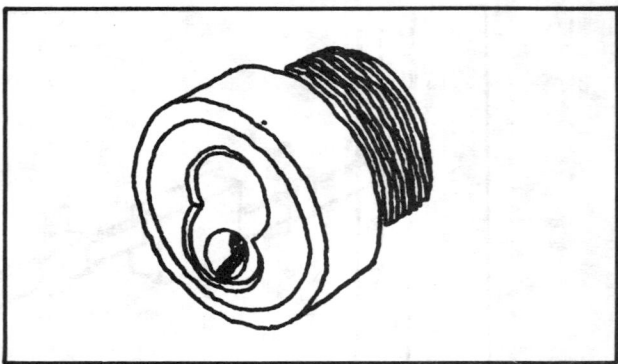

Fig. 24 Spinner ring.

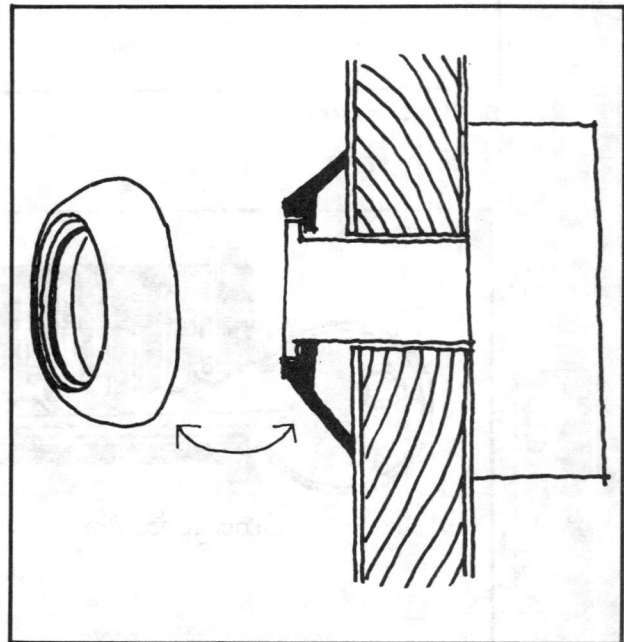

Fig. 25 Bevelled ring.

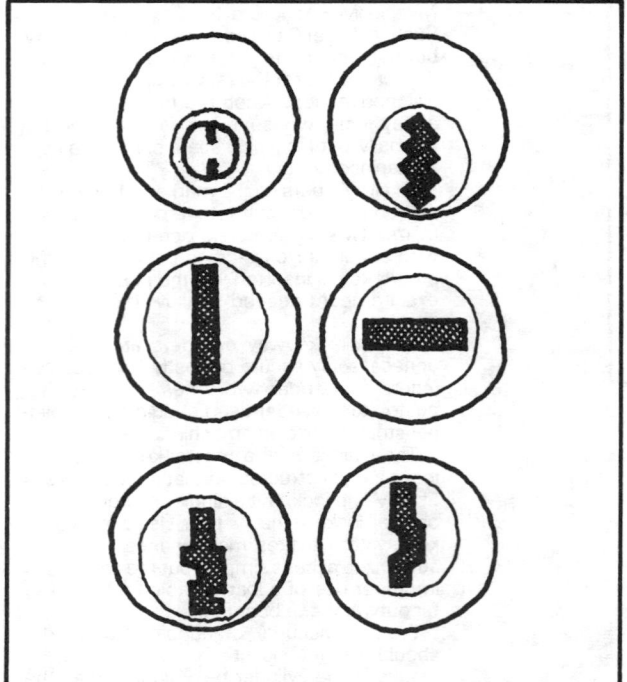

Fig. 23 Keyways.

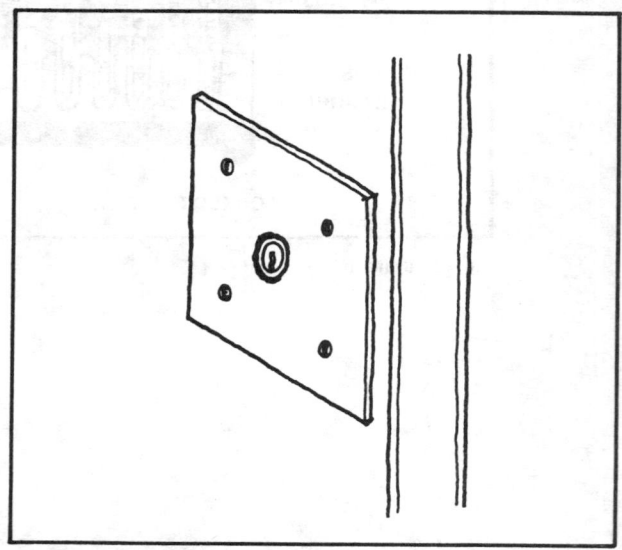

Fig. 26 Escutcheon plate covering cylinder mortise lock.

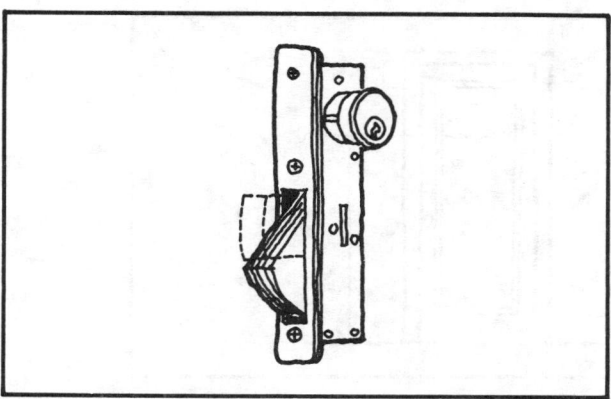

Fig. 27 Segal lock.

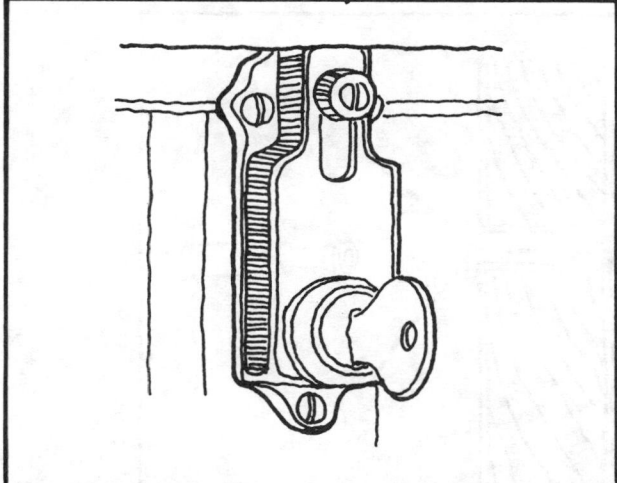

Fig. 28 Loxem Sli-door lock.

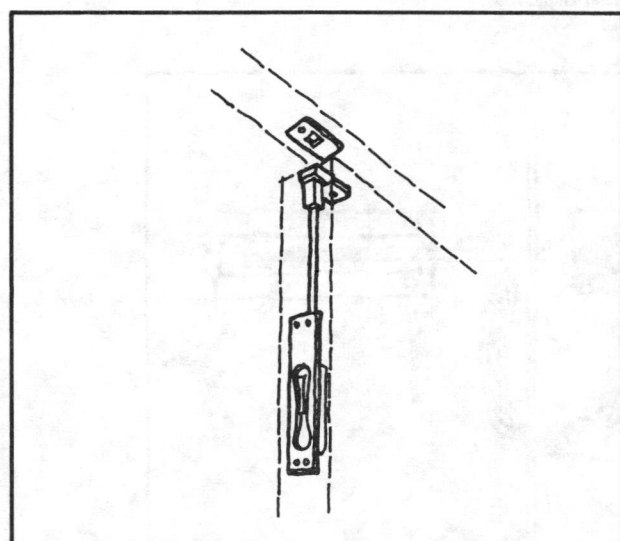

Fig. 29 Flush bolt on double door.

Doors with Large Glass Panels

Exterior doors containing panes of glass are not recommended for security. French doors that open out should have hinges with nonremovable pins. The vertical stile incorporating the lock should withstand a concentrated horizontal load of 300 pounds. The doors should contain a mortise-type lock that is key operated from the inside and outside. The lock should contain a pin-tumbler cylinder with at least six pins (a pick-resistant cylinder can be used for extra protection).

Even when fitted with key-operated locks inside and outside, doors with large panes of glass are a security problem. Use of break-resistant glass substitutes is one modification. Bars or metal grilles, while providing good security, may be aesthetically unacceptable. Alarms may also be used on these vulnerable doors.

Double Doors

On double doors, the active leaf should be equipped with a mortise-type lock. The inactive leaf should be equipped with flush bolts with at least a ¾-inch throw at head and foot (see Fig. 24).

Private Garage Doors

Many rolling overhead doors operated by electric motors offer adequate security because the motors are controlled by a key switch inside the garage or by a low-power radio transmittor. Manually operated doors should be provided with side bolts on the bottom bar (see Fig. 30). Chair-operated doors should be provided with a cast-iron keeper and pin for securing the hardened-steel chain.

Door Interviewers

Interviewers are devices installed on an opaque door to allow residents to see and hear who is outside the door without opening it.

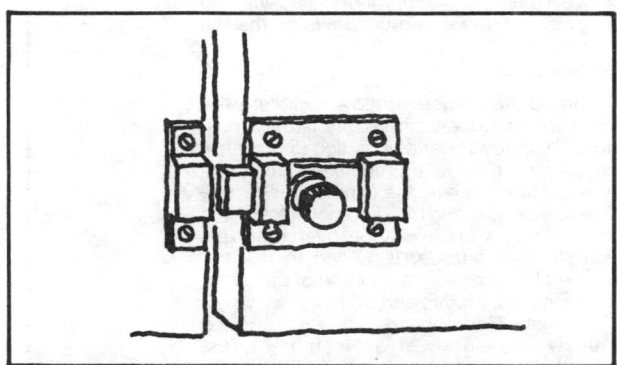

Fig. 30 Slide bolt on garage door.

An optical interviewer (peephole) should be installed on each door that provides entry into private dwellings. Many types of interviewers are available, ranging in diameter from two-tenths of an inch to 3 inches. Optics of the interviewer include one-way glass, plastic, and wide-angle glass.

Interviewers with openings of over one-quarter of an inch are not recommended. Larger interviewers can easily be punched out to allow insertion of tools to open the door from the inside. Someone also may stick a knife, wire, or gun through the hole while the person is looking through it. Interviewers are located approximately 4 feet 9 inches from the floor (see Fig. 31). The best interviewers contain a double glass for safety. Wide-angle glass allows maximum visibility. Although a wide-angle lens does produce a curved, "fisheye" image, clarity of the image is not impaired. If wide-angle glass is not used, the person outside cannot be seen unless he is standing in a direct line with the interviewer (see Fig. 32).

Instead of an optical interviewer, a case-hardened steel chain which fits into a horizontally mounted slide track on one end of the door jamb may be installed (see Fig. 33). The chain allows the door to open slightly (preferably not more than 2 inches) to permit easy conversation without fully unlocking the door. These chains should be used for interviewing only, not to protect a locked door. The swing of the door, even if only 2 inches, allows the criminal to exert strong force with momentum, which breaks most chain devices. The interviewing space also allows insertion and use of tools. Some slide chains have a locking mechanism which prevents use of a thumb tack (or piece of tape) and rubber band to pull back the slide mechanism and remove the chain from the track. Even when equipped with a locking mechanism, steel chains and slides are readily overcome by simple tools and brute force.

Window Materials

Because windows contain large sections of glass, they naturally impose a security problem. Windows most vulnerable are those on the first floor (or otherwise accessible from the ground) and those leading to fire escapes. Less vulnerable, but still easily reached, are windows over a canopy (as above a main entrance), windows adjacent to stairwell windows, and windows on the top floor.

Window Locks

Among the common window locks are the crescent sash lock, often standard on residential windows; various friction or pressure devices, such as the thumb-screw latch; pin-type latches, such as the simple steel pin-in-the-hole device; and the slide-bolt latch. All of these devices can easily be overcome, especially if an intruder is willing to risk the noise of breaking a small section of the glass. (See Figs. 34, 35, 36, and 37.)

Normal windowpane glass is approximately one-eighth of an inch thick, extremely brittle, and breaks easily. Plate glass is usually one-quarter of an inch thick and tempered to withstand an accidental knock. Plate glass is used for larger areas because of its greater strength and because the initial cost is worth the extra protection. Tempered

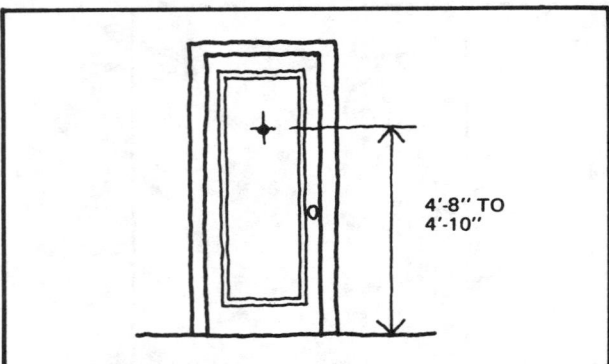

Fig. 31 Interviewer location.

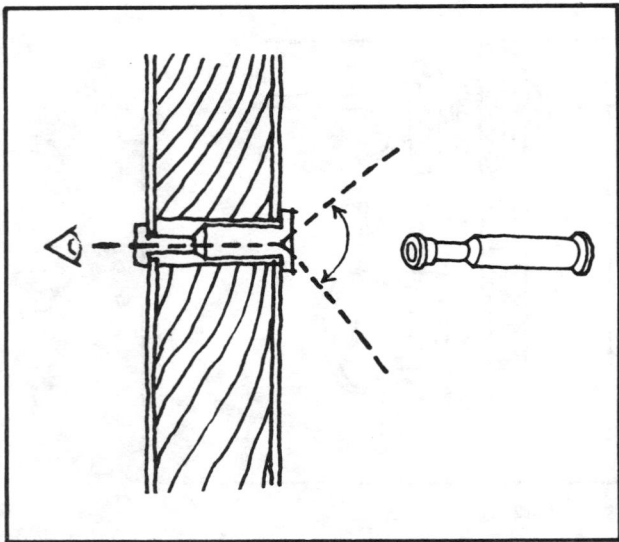

Fig. 32 Interviewer angles.

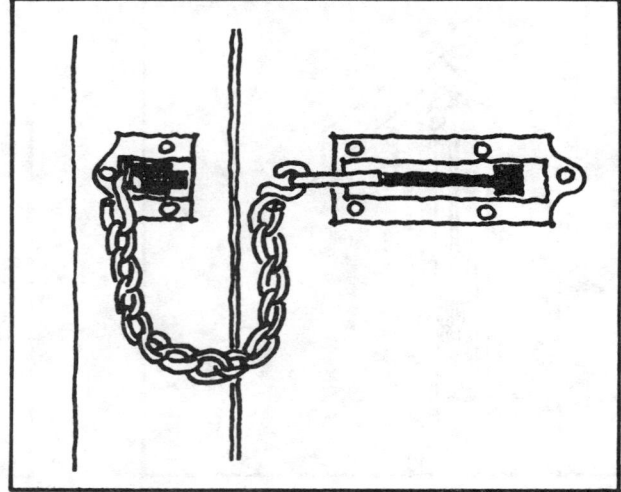

Fig. 33 Chain lock.

glass has a thin, hardening coating and, while no stronger than plate glass, will not cut someone who breaks it.

Several companies have developed unbreakable, transparent polycarbonate materials which look like glass but are very difficult to break. GE's Lexan, for example, is guaranteed unbreakable. It costs two to three times as much as glass and has low resistance to scratching. An improved material, Lexan MR-4000, is slightly more expensive but is much less easily scratched. These polycarbonate materials have not yet been extensively used for private dwellings.

Another type of durable "glass" is fabricated much like the safety glass used in automobiles: two layers of high-quality glass are bonded together with a layer of tough vinyl between. This is sold by one company as Secur-lite. While Secur-lite can eventually be broken, the noise and trouble required to do so are considerable deterrents.

Oversized glazed areas should be avoided. Anything beyond standard size (6 feet by 8 feet for glass, for example) is expensive and may be difficult to obtain.

The only reliable devices are those with a key-operated locking mechanism. Yale and Ideal Security manufacture a window lock which is a modification of the pin-type lock. It can be locked in either of two positions, one of which allows the window to be open slightly at the bottom for ventilation (see Fig. 38). Fox makes a window lock combining a pin-type lock and a hasp and padlock. Although somewhat unsightly, it provides excellent protection. Ideal Security manufactures a modification of the crescent sash lock which requires a key to operate.

All of these devices provide adequate security for normal residential use. A set of keys should be convenient to the window for use in emergencies but far enough away so that a burglar cannot reach them.

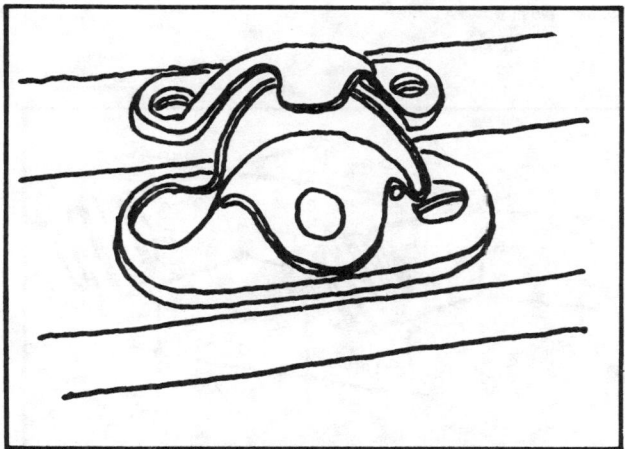

Fig. 34   Crescent sash lock.

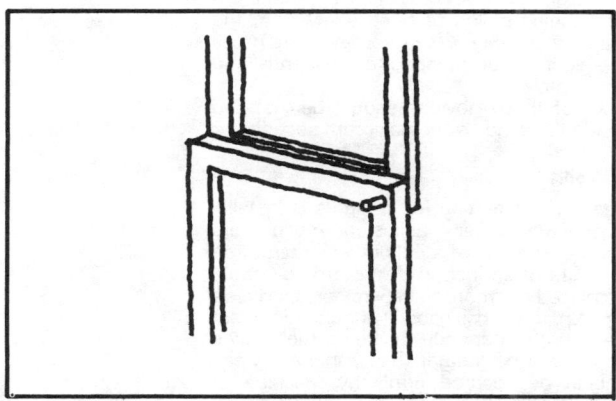

Fig. 36   Pin latch.

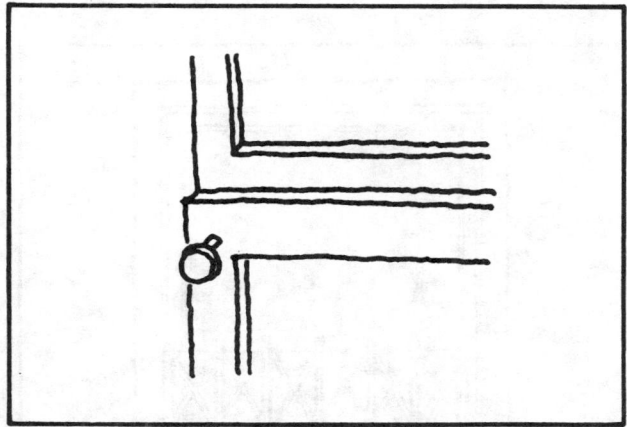

Fig. 35   Thumb screw lock

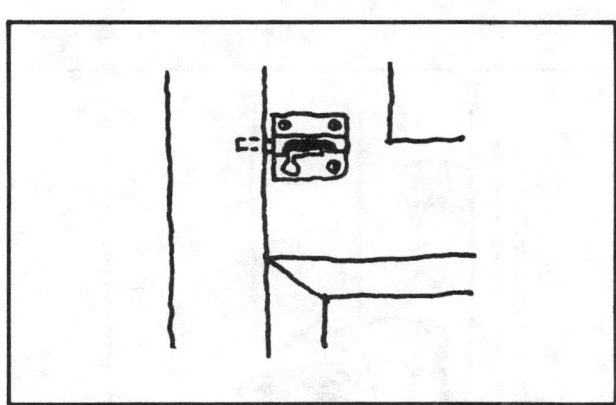

Fig. 37   Slide bolt.

SECURITY
Windows and Hardware

Window Bars, Grilles, and Gates

Where tighter security is desired, metal bars, grilles, and gates have proven most reliable. If a wire mesh grille is used, the metal should be at least one-eighth of an inch in diameter and the openings should not exceed 2 inches (see Figs. 39 and 40). The grille should be attached to the window frame with machine or roundhead bolts which cannot be removed from the outside.

If bars are used, they should be placed not more than 5 inches apart. The bars should have a diameter of at least three-quarters of an inch and be set at least 3 inches into the masonry.

Sliding gates afford excellent protection and can be pushed aside or opened for emergency exit. The gates should be set in tracks on the top and bottom to prevent them from being pulled or pried away from the window (see Fig. 41). Protect-A-Guard gates are highly recommended for residential and commercial use.

All of these devices should be installed inside the window for maximum security.

Skylights

The best protection for skylights is installation of metal bars, grilles, or mesh. Bars should be made of steel not less than three quarters of an inch in diameter and should be placed not more than 5 inches apart (see Fig. 42). If mesh is used, it should be at least one-eighth of an inch thick and the spaces should not be greater than 2 inches. Mesh should be secured firmly by machine or roundhead bolts that cannot be removed from the outside.

If metal is undesirable, a securely fastened hasp and padlock will discourage entry and exit through the roof, if the glass is not removed.

Both hook-in-eye and sliding-bolt devices are unacceptable security measures for skylights.

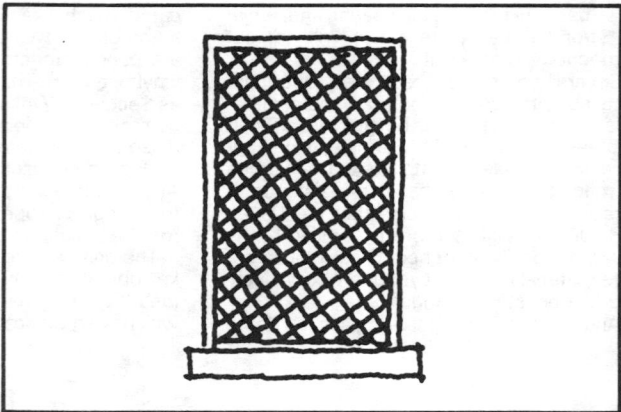

Fig. 39   Mesh window grille.

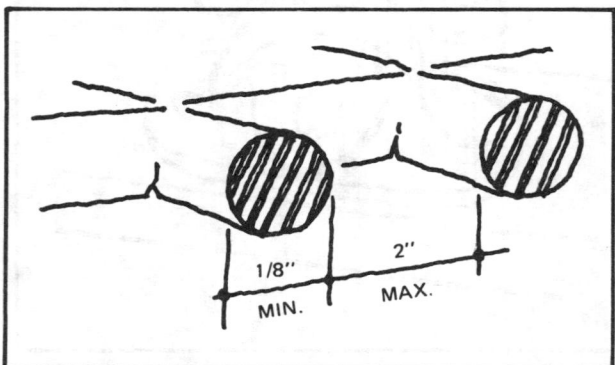

Fig. 40   Wire mesh dimensions.

Fig. 38   Keyed window lock.

Fig. 41   Window guard.

MULTIFAMILY DWELLINGS

Lobby Doors and Walls

All lobby entrance doors should provide maximum visibility of the lobby. This often requires large glass areas in the lobby doors. Where there is a high degree of vandalism and crime, use of Lexan is recommended. In all cases, oversized glass sheet should be avoided. Glazed areas should be divided so that sheets larger than 6 by 8 feet are not needed. The doorframe should be constructed of rugged, heavy-duty metal. The vertical jamb incorporating the lock should withstand a concentrated load of 500 pounds and be a minimum of 5 inches thick so that it can receive heavy-duty mortise lock sets.

The main outer lobby door should have a key-operated lock with a pin-tumbler cylinder containing at least six pins. The key for this lock should not open any other door (such as an apartment door) as this makes the lobby-door cylinder susceptible to picking. An anti-friction latch (see Fig. 43) and a sturdy door closer should be used in conjunction with the lock.

Lobby doors, especially if locked or equipped with intercoms, should open out for fire safety and to reduce vandalism (tenants who have misplaced their keys can kick an in-swinging door hard enough to break the locking mechanism).

Secondary Exits

In multifamily dwellings, exit doors leading to fire stairwells on each landing should have self-locking deadlatches to allow free egress while prohibiting entry. The stairside surface of the door should be free of hardware to prevent access to one floor from another via the stairwell. Hardware should limit access to the roof or ground-floor exits via the stairwell.

Panic hardware, if required, should be in the form of vertical-bolt latches on the top and bottom of the door. This hardware makes the door more sturdy and makes entry from the outside difficult (see Fig. 44).

Doors leading into the buildings from garage areas should have self-locking deadlatches with a minimum throw of one-half inch that allow free egress but require a key for entry into the building. The door should be protected in the area of the strike. All exit doors should be equipped with a self-closing apparatus that can be adjusted to the desired tension.

Since fire doors are required by law to be operable from the inside, they are often a means of escape. Exit alarms (see Fig. 45) bring immediate attention to fire doors that are opened when there is no apparent fire. A panic bar or other device simultaneously opens the door and sounds a local alarm. However, effectiveness of the alarm as a security measure depends upon the speed and consistence of response to the signal.

Exit alarms on fire exits leading to roofs keep burglars from using the roof for escape or for access to top-floor apartments. However, the alarm may prove more a nuisance than a good security measure if teenage vandalism is prevalent. Teenagers often set off the alarm to harass the local official, who must respond to the signal and reset the alarm.

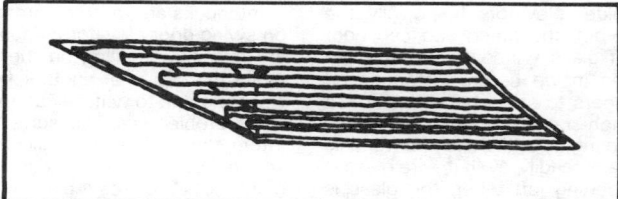

Fig. 42 Skylight protection.

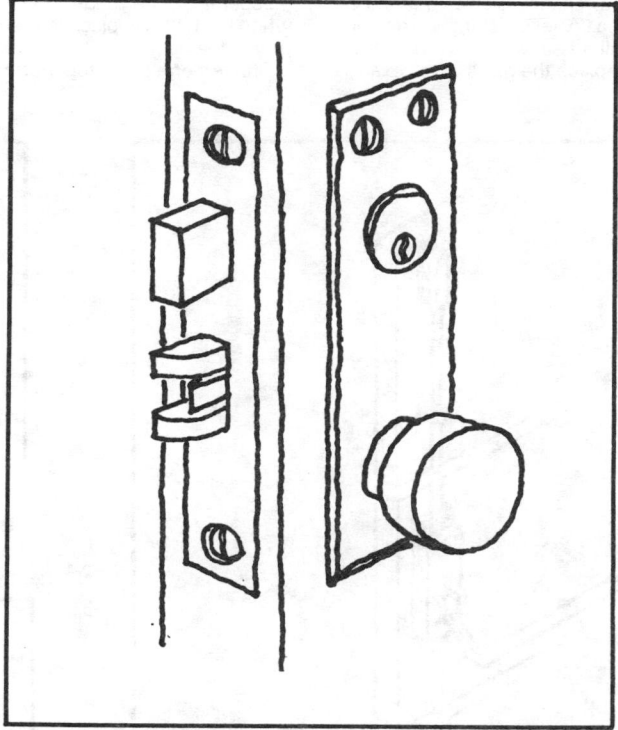

Fig. 43 Antifriction latch bolt.

Elevators

In most middle-income multifamily dwellings, vandalism of elevators is relatively rare. However, in many high-crime areas and low-income housing developments, this vandalism is reaching a critical level. In New York City Housing Authority projects, vandalism to elevators and elevator equipment is responsible for almost 60 percent of elevator outages. Parts of the elevator most commonly vandalized are the hall buttons, indicator lights, hatch door glass, hatch door interlock, and buttons located inside the cab, especially the emergency and light switches.

Hall buttons are most commonly vandalized because of their accessibility. Impatient tenants push the buttons excessively and often kick or smash them in frustration. To prevent damage to the button and the electrical contacts inside, a stainless steel mushroom-type button should be used (see Fig. 46). The shape of the button prevents the contacts from being damaged by the button's being pushed too heavily against them. Another stainless steel button has been developed on the same principle, except that the stopper is inside the mechanism so that the button has the more familiar stunted-cone appearance.

Use of indicator lights for the lobby, the cab, and the other floors should be decided by the management. In some projects, indicator lights are so vandalized that it is easier to eliminate them. In other developments, indicator lights dampen user impatience and the result is less wear and tear on the buttons. If indicator lights are used, they should be protected by a heavy-duty plastic shield.

There are two types of elevator doors: swing and slide. This nomenclature refers to the doors on each floor; the cab door is always a slide door. Slide doors, which are automatic, are becoming increasingly popular despite higher initial cost, because they increase protection against vandalism. Swing doors are inconvenient and more subject to vandalism (short-circuiting of door interlocks, jamming of closing mechanisms, and joyriding on top of cabs).

In many older elevators (especially the swing-door type), the hatch and cab door contain small glass windows which allow people to see inside before entering and allow passengers to see what floor they're passing. In high-crime areas, this glass has proven more dangerous than helpful. Vandals smash the glass readily, even if wire glass is used. The opening left when the glass is broken presents a very dangerous situation. Hatch door glass should be eliminated by welding or bolting a piece of metal over the opening. Where this is prohibited by a strict building code, a variance is often granted in a high-crime area. A less desirable modification is to install a heavy steel grille over the opening and replace the glass with Lexan.

Interlocks are more commonly vandalized on swing-door elevators. Causes of damage are excessive pulling on the elevator door while the cab is at another floor and short circuiting due to water or urine damage. The latter problem can be solved by installing interlocks with hydrophilic (non-water-absorbing) contacts. When damaged, this type of interlock requires replacement of only the contact plates rather than the entire mechanism. Damage caused by excessive pulling may be alleviated by signs cautioning tenants against such pulling. Closing mechanisms (keepers) can be made to fit more securely when the bolt is in place to prevent too much play in the door.

The emergency stop button presents a problem because it is often misused. The button may be activated to stop the elevator between floors to commit crimes such as mugging, rape, and drug abuse. Because every elevator has several automatic safety mechanisms that prevent if from falling freely down the shaft, the stop button is primarily a psychological comfort to passengers. Wherever possible, the stop button should be eliminated. The building code requirement for stop buttons is being challenged in New York and several other cities. If code change is unlikely, a variance should be applied for where elevator crime is common. A constant-pressure alarm switch is also somewhat better than the conventional toggle switch.

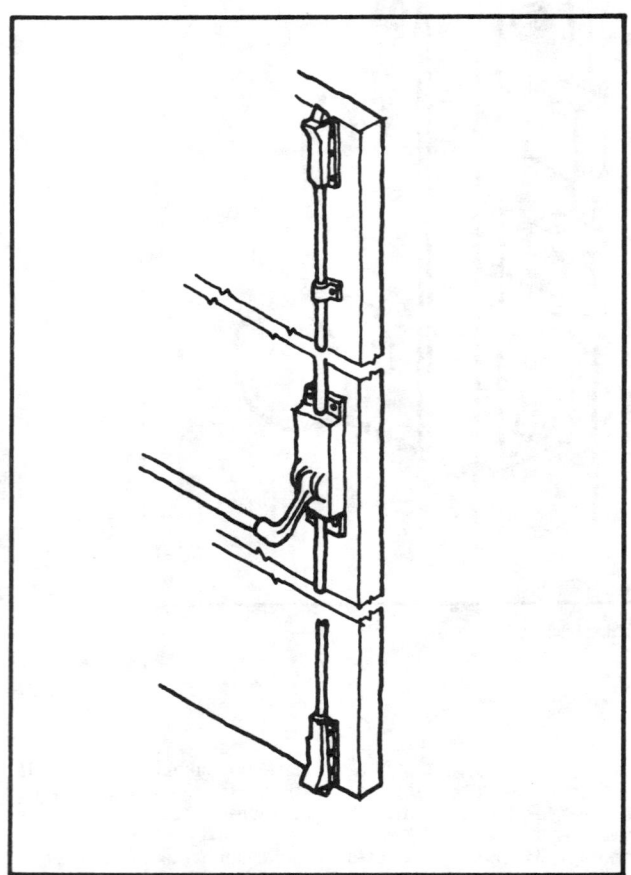

Fig. 44 Vertical bolt on exit door.

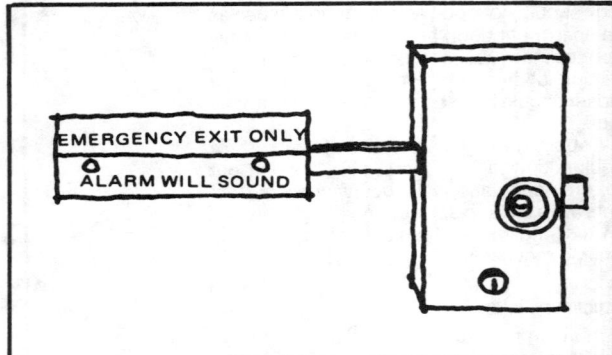

Fig. 45 Exit alarm.

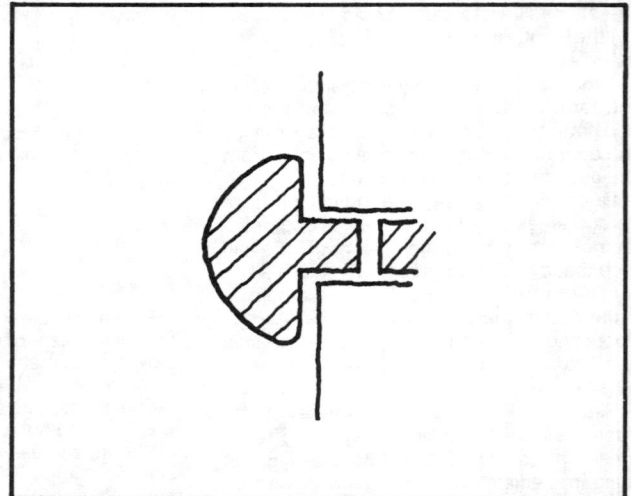

Fig. 46 Mushroom button.

Secer Light and Kendall are among the manufacturers of elevator dome lights that are highly vandal resistant (see Fig. 47). They are constructed of durable steel and contain a shatterproof plastic plate to protect the bulb. Where use of these lights is economically prohibitive, Lexan or an equivalent should be used to protect the light bulb.

Aside from vandalism, joyriding on top of elevator cabs is becoming prevalent in high-crime areas. Injury occurs most often when children are struck by the counterweight when the cab and counterweight pass each other. In other cases, children are crushed between cabs, struck by dividing beams, or squashed under a cab in the pit.

There are numerous means of access to elevator roofs and shafts: door interlocks are jammed by using simple household tools;

emergency stop switches are abused; and roof escape hatch doors are forced. Once on top, children often abuse passengers inside the cabs and interfere with normal elevator operation.

It is difficult to prevent crime by modifying elevator equipment. Restricted access to the building through the use of a buzzer-reply system, tenant patrol groups, or doormen is more likely to be effective. Closed-circuit television and audio-intercom systems mounted on elevators are other possible crime control devices.

A common device used to increase visibility in an elevator is a convex mirror placed in the upper back corner of the elevator. This allows a person to see if anyone is waiting inside the elevator *before* he walks into a possible assault situation (see Fig. 48).

An elevator modification that may deter crime is the up-discharge, down-collect system. When controlled in this way, an elevator will only stop for a person who has selected "up" (discharge) at the ground-floor level. Passengers on the upper floor can only enter the elevator on its way down (collect). The advantage is that a person entering the elevator on the first floor can be assured that the elevator will not stop at another floor to allow a suspicious person to enter. Such a system may be inconvenient for residents—a person wishing to go from the fifth to the seventh floor would have to travel down to the ground floor and then up again. The system is far from foolproof, as criminals can operate in other ways; but the modification is inexpensive and may deter crime in buildings without security personnel.

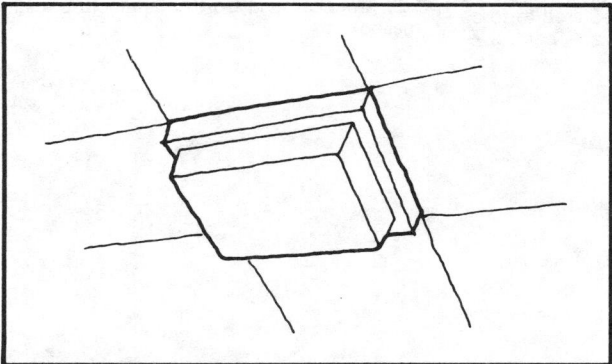

Fig. 47   Unbreakable light fixture.

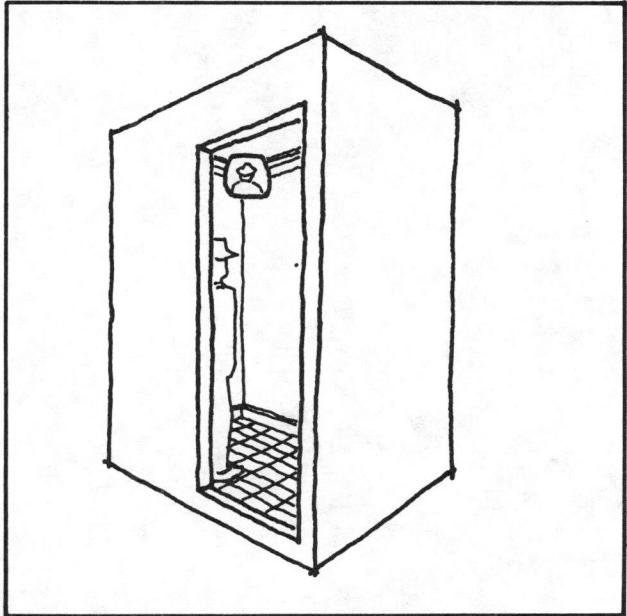

Fig. 48   Elevator mirror.

Garage Doors and Secondary Entries

Doors to interior garages provide a means of entry that circumvents many security precautions. If access to the building is to be limited, entry through the garage door must be carefully controlled.

The most practical solution is to have a locked door which tenants can open but which automatically closes behind them, usually within 15 seconds. A large number of manufacturers provide such self-closing doors. The major variation is the means for opening the garage door. Radio-controlled devices, requiring each auto to have a transistor, are expensive and far from foolproof. If a device is stolen from one car, all the devices should be replaced (an expensive procedure). A convenient and less elaborate system has a key-operated switch mounted on the driver's side of the garage, allowing the driver to use a key without leaving his car.

Despite these controls, the garage door should be monitored by tenants, security personnel, or electronic equipment if a build-ing is to retain a high level of security.

A door leading directly from a parking area to the building interior must be treated the same as a main entry. Such a door will be used continually, and requires equivalent security measures.

The secondary lock recommended for storage rooms containing valuables is the Fox double-bar lock.

Mailboxes and Mailbox Rooms

Mailboxes are a major target for criminals within multifamily dwellings, particularly in low-income communities. The mail includes welfare, social security, and veterans' checks as well as others. These checks are particularly vulnerable because they arrive on set days of the month.

The bank of mailboxes should be located in the most secure and easily surveyed space available. Some brands of mailboxes do provide security, but any mailbox can be opened in the 10 minutes required to force open the door. If there is any control of access to the building (intercom or doorman), mailboxes should be located inside the protected area.

Mailboxes may be located in a locked room. Such a room must contain a large window to make it visible from the lobby, and be lighted 24 hours a day to reduce its potential as a location for muggings and other crimes. The door to a mailbox room should have sturdy self-locking hardware. Where back-loading mailboxes (generally secure) are used, a separate mail-loading room is often provided (see Fig. 49).

The better mailboxes are constructed of 16-gauge metal. The doors are tightly fitted and without holes to prevent prying them open and to prevent matches from being dropped in. The metal may be corrugated for additional strength. Cylinder locks with at least five pins should be used. Door size should be kept to a minimum to further limit the possibility of prying doors open (see Fig. 50). American and Gorth manufacture such mailboxes.

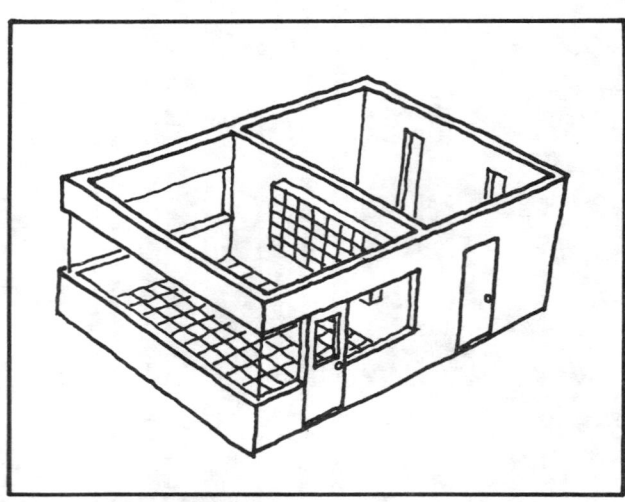

Fig. 49 Mailroom and loading room.

LIGHTING

Good lighting in a residential development permits adequate visibility and surveillance. Generally, the higher the lighting level, the better the security. An appropriate level of lighting should be provided in each area; the light should be without excessive glare and generate no heavy shadows; and lighting should be resistant to vandalism and easy to maintain.

Fluorescent lamps are tubular glass lights that require special current-control devices called ballasts. Operating costs of fluorescent lamps are significantly lower than for incandescent bulbs: fluorescent tubes typically produce 3 to 4 times as much light per watt and operate 7 to 10 times longer than incandescent bulbs (due in part to lower operating temperatures).

Interior Lighting

Lobbies, elevators, stairwells, and corridors must be well lit. Interior lighting normally requires only conventional incandescent bulbs, but low-glare or "frosted" incandescent or fluorescent luminaries are preferable. Low wattages of 25 to 200 watts generally suffice. It is usually desirable to install low-wattage fixtures at close intervals to minimize shadows and glare.

The most common problem of interior lighting is vandalism. Naked bulbs provide maximum illumination at minimal installation cost, but they are so often and so easily broken that maintenance costs are very high, and crime is encouraged by lack of lights. Recessed lighting suffers less from accidental breakage and vandalism. Transparent bulb protectors allow nearly total passage of light, but since the bulb can be seen, a vandal will likely try to break it. Translucent bulb covers are therefore preferable, even though some of the light is blocked by the cover.

Secer and Kendall have developed fixtures that are vandal resistant. They are made of plastic and come in a variety of shapes and sizes.

Exterior Lighting

All heavily used spaces such as paths, entries, and parking areas should be lit by 5- to 10-foot candles. Higher fixture locations have a variety of advantages. As a general rule, the useful ground coverage of an elevated light fixture is roughly twice the height of the fixture. Thus, a 150-watt incandescent lamp mounted 8 feet above the ground can provide adequate light for 16 feet along a walk. Higher luminaries are safer from vandalism. However, lighting fixtures mounted higher than the second floor may create a feeling of being in a "compound."

A variety of specialized, high-intensity light sources can illuminate large outdoor areas such as recreation facilities and parking lots. Mercury-vapor and sodium-vapor lamps are available in sizes up to 1500 watts; the eerie bluish light of early mercury-vapor lamps may be avoided by selecting one of the newer "color-corrected" models. Once again, the point is to provide an appropriate level of light without creating glare or shadows.

Lamp and fixture breakage can be controlled in part by installing fixtures of tough, break-resistant plastic. The spherical, white glass fixtures so common today are less vulnerable, though not as tough as the more expensive plastic models.

A final comment on lighting is specifically relevant to a building or residential development inhabited primarily by the elderly. The pupil in the human eye gradually decreases in size due to advancing age. As a result, about twice as much actual brightness is required to create the same degree of brightness on the retina of a 60-year-old as on the retina of a 20-year-old (the ratio reaches 3 by age 75). Therefore, lighting levels in residences for the elderly should be well in excess of conventional standards and much higher than what seems adequate to a (younger) management staff.

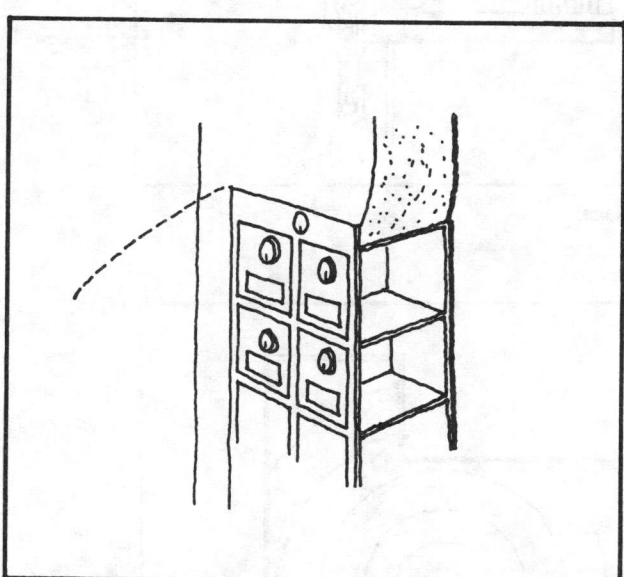

Fig. 50   Mailboxes.

Electronic security equipment includes alarms designed to detect unauthorized entrance; closed-circuit television systems, apartment-to-lobby intercom locks, and various audio equipment. While the initial cost of many of these systems is high, each could reasonably be installed in moderate-income residential complexes and could prevent future need for more costly measures.

ALARMS

An alarm performs two functions: it detects the presence of an intruder, and it reports the intrusion. The quality of an alarm mechanism is measured by its ability to perform these two functions.

A wide range of devices detect intrusion of a criminal into a building. These fall roughly into two categories: contact devices and motion-detection devices.

Contact Devices

Contact devices are mechanical switches that detect movement or perhaps the breakage of glass. A common type consists of a contact on the door (or window) and a contact on the frame. When the door is closed, the two contacts form part of an electrical circuit. When the door is opened, the contact is broken, the ciruit is opened, and the alarm circuit is activated (see Fig. 51). A similar device, called a string-pull alarm, employs a slight variation in that the opening of the door pulls a string, which closes a switch that trips the alarm. Many contact devices are purely mechanical (as just described), while others include magnetic and mercury switches.

Usefulness of a contact depends upon its sensitivity (how much the device can be jarred without being activated) and its reliability. Most situations call for a device sufficiently sensitive that a skilled burglar cannot enter without setting off the alarm, but not so delicate that an innocent jostling will disturb it.

Foil strips are a related mechanism used primarily to detect breakage of glass in windows and doors. A delicate strip of metal foil is glued or taped to the glass. The foil strip acts as one long, continuous electrical circuit. If the glass is broken, the foil is broken, which interrupts the circuit and activates the alarm. Foil can be circumvented if it is possible to break the glass or release a lock without breaking the foil. Primarily because of their unattractiveness, foil strips are seldom installed in residences.

Contact devices can be made part of a lock mechanism (see Fig. 52). This type of alarm is set off whenever an attempt is made to force or pick the lock.

Contact devices themselves are very inexpensive; a simple magnetic contact pair costs about $2. But each contact device can protect only one opening; therefore, even a single-family house requires several devices to protect all points of entry. In addition, it is often expensive to install the alarms and connect them to an alarm-reporting device.

Contacts may be hidden so criminals cannot locate and dismantle them easily. Hiding an alarm system lessens its value as a deterrent, but increases the criminal's chances of being apprehended while com-

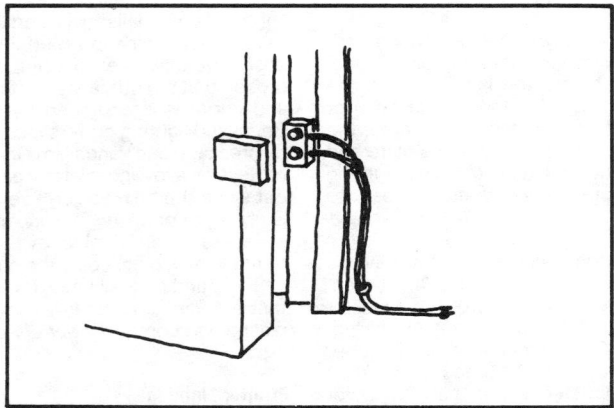

Fig. 51   Contact switch on door.

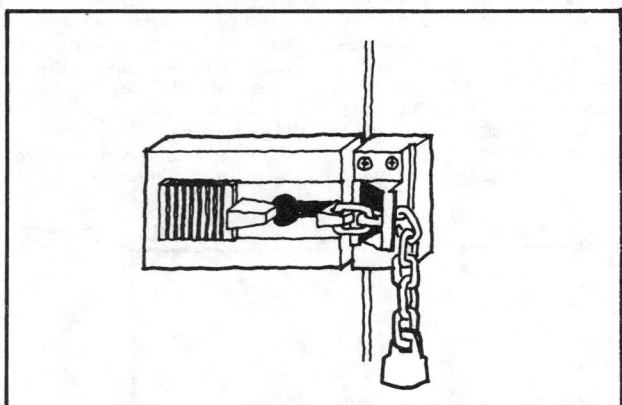

Fig. 52   Lock alarm.

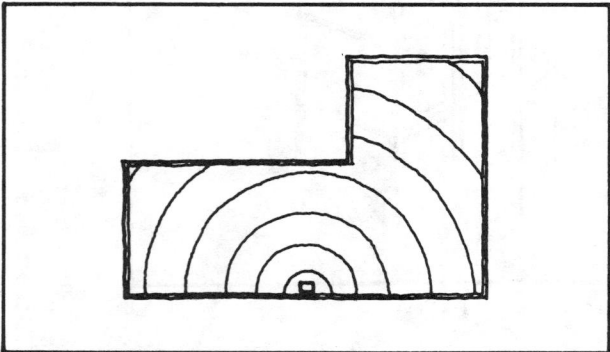

Fig. 53   Ultrasonic detector.

mitting a crime. Since deterrence is the primary goal of residential security efforts, it is quite common to advertise the existence of an alarm without revealing the location of the mechanisms. This advertising is sometimes done where no alarm system exists. Considering the minimal expense involved in such a ruse, it may be worth the cost, but even very unsophisticated criminals can pick out such fake systems.

Heat-sensitive devices are sometimes combined with contact switches to provide an inexpensive fire-security alarm system.

Motion-Detection Devices

These devices detect the motion of an intruder as he moves about the protected space. This detection can be accomplished in a variety of ways. Seismographic devices are turned on by vibrations or weight upon the floor (these devices have been perfected so they are not triggered by a passing truck). Photoelectric cells ("seeing-eye" mechanisms) use a beam of light to detect any motion across a protected span. Ultrasonic devices send inaudible sound waves through a room (see Fig. 53). Movement by an intruder changes the pattern of reflected sound waves and thus triggers an alarm. Increased sensitivity improves the effectiveness of each of these systems, but also raises their costs.

Motion detectors are far more expensive than contact devices, but one motion device can protect an entire area, regardless of the number of points of entry. Installation costs are often minimal, as the detection device need not be connected to any part of the structure. Motion detectors are most useful in spaces not used during scheduled periods of time, such as in commercial establishments which are totally empty at night and in homes left empty during vacation. More expensive motion-detection devices can protect limited areas, such as a single door or window.

Alarm Reporting Systems

The term "alarm-reporting system" describes the mechanism that receives the message of an intrusion and reacts. Essentially, there are only two kinds of alarm-reporting systems: Intrusion is reported either by a loud alarm on the premises (called a local alarm) or via wires to a security force which is prepared to react when notified (called a central alarm or silent alarm).

A local alarm has a bell or buzzer connected to the intrusion device which produces a loud audio signal on the premises when the alarm is activated. This is the simplest type of alarm and can be installed readily. The deterrent effect is dependent upon the burglar's being intimidated and driven off immediately by the noise. Noise of the local alarm can also stop a crime in progress and aid in apprehension if someone responds to the alarm. Local alarms are often operated by batteries (see Fig. 54). Instead of an alarm being sounded, lights in the building can be turned on by an alarm system, or lights and alarm can both be activated.

This local system also protects people sleeping in a house by alerting them that a break-in is being attempted. Generally, keys are required to shut off local alarms.

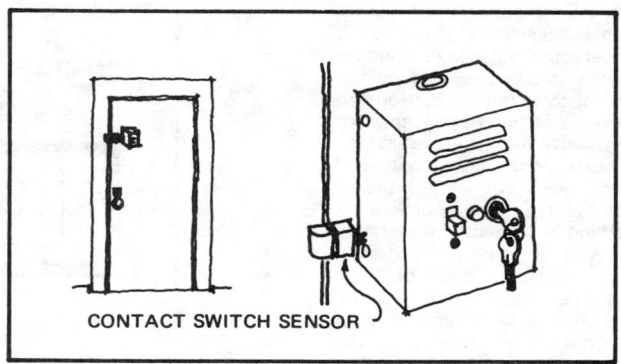

CONTACT SWITCH SENSOR

Fig. 54 Local alarm.

A central alarm-reporting system sounds an alarm at a remote point usually connected to the detection device by wires (telephone lines are used in many cases). The remote point is sometimes the residence of the owner of a protected business establishment and sometimes the local police station; but generally, it is the headquarters of a private protective agency. These agencies have guards stationed at this headquarters who will respond to the alarm signal. Usefulness of the alarm system is dependent upon the speed and reliability of the response.

A local alarm signal is often activated at the same time as a central alarm, thus simultaneously frightening the criminal and alerting the authorities. If only a central alarm-reporting system is activated, the criminal is not warned that an alarm has been sent. This system (called a "silent" alarm) increases the possibility of apprehension while eliminating the possibility of driving the intruder off with noise.

A variation on this central-alarm arrangement is to utilize regular city police to respond to the central alarm. In high-income, low-density, high-burglary-risk communities, the city police allow alarms to be hooked up to the police headquarters, where the dispatcher serves as monitor. Another arrangement is for the detection device to trigger a tape-recorded message that is automatically telephoned to the police, telling them the location of a burglary in progress.

The single major problem of all alarm systems is the possibility of false alarms. They can be caused by defects in the intrusion-detection device or the reporting system. False alarms diminish the credibility of the entire system.

If neighbors experience repeated false alarms, if security guards are called out unnecessarily, or if police are accidentally telephoned a tape-recorded message, response by all of these persons slows dramatically and will eventually cease. Thus, the intrusion device must be designed so that it is not accidentally activated by noncriminal occurrences.

Related to the false alarm issue is the question of how the alarm is turned off. The most common method is for the alarm to operate after a 20-second delay; that is, the alarm will not sound for 20 seconds after a contact is broken or motion detected, allow-

ing the resident a brief period in which to switch off the entire system. The switch can be simply a button located in a hidden place. A key-operated switch is more secure, but the possibility of false alarms increases because residents often forget or cannot locate their keys. However, the turnoff mechanism should not be so simple or accessible that the criminal can activate it.

Selecting Alarm Systems

The security alarm business is large and complex. It is therefore impossible to specify manufacturers or even types of alarm systems for general use. The quality of installation and the maintenance program that backs up the system are crucial elements that should outweigh initial price in the selection of equipment. The best advice is to deal with firms that have a verifiable history of quality installation, a reliable guarantee/warranty record, and an established repair and maintenance program.

The concept of a consistent "level of security" avoids excessive expenditures for one piece of equipment while other means of entry are unprotected. Equipment characteristics should fit specific installation situations. It is often difficult to install contact switches in older houses because window frames often have warped or buckled. String-pull devices have to be set from the inside and therefore cannot be used for a normal exit door.

Selection of alarm equipment should be based on specific system characteristics desired: Is deterrence of crime or apprehension of criminals the primary goal? Should the system be visible to deter attempted burglary, or should it be hidden to increase the likelihood of apprehending a burglar?

CLOSED-CIRCUIT TELEVISION

When used in residential settings, closed-circuit television (CCTV) is intended to provide "electronic windows"; that is, a visual surveillance where physical design has obviated unaided surveillance. The purpose is to create an environment in which residents know that normal restraints of surveillance by citizens and their authorized agents exist, albeit aided by electronics. While initially costly, CCTV often reduces security personnel requirements or obviates the need for expensive redesign of existing structures.

Electronically aided surveillance is not equal to personal surveillance. A corrective response to a detected crime is obviously a step further away if the viewer sees the crime on a TV receiver rather than on the spot. The deterrent of having a policeman or other person on hand is lost. There is also the possibility of equipment malfunction. But CCTV has a quality of its own: being watched while unable to ascertain who, if anyone, is doing the watching is somehow unnerving, and definitely is a deterrent. A remotely controlled surveillance camera can be fitted with an automatic panning device so that the camera swings from side to side continuously, even when no one is monitoring the system.

CCTV System Requirements

In general, a CCTV system should perform at approximately the same level as commercial broadcast receivers. Specific equipment and the quality of image needed are determined by characteristics of the area under surveillance, schedules of operation, makeup of the monitoring staff and their expected responses to emergencies, and use of special equipment.

American and foreign manufacturers have TV cameras suitable for security work. All equipment should meet the standards of the Electronic Industries Association for CCTV. Service and maintenance are generally more difficult and expensive than installation; therefore, the capability and reputation of a local supplier is crucial. City police or traffic departments often have had experience with manufacturers, suppliers, and maintenance operations. To encourage reliance on the system by users, and to prevent criminals from taking advantage of a lapse, the CCTV system should break down as infrequently as possible and be repaired quickly in the event of a breakdown.

Picture resolution depends primarily on camera quality and lighting levels: Higher lighting levels permit the use of less sensitive, less expensive cameras.

The entire system should operate unattended. This requires electronically stable equipment, meaning, for example, that no one should be required to constantly adjust the lens of the camera.

It is difficult to project costs of CCTV systems because of the variety of system sizes and configurations and the range of equipment costs. Camera prices start as low as $200, but more sophisticated models, such as those sensitive to very low light levels, cost up to $10,000 each. Complicated accessories including zoom lenses, remote pan (side-to-side movement) and tilt (up-and-down movement) mechanisms, and low-light equipment can increase installation and maintenance costs tremendously. The cost of monitoring equipment can be as low as the cost of a conventional television receiver, but more specialized and sensitive equipment is far more expensive.

Camera Locations

Locations of a CCTV camera and the light level at that point are key cost-effectiveness factors. A camera's location defines the area to be observed by the camera, and the nature of the location greatly influences the camera's vulnerability to theft and vandalism.

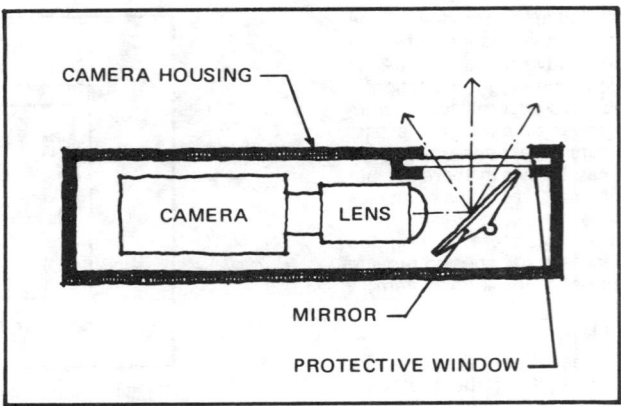

Fig. 55   Recessed camera.

Available lighting dictates the type of camera needed to produce a final image of adequate quality. Of course, supplemental lighting may be provided at additional cost.

The camera must be able to view an area that is significant in terms of crime control. Wide-angle or other special lenses should be avoided by choosing a different camera location. Most importantly, the camera itself must be protected from theft and vandalism. This means that the body and lens of the camera should be in an inaccessible place. A mirror is often used to reflect the image into the lens, so that the expensive lens will not be broken by pointed instruments, thrown objects, or bullets (see Fig. 55). All interior cameras should be placed inside sturdy housings which are installed with tamper-proof connectors. Cameras must be accessible for maintenance and repair, however.

A number of locations meet all of these requirements. An elevator in a high-rise building is often protected by CCTV. The camera is generally mounted on the outside of the elevator cab wall so that the image passes via a mirror in a corner of the elevator to the protected lens. In case of camera failure, the elevator must be stopped so that the camera maintenance man can step onto the top of the cab and reach over the side to repair the units. This is not overly inconvenient for repairmen, but it does make access to the camera more difficult for a potential thief.

Building lobbies are another common location of interior cameras. Lobby cameras are commonly hung from the ceiling or recessed into the ceiling. The elevated locations require that the repairmen use a ladder. Use of a ladder, however, would make a thief very conspicuous.

Outdoor locations usually depend upon inaccessibility to protect equipment from theft and vandalism. Cameras are located atop steel poles or on poles extending from roofs or walls. An alternative is to place the camera in a wall or window of an accessible apartment.

Lighting for CCTV Systems

Lighting plays a key role in the cost and effectiveness of a CCTV system. For camera locations inside buildings, it is almost always less expensive to raise the light level than to use low-light-level equipment. The required

lighting level is only slightly higher than normal for building interiors, can be achieved without glare, and has an intrinsic value as a crime deterrent.

Exterior lighting can be very expensive. Cameras used outdoors are almost always more flexible and sensitive, being capable of adapting to full sun, cloudiness, and dusk. But as indicated earlier, camera costs rise dramatically for low-light-level equipment. While increasing of lighting levels is also expensive, well-designed extra lighting again has an intrinsic value as a crime deterrent.

Monitoring of CCTV Systems

Effectiveness of CCTV depends on the nature and quality of monitoring. Many people may be used as monitors: city police, project security personnel, members of organized tenant patrols, tenants acting as individuals, and various combinations of these groups. The choice depends principally upon availability of personnel and their monitoring costs.

City police will monitor CCTV systems only if they believe it is the most efficient use of manpower. Thus an area being surveyed must suffer large numbers of crimes to warrant hiring a policeman or civilian whose function is simply sitting, watching, and adjusting. Crime reduction or criminal apprehension through CCTV monitoring would have to be substantial to justify continued use of such manpower. Police use of CCTV systems is generally limited to shopping districts and city-center areas. Police normally monitor large systems that include several cameras (each equipped with pan, tilt, and zoom capability) and a monitoring console, so that the viewer can watch activity in several places at once and adjust his equipment to concentrate on a particular place, incident, or individual.

Commercial and industrial facilities often hire private security personnel to monitor CCTV systems. Guards are used less frequently in residential complexes. The major advantage of use of guards is that a single guard can control several entrances to a building or complex of buildings. Usually the guard can see all entrance doors, the lobby, and the elevator interiors on the monitor screens. He can be given audio contact with the lobby area. With the use of an intercom system, he can also control garage and front door entrances. He can also be given the ability to stop the elevator in midflight. Thus the security guard can see and hear every person entering the premises; he can prevent them from entering; and he can even exert some control after they enter.

It is also possible to staff a monitoring panel with members of tenant patrols. Use of volunteer personnel eliminates payment of guard salaries. Because they are personally acquainted with the project residents, tenant monitors can easily pick out strangers and perhaps distinguish a minor argument among friends from an impending fight.

But, there are serious drawbacks in using tenant monitors. It is difficult to guarantee the performance of unpaid people. The novelty of working with TV monitors will wear off quickly, and declining interest increases the likelihood of patrol members simply not showing up. Additionally, tenant patrol members are not equipped or empowered to take much action. The tenant monitoring the CCTV has no real authority over police or security personnel. Finally, there is the problem of tenant patrol members using their position to harass or intimidate other tenants.

An alternative is in-apartment tenant monitoring. Tenants of a building or housing project can monitor CCTV on their home TV screens. By connecting CCTV equipment to a master antenna within a building, tenants can have the option of tuning into unused TV channels to monitor lobby, elevator, playground, or parking lot activity. Tenants may watch CCTV when they are expecting someone to arrive, or when a child is playing within viewing range of a camera in a playground area. Older people may watch for less specific reasons. Obviously, this does not assure continuous monitoring, but if one or more of 200 tennats is watching, it would be risky for intruders to take chances.

An in-apartment tenant monitoring system requires that a cable TV or master antenna system be in operation in the building. CCTV is clearly most suited to large, high-rise dwellings. Picture quality of the CCTV systems should be comparable to that of commercial broadcasting to promote tenant usage. While some picture disintegration may be acceptable in a conventionally monitored CCTV system, there should be no distortion in a system designed for in-apartment monitoring. It is desirable (and generally not expensive) to install a microphone system so that sound accompanies the TV picture, which makes the system more interesting and enjoyable.

It is possible to organize a voluntary in-apartment monitoring program to improve coverage. A tenant organization could arrange for persons to watch CCTV in their homes during specified hours. Such a scheduled system would promote better coverage and facilitate participation because there would be no requirement that residents leave their apartments.

Also, CCTV monitors should be placed where responsible individuals, such as management staff and patrolling guards, are at work or pass by continually.

INTERCOM SYSTEMS

Most urban multifamily dwellings are equipped with buzzer-reply systems to limit access to the building to tenants and to people who have been interviewed by tenants on an intercom system. A typical buzzer-reply intercom system in an apartment building functions as follows: A panel located outside the lobby entrance door lists the names and apartment numbers of all tenants in the building. Next to each tenant's name is a call button that when pressed rings a bell or buzzer within that tenant's apartment. The tenant responds to the call by walking to a panel mounted on the wall of his apartment and speaking via an intercom system to the person outside the door. When identification is satisfactorily established, the tenant pushes a button on the panel which momentarily allows the entrance door to be opened without a key. Because the costs involved in installing wiring for such a system in an existing building are very high, buzzer-reply systems should be installed in all new buildings during the construction phase.

A modified version of the traditional buzzer-reply system has recently come into use. Local telephone companies install and service front-door intercom systems that use existing telephone wires instead of a separately wired system. The panel mounted outside the lobby door differs from a conventional panel in that it is supplied with a telephone receiver, and the list of residents has a three-digit number next to each name. A person wishing to enter the building dials the appropriate three-digit number, which makes the phone of the tenant buzz (not ring). The tenant then speaks with the person over the phone. If recognition is established, the tenant dials "4" to open the front door. If a tenant is speaking on the phone when the buzzer sounds, he can depress the receiver once, speak to the person in the lobby, buzz him in by dialing "4," and then depress the receiver again to return to his initial telephone conversation. For tenants without telephones, a special unit that can be used only for the intercom can be installed. Fees for installation and service are billed by the phone company and added to the tenants' monthly rent.

ELEVATOR AUDIO SYSTEMS

Use of audio systems in elevators is rapidly increasing. An elevator audio system is an uncomplicated sound-transmission installation consisting of a microphone and speaker located in the elevator cab and connected to similar devices near the elevator doors on each floor. The system allows someone inside the elevator to speak to anyone standing in the elevator waiting area, and vice versa. In office buildings or high-income residential buildings, an additional connection is made so that a doorman, guard, or maintenance man can respond to persons inside the elevator. In low-income housing, the equipment in the cab is simply connected to the elevator on each floor.

Some systems are designed to remain on at all times, but most require the person in the cab to push a button before he can talk to the outside location. A continuous voice relay system reassures the elevator rider that he can communicate with the outside if any trouble arises, whereas the need to push a button limits the usefulness of a noncontinuous audio system in crime situations. Any elevator audio device is useful when breakdowns occur and someone is trapped inside the cab.

COLOR THEORY

Primary colors The longest extended slices on the color wheel (Fig. 1) show the three primary colors — red, yellow, and blue. They're called primary because all the other colors come from combinations of these three colors.

Secondary colors Mix any two primary colors and you get the secondary colors:

Orange (red and yellow)
Violet (red and blue)
Green (blue and yellow)

Tertiary colors All of the other six colors on the wheel are called tertiary, or intermediate, colors. They are a mixture of the primary colors plus an adjacent secondary color. Thus:

Yellow orange (yellow and orange)
Yellow green (yellow and green)
Blue green (blue and green)
Blue violet (blue and violet)
Red violet (red and violet)
Red orange (red and orange)

Color has three dimensions: the *hue*, distinguishing one color from another — such as red, green, blue, etc.; the *value*, denoting lightness or darkness; and the *tone* or *intensity*, which is the brightness or dullness.

These hues, values, and intensities can appear to change when different ones are used together. Two or more light values combined afford little contrast; nor will darker values in combination provide much interest. But, when a light value is used with a dark, the light appears lighter while the dark appears darker. White is the lightest of all colors, and values range from it through varying gradations of gray to black. Colors that are nearer white in value are called *tints* and colors that are closer to black in value are called *shades*.

Intensities or tones also have similar effects. A brightly upholstered chair will appear brighter and will stand out when used with a carpet of dull color, as it will produce a spot of interest. In contrast, a few dull-colored pieces of furniture will sink into the background if the room contains brighter-colored rugs, draperies, and other furnishings.

Contrasting or opposite hues will emphasize one another. Red with green will make the red look redder and the green appear more orange, while the red-purple will take on a bluish tone.

There are many ways of combining colors for interest. Related color schemes such as reds, purples, and blues together can produce very pleasing effects. Contrasting hues, such as blues with oranges, can also be combined to give more vibrant results.

Some people enjoy excitement. Warm colors such as yellow, orange, and red are exciting because they are associated with things like sunshine, fire, heat, and even blood. Warm colors tend to "advance," and a predominantly warm-colored wall will seem to come forward. They are especially effective in rooms that are on the east or north side of a house, because light entering from those directions seems to be a cool light. The warm colors and cool light complement each other and make the room seem cozier and warmer.

Cool colors are those associated with water, verdure, and the sky — blues, greens, and violets. These tend to "recede," and under most conditions, light, cool-colored walls will create an illusion of greater space. They are good choices for rooms on the south and west side of the house, since these areas receive a lot of sunlight all year around. Theirs is a cooling effect in the warm-light areas, another complementary association.

Black, white, gray, and brown — and the tones of the latter two, known as griege and beige — are not considered to be colors so much as *neutrals*. In practice, they are the "no-color" colors, which are used with other colors to modify them or to contrast with them. But they are far from being negative. As you work with color, you will find that all colors are influenced by the company they keep. This is particularly true of the tints, shades, and so-called neutral colors. A juxtaposition of two muted colors, such as a gray and a tan, will bring out latent greens, lavenders, and pinks you did not see before. Colors also have visual weights. Dark and bright appear heavy, while light or dull seem to weigh less. Remember that a dominant color is the one that "controls" a room, while the others are accents.

Basic Color-Scheme Planning

Successful decorating often depends on how well the total effect is anticipated. Here are four types of schemes that professional decorators have in mind when they start to plan a job. They are no guarantee of perfect results, but they do make an unwieldy subject easier to handle.

Monochromatic This scheme is built around one color, using it somewhere in its full intensity, and then varying it with a number of shades, and tints of the same color. For example, in a monochromatic scheme of yellow, the range could be from dark shades of gold, through clear yellow, to light, pale-yellow tints. A monochromatic color scheme can be restful, create a feeling of spaciousness, and provides a good background for art objects, collections or similar decorations. But generally, when employing a monochromatic color scheme, the interest of the room comes through by using a variety of textures and patterns.

Analogous or related Because it's the easiest color scheme to work with, an analogous scheme is the one that enjoys the greatest popularity at the present time. It is based on two or three colors, such as yellow, yellow orange, and red orange, that lie close to each other on the color wheel, with "relief" provided by tints and shades of the same that have been tinged with adjacent greens or vermilion. The analogous color scheme is restful and refreshing also, and the colors are more interesting because of their variations in intensity and value. It is the kind of color scheme that is easily changed; a slight shift of emphasis here and there is all that is necessary to completely change the character of the room.

Complementary or contrasting This scheme, which is rapidly coming into favor, uses colors that are opposite each other on the color wheel — blue and orange, red and green, yellow and violet. One color is usually a primary color and the other a secondary color. Using such contrasting colors will give a lively and vibrant room, but it is a color scheme that must be used with caution. One color should always dominate, with the others being primarily dramatic accents. The "shock" impact of a complementary color scheme can be softened by selecting unexpected shades and tints of the two colors. That is, a vivid color and its complement can be quieted, if you prefer, by graying them, or reducing their values. Employing a pair of opposites in this manner means that there will be both cool and warm colors in a room, which makes a mutually complementary association. A complementary color scheme tends to make a room seem smaller.

Accented This is a combination of adjacent, related, or analogous colors — call them what you will — accented by a bold touch of color from the opposite side of the wheel. An example would be a scheme ranging through a number of strong, soft, and grayed yellows, spiked with purple or violet.

There are also other color schemes, such as *triad* and *split-complementary* that you can adapt from the color wheel, but the four suggested above are the easiest to visualize and to carry out.

In whatever basic scheme you use do not forget the neutrals: black, white, the grays, and browns — to which you might add metallic gold and silver. Since they will appear, of themselves, in the wood and metal of your furnishings, they must at all times be considered for the part they play in the total effect. If you wish, the neutrals can constitute a fifth, and very sophisticated, color scheme of their own! But usually they must be more or less just "accepted," and played up or played down by the colors you combine them with. Incidentally, some black and white is an asset to almost any color scheme, but too many and indefinite neutrals, used with stronger colors, tend to compromise a color scheme and make it look confused or merely drab. It is best to think of any neutral as a distinctive note of color, whether it is the fieldstone of a fireplace or a hardwood floor.

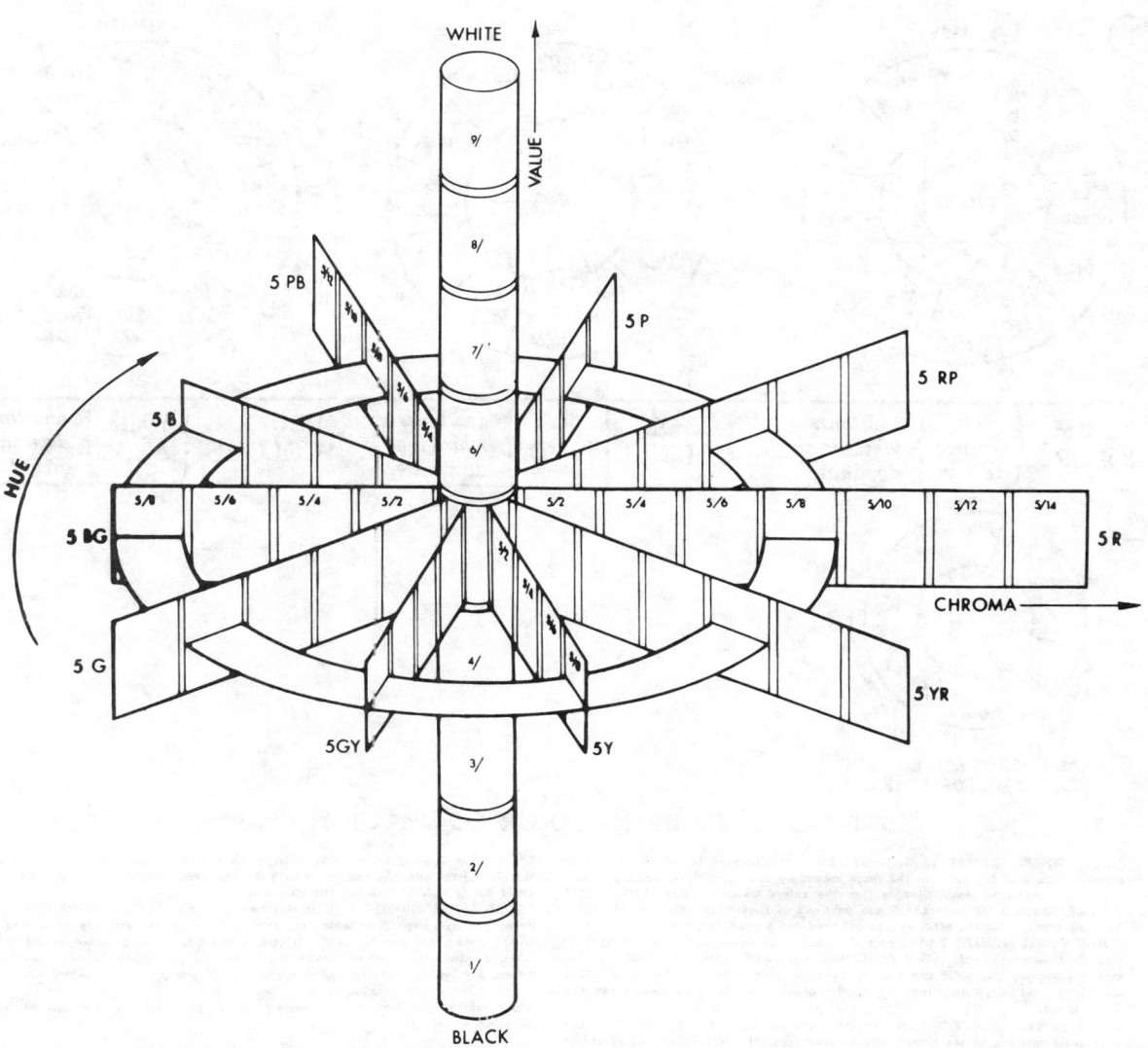

Fig. 1 The basic wheel with a three-dimensional projection of the attributes of color — hue, value, and intensity — as shown in their relation to one another. The circular band represents the hues: G, green; B, blue; P, purple; R, red; and Y, yellow. The upright center axis is the scale of value. Paths leading from the center indicate color intensity.

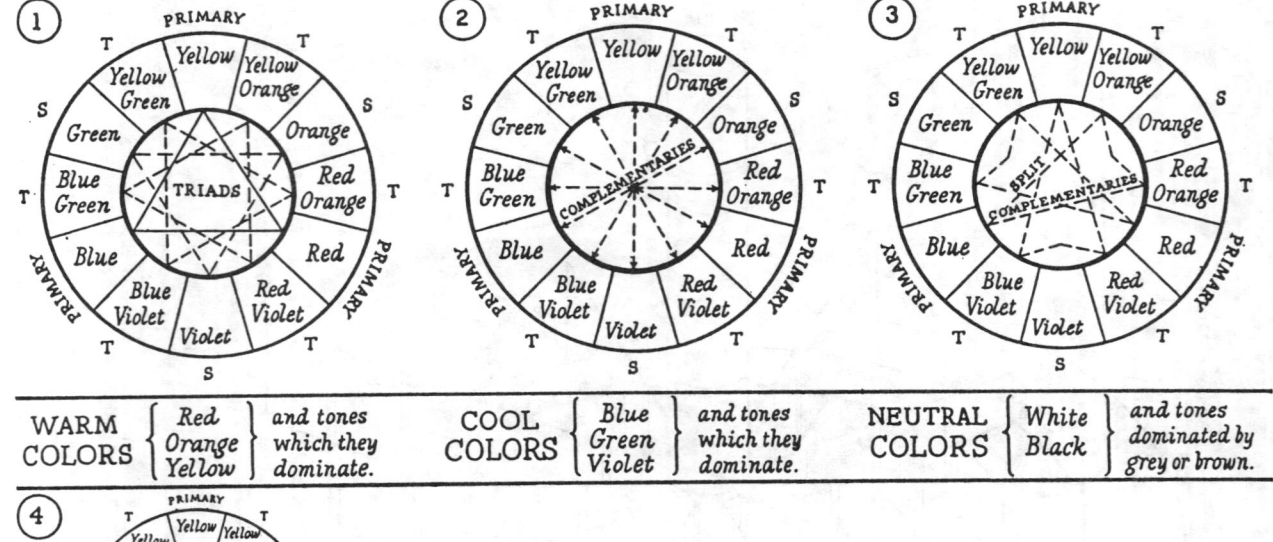

| WARM COLORS | Red Orange Yellow | and tones which they dominate. | COOL COLORS | Blue Green Violet | and tones which they dominate. | NEUTRAL COLORS | White Black | and tones dominated by grey or brown. |

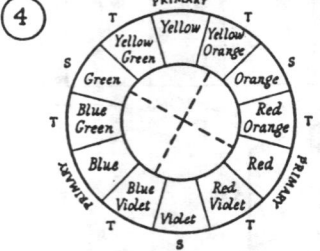

EXAMPLES OF ANALOGOUS
(RELATED) COLOR SCHEMES

DIRECTIONS FOR USING COLOR COMBINATION CHARTS

COLOR WHEEL NUMBER 1 illustrates color combinations in which the three primaries are used together, or the three secondary colors, or three tertiary colors. The three points of each triangle link the colors used in this TRIAD COLOR SCHEME. The rule for success is to use only one of them in a strong, bright tone, in small areas, with the other two in softened (or grayed) tones.

COLOR WHEEL NUMBER 2 illustrates the color pairs which are effective together through contrast. This is called the COMPLEMENTARY COLOR SCHEME. As the arrows indicate, the pairs are exactly opposite each other on the wheel. One should be used in a bright tone for smaller areas, the other in grayed tones and larger areas.

COLOR WHEEL NUMBER 3 illustrates the use of a color with the two which are next to its opposite on the wheel, one on each side. This SPLIT COMPLEMENTARY COLOR SCHEME follows the rule for complementaries, and may include the direct contrast color also, if desired. For example, yellow may be used with blue-violet, and red-violet, with or without the true violet shade which comes between them.

To avoid confusion, not all of the triangles are indicated. Cut a piece of paper the size of the triangle and lay it with the top point at any color you choose. The other points will rest on the correct colors.

COLOR WHEEL NUMBER 4 illustrates how an ANALOGOUS COLOR SCHEME is developed by using colors which are related because they are side by side on the wheel. Any group can be used, all around the wheel, as indicated by the dotted lines. For an accent color you can use a contrast color opposite any one of your group. For instance, in the yellow-orange to red group, complementary blue could be used for accent (shown on color wheel 2).

Black, white, gray and other definitely neutral tones can be used with any combination of colors.

BASIC PRINCIPLES FOR WORKING OUT A COLOR SCHEME

1. DOMINANT OR CONTROLLING COLOR

Decide on your dominant or controlling color, which may dominate by covering a large area or by strength of color in a smaller area. Decide whether your foundation or background color is to be the dominant or a secondary color. Plan to use a large amount of quiet background color, a small amount of bold, strong color. All large foundation areas should be in light or grayed tones.

2. GRAYING

Clear colors are gayer, more cheerful, but grayed tones are more restful, their harmonies more subtle. Mixing gray with bright colors brings them into relation with other colors in the room. As . . . red and yellow in bright tones seem to clash. Mixed with gray, they become rose and tan and go very well together. Use this principle also in buying materials. Avoid too much graying. It gives muddy tones, dirty grays, flat greens. A little gray goes far.

3. RELIEF AND CONTRAST COLORS

Decide on relief and contrast colors and bring them into all parts of the room composition. Remember the order in the amount of space allowed each one—foundation, then relief, then contrast. All colors—including background colors—should be keyed to the dominant color. Soften strong contrast colors

with white. Contrast is less in lighter tints. Soften darker contrasts with gray.

4. ACCENT COLORS

Use pure bright intense colors only in accessories, etc. Distribute them so they will not be spotty. The smaller the area the brighter the color may be. The larger the area the softer the tone should be. Don't use large amounts of pure bright color.

5. KEYING

This is another means of creating harmony. A key color is the one about which the color scheme is built—the dominant, or controlling color. All other colors in the room must be "keyed" with it—harmonized. Two colors in which any part of a third color is present will be linked together. Example: To key red and yellow to each other, mix them both with a little of the third primary hue—blue. Violet and green will result, and these are harmonious to use with your strong tones. Remember this principle in buying as well as mixing colors. A lovely print or art object will have these tones keyed for you, and you can use them for your own composition. The safe rule is to avoid too many colors and too strong tones except in accents, etc. Most colors will "go together" if you soften them.

WHAT DECORATORS MEAN
WHEN THEY USE THESE COLOR TERMS

HUE: Each section in the color wheel is called a hue. To change a hue, another color (not black, white or pure gray) must be added to it. Every hue has a different wave length from every other hue. Mixed with its complement equally it produces gray.

PRIMARY COLORS: Also called "normal," also "fundamental." Primaries are the three pigment colors which cannot be produced by any mixture of other pigments. These are red like that of a geranium flower, yellow like that of ripe lemons, blue like the deep clear hue of a sunny southern sky.

SECONDARY COLORS: Secondaries are the three colors which are produced by mixing two of the three primaries in equal amounts. Red + yellow = orange; red + blue = purple (or violet); yellow + blue = green.

TERTIARY COLORS: Tertiaries are the colors produced by mixing a primary with a secondary, the exact shade depending upon the proportion. Red + orange produces shades such as russet, burnt orange, coral, etc. Red + purple—mulberry, amethyst, orchid, etc. Blue + purple—heliotrope, periwinkle, lavender, etc. Blue + green—turquoise, aquamarine, bottle green, etc. Yellow + orange—maize, primrose, flame, etc. Yellow + green—jade, Nile, olive, chartreuse, etc. Mixtures of complementaries not included because these produce shades of gray—a neutral. Some authorities consider, also, the shades produced by mixing two secondaries as tertiaries, such as slate, citron, buff, sage, etc.

COMPLEX COLORS: All colors which are made up of more complicated mixtures than those producing secondary and tertiary colors are called complex.

NEUTRAL COLORS: Black and white are considered neutral. Also all those tints and shades in which tones of gray or brown predominate.

TINTS: The light tones resulting when white is mixed with a color. Much white makes a color cold.

SHADES: The dark tones resulting when black is mixed with a color. Much black deadens the color.

TONE: Each hue has many tones. By tone—or tonal value—we mean the relative strength of the hue as it approaches black or white at the opposite ends of the value scale. Mixed with white, a color is "pale" in tone; mixed with black, it is "dark" in tone. The upper and lower extremes of any color would be white (or very pale gray), and black.

CHROMA: This term is used interchangeably with value, tonal value, and intensity. The chroma of a color such as yellow is "light"; the chroma of a color such as Navy blue is "dark." When a color fades, it loses chroma.

LUMINOSITY: This term is used to describe a quality of warm clear colors in light-reflecting tones and finishes, such as light golden-yellow. Clear white is also luminous. Literally "luminous" are only metals in gold, silver, platinum, or clear plastics.

COLOR	SUGGESTED COLOR GROUPS TO USE WITH IT
RED	Green, gray, blue (for accent)
SCARLET	Light blue, ecru (or Navy and taupe)
CRIMSON	Pearl gray, mauve
GARNET	Sapphire blue, mauve, pearl gray
CARDINAL	Marine blue, turquoise, gray
WINE	Black, old blue, beige
ROSE	Flesh, light blue, green
OLD ROSE	Blue in various shades
CEDAR ROSE	Blue, cream
PINK	Green, orchid, blue for accent
ORANGE	Violet, light blue, indigo for accent
BURNT ORANGE	Electric blue, light brown
SALMON	Turquoise, lavender
HENNA	Peacock green, royal blue, gray
PEACH	Rust, blue, tan
MAIZE	Powder blue, pink
YELLOW	Violet, blue, green
PRIMROSE	Lavender, dusty rose, soft green
SOFT YELLOW	Brown, French blue
GOLD	Soft gray-green, deep red
DARK GREEN	Brown, beige (or sage green and gold)
MYRTLE	Heliotrope, yellow
SOFT GREEN	Rosewood, deep violet
TARRAGON	Heliotrope, pearl grey
CHINESE JADE	Rose, ivory
NILE	Cornflower, orange
LIGHT GREEN	Rose, dark green, mauve
BLUE	Yellow, sand, orange for accent
COPENHAGEN BLUE	Burgundy, gray
FLEMISH BLUE	Olive-green, cardinal
LIGHT BLUE	Orchid, champagne
DEEP PURPLE	Orange, gray
VIOLET	Green, light and dark shades
LAVENDER	Green, mauve, gray
HELIOTROPE	Light blue, cream
HYDRANGEA	Old rose, primrose yellow
MAUVE	Emerald green, dark red, brown
BROWN	Orange, tan, cardinal for accent
GRAY	Violet, crimson, lavender.

COLOR AREAS AND SAMPLES

PROPORTIONATE SAMPLE SIZES

1. WALLS	24" x 24"
2. FLOOR	18" x 18"
3. DRAPERIES	16" x 16"
4. CEILING	14" x 14"
5. COUCH, ETC.	12" x 14"
6. WOODWORK	10" x 14"
7. LARGE CHAIR	8" x 8"
8. LARGE CHAIR	6" x 8"
9. SMALL CHAIR	6" x 7"
10. ACCESSORIES	6" x 7"
11. ACCENTS	5" x 6"
12. TRIMMINGS	5" x 6"

VARIED as used here means choice of light, dark, or medium tones, clear or grayed colors.

POINTS TO REMEMBER IN MATCHING SAMPLES FOR COLOR

1. Use larger samples if possible, especially in patterned materials, but keep approximate proportions of chart. Sizes are determined according to area and interest. Ceiling and floor areas, for example, are equal—but floor interest is greater, hence the larger sample. If several items are the same color add them to make one sample.

2. Make allowance for texture. Soft rough surface in paint, paper, or fabric makes colors appear darker. Hard glossy surfaces appear lighter.

3. Make allowance for distance. Colors look brighter when they are close; farther away they seem softer, grayed by atmosphere. Colors which match exactly 1 ft. away may seem quite different at 15 ft. This is important in a large high-ceilinged room.

4. Make allowance for proximity. When side by side: Complementary colors brighten each other; related colors, when both light or both dark, deaden each other; neutral colors brighten clear colors, but pure strong primary colors deaden neutrals such as grays, browns, etc.; light and dark tones brighten each other, especially white for dark colors and black for light tones; one color may seem to change another's hue as when a strong clear color gives a tinge of its complementary to a neutral —red, for example, may give a greenish cast to gray unless a little red has been mixed with the gray.

5. Make allowance for proportion. The larger the area the darker the color will appear. Choose a wall color slightly lighter than you really want it. Don't decide exact shade of a painted wall until all other materials have been chosen. It is easier to match paint to fabric and paper than the other way around.

WALLS — MEDIUM TO LIGHT

FLOORS — DARK TO MEDIUM

DRAPERY — VARIED

CEILING — LIGHT

LARGE COUCH BED SOFA — VARIED

WOODWORK — VARIED

LARGE CHAIR — VARIED

LARGE CHAIR

SMALL CHAIR — BRIGHT

ACCESSORIES

ACCENTS — BRIGHT

TRIMMINGS

1 2 3 4 5 6 7 8 9 10 11 12

# COLOR COMBINATION CHARTS
S = SECONDARY ..... T = TERTIARY

COLOR THEORY
Munsell System of Color

One of the best-known and widely respected systems of color standardization used in the United States today is that developed by Albert H. Munsell. He became greatly interested in the practical application of color and was disturbed by the fact that the popular names for colors did not describe them adequately for professional purposes. They are named after flowers or plants, such as violet, indigo, old rose, primrose; after fruits, such as peach, pomegranate, grape, avocado, plum; after places such as french blue, naples yellow, or prussian blue; or after persons, such as Davy's gray or Hooker's green.

Essentially the system consists of an orderly arrangement of colors in the shape of a three-dimensional color solid. The system is based on a color circle of ten major hues made up of five principal hues, red, yellow, green, blue, and purple, and five intermediate hues, yellow-red, green-yellow, blue-green, purple-blue, and red-purple. Each hue is indicated by a symbol as follows:

Red: R
Yellow: Y
Green: G
Blue: B
Purple: P
Yellow-red: YR
Green-yellow: GY
Blue-green: BG

Purple-blue: PB
Red-purple: RP

Each of the above major hues has been given a value of 5 in the inner scale around the hue circle (see Fig. 2, hue symbols), i.e., 5 R, 5 YR, 5 Y, 5 GY, 5 G, 5 BG, 5 B, 5 PB, 5 P, and 5 RP. Between each of the major hues are values of 2.5, 10, and 7.5 for rough indication of hue. The outer scale of the hue circuit is divided into 100 segments to provide greater accuracy for indicating hue where needed.

In the Munsell color tree each hue (H) is allotted ten segments of the hue circle, making 100 hues, and these hues form the horizontal center, or equator, of the color solid. The center segment of each hue is considered the true color, and the remaining segments in each hue section vary according to their proximity to adjoining colors; for example, as red gets closer to yellow it contains more yellow, and this is indicated by the numerical designation.

The value (V) notation denotes the lightness or darkness of a hue, which is determined by a neutral core at the center of the hue circle. The core contains ten gradations from a supposedly perfect white (one having 100 percent reflectance) at the top to 0, a perfect black (having 0 percent reflectance) at the bottom.

The chroma (C) notation indicates the saturation of the hue, or the strength of the color. The chroma scale extends outward from the central core or axis, and the increments vary from 0 at a neutral gray to as high as 16, according to the amount of saturation produced by a given hue at a given value level. Since colors vary in chroma, or saturation, some colors extend farther from the neutral axis than others, and the solid is therefore not symmetrical. Pure red, with a chroma of 14, for instance, extends farther than blue-green, with a chroma of only 6 (see Fig. 1).

A Munsell notation indicating hue, value, and chroma (H V/C) might be given as follows:

Vermilion: 5R 5/14
Rose: 5R 5/4

With this information it is possible to describe exactly any given hue and to locate its place in the color solid. Furthermore, as Munsell stated, one can "select one familiar color, and study what others will combine with it to please the eye," by the use of three typical paths: one vertical, with rapid change of value; another lateral, with rapid change of hue; and a third, inward, through the neutral center, to seek out the opposite color field. All other paths are combined by two or three of these typical directions in the color solid.

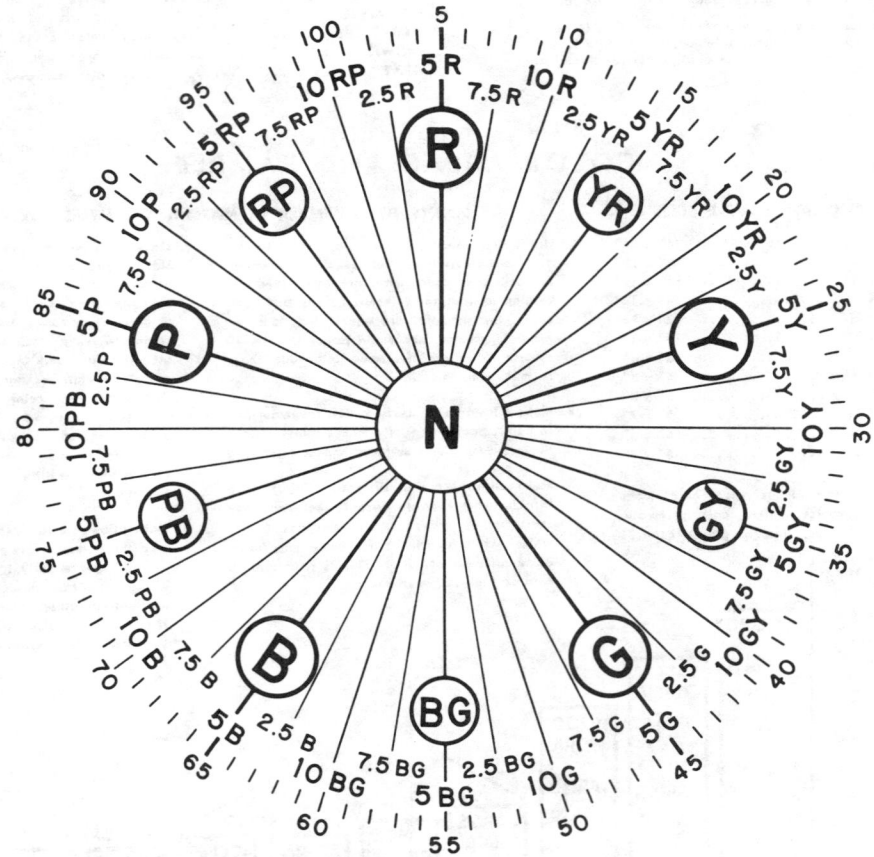

Fig. 2   Munsell hue symbols and their relation to one another.

THE RED FAMILY

REPRESENTATIVE MEMBERS OF THE RED FAMILY ... ROSE ... DUSTY ROSE ... OLD ROSE ... MAROON ... BURGUNDY OR WINE RED ... MAROON ... ETC. ... FLESH ... DUSTY-PINK ... SHELL-PINK ... CARDINAL OR CRIMSON ... RASPBERRY ... RED-

CHARACTERISTICS ... Warm, advancing ... Cheerful, hospitable, active ... In strong tones, stimulating, bold, vital, dramatic, exciting.

WHAT THEY CAN DO ... Make objects seem closer, larger ... Make room seem smaller by bringing background closer ... Focus attention on wall or object ... Bring life, brightness, warmth, to drab, dark or too-cool rooms.

CORRECT USES ... In light tints, charming background for fairly light, large rooms ... In bright tones, highly decorative when used for comparatively small areas, as in accessories, accents, etc. ... In darker shades, rich and warm for draperies, carpets, upholstery, especially in large rooms with heavy furniture.

CAUTION ... Do not use too much red—especially in clear, bright tones, and in light rooms ... Safer to soften a little by "graying," except when used for accent ... Do not use the Red Family for background of a room that is small or crowded ... Do not use bright red for large objects, unless you want to call attention to them ... Do not forget when using the Red Family to include cool colors in your color schemes ... It takes two cool colors, or a large area of one cool color, to balance red.

SUGGESTED COLOR SCHEMES IN WHICH MEMBERS OF RED FAMILY PLAY A DOMINANT ROLE

DOMINANT COLOR	MAJOR WALL COLOR	MAJOR FLOOR COLOR	DRAPERIES AND UPHOLSTERY	ACCENT COLORS	REMARKS
SHELL-PINK	Shell-pink	Light Blue	Off-white background, powder-blue and shell-pink in pattern	Italian Red	Charming for bedroom. In slightly darker tones of same colors, could be adapted to living rooms. Feminine feeling
MELON PINK (like Pompeiian terra cotta)	Melon Pink	Brown	Light tan background, melon-pink with green olive in design	Green Olive	Good for living or dining room with mahogany or walnut furniture
VENETIAN PINK	Venetian Pink	Patterned rug, soft tones, green, mauve, red	Draperies, yellow and white stripes. Upholstery, green and dull pink stripes	Red	Good for living room with 18th Century furniture
DUSTY PINK	Dusty Pink Woodwork, cocoa brown	Deep Brown	Draperies, pale aquamarine (dusty pink curtains) Chair and bed covers, cocoa and pink stripes with cocoa brown trimming	White	Interesting for modern bedroom with furniture in cocoa tones
BOIS DE ROSE	Bois de Rose	Sage Green	Draperies, pearl gray, trimmed with bois de rose. Upholstery, pale gray with sulphur yellow	Green and Sulphur yellow	Living room color scheme with feminine feeling
DAWN ROSE	Dawn Rose	Dark Green	Neutral background, dawn rose and leaf-green in pattern	Wet Leaf-green	Attractive for bedroom
LIGHT ROSE	Light Rose	Deep Blue-green	Draperies, dusty rose background, blue-green and foliage tones in design. Upholstery, blue, blue-green and green, plain, pattern and stripes	Blue	Suitable for fairly large room with average light
ROSE (1)	Warm Gray	Rose Taupe	Draperies, rose. Upholstery, rose and cream stripes	Blue or Green	Appropriate for almost any living or bedroom
ROSE (2)	Oyster White	Rose Red	Draperies, oyster white. Upholstery, oyster white with reds, blues and soft green	Red	Charming for bedroom or woman's living room
ASHES OF ROSES	Ashes of Roses	Cafe au lait	White	Strong Blue	Adaptable to bedroom or living room
DUSTY ROSE (1)	Deep dusty Rose	Brown	Lighter dusty rose, white and brown	Silver	Good color scheme for living room or dining room
DUSTY ROSE (2)	Pickled wood	Pinkish Beige	Draperies, dusty rose. Upholstery, foam green and natural	Pale Green	Adaptable to living room, traditional or modern
OLD ROSE (1)	Old Rose	Warm Gray	Blue and pale yellow, with touch of old rose	Jade Green	This color scheme is charming and delicate, suitable for bedrooms and dressing rooms
OLD ROSE (2)	Paper, Old Rose, cream and gray	Mulberry	Old rose and gray	Blue and Silver	With woodwork painted warm gray, this scheme would be attractive for bedroom or dressing room
OLD ROSE (3)	Paper, Blue and rose pattern	Ivory	Draperies, ivory background, rose, blue and green in pattern. Upholstery, old rose, and drapery fabric	Green	Attractive for formal living room
RED (1)	Soft grayed Green	Patterned rug with red background	Draperies, pale gray background, red in pattern. Upholstery, plain green, red and green stripes	Blue and Orange	Suitable living room or dining room

COLOR THEORY

Color Families: Red

Color	Walls / Woodwork	Floor / Rug	Draperies / Upholstery	Accent	Remarks
RED (2)	Paper, granite flecked with red	Patterned rug, red predominating	Chintz, red predominating in pattern	Green and Pewter	Good for Early American room, with pine or maple
RED (3)	Paper, red toile design; woodwork, white	Hooked rugs Floors, painted blue	Draperies, textured beige Upholstery, textured beige trimmed with red	Blue (chairs painted blue)	Colonial type living room or library
RED (4)	Old white Woodwork, dark green	Red rug	Red and white brocade	Green	Living room in period feeling with walnut furniture
RED (5)	Paper, light background, red with green and brown in pattern	Dark blue	Red	Blue	Early American dining room, with pine and maple
SOFT RED (1)	Neutral	Soft Red	Draperies, blue-green background, deep red in design Upholstery, blue-green	Yellow	Nice for living room
SOFT RED (2)	White	Rug, blue, red and white pattern	Draperies, linen color with red in pattern Upholstery, chair seats, blue	Silver	18th Century dining room
CRIMSON (1)	Bone white	Crimson	White background, floral design in red and soft green	White	Mahogany furniture of very nice design would be lovely with white walls
CRIMSON (2)	Soft Gray	Crimson	Draperies, white, gray and crimson Upholstery, white, trimmed with crimson	Black	A smart sophisticated color scheme
CRIMSON (3)	Slate Gray	Soft Crimson	Draperies, bluish white, trimmed with soft crimson Upholstery, bluish white	Gold	Adaptable to modern styles
CHINESE RED	Grayed soft Green	Chinese Red	Draperies, grayed soft green Upholstery, deep beige	Light Beige	Good for living room or dining room
LACQUER RED (1)	Gray	Brown	Gray and lacquer red	Green	Colorful living room with some red lacquer furniture
LACQUER RED (2)	Paneling, Red Lacquer, silver trim	Black	Silver gray, with red and black in design	Silver	Modern library
ITALIAN RED	Yellow	Floor, stained dark Patterned rug in old reds and dark blues, red predominating	Draperies, Italian red damask. Upholstery, red damask, yellow, glazed chintz with white ground and red in design	Gold	Living room English in feeling; also good for Federal American
CRANBERRY RED	Paper with light ground and cranberry pattern Paneled fireplace and painted blue	Deep soft red	Draperies, rose Upholstery, blue, and chintz-like wallpaper pattern	Green	Cheerful living room color scheme
WINE RED (1)	Green	Wine Red	Draperies, wine red Upholstery, grayed green and off white	Crystal	Attractive for living room with cool North or East light
WINE RED (2)	Soft grayed Blue	Deep Gray	Draperies, wine red Upholstery, wine red, grayed white and blue	Silver	For fairly formal living room, average size
WINE RED (3)	Paper in yellow, pale gray and white	Dark Wine Red	Draperies, Ruby taffeta Upholstery, glazed maroon chintz with yellow flowers Chair seats, bright yellow leather	Gold	Specially appropriate for Victorian dining room
AMERICAN BEAUTY	Linen color	Fawn	Draperies, fawn and American beauty Upholstery, American beauty, fawn, blue and gray	Blue	Dramatic color scheme for fairly large living room
RED DAHLIA	Gray	Red Dahlia	Draperies, light neutral background with dahlia and melon green in pattern Upholstery, melon green	Larkspur Blue	Adaptable to various types of living rooms
OLD RED	Soft light shade Old Red	Deep Old Red	Draperies, old red, beige and white stripes Upholstery, light tan	Copper	Warm, colorful plan for a room inclined to be cold
BURGUNDY (1)	Pale clear yellow	Burgundy	Draperies, white, valance and trimming Upholstery, burgundy and white	Gold	Rich color scheme for formal room
BURGUNDY (2)	Burgundy	Darker Burgundy	Burgundy and natural	Chartreuse	For large room, living room or library
BURGUNDY (3)	Warm Gray with pinkish cast	Burgundy	Draperies, primrose yellow Upholstery, pale grayed blue and white	White	Good for any room not too small or too sunny
BURGUNDY (4)	Beige with pinkish cast	Burgundy	Draperies, beige background, shell pink and burgundy in pattern Upholstery, shell pink	Grayed White	Same as above

THE ORANGE FAMILY

REPRESENTATIVE MEMBERS OF THE ORANGE FAMILY ... IVORY ... PEACH ... CORAL ... BEIGE RUST ... TERRA COTTA ... WARM BROWN.

CHARACTERISTICS ... Always warm, advancing ... Cheerful, welcoming, gay, vibrant, glowing ... In strong tones, akin to red ... In softer tones, a good mixer.

WHAT THEY CAN DO ... In slightly less degree, Orange repeats the activities of the Red Family ... Effective for "toning" up a room in too dull or quiet colors, or warming a cold room.

CORRECT USES ... Best in off shades, except for accent ... In softened tones, excellent background color for dark or cold rooms ... Wonderful accent color in proper combinations.

CAUTION ... Do not use too much of the clear color ... In large areas it has the disturbing quality of red ... Do not use for background of small room unless you want it to be very "cozy."

SUGGESTED COLOR SCHEMES IN WHICH MEMBERS OF ORANGE FAMILY PLAY A DOMINANT ROLE

DOMINANT COLOR	MAJOR WALL COLOR	MAJOR FLOOR COLOR	DRAPERIES AND UPHOLSTERY	ACCENT COLORS	REMARKS
IVORY	Ivory Woodwork, Ivory	Floor, painted ivory Rug, Jade Green	Ivory background, rose and blue green in pattern	Rose and Jade Green	Charming for bedroom or lady's sitting room with ivory painted furniture
PEACH (1)	Peach	Peach	Apple green	Bittergreen	Attractive for bedroom, modern or traditional
PEACH (2)	Peach	Old Green	Draperies and upholstery, peach, with old blue	Old Blue	For a room that needs warming up, with cool touches
PEACH (3)	Peach	Warm Brown	Draperies, brown and coral stripes Upholstery, brown background, with coral, beige and tan	Copper	Modern color scheme appropriate for living room or library
PEACH (4)	Paper, shades of yellow, through peach to brown	Brown	Draperies, brown Upholstery, light and dark peach	Yellow	Good modern living room color scheme
PEACH (5)	Floral pattern paper, white ground, peach and green	Rust	Draperies, peach Upholstery (chair seats), green	Green	Very good for late Colonial dining room with Duncan Phyfe style furniture
PEACH (6)	Yellowish Pink	Eggplant	Draperies, peach background, blue in design Upholstery, peach and blue	Coral and yellow	Good color scheme to lighten dark bedroom
APRICOT	Apricot	Rose and Cream	Draperies, old rose Bed and furniture covering, apricot, trimmed with black	Orchid	Charming for young girl's room
CORAL (1)	Paper, silver ground, coral-rose design; Woodwork, coral	Aquamarine	Aquamarine	Aquamarine and Silver	Charming for woman's bedroom
CORAL (2)	Coral Woodwork, soft Blue	Gray Blue	Draperies, off-white background rose and green in design, Coral valance; Bed and furniture covering, copper rose and same chintz used for hangings	Off-white	Attractive for bedroom with furniture painted blue
WARM BEIGE (1)	Warm Beige	Warm Beige	Brown and Copper	Bright Green	Modern living room or library
WARM BEIGE (2)	Pink and Beige wallpaper	Warm Beige	Draperies, old white and beige Upholstery, dusty pink and pale olive green	Terra Cotta	Restful living room color scheme
WARM BEIGE (3)	Warm Beige	Warm Beige	Draperies, burgundy background, white and beige in design; Upholstery, burgundy and natural	White	Good for living room, library, or man's bedroom
WARM BEIGE (4)	Warm Beige	Dark Taupe	Draperies, russet (beige glass curtains) Upholstery, brown with tan cushions	Tan	Restful, chromatic color scheme
WARM BEIGE (5)	Beige with pink cast	Light warm beige	Brown, beige and white stripes or checks	Sky Blue	Appropriate for informal living room or boy's room
HENNA (1)	Grass cloth, tan and gold	Henna and black	Henna, green and gray	Gold	Living room or man's bedroom
HENNA (2)	Mint Green Woodwork, Cream	Henna	Draperies, henna with valance of bedspread material Bedspread, henna, light and dark green and tan stripes Upholstery, same combination in patterned material	White	Man's bedroom
TERRA COTTA	Pink Terra Cotta	Eggplant	Draperies, pinkish yellow, trimmed with terra cotta Upholstery, bois de rose	Pale Green	Charming for dining room in Directoire feeling with furniture painted yellow and gold
COPPER (1)	Pine paneled	Floor, Pine Rugs (hooked) In tones of orange, yellow, green	Draperies, copper toned background with orange, yellow and green in pattern	Blue and copper	Appropriate for living room in Early American feeling with Early American style furniture
COPPER (2)	Rough plaster with oak paneling	Oak plank floor Patterned rug, tones of brown, green, copper	Draperies, copper colored, coarsely woven material Upholstery, neutral green, trimmed with brown and copper	Green	Good color scheme for large, formal, English-style living room, with furniture in natural oak and walnut
BURNT ORANGE	Neutral Woodwork, walnut	Rug, greenish background, with burnt orange and henna	Burnt orange and henna	Blue	Good for dining room with walnut furniture
WARM BROWN (1)	Tobacco Brown	Warm Beige	Chintz in clear yellow, beige and warm brown in design	White	Modern living room or library
WARM BROWN (2)	Tan	Warm Brown	Draperies, copper and topaz; Upholstery, warm browns	Orange, French Blue	Appropriate for boy's room
WARM BROWN (3)	Yellow Brown	Orange Brown	Burnt orange and apple green	Greenish Blue	Restful, cheerful color scheme for library
WARM BROWN (4)	Pale Yellow	Orange Brown	Shades of warm browns and orange	Silver	Attractive for modern living room or dining room

COLOR THEORY
Color Families: Yellow

THE YELLOW FAMILY

REPRESENTATIVE MEMBERS OF THE YELLOW FAMILY . . . CREAM . . . BUFF . . . STRAW . . . CANARY . . . GOLD . . . TAN . . . BROWN.

CHARACTERISTICS . . . Warm, somewhat advancing . . . The sunlight color—gay, happy, bright, cheerful . . . In light tones, luminous, radiant.

WHAT THEY CAN DO . . . Diffuse and increase light by reflection, making dark rooms seem lighter and brighter . . . In pale tints, yellow lights up a small room without making it seem smaller because reflective radiance of yellow balances its advancing quality as a warm color. . . . In light tints, best wall-background for all average rooms . . . In light tints, best wall-background for poorly lighted rooms . . . In clear, bright tones, safe accent color almost everywhere.

CORRECT USES . . . Excellent background for all average rooms . . . In light tints, best wall-background for poorly lighted rooms . . . In clear, bright tones, safe accent color almost everywhere.

CAUTION . . . Do not use yellow without testing under artificial light, and providing lamp shades to offset color changes . . . Don't use in wide expanses in a very sunny room . . . Don't use bright tones without restful combination color.

SUGGESTED COLOR SCHEMES IN WHICH MEMBERS OF YELLOW FAMILY PLAY A DOMINANT ROLE

DOMINANT COLOR	MAJOR WALL COLOR	MAJOR FLOOR COLOR	DRAPERIES AND UPHOLSTERY	ACCENT COLORS	REMARKS
CREAM	Cream Woodwork, cream	Patterned rug, mulberry, green and cream	Draperies, green, cream trimming; Upholstery, green and green yellow	Mulberry	Appropriate for bedroom, especially in Directoire feeling with cream and gold furniture
BUFF	Buff	Buff	Copenhagen blue and burgundy	Orange, Tete de Negre	Glowing color scheme for living room or man's bedroom
PALE YELLOW (1)	Pale Yellow	Soft Beige	Draperies, light yellow background, soft reds, greens and blue in pattern; Upholstery, soft blue, chintz of draperies	Green and Red	Good color scheme for medium-sized dark room
PALE YELLOW (2)	Pale Yellow	Pale Yellow	Turquoise	Coral	Colorful for bedroom or small sitting room
BRIGHT LEMON (1)	Bright Lemon	Beige	Draperies, beige background, yellow green and lavender; Seat covers, wet leaf green	Wet Leaf Green	This color scheme will brighten up a dark dining room
PALE LEMON (2)	Pale Lemon Yellow Woodwork, white	Tobacco Brown	Draperies, white with yellow trimming; Upholstery, emerald green; some pieces white, yellow, dull orange	Orange	Suitable for living room with north light
JONQUIL YELLOW (1)	Jonquil Yellow	Gray	Draperies, white, trimmed with Chinese red; Upholstery, warm gray and white	Chinese Red	Charming for living room, modern or traditional
JONQUIL YELLOW (2)	Jonquil Yellow	Soft Blue-Green	Draperies, white and yellow; Upholstery, soft blue, green and white	White	Good for any room without too much light
YELLOW (1)	Yellow	Brown	Blue and apple green	Black	Good for room with cold light
YELLOW (2)	Yellow	Brown	Dutch blue and white	Bright Red	Attractive for informal living room
YELLOW (3)	Marbleized yellow paper Woodwork, deep green	Deep Green	Draperies, green, yellow trimming; Chair seat upholstery, yellow	Blue	Charming for dining room, especially in Directoire feeling
YELLOW (4)	Paper in Yellow and Ivory stripes, divided by narrow plum lines	Yellow Tan	Draperies, gray background, yellow, plum and rose in pattern; Upholstery, blue and light tan	Old Gold	Good combination for dark maple woodwork
GRAYED YELLOW	Grayed Yellow	Brown	Draperies, brown and beige stripes; Upholstery, yellow, beige, moss green	White	Pleasant for living room or man's bedroom
SOFT YELLOW	Soft Yellow	Deep Brown	Draperies, yellow; Upholstery, cinnamon brown	Chartreuse	Attractive and restful for library or living room
EMPIRE YELLOW	Slate Gray	Lime Green	Draperies, Empire yellow; Upholstery, Strong clear yellow	Silver	Suitable for living room or dining room
CITRON YELLOW	Citron Yellow	Citron Yellow	Coral	Silver	Modern or traditional living room
LEMON YELLOW	Lemon Yellow	Tete de Negre	Brown and henna	Orange	Distinctive for modern living room
SULPHUR YELLOW	Sulphur Yellow	Olive Green	Shades of green and sulphur	Coral	Colorful modern living room

	Deep Yellow	Red	Draperies / Upholstery	Gold	
DEEP YELLOW			Draperies, gold damask Upholstery, plum, wine red, gold with red, blue, lavender in pattern		Suitable for period room with Queen Anne, Sheraton, and other Georgian style furniture
MUTED GOLD	Caramel	Bleached wood, rubbed with gold and waxed	Draperies, soft caramel taffeta, trimmed with brown Upholstery, brown and yellow	Ebony	Unusual modern living room scheme where there is plenty of light
GOLD (1)	Yellow, flat finish Woodwork, Olive Green	Old gold carpet	Draperies, old gold, trimmed with green Upholstery, olive green and paprika	Light Green	Charming for modern living room with blond wood
GOLD (2)	Gray and pale Yellow paper	Harvest Gold and Gray	Draperies, oyster white, trimmed with multi-color fringe Upholstery, rust-shot silk	Brass	Traditional or modern dining room
TAN (1)	Neutral Tan	Dark Tan	Draperies, burnt orange Upholstery, brown and burnt orange	Rich Chocolate	Good with natural wood tones
TAN (2)	Tan linen color	Light and dark Tan	Draperies, tan and rose stripes Upholstery, linen color with rose, tan, gray and blue in pattern	Rose	Attractive for living room or library with walnut woodwork and furniture
TAN (3)	Tan	Brown Taupe	Dark green and vermilion	Brown	Rich, warm color scheme for living room or library, especially with walnut furniture and paintings
TAN (4)	Brownish Tan	Floor, Oak Multi-colored scatter rugs	Draperies, brown with red, yellow and blue pattern Upholstery, old red and yellow chintz	Blue	Suitable for bedroom with oak furniture in Early English feeling
BROWN (1)	Brown paneled	Deep Brown	Beige background with brilliant gold, scarlet and orange tones of fall foliage	Blue	Attractive for living room with plenty of light
BROWN (2)	Pine paneled	Pine	Old chintz in blue and brown	Silver and Pewter	Dining room in French Provincial style
BROWN (3)	Warm Beige with brown cast	Brown	Draperies, brown, beige and dusty pink Upholstery, brown and off-white	White	Appropriate for modern living room
BROWN (4)	Pine paneled	Hooked Rugs	Yellow, copper and blue chintz	Green	Suitable Early American living room with maple furniture
BROWN (5)	Chalk White	Brown	Turquoise	Peach	Charming bedroom color scheme
SABLE BROWN (1)	Sable Brown	Off-white	Draperies, off-white with turquoise Upholstery, shell pink and off-white	Turquoise	Distinctive modern living room
SABLE BROWN (2)	Sable Brown	Deep warm Beige	Draperies, bright yellow Upholstery, plain chartreuse with white pattern	Earth Brown	Same as above
CHESTNUT BROWN	Fawn	Chestnut Brown	Champagne background, beaver, turquoise and apricot in pattern and trimming	Turquoise	Appropriate for living or dining room
TAWNY BROWN	Tawny Brown Pine	Light beige and taupe	Blue on light ground	Yellow	Good for dining room in French period feeling
GOLDEN BROWN	Knotty Pine	Golden Brown Navajo rug	Draperies, colorful hunting print Upholstery, red leather	Blue and Green	Library or Den
NUT BROWN	Nut Brown Pine	Moss Green	Draperies, dark linen Upholstery, green, brown and white	Yellow	Restful living room color scheme
TOBACCO BROWN	Tobacco Brown	Beige	Clear yellow chintz with beige and dark brown in design	White	Suitable modern dining room with much sunlight
CHOCOLATE BROWN	Chocolate Brown	Eggshell	Draperies, white Upholstery, chartreuse, brown and eggshell	Chartreuse	Interesting modern color scheme for living room or dining room
DARK BROWN (1)	Deep Beige	Dark Brown	Draperies, pale, clear blue Upholstery, cinnamon brown	Pale Clear Blue	Good for dining room or living room
DARK BROWN (2)	Light Chartreuse	Dark Brown	Light tan and brown	White	Good for modern living room
BROWNS	Light Brown	Deep Brown	Draperies, off-white Upholstery, Wedgwood green and off-white	Gold	Suitable for living or dining room

COLOR THEORY
Color Families: Green

THE GREEN FAMILY

REPRESENTATIVE MEMBERS OF THE GREEN FAMILY ... NILE ... LETTUCE ... PEA ... GRASS ... SEA ... OLIVE ... BOTTLE ... ETC.

CHARACTERISTICS ... Cool, receding—except when mixed with a warm color ... Most restful color ... Friendly with all other colors, refreshing, versatile ... Endless variety of tones and combinations.

WHAT THEY CAN DO ... In light, soft tints, makes rooms seem larger because the wall seems farther away ... Makes objects seem farther away, therefore smaller ... Brings atmosphere of rest and relaxation to room.

CORRECT USES ... One of best background colors for average room, especially where restfulness is important ... Great corrective value for rooms too small or too warm ... Suitable in proper tones for background in any part of room—floor, walls, ceiling.

CAUTION ... Do not use in quantity in cold, dark or overlarge rooms—choose warm, advancing colors for backgrounds, keeping green for smaller areas.

SUGGESTED COLOR SCHEMES IN WHICH MEMBERS OF GREEN FAMILY PLAY A DOMINANT ROLE

DOMINANT COLOR	MAJOR WALL COLOR	MAJOR FLOOR COLOR	DRAPERIES AND UPHOLSTERY	ACCENT COLORS	REMARKS
PALE GREEN (1)	Pale Green	Dark Green	Draperies, off-white background, with pale blues, greens, and mauve in pattern; Upholstery, darker blue	Mauve and Violet	Appropriate for average living room and bedroom
PALE GREEN (2)	Pale Green	Plum	Draperies, natural linen color, with flowered plum and green in design; Upholstery, plum, gold, green	Gold	Especially good for traditional living room
LIGHT GREEN (1)	White	Light Green	Draperies, white with dark green pattern; Upholstery, dark green and white	Yellow	Pleasant color scheme for modern room
LIGHT GREEN (2)	Pickled Pine	Light Green	Draperies, off-white and light green; Upholstery, light green	Brown	Attractive for living room or library
LIGHT GREEN (3)	Off-white	Soft Light Green	Shell-pink, green and off-white	Crystal	Charming and cool for small living room or sitting room
APPLE GREEN (1)	Apple Green	Plum	Draperies, apple green; Upholstery, gold, yellow and ivory	Gold	Good for small living room
APPLE GREEN (2)	Apple Green	Yellow Green	Gray, blue, and touches of light yellow	Light Yellow	This combination makes cool room
APPLE GREEN (3)	Pale Apple Green	Floor, brown walnut; Rug, blue and tan	Draperies, royal blue background, with rose and green leaves in pattern; Upholstery, same drapery chintz, also rose, antique salmon, apple green and cream stripes	Black, gold, white and ruby	Early American living room with maple or cherry furniture
SOFT GREEN (1)	Soft Green	Deeper Green	Draperies, plum background with beige and green in pattern; Upholstery, plum, beige and green	Orange	Restful Color Scheme
SOFT GREEN (2)	Soft Grayed Green	Deeper Green	Draperies, corn yellow; Upholstery, grayed green and off-white	Pine Green	Adaptable to living room, dining room or bedroom
SOFT GREEN (3)	Pale Soft Grayed Green	Ivy Green	Draperies, soft grayed green; Upholstery, golden yellow and white	Lacquer Red	Excellent to add feeling of space to small room
FOAM GREEN	Slate Gray	Foam Green	Draperies, lemon yellow and white; Upholstery, lemon yellow and gray	Gold	Good modern color scheme
IVY GREEN	Clear Beige	Ivy Green	Draperies, beige with light and dark green floral design; Upholstery, same chintz and some clear beige	Black	Appropriate for living room
DEEP LIME	Deep Lime	Deep Lime	White, green and melon pink	White	Dramatic modern scheme, especially good with blond wood

NILE GREEN	Nile Green	Green	Glazed chintz with green background and white in design, red lining and trimming	Crystal	Cool, airy bedroom
MINT GREEN	Pure White Woodwork, white	Painted Mint Green, spatter-dashed with turquoise and yellow	Turquoise, yellow and mint green	White	Adaptable for informal living room, dining room or bedroom
JADE GREEN	Pale Jade	Dark Blue	Draperies, blue / Upholstery, blue and jade green	Silver	Attractive for modern living room
SAGE	Slate Gray	Soft Deep Sage	Gray and blue with green touches	Silver	Excellent color to make small sunny room seem larger and cooler
BOTTLE GREEN	Pale Apricot	Bottle Green	Green, apricot and topaz	Topaz	Good for living room or dining room
CHARTREUSE GREEN	Chartreuse Green	Shades of Tete de Negre	Draperies, chartreuse green / Upholstery, shades of heliotrope	Silver	Modern bedroom. Good with furniture painted chartreuse
CHARTREUSE GREEN	Gray	Chartreuse	Chartreuse and bright blue	Silver	Adaptable to any modern room
TURQUOISE	Light Turquoise	Patterned rug, Green with Moss Rose	Draperies, turquoise, green and rose stripes / Upholstery, turquoise	Rose	Attractive for bedroom with mahogany furniture
BLUE GREEN (1)	Deep Cream	Blue Green	Apple green, greenish blue, touch of burnt orange	Burnt Orange	Versatile color scheme for average room
BLUE GREEN (2)	Blue Green	Blue Green	Draperies, light grayish tan background, turquoise, rose and green in pattern / Upholstery, same print and some soft rose	Green	Very restful for living room or bedroom
BLUE GREEN (3)	Dull Blue Green	Rug, light field, red violet and green leaves in pattern	Draperies, white / Upholstery, red violet	Dark Green	Dining room in period feeling with walnut furniture
WET LEAF GREEN	Deep Lime	Bronze	White background, wet leaf green, dawn rose and bright lemon in pattern	Rose	Sophisticated modern color scheme
DEEP GREEN (1)	Deep Green	Gray	Draperies, sky blue chintz with rose and green pattern / Upholstery, emerald green and gray	Gold and Rose	Suitable for living room or man's bedroom
DEEP GREEN (2)	Gray and White paper, Block pattern	Deep Green	Draperies, yellow / Upholstery, yellow flowers and pale green leaves on gray background	White and Green	Modern living room or dining room
DEEP GREEN (3)	Green, lighter than carpet	Deep Soft Green	Draperies, off-white / Upholstery, off-white and Wedgwood green	Yellow	Very cool and fresh
DEEP GREEN (4)	Greenish Gray	Deep Green	Draperies, apple green / Upholstery, grayed greens and white	Salmon	Good combination to make small room seem larger
DEEP GREEN (5)	Deep Soft Green	Light Brown	Golden yellow and white	White	Modern or traditional setting
GEORGIAN GREEN	Deep Georgian Green	Deep Green	Draperies, soft golden yellow / Upholstery, golden yellow and deep green	Gold	Very cool and restful for period living room or library
DARK GREEN (1)	Ivory Green	Dark Green	Draperies, white with dark green pattern / Upholstery, off-red, off-white and dark green	Black	Subtle color combination. Good for living room or dining room
DARK GREEN (2)	Warm Gray	Dark Green	Draperies, dark green or gray background / Upholstery, light green	Yellow	Cool and restful for living room
DARK GREEN (3)	Dark Green	Tan	Draperies, chintz in blue-green and soft red / Upholstery, same chintz, also some soft red	Copper	Charming for sunny living room
GREEN OLIVE	Green Olive	Red-Coral	Lime green, red-coral, antique white	Coral and White	Daring modern color scheme. Good with traditional or modern furniture in light finish

COLOR THEORY
Color Families: Blue

THE BLUE FAMILY

REPRESENTATIVE MEMBERS OF THE BLUE FAMILY . . . PALE . . . BABY . . . SKY . . . POWDER . . . NAVY . . . MIDNIGHT . . . ETC.

CHARACTERISTICS . . . Coldest, most receding, unless mixed with warm colors . . . Serene, quiet, "spacious" . . . Much-loved hue . . . Too much of it in dull tones may be depressing.

WHAT THEY CAN DO . . . Make room seem larger, cooler, more airy and spacious . . . Make objects look smaller because they seem more distant . . . In dark tones, make lighter contrast colors more luminous.

CORRECT USES . . . In light tones, excellent background for small, dark, warm rooms . . . Good combining color, especially in soft tones . . . Effective background for many other colors.

CAUTION . . . Do not use in quantity in cold or dark or over-large rooms . . . Do not use too much in dull shades . . . Do not use without some warm bright accent color.

SUGGESTED COLOR SCHEMES IN WHICH MEMBERS OF BLUE FAMILY PLAY A DOMINANT ROLE

DOMINANT COLOR	MAJOR WALL COLOR	MAJOR FLOOR COLOR	DRAPERIES AND UPHOLSTERY	ACCENT COLORS	REMARKS
PALE BLUE (1)	Pale Blue	Dark Blue	Tan draperies and upholstery	Silver	Modern color scheme for bedroom with furniture in lemon color
SKY BLUE	Garden Sky Blue	Champagne	Champagne, sky blue and orchid	Orchid	Modern color scheme, good with light natural finish woods
POWDER BLUE (1)	Powder Blue	Delft Blue	Draperies, canary yellow Upholstery, yellow and powder blue	Off-white	Cool and fresh for bedroom
POWDER BLUE (2)	Powder Blue	Powder Blue	White draperies and upholstery	Peach	Dainty feminine bedroom
LARKSPUR BLUE (1)	Larkspur Blue	Pale Gray	Draperies, wine, trimmed with white Upholstery, deep blue and white	Deep Blue and Wine	Good modern living room combination
LARKSPUR BLUE (2)	Larkspur Blue	Blue	Neutral background, blue and pink in pattern	Red Dahlia	Any period room with enough light
BLUE (1)	Pale Blue, deep Rose and Ivory paper	Blue	Blue, gold and rose with touches of black—in stripes or plain	Black	Attractive for traditional living room
BLUE (2)	Faded Blue (middle value)	Floor, dark Brown Carpet, Gray and Yellow	Draperies, old yellow Upholstery, yellow, old yellow, and touch of Venetian red, also some blue	Blue	Bedroom with Directoire feeling and walnut furniture
BLUE (3)	Striped wallpaper in tones of light and medium blue and White	Dark Blue	Draperies, blue with white in pattern and trimming Upholstery, lemon yellow	Dark Blue	Good for small, low-ceilinged but light room
HYDRANGEA BLUE (1)	Pale Hydrangea Blue	Eggplant	Draperies, peach background with white, copper, gold and hydrangea blue in design Upholstery, some chintz, also old blue	Old Blue	Good for room with strong light, especially with 18th Century furniture
HYDRANGEA BLUE (2)	Hydrangea Blue	Deeper Blue	Draperies, salmon pink Chair seats, black and gold	Gold	Dining room with Directoire feeling
COPENHAGEN BLUE	Copenhagen Blue	Burgundy	Gray with blue and burgundy	Rose and Silver	Attractive for traditional living room
PENCIL BLUE	Lemon Yellow	Pencil Blue	Blue background with yellow in pattern and trim	Silver	Setting for dining room with modern furniture

Color	Wall/Ground	Floor/Rug	Draperies & Upholstery	Accents	Notes
MEDIUM BLUE (1)	Blue	Mulberry ground	Draperies, cherry red / Upholstery, chintz in blue, rose and mauve, some pieces in cherry red and gold	Gold	Good for living room, especially in 18th Century French feeling
MEDIUM BLUE (2)	Blue	Mole	Lavender, gray, and some rose	Rose	Adaptable for lady's bedroom in lighter blues, also to living room in darker shades of duller blues
MEDIUM BLUE (3)	Cream	Blue	French Blue	Jade Green	Good for south living room or bedroom
DUSTY BLUE	Dusty Blue	Dark Burgundy	Draperies, gray, trimmed with soft blue / Upholstery, soft blue and gray	Crystal	Restful for living room or dining room
SOFT DULL BLUE	Ivory	Soft Dull Blue	Ivory background with blue, rose and green in design, some pieces in old rose	Green	Bedroom or informal living room
OLD BLUE	Old Blue	Deeper Blue	Faded Pink, or chintz with blue, green and pink	Green	Charming for living room or bedroom
GRAYED BLUE	Gray Blue	Deeper grayed Blue	Yellow, white, and gold	Red	Dining room in Directoire feeling with mahogany
TURQUOISE BLUE	Pale Turquoise Blue	Turquoise	Draperies, golden yellow / Upholstery, golden yellow and white	White	Any room not too large or too dark
TURQUOISE BLUE	Grayed Turquoise	Grayed Turquoise	Wine and ivory	Polished Brass	Dignified but friendly living room
GREEN BLUE	Green Blue	Plum rug; flowered pattern	Draperies, peach / Upholstery, green-blue with some plum	Peach	Simple living room in French Provincial feeling
ROYAL BLUE (1)	Walls, Silver Woodwork, Royal Blue	Floor, painted Gray Rug, Blue	Draperies, blue, trimmed with silver / Upholstery (chairs), silver and blue leather	Silver and Black	Distinctive modern dining room
ROYAL BLUE (2)	Old White	Royal Blue	Clear yellow	Silver	Modern living or dining room
ROYAL BLUE (3)	Dull White	Rug, Deep Blue ground with honey-yellow in pattern	Draperies, royal blue / Chair Seats, royal blue Morocco	Silver	Attractive for modern dining room, especially with lemon wood furniture
DEEP BLUE (1)	Pale Amethyst	Deep Blue	Deep blue, trimmed with gold	Amethyst and Gold	Cool and charming for living room not too dark
DEEP BLUE (2)	Deep Blue Woodwork, Ivory	Dark Blue rug with Tan and Rose in pattern	Draperies, dull ivory / Upholstery (chairs), ivory or rosy red leather	Red	Colorful for dining room with plenty of light
DEEP BLUE (3)	Deep Blue	Deep Blue	Draperies, deep sea blue / Upholstery, canary yellow	White	Modern living room or dining room
DEEP BLUE (4)	Pale Yellow	Natural	Draperies, deep sea blue (gold gauze glass curtains) / Upholstery, deep blue	White	Good when blue is dominant color in a dark room
DEEP BLUE (5)	Creamy White	Blue	Draperies, deep blue / Upholstery, yellow with dash of white	Gold, Rose-Pink and Blue	Good for bedroom, furniture painted blue with flower decorations, and some smaller oyster white pieces
GARDEN POOL BLUE	Ivory	Garden Pool Blue	Draperies, garden pool blue / Chair Seats, red leather	White and Silver	Dramatic modern living room with furniture in rich mahogany or walnut tones
DARK BLUE	Cream and beige paper	Dark Blue rug with rose and tan in pattern	Draperies, linen color with blues, greens and rosy reds in pattern / Chair Seats, dark blue	Blue and Silver	Good for dining room where light is needed

COLOR THEORY

Color Families: Violet/Purple

THE VIOLET (OR PURPLE) FAMILY

REPRESENTATIVE MEMBERS OF THE VIOLET FAMILY . . . ORCHID . . . LAVENDER . . . MAUVE . . . Create restful, quiet atmosphere when used in soft tones.
VIOLET . . . PLUM . . . PURPLE.
CHARACTERISTICS . . . Cool when mixed with blue, warm when mixed with red . . . In pure form, cold and formal . . . In purple tones, rich and dignified but not friendly . . . May be depressing.
WHAT THEY CAN DO . . . Add to impression of room size and coolness, especially when mixed with blue

CORRECT USES . . . In light, soft tints, excellent wall and ceiling background for an average room . . . Strong shades good for accent . . . In deep, soft tones, attractive for carpets, upholstery, draperies.
CAUTION . . . Do not use blue tones of violet in cold, dark, over-large rooms . . . Be careful when using strong shades for dominant color . . . Do not use without some warm contrast.

SUGGESTED COLOR SCHEMES IN WHICH MEMBERS OF VIOLET FAMILY PLAY A DOMINANT ROLE

DOMINANT COLOR	MAJOR WALL COLOR	MAJOR FLOOR COLOR	DRAPERIES AND UPHOLSTERY	ACCENT COLORS	REMARKS
ORCHID (1)	Orchid	Blue	Champagne, orchid and blue	Black and Silver	Attractive for living room
ORCHID (2)	Paneled paper in Orchid and Pale Yellow	Mulberry	Green, yellow and orchid chintz	Green	Cool, airy bedroom
LAVENDER (1)	Lavender	Lavender with mauve border	Gray, light blue and touches of jade green	Jade Green	Good for sunny room
LAVENDER (2)	Lavender, Blue and White paper	Plum	Lavender	Rose	Feminine bedroom
LAVENDER (3)	Pale Lavender	Rose	Pink, lavender and white	Lavender	Bedroom with warm light
HELIOTROPE (1)	Gray	Beige	Heliotrope draperies and upholstery	Violet and Silver	Lovely color scheme for woman with gray hair
MAUVE (1)	Gray	Mauve	Light blue, Nile green, some rose	Rose	Good for sunny bedroom
MAUVE (2)	Paneled wall painted Pale Mauve	Deep Violet	Mauve and yellow	Crystal and Sepia	Especially attractive for Louis XVI style bedroom with walnut furniture
HELIOTROPE (2)	Pearl Gray	Heliotrope	Draperies, heliotrope trimmed with silver / Upholstery, Tarragon green, gray and heliotrope	Green	Cool and restful living room
VIOLET	Dove Gray	Black and White	Draperies, violet / Upholstery, coral and old gold	Silver and Black	Attractive with silver gray painted woodwork and violet lines, also white and gold furniture
MULBERRY (1)	Dusty Mulberry	Mahogany	Draperies, clear blue chintz with mulberry and brown in pattern / Upholstery, clear blue	White	Very good for traditional living room or dining room
MULBERRY (2)	Dusty Mulberry	Ebony	Draperies, creamy peach chintz with gray, old rose and ebony design / Upholstery, creamy peach	Black	Good for sunny living room or dining room
MULBERRY (3)	Scenic paper Woodwork, walnut	Deep Mulberry	Mulberry	Orange	Traditional dining room
PURPLE	Paper in Gray and soft Purple stripes	Gray	Purple, with blue, green and gray	Burnt Orange	Hall or living room

TABLE 1 Reflective Values

Color	Approx. percent of reflection
White, dull or flat	75–85
White, gloss	85–90
Light tints	
Cream or eggshell	79
Ivory	75
Pale pink and pale yellow	75–80
Light green, light blue, light orchid	70–75
Soft pink, light peach	69
Light beige, pale grey	70
Medium tones	
Apricot	56–62
Pink	64
Tan, yellow gold	55
Light greys	35–50
Medium turquoise	44
Medium light blue	42
Yellow green	45
Old gold, pumpkin	34
Rose	29
Deep tones	
Cocoa brown, mauve	24
Medium green, medium blue	21
	20
Unsuitable dark colors	
Dark brown, dark grey	10–15
Olive green	12
Dark blue, blue green	5–10
Forest green	7
Natural wood tones	
Birch and beech	35–50
Light maple	25–35
Light oak	25–35
Dark oak, cherry	10–15
Redwood	10–15
Black walnut, mahogany	5–15

Recommended ceiling values should be in the range of 60–90%. Floor reflection values should be in the range of 15–35%. Overall reflection values of a room should be in the 35–60% range.

Safety Color Guides

Physical hazards:
Red: Fire protection equipment and apparatus; danger; stop
Orange: Dangerous parts of moving machinery
Yellow: Physical hazards that might cause stumbling, falling, etc.
Green: Safety – first-aid dispensary or kits, stretchers, safety deluge showers, etc.
Blue: Caution against movement or use of equipment being worked on such as elevators, scaffolding, etc.
Black and White: Traffic direction; sanitation

Equipment in industrial plants:
Red: Fire protection systems and equipment
Orange: Dangerous materials, nonflammable, such as acids, alkalis, toxic materials, gases, oxygen
Yellow: Dangerous materials, flammable, such as fuel oil, gasoline, kerosene, alcohol, propane, butane, acetylene, hydrogen, and solvent
Green: Safe materials, such as drinking water, service water, brine
Blue: Protective materials
Violet: Valuable materials
Black: Electrical conduit

COLOR THEORY
Color Effect

TABLE 2

			Color Effects of White Fluorescent Lamps				
	Cool* White	Deluxe* Cool White	Warm† White	Deluxe† Warm White	Daylight	White	Soft White— Natural
Lamp appearance; effect on neutral surfaces	White	White	Yellowish white	Yellowish white	Bluish white	Pale yellowish white	Pinkish white
Effect on "atmosphere"	Neutral to moderately cool	Neutral to moderately cool	Warm	Warm	Very cool	Moderately warm	Warm, pinkish
Colors strengthened	Orange, yellow, blue	All nearly equal	Orange, yellow	Red, orange, yellow, green	Green, blue	Orange, yellow	Red, orange
Colors grayed	Red	None appreciably	Red, green, blue	Blue	Red, orange	Red, green, blue	Green, blue
Remarks	Blends with natural daylight	Best overall color rendition; simulates natural daylight	Blends with incandescent light	Excellent color rendition; simulates incandescent light	Usually replaceable with CW	Usually replaceable with CW or WW	Usually replaceable with CWX or WWX

		Color Effects of Mercury and Filament Lamps			
	Mercury	White Mercury	Color-Improved Mercury	Deluxe White Mercury	Filament
Lamp appearance; effect on neutral surfaces	Greenish blue white	Greenish white	Yellowish white	White	Yellowish white
Effect on "atmosphere"	Very cool, greenish	Moderately cool, greenish	Warm, yellowish	Moderately cool	Warm
Colors strengthened	Yellow, green, blue	Yellow, green, blue	Yellow, green	Orange, yellow, blue	Red, orange, yellow
Colors grayed	Red, orange	Red, orange	Blue	Green	Blue
Remarks	Poor overall color rendering		Color rendering often acceptable, but not equal to any white fluorescent	Color rendering good; compares favorably with CWX fluorescent	Excellent color rendering

* Greater preference at higher levels.
† Greater preference at lower levels.

Windows are available in many types, each having advantages. The principal types are double-hung, casement, stationary, awning, and horizontal sliding. They may be made of wood or metal. Heat loss through metal frames and sash is much greater than through similar wood units. Glass blocks are sometimes used for admitting light in places where transparency or ventilation is not required.

Insulated glass, used both for stationary and moveable sash, consists of two or more sheets of spaced glass with hermetically-sealed edges. This type has more resistance to heat loss than a single thickness and is often used without a storm sash.

Wood sash and door and window frames should be made from a clear grade of all-heartwood stock of a decay resistant wood species or from wood which is given a preservative treatment. Species commonly used include ponderosa and other pines, the cedars, cypress, redwood, and the spruces.

Double-Hung Windows

The double-hung window is perhaps the most familiar window type. It consists of an upper and lower sash that slide vertically in separate grooves in the side jambs or in full-width metal weatherstripping. This type of window provides a maximum face opening for ventilation of one-half the total window area. Each sash is provided with springs, balances, or *compression weatherstripping* to hold it in place in any location. Compression weatherstripping, for example, prevents air infiltration, provides tension, and acts as a counterbalance; several types allow the sash to be removed for easy painting or repair.

The *jambs* (sides and top of the frames) are made of nominal 1-inch lumber; the width provides for use with dry-wall or plastered interior finish. Sills are made from nominal 2-inch lumber and sloped at about 3 in 12 for good drainage. Sash are normally 1⅜ inches thick and wood combination storm and screen windows are usually 1⅛ inches thick.

Sash may be divided into a number of lights by small wood members called *muntins*. A ranch-type house may provide the best appearance with top and bottom sash divided into two horizontal lights. A colonial or Cape Code house usually has each sash divided into six or eight lights. Some manufacturers provided preassembled dividers which snap in place over a single light, dividing it into six or eight lights. This simplifies painting and other maintenance.

Assembled frames are placed in the rough opening over strips of building paper put around the perimeter to minimize air infiltration. The frame is plumbed and nailed to side studs and header through the casings or the blind at the sides. Where nails are exposed, such as on the casing, use the corrosion-resistant type.

Hardware for double-hung windows includes the sash lifts that are fastened to the bottom rail, although they are sometimes eliminated by providing a finger groove in the rail. Other hardware consists of sash locks or fasteners located at the meeting rail. They not only lock the window, but draw the sash together to provide a "windtight" fit.

Double-hung windows can be arranged in a number of ways — as a single unit, doubled (or mullion) type, or in groups of three or more. One or two double-hung windows on each side of a large stationary insulated window are often used to effect a window wall. Such large openings must be framed with headers large enough to carry roofloads.

Casement Windows

Casement windows consist of side-hinged sash, usually designed to swing outward because this type can be made more weathertight than the inswinging style. Screens are located inside these outswinging windows and winter protection is obtained with a storm sash or by using insulated glass in the sash. One advantage of the casement window over the double-hung type is that the entire window area can be opened for ventilation.

Weatherstripping is also provided for this type of window, and units are usually received from the factory entirely assembled with hardware in place. Closing hardware consists of a rotary operator and sash lock. As in the double-hung units, casement sash can be used in a number of ways — as a pair or in combinations of two or more pairs. Style variations are achieved by divided lights. Snap-in muntins provided a small, multiple-pane appearance for traditional styling.

Metal sash are sometimes used but, because of low insulating value, should be installed carefully to prevent condensation and frosting on the interior surfaces during cold weather. A full storm-window unit is sometimes necessary to eliminate this problem in cold climates.

Stationary Windows

Stationary windows used alone or in combination with double-hung or casement windows usually consist of a wood sash with a large single light of insulated glass. They are designed to provide light as well as for attractive appearance, and are fastened permanently into the frame. Because of their size (sometimes 6 to 8 feet wide), 1¾-inch-thick sash is used to provide strength. The thickness is usually required because of the thickness of the insulating glass.

OPERATION		VENTILATION	REMARKS

Double-hung window: upper and lower sections slide vertically to open; spring balance; lock at meeting rail

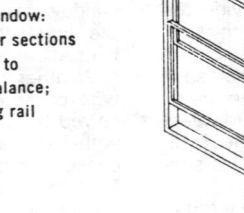

Substantial airflow, but not directed well; drafty without a shield

No parts project even when open; sometimes difficult to open if schoolroom has usual shelving at sill level; usually a glass deflector is installed to prevent drafts

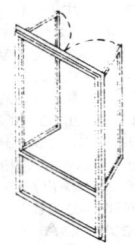

Casement window: with fixed glass section at bottom, two swing-out sections at top; crank-operated

Substantial airflow, but not directed well; drafts are difficult to avoid

Easily operated; shades can be drawn without obstruction when window is open (but they will billow in breeze); these windows must be placed carefully—there is danger of children running into them outdoors if open; rarely used in schools

Projected window: with fixed upper section of glass, vent (hopper type) at bottom opening in; crank-operated

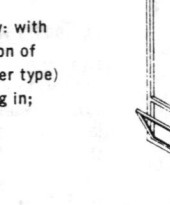

Adequate airflow in most climates; well directed, not drafty

Easily operated, can be used with shades or blinds closed over most of its area; view is unobstructed, even when window is closed

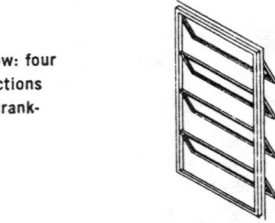

Projected window: with sections opening out at top, in at bottom; crank-operated

Very good airflow, both in quantity and quality (not drafty)

Easily operated; does provide some ventilation even when partially shaded; view through this type is almost unhindered with few obstructions at eye level

Awning window: four horizontal sections project out; crank-operated

Large quantities of airflow are easily controlled, with fairly good draft control

Can be opened quite wide even during rainstorms; is easily operated; shades can be drawn without obstruction; framing does obstruct outdoor view somewhat whether window is open or closed

Sliding window with lower fixed section

Substantial airflow, but hard to control, drafty

No parts project either inward or outward when open, but window is sometimes difficult to slide with the usual schoolroom shelf at sill level

Combination window: upper section is of glass block, supported on angle and channel girts attached to columns; lower section is half fixed glass, and half hopper (crank-operated)

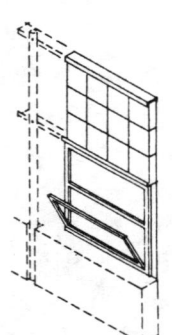

Adequate, well directed air flow for most climates

Some types of glass block refract light to ceiling, providing good light distribution across classroom and eliminating need for shades or blinds; however, designer must take care to use properly; this type does not always meet brightness tests for good schoolroom lighting

TYPE	DESCRIPTION

SIDE HINGED

CASEMENT

 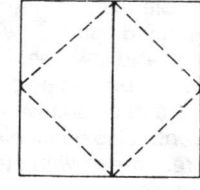

materials	• wood, steel, aluminum
use	• common in residences and apartments
operation	• rotary crank or lever operators hold the vent open to desired position, up to 180°, but usually 90°
note	• available also as a single vent
	• generally allow exterior of glazing to be cleaned from inside when outswinging.
	• provide 100 percent opening in the ventilation area
	• will be subject to wind pressures when opened.

CASEMENT-HOPPER

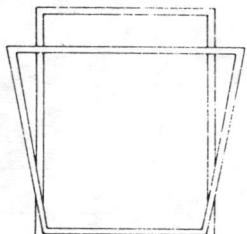 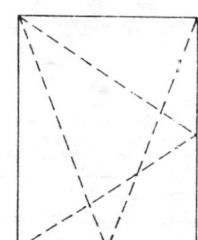

materials	• wood, aluminum
use	• especially appropriate for high-rise, life safety installations
operation	• sophisticated hardware
note	• no protection from rain when open
	• available to limited extent as "tilt and turn" type which acts as a bottom hung window in normal use, but which can be converted by use of secondary hinges into a side-hung, inswinging type, allowing for easy cleaning.

CASEMENT-COMBINATION

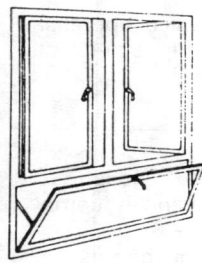 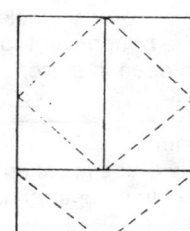

materials	• wood, aluminum, steel in varied quality grades
use	• commonly known as the "classroom window"
operation	• combination of in-swinging hopper and out-swinging casement vents offer flexibility for ventilation control

BOTTOM HINGED

HOPPER

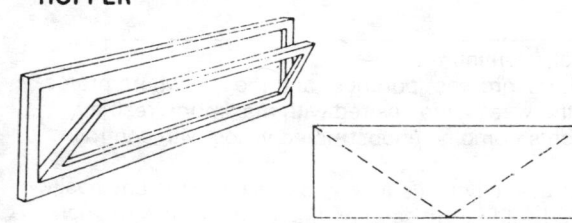

materials	• wood, aluminum and steel
use	• where vent will not interfere with interior conditions
	• lower cost utility quality is commonly used for residential basements
note	• no protection from rain when open

WINDOW TREATMENTS
Window Types

TYPE	DESCRIPTION

BOTTOM HINGED, continued

HOPPER-SPECIAL

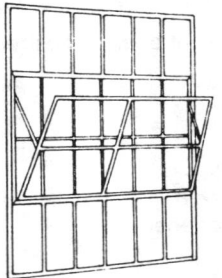 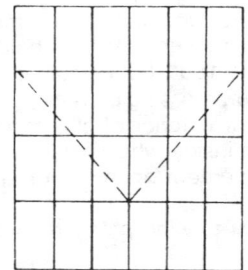

materials • steel, stainless steel
use • in commercial and industrial buildings where appearance is not of major importance and resistance to forced entry is
• to prevent forcible exit; sometimes called "guard" windows
operation • combined with fixed lights or with projecting vents above, which offer high and low openings that are best for natural-air circulation (due to principles of stratification)
• separate vent frames usually swing in as hoppers
• jalousie-like vents also available
• frames often reinforced with steel rods
notes • vents limited in size
• muntins usually separate openings of 88 inches square

HOPPER-MULTIPLE

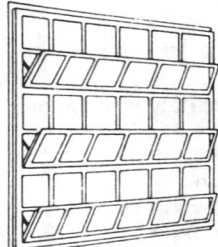 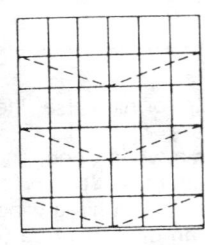

materials • steel
use • in housing for mental patients, to provide protection against exit while minimizing appearance of restraint
note • vents have a maximum clear opening of about 6 inches

TOP HINGED

AWNING

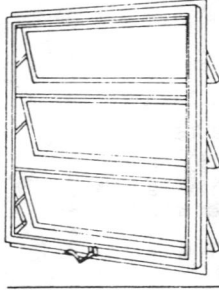 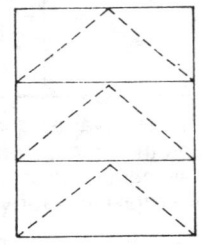

materials • wood, steel, aluminum
use • multiple assemblies are used mostly in steel for industrial buildings
• separate units are commonly combined with fixed lights, or with hoppers for maximum stratification ventilation (These are available also in wood and aluminum.)
operation • are out-swinging projected windows that create a "canopy" against rain penetration
• when in multiple, vertical stacks, the mechanical operation will allow for the bottom vent to open before the other vents, which will then open in unison

PROJECTED

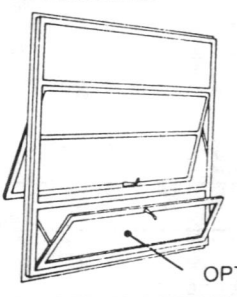 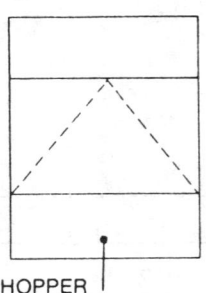

OPTIONAL HOPPER

materials • steel or aluminum
use • medium quality grade is called "intermediate" and is commonly used in commercial, institutional and industrial type buildings
• architectural windows are frequently used for schools, hospitals, office buildings, etc.
operation • similar to awning windows but with optional fixed glass lights and/or hoppers.

JALOUSIE

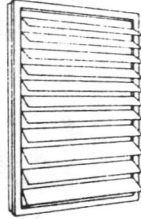 

materials • wood, steel, aluminum
use • primarily for sunrooms, porches, and the like where protection from the weather is desired with maximum fresh air
operation • multiple vents combine unobstructed vision with controlled ventilation
• the louvers are fully adjustable and can be set in any position
note • can be fitted with storm sash on the inside to provide more weather tightness
• screens, interchangeable with storm sash, are furnished
• various types of glass, including obscure and colored, often are used for privacy or decoration

TYPES		DESCRIPTION

GLIDING

DOUBLE-HUNG

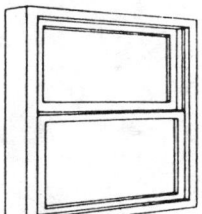 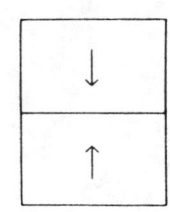

materials • wood, aluminum, steel in different designs and weights to meet various service requirements for all types of buildings

use • with combination of fixed windows for maximum window openings
• use in buildings other than residential and light commercial has been declining

operation • top and bottom openings optimize natural stratification ventilation

note • also available in single-hung (only one sash operating) and triple hung (three operable sash)

SLIDING

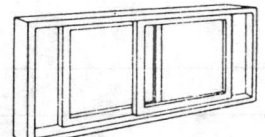 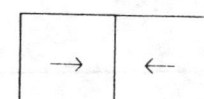

materials • wood, aluminum (with various coatings and claddings)

use • mostly in residential buildings

operation • provide only one half of opening for ventilation;
• sash height to width ratio should not exceed 1 to 2 for good operation

note • sash usually removable for cleaning and may be very large

DUAL-VENT

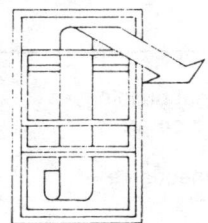 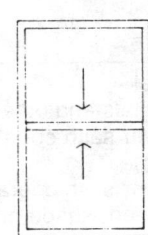

materials • aluminum

use • mostly in hospitals

operation • essentially two sets of double-hung sash—air circulates through the bottom outer sash and then through the top inner sash

note • provides ventilation while protecting from rain and drafts
• check cost

PIVOT

VERTICAL PIVOT

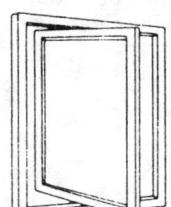 

materials • wood, aluminum and steel

use • mostly in air conditioned buildings

operation • consists of large vent, usually pivoted in the center of the head and sill of the main frame, which rotates 180° or 360° around its vertical axis for cleaning

note • not primarily designed for ventilation, although may be held open up to 4'' with special hardware (unless unlocked by maintenance personnel)

WINDOW TREATMENTS
Window Types

TYPES	DESCRIPTION

PIVOT, continued

HORIZONTAL PIVOT

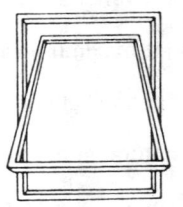 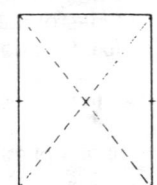

operation • similar to vertically pivoted but rotates around a horizontal axis

INDUSTRIAL PIVOT

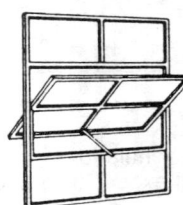 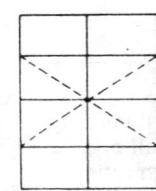

materials • steel, aluminum
use • often used horizontally and vertically to form entire walls
• lower cost for use in industrial and utilitarian buildings
note • mechanical operators are available

SPECIAL

CONTINUOUS

 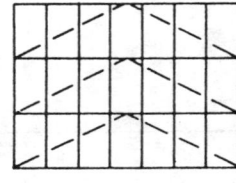

materials • steel
use • for top lighting and ventilation in monitor and sawtooth roof construction
operation • hinged at the top to the structural-steel framing members of the building and swing outward at the bottom
• two-floor lengths are connected end to end on the job
note • mechanical operators may be either manual or motor-powered

AUSTRAL

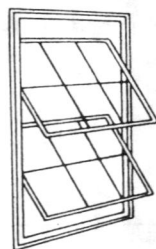 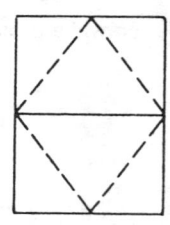

materials • wood and steel
use • schools, hospitals and other institutional buildings
• upper and lower sash counterbalanced on arms pivoted to frame
• upper and lower sash operate simultaneously
note • difficult to screen, shade or curtain

REVERSIBLE

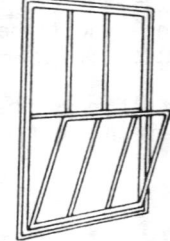 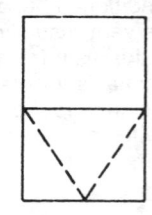

materials • wood and steel
use • residential and industrial buildings
operation • similar to double-hung in appearance, but may be tilted for better control of ventilation, or reversed for cleaning
note • not universally available

CUSTOM TYPES
VARIOUS CONFIGURATIONS

materials • aluminum, steel, stainless steel
use • special types for windows in houses of worship, mausoleums, and memorial buildings
operation • various arrangements available

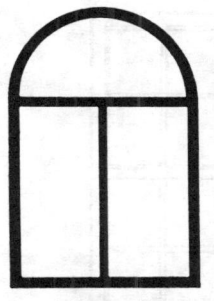

1. Round Top
over casements

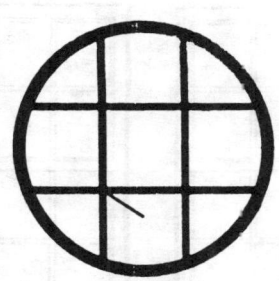

2. Full Round
with operating center

3. Round Top
with authentic divided lites

4. Separated
Round Top

5. Eyebrow
with Gothic divided lites

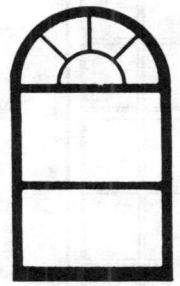

6. Round Top
over double-hung

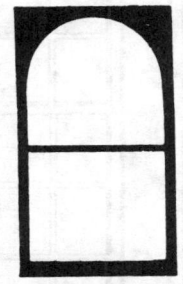

7. Simulated
Round Top

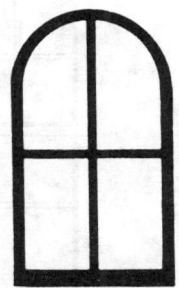

8. Round Top
with quarter panes

9. Transom Round Top.

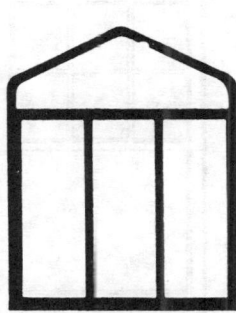

10. 3 point Round Top

11. Quarter Rounds

12. Round Top
over picture window

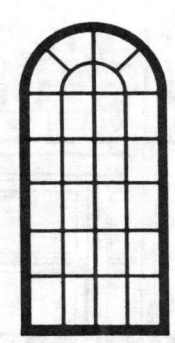

13. 12 foot Round Top
with decorative divided lites

14. Inverted
corners

15. 12 foot wide Round Top
with operating center

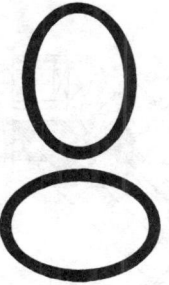

16. Ovals

17. Spider Web

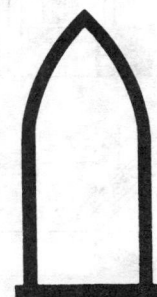

18. Gothic head

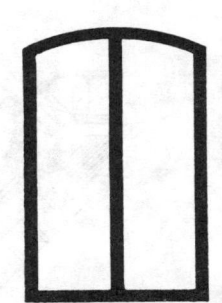

19. Rounded casements

20. Rounded double
hung with Gothic
lite pattern.

WINDOW TREATMENTS

Window Types

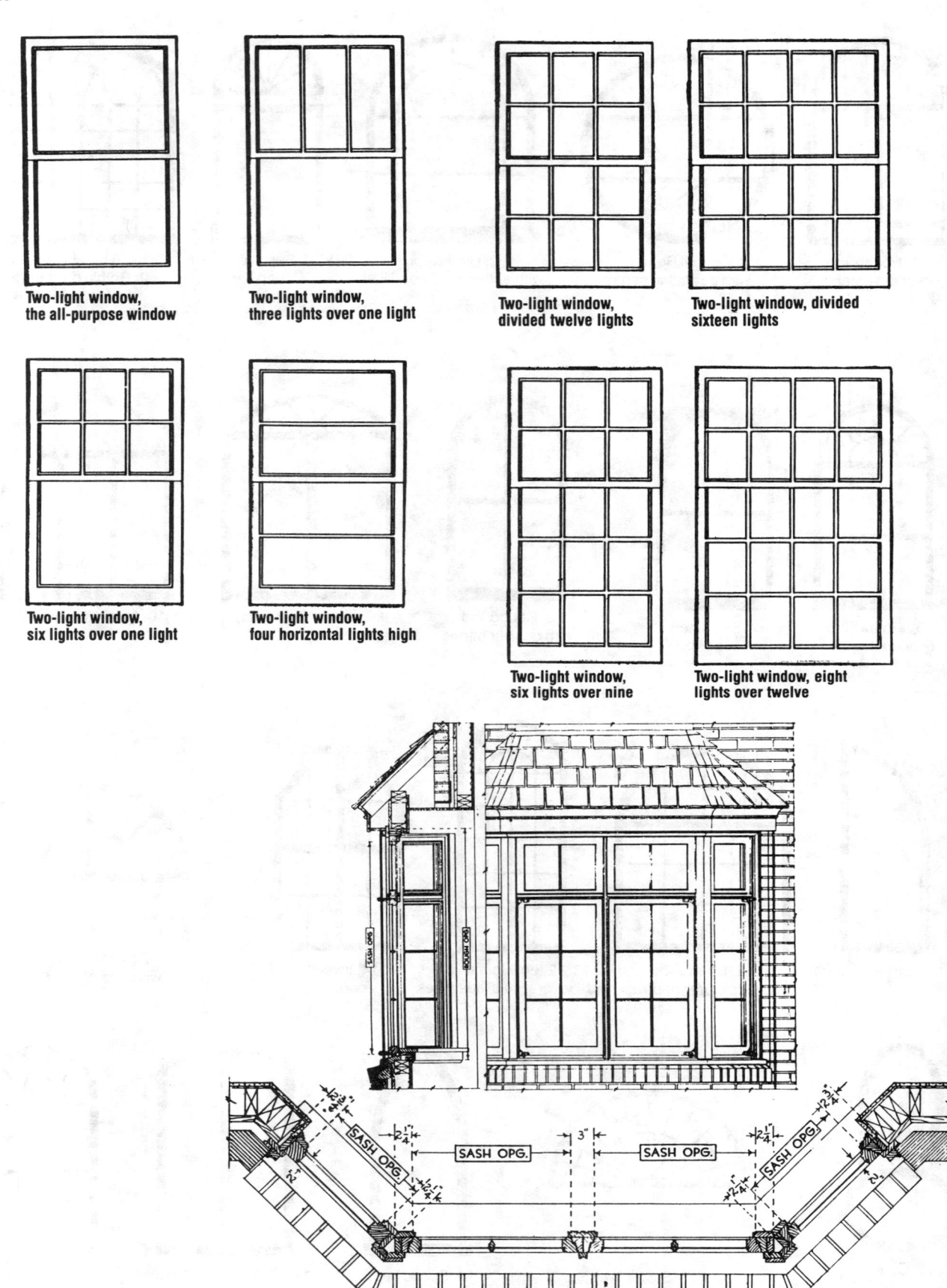

Two-light window,
the all-purpose window

Two-light window,
three lights over one light

Two-light window,
divided twelve lights

Two-light window, divided
sixteen lights

Two-light window,
six lights over one light

Two-light window,
four horizontal lights high

Two-light window,
six lights over nine

Two-light window, eight
lights over twelve

Typical styles of windows

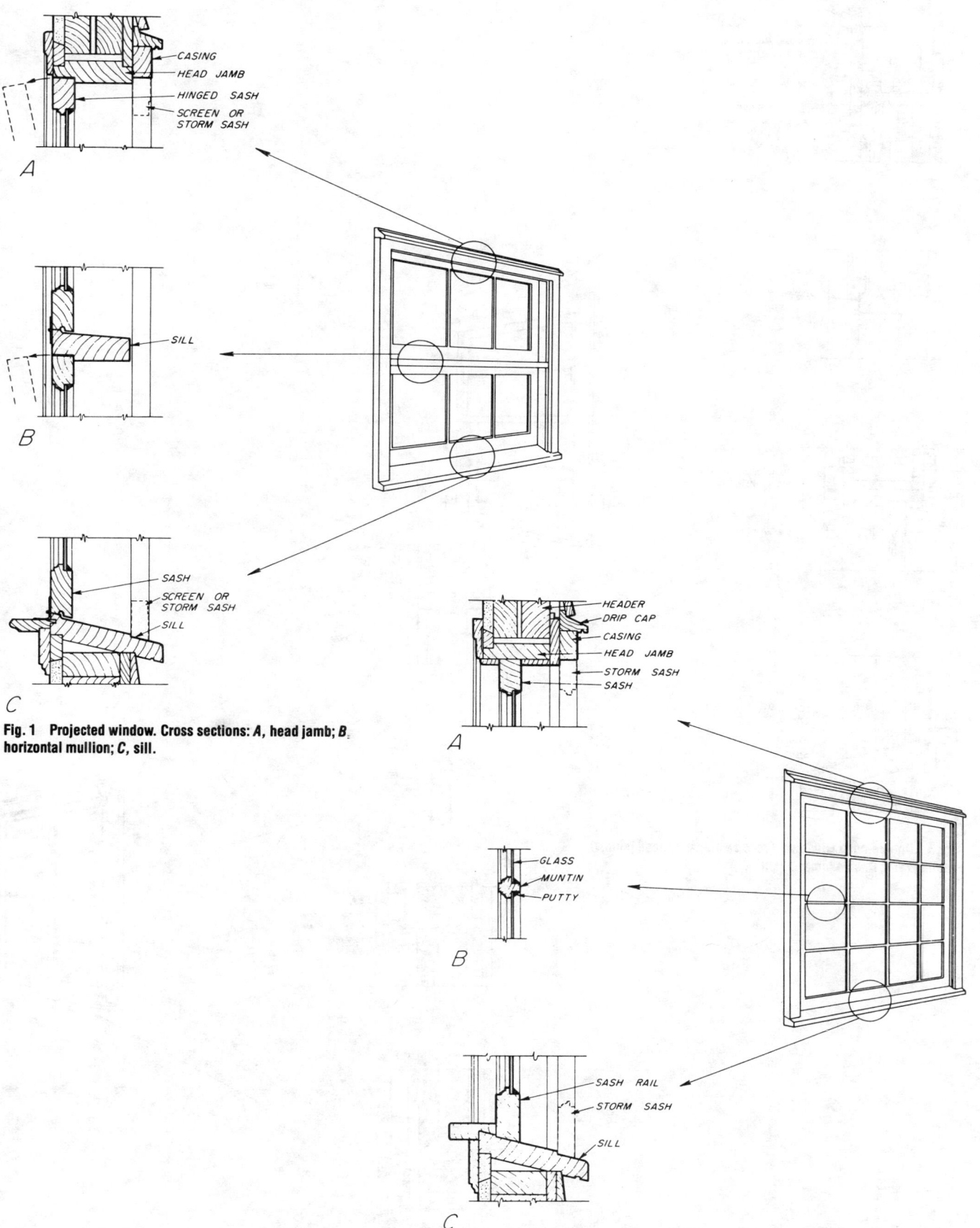

CASING
HEAD JAMB
HINGED SASH
SCREEN OR STORM SASH

A

SILL

B

SASH
SCREEN OR STORM SASH
SILL

C

Fig. 1 Projected window. Cross sections: *A*, **head jamb;** *B*, **horizontal mullion;** *C*, **sill.**

HEADER
DRIP CAP
CASING
HEAD JAMB
STORM SASH
SASH

A

GLASS
MUNTIN
PUTTY

B

SASH RAIL
STORM SASH
SILL

C

Fig. 2 Stationary window. Cross sections: *A*, **head jamb;** *B*, **muntin;** *C*, **sill.**

WINDOW TREATMENTS

Window Types: Double-Hung and Casement

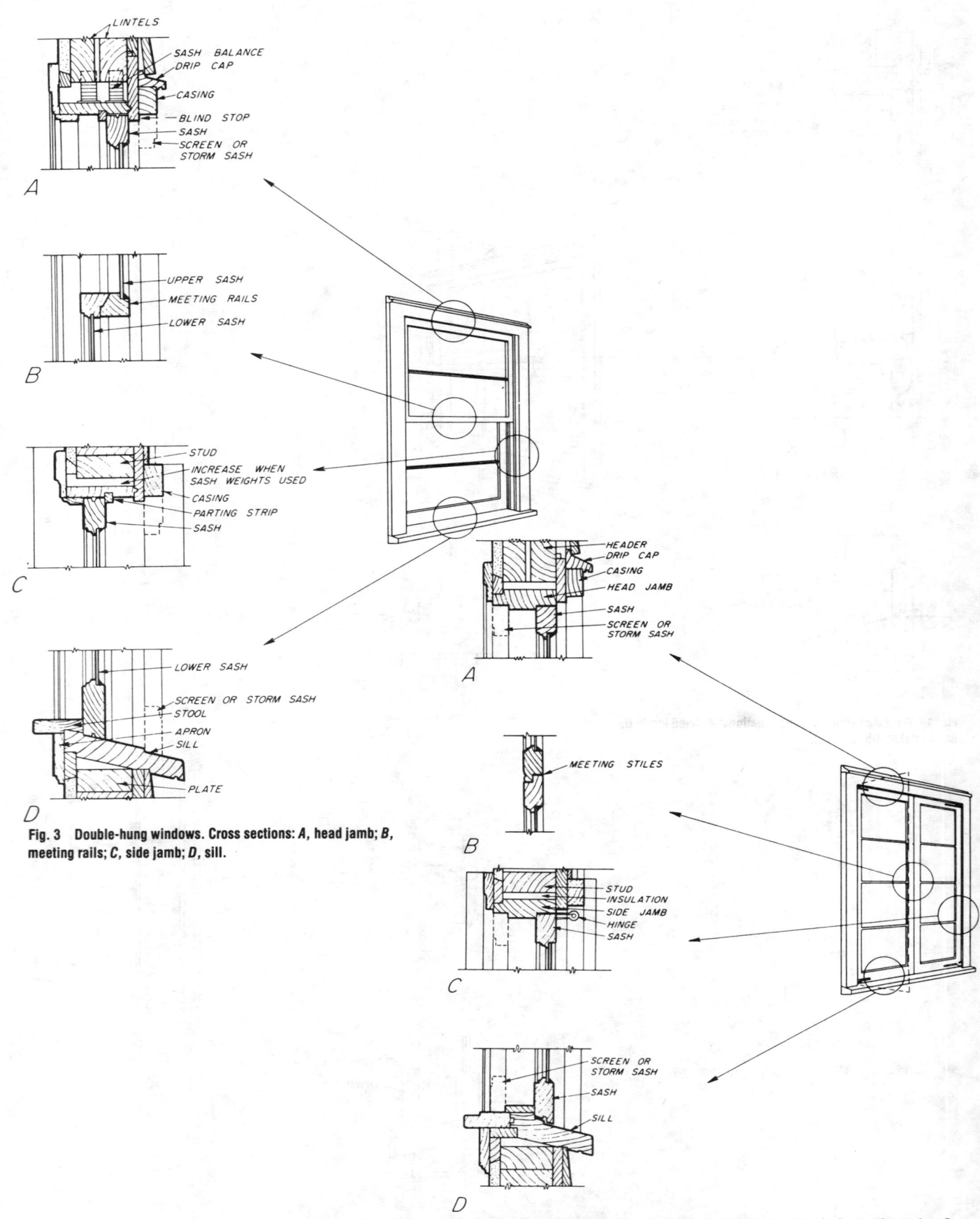

LINTELS
SASH BALANCE
DRIP CAP
CASING
BLIND STOP
SASH
SCREEN OR STORM SASH

A

UPPER SASH
MEETING RAILS
LOWER SASH

B

STUD
INCREASE WHEN SASH WEIGHTS USED
CASING
PARTING STRIP
SASH

C

LOWER SASH
SCREEN OR STORM SASH
STOOL
APRON
SILL
PLATE

D

Fig. 3 Double-hung windows. Cross sections: *A*, head jamb; *B*, meeting rails; *C*, side jamb; *D*, sill.

HEADER
DRIP CAP
CASING
HEAD JAMB
SASH
SCREEN OR STORM SASH

A

MEETING STILES

B

STUD
INSULATION
SIDE JAMB
HINGE
SASH

C

SCREEN OR STORM SASH
SASH
SILL

D

Fig. 4 Outswinging casement sash. Cross sections: *A*, head jamb; *B*, meeting styles; *C*, side jambs; *D*, sill.

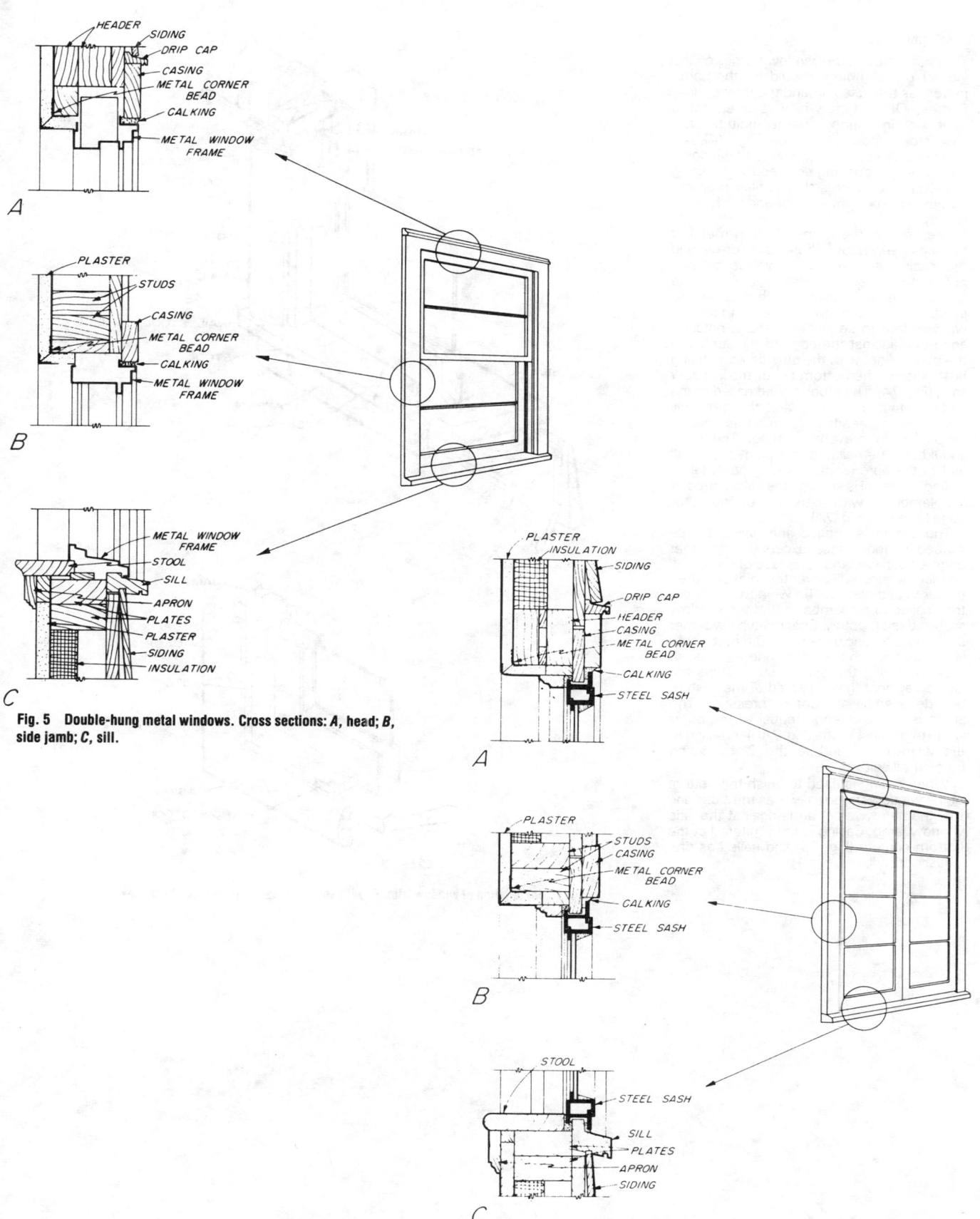

Fig. 5 Double-hung metal windows. Cross sections: *A*, head; *B*, side jamb; *C*, sill.

Fig. 6 Solid-section steel outswinging casement sash. Cross sections: *A*, head jamb; *B*, side jamb; *C*, sill.

WINDOW TREATMENTS
Window Types

Wood Trim

The casing around the window frames on the interior of the house should be the same pattern as that used around the interior door frames. Other trim which is used for a double-hung window frame includes the sash stops, stool, and apron (Fig. 7A). Another method of using trim around windows has the entire opening enclosed with casing (Fig. 7B). The stool is then a filler member between the bottom sash rail and the bottom casing.

The *stool* is the horizontal trim member that laps the window sill and extends beyond the casing at the sides, with each end notched against the plastered wall. The *apron* serves as a finish member below the stool. The window stool is the first piece of window trim to be installed and is notched and fitted against the edge of the jamb and the plaster line, with the outside edge being flush against the bottom rail of the window sash (Fig. 7A). The stool is blind-nailed at the ends so that the casing and the stop will cover the nailheads. Predrilling is usually necessary to prevent splitting. The stool should also be nailed at midpoint to the sill and to the apron with finishing nails. Face-nailing to the sill is sometimes substituted or supplemented with toenailing of the outer edge to the sill (Fig. 7A).

The casing is applied and nailed as described for doorframes, except that the inner edge is flush with the inner face of the jambs so that the stop will cover the joint between the jamb and casing. The window stops are then nailed to the jambs so that the window sash slides smoothly. Channel-type weather stripping often includes full-width metal sub-jambs into which the upper and lower sash slide, replacing the parting strip. Stops are located against these instead of the sash to provide a small amount of pressure. The apron is cut to a length equal to the outer width of the casing line (Fig. 7A). It is nailed to the window sill and to the 2- by 4-inch framing sill below.

When casing is used to finish the bottom of the window frame as well as the sides and top, the narrow stool butts against the side window jamb. Casing is then mitered at the bottom corners (Fig. 7B) and nailed as previously described.

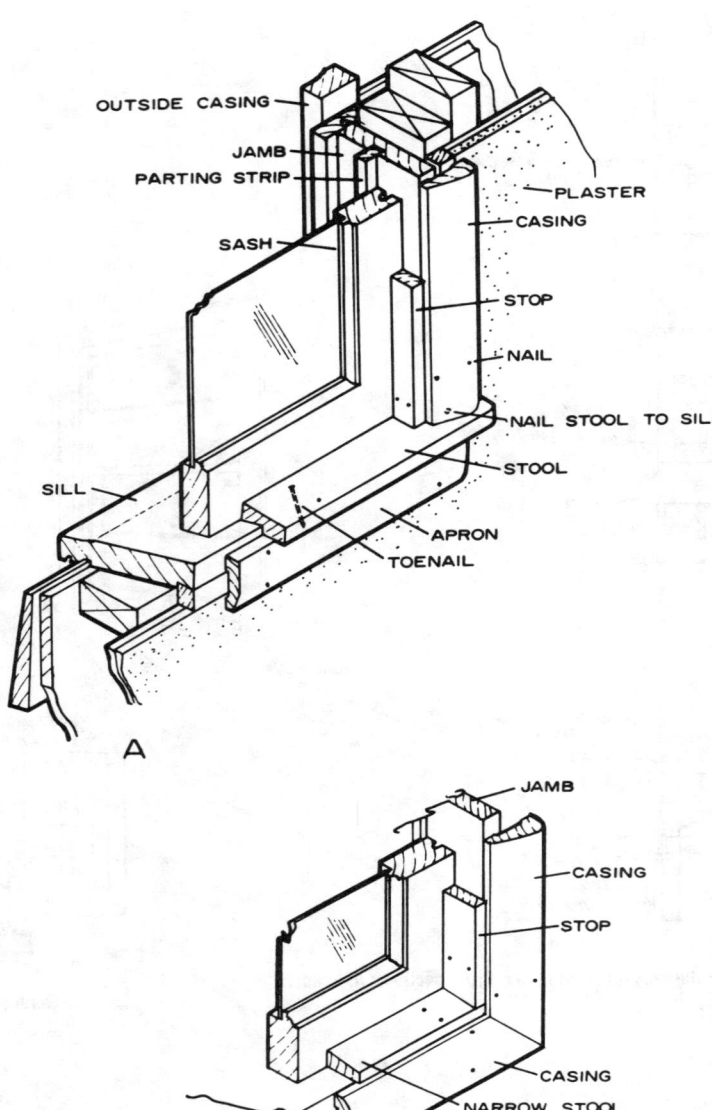

Fig. 7 Installation of window trim: *A*, with stool and apron; *B*, enclosed with casing.

CURTAINS

Curtains are soft window coverings that generally are shirred (gathered onto a rod) or have headings attached to solid-wood rods, round or oval metal rods, or café rods rather than cord-operated traverse rods. Curtains may be either stationary fabric panels or slid open and closed by hand. They are flexible in that they can be short or long, layered or tiered, or used alone or in combination with other soft, or with hard treatments. *Curtain* is traditionally a term for informal treatments, such as café curtains. However, curtains also may be quite formal, as are shirred and elegant tied-back fabric treatments.

Even though curtains are generally thought to be shirred treatments, other headings might be included in this category. Indeed, there is a crossover of terminology between draperies and curtains. Generally draperies are installed on cord-operated traverse rods, although they may be stationary pleated panels. Curtains may be installed on traverse rods (as in a pleated café curtain, for example), and headings such as the pencil pleat; drawstring pencil pleat; shirred, spaced pencil pleat; alternate pencil pleat; ruffled shirring tape heading; and smocked heading may be called either curtain or drapery treatments.

DRAPERIES

Draperies are made with pleats. They are hung with drapery hoods onto carriers of conventional, architectural, or decorative traverse rods or into the rings of wood rods or café curtain rods; or they may thread onto spring-system traverse rods. Generally draperies are either hung straight to the floor or tied back. Thus they operate, or "draw," by opening and closing with a cord or a wand or by hand. The exception is tied-back draperies, which sometimes are let down at night. However, tied-back draperies are trained to tie back at an angle and therefore should not be handled to any extent. Draperies draw in a pair and meet in the center (center-meet) or draw one way from left to right or from right to left. One-way draw draperies require one-way traverse rods.

Draperies that hang at a doorway rather than at a window are called portières. They may be pleated in any fashion or shirred. They may be placed on a traverse rod, but historically (and they were used extensively in the Victorian era), they were tied-back stationary panels made of a heavy fabric that were let down when privacy or insulation was needed.

Draperies can be made of any fabric. The selection will depend on the style, use, and needs. Sheer fabrics do best as diffusers of glare and as providers of daytime privacy. Medium- to heavyweight fabrics are excellent choices for overdraperies and plain tieback draperies. Lining fabrics are the right weight for privacy liners or underdraperies. If a drapery is given a ruffled edge or a banding, that trim should be a lightweight, semi-crisp, flexible fabric, not a heavy, stiff fabric or a sheer, slippery fabric.

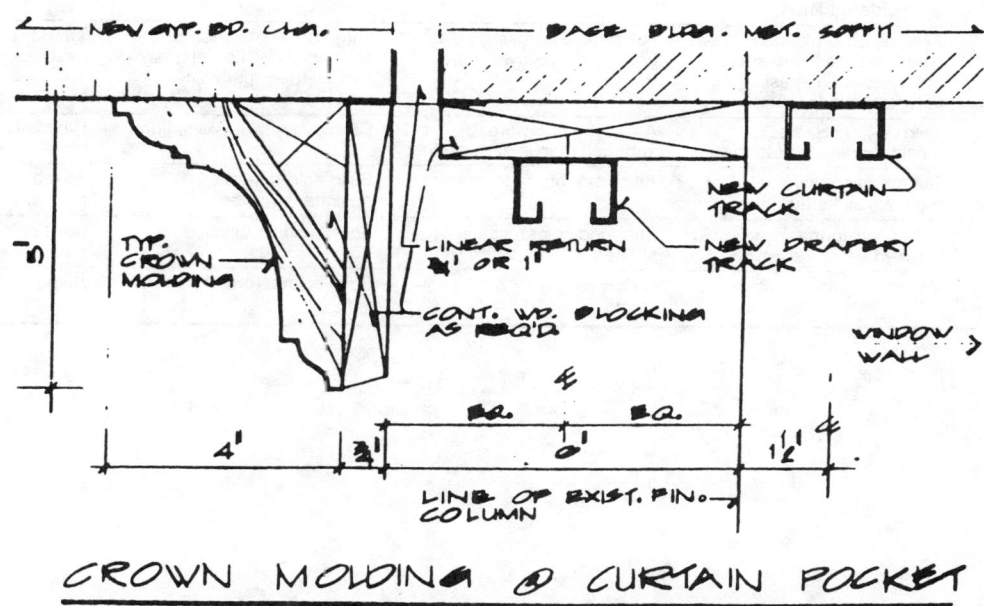

CROWN MOLDING @ CURTAIN POCKET

TABLE 1 Draperies

Period style	Fabric	Colors	Design	Upholstery fabrics
Early English Tudor Jacobean Charles II	Crewel, embroideries, hand-blocked linen, silk and worsted damask, velvet, brocade	Full-bodied crimson, green, and yellow	Large bold patterns: tree branch, fruits, flowers, oak leaf, animals, heraldic designs	Tapestry, leather, needlework, velvet, brocade
Anglo-Dutch William & Mary Queen Anne	Crewel, embroideries, hand-blocked linen, silk and worsted damask, velvet, brocade, India print	Full-bodied crimson, green, and yellow	Large bold patterns: tree branch, fruits, flowers, oak leaf, animals, heraldic designs	Tapestry, leather, needlework, velvet, brocade
Early Georgian Chippendale	Crewel, embroideries, hand-blocked linen, silk and worsted damask, velvet, brocade, Indian print	Full-bodied crimson, green, and yellow	Jacobean motifis, classic medallions and garlands	Tapestry, leather, needlepoint, velvet, brocade
Late Georgian Adam Hepplewhite Sheraton Empire Federal	Brocade, damask, chintz, taffeta, satin, toile de jouy	Delicate subdued hues of rose, yellow, mauve, green, and gray	Classic designs, small in scale: garlands, urns, floral, animals, etc.	Damask, brocade, velour, satin, petit point, leather in libraries
Louis XIV Louis XV Louis XVI	Silk, satin, damask, taffeta, muslin, brocade, toile de jouy	Delicate powder blue, oyster white, pearl, rose, pale greens, mauve, yellow	Stripes sprinkled with ribbons, flowers, medallions, lyres, and other classic motifs	Petit point, satin, moire, velour, chintz, damask, brocade, tapestry
Spanish renaissance	Velvet, damask, crewel, India print, printed and embroidered linen	Rich vigorous colors, red, green, and gold	Bold patterns in classic and heraldic designs; also arabesques	Leather, tapestry, velvet, linen, brocatelle
Early colonial	Crewel, embroideries, hand-blocked linen, silk and worsted damask, velvet, brocade	Full-bodied crimson, green, and yellow	Large bold patterns: tree branch, fruits, flowers, oak leaf, animals, heraldic designs	Tapestry, leather, needlepoint, velvet, brocade
Early American	Toile de jouy, damask, chintz, organdy, cretonne	All colors, but more subdued than in early period	Scenic, birds, animals, floral	Haircloth, mohair, linen, chintz, velours
Modern	Textured and novelty weaves, all fabrics	All colors, bright to pastel	Solid colors, modern designs, stripes	All fabrics, novelty weaves, plastics
French provincial	Chintz, cretonne, hand-blocked linen, velvet	Subdued colors, pastel shades	Screen prints, block prints	Solid colors, textured weaves, tapestry
Victorian	Velvet, brocade, damask	Turkey red, other rich colors	Solid colors, formal patterns	Haircloth, needlework

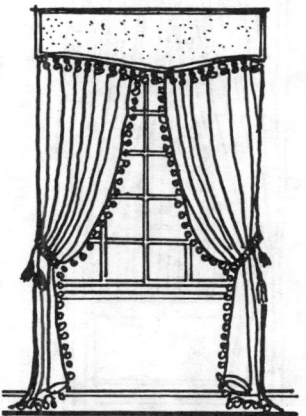

18th-century colonial: tieback damask drapery with balled fringe

18th-century colonial: staggered tieback with plain edge asymmetric panels

18th-century colonial: swagged valance over bishop sleeve draperies over holdback

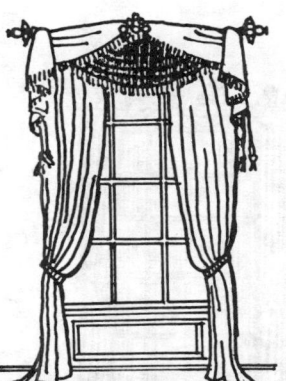

Federal: tieback panels with fringed raised valance of contrasting color

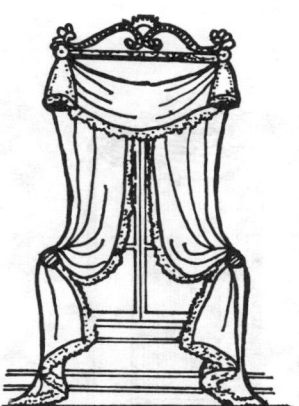

Federal: waterfall over holdback with draped valance

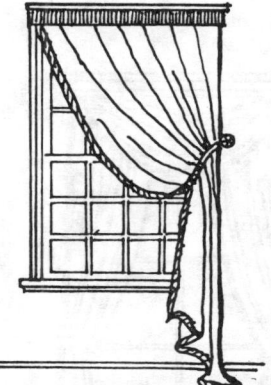

Federal: asymmetric tieback with fringed valance

Federal: heavy valance over straight draperies

WINDOW TREATMENTS
Curtains/Draperies of Georgian and Directoire Periods

Georgian: tieback drapery with Austrian valance with fringes

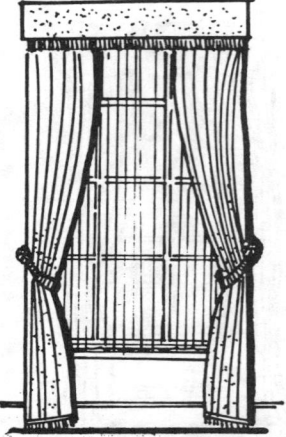

Georgian: tieback heavy woven drapery with fabric-covered heading — sheer curtains behind

Georgian: tieback drapery with tapered French pleat heading

Late Georgian: curved fabric cartridge valance over holdback draperies

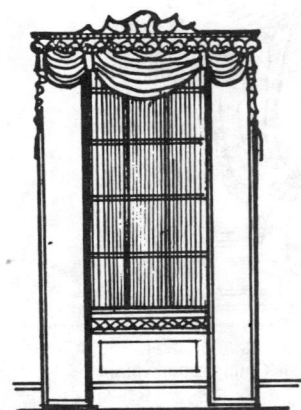

Late Georgian: gilt wood cornice over fixed lambrequins and sheer curtains

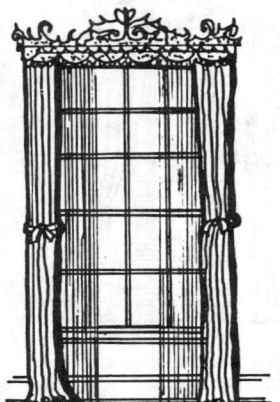

Late Georgian: gilt metal cornice over fixed tieback draperies and sheer curtains

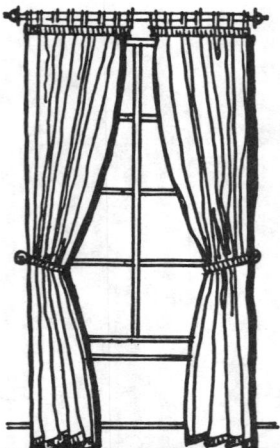

Directoire: tieback draperies with contrasting edging on decorative brass rod

Directoire: fringed overdrapery valance on fringed sleeved tiebacks and fringed drapery

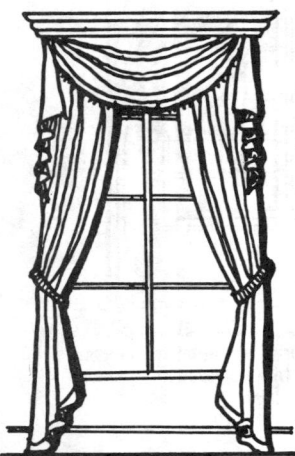

Directoire: painted stepped wood cornice over swag with twin cascades and tieback draperies

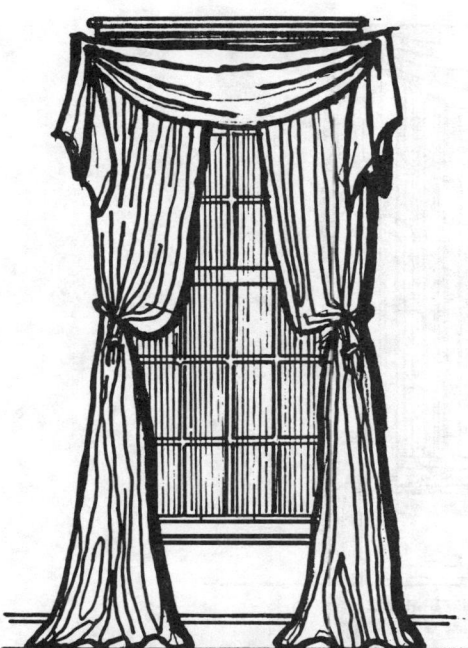

Mid-19th-century Victorian: central swag with twin cascades over heavy draperies with braided tieback over sheer undercurtain

Late-19th-century Victorian: looped festoon over decorative brass rod

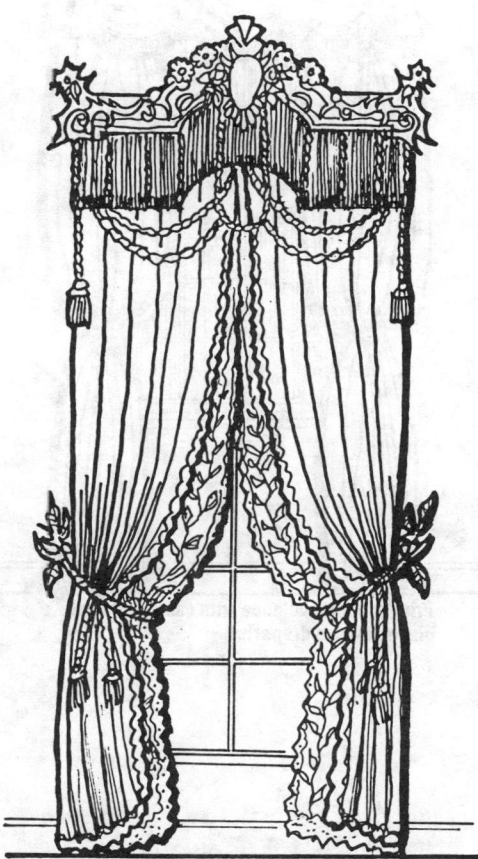

Late-19th-century Victorian: neo-Greek-style cornice with fringed valance over tieback fringed fabric with lace undercurtains

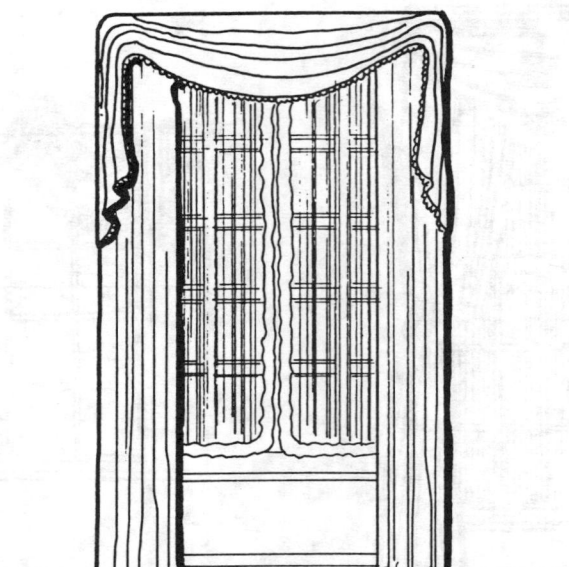

Fringed finger festoon over brackets over straight line draperies with sheer undercurtains

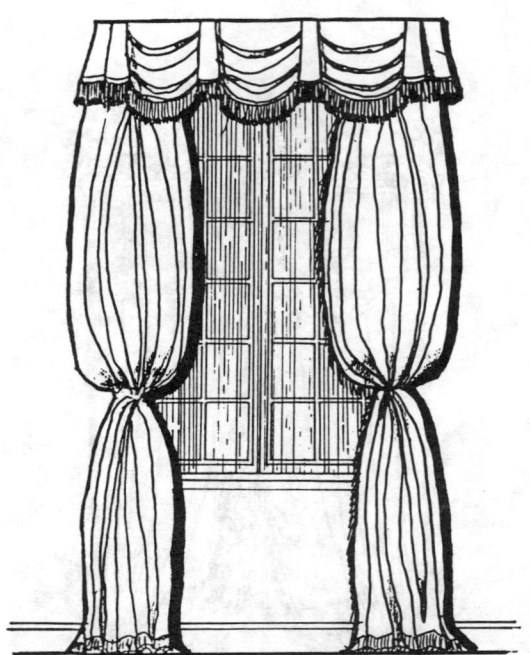

Fringed fabric valance with cascades over bishop sleeve draperies

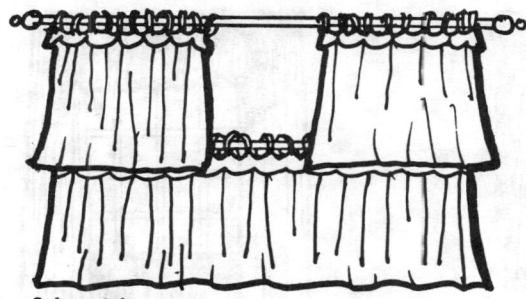

Cafe curtains

Ruffled tieback curtains

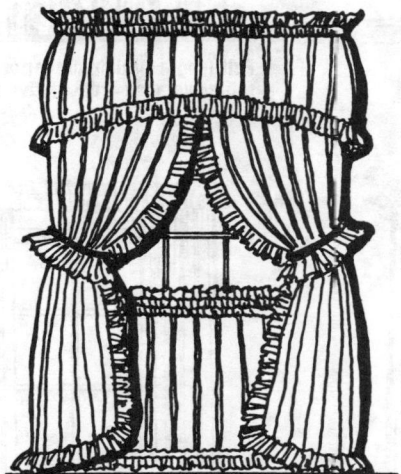

Fringed segmented valance with ruffled trim — tieback draperies over café curtains

Fabric-wrapped-pole draped valance

Café curtains with gathered valance and ball fringe trim

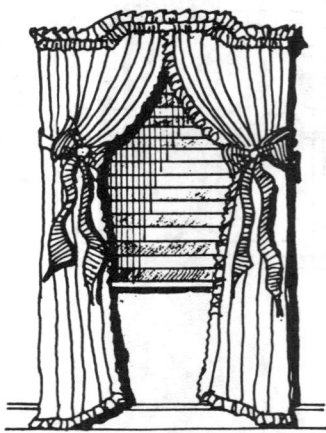

Tieback draperies with ruffles on center arch rod — pleated shade beneath

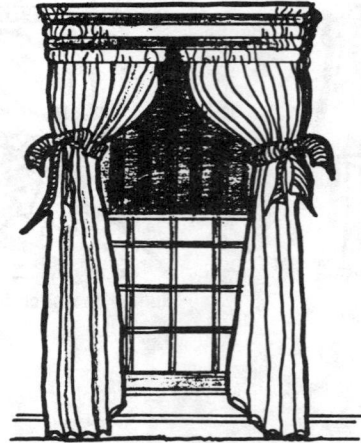

High tieback draperies with ruffled multirow valance — woven shade beneath

Full-length straight draperies with ruffled valance — decorative bows

Shirred, ruffled balloon valance over ruffled, shirred heading on narrow rod

Shirred heading on brass pole — fixed draperies with rosette tieback

Shirred heading on brass pole — fixed panel draperies

Shirred balance with shirred tieback draperies over blinds

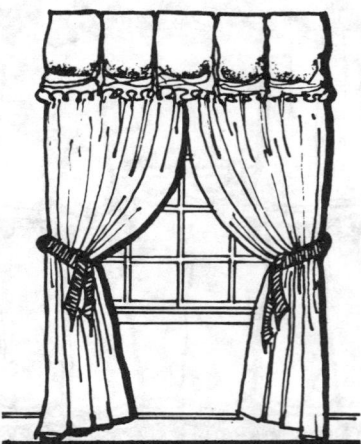

Penta balloon valance over ribbon tieback draperies

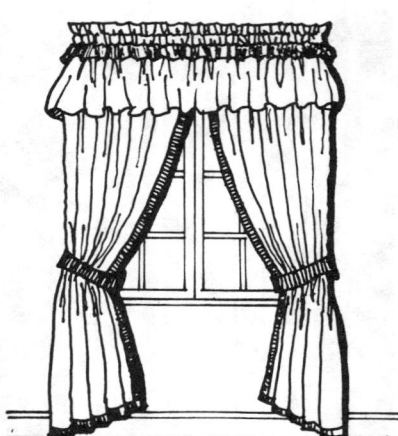

Shirred valance with horizontal accent banding — tieback draperies with matching edge banding

Bishop sleeve fringed-tip valance with ribbon tieback draperies

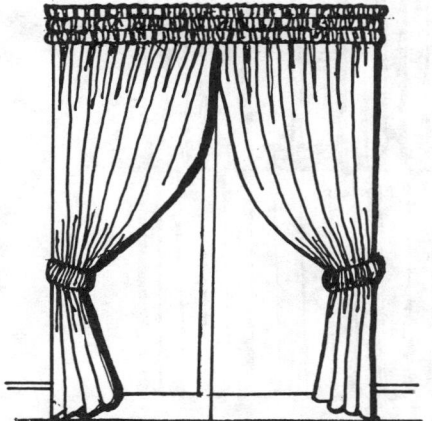

Triple-row fringed heading with shirred tieback draperies

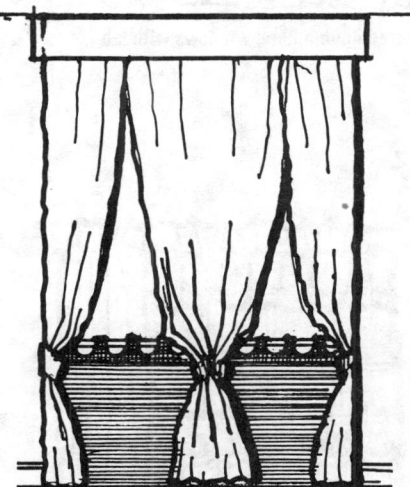

Fabric-covered straight cornice over paired tieback draperies and scalloped curtain on brass rod

Pinch pleated draperies with horizontal tiebacks over standard roller shades

WINDOW TREATMENTS

Curtains/Draperies

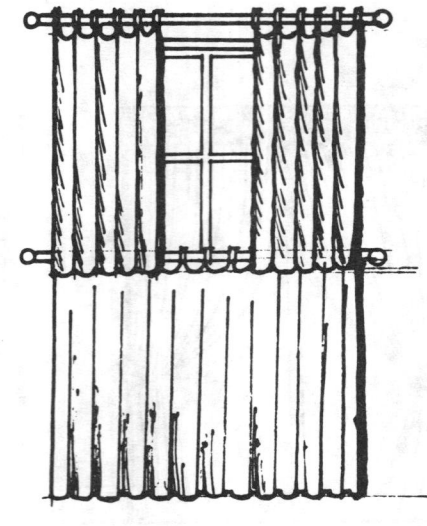

Café curtains with scalloped edges on
brass rods

Single pleated draperies over paired double hung windows with tab
headed café curtains on rod

Fabric-covered cornice board valance — ribbon tiebacks on
drapery

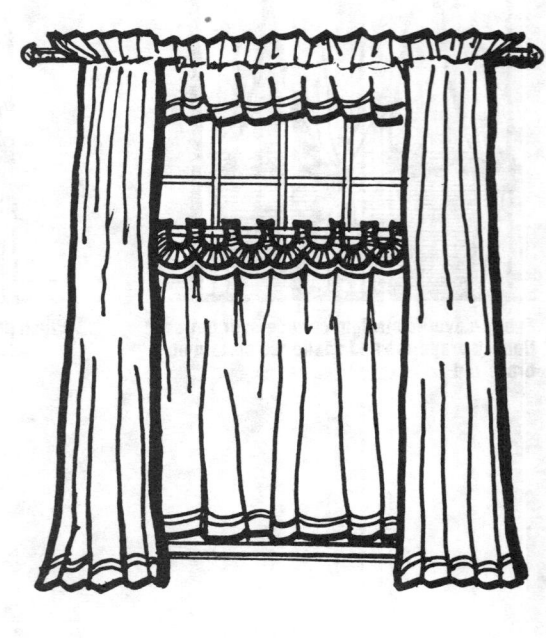

Ruffled valance heading over brass rod with straight draperies
over scalloped café curtain

**Simple traditional swag with
cascade draperies**

**Rosette tieback priscilla curtains
with continental heading**

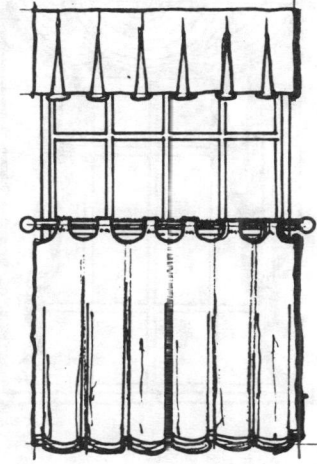

**Scalloped café curtains on brass rod
with pleated valance**

**Bow tieback curtains with fringed trim
and gathered valance**

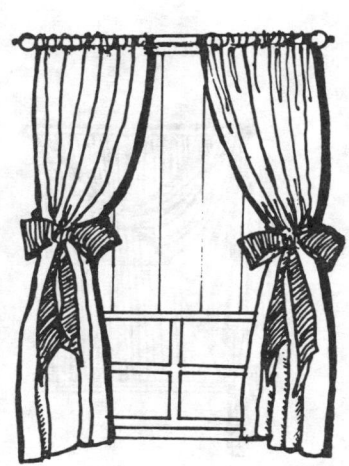

**Bow tieback gathered curtains
on brass rod**

Overlapping swag on rod with ball-fringed cascades

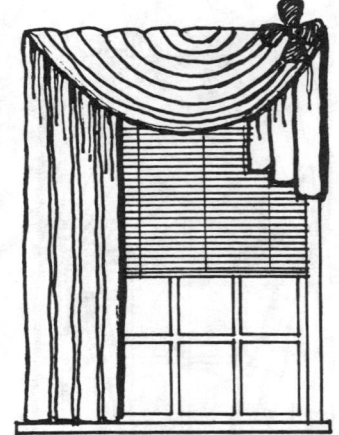

Swag with bow and assymmetric cascades

Symmetrical swags and cascades with center rosette

Symmetrical draped swag over brass rod

Asymmetrical swag drapery over brass rod with sheer curtain

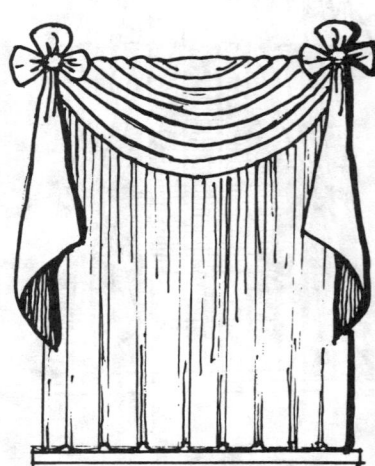

Symmetrical draped swag on rod with ties at end over sheer or solid curtain

Triple-tail cascades with dual swags and rosette holds

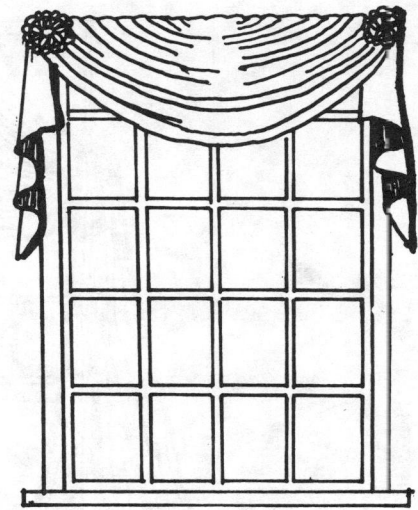

Swag over rod with rosette holds

Swag, draped valance, cascading ends

Asymmetrical double-rod-supported swags and draperies — contemporary

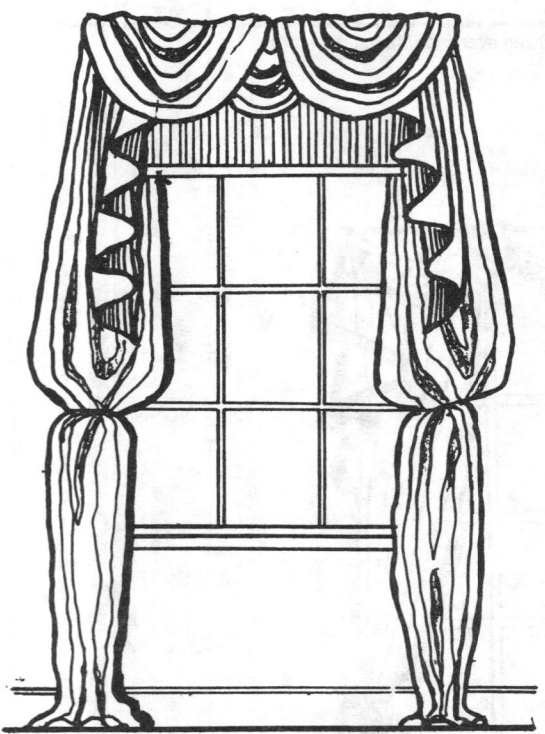

Symmetrical long cascades and swags with center swag and bishop sleeve draperies

Overlapped double swag thrown over door-high holdbacks, with draperies billowed at floor

Flared cornice box with geometric trimmed scallops over reverse swags and asymmetric floor-tip cascades

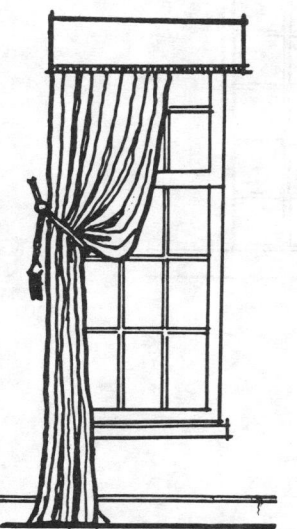

Trimmed cornice box over asymmetric tieback drapery

Symmetrical box-pleated draperies on brass rod with double-tiered rosette holdbacks

WINDOW TREATMENTS

Curtains/Draperies

Pleated shade

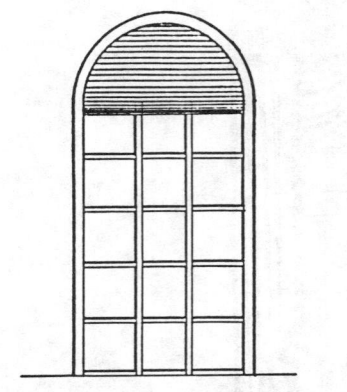

Miniblind — custom fitted

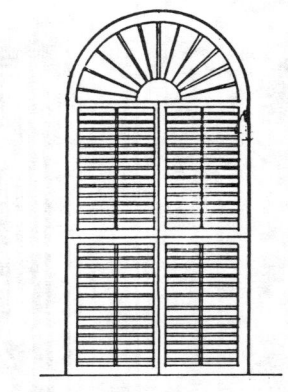

Wooden shutters

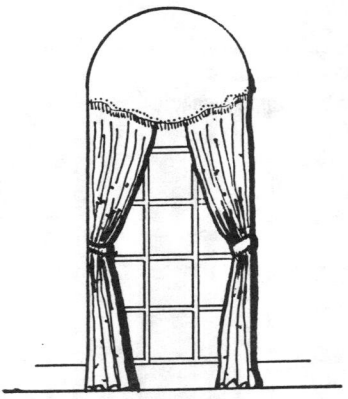

Rounded valance with drapery

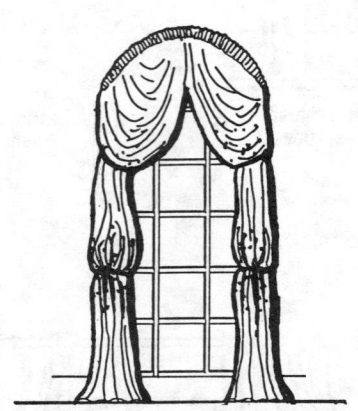

Double swags with balloon drapery

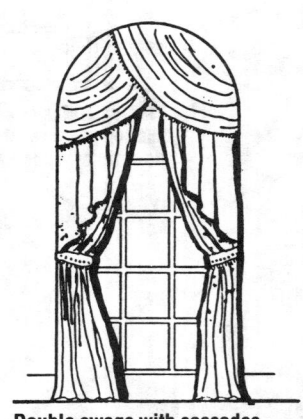

Double swags with cascades and drapery

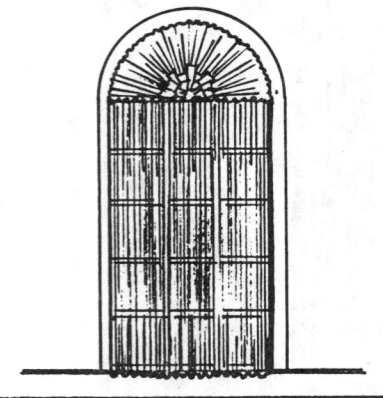

Shirred curtain with sunburst

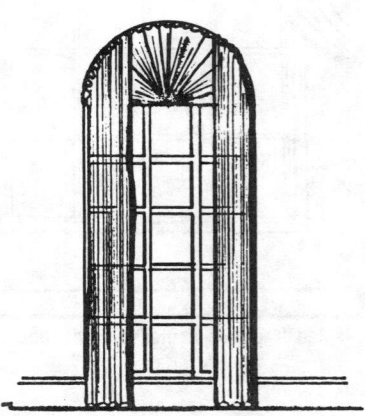

Pleated shade with shirred curtain

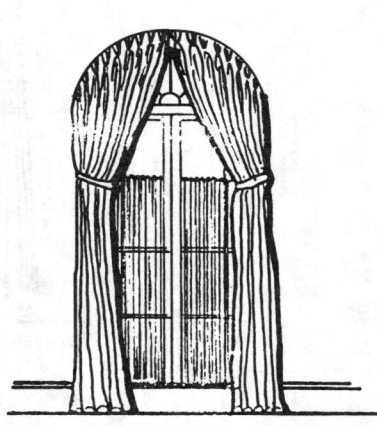

French pleats with shaped top under curtain

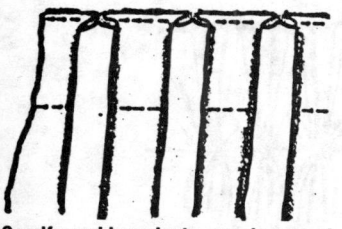

Semiformal box pleats, evenly spaced

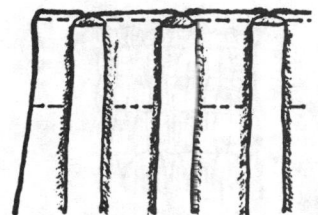

Cartridge pleat, evenly spaced

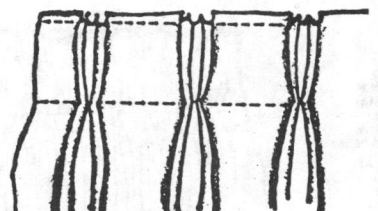

Triple pleat heading, evenly spaced

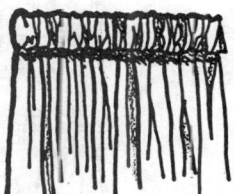

Shirred heading on a narrow rod

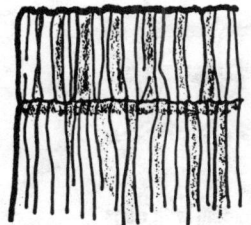

Shirred heading gathering on a wide rod

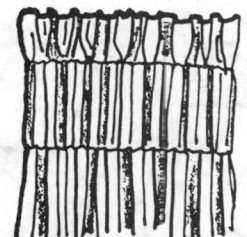

Ruffled shirred heading on an extra-wide rod

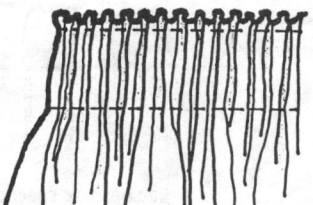

Pencil heading on a wide rod

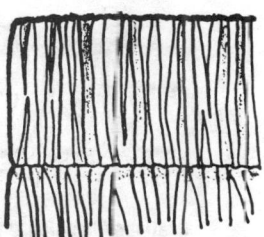

Shirred heading gathered on an extra-wide rod

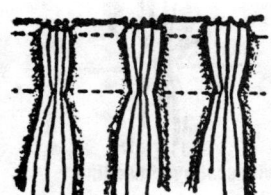

Cluster heading, spaced evenly

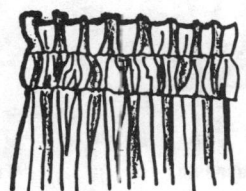

Ruffled shirred heading on a narrow rod

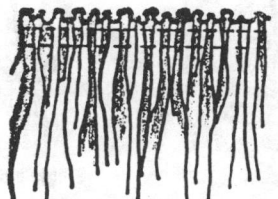

Standard heading on a narrow rod

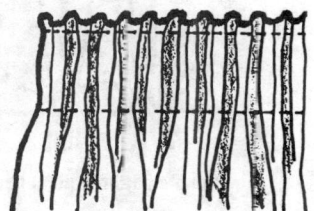

Spaced pencil pleats heading on a wide rod

WINDOW TREATMENTS

Headings

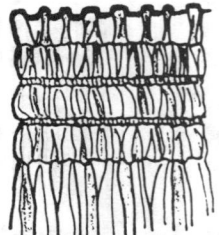

Triple shirred heading with ruffle gathered on 3 narrow rods

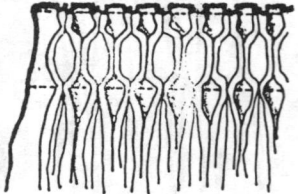

Decorative heading on a wide rod

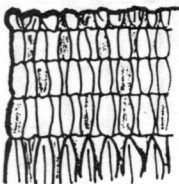

Triple shirred heading gathered on 3 narrow rods

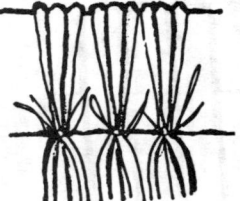

Grouped French pleats

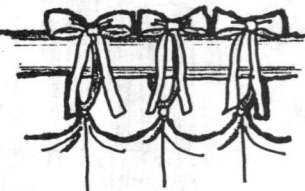

Scalloped heading with rings and bows

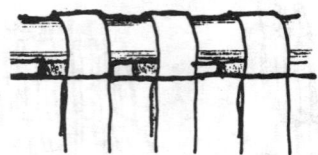

Tab heading spaced evenly on rod

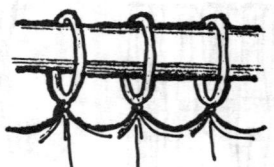

Scalloped heading with rings

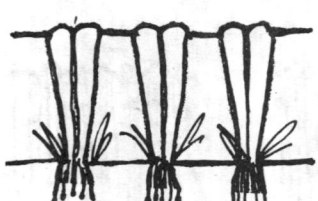

Double butterfly pleat heading

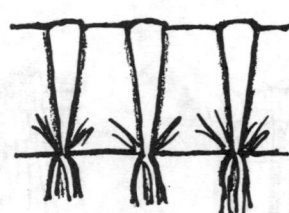

Single butterfly pleat heading

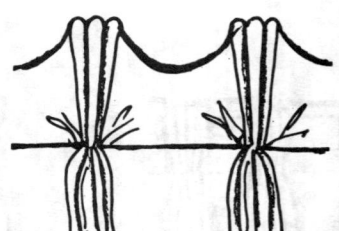

French pleats with scalloped heading

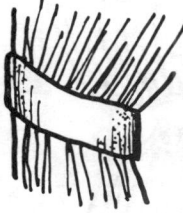

Straight

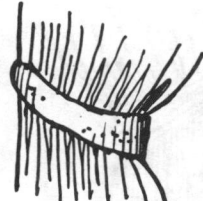

Tapered

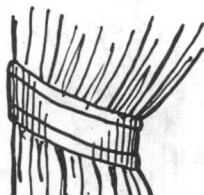

Banded

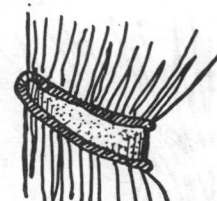

Tapered with welting

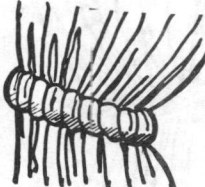

Oversized welting

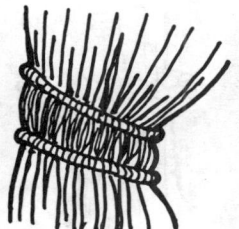

Shirred with welting

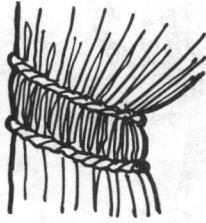

Shirred with braided trim

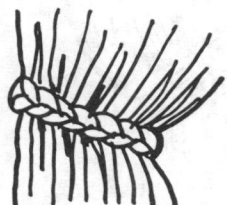

Braided

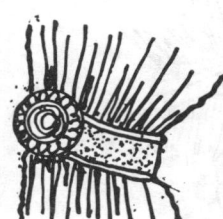

Rosette

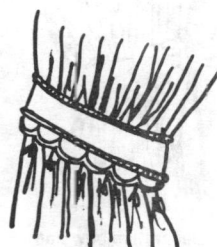

Fringed with welting

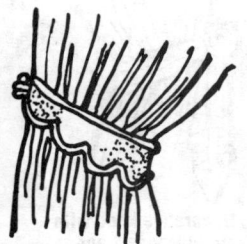

Scalloped

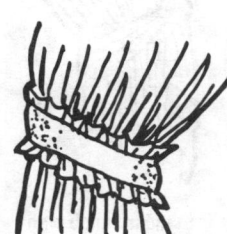

Frilled

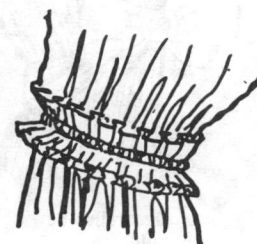

Twin ruffles

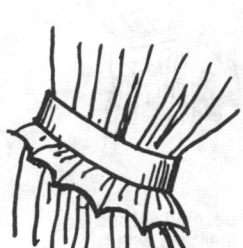

Straight with scallops

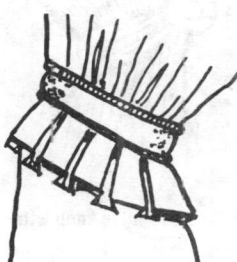

Twin welting with box pleating

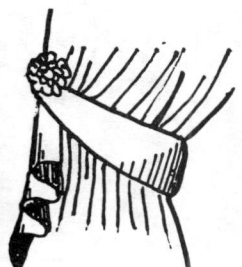

Rosette with cascade

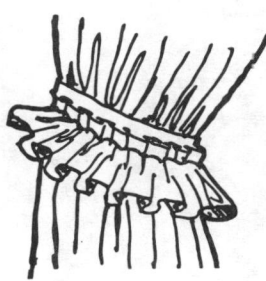

Ruffles

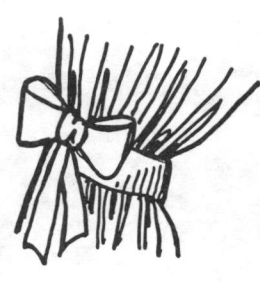

Bow/ribbon

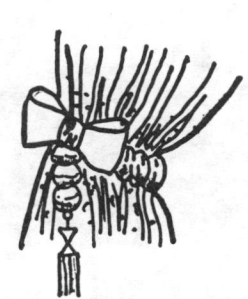

Bow with welting and tassel

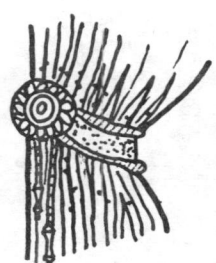

Tapered with welting, rosette, and tassels

WINDOW TREATMENTS

Tiebacks and Holdbacks

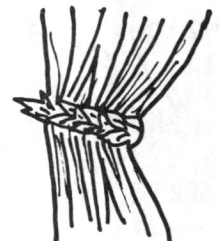

Leaf motif

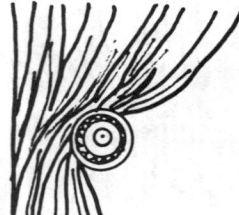

Decorative holdback

Scalloped with welting

Layered with pleats

Decorative with tassel

Decorative bow and ribbon

Square holdback with insert

Decorative knob with 2 inserts

Decorative knob holdback with tassel

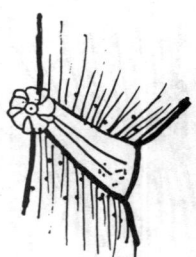

Stylized rosette

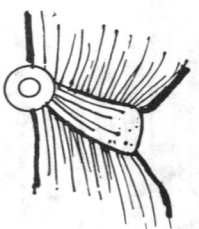

Decorative knob with inserts

Decorative knob holdback with two tassels

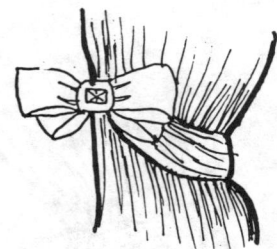

Decorative bow holdback

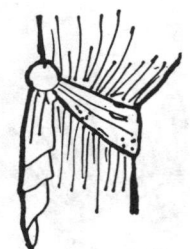

Standard knob with cascade

Decorative knob with circular insert and cascade

MOUNTS

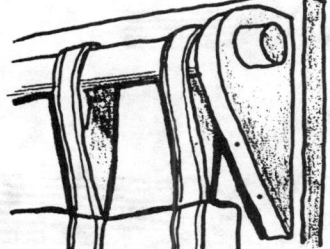

Flush mount — closed top

Outside mount — open top

Outside mount — closed side

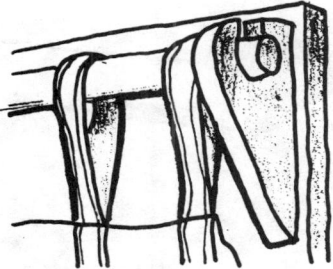

Flush mount — open top

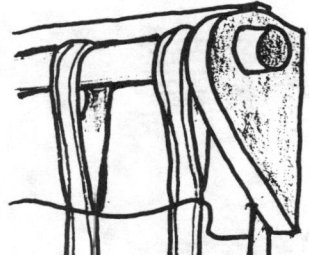

Outside mount — closed top

Inside mount bracket

BRACKETS

Flush extra-projection bracket

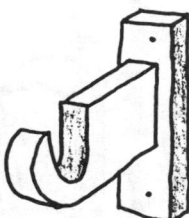

Base-mounted extra-projection bracket

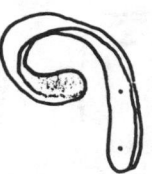

Curved bracket

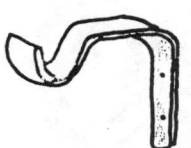

Support bracket

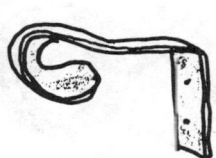

Curved support bracket

Double rod bracket

COUPLERS

Extra-projection base-mounted coupler

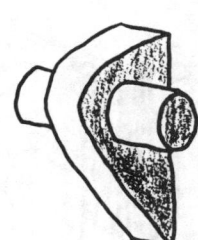

Base-mounted coupler

WINDOW TREATMENTS
Finials, Rings, and Hooks

FINIALS

 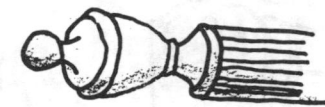 

RINGS

Plain ring   Round eyelet ring   Oval eyelet ring   Square eyelet ring   Round clip-on ring   Oval clip-on ring   Rounded-end clip-on ring

HOOKS

  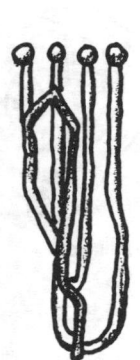 

Metal and plastic hooks for standard tapes

Metal hooks for decorative tapes

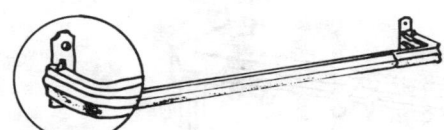

Flat curtain rod

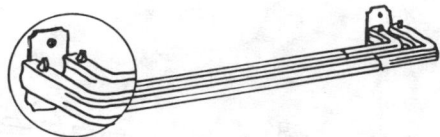

Double flat curtain rod

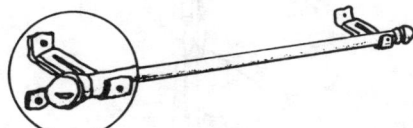

Cafe curtain rod

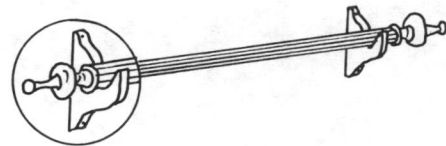

Fluted wood rod

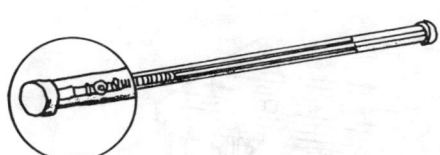

Tension rod with adjustable screw

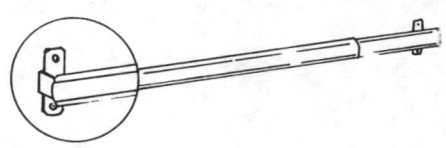

Sash rods

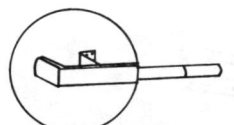

Separated curtain rod

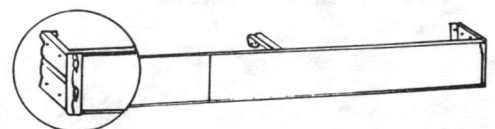

Extra wide telescoping projection rod

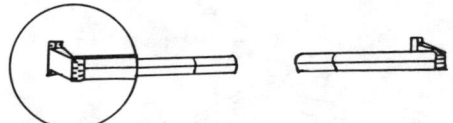

Swinging arm separated rod

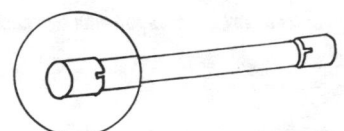

Polyvinyl chloride (PVC) with end caps
curtain rod

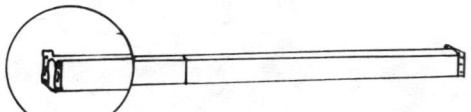

Wide telescoping curtain rod

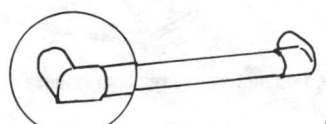

PVC pipe with elbows for projection

WINDOW TREATMENTS
Traverse Rods

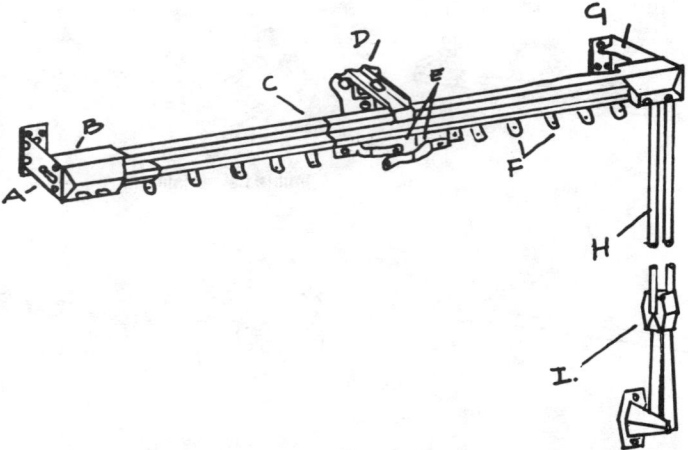

Conventional single hung traverse rod — A, projecting end brackets; B, end housing; C, telescoping rod; D, center support; E, master carriers; F, carriers; G, end bracket; H, cord; I, tension pulley

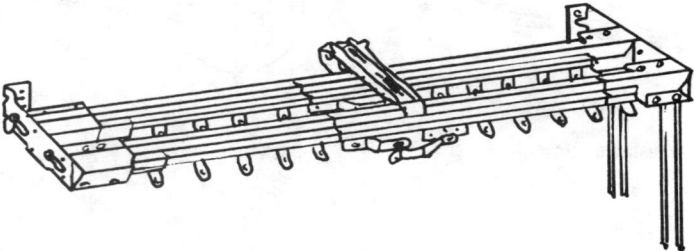

Double traverse rod

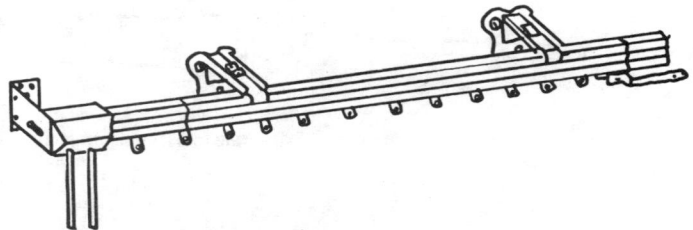

One-way traverse rod with two center supports

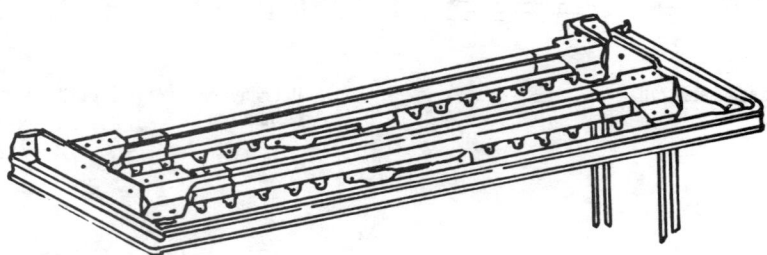

Double traverse rod with valence

TABLE 2 Fabric Panel Widths and Pleating Guidelines

Desired pleated panel coverage	Flat fabric without hems	Hemmed flat fabric	Number of 4" flat spaces between pleats	Number of pleats	Width of fabric in each pleat
16"	43"	39"	4	5	3⅛"
20"	51"	47"	5	6	3¼"
24"	59"	55"	6	7	3⅜"
28"	67"	63"	7	8	3½"
32"	75"	71"	8	9	3½"
36"	83"	79"	9	10	3⁹⁄₁₆"
40"	91"	87"	10	11	3⅝"
44"	99"	95"	11	12	3⅝"
48"	107"	103"	12	13	3⅝"
52"	115"	111"	13	14	3⅝"
56"	123"	119"	14	15	3¾"
60"	131"	127"	15	16	3¾"
64"	139"	135"	16	17	3¾"
68"	147"	143"	17	18	3¾"
72"	155"	151"	18	19	3¾"
76"	163"	159"	19	20	3¾"
80"	171"	167"	20	21	3¾"
84"	179"	175"	21	22	3¾"
88"	187"	183"	22	23	3¾"
92"	195"	191"	23	24	3¾"
96"	203"	199"	24	25	3¾"
100"	211"	207"	25	26	3¾"
104"	219"	215"	26	27	3¾"
108"	227"	223"	27	28	3¾"
112"	235"	231"	28	29	3¾"
116"	243"	239"	29	30	3¾"
120"	251"	247"	30	31	3⅞"
124"	259"	254"	31	32	3⅞"
128"	267"	263"	32	33	3⅞"

TABLE 3 Rod Lengths Needed for Various Widths of Windows and Stackback Spaces

If the glass is	The stackback* should be	Your rod length and drapery coverage should be (add for overlaps and returns)
38"	26"	64"
44"	28"	72"
50"	30"	80"
56"	32"	88"
62"	34"	96"
68"	36"	104"
75"	37"	112"
81"	39"	120"
87"	41"	128"
94"	42"	136"
100"	44"	144"
106"	46"	152"
112"	48"	160"
119"	49"	168"
125"	51"	176"
131"	53"	184"
137"	55"	192"
144"	56"	200"
150"	58"	208"
156"	60"	216"
162"	62"	224"
169"	63"	232"
175"	65"	240"
181"	67"	248"
187"	69"	256"

*For one-way draws, deduct 7" from stackback.
 Note: Figures are based on average pleating and medium-weight fabric. For extra bulky fabrics, add to stackback to compensate for the additional space they require.

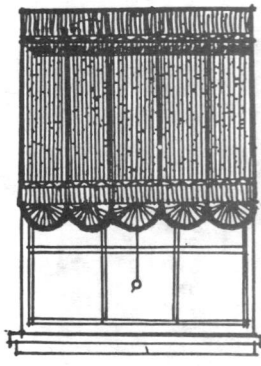

Overlapping trimmed valance over scalloped shade

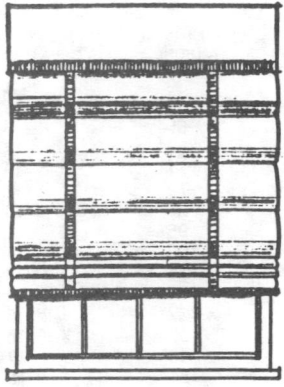

Banded valance over Roman shade

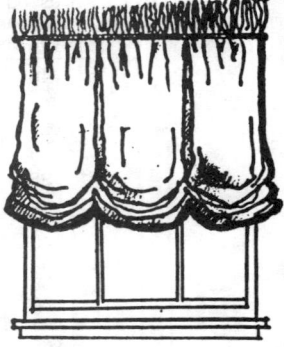

Shirred cornice box over tri-part balloon shade

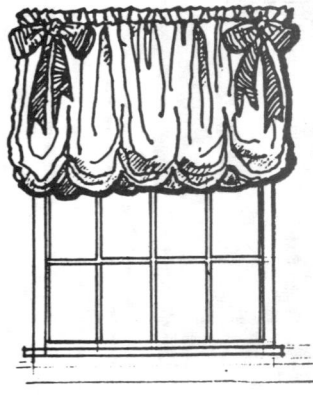

Twin bow cloud shade with gathered heading

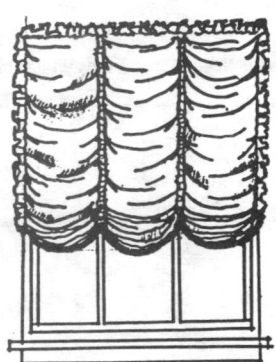

Inset flush Roman shade with horizontal folds

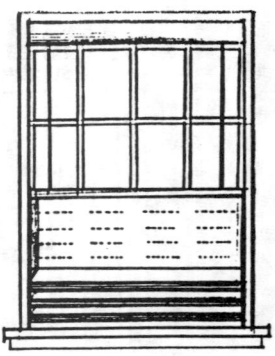

Tri-part Austrian shade with ruffled trim

Inset flush bottom pull Roman shade with horizontal folds

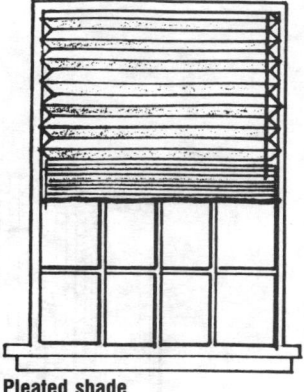

Pleated shade

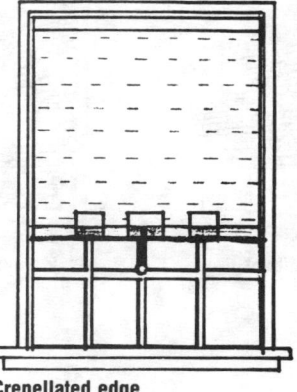

Crenellated edge

Shirred shade

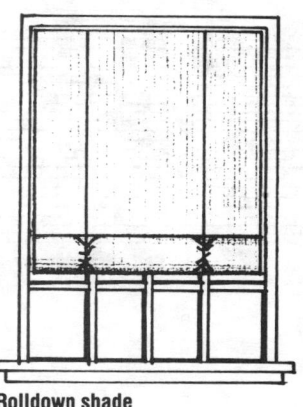

Rolldown shade

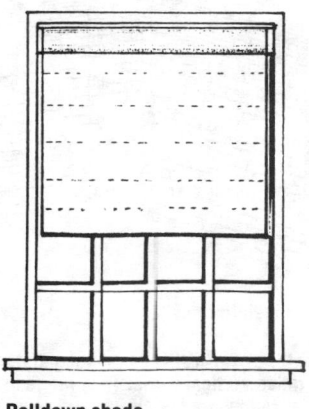

Rolldown shade

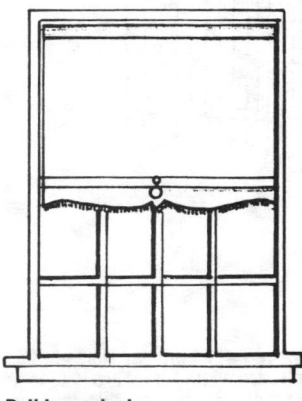

Pulldown shade

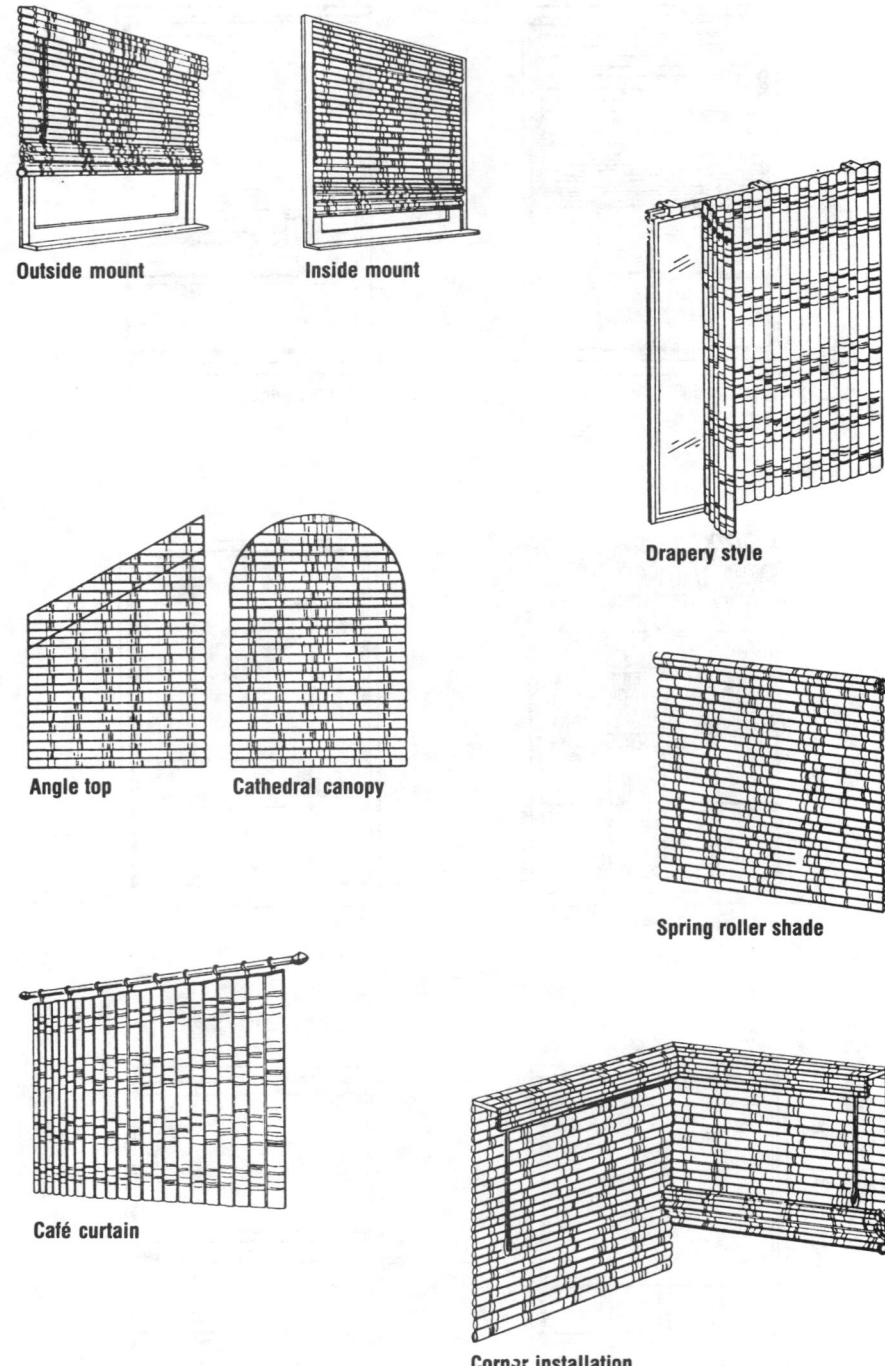

Outside mount   Inside mount

Drapery style

Angle top   Cathedral canopy

Spring roller shade

Café curtain

Corner installation

Fig. 8   Woven wood blinds. These blinds have horizontal or vertical reeds — long slats of wood from ¼ to 1 inch width — that are held together by decorative vertical yarns. They range in designs from those that are made mostly from exposed wood to those that are mainly yarns of several colors creating various interesting effects. Woven wood blinds can be used with many window treatments including draperies and café curtains, and such shade types as Roman-fold, spring-rolls, cord and pulley, and duo-fold. Top treatments include canopies, valances, and arches, while scallops, fringes, and trims are suitable for the bottom. Because woven wood blinds add color and texture to a window, they are particularly adaptable to the "natural" look in decorating.

Louvers: 1⅛″,
2½″, 3½″, 4½″;
thickness: 1¼″;
width of stile: 2″;
width: 8″ to 36″ in
¼″ increments

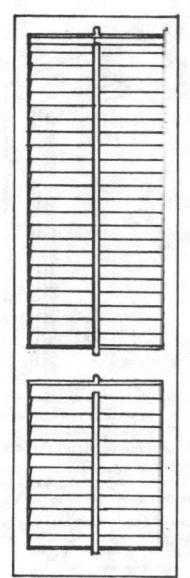

Louvers: 1⅛″,
2½″, 3½″, 4½″;
thickness: 1¼″;
width of stile: 2″;
width: 8″ to 36″ in
¼″ increments.

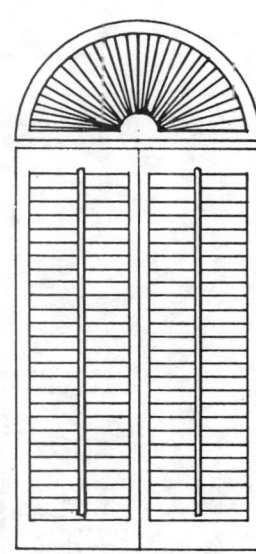

Louvers:
2½″.

Fan top (nonadjustable
louvers); louvers: 2½″;
thickness: 1¼″.

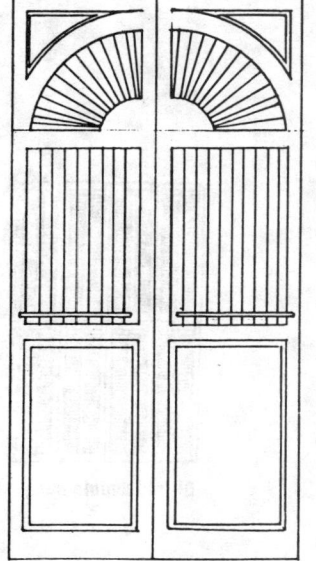

Louvers: 2½″; thickness: 1¼″.

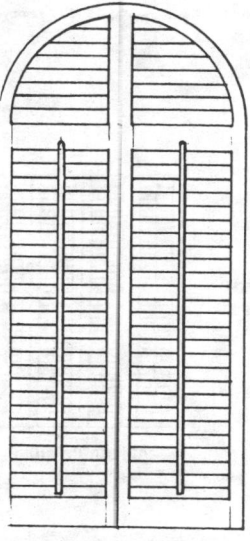

Louvers: 2½″; thickness:
1¼″.

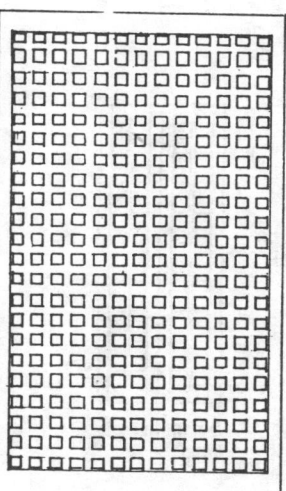

Louver grid. Standard:
4′ x 8″ unframed; standard
framing: 1⅟₁₆″ wide x 2¼″
thick.

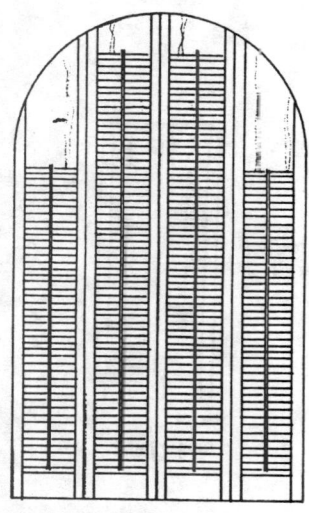

Traditional/Dixie panel;
louvers: 1¼″; thickness: 1⅛″.

Fig. 9 Inside shutters can be used next to windows in place of curtains. Some are put under curtains or draperies; others are used café style either above or beneath café curtains. Shutters may be made from wood or metal. Natural wood tones are often used to enhance the beauty of the shutters. The inside section may be made from any of the following materials: fabric mesh, cane, grill cloth, or screening.

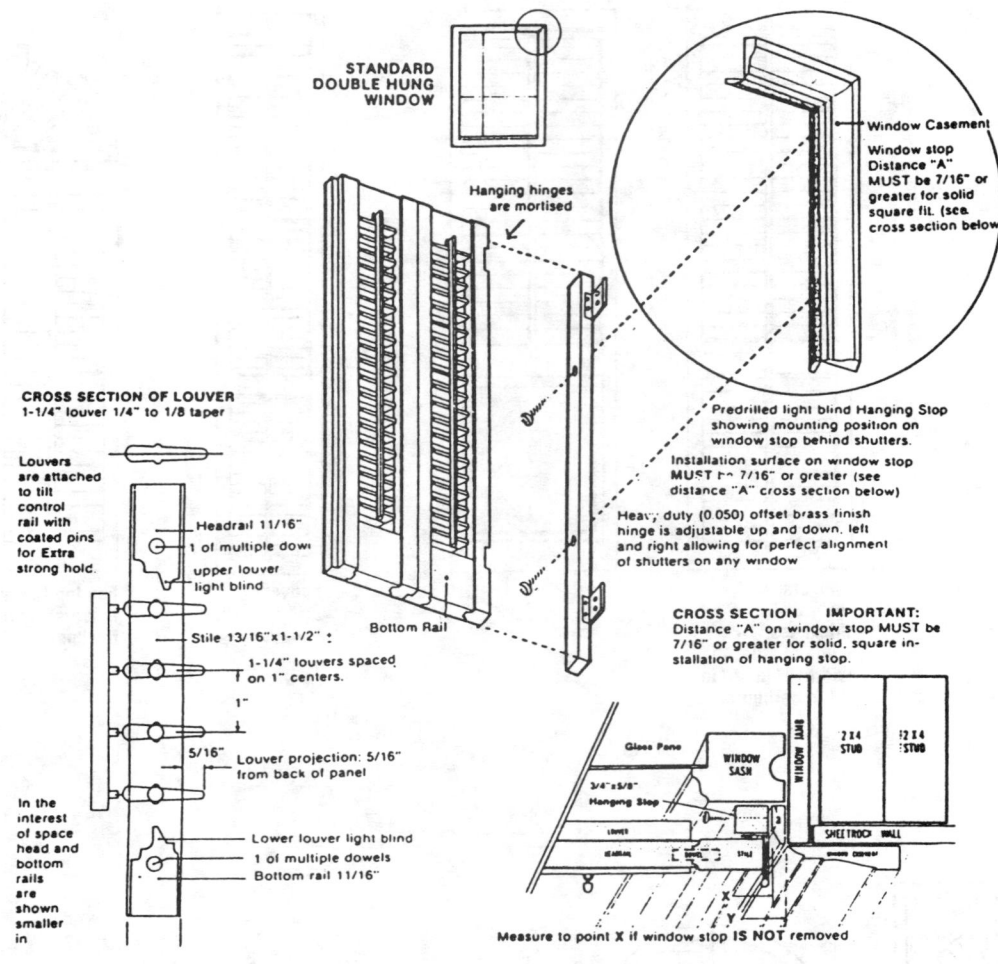

STANDARD
DOUBLE HUNG
WINDOW

Hanging hinges
are mortised

Window Casement

Window stop
Distance "A"
MUST be 7/16" or
greater for solid
square fit. (see
cross section below)

CROSS SECTION OF LOUVER
1-1/4" louver 1/4" to 1/8 taper

Louvers
are attached
to tilt
control
rail with
coated pins
for **Extra**
strong hold.

Headrail 11/16"
1 of multiple dowels

upper louver
light blind

Stile 13/16"x1-1/2"

1-1/4" louvers spaced
on 1" centers.

1"

Bottom Rail

5/16"   Louver projection: 5/16"
from back of panel

In the
interest
of space
head and
bottom
rails
are
shown
smaller
in

Lower louver light blind
1 of multiple dowels
Bottom rail 11/16"

Predrilled light blind Hanging Stop
showing mounting position on
window stop behind shutters.

Installation surface on window stop
MUST be 7/16" or greater (see
distance "A" cross section below)

Heavy duty (0.050) offset brass finish
hinge is adjustable up and down, left
and right allowing for perfect alignment
of shutters on any window

CROSS SECTION   IMPORTANT:
Distance "A" on window stop MUST be
7/16" or greater for solid, square installation of hanging stop.

Glass Pane

WINDOW
SASH

2 X 4
STUD

2 X 4
STUD

3/4" ±5/8"
Hanging Stop

SHEETROCK WALL

LOUVER

HEADRAIL

DOWEL   STILE

Measure to point **X** if window stop **IS NOT** removed

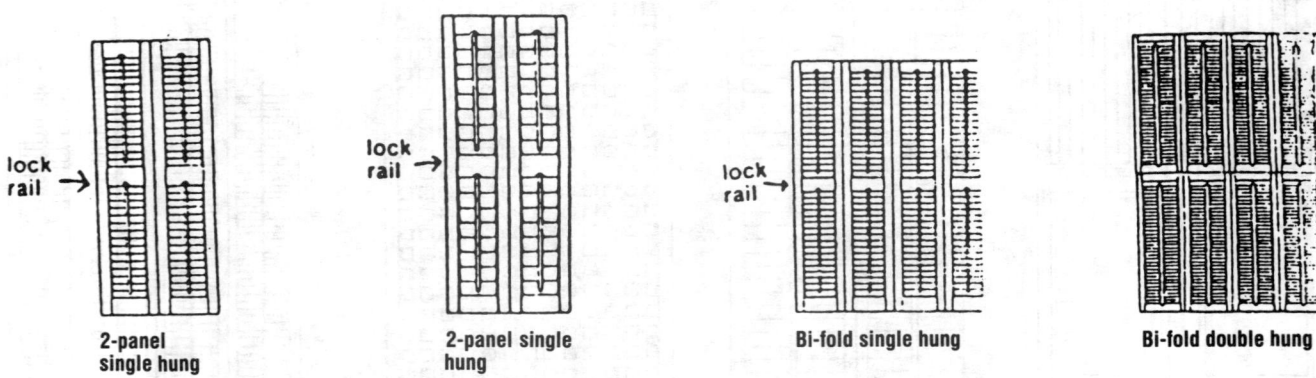

lock
rail →

2-panel
single hung

lock
rail →

2-panel single
hung

lock
rail →

Bi-fold single hung

Bi-fold double hung

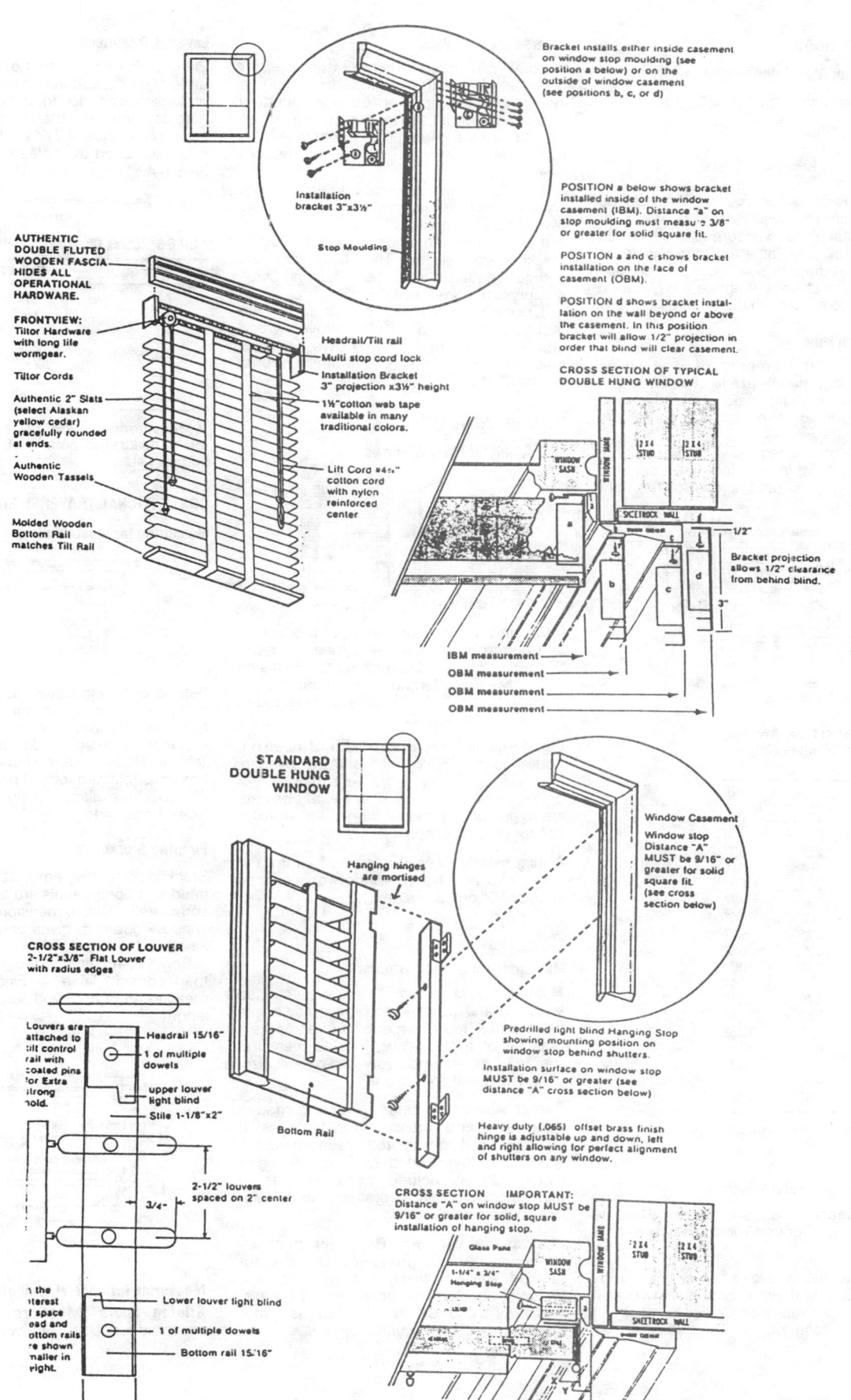

Bracket installs either inside casement on window stop moulding (see position a below) or on the outside of window casement (see positions b, c, or d)

Installation bracket 3"x3½"

Stop Moulding

POSITION a below shows bracket installed inside of the window casement (IBM). Distance "a" on stop moulding must measure 3/8" or greater for solid square fit.

POSITION a and c shows bracket installation on the face of casement (OBM).

POSITION d shows bracket installation on the wall beyond or above the casement. In this position bracket will allow 1/2" projection in order that blind will clear casement.

CROSS SECTION OF TYPICAL DOUBLE HUNG WINDOW

AUTHENTIC DOUBLE FLUTED WOODEN FASCIA HIDES ALL OPERATIONAL HARDWARE.

FRONTVIEW:
Tiltor Hardware with long life wormgear.

Tiltor Cords

Authentic 2" Slats (select Alaskan yellow cedar) gracefully rounded at ends.

Authentic Wooden Tassels

Molded Wooden Bottom Rail matches Tilt Rail

Headrail/Tilt rail

Multi stop cord lock

Installation Bracket 3" projection x3½" height

1½"cotton web tape available in many traditional colors.

Lift Cord #4½" cotton cord with nylon reinforced center.

1/2"

Bracket projection allows 1/2" clearance from behind blind.

3"

IBM measurement

OBM measurement

OBM measurement

OBM measurement

STANDARD DOUBLE HUNG WINDOW

Hanging hinges are mortised

Window Casement

Window stop Distance "A" MUST be 9/16" or greater for solid square fit. (see cross section below)

CROSS SECTION OF LOUVER
2-1/2"x3/8" Flat Louver with radius edges

Louvers are attached to tilt control rail with coated pins for Extra strong hold.

Headrail 15/16"

1 of multiple dowels

upper louver light blind

Stile 1-1/8"x2"

Bottom Rail

Predrilled light blind Hanging Stop showing mounting position on window stop behind shutters.

Installation surface on window stop MUST be 9/16" or greater (see distance "A" cross section below)

Heavy duty (.065) offset brass finish hinge is adjustable up and down, left and right allowing for perfect alignment of shutters on any window.

2-1/2" louvers spaced on 2" center

3/4"

in the interest of space head and bottom rails are shown smaller in right.

Lower louver light blind

1 of multiple dowels

Bottom rail 15/16"

1-1/8"

CROSS SECTION   IMPORTANT:
Distance "A" on window stop MUST be 9/16" or greater for solid, square installation of hanging stop.

Glass Pane

1-1/4" x 3/4" Hanging Stop

WINDOW SASH

2 X 4 STUD

2 X 4 STUD

SHEETROCK WALL

Measure to point X if window stop IS NOT removed.

Measure to point Y if window stop IS removed

WINDOW TREATMENTS
Guidelines

DECORATIVE RODS

Measuring for Most Windows

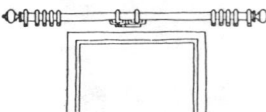

Outside mount Decorative rods should be mounted on the wall. Measure width of glass; if total glass exposure is desired, add for stackback (see Table 4). Rods should be hung so that drapery headings (pleated tops of panels) are at least 4" above the glass, so they can't be seen from the outside.

Figuring Stackback

Stackback is the amount of wall space needed if open panels are to clear the glass completely. This dimension, added to the window opening, gives you the proper rod length.

Begin by measuring the window opening, then consult Table 4. Find your opening measurement and read across for the right rod length.

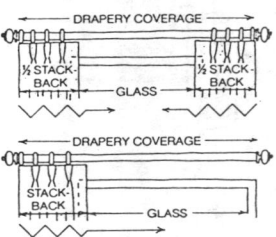

TABLE 4   Stackback: Average Pleating and Medium Weight Fabric

Window opening	Stackback*	Rod length
24"	21"	45"
30"	23"	53"
36"	25"	61"
42"	26"	68"
48"	29"	77"
54"	30"	84"
60"	31"	91"
66"	32"	98"
72"	34"	106"
78"	36"	114"
84"	37"	121"
90"	38"	128"
96"	39"	135"
102"	42"	144"
108"	44"	152"
114"	45"	159"
120"	48"	168"

*Deduct 7" for one-way draw.

Measuring for Special Windows

Sliding doors Measure as for outside mounted rod. Convert rod from two to one-way draw.

Corner and bay windows Decorative rods may be used at these windows. However, it is best to consult your dealer or designer about the measuring.

Layered Treatments

Decorative traverse rods are often used for overtreatments. If the undertreatment is inside mounted or is an outside mounted mini-blind, pleated shade, Romanette woven wood or a cafe curtain, set the brackets for maximum clearance. Drapery returns will be 4½".

If you are using an undercurtain, you will want a utility curtain rod. It comes with its own bracket-supports.

If you are using underdraperies, double brackets are available. They hold both rods and automatically align the headings. Overdrapery returns will be 6" to 7".

If using a decorative rod over an outside mounted vertical blind or a woven wood shade other than Romanette, special brackets are available. Overdrapery returns will be 6" to 7".

PLEATED SHADES

Measuring for Most Windows

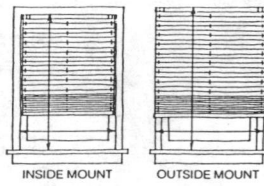

Inside mount Measure width at top, center and bottom. Use narrowest measurement. Shades will be made narrower to slip inside easily. Measure length from inside top of opening to sill. A 1⅝" deep recess is needed for flush mounting. 2¼" for Duette in ¾.

Outside mount Measure width of opening. Add at least 1½" on each side for overlap. Measure from top of frame to sill or 1½" below opening if there is no sill. (If brackets are to go above window frame, add an extra 1½" for bracket bases.)

Ceiling mount Measure desired width and length of blind. Overlap window openings by at least 1½" on each side.

Measuring for Special Windows

Multiple shades At very wide or sectioned windows and at sliding doors, it's wise to use two shades hung from one headrail. Make a drawing of the window; include measurements of glass, woodwork and overall size. Your dealer will do the rest.

Corner windows Inside-mounted shades need no special measuring instructions. If outside or ceiling-mounted shades are used, they can be overlapped. Make a drawing of the windows; include measurements of glass, woodwork and overall size. Your dealer will do the rest.

Other special windows Bays and other unusual windows can frequently be fitted for pleated shades. Make a drawing of the window; include measurements of glass, woodwork and overall size. Or ask your dealer to do the measuring for you.

Layered Treatments

Pleated shades are most often used with an undertreatment. If inside mounted, no extra projection is needed for the overtreatment. If outside mounted, the overtreatment must have a clearance of 2½" to clear the headrail. A cornice used over pleated shades should have a 4½" return.

STACK UP

TABLE 5   Stack Chart

Shade length	Stack
24"	1¾"
36"	1⅞"
48"	2"
60"	2⅛"
72"	2¼"
84"	2⅜"
96"	2½"

Measurements are from top of headrail to bottom of bottom rail.

CONVENTIONAL TRAVERSE RODS

Measuring for Most Windows

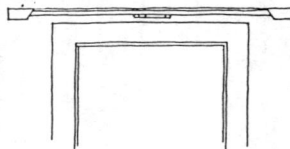

Outside or ceiling mount Conventional rods may be mounted on the wall or ceiling. Measure the width of glass; if total glass exposure is desired, add for stackback (see Table 4). Rods should be hung so that drapery headings (pleated tops of panels) are at least 4" above the glass, so they can't be seen from the outside.

Figuring Stackback

Stackback is the amount of wall space needed if open panels are to clear the glass completely. This dimension, added to the window opening, gives you the proper rod length.

Begin by measuring the window opening, then consult Table 4. Find your opening measurement and read across the right rod length.

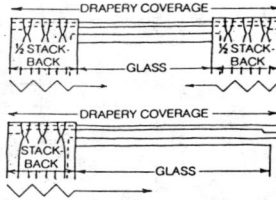

Measuring for Special Windows

Sliding doors Measure as for outside mounted rod. Use a one-way draw rod.

Corner and bay windows Measure each window as if it were set flat into the wall. At corners, run one rod into the corner and butt the other into it. At bays, butt all rods. Use either one or two-way draw rods for corners. For bays, use three two-way rods or two one-ways with a two-way in the center.

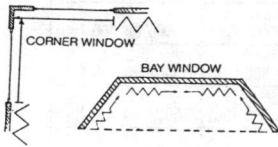

CORNER WINDOW
BAY WINDOW

Layered Treatments

Conventional traverse rods come in sets specifically for layered treatments. If you are using an undercurtain, you will want a traverse and plain rod set; both rods are on one set of brackets. Overdrapery returns will be 4½" to 5½".

If you are using underdraperies, use a double traverse rod set. Again, one set of brackets holds both rods. Overdrapery returns will be 5½" to 6½".

If the undertreatment is inside mounted or is an outside mounted mini-blind, pleated shade, Romanette woven wood or a cafe curtain, use a single rod and set the brackets for maximum clearance. Drapery returns will be 4½".

If the undertreatment is an outside-mounted vertical blind or a woven wood shade other than Romanette, special extender plates for brackets and supports are available. Overdrapery returns will be 5½" to 6½".

Remember, whenever you change the clearance of the brackets, you also change the drapery return.

VERTICAL BLINDS

Measuring for Most Windows

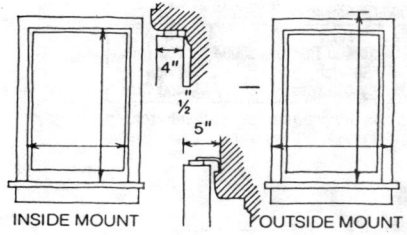

INSIDE MOUNT   OUTSIDE MOUNT

Inside mount Measure width at top, center and bottom. Use narrowest measurement. Verticals will be made slightly narrower to slip inside easily. Measure length from inside top of opening to sill. A minimum 3¼" recess is required for track; 4½" if open vanes are to be flush with front of opening.

Outside mount Measure width of opening. Add for stackback (see Tables 6 and 7). Measure from a point 2½" above top of frame to sill or floor; deduct ¾" for clearance.

Minimum projection of front of vane from wall is 5"; maximum is 6½". Minimum clearance of back of vane from wall is 1"; maximum is 2½".

Ceiling mount Measure desired width and length of verticals; deduct at least ¾" for floor clearance.

Cirmosa 2000 Ask your designer, decorator, or store to measure for you.

Measuring for Special Windows

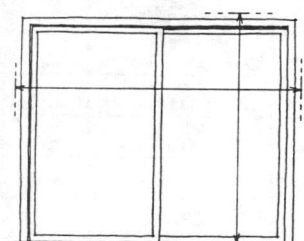

Sliding doors Use a one-way draw. Measure width from trim to trim. Add to this measurement desired extra width for overlap beyond door. If total glass exposure is desired, also add for stackback (see Tables 6 and 7). Measure from a point 2½" above door trim to floor; deduct ¾" for clearance.

Layered Treatments

When layered, verticals are most often used as an undertreatment. If inside mounted, no extra clearance is needed for the overtreatment. If outside mounted, the overtreatment must have a clearance of 6" to clear the open vanes. A cornice used over verticals should have a 6" return.

Figuring Stackback

Stackback is the amount of wall space needed if open verticals are to clear the glass completely. This dimension, added to the window opening, gives you the proper track length.

Begin by measuring the window opening, then consult Table 6 or 7 for the type of treatment you desire — one- or two-way draw. Find your opening measurement and read across for the right track. *(Note: Stackback figure for two-way draw is total stack; one-half of this is on each side of the window.)*

If your window opening is somewhere in between the measurements in the tables, go to the next smallest opening. Add the stackback listed there to your opening dimension.

TABLE 6 Two-Way Draw Stackback

Window opening	Stackback	Track
24"	9"	33"
30"	10"	40"
36"	11"	47"
42"	12"	54"
48"	14"	62"
54"	15"	69"
60"	16"	76"
66"	17"	83"
72"	19"	91"
78"	20"	98"
84"	21"	105"
90"	22"	112"
96"	23"	119"
102"	25"	127"
108"	26"	134"
114"	27"	141"
120"	29"	149"

TABLE 7 One-Way Draw Stackback

Window opening	Stackback	Track
24"	7"	31"
30"	8"	38"
36"	9"	45"
42"	11"	53"
48"	12"	60"
54"	13"	67"
60"	14"	74"
66"	15"	81"
72"	17"	89"
78"	18"	96"
84"	19"	103"
90"	20"	110"
96"	21"	117"
102"	22"	124"
108"	23"	131"
114"	25"	139"
120"	26"	146"

MINI BLINDS

Measuring for Most Windows

Inside mount Measure width at top, center and bottom. Use narrowest measurement. Blinds will be made slightly narrower to slip inside easily. Measure length from inside top of open to sill. A 1⅜" deep recess is needed for flush mounting of Mono-Rail minis; however, a difference of ¼" is not objectionable.

Outside mount Measure height and width of area to be covered. It is recommended that blinds overlap window opening by at least 1½" on each side. Measure from top of frame to sill or 1½" below opening if there is no sill.

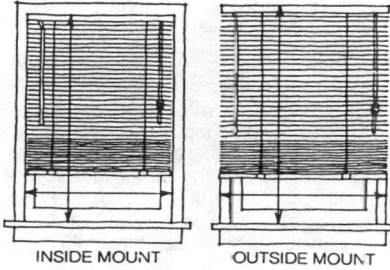

INSIDE MOUNT   OUTSIDE MOUNT

Ceiling mount Measure desired width and length of blind. Overlap window openings by at least 1½" on each side.

TABLE 8 Stack Chart

Blind length	Mini stack	Micro stack
36"	3"	3¼"
48"	3½"	3¾"
60"	4"	4¼"
72"	4¼"	4¾"
84"	4¾"	5¼"
96"	5¼"	5¾"
108"	5½"	6¼"

Measurements are from top of headrail to bottom of bottomrail.

ELEVATORS
Elevator Types and Planning

ELEVATOR TYPES

Hydraulic: For low-rise buildings — speeds up to 200 ft/min. Ideal where design limitations preclude overhead supports and machine rooms. Economical to install and maintain; no penthouse or load-bearing walls required.

Geared traction: For low- to medium-rise buildings — speeds up to 400 ft/min. Recommended for all types of buildings where higher speeds are not essential.

Gearless traction: Recommended for high-rise applications requiring the ultimate in service — speeds of 500 ft/min and up.

ELEVATOR PLANNING

Starting Point Recommendations for All Types of Buildings

When preparing schematics for a particular type of building, select the quantity, capacity, and speed from one of Tables 1 to 4 and keep in mind that generally speaking:

■ Passenger elevators should be wide and shallow with center-opening or single slide doors.

■ Service elevators should be narrow and deep with two-speed doors.

■ Combination passenger/service elevators should be almost square with either center-opening or two-speed center-opening doors.

■ Freight elevator size and shape should be determined by the dimensions of goods to be carried and by the loading/unloading methods used. Doors should be of the vertical bi-parting type.

The data contained in Tables 1 to 4 are based upon the following criteria.

Office buildings 100 square feet per person; an interval of 30 sec.; net rentable area = 80% of gross area; 5 minute carrying capacity of 12% of building population; typical floor heights were estimated at 12' and the main floor at 18'. When the building exceeds 250,000 square feet total, it is suggested that consideration be given to the use of separate freight elevators which are not included in Table 1.

Hospitals 5 minute vehicular demand = .04 × the number of beds; interval of 35–50 seconds for vehicular traffic; visitor and staff population = 3 × number of beds; 5 minute carrying capacity equal to 12% of building population.

Hotels Registration during conventions = 1.5 × the total number of rooms; maximum 1 hour peak is 1.15 × total registrations; 5 minute carrying capacity = 10% of total 1 hour peak load.

Apartments Population est. @ 2 persons per bedroom; 5 minute carrying capacity of 7%; maximum waiting interval of 60–90 seconds; average of 9'0" floor height. Further, Table 4 applies only for average or middle income apartments. For applications beyond the scope of the table such as local-express arrangements, luxury apartment buildings and other considerations, please consult your local elevator company representative.

Note: If a restaurant or general assembly area is located in your building (on any but the main floor) and is not served by a separate elevator, the information contained in Tables 1 to 4 may not apply.

TABLE 1 Office Buildings — Passenger Elevators Only

Number of Floors, Including Main	GROSS SQUARE FOOTAGE/FLOOR			
	5000 Sq. Ft.	8000 Sq. Ft.	12000 Sq. Ft.	16000 Sq. Ft.
5 floors	2 Elev. 2500# @ 250 fpm	2 Elev. 2500# @ 250 fpm	3 Elev. 2500# @ 250 fpm	3 Elev. 2500# @ 300 fpm
6 to 8 floors	3 Elev. 2500# @ 350 fpm	3 Elev. 2500# @ 350 fpm	3 Elev. 2500# @ 400 fpm	4 Elev. 2500# @ 400 fpm
9 to 12 floors	4 Elev. 2500# @ 400-500 fpm	4 Elev. 2500# @ 400-500 fpm	4 Elev. 3000# @ 500 fpm	5 Elev. 3500# @ 600 fpm
13 to 15 floors	4 Elev. 2500# @ 600 fpm	4 Elev. 2500# @ 600 fpm	5 Elev. 3000# @ 700 fpm	6 Elev. 3500# @ 700 fpm
16 to 19 floors	5 Elev. 2500# @ 700 fpm	6 Elev. 2500# @ 700 fpm	*	*
20 to 22 floors	5 Elev. 2500# @ 800 fpm	6 Elev. 3000# @ 800 fpm	*	*

* Because of the complexities such as local and express arrangements and service requirements inherent in taller and larger buildings, we suggest you contact your Armor representative when the limitations of this chart are exceeded.

TABLE 2 Hospitals

Number of Floors	BEDS/FLOOR			
	Up to 20 Beds	21 to 30 Beds	31 to 40 Beds	41 to 50 Beds
Up to 6 Floors	3 Elev. 4500# @ 200 fpm	4 Elev. 2-3000# @ 300 fpm 2-4500# @ 300 fpm	5 Elev. 2-3000# @ 350 fpm 3-4500# @ 350 fpm	5 Elev. 2-3000# @ 350 fpm 3-4500# @ 350 fpm
7 to 9 floors	6 Elev. 3-3000# @ 500 fpm 3-4500# @ 500 fpm	7 Elev. 3-3000# @ 500 fpm 4-4500# @ 500 fpm	8 Elev. 4-3000# @ 500 fpm 4-4500# @ 500 fpm	9 Elev. 4-3000# @ 500 fpm 5-4500# @ 500 fpm
10 to 12 floors	7 Elev. 3-3000# @ 500 fpm 4-4500# @ 500 fpm	8 Elev. 4-3000# @ 500 fpm 4-4500# @ 500 fpm	9 Elev. 4-3000# @ 500 fpm 5-4500# @ 500 fpm	10 Elev. 4-3000# @ 500 fpm 6-4500# @ 500 fpm

NOTE: The number of elevators listed above will most likely be reduced if automatic cart and/or container handling equipment for food, laundry, surgical instrument and central supply distribution is used.

TABLE 3 Hotel Buildings — Passenger Elevators Only

Number of Floors	UNITS/FLOOR			
	Up to 14 Units	15 to 20 Units	21 to 28 Units	29 to 32 Units
4 to 5 floors	2 Elev. 3000# @ 150 fpm	2 Elev. 3000# @ 175 fpm	2 Elev. 3000# @ 200 fpm	2 Elev. 3000# @ 200 fpm
6 to 9 floors	2 Elev. 3000# @ 300 fpm	2 Elev. 3000# @ 350 fpm	2 Elev. 3000# @ 400 fpm	3 Elev. 3000# @ 300 fpm
10 to 12 floors	3 Elev. 3000# @ 300 fpm	3 Elev. 3000# @ 350 fpm	4 Elev. 3000# @ 350 fpm	4 Elev. 3000# @ 350 fpm
13 to 15 floors	4 Elev. 3000# @ 350 fpm	4 Elev. 3000# @ 350 fpm	4 Elev. 3000# @ 350 fpm	4 Elev. 3000# @ 350 fpm
16 to 20 floors	4 Elev. 3000# @ 350 fpm	4 Elev. 3000# @ 400 fpm	4 Elev. 3000# @ 400 fpm +1 Service 3500# @ 400 fpm	4 Elev. 3000# @ 400 fpm +2 Service 3500# @ 400 fpm

NOTE: Because of the complexities such as local and express and service requirements inherent in taller and larger hotels, we suggest that you contact your Armor representatives when the limitations of this chart are exceeded.

TABLE 4 Apartment Buildings — Passenger Elevators Only

Number of Floors Including Main	BEDROOMS/FLOOR			
	10 Bedrooms	16 Bedrooms	22 Bedrooms	30 Bedrooms
6 floors	1 Elev. 2000# @ 150 fpm	1 Elev. 2000# @ 150 fpm	2 Elev. 2000# @ 150 fpm	2 Elev. 2000# @ 150 fpm
12 floors	2 Elev. 2000# @ 200 fpm	2 Elev. 2000# @ 200 fpm	2 Elev. 2500# @ 250 fpm	3 Elev. 2500# @ 250 fpm
18 floors	3 Elev. 2000# @ 350 fpm	3 Elev. 2000# @ 350 fpm	3 Elev. 2500# @ 350 fpm	4 Elev. 2500# @ 350 fpm
25 floors	3 Elev. 2500# @ 400 fpm	3 Elev. 2500# @ 400 fpm	4 Elev. 2500# @ 400 fpm	*
32 floors	3 Elev. 2500# @ 500 fpm	4 Elev. 2500# @ 500 fpm	*	*
40 floors	4 Elev. 2500# @ 700 fpm	*	*	*

HYDRAULIC ELEVATORS

Ideal for use in buildings up to six floors. Supported and raised by a powerful hydraulic plunger, the Oildraulic is renowned for smooth performance, quiet operation, and accurate floor leveling. And since it's supported from below, no vertical load is placed on the building. That means hoistways can be of lighter construction and no penthouse is needed. The machine room can be located nearly anywhere to let you maintain a flat roof line *and* save money on construction.

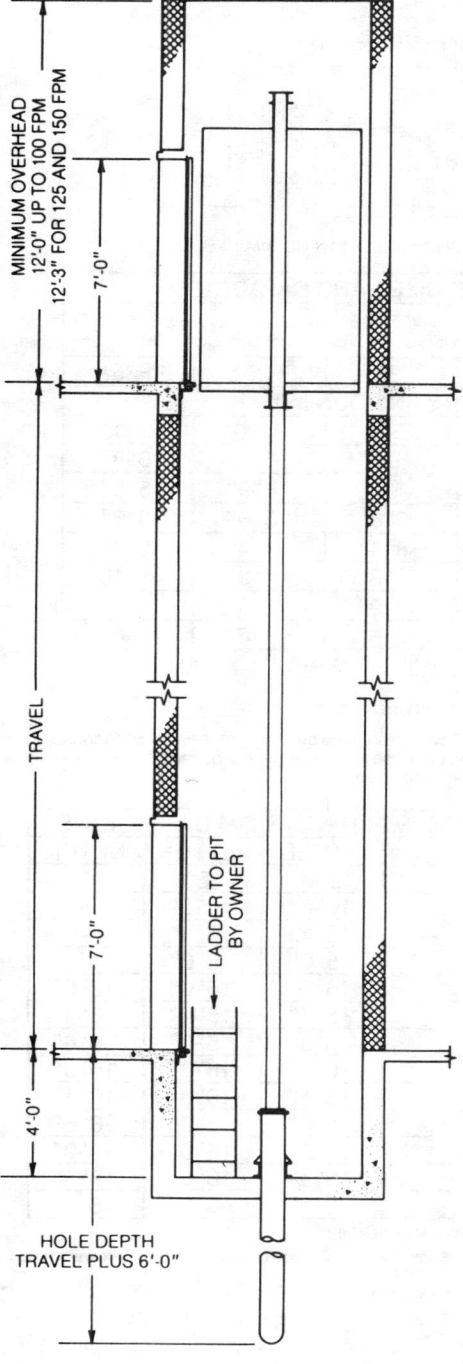

MINIMUM OVERHEAD 12'-0" UP TO 100 FPM 12'-3" FOR 125 AND 150 FPM

7'-0"

TRAVEL

7'-0"

4'-0"

LADDER TO PIT BY OWNER

HOLE DEPTH TRAVEL PLUS 6'-0"

HOISTWAY PLAN

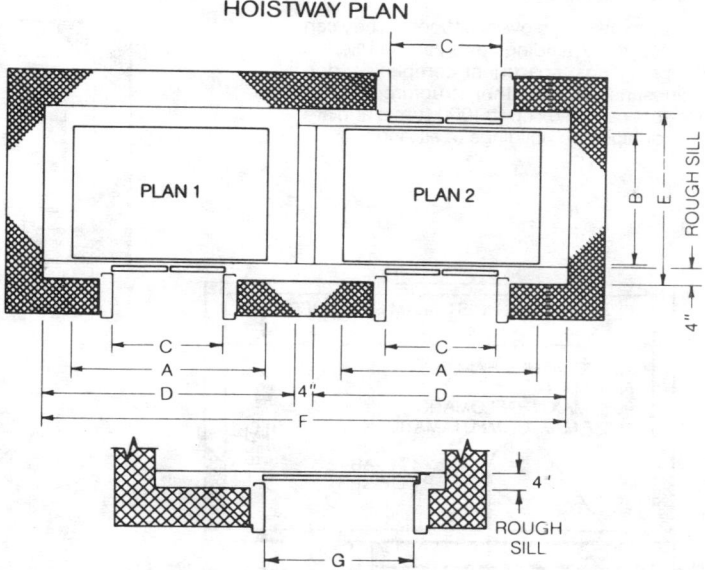

RIGHT HAND DOOR SHOWN; LEFT HAND AVAILABLE

RECOMMENDED SIZES AND CAPACITIES					
TYPE BUILDING	APART-MENT	AVERAGE OFFICE/HOTEL		LARGE OFFICE/STORE	
MODEL	FLEET-WOOD 21-H	PLAN 1 MARQUIS-25	PLAN 2 MARQUIS-25	SEVILLE-30	SEVILLE-35
CAPACITY (IN POUNDS)					
DIMENSIONS	2100 ♿	2500 ♿	2500 ♿	3000 ♿	3500 ♿
A[1]	5'-8"	6'-8"	6'-8"	6'-8"	6'-8"
B[1]	4'-3"	4'-3"	4'-3 1/2"	4'-9"	5'-5"
C	—	3'-6"	3'-6"	3'-6"	3'-6"
D[2]	7'-4"	8'-4"	8'-4"	8'-4"	8'-4"
E	5'-9"	5'-9"	6'-8 3/4"	6'-3"	6'-11"
F	15'-0"	17'-0"	17'-0"	17'-0"	17'-0"
G	3'-0"	3'-6"	3'-6"	3'-6"	3'-6"

[1] Inside dimensions.
[2] Single car dimensions.
♿ These models meet minimum size for handicapped use.
Hoistway dimensions are based on no provisions for seismic conditions and 8'-0" O.A. nominal cab height.
Standard speeds available: 75, 100, 125 150 FPM.

POWER UNIT (MACHINE) LOCATION: The most desirable machine room location is on the lowest floor, adjacent to the elevator hoistway. It may, however, be located remote from hoistway if necessary. Typical size for one-car installation: 7'-10" x 5'-6" x 8'-0" high; for two cars: 10'-9" x 6'-6" x 8'-0" high. Enclosure to meet local code requirements must be provided. A sound-isolated machine room is recommended for quietest operation. Adequate heating and ventilation of machine spaces must be provided.

ELEVATORS
High-Rise Elevators

TRACTION ELEVATORS

For use in buildings over six floors. They can serve up to 27 landings and can be used in office buildings, apartment complexes, dormitories, hotels, and other structures. These elevators can travel up to 1000 ft/min and are ideal for high-rise buildings of all kinds.

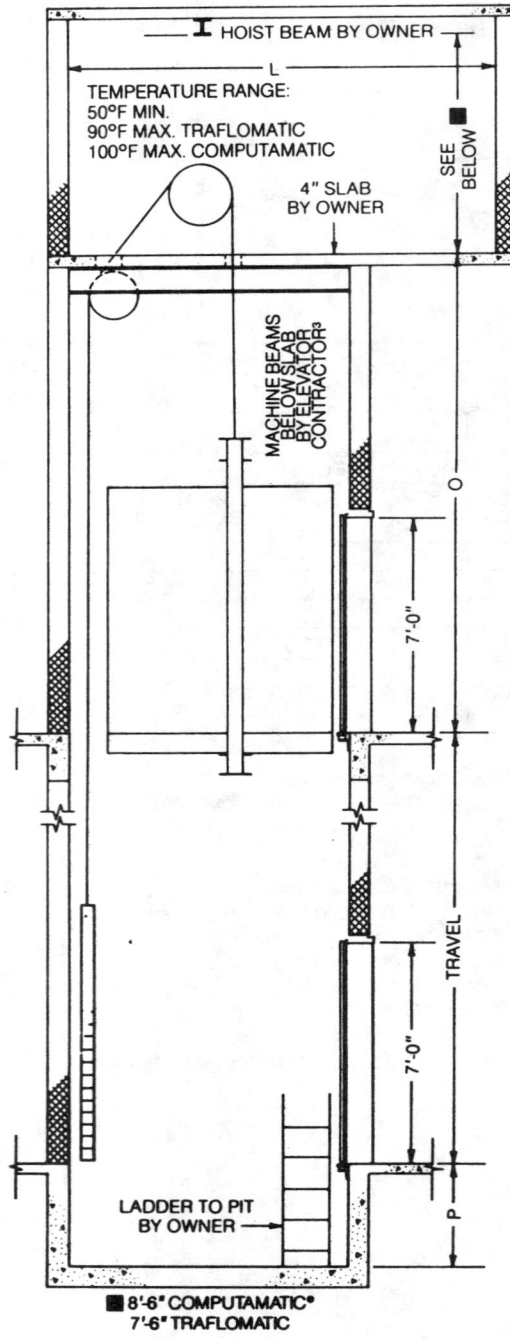

- I HOIST BEAM BY OWNER
- TEMPERATURE RANGE:
  50°F MIN.
  90°F MAX. TRAFLOMATIC
  100°F MAX. COMPUTAMATIC
- 4" SLAB BY OWNER
- SEE BELOW
- MACHINE BEAMS BELOW SLAB BY ELEVATOR CONTRACTOR³
- LADDER TO PIT BY OWNER
- 8'-6" COMPUTAMATIC•
- 7'-6" TRAFLOMATIC

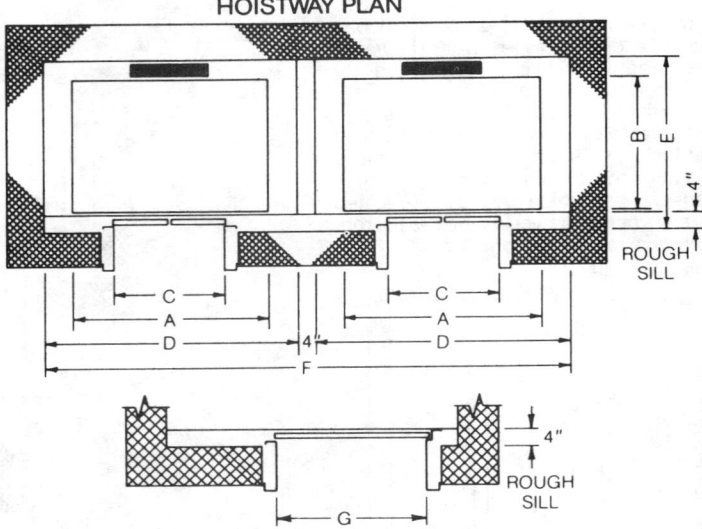

HOISTWAY PLAN

ROUGH SILL

RIGHT HAND DOOR SHOWN: LEFT HAND AVAILABLE

RECOMMENDED SIZES AND CAPACITIES

TYPE BUILDING	SMALL OFFICE/ APARTMENT	AVERAGE OFFICE/HOTEL	LARGE OFFICE/STORE	
MODEL	SPF21-H ♿	SPF25 ♿	SPF30 ♿	SPF35 ♿
CAPACITY (IN POUNDS)				
DIMENSIONS	2100	2500	3000	3500
A¹	5'-8"	6'-8"	6'-8"	6'-8"
B¹	4'-3"	4'-3"	4'-9"	5'-5"
C	–	3'-6"	3'-6"	3'-6"
D²	7'-4"	8'-4"	8'-4"	8'-4"
E	6'-8"	6'-8"	7'-2"	7'-10"
F	15'-0"	17'-0"	17'-0"	17'-0"
G	3'-0"	3'-6"	3'-6"	3'-6"

¹ Inside dimensions
² Single car dimensions
♿ These models meet minimum size for handicapped use.

Hoistway dimensions are based on 1" out of plumb, no provisions for seismic conditions, and no occupied space below hoistway. If these conditions cannot be met, then consideration must be given for additional required space.

MINIMUM PIT, OVERHEAD, MACHINE ROOM DIMENSIONS

CAPACITY (IN LBS.)	DIMENSIONS	SPEED (FEET PER MINUTE)		
		200	350	450
2100	L	16'-0"	16'-0"	–
	O	15'-4"	15'-4"	–
	P⁴	5'-0"	5'-0"	–
2500	L	16'-0"	16'-0"	16'-0"
	O	15'-4"	15'-4"	16'-4"
	P⁴	5'-0"	5'-0"	6'-6"
3000	L	16'-0"	16'-0"	16'-0"
	O	15'-4"	16'-0"	16'-4"
	P⁴	5'-0"	5'-0"	6'-6"
3500	L	16'-0"	16'-0"	16'-0"
	O	15'-4"	16'-0"	17'-6"
	P⁴	5'-0"	5'-0"	6'-6"

Overhead "O" based on 8'-0" O.A. nominal cab height.
³ Machine beams designed per ANSI/ASME code A17.1 and does not include floor weight and loads on floor.
⁴ 6'-0" min. "P" travel above 250'-0" SPF21 SPF25
travel above 225'-0" SPF30 } for speeds up to 350 F/M
travel above 200'-0" SPF35

HOISTWAY PLAN

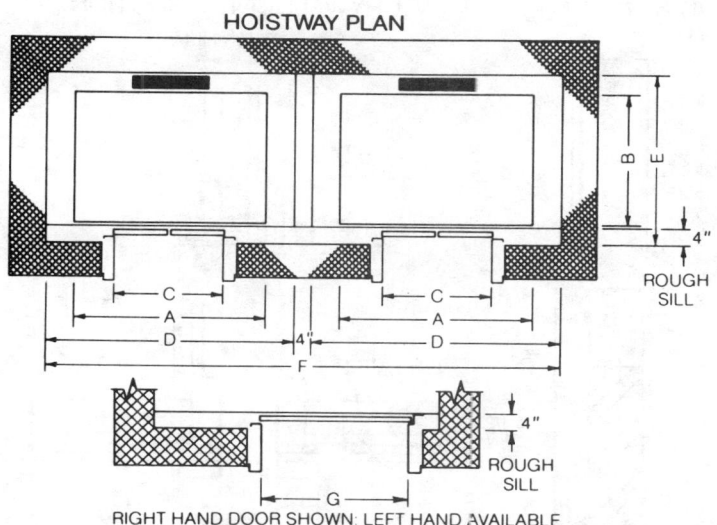

RIGHT HAND DOOR SHOWN: LEFT HAND AVAILABLE

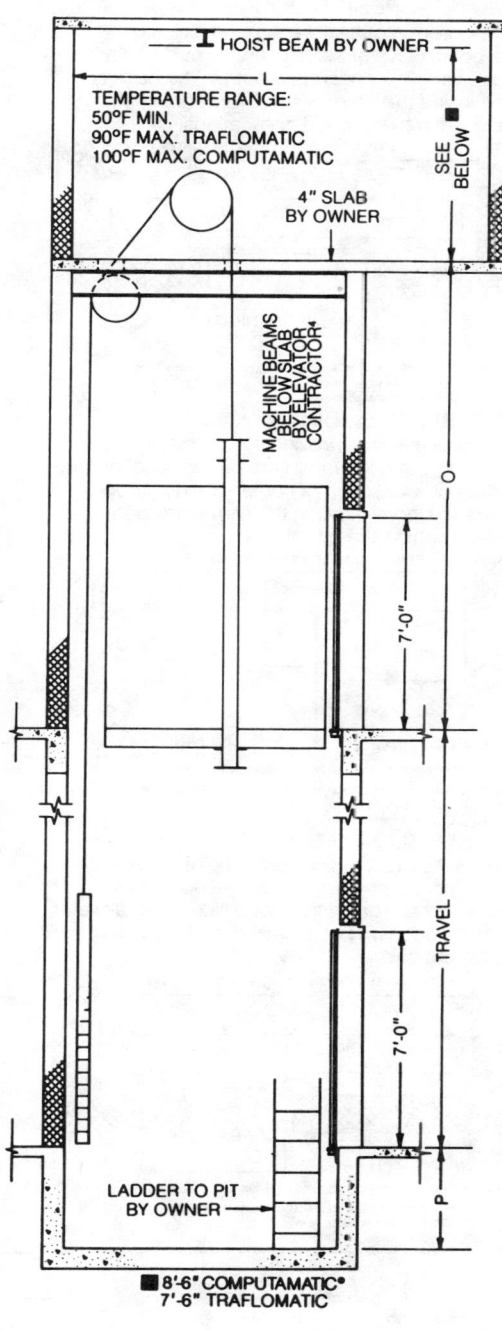

TEMPERATURE RANGE:
50°F MIN.
90°F MAX. TRAFLOMATIC
100°F MAX. COMPUTAMATIC

HOIST BEAM BY OWNER

4" SLAB BY OWNER

MACHINE BEAMS BELOW SLAB BY ELEVATOR CONTRACTOR[4]

LADDER TO PIT BY OWNER

■ 8'-6" COMPUTAMATIC®
7'-6" TRAFLOMATIC

RECOMMENDED SIZES AND CAPACITIES

TYPE BUILDING	SMALL OFFICE/APARTMENT		AVERAGE OFFICE/HOTEL		LARGE OFFICE/STORE	
DIMENSIONS	CAPACITY (IN POUNDS)					
	2000 ♿	2100 ♿	2500 ♿	3000 ♿	3500 ♿	4000 ♿
A[1]	6'-0"	5'-8"	6'-8"	6'-8"	6'-8"	7'-8"
B[1]	3'-7"	4'-3"	4'-3"	4'-9"	5'-5"	5'-5"
C	3'-0"	—	3'-6"	3'-6"	3'-6"	4'-0"
D[2]	7'-8"	7'-4"	8'-4"	8'-4" ▲	8'-4" ▲	9'-4" ▲
E[3]	6'-0"	6'-8"	6'-8"	7'-2"	7'-10"	7'-10"
F	15'-8"	15'-0"	17'-0"	17'-0" ●	17'-0" ●	19'-0" ●
G	—	3'-0"	3'-6"	3'-6"	3'-6"	4'-0"

[1] Inside dimensions   [2] Single car dimensions   [3] Add 3" when speed = 500 FPM or above
▲ Add 2" when speed = 1000 FPM   ● Add 4" when speed = 1000 FPM

Hoistway dimensions are based on 1" out of plumb, no provisions for seismic conditions, and no occupied space below hoistway. If these conditions cannot be met then consideration must be given for additional required space.

MINIMUM PIT, OVERHEAD, MACHINE ROOM DIMENSIONS

CAPACITY (IN LBS.)	DIMENSIONS	SPEED (FEET PER MINUTE)						
		200	350	450	500	700	800	1000
2000	L	16'-0"	16'-0"	16'-0"				
	O	15'-4"	15'-4"	16'-4"				
	P[5]	5'-0"	5'-0"	6'-5"				
2100	O	16'-0"	16'-0"	16'-0"				
	O	15'-4"	15'-4"	16'-4"				
	P[5]	5'-0"	5'-0"	6'-5"				
2500	L	16'-0"	16'-0"	16'-0"	16'-6"	16'-6"		
	O	15'-4"	15'-4"	16'-4"	18'-6"	20'-6"		
	P[5]	5'-0"	5'-0"	6'-6"	10'-1"	11'-5"		
3000	L	16'-0"	16'-0"	16'-0"	17'-0"	17'-0"	18'-0"	18'-0"
	O	15'-4"	16'-0"	16'-4"	18'-6"	20'-6"	20'-0"	20'-0"
	P[5]	5'-0"	5'-0"	6'-6"	10'-1"	11'-5"	11'-6"	11'-6"
3500 4000	L	16'-0"	16'-0"	16'-0"	17'-0"	17'-0"	18'-0"	18'-0"
	O	15'-4"	16'-0"	17'-6"	18'-6"	20'-6"	20'-6"	20'-6"
	P[5]	5'-0"	5'-0"	6'-6"	10'-1"	11'-5"	11'-6"	11'-6"

NOTE: These dimensions are for general application to custom designed elevators.
Overhead "O" based on 8'-0" O.A. nominal cab height.

[4] Machine beams designed per ANSI/ASME code A17.1 and does not include floor weight and loads on floor.

CENTER-OPENING DOORS
These permit quickest entry and exit, thus speeding elevator service, and provide an attractive balanced appearance both in the hallway and inside the elevator car. They should always be used in high-speed applications.

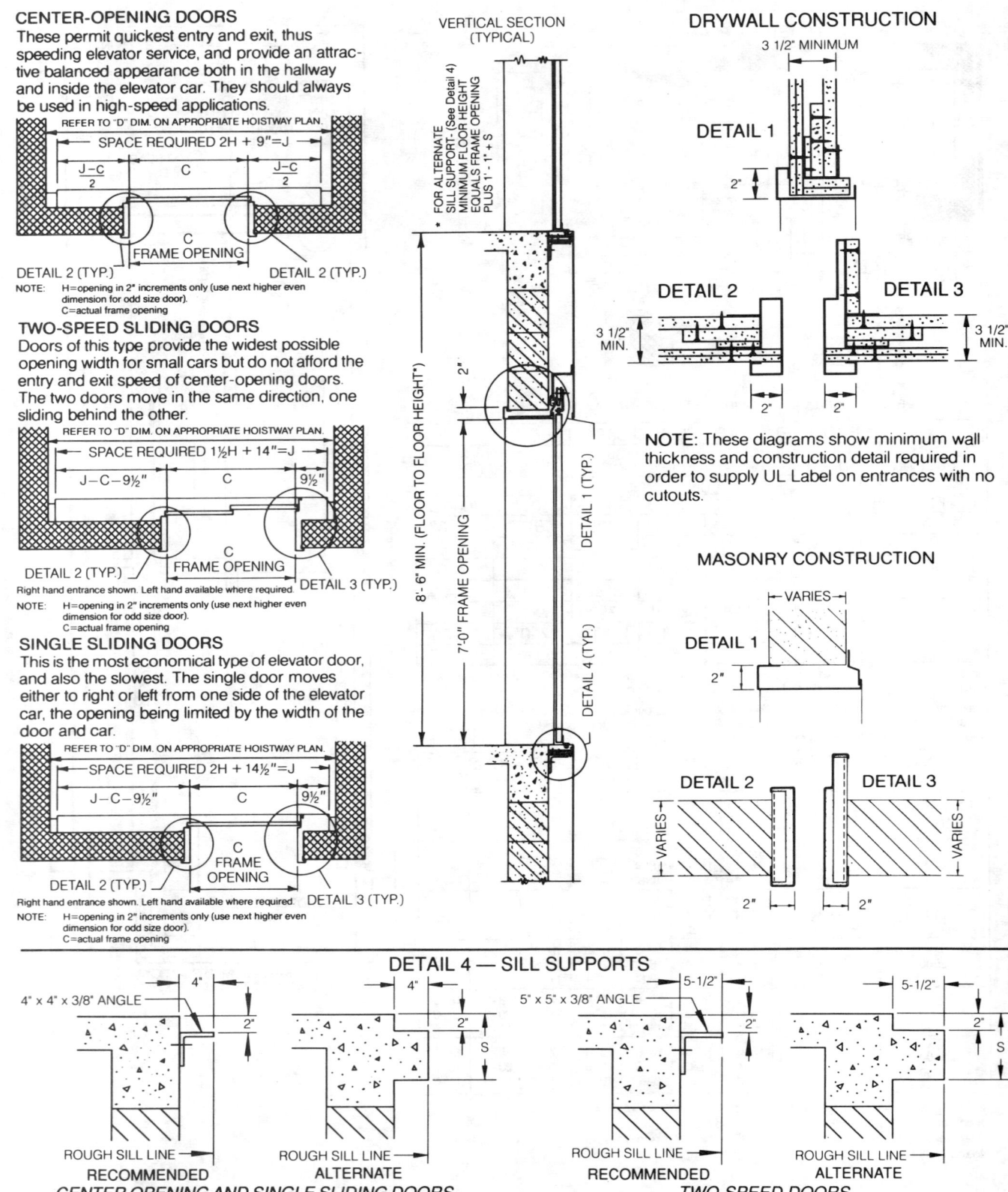

REFER TO "D" DIM. ON APPROPRIATE HOISTWAY PLAN.

SPACE REQUIRED 2H + 9"=J

$\frac{J-C}{2}$ C $\frac{J-C}{2}$

C
FRAME OPENING

DETAIL 2 (TYP.)   DETAIL 2 (TYP.)

NOTE: H=opening in 2" increments only (use next higher even dimension for odd size door).
C=actual frame opening

TWO-SPEED SLIDING DOORS
Doors of this type provide the widest possible opening width for small cars but do not afford the entry and exit speed of center-opening doors. The two doors move in the same direction, one sliding behind the other.

REFER TO "D" DIM. ON APPROPRIATE HOISTWAY PLAN.

SPACE REQUIRED 1½H + 14"=J

J−C−9½"   C   9½"

C
FRAME OPENING

DETAIL 2 (TYP.)   DETAIL 3 (TYP.)

Right hand entrance shown. Left hand available where required.

NOTE: H=opening in 2" increments only (use next higher even dimension for odd size door).
C=actual frame opening

SINGLE SLIDING DOORS
This is the most economical type of elevator door, and also the slowest. The single door moves either to right or left from one side of the elevator car, the opening being limited by the width of the door and car.

REFER TO "D" DIM. ON APPROPRIATE HOISTWAY PLAN.

SPACE REQUIRED 2H + 14½"=J

J−C−9½"   C   9½"

C
FRAME OPENING

DETAIL 2 (TYP.)   DETAIL 3 (TYP.)

Right hand entrance shown. Left hand available where required.

NOTE: H=opening in 2" increments only (use next higher even dimension for odd size door).
C=actual frame opening

VERTICAL SECTION
(TYPICAL)

FOR ALTERNATE SILL SUPPORT- (See Detail 4)
*MINIMUM FLOOR HEIGHT EQUALS FRAME OPENING PLUS 1'- 1" + S

2"

8'- 6" MIN. (FLOOR TO FLOOR HEIGHT*)

7'-0" FRAME OPENING

DETAIL 1 (TYP.)

DETAIL 4 (TYP.)

DRYWALL CONSTRUCTION

3 1/2" MINIMUM

DETAIL 1

2"

DETAIL 2   DETAIL 3

3 1/2" MIN.   3 1/2" MIN.

2"   2"

NOTE: These diagrams show minimum wall thickness and construction detail required in order to supply UL Label on entrances with no cutouts.

MASONRY CONSTRUCTION

VARIES

DETAIL 1

2"

DETAIL 2   DETAIL 3

VARIES   VARIES

2"   2"

DETAIL 4 — SILL SUPPORTS

4" x 4" x 3/8" ANGLE
4"
2"

4"
2"
S

5" x 5" x 3/8" ANGLE
5-1/2"
2"

5-1/2"
2"
S

ROUGH SILL LINE   ROUGH SILL LINE
RECOMMENDED   ALTERNATE
CENTER OPENING AND SINGLE SLIDING DOORS

ROUGH SILL LINE   ROUGH SILL LINE
RECOMMENDED   ALTERNATE
TWO-SPEED DOORS

Floor plan of elevator cars The floor area of elevator cars shall provide space for wheelchair users to enter the car, maneuver within reach of controls, and exit from the car. Acceptable door opening and inside dimensions shall be as shown in Fig. 1. The clearance between the car platform sill and the edge of any hoistway landing shall be no greater than 1¼ in (32 mm).

Illumination levels The level of illumination at the car controls, platform, and car threshold and landing sill shall be at least 5 footcandles (53.8 lux).

Car controls Elevator control panels shall have the following features:

1. Buttons. All control buttons shall be at least ¾ in (19 mm) in their smallest dimension. They may be *raised* or flush.

2. Tactile and visual control indicators. All control buttons shall be designated by *raised* standard alphabet characters for letters, arabic characters for numerals, or standard symbols as shown in Fig. 3(*a*), and as required in ANSI A17.1-1978 and A17.1a-1979. The call button for the main entry floor shall be designated by a *raised* star at the left of the floor designation [see Fig. 3(*a*)]. All *raised* designations for control buttons shall be placed immediately to the left of the button to which they apply. Applied plates, permanently attached, are an acceptable means to provide *raised* control designations. Floor buttons shall be provided with visual indicators to show when each call is registered. The visual indicators shall be extinguished when each call is answered.

3. Height. All floor buttons shall be no higher than *48 in (1220 mm), unless there is a substantial increase in cost, in which case the maximum mounting height may be increased to 54 in (1370 mm),* above the floor. Emergency controls, including the emergency alarm and emergency stop, shall be grouped at the bottom of the panel and shall have their centerlines no less than 35 in (890 mm) above the floor [see Fig. 3(*a*) and (*b*)].

4. Location. Controls shall be located on a front wall if cars have center opening doors, and at the side wall or at the front wall next to the door if cars have side opening doors [see Fig. 3(*c*) and (*d*)].

Car position indicators In elevator cars, a visual car position indicator shall be provided above the car control panel or over the door to show the position of the elevator in the hoistway. As the car passes or stops at a floor served by the elevators, the corresponding numerals shall illuminate, and an audible signal shall sound. Numerals shall be a minimum of ½ in (13 mm) high. The audible signal shall be no less than 20 decibels with a frequency no higher than 1500 Hz. An automatic verbal announcement of the floor number at which a car stops or which a car passes may be substituted for the audible signal.

Emergency communications If provided, emergency two-way communication systems between the elevator and a point outside the hoistway shall comply with ANSI A17.1-1978 and A17.1a-1979. The highest operable part of a two-way communication system shall be a maximum of 48 in (1220 mm) from the floor of the car. It shall be identified by a raised or recessed symbol and located adjacent to the device. If the system uses a handset, then the length of the cord from the panel to the handset shall be at east 29 in (735 mm). The emergency intercommunication system shall not require voice communication.

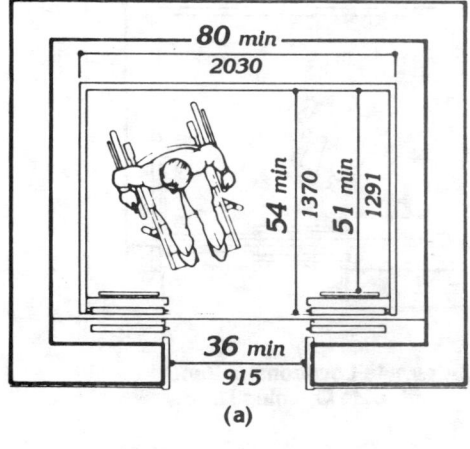

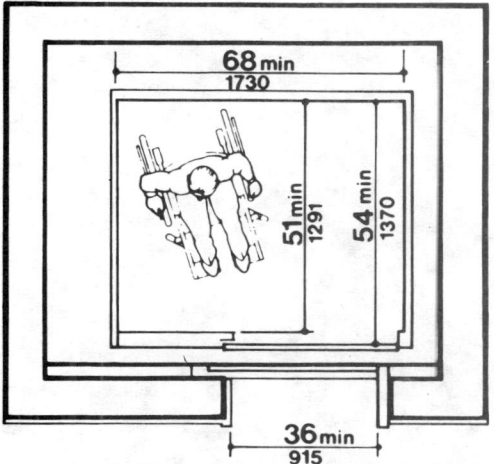

Fig. 1   Minimum dimensions of elevator cars.

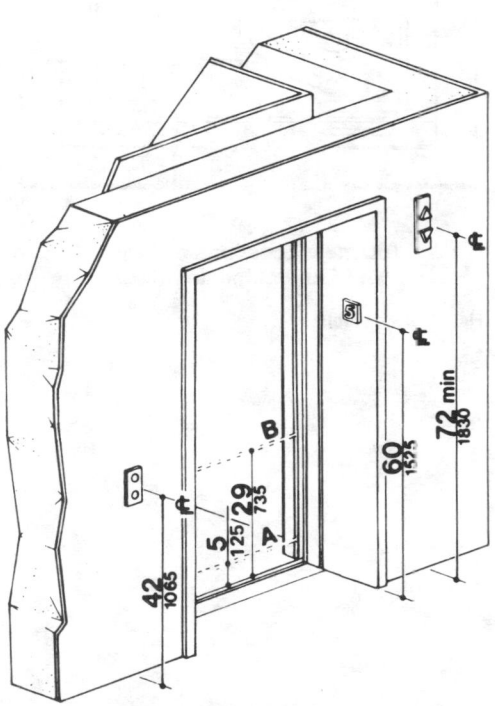

NOTE: The automatic door reopening device is activated if an object passes through either line A or line B. Line A and line B represent the vertical locations of the door reopening device not requiring contact.

Fig. 2   Hoistway and elevator entrances.

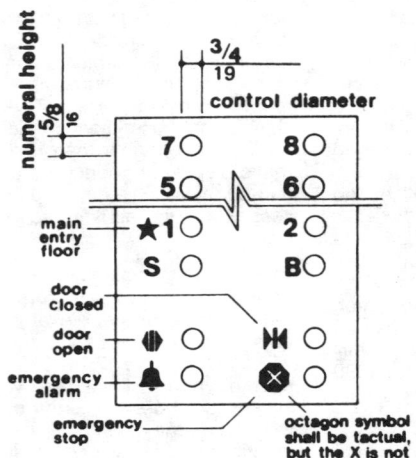

(a)
Panel Detail

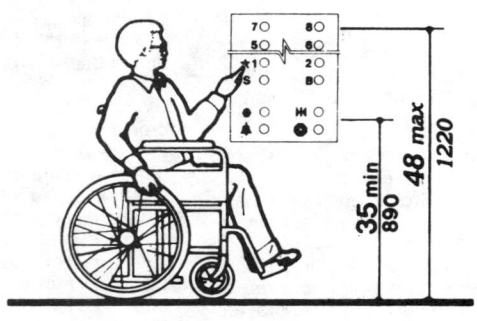

(b)
Control Height

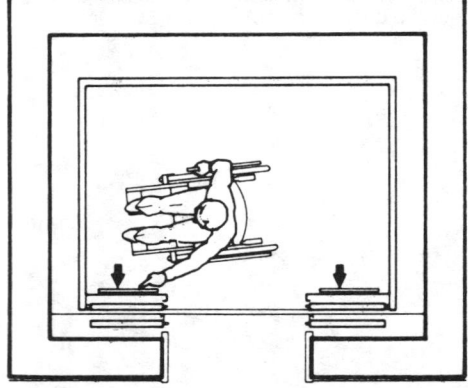

(c)
**Alternate Locations of Panel
with Center Opening Door**

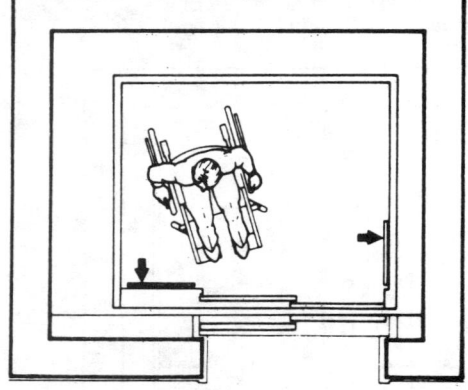

(d)
**Alternate Locations of Panel
with Side Opening Door**

Fig. 3   Car controls.

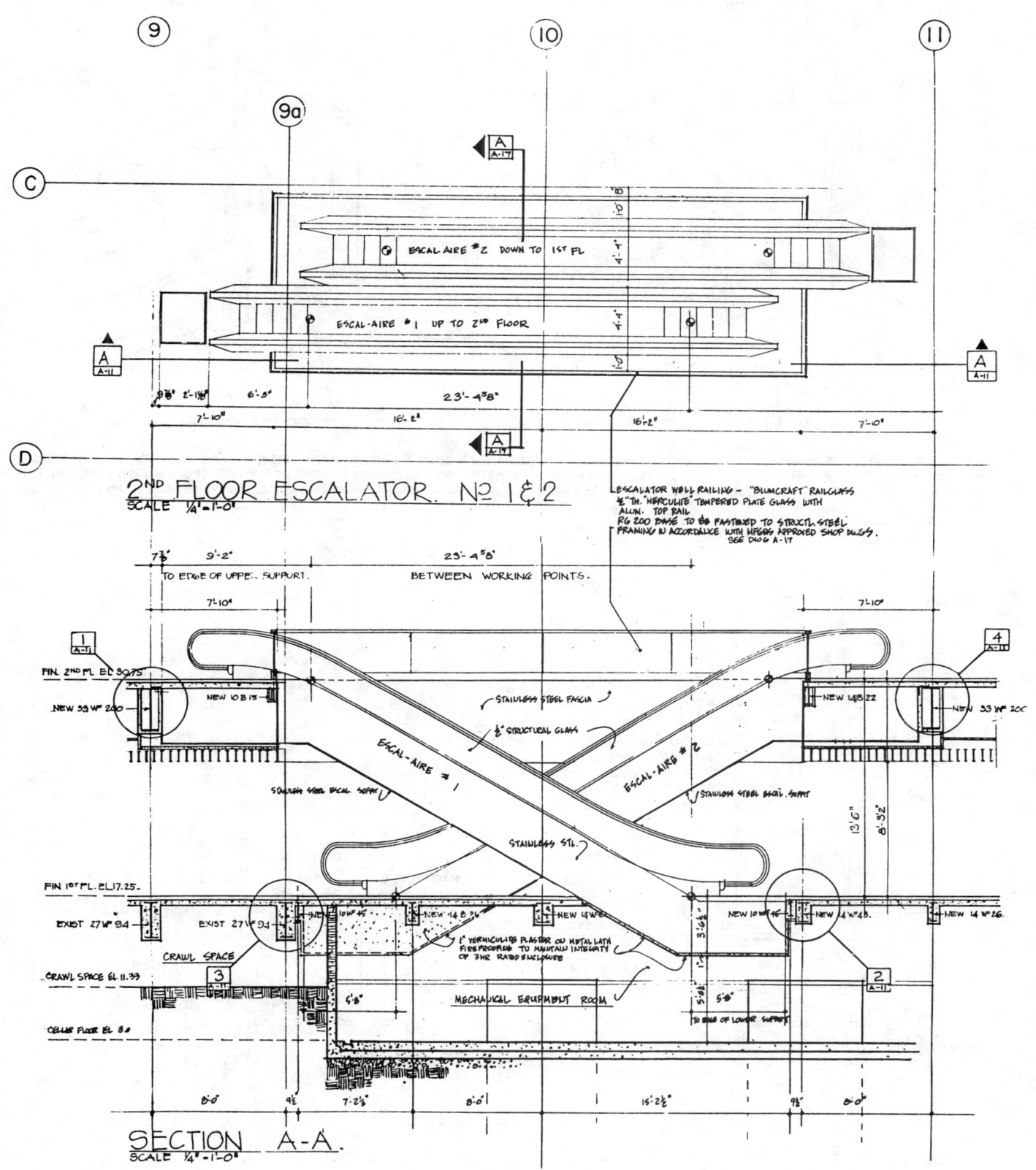

2ND FLOOR ESCALATOR. N° 1 & 2
SCALE ¼"=1'-0"

ESCAL-AIRE #2 DOWN TO 1ST FL

ESCAL-AIRE #1 UP TO 2ND FLOOR

ESCALATOR WELL RAILING – "BLUMCRAFT" RAILGLASS
½" TH. HERCULITE TEMPERED PLATE GLASS WITH
ALUM. TOP RAIL
RG 200 BASE TO BE FASTENED TO STRUCT. STEEL
FRAMING IN ACCORDANCE WITH MFGRS APPROVED SHOP DWGS.
SEE DWG A-17

TO EDGE OF UPPER SUPPORT.   BETWEEN WORKING POINTS.

FIN. 2ND FL EL 30.75

NEW 33 W° 200   NEW 10 B 15

STAINLESS STEEL FASCIA

½" STRUCTURAL GLASS

ESCAL-AIRE #1

ESCAL-AIRE #2

STAINLESS STEEL ESCAL. SOFFIT

STAINLESS STEEL ESCAL. SOFFIT

NEW 14 B 22   NEW 33 W° 200

STAINLESS STL.

FIN. 1ST FL. EL 17.25.

EXIST 27 W° 94   EXIST 27 W° 94   NEW 10 W° 45   NEW 14 B 26   NEW 14 W°   NEW 10 W° 45   NEW 14 W° 43.   NEW 14 W° 26.

CRAWL SPACE

CRAWL SPACE EL 11.33

CELLAR FLOOR EL 8.0

1" VERMICULITE PLASTER ON METAL LATH
FIREPROOFING TO MAINTAIN INTEGRITY
OF 3 HR RATED ENCLOSURE

MECHANICAL EQUIPMENT ROOM

TO EDGE OF LOWER SUPPORT

SECTION A-A.
SCALE ¼"=1'-0"

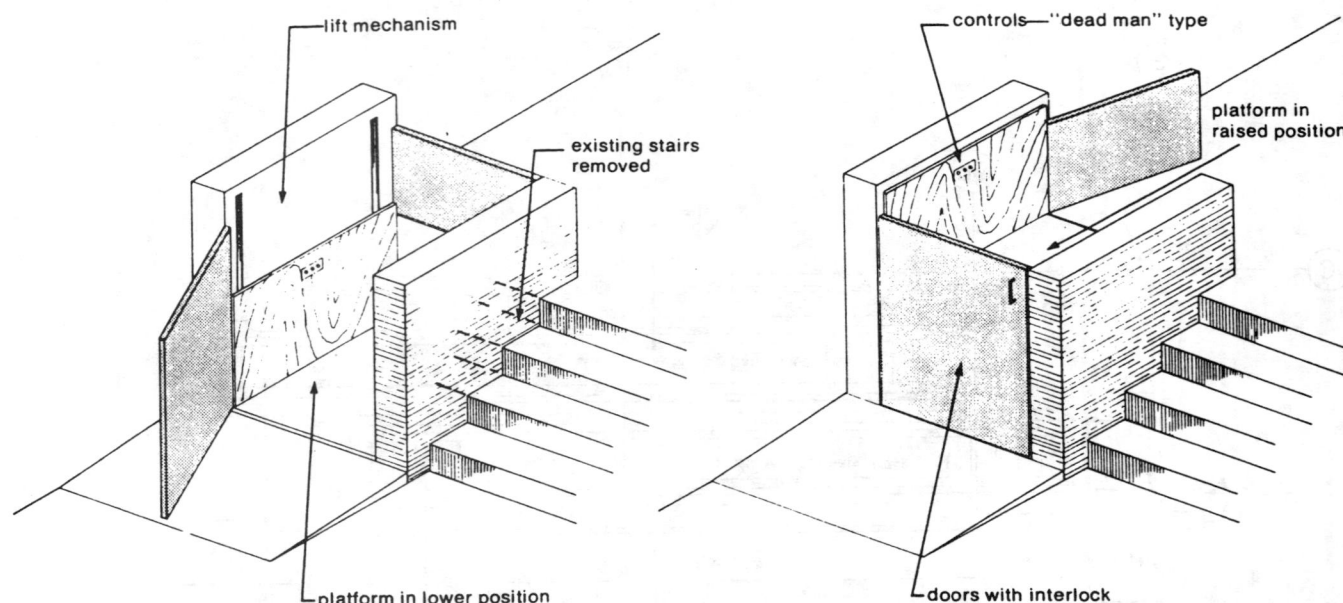

Fig. 4   Wheelchair lift. In certain installations where ramps may be impossible due to space limitations, small mechanical wheelchair lifts can be installed to overcome level changes. Manufactured lifts have a lift range from two to several feet and are either electro-mechanical, hydraulic, or pneumatically operated. Lifts can be semi-enclosed and equipped with entrance interlocks for safety, and either key-operated for limited use or button-type. "Dead-man" controls are recommended for safety.

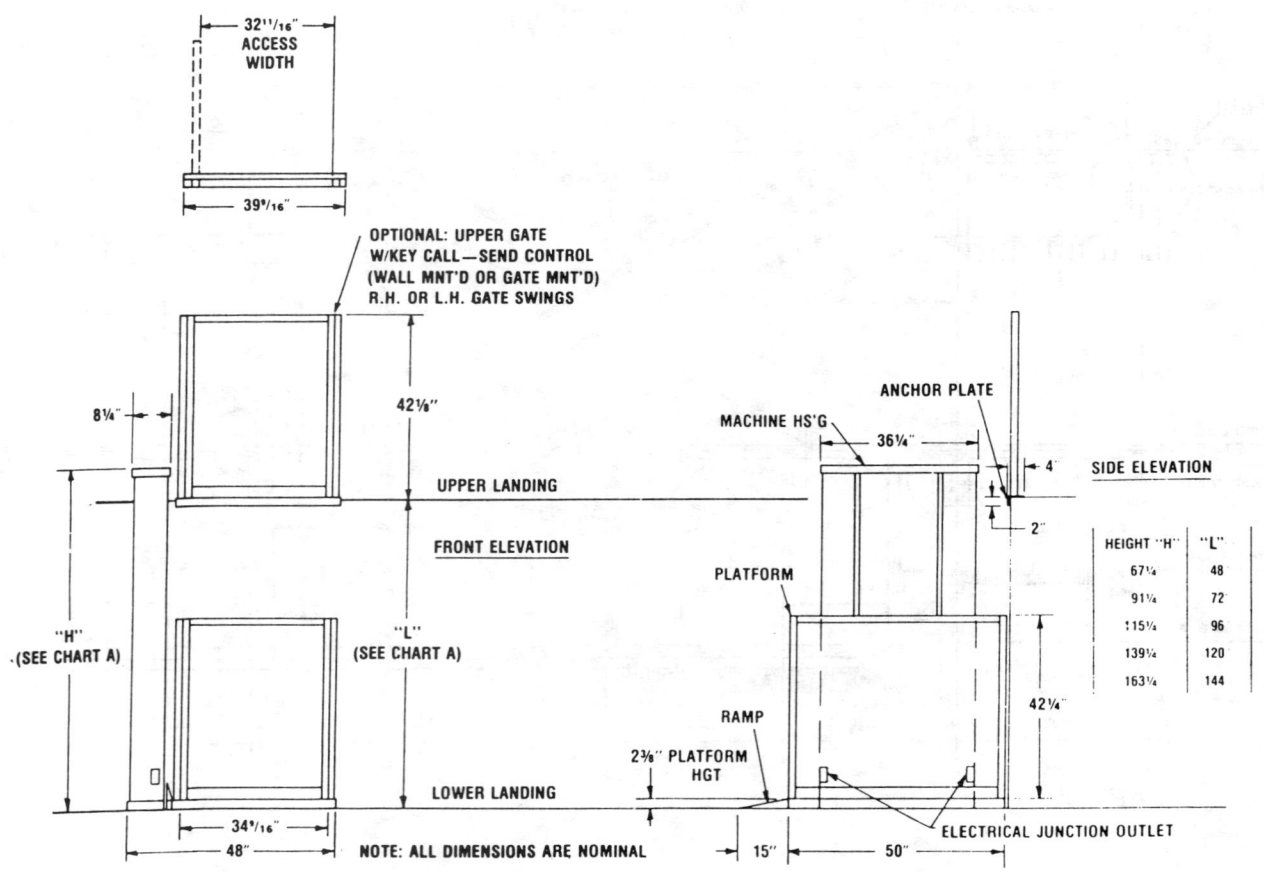

HEIGHT "H"	"L"
67¼	48
91¼	72
115¼	96
139¼	120
163¼	144

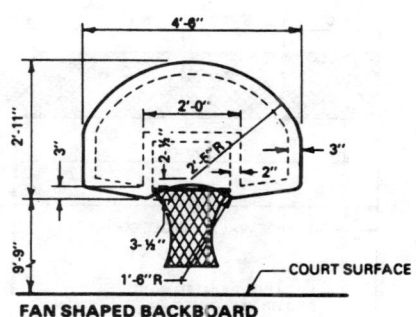

FAN SHAPED BACKBOARD

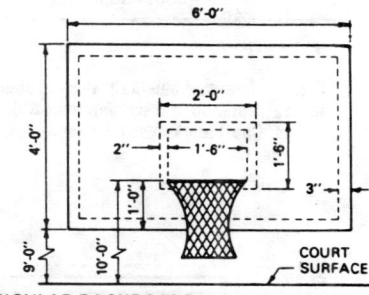

RECTANGULAR BACKBOARD

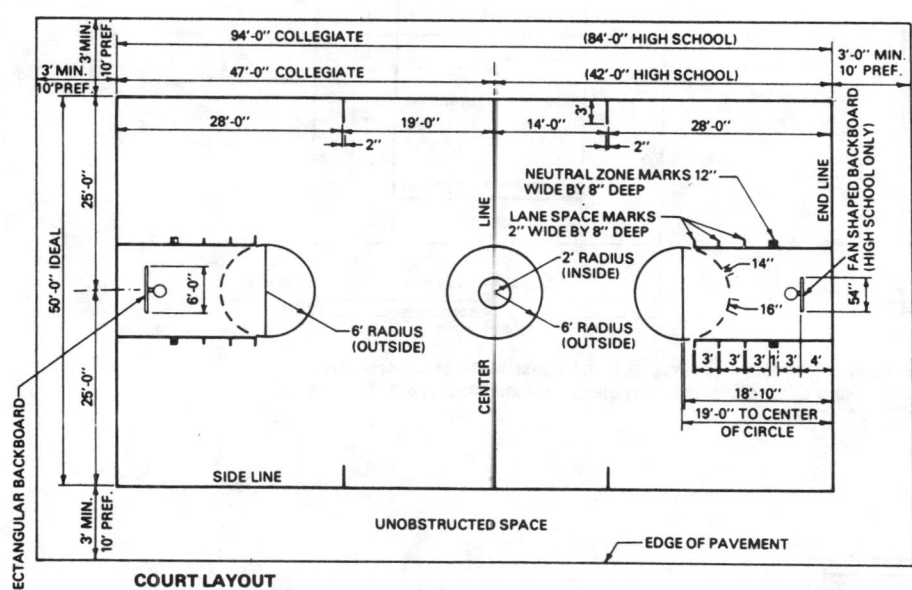

COURT LAYOUT

Fig. 1 NCAA basketball. The color of the lane space marks and neutral zone marks shall contrast with the color of the bounding lines. The midcourt marks shall be the same color as the bounding lines. All lines shall be 2 in wide (neutral zone excluded). All dimensions are to inside edge of lines except as noted. Backboard shall be of any rigid weather-resistant material. The front surface shall be flat and painted white unless it is transparent. If the backboard is transparent, it shall be marked with a 3-in wide white line around the border and an 18 x 24-in target area bounded with a 2-in wide white line. [High school recommended court is 84 x 50 ft with a 10-ft unobstructed space on all sides (3 ft minimum). Collegiate recommended court is 94 x 50 ft with a 10-ft unobstructed space on all sides (3 ft minimum).]

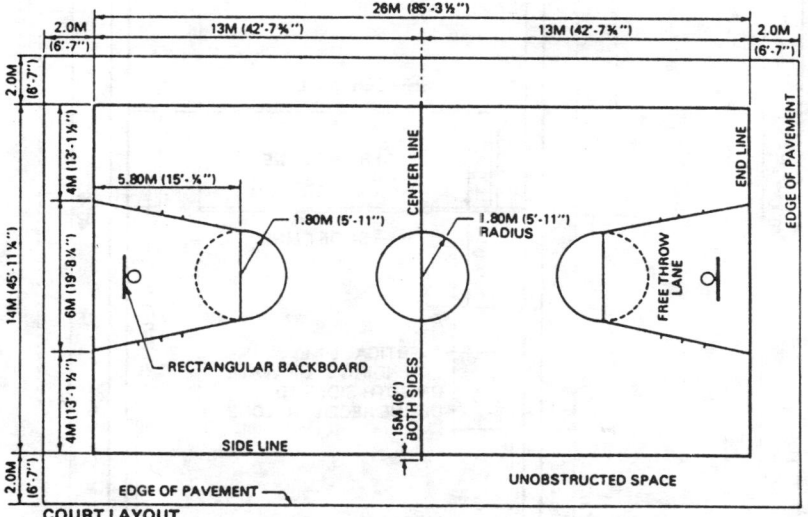

COURT LAYOUT

Fig. 2 AAU basketball court. All dimensions are to inside edge of lines except as noted. All lines to be .05 m (2") wide. Backboard shall be of any rigid weather-resistant material. The front shall be flat and painted white unless it is transparent. If the backboard is transparent, it shall be marked with a .05-m-wide white line around the border and a .45 x .59-m target area bounded with a .05-m-wide white line.

INDOOR RECREATION

One-, Three-, and Four-Wall Handball

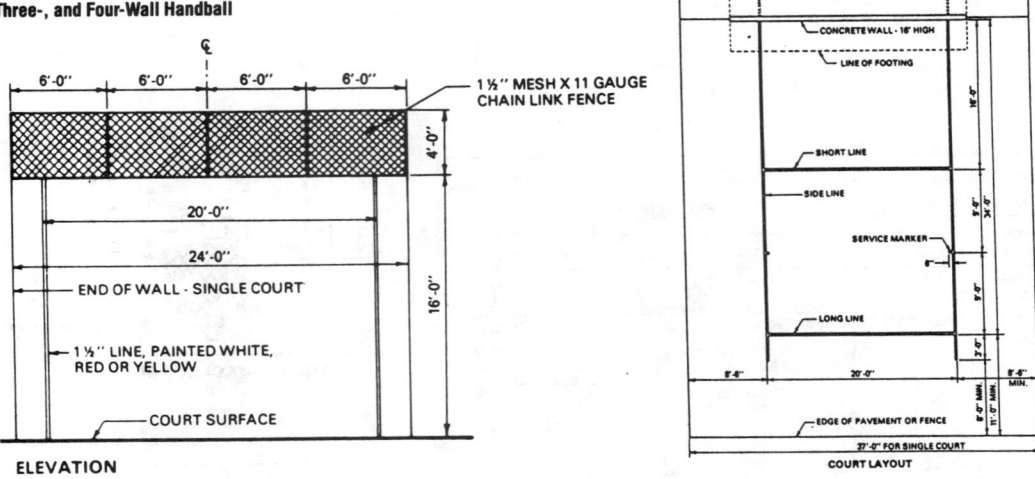

ELEVATION

Fig. 3 One-wall handball. Playing court is 20'0" wide by 34'0" long plus a required 11'0" minimum width of surfaced area to the rear and a recommended 8'6" minimum width on each side. Courts in battery are to be a minimum of 6'0" between courts. Court markings: 1½-in-wide lines painted white, red, or yellow.

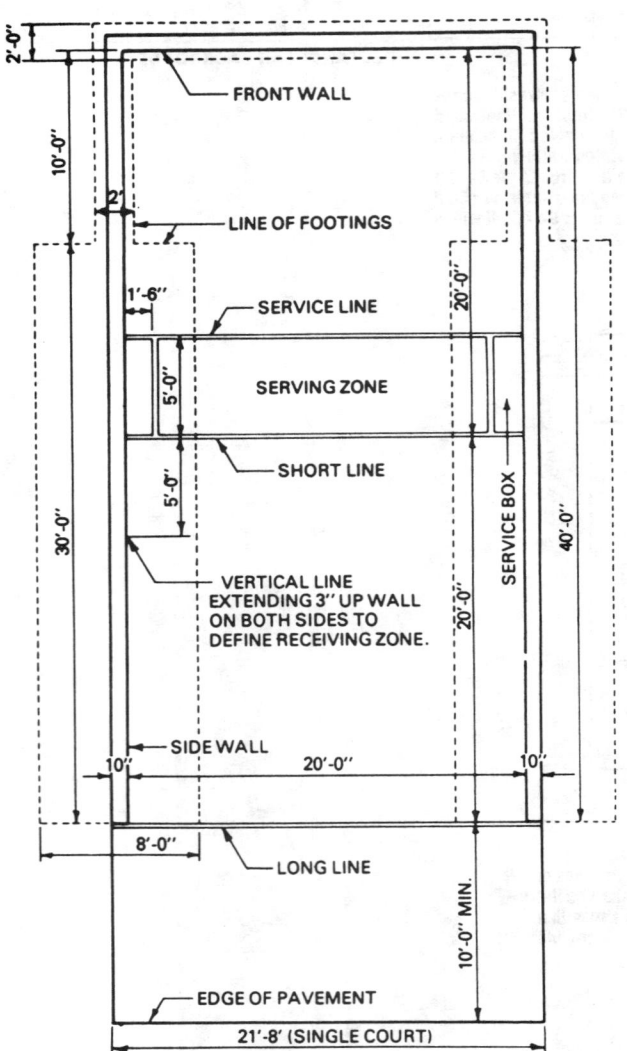

Fig. 4 Handball court layout — four-wall. All court markings to be 1½ in wide and painted white, red, or yellow.

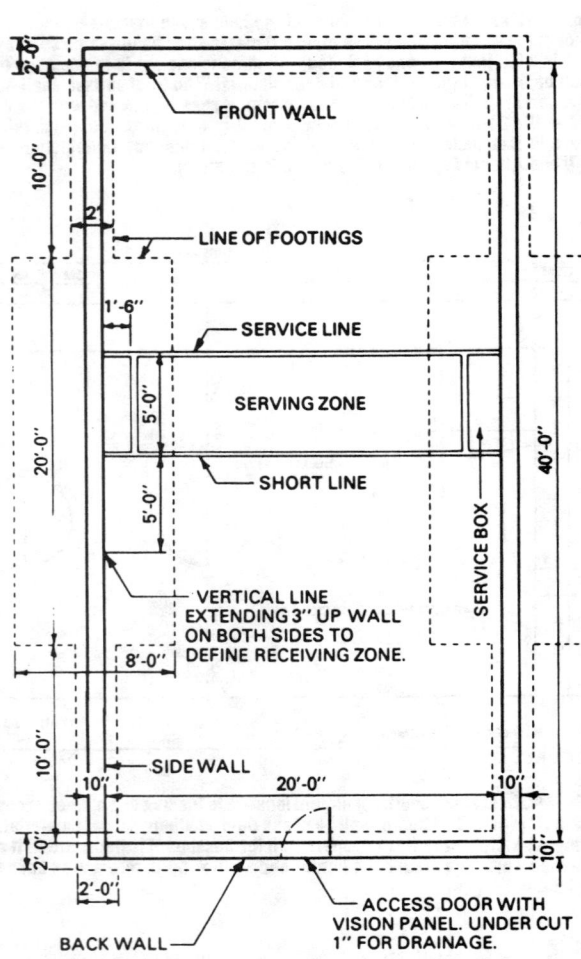

Fig. 5 Handball court layout — three-wall. All court markings to be 1½ in wide and painted white, red, or yellow. Playing court is 20'0" wide by 40'0" long plus a minimum 10'0" to the rear of the three-wall court. Overhead clearance required is 20'0" minimum.

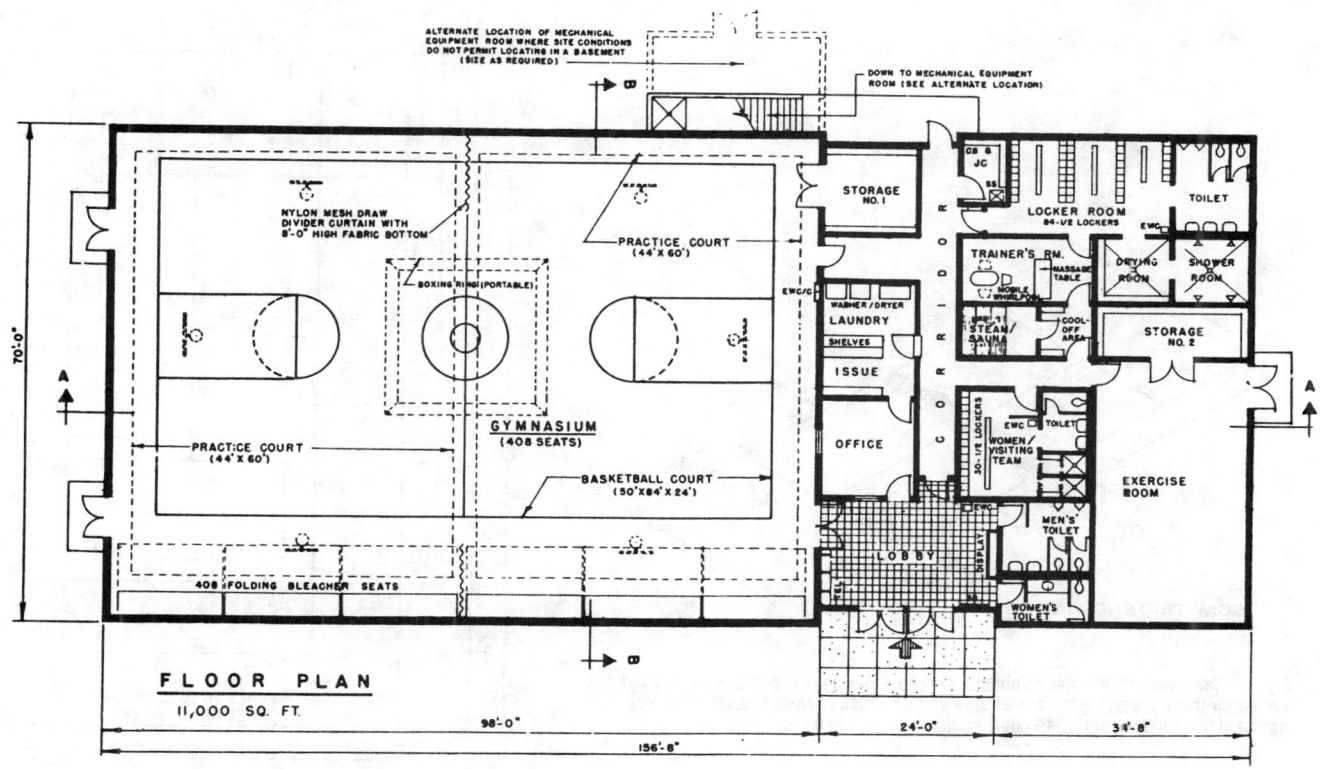

FLOOR PLAN

11,000 SQ. FT.

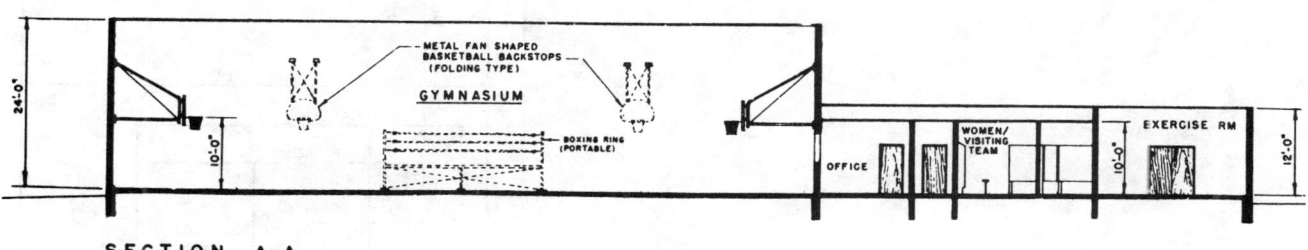

SECTION A-A

Fig. 6 Gymnasium plan and section.

COURT LAYOUT

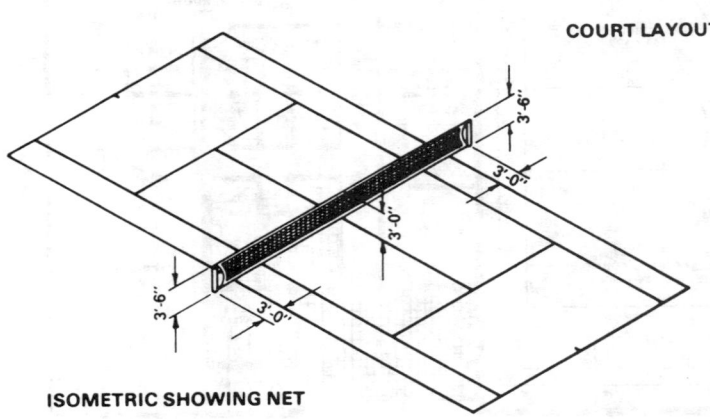

ISOMETRIC SHOWING NET

Fig. 7 Tennis court. All measurements for court markings are to the outside of lines except for those involving the center service line which is equally divided between the right and left service courts. All court markings to be 2 in wide.

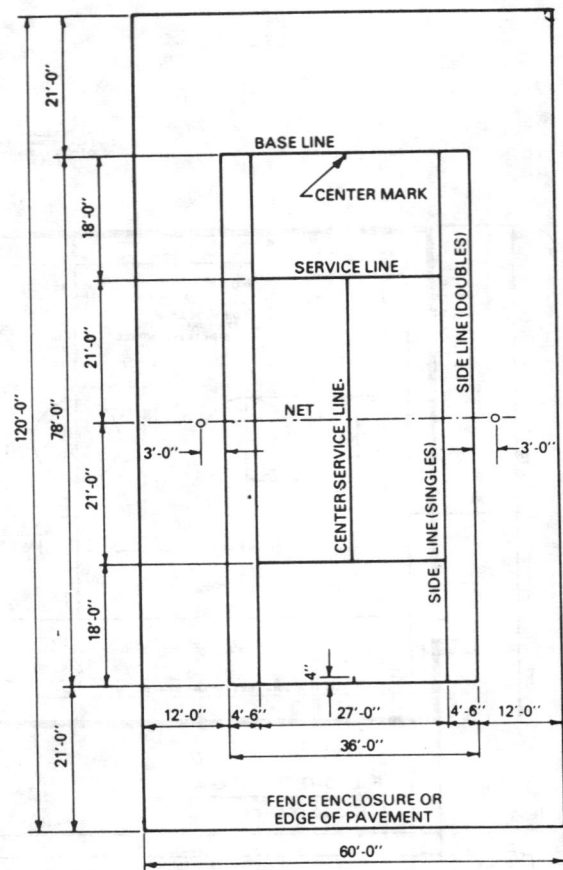

COURT LAYOUT

FENCE ENCLOSURE OR
EDGE OF PAVEMENT

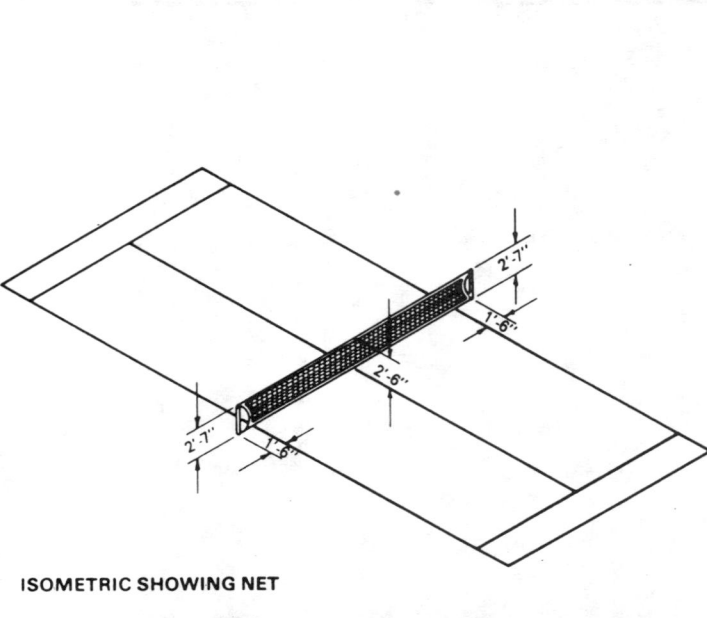

ISOMETRIC SHOWING NET

Fig. 8 Paddle tennis court. All measurements for court markings are to the outside of lines except for those involving the center service line, which is equally divided between right and left service court. All court markings to be 1½ in wide.

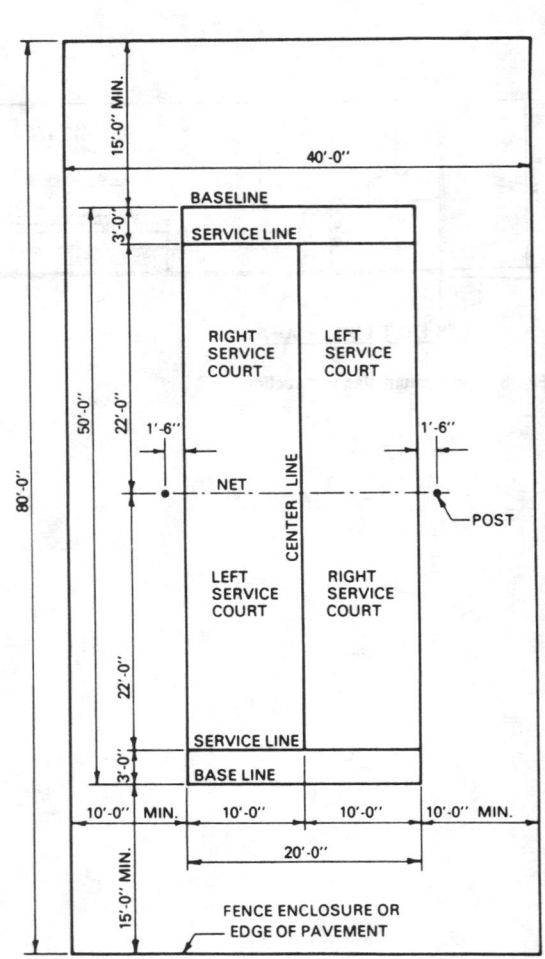

COURT LAYOUT

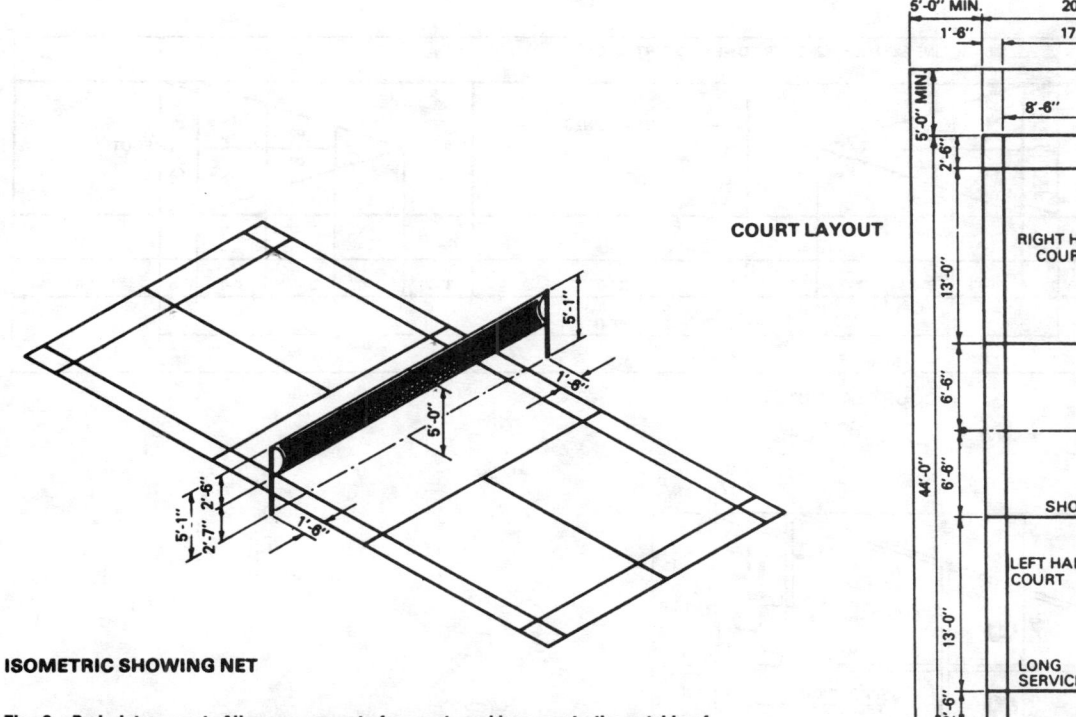

COURT LAYOUT

5'-0'' MIN. 20'-0'' (DOUBLES) 5'-0''MIN.
1'-6'' 17'-0'' (SINGLES) 1'-6''
8'-6'' 8'-6''
5'-0'' MIN.
2'-6''
RIGHT HALF COURT LEFT HALF COURT
SIDE BOUNDARY LINE (DOUBLES)
13'-0''
6'-6''
44'-0'' NET 1'-6''
6'-6'' POST
SHORT SERVICE LINE
SIDE BOUNDARY LINE (SINGLES)
LEFT HALF COURT RIGHT HALF COURT
CENTER LINE
13'-0''
LONG SERVICE LINE (DOUBLES)
2'-6''
BACK BOUNDARY LINE
5'-0'' MIN.
EDGE OF PAVEMENT

ISOMETRIC SHOWING NET

5'-1''
1'-6''
5'-0''
5'-1'' 2'-6'' 1'-6''
2'-7''

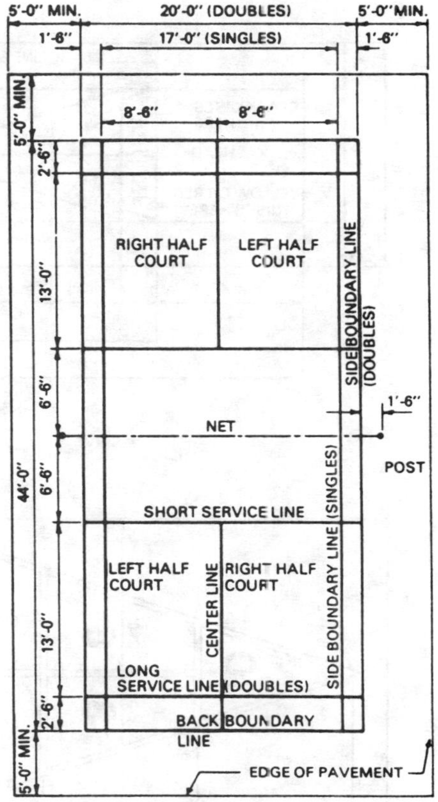

Fig. 9 Badminton court. All measurements for court markings are to the outside of lines except for those involving the center service line which is equally divided between right and left service courts. All court markings to be 1½'' wide and preferably white or in color. Minimum distance between sides of parallel courts to be 5'0''.

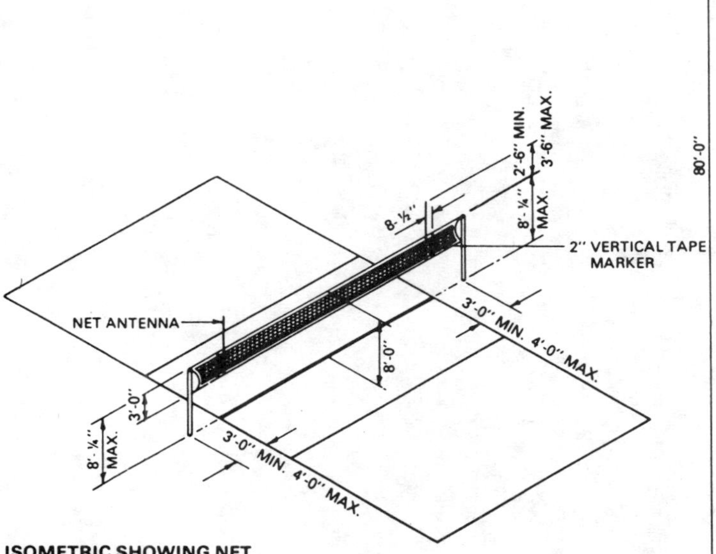

30'-0''
10'-0''
10'-0'' SERVICE AREA
10'-0'' 10'-0''
30'-0''
2'' SPIKING LINE
10'-0''
80'-0'' 4'' CENTER LINE POST
3'-0'' MIN.
10'-0''
2'' SPIKING LINE
30'-0''
SIDE LINE
EDGE OF PAVEMENT
8''
END LINE
10'-0'' 6''
EDGE OF PAVEMENT
50'-0''

COURT LAYOUT

ISOMETRIC SHOWING NET

2'-6'' MIN. 3'-6'' MAX.
8'-¼'' MAX.
8'-½''
2'' VERTICAL TAPE MARKER
NET ANTENNA
3'-0'' MIN. 4'-0'' MAX.
8'-0''
3'-0''
8'-¼'' MAX.
3'-0'' MIN. 4'-0'' MAX.

Fig. 10 Volleyball court. All measurements for court markings are to the outside of lines except for the centerline. All court markings to be 2 in wide except as noted.

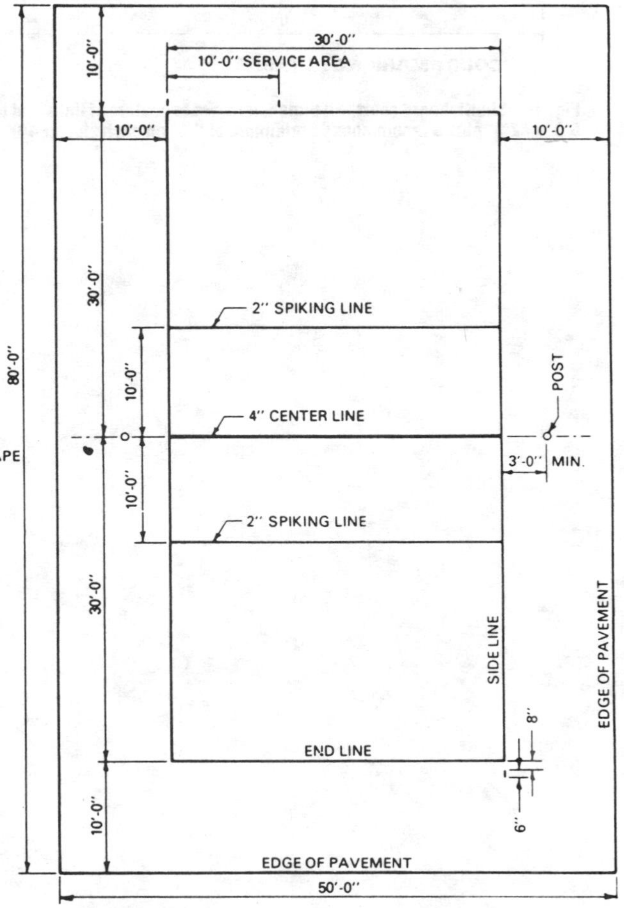

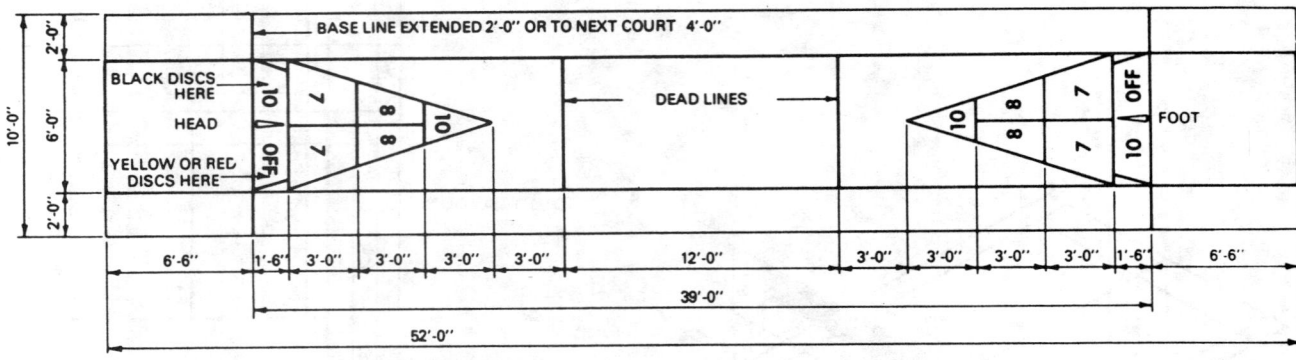

BASE LINE EXTENDED 2'-0" OR TO NEXT COURT 4'-0"

BLACK DISCS HERE

HEAD

YELLOW OR RED DISCS HERE

DEAD LINES

FOOT

COURT LAYOUT

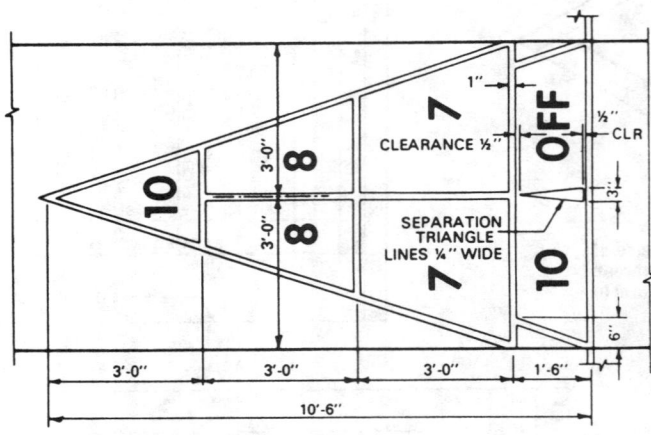

CLEARANCE ½"

SEPARATION TRIANGLE LINES ¼" WIDE

COURT MARKING DETAIL

Fig. 11 Shuffleboard court. All dimensions are to centers of lines and to edge of court. Maximum line width 1½ in, minimum ¾ in. Playing court is 6'0" x 52'0" plus a recommended minimum of 2'0" on each side or 4'0" between courts in battery.

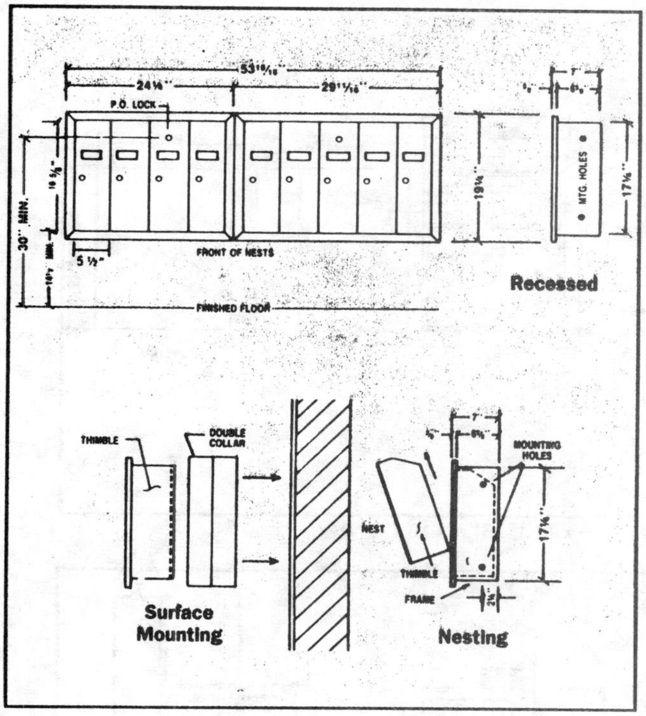
53 15/16"
24¼"
29 11/16"
P.O. LOCK
30" MIN.
5½"
FRONT OF NESTS
19¼"
MTG. HOLES
17¼"
7"
FINISHED FLOOR
Recessed
THIMBLE
DOUBLE COLLAR
Surface Mounting
MOUNTING HOLES
NEST
THIMBLE
FRAME
17¼"
Nesting

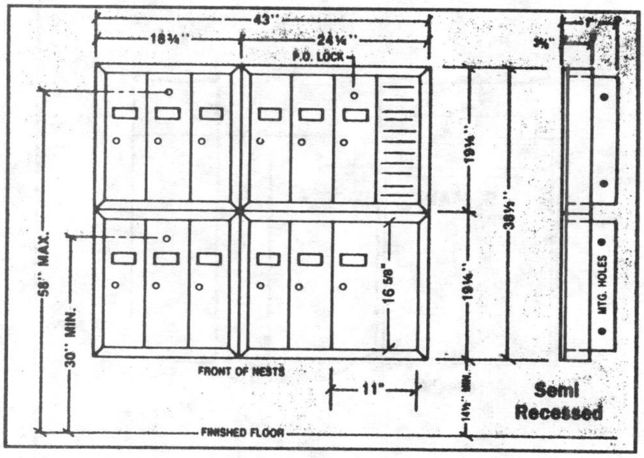
43"
18¾"
24¼"
P.O. LOCK
7"
19¼"
38½"
58" MAX.
30" MIN.
16 5/8"
19¼"
MTG. HOLES
FRONT OF NESTS
11"
FINISHED FLOOR
Semi Recessed

NO. OF OPENINGS — FOR 3-4 & 5 WIDE NESTS — All dimensions in inches.

SINGLE	DOUBLE	SUGGESTED ARRANGEMENT	ROUGH OPENING	CABINET	NET OVERALL WIDTH
3	6	3	17¾	16¾	18¾
4	8	4	23¼	22¼	24¼
5	10	5	28 11/16	27 11/16	29 11/16
6	12	3-3	36½	35½	37½
7	14	3-4	42	41	43
8	16	4-4	47½	46½	48½
9	18	4-5	52 15/16	51 15/16	53 15/16
10	20	5-5	58⅜	57⅜	59⅜
11	22	4-3-4	66¼	65¼	67¼
12	24	4-4-4	71¾	70¾	72¾
13	26	4-5-4	77 3/16	76 3/16	78 3/16
14	28	5-4-5	82⅝	81⅝	83⅝
15	30	5-5-5	88 1/16	87 1/16	89 1/16
16	32	4-4-4-4	96	95	97
17	34	5-4-4-4	101 7/16	100 7/16	102 7/16
18	36	5-4-4-5	106⅞	105⅞	107⅞
19	38	5-4-5-5	112 5/16	111 5/16	113 5/16
20	40	5-5-5-5	117¾	116¾	118¾
21	42	4-4-5-4-4	125 11/16	124 11/16	126 11/16
22	44	5-4-4-4-5	131⅛	130⅛	132⅛
23	46	5-5-3-5-5	136½	135½	137½
24	48	5-5-4-5-5	142	141	143
25	50	5-5-5-5-5	147 7/16	146 7/16	148 7/16
26	52	5-4-4-4-4-5	155⅜	154⅜	156⅜
27	54	5-4-5-4-5-4	160 13/16	159 13/16	161 13/16
28	56	5-5-4-4-5-5	166¼	165¼	167¼
29	58	5-5-4-5-5-5	171 11/16	170 11/16	172 11/16
30	60	5-5-5-5-5-5	177⅛	176⅛	178⅛
31	62	5-4-4-5-4-4-5	185 1/16	184 1/16	186 1/16
32	64	5-5-4-4-4-5-5	190½	189½	191½
33	66	5-5-4-5-4-5-5	195 15/16	194 15/16	196 15/16
34	68	5-5-5-4-5-5-5	201⅜	200⅜	202⅜
35	70	5-5-5-5-5-5-5	206 13/16	205 13/16	207 13/16
36	72	5-5-4-4-4-4-5-5	214¾	213¾	215¾
37	74	5-5-5-4-4-4-5-5	220 3/16	219 3/16	221 3/16
38	76	5-5-5-4-4-5-5-5	225⅝	224⅝	226⅝
39	78	5-5-5-5-4-5-5-5	231 1/16	230 1/16	232 1/16
40	80	5-5-5-5-5-5-5-5	236½	235½	237½
41	82	4-4-5-5-5-5-5-4-4	244 7/16	243 7/16	245 7/16
42	84	5-5-5-4-4-4-5-5-5	249⅞	248⅞	250⅞
43	86	5-5-5-5-3-5-5-5-5	255¼	254¼	256¼
44	88	5-5-5-5-4-5-5-5-5	260¾	259¾	261¾
45	90	5-5-5-5-5-5-5-5-5	266 3/16	265 3/16	267 3/16

ACCESSORIES
Mail Collection Boxes

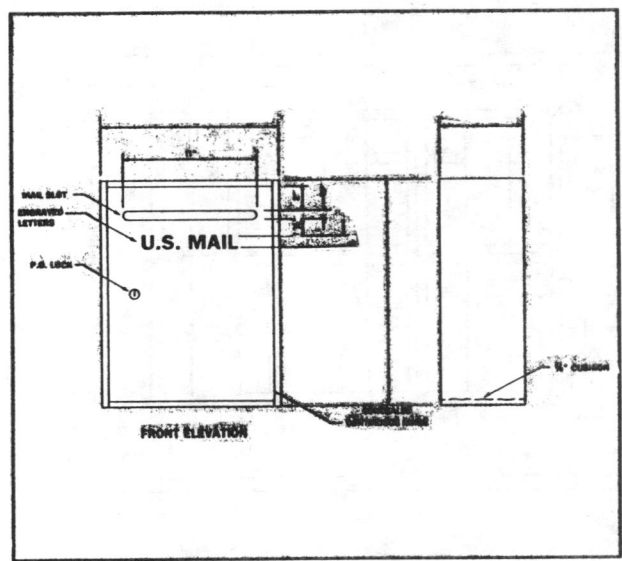

19 1/4" H x 14 3/8" W x 6" D

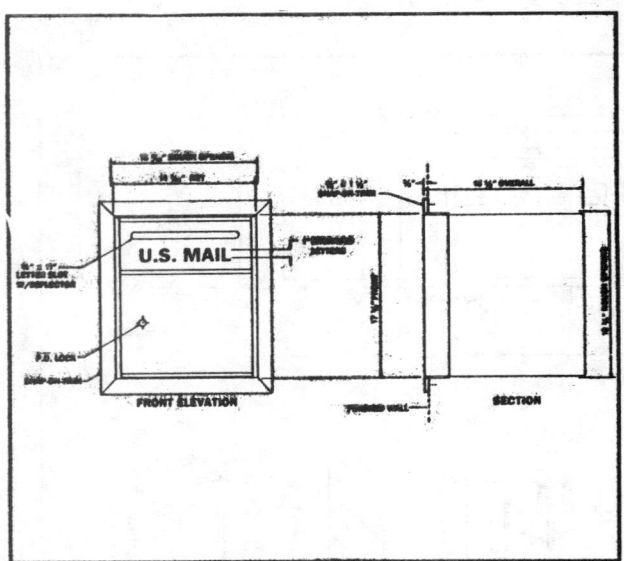

17 1/8" H x 14 1/16" W x 16 1/8" D

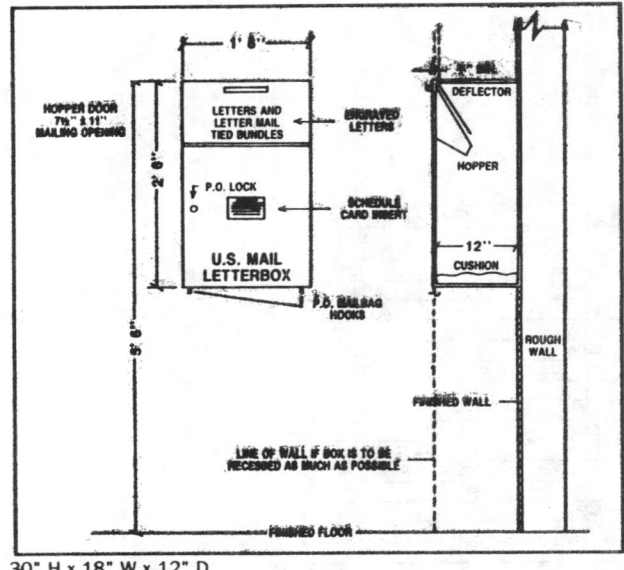

30" H x 18" W x 12" D

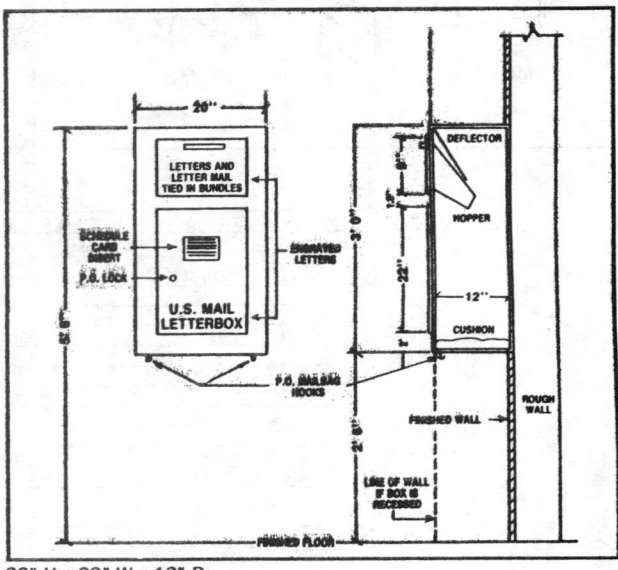

36" H x 20" W x 12" D

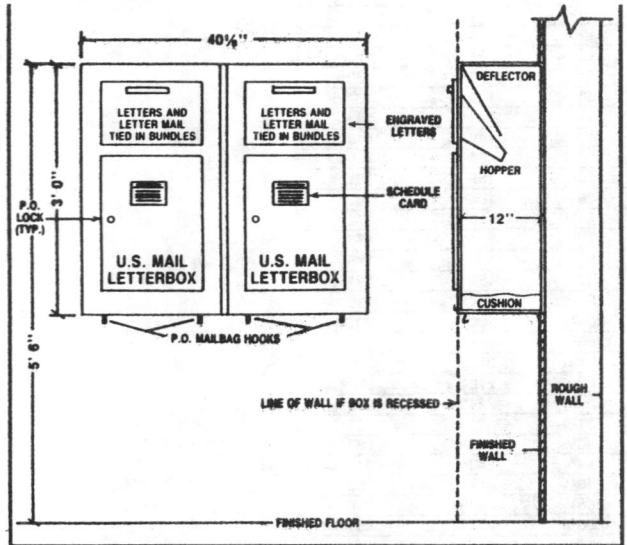

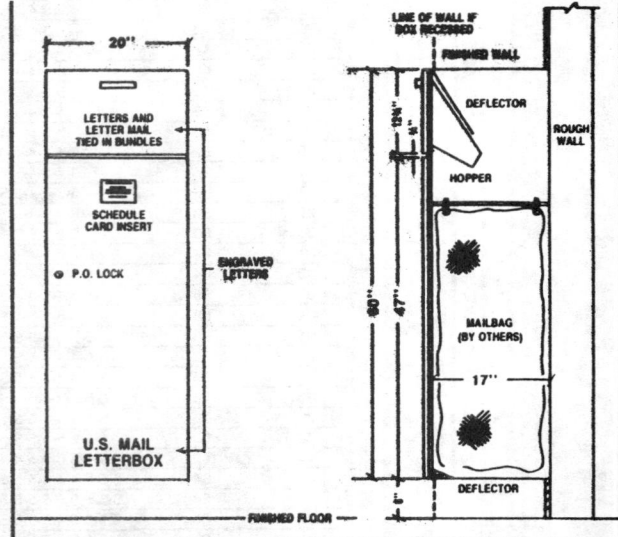

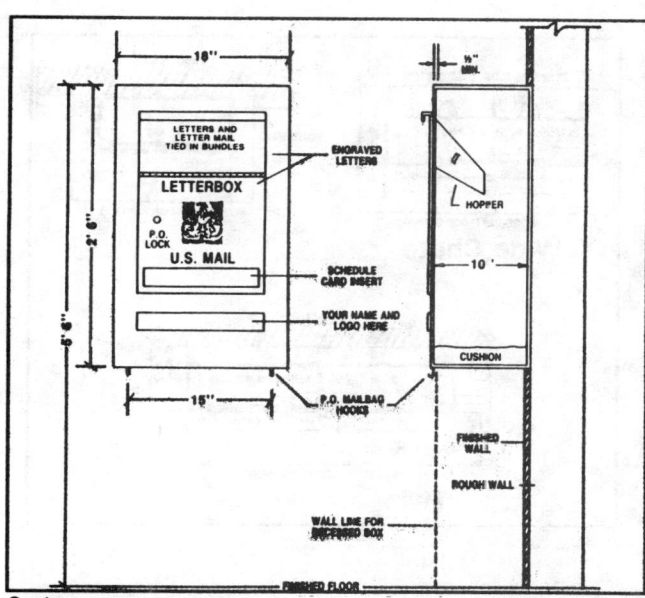

Contemporary
30" H x 18" W x 10" D

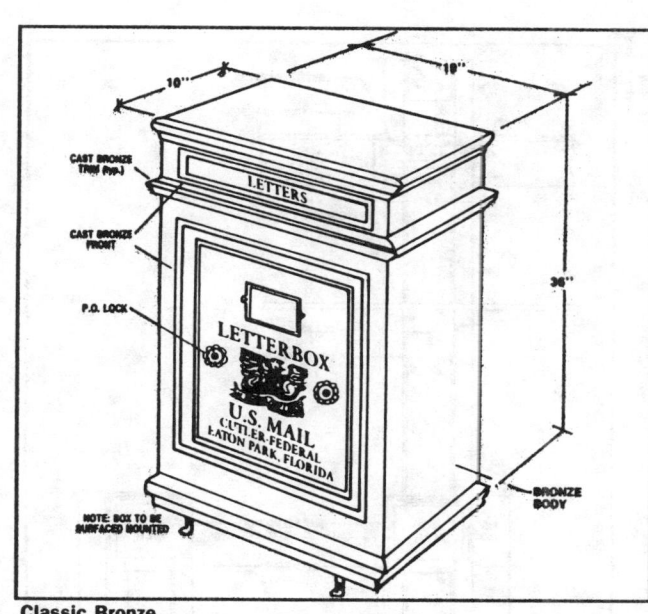

Classic Bronze
36" H x 19" W x 10" D

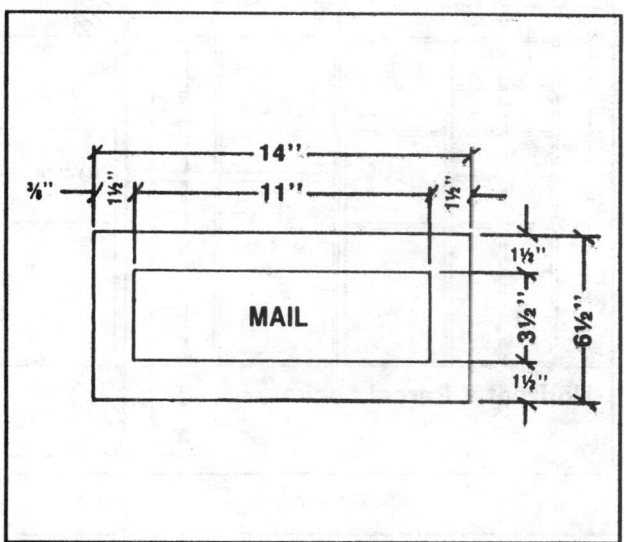

Letterslot
6 1/2" H x 14" W

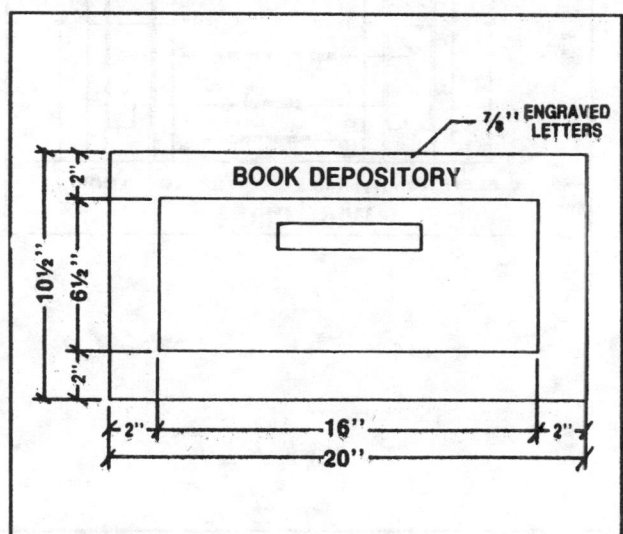

Book Depository
10 1/2" H x 20" W

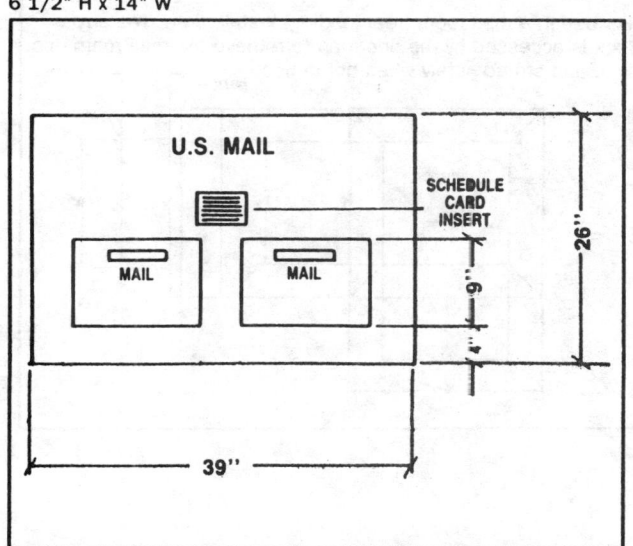

Plate Front
26"H x 39"W

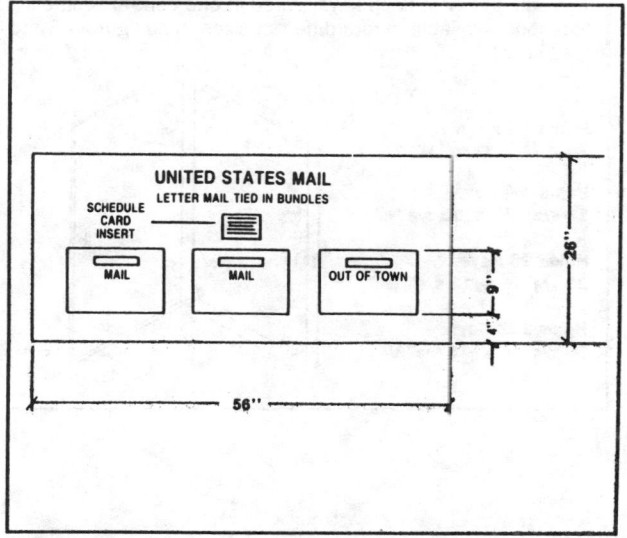

Plate Front
26" H x 56" W

ACCESSORIES
Mail Chutes, Parcel Lockers, and Key Cabinets

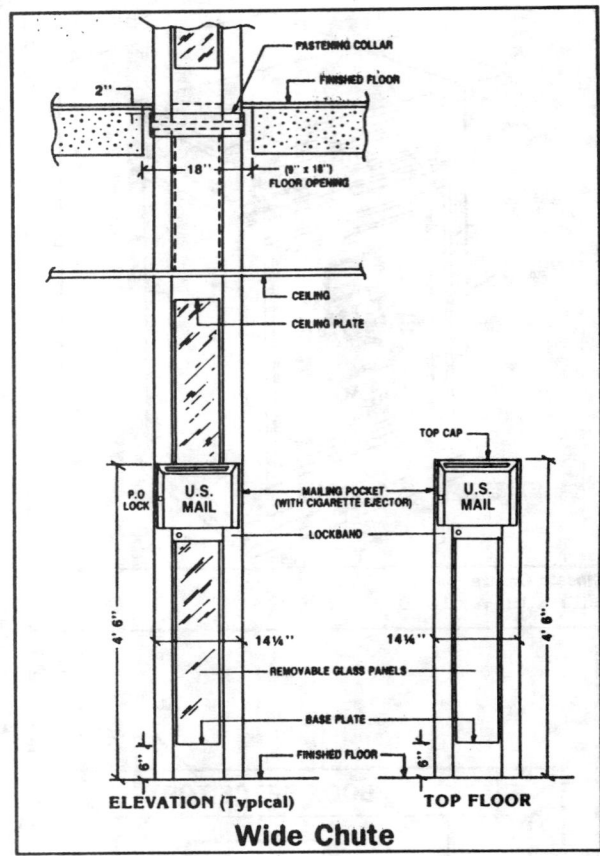

Wide Chute

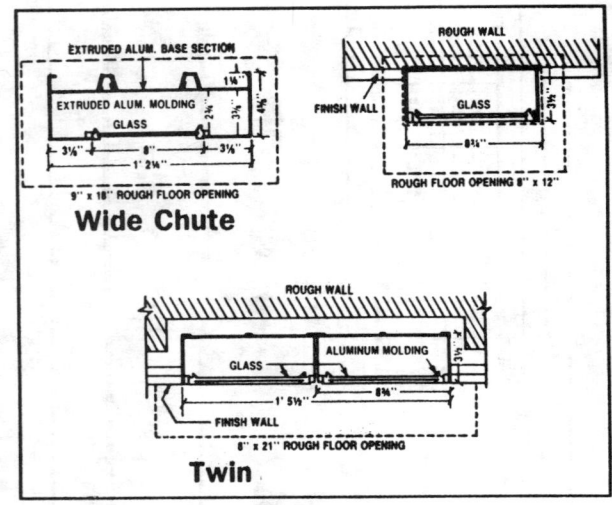

Wide Chute

Twin

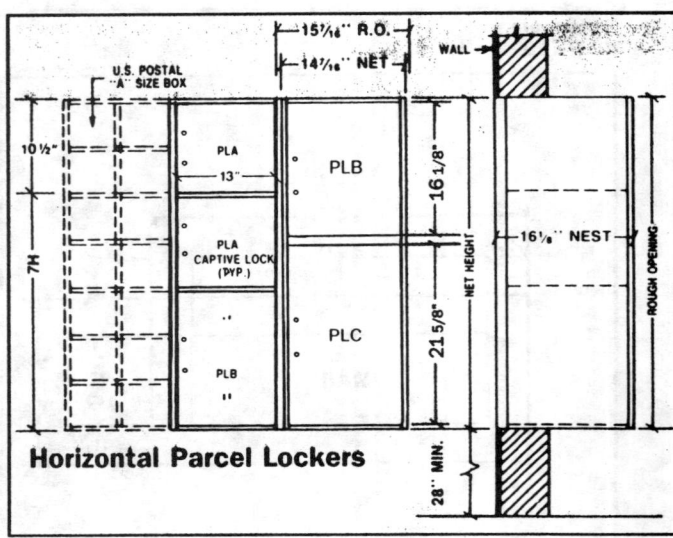

Horizontal Parcel Lockers

Key Storage Cabinet

The safest way to keep keys stored in one central secure location. Available in four different sizes, holding from 32 to 128 keys.

Holds 32 Keys
9 1/4" H x 13 5/8" W

Holds 64 Keys
16 5/16" H x 13 5/8" W

Holds 96 Keys
23 1/4" H x 13 5/8" W

Holds 128 Keys
30 1/4" H x 13 5/8" W

Key Keeper

For use in a mail room (rear loading) installation. The arrow lock is accessed by the postman to retrieve the mail room door key, and stored safely when not in use.

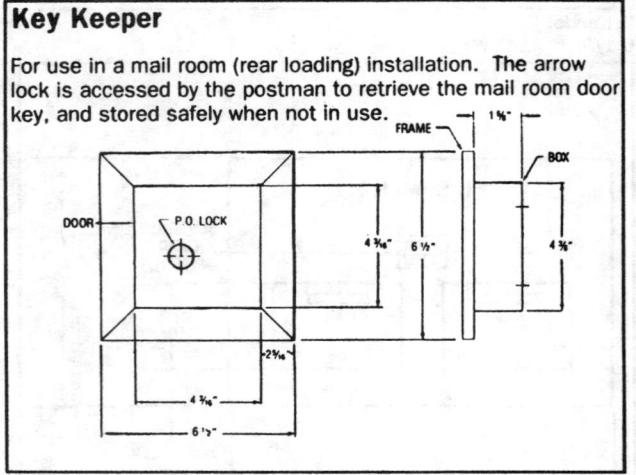

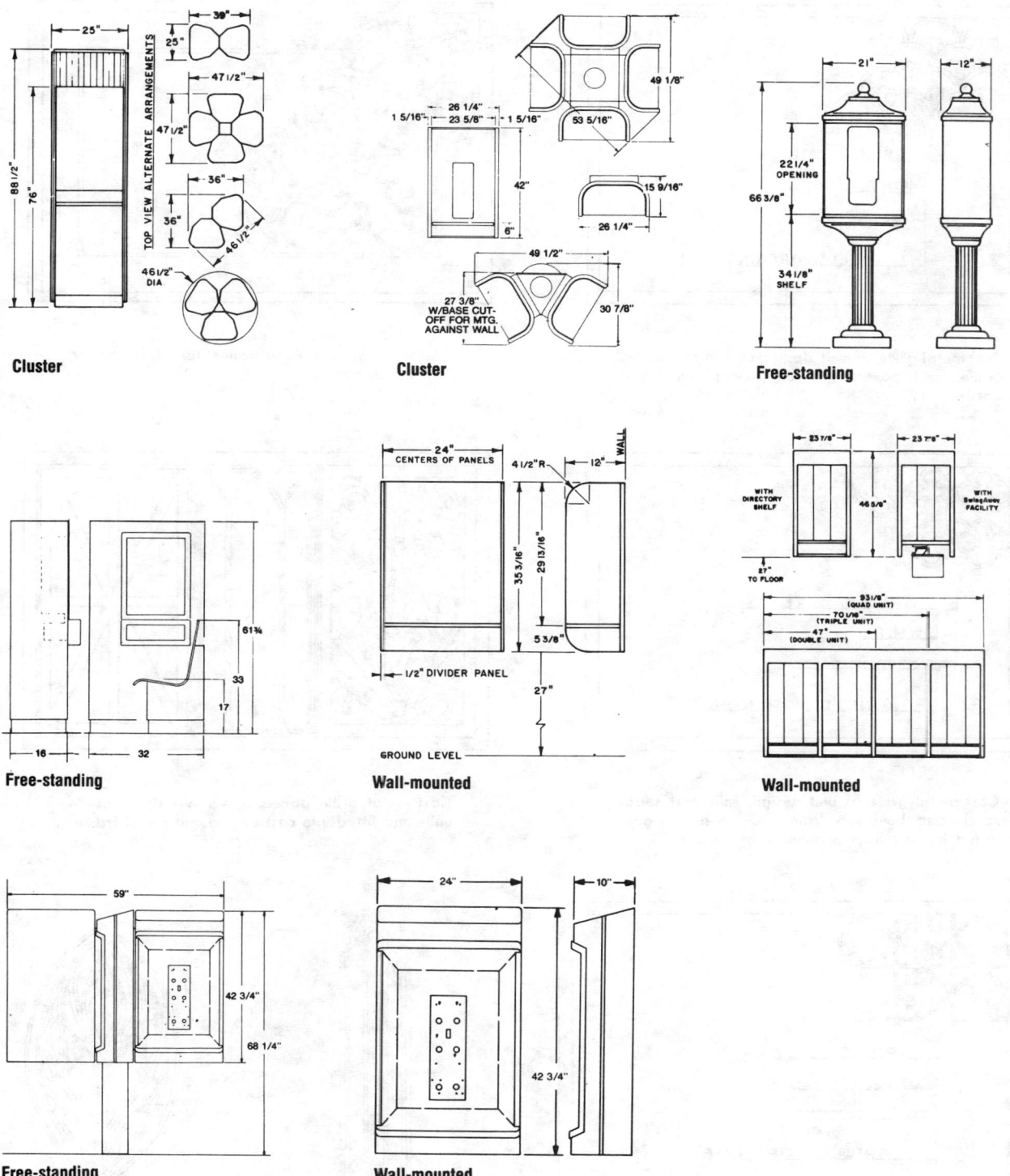

Cluster

Cluster

Free-standing

Free-standing

Wall-mounted

Wall-mounted

Free-standing

Wall-mounted

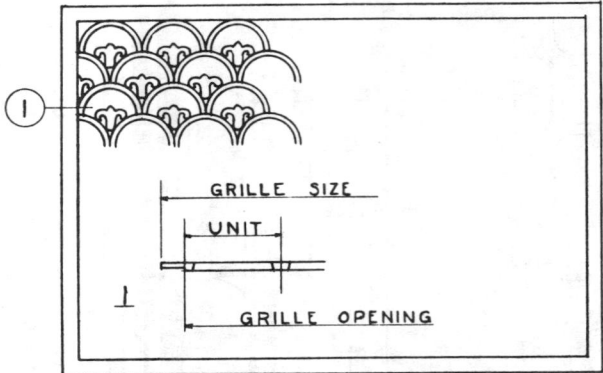

Cast metal grille of unit design, cast in one piece. Grille size is governed by unit sizes plus width of border.

Cast metal grille of Renaissance design, ferrous or non-ferrous metal.

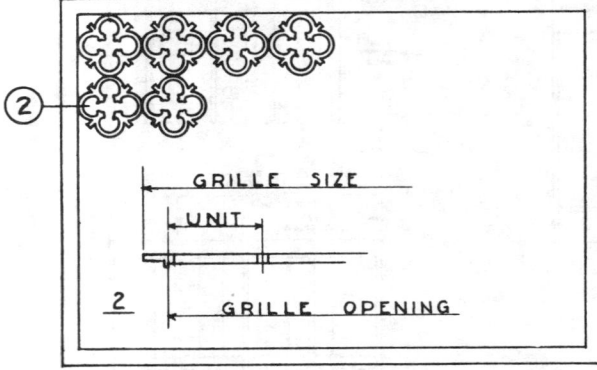

Cast metal grille of unit design, units cast separately and built into frame. Grille size is governed by unit sizes plus width of border.

Cast metal grille panels of various sizes cast in units and fitted into cast or wrought metal frame.

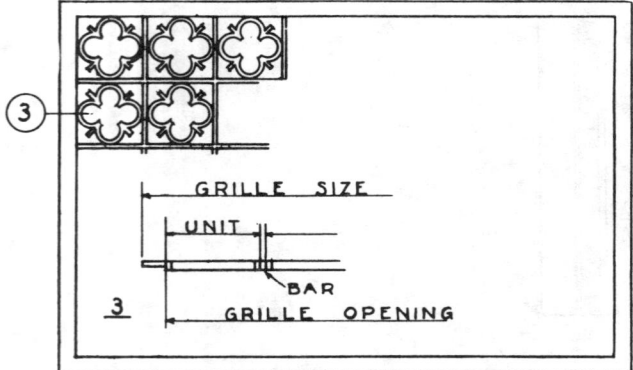

Cast metal grille of unit design. Units cast separately and built into grille spaces. Grille size must conform to unit sizes plus widths of bars and borders.

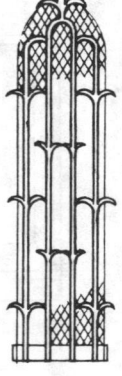

Cast metal grille for ventilator opening; may be fitted with metal screen and may be formed to curved wall or cove.

Cast metal grille for ventilator opening of special architectural form.

Fig. 1   Cast metal grilles may be designed and built in various combinations. They may be made in small units cast separately or as one complete piece.

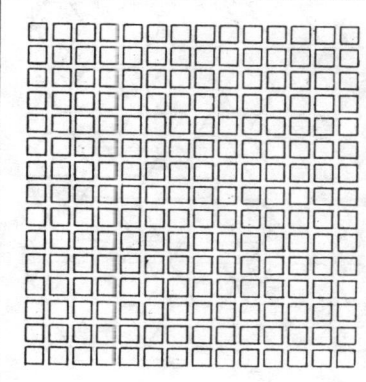

Stamped metal grille, square holes. Holes may be from ¼" to 1½" or larger, in ⅛" steps, with bars or frets from ⅛" to ⅜" or greater.

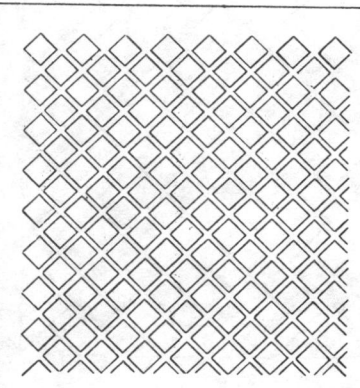

Stamped metal grille, square holes diagonally arranged.

Stamped metal grille, Grecian or Union Jack design, made in a number of unit sizes and variations.

Stamped metal grille, shell or fish scale design, made in several unit sizes and variations.

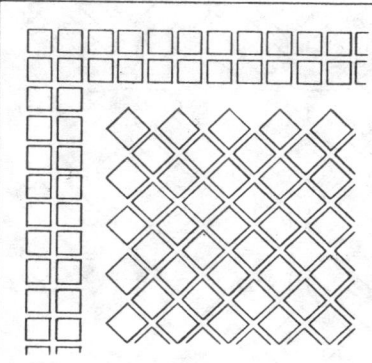

Stamped metal grille, square holes arranged to form plain border with diagonal center.

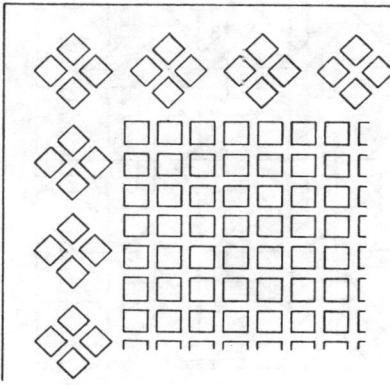

Stamped metal grille, square holes arranged to form diagonal border, with plain center.

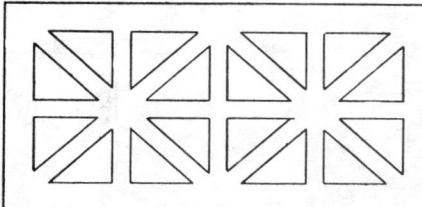

Foundation or Bulkhead Grille

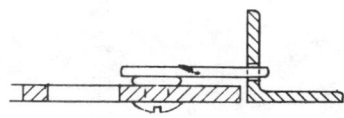

Screwdriver Operated Catch

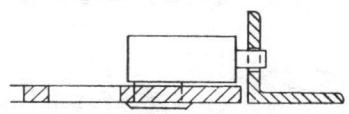

Lock and Dead Bolt

SCALE 1½" = 1'-0" AND ½" = 1"

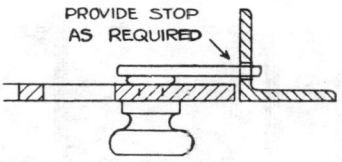

PROVIDE STOP AS REQUIRED

Thumb Latch

SPECIFY:
Sizes of holes or unit stampings
Thickness
Metal and finish
Approximate width of margins
Method of fastening
Hinges and locks where required
Invisible hand hole doors.

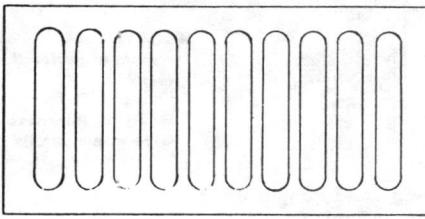

Foundation or Bulkhead Grille

Fig. 2 Stamped metal grilles are produced in a great variety of designs, metals, thicknesses, and sizes. Percentage of free area of stamped grilles may vary from about 25% to over 70%, with a great many designs in the 55% to 65% range. Margin widths can be made to accord with requirements of particular installations, consideration being given to duct openings and overall dimensions. Metal may be steel, painted or otherwise finished, bronze, aluminum, monel metal, or other nonferrous metals, in thicknesses from 16 gauge to ¼".

ACCESSORIES
Types of Grilles

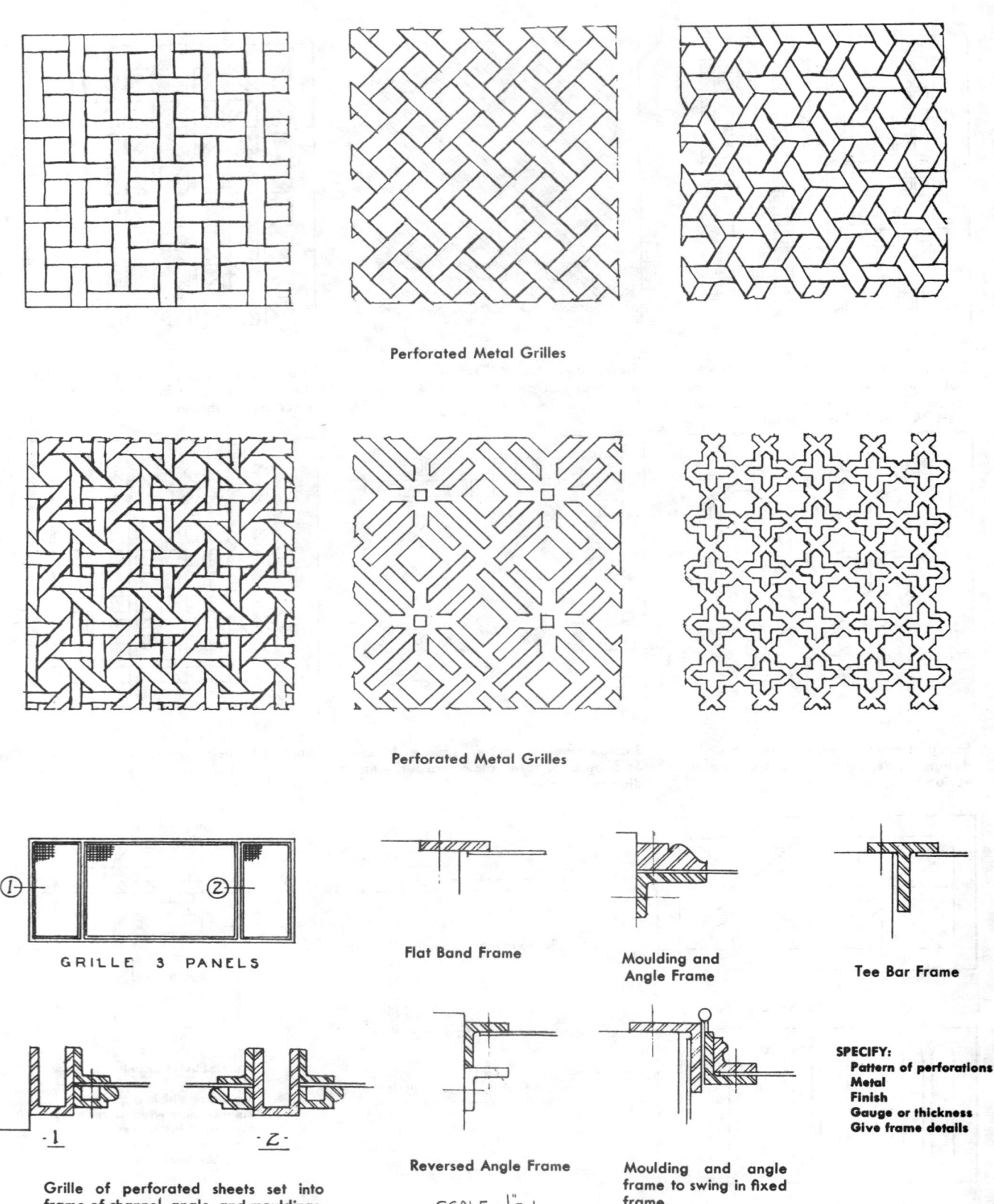

Perforated Metal Grilles

Perforated Metal Grilles

GRILLE 3 PANELS

Flat Band Frame

Moulding and Angle Frame

Tee Bar Frame

-1-   -2-

Reversed Angle Frame

SCALE $\frac{1}{2}$" = 1

Moulding and angle frame to swing in fixed frame.

Grille of perforated sheets set into frame of channel, angle, and mouldings.

SPECIFY:
Pattern of perforations
Metal
Finish
Gauge or thickness
Give frame details

Fig. 3 Perforated metal grilles may be obtained in several designs and are produced of 19 gauge steel in sheets of standard sizes. Sheets may be cut to any size and placed in frames of metal or other material. Perforated metal grilles are used for vent openings, panels, covers, shelves, partitions, cabinets, metal furniture, boxes, machinery guards, enclosures and many other purposes. They are also available in many other patterns in any ferrous or nonferrous metal that can be perforated, and in thicknesses from about 24 gauge in the smaller perforations to ¼" or ⅜" in the larger perforations.

Wrought metal grille of heavy close construction, for radiator or ventilator openings.

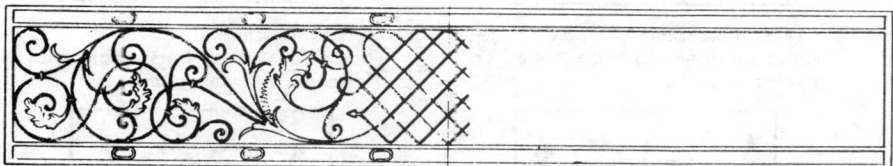

Wrought metal grille for railing or ornamental construction.

Wrought metal grille for glass door.

Wrought metal grille of light construction, with silhouette work, leaves, flowers, and husks, for arch decoration.

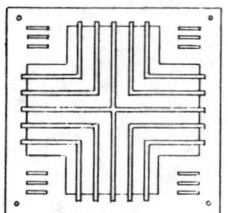

Wrought metal grille of sheet and flat bars, for ventilating opening.

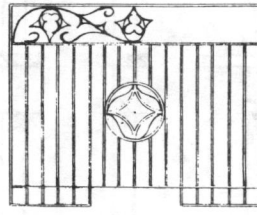

Wrought metal grille for counter.

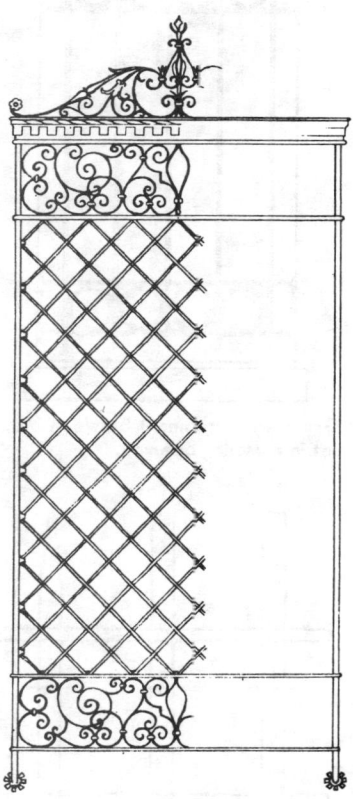

Wrought metal grille for large window or opening.

Fig. 4 Design of wrought metal grilles includes the use of other metal forms, such as sheets, extruded mouldings, castings, and stampings. Thus, in addition to plain bar sections and forged items, use is made of the unlimited number of extruded mouldings in non-ferrous metals; stamped leaves, rosettes, and ornaments of many kinds; cast iron, bronze, nickel silver, and aluminum items of every character; and rolled or drawn sections of many shapes.

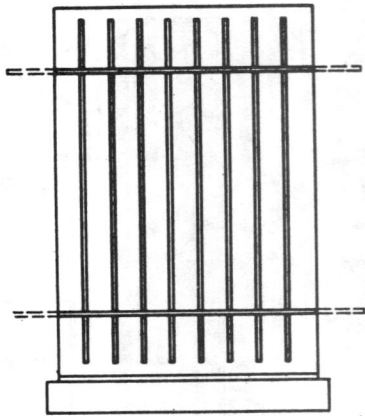

Grille of round or square vertical bars welded to horizontal bars set in masonry.

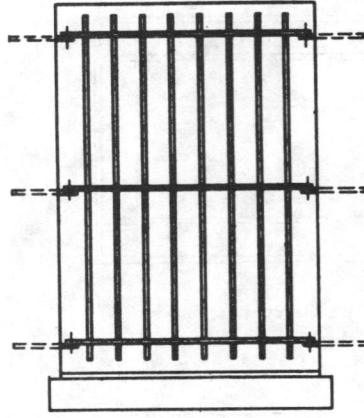

Grille with anchors set in masonry and grille bolted or riveted to anchors.

Grille with short alternate vertical bars, angle clips fastened to opening jambs.

Grille, with ornament between bars, set in masonry opening.

Grille of welded construction set on face of wall.

Grille of welded construction set on face of wall.

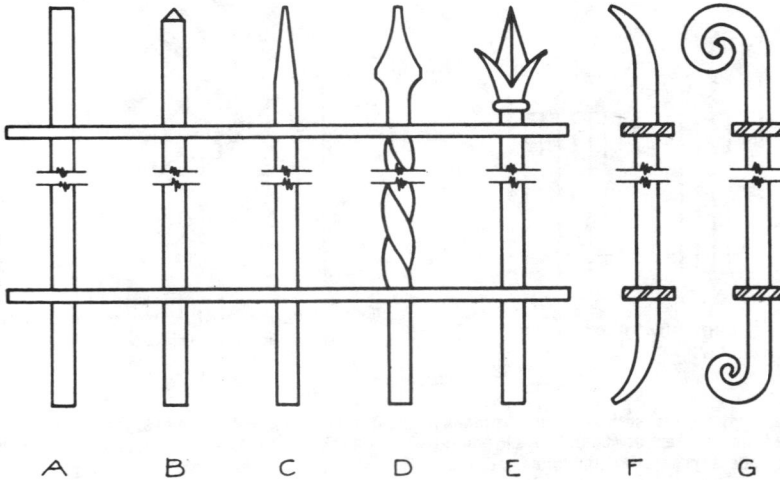

A   B   C   D   E   F   G

Methods of forming vertical bars.

Fig. 5 Window grilles are of plain construction when used for protection only, and when used for ornamental effect, may be designed with many unique and interesting ideas. Window grilles may be set in the masonry openings or on the face of the wall, with either plain or ornamental brackets or supports. They may also be attached to window frames, or may be arranged to swing, with hinges and locks. Material sizes in window grilles may vary according to the degree of protection required, and in proportion to the size of the grille.

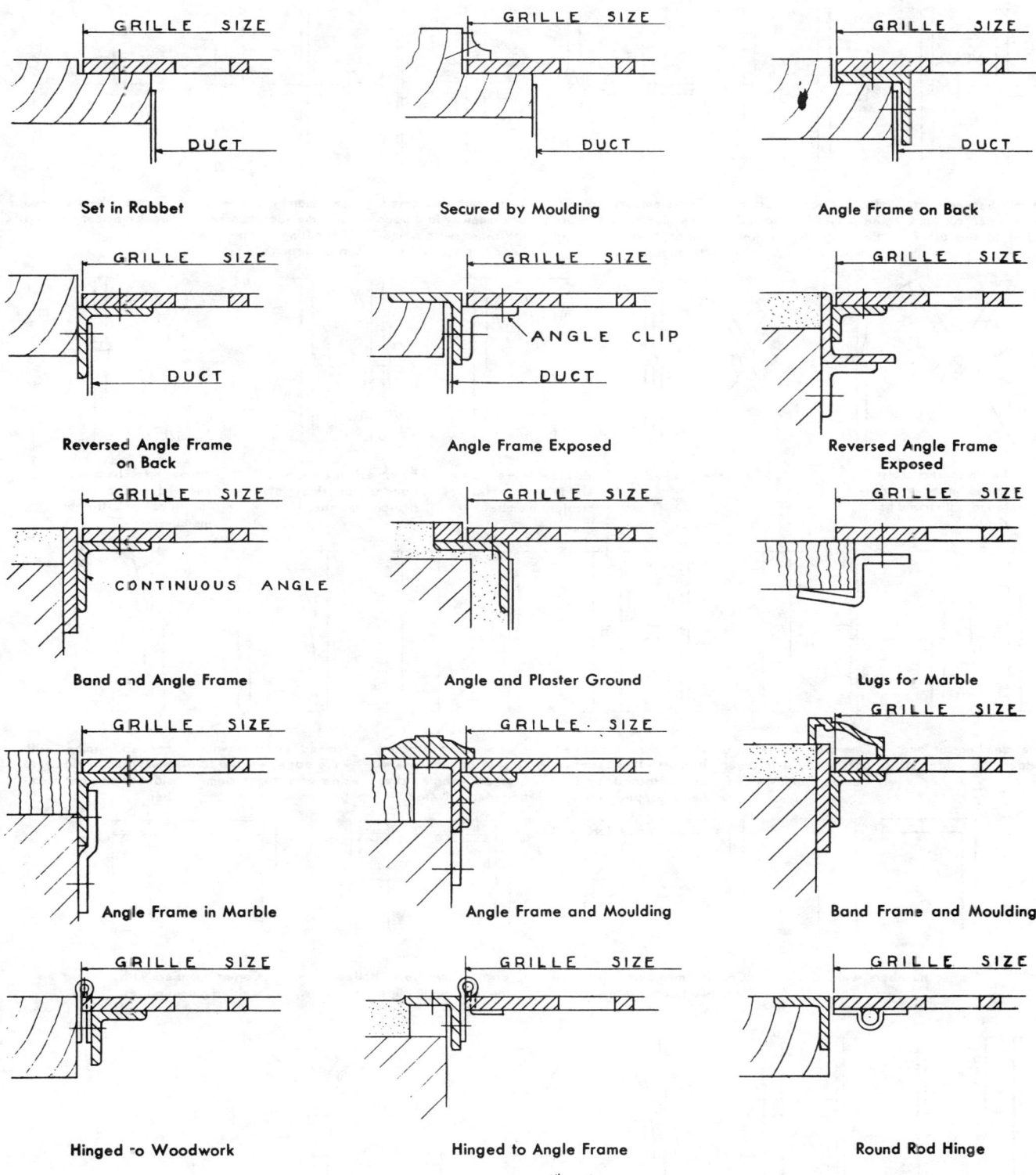

Fig. 6 Methods of fastening grilles. Cast and stamped metal grilles may be fastened by screws or hinges and locks to walls of wood, plaster, marble, or other material in a variety of ways, depending upon the type of the grille, the type of framing to be used around the grille, and the appearance or effect desired. These methods show a number of ways in which cast and stamped grilles may be fastened. In selecting the method desired, consideration should be given to whether or not the grille will require frequent removal. The size and weight of the grille will have a bearing upon the size of frames, screws, and hinges.

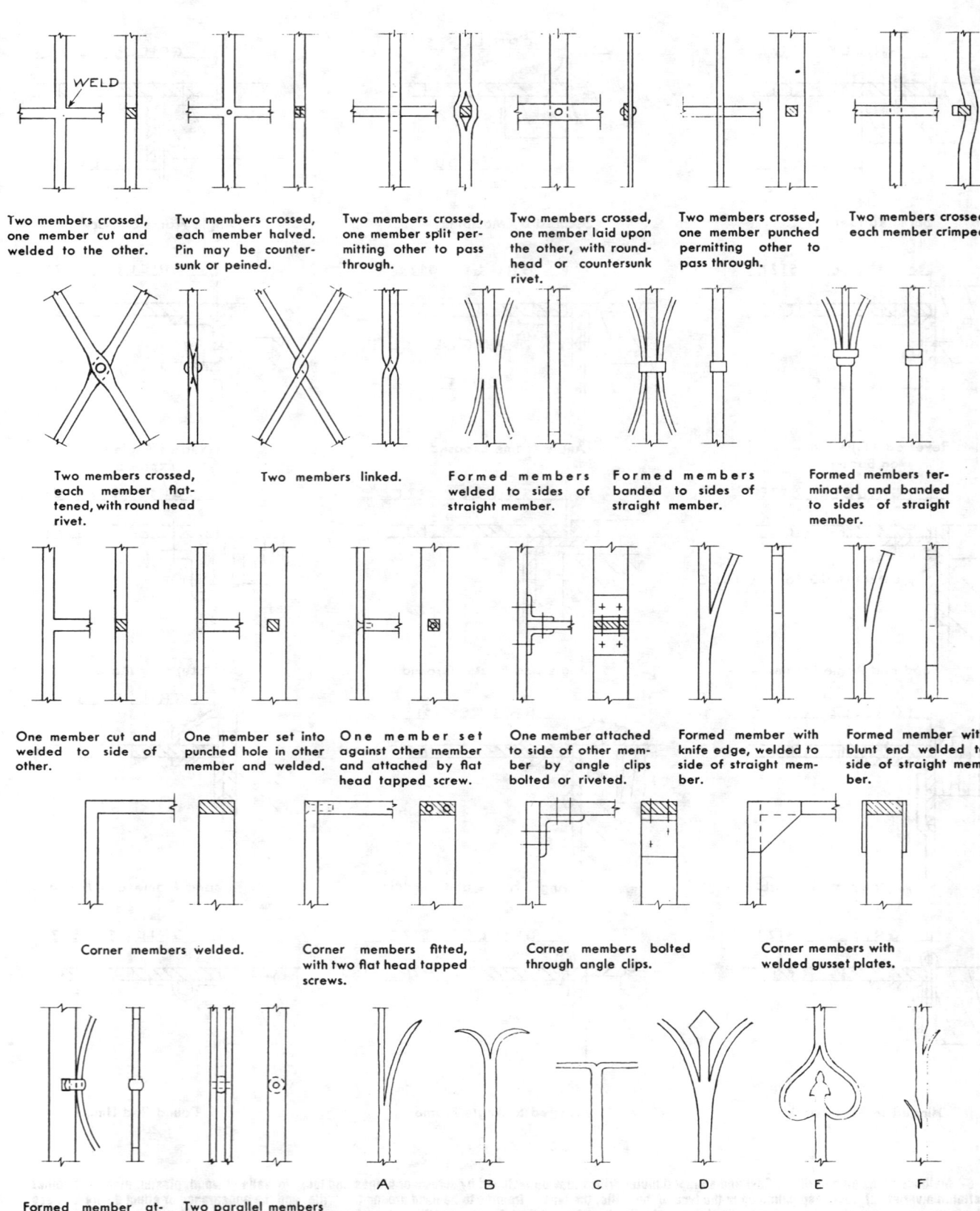

Two members crossed, one member cut and welded to the other.

Two members crossed, each member halved. Pin may be countersunk or peined.

Two members crossed, one member split permitting other to pass through.

Two members crossed, one member laid upon the other, with round-head or countersunk rivet.

Two members crossed, one member punched permitting other to pass through.

Two members crossed, each member crimped.

Two members crossed, each member flattened, with round head rivet.

Two members linked.

Formed members welded to sides of straight member.

Formed members banded to sides of straight member.

Formed members terminated and banded to sides of straight member.

One member cut and welded to side of other.

One member set into punched hole in other member and welded.

One member set against other member and attached by flat head tapped screw.

One member attached to side of other member by angle clips bolted or riveted.

Formed member with knife edge, welded to side of straight member.

Formed member with blunt end welded to side of straight member.

Corner members welded.

Corner members fitted, with two flat head tapped screws.

Corner members bolted through angle clips.

Corner members with welded gusset plates.

Formed member attached to the other member by band in slot.

Two parallel members attached by spool and pin.

A   B   C   D   E   F

Methods of splitting members and forming into scrolls, ends, ornaments, or structural elements.

SCALE 1½ = 1-0"

Fig. 7 Wrought metal grilles are fabricated by the use of a great many different methods of crossing and joining members. Some of the more widely employed of these methods are shown here.

VINYL WALL PROTECTION GUARDS

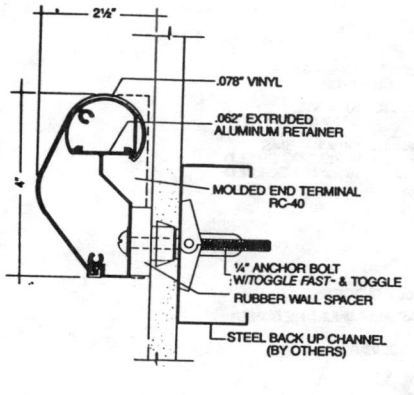

.078" VINYL
.062" EXTRUDED ALUMINUM RETAINER
MOLDED END TERMINAL RC-40
¼" ANCHOR BOLT W/TOGGLE FAST- & TOGGLE
RUBBER WALL SPACER
STEEL BACK UP CHANNEL (BY OTHERS)

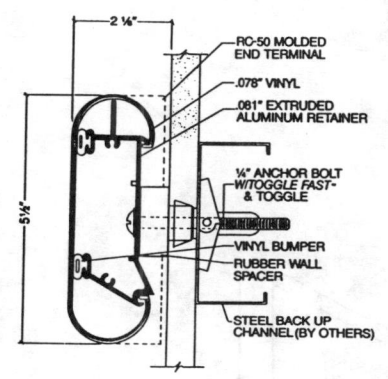

RC-50 MOLDED END TERMINAL
.078" VINYL
.081" EXTRUDED ALUMINUM RETAINER
¼" ANCHOR BOLT W/TOGGLE FAST- & TOGGLE
VINYL BUMPER
RUBBER WALL SPACER
STEEL BACK UP CHANNEL (BY OTHERS)

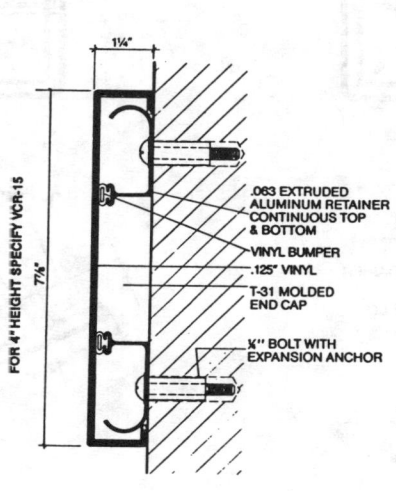

FOR 4" HEIGHT SPECIFY VCR-15

.063 EXTRUDED ALUMINUM RETAINER CONTINUOUS TOP & BOTTOM
VINYL BUMPER
.125" VINYL
T-31 MOLDED END CAP
¼" BOLT WITH EXPANSION ANCHOR

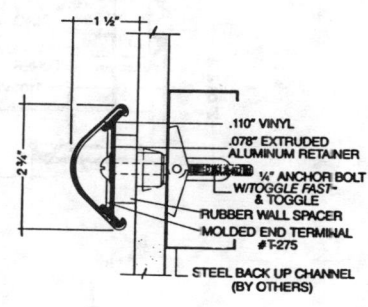

.110" VINYL
.078" EXTRUDED ALUMINUM RETAINER
¼" ANCHOR BOLT W/TOGGLE FAST- & TOGGLE
RUBBER WALL SPACER
MOLDED END TERMINAL #T-275
STEEL BACK UP CHANNEL (BY OTHERS)

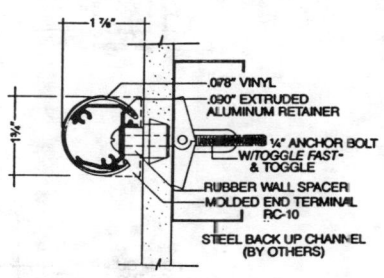

.078" VINYL
.090" EXTRUDED ALUMINUM RETAINER
¼" ANCHOR BOLT W/TOGGLE FAST- & TOGGLE
RUBBER WALL SPACER
MOLDED END TERMINAL RC-10
STEEL BACK UP CHANNEL (BY OTHERS)

ALUMINUM WALL PROTECTION GUARDS

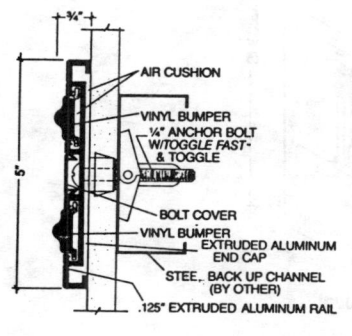

AIR CUSHION
VINYL BUMPER
¼" ANCHOR BOLT W/TOGGLE FAST- & TOGGLE
BOLT COVER
VINYL BUMPER
EXTRUDED ALUMINUM END CAP
STEEL BACK UP CHANNEL (BY OTHER)
.125" EXTRUDED ALUMINUM RAIL

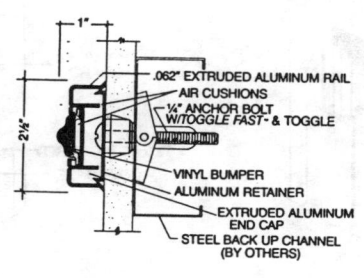

.062" EXTRUDED ALUMINUM RAIL
AIR CUSHIONS
¼" ANCHOR BOLT W/TOGGLE FAST- & TOGGLE
VINYL BUMPER
ALUMINUM RETAINER
EXTRUDED ALUMINUM END CAP
STEEL BACK UP CHANNEL (BY OTHERS)

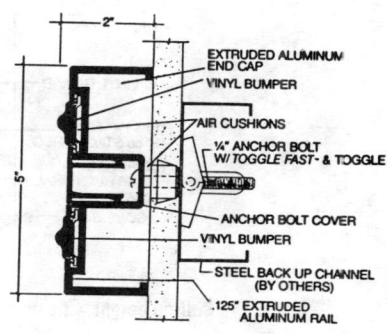

EXTRUDED ALUMINUM END CAP
VINYL BUMPER
AIR CUSHIONS
¼" ANCHOR BOLT W/ TOGGLE FAST- & TOGGLE
ANCHOR BOLT COVER
VINYL BUMPER
STEEL BACK UP CHANNEL (BY OTHERS)
.125" EXTRUDED ALUMINUM RAIL

FLUSH-MOUNTED CORNER PROTECTION GUARDS

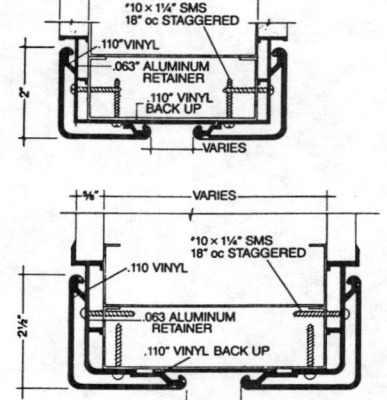

VARIES
#10 × 1¼" SMS 18" oc STAGGERED
.110" VINYL
.063" ALUMINUM RETAINER
.110" VINYL BACK UP
VARIES
#10 × 1¼" SMS 18" oc STAGGERED
.110" VINYL
.063 ALUMINUM RETAINER
.110" VINYL BACK UP
VARIES

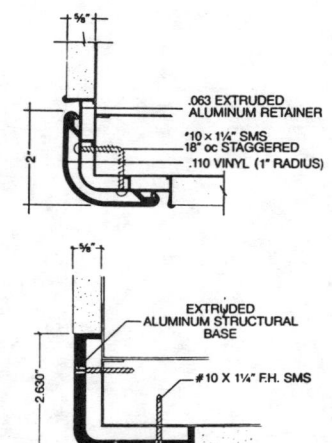

.063 EXTRUDED ALUMINUM RETAINER
#10 × 1¼" SMS 18" oc STAGGERED
.110 VINYL (1" RADIUS)
EXTRUDED ALUMINUM STRUCTURAL BASE
#10 × 1¼" F.H. SMS

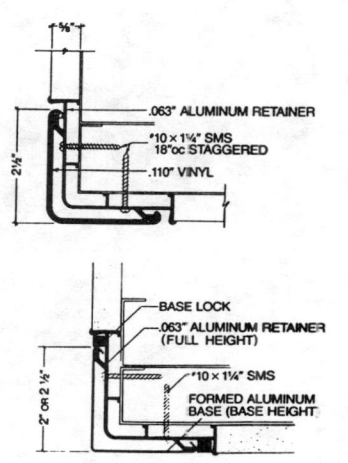

.063" ALUMINUM RETAINER
#10 × 1¼" SMS 18" oc STAGGERED
.110" VINYL
BASE LOCK
.063" ALUMINUM RETAINER (FULL HEIGHT)
#10 × 1¼" SMS
FORMED ALUMINUM BASE (BASE HEIGHT)

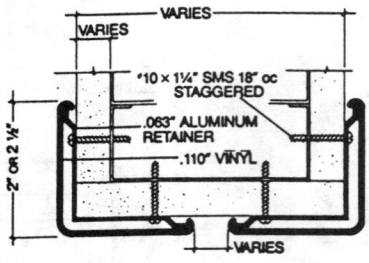

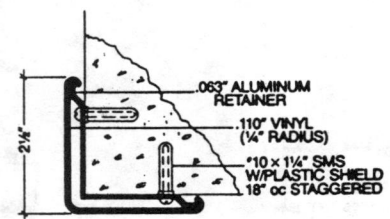

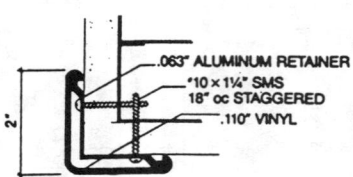

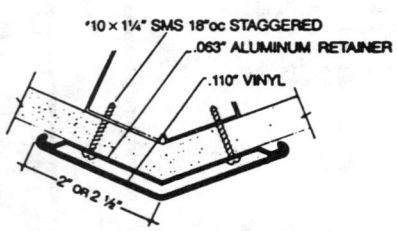

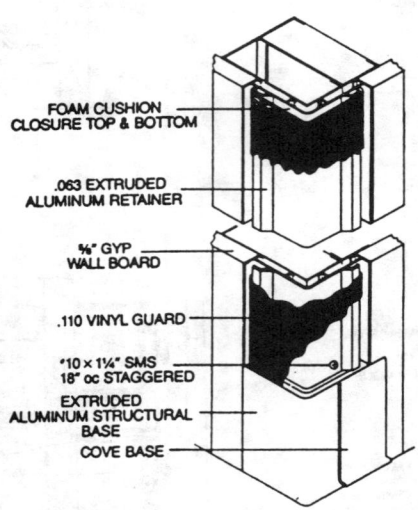

Ceiling height — flush mount

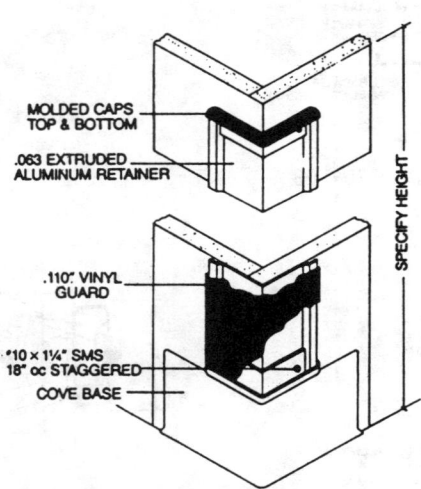

Wainscot installation — surface mount

VINYL HANDRAILS

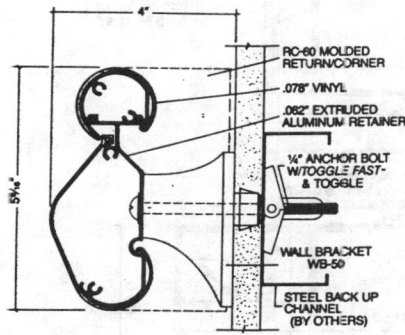

4"
5⅞₁₆"

RC-60 MOLDED RETURN/CORNER
.078" VINYL
.062" EXTRUDED ALUMINUM RETAINER
¼" ANCHOR BOLT W/TOGGLE FAST- & TOGGLE
WALL BRACKET WB-50
STEEL BACK UP CHANNEL (BY OTHERS)

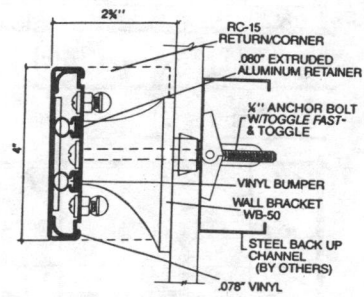

2¾"
4"

RC-15 RETURN/CORNER
.080" EXTRUDED ALUMINUM RETAINER
¼" ANCHOR BOLT W/TOGGLE FAST- & TOGGLE
VINYL BUMPER
WALL BRACKET WB-50
STEEL BACK UP CHANNEL (BY OTHERS)
.078" VINYL

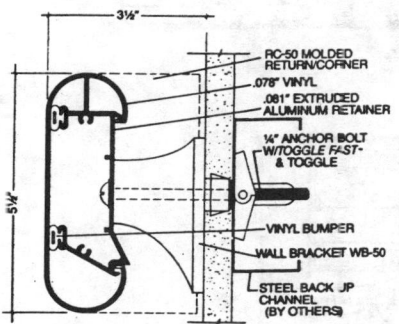

3½"
5¼"

RC-50 MOLDED RETURN/CORNER
.078" VINYL
.081" EXTRUDED ALUMINUM RETAINER
¼" ANCHOR BOLT W/TOGGLE FAST- & TOGGLE
VINYL BUMPER
WALL BRACKET WB-50
STEEL BACK UP CHANNEL (BY OTHERS)

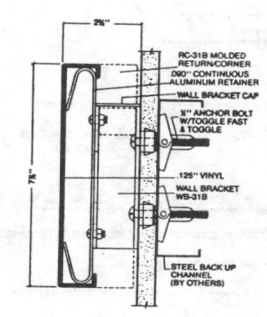

2⅝"
7⅞"

RC-31B MOLDED RETURN/CORNER
.090" CONTINUOUS ALUMINUM RETAINER
WALL BRACKET CAP
¼" ANCHOR BOLT W/TOGGLE FAST & TOGGLE
.125" VINYL
WALL BRACKET WB-31B
STEEL BACK UP CHANNEL (BY OTHERS)

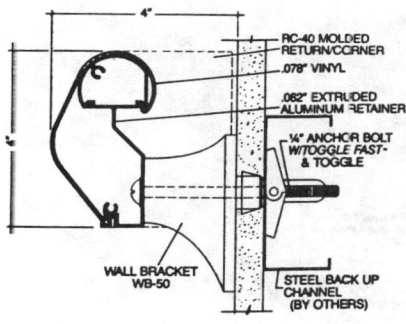

4"
4"

RC-40 MOLDED RETURN/CORNER
.078" VINYL
.062" EXTRUDED ALUMINUM RETAINER
¼" ANCHOR BOLT W/TOGGLE FAST- & TOGGLE
WALL BRACKET WB-50
STEEL BACK UP CHANNEL (BY OTHERS)

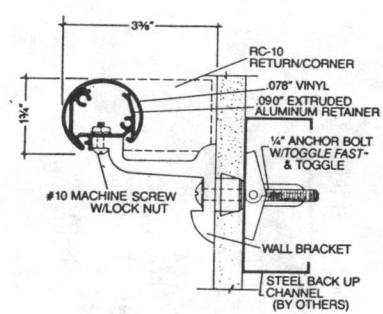

3⅜"
1¾"

RC-10 RETURN/CORNER
.078" VINYL
.090" EXTRUDED ALUMINUM RETAINER
¼" ANCHOR BOLT W/TOGGLE FAST- & TOGGLE
#10 MACHINE SCREW W/LOCK NUT
WALL BRACKET
STEEL BACK UP CHANNEL (BY OTHERS)

ALUMINUM HANDRAILS

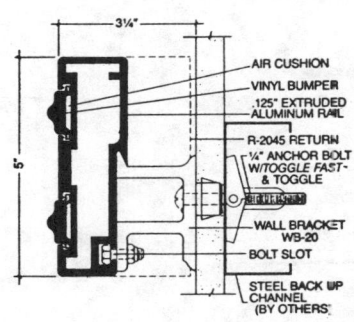

3¼"
5"

AIR CUSHION
VINYL BUMPER
.125" EXTRUDED ALUMINUM RAIL
R-2045 RETURN
¼" ANCHOR BOLT W/TOGGLE FAST- & TOGGLE
WALL BRACKET WB-20
BOLT SLOT
STEEL BACK UP CHANNEL (BY OTHERS)

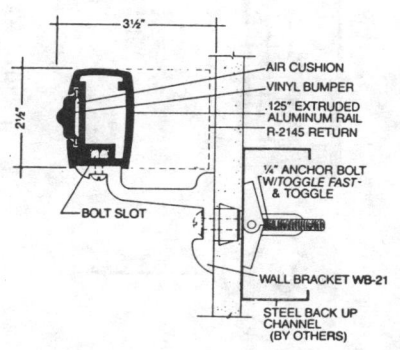

3½"
2½"

AIR CUSHION
VINYL BUMPER
.125" EXTRUDED ALUMINUM RAIL
R-2145 RETURN
¼" ANCHOR BOLT W/TOGGLE FAST- & TOGGLE
BOLT SLOT
WALL BRACKET WB-21
STEEL BACK UP CHANNEL (BY OTHERS)

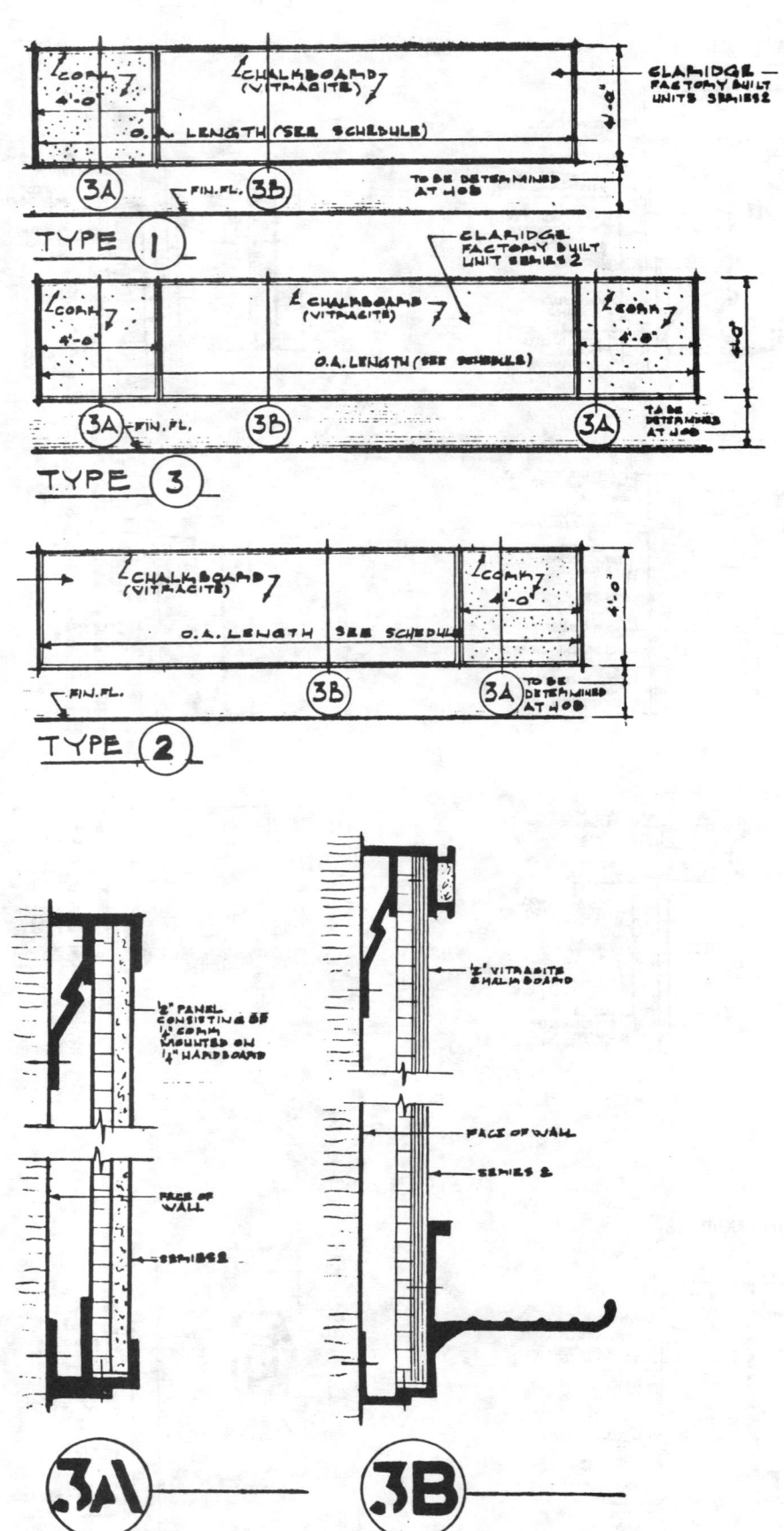

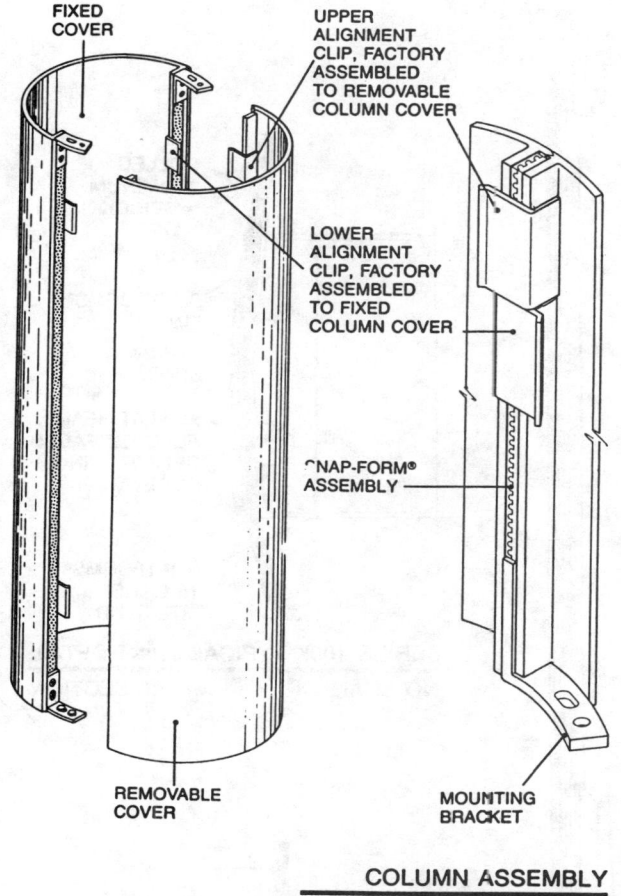

FIXED COVER

UPPER ALIGNMENT CLIP, FACTORY ASSEMBLED TO REMOVABLE COLUMN COVER

LOWER ALIGNMENT CLIP, FACTORY ASSEMBLED TO FIXED COLUMN COVER

SNAP-FORM® ASSEMBLY

REMOVABLE COVER

MOUNTING BRACKET

COLUMN ASSEMBLY
PERSPECTIVE

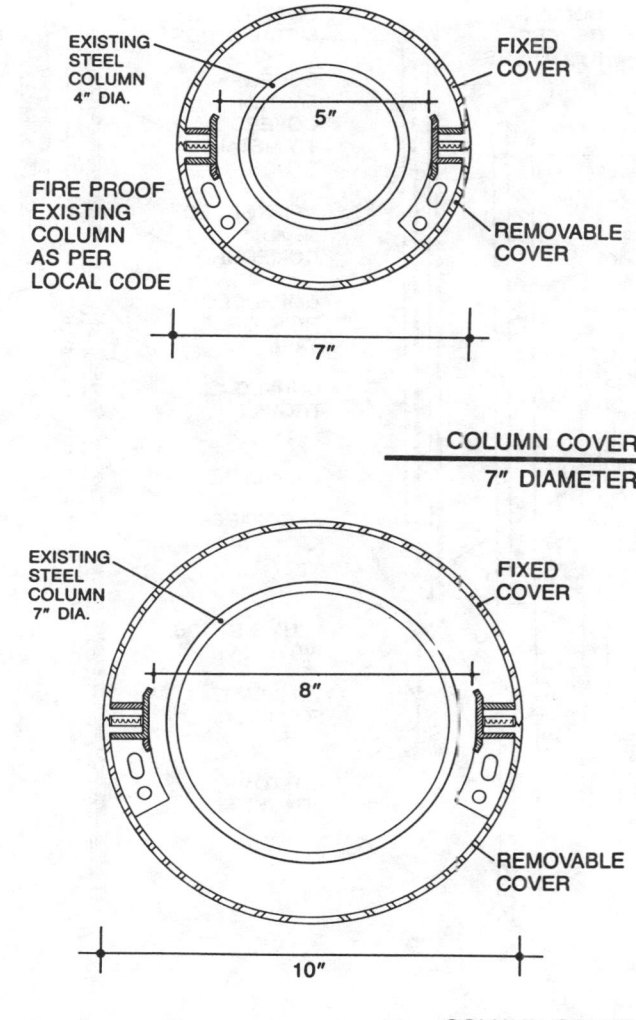

EXISTING STEEL COLUMN 4" DIA.

FIXED COVER

5"

FIRE PROOF EXISTING COLUMN AS PER LOCAL CODE

REMOVABLE COVER

7"

COLUMN COVER
7" DIAMETER

EXISTING STEEL COLUMN 7" DIA.

FIXED COVER

8"

REMOVABLE COVER

10"

COLUMN COVER
10" DIAMETER

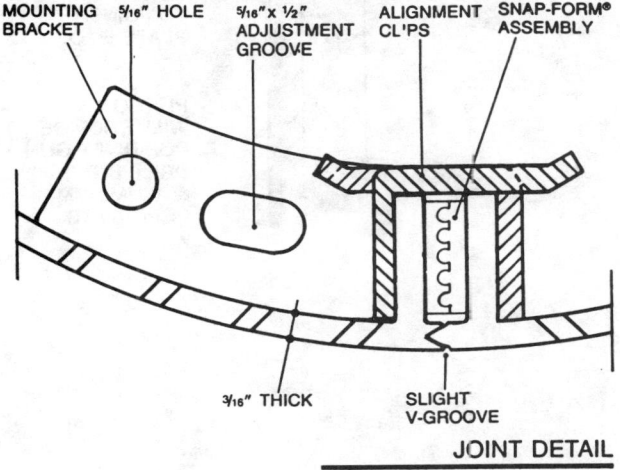

MOUNTING BRACKET

5/16" HOLE

5/16" x 1/2" ADJUSTMENT GROOVE

ALIGNMENT CL'PS

SNAP-FORM® ASSEMBLY

3/16" THICK

SLIGHT V-GROOVE

JOINT DETAIL
PLAN

ACCESSORIES

Column Covers

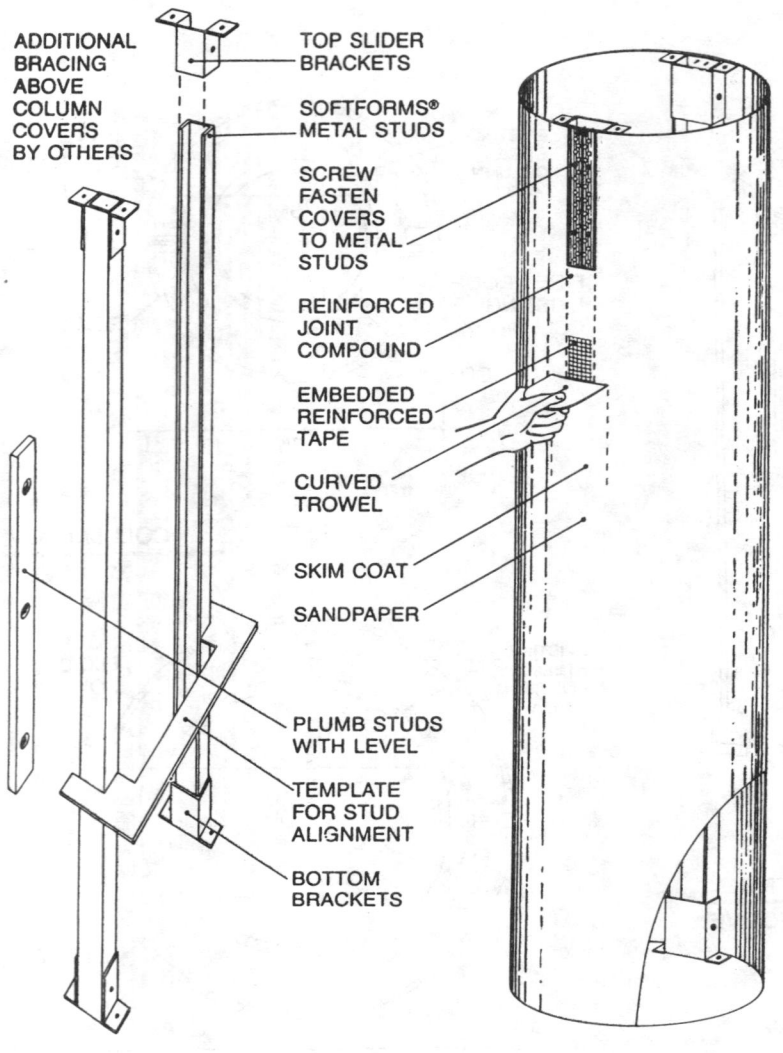

ADDITIONAL BRACING ABOVE COLUMN COVERS BY OTHERS

TOP SLIDER BRACKETS

SOFTFORMS® METAL STUDS

SCREW FASTEN COVERS TO METAL STUDS

REINFORCED JOINT COMPOUND

EMBEDDED REINFORCED TAPE

CURVED TROWEL

SKIM COAT

SANDPAPER

PLUMB STUDS WITH LEVEL

TEMPLATE FOR STUD ALIGNMENT

BOTTOM BRACKETS

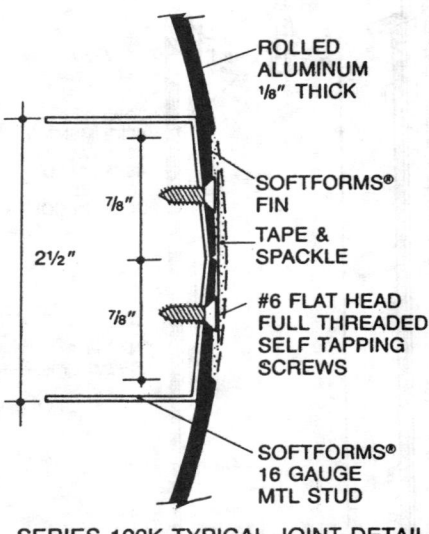

ROLLED ALUMINUM ⅛" THICK

SOFTFORMS® FIN

TAPE & SPACKLE

#6 FLAT HEAD FULL THREADED SELF TAPPING SCREWS

SOFTFORMS® 16 GAUGE MTL STUD

⅞"

2½"

⅞"

SERIES 100K TYPICAL JOINT DETAIL

NO SCALE   SECTION

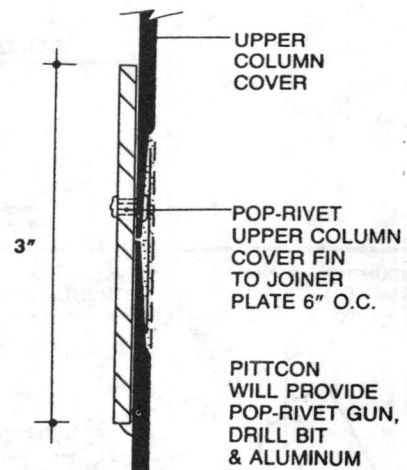

UPPER COLUMN COVER

POP-RIVET UPPER COLUMN COVER FIN TO JOINER PLATE 6" O.C.

PITTCON WILL PROVIDE POP-RIVET GUN, DRILL BIT & ALUMINUM POP-RIVETS

3"

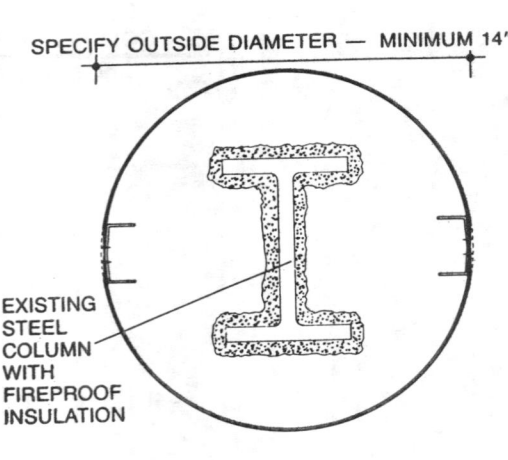

SPECIFY OUTSIDE DIAMETER — MINIMUM 14"

EXISTING STEEL COLUMN WITH FIREPROOF INSULATION

SOFTFORMS® COLUMN COVERS

SECTION

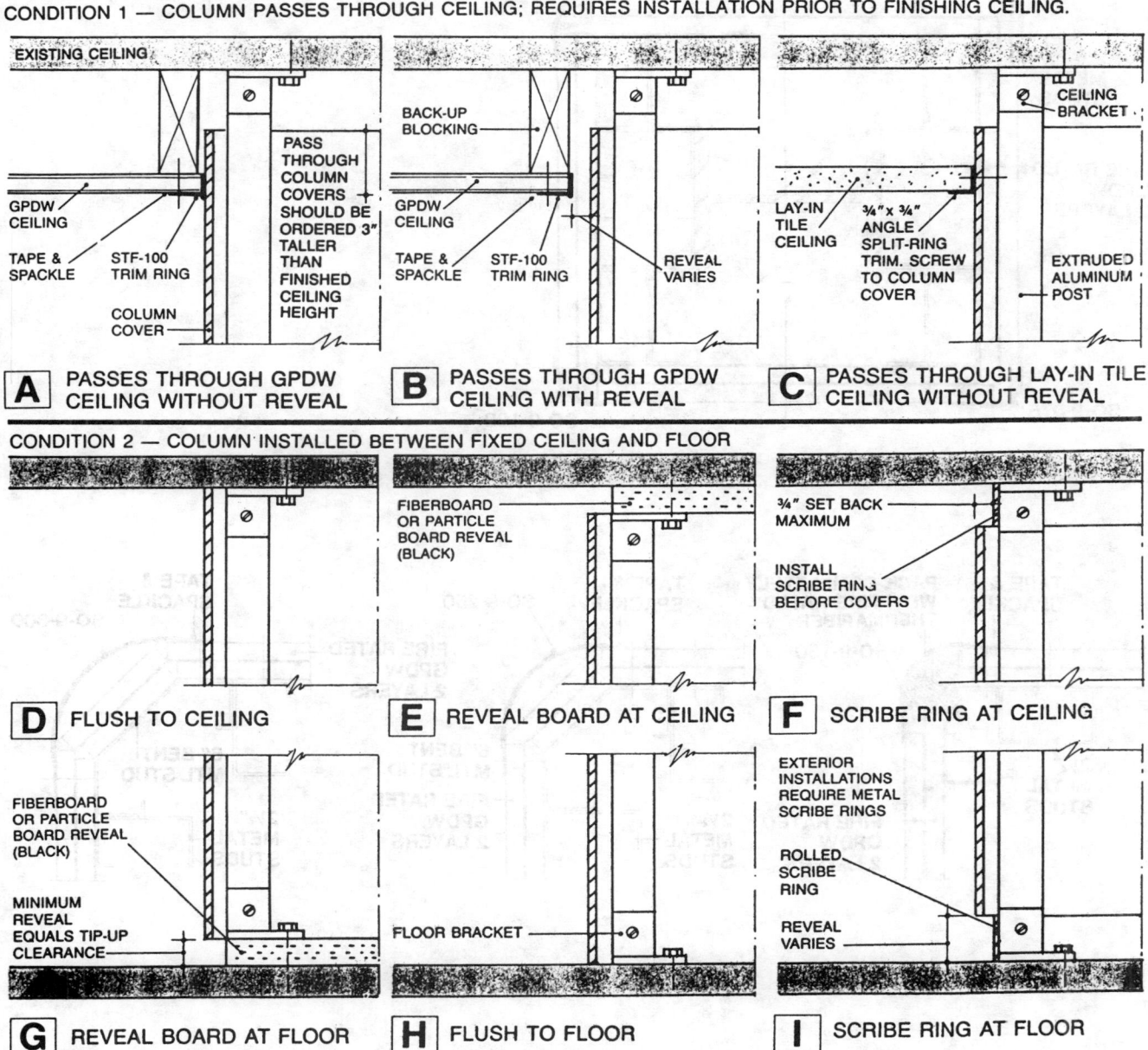

CONDITION 1 — COLUMN PASSES THROUGH CEILING; REQUIRES INSTALLATION PRIOR TO FINISHING CEILING.

EXISTING CEILING

GPDW CEILING

TAPE & SPACKLE

STF-100 TRIM RING

COLUMN COVER

PASS THROUGH COLUMN COVERS SHOULD BE ORDERED 3" TALLER THAN FINISHED CEILING HEIGHT

A PASSES THROUGH GPDW CEILING WITHOUT REVEAL

BACK-UP BLOCKING

GPDW CEILING

TAPE & SPACKLE

STF-100 TRIM RING

REVEAL VARIES

B PASSES THROUGH GPDW CEILING WITH REVEAL

CEILING BRACKET

LAY-IN TILE CEILING

¾" x ¾" ANGLE SPLIT-RING TRIM. SCREW TO COLUMN COVER

EXTRUDED ALUMINUM POST

C PASSES THROUGH LAY-IN TILE CEILING WITHOUT REVEAL

CONDITION 2 — COLUMN INSTALLED BETWEEN FIXED CEILING AND FLOOR

D FLUSH TO CEILING

FIBERBOARD OR PARTICLE BOARD REVEAL (BLACK)

E REVEAL BOARD AT CEILING

¾" SET BACK MAXIMUM

INSTALL SCRIBE RING BEFORE COVERS

F SCRIBE RING AT CEILING

FIBERBOARD OR PARTICLE BOARD REVEAL (BLACK)

MINIMUM REVEAL EQUALS TIP-UP CLEARANCE

G REVEAL BOARD AT FLOOR

FLOOR BRACKET

H FLUSH TO FLOOR

EXTERIOR INSTALLATIONS REQUIRE METAL SCRIBE RINGS

ROLLED SCRIBE RING

REVEAL VARIES

I SCRIBE RING AT FLOOR

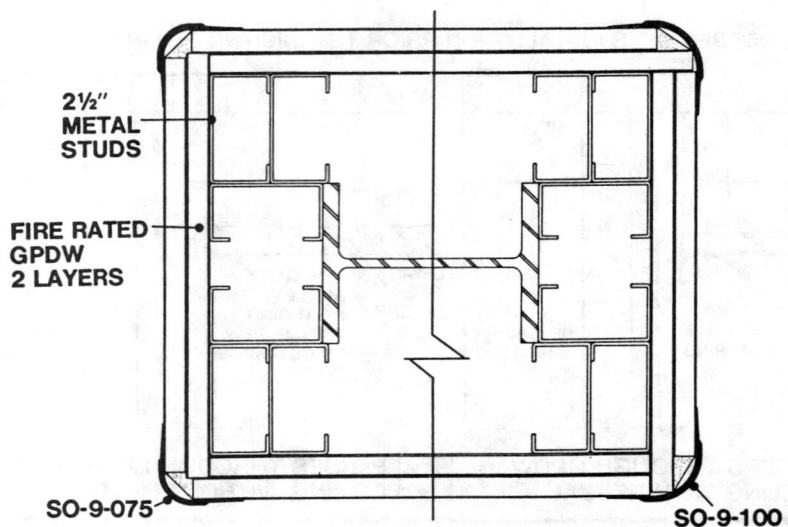

2½″ METAL STUDS

FIRE RATED GPDW 2 LAYERS

SO-9-075

SO-9-100

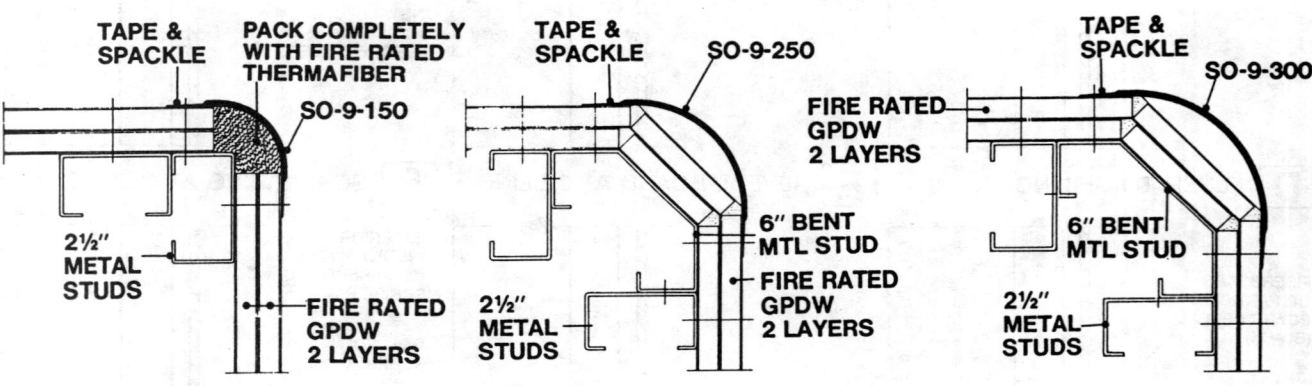

TAPE & SPACKLE

PACK COMPLETELY WITH FIRE RATED THERMAFIBER

SO-9-150

2½″ METAL STUDS

FIRE RATED GPDW 2 LAYERS

TAPE & SPACKLE

SO-9-250

2½″ METAL STUDS

6″ BENT MTL STUD

FIRE RATED GPDW 2 LAYERS

TAPE & SPACKLE

FIRE RATED GPDW 2 LAYERS

SO-9-300

6″ BENT MTL STUD

2½″ METAL STUDS

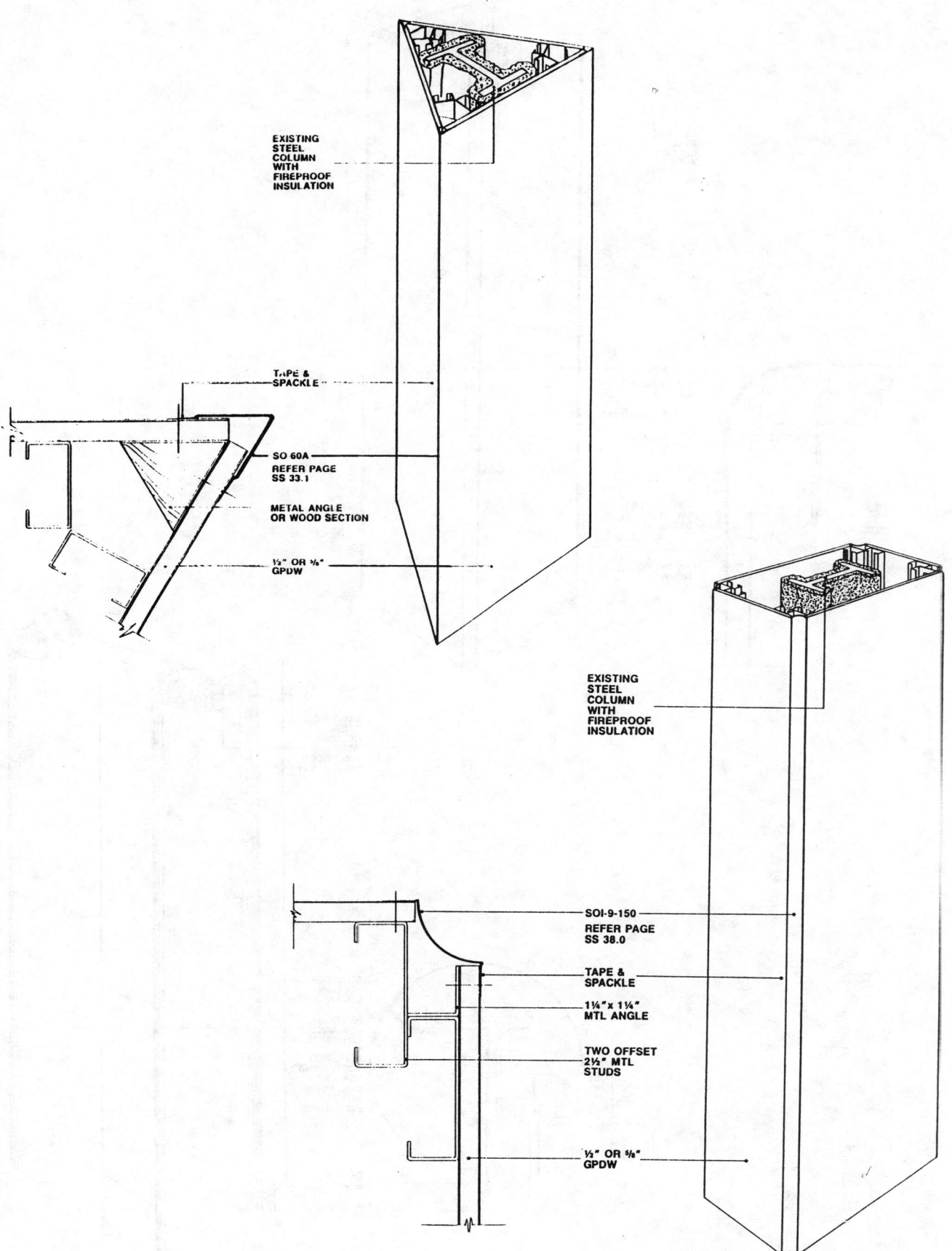

EXISTING
STEEL
COLUMN
WITH
FIREPROOF
INSULATION

TAPE &
SPACKLE

SO 60A
REFER PAGE
SS 33.1

METAL ANGLE
OR WOOD SECTION

½" OR ⅝"
GPDW

EXISTING
STEEL
COLUMN
WITH
FIREPROOF
INSULATION

SOI-9-150
REFER PAGE
SS 38.0

TAPE &
SPACKLE

1¼" x 1¼"
MTL ANGLE

TWO OFFSET
2½" MTL
STUDS

½" OR ⅝"
GPDW

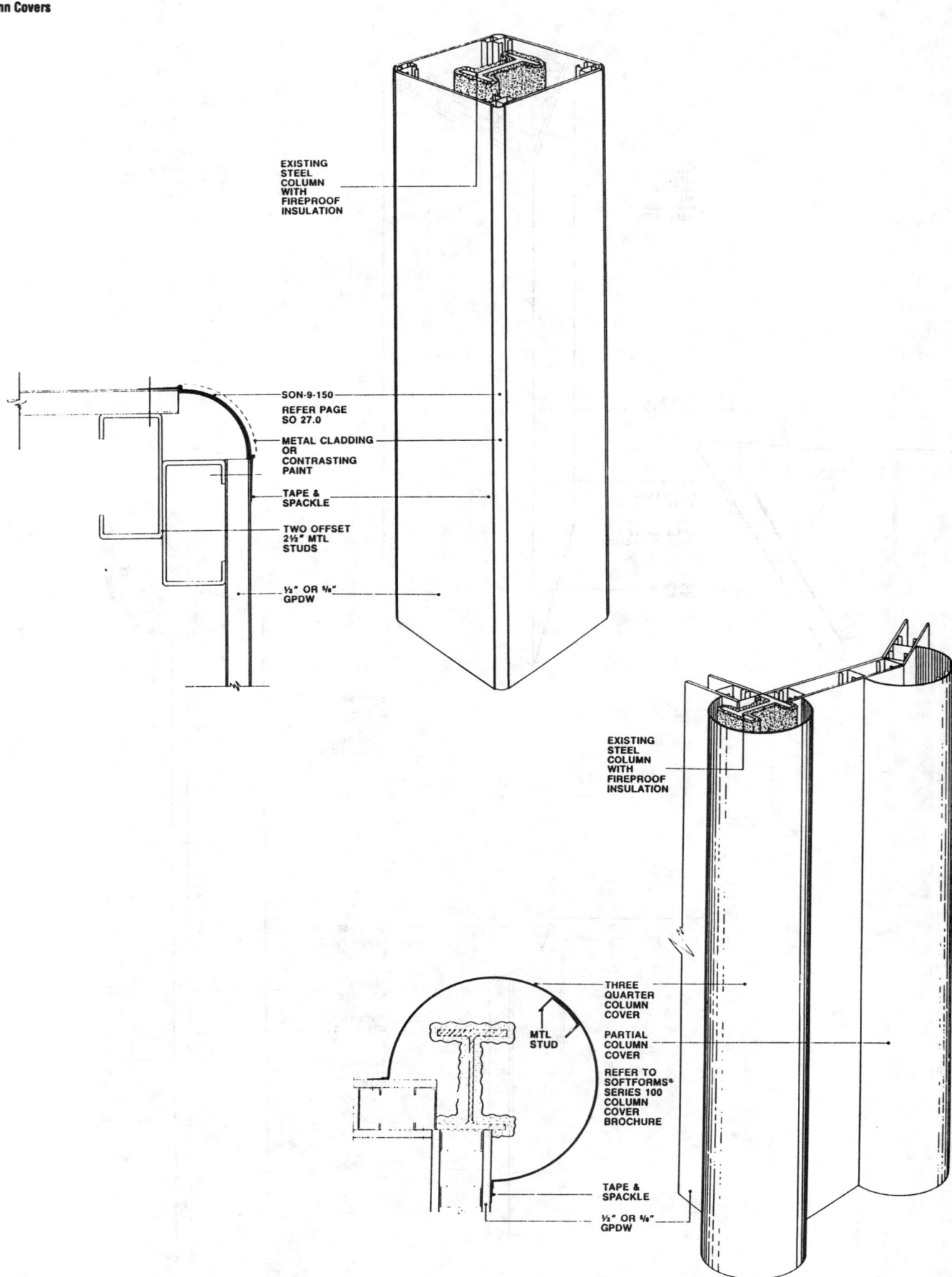

EXISTING
STEEL
COLUMN
WITH
FIREPROOF
INSULATION

SON-9-150
REFER PAGE
SO 27.0

METAL CLADDING
OR
CONTRASTING
PAINT

TAPE &
SPACKLE

TWO OFFSET
2½" MTL
STUDS

½" OR ⅝"
GPDW

EXISTING
STEEL
COLUMN
WITH
FIREPROOF
INSULATION

THREE
QUARTER
COLUMN
COVER

MTL
STUD

PARTIAL
COLUMN
COVER

REFER TO
SOFTFORMS®
SERIES 100
COLUMN
COVER
BROCHURE

TAPE &
SPACKLE

½" OR ⅝"
GPDW

3-ARM HIGH-TRAFFIC MANUAL AND ELECTRIC TURNSTILES

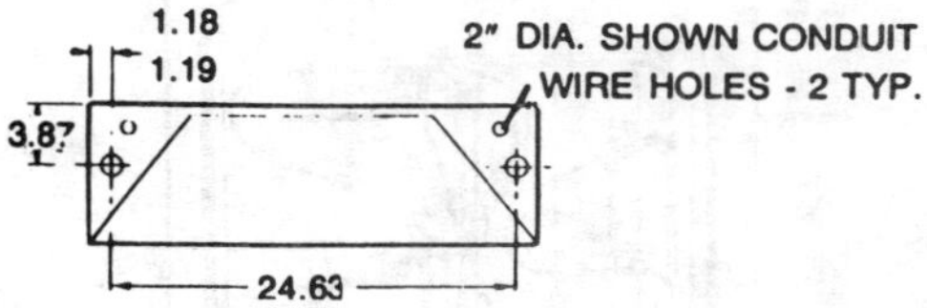

1.18
1.19
3.87

2″ DIA. SHOWN CONDUIT WIRE HOLES - 2 TYP.

24.63

Plan

A

A

FINISHED FLOOR

SEE DETAIL "B"

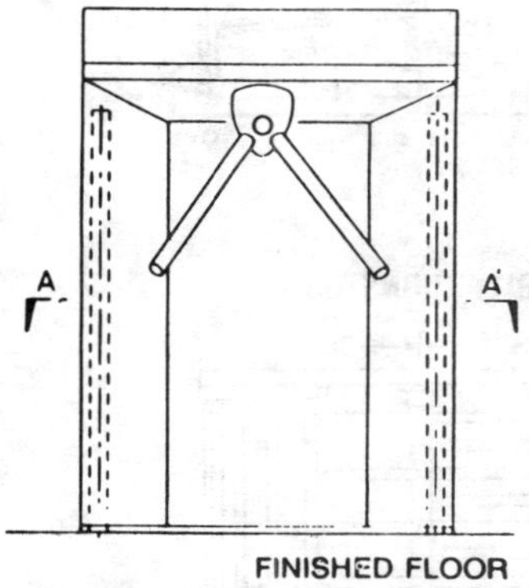

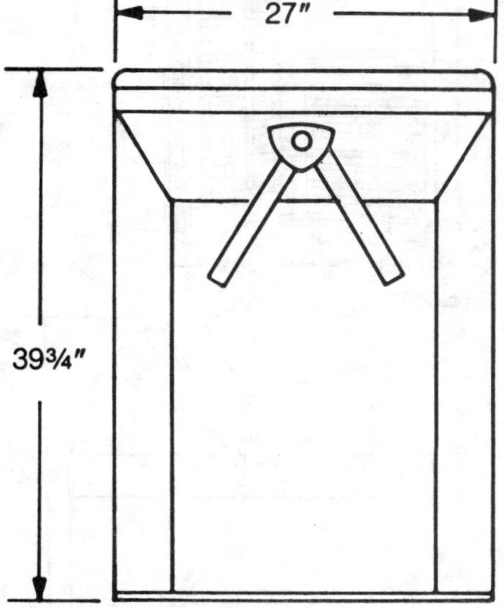

Side elevation

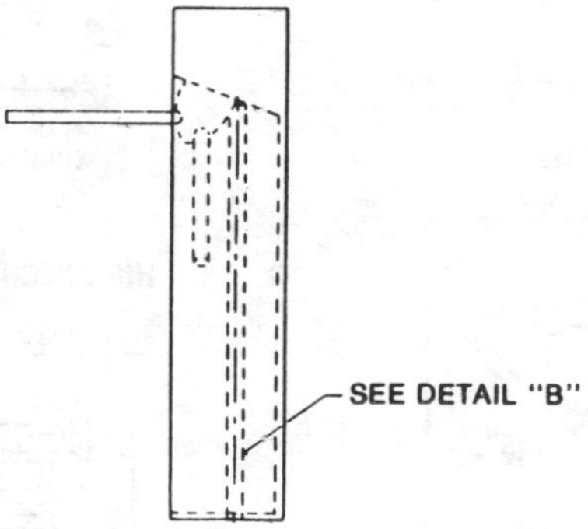

Front elevation

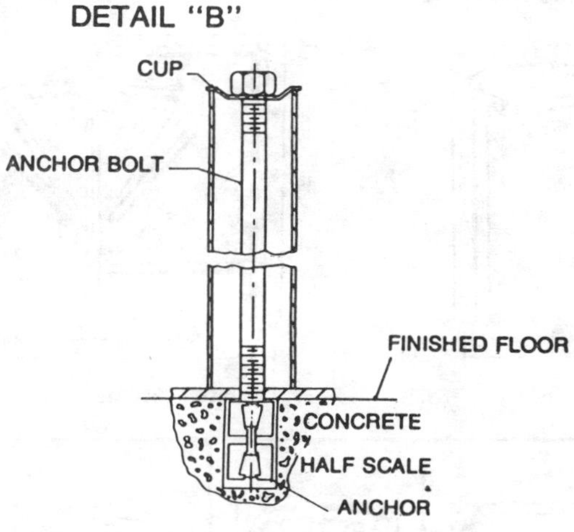

DETAIL "B"

CUP

ANCHOR BOLT

FINISHED FLOOR

CONCRETE

HALF SCALE

ANCHOR

Vertical section

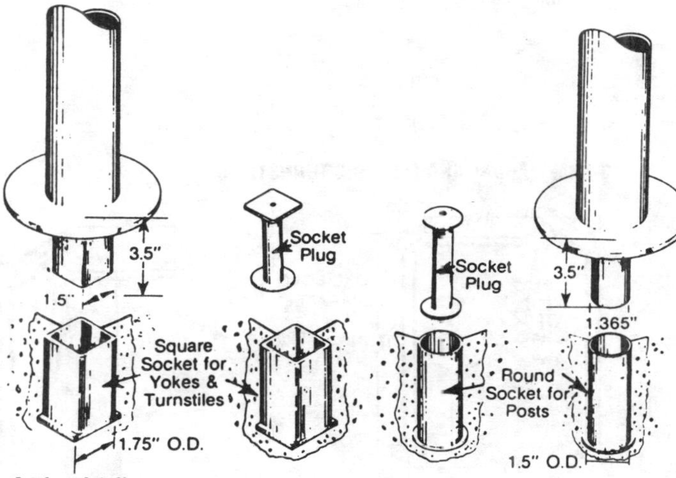

25″

15½″

Plan

3.5″

1.5″

Socket Plug

Socket Plug

3.5″

1.365″

Square Socket for Yokes & Turnstiles

1.75″ O.D.

Round Socket for Posts

1.5″ O.D.

Anchor details

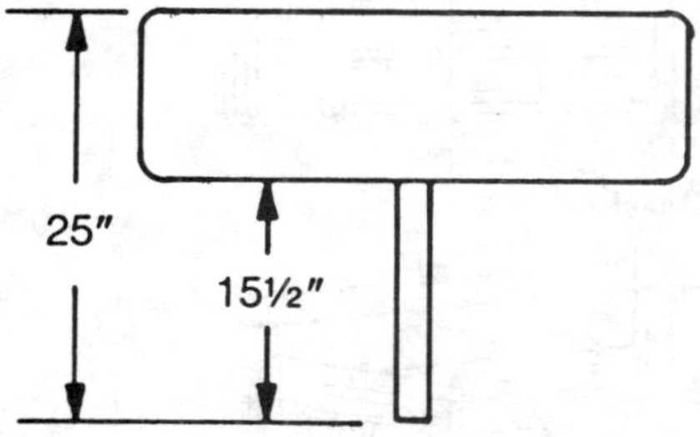

27″

39¾″

Side elevation

55°

90°

34″

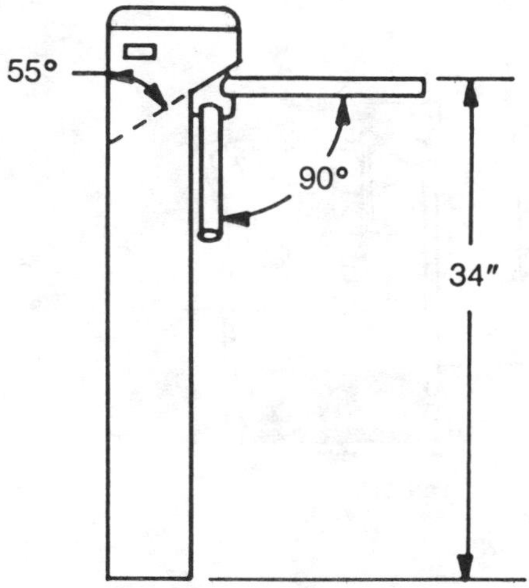

Front elevation

4-ARM MANUAL AND ELECTRIC TURNSTILES

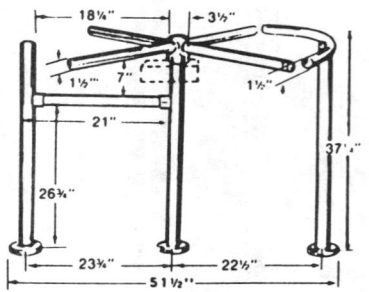

Basic customer security

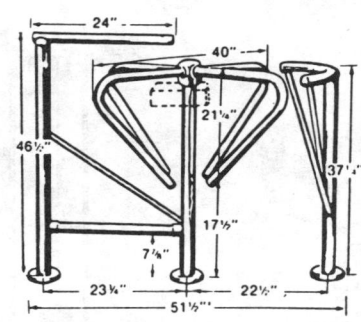

Enhanced security

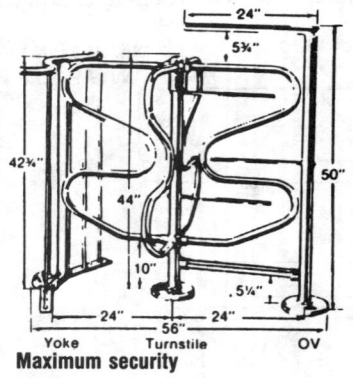

Yoke   Turnstile   OV

Maximum security

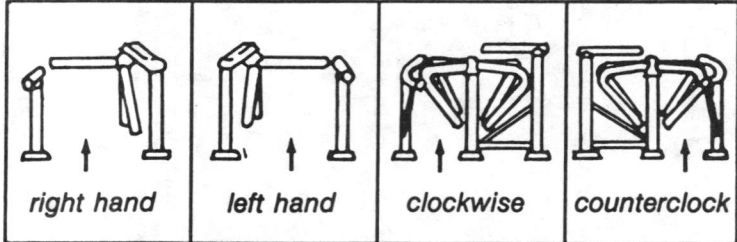

right hand   *left hand*   *clockwise*   *counterclock*

Rotation guide

HIGH-SECURITY TURNSTILES

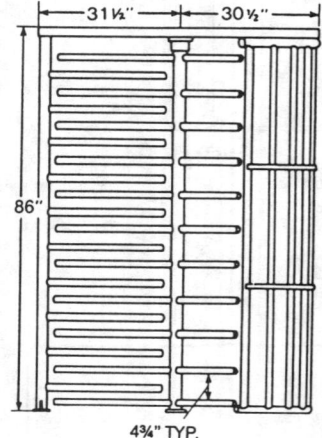

4¾" TYP.

Manual

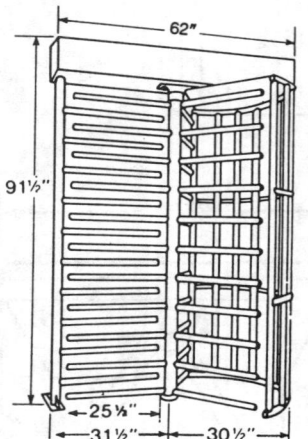

Electric

3-ARM MANUAL AND ELECTRIC TURNSTILES

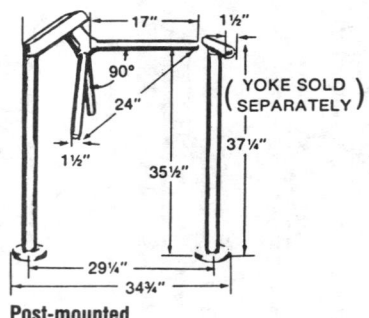

(YOKE SOLD SEPARATELY)

Post-mounted

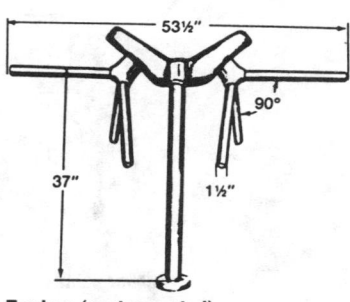

Tandem (post-mounted)

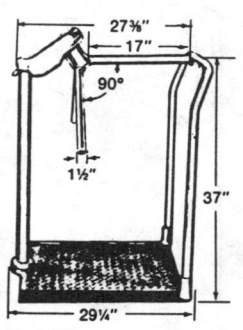

Wall-mounted   **Portable**

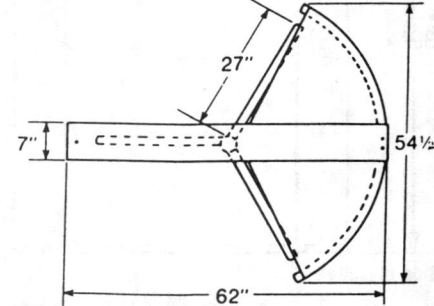

Plan of electric type configuration

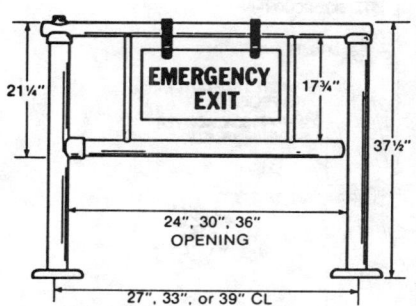

Emergency — quick release

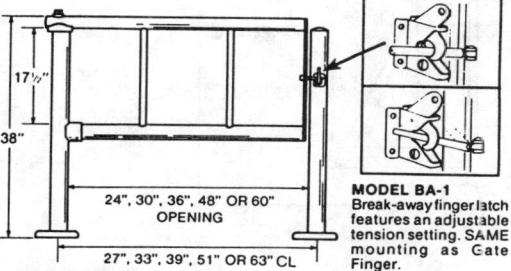

MODEL BA-1
Break-away finger latch
features an adjustable
tension setting. SAME
mounting as Gate
Finger.

Finger latch

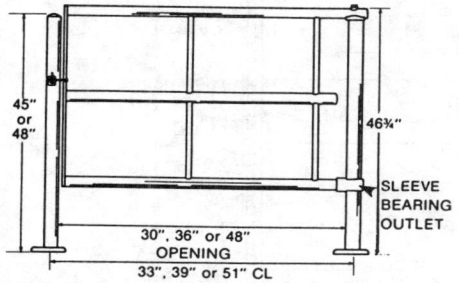

SLEEVE
BEARING
OUTLET

Triple rail — finger latch

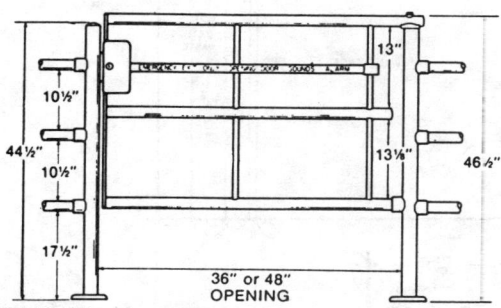

Triple rail — alarm system

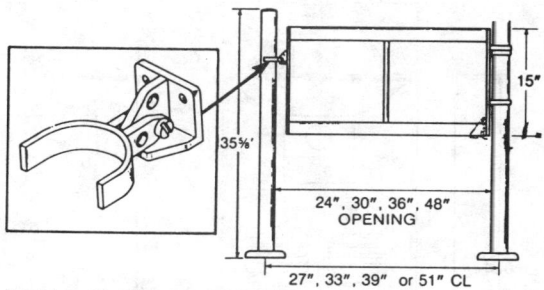

Double rail — flip sleeve latch

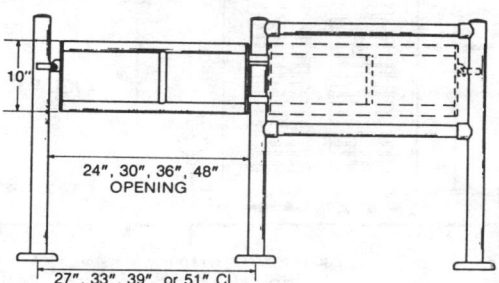

Double rail — aisle closure with flip sleeve latch

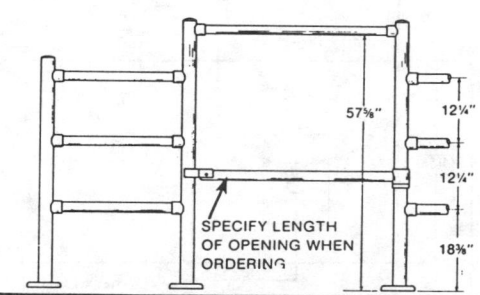

SPECIFY LENGTH
OF OPENING WHEN
ORDERING

Single rail — cart security with flip sleeve latch

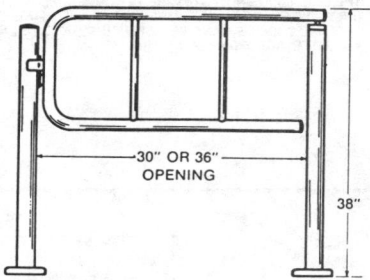

**Single section welded rail —
electrically controlled gate latch,
wheelchair access**

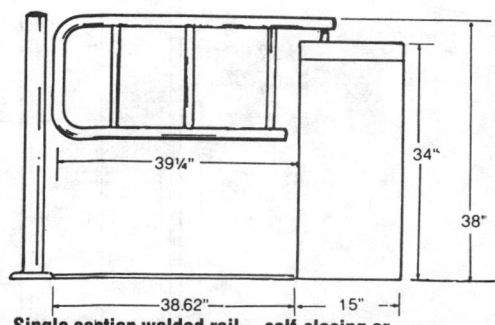

Double rail

**Single section welded rail — self-closing or
self-opening**

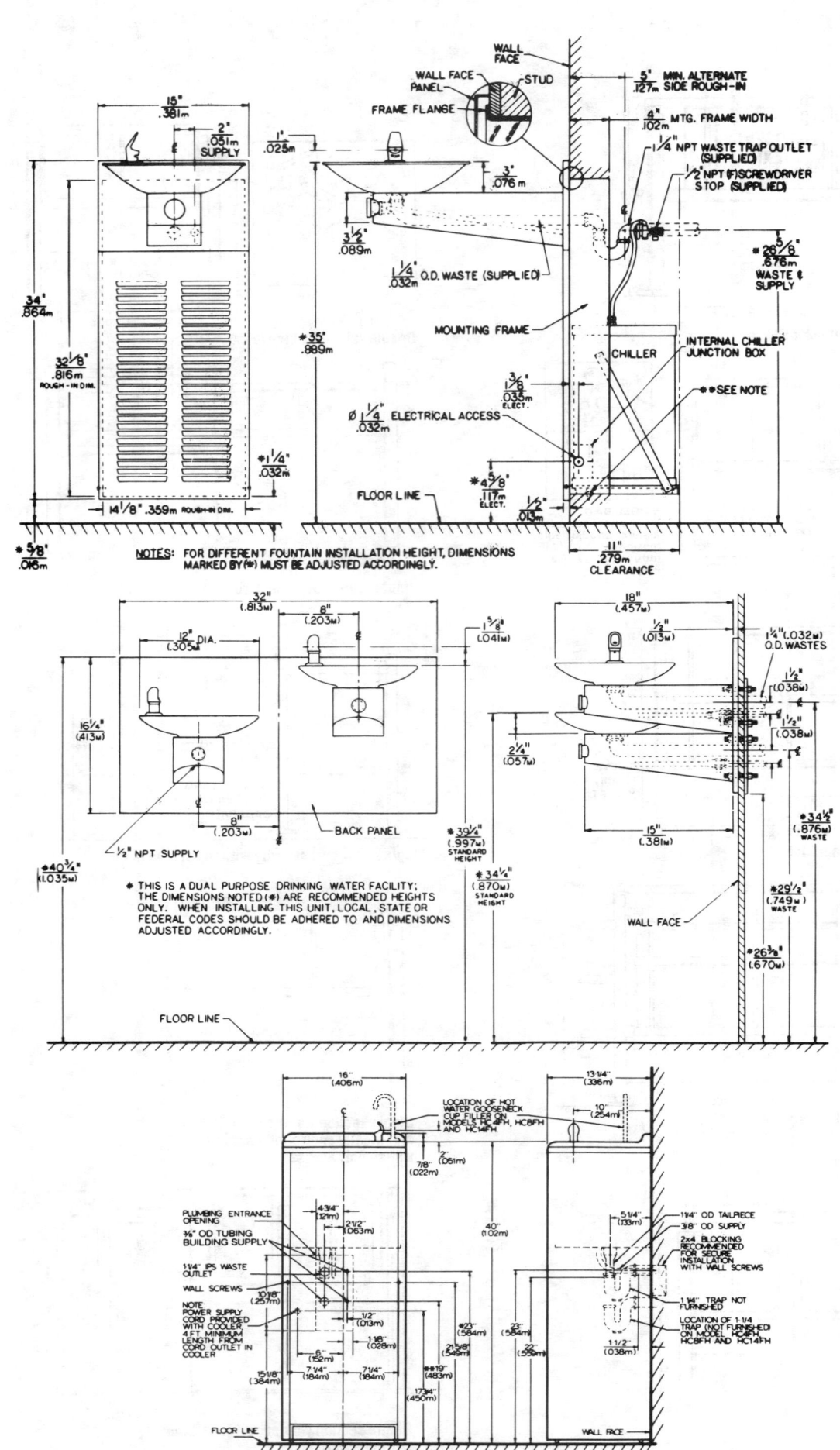

NOTES: FOR DIFFERENT FOUNTAIN INSTALLATION HEIGHT, DIMENSIONS MARKED BY (*) MUST BE ADJUSTED ACCORDINGLY.

* THIS IS A DUAL PURPOSE DRINKING WATER FACILITY; THE DIMENSIONS NOTED (*) ARE RECOMMENDED HEIGHTS ONLY. WHEN INSTALLING THIS UNIT, LOCAL, STATE OR FEDERAL CODES SHOULD BE ADHERED TO AND DIMENSIONS ADJUSTED ACCORDINGLY.

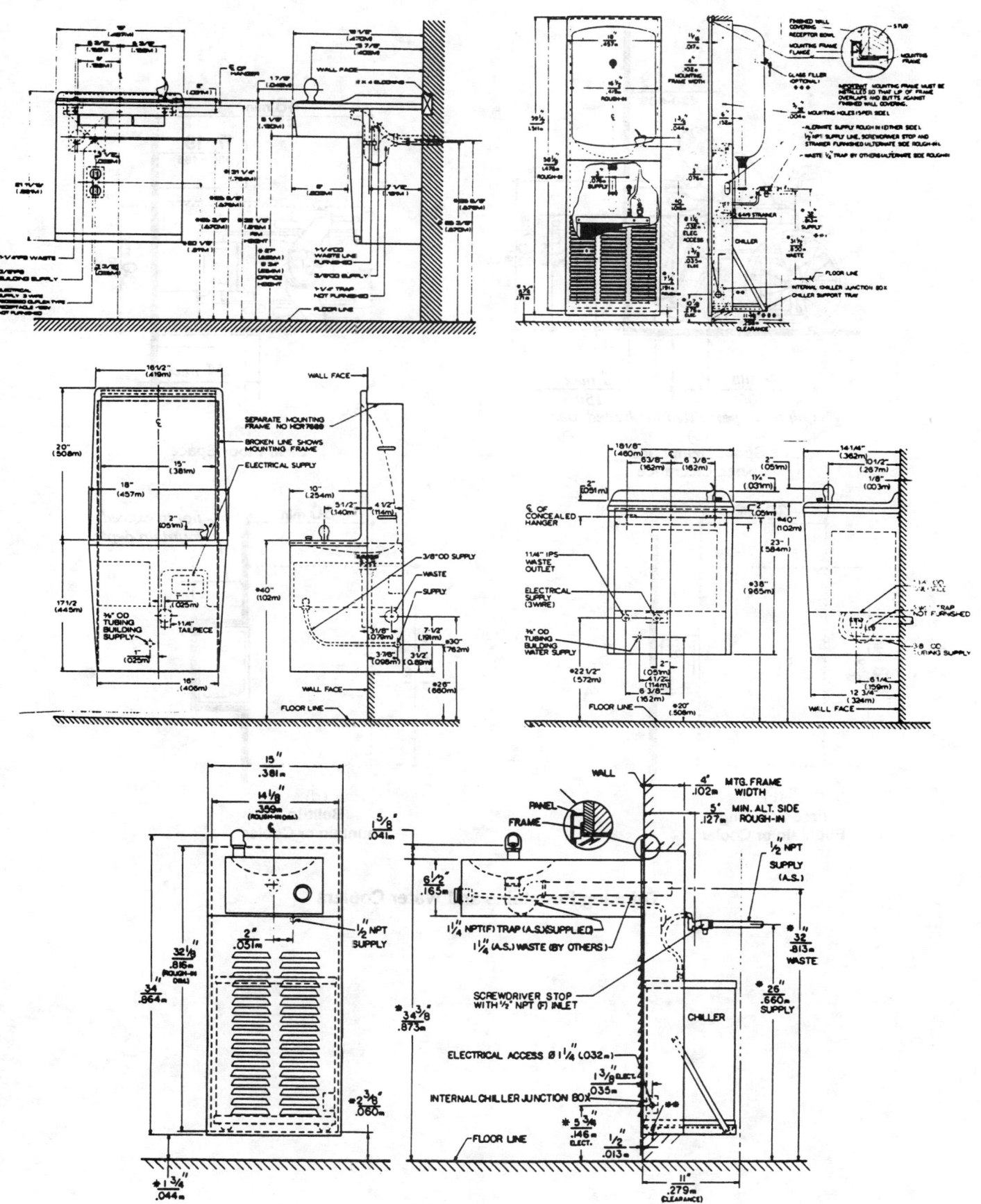

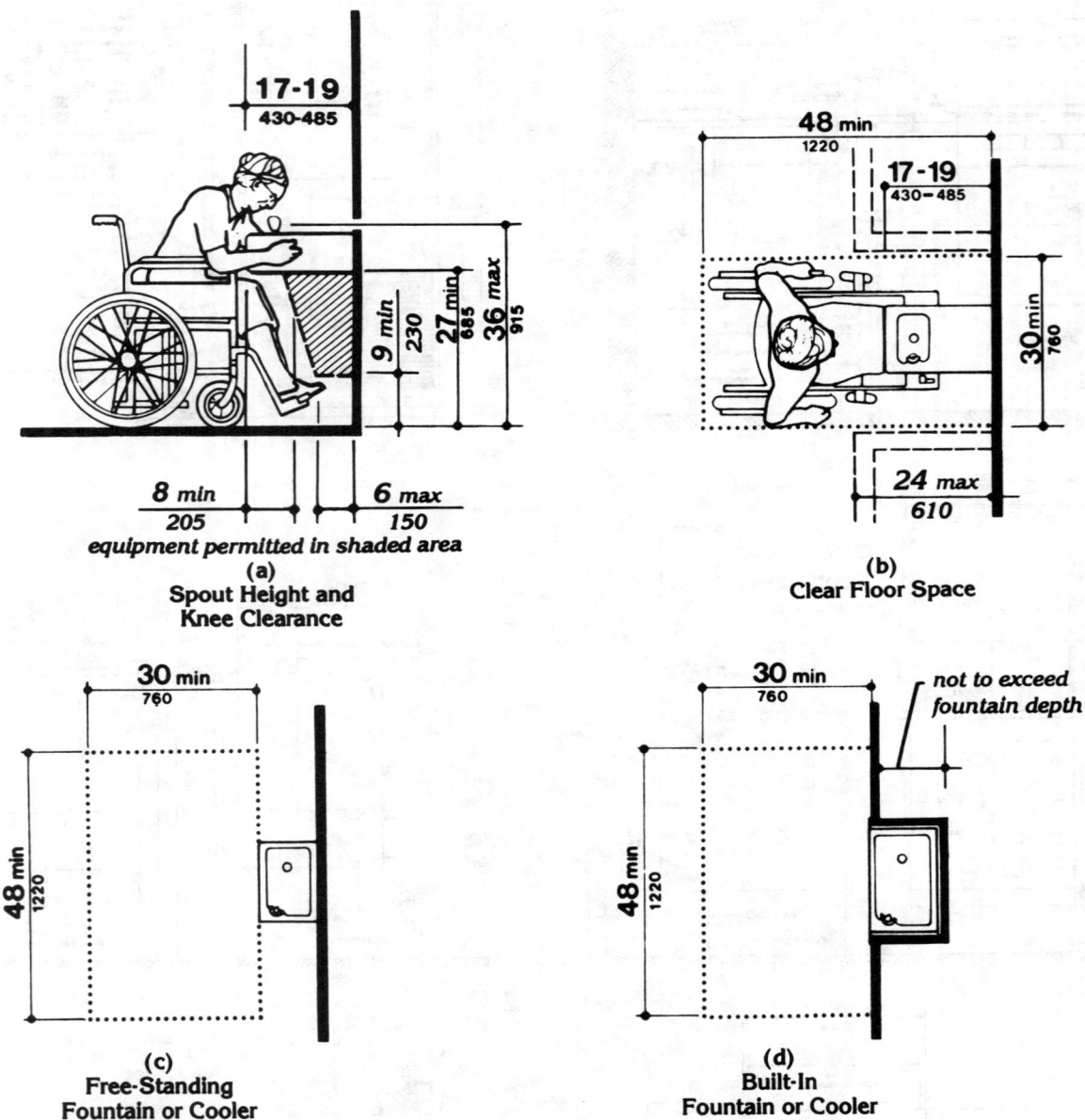

(a)
Spout Height and
Knee Clearance

equipment permitted in shaded area

(b)
Clear Floor Space

(c)
Free-Standing
Fountain or Cooler

(d)
Built-In
Fountain or Cooler

not to exceed
fountain depth

Drinking Fountains and Water Coolers

5

General Reference Data

General Reference Data

This section provides a variety of time-saving reference material in the form of tables, charts, formulas, and planning guidelines. Included are area requirements for the preliminary space planning of various building types and human factors data related to anthropometrics, space, and acoustics. Also included are a number of tables for determining carpet and wall covering yardage quantities. In addition, a series of tables dealing with electrical data provides typical amperage ratings for office and electronic equipment and for residential appliances. Still other tables and charts contain mathematical data relative to functions of numbers, metric system conversions, and areas of plane figures.

SPACE PLANNING
Area Requirements By Use

The first portion of Table 1 shows some of the planning guidelines for several types of office use. Of course, usable areas per employee vary greatly depending on the type of work performed and types of support space and common areas required, such as file rooms, data processing, conference rooms, and so forth.

Rules of Thumb

Office use: 125 to 150 net sq. ft. area per person.

Retail space: 30 net sq. ft. per person on ground floor; 50 net sq. ft. per person on upper floors.

Classrooms: 20 net sq. ft. per pupil.

TABLE 1 Space Planning By Building Type

Building/Use Type	Sq. Ft. per Unit		Area Basis
Office buildings, all types	100–250	net	usable
Work station, minimum clerical	40	person	usable
Work station, clerical with VDT	55	person	usable
Work station, with visitor space	65	person	usable
Work station, supervisor	100	person	usable
Manager, private office	150–225	person	usable
Law firm	450	attorney	total usable
Law firm library	25–30	attorney	usable
Law firm conference	25–30	attorney	usable
Insurance company, branch	100 average	work station	usable
Insurance company, branch Total, includes common areas and circulation	155–165	employee	total usable
Energy company	255	employee	total usable
Conference and dining rooms	15	person	net

Restaurants			
Dining areas (includes dining room but not waiting, coat room, etc.)			
Banquet	10–15	seat	net
Cafeteria, college	12–15	seat	net
Cafeteria, commercial	16–18	seat	net
Counter service	18–20	seat	net
Table service, hotel or restaurant	15–18	seat	net
Table service, minimum	11–14	seat	net

Kitchens

Type	< 200	200–400	400–800	800–1300
		Meals per Hour		
Cafeterias	7.5–5.0	5.0–4.0	4.0–3.5	3.5–3.0
Hotels	18.0–4.0	7.5–3.0	6.0–3.0	4.0–3.0
Restaurants	7.0–4.0	5.0–3.6	5.0–3.6	5.0–3.0
Serving and service areas				
Cafeterias		6	person	net
Restaurants		5	person	net
Add to totals space for food storage, administration, waiting.				

TABLE 1   Space Planning By Building Type *(Continued)*

Building/Use Type	Sq. Ft. per Unit		Area Basis
Night clubs	25	person	net
Bars	18	person	net
Hotel			
1.5 persons per room without extensive conferencing facilities	550–600	room	gross
Retail			
Large stores	30–50	person	net
Cultural			
Public library			
Stack space	0.08	bound vols.	net
Reading rooms	20–35	user	net
Staff space	100	staff person	net
Overall	50	person	net
Museums, exhibition areas	15	person	net
Theater and assembly areas			
Seating area, fixed seats	7.5	seat	net
Seating, movable seating	15	seat	net
Theaters, fixed seating (Does not include stage, lobby, etc.)	8–12	seat	net
Stage/backstage Performing arts theater	100%	seating area	
Lobbies	3	person	net
Lobbies	30%	seating area	
Educational			
Elementary			
The following figures are based on the number of students in the particular space listed.			
Small classrooms	20–30	student	net
Library	40	student	net
Art room	40	student	net
Secondary			
The following figures are based on the number of students in the particular space listed.			
Cafeteria	12–15	student	1/3 of total
Small classrooms	20–25	student	net
Large classrooms	15	student	net
Art classrooms	50–60	student	net
Home economics	50–60	student	net
Laboratory classrooms	55–70	student	net
Library	40	student	20% of total
Music rooms	30–35	student	net
Physical education	125	student	net
Shops/vocational rooms small	50	student	net
Shops/vocational rooms wood, metal, etc.	120–140	student	net
University			
Classrooms, small	20	student	net
Classrooms, large	12–15	student	net

TABLE 1   Space Planning By Building Type *(Continued)*

Building/Use Type	Sq. Ft. per Unit		Area Basis
Lecture halls	9–12	seat	net
Dormitory, no dining	160	student	net
Dormitory, no dining	210–240	student	gross
Dormitory, dining	235–260	student	gross
Food service, table service	18–26	seat	net, all areas
Food service, cafeteria	14–19	seat	net, all areas
Laboratories	34–45	student	net
Laboratory storage	6–10	student	net
Library			
Book stacks, less than 300,000 volumes	0.10	volume	net
Book stacks, 300,000– 1,000,000 volumes	0.7–0.8	volume	net
Book stacks, over 1,000,000 volumes	0.5	volume	net
Reading, study	25–35	station	net
(provide stations equal to 25% to 40% of student population):			
	6.25–10	student	net
Total service space	25%	of reading	net

Residential

Apartments	250	Occupant	net
Senior citizen housing			
Living units	300–380	1-person unit	net
Living units	350–425	2-person unit	net
Living units	400–600	unit	gross
Dining, lounge, lobby, administration, etc.	33%–45% of living unit space, gross area		

Health Care Facilities

General hospital	1000	bed	gross
Medical center	1100	bed	gross

The above figures are based on *usable* square footage, which in the language of leasing includes the area within the boundaries of the leased space. Most building owners lease space based on the *rentable* area, which includes a tenant's prorated share of common areas such as toilet rooms, elevator lobby, public corridors, and so on. The multiplying figure can be obtained from the building owner, or a figure of 1.1 to 1.15 can be used as an estimated multiplying factor.

TABLE 2   Gross to Net Ratios for Common Building Types

Building Type	Multiplying Factor	Building Type	Multiplying Factor
Office	1.25–1.35	Library reading space	1.5
Retail	1.35	Museum	1.2
Bank	1.4	Theater	1.3–1.7
Restaurant, table service	1.4–1.5	School, classroom	1.5–1.65
Restaurant, cafeteria	1.5	School, dormitory	1.5–1.8
Bars, nightclubs	1.3–1.4	School, laboratory	1.7
Hotel	1.4–1.6	School, gymnasium	1.4–1.45
Public library	1.25–1.3	Apartment	1.25–1.5
Library stack space	1.1–1.3	Hospital	1.5–1.85

LIBRARY PLANNING

Libraries represent a unique building type in that a majority of space is devoted to housing books and not people. The number of volumes to be housed becomes the primary planning parameter, rather than numbers of people. For a detailed layout of book stacks, you can use the figures given in Table 3. For preliminary planning, the following general guidelines are useful.

Rules of Thumb

Public library: 12–18½ volumes per sq. ft.

Law library: 5–7 volumes per sq. ft.

To stack space, add a "configuration loss" of from 6% to 20%, to account for inefficiencies in stack layout.

Minimum aisle between open stacks: 3 ft. 0 in.

Staff spaces: 100 net sq. ft. per person.

Reading room seating: 15–35 sq. ft. per person plus 6% configuration loss.

Net/gross multiplier: 1.25.

Maximum of 15,000–20,000 sq. ft. per floor.

Example
A 100,000 volume public library is planned. How much space should be devoted to open stacks?

Plan about 15 volumes per sq. ft. (100,000 ÷ 15 = 6667 sq. ft.). Add a configuration loss of 10%, to give a total area of 6667 + 667, or 7333 sq. ft. of stack space.

TABLE 3   Library Shelving — Volumes per Linear Foot of Shelf Based on Subject

(Standard stack section 3 ft wide x 7½ ft high with 7 shelves)

Subject	Volumes per foot of shelf	Volumes per single face section
Art (excluding oversize)	7	147
Circulating, nonfiction	8	168
Economics	8	168
Fiction	8	168
General literature	7	147
History	7	147
Law	4	84
Medical	5	105
Periodicals, bound	5	105
Public documents	5	105
Technical and scientific	6	126
Average for overall estimating		125

These figures should be reduced by at least 10% to avoid overcrowding and to allow for expansion.

APPROPRIATENESS

It is essential, due to the many variables involved, that the data selected be appropriate to the user of the space or furniture to be designed. It becomes necessary, therefore, for the intended user population to be properly defined in terms of such factors as age, sex, occupation, and ethnicity. If the user is an individual, or constitutes a very small group, it may, in certain situations, be feasible to develop your own primary anthropometric data by actually having individual body measurements taken. Surely, if one is prepared to take the time to be fitted for a dress or a suit, one should be willing to spend the time to be fitted for an interior environment or components of that environment, particularly since, in most cases, the latter will reflect a far greater financial investment. The measurements, in the event individual data are generated, should, however, be taken with proper instruments by a trained observer. In situations where specific body dimensions or other data for a particular user population are unavailable, and both time and funds prevent undertaking sophisticated studies, an engineering anthropometrist can be consulted to discuss the statistical methods of obtaining the necessary information.

"AVERAGE MAN" FALLACY

As suggested previously, a very serious error in the application of data is to assume that the 50th percentile dimensions represent the measurements of an "average man" and to create a design to accommodate 50th percentile data. The fallacy in such an assumption is that by prior definition 50 percent of the group may suffer. There simply is no "average man." Depending on the nature of the design problem, the design should usually be conceived to accommodate the 5th or the 95th percentile, so that the greatest portion of the population is served.

Dr. H.T.E. Hertzberg, one of the country's most distinguished research physical anthropologists, in discussing the so-called average man, indicated, "there is really no such thing as an 'average' man or woman. There are men who are average in weight, or in stature, or in sitting height, but the men who are average in two dimensions constitute only about 7 percent of the population; those in three, only about 3 percent; those in four, less than 2 percent. There are no men average in as few as 10 dimensions. Therefore, the concept of the 'average' man is fundamentally incorrect, because no such creature exists. Work places to be efficient should be designed according to the measured range of body size."

REACH, CLEARANCE, AND ADJUSTABILITY

The selection of appropriate anthropometric data is based on the nature of the particular design problem under consideration. If the design requires the user to reach from a seated or standing position, the 5th percentile data should be utilized. Such data for arm reach indicates that 5 percent of the population would have an arm reach of short (or shorter) dimension, while 95 percent of the population, the overwhelming majority, would have longer arm reaches. If the design

in a reach situation can accommodate the user with the shortest arm reach, obviously it will function for the users with longer reaches as well; it is equally obvious that the opposite is not true, as shown in Fig. 1(a).

In designs where clearance is the primary consideration, the larger or 95th percentile data should be used. The logic is simple. If the design will allow adequate clearance for the users with the largest body size, it would also allow clearance for those users with smaller body size. Here, too, it can be seen from Fig. 1(b) that the opposite is not true.

In other situations it may be desirable to

provide the design with a built-in adjustment capability. Certain chair types, adjustable shelves, etc., are examples of such. The range of adjustment should be based on the anthropometrics of the user, the nature of the task, and the physical or mechanical limitations involved. The range should allow the design to accommodate at least 90 percent of the user population involved, or more.

It should be noted that all the foregoing examples were used primarily to illustrate the basic logic underlying the selection of the body dimensions involved and the particular percentiles to be accommodated. Wherever possible, however, it is naturally more desir-

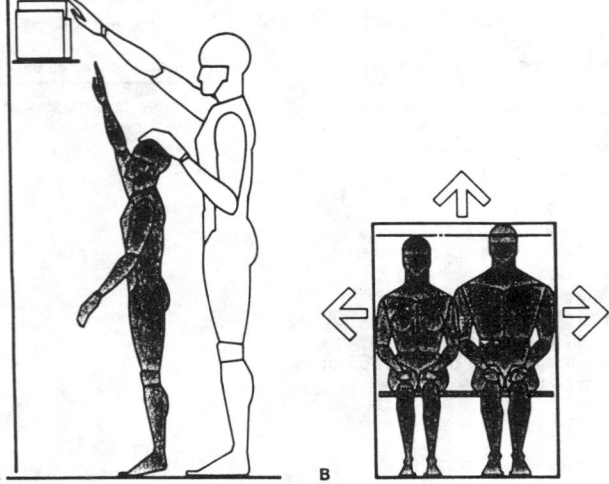

Fig. 1 *(a)* **People of smaller body dimensions and, correspondingly, the lower-range percentile data should be used to establish dimensions where reach is the determining factor.** *(b)* **Larger-size people and, correspondingly, the high percentile range data should be used in establishing clearance dimensions.**

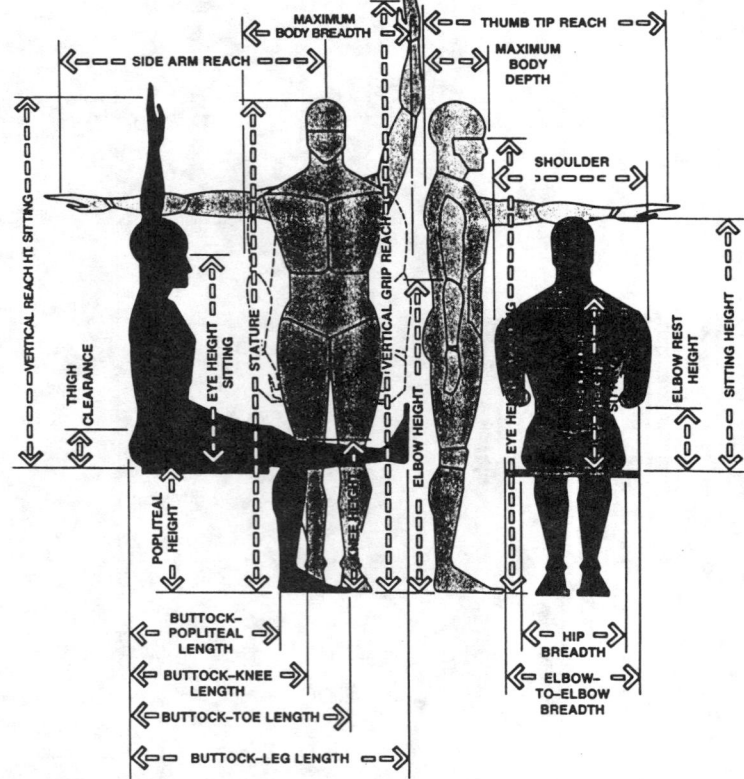

Fig. 2   Body measurements of most use to the designer of interior spaces.

Adult Male and Female Miscellaneous Structural Body Dimensions in Inches and Centimeters by Age and Selected Percentiles

		A		B		C		D		E		F		G	
		in	cm	in	cm	in	cm	in	cm	in	cm	in	cm	in	cm
95	MEN	36.2	91.9	47.3	120.1	68.6	174.2	20.7	52.6	27.3	69.3	37.0	94.0	33.9	86.1
	WOMEN	32.0	81.3	43.6	110.7	64.1	162.8	17.0	43.2	24.6	62.5	37.0	94.0	31.7	80.5
5	MEN	30.8	78.2	41.3	104.9	60.8	154.4	17.4	44.2	23.7	60.2	32.0	81.3	30.0	76.2
	WOMEN	26.8	68.1	38.6	98.0	56.3	143.0	14.9	37.8	21.2	53.8	27.0	68.6	28.1	71.4

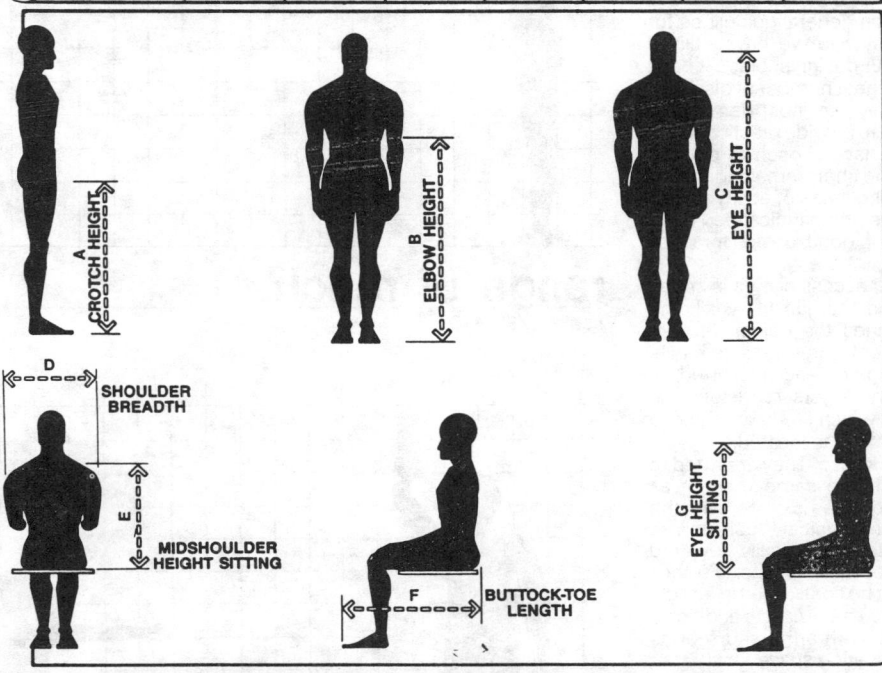

Adult Male and Female Functional Body Dimensions in Inches and Centimeters by Age, Sex, and Selected Percentiles

		A		B		C		D		E		F	
		in	cm	in	cm	in	cm	in	cm	in	cm	in	cm
95	MEN	38.3	97.3	46.1	117.1	51.6	131.1	35.0	88.9	39.0	86.4	88.5	224.8
	WOMEN	36.3	92.2	49.0	124.5	49.1	124.7	31.7	80.5	38.0	96.5	84.0	213.4
5	MEN	32.4	82.3	39.4	100.1	59.0	149.9	29.7	75.4	29.0	73.7	76.8	195.1
	WOMEN	29.9	75.9	34.0	86.4	55.2	140.2	26.6	67.6	27.0	68.6	72.9	185.2

able to accommodate the greatest percentage of the user population. In this regard, there is no substitute for common sense. If a shelf can just as easily be placed an inch or two lower, without significantly impacting on other design or cost factors, thereby accommodating 98 or 99 percent of the user population, obviously that is the correct design decision.

The clearances shown in Fig. 3 are intended to introduce general guidelines for barrier-free design. While we have utilized the wheelchair as our design subject, it does not represent the largest number of disabled. However, it is usually the most demanding for which to design. To provide practical limits for this design, we have chosen to plot the range of reach for the short female to the tall male. The overlapping areas of ability for the handicapped and the non-handicapped demonstrate the field of good design practice common to both.

When planning for accessibility, it is important to consider the attitude at which the wheelchair approaches the object desired. Reach limits differ for frontal and side reach. Because of this, range of reach is plotted for each. The elevation targets represent the maximum height at which controls requiring manual dexterity should be located.

Wheelchairs vary in size. They are fitted to their users in much the same manner as clothing is. A range of sizes is given, with the dimensions for the "typical" collapsible, manual chair indicated. Electrically powered wheelchairs require more space. Further, the wheelchair must be considered in its "occupied" state, as the user imparts additional space requirements with arms and feet as well as basic maneuvering space.

We consider the basic space requirement for an occupied wheelchair to function to be 3 ft wide by 4 ft deep. This same space will accommodate most people who use canes, crutches, and walkers. Blind people using the cane technique for perceiving obstacles can also be accommodated in this space. For a person in a wheelchair to make a complete turn, an area of approximately 5 ft by 5 ft is required. As the elevations of surrounding surfaces change, so do the space requirements. The length of time that one is confronted by close quarters also affects the required clearance. An opening through a wall may be 2 ft 8 in clear as it represents only a short time involvement. As travel distance and traffic increase, passage width must also.

The complexity of space also affects minimum clearance. To make a simple 90° turn, adjoining passages 3 ft wide are required (and 3 ft 6 in preferred if a normal walking is to be maintained). A 180° turn around a fixed partition requires more space.

As clearances relate to general circulation requirements, space needs again increase with traffic speed and volume. Narrow corridors (4 ft) should be restricted to basically short, one-directional traffic patterns. Generally, maintain at least 5 ft clearances or more as determined by code.

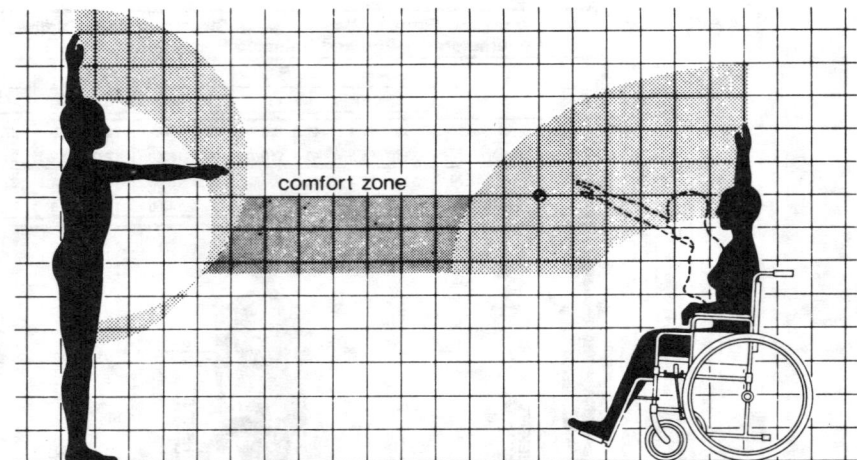

range of reach
scale: 3/8"= 1'-0"

a / 1

range of reach
scale: 3/8"= 1'-0"

b / 1

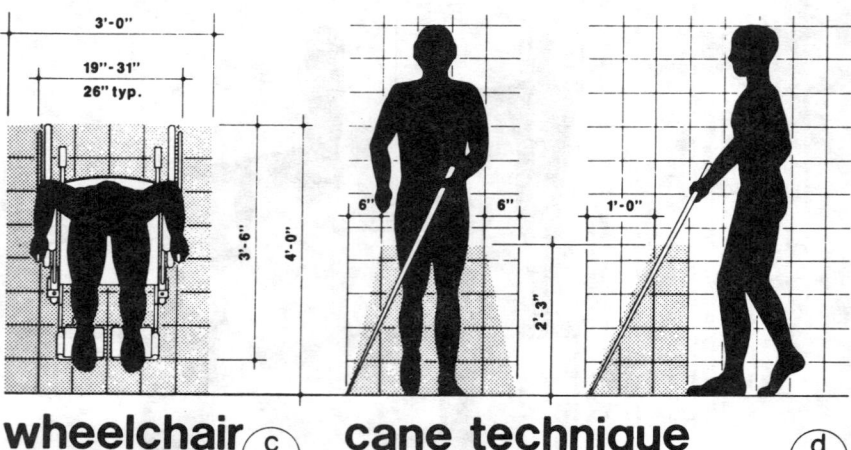

wheelchair
scale: 3/8"= 1'-0"

c / 1

cane technique
scale: 3/8"= 1'-0"

d / 1

Fig. 3

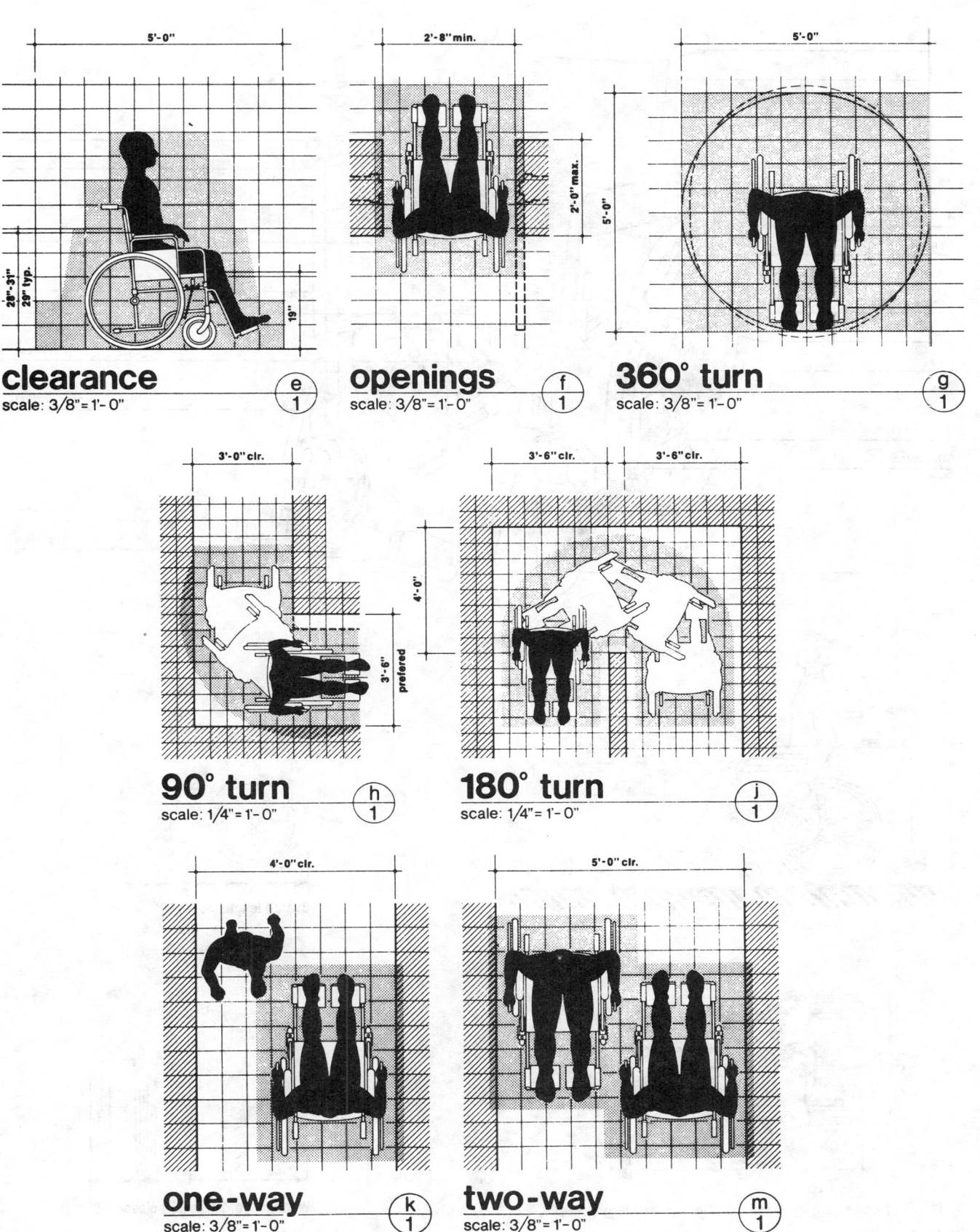

5'-0"

clearance e/1
scale: 3/8"= 1'- 0"

2'- 8" min.

openings f/1
scale: 3/8"= 1'- 0"

5'-0"

360° turn g/1
scale: 3/8"= 1'- 0"

3'-0" clr.

90° turn h/1
scale: 1/4"= 1'- 0"

3'-6" clr.   3'-6" clr.

180° turn j/1
scale: 1/4"= 1'- 0"

4'-0" clr.

one-way k/1
scale: 3/8"= 1'- 0"

5'-0" clr.

two-way m/1
scale: 3/8"= 1'- 0"

Fig. 3 *(Continued)*

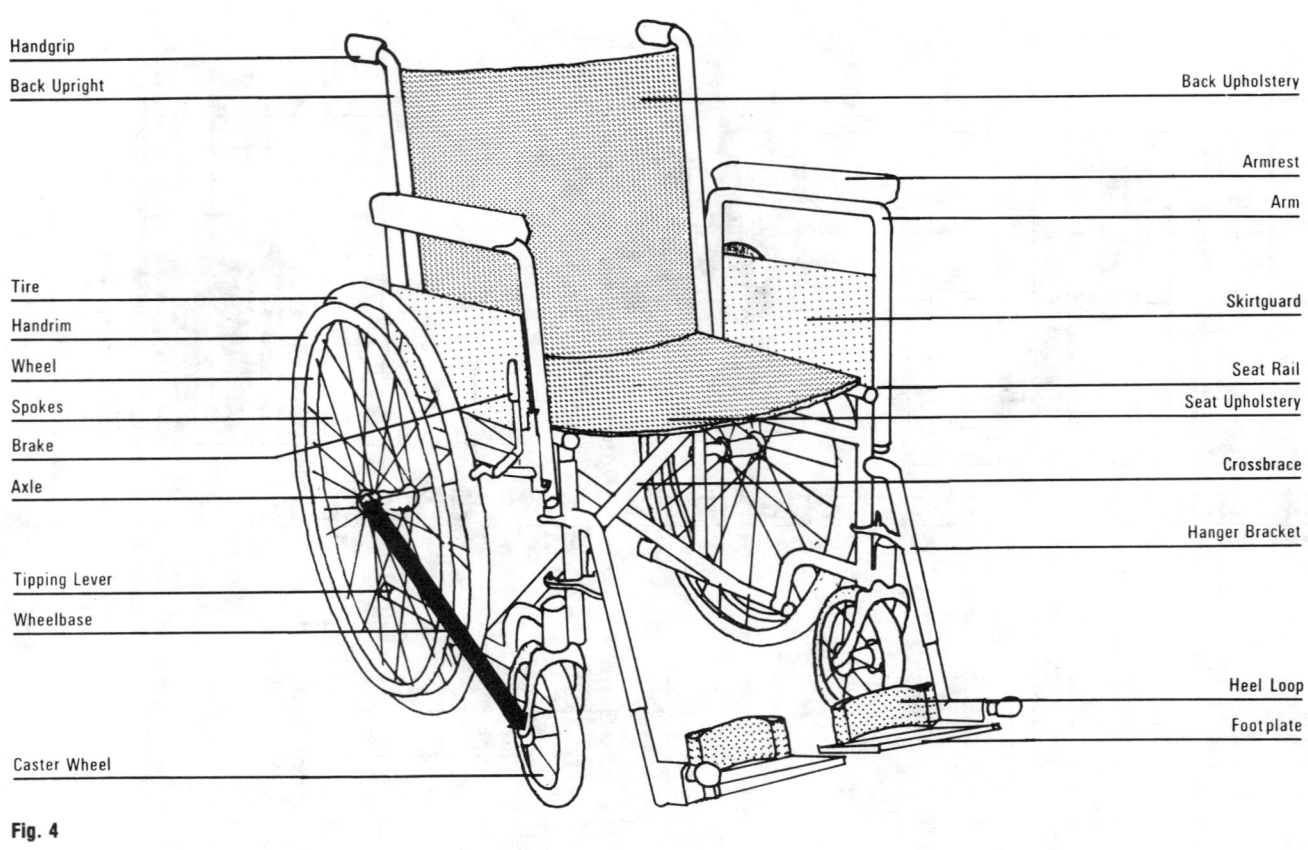

Handgrip
Back Upright

Tire
Handrim
Wheel
Spokes
Brake
Axle

Tipping Lever
Wheelbase

Caster Wheel

Back Upholstery

Armrest
Arm

Skirtguard

Seat Rail
Seat Upholstery

Crossbrace

Hanger Bracket

Heel Loop
Footplate

Fig. 4

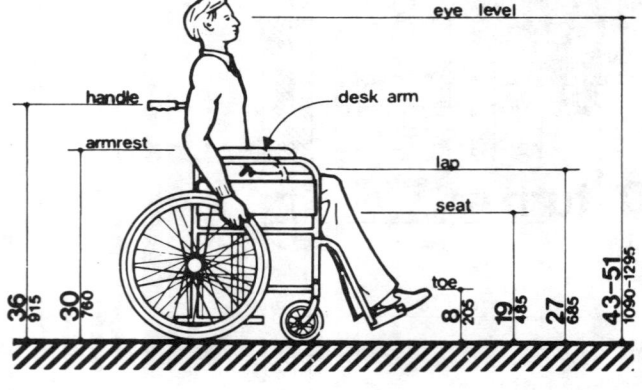

eye level
handle
desk arm
armrest
lap
seat
toe

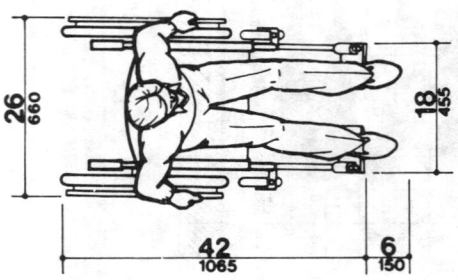

NOTE: Footrests may extend further for very large people.

Fig. 5   Dimensions of adult-sized wheelchairs.

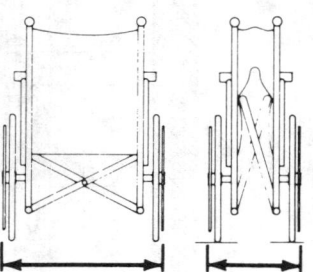

Overall length: 40" to 50"

Width: open, 24" to 25"; closed, 10"

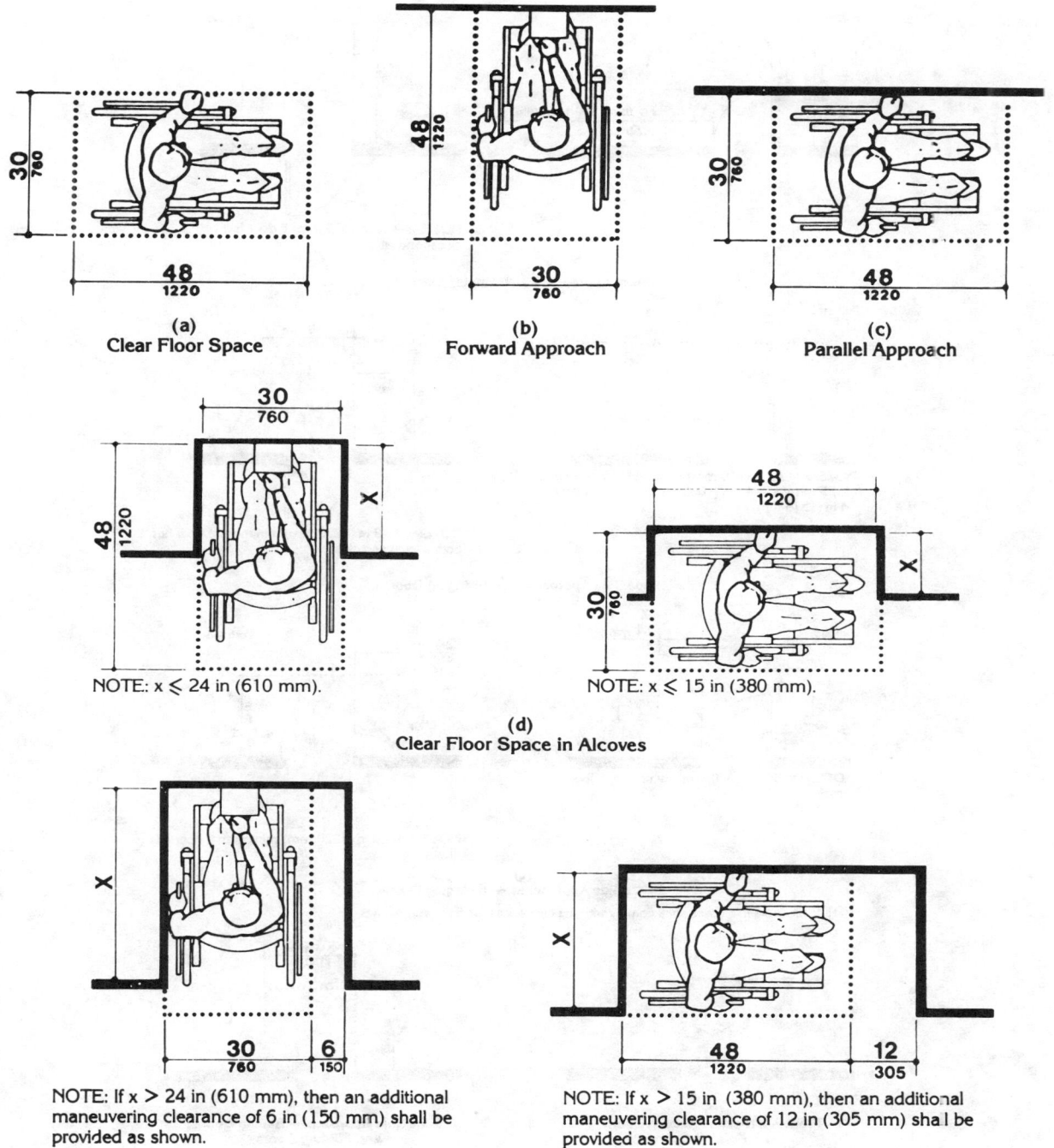

(a)
Clear Floor Space

(b)
Forward Approach

(c)
Parallel Approach

NOTE: x ≤ 24 in (610 mm).

NOTE: x ≤ 15 in (380 mm).

(d)
Clear Floor Space in Alcoves

NOTE: If x > 24 in (610 mm), then an additional maneuvering clearance of 6 in (150 mm) shall be provided as shown.

NOTE: If x > 15 in (380 mm), then an additional maneuvering clearance of 12 in (305 mm) shall be provided as shown.

(e)
Additional Maneuvering Clearances for Alcoves

Fig. 6   Minimum clear floor space for wheelchairs.

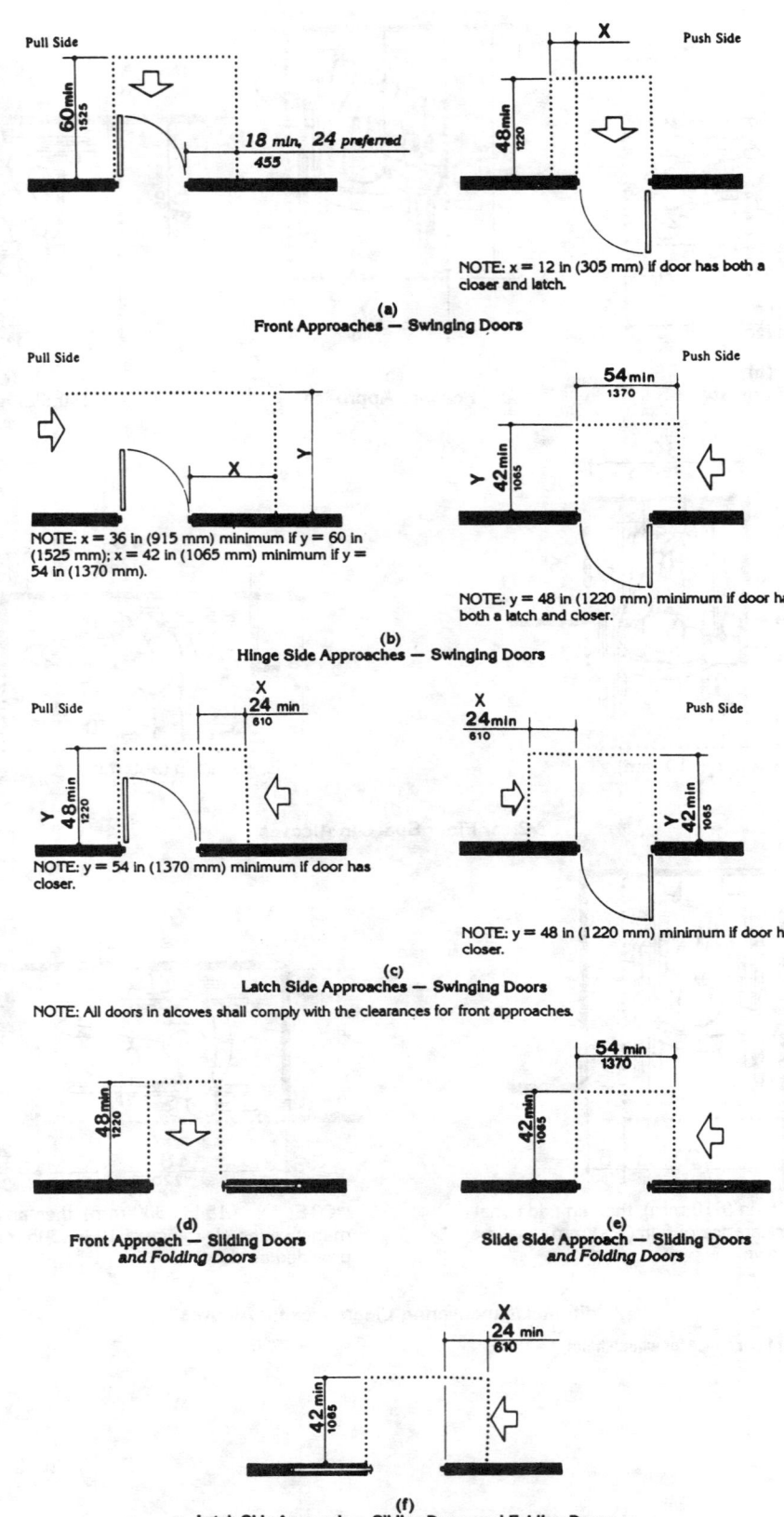

(a)
Front Approaches — Swinging Doors

NOTE: x = 12 in (305 mm) if door has both a closer and latch.

NOTE: x = 36 in (915 mm) minimum if y = 60 in (1525 mm); x = 42 in (1065 mm) minimum if y = 54 in (1370 mm).

NOTE: y = 48 in (1220 mm) minimum if door has both a latch and closer.

(b)
Hinge Side Approaches — Swinging Doors

NOTE: y = 54 in (1370 mm) minimum if door has closer.

NOTE: y = 48 in (1220 mm) minimum if door has closer.

(c)
Latch Side Approaches — Swinging Doors

NOTE: All doors in alcoves shall comply with the clearances for front approaches.

(d)
Front Approach — Sliding Doors and Folding Doors

(e)
Slide Side Approach — Sliding Doors and Folding Doors

(f)
Latch Side Approach — Sliding Doors and Folding Doors

NOTE: All doors in alcoves shall comply with the clearances for front approaches.

Fig. 7   Maneuvering clearances at doors.

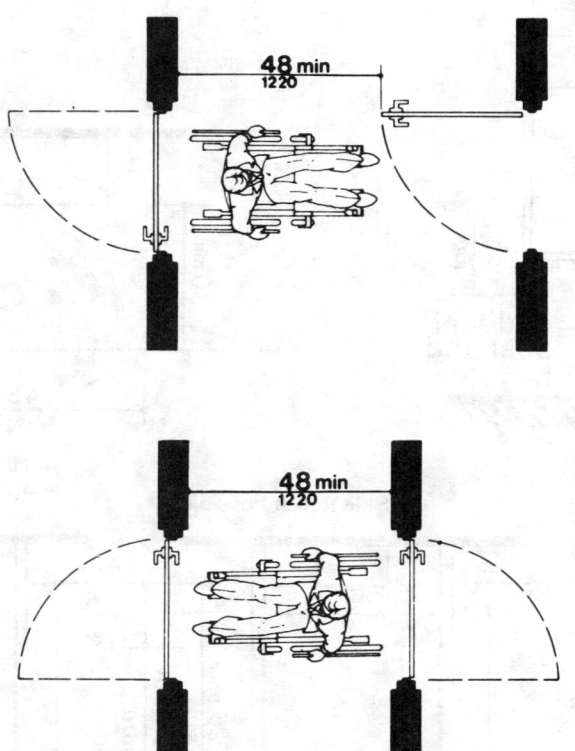

Fig. 8   Two hinged doors in series.

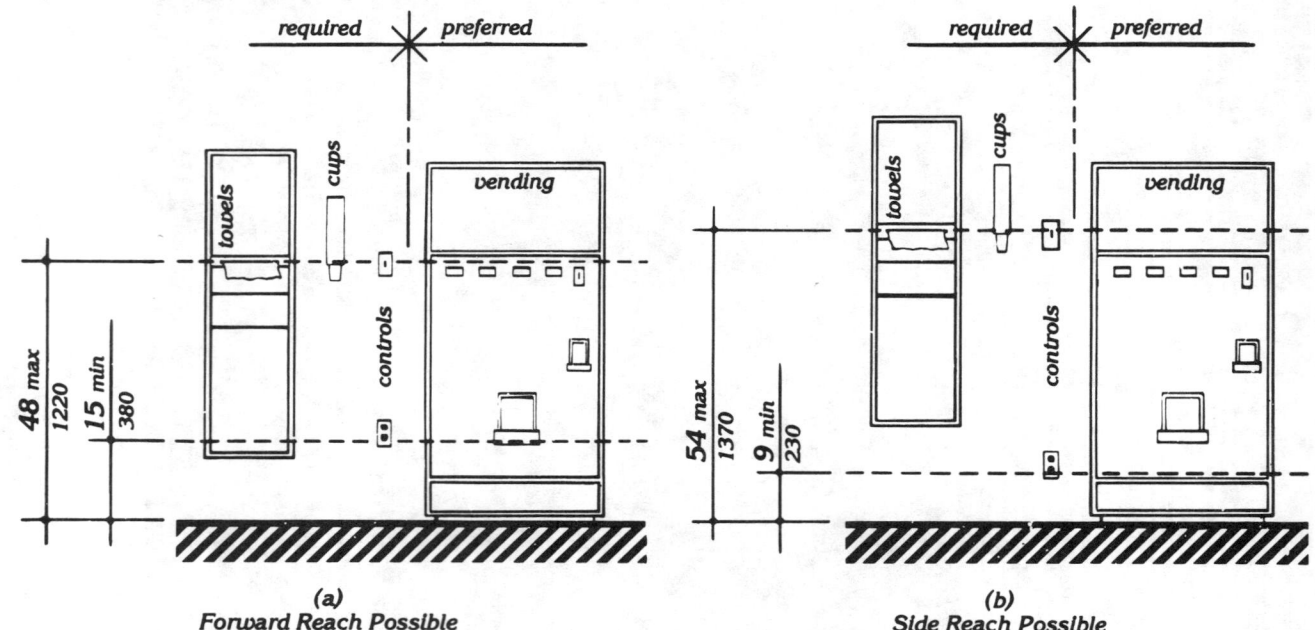

HUMAN FACTORS

Telephone Mounting Heights; Control Reach

Any width
*
54 max
1366
27 or below
685
optional post and base
Elevation
30 min
760
10 max
255
48 min
1220
Plan
(a)
Side Reach Possible
see Plans
*
48 max
1220
27 or below
685
Elevation
48
1220
20 max
510
24 max
610
30 min
760
48
1220
20 max
510
more than 24
610
30
760
6 min
150
Plans
(b)
Forward Reach Required

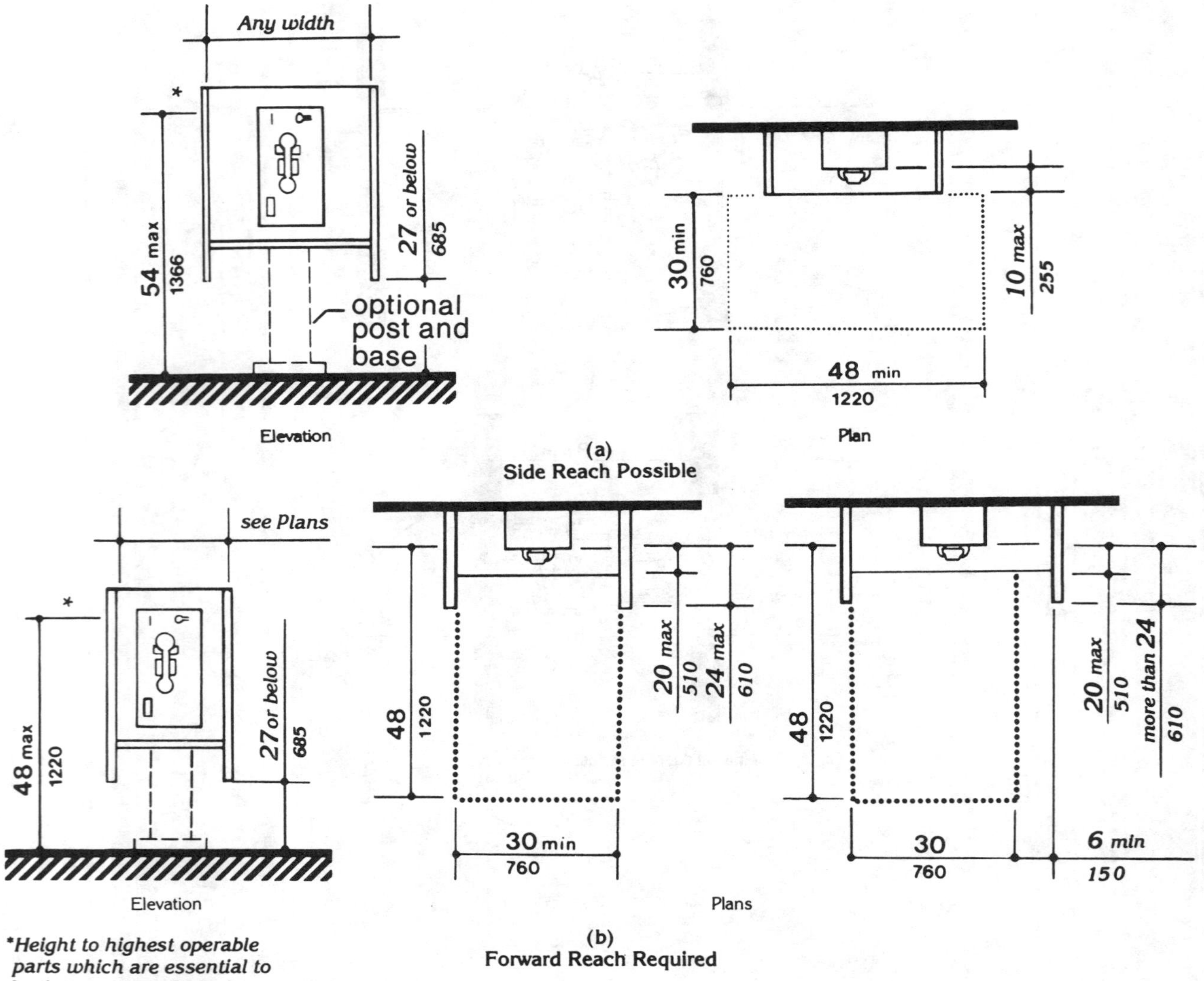

Height to highest operable parts which are essential to basic operation of telephone.

Fig. 9 Mounting heights and clearances for telephones.

required
preferred
towels
cups
vending
controls
48 max
1220
15 min
380
(a)
Forward Reach Possible
required
preferred
towels
cups
vending
controls
54 max
1370
9 min
230
(b)
Side Reach Possible

Fig. 10 Control reach limitations.

TYPES OF SPACE

Besides needing enough space in order to move about and perform various tasks, people react to space in a variety of ways. Several researchers have defined the space surrounding the individual in terms of the limits within which people categorically respond (see Figs. 11 and 12). *Intimate space* is that area in which a person tends not to allow anyone to intrude unless intimate relationships are expected. *Personal space* is that area within which a person allows only selected friends or fellow workers with whom personal discussion is mandatory. *Social space* is that area within which the individual expects to make purely social contacts on a temporary basis. And, finally, *public space* is that area within which the individual does not expect to have direct contact with others. Obviously, the more intimate the spatial relationship becomes, the more people resist intrusion by others. Personal space factors are important in establishing the privacy requirements for architectural design.

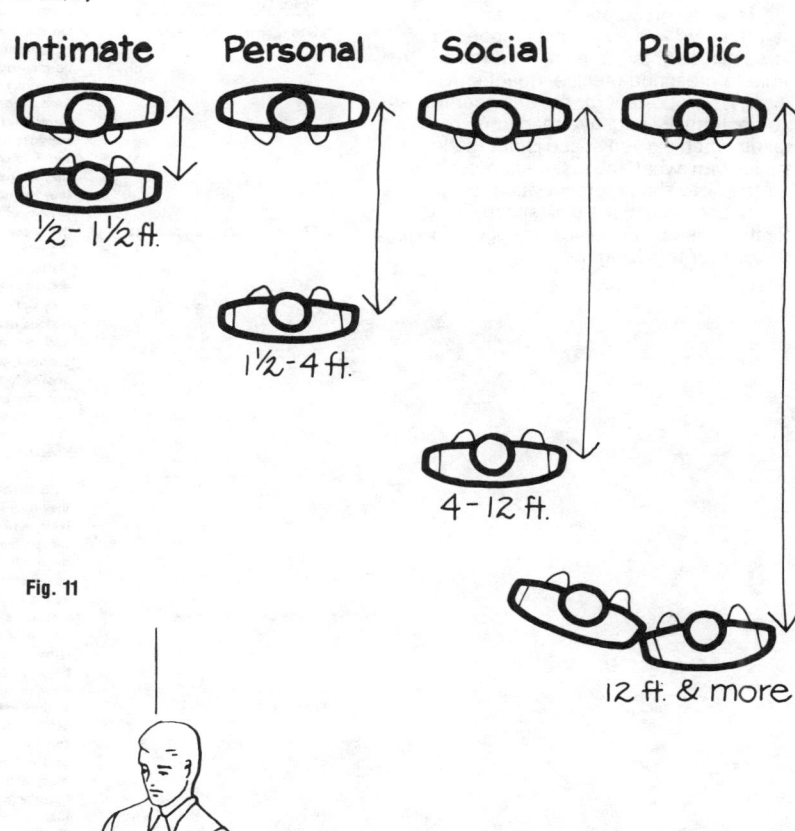

Distance Relationships Among People
(Hall)

Intimate   Personal   Social   Public

½ – 1½ ft.

1½ – 4 ft.

4 – 12 ft.

12 ft. & more

Fig. 11

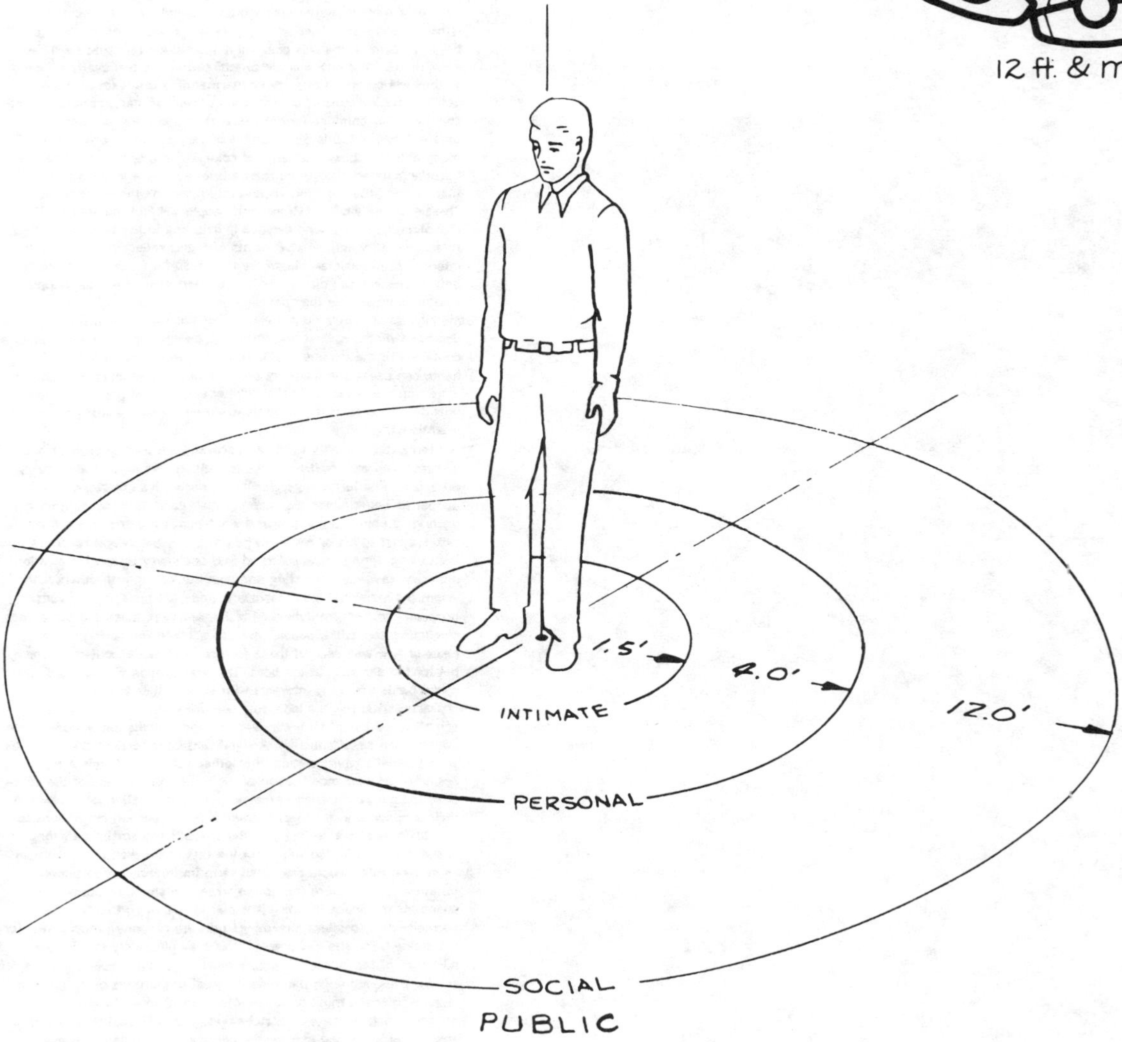

INTIMATE

1.5'

4.0'

12.0'

PERSONAL

SOCIAL

PUBLIC

Fig. 12

TYPICAL SUBJECTIVE RESPONSES TO SELECTED SPATIAL FEATURES

Although few research data have been generated with regard to how people respond to specific spatial factors (at least in terms of being able to prescribe precise, quantitative guidelines), it is important for the designer to reflect on potentially negative reactions that often result when a given space is not made compatible with what the user expects in terms of the size, shape, organization, color, and illumination of a particular space. The considerations listed in Table 4 are suggested as a checklist for the designer.

TABLE 4

Space Characteristic	Probable Response
Size (generally volume)	If the space is too small for the number of people, furnishings, equipment, or other objects that occupy it, people will consider it to be crowded. Although they may accept a crowded condition on a temporary basis, they will object to living or working in such a space for extended periods of time. If the space is too large for the people, furnishings, equipment, or other objects that occupy it, people will consider it "unfriendly," inconvenient, and/or overly demanding in terms of communicating, travel distance, maintenance, etc. Although they may accept the "barnlike" atmosphere for temporary periods, they will object to living or working in such a space for extended periods of time.
Shape (generally proportion)	If the space is out of proportion (too narrow, wide, long, high, etc.) for the intended use, people will consider it awkward and often distracting or oppressive. Although they may accept proportional distortion on a short-term basis (i.e., as they pass through briefly), they will object to living or working in such a space for extended periods of time. If the space contains such distortions as all curved surfaces, acute wall junctures, and too many projections or surface changes, people will consider it confusing and difficult to maneuver in and/or furnish. Although they may accept such distortions (or even consider them interesting) on a temporary or one-time basis, they will object to living or working in such a space for extended periods of time. It should also be noted that blind people depend on the constant proportions of right-angle corners to aid them in negotiating a space; such individuals are easily confused by curved surfaces, walls that are not at right angles, and periodic projections that imply they may have reached a turning point. When a ceiling is extremely high relative to the lateral dimension of a space, people feel as though they are working in a pit and that the walls are closing in on them. When a ceiling is extremely low and the space in front of the observer is very long, people feel as though the room is "endless" or as if they will hit their heads unless they duck.
Color and illumination	If a space is dark (unless this is required for a particular operation, such as a motion picture presentation), people tend to become lethargic and less active, or they may feel anxious. As a rule, the less bright a room is, the less cheerful it seems. A small space will seem even smaller. If a space is too bright, people will feel overly exposed, or they will complain of glare or thermal discomfort (even though actual glare in terms of accepted light levels or inappropriate thermal conditions for comfort are not present). If there are too many different colors, too large expanses of very saturated color, or too many and too "busy" patterns of color within a space, most people become irritated after more than a brief exposure to the space. If there is too little color, no visual pattern, or no other decorative "break" in the visual environment, people will find the space monotonous, boring, and eventually irritating to the point of wanting to escape. Although isolated points of highly reflective surface provide interest, all-metallic and highly reflective surface treatments create both subjective and directly objective interference for most people who have to work in the space.
Windows	Generally, most people do not like to live and work in a space that is devoid of windows. First and foremost, people seem to need visual contact with the outside world. Too many windows, on the other hand, can cause the following possible negative reactions: too much glare, too much exposure (fishbowl effect), lack of protection from outside elements, true anxiety (caused by floor-to-ceiling glass at high elevations).
Space organization	The internal components within a space and the traffic corridors and entrance and exit locations will seem either well organized or badly organized. The furnishings, partitions, decorative objects, etc., will appear as being either organized or disorganized, depending on the observer's ability to comprehend what things are and where they are with respect to his or her vantage point. Key behavioral response issues are: apparent capability to find one's way to specific locations, apparent ease for interacting and communicating with others with whom the individual must associate, apparent privacy provisions necessary to perform individual tasks. Although these are sometimes conflicting needs, the people who use a space will perform on the basis of how well each of these factors has been executed for *them*, not for the designer or the boss. The organization of internal space components obviously interacts with all the other space characteristics; i.e., the individual perceives and reacts to the combined effects of size, shape, color and illumination, windows, and organization simultaneously. A significant behavioral response will be an individual's interpretation of whether sufficient options are available for local modification of his or her own portion of the space. Even though people may never require a modification, they react to their own space in terms of permanently established restrictions that eventually elicit the feeling that the space is too small, the wrong shape, too dark, or isolated from the rest of the world, for example.
Furnishings	As a general rule, people are sensitive to improperly proportioned furniture, i.e., furniture that is too large, too small, or the wrong shape for the space in which it is placed. Although the designer normally tries to select furnishings that are properly proportioned for the space he or she has created, this may ultimately restrict the efficiency of the individual (e.g., a desk or storage cabinet may be too small). Thus, although the general visual proportions of furniture in relation to space must be taken into account to avoid negative observational responses, shortchanging the individual in terms of specific furniture and use requirements soon stimulates an even stronger negative response.

TABLE 5 Comparison of Sound Pressure Levels and Loudness Sensations

Sound Pressure Level (decibels—A scale)	Source	Sensation
130	Jet Aircraft at 100'	
	Bass Drum at 3'	Physical Pain
	Auto Horn at 3'	
120		
	Thunder, Artillery, Nearby Riveter	
110		Deafening
	Elevated Train	
	Discotheque	
100		
	Loud Street Noise	
	Noisy Factory	
90		Very Loud
	Truck Unmuffled	
	Police Whistle	
80		
	Cocktail Party	
	Noisy Office	
	Average Street Noise	
70		Loud
	Average Radio	
	Average Factory	
60		
	Noisy Home	
	Inside General Office	
50		Moderate
	Face to Face Conversation	
	Quiet Radio	
40		
	Quiet Home	
	Private Office	
30		Faint
	Empty Auditorium	
	Quiet Conversation	
20		
	Rustle of Leaves	
10	Whisper	Very Faint
	Soundproof Room	
0	Threshold of Audibility	

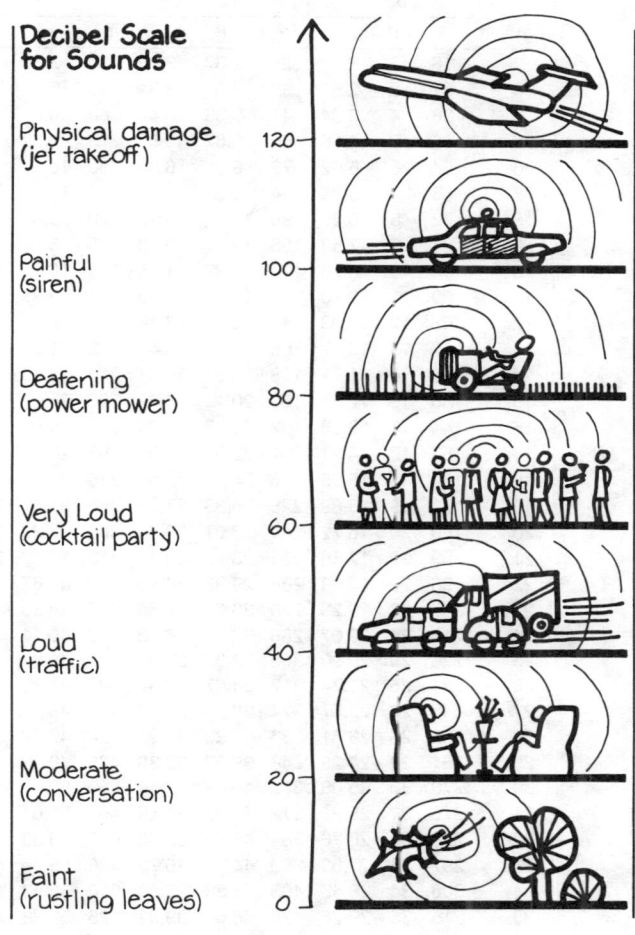

Decibel Scale for Sounds

Physical damage (jet takeoff) — 120

Painful (siren) — 100

Deafening (power mower) — 80

Very Loud (cocktail party) — 60

Loud (traffic) — 40

Moderate (conversation) — 20

Faint (rustling leaves) — 0

Fig. 13

TABLE 6 Speech-Interference Levels that Barely Permit Reliable Conversation

Distance between talker and listener, ft	Speech-interference level, dB			
	Normal	Raised	Very loud	Shouting
0.5	71	77	83	89
1.0	65	71	77	83
2.0	59	65	71	77
3.0	55	61	67	73
4.0	53	59	65	71
5.0	51	57	63	69
6.0	49	55	61	67
12.0	43	49	55	61

TABLE 7 Speech Interference Levels (SIL) and Noise Criteria (NC) Recommended for Rooms

Type of room	Maximum permissible level (measured in vacant rooms)	
	SIL	NC
Secretarial offices, typing	60	50–55
Coliseum for sports only (amplification)	55	50
Small private office	45	30–35
Conference room for 20	35	30
Movie theater	35	30
Conference room for 50	30	20–30
Theaters for drama, 500 seats (no amplification)	30	20–25
Homes, sleeping areas	30	20–25
Assembly halls (no amplification)	30	
Schoolrooms	30	25
Concert halls (no amplification)	25	15–20

FLOOR AND WALL COVERING
Length and Width of Carpet Roll Converted to Area

TABLE 8 Length and Width of Carpet Roll Converted to Area

Length, ft	9 ft ft²	9 ft yd²	9 ft m²	12 ft ft²	12 ft yd²	12 ft m²	15 ft ft²	15 ft yd²	15 ft m²	Length, ft	9 ft ft²	9 ft yd²	9 ft m²	12 ft ft²	12 ft yd²	12 ft m²	15 ft ft²	15 ft yd²	15 ft m²
2	18	2	1.67	24	2.67	2.23	30	3.33	2.79	51	459	51	42.64	612	68	56.86	765	85	71.07
3	27	3	2.51	36	4	3.34	45	5	4.18	52	468	52	43.48	624	69.33	57.97	780	86.67	72.46
4	36	4	3.34	48	5.33	4.46	60	6.67	5.57	53	477	53	44.31	636	70.67	59.09	795	88.33	73.86
5	45	5	4.18	60	6.67	5.57	75	8.33	6.97	54	486	54	45.15	648	72	60.20	810	90	75.25
6	54	6	5.02	72	8	6.69	90	10	8.36	55	495	55	45.99	660	73.33	61.32	825	91.67	76.64
7	63	7	5.85	84	9.33	7.80	105	11.67	9.76	56	504	56	46.82	672	74.67	62.43	840	93.33	78.04
8	72	8	6.69	96	10.67	8.92	120	13.33	11.15	57	513	57	47.66	684	76	63.55	855	95	79.43
9	81	9	7.52	108	12	10.03	135	15	12.54	58	522	58	48.49	696	77.33	64.66	870	96.67	80.83
10	90	10	8.36	120	13.33	11.15	150	16.67	13.94	59	531	59	49.33	708	78.67	65.77	885	98.33	82.22
11	99	11	9.20	132	14.67	12.26	165	18.33	15.33	60	540	60	50.17	720	80	66.89	900	100	83.61
12	108	12	10.03	144	16	13.38	180	20	16.72	61	549	61	51	732	81.33	68	915	101.67	85.01
13	117	13	10.87	156	17.33	14.47	195	21.67	18.12	62	558	62	51.84	744	82.67	69.12	930	103.33	86.40
14	126	14	11.71	168	18.67	15.61	210	23.33	19.51	63	567	63	52.68	756	84	70.23	945	105	87.79
15	135	15	12.54	180	20	16.72	225	25	20.90	64	576	64	53.51	768	85.33	71.35	960	106.67	89.19
16	144	16	13.38	192	21.33	17.84	240	26.67	22.30	65	585	65	54.35	780	86.67	72.46	975	108.33	90.58
17	153	17	14.21	204	22.67	18.95	255	28.33	23.69	66	594	66	55.18	792	88	73.58	990	110	91.97
18	162	18	15.05	216	24	20.07	270	30	25.08	67	603	67	56.02	804	89.33	74.69	1005	111.67	93.37
19	171	19	15.89	228	25.33	21.18	285	31.67	26.48	68	612	68	56.86	816	90.67	75.81	1020	113.33	94.76
20	180	20	16.72	240	26.67	22.30	300	33.33	27.87	69	621	69	57.69	828	92	76.92	1035	115	96.15
21	189	21	17.55	252	28	23.41	315	35	29.26	70	630	70	58.53	840	93.33	78.04	1050	116.67	97.55
22	198	22	18.39	264	29.33	24.53	330	36.67	30.66	71	639	71	59.36	852	94.67	79.15	1065	118.33	98.94
23	207	23	19.23	276	30.67	25.64	345	38.33	32.05	72	648	72	60.20	864	96	80.27	1080	120	100.33
24	216	24	20.07	288	32	26.76	360	40	33.44	73	657	73	61.04	876	97.33	81.38	1095	121.67	101.73
25	225	25	20.90	300	33.33	27.87	375	41.67	34.84	74	666	74	61.87	888	98.67	82.50	1110	123.33	103.12
26	234	26	21.74	312	34.67	28.99	390	43.33	36.23	75	675	75	62.71	900	100	83.61	1125	125	104.52
27	243	27	22.57	324	36	30.10	405	45	37.63	76	684	76	63.55	912	101.33	84.73	1140	126.67	105.91
28	252	28	23.41	336	37.33	31.21	420	46.67	39.02	77	693	77	64.30	924	102.67	85.84	1155	128.33	107.30
29	261	29	24.25	348	38.67	32.33	435	48.33	40.41	78	702	78	65.22	936	104	86.96	1170	130	108.70
30	270	30	25.08	360	40	33.44	450	50	41.81	79	711	79	66.05	948	105.33	88.07	1185	131.67	110.09
31	279	31	25.92	372	41.33	34.56	465	51.67	43.20	80	720	80	66.89	960	106.67	89.19	1200	133.33	111.48
32	288	32	26.76	384	42.67	35.68	480	53.33	44.59	81	729	81	67.73	972	108	90.30	1215	135	112.88
33	297	33	27.59	396	44	36.79	495	55	45.99	82	738	82	68.56	984	109.33	91.42	1230	136.67	114.27
34	306	34	28.43	408	45.33	37.90	510	56.67	47.38	83	747	83	69.40	996	110.67	92.53	1245	138.33	115.66
35	315	35	29.26	420	46.67	39.02	525	58.33	48.77	84	756	84	70.23	1008	112	93.65	1260	140	117.06
36	324	36	30.10	432	48	40.13	540	60	50.17	85	765	85	71.07	1020	113.33	94.76	1275	141.67	118.45
37	333	37	30.94	444	49.33	41.25	555	61.67	51.56	86	774	86	71.91	1032	114.67	95.88	1290	143.33	119.84
38	342	38	31.77	456	50.67	42.36	570	63.33	52.95	87	783	87	72.74	1044	116	96.99	1305	145	121.24
39	351	39	32.61	468	52	43.48	585	65	54.35	88	792	88	73.58	1056	117.33	98.11	1320	146.67	122.63
40	360	40	33.44	480	53.33	44.59	600	66.67	55.74	89	801	89	74.41	1068	118.67	99.22	1335	148.33	124.03
41	369	41	34.28	492	54.67	45.71	615	68.33	57.13	90	810	90	75.25	1080	120	100.33	1350	150	125.42
42	378	42	35.12	504	56	46.82	630	70	58.53	91	819	91	76.09	1092	121.33	101.45	1365	151.67	126.81
43	387	43	35.95	516	57.33	47.94	645	71.67	59.92	92	828	92	76.92	1104	122.67	102.56	1380	153.33	128.21
44	396	44	36.79	528	58.67	49.05	660	73.33	61.32	93	837	93	77.76	1116	124	103.68	1395	155	129.60
45	405	45	37.63	540	60	50.17	675	75	62.71	94	846	94	78.6	1128	125.33	104.79	1410	156.67	130.99
46	414	46	38.46	552	61.33	51.28	690	76.67	64.10	95	855	95	79.43	1140	126.67	105.91	1425	158.33	132.39
47	423	47	39.30	564	62.67	52.40	705	78.33	65.50	96	864	96	80.27	1152	128	107.02	1440	160	133.78
48	432	48	40.13	576	64	53.51	720	80	66.89	97	873	97	81.10	1164	129.33	108.14	1455	161.67	135.17
49	441	49	40.97	588	65.33	54.63	735	81.67	68.28	98	882	98	81.94	1176	130.67	109.25	1470	163.33	136.57
50	450	50	41.81	600	66.67	55.74	750	83.33	69.68	99	891	99	82.78	1188	132	110.37	1485	165	137.96
										100	900	100	83.61	1200	133.33	111.48	1500	166.67	139.36

TABLE 9 Paperhanging Walls and Ceilings

Size of room, ft	Height of ceiling			Yards of border	Rolls of ceiling
	8 ft	9 ft	10 ft		
	Single rolls for walls				
4 × 8	6	7	8	9	2
4 × 10	7	8	9	11	2
4 × 12	8	9	10	12	2
6 × 10	8	9	10	12	2
6 × 12	9	10	11	13	3
8 × 12	10	11	13	15	4
8 × 14	11	12	14	16	4
10 × 14	12	14	15	18	5
10 × 16	13	15	16	19	6
12 × 16	14	16	17	20	7
12 × 18	15	17	19	22	8
14 × 18	16	18	20	23	8
14 × 22	18	20	22	26	10
15 × 16	15	17	19	23	8
15 × 18	16	18	20	24	9
15 × 20	17	20	22	25	10
15 × 23	19	21	23	28	11
16 × 18	17	19	21	25	10
16 × 20	18	20	22	26	10
16 × 22	19	21	23	28	11
16 × 24	20	22	25	29	12
16 × 26	21	23	26	31	13
17 × 22	19	22	24	28	12
17 × 25	21	23	26	31	13
17 × 28	22	25	28	32	15
17 × 32	24	27	30	35	17
17 × 35	26	29	32	37	18
18 × 22	20	22	25	29	12
18 × 25	21	24	27	31	14
18 × 28	23	26	28	33	16
20 × 26	23	28	28	33	17
20 × 28	24	27	30	34	18
30 × 34	27	30	33	39	21

Allowance for waste is included in all figures.
Deduct one roll for every 36 sq ft of openings.
Deduct one roll for every 2 doors.
Deduct for windows as area of each opening.
One roll of wallpaper equals 36 sq ft (24 ft by 18 in.).

TABLE 10 Covering Capacity

Material	Surface or use	Coverage per gallon, sq ft
Exterior Painting		
Priming paint	Wood	450
	Metal	500
Flat house paint	Over primer	500
	Repainting 1 coat	400
Oil paint	Masonry	300
	Concrete	250
	Stucco (smooth)	200
	Stucco (rough)	150
Stain	Wood shingle siding, first coat	150
	Wood shingle siding, second coat	200
Interior Painting		
Priming paint	Wood	500
Metal primer	Metal	600
Undercoat (enamel)	Over primer	400
Flat	Finish coat	500
Semigloss enamel	Finish coat	450
Satin-gloss enamel	Finish coat	450
Gloss enamel	Finish coat	400
Floor enamel	Floors	500
Aluminum paint	Aluminum, first coat	600
	Aluminum, second coat	700
Spar varnish	Finishing woodwork	600
Clear gloss varnish	Finishing woodwork	600
Lacquer	Over stain	450
Interior stain	Woodwork, first coat	500
	Woodwork, second coat	600
	Woodwork, third coat	700
Miscellaneous		
Barn red oil paint	Repaint barn	450
Rust inhibitor (zinc paint)	Metal	650
Furniture sealer and stain	Unpainted furniture	600

TABLE 11 Flooring Tile

(Net covering capacity per 100 sq ft)

Tile size, in.	No. of pieces per 100 sq ft	No. of pieces per sq ft
6 × 6	400	4.00
6 × 12	200	2.00
9 × 9	178	1.78
12 × 12	100	1.00
12 × 24	50	0.50
18 × 18	45	0.45
18 × 24	34	0.33
18 × 36	23	0.23
36 × 36	11	0.11

FLOOR AND WALL COVERING

Wall Areas of Rooms

TABLE 12 Wall Area of Rooms (8-ft ceiling), ft²

Feet	3	4	5	6	7	8	9	10	11
3	96	112	128	144	160	176	192	208	224
4	112	128	144	160	176	192	208	224	240
5	128	144	160	176	192	208	224	240	256
6	144	160	176	192	208	224	240	256	272
7	160	176	192	208	224	240	256	272	288
8	176	192	208	224	240	256	272	288	304
9	192	208	224	240	256	272	288	304	320
10	208	224	240	256	272	288	304	320	336
11	224	240	256	272	288	304	320	336	352
12	240	256	272	288	304	320	336	352	368
13	256	272	288	304	320	336	352	368	384
14	272	288	304	320	336	352	368	384	400
15	288	304	320	336	352	368	384	400	416
16	304	320	336	352	368	384	400	416	432
17	320	336	352	368	384	400	416	432	448
18	336	352	368	384	400	416	432	448	464
19	352	368	384	400	416	432	448	464	480
20	368	384	400	416	432	448	464	480	496
21	384	400	416	432	448	464	480	496	512
22	400	416	432	448	464	480	496	512	528
23	416	432	448	464	480	496	512	528	544
24	432	448	464	480	496	512	528	544	560
25	448	464	480	496	512	528	544	560	576

Feet	12	13	14	15	16	17	18	19	20
3	240	256	272	288	304	320	336	352	368
4	256	272	288	304	320	336	352	368	384
5	272	288	304	320	336	352	368	384	400
6	288	304	320	336	352	368	384	400	416
7	304	320	336	352	368	384	400	416	432
8	320	336	352	368	384	400	416	432	448
9	336	352	368	384	400	416	432	448	464
10	352	368	384	400	416	432	448	464	480
11	368	384	400	416	432	448	464	480	496
12	384	400	416	432	448	464	480	496	512
13	400	416	432	448	464	480	496	512	528
14	416	432	448	464	480	496	512	528	544
15	432	448	464	480	496	512	528	544	560
16	448	464	480	496	512	528	544	560	576
17	464	480	496	512	528	544	560	576	592
18	480	496	512	528	544	560	576	592	608
19	496	512	528	544	560	576	592	608	624
20	512	528	544	560	576	592	608	624	640
21	528	544	560	576	592	608	624	640	656
22	544	560	576	592	608	624	640	656	672
23	560	576	592	608	624	640	656	672	688
24	576	592	608	624	640	656	672	688	704
25	592	608	624	640	656	672	688	704	720

TABLE 13 Wall Area of Rooms (9-ft Ceiling), ft²

Feet	3	4	5	6	7	8	9	10	11
3	108	126	144	162	180	198	216	234	252
4	126	144	162	180	198	216	234	252	270
5	144	162	180	198	216	234	252	270	288
6	162	180	198	216	234	252	270	288	306
7	180	198	216	234	252	270	288	306	324
8	198	216	234	252	270	288	306	324	342
9	216	234	252	270	288	306	324	342	360
10	234	252	270	288	306	324	342	360	378
11	252	270	288	306	324	342	360	378	396
12	270	288	306	324	342	360	378	396	414
13	288	306	324	342	360	378	396	414	432
14	306	324	342	360	378	396	414	432	450
15	324	342	360	378	396	414	432	450	468
16	342	360	378	396	414	432	450	468	486
17	360	378	396	414	432	450	468	486	504
18	378	396	414	432	450	468	486	504	522
19	396	414	432	450	468	486	504	522	540
20	414	432	450	468	486	504	522	540	558
21	432	450	468	486	504	522	540	558	576
22	450	468	486	504	522	540	558	576	594
23	468	486	504	522	540	558	576	594	612
24	486	504	522	540	558	576	594	612	630
25	504	522	540	558	576	594	612	630	648

Feet	12	13	14	15	16	17	18	19	20
3	270	288	306	324	342	360	378	396	414
4	288	306	324	342	360	378	396	414	432
5	306	324	342	360	378	396	414	432	450
6	324	342	360	378	396	414	432	450	468
7	342	360	378	396	414	432	450	468	486
8	360	378	396	414	432	450	468	486	504
9	378	396	414	432	450	468	486	504	522
10	396	414	432	450	468	486	504	522	540
11	414	432	450	468	486	504	522	540	558
12	432	450	468	486	504	522	540	558	576
13	450	468	486	504	522	540	558	576	594
14	468	486	504	522	540	558	576	594	612
15	486	504	522	540	558	576	594	612	630
16	504	522	540	558	576	594	612	630	648
17	522	540	558	576	594	612	630	648	666
18	540	558	576	594	612	630	648	666	684
19	558	576	594	612	630	648	666	684	702
20	576	594	612	630	648	666	684	702	720
21	594	612	630	648	666	684	702	720	738
22	612	630	648	666	684	702	720	738	756
23	630	648	666	684	702	720	738	756	774
24	648	666	684	702	720	738	756	774	792
25	666	684	702	720	738	756	774	792	810

TABLE 14 Wall Area of Rooms (10-ft Ceiling), ft²

Feet	Feet									Feet	Feet								
	3	4	5	6	7	8	9	10	11		12	13	14	15	16	17	18	19	20
3	120	140	160	180	200	220	240	260	280	3	300	320	340	360	380	400	420	440	460
4	140	160	180	200	220	240	260	280	300	4	320	340	360	380	400	420	440	460	480
5	160	180	200	220	240	260	280	300	320	5	340	360	380	400	420	440	460	480	500
6	180	200	220	240	260	280	300	320	340	6	360	380	400	420	440	460	480	500	520
7	200	220	240	260	280	300	320	340	360	7	380	400	420	440	460	480	500	520	540
8	220	240	260	280	300	320	340	360	380	8	400	420	440	460	480	500	520	540	560
9	240	260	280	300	320	340	360	380	400	9	420	440	460	480	500	520	540	560	580
10	260	280	300	320	340	360	380	400	420	10	440	460	480	500	520	540	560	580	600
11	280	300	320	340	360	380	400	420	440	11	460	480	500	520	540	560	580	600	620
12	300	320	340	360	380	400	420	440	460	12	480	500	520	540	560	580	600	620	640
13	320	340	360	380	400	420	440	460	480	13	500	520	540	560	580	600	620	640	660
14	340	360	380	400	420	440	430	480	500	14	520	540	560	580	600	620	640	660	680
15	360	380	400	420	440	460	430	500	520	15	540	560	580	600	620	640	660	680	700
16	380	400	420	440	460	480	500	520	540	16	560	580	600	620	640	660	680	700	720
17	400	420	440	460	480	500	520	540	560	17	580	600	620	640	660	680	700	720	740
18	420	440	460	480	500	520	540	560	580	18	600	620	640	660	680	700	720	740	760
19	440	460	480	500	520	540	560	580	600	19	620	640	660	680	700	720	740	760	780
20	460	480	500	520	540	560	580	600	620	20	640	660	680	700	720	740	760	780	800
21	480	500	520	540	560	580	600	620	640	21	660	680	700	720	740	760	780	800	820
22	500	520	540	560	580	600	620	640	660	22	680	700	720	740	760	780	800	820	840
23	520	540	560	580	600	620	640	660	680	23	700	720	740	760	780	800	820	840	860
24	540	560	580	600	620	640	660	680	700	24	720	740	760	780	800	820	840	860	880
25	560	580	600	620	640	660	680	700	720	25	740	760	780	800	820	840	860	880	900

FLOOR AND WALL COVERING

Panel Conversion Chart

TABLE 15   Standard Modular Panel Conversion Chart
(For plywood, architectural woodwork, sheathing, plastic laminate, gypsum board, and other modular wall components)

No. of units	Size (areas in square feet)				No. of units	Size (areas in square feet)			
	4' x 8'	4' x 10'	4' x 12'	4' x 14'		4' x 8'	4' x 10'	4' x 12'	4' x 14'
10	320	400	480	560					
11	352	440	528	616	36	1152	1440	1728	2016
12	384	480	576	672	37	1184	1480	1776	2072
13	416	520	624	728	38	1216	1520	1824	2128
14	448	560	672	784	39	1248	1560	1872	2184
15	480	600	720	840	40	1280	1600	1920	2240
16	512	640	768	896	41	1312	1640	1968	2296
17	544	680	816	952	42	1344	1680	2016	2352
18	576	720	864	1008	43	1376	1720	2064	2408
19	608	760	912	1064	44	1408	1760	2112	2464
20	640	800	960	1120	45	1440	1800	2160	2520
21	672	840	1008	1176	46	1472	1840	2208	2576
22	704	880	1056	1232	47	1504	1880	2256	2632
23	736	920	1104	1288	48	1536	1920	2304	2688
24	768	960	1152	1344	49	1568	1960	2352	2744
25	800	1000	1200	1400	50	1600	2000	2400	2800
26	832	1040	1248	1456	51	1632	2040	2448	2856
27	864	1080	1296	1512	52	1664	2080	2496	2912
28	896	1120	1344	1568	53	1696	2120	2544	2968
29	928	1160	1392	1624	54	1728	2160	2592	3024
30	960	1200	1440	1680	55	1760	2200	2640	3080
31	992	1240	1488	1736	56	1792	2240	2688	3136
32	1024	1280	1536	1792	57	1824	2280	2736	3192
33	1056	1320	1584	1848	58	1856	2320	2784	3248
34	1088	1360	1632	1904	59	1888	2360	2832	3304
35	1120	1400	1680	1960	60	1920	2400	2880	3360

ESTIMATING THE AMOUNT OF HARDWOOD STRIP FLOORING REQUIRED

An allowance for side-matching, plus 5% for end-matching and normal waste are incorporated in these percentages.

Take the Square Footage and ADD the percentage below opposite the size strip flooring to be used.

When using		
3/4x1-1/2" Strip ADD	55%
3/4x2"	42-1/2%
3/4x2-1/4"	38-1/3%
3/4x3-1/4"	29%
3/8x1-1/2"	38-1/3%
3/8x2"	30%
1/2x2-1/2"	38-1/3%
1/2x2"	30%

Above percentages are for laying flooring straight across the room. Additional flooring should be estimated for diagonal applications and bay windows or other projections.

CONVERTING SQUARE FEET OF FLOOR SPACE
To Board Feet of Strip Flooring Required.

FLOOR SPACE	BOARD FEET REQUIRED (5% Cutting Waste Included)				
Square Feet	3/4x2¼"	3/4x1½"	3/4x3¼"	1/2x2"	3/8x1½"
5	7	8	6	7	7
10	14	16	13	13	14
20	28	31	26	26	28
30	42	47	39	39	42
40	55	62	52	52	55
50	69	78	65	65	69
60	83	93	77	78	83
70	97	109	90	91	97
80	111	124	103	104	111
90	125	140	116	117	125
100	138	155	129	130	138
200	277	310	258	260	277
300	415	465	387	390	415
400	553	620	516	520	553
500	692	775	645	650	692
600	830	930	774	780	830
700	968	1085	903	910	968
800	1107	1240	1032	1040	1107
900	1245	1395	1161	1170	1245
1000	1383	1550	1290	1300	1383

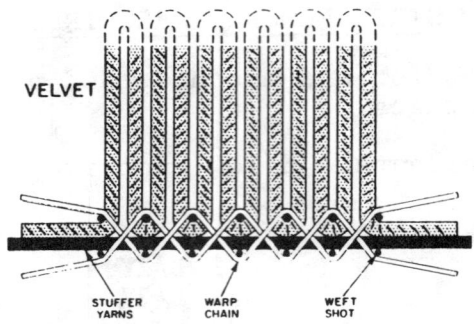

(a) Velvet weave

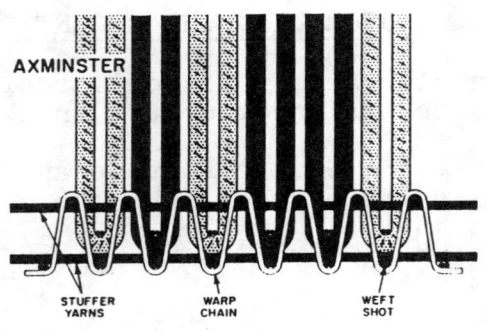

(c) Axminster weave

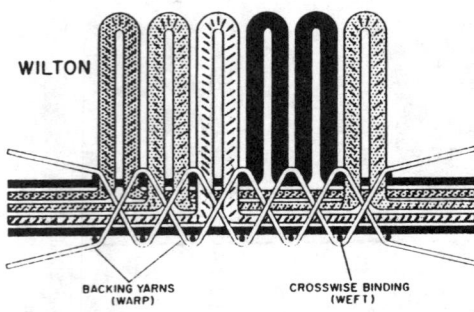

(b) Wilton weave

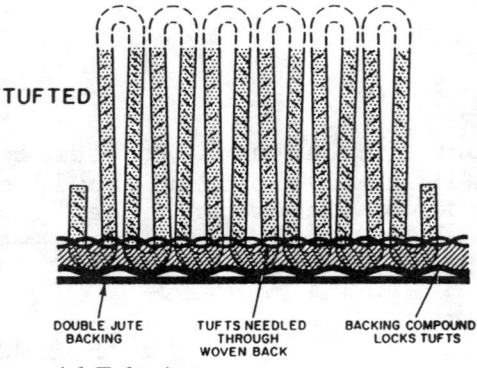

(d) Tufted process

Fig. 14

Carpets are manufactured in three different ways: woven, knitted, or tufted.

Woven carpet The surface pile and backing of woven carpet are interwoven at the same time, creating a single fabric. Due to the interweaving, which locks all of the yarns together in the single woven fabric, the pile yarns cannot be pulled out. Some carpet weaves presently available are velvet, wilton, and axminster. Velvet is best suited for solid-color carpet; however, tweeds, stripes, and salt-and-pepper effects can be produced on velvet looms. The usual velvet is a solid-color carpet with smooth surface and even pile. Sometimes the pile is cut to produce a plushlike surface [see Fig. 14(a)]. It may also be had in loop pile, or twist.

Wilton weave comes in almost unlimited numbers of textures and sculptured effects, as well as patterns. The pile is sometimes cut, sometimes left uncut; a combination of cut and uncut may also be obtained. In multicolor wiltons, one color may be seen on the surface pile, while other colors are hidden in the body of the carpet. Embossed and sculptured effects are also made by the wilton looms, and cut and uncut pile can be combined with cut pile for the top level, with loops at other levels. Another variation is to have some pile yarn straight and others twisted [see Fig. 14(b)].

In the axminster weave, which is similar in appearance to handweaving, we find a complete flexibility in the use of color. In this method each tuft is inserted separately and while solid-color carpets can be made by this method, it is nearly always used for multi-colored pattern carpet such as orientals, or modern and geometric designs [see Fig. 14(c)].

Tufted carpet In the tufted process, which was only recently perfected, the tufts are attached to a previously made backing, as compared with the methods described above in which the backing and pile are integral. The tufts are held in place by a heavy coating of latex applied to the backing, which is usually cotton, jute, or kraft cord. By the use of this method, a wide variety of textures is possible. For example, the tufted pile can be made in several levels; it can be cut or uncut; and carved or striated effects can be obtained. The pile can be looped or plush. Tufted carpets are made in multicolor patterns with an increasing number of textural effects and refinements [see Fig. 14(d)].

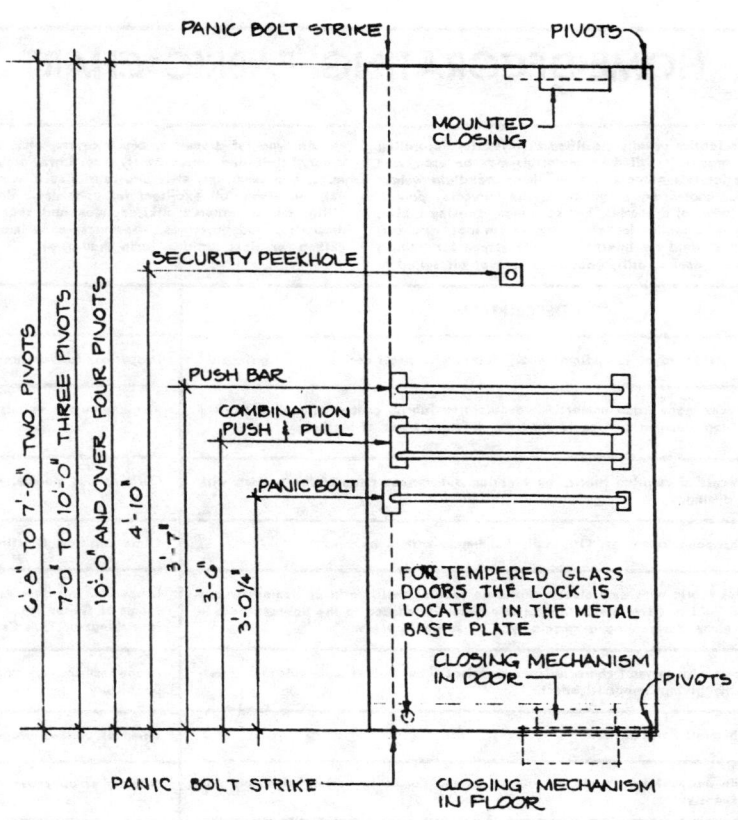

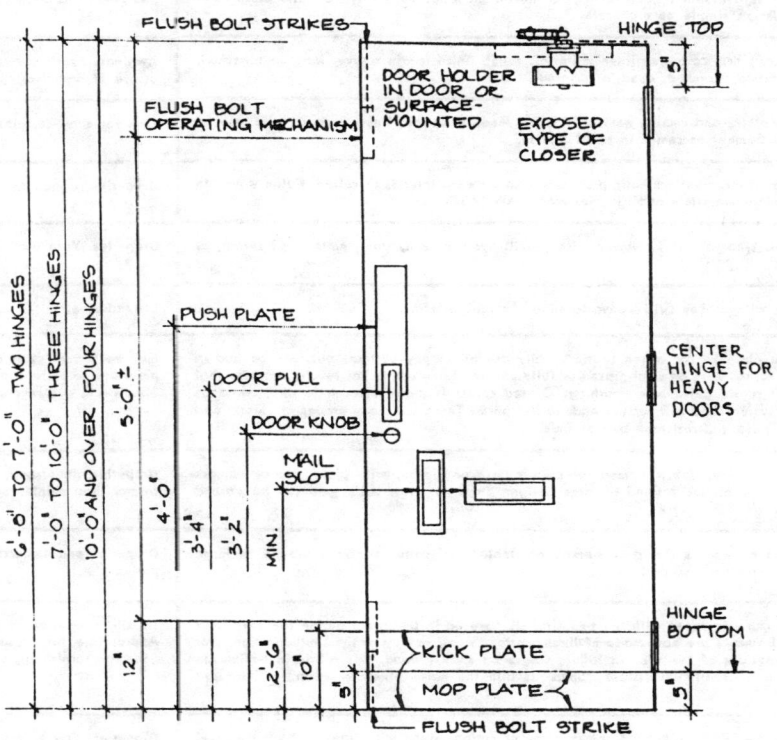

FINISH HARDWARE LOCATION FOR
ALL TYPES of DOORS

HOME-DECORATING FABRIC CHART

In the chart below are listed the fabrics usually classified as primarily decorating materials. In addition to these, practically all dress materials may be used, and are often woven in extra widths for this purpose. Among these are: light weight cottons such as cambric, challis, chambray, gingham, muslin, percale, poplin, seersucker, silkaline all used for informal draperies, bed coverings, dressing tables, etc.; stiff fabrics such as buckram and crinoline for interlining curtain tops, valances, etc.; cottons such as Canton flannel used for interlinings, and sateen for linings; heavy utility cottons such as crash, denim, drill, gabardine, pique, all suited to certain types of draperies, couch covers, etc.; sheer cottons such as cheesecloth, dimity, plain and dotted Swiss, lace, lawn, organdy, voile, all used for glass curtains, bed coverings, etc.; pile fabrics such as corduroy, panne velet, velour, velvet, velveteen, all excellent for upholstery, draperies, etc.; silk fabrics such as faille, moire (watered silk), pongee and shantung, satin, taffeta, all used for draperies, bed coverings, slipcovers, sometimes upholstery; sheer silks such as chiffon for glass curtains, lamp shades, etc.

FABRIC	DESCRIPTION	SUITABLE FOR
ARMURE	Ribbed silk, cotton, rayon (sometimes wool), fabric with small design on the surface.	Draperies. Medium-weight upholstery.
ARTIFICIAL LEATHER	Available under many trade names. A woven cotton fabric, coated with nitrocellulose preparation and stamped surface to simulate different kinds of leather.	Medium-weight upholstery. Panels. Other decorative uses.
BATIK	Javanese process of coloring fabrics by blocking out various parts of the pattern with wax before dyeing.	Curtains and panels. Other decorative effects.
BOBBINET	Net with hexagonal openings. Originally handmade with a bobbin.	Glass curtains. Dressing table skirts, etc.
BROCADE	Rich, colorful fabric with embroidery effects on taffeta, twill, satin or damask weave background. Gold or silver metal threads sometimes introduced in the figures. Brocade is also the name designating a certain type of Jacquard weave.	Draperies. Medium-weight upholstery. Especially good for rooms of Queen Anne, Chippendale, Hepplewhite or Sheraton furnishings of 18th Century.
BROCATELLE	A heavy fabric with general characteristics of damask, but figures more raised and velvety in quality giving embossed effect.	Draperies on very large studio-size windows. Heavy-weight upholstery.
BROCHE	Brocade with small floral pattern.	Lined or unlined draperies. Medium-weight upholstery.
BURLAP	Coarse, plain-weave fabric made of jute or hemp. Comes in variety of colors and widths. Inexpensive.	Drapery or upholstery purposes.
CALICO	Light-weight cotton fabric in plain weave. May be printed, plain or patterned, in deep colors. Designs usually small. (Also for dresses.)	Curtains, draperies, bedspreads, comfortables. Excellent with Early American or French Provincial furnishings.
CANDLEWICK	Cotton yarn used for hand tufting on muslin sheeting. Yarn may be white or in color and design simple or elaborate.	Bedspreads, draperies, and other decorative purposes.
CANVAS	A coarse, firm cotton or linen material, rough finish, plain weave. May be bleached, unbleached, starched, dyed, or printed.	Awnings, couch covers, etc.; also used for stiff interlining as at top of draperies.
CASEMENT CLOTH	Light, plain, and usually neutral in color. Made in cotton, linen, mohair, silk, wool or rayon. Sometimes comes in small figures.	Fine for draw-curtains; also glass curtains in sheer textures.
CELLOPHANE	Glossy, transparent synthetic product woven on warp threads of cotton. Often woven in with other materials and used for many novelty effects.	Draperies in modern interiors. Trimmings, etc.
CHENILLE	Various types of fabrics woven with chenille yarn of silk, wool, mercerized cotton, or rayon.	Draperies. Yarn used for tufting, fringes, etc.
CHEVRON CLOTH	Fabric with broken twill weave forming chevron pattern.	Draperies, etc.
CHINTZ	A firm plain weave cotton fabric usually printed in gay pattern, but may be had in plain colors. May be semi-glazed or fully glazed. Some chintz has special finish so that it will retain glaze after washing. Glazed chintz is more resistant to dirt, while its shiny surface and stiff texture adds to its charm. There are many grades of chintz, and many have soil-resistant special finish.	May be formal or informal in pattern. Suitable to any room according to pattern, quality and treatment. Used for draperies, upholstery, slip covers, lamp shades, etc.
CRETONNE	Cotton or linen fabric named for French town of Creton, with plain, rep or damask weave background printed in large designs. Does not muss easily and can be washed often.	Draperies, upholstery, slip covers, bed covers, etc. Often more formal than chintz.
CREWEL EMBROIDERY	A type of wool embroidery worked on unbleached cotton or linen ground in large floral, bird, or tree designs.	Draperies and upholstery. Used extensively during Jacobean period.
DAMASK	The name originated with the beautiful silks woven in Damascus during the 12th Century. Damasks are now made of linen, cotton, wool, or any of the synthetic fibers, or combinations of the two. In taffeta weave on satin ground, this fabric in flat woven pattern is usually reversible. Damask is also the name given to a kind of Jacquard weave.	In silk or cotton it is used for draperies and upholstery. Appropriate for Queen Anne, Chippendale, Hepplewhite or Sheraton furnishings of 18th Century.
DRUID'S CLOTH	A fabric of loosely twisted cotton yarn, or cotton mixed with jute, in basket weave. Something like monk's cloth but not as rough in texture.	Draperies. Couch covers.
DUCK	Heavy plain weave cotton fabric.	Outdoor cushions, etc.
FELT	A material made by matting together, under heat or pressure, woolen fibers, mohair, cowhair, or mixed fibers.	Upholstery and couch covers. Rugs.

HOME-DECORATING FABRIC CHART CONTINUED

FABRIC	DESCRIPTION	SUITABLE FOR
FILET NET	Cotton or linen net with square mesh. Hand netted filet has a knot at each corner of square mesh.	Curtains, tablecloths, scarves, etc.
FORTUNY PRINTS	Fabrics produced in Venice by a secret printing process which gives cotton cloth the effect of antique brocades and damasks. Comes in beautiful color combinations.	Draperies. Wall hangings, screens, etc.
FRIAR'S CLOTH	Like druid's cloth but with finer basket weave.	Same as druid's cloth.
FRISE	Uncut pile fabric of wool, mohair, cotton or linen. Patterns may be printed or produced by using yarns of different colors, or by cutting some of the loops to give sculptured effect. Very durable.	Upholstery.
GAUZE	Thin, sheer transparent fabric of plain weave, sometimes printed. May be all silk, or cotton, linen, wool, mohair, synthetic fibers, or combinations.	Glass curtains.
HAIR CLOTH	A fabric with warp of cotton, worsted, or linen, and horsehair weft, woven plain, striped or patterned. May now be obtained in colors and variety of woven designs.	Upholstery. Used extensively in England and America during middle of 19th Century.
HOMESPUN	Coarse hand-woven woolen, cotton or linen fabrics. Also trade name given to imitations made on power looms.	Curtains and upholstery in informal rooms. Bedspreads in cotton.
INDIA PRINTS	Printed cotton cloth with clear colors and characteristic designs of India or Persia. Handprinted with many colors on white or natural background.	Draperies. Wall hangings. Bed coverings, etc.
JASPE	Fabrics having warp threads of different colors giving material streaked or mottled effect, resembling jasper.	Draperies and other decorative effects.
LAME	A fabric with silk and metal threads in plain weave or with a woven pattern.	Drapery. Panels.
LAMPAS	A fabric similar to damask in appearance and brocatelle in weave. Generally all silk with multi-colored pattern on plain background, often classic in design.	Used as damask is used.
MARQUISETTE	Sheer cloth in gauze weave of cotton, silk, rayon, often with woven figure. It comes in wide range of colors, and may be dyed or printed.	Excellent for glass curtains. Fluffy, dainty, tailored spreads.
METALASSE	Fabric with brocaded pattern in raised, padded or blistered effect.	Draperies.
MOHAIR	Various types of fabrics made from the fleece of the Angora goat. Most durable of all textiles. Now woven in combination with cotton, linen, silk or wool into many types of plain, twill or pile fabrics.	Very durable and widely used for upholstery.
MONK'S CLOTH	Heavy cotton fabric of coarse basket weave.	Drapery material.
MOQUETTE	Pile fabric resembling frise, woven on Jacquard loom with small set pattern in different colors.	Used for upholstery in mohair, wool, or heavy cotton.
NINON	A semi-transparent fabric of silk or rayon.	Glass curtains.
PLUSH	High pile fabric resembling fur, made of silk, wool, cotton or any synthetic fiber. Pile may be cut or uncut.	Upholstery.
REP	Plain weave fabric of heavy rib made of silk, cotton or wool, or synthetic fibers. Unpatterned and reversible.	Draperies. Upholstery.
SAIL CLOTH	Stout, firm, plain weave cotton material similar to canvas in construction but lighter. Has a stiff, hard texture and is printed in gay, bright colors.	Draperies. Slip covers. Bedspreads, etc.
SLIPPER SATIN	Sleek, smooth very heavy satin in rayon or silk; may be slightly stiff because of thickness.	Drapery and upholstery, bed coverings, etc. Suitable in formal and period rooms for draperies.
SCRIM	Fabric of coarse two-ply yarns in plain, open weave. Often mercerized.	Curtains, bedspreads, etc.
STRIE	Term used to designate fabric with uneven streaked effect. This process gives two-toned appearance to taffeta, satin, etc.	According to fabric.
TERRY CLOTH	Light cotton fabric similar to bath toweling. Woven with uncut loops. May be dyed or printed, in designs of one or two colors. Rich texture and reversible.	Draperies. Draw-curtains.
THEATRICAL GAUZE	Loosely woven, transparent plain-weave fabric of cotton or linen. Obtainable in brilliant as well as soft colors. Inexpensive.	Glass curtains.
TOILES DE JOUY	Printed cotton material with repeat designs showing landscapes, or historical scenes. Reproductions of famous printed fabric woven at Jouy, near Paris, France. Designs and figure groups usually in colors on white or cream background.	Draperies, wall hangings, upholstery, bed coverings. Excellent for French, English and American period rooms of late 18th Century and early 19th Century; also French Provincial.
TWEED WEAVES	Term applied to a large group of woolen goods made from worsted yarns, woven in plain, twill, or herringbone twill weaves in homespun type.	Draperies and upholstery. Very good for modern or masculine rooms.
VELOUR	Really a French word for velvet. Through common usage, a short-pile velvet.	Same as velvet.

ELECTRICAL
Office and Electronic Equipment

TABLE 16 Typical Amperage Ratings

Equipment	Amperage	Equipment	Amperage
Electronic Equipment'		**Electronic Equipment**	
Video Display Terminals (Detached Keyboards)		Memory Storage Devices (Desk Top)	
Normal maximum	2.50	Wang/5503 Disk	4.00
Burroughs/MT 983 TP110	.08	Xerox/8000 NS	12.00
Digital/VT 278 Decmate	1.25	Digital Equipment/RX02	3.00
Form-Phase Systems/8115-2	.48	Hewlett-Packard/8290 ZM	1.00
Harris/8680A	1.00	Hewlett-Packard/9895A	1.60
Hewlett-Packard/2382A	.75	Sperry-Univac/8406	1.50
IBM/3101	1.20	Texas Instruments/WD-500	3.00
IBM/3278 or 3276	1.33	Bell/Western Electric/Dataphone 300/1200	.08
IBM/3279	2.50		
IBM/5251 Model 11	2.10	**Office Equipment***	
IBM/6580	4.80	General	
ITT Courier/2790-2A	1.50	Typewriter	1.50
Perkin/Elmer/1251	1.30	Transcriber	.15
Prime/PT-45	1.00	Microfiche	.85
Raytheon/PTS100	.80	Manuscript holder	.75
Sperry-Univac/UTS20 (313)	.50	Calculator	.25
Texas Instruments/940/200	2.00	A.C. adapter	.05
Texas Instruments/DS990	2.20	Electric eraser	.25
Wang/5503	3.00	Pencil sharpener	.25
Xerox/8000 Series	.50	Fan	1.00
Video Display Terminals (Integrated Keyboard)		Space heater (1,000 watts)	8.50
Normal maximum	3.00	Space heater (1,250 watts)	10.50
Hewlett-Packard/HP-9845A	4.50	Space heater (1,500 watts)	12.50
Lear Siegler/ADM31	.50	Coffee pots	10.00
NCR/7900-01	.60	Copy machine	15.00
Perkin-Elmer/550B	.80	Clock	.03
Tektronics/4112	3.00	CRT (average)	1.50
Wang/5536	2.00	Printer (average)	3.50
Printers (Stand Alone)		Lighting	
Digital Equipment/LA-120AA	3.00	Adjustable task light	.80
Wang/5503	4.00	2" task light (20 watt)	.27
Xerox/8000 Print Server	11.00	2" task light (30 watt)	.40
Printers (Desk Top)		2" task light (40 watt)	.48
Normal maximum	3.50	2" task light (35 watt, energy-saving ballast)	.38
Centronics/7030	1.50	Indirect ambient light	
Digital Equipment/Decwriter IV	1.30	(30 watt/2 lamp)	.68
Form-Phase Systems/8125	1.60	(30 watt/3 lamp)	1.08
Hewlett-Packard/7221B	1.00	(40 watt/2 lamp)	.80
Hewlett-Packard/HP7240A	2.50	(40 watt/3 lamp)	1.28
IBM/3287	2.36	(35 watt/2 lamp)	.63
IBM/5256	4.70	(35 watt/3 lamp with energy-saving ballast)	1.01
Epson/FX 185	.70	HID light (400 watt)	4.00
NEC/3510	2.50	(250 watt)	2.50
ITT Courier/8700	1.60	(175 watt)	1.80
Lear Siegler/300 Series	1.60	PLP light (20 watt)	.65
Perkin-Elmer/650	1.50	(40 watt)	.80
Raytheon/PTS 1200 3472	1.50		
Sperry-Univac/0786	4.00		
Tektronix/4612	3.30		
Texas Instruments/Omni-800 810R0	5.00		
Wang/5531-2 w/floor mount	1.70		
Wang/5577 (DW-20 Series)	1.20		

Note: These figures are for quick reference only. For specific information consult the manufacturer.

*Some appliances — such as large copiers, coffee makers, or space heaters — require most of the current available on a 20-amp circuit. It is recommended that such devices be supplied with their own receptacle, directly from the building. This leaves the capacity of Series 9000 circuits available for the more dynamic requirements of the office occupants.

Receptacle required if any wall width is 2 ft or more

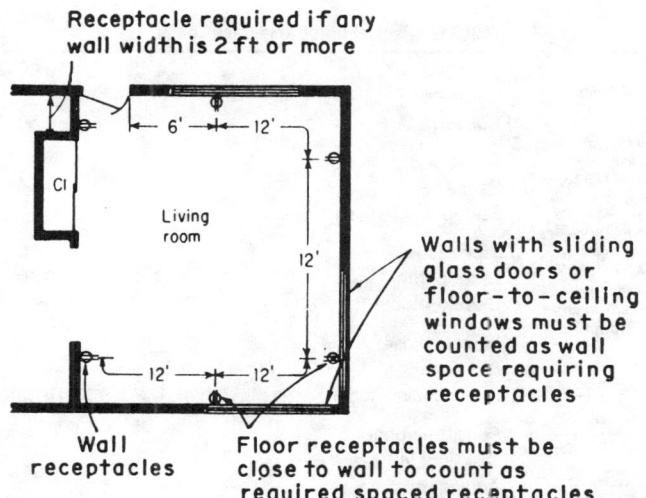

Walls with sliding glass doors or floor-to-ceiling windows must be counted as wall space requiring receptacles

Wall receptacles

Floor receptacles must be close to wall to count as required spaced receptacles

Fig. 15 From any point along wall, at floor line, a receptacle must be not more than 6 ft away.

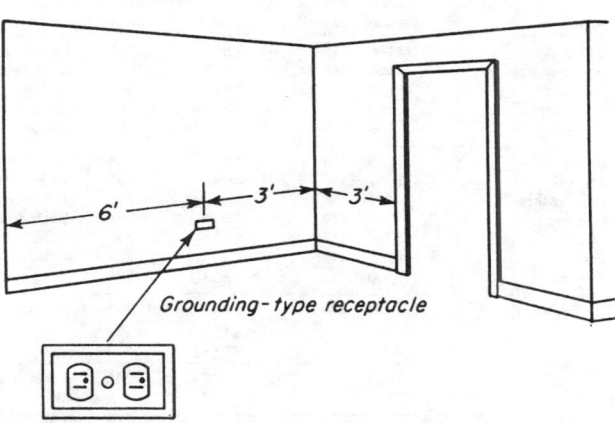

Grounding-type receptacle

Fig. 16 Location of the receptacle as shown will permit the plugging in of a lamp or appliance located 6 ft on either side of the receptacle.

Receptacle required at each counter space wider than 12 in.

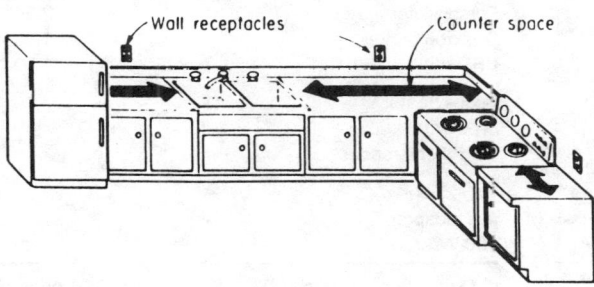

Wall receptacles   Counter space

COUNTER SPACES in kitchen and dining rooms such as shown by arrows (above) must be supplied with receptacles if they are over 12 in. wide Appliances are frequently used even on narrow counter widths; this requirement is designed to remove the dangerous practice of stretching cords across sinks, behind ranges, etc., to feed such appliances.

Inaccessible receptacles.

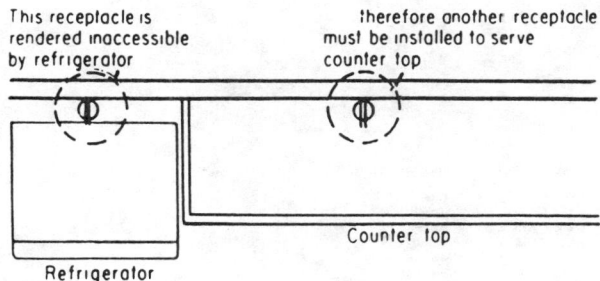

This receptacle is rendered inaccessible by refrigerator

therefore another receptacle must be installed to serve counter top

Counter top

Counter top

Refrigerator

RECEPTACLE LOCATED behind an appliance, making the receptacle inaccessible, does not count as one of the required "counter-top" receptacles. (Neither does it count as one of the appliance-circuit receptacles required to be located every 12 ft.)

Fig. 17 Countertop receptacles are needed and must be accessible.

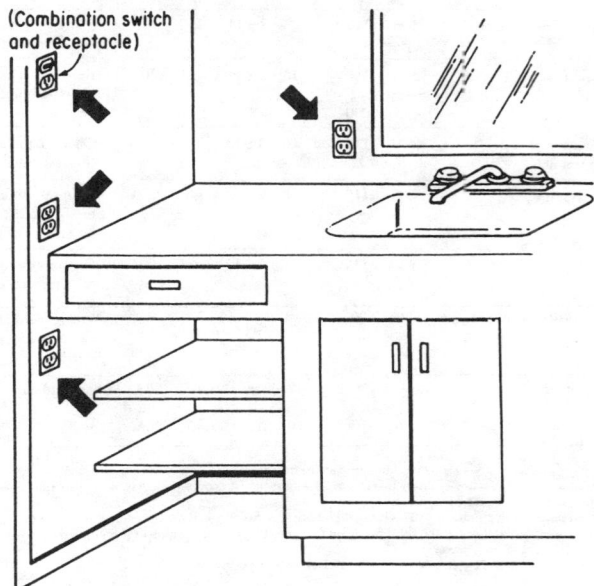

(Combination switch and receptacle)

LOCATION of receptacle will vary, depending upon available wall space. Arrows show several possibilities. A receptacle in a medicine cabinet or in the bathroom lighting fixture does not satisfy this rule.

Fig. 18 Receptacle required adjacent to wash basin in residence.

ELECTRICAL
Appliance Loads and House Circuits

TABLE 17   Residential Appliance, Load, and Circuit Chart*

Appliance	Typical wattage	Voltage needed	Amps load	Wires and size†	Size fuse or breaker‡	Type of circuit and comments
Range	12,000	115/230	52	3#6	50A	Separate circuit—grounded
Countertop range	6,000	115/230	26	3#10	30A	Separate circuit—grounded
Oven built-in	5,000	115/230	22	3#10	30A	Separate circuit—grounded
Dishwasher	1,200	115	10	2#12 w/grd§	20A	These two can be connected on one
Waste disposal	500	115	5	2#12 w/grd	20A	circuit; must be grounded.
Broiler	1,500	115	13	2#12	20A	Two or more 20-amp circuits needed
Fryer	1,300	115	11	2#12	20A	for these appliances depending on
Coffeemaker	800	115	7	2#12	20A	number used at once. A 115/230 V
Refrigerator	400	115	4	2#12	20A	"splitwired" circuit provides capac-
Toaster	1,100	115	10	2#12	20A	ity of two ordinary circuits at any
Frypan	1,200	115	10	2#12	20A	outlet. Ask your wiring inspector
Roaster	1,500	115	13	2#12	20A	about this.
Clothes dryer	5,000 to 9,000	115/230	25	3#10 to 3#6	30A to 45A	Separate circuit—grounded.
Washer	500	115	9	2#12 w/grd	20A	Grounded—advise fused outlet for motor protection.
Hand iron	1,000	115	9	2#12 w/grd	20A	A 20-A circuit will carry
Hot plate	1,500	115	13	2#12 w/grd	20A	only one of these in addition
Ironer	1,650	115	15	2#12 w/grd	20A	to washer.
Workshop	――	115	―	2#12	20A	Separate circuit grounded.
Portable heater	1,500	115	13	2#12	20A	
Television	300	115	3	2#14	15A	Use on general-use circuits.
Portable lights—(up to)	300	115	3	2#14	15A	
Lighting, general (each)	100	115	1½	2#14	15A	(Not over 9 per circuit, including convenience outlets.)
Air conditioner (window unit)	1,500	115 or 230	13 or 7	2#12 w/grd	20A	Requires separate circuit; 230 volt operation preferred.
Air conditioner (central unit)	3,400	115/230	20	3#10	—	Check manufacturer's recommendations; should be grounded.
Water system	500	115	5	2#12 w/grd	20A	Separate circuit—grounded. Provide motor protection (230V. for ½ hp. or larger).
Heating plant	600	115	6	2#12 w/grd	20A	Separate circuit—grounded. Provide motor protection.
Electric heaters (built-in)	750 to 4,500	230	—	—	—	Wiring should be planned with heating. Provide separate circuits for heating.
Water heater	1,500 to 4,500	230	7 to 20	2#12 w/grd 2#10 w/grd	20A to 30A	Separate circuit—grounded.

† Wire sizes are for copper wire. For aluminum, use next larger size.
‡ Fustats advised in place of ordinary fuses up to 30 amp as they do not blow on harmless short-time overloads and cannot be replaced by a larger size.
§ W/grd means with groundwire. This is usually a bare wire run inside the same cable but can be installed separately. Portable equipment is grounded through the third prong on the plug. Permanent equipment is grounded by direct connection of the third wire to the frame of the appliance.
* Courtesy Agricultural Extension Service, South Dakota State University.

TABLE 18   Typical Office Amperage Loads

CAD station*	10.00–20.00
Calculator	.25
Coffee pot*	8.50–15.00
Clock	.03
Radio	.03
Stereo	.33
Tape recorder	.07
Laser printer*	6.00–10.00
Desktop copier*	10.00–15.00
Electric eraser	.25
Fan	1.10
Freestanding copier*	15.00–20.00
Pencil sharpener	1.00
Task light (4')	.67
Adding machine	.35
Letter opener	1.90
Dictaphone	.25
Telecopier	.50
Word processor	1.50– 3.00
Postage meter	2.80
Tape dispenser	1.80
Personal computer	3.50– 8.00
Desktop printer	1.50– 5.00
CRT	1.00– 3.00
Space heater*	12.50
Typewriter	1.50
Microfiche reader	.85
Transcriber	.15
A.C. adapter	.05
100-W lamp	.80

*Some appliances such as coffee pots, copiers, printers, and heaters consume most of the amperage available on a circuit. It is recommended that these devices be connected directly to the building power supply, leaving flexibility for other circuit planning.

TABLE 19   Common House Circuits

Type	Wire size	Ampere rating of fuse or circuit breaker	Volts	Load capacity in watts	Use of circuit	Types of outlets
General purpose	minimum #14 recommended #12	15 20	115–120	1725–1800	Installed lighting, outlets for lamps and low wattage appliances all over the house	Those for attached light fixtures; ordinary convenience outlets
Appliance	minimum #12 recommended #10	20 25	115–120	2300–2400 2875–3000	Portable appliances in kitchen, dining room, work room, laundry	Ordinary or grounded convenience outlets
Individual appliance	#12	20	115–120	2300–2400	Automatic washer, refrigerator, freezer	Ordinary or grounded convenience outlets
Individual power	#6 or #8	30–60	220–240	6600–14400	Range, water heater, clothes dryer	Receptacle for plug with 3 heavy prongs or appliances may be attached

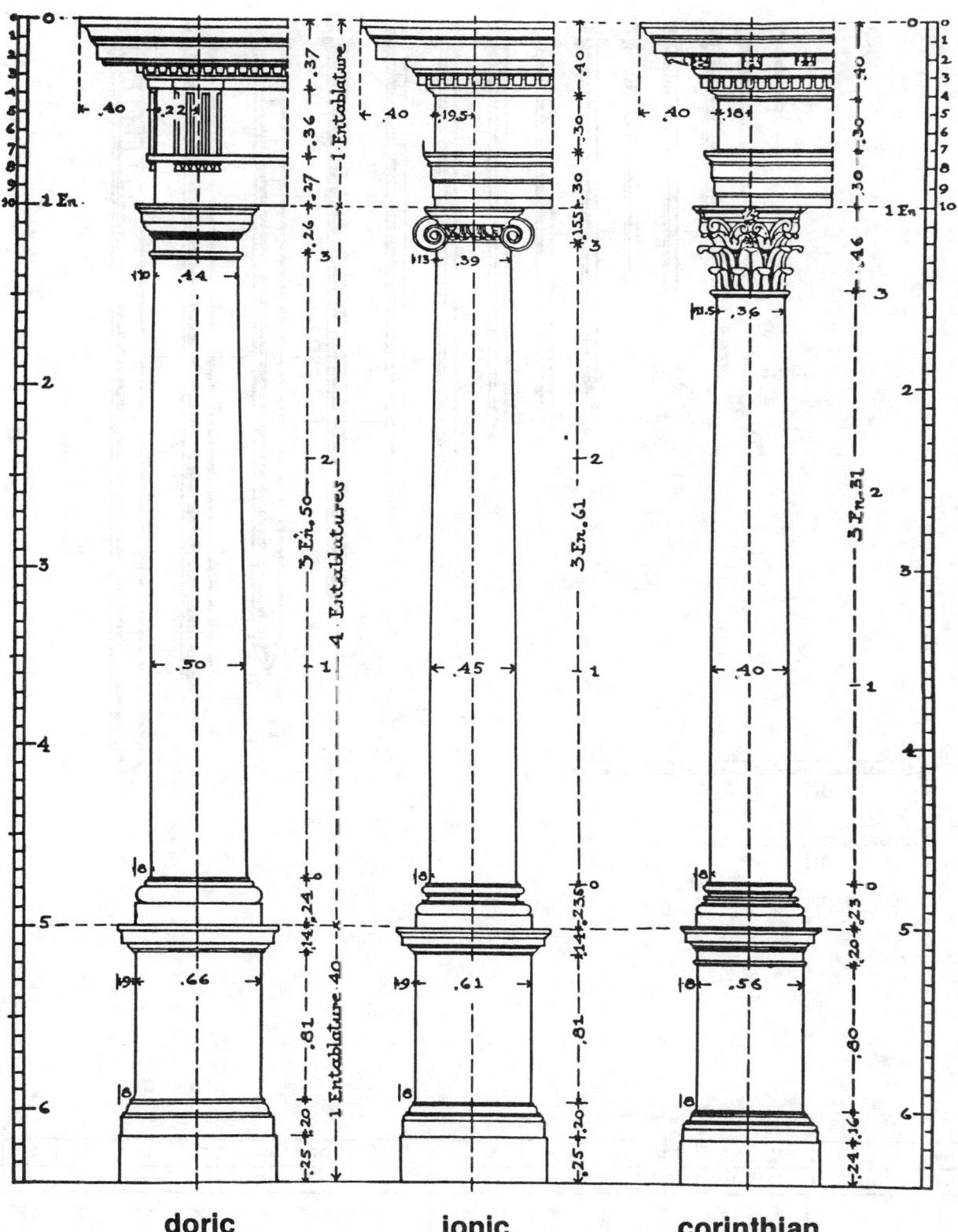

doric   **ionic**   **corinthian**

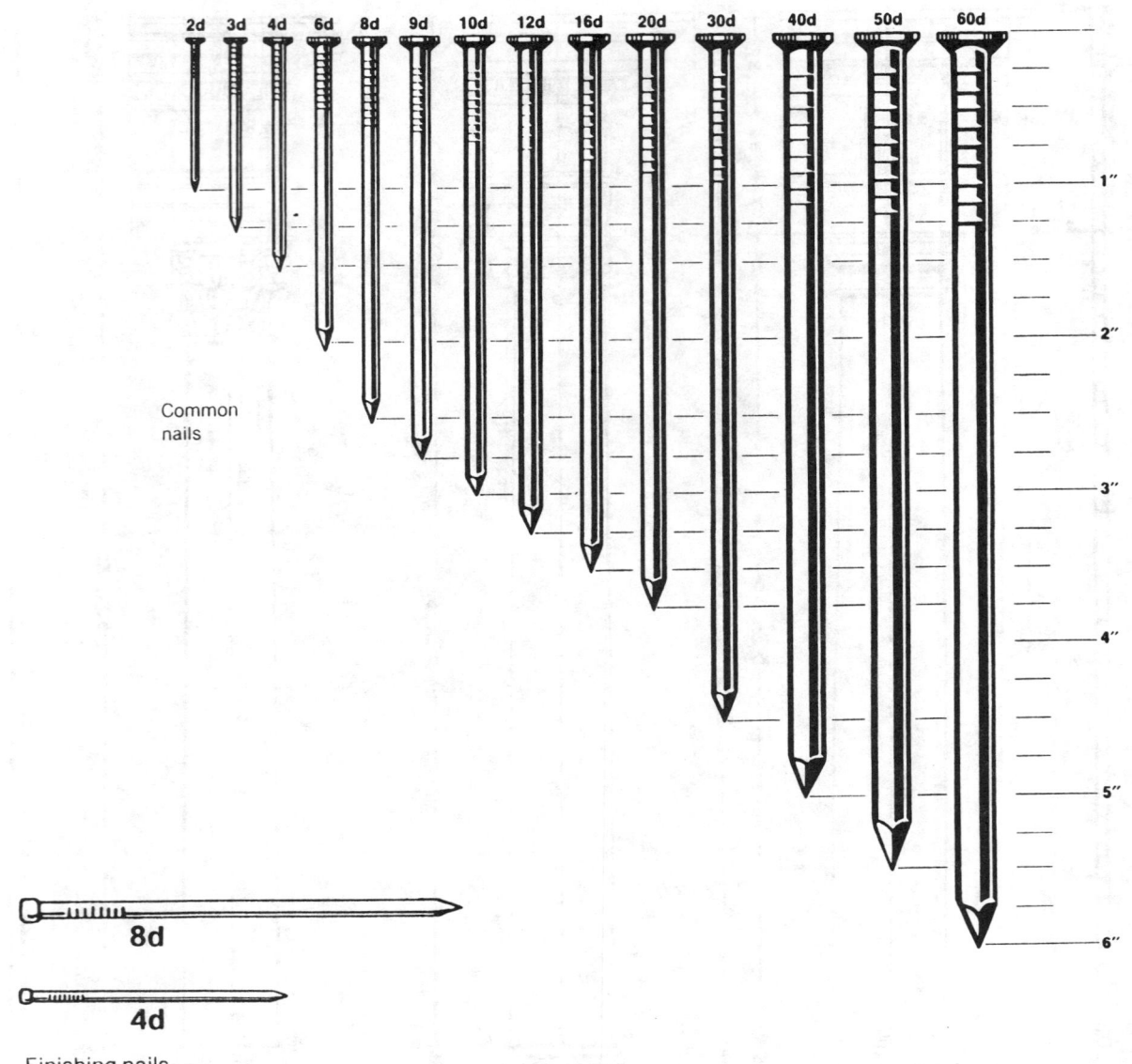

2d 3d 4d 6d 8d 9d 10d 12d 16d 20d 30d 40d 50d 60d

Common
nails

1″
2″
3″
4″
5″
6″

8d

4d

Finishing nails

Nos.	1	1-1/2	2	2-1/2	3	4	6	8	10	12	14	16	18	20	22	24
Ins.	3/16″	7/32″	1/4″	5/16″	3/8″	7/16″	1/2″	9/16″	5/8″	11/16″	3/4″	13/16″	7/8″	15/16″	1″	1-1/8″

STANDARD TACK SIZES

ESTABLISHED LENGTHS OF TACKS MEASURED UNDER THE HEAD

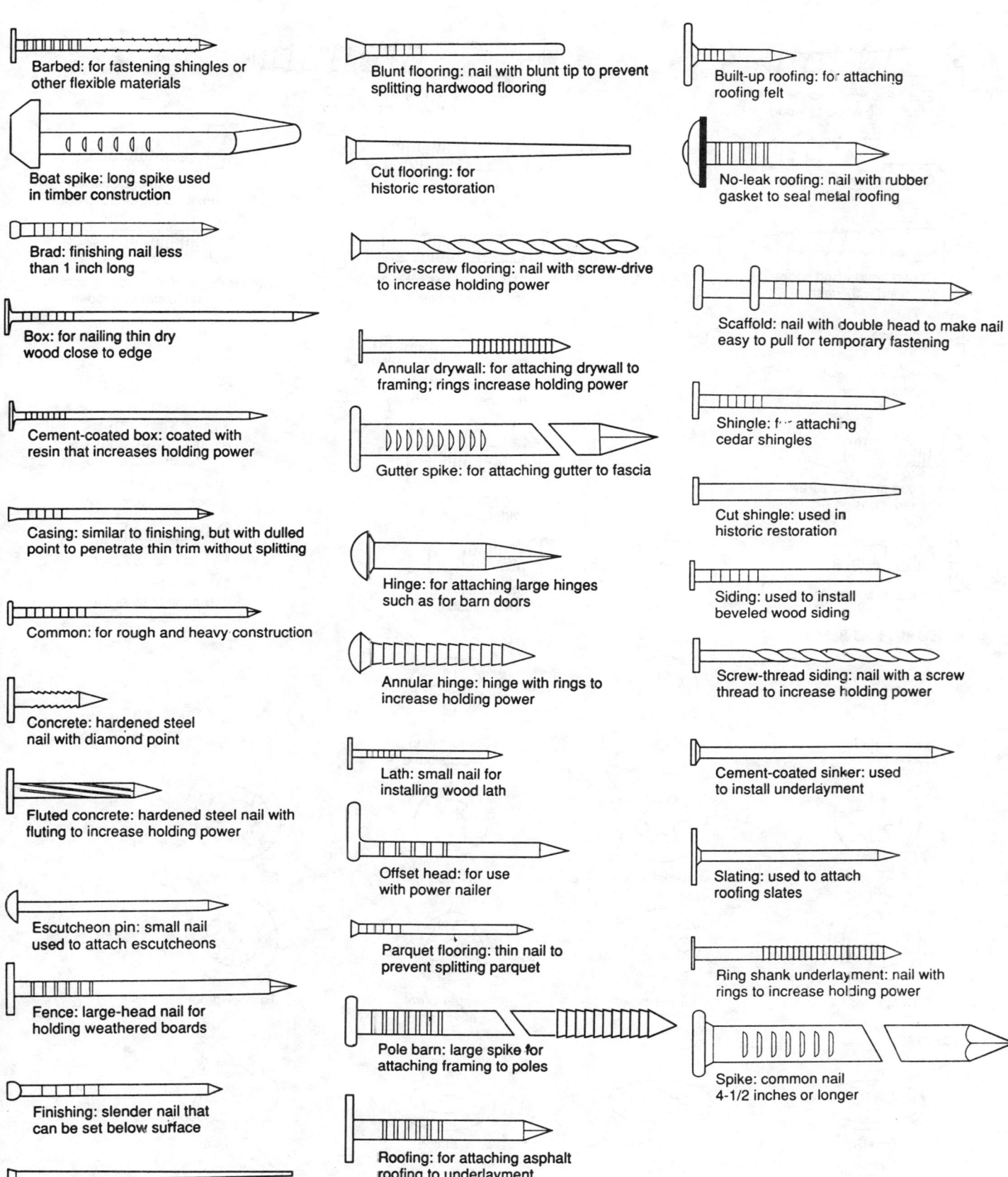

Barbed: for fastening shingles or other flexible materials

Boat spike: long spike used in timber construction

Brad: finishing nail less than 1 inch long

Box: for nailing thin dry wood close to edge

Cement-coated box: coated with resin that increases holding power

Casing: similar to finishing, but with dulled point to penetrate thin trim without splitting

Common: for rough and heavy construction

Concrete: hardened steel nail with diamond point

Fluted concrete: hardened steel nail with fluting to increase holding power

Escutcheon pin: small nail used to attach escutcheons

Fence: large-head nail for holding weathered boards

Finishing: slender nail that can be set below surface

Cut finishing: finishing nail used in historic restoration

Blunt flooring: nail with blunt tip to prevent splitting hardwood flooring

Cut flooring: for historic restoration

Drive-screw flooring: nail with screw-drive to increase holding power

Annular drywall: for attaching drywall to framing; rings increase holding power

Gutter spike: for attaching gutter to fascia

Hinge: for attaching large hinges such as for barn doors

Annular hinge: hinge with rings to increase holding power

Lath: small nail for installing wood lath

Offset head: for use with power nailer

Parquet flooring: thin nail to prevent splitting parquet

Pole barn: large spike for attaching framing to poles

Roofing: for attaching asphalt roofing to underlayment

Built-up roofing: for attaching roofing felt

No-leak roofing: nail with rubber gasket to seal metal roofing

Scaffold: nail with double head to make nail easy to pull for temporary fastening

Shingle: for attaching cedar shingles

Cut shingle: used in historic restoration

Siding: used to install beveled wood siding

Screw-thread siding: nail with a screw thread to increase holding power

Cement-coated sinker: used to install underlayment

Slating: used to attach roofing slates

Ring shank underlayment: nail with rings to increase holding power

Spike: common nail 4-1/2 inches or longer

NAILS, SCREWS, AND BOLTS

Screws and Bolts

SCREWS

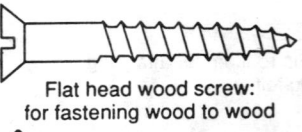

Flat head wood screw:
for fastening wood to wood

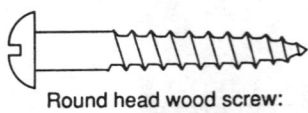

Oval head wood screw:
decorative

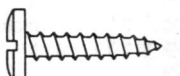

Round head wood screw:
used with washer

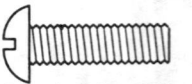

Sheet metal screw:
for thin metal

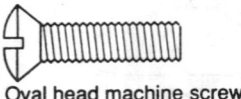

Oven head machine screw:
older design

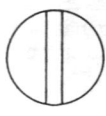

Oval head machine screw:
attractive

Lag bolt:
for heavy loads in wood

Carriage bolt:
bolt will not turn

Hex head bolt:
for heavy loads

Square head bolt:
replaced by hex head

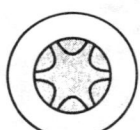

Round head bolt:
older design

Stove bolt:
finishes flush

Fillister head cap screw:
small, strong-headed

Fillister head machine screw:
small, strong-headed

Step bolt:
bolt won't turn

Plow bolt:
for steel to steel

SCREW AND BOLT HEADS

Slotted

Phillips

Combination
Phillips/slotted

Square

Frearson

Internal torx

Clutch

External torx

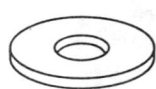

Tamper-proof

Tamper-proof

Tamper-proof
hexagon

Tamper-proof
torx

WASHERS

Flat USS

Flat SAE

Finish

Torque

Internal-
tooth

External-
tooth

Internal-external-
tooth

Split-
lock

LINEAR MEASURE

Measures of Length

12 inches	= 1 foot
3 feet	= 1 yard
5½ yards = 16½ feet	= 1 rod, pole or perch
40 poles = 220 yards	= 1 furlong
8 furlongs = 1760 yards = 5280 feet	= 1 mile
3 miles	= 1 league
4 inches	= 1 hand
9 inches	= 1 span

Nautical Units

6080.20 feet	= 1 nautical mile
6 feet	= 1 fathom
120 fathoms	= 1 cable length
1 nautical mile per hr.	= 1 knot

Surveyor's or Gunter's Measure

7.92 inches	= 1 link
100 links = 66 ft. = 4 rods	= 1 chain
80 chains	= 1 mile
33⅓ inches	= 1 vara (Texas)

Length Equivalents

Centi-meters	Inches	Feet	Yards	Meters	Chains	Kilo-meters	Miles
1	0.3937	0.03281	0.01094	0.01	0.0₃4971	10⁻⁵	0.0₅6214
2.540	**1**	0.08333	0.02778	0.0254	0.001263	0.0₄254	0.0₄1578
30.48	12	**1**	0.3333	0.3048	0.01515	0.0₃3048	0.0₃1894
91.44	36	3	**1**	0.9144	0.04545	0.0₃9144	0.0₃5682
100	39.37	3.281	1.0936	**1**	0.04971	0.001	0.0₃6214
2012	792	66	22	20.12	**1**	0.02012	0.0125
100000	39370	3281	1093.6	1000	49.71	**1**	0.6214
160935	63360	5280	1760	1609	80	1.609	**1**

Subscripts after any figure, 0₃, 9₄, etc., mean that that figure is to be repeated the indicated number of times.

MEASURES OF AREA

144	square inches	= 1 square foot
9	square feet	= 1 square yard
30¼	square yards	= 1 square rod, pole or perch

160 square rods
= 10 square chains
= 43,560 sq. ft. } = 1 acre
= 5645 sq. varas (Texas)

640 acres = 1 square mile = 1 "section" of U. S. Govt. surveyed land

Area Equivalents

Square Meters	Square Inches	Square Feet	Square Yards	Square Rods	Square Chains	Roods	Acres	Square Miles or Sections
1	1550	10.76	1.196	0.0395	0.002471	0.0₃9834	0.0₃2471	0.0₆3861
0.0₃6452	**1**	0.006944	0.0₃7716	0.0₄2551	0.0₅1594	0.0₆6377	0.0₆1594	0.0₉2491
0.09290	144	**1**	0.1111	0.003673	0.0₃2296	0.0₄9184	0.0₄2296	0.0₇3587
0.8361	1296	9	**1**	0.03306	0.002066	0.0₃8264	0.0002066	0.0₆3228
25.29	39204	272.25	30.25	**1**	0.0625	0.02500	0.00625	0.0₅9766
404.7	627264	4356	484	16	**1**	0.4	0.1	0.0001562
1012	1568160	10890	1210	40	2.5	**1**	0.25	0.0₃3906
4047	6272640	43560	4840	160	10	4	**1**	0.001562
2589998	......	27878400	3097600	102400	6400	2560	640	**1**

(1 hectare = 100 ares = 10,000 centiares or square meters)

Subscripts after any figure 0₃, 9₄, etc., mean that that figure is to be repeated the indicated number of times.

VOLUMETRIC MEASURE

Measures of Volume

1728 cubic inches	= 1 cubic foot
27 cubic feet	= 1 cubic yard
1 cord of wood	= 128 cu. ft.
1 perch of masonry	= 16½ to 25 cu. ft.

Dry Measure

2 pints	= 1 quart
8 quarts	= 1 peck
4 pecks	= 1 bushel

1 std. bbl. for fruits and vegetables = 7056 cu. in. or 105 dry quarts, struck measure

Board Measure

1 board foot = { 144 cu. in. = volume of board 1 ft. sq. and 1 in. thick.

No. of board feet in a log = [¼(d−4)]²L, where d = diam. of log (usually taken inside the bark at small end), in., and L = length of log, ft. The 4 in. deducted are an allowance for slab. This rule is variously known as the Doyle, Conn. River, St. Croix, Thurber, Moore and Beeman, and the Scribner rule.

Liquid or Fluid Measure

4 gills	= 1 pint
2 pints	= 1 quart
4 quarts	= 1 gallon
7.4805 gallons	= 1 cubic foot

(There is no standard liquid barrel; by trade custom, 1 bbl. of petroleum oil, unrefined = 42 gal.)

Volume and Capacity Equivalents

Cubic inches	Cubic feet	Cubic yards	U.S. Apothecary liquid ounces	U.S. quarts Liquid	U.S. quarts Dry	U.S. gallons Liquid	U.S. gallons Dry	Bushels U.S.	Liters (1)
1	0.0₃5787	0.0₄2143	0.5541	0.01732	0.01488	0.0₂4329	0.0₂3720	0.0₃4650	0.01639
1728	**1**	0.03704	957.5	29.92	25.71	7.481	6.429	0.8036	28.32
46656	27	**1**	25853	807.9	694.3	202.0	173.6	21.70	764.6
1.805	0.001044	0.0₄3868	**1**	0.03125	0.02686	0.007813	0.006714	0.0₃8392	0.02957
57.75	0.03342	0.001238	32	**1**	0.8594	0.25	0.2148	0.02686	0.9464
67.20	0.03889	0.001440	37.24	1.164	**1**	0.2909	0.25	0.03125	1.101
231	0.1337	0.004951	128	4	3.437	**1**	0.8594	0.1074	3.785
268.8	0.1556	0.005761	148.9	4.655	4	1.164	**1**	0.125	4.405
2150	1.244	0.04609	1192	37.24	32	9.309	8	**1**	35.24
61.02	0.03531	0.001308	33.81	1.057	0.9081	0.2642	0.22₂70	0.02838	**1**

Subscripts after any figure, 0₃, 9₄, etc., mean that that figure is to be repeated the indicated number of times.

MEASURES OF WEIGHT

Weights
(The grain is the same in all systems)

Avoirdupois Weight

16 drams = 437.5 grains		= 1 ounce
16 ounces = 7000 grains		= 1 pound
100 pounds		= 1 cental
2000 pounds		= 1 short ton
2240 pounds		= 1 long ton
1 std. lime bbl., small		= 180 lb. net
1 std. lime bbl., large		= 280 lb. net

Also (in Great Britain):

14 pounds	= 1 stone
2 stone = 28 lb.	= 1 quarter
4 quarters = 112 lb.	= 1 hundred-weight (cwt.)
20 hundredweight	= 1 long ton

Troy Weight

24 grains	= 1 penny-weight (dwt.)
20 pennyweights = 480 grains	= 1 ounce
12 ounces = 5760 grains	= 1 pound

1 Assay Ton = 29,167 milligrams, or as many milligrams as there are troy ounces in a ton of 2000 lb. avoirdupois. Consequently, the number of milligrams of precious metal yielded by an assay ton of ore gives directly the number of troy ounces that would be obtained from a ton of 2000 lb. avoirdupois

Apothecaries' Weight

20 grains	= 1 scruple ℈
3 scruples = 60 grains	= 1 dram ℨ
8 drams	= 1 ounce ℥
12 ounces = 5760 grains	= 1 pound

Mass Equivalents

Kilograms	Grains	Ounces Troy and apoth.	Ounces Avoir-dupois	Pounds Troy and apoth.	Pounds Avoir-dupois	Tons Short	Tons Long	Tons Metric
1	15432	32.15	35.27	2.6792	2.205	0.0₂1102	0.0₃9842	0.001
0.0₄6480	**1**	0.0₂2083	0.0₂2286	0.0₃1736	0.0₃1429	0.0₇7143	0.0₇6378	0.0₇6480
0.03110	480	**1**	1.09714	0.08333	0.06857	0.0₄3429	0.0₄3061	0.0₄3110
0.02835	437.5	0.9115	**1**	0.07595	0.0625	0.0₄3125	0.0₄2790	0.0₄2835
0.3732	5760	12	13.17	**1**	0.8229	0.0₃4114	0.0₃3673	0.0₃3732
0.4536	7000	14.58	16	1.215	**1**	0.0005	0.0₃4464	0.0₃4536
907.2	140₆	29167	320₃	2431	2000	**1**	0.8929	0.9072
1016	15680₄	32667	35840	2722	2240	1.12	**1**	1.016
1000	15432356	32151	35274	2679	2205	1.102	0.9842	**1**

Subscripts after any figure, 0₃, 9₄, etc., mean that that figure is to be repeated the indicated number of times.

MATHEMATICAL DATA AND FORMULAS
Metric Conversion Tables

METRIC WEIGHT

		Avoirdupois
1 milligram (mg)		= 0.0154 gr.
1 centigram (cg)	= 10 mg	= 0.1543 gr.
1 decigram (dg)	= 10 cg	= 1.5432 gr.
1 gram (g)	= 10 dg	= 15.4323 gr.
1 dekagram (dag)	= 10 g	= 0.3527 oz.
1 hectogram (hg)	= 10 dag	= 3.5274 oz.
1 kilogram (kg)	= 10 hg	= 2.2046 lb.
1 quintal (q)	= 100 kg	= 220.46 lb.
1 metric ton (M.T.)	= 10 q or 1,000 kg	= 2,204.62 lb.

AVOIRDUPOIS WEIGHT

		Metric
1 grain (gr.)		= 0.0648 g
1 dram (dr.)	= 27.34375 gr.	= 1.7718 g
1 ounce (oz.)	= 16. dr.	= 28.3495 g
1 pound (lb.)	= 16 oz.	= 453.5924 g or 0.4536 kg
1 hundredweight (cwt.)	= 100 lb.	= 45.3592 kg
1 short ton (s.t.)	= 2,000 lb.	= 907.18 kg or 0.9072 M.T.

WOOD MEASUREMENTS

	Customary	Metric
1 board foot (bd. ft.)	= 144 cu. in. (1 ft. x 1 ft. x 1 in.)	= .00236 m³
1 cord foot (cd. ft.)	= 16 cu. ft. (4 ft. x 4 ft. x 1 ft.)	= .4528 m³
1 cord (cd.)	= 8 cd. ft. (4 ft. x 4 ft. x 8 ft.)	= 3.625 m³

	Metric	Customary
1 stere	1 m³	1.3079 cu. yd. or 0.2759 cord

LENGTH AND DISTANCE

	Customary	Metric
1 inch (in.)		= 2.54 cm
1 foot (ft.)	= 12 in.	= 30.48 cm
1 yard (yd.)	= 3 ft.	= 0.9144 m
1 rod (rd.)	= 5½ yd.	= 5.0292 m
1 furlong (fur.)	= 40 rd. or ⅛ mi.	= 201.168 m
1 statute mile (mi.)	= 5,280 ft.	= 1.6093 km
1 league	= 3 mi.	= 4.8280 km

	Metric	Customary
1 millimeter (mm)		= 0.03937 in.
1 centimeter (cm)	= 10 mm	= 0.3937 in.
1 decimeter (dm)	= 10 cm	= 3.937 in.
1 meter (m)	= 10 dm	= 39.37 in.
1 dekameter (dam)	= 10 m	= 393.7 in.
1 hectometer (hm)	= 10 dam	= 328.0833 ft.
1 kilometer (km)	= 10 hm	= 0.62137 mi.

SURFACE OR AREA

	Customary	Metric
1 square inch (sq. in.)		= 6.4516 cm²
1 square foot (sq. ft.)	= 144 sq. in.	= 0.0929 m²
1 square yard (sq. yd.)	= 9 sq. ft.	= 0.8361 m²
1 square rod (sq. rd.)	= 30¼ sq. yd.	= 25.293 m²
1 acre (A.)	= 160 sq. rd.	= 0.4047 ha
1 square mile (sq. mi.)	= 640 A.	= 258.998 ha or 2.5899 km²

	Metric	Customary
1 square millimeter (mm²)		= 0.002 sq. in.
1 square centimeter (cm²)	= 100 mm²	= 0.1549 sq. in
1 square decimeter (dm²)	= 100 cm²	= 15.499 sq. in.
1 square meter (m²)	= 100 dm²	= 1.549 sq. in.
1 square dekameter (dam²)	= 100 m²	= 119.6 sq. yd.
1 square hectometer (hm²)	= 100 dam²	= 2.4710 A.
1 square kilometer (km²)	= 100 hm²	= 247.104 A. or 0.3861 sq. mi.

METRIC LAND MEASUREMENTS

	Metric	Customary
1 centiare (ca)		= 1.549 sq. in.
1 are (a)	= 100 ca	= 119.6 sq. yd.
1 hectare (ha)	= 100 a	= 2.4710 A.
1 square kilometer (km²)	= 100 ha	or 0.3861 sq. mi.

VOLUME MEASUREMENTS

	Customary	Metric
1 cubic inch (cu. in.)		= 16.387 cm³
1 cubic foot (cu. ft.)	= 1,728 cu. in.	= 0.0283 m³
1 cubic yard (cu. yd.)	= 27 cu. ft.	= 0.7646 m³

	Metric	Customary
1 cubic millimeter (mm³)		= 0.00006 cu. in.
1 cubic centimeter (cm³)	= 1,000 mm³	= 0.0610 cu. in.
1 cubic decimeter (dm³)	= 1,000 cm³	= 0.0353 cu. ft.
1 cubic meter (m³)	= 1,000 dm³	= 1.3079 cu. yd.
1 cubic dekameter (dam³)	= 1,000 m³	= 1,307.9 cu. yd.
1 cubic hectometer (hm³)	= 1,000 dam³	= 1,307,9000 cu. yd.

METRIC CAPACITY MEASUREMENTS

	Metric	Customary
1 milliliter (ml)		= 0.0610 cu. in.
1 centiliter (cl)	= 10 ml	= 0.6102 cu. in.
1 deciliter (dl)	= 10 cl	= 6.1025 cu. in.
1 liter (l)	= 10 dl	= 61.025 cu. in.
		or 1.057 liquid qt.
		or 0.908 dry
1 dekaliter (dal)	= 10 l	= 610.25 cu. in.
1 hectoliter (hl)	= 10 dal	= 6,102.50 cu. in.
1 kiloliter (kl)	= 10 hl	= 35.315 cu. ft.
		or 264.178 gal.
		or 28.38 bu.

HOUSEHOLD CAPACITY MEASUREMENTS

	Customary		Metric
1 teaspoon		= ⅙ fl. oz.	= 4.9 ml
1 tablespoon	= 3 teaspoons	= ½ fl. oz.	= 14.8 ml
1 cup	= 16 tablespoons	= 8 fl. oz.	= 236.6 ml
1 pint	= 2 cups	= 16 fl. oz.	= 473.2 ml
1 quart	= 2 pints	= 32 fl. oz.	= 946.4 ml
1 gallon	= 4 quarts	= 128 fl. oz.	= 3.785 l

LIQUID CAPACITY MEASUREMENTS

	Customary		Metric
1 gill (gi.)		= 7.219 cu. in.	= 0.1183 l
1 pint (pt.)	= 4 gi.	= 28.875 cu. in.	= 0.4732 l
1 quart (qt.)	= 2 pt.	= 57.75 cu. in.	= 0.9463 l
1 gallon (gal.)	= 4 qt.	= 231 cu. in.	= 3.7853 l
1 barrel (liquids) (bbl.)	= 31.5 gal.	= 4.21 cu. ft.	= 119.24 l
1 barrel (petroleum) (bbl.)	= 42 gal.	= 5.61 cu. ft.	= 158.98 l

Imperial	Customary		Metric
1 imperial quart	= 1.2009 U.S. qt.	= 69.355 cu. in.	= 1.13649 l
1 imperial gallon	= 1.2009 U.S. gal.	= 277.420 cu. in.	= 4.54596 l

DRY CAPACITY MEASUREMENTS

	Customary		Metric
1 pint (pt.)		= 33.600 cu. in.	= 550.60 cm³
1 quart (qt.)	= 2 pt.	= 67.20 cu. in.	= 1,101.21 cm³
1 peck (pk.)	= 8 qt.	= 537.61 cu. in.	= 8,809.85 cm³
1 bushel (bu.)	= 4 pk.	= 2,150.42 cu. in.	= 0.035239 m³
1 barrel (bbl.)		= 4.08 cu. ft.	= 0.115627 m³

Imperial	Customary		Metric
1 imperial dry quart	= 1.032 U.S. qt.	= 69.354 cu. in.	= 1,136.5 cm³
1 imperial bushel	= 1.032 U.S. bu.	= 1.284 cu. ft.	= 0.03636 m³

DECIMAL OF AN INCH AND OF A FOOT

Fractions of Inch or Foot		Inch Equiv. to Foot Fractions	Fractions of Inch or Foot		Inch Equiv. to Foot Fractions	Fractions of Inch or Foot		Inch Equiv. to Foot Fractions	Fractions of Inch or Foot		Inch Equiv. to Foot Fractions
	.0052	1/16		.2552	3 1/16		.5052	6 1/16		.7552	9 1/16
	.0104	1/8		.2604	3 1/8		.5104	6 1/8		.7604	9 1/8
1/64	.015625	3/16	17/64	.265625	3 3/16	33/64	.515625	6 3/16	49/64	.765625	9 3/16
	.0208	1/4		.2708	3 1/4		.5208	6 1/4		.7708	9 1/4
	.0260	5/16		.2760	3 5/16		.5260	6 5/16		.7760	9 5/16
1/32	.03125	3/8	9/32	.28125	3 3/8	17/32	.53125	6 3/8	25/32	.78125	9 3/8
	.0365	7/16		.2865	3 7/16		.5365	6 7/16		.7865	9 7/16
	.0417	1/2		.2917	3 1/2		.5417	6 1/2		.7917	9 1/2
3/64	.046875	9/16	19/64	.296875	3 9/16	35/64	.546875	6 9/16	51/64	.796875	9 9/16
	.0521	5/8		.3021	3 5/8		.5521	6 5/8		.8021	9 5/8
	.0573	11/16		.3073	3 11/16		.5573	6 11/16		.8073	9 11/16
1/16	.0625	3/4	5/16	.3125	3 3/4	9/16	.5625	6 3/4	13/16	.8125	9 3/4
	.0677	13/16		.3177	3 13/16		.5677	6 13/16		.8177	9 13/16
	.0729	7/8		.3229	3 7/8		.5729	6 7/8		.8229	9 7/8
5/64	.078125	15/16	21/64	.328125	3 15/16	37/64	.578125	6 15/16	53/64	.828125	9 15/16
	.0833	1		.3333	4		.5833	7		.8333	10
	.0885	1 1/16		.3385	4 1/16		.5885	7 1/16		.8385	10 1/16
3/32	.09375	1 1/8	11/32	.34375	4 1/8	19/32	.59375	7 1/8	27/32	.84375	10 1/8
	.0990	1 3/16		.3490	4 3/16		.5990	7 3/16		.8490	10 3/16
	.1042	1 1/4		.3542	4 1/4		.6042	7 1/4		.8542	10 1/4
7/64	.109375	1 5/16	23/64	.359375	4 5/16	39/64	.609375	7 5/16	55/64	.859375	10 5/16
	.1146	1 3/8		.3646	4 3/8		.6146	7 3/8		.8646	10 3/8
	.1198	1 7/16		.3698	4 7/16		.6198	7 7/16		.8698	10 7/16
1/8	.1250	1 1/2	3/8	.3750	4 1/2	5/8	.6250	7 1/2	7/8	.8750	10 1/2
	.1302	1 9/16		.3802	4 9/16		.6302	7 9/16		.8802	10 9/16
	.1354	1 5/8		.3854	4 5/8		.6354	7 5/8		.8854	10 5/8
9/64	.140625	1 11/16	25/64	.390625	4 11/16	41/64	.640625	7 11/16	57/64	.890625	10 11/16
	.1458	1 3/4		.3958	4 3/4		.6458	7 3/4		.8958	10 3/4
	.1510	1 13/16		.4010	4 13/16		.6510	7 13/16		.9010	10 13/16
5/32	.15625	1 7/8	13/32	.40625	4 7/8	21/32	.65625	7 7/8	29/32	.90625	10 7/8
	.1615	1 15/16		.4115	4 15/16		.6615	7 15/16		.9115	10 15/16
	.1667	2		.4167	5		.6667	8		.9167	11
11/64	.171875	2 1/16	27/64	.421875	5 1/16	43/64	.671875	8 1/16	59/64	.921875	11 1/16
	.1771	2 1/8		.4271	5 1/8		.6771	8 1/8		.9271	11 1/8
	.1823	2 3/16		.4323	5 3/16		.6823	8 3/16		.9323	11 3/16
3/16	.1875	2 1/4	7/16	.4375	5 1/4	11/16	.6875	8 1/4	15/16	.9375	11 1/4
	.1927	2 5/16		.4427	5 5/16		.6927	8 5/16		.9427	11 5/16
	.1979	2 3/8		.4479	5 3/8		.6979	8 3/8		.9479	11 3/8
13/64	.203125	2 7/16	29/64	.453125	5 7/16	45/64	.703125	8 7/16	61/64	.953125	11 7/16
	.2083	2 1/2		.4583	5 1/2		.7083	8 1/2		.9583	11 1/2
	.2135	2 9/16		.4635	5 9/16		.7135	8 9/16		.9635	11 9/16
7/32	.21875	2 5/8	15/32	.46875	5 5/8	23/32	.71875	8 5/8	31/32	.96875	11 5/8
	.2240	2 11/16		.4740	5 11/16		.7240	8 11/16		.9740	11 11/16
	.2292	2 3/4		.4792	5 3/4		.7292	8 3/4		.9792	11 3/4
15/64	.234375	2 13/16	31/64	.484375	5 13/16	47/64	.734375	8 13/16	63/64	.984375	11 13/16
	.2396	2 7/8		.4896	5 7/8		.7396	8 7/8		.9896	11 7/8
	.2448	2 15/16		.4948	5 15/16		.7448	8 15/16		.9948	11 15/16
1/4	.2500	3	1/2	.5000	6	3/4	.7500	9	1	1.0000	12

METRIC CONVERSION FACTORS

METRIC TO AMERICAN

Millimeters ÷ 25.4 = inches
Centimeters × 0.3937 = inches
Meters × 39.27 = inches
Millimeters × 0.003281 = feet
Centimeters × 0.03281 = feet
Meters × 3.281 = feet
Meters × 1.094 = yards
Kilometers × 0.621 = miles
Kilometers × 3280.7 = feet
Square millimeters ÷ 645.1 = square inches
Square centimeters ÷ 6.451 = square inches
Square meters × 10.764 = square feet
Square kilometers × 247.1 = acres
Hectares × 2.471 = acres
Cubic centimeters ÷ 16.383 = cubic inches
Cubic meters × 35.315 = cubic feet
Cubic meters × 1.308 = cubic yards
Cubic meters × 264.2 = gallons
Liters × 61.022 = cubic inches
Liters × 0.2642 = gallons
Liters ÷ 28.316 = cubic feet
Hectoliters × 3.531 = cubic feet
Hectoliters × 2.84 = bushels
Hectoliters × 0.131 = cubic yards
Hectoliters × 26.42 = gallons
Kilograms × 2.2046 = pounds
Kilograms ÷ 1102.3 = tons

AMERICAN TO METRIC

Inches × 25.4 = millimeters
Inches × 2.54 = centimeters
Inches × 0.0254 = meters
Feet × 304.8 = millimeters
Feet × 30.48 = centimeters
Feet × 0.3048 = meters
Yards × 0.9143 = meters
Miles × 1.6093 = kilometers
Feet ÷ 3280.7 = kilometers
Square inches × 645.1 = square millimeters
Square inches × 6.451 = square centimeters
Square feet ÷ 10.764 = square meters
Acres ÷ 247.1 = square kilometers
Acres ÷ 2.471 = hectares
Cubic inches × 16.383 = cubic centimeters
Cubic feet ÷ 35.315 = cubic meters
Cubic yards ÷ 1.308 = cubic meters
Gallons (231 cu. in.) ÷ 264.2 = cubic meters
Cubic inches ÷ 61.022 = liters
Gallons × 3.78 = liters
Cubic feet × 28.316 = liters
Cubic feet ÷ 3.531 = hectoliters
Bushels ÷ 2.84 = hectoliters
Cubic yards ÷ 0.131 = hectoliters
Gallons ÷ 26.42 = hectoliters
Pounds ÷ 2.2046 = kilograms
Tons × 1102.3 = kilograms

METRIC MEASURES

Linear	Liquid and Dry	Weights
10 millimeters = 1 centimeter	10 milliliters = 1 centiliter	10 milligrams = 1 centigram
10 centimeters = 1 decimeter	10 centiliters = 1 deciliter	10 centigrams = 1 decigram
10 decimeters = 1 METER (m)	10 deciliters = 1 LITER (l)	10 decigrams = 1 GRAM (g)
10 meters = 1 decameter	10 liters = 1 decaliter	10 grams = 1 decagram
10 decameters = 1 hectometer	10 decaliters = 1 hectoliter	10 decagrams = 1 hectogram
10 hectometers = 1 kilometer	10 hectoliters = 1 kiloliter	10 hectograms = 1 kilogram

MATHEMATICAL DATA AND FORMULAS
Areas of Plane Figures

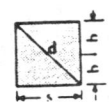

Square

Diagonal $= d = s\sqrt{2}$.
Area $= s^2 = 4b^2 = 0.5d^2$.
Example. $s = 6$; $b = 3$. Area $= (6)^2 = 36$ Ans.
$d = 6 \times 1.414 = 8.484$ Ans.

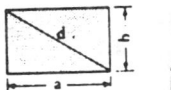

Rectangle and Parallelogram

Area $= ab$ or $b\sqrt{d^2 - b^2}$
Example. $a = 6$; $b = 3$.
Area $= 3 \times 6 = 18$ Ans

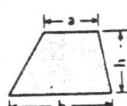

Trapezoid

Area $= \frac{1}{2}h(a + b)$
Example. $a = 2$; $b = 4$; $h = 3$.
Area $= \frac{1}{2} \times 3(2 + 4) = 9$. Ans.

Trapezium

Area $= \frac{1}{2}[a(h + h^1) + bh^1 + ch]$
Example. $a = 4$; $b = 2$; $c = 2$; $h = 3$; $h^1 = 2$.
Area $= \frac{1}{2}[4(3 + 2) + (2 \times 2) + (2 \times 3)] = 15$.
Ans.

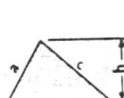

Triangles

Both formulas apply to both figures
Area $= \frac{1}{2}bh$.
Example. $h = 3$; $b = 5$.
Area $= \frac{1}{2}(3 \times 5) = 7\frac{1}{2}$. Ans.

Area $= \sqrt{S(S - a)(S - b)(S - c)}$ when $S = \frac{a + b + c}{2}$

Example. $a = 2$; $b = 3$; $c = 4$.
$S = \frac{2 + 3 + 4}{2} = 4.5$
Area $= \sqrt{4.5(4.5 - 2)(4.5 - 3)(4.5 - 4)} = 2.9$.
Ans.

Regular Polygons

Area
$\begin{cases}
5 \text{ sides} = 1.720477\ S^2 = 3.63271\ r^2 \\
6\ " = 2.598150\ S^2 = 3.46410\ r^2 \\
7\ " = 3.633875\ S^2 = 3.37101\ r^2 \\
8\ " = 4.828427\ S^2 = 3.31368\ r^2 \\
9\ " = 6.181875\ S^2 = 3.27573\ r^2 \\
10\ " = 7.694250\ S^2 = 3.24920\ r^2 \\
11\ " = 9.365675\ S^2 = 3.22993\ r^2 \\
12\ " = 11.196300\ S^2 = 3.21539\ r^2
\end{cases}$

n = number of sides; r = short radius;
S = length of side; R = long radius.

Area $= \frac{n}{4}S^2 \cot \frac{180°}{n} = \frac{n}{2}R^2 \sin \frac{360°}{n}$

$= nr^2 \tan \frac{180°}{n}$

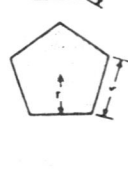

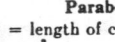

Spandrel

Area $= 0.2146r^2 = 0.1073c^2$
Example. $r = 3$
Area $= 0.2146 \times 3^2 = 1.9314$. Ans

Parabola

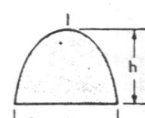

l = length of curved line = periphery − s
$l = \frac{s^2}{8h}[\sqrt{c(1+c)} + 2.0326 \times \log(\sqrt{c} + \sqrt{1+c})]$
in which $c = \left(\frac{4h}{s}\right)^2$

Area $= \frac{2}{3}sh$
Example. $s = 3$; $h = 4$
Area $= \frac{2}{3} \times 3 \times 4 = 8$. Ans.

Ellipse

Area $= \pi\,ab = 3.1416ab$

Circum. $= 2\pi\sqrt{\frac{a^2 + b^2}{2}}$ (close approximation)

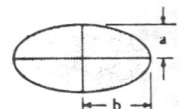

Example. $a = 3$; $b = 4$.
Area $= 3.1416 \times 3 \times 4 = 37.6992$. Ans.

Circum. $= 2 \times 3.1416\sqrt{\frac{(3)^2 + (4)^2}{2}}$
$= 6.2832 \times 3.5355 = 22.21$ Ans.

Circle

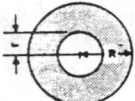

$\pi = 3.1416$; A = area; d = diameter; p = circumference or periphery; r = radius.

$p = \pi d = 3.1416d$. $p = 2\sqrt{\pi A} = 3.54\sqrt{A}$

$p = 2\pi r = 6.2832r$. $p = \frac{2A}{r} = \frac{4A}{d}$

$d = \frac{p}{\pi} = \frac{p}{3.1416}$ $d = 2\sqrt{\frac{A}{\pi}} = 1.128\sqrt{A}$

$r = \frac{p}{2\pi} = \frac{p}{6.2832}$ $r = \sqrt{\frac{A}{\pi}} = 0.564\sqrt{A}$

$A = \frac{\pi d^2}{4} = 0.7854d^2$ $A = \frac{p^2}{4\pi} = \frac{p^2}{12.57}$

$A = \pi r^2 = 3.1416r^2$ $A = \frac{pr}{2} = \frac{pd}{4}$

Circular Ring

Area $= \pi(R^2 - r^2) = 3.1416(R^2 - r^2)$
Area $= 0.7854(D^2 - d^2) = 0.7854(D - d)(D + d)$
Area = difference in areas between the inner and outer circles.
Example. $R = 4$; $r = 2$.
Area $= 3.1416(4^2 - 2^2) = 37.6992$. Ans.

Quadrant

Area $= \frac{\pi r^2}{4} = 0.7854r^2 = 0.3927c^2$.

Example. $r = 3$. c = chord.
Area $= .7854 \times 3^2 = 7.0686$. Ans.

Segment

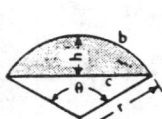

b = length of arc. θ = angle in degrees
c = chord $= \sqrt{4(2hr - h^2)}$
Area $= \frac{1}{2}[br - c(r - h)]$
$= \pi r^2 \frac{\theta}{360} - \frac{c(r - h)}{2}$

When θ is greater than 180° then $\frac{c}{2} \times$ difference

between r and h is added to the fraction $\frac{\pi r^2 \theta}{360}$

Example. $r = 3$; $\theta = 120°$; $h = 1.5$
Area $= 3.1416 \times 3^2 \times \frac{120}{360} - \frac{5.196(3 - 1.5)}{2}$
$= 5.5278$. Ans.

Sector

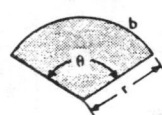

Area $= \frac{br}{2} = \pi r^2 \frac{\theta}{360°}$

θ = angle in degrees; b = length of arc.
Example. $r = 3$; $\theta = 120°$
Area $= 3.1416 \times 3^2 \times \frac{120}{360} = 9.4248$. Ans.

FORM			METHOD OF FINDING AREAS
TRIANGLE			Base × ½ perpendicular height. $\sqrt{s(s-a)(s-b)(s-c)}$, s = ½ sum of the three sides a, b, c.
TRÁPEZIUM			Sum of area of the two triangles
TRAPEZOID			½ sum of parallel sides × perpendicular height.
PARALLELOGRAM			Base × perpendicular height.
REG. POLYGON			½ sum of sides × inside radius.
CIRCLE			$\pi r^2 = 0.78540 \times$ diam^2. = 0.07958 × circumference
SECTOR OF A CIRCLE			$\frac{\pi r^2 A°}{360} = 0.0087266\ r^2 A°$, = arc × ½ radius
SEGMENT OF A CIRCLE			$\frac{r^2}{2}\left(\frac{\pi A}{180} - \sin A°\right)$
CIRCLE of same area as a square			Diameter = side × 1.12838
SQUARE of same area as a circle			Side = diameter × 0.88623
ELLIPSE			Long diameter × short diameter × 0.78540
PARABOLA			Base × ⅔ perpendicular height.

TABLE 20   Functions of Numbers

NO.	SQUARE	CUBE	SQUARE ROOT	CUBE ROOT	LOGARITHM	1000 x RECIPROCAL	NO. - DIAMETER CIRCUM.	AREA
1	1	1	1.0000	1.0000	0.00000	1000.000	3.142	0.7854
2	4	8	1.4142	1.2599	0.30103	500.000	6.283	3.1416
3	9	27	1.7321	1.4422	0.47712	333.333	9.425	7.0686
4	16	64	2.0000	1.5874	0.60206	250.000	12.566	12.5664
5	25	125	2.2361	1.7100	0.69897	200.000	15.708	19.6350
6	36	216	2.4495	1.8171	0.77815	166.667	18.850	28.2743
7	49	343	2.6458	1.9129	0.84510	142.857	21.991	38.4845
8	64	512	2.8284	2.0000	0.90309	125.000	25.133	50.2655
9	81	729	3.0000	2.0801	0.95424	111.111	28.274	63.6173
10	100	1000	3.1623	2.1544	1.00000	100.000	31.416	78.5398
11	121	1331	3.3166	2.2240	1.04139	90.9091	34.558	95.0332
12	144	1728	3.4641	2.2894	1.07918	83.3333	37.699	113.097
13	169	2197	3.6056	2.3513	1.11394	76.9231	40.841	132.732
14	196	2744	3.7417	2.4101	1.14613	71.4286	43.982	153.938
15	225	3375	3.8730	2.4662	1.17609	66.6667	47.124	176.715
16	256	4096	4.0000	2.5198	1.20412	62.5000	50.265	201.062
17	289	4913	4.1231	2.5713	1.23045	58.8235	53.407	226.980
18	324	5832	4.2426	2.6207	1.25527	55.5556	56.549	254.469
19	361	6859	4.3589	2.6684	1.27875	52.6316	59.690	283.529
20	400	8000	4.4721	2.7144	1.30103	50.0000	62.832	314.159
21	441	9261	4.5826	2.7589	1.32222	47.6190	65.973	346.361
22	484	10648	4.6904	2.8020	1.34242	45.4545	69.115	380.133
23	529	12167	4.7958	2.8439	1.36173	43.4783	72.257	415.476
24	576	13824	4.8990	2.8845	1.38021	41.6667	75.398	452.389
25	625	15625	5.0000	2.9240	1.39794	40.0000	78.540	490.874
26	676	17576	5.0990	2.9625	1.41497	38.4615	81.681	530.929
27	729	19683	5.1962	3.0000	1.43136	37.0370	84.823	572.555
28	784	21952	5.2915	3.0366	1.44716	35.7143	87.965	615.752
29	841	24389	5.3852	3.0723	1.46240	34.4828	91.106	660.520
30	900	27000	5.4772	3.1072	1.47712	33.3333	94.248	706.858
31	961	29791	5.5678	3.1414	1.49136	32.2581	97.389	754.768
32	1024	32768	5.6569	3.1748	1.50515	31.2500	100.531	804.248
33	1089	35937	5.7446	3.2075	1.51851	30.3030	103.673	855.299
34	1156	39304	5.8310	3.2396	1.53148	29.4118	106.814	907.920
35	1225	42875	5.9161	3.2711	1.54407	28.5714	109.956	962.113
36	1296	46656	6.0000	3.3019	1.55630	27.7778	113.097	1017.88
37	1369	50653	6.0828	3.3322	1.56820	27.0270	116.239	1075.21
38	1444	54872	6.1644	3.3620	1.57978	26.3158	119.381	1134.11
39	1521	59319	6.2450	3.3912	1.59106	25.6410	122.522	1194.59
40	1600	64000	6.3246	3.4200	1.60206	25.0000	125.66	1256.64
41	1681	68921	6.4031	3.4482	1.61278	24.3902	128.81	1320.25
42	1764	74088	6.4807	3.4760	1.62325	23.8095	131.95	1385.44
43	1849	79507	6.5574	3.5034	1.63347	23.2558	135.09	1452.20
44	1936	85184	6.6332	3.5303	1.64345	22.7273	138.23	1520.53
45	2025	91125	6.7082	3.5569	1.65321	22.2222	141.37	1590.43

TABLE 20   Functions of Numbers *(Continued)*

NO.	SQUARE	CUBE	SQUARE ROOT	CUBE ROOT	LOGARITHM	1000 x RECIPROCAL	NO. = DIAMETER CIRCUM.	AREA
46	2116	97336	6.7823	3.5830	1.66276	21.7391	144.51	1661.90
47	2209	103823	6.8557	3.6088	1.67210	21.2766	147.65	1734.94
48	2304	110592	6.9282	3.6342	1.68124	20.8333	150.80	1809.56
49	2401	117649	7.0000	3.6593	1.69020	20.4082	153.94	1885.74
50	2500	125000	7.0711	3.6840	1.69897	20.0000	157.08	1963.50
51	2601	132651	7.1414	3.7084	1.70757	19.6078	160.22	2042.82
52	2704	140608	7.2111	3.7325	1.71600	19.2308	163.36	2123.72
53	2809	148877	7.2801	3.7563	1.72428	18.8679	166.50	2206.18
54	2916	157464	7.3485	3.7798	1.73239	18.5185	169.65	2290.22
55	3025	166375	7.4162	3.8030	1.74036	18.1818	172.79	2375.83
56	3136	175616	7.4833	3.8259	1.74819	17.8571	175.93	2463.01
57	3249	185193	7.5498	3.8485	1.75587	17.5439	179.07	2551.76
58	3364	195112	7.6158	3.8709	1.76343	17.2414	182.21	2642.08
59	3481	205379	7.6811	3.8930	1.77085	16.9492	185.35	2733.97
60	3600	216000	7.7460	3.9149	1.77815	16.6667	188.50	2827.43
61	3721	226981	7.8102	3.9365	1.78533	16.3934	191.64	2922.47
62	3844	238328	7.8740	3.9579	1.79239	16.1290	194.78	3019.07
63	3969	250047	7.9373	3.9791	1.79934	15.8730	197.92	3117.25
64	4096	262144	8.0000	4.0000	1.80618	15.6250	201.06	3216.99
65	4225	274625	8.0623	4.0207	1.81291	15.3846	204.20	3318.31
66	4356	287496	8.1240	4.0412	1.81954	15.1515	207.35	3421.19
67	4489	300763	8.1854	4.0615	1.82607	14.9254	210.49	3525.65
68	4624	314432	8.2462	4.0817	1.83251	14.7059	213.63	3631.68
69	4761	328509	8.3066	4.1016	1.83885	14.4928	216.77	3739.28
70	4900	343000	8.3666	4.1213	1.84510	14.2857	219.91	3848.45
71	5041	357911	8.4261	4.1408	1.85126	14.0845	223.05	3959.19
72	5184	373248	8.4853	4.1602	1.85733	13.8889	226.19	4071.50
73	5329	389017	8.5440	4.1793	1.86332	13.6986	229.34	4185.39
74	5476	405224	8.6023	4.1983	1.86923	13.5135	232.48	4300.84
75	5625	421875	8.6603	4.2172	1.87506	13.3333	235.62	4417.86
76	5776	438976	8.7178	4.2358	1.88081	13.1579	238.76	4536.46
77	5929	456533	8.7750	4.2543	1.88649	12.9870	241.90	4656.63
78	6084	474552	8.8318	4.2727	1.89209	12.8205	245.04	4778.36
79	6241	493039	8.8882	4.2908	1.89763	12.6582	248.19	4901.67
80	6400	512000	8.9443	4.3089	1.90309	12.5000	251.33	5026.55
81	6561	531441	9.0000	4.3267	1.90849	12.3457	254.47	5153.00
82	6724	551368	9.0554	4.3445	1.91381	12.1951	257.61	5281.02
83	6889	571787	9.1104	4.3621	1.91908	12.0482	260.75	5410.61
84	7056	592704	9.1652	4.3795	1.92428	11.9048	263.89	5541.77
85	7225	614125	9.2195	4.3968	1.92942	11.7647	267.04	5674.50
86	7396	636056	9.2736	4.4140	1.93450	11.6279	270.18	5808.80
87	7569	658503	9.3274	4.4310	1.93952	11.4943	273.32	5944.68
88	7744	681472	9.3808	4.4480	1.94448	11.3636	276.46	6082.12
89	7921	704969	9.4340	4.4647	1.94939	11.2360	279.60	6221.14
90	8100	729000	9.4868	4.4814	1.95424	11.1111	282.74	6361.73

Credits

1. Planning and Design of Interior Spaces

Residential Spaces

Pages 5–28: *House and Garden's Complete Guide to Interior Decoration,* edited by Richardson Wright, Simon and Schuster, New York, 1942 (copyright renewed 1970 by The Condé Nast Publications Inc.).

Pages 29–42: Gottshall, Franklin H., *How to Design and Construct Period Furniture,* Bonanza Books, New York, 1989.

Page 43: *The House and Home Book of Interior Design,* McGraw-Hill, New York, 1976.

Page 49: *New Spaces for Learning,* Educational Facilities Lab, New York, 1966.

Pages 56–60: Ramsey, Charles George, and Harold Reeve Sleeper, *Architectural Graphic Standards,* 2d Edition, Wiley, New York, 1936.

Pages 62, 63, 81, 83, 84, 196, 197, 199: *Architectural Forum,* October 1937.

Pages 65–68, 71, 72, 96, 118–124, 164: Thompson, Robinson, Toraby.

Page 69: Verna Cook Salomonsky, Architect.

Page 70: Ulrich Franzen, Architect; *Selected Architectural Details,* Reinhold, New York.

Pages 73–76: Parrish Hadley Associates.

Page 80: U.S. Department of Housing and Urban Development, Washington, D.C.

Pages 82, 104, 105, 152: *House Planning Handbook,* 2d Edition, MWPS–16, Midwest Plan Service, Ames, Iowa, 1988 (reproduced with permission).

Pages 85, 86: Lehigh Furniture Company.

Pages 88, 89, 153, 154: *Manual of Acceptable Practices,* U.S. Department of Housing and Urban Development, Washington, D.C.

Pages 89, 201: *Internal Spaces of the Dwelling,* Canada Mortgage and Housing Corporation, 1984.

Pages 90–93, 125–127, 135, 166, 167: Bromley/Jacobsen.

Page 94: Knobloch, Philip G., *Good Practice in Construction,* Pencil Points Press, New York, 1931.

Page 95: *Comparative Architectural Details,* Pencil Points Series (Francis Y. Joannes, Architect), 1935.

Page 97: Gensler Associates; ISD; Bromley/Jacobson.

Pages 98, 99: *American Architect and Architecture,* January 1937.

Pages 100, 101, 149, 150, 206: Panero, Julius, and Martin Zelnik, *Human Dimension & Interior Space,* Whitney Library of Design/Watson-Guptill Publications, New York, 1979.

Pages 102, 103, 202–204: *Time-Saver Standards: A Manual of Essential Architectural Data,* F. W. Dodge Corporation, New York, 1946.

Pages 106–108: Kohler.

Pages 109, 110, 114, 170 (bottom): Eljer.

Pages 111–113, 115, 116, 170 (top): American Standard.

Pages 117, 194, 198: Hornbostel, Caleb, *Architectural Detailing Simplified,* Prentice-Hall, Englewood Cliffs, N.J., 1986.

Pages 128, 156: *A Design Guide for Home Safety,* U.S. Department of Housing and Urban Development, Washington, D.C., 1972.

Page 129: Space Design Group.

Pages 130, 131: Marble Institute of America.

Pages 132–134, 136: *Handbook for Ceramic Tile Installation,* Tile Council of America, Princeton, N.J., 1987.

Pages 137–140, 181–186: *Adaptable Housing,* Office of Policy Development and Research, U.S. Department of Housing and Urban Development, 1987.

Pages 141, 142, 179, 180: New York City Building Code.

Pages 143, 146, 147, 178: *Uniform Federal Accessibility Standards,* 1985-494-187, U.S. Government Printing Office, Washington, D.C., 1985.

Pages 144, 187: *Handbook for Design,* Veterans Administration, Washington, D.C.

Pages 145, 148, 165, 168, 169, 188, 189, 191, 192: Jerry Caldari, Architect.

Pages 357, 358, 362: *Interiors,* July 1985.

Page 360: *Selected Architectural Details,* Reinhold, New York.

Pages 361, 369, 370, 373, 381, 382: *Design Solutions,* Architectural Woodworking Institute, Spring 1990.

Pages 371, 372: Hochheiser-Elias Design Group.

Pages 374, 376: De Chiara, Joseph, and John Hancock Callender (eds.), *Time-Saver Standards for Building Types,* 3d Edition, McGraw-Hill, New York, 1990.

Retail Spaces

Pages 387–389: Panero, Julius, and Martin Zelnik, *Human Dimension & Interior Space,* Whitney Library of Design/Watson-Guptill Publications, New York, 1979.

Pages 390, 394, 400: *Selected Architectural Details,* Reinhold, New York.

Pages 391, 392, 396–399: *Design Solutions,* Architectural Woodworking Institute, Winter 1987, Summer 1988.

Pages 393, 401–411: Walker Group/CNI.

Page 395: Marble Institute of America.

Pages 412–417: Panero Zelnik Associates.

Pages 418–422: PAM International Co., Inc.

Public Restrooms, Toilets, and Coatrooms

Page 425: New York City Building Code.

Pages 427–430: General Services Administration.

Pages 431–438, 465: Bertram Bassuk, FAIA.

Page 439: William Morgan, FAIA.

Pages 440–445: DeChiara, Joseph, *Handbook of Architectural Details for Commercial Buildings,* McGraw-Hill, New York, 1980.

Page 446: Toni Chi and Associates.

Pages 447, 448: American Sanitary Partition Corporation.

Pages 449–451: *Access America,* Architectural and Transportation Barriers Compliance Board, Washington, D.C., 1980.

Page 452: *Uniform Federal Accessibility Standards,* 1985-494-187, U.S. Government Printing Office, Washington, D.C., 1985.

Page 453: A & J Washroom Accessories.

Pages 454–457: Parker/Nutone.

Pages 458, 459: American Specialties, Inc.

Pages 461–463: Railex.

Page 464: Jerry Caldari, Architect.

2. Construction Details and Finishes

Pages 471, 472, 518, 542, 547, 660–664, 727: *Time-Saver Standards: A Manual of Essential Architectural Data,* F. W. Dodge Corp., New York, 1946.

Pages 470, 517: McQuade, Walter (ed.), *Schoolhouse,* Simon and Schuster, New York, 1958.

Pages 473, 475–477: New York State Building Code.

Pages 474, 478, 565: Hornung, William J., *Reinhold Data Sheets,* Reinhold, New York, 1965.

Pages 480, 487, 489, 491, 497, 500–502, 512–515, 522–526, 532, 540, 541 (top), 577–579, 581–588, 601, 606, 608, 609, 614, 617, 629, 630–632, 648, 657, 658, 692 (bottom), 698, 708, 714, 721, 722, 751 (bottom): Bertram Bassuk, FAIA.

Pages 481–483, 484 (bottom), 490 (bottom), 629, 649, 651 (top), 652, 754, 755 (top): ISD.

Pages 484 (top), 485, 488, 492, 493, 495, 496, 529, 530, 534, 564, 653, 654, 656, 751 (top), 752, 753: Gensler Associates.

Pages 486, 580, 605, 659, 669 (top): William Morgan, FAIA.

Pages 490 (top), 650, 651 (bottom): Charles D. Flayhan Associates.

Pages 491, 754 (top), 755 (bottom): Michael Lynn Associates.

Pages 494, 543, 548, 549, 627, 628, 634: Anderson, L. O., *Wood-Frame House Construction,* Department of Agriculture Handbook No. 73, U.S. Government Printing Office, Washington, D.C., 1970.

Pages 498, 550: *Wood Frame Design,* Western Wood Products Association.

Pages 499, 504, 758, 759: Panero Zelnik Associates.

Pages 503, 508, 510, 616, 633, 665, 704, 705, 738: Knobloch, Philip G., *Good Practice in Construction,* Pencil Points Press, New York, 1931.

Pages 505, 506, 561–563: *Handbook for Ceramic Tile Installation,* Tile Council of America, Princeton, N.J., 1988.

Pages 507, 554–560:   American Olean Tile.

Pages 509, 520, 715, 733–735:   Marble Institute of America.

Page 519:   Radford, William, *Architectural Details*, R. D. Radford, Chicago, 1938.

Pages 521, 749, 750:   Callender, John Hancock (ed.), *Time-Saver Standards for Architectural Design Data*, 6th Edition, McGraw-Hill, New York, 1982.

Pages 527, 528 (top):   Walker Group/CNI.

Pages 531, 551:   Roppe Rubber Corp.

Page 533:   *American Architect and Architecture*, May 1932.

Pages 535–539:   National Terrazzo and Mosaic Association, Inc.

Page 541:   Buckingham Virginia Slate Co.

Page 544:   American Parquet Association.

Page 545:   Hoboken Wood Flooring Co.

Page 546:   Tarkett.

Page 553:   Franciscan Tile Company.

Pages 566–571, 574–576, 589–599, 607:   Hollow Metal Manufacturers Association.

Pages 572, 670, 671, 706:   Jerry Caldari, Architect.

Page 573:   *Methods and Materials of Commercial Construction.*

Page 600:   *New York State Construction Handbook.*

Pages 602, 603, 678–684, 687, 689, 695, 696, 710, 711, 742:   Baker, Earl P., and Harold S. Langland, *Architectural Metal Handbook*, National Association of Ornamental Metal Manufacturers, Washington, D.C., 1947.

Page 604:   General Services Administration.

Page 610:   Eggers Industries.

Pages 611, 675:   Raymond, Antonin, *Architectural Details*, Architectural Book Publishing Co., Inc., 1947.

Pages 612, 666:   Burbank, Nelson L., *House Construction Details*, 3d Edition, Simmons-Boardman Publishing Corp., New York, 1952.

Page 615:   Thompson, Robinson, Toraby.

Page 618:   *Progressive Architecture*, April 1971.

Pages 620–626:   *Comparative Architectural Details*, Pencil Points Series (Frank J. Forster, Architect), 1935.

Pages 637–640:   Schlage.

Pages 641–643:   New York City Building Code.

Pages 644–647:   Sweet's Catalog.

Pages 655, 707, 769, 771–773:   Toni Chi and Associates.

Page 667:   *Design Solutions*, Architectural Woodworking Institute.

Page 668:   Simon B. Zelnik, FAIA.

Page 672:   *Interiors*, April 1985.

Page 673:   Feirer, John L., *Cabinet Making and Millwork*, Charles A. Bennet Co., Peoria, Ill.

Page 674:   Ascente.

Page 676, 712:   *Selected Architectural Details*, Reinhold, New York.

Pages 677, 685, 686, 688, 690, 691, 692 (top), 693, 694, 697, 699–703, 709:   National Association of Architectural Manufacturers.

Page 713:   New York City Housing Authority.

Page 716:   Slate Institute.

Page 717:   *Manual of School Planning*, New York City Board of Education.

Pages 718, 719, 723:   *Uniform Federal Accessibility Standards*, 1985-494-187, U.S. Government Printing Office, Washington, D.C., 1985.

Page 720:   Lapeyre Stair.

Page 726:   *Farmers Bulletin #1889*, U.S. Department of Agriculture, Washington, D.C., 1971.

Pages 728, 729:   *Handbook of Successful Fireplaces*, Dunley Bros. Co., Cleveland, Ohio, 1961.

Page 731:   *Pencil Points* (Ely Jacques Kahn, Architect), October 1938.

Page 732:   *Pencil Points* (Richard Neutra, Architect), 1938.

Page 736:   *Pencil Points* (Frank Forster, Architect).

Page 737:   *Pencil Points* (Walker & Gillette, Architects).

Pages 739–741:   Architectural Paneling, Inc.

Pages 743, 744, 778:   General Electric Company.

Pages 745–748:   Nessen Lamp Company.

Pages 756, 757:   Horton Lees Lighting Designs, Inc.

Pages 760–762:   Space Design Group.

Pages 763, 764:   Bromley/Jacobsen.

Page 765:   *Architectural Lighting*, September 1987.

Pages 766, 768:   Roberts Step Lite Systems, Inc.

Pages 767, 770, 774:   National Cathode Corp.

Page 775:   Philips Lighting Co.

Pages 776, 777:   Just Bulbs Ltd.

3. Architectural Woodwork

Pages 781, 785–787: *Time-Saver Standards: A Manual of Essential Architectural Data,* F. W. Dodge Corp., New York, 1946.

Pages 782–784, 788–797, 801–803: Woodworking Institute of California.

Pages 798–800, 872, 873, 877, 879, 881–883: Architectural Woodwork Institute.

Page 804: Leroy P. Ward, Architect.

Page 806: *Comparative Architectural Details,* Pencil Points Series (Frank J. Forster, Architect), 1935.

Page 807: *Comparative Architectural Details,* Pencil Points Series (Evans, Moore, Peterson & Woodbridge, Architects), 1935.

Pages 812, 813, 839 (right), 842, 845, 847, 848, 849 (bottom), 853–856, 859, 862–864: *Design Solutions.*

Pages 814, 815: Space Design Group; ISD.

Page 816: *Selected Architectural Details,* Progressive Architecture (Perkins & Wills, Architects).

Pages 808–810, 851: Knobloch, Philip G., *Good Practice in Construction,* Pencil Points Press, New York, 1931.

Page 818: Thompson, Robinson, Cecil, Inc.

Pages 819–823, 829, 831–835: Bertram Bassuk, FAIA.

Pages 824, 828, 836–838: Charles D. Flayhan Associates.

Page 825: ISD.

Page 826, 827, 830, 839 (left), 846: Gensler Associates.

Pages 840, 841: Winebarger Church Furniture.

Page 843: Panero Zelnik Associates.

Page 844: Hochheiser-Elias.

Pages 849 (top), 852: General Services Administration.

Page 850: Roger H. Ballard, Architect.

Page 857: Hyde and Shepherd, Architects.

Page 858: Howard and Frenaye, Architects.

Pages 860, 861: *Comparative Architectural Details,* Pencil Points.

Page 865: *Manual of Millwork,* Woodworking Institute of California.

Pages 866–870, 886: Architectural Paneling, Inc.

Pages 871, 873–878, 880–885: Camden Window and Millwork.

Pages 887–889: Joyce, Ernest, *Encyclopedia of Furniture Making,* Sterling Publishing Co., Inc., New York, 1987.

Pages 890–902: Hafele.

4. Specialties

Pages 906–915: Everett Conklin and Susan Korner, in Alpern, Andrew (ed.), *Handbook of Specialty Elements in Architecture,* McGraw-Hill, New York, 1982.

Pages 916–922, 923 (top): *The Green Scene,* National Park Service, U.S. Department of the Interior, Washington, D.C., 1973.

Pages 923 (bottom), 924–926, 929, 930: Engel/GGP.

Pages 927, 928: Hornbostel, Caleb, *Architectural Detailing Simplified,* Prentice-Hall, Englewood Cliffs, N.J., 1986.

Pages 931–935, 940, 941, 943, 945–948: Fred T. Knowles, in Alpern, Andrew (ed.), *Handbook of Specialty Elements in Architecture,* McGraw-Hill, New York, 1982.

Pages 936–939: Designers Sign Company/Frank Rispoli.

Pages 942–944: U.S. Department of Transportation, Washington, D.C.

Pages 949–957: Jerome Menell, in Alpern, Andrew (ed.), *Handbook of Specialty Elements in Architecture,* McGraw-Hill, New York, 1982.

Pages 961–964: Hussey Seating Company.

Pages 965, 966, 968–976: J.G. Furniture Systems.

Page 967: *Design Guide for Music and Drama Centers,* Department of the Army, Washington, D.C., 1981.

Pages 977–997: *A Design Guide for Improving Residential Security,* U.S. Department of Housing and Urban Development, Washington, D.C., 1973.

Pages 998, 1002, 1028: *The House and Home Book of Interior Design,* McGraw-Hill, New York, 1979.

Pages 999, 1013, 1014: Halse, *The Use of Color in Interiors,* McGraw-Hill, New York, 1968.

Pages 1000, 1001, 1003–1012: Derieux, Mary, and Isabelle Stevenson, *The Complete Book of Interior Decorating,* Greystone Press, New York, 1950.

Pages 1023–1026: Anderson, L. O., *Wood-Frame House Construction,* Department of Agriculture Handbook No. 73, U.S. Government Printing Office, Washington, D.C., 1970.

Page 1016: McQuade, Walter (ed.), *Schoolhouse,* Simon and Schuster, New York, 1958.

Pages 1017–1020: Sweet's Catalog.

Page 1021: Marvin Windows.

Pages 1056–1059: Kirsch.

Page 1060: Armor Elevator.

Pages 1061–1064: Dover Elevator Co.

Pages 1065, 1066, 1102: *Uniform Federal Accessibility Standards,* 1985-494-187, U.S. Government Printing Office, Washington, D.C., 1985.

Page 1067: Panero Zelnik Associates.

Pages 1067–1074: *Outdoor Sports Facilities,* Departments of the Army, Navy, and Air Force, Washington, D.C.

Page 1068 (top): Mace, Ronald L., *An Illustrated Handbook of the Handicapped Section of the North Carolina State Building Code,* Raleigh, N.C., 1974.

Pages 1075–1078: Cutler Manufacturing.

Page 1079: Phillips and Brooks, Inc.

Pages 1080–1086: Baker, Earl P., and Harold S. Langland, *Architectural Metal Handbook,* National Association of Ornamental Metal Manufacturers, Washington, D.C., 1947.

Pages 1087–1089: Brown Manufacturing Co.

Page 1090: Bertram Bassuk, FAIA.

Pages 1091–1096: Pittcon Softforms.

Pages 1097–1099: Alvarado Manufacturing Co.

Pages 1100–1101: Haws.

5. General Reference Data

Pages 1106–1109: Ballast, David Kent, *Architect's Handbook of Formulas, Tables, and Mathematical Calculations,* Prentice-Hall, Englewood Cliffs, N.J., 1988.

Pages 1110, 1111: Panero, Julius, and Martin Zelnik, *Human Dimension & Interior Space,* Whitney Library of Design/Watson-Guptill Publications, New York, 1979.

Pages 1112, 1113: *Access America,* Washington, D.C.

Pages 1114 (top): Sister Kenny Institute.

Pages 1114 (bottom), 1115–1118: *Uniform Federal Accessibility Standards,* 1985-494-187, U.S. Government Printing Office, Washington, D.C., 1985.

Pages 1119, 1120: Woodson, W. E., *Human Factors Design Handbook,* McGraw-Hill, New York, 1981.

Page 1121: *Building for People,* U.S. Department of Commerce, Washington, D.C.

Pages 1123–1125: Foster, Norman, *Practical Tables for Building Construction,* McGraw-Hill, New York, 1963.

Page 1128: Halse, *The Use of Color in Interiors,* McGraw-Hill, New York, 1968.

Page 1129: Hornbostel, Caleb, *Architectural Detailing Simplified,* Prentice-Hall, Englewood Cliffs, N.J., 1986.

Pages 1130, 1131: Derieux, Mary, and Isabelle Stevenson, *The Complete Book of Interior Decorating,* Greystone Press, New York, 1950.

Pages 1132, 1134: Steelcase.

Page 1133: *National Electrical Code Book,* McGraw-Hill, New York, 1981.

Page 1135: Indiana Limestone Institute.

Pages 1137, 1138: Wing, Charles, *The Visual Handbook of Building and Remodeling,* Rodale Press, 1990.

Pages 1139–1142: *Time-Saver Standards: A Manual of Essential Architectural Data,* F. W. Dodge Corp., New York, 1946.

Index

About the Editors

JOSEPH DE CHIARA is a practicing architect and city planner in New York City. He has taught at Columbia University, Pratt Institute, Cooper Union, the New York Institute of Technology, and the State University of New York at Farmingdale. He is coauthor of *Time-Saver Standards for Site Planning* and the author of *Handbook of Architectural Details for Commercial Buildings* and *Time-Saver Standards for Building Types*, all published by McGraw-Hill. De Chiara received a Bachelor of Architecture degree from Pratt Institute and a Master's degree in Urban Planning from Columbia University.

JULIUS PANERO, AIA, ASID, is a practicing architect, interior designer, and Professor of Interior Design at the Fashion Institute of Technology in New York City. He has taught interior design for the past 32 years and was a former chairperson of the interior design department at FIT. A graduate of Pratt Institute, where he received a Bachelor of Architecture, and Columbia University, where he received a Master of Science in Urban Planning, Panero is a member of the American Institute of Architects and the American Society of Interior Designers.

Licensed to practice architecture in New York, Panero is a principal in the architectural and consulting firm of Panero Zelnik Associates, Architects/Interior Designers. He is coauthor of *Human Dimension & Interior Space*, a sourcebook of design reference standards. In 1986, he was awarded the prestigious ASID Joel Polsky Prize for this book. He is also the author of *Anatomy for Interior Designers* and a contributing author to the *Time-Saver Standards* series.

MARTIN ZELNIK, AIA, ASID, IDEC, is a practicing architect, interior designer, and Professor of Interior Design at the Fashion Institute of Technology in New York City, where he has taught interior design for the past 23 years. He served as chairperson of the interior design department from 1983 to 1986. He is a graduate of Brandeis University, where he received a Bachelor of Fine Arts degree, and

Columbia University, where he earned a Master of Architecture degree. Zelnik is a member of the Interior Design Educators Council, the American Society of Interior Designers, and the American Institute of Architects; has served as a special consultant to the National Council of Interior Design Qualifications; and holds certification with the National Council of Architectural Registration Boards.

He has been a principal in the New York City–based architectural and consulting firm of Panero Zelnik Associates, Architects/Interior Designers, for over 18 years. The firm specializes in institutional, religious, and transportation facilities, and corporate interiors. Zelnik is coauthor of *Human Dimension & Interior Space*, a sourcebook of design reference standards. In 1986, he was awarded the prestigious ASID Joel Polsky Prize for this book.

Rs. 1930'30

Rs. 1930'30